HOLT SCIENCE & TECHNOLOGY

Life Science

Teacher Edition WALK-THROUGH

Student Edition CONTENTS IN BRIEF

HOLT, RINEHART AND WINSTON

A Harcourt Education Company

Orlando • **Austin** • New York • San Diego • Toronto • London

Designed to meet the needs of all students

Holt Science & Technology reflects current curriculum developments and includes the strongest skills-development strand of any middle school science series. This comprehensive middle school program provides students with a solid foundation in life science, Earth science, and physical science fundamentals. Students of all abilities will develop skills that they can use both in science as well as in other courses.

STUDENTS OF ALL ABILITIES RECEIVE THE READING HELP AND TAILORED INSTRUCTION THEY NEED.

- The *Student Edition* is accessible with a clean, easy-to-follow design and highlighted vocabulary words.
- Inclusion strategies and different learning styles are addressed to support all learners.
- Comprehensive Section and Chapter Reviews and Standardized Test Preparation allow students to practice their test-taking skills.
- Reading Comprehension Guide and Guided Reading Audio CDs help students better understand the content.

CROSS-DISCIPLINARY CONNECTIONS LET STUDENTS SEE HOW SCIENCE RELATES TO OTHER DISCIPLINES.

- Mathematics, reading, and writing skills are integrated throughout the program.
- Cross-discipline Connection To features show students how science relates to language arts, social studies, and other sciences.

A FLEXIBLE LABORATORY PROGRAM HELPS STUDENTS BUILD IMPORTANT INQUIRY AND CRITICAL-THINKING SKILLS.

- The laboratory program includes labs in each chapter, labs in the **LabBook** at the end of the text, six different lab books, and **Video Labs.**
- All labs are teacher-tested and rated by difficulty in the *Teacher Edition,* so you can be sure the labs will be appropriate for your students.
- A variety of labs, from Inquiry Labs to Skills Practice Labs, helps you meet the needs of your curriculum and work within the time constraints of your teaching schedule.

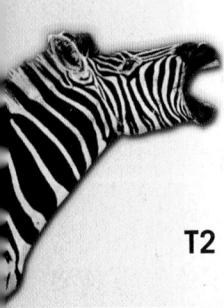

INTEGRATED TECHNOLOGY AND ONLINE RESOURCES EXPAND LEARNING BEYOND CLASSROOM WALLS.

- An **Enhanced Online Edition** or **CD-ROM Version** of the student text lightens your students' load.

- **SciLinks,** a Web service developed and maintained by the National Science Teachers Association (NSTA), contains current prescreened links directly related to the textbook.

- **Brain Food Video Quizzes** on videotape and DVD are game-show style quizzes that assess students' progress and motivate them to study.

- The **One-Stop Planner® CD-ROM** with **ExamView® Test Generator** contains all of the resources you need including an Interactive Teacher Edition, worksheets, customizable lesson plans, **Holt Calendar Planner,** a powerful test generator, **Lab Materials QuickList Software,** and more.

Special Needs Workbook

Study Guide

Life Science

CHAPTERS

1 The World of Life Science
2 It's Alive!! Or Is It?
3 Cells: The Basic Units of Life
4 The Cell in Action
5 Heredity

13 Plant Processes
14 Animals and Behavior
15 Invertebrates
16 Fishes, Amphibians, and Reptiles
17 Birds and Mammals

One-Stop Planner®
with Test Generator
CD-ROM for Macintosh® and Windows®

Printable
Teaching Resources
Special Needs Resources
Customizable
Lesson Plans
Holt Calendar Planner
PowerPoint® LectureNotes
Powerful
Test Generator
Lab Materials QuickList
Holt PuzzlePro
Interactive Teacher Edition

Chapter Resource File 1

The World of Life Science

Skills Worksheets
Directed Reading A 1
Directed Reading B 11
Vocabulary & Notes 25
Section Reviews 31
Chapter Review 39
Reinforcement 45
Critical Thinking 48

Assessments
Section Quizzes 50
Chapter Test A 54
Chapter Test B 58
Chapter Test C 62
Performance-Based Assessment 66
Standardized Test Preparation 68

Labs and Activities
Datasheet for In-Text Labs: Does It All Add Up? 72
Datasheets for Quick Labs: Measure Up 76
Datasheets for LabBook: Graphing Data 80
Vocabulary Activity 84
SciLinks® Activity 86

Teacher Resources
Teacher Notes for Performance-Based Assessment 87
Lab Notes and Answers 90
Answer Keys 97
Lesson Plans 112
Test Item Listing for ExamView® Test Generator T1
Teaching Transparencies
Scientific Methods
Compound Light Microscope
Common SI Units and Conversions
Chapter Starter Transparencies
Bellringer Transparencies
Concept Mapping Transparencies

Guided Reading Audio CD Program

Life Science

Direct read of the student text

T3

The skills students need for science success

A WELL-DESIGNED TEXT MAKES SCIENCE ENGAGING AND ACCESSIBLE.

A preview of the upcoming content guides students' reading.

Pre-Reading Activity includes a **FoldNote** or **Graphic Organizer** to help students organize their ideas and improve their comprehension and retention.

Accessible navigation engages students with outline-style headings, content grouped into small chunks, and text that doesn't break between pages.

Reading Strategy gives students additional reading guidance with a **Reading Organizer, Prediction Guide, Discussion, Paired Summarizing, Brainstorming, or Mnemonics tip.**

Visuals are engaging and closely related to the text narrative.

An engaging photo and hands-on **Start-Up Activity** motivate students.

Objectives and Terms to Learn help focus students' attention and develop reading skills.

Key Terms are highlighted in yellow and defined in the margin to develop students' vocabulary skills.

Reading Check allows students to check their understanding at least once every two-page spread. Answers are found in the **Appendix.**

RELEVANT AND EXCITING FEATURES PROMOTE STUDENTS' INTEREST.

Science in Action grabs students' attention with three short articles and online extensions.

Current Science connects students to interesting online articles from *Current Science*® magazine.

SciLinks refers students to the NSTA Web site for up-to-date links, information, and activities.

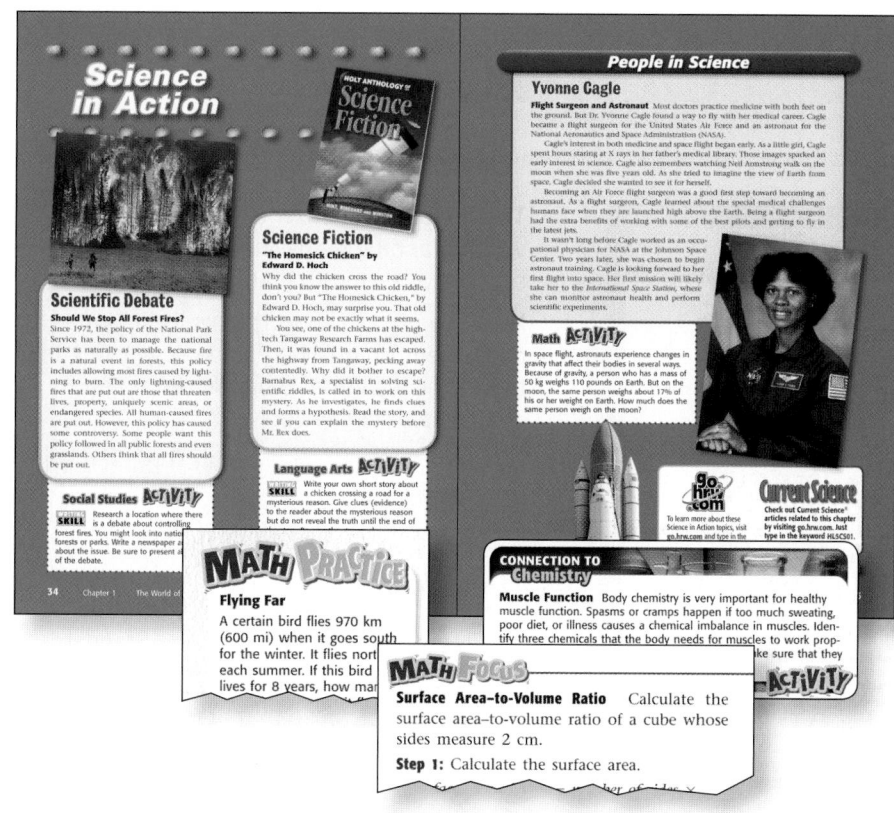

CROSS-DISCIPLINARY FEATURES CONNECT SCIENCE TO OTHER SUBJECTS.

Math Practice and Math Focus help build students' math skills.

Connection shows how science relates to social studies, language arts, or other sciences.

Writing skills are developed and highlighted throughout the program, including in the Science Journal.

Social Studies, Language Arts, and Math Activity are included in the **Science in Action** feature at the end of every chapter.

LABS AND ACTIVITIES MAKE LEARNING HANDS-ON.

Internet Activity sends students online for a variety of projects, such as creating scientist biographies and writing articles.

Quick Lab and School to Home Activity require few materials and reinforce science concepts.

Chapter Lab includes **Inquiry**, **Model-Making**, and **Skills Practice labs.** Additional labs are located in the **LabBook** at the end of the book.

Observe a Mushroom
1. Identify the stalk, cap, and gills on a **mushroom** that your teacher has provided.

REVIEW FOR TEST-READINESS

Section Review includes a comprehensive assessment of the Section's **Objectives.**

Chapter Review checks students' understanding of all of the Chapter **Objectives** with vocabulary, multiple-choice, short answer, **Critical-Thinking,** and **Interpreting Graphics** questions.

Standardized Test Preparation gives students skill practice in reading, math, and interpreting graphics.

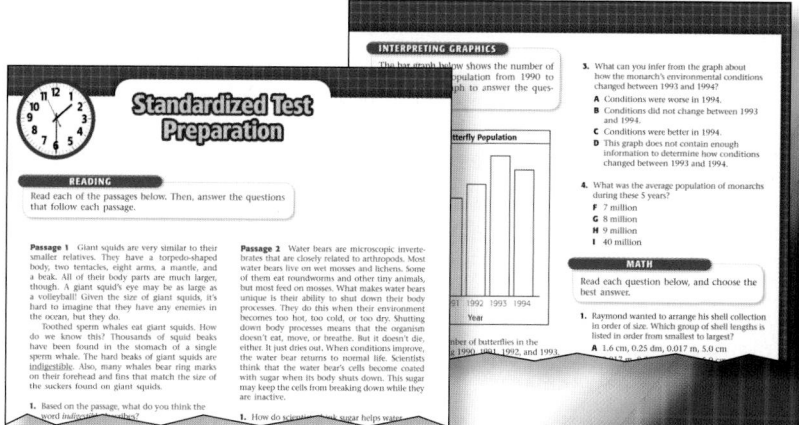

A Teacher Edition that is functional and easy-to-use

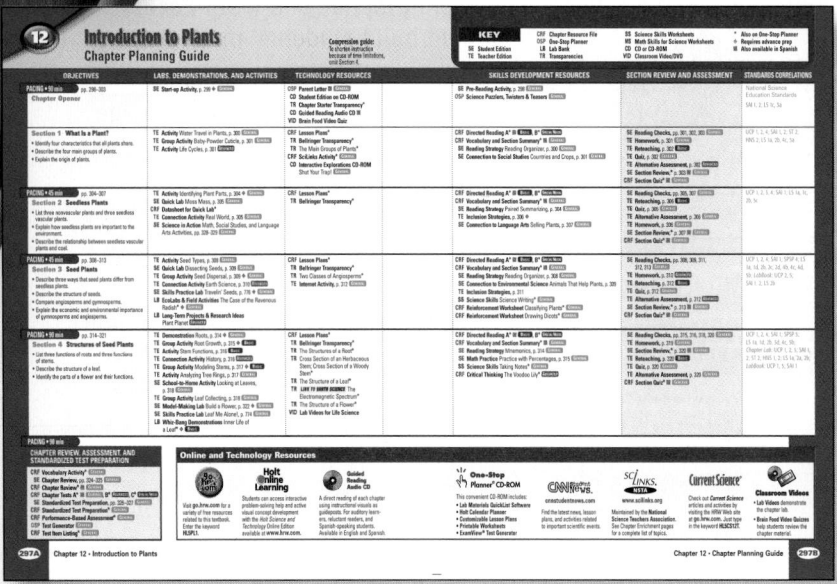

The **Chapter Organizer** is an easy-to-follow visual planning guide that provides the support you need to plan your lessons.

You'll be glad to know that we've included a convenient time-saving guide suggesting how to use the wealth of program resources. The **Chapter Organizer:**

- integrates all labs, technology, and print resources.
- is organized according to time requirements.
- includes section correlations to the National Science Education Standards.
- rates activities by ability level to help you select those that are appropriate for your class.

Chapter Resources and Worksheets are shown as reduced pages to make choosing appropriate worksheets easy. Available resources and worksheets are grouped by

- Visual Resources
- Meeting Individual Needs
- Review and Assessment
- Applications and Extensions

Chapter Enrichment provides additional information for each section in the chapter, including interesting facts that spark student interest. Also included is a selection of **SciLinks** for more information about the topics listed.

The **Lesson Cycle** provides a structure for the teaching strategies included in the Teacher's wrap. **Focus** uses objectives to focus student attention on the upcoming content; **Motivate** includes activities and discussions to get students excited about learning; **Teach** includes **Teaching** and **Reading Strategies;** and **Close** provides additional assessment including **Alternative Assessment.**

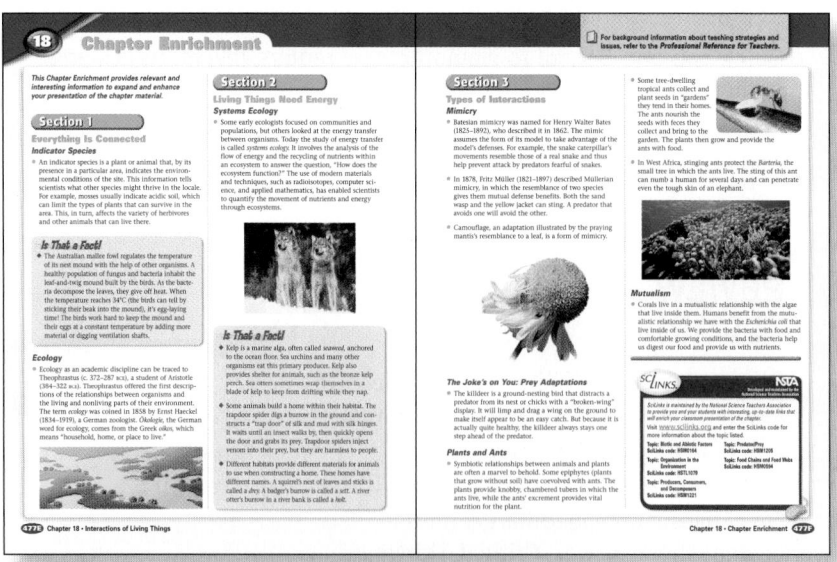

ACTIVITIES AND DEMONSTRATIONS FOR EVERY LEARNING LEVEL

Activities in the teacher's wrap are labeled by ability level—Basic, General, and Advanced—helping you choose appropriate activities for each student.

- Basic activities are designed to be accessible to all students.

- General activities are appropriate for most students and require more critical-thinking skills than Basic activities.

- Advanced activities are more challenging than General activities and can be used to extend learning.

Learning styles—Interpersonal, Intrapersonal, Auditory, Kinesthetic, Logical, Visual, and Verbal—are addressed throughout so you can adapt material to different ways of learning. In addition, some labels identify the activities that help with Co-op Learning and English Language Learners.

Bellringer activities begin each section with an activity designed to get students thinking. Bellringers are also available on transparency.

Bellringer

Have students make a list of the ways that pathogens might enter the body. (Examples include through the mouth, ears, nose, and cuts in the skin. Pathogens can travel in the water, in the air, and in food.)

Activity, Group Activity, Connection Activity, Demonstrations, and Homework provide more quick activities that you can integrate into your lesson.

ACTIVITY — BASIC

Plant Identification Have students work together in small groups to find pictures in magazines of ferns and flowering plants that grow in North America. Provide resource books for the students to use to identify the plants. Then, have students mount the plant pictures on poster board and label them. English Language Learners
LS Visual

BRAIN FOOD

Classifying Ideas Have students consider the importance of classification to human thought. Ask students to try to think of something that cannot be classified in some way. Suggest that they test any item or concept they come up with by placing the following sentence:

(A) _____ is a type of _____.
For example, if the word is *speech*, the sentence can be filled in as follows:

Speech is a type of communication.

You may wish to hold a test or have students share their examples in class.
LS Logical/Verbal

MISCONCEPTION ALERT

It Never Fails Students may believe that an experiment is a failure if their hypothesis is not supported by the data gathered. Remind them that the point of conducting experiments is to investi... ... learn from ... be learned ... prove a ... questions. ...ntless if we ...

Teach

READING STRATEGY — BASIC

Mnemonics Have students create a mnemonic device that will remind them of the names of the bases and the way the bases form pairs. Examples such as "**A**toms are **T**iny" or "**A**dam is **T**errific" might help remind students that **a**denine pairs with **t**hymine. "**C**athy is **G**reat" might remind them that **c**ytosine pairs with **g**uanine.
LS Verbal/Logical

TEACHING TIPS AND ENGAGING FEATURES KEEP STUDENTS INTERESTED AND INVOLVED.

- Reading and Teaching Strategies
- Misconception Alert
- Cultural Awareness
- Scientists at Odds
- Weird Science
- Brain Food
- Connections to other disciplines and sciences
- Science Humor
- Is That a Fact!

INCLUSION STRATEGIES MAKE MATERIAL ACCESSIBLE TO ALL.

Written by professionals in the field of special needs education, **Inclusion Strategies** address many different learning exceptionalities in the classroom.

- Hearing Impaired
- Visually Impaired
- Developmentally Delayed
- Attention Deficit Disorder
- Behavior Control Issues
- Gifted and Talented

INCLUSION Strategies

- *Visually Impaired*
- *Learning Disabled*
- *Developmentally Delayed*

Assist students in understanding the concepts in **Figure 4** by creating a cardboard replica of each of the continents. Let students experiment with fitting the pieces together. Then, have them approximate the shape of Pangaea, as shown in **Figure 4**. English Language Learners
LS Kinesthetic

Complete assessment every step of the way

Holt Science & Technology provides many ways to accurately measure students' mastery of content.

CUSTOM ASSESSMENT WITH THE ONE-STOP PLANNER CD-ROM WITH TEST GENERATOR

With Holt's *One-Stop Planner CD-ROM* create, revise, and edit quizzes, section and chapter reviews, and chapter tests. Thousands of questions, organized by chapter and linked to chapter objectives, allow you to customize tests for your classroom. **Performance-Based Assessment** is also included.

SECTION ASSESSMENT

Reading Check is found at least once on each two-page spread. Students are encouraged to check their understanding of content by answering these questions found throughout the chapter and comparing their answers to the answer key in the **Appendix.**

Section Review provides a summary of the section and a comprehensive assessment of students' understanding of Section **Objectives. Math, Interpreting Graphics,** and **Critical Thinking** questions are included.

Section Quiz in the *Teacher Edition* and the *Chapter Resource Files* provides additional questions to check students' understanding.

Alternative Assessment gives you different evaluation options, such as expository writing and concept mapping, to ensure a thorough assessment.

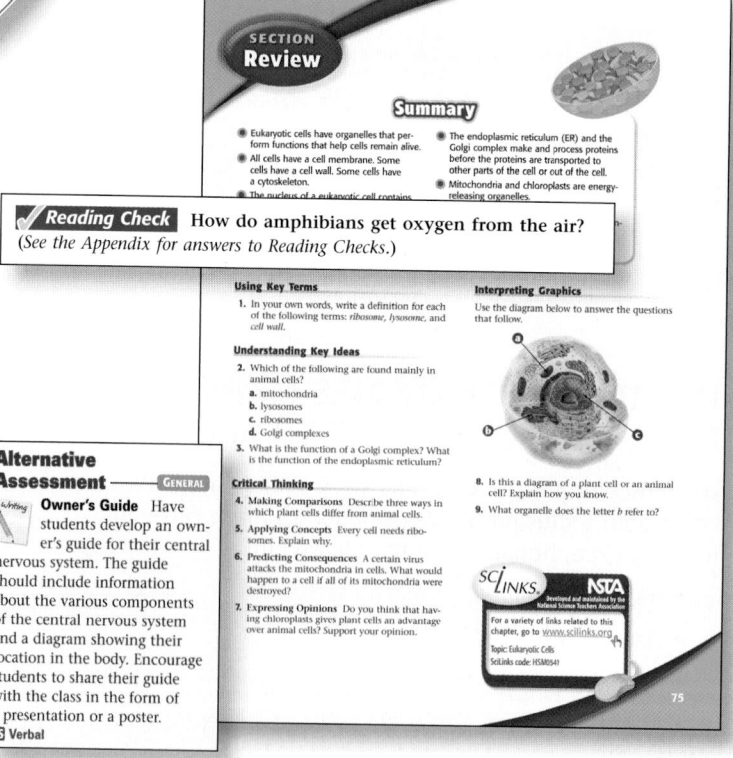

CHAPTER ASSESSMENT

Chapter Review checks students' understanding of all of the Section **Objectives** with vocabulary, multiple-choice, short-answer, critical-thinking, and interpreting graphics questions. Question types are similar to those found on **Chapter Tests,** making this an excellent resource for pretest practice.

- **Assignment Guide** in the Teacher Edition lets you see which review questions correlate with a specific section's content.
- **Study Guide** provides blackline masters of the **Section** and **Chapter Reviews** to help students prepare for testing.

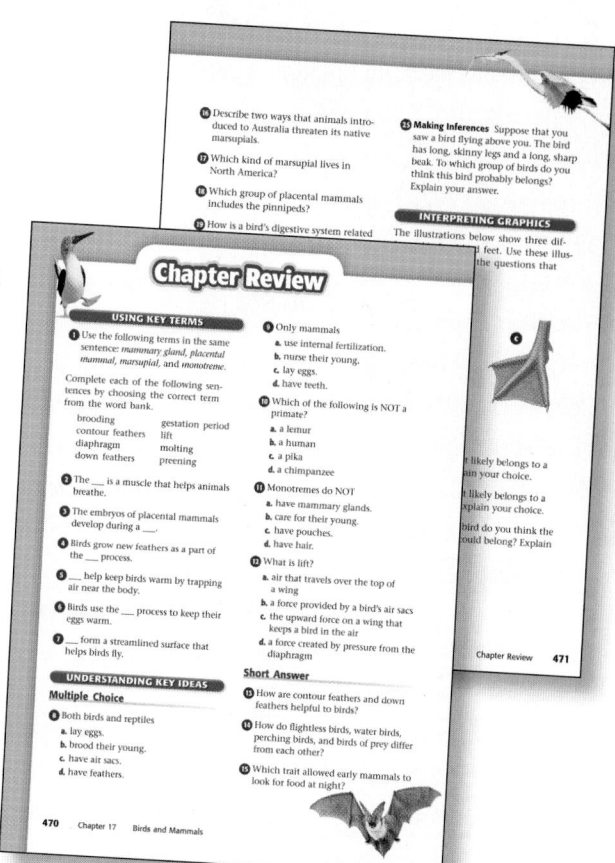

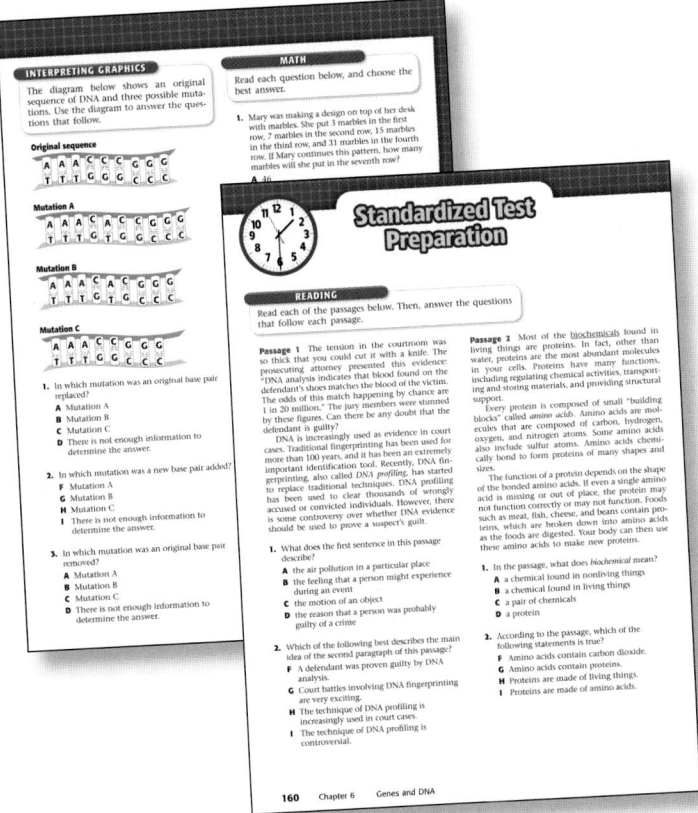

Standardized Test Preparation helps students prepare for testing with skill practice in reading, math, and interpreting graphics. There are two full pages of test preparation in the *Student Edition* and additional practice in the *Chapter Resource Files.*

Test Doctor in the *Teacher Edition* helps you diagnose why a student answered a **Standardized Test Preparation** question incorrectly.

Chapter Resource Files include **Performance-Based Assessment** plus three levels of **Chapter Tests** to meet the needs of your classroom—Special Needs, General, and Advanced. In addition, a **Test Item Listing** is available so you can quickly see all of the available test items located on the **One-Stop Planner CD-ROM.**

Assessment Checklists & Rubrics provide guidelines for evaluating your students' progress. You can create a customized checklist for each class to help you gather daily scores and determine grades.

Resources to make teaching easier

CHAPTER RESOURCE FILES

A *Chapter Resource File* is provided for each chapter of **Holt Science & Technology.** Each *Chapter Resource File* provides everything you need to plan and manage your lessons for the chapter in a convenient, time-saving format. Also included is a **Program Resource Introduction File,** your guide to the resources in each *Chapter Resource File. Chapter Resource Files* include the following:

Skills Worksheets
- Directed Reading A: Basic
- Directed Reading B: Special Needs
- Vocabulary and Section Summary
- Section Reviews
- Chapter Review
- Reinforcement
- Critical Thinking

Assessments
- Section Quizzes
- Chapter Test A: General
- Chapter Test B: Advanced
- Chapter Test C: Special Needs
- Performance-Based Assessment
- Standardized Test Preparation

Labs and Activities
- Datasheet for Chapter Lab
- Datasheets for Quick Labs
- Datasheets for LabBook Labs
- Vocabulary Activity
- SciLinks Activity

Teacher Resources
- Teacher Notes for Performance-Based Assessment
- Lab Notes and Answers
- Answer Keys
- Lesson Plans
- Test Item Listing for ExamView® Test Generator

All of these additional resources can also be found in one place on Holt's **One-Stop Planner CD-ROM.** Also included on this *CD-ROM* is a **Test Generator** that allows you to customize your quizzes and tests.

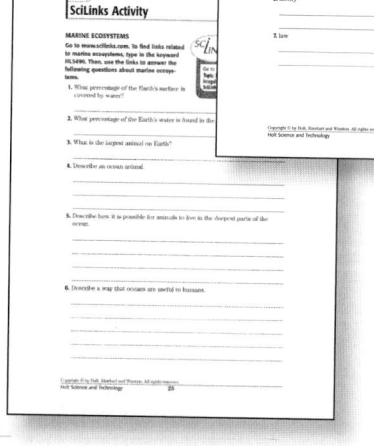

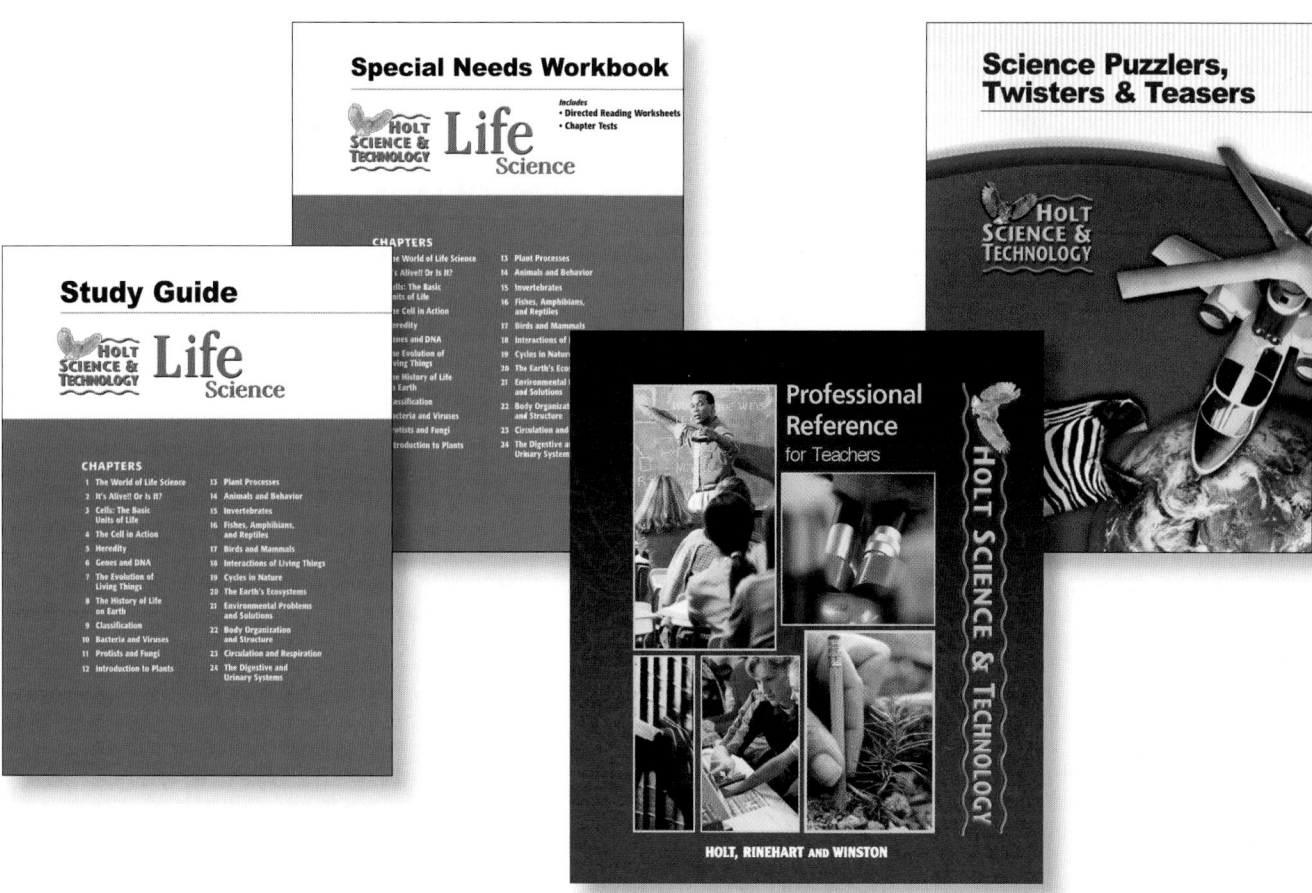

Study Guide contains **Section** and **Chapter Review Worksheets.** Answers are contained in the corresponding *Chapter Resource File.*

Reading Comprehension Guide includes **Directed Reading Worksheets** and **Vocabulary** and **Section Summary** worksheets to improve students' understanding of the text.

Special Needs Workbook includes **Special Needs Directed Reading Worksheets** and the **Special Needs Chapter Tests.**

Program Teaching Resources includes a variety of resources for additional skill development—Science Puzzlers, Twisters & Teasers; Science Skills Worksheets; Math Skills for Science; Science Fair Guide; Assessment Checklists & Rubrics.

Professional Reference for Teachers provides current information about issues in science education today. In professional articles, you can learn more about the National Education Standards, block scheduling, classroom management, and more.

Holt Science Posters includes seven colorful posters.

Holt Anthology of Science Fiction sparks your students' imaginations.

Holt Science Skills Workshop: Reading in the Content Area contains exercises that target key reading skills using excerpts from Holt's science textbooks.

Transparencies visually reinforce important science concepts with 300 *Teaching Transparencies* plus *Bellringer, Chapter Starter,* and *Concept Mapping Transparencies.*

SPANISH RESOURCES BRING HOLT SCIENCE & TECHNOLOGY TO ENGLISH-LANGUAGE LEARNERS.

These translations open the door to students who are frequently locked out.

- *Student Edition* in Spanish
- Spanish glossary in both the English and Spanish *Student Edition*
- **Study Guide** in Spanish
- **Reading Comprehension Guide** in Spanish
- **Assessments** in Spanish
- **Guided Reading Audio CD Program** in Spanish

Technology that expands your teaching options

One-Stop Planner CD-ROM® with Test Generator

Holt Science & Technology provides the correct combination of integrated technology resources—including CD-ROMs, videotapes, and DVD products—to make teaching more effective, efficient, and creative.

Planning and managing lessons has never been easier than with this convenient, all-in-one CD-ROM that includes the following time-saving features:

Printable:

• Teaching Resources

• Transparency Masters

• Special Needs Resources

Customizable:

• **Lesson Plans:** traditional and block-scheduling lesson plans in several word-processing formats

• **Holt Calendar Planner:** a tool that allows you to manage your time and resources by the day, week, month, or year

• **PowerPoint® LectureNotes:** graphic organizers and key concepts for each section that teachers can use to develop their own customized lectures

Powerful:

• **ExamView® Test Generator:** test items organized by chapter, plus thousands of editable questions, so you can put together your own tests and quizzes

• **Lab Materials QuickList Software:** a tool to easily create a customizable list of lab materials you need

• **Holt PuzzlePro:** an easy way to create crossword puzzles and word searches that make learning vocabulary fun

• **Interactive** *Teacher Edition:* the entire teacher text, with links to related Teaching Resources; planning has never been easier

HOLT SCIENCE & TECHNOLOGY **Life** Science

with Interactive Teacher Edition

One-Stop Planner® with Test Generator

CD-ROM for Macintosh® and Windows®

Printable
Teaching Resources
Special Needs Resources
Customizable
Lesson Plans
Holt Calendar Planner
PowerPoint® LectureNotes
Powerful
Test Generator
Lab Materials QuickList
Holt PuzzlePro
Interactive Teacher Edition

CD-ROM RESOURCES

Guided Reading Audio CD Program provides a direct reading of each chapter in English and in Spanish. This program helps struggling readers and English-language learners better understand the text.

Interactive Explorations CD-ROM turns a computer into a virtual laboratory where students help solve a selection of real-world problems.

Science Tutor CD-ROM serves as a personal tutor to help students practice what they learn. Immediate feedback is provided.

Student Edition on CD-ROM provides students with the entire textbook on a CD-ROM so that they have less to carry home.

Visual Concepts CD-ROM provides you with graphics, animations, and movie clips that demonstrate key chapter concepts. Visual Concepts work well as a student tutor or a teacher-presentation tool.

VIDEO RESOURCES

Lab Videos (on videotape or DVD) make it easier for you to integrate more experiments into your lessons without the preparation time and costs of a traditional laboratory setup.

Brain Food Video Quizzes (on videotape or DVD) are game-show style quizzes that assess students' progress and motivate students to study.

HRW Earth Science Videotape takes your students on a geology "field trip" with full-motion video.

CNN Presents Science in the News: Video Library allows your students to see the impact of science in their everyday lives with the following videos: Scientists in Action, Multicultural Connections, Science, Technology & Society, and Eye on the Environment. This program includes a **Teacher's Guide** and **Critical-Thinking Worksheets.**

Online resources available anytime, anywhere!

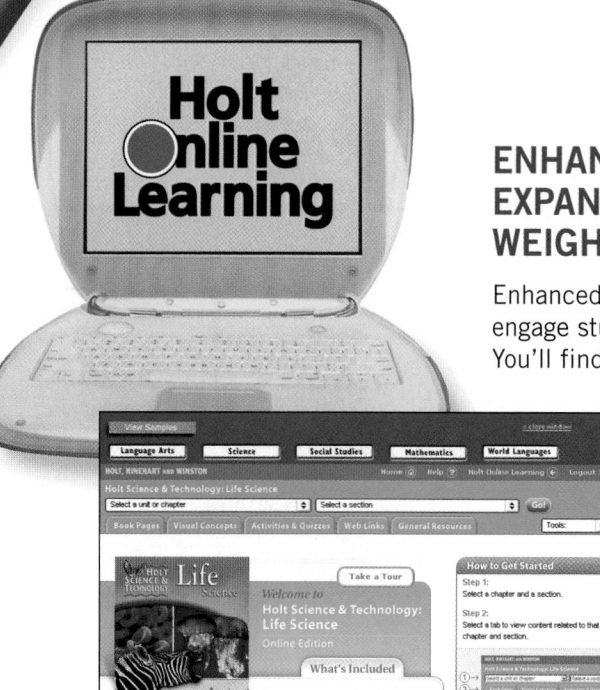

ENHANCED ONLINE EDITIONS ARE PORTABLE, EXPANDABLE, AND INTERACTIVE, AND YET WEIGH NOTHING AT ALL.

Enhanced Online Editions of *Holt Science & Technology* engage students in ways that were never before possible. You'll find the following:

- Entire *Student Edition* online
- Interactive exercises, quizzes, and a science tutor with immediate feedback
- Web links
- **Visual Concepts** for student study or teacher presentation
- General tools, such as a glossary
- **Classroom Manager** and **One-Stop Planner** to create a lesson and manage resources.

This web service, developed and maintained by the National Science Teachers Association, contains a large collection of prescreened links that include current information and activities directly related to chapter topics.

- Prescreening saves you valuable time searching for relevant and up-to-date Web sites.
- Sites are reviewed by science-content experts and educators.
- **Internet Connect** boxes within each chapter offer opportunities to enrich, enhance, and extend learning.
- Each topic leads to many links.

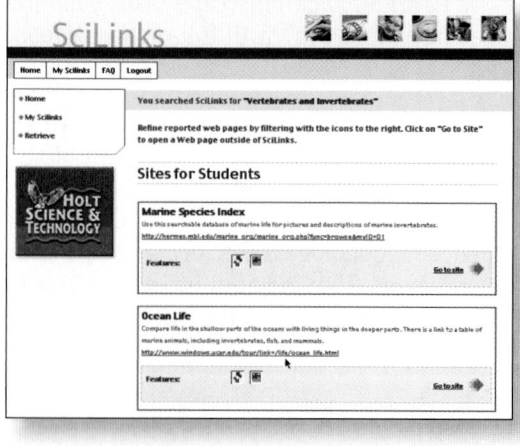

Current Science

Current Science is a science magazine with articles that speak directly to middle school students and relate to students' lives. A collection of articles and activities have been placed online and are correlated to the text.

student CNN News

cnnstudentsnews.com is the ultimate news and information Web site for both teachers and students. The site includes news as it happens, classroom resources, activities, and lesson plans.

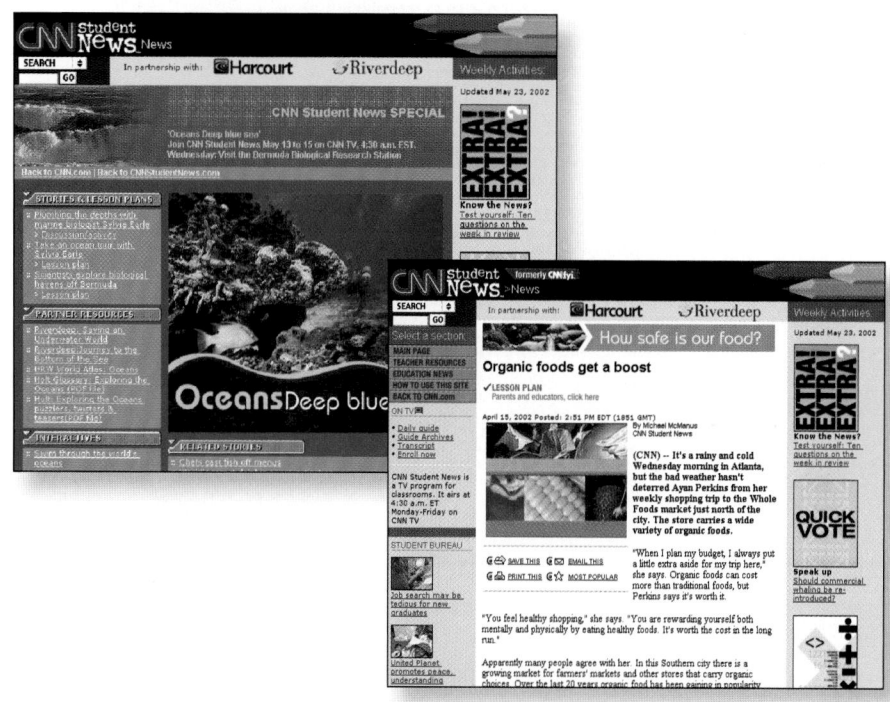

go.hrw.com

go.hrw.com enriches student learning with activities and resources keyed to the chapters in the textbook.

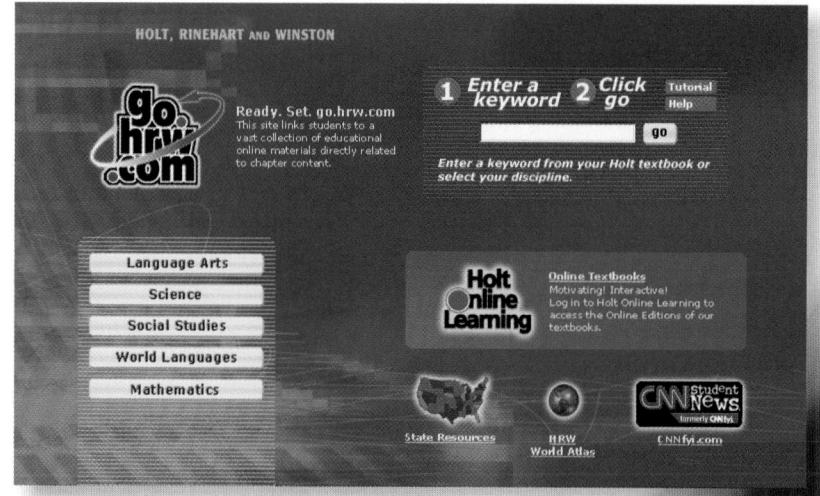

A complete lab program that makes learning meaningful

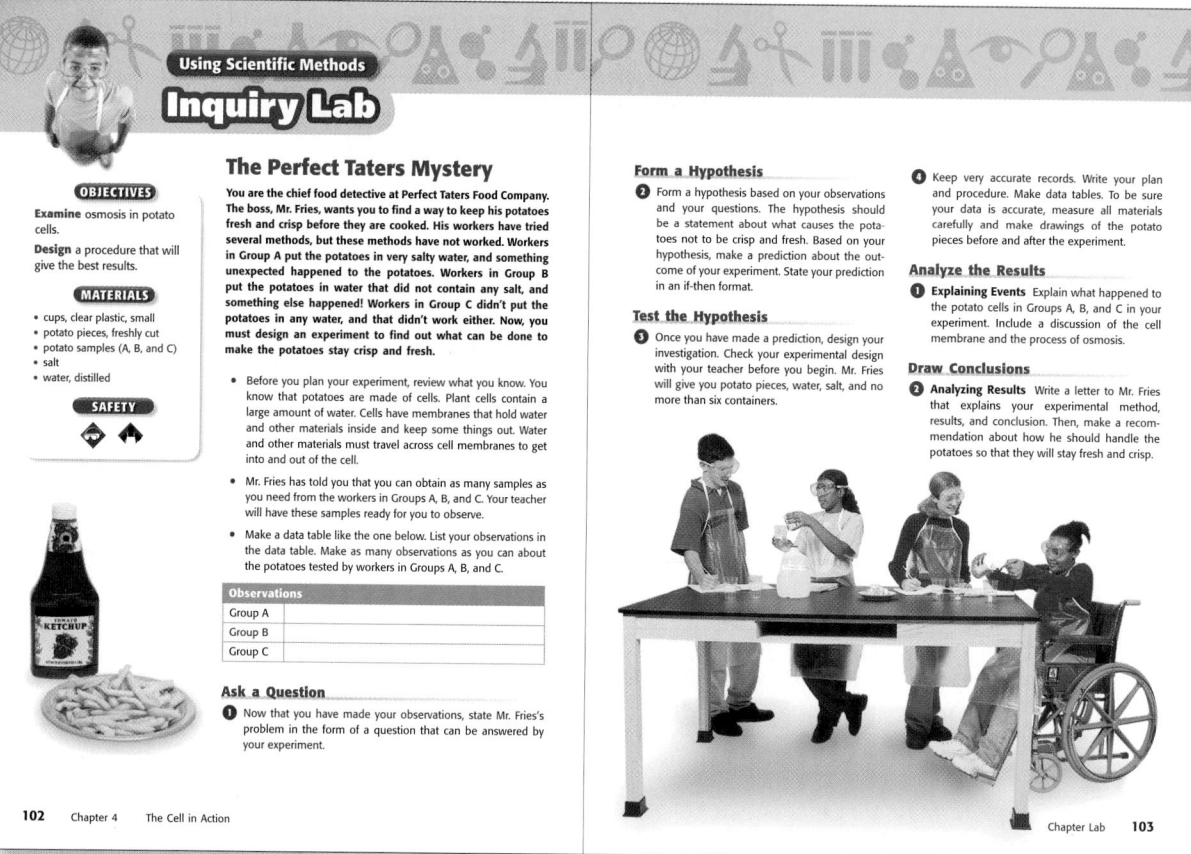

Using Scientific Methods

Inquiry Lab

The Perfect Taters Mystery

You are the chief food detective at Perfect Taters Food Company. The boss, Mr. Fries, wants you to find a way to keep his potatoes fresh and crisp before they are cooked. His workers have tried several methods, but these methods have not worked. Workers in Group A put the potatoes in very salty water, and something unexpected happened to the potatoes. Workers in Group B put the potatoes in water that did not contain any salt, and something else happened! Workers in Group C didn't put the potatoes in any water, and that didn't work either. Now, you must design an experiment to find out what can be done to make the potatoes stay crisp and fresh.

OBJECTIVES

Examine osmosis in potato cells.

Design a procedure that will give the best results.

MATERIALS

- cups, clear plastic, small
- potato pieces, freshly cut
- potato samples (A, B, and C)
- salt
- water, distilled

SAFETY

- Before you plan your experiment, review what you know. You know that potatoes are made of cells. Plant cells contain a large amount of water. Cells have membranes that hold water and other materials inside and keep some things out. Water and other materials must travel across cell membranes to get into and out of the cell.
- Mr. Fries has told you that you can obtain as many samples as you need from the workers in Groups A, B, and C. Your teacher will have these samples ready for you to observe.
- Make a data table like the one below. List your observations in the data table. Make as many observations as you can about the potatoes tested by workers in Groups A, B, and C.

Observations	
Group A	
Group B	
Group C	

Ask a Question

1. Now that you have made your observations, state Mr. Fries's problem in the form of a question that can be answered by your experiment.

Form a Hypothesis

2. Form a hypothesis based on your observations and your questions. The hypothesis should be a statement about what causes the potatoes not to be crisp and fresh. Based on your hypothesis, make a prediction about the outcome of your experiment. State your prediction in an if-then format.

Test the Hypothesis

3. Once you have made a prediction, design your investigation. Check your experimental design with your teacher before you begin. Mr. Fries will give you potato pieces, water, salt, and no more than six containers.

4. Keep very accurate records. Write your plan and procedure. Make data tables. To be sure your data is accurate, measure all materials carefully and make drawings of the potato pieces before and after the experiment.

Analyze the Results

1. **Explaining Events** Explain what happened to the potato cells in Groups A, B, and C in your experiment. Include a discussion of the cell membrane and the process of osmosis.

Draw Conclusions

2. **Analyzing Results** Write a letter to Mr. Fries that explains your experimental method, results, and conclusion. Then, make a recommendation about how he should handle the potatoes so that they will stay fresh and crisp.

102   Chapter 4   The Cell in Action

Chapter Lab   103

Holt Science & Technology provides a strong and flexible lab program that meets lab science requirements, regardless of lab equipment limits or time restrictions.

Chapter Labs—**Inquiry Labs, Skills Practice Labs,** and **Model Making Labs**—include clear procedures, demonstrate scientific concepts, and help develop students' understanding of scientific methods. All labs have been classroom-tested and reviewed for reliability, safety, and efficiency. Labs are rated in the *Teacher Edition,* making it easy for you to select labs that are appropriate for your classroom.

Video Labs (on videotape or DVD) demonstrate the **Chapter Labs,** making it easy for you to integrate more experiments into your lessons without the preparation time and costs of a traditional laboratory setup. **Video Labs** can also provide reinforcement and reteaching opportunities for students.

LabBook provides additional experiments at the end of the *Student Edition,* giving you even more full-length labs to choose from.

Datasheets for all **Quick Labs, Chapter Labs,** and **LabBook Labs** are available in the *Chapter Resource Files.*

Making Rain

Do you have the power to make rain? Yes!—on a small scale. In this activity, you will cause water to change state in the same way that rain is formed. This process is one way that water is reused on Earth.

Start-Up Activity is an engaging activity at the beginning of the chapter that motivates students to learn.

Diaphragm Demo

1. Place your hand under your rib cage to feel your

Quick Lab is easy to execute and requires minimal time and materials—great for an in-class activity, teacher demonstration, or group presentation.

How You Measure Matters

Measure the length and width of a desk or table, but do not use a ruler. Pick

School-to-Home Activity provides an opportunity for parents or guardians to get involved with student learning. These activities require little or no equipment and do not require safety precautions.

INTERNET ACTIVITY

For another activity related to this chapter, go to **go.hrw.com** and type in the keyword **HL5INTW.**

Internet Activity sends students online for a variety of projects, such as creating scientist biographies and writing science articles.

Language Arts ACTIVITY

WRITING SKILL Write your own short story about a mysterious to the reade but do not the story. Be

Social Studies ACTIVITY

WRITING SKILL Research a location where there is forest fires. forests or pa about the is of the debat

Math ACTIVITY

In space flight, astronauts experience changes in gravity that affect their bodies in several ways. Because of gravity, a person who has a mass of 50 kg weighs 110 pounds on Earth. But on the

Cross-Disciplinary Activity gives students the opportunity to see how science relates to social studies, language arts, or mathematics.

Teach

Demonstration —— BASIC

Cell Walls and Cell Membranes

Using a stick and your own hand, you can illustrate the difference between a rigid cell

You can also integrate additional activities from the *Teacher Edition* into your lessons— **Activity, Group Activity, Connection Activity, Demonstration,** and **Homework.**

Lab options for every need

Calculator-Based Labs
for use with graphing calculators, probes, and computers

Whiz-Bang Demonstrations

Labs You Can Eat

Inquiry Labs

EcoLabs

Long-term Projects

Holt Science & Technology provides a variety of additional meaningful activities that are cost effective and fun. A variety of ancillary materials complement and complete your presentations.

Calculator-Based Labs integrate calculator use into science labs, providing a link to help students develop mathematics skills. **20 labs in all!**

Whiz-Bang Demonstrations include compelling demonstrations that students will enjoy—proving that learning science can be fun, as well as meaningful. **65 labs in all!**

Labs You Can Eat spark student interest, while explaining important scientific concepts. **25 labs in all!**

Inquiry Labs introduce students to the world of science inquiry and foster the skills necessary to develop hands-on science literacy. **23 labs in all!**

EcoLabs & Field Activities provide students with ideas for exploring the world of science outside the classroom. **23 labs in all!**

Long-Term Projects and Research Ideas help students think about science as a long-term process. Students are encouraged to study topics they find intriguing and to construct their own types of investigation. **2 for every chapter!**

Materials ordering made easy

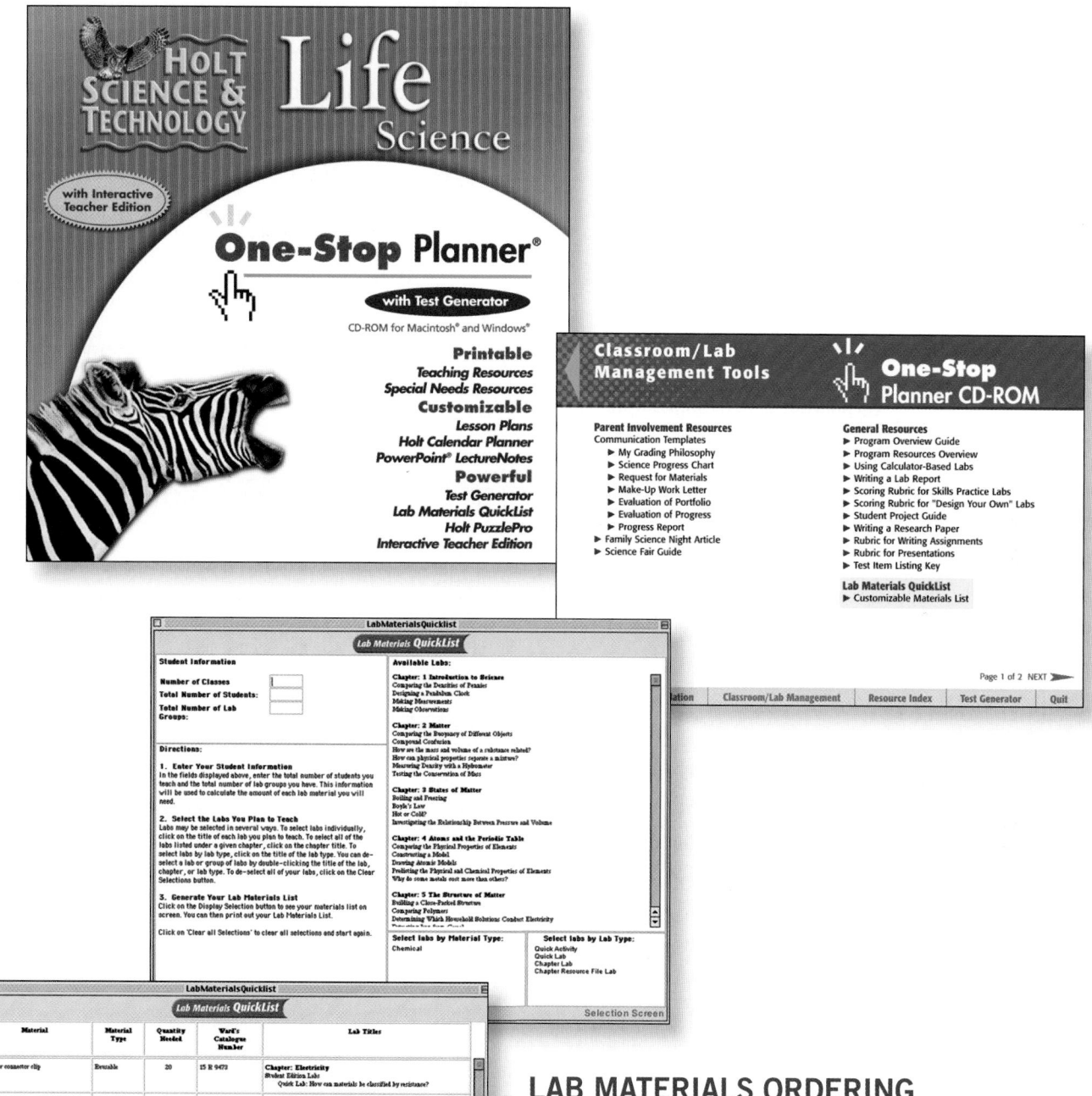

LAB MATERIALS ORDERING

Now it's easier to order your laboratory materials!

Lab Materials QuickList Software saves you time:

- See all materials needed for in-text labs.
- Create a customized list of materials.
- Quickly create a list of the items you need.
- Find everything conveniently located on the *One-Stop Planner CD-ROM.*

Meeting Individual Needs

Students have a wide range of abilities and learning exceptionalities. These pages show you how *Holt Science & Technology* provides resources and strategies to help you tailor your instruction to engage every student in your classroom. Furthermore, activities in the *Teacher Edition* are labeled with one or more learning styles designed to engage a variety of skills and strengths in every student.

LS Visual activities emphasize learning through pictures, colors, and shapes.

LS Verbal activities emphasize learning through words.

LS Logical activities emphasize learning through patterns, reason, or numbers.

LS Kinesthetic activities emphasize learning through physical activity and touch.

LS Auditory activities emphasize learning through sound.

LS Interpersonal activities emphasize learning through interactions with others.

LS Intrapersonal activities emphasize learning through independent work and reflection.

Learning exceptionality	Inclusion Strategies and Activities	
Learning Disabilities and Slow Learners Students who have dyslexia or dysgraphia, students reading below grade level, students having difficulty understanding abstract or complex concepts, and slow learners	• Inclusion Strategies labeled *Learning Disabled* • Activities and Alternative Assessments labeled *Basic* • *Reteaching* activities	• Activities labeled *Visual, Kinesthetic, or Auditory* • Hands-on activities or projects • Oral presentations instead of written tests or assignments
Developmental Delays Students who are functioning far below grade level because of mental retardation, autism, or brain injury; goals are to learn or retain basic concepts	• Inclusion Strategies labeled *Developmentally Delayed* • Activities and Alternative Assessments labeled *Basic*	• *Reteaching* activities • Project-based activities
Attention Deficit Disorders Students experiencing difficulty completing a task that has multiple steps, difficulty handling long assignments, or difficulty concentrating without sensory input from physical activity	• Inclusion Strategies labeled *Attention Deficit Disorder* • Activities and Alternative Assessments labeled *Basic* • *Reteaching* activities • Activities labeled *Co-op Learning*	• Activities labeled *Visual, Kinesthetic, or Auditory* • Concepts broken into small chunks • Oral presentations instead of written tests or assignments
English as a Second Language Students learning English	• Activities labeled *English-Language Learners* • Activities labeled *Basic*	• *Reteaching* activities • Activities labeled *Visual*
Gifted and Talented Students who are performing above grade level and demonstrate aptitude in crosscurricular assignments	• Inclusion Strategies labeled *Gifted and Talented* • Activities and Alternative Assessments labeled *Advanced*	• *Connection* activities • Activities that involve multiple tasks, a strong degree of independence, and student initiative
Hearing Impairments Students who are deaf or who have difficulty hearing	• Inclusion Strategies labeled *Hearing Impaired* • Activities labeled *Visual*	• Activities labeled *Co-op Learning* • Assessments that use written presentations
Visual Impairments Students who are blind or who have difficulty seeing	• Inclusion strategies labeled *Visually Impaired* • Activities labeled *Auditory*	• Activities labeled *Co-op Learning* • Assessments that use oral presentations
Behavior Control Issues Students learning to manage their behavior	• Inclusion Strategies labeled *Behavior Control Issues* • Activities labeled *Basic*	• Assignments that actively involve students and help students develop confidence and improved behaviors

GENERAL INCLUSION STRATEGIES

The following strategies can help you modify instruction to help students who struggle with common classroom difficulties.

A student experiencing difficulty with...	May benefit if you...	
Beginning assignments	• Assign work in small amounts • Have the student use cooperative or paired learning • Provide varied and interesting activities	• Allow choice in assignments or projects • Reinforce participation • Seat the student closer to you
Following directions	• Gain the student's attention before giving directions • Break up the task into small steps • Give written directions rather than oral directions • Use short, simple phrases	• Stand near the student when you are giving directions • Have the student repeat directions to you • Prepare the student for changes in activity • Give visual cues by posting general routines • Reinforce improvement in or approximation of following directions
Keeping track of assignments	• Have the student use folders for assignments • Have the student use assignment notebooks	• Have the student keep a checklist of assignments and highlight assignments when they are turned in
Reading the textbook	• Provide outlines of the textbook content • Reduce the length of required reading • Allow extra time for reading • Have the students read aloud in small groups	• Have the student use peer or mentor readers • Have the student use books on tape or CD • Discuss the content of the textbook in class after reading
Staying on task	• Reduce distracting elements in the classroom • Provide a task-completion checklist • Seat the student near you	• Provide alternative ways to complete assignments, such as oral projects taped with a buddy
Behavioral or social skills	• Model the appropriate behaviors • Establish class rules, and reiterate them often • Reinforce positive behavior • Assign a mentor as a positive role model to the student • Contract with the student for expected behaviors • Reinforce the desired behaviors or any steps toward improvement	• Separate the student from any peer who stimulates the inappropriate behavior • Provide a "cooling off" period before talking with the student • Address academic/instructional problems that may contribute to disruptive behaviors • Include parents in the problem-solving process through conferences, home visits, and frequent communication
Attendance	• Recognize and reinforce attendance by giving incentives or verbal praise • Emphasize the importance of attendance by letting the student know that he or she was missed when he or she was absent	• Encourage the student's desire to be in school by planning activities that are likely to be enjoyable, giving the student a preferred responsibility to be performed in class, and involving the student in extracurricular activities • Schedule problem-solving meeting with parents, faculty, or both
Test-taking skills	• Prepare the student for testing by teaching ways to study in pairs, such as using flashcards, practice tests, and study guides, and by promoting adequate sleep, nourishment, and exercise • Decrease visual distraction by improving the visual design of the test through use of larger type, spacing, consistent layout, and shorter sentences	• During testing, allow the student to respond orally on tape or to respond using a computer; to use notes; to take breaks; to take the test in another location; to work without time constraints; or to take the test in several short sessions

Reading features that foster understanding

Holt Science & Technology makes instruction accessible to all students—advanced learners, students having difficulty mastering content, and those needing more practice or hands-on experiences.

Every page begins with a new head, making the text easy to navigate and more accessible.

Each section begins with a Reading Warm-up that lists objectives and terms covered in the section. This feature helps students focus on the content being presented and understand what they read.

Reading Strategy helps students better understand what they read. Strategies provided include the following: **Reading Organizer, Prediction Guide, Discussion, Paired Summarizing, Brainstorming, and Mnemonics.**

Key Terms are highlighted in yellow and defined in the margin, helping students increase their science vocabulary.

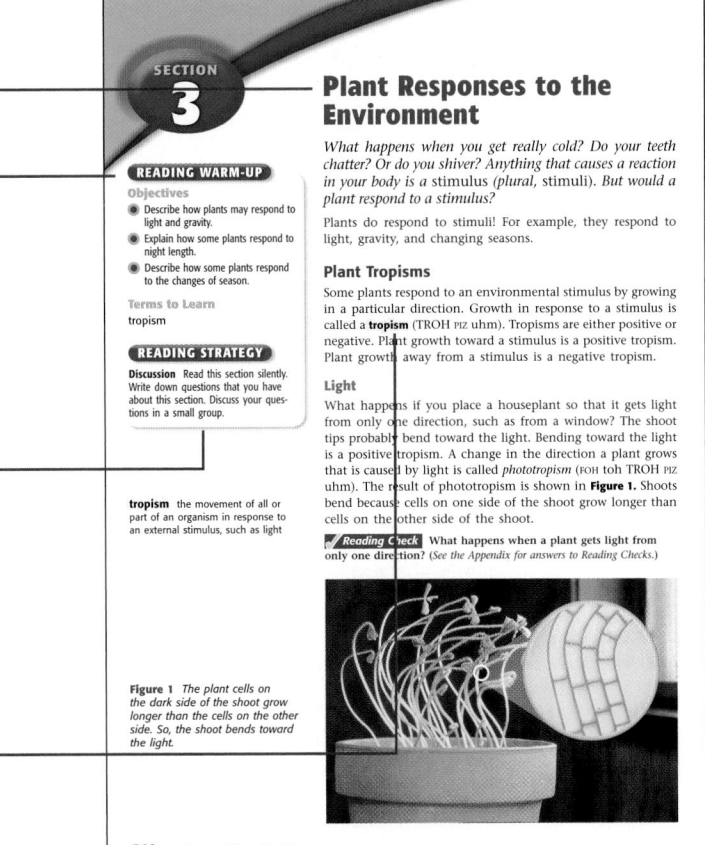

SECTION 3

Plant Responses to the Environment

What happens when you get really cold? Do your teeth chatter? Or do you shiver? Anything that causes a reaction in your body is a stimulus (plural, stimuli). But would a plant respond to a stimulus?

Plants do respond to stimuli! For example, they respond to light, gravity, and changing seasons.

Plant Tropisms

Some plants respond to an environmental stimulus by growing in a particular direction. Growth in response to a stimulus is called a **tropism** (TROH PIZ uhm). Tropisms are either positive or negative. Plant growth toward a stimulus is a positive tropism. Plant growth away from a stimulus is a negative tropism.

Light

What happens if you place a houseplant so that it gets light from only one direction, such as from a window? The shoot tips probably bend toward the light. Bending toward the light is a positive tropism. A change in the direction a plant grows that is caused by light is called *phototropism* (FOH toh TROH PIZ uhm). The result of phototropism is shown in **Figure 1.** Shoots bend because cells on one side of the shoot grow longer than cells on the other side of the shoot.

Reading Check What happens when a plant gets light from only one direction? (*See the Appendix for answers to Reading Checks.*)

READING WARM-UP

Objectives
- Describe how plants may respond to light and gravity.
- Explain how some plants respond to night length.
- Describe how some plants respond to the changes of season.

Terms to Learn
tropism

READING STRATEGY

Discussion Read this section silently. Write down questions that you have about this section. Discuss your questions in a small group.

tropism the movement of all or part of an organism in response to an external stimulus, such as light

Figure 1 The plant cells on the dark side of the shoot grow longer than the cells on the other side. So, the shoot bends toward the light.

340   Chapter 13   Plant Processes

PRE-READING ACTIVITY

FOLDNOTES **Booklet** Before you read the chapter, create the FoldNote entitled "Booklet" described in the **Study Skills** section of the Appendix. Label each page of the booklet with a main idea from the chapter. As you read the chapter, write what you learn about each main idea on the appropriate page of the booklet.

READING STRATEGY

Reading Organizer As you read this section, create an outline of the section. Use the headings from the section in your outline.

READ FOR UNDERSTANDING

Each chapter provides suggestions to help your students read for understanding.

- **Pre-Reading Activity** provides **FoldNotes** or **Graphic Organizer** activities to help students organize information presented in the chapter. Students are encouraged to take notes and then categorize what they read. In addition, the **Appendix** provides complete instruction on how to create and use the reading strategies suggested in pre-reading activities.

- **Reading Check** provides students with opportunities to check their comprehension as they read. Answers are included in the **Appendix.**

- Additional **Reading Strategies** in the *Teacher Edition* emphasize key concepts in order to guide reading and ensure comprehension.

- **Standardized Test Preparation** enables students to test their comprehension skills by reading a passage and answering a series of questions in a standardized test format. Practice is included at the end of each chapter and a blackline master of the test is located in the *Chapter Resource Files.*

ADDITIONAL RESOURCES HELP STUDENTS DEVELOP READING COMPREHENSION SKILLS.

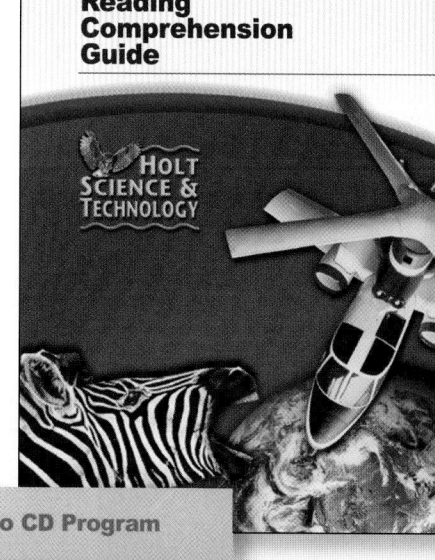

Reading Comprehension Guide includes **Directed Reading Worksheets** and **Vocabulary** and **Section Summary Worksheets** that make reading an active process.

- **Directed Reading Worksheets** guide students through each section and focus their attention on key elements. Available in two levels: Basic and Special Needs.

- **Vocabulary** and **Section Summary** worksheets help students review vocabulary words and provide a bulleted list of main topics from each section.

Reinforcement Worksheets, found in the *Chapter Resource Files,* make reviewing and reinforcing chapter content easy.

Guided Reading Audio CD Program, a direct reading of the student text, is helpful to students who benefit from different learning modalities. Available in English and Spanish.

Special Needs Workbook provides special needs directed reading worksheets and special needs **Chapter Tests** to give special needs students additional practice opportunities.

HOLT SCIENCE SKILLS WORKSHOP: READING IN THE CONTENT AREA

Target the reading skills specific to the comprehension of science texts with these activities and exercises. Students learn to analyze text structures, recognize patterns, and organize information in ways that help them construct meaning.

Linking science to other disciplines

Science does not occur in a vacuum. It is an integral part of the human quest to understand the world. Connection features help students become more aware of the interconnectedness of their school studies and prepare them for standardized testing.

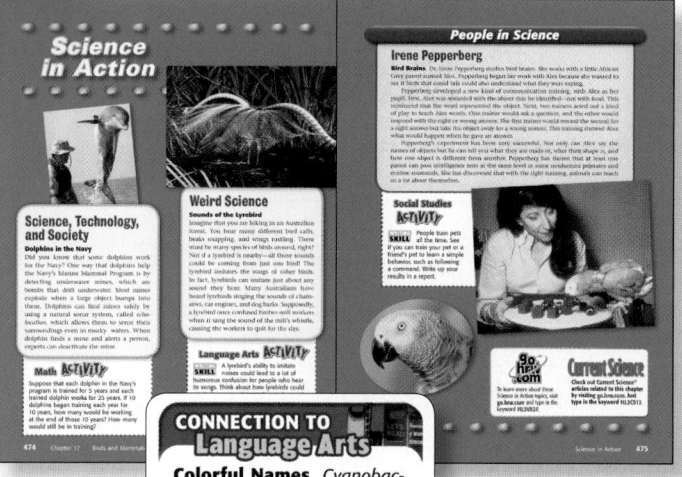

Science in Action features provide short articles designed to spark students' interest in science topics. Cross-Disciplinary activities including social studies, language arts, and math activities are also included for each article. Students can extend their learning by visiting **go.hrw.com.**

Connection to Language Arts links science with various language arts skills.

Holt Anthology of Science Fiction connects science to literature with interesting and relevant stories.

Writing Skills icon occurs in any activity that requires students to practice their writing skills.

WRITING SKILL

Connection to Social Studies links science to social studies, presenting students with opportunities to see how science relates to history, geography, and wider society concerns.

Connection to Science links various sciences to explain phenomena in the natural world. This feature provides students with opportunities to recognize and explore important links to sciences such as environmental science, geology, physics, and oceanography.

CONNECTION TO Language Arts

Colorful Names *Cyanobacteria* means "blue bacteria." Many other names also refer to colors. You might not recognize these colors because the words for the colors are in another language. Look at the list of Greek color words below. Write down two English words that have one of the color roots in them. (Hint: Many words have the color as the first part of the word.)

melano = black

chloro = green

erythro = red

leuko = white

CONNECTION TO Chemistry

Round and Wrinkled Round seeds may look better, but wrinkled seeds taste sweeter. The dominant a[llele] causes sugar to be changed into starch (v[...] ecule for sugar). This change makes the s[...] the genotype *rr* do not make or store this [...] sugar has not been changed into starch, t[...] you had a pea plant with round seeds (*R[...]*) it with to get some offspring with wrinkle[d ...] square showing your cross.

CONNECTION TO Social Studies

Disease and History Many diseases have shaped history. For example, yellow fe[ver] which is caused by a [...] is spread by mosquito[...] one of the obstacles i[...] ing the Panama Canal[...] after people learned h[...] prevent the spread of [...] low fever virus could [...] be completed.

Use information fro[m ...] net and library researc[h ...] create a poster describ[ing ...] one infectious disease [...] history.

ACTIVITY

CONNECTION ACTIVITY Earth Science — GENERAL

Ancient Mountains Provide a large wall map of the world, and provide map pins o[r] tacks in three colors. Have students locate the following mountain ranges on a map. Have students place pins on the map for each range to match the eras when each range was formed. Use the following list for reference:

CONNECTION to Math — GENERAL

Energy Loss There are 12,000 units of the sun's energy available to grass, which occupies the base of an energy pyramid. Grass stores this 10% of available energy in its tissues. This energy becomes available to the next consumer, a prairie dog. In turn, the prairie dog, a consumer of grass, stores 10% of the energy that was stored in the grass. A coyote, a consumer of prairie dogs, stores 10% of the energy that was stored in the prairie dog. Calculate the units of food energy stored in the grass, the prairie dog, and the

dian (New [...] rth

(western [...]

urope),

ADDITIONAL MATH CONNECTIONS

Math Practice provides practice in simple mathematical computations. Students can hone math skills by using the exercises provided in this feature.

Math Focus feature links mathematics directly to the science being presented. Problems are solved to show students the natural links between these two disciplines. Following the solved problem, students are presented with an application that checks their understanding.

Math Activity in **Science in Action** provides additional integrated exposure to mathematics problems.

Math Skills problem is presented in most Section Reviews, providing additional math practice.

Standardized Test Preparation tests students' math abilities with questions in a standardized test format. Practice is included at the end of each chapter, and a blackline master is located in the *Chapter Resource Files.*

Math Refresher, found in the **Appendix**, reviews basic math skills such as averages, ratios, percentages, and more.

Math Skills for Science helps students develop and apply basic math skills to scientific problems.

Averages

Finding the average, or mean, of a group of numbers is a common way to analyze data.

For example, three seeds were kept at 25°C and sprouted in 8, 8, and 5 days. To find the average number of days that it took the seed to sprout, add 8, 8, and 5

MATH FOCUS

Probability If you roll a pair of dice, what is the probability that you will roll 2 threes?

Step 1: Count the number of faces on a single die. Put this number in the denominator: 6.

Step 2: Count how many ways you can roll a three with one die. Put this number in the numerator: 1/6.

Step 3: To find the probability that you will throw 2 threes, multiply the probability of throwing the first three by the probability of throwing the second three: $1/6 \times 1/6 = 1/36$.

Now It's Your Turn

If you roll a single die, what is the probability that you will roll an even number?

Math ACTIVITY

Suppose that each dolphin in the Navy's program is trained for 5 years and each trained dolphin works for 25 years. If 10 dolphins began training each year for 10 years, how many would be working at the end of those 10 years? How m would still be in training?

Math Skills

9. A certain toad species spends 2 months of its life as a tadpole and 3 years of its life as an adult. What percentage of its life is spent in the water? What percentage is spent on land?

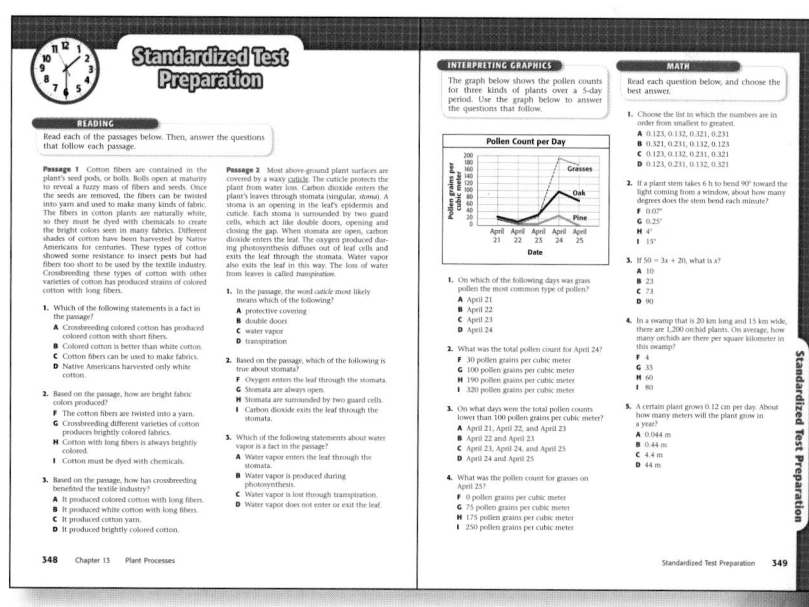

Science and Math Skills Worksheets

The **Holt Science & Technology** program helps you meet the needs of a wide variety of students, regardless of their skill level. The following pages provide examples of the worksheets available to improve your students' science and math skills whether they already have a strong science and math background or are weak in these areas. Samples of assessment checklists and rubrics are also provided.

In addition to the skills worksheets represented here, **Holt Science & Technology** provides a variety of worksheets that are correlated directly with each chapter of the program. Representations of these worksheets are found at the beginning of each chapter in this *Teacher Edition*.

Many worksheets are also available on the Holt Web site. The address is **go.hrw.com**.

Science Skills Worksheets: Thinking Skills

BEING FLEXIBLE

USING YOUR SENSES

THINKING OBJECTIVELY

UNDERSTANDING BIAS

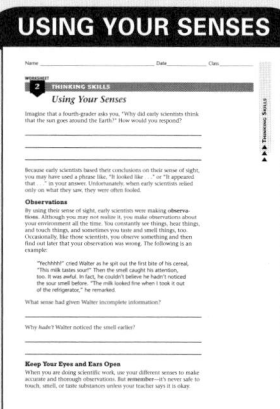
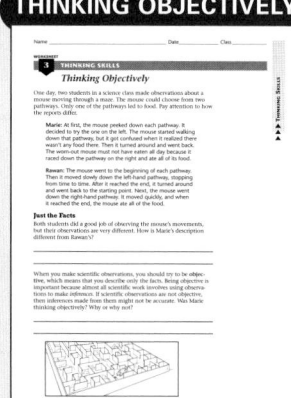
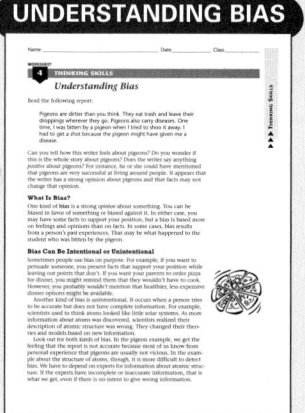

USING LOGIC

BOOSTING YOUR MEMORY

IMPROVING YOUR STUDY HABITS

READING A SCIENCE TEXTBOOK

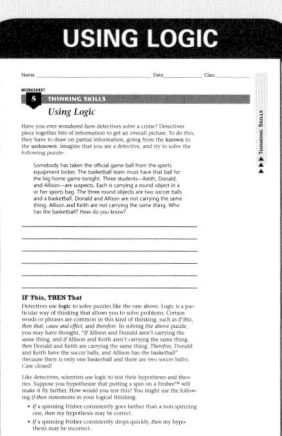
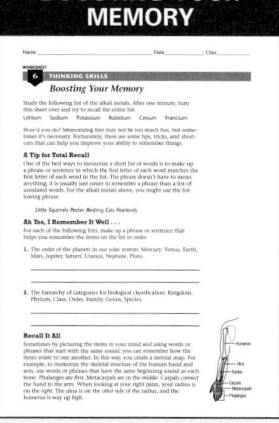
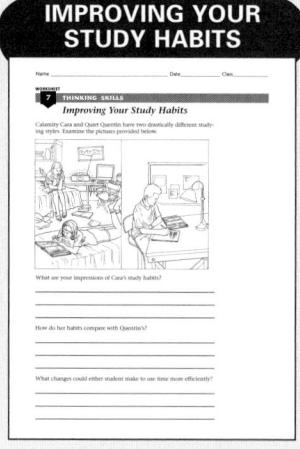
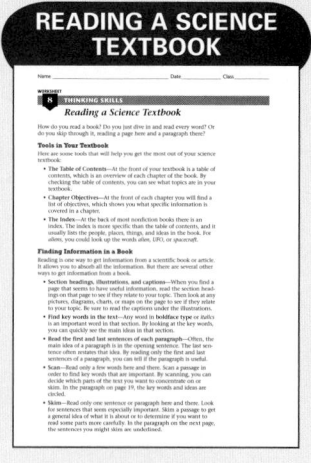

Science Skills Worksheets: Experimenting Skills

SAFETY RULES!
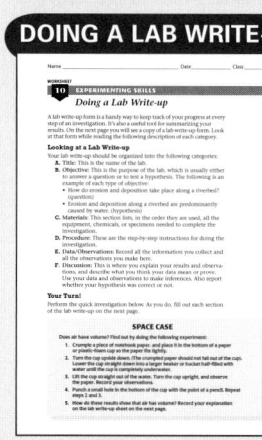

DOING A LAB WRITE-UP
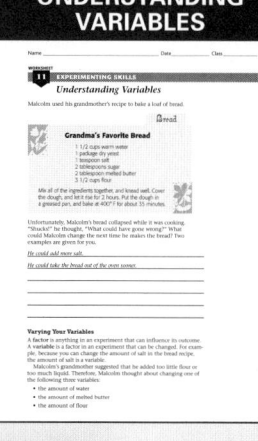

UNDERSTANDING VARIABLES

WORKING WITH HYPOTHESES
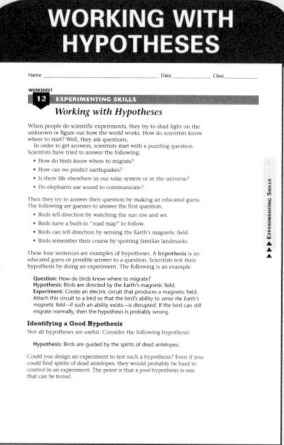

DESIGNING AN EXPERIMENT
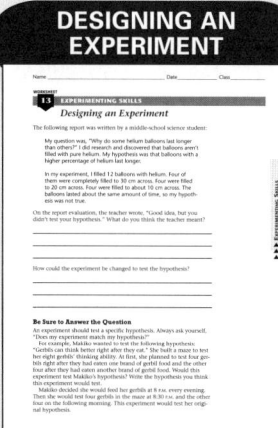

USING THE INTERNATIONAL SYSTEM OF UNITS (SI)
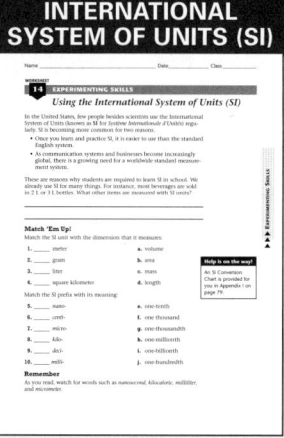

MEASURING
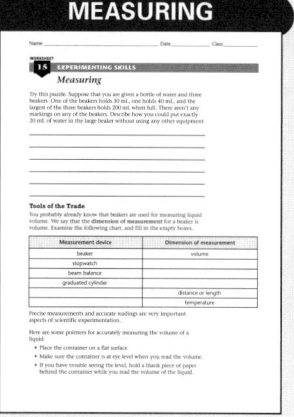

Science Skills Worksheets: Researching Skills

CHOOSING YOUR TOPIC
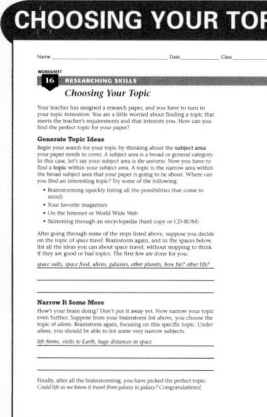

ORGANIZING YOUR RESEARCH
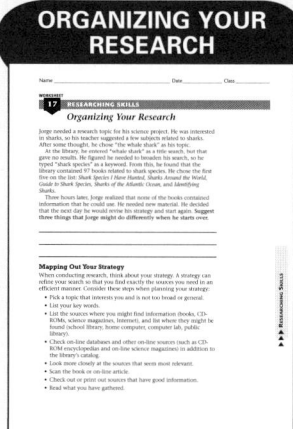

FINDING USEFUL SOURCES
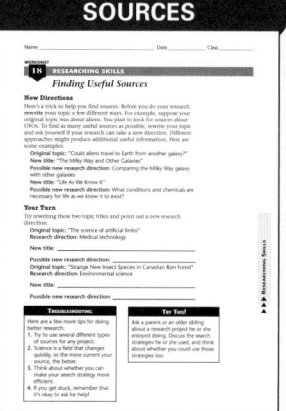

RESEARCHING ON THE WEB
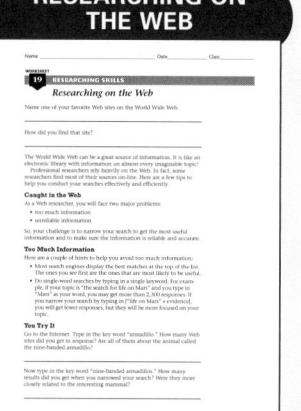

Science Skills Worksheets: Researching Skills (continued)

IDENTIFYING BIAS

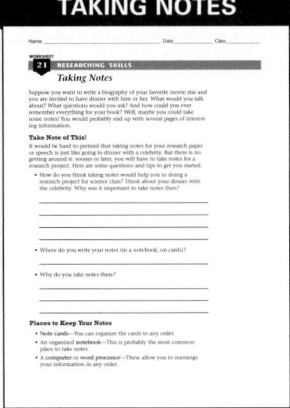

TAKING NOTES

Science Skills Worksheets: Communicating Skills

SCIENCE WRITING

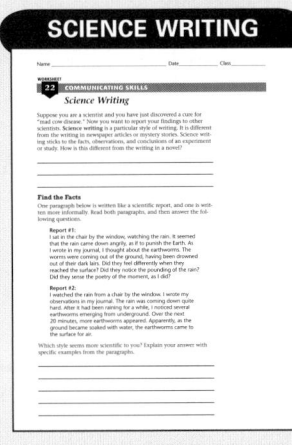

SCIENCE DRAWING

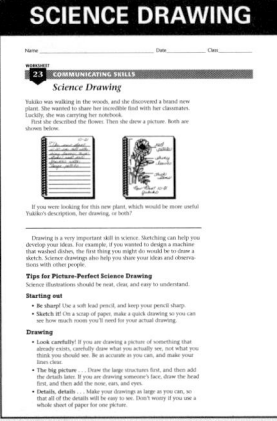

USING MODELS TO COMMUNICATE

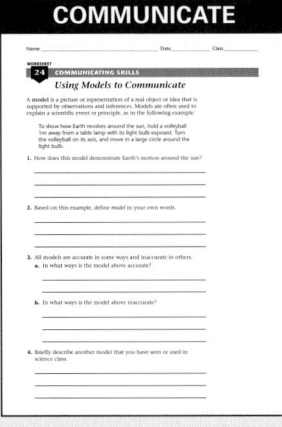

INTRODUCTION TO GRAPHS

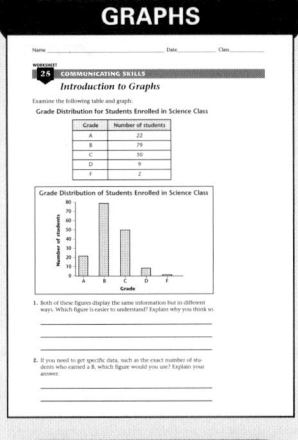

GRASPING GRAPHING

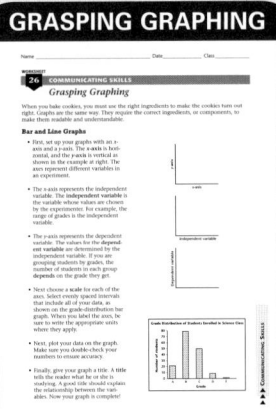

INTERPRETING YOUR DATA

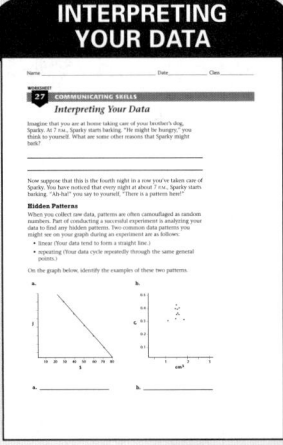

RECOGNIZING BIAS IN GRAPHS

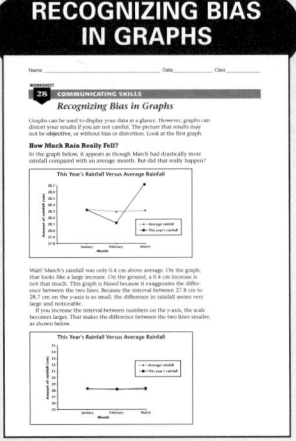

MAKING DATA MEANINGFUL

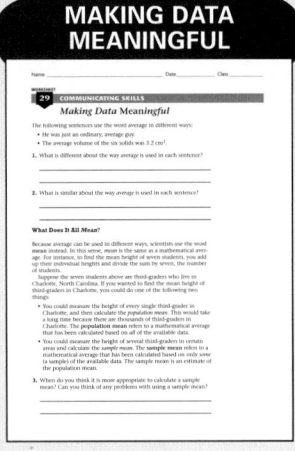

HINTS FOR ORAL PRESENTATIONS

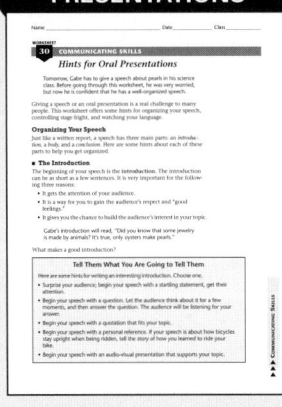

Math Skills for Science

ADDITION AND SUBTRACTION

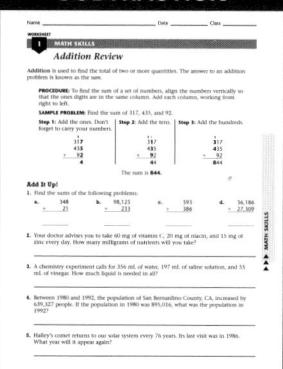

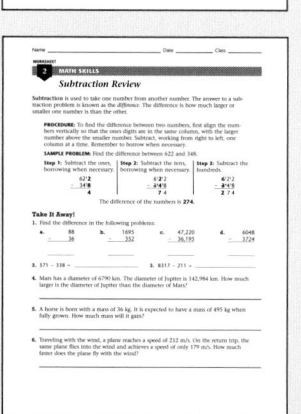

MULTIPLICATION

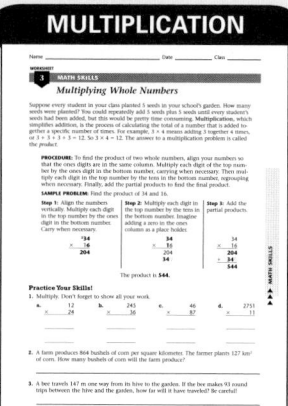

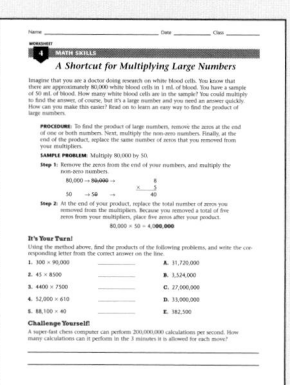

DIVISION

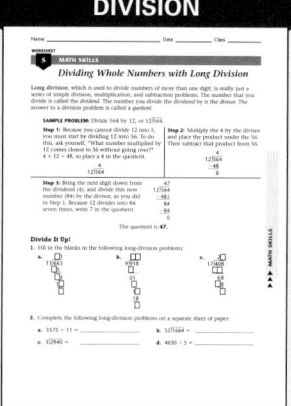

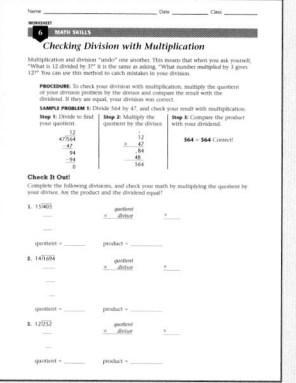

AVERAGES

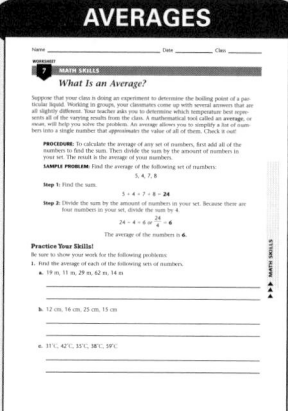

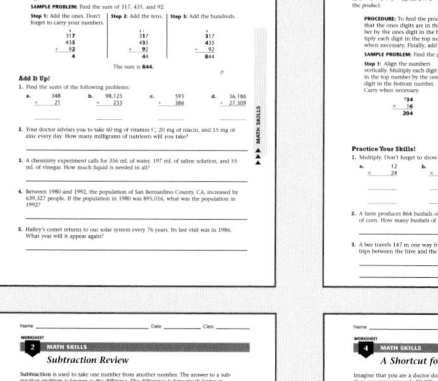

POSITIVE AND NEGATIVE NUMBERS

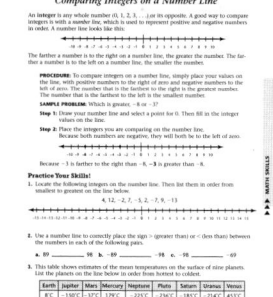

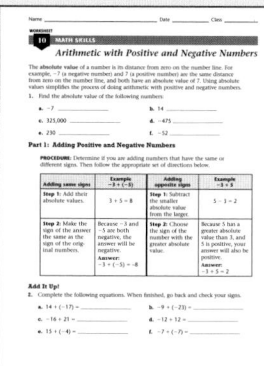

FRACTIONS

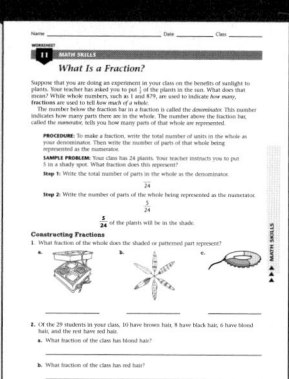

Math Skills for Science (continued)

RATIOS AND PROPORTIONS

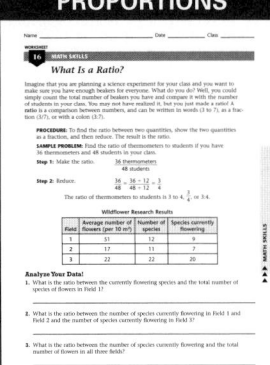

DECIMALS

PERCENTAGES

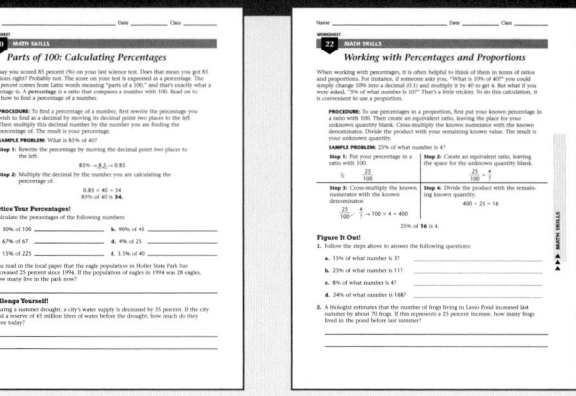

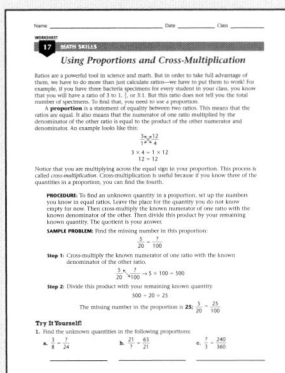

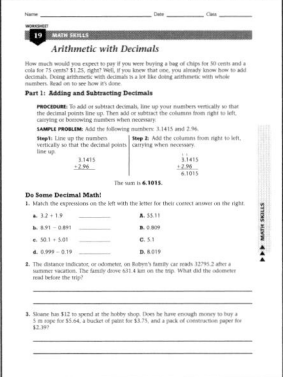

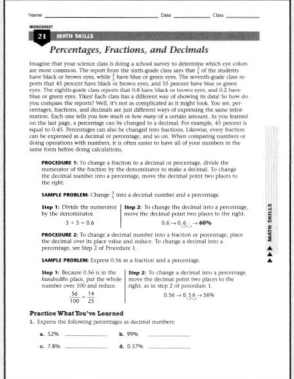

POWERS OF 10

SCIENTIFIC NOTATION

SI MEASUREMENT AND CONVERSION

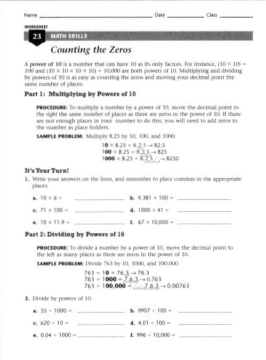

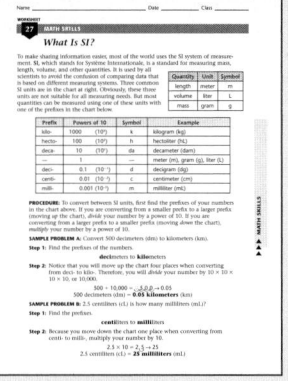

Math Skills for Science (continued)

GEOMETRY

THE UNIT FACTOR AND DIMENSIONAL ANALYSIS

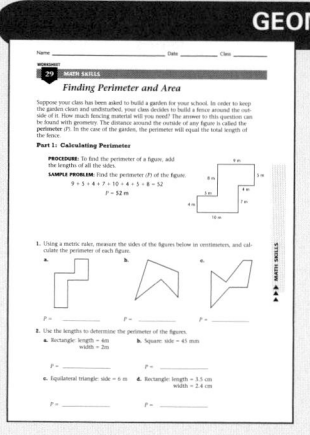

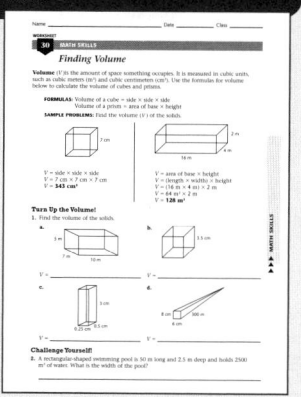

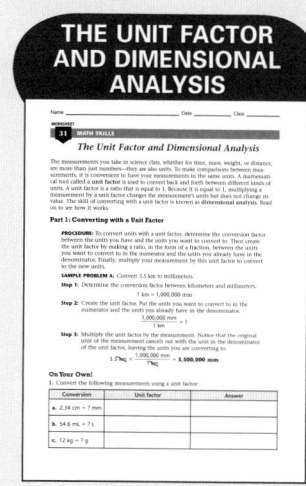

MATH IN SCIENCE: INTEGRATED SCIENCE

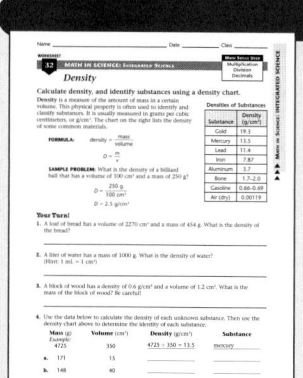

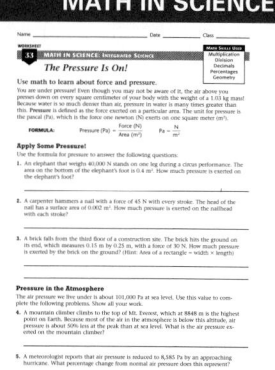

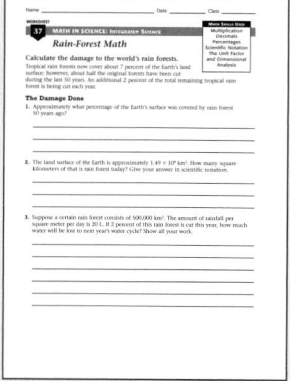

Math Skills for Science (continued)

MATH IN SCIENCE: LIFE SCIENCE

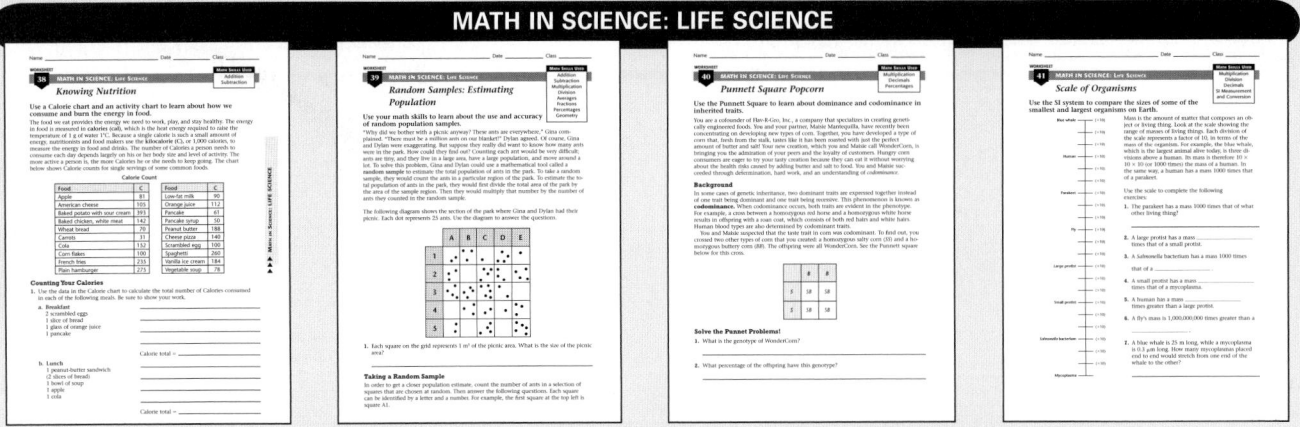

38 — MATH IN SCIENCE: LIFE SCIENCE
Knowing Nutrition

39 — MATH IN SCIENCE: LIFE SCIENCE
Random Samples: Estimating Population

40 — MATH IN SCIENCE: LIFE SCIENCE
Punnett Square Popcorn

41 — MATH IN SCIENCE: LIFE SCIENCE
Scale of Organisms

MATH IN SCIENCE: EARTH SCIENCE

42 — MATH IN SCIENCE: EARTH SCIENCE
Sedimentation in the Grand Canyon

43 — MATH IN SCIENCE: EARTH SCIENCE
Earthquake Power!

44 — MATH IN SCIENCE: EARTH SCIENCE
Distances in Space

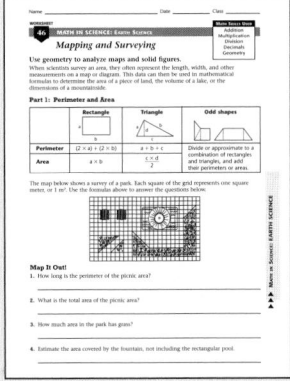

45 — MATH IN SCIENCE: EARTH SCIENCE
Geologic Time Scale

46 — MATH IN SCIENCE: EARTH SCIENCE
Mapping and Surveying

Math Skills for Science (continued)

MATH IN SCIENCE: PHYSICAL SCIENCE

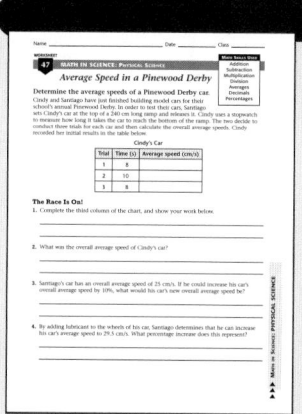

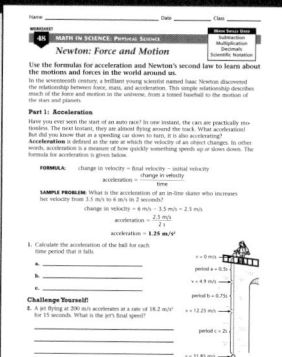

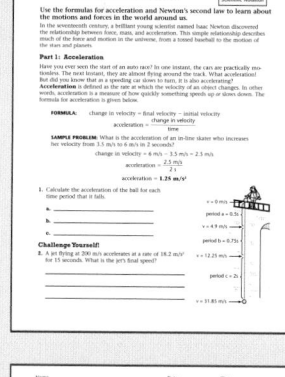

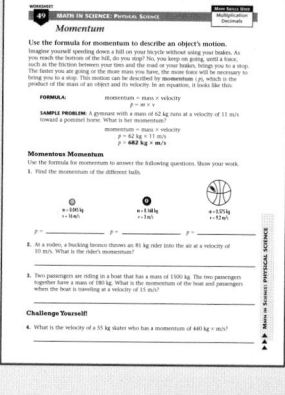

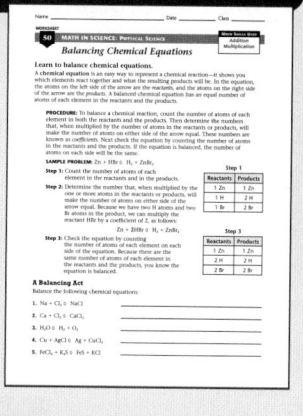

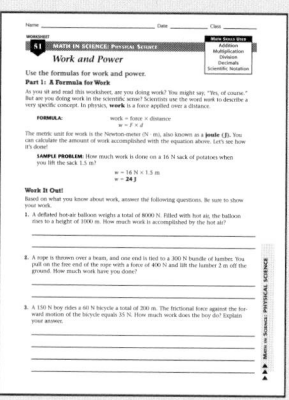

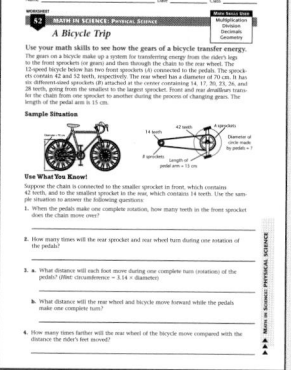

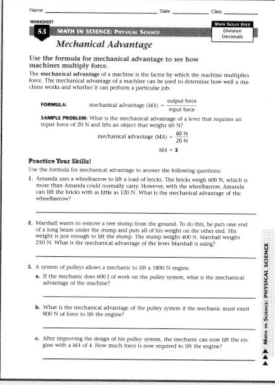

Assessment Checklist & Rubrics

The following is just a sample of over 50 checklists and rubrics contained in this booklet.

RUBRICS FOR WRITTEN WORK

RUBRIC FOR EXPERIMENTS

TEACHER EVALUATION OF COOPERATIVE LEARNING

TEACHER EVALUATION OF STUDENT PROGRESS

Pacing and Compression Guide

Pacing Each **Chapter Planning Guide** breaks down the chapter into instructional blocks. Each instructional block consists of sections and labs that you can cover in 45 or 90 minutes. The **Chapter Planning Guide** also lists activities, demonstrations, and resources that are available to accompany each section.

12 Introduction to Plants
Chapter Planning Guide

Compression guide: To shorten instruction because of time limitations, omit Section 4.

OBJECTIVES	LABS, DEMONSTRATIONS, AND ACTIVITIES	TECHNOLOGY RESOURCES
PACING • 90 min pp. 298–303 **Chapter Opener**	SE **Start-up Activity,** p. 299 ◆ GENERAL	OSP **Parent Letter** ■ GENERAL CD **Student Edition on CD-ROM** TR **Chapter Starter Transparency*** CD **Guided Reading Audio CD** ■ VID **Brain Food Video Quiz**
Section 1 What Is a Plant? • Identify four characteristics that all plants share. • Describe the four main groups of plants. • Explain the origin of plants.	TE **Activity** Water Travel in Plants, p. 300 GENERAL TE **Group Activity** Baby-Powder Cuticle, p. 301 GENERAL TE **Activity** Life Cycles, p. 301 ADVANCED	CRF **Lesson Plans*** TR **Bellringer Transparency*** TR **The Main Groups of Plants*** CRF **SciLinks Activity*** GENERAL CD **Interactive Explorations CD-ROM** Shut Your Trap! GENERAL
PACING • 45 min pp. 304–307 **Section 2 Seedless Plants** • List three nonvascular plants and three seedless vascular plants. • Explain how seedless plants are important to the environment. • Describe the relationship between seedless vascular plants and coal.	TE **Activity** Identifying Plant Parts, p. 304 ◆ GENERAL SE **Quick Lab** Moss Mass, p. 305 GENERAL CRF **Datasheet for Quick Lab*** TE **Connection Activity** Real World, p. 305 GENERAL SE **Science in Action** Math, Social Studies, and Language Arts Activities, pp. 328–329 GENERAL	CRF **Lesson Plans*** TR **Bellringer Transparency***
PACING • 45 min pp. 308–313 **Section 3 Seed Plants** • Describe three ways that seed plants differ from seedless plants. • Describe the structure of seeds. • Compare angiosperms and gymnosperms. • Explain the economic and environmental importance of gymnosperms and angiosperms.	TE **Activity** Seed Types, p. 308 GENERAL SE **Quick Lab** Dissecting Seeds, p. 309 GENERAL TE **Group Activity** Seed Dispersal, p. 309 ◆ GENERAL TE **Connection Activity** Earth Science, p. 310 ADVANCED SE **Skills Practice Lab** Travelin' Seeds, p. 776 ◆ GENERAL LB **EcoLabs & Field Activities** The Case of the Ravenous Radish* ◆ GENERAL LB **Long-Term Projects & Research Ideas** Plant Planet ADVANCED	CRF **Lesson Plans*** TR **Bellringer Transparency*** TR **Two Classes of Angiosperms*** TE **Internet Activity,** p. 312 GENERAL
PACING • 90 min pp. 314–321 **Section 4 Structures of Seed Plants** • List three functions of roots and three functions of stems. • Describe the structure of a leaf. • Identify the parts of a flower and their functions.	TE **Demonstration** Roots, p. 314 ◆ GENERAL TE **Group Activity** Root Growth, p. 315 ◆ BASIC TE **Activity** Stem Functions, p. 316 BASIC TE **Connection Activity** History, p. 316 ADVANCED TE **Group Activity** Modeling Stems, p. 317 ◆ BASIC TE **Activity** Analyzing Tree Rings, p. 317 GENERAL SE **School-to-Home Activity** Looking at Leaves, p. 318 GENERAL TE **Group Activity** Leaf Collecting, p. 318 GENERAL SE **Model-Making Lab** Build a Flower, p. 322 ◆ GENERAL SE **Skills Practice Lab** Leaf Me Alone!, p. 774 GENERAL LB **Whiz-Bang Demonstrations** Inner Life of a Leaf* ◆ BASIC	CRF **Lesson Plans*** TR **Bellringer Transparency*** TR **The Structures of a Root*** TR **Cross Section of an Herbaceous Stem; Cross Section of a Woody Stem*** TR **The Structure of a Leaf*** TR ***LINK TO EARTH SCIENCE*** The Electromagnetic Spectrum*** TR **The Structure of a Flower*** VID **Lab Videos for Life Science**

PACING • 90 min

CHAPTER REVIEW, ASSESSMENT, AND STANDARDIZED TEST PREPARATION

CRF **Vocabulary Activity*** GENERAL
SE **Chapter Review,** pp. 324–325 GENERAL
CRF **Chapter Review*** ■ GENERAL
CRF **Chapter Tests A*** GENERAL, **B*** ADVANCED, **C*** SPECIAL NEEDS
SE **Standardized Test Preparation,** pp. 326–327 GENERAL
CRF **Standardized Test Preparation*** GENERAL
CRF **Performance-Based Assessment*** GENERAL
OSP **Test Generator** GENERAL
CRF **Test Item Listing*** GENERAL

Online and Technology Resources

Visit **go.hrw.com** for a variety of free resources related to this textbook. Enter the keyword **HL5PL1.**

Students can access interactive problem-solving help and active visual concept development with the *Holt Science and Technology* Online Edition available at www.hrw.com.

Guided Reading Audio CD

A direct reading of each chapter using instructional visuals as guideposts. For auditory learners, reluctant readers, and Spanish-speaking students. Available in English and Spanish.

297A   Chapter 12 · Introduction to Plants

Assessment
Each chapter includes enough chapter assessment material to fill two 45-minute periods.

Compression In many cases, a chapter contains more material than you will have time to teach. The Compression Guide in each **Chapter Planning Guide** suggests sections or labs you can omit if you are short on time. The sections or labs that can be omitted often contain advanced material. You may wish to also consider using the material suggested for omission as extension material for advanced students.

KEY		
SE Student Edition	**CRF** Chapter Resource File	**SS** Science Skills Worksheets
TE Teacher Edition	**OSP** One-Stop Planner	**MS** Math Skills for Science Worksheets
	LB Lab Bank	**CD** CD or CD-ROM
	TR Transparencies	**VID** Classroom Video/DVD

* Also on One-Stop Planner
♦ Requires advance prep
■ Also available in Spanish

SKILLS DEVELOPMENT RESOURCES	SECTION REVIEW AND ASSESSMENT	STANDARDS CORRELATIONS
SE Pre-Reading Activity, p. 298 GENERAL **OSP Science Puzzlers, Twisters & Teasers** GENERAL		National Science Education Standards SAI 1, 2; LS 1c, 3a
CRF Directed Reading A* ■ BASIC, **B*** SPECIAL NEEDS **CRF Vocabulary and Section Summary*** ■ GENERAL **SE Reading Strategy** Reading Organizer, p. 300 GENERAL **SE Connection to Social Studies** Countries and Crops, p. 301 GENERAL	**SE Reading Checks,** pp. 301, 302, 303 GENERAL **TE Homework,** p. 301 GENERAL **TE Reteaching,** p. 302 BASIC **TE Quiz,** p. 302 GENERAL **TE Alternative Assessment,** p. 302 ADVANCED **SE Section Review,*** p. 303 ■ GENERAL **CRF Section Quiz*** ■ GENERAL	UCP 1, 2, 4; SAI 1, 2; ST 2; HNS 2; LS 1a, 2b, 4c, 5a
CRF Directed Reading A* ■ BASIC, **B*** SPECIAL NEEDS **CRF Vocabulary and Section Summary*** ■ GENERAL **SE Reading Strategy** Paired Summarizing, p. 304 GENERAL **TE Inclusion Strategies,** p. 306 ♦ **SE Connection to Language Arts** Selling Plants, p. 307 GENERAL	**SE Reading Checks,** pp. 305, 307 GENERAL **TE Reteaching,** p. 306 BASIC **TE Quiz,** p. 306 GENERAL **TE Alternative Assessment,** p. 306 GENERAL **TE Homework,** p. 306 GENERAL **SE Section Review,*** p. 307 ■ GENERAL **CRF Section Quiz*** ■ GENERAL	UCP 1, 2, 3, 4; SAI 1; LS 1a, 1c, 2b, 5c
CRF Directed Reading A* ■ BASIC, **B*** SPECIAL NEEDS **CRF Vocabulary and Section Summary*** ■ GENERAL **SE Reading Strategy** Reading Organizer, p. 308 GENERAL **SE Connection to Environmental Science** Animals That Help Plants, p. 309 GENERAL **TE Inclusion Strategies,** p. 311 **SS Science Skills** Science Writing* GENERAL **CRF Reinforcement Worksheet** Classifying Plants* GENERAL **CRF Reinforcement Worksheet** Drawing Dicots* GENERAL	**SE Reading Checks,** pp. 308, 309, 311, 312, 313 GENERAL **TE Homework,** p. 310 ADVANCED **TE Reteaching,** p. 312 BASIC **TE Quiz,** p. 312 GENERAL **TE Alternative Assessment,** p. 312 ADVANCED **SE Section Review,*** p. 313 ■ GENERAL **CRF Section Quiz*** ■ GENERAL	UCP 1, 2, 4; SAI 1; SPSP 4; LS 1a, 1d, 2b, 2c, 2d, 4b, 4c, 4d, 5b; *LabBook:* UCP 2, 5; SAI 1, 2; LS 2b
CRF Directed Reading A* ■ BASIC, **B*** SPECIAL NEEDS **CRF Vocabulary and Section Summary*** ■ GENERAL **SE Reading Strategy** Mnemonics, p. 314 GENERAL **SE Math Practice** Practice with Percentages, p. 315 GENERAL **SS Science Skills** Taking Notes* GENERAL **CRF Critical Thinking** The Voodoo Lily* ADVANCED	**SE Reading Checks,** pp. 315, 316, 318, 320 GENERAL **TE Homework,** p. 319 GENERAL **SE Section Review,*** p. 320 ■ GENERAL **TE Reteaching,** p. 320 BASIC **TE Quiz,** p. 320 GENERAL **TE Alternative Assessment,** p. 320 GENERAL **CRF Section Quiz*** ■ GENERAL	UCP 1, 2, 4; SAI 1; SPSP 5; LS 1a, 1d, 2b, 3d, 4c, 5b; *Chapter Lab:* UCP 1, 2, 5; SAI 1, 2; ST 2; HNS 1, 2; LS 1a, 2a, 2b; *LabBook:* UCP 1, 5; SAI 1

⚡ One-Stop Planner® CD-ROM

This convenient CD-ROM includes:
- Lab Materials QuickList Software
- Holt Calendar Planner
- Customizable Lesson Plans
- Printable Worksheets
- ExamView® Test Generator

CNN student News™

cnnstudentnews.com

Find the latest news, lesson plans, and activities related to important scientific events.

SCiLINKS.
NSTA

www.scilinks.org

Maintained by the **National Science Teachers Association.** See Chapter Enrichment pages for a complete list of topics.

Current Science®

Check out *Current Science* articles and activities by visiting the HRW Web site at go.hrw.com. Just type in the keyword **HL5CS12T.**

Classroom Videos
- **Lab Videos** demonstrate the chapter lab.
- **Brain Food Video Quizzes** help students review the chapter material.

Chapter 12 • Chapter Planning Guide 297B

Safety in your laboratory

RISK ASSESSMENT

MAKING YOUR LABORATORY A SAFE PLACE TO WORK AND LEARN

Concern for safety must begin before any activity in the classroom and before students enter the lab. A careful review of the facilities should be a basic part of preparation for each school term. You should investigate the physical environment, identify any safety risks, and inspect your work areas for compliance with safety regulations.

The review of the lab should be thorough, and all safety issues must be addressed immediately. Keep a file of your review, and add to the list each year. This will allow you to continue to raise the standard of safety in your lab and classroom.

Many classroom experiments, demonstrations, and other activities are classics that have been used for years. This familiarity may lead to a comfort that can obscure inherent safety concerns. Review all experiments, demonstrations, and activities for safety concerns before presenting them to the class. Identify and eliminate potential safety hazards.

1. **Identify the Risks**

   Before introducing any activity, demonstration, or experiment to the class, analyze it and consider what could possibly go wrong. Carefully review the list of materials to make sure they are safe. Inspect the equipment in your lab or classroom to make sure it is in good working order. Read the procedures to make sure they are safe. Record any hazards or concerns you identify.

2. **Evaluate the Risks**

   Minimize the risks you identified in the last step without sacrificing learning. Remember that no activity you perform in the lab or classroom is worth risking injury. Thus, extremely hazardous activities, or those that violate your school's policies, must be eliminated. For activities that present smaller risks, analyze each risk carefully to determine its likelihood. If the pedagogical value of the activity does not outweigh the risks, the activity must be eliminated.

3. **Select Controls to Address Risks**

   Even low-risk activities require controls to eliminate or minimize the risks. Make sure that in devising controls you do not substitute an equally or more hazardous alternative. Some control methods include the following:

   - Explicit verbal and written warnings may be added or posted.
   - Equipment may be rebuilt or relocated, parts may be replaced, or equipment be replaced entirely by safer alternatives.
   - Risky procedures may be eliminated.
   - Activities may be changed from student activities to teacher demonstrations.

4. **Implement and Review Selected Controls**

   Controls do not help if they are forgotten or not enforced. The implementation and review of controls should be as systematic and thorough as the initial analysis of safety concerns in the lab and laboratory activities.

SOME SAFETY RISKS AND PREVENTATIVE CONTROLS

The following list describes several possible safety hazards and controls that can be implemented to resolve them. This list is not complete, but it can be used as a starting point to identify hazards in your laboratory.

Identified risk	Preventative control
Facilities and Equipment	
Lab tables are in disrepair, room is poorly lighted and ventilated, faucets and electrical outlets do not work or are difficult to use because of their location.	Work surfaces should be level and stable. There should be adequate lighting and ventilation. Water supplies, drains, and electrical outlets should be in good working order. Any equipment in a dangerous location should not be used; it should be relocated or rendered inoperable.
Wiring, plumbing, and air circulation systems do not work or do not meet current specifications.	Specifications should be kept on file. Conduct a periodic review of all equipment, and document compliance. Damaged fixtures must be labeled as such and must be repaired as soon as possible.
Eyewash fountains and safety showers are present, but no one knows anything about their specifications.	Ensure that eyewash fountains and safety showers meet the requirements of the ANSI standard (Z358.1).
Eyewash fountains are checked and cleaned once at the beginning of each school year. No records are kept of routine checks and maintenance on the safety showers and eyewash fountains.	Flush eyewash fountains for 5 min. every month to remove any bacteria or other organisms from pipes. Test safety showers (measure flow in gallons per min.) and eyewash fountains every 6 months and keep records of the test results.
Labs are conducted in multipurpose rooms, and equipment from other courses remains accessible.	Only the items necessary for a given activity should be available to students. All equipment should be locked away when not in use.
Students are permitted to enter or work in the lab without teacher supervision.	Lock all laboratory rooms whenever a teacher is not present. Supervising teachers must be trained in lab safety and emergency procedures.
Safety equipment and emergency procedures	
Fire and other emergency drills are infrequent, and no records or measurements are made of the results of the drills.	Always carry out critical reviews of fire or other emergency drills. Be sure that plans include alternate routes. Don't wait until an emergency to find the flaws in your plans.
Emergency evacuation plans do not include instructions for securing the lab in the event of an evacuation during a lab activity.	Plan actions in case of emergency: establish what devices should be turned off, which escape route to use, and where to meet outside the building.
Fire extinguishers are in out-of-the-way locations, not on the escape route.	Place fire extinguishers near escape routes so that they will be of use during an emergency.
Fire extinguishers are not maintained. Teachers are not trained to use them.	Document regular maintenance of fire extinguishers. Train supervisory personnel in the proper use of extinguishers. Instruct students not to use an extinguisher but to call for a teacher.

Identified risk	Preventative control
Safety equipment and emergency procedures, *continued*	
Teachers in labs and neighboring classrooms are not trained in CPR or first aid.	Teachers should receive training. The American Red Cross and other groups offer training. Certifications should be kept current with frequent refresher courses.
Teachers are not aware of their legal responsibilities in case of an injury or accident.	Review your faculty handbook for your responsibilities regarding safety in the classroom and laboratory. Contact the legal counsel for your school district to find out the extent of their support and any rules, regulations, or procedures you must follow.
Emergency procedures are not posted. Emergency numbers are kept only at the switchboard or main office. Instructions are given verbally only at the beginning of the year.	Emergency procedures should be posted at all exits and near all safety equipment. Emergency numbers should be posted at all phones, and a script should be provided for the caller to use. Emergency procedures must be reviewed periodically, and students should be reminded of them at the beginning of each activity.
Spills are handled on a case-by-case basis and are cleaned up with whatever materials happen to be on hand.	Have the appropriate equipment and materials available for cleaning up; replace them before expiration dates. Make sure students know to alert you to spilled chemicals, blood, and broken glass.
Work habits and environment	
Safety wear is only used for activities involving chemicals or hot plates.	Aprons and goggles should be worn in the lab at all times. Long hair, loose clothing, and loose jewelry should be secured.
There is no dress code established for the laboratory; students are allowed to wear sandals or open-toed shoes.	Open-toed shoes should never be worn in the laboratory. Do not allow any footwear in the lab that does not cover feet completely.
Students are required to wear safety gear, but teachers and visitors are not.	Always wear safety gear in the lab. Keep extra equipment on hand for visitors.
Safety is emphasized at the beginning of the term but is not mentioned later in the year.	Safety must be the first priority in all lab work. Students should be warned of risks and instructed in emergency procedures for each activity.
There is no assessment of students' knowledge and attitudes regarding safety.	Conduct frequent safety quizzes. Only students with perfect scores should be allowed to work in the lab.
You work alone during your preparation period to organize the day's labs.	Never work alone in a science laboratory or a storage area.
Safety inspections are conducted irregularly and are not documented. Teachers and administrators are unaware of what documentation will be necessary in case of a lawsuit.	Safety reviews should be frequent and regular. All reviews should be documented, and improvements must be implemented immediately. Contact legal counsel for your district to make sure your procedures will protect you in case of a lawsuit.

Identified risk	Preventative control
Purchasing, storing, and using chemicals	
The storeroom is too crowded, so you decide to keep some equipment on the lab benches.	Do not store reagents or equipment on lab benches and keep shelves organized. Never place reactive chemicals (in bottles, beakers, flasks, wash bottles, etc.) near the edges of a lab bench.
You prepare solutions from concentrated stock to save money.	Reduce risks by ordering diluted instead of concentrated substances.
You purchase plenty of chemicals to be sure that you won't run out or to save money.	Purchase chemicals in class-size quantities. Do not purchase or have on hand more than one year's supply of each chemical.
You don't generally read labels on chemicals when preparing solutions for a lab because you already know about a chemical.	Read each label to be sure it states the hazards and describes the precautions and first aid procedures (when appropriate) that apply to the contents in case someone else has to deal with that chemical in an emergency.
You never read the Material Safety Data Sheets (MSDSs) that come with your chemicals.	Always read the Material Safety Data Sheet (MSDS) for a chemical before using it and follow the precautions described. File and organize MSDSs for all chemicals where they can be found easily in case of an emergency.
The main stockroom contains chemicals that haven't been used for years.	Do not leave bottles of chemicals unused on the shelves of the lab for more than one week or unused in the main stockroom for more than one year. Dispose of or use up any leftover chemicals.
No extra precautions are taken when flammable liquids are dispensed from their containers.	When transferring flammable liquids from bulk containers, ground the container, and before transferring to a smaller metal container, ground both containers.
Students are told to put their broken glass and solid chemical wastes in the trash can.	Have separate containers for trash, for broken glass, and for different categories of hazardous chemical wastes.
You store chemicals alphabetically instead of by hazard class. Chemicals are stored without consideration of possible emergencies (fire, earthquake, flood, etc.), which could compound the hazard.	Use MSDSs to determine which chemicals are incompatible. Store chemicals by the hazard class indicated on the MSDS. Store chemicals that are incompatible with common fire-fighting media like water (such as alkali metals) or carbon dioxide (such as alkali and alkaline-earth metals) under conditions that eliminate the possibility of a reaction with water or carbon dioxide if it is necessary to fight a fire in the storage area.
Corrosives are kept above eye level, out of reach from anyone who is not authorized to be in the storeroom.	Always store corrosive chemicals on shelves below eye level. Remember, fumes from many corrosives can destroy metal cabinets and shelving.
Chemicals are kept on the stockroom floor on the days that they will be used so that they are easy to find.	Never store chemicals or other materials on floors or in the aisles of the laboratory or storeroom, even for a few minutes.

Safety symbols and safety guidelines for students

 **EYE PROTECTION**

- Wear safety goggles, and know where the eyewash station is located and how to use it.
- Avoid swinging objects, which can cause serious injury.
- Avoid directly looking at a light source, as this may cause permanent eye damage.

 **HAND SAFETY**

- Wear latex or nitrile gloves to protect yourself from chemicals in the lab.
- Use a hot mitt to handle resistors, light sources, and other equipment that may be hot. Allow equipment to cool before handling it and storing it.

 **CLOTHING PROTECTION**

- Wear a laboratory apron to protect your clothing.
- Tie back long hair, secure loose clothing, and remove loose jewelry to prevent their getting caught in moving parts or coming in contact with chemicals.

 **HEATING SAFETY**

- When using a Bunsen burner or a hot plate, always wear safety goggles and a laboratory apron to protect your eyes and clothing. Tie back long hair, secure loose clothing, and remove loose jewelry.
- Never leave a hot plate unattended while it is turned on.
- If your clothing catches on fire, walk to the emergency lab shower, and use the shower to put out the fire.
- Wire coils may heat up rapidly during experiments. If heating occurs, open the switch immediately, and handle the equipment with a hot mitt.
- Allow all equipment to cool before storing it.

CHEMICAL SAFETY

- Do not eat or drink anything in the lab. Never taste chemicals.
- If a chemical gets on your skin or clothing or in your eyes, rinse it immediately with lukewarm water, and alert your teacher.
- If a chemical is spilled, tell your teacher, but do not clean it up yourself unless your teacher says it is OK to do so.

ELECTRICAL SAFETY

- Never close a circuit until it has been approved by your teacher. Never rewire or adjust any element of a closed circuit.
- Never work with electricity near water; be sure the floor and all work surfaces are dry.
- If the pointer of any kind of meter moves off the scale, open the circuit immediately by opening the switch.
- Light bulbs or wires that are conducting electricity can become very hot.
- Do not work with any batteries, electrical devices, or magnets other than those provided by your teacher.

ANIMAL SAFETY

- Handle animals only as directed by your teacher.
- Always treat animals carefully and with respect.
- Wash your hands thoroughly after handling any animal.

PLANT SAFETY

- Wash your hands thoroughly after handling any part of a plant.

SHARP/POINTED OBJECTS

- Use knives and other sharp instruments with extreme care.
- Do not cut an object while holding it in your hands. Instead, place it on a suitable work surface for cutting.

National Science Education Standards

The following lists show the chapter correlation of *Holt Science & Technology: Life Science* with the *National Science Education Standards* (grades 5–8).

The chapter correlations for the Life Science Content Standards begin on page T45.

Unifying Concepts and Processes

Standard	Chapter Correlation			
Systems, order, and organization Code: UCP 1	Chapter 1	1.1	Chapter 15	15.1, 15.2
	Chapter 2	2.1	Chapter 16	16.1, 16.2, 16.3
	Chapter 3	3.2, 3.3	Chapter 17	17.1
	Chapter 4	4.1, 4.2	Chapter 18	18.2, 18.3
	Chapter 5	5.1	Chapter 19	19.1, 19.2
	Chapter 6	6.2	Chapter 22	22.1, 22.3
	Chapter 7	7.2, 7.3	Chapter 23	23.1, 23.2, 23.3, 23.4
	Chapter 8	8.1, 8.2	Chapter 24	24.1, 24.2
	Chapter 9	9.1	Chapter 25	25.1, 25.3
	Chapter 10	10.1, 10.3	Chapter 26	26.2, 26.3
	Chapter 12	12.1, 12.2, 12.3, 12.4	Chapter 27	27.2
	Chapter 13	13.1, 13.3	Chapter 28	28.1
	Chapter 14	14.1, 14.2, 14.3		
Evidence, models, and explanation Code: UCP 2	Chapter 1	1.2, 1.3	Chapter 15	15.2, 15.3
	Chapter 2	2.1, 2.2	Chapter 16	16.3
	Chapter 3	3.3	Chapter 17	17.1
	Chapter 4	4.1	Chapter 20	20.1, 20.2, 20.3
	Chapter 5	5.1, 5.2	Chapter 21	21.2
	Chapter 6	6.1	Chapter 22	22.2, 22.3
	Chapter 7	7.1, 7.2	Chapter 23	23.1, 23.4
	Chapter 8	8.1, 8.2, 8.3	Chapter 24	24.1, 24.2
	Chapter 10	10.2, 10.3	Chapter 25	25.1, 25.2
	Chapter 12	12.1, 12.2, 12.3, 12.4	Chapter 26	26.3
	Chapter 13	13.1, 13.2, 13.3	Chapter 27	27.2
Change, constancy, and measurement Code: UCP 3	Chapter 1	1.2, 1.3, 1.4	Chapter 16	16.1
	Chapter 3	3.1	Chapter 19	19.1, 19.2
	Chapter 4	4.1, 4.2	Chapter 20	20.2, 20.3
	Chapter 5	5.2	Chapter 21	21.1, 21.2
	Chapter 7	7.3	Chapter 22	22.1, 22.2, 22.3, 22.4
	Chapter 8	8.2	Chapter 23	23.1
	Chapter 10	10.1, 10.2	Chapter 24	24.2
	Chapter 12	12.2	Chapter 25	25.1, 25.3
	Chapter 13	13.1, 13.2, 13.3	Chapter 26	26.3
	Chapter 14	14.2	Chapter 27	27.2
	Chapter 15	15.2, 15.3	Chapter 28	28.3

Unifying Concepts and Processes (cont.)

Standard	Chapter Correlation			
Evolution and equilibrium Code: UCP 4	Chapter 3	3.2	Chapter 18	18.3
	Chapter 4	4.1, 4.2	Chapter 19	19.1, 19.2
	Chapter 5	5.3	Chapter 20	20.1, 20.3
	Chapter 6	6.2	Chapter 21	21.2
	Chapter 7	7.1, 7.2, 7.3	Chapter 22	22.1, 22.3
	Chapter 8	8.1, 8.2, 8.3	Chapter 23	23.4
	Chapter 10	10.2	Chapter 24	24.2
	Chapter 12	12.1, 12.2, 12.3, 12.4	Chapter 25	25.1, 25.2, 25.3
	Chapter 13	13.1, 13.2	Chapter 27	27.2
	Chapter 15	15.1	Chapter 28	28.1
Form and function Code: UCP 5	Chapter 3	3.1, 3.2, 3.3	Chapter 15	15.1, 15.2, 15.3, 15.4
	Chapter 4	4.2	Chapter 16	16.1, 16.2, 16.3
	Chapter 5	5.3	Chapter 17	17.1, 17.2, 17.3, 17.4, 17.5
	Chapter 6	6.1, 6.2		
	Chapter 7	7.1, 7.2	Chapter 20	20.1
	Chapter 8	8.3	Chapter 22	22.2, 22.4
	Chapter 9	9.2	Chapter 23	23.1, 23.3, 23.4
	Chapter 10	10.1, 10.2, 10.3	Chapter 24	24.1, 24.2
	Chapter 11	11.1, 11.2, 11.3	Chapter 25	25.1, 25.2
	Chapter 13	13.1, 13.2	Chapter 26	26.2
	Chapter 14	14.2	Chapter 27	27.2

Science as Inquiry

Standard	Chapter Correlation			
Abilities necessary to do scientific inquiry Code: SAI 1	Chapter 1	1.1, 1.2, 1.3, 1.4	Chapter 14	14.1, 14.2, 14.3
	Chapter 3	3.1	Chapter 16	16.1, 16.2, 16.3
	Chapter 4	4.1, 4.2, 4.3	Chapter 18	18.1, 18.2
	Chapter 5	5.1, 5.3	Chapter 19	19.1
	Chapter 6	6.1, 6.2	Chapter 20	20.1, 20.2, 20.3
	Chapter 7	7.2	Chapter 21	21.1, 21.2
	Chapter 8	8.1, 8.2, 8.3	Chapter 22	22.2, 22.3
	Chapter 9	9.2	Chapter 24	24.1, 24.2
	Chapter 10	10.1, 10.3	Chapter 25	25.1, 25.2
	Chapter 11	11.3	Chapter 26	26.2, 26.3
	Chapter 12	12.1, 12.2, 12.3, 12.4	Chapter 27	27.1, 27.2
	Chapter 13	13.1, 13.2, 13.3	Chapter 28	28.1, 28.2, 28.3
Understandings about scientific inquiry Code: SAI 2	Chapter 1	1.1, 1.2, 1.3, 1.4	Chapter 12	12.1
	Chapter 2	2.2	Chapter 13	13.1, 13.2, 13.3
	Chapter 3	3.1	Chapter 15	15.3
	Chapter 4	4.2	Chapter 18	18.1
	Chapter 5	5.1	Chapter 19	19.1, 19.2
	Chapter 6	6.1, 6.2	Chapter 20	20.2
	Chapter 7	7.1, 7.2	Chapter 21	21.1
	Chapter 8	8.1, 8.3	Chapter 22	22.3, 22.4
	Chapter 9	9.1	Chapter 24	24.1, 24.2
	Chapter 10	10.3	Chapter 25	25.1
	Chapter 11	11.1	Chapter 27	27.1

Science and Technology

Standard	Chapter Correlation					
Abilities of technological design Code: ST 1	Chapter 1	1.4			Chapter 10	10.2
	Chapter 6	6.1			Chapter 20	20.1
	Chapter 8	8.3				
Understandings about science and technology Code: ST 2	Chapter 1	1.1, 1.3, 1.4	Chapter 6	6.1, 6.2	Chapter 21	21.1, 21.2
	Chapter 3	3.1	Chapter 8	8.3	Chapter 26	26.3
	Chapter 4	4.2	Chapter 10	10.2	Chapter 27	27.1
	Chapter 5	5.1	Chapter 12	12.1		

Science in Personal Perspectives

Standard	Chapter Correlation					
Personal health Code: SPSP 1	Chapter 1	1.1			Chapter 24	24.1
	Chapter 4	4.2			Chapter 25	25.1
	Chapter 22	22.2, 22.3, 22.4			Chapter 26	26.2
	Chapter 23	23.1, 23.2			Chapter 28	28.1, 28.2, 28.3
Populations, resources, and environments Code: SPSP 2	Chapter 1	1.1, 1.2			Chapter 19	19.1, 19.2
	Chapter 7	7.2			Chapter 20	20.1, 20.2, 20.3
	Chapter 13	13.3			Chapter 21	21.1, 21.2
	Chapter 18	18.1, 18.2				
Natural hazards Code: SPSP 3	Chapter 13	13.1, 13.3			Chapter 20	20.1
	Chapter 19	19.2			Chapter 21	21.1
Risks and benefits Code: SPSP 4	Chapter 1	1.1	Chapter 12	12.3	Chapter 23	23.1
	Chapter 4	4.2	Chapter 13	13.2	Chapter 26	26.2
	Chapter 6	6.2	Chapter 19	19.1	Chapter 28	28.1, 28.2, 28.3
	Chapter 7	7.3	Chapter 21	21.1, 21.2		
	Chapter 10	10.3	Chapter 22	22.2		
Science and technology in society Code: SPSP 5	Chapter 1	1.1, 1.2, 1.3	Chapter 10	10.2, 10.3	Chapter 21	21.1, 21.2
	Chapter 3	3.1	Chapter 11	11.3	Chapter 23	23.1, 23.2
	Chapter 4	4.2	Chapter 12	12.4	Chapter 27	27.1
	Chapter 5	5.1, 5.3	Chapter 13	13.3	Chapter 28	28.2, 28.3
	Chapter 6	6.1, 6.2	Chapter 17	17.5		
	Chapter 7	7.2, 7.3	Chapter 19	19.1		

History and Nature of Science

Standard	Chapter Correlation					
Science as a human endeavor Code: HNS 1	Chapter 1	1.1, 1.2, 1.3	Chapter 7	7.2	Chapter 13	13.1, 13.2
	Chapter 5	5.1	Chapter 8	8.1	Chapter 24	24.1, 24.2
	Chapter 6	6.1	Chapter 9	9.1, 9.2	Chapter 27	27.1
Nature of science Code: HNS 2	Chapter 1	1.1, 1.2, 1.3	Chapter 7	7.1, 7.2	Chapter 12	12.1
	Chapter 5	5.1, 5.3	Chapter 8	8.1, 8.3	Chapter 13	13.1, 13.3
	Chapter 6	6.1	Chapter 9	9.1, 9.2	Chapter 21	21.2
History of science Code: HNS 3	Chapter 1	1.1, 1.2, 1.3	Chapter 8	8.1, 8.3	Chapter 21	21.1
	Chapter 5	5.1, 5.3	Chapter 9	9.1	Chapter 27	27.1, 27.2
	Chapter 6	6.1	Chapter 10	10.2		
	Chapter 7	7.2	Chapter 14	14.1		

Life Science Content Standards

Structure and Function in Living Systems

Standard	Chapter Correlation			
Living systems at all levels of organization demonstrate the complementary nature of structure and function. Important levels of organization for structure and function include cells, organs, tissues, organ systems, whole organisms, and ecosystems. Code: LS 1a	**Chapter 2** 2.2 **Chapter 3** 3.1, 3.2, 3.3 **Chapter 4** 4.1 **Chapter 6** 6.1 **Chapter 8** 8.1, 8.2, 8.3 **Chapter 11** 11.2, 11.3 **Chapter 12** 12.1, 12.2, 12.3, 12.4 **Chapter 13** 13.1, 13.2 **Chapter 14** 14.1, 14.2, 14.3 **Chapter 15** 15.1, 15.2, 15.3, 15.4		**Chapter 16** 16.1, 16.2, 16.3 **Chapter 17** 17.1, 17.2, 17.3, 17.4, 17.5 **Chapter 19** 19.2 **Chapter 20** 20.1, 20.2, 20.3 **Chapter 22** 22.1 **Chapter 23** 23.3 **Chapter 24** 24.1, 24.2 **Chapter 25** 25.1, 25.2, 25.3 **Chapter 26** 26.3	
All organisms are composed of cells—the fundamental unit of life. Most organisms are single cells; other organisms, including humans, are multicellular. Code: LS 1b	**Chapter 2** 2.1 **Chapter 3** 3.1, 3.2 **Chapter 8** 8.2 **Chapter 9** 9.2		**Chapter 10** 10.1 **Chapter 11** 11.1, 11.2, 11.3 **Chapter 14** 14.1 **Chapter 27** 27.2	
Cells carry on the many functions needed to sustain life. They grow and divide, thereby producing more cells. This requires that they take in nutrients, which they use to provide energy for the work that cells do and to make the materials that a cell or an organism needs. Code: LS 1c	**Chapter 2** 2.1, 2.2 **Chapter 3** 3.1, 3.2 **Chapter 4** 4.1, 4.2, 4.3 **Chapter 5** 5.3 **Chapter 6** 6.2 **Chapter 10** 10.1 **Chapter 11** 11.1		**Chapter 12** 12.2 **Chapter 13** 13.1 **Chapter 19** 19.1 **Chapter 22** 22.4 **Chapter 23** 23.3 **Chapter 24** 24.2 **Chapter 26** 26.3	
Specialized cells perform specialized functions in multicellular organisms. Groups of specialized cells cooperate to form a tissue, such as a muscle. Different tissues are in turn grouped together and form larger functional units, called organs. Each type of cell, tissue, and organ has a distinct structure and set of functions that serve the organism as a whole. Code: LS 1d	**Chapter 2** 2.1 **Chapter 3** 3.3 **Chapter 5** 5.3 **Chapter 11** 11.3 **Chapter 12** 12.3, 12.4 **Chapter 14** 14.1 **Chapter 15** 15.1, 15.2, 15.3, 15.4 **Chapter 16** 16.1, 16.3		**Chapter 17** 17.1, 17.3, 17.4, 17.5 **Chapter 22** 22.1, 22.2, 22.3, 22.4 **Chapter 23** 23.3 **Chapter 24** 24.1, 24.2 **Chapter 25** 25.1, 25.2, 25.3 **Chapter 26** 26.2, 26.3 **Chapter 27** 27.2	
The human organism has systems for digestion, respiration, reproduction, circulation, excretion, movement, control and coordination, and protection from disease. These systems interact with one another. Code: LS 1e	**Chapter 3** 3.3 **Chapter 6** 6.2 **Chapter 22** 22.2, 22.3, 22.4 **Chapter 23** 23.3		**Chapter 24** 24.1, 24.2 **Chapter 25** 25.1, 25.2, 25.3 **Chapter 26** 26.2, 26.3 **Chapter 27** 27.2	
Disease is the breakdown in structures or functions of an organism. Some diseases are the result of intrinsic failures of the system. Others are the result of damage by infection by other organisms. Code: LS 1f	**Chapter 6** 6.2 **Chapter 9** 9.2 **Chapter 10** 10.2, 10.3 **Chapter 11** 11.1, 11.2, 11.3 **Chapter 15** 15.1, 15.3		**Chapter 22** 22.4 **Chapter 23** 23.3 **Chapter 24** 24.1, 24.2 **Chapter 26** 26.2 **Chapter 27** 27.1, 27.2	

Reproduction and Heredity

Standard	Chapter Correlation			
Reproduction is a characteristic of all living systems; because no living organism lives forever, reproduction is essential to the continuation of every species. Some organisms reproduce asexually. Others reproduce sexually. Code: LS 2a	Chapter 2 Chapter 5 Chapter 7 Chapter 9 Chapter 10 Chapter 11	2.1 5.2, 5.3 7.2, 7.3 9.2 10.1, 10.3 11.1, 11.3	Chapter 13 Chapter 14 Chapter 15 Chapter 16 Chapter 17	13.2 14.1 15.1 16.1, 16.2, 16.3 17.1, 17.3, 17.4, 17.5
In many species, including humans, females produce eggs and males produce sperm. Plants also reproduce sexually—the egg and sperm are produced in the flowers of flowering plants. An egg and sperm unite to begin development of a new individual. The individual receives genetic information from its mother (via the egg) and its father (via the sperm). Sexually produced offspring never are identical to either of their parents. Code: LS 2b	Chapter 2 Chapter 5 Chapter 6 Chapter 7 Chapter 12	2.1 5.1, 5.2, 5.3 6.2 7.2 12.1, 12.2, 12.3, 12.4	Chapter 13 Chapter 14 Chapter 16 Chapter 26	13.2, 13.3 14.1 16.3 26.3
Every organism requires a set of instructions for specifying its traits. Heredity is the passage of these instructions from one generation to another. Code: LS 2c	Chapter 2 Chapter 3 Chapter 5	2.1, 2.2 3.1 5.2, 5.3	Chapter 6 Chapter 12 Chapter 13	6.2 12.3 13.3
Hereditary information is contained in the genes, located in the chromosomes of each cell. Each gene carries a single unit of information. An inherited trait of an individual can be determined by one or by many genes, and a single gene can influence more than one trait. A human cell contains many thousands of different genes. Code: LS 2d	Chapter 4 Chapter 5 Chapter 6	4.3 5.2, 5.3 6.1, 6.2	Chapter 7 Chapter 12 Chapter 13	7.2 12.3 13.2
The characteristics of an organism can be described in terms of a combination of traits. Some traits are inherited and others result from interactions with the environment. Code: LS 2e	Chapter 5 Chapter 6 Chapter 7	5.1, 5.2 6.2 7.1, 7.2, 7.3		

Regulation and Behavior

Standard	Chapter Correlation			
All organisms must be able to obtain and use resources, grow, reproduce, and maintain stable internal conditions while living in a constantly changing external environment. Code: LS 3a	Chapter 2 Chapter 3 Chapter 7 Chapter 10 Chapter 11 Chapter 13 Chapter 14 Chapter 15 Chapter 16	2.1, 2.2 3.2 7.1 10.1 11.2 13.3 14.2 15.1, 15.2, 15.4 16.1, 16.2, 16.3	Chapter 17 Chapter 18 Chapter 20 Chapter 21 Chapter 22 Chapter 23 Chapter 24 Chapter 25 Chapter 27	17.1, 17.2, 17.3, 17.4, 17.5 18.3 20.1 21.1 22.1, 22.4 23.2 24.2 25.2 27.2

Regulation and Behavior (cont.)

Standard	Chapter Correlation			
Regulation of an organism's internal environment involves sensing the internal environment and changing physiological activities to keep conditions within the range required to survive. Code: LS 3b	Chapter 2 Chapter 3 Chapter 10 Chapter 14 Chapter 16 Chapter 17	2.1 3.1 10.1 14.2 16.1 17.1, 17.3	Chapter 22 Chapter 23 Chapter 24 Chapter 25 Chapter 27	22.4 23.1, 23.2 24.1, 24.2 25.1 27.2
Behavior is one kind of response an organism can make to an internal or environmental stimulus. A behavioral response requires coordination and communication at many levels, including cells, organ systems, and whole organisms. Behavioral response is a set of actions determined in part by heredity and in part from experience. Code: LS 3c	Chapter 2 Chapter 13 Chapter 14 Chapter 15 Chapter 16 Chapter 17	2.1 13.1, 13.3 14.2, 14.3 15.1 16.1, 16.2, 16.3 17.1, 17.2, 17.3, 17.4, 17.5	Chapter 18 Chapter 20 Chapter 25	18.3 20.1 25.1
An organism's behavior evolves through adaptation to its environment. How a species moves, obtains food, reproduces, and responds to danger are based in the species' evolutionary history. Code: LS 3d	Chapter 2 Chapter 7 Chapter 8 Chapter 12 Chapter 13	2.2 7.1, 7.2, 7.3 8.1, 8.2, 8.3 12.4 13.3	Chapter 14 Chapter 16 Chapter 18 Chapter 20	14.2, 14.3 16.2, 16.3 18.3 20.1, 20.2, 20.3

Population and Ecosystems

Standard	Chapter Correlation			
A population consists of all individuals of a species that occur together at a given place and time. All populations living together and the physical factors with which they interact compose an ecosystem. Code: LS 4a	Chapter 7 Chapter 14 Chapter 18 Chapter 20	7.1 14.3 18.1, 18.2 20.2, 20.3		
Populations of organisms can be categorized by the functions they serve in an ecosystem. Plants and some micro-organisms are producers—they make their own food. All animals, including humans, are consumers, which obtain their food by eating other organisms. Decomposers, primarily bacteria and fungi, are consumers that use waste materials and dead organisms for food. Food webs identify the relationship among producers, consumers, and decomposers in an ecosystem. Code: LS 4b	Chapter 2 Chapter 9 Chapter 10 Chapter 11 Chapter 12	2.2 9.2 10.1 11.1, 11.3 12.3	Chapter 14 Chapter 18 Chapter 19 Chapter 20	14.1 18.1, 18.2, 18.3 19.1 20.1, 20.2, 20.3
For ecosystems, the major source of energy is sunlight. Energy entering ecosystems as sunlight is transferred by producers into chemical energy through photosynthesis. That energy passes from organism to organism in food webs. Code: LS 4c	Chapter 2 Chapter 4 Chapter 9 Chapter 12 Chapter 13	2.2 4.2 9.2 12.1, 12.3, 12.4 13.1	Chapter 18 Chapter 19 Chapter 20	18.1, 18.2 19.1 20.1, 20.2, 20.3

Population and Ecosystems (cont.)

Standard	Chapter Correlation		
The number of organisms an ecosystem can support depends on the resources available and abiotic factors, such as the quantity of light and water, range of temperatures, and soil composition. Given adequate biotic and abiotic resources and no disease or predators, populations (including humans) increase at rapid rates. Lack of resources and other factors, such as predation and climate, limit the growth of populations in specific niches in the ecosystem. Code: LS 4d	**Chapter 2** 2.2 **Chapter 7** 7.3 **Chapter 12** 12.3 **Chapter 18** 18.1, 18.2, 18.3 **Chapter 19** 19.2 **Chapter 20** 20.1, 20.2, 20.3 **Chapter 21** 21.1		

Diversity and Adaptations of Organisms

Standard	Chapter Correlation		
Millions of species of animals, plants, and microorganisms are alive today. Although different species might look dissimilar, the unity among organisms becomes apparent from an analysis of internal structures, the similarity of their chemical processes, and the evidence of common ancestry. Code: LS 5a	**Chapter 3** 3.1, 3.2 **Chapter 6** 6.1 **Chapter 7** 7.1, 7.2 **Chapter 8** 8.2, 8.3 **Chapter 9** 9.1 **Chapter 11** 11.1, 11.2, 11.3 **Chapter 12** 12.1 **Chapter 14** 14.1	**Chapter 15** 15.1, 15.2, 15.3, 15.4 **Chapter 16** 16.1, 16.2, 16.3 **Chapter 17** 17.1, 17.2, 17.3, 17.4, 17.5 **Chapter 19** 19.1 **Chapter 20** 20.1	
Biological evolution accounts for the diversity of species developed through gradual processes over many generations. Species acquire many of their unique characteristics through biological adaptation, which involves the selection of naturally occurring variations in populations. Biological adaptations include changes in structures, behaviors, or physiology that enhance survival and reproductive success in a particular environment. Code: LS 5b	**Chapter 6** 6.2 **Chapter 7** 7.1, 7.2, 7.3 **Chapter 8** 8.1, 8.2, 8.3 **Chapter 9** 9.2 **Chapter 12** 12.3, 12.4	**Chapter 13** 13.2, 13.3 **Chapter 14** 14.2 **Chapter 16** 16.2, 16.3 **Chapter 17** 17.1, 17.2 **Chapter 20** 20.1	
Extinction of a species occurs when the environment changes and the adaptive characteristics of a species are insufficient to allow its survival. Fossils indicate that many organisms that lived long ago are extinct. Extinction of species is common; most of the species that have lived on Earth no longer exist. Code: LS 5c	**Chapter 7** 7.1 **Chapter 8** 8.1, 8.2, 8.3 **Chapter 12** 12.2 **Chapter 16** 16.1, 16.3 **Chapter 17** 17.5 **Chapter 21** 21.2		

HOLT SCIENCE & TECHNOLOGY

Life Science

HOLT, RINEHART AND WINSTON

A Harcourt Education Company

Orlando • Austin • New York • San Diego • Toronto • London

Acknowledgments

Contributing Authors

Katy Z. Allen
Science Writer
Wayland, Massachusetts

Linda Ruth Berg, Ph.D.
Adjunct Professor
Natural Sciences
St. Petersburg College
St. Petersburg, Florida

Barbara Christopher
Science Writer and Editor
Austin, Texas

Jennie Dusheck
Science Writer
Santa Cruz, California

Mark F. Taylor, Ph.D.
Associate Professor of Biology
Biology Department
Baylor University
Waco, Texas

Inclusion Specialist

Ellen McPeek Glisan
Special Needs Consultant
San Antonio, Texas

Safety Reviewer

Jack Gerlovich, Ph.D.
Associate Professor
School of Education
Drake University
Des Moines, Iowa

Academic Reviewers

Glenn Adelson
Instructor
Biology Undergraduate
Program
Harvard University
Cambridge, Massachusetts

Christopher B. Boyko, Ph.D.
Research Associate
Division of Invertebrate
Zoology
American Museum of
Natural History
New York, New York

John Brockhaus, Ph.D.
*Professor of Geospatial
Information Science and
Director of Geospatial
Information Science
Program*
Department of Geography
and Environmental
Engineering
United States Military
Academy
West Point, New York

Ruth E. Buskirk, Ph.D.
Senior Lecturer
Biological Sciences
The University of Texas
at Austin
Austin, Texas

Michael Carleton, Ph.D.
Curator of Mammals
Smithsonian Museum
of Natural History
Washington, D.C.

Joe W. Crim, Ph.D.
*Professor and Head of
Cellular Biology*
Department of Cellular
Biology
University of Georgia
Athens, Georgia

Jim Denbow, Ph.D.
*Associate Professor of
Archaeology*
Department of
Anthropology
and Archaeology
The University of Texas
at Austin
Austin, Texas

William E. Dunscombe
Chairman
Biology Department
Union County College
Cranford, New Jersey

William Grisham, Ph.D.
Lecturer
Psychology Department
University of California,
Los Angeles
Los Angeles, California

David Haig, Ph.D.
Professor of Biology
Organismic and
Evolutionary Biology
Harvard University
Cambridge, Massachusetts

David Hershey, Ph.D.
Education Consultant
Hyattsville, Maryland

Ping H. Johnson, M.D., Ph.D., CHES
*Assistant Professor of
Health Education*
Department of Health,
Physical Education
and Sport Science
Kennesaw State University
Kennesaw, Georgia

Linda Jones
Program Manager
Texas Department
of Public Health
Austin, Texas

Jamie Kneitel, Ph.D.
Postdoctoral Associate
Department of Biology
Washington University
St. Louis, Missouri

John Krenz, Ph.D.
Associate Professor
Biological Sciences
Minnesota State University
Mankato, Minnesota

Nancy L. McQueen, Ph.D.
Professor of Microbiology
Department of Biological
Sciences
California State University,
Los Angeles
Los Angeles, California

Gerald J. Niemi, Ph.D.
Professor and Center Director
Biology and Center
for Water and the
Environment
Natural Resources Research
Institute
University of Minnesota
Duluth, Minnesota

Acknowledgments
continued on page 874

Printed in the United States of America

ISBN 0-03-066477-2

2 3 4 5 6 7 048 08 07 06 05 04

Contents in Brief

Contents

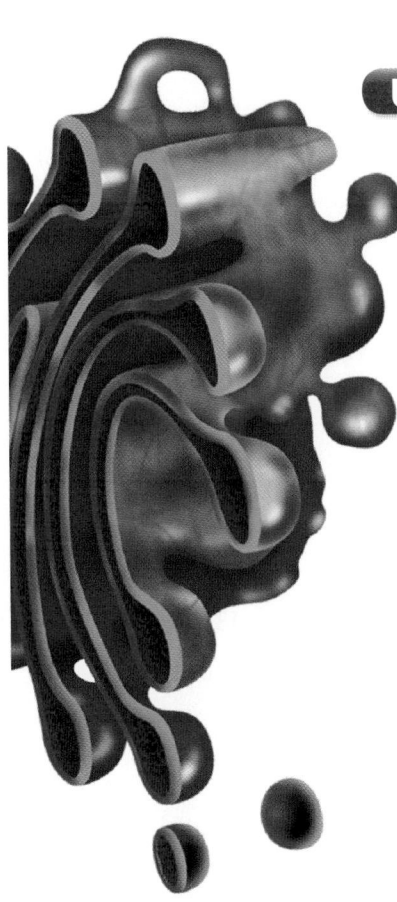

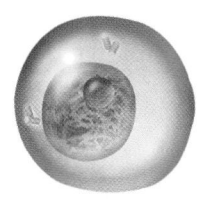 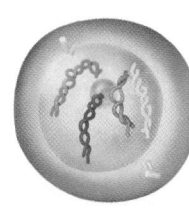  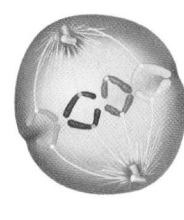

UNIT 3 ··· Heredity, Evolution, and Classification

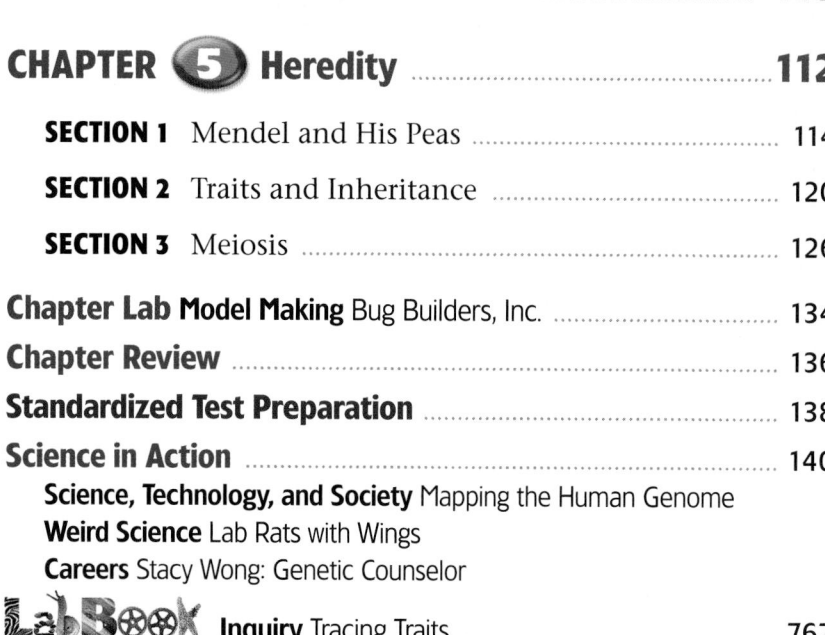

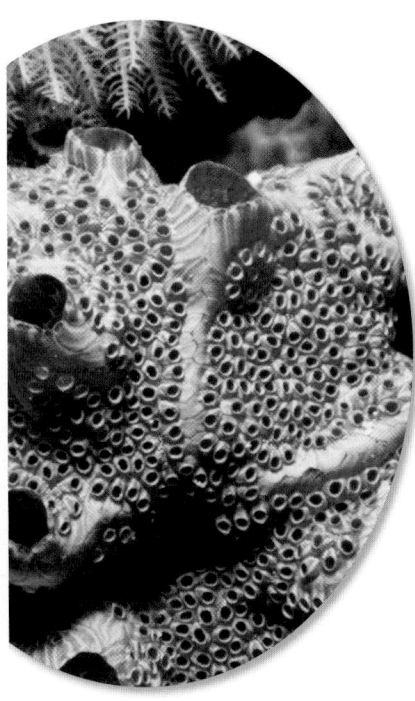

Contents   **xi**

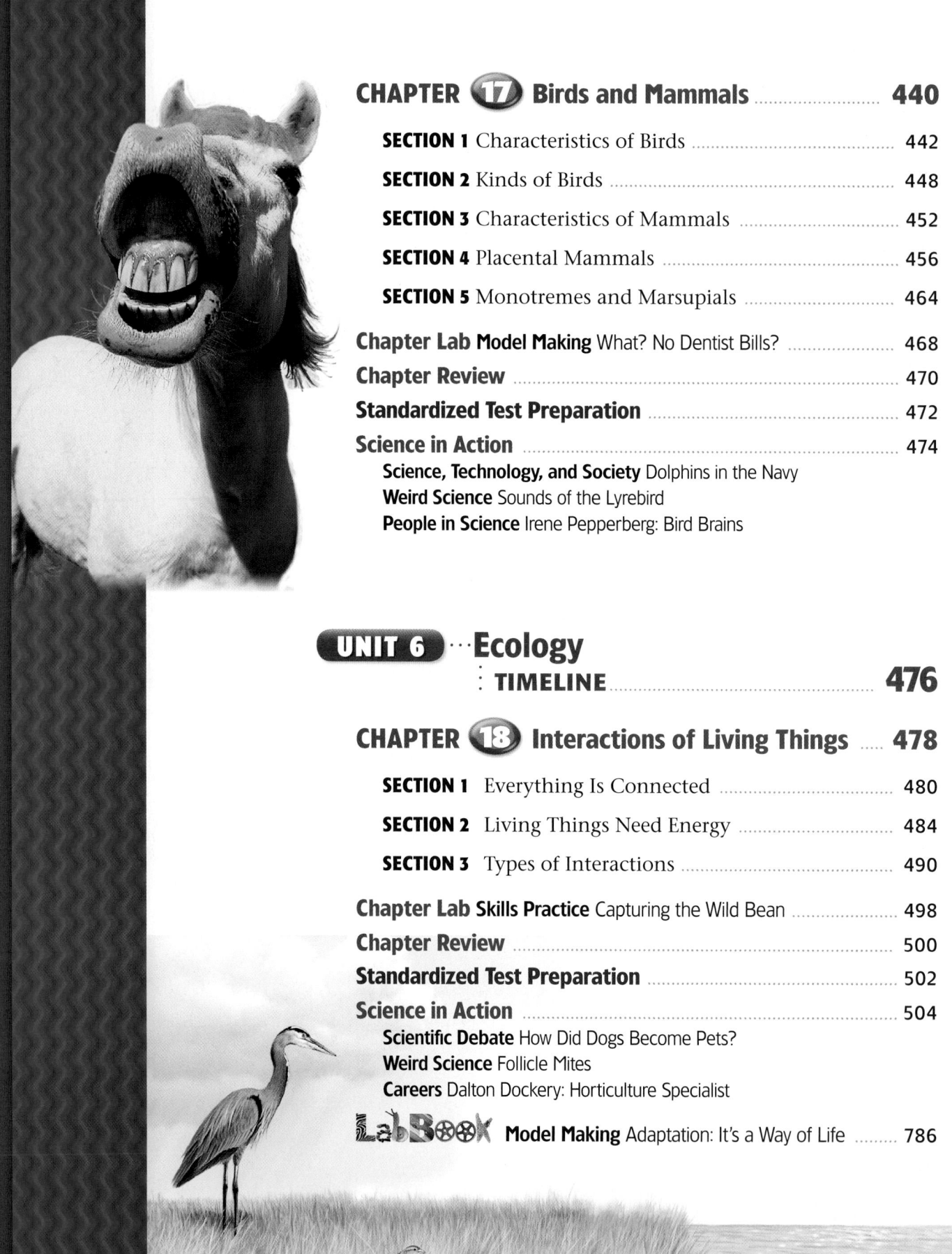

Contents   **xiii**

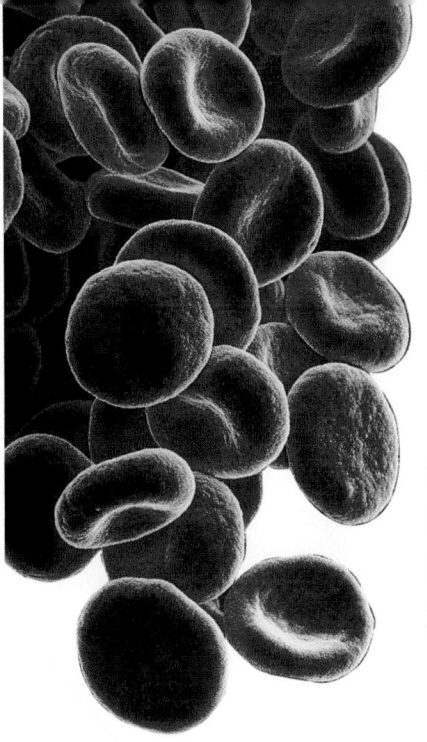

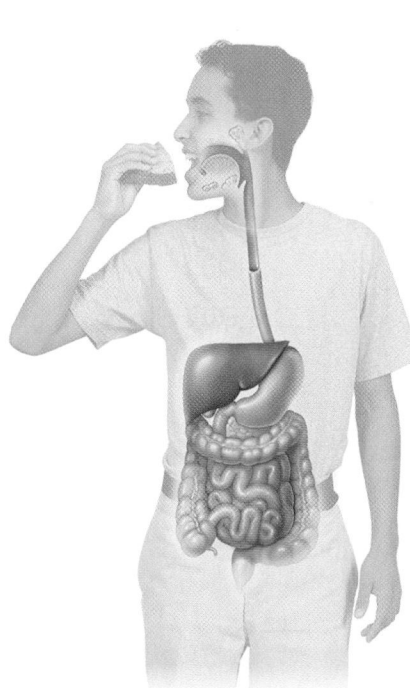

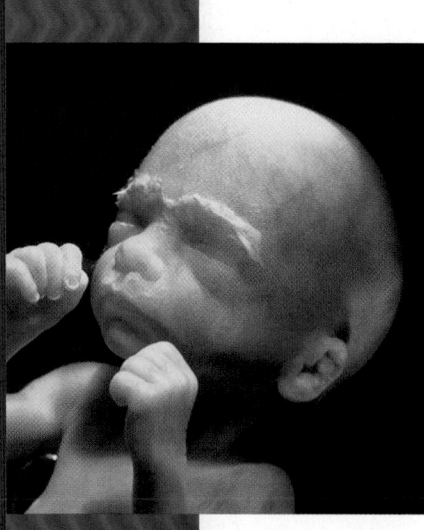

Chapter Labs and LabBook

The more labs, the better!

Take a minute to browse the variety of exciting **labs** in this textbook. Labs appear within the chapters and in a special LabBook in the back of the textbook. All labs are designed to help you experience science firsthand. But please don't forget to be safe. Read the Safety First! section before starting any of the labs.

Start your engines with an activity!

Get motivated to learn by doing the two activities at the beginning of each chapter. The **Pre-Reading Activity** helps you organize information as you read the chapter. The **Start-up Activity** helps you gain scientific understanding of the topic through hands-on experience.

PRE-READING ACTIVITY

FOLDNOTES

Graphic Organizer

START-UP ACTIVITY

READING STRATEGY

Remembering what you read doesn't have to be hard!

A **Reading Strategy** at the beginning of every section provides tips to help you remember and/or organize the information covered in the section.

Quick Lab

School to Home

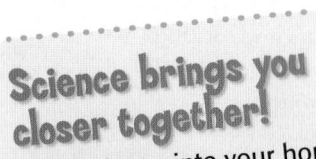

Science brings you closer together!
Bring science into your home by doing **School-to-Home Activities** with a parent or another adult in your household.

INTERNET ACTIVITY

MATH PRACTICE

MATH FOCUS

Science and math go hand in hand.

The **Math Focus** and **Math Practice** items show you many ways that math applies directly to science and vice versa.

Connection to . . .

One subject leads to another.

You may not realize it at first, but different subjects are related to each other in many ways. Each **Connection** explores a topic from the viewpoint of another discipline. In this way, all of the subjects you learn about in school merge to improve your understanding of the world around you.

Science in Action

How to Use Your Textbook

Your Roadmap for Success with Holt Science and Technology

Reading Warm-Up

A Reading Warm-Up at the beginning of every section provides you with the section's objectives and key terms. The objectives tell you what you'll need to know after you finish reading the section.

Key terms are listed for each section. Learn the definitions of these terms because you will most likely be tested on them. Each key term is highlighted in the text and is defined at point of use and in the margin. You can also use the glossary to locate definitions quickly.

STUDY TIP Reread the objectives and the definitions to the key terms when studying for a test to be sure you know the material.

Get Organized

A Reading Strategy at the beginning of every section provides tips to help you organize and remember the information covered in the section. Keep a science notebook so that you are ready to take notes when your teacher reviews the material in class. Keep your assignments in this notebook so that you can review them when studying for the chapter test.

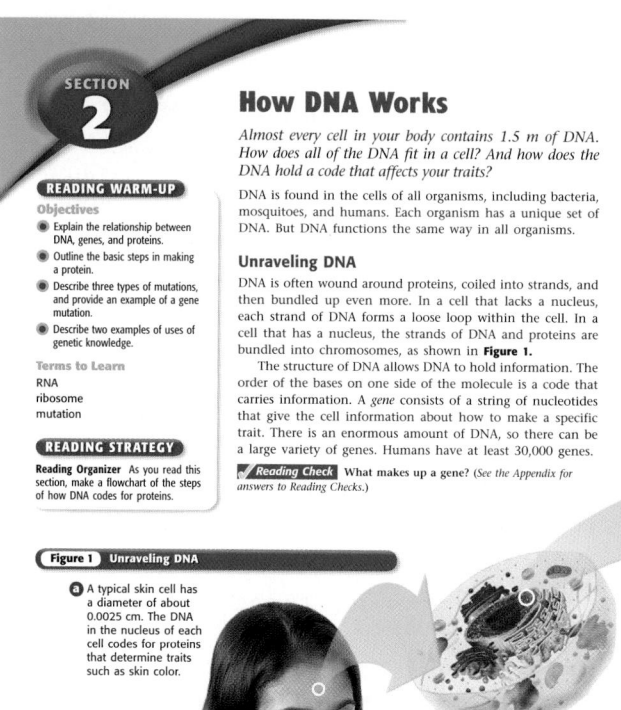

SECTION 2

How DNA Works

Almost every cell in your body contains 1.5 m of DNA. How does all of the DNA fit in a cell? And how does the DNA hold a code that affects your traits?

DNA is found in the cells of all organisms, including bacteria, mosquitoes, and humans. Each organism has a unique set of DNA. But DNA functions the same way in all organisms.

Unraveling DNA

DNA is often wound around proteins, coiled into strands, and then bundled up even more. In a cell that lacks a nucleus, each strand of DNA forms a loose loop within the cell. In a cell that has a nucleus, the strands of DNA and proteins are bundled into chromosomes, as shown in **Figure 1.**

The structure of DNA allows DNA to hold information. The order of the bases on one side of the molecule is a code that carries information. A *gene* consists of a string of nucleotides that give the cell information about how to make a specific trait. There is an enormous amount of DNA, so there can be a large variety of genes. Humans have at least 30,000 genes.

Reading Check What makes up a gene? (*See the Appendix for answers to Reading Checks.*)

READING WARM-UP

Objectives
- Explain the relationship between DNA, genes, and proteins.
- Outline the basic steps in making a protein.
- Describe three types of mutations, and provide an example of a gene mutation.
- Describe two examples of uses of genetic knowledge.

Terms to Learn
RNA
ribosome
mutation

READING STRATEGY
Reading Organizer As you read this section, make a flowchart of the steps of how DNA codes for proteins.

Figure 1 Unraveling DNA

ⓐ A typical skin cell has a diameter of about 0.0025 cm. The DNA in the nucleus of each cell codes for proteins that determine traits such as skin color.

ⓑ The DNA in the nucleus is part of a material called *chromatin*. Long strands of chromatin are usually bundled loosely within the nucleus.

148 Chapter 6

Be Resourceful—Use the Web

SCILINKS®

Internet Connect boxes in your textbook take you to resources that you can use for science projects, reports, and research papers. Go to scilinks.org, and type in the SciLinks code to get information on a topic.

go.hrw.com

Visit go.hrw.com Find worksheets, **Current Science®** magazine articles online, and other materials that go with your textbook at **go.hrw.com.** Click on the textbook icon and the table of contents to see all of the resources for each chapter.

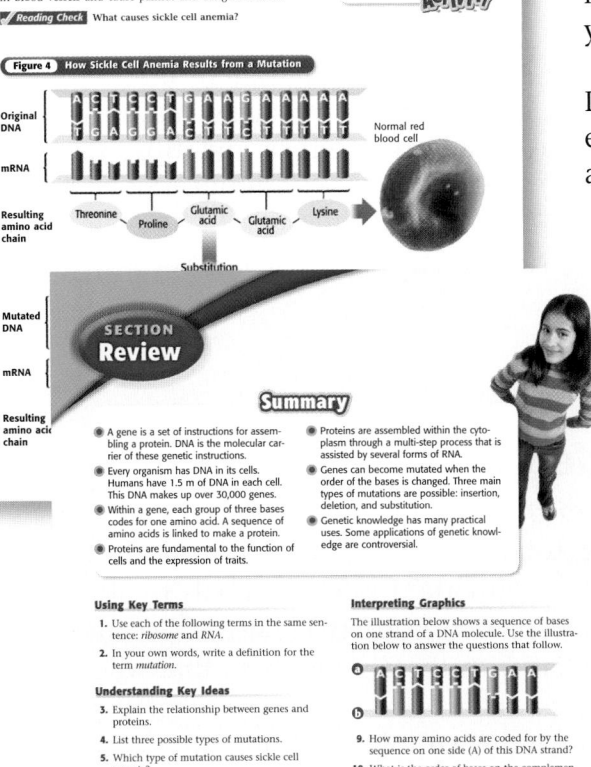

An Example of a Substitution

A mutation, such as a substitution, can be harmful because it may cause a gene to produce the wrong protein. Consider the DNA sequence GAA. When copied as mRNA, this sequence gives the instructions to place the amino acid glutamic acid into the growing protein. If a mistake happens and the original DNA sequence is changed to GTA, the sequence will code for the amino acid valine instead.

This simple change in an amino acid can cause the disease *sickle cell anemia*. Sickle cell anemia affects red blood cells. When valine is substituted for glutamic acid in a blood protein, as shown in **Figure 4**, the red blood cells are changed into a sickle shape.

The sickle cells are not as good at carrying oxygen as normal red blood cells are. Sickle cells are also likely to get stuck in blood vessels and cause painful and dangerous clots.

Reading Check What causes sickle cell anemia?

SCHOOL to HOME

An Error in the Message

The sentence below is the result of an error similar to a DNA mutation. The original sentence was made up of three-letter words, but an error was made in this copy. Explain the idea of mutations to your parent. Then, work together to find the mutation, and write the sentence correctly.

THE IGB ADC ATA TET HEB IGR EDR AT.

ACTIVITY

Figure 4 How Sickle Cell Anemia Results from a Mutation

SECTION Review

Summary

- A gene is a set of instructions for assembling a protein. DNA is the molecular carrier of these genetic instructions.
- Every organism has DNA in its cells. Humans have 1.5 m of DNA in each cell. This DNA makes up over 30,000 genes.
- Within a gene, each group of three bases codes for one amino acid. A sequence of amino acids is linked to make a protein.
- Proteins are fundamental to the function of cells and the expression of traits.
- Proteins are assembled within the cytoplasm through a multi-step process that is assisted by several forms of RNA.
- Genes can become mutated when the order of the bases is changed. Three main types of mutations are possible: insertion, deletion, and substitution.
- Genetic knowledge has many practical uses. Some applications of genetic knowledge are controversial.

Using Key Terms

1. Use each of the following terms in the same sentence: *ribosome* and *RNA*.
2. In your own words, write a definition for the term *mutation*.

Understanding Key Ideas

3. Explain the relationship between genes and proteins.
4. List three possible types of mutations.
5. Which type of mutation causes sickle cell anemia?
   a. substitution   c. deletion
   b. insertion   d. mutagen

Math Skills

6. A set of 23 chromosomes in a human cell contains 3.2 billion pairs of DNA bases in sequence. On average, about how many pairs of bases are in each chromosome?

Critical Thinking

7. **Applying Concepts** In which cell type might a mutation be passed from generation to generation? Explain.
8. **Making Comparisons** How is genetic engineering different from natural reproduction?

Interpreting Graphics

The illustration below shows a sequence of bases on one strand of a DNA molecule. Use the illustration below to answer the questions that follow.

9. How many amino acids are coded for by the sequence on one side (A) of this DNA strand?
10. What is the order of bases on the complementary side (B), from left to right?
11. If a G were inserted as the first base on the top side (A), what would the order of bases be on the complementary side (B)?

SCLINKS.

For a variety of links related to this chapter, go to www.scilinks.org

Topic: Genetic Engineering
SciLinks code: HSM0654

155

Use the Illustrations and Photos

Art shows complex ideas and processes. Learn to analyze the art so that you better understand the material you read in the text.

Tables and graphs display important information in an organized way to help you see relationships.

A picture is worth a thousand words. Look at the photographs to see relevant examples of science concepts that you are reading about.

Answer the Section Reviews

Section Reviews test your knowledge of the main points of the section. Critical Thinking items challenge you to think about the material in greater depth and to find connections that you infer from the text.

STUDY TIP When you can't answer a question, reread the section. The answer is usually there.

Do Your Homework

Your teacher may assign worksheets to help you understand and remember the material in the chapter.

STUDY TIP Don't try to answer the questions without reading the text and reviewing your class notes. A little preparation up front will make your homework assignments a lot easier. Answering the items in the Chapter Review will help prepare you for the chapter test.

Holt Online Learning

Visit Holt Online Learning

If your teacher gives you a special password to log onto the Holt Online Learning site, you'll find your complete textbook on the Web. In addition, you'll find some great learning tools and practice quizzes. You'll be able to see how well you know the material from your textbook.

CNN Student News™

Visit CNN Student News
You'll find up-to-date events in science at **cnnstudentnews.com.**

SAFETY FIRST!

Exploring, inventing, and investigating are essential to the study of science. However, these activities can also be dangerous. To make sure that your experiments and explorations are safe, you must be aware of a variety of safety guidelines. You have probably heard of the saying, "It is better to be safe than sorry." This is particularly true in a science classroom where experiments and explorations are being performed. Being uninformed and careless can result in serious injuries. Don't take chances with your own safety or with anyone else's.

The following pages describe important guidelines for staying safe in the science classroom. Your teacher may also have safety guidelines and tips that are specific to your classroom and laboratory. Take the time to be safe.

Safety Rules!

Start Out Right

Always get your teacher's permission before attempting any laboratory exploration. Read the procedures carefully, and pay particular attention to safety information and caution statements. If you are unsure about what a safety symbol means, look it up or ask your teacher. You cannot be too careful when it comes to safety. If an accident does occur, inform your teacher immediately regardless of how minor you think the accident is.

Safety Symbols

All of the experiments and investigations in this book and their related worksheets include important safety symbols to alert you to particular safety concerns. Become familiar with these symbols so that when you see them, you will know what they mean and what to do. It is important that you read this entire safety section to learn about specific dangers in the laboratory.

If you are instructed to note the odor of a substance, wave the fumes toward your nose with your hand. Never put your nose close to the source.

Eye protection

Clothing protection

Hand safety

Heating safety

Electric safety

Chemical safety

Animal safety

Sharp object

Plant safety

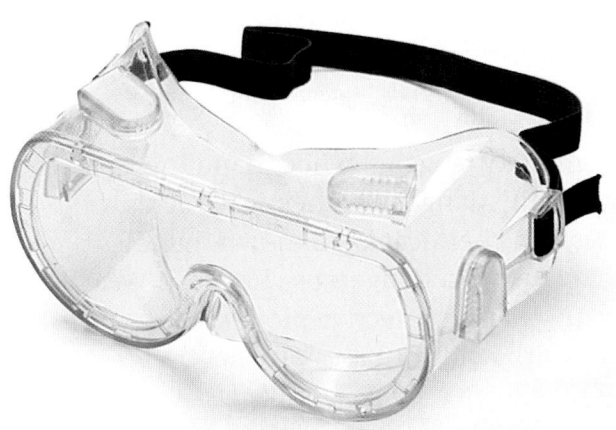

Eye Safety

Wear safety goggles when working around chemicals, acids, bases, or any type of flame or heating device. Wear safety goggles any time there is even the slightest chance that harm could come to your eyes. If any substance gets into your eyes, notify your teacher immediately and flush your eyes with running water for at least 15 minutes. Treat any unknown chemical as if it were a dangerous chemical. Never look directly into the sun. Doing so could cause permanent blindness.

Avoid wearing contact lenses in a laboratory situation. Even if you are wearing safety goggles, chemicals can get between the contact lenses and your eyes. If your doctor requires that you wear contact lenses instead of glasses, wear eye-cup safety goggles in the lab.

Safety Equipment

Know the locations of the nearest fire alarms and any other safety equipment, such as fire blankets and eyewash fountains, as identified by your teacher, and know the procedures for using the equipment.

Neatness

Keep your work area free of all unnecessary books and papers. Tie back long hair, and secure loose sleeves or other loose articles of clothing, such as ties and bows. Remove dangling jewelry. Don't wear open-toed shoes or sandals in the laboratory. Never eat, drink, or apply cosmetics in a laboratory setting. Food, drink, and cosmetics can easily become contaminated with dangerous materials.

Certain hair products (such as aerosol hair spray) are flammable and should not be worn while working near an open flame. Avoid wearing hair spray or hair gel on lab days.

Sharp/Pointed Objects

Use knives and other sharp instruments with extreme care. Never cut objects while holding them in your hands. Place objects on a suitable work surface for cutting.

Be extra careful when using any glassware. When adding a heavy object to a graduated cylinder, tilt the cylinder so the object slides slowly to the bottom.

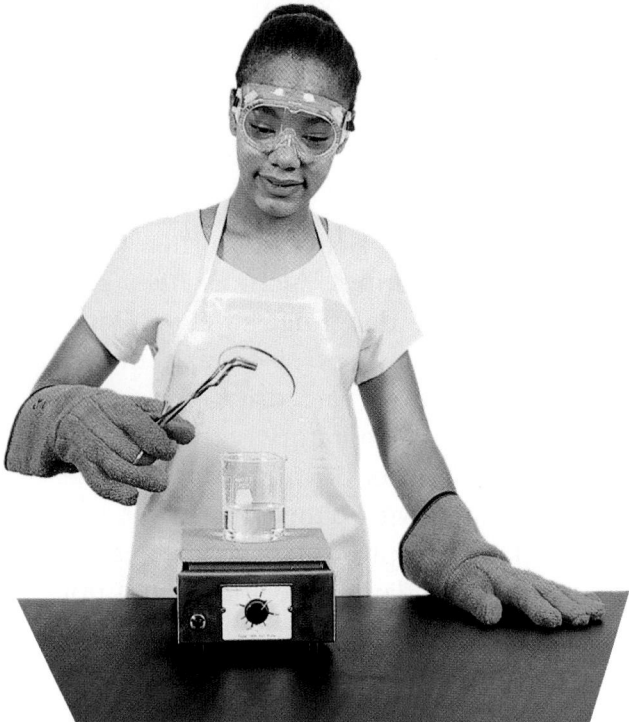

Heat

Wear safety goggles when using a heating device or a flame. Whenever possible, use an electric hot plate as a heat source instead of using an open flame. When heating materials in a test tube, always angle the test tube away from yourself and others. To avoid burns, wear heat-resistant gloves whenever instructed to do so.

Electricity

Be careful with electrical cords. When using a microscope with a lamp, do not place the cord where it could trip someone. Do not let cords hang over a table edge in a way that could cause equipment to fall if the cord is accidentally pulled. Do not use equipment with damaged cords. Be sure that your hands are dry and that the electrical equipment is in the "off" position before plugging it in. Turn off and unplug electrical equipment when you are finished.

Chemicals

Wear safety goggles when handling any potentially dangerous chemicals, acids, or bases. If a chemical is unknown, handle it as you would a dangerous chemical. Wear an apron and protective gloves when you work with acids or bases or whenever you are told to do so. If a spill gets on your skin or clothing, rinse it off immediately with water for at least 5 minutes while calling to your teacher.

Never mix chemicals unless your teacher tells you to do so. Never taste, touch, or smell chemicals unless you are specifically directed to do so. Before working with a flammable liquid or gas, check for the presence of any source of flame, spark, or heat.

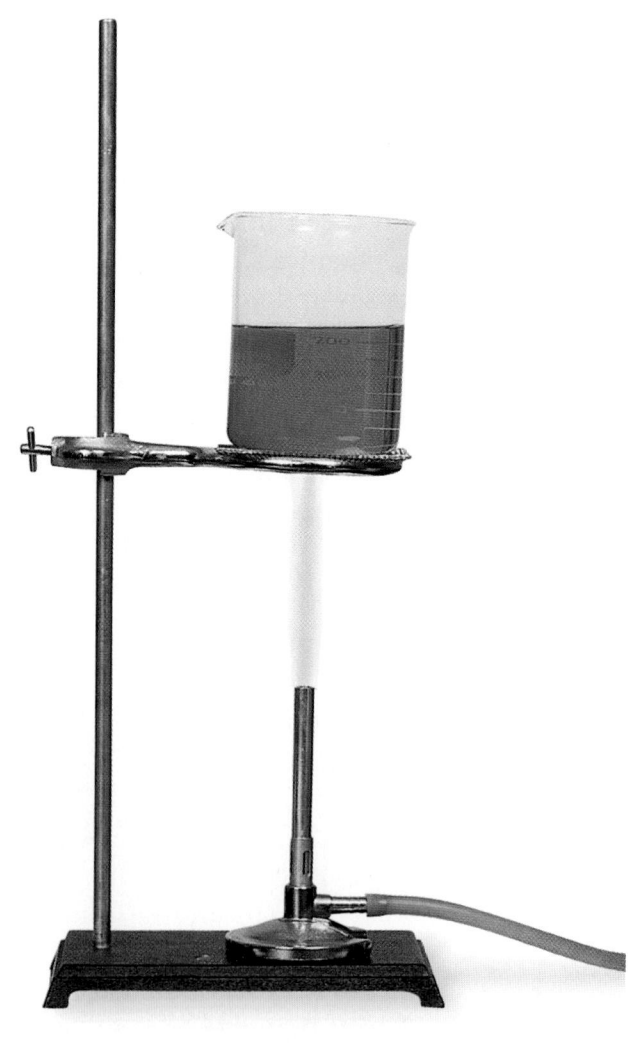

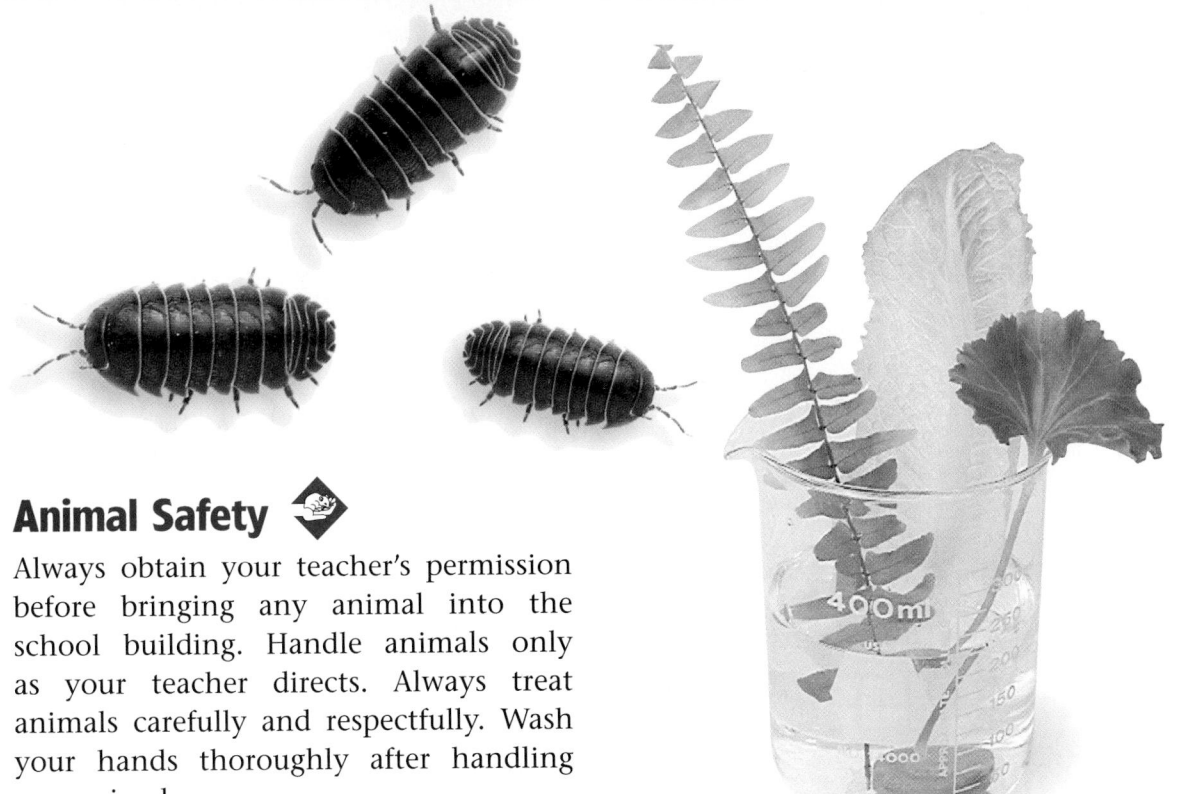

Animal Safety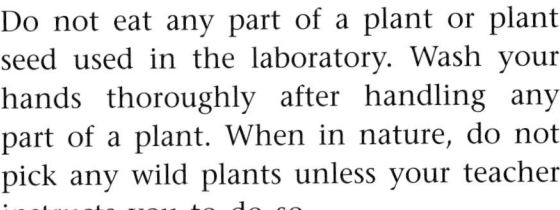

Always obtain your teacher's permission before bringing any animal into the school building. Handle animals only as your teacher directs. Always treat animals carefully and respectfully. Wash your hands thoroughly after handling any animal.

Plant Safety

Do not eat any part of a plant or plant seed used in the laboratory. Wash your hands thoroughly after handling any part of a plant. When in nature, do not pick any wild plants unless your teacher instructs you to do so.

Glassware

Examine all glassware before use. Be sure that glassware is clean and free of chips and cracks. Report damaged glassware to your teacher. Glass containers used for heating should be made of heat-resistant glass.

UNIT 1

TIMELINE

The Study of Living Things

Life science is the study of living things—from the tiniest bacterium to the largest tree! In this unit, you will discover the similarities of all living things. You will learn about the tools that life scientists use, and you'll learn to ask your own questions about the living world around you.

People have always searched for answers about life. This timeline includes a few of the many people who have studied living things and a few events that have shaped the history of life science. And there's always more to be learned, so keep your eyes open.

Around 2700 BCE

Si Ling-Chi, empress of China, observes silkworms in her garden and develops a process to cultivate them and make silk.

1931

The first electron microscope is developed.

1934

Dorothy Crowfoot Hodgkin uses X-ray techniques to determine the protein structure of insulin.

1970

Floppy disks for computer data storage are introduced.

1983

Dian Fossey writes *Gorillas in the Mist*, a book about her research on mountain gorillas in Africa and her efforts to save them from poachers.

Around 1000

Arab mathematician and physicist Ibn al Haytham discovers that vision is caused by the reflection of light from objects into the eye.

1684

Improvements to microscopes allow the first observation of red blood cells.

1914

His studies on agriculture and soil conservation lead George Washington Carver to perform research on peanuts.

1944

Oswald T. Avery demonstrates that DNA is the material that carries genetic properties in living organisms.

1946

ENIAC, the first entirely electronic computer, is built. It weighs 30 tons.

1967

Dr. Christiaan Barnard performs the first successful human heart transplant.

1984

A process known as DNA fingerprinting is developed by Alec Jeffreys.

1998

In China, scientists discover a fossil of a dinosaur that had feathers.

2001

A team of scientists led by Philippa Uwins announces that tiny nanobes that are 20 to 150 nanometers wide have been found in Australia. Scientists debate whether these particles are living.

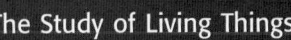

Compression guide:
To shorten instruction because of time limitations, omit Section 1.

OBJECTIVES	LABS, DEMONSTRATIONS, AND ACTIVITIES	TECHNOLOGY RESOURCES
PACING • 90 min pp. 4–9 **Chapter Opener**	SE **Start-up Activity**, p. 5 ◆ GENERAL	OSP **Parent Letter** ■ GENERAL CD **Student Edition on CD-ROM** CD **Guided Reading Audio CD** ■ TR **Chapter Starter Transparency*** VID **Brain Food Video Quiz**
Section 1 Asking About Life • Explain the importance of asking questions in life science. • State examples of life scientists at work. • List three ways life science is beneficial to living things.	TE **Group Activity** Local Life Scientists, p. 6 ◆ GENERAL TE **Group Activity** Wildlife Safari, p. 7 ◆ GENERAL TE **Connection Activity** Environmental Science, p. 8 ◆ BASIC LB **Long-Term Projects & Research Ideas** The Length of a Fethel* ADVANCED	CRF **Lesson Plans*** TR **Bellringer Transparency*** TE **Internet Activity** p. 6 GENERAL
PACING • 90 min pp. 10–17 **Section 2 Scientific Methods** • Describe scientific methods. • Determine the appropriate design of a controlled experiment. • Use information in tables and graphs to analyze experimental results. • Explain how scientific knowledge can change.	TE **Activity** Now You See It, p. 10 ◆ GENERAL TE **Connection Activity** Social Studies, p. 11 GENERAL TE **Demonstration** Frog Call, p. 12 ◆ GENERAL TE **Activity** Test a Hypothesis, p. 12 ADVANCED TE **Activity** Roots of Words, p. 13 BASIC TE **Activity** Writing Predictions, p. 13 GENERAL TE **Connection Activity** Math, p. 16 BASIC SE **Skills Practice Lab** Does It All Add Up?, p. 28 ◆ GENERAL SE **Skills Practice Lab** Graphing Data, p. 760 BASIC LB **Whiz-Bang Demonstrations** Air Ball* ◆ GENERAL LB **Whiz-Bang Demonstrations** Getting to the Point* ◆ GENERAL	CRF **Lesson Plans*** TR **Bellringer Transparency*** TR **Scientific Methods*** VID **Lab Videos for Life Science**
PACING • 45 min pp. 18–21 **Section 3 Scientific Models** • Give examples of three types of models. • Identify the benefits and limitations of models. • Compare the ways that scientists use hypotheses, theories, and laws.	TE **Group Activity** Classifying, p. 19 ◆ GENERAL SE **Model-Making Lab** A Window to a Hidden World, p. 761 ◆ GENERAL CRF **Datasheet for LabBook*** LB **Inquiry Lab** One Side or Two?* ◆ GENERAL SE **Science in Action** Math, Social Studies, and Language Arts Activities, pp. 34–35 GENERAL	CRF **Lesson Plans*** TR **Bellringer Transparency***
PACING • 45 min pp. 22–27 **Section 4 Tools, Measurement, and Safety** • Give three examples of how life scientists use computers and technology. • Describe three tools life scientists use to observe organisms. • Explain the importance of the International System of Units, and give four examples of SI units.	TE **Demonstration** Tools for Seeing, p. 22 ◆ GENERAL TE **Activity** Using a Microscope, p. 23 ◆ GENERAL TE **Group Activity** X Rays, p. 23 GENERAL SE **School-to-Home Activity** How You Measure Matters, p. 24 GENERAL TE **Demonstration** Measuring Mass and Volume, p. 25 ◆ BASIC SE **Quick Lab** Measure Up!, p. 26 ◆ GENERAL CRF **Datasheet for Quick Lab***	CRF **Lesson Plans*** TR **Bellringer Transparency*** TR **Compound Light Microscope*** TR **Common SI Units and Conversions*** TR **LINK TO PHYSICAL SCIENCE** Three Temperature Scales* CRF **SciLinks Activity*** GENERAL CD **Interactive Explorations CD-ROM** Something's Fishy! GENERAL

PACING • 90 min

CHAPTER REVIEW, ASSESSMENT, AND STANDARDIZED TEST PREPARATION

CRF **Vocabulary Activity*** GENERAL
SE **Chapter Review**, pp. 30–31 GENERAL
CRF **Chapter Review*** ■ GENERAL
CRF **Chapter Tests A*** ■ GENERAL, **B*** ADVANCED, **C*** SPECIAL NEEDS
SE **Standardized Test Preparation**, pp. 32–33 GENERAL
CRF **Standardized Test Preparation*** GENERAL
CRF **Performance-Based Assessment*** GENERAL
OSP **Test Generator** GENERAL
CRF **Test Item Listing*** GENERAL

Online and Technology Resources

Visit **go.hrw.com** for a variety of free resources related to this textbook. Enter the keyword **HL5LIV**.

Students can access interactive problem-solving help and active visual concept development with the *Holt Science and Technology* Online Edition available at **www.hrw.com**.

 Guided Reading Audio CD
Also in Spanish

A direct reading of each chapter for auditory learners, reluctant readers, and Spanish-speaking students.

 Science Tutor CD-ROM

Excellent for remediation and test practice.

SKILLS DEVELOPMENT RESOURCES	SECTION REVIEW AND ASSESSMENT	STANDARDS CORRELATIONS
SE Pre-Reading Activity, p. 4 GENERAL **OSP** Science Puzzlers, Twisters & Teasers GENERAL **SS** Science Skills Reading a Science Textbook* ADVANCED		National Science Education Standards UCP 2; SAI 1, 2; HNS 1, 2, 3; LS 1f
CRF Directed Reading A* ■ BASIC, B* SPECIAL NEEDS **CRF** Vocabulary and Section Summary* ■ GENERAL **SE** Reading Strategy Paired Summarizing, p. 6 GENERAL **SE** Connection to Language Arts Profile of a Life Scientist, p. 7 GENERAL **TE** Inclusion Strategies, p. 8	**SE** Reading Checks, pp. 6, 9 GENERAL **TE** Homework, p. 8 GENERAL **SE** Section Review,* p. 9 ■ GENERAL **TE** Reteaching, p. 9 BASIC **TE** Quiz, p. 9 GENERAL **TE** Alternative Assessment, p. 9 GENERAL **CRF** Section Quiz* ■ GENERAL	UCP 1; SAI 1, 2; ST 2; SPSP 1, 2, 4, 5; HNS 1, 2, 3
CRF Directed Reading A* ■ BASIC, B* SPECIAL NEEDS **CRF** Vocabulary and Section Summary* ■ GENERAL **SE** Reading Strategy Reading Organizer, p. 10 GENERAL **TE** Reading Strategy Mnemonics, p. 11 BASIC **SE** Connection to Environmental Science Vanishing Amphibians, p. 12 GENERAL **SE** Connection to Language Arts Have Aliens Landed?, p. 13 GENERAL **SE** Math Practice Averages, p. 16 GENERAL **MS** Math Skills for Science What Is an Average?* GENERAL **CRF** Reinforcement Worksheet The Mystery of the Bubbling Top* BASIC **CRF** Critical Thinking The Case of the Bulge* ADVANCED	**SE** Reading Checks, pp. 10, 12, 14, 16 GENERAL **TE** Homework, p. 12 GENERAL **TE** Reteaching, p. 16 BASIC **TE** Quiz, p. 16 GENERAL **TE** Alternative Assessment, p. 16 ADVANCED **SE** Section Review,* p. 17 ■ GENERAL **CRF** Section Quiz* ■ GENERAL	UCP 2, 3; SAI 1, 2; SPSP 2, 5; HNS 1, 2, 3; *Chapter Lab:* UCP 2; SAI 1, 2; HNS 1, 2; *LabBook:* SAI 1
CRF Directed Reading A* ■ BASIC, B* SPECIAL NEEDS **CRF** Vocabulary and Section Summary* ■ GENERAL **SE** Reading Strategy Reading Organizer, p. 18 GENERAL **SE** Connection to Social Studies Gregor Mendel, p. 19 GENERAL **TE** Reading Strategy Paired Reading, p. 19 BASIC **SE** Connection to Physics The Laws of Physics, p. 21 GENERAL **SS** Science Skills Study Habits GENERAL **MS** Math Skills for Science Arithmetic with Decimals* GENERAL	**SE** Reading Checks, pp. 19, 20 GENERAL **TE** Reteaching, p. 20 BASIC **TE** Quiz, p. 20 GENERAL **TE** Homework, p. 20 ADVANCED **TE** Alternative Assessment, p. 20 GENERAL **SE** Section Review,* p. 21 ■ GENERAL **CRF** Section Quiz* ■ GENERAL	UCP 2, 3; SAI 1, 2; ST 2; SPSP 5; HNS 1, 2, 3; *LabBook:* SAI 1, 2; ST 1, 2; HNS 2, 3
CRF Directed Reading A* ■ BASIC, B* SPECIAL NEEDS **CRF** Vocabulary and Section Summary* ■ GENERAL **SE** Reading Strategy Reading Organizer, p. 22 GENERAL **TE** Inclusion Strategies, p. 25 ◆ **MS** Math Skills for Science A Formula for SI Catch-up* GENERAL **MS** Math Skills for Science What Is SI?* GENERAL **MS** Math Skills for Science Finding Perimeter and Area* GENERAL **MS** Math Skills for Science Finding Volume* GENERAL **SS** Science Skills Safety Rules! GENERAL	**SE** Reading Checks, pp. 23, 25, 26 GENERAL **TE** Reteaching, p. 26 BASIC **TE** Quiz, p. 26 GENERAL **TE** Alternative Assessment, p. 26 BASIC **TE** Homework, p. 26 BASIC **SE** Section Review,* p. 27 ■ GENERAL **CRF** Section Quiz* ■ GENERAL	UCP 3; SAI 1, 2; ST 1, 2

One-Stop Planner® CD-ROM

This convenient CD-ROM includes:
- Lab Materials QuickList Software
- Holt Calendar Planner
- Customizable Lesson Plans
- Printable Worksheets
- ExamView® Test Generator

cnnstudentnews.com

Find the latest news, lesson plans, and activities related to important scientific events.

www.scilinks.org

Maintained by the **National Science Teachers Association.** See Chapter Enrichment pages for a complete list of topics.

Check out *Current Science* articles and activities by visiting the HRW Web site at **go.hrw.com.** Just type in the keyword **HL5CS01T.**

Classroom Videos

- **Lab Videos** demonstrate the chapter lab.
- **Brain Food Video Quizzes** help students review the chapter material.
- **CNN Videos** bring science into your students' daily life.

Chapter Resources

Visual Resources

CHAPTER STARTER TRANSPARENCY

The World of Life Science · CHAPTER STARTER

Imagine . . .

You are walking through a field with some classmates. Suddenly you notice that there are frogs hopping around all over the place! You and your classmates start catching the frogs with a net. As you lift the first frog from the net, you notice something. Its legs seem to be broken. You look at your friend's frog. It seems to be injured, too. You look at another. A frog with no eyes? Wait a minute! These frogs aren't injured. They're deformed! What are these, aliens from outer space?

Believe it or not, this really happened to a group of students from Le Sueur, Minnesota, during a visit to a wildlife refuge. About half of the frogs they collected were deformed. The students and their teacher were stunned by what they found. What could have caused these deformities? Was it just some weird natural phenomenon, or were the frogs

exposed to some sort of chemical? The students gathered more information on the frogs and alerted local scientists. Students and scientists from all over the country are now working together to solve the mystery of the freaky frogs.

The students, like almost all scientists, began their research by noticing something about the natural world and then asking questions about what they observed. In this chapter, you will learn how questions fuel the study of science and how scientists go about finding answers to these questions.

Copyright © by Holt, Rinehart and Winston. All rights reserved.

BELLRINGER TRANSPARENCIES

The World of Life Science · BELLRINGER TRANSPARENCY

Section: Asking About Life
Have you ever wondered how homing pigeons find their way home? Do you know why the dinosaurs went extinct? Write five questions about the natural world that you hope to have answered in this class.

Record your questions in your **science journal.**

Section: Scientific Methods
Which do you think is more important: imagination or knowledge? Can one exist without the other?

Reflect on this in your **science journal.** You may want to think of some famous scientists to write about in your answer. Then share your answer with the class and have a debate.

Copyright © by Holt, Rinehart and Winston. All rights reserved.

TEACHING TRANSPARENCIES

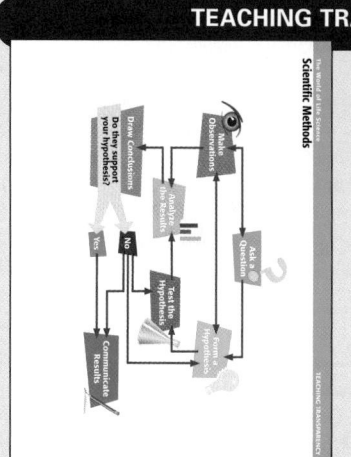

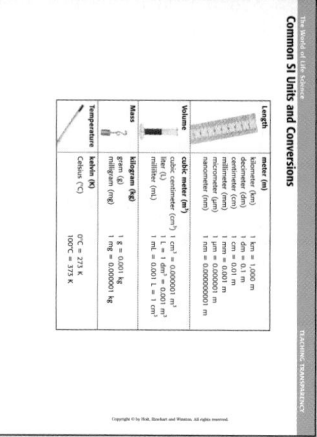

TEACHING TRANSPARENCIES

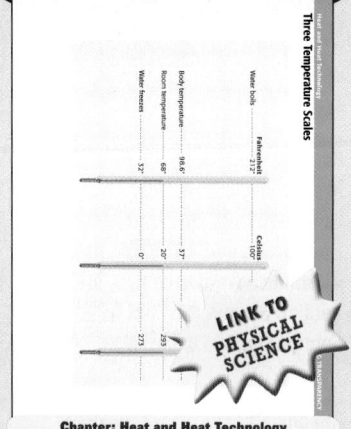

Chapter: Heat and Heat Technology

CONCEPT MAPPING TRANSPARENCY

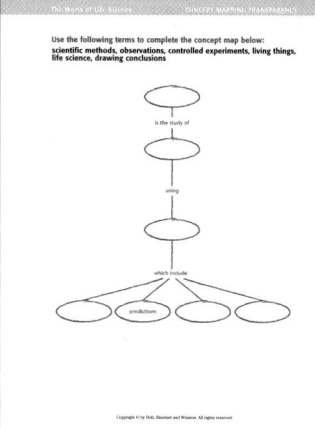

Use the following terms to complete the concept map below: **scientific methods, observations, controlled experiments, living things, life science, drawing conclusions**

Copyright © by Holt, Rinehart and Winston. All rights reserved.

Planning Resources

LESSON PLANS

Lesson Plan   SAMPLE

Section: Waves

Pacing
Regular Schedule: with lab(s):2 days   without lab(s):2 days
Block Schedule: with lab(s):1 1/2 days without lab(s):1 day

Objectives
1. Relate the seven properties of life to a living organism.
2. Describe seven themes that can help you to organize what you learn about biology.
3. Identify the tiny structures that make up all living organisms.
4. Differentiate between reproduction and heredity and between metabolism and homeostasis.

National Science Education Standards Covered
LSInter:Cells have particular structures that underlie their functions.
LSMat1:Most cell functions involve chemical reactions.
LSBeh1:Cells store and use information to guide their functions.
UCP1:Cell functions are regulated.
SI1: Cells can differentiate and form complete multicellular organisms.
PS1: Species evolve over time.
ESS1: The great diversity of organisms is the result of more than 3.5 billion years of evolution.
ESS2: Natural selection and its evolutionary consequences provide a scientific explanation for the fossil record of ancient life forms as well as for the striking molecular similarities observed among the diverse species of living organisms.
ST1: The millions of different species of plants, animals, and microorganisms that live on Earth today are related by descent from common ancestors.
ST2: The energy for life primarily comes from the sun.
SPSP1: The complexity and organization of organisms accommodates the need for obtaining, transforming, transporting, releasing, and eliminating the matter and energy used to sustain the organism.
SPSP6: As matter and energy flows through different levels of organization of living systems—cells, organs, communities—and between living systems and the physical environment, chemical elements are described in different ways.
HNS1: Organisms have behavioral responses to internal changes and to external stimuli.

PARENT LETTER

                                        SAMPLE
Dear Parent,

Your son's or daughter's science class will soon begin exploring the chapter entitled "The World of Physical Science." In this chapter, students will learn about how the scientific method applies to the world of physical science and the role of physical science in the world. By the end of the chapter, students should demonstrate a clear understanding of the chapter's main ideas and be able to discuss the following topics:

1. physical science as the study of energy and matter (Section 1)
2. the role of physical science in the world around them (Section 1)
3. careers that rely on physical science (Section 1)
4. the steps used in the scientific method (Section 2)
5. examples of technology (Section 2)
6. how the scientific method is used to answer questions and solve problems (Section 2)
7. how our knowledge of science changes over time (Section 2)
8. how models represent real objects or systems (Section 3)
9. examples of different ways models are used in science (Section 3)
10. the importance of the International System of Units (Section 4)
11. the appropriate units to use for particular measurements (Section 4)
12. how area and density are derived quantities (Section 4)

Questions to Ask Along the Way

You can help your son or daughter learn about these topics by asking interesting questions such as the following:

• What are some surprising careers that use physical science?
• What is a characteristic of a good hypothesis?
• When is it a good idea to use a model?
• Why do Americans measure things in terms of inches and yards and meters ?

ALSO IN SPANISH

TEST ITEM LISTING

TEST ITEM LISTING
The World of Science   SAMPLE

MULTIPLE CHOICE
1. A limitation of models is that
   a. they are large enough to see.
   b. they do not act exactly like the things that they model.
   c. they are smaller than the things that they model.
   d. they model unfamiliar things.
   Answer: B   Difficulty: 1   Section: 1   Objective: 2

2. The length 10 m is equal to
   a. 100 cm.   c. 10,000 mm.
   b. 1,000 cm.   d. Both (b) and (c).
   Answer: B   Difficulty: 1   Section: 3   Objective: 2

3. To be valid, a hypothesis must be
   a. testable.   c. made into a law.
   b. supported by evidence.   d. observation.
   Answer: B   Difficulty: 1   Section: 3   Objective: 2 1

4. The statement "Sheila has a stain on her shirt" is an example of a(n)
   a. law.   c. observation.
   b. hypothesis.   d. prediction.
   Answer: B   Difficulty: 1   Section: 2   Objective: 2

5. A hypothesis is often developed out of
   a. observations.   c. laws.
   b. experiments.   d. Both (a) and (b)
   Answer: B   Difficulty: 1   Section: 2   Objective: 2

6. How many milliliters are in 3.5 kL?
   a. 3,500 mL.   c. 3,300, 000 mL.
   b. 0.0035 mL.   d. 35,000 mL.
   Answer: B   Difficulty: 1   Section: 3   Objective: 2

7. A map of Seattle is an example of a
   a. law.   c. model.
   b. theory.   d. unit.
   Answer: B   Difficulty: 1   Section: 3   Objective: 2

8. A lab has the safety icons shown below. These icons mean that you should wear
   a. safety goggles.   c. safety goggles and a lab apron.
   b. only a lab apron.   d. safety goggles, a lab apron, and gloves.
   Answer: B   Difficulty: 1   Section: 3   Objective: 2

9. The law of conservation of mass says the kit al mass before a chemical change is
   a. more than the total mass after the change.
   b. less than the total mass after the change.
   c. the same as the total mass after the change.
   d. not the same as the total mass after the change.
   Answer: B   Difficulty: 1   Section: 3   Objective: 2

10. In which of the following areas might you find a geochemical at work?
    a. studying the chemistry of rocks   c. studying fishes
    b. studying forestry   d. studying the atmosphere
    Answer: B   Difficulty: 1   Section: 3   Objective: 2

One-Stop Planner® CD-ROM

This CD-ROM includes all of the resources shown here and the following time-saving tools:

• *Lab Materials QuickList Software*
• *Customizable lesson plans*
• *Holt Calendar Planner*
• *The powerful ExamView® Test Generator*

Meeting Individual Needs

DIRECTED READING A
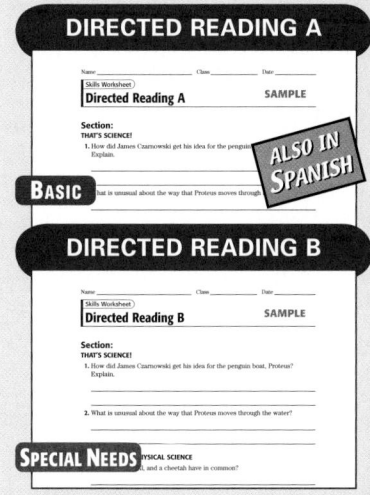

Directed Reading A — SAMPLE

Section: THAT'S SCIENCE!
1. How did James Czarnowski get his idea for the penguin boat? Explain.

ALSO IN SPANISH

BASIC

DIRECTED READING B

Directed Reading B — SAMPLE

Section: THAT'S SCIENCE!
1. How did James Czarnowski get his idea for the penguin boat, Proteus? Explain.

2. What is unusual about the way that Proteus moves through the water?

SPECIAL NEEDS

VOCABULARY ACTIVITY
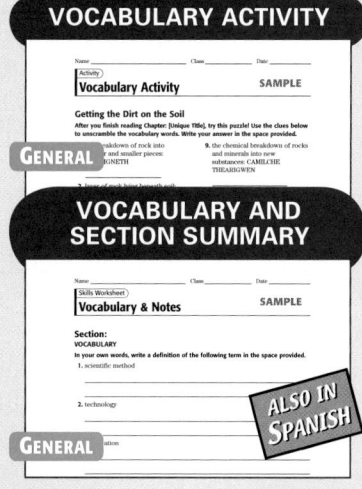

Vocabulary Activity — SAMPLE

Getting the Dirt on the Soil

GENERAL

VOCABULARY AND SECTION SUMMARY

Vocabulary & Notes — SAMPLE

Section: VOCABULARY
In your own words, write a definition of the following term in the space provided.
1. scientific method

2. technology

ALSO IN SPANISH

GENERAL

REINFORCEMENT
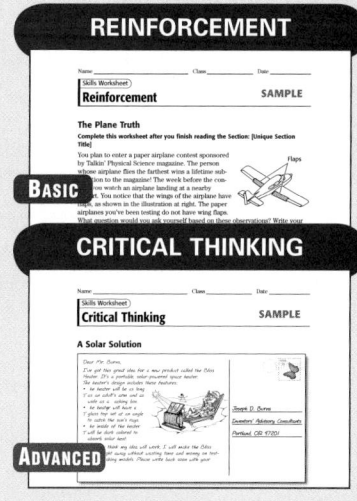

Reinforcement — SAMPLE

The Plane Truth
Complete this worksheet after you finish reading the Section: [Unique Section Title]

BASIC

CRITICAL THINKING

Critical Thinking — SAMPLE

A Solar Solution

ADVANCED

SCILINKS ACTIVITY

SciLinks Activity — SAMPLE

MARINE ECOSYSTEMS

GENERAL

SCIENCE PUZZLERS, TWISTERS & TEASERS

CHAPTER 1 — SCIENCE PUZZLERS, TWISTERS & TEASERS
The World of Life Science

Listening In
1. Figure out what step in the scientific method the scientists are practicing. Write the name of the step in the blank.
   a. "Wow! I can't believe how green the grass is over there. Why isn't it brown like on our side of the mountain?"

   b. "All right, Nan, flip that switch and cross your fingers."

GENERAL

Labs and Activities

LONG-TERM PROJECTS & RESEARCH IDEAS
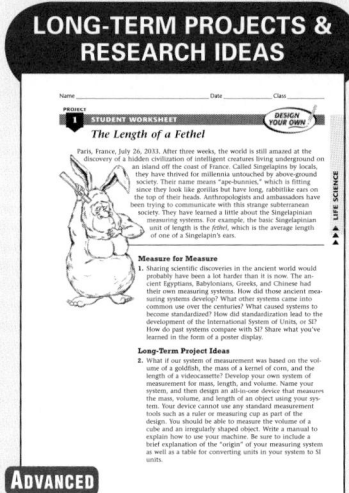

PROJECT 1 — STUDENT WORKSHEET — DESIGN YOUR OWN
The Length of a Fethel

ADVANCED

WHIZ-BANG DEMONSTRATIONS
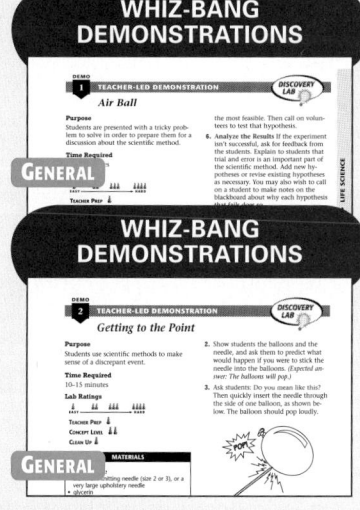

DEMO 1 — TEACHER-LED DEMONSTRATION — DISCOVERY LAB
Air Ball

GENERAL

WHIZ-BANG DEMONSTRATIONS

DEMO 2 — TEACHER-LED DEMONSTRATION — DISCOVERY LAB
Getting to the Point

GENERAL — MATERIALS

INQUIRY LABS
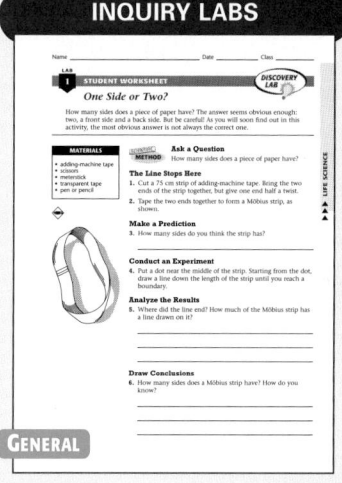

LAB 1 — STUDENT WORKSHEET — DISCOVERY LAB
One Side or Two?

GENERAL

DATASHEETS FOR QUICK LABS

TEACHER RESOURCE PAGE

Quick Lab — DATASHEET FOR QUICK LAB
Reaction to Stress — SAMPLE

Background

DATASHEETS FOR CHAPTER LABS

TEACHER RESOURCE PAGE

Skills Practice Lab — DATASHEET FOR CHAPTER LAB
Using Scientific Methods — SAMPLE

Teacher's Notes
TIME REQUIRED
One 45-minute class period.

DATASHEETS FOR LABBOOK

TEACHER RESOURCE PAGE

Skills Practice Lab — DATASHEET FOR LABBOOK LAB
Does It All Add Up? — SAMPLE

Teacher's Notes
TIME REQUIRED
One 45-minute class period.

Review and Assessments

SECTION QUIZ
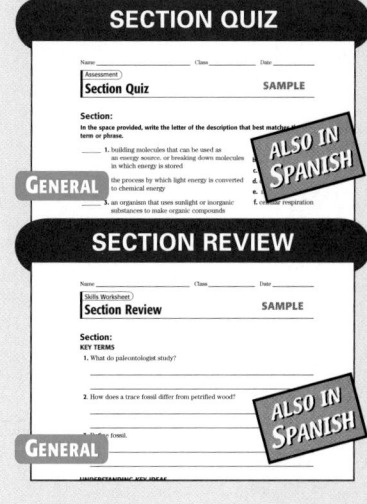

Section Quiz — SAMPLE

ALSO IN SPANISH

GENERAL

SECTION REVIEW

Section Review — SAMPLE

Section: KEY TERMS
1. What do paleontologist study?

2. How does a trace fossil differ from petrified wood?

ALSO IN SPANISH

GENERAL

CHAPTER REVIEW
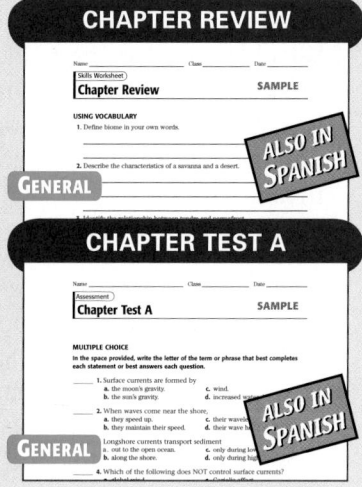

Chapter Review — SAMPLE

USING VOCABULARY
1. Define biome in your own words.

2. Describe the characteristics of a savanna and a desert.

ALSO IN SPANISH

GENERAL

CHAPTER TEST A

Chapter Test A — SAMPLE

MULTIPLE CHOICE
In the space provided, write the letter of the term or phrase that best completes each statement or best answers each question.
1. Surface currents are formed by
   a. the moon's gravity.   c. wind.
   b. the sun's gravity.   d. increased water density.
2. When waves come near the shore,
   a. they speed up.   c. their wavelength increases.
   b. they maintain their speed. d. their wave height increases.

ALSO IN SPANISH

GENERAL

CHAPTER TEST B
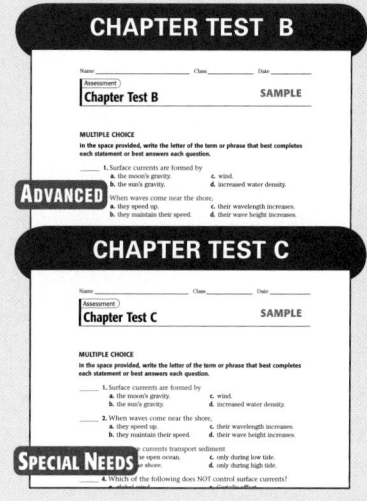

Chapter Test B — SAMPLE

MULTIPLE CHOICE
In the space provided, write the letter of the term or phrase that best completes each statement or best answers each question.
1. Surface currents are formed by
   a. the moon's gravity.   c. wind.
   b. the sun's gravity.   d. increased water density.
When waves come near the shore,
   a. they speed up.   c. their wavelength increases.
   b. they maintain their speed. d. their wave height increases.

ADVANCED

CHAPTER TEST C

Chapter Test C — SAMPLE

MULTIPLE CHOICE
In the space provided, write the letter of the term or phrase that best completes each statement or best answers each question.
1. Surface currents are formed by
   a. the moon's gravity.   c. wind.
   b. the sun's gravity.   d. increased water density.

SPECIAL NEEDS

STANDARDIZED TEST PREPARATION
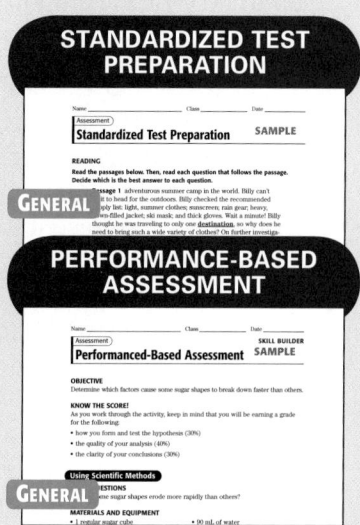

Standardized Test Preparation — SAMPLE

READING
Read the passages below. Then, read each question that follows the passage. Decide which is the best answer to each question.

GENERAL

PERFORMANCE-BASED ASSESSMENT

Performanced-Based Assessment — SKILL BUILDER SAMPLE

OBJECTIVE
Determine which factors cause some sugar shapes to break down faster than others.

KNOW THE SCORE!

Using Scientific Methods

GENERAL

This Chapter Enrichment provides relevant and interesting information to expand and enhance your presentation of the chapter material.

Section 1

Asking About Life
Deformed Frogs

- The discovery of deformed frogs by Minnesota middle school students in 1995 sparked much attention around the country. Since that summer, reports of amphibian deformations have poured into agencies from many parts of the continent.

- The reported deformities include extra limbs, malformed or missing limbs, and facial malformations. Deformities have been documented in 44 states and involve nearly 60 species. In some local populations, up to 60% of the amphibians exhibit deformities.

Dr. Pepperberg's Studies on Parrots

- Parrots, or psittacids, are rarely mentioned during discussions of animal intelligence, but recent studies indicate that they are intelligent animals. Dr. Irene Pepperberg, while an associate professor at the University of Arizona's Department of Ecology and Evolutionary Biology, demonstrated that African gray parrots can process information and make decisions.

- Pepperberg has studied Alex, an African gray parrot, for more than 20 years. Pepperberg says that she has used a variety of techniques to establish a form of interspecies communication with Alex. "The existence of such behavior," she says, "demonstrates that at least one avian species is capable of interactive, referential communication."

- Alex can count and identify more than 35 objects, such as paper, a key, wood, and grain; recognize seven colors; identify five different shapes; and combine names to identify, request, refuse, and categorize more than 100 objects. Alex even learned to boss around lab assistants in order to modify his environment.

Is That a Fact!

- ◆ In this century, the Siberian, or Amur, tiger, has survived wars, revolutions, and deforestation in eastern Asia. Its numbers in the wild were below 100 in the 1940s, but conservation efforts have brought numbers to around 400. There are now over 4,500 km² of protected areas for these tigers in Russia. About 500 additional Siberian tigers live in captivity.

Section 2

Scientific Methods
Vanishing Amphibians

- Scientists are perplexed by steady declines in the world's amphibian populations since the mid-1980s. What's causing these mysterious declines? Scientists conducting field research have produced evidence that the causes may include habitat loss, climate change, UV radiation, contaminants and pollutants, disease and parasitism, and predation by invasive species.

- Alarmingly, declines are not simply occurring in places where human impacts are obvious; some of the most dramatic declines are happening in wilderness areas and parks. In the United States, declines are particularly serious in California, the Rocky Mountains, the Southwest, and Puerto Rico. Worldwide, areas of concern include Australia and Central America.

- The scientific community suspects that there is no single reason for the declines. Different possible causes seem to be at work in different parts of the world. The cause is clear in some cases but not in others. Many researchers believe that multiple causes are adding up to endanger the world's amphibians.

Is That a Fact!

◆ The continental United States is home to at least 230 amphibian species.

Section 3

Scientific Models
Modeling Dinosaurs

- In 1995, the unearthing of a rare fossil *Parasaurolophus* skull prompted a unique form of computer-based modeling. Scientists hypothesized that the cavity-filled crest atop the skull might have been used to produce a low-frequency sound that could vary in pitch. In 1997, scientists in New Mexico used computed tomography scans and powerful computers to simulate the sounds that the crest could have produced. The same techniques may be used in other engineering applications, such as predicting the stength of structural materials.

A Model Birthday

- In 1953, scientists James Watson and Francis Crick assembled the first accurate model of a DNA molecule. Their discovery of DNA's structure was celebrated as one of the key scientific achievements of the 20th century. Fifty years later, the anniversary of this event was marked by a variety of commemorative events. Art historian Martin Kemp dubbed the double helix "the Mona Lisa of modern science."

Section 4

Tools, Measurement, and Safety
How Does MRI Work?

- Magnetic resonance imaging (MRI) utilizes large magnets, radio-frequency signals, and computers to capture images of internal body structures. When a body is placed in a magnet, hydrogen protons in the body (which is mostly water) align themselves with the magnetic field. A radio-frequency signal is then transmitted through the body. An interaction between the newly aligned protons and the radio-frequency signal produces a new signal, which is then received by a computer. The computer uses the data to produce detailed magnetic resonance images.

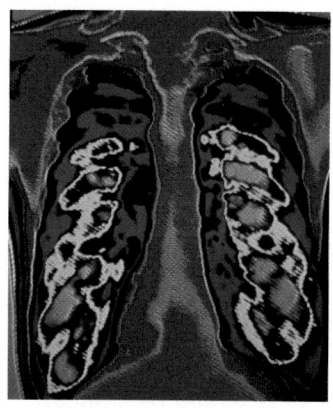

Is That a Fact!

◆ Almost every country in the world has officially adopted the International System of Units (SI). The only countries that have not are Bangladesh and Liberia. All other countries either use the SI or are in the process of making the transition.

SCiLINKS®

NSTA
Developed and maintained by the
National Science Teachers Association

SciLinks is maintained by the National Science Teachers Association to provide you and your students with interesting, up-to-date links that will enrich your classroom presentation of the chapter.

Visit www.scilinks.org and enter the SciLinks code for more information about the topic listed.

Topic: Careers in Life Science
SciLinks code: HSM0224

Topic: Deformed Frogs
SciLinks code: HSM0383

Topic: Scientific Methods
SciLinks code: HSM1359

Topic: Tools of Life Science
SciLinks code: HSM1535

Topic: SI Units
SciLinks code: HSM1390

Topic: Using Models
SciLinks code: HSM1588

Topic: Safety in the Laboratory
SciLinks code: HSM1341

Overview

Tell students that this chapter will introduce them to the world of life science—the world of plants, animals, bacteria, mushrooms, health, disease, and anything related to living organisms. Students will see that science is about asking questions and using scientific methods to find answers and build knowledge. Science is also about using models and tools to investigate questions and share answers.

Assessing Prior Knowledge

Students should be familiar with the following topics:

• measurement
• basic arithmetic

Identifying Misconceptions

As students approach life science, they may have very limited ideas about what "life" and "living" mean. Research shows that even after a significant amount of direct instruction, students often maintain misconceptions, such as the idea that anything that moves is alive. Also, students may have prior conceptions that science is too boring or too hard or that it always involves conducting elaborate experiments in a lab. As you begin this chapter, observe and query students about their conceptions of life science.

1
The World of Life Science

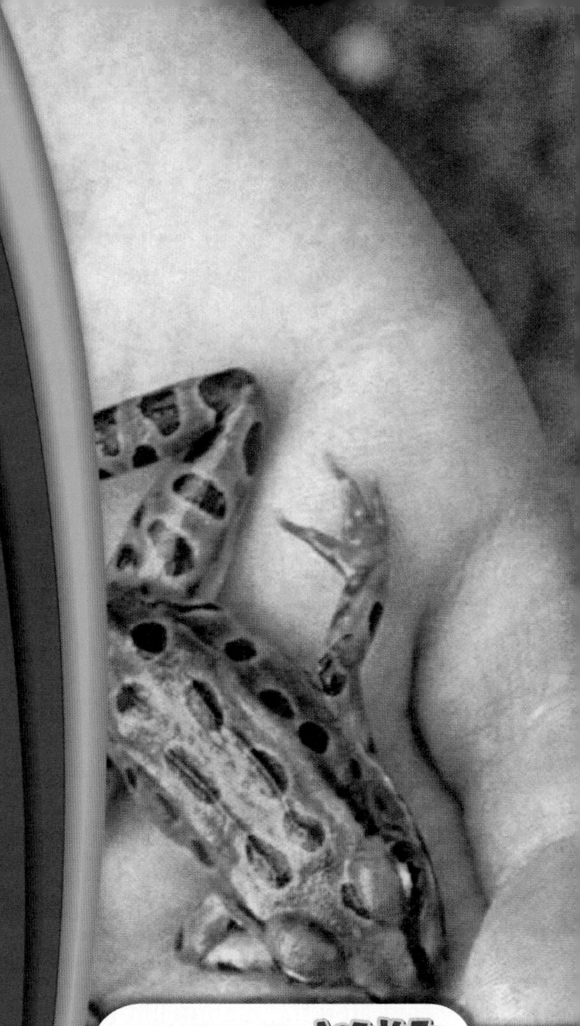

About the PHOTO

What happened to the legs of these frogs? Life science can help answer this question. Deformed frogs, such as the ones in this photo, have been found in the northern United States and southern Canada. Scientists and students like you have been using life science to find out how frogs can develop deformities.

PRE-READING ACTIVITY

FOLDNOTES **Layered Book** Before you read the chapter, create the FoldNote entitled "Layered Book" described in the **Study Skills** section of the Appendix. Label the tabs of the layered book with "Examples of life scientists," "Scientific methods," "Scientific models," and "Tools, measurement, and safety." As you read the chapter, write information you learn about each category under the appropriate tab.

Standards Correlations

National Science Education Standards

The following codes indicate the National Science Education Standards that correlate to this chapter. The full text of the standards is at the front of the book.

Chapter Opener
UCP 2; SAI 1, 2; HNS 1, 2, 3; LS 1f

Section 1 Asking About Life
UCP 1; SAI 1, 2; ST 2; SPSP 1, 2, 4, 5; HNS 1, 2, 3

Section 2 Scientific Methods
UCP 2, 3; SAI 1, 2; SPSP 2, 5; HNS 1, 2, 3

Section 3 Scientific Models
UCP 2, 3; SAI 1, 2; ST 2; SPSP 5; HNS 1, 2, 3

Section 4 Tools, Measurement, and Safety
UCP 3; SAI 1, 2; ST 1, 2

Chapter Lab
UCP 2; SAI 1, 2; HNS 1, 2

Chapter Review
UCP 1, 2, 3; SAI 1, 2; HNS 2

Science in Action
UPC 1, 2, 3; SAI 2; SPSP 4, 5; HNS 1, 3; LS 3a

START-UP ACTIVITY
MATERIALS
FOR EACH STUDENT PAIR
- can, coffee, 1/2–1 lb size, empty
- objects, various, small (such as rocks, nuts, washers, pencils, silverware, small toys, dried fruit, crumpled paper, or paper clips)
- sock, sport, long

Safety Caution: Cover any sharp edges around the rim of the cofee cans with tape. Be sure that the objects placed in the cans are safe to handle. Students should wear safety gloves.

Teacher's Notes: You must prepare this activity ahead of time. Fill the cans with four or five small objects. Try to choose some common and some uncommon objects that would require more than one of the senses to identify. To assemble each setup, cut the toe out of a sport sock, stretch the open toe around the open end of the coffee can, and use duct tape to secure the sock to the can.

Answers

1. Students may guess wrong based on assumptions made from the first thing they notice (such as the sound or shape of the object).

2. Students are likely to make observations using hearing, touch (including sensing weight), and perhaps smell but not sight or taste.

START-UP ACTIVITY

A Little Bit of Science

In this activity, you'll find out that you can learn about the unknown without having to see it.

Procedure

1. Your teacher will give you a **coffee can** to which a **sock** has been attached. Do not look into the can.

2. Reach through the opening in the sock. You will feel **several objects** inside the can.

3. Record observations you make about the objects by feeling them, shaking the can, and so on.

4. What do you think is in the can? List your guesses. State some reasons for your guesses.

5. Pour the contents of the can onto your desk. Compare your list with what was in the can.

Analysis

1. Did you guess the contents of the can correctly? What might have caused you to guess wrongly?

2. What observations did you make about each of the objects while they were in the can? Which of your senses did you use?

Chapter Starter Transparency
Use this transparency to help students begin thinking about the world of life science and using scientific methods.

CHAPTER RESOURCES

Technology

 **Transparencies**
- Chapter Starter Transparency

READING SKILLS

Student Edition on CD-ROM

Guided Reading Audio CD
- English or Spanish

Classroom Videos
- Brain Food Video Quiz

Workbooks

 Science Puzzlers, Twisters & Teasers
- The World of Life Science **GENERAL**

Focus

Overview

This section provides students with an introduction to the life sciences. Students discover that the first step in learning about the living world around us is to ask questions. Students also learn about areas of study in the life sciences and about scientists who are conducting important studies in their fields.

🎵 Bellringer

Have students write five questions about the natural world. (Examples might include the following: How do insects find food? Do trees breathe? Why are dinosaurs extinct?) Ask several students to share their questions with the class.

Motivate

Group ACTiViTY — GENERAL

Local Life Scientists
Organize the class into groups. Have the groups brainstorm about what types of people in their community might be using life science. Have each group choose a professional to interview by phone or e-mail. Encourage students to consider a variety of life science–related professions. Each group should prepare and present a brief report. **LS** Verbal Co-op Learning

---

READING WARM-UP

Objectives

● Explain the importance of asking questions in life science.
● State examples of life scientists at work.
● List three ways life science is beneficial to living things.

Terms to Learn

life science

READING STRATEGY

Paired Summarizing Read this section silently. In pairs, take turns summarizing the material. Stop to discuss ideas that seem confusing.

life science the study of living things

Asking About Life

Imagine that it's summer. You are lying in the grass at the park, casually looking around. Three dogs are playing on your left. A few bumblebees are visiting nearby flowers. And an ant is carrying a crumb away from your sandwich.

Suddenly, a question pops into your head: How do ants find food? Then, you think of another question: Why do the bees visit the yellow flowers but not the red ones? Congratulations! You have just taken the first steps toward becoming a life scientist. How did you do it? You observed the living world around you. You were curious, and you asked questions about your observations. Those steps are what science is all about. **Life science** is the study of living things.

✔ **Reading Check** **What is life science?** (*See the Appendix for answers to Reading Checks.*)

It All Starts with a Question

The world around you is full of an amazing diversity of life. Single-celled algae float unseen in ponds. Giant redwood trees seem to touch the sky. And 40-ton whales swim through the oceans. For every living thing, or organism, that has ever lived, you could ask many questions. Those questions could include (1) How does the organism get its food? (2) Where does it live? and (3) Why does it behave in a particular way?

In Your Own Backyard

Questions are easy to think of. Take a look around your room, your home, and your neighborhood. What questions about life science come to mind? The student in **Figure 1** has questions about some very familiar organisms. Do you know the answer to any of his questions?

Touring the World

The questions you can ask about your neighborhood are just a sample of all the questions you could ask about the world. The world is made up of many different places to live, such as deserts, forests, coral reefs, and tide pools. Just about anywhere you go, you will find some kind of living organism. If you observe these organisms, you can easily think of questions to ask about them.

Figure 1 *Part of science is asking questions about the world around you.*

CHAPTER RESOURCES

Chapter Resource File

📁 • Lesson Plan
• Directed Reading A **BASIC**
• Directed Reading B **SPECIAL NEEDS**

Technology

💾 **Transparencies**
• Bellringer

INTERNET ACTiViTY

Essay ———————— GENERAL

For an internet activity related to this chapter, have students go to **go.hrw.com** and type in the keyword **HL5LIVW.**

Irene Duhart Long asks, "How does the human body respond to space travel?"

Geerat Vermeij asks, "How have shells changed over time?"

Irene Pepperberg asks, "Are parrots smart enough to learn human language?"

Figure 2 *Life scientists ask many different kinds of questions about living things.*

Life Scientists

Close your eyes for a moment, and imagine a life scientist. What do you see? Do you see someone who is in a laboratory and peering into a microscope? Which of the people in **Figure 2** do you think are life scientists?

Anyone

If you guessed that all of the people in **Figure 2** are life scientists, then you are right. Anyone can investigate the world around us. Women and men from any cultural or ethnic background can become life scientists.

Anywhere

Making investigations in a laboratory is an important part of life science, but life science can be studied in many other places, too. Life scientists carry out investigations on farms, in forests, on the ocean floor—even in space. They work for businesses, hospitals, government agencies, and universities. Many are also teachers.

Anything

What a life scientist studies is determined by one thing—his or her curiosity. Life scientists specialize in many different areas of life science. They may study how organisms function and behave. Or they may study how organisms interact with each other and with their environment. Some life scientists explore how organisms reproduce and pass traits from one generation to the next. Some life scientists investigate the ancient origins of organisms and the ways in which organisms have changed over time.

CONNECTION TO Language Arts

WRITING SKILL **Profile of a Life Scientist** Research some of the life scientists named in this chapter. Choose the scientist who interests you the most. In your **science journal,** write a short biography, career feature, or informational piece about your chosen scientist and the work he or she does. Style the article as a newspaper or magazine article.

SCIENCE HUMOR

Q: What's the difference between a friendly dog and a marine biologist?

A: One's a tail wagger; the other's a whale tagger.

Answer to Connection to Language Arts
Students' articles should be styled as short magazine articles that profile the scientist, with a focus on the scientist's life history, interesting research, or type of work as a career opportunity. If it is early in the course, give students as much positive and encouraging feedback as possible regarding their articles.

Teach

Answer to Reading Check
the study of living things

Discussion ——— BASIC

Writing **Why Ask Why?** Ask students to write a paragraph that explains the benefit of studying how the human body responds to space travel. Why might that be important? Write the reasons on the board as students read their paragraphs. **LS** Verbal/Intrapersonal

Group ACTIVITY — GENERAL

Wildlife Safari Arrange a visit to a local zoo or wildlife area, and guide students in a fact-finding mission about the kinds of animals found there. Encourage students to compile a list of questions in advance that they can ask the caretakers. Discuss your fact-finding mission when you return to class. **LS** Verbal/Kinesthetic

CONNECTION to Real World ——— GENERAL

Crime-Fighting Bugs Dr. Neal Haskell is a forensic entomologist—a scientist trained in getting information about crimes from insects. Insects develop and grow at rapid—but regular—rates. When Dr. Haskell finds particular larvae on a corpse, he can calculate exactly how long ago a person must have died. When a man was murdered and left in a junk pile in Oklahoma, Dr. Haskell was asked to establish the time of death by using photographs, case reports, and a few vials of fly larvae. Using this information, Dr. Haskell determined exactly when the murder took place. This information was crucial to the team that solved the crime.

Historic Disease Researcher
Shibasaburo Kitasato was an important Japanese life scientist in the late 1800s and early 1900s. Kitasato was one of the first scientists to discover the bacteria for tetanus, diphtheria, and the bubonic plague. Kitasato accomplished what many thought was impossible: He developed a procedure to grow pure tetanus bacteria. This success led him to develop treatments for tetanus infections and discover new ways to fight diphtheria and plague. Ask students if they have had shots or treatments for these diseases. (Diphtheria and plague have been almost eradicated, but most students have been vaccinated for diphtheria. Some may have been vaccinated or treated for tetanus.) **LS** Verbal

INCLUSION Strategies

• *Gifted and Talented*
Ask students to extend their understanding of polio and other diseases by researching these questions:
• What are the symptoms of a person with polio?
• When was polio common?
• Why did people stop getting polio?
• What other diseases used to be more serious threats than they are now?
LS Verbal

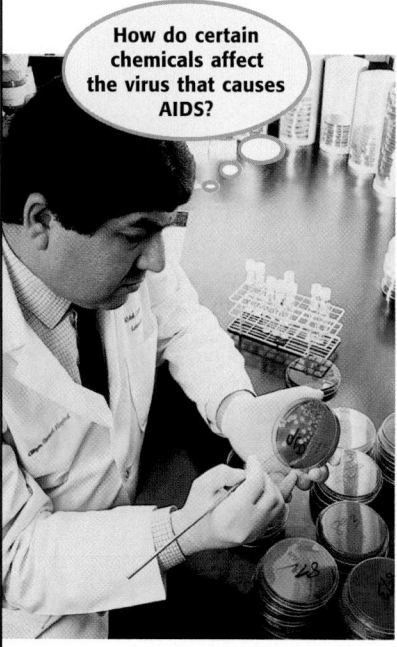

Figure 3 *Abdul Lakhani studies AIDS to try to find a cure for the disease.*

Why Ask Questions?

What is the point of asking all these questions? Life scientists might find some interesting answers, but do any of the answers really matter? Will the answers affect *your* life? Absolutely! As you study life science, you will see how the investigations of life science affect you and all the living things around you.

Fighting Diseases

Polio is a disease that causes paralysis by affecting the brain and nerves. Do you know anyone who has had polio? Probably not. The polio virus has been eliminated from most of the world. But at one time, it was much more common. In 1952, before life scientists discovered ways to prevent the spread of the polio virus, it infected 58,000 Americans.

Today, life scientists continue to search for ways to fight diseases. Acquired immune deficiency syndrome (AIDS) is a disease that kills millions of people every year. The scientist in **Figure 3** is trying to learn more about AIDS. Life scientists have discovered how the virus that causes AIDS is carried from one person to another. Scientists have also learned about how the virus affects the body. By learning more about the virus, scientists may find a cure for this deadly disease.

Understanding Inherited Diseases

Some diseases, such as cystic fibrosis, are inherited. They are passed from parents to children. Most of the information that controls an organism's cells is inherited as coded information. Changes in small parts of this information may cause the organism to be born with or to develop certain diseases. The scientist in **Figure 4** is one of the many scientists worldwide who are studying the way humans inherit the code that controls their cells. By learning about this code, scientists hope to find ways to cure or prevent inherited diseases.

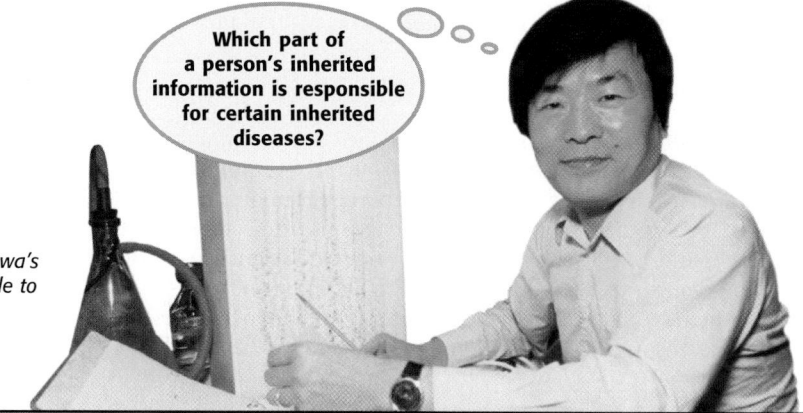

Figure 4 *Susumu Tonegawa's work may help in the battle to fight inherited diseases.*

Pollution Demonstration To help students understand how air pollution is spread from one area to the next, squeeze or peel a lemon or an orange in front of the class. Tell students to raise their hand when they can smell the fragrance. **LS** Kinesthetic   English Language Learners

Writing **Critter Comics** Have students create an imaginary organism and an environment in which it can live. Then, have them create a comic book about it. Students should consider how the organism will eat, which other organisms will live near it, and how the organisms will coexist. English Language Learners
LS Visual   PORTFOLIO

Protecting the Environment

Life scientists also study environmental problems on Earth. Many environmental problems are caused by people's misuse of natural resources. Understanding how we affect the world around us is the first step in finding solutions to problems such as pollution and the extinction of wildlife.

Why should we try to decrease pollution? Pollution can harm our health and the health of other organisms. Water pollution may be a cause of frog deformities seen in Minnesota and other states. Pollution in oceans kills marine mammals, birds, and fish. By finding ways to produce less pollution, we can help make the world a healthier place.

When we cut down trees to clear land for crops or for lumber, we change and sometimes destroy habitats. The man in **Figure 5** is part of a team of Russian and American scientists studying the Siberian tiger. Hunting and loss of forests have caused the tigers to become almost extinct. By learning about the tigers' food and habitat needs, the scientists hope to develop a plan that will ensure their survival.

✔ **Reading Check** Give an example of a pollution problem.

How much space does a tiger need in order to survive?

Figure 5 *To learn how much land area is used by an individual Siberian tiger, Dale Miquelle puts radio-transmitting collars on the tigers.*

SECTION Review

Summary

- Science is a process of gathering knowledge about the natural world. Science includes making observations and asking questions about those observations. Life science is the study of living things.

- A variety of people may become life scientists for a variety of reasons.

- Life science can help solve problems such as disease or pollution, and it can be applied to help living things survive.

Using Key Terms

1. In your own words, write a definition for the term *life science*.

Understanding Key Ideas

2. Life scientists may study any of the following EXCEPT
   a. things that were once living.
   b. environmental problems.
   c. stars in outer space.
   d. diseases that are not inherited by humans.

3. What is the importance of asking questions in life science?

4. Where do life scientists work? What do life scientists study?

Math Skills

5. Students in a science class collected 50 frogs from a pond and found that 15 of these frogs had deformities. What percentage of the frogs had deformities?

Critical Thinking

6. **Identifying Relationships** Make a list of five things you do or deal with daily. Give an example of how life science might relate to each of these things.

7. **Applying Concepts** Look at **Figure 5**. Propose five questions about what you see. Share one of your questions with your classmates.

SCiLINKS® NSTA
Developed and maintained by the National Science Teachers Association

For a variety of links related to this chapter, go to www.scilinks.org

Topic: Careers in Life Science
SciLinks code: HSM0244

Answer to Reading Check

Sample answers: ocean pollution that harms mammals, birds, and fish

---

CHAPTER RESOURCES

Chapter Resource File

- Section Quiz GENERAL
- Section Review GENERAL
- Vocabulary and Section Summary GENERAL

Close

Reteaching ——— BASIC

Asking Questions Display a picture of a scene with organisms in it, or take students outside. Challenge them to write as many questions as they can think of about the organisms. 🄛 Verbal/Visual

Quiz ——— GENERAL

1. Who can be a life scientist? (Anyone from any background can learn to be a life scientist.)

2. Why is polio a less serious health concern now? (Scientists developed a vaccine.)

Alternative Assessment ——— GENERAL

 Writing

Habitat Helpers Ask students to develop ideas about what they can do to help preserve wildlife habitats in their area. Suggest that they contact local environmental organizations for information. Have the students prepare a poster on what they learned. 🄛 Intrapersonal PORTFOLIO

Answers to Section Review

1. Sample answer: Life science is the study of living things.
2. c
3. Scientific investigations usually start with a question.
4. anywhere; anything having to do with living things
5. 15/50 = 30%
6. Sample answer: eat lunch—how digestion works; play with the dog—how animals behave; drive to school—environmental problems; play soccer—how muscles work; play chess—how the brain works
7. Sample answer: How does the scientist get close to the tiger? Where do Siberian tigers live? What do Siberian tigers eat? Do Siberian tigers get cold? Are Siberian tigers the same as other tigers?

Focus

Overview

This section introduces scientific methods used by scientists through a case study of an actual investigation of deformed frogs. The section also demonstrates the development of testable hypotheses and the importance of sharing information among scientists.

Bellringer

Ask students to write a brief response to this question:

"Which is more important, imagination or knowledge?"

Have students share their responses and then debate this question. Raise the point that many important scientists were known for their original thinking and sometimes faced resistance to their new ideas.

Motivate

ACTIVITY — GENERAL

Now You See It As an exercise in observation, display a collection of assorted shapes on the overhead projector. Allow the students to look at the shapes for 15 seconds. Turn the projector off, and have the students spend 5 minutes describing or drawing as many of the shapes as they can in their **science journal.** **Visual/Intrapersonal**

READING WARM-UP

Objectives
- Describe scientific methods.
- Determine the appropriate design of a controlled experiment.
- Use information in tables and graphs to analyze experimental results.
- Explain how scientific knowledge can change.

Terms to Learn
scientific methods
hypothesis
controlled experiment
variable

READING STRATEGY

Reading Organizer As you read this section, make a flowchart of the possible steps in scientific methods.

---

scientific methods a series of steps followed to solve problems

---

Figure 1 *Scientific methods often include the same steps, but the steps are not always used in the same order.*

Scientific Methods

Imagine that your class is on a field trip to a wildlife refuge. You discover several deformed frogs. You wonder what could be causing the frogs' deformities.

A group of students from Le Sueur, Minnesota, actually made this discovery! By making observations and asking questions about the observations, the students used scientific methods.

What Are Scientific Methods?

When scientists observe the natural world, they often think of a question or problem. But scientists don't just guess at answers. They use scientific methods. **Scientific methods** are the ways in which scientists follow steps to answer questions and solve problems. The steps used for all investigations are the same. But the order in which the steps are followed may vary, as shown in **Figure 1.** Scientists may use all of the steps or just some of the steps during an investigation. They may even repeat some of the steps. The order depends on what works best to answer their question. No matter where life scientists work or what questions they try to answer, all life scientists have two things in common. They are curious about the natural world, and they use similar methods to investigate it.

✔ **Reading Check** What are scientific methods? (*See the Appendix for answers to Reading Checks.*)

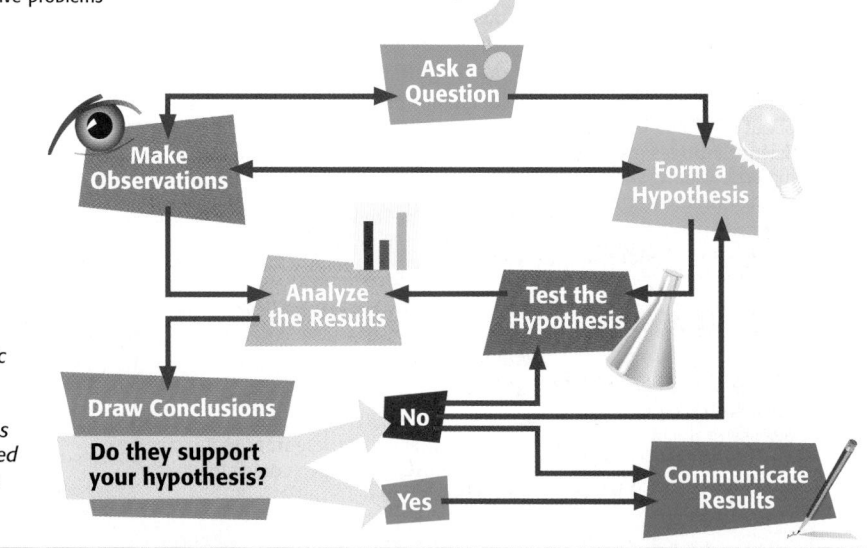

CHAPTER RESOURCES

Chapter Resource File

- Lesson Plan
- Directed Reading A **BASIC**
- Directed Reading B **SPECIAL NEEDS**

Technology

Transparencies
- Bellringer
- Scientific Methods

Answer to Reading Check

a series of steps used by scientists to solve problems

Ask a Question

Have you ever observed something out of the ordinary or difficult to explain? Such an observation usually raises questions. For example, you might ask, "Could something in the water be causing the frog deformities?" Looking for answers may include making more observations.

Make Observations

After the students from Minnesota realized something was wrong with the frogs, they decided to make additional, careful observations, as shown in **Figure 2.** They counted the number of deformed frogs and the number of normal frogs they caught. The students also photographed the frogs, took measurements, and wrote a thorough description of each frog.

In addition, the students collected data on other organisms living in the pond. They also conducted many tests on the pond water, measuring things such as the level of acidity. The students carefully recorded their data and observations.

Accurate Observations

Any information you gather through your senses is an observation. Observations can take many forms. They may be measurements of length, volume, time, or speed or of how loud or soft a sound is. They may describe the color or shape of an organism. Or they may record the behavior of organisms in an area. The range of observations a scientist can make is endless. But no matter what observations reveal, they are useful only if they are accurately made and recorded. Scientists use many standard tools and methods to make and record observations. Examples of these tools are shown in **Figure 3.**

Figure 2 *Making careful observations is often the first step in an investigation.*

Figure 3 *Microscopes, rulers, and thermometers are some of the many tools scientists use to collect information. Scientists also record their observations carefully.*

Teach

📖 **READING STRATEGY** ──── BASIC

Mnemonics Have students develop a mnemonic device that will remind them of the six steps of scientific methods: **A**sk a question, **F**orm a hypothesis, **T**est the hypothesis, **A**nalyze results, **D**raw conclusions, and **C**ommunicate results. An example is "**A**nne **F**ound **T**wenty **A**dorable **D**ogs and **C**ats."
🔊 Verbal/Auditory   English Language Learners

CONNECTION ACTiViTY
Social Studies ──── GENERAL

A Lifetime of Discoveries To help students become aware of how science and technology affect their lives, have them work together to develop a timeline of discoveries that have occurred during their lifetime. Divide the class into small groups, and assign each group a year. Have them use library resources or the Internet to research their year. Each student will be responsible for selecting two events, preparing a note card for each event, and illustrating at least one of the events. The cards should include the year, the discovery, and a few descriptive sentences about the discovery and its significance. Have several volunteers assemble the timeline on a bulletin board.
🔊 Intrapersonal   English Language
Co-op Learning   Learners

WEiRD SCIENCE

Frog Legs In 1786, Luigi Galvani noted that the legs of a dead frog jerked when he touched them with a brass hook. The hook created a small electric current, which stimulated the nerve. The nerve in turn stimulated the muscle. With these observations, Galvani helped to establish the fields of neurophysiology and clinical neurology.

BRAIN FOOD

Imagination Albert Einstein said, "Imagination is more important than knowledge. Knowledge is limited. Imagination encircles the world." He also said, "Logic will get you from A to B. Imagination will take you everywhere."

Demonstration —— GENERAL

Frog Call Scientists who study frogs often locate the frogs by their calls. The northern leopard frog, which inhabits the pond that was studied by the Minnesota students, has quite a peculiar call—a mixture of grunts, snores, and squeaks that sounds like a wet palm being rubbed across an inflated balloon. Ask a volunteer to use a balloon to demonstrate the frog's call for the class.
LS Auditory

Answer to Reading Check

the possibility that an experiment can be designed to test the hypothesis.

Discussion —— BASIC

Testing Hypotheses Answers to questions in many areas of life can be found by forming and testing a hypothesis. Have students form a hypothesis based on the following observation:

The black pavement is hotter than the concrete sidewalk.

Ask students how such a hypothesis might be tested. (Sample hypothesis: A dark surface heats up under the sun faster than a light surface; Sample test: Place dark and light paper in sunlight at the same time and measure temperature over time.) **English Language Learners**
LS Verbal/Logical

CONNECTION TO Environmental Science

WRITING SKILL **Vanishing Amphibians**
Since the 1980s, scientists have been concerned about a steady worldwide decline in the number of amphibians, such as frogs and salamanders. Scientists have studied several possible causes, including UV radiation, chemical pollutants, parasites, and skin fungi. Find a recent news article about one such study, and write a short summary of the article.

Form a Hypothesis

After asking questions and making observations, scientists may form a hypothesis. A **hypothesis** (hie PAHTH uh sis) is a possible explanation or answer to a question. A good hypothesis is based on observation and can be tested. When scientists form hypotheses, they think logically and creatively and consider what they already know.

To be useful, a hypothesis must be testable. A hypothesis is testable if an experiment can be designed to test the hypothesis. Yet, if a hypothesis is not testable, it is not always wrong. An untestable hypothesis is simply one that cannot be supported or disproved. Sometimes, it may be impossible to gather enough observations to test a hypothesis.

Scientists may form different hypotheses for the same problem. In the case of the Minnesota frogs, scientists formed the hypotheses shown in **Figure 4.** Were any of these explanations correct? To find out, each hypothesis had to be tested.

✓ **Reading Check** What makes a hypothesis testable?

hypothesis an explanation that is based on prior scientific research or observations and that can be tested

Figure 4
More than one hypothesis can be made for a single question.

Hypothesis 1:
The deformities were caused by one or more chemical pollutants in the water.

Hypothesis 2:
The deformities were caused by attacks from parasites or other frogs.

Hypothesis 3:
The deformities were caused by an increase in exposure to ultraviolet light from the sun.

Homework —— GENERAL

Writing **Investigate Your Area** Have students observe the daily activities in and around a local pond, woods, or garden over a period of several weeks. Tell students to record their observations in their **science journal.**

LS Visual/Intrapersonal

ACTIVITY —— ADVANCED

PORTFOLIO **Test a Hypothesis** Encourage students to come up with a very simple hypothesis that they can easily test themselves. Require students to have you approve the design of their experiment before they begin. **LS Logical/Intrapersonal**

Predictions

Before scientists can test a hypothesis, they must first make predictions. A prediction is a statement of cause and effect that can be used to set up a test for a hypothesis. Predictions are usually stated in an if-then format, as shown in **Figure 5.**

More than one prediction may be made for each hypothesis. For each of the hypotheses on the previous page, the predictions shown in **Figure 5** were made. After predictions are made, scientists can conduct experiments to see which predictions, if any, prove to be true and support the hypotheses.

Figure 5 *More than one prediction may be made for a single hypothesis.*

Hypothesis 1:
Prediction: If a substance in the pond water is causing the deformities, then the water from ponds that have deformed frogs will be different from the water from ponds in which no abnormal frogs have been found.
Prediction: If a substance in the pond water is causing the deformities, then some tadpoles will develop deformities when they are raised in pond water collected from ponds that have deformed frogs.

Hypothesis 2:
Prediction: If a parasite is causing the deformities, then this parasite will be found more often in frogs that have deformities.

Hypothesis 3:
Prediction: If an increase in exposure to ultraviolet light is causing the deformities, then some frog eggs exposed to ultraviolet light in a laboratory will develop into deformed frogs.

CONNECTION TO Language Arts

WRITING SKILL **Have Aliens Landed?** Suppose that you and a friend are walking through a heavily wooded park. Suddenly, you come upon a small cluster of trees lying on the ground. What caused them to fall over? Your friend thinks that extraterrestrials knocked the trees down. Write a dialogue of the debate you might have with your friend about whether this hypothesis is testable.

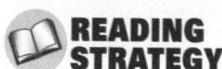

READING STRATEGY — Basic

Roots of Words Have students use a dictionary to find the definition and root origins of the word *hypothesis*. Have volunteers write on the board the information they find. Small groups of students could then compile lists of words that contain the word roots *hypo-* or *-thesis,* as an alternative or additional activity. Example words include *hypothermia, hypoallergenic, synthesis, prosthesis,* and *photosynthesis*. English Language Learners
LS Verbal/Auditory

ACTIVITY — General

Writing Predictions Have students practice writing predictions as "if–then" statements. Some questions they can consider when writing their predictions are the following:

- Is an unknown liquid water or rubbing alcohol? (Sample prediction: If the liquid is alcohol, then it will have an odor.)
- Can plants sense which way is up? (Sample prediction: If the plant is laid on its side for several days, then the stem will begin to curve upward.)
- Do cardinals prefer sunflower seeds to millet? (Sample prediction: If cardinals are offered both sunflower seeds and millet, then they will eat the sunflower seeds first.)

English Language Learners
LS Verbal/Logical

MISCONCEPTION ALERT

It Never Fails Students may believe that an experiment is a failure if their hypothesis is not supported by the data gathered. Remind them that the point of conducting experiments is to investigate the hypothesis and to learn from the data. Often, much can be learned from experiments that disprove a hypothesis or create new questions. Experiments would be pointless if we already knew the outcome.

Answer to Connection to Language Arts

Answers may vary. Sample answer: The hypothesis that extraterrestrials caused the trees to fall is not testable because there is no way to support or disprove the hypothesis. No observations or experiments can be performed to test this hypothesis if the extraterrestrials do not exist or if they are simply gone. A testable hypothesis is that a volcanic eruption knocked the trees down. We can observe volcanoes in action in several places on the planet.

Discussion ————— GENERAL

Are We Next?   At the forefront of the deformed-frog situation are these concerns:

> Is human health at risk? Do the malformed frogs signal a widespread environmental problem?

Discuss these concerns with students, and pose this question: "What steps can scientists take to find out whether humans are also at risk?" **LS** Verbal

Using the Table ——— BASIC

Experimental Factors   Have students study the table on this page. Ask them the following questions:

- What is the only factor that differs between the control group and the experimental groups? (the variable, which is exposure time to UV light)

- What would happen if the temperature varied for each of the groups? (The experiment would not be controlled, because there is more than one variable.)

- How should the experiment be altered if we wanted to test the effect of temperature? (Have a different temperature of water for each group, but do not expose any of them to UV light. Leave the other factors the same.)
LS Verbal/Logical

Answer to Reading Check

only one

Figure 6 *Many factors affect this tadpole in the wild. These factors include chemicals, light, temperature, and parasites.*

controlled experiment   an experiment that tests only one factor at a time by using a comparison of a control group with an experimental group

variable   a factor that changes in an experiment in order to test a hypothesis

Test the Hypothesis

After scientists make a prediction, they test the hypothesis. Scientists try to design experiments that will clearly show whether a particular factor caused an observed outcome. A *factor* is anything in an experiment that can influence the experiment's outcome. Factors can be anything from temperature to the type of organism being studied.

Under Control

Scientists studying the frogs in Minnesota observed many factors that affect the development of frogs in the wild, as shown in **Figure 6.** But it was hard to tell which factor could be causing the deformities. To sort factors out, scientists perform controlled experiments. A **controlled experiment** tests only one factor at a time and consists of a control group and one or more experimental groups. All of the factors for the control group and the experimental groups are the same except for one. The one factor that differs is called the **variable.** Because only the variable differs between the control group and the experimental groups, any differences observed in the outcome of the experiment are probably caused by the variable.

✓ **Reading Check**   How many factors should an experiment test?

Designing an Experiment

Designing a good experiment requires planning. Every factor should be considered. Examine the prediction for Hypothesis 3: *If an increase in exposure to ultraviolet light is causing the deformities, then some frog eggs exposed to ultraviolet light in a laboratory will develop into deformed frogs.* An experiment to test this hypothesis is summarized in **Table 1.** In this case, the variable is the length of time the eggs are exposed to ultraviolet (UV) light. All other factors, such as the temperature of the water, are the same in the control group and in the experimental groups.

Table 1 Experiment to Test Effect of UV Light on Frogs				
	Control factors			**Variable**
Group	**Kind of frog**	**Number of Eggs**	**Temperature of water**	**UV light exposure**
#1 (control)	leopard frog	100	25°C	0 days
#2 (experimental)	leopard frog	100	25°C	15 days
#3 (experimental)	leopard frog	100	25°C	24 days

Is That a Fact!

Evidence suggests that UV light levels are highest in late spring and early summer, the time of year when Minnesota's frog population is laying eggs. Such evidence points to a need for UV experiments in natural environments at various times of the year.

Figure 7 UV Light Experiment

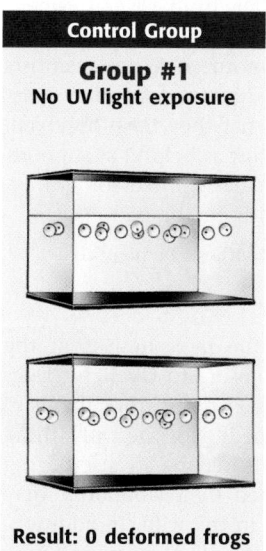

Control Group

Group #1
No UV light exposure

Result: 0 deformed frogs

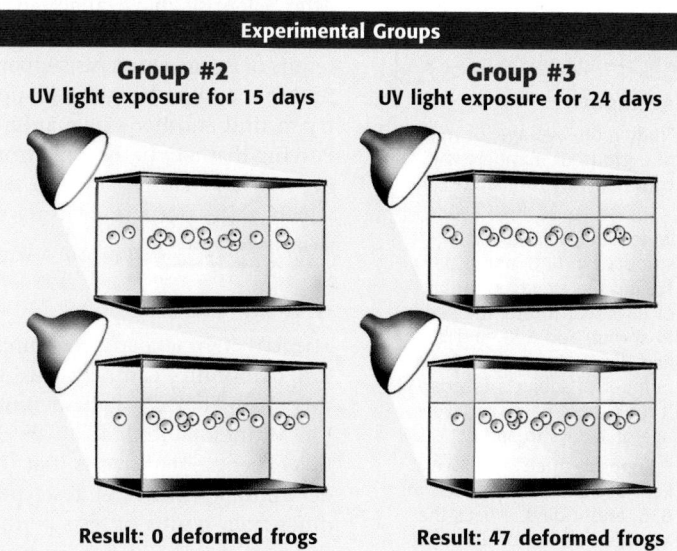

Experimental Groups

Group #2
UV light exposure for 15 days

Result: 0 deformed frogs

Group #3
UV light exposure for 24 days

Result: 47 deformed frogs

Collecting Data

As **Table 1** shows, each group in the experiment contains 100 eggs. Scientists always try to test many individuals. The more organisms tested, the more certain scientists can be of the data they collect in an experiment. They want to be certain that differences between control and experimental groups are actually caused by differences in the variable and not by any differences among the individuals. Scientists also support their conclusions by repeating their experiments. If an experiment produces the same results again and again, scientists can be more certain about the effect the variable has on the outcome of the experiment. The experimental setup to test Hypothesis 3 is illustrated in **Figure 7.** The results are also shown.

Analyze the Results

A scientist's work does not end when an experiment is finished. After scientists finish their tests, they must analyze the results. Scientists must organize the data so that they can be analyzed. For example, scientists may organize the data in a table or a graph. The data collected from the UV light experiment are shown in the bar graph in **Figure 8.** Analyzing results helps scientists explain and focus on the effect of the variable. For example, the graph shows that the length of UV exposure has an effect on the development of frog deformities.

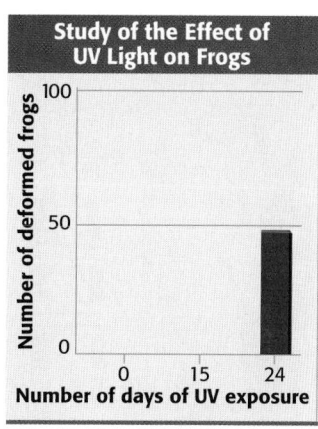

Study of the Effect of UV Light on Frogs

Number of deformed frogs

100

50

0

0   15   24

Number of days of UV exposure

Figure 8 *This graph shows that 24 days of UV exposure had an effect on frog deformities, while less exposure had no effect.*

CONNECTION to
Real Life ——— GENERAL

Frog Investigations In August 1995, students from the Minnesota New Country School in Le Sueur, Minnesota, noticed deformed frogs while on a field trip to a nearby wetland area. The school notified local authorities, fueling a wave of public attention and scientific investigations. The UV light experiment described in this section is an actual example. Have students use the Internet to find other studies on frog deformities. **LS** Intrapersonal/Logical

Using the Figure— BASIC

Control Group Have students carefully examine the experimental setup depicted in **Figure 7.** Be sure that they observe how the setup matches the information in **Table 1.** Ask the following questions:

- Which of the aquariums shown are part of the control group, and which are experimental? (The control group includes the two aquariums shown under #1, in the left-hand column; the experimental groups are the two groups of two aquariums each under #2 and #3 in the right-hand columns.)

- If it was not labeled, how could you tell which group was the control group? (It is the group that does not have any exposure to UV light. The other groups have differing amounts of this variable.)

- Other than the variable, what differences are there between the groups? (none—or at least there shouldn't be—other than the different results for group #3) **English Language**
LS Visual/Logical **Learners**

Discussion ——— ADVANCED

Experimental Setup Discuss the conditions within each of the aquariums in the experiment in **Figure 7.** Ask students to think about any steps that should be taken before the eggs are put in the aquariums. Consider such factors as bottom material (rocks, grass), the cleanliness of each aquarium (were they all washed with the same cleaners?), and so on. Ask students, "How might the experiment be ruined if the environments varied in any significant way?" (A new variable might accidentally be introduced, so the experiment would not be valid.)
LS Visual/Logical

Close

Averages

Finding the average, or mean, of a group of numbers is a common way to analyze data.

For example, three seeds were kept at 25°C and sprouted in 8, 8, and 5 days. To find the average number of days that it took the seeds to sprout, add 8, 8, and 5 and divide the sum by 3, the number of subjects (seeds). It took these seeds an average of 7 days to sprout.

Suppose three seeds were kept at 30°C and sprouted in 6, 5, and 4 days. What's the average number of days that it took these seeds to sprout?

Figure 9 *This student scientist is communicating the results of his investigation at a science fair.*

Draw Conclusions

After scientists have analyzed the data from several experiments, they can draw conclusions. They decide whether the results of the experiments support a hypothesis. When scientists find that a hypothesis is not supported by the tests, they must try to find another explanation for what they have observed. Proving that a hypothesis is wrong is just as helpful as supporting it. Why? Either way, the scientist has learned something, which is the purpose of using scientific methods.

✓ **Reading Check** How can a wrong hypothesis be helpful?

Is It the Answer?

The UV light experiment supports the hypothesis that the frog deformities can be caused by exposure to UV light. Does this mean that UV light definitely caused the frogs living in the Minnesota wetland to be deformed? No, the only thing this experiment shows is that UV light may be a cause of frog deformities. Results of tests performed in a laboratory may differ from results of tests performed in the wild. In addition, the experiment did not investigate the effects of parasites or some other substance on the frogs. In fact, many scientists now think that more than one factor could be causing the deformities.

Puzzles as complex as the deformed-frog mystery are rarely solved with a single experiment. The quest for a solution may continue for years. Finding an answer doesn't always end an investigation. Often, that answer begins another investigation. In this way, scientists continue to build knowledge.

Communicate Results

Scientists form a global community. After scientists complete their investigations, they communicate their results to other scientists. The student in **Figure 9** is explaining the results of a science project.

There are several reasons scientists regularly share their results. First, other scientists may then repeat the experiments to see if they get the same results. Second, the information can be considered by other scientists with similar interests. The scientists can then compare hypotheses and form consistent explanations. New data may strengthen existing hypotheses or show that the hypotheses need to be altered. There are many paths from observations and questions to communicating results.

SECTION Review

Summary

- Scientific methods are the ways in which scientists follow steps to answer questions and solve problems.
- Any information you gather through your senses is an observation. Observations often lead to the formation of questions and hypotheses.
- A hypothesis is a possible explanation or answer to a question. A well-formed hypothesis is testable by experiment.

- A controlled experiment tests only one factor at a time and consists of a control group and one or more experimental groups.
- After testing a hypothesis, scientists analyze the results and draw conclusions about whether the hypothesis is supported.
- Communicating results allows others to check the results, add to their knowledge, and design new experiments.

Using Key Terms

1. Use the following terms in the same sentence: *hypothesis, controlled experiment,* and *variable.*

Understanding Key Ideas

2. The steps of scientific methods
   a. are exactly the same in every investigation.
   b. must always be used in the same order.
   c. are not always used in the same order.
   d. always end with a conclusion.

3. What are the essential parts of a controlled experiment?

4. What causes scientific knowledge to change?

Math Skills

5. Calculate the average of the following values: 4, 5, 6, 6, 9.

Critical Thinking

6. **Analyzing Methods** Why was UV light chosen to be the variable in the frog experiment?

7. **Analyzing Processes** Why are there many ways to follow the steps of scientific methods?

8. **Making Inferences** Why might two scientists working on the same problem draw different conclusions?

9. **Identifying Bias** Investigations often begin with observation. How does observation limit what scientists can study?

Interpreting Graphics

10. The table below shows how long it takes for one bacterium to divide and become two bacteria. Plot this information on a graph, with temperature on the *x*-axis and the time to double on the *y*-axis. Do not graph values for which there is no growth. What temperature allows the bacteria to multiply most quickly?

Temperature (°C)	Time to double (min)
10	130
20	60
25	40
30	29
37	17
40	19
45	32
50	no growth

For a variety of links related to this chapter, go to www.scilinks.org

Topic: Scientific Methods; Deformed Frogs
SciLinks code: HSM1359; HSM0383

Answers to Section Review

1. Sample answer: A good controlled experiment will test a single hypothesis and a single variable at a time.

2. c

3. a control group and one or more experiemental groups that differ by only one factor—the variable.

4. Scientific knowledge changes because scientists conduct new experiments to test new hypotheses, then share their results and build upon existing knowledge.

5. $[(4 + 5 + 6 + 6 + 9) \div 5] = [30 \div 5] = 6$

6. Sample answer: Because the scientists were trying to test the hypothesis that UV light causes deformities, UV light was the factor that needed to be varied—the variable.

7. Sample answer: because sometimes scientists need to go back and change a step, and sometimes they may be able to skip a step if someone else has already done it

8. Sample answer: In addition to the variable being tested, other factors for the control group and the experimental group were not the same.

9. Sample answer: Observations are limited to our human senses or to what we have the technology to observe.

10. See sample graph below. The temperature that allows the bacteria to multiply most quickly is 37°C.

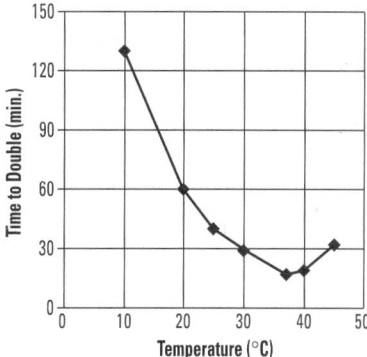

CHAPTER RESOURCES

Chapter Resource File

- Section Quiz GENERAL
- Section Review GENERAL
- Vocabulary and Section Summary GENERAL
- Reinforcement Worksheet BASIC
- Critical Thinking ADVANCED

Workbooks

Math Skills for Science
- What Is an Average? BASIC

Focus

Overview

This section discusses the importance of models in science and defines physical, mathematical, and conceptual models. Students also describe theories and laws.

Bellringer

Have students write answers to the following in their **science journal:**

• What is a model?

• Name several types of models.

• What models have you used?

Discuss students' answers.

Motivate

Discussion ——— GENERAL

Toys as Models Children's toys are often physical models of everyday objects. Have students pass around a variety of toys, such as cars, dolls, and stuffed animals. Discuss how the toys are similar to the objects they represent and how they are different. Discuss the limitations of the toys. (The toys may look similar to the objects they represent, but may be smaller and have simpler features. The limitations of toys as models may be good or bad—the models may be safer, easier to handle, or more durable but not as useful as the real thing.) **English Language**
LS Visual/Kinesthetic **Learners**

READING WARM-UP

Objectives

● Give examples of three types of models.

● Identify the benefits and limitations of models.

● Compare the ways that scientists use hypotheses, theories, and laws.

Terms to Learn

model
theory
law

READING STRATEGY

Reading Organizer As you read this section, create an outline of the section. Use the headings from the section in your outline.

model a pattern, plan, representation, or description designed to show the structure or workings of an object, system, or concept

Scientific Models

How can you see the parts of a cell? Unless you had superhuman eyesight, you couldn't see inside most cells without a microscope.

How do you learn about the parts of the cell if you don't have a microscope? You can look at a model of a cell. A model can help you understand what the parts of a cell look like.

Types of Scientific Models

A **model** is a representation of an object or a system. Models are used in science to help explain how something works or to describe how something is structured. Models can also be used to make predictions or to explain observations. However, models have limitations. A model is never exactly like the real thing—if it were, it would no longer be a model. There are many kinds of scientific models. Some examples are physical models, mathematical models, and conceptual models.

Physical Models

A toy rocket and a plastic skeleton are examples of physical models. Many physical models, such as the model of a human body in **Figure 1,** look like the thing they model. However, a limitation of the model of a body is that it is not alive and doesn't act exactly like a human body. But the model is useful for understanding how the body works. Other physical models may look and act more like or less like the thing they represent than the model in **Figure 1** does. Scientists often use the model that is simplest to use but that still serves their purpose.

Figure 1 *This model looks a lot like a real human body. However, it doesn't act like a real human, which is both a benefit and a limitation.*

CHAPTER RESOURCES

Chapter Resource File

 • Lesson Plan
• Directed Reading A BASIC
• Directed Reading B SPECIAL NEEDS

Technology

 Transparencies
• Bellringer

Workbooks

 Science Skills
• Study Habits GENERAL

 Math Skills for Science
• Arithmetic with Decimals BASIC

Is That a Fact!

Most animal cells are only 10–20 μm long—too small to see with the naked eye. However, some cells are easily seen without the aid of a microscope. An ostrich egg is a single cell that can be as big as 25 cm in diameter!

Figure 2 Mathematical Model: A Punnett Square

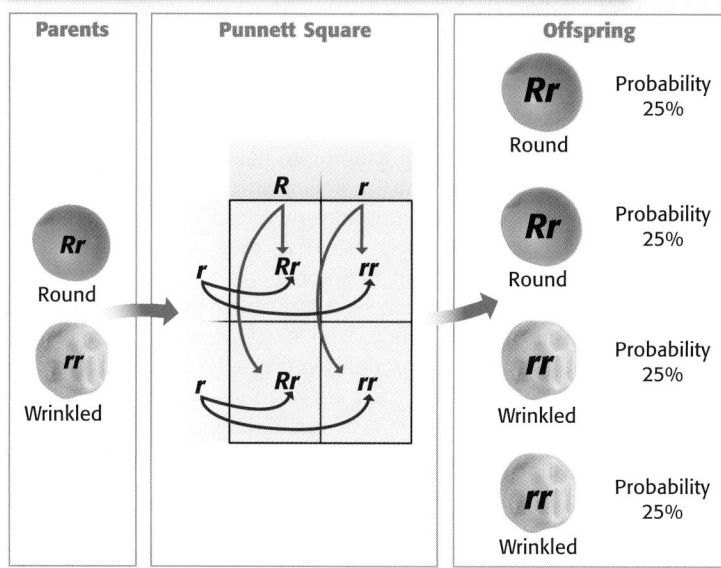

| Parents | Punnett Square | Offspring |

Round

Rr Probability 25% Round

Rr Probability 25% Round

rr Probability 25% Wrinkled

rr Probability 25% Wrinkled

Mathematical Models

A mathematical model may be made up of numbers, equations, or other forms of data. Some mathematical models are simple and can be used easily. The Punnett square shown in **Figure 2** is a model of how traits may be passed from parents to offspring. Using this model, scientists can predict how often certain traits will appear in the offspring of certain parents.

Computers are very useful for creating and manipulating mathematical models. They make fewer mistakes and can keep track of more variables than a human can. But a computer model can be incorrect in many ways. The more complex a model is, the more carefully scientists must build the model.

✓ **Reading Check** What type of model is a Punnett square? (*See the Appendix for answers to Reading Checks.*)

Conceptual Models

The third type of model is the conceptual model. Some conceptual models represent systems of ideas. Others compare unfamiliar things with familiar things. These comparisons help explain unfamiliar ideas. The idea that life originated from chemicals is a conceptual model. Scientists also use conceptual models to classify behaviors of animals. Scientists can then predict how an animal might respond to a certain action based on the behaviors that have already been observed.

CONNECTION TO Social Studies

Gregor Mendel About 150 years ago, Gregor Mendel studied the passing of traits in pea plants. After studying biology at a university, Mendel entered a monastery. His work with peas in the monastery garden started the field of life science called *genetics*.

Use the library or the Internet to research Gregor Mendel. Also, research the time and place where he lived. Discuss the following questions with your classmates: What made Mendel unique in his time? In what ways was Mendel a great life scientist?

ACTIVITY

Science Bloopers

Bridge Breakup On November 7, 1940, the Tacoma Narrows Bridge in Washington broke apart and crashed into the river below after twisting violently for several hours. Because the bridge was destroyed, scientists had to use complex mathematical models and scale models of the bridge to determine the cause of the accident. Both physicists and engineers studied the bridge extensively. Their work led to better construction guidelines and safer bridges.

Answer to Connection to Social Studies

Gregor Mendel lived in Austria in the 1800s and discovered how characteristics of pea plants were inherited. He cross-fertilized pea plants with different characteristics and analyzed the characteristics of the offspring. Once he observed patterns, he used mathematical models to predict the results of future crosses. Mendel was a great scientist in that he made careful observations, designed experiments to test variables individually, and kept careful records. Unfortunately, his work was not shared widely with other scientists for many years.

Reteaching ——— BASIC

Models Ask students to brainstorm a list of items that function as models. For each item, ask whether it is used by scientists, and if so, ask which type of model it is. **Auditory**

Quiz ——————— GENERAL

1. How is a scientific theory different from a scientific law? (A theory is an explanation for a range of information, and a law is simply a summary of a specific set of observations.)

2. What kind of model is a globe, and what are some of its limitations? (A globe is a physical model of Earth. Its limitations include that it does not support life and that it may not have relief features like those of Earth.)

Alternative Assessment ——— GENERAL

Tour-Guide Talk Ask students to write a speech for a tour guide who will lead a group of visitors through a giant model of an organism, organ, or cell. Descriptions of the functions of the parts should be included. Students should also address why the model is important to the understanding of biology and what the limitations of the model are. Students can give their speeches to each other in groups of five or six, and the students in the audience should ask questions and fill in omitted ideas. **Verbal/Interpersonal**

Figure 3 *This computer-generated model doesn't just look like a dinosaur. This model includes the movement of bones and muscles.*

theory an explanation that ties together many hypotheses and observations

law a summary of many experimental results and observations; a law tells how things work

Benefits of Models

Models are often used to represent things that are very small or very large. Models may also represent things that are very complicated or things that no longer exist. For example, **Figure 3** is a model of a dinosaur. Such computer models have been used for many things, including to make movies about prehistoric life on Earth. Models are used, of course, because filming a real dinosaur in action is impossible. But in building models, scientists may discover things they hadn't thought of before.

A model can be a kind of hypothesis and can be tested. To build a model of an organism, scientists must gather information learned from fossils and other observations. Then, they can test whether their model fits with their ideas about how an organism might have moved or what it might have eaten.

Building Scientific Knowledge

Sometimes, scientists may draw different conclusions from the same data. Other times, new results show that old conclusions are wrong. Sometimes, more information is needed. Life scientists are always asking new questions or looking at old questions from a new angle. As they find new answers, scientific knowledge continues to grow and change.

Scientific Theories

For every hypothesis, more than one prediction can be made. Each time another prediction is proven true, the hypothesis gains more support. Over time, scientists try to tie together all they have learned. An explanation that ties together many related facts, observations, and tested hypotheses is called a **theory.** Theories are conceptual models that help to organize scientific thinking. Theories are used to explain observations and also to predict what might happen in the future.

✓ Reading Check How do scientists use theories?

Scientific Laws

The one kind of scientific idea that rarely changes is called a *scientific law*. In science, a **law** is a summary of many experimental results and observations. Unlike traffic laws, scientific laws are not based on what people may want to happen. Instead, scientific laws are statements of what *will* happen in a specific situation. And unlike theories, scientific laws tell you only what happens, not why it happens.

Answer to Reading Check

to explain a broad range of observations, facts, and tested hypotheses, to predict what might happen, and to organize scientific thinking

Homework ——— ADVANCED

Computer-Generated Models Have students search the Internet for images of computer-generated, three-dimensional models of prehistoric organisms. Also, look for information about animated models of prehistoric animals that were created for movies. Have students find out who created the models and how. (Often, a team of scientists, artists, and computer programmers collaborate to create such models, using a variety of tools and experimenting as they go.) **Visual/Logical**

Combining Scientific Ideas

Scientific laws are at work around you every day. For example, the law of gravity is at work when we see a leaf fall to the ground. The law of gravity tells us that objects always fall toward the center of the Earth. Many laws of chemistry are at work inside your cells. However, living organisms are very complex. So, there are very few laws within life science. But some theories are very important in life science and are widely accepted. An example is the theory that all living things are made up of cells.

Scientific Change

History shows that new scientific ideas take time to develop into theories or to become accepted as facts or laws. Scientists should be open to new ideas, but they should always test those ideas with scientific methods. And if new evidence contradicts an accepted idea, scientists must be willing to re-examine the evidence and re-evaluate their reasoning. The process of building scientific knowledge never ends.

CONNECTION TO Physics

The Laws of Physics Part of understanding a scientific law is knowing the conditions under which it is true. Many of the laws of physics deal with a simple set of conditions. For example, Newton's laws of motion are used to predict how objects, such as planets, will move through space. The same laws apply on Earth, but predicting the motion of objects on Earth is more complex. Look up Newton's laws, and then brainstorm ways in which the conditions in space differ from the conditions on Earth.

ACTIVITY

SECTION Review

Summary

● A model is a representation of an object or system. Models often use familiar things to represent unfamiliar things. Three main types of models are physical, mathematical, and conceptual. Models have limitations but are useful and can be changed based on new evidence.

● Scientific knowledge is built as scientists form and revise scientific hypotheses, models, theories, and laws.

Using Key Terms

In each of the following sentences, replace the incorrect term with the correct term from the word bank.

  theory   law

1. A conclusion is an explanation that matches many hypotheses but may still change.

2. A model tells you exactly what to expect in certain situations.

Understanding Key Ideas

3. A limitation of models is that
   a. they are large enough to see.
   b. they do not act exactly like the things that they model.
   c. they are smaller than the things that they model.
   d. they model unfamiliar things.

4. What are three types of models? Give an example of each type.

5. Compare how scientists use theories with how they use laws.

Math Skills

6. If Jerry is 2.1 m tall, how tall is a scale model of Jerry that is 10% of his size?

Critical Thinking

7. **Applying Concepts** You are making a three-dimensional model of an extinct plant. Describe some of the potential uses for your model. What are some limitations of your model?

SCLINKS **NSTA**
Developed and maintained by the National Science Teachers Association

For a variety of links related to this chapter, go to www.scilinks.org

Topic: Using Models
SciLinks code: HSM1588

Answers to Section Review

1. A theory is an explanation that matches many hypotheses but may still change.

2. A law tells you exactly what to expect in certain situations.

3. b

4. Sample answer: physical model: a plastic human body; mathematical model: a Punnett square; conceptual model: cell theory

5. Sample answer: Scientists use laws to predict what will happen under specific conditions but not to explain why. Scientists use theories to make general predictions and explain why they think something happens.

6. 0.21 m or 21 cm

7. Sample answer: The plant model could be used to determine if a certain prehistoric animal was tall enough to reach the leaves of the plant or to show what the environment of a certain prehistoric area looked like. A limitation of the model is that it might not smell or taste like the real plant did.

Answer to Connection to Physics

Sample answer: Moving objects on Earth's surface do not always seem to obey Newton's laws. For example, an object in motion does not always stay in motion. On the surface of Earth, there is a strong force of gravity pulling things towards Earth's center. This force acts on objects at all times, and may change the direction of motion of an object. In addition, Earth has an atmosphere made up of gases. Moving objects experience friction from these gases. Objects moving along the ground experience additional friction.

CHAPTER RESOURCES

Chapter Resource File

• **Section Quiz** GENERAL
• **Section Review** GENERAL
• **Vocabulary and Section Summary** GENERAL

Focus

Overview

This section describes several tools that scientists use to gather information. Students also learn about the International System of Units (SI), a unified global measurement system. They learn the units and tools associated with quantities such as mass and volume. Finally, students learn about lab safety and safety symbols and their meanings.

 Bellringer

Have students write an answer to the following question:

"Why do you think scientists use tools such as graduated cylinders and stopwatches?"

Ask students to share their answers with the class, and briefly discuss their responses.

Motivate

Demonstration ── GENERAL

Tools for Seeing Assemble a collection of images of ordinary objects that were made with light and electron microscopes, X rays, MRI, and CAT scans. Display the images on an overhead projector. Challenge students to identify the objects.
LS Visual   English Language Learners

READING WARM-UP

Objectives
- Give three examples of how life scientists use computers and technology.
- Describe three tools life scientists use to observe organisms.
- Explain the importance of the International System of Units, and give four examples of SI units.

Terms to Learn
technology
compound light microscope
electron microscope
area
volume
mass
temperature

READING STRATEGY

Reading Organizer As you read this section, make a concept map by using the terms above.

technology the application of science for practical purposes; the use of tools, machines, materials, and processes to meet human needs

---

Tools, Measurement, and Safety

Would you use a hammer to tighten a bolt on a bicycle? You probably wouldn't. To be successful in many tasks, you need the correct tools.

Life scientists use various tools to help them in their work. These tools are used to make observations and to gather, store, and analyze information. Choosing and using tools properly are important parts of scientific work.

Computers and Technology

The application of science for practical purposes is called **technology.** By using technology, life scientists are able to find information and solve problems in new ways. New technology allows scientists to get information that wasn't available previously.

Since the first electronic computer was built in 1946, improvements in technology have made computers more powerful and easier to use. Computers can be used to create graphs, solve complex equations, and analyze data. Computers also help scientists share data and ideas with each other and publish reports about their research.

Tools for Seeing

It's difficult to make accurate observations of things that cannot be seen. When the first microscopes were invented, scientists were able to see into a whole new world. Today, the workings of tiny cells and organisms are well understood. New tools and technologies allow us to see inside organisms in new ways. For example, the images shown in **Figure 1** were created by sending electromagnetic waves through human bodies.

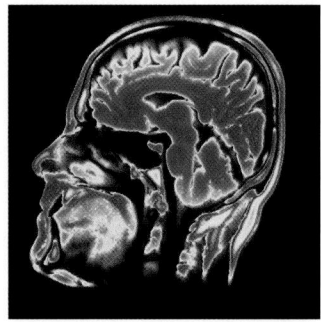 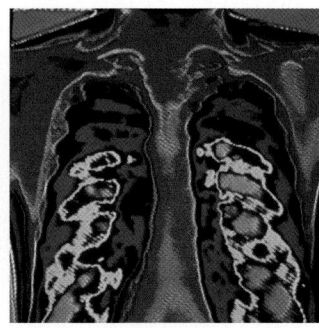

Figure 1 *The image on the left is a computerized axial tomography scan (CAT scan). The image on the right was made with magnetic resonance imagery (MRI).*

CHAPTER RESOURCES

Chapter Resource File

- **Lesson Plan**
- **Directed Reading A** BASIC
- **Directed Reading B** SPECIAL NEEDS

Technology

Transparencies
- Bellringer
- Compound Light Microscope

Science Bloopers

In the 1940s and 1950s, many shoe stores had an X-ray unit designed to assist in fitting shoes. Although the machines were popular, they exposed users to dangerous amounts of radiation. Regulations removed most of the machines by 1970. A few might still be in existence. One was discovered in a department store in 1981 and was promptly removed.

Figure 2 Types of Microscopes

Compound Light Microscope
Light passes through the specimen and produces a flat image.

Transmission Electron Microscope Electrons pass through the specimen and produce a flat image.

Scanning Electron Microscope Electrons bounce off the surface of the specimen and produce a three-dimensional (3-D) image.

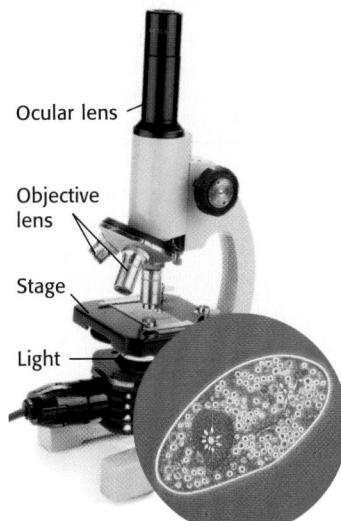

Ocular lens

Objective lens

Stage

Light

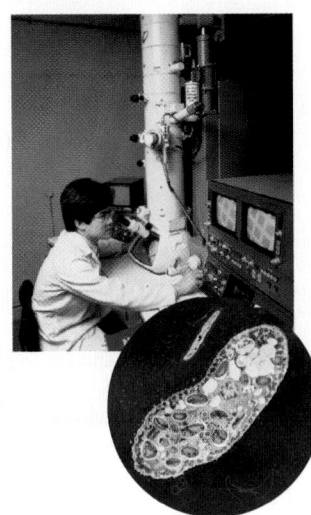

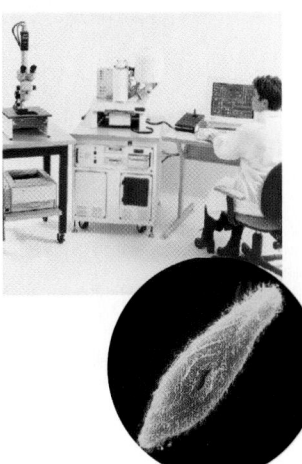

Compound Light Microscope

The compound light microscope is a common tool in a life science laboratory. A **compound light microscope** is an instrument that magnifies small objects so that they can be seen easily. It has three main parts—a tube with two or more lenses, a stage, and a light. Items viewed through a compound microscope may be colored with special dyes to make them more visible. Items are placed on the stage so that the light passes through them. The lenses at each end of the tube magnify the image.

Electron Microscopes

Not all microscopes use light. In **electron microscopes,** tiny particles called *electrons* are used to produce magnified images. The images produced are clearer and more detailed than those made by light microscopes. However, living things cannot be viewed with electron microscopes because the preparation process kills them. There are two kinds of electron microscopes used in life science—the transmission electron microscope (TEM) and the scanning electron microscope (SEM). **Figure 2** shows each kind of microscope, describes the specialized purpose of each, and shows an example of the images each can produce.

Reading Check How are SEMs different from TEMs? (*See the Appendix for answers to Reading Checks.*)

compound light microscope
an instrument that magnifies small objects so that they can be seen easily by using two or more lenses

electron microscope a microscope that focuses a beam of electrons to magnify objects

Debate — GENERAL

SI in U.S. Explain to students that the United States does not use SI to the extent that most other countries do. Have students debate the issue of whether the government should force citizens to use SI for all types of measurement. Suggest that students support their arguments with examples from the history of the English system and SI. **LS** Interpersonal/Verbal

CONNECTION to Math — GENERAL

International System of Units

To help students understand SI conversions, have them answer the following questions:

1. How many meters are there in 2.5 km? (2,500 m)

2. How many centimeters are in 3.1 m? (310 cm)

3. What is 20 km in millimeters? (20,000,000 mm)   English Language Learners
LS Logical

Answer to School-to-Home Activity

Measurements will vary, depending on the standard of measurement chosen. Some units might include hand width, hand length, finger width, or pencil length. (By comparing their units and measurements with others, students should recognize that a standard of measurement is important in order to communicate data and be understood.)

SCHOOL to HOME

How You Measure Matters

Measure the length and width of a desk or table, but do not use a ruler. Pick a common object to use as your unit of measurement. It could be a pencil, your hand, or anything else. Use that unit to determine the area of the desk or table.

To calculate the area of a rectangle, first measure the length and width. Then, use the following equation:

$area = length \times width$

Ask your parent or sibling to do this activity on their own. When they are finished, compare your area calculation with theirs. **ACTIVITY**

Table 1	Common SI Units and Conversions	
Length 	**meter (m)**	
	kilometer (km)	1 km = 1,000 m
	decimeter (dm)	1 dm = 0.1 m
	centimeter (cm)	1 cm = 0.01 m
	millimeter (mm)	1 mm = 0.001 m
	micrometer (μm)	1 μm = 0.000001 m
	nanometer (nm)	1 nm = 0.000000001 m
Volume	**cubic meter (m³)**	
	cubic centimeter (cm³)	1 cm³ = 0.000001 m³
	liter (L)	1 L = 1 dm³ = 0.001 m³
	milliliter (mL)	1 mL = 0.001 L = 1 cm³
Mass	**kilogram (kg)**	
	gram (g)	1 g = 0.001 kg
	milligram (mg)	1 mg = 0.000001 kg
Temperature	**kelvin (K)**	
	Celsius (°C)	0°C = 273 K
		100°C = 373 K

Measurement

The ability to make reliable measurements is an important skill in science. But different standards of measurement have developed throughout the world. Ancient measurement units were based on parts of the body, such as the foot, or on objects, such as grains of wheat. Such systems were not very reliable. Even as better standards were developed, they varied from country to country.

The International System of Units

In the late 1700s, the French Academy of Sciences began to form a global measurement system now known as the *International System of Units* (also called *SI,* or *Système International d'Unités*). Today, most scientists and almost all countries use this system. One advantage of using SI measurements is that it helps scientists share and compare their observations and results.

Another advantage of SI units is that almost all units are based on the number 10, which makes conversions from one unit to another easier. **Table 1** contains commonly used SI units for length, volume, mass, and temperature. Notice how the prefix of each SI unit relates to a base unit.

CHAPTER RESOURCES
Technology
Transparencies
• Common SI Units and Conversions
Workbooks
Math Skills for Science
• What Is SI? GENERAL
• A Formula for SI Catch-Up GENERAL
• Finding Perimeter and Area GENERAL
• Finding Volume GENERAL
Science Skills
• Safety Rules! GENERAL

Is That a Fact!

The International System of Units is abbreviated SI because it stands for the French version of the phrase—*Système International d'Unités.*

Length

How long is an ant? A life scientist would probably use millimeters (mm) to describe an ant's length. If you divide 1 m into 1,000 parts, each part equals 1 mm. So, 1 mm is one-thousandth of a meter. Although millimeters seem small, some organisms and structures are so tiny that even smaller units—micrometers (μm) or nanometers (nm)—must be used.

Area

How much paper would you need to cover your desktop? To answer this question, you must find the area of the desk. **Area** is a measure of how much surface an object has. Area can be calculated from measurements such as length and width. Area is stated in square units, such as square meters (m^2), square centimeters (cm^2), and square kilometers (km^2).

✓ *Reading Check* What kinds of units describe area?

area a measure of the size of a surface or a region

volume a measure of the size of a body or region in three-dimensional space

Volume

How many books will fit into a backpack? The answer depends on the volume of the backpack and the volume of each book. **Volume** is a measure of the size of something in three-dimensional space.

The volume of a liquid is most often described in liters (L). Liters are based on the meter. A cubic meter (1 m^3) is equal to 1,000 L. So 1,000 L will fit into a box measuring 1 m on each side. A milliliter (mL) will fit into a box that is 1 cm on each side. So, 1 mL = 1 cm^3. Graduated cylinders are used to measure the volume of liquids, as shown in **Figure 3.**

The volume of a solid object is given in cubic units, such as cubic meters (m^3), cubic centimeters (cm^3), or cubic millimeters (mm^3). To find the volume of a box-shaped object, multiply the object's length by its width and height. As **Figure 3** shows, the volume of an irregularly shaped object is found by measuring the volume of liquid that the object displaces.

Figure 3 *A rock added to a graduated cylinder raised the level of water from 70 mL to 80 mL of water. Because the rock displaced 10 mL of water and because 1 mL = 1 cm^3, the volume of the rock is 10 cm^3.*

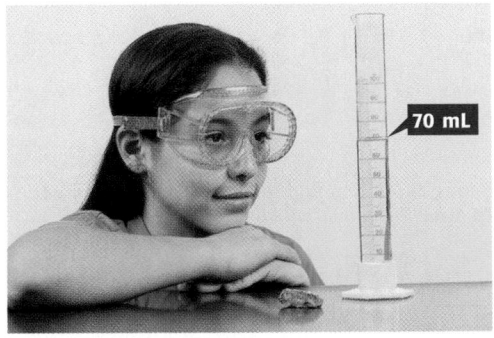
70 mL

80 mL

Close

Answer to Reading Check

how hot or cold it is or how much energy it has

Reteaching — BASIC

SI Estimation Display or name various objects one at a time. For each object, call on a different student to estimate some measurement of the object in SI units. Have another student verify the measurement. **LS** Logical

Quiz — GENERAL

1. What is the SI unit for length? for mass? for temperature? (meter; kilogram; kelvin or degrees Celsius)

2. What is the area of a compact disc case with sides measuring 14 cm and 12.5 cm? (14 cm × 12.5 cm = 175 cm²)

3. How could you find the volume of an irregularly shaped pebble? (Use a graduated cylinder to measure the amount of water that the pebble displaces.)

4. What is temperature? (Temperature is a measure of how hot or cold something is.)

Alternative Assessment — BASIC

 **Draw It** Have students create an illustrated dictionary of key terms that were used in this section. Students can share their dictionaries with the rest of the class. **LS** Visual *English Language Learners*

Measure Up!

1. For each of the following tasks, find a different item to measure. With permission from your teacher or parent, you may choose items within your classroom, school, or home.
   a. Measure length with a **meterstick.**
   b. Measure length with a **metric ruler.**
   c. Measure and calculate area in square meters.
   d. Measure volume with a **graduated cylinder.**
   e. Measure and calculate volume in cubic meters.
   f. Measure mass with a **balance.**
   g. Measure temperature with a **thermometer.**

2. Make a **poster** to present your measurements. Include drawings showing how you measured each item and tips stating how to use the measurement tools properly.

mass a measure of the amount of matter in an object

temperature a measure of how hot (or cold) something is

Mass

How much matter is in an apple? **Mass** is a measure of the amount of matter in an object. The kilogram (kg) is the basic unit for mass. The mass of a very large object is described in kilograms or metric tons. A metric ton equals 1,000 kg. The mass of a small object may be described in grams (g). A kilogram equals 1,000 g; therefore, a gram is one-thousandth of a kilogram. A medium-sized apple has a mass of about 100 g. Mass can be measured by using a balance.

Temperature

How much should food be heated to kill any bacteria in the food? To answer this question, a life scientist would measure the temperature at which bacteria die. **Temperature** is a measure of how hot or cold something is. Temperature is actually an indication of the amount of energy within matter. You are probably used to describing temperature in degrees Fahrenheit (°F). Scientists commonly use degrees Celsius (°C), although the kelvin (K) is the official SI base unit for temperature. You will use degrees Celsius in this book. The thermometer in **Figure 4** shows how two of these scales compare.

✓ **Reading Check** What does temperature indicate about matter?

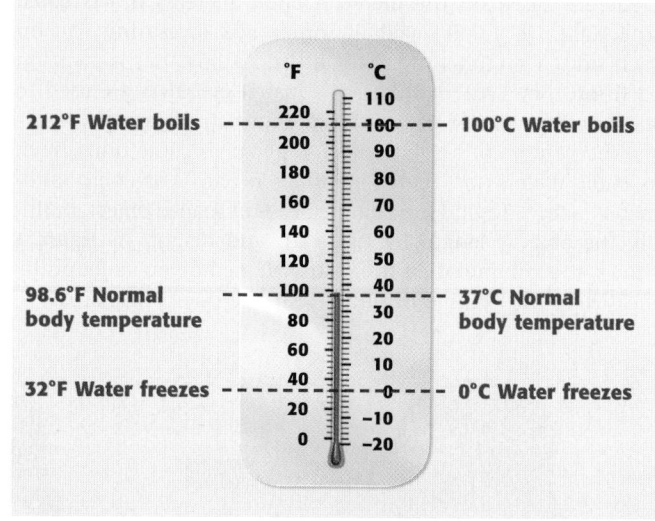

Figure 4 Water freezes at 0°C and boils at 100°C. Your normal body temperature is 37°C, which is equal to 98.6°F.

MATERIALS

FOR EACH GROUP
- balance or scale, metric
- graduated cylinder, 100 mL
- markers, assorted colors
- meterstick
- poster board
- ruler, metric
- thermometer, safety, Celsius

Safety Caution: Supervise and direct students carefully in the safe and responsible use of all equipment. Non-mercury safety thermometers and plastic graduated cylinders are recommended.

Answers

1. Check that students record their observations accurately.

2. Check that student posters portray correct procedures.

Safety Rules!

Life science is exciting and fun, but it can also be dangerous. So, don't take any chances! Always follow your teacher's instructions, and don't take shortcuts—even when you think there is no danger in doing so. Before starting an experiment, get your teacher's permission, and read the lab procedures carefully. Pay particular attention to safety information and caution statements. **Figure 5** shows the safety symbols used in this book. Get to know these symbols and their meanings by reading the safety information in the front of this book. **This is important!** If you are still unsure about what a safety symbol means, ask your teacher.

Figure 5 Safety Symbols

 Eye protection   Clothing protection   Hand safety

 Heating safety   Electric safety   Sharp object

 Chemical safety Animal safety Plant safety

Answers to Section Review

1. area
2. mass
3. volume
4. b
5. Temperature is an indication of the amount of energy within matter.
6. the gram or the milligram
7. 3.0 L = 3,000 mL = 3,000 cm^3
8. 2,194.5 cm^3 or about 2,195 cm^3
9. a SEM; You can tell by the magnification and by the visible three-dimensional features.
10. Sample answer: You could get hurt by an unknown chemical.

SECTION Review

Summary

- Life scientists use computers to collect, store, organize, analyze, and share data.
- Life scientists commonly use light microscopes and electron microscopes to make observations of things that are too small to be seen without help. Electromagnetic waves are also used in other ways to create images.
- The International System of Units (SI) is a simple and reliable system of measurement that is used by most scientists.

Using Key Terms

Complete each of the following sentences by choosing the correct term from the word bank.

mass	area
volume	temperature

1. The measure of the surface of an object is called ___.
2. Life scientists use kilograms when measuring an object's ___.
3. The ___ of a liquid is usually described in liters.

Understanding Key Ideas

4. SI units are
   a. always based on standardized measurements of body parts.
   b. almost always based on the number 10.
   c. used only to measure length.
   d. used only in France.
5. How is temperature related to energy?
6. If you were going to measure the mass of a fly, which SI unit would be most appropriate?

Math Skills

7. Convert 3.0 L into cubic centimeters.

8. Calculate the volume of a textbook that is 28.5 cm long, 22 cm wide, and 3.5 cm thick.

Critical Thinking

9. **Making Inferences** The mite shown below is about 500 μm long in real life. What tool was probably used to produce this image? How can you tell?

10. **Applying Concepts** Give an example of what could happen if you do not follow safety rules.

 SCiLINKS. NSTA
Developed and maintained by the National Science Teachers Association

For a variety of links related to this chapter, go to www.scilinks.org

Topic: Tools of Science; SI Units
SciLinks code: HSM1535; HSM1390

CONNECTION to Physical Science—GENERAL

How Hot? Although students might be most familiar with the Fahrenheit temperature scale, remind them that they will be using the Celsius scale in their science class. Use the teaching transparency "Three Temperature Scales" to demonstrate the importance of paying attention to the units in which a temperature is given. Logical/Visual   English Language Learners

CHAPTER RESOURCES

Chapter Resource File

- Section Quiz GENERAL
- Section Review GENERAL
- Vocabulary and Section Summary GENERAL
- SciLinks Activity GENERAL
- Datasheet for Quick Lab

Technology

 Transparencies
- *LINK TO PHYSICAL SCIENCE* Three Temperature Scales

Interactive Explorations CD-ROM
- Something's Fishy GENERAL

Does It All Add Up?

Teacher's Notes

Time Required
One 45-minute class period

Lab Ratings

EASY ——————————→ HARD

Teacher Prep 🧪🧪
Student Set-Up 🧪
Concept Level 🧪🧪
Clean Up 🧪

MATERIALS

The materials listed on the student page are enough for a group of 2–3 students. Prepare a jug of plain water labeled "Liquid A" and a jug of either isopropyl alcohol (2-propanol, $CH_3CH(OH)CH_3$) or denatured ethyl alcohol (95% ethanol, CH_3CH_2OH) labeled "Liquid B." Safety thermometers are recommended.

Safety Caution

Remind students to review all safety cautions and icons before beginning this lab activity. Caution students to handle thermometers with care and to treat all unknown chemicals as dangerous. Alcohol is flammable and poisonous. Students should wear goggles and aprons at all times. A fire extinguisher and fire blanket should be nearby. Know how to use them. The room should be well ventilated, and students should be familiar with evacuation procedures.

Using Scientific Methods
Skills Practice Lab

Does It All Add Up?

Your math teacher won't tell you this, but did you know that sometimes 2 + 2 does not appear to equal 4?! In this experiment, you will use scientific methods to predict, measure, and observe the mixing of two unknown liquids. You will learn that a scientist does not set out to prove a hypothesis but to test it and that sometimes the results just don't seem to add up!

OBJECTIVES

Apply scientific methods to predict, measure, and observe the mixing of two unknown liquids.

MATERIALS

- beakers, 100 mL (2)
- Celsius thermometer
- glass-labeling marker
- graduated cylinders, 50 mL (3)
- liquid A, 75 mL
- liquid B, 75 mL
- protective gloves

SAFETY

Make Observations

1 Put on your safety goggles, gloves, and lab apron. Examine the beakers of liquids A and B provided by your teacher. Write down as many observations as you can about each liquid. **Caution:** Do not taste, touch, or smell the liquids.

2 Pour exactly 25 mL of liquid A from the beaker into each of two 50 mL graduated cylinders. Combine these samples in one of the graduated cylinders. Record the final volume. Pour the liquid back into the beaker of liquid A. Rinse the graduated cylinders. Repeat this step for liquid B.

Form a Hypothesis

3 Based on your observations and on prior experience, formulate a testable hypothesis that states what you expect the volume to be when you combine 25 mL of liquid A with 25 mL of liquid B.

4 Make a prediction based on your hypothesis. Use an if-then format. Explain why you made your prediction.

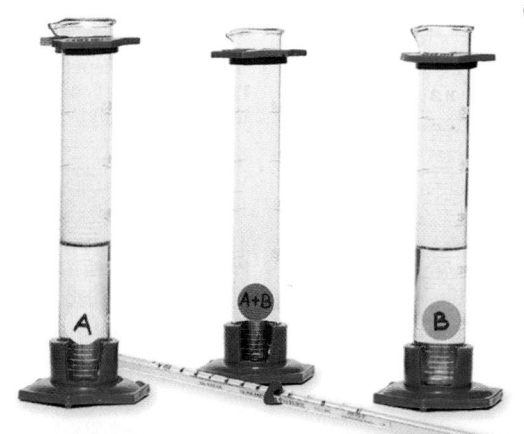

Kevin McCurdy
Elmwood Junior High School
Rogers, Arkansas

CHAPTER RESOURCES

Chapter Resource File

- **Datasheet for Chapter Lab**
- **Lab Notes and Answers**

Technology

Classroom Videos
- Lab Video

- Graphing Data
- A Window to a Hidden World

Data Table				
	Contents of cylinder A	Contents of cylinder B	Mixing results: predictions	Mixing results: observations
Volume				
Appearance		DO NOT WRITE IN BOOK		
Temperature				

Test the Hypothesis

5 Make a data table like the one above.

6 Mark one graduated cylinder "A." Carefully pour exactly 25 mL of liquid A into this cylinder. In your data table, record its volume, appearance, and temperature.

7 Mark another graduated cylinder "B." Carefully pour exactly 25 mL of liquid B into this cylinder. Record its volume, appearance, and temperature in your data table.

8 Mark the empty third cylinder "A + B."

9 In the "Mixing results: predictions" column in your table, record the prediction you made earlier. Each classmate may have made a different prediction.

10 Carefully pour the contents of both cylinders into the third graduated cylinder.

11 Observe and record the total volume, appearance, and temperature in the "Mixing results: observations" column of your table.

Analyze the Results

1 **Analyzing Data** Discuss your predictions as a class. How many different predictions were there? Which predictions were supported by testing? Did any measurements surprise you?

Draw Conclusions

2 **Drawing Conclusions** Was your hypothesis supported or disproven? Either way, explain your thinking. Describe everything that you think you learned from this experiment.

3 **Analyzing Methods** Explain the value of incorrect predictions.

Disposal Informations

Set out a disposal container. Have students pour their water-alcohol mix and any alcohol they have left over into the container at the end of the procedure. Make sure the pH is between 5 and 9, dilute it with 10 times as much water, and pour it down the drain.

Lab Notes

Do not reveal the identity of the liquids until the end of the lab! In this lab, students will likely be surprised to discover that 25 mL of liquid A (water) plus 25 mL of liquid B (an alcohol) do not make 50 mL of the mixture. Spaces between molecules of alcohol become filled with water molecules, resulting in a lower total volume. The water-alcohol mixture will be cloudy and bubbly for a brief time after mixing and may emit some heat. Have students record observations until the mixture becomes clear and then make their final measurements and observations.

Try the following demonstration in order to model the mixing of water and alcohol molecules for your students. Mix 25 mL of marbles with 25 mL of round BB-gun pellets. The BBs will settle between the marbles, and the result will be a total volume less than 50 mL.

Analyze the Results

Note: All answers in this lab are based on student observations and may vary.

1. Students may make some unusual predictions. You may want to lead them into questions about volume. Encourage them to think of many ways to observe and characterize the two liquids. Avoid giving away the explanation too quickly.

Draw Conclusions

2. Check that students are clear about whether or not their hypothesis was supported and in what ways their observations supported or disproved their hypothesis.

3. Incorrect predictions can lead to new questions and a new understanding of the way things work.

Assignment Guide

SECTION	QUESTIONS
1	12
2	2, 6, 7, 13, 18–21
3	3, 15, 16
4	4, 5, 8–11, 14, 17, 22, 23
1 and 2	1

ANSWERS

Using Key Terms

1. Sample answer: You can use scientific methods to study life science.

2. Sample answer: A variable is a part of a controlled experiment.

3. Sample answer: A theory is an explanation for a broad range of observations and hypotheses. A hypothesis is an explanation of a specific set of observations and can be tested.

4. Sample answer: A compound light microscope uses light to create an image of an object. An electron microscope uses electrons.

5. Sample answer: Area is a measure of a surface. Volume is a measure of space or size in three dimensions.

USING KEY TERMS

1 Use the following terms in the same sentence: *life science* and *scientific methods*.

2 Use the following terms in the same sentence: *controlled experiment* and *variable*.

For each pair of terms, explain how the meanings of the terms differ.

3 *theory* and *hypothesis*

4 *compound light microscope* and *electron microscope*

5 *area* and *volume*

UNDERSTANDING KEY IDEAS

Multiple Choice

6 The steps of scientific methods
   a. must all be used in every scientific investigation.
   b. must always be used in the same order.
   c. often start with a question.
   d. always result in the development of a theory.

7 In a controlled experiment,
   a. a control group is compared with one or more experimental groups.
   b. there are at least two variables.
   c. all factors should be different.
   d. a variable is not needed.

8 Which of the following tools is best for measuring 100 mL of water?
   a. 10 mL graduated cylinder
   b. 150 mL graduated cylinder
   c. 250 mL beaker
   d. 500 mL beaker

9 Which of the following is NOT an SI unit?
   a. meter
   b. foot
   c. liter
   d. kilogram

10 A pencil is 14 cm long. How many millimeters long is it?
   a. 1.4 mm
   b. 140 mm
   c. 1,400 mm
   d. 1,400,000 mm

11 The directions for a lab include the safety icons shown below. These icons mean that

   a. you should be careful.
   b. you are going into the laboratory.
   c. you should wash your hands first.
   d. you should wear safety goggles, a lab apron, and gloves during the lab.

Short Answer

12 List three ways that science is beneficial to living things.

13 Why do hypotheses need to be testable?

Understanding Key Ideas

6. c
7. a
8. b
9. b
10. b
11. d

12. Sample answer: Science can be used to find cures for diseases, to understand animal behavior, and to solve environmental problems.

13. Hypotheses need to be testable in order to be useful. If no information can be gathered to either support or disprove a hypothesis, then it is merely an idea that cannot be built upon scientifically.

14. Sample answer: A life scientist studying animals might use a radio collar to track the animal's location, a computer database program to record data, and a computer mapping program to draw maps.

14 Give an example of how a life scientist might use computers and technology.

15 List three types of models, and give an example of each.

16 What are some advantages and limitations of models?

17 Which SI units can be used to describe the volume of an object? Which SI units can be used to describe the mass of an object?

18 In a controlled experiment, why should there be several individuals in the control group and in each of the experimental groups?

CRITICAL THINKING

19 Concept Mapping Use the following terms to create a concept map: *observations, predictions, questions, controlled experiments, variable,* and *hypothesis.*

20 Making Inferences Investigations often begin with observation. What limits are there to the observations that scientists can make?

21 Forming Hypotheses A scientist who studies mice observes that on the day the mice are fed vitamins with their meals, they perform better in mazes. What hypothesis would you form to explain this phenomenon? Write a testable prediction based on your hypothesis.

INTERPRETING GRAPHICS

The pictures below show how an egg can be measured by using a beaker and water. Use the pictures to answer the questions that follow.

Before: 125 mL   After: 200 mL

22 What kind of measurement is being taken?

a. area

b. length

c. mass

d. volume

23 Which of the following is an accurate measurement of the egg in the picture?

a. 75 cm^3

b. 125 cm^3

c. 125 mL

d. 200 mL

24 Make a double line graph from the data in the following table.

Number of Frogs		
Date	**Normal**	**Deformed**
1995	25	0
1996	21	0
1997	19	1
1998	20	2
1999	17	3
2000	20	5

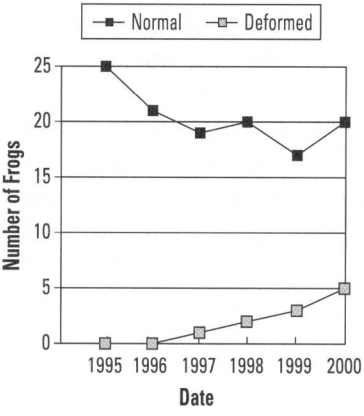

Standardized Test Preparation

Teacher's Note

To provide practice under more realistic testing conditions, give students 20 minutes to answer all of the questions in this Standardized Test Preparation.

> **MISCONCEPTION ALERT**
>
> Answers to the standardized test preparation can help you identify student misconceptions and misunderstandings.

READING

Passage 1

1. C
2. F
3. C

🞣 TEST DOCTOR

Question 2: Answering this question correctly requires the reader to pick up context clues from the sentence and yet not overgeneralize the contents of the entire passage. In the first sentence in which the word *naturalist* is used, the person is strongly associated with both animals and plants, supporting answer F. The second use of the word *naturalist* is associated with the word *theory* (answer H), but a specific theory is named, so the association is not strong.

Standardized Test Preparation

READING

Read each of the passages below. Then, answer the questions that follow the passage.

Passage 1 Zoology is the study of animals. Zoology dates back more than 2,300 years, to ancient Greece. There, the philosopher Aristotle observed and theorized about animal behavior. About 200 years later, Galen, a Greek physician, began dissecting and experimenting with animals. However, there were few advances in zoology until the 1700s and 1800s. During this period, the Swedish naturalist Carolus Linnaeus developed a classification system for plants and animals, and British naturalist Charles Darwin published his theory of evolution by natural selection.

1. According to the passage, when did major advances in Zoology begin?
   - **A** About 2,300 years ago
   - **B** About 2,100 years ago
   - **C** During the 1700s and 1800s
   - **D** Only during recent history

2. Which of the following is a possible meaning of the word *naturalist,* as used in the passage?
   - **F** a scientist who studies plants and animals
   - **G** a scientist who studies animals
   - **H** a scientist who studies theory
   - **I** a scientist who studies animal behavior

3. Which of the following is the **best** title for this passage?
   - **A** Greek Zoology
   - **B** Modern Zoology
   - **C** The Origins of Zoology
   - **D** Zoology in the 1700s and 1800s

Passage 2 When looking for answers to a problem, scientists build on existing knowledge. For example, scientists have wondered if there is some relationship between Earth's core and Earth's magnetic field. To form a hypothesis, scientists started with what they knew: Earth has a dense, solid inner core and a molten outer core. Scientists then created a computer model to simulate how Earth's magnetic field might be generated.

They tried different things with their model until the model produced a magnetic field that matched that of the real Earth. The model predicted that Earth's inner core spins in the same direction as the rest of the Earth, but the inner core spins slightly faster than Earth's surface. If the hypothesis is correct, it might explain how Earth's magnetic field is produced. Although scientists cannot reach the Earth's core to examine it directly, they can test whether other observations match what is predicted by their hypothesis.

1. What does the word *model* refer to in this passage?
   - **A** a giant plastic globe
   - **B** a representation of the Earth created on a computer
   - **C** a computer terminal
   - **D** a technology used to drill into the Earth's core

2. Which of the following is the **best** summary of the passage?
   - **F** Scientists can use models to help them answer difficult and complex questions.
   - **G** Scientists have discovered the source of Earth's magnetic field.
   - **H** The spinning of Earth's molten inner core causes Earth's magnetic field.
   - **I** Scientists make a model of a problem and then ask questions about the problem.

Passage 2

1. B
2. I

🞣 TEST DOCTOR

Question 2: The question requires the reader to choose the statement that best encompasses all of the ideas presented in the passage. Answers G and H state information that was presented in the passage, but in these cases the information was supporting detail and not the focus of the passage. Answer F is supported by the passage but does not summarize the narrative of the passage as accurately as answer I does. For this type of question, suggest that students look for the answer that best tells the "story" of the passage.

The table below shows the plans for an experiment in which bees will be observed visiting flowers. Use the table to answer the questions that follow.

Bee Experiment

Group	Type of bee	Time of day	Type of plant	Flower color
#1	Honey-bee	9:00 A.M.–10:00 A.M.	Portland rose	red
#2	Honey-bee	9:00 A.M.–10:00 A.M.	Portland rose	yellow
#3	Honey-bee	9:00 A.M.–10:00 A.M.	Portland rose	white
#4	Honey-bee	9:00 A.M.–10:00 A.M.	Portland rose	pink

1. Which factor is the variable in this experiment?
   A the type of bee
   B the time of day
   C the type of plant
   D the color of the flowers

2. Which of the following hypotheses could be tested by this experiment?
   F Honeybees prefer to visit rose plants.
   G Honeybees prefer to visit red flowers.
   H Honeybees prefer to visit flowers in the morning.
   I Honey bees prefer to visit Portland rose flowers between 9 and 10 A.M.

3. Which of the following is the **best** reason why the Portland rose plant is included in all of the groups to be studied?
   A The type of plant is a control factor; any type of flowering plant could be used as long as all plants were of the same type.
   B The experiment will test whether bees prefer the Portland rose over other flowers.
   C An experiment should always have more than one variable.
   D The Portland rose is a very common plant.

Read each question below, and choose the best answer.

1. A survey of students was conducted to find out how many people were in each student's family. The replies from five students were as follows: 3, 3, 4, 4, and 6. What was the average family size?
   A 3
   B 3.5
   C 4
   D 5

2. In the survey above, if one more student were surveyed, which reply would make the average lower?
   F 3
   G 4
   H 5
   I 6

3. If an object that is 5 µm long were magnified by 1,000, how long would that object then appear?
   A 5 µm
   B 5 mm
   C 1,000 µm
   D 5,000 mm

4. How many meters are in 50 km?
   F 50 m
   G 500 m
   H 5,000 m
   I 50,000 m

5. What is the area of a square whose sides measure 4 m each?
   A 16 m
   B 16 m^2
   C 32 m
   D 32 m^2

Standardized Test Preparation

1. D
2. G
3. A

 TEST DOCTOR

Question 1: This question requires students to understand the meaning of the term *variable* for a scientific experiment. The variable should be the one factor that varies in the experiment. The table indicates that the type of bee (answer A), the time of day (answer B), and the type of plant (answer C) were the same for all groups and thus could not be the variable.

1. C
2. F
3. B
4. I
5. B

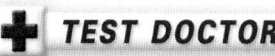 **TEST DOCTOR**

Question 2: To answer this question, the student could recalcualte the average for each of the possible values. There is also a shortcut: because the average is already 4, the only value that would lower the average would be one that is less than 4. Regardless of the method, remind students to check their answer by recalculating with their chosen value to ensure that their answer meets the requirements.

Question 3: This question merely requires knowledge of the standard prefixes used in SI. The symbol μ represents the prefix *micro-* and indicates 1/1,000,000th; the symbol *m* represents the prefix *milli-* and indicates 1/1,000th. Thus, 1 µm is 1/1,000th of 1 mm and 5 µm × 1,000 = 5 mm. Many standardized tests provide a table of SI units and conversions for reference during the test.

CHAPTER RESOURCES

Chapter Resource File

 • Standardized Test Preparation GENERAL

State Resources

 For specific resources for your state, visit **go.hrw.com** and type in the keyword **HSMSTR**.

Scientific Debate

Background

There are three main ingredients of a fire: oxygen, heat, and fuel. Firefighters call this the *fire triangle*, and their goal is to eliminate at least one ingredient. Two groups of firefighters are sent into a forest fire: *hotshots* and *smokejumpers*. Hotshots build a *firebreak* in order to stop the spread of the fire. They clear an area of land of anything that could become fuel for the fire, such as trees, bushes, and grass. The smokejumpers jump from airplanes into remote places to fight small blazes or to start *backfires* in order to eliminate fuel from an oncoming fire.

Science Fiction

ACTiViTY ——— GENERAL

Further Reading If students liked this story, recommend other stories by Edward D. Hoch, such as the following:

- *The Monkey's Clue*
- *The Stolen Sapphire*
- *The Night, My Friend: Stories of Crime & Suspense*

Science in Action

HOLT ANTHOLOGY OF
Science Fiction
HOLT, RINEHART AND WINSTON

Scientific Debate

Should We Stop All Forest Fires?
Since 1972, the policy of the National Park Service has been to manage the national parks as naturally as possible. Because fire is a natural event in forests, this policy includes allowing most fires caused by lightning to burn. The only lightning-caused fires that are put out are those that threaten lives, property, uniquely scenic areas, or endangered species. All human-caused fires are put out. However, this policy has caused some controversy. Some people want this policy followed in all public forests and even grasslands. Others think that all fires should be put out.

Social Studies ACTiViTY

WRITING SKILL Research a location where there is a debate about controlling forest fires. You might look into national forests or parks. Write a newspaper article about the issue. Be sure to present all sides of the debate.

Science Fiction

"The Homesick Chicken" by Edward D. Hoch
Why did the chicken cross the road? You think you know the answer to this old riddle, don't you? But "The Homesick Chicken," by Edward D. Hoch, may surprise you. That old chicken may not be exactly what it seems.

You see, one of the chickens at the high-tech Tangaway Research Farms has escaped. Then, it was found in a vacant lot across the highway from Tangaway, pecking away contentedly. Why did it bother to escape? Barnabus Rex, a specialist in solving scientific riddles, is called in to work on this mystery. As he investigates, he finds clues and forms a hypothesis. Read the story, and see if you can explain the mystery before Mr. Rex does.

Language Arts ACTiViTY

WRITING SKILL Write your own short story about a chicken crossing a road for a mysterious reason. Give clues (evidence) to the reader about the mysterious reason but do not reveal the truth until the end of the story. Be sure the story makes sense scientifically.

Answer to Social Studies Activity
Student articles should reflect objective, journalistic style and present more than one perspective on the issue. Encourage students to research areas that are close to where they live.

Answer to Language Arts Activity
Student stories should include logical clues and have a logical ending. Encourage students to read each other's stories and give each other feedback on the use of scientific reasoning in the story.

People in Science

Yvonne Cagle

Flight Surgeon and Astronaut Most doctors practice medicine with both feet on the ground. But Dr. Yvonne Cagle found a way to fly with her medical career. Cagle became a flight surgeon for the United States Air Force and an astronaut for the National Aeronautics and Space Administration (NASA).

Cagle's interest in both medicine and space flight began early. As a little girl, Cagle spent hours staring at X rays in her father's medical library. Those images sparked an early interest in science. Cagle also remembers watching Neil Armstrong walk on the moon when she was five years old. As she tried to imagine the view of Earth from space, Cagle decided she wanted to see it for herself.

Becoming an Air Force flight surgeon was a good first step toward becoming an astronaut. As a flight surgeon, Cagle learned about the special medical challenges humans face when they are launched high above the Earth. Being a flight surgeon had the extra benefits of working with some of the best pilots and getting to fly in the latest jets.

It wasn't long before Cagle worked as an occupational physician for NASA at the Johnson Space Center. Two years later, she was chosen to begin astronaut training. Cagle is looking forward to her first flight into space. Her first mission will likely take her to the *International Space Station*, where she can monitor astronaut health and perform scientific experiments.

Math

In space flight, astronauts experience changes in gravity that affect their bodies in several ways. Because of gravity, a person who has a mass of 50 kg weighs 110 pounds on Earth. But on the moon, the same person weighs about 17% of his or her weight on Earth. How much does the same person weigh on the moon?

go.hrw.com

To learn more about these Science in Action topics, visit **go.hrw.com** and type in the keyword **HL5LIVF**.

Current Science

Check out Current Science® articles related to this chapter by visiting go.hrw.com. Just type in the keyword **HL5CS01**.

Answer to Math Activity
17% of 110 lb is 18.7 lb.

People in Science

ACTIVITY ——— GENERAL

Flight surgeons work to prevent illness in the abnormal environment of flight. Arrange students into groups, and have them use the Internet to research the medical risks of flight. Have them focus on environmental conditions that can cause problems and ways to prevent those problems. Have each group organize their findings on a poster.

(Low oxygen, decreased pressure, high acceleration, extreme heat or cold, high noise levels, and bright sun can cause medical problems during or after flight. These problems can be prevented with oxygen masks, a pressurized cabin, pressurized suits, and protective masks and clothing.)

MISCONCEPTION ALERT

Mass Confusion Students may confuse density with mass or weight. Ask students the question "Which has more mass: 1 kg of feathers or 1 kg of lead?" (They both have the same mass.) Remind students that the kilogram is a unit for mass, so the masses are the same. Remind students that density involves both mass and volume. Because feathers have a much lower density than lead, 1 kg of feathers would have a much larger volume than 1 kg of lead. Ask students: "In space, if you threw 1 kg of feathers and 1 kg of lead with the same force at the same time, which would move farther or faster?" (Again, note that the two objects have the same mass and were moved with the same force. Thus, according to Newton's laws, the two objects would move at the same speed and keep going until they bump into something or another force acts upon them.)

It's Alive!! Or Is It?
Chapter Planning Guide

Compression guide:
To shorten instruction because of time limitations, omit the Chapter Lab.

OBJECTIVES	LABS, DEMONSTRATIONS, AND ACTIVITIES	TECHNOLOGY RESOURCES
PACING • 90 min pp. 36–41 **Chapter Opener**	**SE** Start-up Activity, p. 37 GENERAL	**OSP** Parent Letter ■ GENERAL **CD** Student Edition on CD-ROM **CD** Guided Reading Audio CD ■ **TR** Chapter Starter Transparency* **VID** Brain Food Video Quiz
Section 1 Characteristics of Living Things • Describe the six characteristics of living things. • Describe how organisms maintain stable internal conditions. • Explain how asexual reproduction differs from sexual reproduction.	**SE** Connection to Physics Temperature Regulation, p. 39 GENERAL **TE** Activity Poster Project, p. 39 GENERAL **TE** Connection Activity Math, p. 40 GENERAL **SE** Skills Practice Lab Roly-Poly Races, p. 48 ◆ GENERAL **CRF** Datasheet for Chapter Lab*	**CRF** Lesson Plans* **TR** Bellringer Transparency* **VID** Lab Videos for Life Science
PACING • 45 min pp. 42–47 **Section 2 The Necessities of Life** • Explain why organisms need food, water, air, and living space. • Describe the chemical building blocks of cells.	**TE** Demonstration Fire and Life, p. 43 BASIC **TE** Activity Poster Project, p. 43 GENERAL **SE** School-to-Home Activity Pen a Menu, p. 44 GENERAL **TE** Activity Vocabulary Review, p. 44 BASIC **SE** Quick Lab Starch Search, p. 45 GENERAL **CRF** Datasheet for Quick Lab* **SE** Connection to Social Studies Whaling, p. 46 GENERAL **SE** Skills Practice Lab The Best-Bread Bakery Dilemma, p. 762 ◆ GENERAL **CRF** Datasheet for LabBook* **LB** Labs You Can Eat Say Cheese!* GENERAL **LB** Long-Term Projects & Research Ideas I Think, Therefore I Live* ADVANCED	**CRF** Lesson Plans* **TR** Bellringer Transparency* **TR** *LINK TO EARTH SCIENCE* The Earth's Land Biomes* **TR** Phospholipid Molecule and Cell Membrane* **CRF** SciLinks Activity* GENERAL **TE** Internet Activity, p. 43 GENERAL

PACING • 90 min

CHAPTER REVIEW, ASSESSMENT, AND STANDARDIZED TEST PREPARATION

CRF Vocabulary Activity* GENERAL
SE Chapter Review, pp. 50–51 GENERAL
CRF Chapter Review* ■ GENERAL
CRF Chapter Tests A* ■ GENERAL, B* ADVANCED, C* SPECIAL NEEDS
SE Standardized Test Preparation, pp. 52–53 GENERAL
CRF Standardized Test Preparation* GENERAL
CRF Performance-Based Assessment* GENERAL
OSP Test Generator GENERAL
CRF Test Item Listing* GENERAL

Online and Technology Resources

Visit **go.hrw.com** for a variety of free resources related to this textbook. Enter the keyword **HL5ALV.**

 **Holt Online Learning**

Students can access interactive problem-solving help and active visual concept development with the *Holt Science and Technology* Online Edition available at **www.hrw.com.**

 Guided Reading Audio CD
Also in Spanish

A direct reading of each chapter for auditory learners, reluctant readers, and Spanish-speaking students.

 Science Tutor CD-ROM

Excellent for remediation and test practice.

KEY

SE Student Edition
TE Teacher Edition

CRF Chapter Resource File
OSP One-Stop Planner
LB Lab Bank
TR Transparencies

SS Science Skills Worksheets
MS Math Skills for Science Worksheets
CD CD or CD-ROM
VID Classroom Video/DVD

* Also on One-Stop Planner
◆ Requires advance prep
■ Also available in Spanish

SKILLS DEVELOPMENT RESOURCES	SECTION REVIEW AND ASSESSMENT	STANDARDS CORRELATIONS
SE **Pre-Reading Activity**, p. 36 `GENERAL` OSP **Science Puzzlers, Twisters & Teasers*** `GENERAL`		National Science Education Standards UCP 5; SAI 1; LS 3c
CRF **Directed Reading A*** ■ `BASIC` , **B*** `SPECIAL NEEDS` CRF **Vocabulary and Section Summary*** ■ `GENERAL` SE **Reading Strategy** Prediction Guide, p. 38 `GENERAL` TE **Inclusion Strategies**, p. 39 MS **Math Skills for Science** A Shortcut for Multiplying Large Numbers* `GENERAL` MS **Math Skills for Science** Multiplying and Dividing in Scientific Notation* `GENERAL` MS **Math Skills for Science** Decimals and Fractions* `GENERAL` MS **Math Skills for Science** Percentages, Fractions, and Decimals* `GENERAL` CRF **Critical Thinking** Intergalactic Planetary Mission* `ADVANCED`	SE **Reading Checks**, pp. 39, 40 `GENERAL` TE **Reteaching**, p. 40 `BASIC` TE **Quiz**, p. 40 `GENERAL` TE **Alternative Assessment**, p. 40 `ADVANCED` SE **Section Review,*** p. 41 ■ `GENERAL` CRF **Section Quiz*** ■ `GENERAL`	UCP 1, 2; LS 1b, 1c, 1d, 2a, 2b, 2c, 3a, 3b, 3c; *Chapter Lab:* UCP 2; SAI 1
CRF **Directed Reading A*** ■ `BASIC` , **B*** `SPECIAL NEEDS` CRF **Vocabulary and Section Summary*** ■ `GENERAL` SE **Reading Strategy** Discussion, p. 42 `GENERAL` TE **Connection to Earth Science** Adaptation, p. 43 `GENERAL` SE **Math Practice** How Much Oxygen?, p. 45 `GENERAL` TE **Inclusion Strategies**, p. 46 CRF **Reinforcement Worksheet** Amazing Discovery* `BASIC` CRF **Reinforcement Worksheet** Building Blocks* `BASIC`	SE **Reading Checks**, pp. 42, 45, 46 `GENERAL` TE **Reteaching**, p. 46 `BASIC` TE **Quiz**, p. 46 `GENERAL` TE **Alternative Assessment**, p. 46 `ADVANCED` SE **Section Review,*** p. 47 ■ `GENERAL` CRF **Section Quiz*** ■ `GENERAL`	UCP 1, 2; LS 1b, 1c, 1d, 2a, 2b, 2c, 3a, 3b, 3c

One-Stop Planner® CD-ROM

This convenient CD-ROM includes:
• Lab Materials QuickList Software
• Holt Calendar Planner
• Customizable Lesson Plans
• Printable Worksheets
• ExamView® Test Generator

CNN student News™

cnnstudentnews.com

Find the latest news, lesson plans, and activities related to important scientific events.

SCiLINKS.
NSTA

www.scilinks.org

Maintained by the **National Science Teachers Association.** See Chapter Enrichment pages for a complete list of topics.

Current Science®

Check out **Current Science** articles and activities by visiting the HRW Web site at **go.hrw.com.** Just type in the keyword **HL5CS02T.**

Classroom Videos

• **Lab Videos** demonstrate the chapter lab.
• **Brain Food Video Quizzes** help students review the chapter material.
• **CNN Videos** bring science into your students' daily life.

Visual Resources

CHAPTER STARTER TRANSPARENCY

Imagine . . .

The Movile Cave, in Romania, is one of the spookiest, slimiest, and smelliest places on Earth. For more than 5 million years, the cave and its inhabitants were sealed off from the outside world. Many of the creepiest organisms known to science inhabit the Movile Cave.

Poisonous water scorpions lurk in murky pools and breathe through snorkels attached to their stomach. Predatory centipedes zero in on smaller bugs and inject them with a paralyzing toxin. Wolf spiders move on spindly legs in pursuit of millipedes, pill bugs, and even their own young!

Almost all living things get their energy either directly or indirectly from the sun. But what about the inhabitants of the Movile Cave, a place where sunlight never enters? The supply of energy that fuels life in the Movile Cave comes from organisms that can't be seen. These microorganisms don't feed on other creepy crawlies; they feed on hydrogen sulfide. This chemical, which smells like rotten eggs, is abundant in the cave. The hydrogen sulfide provides the microorganisms with the energy they need for life. When the microorganisms are eaten, their energy is transferred to other organisms.

Using energy is just one of the characteristics of life. Read on to find out what else all living things have in common.

BELLRINGER TRANSPARENCIES

Section: Characteristics of Living Things
What are four living and nonliving things that you interact with every day? How do you know whether each is living or nonliving? Do you know what the word *inanimate* means? If so, write out a definition. Does *nonliving* mean the same thing as *dead*? Explain your answer.

Write your answers in your **science journal**.

Section: The Necessities of Life
What do you think your mass would be if there were no water in your body? What else besides water is your body composed of? Where do you think you get the minerals that make up your body mass?

Record your answers in your **science journal**.

TEACHING TRANSPARENCIES

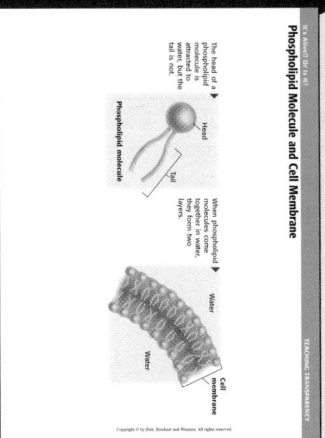

Phospholipid Molecule and Cell Membrane

TEACHING TRANSPARENCIES

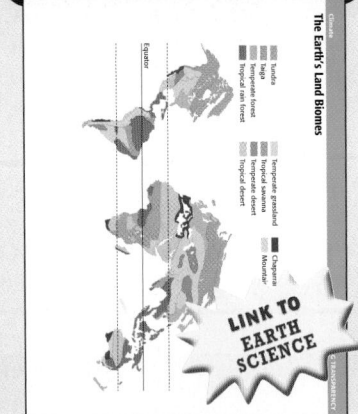

The Earth's Land Biomes

Chapter: Climate

CONCEPT MAPPING TRANSPARENCY

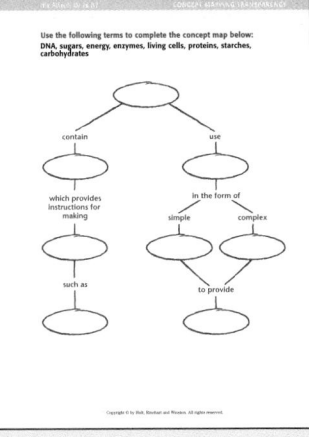

Use the following terms to complete the concept map below: DNA, sugars, energy, enzymes, living cells, proteins, starches, carbohydrates

Planning Resources

LESSON PLANS

Lesson Plan SAMPLE

Section: Waves

Pacing
Regular Schedule: with lab(s):2 days   without lab(s):2 days
Block Schedule: with lab(s):1 1/2 days   without lab(s):3 day

Objectives
1. Relate the seven properties of life to a living organism.
2. Describe seven themes that can help you to organize what you learn about biology.
3. Identify the tiny structures that make up all living organisms.
4. Differentiate between reproduction and heredity and between metabolism and homeostasis.

National Science Education Standards Covered
LSInter6:Cells have particular structures that underlie their functions.
LSMat1:Most cell functions involve chemical reactions.
LSBeh1:Cells store and use information to guide their functions.
UCP1:Cell functions are regulated.
SI1:Cells can differentiate and form complete multicellular organisms.
PS1:Species evolve over time.
ESS1: The great diversity of organisms is the result of more than 3.5 billion years of evolution.
ESS2: Natural selection and its evolutionary consequences provide a scientific explanation for the fossil record of ancient life forms as well as for the striking molecular similarities observed among the diverse species of living organisms.
ST1: The millions of different species of plants, animals, and microorganisms that live on Earth today are related by descent from common ancestors.
ST2: The energy for life primarily comes from the sun.
SPSP1: The complexity and organization of organisms accommodates the need for obtaining, transforming, transporting, releasing, and eliminating the matter and energy used to sustain the organism.
SPSP6: As matter and energy flows through different levels of organization of living systems—cells, organs, communities—and between living systems and the physical environment, chemical elements are recombined in different ways.
HNS1: Organisms have behavioral responses to internal changes and to external stimuli.

PARENT LETTER

SAMPLE

Dear Parent,

Your son's or daughter's science class will soon begin exploring the chapter entitled "The World of Physical Science." In this chapter, students will learn about how the scientific method applies to the world of physical science and the role of physical science in the world. By the end of the chapter, students should demonstrate a clear understanding of the chapter's main ideas and be able to discuss the following topics:

1. physical science is the study of energy and matter (Section 1)
2. the role of physical science in the world around them (Section 1)
3. careers that rely on physical science (Section 1)
4. the steps used in the scientific method (Section 2)
5. examples of technology (Section 2)
6. how the scientific method is used to answer questions and solve problems (Section 2)
7. how our knowledge of science changes over time (Section 2)
8. how models represent real objects or systems (Section 3)
9. examples of different ways models are used in science (Section 3)
10. the importance of the International System of Units (Section 4)
11. the appropriate units to use for particular measurements (Section 4)
12. how area and density are derived quantities (Section 4)

Questions to Ask Along the Way

You can help your son or daughter learn about these topics by asking interesting questions such as the following:

• What are some surprising careers that use physical science?
• What is a characteristic of a good hypothesis?
• When is it a good idea to use a model?
• Why do Americans measure things in terms of inches and yards and meters ?

ALSO IN SPANISH

TEST ITEM LISTING

TEST ITEM LISTING
The World of Science   SAMPLE

MULTIPLE CHOICE

1. A limitation of models is that
   a. they are large enough to see.
   b. they do not act exactly like the things that they model.
   c. they are smaller than the things that they model.
   d. they model unfamiliar things.
   Answer: B   Difficulty: 1   Section: 3   Objective: 2

2. The length 10 m is equal to
   a. 100 cm.   c. 10,000 mm.
   b. 1,000 cm.   d. Both (b) and (c)
   Answer: B   Difficulty: 1   Section: 1   Objective: 2

3. To be valid, a hypothesis must be
   a. testable.   c. made into a law.
   b. supported by evidence.   d. Both (a) and (b)
   Answer: B   Difficulty: 1   Section: 2   Objective: 2

4. The statement "Sheila has a stain on her shirt" is an example of a(n)
   a. law.   c. observation.
   b. hypothesis.   d. prediction.
   Answer: B   Difficulty: 1   Section: 3   Objective: 2

5. A hypothesis is often developed out of
   a. observations.   c. laws.
   b. experiments.   d. Both (a) and (b)
   Answer: B   Difficulty: 1   Section: 2   Objective: 2

6. How many milliliters are in 3.5 kL?
   a. 3,500 mL   c. 3,500, 000 mL
   b. 0.0035 mL   d. 35,000 mL
   Answer: B   Difficulty: 1   Section: 3   Objective: 2

7. A map of Seattle is an example of a
   a. law.   c. model.
   b. theory.   d. unit.
   Answer: B   Difficulty: 1   Section: 3   Objective: 2

8. A lab has the safety icons shown below. These icons mean that you should wear
   a. only safety goggles.   c. safety goggles and a lab apron.
   b. only a lab apron.   d. safety goggles, a lab apron, and gloves.
   Answer: B   Difficulty: 1   Section: 3   Objective: 2

9. The law of conservation of mass says the lot al mass before a chemical change is
   a. more than the total mass after the change.
   b. less than the total mass after the change.
   c. the same as the total mass after the change.
   d. not the same as the total mass after the change.
   Answer: B   Difficulty: 1   Section: 3   Objective: 2

10. In which of the following areas might you find a geochemist at work?
    a. studying the chemistry of rocks   c. studying fishes
    b. studying forestry   d. studying the atmosphere
    Answer: B   Difficulty: 1   Section: 3   Objective: 3

One-Stop Planner® CD-ROM

This CD-ROM includes all of the resources shown here and the following time-saving tools:

• *Lab Materials QuickList Software*
• *Customizable lesson plans*
• *Holt Calendar Planner*
• *The powerful ExamView® Test Generator*

Meeting Individual Needs

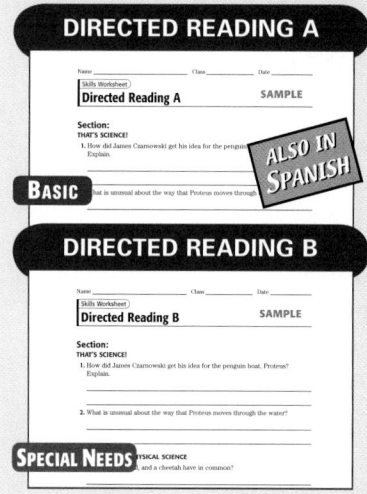

DIRECTED READING A

DIRECTED READING B

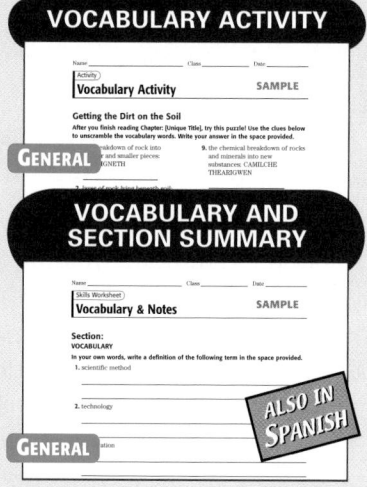

VOCABULARY ACTIVITY

VOCABULARY AND SECTION SUMMARY

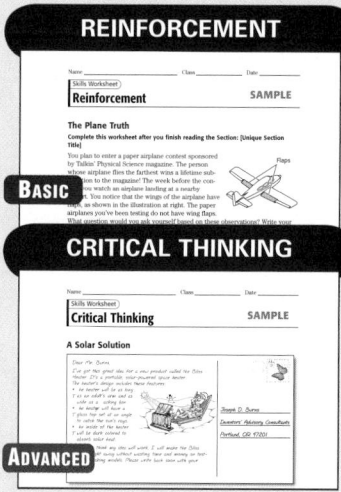

REINFORCEMENT

CRITICAL THINKING

SCILINKS ACTIVITY

SCIENCE PUZZLERS, TWISTERS & TEASERS

Labs and Activities

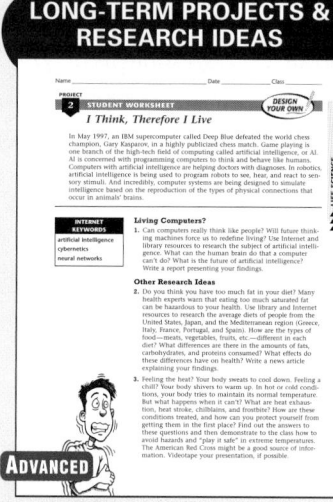

LONG-TERM PROJECTS & RESEARCH IDEAS

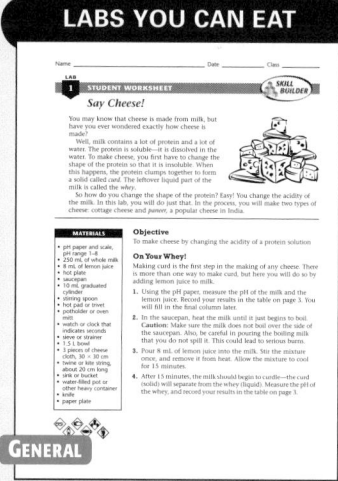

LABS YOU CAN EAT

DATASHEETS FOR QUICK LABS

DATASHEETS FOR CHAPTER LABS

DATASHEETS FOR LABBOOK

Review and Assessments

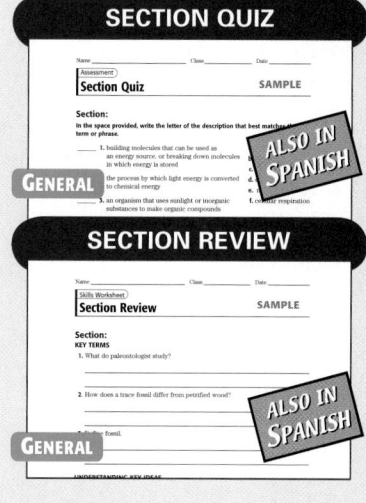

SECTION QUIZ

SECTION REVIEW

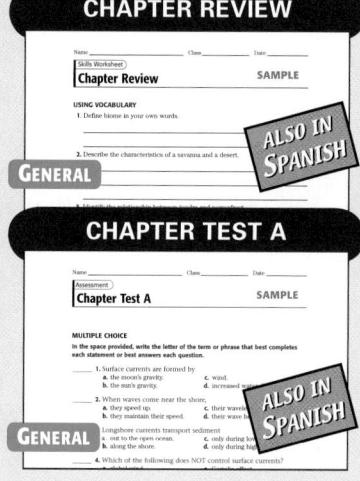

CHAPTER REVIEW

CHAPTER TEST A

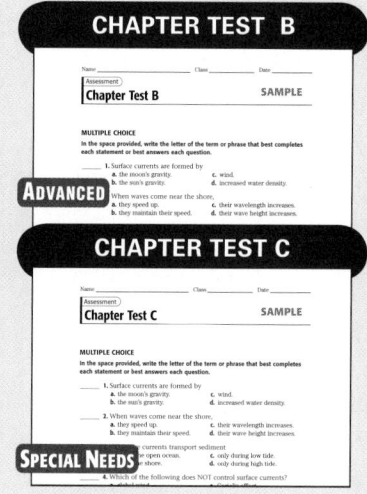

CHAPTER TEST B

CHAPTER TEST C

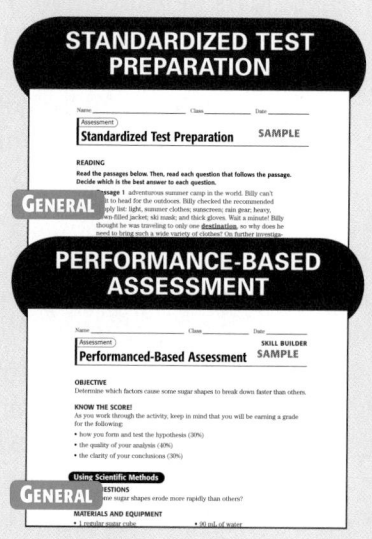

STANDARDIZED TEST PREPARATION

PERFORMANCE-BASED ASSESSMENT

This Chapter Enrichment provides relevant and interesting information to expand and enhance your presentation of the chapter material.

Section 1

Characteristics of Living Things

Biogenesis

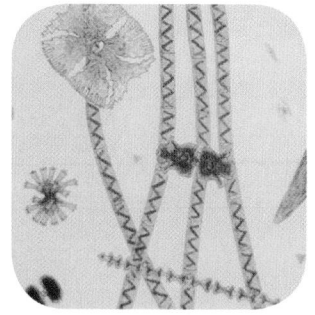

- The theory of biogenesis states that living things come only from other living things. However, until the late 1600s, people generally believed in *spontaneous generation*, the theory that lower forms of life, such as insects, come from nonliving things.

- The first evidence disproving spontaneous generation came from controlled experiments conducted in 1667 by Italian scientist Francesco Redi. Redi showed that maggots will appear on meat in an uncovered jar but not on meat in a closed container. Why? The maggots came from eggs laid by flies that had access to the uncovered meat.

Robert Hooke

- Robert Hooke was one of the greatest scientists of his time. In 1665, he discovered cells with the compound microscope. Hooke was also involved in physics, astronomy, chemistry, geology, and architecture. Hooke applied his discovery of the law of elasticity (which states that the stretching of a solid material is proportional to the force applied to it) to the design of balance springs for watches and clocks. His sketches of Mars were used 200 years later to determine that planet's rate of rotation. In 1672, he developed the wave theory of light to explain diffraction, which he had also discovered. Hooke was the first person to examine fossils with a microscope and to recognize, 200 years before Charles Darwin was born, that fossils provide evidence of changes in organisms on Earth over millions of years.

Is That a Fact!

- ◆ Different cells in the human body have different life spans, which range from a few days for intestinal cells to about 120 days for red blood cells and years for brain cells.

Section 2

The Necessities of Life

A Place to Call Home

- Every organism needs a place to live, and the places where some organisms thrive are surprising.

- Antarctica is a harsh environment. Most of the subantarctic islands are solid rock, and 98% of the continent is covered with ice, but it is home to more than 400 types of lichens and 85 mosses. Lichens can tolerate low temperatures and little moisture. Moss grows on the few patches of soil that exist.

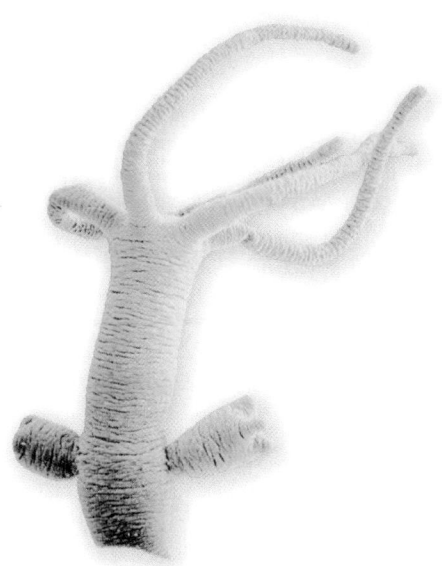

- In Death Valley National Park, summertime temperatures routinely reach 50°C (122°F), and rainfall averages 3.8 cm per year. Yet, more than 900 types of plants live there. More than 400 animal species, including bats, kangaroo rats, bighorn sheep, lizards, tortoises, snakes, spiders, scorpions, beetles, turkey vultures, and roadrunners, also live in this region

- Three to four kilometers into the ocean depths, the pressure is 275 times that at sea level, and it is cold and dark. Huge yellow jellyfish, giant clams, blind fish, and red worms that are 2 m long can be found here. These animals live near deep-sea vents. Water that is heated by volcanic activity to as much as 300°C escapes through these vents. The cold ocean cools the water around the vents to about 13°C. Because there is no sunlight at this depth, the animals use the chemicals in the water for energy through a process called *chemosynthesis.*

Is That a Fact!

◆ The sand grouse of Chad, in northern Africa, builds its nest many miles from water. When the chicks hatch, the parents fly to Lake Chad, where they soak their breast feathers before flying back to their chicks. The chicks then drink the water from their parents' feathers to both feed and cool themselves.

Chemical Menu

● Carbohydrates are the body's primary source of energy. Simple carbohydrates, or sugars, are found in fruits, some vegetables, and milk. Complex carbohydrates, which include starches, are obtained from pasta, seeds, nuts, and vegetables such as peas, beans, and potatoes.

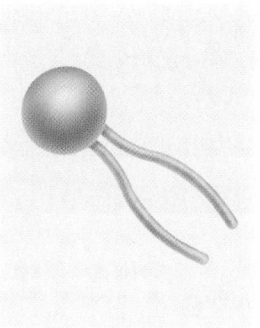
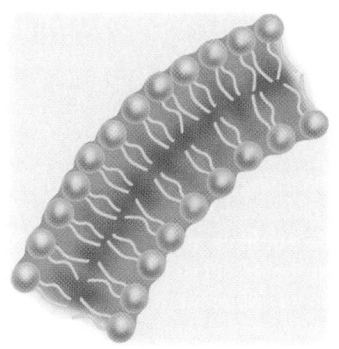

● Lipids include saturated and polyunsaturated fats. Saturated fats are present in greater amounts in animal products. Vegetable-based oils have more polyunsaturated fats.

● Nucleic acids are composed of thousands of nucleotides. The sequence of the nucleotides contains the information for the construction of proteins.

● Proteins are made of 20 different amino acids. Our cells arrange these amino acids in different sequences to make all the proteins in our body.

Is That a Fact!

◆ If stretched out end to end, the DNA in an average human body would measure 20 billion kilometers.

◆ For about 100 years, beginning in the late 1700s, sperm whales were a major source of oil for lubricants and fuel for lamps. These huge animals grow to 18 m long. Whaling made sperm whales nearly extinct.

Metabolism

● Biochemical reactions that take place within a cell are collectively known as *metabolism*. Enzymes, which are proteins, catalyze or accelerate most of the chemical reactions within a cell. Each type of reaction is catalyzed by a specific enzyme.

● A *metabolic pathway* is the sequence of chemical reactions needed to make a particular biological molecule. If a disruption occurs somewhere along the pathway, then the organism might develop an illness or suffer a deficiency.

Is That a Fact!

◆ When bears sleep in their dens during winter, their body temperature decreases several degrees. The lower body temperature reduces energy requirements, so bears can sleep for weeks or months without eating.

SciLinks is maintained by the National Science Teachers Association to provide you and your students with interesting, up-to-date links that will enrich your classroom presentation of the chapter.

Visit www.scilinks.org and enter the SciLinks code for more information about the topic listed.

Topic: Characteristics of Living Things
SciLinks code: HSM0258

Topic: The Necessities of Life
SciLinks code: HSM1018

Topic: Chemistry of Life
SciLinks code: HSM0278

Topic: Life on Other Planets?
SciLinks code: HSM0875

Overview

Tell students that this chapter will help them learn about the characteristics of living things. The chapter also describes the basic nutrient needs of living things and describes some of the molecules cells use for energy and for passing on information.

Assessing Prior Knowledge

Students should be familiar with the following topic:

• scientific methods

Identifying Misconceptions

As students learn the material in this chapter, some of them may be confused about the difference between living and nonliving things. For example, students may think that clouds are living because clouds move and change shape. Many students also mistakenly think that fire is alive. Students often assign intentions to nonliving things and phenomena. For example, students may think that the sun or sunshine *wants* to keep people warm. Students may also confuse cells and molecules. Help them understand that molecules are not alive, that molecules are much smaller than cells, and that cells are made of molecules.

It's Alive!! Or Is It?

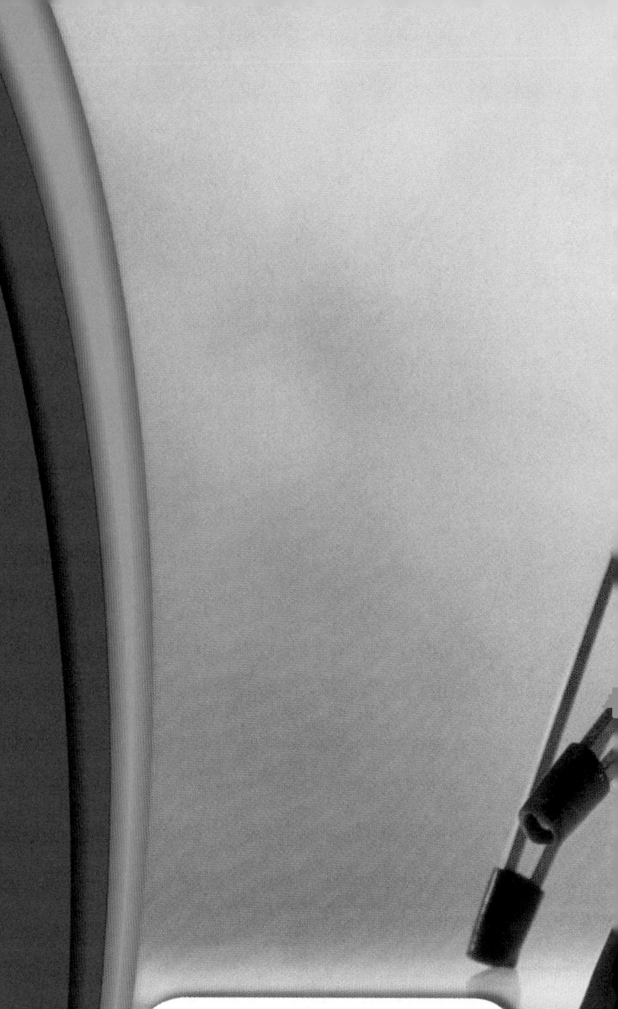

About the PHOTO

What does it mean to say something is *alive*? Machines have some of the characteristics of living things, but machines do not have all of these characteristics. This amazing robot insect can respond to changes in its environment. It can walk over obstacles. It can perform some tasks. But it is still not alive. How is it like and unlike a living insect?

PRE-READING ACTIVITY

Graphic Organizer

Concept Map Before you read the chapter, create the graphic organizer entitled "Concept Map" described in the **Study Skills** section of the Appendix. As you read the chapter, fill in the concept map with details about the characteristics of living things.

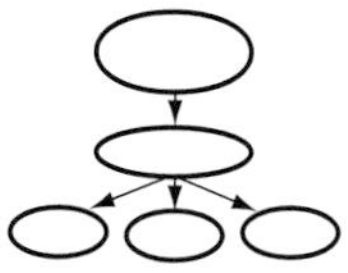

Standards Correlations

National Science Education Standards

The following codes indicate the National Science Education Standards that correlate to this chapter. The full text of the standards is at the front of the book.

Chapter Opener
UCP 5; SAI 1; LS 3c

Section 1 Characteristics of Living Things
UCP 1, 2; LS 1b, 1c, 1d, 2a, 2b, 2c, 3a, 3b, 3c

Section 2 The Necessities of Life
UCP 1, 2; LS 1b, 1c, 1d, 2a, 2b, 2c, 3a, 3b, 3c

Chapter Lab
UCP 2; SAI 1

Chapter Review
LS 1a, 1c, 3a, 3c, 3d, 4b, 4c, 4d

Science in Action
HNS 1

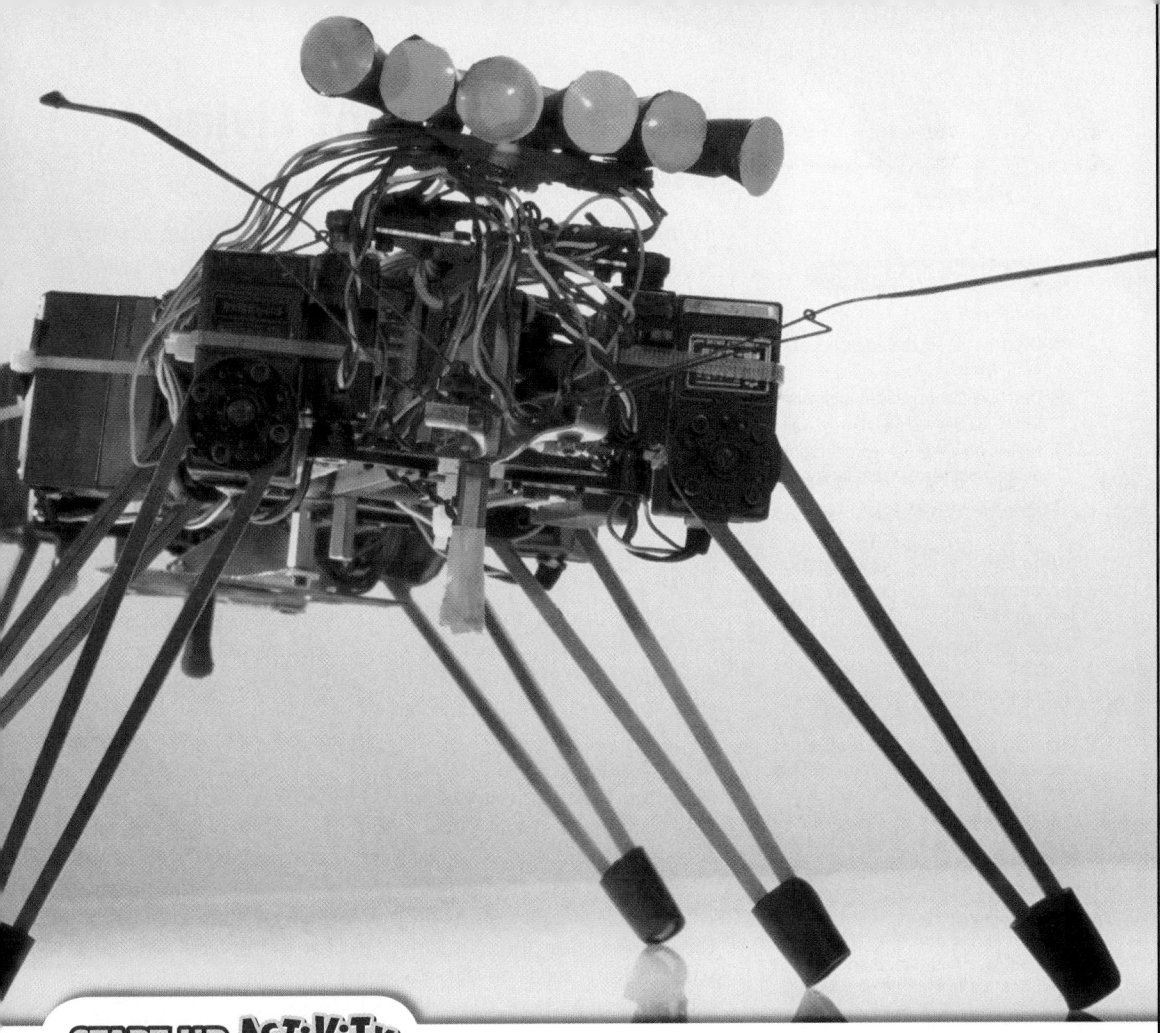

Safety Caution: Students must not use the sun as a source of light.

Answers

1. Sample answer: Pupils were smaller when exposed to light. Pupils became enlarged when light was taken away.

2. Sample answer: In a dark environment, pupils become larger, so more light enters the eye. The surroundings appear brighter and can be more easily seen. In a bright environment, the pupils become smaller, and less light enters the eye. The surroundings are clearly visible without extra light entering the eye. Otherwise, too much light might over-stimulate the eye.

START-UP ACTIVITY

Lights On!

In this activity, you will work with a partner to see how eyes react to changes in light.

Procedure

1. Observe a classmate's eyes in a lighted room. Note the size of your partner's pupils.

2. Have your partner keep both eyes open. Ask him or her to cover each one with a cupped hand. Wait about one minute.

3. Instruct your partner to pull away both hands quickly. Immediately, look at your partner's pupils. Record what happens.

4. Now, briefly shine a **flashlight** into your partner's eyes. Record how this affects your partner's pupils. **Caution:** Do not use the sun as the source of the light.

5. Change places with your partner, and repeat steps 1–4 so that your partner can observe your eyes.

Analysis

1. How did your partner's eyes respond to changes in the level of light?

2. How did changes in the size of your pupils affect your vision? What does this tell you about why pupils change size?

Imagine . . .

The Movile Cave, in Romania, is one of the spookiest, slimiest, and smelliest places on Earth. For more than 5 million years, the cave and its inhabitants were sealed off from the outside world. Many of the creepiest organisms known to science inhabit the Movile Cave.

Poisonous water scorpions lurk in murky pools and breathe through snorkels attached to their stomach. Predatory centipedes zero in on smaller bugs and inject them with a paralyzing toxin. Wolf spiders move on spindly legs in pursuit of millipedes, pill bugs, and even their own young!

Almost all living things get their energy either directly or indirectly from the sun. But what about the inhabitants of the Movile Cave, a place where sunlight never enters? The supply of energy that fuels life in the Movile Cave comes from organisms that can't be seen. These microorganisms don't feed on other creepy crawlies; they feed on hydrogen sulfide. This chemical, which smells like rotten eggs, is abundant in the cave. The hydrogen sulfide provides the microorganisms with the energy they need for life. When the

Chapter Starter Transparency
Use this transparency to help students begin thinking about how living things get energy.

CHAPTER RESOURCES

Technology

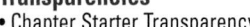 **Transparencies**
• Chapter Starter Transparency

READING SKILLS

Student Edition on CD-ROM

Guided Reading Audio CD
• English or Spanish

Classroom Videos
• Brain Food Video Quiz

Workbooks

 Science Puzzlers, Twisters & Teasers
• It's Alive!! Or Is It? **GENERAL**

Focus

Overview

This section describes the characteristics of living things. Students will learn that living things have cells, sense and respond to stimuli, reproduce, have DNA, use energy, and grow and develop.

Bellringer

Display this question on the board or an overhead projector: "What are four living and four nonliving things that you interact with or see every day?" (Sample answer: living: family members, pets, house plants, trees; nonliving: clothes, books, furniture, radio)

Motivate

Discussion ——— GENERAL

Stimuli Ask students what they do when they go outside and the air is cold. (They put on a jacket or go back inside.) Explain to students that feeling cold is a stimulus and that their reaction to the cold is a response. Ask students how people use technology to improve their ability to respond to environmental stimuli. (Sample answer: furnaces to heat buildings, air conditioners to cool buildings, and sunglasses to shield eyes from bright sunlight)
LS Verbal

SECTION
1

Characteristics of Living Things

While outside one day, you notice something strange in the grass. It's slimy, bright yellow, and about the size of a dime. You have no idea what it is. Is it a plant part that fell from a tree? Is it alive? How can you tell?

An amazing variety of living things exists on Earth. But living things are all alike in several ways. What does a dog have in common with a bacterium? What does a fish have in common with a mushroom? And what do *you* have in common with a slimy, yellow blob, known as a *slime mold*? Read on to find out about the six characteristics that all organisms share.

Living Things Have Cells

All living things, such as those in **Figure 1,** are composed of one or more cells. A **cell** is a membrane-covered structure that contains all of the materials necessary for life. The membrane that surrounds a cell separates the contents of the cell from the cell's environment. Most cells are too small to be seen with the naked eye.

Some organisms are made up of trillions of cells. In an organism with many cells, different kinds of cells perform specialized functions. For example, your nerve cells transport signals, and your muscle cells are specialized for movement.

In an organism made up of only one cell, different parts of the cell perform different functions. For example, a one-celled paramecium needs to eat. So, some parts of the cell take in food. Other parts of the cell break down the food. Still other parts of the cell excrete wastes.

READING WARM-UP

Objectives
- Describe the six characteristics of living things.
- Describe how organisms maintain stable internal conditions.
- Explain how asexual reproduction differs from sexual reproduction.

Terms to Learn

cell
stimulus
homeostasis
sexual
  reproduction
asexual
  reproduction
heredity
metabolism

READING STRATEGY

Prediction Guide Before reading this section, write the title of each heading in this section. Next, under each heading, write what you think you will learn.

cell the smallest unit that can perform all life processes; cells are covered by a membrane and have DNA and cytoplasm

Figure 1 *Some organisms, such as the protists on the right, are made of one cell or a few cells. The monkeys on the left are made up of trillions of cells.*

CHAPTER RESOURCES

Chapter Resource File

- **Lesson Plan**
- **Directed Reading A** BASIC
- **Directed Reading B** SPECIAL NEEDS

Technology

Transparencies
- Bellringer

 **SCIENCE**

An early indication that the pancreas was the organ that secreted insulin, the compound that regulates sugar levels in the blood, came when flies were noticed swarming over the urine of a dog whose pancreas was damaged. The flies were attracted to the excess sugar in the urine.

Figure 2 *The touch of an insect triggers the Venus' flytrap to close its leaves quickly.*

Living Things Sense and Respond to Change

All organisms have the ability to sense change in their environment and to respond to that change. When your pupils are exposed to light, they respond by becoming smaller. A change that affects the activity of the organism is called a **stimulus** (plural, *stimuli*).

Stimuli can be chemicals, gravity, light, sounds, hunger, or anything that causes organisms to respond in some way. A gentle touch causes a response in the plant shown in **Figure 2.**

Homeostasis

Even though an organism's outside environment may change, conditions inside an organism's body must stay the same. Many chemical reactions keep an organism alive. These reactions can take place only when conditions are exactly right, so an organism must maintain stable internal conditions to survive. The maintenance of a stable internal environment is called **homeostasis** (HOH mee OH STAY sis).

Responding to External Changes

Your body maintains a temperature of about 37°C. When you get hot, your body responds by sweating. When you get cold, your muscles twitch in an attempt to warm you up. This twitching is called *shivering*. Whether you are sweating or shivering, your body is trying to return itself to normal.

Other animals also need to have stable internal conditions. But many cannot respond the way you do. They have to control their body temperature by moving from one environment to another. If they get too warm, they move to the shade. If they get too cool, they move out into the sunlight.

✔ Reading Check How do some animals maintain homeostasis?
(See the Appendix for answers to Reading Checks.)

stimulus anything that causes a reaction or change in an organism or any part of an organism

homeostasis the maintenance of a constant internal state in a changing environment

CONNECTION TO Physics

Temperature Regulation
Your body temperature does not change very much throughout the day. When you exercise, you sweat. Sweating helps keep your body temperature stable. As your sweat evaporates, your skin cools. Given this information, why do you think you feel cooler faster when you stand in front of a fan?

Answer to Reading Check
Sample answer: They control their body temperature by moving from one environment to another. If they get too warm, they move to the shade. If they get too cool, they move out into the sunlight.

Answer to Connection To Physics
Sample answer: When a fan is blowing on the skin, more air is passing over it per minute. So, the rate of evaporation increases, allowing more thermal energy to leave the body.

Close

Reteaching — BASIC

Asexual Reproduction Tell students to look at **Figure 4.** Ask them to find the buds that will become new hydras. (Students can find two buds forming close to the base of the hydra.) **LS** Visual

Quiz — GENERAL

1. Explain how you can tell that an apple tree is a living thing. (Apple trees have the six characteristics of living things: they have cells, they sense and respond to change, they have DNA, they can reproduce, they use energy, and they grow.)

2. What is the difference between growth and development? (Growth is an increase in size. Development is a change in the form of an organism that happens as it grows.)

3. Name three activities of an organism that require energy. (Sample answer: Organisms need energy to break down food, to move materials into and out of cells, and to build cell parts.)

Alternative Assessment — ADVANCED

Writing **Responding** Have students read a story of their choice and find five examples of stimuli and responses. Then, have students write an explanation of why the ability to respond to all of these stimuli is important. **LS** Verbal

Figure 3 *Like most animals, bears produce offspring by sexual reproduction.*

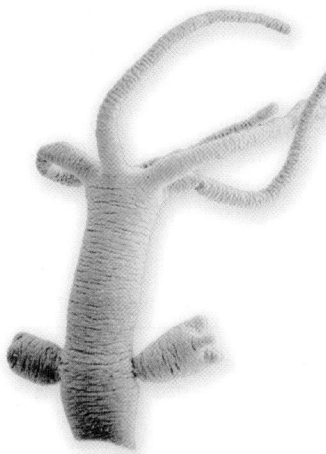

Figure 4 *The hydra can reproduce asexually by forming buds that break off and grow into new individuals.*

sexual reproduction reproduction in which the sex cells from two parents unite, producing offspring that share traits from both parents

asexual reproduction reproduction that does not involve the union of sex cells and in which one parent produces offspring identical to itself

heredity the passing of genetic traits from parent to offspring

metabolism the sum of all chemical processes that occur in an organism

Living Things Reproduce

Organisms make other organisms similar to themselves. They do so in one of two ways: by sexual reproduction or by asexual reproduction. In **sexual reproduction,** two parents produce offspring that will share characteristics of both parents. Most animals and plants reproduce in this way. The bear cubs in **Figure 3** were produced sexually by their parents.

In **asexual reproduction,** a single parent produces offspring that are identical to the parent. **Figure 4** shows an organism that reproduces asexually. Most single-celled organisms reproduce in this way.

Living Things Have DNA

The cells of all living things contain the molecule **d**eoxyribo**n**ucleic (dee AHKS uh RIE boh noo KLEE ik) acid, or DNA. *DNA* controls the structure and function of cells. When organisms reproduce, they pass copies of their DNA to their offspring. Passing DNA ensures that offspring resemble parents. The passing of traits from one generation to the next is called **heredity.**

Living Things Use Energy

Organisms use energy to carry out the activities of life. These activities include such things as making food, breaking down food, moving materials into and out of cells, and building cells. An organism's **metabolism** (muh TAB uh LIZ uhm) is the total of all of the chemical activities that the organism performs.

✓ *Reading Check* **Name four chemical activities in living things that require energy.**

CONNECTION ACTIVITY
Math — GENERAL

Calculating Distance The red kangaroo can cover 12 m in a single jump. The African sharp-nosed frog can jump about 5.4 m. What percentage of the kangaroo's jump is the frog's leap? ($5.4 \div 12 \times 100 = 45\%$) **LS** Logical

Answer to Reading Check

making food, breaking down food, moving materials into and out of cells, and building cells

---

40 **Chapter 2 • It's Alive!! Or Is It?**

Living Things Grow and Develop

All living things, whether they are made of one cell or many cells, grow during periods of their lives. In a single-celled organism, the cell gets larger and divides, making other organisms. In organisms made of many cells, the number of cells gets larger, and the organism gets bigger.

In addition to getting larger, living things may develop and change as they grow. Just like the organisms in **Figure 5,** you will pass through different stages in your life as you develop into an adult.

Figure 5 *Over time, acorns develop into oak seedlings, which become oak trees.*

SECTION
Review

Summary

- Organisms are made of one or more cells.
- Organisms detect and respond to stimuli.
- Organisms make more organisms like themselves by reproducing either asexually or sexually.
- Organisms have DNA.
- Organisms use energy to carry out the chemical activities of life.
- Organisms grow and develop.

Using Key Terms

Complete each of the following sentences by choosing the correct term from the word bank.

cells	stimulus
homeostasis	metabolism

1. Sunlight can be a ___.

2. Living things are made of ___.

Understanding Key Ideas

3. Homeostasis means maintaining
   a. stable internal conditions.
   b. varied internal conditions.
   c. similar offspring.
   d. varied offspring.

4. Explain the difference between asexual and sexual reproduction.

5. Describe the six characteristics of living things.

Math Skills

6. Bacteria double every generation. One bacterium is in the first generation. How many are in the sixth generation?

Critical Thinking

7. **Applying Concepts** How do you respond to some stimuli in your environment?

8. **Identifying Relationships** What does the fur coat of a bear have to do with homeostasis?

SCLINKS® **NSTA**
Developed and maintained by the National Science Teachers Association

For a variety of links related to this chapter, go to www.scilinks.org

Topic: Characteristics of Living Things
SciLinks code: HSM0258

Answers to Section Review

1. stimulus

2. cells

3. a

4. Sample answer: In asexual reproduction, there is one parent, and the offspring are identical to the parent. In sexual reproduction, there are two parents, and offspring share the characteristics of both parents.

5. Sample answer: Organisms are made of cells, detect and respond to stimuli, reproduce, have DNA, use energy, and grow and develop.

6. 64 bacteria

first generation:	1
second generation	2
third generation	4
fourth generation	8
fifth generation	16
sixth generation	32

7. Sample answer: I sweat or shiver to maintain a constant body temperature. I go inside or put on a coat if I get cold. I squint my eyes when the sun is too bright.

8. Sample answer: The fur coat of a bear helps keep the bear's body warm during cold weather. By keeping the bear warm, the coat helps the bear maintain homeostasis.

CHAPTER RESOURCES

Chapter Resource File

- Section Quiz GENERAL
- Section Review GENERAL
- Vocabulary and Section Summary GENERAL
- Critical Thinking ADVANCED

Focus

Overview

This section identifies the things that an organism needs to live. Students will learn the roles that food, water, and air play in an organism's survival. They will also learn that where an organism lives is related to its ability to obtain the necessities of life. Students will also learn about the chemical building blocks and processes necessary for life.

Bellringer

Have students answer the following question in their **science journal:** "What do you think your mass would be if there were no water in your body?" (Sample answer: If a student has a mass of 40 kg, the water's mass is 40 kg × 0.70 = 28 kg. The student's mass without water would be 40 kg − 28 kg = 12 kg.)

Answer to Reading Check

photosynthesis

READING WARM-UP

Objectives

● Explain why organisms need food, water, air, and living space.

● Describe the chemical building blocks of cells.

Terms to Learn

producer   lipid
consumer   phospholipid
decomposer   ATP
protein   nucleic acid
carbohydrate

READING STRATEGY

Discussion Read this section silently. Write down questions that you have about this section. Discuss your questions in a small group.

The Necessities of Life

Would it surprise you to learn that you have the same basic needs as a tree, a frog, and a fly?

In fact, almost every organism has the same basic needs: water, air, a place to live, and food.

Water

You may know that your body is made mostly of water. In fact, your cells and the cells of almost all living organisms are approximately 70% water. Most of the chemical reactions involved in metabolism require water.

Organisms differ greatly in terms of how much water they need and how they get it. You could survive for only about three days without water. You get water from the fluids you drink and the food you eat. The desert-dwelling kangaroo rat never drinks. It gets all of its water from its food.

Air

Air is a mixture of several different gases, including oxygen and carbon dioxide. Most living things use oxygen in the chemical process that releases energy from food. Organisms living on land get oxygen from the air. Organisms living in water either take in dissolved oxygen from the water or come to the water's surface to get oxygen from the air. The European diving spider in **Figure 1** goes to great lengths to get oxygen.

Green plants, algae, and some bacteria need carbon dioxide gas in addition to oxygen. These organisms produce food and oxygen by using photosynthesis (FOHT oh SIN thuh sis). In *photosynthesis*, green organisms convert the energy in sunlight to energy stored in food.

Reading Check What process do plants use to make food? (*See the Appendix for answers to Reading Checks.*)

Figure 1 *This spider surrounds itself with an air bubble that provides the spider with a source of oxygen underwater.*

CHAPTER RESOURCES

Chapter Resource File

● **Lesson Plan**
● **Directed Reading A** BASIC
● **Directed Reading B** SPECIAL NEEDS

Technology

Transparencies
● Bellringer
● *LINK TO EARTH SCIENCE* The Earth's Land Biomes

Is That a Fact!

Camels in the Sahara don't need to drink water at all during the winter months. They get enough water from the plants they eat. During the hottest part of the summer, they can go a week without drinking water. When a water source is available, they can drink up to 190 L (50 gal) at a time!

A Place to Live

All organisms need a place to live that contains all of the things they need to survive. Some organisms, such as elephants, require a large amount of space. Other organisms may live their entire life in one place.

Space on Earth is limited. So, organisms often compete with each other for food, water, and other necessities. Many animals, including the warbler in **Figure 2,** will claim a particular space. After claiming a space, they try to keep other animals away.

Food

All living things need food. Food gives organisms energy and the raw materials needed to carry on life processes. Organisms use nutrients from food to replace cells and build body parts. But not all organisms get food in the same way. In fact, organisms can be grouped into three different groups based on how they get their food.

Making Food

Some organisms, such as plants, are called producers. **Producers** can make their own food. Like most producers, plants use energy from the sun to make food from water and carbon dioxide. Some producers get energy and food from the chemicals in their environment.

Taking Food

Other organisms are called **consumers** because they must eat (consume) other organisms to get food. The frog in **Figure 3** is an example of a consumer. It gets the energy it needs by eating insects and other organisms.

Some consumers are decomposers. **Decomposers** are organisms that get their food by breaking down the nutrients in dead organisms or animal wastes. The mushroom in **Figure 3** is a decomposer.

Figure 2 *A warbler's song is more than just a pretty tune. The warbler is protecting its home by telling other warblers to stay out of its territory.*

producer an organism that can make its own food by using energy from its surroundings

consumer an organism that eats other organisms or organic matter

decomposer an organism that gets energy by breaking down the remains of dead organisms or animal wastes and consuming or absorbing the nutrients

Figure 3 *The frog is a consumer. The mushroom is a decomposer. The green plants are producers.*

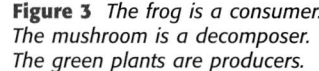

ACTIVITY ———— GENERAL

Writing **Poster Project** Have students collect pictures from magazines and create a poster that shows the home of a plant and the home of an animal with all the necessities of life that were discussed in this section. **LS Visual**

INTERNET ACTIVITY
Short Story ———— GENERAL

For an internet activity related to this chapter, have students go to **go.hrw.com** and type in the keyword **HL5ALVW.**

ACTIVITY — BASIC

Vocabulary Review Have students unscramble the following words and then use all four in a single sentence.

cdporesru (producers)
gnreey (energy)
dofo (food)
rwtea (water)

(Sample sentence: Producers use energy from the sun to make food from carbon dioxide and water.)

LS Logical/Verbal

Using the Figure — BASIC

Protein Structures

Writing Have students discuss or describe in writing the characteristics of each of the protein structures illustrated in **Figure 4.** Ask students the following question: "How can all of these structures be proteins and have such different properties?" (Sample answer: Most proteins are made from different combinations of the same 20 amino acids. Different combinations of amino acids create proteins with different characteristics.)

LS Auditory/Verbal

SCHOOL to HOME

Pen a Menu

WRITING SKILL With a parent, write a menu for a favorite meal. Using Nutrition Facts labels, find out which items on your menu include proteins, carbohydrates, and fats. Try making the meal.

ACTIVITY

protein a molecule that is made up of amino acids and that is needed to build and repair body structures and to regulate processes in the body

Putting It All Together

Some organisms make their own food. Some organisms get food from eating other organisms. But all organisms need to break down that food in order to use the nutrients in it.

Nutrients are made up of molecules. A *molecule* is a substance made when two or more atoms combine. Molecules made of different kinds of atoms are *compounds*. Molecules found in living things are usually made of different combinations of six elements: carbon, hydrogen, nitrogen, oxygen, phosphorus, and sulfur. These elements combine to form proteins, carbohydrates, lipids, ATP, and nucleic acids.

Proteins

Almost all of the life processes of a cell involve proteins. **Proteins** are large molecules that are made up of smaller molecules called *amino acids*.

Making Proteins

Organisms break down the proteins in food to supply their cells with amino acids. These amino acids are then linked together to form new proteins. Some proteins are made up of only a few amino acids, but others contain more than 10,000 amino acids.

Proteins in Action

Proteins have many different functions. Some proteins form structures that are easy to see, such as those in **Figure 4.** Other proteins are very small and help cells do their jobs. Inside red blood cells, the protein hemoglobin (HEE moh GLOH bin) binds to oxygen to deliver and release oxygen throughout the body. Some proteins protect cells. Other proteins, called *enzymes* (EN ZIEMZ), start or speed up chemical reactions in cells.

Figure 4 *Spider webs, hair, horns, and feathers are all made from proteins.*

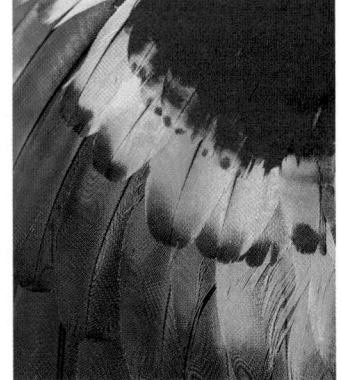

Cultural Awareness — GENERAL

Staple Crops Hunters and gatherers of all races historically required very large areas of land to sustain themselves. Most cultures later developed farming and herding techniques that made higher population densities possible. Staple crops vary around the world, but the millet and sorghum grains of Africans, the wheat and barley of Europeans, the corn and squash of Native Americans, and the rice and soybeans of Asians, in correct amounts and supplemented with other foods, are all equally nutritious. Have interested students research the diet of another culture and compose a menu representing the food of that culture. **LS** Verbal

Figure 5 *The extra sugar in a potato plant is stored in the potato as starch, a complex carbohydrate.*

Carbohydrates

Molecules made of sugars are called **carbohydrates.** Cells use carbohydrates as a source of energy and for energy storage. An organism's cells break down carbohydrates to release the energy stored in them. There are two kinds of carbohydrates—simple carbohydrates and complex carbohydrates.

Simple Carbohydrates

Simple carbohydrates are made up of one sugar molecule or a few sugar molecules linked together. Table sugar and the sugar in fruits are examples of simple carbohydrates.

Complex Carbohydrates

When an organism has more sugar than it needs, its extra sugar may be stored as complex carbohydrates. *Complex carbohydrates* are made of hundreds of sugar molecules linked together. Plants, such as the potato plant in **Figure 5,** store extra sugar as starch. When you eat mashed potatoes, you are eating a potato plant's stored starch. Your body then breaks down this complex carbohydrate to release the energy stored in the potato.

Reading Check What is the difference between simple carbohydrates and complex carbohydrates?

carbohydrate a class of energy-giving nutrients that includes sugars, starches, and fiber; contains carbon, hydrogen, and oxygen

How Much Oxygen?

Each red blood cell carries about 250 million molecules of hemoglobin. How many molecules of oxygen could a single red blood cell deliver throughout the body if every hemoglobin molecule attached to four oxygen molecules?

Starch Search

1. Obtain several **food samples** from your teacher.
2. Put **a few drops of iodine** on each sample. Record your observations. **Caution:** Iodine can stain clothing.
3. When iodine comes into contact with starch, a black substance appears. Which samples contain starch?

Answer to Reading Check

Simple carbohydrates are made of one sugar. Complex carbohydrates are made of many sugars linked together.

Quiz ─────────── GENERAL

1. Give an example of a producer, consumer, and a decomposer. (Sample answer: producer: plants; consumer: animals; decomposer: fungi)

2. Name two functions of lipids. (Some lipids store energy, and others form the cell membrane.)

3. How are proteins used by an organism? (An organism breaks down proteins and uses their amino acids to build other proteins. These other proteins are used to carry out chemical reactions in cells, transport materials, and protect the cell.)

Alternative Assessment ─── ADVANCED

Writing
Job Description Have students write a job description for one of the cell's basic chemical building blocks. Tell students to describe the required job responsibilities. Have them include a description of the expected workload by explaining whether the building block will have to work constantly or sporadically. Finally, indicate whether the building block will work independently or with other cell components.
🔲 Verbal

Figure 6 **Phospholipid Membranes**

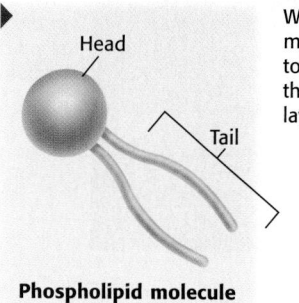

The head of a phospholipid molecule is attracted to water, but the tail is not.

Head

Tail

Phospholipid molecule

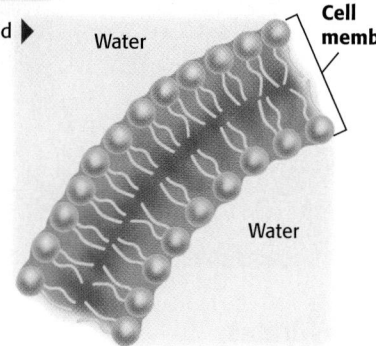

When phospholipid molecules come together in water, they form two layers.

Water

Cell membrane

Water

---

lipid a type of biochemical that does not dissolve in water; fats and steroids are lipids

phospholipid a lipid that contains phosphorus and that is a structural component in cell membranes

ATP **a**denosine **trip**hosphate, a molecule that acts as the main energy source for cell processes

---

CONNECTION TO
Social Studies

Whaling In the 1900s, whales were hunted and killed for their oil. Whale oil was often used as fuel for oil lamps. Most of the oil taken from whales was taken from their fat, or *blubber*. Some whales had blubber over 18 in. thick, producing over 40 barrels of oil per whale. Research whether anyone still hunts whales or uses whale oil. Make a presentation to the class on your findings.

Lipids

Lipids are compounds that cannot mix with water. Lipids have many important jobs in the cell. Like carbohydrates, some lipids store energy. Other lipids form the membranes of cells.

Phospholipids

All cells are surrounded by a cell membrane. The cell membrane helps protect the cell and keep the internal conditions of the cell stable. **Phospholipids** (FAHS foh LIP idz) are the molecules that form much of the cell membrane. The head of a phospholipid molecule is attracted to water. The tail is not. Cells are mostly water. When phospholipids are in water, the tails come together, and the heads face out into the water. **Figure 6** shows how phospholipid molecules form two layers in water.

Fats and Oils

Fats and oils are lipids that store energy. When an organism has used up most of its carbohydrates, it can get energy from these lipids. The structures of fats and oils are almost the same, but at room temperature, most fats are solid, and most oils are liquid. Most of the lipids stored in plants are oils. Most of the lipids stored in animals are fats.

✓ **Reading Check** What is one difference between oils and fats?

ATP

Adenosine **trip**hosphate (uh DEN uh SEEN trie FAHS FAYT), also called ATP, is another important molecule. **ATP** is the major energy-carrying molecule in the cell. The energy in carbohydrates and lipids must be transferred to ATP, which then provides fuel for cellular activities.

Nucleic Acids

Nucleic acids are sometimes called the blueprints of life because they have all the information needed for a cell to make proteins. **Nucleic acids** are large molecules made up of molecules called *nucleotides* (NOO klee oh TIEDZ). A nucleic acid may have thousands of nucleotides. The order of those nucleotides stores information. DNA is a nucleic acid. A DNA molecule is like a recipe book entitled *How to Make Proteins*. When a cell needs to make a certain protein, the cell gets information from the order of the nucleotides in DNA. This order of nucleotides tells the cell the order of the amino acids that are linked together to make that protein.

nucleic acid a molecule made up of subunits called *nucleotides*

SECTION Review

Summary

- Organisms need water for cellular processes.
- Organisms need oxygen to release the energy contained in their food.
- Organisms must have a place to live.
- Cells store energy in carbohydrates, which are made of sugars.
- Proteins are made up of amino acids. Some proteins are enzymes.
- Fats and oils store energy and make up cell membranes.
- Cells use molecules of ATP to fuel their activities.
- Nucleic acids, such as DNA, are made up of nucleotides.

Using Key Terms

For each pair of terms, explain how the meanings of the terms differ.

1. *producer* and *consumer*
2. *lipid* and *phospholipid*

Understanding Key Ideas

3. Plants store extra sugar as
   a. proteins.
   b. starch.
   c. nucleic acids.
   d. phospholipids.

4. Explain why organisms need food, water, air, and living space.

5. Describe the chemical building blocks of cells.

6. Why are decomposers categorized as consumers? How do they differ from producers?

7. What are the subunits of proteins?

Math Skills

8. Protein A is a chain of 660 amino acids. Protein B is a chain of 11 amino acids. How many times more amino acids does protein A have than protein B?

Critical Thinking

9. **Making Inferences** Could life as we know it exist on Earth if air contained only oxygen? Explain.

10. **Identifying Relationships** How might a cave, an ant, and a lake each meet the needs of an organism?

11. **Predicting Consequences** What would happen to the supply of ATP in your cells if you did not eat enough carbohydrates? How would this affect your cells?

12. **Applying Concepts** Which resource do you think is most important to your survival: water, air, a place to live, or food? Explain your answer.

For a variety of links related to this chapter, go to www.scilinks.org

Topic: The Necessities of Life
SciLinks code: HSM1018

Answer to Reading Check

Most fats are solid, and most oils are liquid.

CHAPTER RESOURCES

Chapter Resource File

- Section Quiz GENERAL
- Section Review GENERAL
- Vocabulary and Section Summary GENERAL
- Reinforcement Worksheet BASIC
- SciLinks Activity GENERAL
- Datasheet for Quick Lab

Technology

Transparencies
- Phospholipid Molecule and Cell Membrane

Answers to Section Review

1. Sample answer: Producers can make their own food. Consumers must eat other organisms to get food.

2. Sample answer: A phospholipid contains phosphorous and forms cell membranes.

3. b

4. Sample answer: Most of the chemical reactions involved in metabolism require water. Most living things need oxygen from air to release energy from food. Plants and other organisms need carbon dioxide from air to make food. Food gives organisms the energy they need to carry out life processes. Organisms need a place to live that contains the things they need to survive.

5. Sample answer: Proteins contain amino acids, which are used to build other proteins. Carbohydrates provide energy. Lipids are energy-storage molecules and form cell membranes.

6. Sample answer: Decomposers cannot make their own food, as producers can, so decomposers consume dead organisms.

7. amino acids

8. $660 \div 11 = 60$ times

9. Sample answer: Green plants, algae, and some bacteria need carbon dioxide gas as well as oxygen. Without the carbon dioxide, these organisms could not survive, and other organisms could not rely on them as a food source.

10. Sample answer: A cave provides shelter. An ant could be food. A lake provides water.

11. Sample answer: The supply of ATP would decrease. A decrease in ATP would cause a cell to have less energy than it needs to carry out its activities. Your body would have to get ATP from other sources, such as lipids.

12. Sample answer: They are all equally important. An organism could not survive without any one resource.

Roly-Poly Races

Teacher's Notes

Time Required

One or two 45-minute class periods

Lab Ratings

EASY ———————→ HARD

Teacher Prep 🧪🧪
Student Set-Up 🧪🧪
Concept Level 🧪
Clean Up 🧪

M A T E R I A L S

The materials listed on the student page are enough for 1 or 2 students. Remind students that they are handling living things that should be treated with respect. The soil used in this lab should be sterilized potting soil to avoid causing allergic reactions among the students.

Safety Caution

Remind students to review all safety cautions and icons before beginning this lab activity.

Roly-Poly Races

Have you ever watched a bug run? Did you wonder why it was running? The bug you saw running was probably reacting to a stimulus. In other words, something happened to make the bug run! One characteristic of living things is that they respond to stimuli. In this activity, you will study the movement of roly-polies. Roly-polies are also called *pill bugs*. But they are not really bugs; they are land-dwelling animals called *isopods*. Isopods live in dark, moist areas under rocks or wood. You will provide stimuli to determine how fast your isopod can move and what affects its speed and direction. Remember that isopods are living things and must be treated gently and respectfully.

OBJECTIVES

Observe responses to stimuli.

Analyze responses to stimuli.

MATERIALS

- chalk (1 stick)
- container, plastic, small, with lid
- gloves, protective
- isopod (4)
- potato, raw (1 small slice)
- ruler, metric
- soil (8 oz)
- stopwatch

SAFETY

Ask a Question

❶ Ask a question such as, "Which stimuli cause pill bugs to run?"

Form a Hypothesis

❷ Using your question as a guide, form a hypothesis. For example, you could form the following hypothesis: "Light, sound, and touch stimulate pill bugs to run."

Test the Hypothesis

❸ Choose a partner, and decide together how you will run your roly-poly race. Discuss some gentle ways to stimulate your isopods to move. Choose five or six things that might cause movement, such as a gentle nudge or a change in temperature, sound, or light. Check your choices with your teacher.

❹ Make a data table similar to the table below. Label the columns with the stimuli that you've chosen. Label the rows "Isopod 1," "Isopod 2," "Isopod 3," and "Isopod 4."

Isopod Responses			
	Stimulus 1	Stimulus 2	Stimulus 3
Isopod 1			
Isopod 2			
Isopod 3		DO NOT WRITE IN BOOK	
Isopod 4			

Lab Notes

Isopods were selected for this lab because they are very common in most areas and can be collected and released in natural areas. If you choose to use other animals that you can obtain at a pet store, such as mealworms, be sure to have a plan for appropriate disposal after the lab.

CHAPTER RESOURCES

Chapter Resource File

📑 • Datasheet for Chapter Lab
   • Lab Notes and Answers

Technology

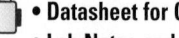 **Classroom Videos**
   • Lab Video

• The Best-Bread Bakery Dilemma

5. Place a layer of soil that is 1 cm or 2 cm deep in a small plastic container. Add a small slice of potato and a piece of chalk. Your isopods will eat these items.

6. Place four isopods in your container. Observe them for a minute or two before you perform your tests. Record your observations.

7. Decide which stimulus you want to test first. Carefully arrange the isopods at the "starting line." The starting line can be an imaginary line at one end of the container.

8. Gently stimulate each isopod at the same time and in the same way. In your data table, record the isopods' responses to the stimulus. Be sure to record the distance that each isopod travels. Don't forget to time the race.

9. Repeat steps 7–8 for each stimulus. Be sure to wait at least 2 min between trials.

Analyze the Results

1. **Describing Events** Describe the way that isopods move. Do their legs move together?

2. **Analyzing Results** Did your isopods move before or between the trials? Did the movement seem to have a purpose, or were the isopods responding to a stimulus? Explain.

Draw Conclusions

3. **Interpreting Information** Did any of the stimuli make the isopods move faster or go farther? Explain.

> ## Applying Your Data
> Like isopods and all other living things, humans react to stimuli. Describe three stimuli that might cause humans to run.

CLASSROOM TESTED & APPROVED

Gladys Cherniak
St. Paul's Episcopal School
Mobile, Alabama

Disposal Information
When the lab has been completed, the isopods can be disposed of according to your policy or can be released into a natural area if the isopods are native to that area.

Analyze the Results
1. Isopods move their legs in sequence.

2. Answers may vary based on students' observations. Some students may note that the isopods "roll up" rather than move in response to some stimuli.

Draw Conclusions
3. Answers may vary based on the stimuli tested and students' observations.

Applying Your Data
Sample answer: Something that is dangerous, such as a fire or a wild animal, may make a person run. Pain, such as that caused by walking barefoot on hot sand, may make a person run. Being late may make a person run. An alarm may make a person run. Hearing a parent or friend calling may make a person run. A person may also run if he or she wants exercise.

Chapter Review

Assignment Guide

SECTION	QUESTIONS
1	1–2, 6–7, 9, 13, 17, 19–21
2	3–5, 8, 10–12, 14–16, 18

ANSWERS

Using Key Terms

1. homeostasis
2. heredity
3. consumer
4. carbohydrate
5. lipid

Understanding Key Ideas

6. d
7. b
8. a
9. b
10. c
11. c
12. a

USING KEY TERMS

Complete each of the following sentences by choosing the correct term from the word bank.

lipid	carbohydrate
consumer	heredity
homeostasis	producer

1 The process of maintaining a stable internal environment is known as ___.

2 Offspring resemble their parents because of ___.

3 A ___ obtains food by eating other organisms.

4 Starch is a ___ and is made up of sugars.

5 Fat is a ___ that stores energy for an organism.

UNDERSTANDING KEY IDEAS

Multiple Choice

6 Which of the following statements about cells is true?

  a. Cells are the structures that contain all of the materials necessary for life.

  b. Cells are found in all organisms.

  c. Cells are sometimes specialized for particular functions.

  d. All of the above

7 Which of the following statements about all living things is true?

  a. All living things reproduce sexually.

  b. All living things have one or more cells.

  c. All living things must make their own food.

  d. All living things reproduce asexually.

8 Organisms must have food because

  a. food is a source of energy.

  b. food supplies cells with oxygen.

  c. organisms never make their own food.

  d. All of the above

9 A change in an organism's environment that affects the organism's activities is a

  a. response.   **c.** metabolism.

  b. stimulus.   **d.** producer.

10 Organisms store energy in

  a. nucleic acids.   **c.** lipids.

  b. phospholipids.   **d.** water.

11 The molecule that contains the information about how to make proteins is

  a. ATP.

  b. a carbohydrate.

  c. DNA.

  d. a phospholipid.

12 The subunits of nucleic acids are

  a. nucleotides.

  b. oils.

  c. sugars.

  d. amino acids.

Short Answer

13 What is the difference between asexual reproduction and sexual reproduction?

14 In one or two sentences, explain why living things must have air.

15 What is ATP, and why is it important to a cell?

CRITICAL THINKING

16 Concept Mapping Use the following terms to create a concept map: *cell, carbohydrates, protein, enzymes, DNA, sugars, lipids, nucleotides, amino acids,* and *nucleic acid.*

17 Analyzing Ideas A flame can move, grow larger, and give off heat. Is a flame alive? Explain.

18 Applying Concepts Based on what you know about carbohydrates, lipids, and proteins, why is it important for you to eat a balanced diet?

19 Evaluating Hypotheses Your friend tells you that the stimulus of music makes his goldfish swim faster. How would you design a controlled experiment to test your friend's claim?

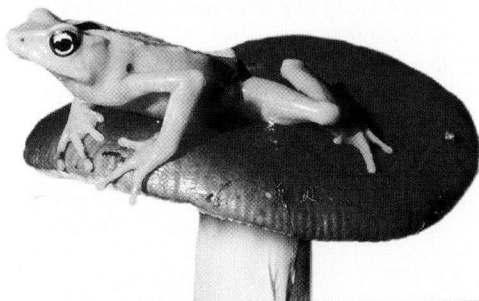

INTERPRETING GRAPHICS

The pictures below show the same plant over a period of 3 days. Use the pictures below to answer the questions that follow.

Day 1

Day 2

Day 3

20 What is the plant doing?

21 What characteristic(s) of living things is the plant exhibiting?

Critical Thinking

16. An answer to this exercise can be found at the end of this book.

17. Sample answer: The flame is not alive. Although a flame can move, grow, and give off heat, it does not have all of the characteristics of a living organism. For example, a flame is not made up of cells and does not contain DNA.

18. Sample answer: Cells use carbohydrates as a source of energy and for energy storage. Eating protein supplies the body with amino acids. The body uses these amino acids to make its own proteins. Proteins have many functions. For example, the protein hemoglobin helps deliver oxygen throughout the body. Other proteins called *enzymes* help speed up chemical reactions. Lipids store energy and form the membranes of cells. If you eat an unbalanced diet, you may lack one or more of these three nutrients, and your cells will not be able to function properly as a result.

19. Answers may vary. Sample answer: I could put the goldfish bowl in a box, making sure that the fish does not see anything outside the bowl. I would make sure that the fish gets light, air, and food in regulated amounts. Then, I would observe the fish without the stimulus of music and with the stimulus of music to see what happens.

Interpreting Graphics

20. The plant is bending toward the light coming through the window.

21. Sample answer: The plant is sensing a stimulus (the light) and is responding to it.

13. In sexual reproduction, two parents produce offspring that will share characteristics of both parents. In asexual reproduction, a single parent produces offspring that are identical to the parent.

14. Sample answer: Most organisms need oxygen from air to release energy from food. Green plants, algae, and some bacteria need carbon dioxide from air for photosynthesis.

15. ATP is the energy-containing molecule in a cell. It provides fuel for cellular activities.

Teacher's Note

To provide practice under more realistic testing conditions, give students 20 minutes to answer all of the questions in this Standardized Test Preparation.

MISCONCEPTION ALERT

Answers to the standardized test preparation can help you identify student misconceptions and misunderstandings.

READING

Passage 1

1. A
2. G
3. C
4. G

TEST DOCTOR

Question 4: Some students may answer that the difference between sexual and asexual reproduction pertains to the number of offspring produced or the number that survive. However, the passage does not discuss either. Some students may infer that sexual reproduction produces more traits because two parents are involved rather than one parent as in asexual reproduction. Again, this idea is not discussed in the passage.

Passage 2

1. C
2. F

READING

Read each of the passages below. Then, answer the questions that follow each passage.

Passage 1 Organisms make other organisms similar to themselves. They do so in one of two ways: by sexual reproduction or by <u>asexual reproduction</u>. In sexual reproduction, two parents produce offspring that will share characteristics of both parents. Most animals and plants reproduce in this way. In asexual reproduction, a single parent produces offspring that are identical to the parent. Most single-celled organisms reproduce in this way.

1. In the passage, what does the term *asexual reproduction* mean?
   A A single parent produces offspring.
   B Two parents make identical offspring.
   C Plants make offspring.
   D Animals make offspring.

2. What is characteristic of offspring produced by sexual reproduction?
   F They are identical to both parents.
   G They share the traits of both parents.
   H They are identical to one parent.
   I They are identical to each other.

3. What is characteristic of offspring produced by asexual reproduction?
   A They are identical to both parents.
   B They share the traits of both parents.
   C They are identical to one parent.
   D They are usually plants.

4. What is the difference between sexual and asexual reproduction?
   F the number of offspring produced
   G the number of parents needed to produce offspring
   H the number of traits produced
   I the number of offspring that survive

Passage 2 In 1996, a group of researchers led by NASA scientists studied a 3.8-billion-year-old meteorite named ALH84001. These scientists agree that ALH84001 is a potato-sized piece of the planet Mars. They also agree that it fell to Earth about 13,000 years ago. It was discovered in Antarctica in 1984. According to the NASA team, ALH84001 brought with it evidence that life once existed on Mars.

Scientists found certain kinds of organic molecules (molecules containing carbon) on the surface of ALH84001. These molecules are similar to those left behind when living things break down substances for food. When these scientists examined the interior of the meteorite, they found the same organic molecules throughout. Because these molecules were spread throughout the meteorite, scientists concluded that the molecules were not contamination from Earth. The NASA team believes that these organic compounds are strong evidence that tiny organisms similar to bacteria lived, ate, and died on Mars millions of years ago.

1. How old is the meteorite named ALH84001?
   A 13,000 years old
   B millions of years old
   C 3.8 billion years old
   D 3.8 trillion years old

2. Which of the following would best support a claim that life might have existed on Mars?
   F remains of organisms
   G water
   H meteorite temperatures similar to Earth temperatures
   I oxygen

TEST DOCTOR

Question 1: Some students may answer 13,000 years old because the passage states that the meteorite fell to Earth about 13,000 years ago. Some students may answer millions of years old because the passage mentions life that lived millions of years ago, but the passage gives the meteorite's age as 3.8 billion years old. Students may answer 3.8 trillion years old if they misread the passage or the answers.

The graph below shows an ill person's body temperature. Use the graph below to answer the questions that follow.

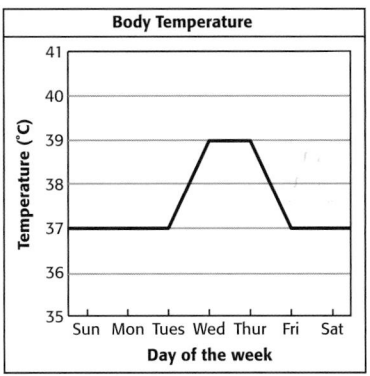

Body Temperature

1. A fever is a spike in temperature. On which day does this person have a fever?
   - **A** Sunday
   - **B** Monday
   - **C** Wednesday
   - **D** Saturday

2. A body with a fever is often fighting an infection. Fevers help eliminate the pathogens that cause the infection. According to the chart, when does this person probably have the highest fever?
   - **F** Sunday
   - **G** Monday
   - **H** Wednesday
   - **I** Saturday

3. What is the highest temperature that this fever reaches?
   - **A** 37°C
   - **B** 38°C
   - **C** 39°C
   - **D** 40°C

4. What is probably this person's normal body temperature?
   - **F** 37°C
   - **G** 38°C
   - **H** 39°C
   - **I** 40°C

Read each question below, and choose the best answer.

1. An aquarium is a place where fish can live. What is the volume of the aquarium shown below?

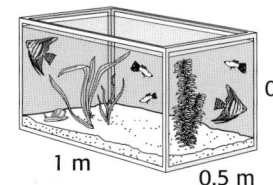
0.5 m

1 m

0.5 m

   - **A** 0.25 m
   - **B** 0.25 m²
   - **C** 0.25 m³
   - **D** 0.52 m³

2. The cost of admission to a natural history museum is $7 per adult. What is the total cost of admission for a group of five adults?
   - **F** $25
   - **G** $35
   - **H** $45
   - **I** $55

3. Lee biked 25.3 km on Monday, 20.7 km on Tuesday, and 15.6 km on Wednesday. How many kilometers did Lee bike during those three days?
   - **A** 66.1 km
   - **B** 61.6 km
   - **C** 51.6 km
   - **D** 16.6 km

4. Laura collected 24 leaves. One-third of the leaves were oak leaves. How many oak leaves did Laura collect?
   - **F** 6
   - **G** 8
   - **H** 12
   - **I** 24

Standardized Test Preparation

1. C
2. H
3. C
4. F

✚ TEST DOCTOR

Question 4: Students may answer 38°C if they find the value between 37°C and 39°C rather than observe that 37°C is the person's temperature when not feverish. Some students may answer 39°C if they don't realize that this temperature is the person's fever, not the person's normal body temperature. Finally, 40°C is above even the fever temperature, so this answer is incorrect.

1. C
2. G
3. B
4. G

✚ TEST DOCTOR

Question 1: Students may answer 0.25 m or 0.25 m² if they forget that the correct units for volume are m³. If they transpose the 2 and the 5 in the answer, they will incorrectly answer 0.52 m³. You may want to show students how to do this problem on the board so that they understand where m³ comes from (m × m × m = m³).

Question 3: Some students may answer 51.6 km if they forget to carry the 1 to the tens column. Some students may answer 66.1 or 16.6 km if they transpose numbers in the correct answer.

CHAPTER RESOURCES

Chapter Resource File

 • Standardized Test Preparation GENERAL

State Resources

 For specific resources for your state, visit **go.hrw.com** and type in the keyword **HSMSTR**.

Science, Technology, and Society

Teaching Strategy—GENERAL

Students may not be familiar with the game of chess. Understanding how chess is played may assist students in understanding the complexity of chess playing computers. Encourage students who know how to play chess to demonstrate the game to the other students.

Students who are interested in the history of science may be interested in creating a timeline showing the achievements in the development of chess-playing computers.

Science Fiction

Background

Terry Bisson has written comic books, short stories, novels, plays, how-to articles about writing, and news editorials. In 1991, Bisson's short story "Bears Discover Fire" received the highest honors possible for science fiction writers—both the Nebula Award and the Hugo Award.

Science in Action

Science, Technology, and Society

Chess-Playing Computers

Computers can help us explore how humans think. One way to explore how humans think is to study how people and computers play chess against each other.

A computer's approach to chess is straightforward. By calculating each piece's possible board position for the next few moves, a computer creates what is called a *position tree*. A position tree shows how each move can lead to other moves. This way of playing requires millions of calculations.

Human chess champions play differently. Humans calculate only three or four moves every minute. Even so, human champions are still a match for computer opponents. By studying the ways that people and computers play chess, scientists are learning how people think and make choices.

Math ACTiViTY

A chess-playing computer needs to evaluate 3 million positions before a move. If you could evaluate two positions in 1 min, how long would it take you to evaluate 3 million possible positions?

Science Fiction

"They're Made Out of Meat" by Terry Bisson

Two space explorers millions of light-years from home are visiting an uncharted sector of the universe to find signs of life. Their mission is to contact, welcome, and log any and all beings in this part of the universe.

During their mission, they encounter a life-form quite unlike anything they have ever seen before. It looked too strange and, well, disgusting. The explorers have very strong doubts about adding this new organism to the list. But the explorers' official duty is to contact and welcome all life-forms no matter how ugly they are. Can the explorers bring themselves to perform their duty?

You'll find out by reading "They're Made Out of Meat," a short story by Terry Bisson. This story is in the *Holt Anthology of Science Fiction*.

Language Arts ACTiViTY

WRITING SKILL Write a story about what happens when the explorers next meet the creatures on the star in G445 zone.

Answer to Math Activity
1,500,000 minutes
(3,000,000 ÷ 2 = 1,500,000 minutes)

Answer to Language Arts Activity
Answers may vary.

People in Science

Janis Davis-Street

NASA Nutritionist Do astronauts eat shrimp cocktail in space? Yes, they do! Shrimp cocktail is nutritious and tastes so good that it is one of the most popular foods in the space program. And eating a proper diet helps astronauts stay healthy while they are in space.

But who figures out what astronauts need to eat? Janis Davis-Street is a nutritionist and laboratory supervisor for the Nutritional Biochemistry Laboratory at the Johnson Space Center in Houston, Texas. She was born in Georgetown, Guyana, on the northeastern coast of South America. She was educated in Canada.

Davis-Street is part of a team that uses their knowledge of nutrition, biology, and chemistry to figure out the nutritional requirements for spaceflight. For example, they determine how many calories and other nutrients each astronaut needs per day during spaceflight.

The Nutritional Biochemistry Laboratory's work on the space shuttle missions and *Mir* space station developed into tests that allow NASA to help ensure astronaut health before, during, and after flight. These tests are important for understanding how the human body adapts to long space missions, and for determining whether treatments for preventing bone and muscle loss during spaceflight are working.

Social Studies ACTIVITY

Scientists from more than 30 countries have been on space missions. Research which countries have provided astronauts or cosmonauts for space missions. Using a map, place self-stick notes on countries that have provided scientists for space missions. Write the names of the appropriate scientists on the self-stick notes.

go.hrw.com

To learn more about these Science in Action topics, visit **go.hrw.com** and type in the keyword **HL5ALVF.**

Current Science

Check out Current Science® articles related to this chapter by visiting **go.hrw.com.** Just type in the keyword **HL5CS02.**

People in Science

Background

One of the reasons to conduct nutritional tests in space is to determine potential benefits for disease research and medicine on earth. One of Davis-Street's current tests is Experiment E381, "Calcium Kinetics During Space Flight." Experiment E381 addresses bone health and bone loss during space missions.

Calcium may be lost from bones during space flight partly as a result of insufficient levels of vitamin D in the body. Vitamin D is critical to calcium absorption and metabolism. Vitamin D is synthesized using sunlight and ultraviolet radiation, and spaceships are heavily shielded from any ultraviolet light. Calcium kinetics will track the movement of calcium tracers through an astronaut's body, from the absorption from food to the formation and breakdown of bones.

If the rate of bone loss during flight and the recovery rate on the ground are constant, scientists predict it will take 2.5 times the mission length to recover lost bone mass. Understanding bone and calcium dynamics in accelerated contexts such as space might help us to better understand earth bone diseases, such as osteoporosis.

Answer to Social Studies Activity

Answers may vary. Some of the countries from which astronauts or cosmonauts have come include the United States, Russia, Israel, India, Japan, Canada, Brazil, Germany, Italy, Switzerland, France, and Sweden.

TIMELINE

Cells

Cells are everywhere. Even though most cells can't be seen with the naked eye, they make up every living thing. Your body alone contains trillions of cells.

In this unit, you will learn about cells. You will learn the difference between animal cells, plant cells, and bacterial cells. You will learn about the parts of a cell and will see how they work together.

Since cells were discovered in 1665, we have learned a lot about cells and the way they work. This timeline shows some of the discoveries that have been made along the way, but there is still a lot to learn about the fascinating world of cells!

1620
The Pilgrims settle Plymouth Colony.

1665
Robert Hooke discovers cells after observing a thin piece of cork under a microscope.

1861
The American Civil War begins.

1952
Martha Chase and Alfred Hershey demonstrate that DNA is the hereditary material.

1831

Robert Brown discovers the nucleus in a plant cell.

1838

Matthias Schleiden discovers that all plant tissue is made up of cells.

1839

Theodor Schwann shows that all animal tissue is made up of cells.

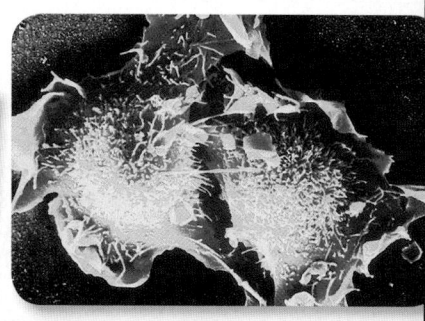

1858

Rudolf Virchow determines that all cells are produced from cells.

1873

Anton Schneider observes and accurately describes mitosis.

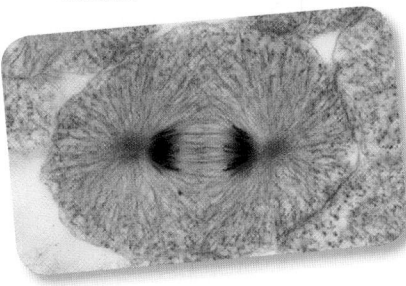

1937

The Golden Gate Bridge opens in San Francisco.

1941

George Beadle and Edward Tatum discover that genes control the chemical reactions in cells by directing protein production.

1956

The manufacture of protein in the cell is found to occur in ribosomes.

1971

Lynn Margulis proposes the endosymbiotic theory of the origin of cell organelles.

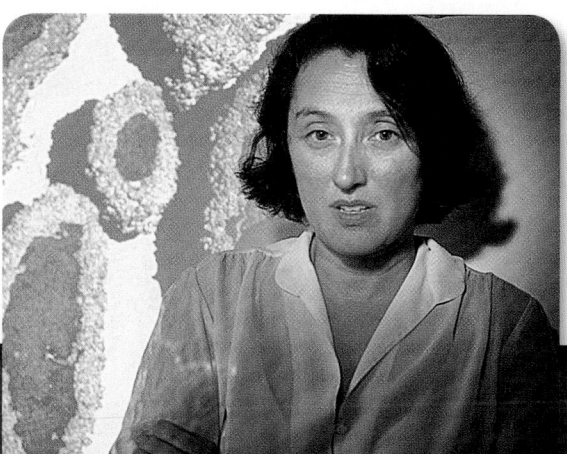

1997

A sheep named Dolly becomes the first animal to be cloned from a single body cell.

2002

Scientists test a cancer vaccine that can be given orally. Tests on mice lead scientists to be hopeful that the vaccine can be tested on humans.

Compression guide:
To shorten instruction because of time limitations, omit the Chapter Lab.

OBJECTIVES	LABS, DEMONSTRATIONS, AND ACTIVITIES	TECHNOLOGY RESOURCES
PACING • 90 min pp. 58–67 **Chapter Opener**	**SE** Start-up Activity, p. 59 ◆ GENERAL	**OSP** Parent Letter ■ GENERAL **CD** Student Edition on CD-ROM **CD** Guided Reading Audio CD ■ **TR** Chapter Starter Transparency* **VID** Brain Food Video Quiz
Section 1 The Diversity of Cells • State the parts of the cell theory. • Explain why cells are so small. • Describe the parts of a cell. • Describe how eubacteria are different from archaebacteria. • Explain the difference between prokaryotic cells and eukaryotic cells.	**TE** Activity Modeling Cell Discovery, p. 60 ◆ GENERAL **SE** Connection to Physics Microscopes, p. 61 GENERAL **SE** Quick Lab Bacteria in Your Lunch?, p. 64 ◆ GENERAL **CRF** Datasheet for Quick Lab* **TE** Group Activity Archaebacteria, p. 64 ADVANCED **SE** Connection to Social Studies Where Do They Live?, p. 65 GENERAL **SE** Skills Practice Labs Elephant-Sized Amoebas?, p. 80 ◆ GENERAL **CRF** Datasheet for Chapter Lab*	**CRF** Lesson Plans* **TR** Bellringer Transparency* **TR** Math Focus: Surface Area–to-Volume Ratio* **TR** A Typical Eukaryotic Cell* **VID** Lab Videos for Life Science **TE** Internet Activity, p. 66 GENERAL
PACING • 45 min pp. 68–75 **Section 2 Eukaryotic Cells** • Identify the different parts of a eukaryotic cell. • Explain the function of each part of a eukaryotic cell.	**TE** Demonstration Cell Walls and Cell Membranes, p. 69 BASIC **TE** Activity Cellular Sieve, p. 69 ◆ BASIC **TE** Group Activity Drawing Cells, p. 70 BASIC **TE** Activity Cell Models, p. 71 GENERAL **TE** Activity Vacuole Model, p. 74 ◆ BASIC **SE** Skills Practice Lab Cells Alive!, p. 764 ◆ GENERAL **CRF** Datasheet for LabBook* **LB** Whiz-Bang Demonstrations Grand Strand* ◆ GENERAL **LB** Labs You Can Eat The Incredible Edible Cell* ◆ ADVANCED **LB** Long-Term Projects & Research Ideas Ewe Again, Dolly?* ◆ ADVANCED	**CRF** Lesson Plans* **TR** Bellringer Transparency* **TR** *LINK TO PHYSICAL SCIENCE* Structural Formulas* **TR** Organelles and Their Functions* **CRF** SciLinks Activity* GENERAL
PACING • 45 min pp. 76–79 **Section 3 The Organization of Living Things** • List three advantages of being multicellular. • Describe the four levels of organization in living things. • Explain the relationship between the structure and function of a part of an organism.	**TE** Activity Concept Mapping, p. 76 ◆ GENERAL **TE** Activity Explain It to a Friend, p. 79 BASIC **SE** Science in Action Math, Social Studies, and Language Arts Activities, pp. 86–87 GENERAL	**CRF** Lesson Plans* **TR** Bellringer Transparency* **TR** Levels of Organization in the Cardiovascular System*

PACING • 90 min

CHAPTER REVIEW, ASSESSMENT, AND STANDARDIZED TEST PREPARATION

CRF Vocabulary Activity* GENERAL
SE Chapter Review, pp. 82–83 GENERAL
CRF Chapter Review* ■ GENERAL
CRF Chapter Tests A* ■ GENERAL, B* ADVANCED, C* SPECIAL NEEDS
SE Standardized Test Preparation, pp. 84–85 GENERAL
CRF Standardized Test Preparation* GENERAL
CRF Performance-Based Assessment* GENERAL
OSP Test Generator GENERAL
CRF Test Item Listing* GENERAL

Online and Technology Resources

Visit **go.hrw.com** for a variety of free resources related to this textbook. Enter the keyword **HL5CEL**.

Holt Online Learning

Students can access interactive problem-solving help and active visual concept development with the *Holt Science and Technology* Online Edition available at **www.hrw.com**.

 Guided Reading Audio CD
Also in Spanish

A direct reading of each chapter for auditory learners, reluctant readers, and Spanish-speaking students.

 Science Tutor CD-ROM

Excellent for remediation and test practice.

SKILLS DEVELOPMENT RESOURCES	SECTION REVIEW AND ASSESSMENT	STANDARDS CORRELATIONS
SE Pre-Reading Activity, p. 58 `GENERAL` **OSP** Science Puzzlers, Twisters & Teasers `GENERAL`		National Science Education Standards UCP 4; HNS 3; LS 1b, 5b
CRF Directed Reading A* ■ `BASIC`, B* `SPECIAL NEEDS` **CRF** Vocabulary and Section Summary* ■ `GENERAL` **SE** Reading Strategy Reading Organizer, p. 60 `GENERAL` **TE** Inclusion Strategies, p. 61 **SE** Math Focus Surface Area-to-Volume Ratio, p. 62 `GENERAL` **TE** Reading Strategy Prediction Guide, p. 62 `GENERAL` **TE** Reading Strategy Prediction Guide, p. 63 `GENERAL` **TE** Research Be a Good Host, p. 65 `GENERAL` **MS** Math Skills for Science What Is a Ratio?* `GENERAL` **MS** Math Skills for Science Finding Perimeter and Area* `GENERAL` **MS** Math Skills for Science Finding Volume* `GENERAL`	**SE** Reading Checks, pp. 61, 62, 63, 65, 66 `GENERAL` **TE** Reteaching, p. 66 `BASIC` **TE** Quiz, p. 66 `GENERAL` **TE** Alternative Assessment, p. 66 `GENERAL` **SE** Section Review,* p. 67 ■ `GENERAL` **CRF** Section Quiz* ■ `GENERAL`	UCP 3, 5; SAI 1, 2; ST 2; SPSP 5; LS 1a, 1b, 1c, 2c, 3b, 5a; *Chapter Lab:* UCP 1, 2, 3; SAI 2; LS 1b, 1c, 3a, 3b
CRF Directed Reading A* ■ `BASIC`, B* `SPECIAL NEEDS` **CRF** Vocabulary and Section Summary* ■ `GENERAL` **SE** Reading Strategy Reading Organizer, p. 68 `GENERAL` **SE** Connection to Language Arts The Great Barrier, p. 69 `GENERAL` **TE** Inclusion Strategies, p. 70 **TE** Reading Strategy Prediction Guide, p. 72 `GENERAL` **CRF** Critical Thinking Cellular Construction* `ADVANCED` **CRF** Reinforcement Worksheet Building a Eukaryotic Cell* `BASIC`	**SE** Reading Checks, pp. 68, 69, 70, 72, 74 `GENERAL` **TE** Homework, p. 69 `GENERAL` **TE** Homework, p. 71 `GENERAL` **TE** Homework, p. 73 `GENERAL` **TE** Reteaching, p. 74 `BASIC` **TE** Quiz, p. 74 `GENERAL` **TE** Alternative Assessment, p. 74 `GENERAL` **SE** Section Review,* p. 75 ■ `GENERAL` **CRF** Section Quiz* ■ `GENERAL`	UCP 1, 4, 5; LS 1b, 1c, 3a, 5a, 5b; *LabBook:* UCP 1, 2, 5; SAI 1; ST 2; SPSP 5; HNS 1, 3; LS 1a, 1b, 1c, 1d, 2c, 3a, 5a
CRF Directed Reading A* ■ `BASIC`, B* `SPECIAL NEEDS` **CRF** Vocabulary and Section Summary* ■ `GENERAL` **SE** Reading Strategy Paired Summarizing, p. 76 `GENERAL` **SE** Math Practice A Pet Protist, p. 77 `GENERAL`	**SE** Reading Checks, pp. 76, 77, 78 `GENERAL` **TE** Homework, p. 77 `GENERAL` **TE** Reteaching, p. 78 `BASIC` **TE** Quiz, p. 78 `GENERAL` **TE** Alternative Assessment, p. 78 `GENERAL` **SE** Section Review,* p. 79 ■ `GENERAL` **CRF** Section Quiz* ■ `GENERAL`	UCP 1, 2, 5; LS 1a, 1b, 1d

One-Stop Planner® CD-ROM

This convenient CD-ROM includes:
- Lab Materials QuickList Software
- Holt Calendar Planner
- Customizable Lesson Plans
- Printable Worksheets
- ExamView® Test Generator

CNN student News™

cnnstudentnews.com

Find the latest news, lesson plans, and activities related to important scientific events.

SCiLINKS® NSTA

www.scilinks.org

Maintained by the **National Science Teachers Association.** See Chapter Enrichment pages for a complete list of topics.

Current Science®

Check out *Current Science* articles and activities by visiting the HRW Web site at go.hrw.com. Just type in the keyword **HL5CS03T.**

Classroom Videos

- **Lab Videos** demonstrate the chapter lab.
- **Brain Food Video Quizzes** help students review the chapter material.
- **CNN Videos** bring science into your students' daily life.

Visual Resources

CHAPTER STARTER TRANSPARENCY

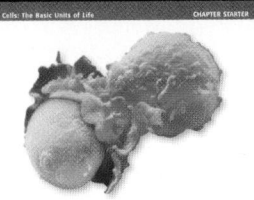

What If . . . ?

Imagine this scene from a horror film. A young man sits down to dinner to find that his mother has made prepared asparagus stalks. The young man eats the dreaded asparagus stalks. Later, he finds out that instead of being digested, one of the stalks has taken up residence inside his body and is very much alive! Too horrifying to think about? What if the asparagus began to do wonderful things for the young man, such as giving him more energy than he had ever dreamed possible? Lynn Margulis, a scientist, thinks that something similar may have happened to certain one-celled organisms that lived more than a billion years ago, giving rise to the kinds of cells that we are made of today.

According to Margulis's theory, about 1.2 billion years ago, some larger cells began eating smaller cells for dinner. Like the white blood cell on this page, these larger cells trapped the smaller cells with extensions of their cell body. But some of these smaller cells resisted being digested. In fact, they began to do very well in their new homes. The larger cells also benefited from their new guests. The smaller cells released large amounts of energy from food taken in by the larger cells. Other kinds of small cells used the energy in sunlight to make enough food to feed themselves and the larger cell. The energy-producing structures of most cells, including yours, are thought to have descended from these smaller cells. In this chapter, you will learn more about cells and their structures.

BELLRINGER TRANSPARENCIES

Section: The Diversity of Cells
Why do you think cells weren't discovered until 1665? What invention do you think made their discovery possible? Do you think people can ever see cells with the naked eye? Explain your answer.

Write your responses in your **science journal.**

Section: Eukaryotic Cells
List three differences between *prokaryotic* and *eukaryotic* cells. Draw two diagrams illustrating the differences.

Write your responses in your **science journal.**

TEACHING TRANSPARENCIES

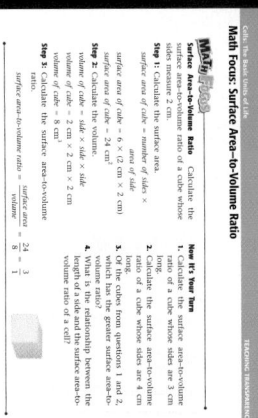

Math Focus: Surface Area-to-Volume Ratio

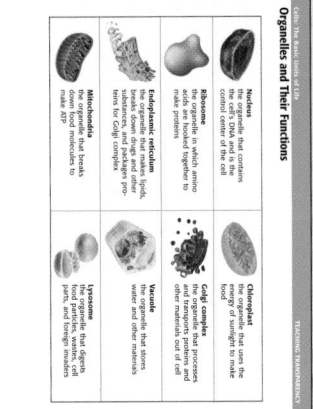

Organelles and Their Functions

TEACHING TRANSPARENCIES

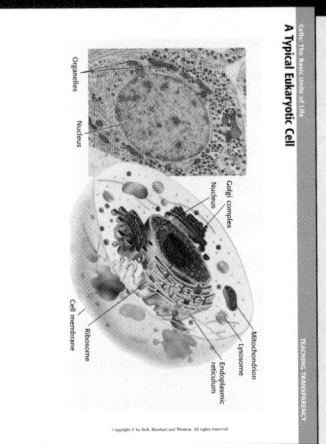

A Typical Eukaryotic Cell

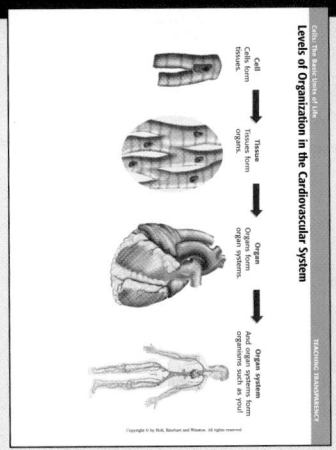

Levels of Organization in the Cardiovascular System

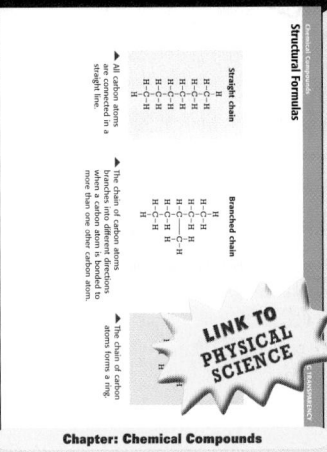

Structural Formulas

Chapter: Chemical Compounds

CONCEPT MAPPING TRANSPARENCY

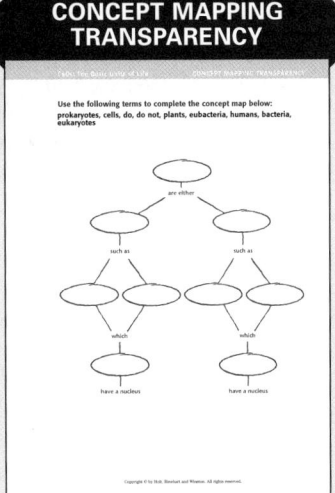

Use the following terms to complete the concept map below: prokaryotes, cells, do, do not, plants, eubacteria, humans, bacteria, eukaryotes

Planning Resources

LESSON PLANS

Lesson Plan   SAMPLE

Section: Waves

Pacing

Regular Schedule:	with lab(s):2 days	without lab(s):2 days
Block Schedule:	with lab(s):1 1/2 days	without lab(s):1 day

Objectives
1. Relate the seven properties of life to a living organism.
2. Describe seven themes that can help you to organize what you learn about biology.
3. Identify the tiny structures that make up all living organisms.
4. Differentiate between reproduction and heredity and between metabolism and homeostasis.

National Science Education Standards Covered

LSInter4: Cells have particular structures that underlie their functions.
LSMat1: Most cell functions involve chemical reactions.
LSBeh1: Cells store and use information to guide their functions.
UCP1: Cell functions are regulated.
SI1: Cells can differentiate and form complete multicellular organisms.
PS1: Species evolve over time.
ES51: The great diversity of organisms is the result of more than 3.5 billion years of evolution.
ES52: Natural selection and its evolutionary consequences provide a scientific explanation for the fossil record of ancient life forms as well as for the striking molecular similarities observed among the diverse species of living organisms.
ST1: The millions of different species of plants, animals, and microorganisms that live on Earth today are related by descent from common ancestors.
ST2: The energy for life primarily comes from the sun.
SPSP1: The complexity and organization of organisms accommodates the need for obtaining, transforming, transporting, releasing, and using the matter and energy used to sustain the organism.
SPSP6: As matter and energy flows through different levels of organization of living systems—cells, organs, communities—and between living systems and the physical environment, chemical elements are recombined in different ways.
HNS1: Organisms have behavioral responses to internal changes and to external stimuli.

PARENT LETTER

SAMPLE

Dear Parent,

Your son's or daughter's science class will soon begin exploring the chapter entitled "The World of Physical Science." In this chapter, students will learn about how the scientific method applies to the world of physical science and the role of physical science in the world. By the end of the chapter, students should demonstrate a clear understanding of the chapter's main ideas and be able to discuss the following topics:

1. physical science is the study of energy and matter (Section 1)
2. the role of physical science in the world around them (Section 1)
3. careers that rely on physical science (Section 1)
4. the steps used in the scientific method (Section 2)
5. examples of technology (Section 2)
6. how the scientific method is used to answer questions and solve problems (Section 2)
7. how our knowledge of science changes over time (Section 2)
8. how models represent real objects or systems (Section 3)
9. examples of different ways models are used in science (Section 3)
10. the importance of the International System of Units (Section 4)
11. the appropriate units to use for particular measurements (Section 4)
12. how area and density are derived quantities (Section 4)

Questions to Ask Along the Way

You can help your son or daughter learn about these topics by asking interesting questions such as the following:

• What are some surprising careers that use physical science?
• What is a characteristic of a good hypothesis?
• When is it a good idea to use a model?
• Why do Americans measure things in terms of inches and yards and meters?

ALSO IN SPANISH

TEST ITEM LISTING

TEST ITEM LISTING
The World of Science   SAMPLE

MULTIPLE CHOICE

1. A limitation of models is that
   a. they are large enough to see.
   b. they do not act exactly like the things that they model.
   c. they are smaller than the things that they model.
   d. they model unfamiliar things.
   Answer: B   Difficulty: 1   Section: 3   Objective: 2

2. The length 10 m is equal to
   a. 100 cm.
   b. 1,000 cm.
   c. 10,000 mm.
   d. Both (b) and (c)
   Answer: B   Difficulty: 1   Section: 3   Objective: 2

3. To be valid, a hypothesis must be
   a. testable.
   b. supported by evidence.
   c. unproven a law.
   d. Both (a) and (b)
   Answer: B   Difficulty: 1   Section: 3   Objective: 2

4. The statement "Sheila has a stain on her shirt" is an example of a(n)
   a. law.
   b. hypothesis.
   c. observation.
   d. prediction.
   Answer: B   Difficulty: 1   Section: 3   Objective: 2

5. A hypothesis is often developed out of
   a. observations.
   b. experiments.
   c. laws.
   d. Both (a) and (b)
   Answer: B   Difficulty: 1   Section: 3   Objective: 2

6. How many milliliters are in 3.5 kL?
   a. 3,500 mL
   b. 0.0035 mL
   c. 3,500,000 mL
   d. 3,500 mL
   Answer: B   Difficulty: 1   Section: 3   Objective: 2

7. A map of beattle is an example of a
   a. law.
   b. theory.
   c. model.
   d. unit.
   Answer: B   Difficulty: 1   Section: 3   Objective: 2

8. A lab has the safety icons shown below. These icons mean that you should wear
   a. only safety goggles.
   b. only a lab apron.
   c. safety goggles and a lab apron.
   d. safety goggles, a lab apron, and gloves.
   Answer: B   Difficulty: 1   Section: 3   Objective: 2

9. The law of conservation of mass says the tot al mass before a chemical change is
   a. more than the total mass after the change.
   b. less than the total mass after the change.
   c. the same as the total mass after the change.
   d. not the same as the total mass after the change.
   Answer: B   Difficulty: 1   Section: 3   Objective: 2

10. In which of the following areas might you find a geochemist at work?
    a. studying the chemistry of rocks
    b. studying fishes
    c. studying chemistry
    d. studying the atmosphere
    Answer: B   Difficulty: 1   Section: 3   Objective: 2

One-Stop Planner® CD-ROM

This CD-ROM includes all of the resources shown here and the following time-saving tools:

• Lab Materials QuickList Software
• Customizable lesson plans
• Holt Calendar Planner
• The powerful ExamView® Test Generator

Meeting Individual Needs

DIRECTED READING A
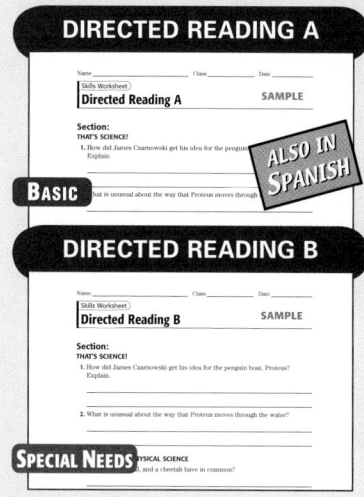
BASIC — ALSO IN SPANISH

DIRECTED READING B
SPECIAL NEEDS

VOCABULARY ACTIVITY
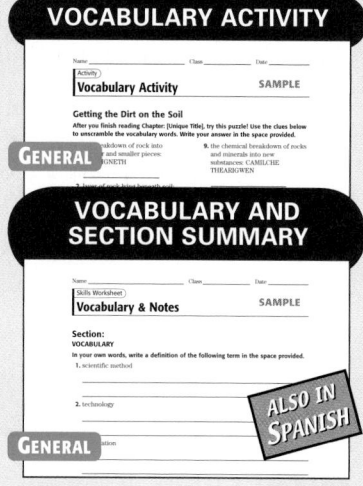
GENERAL

VOCABULARY AND SECTION SUMMARY
GENERAL — ALSO IN SPANISH

REINFORCEMENT
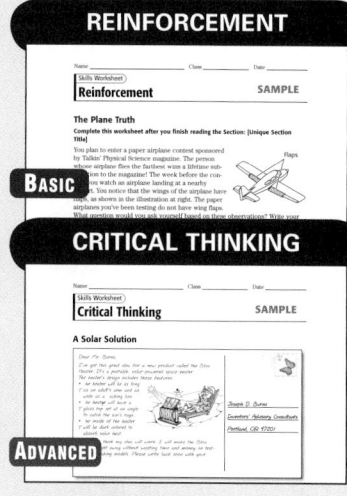
BASIC

CRITICAL THINKING
ADVANCED

SCILINKS ACTIVITY

GENERAL

SCIENCE PUZZLERS, TWISTERS & TEASERS
GENERAL

Labs and Activities

LONG-TERM PROJECTS & RESEARCH IDEAS
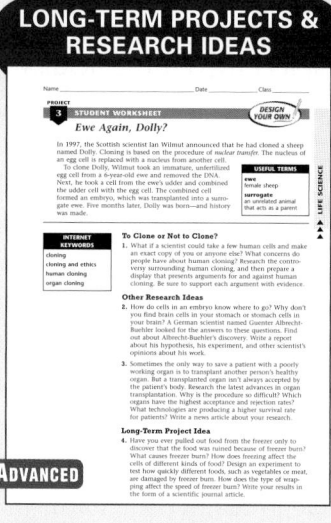
ADVANCED

WHIZ-BANG DEMONSTRATIONS
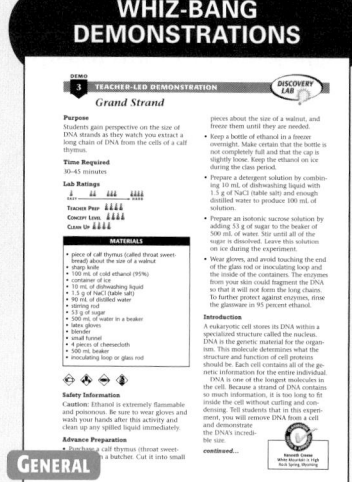
GENERAL

LABS YOU CAN EAT
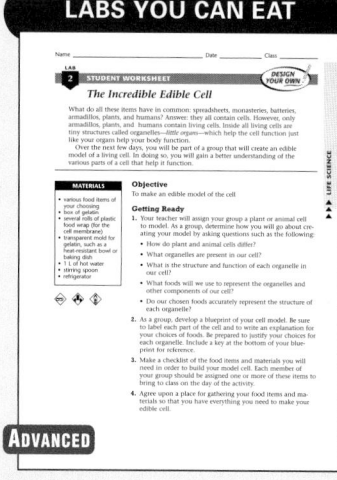
ADVANCED

DATASHEETS FOR QUICK LABS

DATASHEETS FOR CHAPTER LABS

DATASHEETS FOR LABBOOK

Review and Assessments

SECTION QUIZ
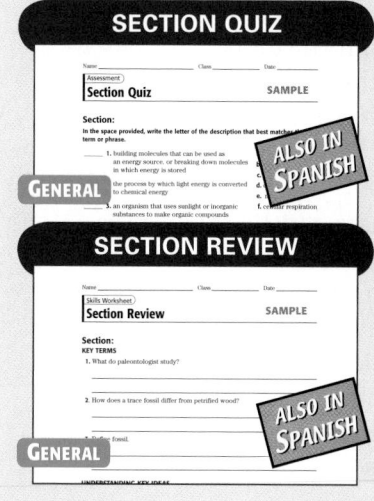
GENERAL — ALSO IN SPANISH

SECTION REVIEW
GENERAL

CHAPTER REVIEW
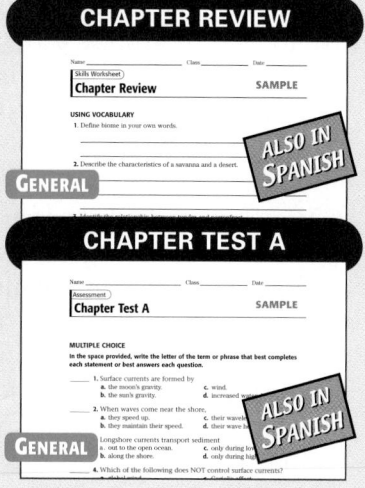
GENERAL — ALSO IN SPANISH

CHAPTER TEST A
GENERAL — ALSO IN SPANISH

CHAPTER TEST B
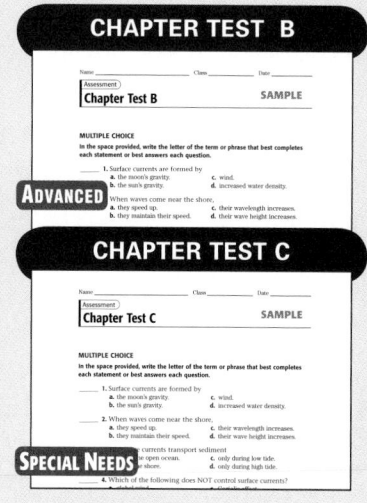
ADVANCED

CHAPTER TEST C
SPECIAL NEEDS

STANDARDIZED TEST PREPARATION
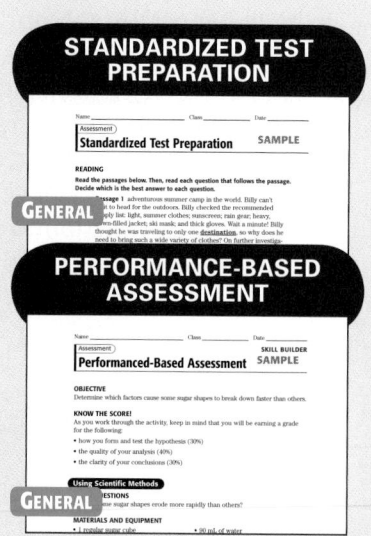
GENERAL

PERFORMANCE-BASED ASSESSMENT
GENERAL

This Chapter Enrichment provides relevant and interesting information to expand and enhance your presentation of the chapter material.

Section 1

The Diversity of Cells
Microtomy

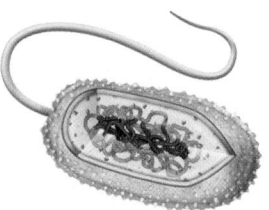

- The development of high-magnification microscopes required that the preparation of specimens for viewing also become more sophisticated. Microtomy once referred only to specimen cutting, because a microtome is the instrument used to slice tissue sections. Today, microtomy refers collectively to the art of preparing specimens by any number of techniques.

- When microscopic organisms are viewed as whole- mounts, they are preserved, stained, dried (alcohol removes the water), and made transparent with clove or cedar oil. Then, the organism is mounted in a drop of resin on a glass slide and covered with a piece of glass only 0.005 mm thick.

Physiology and the Cell Theory

- The development of the cell theory aided research in other fields. In the mid-1800s, French physiologist Claude Bernard proposed that plants and animals are composed of sets of control mechanisms that work to maintain the internal conditions necessary for life. He recognized that a mammal can sustain a constant body temperature regardless of the outside temperature. Today, we recognize the ability of organisms to regulate their physiological processes to maintain specific conditions as *homeostasis*. But at the time, no one knew what the "organized sets of control mechanisms" were. The discovery of cells and the way their many components function to sustain life in an organism gave credence to Bernard's position.

Is That a Fact!

- The Earth is 4.5 billion years old, and the oldest cell-like fossils are about 3.5 billion years old!

- Aeolid nudibranchs are mollusks that eat hydroids, small polyps that have protective stinging cells. The nudibranch's digestive system carefully sorts out the hydroid's stinging cells and sends them to the protective tentacles on the nudibranch's own back.

Section 2

Eukaryotic Cells
"Protein" Therapy

- Decades of investigation into cell biology have produced what scientists call *gene therapy,* which refers to the use of genetic material to cure disease. It might be more appropriate to call this rapidly expanding field of science *protein therapy.*

- The gene can be thought of as a recipe for the proteins essential to life. For example, people with Duchenne muscular dystrophy lack dystrophin, an essential muscle protein that maintains the structure of muscle cells. Researchers have been able to remove the harmful genetic components of a virus and replace them with the gene for dystrophin. Their plan is to inject the dystrophin gene (the gene that codes for the dystrophin protein) directly into the muscles of Duchenne muscular dystrophy patients. If the process is successful, the dystrophin gene in the virus will compensate for patients' faulty dystrophin gene.

Tiny Scientists?

- Microbiologists study the characteristics of bacteria and other microorganisms to understand how they interact with other organisms. Virologists investigate viruses, which are active only inside a living host cell. Mycologists study fungi, which include molds and yeasts. Environmental microbiologists inspect the water in rivers and lakes. Microbiologists in agriculture study organisms that affect soil quality and crops.

Is That a Fact!

◆ The oldest unquestionably eukaryotic fossil is about 2.1 billion years old.

Section 3

The Organization of Living Things

In a Heartbeat

• The heart will function properly only if the cells that form the connective tissue and muscle perform their jobs in coordination. Scientists can use an enzyme to dissolve an embryonic heart into its individual cells. When placed in a dish, these cells, called *myocytes,* will continue to beat, although they are out of sync with each other. After a couple of days, sheets of interconnected cells form, and the myocytes beat in unison. Why do these changes happen? Openings develop between cells that touch, and their cytoplasms connect, which allows the cells to communicate directly with each other.

Organs: Delicate Workhorses

• The most frequently transplanted organ is the kidney, followed by the liver, the heart, and the lung. Most transplants must be done within a few hours after the organ is removed from a donor because organs are too delicate to survive current long-term storage procedures.

• Cryobiologists, scientists who study how life systems tolerate low temperatures, are studying the possibility of storing organs and organ systems at subfreezing temperatures. They are investigating the fluids that keep insects and some frogs alive during subfreezing temperatures. Cryobiologists hope that this knowledge can be applied to human organs.

Development

• In a multicellular organism, almost every cell has the same set of genes. (Some specialized cells delete or duplicate sections of their DNA.) Yet, different cell types are structurally distinct and perform widely different functions. Part of the reason is that each cell expresses some genes but not others. Sometimes, genes can be expressed in tissues where they should not be. Doctors have occasionally operated on people and removed tumors that had hair and teeth!

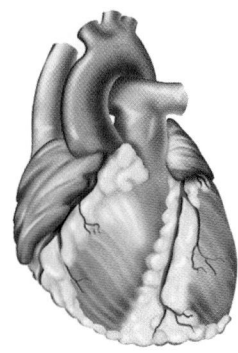

Is That a Fact!

◆ The oldest fossils of multicellular organisms are fossils of tiny algae approximately 1.2 billion years old.

◆ In 1931, a doctor removed a patient's parathyroid glands in error. These glands control the amount of calcium in the blood, which in turn regulates the heart. As a last-ditch effort to save the patient, a cow's parathyroid glands were ground up and injected into the patient. The patient recuperated and lived another 30 years with similar treatments.

SciLINKS®

NSTA
Developed and maintained by the
National Science Teachers Association

SciLinks is maintained by the National Science Teachers Association to provide you and your students with interesting, up-to-date links that will enrich your classroom presentation of the chapter.

Visit www.scilinks.org and enter the SciLinks code for more information about the topic listed.

Topic: Prokaryotic Cells
SciLinks code: HSM1225

Topic: Archaebacteria
SciLinks code: HSM0091

Topic: Eukaryotic Cells
SciLinks code: HSM0541

Topic: Organization of Life
SciLinks code: HSM1080

Topic: Cell Structures
SciLinks code: HSM0240

Topic: Body Systems
SciLinks code: HSM0184

Overview

This chapter will help students understand the great diversity of cells. The chapter will take students from the time when cells were unknown through the discovery of cells to the understanding of the tremendous diversity of cells. Students will learn about cell structures and will also learn how cells, tissues, and organs form organisms.

Assessing Prior Knowledge

Students should be familiar with the following topic:

• characteristics of a living thing

Identifying Misconceptions

Students may not understand that all cells and organisms have the same basic structures. Also, students may not have a sense of scale. When asked to draw a molecule, most students will draw something that resembles a cell. Instruction should emphasize the relationship between molecules and cells. For example, many students believe that proteins and molecules are bigger than cells.

Cells: The Basic Units of Life

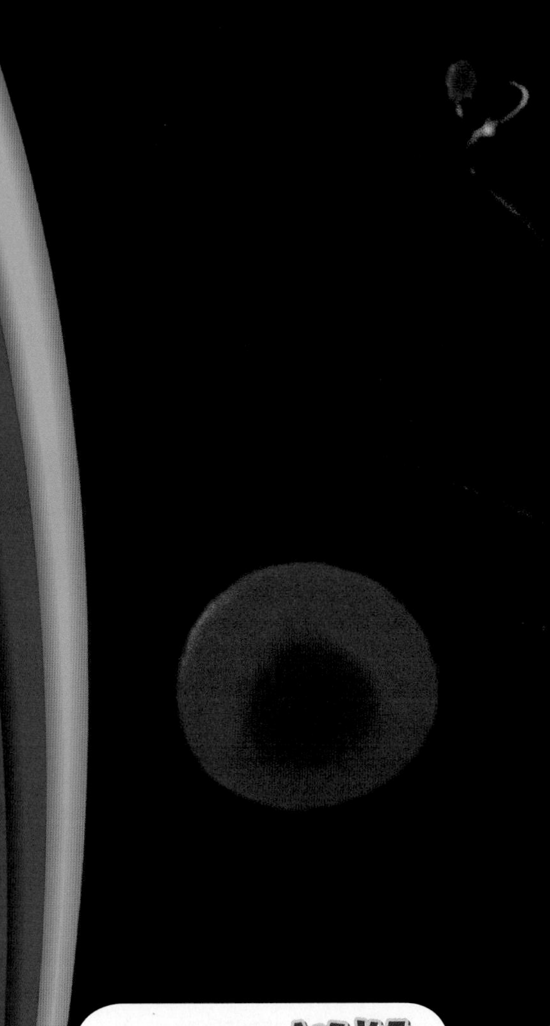

About the PHOTO

Harmful bacteria may invade your body and make you sick. But wait—your white blood cells come to the rescue! In this image, a white blood cell (the large, yellowish cell) reaches out its pseudopod to destroy bacteria (the purple cells). The red discs are red blood cells.

PRE-READING ACTIVITY

FOLDNOTES **Key-Term Fold** Before you read the chapter, create the FoldNote entitled "Key-Term Fold" described in the **Study Skills** section of the Appendix. Write a key term from the chapter on each tab of the key-term fold. Under each tab, write the definition of the key term.

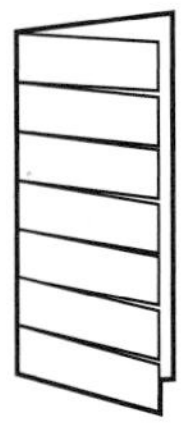

Standards Correlations

National Science Education Standards

The following codes indicate the National Science Education Standards that correlate to this chapter. The full text of the standards is at the front of the book.

Chapter Opener
UCP 1; HNS 3; LS 1b, 5b

Section 1 The Diversity of Cells
UCP 4, 5; SAI 1, 2; ST 2; SPSP 5; LS 1a, 1b, 1c, 2c, 3b, 5a; *LabBook:* UCP 1, 2, 5; SAI 1; ST 2; SPSP 5; HNS 1, 3; LS 1a, 1b, 1c, 1d, 2c, 3a, 5a

Section 2 Eukaryotic Cells
UCP 1, 4, 5; LS 1b, 1c, 3a, 5a, 5b

Section 3 The Organization of Living Things
UCP 1, 2, 5; LS 1a, 1b, 1d

Chapter Lab
UCP 1, 2, 3; SAI 2; LS 1b, 1c, 3a, 3b

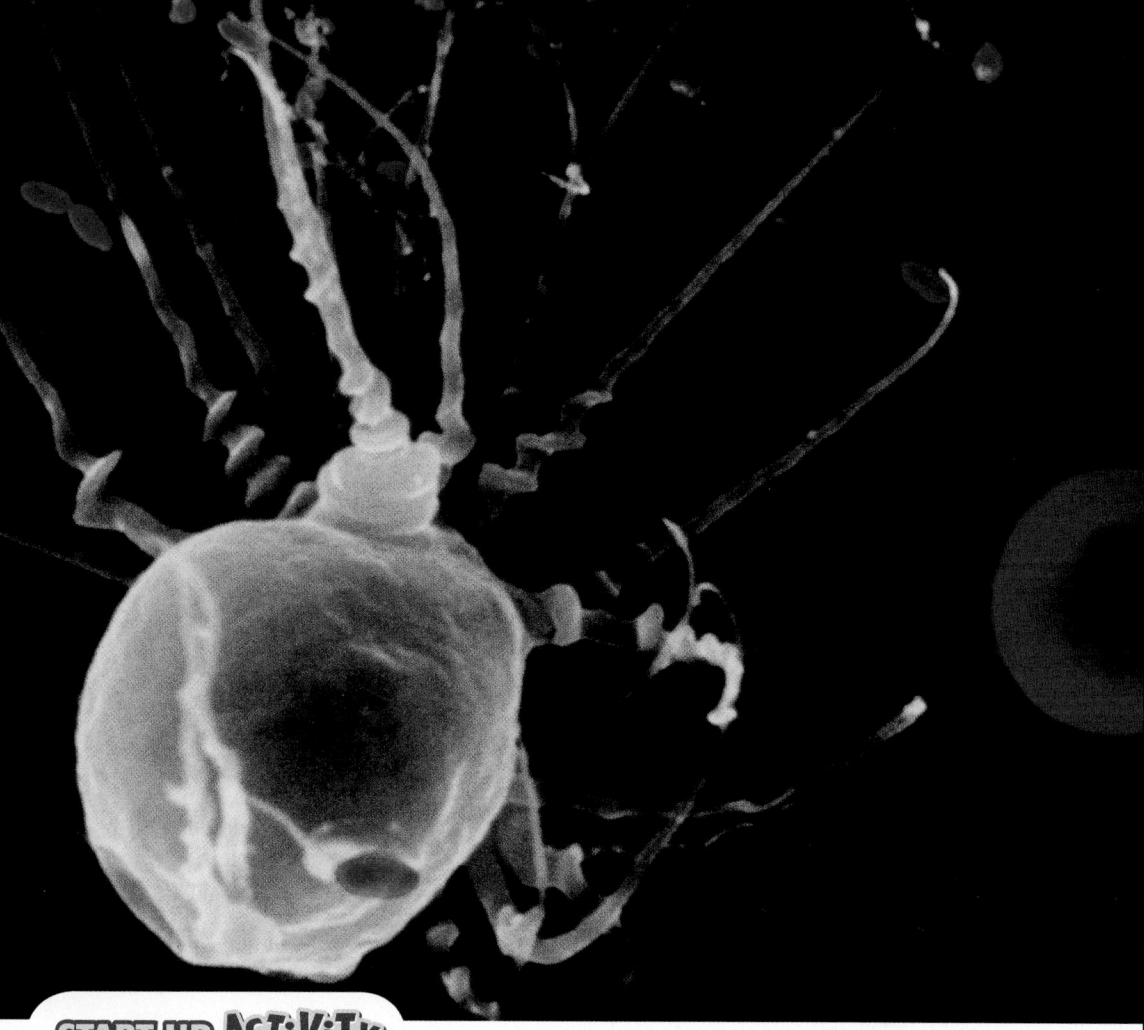

START-UP ACTIVITY
MATERIALS
FOR EACH STUDENT
- coverslip, plastic
- *Elodea*, small leaf
- forceps
- microscope
- microscope slide, plastic
- water

Safety Caution: Remind students to review all safety cautions and icons before beginning this activity.

Answers

1. Students should be able to describe accurately the cells that they see. Students should observe that all of the cells share similar structures but the cells may not be exactly the same.

2. Accept all reasonable responses. Students may note that plant cells differ from human body cells but that plant and animal cells share many of the same structures.

START-UP ACTIVITY

What Are Plants Made Of?

All living things, including plants, are made of cells. What do plant cells look like? Do this activity to find out.

Procedure

1. Tear off a **small leaf** from near the tip of an **Elodea sprig.**

2. Using **forceps,** place the whole leaf in a **drop of water** on a **microscope slide.**

3. Place a **coverslip** on top of the water drop by putting one edge of the coverslip on the slide near the water drop. Next, lower the coverslip slowly so that the coverslip does not trap air bubbles.

4. Place the slide on your **microscope.**

5. Using the lowest-powered lens first, find the plant cells. When you can see the cells under the lower-powered lens, switch to a higher-powered lens.

6. Draw a picture of what you see.

Analysis

1. Describe the shape of the *Elodea* cells. Are all of the cells in the *Elodea* the same?

2. Do you think human cells look like *Elodea* cells? How do you think they are different? How might they be similar?

Chapter Review
UCP 1; SAI 1; HNS 1; LS 1a, 1b, 1c, 1d, 3a, 3b

Science in Action
SAI 2; ST 2; SPSP 5; HNS 1; LS 3a, 3c

Cells: The Basic Units of Life   CHAPTER STARTER

What If . . . ?

Imagine this scene from a horror film. A young man sits down to dinner to find that his mother has made asparagus again. The young man eats the dreaded asparagus stalks. Later, he finds out that instead of being digested, one of the stalks has taken up residence inside his body and is very much alive! Too horrifying to think about? What if the asparagus began to do wonderful things for the young man, such as giving him more energy than he ever dreamed possible? Lynn Margulis, a scientist, thinks that something similar may have

According to Margulis's theory, about 1.2 billion years ago, some larger cells began eating smaller cells for dinner. Like the white blood cell on this page, these larger cells trapped the smaller cells with extensions of their cell body. But some of these smaller cells resisted being digested. In fact, they began to do very well in their new homes. The larger cells also benefited from their new guests. The smaller cells released large amounts of energy from food taken in by the larger cells. Other kinds of small cells used the energy in sunlight to make enough food

Chapter Starter Transparency
Use this transparency to help students begin thinking about cells, cell structures, and organisms.

CHAPTER RESOURCES

Technology

Transparencies
- Chapter Starter Transparency

READING SKILLS

Student Edition on CD-ROM

Guided Reading Audio CD
- English or Spanish

Classroom Videos
- Brain Food Video Quiz

Workbooks

Science Puzzlers, Twisters & Teasers
- Cells: The Basic Units of Life GENERAL

SECTION
1

Focus

Overview

This section introduces students to cells, their discovery, and their diversity. Students will learn about the parts of a cell and the reason that cells are so small. Finally, students will learn about eubacterial, archaebacterial, and eukaryotic cells.

🔊 Bellringer

Write the following questions on the board:

Why weren't cells discovered until 1665? What invention made their discovery possible? (Cells weren't discovered until 1665 because almost all cells are too small to be seen with the naked eye. The microscope is the invention that made their discovery possible.)

Motivate

ᴀᴄᴛɪᴠɪᴛʏ ——————— GENERAL

Modeling Cell Discovery Before students begin this section, have them model Robert Hooke's discovery. Organize the class into small groups. Provide each group with a microscope and a prepared slide of cork cells. Have students describe and sketch their observations. **LS** Visual

---

The Diversity of Cells

Most cells are so small they can't be seen by the naked eye. So how did scientists find cells? By accident, that's how! The first person to see cells wasn't even looking for them.

All living things are made of tiny structures called cells. A **cell** is the smallest unit that can perform all the processes necessary for life. Because of their size, cells weren't discovered until microscopes were invented in the mid-1600s.

Cells and the Cell Theory

Robert Hooke was the first person to describe cells. In 1665, he built a microscope to look at tiny objects. One day, he looked at a thin slice of cork. Cork is found in the bark of cork trees. The cork looked like it was made of little boxes. Hooke named these boxes *cells,* which means "little rooms" in Latin. Hooke's cells were really the outer layers of dead cork cells. Hooke's microscope and his drawing of the cork cells are shown in **Figure 1.**

Hooke also looked at thin slices of living plants. He saw that they too were made of cells. Some cells were even filled with "juice." The "juicy" cells were living cells.

Hooke also looked at feathers, fish scales, and the eyes of houseflies. But he spent most of his time looking at plants and fungi. The cells of plants and fungi have cell walls. This makes them easy to see. Animal cells do not have cell walls. This absence of cell walls makes it harder to see the outline of animal cells. Because Hooke couldn't see their cells, he thought that animals weren't made of cells.

READING WARM-UP

Objectives
- State the parts of the cell theory.
- Explain why cells are so small.
- Describe the parts of a cell.
- Describe how eubacteria are different from archaebacteria.
- Explain the difference between prokaryotic cells and eukaryotic cells.

Terms to Learn

cell	nucleus
cell membrane	prokaryote
organelle	eukaryote

READING STRATEGY

Reading Organizer As you read this section, create an outline of the section. Use the headings from the section in your outline.

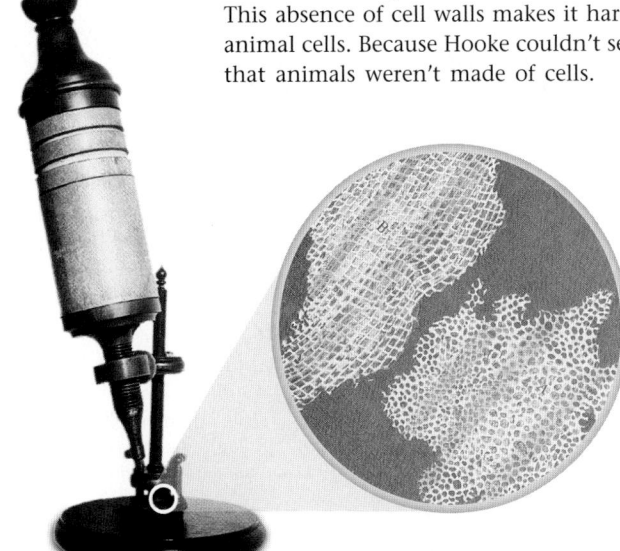

Figure 1 *Hooke discovered cells using this microscope. Hooke's drawing of cork cells is shown to the right of his microscope.*

CHAPTER RESOURCES

Chapter Resource File

 • Lesson Plan
- Directed Reading A **BASIC**
- Directed Reading B **SPECIAL NEEDS**

Technology

 Transparencies
- Bellringer

Cultural Awareness   GENERAL

Yeast Yeast is a fungus. Yeast used in baking is related to wild fungi living in the air around us. Strains of native yeasts vary regionally. For example, sourdough from San Francisco has its characteristic taste because bakers there use a yeast that is common in the air around that city. Not all breads require yeast. Many cultures have flat breads, such as tortillas from Mexico.

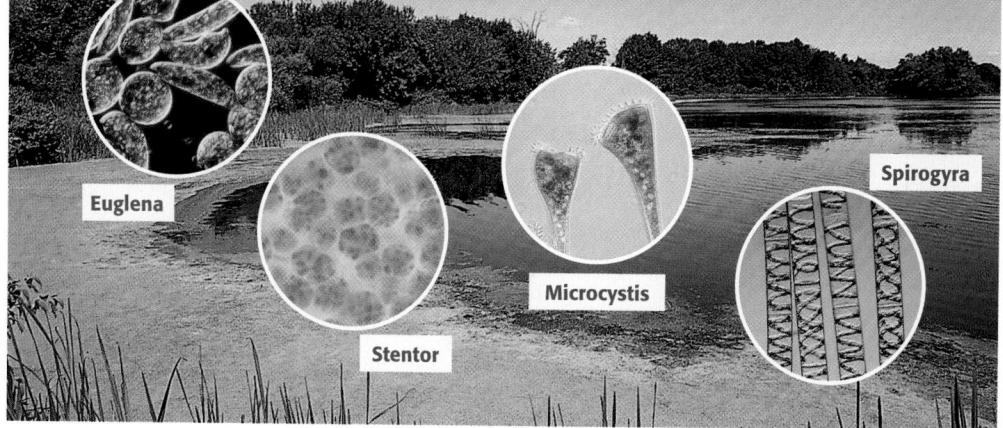

Euglena

Spirogyra

Microcystis

Stentor

Finding Cells in Other Organisms

In 1673, Anton van Leeuwenhoek (LAY vuhn HOOK), a Dutch merchant, made his own microscopes. Leeuwenhoek used one of his microscopes to look at pond scum. Leeuwenhoek saw small organisms in the water. He named these organisms *animalcules,* which means "little animals." Today, we call these single-celled organisms protists (PROH tists). Pond scum and some of the protists it contains are shown in **Figure 2.**

Leeuwenhoek also looked at animal blood. He saw differences in blood cells from different kinds of animals. For example, blood cells in fish, birds, and frogs are oval. Blood cells in humans and dogs are round and flat. Leeuwenhoek was also the first person to see bacteria. And he discovered that yeasts that make bread dough rise are single-celled organisms.

The Cell Theory

Almost 200 years passed before scientists concluded that cells are present in all living things. Scientist Matthias Schleiden (mah THEE uhs SHLIE duhn) studied plants. In 1838, he concluded that all plant parts were made of cells. Theodor Schwann (TAY oh dohr SHVAHN) studied animals. In 1839, Schwann concluded that all animal tissues were made of cells. Soon after that, Schwann wrote the first two parts of what is now known as the *cell theory.*

- All organisms are made of one or more cells.
- The cell is the basic unit of all living things.

Later, in 1858, Rudolf Virchow (ROO dawlf FIR koh), a doctor, stated that all cells could form only from other cells. Virchow then added the third part of the cell theory.

- All cells come from existing cells.

✓ Reading Check What are the three parts of the cell theory? *(See the Appendix for answers to Reading Checks.)*

Figure 2 *The green area at the edge of the pond is a layer of pond scum. This pond scum contains organisms called protists, such as those shown above.*

cell in biology, the smallest unit that can perform all life processes; cells are covered by a membrane and have DNA and cytoplasm

CONNECTION TO Physics

Microscopes The microscope Hooke used to study cells was much different from microscopes today. Research different kinds of microscopes, such as light microscopes, scanning electron microscopes (SEMs), and transmission electron microscopes (TEMs). Select one type of microscope. Make a poster or other presentation to show to the class. Describe how the microscope works and how it is used. Be sure to include images.

ACTiViTy

Answer to Reading Check
All organisms are made of one or more cells, the cell is the basic unit of all living things, and all cells come from existing cells.

Teach

INCLUSION Strategies

- *Learning Disabled*
- *Attention Deficit Disorder*
- *Behavior Control Issues*

Give students a chance to associate dates with specific familiar reference points. Draw a timeline on the board. On opposite ends of the timeline, place "1492, Columbus sails to America" and "1879, Edison invents the electric light bulb." Tell students to add dates and information for five major cell discoveries that happened between 1492 and 1879. Ask students with behavior control issues to add their teams' information to the timeline. **LS Interpersonal** English Language Learners

CONNECTION to Astronomy ———— GENERAL

Writing **Magnifiers** Both biologists and astronomers use magnifiers. Biologists use microscopes to see things that are too small to see with the unaided eye. Astronomers use telescopes to see planets, moons, and stars that are huge but too far away to view otherwise. Ask students to write a list of words that have the prefixes *micro-* and *tele-* and to use their examples to define those prefixes. **LS Verbal** English Language Learners

Teach, *continued*

 READING STRATEGY — GENERAL

Prediction Guide Before students read this page, ask them to choose one of the following reasons for why they think cells are so small:

1. There isn't enough microscopic food available for them.

2. There isn't enough room in a multicellular organism.

3. another reason (ask for suggestions)

Have students evaluate their answer after they read the page. **LS** Logical

---

MISCONCEPTION ALERT

Molecular Mix-Up The physical relationship between molecules and cells may be confusing to students. Molecules are not alive and are much smaller than cells. Cells and cell structures are made of molecules.

Answer to Reading Check

If a cell's volume gets too large, the cell's surface area will not be able to take in enough nutrients or get rid of wastes fast enough to keep the cell alive.

Cell Size

Most cells are too small to be seen without a microscope. It would take 50 human cells to cover the dot on this letter *i*.

A Few Large Cells

Most cells are small. A few, however, are big. The yolk of a chicken egg, shown in **Figure 3**, is one big cell. The egg can be this large because it does not have to take in more nutrients.

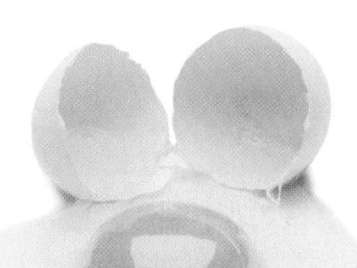

Figure 3 *The white and yolk of this chicken egg provide nutrients for the development of a chick.*

Many Small Cells

There is a physical reason why most cells are so small. Cells take in food and get rid of wastes through their outer surface. As a cell gets larger, it needs more food and produces more waste. Therefore, more materials pass through its outer surface.

As the cell's volume increases, its surface area grows too. But the cell's volume grows faster than its surface area. If a cell gets too large, the cell's surface area will not be large enough to take in enough nutrients or pump out enough wastes. So, the area of a cell's surface—compared with the cell's volume—limits the cell's size. The ratio of the cell's outer surface area to the cell's volume is called the *surface area–to-volume ratio*, which can be calculated by using the following equation:

$$\text{surface area–to-volume ratio} = \frac{\text{surface area}}{\text{volume}}$$

✓ Reading Check Why are most cells small?

MATH FOCUS

Surface Area-to-Volume Ratio Calculate the surface area–to-volume ratio of a cube whose sides measure 2 cm.

Step 1: Calculate the surface area.

surface area of cube = number of sides × area of side

surface area of cube = 6 × (2 cm × 2 cm)

surface area of cube = 24 cm²

Step 2: Calculate the volume.

volume of cube = side × side × side

volume of cube = 2 cm × 2 cm × 2 cm

volume of cube = 8 cm³

Step 3: Calculate the surface area–to-volume ratio.

$$\text{surface area–to-volume ratio} = \frac{\text{surface area}}{\text{volume}} = \frac{24}{8} = \frac{3}{1}$$

Now It's Your Turn

1. Calculate the surface area–to-volume ratio of a cube whose sides are 3 cm long.

2. Calculate the surface area–to-volume ratio of a cube whose sides are 4 cm long.

3. Of the cubes from questions 1 and 2, which has the greater surface area–to-volume ratio?

4. What is the relationship between the length of a side and the surface area–to-volume ratio of a cell?

CHAPTER RESOURCES

Technology

Transparencies
• Math Focus: Surface Area–to-Volume Ratio

Answers to Math Focus

1. Surface area of cube (SA) =
   (3 cm × 3 cm) × 6 = 54 cm²
   Volume of cube (V) =
   3 cm × 3 cm × 3 cm = 27 cm³
   SA:V ratio = 54:27 or 2:1

2. SA = (4 cm × 4 cm) × 6 = 96 cm²
   V = 4 cm × 4 cm × 4 cm = 64 cm³
   SA:V = 96:64 or 1.5:1

3. the cube whose sides are 3 cm long

4. The larger the cell is, the smaller the surface-to-volume ratio is.

Parts of a Cell

Cells come in many shapes and sizes. Cells have many different functions. But all cells have the following parts in common.

The Cell Membrane and Cytoplasm

All cells are surrounded by a cell membrane. The **cell membrane** is a protective layer that covers the cell's surface and acts as a barrier. It separates the cell's contents from its environment. The cell membrane also controls materials going into and out of the cell. Inside the cell is a fluid. This fluid and almost all of its contents are called the *cytoplasm* (SIET oh PLAZ uhm).

Organelles

Cells have organelles that carry out various life processes. **Organelles** are structures that perform specific functions within the cell. Different types of cells have different organelles. Most organelles are surrounded by membranes. For example, the algal cell in **Figure 4** has membrane-bound organelles. Some organelles float in the cytoplasm. Other organelles are attached to membranes or other organelles.

Reading Check What are organelles?

Genetic Material

All cells contain DNA (**d**eoxyribo**n**ucleic **a**cid) at some point in their life. *DNA* is the genetic material that carries information needed to make new cells and new organisms. DNA is passed on from parent cells to new cells and controls the activities of a cell. **Figure 5** shows the DNA of a bacterium.

In some cells, the DNA is enclosed inside an organelle called the **nucleus.** For example, your cells have a nucleus. In contrast, bacterial cells do not have a nucleus.

In humans, mature red blood cells lose their DNA. Red blood cells are made inside bones. When red blood cells are first made, they have a nucleus with DNA. But before they enter the bloodstream, red blood cells lose their nucleus and DNA. They survive with no new instructions from their DNA.

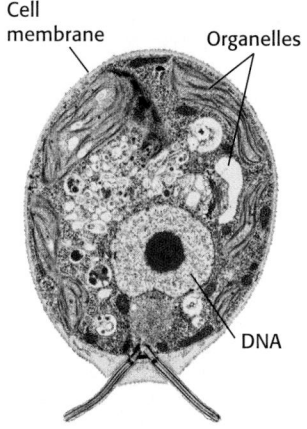

Cell membrane — Organelles

DNA

Figure 4 *This green alga has organelles. The organelles and the fluid surrounding them make up the cytoplasm.*

cell membrane a phospholipid layer that covers a cell's surface; acts as a barrier between the inside of a cell and the cell's environment

organelle one of the small bodies in a cell's cytoplasm that are specialized to perform a specific function

nucleus in a eukaryotic cell, a membrane-bound organelle that contains the cell's DNA and that has a role in processes such as growth, metabolism, and reproduction

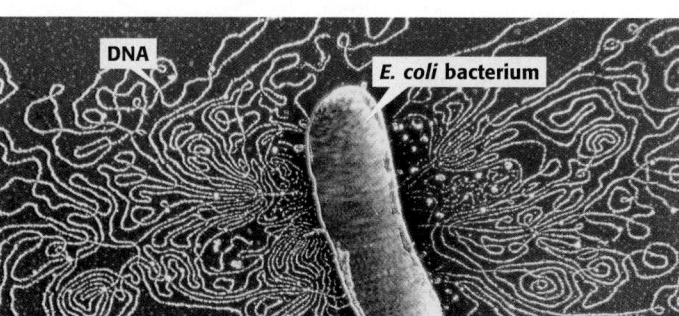

DNA

E. coli bacterium

Figure 5 *This photo shows an* Escherichia coli *bacterium. The bacterium's cell membrane has been treated so that the cell's DNA is released.*

READING STRATEGY — GENERAL

Prediction Guide Before students read this page, ask them if the following statement is true or false: At some point, all cells contain DNA. (true; Even though some cells, such as red blood cells, lose their DNA when they mature, all cells have DNA at some point.)

Ask students to explain the reasons for their answer. Have students evaluate their answer after they read the page. **LS** Verbal

MISCONCEPTION ALERT

DNA and Complexity
Students may believe that larger or more-complex organisms have more DNA. This is not the case. In general, eukaryotes have more DNA than bacteria or viruses do. Among eukaryotes however, there is no strong correlation between body size or measures of complexity and DNA content. Although the fruit fly *Drosophila melanogaster* has about one-fourth as much DNA as a human, the protist *Amoeba dubia* has about 200 times more DNA than a human being does! Part of the reason for this apparent discrepancy is that some DNA does not code for any genes. Species with very large genomes have a lot of non-coding DNA.

CONNECTION to Language Arts — GENERAL

Writing **Smallest Living Thing** Is the smallest living thing an organism called a *Mycoplasma genitalium*? Or is it something called a "nanobacteria"? Have students conduct Internet or library research and write a report on the smallest living thing. (Scientists are not certain. "Nanobacteria" do not always show all the characteristics of living things. More research may settle the issue.) **LS** Verbal/Logical

Answer to Reading Check
Organelles are structures within a cell that perform specific functions for the cell.

MATERIALS

FOR EACH STUDENT
- cotton swab
- coverslip, plastic
- microscope
- microscope slide, plastic
- water
- yogurt with active culture

Answer

4. Drawings should depict rod-shaped bacteria.

CONNECTION to Earth Science —— GENERAL

Writing

Subsurface Cells Astronomers are interested in the work of scientists who investigate bacteria and other microscopic organisms in Earth's crust. Microbiologists have drilled deep into the crust and found microbes nearly 3 km below the surface, where the temperature is 75°C (167°F). Because other planets have surface conditions similar to the harsh environment within the Earth's crust, astronomers believe that microbes may live elsewhere in the solar system. Have students research and write a brief report on the conditions in Earth's crust, and have students learn about the organisms that live there. **LS Verbal**

Quick Lab

Bacteria in Your Lunch?

Most of the time, you don't want bacteria in your food. Many bacteria make toxins that will make you sick. However, some foods—such as yogurt—are supposed to have bacteria in them! The bacteria in these foods are not dangerous.

In yogurt, masses of rod-shaped bacteria feed on the sugar (lactose) in milk. The bacteria convert the sugar into lactic acid. Lactic acid causes milk to thicken. This thickened milk makes yogurt.

1. Using a **cotton swab,** put a **small dot of yogurt** on a **microscope slide.**
2. Add a **drop of water.** Use the cotton swab to stir.
3. Add a **coverslip**.
4. Use a **microscope** to examine the slide. Draw what you observe.

prokaryote an organism that consists of a single cell that does not have a nucleus

Two Kinds of Cells

All cells have cell membranes, organelles, cytoplasm, and DNA in common. But there are two basic types of cells—cells without a nucleus and cells with a nucleus. Cells with no nucleus are *prokaryotic* (proh KAR ee AHT ik) *cells.* Cells that have a nucleus are *eukaryotic* (yoo KAR ee AHT ik) *cells.* Prokaryotic cells are further classified into two groups: *eubacteria* (yoo bak TIR ee uh) and *archaebacteria* (AHR kee bak TIR ee uh).

Prokaryotes: Eubacteria and Archaebacteria

Eubacteria and archaebacteria are prokaryotes (pro KAR ee OHTS). **Prokaryotes** are single-celled organisms that do not have a nucleus or membrane-bound organelles.

Eubacteria

The most common prokaryotes are eubacteria (or just *bacteria*). Bacteria are the world's smallest cells. These tiny organisms live almost everywhere. Bacteria do not have a nucleus, but they do have DNA. A bacteria's DNA is a long, circular molecule, shaped sort of like a rubber band. Bacteria have no membrane-covered organelles. But they do have ribosomes. *Ribosomes* are tiny, round organelles made of protein and other material.

Bacteria also have a strong, weblike exterior cell wall. This wall helps the cell retain its shape. A bacterium's cell membrane is just inside the cell wall. Together, the cell wall and cell membrane allow materials into and out of the cell.

Some bacteria live in the soil and water. Others live in, or on, other organisms. For example, you have bacteria living on your skin and teeth. You also have bacteria living in your digestive system. These bacteria help the process of digestion. A typical bacterial cell is shown in **Figure 6.**

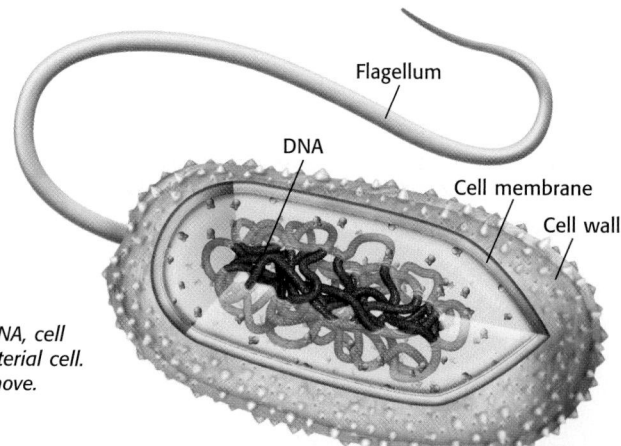

Figure 6 *This diagram shows the DNA, cell membrane, and cell wall of a eubacterial cell. The flagellum helps the bacterium move.*

Group ACTIVITY — ADVANCED

Archaebacteria Have students work in pairs to find out if archaebacteria are more similar to eubacteria or eukaryotes. What kinds of evidence do scientists use to answer this question? Have students make a poster or other visual presentation of their results. **LS Visual/Interpersonal**

WEIRD SCIENCE

In 1969, the *Apollo 12* crew retrieved a space probe from the moon that had been launched nearly 3 years earlier. NASA scientists found a stowaway in the probe's camera. The bacterium *Streptococcus mitis* had traveled to the moon and back. Despite the rigors of space travel, more than 2.5 years of radiation exposure, and freezing temperatures, the *Streptococcus mitis* was successfully reconstituted.

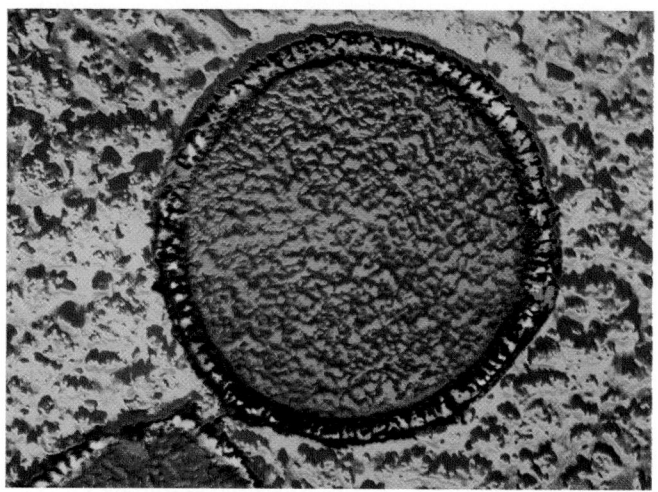

Figure 7 *This photograph, taken with an electron microscope, is of an archaebacterium that lives in the very high temperatures of deep-sea volcanic vents. The photograph has been colored so that the cell wall is green and the cell contents are pink.*

Archaebacteria

The second kind of prokaryote are the archaebacteria. These organisms are also called *archaea* (ahr KEE uh). Archaebacteria are similar to bacteria in some ways. For example, both are single-celled organisms. Both have ribosomes, a cell membrane, and circular DNA. And both lack a nucleus and membrane-bound organelles. But archaebacteria are different from bacteria. For example, archaebacterial ribosomes are different from eubacterial ribosomes.

Archaebacteria are similar to eukaryotic cells in some ways, too. For example, archaebacterial ribosomes are more like the ribosomes of eukaryotic cells. But archaebacteria also have some features that no other cells have. For example, the cell wall and cell membranes of archaebacteria are different from the cell walls of other organisms. And some archaebacteria live in places where no other organisms could live.

Three types of archaebacteria are *heat-loving*, *salt-loving*, and *methane-making*. Methane is a kind of gas frequently found in swamps. Heat-loving and salt-lovng archaebacteria are sometimes called extremophiles. *Extremophiles* live in places where conditions are extreme. They live in very hot water, such as in hot springs, or where the water is extremely salty. **Figure 7** shows one kind of methane-making archaebacteria that lives deep in the ocean near volcanic vents. The temperature of the water from those vents is extreme: it is above the boiling point of water at sea level.

 **Reading Check** What is one difference between eubacteria and archaebacteria?

CONNECTION TO Social Studies

Where Do They Live?
While most archaebacteria live in extreme environments, scientists have found that archaebacteria live almost everywhere. Do research about archaebacteria. Select one kind of archaebacteria. Create a poster showing the geographical location where the organism lives, describing its physical environment, and explaining how it survives in its environment.

ACTIVITY

Answer to Reading Check
One difference between eubacteria and archaea is that bacterial ribosomes are different from archaebacterial ribosomes.

CONNECTION to Earth Science — GENERAL

Writing **Discovering Ancient Earth** The work of paleontologists helps us understand the antiquity of unicellular and multicellular life on Earth. Some paleontologists specialize in ancient plant life, and some specialize in ancient climates. Have students conduct Internet or library research and write a report on different types of paleontologists. **LS** Verbal

MISCONCEPTION ALERT

Extreme Bacteria? Students may believe that all archaebacteria live in extreme environments because biology books often highlight the unusual and extreme environments in which some archaebacteria live. In these environments, other types of organisms cannot survive. In fact, many archaebacteria live in "normal" environments along with other eubacterial and eukaryotic species.

Research — GENERAL

Writing **Be a Good Host** Have students select one type of bacterium (such as the *Streptococcus mutans*, which causes tooth decay) that lives on or in the body, conduct Internet or library research on it, and then write and illustrate a report on the bacterium they have selected. **LS** Verbal/Visual

Close

eukaryote an organism made up of cells that have a nucleus enclosed by a membrane; eukaryotes include animals, plants, and fungi, but not archaebacteria or eubacteria

Eukaryotic Cells and Eukaryotes

Eukaryotic cells are the largest cells. Most eukaryotic cells are still microscopic, but they are about 10 times larger than most bacterial cells. A typical eukaryotic cell is shown in **Figure 8.**

Unlike bacteria and archaebacteria, eukaryotic cells have a nucleus. The nucleus is one kind of membrane-bound organelle. A cell's nucleus holds the cell's DNA. Eukaryotic cells have other membrane-bound organelles as well. Organelles are like the different organs in your body. Each kind of organelle has a specific job in the cell. Together, organelles, such as the ones shown in **Figure 8,** perform all the processes necessary for life.

All living things that are not bacteria or archaebacteria are made of one or more eukaryotic cells. Organisms made of eukaryotic cells are called **eukaryotes.** Many eukaryotes are multicellular. *Multicellular* means "many cells." Multicellular organisms are usually larger than single-cell organisms. So, most organisms you see with your naked eye are eukaryotes. There are many types of eukaryotes. Animals, including humans, are eukaryotes. So are plants. Some protists, such as amoebas, are single-celled eukaryotes. Other protists, including some types of green algae, are multicellular eukaryotes. Fungi are organisms such as mushrooms or yeasts. Mushrooms are multicellular eukaryotes. Yeasts are single-celled eukaryotes.

✓ *Reading Check* How are eukaryotes different from prokaryotes?

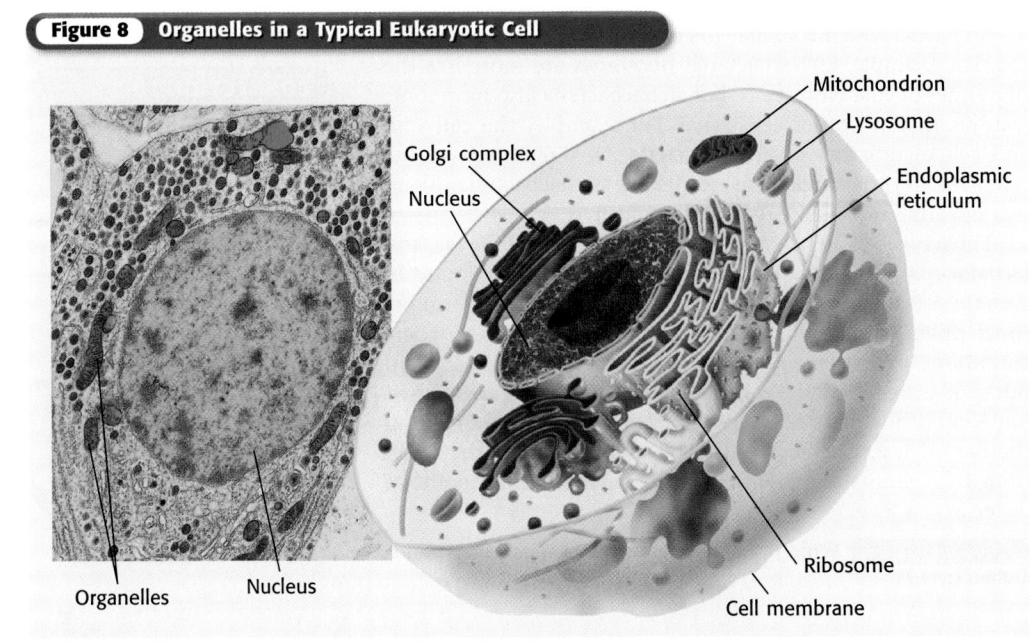

Figure 8 Organelles in a Typical Eukaryotic Cell

Golgi complex
Nucleus
Mitochondrion
Lysosome
Endoplasmic reticulum
Ribosome
Cell membrane
Organelles
Nucleus

SECTION Review

Summary

- Cells were not discovered until microscopes were invented in the 1600s.
- Cell theory states that all organisms are made of cells, the cell is the basic unit of all living things, and all cells come from other cells.
- All cells have a cell membrane, cytoplasm, and DNA.
- Most cells are too small to be seen with the naked eye. A cell's surface area–to-volume ratio limits the size of a cell.

- The two basic kinds of cells are prokaryotic cells and eukaryotic cells. Eukaryotic cells have a nucleus and membrane-bound organelles. Prokaryotic cells do not.
- Prokaryotes are classified as archaebacteria and eubacteria.
- Archaebacterial cell walls and ribosomes are different from the cell walls and ribosomes of other organisms.
- Eukaryotes can be single-celled or multicellular.

Using Key Terms

1. In your own words, write a definition for the term *organelle*.

2. Use the following terms in the same sentence: *prokaryotic, nucleus,* and *eukaryotic*.

Understanding Key Ideas

3. Cell size is limited by the
   a. thickness of the cell wall.
   b. size of the cell's nucleus.
   c. cell's surface area–to-volume ratio.
   d. amount of cytoplasm in the cell.

4. What are the three parts of the cell theory?

5. Name three structures that every cell has.

6. Give two ways in which archaebacteria are different from bacteria.

Critical Thinking

7. **Applying Concepts** You have discovered a new single-celled organism. It has a cell wall, ribosomes, and long, circular DNA. Is it a eukaryote or a prokaryote cell? Explain.

8. **Identifying Relationships** One of your students brings you a cell about the size of the period at the end of this sentence. It is a single cell, but it also forms chains. What characteristics would this cell have if the organism is a eukaryote? If it is a prokaryote? What would you look for first?

Interpreting Graphics

The picture below shows a particular organism. Use the picture to answer the questions that follow.

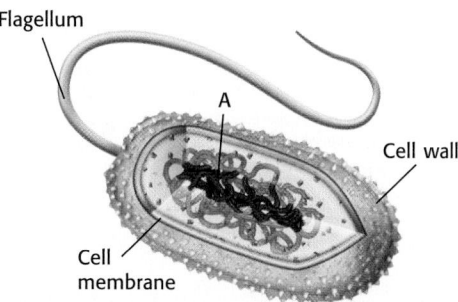

Flagellum · A · Cell wall · Cell membrane

9. What type of organism does the picture represent? How do you know?

10. Which structure helps the organism move?

11. What part of the organism does the letter *A* represent?

SCiLINKS

NSTA
Developed and maintained by the
National Science Teachers Association

For a variety of links related to this chapter, go to www.scilinks.org
Topic: Prokaryotic Cells
SciLinks code: HSM1225

Answers to Section Review

1. Sample answer: An organelle is a structure inside a cell that performs a specific function for the cell.

2. Sample answer: Eukaryotic cells have a nucleus, but prokaryotic cells do not.

3. c

4. All organisms are made of one or more cells, the cell is the basic unit of all living things, and all cells come from existing cells.

5. Every cell has a cell membrane, DNA, and cytoplasm.

6. Sample answer: The cell walls and the ribosomes of archaebacteria are different from those structures in eubacteria.

7. Sample answer: The cell is probably a prokaryote; The key is that it does not appear to have a nucleus and its DNA is long and circular.

8. Sample answer: eukaryote: whether the chains were a multicellular organism or a collection of individual cells, membrane-bound organelles, certain types of ribosomes and certain materials in the cell membranes, where the DNA is located, and a nucleus; prokaryote: other types of ribosomes and cell membrane materials, the structure of the DNA, and a nucleus; The first thing I would look for is a nucleus.

9. a typical eubacterial cell; It has no nucleus, and its DNA is long and circular.

10. the flagellum

11. the cell's DNA

CHAPTER RESOURCES

Chapter Resource File

- Section Quiz GENERAL
- Section Review GENERAL
- Vocabulary and Section Summary GENERAL
- Reinforcement Worksheet BASIC

Technology

Transparencies
- A Typical Eukaryotic Cell

Focus

Overview

In this section, students will learn the names and functions of the cell structures, called *organelles*, in a eukaryotic cell.

🔊 Bellringer

On the board, write the following:

List three differences between prokaryotic and eukaryotic cells. (Prokaryotic cells have circular DNA, no nucleus, and no membrane-covered organelles. Eukaryotic cells have linear DNA, a nucleus, and membrane-covered organelles.)

Motivate

Discussion ——— GENERAL

Cellular Activity Ask students if they can feel the flurry of activity within their cells that keeps them alive. (no; But even though students can't feel activity in the cells, they can feel the heat produced by cellular activity. Students are not likely to know this.)

Ask students how they know their cells are working. (The students are alive: they can breathe, digest food, and move.) **LS Logical/Intrapersonal**

Answer to Reading Check

Plant, algae, and fungi cells have cell walls.

READING WARM-UP

Objectives

● Identify the different parts of a eukaryotic cell.

● Explain the function of each part of a eukaryotic cell.

Terms to Learn

cell wall   mitochondrion
ribosome   Golgi complex
endoplasmic   vesicle
    reticulum   lysosome

READING STRATEGY

Reading Organizer As you read this section, make a table comparing plant cells and animal cells.

cell wall a rigid structure that surrounds the cell membrane and provides support to the cell

---

Eukaryotic Cells

Most eukaryotic cells are small. For a long time after cells were discovered, scientists could not see what was going on inside cells. They did not know how complex cells are.

Now, scientists know a lot about eukaryotic cells. These cells have many parts that work together and keep the cell alive.

Cell Wall

Some eukaryotic cells have cell walls. A **cell wall** is a rigid structure that gives support to a cell. The cell wall is the outermost structure of a cell. Plants and algae have cell walls made of cellulose (SEL yoo LOHS) and other materials. *Cellulose* is a complex sugar that most animals can't digest.

The cell walls of plant cells allow plants to stand upright. In some plants, the cells must take in water for the cell walls to keep their shape. When such plants lack water, the cell walls collapse and the plant droops. **Figure 1** shows a cross section of a plant cell and a close-up of the cell wall.

Fungi, including yeasts and mushrooms, also have cell walls. Some fungi have cell walls made of *chitin* (KIE tin). Other fungi have cell walls made from a chemical similar to chitin. Eubacteria and archaebacteria also have cell walls, but those walls are different from plant or fungal cell walls.

✓ **Reading Check** What types of cells have cell walls? (*See the Appendix for answers to Reading Checks.*)

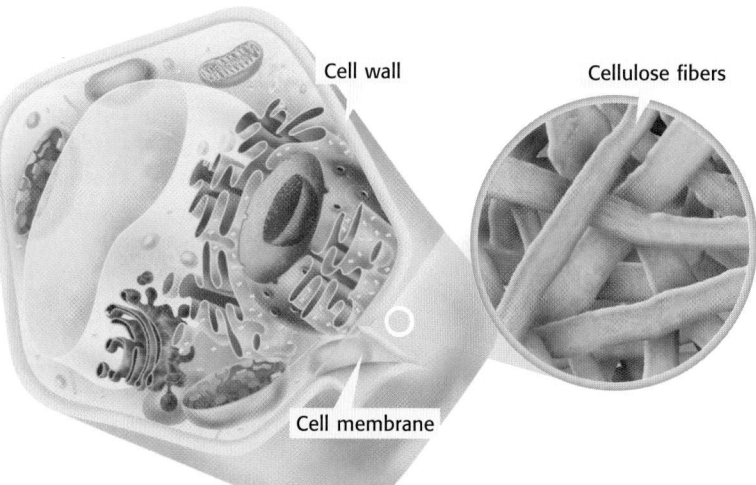

Figure 1 *The cell walls of plant cells help plants retain their shape. Plant cell walls are made of cellulose.*

Cell wall   Cellulose fibers

Cell membrane

CHAPTER RESOURCES

Chapter Resource File

• **Lesson Plan**
   • **Directed Reading A** BASIC
   • **Directed Reading B** SPECIAL NEEDS

Technology

Transparencies
• Bellringer

MISCONCEPTION
///ALERT\\\

Cells Are Three-Dimensional Students often think of cells as flat. Looking at pictures and even viewing cells in a microscope can reinforce that misconception. Make sure that students understand that even though most cells are very small, they do have three dimensions, and they do take up space.

Cell Membrane

All cells have a cell membrane. The *cell membrane* is a protective barrier that encloses a cell. It separates the cell's contents from the cell's environment. The cell membrane is the outermost structure in cells that lack a cell wall. In cells that have a cell wall, the cell membrane lies just inside the cell wall.

The cell membrane contains proteins, lipids, and phospholipids. *Lipids,* which include fats and cholesterol, are a group of compounds that do not dissolve in water. The cell membrane has two layers of phospholipids (FAHS foh LIP idz), shown in **Figure 2.** A *phospholipid* is a lipid that contains phosphorus. Lipids are "water fearing," or *hydrophobic.* Lipid ends of phospholipids form the inner part of the membrane. Phosphorus-containing ends of the phospholipids are "water loving," or *hydrophilic.* These ends form the outer part of the membrane.

Some of the proteins and lipids control the movement of materials into and out of the cell. Some of the proteins form passageways. Nutrients and water move into the cell, and wastes move out of the cell, through these protein passageways.

Reading Check What are two functions of a cell membrane?

CONNECTION TO

Language Arts

WRITING SKILL **The Great Barrier** In your **science journal,** write a science fiction story about tiny travelers inside a person's body. These little explorers need to find a way into or out of a cell to solve a problem. You may need to do research to find out more about how the cell membrane works. Illustrate your story.

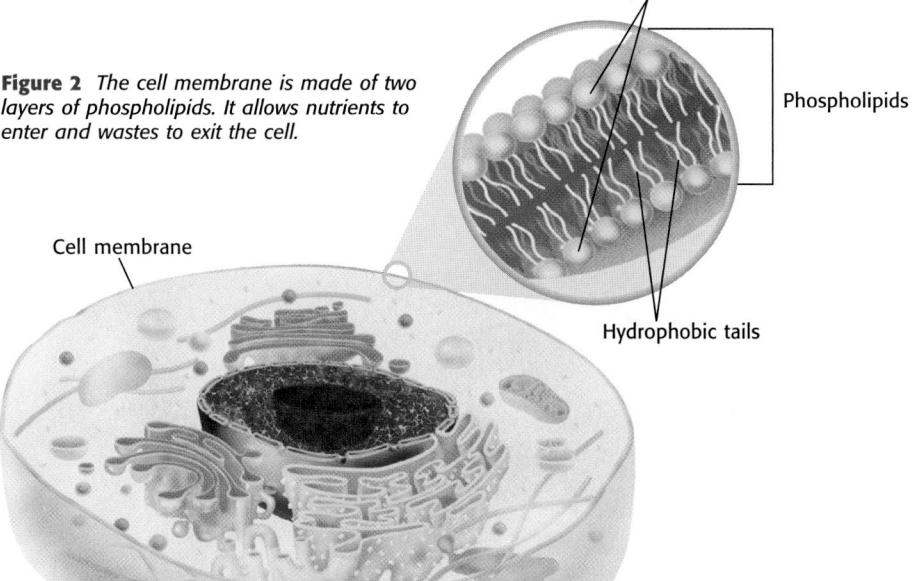

Hydrophilic heads

Phospholipids

Figure 2 *The cell membrane is made of two layers of phospholipids. It allows nutrients to enter and wastes to exit the cell.*

Cell membrane

Hydrophobic tails

Homework — GENERAL

Poster Project Have students investigate red blood cells and create a poster comparing red blood cells with other human cells. (RBCs are the only cells in the human body that do not have a nucleus or mitochondria when they are mature. Without a nucleus, RBCs cannot divide and reproduce. They live for only about 120 days, but new RBCs are made by bone marrow at the rate of up to 200 billion per day.) **LS Visual**

Answer to Reading Check

A cell membrane encloses the cell and separates and protects the cell's contents from the cell's environment. The cell membrane also controls movement of materials into and out of the cell.

Teach

Demonstration — BASIC

Cell Walls and Cell Membranes
Using a stick and your own hand, you can illustrate the difference between a rigid cell wall, found in plant cells, and a flexible cell membrane, found in human skin cells. Bend the stick, and it will break. Make a fist, and your skin stretches to accommodate the flexing of muscles and bone joints. If we had rigid cell walls, we would find moving extremely difficult. English Language
LS Visual   Learners

ACTIVITY — BASIC

MATERIALS

FOR EACH GROUP
- food strainer, wire mesh
- gravel (such as gravel used to line aquaria), 250 mL
- marbles (or pebbles), 250 mL
- pan (to place under strainer)
- sand, 250 mL
- water, 250 mL

Cellular Sieve Have students place each material into the strainer, and have them observe and explain the results. Lead students to understand that a cell membrane functions somewhat like the strainer. The cell membrane lets some materials pass through but not others. Also, explain that the process works in both directions.

Teacher's Note: The effects demonstrated by this Activity also apply to the membranes of organelles within the cell.
LS Kinesthetic/Visual

ACTIVITY — BASIC

Drawing Cells Arrange students in pairs. Tell each pair to draw a plant or animal cell based on information presented in the tet. Instruct students not to label the cell's parts. Then, have students echange drawings with another pair. Students should put the proper labels on their classmates' picture. inally , have each group of two pairs compare and discuss each other's work. **LS** Visual/Interpersonal

Answer to Reading Check

The cytoskeleton is a web of proteins in the cytoplasm. It gives the cell support and structure.

Physical Science — GENERAL

Studying Cells Biophysics uses tools and techniues of physics to study the life processes of cells. Biophysicists are interested in the relationship between a molecule's structure and its function. Sophisticated techniues, such as electron microscopy, -ray diffraction, magnetic resonance spectroscopy, and electrophoresis, allow biophysicists to study the structure of proteins, nucleic acids, and even parts of cells, such as ribosomes. se the teaching transparency Structural ormulas to illustrate molecular structure.
LS Visual

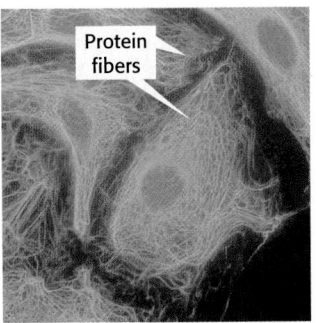

Figure 3 *The cytoskeleton, made of protein fibers, helps a cell retain its shape, move in its environment, and move its organelles.*

Figure 4 *The nucleus contains the cell's DNA. Pores allow materials to move between the nucleus and the cytoplasm.*

Cytoskeleton

The *cytoskeleton* (SIET oh SKEL uh tuhn) is a web of proteins in the cytoplasm. The cytoskeleton, shown in **Figure 3,** acts as both a muscle and a skeleton. It keeps the cell's membranes from collapsing. The cytoskeleton also helps some cells move.

The cytoskeleton is made of three types of protein. One protein is a hollow tube. The other two are long, stringy fibers. One of the stringy proteins is also found in muscle cells.

✔ Reading Check What is the cytoskeleton?

Nucleus

All eukaryotic cells have the same basic membrane-bound organelles, starting with the nucleus. The *nucleus* is a large organelle in a eukaryotic cell. It contains the cell's DNA, or genetic material. DNA contains the information on how to make a cell's proteins. Proteins control the chemical reactions in a cell. They also provide structural support for cells and tissues. But proteins are not made in the nucleus. Messages for how to make proteins are copied from the DNA. These messages are then sent out of the nucleus through the membranes.

The nucleus is covered by two membranes. Materials cross this double membrane by passing through pores. **Figure 4** shows a nucleus and nuclear pores. The nucleus of many cells has a dark area called the nucleolus (noo KLEE uh luhs). The *nucleolus* is where a cell begins to make its ribosomes.

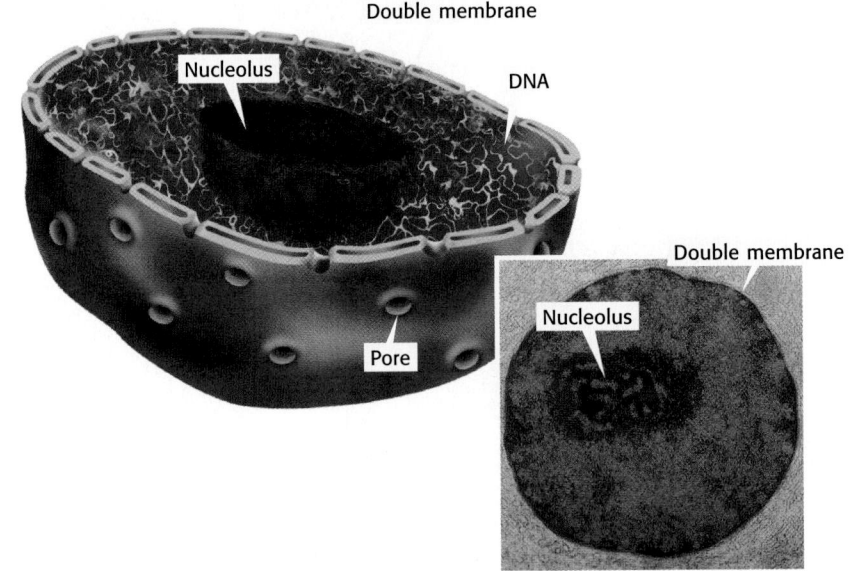

Double membrane

Nucleolus

DNA

Pore

Double membrane

Nucleolus

CHAPTER RESOURCES

Technology

 Transparencies
• **LINK TO PHYSICAL SCIENCE** Structural Formulas

Strategies

• *Developmentally Delayed*
• *Attention Deficit Disorder*
• *Behavior Control Issues*

ave si volunteers line up at the front of the room. Then, write AB order on the board, and ask students to line up correctly. Net, add by last letter of first name, and ask them to line up correctly . Discuss that having DNA in cells is like having complete, specific directions. **LS** Kinesthetic   English Language Learners

Ribosomes

Organelles that make proteins are called **ribosomes.** Ribosomes are the smallest of all organelles. And there are more ribosomes in a cell than there are any other organelles. Some ribosomes float freely in the cytoplasm. Others are attached to membranes or the cytoskeleton. Unlike most organelles, ribosomes are not covered by a membrane.

Proteins are made within the ribosomes. Proteins are made of amino acids. An *amino acid* is any one of about 20 different organic molecules that are used to make proteins. All cells need proteins to live. All cells have ribosomes.

Endoplasmic Reticulum

Many chemical reactions take place in a cell. Many of these reactions happen on or in the endoplasmic reticulum (EN doh PLAZ mik ri TIK yuh luhm). The **endoplasmic reticulum,** or ER, is a system of folded membranes in which proteins, lipids, and other materials are made. The ER is shown in **Figure 5.**

The ER is part of the internal delivery system of the cell. Its folded membrane contains many tubes and passageways. Substances move through the ER to different places in the cell.

Endoplasmic reticulum is either rough ER or smooth ER. The part of the ER covered in ribosomes is rough ER. Rough ER is usually found near the nucleus. Ribosomes on rough ER make many of the cell's proteins. The ER delivers these proteins throughout the cell. ER that lacks ribosomes is smooth ER. The functions of smooth ER include making lipids and breaking down toxic materials that could damage the cell.

ribosome cell organelle composed of RNA and protein; the site of protein synthesis

endoplasmic reticulum a system of membranes that is found in a cell's cytoplasm and that assists in the production, processing, and transport of proteins and in the production of lipids

Figure 5 *The endoplasmic reticulum (ER) is a system of membranes. Rough ER is covered with ribosomes. Smooth ER does not have ribosomes.*

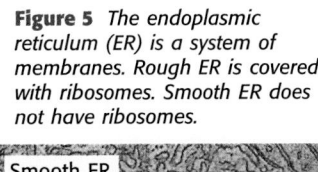

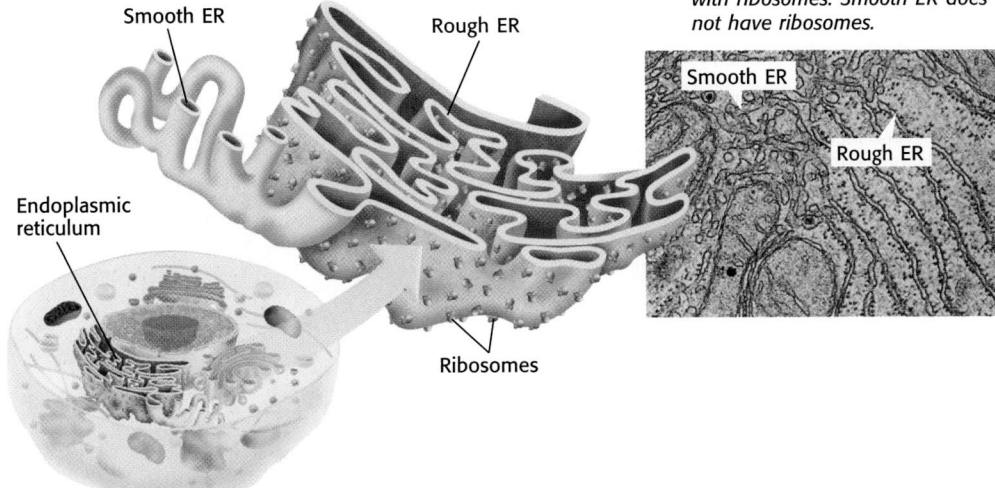

Smooth ER

Rough ER

Endoplasmic reticulum

Ribosomes

Homework ——— GENERAL

Cell Search Have students search the Internet for images (photomicrographs) of cells. Encourage students to compare images of cells from different types of organisms. Also, have students compare images of the same type of cell made by different microscopes, such as light microscopes, scanning electron microscopes, and transmission electron microscopes. Have students describe the cells that they find. **LS Logical/Visual**

ACTiViTY ——— GENERAL

Cell Models Students will be making edible models of cells. Students can bring edible items for the cell wall or cell membrane, such as crackers or pita bread. They can also bring items to represent organelles within the cell, such as small pieces of different kinds of candy (the hard candy shell on some candies may represent an organelle's membrane), olives, or other items. Have students explain the way they have represented the cell's structure in food. Pictures of the edible cells can be displayed in the classroom. English Language Learners **LS Kinesthetic**

CONNECTION to Chemistry ——— ADVANCED

Ribosome Structure Ribosomes make proteins. The structure of ribosomes has been intensely studied. Scientists now know how ribosome structure relates to ribosome function. Have students research and report on how ribosomes work. Their report should include a diagram of ribosome structure and its relationship to ribosome function. **LS Verbal/Visual**

CONNECTION to Language Arts ——— ADVANCED

No Energy? Mitochondrial diseases are a group of illnesses caused by malfunctioning mitochondria. These diseases can be caused by genes in the mitochondria or genes in the cell. Any activity or organ that requires energy is affected by these diseases. Have students conduct Internet or library research on mitochondrial diseases. Have them create a brochure or a pamphlet explaining one or more of these diseases. (Interested students may want to read *A Wind in the Door,* by Madeleine L'Engle, which is a story about a little boy with mitochondrial disease.) **LS Verbal**

Section 2 · Eukaryotic Cells **71**

Prediction Guide Before students read this page, ask them if the following statement is true or false: Animal cells are completely different from plant cells. (false; Animal cells and plant cells have many features in common, such as membrane-covered organelles and a cell membrane. The main difference between animal and plant cells is that animal cells do not have a cell wall and they do not have chloroplasts and chlorophyll.)

Have students explain their answer. Then, have them evaluate their answer after they read the page. **LS** Logical

Answer to Reading Check

Most of a cell's ATP is made in the cell's mitochondria.

CONNECTION to Language Arts — ADVANCED

Far-Out Fiction Have students write a story about an animal whose cells are invaded by chloroplasts. Students should describe how the animal's life processes at the cellular level would be affected. Students may also describe how the animal might use this chloroplast invasion to its advantage. Encourage students to write about an animal other than a mammal (corals might be an interesting subject). **LS** Verbal/Logical

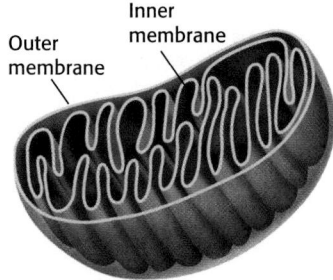

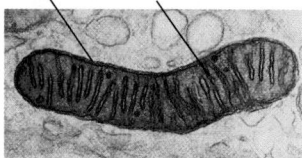

Figure 6 *Mitochondria break down sugar and make ATP. ATP is produced on the inner membrane.*

mitochondrion in eukaryotic cells, the cell organelle that is surrounded by two membranes and that is the site of cellular respiration

Figure 7 *Chloroplasts harness and use the energy of the sun to make sugar. A green pigment—chlorophyll—traps the sun's energy.*

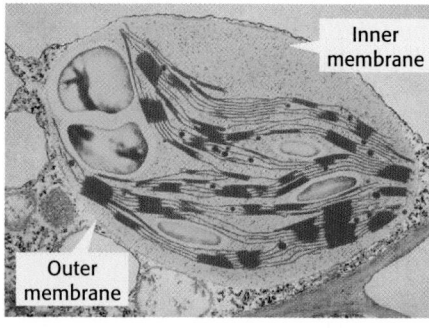

Mitochondria

A mitochondrion (MIET oh KAHN dree uhn) is the main power source of a cell. A **mitochondrion** is the organelle in which sugar is broken down to produce energy. Mitochondria are covered by two membranes, as shown in **Figure 6.** Energy released by mitochondria is stored in a substance called *ATP* (**a**denosine **trip**hosphate). The cell then uses ATP to do work. ATP can be made at several places in a cell. But most of a cell's ATP is made in the inner membrane of the cell's mitochondria.

Most eukaryotic cells have mitochondria. Mitochondria are the size of some bacteria. Like bacteria, mitochondria have their own DNA, and mitochondria can divide within a cell.

✓ **Reading Check** Where is most of a cell's ATP made?

Chloroplasts

Animal cells cannot make their own food. Plants and algae are different. They have chloroplasts (KLAWR uh PLASTS) in some of their cells. *Chloroplasts* are organelles in plant and algae cells in which photosynthesis takes place. Like mitochondria, chloroplasts have two membranes and their own DNA. A chloroplast is shown in **Figure 7.** *Photosynthesis* is the process by which plants and algae use sunlight, carbon dioxide, and water to make sugar and oxygen.

Chloroplasts are green because they contain *chlorophyll,* a green pigment. Chlorophyll is found inside the inner membrane of a chloroplast. Chlorophyll traps the energy of sunlight, which is used to make sugar. The sugar produced by photosynthesis is then used by mitochondria to make ATP.

SCIENTISTS AT ODDS

Acquiring Genomes Dr. Lynn Margulis knew that mitochondria and chloroplasts have their own DNA and divide by binary fission. She proposed that these organelles were once bacteria that entered organisms and became parts of those cells. Other scientists disagreed, but research proved Dr. Margulis right. Now, Margulis proposes that all eukaryotes developed as a result of genetic mergers between different kinds of organisms. And other scientists disagree. Only more research will settle the debate.

Is That a Fact!

About 100 eukaryotic species do not have mitochondria. *Giardia* is a freshwater protist that lacks mitochondria. *Giardia* can make people sick if they drink water from an infected lake or stream.

Golgi Complex

The organelle that packages and distributes proteins is called the **Golgi complex** (GOHL jee KAHM PLEKS). It is named after Camillo Golgi, the Italian scientist who first identified the organelle.

The Golgi complex looks like smooth ER, as shown in **Figure 8.** Lipids and proteins from the ER are delivered to the Golgi complex. There, the lipids and proteins may be modified to do different jobs. The final products are enclosed in a piece of the Golgi complex's membrane. This membrane pinches off to form a small bubble. The bubble transports its contents to other parts of the cell or out of the cell.

Cell Compartments

The bubble that forms from the Golgi complex's membrane is a vesicle. A **vesicle** (VES i kuhl) is a small sac that surrounds material to be moved into or out of a cell. All eukaryotic cells have vesicles. Vesicles also move material within a cell. For example, vesicles carry new protein from the ER to the Golgi complex. Other vesicles distribute material from the Golgi complex to other parts of the cell. Some vesicles form when part of the cell membrane surrounds an object outside the cell.

Golgi complex cell organelle that helps make and package materials to be transported out of the cell

vesicle a small cavity or sac that contains materials in a eukaryotic cell

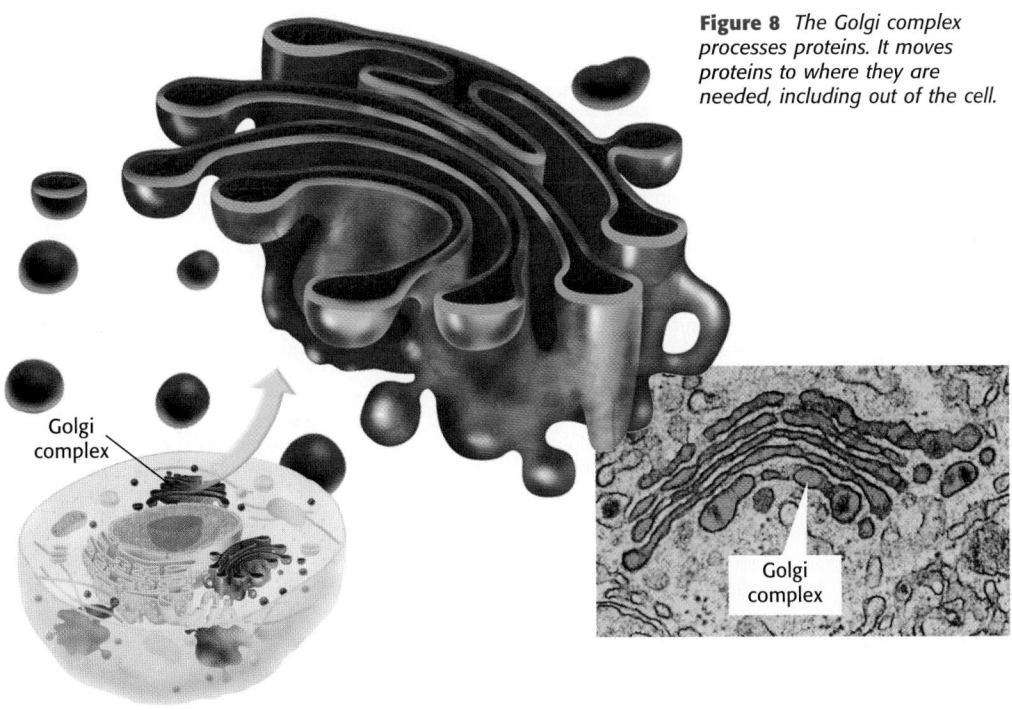

Figure 8 *The Golgi complex processes proteins. It moves proteins to where they are needed, including out of the cell.*

Golgi complex

Golgi complex

SCIENTISTS AT ODDS

Is It There or Not? Many scientists did not believe Golgi's claims about the organelle he observed and described. Those scientists thought that Golgi just saw tiny globs of the staining material. The existence of the organelle that was eventually named the *Golgi complex* was finally confirmed in the mid-1950s with the aid of the electron microscope.

Close

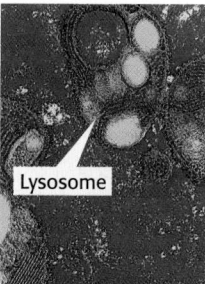

Figure 9
Lysosomes digest materials inside a cell. In plant and fungal cells, vacuoles often perform the same function.

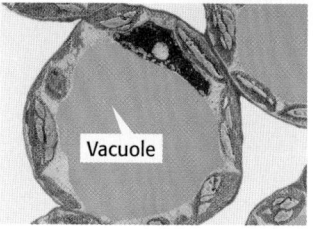

lysosome a cell organelle that contains digestive enzymes

Cellular Digestion

Lysosomes (LIE suh SOHMZ) are vesicles that are responsible for digestion inside a cell. **Lysosomes** are organelles that contain digestive enzymes. They destroy worn-out or damaged organelles, get rid of waste materials, and protect the cell from foreign invaders. Lysosomes, which come in a wide variety of sizes and shapes, are shown in **Figure 9.**

Lysosomes are found mainly in animal cells. When eukaryotic cells engulf particles, they enclose the particles in vesicles. Lysosomes bump into these vesicles and pour enzymes into them. These enzymes digest the particles in the vesicles.

✓ **Reading Check** Why are lysosomes important?

Vacuoles

A *vacuole* (VAK yoo OHL) is a large vesicle. In plant and fungal cells, some vacuoles act like large lysosomes. They store digestive enzymes and aid in digestion within the cell. Other vacuoles in plant cells store water and other liquids. Vacuoles that are full of water, such as the one in **Figure 9,** help support the cell. Some plants wilt when their vacuoles lose water. **Table 1** shows some organelles and their functions.

Table 1 Organelles and Their Functions			
	**Nucleus** the organelle that contains the cell's DNA and is the control center of the cell		**Chloroplast** the organelle that uses the energy of sunlight to make food
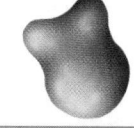	**Ribosome** the organelle in which amino acids are hooked together to make proteins		**Golgi complex** the organelle that processes and transports proteins and other materials out of cell
	**Endoplasmic reticulum** the organelle that makes lipids, breaks down drugs and other substances, and packages proteins for Golgi complex		**Vacuole** the organelle that stores water and other materials
	**Mitochondria** the organelle that breaks down food molecules to make ATP		**Lysosome** the organelle that digests food particles, wastes, cell parts, and foreign invaders

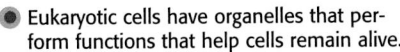

SECTION Review

Summary

- Eukaryotic cells have organelles that perform functions that help cells remain alive.
- All cells have a cell membrane. Some cells have a cell wall. Some cells have a cytoskeleton.
- The nucleus of a eukaryotic cell contains the cell's genetic material, DNA.
- Ribosomes are the organelles that make proteins. Ribosomes are not covered by a membrane.

- The endoplasmic reticulum (ER) and the Golgi complex make and process proteins before the proteins are transported to other parts of the cell or out of the cell.
- Mitochondria and chloroplasts are energy-producing organelles.
- Lysosomes are organelles responsible for digestion within a cell. In plant cells, organelles called *vacuoles* store cell materials and sometimes act like large lysosomes.

Using Key Terms

1. In your own words, write a definition for each of the following terms: *ribosome, lysosome,* and *cell wall.*

Understanding Key Ideas

2. Which of the following are found mainly in animal cells?
   a. mitochondria
   b. lysosomes
   c. ribosomes
   d. Golgi complexes

3. What is the function of a Golgi complex? What is the function of the endoplasmic reticulum?

Critical Thinking

4. **Making Comparisons** Describe three ways in which plant cells differ from animal cells.

5. **Applying Concepts** Every cell needs ribosomes. Explain why.

6. **Predicting Consequences** A certain virus attacks the mitochondria in cells. What would happen to a cell if all of its mitochondria were destroyed?

7. **Expressing Opinions** Do you think that having chloroplasts gives plant cells an advantage over animal cells? Support your opinion.

Interpreting Graphics

Use the diagram below to answer the questions that follow.

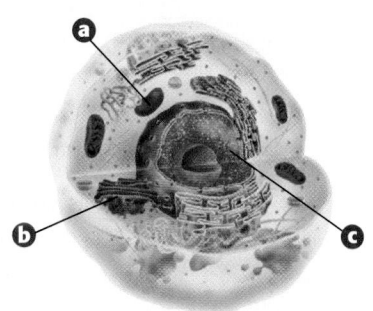

8. Is this a diagram of a plant cell or an animal cell? Explain how you know.

9. What organelle does the letter *b* refer to?

For a variety of links related to this chapter, go to www.scilinks.org

Topic: Eukaryotic Cells
SciLinks code: HSM0541

CHAPTER RESOURCES

Chapter Resource File

- Section Quiz **GENERAL**
- Section Review **GENERAL**
- Vocabulary and Section Summary **GENERAL**
- SciLinks Activity **GENERAL**

Technology

Transparencies
- Organelles and Their Functions

Answers to Section Review

1. Sample answer: Ribosomes are organelles where amino acids are joined together to make proteins. Lysosomes are organelles that carry out cellular digestion. The cell wall is the outermost structure in cells of plants, fungi, and algae.

2. b

3. Sample answer: Golgi complex: packages and distributes proteins within a cell; endoplasmic reticulum: a series of folded membranes on which lipids, proteins, and other materials are made, and through which those materials are delivered to other places in the cell

4. Sample answer: Plant cells have cell walls, but animal cells do not. Plant cells have chloroplasts, which animal cells do not have. Plant cells do not seem to have small lysosomes (they have large vacuoles instead), which animal cells do have.

5. Sample answer: Ribosomes are the organelles where proteins are made. All cells need protein in order to live.

6. Sample answer: Mitochondria are organelles that produce most of a cell's energy. If its mitochondria were destroyed, a cell would eventually die because it would not be able to produce enough energy to survive.

7. Sample answer: I think plants have an advantage over animals because plants can make their own food just by using sunlight and other nutrients. Animals have to wait for plants to grow in order to get food.

8. This diagram is of an animal cell; the first clue is that the cell has no cell wall.

9. the Golgi complex

SECTION
3

Focus

Overview

In this section, students will learn that a cell is the smallest unit of life. In most multicellular organisms, groups of cells form tissues that compose organs. Two or more organs can interact to form an organ system.

🔊 Bellringer

Write the following questions on the board for students to answer:

Why can't you use your teeth to breathe? Why can't you use your arm muscles to digest food?

Motivate

ACTiViTY ——— GENERAL

Concept Mapping Organize the class into small groups. Provide each group with pictures of tissues, organs, and organ systems. Have students arrange the pictures into concept maps. Encourage students to notice similarities and differences between organs. For example, the stomach and the heart are very different organs, but both are made of muscle tissue, and both function by holding and moving substances through their cavities. **LS Intrapersonal/ Visual Co-op Learning**

📖 READING WARM-UP

Objectives

● List three advantages of being multicellular.

● Describe the four levels of organization in living things.

● Explain the relationship between the structure and function of a part of an organism.

Terms to Learn

tissue	organism
organ	structure
organ system	function

📖 READING STRATEGY

Paired Summarizing Read this section silently. In pairs, take turns summarizing the material. Stop to discuss ideas that seem confusing.

The Organization of Living Things

In some ways, organisms are like machines. Some machines have just one part. But most machines have many parts. Some organisms exist as a single cell. Other organisms have many—even trillions—of cells.

Most cells are smaller than the period that ends this sentence. Yet, every cell in every organism performs all the processes of life. So, are there any advantages to having many cells?

The Benefits of Being Multicellular

You are a *multicellular organism.* This means that you are made of many cells. Multicellular organisms grow by making more small cells, not by making their cells larger. For example, an elephant is bigger than you are, but its cells are about the same size as yours. An elephant just has more cells than you do. Some benefits of being multicellular are the following:

● **Larger Size** Many multicellular organisms are small. But they are usually larger than single-celled organisms. Larger organisms are prey for fewer predators. Larger predators can eat a wider variety of prey.

● **Longer Life** The life span of a multicellular organism is not limited to the life span of any single cell.

● **Specialization** Each type of cell has a particular job. Specialization makes the organism more efficient. For example, the cardiac muscle cell in **Figure 1** is a specialized muscle cell. Heart muscle cells contract and make the heart pump blood.

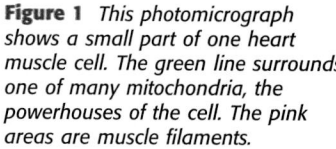 **Reading Check** List three advantages of being multicellular. *(See the Appendix for answers to Reading Checks.)*

Figure 1 *This photomicrograph shows a small part of one heart muscle cell. The green line surrounds one of many mitochondria, the powerhouses of the cell. The pink areas are muscle filaments.*

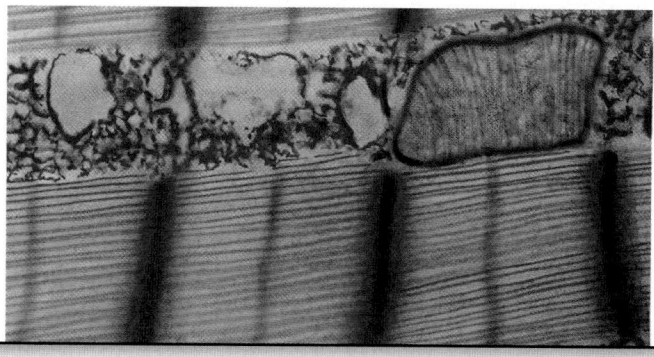

CHAPTER RESOURCES

Chapter Resource File

- Lesson Plan
- Directed Reading A BASIC
- Directed Reading B SPECIAL NEEDS

Technology

Transparencies
- Bellringer
- Levels of Organization in the Cardiovascular System

Answer to Reading Check

Sample answer: larger size, longer life, cell specialization

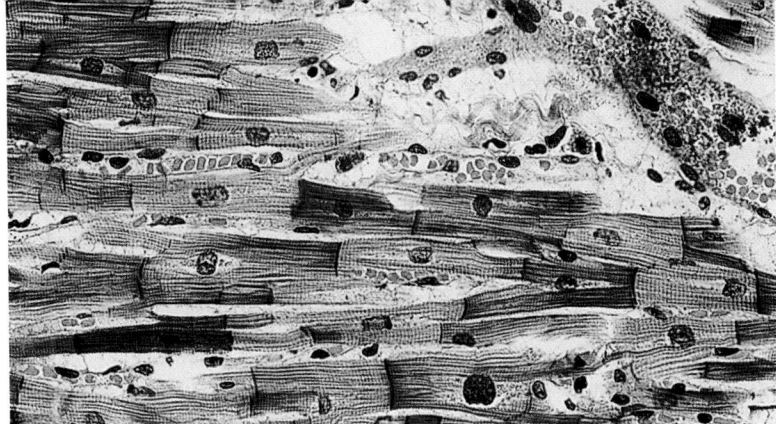

Figure 2 *This photomicrograph shows cardiac muscle tissue. Cardiac muscle tissue is made up of many cardiac cells.*

Cells Working Together

A **tissue** is a group of cells that work together to perform a specific job. The material around and between the cells is also part of the tissue. The cardiac muscle tissue, shown in **Figure 2,** is made of many cardiac muscle cells. Cardiac muscle tissue is just one type of tissue in a heart.

Animals have four basic types of tissues: nerve tissue, muscle tissue, connective tissue, and protective tissue. In contrast, plants have three types of tissues: transport tissue, protective tissue, and ground tissue. Transport tissue moves water and nutrients through a plant. Protective tissue covers the plant. It helps the plant retain water and protects the plant against damage. Photosynthesis takes place in ground tissue.

Tissues Working Together

A structure that is made up of two or more tissues working together to perform a specific function is called an **organ.** For example, your heart is an organ. It is made mostly of cardiac muscle tissue. But your heart also has nerve tissue and tissues of the blood vessels that all work together to make your heart the powerful pump that it is.

Another organ is your stomach. It also has several kinds of tissue. In the stomach, muscle tissue makes food move in and through the stomach. Special tissues make chemicals that help digest your food. Connective tissue holds the stomach together, and nervous tissue carries messages back and forth between the stomach and the brain. Other organs include the intestines, brain, and lungs.

Plants also have different kinds of tissues that work together as organs. A leaf is a plant organ that contains tissue that traps light energy to make food. Other examples of plant organs are stems and roots.

Reading Check What is an organ?

tissue a group of similar cells that perform a common function

organ a collection of tissues that carry out a specialized function of the body

A Pet Protist

Imagine that you have a tiny box-shaped protist for a pet. To care for your pet protist properly, you have to figure out how much to feed it. The dimensions of your protist are roughly 25 μm × 20 μm × 2 μm. If seven food particles per second can enter through each square micrometer of surface area, how many particles can your protist eat in 1 min?

Is That a Fact!

In your lifetime, your body will shed about 18 kg (almost 40 lb) of dead skin.

Teach

Discussion ——— GENERAL

Muscles Ask students to list all of the ways they use their muscles. Responses will probably include walking, riding a bike, swimming, and throwing or kicking a ball. Lead students to understand that muscles are also involved in swallowing food (tongue and esophagus), digestion (stomach and intestines), and blinking eyes (eyelids). Also, help students understand that sometimes muscles act voluntarily (jumping, writing), and sometimes they act involuntarily (heart beating). **LS** **Auditory/Logical**

Homework ——— GENERAL

Respiration Variations Not all living things have the same kinds of tissues and organs. Yet, all must perform similar life processes. Have students do research in order to compare the structures a fish uses to breathe with those that a human uses. Students' reports should also answer the question, What parts of the human and fish respiratory systems are similar? (Even though a fish has gills and a human has lungs, both have cells that exchange and transport oxygen and carbon dioxide.) **LS** **Logical**

Answer to Math Practice

The surface area of the protist is [(25 μm × 20 μm) + (25 μm × 2 μm) + (20 μm × 2 μm)] × 2 = 1,180 μm², so it can eat 1,180 μm² × 7 particles per second = 8,260 particles of food every second, or 60 s/min × 8,260 particles/s = 495,600 particles of food per minute.

Answer to Reading Check

An organ is a structure of two or more tissues working together to perform a specific function in the body.

organ system a group of organs that work together to perform body functions

organism a living thing; anything that can carry out life processes independently

structure the arrangement of parts in an organism

function the special, normal, or proper activity of an organ or part

Organs Working Together

A group of organs working together to perform a particular function is called an **organ system.** Each organ system has a specific job to do in the body.

For example, the digestive system is made up of several organs, including the stomach and intestines. The digestive system's job is to break down food into small particles. Other parts of the body then use these small particles as fuel. In turn, the digestive system depends on the respiratory and cardiovascular systems for oxygen. The cardiovascular system, shown in **Figure 3,** includes organs and tissues such as the heart and blood vessels. Plants also have organ systems. They include leaf systems, root systems, and stem systems.

✓ Reading Check List the levels of organization in living things.

Organisms

Anything that can perform life processes by itself is an **organism.** An organism made of a single cell is called a *unicellular organism.* Bacteria, most protists, and some kinds of fungi are unicellular. Although some of these organisms live in colonies, they are still unicellular. They are unicellular organisms living together, and all of the cells in the colony are the same. Each cell must carry out all life processes in order for that cell to survive. In contrast, even the simplest multicellular organism has specialized cells that depend on each other for the organism to survive.

Figure 3 Levels of Organization in the Cardiovascular System

Cell
Cells form tissues.

Tissue
Tissues form organs.

Organ
Organs form organ systems.

Organ system
And organ systems form organisms such as you!

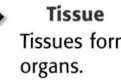

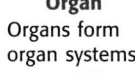
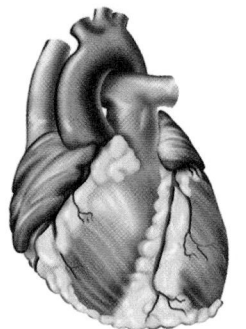
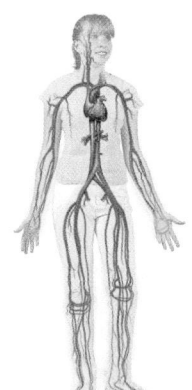

Is That a Fact!

An elephant's trunk is constructed of 135 kg (300 lb) of hair, skin, connective tissue, nerves, and muscles. The muscle tissue is composed of 150,000 tiny subunits of muscle, each of which is coordinated with the others to enable an elephant to greet its friends, breathe, grab, and drink.

Answer to Reading Check
cell, tissue, organ, organ system, organism

Structure and Function

In organisms, structure and function are related. **Structure** is the arrangement of parts in an organism. It includes the shape of a part and the material of which the part is made. **Function** is the job the part does. For example, the structure of the lungs is a large, spongy sac. In the lungs, there are millions of tiny air sacs called *alveoli*. Blood vessels wrap around the alveoli, as shown in **Figure 4.** Oxygen from air in the alveoli enters the blood. Blood then brings oxygen to body tissues. Also, in the alveoli, carbon dioxide leaves the blood and is exhaled.

The structures of alveoli and blood vessels enable them to perform a function. Together, they bring oxygen to the body and get rid of its carbon dioxide.

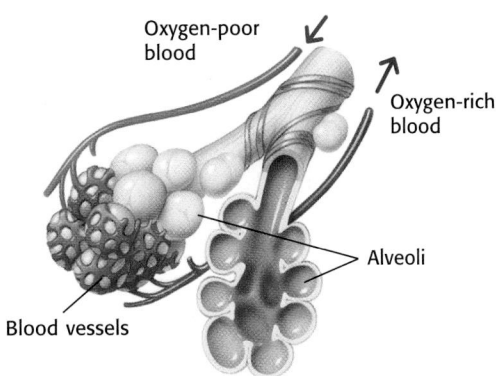

Figure 4 The Structure and Function of Alveoli

Oxygen-poor blood

Oxygen-rich blood

Alveoli

Blood vessels

SECTION Review

Summary

- Advantages of being multicellular are larger size, longer life, and cell specialization.
- Four levels of organization are cell, tissue, organ, and organ system.
- A *tissue* is a group of cells working together. An *organ* is two or more tissues working together. An *organ system* is two or more organs working together.
- In organisms, a part's structure and function are related.

Using Key Terms

1. Use each of the following terms in a separate sentence: *tissue, organ,* and *function.*

Understanding Key Ideas

2. What are the four levels of organization in living things?
   a. cell, multicellular, organ, organ system
   b. single cell, multicellular, tissue, organ
   c. larger size, longer life, specialized cells, organs
   d. cell, tissue, organ, organ system

Math Skills

3. One multicellular organism is a cube. Each of its sides is 3 cm long. Each of its cells is 1 cm³. How many cells does it have? If each side doubles in length, how many cells will it then have?

Critical Thinking

4. **Applying Concepts** Explain the relationship between structure and function. Use alveoli as an example. Be sure to include more than one level of organization.

5. **Making Inferences** Why can multicellular organisms be more complex than unicellular organisms? Use the three advantages of being multicellular to help explain your answer.

For a variety of links related to this chapter, go to www.scilinks.org

Topic: Organization of Life
SciLinks code: HSM1080

CHAPTER RESOURCES

Chapter Resource File

- **Section Quiz** GENERAL
- **Section Review** GENERAL
- **Vocabulary and Section Summary** GENERAL
- **Reinforcement Worksheet** BASIC
- **Critical Thinking** ADVANCED

Answers to Section Review

1. Sample answer: The body has several different kinds of tissue. I think that the most important organ in the body is the brain. Sometimes a part of the body with a certain structure performs more than one function.

2. d

3. 3 cm × 3 cm × 3 cm = 27 cm³ 27 cm³ ÷ 1 cm³ = 27 cells; If each side doubles in length, the organism will have 216 cells (6 × 6 × 6 = 216).

4. Sample answer: Alveoli are tiny sacs whose function is to contain and exchange gases such as oxygen and carbon dioxide. The structure of alveoli, as tiny sacs surrounded by tiny blood vessels, includes the cells that make up the tissue of the alveoli and the tissue that joins the alveoli to the bronchioles, which are part of the lung. The lungs are made of several kinds of tissue, such as the bronchi, bronchioles, and alveoli.

5. Sample answer: The main reason that multicellular organisms can be more complex than unicellular organisms is that multicellular organisms have cell specialization. Specialization allows some cells to do only digestion while others do respiration or circulation. Therefore, the organism is more efficient. Being multicellular also means that an organism may grow larger than a unicellular organism. Size is an advantage because, in general, the larger the organism is, the fewer predators it faces. Finally, being unicellular means that when your one cell dies, you are dead. In a multicellular organism, the death of one cell does not mean the death of the organism.

Teacher's Note: In fact, only multicellular organisms can have an efficient vascular system, which is the key to efficient delivery of materials to cells and removal of wastes from cells. Most students will probably not know this, but some advanced or interested students may grasp this idea.

Elephant-Sized Amoebas?

Teacher's Notes

Time Required
Two 45-minute class periods

Lab Ratings

EASY —————————→ HARD

Teacher Prep 🧪🧪
Student Set-Up 🧪🧪
Concept Level 🧪🧪🧪
Clean Up 🧪

Safety Caution
Remind students to review all safety cautions and icons before beginning this lab activity.

Preparation Notes
Some students may find it difficult to work with a nonspecific unit of measurement. If so, the cube models easily convert to centimeters. You may want to add some small items, such as peas, beans, popcorn, or peppercorns, to the sand to represent organelles floating in the cytoplasm. Some students may need to review what a ratio is and how ratios are used.

Model-Making Lab

OBJECTIVES

Explore why a single-celled organism cannot grow to the size of an elephant.

Create a model of a cell to illustrate the concept of surface area–to-volume ratio.

MATERIALS

- calculator (optional)
- cubic cell patterns
- heavy paper or poster board
- sand, fine
- scale or balance
- scissors
- tape, transparent

SAFETY

Elephant-Sized Amoebas?

An amoeba is a single-celled organism. Like most cells, amoebas are microscopic. Why can't amoebas grow as large as elephants? If an amoeba grew to the size of a quarter, the amoeba would starve to death. To understand how this can be true, build a model of a cell and see for yourself.

Procedure

1 Use heavy paper or poster board to make four cube-shaped cell models from the patterns supplied by your teacher. Cut out each cell model, fold the sides to make a cube, and tape the tabs on the sides. The smallest cell model has sides that are each one unit long. The next larger cell has sides of two units. The next cell has sides of three units, and the largest cell has sides of four units. These paper models represent the cell membrane, the part of a cell's exterior through which food and wastes pass.

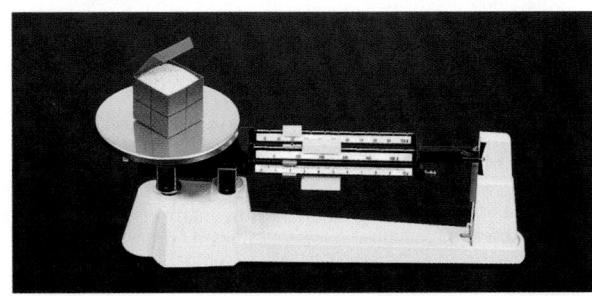

Data Table for Measurements				
Length of side	Area of one side ($A = S \times S$)	Total surface area of cube cell ($TA = S \times S \times 6$)	Volume of cube cell ($V = S \times S \times S$)	Mass of filled cube cell
1 unit	1 unit^2	6 unit^2	1 unit^3	
2 unit				
3 unit				
4 unit				

DO NOT WRITE IN BOOK

Key to Formula Symbols

S = the length of one side

A = area

6 = number of sides

V = volume

TA = total area

2 Copy the data table shown above. Use each formula to calculate the data about your cell models. Record your calculations in the table. Calculations for the smallest cell have been done for you.

3 Carefully fill each model with fine sand until the sand is level with the top edge of the model. Find the mass of the filled models by using a scale or a balance. What does the sand in your model represent?

4 Record the mass of each filled cell model in your Data Table for Measurements. (Always remember to use the appropriate mass unit.)

Analyze the Results

1 **Constructing Tables** Make a data table like the one shown at right.

2 **Organizing Data** Use the data from your Data Table for Measurements to find the ratios for each of your cell models. For each of the cell models, fill in the Data Table for Ratios .

Draw Conclusions

3 **Interpreting Information** As a cell grows larger, does the ratio of total surface area to volume increase, decrease, or stay the same?

4 **Interpreting Information** As a cell grows larger, does the total surface area–to-mass ratio increase, decrease, or stay the same?

5 **Drawing Conclusions** Which is better able to supply food to all the cytoplasm of the cell: the cell membrane of a small cell or the cell membrane of a large cell? Explain your answer.

6 **Evaluating Data** In the experiment, which is better able to feed all of the cytoplasm of the cell: the cell membrane of a cell that has high mass or the cell membrane of a cell that has low mass? You may explain your answer in a verbal presentation to the class, or you may choose to write a report and illustrate it with drawings of your models.

Data Table for Ratios		
Length of side	Ratio of total surface area to volume	Ratio of total surface area to mass
1 unit		
2 unit		
3 unit		
4 unit		

DO NOT WRITE IN BOOK

Cell Model Template

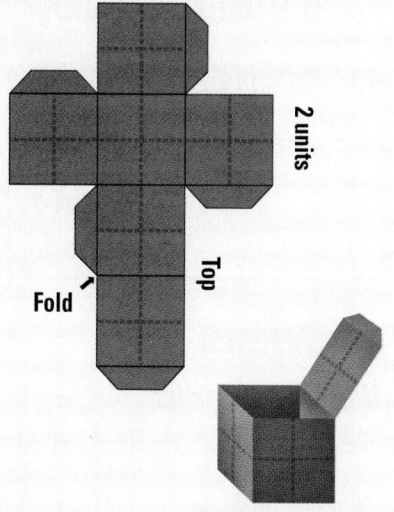

2 units

Top

Fold

Two-unit cell model

Using the template above, prepare four patterns for students to use to make their cubes. Make one cube 1 unit wide, one cube 2 units wide, one cube 3 units wide, and one cube 4 units wide. The unit can be the size of your choosing.

Procedure

3. The sand represents cytoplasm.

4. Masses may vary.

Analyze the Results

2. See the tables below.

Draw Conclusions

3. decreases

4. decreases

5. the cell membrane of a small cell. A small cell has a higher surface-area-to-volume ratio than a large cell has, so more nutrients per cubic unit of volume can enter a small cell.

6. the cell membrane of a cell with low mass

Data Table for Measurements				
Length of side S	Area of one side (square units)	Total surface area of cube cell (square units)	Volume of cube cell (cubic units)	Mass of cube cell (sample answer, in grams)
1	1	6	1	4.5
2	4	24	8	30
3	9	54	27	105
4	16	96	64	230

Data Table for Ratios		
Length of side S	Total surface area-to-volume ratio	Total surface area-to-mass ratio (sample answer)
1	6:1	6:4.5 = 1.33:1
2	24:8 = 3:1	24:30 = 0.80:1
3	54:27 = 2:1	54:105 = 0.51:1
4	96:64 = 1.5:1	96:230 = 0.42:1

CLASSROOM TESTED & APPROVED

Terry Rakes
Elmwood Junior High School
Rogers, Arkansas

Chapter Review

Assignment Guide

Section	Questions
1	1, 4, 10–13, 23
2	3, 6, 9, 16–19, 22, 24–26
3	2, 5, 7–8, 14–15, 20–21

ANSWERS

Using Key Terms

1. cell
2. function
3. organelles
4. eukaryote
5. tissue
6. cell wall

Understanding Key Ideas

7. c
8. d
9. a
10. b
11. b
12. c

USING KEY TERMS

Complete each of the following sentences by choosing the correct term from the word bank.

cell	organ
cell membrane	prokaryote
organelles	eukaryote
cell wall	tissue
structure	function

1 A(n) ___ is the most basic unit of all living things.

2 The job that an organ does is the ___ of that organ.

3 Ribosomes and mitochondria are types of ___.

4 A(n) ___ is an organism whose cells have a nucleus.

5 A group of cells working together to perform a specific function is a(n) ___.

6 Only plant cells have a(n) ___.

UNDERSTANDING KEY IDEAS

Multiple Choice

7 Which of the following best describes an organ?

a. a group of cells that work together to perform a specific job

b. a group of tissues that belong to different systems

c. a group of tissues that work together to perform a specific job

d. a body structure, such as muscles or lungs

8 The benefits of being multicellular include

a. small size, long life, and cell specialization.

b. generalized cells, longer life, and ability to prey on small animals.

c. larger size, more enemies, and specialized cells.

d. longer life, larger size, and specialized cells.

9 In eukaryotic cells, which organelle contains the DNA?

a. nucleus   c. smooth ER

b. Golgi complex   d. vacuole

10 Which of the following statements is part of the cell theory?

a. All cells suddenly appear by themselves.

b. All cells come from other cells.

c. All organisms are multicellular.

d. All cells have identical parts.

11 The surface area–to-volume ratio of a cell limits

a. the number of organelles that the cell has.

b. the size of the cell.

c. where the cell lives.

d. the types of nutrients that a cell needs.

12 Two types of organisms whose cells do not have a nucleus are

a. prokaryotes and eukaryotes.

b. plants and animals.

c. eubacteria and archaebacteria.

d. single-celled and multicellular organisms.

13. Cells must be small in order to have a large enough surface area–to-volume ratio to get sufficient nutrients to survive and to get rid of wastes.

14. Cells are the smallest unit of all living things. Cells combine to make tissues. Different tissues combine to make organs, which have specialized jobs in the body. Organs work together in organ systems, which perform body functions.

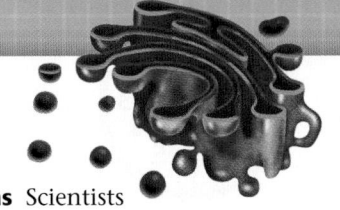

Short Answer

13 Explain why most cells are small.

14 Describe the four levels of organization in living things.

15 What is the difference between the structure of an organ and the function of the organ?

16 Name two functions of a cell membrane.

17 What are the structure and function of the cytoskeleton in a cell?

18 **Concept Mapping** Use the following terms to create a concept map: *cells, organisms, Golgi complex, organ systems, organs, nucleus, organelle,* and *tissues.*

19 **Making Comparisons** Compare and contrast the functions of the endoplasmic reticulum and the Golgi complex.

20 **Identifying Relationships** Explain how the structure and function of an organism's parts are related. Give an example.

21 **Evaluating Hypotheses** One of your classmates states a hypothesis that all organisms must have organ systems. Is your classmate's hypothesis valid? Explain your answer.

22 **Predicting Consequences** What would happen if all of the ribosomes in your cells disappeared?

23 **Expressing Opinions** Scientists think that millions of years ago the surface of the Earth was very hot and that the atmosphere contained a lot of methane. In your opinion, which type of organism, a eubacterium or an archaebacterium, is the older form of life? Explain your reasoning.

INTERPRETING GRAPHICS

Use the diagram below to answer the questions that follow.

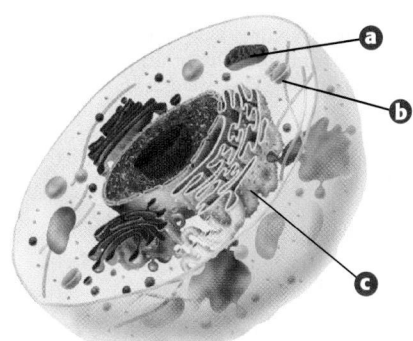

24 What is the name of the structure identified by the letter *a*?

25 Which letter identifies the structure that digests food particles and foreign invaders?

26 Which letter identifies the structure that makes proteins, lipids, and other materials and that contains tubes and passageways that enable substances to move to different places in the cell?

Critical Thinking

18. 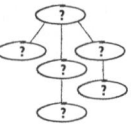 An answer to this exercise can be found at the end of this book.

19. Sample answer: The endoplasmic reticulum (ER) is a series of folded membranes within a cell where many proteins, lipids, and other materials are made in the cell. The smooth ER also helps break down toxic materials. The ER is the part of the internal delivery system in a cell. The Golgi complex modifies, packages, and distributes proteins to other parts of the cell. It takes materials from the ER and encloses them in a small bubble of membrane. Then, it delivers them to where they are needed in other parts of the cell as well as outside the cell.

20. Sample answer: The structure of a part is its shape and the material it is made of. The function of a part is what that shape and material enable that part to do in the body; for example, alveoli are tiny sacs in the lungs that hold gases. Alveoli are made of a membrane that enables oxygen and carbon dioxide to pass into and out of the blood.

21. Sample answer: not valid; Some organisms are unicellular and have no tissues, organ, or organ systems.

22. Ribosomes make proteins, which all cells and all organisms need to survive. If your ribosomes disappeared, you would die.

23. Sample answer: Archaebacteria are older because there are many types of methane-making archaebacteria and because many types of archaebacteria live in very hot places.

Interpreting Graphics

24. mitochondrion

25. b

26. c

---

15. Structure is the shape of a part. Function is the job a part does.

16. The cell membrane separates the cell's contents from the outside environment and controls the flow of nutrients, wastes, and other materials into and out of the cell.

17. The cytoskeleton is a web of tubular and stringy proteins. The cytoskeleton helps give the cell its shape, helps the cell move in its environment, and helps the cell move its organelles around.

CHAPTER RESOURCES

Chapter Resource File

- Chapter Review GENERAL
- Chapter Test A GENERAL
- Chapter Test B ADVANCED
- Chapter Test C SPECIAL NEEDS
- Vocabulary Activity GENERAL

Workbooks

Study Guide
- Assessment resources are also available in Spanish.

Teacher's Note

To provide practice under more realistic testing conditions, give students 20 minutes to answer all of the questions in this Standardized Test Preparation.

MISCONCEPTION ALERT

Answers to the standardized test preparation can help you identify student misconceptions and misunderstandings.

READING

Passage 1

1. D
2. G
3. B

✚ **TEST DOCTOR**

Question 1: Students may select incorrect answer B if they misread the part of the passage about snottites eventually becoming rock. Snottites themselves are a mixture of bacteria, sticky fluids, and minerals.

Question 2: Students may select incorrect answer I if, again, they misread the part of the passage about snottites eventually hardening into rock structures. Snottites do not create other structures in caves. The best answer is that snottite bacteria do not need sunlight because snottites live deep underground and are acidophiles that do not depend on sunlight for food.

READING

Read each of the passages below. Then, answer the questions that follow each passage.

Passage 1 Exploring caves can be dangerous but can also lead to interesting discoveries. For example, deep in the darkness of Cueva de Villa Luz, a cave in Mexico, are slippery formations called *snottites*. They were named snottites because they look just like a two-year-old's runny nose. If you use an electron microscope to look at them, you see that snottites are bacteria; thick, sticky fluids; and small amounts of minerals produced by the bacteria. As tiny as they are, these bacteria can build up snottite structures that may eventually turn into rock. Formations in other caves look like hardened snottites. The bacteria in snottites are acidophiles. Acidophiles live in environments that are highly acidic. Snottite bacteria produce sulfuric acid and live in an environment that is similar to the inside of a car battery.

1. Which statement best describes snottites?
   - **A** Snottites are bacteria that live in car batteries.
   - **B** Snottites are rock formations found in caves.
   - **C** Snottites were named for a cave in Mexico.
   - **D** Snottites are made of bacteria, sticky fluids, and minerals.

2. Based on this passage, which conclusion about snottites is most likely to be correct?
   - **F** Snottites are found in caves everywhere.
   - **G** Snottite bacteria do not need sunlight.
   - **H** You could grow snottites in a greenhouse.
   - **I** Snottites create other bacteria in caves.

3. What is the main idea of this passage?
   - **A** Acidophiles are unusual organisms.
   - **B** Snottites are strange formations.
   - **C** Exploring caves is dangerous.
   - **D** Snottites are large, slippery bacteria.

Passage 2 The world's smallest mammal may be a bat about the size of a jelly bean. The scientific name for this tiny animal, which was unknown until 1974, is *Craseonycteris thonglong-yai*. It is so small that it is sometimes called the *bumblebee bat*. Another name for this animal is the *hog-nosed bat*. Hog-nosed bats were given their name because one of their distinctive features is a piglike muzzle. Hog-nosed bats differ from other bats in another way: they do not have a tail. But, like other bats, hog-nosed bats do eat insects that they catch in mid-air. Scientists think that the bats eat small insects that live on the leaves at the tops of trees. Hog-nosed bats live deep in limestone caves and have been found in only one country, Thailand.

1. According to the passage, which statement about hog-nosed bats is most accurate?
   - **A** They are the world's smallest animal.
   - **B** They are about the size of a bumblebee.
   - **C** They eat leaves at the tops of trees.
   - **D** They live in hives near caves in Thailand.

2. Which of the following statements describes distinctive features of hog-nosed bats?
   - **F** The bats are very small and eat leaves.
   - **G** The bats live in caves and have a tail.
   - **H** The bats live in Thailand and are birds.
   - **I** The bats have a piglike muzzle and no tail.

3. From the information in this passage, which conclusion is most likely to be correct?
   - **A** Hog-nosed bats are similar to other bats.
   - **B** Hog-nosed bats are probably rare.
   - **C** Hog-nosed bats can sting like a bumblebee.
   - **D** Hog-nosed bats probably eat fruit.

Passage 2

1. B
2. I
3. B

✚ **TEST DOCTOR**

Question 1: Students may select incorrect answer A if they misread "world's smallest mammal" as being "world's smallest animal."

Question 3: Students may select incorrect answer A if they overlook information in the passage that describes how hog-nosed bats are both similar to and different from other bats.

The diagrams below show two kinds of cells. Use these cell diagrams to answer the questions that follow.

Cell 1

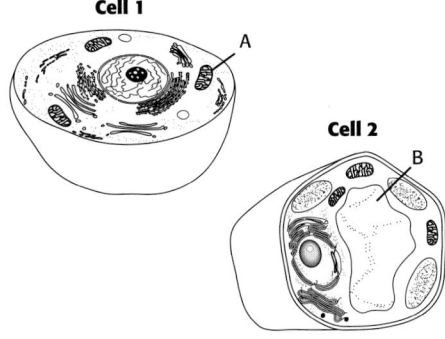

Cell 2

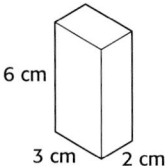

1. What is the name of the organelle labeled *A* in Cell 1?
   A endoplasmic reticulum
   B mitochondrion
   C vacuole
   D nucleus

2. What type of cell is Cell 1?
   F a bacterial cell
   G a plant cell
   H an animal cell
   I a prokaryotic cell

3. What is the name and function of the organelle labeled *B* in Cell 2?
   A The organelle is a vacuole, and it stores water and other materials.
   B The organelle is the nucleus, and it contains the DNA.
   C The organelle is the cell wall, and it gives shape to the cell.
   D The organelle is a ribosome, where proteins are put together.

4. What type of cell is Cell 2? How do you know?
   F prokaryotic; because it does not have a nucleus
   G eukaryotic; because it does not have a nucleus
   H prokaryotic; because it has a nucleus
   I eukaryotic; because it has a nucleus

Read each question below, and choose the best answer.

1. What is the surface area–to-volume ratio of the rectangular solid shown in the diagram below?

6 cm
3 cm   2 cm

   A 0.5:1
   B 2:1
   C 36:1
   D 72:1

2. Look at the diagram of the cell below. Three molecules of food per cubic unit of volume per minute are required for the cell to survive. One molecule of food can enter through each square unit of surface area per minute. What will happen to this cell?

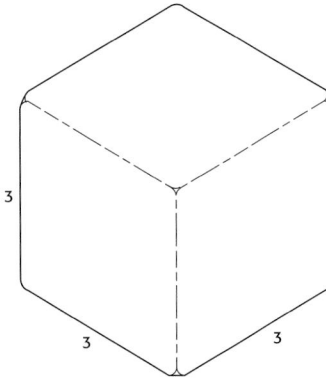

3

3   3

   F The cell is too small, and it will starve.
   G The cell is too large, and it will starve.
   H The cell is at a size that will allow it to survive.
   I There is not enough information to determine the answer.

Standardized Test Preparation

1. B
2. H
3. A
4. I

TEST DOCTOR

Question 2: The cell is not a bacterium or a prokaryotic cell because it has a nucleus, and it is not a plant cell because it has no cell wall.

Question 4: The cell has a nucleus, and only eukaryotic cells have a nucleus. Answer I is the only answer that has that combination of facts.

1. B
2. G

TEST DOCTOR

Question 2: When students calculate the cell's surface area–to-volume ratio, they will find that it is 2.00:1. Therefore, only 2.00 food molecules can enter per minute. Because the cell needs 3 molecules of food per minute, the cell is too large, and it will starve. It may help students to understand how the surface area–to-volume ratio affects survival by showing students a variety of three-dimensional models.

CHAPTER RESOURCES

Chapter Resource File

• Standardized Test Preparation GENERAL

State Resources

For specific resources for your state, visit **go.hrw.com** and type in the keyword **HSMSTR**.

Weird Science

Background

Within the last 20 years, biologists' ideas of which environments would be suitable for life have increased dramatically. Discoveries of organisms that live under extreme conditions of temperature and pressure have led to the use of the word *extremophile* for these life-forms.

Scientific Discoveries

Background

It is important to note that stem cells are very different from other cells. All stem cells—embryonic or adult—have three unique characteristics. First, stem cells are unspecialized. So, a stem cell in its original form cannot perform the function of a muscle cell or a blood cell. But these unspecialized cells can give rise to specialized cells and then can perform these functions. Second, stem cells can divide and renew for long periods of time. Scientists have shown that as long as a stem cell remains unspecialized, it can continue to divide for an extended period of time. Third, stem cells can evolve into specialized cells through the process of differentiation.

Science in Action

Scientific Discoveries

Discovery of the Stem Cell

What do Parkinson's disease, diabetes, aplastic anemia, and Alzheimer's disease have in common? All of these diseases are diseases for which stem cells may provide treatment or a cure. Stem cells are unspecialized cells from which all other kinds of cells can grow. And research on stem cells has been going on almost since microscopes were invented. But scientists have been able to culture, or grow, stem cells in laboratories for only about the last 20 years. Research during these 20 years has shown scientists that stem cells can be useful in treating—and possibly curing—a variety of diseases.

Language Arts ACTiViTY

WRITING SKILL Imagine that you are a doctor who treats diseases such as Parkinson's disease. Design and create a pamphlet or brochure that you could use to explain what stem cells are. Include in your pamphlet a description of how stem cells might be used to treat one of your patients who has Parkinson's disease. Be sure to include information about Parkinson's disease.

Weird Science

Extremophiles

Are there organisms on Earth that can give scientists clues about possible life elsewhere? Yes, there are! These organisms are called *extremophiles,* and they live where the environment is extreme. For example, some extremophiles live in the hot volcanic thermal vents deep in the ocean. Other extremophiles live in the extreme cold of Antarctica. But these organisms do not live only in extreme environments. Research shows that extremophiles may be abundant in plankton in the ocean. And not all extremophiles are archaebacteria; some extremophiles are eubacteria.

Social Studies ACTiViTY

Choose one of the four types of extremophiles. Do some research about the organism you have chosen and make a poster showing what you learned about it, including where it can be found, under what conditions it lives, how it survives, and how it is used.

Answer to Social Studies Activity

Students' posters should reflect the research they have done. For example, a student who chooses methanogens may show that these extremophiles live in a wide variety of places and in a large number of geographical locations. The poster may also include an explanation of how these organisms get nutrients and how the metabolism of methanogens is different from human metabolism. Students should also show any commercial, industrial, or medical uses of whichever organism they have chosen.

Answer to Language Arts Activity

Students' pamphlets or brochures should present a basic explanation of what stem cells are, where they come from, why they are useful, and how they may be used specifically to treat Parkinson's disease. So, the student will also have to include a little information about Parkinson's disease.

Caroline Schooley

Microscopist Imagine that your assignment is the following: Go outside. Look at 1 ft² of the ground for 30 min. Make notes about what you observe. Be prepared to describe what you see. If you look at the ground with just your naked eyes, you may quickly run out of things to see. But what would happen if you used a microscope to look? How much more would you be able to see? And how much more would you have to talk about? Caroline Schooley could tell you.

Caroline Schooley joined a science club in middle school. That's when her interest in looking at things through a microscope began. Since then, Schooley has spent many years studying life through a microscope. She is a microscopist. A *microscopist* is someone who uses a microscope to look at small things. Microscopists use their tools to explore the world of small things that cannot be seen by the naked eye. And with today's powerful electron microscopes, microscopists can study things we could never see before, things as small as atoms.

Math ACTIVITY

An average bacterium is about 0.000002 m long. A pencil point is about 0.001 m wide. Approximately how many bacteria would fit on a pencil point?

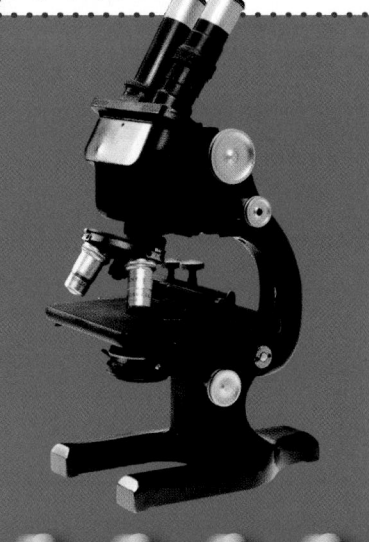

go.hrw.com
To learn more about these Science in Action topics, visit go.hrw.com and type in the keyword **HL5CELF.**

Current Science
Check out Current Science® articles related to this chapter by visiting go.hrw.com. Just type in the keyword **HL5CS03.**

People in Science
Background

Caroline Schooley wants students to think about microscopes and microscopy. The field is changing. One of the newest uses of microscopy is in nanotechnology. *Nanotechnology* is the science of manipulating materials on an atomic or molecular level to build microscopic devices. To do so, scientists will develop tiny machines (called *assemblers*) that can manipulate atoms and molecules as directed. Tiny nanomachines (called *replicators*) will be then programmed to build more assemblers. Nanotechnology can be thought of as molecular manufacturing.

Answer to Math Activity

0.001 m (size of pencil point) ÷ 0.000002 m (size of bacteria) = 500

So, approximately 500 bacteria could fit on a pencil point.

The Cell in Action
Chapter Planning Guide

Compression guide:
To shorten instruction because of time limitations, omit the Chapter Lab.

OBJECTIVES	LABS, DEMONSTRATIONS, AND ACTIVITIES	TECHNOLOGY RESOURCES
PACING • 135 min pp. 88–93 **Chapter Opener**	SE **Start-up Activity**, p. 89 ◆ `GENERAL`	OSP **Parent Letter** ■ `GENERAL` CD **Student Edition on CD-ROM** CD **Guided Reading Audio CD** ▣ TR **Chapter Starter Transparency*** VID **Brain Food Video Quiz**
Section 1 Exchange with the Environment • Explain the process of diffusion. • Describe how osmosis occurs. • Compare passive transport with active transport. • Explain how large particles get into and out of cells.	TE **Demonstration** Membrane Model, p. 90 ◆ `GENERAL` SE **Quick Lab** Bead Diffusion, p. 91 ◆ `GENERAL` CRF **Datasheet for Quick Lab*** TE **Demonstration** Crossing Membranes, p. 91 ◆ `GENERAL` SE **Inquiry Labs** The Perfect Taters Mystery, p. 102 ◆ `GENERAL` CRF **Datasheet for Chapter Lab*** LB **Inquiry Labs** Fish Farms in Space* ◆ `GENERAL` LB **Whiz-Bang Demonstrations** It's in the Bag!* ◆ `BASIC`	CRF **Lesson Plans*** TR **Bellringer Transparency*** TR **Passive Transport and Active Transport*** TR **Endocytosis and Exocytosis*** CRF **SciLinks Activity*** `GENERAL` VID **Lab Videos for Life Science** CD **Interactive Explorations CD-ROM** The Nose Knows `GENERAL`
PACING • 45 min pp. 94–97 **Section 2 Cell Energy** • Describe photosynthesis and cellular respiration. • Compare cellular respiration with fermentation.	TE **Demonstration** Leaves and Light, p. 94 `GENERAL` SE **Connection to Chemistry**, Earth's Early Atmosphere p. 95 `GENERAL` TE **Group Activity** Recycling Carbon, p. 95 `GENERAL` TE **Group Activity** Photosynthesis and Cellular Respiration, p. 96 `GENERAL` SE **Skills Practice Lab** Stayin' Alive!, p. 765 `GENERAL` CRF **Datasheet for LabBook***	CRF **Lesson Plans*** TR **Bellringer Transparency*** TR **The Connection Between Photosynthesis and Respiration*** TR ***LINK TO PHYSICAL SCIENCE*** Solar Heating Systems*
PACING • 45 min pp. 98–101 **Section 3 The Cell Cycle** • Explain how cells produce more cells. • Describe the process of mitosis. • Explain how cell division differs in animals and plants.	TE **Activity** Making Models, p. 98 `GENERAL` SE **Connection to Language Arts** Picking Apart Vocabulary, p. 99 `GENERAL` TE **Connection Activity** Math, p. 99 `ADVANCED` LB **Labs You Can Eat** The Mystery of the Runny Gelatin* ◆ `GENERAL` LB **Whiz-Bang Demonstrations** Stop Picking on My Enzyme* ◆ `BASIC` LB **Long-Term Projects & Research Ideas** Taming the Wild Yeast* ◆ `ADVANCED` SE **Science in Action** Math, Social Studies, and Language Arts Activities, pp. 108–109 `GENERAL`	CRF **Lesson Plans*** TR **Bellringer Transparency*** TR **The Cell Cycle*** TE **Internet Activity**, p. 100 `GENERAL`

PACING • 90 min

CHAPTER REVIEW, ASSESSMENT, AND STANDARDIZED TEST PREPARATION

CRF **Vocabulary Activity*** `GENERAL`
SE **Chapter Review**, pp. 104–105 `GENERAL`
CRF **Chapter Review*** ■ `GENERAL`
CRF **Chapter Tests A*** ■ `GENERAL`, **B*** `ADVANCED`, **C*** `SPECIAL NEEDS`
SE **Standardized Test Preparation**, pp. 106–107 `GENERAL`
CRF **Standardized Test Preparation*** `GENERAL`
CRF **Performance-Based Assessment*** `GENERAL`
OSP **Test Generator** `GENERAL`
CRF **Test Item Listing*** `GENERAL`

Online and Technology Resources

Visit **go.hrw.com** for a variety of free resources related to this textbook. Enter the keyword **HL5ACT.**

Holt Online Learning

Students can access interactive problem-solving help and active visual concept development with the *Holt Science and Technology* Online Edition available at **www.hrw.com.**

Guided Reading Audio CD
Also in Spanish

A direct reading of each chapter for auditory learners, reluctant readers, and Spanish-speaking students.

Science Tutor CD-ROM

Excellent for remediation and test practice.

SKILLS DEVELOPMENT RESOURCES	SECTION REVIEW AND ASSESSMENT	STANDARDS CORRELATIONS
SE Pre-Reading Activity, p. 88 `GENERAL` **OSP** Science Puzzlers, Twisters & Teasers `GENERAL`		National Science Education Standards UCP 3; SAI 1; SPSP 5; LS 1b
CRF Directed Reading A* ■ `BASIC`, B* `SPECIAL NEEDS` **CRF** Vocabulary and Section Summary* ■ `GENERAL` **SE** Reading Strategy Reading Organizer, p. 90 `GENERAL` **TE** Inclusion Strategies, p. 91 **CRF** Reinforcement Worksheet Into and Out of the Cell* `BASIC` **SS** Science Skills Doing a Lab Write-Up* `BASIC` **SS** Science Skills Taking Notes* `BASIC` **MS** Math Skills for Science Multiplying Whole Numbers* `BASIC` **MS** Math Skills for Science Dividing Whole Numbers with Long Division* `BASIC`	**SE** Reading Checks, pp. 91, 93 `GENERAL` **TE** Reteaching, p. 92 `BASIC` **TE** Quiz, p. 92 `GENERAL` **TE** Alternative Assessment, p. 92 `ADVANCED` **TE** Homework, p. 92 `GENERAL` **SE** Section Review,* p. 93 `GENERAL` **CRF** Section Quiz* ■ `GENERAL`	UCP 1, 2, 3, 4; LS 1c; *Chapter Lab:* UCP 2; SAI 1
CRF Directed Reading A* ■ `BASIC`, B* `SPECIAL NEEDS` **CRF** Vocabulary and Section Summary* ■ `GENERAL` **SE** Reading Strategy Discussion, p. 94 `GENERAL` **CRF** Reinforcement Worksheet Activities of the Cell* `BASIC` **CRF** Critical Thinking A Celluloid Thriller* `ADVANCED` **SS** Science Skills Using Logic* `BASIC` **SS** Science Skills Identifying Bias* `GENERAL`	**SE** Reading Checks, pp. 95, 97 `GENERAL` **TE** Reteaching, p. 96 `BASIC` **TE** Quiz, p. 96 `GENERAL` **TE** Alternative Assessment, p. 96 `GENERAL` **TE** Homework, p. 96 `ADVANCED` **SE** Section Review,* p. 97 ■ `GENERAL` **CRF** Section Quiz* ■ `GENERAL`	UCP 1, 3, 4, 5; SAI 2; ST 2; SPSP 4; LS 1c, 4c; *LabBook:* SAI 1; SPSP 1; LS 1c
CRF Directed Reading A* ■ `BASIC`, B* `SPECIAL NEEDS` **CRF** Vocabulary and Section Summary* ■ `GENERAL` **SE** Reading Strategy Paired Summarizing, p. 98 `GENERAL` **TE** Connection to Math Cell Multiplication, p. 98 `BASIC` **TE** Reading Strategy Prediction Guide, p. 99 `GENERAL` **TE** Inclusion Strategies, p. 100 **MS** Math Skills for Science Multiplying Whole Numbers* `GENERAL` **MS** Math Skills for Science Grasping Graphing* `GENERAL` **SS** Science Skills Organizing Your Research* `GENERAL` **SS** Science Skills Researching on the Web* `BASIC` **CRF** Reinforcement Worksheet This Is Radio KCEL* `BASIC`	**SE** Reading Checks, pp. 99, 100 `GENERAL` **TE** Reteaching, p. 100 `BASIC` **TE** Quiz, p. 100 `GENERAL` **TE** Alternative Assessment, p. 100 `GENERAL` **SE** Section Review,* p. 101 ■ `GENERAL` **CRF** Section Quiz* ■ `GENERAL`	SAI 1; LS 1c, 2d

---

One-Stop Planner® CD-ROM

This convenient CD-ROM includes:
- Lab Materials QuickList Software
- Holt Calendar Planner
- Customizable Lesson Plans
- Printable Worksheets
- ExamView® Test Generator

cnnstudentnews.com

Find the latest news, lesson plans, and activities related to important scientific events.

SCiLINKS®
NSTA
www.scilinks.org

Maintained by the **National Science Teachers Association.** See Chapter Enrichment pages for a complete list of topics.

Current Science®

Check out *Current Science* articles and activities by visiting the HRW Web site at **go.hrw.com.** Just type in the keyword **HL5CS04T.**

Classroom Videos

- **Lab Videos** demonstrate the chapter lab.
- **Brain Food Video Quizzes** help students review the chapter material.
- **CNN Videos** bring science into your students' daily life.

Visual Resources

CHAPTER STARTER TRANSPARENCY

Happy 140th Birthday!

What If . . . ?

How long would you like to live? What if you could live to be 120 years old? or 150 and beyond? Since ancient times, people have searched in vain for a magical fountain or potion that could give them eternal youth. No one has yet found the secret of immortality, but scientists have recently made a startling discovery that may help extend people's lives.

In January of 1998, researchers at the University of Texas reported that they had found an enzyme in the body that acts like a "cellular fountain of youth." In the laboratory, the enzyme enables human cells to stay young and multiply long

past the time when cells would normally stop dividing and die. Researchers hope that the enzyme can someday be used to understand and treat certain cancers and other incurable diseases. Although the so-called immortalizing enzyme won't help people live forever, it may help them live longer, healthier lives.

Every living thing is made of cells. In this chapter you will learn how cells grow and how they make more cells. You will also learn how cells transport materials and obtain the energy they need to survive.

BELLRINGER TRANSPARENCIES

Section: Exchange with the Environment
Which of the following best describes a living cell:
a) building block
b) a living organism
c) a complex factory
d) all of the above

Write a paragraph in your **science journal** defending your choice.

Section: Cell Energy
Make a list of all the different types of cells that you can think of and the jobs they do. Then make a list of all the reasons that a cell needs energy.

Write your answers in your **science journal**.

TEACHING TRANSPARENCIES

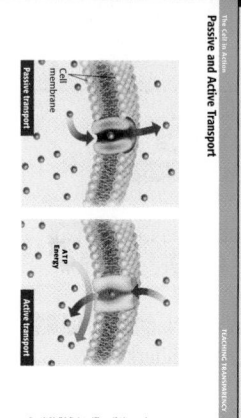

Passive and Active Transport

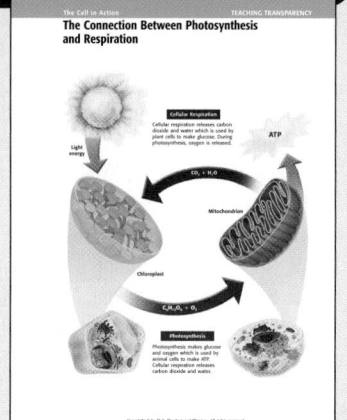

The Connection Between Photosynthesis and Respiration

TEACHING TRANSPARENCIES

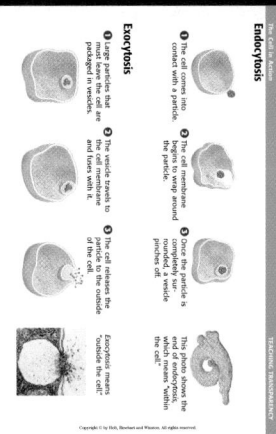

Exocytosis / Endocytosis

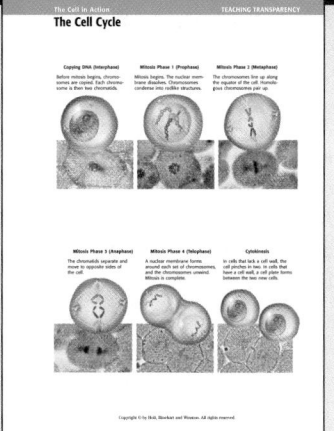

The Cell Cycle

Solar Heating Systems

LINK TO PHYSICAL SCIENCE

Chapter: Heat and Heat Technology

CONCEPT MAPPING TRANSPARENCY

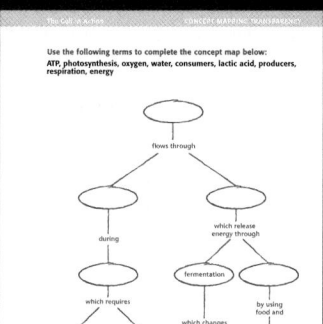

Use the following terms to complete the concept map below:
ATP, photosynthesis, oxygen, water, consumers, lactic acid, producers, respiration, energy

Planning Resources

LESSON PLANS

Lesson Plan   SAMPLE

Section: Waves

Pacing
Regular Schedule: with lab(s):2 days   without lab(s):2 days
Block Schedule: with lab(s): 1 1/2 days   without lab(s):1 day

Objectives
1. Relate the seven properties of life to a living organism.
2. Compare seven themes that can help you to organize what you learn about biology.
3. Identify the tiny structures that make up all living organisms.
4. Differentiate between reproduction and heredity and between metabolism and homeostasis.

National Science Education Standards Covered
LSInter6:Cells have particular structures that underlie their functions.
LSMat1:Most cell functions involve chemical reactions.
LSBeh1:Cells store and use information to guide their functions.
UCP1:Cell functions are regulated.
SI1:Cells can differentiate and form complete multicellular organisms.
PS1:Species evolve over time.
ESS3: The great diversity of organisms is the result of more than 3.5 billion years of evolution.
ESS2: Natural selection and its evolutionary consequences provide a scientific explanation for the fossil record of ancient life forms as well as for the striking molecular similarities observed among the diverse species of living organisms.
ST1: The millions of different species of plants, animals, and microorganisms that live on Earth today are related by descent from common ancestors.
ST2: The energy for life primarily comes from the sun.
SPSP1: The complexity and organization of organisms accommodates the need for obtaining, transforming, transporting, releasing, and eliminating the matter and energy used to sustain the organism.
SPSP6: As matter and energy flows through different levels of organization of living systems—cells, organs, communities—and between living systems and the physical environment, chemical elements are recombined in different ways.
HNS1: Organisms have behavioral responses to internal change and to external stimuli.

PARENT LETTER

    SAMPLE

Dear Parent,

Your son's or daughter's science class will soon begin exploring the chapter entitled "The World of Physical Science." In this chapter, students will learn about how the scientific method applies to the world of physical science and the role of physical science in the world. By the end of the chapter, students should demonstrate a clear understanding of the chapter's main ideas and be able to discuss the following topics:

1. physical science is the study of energy and matter (Section 1)
2. the role of physical science in the world around them (Section 1)
3. careers that rely on physical science (Section 1)
4. the steps used in the scientific method (Section 2)
5. examples of technology (Section 2)
6. how the scientific method is used to answer questions and solve problems (Section 2)
7. how our knowledge of science changes over time (Section 2)
8. how models represent real objects or systems (Section 3)
9. examples of different ways models are used in science (Section 3)
10. the importance of the International System of Units (Section 4)
11. the appropriate units to use for particular measurements (Section 4)
12. how area and density are derived quantities (Section 4)

Questions to Ask Along the Way

You can help your son or daughter learn about these topics by asking interesting questions such as the following:

• What are some surprising careers that use physical science?
• What is a characteristic of a good hypothesis?
• When is it a good idea to use a model?
• Why do Americans measure things in terms of inches and feet and meters?

ALSO IN SPANISH

TEST ITEM LISTING

TEST ITEM LISTING
The World of Science   SAMPLE

MULTIPLE CHOICE

1. A limitation of models is that
   a. they are large enough to see.
   b. they do not act exactly like the things that they model.
   c. they are smaller than the things that they model.
   d. they model unfamiliar things.
   Answer: B   Difficulty: 1   Section: 3   Objective: 2
2. The length 10 m is equal to
   a. 100 cm.   c. 10,000 mm.
   b. 1,000 cm.   d. Both (b) and (c)
   Answer: B   Difficulty: 1   Section: 3   Objective: 2
3. To be valid, a hypothesis must be
   a. testable.   c. made into a law.
   b. supported by evidence.   d. Both (a) and (b)
   Answer: B   Difficulty: 1   Section: 3   Objective: 2
4. The statement "Sheila has a stain on her shirt" is an example of a(n)
   a. law.   c. observation.
   b. hypothesis.   d. prediction.
   Answer: B   Difficulty: 1   Section: 2   Objective: 2
5. A hypothesis is often developed out of
   a. observations.   c. experiments.
   b. experiments.   d. Both (a) and (b)
   Answer: B   Difficulty: 1   Section: 2   Objective: 2
6. How many milliliters are in 3.5 kL?
   a. 3,500 mL   c. 3,500,000 mL
   b. 0.0035 mL.   d. 35,000 mL.
   Answer: B   Difficulty: 1   Section: 3   Objective: 2
7. A map of Seattle is an example of a
   a. law.   c. model.
   b. theory.   d. unit.
   Answer: B   Difficulty: 1   Section: 3   Objective: 2
8. A lab has the safety icons shown below. These icons mean that you should wear
   a. only safety goggles.   c. safety goggles and a lab apron.
   b. only a lab apron.   d. safety goggles, a lab apron, and gloves.
   Answer: B   Difficulty: 1   Section: 1   Objective: 2
9. The law of conservation of mass says the tot al of mass before a chemical change is
   a. more than the total mass after the change.
   b. less than the total mass after the change.
   c. the same as the total mass after the change.
   d. not the same as the total mass after the change.
   Answer: B   Difficulty: 1   Section: 2   Objective: 2
10. In which of the following areas might you find a geochemist at work?
    a. studying the chemistry of rocks   c. studying fishes
    b. studying forestry   d. studying the atmosphere
    Answer: B   Difficulty: 1   Section: 2   Objective: 2

One-Stop Planner® CD-ROM

This CD-ROM includes all of the resources shown here and the following time-saving tools:

• Lab Materials QuickList Software
• Customizable lesson plans
• Holt Calendar Planner
• The powerful ExamView® Test Generator

Meeting Individual Needs

DIRECTED READING A
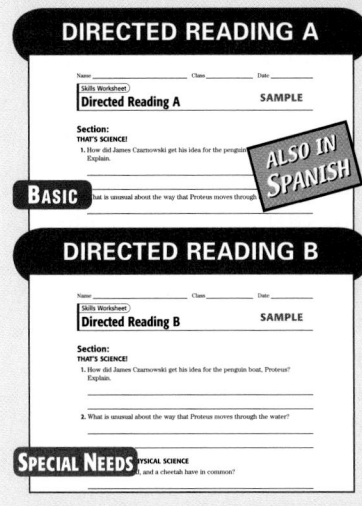

Skills Worksheet
Directed Reading A — SAMPLE

Section:
THAT'S SCIENCE!
1. How did James Czarnowski get his idea for the penguin boat, Proteus? Explain.

ALSO IN SPANISH

BASIC

DIRECTED READING B

Skills Worksheet
Directed Reading B — SAMPLE

Section:
THAT'S SCIENCE!
1. How did James Czarnowski get his idea for the penguin boat, Proteus? Explain.

2. What is unusual about the way that Proteus moves through the water?

SPECIAL NEEDS PHYSICAL SCIENCE

VOCABULARY ACTIVITY
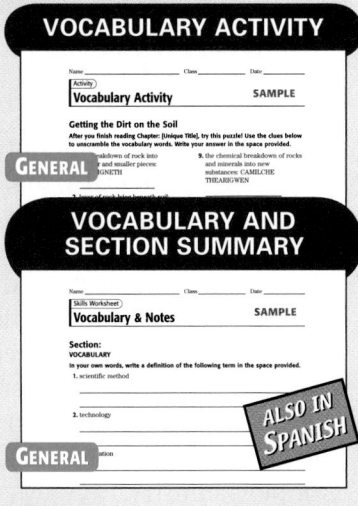

Activity
Vocabulary Activity — SAMPLE

Getting the Dirt on the Soil
After you finish reading Chapter: [Unique Title], try this puzzle! Use the clues below to unscramble the vocabulary words. Write your answer in the space provided.

GENERAL

VOCABULARY AND SECTION SUMMARY

Skills Worksheet
Vocabulary & Notes — SAMPLE

Section:
VOCABULARY
In your own words, write a definition of the following term in the space provided.
1. scientific method

2. technology

ALSO IN SPANISH

GENERAL

REINFORCEMENT
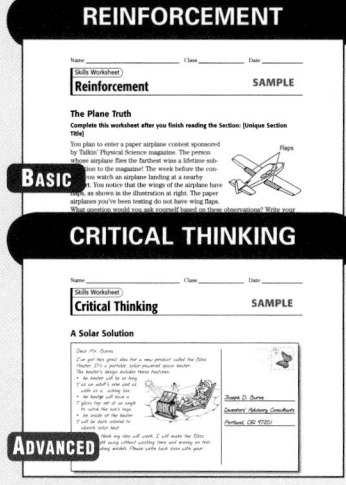

Skills Worksheet
Reinforcement — SAMPLE

The Plane Truth
Complete this worksheet after you finish reading the Section: [Unique Section Title]

BASIC

CRITICAL THINKING

Skills Worksheet
Critical Thinking — SAMPLE

A Solar Solution

ADVANCED

SCILINKS ACTIVITY
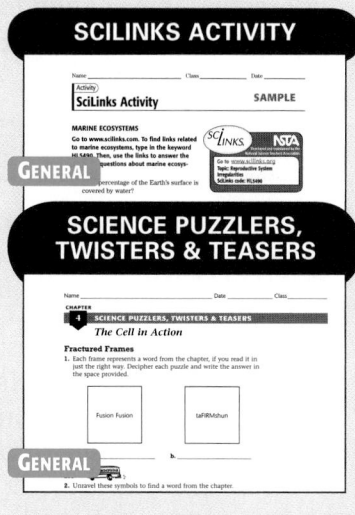

Activity
SciLinks Activity — SAMPLE

MARINE ECOSYSTEMS
Go to www.scilinks.com. To find links related to marine ecosystems, type in the keyword HL5496. Then, use the links to answer the questions about marine ecosys-

GENERAL

SCIENCE PUZZLERS, TWISTERS & TEASERS

CHAPTER 4
SCIENCE PUZZLERS, TWISTERS & TEASERS
The Cell in Action

Fractured Frames
1. Each frame represents a word from the chapter. If you read it in just the right way, you can decipher each puzzle and write the answer in the space provided.

Fusion Fusion | taFIRMshun

2. Unravel these symbols to find a word from the chapter.

GENERAL

Labs and Activities

LONG-TERM PROJECTS & RESEARCH IDEAS
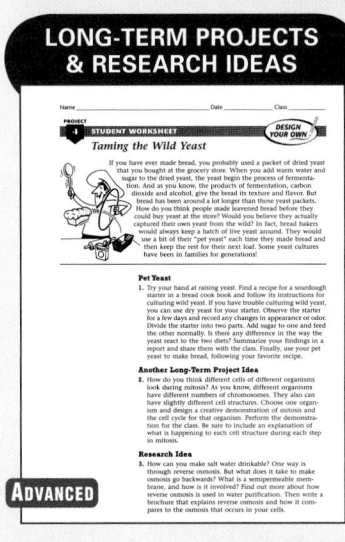

PROJECT
STUDENT WORKSHEET — *DESIGN YOUR OWN*
Taming the Wild Yeast

Pet Yeast
1. Try your hand at raising yeast. Find a recipe for a sourdough starter from a bread cook book and follow its instructions for culturing wild yeast.

Another Long-Term Project Idea
2. How do you think different cells of different organisms look during mitosis?

Research Idea
3. How can you make salt water drinkable? One way is through reverse osmosis.

ADVANCED

WHIZ-BANG DEMONSTRATIONS
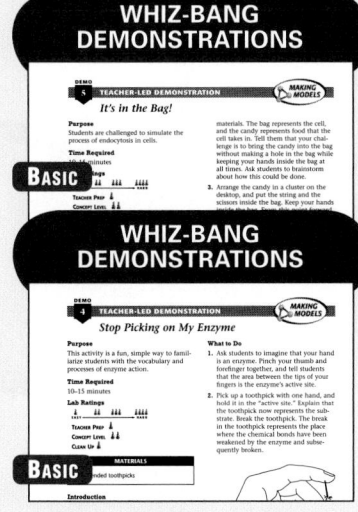

DEMO
TEACHER-LED DEMONSTRATION — *MAKING MODELS*
It's in the Bag!

Purpose
Students are challenged to simulate the process of endocytosis in cells.

Time Required

BASIC

WHIZ-BANG DEMONSTRATIONS

DEMO
TEACHER-LED DEMONSTRATION — *MAKING MODELS*
Stop Picking on My Enzyme

Purpose
This activity is a fun, simple way to familiarize students with the vocabulary and processes of enzyme action.

Time Required
10–15 minutes

MATERIALS

Introduction

BASIC

INQUIRY LABS
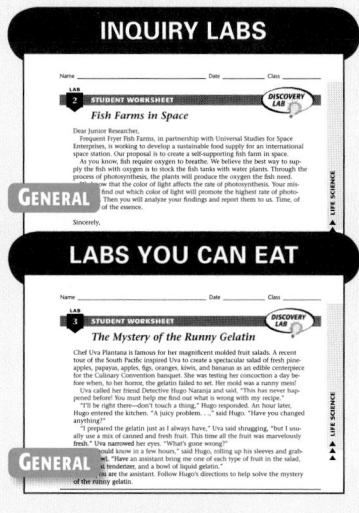

LAB
STUDENT WORKSHEET — *DISCOVERY LAB*
Fish Farms in Space

Dear Junior Researcher,
Frequent Fryer Fish Farms, in partnership with Universal Studios for Space Enterprises, is working to develop a sustainable food supply for an international space station.

Sincerely,

GENERAL

LABS YOU CAN EAT

LAB
STUDENT WORKSHEET — *DISCOVERY LAB*
The Mystery of the Runny Gelatin

Chef Uva Plantana is famous for her magnificent molded fruit salads.

GENERAL

DATASHEETS FOR QUICK LABS
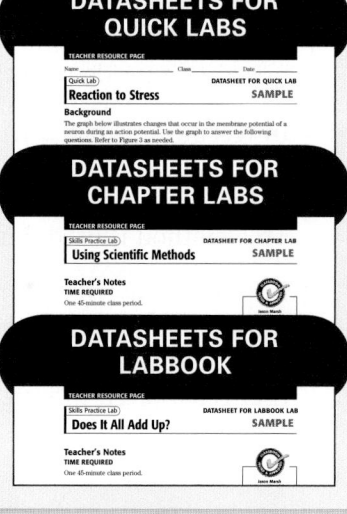

TEACHER RESOURCE PAGE

Quick Lab
Reaction to Stress — SAMPLE

Background
The graph below illustrates changes that occur in the membrane potential of a neuron during an action potential. Use the graph to answer the following questions. Refer to Figure 3 as needed.

DATASHEETS FOR CHAPTER LABS

TEACHER RESOURCE PAGE

Skills Practice Lab
Using Scientific Methods — SAMPLE

Teacher's Notes
TIME REQUIRED
One 45-minute class period.

DATASHEETS FOR LABBOOK

TEACHER RESOURCE PAGE

Skills Practice Lab
Does It All Add Up? — SAMPLE

Teacher's Notes
TIME REQUIRED
One 45-minute class period.

Review and Assessments

SECTION QUIZ
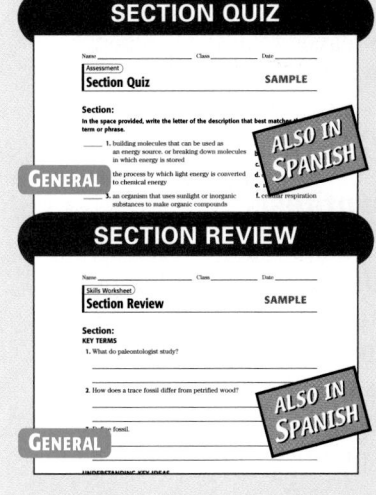

Assessment
Section Quiz — SAMPLE

Section:
In the space provided, write the letter of the description that best matches the term or phrase.

1. an energy source or breaking down molecules in which energy is stored
2. the process by which light energy is converted to chemical energy
3. an organism that uses sunlight or inorganic substances to make organic compounds

ALSO IN SPANISH

GENERAL

SECTION REVIEW

Skills Worksheet
Section Review — SAMPLE

Section:
KEY TERMS
1. What do paleontologists study?

2. How does a trace fossil differ from petrified wood?

GENERAL

CHAPTER REVIEW
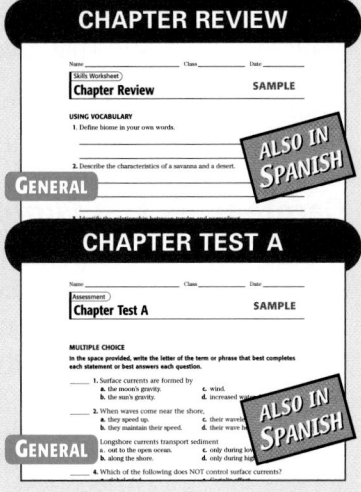

Skills Worksheet
Chapter Review — SAMPLE

USING VOCABULARY
1. Define biome in your own words.

2. Describe the characteristics of a savanna and a desert.

ALSO IN SPANISH

GENERAL

CHAPTER TEST A

Assessment
Chapter Test A — SAMPLE

MULTIPLE CHOICE
In the space provided, write the letter of the term or phrase that best completes each statement or best answers each question.

1. Surface currents are formed by
   a. the moon's gravity.   c. wind.
   b. the sun's gravity.   d. increased water density.
2. When waves come near the shore,
   a. they speed up.   c. their wavelength increases.
   b. they maintain their speed. d. their wave height increases.
   Longshore currents transport sediment
   a. out to the open ocean.   c. only during low tide.
   b. along the shore.   d. only during high tide.
4. Which of the following does NOT control surface currents?

ALSO IN SPANISH

GENERAL

CHAPTER TEST B
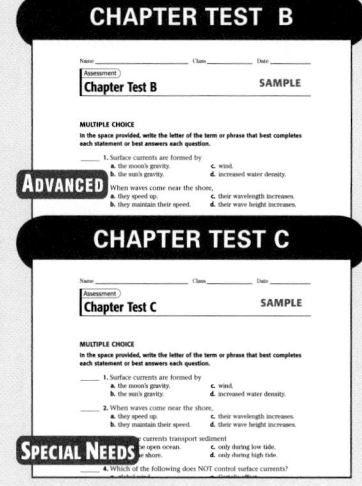

Assessment
Chapter Test B — SAMPLE

MULTIPLE CHOICE
In the space provided, write the letter of the term or phrase that best completes each statement or best answers each question.

1. Surface currents are formed by
   a. the moon's gravity.   c. wind.
   b. the sun's gravity.   d. increased water density.
2. When waves come near the shore,
   a. they speed up.   c. their wavelength increases.
   b. they maintain their speed. d. their wave height increases.

ADVANCED

CHAPTER TEST C

Assessment
Chapter Test C — SAMPLE

MULTIPLE CHOICE
In the space provided, write the letter of the term or phrase that best completes each statement or best answers each question.

1. Surface currents are formed by
   a. the moon's gravity.   c. wind.
   b. the sun's gravity.   d. increased water density.
2. When waves come near the shore,
   a. they speed up.   c. their wavelength increases.
   b. they maintain their speed. d. their wave height increases.
   currents transport sediment
   a. out to the open ocean.   c. only during low tide.
   b. along the shore.   d. only during high tide.
4. Which of the following does NOT control surface currents?

SPECIAL NEEDS

STANDARDIZED TEST PREPARATION
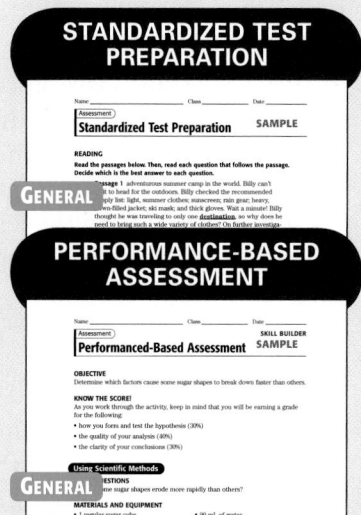

Assessment
Standardized Test Preparation — SAMPLE

READING
Read the passages below. Then, read each question that follows the passage. Decide which is the best answer to each question.

Passage 1 I adventurous summer camp in the world. Billy can't wait to head for the outdoors. Billy checked the recommended supply list: light, summer clothes; sunscreen; rain gear; heavy, warm-filled jacket; ski mask; and thick gloves. Wait a minute! Billy thought he was traveling to only one *destination*, so why does he need to bring such a wide variety of clothes? On further investiga-

GENERAL

PERFORMANCE-BASED ASSESSMENT

Assessment
Performanced-Based Assessment — SKILL BUILDER SAMPLE

OBJECTIVE
Determine which factors cause some sugar shapes to break down faster than others.

KNOW THE SCORE!
As you work through the activity, keep in mind that you will be earning a grade for the following
• how you form and test the hypothesis (30%)
• the quality of your analysis (40%)
• the clarity of your conclusions (30%)

Using Scientific Methods

QUESTIONS
Do some sugar shapes erode more rapidly than others?

MATERIALS AND EQUIPMENT
• 1 regular sugar cube   • 90 mL of water

GENERAL

This Chapter Enrichment provides relevant and interesting information to expand and enhance your presentation of the chapter material.

Section 1

Exchange with the Environment

Endocytosis

- There are three different mechanisms of endocytosis: phagocytosis, receptor-mediated endocytosis, and pinocytosis. These processes allow a substance to enter a cell without passing through the cell membrane. The substance involved determines which method is used.

- Large particles such as bacteria enter the cell by phagocytosis. The host cell changes shape, and the membrane sends out projections called *pseudopods,* meaning "false feet," which surround the particle, bringing it inside the cell.

- In receptor-mediated endocytosis, receptors on the membrane that are specific for a given substance bind to the substance before the endocytotic process begins. This method is used during cholesterol metabolism.

- In pinocytosis, the cell membrane surrounds the substance and forms a vesicle to bring the material into the cell. Pinocytosis usually involves material that is dissolved in water.

 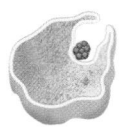 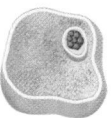

Reverse Osmosis

- Reverse osmosis is a process that forces water across semipermeable membranes under high pressure. The high pressure reverses the natural tendency of the solutes on the more concentrated side of the membrane to pass through to the less-concentrated side. In this way, water passing through the membrane is purified.

Is That a Fact!

◆ The largest single-celled organism that ever lived was a protozoan that measured 20 cm in diameter. It is now extinct.

Section 2

Cell Energy

Early Plant Scientists

- Jan Baptista Van Helmont (1580–1644) was a Belgian chemist, physiologist, and physician who coined the word *gas*. Van Helmont was the first scientist to comprehend the existence of gases separate from the atmospheric air. Although he didn't know that it was carbon dioxide, van Helmont stated that the *spiritus sylvestre,* or "wild spirit," emitted by burning charcoal was the same as that given off by fermenting grape juice. He applied chemistry to the study of physiological processes, and for this he is known as the "father of biochemistry."

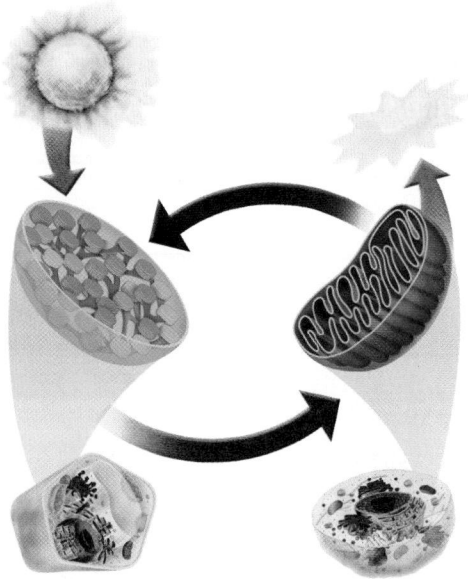

- Joseph Priestley (1733–1804) was an English clergyman and physical scientist who was one of the discoverers of oxygen. He also observed that light was vital for plant growth and that green leaves released oxygen.

- Jan Ingenhousz (1730–1799), a Dutch-born British physician and scientist, discovered photosynthesis.

Carotenoids and Photosynthesis

- Carotenoids are responsible for the orange colors in plants. Carotenoids are usually masked by chlorophyll which is more abundant until autumn. They are sensitive to wavelengths of light to which chlorophyll cannot respond. Carotenoids absorb wavelengths and transfer the energy to chlorophyll, which then incorporates that energy into the photosynthetic pathway.

Section 3

The Cell Cycle

Cytogenetics

- Cytogeneticists study the role of human chromosomes in health and disease. Chromosome studies can reveal abnormalities such as whether a person is carrying the genetic material for a genetically linked disease.

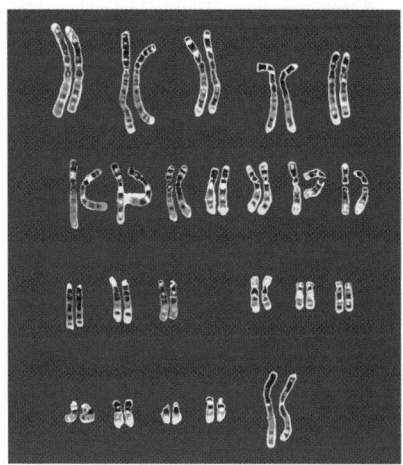

Cell Division

- The frequency of cell division varies a great deal. Fruit-fly embryo cells divide about every eight minutes. Human liver cells may not divide for up to one year. Scientists are still trying to determine what orchestrates growth and regulates cell division. This information would help scientists understand diseases of unregulated cell division, such as cancer.

- DNA and chromosomes are related but are not the same thing. A chromosome is made up of DNA that has been wound up and organized with proteins that hold it all together. For much of the cell cycle, DNA is loose and not very visible.

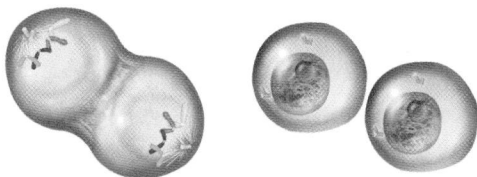

Is That a Fact!

- ◆ In an adult human body, cell division happens at least 10 million times every second.

Cell Adhesion

- Blood cells exist individually in the body, but most other cells are connected to each other. Usually this involves special adhesion proteins, such as adherins, cadherins, catenins, and integrins. These proteins connect adjoining cells by physically locking the cells together, fastening one cell to the next. Sometimes these junctions are outside the cell, and sometimes they are inside. Adhesion proteins can span the cell membranes and connect the inside of one cell to the inside of its neighbor cell.

Is That a Fact!

- ◆ In a healthy body, cells reproduce at exactly the same rate at which cells die. However, some agents make cells reproduce uncontrollably, causing a disease known as cancer. One of these carcinogenic agents is ultraviolet radiation, which is emitted by the sun and ultraviolet lamps. People who spend excessive amounts of time in the sun run the risk of developing skin cancer.

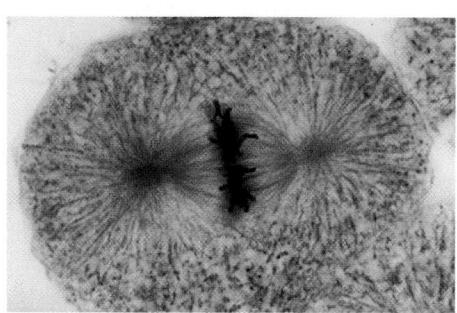

SciLINKS

NSTA
Developed and maintained by the
National Science Teachers Association

SciLinks is maintained by the National Science Teachers Association to provide you and your students with interesting, up-to-date links that will enrich your classroom presentation of the chapter.

Visit www.scilinks.org and enter the SciLinks code for more information about the topic listed.

Topic: Diffusion	**Topic:** Photosynthesis
SciLinks code: HSM0406	**SciLinks code:** HSM1140
Topic: Osmosis	**Topic:** Cell Cycle
SciLinks code: HSM1090	**SciLinks code:** HSM0235
Topic: Cell Energy	**Topic:** Cell Structures
SciLinks code: HSM0237	**SciLinks code:** HSM0240

Overview
In this chapter, students will learn about how cells interact with their environment, how cells get nutrients and get rid of wastes, and where cells get the energy from to carry out all the activities of life. Students will also learn about how cells produce more cells.

Assessing Prior Knowledge
Students should be familiar with the following topic:
• cells as the basic units of life

Identifying Misconceptions
Students may not think of cells as self-contained units of life. It is important for students to realize that cells, just like multicellular organisms, live in an environment and must perform all the activities—such as taking in nutrients, producing energy, and getting rid of wastes—necessary to stay alive and reproduce. Students may also be confused about the difference between cells and molecules. Emphasize the relationship between cells and molecules, and that proteins, carbohydrates, and other substances are made of molecules. These molecules must be smaller than the cells they enter and leave. Many students believe that proteins and other molecules are bigger than cells.

4

The Cell in Action

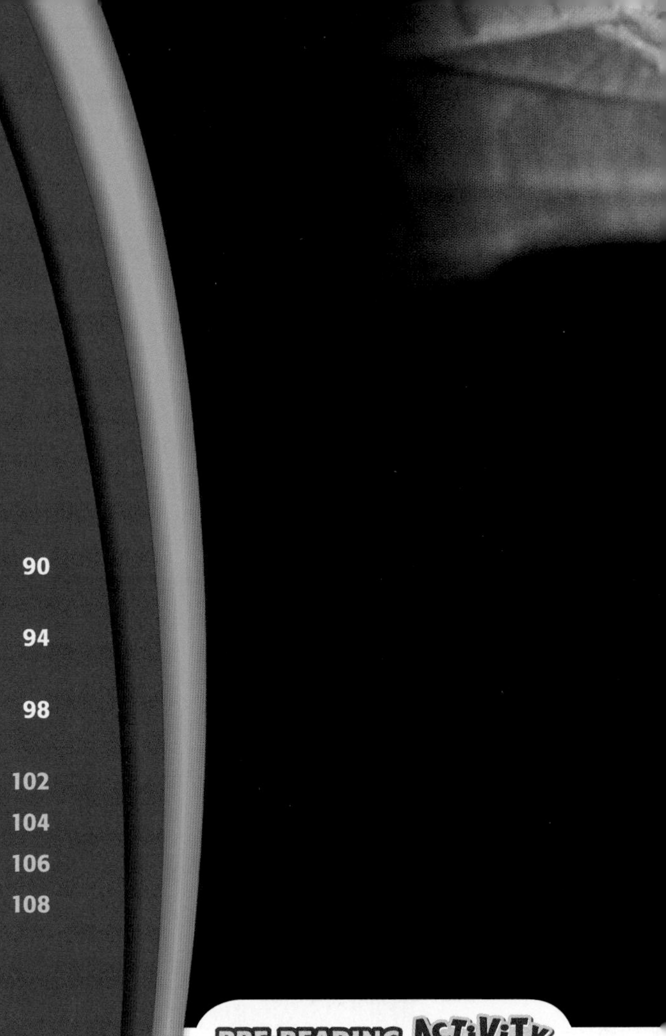

About the PHOTO
This adult katydid is emerging from its last immature, or nymph, stage. As the katydid changed from a nymph to an adult, every structure of its body changed. To grow and change, an organism must produce new cells. When a cell divides, it makes a copy of its genetic material.

PRE-READING ACTIVITY

FOLDNOTES **Tri-Fold** Before you read the chapter, create the FoldNote entitled "Tri-Fold" described in the **Study Skills** section of the Appendix. Write what you know about the actions of cells in the column labeled "Know." Then, write what you want to know in the column labeled "Want." As you read the chapter, write what you learn about the actions of cells in the column labeled "Learn."

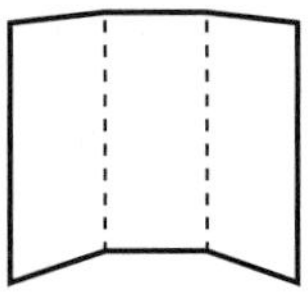

Standards Correlations

National Science Education Standards

The following codes indicate the National Science Education Standards that correlate to this chapter. The full text of the standards is at the front of the book.

Chapter Opener
UCP 3; SAI 1; SPSP 5; LS 1b

Section 1 Exchange with the Environment
UCP 1, 2, 3, 4; LS 1c

Section 2 Cell Energy
UCP 1, 3, 4, 5; SAI 2; ST 2; SPSP 4; LS 1c, 4c;
LabBook: SAI 1; SPSP1; LS 1c

Section 3 The Cell Cycle
SAI 1; LS 1c, 2d

Chapter Lab
UCP 2; SAI 1

Chapter Review
UCP 1, 2, 3, 4, 5; SAI 1, 2; ST 2; SPSP 4, 5; LS 1b, 1c, 2d, 4c

Science in Action
UCP 1, 2, 3, 5; SAI 1, 2; ST 1, 2; SPSP 5; LS 1d, 1e, 1f

START-UP ACTIVITY

MATERIALS

FOR EACH STUDENT
- cup, small plastic
- ruler
- stirring rod
- sugar solution
- test tube, large plastic
- test-tube rack
- test tube, small plastic
- yeast-and-water mixture

Safety Caution: Remind students to review all safety cautions and icons before beginning this lab activity. Students should wear safety goggles at all times and wash their hands when they are finished. Students should not taste the solutions.

Teacher's Notes: The yeast suspension is prepared by mixing one package of dry yeast in 250 mL of water. The sugar solution is prepared by dissolving 30 mL (2 tbsp) of sugar in 100 mL of water.

Answers

1. Answers may vary. Students should subtract the first measurement from the second measurement.

2. When the yeast cells released the energy in sugar, the CO_2 that the cells produced increased the volume of air in the smaller tube and pushed more yeast-and-sugar mixture into the larger tube, increasing the height of the liquid in the larger tube.

START-UP ACTIVITY

Cells in Action

Yeast are single-celled fungi that are an important ingredient in bread. Yeast cells break down sugar molecules to release energy. In the process, carbon dioxide gas is produced, which causes bread dough to rise.

Procedure

1. Add **4 mL of a sugar solution** to **10 mL of a yeast-and-water mixture**. Use a **stirring rod** to thoroughly mix the two liquids.
2. Pour the stirred mixture into a small test tube.
3. Place a slightly **larger test tube** over the **small test tube**. The top of the small test tube should touch the bottom of the larger test tube.
4. Hold the test tubes together, and quickly turn both test tubes over. Place the test tubes in a test-tube rack.
5. Use a **ruler** to measure the height of the fluid in the large test tube. Wait 20 min, and then measure the height of the liquid again.

Analysis

1. What is the difference between the first height measurement and the second height measurement?
2. What do you think caused the change in the fluid's height?

Chapter Starter Transparency
Use this transparency to help students begin thinking about the relationship between cells and their environment.

CHAPTER RESOURCES

Technology

 **Transparencies**
- Chapter Starter Transparency

READING SKILLS

 Student Edition on CD-ROM

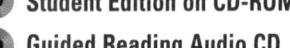 **Guided Reading Audio CD**
- English or Spanish

 Classroom Videos
- Brain Food Video Quiz

Workbooks

 Science Puzzlers, Twisters & Teasers
- The Cell in Action **GENERAL**

Focus

Overview

This section explains the processes of diffusion and osmosis. Students will compare the passive and active transport of particles into and out of cells.

Bellringer

Write the following on the board:

Which of the following best describes a living cell: a building block, a living organism, a complex factory, or all of the above? Explain your choice.

Motivate

Demonstration — GENERAL

Membrane Model Blow soap bubbles for the class. Explain that soap bubbles have properties, such as flexibility, that are similar to biological membranes. Components of soap film and of cell membranes move around freely. Soap bubbles and membranes are self-sealing. If two bubbles or membranes collide, they fuse. If one is cut in half, two smaller but whole bubbles or membranes form.

English Language Learners

LS Visual

READING WARM-UP

Objectives

- Explain the process of diffusion.
- Describe how osmosis occurs.
- Compare passive transport with active transport.
- Explain how large particles get into and out of cells.

Terms to Learn

diffusion
osmosis
passive transport
active transport
endocytosis
exocytosis

READING STRATEGY

Reading Organizer As you read this section, make a table comparing active transport and passive transport.

diffusion the movement of particles from regions of higher density to regions of lower density

Exchange with the Environment

What would happen to a factory if its power were shut off or its supply of raw materials never arrived? What would happen if the factory couldn't get rid of its garbage?

Like a factory, an organism must be able to obtain energy and raw materials and get rid of wastes. An organism's cells perform all of these functions. These functions keep cells healthy so that they can divide. Cell division allows organisms to grow and repair injuries.

The exchange of materials between a cell and its environment takes place at the cell's membrane. To understand how materials move into and out of the cell, you need to know about diffusion.

What Is Diffusion?

What happens if you pour dye on top of a layer of gelatin? At first, it is easy to see where the dye ends and the gelatin begins. But over time, the line between the two layers will blur, as shown in **Figure 1.** Why? Everything, including the gelatin and the dye, is made up of tiny moving particles. Particles travel from where they are crowded to where they are less crowded. This movement from areas of high concentration (crowded) to areas of low concentration (less crowded) is called **diffusion** (di FYOO zhuhn). Dye particles diffuse from where they are crowded (near the top of the glass) to where they are less crowded (in the gelatin). Diffusion also happens within and between living cells. Cells do not need to use energy for diffusion.

Figure 1 *The particles of the dye and the gelatin slowly mix by diffusion.*

CONNECTION to Math — GENERAL

Gas Diffusion Have students solve the following problem in class or as part of their homework:

Gases diffuse about 10,000 times faster in air than in water. If a gas diffuses to fill a room completely in 6 min, how long would it take the gas to fill a similar volume of still water? (60,000 min) How many hours would that be? (1,000 h) How many days? (41.67 days) **LS** Logical

Figure 2 Osmosis

❶ The side that holds only pure water has the higher concentration of water particles.

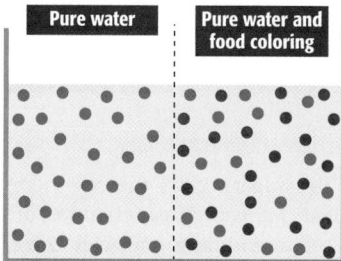

| Pure water | Pure water and food coloring |

❷ During osmosis, water particles move to where they are less concentrated.

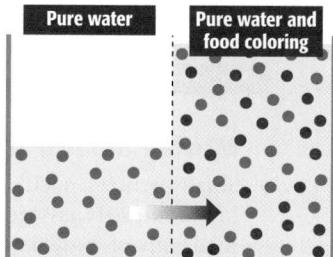

| Pure water | Pure water and food coloring |

Diffusion of Water

The cells of organisms are surrounded by and filled with fluids that are made mostly of water. The diffusion of water through cell membranes is so important to life processes that it has been given a special name—**osmosis** (ahs MOH sis).

Water is made up of particles, called *molecules*. Pure water has the highest concentration of water molecules. When you mix something, such as food coloring, sugar, or salt, with water, you lower the concentration of water molecules. **Figure 2** shows how water molecules move through a membrane that is semi-permeable (SEM i PUHR mee uh buhl). *Semipermeable* means that only certain substances can pass through. The picture on the left in **Figure 2** shows liquids that have different concentrations of water. Over time, the water molecules move from the liquid with the high concentration of water molecules to the liquid with the lower concentration of water molecules.

The Cell and Osmosis

Osmosis is important to cell functions. For example, red blood cells are surrounded by plasma. Plasma is made up of water, salts, sugars, and other particles. The concentration of these particles is kept in balance by osmosis. If red blood cells were in pure water, water molecules would flood into the cells and cause them to burst. When red blood cells are put into a salty solution, the concentration of water molecules inside the cell is higher than the concentration of water outside. This difference makes water move out of the cells, and the cells shrivel up. Osmosis also occurs in plant cells. When a wilted plant is watered, osmosis makes the plant firm again.

✔ **Reading Check** Why would red blood cells burst if you placed them in pure water? (*See the Appendix for answers to Reading Checks.*)

osmosis the diffusion of water through a semipermeable membrane

Bead Diffusion

1. Put three groups of **colored beads** on the bottom of a **plastic bowl.** Each group should be made up of five beads of the same color.

2. Stretch some **clear plastic wrap** tightly over the top of the bowl. Gently shake the bowl for 10 seconds while watching the beads.

3. How is the scattering of the beads like the diffusion of particles? How is it different from the diffusion of particles?

Answer to Reading Check

Red blood cells would burst in pure water because water particles move from outside, where particles were dense, to inside the cell, where particles were less dense. This movement of water would cause red blood cells to fill up and burst.

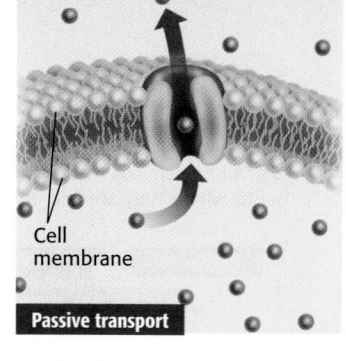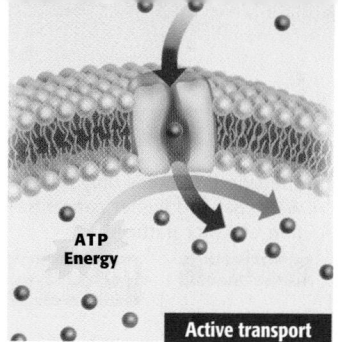

Figure 3 *In passive transport, particles travel through proteins to areas of lower concentration. In active transport, cells use energy to move particles, usually to areas of higher concentration.*

Cell membrane

ATP Energy

Passive transport

Active transport

Close

Reteaching ——————— BASIC

Writing **Cell Transport Instructions** Have students write an instruction manual that tells a cell how to transport both a large molecule and a small molecule through the cell membrane. **LS** Logical

Quiz ——————— GENERAL

1. What part of the cell do materials pass through to get into and out of the cell? (the cell membrane)

2. What is osmosis? (the diffusion of water through a semipermeable membrane)

Alternative Assessment ——— ADVANCED

Writing **Science Biography** Have students write a brief biography of Albert Claude (1898–1983), who used the electron microscope to study cells. (Claude shared the 1974 Nobel Prize for physiology with his student George Palade and with Christian de Duve.) **LS** Verbal

passive transport the movement of substances across a cell membrane without the use of energy by the cell

active transport the movement of substances across the cell membrane that requires the cell to use energy

endocytosis the process by which a cell membrane surrounds a particle and encloses the particle in a vesicle to bring the particle into the cell

Moving Small Particles

Small particles, such as water and sugars, cross the cell membrane through passageways called *channels*. These channels are made up of proteins in the cell membrane. Particles travel through these channels by either passive or active transport. The movement of particles across a cell membrane without the use of energy by the cell is called **passive transport**, and is shown in **Figure 3**. During passive transport, particles move from an area of high concentration to an area of low concentration. Diffusion and osmosis are examples of passive transport.

A process of transporting particles that requires the cell to use energy is called **active transport.** Active transport usually involves the movement of particles from an area of low concentration to an area of high concentration.

Moving Large Particles

Small particles cross the cell membrane by diffusion, passive transport, and active transport. Large particles move into and out of the cell by processes called *endocytosis* and *exocytosis*.

Endocytosis

The active-transport process by which a cell surrounds a large particle, such as a large protein, and encloses the particle in a vesicle to bring the particle into the cell is called **endocytosis** (EN doh sie TOH sis). *Vesicles* are sacs formed from pieces of cell membrane. **Figure 4** shows endocytosis.

Figure 4 **Endocytosis**

 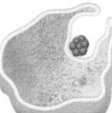 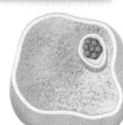 

❶ The cell comes into contact with a particle.

❷ The cell membrane begins to wrap around the particle.

❸ Once the particle is completely surrounded, a vesicle pinches off.

This photo shows the end of *endocytosis*, which means "within the cell."

CHAPTER RESOURCES

Technology

Transparencies
• Passive Transport and Active Transport
• Endocytosis/Exocytosis

Homework ——————— GENERAL

 Transport Ask students to describe how each of the following materials would get through a cell membrane and into a cell.

a. pure water (osmosis)

b. sugar entering a cell that already contains a high concentration of particles (active transport)

c. sugar entering a cell that has a low concentration of particles (diffusion or passive transport)

d. a protein (active transport or endocytosis)

LS Logical

Figure 5 Exocytosis

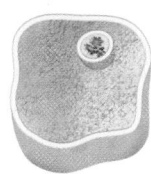
1 Large particles that must leave the cell are packaged in vesicles.

2 The vesicle travels to the cell membrane and fuses with it.

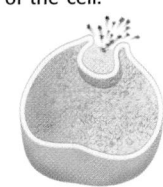
3 The cell releases the particle to the outside of the cell.

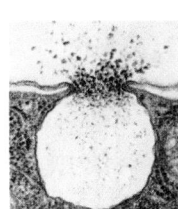
Exocytosis means "outside the cell."

Exocytosis

When large particles, such as wastes, leave the cell, the cell uses an active-transport process called **exocytosis** (EK soh sie TOH sis). During exocytosis, a vesicle forms around a large particle within the cell. The vesicle carries the particle to the cell membrane. The vesicle fuses with the cell membrane and releases the particle to the outside of the cell. **Figure 5** shows exocytosis.

exocytosis the process in which a cell releases a particle by enclosing the particle in a vesicle that then moves to the cell surface and fuses with the cell membrane

✔ *Reading Check* What is exocytosis?

SECTION Review

Summary

- Diffusion is the movement of particles from an area of high concentration to an area of low concentration.
- Osmosis is the diffusion of water through a semipermeable membrane.
- Cells move small particles by diffusion, which is an example of passive transport, and by active transport.
- Large particles enter the cell by endocytosis, and exit the cell by exocytosis.

Using Key Terms

For each pair of terms, explain how the meanings of the terms differ.

1. *diffusion* and *osmosis*

2. *active transport* and *passive transport*

3. *endocytosis* and *exocytosis*

Understanding Key Ideas

4. The movement of particles from a less crowded area to a more crowded area requires
   a. sunlight.   **c.** a membrane.
   b. energy.   **d.** osmosis.

5. What structures allow small particles to cross cell membranes?

Math Skills

6. The area of particle 1 is 2.5 mm². The area of particle 2 is 0.5 mm². The area of particle 1 is how many times as big as the area of particle 2?

Critical Thinking

7. **Predicting Consequences** What would happen to a cell if its channel proteins were damaged and unable to transport particles? What would happen to the organism if many of its cells were damaged in this way? Explain your answer.

8. **Analyzing Ideas** Why does active transport require energy?

SCLINKS **NSTA**
Developed and maintained by the National Science Teachers Association

For a variety of links related to this chapter, go to www.scilinks.org

Topics: Diffusion; Osmosis
SciLinks code: HSM0406; HSM1090

Answer to Reading Check
Exocytosis is the process by which a cell moves large particles to the outside of the cell.

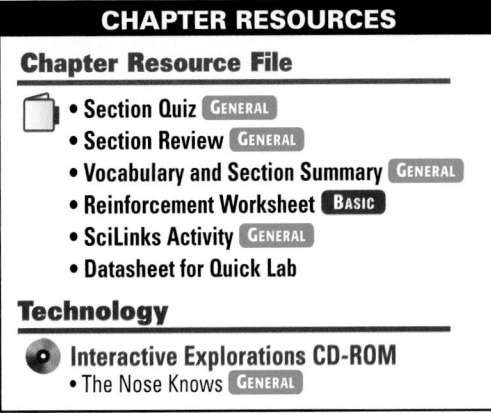
CHAPTER RESOURCES

Chapter Resource File
- Section Quiz GENERAL
- Section Review GENERAL
- Vocabulary and Section Summary GENERAL
- Reinforcement Worksheet BASIC
- SciLinks Activity GENERAL
- Datasheet for Quick Lab

Technology
- Interactive Explorations CD-ROM
  - The Nose Knows GENERAL

Overview

This section introduces energy and the cell. Students learn about solar energy and the process of photosynthesis. Finally, students learn about cellular respiration and fermentation.

🔊 Bellringer

Ask students to make a list of all the reasons why a cell might need energy. Remind students that there are many types of cells doing many different jobs.

Motivate

Demonstration — GENERAL

Leaves and Light Ask students what they think would happen if a plant could not get sunlight. A few days before teaching this section, cut out a square from black construction paper. Fold the square over a leaf of any common plant, such as a geranium. Affix the square with a paper clip. Be sure the leaf does not receive any sunlight. Leave the leaf covered for about one week. Remove the black square. The leaf will be paler than the other leaves. In the absence of sunlight, chlorophyll is depleted and not replenished. The leaf's green color will have faded. English Language Learners
 Visual

SECTION 2

Cell Energy

Why do you get hungry? Feeling hungry is your body's way of telling you that your cells need energy.

All cells need energy to live, grow, and reproduce. Plant cells get their energy from the sun. Many animal cells get the energy they need from food.

From Sun to Cell

Nearly all of the energy that fuels life comes from the sun. Plants capture energy from the sun and change it into food through a process called **photosynthesis.** The food that plants make supplies them with energy. This food also becomes a source of energy for the organisms that eat the plants.

Photosynthesis

Plant cells have molecules that absorb light energy. These molecules are called *pigments*. Chlorophyll (KLAWR uh FIL), the main pigment used in photosynthesis, gives plants their green color. Chlorophyll is found in chloroplasts.

Plants use the energy captured by chlorophyll to change carbon dioxide and water into food. The food is in the form of the simple sugar glucose. Glucose is a carbohydrate. When plants make glucose, they convert the sun's energy into a form of energy that can be stored. The energy in glucose is used by the plant's cells. Photosynthesis also produces oxygen. Photosynthesis is summarized in **Figure 1.**

READING WARM-UP

Objectives
- Describe photosynthesis and cellular respiration.
- Compare cellular respiration with fermentation.

Terms to Learn
photosynthesis
cellular respiration
fermentation

READING STRATEGY

Discussion Read this section silently. Write down questions that you have about this section. Discuss your questions in a small group.

photosynthesis the process by which plants, algae, and some bacteria use sunlight, carbon dioxide, and water to make food

Photosynthesis

$$6CO_2 + 6H_2O + \text{Light energy} \longrightarrow C_6H_{12}O_6 + 6O_2$$

Carbon dioxide   Water   Glucose   Oxygen

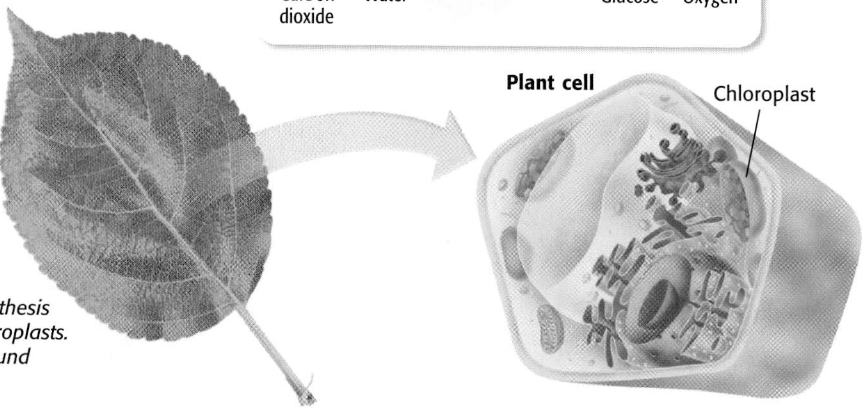

Plant cell

Chloroplast

Figure 1 *Photosynthesis takes place in chloroplasts. Chloroplasts are found inside plant cells.*

CHAPTER RESOURCES

Chapter Resource File

- **Lesson Plan**
- **Directed Reading A** BASIC
- **Directed Reading B** SPECIAL NEEDS

Technology

- **Transparencies**
- Bellringer
- *LINK TO PHYSICAL SCIENCE* Solar Heating Systems

Workbooks

- **Science Skills**
- Using Logic GENERAL
- Identifying Bias GENERAL

MISCONCEPTION /// ALERT \\\

Not the Only Steps The processes of photosynthesis and respiration are complex chemical reactions that involve several steps shown by many chemical reactions. The much-simpler equations shown for the processes of respiration and photosynthesis in this chapter are the *net* equations for those reactions.

Getting Energy from Food

Animal cells have different ways of getting energy from food. One way, called **cellular respiration,** uses oxygen to break down food. Many cells can get energy without using oxygen through a process called **fermentation.** Cellular respiration will release more energy from a given food than fermentation will.

Cellular Respiration

The word *respiration* means "breathing," but cellular respiration is different from breathing. Breathing supplies the oxygen needed for cellular respiration. Breathing also removes carbon dioxide, which is a waste product of cellular respiration. But cellular respiration is a chemical process that occurs in cells.

Most complex organisms, such as the cow in **Figure 2,** obtain energy through cellular respiration. During cellular respiration, food (such as glucose) is broken down into CO_2 and H_2O, and energy is released. Most of the energy released maintains body temperature. Some of the energy is used to form adenosine triphosphate (ATP). ATP supplies energy that fuels cell activities.

Most of the process of cellular respiration takes place in the cell membrane of prokaryotic cells. But in the cells of eukaryotes, cellular respiration takes place mostly in the mitochondria. The process of cellular respiration is summarized in **Figure 2.** Does the equation in the figure remind you of the equation for photosynthesis? **Figure 3** on the next page shows how photosynthesis and respiration are related.

Reading Check What is the difference between cellular respiration and breathing? (*See the Appendix for answers to Reading Checks.*)

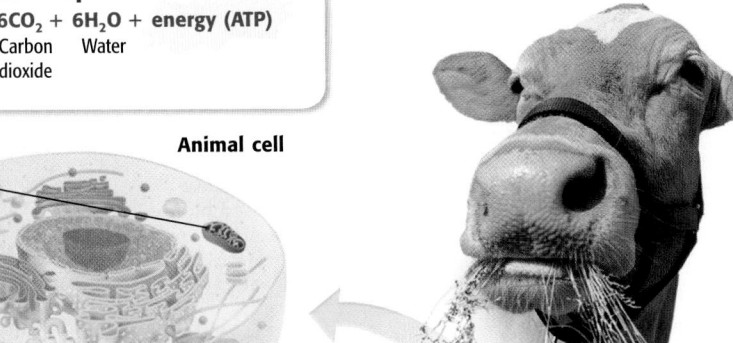

Cellular Respiration

$$C_6H_{12}O_6 + 6O_2 \rightarrow 6CO_2 + 6H_2O + \text{energy (ATP)}$$

Glucose   Oxygen   Carbon dioxide   Water

Mitochondria   **Animal cell**

<img style omitted>

CONNECTION TO Chemistry

Earth's Early Atmosphere

Scientists think that Earth's early atmosphere lacked oxygen. Because of this lack of oxygen, early organisms used fermentation to get energy from food. When organisms began to photosynthesize, the oxygen they produced entered the atmosphere. How do you think this oxygen changed how other organisms got energy?

cellular respiration the process by which cells use oxygen to produce energy from food

fermentation the breakdown of food without the use of oxygen

Figure 2 *The mitochondria in the cells of this cow will use cellular respiration to release the energy stored in the grass.*

Answer to Reading Check

Cellular respiration is a chemical process by which cells produce energy from food. Breathing supplies oxygen for cellular respiration and removes the carbon dioxide produced by cellular respiration.

Teach

Group ACTiViTY — GENERAL

Writing **Recycling Carbon**

Organize the class into groups of three or four. Have each group write the story of a carbon atom as it is used throughout time. Stories should begin with a molecule of carbon dioxide. Ask: "What plant uses it for photosynthesis? What animals swallow it and use it to fuel respiration?" Have students share their stories if time allows. **LS Verbal/Interpersonal**

Answer to Connection to Chemistry

The presence of oxygen gave other organisms the opportunity to get energy in other ways besides fermentation. Most organisms would eventually use cellular respiration to get energy from food.

CONNECTION to Physical Science — ADVANCED

Solar Heating Conventional solar heating is a much simpler process than photosynthesis. The sun's energy heats either the house itself, or it heats water, which then circulates through the house. If students have ever felt the warm water from a hose that has been left in the sun, they have felt stored solar energy. Use the teaching transparency titled "Solar Heating Systems" to illustrate how solar energy can be used to heat a home. **LS Visual**

Close

Reteaching — BASIC

Concept Mapping Have students draw a concept map of energy transfer using the following images:

> sunshine; tree, for firewood; sugar cane; yeast consuming sugar, making bread rise; person chopping firewood, for baking oven; person eating bread

Students should note on their maps which organisms use photosynthesis, which use respiration, and which use fermentation. **LS Visual**

Quiz — GENERAL

Ask students whether the following statements are true or false.

1. Plants and animals capture their energy from the sun. (false)

2. Cellular respiration describes how a cell breathes. (false)

3. Fermentation in animals produces ATP and lactic acid. (true)

Alternative Assessment — GENERAL

Lungs of the Earth Tell students that plants are sometimes called the "lungs of the Earth." Ask students to think about this and to prepare an illustrated presentation for the class. Students may want to research the role that rain forests play as Earth's "lungs" and explain the contributions rain forests make to the health of the planet. **LS Verbal/Visual**

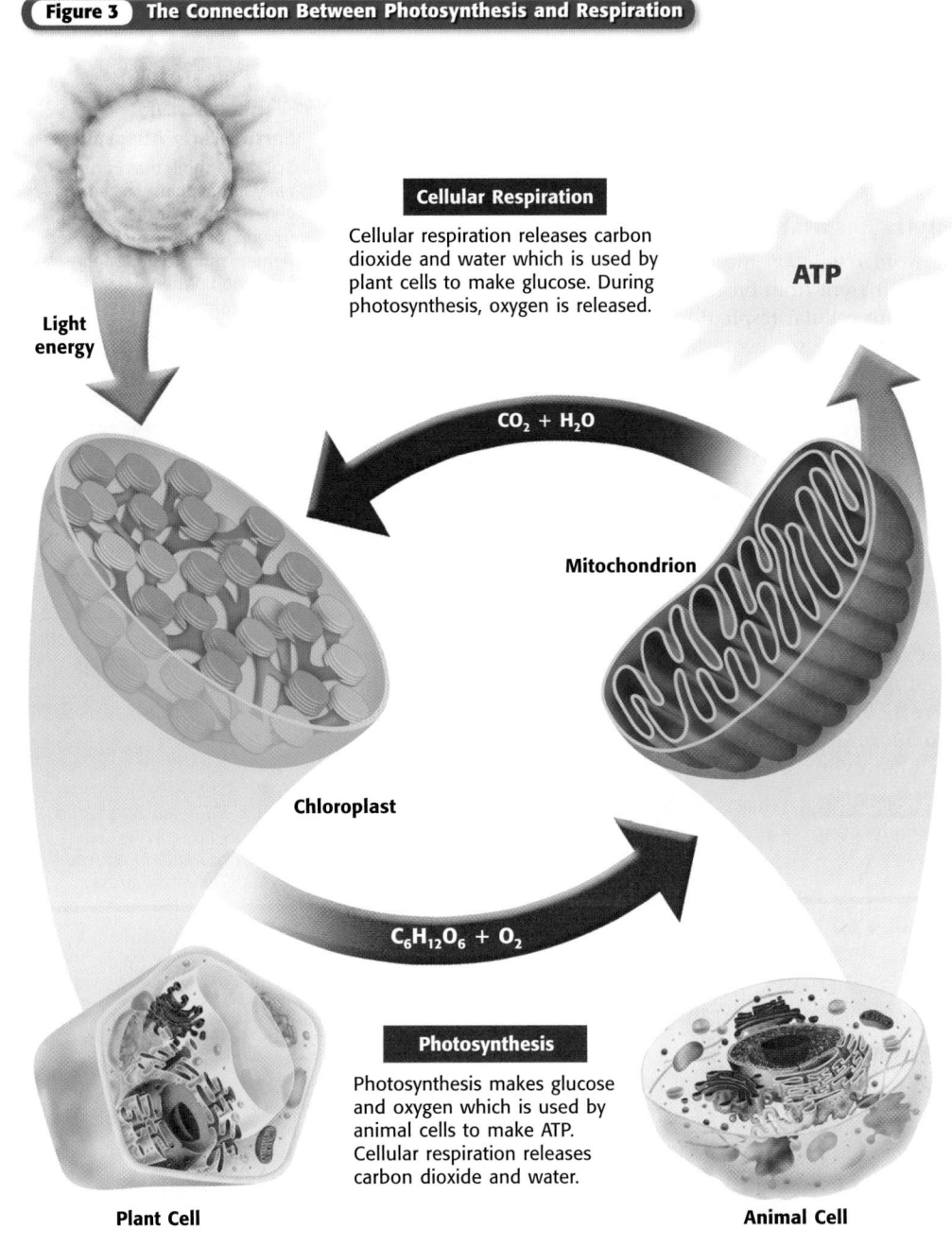

Figure 3 The Connection Between Photosynthesis and Respiration

Light energy

Cellular Respiration
Cellular respiration releases carbon dioxide and water which is used by plant cells to make glucose. During photosynthesis, oxygen is released.

ATP

$CO_2 + H_2O$

Mitochondrion

Chloroplast

$C_6H_{12}O_6 + O_2$

Photosynthesis
Photosynthesis makes glucose and oxygen which is used by animal cells to make ATP. Cellular respiration releases carbon dioxide and water.

Plant Cell

Animal Cell

Group ACTIVITY — GENERAL

Photosynthesis and Cellular Respiration Have students work in pairs and refer to the diagram on this page. Have each pair compare and contrast photosynthesis and respiration. Ask students to answer the following questions: "What happens to the ATP? Where does the ATP go? How is ATP used by the cell? How is the cell's use of CO_2 and H_2O similar to people's recycling of paper and glass bottles?" **LS Interpersonal/Logical**

Homework — ADVANCED

Comparing Cell Processes Newer kinds of solar cells simulate photosynthesis more closely than older solar cells do. Just as plant cells use energy from the sun to change water and carbon dioxide into energy-rich sugars, these new solar cells use the sun's energy to convert water into energy-rich hydrogen gas, which can be used as fuel. The byproduct of this process is oxygen. Have students research these newer solar cells and make a poster showing how they work. **LS Visual**

Connection Between Photosynthesis and Respiration

As shown in **Figure 3,** photosynthesis transforms energy from the sun into glucose. During photosynthesis, cells use CO_2 to make glucose, and the cells release O_2. During cellular respiration, cells use O_2 to break down glucose and release energy and CO_2. Each process makes the materials that are needed for the other process to occur elsewhere.

Fermentation

Have you ever felt a burning sensation in your leg muscles while you were running? When muscle cells can't get the oxygen needed for cellular respiration, they use the process of fermentation to get energy. One kind of fermentation happens in your muscles and produces lactic acid. The buildup of lactic acid contributes to muscle fatigue and causes a burning sensation. This kind of fermentation also happens in the muscle cells of other animals and in some fungi and bacteria. Another type of fermentation occurs in some types of bacteria and in yeast as described in **Figure 4.**

Reading Check What are two kinds of fermentation?

Figure 4 *Yeast forms carbon dioxide during fermentation. The bubbles of CO_2 gas cause the dough to rise and leave small holes in bread after it is baked.*

SECTION Review

Summary

- Most of the energy that fuels life processes comes from the sun.
- The sun's energy is converted into food by the process of photosynthesis.
- Cellular respiration breaks down glucose into water, carbon dioxide, and energy.
- Fermentation is a way that cells get energy from their food without using oxygen.

Using Key Terms

1. In your own words, write a definition for the term *fermentation*.

Understanding Key Ideas

2. O_2 is released during
   a. cellular respiration.
   b. photosynthesis.
   c. breathing.
   d. fermentation.

3. How are photosynthesis and cellular respiration related?

4. How are respiration and fermentation similar? How are they different?

Math Skills

5. Cells of plant A make 120 molecules of glucose an hour. Cells of plant B make half as much glucose as plant A does. How much glucose does plant B make every minute?

Critical Thinking

6. **Analyzing Relationships** Why are plants important to the survival of all other organisms?

7. **Applying Concepts** You have been given the job of restoring life to a barren island. What types of organisms would you put on the island? If you want to have animals on the island, what other organisms must you bring? Explain your answer.

SC*LINKS*

NSTA
Developed and maintained by the National Science Teachers Association

For a variety of links related to this chapter, go to www.scilinks.org

Topic: Cell Energy; Photosynthesis
SciLinks code: HSM0237; HSM1140

SECTION
3

Focus

Overview

This section introduces the life cycle of a cell. Students will learn how cells reproduce and how mitosis is important. Finally, students will learn how cell division differs in plants and animals.

Bellringer

On the board, write the following:

Biology is the only science in which multiplication means the same thing as division.

Have students write an explanation of this sentence. (When cells divide, they are multiplying. Some students may point out that multiplying a number by a fraction is the same as division.)

Motivate

ACTIVITY ——————— GENERAL

Making Models Have pairs of students use string for the cell membrane and pieces of pipe cleaners for chromosomes to demonstrate the basic steps of mitosis, as described in this section. **LS** Visual/Interpersonal

---

READING WARM-UP

Objectives

- Explain how cells produce more cells.
- Describe the process of mitosis.
- Explain how cell division differs in animals and plants.

Terms to Learn

cell cycle
chromosome
homologous chromosomes
mitosis
cytokinesis

READING STRATEGY

Paired Summarizing Read this section silently. In pairs, take turns summarizing the material. Stop to discuss ideas that seem confusing.

cell cycle the life cycle of a cell

chromosome in a eukaryotic cell, one of the structures in the nucleus that are made up of DNA and protein; in a prokaryotic cell, the main ring of DNA

The Cell Cycle

In the time that it takes you to read this sentence, your body will have made millions of new cells! Making new cells allows you to grow and replace cells that have died.

The environment in your stomach is so acidic that the cells lining your stomach must be replaced every few days. Other cells are replaced less often, but your body is constantly making new cells.

The Life of a Cell

As you grow, you pass through different stages in life. Your cells also pass through different stages in their life cycle. The life cycle of a cell is called the **cell cycle.**

The cell cycle begins when the cell is formed and ends when the cell divides and forms new cells. Before a cell divides, it must make a copy of its deoxyribonucleic acid (DNA). DNA is the hereditary material that controls all cell activities, including the making of new cells. The DNA of a cell is organized into structures called **chromosomes.** Copying chromosomes ensures that each new cell will be an exact copy of its parent cell. How does a cell make more cells? It depends on whether the cell is prokaryotic (with no nucleus) or eukaryotic (with a nucleus).

Making More Prokaryotic Cells

Prokaryotic cells are less complex than eukaryotic cells are. Bacteria, which are prokaryotes, have ribosomes and a single, circular DNA molecule but don't have membrane-enclosed organelles. Cell division in bacteria is called *binary fission*, which means "splitting into two parts." Binary fission results in two cells that each contain one copy of the circle of DNA. A few of the bacteria in **Figure 1** are undergoing binary fission.

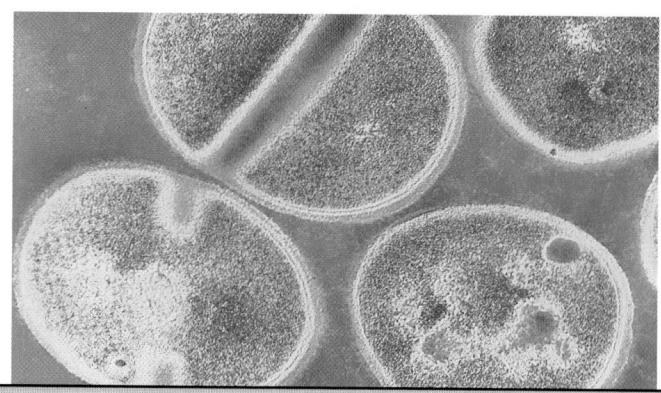

Figure 1 *Bacteria reproduce by binary fission.*

CHAPTER RESOURCES

Chapter Resource File

- • Lesson Plan
- • Directed Reading A BASIC
- • Directed Reading B SPECIAL NEEDS

Technology

Transparencies
- • Bellringer
- • The Cell Cycle

Workbooks

Math Skills for Science
- • Multiplying Whole Numbers BASIC
- • Grasping Graphing GENERAL

CONNECTION to Math ——————— BASIC

Cell Multiplication It takes Cell A 1 h to complete its cell cycle and produce two cells. The cell cycle of Cell B takes 2 h. How many more cells would be formed from Cell A than from Cell B in 6 h?

(After 6 h, Cell A would have formed 64 cells, and Cell B would have formed 8 cells. Cell A would have formed 56 cells more than Cell B.) **LS** Logical/Verbal

---

Eukaryotic Cells and Their DNA

Eukaryotic cells are more complex than prokaryotic cells are. The chromosomes of eukaryotic cells contain more DNA than those of prokaryotic cells do. Different kinds of eukaryotes have different numbers of chromosomes. More-complex eukaryotes do not necessarily have more chromosomes than simpler eukaryotes do. For example, fruit flies have 8 chromosomes, potatoes have 48, and humans have 46. **Figure 2** shows the 46 chromosomes of a human body cell lined up in pairs. These pairs are made up of similar chromosomes known as **homologous chromosomes** (hoh MAHL uh guhs KROH muh SOHMZ).

✔ *Reading Check* Do more-complex organisms always have more chromosomes than simpler organisms do? (*See the Appendix for answers to Reading Checks.*)

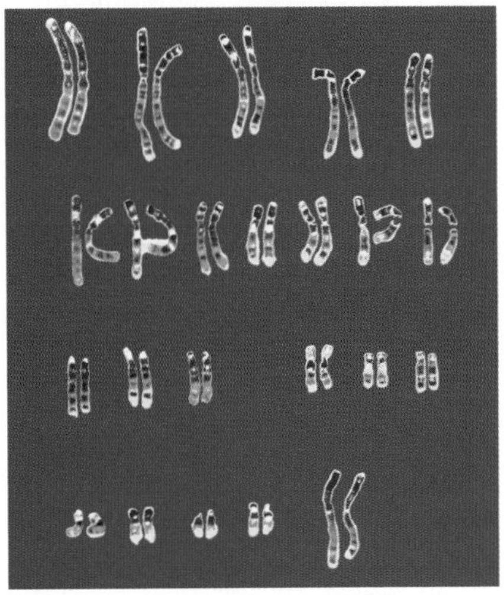

Figure 2 *Human body cells have 46 chromosomes, or 23 pairs of chromosomes.*

Making More Eukaryotic Cells

The eukaryotic cell cycle includes three stages. In the first stage, called *interphase*, the cell grows and copies its organelles and chromosomes. After each chromosome is duplicated, the two copies are called *chromatids*. Chromatids are held together at a region called the *centromere*. The joined chromatids twist and coil and condense into an X shape, as shown in **Figure 3**. After this step, the cell enters the second stage of the cell cycle.

In the second stage, the chromatids separate. The complicated process of chromosome separation is called **mitosis**. Mitosis ensures that each new cell receives a copy of each chromosome. Mitosis is divided into four phases, as shown on the following pages.

In the third stage, the cell splits into two cells. These cells are identical to each other and to the original cell.

homologous chromosomes chromosomes that have the same sequence of genes and the same structure

mitosis in eukaryotic cells, a process of cell division that forms two new nuclei, each of which has the same number of chromosomes

Figure 3 *This duplicated chromosome consists of two chromatids. The chromatids are joined at the centromere.*

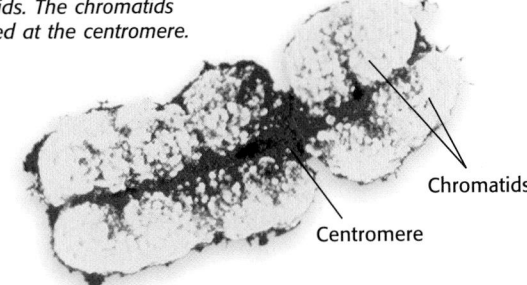

Chromatids

Centromere

CONNECTION TO Language Arts

Picking Apart Vocabulary
Brainstorm what words are similar to the parts of the term *homologous chromosome*. What can you guess about the meaning of the term's root words? Look up the roots of the words, and explain how they help describe the concept.

ACTIVITY

Is That a Fact!
Before sophisticated microscopes were available, scientists could not see cells pinching and dividing. Many scientists believed that cells came into existence spontaneously—as though crystallizing out of bodily fluids.

Reteaching — BASIC

Biography of a Cell
Have students write and illustrate the biography of a cell. It can be humorous or serious, but it should include accurate descriptions of how materials are transported into and out of the cell and how cells reproduce. **LS** Visual/Verbal

Quiz — GENERAL

1. What is cell division? (It is the process by which cells reproduce themselves.)

2. How do prokaryotic cells make more cells? (binary fission)

3. How do eukaryotic cells make more cells? (mitosis and cytokinesis)

Alternative Assessment — GENERAL

Mitosis and Cancer
Have students research the role of mitosis in cancer and write a report or create a poster or other visual presentation on what they learn. Students' reports should include information about various cancer treatments, such as radiation, chemotherapy, and surgery. **LS** Verbal/Visual

Answer to Reading Check

During cytokinesis in plant cells, a cell plate is formed. During cytokinesis in animal cells, a cell plate does not form.

Figure 4 The Cell Cycle

Copying DNA (Interphase)
Before mitosis begins, chromosomes are copied. Each chromosome is then two chromatids.

Mitosis Phase 1 (Prophase)
Mitosis begins. The nuclear membrane dissolves. Chromosomes condense into rodlike structures.

Mitosis Phase 2 (Metaphase)
The chromosomes line up along the equator of the cell. Homologous chromosomes pair up.

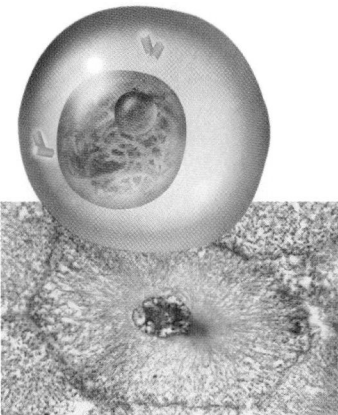 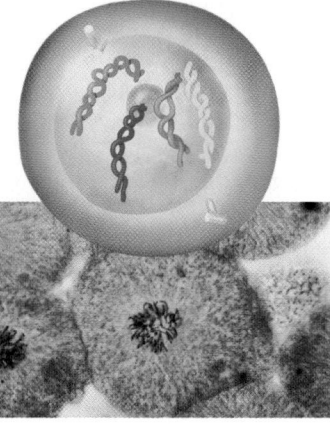 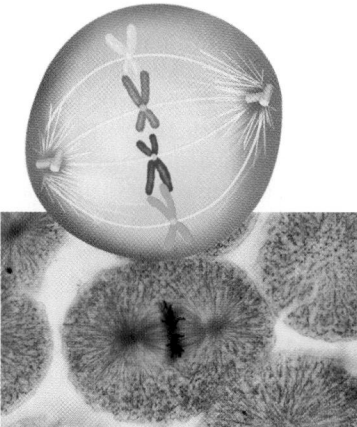

cytokinesis the division of the cytoplasm of a cell

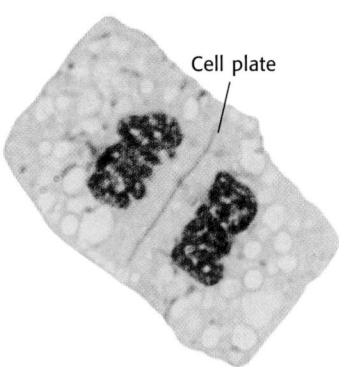

Cell plate

Figure 5 When a plant cell divides, a cell plate forms and the cell splits into two cells.

Mitosis and the Cell Cycle

Figure 4 shows the cell cycle and the phases of mitosis in an animal cell. Mitosis has four phases that are shown and described above. This diagram shows only four chromosomes to make it easy to see what's happening inside the cell.

Cytokinesis

In animal cells and other eukaryotes that do not have cell walls, division of the cytoplasm begins at the cell membrane. The cell membrane begins to pinch inward to form a groove, which eventually pinches all the way through the cell, and two daughter cells form. The division of cytoplasm is called **cytokinesis** and is shown at the last step of **Figure 4.**

Eukaryotic cells that have a cell wall, such as the cells of plants, algae, and fungi, reproduce differently. In these cells, a *cell plate* forms in the middle of the cell. The cell plate contains the materials for the new cell membranes and the new cell walls that will separate the new cells. After the cell splits into two, a new cell wall forms where the cell plate was. The cell plate and a late stage of cytokinesis in a plant cell are shown in **Figure 5.**

✓ **Reading Check** What is the difference between cytokinesis in an animal cell and cytokinesis in a plant cell?

INCLUSION Strategies

- *Developmentally Delayed*   - *Hearing Impaired*
- *Learning Disabled*

Make a three-column table with these column headings: *Characteristics, Prokaryotic Cells,* and *Eukaryotic Cells.* Under Characteristics, use these five row headings: *Small or large?, Complex or simple?, More or less DNA?, Has organelles?,* and *Number of stages in cell division.* Have students copy the table and fill it in. **LS** Logical/Visual

INTERNET ACTiViTY

Sequence Board — GENERAL

For an internet activity related to this chapter, have students go to **go.hrw.com** and type in the keyword **HL5ACTW.**

Mitosis Phase 3 (Anaphase)

The chromatids separate and move to opposite sides of the cell.

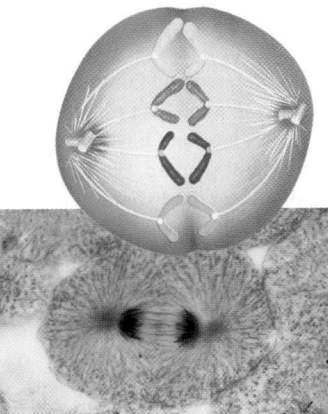

Mitosis Phase 4 (Telophase)

A nuclear membrane forms around each set of chromosomes, and the chromosomes unwind. Mitosis is complete.

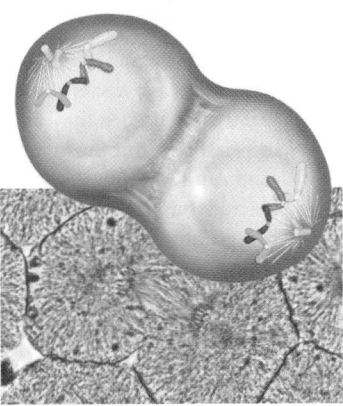

Cytokinesis

In cells that lack a cell wall, the cell pinches in two. In cells that have a cell wall, a cell plate forms between the two new cells.

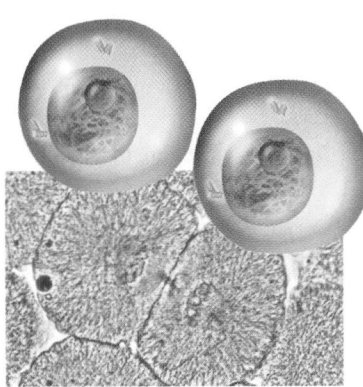

SECTION Review

Summary

- A cell produces more cells by first copying its DNA.
- Eukaryotic cells produce more cells through the four phases of mitosis.
- Mitosis produces two cells that have the same number of chromosomes as the parent cell.
- At the end of mitosis, a cell divides the cytoplasm by cytokinesis.
- In plant cells, a cell plate forms between the two new cells during cytokinesis.

Using Key Terms

1. In your own words, write a definition for each of the following terms: *cell cycle* and *cytokinesis*.

Understanding Key Ideas

2. Eukaryotic cells
   a. do not divide.
   b. undergo binary fission.
   c. undergo mitosis.
   d. have cell walls.

3. Why is it important for chromosomes to be copied before cell division?

4. Describe mitosis.

Math Skills

5. Cell A takes 6 h to complete division. Cell B takes 8 h to complete division. After 24 h, how many more copies of cell A would there be than cell B?

Critical Thinking

6. **Predicting Consequences** What would happen if cytokinesis occurred without mitosis?

7. **Applying Concepts** How does mitosis ensure that a new cell is just like its parent cell?

8. **Making Comparisons** Compare the processes that animal cells and plant cells use to make new cells. How are the processes different?

SCi LINKS®

NSTA
Developed and maintained by the National Science Teachers Association

For a variety of links related to this chapter, go to www.scilinks.org

Topic: Cell Cycle
SciLinks code: HSM0235

CHAPTER RESOURCES

Chapter Resource File

- Section Quiz GENERAL
- Section Review GENERAL
- Vocabulary and Section Summary GENERAL
- Reinforcement Worksheet BASIC

Workbooks

Science Skills
- Researching on the Web BASIC
- Organizing Your Research GENERAL

The Perfect Taters Mystery

Teacher's Notes

Time Required
Two 45-minute class periods

Lab Ratings

🍶 EASY	🍶🍶	🍶🍶🍶	🍶🍶🍶🍶 HARD

Teacher Prep 🍶🍶
Student Set-Up 🍶🍶
Concept Level 🍶🍶🍶
Clean Up 🍶

MATERIALS
The materials listed on the student pages are enough for one class of students. You will need one or two potatoes per class. Do not allow students to cut or peel potatoes. You will need to do this ahead of time. Allow students to choose the number of containers they will need for the experiment. They may wish to test several salt concentrations.

Safety Caution
Remind students to review all safety cautions and icons before beginning this lab activity.

Avoid including green or discolored parts of the potato in the pieces students work with. These could cause illness.

The Perfect Taters Mystery

You are the chief food detective at Perfect Taters Food Company. The boss, Mr. Fries, wants you to find a way to keep his potatoes fresh and crisp before they are cooked. His workers have tried several methods, but these methods have not worked. Workers in Group A put the potatoes in very salty water, and something unexpected happened to the potatoes. Workers in Group B put the potatoes in water that did not contain any salt, and something else happened! Workers in Group C didn't put the potatoes in any water, and that didn't work either. Now, you must design an experiment to find out what can be done to make the potatoes stay crisp and fresh.

OBJECTIVES

Examine osmosis in potato cells.

Design a procedure that will give the best results.

MATERIALS

- cups, clear plastic, small
- potato pieces, freshly cut
- potato samples (A, B, and C)
- salt
- water, distilled

SAFETY

- Before you plan your experiment, review what you know. You know that potatoes are made of cells. Plant cells contain a large amount of water. Cells have membranes that hold water and other materials inside and keep some things out. Water and other materials must travel across cell membranes to get into and out of the cell.

- Mr. Fries has told you that you can obtain as many samples as you need from the workers in Groups A, B, and C. Your teacher will have these samples ready for you to observe.

- Make a data table like the one below. List your observations in the data table. Make as many observations as you can about the potatoes tested by workers in Groups A, B, and C.

Observations	
Group A	
Group B	
Group C	

Ask a Question

1 Now that you have made your observations, state Mr. Fries's problem in the form of a question that can be answered by your experiment.

Lab Notes
Osmosis is often a confusing and misunderstood concept in life science. Quite often, students can repeat the definition of the process but are unable to apply the concept to explain the movement of water in different osmotic environments. In this lab, students will have an opportunity to observe osmosis in a model and obtain measurable results. This lab can be done as a class demonstration if materials and space are limited. The purpose of this lab is to reinforce comprehension of osmosis and to practice the scientific method.

CHAPTER RESOURCES

Chapter Resource File
- 📁 • Datasheet for Chapter Lab
  - • Lab Notes and Answers

Technology
- 📹 Classroom Videos
  - • Lab Video

LabBook
- • Stayin' Alive!

Form a Hypothesis

2 Form a hypothesis based on your observations and your questions. The hypothesis should be a statement about what causes the potatoes not to be crisp and fresh. Based on your hypothesis, make a prediction about the outcome of your experiment. State your prediction in an if-then format.

Test the Hypothesis

3 Once you have made a prediction, design your investigation. Check your experimental design with your teacher before you begin. Mr. Fries will give you potato pieces, water, salt, and no more than six containers.

4 Keep very accurate records. Write your plan and procedure. Make data tables. To be sure your data is accurate, measure all materials carefully and make drawings of the potato pieces before and after the experiment.

Analyze the Results

1 **Explaining Events** Explain what happened to the potato cells in Groups A, B, and C in your experiment. Include a discussion of the cell membrane and the process of osmosis.

Draw Conclusions

2 **Analyzing Results** Write a letter to Mr. Fries that explains your experimental method, results, and conclusion. Then, make a recommendation about how he should handle the potatoes so that they will stay fresh and crisp.

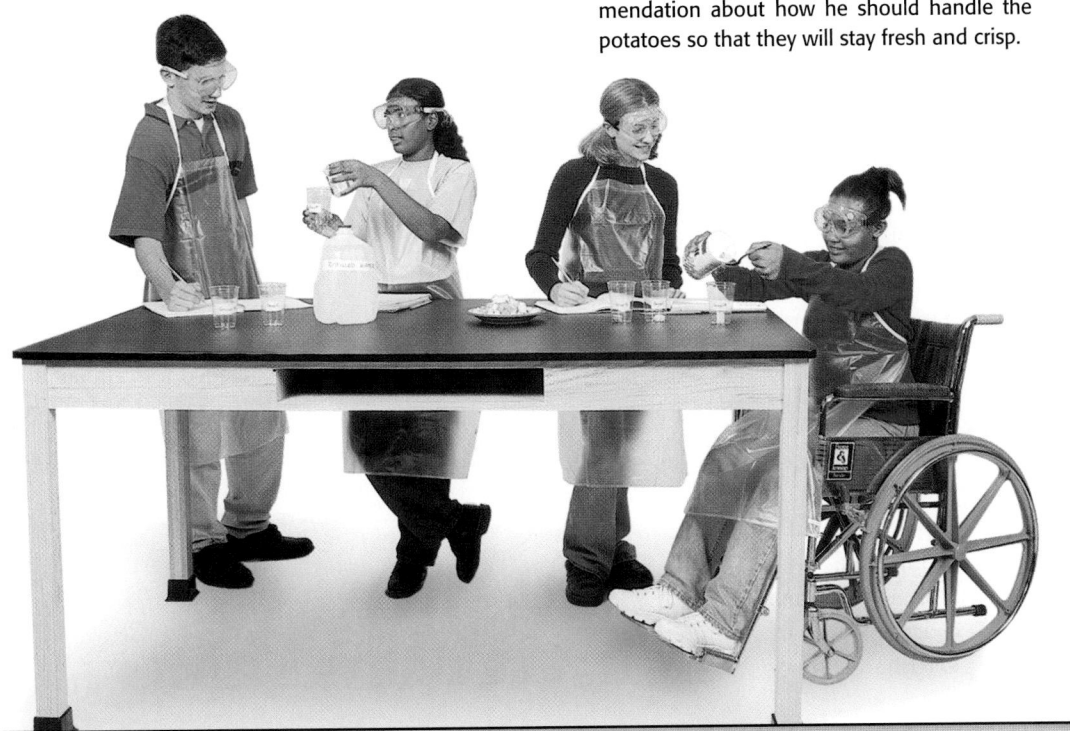

Analyze the Results

1. The potato cells in Group A were placed in very salty water. The potatoes shriveled up because water moved out of the cell and into the salty water (from an area of high concentration of water to an area of low concentration of water). This may be confusing to some students, who may think that because the concentration of salt is high outside the potato, the salt should move to the area of lower concentration. Explain that although water can move through a cell membrane by osmosis, salt must be moved across a cell membrane by a process that requires energy.

The potato cells in Group B were placed in water with no salt. The potatoes swelled because the concentration of water was lower inside the cell. (The concentration of salt and other molecules was higher inside the potato cell.)

The potato cells in Group C turned brown and dried up because the water concentration outside the cell was low. In fact, there wasn't any water at all. The water evaporated as soon as it left the cell membrane. The potato cells turned brown because of chemical reactions with the air.

Draw Conclusions

2. Letters to Mr. Fries will vary according to each student's results. However, all students should explain that through trial and error they found one salt concentration that was closest to the concentration of salt and other molecules inside the potato. This is the concentration that should be used to maintain an osmotic balance in the potato. Furthermore, some students will realize that the potatoes must be kept in water to prevent them from turning brown.

CLASSROOM TESTED & APPROVED

Susan Gorman
North Ridge Middle School
North Richland Hills, Texas

Chapter Review

Assignment Guide

Section	Questions
1	1, 2, 6, 8, 12, 16
2	3, 4, 7, 10, 13, 17
3	5, 9, 11, 14, 15, 18–22

ANSWERS

Using Key Terms

1. Sample answer: Osmosis is the diffusion of water through a semipermeable membrane.

2. Sample answer: Exocytosis is the process cells use to remove large particles; endocytosis is the process cells use to move large particles into a cell

3. photosynthesis

4. cellular respiration

5. Cytokinesis is the division of just the cytoplasm. Mitosis is the process in eukaryotic cells in which the nuclear material splits to form two new nuclei.

6. Active transport requires the cell to use energy to move substances. Passive transport does not require the cell to use any energy.

7. Cellular respiration releases stored energy by using oxygen. Fermentation releases stored energy without using oxygen.

Understanding Key Ideas

8. c

9. a

10. d

11. c

USING KEY TERMS

1 Use the following terms in the same sentence: *diffusion* and *osmosis*.

2 In your own words, write a definition for each of the following terms: *exocytosis* and *endocytosis*.

Complete each of the following sentences by choosing the correct term from the word bank.

> cellular respiration
> photosynthesis
> fermentation

3 Plants use ___ to make glucose.

4 During ___, oxygen is used to break down food molecules releasing large amounts of energy.

For each pair of terms, explain how the meanings of the terms differ.

5 *cytokinesis* and *mitosis*

6 *active transport* and *passive transport*

7 *cellular respiration* and *fermentation*

UNDERSTANDING KEY IDEAS

Multiple Choice

8 The process in which particles move through a membrane from a region of low concentration to a region of high concentration is
- **a.** diffusion.
- **b.** passive transport.
- **c.** active transport.
- **d.** fermentation.

9 What is the result of mitosis and cytokinesis?
- **a.** two identical cells
- **b.** two nuclei
- **c.** chloroplasts
- **d.** two different cells

10 Before the energy in food can be used by a cell, the energy must first be transferred to molecules of
- **a.** proteins.
- **b.** carbohydrates.
- **c.** DNA.
- **d.** ATP.

11 Which of the following cells would form a cell plate during the cell cycle?
- **a.** a human cell
- **b.** a prokaryotic cell
- **c.** a plant cell
- **d.** All of the above

Short Answer

12 Are exocytosis and endocytosis examples of active or passive transport? Explain your answer.

13 Name the cell structures that are needed for photosynthesis and the cell structures that are needed for cellular respiration.

14 Describe the three stages of the cell cycle of a eukaryotic cell.

12. Endocytosis and exocytosis are examples of active transport. In both processes the cell must change shape, wrap around a particle, and make other movements that require the cell to use energy.

13. Chloroplasts are needed for photosynthesis. Cellular respiration requires mitochondria.

14. The first stage is cell growth and copying of DNA (duplication). The second stage is mitosis, which involves separating the duplicated chromosomes. The third stage is cytokinesis (cell division), which results in two separate, identical cells.

CRITICAL THINKING

15. Concept Mapping Use the following terms to create a concept map: *chromosome duplication, cytokinesis, prokaryote, mitosis, cell cycle, binary fission,* and *eukaryote.*

16. Making Inferences Which one of the plants pictured below was given water mixed with salt, and which one was given pure water? Explain how you know, and be sure to use the word *osmosis* in your answer.

17. Identifying Relationships Why would your muscle cells need to be supplied with more food when there is a lack of oxygen than when there is plenty of oxygen present?

18. Applying Concepts A parent cell has 10 chromosomes.

  a. Will the cell go through binary fission or mitosis and cytokinesis to produce new cells?

  b. How many chromosomes will each new cell have after the parent cell divides?

INTERPRETING GRAPHICS

The picture below shows a cell. Use the picture below to answer the questions that follow.

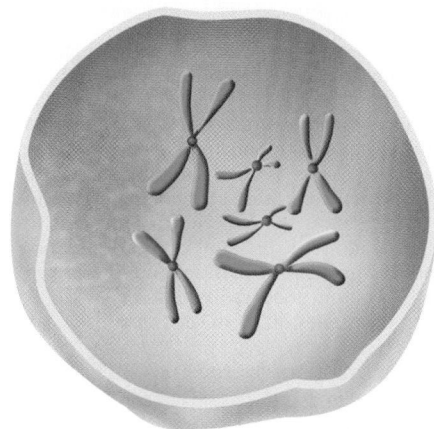

19 Is the cell prokaryotic or eukaryotic?

20 Which stage of the cell cycle is this cell in?

21 How many chromatids are present? How many pairs of homologous chromosomes are present?

22 How many chromosomes will be present in each of the new cells after the cell divides?

Critical Thinking

15. An answer to this exercise can be found at the end of this book.

16. The plant on the left was given pure water. The plant on the right was given salt water. Osmosis occurred in both plants. In the plant on the right, water moved into the plant because the concentration of water was lower in the plant than in the soil. So, the plant on the right did not wilt. In the plant on the left, the water in the plant moved into the soil, where the concentration of water was lower. The concentration of water in the soil was lower because the water contained salt. As a result, the plant on the left wilted.

17. When there is plenty of oxygen, the cells can get energy from cellular respiration. When there is a lack of oxygen, the cells must use fermentation, which doesn't produce as much energy. For fermentation to produce more energy, more food would be required.

18. a. The cell is a eukaryotic cell and will go through mitosis and cytokinesis. Prokaryotic cells have only one chromosome.

  b. Each new cell will receive a copy of each chromosome, so each new cell will have 10 chromosomes.

Interpreting Graphics

19. The cell is eukaryotic because it shows chromatids held together at a centromere. Prokaryotic cells do not have chromatids.

20. The cell is in mitosis because the chromosomes have already duplicated.

21. There are 12 chromatids. There are three pairs of homologous chromosomes.

22. There will be six chromosomes in each new cell.

CHAPTER RESOURCES

Chapter Resource File

- Chapter Review GENERAL
- Chapter Test A GENERAL
- Chapter Test B ADVANCED
- Chapter Test C SPECIAL NEEDS
- Vocabulary Activity GENERAL

Workbooks

Study Guide
• Assessment resources are also available in Spanish.

Teacher's Note

To provide practice under more realistic testing conditions, give students 20 minutes to answer all of the questions in this Standardized Test Preparation.

MISCONCEPTION ALERT

Answers to the standardized test preparation can help you identify student misconceptions and misunderstandings.

READING

Passage 1
1. C
2. G
3. A

➕ **TEST DOCTOR**

Question 1: Students may choose wrong answers A and B if they mistakenly read the passage to say that burning a log is the same as the release of energy in a cell during cellular respiration.

Question 3: Students may choose wrong answer B if they already know that heat is released during cellular respiration. While this may be true, the information is not contained anywhere in this passage. The correct answer, based on the passage, is A.

READING

Read each of the passages below. Then, answer the questions that follow each passage.

Passage 1 Perhaps you have heard that jogging or some other kind of exercise "burns" a lot of Calories. The word *burn* is often used to describe what happens when your cells release stored energy from food. The burning of food in living cells is not the same as the burning of logs in a campfire. When logs burn, the energy stored in wood is released as thermal energy and light in a single reaction. But this kind of reaction is not the kind that happens in cells. Instead, the energy that cells get from food molecules is released at each step of a series of chemical reactions.

1. According to the passage, how do cells release energy from food?
   A in a single reaction
   B as thermal energy and light
   C in a series of reactions
   D by burning

2. Which of the following statements is a fact in the passage?
   F Wood burns better than food does.
   G Both food and wood have stored energy.
   H Food has more stored energy than wood does.
   I When it is burned, wood releases only thermal energy.

3. According to the passage, why might people be confused between what happens in a living cell and what happens in a campfire?
   A The word *burn* may describe both processes.
   B Thermal energy is released during both processes.
   C Wood can be burned and broken down by living cells.
   D Jogging and other exercises use energy.

Passage 2 The word *respiration* means "breathing," but cellular respiration is different from breathing. Breathing supplies your cells with the oxygen that they need for cellular respiration. Breathing also rids your body of carbon dioxide, which is a waste product of cellular respiration. Cellular respiration is the chemical process that releases energy from food. Most organisms obtain energy from food through cellular respiration. During cellular respiration, oxygen is used to break down food (glucose) into CO_2 and H_2O, and energy is released. In humans, most of the energy released is used to maintain body temperature.

1. According to the passage, what is glucose?
   A a type of chemical process
   B a type of waste product
   C a type of organism
   D a type of food

2. According to the passage, how does cellular respiration differ from breathing?
   F Breathing releases carbon dioxide, but cellular respiration releases oxygen.
   G Cellular respiration is a chemical process that uses oxygen to release energy from food, but breathing supplies cells with oxygen.
   H Cellular respiration requires oxygen, but breathing does not.
   I Breathing rids your body of waste products, but cellular respiration stores wastes.

3. According to the passage, how do humans use most of the energy released?
   A to break down food
   B to obtain oxygen
   C to maintain body temperature
   D to get rid of carbon dioxide

Passage 2
1. D
2. G
3. C

➕ **TEST DOCTOR**

Question 2: Students may choose wrong answer F if they mistakenly read the passage to say that cellular respiration "releases" oxygen instead of "requires" oxygen. Cellular respiration releases carbon dioxide and water.

Question 3: The passage talks about the release of energy from food. Students may choose wrong answer A if they mistakenly read the passage to say that most of the energy is used to break down food. Most of the food energy is used to maintain body temperature.

The graph below shows the cell cycle. Use this graph to answer the questions that follow.

The Cell Cycle

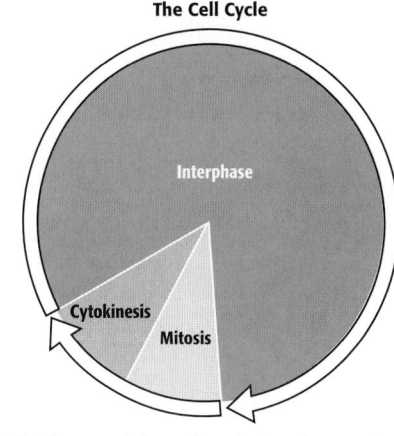

1. Which part of the cell cycle lasts longest?
   A interphase
   B mitosis
   C cytokinesis
   D There is not enough information to determine the answer.

2. Which of the following lists the parts of the cell cycle in the proper order?
   F mitosis, cytokinesis, mitosis
   G interphase, cytokinesis, mitosis
   H interphase, mitosis, interphase
   I mitosis, cytokinesis, interphase

3. Which part of the cell cycle is the briefest?
   A interphase
   B cell division
   C cytokinesis
   D There is not enough information to determine the answer.

4. Why is the cell cycle represented by a circle?
   F The cell cycle is a continuous process that begins again after it finishes.
   G The cell cycle happens only in cells that are round.
   H The cell cycle is a linear process.
   I The cell is in interphase for more than half of the cell cycle.

Read each question below, and choose the best answer.

1. A normal cell spends 90% of its time in interphase. How is 90% expressed as a fraction?
   A 3/4
   B 4/5
   C 85/100
   D 9/10

2. If a cell lived for 3 weeks and 4 days, how many days did it live?
   F 7
   G 11
   H 21
   I 25

3. How is $2 \times 3 \times 3 \times 3 \times 3$ expressed in exponential notation?
   A 3×2^4
   B 2×3^3
   C 3^4
   D 2×3^4

4. Cell A has 3 times as many chromosomes as cell B has. After cell B's chromosomes double during mitosis, cell B has 6 chromosomes. How many chromosomes does cell A have?
   F 3
   G 6
   H 9
   I 18

5. If $x + 2 = 3$, what does $x + 1$ equal?
   A 4
   B 3
   C 2
   D 1

6. If $3x + 2 = 26$, what does $x + 1$ equal?
   F 7
   G 8
   H 9
   I 10

Standardized Test Preparation

1. A
2. I
3. D
4. F

 TEST DOCTOR

Question 2: Students may select incorrect answers F and H if they follow the arrow but skip a step on the graph. They may select incorrect answer G if they ignore the direction of the arrow. Only answer I has the steps of the cell cycle in proper sequence.

1. D
2. I
3. D
4. H
5. C
6. H

 **TEST DOCTOR**

Question 4: Students may have trouble converting this word problem into a numerical statement because they may confuse what is happening to cell B (its chromosomes are doubling in number to 6, which means that it starts with 3) with what is happening to cell A (nothing). Students may select incorrect answer I because 3 times 6 is 18. Students who are struggling may want to create a small data table that shows what they "know" (the information given in the word problem) and what they are trying to find out (what the question asks). Word problems are a challenge for many students, and often a table or chart will help them keep the information straight.

CHAPTER RESOURCES

Chapter Resource File

 • Standardized Test Preparation GENERAL

State Resources

 For specific resources for your state, visit **go.hrw.com** and type in the keyword **HSMSTR**.

Scientific Discovery

Background

The release of energy from food is called *cellular respiration.* Cellular respiration takes place in two stages. The end result of the process is that energy is stored in the cell in the form of ATP (adenosine triphosphate) molecules.

In the microbial battery, scientists harvest some of this energy and transfer it into electricity that can be readily used.

One of the benefits of the microbial battery is its ability to make use of waste products. Ask students to consider the effect this might have on the energy demands of nations that have limited access to fossil fuels.

Science Fiction

Teaching Strategy— BASIC

This is a relatively long story, containing quite a few medical terms. Students may find it easier to read if the class discusses some of the unfamiliar terms before they start reading the story.

Science in Action

HOLT ANTHOLOGY OF
Science
Fiction

HOLT, RINEHART AND WINSTON

Scientific Discoveries

Electrifying News About Microbes

Your car is out of fuel, and there isn't a service station in sight. This is not a problem! Your car's motor runs on electricity supplied by trillions of microorganisms. Some chemists think that "living" batteries will someday operate everything from watches to entire cities. A group of scientists at King's College in London have demonstrated that microorganisms can convert food into usable electrical energy. The microorganisms convert foods such as table sugar and molasses most efficiently. An efficient microorganism can convert more than 90% of its food into compounds that will fuel an electric reaction. A less efficient microbe will only convert 50% of its food into these types of compounds.

Math ACTIVITY

An efficient microorganism converts 90% of its food into fuel compounds, and an inefficient microorganism converts only 50%. If the inefficient microorganism makes 60 g of fuel out of a possible 120 g of food, how much fuel would an efficient microorganism make out of the same amount of food?

Science Fiction

"Contagion" by Katherine MacLean

A quarter mile from their spaceship, the *Explorer,* a team of doctors walk carefully along a narrow forest trail. Around them, the forest looks like a forest on Earth in the fall—the leaves are green, copper, purple, and fiery red. But it isn't fall. And the team is not on Earth.

Minos is enough like Earth to be the home of another colony of humans. But Minos might also be home to unknown organisms that could cause severe illness or death among the crew of *Explorer*. These diseases might be enough like diseases on Earth to be contagious, but they might be different enough to be very difficult to treat.

Something large moves among the shadows—it looks like a man. What happens next? Read Katherine's MacLean's "Contagion" in the *Holt Anthology of Science Fiction* to find out.

Language Arts ACTIVITY

WRITING SKILL Write two to three paragraphs that describe what you think might happen next in the story.

Answer to Math Activity

An efficient microbe converts 90% of its food to fuel compounds; 90% of 120 g is 108 g of fuel compounds.

Answer to Language Arts Activity

Students' predictions will vary. Whatever a student predicts, the prediction should be reasonably related to the information that the student has from reading this introductory paragraph.

Careers

Jerry Yakel

Neuroscientist Jerry Yakel credits a sea slug for making him a neuroscientist. In a college class studying neurons, or nerve cells, Yakel got to see firsthand how ions move across the cell membrane of *Aplysia californica,* also known as a sea hare. He says, "I was totally hooked. I knew that I wanted to be a neurophysiologist then and there. I haven't wavered since."

Today, Yakel is a senior investigator for the National Institutes of Environmental Health Sciences, which is part of the U.S. government's National Institutes of Health. "We try to understand how the normal brain works," says Yakel of his team. "Then, when we look at a diseased brain, we train to understand where the deficits are. Eventually, someone will have an idea about a drug that will tweak the system in this or that way."

Yakel studies the ways in which nicotine affects the human brain. "It is one of the most prevalent and potent neurotoxins in the environment," says Yakel. "I'm amazed that it isn't higher on the list of worries for the general public."

Social Studies ACTiViTY

WRITING SKILL Research a famous or historical figure in science. Write a short report that outlines how he or she became interested in science.

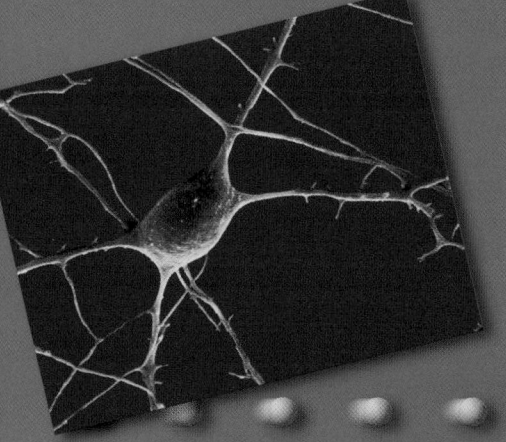

To learn more about these Science in Action topics, visit **go.hrw.com** and type in the keyword **HL5ACTF.**

Current Science

Check out Current Science® articles related to this chapter by visiting go.hrw.com. Just type in the keyword **HL5CS04.**

Answer to Social Studies Activity

Students may write about any historical figure in science. Some students may go back as far as Archimedes; others may choose Hypatia (the first woman to be a true astronomer), Benjamin Franklin, Marie Curie, Albert Einstein, Rosalind Franklin, or one of hundreds of other people. The important issues for the student are why the person is important to science and how the person became interested in science.

Careers

Background

Jerry Yakel grew up in Ventura County, California. After graduating from high school, he attended a nearby community college "ostensibly to continue running track, figuring out life." Eventually, he relocated to Oregon State University, where he obtained a B.S. in 1982. He was accepted into UCLA in 1983 and received a Ph.D. in 1988.

Working for the NIH was not something Yakel originally expected to do. "Most of us trained in universities think we will work there," he says. He does enjoy some aspects of being outside the typical university setting. "In the NIH, we are supposed to take more risks in our research." He also enjoys the focus he is able to bring to his work. "I miss having students to teach, but then again I get to spend more time doing research," Yakel says. His choice of environment hasn't affected his passion. "Honestly, the type of research I [would] do actually is the same."

UNIT 3

TIMELINE

Heredity, Evolution, and Classification

The differences and similarities between living things are the subject of this unit. You will learn how characteristics are passed from one generation to another, how living things are classified based on their characteristics, and how these characteristics help living things survive.

Scientists have not always understood these topics, and there is still much to be learned. This timeline will give you an idea of some things that have been learned so far.

1753

Carolus Linnaeus publishes the first of two volumes containing the classification of all known species.

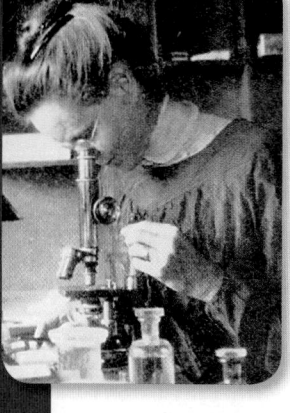

1905

Nettie Stevens describes how human gender is determined by the X and Y chromosomes.

1930

The planet Pluto is discovered.

1969

Apollo 11 lands on the moon. Neil Armstrong becomes the first person to walk on the lunar surface.

1859

Charles Darwin suggests that natural selection is a mechanism of evolution.

1860

Abraham Lincoln is elected the 16th president of the United States.

1865

Gregor Mendel publishes the results of his studies of genetic inheritance in pea plants.

1951

Rosalind Franklin photographs DNA.

1953

James Watson and Francis Crick figure out the structure of DNA.

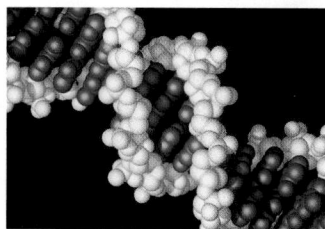

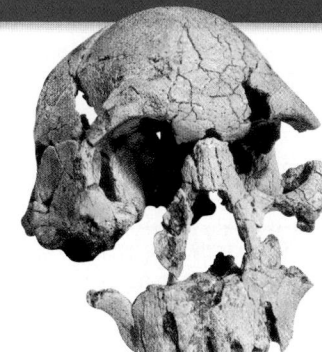

1960

Mary and Jonathan Leakey discover fossil bones of the human ancestor *Homo habilis* in Olduvai Gorge, Tanzania.

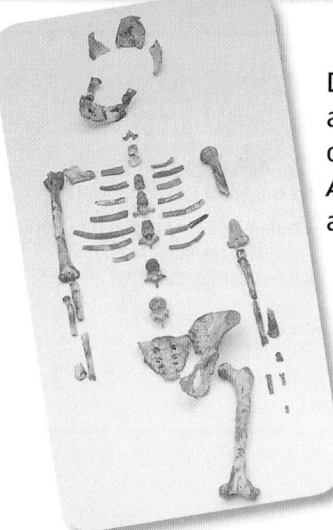

1974

Donald Johanson discovers a fossilized skeleton of one of the first hominids, *Australopithecus afarensis*, also called "Lucy."

1990

Ashanti DeSilva's white blood cells are genetically engineered to treat her immune deficiency disease.

2003

The Human Genome Project is completed. Scientists spent 13 years mapping out the 3 billion DNA subunits of chromosomes.

Compression guide:
To shorten instruction
because of time limitations,
omit the Chapter Lab.

OBJECTIVES	LABS, DEMONSTRATIONS, AND ACTIVITIES	TECHNOLOGY RESOURCES
PACING • 90 min pp. 112–119 **Chapter Opener**	SE **Start-up Activity**, p. 113 ◆ (GENERAL)	OSP **Parent Letter** ■ (GENERAL) CD **Student Edition on CD-ROM** CD **Guided Reading Audio CD** ■ TR **Chapter Starter Transparency*** VID **Brain Food Video Quiz**
Section 1 Mendel and His Peas • Explain the relationship between traits and heredity. • Describe the experiments of Gregor Mendel. • Explain the difference between dominant and recessive traits.	TE **Activity** Trait Trends, p. 114 (GENERAL) SE **School-to-Home Activity** Describing Traits, p. 115 (GENERAL) TE **Demonstration** Flower Dissection, p. 116 ◆ (BASIC) TE **Activity** Mendelian Crosses, p. 116 (ADVANCED) SE **Science in Action** Math, Science, and Social Studies Activities, pp. 140-141 (GENERAL)	CRF **Lesson Plans*** TR **Bellringer Transparency*** CRF **SciLinks Activity*** (GENERAL)
PACING • 90 min pp. 120–125 **Section 2 Traits and Inheritance** • Explain how genes and alleles are related to genotype and phenotype. • Use the information in a Punnett square. • Explain how probability can be used to predict possible genotypes in offspring. • Describe three exceptions to Mendel's observations.	TE **Demonstration**, p. 120 ◆ (BASIC) SE **Quick Lab** Making a Punnett Square, p. 121 (GENERAL) CRF **Datasheet for Quick Lab*** SE **Quick Lab** Taking Your Chances, p. 122 ◆ (GENERAL) CRF **Datasheet for Quick Lab*** TE **Connection Activity** Math, p. 122 (ADVANCED) SE **Connection to Chemistry** Round and Wrinkled, p. 123 (GENERAL) SE **Model-Making Lab** Bug Builders, Inc., p. 134 ◆ (GENERAL) CRF **Datasheet for Chapter Lab***	CRF **Lesson Plans*** TR **Bellringer Transparency*** TR **Punnett Squares** TR **LINK TO PHYSICAL SCIENCE** The Periodic Table of the Elements*** VID **Lab Videos for Life Science**
PACING • 45 min pp. 126–133 **Section 3 Meiosis** • Explain the difference between mitosis and meiosis. • Describe how chromosomes determine sex. • Explain why sex-linked disorders occur in one sex more often than in the other. • Interpret a pedigree.	TE **Activity** Crosses, p. 126 (GENERAL) TE **Connection Activity** Math, p. 126 (ADVANCED) TE **Activity** Describing Meiosis, p. 129 (BASIC) TE **Connection Activity** Math, p. 129 (GENERAL) TE **Group Activity** Comparing Mitosis and Meiosis, p. 130 (GENERAL) TE **Connection Activity** Language Arts, p. 131 (ADVANCED) SE **Inquiry Lab** Tracing Traits, p. 767 (GENERAL) CRF **Datasheet for LabBook*** LB **Long-Term Projects & Research Ideas** Portrait of a Dog* (ADVANCED)	CRF **Lesson Plans*** TR **Bellringer Transparency*** TR **The Steps of Meiosis: A*** TR **The Steps of Meiosis: B*** TR **Meiosis and Dominance*** TE **Internet Activity**, p.133 (GENERAL)

PACING • 90 min

CHAPTER REVIEW, ASSESSMENT, AND STANDARDIZED TEST PREPARATION

CRF **Vocabulary Activity*** (GENERAL)
SE **Chapter Review**, pp. 136–137 (GENERAL)
CRF **Chapter Review*** ■ (GENERAL)
CRF **Chapter Tests A*** (GENERAL), **B*** (ADVANCED), **C*** (SPECIAL NEEDS)
SE **Standardized Test Preparation**, pp. 138–139 (GENERAL)
CRF **Standardized Test Preparation*** (GENERAL)
CRF **Performance-Based Assessment*** (GENERAL)
OSP **Test Generator** (GENERAL)
CRF **Test Item Listing*** (GENERAL)

Online and Technology Resources

Visit **go.hrw.com** for a variety of free resources related to this textbook. Enter the keyword **HL5HER**.

Holt Online Learning

Students can access interactive problem-solving help and active visual concept development with the *Holt Science and Technology* Online Edition available at **www.hrw.com**.

 Guided Reading Audio CD Also in Spanish

A direct reading of each chapter for auditory learners, reluctant readers, and Spanish-speaking students.

 Science Tutor CD-ROM

Excellent for remediation and test practice.

SKILLS DEVELOPMENT RESOURCES	SECTION REVIEW AND ASSESSMENT	STANDARDS CORRELATIONS
SE Pre-Reading Activity, p. 112 GENERAL **OSP** Science Puzzlers, Twisters & Teasers* GENERAL		National Science Education Standards UCP 2, 3; LS 1d, 2c
CRF Directed Reading A* ■ BASIC, B* SPECIAL NEEDS **CRF** Vocabulary and Section Summary* ■ GENERAL **SE** Reading Strategy Brainstorming, p. 114 GENERAL **SE** Math Practice Understanding Ratios, p. 118 GENERAL **TE** Reading Strategy Paired Reading, p. 115 BASIC **TE** Inclusion Strategies, p. 117 ◆ **MS** Math Skills for Science What Is a Ratio?* GENERAL **SS** Science Skills Finding Useful Sources* GENERAL **CRF** Critical Thinking A Bittersweet Solution* ADVANCED	**SE** Reading Checks, pp. 114, 117, 118 GENERAL **TE** Reteaching, p. 118 BASIC **TE** Quiz, p. 118 GENERAL **TE** Alternative Assessment, p. 118 ADVANCED **SE** Section Review,* p. 119 ■ GENERAL **TE** Homework, p. 119 GENERAL **CRF** Section Quiz* ■ GENERAL	UCP 1, 2; SAI 1, 2; ST 2; SPSP 5; HNS 1, H2, 3; LS 2b, 2e; *Chapter Lab:* SAI 1; HNS 2; LS 2c, 2e; *LabBook:* UCP 2; SAI 1; HNS 2; LS 2b, 2c, 2e
CRF Directed Reading A* ■ BASIC, B* SPECIAL NEEDS **CRF** Vocabulary and Section Summary* ■ GENERAL **SE** Reading Strategy Paired Summarizing, p. 120 GENERAL **SE** Math Focus Probability, p. 123 GENERAL **MS** Math Skills for Science Punnett Square Popcorn* GENERAL **CRF** Reinforcement Worksheet Dimples and DNA* BASIC	**SE** Reading Checks, pp. 120, 122, 124 GENERAL **TE** Homework, p. 123 GENERAL **TE** Reteaching, p. 124 BASIC **TE** Quiz, p. 124 GENERAL **TE** Alternative Assessment, p. 125 GENERAL **SE** Section Review,* p. 125 ■ GENERAL **CRF** Section Quiz* ■ GENERAL	UCP 2, 3; LS 2a, 2b, 2c, 2d, 2e
CRF Directed Reading A* ■ BASIC, B* SPECIAL NEEDS **CRF** Vocabulary and Section Summary* ■ GENERAL **SE** Reading Strategy Reading Organizer, p. 126 GENERAL **SE** Connection to Language Arts Greek Roots, p. 127 GENERAL **TE** Reading Strategy Prediction Guide, p. 128 GENERAL **TE** Inclusion Strategies, p. 130 **CRF** Reinforcement Worksheet Vocabulary Garden* BASIC	**SE** Reading Checks, pp. 127, 128 GENERAL **TE** Reteaching, p. 132 BASIC **TE** Quiz, p. 132 GENERAL **TE** Alternative Assessment, p. 132 GENERAL **TE** Homework, p. 132 ADVANCED **SE** Section Review,* p. 133 ■ GENERAL **CRF** Section Quiz* ■ GENERAL	UCP 4, 5; SAI 1; SPSP 5; HNS 2, 3; LS 1c, 1d, 2a, 2b, 2c, 2d

One-Stop Planner® CD-ROM

This convenient CD-ROM includes:
- **Lab Materials QuickList Software**
- **Holt Calendar Planner**
- **Customizable Lesson Plans**
- **Printable Worksheets**
- **ExamView® Test Generator**

cnnstudentnews.com

Find the latest news, lesson plans, and activities related to important scientific events.

www.scilinks.org

Maintained by the **National Science Teachers Association.** See Chapter Enrichment pages for a complete list of topics.

Current Science®

Check out *Current Science* articles and activities by visiting the HRW Web site at **go.hrw.com.** Just type in the keyword **HL5CS05T.**

 Classroom Videos

- **Lab Videos** demonstrate the chapter lab.
- **Brain Food Video Quizzes** help students review the chapter material.
- **CNN Videos** bring science into your students' daily life.

Visual Resources

CHAPTER STARTER TRANSPARENCY

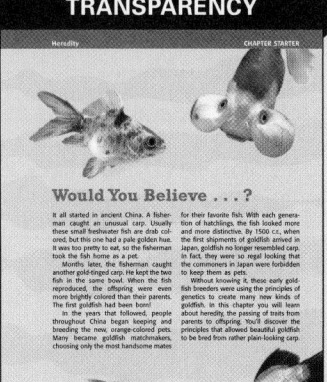

BELLRINGER TRANSPARENCIES

Section: Mendel and His Peas
You have probably noticed that different people have different characteristics, such as eye color, hair color, or whether or not their ear lobes attach directly to their head or hang down loosely. These characteristics are called traits. Where do you think people get these different traits? How do you think they are passed from one generation to the next?

Write your answers in your **science journal.**

Section: Traits and Inheritance
If you flip a coin, what are the chances that it will land on heads? tails? Suppose that you flip the coin, get heads, and then flip again. What are the chances that you will get heads again? What are the chances you will get heads two times in a row? five times?

Record your answers in your **science journal.**

TEACHING TRANSPARENCIES

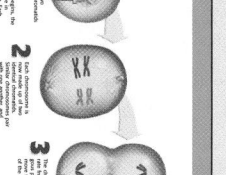

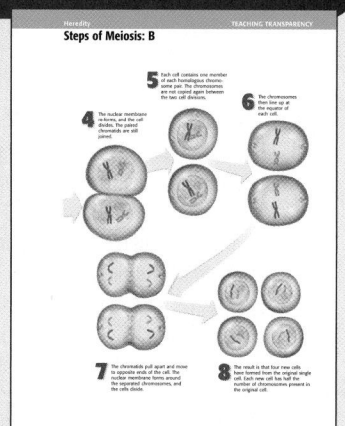

TEACHING TRANSPARENCIES

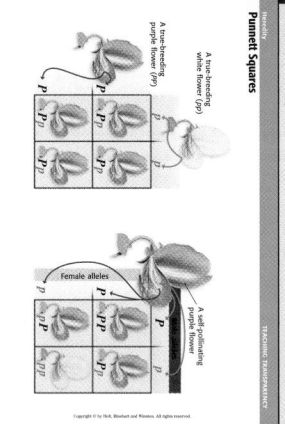

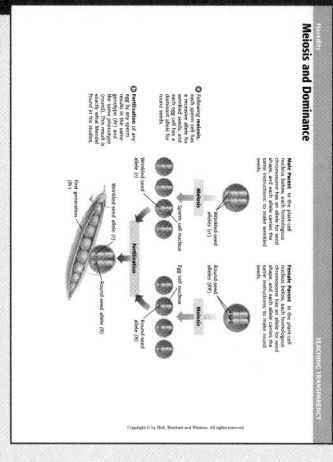

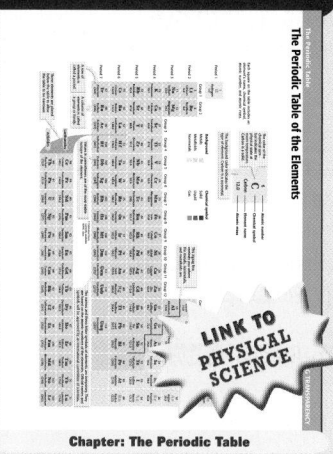

CONCEPT MAPPING TRANSPARENCY

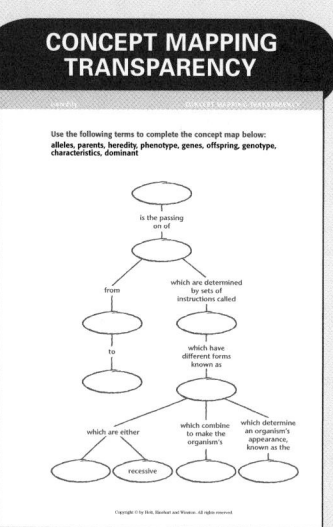

Planning Resources

LESSON PLANS

Lesson Plan   SAMPLE

Section: Waves

Pacing
Regular Schedule: with labs\:2 days   without labs\:2 days
Block Schedule: with labs\:1 1/2 days   without labs\:1 day

Objectives
1. Relate the seven properties of life to a living organism.
2. Describe seven themes that can help you to organize what you learn about biology.
3. Identify the tiny structures that make up all living organisms.
4. Differentiate between reproduction and heredity and between metabolism and homeostasis.

National Science Education Standards Covered
LSInter1:Cells have particular structures that underlie their functions.
LSMat1:Most cell functions involve chemical reactions.
LSBeh1:Cells store and use information to guide their functions.
UCP1:Cell functions are regulated.
SI1: Cells can differentiate and form complete multicellular organisms.
PS1: Species evolve over time.
ESS1: The great diversity of organisms is the result of more than 3.5 billion years of evolution.
ESS2: Natural selection and its evolutionary consequences provide a scientific explanation for the fossil record of ancient life as well as for the striking molecular similarities observed among the diverse species of living organisms.
ST1: The millions of different species of plants, animals, and microorganisms that live on Earth today are related by descent from common ancestors.
ST2: The energy for life primarily comes from the sun.
SPSP1: The complexity and organization of organisms accommodates the need for obtaining, transforming, transporting, releasing, and eliminating the matter and energy used to sustain the organism.
SPSP6: As matter and energy flows through different levels of organization of living systems—cells, organs, communities—and between living systems and the physical environment, chemical elements are recombined in different ways.
HNS1: Organisms have behavioral responses to internal changes and to external stimuli.

PARENT LETTER

SAMPLE

Dear Parent,

Your son's or daughter's science class will soon begin exploring the chapter entitled "The World of Physical Science." In this chapter, students will learn about how the scientific method applies to the world of physical science and the role of physical science in the world. By the end of the chapter, students should demonstrate a clear understanding of the chapter's main ideas and be able to discuss the following topics:

1. physical science as the study of energy and matter (Section 1)
2. the role of physical science in the world around them (Section 1)
3. careers that rely on physical science (Section 1)
4. the steps used in the scientific method (Section 2)
5. examples of technology (Section 2)
6. how the scientific method is used to answer questions and solve problems (Section 2)
7. how our knowledge of science changes over time (Section 2)
8. how models represent real objects or systems (Section 3)
9. examples of different ways models are used in science (Section 3)
10. the importance of the International System of Units (Section 4)
11. the appropriate units to use for particular measurements (Section 4)
12. how area and density are derived quantities (Section 4)

Questions to Ask Along the Way

You can help your son or daughter learn about these topics by asking interesting questions such as the following:

• What are some surprising careers that use physical science?
• What is a characteristic of a good hypothesis?
• When is it a good idea to use a model?
• Why do Americans measure things in terms of inches and yards and meters ?

ALSO IN SPANISH

TEST ITEM LISTING

TEST ITEM LISTING
The World of Science   SAMPLE

MULTIPLE CHOICE
1. A limitation of models is that
   a. they are large enough to see.
   b. they do not act exactly like the things that they model.
   c. they are smaller than the things that they model.
   d. they model unfamiliar things.
   Answer: B   Difficulty: 1   Section: 3   Objective: 2
2. The length 10 m is equal to
   a. 100 cm.   c. 10,000 mm.
   b. 1,000 cm.   d. Both (b) and (c)
   Answer: B   Difficulty: 1   Section: 3   Objective: 2
3. To be valid, a hypothesis must be
   a. testable.   c. made into a law
   b. supported by evidence.   d. Both (a) and (b)
   Answer: D   Difficulty: 1   Section: 3   Objective: 2
4. The statement "Sheila has a stain on her shirt" is an example of a(n)
   a. law.   c. observation.
   b. hypothesis.   d. prediction.
   Answer: B   Difficulty: 1   Section: 1   Objective: 2
5. A hypothesis is often developed out of
   a. observations.   c. laws.
   b. experiments.   d. Both (a) and (b)
   Answer: B   Difficulty: 1   Section: 3   Objective: 2
6. How many milliliters are in 3.5 kL?
   a. 3,500 mL   c. 3,500, 000 mL
   b. 0.0035 mL   d. 35,000 mL.
   Answer: B   Difficulty: 1   Section: 3   Objective: 2
7. A model of a beetle is an example of a
   a. law.   c. model.
   b. theory.   d. unit.
   Answer: B   Difficulty: 1   Section: 3   Objective: 2
8. A lab has the safety icons shown below. These icons mean that you should wear
   a. only safety goggles.   c. safety goggles and a lab apron.
   b. only a lab apron.   d. safety goggles, a lab apron, and gloves.
   Answer: B   Difficulty: 1   Section: 3   Objective: 2
9. The law of conservation of mass says that the total mass before a chemical change is
   a. more than the total mass after the change.
   b. less than the total mass after the change.
   c. the same as the total mass after the change.
   d. not the same as the total mass after the change.
   Answer: B   Difficulty: 1   Section: 3   Objective: 2
10. In which of the following areas might you find a geochemist at work?
    a. studying the chemistry of rocks   c. studying fishes
    b. studying forests   d. studying the atmosphere
    Answer: B   Difficulty: 1   Section: 3   Objective: 2

One-Stop Planner® CD-ROM

This CD-ROM includes all of the resources shown here and the following time-saving tools:

• *Lab Materials QuickList Software*

• *Customizable lesson plans*

• *Holt Calendar Planner*

• *The powerful ExamView® Test Generator*

Meeting Individual Needs

DIRECTED READING A
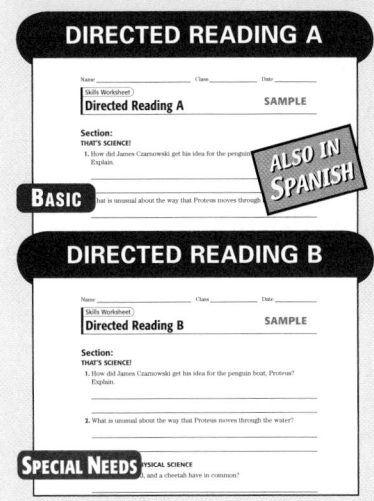

DIRECTED READING B

VOCABULARY ACTIVITY
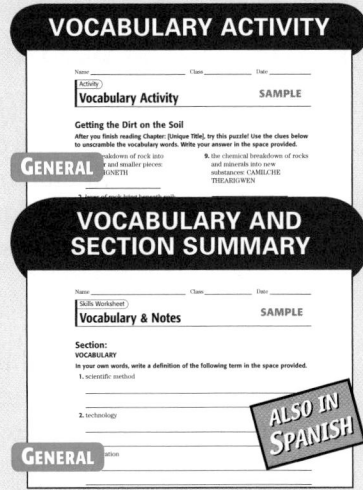

VOCABULARY AND SECTION SUMMARY

REINFORCEMENT
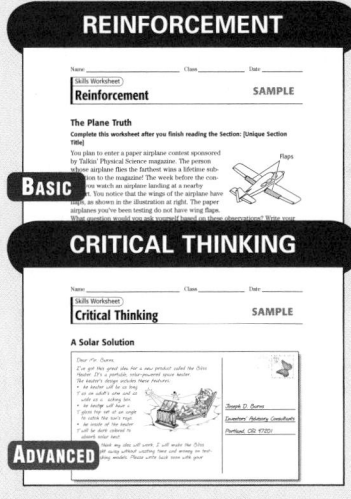

CRITICAL THINKING

SCILINKS ACTIVITY
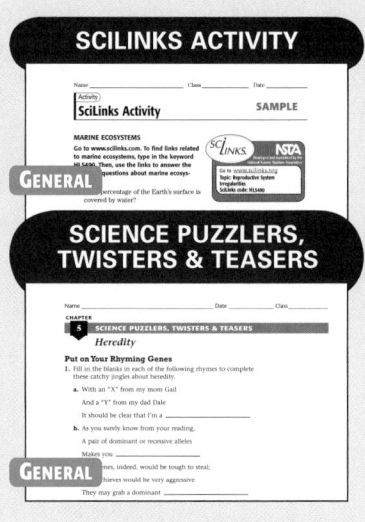

SCIENCE PUZZLERS, TWISTERS & TEASERS

Labs and Activities

LONG-TERM PROJECTS & RESEARCH IDEAS
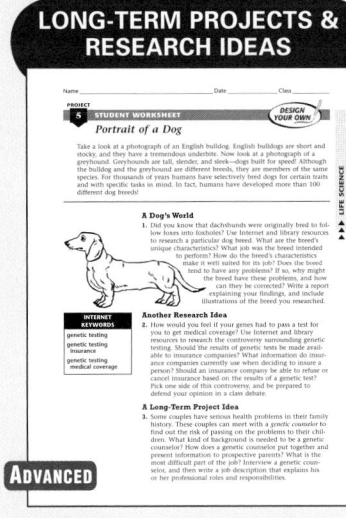

DATASHEETS FOR QUICK LABS
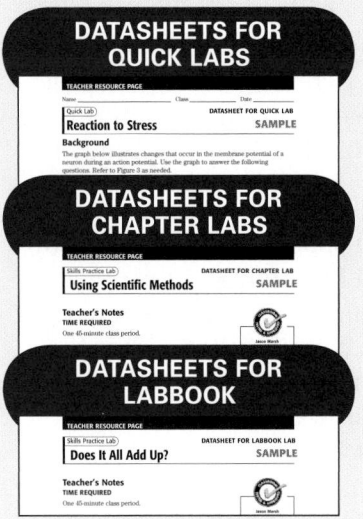

DATASHEETS FOR CHAPTER LABS

DATASHEETS FOR LABBOOK

Review and Assessments

SECTION QUIZ

SECTION REVIEW

CHAPTER REVIEW
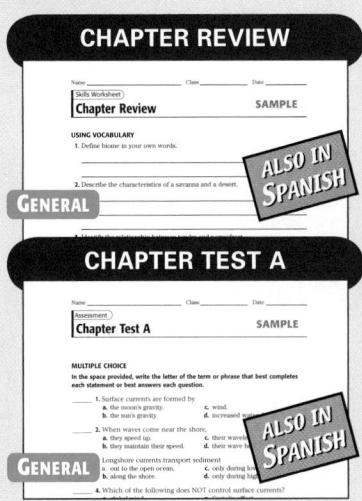

CHAPTER TEST A

CHAPTER TEST B
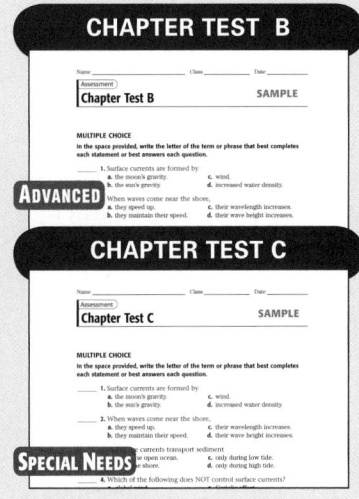

CHAPTER TEST C

STANDARDIZED TEST PREPARATION
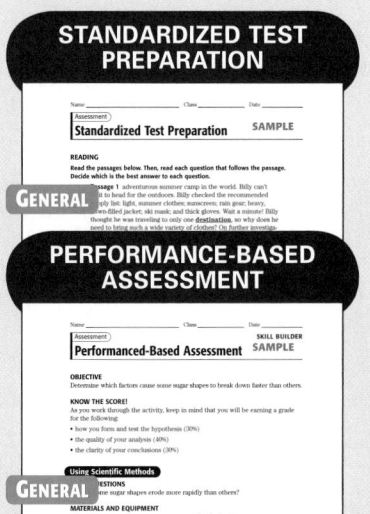

PERFORMANCE-BASED ASSESSMENT

This Chapter Enrichment provides relevant and interesting information to expand and enhance your presentation of the chapter material.

Section 1

Mendel and His Peas

Gregor Mendel

- In 1843, in the city of Brünn, Austria (which is now Brno, a city in the Czech Republic), Gregor Mendel (1822–1884) entered a monastery. In 1865, Mendel published the results of his garden-pea experiments. Although Mendel's ideas are widespread today, few scientists learned of his work during his lifetime because there were few ways to distribute information. Mendel presented his findings in two lectures, and only 40 copies of his work were printed in his lifetime.

- When Mendel was elected abbot of the monastery in 1868, his duties prevented him from visiting other scientists or attending conferences where he could have discussed his results. Not until 1900, when Mendel's work was rediscovered by scientists in Holland, Germany, and Austria-Hungary, were his theories spread through the scientific community.

- Mendel's work was used to support Darwin's theory of evolution by natural selection and is considered to be the foundation of modern genetics. Mendel also made contributions to beekeeping, horticulture, and meteorology. In 1877, Mendel became interested in weather and began issuing weather reports to local farmers.

Is That a Fact!
- From 1856 to 1863, while studying inheritance, Mendel grew almost 30,000 pea plants!

Section 2

Traits and Inheritance

Punnett and His Squares

- Punnett squares are named after their inventor, R. C. Punnett. Punnett explored inheritance by crossing different breeds of chickens in the early 1900s, soon after Mendel's work was rediscovered.

Pollination

- Pollen can be transferred between plants by wind, insects, and a variety of animals. Some common pollinators are bees, butterflies, moths, flies, bats, and birds. Animals are attracted to the color of the flower, the patterns found on the petals, or the flower's fragrance. Pollen is an excellent food for some animals.

Is That a Fact!
- Male bees have only half the number of chromosomes that female bees have.

Section 3

Meiosis

Chromosomes

- Chromosomes are composed of genes, the sequences of DNA that provide the instructions for making all the proteins in an organism. During cell division, the duplicated chromosomes separate so that one copy of each chromosome is present in the two new cells.

Walther Flemming

- Walther Flemming (1843–1905), a German physician and anatomist, was the first to use a microscope and special dyes to study cell division. Flemming used the term *mitosis* to describe the process he observed.

Mitosis

- In mitosis, a cell divides to form two identical cells. The steps of the process are similar in almost all living organisms. In addition to enabling growth, mitosis allows organisms to replace cells that have died or malfunctioned. Mitosis can take anywhere from a few minutes to a few hours, and it may be affected by characteristics of the environment, such as light and temperature.

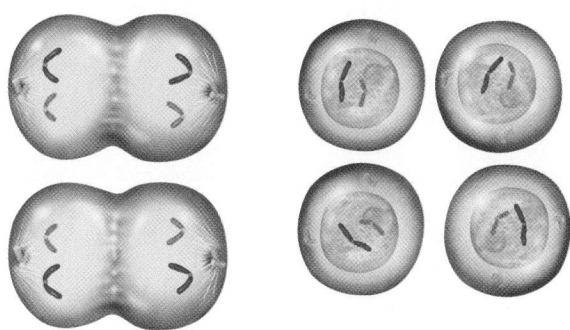

Meiosis

- Meiosis is not the same in all organisms. In humans, meiosis is very different in males and females. In males, meiosis results in four similar sperm cells. In females, however, only one functional egg is produced. The other resulting cells, which are known as *polar bodies,* are formed during the division of the original cell but do not mature.

Genetic Disorders

- A genetic disorder results from an inherited disruption in an organism's DNA. These inherited disruptions can take several forms, including a change in the number of chromosomes and the deletion or duplication of entire chromosomes or parts of chromosomes. Often, the change responsible for a disorder is the alteration of a single specific gene. However, some genetic disorders result from several of these genetic alterations occurring simultaneously. Diseases resulting from these alterations cause a wide variety of physical malfunctions and developmental problems.

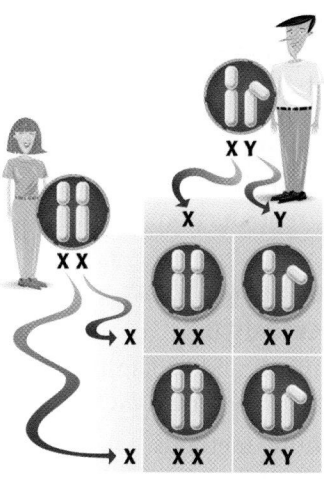

- Cystic fibrosis (CF) is a disease for which one in 31 Americans carries a recessive trait. If two of these people have children together, there is a 25% chance that any child born to them will have the disease. CF affects the intestinal, bronchial, and sweat glands. In people with CF, these glands secrete thick, sticky fluids that are difficult for the body to process, impeding breathing and digestion. Due to improvements in diagnosis and treatment, median life expectancy for those with CF has improved from under 10 years in 1960 to an estimated 40 years for those born in 1990.

- Rubinstein-Taybi syndrome (RTS) is a complex genetic disorder whose characteristics include broad thumbs and toes, mental retardation, and distinctive facial features. This wide range of characteristics is believed to be linked to any one of a number of mutations in a gene responsible for providing the body with a protein called *CBP.* CBP is thought to be vital to the body's delicate metabolism. Because CBP greatly influences body processes, people with a problem producing CBP have a wide range of difficulties. Children with RTS can benefit from proper nutrition and early intervention with therapies and special education.

SCILINKS®

NSTA

Developed and maintained by the National Science Teachers Association

SciLinks is maintained by the National Science Teachers Association to provide you and your students with interesting, up-to-date links that will enrich your classroom presentation of the chapter.

Visit www.scilinks.org and enter the SciLinks code for more information about the topic listed.

Topic: Heredity
SciLinks code: HSM0738

Topic: Dominant and Recessive Traits
SciLinks code: HSM0423

Topic: Genotypes
SciLinks code: HSM0664

Topic: Phenotypes
SciLinks code: HSM1135

Topic: Meiosis
SciLinks code: HSM0935

Topic: Genetic Diseases, Screening, Counseling
SciLinks code: HSM0651

Overview

Tell students that this chapter will introduce heredity—the ways that traits are passed from parents to offspring. The chapter describes the ways scientists study heredity and the role of sexual reproduction.

Assessing Prior Knowledge

Students should be familiar with the following topics:

- scientific methods
- cells
- mitosis

Identifying Misconceptions

Students often hold onto misconceptions about inheritance, even after instruction. For example, they may believe that traits are inherited from only one parent or that environmentally caused characteristics may be passed on to offspring. Students tend to understand phenotype (physical traits) more easily than genotype. Finally, the process of meiosis, as it relates to the structure and location of chromosomes, is very complex. Most students require time and repeated exposure in order to comprehend all the parts and steps of meiosis. Assure students that the concepts of heredity are a foundation that will be built upon throughout their studies of life science.

5

Heredity

About the PHOTO

The guinea pig in the middle has dark fur, and the other two have light orange fur. The guinea pig on the right has longer hair than the other two. Why do these guinea pigs look different from one another? The length and color of their fur was determined before they were born. These are just two of the many traits determined by genetic information. Genetic information is passed on from parents to their offspring.

PRE-READING ACTIVITY

FOLDNOTES **Key-Term Fold** Before you read the chapter, create the FoldNote entitled "Key-Term Fold" described in the **Study Skills** section of the Appendix. Write a key term from the chapter on each tab of the key-term fold. Under each tab, write the definition of the key term.

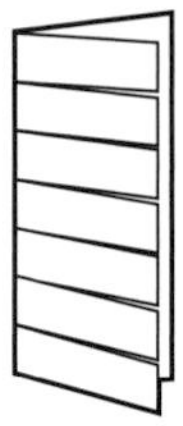

Standards Correlations

National Science Education Standards

The following codes indicate the National Science Education Standards that correlate to this chapter. The full text of the standards is at the front of the book.

Chapter Opener
UCP 2, 3; LS 1d, 2c

Section 1 Mendel and His Peas
UCP 1, 2; SAI 1, 2; ST 2; SPSP 5; HNS 1, 2, 3; LS 2b, 2e

Section 2 Traits and Inheritance
UCP 2, 3; LS 2a, 2b, 2c, 2d, 2e

Section 3 Meiosis
UCP 4, 5; SAI 1; SPSP 5; HNS 2, 3; LS 1c, 1d, 2a, 2b, 2c, 2d

Chapter Lab
SAI 1; HNS 2; LS 2c, 2e

Chapter Review
LS 1c, 2a, 2b, 2c, 2d, 2e

Science in Action
ST 2; SPSP 5

FOR EACH GROUP
• boxes large, (3)
• gloves different types, (5)
• hats different types, (5)
• scarves different types, (5)

Safety Caution: Infestations of head lice are a common problem in schools. Sharing hats should be avoided during such a period. Jackets or sweatshirts could be substituted for hats in this exercise.

Answers

1. Answers may vary. There should be many different combinations. It is not likely that students will see all of the possible combinations.

2. Sample answer: eight new combinations (taken from the outfits of the two "parents") would be possible for the third person ("offspring"). This process is like inheritance because you are choosing combinations of hats, scarves, and gloves randomly. Traits are also passed from parent to offspring randomly. By combining the traits (outfits) of two "parents" (partners), there are many possible combinations of traits in the "offspring" (third person).

3. Sample answer: The number of possible genetic combinations is huge because we have so many genes.

START-UP **ACTIVITY**

Clothing Combos

How do the same parents have children with many different traits?

Procedure

1. Gather **three boxes**. Put **five hats** in the first box, **five gloves** in the second, and **five scarves** in the third.

2. Without looking in the boxes, select one item from each box. Repeat this process, five students at a time, until the entire class has picked "an outfit." Record what outfit each student chooses.

Analysis

1. Were any two outfits exactly alike? Did you see all possible combinations? Explain your answer.

2. Choose a partner. Using your outfits, how many different combinations could you make by giving a third person one hat, one glove, and one scarf? How is this process like parents passing traits to their children?

3. After completing this activity, why do you think parents often have children who look very different from each other?

Chapter Starter Transparency
Use this transparency to help students begin thinking about heredity.

Focus

Overview

This section introduces the genetic experiments of Gregor Mendel. Students explore how crosses between different parent plants produce different off-spring. Students are also introduced to genetic probability.

🔊 Bellringer

Present the following prompt to your students: "You have probably noticed that different people have different traits, such as eye color, hair color, and ear lobes that do or do not attach directly to their head. Where do people get these different traits?" (Many traits are inherited from parents and passed from parents to offspring through genes.)

Motivate

ACTiViTY ———— GENERAL

Trait Trends Create a large table to record the number of students with the following traits: widow's peak, ability to roll tongue, and attached earlobes. Have pairs of students enter data for each other by adding tick marks on the table. Ask students if they can see any trends in the class data. If possible, compile data from several classes. **LS** Kinesthetic/Interpersonal

READING WARM-UP

Objectives

● Explain the relationship between traits and heredity.

● Describe the experiments of Gregor Mendel.

● Explain the difference between dominant and recessive traits.

Terms to Learn

heredity
dominant trait
recessive trait

READING STRATEGY

Brainstorming The key idea of this section is heredity. Brainstorm words and phrases related to heredity.

heredity the passing of genetic traits from parent to offspring

Figure 1 *Gregor Mendel discovered the principles of heredity while studying pea plants.*

CHAPTER RESOURCES

Chapter Resource File

• Lesson Plan
• Directed Reading A **BASIC**
• Directed Reading B **SPECIAL NEEDS**

Technology

Transparencies
• Bellringer

Mendel and His Peas

Why don't you look like a rhinoceros? The answer to this question seems simple: Neither of your parents is a rhinoceros. But there is more to this answer than meets the eye.

As it turns out, **heredity,** or the passing of traits from parents to offspring, is more complicated than you might think. For example, you might have curly hair, while both of your parents have straight hair. You might have blue eyes even though both of your parents have brown eyes. How does this happen? People have investigated this question for a long time. About 150 years ago, Gregor Mendel performed important experiments. His discoveries helped scientists begin to find some answers to these questions.

✓ **Reading Check** What is heredity? (*See the Appendix for answers to Reading Checks.*)

Who Was Gregor Mendel?

Gregor Mendel, shown in **Figure 1,** was born in 1822 in Heinzendorf, Austria. Mendel grew up on a farm and learned a lot about flowers and fruit trees.

When he was 21 years old, Mendel entered a monastery. The monks taught science and performed many scientific experiments. From there, Mendel was sent to Vienna where he could receive training in teaching. However, Mendel had trouble taking tests. Although he did well in school, he was unable to pass the final exam. He returned to the monastery and put most of his energy into research. Mendel discovered the principles of heredity in the monastery garden.

Unraveling the Mystery

From working with plants, Mendel knew that the patterns of inheritance were not always clear. For example, sometimes a trait that appeared in one generation (parents) was not present in the next generation (offspring). In the generation after that, though, the trait showed up again. Mendel noticed these kinds of patterns in several other living things, too. Mendel wanted to learn more about what caused these patterns.

To keep his investigation simple, Mendel decided to study only one kind of organism. Because he had studied garden pea plants before, they seemed like a good choice.

Answer to Reading Check

the passing of traits from parents to offspring

Self-Pollinating Peas

In fact, garden peas were a good choice for several reasons. Pea plants grow quickly, and there are many different kinds available. They are also able to self-pollinate. A *self-pollinating plant* has both male and female reproductive structures. So, pollen from one flower can fertilize the ovule of the same flower or the ovule of another flower on the same plant. The flower on the right side of **Figure 2** is self-pollinating.

Why is it important that pea plants can self-pollinate? Because eggs (in an ovule) and sperm (in pollen) from the same plant combine to make a new plant, Mendel was able to grow true-breeding plants. When a *true-breeding plant* self-pollinates, all of its offspring will have the same trait as the parent. For example, a true-breeding plant with purple flowers will always have offspring with purple flowers.

Pea plants can also cross-pollinate. In *cross-pollination*, pollen from one plant fertilizes the ovule of a flower on a different plant. There are several ways that this can happen. Pollen may be carried by insects to a flower on a different plant. Pollen can also be carried by the wind from one flower to another. The left side of **Figure 2** shows these kinds of cross-pollination.

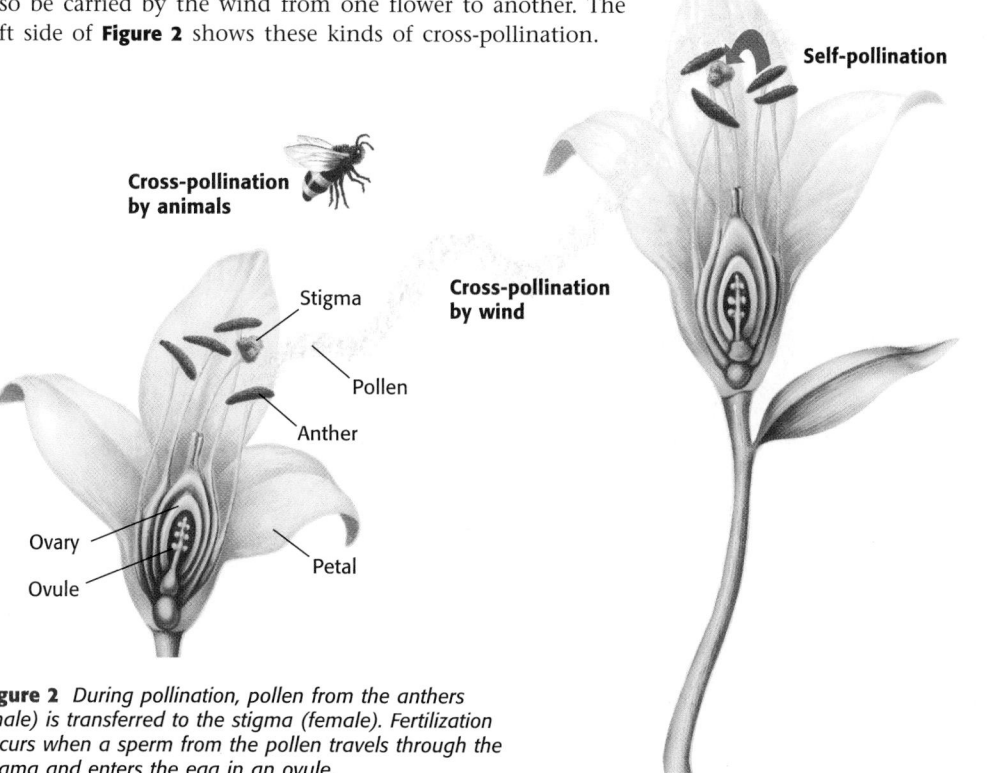

Self-pollination

Cross-pollination by animals

Cross-pollination by wind

Stigma

Pollen

Anther

Ovary

Ovule

Petal

Figure 2 *During pollination, pollen from the anthers (male) is transferred to the stigma (female). Fertilization occurs when a sperm from the pollen travels through the stigma and enters the egg in an ovule.*

Is That a Fact!

Although Mendel was brilliant, he had difficulty learning from scientific texts. In the monastery gardens, Mendel explored the scientific ideas he had trouble with in school. While trying to grow better peas, he discovered genetics, an entirely new field of science!

CONNECTION to Physical Science— GENERAL

Seeing Flower Color Flower color depends on which wavelength of light is reflected by the petals. For example, red absorbs all of the wavelengths except those for red. Display a color spectrum to illustrate that white light is composed of a "rainbow" gradient of colors. Show students different colors, and ask them which colors of light are being absorbed and which are being reflected to our eye. **LS** Visual

Teach

READING STRATEGY — BASIC

Paired Reading Have students read the section silently. As they read, students should make notes or write questions about any section that is confusing or hard to understand. Then, have students discuss the section with a partner, and allow students to help each other understand the material from this section. **LS** Verbal/Interpersonal

Using the Figure— BASIC

Flower Fertilization Discuss the physical processes involved in the fertilization of the flowers illustrated in **Figure 2.** These flowers can be fertilized by another flower or can fertilize themselves. Compare this figure with **Figure 4** on the next page, and point out that removing the anthers from the flower makes it impossible for the plant to self-pollinate. **LS** Visual/Verbal

CONNECTION to Real World— GENERAL

Rapidly Growing Organisms Mendel favored the garden pea because it grows quickly, allowing him to produce many generations within a short time span. Modern scientists favor yeast, bacteria, fruit flies, and mice for studies of heredity and genetics. Each of these organisms has a rapid rate of reproduction. However, rapidly-growing organisms can pose problems. For example, medical scientists face ongoing threats from strains of bacteria that develop resistance to common antibiotics. In some cases, medications that were once widely prescribed are no longer effective. **LS** Logical/Intrapersonal

Discussion — GENERAL

Scientific Methods Have students identify the use of scientific methods in Mendel's work.

• **Ask a question:** How are traits inherited?

• **Form a hypothesis:** Inheritance has a pattern.

• **Test the hypothesis:** Cross true-breeding plants and offspring.

• **Analyze the results:** Identify patterns in inherited traits.

• **Draw conclusions:** Traits are inherited in predictable patterns.

• **Communicate the results:** Publish the results for peer review.

Ask students, "Why weren't Mendel's ideas accepted for so many years?" (because of problems with the last step—other scientists could not easily read or understand his findings)
LS Logical/Verbal

Demonstration — BASIC

Flower Dissection Obtain a flower that has anthers and a stigma, such as a pea flower, a tulip, or a lily. Be careful because pollen can stain clothing and cause allergic reactions. Dissect the flower, and show students the anthers and the stigma. Ask students if this flower could self-pollinate. (yes, because it has both anthers and a stigma) Demonstrate how Mendel removed the anthers of his flowers and then used a small brush to transfer pollen from plant to plant.   English Language
LS Kinesthetic   Learners

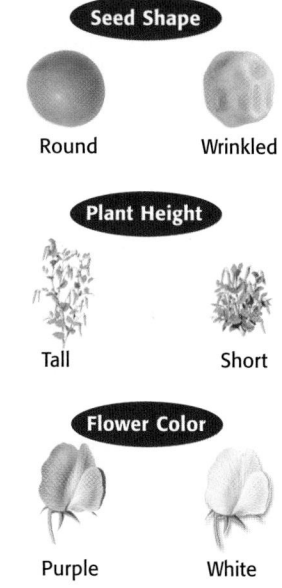

Seed Shape

Round   Wrinkled

Plant Height

Tall   Short

Flower Color

Purple   White

Figure 3 *These are some of the plant characteristics that Mendel studied.*

Characteristics

Mendel studied only one characteristic at a time. A *characteristic* is a feature that has different forms in a population. For example, hair color is a characteristic in humans. The different forms, such as brown or red hair, are called *traits*. Mendel used plants that had different traits for each of the characteristics he studied. For instance, for the characteristic of flower color, he chose plants that had purple flowers and plants that had white flowers. Three of the characteristics Mendel studied are shown in **Figure 3.**

Mix and Match

Mendel was careful to use plants that were true breeding for each of the traits he was studying. By doing so, he would know what to expect if his plants were to self-pollinate. He decided to find out what would happen if he bred, or crossed, two plants that had different traits of a single characteristic. To be sure the plants cross-pollinated, he removed the anthers of one plant so that the plant could not self-pollinate. Then, he used pollen from another plant to fertilize the plant, as shown in **Figure 4.** This step allowed Mendel to select which plants would be crossed to produce offspring.

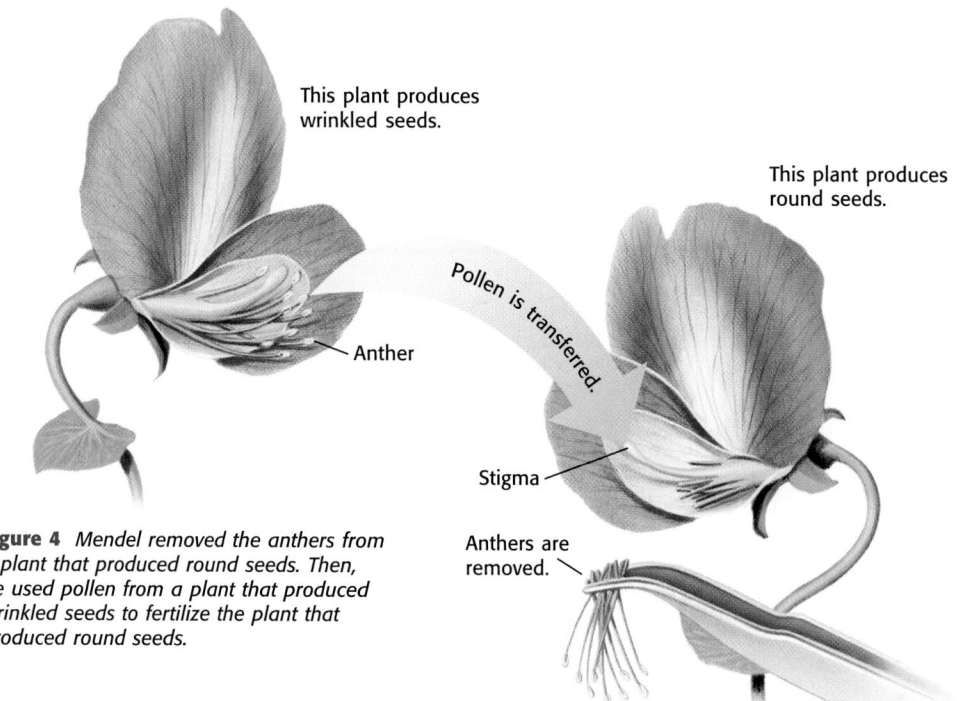

This plant produces wrinkled seeds.

This plant produces round seeds.

Pollen is transferred.

Anther

Stigma

Anthers are removed.

Figure 4 *Mendel removed the anthers from a plant that produced round seeds. Then, he used pollen from a plant that produced wrinkled seeds to fertilize the plant that produced round seeds.*

ACTiViTy — ADVANCED

Mendelian Crosses Give each student a purple bead (*P*) and a white bead (*p*), and ask students to perform a Mendelian cross. Tell students to begin the first generation with the allele combination *Pp*. Have students randomly "pollinate" with 10 other members of the class. To pollinate, one student should hide one bead in each hand. The partner should pick a hand. That hand holds the allele from one parent. Partners should switch roles and repeat this step to determine the allele from the second parent. Students should record the genotype for each pollination. Have students tally the results and determine the ratio of white-flowering plants to purple-flowering plants that results from the matches.
LS Kinesthetic/Interpersonal Co-op Learning

Mendel's First Experiments

In his first experiments, Mendel crossed pea plants to study seven different characteristics. In each cross, Mendel used plants that were true breeding for different traits for each characteristic. For example, he crossed plants that had purple flowers with plants that had white flowers. This cross is shown in the first part of **Figure 5.** The offspring from such a cross are called *first-generation plants.* All of the first-generation plants in this cross had purple flowers. Are you surprised by the results? What happened to the trait for white flowers?

Mendel got similar results for each cross. One trait was always present in the first generation, and the other trait seemed to disappear. Mendel chose to call the trait that appeared the **dominant trait.** Because the other trait seemed to fade into the background, Mendel called it the **recessive trait.** (To *recede* means "to go away or back off.") To find out what might have happened to the recessive trait, Mendel decided to do another set of experiments.

Mendel's Second Experiments

Mendel allowed the first-generation plants to self-pollinate. **Figure 5** also shows what happened when a first-generation plant with purple flowers was allowed to self-pollinate. As you can see, the recessive trait for white flowers reappeared in the second generation.

Mendel did this same experiment on each of the seven characteristics. In each case, some of the second-generation plants had the recessive trait.

✓ **Reading Check** Describe Mendel's second set of experiments.

dominant trait the trait observed in the first generation when parents that have different traits are bred

recessive trait a trait that reappears in the second generation after disappearing in the first generation when parents with different traits are bred

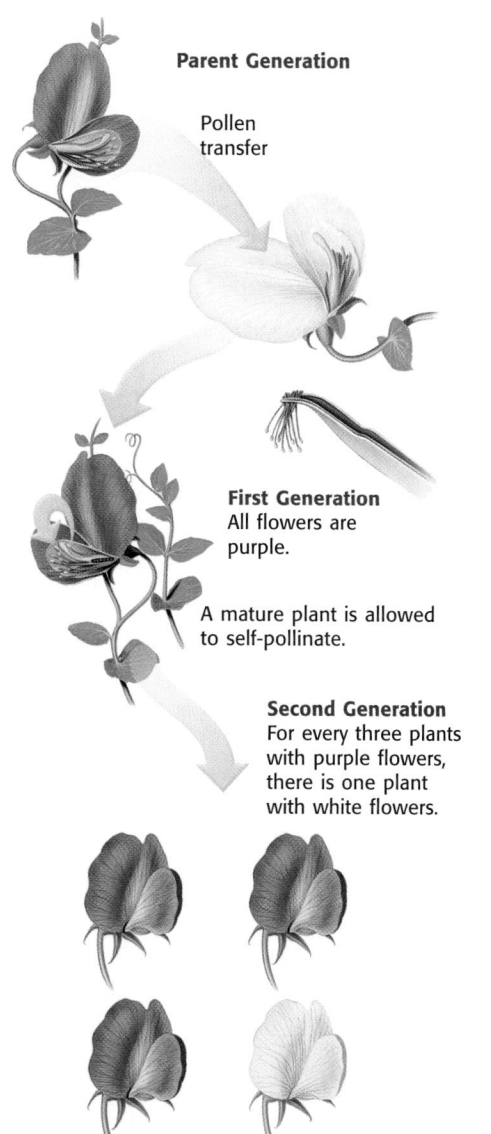

Parent Generation

Pollen transfer

First Generation
All flowers are purple.

A mature plant is allowed to self-pollinate.

Second Generation
For every three plants with purple flowers, there is one plant with white flowers.

Figure 5 *Mendel used the pollen from a plant with purple flowers to fertilize a plant with white flowers. Then, he allowed the offspring to self-pollinate.*

Answer to Reading Check

During his second set of experiments, Mendel allowed the first-generation plants, which resulted from his first set of experiments, to self-pollinate. The recessive trait reappeared in the second generation.

Answers for Table 1 Ratios

Seed color	3.00:1
Seed shape	2.96:1
Pod color	2.82:1
Pod shape	2.95:1
Flower position	3.14:1
Plant height	2.84:1

Reteaching — BASIC

Mendel's Experiments Have students re-enact Mendel's experiments using cups (to represent a plant), colored buttons or chips (to represent various alleles or genotypes), and colored strips of paper (to represent visible traits or phenotypes). Have students perform crosses by taking alleles from "parent" cups and creating "offspring" cups, deciding which traits would then become visible. **English Language Learners**
LS Kinesthetic/Logical

Quiz — GENERAL

1. What did Mendel call the trait that appeared in all of his first-generation plants? (the dominant trait)

2. What is the probability of getting heads in a coin toss? (1/2)

Alternative Assessment — ADVANCED

Story of a Scientist Have students create a comic book or short video drama about Mendel's life and work. Tell students to highlight his use of the scientific method and his habits as a scientist. **LS Interpersonal**

MATH PRACTICE

Understanding Ratios

A ratio is a way to compare two numbers. Look at **Table 1**. The ratio of plants with purple flowers to plants with white flowers can be written as 705 to 224 or 705:224. This ratio can be reduced, or simplified, by dividing the first number by the second as follows:

$$\frac{705}{224} = \frac{3.15}{1}$$

which is the same thing as a ratio of 3.15:1.

For every 3 plants with purple flowers, there will be roughly 1 plant with white flowers. Try this problem:

In a box of chocolates, there are 18 nougat-filled chocolates and 6 caramel-filled chocolates. What is the ratio of nougat-filled chocolates to caramel-filled chocolates?

Mendel then decided to count the number of plants with each trait that turned up in the second generation. He hoped that this might help him explain his results. Take a look at Mendel's results, shown in **Table 1.**

As you can see, the recessive trait did not show up as often as the dominant trait. Mendel decided to figure out the ratio of dominant traits to recessive traits. A *ratio* is a relationship between two different numbers that is often expressed as a fraction. Calculate the dominant-to-recessive ratio for each characteristic. (If you need help, look at the Math Practice at left.) Do you notice anything interesting about the ratios? Round to the nearest whole number. Are the ratios all the same, or are they different?

✔ **Reading Check** What is a ratio?

Table 1 Mendel's Results

Characteristic	Dominant traits	Recessive traits	Ratio
Flower color	705 purple	224 white	3.15:1
Seed color	6,002 yellow	2,001 green	?
Seed shape	5,474 round	1,850 wrinkled	?
Pod color	428 green	152 yellow	?
Pod shape	882 smooth	299 bumpy	?
Flower position	651 along stem	207 at tip	?
Plant height	787 tall	277 short	?

Answer to Math Practice

The ratio of nougat-filled chocolates to caramel-filled chocolates is 18:6, or 18/6, which can be reduced to 3/1. This fraction can be rewritten as 3:1 or 3 to 1.

Answers to questions on student page

All the ratios are about the same. They can be rounded to 3:1.

Answer to Reading Check

A ratio is a relationship between two different numbers that is often expressed as a fraction.

Gregor Mendel—Gone but Not Forgotten

Mendel realized that his results could be explained only if each plant had two sets of instructions for each characteristic. Each parent would then donate one set of instructions. In 1865, Mendel published his findings. But good ideas are sometimes overlooked or misunderstood at first. It wasn't until after his death, more than 30 years later, that Mendel's work was widely recognized. Once Mendel's ideas were rediscovered and understood, the door was opened to modern genetics. Genetic research, as shown in **Figure 6,** is one of the fastest changing fields in science today.

Figure 6 *This researcher is continuing the work started by Gregor Mendel more than 100 years ago.*

SECTION Review

Summary

- Heredity is the passing of traits from parents to offspring.
- Gregor Mendel made carefully planned experiments using pea plants that could self-pollinate.
- When parents with different traits are bred, dominant traits are always present in the first generation. Recessive traits are not visible in the first generation but reappear in the second generation.
- Mendel found a 3:1 ratio of dominant-to-recessive traits in the second generation.

Using Key Terms

1. Use each of the following terms in a separate sentence: *heredity, dominant trait,* and *recessive trait.*

Understanding Key Ideas

2. A plant that has both male and female reproductive structures is able to
   a. self-replicate.
   b. self-pollinate.
   c. change colors.
   d. None of the above

3. Explain the difference between self-pollination and cross-pollination.

4. What is the difference between a trait and a characteristic? Give one example of each.

5. Describe Mendel's first set of experiments.

6. Describe Mendel's second set of experiments.

Math Skills

7. In a bag of chocolate candies, there are 21 brown candies and 6 green candies. What is the ratio of brown to green? What is the ratio of green to brown?

Critical Thinking

8. **Predicting Consequences** Gregor Mendel used only true-breeding plants. If he had used plants that were not true breeding, do you think he would have discovered dominant and recessive traits? Explain.

9. **Applying Concepts** In cats, there are two types of ears: normal and curly. A curly-eared cat mated with a normal-eared cat, and all of the kittens had curly ears. Are curly ears a dominant or recessive trait? Explain.

10. **Identifying Relationships** List three other fields of study that use ratios.

For a variety of links related to this chapter, go to www.scilinks.org
Topic: Heredity; Dominant and Recessive Traits
SciLinks code: HSM0738; HSM0423

Homework — GENERAL

Poster Project Have students create posters to illustrate Mendel's first and second experiments. Have each student demonstrate one of the seven traits that Mendel studied. Encourage students to use materials such as flowers, yellow and green seeds, or wrinkled and round peas. Each project should clearly identify the parents, the first generation, and the second generation. **LS Visual/Logical**

Overview

In this section, students distinguish between genotype and phenotype and use mathematical models to predict the results of genetic crosses. They also learn some exceptions to Mendel's rules of inheritance.

Bellringer

Have students respond to the following prompts: "If you flip a coin, what are the chances that it will land on heads?" (1/2 or 50%) "tails?" (same) "Suppose you flip the coin once, get heads, and then flip it again. What are the chances that you will get heads again?" (still 1/2 or 50%) "Explain." (Each flip of the coin is independent of the last. The chances are the same on each flip.)

Demonstration — BASIC

Ratios To review fractions and ratios, display three pennies and one nickel, and then ask students the following questions: "How many coins are there in all?" (4) "What fraction of the coins are pennies?" (3/4) "What fraction of the coins are nickels?" (1/4) "What is the ratio of pennies to nickels?" (3 to 1)
 Visual/Verbal

READING WARM-UP

Objectives
- Explain how genes and alleles are related to genotype and phenotype.
- Use the information in a Punnett square.
- Explain how probability can be used to predict possible genotypes in offspring.
- Describe three exceptions to Mendel's observations.

Terms to Learn

gene	genotype
allele	probability
phenotype	

READING STRATEGY

Paired Summarizing Read this section silently. In pairs, take turns summarizing the material. Stop to discuss ideas that seem confusing.

---

gene one set of instructions for an inherited trait

allele one of the alternative forms of a gene that governs a characteristic, such as hair color

phenotype an organism's appearance or other detectable characteristic

---

Traits and Inheritance

Mendel calculated the ratio of dominant traits to recessive traits. He found a ratio of 3:1. What did this tell him about how traits are passed from parents to offspring?

A Great Idea

Mendel knew from his experiments with pea plants that there must be two sets of instructions for each characteristic. The first-generation plants carried the instructions for both the dominant trait and the recessive trait. Scientists now call these instructions for an inherited trait **genes.** Each parent gives one set of genes to the offspring. The offspring then has two forms of the same gene for every characteristic—one from each parent. The different forms (often dominant and recessive) of a gene are known as **alleles** (uh LEELZ). Dominant alleles are shown with a capital letter. Recessive alleles are shown with a lowercase letter.

✔ **Reading Check** What is the difference between a gene and an allele? (*See the Appendix for answers to Reading Checks.*)

Phenotype

Genes affect the traits of offspring. An organism's appearance is known as its **phenotype** (FEE noh TIEP). In pea plants, possible phenotypes for the characteristic of flower color would be purple flowers or white flowers. For seed color, yellow and green seeds are the different phenotypes.

Phenotypes of humans are much more complicated than those of peas. Look at **Figure 1** below. The man has an inherited condition called *albinism* (AL buh NIZ uhm). Albinism prevents hair, skin, and eyes from having normal coloring.

Figure 1 *Albinism is an inherited disorder that affects a person's phenotype in many ways.*

CHAPTER RESOURCES

Chapter Resource File
- Lesson Plan
- Directed Reading A BASIC
- Directed Reading B SPECIAL NEEDS

Technology

Transparencies
- Bellringer
- Punnett Squares
- *LINK TO PHYSICAL SCIENCE* The Periodic Table of the Elements

---

Answer to Reading Check

A gene contains the instructions for an inherited trait. the different versions of a gene are called *alleles.*

Genotype

Both inherited alleles together form an organism's **genotype.** Because the allele for purple flowers (*P*) is dominant, only one *P* allele is needed for the plant to have purple flowers. A plant with two dominant or two recessive alleles is said to be *homozygous* (HOH moh ZIE guhs). A plant that has the genotype *Pp* is said to be *heterozygous* (HET uhr OH ZIE guhs).

Punnett Squares

A Punnett square is used to organize all the possible combinations of offspring from particular parents. The alleles for a true-breeding, purple-flowered plant are written as *PP*. The alleles for a true-breeding, white-flowered plant are written as *pp*. The Punnett square for this cross is shown in **Figure 2.** All of the offspring have the same genotype: *Pp*. The dominant allele, *P,* in each genotype ensures that all of the offspring will be purple-flowered plants. The recessive allele, *p,* may be passed on to the next generation. This Punnett square shows the results of Mendel's first experiments.

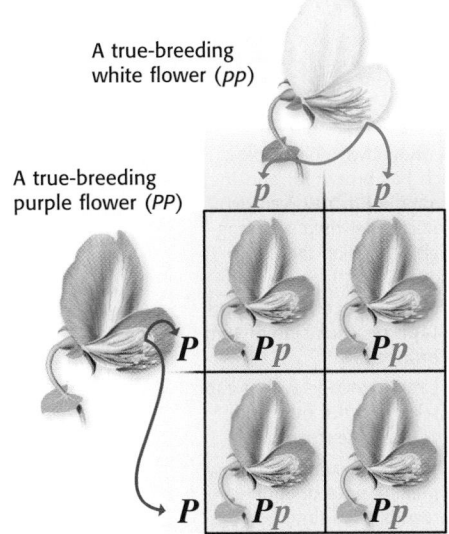

A true-breeding white flower (*pp*)

A true-breeding purple flower (*PP*)

Figure 2 *All of the offspring for this cross have the same genotype—Pp.*

genotype the entire genetic makeup of an organism; also the combination of genes for one or more specific traits

Making a Punnett Square

1. Draw a square, and divide it into four sections.
2. Write the letters that represent alleles from one parent along the top of the box.
3. Write the letters that represent alleles from the other parent along the side of the box.
4. The cross shown at right is between two plants that produce round seeds. The genotype for each is *Rr*. Round seeds are dominant, and wrinkled seeds are recessive. Follow the arrows to see how the inside of the box was filled. The resulting alleles inside the box show all the possible genotypes for the offspring from this cross. What would the phenotypes for these offspring be?

SCIENCE **HUMOR**

Q: What do you get when you cross a bridge with a bicycle?

A: to the other side

Teach, *continued*

Answers to Quick Lab

4. Students should get *bb* on average 1/4 or 25% of the time.
5. 1/4 or 25%
6. 1/4 (If brown fur results from genotype *Bb*, then brown fur is dominant, and white fur will result from the genotype *bb*.)

CONNECTION ACTIVITY
Math — ADVANCED

Probability of Independent Events The probability of two or more independent events is the product of the individual probabilities. For example, the probability of getting heads in a coin toss is 1/2, but the probability of getting heads twice in a row is $1/2 \times 1/2$, or 1/4. Have students consider the following parent genotypes for pea plants: *PpRr* and *Pprr*. Work out and discuss the probability of each possible combined phenotype. (For example, the probability of a plant with white flowers and round seeds is $1/4 \times 1/2 = 1/8$.) **LS Logical**

Answer to Reading Check

Probability is the mathematical chance that something will happen.

Quick Lab

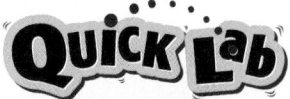

Taking Your Chances

You have two guinea pigs. Each has brown fur and the genotype *Bb*. You want to predict what their offspring might look like. Try this to find out.

1. Stick a **piece of masking tape** on each side of **two quarters.**
2. Label one side with a capital *B* and the other side with a lowercase *b*.
3. Toss both coins 10 times, making note of your results each time.
4. How many times did you get the *bb* combination?
5. What is the probability that the next toss will result in *bb*?
6. What are the chances that the guinea pigs' offspring will have white fur (with the genotype *bb*)?

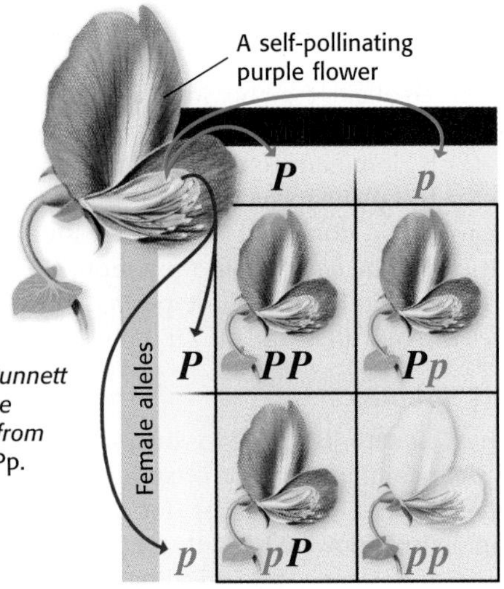

Figure 3 *This Punnett square shows the possible results from the cross* Pp × Pp.

More Evidence for Inheritance

In Mendel's second experiments, he allowed the first generation plants to self-pollinate. **Figure 3** shows a self-pollination cross of a plant with the genotype *Pp*. What are the possible genotypes of the offspring?

Notice that one square shows the genotype *Pp*, while another shows *pP*. These are exactly the same genotype. The other possible genotypes of the offspring are *PP* and *pp*. The combinations *PP, Pp,* and *pP* have the same phenotype—purple flowers. This is because each contains at least one dominant allele (*P*).

Only one combination, *pp,* produces plants that have white flowers. The ratio of dominant to recessive is 3:1, just as Mendel calculated from his data.

What Are the Chances?

Each parent has two alleles for each gene. When these alleles are different, as in *Pp,* offspring are equally likely to receive either allele. Think of a coin toss. There is a 50% chance you'll get heads and a 50% chance you'll get tails. The chance of receiving one allele or another is as random as a coin toss.

Probability

The mathematical chance that something will happen is known as **probability.** Probability is most often written as a fraction or percentage. If you toss a coin, the probability of tossing tails is 1/2—you will get tails half the time.

probability the likelihood that a possible future event will occur in any given instance of the event

Reading Check What is probability?

MISCONCEPTION ALERT

The Role of Chance Students' lack of understanding of mathematical probability may block their understanding of the random and independent sorting of genes that occurs during meiosis. Be careful that students do not overextend mathematical probabilities to predict the outcome of single events. It is correct to predict that an average of many outcomes will be similar to, but not exactly match, a probability ratio.

SCIENCE HUMOR

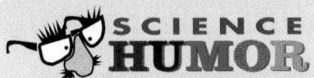

Q: What do you get when you cross a crocodile with an abalone?

A: a crocabaloney

MATH FOCUS

Probability If you roll a pair of dice, what is the probability that you will roll 2 threes?

Step 1: Count the number of faces on a single die. Put this number in the denominator: 6.

Step 2: Count how many ways you can roll a three with one die. Put this number in the numerator: 1/6.

Step 3: To find the probability that you will throw 2 threes, multiply the probability of throwing the first three by the probability of throwing the second three: $1/6 \times 1/6 = 1/36$.

Now It's Your Turn

If you roll a single die, what is the probability that you will roll an even number?

Calculating Probabilities

To find the probability that you will toss two heads in a row, multiply the probability of tossing the first head (1/2) by the probability of tossing the second head (1/2). The probability of tossing two heads in a row is 1/4.

Genotype Probability

To have white flowers, a pea plant must receive a *p* allele from each parent. Each offspring of a *Pp* × *Pp* cross has a 50% chance of receiving either allele from either parent. So, the probability of inheriting two *p* alleles is $1/2 \times 1/2$, which equals 1/4, or 25%. Traits in pea plants are easy to predict because there are only two choices for each trait, such as purple or white flowers and round or wrinkled seeds. Look at **Figure 4.** Do you see only two distinct choices for fur color?

Figure 4 *These kittens inherited one allele from their mother for each trait.*

CONNECTION TO Chemistry

Round and Wrinkled Round seeds may look better, but wrinkled seeds taste sweeter. The dominant allele for seed shape, *R*, causes sugar to be changed into starch (which is a storage molecule for sugar). This change makes the seed round. Seeds with the genotype *rr* do not make or store this starch. Because the sugar has not been changed into starch, the seed tastes sweeter. If you had a pea plant with round seeds (*Rr*), what would you cross it with to get some offspring with wrinkled seeds? Draw a Punnett square showing your cross.

ACTIVITY

WEIRD SCIENCE

Many ordinary fruits and vegetables carry recessive genes for bizarre traits. For instance, a recessive gene in tomatoes causes the skin to be covered with fuzzy hair!

Answer to Math Focus

3/6 or 1/2

Answer to Connection to Chemistry

You would cross it with a plant with wrinkled seeds (*rr*). Students should draw a Punnett square showing this cross.

	R	r
r	Rr	rr
r	Rr	rr

MISCONCEPTION // ALERT \\\\

Exception to Mendel's Rules Caution students not to assume that all inherited traits follow the examples studied by Mendel. For instance, a cross between a red-haired horse and a white-haired horse can produce a horse with both red and white hair. Such a horse is said to have a roan coat. This is an example of *codominance*—the expression of two phenotypes at the same time within the same organism. As in the case of incomplete dominance (which is when a heterozygote shows a phenotype that is intermediate between the homozygous traits), both alleles are visible in the offspring, and therefore neither allele is purely dominant.

Reteaching — BASIC

Exceptions Have students describe three exceptions to Mendel's heredity principles in their **science journal.** LS Verbal

Quiz — GENERAL

In rabbits, the allele for black fur, *B*, is dominant over the allele for white fur, *b*. Suppose two black parents produce one white and three black bunnies.

1. What are the genotypes of the parents? (The parents must both have the recessive allele, so they are both genotype *Bb*.)

2. What are the possible genotypes of all four siblings? (White has genotype *bb*, and black may have *BB* or *Bb*.)

Alternative Assessment — GENERAL

Tracing Traits Ask students to imagine two true-breeding animal parents that have different genetic traits. Have them assign three characteristics, such as tall or short and red nosed or blue nosed, to each parent. Have students label each characteristic as either dominant or recessive. Then, have students use Punnett squares to determine the possible genotypes and phenotypes for each trait in the parents' offspring and in a possible second generation.
LS Logical/ Interpersonal   English Language Learners

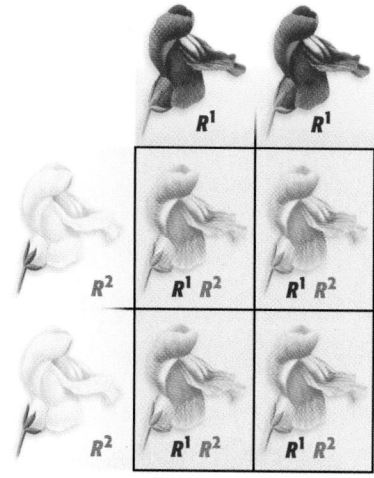

Figure 5 *Cross-breeding two true-breeding snapdragons provides a good example of incomplete dominance.*

More About Traits

As you may have already discovered, things are often more complicated than they first appear to be. Gregor Mendel uncovered the basic principles of how genes are passed from one generation to the next. But as scientists learned more about heredity, they began to find exceptions to Mendel's principles. A few of these exceptions are explained below.

Incomplete Dominance

Since Mendel's discoveries, researchers have found that sometimes one trait is not completely dominant over another. These traits do not blend together, but each allele has its own degree of influence. This is known as *incomplete dominance.*

One example of incomplete dominance is found in the snapdragon flower. **Figure 5** shows a cross between a true-breeding red snapdragon (R^1R^1) and a true-breeding white snapdragon (R^2R^2). As you can see, all of the possible phenotypes for their offspring are pink because both alleles of the gene have some degree of influence.

✓ Reading Check What is incomplete dominance?

One Gene, Many Traits

Sometimes one gene influences more than one trait. An example of this phenomenon is shown by the white tiger in **Figure 6.** The white fur is caused by a single gene, but this gene influences more than just fur color. Do you see anything else unusual about the tiger? If you look closely, you'll see that the tiger has blue eyes. Here, the gene that controls fur color also influences eye color.

Figure 6 *The gene that gave this tiger white fur also influenced its eye color.*

BRAIN FOOD

Round Peas Mendel found that round seeds were dominant over wrinkled seeds. However, at the microscopic level, this is a case of incomplete dominance. The *R* and *r* alleles actually seem to affect the amount of starch produced in the pea. *RR* seeds have many starch grains that give them a full, round shape, but *rr* seeds have few starch grains and a wrinkled shape. *Rr* seeds have an intermediate number of starch grains—but enough for the pea to be full and round.

Many Genes, One Trait

Some traits, such as the color of your skin, hair, and eyes, are the result of several genes acting together. Therefore, it's difficult to tell if some traits are the result of a dominant or a recessive gene. Different combinations of alleles result in different eye-color shades, as shown in **Figure 7.**

The Importance of Environment

Genes aren't the only influences on traits. A guinea pig could have the genes for long fur, but its fur could be cut. In the same way, your environment influences how you grow. Your genes may make it possible that you will grow to be tall, but you need a healthy diet to reach your full potential height.

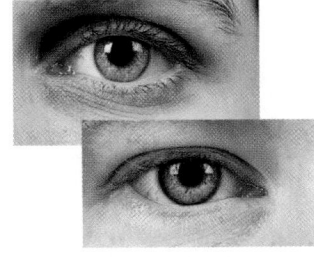

Figure 7 *At least two genes determine human eye color. That's why many shades of a single color are possible.*

SECTION Review

Summary

- Instructions for an inherited trait are called *genes*. For each gene, there are two alleles, one inherited from each parent. Both alleles make up an organism's genotype. Phenotype is an organism's appearance.

- Punnett squares show all possible offspring genotypes.

- Probability can be used to describe possible outcomes in offspring and the likelihood of each outcome.

- Incomplete dominance occurs when one allele is not completely dominant over the other allele.

- Some genes influence more than one trait.

Using Key Terms

1. Use the following terms in the same sentence: *gene* and *allele*.

2. In your own words, write a definition for each of the following terms: *genotype* and *phenotype*.

Understanding Key Ideas

3. Use a Punnett square to determine the possible genotypes of the offspring of a *BB* × *Bb* cross.
   - **a.** all *BB*
   - **b.** *BB, Bb*
   - **c.** *BB, Bb, bb*
   - **d.** all *bb*

4. How are genes and alleles related to genotype and phenotype?

5. Describe three exceptions to Mendel's observations.

Math Skills

6. What is the probability of rolling a five on one die three times in a row?

Critical Thinking

7. **Applying Concepts** The allele for a cleft chin, *C*, is dominant among humans. What are the results of a cross between parents with genotypes *Cc* and *cc*?

Interpreting Graphics

The Punnett square below shows the alleles for fur color in rabbits. Black fur, *B*, is dominant over white fur, *b*.

	?	?
?	*Bb*	*Bb*
?	*Bb*	*Bb*

8. Given the combinations shown, what are the genotypes of the parents?

9. If black fur had incomplete dominance over white fur, what color would the offspring be?

SC*LINKS* NSTA
Developed and maintained by the National Science Teachers Association

For a variety of links related to this chapter, go to www.scilinks.org

Topic: Genotypes; Phenotypes
SciLinks code: HSM0664; HSM1135

Focus

Overview

In this section, students are introduced to meiosis and relate it to Mendel's findings. Students also learn about sex chromosomes and hereditary disorders.

🔊 Bellringer

Ask students to write a sentence for each of the following terms: *heredity, genotype, phenotype.* (Sample answer: Heredity is the passing of traits from parents to offspring. The combination of an organism's alleles is its genotype. All of an organism's physical traits are its phenotype.)

Motivate

ACTiViTY ——————— GENERAL

Crosses Have students model a cross between an organism with one pair of chromosomes and a member of the opposite sex of its species. Show the chromosomes in the cross as "$F_1F_2 \times M_1M_2$." Explain that F_1 and F_2 represent the father's chromosomes, and M_1 and M_2 represent the mother's chromosomes. Ask students, "If each parent contributes only one chromosome from his or her own pair to the offspring, what are the possible combinations in the offspring?" (F_1M_1, F_1M_2, F_2M_1, and F_2M_2) **LS** Logical/Visual

---

READING WARM-UP

Objectives

- Explain the difference between mitosis and meiosis.
- Describe how chromosomes determine sex.
- Explain why sex-linked disorders occur in one sex more often than in the other.
- Interpret a pedigree.

Terms to Learn

homologous chromosomes
meiosis
sex chromosome
pedigree

READING STRATEGY

Reading Organizer As you read this section, make a flowchart of the steps of meiosis.

homologous chromosomes chromosomes that have the same sequence of genes and the same structure

meiosis a process in cell division during which the number of chromosomes decreases to half the original number by two divisions of the nucleus, which results in the production of sex cells

---

Meiosis

Where are genes located, and how do they pass information? Understanding reproduction is the first step to finding the answers.

There are two kinds of reproduction: asexual and sexual. Asexual reproduction results in offspring with genotypes that are exact copies of their parent's genotype. Sexual reproduction produces offspring that share traits with their parents but are not exactly like either parent.

Asexual Reproduction

In *asexual reproduction,* only one parent cell is needed. The structures inside the cell are copied, and then the parent cell divides, making two exact copies. This type of cell reproduction is known as *mitosis.* Most of the cells in your body and most single-celled organisms reproduce in this way.

Sexual Reproduction

In sexual reproduction, two parent cells join together to form offspring that are different from both parents. The parent cells are called *sex cells.* Sex cells are different from ordinary body cells. Human body cells have 46, or 23 pairs of, chromosomes. One set of human chromosomes is shown in **Figure 1.** Chromosomes that carry the same sets of genes are called **homologous** (hoh MAHL uh guhs) **chromosomes.** Imagine a pair of shoes. Each shoe is like a homologous chromosome. The pair represents a homologous pair of chromosomes. But human sex cells are different. They have 23 chromosomes—half the usual number. Each sex cell has only one of the chromosomes from each homologous pair. Sex cells have only one "shoe."

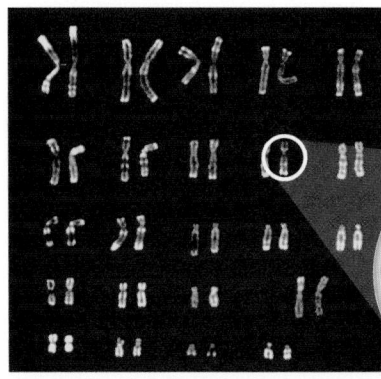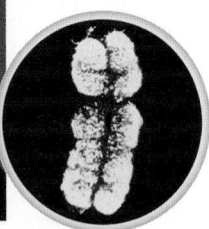

Figure 1 *Human body cells have 23 pairs of chromosomes. One member of a pair of homologous chromosomes is shown below.*

CHAPTER RESOURCES

Chapter Resource File

 • Lesson Plan
  • Directed Reading A **BASIC**
  • Directed Reading B **SPECIAL NEEDS**

Technology

 Transparencies
  • Bellringer

CONNECTION ACTiViTY
Math ——————— ADVANCED

Crosses In algebraic multiplication, some students use the mnemonic device FOIL (**f**irst, **o**uter, **i**nner, **l**ast). This device can be used to calculate genotype crosses. For example, the cross $X_1X_2 \times Y_1Y_2$ yields:

First: X_1X_2

Outer: X_1Y_2

Inner: X_2Y_1

Last: Y_1Y_2

LS Logical/Auditory

Meiosis

Sex cells are made during meiosis (mie OH sis). **Meiosis** is a copying process that produces cells with half the usual number of chromosomes. Each sex cell receives one-half of each homologous pair. For example, a human egg cell has 23 chromosomes, and a sperm cell has 23 chromosomes. The new cell that forms when an egg cell and a sperm cell join has 46 chromosomes.

✓ **Reading Check** How many chromosomes does a human egg cell have? (*See the Appendix for answers to Reading Checks.*)

Genes and Chromosomes

What does all of this have to do with the location of genes? Not long after Mendel's work was rediscovered, a graduate student named Walter Sutton made an important observation. Sutton was studying sperm cells in grasshoppers. Sutton knew of Mendel's studies, which showed that the egg and sperm must each contribute the same amount of information to the offspring. That was the only way the 3:1 ratio found in the second generation could be explained. Sutton also knew from his own studies that although eggs and sperm were different, they did have something in common: Their chromosomes were located inside a nucleus. Using his observations of meiosis, his understanding of Mendel's work, and some creative thinking, Sutton proposed something very important:

Genes are located on chromosomes!

Understanding meiosis was critical to finding the location of genes. Before you learn about meiosis, review mitosis, shown in **Figure 2**. Meiosis is outlined in **Figure 3** on the next two pages.

CONNECTION TO Language Arts

Greek Roots The word *mitosis* is related to a Greek word that means "threads." Threadlike spindles are visible during mitosis. The word *meiosis* comes from a Greek word that means "to make smaller." How do you think meiosis got its name?

Figure 2 Mitosis Revisited

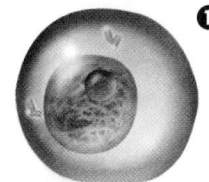
❶ Each chromosome is copied.

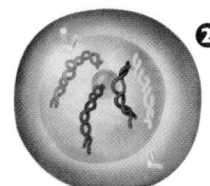
❷ The chromosomes thicken and shorten. Each chromosome consists of two identical copies, called *chromatids.*

❸ The nuclear membrane dissolves. The chromatids line up along the equator (center) of the cell.

❹ The chromatids pull apart.

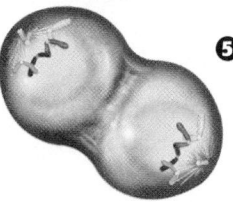
❺ The nuclear membrane forms around the separated chromatids. The chromosomes unwind, and the cell divides.

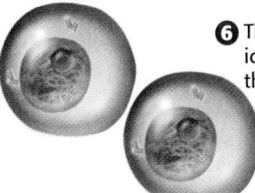
❻ The result is two identical copies of the original cell.

Answer to Connection to Language Arts

Sample answer: Meiosis makes each of the daughter cells smaller than the parent cell. Also, there are fewer chromosomes in the daughter cells than in the parent cell.

Science Bloopers

Wrong Number In 1918, a prominent scientist miscounted the number of chromosomes in a human cell. He counted 48. For almost 40 years, scientists thought this number was correct. In fact, not until 1956 were chromosomes counted correctly and found to number only 46.

Using the Figure — BASIC

Mitosis and Meiosis Have students examine **Figures 2** and **3** to compare what happens in each type of cell division. On the board, draw two identical cells, each of which contains four chromosomes. Label one cell "Mitosis," and label the other "Meiosis." Have students describe what happens in each stage of mitosis, and have them illustrate the stages on the board and in their **science journal.** (Using colored chalk might help distinguish between the dividing chromosomes.) Repeat the process for meiosis. Point out that mitosis results in two identical cells, each of which contains four chromosomes, and meiosis results in four cells, each of which contains two chromosomes. **LS Visual**

Answer to Reading Check

23 chromosomes

CONNECTION to Real World — ADVANCED

Aging and Cell Division Research suggests a connection between aging, cell division, and mitosis. The ends of the chromosomes are protected by special sequences of DNA that do not seem to code for proteins but rather serve a function similar to that of the plastic tips on the ends of shoelaces. These structures, called *telomeres,* act as protective caps on the ends of the long strand of DNA that makes up each chromosome. However, with each cell division, the telomeres lose a little bit of material. At some point, the telomeres become so short that the cell can no longer divide. Eventually, the cell dies, which brings the organism one step closer to its inevitable end.

READING STRATEGY — GENERAL

Prediction Guide Before students read the passage about meiosis, ask them whether the following statements are true or false. Students will discover the answers as they explore the rest of the section.

• Mitosis is the only type of cell division. (false)

• Only cells that produce sex cells undergo meiosis. (true)

• Sex cells contain half the number of chromosomes that other body cells do. (true)

LS Verbal/Auditory

Answer to Reading Check

During meiosis, one parent cell makes four new cells.

Discussion — GENERAL

Predicting Problems Ask students what they think would happen if something went wrong during cell division and the sperm or egg cell ended up with either too few or too many chromosomes? (The fertilized egg, with too few or too many chromosomes, may die, or the growing embryo may have birth defects. Down syndrome occurs in humans when the offspring receives an extra twenty-first chromosome.)

LS Verbal/Logical

The Steps of Meiosis

During mitosis, chromosomes are copied once, and then the nucleus divides once. During meiosis, chromosomes are copied once, and then the nucleus divides twice. The resulting sperm and eggs have half the number of chromosomes of a normal body cell. **Figure 3** shows all eight steps of meiosis. Read about each step as you look at the figure. Different types of living things have different numbers of chromosomes. In this illustration, only four chromosomes are shown.

✓ **Reading Check** How many cells are made from one parent cell during meiosis?

Figure 3 Steps of Meiosis

Read about each step as you look at the diagram. Different types of living things have different numbers of chromosomes. In this diagram, only four chromosomes are shown.

One pair of homologous chromosomes / Two chromatids

1 Before meiosis begins, the chromosomes are in a threadlike form. Each chromosome makes an exact copy of itself, forming two halves called *chromatids*. The chromosomes then thicken and shorten into a form that is visible under a microscope. The nuclear membrane disappears.

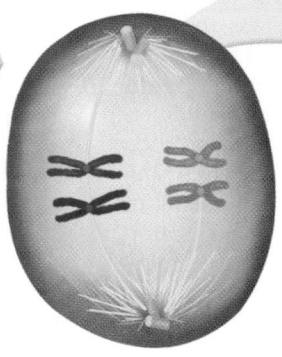

2 Each chromosome is now made up of two identical chromatids. Similar chromosomes pair with one another, and the paired homologous chromosomes line up at the equator of the cell.

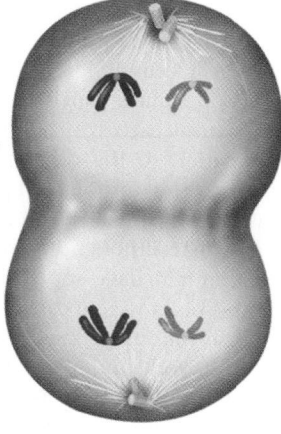

3 The chromosomes separate from their homologous partners and then move to opposite ends of the cell.

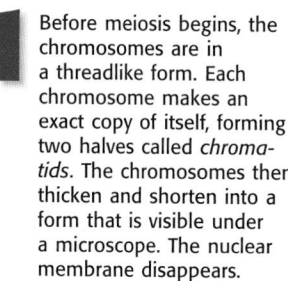

Is That a Fact!

There are many organisms that have more chromosomes than humans do.

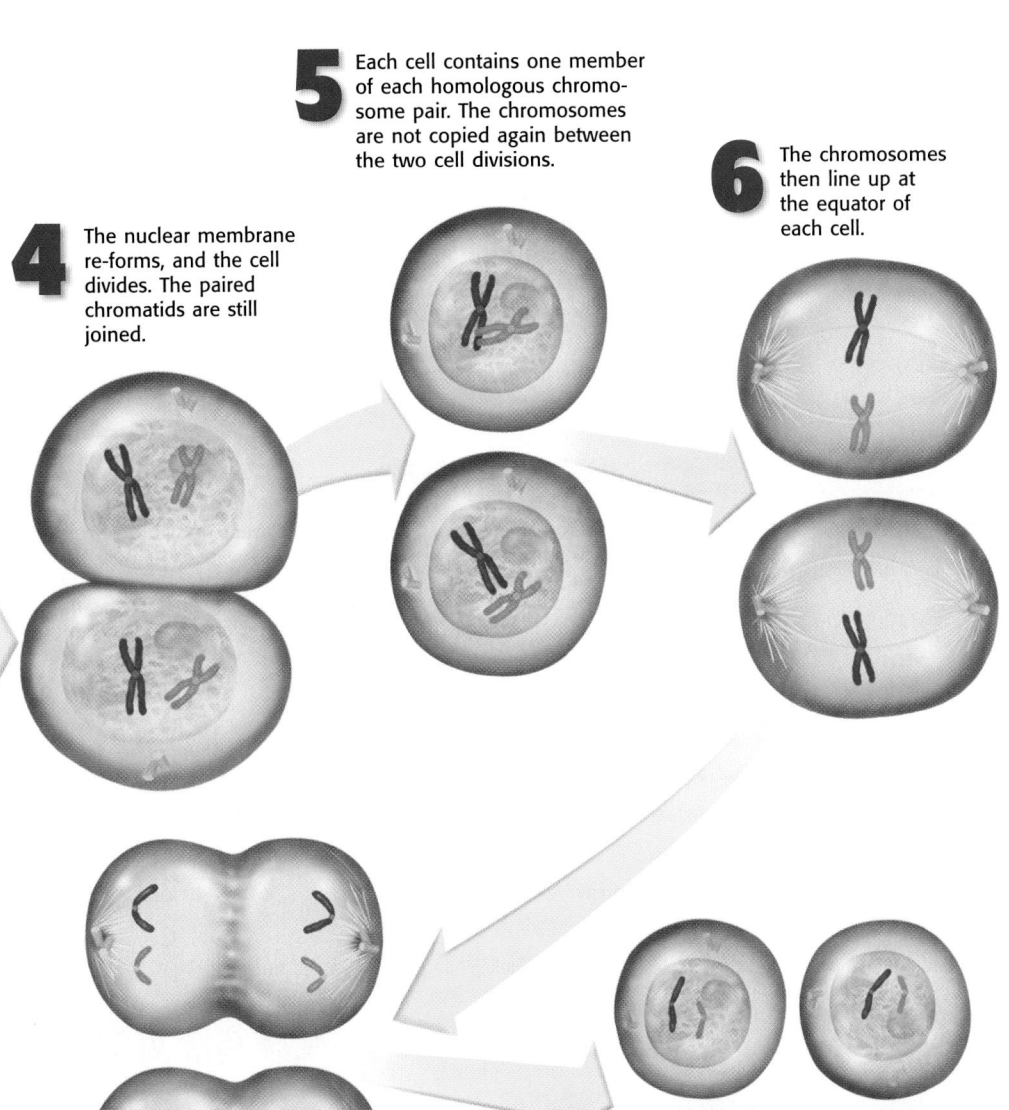

5 Each cell contains one member of each homologous chromosome pair. The chromosomes are not copied again between the two cell divisions.

6 The chromosomes then line up at the equator of each cell.

4 The nuclear membrane re-forms, and the cell divides. The paired chromatids are still joined.

7 The chromatids pull apart and move to opposite ends of the cell. The nuclear membrane forms around the separated chromosomes, and the cells divide.

8 The result is that four new cells have formed from the original single cell. Each new cell has half the number of chromosomes present in the original cell.

SCIENCE HUMOR

Q: If human sex cells are created by meiosis, how are cat sex cells produced?

A: by meow-sis

MISCONCEPTION ///ALERT

Chromatids and Chromosome Pairing Students often have difficulty keeping track of the differences between the way that chromatids and chromosome pairs move during mitosis as compared to meiosis. Caution students to note these differences as they compare mitosis and meiosis, and to analyze the ways that these differences are critical to each process.

ACTIVITY ———— **BASIC**

Describing Meiosis Have students write their own captions for the steps of meiosis illustrated here. They should use language and descriptions that will help them understand and remember the material.
LS Verbal/Visual

CONNECTION ACTIVITY
Math ———— **GENERAL**

Chromosome Number Meiosis and sexual reproduction have benefits for organisms because these processes maintain a variety of traits within a population. Meiosis and sexual recombination reshuffle the genetic material in each generation. Furthermore, the division of chromosomes during meiosis ensures that when the egg and sperm combine, the new organism has the same number of chromosomes as its parents. To explore these concepts, ask students the following questions:

• If the normal number of chromosomes for a certain organism is 30, how many chromosomes would be found in the egg or sperm cells? (15)

• What would happen if eggs and sperm were produced by mitosis instead of by meiosis? (The organism would produce sex cells with a full set of 30 chromosomes.)

• If the organism described above were to have offspring that also produced sex cells by mitosis, how many chromosomes would be found in the descendants after four generations? (first generation: 60; second generation: 120; third generation: 240; fourth generation: 480)
LS Verbal/Logical

- *Learning Disabled*
- *Attention Deficit Disorder*

Have students make a flip book that animates the phases of meiosis. First, have students draw the events of meiosis in at least 15 sketches on sturdy cards. Explain that each drawing should vary only slightly from the one before it. When the book is flipped through quickly, the images should appear to be in motion, and students will be able to watch meiosis in action. This activity could be repeated to demonstrate mitosis.

English Language Learners

LS Visual

Group ACTIVITY — GENERAL

Comparing Mitosis and Meiosis Organize the class into small groups. Instruct each group to create a table listing the similarities and differences between mitosis and meiosis. Challenge groups to make the longest list possible in a limited time period. After their time is up, have groups report items from their lists. Discuss and correct items as you compile a single, large table for display in the classroom.

English Language Learners

LS Visual/Verbal

Meiosis and Mendel

As Walter Sutton figured out, the steps in meiosis explained Mendel's results. **Figure 4** shows what happens to a pair of homologous chromosomes during meiosis and fertilization. The cross shown is between a plant that is true breeding for round seeds and a plant that is true breeding for wrinkled seeds.

Each fertilized egg in the first generation had one dominant allele and one recessive allele for seed shape. Only one genotype was possible because all sperm formed by the male parent during meiosis had the wrinkled-seed allele, and all of the female parent's eggs had the round-seed allele. Meiosis also helped explain other inherited characteristics.

Figure 4 Meiosis and Dominance

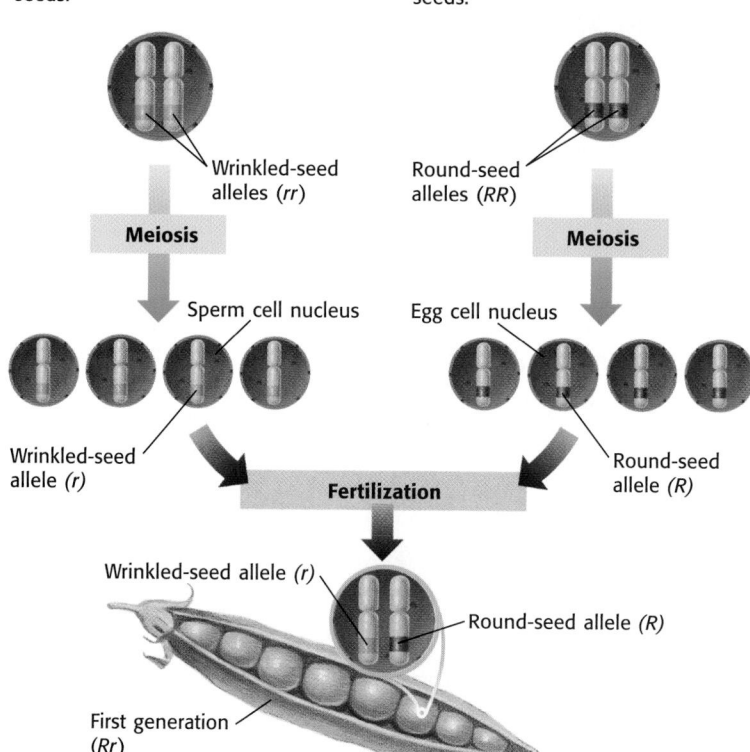

Male Parent In the plant-cell nucleus below, each homologous chromosome has an allele for seed shape, and each allele carries the same instructions: to make wrinkled seeds.

Female Parent In the plant-cell nucleus below, each homologous chromosome has an allele for seed shape, and each allele carries the same instructions: to make round seeds.

Wrinkled-seed alleles (*rr*)

Round-seed alleles (*RR*)

Meiosis

Meiosis

Sperm cell nucleus

Egg cell nucleus

a Following **meiosis**, each sperm cell has a recessive allele for wrinkled seeds, and each egg cell has a dominant allele for round seeds.

Wrinkled-seed allele (*r*)

Round-seed allele (*R*)

b **Fertilization** of any egg by any sperm results in the same genotype (*Rr*) and the same phenotype (round). This result is exactly what Mendel found in his studies.

Fertilization

Wrinkled-seed allele (*r*)

Round-seed allele (*R*)

First generation (*Rr*)

CHAPTER RESOURCES

Technology

Transparencies
- Meiosis and Dominance

Is That a Fact!

Martin-Bell syndrome is a genetic disorder also known as *Fragile X syndrome*. It is one of the most common forms of inherited mental retardation. This disorder is a genetic condition associated with mental retardation and autism. The disorder is identified by flaws apparent in the long arm of the X chromosome.

Sex Chromosomes

Information contained on chromosomes determines many of our traits. **Sex chromosomes** carry genes that determine sex. In humans, females have two X chromosomes. But human males have one X chromosome and one Y chromosome.

During meiosis, one of each of the chromosome pairs ends up in a sex cell. Females have two X chromosomes in each body cell. When meiosis produces the egg cells, each egg gets one X chromosome. Males have both an X chromosome and a Y chromosome in each body cell. Meiosis produces sperm with either an X or a Y chromosome. An egg fertilized by a sperm with an X chromosome will produce a female. If the sperm contains a Y chromosome, the offspring will be male, as shown in **Figure 5.**

Sex-Linked Disorders

The Y chromosome does not carry all of the genes of an X chromosome. Females have two X chromosomes, so they carry two copies of each gene found on the X chromosome. This makes a backup gene available if one becomes damaged. Males have only one copy of each gene on their one X chromosome. The genes for certain disorders, such as colorblindness, are carried on the X chromosome. These disorders are called *sex-linked disorders*. Because the gene for such disorders is recessive, men are more likely to have sex-linked disorders.

People who are colorblind can have trouble distinguishing between shades of red and green. To help the colorblind, some cities have added shapes to their street lights, as shown in **Figure 6.** Hemophilia (HEE moh FIL ee uh) is another sex-linked disorder. Hemophilia prevents blood from clotting, and people with hemophilia bleed for a long time after small cuts. Hemophilia can be fatal.

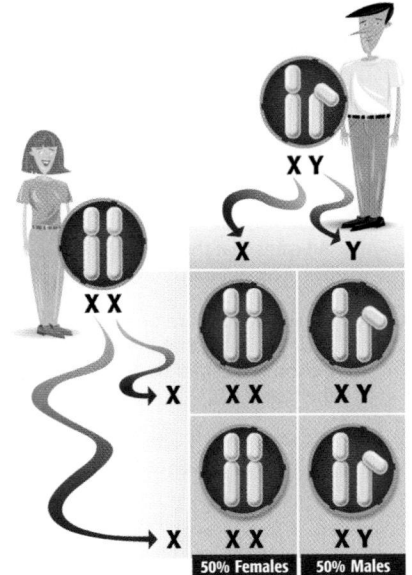

Figure 5 *Egg and sperm combine to form either the XX or XY combination.*

sex chromosome one of the pair of chromosomes that determine the sex of an individual

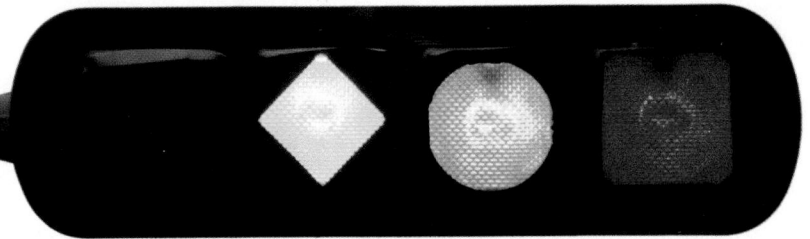

Figure 6 *This stoplight in Canada is designed to help the colorblind see signals easily. This photograph was taken over a few minutes to show all three shapes.*

Reteaching ——— BASIC

Modeling Mates Have students use Punnett squares to model several possible combinations of parents with sex-linked traits that are variously dominant and recessive.

LS Logical/ Kinesthetic   English Language Learners

Quiz ——— GENERAL

Are the following statements true or false?

1. Every one of the chromosomes is different between men and women. (false)

2. Men and women each have different numbers of chromosomes in their sex cells. (false)

3. If you looked inside a cell during mitosis and you could see the chromosomes lining up, you could tell whether the cell belongs to a man or a woman. (true)

Alternative Assessment ——— GENERAL

Writing **Meiosis versus Mitosis** Tell students that there will be a mock debate to decide whether mitosis or meiosis is "better." First, have the class discuss and agree upon a definition of "better." Then, have students choose a "side" and prepare a written argument that is supported by scientific facts. You may wish to allow volunteers to act out such a debate. **LS** Verbal

---

Figure 7 Pedigree for a Recessive Disease

☐ Males   ○ Females

Vertical lines connect children to their parents.

■ or ● A solid square or circle indicates that the person has a certain trait.

◨ or ◑ A half-filled square or circle indicates that the person is a carrier of the trait.

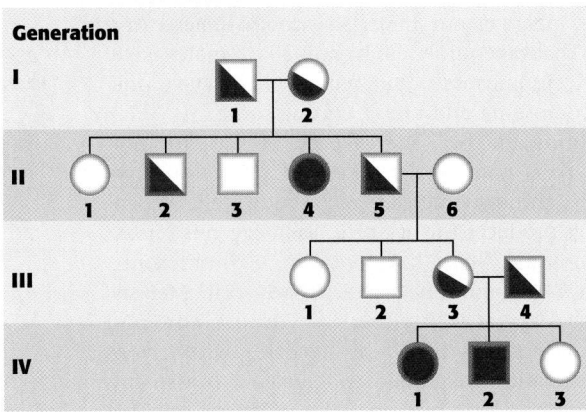

pedigree a diagram that shows the occurrence of a genetic trait in several generations of a family

Figure 8 *Roses have been selectively bred to create large, bright flowers.*

Genetic Counseling

Hemophilia and other genetic disorders can be traced through a family tree. If people are worried that they might pass a disease to their children, they may consult a genetic counselor. These counselors often make use of a diagram known as a **pedigree,** which is a tool for tracing a trait through generations of a family. By making a pedigree, a counselor can often predict whether a person is a carrier of a hereditary disease. The pedigree shown in **Figure 7** traces a disease called *cystic fibrosis* (SIS tik FIE broh sis). Cystic fibrosis causes serious lung problems. People with this disease have inherited two recessive alleles. Both parents need to be carriers of the gene for the disease to show up in their children.

Pedigrees can be drawn up to trace any trait through a family tree. You could even draw a pedigree that would show how you inherited your hair color. Many different pedigrees could be drawn for a typical family.

Selective Breeding

For thousands of years, humans have seen the benefits of the careful breeding of plants and animals. In *selective breeding,* organisms with desirable characteristics are mated. You have probably enjoyed the benefits of selective breeding, although you may not have realized it. For example, you have probably eaten an egg from a chicken that was bred to produce more eggs. Your pet dog may be a result of selective breeding. Roses, like the one shown in **Figure 8,** have been selectively bred to produce large flowers. Wild roses are much smaller and have fewer petals than roses that you could buy at a nursery.

WEIRD SCIENCE

Gene therapy is an experimental field of medical research in which defective genes are replaced with healthy genes. One way to insert healthy genes involves using a delivery system called a *gene gun* to inject microscopic gold bullets coated with genetic material.

Homework ——— ADVANCED

Pet Pedigrees Have students obtain a copy of the pedigree of a thoroughbred animal from a professional breeder of dogs, cats, horses, or other animals. Ask students to write a paragraph explaining what information the pedigree provides about the animal and its ancestors. **LS** Verbal/Interpersonal

SECTION Review

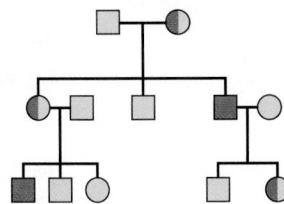

Summary

- In mitosis, chromosomes are copied once, and then the nucleus divides once. In meiosis, chromosomes are copied once, and then the nucleus divides twice.
- The process of meiosis produces sex cells, which have half the number of chromosomes. These two halves combine during reproduction.

- In humans, females have two X chromosomes. So, each egg contains one X chromosome. Males have both an X and a Y chromosome. So, each sperm cell contains either an X or a Y chromosome.
- Sex-linked disorders occur in males more often than in females. Colorblindness and hemophilia are examples of sex-linked disorders.
- A pedigree is a diagram used to trace a trait through many generations of a family.

Using Key Terms

1. Use each of the following terms in the same sentence: *meiosis* and *sex chromosomes*.

In each of the following sentences, replace the incorrect term with the correct term from the word bank.

pedigree   homologous chromosomes

meiosis   mitosis

2. During fertilization, chromosomes are copied, and then the nucleus divides twice.

3. A Punnett square is used to show how inherited traits move through a family.

4. During meiosis, sex cells line up in the middle of the cell.

Understanding Key Ideas

5. Genes are found on
   a. chromosomes.
   b. proteins.
   c. alleles.
   d. sex cells.

6. If there are 14 chromosomes in pea plant cells, how many chromosomes are present in a sex cell of a pea plant?

7. Draw the eight steps of meiosis. Label one chromosome, and show its position in each step.

Interpreting Graphics

Use this pedigree to answer the question below.

8. Is this disorder sex linked? Explain your reasoning.

Critical Thinking

9. **Identifying Relationships** Put the following in order of smallest to largest: chromosome, gene, and cell.

10. **Applying Concepts** A pea plant has purple flowers. What alleles for flower color could the sex cells carry?

 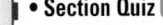

Developed and maintained by the
National Science Teachers Association

For a variety of links related to this chapter, go to www.scilinks.org
Topic: Meiosis; Genetic Diseases, Screening, Counseling
SciLinks code: HSM0935; HSM0651

Answers to Section Review

1. Sample answer: At the end of meiosis, each sex cell will contain only one sex chromosome (either X or Y).

2. During meiosis, chromosomes are copied, and then the nucleus divides twice.

3. A pedigree is used to show how inherited traits move through a family.

4. During meiosis, homologous chromosomes line up in the middle of the cell.

5. a

6. 7

7. Answers may vary. Students' drawings should be similar to the diagram of meiosis in the student text.

8. Sample answer: yes; The disorder seems to be sex linked because the females are carriers of the disease but only males have the disease itself.

9. gene, chromosome, cell

10. Sample answer: Because the purple gene (*P*) is dominant over the white gene (*p*), the genotype of the purple-flowered pea plant could be either *PP* or *Pp*. Thus, the possible alleles carried by the sex cells would be *P* or *p*.

INTERNET ACTiViTy
Essay   GENERAL

For an internet activity related to this chapter, have students goto **go.hrw.com** and type in the keyword **HL5DNAW.**

CHAPTER RESOURCES

Chapter Resource File

- Section Quiz GENERAL
- Section Review GENERAL
- Vocabulary and Section Summary GENERAL
- Reinforcement Worksheet BASIC

Bug Builders, Inc.

Teacher's Notes

Time Required

Two 45-minute class periods

Lab Ratings

EASY ————————→ HARD

Teacher Prep 🧪🧪🧪
Student Set-Up 🧪🧪
Concept Level 🧪🧪🧪
Clean Up 🧪

MATERIALS

The materials listed on the student page are enough for a group of 3–4 students. For step 3, prepare 14 small paper sacks—representing paired parent alleles for each of seven characteristics—as follows:

1. Use the table in step 6 to decide the genotypes for each of the parent bugs' characteristics.

2. Cut 1 in. squares of paper to represent alleles. Use seven colors of paper—a different color for each characteristic. Cut enough squares so that each student will receive two alleles for each characteristic.

3. Label the alleles for each characteristic according to the genotypes you chose.

4. Label each pair of sacks with one of the seven characteristics. Place an equal number of alleles in each sack.

5. For each characteristic, label one sack "Mom" and the other sack "Dad." Have students draw one allele from each sack.

OBJECTIVES

Build models to further your understanding of inheritance.

Examine the traits of a population of offspring.

MATERIALS

- allele sacks (14) (supplied by your teacher)
- gumdrops, green and black (feet)
- map pins (eyes)
- marshmallows, large (head and body segments)
- pipe cleaners (tails)
- pushpins, green and blue (noses)
- scissors
- toothpicks, red and green (antennae)

SAFETY

Bug Builders, Inc.

Imagine that you are a designer for a toy company that makes toy alien bugs. The president of Bug Builders, Inc., wants new versions of the wildly popular Space Bugs, but he wants to use the bug parts that are already in the warehouse. It's your job to come up with a new bug design. You have studied how traits are passed from one generation to another. You will use this knowledge to come up with new combinations of traits and assemble the bug parts in new ways. Model A and Model B, shown below, will act as the "parent" bugs.

Ask a Question

① If there are two forms of each of the seven traits, then how many possible combinations are there?

Form a Hypothesis

② Write a hypothesis that is a possible answer to the question above. Explain your reasoning.

Test the Hypothesis

③ Your teacher will display 14 allele sacks. The sacks will contain slips of paper with capital or lowercase letters on them. Take one piece of paper from each sack. (Remember: Capital letters represent dominant alleles, and lowercase letters represent recessive alleles.) One allele is from "Mom," and one allele is from "Dad." After you have recorded the alleles you have drawn, place the slips of paper back into the sack.

Model A ("Mom")
- red antennae
- 3 body segments
- curly tail
- 2 pairs of legs
- green nose
- black feet
- 3 eyes

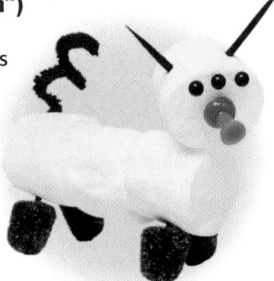

Model B ("Dad")
- green antennae
- 2 body segments
- straight tail
- 3 pairs of legs
- blue nose
- green feet
- 2 eyes

Safety Caution

Remind students to review all safety cautions and icons before beginning this lab activity. Students should use caution with toothpicks and should not eat any of the materials used.

CHAPTER RESOURCES

Chapter Resource File

- Datasheet for Chapter Lab
- Lab Notes and Answers

Technology

Classroom Videos
- Lab Video

- Tracing Traits

Bug Family Traits				
Trait	Model A "Mom" allele	Model B "Dad" allele	New model "Baby" genotype	New model "Baby" phenotype
Antennae color				
Number of body segments				
Tail shape				
Number of leg pairs				
Nose color				
Foot color				
Number of eyes				

DO NOT WRITE IN BOOK

❹ Create a table like the one above. Fill in the first two columns with the alleles that you selected from the sacks. Next, fill in the third column with the genotype of the new model ("Baby").

❺ Use the information below to fill in the last column of the table.

Genotypes and Phenotypes	
RR or *Rr*—red antennae	*rr*—green antennae
SS or *Ss*—3 body segments	*ss*—2 body segments
CC or *Cc*—curly tail	*cc*—straight tail
LL or *Ll*—3 pairs of legs	*ll*—2 pairs of legs
BB or *Bb*—blue nose	*bb*—green nose
GG or *Gg*—green feet	*gg*—black feet
EE or *Ee*—2 eyes	*ee*—3 eyes

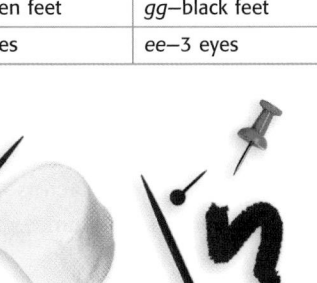

❻ Now that you have filled out your table, you are ready to pick the parts you need to assemble your bug. (Toothpicks can be used to hold the head and body segments together and as legs to attach the feet to the body.)

Analyze the Results

❶ **Organizing Data** Take a poll of the traits of the offspring. What are the ratios for each trait?

❷ **Examining Data** Do any of the new models look exactly like the parents? Explain.

Draw Conclusions

❸ **Interpreting Information** What are the possible genotypes of the parent bugs?

❹ **Making Predictions** How many different genotypes are possible in the offspring?

> ### Applying Your Data
> Find a mate for your "Baby" bug. What are the possible genotypes and phenotypes of the offspring from this match?

Analyze the Results
1. Student ratios should be similar to the ratios determined when the alleles were selected by the teacher.

2. If any students have offspring bugs that look like one of the parents, have students compare the genotype of the offspring with the genotype of the parents. The offspring and parents look alike but still have different genotypes for some traits.

Draw Conclusions
3. Student answers should reflect the data on parent alleles that were recorded in step 6.

4. Students' answers should include Punnett squares based on the parental traits. Except for the results obtained by parental genotypes that are all homozygous recessive, students will see other possibilities for genotypes and phenotypes from the same parents.

Applying Your Data
Students should create Punnett squares to show the possible genotypes and describe phenotypes that follow the rules of dominance for each characteristic.

CHAPTER RESOURCES

Workbooks

 Long-Term Projects & Research Ideas
• Portrait of a Dog ADVANCED

CLASSROOM TESTED & APPROVED

Kathy LaRoe
East Valley Middle School
East Helena, Montana

Chapter Review

Assignment Guide

Section	Questions
1	7, 13, 18
2	2, 4, 5, 8, 9, 11, 19–23
3	1, 3, 6, 10, 12, 14–17

ANSWERS

Using Key Terms

1. sex cells
2. phenotype, genotype
3. Meiosis
4. alleles

Understanding Key Ideas

5. d
6. c
7. b
8. b
9. c
10. c
11. b

USING KEY TERMS

Complete each of the following sentences by choosing the correct term from the word bank.

sex cells   genotype
sex chromosomes   alleles
phenotype   meiosis

1 Sperm and eggs are known as _____.

2 The _____ is the expression of a trait and is determined by the combination of alleles called the _____.

3 _____ produces cells with half the normal number of chromosomes.

4 Different versions of the same genes are called _____.

UNDERSTANDING KEY IDEAS

Multiple Choice

5 Genes carry information that determines

a. alleles.
b. ribosomes.
c. chromosomes.
d. traits.

6 The process that produces sex cells is

a. mitosis.
b. photosynthesis.
c. meiosis.
d. probability.

7 The passing of traits from parents to offspring is called

a. probability.
b. heredity.
c. recessive.
d. meiosis.

8 If you cross a white flower with the genotype *pp* with a purple flower with the genotype *PP*, the possible genotypes in the offspring are

a. *PP* and *pp*.
b. all *Pp*.
c. all *PP*.
d. all *pp*.

9 For the cross in item 8, what would the phenotypes be?

a. all white
b. 3 purple and 1 white
c. all purple
d. half white, half purple

10 In meiosis,

a. chromosomes are copied twice.
b. the nucleus divides once.
c. four cells are produced from a single cell.
d. two cells are produced from a single cell.

11 When one trait is not completely dominant over another, it is called

a. recessive.
b. incomplete dominance.
c. environmental factors.
d. uncertain dominance.

Short Answer

12 Which sex chromosomes do females have? Which do males have?

13 In one or two sentences, define the term *recessive trait* in your own words.

14 How are sex cells different from other body cells?

15 What is a sex-linked disorder? Give one example of a sex-linked disorder that is found in humans.

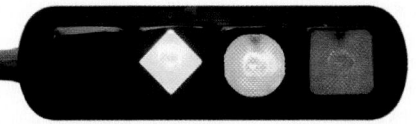

16 Concept Mapping Use the following terms to create a concept map: *meiosis, eggs, cell division, X chromosome, mitosis, Y chromosome, sperm,* and *sex cells.*

17 Identifying Relationships If you were a carrier of one allele for a certain recessive disorder, how could genetic counseling help you prepare for the future?

18 Applying Concepts If a child has blond hair and both of her parents have brown hair, what does that tell you about the allele for blond hair? Explain.

19 Applying Concepts What is the genotype of a pea plant that is true-breeding for purple flowers?

INTERPRETING GRAPHICS

Use the Punnett square below to answer the questions that follow.

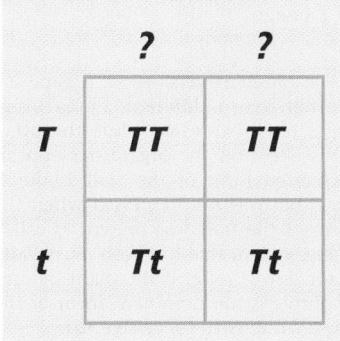

	?	?
T	**TT**	**TT**
t	**Tt**	**Tt**

20 What is the unknown genotype?

21 If *T* represents the allele for tall pea plants and *t* represents the allele for short pea plants, what is the phenotype of each parent and of the offspring?

22 If each of the offspring were allowed to self-fertilize, what are the possible genotypes in the next generation?

23 What is the probability of each genotype in item 22?

Critical Thinking

16. 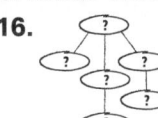 An answer to this exercise can be found at the end of this book.

17. Sample answer: A genetic counselor could test my spouse to see if my spouse is also a carrier of the recessive allele. The counselor could then predict what the chances are that we could have a child with the recessive disorder.

18. The allele for blomd hair is recessive.

19. *PP*

Interpreting Graphics

20. *TT*

21. All the parents and offspring are tall pea plants.

22. Students should make two new Punnett squares. Self-fertilization of *TT* (*TT* × *TT*) will yield offspring that are all *TT*. Self fertilization of *Tt* (*Tt* × *Tt*) will yield offspring that are *TT*, *Tt*, and *tt*.

23. *TT* has a 100% probability with a *TT* parent and a 25% probability with a *Tt* parent. *Tt* has a 50% probability with a *Tt* parent and a 0% probability with a *TT* parent. The genotype *tt* has a 25% probability with a *Tt* parent and a 0% probability with a *TT* parent.

---

12. Females have two X chromosomes. Males have one X and one Y chromosome.

13. Sample answer: A recessive trait is a genetic trait that is expressed only if there is not a dominant allele present.

14. Sex cells have half the number of chromosomes as other body cells.

15. Sample answer: A sex-linked disorder is a disorder that is caused by a gene on one of the sex chromosomes and so is expressed in one sex more than the other. Color blindness is a sex-linked disorder found in humans.

CHAPTER RESOURCES

Chapter Resource File

- Chapter Review **GENERAL**
- Chapter Test A **GENERAL**
- Chapter Test B **ADVANCED**
- Chapter Test C **SPECIAL NEEDS**
- Vocabulary Activity **GENERAL**

Workbooks

Study Guide
- Assessment resources are also available in Spanish.

Standardized Test Preparation

Teacher's Note

To provide practice under more realistic testing conditions, give students 20 minutes to answer all of the questions in this Standardized Test Preparation.

MISCONCEPTION
///ALERT

Answers to the standardized test preparation can help you identify student misconceptions and misunderstandings.

READING

Passage 1

1. C
2. F
3. C

✚ TEST DOCTOR

Question 2: This question primarily requires the reader to re-read the sentence in which the word is used, which clearly serves to define the word. Then, the reader must look among the possible answers for the one that most closely matches the meaning given in the sentence.

Question 3: This question requires a simple deduction from the final two sentences of the passage. The uses of "if," "then," and "therefore" are clear indicators of logical reasoning. Remind students to look for these kinds of indicators for these types of test questions.

READING

Read the passages below. Then, answer the questions that follow each passage.

Passage 1 The different versions of a gene are called *alleles*. When two different alleles occur together, one is often expressed while the other has no obvious effect on the organism's appearance. The expressed form of the trait is dominant. The trait that was not expressed when the dominant form of the trait was present is called *recessive*. Imagine a plant that has both purple and white alleles for flower color. If the plant blooms purple, then purple is the dominant form of the trait. Therefore, white is the recessive form.

1. According to the passage, which of the following statements is true?
   A All alleles are expressed all of the time.
   B All traits for flower color are dominant.
   C When two alleles are present, the expressed form of the trait is dominant.
   D A recessive form of a trait is always expressed.

2. According to the passage, a trait that is not expressed when the dominant form is present is called
   F recessive.
   G an allele.
   H heredity.
   I a gene.

3. According to the passage, which allele for flower color is dominant?
   A white
   B pink
   C purple
   D yellow

Passage 2 Sickle cell anemia is a recessive genetic disorder. People inherit this disorder only when they inherit the disease-causing recessive allele from both parents. The disease causes the body to make red blood cells that bend into a sickle (or crescent moon) shape. The sickle-shaped red blood cells break apart easily. Therefore, the blood of a person with sickle cell anemia carries less oxygen. Sickle-shaped blood cells also tend to get stuck in blood vessels. When a blood vessel is blocked, the blood supply to organs can be cut off. But the sickle-shaped blood cells can also protect a person from malaria. Malaria is a disease caused by an organism that invades red blood cells.

1. According to the passage, sickle cell anemia is a
   A recessive genetic disorder.
   B dominant genetic disorder.
   C disease caused by an organism that invades red blood cells.
   D disease also called *malaria*.

2. According to the passage, sickle cell anemia can help protect a person from
   F blocked blood vessels.
   G genetic disorders.
   H malaria.
   I low oxygen levels.

3. Which of the following is a fact in the passage?
   A When blood vessels are blocked, vital organs lose their blood supply.
   B When blood vessels are blocked, it causes the red blood cells to bend into sickle shapes.
   C The blood of a person with sickle cell anemia carries more oxygen.
   D Healthy red blood cells never get stuck in blood vessels.

Passage 2

1. A
2. H
3. A

✚ TEST DOCTOR

Question 2: The answer to this question comes from the second-to-last sentence in the passage. Weak readers often miss details from the middle parts of passages, and standardized tests sometimes probe for this kind of mistake with such questions. One strategy for this type of question is to form a question such as "From what problem can sickle cell anemia protect a person?" and then re-read or skim the passage with this question in mind.

The Punnett square below shows a cross between two flowering plants. Use this Punnett square to answer the questions that follow.

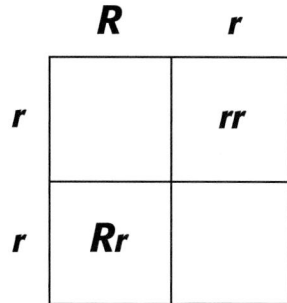

1. What is the genotype of the offspring represented in the upper left-hand box of the Punnett square?

   A *RR*

   B *Rr*

   C *rr*

   D *rrr*

2. What is the genotype of the offspring represented in the lower right-hand box of the Punnett square?

   F *RR*

   G *Rr*

   H *rr*

   I *rrr*

3. What is the ratio of *Rr* (purple-flowered plants) to *rr* (white-flowered plants) in the offspring?

   A 1:3

   B 2:2

   C 3:1

   D 4:0

Read each question below, and choose the best answer.

1. What is another way to write $4 \times 4 \times 4$?

   A 4^2

   B 4^3

   C 3^3

   D 3^4

2. Jane was making a design on top of her desk with pennies. She put 4 pennies in the first row, 7 pennies in the second row, and 13 pennies in the third row. If Jane continues this pattern, how many pennies will she put in the sixth row?

   F 25

   G 49

   H 97

   I 193

3. In which of the following lists are the numbers in order from smallest to greatest?

   A 0.012, 0.120, 0.123, 1.012

   B 1.012, 0.123, 0.120, 0.012

   C 0.123, 0.120, 0.012, 1.012

   D 0.123, 1.012, 0.120, 0.012

4. In which of the following lists are the numbers in order from smallest to greatest?

   F $-12.0, -15.5, 2.2, 4.0$

   G $-15.5, -12.0, 2.2, 4.0$

   H $-12.0, -15.5, 4.0, 2.2$

   I $2.2, 4.0, -12.0, -15.5$

5. Which of the following is equal to -11?

   A $7 + 4$

   B $-4 + 7$

   C $-7 + 4$

   D $-7 + -4$

6. Catherine earned $75 for working 8.5 h. How much did she earn per hour?

   F $10.12

   G $9.75

   H $8.82

   I $8.01

Standardized Test Preparation

1. B

2. H

3. B

➕ TEST DOCTOR

Questions 1 and 2: These questions require understanding of the term *genotype* and the ability to complete a Punnett square. Students who miss these questions may need to review these concepts.

Question 3: This question asks for the ratio of the genotype *Rr* to the genotype *rr*. If completed, the Punnett square would show 2 *Rr* and 2 *rr* genotypes. Thus, the ratio would be 2:2 (answer B). Students who miss this question may need to review the concept of ratios.

1. B

2. H

3. A

4. G

5. D

6. H

➕ TEST DOCTOR

Question 6: This question is essentially a simple long-division problem, but students may get confused or discouraged by long division when the calculation extends for many decimal places. For this problem, students can save time if they recognize that they need only to find the answer in dollars and cents. Thus, they need to calculate to the thousandths place ($8.823) and then round their answer to the nearest cent.

CHAPTER RESOURCES

Chapter Resource File

📁 • Standardized Test Preparation GENERAL

State Resources

For specific resources for your state, visit **go.hrw.com** and type in the keyword **HSMSTR**.

Science, Technology, and Society

Background

Genetic research has spawned a flurry of debate over ethical, social, and legal issues surrounding the use of genetic information. These issues include the privacy and ownership of personal genetic information and the possibility that people will selectively breed or control the birth of their children based on genetic knowledge.

Weird Science

Teaching Strategy—GENERAL

Offer the following analogies to help students grasp the concepts discussed in this article.

- Blueprints: Show students sample construction blueprints. Explain that genes are like these plans for a building and that mutations are like mistakes in copying, reading, or building from the blueprints.

- Recipes: Show students a book of cake recipes. Genes are like recipes, and an organism is like a cake made according to a recipe. A mutation is like using a different ingredient or a different amount of an ingredient. The mutation may or may not "ruin" the "cake."

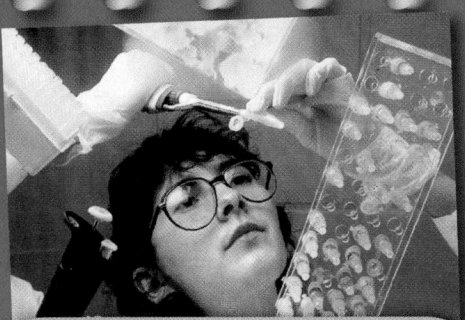

Science in Action

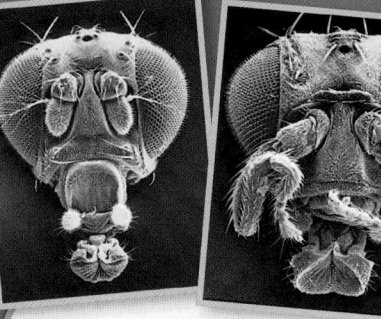

This is a normal fruit fly under a scanning electron microscope.

This fruit fly has legs growing where its antennae should be.

Science, Technology, and Society

Mapping the Human Genome

In 2003, scientists finished one of the most ambitious research projects ever. Researchers with the Human Genome Project (HGP) mapped the human body's complete set of genetic instructions, which is called the *genome*. You might be wondering whose genome the scientists are decoding. Actually, it doesn't matter—only 0.1% of each person's genetic material is unique. The researchers' goals are to identify how tiny differences in that 0.1% make each of us who we are and to begin to understand how some differences can cause disease. Scientists are already using the map to think of new ways to treat genetic diseases, such as asthma, diabetes, and kidney disease.

Social Studies ACTIVITY

WRITING SKILL Research DNA fingerprinting. Write a short report describing how DNA fingerprinting has affected the way criminals are caught.

Weird Science

Lab Rats with Wings

Drosophila melanogaster (droh SAHF i luh muh LAN uh GAS tuhr) is the scientific name for the fruit fly. This tiny insect has played a big role in helping scientists understand many illnesses. Because fruit flies reproduce every 2 weeks, scientists can alter a fruit fly gene and see the results of the experiment very quickly. Another important reason for using these "lab rats with wings" is that their genetic code is simple and well understood. Fruit flies have 12,000 genes, but humans have more than 25,000. Scientists use fruit flies to find out about diseases like cancer, Alzheimer's, and muscular dystrophy.

Language Arts ACTIVITY

WRITING SKILL The mythical creature called the *Chimera* (kie MIR uh) was said to be part lion, part goat, and part serpent. According to legend, the Chimera terrorized people for years until it was killed by a brave hero. The word *chimera* now refers to any organism that has parts from many organisms. Write a short story about the Chimera that describes what it looks like and how it came to be.

Answer to Social Studies Activity

Sample answer: DNA fingerprinting has made it much easier to match genetic material (evidence) at a crime scene to the genetic information of one particular individual. DNA can be found in hair, saliva, blood, and small skin cells. The DNA is analyzed and then compared to the DNA fingerprint of particular individuals. When the DNA fingerprints match, police can be sure that the person was at the scene of the crime.

Answer to Language Arts Activity

The Chimera (or Chimaera) was said to be a savage beast that spat fire from its mouth. In classical Greco-Roman stories, it wreaked havoc on the ancient lands until it was killed by the hero Bellerophon, who rode his winged horse Pegasus. This basic story is among the most ancient myths and appears in many texts from Homer's *Iliad* to traditional fairy tales.

Careers

Stacey Wong

Genetic Counselor If your family had a history of a particular disease, what would you do? Would you eat healthier foods, get more exercise, or visit your doctor regularly? All of those are good ideas, but Stacey Wong went a step farther. Her family's history of cancer helped her decide to become a genetic counselor. "Genetic counselors are usually part of a team of health professionals," she says, which can include physicians, nurses, dieticians, social workers, laboratory personnel, and others. "If a diagnosis is made by the geneticist," says Wong, "then I provide genetic counseling." When a patient visits a genetic counselor, the counselor asks many questions and builds a family medical history. Although counseling involves discussing what it means to have a genetic condition, Wong says "the most important part is to get to know the patient or family we are working with, listen to their concerns, gain an understanding of their values, help them to make decisions, and be their advocate."

Math ACTiViTY

The probability of inheriting genetic disease *A* is 1/10,000. The probability of inheriting genetic disease *B* is also 1/10,000. What is the probability that one person would inherit both genetic diseases *A* and *B*?

To learn more about these Science in Action topics, visit go.hrw.com and type in the keyword **HL5HERF**.

Current Science

Check out Current Science® articles related to this chapter by visiting go.hrw.com. Just type in the keyword **HL5CS05**.

Careers

Background

Stacey Wong was born in Oakland, California, and grew up in the nearby suburb of Alameda. She received a B.S. in cell and molecular biology from UCLA and an M.S. in genetic counseling from California State University Northridge. More information about genetic-counseling careers can be obtained from the National Society of Genetic Counselors.

Answer to Math Activity

1/10,000 × 1/10,000 = 1/100,000,000

Genes and DNA
Chapter Planning Guide

Compression guide:
To shorten instruction because of time limitations, omit the Chapter Lab.

OBJECTIVES	LABS, DEMONSTRATIONS, AND ACTIVITIES	TECHNOLOGY RESOURCES
PACING • 90 min pp. 142–147 **Chapter Opener**	**SE** Start-up Activity, p. 143 ◆ `GENERAL`	**OSP** Parent Letter ■ `GENERAL` **CD** Student Edition on CD-ROM **CD** Guided Reading Audio CD ■ **TR** Chapter Starter Transparency* **VID** Brain Food Video Quiz
Section 1 What Does DNA Look Like? • List three important events that led to understanding the structure of DNA. • Describe the basic structure of a DNA molecule. • Explain how DNA molecules can be copied.	**TE** Activity Modeling Code, p. 144 `GENERAL` **TE** Group Activity A Place in History, p. 145 `GENERAL` **SE** Quick Lab Making a Model of DNA, p. 146 ◆ `GENERAL` **CRF** Datasheet for Quick Lab* **SE** Science in Action Math, Social Studies, and Language Arts Activities, pp. 162–163 `GENERAL` **SE** Model-Making Lab Base-Pair Basics, p. 156 ◆ `GENERAL` **CRF** Datasheet for Chapter Lab* **LB** Whiz-Bang Demonstrations Grand Strand* `GENERAL`	**CRF** Lesson Plans* **TR** Bellringer Transparency* **TR** DNA Structure* **CRF** SciLinks Activity* `GENERAL` **VID** Lab Videos for Life Science
PACING • 45 min pp. 148–155 **Section 2 How DNA Works** • Explain the relationship between DNA, genes, and proteins. • Outline the basic steps in making a protein. • Describe three types of mutations, and provide an example of a gene mutation. • Describe two examples of uses of genetic knowledge.	**TE** Demonstration A Tight Fit, p. 148 ◆ `GENERAL` **TE** Connection Activity Chemistry, p. 150 `ADVANCED` **TE** Group Activity Skit, p. 150 `GENERAL` **TE** Connection Activity Math, p. 151 ◆ `GENERAL` **TE** Activity Complementary Code, p. 152 `GENERAL` **SE** School-to-Home Activity An Error in the Message, p. 153 `GENERAL` **TE** Connection Activity Social Studies, p. 154 `ADVANCED` **LB** Long-Term Projects & Research Ideas The Antifreeze Protein* `ADVANCED` **LB** Long-Term Projects & Research Ideas Ewe Again, Dolly?* `ADVANCED`	**CRF** Lesson Plans* **TR** Bellringer Transparency* **TR** Unraveling DNA* **TR** The Making of a Protein: A* **TR** The Making of a Protein: B* **TR** *LINK TO EARTH SCIENCE* The Formation of Smog* **TR** How Sickle Cell Anemia Results from a Mutation* **SE** Internet Activity, p. 150 `GENERAL` **CD** Interactive Explorations CD-ROM DNA Pawprints `GENERAL`

PACING • 90 min

CHAPTER REVIEW, ASSESSMENT, AND STANDARDIZED TEST PREPARATION

CRF Vocabulary Activity* `GENERAL`
SE Chapter Review, pp. 158–159 `GENERAL`
CRF Chapter Review* ■ `GENERAL`
CRF Chapter Tests A* ■ `GENERAL`, B* `ADVANCED`, C* `SPECIAL NEEDS`
SE Standardized Test Preparation, pp. 160–161 `GENERAL`
CRF Standardized Test Preparation* `GENERAL`
CRF Performance-Based Assessment* `GENERAL`
OSP Test Generator `GENERAL`
CRF Test Item Listing* `GENERAL`

Online and Technology Resources

Visit **go.hrw.com** for a variety of free resources related to this textbook. Enter the keyword **HL5DNA**.

Students can access interactive problem-solving help and active visual concept development with the *Holt Science and Technology* Online Edition available at **www.hrw.com**.

 Guided Reading Audio CD
Also in Spanish

A direct reading of each chapter for auditory learners, reluctant readers, and Spanish-speaking students.

 Science Tutor
CD-ROM

Excellent for remediation and test practice.

SKILLS DEVELOPMENT RESOURCES	SECTION REVIEW AND ASSESSMENT	STANDARDS CORRELATIONS
SE Pre-Reading Activity, p. 142 GENERAL **OSP** Science Puzzlers, Twisters & Teasers GENERAL		National Science Education Standards UCP 5; SAI 1, 2; ST 2; LS 2e
CRF Directed Reading A* ■ BASIC, B* SPECIAL NEEDS **CRF** Vocabulary and Section Summary* ■ GENERAL **SE** Reading Strategy Prediction Guide, p. 144 GENERAL **SE** Connection to Chemistry Linus Pauling, p. 145 GENERAL **TE** Reading Strategy Mnemonics, p. 145 BASIC **TE** Inclusion Strategies, p. 145 **MS** Math Skills for Science A Shortcut for Multiplying Large Numbers* GENERAL **SS** Science Skills Science Drawing* GENERAL	**SE** Reading Checks, pp. 145, 147 GENERAL **TE** Reteaching, p. 146 BASIC **TE** Quiz, p. 147 GENERAL **TE** Alternative Assessment, p. 147 GENERAL **SE** Section Review,* p. 147 ■ GENERAL **CRF** Section Quiz* ■ GENERAL	UCP 2, 5; SAI 1, 2; ST 1, 2; SPSP 5; HNS 1, 2, 3; LS 1a, 2d, 5a; *Chapter Lab:* UCP 2, 5; SAI 1, 2; HNS 1; LS 1a
CRF Directed Reading A* ■ BASIC, B* SPECIAL NEEDS **CRF** Vocabulary and Section Summary* ■ GENERAL **SE** Reading Strategy Reading Organizer, p. 148 GENERAL **SE** Math Practice Code Combinations, p. 151 GENERAL **TE** Inclusion Strategies, p. 153 **SE** Connection to Social Studies Genetic Property, p. 154 GENERAL **CRF** Reinforcement Worksheet DNA Mutations* BASIC **CRF** Critical Thinking The Perfect Parrot* ADVANCED	**SE** Reading Checks, pp. 148, 151, 152, 153, 154 GENERAL **TE** Homework, p. 150 GENERAL **TE** Homework, p. 153 GENERAL **TE** Reteaching, p. 154 BASIC **SE** Section Review,* p. 155 ■ GENERAL **TE** Quiz, p. 154 GENERAL **TE** Alternative Assessment, p. 154 GENERAL **CRF** Section Quiz* ■ GENERAL	UCP 1, 4, 5; SAI 1, 2; ST 2; SPSP 4, 5; LS 1c, 1e, 1f, 2b, 2c, 2d, 2e, 5b

Visual Resources

CHAPTER STARTER TRANSPARENCY

BELLRINGER TRANSPARENCIES

Section: What Does DNA Look Like?
Can you explain the difference between traits and characteristics? Which is more closely associated with DNA and genes? Where do you think DNA and genes are usually found?

Write your answers in your **science journal.**

Section: How DNA Works
Unscramble the following words:
tpsoneir
neesg
Now think of three words you associate with each of the above words and use them all in a paragraph that highlights what you know about DNA.

Write your paragraph in your **science journal.**

TEACHING TRANSPARENCIES

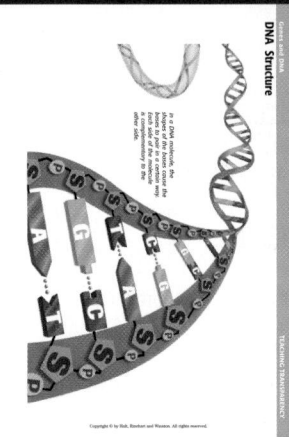

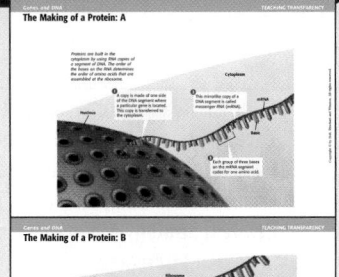

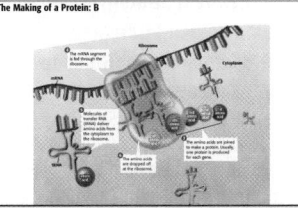

TEACHING TRANSPARENCIES

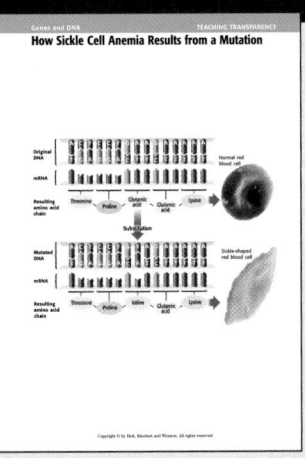

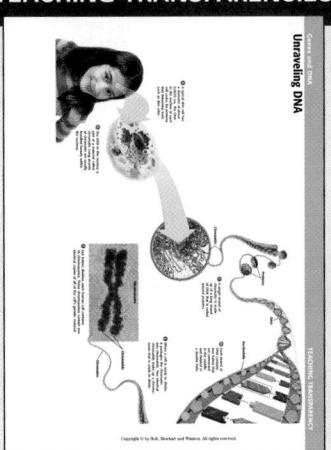

Chapter: The Atmosphere

CONCEPT MAPPING TRANSPARENCY

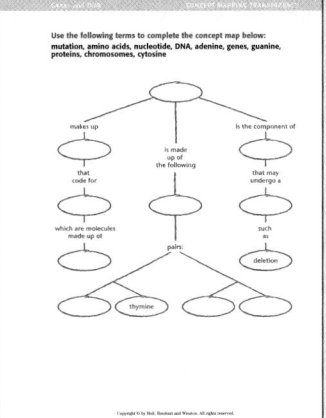

Planning Resources

LESSON PLANS

Lesson Plan   SAMPLE

Section: Waves

Pacing
Regular Schedule: with lab(s):2 days   without lab(s):1 days
Block Schedule: with lab(s):1 1/2 days   without lab(s):1 day

Objectives
1. Relate the seven properties of life to a living organism.
2. Describe seven themes that can help you to organize what you learn about biology.
3. Identify the tiny structures that make up all living organisms.
4. Differentiate between reproduction and heredity and between metabolism and homeostasis.

National Science Education Standards Covered
LSInter6:Cells have particular structures that underlie their functions.
LSMat1:Most cell functions involve chemical reactions.
LSBeh1:Cells store and use information to guide their functions.
UCP1:Cell functions are regulated.
SI1: Cells can differentiate and form complete multicellular organisms.
PS1: Species evolve over time.
ESS1: The great diversity of organisms is the result of more than 3.5 billion years of evolution.
ESS2: Natural selection and its evolutionary consequences provide a scientific explanation for the fossil record of ancient life forms as well as for the striking molecular similarities observed among the diverse species of living organisms.
ST1: The millions of different species of plants, animals, and microorganisms that live on Earth today are related by descent from common ancestors.
ST2: The energy for life primarily comes from the sun.
SPSP1: The complexity and organization of organisms accommodates the need for obtaining, transforming, transporting, releasing, and eliminating the matter and energy used to sustain the organism.
SPSP6: As matter and energy flows through different levels of organization of living systems—cells, organs, communities—and between living systems and the physical environment, chemical elements are recombined in different ways.
HNS1: Organisms have behavioral responses to internal and external stimuli.

PARENT LETTER

SAMPLE

Dear Parent,

Your son's or daughter's science class will soon begin exploring the chapter entitled "The World of Physical Science." In this chapter, students will learn about how the scientific method applies to the world of physical science and the role of physical science in the world. By the end of the chapter, students should demonstrate a clear understanding of the chapter's main ideas and be able to discuss the following topics:

1. physical science as the study of energy and matter (Section 1)
2. the role of physical science in the world around them (Section 1)
3. careers that rely on physical science (Section 1)
4. the steps used in the scientific method (Section 2)
5. examples of technology (Section 2)
6. how the scientific method is used to answer questions and solve problems (Section 2)
7. how our knowledge of science changes over time (Section 2)
8. how models represent real objects or systems (Section 3)
9. examples of different ways models are used in science (Section 3)
10. the importance of the International System of Units (Section 4)
11. the appropriate units to use for particular measurements (Section 4)
12. how area and density are derived quantities (Section 4)

Questions to Ask Along the Way

You can help your son or daughter learn about these topics by asking interesting questions such as the following:

• What are some surprising careers that use physical science?
• What is a characteristic of a good hypothesis?
• Where is it a good idea to use a model?
• Why do Americans measure things in terms of inches and yards and meters ?

ALSO IN SPANISH

TEST ITEM LISTING

TEST ITEM LISTING
The World of Science   SAMPLE

MULTIPLE CHOICE
1. A limitation of models is that
   a. they are large enough to see.
   b. they do not act exactly like the things that they model.
   c. they are smaller than the things that they model.
   d. they model unfamiliar things.
   Answer: B   Difficulty: 1   Section: 3   Objective: 2
2. The length 10 m is equal to
   a. 100 cm.   c. 10,000 mm.
   b. 1,000 cm.   d. Both (b) and (c)
   Answer: B   Difficulty: 1   Section: 3   Objective: 2
3. To be valid, a hypothesis must be
   a. testable.   c. made into a law
   b. supported by evidence.   d. Both (a) and (b)
   Answer: B   Difficulty: 1   Section: 3   Objective: 2 1
4. The statement "Sheila has a stain on her shirt" is an example of a(n)
   a. law.   c. observation.
   b. hypothesis.   d. prediction.
   Answer: B   Difficulty: 1   Section: 3   Objective: 2
5. A hypothesis is often developed out of
   a. observations.   c. laws.
   b. experiments.   d. Both (a) and (b)
   Answer: B   Difficulty: 1   Section: 3   Objective: 2
6. How many milliliters are in 3.5 kL?
   a. 3,500 mL.   c. 3,500, 000 mL.
   b. 0.0035 mL.   d. 35,000 mL.
   Answer: B   Difficulty: 1   Section: 3   Objective: 2
7. A map of Seattle is an example of a
   a. law.   c. model.
   b. theory.   d. unit.
   Answer: B   Difficulty: 1   Section: 3   Objective: 2
8. A lab has the safety icons shown below. These icons mean that you should wear
   a. only safety goggles.   c. safety goggles and a lab apron.
   b. only a lab apron.   d. safety goggles, a lab apron, and gloves.
   Answer: B   Difficulty: 1   Section: 3   Objective: 2
9. The law of conservation of mass says the lot al mass before a chemical change is
   a. more than the total mass after the change.
   b. less than the total mass after the change.
   c. the same as the total mass after the change.
   d. not the same as the total mass after the change.
   Answer: B   Difficulty: 1   Section: 3   Objective: 2
10. In which of the following areas might you find a geochemist at work?
    a. studying the chemistry of rocks   c. studying fishes
    b. studying forestry   d. studying the atmosphere
    Answer: B   Difficulty: 1   Section: 3   Objective: 2

One-Stop Planner® CD-ROM

This CD-ROM includes all of the resources shown here and the following time-saving tools:

• *Lab Materials QuickList Software*
• *Customizable lesson plans*
• *Holt Calendar Planner*
• *The powerful ExamView® Test Generator*

For a preview of available worksheets covering math and science skills, see pages T26–T33. All of these resources are also on the One-Stop Planner®.

Meeting Individual Needs

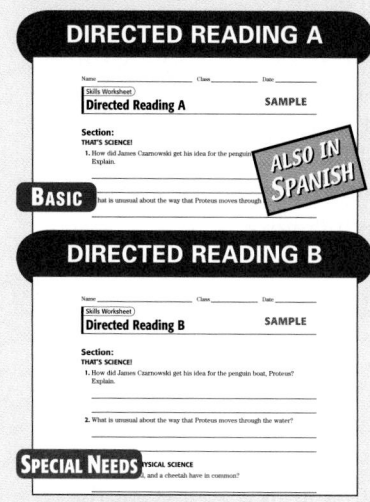
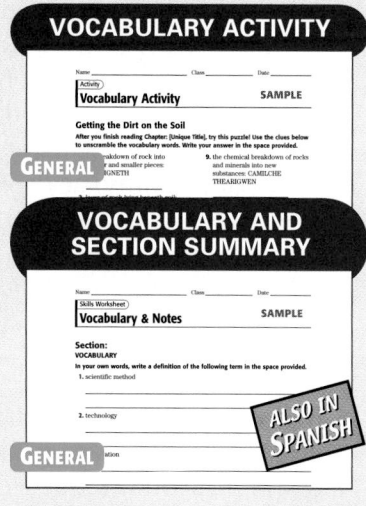
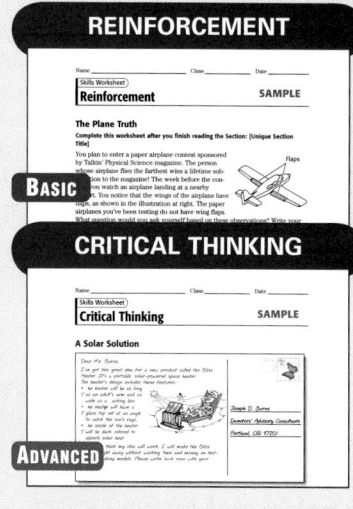

Labs and Activities

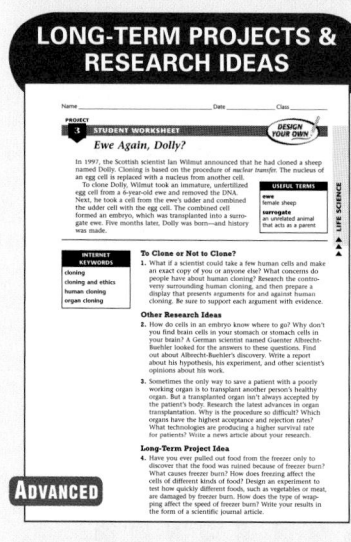
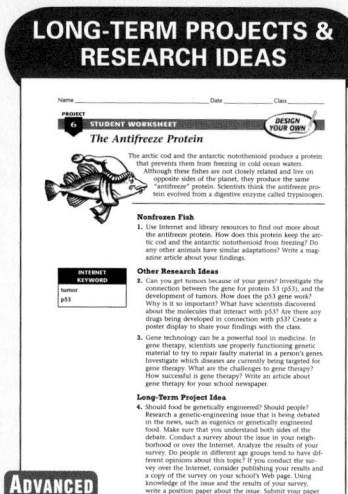
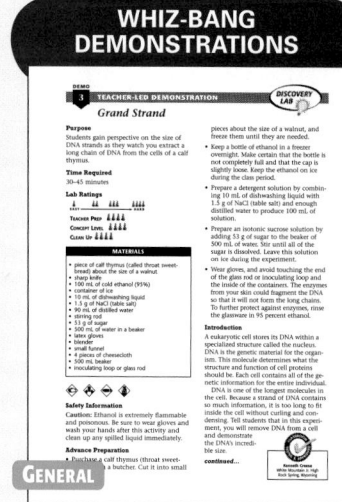

Review and Assessments

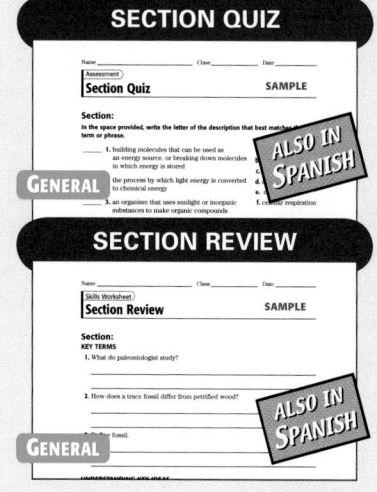
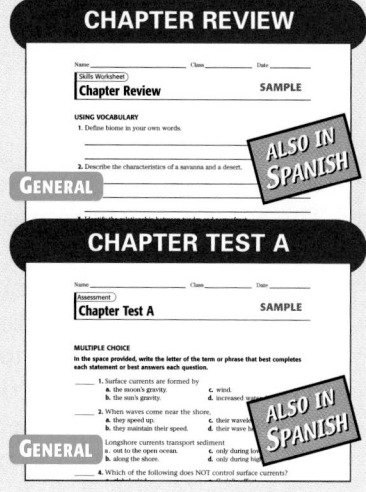
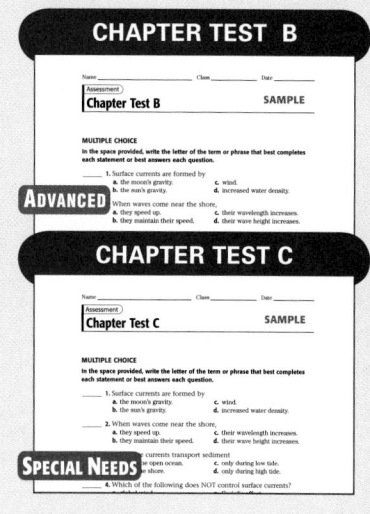
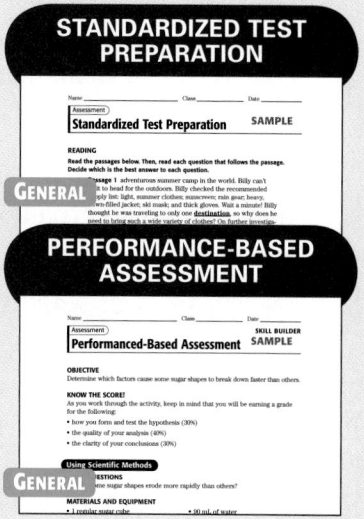

This Chapter Enrichment provides relevant and interesting information to expand and enhance your presentation of the chapter material.

Section 1

What Does DNA Look Like?

Discovering DNA

- In 1869, long before the time of Watson and Crick, a 22-year-old Swiss scientist isolated DNA from a cell nucleus. Unfortunately, he had no idea of its function, much less of its role in inheritance. It was not until 75 years later, in 1944, that an American geneticist named Oswald T. Avery found evidence that DNA is the carrier of genetic information.

Section 2

How DNA Works

Cracking the Genetic Code

- In the 1960s, scientists cracked the genetic code—the translation between codons (sequences of three bases) and amino acids. They have found that the genetic code is similar in all living organisms. If a codon aligns with a particular amino acid in humans, the same codon aligns with the same amino acid in bacteria. This similarity suggests that all life-forms have a common evolutionary ancestor.

Is That a Fact!

- ◆ Human DNA consists of about 3 billion base pairs. If you could print a book with all the genetic information carried in just one human cell, it would be 500,000 pages long.

Amino Acids

- All known organisms produce proteins using only 20 amino acids as building blocks (some use a rare 21st amino acid). The human body can manufacture 10 of these amino acids. The other 10 must be obtained from proteins in the diet and for this reason are called the *essential* amino acids. Foods that contain all the essential amino acids at once include eggs, milk, seafood, and meat. However, all amino acids can be obtained from a varied diet.

Protein Synthesis

- It took many years for scientists to determine how protein is synthesized in the cell. The discovery that DNA's nucleotide sequence corresponds to a certain amino acid sequence was a key step in unlocking this mystery. This link was conclusively proven by Charles Yanofsky and Sydney Brenner in 1964.

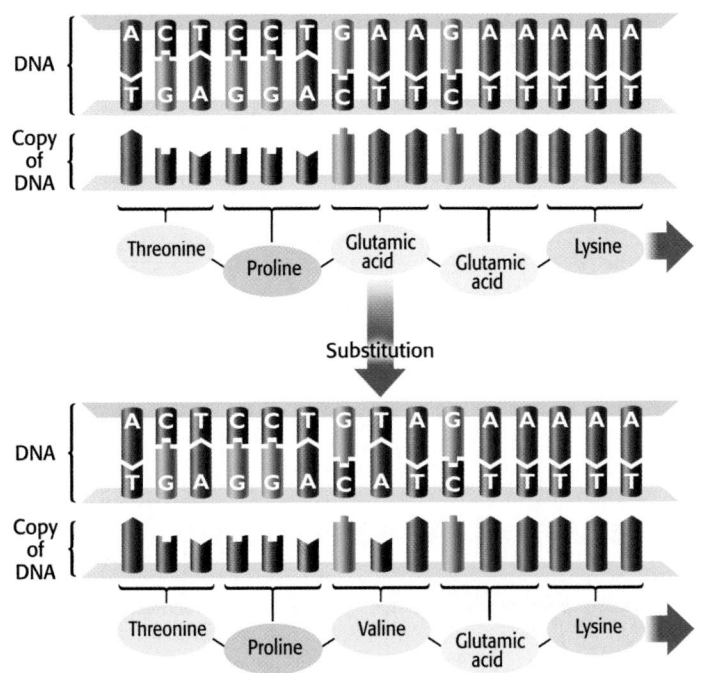

- The genetic sequences used to make proteins can be compared to sentences. Where each three-letter "word" in the genetic "sentence" starts and stops is very important for constructing a protein. For example, suppose the sentence to code for a particular protein read "PAT SAW THE FAT CAT." If you start just one base pair too late, the sentence would read "ATS AWT HEF ATC AT," which is meaningless.

Is That a Fact!

◆ If uncoiled, the DNA in the 46 chromosomes of a human body cell is about 2 m long. Within chromosomes, this DNA is so tightly coiled that if all 46 chromosomes were lined up end to end, they would span less than 0.5 cm.

Genetic Engineering

● Genetically engineered hybrid organisms are often called *chimeras*. The word *chimera* comes from Greek mythology, in which the Chimera was a fire-breathing monster, usually depicted as a composite of a lion, a goat, and a serpent.

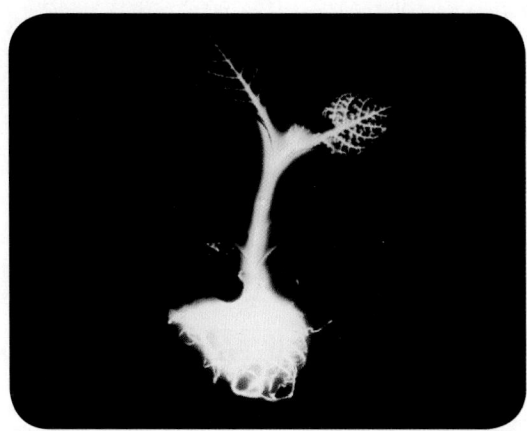

● Scientists often disagree about the ethics of genetic engineering and about the safety risks involved. Dr. Maxine Frank Singer was one of the first scientists to warn the National Academy of Science of the potential hazards of genetic engineering. Because of the efforts of Dr. Singer and her colleagues, the National Institute of Health began to develop specific guidelines for genetic research as early as 1976. These guidelines, now regularly amended, continue to regulate the production and use of DNA and genetically engineered organisms.

The Human Genome Project

● The Human Genome Project (HGP) was started in 1990 as an international collaboration of scientists with the goal of mapping the entire sequence of DNA found in humans. In April 2003, in conjunction with the anniversary of the historic publication by Watson and Crick of DNA's molecular structure, the HGP announced that its work was mostly done. The HGP had completed mapping 99% of the human genetic code. Some mystery remained about the area of chromosomes called the *centromere*.

● Many potential benefits are predicted to result from the Human Genome Project, and some benefits have already been realized. Scientists working on the HGP have developed faster methods of determining the sequences within DNA samples. Also, scientists have improved methods of finding and tracking the functions of specific genes within cells. Such advances have made it easier to study the genetics of all kinds of organisms and to find the genetic indicators of specific kinds of cancer and other diseases.

DNA Fingerprints

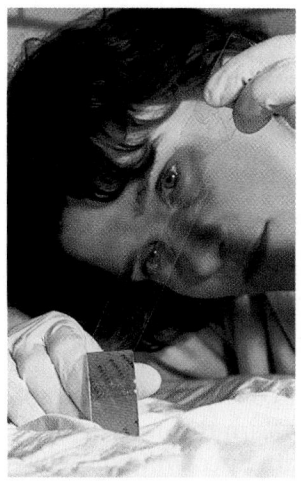

● DNA fingerprints are frequently used in criminal investigations. The DNA can come from hair, skin cells, blood, or other body fluids left at the crime scene by the perpetrator. Scientists use enzymes to make copies of specific DNA sections from different locations on different chromosomes. The copied fragments are separated by size and other characteristics on a gel, and they are stained to yield a unique set of dark bands on the gel. This set of bands is known as a *DNA fingerprint*. The fingerprint is then compared with the DNA fingerprint of the suspect to help determine innocence or guilt.

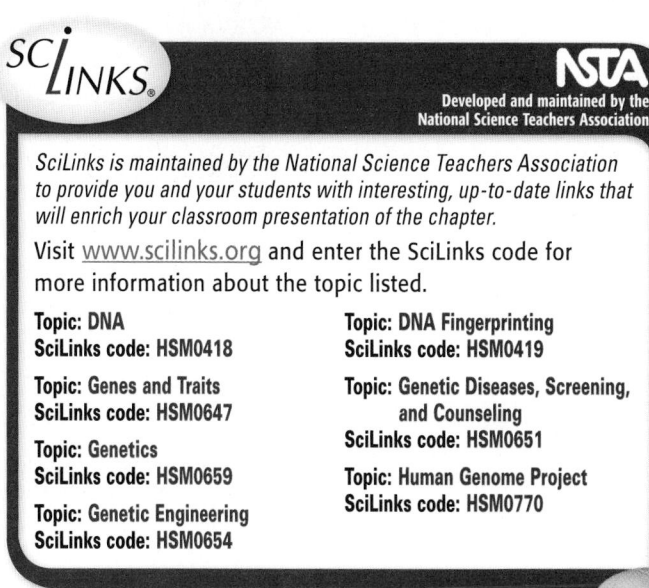

SciLinks is maintained by the National Science Teachers Association to provide you and your students with interesting, up-to-date links that will enrich your classroom presentation of the chapter.

Visit www.scilinks.org and enter the SciLinks code for more information about the topic listed.

Topic: DNA
SciLinks code: HSM0418

Topic: Genes and Traits
SciLinks code: HSM0647

Topic: Genetics
SciLinks code: HSM0659

Topic: Genetic Engineering
SciLinks code: HSM0654

Topic: DNA Fingerprinting
SciLinks code: HSM0419

Topic: Genetic Diseases, Screening, and Counseling
SciLinks code: HSM0651

Topic: Human Genome Project
SciLinks code: HSM0770

Overview

Tell students that this chapter is about DNA—the substance that makes up genes—and about how DNA works within cells to direct the growth and functioning of every organism.

Assessing Prior Knowledge

Students should be familiar with the following topics:

- cell structure
- mitosis and meiosis
- basic rules of heredity
- chromosomes

Identifying Misconceptions

The roles of DNA, RNA, and proteins in cells are very complex, and many puzzles remain. Students may tend to simplify their concept of the "rules" as they learn them. Students may remain unconvinced of the role of chance and probability in heredity. Also, students may have difficulty linking their knowledge of the functions of DNA at the cellular level to what they have learned and will learn about the functioning of tissues and organs within an entire organism.

6

Genes and DNA

About the PHOTO

These adult mice have no hair—not because their hair was shaved off but because these mice do not grow hair. In cells of these mice, the genes that normally cause hair to grow are not working. The genes were "turned off" by scientists who have learned to control the function of some genes. Scientists changed the genes of these mice to research medical problems such as cancer.

PRE-READING ACTIVITY

Graphic Organizer

Concept Map Before you read the chapter, create the graphic organizer entitled "Concept Map" described in the **Study Skills** section of the Appendix. As you read the chapter, fill in the concept map with details about DNA.

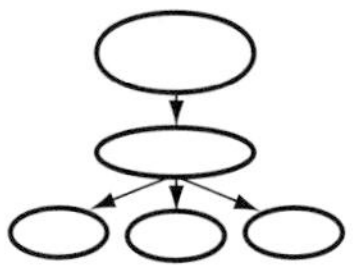

Standards Correlations

National Science Education Standards

The following codes indicate the National Science Education Standards that correlate to this chapter. The full text of the standards is at the front of the book.

Chapter Opener
UCP 5; SAI 1, 2; ST 2; LS 2e

Section 1 What Does DNA Look Like?
UCP 2, 5; SAI 1, 2; ST 1, 2; SPSP 5; HNS 1, 2, 3; LS 1a, 2d, 5a

Section 2 How DNA Works
UCP 1, 4, 5; SAI 1, 2; ST 2; SPSP 4, 5; LS 1c, 1e, 1f, 2b, 2c, 2d, 2e, 5b

Chapter Lab
UCP 2, 5; SAI 1, 2; HNS 1; LS 1a

Chapter Review
UCP 1, 2, 5; SAI 1, 2; ST 2; SPSP 4; HNS 2, 3; LS 1a, 1c, 1e, 1f, 2c, 2d, 2e, 5a, 5b

Science In Action
UCP 1, 2, 5; ST 2; SPSP 4 ,5; HNS 1, 2, 3; LS 1f

START-UP ACTIVITY
MATERIALS
FOR EACH GROUP
- magnifying lens
- paper, tracing (1 sheet)
- paper, white (1 sheet for each student)
- pencil or piece of charcoal
- tape, transparent

Safety Caution: Remind students to review all safety cautions and icons before beginning this lab activity. Charcoal is nontoxic, but it can stain clothes.

Teacher's Notes: The loop pattern is found in about 65% of the population, the whorl in about 30%, and the arch in about 5%.

Answers
1. The number of fingerprint types will vary for each class. No two students should have the same fingerprint (those of identical twins may be similar but still unique). Accept any reasonable explanation that incorporates variation in inherited traits among populations.

START-UP ACTIVITY

Fingerprint Your Friends

One way to identify people is by taking their fingerprints. Does it really work? Are everyone's fingerprints unique? Try this activity to find out.

Procedure

1. Rub the tip of a **pencil** back and forth across a **piece of tracing paper.** Make a large, dark mark.
2. Rub the tip of one of your fingers on the pencil mark. Then place a small **piece of transparent tape** over the darkened area on your finger.
3. Remove the tape, and stick it on **a piece of white paper.** Repeat steps 1–3 for the rest of your fingers.
4. Look at the fingerprints with a **magnifying lens.** What patterns do you see? Is the pattern the same on every finger?

Analysis

1. Compare your fingerprints with those of your classmates. Do any two people in your class have the same prints? Try to explain your findings.

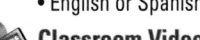

Chapter Starter Transparency
Use this transparency to help students begin thinking about genes and DNA.

CHAPTER RESOURCES

Technology

- **Transparencies**
  - Chapter Starter Transparency — READING SKILLS
- **Student Edition on CD-ROM**
- **Guided Reading Audio CD**
  - English or Spanish
- **Classroom Videos**
  - Brain Food Video Quiz

Workbooks

- **Science Puzzlers, Twisters & Teasers**
  - Genes and DNA GENERAL

Focus

Overview

This section introduces students to the structure and function of DNA and to the process of DNA replication.

🔊 Bellringer

To test prior knowledge, have students answer the following questions:

1. Give an example of the difference between traits and characteristics. (Sample answer: Eye color is a characteristic, while having blue eyes is a trait.)

2. Where are genes found in cells? (in chromosomes; in cells that have nuclei, chromosomes are within the nucleus)

Motivate

ACTIVITY ——— GENERAL

Modeling Code Create a code by pairing each letter of the alphabet with a numeral. For example, the numeral 1 could represent the letter *a*. Have students encode a brief message. Then, have students exchange and decode the message. Explain that a code is simply another way to represent information and that there are many types of codes. The genetic code is based on sequences of the four nucleotide bases of DNA. **English Language Learners**

LS Logical

READING WARM-UP

Objectives

● List three important events that led to understanding the structure of DNA.

● Describe the basic structure of a DNA molecule.

● Explain how DNA molecules can be copied.

Terms to Learn

DNA
nucleotide

READING STRATEGY

Prediction Guide Before reading this section, write the title of each heading in this section. Next, under each heading, write what you think you will learn.

DNA **d**eoxyribo**n**ucleic **a**cid, a molecule that is present in all living cells and that contains the information that determines the traits that a living thing inherits and needs to live

nucleotide in a nucleic-acid chain, a subunit that consists of a sugar, a phosphate, and a nitrogenous base

---

What Does DNA Look Like?

For many years, the structure of a DNA molecule was a puzzle to scientists. In the 1950s, two scientists deduced the structure while experimenting with chemical models. They later won a Nobel Prize for helping solve this puzzle!

Inherited characteristics are determined by genes, and genes are passed from one generation to the next. Genes are parts of chromosomes, which are structures in the nucleus of most cells. Chromosomes are made of protein and DNA. **DNA** stands for *deoxyribonucleic acid* (dee AHKS ee RIE boh noo KLEE ik AS id). DNA is the genetic material—the material that determines inherited characteristics. But what does DNA look like?

The Pieces of the Puzzle

Scientists knew that the material that makes up genes must be able to do two things. First, it must be able to give instructions for building and maintaining cells. Second, it must be able to be copied each time a cell divides, so that each cell contains identical genes. Scientists thought that these things could be done only by complex molecules, such as proteins. They were surprised to learn how much the DNA molecule could do.

Nucleotides: The Subunits of DNA

DNA is made of subunits called nucleotides. A **nucleotide** consists of a sugar, a phosphate, and a base. The nucleotides are identical except for the base. The four bases are *adenine, thymine, guanine,* and *cytosine.* Each base has a different shape. Scientists often refer to a base by the first letter of the base, *A, T, G,* and *C.* **Figure 1** shows models of the four nucleotides.

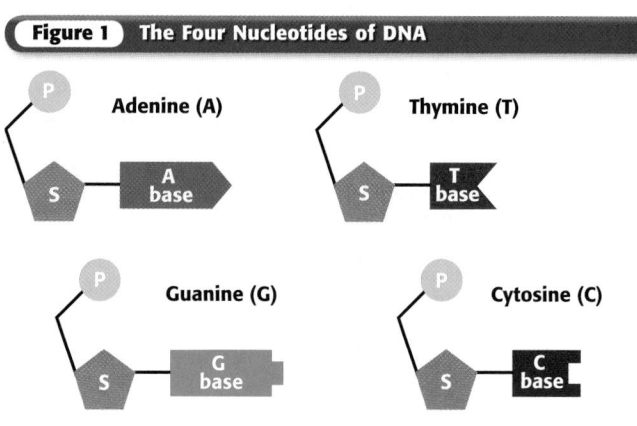

Figure 1 The Four Nucleotides of DNA

CHAPTER RESOURCES

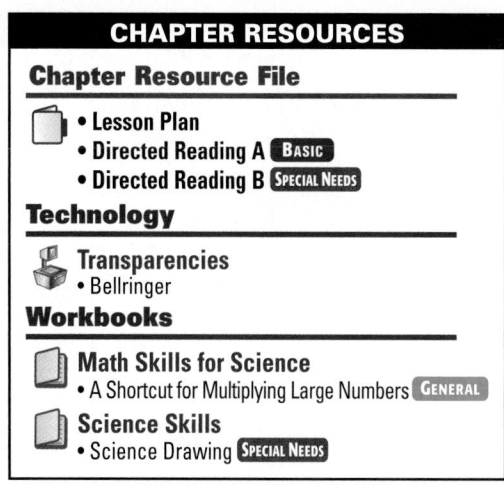

Chapter Resource File

- **Lesson Plan**
- **Directed Reading A** BASIC
- **Directed Reading B** SPECIAL NEEDS

Technology

Transparencies
- Bellringer

Workbooks

Math Skills for Science
- A Shortcut for Multiplying Large Numbers GENERAL

Science Skills
- Science Drawing SPECIAL NEEDS

Chargaff's Rules

In the 1950s, a biochemist named Erwin Chargaff found that the amount of adenine in DNA always equals the amount of thymine. And he found that the amount of guanine always equals the amount of cytosine. His findings are known as *Chargaff's rules*. At the time of his discovery, no one knew the importance of these findings. But Chargaff's rules later helped scientists understand the structure of DNA.

✓ Reading Check Summarize Chargaff's rules. (*See the Appendix for answers to Reading Checks.*)

Franklin's Discovery

More clues about the structure of DNA came from scientists in Britain. There, chemist Rosalind Franklin, shown in **Figure 2**, was able to make images of DNA molecules. She used a process known as *X-ray diffraction* to make these images. In this process, X rays are aimed at the DNA molecule. When an X ray hits a part of the molecule, the ray bounces off. The pattern made by the bouncing rays is captured on film. Franklin's images suggested that DNA has a spiral shape.

Watson and Crick's Model

At about the same time, two other scientists were also trying to solve the mystery of DNA's structure. They were James Watson and Francis Crick, shown in **Figure 3.** After seeing Franklin's X-ray images, Watson and Crick concluded that DNA must look like a long, twisted ladder. They were then able to build a model of DNA by using simple materials from their laboratory. Their model perfectly fit with both Chargaff's and Franklin's findings. The model eventually helped explain how DNA is copied and how it functions in the cell.

CONNECTION TO
Chemistry

WRITING SKILL **Linus Pauling** Many scientists contributed to the discovery of DNA's structure. In fact, some scientists competed to be the first to make the discovery. One of these competitors was a chemist named Linus Pauling. Research and write a paragraph about how Pauling's work helped Watson and Crick.

Figure 2 *Rosalind Franklin used X-ray diffraction to make images of DNA that helped reveal the structure of DNA.*

Figure 3 *This photo shows James Watson (left) and Francis Crick (right) with their model of DNA.*

Answer to Connection to Chemistry

Linus Pauling was an innovator in the use of models to deduce chemical behavior. Whereas some scientists belittled the practice of "playing" with chemical models, Pauling inspired other scientists, such as Watson and Crick, to try this strategy. Watson and Crick's deduction of DNA's ladder structure was partly brought about by manipulating models of nucleotides.

Teach

📖 READING STRATEGY — BASIC

Mnemonics Have students create a mnemonic device that will remind them of the names of the bases and the way the bases form pairs. Examples such as "**A**toms are **T**iny" or "**A**dam is **T**errific" might help remind students that **a**denine pairs with **t**hymine. "**C**athy is **G**reat" might remind them that **c**ytosine pairs with **g**uanine.
LS Verbal/Logical

Answer to Reading Check

Guanine and cytosine always occur in equal amounts in DNA, as do adenine and thymine.

🔵 INCLUSION Strategies

• *Learning Disabled*
• *Attention Deficit Disorder*
• *Behavior Control Issues*
Give students a chance to move around while they learn. Have students group themselves by eye color: all blues together, etc. Then, have students within each eye color group line up from lightest shade to darkest shade. Assign a spokesman within each group to explain how they decided the order for their line up. Also, ask each team to tell the number of unique eye colors within the team.   English Language Learners
LS Kinesthetic

A Place in History Have students imagine that they have just discovered the structure of DNA and must present their findings to a group of scientists. Have small groups of students use a model of DNA, a poster, or another visual aid to briefly describe the structure of DNA to their classmates. **LS** Verbal

DNA's Complementary Strands
To help students understand
how the term *complementary*
relates to the structure of DNA,
point out that the term means
"completing." Using **Figure 4**
and **Figure 5,** explain that complementary base pairs join to
complete each rung on the
spiral-staircase structure of DNA.
Then, point out that complementary strands of DNA join to
complete one DNA molecule.
LS Visual/Verbal

Quiz — GENERAL

1. When is DNA copied? (every
time a cell divides)

2. Name the four types of
nucleotides. (adenine, thymine,
guanine, and cytosine)

Alternative
Assessment — GENERAL

Custom Code Have
students create an alter-
native code that functions like
DNA in the following ways:

- The code is based on four
letters or symbols.

- Coded information can be split
up and then reassembled.

Have students draw and explain
their coding system. **LS** Logical

Quick Lab

Making a Model of DNA

1. Gather assorted simple
materials that you could
use to build a basic
model of DNA. You
might use **clay, string,
toothpicks, paper,
tape, plastic foam,**
or **pieces of food.**

2. Work with a partner or a
small team to build your
model. Use your book and
other resources to check
the details of your model.

3. Show your model to your
classmates. Give your
classmates feedback about
the scientific aspects of
their models.

DNA's Double Structure

The shape of DNA is shown in **Figure 4.** As you can see, a strand
of DNA looks like a twisted ladder. This shape is known as a
double helix (DUB uhl HEE liks). The two sides of the ladder
are made of alternating sugar parts and phosphate parts. The
rungs of the ladder are made of a pair of bases. Adenine on
one side of a rung always pairs with thymine on the other
side. Guanine always pairs with cytosine.

Notice how the double helix structure matches Chargaff's
observations. When Chargaff separated the parts of a sample
of DNA, he found that the matching bases were always present
in equal amounts. To model how the bases pair, Watson and
Crick tried to match Chargaff's observations. They also used
information from chemists about the size and shape of each of
the nucleotides. As it turned out, the width of the DNA ladder
matches the combined width of the matching bases. Only the
correct pairs of bases fit within the ladder's width.

Making Copies of DNA

The pairing of bases allows the cell to *replicate*, or make copies
of, DNA. Each base always bonds with only one other base.
Thus, pairs of bases are *complementary* to each other, and both
sides of a DNA molecule are complementary. For example, the
sequence CGAC will bond to the sequence GCTG.

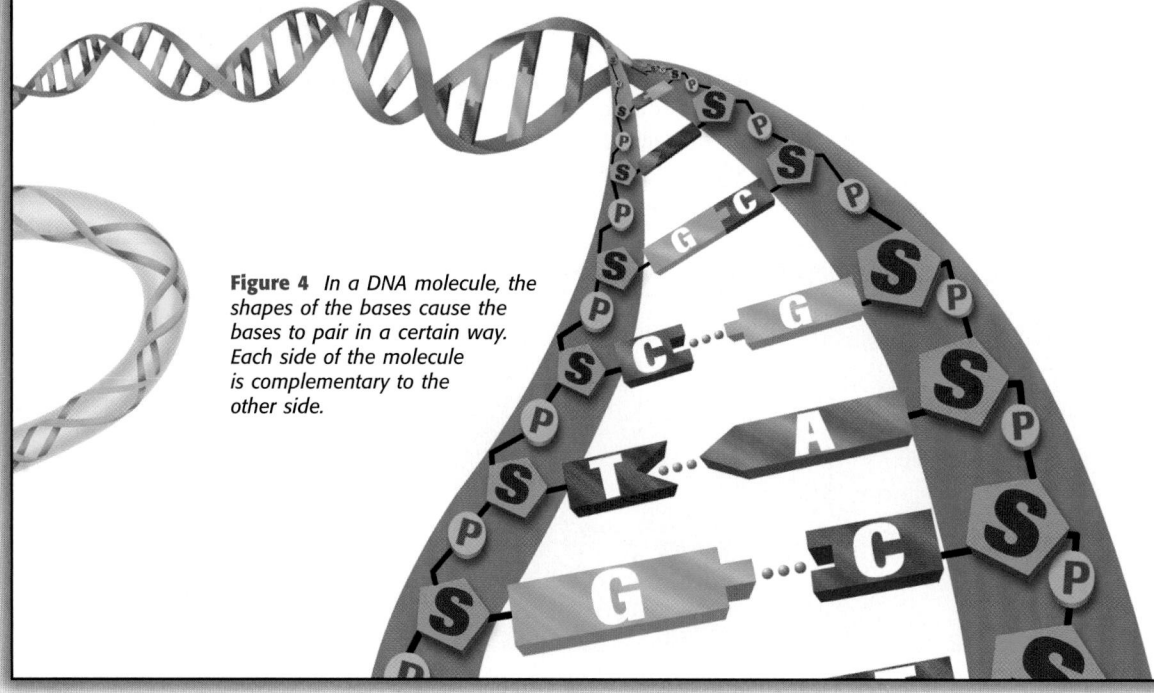

Figure 4 *In a DNA molecule, the
shapes of the bases cause the
bases to pair in a certain way.
Each side of the molecule
is complementary to the
other side.*

Quick Lab

MATERIALS

FOR EACH GROUP
- variety of materials, such as clay, string,
toothpicks, paper, tape, plastic foam, beads
or buttons and pipe cleaners or wire.
- food or candy items could be another option

Teacher's Note: Display student models
within the school. Have students
reevaluate or improve upon them later.

Safety Caution: Advise students to
keep the area around them uncluttered.
Students should exercise caution with
sharp objects. Any food items used should
not be eaten and should be disposed of.

Answers
2. Student models should resemble **Figure 4**
in basic structure but may vary in size,
color, and construction.
3. Students should suggest ways to make
each model more accurate.

How Copies Are Made

During replication, as shown in **Figure 5,** a DNA molecule is split down the middle, where the bases meet. The bases on each side of the molecule are used as a pattern for a new strand. As the bases on the original molecule are exposed, complementary nucleotides are added to each side of the ladder. Two DNA molecules are formed. Half of each of the molecules is old DNA, and half is new DNA.

When Copies Are Made

DNA is copied every time a cell divides. Each new cell gets a complete copy of all the DNA. The job of unwinding, copying, and re-winding the DNA is done by proteins within the cell. So, DNA is usually found with several kinds of proteins. Other proteins help with the process of carrying out the instructions written in the code of the DNA.

✔ **Reading Check** How often is DNA copied?

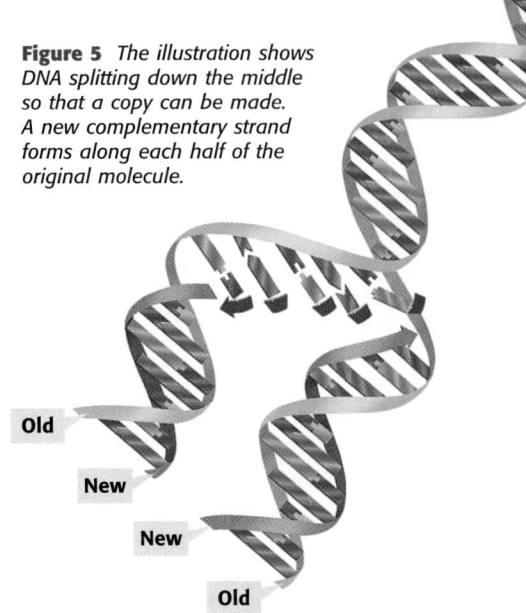

Figure 5 The illustration shows DNA splitting down the middle so that a copy can be made. A new complementary strand forms along each half of the original molecule.

Old

New

New

Old

SECTION Review

Summary

- DNA is the material that makes up genes. It carries coded information that is copied in each new cell.
- The DNA molecule looks like a twisted ladder. The two halves are long strings of nucleotides. The rungs are complementary pairs of bases.
- Because each base has a complementary base, DNA can be replicated accurately.

Using Key Terms

1. Use the term *DNA* in a sentence.

2. In your own words, write a definition for the term *nucleotide.*

Understanding Key Ideas

3. List three important events that led to understanding the structure of DNA.

4. Which of the following is NOT part of a nucleotide?
   a. base
   b. sugar
   c. fat
   d. phosphate

Math Skills

5. If a sample of DNA contained 20% cytosine, what percentage of guanine would be in this sample? What percentage of adenine would be in the sample? Explain.

Critical Thinking

6. **Making Inferences** Explain what is meant by the statement "DNA unites all organisms."

7. **Applying Concepts** What would the complementary strand of DNA be for the sequence of bases below?

   C T T A G G C T T A C C A

8. **Analyzing Processes** How are copies of DNA made? Draw a picture as part of your answer.

Developed and maintained by the National Science Teachers Association

For a variety of links related to this chapter, go to www.scilinks.org

Topic: DNA; Genes and Traits
SciLinks code: HSM0418; HSM0647

Answers to Section Review

1. Sample answer: DNA is the material that makes up genes and is found in all cells.

2. Sample answer: A nucleotide is a subunit of a DNA molecule and consists of a sugar, a phosphate, and a base; there are four kinds of bases and thus four kinds of nucleotides.

3. Sample answers: Scientists thought only complex materials such as proteins could make up genes; Erwin Chargaff discovered the rules of nucleotide base pairing; Rosalind Franklin made images of DNA molecules; Watson and Crick made a correct model of DNA's structure.

4. c

5. 20% guanine, because it should be equal to the amount of cytosine; 30% adenine, because the remaining 60% of the DNA should be made up of equal amounts of adenine and thymine

6. Sample answer: DNA is found in the cells of all organisms.

7. GAATCCGAATGGT

8. DNA copies are made by splitting the molecule down the middle and then adding new nucleotides to each side. (Students' drawings should resemble **Figure 5.**)

Answer to Reading Check
every time a cell divides

CHAPTER RESOURCES

Chapter Resource File

- Section Quiz GENERAL
- Section Review GENERAL
- Vocabulary and Section Summary GENERAL
- SciLinks Activity GENERAL
- Datasheet for Quick Lab

Technology

Transparencies
- DNA Structure

Overview

This section shows how DNA is a part of chromosomes, how DNA is used as a template for making proteins, and how errors in DNA can lead to mutations and genetic disorders.

🎙 Bellringer

Have students unscramble the following words and use them both in one sentence:

tpsoneir (proteins)

neesg (genes)

(Sample answer: Genes contain instructions for making proteins.)

Motivate

Demonstration — GENERAL

A Tight Fit To illustrate the way that DNA is *supercoiled* within chromosomes and cells, hold up a long rubber band or thick piece of string. Begin to twist each end in opposite directions until coils form. Continue twisting until the band is highly compacted. Then, challenge students to fit 2 m of fine thread into a thimble or an empty gelatin capsule. English Language Learners

🔳 Kinesthetic

Answer to Reading Check

a string of nucleotides that give the cell information about how to make a specific trait

---

SECTION
2

How DNA Works

Almost every cell in your body contains about 2 m of DNA. How does all of the DNA fit in a cell? And how does the DNA hold a code that affects your traits?

DNA is found in the cells of all organisms, including bacteria, mosquitoes, and humans. Each organism has a unique set of DNA. But DNA functions the same way in all organisms.

Unraveling DNA

DNA is often wound around proteins, coiled into strands, and then bundled up even more. In a cell that lacks a nucleus, each strand of DNA forms a loose loop within the cell. In a cell that has a nucleus, the strands of DNA and proteins are bundled into chromosomes, as shown in **Figure 1.**

The structure of DNA allows DNA to hold information. The order of the bases on one side of the molecule is a code that carries information. A *gene* consists of a string of nucleotides that give the cell information about how to make a specific trait. There is an enormous amount of DNA, so there can be a large variety of genes.

✓ **Reading Check** What makes up a gene? (*See the Appendix for answers to Reading Checks.*)

READING WARM-UP

Objectives
● Explain the relationship between DNA, genes, and proteins.
● Outline the basic steps in making a protein.
● Describe three types of mutations, and provide an example of a gene mutation.
● Describe two examples of uses of genetic knowledge.

Terms to Learn
RNA
ribosome
mutation

READING STRATEGY

Reading Organizer As you read this section, make a flowchart of the steps of how DNA codes for proteins.

Figure 1 **Unraveling DNA**

ⓐ A typical skin cell has a diameter of about 0.0025 cm. The DNA in the nucleus of each cell codes for proteins that determine traits such as skin color.

ⓑ The DNA in the nucleus is part of a material called *chromatin*. Long strands of chromatin are usually bundled loosely within the nucleus.

⚛ WEIRD SCIENCE

In 2003, the Human Genome Project had successfully mapped 99% of the 3 billion base pairs that make up a set of human DNA. But the project has raised new questions as well. For example, only about 3% of those base pairs are used in making proteins; the other 97% are regulatory sequences, nonfunctioning genes, and sequences with no known function.

Additionally, scientists originally expected to find over 50,000 human genes because human cells produce at least that many proteins. Instead, latest estimates indicate that there are about 25,000 human genes, and many genes code for multiple proteins. In this and other ways, human genes appear to be unique among organisms.

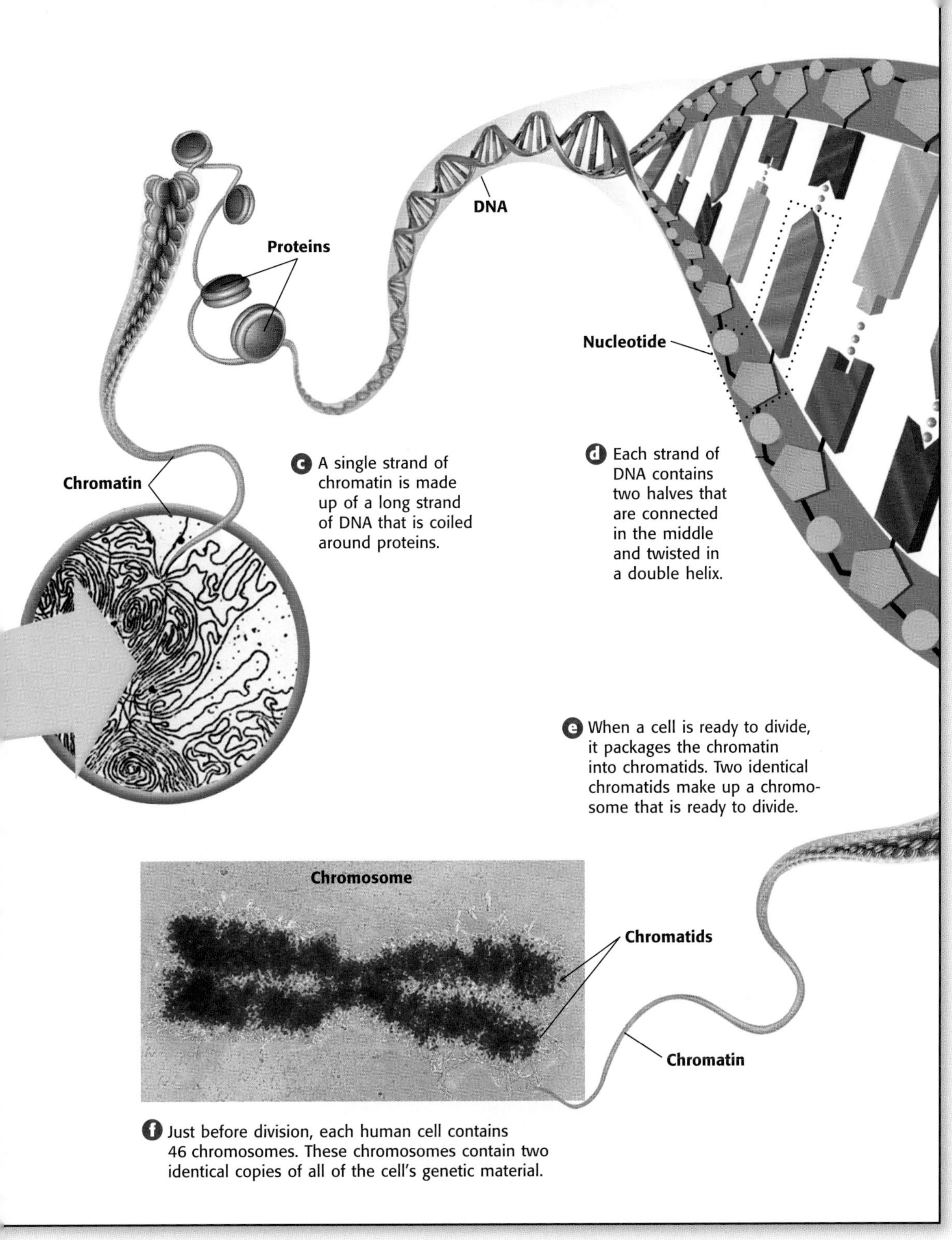

DNA

Proteins

Chromatin

c A single strand of chromatin is made up of a long strand of DNA that is coiled around proteins.

Nucleotide

d Each strand of DNA contains two halves that are connected in the middle and twisted in a double helix.

e When a cell is ready to divide, it packages the chromatin into chromatids. Two identical chromatids make up a chromosome that is ready to divide.

Chromosome

Chromatids

Chromatin

f Just before division, each human cell contains 46 chromosomes. These chromosomes contain two identical copies of all of the cell's genetic material.

Using the Figure—BASIC

Unraveling DNA Have students carefully study **Figure 1.** Remind them that each chromosome is a pair of chromatids, and each chromatid is one long strand of DNA. This DNA strand is usually somewhat wound up around proteins in the form of chromatin. The chromatin may be tightly bundled (and visible) or loose (and not visible) within the nucleus. Most of the time, the chromatin is loose. Ask students the following questions:

- Where is the DNA in your cells? (in the nucleus)
- How does so much DNA fit into the nucleus? (It is coiled up tightly around proteins.)
- What is the name for strands of DNA wound around proteins? (chromatin)
- When do chromosomes become visible in cells? (when the cell is about to divide)
- What are chromatids? (two identical copies of a chromosome that is about to divide)

LS Visual/Auditory

BRAIN FOOD

Hereditary Hearing
Researchers are trying to find out if a gene is responsible for "perfect pitch," the ability to determine any musical note upon hearing it. It is a rare ability—possessed by one in every 2,000 people—found most often among musicians. People with perfect pitch can easily tell the musical note of a dial tone, the hum of a refrigerator, or of any sound they hear. The researchers think that people with perfect pitch may inherit the ability, but an early education in music may also be necessary.

MISCONCEPTION ALERT

DNA from the Dead Can ancient DNA be used to produce dinosaurs? In some science fiction, scientists make dinosaurs by combining fragments of ancient DNA with DNA from modern organisms. In reality, less-ancient fragments of DNA have indeed been found. However, a fragment of DNA is not enough information to make an entire organism. And identifying the owner of a given DNA fragment is difficult.

CHAPTER RESOURCES

Technology

Transparencies
- Unraveling DNA

CONNECTION ACTIVITY
Chemistry ———— ADVANCED

Proteins' Roles
Have the students pair up. Then, have each pair of students select an important human protein to research. Suggest proteins such as insulin, hemoglobin, dopamine, somatostatin, erythropoetin (EPO), Alpha-1 antitrypsin (AAT), and Factor V (blood-clotting protein). Tell students to summarize the role the protein plays in the human body and to find out a disease that is caused by a mutation in the gene that codes for this protein. Have each pair of students present their findings on small placards that can be displayed in the classroom or school. **LS** Logical/Verbal

Group ACTIVITY — GENERAL

Skit Have groups of students write and perform a short skit to demonstrate the formation of a protein. For example, students could play the roles of a ribosome, an amino acid, a transfer RNA, and a DNA copy.
LS Kinesthetic/ Interpersonal   English Language Learners

INTERNET ACTIVITY

For another activity related to this chapter, go to **go.hrw.com** and type in the keyword **HL5DNAW**.

RNA ribonucleic acid, a molecule that is present in all living cells and that plays a role in protein production

Genes and Proteins

The DNA code is read like a book—from one end to the other and in one direction. The bases form the alphabet of the code. Groups of three bases are the codes for specific amino acids. For example, the three bases CCA form the code for the amino acid proline. The bases AGC form the code for the amino acid serine. A long string of amino acids forms a protein. Thus, each gene is usually a set of instructions for making a protein.

Proteins and Traits

How are proteins related to traits? Proteins are found throughout cells and cause most of the differences that you can see among organisms. Proteins act as chemical triggers and messengers for many of the processes within cells. Proteins help determine how tall you grow, what colors you can see, and whether your hair is curly or straight. Proteins exist in an almost limitless variety. A single organism may have thousands of genes that code for thousands of proteins.

Help from RNA

Another type of molecule that helps make proteins is called **RNA**, or *ribonucleic acid* (RIE boh noo KLEE ik AS id). RNA is so similar to DNA that RNA can serve as a temporary copy of a DNA sequence. Several forms of RNA help in the process of changing the DNA code into proteins, as shown in **Figure 2**.

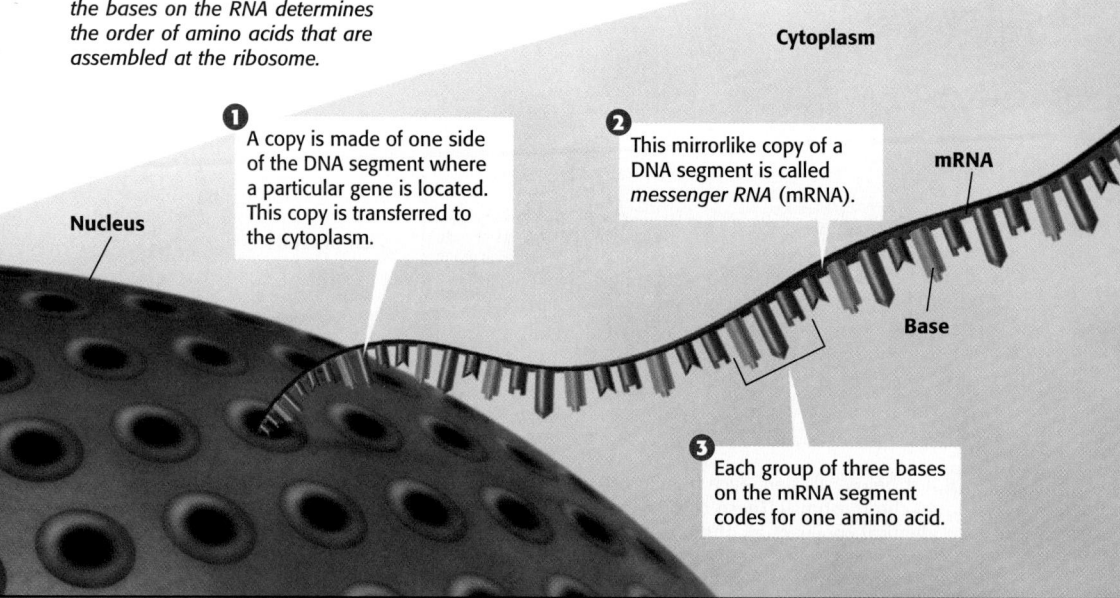

Figure 2 *Proteins are built in the cytoplasm by using RNA copies of a segment of DNA. The order of the bases on the RNA determines the order of amino acids that are assembled at the ribosome.*

Cytoplasm

1 A copy is made of one side of the DNA segment where a particular gene is located. This copy is transferred to the cytoplasm.

Nucleus

2 This mirrorlike copy of a DNA segment is called *messenger RNA* (mRNA).

mRNA

Base

3 Each group of three bases on the mRNA segment codes for one amino acid.

Homework ———— GENERAL

Research Have students collect information on the use of amino acids to gain muscle. Suggest that they look at ads for amino acid supplements in health-food or fitness magazines or at labels of amino acid powdered drinks at the supermarket. Use these materials to discuss issues such as the expense of such supplements and how they might be used by the body. Discuss how amino acids might be acquired in a balanced diet. **LS** Logical

SCIENCE HUMOR

Q: What happens when an amateur-tein gets paid?

A: It becomes a pro-tein.

The Making of a Protein

The first step in making a protein is to copy one side of the segment of DNA containing a gene. A mirrorlike copy of the DNA segment is made out of RNA. This copy of the DNA segment is called *messenger RNA* (mRNA). It moves out of the nucleus and into the cytoplasm of the cell.

In the cytoplasm, the messenger RNA is fed through a protein assembly line. The "factory" that runs this assembly line is known as a ribosome. A **ribosome** is a cell organelle composed of RNA and protein. The messenger RNA is fed through the ribosome three bases at a time. Then, molecules of *transfer RNA* (tRNA) translate the RNA message. Each transfer RNA molecule picks up a specific amino acid from the cytoplasm. Inside the ribosome, bases on the transfer RNA match up with bases on the messenger RNA like pieces of a puzzle. The transfer RNA molecules then release their amino acids. The amino acids become linked in a growing chain. As the entire segment of messenger RNA passes through the ribosome, the growing chain of amino acids folds up into a new protein molecule.

✓ **Reading Check** What do the transfer RNA molecules transfer?

Code Combinations

A given sequence of three bases codes for one amino acid. For example, AGT is one possible sequence. How many different sequences of the four DNA base types are possible? (Hint: Make a list.)

ribosome a cell organelle composed of RNA and protein; the site of protein synthesis

CONNECTION ACTiViTy

Math ——————— GENERAL

Redundant Code Mathematics has a lot to do with how DNA codes for amino acids. Each combination of three nucleotides that codes for one amino acid is called a *codon*. Yet cells use only 20 different amino acids to build proteins. Thus, most amino acids have several, redundant corresponding codons. This redundancy is another reason that mutations in genes do not always result in changes in proteins. To physically model the possible base combinations that make up codons, organize the class into small groups. Give each group four pieces of paper, with one of the following four letters printed on each piece: *A, T, C,* or *G*. Ask students to come up with as many different three-letter "words" as possible by using the four different bases. (There are 4³, or 64, possible three-letter "words"—or codons. For example, the four possible combinations that would start with the bases AA are AAA, AAT, AAG, and AAC.) Check that students realize that the order of letters in each combination also matters. For example, *ATA* is not the same "word" as *AAT*. **LS Kinesthetic/Logical**

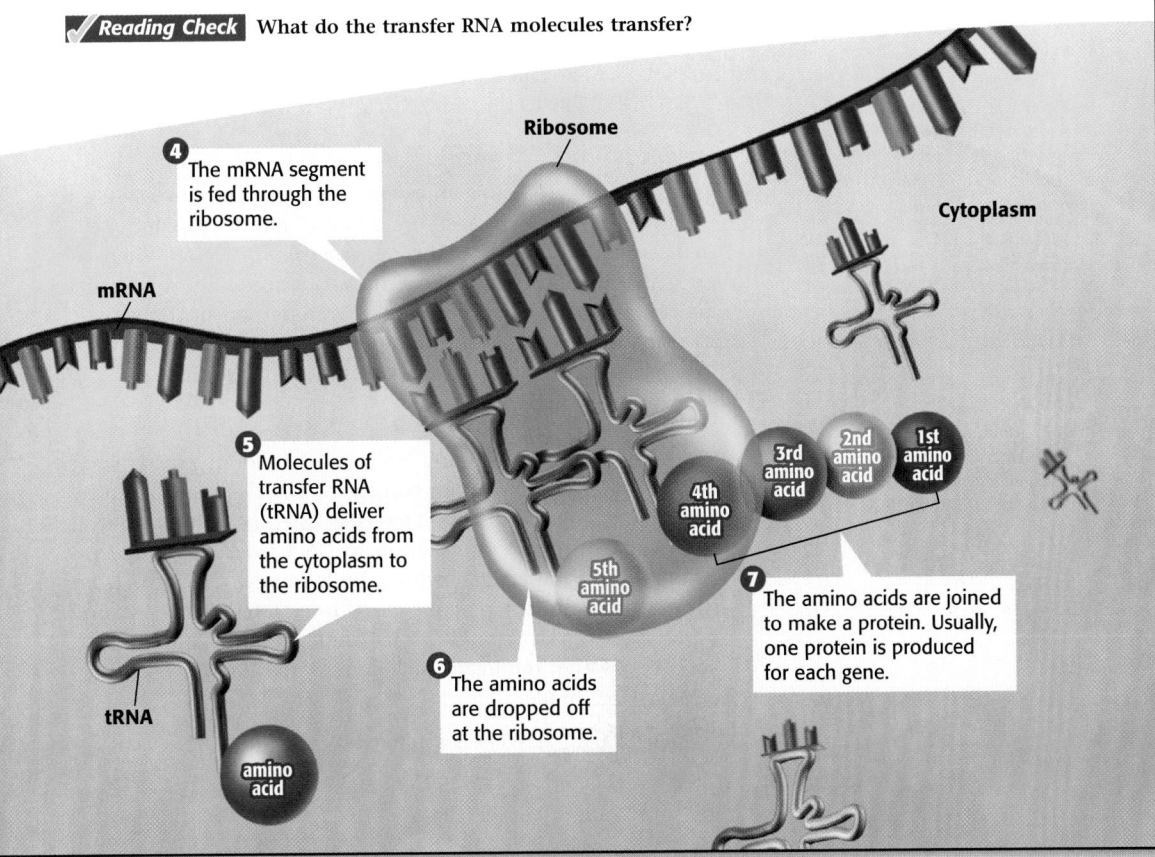

Ribosome

④ The mRNA segment is fed through the ribosome.

Cytoplasm

mRNA

1st amino acid
2nd amino acid
3rd amino acid
4th amino acid
5th amino acid

⑤ Molecules of transfer RNA (tRNA) deliver amino acids from the cytoplasm to the ribosome.

tRNA

amino acid

⑥ The amino acids are dropped off at the ribosome.

⑦ The amino acids are joined to make a protein. Usually, one protein is produced for each gene.

WEiRD SCIENCE

There is a gene located on the X chromosome that causes thick hair to grow on the upper body and face, including the ears, nose, cheeks, forehead, and even eyelids of people who have the gene. This condition is sometimes called *werewolf syndrome* because people who have the condition resemble fictional werewolves. This condition affects only appearance, however, not behavior.

CHAPTER RESOURCES

Technology

📦 **Transparencies**
• The Making of a Protein: A
• The Making of a Protein: B

Complementary Code Write a sequence of DNA bases, such as AACTACGGT, on the board. Ask students to write the complementary base sequence by using base-pairing rules. (TTGATGCCA) Then, ask students to give examples of deletions, insertions, and substitutions. **LS Visual/Verbal**   English Language Learners

---

MISCONCEPTION ///ALERT\\\

Mutants Among Us? Students may think mutations occur rarely, because organisms that are visibly "mutated" appear infrequently. However, scientists estimate that mistakes are made during DNA replication in approximately one out of every 10,000 base pairs. With cellular proofing mechanisms, the final error rate is as low as one in a billion. Still, we inherit hundreds of mutations from our parents' gametes. Many mutations have no apparent effect. For example, a mutation may occur in a cell that does not produce a particular protein or in a "junk" region of DNA that does not code for anything.

Answer to Reading Check

a physical or chemical agent that can cause a mutation in DNA

Original sequence

a **Base pair replaced**

b **Base pair added**

c **Base pair removed**

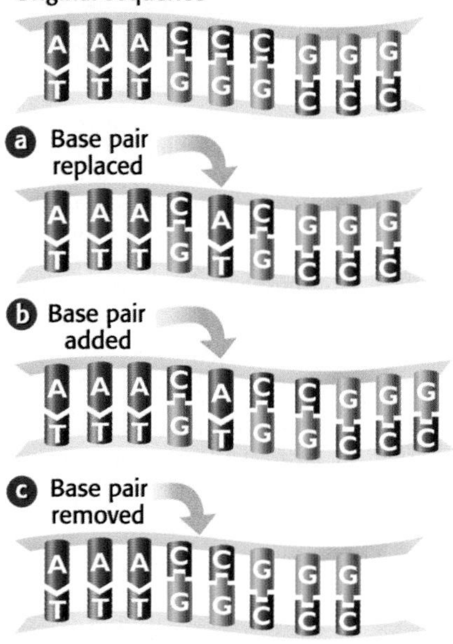

Figure 3 *The original base sequence on the top has been changed to illustrate (a) a substitution, (b) an insertion, and (c) a deletion.*

mutation a change in the nucleotide-base sequence of a gene or DNA molecule

---

Changes in Genes

Imagine that you have been invited to ride on a new roller coaster at the state fair. Before you climb into the front car, you are told that some of the metal parts on the coaster have been replaced by parts made of a different substance. Would you still want to ride this roller coaster? Perhaps a strong metal was used as a substitute. Or perhaps a material that is not strong enough was used. Imagine what would happen if cardboard were used instead of metal!

Mutations

Substitutions like the ones in the roller coaster can accidentally happen in DNA. Changes in the number, type, or order of bases on a piece of DNA are known as **mutations.** Sometimes, a base is left out. This kind of change is known as a *deletion.* Or an extra base might be added. This kind of change is known as an *insertion.* The most common change happens when the wrong base is used. This kind of change is known as a *substitution.* **Figure 3** illustrates these three types of mutations.

Do Mutations Matter?

There are three possible consequences to changes in DNA: an improved trait, no change, or a harmful trait. Fortunately, cells make some proteins that can detect errors in DNA. When an error is found, it is usually fixed. But occasionally the repairs are not accurate, and the mistakes become part of the genetic message. If the mutation occurs in the sex cells, the changed gene can be passed from one generation to the next.

How Do Mutations Happen?

Mutations happen regularly because of random errors when DNA is copied. In addition, damage to DNA can be caused by abnormal things that happen to cells. Any physical or chemical agent that can cause a mutation in DNA is called a *mutagen.* Examples of mutagens include high-energy radiation from X rays and ultraviolet radiation. Ultraviolet radiation is one type of energy in sunlight. It is responsible for suntans and sunburns. Other mutagens include asbestos and the chemicals in cigarette smoke.

✓ Reading Check What is a mutagen?

CHAPTER RESOURCES

Technology

 Transparencies
- *LINK TO EARTH SCIENCE* The Formation of Smog
- How Sickle Cell Anemia Results from a Mutation

CONNECTION to Earth Science ── GENERAL

Pollution and Ozone Ozone is a gas made of three oxygen atoms. High in the atmosphere, ozone absorbs dangerous ultraviolet radiation (the high-energy light that can cause DNA mutations). When produced near the surface of the Earth, however, ozone is a pollutant that affects plant growth and makes breathing more difficult. Use the teaching transparency entitled "The Formation of Smog" to illustrate the process of ozone production. **LS Visual**

An Example of a Substitution

A mutation, such as a substitution, can be harmful because it may cause a gene to produce the wrong protein. Consider the DNA sequence GAA. When copied as mRNA, this sequence gives the instructions to place the amino acid glutamic acid into the growing protein. If a mistake happens and the original DNA sequence is changed to GTA, the sequence will code for the amino acid valine instead.

This simple change in an amino acid can cause the disease *sickle cell disease*. Sickle cell disease affects red blood cells. When valine is substituted for glutamic acid in a blood protein, as shown in **Figure 4,** the red blood cells are changed into a sickle shape.

The sickle cells are not as good at carrying oxygen as normal red blood cells are. Sickle cells are also likely to get stuck in blood vessels and cause painful and dangerous clots.

Reading Check What causes sickle cell disease?

An Error in the Message

The sentence below is the result of an error similar to a DNA mutation. The original sentence was made up of three-letter words, but an error was made in this copy. Explain the idea of mutations to your parent. Then, work together to find the mutation, and write the sentence correctly.

THE IGB ADC ATA TET HEB IGR EDR AT.

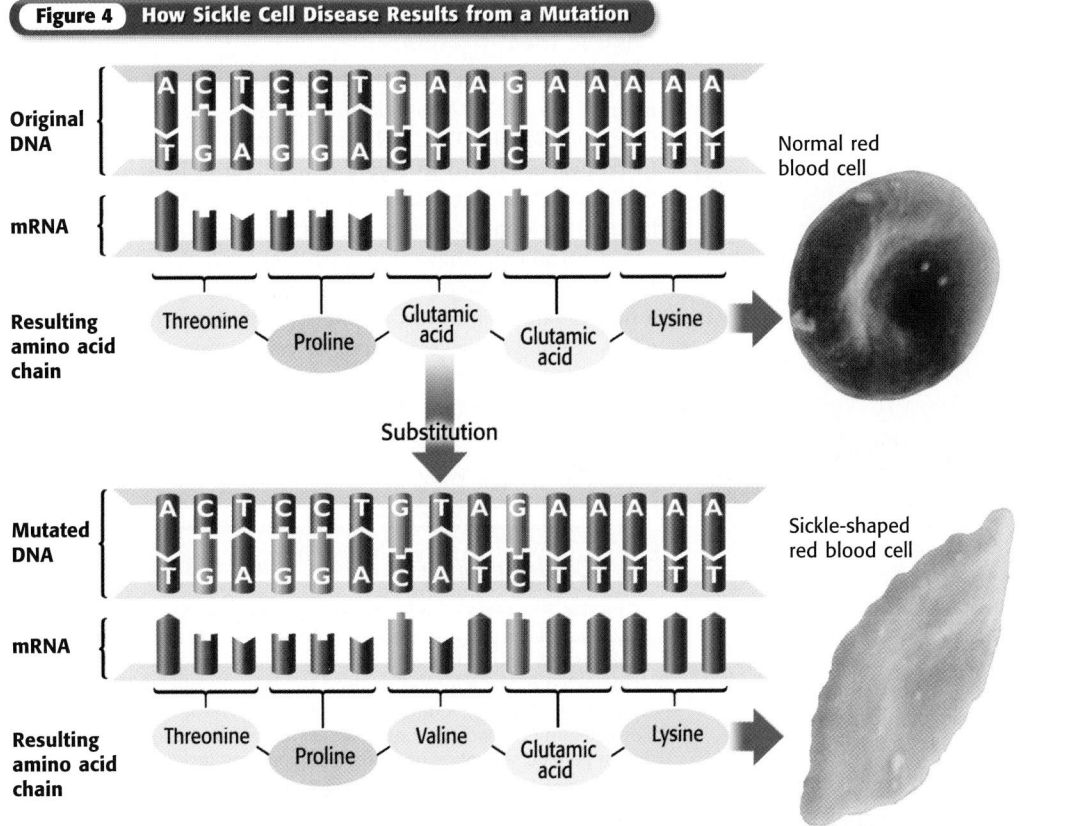

Figure 4 How Sickle Cell Disease Results from a Mutation

Original DNA

mRNA

Resulting amino acid chain: Threonine — Proline — Glutamic acid — Glutamic acid — Lysine

Normal red blood cell

Substitution

Mutated DNA

mRNA

Resulting amino acid chain: Threonine — Proline — Valine — Glutamic acid — Lysine

Sickle-shaped red blood cell

CONNECTION to Real Life — GENERAL

Misunderstood Disease A person who carries a single allele for sickle cell disease is said to have *sickle cell trait.* Only persons with two of these alleles usually develop the disease. In the past, many people did not understand that sickle cell trait and sickle cell disease are not contagious. In some areas, children with the trait were banned from public schools. **LS Verbal**

Answer to Reading Check

Sickle cell disease is caused by a mutation in a single nucleotide of DNA, which then causes the wrong amino acid to be assembled in a protein used in blood cells.

Answer to School-to-Home Activity

The mutation is a deletion. THE BIG BAD CAT ATE THE BIG RED RAT.

INCLUSION Strategies

- **Behavior Control Issues**
- **Attention Deficit Disorder**
- **Visually Impaired**

Many students benefit from small-group work and learn well when actively involved. Divide all but four students into groups of three. Assign a DNA combination to each team (AT, CG, TA, or GC). Have students identify their DNA pairs by taping construction paper to their shirts. Ask students to line up to create a "human" DNA chain. Assign each of the remaining four students one of the four combinations. Have the four "extras" move around to create the three types of mutations: deletions, insertions, and substitutions. **LS Intrapersonal**

Homework — GENERAL

Genetic Diseases

Writing Have students select a genetic disease about which to conduct research and write a report. Suggest diseases such as hemophilia, diabetes, Familial ALS (Amyotrophic Lateral Sclerosis, or Lou Gehrig's Disease), SCID (Severe Combined Immunodeficiency Syndrome, or "Plastic Bubble" syndrome), Huntington's disease, and neurofibromatosis ("elephantitis"). Suggest that their reports focus on historical occurrence of the disease, famous persons that had or have the disease, and treatments that have been tried. **LS Verbal**

Mutations Write a sequence of DNA on the board, and invite students to come up to the board and change the sequence. Then, ask the class to discuss the possible consequences of such a mutation in DNA. (It might cause a different amino acid to be substituted in a protein. This substitution could result in a genetic disorder, an improvement, or no change at all.) Ask how the mutation could be corrected. (Special proteins may find and repair the error.) **LS Auditory**

1. What is the function of the ribosome? (In the ribosome, the mRNA code is translated into proteins.)

2. List some causes of DNA mutations. (Answers may include UV radiation, cigarette smoke, or X rays.)

Writing **DNA How-To** Have students prepare an instruction manual for their DNA. The manual should include instructions for copying their DNA and translating it into proteins. It should also include information about protecting their DNA from mutations by avoiding mutagens and correcting any mutations that occur. **LS Intrapersonal**

English Language Learners PORTFOLIO

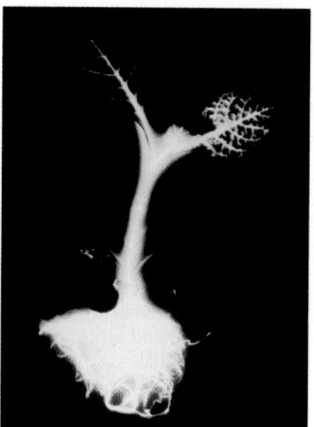

Figure 5 *This genetically engineered tobacco plant contains firefly genes.*

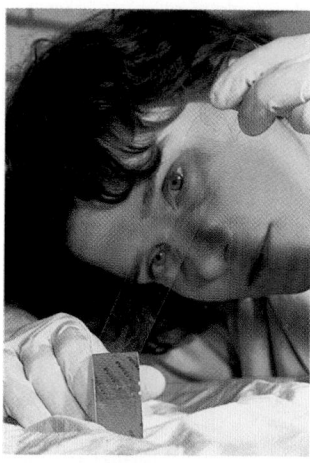

Figure 6 *This scientist is gathering dead skin cells from a crime scene. DNA from the cells could be used as evidence of a criminal's identity.*

Uses of Genetic Knowledge

In the years since Watson and Crick made their model, scientists have learned a lot about genetics. This knowledge is often used in ways that benefit humans. But some uses of genetic knowledge also cause ethical and scientific debates.

Genetic Engineering

Scientists can manipulate individual genes within organisms. This kind of manipulation is called *genetic engineering*. In some cases, genes may be transferred from one type of organism to another. An example of a genetically engineered plant is shown in **Figure 5.** Scientists added a gene from fireflies to this plant. The gene produces a protein that causes the plant to glow.

Scientists may use genetic engineering to create new products, such as drugs, foods, or fabrics. For example, bacteria may be used to make the proteins found in spider's silk. Or cows may be used to produce human proteins. In some cases, this practice could produce a protein that is needed by a person who has a genetic disease. However, some scientists worry about the dangers of creating genetically engineered organisms.

Genetic Identification

Your DNA is unique, so it can be used like a fingerprint to identify you. *DNA fingerprinting* identifies the unique patterns in an individual's DNA. DNA samples are now used as evidence in crimes, as shown in **Figure 6.** Similarities between people's DNA can reveal other information, too. For example, DNA can be used to identify family relations or hereditary diseases.

Identical twins have truly identical DNA. Scientists are now able to create something like a twin, called a clone. A *clone* is a new organism that has an exact copy of another organism's genes. Clones of several types of organisms, including some mammals, have been developed by scientists. However, the possibility of cloning humans is still being debated among both scientists and politicians.

✓ **Reading Check** What is a clone?

CONNECTION TO Social Studies

Genetic Property Could you sell your DNA code? Using current laws and technology, someone could sell genetic information like authors sell books. It is also possible to file a patent to establish ownership of the information used to make a product. Thus, a patent can be filed for a unique sequence of DNA or for new genetic engineering technology. Conduct research to find an existing patent on a genetic sequence or genetic engineering technology.

Answer to Connection to Social Studies

Students should be able to find examples of patents for specially bred or genetically engineered plants and seeds or for procedures that rely on genetic technologies to produce drugs or treat genetic diseases.

Answer to Reading Check

a near-identical copy of another organism, created with the original organism's genes

CONNECTION ACTIVITY Social Studies — ADVANCED

Ethics Debate Have interested students stage a debate about what kinds of regulations should be placed on the practices of genetic manipulation. Suggest students consider issues such as transferring genes between different species, DNA fingerprinting, cloning, and genetic patents. **LS Interpersonal**

SECTION Review

Summary

- A gene is a set of instructions for assembling a protein. DNA is the molecular carrier of these genetic instructions.
- Every organism has DNA in its cells. Humans have about 2 m of DNA in each cell.
- Within a gene, each group of three bases codes for one amino acid. A sequence of amino acids is linked to make a protein.
- Proteins are fundamental to the function of cells and the expression of traits.

- Proteins are assembled within the cytoplasm through a multi-step process that is assisted by several forms of RNA.
- Genes can become mutated when the order of the bases is changed. Three main types of mutations are possible: insertion, deletion, and substitution.
- Genetic knowledge has many practical uses. Some applications of genetic knowledge are controversial.

Using Key Terms

1. Use each of the following terms in the same sentence: *ribosome* and *RNA*.

2. In your own words, write a definition for the term *mutation*.

Understanding Key Ideas

3. Explain the relationship between genes and proteins.

4. List three possible types of mutations.

5. Which type of mutation causes sickle cell anemia?
   a. substitution   c. deletion
   b. insertion   d. mutagen

Math Skills

6. A set of 23 chromosomes in a human cell contains 3.2 billion pairs of DNA bases in sequence. On average, about how many pairs of bases are in each chromosome?

Critical Thinking

7. **Applying Concepts** In which cell type might a mutation be passed from generation to generation? Explain.

8. **Making Comparisons** How is genetic engineering different from natural reproduction?

Interpreting Graphics

The illustration below shows a sequence of bases on one strand of a DNA molecule. Use the illustration below to answer the questions that follow.

9. How many amino acids are coded for by the sequence on one side (A) of this DNA strand?

10. What is the order of bases on the complementary side of the strand (B), from left to right?

11. If a G were inserted as the first base on the top side (A), what would the order of bases be on the complementary side (B)?

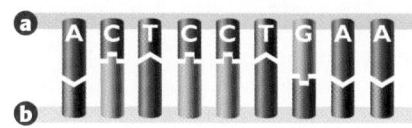

For a variety of links related to this chapter, go to www.scilinks.org

Topic: Genetic Engineering
SciLinks code: HSM0654

Answers to Section Review

1. Sample answer: A ribosome is made of RNA and protein.

2. Sample answer: A mutation is a mistake in the DNA code.

3. Genes are sequences of DNA that code for particular proteins.

4. substitution, insertion, deletion

5. a

6. about 139 million (3,200,000,000 ÷ 23 = 139,130,435)

7. A sex cell (germ cell, sperm cell, or egg cell), because these cells contain the genes from which a new organism is formed.

8. Sample answer: Genetic engineering is deliberately controlled by humans and may involve processes that are rare or impossible in nature.

9. 3

10. TGAGGACTT

11. CTGAGGACTT

WEIRD SCIENCE

Gene therapy is an experimental field of medical research in which defective genes are replaced with healthy genes. One way to insert healthy genes involves using a delivery system called a gene gun to inject microscopic gold bullets coated with genetic material.

CHAPTER RESOURCES

Chapter Resource File

- Section Quiz GENERAL
- Section Review GENERAL
- Vocabulary and Section Summary GENERAL
- Reinforcement Worksheet BASIC
- Critical Thinking ADVANCED

Technology

- Interactive Explorations CD-ROM
  - DNA Pawprints GENERAL

Base-Pair Basics

Teacher's Notes

Time Required
One 45-minute class period

Lab Ratings

Teacher Prep 🧪
Student Set-Up 🧪🧪
Concept Level 🧪
Clean Up 🧪

Safety Caution
Remind students to review all safety cautions and icons before beginning this lab activity. Students should always exercise care when using scissors.

Model-Making Lab

Base-Pair Basics

You have learned that DNA is shaped something like a twisted ladder. The side rails of the ladder are made of sugar parts and phosphate parts. The two side rails are connected to each other by parts called *bases*. The bases join in pairs to form the rungs of the ladder. Within DNA, each base can pair with only one other base. Each of these pairs is called a *base pair*. When DNA replicates, enzymes separate the base pairs, which breaks the rungs of the ladder in half. Then, each half of the DNA ladder can be used as a template for building a new half. In this activity, you will construct a paper model of DNA and use it to model the replication process.

Procedure

1 Trace the models of nucleotides below onto white paper. Label the pieces "A" (**a**denine), "T" (**t**hymine), "C" (**c**ytosine), and "G" (**g**uanine). Draw the pieces again on colored paper. Use a different color for each type of base. Draw the pieces as large as you want, and draw as many of the white pieces and as many of the colored pieces as time will allow.

2 Carefully cut out all of the pieces.

3 Put all of the colored pieces in the classroom into a large paper bag. Spread all of the white pieces in the classroom onto a large table.

4 Remove nine colored pieces from the bag. Arrange the colored pieces in any order in a straight column so that the letters *A, T, C,* and *G* are right side up. Be sure to fit the sugar notches to the phosphate tabs. Draw this arrangement.

5 Find the white bases that correctly pair with the nine colored bases. Remember the base-pairing rules, and pair the bases according to those rules.

6 Pair the pieces by fitting tabs to notches. The letters on the white pieces should be upside down. You now have a model of a double-stranded piece of DNA. The strand contains nine pairs of complementary nucleotides. Draw your model.

OBJECTIVES
Construct a model of a DNA strand.
Model the process of DNA replication.

MATERIALS
- bag, large paper
- paper, colored (4 colors)
- paper, white
- scissors

SAFETY

Nucleotides
 A T
Sugar notch — Phosphate tab
G C

Lab Notes
You may wish to enlarge the nucleotide template for your students so that the models will be easier to cut out. Explain to students that the white pieces and the colored pieces represent the complementary sides of DNA strands. Also, suggest that students refer to the figure depicting DNA replication in their text. Remind students that this is a model of the parts of a DNA molecule and that the parts of real DNA molecules are three-dimensional and have a more complex shape.

CHAPTER RESOURCES

Chapter Resource File

- Datasheet for Chapter Lab
- Lab Notes and Answers

Technology

- Classroom Videos
- Lab Video

Workbooks

Whiz-Bang Demonstrations
- Grand Strand GENERAL

Long-Term Projects & Research Ideas
- The Antifreeze Protein ADVANCED
- Ewe Again, Dolly? ADVANCED

Analyze the Results

1 **Identifying Patterns** Now, separate the two halves of your DNA strand along the middle of the base pair rungs of the ladder. Keep the side rails together by keeping the sugar notches fitted to the phosphate tabs. Draw this arrangement.

2 **Recognizing Patterns** Look at the drawing made in the previous step. Along each strand in the drawing, write the letters of the bases that complement the bases in that strand.

3 **Examining Data** Find all of the bases that you need to complete replication. Find white pieces to pair with the bases on the left, and find colored pieces to pair with the bases on the right. Be sure that the tabs and notches fit and the sides are straight. You have now replicated your model of DNA. Are the two models identical? Draw your results.

Draw Conclusions

4 **Interpreting Information** State the correct base-pairing rules. How do these rules make DNA replication possible?

5 **Evaluating Models** What happens when you attempt to pair thymine with guanine? Do they fit together? Are the sides straight? Do all of the tabs and notches fit? Explain.

Applying Your Data

Construct a 3-D model of a DNA molecule that shows DNA's twisted-ladder structure. Use your imagination and creativity to select materials. You may want to use licorice, gum balls, and toothpicks or pipe cleaners and paper clips.

1. Display your model in your classroom.

2. Take a vote to decide which models are the most accurate and the most creative.

Analyze the Results

1. Student drawings should show an "unzipped" DNA strand.

2. Student responses should always show A matched with T and C matched with G.

3. The two new molecules should exactly match each other and match the original molecule.

Draw Conclusions

4. G and C always pair, and A and T always pair. These pairings allow the two halves of a DNA molecule to be separated and replicated and ensure that identical new molecules can be formed.

5. The joining areas of guanine and thymine don't match up. They don't fit together well. The sides of the DNA molecule would not be straight and the parts would not line up if the bases were forced together in this way.

Applying Your Data

1. Student models should be more accurate than any models of DNA that they have previously constructed. Check for the correct "right-handed" orientation of the double-helix spiral, representation of the four base types, correct matching of the base-pairs and subunits, and overall uniformity of the helix.

2. Before voting, have students brainstorm their criteria for "accurate" and "creative." Take a separate vote for each category.

Debra Sampson
Booker T. Washington Middle School
Elgin, Texas

Assignment Guide

SECTION	QUESTIONS
1	4, 5, 10, 13, 15, 16, 20–22
2	1–3, 6–9, 11, 12, 14, 17–19

ANSWERS

Using Key Terms

1. A mutagen is a substance that can cause a mutation in DNA.
2. nucelotides
3. ribosome

Understanding Key Ideas

4. d
5. b
6. b
7. b
8. a
9. b

USING KEY TERMS

1. Use the following terms in the same sentence: *mutation* and *mutagen*.

The statements below are false. For each statement, replace the underlined term to make a true statement.

2. The information in DNA is coded in the order of <u>amino acids</u> along one side of the DNA molecule.

3. The "factory" that assembles proteins based on the DNA code is called a <u>gene</u>.

UNDERSTANDING KEY IDEAS

Multiple Choice

4. James Watson and Francis Crick
   a. took X-ray pictures of DNA.
   b. discovered that genes are in chromosomes.
   c. bred pea plants to study heredity.
   d. made models to figure out DNA's shape.

5. In a DNA molecule, which of the following bases pair together?
   a. adenine and cytosine
   b. thymine and adenine
   c. thymine and guanine
   d. cytosine and thymine

6. A gene can be all of the following EXCEPT
   a. a set of instructions for a trait.
   b. a complete chromosome.
   c. instructions for making a protein.
   d. a portion of a strand of DNA.

7. Which of the following statements about DNA is NOT true?
   a. DNA is found in all organisms.
   b. DNA is made up of five subunits.
   c. DNA has a structure like a twisted ladder.
   d. Mistakes can be made when DNA is copied.

8. Within the cell, where are proteins assembled?
   a. the cytoplasm
   b. the nucleus
   c. the amino acids
   d. the chromosomes

9. Changes in the type or order of the bases in DNA are called
   a. nucleotides.
   b. mutations.
   c. RNA.
   d. genes.

Short Answer

10. What would be the complementary strand of DNA for the following sequence of bases?

    C T T A G G C T T A C C A

11. If the DNA sequence TGAGCCATGA is changed to TGAGCACATGA, what kind of mutation has occurred?

12. Explain how the DNA in genes relates to the traits of an organism.

13. Why is DNA frequently found associated with proteins inside of cells?

14. What is the difference between DNA and RNA?

10. GAATCCGAATGGT
11. an insertion
12. The DNA in genes codes for specific proteins, and proteins control cells and result in traits.
13. because proteins do much of the work of copying and handling the DNA

14. DNA is deoxyribonucleic acid, and exact copies of a set of DNA are found in each cell of an organism. RNA is ribonucleic acid, which is similar to DNA but is used to carry copies of DNA code around the cell and to build proteins based on this code.

CRITICAL THINKING

15 **Concept Mapping** Use the following terms to create a concept map: *bases, adenine, thymine, nucleotides, guanine, DNA,* and *cytosine.*

16 **Analyzing Processes** Draw and label a picture that explains how DNA is copied.

17 **Analyzing Processes** Draw and label a picture that explains how proteins are made.

18 **Applying Concepts** The following DNA sequence codes for how many amino acids?

T C A G C C A C C T A T G G A

19 **Making Inferences** Why does the government make laws about the use of chemicals that are known to be mutagens?

INTERPRETING GRAPHICS

The illustration below shows the process of replication of a DNA strand. Use this illustration to answer the questions that follow.

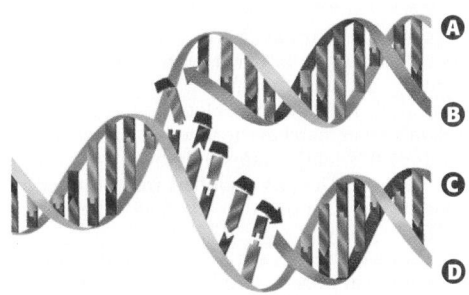

20 Which strands are part of the original molecule?

a. A and B

b. A and C

c. A and D

d. None of the above

21 Which strands are new?

a. A and B

b. B and C

c. C and D

d. None of the above

22 Which strands are complementary?

a. A and C

b. B and C

c. All of the strands

d. None of the strands

Critical Thinking

15. 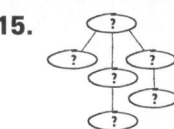 An answer to this exercise can be found at the end of this book.

16. Student drawings should resemble the diagram of replication in their student text and should have appropriate labels.

17. Student drawings should resemble the diagram of protein assembly in their student text and should have appropriate labels.

18. This sequence codes for five amino acids.

19. Sample answer: The government is trying to protect people from the risk of mutagens causing harmful mutations in people's cells—mutations could cause a disease such as cancer.

Interpreting Graphics

20. c

21. b

22. b

CHAPTER RESOURCES

Chapter Resource File

- • Chapter Review GENERAL
- • Chapter Test A GENERAL
- • Chapter Test B ADVANCED
- • Chapter Test C SPECIAL NEEDS
- • Vocabulary Activity GENERAL

Workbooks

Study Guide
- • Assessment resources are also available in Spanish.

Standardized Test Preparation

Teacher's Note

To provide practice under more realistic testing conditions, give students 20 minutes to answer all of the questions in this Standardized Test Preparation.

MISCONCEPTION ALERT

Answers to the standardized test preparation can help you identify student misconceptions and misunderstandings.

READING

Passage 1

1. B
2. H

➕ TEST DOCTOR

Question 2: This question asks for the main idea of the second paragraph. Main ideas are often introduced or summarized in the first sentence of a paragraph, and sometimes summarized or rephrased in the last sentence of a paragraph. The first sentence of the second paragraph is closest in meaning to answer H. Students who chose answer I may have looked for clues in the last sentence of the paragraph but missed the contradiction indicated by the use of "however." For this type of question, advise students to reread the first and last sentences and check for contradictions before choosing an answer.

READING

Read each of the passages below. Then, answer the questions that follow each passage.

Passage 1 The tension in the courtroom was so thick that you could cut it with a knife. The prosecuting attorney presented this evidence: "DNA analysis indicates that blood found on the defendant's shoes matches the blood of the victim. The odds of this match happening by chance are 1 in 20 million." The jury members were stunned by these figures. Can there be any doubt that the defendant is guilty?

DNA is increasingly used as evidence in court cases. Traditional fingerprinting has been used for more than 100 years, and it has been an extremely important identification tool. Recently, DNA fingerprinting, also called *DNA profiling,* has started to replace traditional techniques. DNA profiling has been used to clear thousands of wrongly accused or convicted individuals. However, there is some controversy over whether DNA evidence should be used to prove a suspect's guilt.

1. What does the first sentence in this passage describe?
   A the air pollution in a particular place
   B the feeling that a person might experience during an event
   C the motion of an object
   D the reason that a person was probably guilty of a crime

2. Which of the following best describes the main idea of the second paragraph of this passage?
   F A defendant was proven guilty by DNA analysis.
   G Court battles involving DNA fingerprinting are very exciting.
   H The technique of DNA profiling is increasingly used in court cases.
   I The technique of DNA profiling is controversial.

Passage 2 Most of the <u>biochemicals</u> found in living things are proteins. In fact, other than water, proteins are the most abundant molecules in your cells. Proteins have many functions, including regulating chemical activities, transporting and storing materials, and providing structural support.

Every protein is composed of small "building blocks" called *amino acids.* Amino acids are molecules that are composed of carbon, hydrogen, oxygen, and nitrogen atoms. Some amino acids also include sulfur atoms. Amino acids chemically bond to form proteins of many shapes and sizes.

The function of a protein depends on the shape of the bonded amino acids. If even a single amino acid is missing or out of place, the protein may not function correctly or may not function. Foods such as meat, fish, cheese, and beans contain proteins, which are broken down into amino acids as the foods are digested. Your body can then use these amino acids to make new proteins.

1. In the passage, what does *biochemical* mean?
   A a chemical found in nonliving things
   B a chemical found in living things
   C a pair of chemicals
   D a protein

2. According to the passage, which of the following statements is true?
   F Amino acids contain carbon dioxide.
   G Amino acids contain proteins.
   H Proteins are made of living things.
   I Proteins are made of amino acids.

Passage 2

1. B
2. I

➕ TEST DOCTOR

Question 1: From the first sentence, one can infer that biochemicals are something found in living things and that proteins are one type of biochemical. Hence, the most likely meaning is answer B. Answer A is contradictory to the sentence. Answer C wrongly assumes that the "bi" in "biochemical" means "two." Answer D is a reasonable guess, but answer B best reflects the inference from the first sentence. Remind students to carefully read all answers and compare each with the question and the passage before deciding.

The diagram below shows an original sequence of DNA and three possible mutations. Use the diagram to answer the questions that follow.

Original sequence

Mutation A

Mutation B

Mutation C

1. In which mutation was an original base pair replaced?

  A Mutation A
  B Mutation B
  C Mutation C
  D There is not enough information to determine the answer.

2. In which mutation was a new base pair added?

  F Mutation A
  G Mutation B
  H Mutation C
  I There is not enough information to determine the answer.

3. In which mutation was an original base pair removed?

  A Mutation A
  B Mutation B
  C Mutation C
  D There is not enough information to determine the answer.

MATH

Read each question below, and choose the best answer.

1. Mary was making a design on top of her desk with marbles. She put 3 marbles in the first row, 7 marbles in the second row, 15 marbles in the third row, and 31 marbles in the fourth row. If Mary continues this pattern, how many marbles will she put in the seventh row?

  A 46
  B 63
  C 127
  D 255

2. Bobby walked 3 1/2 km on Saturday, 2 1/3 km on Sunday, and 1 km on Monday. How many kilometers did Bobby walk on those 3 days?

  F 5 1/6
  G 5 5/6
  H 6 1/6
  I 6 5/6

3. Marie bought a new aquarium for her goldfish. The aquarium is 60 cm long, 20 cm wide, and 30 cm high. Which equation could be used to find the volume of water needed to fill the aquarium to 25 cm deep?

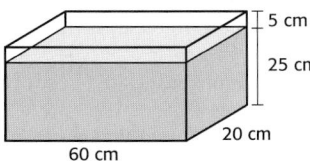

  A $V = 30 \times 60 \times 20$
  B $V = 25 \times 60 \times 20$
  C $V = 30 \times 60 \times 20 - 5$
  D $V = 30 \times 60 \times 25$

4. How is the product of $6 \times 6 \times 6 \times 4 \times 4 \times 4$ expressed in scientific notation?

  F $6^4 \times 3^6$
  G $6^3 \times 4^3$
  H $3^6 \times 3^4$
  I 24^6

Standardized Test Preparation

  1. B
  2. F
  3. C

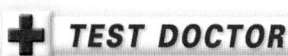

Question 1: The student must recognize that, in Mutation B, the only change from the original sequence is a different base-pair in the middle of the sequence—a replacement. Mutation A is an insertion, and Mutation C is a deletion.

MATH

  1. D
  2. I
  3. B
  4. G

Question 1: The problem requires students to predict the next three values in a patterned sequence of numbers. The pattern is as follows:

  3, 7, 15, 31, . . .

The logic of the pattern is to multiply each number by 2 and then add 1 to get the next number. Thus,

1	3
2	$(3 \times 2) + 1 = 7$
3	$(7 \times 2) + 1 = 15$
4	$(15 \times 2) + 1 = 31$
5	$(31 \times 2) + 1 = 63$
6	$(63 \times 2) + 1 = 127$
7	$(127 \times 2) + 1 = 255$

Question 3: The problem asks for the equation to find the volume of water in the aquarium, which is a rectangular box. The equation for the volume of a rectangular box is *length* $\times$ *width* $\times$ *height* (in any order). The problem and the diagram indicate that the depth of water needed is only 25 cm, so the value to use for *height* is 25 cm. Answer B uses the correct values in the order *height* $\times$ *length* $\times$ *width*.

Science in Action

Scientific Debate

Background

The U.S. Food and Drug Administration began approving genetically modified organisms (GMOs) for consumer use in the 1990s. Some consumer groups have protested and boycotted such foods. Several countries around the world have banned the creation, sale, or importation of GMOs. Some consumer groups have asked that all GMO foods be clearly labeled. The majority of GMO foods being sold in the United States are made with corn or soybeans that contain bacterial genes.

Scientists have mixed opinions about GMOs. However, most scientists recognize that the potential to create new and unknown types of organisms should be undertaken with careful scientific scrutiny, should involve ethical considerations, and should be regulated by governments.

Science Fiction

ACTIVITY ——————— ADVANCED

Further Reading If students liked this story, encourage them to read more of McKillip's stories, such as the following:

- *Fool's Run,* Warner, 1987
- *Something Rich and Strange,* Bantam, 1994
- *Winter Rose,* Ace, 1996

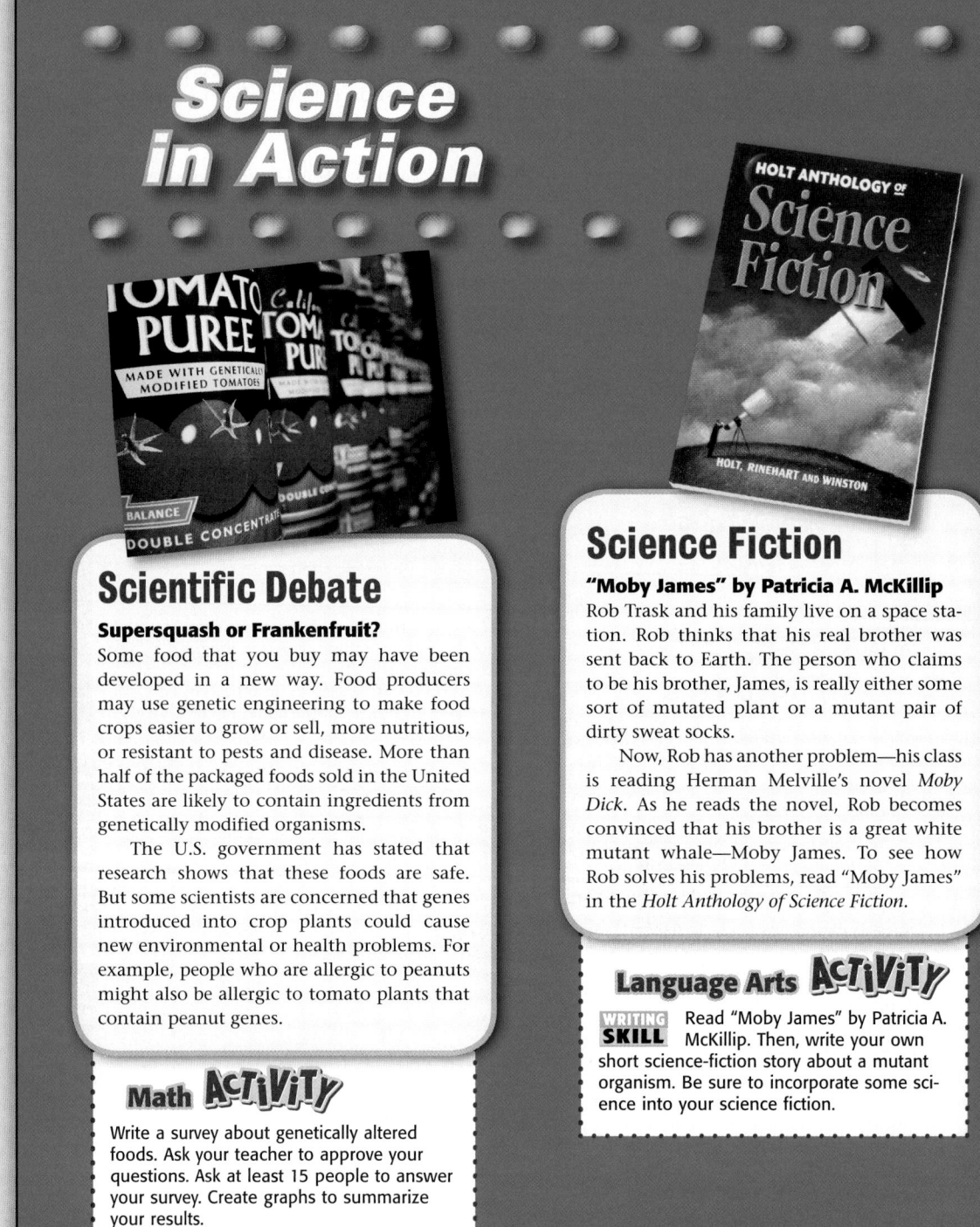

Scientific Debate

Supersquash or Frankenfruit?

Some food that you buy may have been developed in a new way. Food producers may use genetic engineering to make food crops easier to grow or sell, more nutritious, or resistant to pests and disease. More than half of the packaged foods sold in the United States are likely to contain ingredients from genetically modified organisms.

The U.S. government has stated that research shows that these foods are safe. But some scientists are concerned that genes introduced into crop plants could cause new environmental or health problems. For example, people who are allergic to peanuts might also be allergic to tomato plants that contain peanut genes.

Math ACTIVITY

Write a survey about genetically altered foods. Ask your teacher to approve your questions. Ask at least 15 people to answer your survey. Create graphs to summarize your results.

Science Fiction

"Moby James" by Patricia A. McKillip

Rob Trask and his family live on a space station. Rob thinks that his real brother was sent back to Earth. The person who claims to be his brother, James, is really either some sort of mutated plant or a mutant pair of dirty sweat socks.

Now, Rob has another problem—his class is reading Herman Melville's novel *Moby Dick.* As he reads the novel, Rob becomes convinced that his brother is a great white mutant whale—Moby James. To see how Rob solves his problems, read "Moby James" in the *Holt Anthology of Science Fiction.*

Language Arts ACTIVITY

WRITING SKILL Read "Moby James" by Patricia A. McKillip. Then, write your own short science-fiction story about a mutant organism. Be sure to incorporate some science into your science fiction.

Answer to Math Activity

Check that student surveys ask questions for which answers can be easily tallied, such as "Do you think that genetically modified foods should be labeled in the store?" Check that students have kept records and summarized their results accurately. Give them feedback about how well their graphs communicate the data they gathered.

Answer to Language Arts Activity

Instead of collecting and grading students' stories, you may want to have them read their stories to each other or to a family member, and then ask for feedback about how much science is included in their fiction.

People in Science

Lydia Villa-Komaroff

Genetic Researcher When Lydia Villa-Komaroff was young, science represented "a kind of refuge" for her. She grew up in a very large family that lived in a very small house. "I always wanted to find things out. I was one of those kids who took things apart."

In college, Villa-Komaroff became very interested in the process of embryonic development—how a simple egg grows into a complex animal. This interest led her to study genes and the way that genes code for proteins. For example, insulin is a protein that is normally produced by the human body. Often, people who suffer from diabetes lack the insulin gene, so their bodies can't make insulin. These people may need to inject insulin into their blood as a drug treatment.

Before the research by Villa-Komaroff's team was done, insulin was difficult to produce. Villa-Komaroff's team isolated the human gene that codes for insulin. Then, the scientists inserted the normal human insulin gene into the DNA of bacteria. This inserted gene caused the bacteria to produce insulin. This technique was a new and more efficient way to produce insulin. Now, most of the insulin used for diabetes treatment is made in this way. Many genetic researchers dream of making breakthroughs like the one that Villa-Komaroff made in her work with insulin.

Social Studies ACTIVITY

WRITING SKILL Do some research about several women, such as Marie Curie, Barbara McClintock, or Maxine Frank Singer, who have done important scientific research. Write a short biography about one of these women.

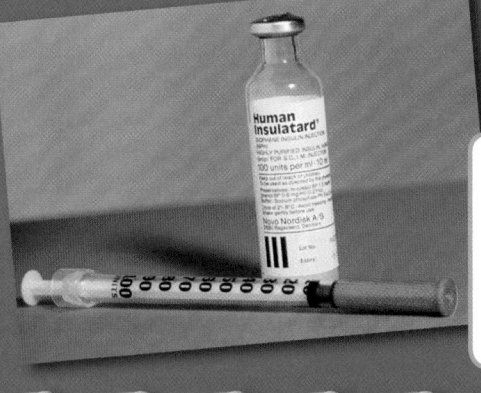

To learn more about these Science in Action topics, visit **go.hrw.com** and type in the keyword **HL5DNAF**.

Check out Current Science® articles related to this chapter by visiting **go.hrw.com**. Just type in the keyword **HL5CS06**.

Answer to Social Studies Activity

Suggest that students do research in the library or on the Internet for information. Additional women scientists to consider are as follows:

- Jewel Plummer Cobb
- Ruth Fulton Benedict
- Emma Perry Carr
- Rosalyn Yalow

Check student biographies for accuracy, and comment on any interesting facts.

People in Science
Background

Lydia Villa-Komaroff grew up in Santa Fe, New Mexico, in a household that loved to tell family stories. One favorite was the story of Villa-Komaroff's grandfather, Encarnacion Villa, and his brush with the Mexican revolutionary Pancho Villa. Encarnacion was going to be killed by Pancho Villa's soldiers when he refused to join their fight. But when Pancho Villa heard the captive's name, he ordered his release but told him he must have many sons. Pancho Villa probably could not imagine that a granddaughter of his former captive would someday become the third Mexican-American woman to earn a Ph.D. in the United States and would go on to make many important contributions to science.

When Lydia Villa-Komaroff and her colleagues inserted the human gene that directs the production of insulin into the DNA of bacteria, they were using recombinant DNA technology. In recombinant DNA technology, researchers identify which segment of DNA is the gene that directs the production of the desired substance, cut this section out of the DNA with special enzymes, and make copies, or clones. The researchers then take one of these clones and insert it, again using special enzymes, into the correct spot on the host DNA. The researchers look for a location on the host DNA that will ensure that the host organism will read the DNA and produce the substance.

The Evolution of Living Things
Chapter Planning Guide

Compression guide:
To shorten instruction because of time limitations, omit Section 3.

OBJECTIVES	LABS, DEMONSTRATIONS, AND ACTIVITIES	TECHNOLOGY RESOURCES
PACING • 90 min pp. 164–173 **Chapter Opener**	SE **Start-up Activity**, p. 165 ◆ GENERAL	OSP **Parent Letter** ■ GENERAL CD **Student Edition on CD-ROM** CD **Guided Reading Audio CD** ■ TR **Chapter Starter Transparency*** VID **Brain Food Video Quiz**
Section 1 Change over Time • Identify two kinds of evidence that show that organisms have evolved. • Describe one pathway through which a modern whale could have evolved from an ancient mammal. • Explain how comparing organisms can provide evidence that they have ancestors in common.	SE **Connection to Geology** Sedimentary Rock, p. 169 ◆ GENERAL TE **Connection Activity** Math, p. 169 ADVANCED TE **Connection Activity** Art, p. 170 ◆ ADVANCED TE **Connection Activity** Geography, p. 171 ADVANCED	CRF **Lesson Plans*** TR **Bellringer Transparency*** TR *LINK TO EARTH SCIENCE* The Rock Cycle* TR **Evidence of Whale Evolution: A*** TR **Evidence of Whale Evolution: B*** TR **Comparing Skeletal Structures***
PACING • 90 min pp. 174–179 **Section 2 How Does Evolution Happen?** • List four sources of Charles Darwin's ideas about evolution. • Describe the four parts of Darwin's theory of evolution by natural selection. • Relate genetics to evolution.	TE **Demonstration** Form and Function, p. 175 ◆ GENERAL TE **Connection Activity** Social Studies, p. 175 ADVANCED TE **Connection Activity** Geography, p. 176 GENERAL SE **Quick Lab** Population Growth Versus Food Supply, p. 177 ◆ GENERAL CRF **Datasheet for Quick Lab*** TE **Activity** Natural Selection, p. 178 BASIC SE **Skills Practice Lab** Survival of the Chocolates, p. 184 GENERAL CRF **Datasheet for Chapter Lab***	CRF **Lesson Plans*** TR **Bellringer Transparency*** TR **Four Parts of Natural Selection*** CRF **SciLinks Activity*** GENERAL VID **Lab Videos for Life Science**
PACING • 45 min pp. 180–183 **Section 3 Natural Selection in Action** • Give three examples of natural selection in action. • Outline the process of speciation.	TE **Connection Activity** Real World, p. 181 GENERAL TE **Group Activity** Amazing Adaptations, p. 181 ADVANCED SE **Science in Action** Math, Social Studies, and Language Arts Activities, p. 190–191 GENERAL LB **Whiz-Bang Demonstrations** Adaptation Behooves You* ◆ GENERAL LB **Long-Term Projects & Research Ideas** Evolution's Explosion* ADVANCED	CRF **Lesson Plans*** TR **Bellringer Transparency*** TR **Evolution of the Galápagos Finches*** TE **Internet Activity**, p. 181 GENERAL

PACING • 90 min

CHAPTER REVIEW, ASSESSMENT, AND STANDARDIZED TEST PREPARATION

CRF **Vocabulary Activity*** GENERAL
SE **Chapter Review**, pp. 186–187 GENERAL
CRF **Chapter Review*** ■ GENERAL
CRF **Chapter Tests A*** ■ GENERAL, **B*** ADVANCED, **C*** SPECIAL NEEDS
SE **Standardized Test Preparation**, pp. 188–189 GENERAL
CRF **Standardized Test Preparation*** GENERAL
CRF **Performance-Based Assessment*** GENERAL
OSP **Test Generator** GENERAL
CRF **Test Item Listing*** GENERAL

Online and Technology Resources

Visit **go.hrw.com** for a variety of free resources related to this textbook. Enter the keyword **HL5EVO.**

Students can access interactive problem-solving help and active visual concept development with the *Holt Science and Technology* Online Edition available at **www.hrw.com.**

 Guided Reading Audio CD
Also in Spanish

A direct reading of each chapter for auditory learners, reluctant readers, and Spanish-speaking students.

 Science Tutor CD-ROM
Excellent for remediation and test practice.

SKILLS DEVELOPMENT RESOURCES	SECTION REVIEW AND ASSESSMENT	STANDARDS CORRELATIONS
SE Pre-Reading Activity, p. 164 `GENERAL` **OSP** Science Puzzlers, Twisters & Teasers* `GENERAL`		National Science Education Standards UCP 2, 5; SAI 1, 2; LS 1a, 5a
CRF Directed Reading A* ■ `BASIC`, B* `SPECIAL NEEDS` **CRF** Vocabulary and Section Summary* ■ `GENERAL` **SE** Reading Strategy Paired Summarizing, p. 166 `GENERAL` **TE** Connection to Earth Science Rock Layers, p. 168 `GENERAL` **SE** Math Practice The Weight of Whales, p. 171 `GENERAL` **TE** Inclusion Strategies, p. 171	**SE** Reading Checks, pp. 166, 168, 170, 172 `GENERAL` **TE** Reteaching, p. 172 `BASIC` **TE** Quiz, p. 172 `GENERAL` **TE** Alternative Assessment, p. 172 `GENERAL` **TE** Homework, p. 173 `GENERAL` **SE** Section Review,* p. 173 ■ `GENERAL` **CRF** Section Quiz* ■ `GENERAL`	UCP 2, 4, 5; SAI 2; HNS 2; LS 2e, 3a, 3d, 4a, 5a, 5b, 5c
CRF Directed Reading A* ■ `BASIC`, B* `SPECIAL NEEDS` **CRF** Vocabulary and Section Summary* ■ `GENERAL` **SE** Reading Strategy Brainstorming, p. 174 `GENERAL` **TE** Connection to Geography Galápagos, p. 175 `GENERAL` **TE** Reading Strategy Prediction Guide, p. 176 `GENERAL` **MS** Math Skills for Science Multiplying Whole Numbers* `GENERAL` **CRF** Reinforcement Worksheet Bicentennial Celebration* `BASIC`	**SE** Reading Checks, pp. 175, 177, 178 `GENERAL` **TE** Homework, p. 174 `GENERAL` **TE** Homework, p. 176 `ADVANCED` **TE** Reteaching, p. 178 `BASIC` **TE** Quiz, p. 178 `GENERAL` **TE** Alternative Assessment, p. 178 `ADVANCED` **SE** Section Review,* p. 179 ■ `GENERAL` **CRF** Section Quiz* ■ `GENERAL`	UCP 1, 2, 4, 5; SAI 1, 2; SPSP 2, 5; HNS 1, 2, 3; LS 2a, 2b, 2d, 2e, 3d, 5a, 5b; *Chapter Lab:* UCP 2, 4; SAI 1, 2
CRF Directed Reading A* ■ `BASIC`, B* `SPECIAL NEEDS` **CRF** Vocabulary and Section Summary* ■ `GENERAL` **SE** Reading Strategy Prediction Guide, p. 180 `GENERAL` **TE** Inclusion Strategies, p. 182 ◆ **CRF** Critical Thinking Taking the Earth's Pulse* `ADVANCED`	**SE** Reading Checks, pp. 181, 182 `GENERAL` **TE** Reteaching, p. 182 `BASIC` **TE** Quiz, p. 182 `GENERAL` **TE** Alternative Assessment, p. 182 `ADVANCED` **SE** Section Review,* p. 183 ■ `GENERAL` **CRF** Section Quiz* ■ `GENERAL`	UCP 1, 3, 4; SPSP 4, 5; LS 2a, 2e, 3d, 4d, 5b

☀ One-Stop Planner® CD-ROM

This convenient CD-ROM includes:
- Lab Materials QuickList Software
- Holt Calendar Planner
- Customizable Lesson Plans
- Printable Worksheets
- ExamView® Test Generator

cnnstudentnews.com

Find the latest news, lesson plans, and activities related to important scientific events.

SCILINKS®
NSTA

www.scilinks.org

Maintained by the **National Science Teachers Association.** See Chapter Enrichment pages for a complete list of topics.

Current Science®

Check out *Current Science* articles and activities by visiting the HRW Web site at **go.hrw.com.** Just type in the keyword **HL5CS07T.**

 Classroom Videos

- **Lab Videos** demonstrate the chapter lab.
- **Brain Food Video Quizzes** help students review the chapter material.
- **CNN Videos** bring science into your students' daily life.

Visual Resources

CHAPTER STARTER TRANSPARENCY

The Evolution of Living Things — CHAPTER STARTER

What If . . . ?

The time is 50 million years ago. The place is a swamp in North America. Imagine yourself trekking through the steamy swamp, sidestepping snakes and spiders. Suddenly, out of the trees dashes a 182 kg giant with a huge head, a thick neck, and long, muscular legs.

What is this beast? A velociraptor? A giant sloth? A prehistoric bear? None of the above. It's a *Diatryma*, a kind of flightless bird that was common during the Cenozoic era of prehistory, 57 to 35 million years ago! *Diatryma* stood over 2 m tall and had an enormous beak and sharp claws.

Scientists know about *Diatryma* from many fossils dug up in Wyoming, New Mexico, and New Jersey. *Diatryma* was probably forced out of existence by large mammals. Though the monster bird is long gone, smaller versions of it live in poultry coops around the world. *Diatryma*'s fossils indicate that it was a distant cousin of the present-day chicken!

BELLRINGER TRANSPARENCIES

The Evolution of Living Things — BELLRINGER TRANSPARENCY

Section: Change Over Time
The cockroach originated on Earth over 250 million years ago and is thriving today all over the world. A giant deer that was 2 m tall first appeared less than 1 million years ago and became extinct around 11,000 years ago. Why do you think one animal thrived and the other one perished?

Record your answer in your **science journal.**

Section: How Does Evolution Happen?
The following are characteristics that almost all humans have in common: upright walking, hair, fingerprints, binocular vision, speech. List the advantages and disadvantages of each characteristic. Do you think the advantages are greater than the disadvantages? Why or why not?

Record your responses in your **science journal.**

TEACHING TRANSPARENCIES

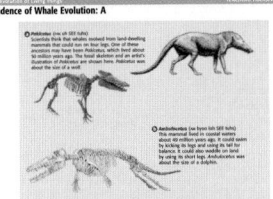

Evidence of Whale Evolution: A

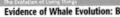
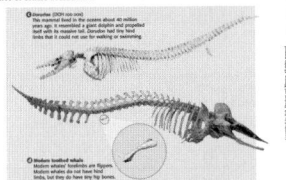

Evidence of Whale Evolution: B

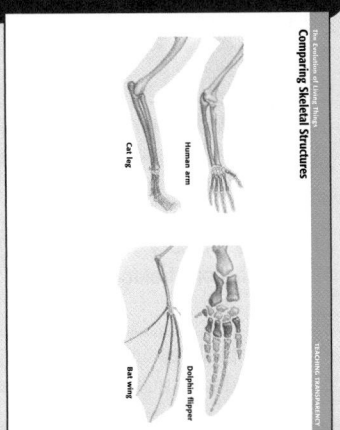

Comparing Skeletal Structures

TEACHING TRANSPARENCIES

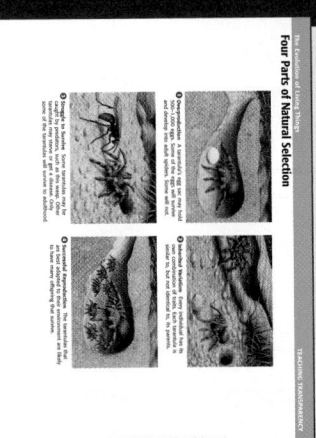

Four Parts of Natural Selection

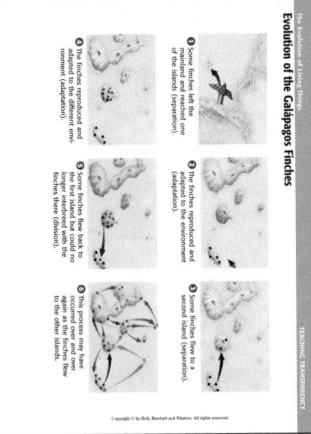

Evolution of the Galápagos Finches

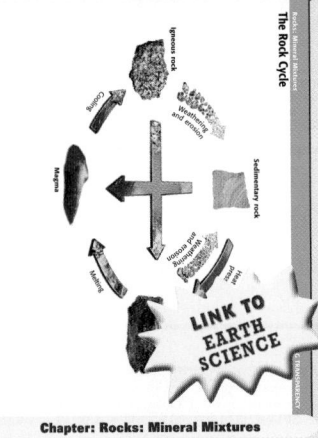

The Rock Cycle

LINK TO EARTH SCIENCE

Chapter: Rocks: Mineral Mixtures

CONCEPT MAPPING TRANSPARENCY

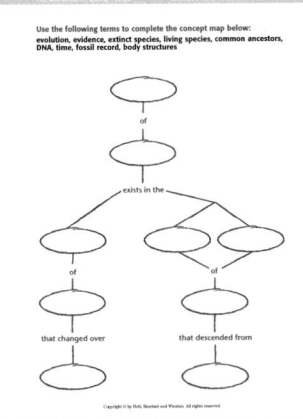

Use the following terms to complete the concept map below:
evolution, evidence, extinct species, living species, common ancestors, DNA, time, fossil record, body structures

Planning Resources

LESSON PLANS

Lesson Plan — SAMPLE

Section: Waves

Pacing
Regular Schedule: with lab(s):2 days / without lab(s):1 day
Block Schedule: with lab(s):1 1/2 days / without lab(s):1 day

Objectives
1. Relate the seven properties of life to a living organism.
2. Describe seven themes that can help you to organizer what you learn about biology.
3. Identify the tiny structures that make up all living organisms.
4. Differentiate between reproduction and heredity and between metabolism and homeostasis.

National Science Education Standards Covered
LSInter4:Cells have particular structures that underlie their functions.
LSMat1:Most cell functions involve chemical reactions.
LSBeh1:Cells store and use information to guide their functions.
UCP1:Cell functions are regulated.
SI1: Cells can differentiate and form complete multicellular organisms.
PS1:Species evolve over time.
ESS1: The great diversity of organisms is the result of more than 3.5 billion years of evolution.
ESS2: Natural selection and its evolutionary consequences provide a scientific explanation for the fossil record of ancient life forms as well as for the striking molecular similarities observed among the diverse species of living organisms.
ST1: The millions of different species of plants, animals, and microorganisms that live on Earth today are related by descent from common ancestors.
ST2: The energy for life primarily comes from the sun.
SPSP1: The complexity and organization of organisms accommodates the need for obtaining, transforming, transporting, releasing, and eliminating the matter and energy used to sustain the organism.
SPSP6: As matter and energy flows through different levels of organization of living systems—cells, organs, communities—and between living systems and the physical environment, chemical elements are recombined in different ways.
HNS1: Organisms have behavioral responses to internal changes and to external stimuli.

PARENT LETTER

SAMPLE

Dear Parent,

Your son's or daughter's science class will soon begin exploring the chapter entitled "The World of Physical Science." In this chapter, students will learn about how the scientific method applies to the world of physical science and the role of physical science in the world. By the end of the chapter, students should demonstrate a clear understanding of the chapter's main ideas and be able to discuss the following topics:

1. physical science is the study of energy and matter (Section 1)
2. the role of physical science in the world around them (Section 1)
3. careers that rely on physical science (Section 1)
4. the steps used in the scientific method (Section 2)
5. examples of technology (Section 2)
6. how the scientific method is used to answer questions and solve problems (Section 2)
7. how our knowledge of science changes over time (Section 2)
8. how models represent real objects or systems (Section 3)
9. examples of different ways models are used in science (Section 3)
10. the importance of the International System of Units (Section 4)
11. the appropriate units to use for particular measurements (Section 4)
12. how area and density are derived quantities (Section 4)

Questions to Ask Along the Way

You can help your son or daughter learn about these topics by asking interesting questions such as the following:

• What are some surprising careers that use physical science?
• What is a characteristic of a good hypothesis?
• When is it a good idea to use a model?
• Why do Americans measure things in terms of inches and yards and meters ?

ALSO IN SPANISH

TEST ITEM LISTING

TEST ITEM LISTING
The World of Science — SAMPLE

MULTIPLE CHOICE

1. A limitation of models is that
   a. they are large enough to see.
   b. they do not act exactly like the things that they model.
   c. they are smaller than the things that they model.
   d. they model unfamiliar things.
   Answer: B   Difficulty: 1   Section: 3   Objective: 2

2. The length 10 m is equal to
   a. 100 cm.   c. 10,000 mm.
   b. 1,000 cm.   d. Both (b) and (c)
   Answer: B   Difficulty: 1   Section: 3   Objective: 2

3. To be valid, a hypothesis must be
   a. testable.   c. made into a law.
   b. supported by evidence. d. Both (a) and (b)
   Answer: D   Difficulty: 1   Section: 2   Objective: 2 1

4. The statement "Sheila has a stain on her shirt" is an example of a(n)
   a. law.   c. observation.
   b. hypothesis.   d. prediction.
   Answer: B   Difficulty: 1   Section: 2   Objective: 2

5. A hypothesis is often developed out of
   a. observations.   c. laws.
   b. experiments.   d. Both (a) and (b)
   Answer: B   Difficulty: 1   Section: 2   Objective: 2

6. How many milliliters are in 3.5 kL?
   a. 3,500 mL   c. 3,500, 000 mL
   b. 0.0035 mL   d. 35,000 mL
   Answer: C   Difficulty: 1   Section: 3   Objective: 2

7. A map of Seattle is an example of a
   a. law.   c. model.
   b. theory.   d. unit.
   Answer: C   Difficulty: 1   Section: 3   Objective: 2

8. A lab has the safety icons shown below. These icons mean that you should wear
   a. only safety goggles.   c. safety goggles and a lab apron.
   b. only a lab apron.   d. safety goggles, a lab apron, and gloves.
   Answer: B   Difficulty: 1   Section: 1   Objective: 2

9. The law of conservation of mass says that the set of mass before a chemical change is
   a. more than the total mass after the change.
   b. less than the total mass after the change.
   c. the same as the total mass after the change.
   d. not the same as the total mass after the change.
   Answer: B   Difficulty: 1   Section: 3   Objective: 2

10. In which of the following areas would you find a geochemist at work?
    a. studying fishes   c. studying fishes
    b. studying forestry   d. studying the atmosphere
    Answer: B   Difficulty: 1   Section: 3   Objective: 2

One-Stop Planner® CD-ROM

This CD-ROM includes all of the resources shown here and the following time-saving tools:

• Lab Materials QuickList Software
• Customizable lesson plans
• Holt Calendar Planner
• The powerful ExamView® Test Generator

Meeting Individual Needs

DIRECTED READING A
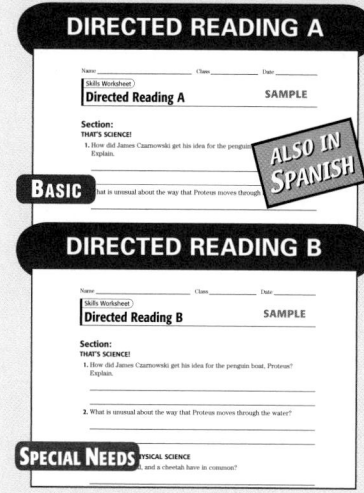
BASIC — *ALSO IN SPANISH*

DIRECTED READING B
SPECIAL NEEDS

VOCABULARY ACTIVITY
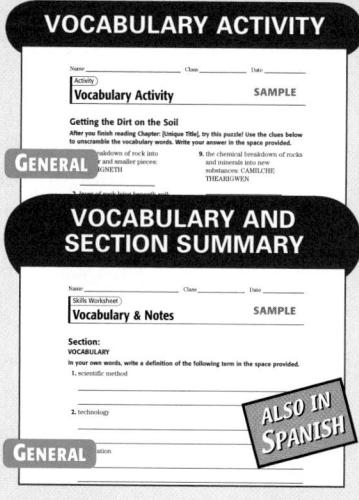
GENERAL

VOCABULARY AND SECTION SUMMARY
GENERAL — *ALSO IN SPANISH*

REINFORCEMENT
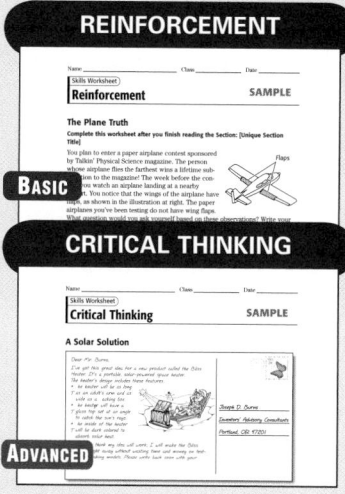
BASIC

CRITICAL THINKING
ADVANCED

SCILINKS ACTIVITY

GENERAL

SCIENCE PUZZLERS, TWISTERS & TEASERS
GENERAL

Labs and Activities

WHIZ-BANG DEMONSTRATIONS
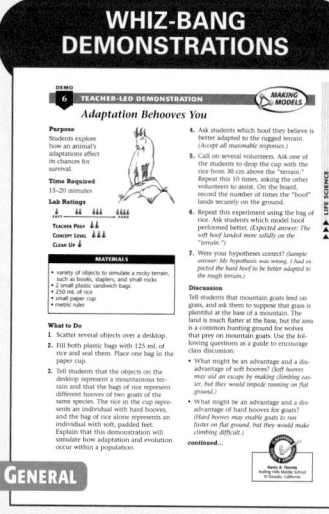
GENERAL

LONG-TERM PROJECTS & RESEARCH IDEAS
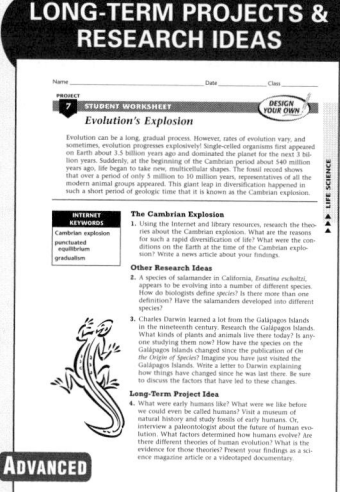
ADVANCED

DATASHEETS FOR QUICK LABS

DATASHEETS FOR CHAPTER LABS

DATASHEETS FOR LABBOOK

Review and Assessments

SECTION QUIZ
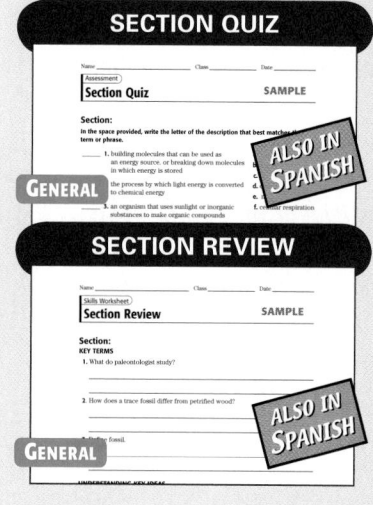
GENERAL — *ALSO IN SPANISH*

SECTION REVIEW
GENERAL — *ALSO IN SPANISH*

CHAPTER REVIEW
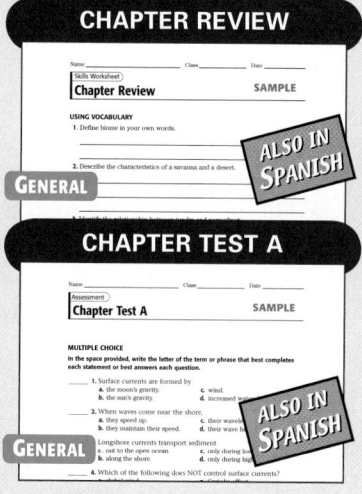
GENERAL — *ALSO IN SPANISH*

CHAPTER TEST A
GENERAL — *ALSO IN SPANISH*

CHAPTER TEST B
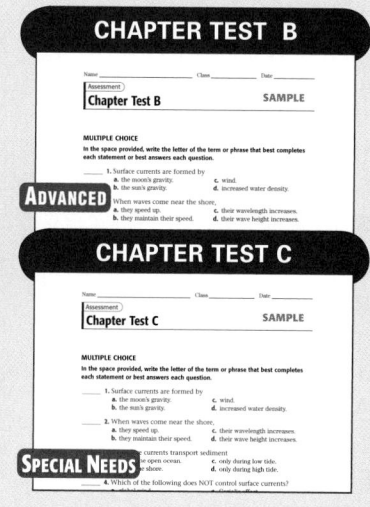
ADVANCED

CHAPTER TEST C
SPECIAL NEEDS

STANDARDIZED TEST PREPARATION
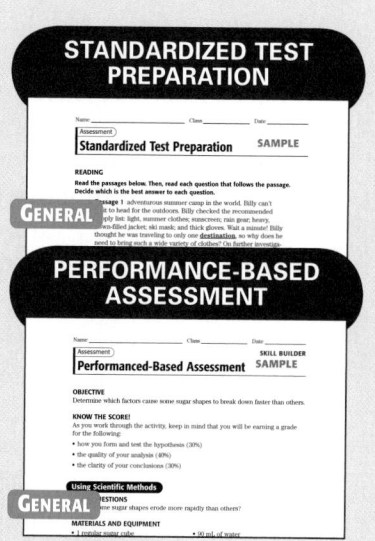
GENERAL

PERFORMANCE-BASED ASSESSMENT
GENERAL

This Chapter Enrichment provides relevant and interesting information to expand and enhance your presentation of the chapter material.

Section 1

Change over Time

Evolution of Whales and Other Mammals

- Scientists think that all mammals evolved from a shrewlike ancestor. This ancestor survived the mass extinction that wiped out the dinosaurs about 65 million years ago. This hypothesis is supported by fossils formed during and after the time of the dinosaurs.

- The first ocean-dwelling mammals appeared in the fossil record about 50 million years ago. Scientists think that these mammals were the ancestors of whales and shared an ancestor with the artiodactyl group (even-toed, hoofed mammals). However, other types of aquatic mammals, such as dugongs, manatees, and sea lions, probably evolved separately and from later branches of the mammal lineage.

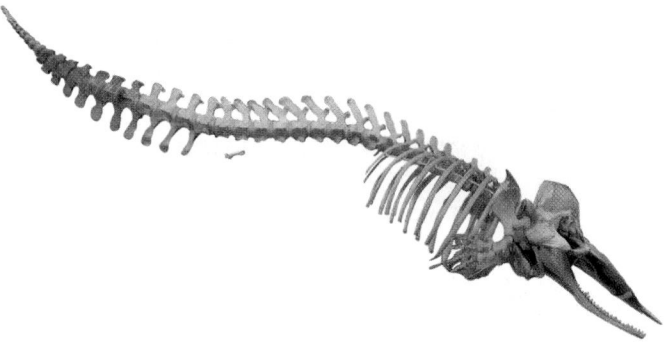

- In many ways, whales are more similar to their hoofed mammal relatives than they are to fish. Similarities include internal structures, behavior, and DNA. Also, whales swim by moving their tails up and down, in a motion similar to a gallop and to the swimming of an otter, whereas fish move their tails sideways.

Homologous Structures

- *Homologous structures* are anatomical features that have similar evolutionary and embryological origins and exhibit similar anatomical patterns. For example, bird wings, human arms, whale flippers, and deer forelimbs are all homologous. However, bird wings and butterfly wings are *analogous structures* because they function similarly but are anatomically dissimilar.

- Cellular components and biochemicals may also be homologous. For example, hemoglobin molecules from different vertebrate species have similar amino-acid sequences. But hemocyanin, which transports oxygen in crabs, has a very different sequence and is therefore analogous to hemoglobin; that is, the two molecules have a similar function but different structure.

Is That a Fact!

- ◆ The California halibut belongs to the family Bothidae, also known as the *left-eyed flounders*. Despite the name, about 40% of California halibut adults have both eyes on the right side of their body.

Convergent Evolution

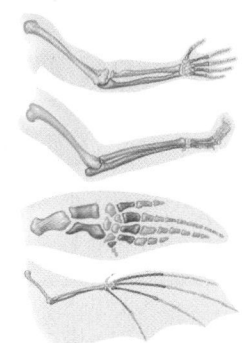

- When scientists study the fossils, skeletons, and DNA of species thought to be related, the scientists sometimes find that the organisms are not related at all. For example, the jerboa and the kangaroo rat look almost identical, but scientists have concluded that they have different ancestors. Such cases illustrate *convergent evolution*, where different species developed similar adaptations to similar environmental conditions and roles.

Frozen Fossils

- In some cases, scientists can obtain DNA from ancient tissues that have not completely decomposed or fossilized. Two Japanese geneticists are hoping to create a mammoth-elephant hybrid by using tissue from a Siberian mammoth that died and was frozen thousands of years ago. However, the chances of finding intact DNA are small, and the genetic structures of mammoths and elephants are not fully compatible.

Is That a Fact!

- ◆ The human appendix is a *vestigial organ,* or an organ that performs little or no apparent function but that is thought to have had a function in ancestors. The appendix is a narrow tube attached to the large intestine. In chimpanzees, gorillas, and orangutans, the appendix is an intestinal sac that helps them digest tough plant material.

Section 2

How Does Evolution Happen?

Alfred Russel Wallace

- Alfred Wallace (1823–1913) was born in England. He came from a poor family and had no formal scientific education. Though originally interested in botany, he began to study insects with the encouragement of British naturalist Henry Walter Bates, whom Wallace met when he was about 20 years old. Bates and Wallace explored the Amazon from 1848 to 1852 and found much evidence to support a theory of evolution by natural selection.

- From 1854 to 1862, Wallace traveled in the Malay Archipelago to find more evidence of evolution. In 1855, he published a preliminary essay, "On the Law Which Has Regulated the Introduction of New Species." Meanwhile, nearly 20 years after Charles Darwin's voyage on the HMS *Beagle*, Darwin was still mulling over his data. In 1858, Wallace mailed an essay to Darwin that explained Wallace's theory that natural selection pressures species to change.

- In July 1858, Wallace's essay was presented along with a paper by Darwin at a meeting of the Linnean Society in London. In the following year, after nearly two decades of delay (because of his doubts and repeated analysis), Darwin published *On the Origin of Species by Means of Natural Selection*.

Charles Lyell

- Charles Lyell (1797–1875), the eldest of 10 children, was born in Scotland and raised in England. His father was a naturalist who traveled with him to collect butterflies and aquatic insects, informal research that Lyell continued throughout college. Lyell's research in geology led him to the belief that natural processes occurring over millions of years have shaped the Earth's features. This idea was known as *uniformitarianism*. Lyell's work influenced Darwin's formulation of his theory of natural selection.

Section 3

Natural Selection in Action

Adaptive Coloration

- Penguins, puffins, killer whales, and blue sharks are just some of the ocean animals that have white bellies and black or dark blue dorsal surfaces. This type of coloration is called *countershading*. When seen from below, the white underside helps the animal blend into the lighter sky above the water. When viewed from above, the dark coloration makes the animal difficult to see against the ocean depths.

Sexual Selection

- *Sexual selection* is the term for the selection of traits brought about by a specific pattern of mating. In many sexual organisms, members of one sex must compete with each other for access to mates. Biologists think this behavior results when one sex's investment in the next generation is greater than that of the other sex. At an extreme, the "choosiness" of one sex may drive the evolution of traits that confer no other apparent advantage to the opposite sex. The long tails and colorful plumage of many male birds are considered examples of such "runaway sexual selection."

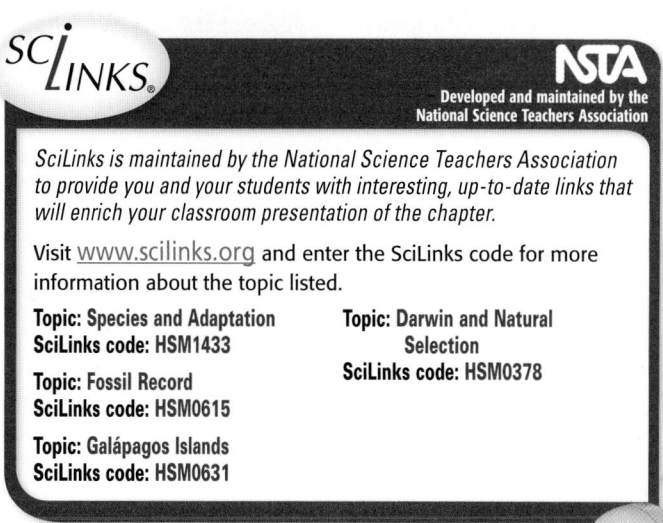

SciLinks is maintained by the National Science Teachers Association to provide you and your students with interesting, up-to-date links that will enrich your classroom presentation of the chapter.

Visit www.scilinks.org and enter the SciLinks code for more information about the topic listed.

Topic: Species and Adaptation
SciLinks code: HSM1433

Topic: Fossil Record
SciLinks code: HSM0615

Topic: Galápagos Islands
SciLinks code: HSM0631

Topic: Darwin and Natural Selection
SciLinks code: HSM0378

Overview

Tell students that this chapter will introduce them to *evolution* —the process by which populations on Earth change over time. Evolution helps explain the variations and adaptations that we see in organisms around us and in evidence of the past.

Assessing Prior Knowledge

Students should be familiar with the following topics:

- scientific methods and models
- heredity and genetics

Identifying Misconceptions

Students may have heard that evolution is "just a theory." But in academic biology, evolution (defined as the process by which species change over time) is accepted in the way that "cell theory" is now accepted. Furthermore, the theory of evolution by natural selection (integrated with modern genetic knowledge) is considered to be strongly supported and widely accepted. Specific models, mechanisms, rates, and other aspects of evolution continue to be investigated and debated among scientists, but few biologists doubt that evolution happens.

7

The Evolution of Living Things

About the PHOTO

What happened to this fish's face? This flounder wasn't born this way, but it did develop naturally. When young, a flounder looks and swims as most fish do. But as it becomes an adult, one of its eyes moves to the other side of its head, and the flounder begins to swim sideways. An adult flounder is adapted to swim and hide along the sandy bottom of coastal areas.

PRE-READING ACTIVITY

Graphic Organizer

Concept Map Before you read the chapter, create the graphic organizer entitled "Concept Map" described in the **Study Skills** section of the Appendix. As you read the chapter, fill in the concept map with details about evolution and natural selection.

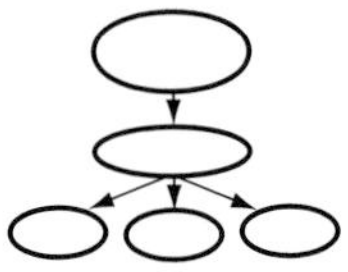

Standards Correlations

National Science Education Standards

The following codes indicate the National Science Education Standards that correlate to this chapter. The full text of the standards is at the front of the book.

Chapter Opener
UCP 2, 5; SAI 1, 2; LS 1a, 5a

Section 1 Change over Time
UCP 2, 4, 5; SAI 2; HNS 2; LS 2e, 3a, 3d, 4a, 5a, 5b, 5c

Section 2 How Does Evolution Happen?
UCP 1, 2, 4, 5; SAI 1, 2; SPSP 2, 5; HNS 1, 2, 3; LS 2a, 2b, 2d, 2e, 3d, 5a, 5b

Section 3 Natural Selection in Action
UCP 1, 3, 4; SPSP 4, 5; LS 2a, 2e, 3d, 4d, 5b

Chapter Lab
UCP 2, 4; SAI 1, 2

Chapter Review
SAI 2; SPSP 4; HNS 1, 2, 3; LS 2e, 3d, 4a, 5a, 5b, 5c

Science in Action
SPSP 2, 4, 5; HNS 1, 3

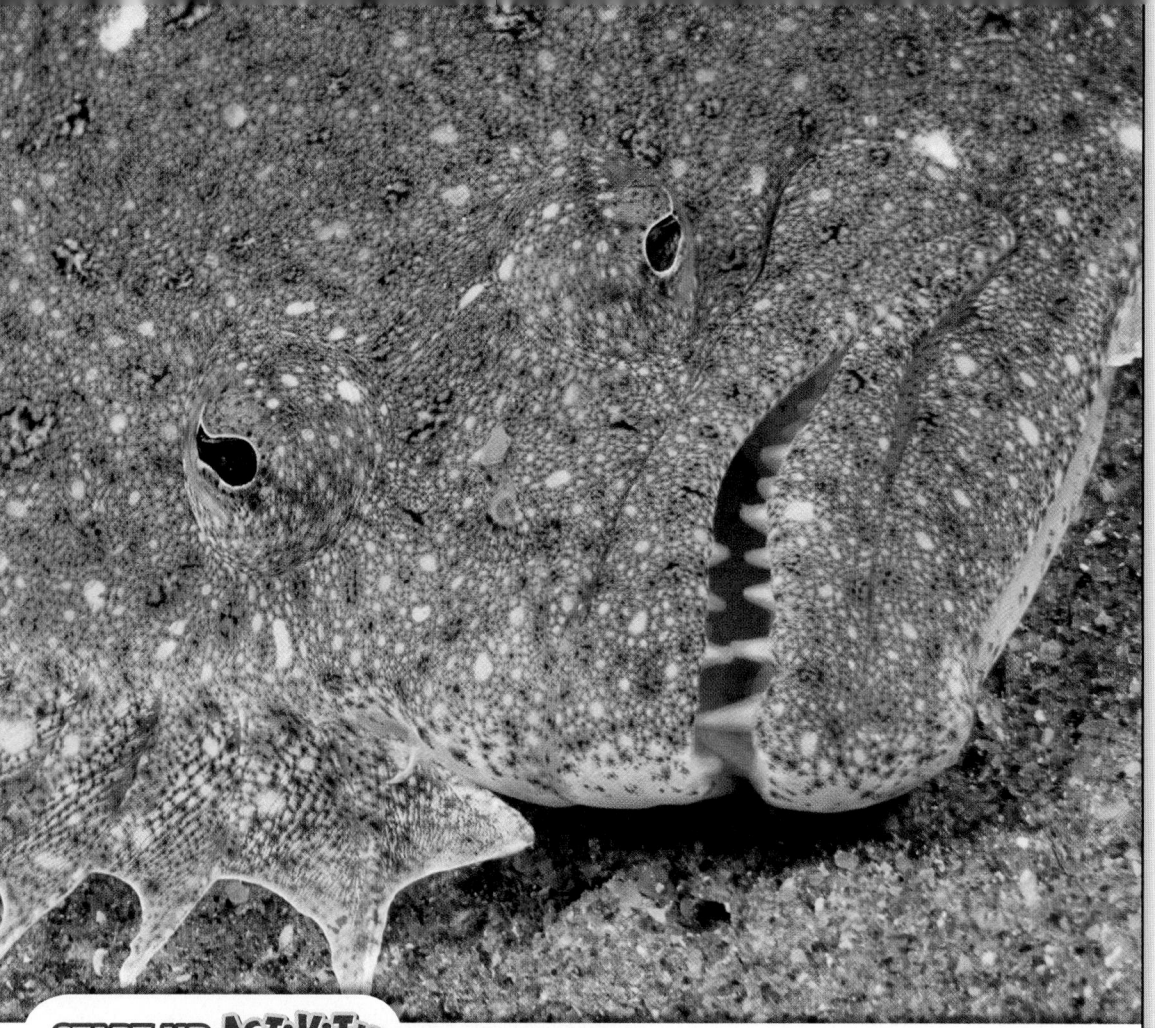

START-UP ACTIVITY
MATERIALS

FOR EACH PAIR
- cloth, white, approximately 20 cm × 20 cm
- marshmallows, colored (all same color), miniature (25)
- marshmallows, white, miniature (25)

Teacher's Note: To avoid the use of marshmallows in this activity, try the following alternative: Instead of using marshmallows, punch 100 holes from the classified advertisement section of a newspaper. Instead of using cloth, use the newspaper for the background. Spread the holes on the paper all at once, and have the "hunter" pick up as many as he or she can in 15 s. Tally the results.

Answers

1. Answers may vary, but students are likely to pick up more colored marshmallows than white ones.

2. Sample answer: The marshmallows represent organisms that could be eaten; the cloth represents the area where they live.

3. Sample answer: Many organisms in the wild blend into their surroundings by having colors or patterns that make them hard to see. This might help them hide from things trying to eat them. A weakness of this model is that it's very simple—a real "wild" environment would be more than two colors and would contain a variety of organisms.

START-UP ACTIVITY

Out of Sight, Out of Mind

In this activity, you will see how traits can affect the success of an organism in a particular environment.

Procedure

1. Count out **25 colored marshmallows** and **25 white marshmallows.**

2. Ask your partner to look away while you spread the marshmallows out on a **white cloth.** Do not make a pattern with the marshmallows. Now, ask your partner to turn around and pick the first marshmallow that he or she sees.

3. Repeat step 2 ten times.

Analysis

1. How many white marshmallows did your partner pick? How many colored marshmallows did he or she pick?

2. What did the marshmallows and the cloth represent in your investigation? What effect did the color of the cloth have?

3. When an organism blends into its environment, the organism is *camouflaged*. How does this activity model camouflaged organisms in the wild? What are some weaknesses of this model?

Chapter Starter Transparency
Use this transparency to help students begin thinking about changes in species over time.

Focus

Overview

This section introduces the concept of evolution as change over time in populations of organisms. Students will survey evidence used to understand evolution and determine ancestry, including the fossil record and comparisons of organisms' physical and genetic traits.

🔊 Bellringer

Have students respond to the following prompt: "The cockroach originated on Earth more than 250 million years ago and is thriving today all over the world. A giant deer (over 2 m tall!) evolved less than 1 million years ago and became extinct around 11,000 years ago. Why do you think one animal thrived and the other perished?" (Accept all reasonable answers.)

Motivate

Discussion ── GENERAL

Adaptation Ask students if a polar bear could live comfortably in Hawaii. Ask if a fish could survive in a forest. Why or why not? Discuss various characteristics of animals, such as physical adaptations, that make the animals well suited for a specific environment. **LS** Verbal

READING WARM-UP

Objectives

● Identify two kinds of evidence that show that organisms have evolved.

● Describe one pathway through which a modern whale could have evolved from an ancient mammal.

● Explain how comparing organisms can provide evidence that they have ancestors in common.

Terms to Learn

adaptation   fossil
species   fossil record
evolution

READING STRATEGY

Paired Summarizing Read this section silently. In pairs, take turns summarizing the material. Stop to discuss ideas that seem confusing.

Change over Time

If someone asked you to describe a frog, you might say that a frog has long hind legs, has bulging eyes, and croaks. But what color skin would you say that a frog has?

Once you start to think about frogs, you realize that frogs differ in many ways. These differences set one kind of frog apart from another. The frogs in **Figures 1, 2,** and **3** look different from each other, yet they may live in the same areas.

Differences Among Organisms

As you can see, each frog has a different characteristic that might help the frog survive. A characteristic that helps an organism survive and reproduce in its environment is called an **adaptation.** Adaptations may be physical, such as a long neck or striped fur. Or adaptations may be behaviors that help an organism find food, protect itself, or reproduce.

Living things that have the same characteristics may be members of the same species. A **species** is a group of organisms that can mate with one another to produce fertile offspring. For example, all strawberry poison arrow frogs are members of the same species and can mate with each other to produce more strawberry poison arrow frogs. Groups of individuals of the same species living in the same place make up a *population*.

✓ **Reading Check** How can you tell that organisms are members of the same species? (*See the Appendix for answers to Reading Checks.*)

▼ **Figure 1** The red-eyed tree frog hides among a tree's leaves during the day and comes out at night.

◀ **Figure 2** The bright coloring of the strawberry poison arrow frog warns predators that the frog is poisonous.

Figure 3 The smoky ▶ jungle frog blends into the forest floor.

CHAPTER RESOURCES

Chapter Resource File

• **Lesson Plan**
• **Directed Reading A** BASIC
• **Directed Reading B** SPECIAL NEEDS

Technology

Transparencies
• Bellringer

Answer to Reading Check

if they mate with each other and produce more of the same type of organism

Do Species Change over Time?

In a single square mile of rain forest, there may be dozens of species of frogs. Across the Earth, there are millions of different species of organisms. The species that live on Earth today range from single-celled bacteria, which lack cell nuclei, to multicellular fungi, plants, and animals. Have these species always existed on Earth?

Scientists think that Earth has changed a great deal during its history, and that living things have changed, too. Scientists estimate that the planet is 4.6 billion years old. Since life first appeared on Earth, many species have died out, and many new species have appeared. **Figure 4** shows some of the species that have existed during Earth's history.

Scientists observe that species have changed over time. They also observe that the inherited characteristics in populations change over time. Scientists think that as populations change over time, new species form. Thus, newer species descend from older species. The process in which populations gradually change over time is called **evolution.** Scientists continue to develop theories to explain exactly how evolution happens.

adaptation a characteristic that improves an individual's ability to survive and reproduce in a particular environment

species a group of organisms that are closely related and can mate to produce fertile offspring

evolution the process in which inherited characteristics within a population change over generations such that new species sometimes arise

Figure 4 *This diagram shows some of the many kinds of organisms that have lived on Earth since the planet formed 4.6 billion years ago.*

Is That a Fact!

There are more than 100,000 living mollusk species, and at least 35,000 extinct forms are known from the fossil record. As a group, mollusks are very successful—there have been mollusks on Earth for nearly 600 million years.

WEIRD SCIENCE

The gastric brooding frogs of Australia, now extinct, incubated their tadpoles in their stomachs and gave birth to their young through their mouths!

Historic Paleontologist
Mary Anning (1799–1847) made some of the most important fossil discoveries of her time. She was born in Lyme Regis in southern Great Britain, an area with many fossils. Her father, a cabinet-maker and amateur fossil collector, died when Anning was 11 years old, leaving the family in debt. Anning's fossil-finding skills provided the family with needed income. Even before she reached her teens, Anning had discovered part of the first *Ichthyosaurus* to be recognized by scientists in London.

In the early 1820s, a professional fossil collector sold his private collection and gave the proceeds to the Anning family. He recognized that they had contributed many specimens for scientific investigation. Soon after, Mary Anning took charge of the family fossil business. However, many of Anning's finds ended up uncredited. Many scientists could not accept that a person of her financial and educational background could have acquired such expertise. Have students research to find out one of Anning's significant fossil finds (For example, she discovered the first plesiosaur fossil.) **LS Verbal**

Answer to Reading Check
by their estimated ages and physical similarities

Figure 5 *The fossil on the left is of a trilobite, an ancient aquatic animal. The fossils on the right are of seed ferns.*

fossil the remains or physical evidence of an organism preserved by geological processes

fossil record a historical sequence of life indicated by fossils found in layers of the Earth's crust

Evidence of Changes over Time

Evidence that evolution has happened is buried within Earth. Earth's crust is arranged in layers. These layers are made up of different kinds of rock and soil stacked on top of each other. These layers form when *sediments*, particles of sand, dust, or soil, are carried by wind and water and are deposited in an orderly fashion. Older layers are deposited before newer layers and are buried deeper within Earth.

Fossils

Sometimes, the remains or imprints of once-living organisms are found in the layers of rock. These remains are called **fossils.** Examples of fossils are shown in **Figure 5.** Fossils can be complete organisms, parts of organisms, or just a set of footprints. Fossils usually form when a dead organism is covered by a layer of sediment. Over time, more sediment settles on top of the organism. Minerals in the sediment may seep into the organism and gradually replace the organism with stone. If the organism rots away completely after being covered, it may leave an imprint of itself in the rock.

The Fossil Record

By studying fossils, scientists have made a timeline of life that is known as the **fossil record.** The fossil record organizes fossils by their estimated ages and physical similarities. Fossils found in newer layers of Earth's crust tend to be similar to present-day organisms. This similarity indicates that the fossilized organisms were close relatives of present-day organisms. Fossils from older layers are less similar to present-day organisms than fossils from newer layers are. The older fossils are of earlier life-forms, which may not exist anymore.

✓ **Reading Check** How does the fossil record organize fossils?

CHAPTER RESOURCES

Technology

 Transparencies
- *LINK TO EARTH SCIENCE* The Rock Cycle

CONNECTION to
Earth Science ——— GENERAL

Rock Layers Using sedimentary layers as reference points, scientists can find the relative age of a fossil. Use the teaching transparency entitled "The Rock Cycle" to illustrate the ways that sedimentary rock is continually formed on Earth. Tell students that a common way for fossils to form is for an organism to be buried under sediment that becomes sedimentary rock. Point out that a layer of sedimentary rock can form only on top of older rock. **LS Visual**

Evidence of Ancestry

The fossil record provides evidence about the order in which species have existed. Scientists observe that all living organisms have characteristics in common and inherit characteristics in similar ways. So, scientists think that all living species descended from common ancestors. Evidence of common ancestors can be found in fossils and in living organisms.

Drawing Connections

Scientists examine the fossil record to figure out the relationships between extinct and living organisms. They draw models, such as the one shown in **Figure 6,** that illustrate their hypotheses. The short horizontal line at the top left in the diagram represents a species that lived in the past. Each branch in the diagram represents a group of organisms that descended from that species.

As shown in **Figure 6,** scientists think that whales and some types of hoofed mammals have a common ancestor. This ancestor was probably a mammal that lived on land between 50 million and 70 million years ago. During this time period, the dinosaurs died out and a variety of mammals appeared in the fossil record. The first ocean-dwelling mammals appeared about 50 million years ago. Scientists think that all mammal species alive today evolved from common ancestors.

Scientists have named and described hundreds of thousands of living and ancient species. Scientists use information about these species to sketch out a "tree of life" that includes all known organisms. But scientists know that their information is incomplete. For example, parts of Earth's history lack a fossil record. In fact, fossils are rare because specific conditions are necessary for fossils to form.

CONNECTION TO Geology

Sedimentary Rock Fossils are most often found in sedimentary rock. *Sedimentary rock* usually forms when rock is broken into sediment by wind, water, and other means. The wind and water move the sediment around and deposit it. Over time, layers of sediment pile up. Lower layers are compressed and changed into rock. Find out if your area has any sedimentary rocks that contain fossils. Mark the location of such rocks on a copy of a local map.

ACTIVITY

Figure 6 *This diagram is a model of the proposed relationships between ancient and modern mammals that have characteristics similar to whales.*

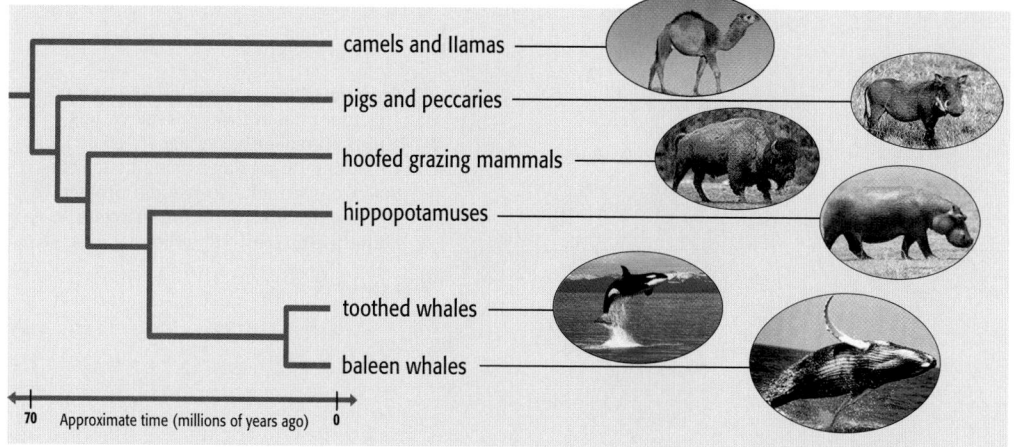

camels and llamas

pigs and peccaries

hoofed grazing mammals

hippopotamuses

toothed whales

baleen whales

70 Approximate time (millions of years ago) 0

BRAIN FOOD

How Many Toes? Hoofed mammals, or *ungulates*, are classified into two major groups. The even-toed *artiodactyls* have either two or four toes on each foot. Examples are pigs, deer, and cows. The odd-toed *perissodactyls* carry their weight on a middle toe. Examples are horses, zebras, tapirs, and rhinoceroses. All ungulates have similar foot and ankle bones.

SCIENCE HUMOR

Q: How did the dinosaurs listen to music?

A: on their fossil records

CONNECTION ACTIVITY Math ──── ADVANCED

Species Countdown Present the following scenario to students: Imagine that you are a scientific time traveler assigned to count the species in your home state 1,000 years from now. You know that, at present, your home state contains 2,300 animal species and 4,500 plant species. But many species are becoming endangered or extinct. Only 55% of the state's species are expected to remain in existence after 1,000 years. How many species should you expect to count during your visit to the future? (Tip: Round your answer to two significant figures.) (Animals: 2,300 × 0.55 = approximately 1,300; Plants: 4,500 × 0.55 = approximately 2,500) **LS Logical**

MISCONCEPTION ALERT

Adaptation on Purpose? Students commonly confuse evolutionary adaptation with intentional change. For example, a student might say that an organism "learns" to adapt or "grows" an adaptation to a changing environment. Explain to students that the evolution of adaptations is something that happens to populations over many generations. Evolution never happens within a single individual. Furthermore, new traits arise by chance and become adaptations in a population only if those traits are both advantageous to individuals and inherited by their offspring. Students may also confuse evolutionary adaptation with acclimation, such as adjustment to seasonal changes. Adaptations that enable organisms to adjust to changing conditions can evolve, but only if those abilities are passed on to future generations.

Evidence of Whale Evolution
Have students examine each of the skeletons in **Figure 7** carefully. Ask them to describe one similarity and one difference between each successive species. (Sample answer: *Pakicetus* and *Ambulocetus* have similar limbs and feet but those of *Ambulocetus* are shorter.)
LS Visual/Logical   English Language Learners

CONNECTION ACTIVITY
Art—————————— ADVANCED

Scientific Illustration The role of a scientific illustrator is to create accurate pictures of organisms and things that scientists study. In the case of long-extinct species, such as dinosaurs, artists must sometimes fill in where science leaves off. Have students look for and compare several examples of illustrations of a specific extinct organism. Have students try to identify ways in which artistic interpretation is used. For comparison, show students examples of similar illustrations from hundreds of years ago, when much less was known about many fossil organisms.
LS Visual   English Language Learners

Answer to Reading Check
a four-legged land mammal

Examining Organisms

Examining an organism carefully can give scientists clues about its ancestors. For example, whales seem similar to fish. But unlike fish, whales breathe air, give birth to live young, and produce milk. These traits show that whales are *mammals*. Thus, scientists think that whales evolved from ancient mammals.

Case Study: Evolution of the Whale

Scientists think that the ancient ancestor of whales was probably a mammal that lived on land and that could run on four legs. A more recent ancestor was probably a mammal that spent time both on land and in water. Comparisons of modern whales and a large number of fossils have supported this hypothesis. **Figure 7** illustrates some of this evidence.

✓ *Reading Check* What kind of organism do scientists think was an ancient ancestor of whales?

Figure 7 Evidence of Whale Evolution

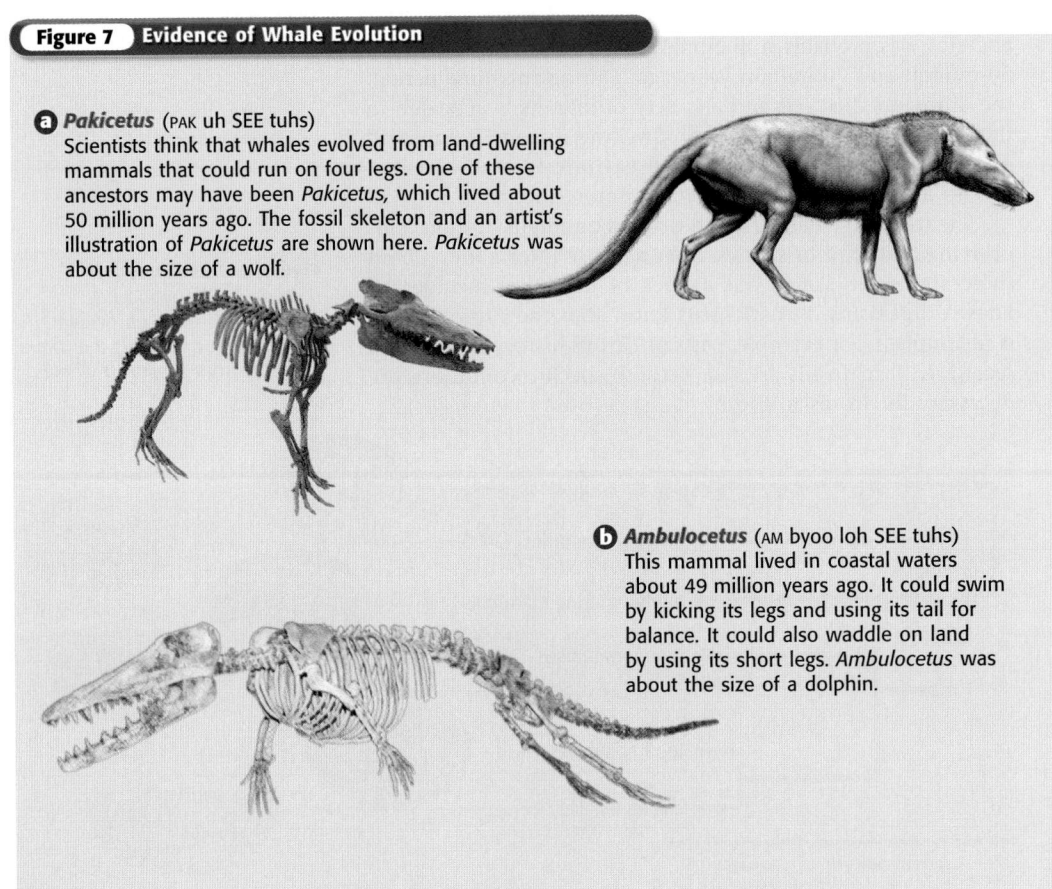

ⓐ *Pakicetus* (PAK uh SEE tuhs)
Scientists think that whales evolved from land-dwelling mammals that could run on four legs. One of these ancestors may have been *Pakicetus,* which lived about 50 million years ago. The fossil skeleton and an artist's illustration of *Pakicetus* are shown here. *Pakicetus* was about the size of a wolf.

ⓑ *Ambulocetus* (AM byoo loh SEE tuhs)
This mammal lived in coastal waters about 49 million years ago. It could swim by kicking its legs and using its tail for balance. It could also waddle on land by using its short legs. *Ambulocetus* was about the size of a dolphin.

CHAPTER RESOURCES

Technology

 Transparencies
• Evidence of Whale Evolution: A
• Evidence of Whale Evolution: B

In 1938, some fishermen near the coast of South Africa caught an unusual fish called a *coelacanth*. Until that time, this type of fish was known only from fossils and was thought to have been extinct.

Walking Whales

The organisms in **Figure 7** form a sequence between ancient four-legged mammals and modern whales. Several pieces of evidence indicate that these species are related by ancestry. Each species shared some traits with an earlier species. However, some species had new traits that were shared with later species. Yet, each species had traits that allowed it to survive in a particular time and place in Earth's history.

Further evidence can be found inside the bodies of living whales. For example, although modern whales do not have hind limbs, inside their bodies are tiny hip bones, as shown in **Figure 7**. Scientists think that these hip bones were inherited from the whales' four-legged ancestors. Scientists often look at this kind of evidence when they want to determine the relationships between organisms.

The Weight of Whales

Whales are the largest animals ever known on Earth. One reason whales can grow so large is that they live in water, which supports their weight in a way that their bones could not. The blue whale—the largest type of whale in existence—is about 24 m long and has a mass of about 99,800 kg. Convert these measurements into feet and pounds, and round to whole numbers.

Answer to Math Practice

length: 24 m × 3.3 ft/m = 79 ft

mass: 99,800 kg × 2.21 lb/kg = 221,000 lb

Note: Final answers should be rounded according to the least number of significant figures used in the starting calculations.

CONNECTION ACTIVITY
Geography — ADVANCED

Inland Whales Explain to students that in 1849, workers constructing a railroad near the town of Charlotte, Vermont, discovered bones that were later identified as those of a beluga whale. Ask students to locate Charlotte on a map and explain why this discovery is so unusual. (Charlotte is more than 150 miles from the nearest ocean.) Ask students what these bones tell us about the history of the land around Charlotte. (It used to be part of an ocean.) Explain that the Champlain Sea, an extension of the ocean, existed for 2,500 years after the last glaciers retreated 12,500 years ago. Recently, many fossils of whale ancestors have been found near the Himalaya Mountains in Pakistan. **LS Visual/Verbal**

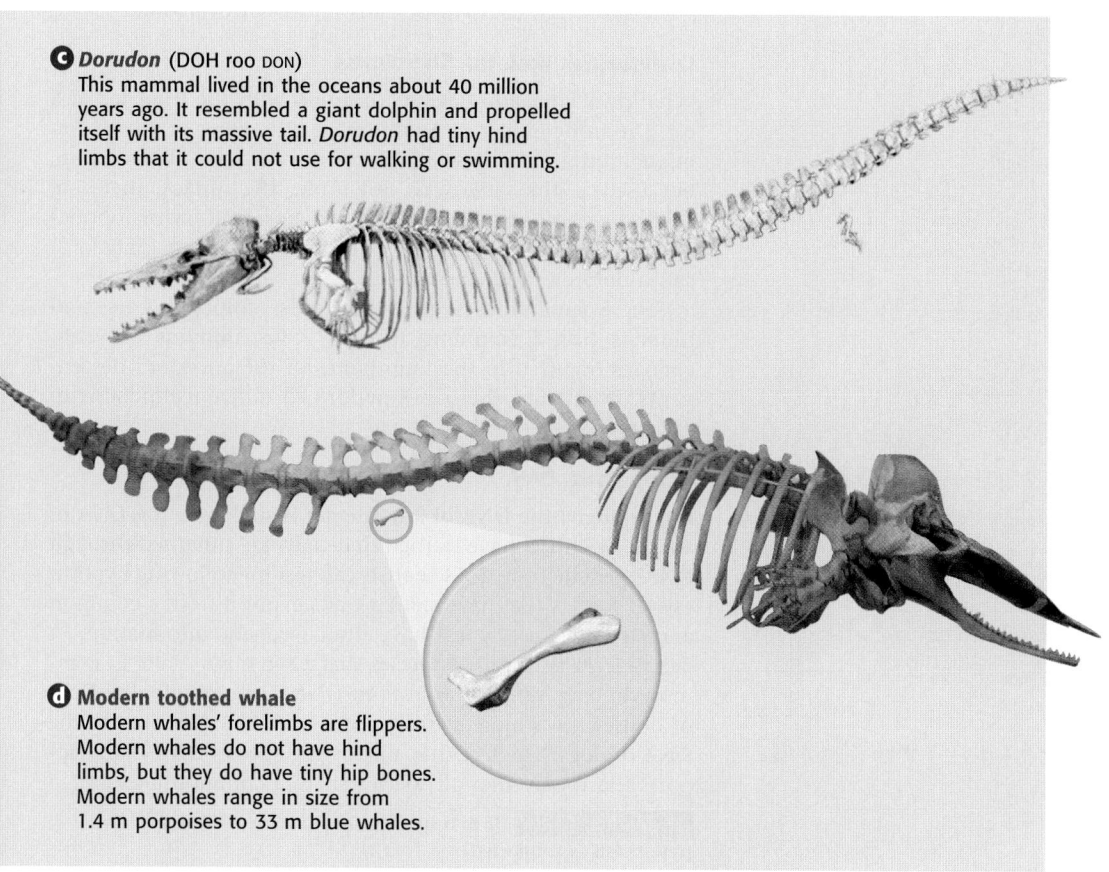

c *Dorudon* (DOH roo DON)
This mammal lived in the oceans about 40 million years ago. It resembled a giant dolphin and propelled itself with its massive tail. *Dorudon* had tiny hind limbs that it could not use for walking or swimming.

d Modern toothed whale
Modern whales' forelimbs are flippers. Modern whales do not have hind limbs, but they do have tiny hip bones. Modern whales range in size from 1.4 m porpoises to 33 m blue whales.

INCLUSION Strategies

• **Gifted and Talented**
Some students benefit from exploring a topic in greater depth. Ask these students to research current theories about the evolution of whales from ancient land mammals. Tell them to include the following at each stage: a picture (skeletons or artists' conception), how it walked or moved, what the animal probably ate, what type of an environment it probably lived in, and how it breathed. **LS Visual/Verbal**

Is That a Fact!

Baby blue whales can weigh about 9 tons (9,000 kg or 20,000 lb) at birth and can grow to 190 tons. Blue whales are baleen whales and are now the largest of all whales. The largest among the toothed whales is the sperm whale. The largest sperm whale on record weighed more than 50 tons. Toothed whales include orcas, dolphins, porpoises, narwhals, belugas, beaked whales, and bottle-nosed whales.

A Vestigial Tail Scientists think that the tailbone in humans is a *vestigial structure*. In other words, it is an inherited remnant of the tails of humans' mammal ancestors.

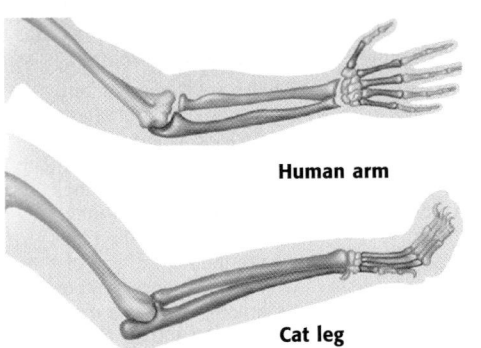 **Human arm**

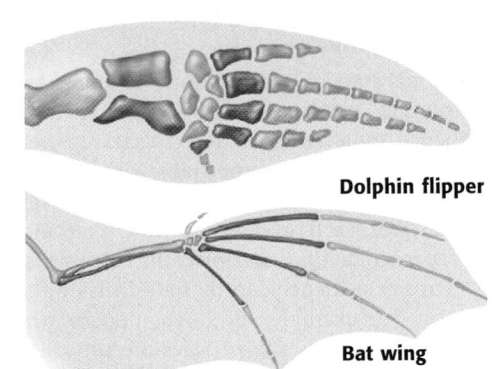 **Dolphin flipper**

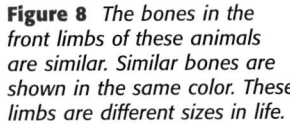 **Cat leg**

Bat wing

Figure 8 *The bones in the front limbs of these animals are similar. Similar bones are shown in the same color. These limbs are different sizes in life.*

Close

Reteaching ─── BASIC
Concept Map While prompting students for input, create a large concept map with key ideas from this chapter. **LS** Visual

Quiz ─── GENERAL
1. Use the words *adaptations*, *population*, and *evolution* together in a sentence. (Sample answer: Evolution is the process by which a population accumulates inherited adaptations over time.)

2. Why are scientists unsure about some parts of the "tree of life" on Earth? (Sample answer: There are many species to consider and incomplete information. Some parts of Earth's history lack a fossil record because fossils are formed only rarely.)

Alternative Assessment ─── ADVANCED

 Writing

Panda Pedigrees
Scientists study animal skeletons and DNA to determine evolutionary relationships and development because merely looking at the outward appearance of a species can be misleading. The giant panda and red panda illustrate this problem. The two pandas seem similar, but scientists now believe that the red panda is more closely related to raccoons than to the giant panda. Have students investigate and write a report based on recent studies on the classification of these two pandas. **LS** Verbal/Logical

Comparing Organisms

Evidence that groups of organisms have common ancestry can be found by comparing the groups' DNA. Because every organism inherits DNA, every organism inherits the traits determined by DNA. Organisms contain evidence that populations and species undergo changes in traits and DNA over time.

Comparing Skeletal Structures

What does your arm have in common with the front leg of a cat, the front flipper of a dolphin, or the wing of a bat? You might notice that these structures do not look alike and are not used in the same way. But under the surface, there are similarities. Look at **Figure 8.** The structure and order of bones of a human arm are similar to those of the front limbs of a cat, a dolphin, and a bat.

These similarities suggest that cats, dolphins, bats, and humans had a common ancestor. Over millions of years, changes occurred in the limb bones of the ancestor's descendants. Eventually, the bones performed different functions in each type of animal.

Comparing DNA

Interestingly, the DNA of a house cat is similar to the DNA of a tiger. Scientists have learned that traits are inherited through DNA's genetic code. So, scientists can test the following hypothesis: If species that have similar traits evolved from a common ancestor, the species will have similar genetic information. In fact, scientists find that species that have many traits in common do have similarities in their DNA. For example, the DNA of house cats is more similar to the DNA of tigers than to the DNA of dogs. The fact that all existing species have DNA supports the theory that all species share a common ancestor.

✓ **Reading Check** If two species have similar DNA, what hypothesis is supported?

Answer to Reading Check
that they have common ancestry

Is That a Fact!
In the late 1990s, analysis of genetic and hereditary molecular material from a variety of mammals showed that whales share more genetic similarities to hippopotamuses than to any other living mammal group.

SECTION Review

Summary

- Evolution is the process in which inherited characteristics within a population change over generations, sometimes giving rise to new species. Scientists continue to develop theories to explain how evolution happens.
- Evidence that organisms evolve can be found by comparing living organisms to each other and to the fossil record. Such comparisons provide evidence of common ancestry.
- Scientists think that modern whales evolved from an ancient, land-dwelling mammal ancestor. Fossil organisms that support this hypothesis have been found.
- Evidence of common ancestry among living organisms is provided by comparing DNA and inherited traits. Species that have a common ancestor will have traits and DNA that are more similar to each other than to those of distantly related species.

Using Key Terms

Complete each of the following sentences by choosing the correct term from the word bank.

adaptation	species
fossil	evolution

1. Members of the same ___ can mate with one another to produce offspring.
2. A(n) ___ helps an organism survive.
3. When populations change over time, ___ has occurred.

Understanding Key Ideas

4. A human's arm, a cat's front leg, a dolphin's front flipper, and a bat's wing
   a. have similar kinds of bones.
   b. are used in similar ways.
   c. are very similar to insect wings and jellyfish tentacles.
   d. have nothing in common.
5. How does the fossil record show that species have changed over time?
6. What evidence do fossils provide about the ancestors of whales?

Critical Thinking

7. **Making Comparisons** Other than the examples provided in the text, how are whales different from fishes?
8. **Forming Hypotheses** Is a person's DNA likely to be more similar to the DNA of his or her biological parents or to the DNA of one of his or her cousins? Explain your answer.

Interpreting Graphics

9. The photograph below shows the layers of sedimentary rock exposed during the construction of a road. Imagine that a species that lived 200 million years ago is found in layer **b.** Would the species' ancestor, which lived 250 million years ago, most likely be found in layer **a** or in layer **c**? Explain your answer.

SCILINKS. NSTA Developed and maintained by the National Science Teachers Association

For a variety of links related to this chapter, go to www.scilinks.org

Topic: Species and Adaptation; Fossil Record

SciLinks code: HSM1433; HSM0615

Answers to Section Review

1. species
2. adaptation
3. evolution
4. a
5. Sample answer: Fossils of types of organisms that no longer exist are found. These fossils form a sequence of change and adaptation of populations of organisms over time.
6. Sample answer: There are fossils of four-legged land mammals that share some characteristics with modern whales and other hoofed mammals. Also, there is a sequence of fossil organisms that have characteristics in between those of the ancient fossils and modern whales.
7. Sample answer: Whales breathe air with lungs (not gills) and breathe through a spout that is like a nasal passage. Whales swim in an up-and-down "galloping" motion, as otters do (not side to side as fish do).
8. Sample answer: A person's DNA is likely to be most similar to that of his or her biological parents, because the parents are most closely related to the person by birth.
9. layer c; That layer is under layer b, so layer c was probably deposited earlier than layer b and is thus older.

Homework GENERAL

Writing **Horse Evolution Report** Have students research to find the four main ancestors of the horse known from the fossil record. (Eohippus, Mesohippus, Merychippus, Pliohippus) Ask students to make a poster that shows each ancestral horse in order of appearance and to write a paragraph about each one, explaining its unique physical characteristics. Students should conclude their reports with an explanation of the origin of wild horses in North America. LS **Verbal**

CHAPTER RESOURCES

Chapter Resource File

- Section Quiz GENERAL
- Section Review GENERAL
- Vocabulary and Section Summary GENERAL

Technology

Transparencies
- Comparing Skeletal Structures

Focus

Overview

This section introduces students to Charles Darwin and his famous life history. Students will learn the observations and ideas that helped Darwin formulate his theory of natural selection. Finally, students will connect concepts of genetics to explanations of evolution.

🔊 Bellringer

Have students respond to the following prompt: "The following are characteristics that almost all humans have in common: upright walking, hair, fingerprints, binocular vision, and speech. List the advantages and disadvantages of each characteristic." (Accept all reasonable answers.)

Motivate

Discussion —— GENERAL

Dinosaurs Ask students to describe a dinosaur. Ask them to explain why there are no dinosaurs alive today. Ask why they think dinosaurs became extinct. (Sample answer: Dinosaurs were well adapted to their environment and lived over 150 million years on Earth. But a catastrophic event changed the environment faster than the dinosaurs could adapt, and they became extinct.) **LS Verbal**

READING WARM-UP

Objectives

● List four sources of Charles Darwin's ideas about evolution.
● Describe the four parts of Darwin's theory of evolution by natural selection.
● Relate genetics to evolution.

Terms to Learn

trait
selective breeding
natural selection

READING STRATEGY

Brainstorming The key idea of this section is natural selection. Brainstorm words and phrases related to natural selection.

How Does Evolution Happen?

Imagine that you are a scientist in the 1800s. Fossils of some very strange animals have been found. And some familiar fossils have been found where you would least expect them. How did seashells end up on the tops of mountains?

In the 1800s, geologists began to realize that the Earth is much older than anyone had previously thought. Evidence showed that gradual processes had changed the Earth's surface over millions of years. Some scientists saw evidence of evolution in the fossil record. However, no one had been able to explain *how* evolution happens—until Charles Darwin.

Charles Darwin

In 1831, 21-year-old Charles Darwin, shown in **Figure 1,** graduated from college. Like many young people just out of college, Darwin didn't know what he wanted to do with his life. His father wanted him to become a doctor, but seeing blood made Darwin sick. Although he eventually earned a degree in theology, Darwin was most interested in the study of plants and animals.

So, Darwin signed on for a five-year voyage around the world. He served as the *naturalist*—a scientist who studies nature—on the British ship the HMS *Beagle,* similar to the ship in **Figure 2.** During the trip, Darwin made observations that helped him form a theory about how evolution happens.

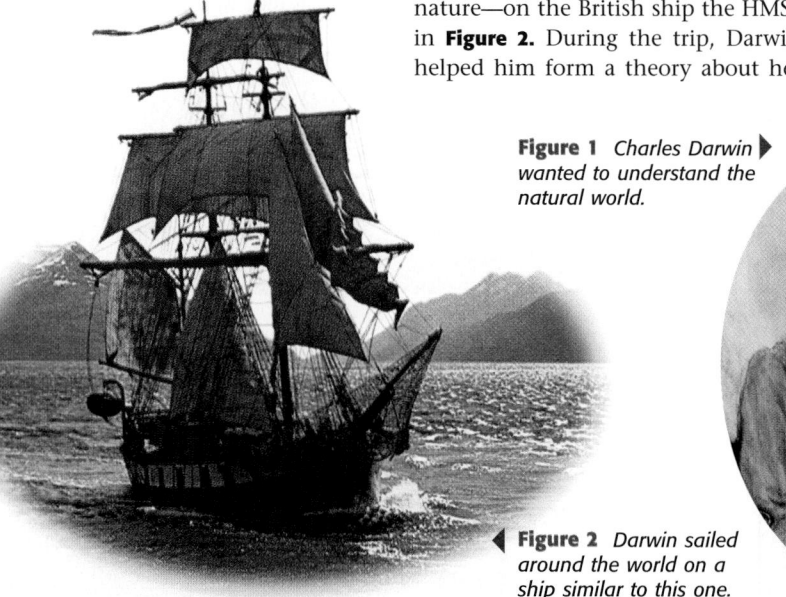

Figure 1 *Charles Darwin* ▶ *wanted to understand the natural world.*

◀ **Figure 2** *Darwin sailed around the world on a ship similar to this one.*

CHAPTER RESOURCES

Chapter Resource File

• Lesson Plan
• Directed Reading A BASIC
• Directed Reading B SPECIAL NEEDS

Technology

Transparencies
• Bellringer

Workbooks

Math Skills for Science
• Multiplying Whole Numbers BASIC

Homework —— GENERAL

Poster Project Have students research the natural history and current status of a specific sea turtle species to find examples for each of the four steps of natural selection. Have them construct a display to present their findings. Require them to include information about the turtle's reproductive habits, physical adaptations, and factors in its environment that affect its success. **LS Verbal/Visual**

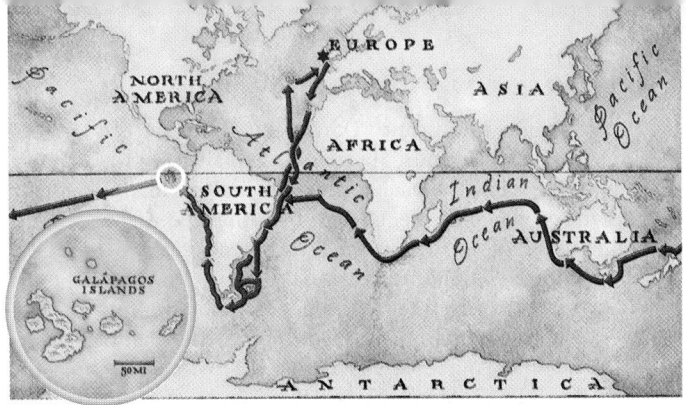

Figure 3 *The course of the HMS Beagle is shown by the red line. The journey began and ended in England.*

Darwin's Excellent Adventure

The *Beagle*'s journey is charted in **Figure 3.** Along the way, Darwin collected thousands of plant and animal samples. He kept careful notes of his observations. One interesting place that the ship visited was the Galápagos Islands. These islands are found 965 km (600 mi) west of Ecuador, a country in South America.

 **Reading Check** Where are the Galápagos Islands? (*See the Appendix for answers to Reading Checks.*)

Darwin's Finches

Darwin noticed that the animals and plants on the Galápagos Islands were a lot like those in Ecuador. However, they were not exactly the same. The finches of the Galápagos Islands, for example, were a little different from the finches in Ecuador. And the finches on each island differed from the finches on the other islands. As **Figure 4** shows, the beak of each finch is adapted to the way the bird usually gets food.

| Figure 4 | Some Finches of the Galápagos Islands |

The **large ground finch** has a wide, strong beak that it uses to crack open big, hard seeds. This beak works like a nutcracker.

The **cactus finch** has a tough beak that it uses for eating cactus parts and insects. This beak works like a pair of needle-nose pliers.

The **warbler finch** has a small, narrow beak that it uses to catch small insects. This beak works like a pair of tweezers.

Is That a Fact!

The giant tortoises of the Galápagos Islands weigh up to 270 kg and can live for more than 150 years.

Answer to Reading Check
965 km (600 mi) west of Ecuador

Teach

Demonstration — GENERAL

Form and Function Present and identify to students the following pieces of clothing: sneaker, dress pump, loafer, necktie, scarf, anklet, knee sock, baseball cap, and ski cap. Discuss the ways that all these items are related and how some are more closely related than others. (Related items are best suited for one particular function.) Explain that this relationship of similarities and differences is what scientists such as Charles Darwin observe in studying organisms. **LS Kinesthetic**

CONNECTION ACTIVITY
Social Studies — ADVANCED

 *Writing* **Darwin's Voyage** Have interested students research in greater detail Darwin's voyage and similar long-distance travel by explorers in the 1800s. Topics for reports include the types of ships used for travel in that era, the kinds of food eaten by the explorers, and the sophistication and thoroughness of maps in the 1800s. **LS Verbal** PORTFOLIO

CONNECTION to
Geography — GENERAL

Galápagos While displaying a world map or atlas, explain the following: The Galápagos Islands are officially part of the country of Ecuador, though they are 1,000 km west of the mainland. They are a group of 19 volcanically formed islands. Though they have a land area of only 8,000 km², they are dispersed over almost 60,000 km² of the Pacific Ocean. Biologists now know that unique new species are likely to arise under these conditions. **LS Visual/Logical**

Prediction Guide Before students read this page, have them answer the following questions:

• Why did the finches Darwin saw on the Galápagos Islands look similar to those he saw in South America?

• Why did they look a little different?

Have students share and evaluate their answers with a partner after they read the page.

LS Verbal/Intrapersonal

Homework ——ADVANCED

Writing **Island Biogeography Report** *Biogeography* is the study of where animals and plants are found and how they came to live in their particular location. Biogeography uses information from the fossil record and integrates ideas from biology, geology, paleontology, and chemistry. Encourage interested students to write a report about island biogeography. Have them include information about how it is used to design and manage terrestrial wildlife refuges. **LS** Verbal/ Intrapersonal

PORTFOLIO

Darwin's Thinking

After returning to England, Darwin puzzled over the animals of the Galápagos Islands. He tried to explain why the animals seemed so similar to each other yet had so many different adaptations. For example, Darwin hypothesized that the island finches were descended from South American finches. The first finches on the islands may have been blown from South America by a storm. Over many generations, the finches may have adapted to different ways of life on the islands.

During the course of his travels, Darwin came up with many new ideas. Before sharing these ideas, he spent several years analyzing his evidence. He also gathered ideas from many other people.

Ideas About Breeding

In Darwin's time, farmers and breeders had produced many kinds of farm animals and plants. These plants and animals had traits that were desired by the farmers and breeders. **Traits** are specific characteristics that can be passed from parent to offspring through genes. The process in which humans select which plants or animals to reproduce based on certain desired traits is called **selective breeding.** Most pets, such as the dogs in **Figure 5,** have been bred for various desired traits.

You can see the results of selective breeding in many kinds of organisms. For example, people have bred horses that are particularly fast or strong. And farmers have bred crops that produce large fruit or that grow in specific climates.

trait a genetically determined characteristic

selective breeding the human practice of breeding animals or plants that have certain desired characteristics

Figure 5 *Over the past 12,000 years, dogs have been selectively bred to produce more than 150 breeds.*

CONNECTION ACTIVITY
Geography ——GENERAL

Bird Barrier Locate the Rocky Mountains on a map. Explain to students that bird-identification guides for North America usually classify birds into those that are east of the Rocky Mountains and those that are west of the Rocky Mountains. Brainstorm reasons why ornithologists might use this system. (Sample answer: because the Rockies present a large geographical barrier.) **LS** Visual/Logical

Is That a Fact!

As a result of selective breeding, the smallest horse is the Falabella, which is only about 76 cm tall. The largest is the Shire, originally bred in England. It can grow more than 1.73 m high at the shoulder and weigh as much as 910 kg.

Quick Lab

Population Growth Versus Food Supply

1. Get an **egg carton** and a **bag of rice**. Use a **marker** to label one row of the carton "Food supply." Then, label the second row "Human population."

2. In the row labeled "Food supply," place one grain of rice in the first cup. Place two grains of rice in the second cup, and place three grains of rice in the third cup. In each subsequent cup, place one more grain than you placed in the previous cup. Imagine that each grain represents enough food for one person's lifetime.

3. In the row labeled "Human population," place one grain of rice in the first cup. Place two grains in the second cup, and place four grains in the third cup. In each subsequent cup, place twice as many grains as you placed in the previous cup. This rice represents people.

4. How many units of food are in the sixth cup? How many "people" are in the sixth cup? If this pattern continued, what would happen?

5. Describe how the patterns in the food supply and in the human population differ. Explain how the patterns relate to Malthus's hypothesis.

Ideas About Population

During Darwin's time, Thomas Malthus wrote a famous book entitled *An Essay on the Principle of Population*. Malthus noted that humans have the potential to reproduce rapidly. He warned that food supplies could not support unlimited population growth. **Figure 6** illustrates this relationship. However, Malthus pointed out that human populations are limited by choices that humans make or by problems such as starvation and disease.

After reading Malthus's work, Darwin realized that any species can produce many offspring. He also knew that the populations of all species are limited by starvation, disease, competition, and predation. Only a limited number of individuals survive to reproduce. Thus, there is something special about the survivors. Darwin reasoned that the offspring of the survivors inherit traits that help the offspring survive in their environment.

Ideas About Earth's History

Darwin had begun to think that species could evolve over time. But most geologists at the time did not think that Earth was old enough to allow for slow changes. Darwin learned new ideas from *Principles of Geology,* a book by Charles Lyell. This book presented evidence that Earth had formed by natural processes over a long period of time. It became clear to Darwin that Earth was much older than anyone had imagined.

Reading Check What did Darwin learn from Charles Lyell?

Malthus's Description of Unlimited Population Growth

Quantity (vertical axis), *Time* (horizontal axis)

Human population

Food supply

Figure 6 *Malthus thought that the human population could increase more quickly than the food supply, with the result that there would not be enough food for everyone.*

Is That a Fact!

The full title of Thomas Malthus's famous essay was "An Essay on the Principle of Population, as it Affects the Future Improvement of Society with Remarks on the Speculations of Mr. Godwin, M. Condorcet, and Other Writers."

Science Bloopers

Malthus's work was important in influencing ecological scientists and prompting social planners to consider the potential problems of rapid population growth. However, Malthus was wrong in his projections of the growth of food supplies. The use of machinery, fossil fuels, and chemicals since Malthus's time enabled food production to increase more rapidly than he thought was possible.

Quick Lab

MATERIALS

FOR EACH STUDENT
- egg carton, 12-egg size, empty (2)
- marker
- rice (about 1 cup) (or lentils or small pebbles)

Answers

4. There are 32 "people" and 6 units of "food." If this pattern continued, there would be a lot more people than food and not enough food to keep the people alive.

5. The human population is growing much faster than the food supply. This pattern is similar to that in Malthus's prediction.

Using the Figure—ADVANCED

Two Kinds of Growth Have students examine **Figure 6.** Ask students to describe the behavior of the graph for food supply. (It rises steadily in a straight line.) Explain that the line graphing food supply represents *linear growth* and increases by *adding* a certain amount in each time interval. Next, ask students to describe the behavior of the graph for human population. (It rises quickly and in a curved line.) Explain that the line graphing human population represents *exponential growth* and increases by *multiplying* by a certain percentage in each time interval. Ask students to suggest alternative titles for this graph. (Sample answer: "Human Population Growth Vs. Food Supply.") **LS Visual/Logical**

Answer to Reading Check

that Earth had been formed by natural processes over a long period of time

Reteaching — BASIC

Writing **Terms** Have students list the key terms and any unfamiliar terms from this chapter. For each term, they should write a definition and then write sample sentences using the term. **LS Verbal**

Quiz — GENERAL

1. Who was Charles Lyell? (He was a British geologist.)

2. What did Darwin learn from Lyell's data about the age of Earth? (Darwin learned from Lyell that Earth was old enough for slow changes to happen in a population.)

Alternative Assessment — ADVANCED

Writing **Darwin's Journal**
Charles Darwin's journals contain notes and records from his travels. Ask students to imagine that they are traveling with Darwin and keeping their own journals. Their notes and drawings should reflect what they see, the questions that arise from their observations, and the hypotheses that they form. Encourage students to write journal entries about other animals on the Galápagos Islands besides the finches, such as the Galápagos tortoise and marine iguanas. **LS Verbal/Intrapersonal**

Answer to Reading Check

On the Origin of Species by Means of Natural Selection

natural selection the process by which individuals that are better adapted to their environment survive and reproduce more successfully than less well adapted individuals do; a theory to explain the mechanism of evolution

Darwin's Theory of Natural Selection

After he returned from his voyage on the HMS *Beagle*, Darwin privately struggled with his ideas for about 20 years. Then, in 1858, Darwin received a letter from a fellow naturalist named Alfred Russel Wallace. Wallace had arrived at the same ideas about evolution that Darwin had. Darwin grew more and more motivated to present his ideas. In 1859, Darwin published a famous book called *On the Origin of Species by Means of Natural Selection*. In his book, Darwin proposed the theory that evolution happens through a process that he called **natural selection.** This process, explained in **Figure 7,** has four parts.

✓ **Reading Check** What is the title of Darwin's famous book?

Figure 7 **Four Parts of Natural Selection**

❶ **Overproduction** A tarantula's egg sac may hold 500–1,000 eggs. Some of the eggs will survive and develop into adult spiders. Some will not.

❷ **Inherited Variation** Every individual has its own combination of traits. Each tarantula is similar to, but not identical to, its parents.

❸ **Struggle to Survive** Some tarantulas may be caught by predators, such as this wasp. Other tarantulas may starve or get a disease. Only some of the tarantulas will survive to adulthood.

❹ **Successful Reproduction** The tarantulas that are best adapted to their environment are likely to have many offspring that survive.

ACTIVITY — BASIC

Natural Selection Have students carefully study **Figure 7** and begin to create their own table, concept map, or other graphic organizer about the four parts of natural selection. For each part of the figure, call on several students to restate the meaning in their own words, and then ask students to write their own version of the explanation on their graphic organizer. Finally, for each part, ask students to describe an additional example of the same process with another organism besides a tarantula. **LS Visual**

Science Bloopers

In 1809, French naturalist Jean Baptiste Lamarck's theory of evolution by *acquired characteristics* stated that if an animal changed a body part through use or nonuse, that change would be inherited by its offspring. For example, larger leg muscles as a result of extensive running would be passed on to the next generation. However, genetic studies in the 1930s and 1940s disproved this mechanism for inheriting traits.

Genetics and Evolution

Darwin lacked evidence for parts of his theory. For example, he knew that organisms inherit traits, but not *how* they inherit traits. He knew that there is great variation among organisms, but not *how* that variation occurs. Today, scientists have found most of the evidence that Darwin lacked. They know that variation happens as a result of differences in genes. Changes in genes may happen whenever organisms produce offspring. Some genes make an organism more likely to survive to reproduce. The process called *selection* happens when only organisms that carry these genes can survive to reproduce. New fossil discoveries and new information about genes add to scientists' understanding of natural selection and evolution.

SECTION Review

Summary

- Darwin explained that evolution occurs through natural selection. His theory has four parts:
  1. Each species produces more offspring than will survive to reproduce.
  2. Individuals within a population have slightly different traits.
  3. Individuals within a population compete with each other for limited resources.
  4. Individuals that are better equipped to live in an environment are more likely to survive to reproduce.

- Modern genetics helps explain the theory of natural selection.

Using Key Terms

1. In your own words, write a definition for the term *trait*.

2. Use the following terms in the same sentence: *selective breeding* and *natural selection*.

Understanding Key Ideas

3. Modern scientific explanations of evolution
   a. have replaced Darwin's theory.
   b. rely on genetics instead of natural selection.
   c. fail to explain how traits are inherited.
   d. combine the principles of natural selection and genetic inheritance.

4. Describe the observations that Darwin made about the species on the Galápagos Islands.

5. Summarize the ideas that Darwin developed from books by Malthus and Lyell.

6. Describe the four parts of Darwin's theory of evolution by natural selection.

7. What knowledge did Darwin lack that modern scientists now use to explain evolution?

Math Skills

8. In a sample of 80 beetles, 50 beetles had 4 spots each, and the rest had 6 spots each. What was the average number of spots per beetle?

Critical Thinking

9. **Making Comparisons** In selective breeding, humans influence the course of evolution. What determines the course of evolution in natural selection?

10. **Predicting Consequences** Suppose that an island in the Pacific Ocean was just formed by a volcano. Over the next million years, how might species evolve on this island?

For a variety of links related to this chapter, go to www.scilinks.org
Topic: Galápagos Islands;
Darwin and Natural Selection
SciLinks code: HSM0631; HSM0378

SCIENTISTS AT ODDS

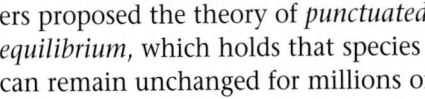

Rate Debate Evolutionary scientists do not yet agree on how often new species arise. *Gradualism*, the theory that Darwin supported, holds that changes in species occur slowly and steadily over thousands of years. In the 1970s, Stephen Jay Gould and others proposed the theory of *punctuated equilibrium*, which holds that species can remain unchanged for millions of years until dramatic environmental changes prompt speciation.

CHAPTER RESOURCES

Chapter Resource File

- Section Quiz GENERAL
- Section Review GENERAL
- Vocabulary and Section Summary GENERAL
- Reinforcement Worksheet BASIC
- SciLinks Activity GENERAL
- Datasheet for Quick Lab

Technology

Transparencies
- Four Parts of Natural Selection

Answers to Section Review

1. Sample answer: A trait is a specific characteristic that is inherited from ancestors.

2. Sample answer: Selective breeding happens when humans choose which organisms will reproduce, and natural selection happens when the environment "chooses."

3. d

4. Darwin observed that many of the species of the Galápagos Islands were similar to those of South America, but they had unique adaptations.

5. From Malthus, Darwin developed the idea that populations are limited by food and other problems. From Lyell, Darwin developed tha idea that conditions on Earth could change slowly over long periods of time.

6. Sample answer: Overproduction means that every organism can produce more offspring than will likely survive; inherited variation means that all offspring will have some differences; struggle to survive means the offspring have to compete with each other and with other organisms around them; and successful reproduction means those that are best adapted will probably have more offsring like themselves.

7. Sample answer: Darwin lacked the knowledge of genetics that helps explain how organisms inherit traits and why there is so much variety in organisms.

8. $\{(50 \times 4) + [(80 - 50) \times 6]\} \div 80 = 4.75$ spots average per beetle

9. Sample answer: natural forces and other organisms

10. Sample answer: Species on the island might evolve in a way similar to those of the Galápagos Islands.

SECTION

3

Focus

Overview

In this section, students will see examples of natural selection at work. They will relate a species' generation time to its ability to adapt. Students will also examine the process of speciation.

Bellringer

Have students respond to the following prompt: "Write the four parts of natural selection, and create a mnemonic device to remember each part by using the first letter of the words." (Sample answer: Overproduction, genetic Variation, Struggle to survive, successful Reproduction; Olga's Vacation Seemed Relaxing.)

Motivate

Debate——— GENERAL

People and Nature During the past several hundred years, a rapidly expanding human population has caused some species to become extinct either from habitat destruction or overhunting. Have students takes sides and debate the following issue: If people are as much a part of the environment as trees and birds, are people's actions just another natural process?

LS Verbal/Intrapersonal

READING WARM-UP

Objectives

● Give three examples of natural selection in action.

● Outline the process of speciation.

Terms to Learn

generation time
speciation

READING STRATEGY

Prediction Guide Before reading this section, write the title of each heading in this section. Next, under each heading, write what you think you will learn.

Natural Selection in Action

Have you ever had to take an antibiotic? Antibiotics are supposed to kill bacteria. But sometimes, bacteria are not killed by the medicine. Do you know why?

A population of bacteria might develop an adaptation through natural selection. Most bacteria are killed by the chemicals in antibiotics. But in some cases, a few bacteria are naturally *resistant* to the chemicals, so they are not killed. These survivors are then able to pass this adaptation to their offspring. This situation is an example of how natural selection works.

Changes in Populations

The theory of natural selection explains how a population changes in response to its environment. If natural selection is always taking place, a population will tend to be well adapted to its environment. But not all individuals are the same. The individuals that are likely to survive and reproduce are those that are best adapted at the time.

Adaptation to Hunting

Changes in populations are sometimes observed when a new force affects the survival of individuals. In Uganda, scientists think that hunting is affecting the elephant population. In 1930, about 99% of the male elephants in one area had tusks. Only 1% of the elephants were born without tusks. Today, as few as 85% of the male elephants in that area have tusks. What happened?

A male African elephant that has tusks is shown in **Figure 1.** The ivory of an elephant's tusks is very valuable. People hunt the elephants for their tusks. As a result, fewer of the elephants that have tusks survive to reproduce, and more of the tuskless elephants survive. When the tuskless elephants reproduce, they pass the tuskless trait to their offspring.

Figure 1 *The ivory tusks of African elephants are very valuable. Some elephants are born without tusks.*

CHAPTER RESOURCES

Chapter Resource File

- **Lesson Plan**
- **Directed Reading A** BASIC
- **Directed Reading B** SPECIAL NEEDS

Technology

- **Transparencies**
  - Bellringer

MISCONCEPTION
///ALERT

Tuskless Elephants It is important to understand that there were always some tuskless elephants in the wild populations. These animals were naturally tuskless—they were born without tusks and never developed tusks. Because the tuskless elephants are not hunted, they are more likely to pass their traits to future generations.

Figure 2   Natural Selection of Insecticide Resistance

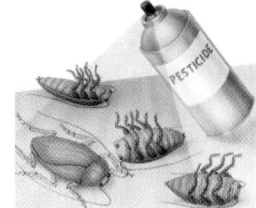

❶ An insecticide will kill most insects, but a few may survive. These survivors have genes that make them resistant to the insecticide.

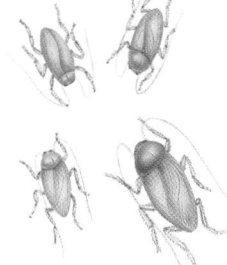

❷ The survivors then reproduce, passing the insecticide-resistance genes to their offspring.

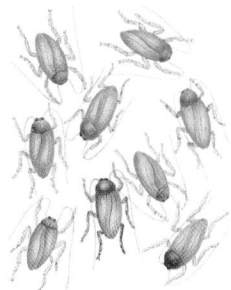

❸ In time, the replacement population of insects is made up mostly of individuals that have the insecticide-resistance genes.

❹ When the same kind of insecticide is used on the insects, only a few are killed because most of them are resistant to that insecticide.

Insecticide Resistance

People have always wanted to control the insect populations around their homes and farms. Many insecticides are used to kill insects. But some chemicals that used to work well do not work as well anymore. Some individual insects within the population are resistant to certain insecticides. **Figure 2** shows how a population of insects might become resistant to common insecticides.

More than 500 kinds of insects are now resistant to certain insecticides. Insects can quickly develop resistance because they often produce many offspring and have short generation times. **Generation time** is the average time between one generation of offspring and the next.

Reading Check Why do insects quickly develop resistance to insecticides? (*See the Appendix for answers to Reading Checks.*)

Competition for Mates

In the process of evolution, survival is simply not enough. Natural selection is at work when individuals reproduce. In organisms that reproduce sexually, finding a mate is part of the struggle to reproduce. Many species have so much competition for mates that interesting adaptations result. For example, the females of many bird species prefer to mate with males that have certain types of colorful feathers.

generation time the period between the birth of one generation and the birth of the next generation

WEIRD SCIENCE

In several species, typical courtship behaviors involve one sex offering food to the other sex. For example, males of the fairy tern fly around the female and offer her a mackerel. In many spider species, males offer an insect carcass to the female. In some spider species, such as the Australian redback spider, the male himself may become a meal!

INTERNET ACTiViTY
Essay——————— GENERAL

For an internet activity related to this chapter, have students go to **go.hrw.com** and type in the keyword **HL5EVOW.**

Reteaching —— BASIC

Selection Have students place 20 black beans and 20 red beans on a piece of black paper. Call the display *Generation 1*. Tell students that the beans are fish and ask which would most likely be eaten first by the bean shark. Then tell them to add 5 black beans and take away 5 red ones. Call this *Generation 2*. Have students predict and model *Generation 3*. **LS Visual**

Quiz —— GENERAL

Concept Mapping Construct a concept map that shows how a population of mosquitoes can develop resistance to a pesticide.

Alternative Assessment —— ADVANCED

Species Report Have each student research and give an oral presentation on how the three steps of speciation (separation, adaptation, and division) worked in providing a particular animal with a distinctive feature. Species of the Galapágos Islands are good examples. **LS Verbal**

Answer to Reading Check

Sample answer: A newly formed canyon, mountain range, or lake could divide the members of a population.

Forming a New Species

Sometimes, drastic changes that can form a new species take place. In the animal kingdom, a *species* is a group of organisms that can mate with each other to produce fertile offspring. A new species may form after a group becomes separated from the original population. This group forms a new population. Over time, the two populations adapt to their different environments. Eventually, the populations can become so different that they can't mate anymore. Each population may then be considered a new species. The formation of a new species as a result of evolution is called **speciation** (SPEE shee AY shuhn). **Figure 3** shows how new species of Galápagos finches may have formed. Speciation may happen in other ways as well.

speciation the formation of new species as a result of evolution

Separation

Speciation often begins when a part of a population becomes separated from the rest. The process of separation can happen in several ways. For example, a newly formed canyon, mountain range, or lake can divide the members of a population.

✓ **Reading Check** How can parts of a population become separated?

Figure 3 The Evolution of Galápagos Finch Species

❶ Some finches left the mainland and reached one of the islands (separation).

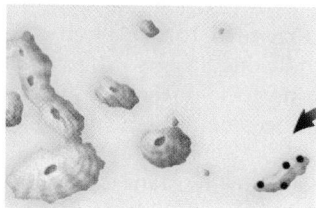
❷ The finches reproduced and adapted to the environment (adaptation).

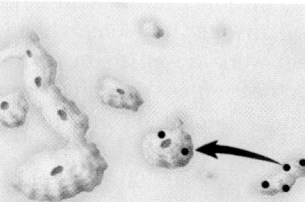
❸ Some finches flew to a second island (separation).

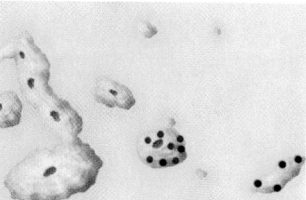
❹ The finches reproduced and adapted to the different environment (adaptation).

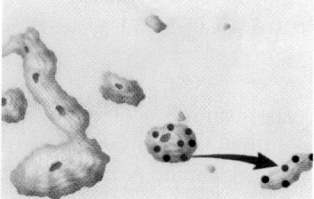
❺ Some finches flew back to the first island but could no longer interbreed with the finches there (division).

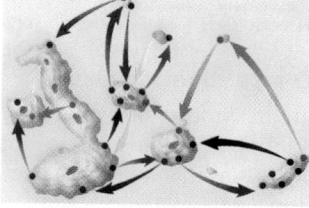
❻ This process may have occurred over and over again as the finches flew to the other islands.

INCLUSION Strategies

- *Learning Disabled*
- *Attention Deficit Disorder*
- *Behavior Control Issues*

Guide students through a simulation. Trace nine rabbit outlines on a single page, and place an X on five of them. For each student, make one copy on each of three colors of paper. Have each student label his or her rabbits. Prompt students through the following stages:

1. Overproduction: Cut out the rabbits.

2. Genetic variation: Spread the rabbits on your desk. Notice the colors.

3. Struggle to survive: For 1 min, try to take rabbits from each other. Yours are "safe" if you are touching them.

4. Successful reproduction: Look at your surviving rabbits. Suppose only those that have an X will reproduce.

As a class, tally and discuss the results.

LS Visual
Co-op Learning

English Language Learners

Adaptation

Populations constantly undergo natural selection. After two groups have separated, natural selection may act on each group in different ways. Over many generations, the separated groups may evolve different sets of traits. If the environmental conditions for each group differ, the adaptations in the groups will also differ.

Division

Over many generations, two separated groups of a population may become very different. Even if a geographical barrier is removed, the groups may not be able to interbreed anymore. At this point, the two groups are no longer the same species.

Figure 4 shows another way that populations may stop interbreeding. Leopard frogs and pickerel frogs probably had the same ancestor species. Then, at some point, some of these frogs began to mate at different times during the year.

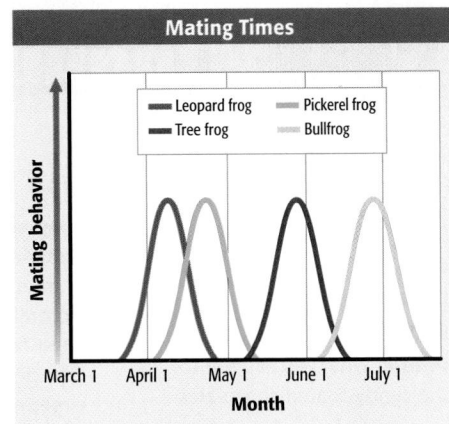

Mating Times

Leopard frog   Pickerel frog
Tree frog   Bullfrog

Figure 4 *The leopard frog and the pickerel frog are similar species. However, leopard frogs do not search for mates at the same time of year that pickerel frogs do.*

SECTION Review

Summary

● Natural selection explains how populations adapt to changes in their environment. A variety of examples of such adaptations can be found.

● Natural selection also explains how one species may evolve into another. Speciation occurs as populations undergo separation, adaptation, and division.

Using Key Terms

1. In your own words, write a definition for the term *speciation*.

Understanding Key Ideas

2. Two populations have evolved into two species when
   a. the populations are separated.
   b. the populations look different.
   c. the populations can no longer interbreed.
   d. the populations adapt.

3. Explain why the number of tuskless elephants in Uganda may be increasing.

Math Skills

4. A female cockroach can produce 80 offspring at a time. If half of the offspring produced by a certain female are female and each female produces 80 offspring, how many cockroaches are there in the third generation?

Critical Thinking

5. **Forming Hypotheses** Most kinds of cactus have leaves that grow in the form of spines. The stems or trunks become thick, juicy pads or barrels. Explain how these cactus parts might have evolved.

6. **Making Comparisons** Suggest an organism other than an insect that might evolve an adaptation to human activities.

For a variety of links related to this chapter, go to www.scilinks.org

Topic: Species and Adaptation
SciLinks code: HSM1433

Answers to Section Review

1. Sample answer: Speciation is one species evolving into two.

2. c

3. Sample answer: The number of tuskless elephants is increasing because hunters are killing off the elephants with tusks before they can breed.

4. 128,000 cockroaches
   Calculations:
   First generation:
       80 cockroaches
   Second generation:
       $(80 \div 2) \times 80 =$
       3,200 cockroaches
   Third generation:
       $(3,200 \div 2) \times 80 =$
       128,000 cockroaches

5. Sample answer: Cactuses evolved from plants with adaptations to dry conditions, such as spiny leaves that keep animals from eating the plant or thick stems that store water.

6. Sample answer: Rodents might adapt to eating our garbage.

Is That a Fact!

Some species that have adapted to live in total darkness no longer even have eyes! Just as whales have evolved into legless forms, these species have completely adapted to life without light, and some have evolved forms lacking eyes altogether. There are blind cave fish, eels, salamanders, worms, shrimp, crayfish, spiders, beetles, and crickets.

CHAPTER RESOURCES

Chapter Resource File

 • Section Quiz GENERAL
   • Section Review GENERAL
   • Vocabulary and Section Summary GENERAL
   • Critical Thinking ADVANCED

Technology

   Transparencies
   • Evolution of the Galápagos Finches

Survival of the Chocolates

Teacher's Notes

Time Required

One or two 45-minute class periods

Lab Ratings

EASY ———————————— HARD

Teacher Prep 🧪
Student Set-Up 🧪🧪
Concept Level 🧪🧪
Clean Up 🧪

Safety Caution

Safety concerns will vary with each design.

Preparation Notes

Be prepared for a variety of experimental designs. For example, students may wish to test which color will crack easiest under physical stress or which color will dissolve more quickly in water. This lab is an opportunity to reinforce scientific methods and practice designing experiments. Encourage students to brainstorm a variety of possible hypotheses and ways of testing the hypotheses. Have students identify scientific methods in their experiments.

Survival of the Chocolates

Imagine a world populated with candy, and hold that delicious thought in your head for just a moment. Try to apply the idea of natural selection to a population of candy-coated chocolates. According to the theory of natural selection, individuals who have favorable adaptations are more likely to survive. In the "species" of candy-coated chocolates you will study in this experiment, the characteristics of individual chocolates may help them "survive." For example, shell strength (the strength of the candy coating) could be an adaptive advantage. Plan an experiment to find out which characteristics of the chocolates are favorable "adaptations."

Ask a Question

❶ What might "survival" mean for a candy-coated chocolate? What are some ways you can test which chocolates are the "strongest" or "most fit" for their environment? Also, write down any other questions that you could ask about the "survival" of the chocolates.

Form a Hypothesis

❷ Form a hypothesis, and make a prediction. For example, if you chose to study candy color, your prediction might be similar to this: If the ___ colored shell is the strongest, then fewer of the chocolates with this color of shell will ___ when ___.

OBJECTIVES

Form a hypothesis about the fate of the candy-coated chocolates.

Predict what will happen to the candy-coated chocolates.

Design and conduct an experiment to test your hypothesis.

MATERIALS

• chocolates, candy-coated, small, in a variety of colors (about 100)
• items to be determined by the students and approved by the teacher

SAFETY

Karma Houston-Hughes
Kyrene Middle School
Tempe, Arizona

CHAPTER RESOURCES

Chapter Resource File

📁 • Datasheet for Chapter Lab
• Lab Notes and Answers

Technology

💿 Classroom Videos
• Lab Video

Test the Hypothesis

3 Design a procedure to determine which type of candy-coated chocolate is most likely to survive. In your plan, be sure to include materials and tools you may need to complete this procedure.

4 Check your experimental design with your teacher before you begin. Your teacher will supply the candy and assist you in gathering materials and tools.

5 Record your results in a data table. Be sure to organize your data in a clear and understandable way.

Analyze the Results

1 **Describing Events** Write a report that describes your experiment. Be sure to include tables and graphs of the data you collected.

Draw Conclusions

2 **Evaluating Data** In your report, explain how your data either support or do not support your hypothesis. Include possible errors and ways to improve your procedure.

Applying Your Data

Can you think of another characteristic of the chocolates that can be tested to determine which type is best adapted to survive? Explain your idea, and describe how you might test it.

CHAPTER RESOURCES

Workbooks

Whiz-Bang Demonstrations
• Adaptation Behooves You GENERAL

Long-Term Projects & Research Ideas
• Evolution's Explosion ADVANCED

Form a Hypothesis

2. Answers may vary. The example statement is only an example for format. Students may wish to investigate a characteristic other than candy shell hardness. Help them make a prediction about their own experiment. Check that all students have formed testable hypotheses.

Test the Hypothesis

4. Answers may vary. Check that students have planned a controlled experiment and that each factor is accounted for. Also, check that they have planned for all materials they will need.

5. Answers may vary. Students should conduct their own experiment and record all procedures, observations, and results. Students should use data tables to record results where appropriate.

Analyze the Results

1. Reports may vary but should describe all parts of the experiment and present the results with tables, diagrams, or graphs as appropriate.

Draw Conclusions

2. Reports may vary but should include a conclusion that the hypothesis was supported or not. Check that student conclusions are directly related to the hypothesis and were logically drawn from the experimental results.

Assignment Guide

Section	Questions
1	2–4, 6, 8, 9, 12, 13, 21, 22
2	5, 10, 11, 14, 15, 17, 23
3	1, 7, 16, 18, 19, 20

ANSWERS

Using Key Terms

1. speciation
2. natural selection
3. species
4. fossil record
5. selective breeding
6. adaptation
7. generation time

Understanding Key Ideas

8. a
9. b
10. b
11. c

USING KEY TERMS

Complete each of the following sentences by choosing the correct term from the word bank.

adaptation
evolution
generation time
species
speciation
fossil record
selective breeding
natural selection

1 When a single population evolves into two populations that cannot interbreed anymore, ___ has occurred.

2 Darwin's theory of ___ explained the process by which organisms become well-adapted to their environment.

3 A group of organisms that can mate with each other to produce offspring is known as a(n) ___.

4 The ___ provides information about organisms that have lived in the past.

5 In ___, humans select organisms with desirable traits that will be passed from one generation to another.

6 A(n) ___ helps an organism survive better in its environment.

7 Populations of insects and bacteria can evolve quickly because they usually have a short ___.

UNDERSTANDING KEY IDEAS

Multiple Choice

8 Fossils are commonly found in
 a. sedimentary rock.
 b. all kinds of rock.
 c. granite.
 d. loose sand.

9 The fact that all organisms have DNA as their genetic material is evidence that
 a. all organisms undergo natural selection.
 b. all organisms may have descended from a common ancestor.
 c. selective breeding takes place every day.
 d. genetic resistance rarely occurs.

10 Charles Darwin puzzled over differences in the ___ of the different species of Galápagos finches.
 a. webbed feet
 b. beaks
 c. bone structure of the wings
 d. eye color

11 Darwin observed variations among individuals within a population, but he did not realize that these variations were caused by
 a. interbreeding.
 b. differences in food.
 c. differences in genes.
 d. selective breeding.

12. Sample answer: Living organisms can be compared in terms of body structures with other living organisms and with organisms from the fossil record. Also, the DNA of living organisms can be compared.

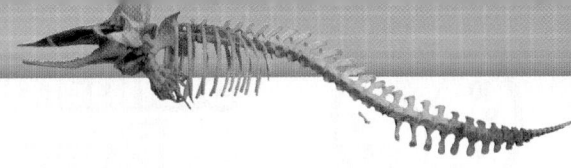

Short Answer

12 Identify two ways that organisms can be compared to provide evidence of evolution from a common ancestor.

13 Describe evidence that supports the hypothesis that whales evolved from land-dwelling mammals.

14 Why are some animals more likely to survive to adulthood than other animals are?

15 Explain how genetics is related to evolution.

16 Outline an example of the process of speciation.

CRITICAL THINKING

17 **Concept Mapping** Use the following terms to create a concept map: *struggle to survive, theory, genetic variation, Darwin, overpopulation, natural selection,* and *successful reproduction.*

18 **Making Inferences** How could natural selection affect the songs that birds sing?

19 **Forming Hypotheses** In Australia, many animals look like mammals from other parts of the world. But most of the mammals in Australia are marsupials, which carry their young in pouches after birth. Few kinds of marsupials are found anywhere else in the world. What is a possible explanation for the presence of so many of these unique mammals in Australia?

20 **Analyzing Relationships** Geologists have evidence that the continents were once a single giant continent. This giant landform eventually split apart, and the individual continents moved to their current positions. What role might this drifting of continents have played in evolution?

INTERPRETING GRAPHICS

The graphs below show information about the infants that are born and the infants that have died in a population. The weight of each infant was measured at birth. Use the graphs to answer the questions that follow.

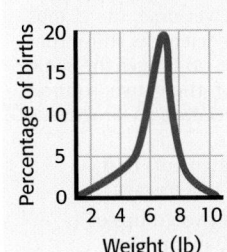
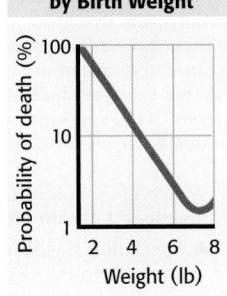

21 What is the most common birth weight?

22 At which birth weight is an infant most likely to survive?

23 How do the principles of natural selection help explain why there are more deaths among babies whose birth weights are low than among babies whose birth weights are average?

---

14. Sample answer: Those animals that are better adapted to the conditions of their environment, including competition with other organisms, are more likely to survive to adulthood.

15. Sample answer: Genetics provides an explanation of what happens inside cells as organisms evolve.

16. Answers may vary. Student answers may resemble the description of the speciation of the Galápagos finches given in the student text.

Critical Thinking

17. 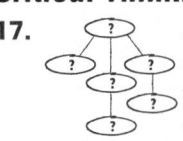 An answer to this exercise can be found at the end of this book.

18. Sample answer: A bird's song could be an advantage if the song helps the bird find mates or food, but the song could be a disadvantage if it attracts predators. So, natural selection would mean that birds whose songs were not an advantage might not survive, and songs would evolve that gave birds some kind of advantage.

19. Sample answer: Australia is an island, so the marsupials there could have evolved separately from other mammals around the world.

20. Sample answer: As the continents drifted apart, populations of species would have been separated and may have had to adapt to new environmental conditions. The separated populations would likely have evolved into separate species over time.

Interpreting Graphics

21. about 7 lb

22. about 7 lb

23. Sample answer: The infants who are best adapted to survive birth are those that weigh about 7 lb at birth.

---

13. Sample answer: Whales share many internal similarities with hoofed land mammals. Ancient fossils of four-legged land mammals exist from times when whales did not exist, but some of these fossils shared characteristics with modern whales and other hoofed mammals. A sequence of fossil organisms shows how the characteristics of modern whales could have evolved from those of ancient land mammals.

CHAPTER RESOURCES

Chapter Resource File

- Chapter Review GENERAL
- Chapter Test A GENERAL
- Chapter Test B ADVANCED
- Chapter Test C SPECIAL NEEDS
- Vocabulary Activity GENERAL

Workbooks

Study Guide
- Assessment resources are also available in Spanish.

Teacher's Note

To provide practice under more realistic testing conditions, give students 20 minutes to answer all of the questions in this Standardized Test Preparation.

MISCONCEPTION
ALERT

Answers to the standardized test preparation can help you identify student misconceptions and misunderstandings.

READING

Passage 1

1. A
2. H

TEST DOCTOR

Question 1: When a test question asks for a main idea, students should re-read the first and last sentences of each paragraph, and then try to summarize the main idea for themselves. In this case, the combination of the first and last sentences of the passage closely matches answer A. If students are still not sure about the best answer from among the options given, they should skim the passage to be sure that the majority of the sentences relate to the possible main idea.

READING

Read each of the passages below. Then, answer the questions that follow each passage.

Passage 1 When the Grand Canyon was forming, a single population of tassel-eared squirrels may have been separated into two groups. Today, descendants of the two groups live on opposite sides of the canyon. The two groups share many characteristics, but they do not look the same. For example, both groups have tasseled ears, but each group has a unique fur color pattern. An important difference between the groups is that the Abert squirrels live on the south rim of the canyon, and the Kaibab squirrels live on the north rim.

The environments on the two sides of the Grand Canyon are different. The north rim is about 370 m higher than the south rim. Almost twice as much precipitation falls on the north rim than on the south rim every year. Over many generations, the two groups of squirrels have adapted to their new environments. Over time, the groups became very different. Many scientists think that the two types of squirrels are no longer the same species. The development of these two squirrel groups is an example of speciation in progress.

1. Which of the following statements **best** describes the main idea of this passage?
   A Speciation is evident in two groups of squirrels in the Grand Canyon area.
   B Two groups of squirrels in the Grand Canyon area are closely related.
   C Two species can form from one species. This process is called *speciation*.
   D There are two groups of squirrels because the Grand Canyon has two sides.

2. Which of the following statements about the two types of squirrels is true?
   F They look the same.
   G They live in similar environments.
   H They have tasseled ears.
   I They can interbreed with each other.

Passage 2 You know from experience that individuals in a <u>population</u> are not exactly the same. If you look around the room, you will see a lot of differences among your classmates. You may have even noticed that no two dogs or two cats are exactly the same. No two individuals have exactly the same adaptations. For example, one cat may be better at catching mice, and another is better at running away from dogs. Observations such as these form the basis of the theory of natural selection. Because adaptations help organisms survive to reproduce, the individuals that are better adapted to their environment are more likely to pass their traits to future generations.

1. In the passage, what does *population* mean?
   A a school
   B some cats and dogs
   C a group of the same type of organism
   D a group of individuals that are the same

2. In this passage, which of the following are given as examples of adaptations?
   F differences among classmates
   G differences among cats
   H differences between cats and dogs
   I differences among environments

3. Which of the following statements about the individuals in a population that survive to reproduce is true?
   A They have the same adaptations.
   B They are likely to pass on adaptations to the next generation.
   C They form the basis of the theory of natural selection.
   D They are always better hunters.

Passage 2

1. C
2. G
3. B

TEST DOCTOR

Question 1: The question asks for an example of a concept that can be found in the passage. A good strategy for the reader is to skim the paragraph for the use of the word *adaptation* and then read the surrounding sentences. In this case, the sentence that begins "For example," clearly offers examples of adaptations. The remaining task is to find the answer (G) that best paraphrases or summarizes the types of examples in that sentence: differences among cats.

The graph below shows average beak sizes of a group of finches on one island over several years. Use the graph to answer the questions that follow.

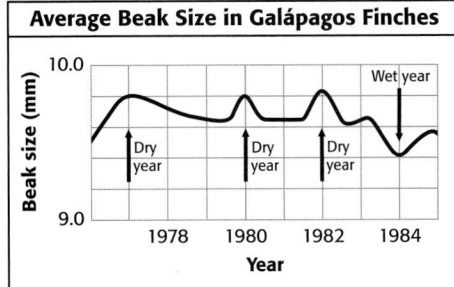

Average Beak Size in Galápagos Finches

1. In which of the years studied was average beak size the largest?
   A 1977
   B 1980
   C 1982
   D 1984

2. If beak size in this group of birds is linked to the amount of rainfall, what can you infer about the year 1976 on this island?
   F The year 1976 was drier than 1977.
   G The year 1976 was drier than 1980.
   H The year 1976 was wetter than 1977.
   I The year 1976 was wetter than 1984.

3. During which year(s) was rainfall probably the lowest on the island?
   A 1978, 1980, and 1982
   B 1977, 1980, 1982, and 1984
   C 1982
   D 1984

4. Which of the following statements **best** summarizes this data?
   F Average beak size stayed about the same except during wet years.
   G Average beak size decreased during dry years and increased during wet years.
   H Average beak size increased during dry years and decreased during wet years.
   I Average beak size changed randomly.

MATH

Read each question below, and choose the best answer.

Island	Average beak length (mm)	Average beak width (mm)	Number of unique species
Verde	9.7	6.5	5
Azul	8.9	8.7	15
Rosa	5.2	8.0	10

Average Beak Measurements of Birds of the Colores Islands

1. What is the ratio of the number of species on Verde Island to the total number of species on all three of the Colores Islands?
   A 1:2
   B 1:5
   C 1:6
   D 5:15

2. What percentage of all bird species on the Colores Islands are on Rosa Island?
   F approximately 15%
   G approximately 30%
   H approximately 50%
   I approximately 80%

3. On which of the islands is the ratio of average beak length to average beak width closest to 1:1?
   A Verde Island
   B Azul Island
   C Rosa Island
   D There is not enough information to determine the answer.

4. On which island does the bird with the smallest beak length live?
   F Verde Island
   G Azul Island
   H Rosa Island
   I There is not enough information to determine the answer.

Standardized Test Preparation

1. C
2. H
3. C
4. H

TEST DOCTOR

Question 1: This question simply requires understanding the labels on the graph. Students who miss this question may have difficulty understanding titles and axis labels.

Question 2: This question asks about a year (1976) that is not directly labeled, so the student needs to count two spaces backward from 1978 in order to determine which part of the data is from 1976. Then, the student needs to infer from the trends in the graph that 1976 was wetter than 1977.

MATH

1. C
2. G
3. B
4. I

TEST DOCTOR

Question 1: The question asks for the ratio of the number in one group to the number in all groups combined. Thus, the ratio is Verde:all or 5:30, which simplifies to 1:6.

Question 3: Because the question asks for a ratio that is close to 1:1, the best strategy is to scan the columns of beak length and beak width, looking for the pair of numbers that are closest in value (Azul Island).

Question 4: For this question, students must recall that an *average* (or mean) does not necessarily indicate the *range* of values that may have been sampled. Thus, there is no way of knowing from the data given in the table what the smallest or largest beak sizes were for each island's set of measurements.

CHAPTER RESOURCES

Chapter Resource File
• Standardized Test Preparation GENERAL

State Resources

For specific resources for your state, visit **go.hrw.com** and type in the keyword **HSMSTR**.

Science, Technology, and Society

Teaching Strategy — GENERAL

To help students understand changes in agriculture, create a table that contrasts traditional and industrial farming practices. Under "Traditional," list phrases such as *smaller scale, few machines, manual labor, more plant varieties,* and m*ainly for sustenance.* Under "Industrial," list phrases such as *larger scale, more mechanized, fewer plant varieties,* and *primarily for profit.* Point out that a shrinking number of farmers practice some form of traditional agriculture. Scientists at seed banks try to obtain samples of traditionally farmed seeds.

Science Fiction

Background

About the Author Scott Sanders (1945–) writes many different kinds of stories. Early in life, he chose to become a writer rather than a scientist, although he still has an interest science. Sanders has written about folklore, physics, the naturalist John James Audubon, and settlers of Indiana. Much of his work is nonfiction. His writing has been published in books and periodicals, such as the *Chicago Sun-Times, Harper's,* and *Omni.*

Science in Action

Science, Technology, and Society

Seed Banks

All over the world, scientists are making deposits in a special kind of bank. These banks are not for money, but for seeds. Why should seeds be saved? Saving seeds saves plants that may someday save human lives. These plants could provide food or medicine in the future. Throughout human history, many medicines have been developed from plants. And scientists keep searching for new chemicals among the incredible variety of plants in the world. But time is running out. Many plant species are becoming extinct before they have even been studied.

Math ACTIVITY

Many drugs were originally developed from plants. Suppose that 100 plants are used for medicines this year, but 5% of plant species become extinct each year. How many of the medicinal plants would be left after 1 year? after 10 years? Round your answers to whole numbers.

Science Fiction

"The Anatomy Lesson" by Scott Sanders

Do you know the feeling you get when you have an important test? A medical student faces a similar situation in this story. The student needs to learn the bones of the human body for an anatomy exam the next day. The student goes to the anatomy library to study. The librarian lets him check out a box of bones that are supposed to be from a human skeleton. But something is wrong. There are too many bones. They are the wrong shape. They don't fit together correctly. Somebody must be playing a joke! Find out what's going on and why the student and the librarian will never be the same after "The Anatomy Lesson." You can read it in the *Holt Anthology of Science Fiction.*

Language Arts ACTIVITY

WRITING SKILL Before you read this story, predict what you think will happen. Write a paragraph that "gives away" the ending that you predict. After you have read the story, listen to some of the predictions made by your classmates. Discuss your opinions about the possible endings.

Answer to Math Activity

year	number of plants
0	100
1	95
5	77
10	60

Answer to Language Arts Activity

Student paragraphs may vary. Have students compare their predictions to the story's ending and to other students' predictions.

People in Science

Raymond Pierotti

Canine Evolution Raymond Pierotti thinks that it's natural that he became an evolutionary biologist. He grew up exploring the desert around his home in New Mexico. He was fascinated by the abundant wildlife surviving in the bleak landscape. "One of my earliest memories is getting coyotes to sing with me from my backyard," he says.

Pierotti now studies the evolutionary relationships between wolves, coyotes, and domestic dogs. Some of his ideas come from the traditions of the Comanches. According to the Comanche creation story, humans came from wolves. Although Pierotti doesn't believe that humans evolved from wolves, he sees the creation story as a suggestion that humans and wolves have evolved together. "Wolves are very similar to humans in many ways," says Pierotti. "They live in family groups and hunt together. It is possible that wolves actually taught humans how to hunt in packs, and there are ancient stories of wolves and humans hunting together and sharing the food. I think it was this relationship that inspired the Comanche creation stories."

Social Studies ACTiViTY

WRITING SKILL Research a story of creation that comes from a Greek, Roman, or Native American civilization. Write a paragraph summarizing the myth, and share it with a classmate.

go.hrw.com
To learn more about these Science in Action topics, visit go.hrw.com and type in the keyword HL5EVOF.

Current Science
Check out Current Science® articles related to this chapter by visiting go.hrw.com. Just type in the keyword HL5CS07.

People in Science

ACTiViTY ——————— GENERAL

Have every student write or present a report on a breed of dog. The report should focus on the origin and evolution of the breed, with particular attention paid to the culture that bred it and why those characteristics were chosen. The report could also explore whether these breeds make good household pets and why. Students can easily find information on dog breeds on the Internet by searching for either the name of a breed or for "dog breeds" and visiting any of several sites that collect information on different breeds.

The History of Life on Earth
Chapter Planning Guide

Compression guide:
To shorten instruction
because of time limitations,
omit Section 3.

OBJECTIVES	LABS, DEMONSTRATIONS, AND ACTIVITIES	TECHNOLOGY RESOURCES
PACING • 90 min pp. 192–199 **Chapter Opener**	SE **Start-up Activity,** p. 193 ◆ GENERAL	OSP **Parent Letter** ■ GENERAL CD **Student Edition on CD-ROM** CD **Guided Reading Audio CD** ■ TR **Chapter Starter Transparency*** VID **Brain Food Video Quiz**
Section 1 Evidence of the Past • Explain how fossils can be formed and how their age can be estimated. • Describe the geologic time scale and the way that scientists use it. • Compare two ways that conditions for life on Earth have changed over time.	TE **Activity** Newspaper Layers, p. 195 ◆ GENERAL SE **Connection to Social Studies** A Place in Time, p. 196 ◆ GENERAL TE **Group Activity** Detailed Geologic Timeline, p. 196 ADVANCED SE **Quick Lab** Making a Geologic Timeline, p. 197 ◆ GENERAL CRF **Datasheet for Quick Lab*** TE **Activity** Rock Collectors, p. 197 GENERAL SE **Skills Practice Lab** The Half-Life of Pennies, p. 769 ◆ GENERAL CRF **Datasheet for LabBook***	CRF **Lesson Plans*** TR **Bellringer Transparency*** TR **Using Half-Lives to Date Fossils*** TR **The Geologic Time Scale*** TR **Moving Continents and Tectonic Plates*** TR *LINK TO EARTH SCIENCE* The South American Plate*
PACING • 45 min pp. 200–205 **Section 2 Eras of the Geologic Time Scale** • Outline the major developments that allowed life to exist on Earth. • Describe the types of organisms that arose during the four major divisions of the geologic time scale.	TE **Connection Activity** Earth Science, p. 201 ◆ GENERAL TE **Activity** Using Maps, p. 201 ◆ GENERAL TE **Group Activity** Ancient Plants, p. 202 GENERAL TE **Connection Activity** Real World, p. 202 ◆ GENERAL LB **Long-Term Projects & Research Ideas** A Horse is a Horse* ADVANCED	CRF **Lesson Plans*** TR **Bellringer Transparency*** SE **Internet Activity,** p. 201 GENERAL CRF **SciLinks Activity*** GENERAL CD **Interactive Explorations CD-ROM** Rock On! GENERAL
PACING • 90 min pp. 206–211 **Section 3 Humans and Other Primates** • Describe two characteristics that all primates share. • Describe three major groups of hominids.	TE **Activity** Exploring Vision, p. 207 GENERAL TE **Activity** Primate Characteristics, p. 208 ◆ BASIC TE **Group Activity** Comparing Hominids, p. 208 ◆ GENERAL SE **School-to-Home Activity** Thumb Through This, p. 209 GENERAL TE **Connection Activity** Art, p. 209 ◆ GENERAL TE **Activity** Classifying Primates, p. 211 ADVANCED SE **Inquiry Lab** Mystery Footprints, p. 212 ◆ GENERAL CRF **Datasheet for LabBook*** SE **Science in Action** Math, Social Studies, and Language Arts Activities, pp. 218–219 GENERAL	CRF **Lesson Plans*** TR **Bellringer Transparency*** TR **Comparison of Primate Skeletons*** VID **Lab Videos for Life Science**

PACING • 90 min

CHAPTER REVIEW, ASSESSMENT, AND STANDARDIZED TEST PREPARATION

CRF **Vocabulary Activity*** GENERAL
SE **Chapter Review,** pp. 214–215 GENERAL
CRF **Chapter Review*** ■ GENERAL
CRF **Chapter Tests A*** ■ GENERAL, **B*** ADVANCED, **C*** SPECIAL NEEDS
SE **Standardized Test Preparation,** pp. 216–217 GENERAL
CRF **Standardized Test Preparation*** GENERAL
CRF **Performance-Based Assessment*** GENERAL
OSP **Test Generator** GENERAL
CRF **Test Item Listing*** GENERAL

Online and Technology Resources

Visit **go.hrw.com** for a variety of free resources related to this textbook. Enter the keyword **HL5HIS.**

Holt Online Learning

Students can access interactive problem-solving help and active visual concept development with the *Holt Science and Technology* Online Edition available at **www.hrw.com.**

 Guided Reading Audio CD
Also in Spanish

A direct reading of each chapter for auditory learners, reluctant readers, and Spanish-speaking students.

 Science Tutor CD-ROM

Excellent for remediation and test practice.

SKILLS DEVELOPMENT RESOURCES	SECTION REVIEW AND ASSESSMENT	STANDARDS CORRELATIONS
SE Pre-Reading Activity, p. 192 GENERAL **OSP Science Puzzlers, Twisters & Teasers** GENERAL		National Science Education Standards UCP 2, 3; SAI 1, 2; SPSP 5; HNS 3
CRF Directed Reading A* ■ BASIC**, B*** SPECIAL NEEDS **CRF Vocabulary and Section Summary*** ■ GENERAL **SE Reading Strategy** Reading Organizer, p. 194 GENERAL **SE Math Practice** Fractions of Fractions, p. 195 GENERAL **SE Connection to Geology** Mid-Atlantic Ridge, p. 199 GENERAL **TE Inclusion Strategies,** p. 198 **MS Math Skills for Science** Radioactive Decay and the Half-Life* GENERAL **MS Math Skills for Science** Geologic Time Scale* GENERAL **CRF Reinforcement Worksheet** Earth Timeline* BASIC	**SE Reading Checks,** pp. 195, 197, 198 GENERAL **TE Homework,** p. 195 GENERAL **TE Homework,** p. 197 GENERAL **TE Reteaching,** p. 198 BASIC **TE Quiz,** p. 198 GENERAL **TE Alternative Assessment,** p. 199 GENERAL **SE Section Review,*** p. 199 ■ GENERAL **CRF Section Quiz*** ■ GENERAL	UCP 1, 2, 4; SAI 1, 2; HNS 1, 2, 3; LS 1a, 3d, 5b, 5c; *LabBook:* UCP 1, 3; SAI 1; LS 5c
CRF Directed Reading A* ■ BASIC**, B*** SPECIAL NEEDS **CRF Vocabulary and Section Summary*** ■ GENERAL **SE Reading Strategy** Mnemonics, p. 200 GENERAL **SE Connection to Oceanography** Prehistoric Marine Organisms, p. 202 GENERAL **TE Inclusion Strategies,** p. 202 **SE Math Focus** Relative Scale, p. 204 GENERAL **TE Connection to Math** Another Time Scale, p. 204 ADVANCED **MS Math Skills for Science** Subtraction Review* GENERAL **CRF Reinforcement Worksheet** Condensed History* GENERAL	**SE Reading Checks,** pp. 200, 203, 204 GENERAL **TE Reteaching,** p. 204 BASIC **TE Quiz,** p. 204 GENERAL **TE Alternative Assessment,** p. 204 GENERAL **SE Section Review,*** p. 205 ■ GENERAL **CRF Section Quiz*** ■	UCP 1, 2, 3, 4; SAI 1; LS 1a, 1b, 3d, 5a, 5b, 5c
CRF Directed Reading A* BASIC**, B*** SPECIAL NEEDS **CRF Vocabulary and Section Summary*** ■ GENERAL **SE Reading Strategy** Discussion, p. 206 GENERAL **CRF Critical Thinking** Fossil Revelations* ADVANCED	**SE Reading Checks,** pp. 207, 208, 211 GENERAL **TE Homework,** p. 210 GENERAL **TE Reteaching,** p. 210 BASIC **TE Quiz,** p. 210 GENERAL **TE Alternative Assessment,** p. 210 GENERAL **SE Section Review,*** p. 211 ■ GENERAL **CRF Section Quiz*** ■ GENERAL	UCP 2, 4, 5; SAI 1, 2; ST 1, 2; HNS 2, 3; LS 1a, 3d, 5a, 5b, 5c; *Chapter Lab:* UCP 2, 5; SAI 1; HNS 2

One-Stop Planner® CD-ROM

This convenient CD-ROM includes:
- Lab Materials QuickList Software
- Holt Calendar Planner
- Customizable Lesson Plans
- Printable Worksheets
- ExamView® Test Generator

CNN student news.

cnnstudentnews.com

Find the latest news, lesson plans, and activities related to important scientific events.

SCILINKS.
NSTA

www.scilinks.org

Maintained by the **National Science Teachers Association.** See Chapter Enrichment pages for a complete list of topics.

Current Science®

Check out *Current Science* articles and activities by visiting the HRW Web site at **go.hrw.com.** Just type in the keyword **HL5CS08T.**

Classroom Videos

- **Lab Videos** demonstrate the chapter lab.
- **Brain Food Video Quizzes** help students review the chapter material.
- **CNN Videos** bring science into your students' daily life.

Visual Resources

CHAPTER STARTER TRANSPARENCY

Imagine . . .

BELLRINGER TRANSPARENCIES

Section: Evidence of the Past
Imagine that you haven't cleaned your room for 30 years and you finally decide to sort through the 2 m pile of stuff on your floor. What might you find on the top of the pile? in the middle? on the bottom?

Write your responses in your **science journal.**

Section: Eras of the Geologic Time Scale
Suppose that electrical energy had never been developed. How would your life differ from what it is like now? What do you do every day that requires electricity?

Write your answers in your **science journal.**

TEACHING TRANSPARENCIES

Using Half-Lives to Date Fossils

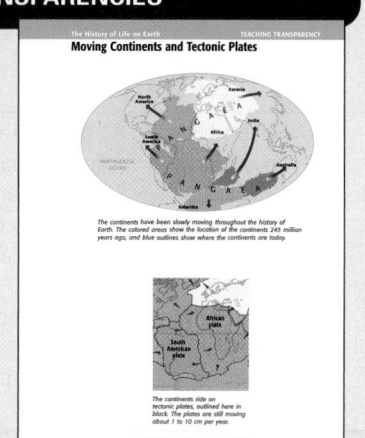

Moving Continents and Tectonic Plates

The continents have been slowly moving throughout the history of Earth. The colored areas show the location of the continents 245 million years ago, and blue outlines show where the continents are today.

The continents ride on tectonic plates, outlined here in black. The plates are still moving about 1 to 10 cm per year.

TEACHING TRANSPARENCIES

The Geologic Time Scale

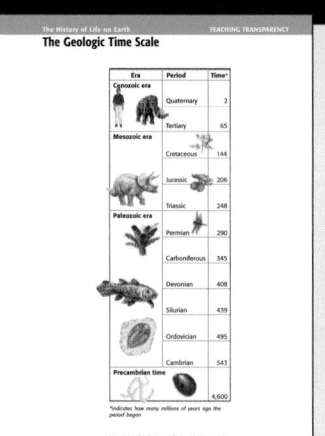

Comparison of Primate Skeletons

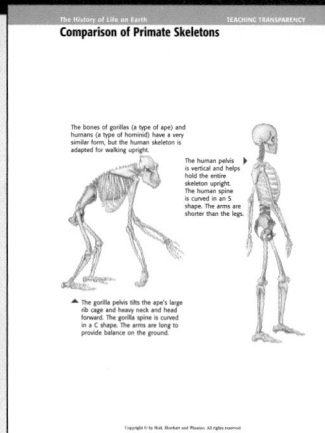

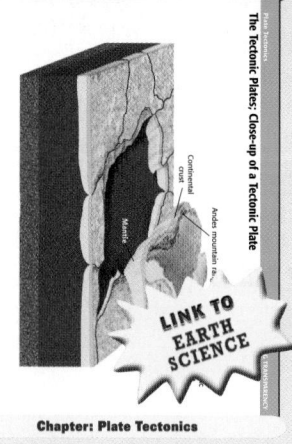

The Tectonic Plates; Close-up of a Tectonic Plate

LINK TO EARTH SCIENCE

Chapter: Plate Tectonics

CONCEPT MAPPING TRANSPARENCY

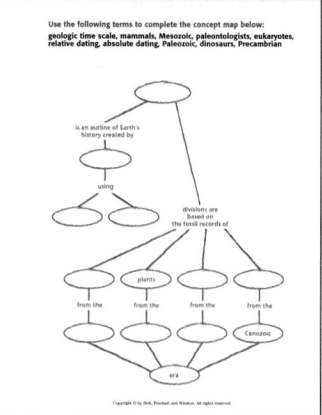

Use the following terms to complete the concept map below:
geologic time scale, mammals, Mesozoic, paleontologists, eukaryotes, relative dating, absolute dating, Paleozoic, dinosaurs, Precambrian

Planning Resources

LESSON PLANS

Lesson Plan SAMPLE

Section: Waves

Pacing
Regular Schedule: with lab(s):2 days   without lab(s):1 days
Block Schedule: with lab(s): 1 1/2 days   without lab(s): day

Objectives
1. Relate the seven properties of life to a living organism.
2. Describe seven themes that can help you to organize what you learn about biology.
3. Identify the tiny structures that make up all living organisms.
4. Differentiate between reproduction and heredity and between metabolism and homeostasis.

National Science Education Standards Covered
LSInter6:Cells have particular structures that underlie their functions.
LSMat1:Most cell functions involve chemical reactions.
LSBeh1:Cells store and use information to guide their functions.
UCP1:Cell functions are regulated.
SI1: Cells can differentiate and form complete multicellular organisms.
PS1: Species evolve over time.
ESS1: The great diversity of organisms is the result of more than 3.5 billion years of evolution.
ESS2: Natural selection and its evolutionary consequences provide a scientific explanation for the fossil record of ancient life forms as well as for the striking molecular similarities observed among the diverse species of living organisms.
ST1: The millions of different species of plants, animals, and microorganism that live on Earth today are related by descent from common ancestors.
ST2: The energy for life primarily comes from the sun.
SPSP1: The complexity of organisms and organisms accommodate the need for obtaining, transforming, transporting, releasing, and eliminating the matter and energy used to sustain the organism.
SPSP6: As matter and energy flows through different levels of organization of living systems—cells, organs, communities—and between living systems and the physical environment, chemical elements are recombined in different ways.
HN1: Organisms have behavioral responses to internal changes and to external stimuli.

PARENT LETTER

Dear Parent,

Your son's or daughter's science class will soon begin exploring the chapter entitled "The World of Physical Science." In this chapter, students will learn about how the scientific method applies to the world of physical science and the role of physical science in the world. By the end of the chapter, students should demonstrate a clear understanding of the chapter's main ideas and be able to discuss the following topics:

1. physical science is the study of energy and matter (Section 1)
2. the role of physical science in the world around them (Section 1)
3. careers that rely on physical science (Section 1)
4. the steps used in the scientific method (Section 2)
5. examples of technology (Section 2)
6. how the scientific method is used to answer questions and solve problems (Section 2)
7. how our knowledge of science changes over time (Section 2)
8. how models represent real objects or systems (Section 3)
9. examples of different ways models are used in science (Section 3)
10. the importance of the International System of Units (Section 4)
11. the appropriate units to use for particular measurements (Section 4)
12. how area and density are derived quantities (Section 4)

Questions to Ask Along the Way
You can help your son or daughter learn about these topics by asking interesting questions such as the following:

* What are some surprising careers that use physical science?
* What is a characteristic of a good hypothesis?
* When is it a good idea to use a model?
* Why do Americans measure things in terms of inches and yards and meters?

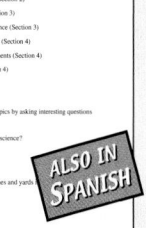
ALSO IN SPANISH

TEST ITEM LISTING

TEST ITEM LISTING
The World of Science SAMPLE

MULTIPLE CHOICE
1. A limitation of models is that
   a. they are large enough to see.
   b. they do not act exactly like the things that they model.
   c. they are smaller than the things that they model.
   d. they model unfamiliar things.
   Answer: B   Difficulty: 1   Section: 3   Objective: 2
2. The length 10 m is equal to
   a. 100 cm.   c. 10,000 mm.
   b. 1,000 cm.   d. Both (b) and (c)
   Answer: B   Difficulty: 1   Section: 3   Objective: 2
3. To be valid, a hypothesis must be
   a. testable.   c. made into a law.
   b. supported by evidence.   d. Both (a) and (b)
   Answer: B   Difficulty: 1   Section: 3   Objective: 2 1
4. The statement "Sheila has a stain on her shirt" is an example of a(n)
   a. law.   c. observation.
   b. hypothesis.   d. prediction.
   Answer: B   Difficulty: 1   Section: 3   Objective: 2
5. A hypothesis is often developed out of
   a. observations   c. laws.
   b. experiments.   d. Both (a) and (b)
   Answer: B   Difficulty: 1   Section: 3   Objective: 2
6. How many milliliters are in 3.5 kL?
   a. 3,500 mL   c. 3,500, 000 mL
   b. 0.0035 mL.   d. 35,000 mL.
   Answer: B   Difficulty: 1   Section: 3   Objective: 2
7. A map of Seattle is an example of a
   a. law.   c. model.
   b. theory.   d. unit.
   Answer: B   Difficulty: 1   Section: 3   Objective: 2
8. A lab has the safety icons shown below. These icons mean that you should wear
   a. safety goggles.   c. safety goggles and a lab apron.
   b. only a lab apron.   d. safety goggles, a lab apron, and gloves.
   Answer: B   Difficulty: 1   Section: 3   Objective: 2
9. The law of conservation of mass says the tot al mass before a chemical change is
   a. more than the total mass after the change.
   b. less than the total mass after the change.
   c. the same as the total mass after the change.
   d. not the same as the total mass after the change.
   Answer: B   Difficulty: 1   Section: 3   Objective: 2
10. In which of the following areas might you find a geochemist at work?
   a. studying the chemistry of rocks   c. studying fishes
   b. studying forestry   d. studying the atmosphere
   Answer: B   Difficulty: 1   Section: 3   Objective: 2

One-Stop Planner® CD-ROM

This CD-ROM includes all of the resources shown here and the following time-saving tools:

* **Lab Materials QuickList Software**
* **Customizable lesson plans**
* **Holt Calendar Planner**
* **The powerful ExamView® Test Generator**

For a preview of available worksheets covering math and science skills, see pages T26–T33. All of these resources are also on the One-Stop Planner®.

Meeting Individual Needs

DIRECTED READING A
Skills Worksheet
Directed Reading A   SAMPLE

Section:
THAT'S SCIENCE!
1. How did James Czarnowski get his idea for the penguin boat, Proteus? Explain.

ALSO IN SPANISH

...that is unusual about the way that Proteus moves through...

BASIC

DIRECTED READING B
Skills Worksheet
Directed Reading B   SAMPLE

Section:
THAT'S SCIENCE!
1. How did James Czarnowski get his idea for the penguin boat, Proteus? Explain.

2. What is unusual about the way that Proteus moves through the water?

SPECIAL NEEDS PHYSICAL SCIENCE

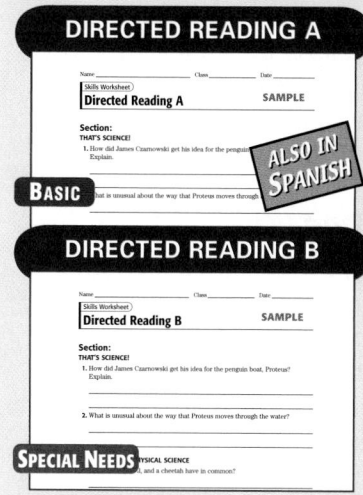

VOCABULARY ACTIVITY
Activity
Vocabulary Activity   SAMPLE

Getting the Dirt on the Soil
After you finish reading Chapter: [Unique Title], try this puzzle! Use the clues below to unscramble the vocabulary words. Write your answer in the space provided.

...breakdown of rock into ...and smaller pieces: ...RGNETH

9. the chemical breakdown of rocks and minerals into new substances: CAMILCHE THEAIRGWEN

GENERAL

VOCABULARY AND SECTION SUMMARY
Skills Worksheet
Vocabulary & Notes   SAMPLE

Section:
VOCABULARY
In your own words, write a definition of the following term in the space provided.
1. scientific method

2. technology

ALSO IN SPANISH

GENERAL

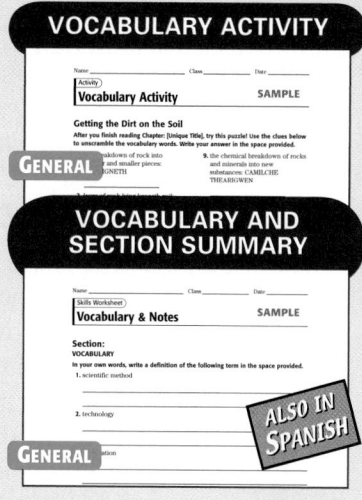

REINFORCEMENT
Skills Worksheet
Reinforcement   SAMPLE

The Plane Truth
You plan to enter a paper airplane contest sponsored by Talkin' Physical Science magazine. The person whose airplane flies the farthest wins a lifetime subscription to the magazine! You watch before the contest to watch an airplane landing at a nearby airport. You notice that the wings of the airplane have flaps, as shown in the illustration at right. The paper airplanes you've been testing do not have wing flaps.
What question would you ask yourself based on these observations? Write your...

Flaps

BASIC

CRITICAL THINKING
Skills Worksheet
Critical Thinking   SAMPLE

A Solar Solution

Dear Mr. Burns,
...

Joseph D. Burns
...Advisory Consultants
Portland, OR 97201

ADVANCED

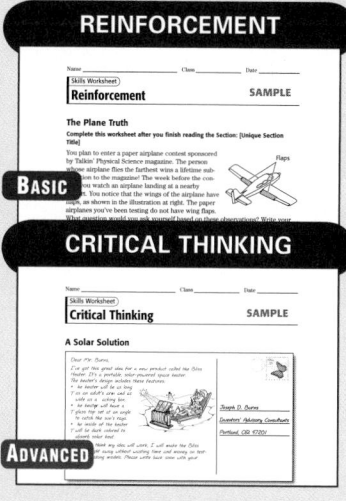

SCILINKS ACTIVITY
Activity
SciLinks Activity   SAMPLE

MARINE ECOSYSTEMS
Go to www.scilinks.com. To find links related to marine ecosystems, type in the keyword HL5400. Then, use the links to answer the questions about marine ecosys-
...percentage of the Earth's surface is covered by water?

SC LINKS   NSTA
Topic: Reproduction System
Irregularities
SciLinks code: HL5400

GENERAL

SCIENCE PUZZLERS, TWISTERS & TEASERS
CHAPTER 8
SCIENCE PUZZLERS, TWISTERS & TEASERS
The History of Life on Earth

Scientific Sleuthing
1. Each of the statements below was made by an organism during the era in which it evolved. Write the correct era in the space provided. The organisms evolved during the following eras: Precambrian, Paleozoic, Mesozoic, or Cenozoic.
a. I've seen the greatest swimmers of my generation destroyed.

b. People often accuse me of monkeying around.

c. Oxygen? What is that?

...and flames have frightened me ever since the day a meteorite came crashing into my backyard.

...My mother had to settle for a potted plant instead of flowers

GENERAL

Labs and Activities

LONG-TERM PROJECTS & RESEARCH IDEAS
PROJECT 8
STUDENT WORKSHEET
A Horse Is a Horse
DESIGN YOUR OWN

Horses haven't always had hooves. In the tropical forests of the Eocene epoch, a many-toed creature about the size of a dog fed on soft tree leaves. Scientists call it *Hyracotherium*, but we also know it as *Eohippus*, the dawn horse. *Hyracotherium* was an ancient ancestor of the modern horse.

An Ancient Ancestor
1. All animals living today are descendants of ancient animals. Some of these animals looked different from their modern descendants. Pick a modern mammal, and trace its evolution. Illustrate its evolution using a family tree. How does the modern animal differ from its ancient ancestor? What other animals have evolved from the same common ancestor? Create a poster of your findings.

USEFUL TERM
paleontologist
a scientist who studies the fossil record

Other Research Ideas
2. Have you ever found a fossil of a plant or animal? Are you interested in the Earth's ancient past? Maybe you would enjoy being a paleontologist? Research the career of a paleontologist, such as Charles Walcott, O. C. Marsh, or E. D. Cope. Write a paper about the paleontologist's life and contributions to the field.

3. Should we do everything possible to protect a species from extinction? Will extinction occur no matter what humans do? Research this issue. Form an opinion and write a position paper defending your opinion. Be sure to include examples of controversial efforts to protect endangered species such as the spotted owl.

4. Did a comet kill the dinosaurs? In 1980, Luis Alvarez hypothesized that every 26 million years an unknown celestial object passes near our solar system, bringing along a host of comets. According to this theory, whenever this object approaches, comets bombard the Earth. The result is mass destruction and extinction of many species. Research the evidence Alvarez used to develop this theory. Write a magazine article about your findings.

Long-Term Project Idea
5. Which part of the history of life on Earth do you find most interesting? Visit a local museum or an on-line natural history museum. Take a look at the exhibits about the history of the Earth. Create either a video documentary or a series of short articles about your favorite exhibits. In your presentation, be sure to explain the scientific information in each exhibit.

ADVANCED

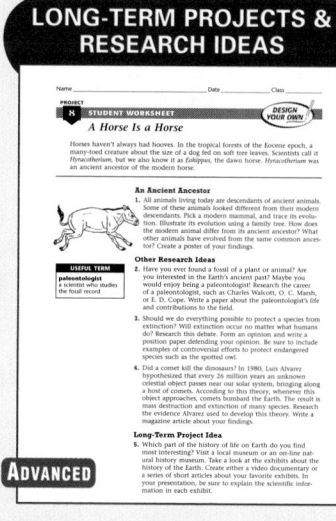

DATASHEETS FOR QUICK LABS
TEACHER RESOURCE PAGE
Quick Lab   DATASHEET FOR QUICK LAB
Reaction to Stress   SAMPLE

Background
The graph below illustrates changes that occur in the membrane potential of a neuron during an action potential. Use the graph to answer the following questions. Refer to Figure 3 as needed.

DATASHEETS FOR CHAPTER LABS
TEACHER RESOURCE PAGE
Skills Practice Lab   DATASHEET FOR CHAPTER LAB
Using Scientific Methods   SAMPLE

Teacher's Notes
TIME REQUIRED
One 45-minute class period.

DATASHEETS FOR LABBOOK
TEACHER RESOURCE PAGE
Skills Practice Lab   DATASHEET FOR LABBOOK LAB
Does It All Add Up?   SAMPLE

Teacher's Notes
TIME REQUIRED
One 45-minute class period.

Review and Assessments

SECTION QUIZ
Assessment
Section Quiz   SAMPLE

Section:
In the space provided, write the letter of the description that best matches the term or phrase.

___ 1. building molecules that can be used as an energy source, or breaking down molecules in which energy is stored
___ 2. the process by which light energy is converted to chemical energy
___ 3. an organism that uses sunlight or inorganic substances to make organic compounds

a. ...
b. ...
c. cellular respiration

ALSO IN SPANISH

GENERAL

SECTION REVIEW
Skills Worksheet
Section Review   SAMPLE

Section:
KEY TERMS
1. What do paleontologist study?

2. How does a trace fossil differ from petrified wood?

...fossil.

ALSO IN SPANISH

GENERAL

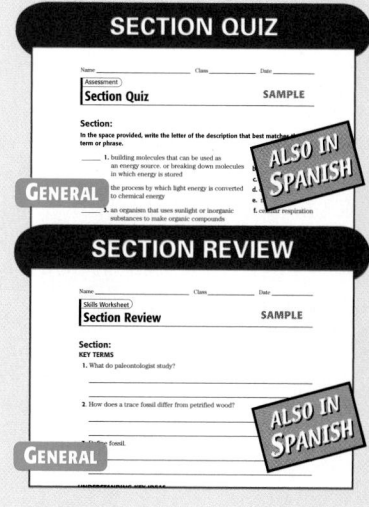

CHAPTER REVIEW
Skills Worksheet
Chapter Review   SAMPLE

USING VOCABULARY
1. Define biome in your own words.

2. Describe the characteristics of a savanna and a desert.

ALSO IN SPANISH

GENERAL

CHAPTER TEST A
Assessment
Chapter Test A   SAMPLE

MULTIPLE CHOICE
In the space provided, write the letter of the term or phrase that best answers each question.

___ 1. Surface currents are formed by
a. the moon's gravity.   c. wind.
b. the sun's gravity.   d. increased water...
___ 2. When waves come near the shore,
a. they speed up.   c. their wavele...
b. they slow down.   d. their wave...
___ 3. Longshore currents transport sediment
a. out to the open ocean.   c. only during low...
b. along the shore.   d. only during...
___ 4. Which of the following does NOT control surface currents?

ALSO IN SPANISH

GENERAL

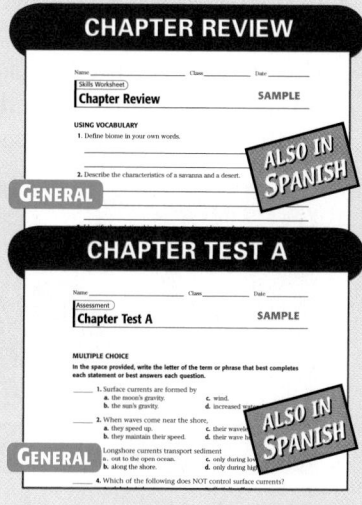

CHAPTER TEST B
Assessment
Chapter Test B   SAMPLE

MULTIPLE CHOICE
In the space provided, write the letter of the term or phrase that best completes each statement or best answers each question.

___ 1. Surface currents are formed by
a. the moon's gravity.   c. wind.
b. the sun's gravity.   d. increased water density.
___ 2. When waves come near the shore,
a. they speed up.   c. their wavelength increases.
b. they maintain their speed. d. their wave height increases.

ADVANCED

CHAPTER TEST C
Assessment
Chapter Test C   SAMPLE

MULTIPLE CHOICE
In the space provided, write the letter of the term or phrase that best completes each statement or best answers each question.

___ 1. Surface currents are formed by
a. the moon's gravity.   c. wind.
b. the sun's gravity.   d. increased water density.
___ 2. When waves come near the shore,
a. they speed up.   c. their wavelength increases.
b. they maintain their speed. d. their wave height increases.
...currents transport sediment
...to the open ocean.   c. only during low tide.
...long the shore.   d. only during high tide.
___ 4. Which of the following does NOT control surface currents?

SPECIAL NEEDS

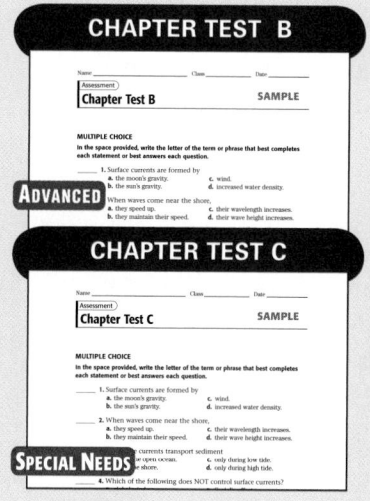

STANDARDIZED TEST PREPARATION
Assessment
Standardized Test Preparation   SAMPLE

READING
Read the passages below. Then, read each question that follows the passage. Decide which is the best answer to each question.

1 adventurous summer camp in the world. Billy can't wait to head for the outdoors. Billy checked the recommended supply list: light, summer clothes; sunscreen; rain gear; heavy, down-filled jacket; ski mask; and thick gloves. Wait a minute! Billy thought he was traveling to only one **destination**, so why does he need to bring such a wide variety of clothes? On further investiga...

GENERAL

PERFORMANCE-BASED ASSESSMENT
Assessment
Performanced-Based Assessment   SKILL BUILDER SAMPLE

OBJECTIVE
Determine which factors cause some sugar shapes to break down faster than others.

KNOW THE SCORE!
As you work through the activity, keep in mind that you will be earning a grade for the following:
• how you form and test the hypothesis (30%)
• the quality of your analysis (40%)
• the clarity of your conclusions (30%)

Using Scientific Methods
...QUESTIONS
...some sugar shapes erode more rapidly than others?

MATERIALS AND EQUIPMENT
1 regular sugar cube   • 90 mL of water

GENERAL

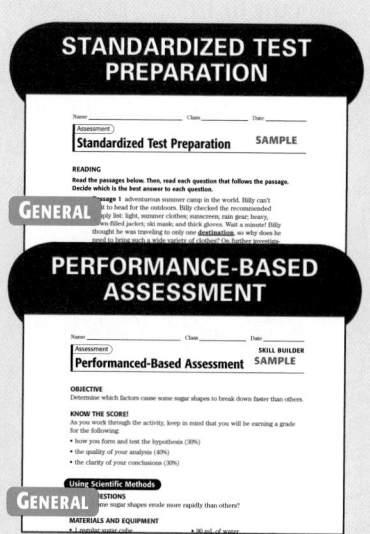

This Chapter Enrichment provides relevant and interesting information to expand and enhance your presentation of the chapter material.

Section 1

Evidence of the Past

Paul Sereno

- Paul Sereno has traveled around the world to study and document dinosaur fossils. He teaches at the University of Chicago and also involves his students in searching museum collections and combing deserts for new fossils. Sereno's teams have made many important finds. One of the first was in 1988 in Argentina, where his team unearthed the skeletons of a primitive 12-foot-long dinosaur called *Herrerasaurus*. The fossils in that area shed light on how and when the Age of Reptiles began. Sereno has continued to map the dinosaur family tree by studying fossils in the Sahara, in Niger, and in Morocco.

Fossils

- Fossils may be mere traces of organisms. Preserved footprints, feces, gnaw marks, and dug-out holes can all be considered fossils. Also, traces or remains of organisms can be preserved in materials other than sedimentary rock, such as amber, tar, or lava.

- Despite what many people think, fossils are not difficult to find. Nearly every state in the United States contains an abundance of fossils. However, scientists think that only a tiny fraction of the countless organisms that lived on Earth has been preserved as fossils. Many organisms have lived and died without leaving evidence of their existence in the fossil record.

Is That a Fact!

◆ The oldest fossils known are structures called *stromatolites* that are more than 3.5 billion years old. These structures are bands of sedimentary rock that are very similar to layered mats formed today by colonies of bacteria and cyanobacteria.

Law of Superposition

- The law of superposition states that in a series of undisturbed sedimentary rock layers, each layer is older than the one above it and younger than the one below it. This law is based on an observation made by Nicolaus Steno, a Danish physician, in 1669.

Methods of Absolute Dating

- Radioisotope dating is the most widely used method for dating a fossil. This method analyzes samples of igneous rock found within the same rock formation as the fossil. The method differs depending on the type of chemical isotope analyzed. The older the rocks are, the less accurate the dating. Isotopes with shorter half-lives provide a more accurate range of possible ages for younger rocks and fossils. Radiocarbon dating by accelerator mass spectrometry (AMS) has become a preferred method to date with high accuracy carbon-based fossils less than 60,000 years old.

Is That a Fact!

◆ The beginning of the Paleozoic era is sometimes called the *Cambrian explosion*. Within the first 100 million years of this period, a large variety of multicellular organisms appeared for the first time on Earth, including most of the major groups of animals.

Modern Mass Extinction

- Because of natural selection, there will always be some extinctions of species within any given time period. Mass extinctions, however, are periods of acceleration of the average rate of extinction. Many scientists think that our planet has entered another era of mass extinction and that human activities are prompting these extinctions. Species all over the Earth are threatened by habitat destruction, pollution, and invasive nonnative species. During the last 200 years, more than 50 species of birds, more than 75 species of mammals, and hundreds of other species have become extinct.

Section 2

Eras of the Geologic Time Scale

Experiment About the Origin of Life

- In 1953, American scientist Stanley Miller devised a famous experiment to simulate life-forming conditions on the early Earth. He mixed together hydrogen, ammonia, and methane (to represent the air) and water (to represent the oceans) in a flask. When he applied electricity to the mixture, amino acids were produced. His experiment demonstrated that the building blocks of life could be created on Earth through simple chemistry. Scientists have since found amino acids in meteorites, confirming that conditions favorable for their formation also exist elsewhere.

Dinosaur Whodunit

- Scientists continue to debate various hypotheses about the cause of the mass extinction that wiped out the dinosaurs at the end of the Cretaceous period of the Mesozoic era. The prime suspect for many scientists is an asteroid that created the 185 km wide Chicxulub crater in the Yucatán area of the Gulf of Mexico. Seismology studies support this hypothesis. However, a sample of rock from the core of this crater contains evidence that the Chicxulub asteroid did not result in sudden climate change. An alternative hypothesis is that a series of asteroid impacts eventually caused climate changes that led to the mass extinction.

Is That a Fact!

- ◆ Dinosaurs are not the biggest animals ever to have lived on Earth. Blue whales are bigger than the largest known dinosaur.

Section 3

Humans and Other Primates

Clues to Migration Route

- Scientists think that people passed through the Nile Valley of Egypt when they migrated from Africa, perhaps as early as 100,000 years ago. The first evidence supporting this idea was an adundance of fossil tools and other artifacts in the Nile Valley area. Then, in 1994, the team of Belgian archaeologist Pierre Vermeersch found an ancient—but clearly human—skeleton in the area. The skeleton appears to have been a child that was ritually buried over 80,000 years ago. The skull and teeth show similarities to those of equally old human remains from East Africa and the Middle East. These similarities show a link between the African and the Middle Eastern populations.

Dawn of Language

- Scientists Matt Cartmill and Richard Kay examined fossil hominid skulls and measured the hole through which the hypoglossal nerve passes in its course from the brain to the tongue. The hypoglossal nerve enables precise control over the tongue movements needed for speech. A large hole suggests a larger nerve. Chimpanzees have much smaller holes in their skulls than do modern humans. Because australopithecine skulls have small holes, like the skulls of chimpanzees, Cartmill and Kay think that australopithecines were unable to form words.

SCiLINKS®

NSTA
Developed and maintained by the
National Science Teachers Association

SciLinks is maintained by the National Science Teachers Association to provide you and your students with interesting, up-to-date links that will enrich your classroom presentation of the chapter.

Visit www.scilinks.org and enter the SciLinks code for more information about the topic listed.

Topic: Evidence of the Past
SciLinks code: HSM0545

Topic: Geologic Time Scale
SciLinks code: HSM0669

Topic: Fossil Record
SciLinks code: HSM0615

Topic: Birds and Dinosaurs
SciLinks code: HSM0169

Topic: Mass Extinctions
SciLinks code: HSM0916

Topic: Human Evolution
SciLinks code: HSM0769

Overview

In this chapter, students will learn about the evidence of the history of life on earth. Students will study the geologic time scale and theories about the evolution of hominids.

Assessing Prior Knowledge

Students should be familiar with the following topics:

• cells
• the basic chemistry of life
• classification
• evolution

Identifying Misconceptions

As students learn the material in this chapter, they may have misconceptions about the length of time living organisms have been on Earth and the length of time needed for geologic processes. For example, mass extinctions are "sudden" on a geologic time scale but may take thousands of years. Furthermore, students may have misconceptions about how long humans have been on Earth. Students may also be unaware of the large amount of evidence scientists have gathered in order to determine the time and order of events in Earth's history.

The History of Life on Earth

About the

What is 23,000 years old and 9 ft tall? The partial remains of the woolly mammoth in this picture! The mammoth was found in the frozen ground in Siberia in 1999. Scientists think that several types of woolly mammoths roamed the northern hemisphere until about 4,000 years ago.

PRE-READING ACTIVITY

FOLDNOTES **Layered Book** Before you read the chapter, create the Foldnote entitled "Layered Book" described in the **Study Skills** section of the Appendix. Label the tabs of the layered book with "Precambrian time," "Paleozoic era," "Mesozoic era," and "Cenozoic era." As you read the chapter, write information you learn about each category under the appropriate tab.

Standards Correlations

National Science Education Standards

The following codes indicate the National Science Education Standards that correlate to this chapter. The full text of the standards is at the front of the book.

Chapter Opener
UCP 2, 3; SAI 1, 2; SPSP 5; HNS 3

Section 1 Evidence of the Past
UCP 1, 2, 4; SAI 1, 2; HNS 1, 2, 3; LS 1a, 3d, 5b, 5c;
LabBook: UCP 1, 3; SAI 1; LS 5c

Section 2 Eras of the Geologic Time Scale
UCP 1, 2, 3, 4; SAI 1; LS 1a, 1b, 3d, 5a, 5b, 5c

Section 3 Humans and Other Primates
UCP 2, 4, 5; SAI 1, 2; ST 1, 2; HNS 2, 3; LS 1a, 3d, 5a, 5b, 5c

Chapter Lab
UCP 2, 5; SAI 1; HNS 2

Chapter Review
LS 1a, 1b, 3d, 5a, 5b, 5c

Science in Action
UCP 2; ST 2; SPSP 5; HNS 1, 3

START-UP ACTIVITY

MATERIALS

FOR EACH STUDENT
• clay, modeling
• leaf or shell
• plaster of Paris
• plate, paper

Teacher's Note: Coating the leaves or shells with a light vegetable oil will help prevent the clay and plaster from sticking.

Answers

1. Sample answer: The crab, the clam, and perhaps the seed will make the best fossils because they have hard parts that would decay slowly and leave clear impressions. The softer objects—the jellyfish, the leaf, and the mushroom—are less likely to make impressions in the sediment and more likely to decay quickly, so they are less likely to form fossils.

2. Sample answer: Like all models, this model cannot encompass all real possibilities. This model does not exactly duplicate the way most fossils are formed. For example, this model does not show how fossils of softer organisms can be formed. Also, in this model, oxygen is present, but the plaster forms into rock quickly, so the objects are not given time to decay. Finally, in this model, the objects do not move on their own, but moving organisms might leave fossils of traces such as footprints.

START-UP ACTIVITY

Making a Fossil

In this activity, you will make a model of a fossil.

Procedure

1. Get a **paper plate,** some **modeling clay,** and a **leaf** or a **shell** from your teacher.

2. Flatten some of the modeling clay on the paper plate. Push the leaf or shell into the clay. Be sure that your leaf or shell has made a mark in the clay. Remove the leaf or shell carefully.

3. Ask your teacher to cover the clay with **plaster of Paris.** Allow the plaster to dry overnight.

4. Carefully remove the paper plate and the clay from the plaster the next day.

Analysis

1. Consider the following objects—a clam, a seed, a jellyfish, a crab, a leaf, and a mushroom. Which of the objects do you think would make good fossils? Explain your answers.

2. In nature, fossils form only under certain conditions. For example, fossils may form when a dead organism is covered by tiny bits of sand or dirt for a long period of time. The presence of oxygen can prevent fossils from forming. Considering these facts, what are some limitations of your model of how a fossil is formed?

Chapter Starter Transparency
Use this transparency to help students begin thinking about evidence of past life on Earth.

CHAPTER RESOURCES

Technology

 Transparencies
• Chapter Starter Transparency

READING SKILLS

Student Edition on CD-ROM

Guided Reading Audio CD
• English or Spanish

Classroom Videos
• Brain Food Video Quiz

Workbooks

Science Puzzlers, Twisters & Teasers
• The History of Life on Earth GENERAL

Focus

Overview

This section introduces students to fossils and how they provide clues to Earth's past. Students learn how fossils most commonly form in sedimentary rock. They explore the methods scientists use to determine the age of fossils. They learn how scientists place events in the Earth's history in the correct order and how mass extinctions mark the boundaries of eras. Finally, they learn how plate tectonics has moved continents slowly and affected life over time.

 Bellringer

Ask students to imagine that they haven't cleaned their room for 30 years. After 30 years, they finally decide to sort through the 2 m pile of stuff on their floor. Ask students, "What might you find on the top of the pile? in the middle? on the bottom?" (The items on the bottom are most likely to be those that were left on the floor at an earlier time than were the items above them.)

READING WARM-UP

Objectives

● Explain how fossils can be formed and how their age can be estimated.

● Describe the geologic time scale and the way that scientists use it.

● Compare two ways that conditions for life on Earth have changed over time.

Terms to Learn

fossil
relative dating
absolute dating
geologic time scale
extinct
plate tectonics

READING STRATEGY

Reading Organizer As you read this section, make a concept map by using the terms above.

fossil the remains or physical evidence of an organism preserved by geological processes

Evidence of the Past

In 1995, scientist Paul Sereno found a dinosaur skull that was 1.5 m long in the Sahara, a desert in Africa. The dinosaur may have been the largest land predator that has ever existed!

Scientists such as Paul Sereno look for clues to help them reconstruct what happened in the past. These scientists, called *paleontologists* (PAY lee uhn TAHL uh jists), use fossils to reconstruct the history of life before humans existed. Fossils show us that life on Earth has changed a great deal. They also provide us clues about how those changes happened.

Fossils

Fossils are traces or imprints of living things—such as animals, plants, bacteria, and fungi—that are preserved in rock. Fossils sometimes form when a dead organism is covered by a layer of sediment. The sediment may later be pressed together to form sedimentary rock. **Figure 1** shows one way that fossils can form in sedimentary rock.

Figure 1   One Way Fossils Can Form

❶ Fossils can form in several ways. The most common way is when an organism dies and becomes buried in sediment.

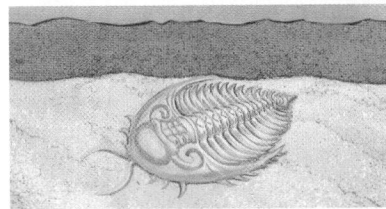

❷ The organism gradually decomposes and leaves a hollow impression, or *mold*, in the sediment.

❸ Over time, the mold fills with sediment, which forms a *cast* of the organism.

CHAPTER RESOURCES

Chapter Resource File

• Lesson Plan
• Directed Reading A **BASIC**
• Directed Reading B **SPECIAL NEEDS**

Technology

Transparencies
• Bellringer
• Using Half-Lives to Date Fossils

SCIENTISTS AT ODDS

Fossil Finds In the 1870s, two American scientists, Edward Drinker Cope and Othniel Charles Marsh, studied dinosaur fossils. They became bitter rivals and often argued. In 1878, Marsh and Cope were both excavating fossils in Wyoming. They had separate excavations and didn't want to share their findings. Both groups found more fossils than they could carry. To prevent the other group from taking their fossils, each group smashed all the fossils that couldn't be carried away.

Figure 2 Using Half-Lives to Date Fossils

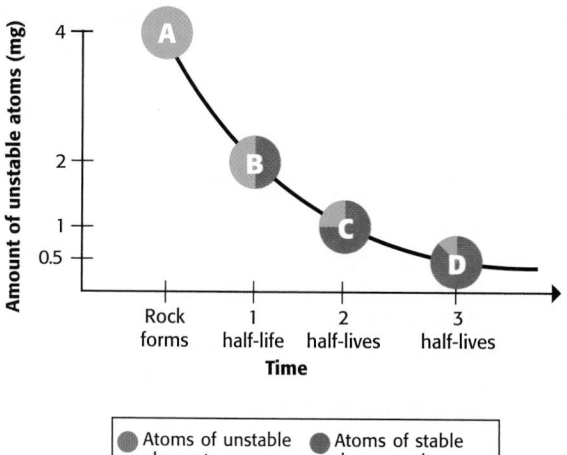

(A) The unstable atoms in this sample of rock have a half-life of 1.3 billion years. The sample contained 4 mg of unstable atoms when it formed.

(B) After 1.3 billion years, (one half-life for this type of unstable atom), 2 mg of the unstable atoms have decayed to become stable atoms, and 2 mg of unstable atoms remain.

(C) After 2.6 billion years (two half-lives for this sample), the rock sample contains 3 mg of stable decay atoms and 1 mg of unstable atoms.

(D) After three half-lives, only 0.5 mg of unstable atoms remain in the rock sample. This is equal to one-eighth of the original amount.

The Age of Fossils

Sedimentary rock has many layers. The oldest layers are usually on the bottom. The newest layers are usually on the top. The layers can tell a scientist the relative age of fossils. Fossils found in the bottom layers are usually older than the fossils in the top layers. So, scientists can determine whether a fossil is older or younger than other fossils based on its position in sedimentary rock. Estimating the age of rocks and fossils in this way is called **relative dating.**

In addition, scientists can determine the age of a fossil more precisely. **Absolute dating** is a method that measures the age of fossils or rocks in years. In one type of absolute dating, scientists examine atoms. *Atoms* are the particles that make up all matter. Atoms, in turn, are made of smaller particles. Some atoms are unstable and will decay by releasing energy, particles, or both. When an atom decays it becomes a different, and more stable, kind of atom. Each kind of unstable atom decays at its own rate. As shown in **Figure 2,** the time it takes for half of the unstable atoms in a sample to decay is the *half-life* of that type of unstable atom. By measuring the ratio of unstable atoms to stable atoms, scientists can determine the approximate age of a sample of rock.

✔ Reading Check Which type of fossil dating is more precise? (*See the Appendix for answers to Reading Checks.*)

relative dating any method of determining whether an event or object is older or younger than other events or objects

absolute dating any method of measuring the age of an object or event in years

Fractions of Fractions

Find the answer to each of the following problems. Be sure to show your work. You may want to draw pictures.
1. 1/2 × 1/2 × 1/2 × 1/2
2. 1/2 × 1/8
3. 1/4 × 1/4

Group **ACTIVITY** —**ADVANCED**

Detailed Geologic Timeline
Table 1 shows that geologic time is divided into *eras,* which are broken into smaller divisions called *periods.* But periods can be divided into *epochs,* and scientists continue to add many more details to this table. Challenge students to construct a giant geologic timeline that identifies all of these divisions. Direct them to scale the size of the divisions relative to time. Allow them to do research in the library or on the Internet for information. **LS** **Visual**

Research ——————— **GENERAL**

Extinct Species Students could research plant and animal species that have become extinct within the last 200 years. Many of the extinctions were caused by human activities. Extinct birds include the dodo, great auk, Labrador duck, moa, and passenger pigeon. Extinct mammals include the Steller's sea cow and the quagga. **LS** **Verbal**

Discussion ——————— **GENERAL**

Abbreviations In geological and paleontological literature, students may encounter the abbreviations *MYA* and *BYA.* Explain to students that *MYA* means "million years ago." Likewise, *BYA* means "billion years ago." Ask students why they think geologists use this form of dating. **LS** **Verbal**

Table 1	Geologic Time Scale	
Era	**Period**	**Time***
Cenozoic era		
	Quaternary	2
	Tertiary	65
Mesozoic era		
	Cretaceous	144
	Jurassic	206
	Triassic	248
Paleozoic era		
	Permian	290
	Carboniferous	345
	Devonian	408
	Silurian	439
	Ordovician	495
	Cambrian	543
Precambrian time		
		4,600

*indicates how many millions of years ago the period began

The Geologic Time Scale

Think about important events that have happened during your lifetime. You usually recall each event in terms of the day, month, or year in which it happened. These divisions of time make it easier to recall when you were born, when you kicked the winning soccer goal, or when you started the fifth grade. Scientists also use a type of calendar to divide the Earth's long history. The span of time from the formation of the Earth to now is very long. Therefore, the calendar is divided into very long units of time.

The calendar scientists use to outline the history of life on Earth is called the **geologic time scale,** shown in **Table 1.** After a fossil is dated, a paleontologist can place the fossil in chronological order with other fossils. This ordering forms a picture of the past that shows how organisms have changed over time.

Divisions in the Geologic Time Scale

Paleontologists have divided the geologic time scale into large blocks of time. Each block may be divided into smaller blocks of time as scientists continue to find more fossil information.

The divisions known as *era*s are characterized by the type of organism that dominated the Earth at the time. For instance, the Mesozoic era—dominated by dinosaurs and other reptiles—is referred to as the *Age of Reptiles.* Eras began with a change in the type of organism that was most dominant.

Paleontologists sometimes adjust and add details to the geologic time scale. For example, the early history of the Earth has been poorly understood. There is little evidence that life existed billions of years ago. So, the earliest part of the geologic time scale is not named as an era. But more evidence of life before the Paleozoic era is being gathered. Scientists have proposed using this evidence to name new eras before the Paleozoic era.

CONNECTION TO
Social Studies

A Place in Time Most of the periods of the Paleozoic era were named by geologists for places where rocks from that period are found. Research the name of each period of the Paleozoic era listed in **Table 1.** On a copy of a world map, label the locations related to each name. **ACTIVITY**

BRAIN FOOD

Private Fossil Collectors In 1997, the most complete skeleton ever found of a *Tyrannosaurus rex* was auctioned. The winning bid was $8.36 million, made by the Field Museum of Natural History in Chicago. Scientists were relieved that a museum won the bid; their fear was that a private collector would buy the skeleton fossil and not allow scientists to study it.

Answer to Connection
to Social Studies

Cambrian: for Cambria, the Latin name for Wales in Great Britain; Ordovician: after the Ordivices, a Celtic tribe; Silurian: after the Silures, a Celtic tribe; Devonian: for Devonshire, England; Carboniferous: for coal-bearing rocks in England; Permian: for the Russian province of Perm

Figure 3 *Scientists think that a meteorite hit Earth about 65 million years ago and caused major climate changes.*

Mass Extinctions

Some of the important divisions in the geologic time scale mark times when rapid changes happened on Earth. During these times, many species died out completely, or became **extinct**. When a species is extinct, it does not reappear. At certain points in the Earth's history, a large number of species disappeared from the fossil record. These periods when many species suddenly become extinct are called *mass extinctions.*

Scientists are not sure what caused each of the mass extinctions. Most scientists think that the extinction of the dinosaurs happened because of extreme changes in the climate on Earth. These changes could have resulted from a giant meteorite hitting the Earth, as shown in **Figure 3**. Or, forces within the Earth could have caused many volcanoes and earthquakes.

geologic time scale the standard method used to divide the Earth's long natural history into manageable parts

extinct describes a species that has died out completely

Reading Check What are mass extinctions?

Making a Geologic Timeline

1. Use a **metric ruler** to mark 10 cm sections on a **strip of paper** that is 46 cm long.

2. Label each 10 cm section in order from top to bottom as follows: 1 bya (billion years ago), 2 bya, etc. The timeline begins at 4.6 bya.

3. Divide each 10 cm section into 10 equal subsections. Divide the top 1 cm into 10 subsections. Calculate the number of years that are represented by 1 mm on this scale.

4. On your timeline, label the following events:
   a. Earth forms. (4.6 billion years ago)
   b. First animals appear. (600 million years ago)
   c. Dinosaurs appear. (251 million years ago)
   d. Dinosaurs are extinct. (65 million years ago)
   e. Humans appear. (160,000 years ago)

5. Label other events from the chapter.

6. Describe what most of the timeline looks like.

7. Compare the length of time dinosaurs existed with the length of time humans have existed.

CHAPTER RESOURCES

Chapter Resource File
• Datasheet for Quick Lab GENERAL

Workbooks

Math Skills for Science
• Geologic Time Scale GENERAL
• Radioactive Decay and the Half-Life GENERAL

Technology

Transparencies
• Geologic Time Scale

ACTIVITY ——————— GENERAL

Rock Collectors If any students have rock collections, ask them to show these collections to the class. Allow students time to observe the different collections and to ask questions about them. **English Language Learners**
LS Interpersonal

Answer to Reading Check

periods of sudden extinction of many species

MATERIALS

FOR EACH GROUP
• paper, adding machine, 46 cm strip
• ruler, metric

Teacher's Note: A fun variation on this activity uses a full roll of perforated toilet paper instead of adding-machine paper. At the scale of 20 million years per perforated sheet, 4.6 billion years would be represented by 230 sheets. This activity variation would best be conducted outdoors or in a long hallway.

Answers

6. Most of the timeline should be blank and should be taken up by Precambrian time.

7. Dinosaurs existed for a much longer time than humans have.

Homework ——————— GENERAL

Poster Project Have students research what their local area was like millions of years ago. They can develop a written report and a poster describing the climate, living things, and landforms at different points in time. **LS Visual**

Reteaching ——— BASIC

Illustrating Drift Have students cut out each continent from a copy of an area-proportionate world map. Have them try to fit the cut-out continents together into one landmass, using **Figure 4** as a model. Then, ask students to model the movements of the continents into their current locations. Finally, ask them to predict where the continents might be in the future if they keep moving in a similar way. (Predictions might include a wider Atlantic Ocean and a shift northward of Africa, Australia, and South America.) **LS Visual/Kinesthetic**

Quiz ——— GENERAL

1. How are fossils most commonly formed? (An organism is buried in sediments that harden into rock.)

2. What can scientists learn about Earth's past from fossils? (how life on Earth has changed over time)

3. Why would fossils found at the top of a canyon probably be younger than those found at the bottom of the canyon? (The upper layers were deposited more recently.)

Answer to Reading Check

the idea that the Earth's continents once formed a single landmass surrounded by oceans

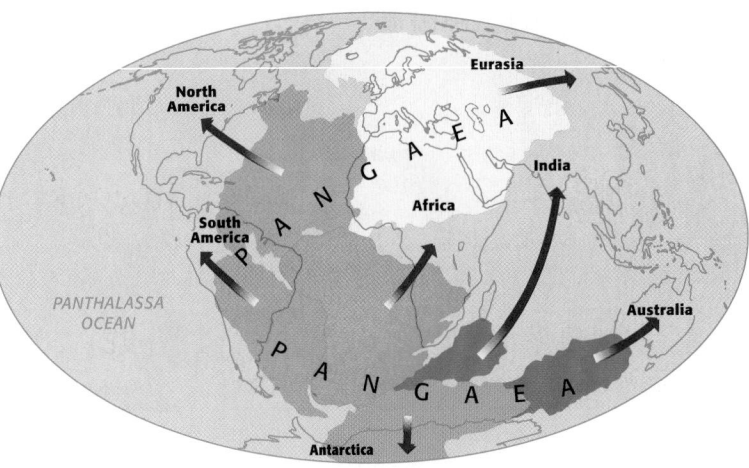

Figure 4 *The continents have been slowly moving throughout the history of Earth. The colored areas show the location of the continents 245 million years ago, and blue outlines show where the continents are today.*

plate tectonics the theory that explains how large pieces of the Earth's outermost layer, called *tectonic plates*, move and change shape

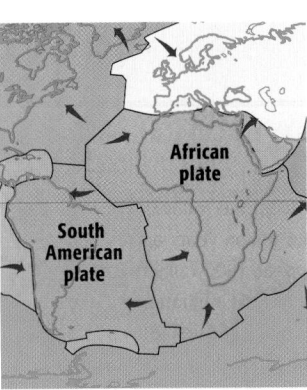

Figure 5 *The continents ride on tectonic plates, outlined here in black. The plates are still moving about 1 to 10 cm per year.*

The Changing Earth

Did you know that fossils of tropical plants have been found in Antarctica? Antarctica, now frozen, must have once had a warm climate to support these plants. The fossils provide evidence that Antarctica was once located near the equator!

Pangaea

Have you ever noticed that the continents look like pieces of a puzzle? German scientist Alfred Wegener had a similar thought in the early 1900s. He proposed that long ago the continents formed one landmass surrounded by a gigantic ocean. Wegener called that single landmass *Pangaea* (pan JEE uh), which means "all Earth." **Figure 4** shows how the continents may have formed from Pangaea.

 **Reading Check** What idea did Alfred Wegener propose?

Do the Continents Move?

In the mid-1960s, J. Tuzo Wilson of Canada came up with the idea that the continents were not moving by themselves. Wilson thought that huge pieces of the Earth's crust were pushed around by forces within the planet. Each huge piece of crust is called a *tectonic plate*. Wilson's theory of how these huge pieces of crust move around the Earth is called **plate tectonics.**

According to Wilson, the outer crust of the Earth is broken into seven large, rigid plates and several smaller ones. The continents and oceans ride on top of these plates. The motion of the plates causes the continents to move. For example, the plates that carry South America and Africa are slowly moving apart, as shown in **Figure 5.**

Cultural Awareness GENERAL

Iceland Tell the class that the Mid-Atlantic Ridge rises above water only in Iceland. Point to Iceland (in the Arctic Circle) on a map. Tell students that Iceland is a place of both extreme cold and extreme heat. Ask students to do some research on what life is like in Iceland. Have them focus on how geologic processes, such as glaciers, geysers, and volcanic activity, affect the lifestyle of the people who live there. **LS Visual**

INCLUSION Strategies

- **Visually Impaired**
- **Learning Disabled**
- **Developmentally Delayed**

Assist students in understanding the concepts in **Figure 4** by creating a cardboard replica of each of the continents. Let students experiment with fitting the pieces together. Then, have them approximate the shape of Pangaea, as shown in **Figure 4.** English Language Learners

LS Kinesthetic

Adaptation to Slow Changes

When conditions on the Earth change, organisms may become extinct. A rapid change, such as a meteorite impact, may cause a mass extinction. But slow changes, such as moving continents, allow time for adaptation.

Anywhere on Earth, you are able to see living things that are well adapted to the location where they live. Yet in the same location, you may find evidence of organisms that lived there in the past that were very different. For example, the animals currently living in Antarctica are able to survive very cold temperatures. But under the frozen surface of Antarctica are the remains of tropical forests. Conditions on Earth have changed many times in history, and life has changed, too.

CONNECTION TO Geology

Mid-Atlantic Ridge In 1947, scientists examined rock from a ridge that runs down the middle of the Atlantic Ocean, between Africa and the Americas. They found that this rock was much younger than the rock on the continents. Explain what this finding indicates about the tectonic plates.

SECTION Review

Summary

- Fossils are formed most often in sedimentary rock. The age of a fossil can be determined using relative dating and absolute dating.

- The geologic time scale is a timeline that is used by scientists to outline the history of Earth and life on Earth.

- Conditions for life on Earth have changed many times. Rapid changes, such as a meteorite impact, might have caused mass extinctions. But many groups of organisms have adapted to changes such as the movement of tectonic plates.

Using Key Terms

1. Use the following terms in the same sentence: *fossil* and *extinct*.

2. In your own words, write a definition for the term *plate tectonics*.

Understanding Key Ideas

3. Explain how a fossil forms in sedimentary rock.

4. What kind of information does the geologic time scale show?

5. About how many years of Earth's history was Precambrian time?

6. What are two possible causes of mass extinctions?

Math Skills

7. The Earth formed 4.6 billion years ago. Modern humans have existed for about 160,000 years. Simple worms have existed for at least 500 million years. For what fraction of the history of Earth have humans existed? have worms existed?

Critical Thinking

8. **Identifying Relationships** Why are both absolute dating and relative dating used to determine the age of fossils?

9. **Making Inferences** Fossils of *Mesosaurus*, the small aquatic reptile shown below, have been found only in Africa and South America. Using what you know about plate tectonics, how would you explain this finding?

Developed and maintained by the National Science Teachers Association

For a variety of links related to this chapter, go to www.scilinks.org

Topic: Evidence of the Past
SciLinks code: HSM0545

CONNECTION to Earth Science —— GENERAL

The South American Plate Have students identify the boundaries of the South American tectonic plate on a map. Ask students, "What kinds of features mark the east side of the plate?" (a rift or canyon down the middle of the Atlantic Ocean) Ask, "Which direction is the plate drifting?" (to the west, away from Africa.) Ask, "What is happening on the west side of the plate?" (the plate is crashing into another plate and pushing up the Andes mountains) **LS Visual**

Alternative Assessment —— GENERAL

Geologic Time Scale Each student in a group receives three blank cards. The group looks at **Table 1** in this section and thinks of questions that could be answered using information from the table. Students write a question on one side of a card. They stack the cards with the blank sides up. In turn, each student draws a card, reads the question on it, and attempts to answer the question. Group members determine if the answer is correct by consulting the table. **LS Visual/Interpersonal**

Answer to Connection to Geology

This finding indicates that the plates are spreading apart as newer rock forms at the center.

Answers to Section Review

1. Sample answer: Scientists can learn about extinct organisms from fossils.

2. Sample answer: Plate tectonics is a theory about how the plates of the Earth's crust move around.

3. A fossil may form when a dead organism is covered by a layer of sediment. Then, these sediments are slowly pressed together to form sedimentary rock.

4. how organisms and Earth have changed over time

5. about 4 billion years

6. meteorite impacts and forces within the Earth

7. Humans have existed for 16/460,000 of the history of Earth. Worms have existed for 5/46 of Earth's history.

8. Sample answer: to compare the results of each method so there can be greater confindence in the conclusions

9. Sample answer: Perhaps *Mesosaurus* evolved after Pangaea broke up but before South America and Africa split apart.

Focus

Overview

This section discusses current theories regarding the origin of life. Students are introduced to the four major divisions of geologic time in chronological order: Precambrian time, the Paleozoic era, the Mesozoic era, and the Cenozoic era. They learn about the organisms that characterize each era.

Bellringer

Ask students to respond to the following question:

> Suppose that electrical energy had never been developed. How would your life differ from what it is like now?

Discuss with students the consequences of great changes over time.

Answer to Reading Check

The early Earth was very different from Earth as it is today. There were violent events and a harsh atmosphere.

READING WARM-UP

Objectives

- Outline the major developments that allowed life to exist on Earth.
- Describe the types of organisms that arose during the four major divisions of the geologic time scale.

Terms to Learn

Precambrian time
Paleozoic era
Mesozoic era
Cenozoic era

READING STRATEGY

Mnemonics As you read this section, create a mnemonic device to help you remember the eras of geologic time.

Precambrian time the period in the geologic time scale from the formation of the Earth to the beginning of the Paleozoic era, from about 4.6 billion to 543 million years ago

Eras of the Geologic Time Scale

The walls of the Grand Canyon are layered with different kinds and colors of rocks. The deeper down into the canyon you go, the older the layers of rocks. Try to imagine a time when the bottom layer was the only layer that existed.

Each layer of rock tells a story about what was happening on Earth when that layer was on top. The rocks and fossils in each layer tell the story. Scientists have compared the stories told by fossils and rocks all over the Earth. From these stories, scientists have divided geologic history into four major parts. These divisions are Precambrian time, the Paleozoic era, the Mesozoic era, and the Cenozoic era.

Precambrian Time

The layers at the bottom of the Grand Canyon are from the oldest part of the geologic time scale. **Precambrian time** (pree KAM bree UHN TIEM) is the time from the formation of Earth 4.6 billion years ago to about 543 million years ago. Life on Earth began during this time.

Scientists think that the early Earth was very different than it is today. The atmosphere was made of gases such as water vapor, carbon dioxide, and nitrogen. Also, the early Earth was a place of great turmoil, as illustrated in **Figure 1.** Volcanic eruptions, meteorite impacts, and violent storms were common. Intense radiation from the sun bombarded Earth's surface.

✓ **Reading Check** Describe the early Earth. (*See the Appendix for answers to Reading Checks.*)

Figure 1 *This illustration shows the conditions under which the first life on Earth may have formed.*

CHAPTER RESOURCES

Chapter Resource File

- **Lesson Plan**
- **Directed Reading A** BASIC
- **Directed Reading B** SPECIAL NEEDS

Technology

Transparencies
- Bellringer

Is That a Fact!

Throughout Earth's history, the forces of erosion have been altering the planet's surface, making it almost impossible to find rocks older than 3.5 billion years. However, a number of rocks dating from about 3.5 billion to 3.9 billion years ago have been found in Canada and Greenland. The oldest was found in the Northwest Territories of Canada in 1989.

How Did Life Begin?

Scientists think that life developed from simple chemicals in the oceans and in the atmosphere. Energy from radiation and storms could have caused these chemicals to react. Some of these reactions formed the complex molecules that made life possible. Eventually, these molecules may have joined to form structures such as cells.

The early atmosphere of the Earth did not contain oxygen gas. The first organisms did not need oxygen to survive. These organisms were *prokaryotes* (proh KAR ee OHTS), or single-celled organisms that lack a nucleus.

Photosynthesis and Oxygen

There is evidence that *cyanobacteria,* a new kind of prokaryotic organism, appeared more than 3 billion years ago. Some cyanobacteria are shown in **Figure 2.** Cyanobacteria use sunlight to produce their own food. Along with doing other things, this process releases oxygen. The first cyanobacteria began to release oxygen gas into the oceans and air.

Eventually, some of the oxygen formed a new layer of gas in the upper atmosphere. This gas, called *ozone,* absorbs harmful radiation from the sun, as shown in **Figure 3.** Before ozone formed, life existed only in the oceans and underground. The new ozone layer reduced the radiation on Earth's surface.

Multicellular Organisms

After about 1 billion years, organisms that were larger and more complex than prokaryotes appeared in the fossil record. These organisms, known as *eukaryotes* (yoo KAR ee OHTS), contain a nucleus and other complex structures in their cells. Eventually, eukaryotic cells may have evolved into organisms that are composed of many cells.

INTERNET ACTIVITY

For another activity related to this chapter, go to **go.hrw.com** and type in the keyword **HL5HISW.**

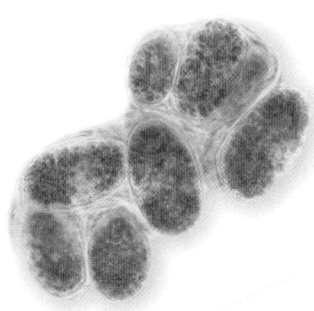

Figure 2 *Cyanobacteria are the simplest living organisms that use the sun's energy to produce their own food.*

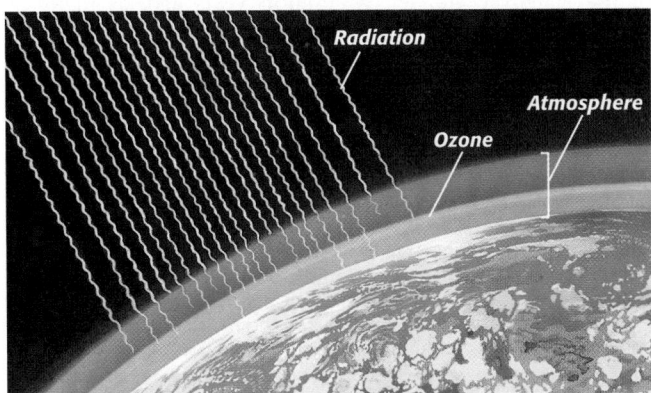

Radiation

Atmosphere

Ozone

Figure 3 *Oxygen in the atmosphere formed a layer of ozone, which helps to absorb harmful radiation from the sun.*

CONNECTION ACTIVITY
Earth Science —— GENERAL

Ancient Mountains Provide a large wall map of the world, and provide map pins or tacks in three colors. Have students locate the following mountain ranges on a map. Have students place pins on the map for each range to match the eras when each range was formed. Use the following list for reference:

Blue (Paleozoic):
• Caledonian (Scandinavia), Acadian (New York), Appalachian (eastern North America), Ural (Russia)

Green (Mesozoic):
• Palisades (New Jersey), Rockies (western North America)

Red (Cenozoic):
• Andes (South America), Alps (Europe), Himalayas (Asia)
LS Visual/Kinesthetic

Group ACTIVITY — GENERAL

Ancient Plants Organize the class into five groups, and assign each group one of the following groups of paleozoic plants: club mosses, ferns, horsetails, ginkos, or conifers.

Have each group use encyclopedias or botany books to look up the plant group and prepare a poster about it. Have students include diagrams of key features of the plant group and pictures of fossils and living examples of the group. **LS Interpersonal/Visual**
Co-op Learning

CONNECTION ACTIVITY
Real World —————— GENERAL

Fossil Fuels The huge plants that grew in forests during the Paleozoic era later became coal. Ask students to research the locations of the world's coal deposits and to mark them on a world map. (Most of the known coal reserves are in Australia, China, Germany, Poland, Great Britain, India, Russia, South Africa, the United States, and Canada.)
LS Visual

Answer to Connection to Oceanography

Descriptions may vary.

Figure 4 *Organisms that first appeared in the Paleozoic era include reptiles, amphibians, fishes, worms, and ferns.*

Paleozoic era the geologic era that followed Precambrian time and that lasted from 543 million to 248 million years ago

The Paleozoic Era

The **Paleozoic era** (PAY lee OH ZOH ik ER uh) began about 543 million years ago and ended about 248 million years ago. Considering the length of Precambrian time, you can see that the Paleozoic era was relatively recent. Rocks from the Paleozoic era are rich in fossils of animals such as sponges, corals, snails, clams, squids, and trilobites. Fishes, the earliest animals with backbones, appeared during this era, and sharks became abundant. **Figure 4** shows an artist's depiction of life in the Paleozoic era.

The word *Paleozoic* comes from Greek words that mean "ancient life." When scientists first named this era, they thought it held the earliest forms of life. Scientists now think that earlier forms of life existed, but less is known about those life-forms. Before the Paleozoic era, most organisms lived in the oceans and left few fossils.

Life on Land

During the 300 million years of the Paleozoic era, plants, fungi, and air-breathing animals slowly colonized land. By the end of the era, forests of giant ferns, club mosses, horsetails, and conifers covered much of the Earth. All major plant groups except for flowering plants appeared during this era. These plants provided food and shelter for animals.

Fossils indicate that crawling insects were some of the first animals to live on land. They were followed by large salamander-like animals. Near the end of the Paleozoic era, reptiles and winged insects appeared.

The largest mass extinction known took place at the end of the Paleozoic era. By 248 million years ago, as many as 90% of all Paleozoic species had become extinct. The mass extinction wiped out entire groups of marine organisms, such as trilobites. The oceans were completely changed.

CONNECTION TO Oceanography

Prehistoric Marine Organisms Find a variety of pictures and descriptions of marine organisms from the Cambrian period of the Paleozoic era. Choose three organisms that you find interesting. Draw or write a description of each organism. Find out whether scientists think the organism is related to any living group of organisms, and add this information to your description.

INCLUSION Strategies

- *Hearing Impaired* • *Learning Disabled*
- *Visually Impaired*

Demonstrate the superposition of geologic layers. Have student teams each use a different color of modeling clay to create a 3 in diameter circle, representing a piece of land. Ask teams to use other pieces of clay to add organisms to the land. Choose one team's model to represent early organisms, and place it where all students can see it. Then, choose a different team's model, and place it on top of the first, squashing the bottom organisms. Continue in this manner until all circles have been stacked. Slice a cross section through the stack for all to see. **LS Kinesthetic**   English Language Learners

The Mesozoic Era

The **Mesozoic era** (MES oh ZOH ik ER uh) began about 248 million years ago and lasted about 183 million years. *Mesozoic* comes from Greek words that mean "middle life." Scientists think that the surviving reptiles evolved into many different species after the Paleozoic era. Therefore, the Mesozoic era is commonly called the *Age of Reptiles*.

Life in the Mesozoic Era

Dinosaurs are the most well known reptiles that evolved during the Mesozoic era. Dinosaurs dominated the Earth for about 150 million years. A great variety of dinosaurs lived on Earth. Some had unique adaptations, such as ducklike bills for feeding or large spines on their bodies for defense. In addition to dinosaurs roaming the land, giant marine lizards swam in the ocean. The first birds also appeared during the Mesozoic era. In fact, scientists think that some of the dinosaurs became the ancestors of birds.

The most important plants during the early part of the Mesozoic era were conifers, which formed large forests. Flowering plants appeared later in the Mesozoic era. Some of the organisms of the Mesozoic era are illustrated in **Figure 5**.

The Extinction of Dinosaurs

At the end of the Mesozoic era, 65 million years ago, dinosaurs and many other animal and plant species became extinct. What happened to the dinosaurs? According to one hypothesis, a large meteorite hit the Earth and generated giant dust clouds and enough heat to cause worldwide fires. The dust and smoke from these fires blocked out much of the sunlight and caused many plants to die out. Without enough plants to eat, the plant-eating dinosaurs died out. And the meat-eating dinosaurs that fed on the plant-eating dinosaurs died. Global temperatures may have dropped for many years. However, some mammals and birds survived.

 **Reading Check** What kind of event happened at the end of both the Paleozoic and Mesozoic eras?

Figure 5 *The Mesozoic era was dominated by dinosaurs. The era ended with the mass extinction of many species.*

Mesozoic era the geologic era that lasted from 248 million to 65 million years ago; also called the *Age of Reptiles*

Answer to Reading Check

a mass extinction

READING STRATEGY — GENERAL

Prediction Guide Before students read the text on this page and the next, ask them to guess whether the following events occurred in the Mesozoic era or in the Cenozoic era:

• Dinosaurs dominated Earth and then died out by the end of this era. (Mesozoic)

• Mammals appeared. (Mesozoic)

• Rock layers close to Earth's surface contain fossils from this era. (Cenozoic)

• The first birds appeared. (Mesozoic)

• Humans appeared. (Cenozoic)

LS Logical/Auditory

Research — GENERAL

Reptile Research Have students research reptiles and list their distinctive characteristics. (Reptiles are ectothermic, or "cold-blooded," they all have a distinctive three-chambered heart and at least one lung, most reptiles have scales but not feathers or fur, many reptiles have claws, all reptiles produce amniotic eggs, and most lay these eggs on land.) Tell students that all living reptiles fall into four main groups—turtles, lizards and snakes, crocodiles and related forms, and the tuatara. Have students investigate these orders and list examples of each. LS Verbal/Logical

Making Models — GENERAL

Dinosaur Models Dinosaurs varied greatly in size and appearance. Have groups of students consult reference books to find information about the many kinds of dinosaurs. Then, have them use art materials to make models of different dinosaurs. Models should include flying and marine reptiles as well as land-dwelling reptiles. LS Kinesthetic   English Language Learners

Close

Reteaching — BASIC

Comparing Organisms Have students compare the characteristics of each of the Paleozoic, Mesozoic, and Cenozoic organisms described in this section with those of a living descendant (if one exists) of each of the organisms. Students can organize the information in the form of a chart. **LS** Visual

Quiz — GENERAL

On index cards, write the names of several types of organisms that appeared in each the four major divisions of geologic time mentioned in this section. Then, on paper strips, write the names of the geologic time divisions, and place the strips on a tabletop. Direct students to classify each organism named on a card by placing the card under the appropriate paper strip.

Alternative Assessment — GENERAL

Diorama Organize students into groups of three or four. Groups should use boxes with covers and art materials to make a diorama of one of the four major divisions of geologic time mentioned in this section. **LS** Interpersonal/Kinesthetic

Answer to Reading Check

"recent life"

Figure 6 *Many types of mammals evolved during the Cenozoic era.*

The Cenozoic Era

The **Cenozoic era** (SEN uh ZOH ik ER uh) began about 65 million years ago and continues today. *Cenozoic* comes from Greek words that mean "recent life." Scientists have more information about the Cenozoic era than about any of the previous eras. Fossils from the Cenozoic era formed recently in geologic time, so they are found in rock layers closer to the Earth's surface. The closer the fossils are to the surface, the easier they are to find.

During the Cenozoic era, many kinds of mammals, birds, insects, and flowering plants appeared. Some organisms that appeared in the Cenozoic era are shown in **Figure 6**.

✓ **Reading Check** What does *Cenozoic* mean?

The Age of Mammals

The Cenozoic era is sometimes called the *Age of Mammals*. Mammals have dominated the Cenozoic era the way reptiles dominated the Mesozoic era. Early Cenozoic mammals were small, forest dwellers. Larger mammals appeared later in the era. Some of these larger mammals had long legs for running, teeth that were specialized for eating different kinds of food, and large brains. Cenozoic mammals have included mastodons, saber-toothed cats, camels, giant ground sloths, and small horses.

MATH FOCUS

Relative Scale It's hard to imagine 4.6 billion years. One way is to use a *relative scale*. For example, we can represent all of Earth's history by using the 12 h shown on a clock. The scale would begin at noon, representing 4.6 billion years ago, and end at midnight, representing the present. Because 12 h represent 4.6 billion years, 1 h represents about 383 million years. (Hint: 4.6 billion ÷ 12 = 383 million) So, what time on the clock represents the beginning of the Paleozoic era, 543 million years ago?

Step 1: Write the ratio.

$$\frac{x}{543,000,000 \text{ years}} = \frac{1 \text{ h}}{383,000,000 \text{ years}}$$

Step 2: Solve for x.

$$x = \frac{543,000,000 \text{ years} \times 1 \text{ h}}{383,000,000 \text{ years}} = 1.42 \text{ h}$$

Step 3: Convert the answer to the clock scale.

$$1.42 \text{ h} = 1 \text{ h} + (0.42 \times 60 \text{ min/h})$$
$$1.42 \text{ h} = 1 \text{ h } 25 \text{ min}$$

So, the Paleozoic era began 1 h 25 min before midnight, at about 10:35.

Now It's Your Turn

1. Use this method to calculate the relative times at which the Mesozoic and Cenozoic eras began.

Answer to Math Focus

Mesozoic:
    12 h − [(348 ÷ 383) × 60] min = 11:21
Cenozoic:
    12 h − [(65 ÷ 383) × 60] min = 11:50

CONNECTION to Math — ADVANCED

Another Time Scale Have students calculate the length of the major divisions of geologic time relative to a 365-day calendar. They should state the month and day that each of the eras began. Use the Math Focus as an example, and provide a calendar for reference. Also, have students calculate the day that humans appeared (about 150,000 years ago). (Precambrian: Jan. 1; Paleozoic: Nov. 16; Mesozoic: Dec. 12; Cenozoic: Dec. 26; humans appeared: Dec. 31) **LS** Logical

The Cenozoic Era Today

We are currently living in the Cenozoic era. Modern humans appeared during this era. The environment and landscapes that we see around us today are part of this era.

However, the climate has changed many times during the Cenozoic era. Earth's history includes some periods called *ice ages,* during which the climate was very cold. During the ice ages, ice sheets and glaciers extended from the Earth's poles. To survive, many organisms migrated toward the equator. Other organisms adapted to the cold or became extinct.

When will the Cenozoic era end? No one knows. In the future, geologists might draw the line at a time when life on Earth again undergoes major changes.

Cenozoic era the most recent geologic era, beginning 65 million years ago; also called the *Age of Mammals*

SECTION Review

Summary

- The Earth is about 4.6 billion years old. Life formed from nonliving matter long ago.
- Precambrian time includes the formation of the Earth and the appearance of simple organisms.
- The first cells did not need oxygen. Later, photosynthetic cells evolved and released oxygen into the atmosphere.
- During the Paleozoic era, animals appeared in the oceans and on land, and plants grew on land.
- Dinosaurs dominated the Earth during the Mesozoic era.
- Mammals have dominated the Cenozoic era. This era continues today.

Using Key Terms

1. Use each of the following terms in a separate sentence: *Precambrian time, Paleozoic era, Mesozoic era,* and *Cenozoic era.*

Understanding Key Ideas

2. Unlike the atmosphere today, the atmosphere 3.5 billion years ago did not contain
   a. carbon dioxide.
   b. nitrogen.
   c. gases.
   d. ozone.

3. How do prokaryotic cells and eukaryotic cells differ?

4. Explain why cyanobacteria were important to the development of life on Earth.

5. Place in chronological order the following events on Earth:
   a. The first cells appeared that could make their own food from sunlight.
   b. The ozone layer formed.
   c. Simple chemicals reacted to form the molecules of life.
   d. Animals appeared.
   e. The first organisms appeared.
   f. Humans appeared.
   g. The Earth formed.

Math Skills

6. Calculate the total number of years that each of the geologic eras lasted, rounding to the nearest 100 million. Then, calculate each of these values as a percentage of the total 4.6 billion years of Earth's history. Round your answer to the units place.

Critical Thinking

7. **Making Inferences** Which chemicals probably made up the first cells on Earth?

8. **Forming Hypotheses** Think of your own hypothesis to explain the disappearance of the dinosaurs. Explain your hypothesis.

SciLINKS.

NSTA
Developed and maintained by the
National Science Teachers Association

For a variety of links related to this chapter, go to www.scilinks.org

Topic: Geologic Time Scale
SciLinks code: HSM0669

Answers to Section Review

1. Sample answer: Most of Earth's history was Precambrian time. The Paleozoic era was the time when life began to colonize land. The Mesozoic era is known as the Age of Reptiles. The Cenozoic era is known as the Age of Mammals.

2. d

3. Eukaryotes have a nucleus and are usually larger and more complex than prokaryotes.

4. Cyanobacteria were the first significant source of atmospheric oxygen on the planet.

5. g, c, e, a, b, d, f

6. Precambrian time: 4,057 million years, 88%; Paleozoic era: 295 million years, 6%; Mesozoic era: 183 million years, 4%; Cenozoic era: 65 million years, 1%

7. Sample answer: carbon dioxide, water, and nitrogen (or carbon, hydrogen, oxygen, and nitrogen)

8. Sample answers: A devastating virus attacked all reptiles on Earth, and only a few survived; a new kind of organism, such as a mammal, began to outcompete the dinosaurs; aliens bombed the Earth with climate-changing gases.

SCIENTISTS AT ODDS

Fire or Ice Scientists continue to debate whether another ice age is coming soon or whether the Earth is overheating. During Earth's history, the climate has changed many times, slowly switching between icy cold and lush warmth. Scientists call the warmer periods *interglacial* because each is usually followed by another ice age. However, in recent decades average temperatures on Earth seem to keep getting warmer.

CHAPTER RESOURCES

Chapter Resource File

- Section Quiz `GENERAL`
- Section Review `GENERAL`
- Vocaulary and Section Summary `GENERAL`
- Reinforcement Worksheet `BASIC`
- SciLinks Activity `GENERAL`

Technology

- Interactive Explorations CD-ROM
  - Rock On! `GENERAL`

Workbooks

Math Skills for Science
- Subtraction Review `BASIC`

Overview

In this section, students will learn that scientists think humans share a common ancestor and common characteristics with other primates, such as apes and monkeys. This section describes the characteristics of hominids and examines trends in their evolution that could have led to modern humans.

🎵 Bellringer

Ask students to write an answer to the following question:

What makes you unique among your family members? (Responses might include food preferences, health condition, physical appearance, and talents.)

Point out that understanding human ancestry requires recognizing similarities and differences, such as those seen in families.

READING WARM-UP

Objectives

● Describe two characteristics that all primates share.

● Describe three major groups of hominids.

Terms to Learn

primate
hominid
Homo sapiens

READING STRATEGY

Discussion Read this section silently. Write down questions that you have about this section. Discuss your questions in a small group.

primate a type of mammal characterized by opposable thumbs and binocular vision

---

Humans and Other Primates

Have you ever heard someone say that humans descended from monkeys or apes? Well, scientists would not exactly say that. The scientific theory is that humans, apes, and monkeys share a common ancestor. This common ancestor probably lived more than 45 million years ago.

Most scientists agree that there is enough evidence to support this theory. Many fossils of organisms have been found that show traits of both humans and apes. Also, comparisons of modern humans and apes support this theory.

Primates

What characteristics make us human? Humans are classified as primates. **Primates** are a group of mammals that includes humans, apes, monkeys, and lemurs. Primates have the characteristics illustrated in **Figure 1.**

The First Primates

The ancestors of primates may have co-existed with the dinosaurs. These ancestors were probably mouselike mammals that were active at night, lived in trees, and ate insects. The first primates did not exist until after the dinosaurs died out. About 45 million years ago, primates that had larger brains appeared. These were the first primates that had traits similar to monkeys, apes, and humans.

Figure 1 Characteristics of Primates

◀ Both eyes are located at the front of the head, and they provide binocular, or three-dimensional, vision.

Almost all primates, such as ▶ these orangutans, have five flexible fingers—four fingers and an opposable thumb. This thumb enables primates to grip objects. Most primates besides humans also have opposable big toes.

CHAPTER RESOURCES

Chapter Resource File

- Lesson Plan
- Directed Reading A BASIC
- Directed Reading B SPECIAL NEEDS

Technology

Transparencies
- Bellringer
- Comparison of Primate Skeletons

Is That a Fact!

Although the skulls of a human and a chimpanzee appear similar, there are significant differences. The cranium of a human skull is domed, whereas the chimpanzee's cranium is flattened. Also, canine teeth in humans do not overlap as they do in chimpanzees. And because humans walk upright, the place where the spine connects to the skull is more centered under the skull in humans.

Apes and Chimpanzees

Scientists think that the chimpanzee, a type of ape, is the closest living relative of humans. This theory does not mean humans descended from chimpanzees. It means that humans and chimpanzees share a common ancestor. Sometime between 5 million and 30 million years ago, the ancestors of humans, chimpanzees, and other apes began to evolve along different lines.

Hominids

Humans are in a family separate from other primates. This family, called **hominids,** includes only humans and their human-like ancestors. The main characteristic that separates hominids from other primates is bipedalism. *Bipedalism* means "walking primarily upright on two feet." Evidence of bipedalism can be seen in a primate's skeletal structure. **Figure 2** shows a comparison of the skeletal features of apes and hominids.

hominid a type of primate characterized by bipedalism, relatively long lower limbs, and lack of a tail

✔ **Reading Check** In which family are humans classified? *(See the Appendix for answers to Reading Checks.)*

Figure 2 | **Comparison of Primate Skeletons**

The bones of gorillas (a type of ape) and humans (a type of hominid) have a very similar form, but the human skeleton is adapted for walking upright.

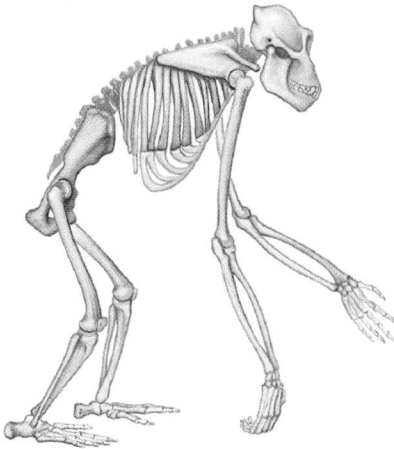

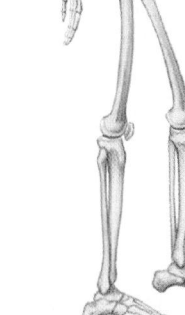

The human pelvis is vertical and helps hold the entire skeleton upright. The human spine is curved in an S shape. The arms are shorter than the legs.

▲ The gorilla pelvis tilts the ape's large rib cage and heavy neck and head forward. The gorilla spine is curved in a C shape. The arms are long to provide balance on the ground.

CONNECTION to Anthropology — ADVANCED

Bipedalism The tendency to walk fully upright distinguishes us from apes. But how do our physical features relate to our posture? Thomas Greiner, a physical anthropologist, developed a computer model that shows how muscle action relates to bone shape. Greiner concluded that in order to regularly walk upright, an ape would need larger gluteus maximus muscles and a larger ileum. These attributes are seen in human bodies.

Answer to Reading Check
the hominid family

Motivate

Discussion — GENERAL

Comparing Primates Display a picture of an ape and a picture of a human for students to compare. Have students identify characteristics that the two organisms have in common. (Answers will probably include references to common physical characteristics.) Then, ask students how the two animals are different from each other. (Answers will probably include references to differences in behavior or abilities.) **LS** Visual/Verbal

Teach

Using the Figure — GENERAL

Binocular Vison Discuss with students how binocular vision, illustrated in **Figure 1,** is important. How is it useful to humans? How is it different in most other animals? (Sample answer: Binocular vision enables humans to perceive depth and thus to judge distances, to hunt, to use tools, to drive vehicles, and to play sports. Except for some predators, most other animals do not have such abilities.) **LS** Visual

ACTIVITY — GENERAL

Exploring Vision Students can explore the utility of binocular vision by making a dot on a sheet of paper and placing the paper on a desktop. Have them stand about half a meter away from the desk and close their right eye. Then, have them try to touch the dot on the paper with the tip of a pencil. Have them repeat the action with their left eye closed and then with both eyes open. (Students should find that it is easier to touch the dot with a pencil when they have both eyes open than when they have one eye closed.) **LS** Visual — English Language Learners

Primate Characteristics Help students identify the characteristics that distinguish primates from other mammal groups. Show them pictures of primate and nonprimate mammals. Ask students to describe how the primates differ from the other animals. (Sample answer: Primates generally have flatter faces than nonprimates. Their eyes are located at the front of the head rather than at the sides, their snouts are small, and their fingers are flexible.) **LS** Visual/Logical

Answer to Reading Check
Africa

Comparing Hominids Create and display a large table to compare the distinguishing characteristics of the primates and hominids discussed in this section. Column heads might include "Binocular vision," "Bipedalism," "Brain size," "Tool use," "Known locations," and "Estimated dates." Call on students to make additions to the table. **LS** Logical/Verbal

Figure 3 *This skull was found in the Sahel desert in Chad, Africa. The skull is estimated to be 6 million to 7 million years old.*

Hominids Through Time

Scientists are constantly filling in pieces of the hominid family picture. They have found many different fossils of ancient hominids and have named at least 18 types of hominids. However, scientists do not agree on the classification of every fossil. Fossils are classified as hominids when they share some of the characteristics of modern humans. But each type of hominid was unique in terms of size, the way it walked, the shape of its skull, and other characteristics.

The Earliest Hominids

The earliest hominids had traits that were more humanlike than apelike. These traits include the ability to walk upright as well as smaller teeth, flatter faces, and larger brains than earlier primates. The oldest hominid fossils have been found in Africa. So, scientists think hominid evolution began in Africa. **Figure 3** shows a fossil that may be from one of the earliest hominids. It is 6 million to 7 million years old.

✓ **Reading Check** Where are the earliest hominid fossils found?

Australopithecines

Many early hominids are classified as *australopithecines* (AW struh LOH PITH uh SEENS). Members of this group were similar to apes but were different from apes in several ways. For example, their brains were slightly larger than the brains of apes. Some of them may have used stone tools. They climbed trees but also walked on two legs.

Fossil evidence of australopithecines has been found in several places in Africa. The fossilized footprints in **Figure 4** were probably made by a member of this group over 3 million years ago. Some skeletons of australopithecines have been found near what appear to be simple tools.

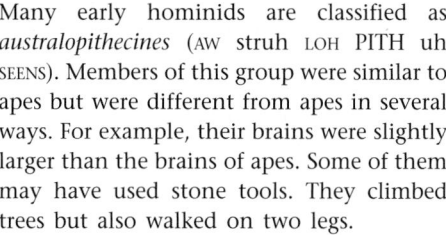

Figure 4 *Anthropologist Mary Leakey discovered these 3.6 million year old footprints in Tanzania, Africa.*

SCIENTISTS AT ODDS

In 1975, fossils of 13 hominids were found in Ethiopia by Donald Johansen, a contemporary of Mary Leakey. These fossils differed in body size and jaw shape. Some anthropologists think that the larger fossils represent the males and the smaller fossils represent the females of a particular species. Johansen and others believe that the differences indicate that the fossils are of two distinct species of australopithecines.

Is That a Fact!

One of the most famous skeletons of an australopithecine was found by Donald Johansen in Ethiopia 1974 and was nicknamed "Lucy." This nickname came from the Beatles' hit song "Lucy in the Sky with Diamonds," which was playing around the time when the fossil was discovered.

A Variety of Early Hominids

Many australopithecines and other types of hominids lived at the same time. Some australopithecines had slender bodies. They had humanlike jaws and teeth but had small, apelike skulls. They probably lived in forests and grasslands and ate a vegetarian diet. Scientists think that some of these types of hominids may have been the ancestors of modern humans.

Some early hominids had large bodies and massive teeth and jaws. They had a unique skull structure and relatively small brains. Most of these types of hominids lived in tropical forests and probably ate tough plant material, such as roots. Scientists do not think that these large-bodied hominids are the ancestors of modern humans.

Global Hominids

About 2.3 million years ago, a new group of hominids appeared. These hominids were similar to the slender australopithecines but were more humanlike. These new hominids had larger and more complex brains, rounder skulls, and flatter faces than early hominids. They showed advanced tool-making abilities and walked upright.

These new hominids were members of the group *Homo*, which includes modern humans. Fossil evidence indicates that several members of the *Homo* group existed at the same time and on several continents. Members of this group were probably scavengers that ate a variety of foods. Some of these hominids may have adapted to climate change by migrating and changing the way they lived.

An early member of this new group was *Homo habilis* (HOH moh HAB uh luhs), which lived about 2 million years ago. In another million years, a hominid called *Homo erectus* (HOH moh i REK tuhs) appeared. This type of hominid could grow as tall as modern humans do. A museum creation of a member of *Homo erectus* is shown in **Figure 5**. No one knows what early hominids looked like. Scientists construct models based on skulls and other evidence.

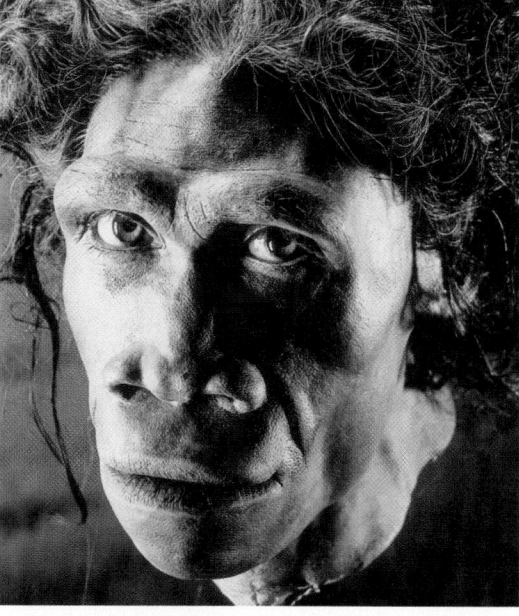

Figure 5 *Fossils of a hominid known as* Homo erectus *have been found in Africa, Europe, and Asia.*

Answers to School-to-Home Activity

3. a. Answers may vary. Most of the tasks will probably be more difficult without the use of the thumb.
   b. Answers may vary. Some people would not like to carry out such a difficult task on a regular basis.

Discussion — GENERAL

Analyzing Tools *Homo habilis* is thought to have made one of the oldest recognizable stone tools. The tool was a pebble with some sharp edges. Ask students how they think the tool was made. (Sample answer: Flakes were chipped off the pebble to sharpen it.) **LS Verbal/Logical**

CONNECTION ACTIVITY ART — GENERAL

Sculpting Sculptors probably helped paleoanthropologists determine the physical appearance of the hominid shown in **Figure 5.** Sculptors can apply their knowledge of anatomy to reconstruct body features. Have students research how sculptors are called upon to reconstruct hominid faces and heads, based on skulls. Then, have interested students use clay to sculpt a model of the head of a hominid. *English Language Learners* **LS Kinesthetic**

MISCONCEPTION ALERT

Students often misunderstand the meaning of the scientific name of the genus *Homo*. This word comes from the greek word for "earth" or "ground" and was later used to mean "man" or "human being" in latin. In some other words, the word root *homo-* comes from the greek word meaning "same."

CONNECTION to History — GENERAL

Insulting Apes? Many cartoons in the 19th century satirized the idea that humans are related to apes. In one such cartoon, Henry Bergh, the founder of the Society for the Prevention of Cruelty to Animals, chided Charles Darwin for insulting apes by suggesting that they are related to humans. Suggest that students look for examples of these historical cartoons. **LS Visual/Interpersonal**

Reteaching ——— BASIC

Timeline Have students make a timeline that shows the order of appearance of the primates discussed in the chapter. When students have finished their timelines, have them review the timeline of another student. **LS Visual**

Quiz ——— GENERAL

Among primates, what is distinctive about hominids? (The main characteristic that distinguishes hominids from other primates is walking upright on two legs as their main way of moving around.)

Alternative Assessment ——— ADVANCED

Hominid Poster Have students construct a poster with a detailed timeline of the appearance of different types of primates and hominids. Ask students to include pictures and information about the distinguishing characteristics of each group. Encourage students to conduct additional research to find the latest discoveries. **LS Visual/Logical**

Homo sapiens the species of hominids that includes modern humans and their closest ancestors and that first appeared about 100,000 to 160,000 years ago

Figure 6 *These photos show museum recreations of early* Homo sapiens.

Recent Hominids

As recently as 30,000 years ago, two types of hominids may have lived in the same areas at the same time. Both had the largest brains of any hominids and made advanced tools, clothing, and art. Scientists think that modern humans may have descended from one of these two types of hominids.

Neanderthals

One recent hominid is known as *Neanderthal* (nee AN duhr TAWL). Neanderthals lived in Europe and western Asia. They may have lived as early as 400,000 years ago. They hunted large animals, made fires, and wore clothing. They also may have cared for the sick and elderly and buried their dead with cultural rituals. About 30,000 years ago, Neanderthals disappeared. No one knows what caused their extinction.

Early and Modern Humans

Modern humans are classified as the species **Homo sapiens** (HOH moh SAY pee UHNZ). The earliest *Homo sapiens* existed in Africa 100,000 to 160,000 years ago. The group migrated out of Africa sometime between 40,000 and 100,000 years ago. Compared with Neanderthals, *Homo sapiens* has a smaller and flatter face, and has a skull that is more rounded. Of all known hominids, only *Homo sapiens* still exists.

Homo sapiens seems to be the first to create art. Early humans produced sculptures, carvings, paintings, and clothing such as that shown in **Figure 6.** The preserved villages and burial grounds of early humans show that they had an organized and complex society.

Homework ——— GENERAL

Writing **Future Scientists** Have students write a page from an anthropologist's journal that will be written 100,000 years in the future. Tell students that the anthropologist is studying an archaeological site that contains the remains or traces of people from today. Suggest that students describe the scientist's thoughts and hypotheses about the site. **LS Visual**

Science Bloopers

A skull of a *Homo sapiens* who had dental problems was found in Zambia. There was a hole in one side of the skull and signs of a partially healed abscess. This skull was made famous by a writer who imagined that the hole was caused by a bullet shot from an interplanetary visitor's gun 120,000 years ago.

Drawing the Hominid Family Tree

Scientists review their hypotheses when they learn something new about a group of organisms and their related fossils. As more hominid fossils are discovered, there are more features to compare. Sometimes, scientists add details to the relationships they see between each group. Sometimes, new groups of hominids are recognized. Human evolution was once thought to be a line of descent from ancient primates to modern humans. But scientists now speak of a "tree" or even a "bush" to describe the evolution of various hominids in the fossil record.

Reading Check What is likely to happen when a new hominid fossil is discovered?

SECTION Review

Summary

● Humans, apes, and monkeys are primates. Almost all primates have opposable thumbs and binocular vision.

● Hominids, a subgroup of primates, include humans and their humanlike ancestors. The oldest known hominid fossils may be 7 million years old.

● Early hominids included australopithecines and the *Homo* group.

● Early *Homo sapiens* did not differ very much from present-day humans. *Homo sapiens* is the only type of hominid living today.

Using Key Terms

1. Use each of the following words in the same sentence: *primate*, *hominid*, and *Homo sapiens*.

Understanding Key Ideas

2. The unique characteristics of primates are
   a. bipedalism and thumbs.
   b. opposable thumbs.
   c. opposable thumbs and binocular vision.
   d. opposable toes and thumbs.

3. Describe the major evolutionary developments from early hominids to modern humans.

4. Compare members of the *Homo* group with australopithecines.

Critical Thinking

5. **Forming Hypotheses** Suggest some reasons why Neanderthals might have become extinct.

6. **Making Inferences** Imagine you are a scientist excavating an ancient campsite. What might you infer about the people who used the site if you found the charred bones of large animals and various stone blades among human fossils?

Interpreting Graphics

The figure below shows a possible ancestral relationships between humans and some modern apes. Use this figure to answer the questions that follow.

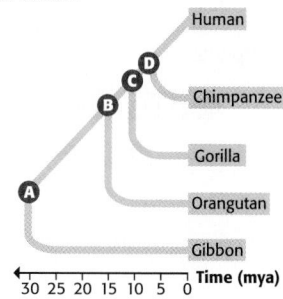

7. Which letter represents the ancestor of all the apes?

8. To which living ape are gorillas most closely related?

For a variety of links related to this chapter, go to www.scilinks.org

Topic: Human Evolution
SciLinks code: HSM0769

Answer to Reading Check

Sample Answer: Scientists will review their ideas about the evolution of hominids.

Answers to Section Review

1. Sample answer: *Homo sapiens* is the only living type of hominid but not the only living type of primate.

2. c

3. walking upright, larger brains, changed diet, using tools, and culture

4. Sample answer: Compared to australopithecines, *Homo* were larger, had larger brains and different skull shapes, moved out of Africa and into other continents, and used tools.

5. Sample answer: They may have been killed off by larger animals, or they may have run out of food and starved to extinction.

6. Sample answer: It is possible that the people had hunted animals for food.

7. A

8. chimpanzee

ACTIVITY — ADVANCED

Classifying Primates Have students find out the family or genus of the apes and hominids mentioned in this section.

- Apes: family Pongidae (great apes; includes orangutans, gorillas, chimpanzees)

- Hominids: family Hominidae

- Australopithecines: genus *Australopithecus* (slender) and genus *Paranthropus* (robust)

- Homo group: genus *Homo* (includes species *Homo habilis*, *Homo erectus*, *Homo neanderthalensis*, and *Homo sapiens*)

LS Verbal

CHAPTER RESOURCES

Chapter Resource File

- Section Quiz GENERAL
- Section Review GENERAL
- Vocabulary and Section Summary GENERAL
- Critical Thinking ADVANCED

Mystery Footprints

Teacher's Notes

Time Required
Two 45-minute class periods

Lab Ratings

EASY ——————————→ HARD

Teacher Prep 🧪🧪🧪
Student Set-Up 🧪🧪
Concept Level 🧪🧪
Clean Up 🧪🧪

Preparation Notes

To set up this lab, you will need to either find a sandy area outside or construct a long, shallow sandbox out of wood or cardboard. You may prefer to perform this activity outside because it is likely to be messy. Ask a boy and a girl (preferably students who are not in your science class) or two adults, one male and one female, to walk through the sand with their bare feet. The sand should be about 16 cm deep, and the area to be walked through should be long enough that three or four footprints can be seen in the sand. Slightly moistened sand will hold the best footprints. You may want to make the footprints more permanent by using plaster of Paris. If you do not have access to sand, look for a type of soil that will hold a footprint.

Mystery Footprints

Sometimes, scientists find clues preserved in rocks that are evidence of the activities of organisms that lived thousands of years ago. Evidence such as preserved footprints can provide important information about an organism. Imagine that your class has been asked by a group of scientists to help study some human footprints. These footprints were found embedded in rocks in an area just outside of town.

Ask a Question

❶ Your teacher will give you some mystery footprints in sand. Examine the mystery footprints. Brainstorm what you might learn about the people who walked on this patch of sand.

Form a Hypothesis

❷ As a class, formulate several testable hypotheses about the people who left the footprints. Form groups of three people, and choose one hypothesis for your group to investigate.

Test the Hypothesis

❸ Draw a table for recording your data. For example, if you have two sets of mystery footprints, your table might look similar to the one below.

Mystery Footprints		
	Footprint set 1	Footprint set 2
Length		
Width		
Depth of toe		
Depth of heel		
Length of stride		

DO NOT WRITE IN BOOK

OBJECTIVES

Form a hypothesis to explain observations of traces left by other organisms.

Design and **conduct** an experiment to test one of these hypotheses.

Analyze and **communicate** the results in a scientific way.

MATERIALS

- ruler, metric or meterstick
- sand, slightly damp
- large box, at least 1 m² or large enough to contain 3 or 4 footprints

SAFETY

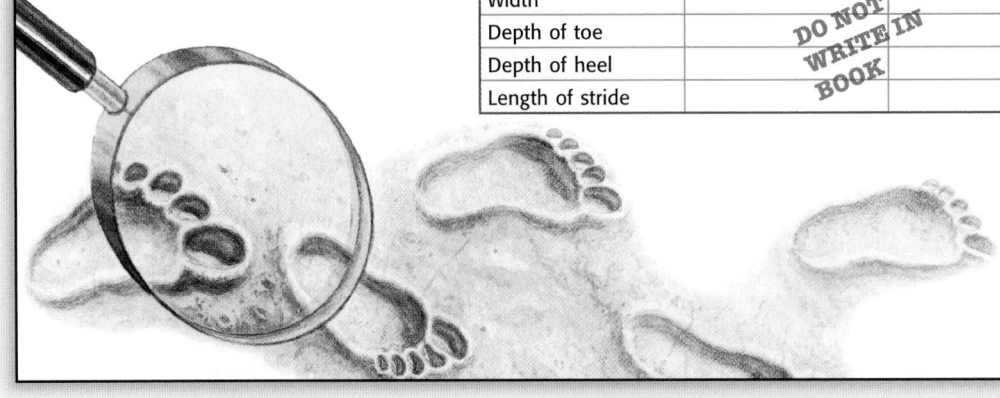

Maurine Marchani
Raymond Park Middle School
Indianapolis, Indiana

CHAPTER RESOURCES

Chapter Resource File

 • Datasheet for Chapter Lab
• Lab Notes and Answers

Technology

 Classroom Videos
• Lab Video

 Lab Book

• The Half-Life of Pennies

④ With the help of your group, you may first want to analyze your own footprints to help you draw conclusions about the mystery footprints. For example, use a meterstick to measure your stride when you are running. Is your stride different when you are walking? What part of your foot touches the ground first when you are running? When you are running, which part of your footprint is deeper?

⑤ Make a list of the kind of footprint each different activity produces. For example, you might write, "When I am running, my footprints are deep near the toe area and 110 cm apart."

Analyze the Results

① **Classifying** Compare the data from your footprints with the data from the mystery footprints. How are the footprints alike? How are they different?

② **Identifying Patterns** How many people do you think made the mystery footprints? Explain your interpretation.

③ **Analyzing Data** Can you tell if the mystery footprints were made by men, women, children, or a combination? Can you tell if they were standing still, walking, or running? Explain your interpretation.

Draw Conclusions

④ **Drawing Conclusions** Do your data support your hypothesis? Explain.

⑤ **Evaluating Methods** How could you improve your experiment?

Communicating Your Data

WRITING SKILL Summarize your group's conclusions in a report for the scientists who asked for your help. Begin by stating your hypothesis. Then, summarize the methods you used to study the footprints. Include the comparisons you made between your footprints and the mystery footprints. Add pictures if you wish. State your conclusions. Finally, offer some suggestions about how you could improve your investigation.

CHAPTER RESOURCES

Workbooks

 **Long-Term Projects & Research Ideas**
• A Horse Is a Horse **ADVANCED**

Answers

The answers for this activity will depend on the footprints your students observe. Students should be able to compare their own activities with variations in the footprints they leave. Then, they should be able to apply what they've learned to the mystery footprints.

Safety Caution

Remind students to review all safety cautions and icons before beginning this lab activity. Supervise students during this activity. Provide students with ample space and a safe location to test walking and running on the sandy area. Remind each group of students to keep out of the way of others. Have students keep shoes, or at least socks, on while walking on the sandy area.

Lab Notes

Tell the students to imagine that a group of scientists wish to analyze human footprints found in the rocks near fossilized remains and that the scientists have contacted the class to help with the investigation. The scientists want to know how the students intend to gather information to make inferences about the humans who left the prints. Explain that a scientist should be able to make the same type of inferences about an organism from fresh tracks as from preserved tracks. Use the mystery footprints in the sand to help students design investigations for gathering data. From the data, students can learn to draw inferences.

A large proportion of research on evolution depends on making scientific inferences and checking for corroboration among different sources of data. To conclude the laboratory experience, lead the students in a discussion about the importance of large sets of data in helping scientists make inferences.

Chapter Review

Assignment Guide

Section	Questions
1	5, 7, 11, 12, 20–22, 26, 27
2	1–4, 8, 9, 13–16, 19, 23, 24
3	6, 10, 17–19, 25

ANSWERS

Using Key Terms

1. Precambrian time
2. Cenozoic era
3. Mesozoic era
4. Paleozoic era
5. Absolute dating tries to determine a specific range of dates, while relative dating determines the order of events but not specific dates.
6. Hominids are a type of primate, but not all primates are hominids.

Understanding Key Ideas

7. d
8. a
9. d
10. d

USING KEY TERMS

Complete each of the following sentences by choosing the correct term from the word bank.

Precambrian time   Paleozoic era
Mesozoic era   Cenozoic era

1. During ___, life is thought to have originated from nonliving matter.

2. The Age of Mammals refers to the ___.

3. The Age of Reptiles refers to the ___.

4. Plants colonized land during the ___.

For each pair of terms, explain how the meanings of the terms differ.

5. *relative dating* and *absolute dating*

6. *primates* and *hominids*

UNDERSTANDING KEY IDEAS

Multiple Choice

7. If the half-life of an unstable element is 5,000 years, what percentage of the parent material will be left after 10,000 years?

   a. 100%
   b. 75%
   c. 50%
   d. 25%

8. The first cells on Earth appeared in

   a. Precambrian time.
   b. the Paleozoic era.
   c. the Mesozoic era.
   d. the Cenozoic era.

9. In which era are we currently living?

   a. Precambrian time
   b. Paleozoic era
   c. Mesozoic era
   d. Cenozoic era

10. Scientists think that the closest living relatives of humans are

    a. lemurs.
    b. monkeys.
    c. gorillas.
    d. chimpanzees.

Short Answer

11. Describe how plant and animal remains can become fossils.

12. What information do fossils provide about the history of life?

13. List three important steps in the early development of life on Earth.

14. List two important groups of organisms that appeared during each of the three most recent geologic eras.

15. Describe the event that scientists think caused the mass extinction at the end of the Mesozoic era.

---

11. Sample answer: The remains of organisms can become fossils when geologic processes preserve them or their traces. An example is sediment covering an organism and the shape becoming hardened into rock.

12. Fossils tell us about the kinds of organisms that existed and the way they changed over time.

13. Simple chemicals reacted to form the molecules that make up life. Simple cells formed. Photosynthetic cells developed and began to produce oxygen.

14. Sample answer: Precambrian: prokaryotes and eukaryotes; Paleozoic: multicellular organisms, plants, insects, and amphibians; Mesozoic: dinosaurs and other reptiles, birds, and small mammals; Cenozoic: large mammals, including humans, and more-diverse birds and insects

15. A giant meteorite hit the Earth, disturbing ecosystems and causing climate change.

16 From which geologic era are fossils most commonly found?

17 Describe two characteristics that are shared by all primates.

18 Which hominid species is alive today?

CRITICAL THINKING

19 **Concept Mapping** Use the following terms to create a concept map: *Earth's history, humans, Paleozoic era, dinosaurs, Precambrian time, land plants, Mesozoic era, cyanobacteria,* and *Cenozoic era.*

20 **Applying Concepts** Can footprints be fossils? Explain your answer.

21 **Making Inferences** If you find rock layers containing fish fossils in a desert, what can you infer about the history of the desert?

22 **Applying Concepts** Explain how an environmental change can threaten the survival of a species. Give two examples.

23 **Analyzing Ideas** Why do scientists think the first cells did not need oxygen to survive?

24 **Identifying Relationships** How does the extinction that occurred at the end of the Mesozoic era relate to the Age of Mammals?

25 **Making Comparisons** Make a table listing the similarities and differences between australopithecines, early members of the group *Homo*, and modern members of the species *Homo sapiens.*

INTERPRETING GRAPHICS

The graph below shows data about fossilized teeth that were found within a series of rock layers. Use this graph to answer the questions that follow.

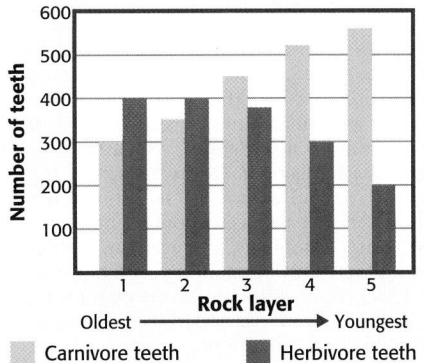

Oldest ——→ Youngest

☐ Carnivore teeth   ■ Herbivore teeth

26 Which of the following statements best describes the information presented in the graph?

  a. Over time, the number of carnivores decreased and the number of herbivores increased.

  b. Over time, the number of carnivores increased and the number of herbivores increased.

  c. Over time, the number of carnivores and herbivores remained the same.

  d. Over time, the number of carnivores increased and the number of herbivores decreased.

27 At what point did carnivore teeth begin to outnumber herbivore teeth?

  a. between layer 1 and layer 2

  b. between layer 2 and layer 3

  c. between layer 3 and layer 4

  d. between layer 4 and layer 5

16. Fossils in the Cenozoic era are most common because they are closer to the surface of Earth and were formed more recently.

17. Primates have opposable thumbs that allow them to grasp objects, and they have eyes positioned at the front of their heads that allow them to tell how far away something is.

18. *Homo sapiens*

Critical Thinking

19. 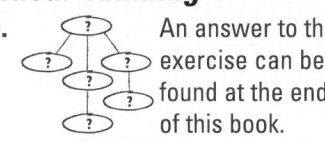 An answer to this exercise can be found at the end of this book.

20. yes; A footprint is a trace left by an organism.

21. that the rocks there may have once been underwater

22. Sample answer: If an environment changes suddenly, species may not be adapted to survive the change. Examples might be a sudden change from a hot to a cold climate or a sudden change from a wet to a dry environment.

23. There was no oxygen available when the first cells developed.

24. After the dinosaurs were wiped out (with the exception of birds), mammals were able to take their place in ecosystems.

25. Sample answer:

	Australo-pithecines	Early homo	Homo sapiens
Bipedalism	yes	yes	yes
Brains	medium	larger	largest
Tools	none	some	many
Art	none	none	a lot
Known locations	Africa	several continents	world-wide

Interpreting Graphics

26. d
27. b

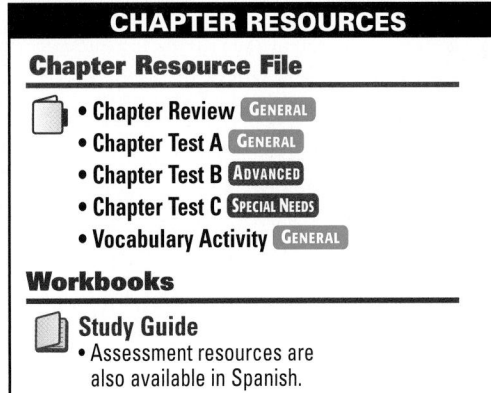

 **Standardized Test Preparation**

Teacher's Note

To provide practice under more realistic testing conditions, give students 20 minutes to answer all of the questions in this Standardized Test Preparation.

MISCONCEPTION ALERT

Answers to the standardized test preparation can help you identify student misconceptions and misunderstandings.

READING

Passage 1

1. D

2. F

3. B

 **TEST DOCTOR**

Question 2: The answer is drawn by inference from the fourth sentence in the passage, ". . . its bladelike teeth meant certain death for its prey." Students who miss this question may have missed the implication or may have difficulty with long sentences.

Question 3: The answer is drawn from the fourth sentence in the passage. Answers A and C are false, given the facts in the passage. Students who chose answer D may have made an incorrect inference from the last sentence in the passage.

READING

Read each of the passages below. Then, answer the questions that follow each passage. Decide which is the best answer to each question.

Passage 1 In 1995, paleontologist Paul Sereno and his team were working in an unexplored region of Morocco when they made an incredible find—an enormous dinosaur skull! The skull measured about 1.6 m in length, which is about the height of a refrigerator. Given the size of the skull, Sereno concluded that the skeleton of the entire animal must have been about 14 m long—about as big as a school bus, and even larger than *Tyrannosaurus rex*. This 90-million-year-old predator most likely chased other dinosaurs by running on large, powerful hind legs, and its bladelike teeth meant certain death for its prey. Sereno named his new discovery *Carcharodontosaurus saharicus*, which means "shark-toothed reptile from the Sahara."

1. Paul Sereno estimated the total size of this *Carcharodontosaurus* based on
  - **A** the size of *Tyrannosaurus rex*.
  - **B** the fact that it was a predator.
  - **C** the fact that it had bladelike teeth.
  - **D** the fact that its skull was 1.6 m long.

2. Which of the following is evidence that the *Carcharodontosaurus* was a predator?
  - **F** It had bladelike teeth.
  - **G** It had a large skeleton.
  - **H** It was found with the bones of a smaller animal nearby.
  - **I** It is 90 million years old.

3. Which of the following is a fact in the passage?
  - **A** *Carcharodontosaurus* was the largest predator that ever existed.
  - **B** *Carcharodontosaurus* had bladelike teeth.
  - **C** *Carcharodontosaurus* was as large as *Tyrannosaurus rex*.
  - **D** *Carcharodontosaurus* was a shark-like reptile.

Passage 2 In 1912, Alfred Wegener proposed a hypothesis called *continental drift*. At the time, many scientists laughed at his idea. Yet Wegener's idea jolted the very foundations of geology.

Wegener used rock, fossil, and glacial evidence from opposite sides of the Atlantic Ocean to support the idea that continents can "drift." For example, Wegener recognized similar rocks and rock structures in the Appalachian Mountains and the Scottish Highlands, as well as similarities between rock layers in South Africa and Brazil. He thought that these striking similarities could be explained only if these geologic features were once part of the same continent. Wegener proposed that because continents are less dense, they float on top of the denser rock of the ocean floor.

Although continental drift explained many of Wegener's observations, he could not find evidence to explain exactly how continents move. But by the 1960s, this evidence was found and continental drift was well understood. However, Wegener's contributions went unrecognized until years after his death.

1. Which of the following did Wegener use as evidence to support his hypothesis?
  - **A** similarities between nearby rock layers
  - **B** similarities between rock layers in different parts of the world
  - **C** a hypothesis that continents float
  - **D** an explanation of how continents move

2. Which of the following statements is supported by the above passage?
  - **F** A hypothesis is never proven.
  - **G** A new hypothesis may take many years to be accepted by scientists.
  - **H** The hypothesis of continental drift was not supported by evidence.
  - **I** Wegener's hypothesis was proven wrong.

Passage 2

1. B

2. G

 **TEST DOCTOR**

Question 1: The answer is drawn from the second paragraph in the passage. Students who missed this question may have failed to distinguish between evidence that supports a hypothesis and other ideas presented in the passage. Answer A is an idea not present in the passage.

Question 2: The answer requires logical reasoning and an inference of the main idea of the passage. Answers H and I are logically inconsistent with the passage. Answer F is a true statement but not supported by the passage.

The map below shows the areas where fossils of certain organisms have been found. Use the map below to answer the questions that follow.

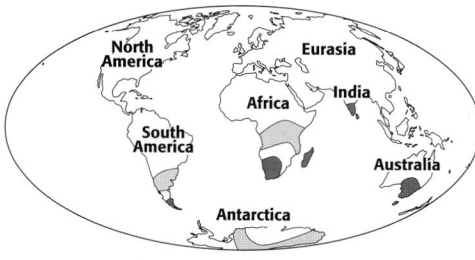

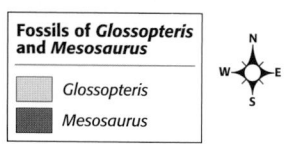

Fossils of *Glossopteris* and *Mesosaurus*

▢ *Glossopteris*

■ *Mesosaurus*

1. *Mesosaurus* was a small, aquatic reptile and *Glossopteris* was an ancient plant species. What do these two have in common?

   A Their fossils have been found on several continents.

   B Their fossils are found in exactly the same places.

   C Their fossils have been found only in North America.

   D Their fossils have only been found near oceans.

2. Which of the following statements is best supported by these findings?

   F All of the continents were once connected to each other.

   G South America was once connected to Africa.

   H *Glossopteris* is adapted to life at the South Pole.

   I *Mesosaurus* could swim.

3. The map provides evidence that the following continents were once connected to each other, with the exception of

   A North America.

   B Africa.

   C Antarctica.

   D South America.

MATH

Read each question below, and choose the best answer.

1. Four students are sharing a birthday cake. The first student takes half of the cake. The second student take half of what remains of the cake. Then, the third student takes half of what remains of the cake. What fraction of the cake is left for the fourth student?

   A 1/2

   B 1/4

   C 1/8

   D 1/16

2. One sixteenth is equal to what percentage?

   F 6.25%

   G 12.5%

   H 25%

   I 50%

3. What is one-half of one-fourth?

   A 1/2

   B 1/4

   C 1/8

   D 1/16

4. Half-life is the time it takes for one-half of the radioactive atoms in a rock sample to decay, or change into different atoms. Carbon-14 is a radioactive isotope with a half-life of 5,730 years. In a sample that is 11,460 years old, what percentage of carbon-14 from the original sample would remain?

   F 100%

   G 50%

   H 25%

   I 12.5%

5. If a sample contains an isotope with a half-life of 10,000 years, how old would the sample be if 1/8 of the original isotope remained in the sample?

   A 5,000 years

   B 10,000 years

   C 20,000 years

   D 30,000 years

Standardized Test Preparation

INTERPRETING GRAPHICS

1. A

2. G

3. A

✚ TEST DOCTOR

Question 1: The answer requires careful viewing of the graphic to find information that supports the correct answer. Simply substituting "the two kinds of shading" for "their fossils" in each statement makes the answer more apparent. Answer A is supported by observing the presence of shading on several continents. Answers B, C, and D are false, as indicated by observing locations where the shading contradicts the statement.

Question 2: The answer requires the student to locate continents in the graphic that have no shading to indicate the presence of either type of fossil. Answers B, C, and D are each false because the continents listed do have some shading on them.

MATH

1. C

2. F

3. C

4. H

5. D

✚ TEST DOCTOR

Question 1: This question is equivalent to the following problem:

$$1 \times \tfrac{1}{2} \times \tfrac{1}{2} \times \tfrac{1}{2}$$

Students who miss this question may have difficulty conceptualizing fractions of fractions or may have multiplied by 1/2 an incorrect number of times.

CHAPTER RESOURCES

Chapter Resource File

 • Standardized Test Preparation `GENERAL`

State Resources

 For specific resources for your state, visit **go.hrw.com** and type in the keyword **HSMSTR**.

Science, Technology, and Society

Background

The computer-generated skull image is reconstructed from the fossil skull of a Neanderthal child. The fossil find is named *Le Moustier 1*; it was excavated from a cave in Le Moustier, France. This site is also important because of the unique types of tools found there. The tools indicate a different form of tool-making than is found in many other Neanderthal sites. One theory related to this finding is that Neanderthals learned new toolmaking techniques from *Homo sapiens* at some point when the two groups came in contact.

Scientific Debate

Discussion ——— GENERAL

Ask students to discuss what they might do if human fossils were discovered in their backyard. Then, discuss a scenario in which a company is prevented or delayed from conducting business when human fossils are discovered on their property. Brainstorm other similar scenarios or research and discuss real scenarios with which the students might be familiar. Ask students to think of ways that these conflicts might be resolved.

Science in Action

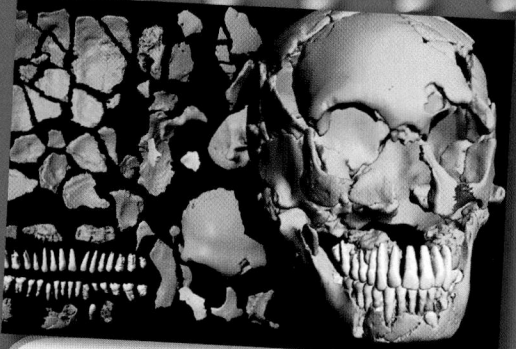

Residents of this neighborhood in Jerusalem, Israel, objected when anthropologists started to dig in the area.

Science, Technology, and Society

Using Computers to Examine Fossils

Paleontologists want to examine fossils without taking apart or damaging the fossils. Fortunately, they can now use a technology called *computerized axial tomography,* or *CAT scanning,* which provides views inside objects without touching the objects. A CAT scan is a series of cross-section pictures of an object. A computer can assemble these "slices" to create a three-dimensional picture of the entire object. Computer graphic programs can also be used to move pictures of fossil pieces around to see how the pieces fit together. The fossil skull above was reconstructed using CAT scans and computers.

Math ACTIVITY

The average volume of a Neanderthal adult's brain was about 1,400 cm^3, while that of an adult gorilla is about 400 cm^3. Calculate how much larger a Neanderthal brain was than a gorilla brain. Express your answer as a percentage.

Scientific Debate

Who Owns the Past?

Does a piece of land include all the layers below it? If you start digging, you may find evidence of past life. In areas that have been inhabited by human ancestors, you may find artifacts that they left behind. But who has the right to dig up these "leftovers" from the past? And who owns them?

In areas that contain many remains of the past, digging up land often leads to conflicts. Landowners may want to build on their own land. But when remains of ancient human cultures are found, living relatives of those cultures may lay claim to the remains. Scientists are often caught in the middle, because they want to study and preserve evidence of past life.

Social Studies ACTIVITY

WRITING SKILL Research an area where there is a debate over what to do with fossils or remains of human ancestors. Write a newspaper article about the issue. Be sure to present all sides of the debate.

Answer to Math Activity

350%
Sample calculation:
$1,400 \div 400 = 3.5$
$3.5 \times 100\% = 350\%$

Answer to Social Studies Activity

Student articles should reflect journalistic style, being both interesting and objective. Check that students have presented more than one side of the issue they have chosen. Almost any large urban area will have some notable archaeological or paleontological sites, and efforts to excavate the sites are often inconvenient to someone. However, if students need help selecting an area, suggest one of the following locations: New York City, New York; Miami, Florida; Rome, Italy; Athens, Greece; Island of Brac, Croatia; Jerusalem, Israel; Ayodhya, India; Kathmandhu, Nepal; or Yangtze River, China.

The Leakey Family

A Family of Fossil Hunters In some families, a business is passed down from one generation to the next. For the Leakey's, the family business is paleoanthropology (PAY lee OH AN thruh PAWL uh jee)—the study of the origin of humans. The first famous Leakey was Dr. Louis Leakey, who was known for his hominid fossil discoveries in Africa in the 1950s. Louis formed many important hypotheses about human evolution. Louis' wife, Mary, made some of the most-important hominid fossil finds of her day.

Louis and Mary's son, Richard, carried on the family tradition of fossil hunting. He found his first fossil, which was of an extinct pig, when he was six years old. As a young man, he went on safari expeditions in which he collected photographs and specimens of African wildlife. Later, he met and married a zoologist named Meave. The photo at right shows Richard (right), Meave (left), and their daughter Louise (middle) Each of the Leakeys has contributed important finds to the study of ancient hominids.

Language Arts ACTiViTY

WRITING SKILL Visit the library and look for a book by or about the Leakey family and other scientists who have worked with them. Write a short book review to encourage your classmates to read the book.

To learn more about these Science in Action topics, visit **go.hrw.com** and type in the keyword **HL5HISF.**

Current Science

Check out Current Science® articles related to this chapter by visiting go.hrw.com. Just type in the keyword **HL5CS08.**

People In Science

Background

In Africa, Richard Leakey may be more widely known for his strong beliefs in political rather than scientific arenas. He has organized and raised money for campaigns against the poaching of wildlife in Kenya. And in 1995, he founded a political party that opposes corruption in the Kenyan government. His political work has been controversial and at times dangerous, as he has received death threats and beatings from opponents.

ACTiViTY ——— GENERAL

Have interested students research and make timelines of major discoveries in hominid evolution. Suggest that they include a map that pinpoints the location of each major discovery. They may wish to present their findings in a poster or Web page.

Answer to Language Arts Activity

Students can find numerous books about members of the Leakey family, books written by some of the Leakeys, and books about their colleagues, such as Dian Fossey, Jane Goodall, Birute Galdikas, and Donald Johanson.

Classification
Chapter Planning Guide

Compression guide:
To shorten instruction because of time limitations, omit the Chapter Lab.

OBJECTIVES	LABS, DEMONSTRATIONS, AND ACTIVITIES	TECHNOLOGY RESOURCES
PACING • 90 min pp. 220–227 **Chapter Opener**	SE **Start-up Activity,** p. 221 `GENERAL`	OSP **Parent Letter** ■ `GENERAL` CD **Student Edition on CD-ROM** CD **Guided Reading Audio CD** ■ TR **Chapter Starter Transparency*** VID **Brain Food Video Quiz**
Section 1 Sorting It All Out • Explain how to classify organisms. • List the seven levels of classification. • Explain scientific names. • Describe how dichotomous keys help in identifying organisms.	TE **Demonstration** Classifying Objects, p. 222 `GENERAL` SE **Quick Lab** A Branching Diagram, p. 223 `GENERAL` CRF **Datasheet for Quick Lab*** TE **Activity** Branching Diagrams, p. 223 `GENERAL` SE **Skills Practice Lab** Shape Island, p. 234 `GENERAL` CRF **Datasheet for Chapter Lab*** LB **EcoLabs & Field Activities** Water Wigglers* `GENERAL`	CRF **Lesson Plans*** TR **Bellringer Transparency*** TR Evolutionary Relationships Among Organisms* TR Levels of Classification* TR A Dichotomous Key* SE **Internet Activity,** p. 224 `GENERAL` VID **Lab Videos for Life Science**
PACING • 45 min pp. 228–233 **Section 2 The Six Kingdoms** • Explain how classification schemes for kingdoms developed as greater numbers of different organisms became known. • Describe each of the six kingdoms.	TE **Activity** Grouping Animals, p. 228 `GENERAL` TE **Connection Activity** Environmental Science, p. 229 `GENERAL` TE **Connection Activity** Real World, p. 230 `ADVANCED` TE **Activity** Plant Identification, p. 231 `BASIC` SE **Connection to Social Studies** Animals That Help, p. 232 `GENERAL` LB **Long-Term Projects & Research Ideas** The Panda Mystery* `ADVANCED` SE **Inquiry Lab** Voyage of the USS *Adventure*, p. 770 `GENERAL` CRF **Datasheet for LabBook***	CRF **Lesson Plans*** TR **Bellringer Transparency*** TR *LINK TO EARTH SCIENCE* Intrusive Igneous Rock Formations* CRF **SciLinks Activity*** `GENERAL`

PACING • 90 min

CHAPTER REVIEW, ASSESSMENT, AND STANDARDIZED TEST PREPARATION

- CRF **Vocabulary Activity*** `GENERAL`
- SE **Chapter Review,** pp. 236–237 `GENERAL`
- CRF **Chapter Review*** ■ `GENERAL`
- CRF **Chapter Tests A*** ■ `GENERAL`, B* `ADVANCED`, C* `SPECIAL NEEDS`
- SE **Standardized Test Preparation,** pp. 238–239 `GENERAL`
- CRF **Standardized Test Preparation*** `GENERAL`
- CRF **Performance-Based Assessment*** `GENERAL`
- OSP **Test Generator** `GENERAL`
- CRF **Test Item Listing*** `GENERAL`

Online and Technology Resources

Visit **go.hrw.com** for a variety of free resources related to this textbook. Enter the keyword **HL5CLS.**

Students can access interactive problem-solving help and active visual concept development with the *Holt Science and Technology* Online Edition available at **www.hrw.com.**

 Guided Reading Audio CD
Also in Spanish

A direct reading of each chapter for auditory learners, reluctant readers, and Spanish-speaking students.

 Science Tutor
CD-ROM

Excellent for remediation and test practice.

219A   **Chapter 9 • Classification**

SKILLS DEVELOPMENT RESOURCES	SECTION REVIEW AND ASSESSMENT	STANDARDS CORRELATIONS
SE Pre-Reading Activity, p. 220 `GENERAL` **OSP** Science Puzzlers, Twisters & Teasers `GENERAL`		National Science Education Standards UCP 1
CRF Directed Reading A* ■ `BASIC`, B* `SPECIAL NEEDS` **CRF** Vocabulary and Section Summary* ■ `GENERAL` **SE** Reading Strategy Reading Organizer, p. 222 `GENERAL` **TE** Connection to Math, p. 223 `BASIC` **TE** Inclusion Strategies, p. 226 **MS** Math Skills for Science A Shortcut for Multiplying Large Numbers* `GENERAL`	**CRF** Critical Thinking A Breach on Planet Biome* `ADVANCED` **SE** Reading Checks, pp. 222, 225, 226 `GENERAL` **TE** Reteaching, p. 226 `BASIC` **TE** Quiz, p. 226 `GENERAL` **TE** Alternative Assessment, p. 226 `GENERAL` **SE** Section Review,* p. 227 ■ `GENERAL` **CRF** Section Quiz* ■ `GENERAL`	UCP 1; SAI 2; HNS 1, 2, 3; LS 5a
CRF Directed Reading A* ■ `BASIC`, B* `SPECIAL NEEDS` **CRF** Vocabulary and Section Summary* ■ `GENERAL` **SE** Reading Strategy Reading Organizer, p. 228 `GENERAL` **TE** Reading Strategy Prediction Guide, p. 229 `BASIC` **SE** Math Practice Ring-Around-the-Sequoia, p. 231 `GENERAL` **TE** Inclusion Strategies, p. 231 **MS** Math Skills for Science Arithmetic with Decimals* `GENERAL` **CRF** Reinforcement Worksheet Keys to the Kingdoms* `GENERAL`	**SE** Reading Checks, pp. 229, 231, 233 `GENERAL` **TE** Homework, p. 230 `ADVANCED` **TE** Reteaching, p. 232 `BASIC` **TE** Quiz, p. 232 `GENERAL` **TE** Alternative Assessment, p. 232 `GENERAL` **SE** Section Review,* p. 233 ■ `GENERAL` **CRF** Section Quiz* ■ `GENERAL`	UCP 5; SAI 1; HNS 1, 2; LS 1b, 1f, 2a, 2c, 4b, 4c, 4d, 5b; *LabBook:* UCP 1; SAI 1

Chapter Resources

9

Visual Resources

CHAPTER STARTER TRANSPARENCY

This Really Happened!

BELLRINGER TRANSPARENCIES

Section: Sorting It All Out

Think about the different ways humans classify things. List five groups of things that humans classify, such as library books, department store merchandise, and addresses. Is there such a thing as too much classification? What happens when you put something in the wrong group? Can objects or ideas belong in more than one group at the same time?

Record your responses in your **science journal.**

Section: The Six Kingdoms

List seven musical artists, bands, or acts. Categorize the names on your list by style of music. Describe the categories you chose, and explain which bands might fit into more than one category.

Record your responses in your **science journal.**

TEACHING TRANSPARENCIES

Levels of Classification

Evolutionary Relationships Between Organisms

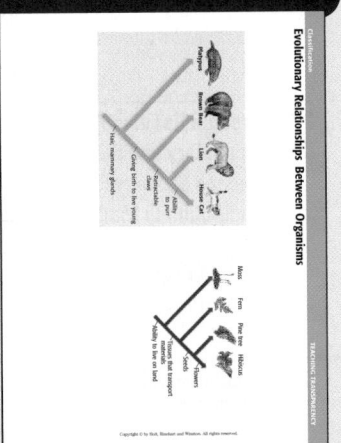

TEACHING TRANSPARENCIES

A Dichotomous Key

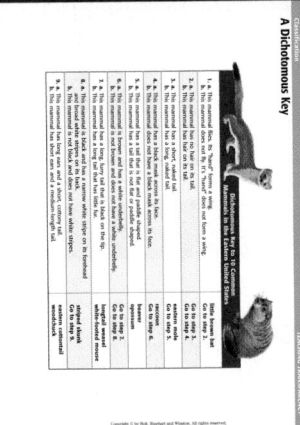

Intrusive Igneous Rock Bodies

LINK TO EARTH SCIENCE

Chapter: Rocks: Mineral Mixtures

CONCEPT MAPPING TRANSPARENCY

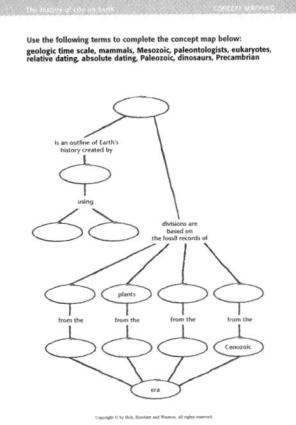

Use the following terms to complete the concept map below: geologic time scale, mammals, Mesozoic, paleontologists, eukaryotes, relative dating, absolute dating, Paleozoic, dinosaurs, Precambrian

Planning Resources

LESSON PLANS

Lesson Plan   SAMPLE

Section: Waves

Pacing
Regular Schedule: with lab(s):2 days   without lab(s):2 days
Block Schedule: with lab(s):1 1/2 days   without lab(s):1 day

Objectives
1. Relate the seven properties of life to a living organisms.
2. Describe seven themes that can help you to organize what you learn about biology.
3. Identify the tiny structures that make up all living organisms.
4. Differentiate between reproduction and heredity and between metabolism and homeostasis.

National Science Education Standards Covered

PARENT LETTER

SAMPLE

Dear Parent,

Your son's or daughter's science class will soon begin exploring the chapter entitled "The World of Physical Science." In this chapter, students will learn about how the scientific method applies to the world of physical science and the role of physical science in the world. By the end of the chapter, students should demonstrate a clear understanding of the chapter's main ideas and be able to discuss the following topics:

ALSO IN SPANISH

TEST ITEM LISTING

TEST ITEM LISTING
The World of Science   SAMPLE

MULTIPLE CHOICE

One-Stop Planner® CD-ROM

This CD-ROM includes all of the resources shown here and the following time-saving tools:

- *Lab Materials QuickList Software*
- *Customizable lesson plans*
- *Holt Calendar Planner*
- *The powerful ExamView® Test Generator*

219C Chapter 9 • Classification

Meeting Individual Needs

DIRECTED READING A
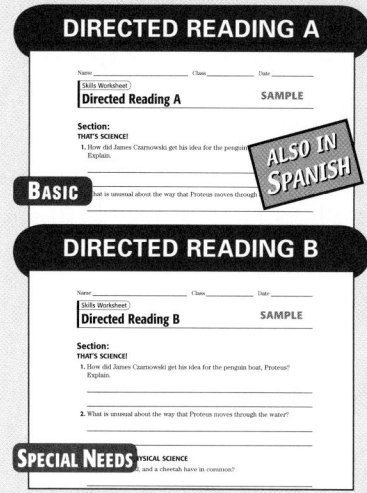

BASIC

DIRECTED READING B

SPECIAL NEEDS

VOCABULARY ACTIVITY
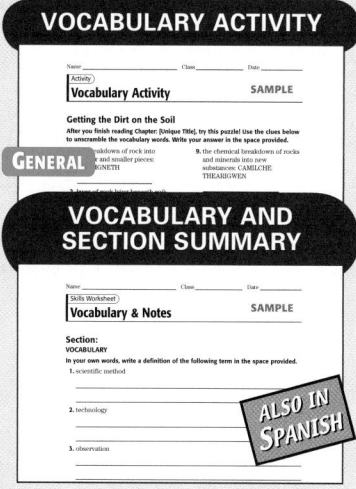

GENERAL

VOCABULARY AND SECTION SUMMARY

GENERAL

REINFORCEMENT
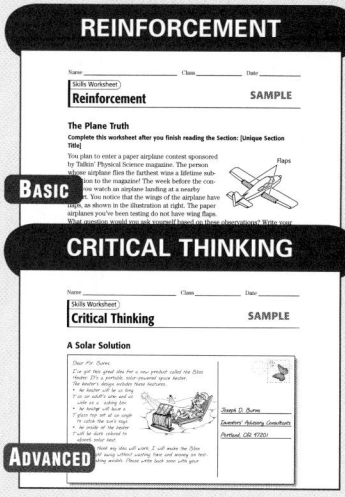

BASIC

CRITICAL THINKING

ADVANCED

SCILINKS ACTIVITY
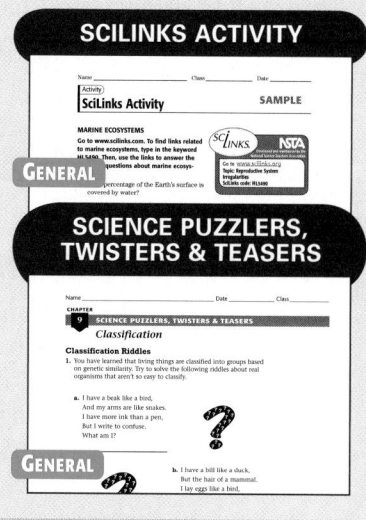

GENERAL

SCIENCE PUZZLERS, TWISTERS & TEASERS

GENERAL

Labs and Activities

ECOLABS & FIELD ACTIVITIES
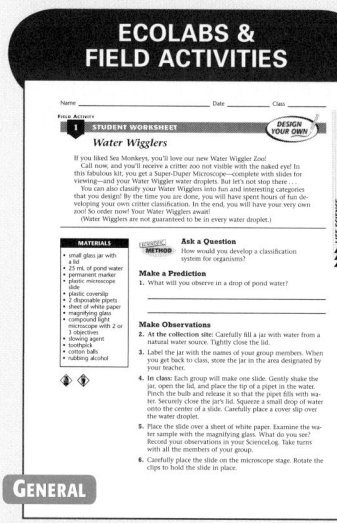

GENERAL

LONG-TERM PROJECTS & RESEARCH IDEAS
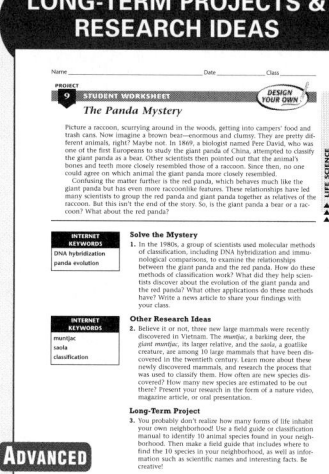

ADVANCED

DATASHEETS FOR QUICK LABS

DATASHEETS FOR CHAPTER LABS

DATASHEETS FOR LABBOOK

Review and Assessments

SECTION QUIZ
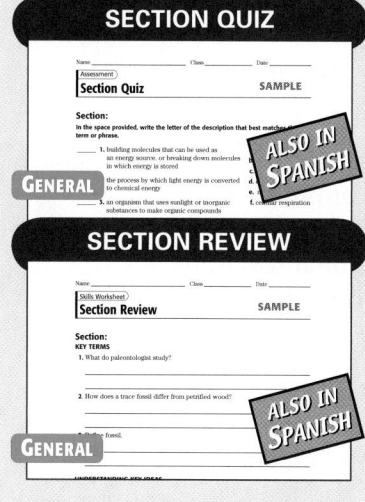

GENERAL

SECTION REVIEW

GENERAL

CHAPTER REVIEW
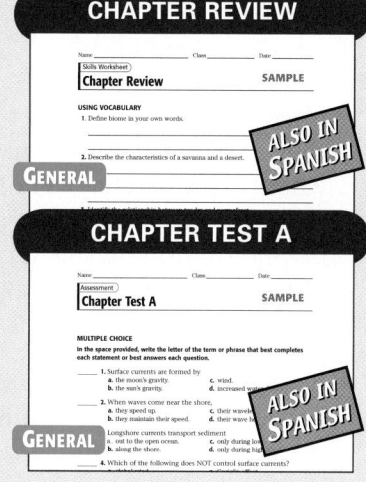

GENERAL

CHAPTER TEST A

GENERAL

CHAPTER TEST B
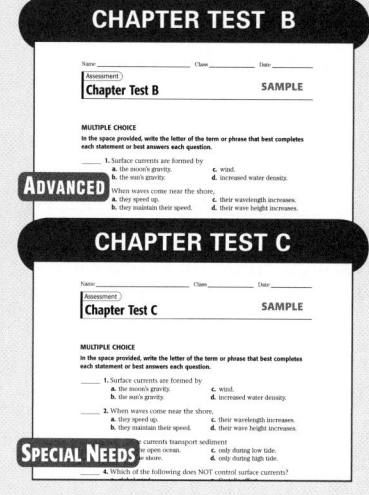

ADVANCED

CHAPTER TEST C

SPECIAL NEEDS

STANDARDIZED TEST PREPARATION
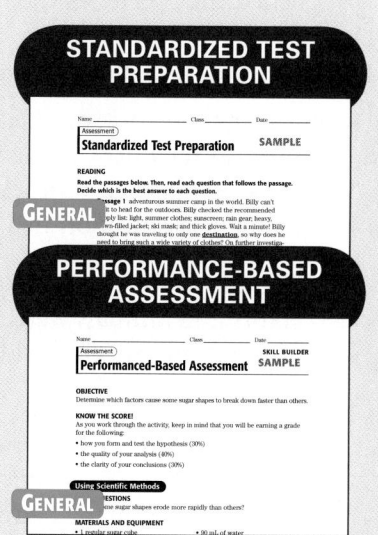

GENERAL

PERFORMANCE-BASED ASSESSMENT

GENERAL

This Chapter Enrichment provides relevant and interesting information to expand and enhance your presentation of the chapter material.

Section 1

Sorting It All Out

Aristotle's Classification System

- The great Greek philosopher and scientist Aristotle (384–322 BCE) began classifying animals into logical groupings more than 2,000 years ago. Although Aristotle did not view different kinds of organisms as being related by descent, he arranged all living things in an ascending ladder with humans at the top.

- Animals were separated into two major groups—those with red blood and those without red blood—that correspond very closely with our modern classification of vertebrates and invertebrates.

- Animals were further classified according to their way of life, their actions, and their body parts.

- Aristotle categorized plants as herbs, shrubs, or trees, based on their size and appearance.

Species in Classification

- In the late 1600s, the English scientist John Ray established the species as the basic unit of classification.

Basis for Modern Classification System

- Our modern system of classification was codified by Swedish scientist Carolus Linnaeus. He published a book on plant classification in 1753 and a book on animal classification in 1758.

- Organisms were classified according to their structure. Plants and animals were arranged into the categories of genus and species, and the categories of class and order were introduced.

- Species were given distinctive two-word names. Linnaeus's system is still in use today, although it has gone through many changes.

- "Carolus Linnaeus" is the Latin translation of the Swedish scientist's given name, Carl von Linné.

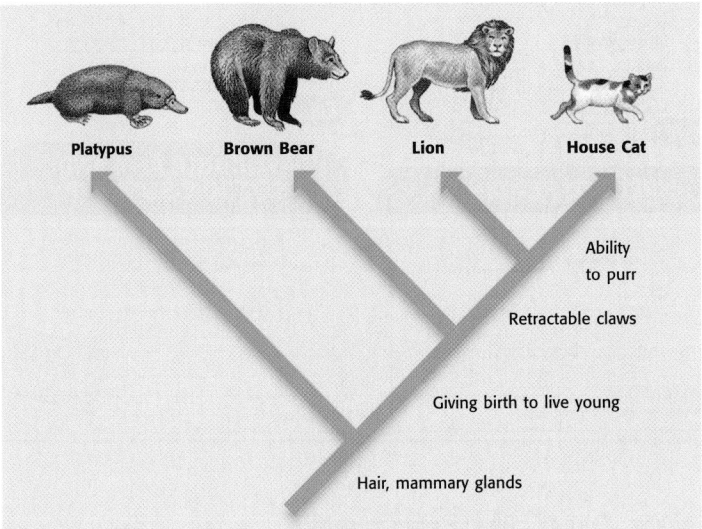

Subgroups in the Animal Kingdom

- Baron Georges Cuvier first divided the animal kingdom into subgroups, such as Vertebrata, Mollusca, Articulata, and Radiata, in 1817.

Section 2

The Six Kingdoms

Variations of the Classification System

- Variations of the five-kingdom classification system introduced by R. H. Whittaker in 1969 are used by some modern scientists. Whittaker's system classifies organisms according to whether they are prokaryotic or eukaryotic, whether they are unicellular or multicellular, and whether they obtain food by photosynthesis, ingestion, or absorption of nutrients from their environment.

- Because studies of DNA indicate significant differences between archaebacteria and eubacteria, many scientists place archaebacteria in a sixth kingdom.

Meeting Individual Needs

DIRECTED READING A
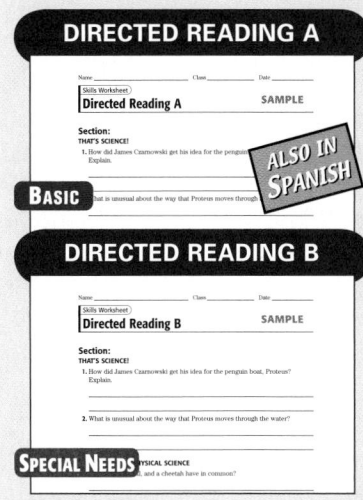
BASIC

DIRECTED READING B
SPECIAL NEEDS

VOCABULARY ACTIVITY
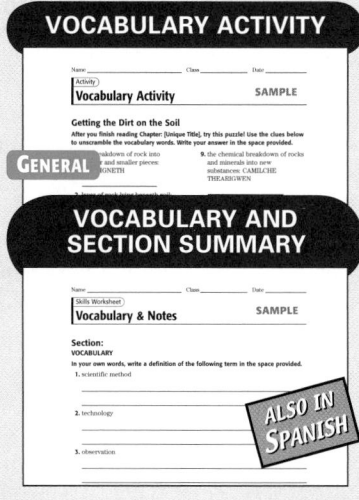
GENERAL

VOCABULARY AND SECTION SUMMARY
GENERAL

REINFORCEMENT
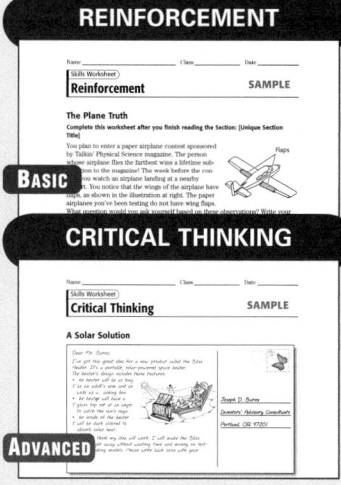
BASIC

CRITICAL THINKING
ADVANCED

SCILINKS ACTIVITY

GENERAL

SCIENCE PUZZLERS, TWISTERS & TEASERS
GENERAL

Labs and Activities

ECOLABS & FIELD ACTIVITIES
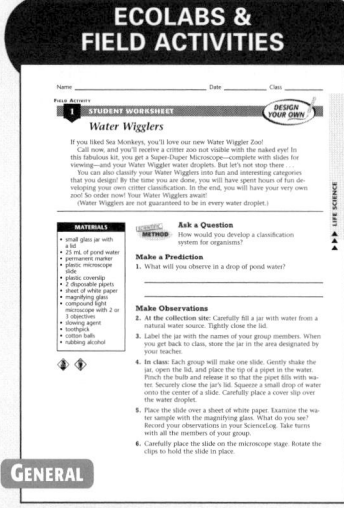
GENERAL

LONG-TERM PROJECTS & RESEARCH IDEAS
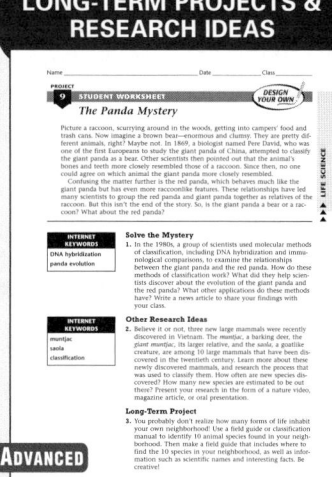
ADVANCED

DATASHEETS FOR QUICK LABS

DATASHEETS FOR CHAPTER LABS

DATASHEETS FOR LABBOOK

Review and Assessments

SECTION QUIZ
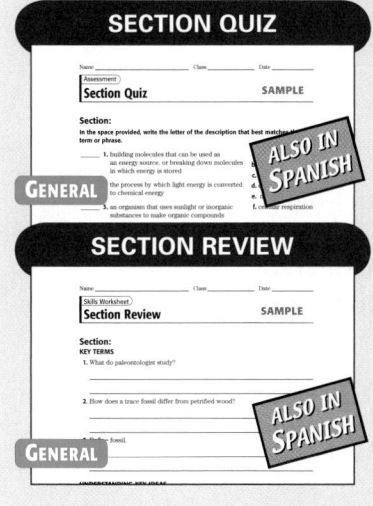
GENERAL

SECTION REVIEW
GENERAL

CHAPTER REVIEW
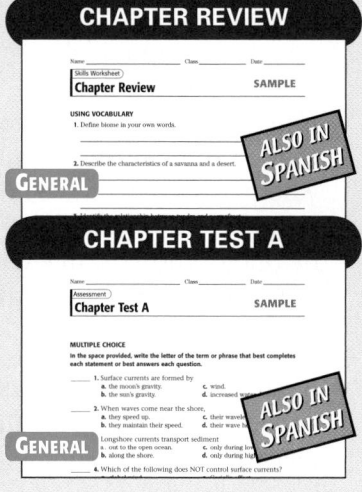
GENERAL

CHAPTER TEST A
GENERAL

CHAPTER TEST B
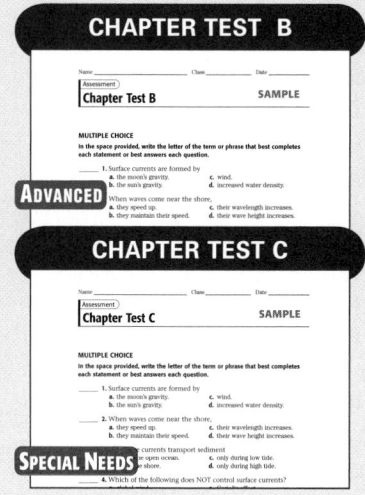
ADVANCED

CHAPTER TEST C
SPECIAL NEEDS

STANDARDIZED TEST PREPARATION
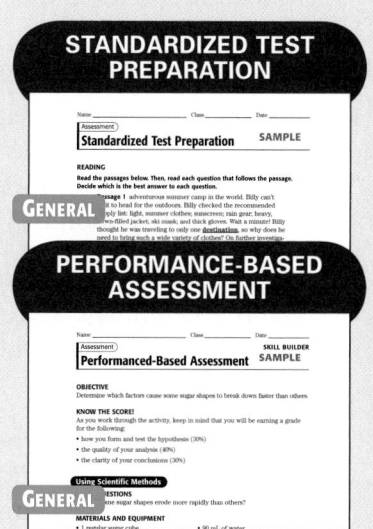
GENERAL

PERFORMANCE-BASED ASSESSMENT
GENERAL

This Chapter Enrichment provides relevant and interesting information to expand and enhance your presentation of the chapter material.

Section 1

Sorting It All Out

Aristotle's Classification System

- The great Greek philosopher and scientist Aristotle (384–322 BCE) began classifying animals into logical groupings more than 2,000 years ago. Although Aristotle did not view different kinds of organisms as being related by descent, he arranged all living things in an ascending ladder with humans at the top.

- Animals were separated into two major groups—those with red blood and those without red blood—that correspond very closely with our modern classification of vertebrates and invertebrates.

- Animals were further classified according to their way of life, their actions, and their body parts.

- Aristotle categorized plants as herbs, shrubs, or trees, based on their size and appearance.

Species in Classification

- In the late 1600s, the English scientist John Ray established the species as the basic unit of classification.

Basis for Modern Classification System

- Our modern system of classification was codified by Swedish scientist Carolus Linnaeus. He published a book on plant classification in 1753 and a book on animal classification in 1758.

- Organisms were classified according to their structure. Plants and animals were arranged into the categories of genus and species, and the categories of class and order were introduced.

- Species were given distinctive two-word names. Linnaeus's system is still in use today, although it has gone through many changes.

- "Carolus Linnaeus" is the Latin translation of the Swedish scientist's given name, Carl von Linné.

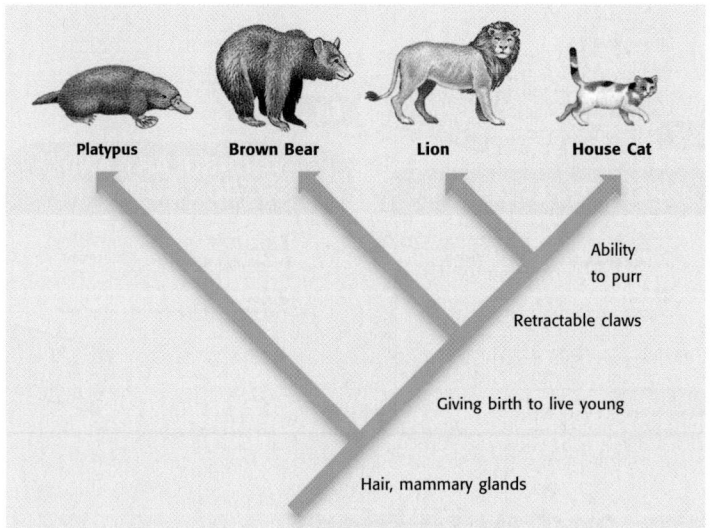

Platypus   Brown Bear   Lion   House Cat

Ability to purr

Retractable claws

Giving birth to live young

Hair, mammary glands

Subgroups in the Animal Kingdom

- Baron Georges Cuvier first divided the animal kingdom into subgroups, such as Vertebrata, Mollusca, Articulata, and Radiata, in 1817.

Section 2

The Six Kingdoms

Variations of the Classification System

- Variations of the five-kingdom classification system introduced by R. H. Whittaker in 1969 are used by some modern scientists. Whittaker's system classifies organisms according to whether they are prokaryotic or eukaryotic, whether they are unicellular or multicellular, and whether they obtain food by photosynthesis, ingestion, or absorption of nutrients from their environment.

- Because studies of DNA indicate significant differences between archaebacteria and eubacteria, many scientists place archaebacteria in a sixth kingdom.

Life Within the Planet

- When we organize life on Earth into categories, it is important to remember that organisms are not equally distributed throughout our classification system. We often think of the Earth's living things in terms of plants and animals—organisms that live above the Earth's surface and within its waters. However, the largest kingdom in terms of the number of individuals and total biomass are bacteria. And bacteria's most common home may be deep within the Earth's crust.

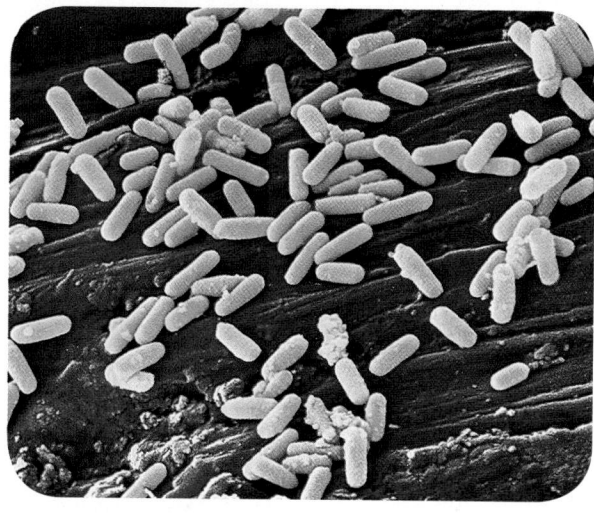

- Scientists have known for some time that bacteria exist all around us and that some have the ability to live in extreme environments. Some bacteria live in hot geysers; other bacteria live in water that has such high salt concentrations that no other organisms can survive in the water. Scientists have also known that many archaebacteria can thrive in anaerobic and high-pressure environments, such as those found underground. But only recently have scientists learned just how far underground archaebacteria are found and just how many archaebacteria live there.

- In 1987, scientists were drilling in the rock beneath the Savannah River in South Carolina to investigate the safety of the drinking water. The cores of the rock they investigated harbored bacteria at a depth of 500 m. Other scientists found bacteria in the ocean at a depth 750 m. A South African gold mine yielded other bacteria from as far down as 5 km.

- Once scientists knew to look deep in the Earth for life-forms, they began looking for—and finding—organisms in the sediment under the ocean. Some scientists predict that further exploration will reveal organisms that live as deep as 15 km within the sediment. If that is the case, then the total biomass of these organisms beneath the surface of the Earth may exceed the total biomass of all the living things on the Earth's surface.

- No one knows exactly how these microorganisms tolerate the tremendous pressures and temperatures of their environment, but scientists have learned that these organisms are meeting their nutritional needs in a variety of ways. Some live on oxidized forms of sulfur; others live on bits of organic matter found in the sediment. Some bacteria have even been found in igneous rocks, where they apparently subsist on the carbon dioxide and hydrogen gas trapped in the rock.

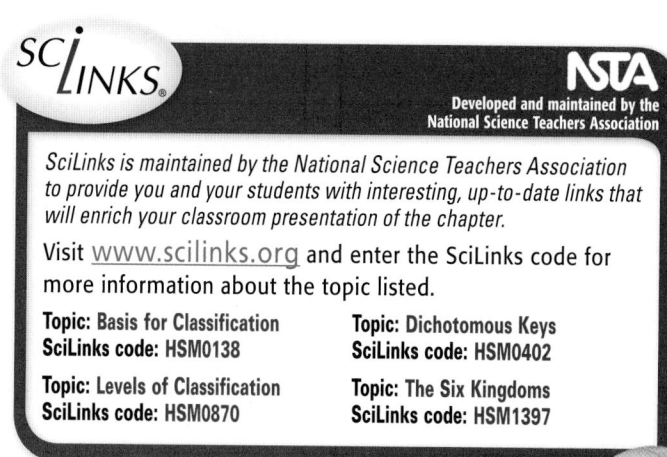

SciLinks is maintained by the National Science Teachers Association to provide you and your students with interesting, up-to-date links that will enrich your classroom presentation of the chapter.

Visit www.scilinks.org and enter the SciLinks code for more information about the topic listed.

Topic: Basis for Classification
SciLinks code: HSM0138

Topic: Dichotomous Keys
SciLinks code: HSM0402

Topic: Levels of Classification
SciLinks code: HSM0870

Topic: The Six Kingdoms
SciLinks code: HSM1397

Overview

Tell students that this chapter will help them learn about classification in life science. The chapter covers methods of classification and the six kingdoms of organisms.

Assessing Prior Knowledge

Students should be familiar with the following topics:

• characteristics of living things

• history of life on Earth

Identifying Misconceptions

As students learn the material in this chapter, some of them may be confused about how scientists classify organisms. Some students categorize by characteristics such as numbers of limbs or the shape of leaves rather than more fundamental distinctions. Furthermore, students often rely on the information found in common names. For example, students may mistakenly categorize a jellyfish as a fish.

9
Classification

About the PHOTO

Look at the katydids, grasshoppers, and mantids in the photo. A scientist is classifying these insects. Every insect has a label describing the insect. These descriptions will be used to help the scientist know if each insect has already been discovered and named. When scientists discover a new insect or other organism, they have to give the organism a name. The name chosen is unique and should help other scientists understand some basic facts about the organism.

PRE-READING ACTIVITY

FOLDNOTES **Booklet** Before you read the chapter, create the FoldNote entitled "Booklet" described in the **Study Skills** section of the Appendix. Label each page of the booklet with a main idea from the chapter. As you read the chapter, write what you learn about each main idea on the appropriate page of the booklet.

Standards Correlations

National Science Education Standards

The following codes indicate the National Science Education Standards that correlate to this chapter. The full text of the standards is at the front of the book.

Chapter Opener
UCP 1

Section 1 Sorting It All Out
UCP 1; SAI 2; HNS 1, 2, 3; LS 5a

Section 2 The Six Kingdoms
UCP 5; SAI 1; HNS 1, 2; LS 1b, 1f, 2a, 2c, 4b, 4c, 4d, 5b;
LabBook: UCP 1; SAI 1

Chapter Lab
UPC 1; SAI 1

Science in Action
HNS 1, 3; LS 5a

MATERIALS

FOR EACH GROUP
- marker
- shoes, 10 different kinds (from class members, a secondhand store, or a garage sale)
- tape, masking

Teacher's Notes: Make certain that students understand that the list of shoe characteristics should be unique to a particular set of 10 shoes.

Characteristics of shoes listed should be those that can easily be observed. For example, whether a shoe belongs to a boy or to a girl is not always obvious to an observer.

You can offer the following as a model for the statement for Procedure step 4:

    a. This is a red sandal.

    b. This is not a red sandal. (Go to step 2.)

Answers

1. Sample answer: Listing the shoes' features helped me find some features that were common and some that were unique.

2. Each student may describe the shoes differently, but the students' descriptions should be clear enough to lead the other students to the same conclusion.

START-UP ACTIVITY

Classifying Shoes

In this group activity, each group will develop a system of classification for shoes.

Procedure

1. Gather **10 shoes.** Number pieces of **masking tape** from 1 to 10. Label the sole of each shoe with a numbered piece of tape.

2. Make a list of shoe features. Make a table that has a column for each feature. Complete the table by describing each shoe.

3. Use the data in the table to make a shoe identification key.

4. The key should be a list of steps. Each step should have two contrasting statements about the shoes. The statements will lead you either to the next step or to a specific shoe.

5. If your shoe is not identified in one step, go on to the next step or steps until the shoe is identified.

6. Trade keys with another group. How did the other group's key help you identify the shoes?

Analysis

1. How was listing the shoe features before making the key helpful?

2. Were you able to identify the shoes using another group's key? Explain.

This Really Happened!

Skunks have been thrown out of their family. It wasn't their awful smell that got them thrown out, though. It was their DNA.

Skunks were once thought to be most closely related to weasels, ferrets, minks, badgers, and otters. Those furry, short-legged, long-bodied, meat-eating mammals are grouped together in a family called Mustelidae (moo STEL i dee). *Mustelidae* is from the Latin word for "mouse." Skunks were classified along with weasels and ferrets because they all share several physical characteristics with mice.

DNA of the other members of Mustelidae. By comparing the DNA of different species, scientists can tell how closely related the species are. The DNA of two closely related animals—a house cat and a tiger, for example—are more similar than the DNA of two animals that are distantly related—such as a house cat and a chicken.

So where does that leave the little striped stinkers? Right in their own, newly created scientific family—Mephitidae (me FIT i dee). *Mephitid* is from the Latin word that means "bad odor"!

Chapter Starter Transparency
Use this transparency to help students begin thinking about classifying organisms.

CHAPTER RESOURCES

Technology

 **Transparencies**
- Chapter Starter Transparency

READING SKILLS

 Student Edition on CD-ROM

 **Guided Reading Audio CD**
- English or Spanish

 **Classroom Videos**
- Brain Food Video Quiz

Workbooks

 Science Puzzlers, Twisters & Teasers
- Classification GENERAL

Focus

Overview

In this section, students learn about the modern biological classification system. The section explains how organisms are classified based on their shared characteristics and how their scientific names are determined. Finally, students learn how to identify animals by using a dichotomous key.

🔊 Bellringer

Ask students to think about the different ways humans classify things. Ask them to list at least five things that humans classify. You may want to give them examples, such as library books, department-store merchandise, and addresses.

Motivate

Demonstration —— GENERAL

Classifying Objects Display a variety of small, solid objects. Ask students for their ideas on ways to put the objects into groups. For each grouping, record the defining characteristic and the objects that belong in the group. Identify objects that fit in more than one grouping. Discuss how putting objects into groups can be helpful. **LS** Visual   English Language Learners

---

SECTION
1

Sorting It All Out

Imagine that you live in a tropical rain forest and must get your own food, shelter, and clothing from the forest. What do you need to know to survive in the forest?

To survive in the rain forest, you need to know which plants are safe to eat and which are not. You need to know which animals you can eat and which might eat you. In other words, you need to study the living things around you and organize them into categories, or classify them. **Classification** is putting things into orderly groups based on similar characteristics.

Why Classify?

For thousands of years, humans have classified living things based on usefulness. The Chácabo people of Bolivia know of 360 types of plants that grow in the forest where they live. Of these 360 plant types, 305 are useful to the Chácabo.

Some biologists, such as those shown in **Figure 1,** classify living and extinct organisms. Scientists classify organisms to help make sense and order of the many kinds of living things in the world. Biologists use a system to classify living things. This system groups organisms according to the characteristics they share. The classification of living things makes it easier for biologists to answer many important questions, such as the following:

- How many known species are there?
- What are the defining characteristics of each species?
- What are the relationships between these species?

✔ *Reading Check* **What are three questions that classifying organisms can help answer?** (*See the Appendix for answers to Reading Checks.*)

classification the division of organisms into groups, or classes, based on specific characteristics

Figure 1 *These biologists are sorting rain-forest plant material.*

CHAPTER RESOURCES

Chapter Resource File
- Lesson Plan
- Directed Reading A **BASIC**
- Directed Reading B **SPECIAL NEEDS**

Technology

Transparencies
- Bellringer
- Evolutionary Relationships Among Organisms

Answer to Reading Check
- How many known species are there?
- What are the defining characteristics of each species?
- What are the relationships between these species?

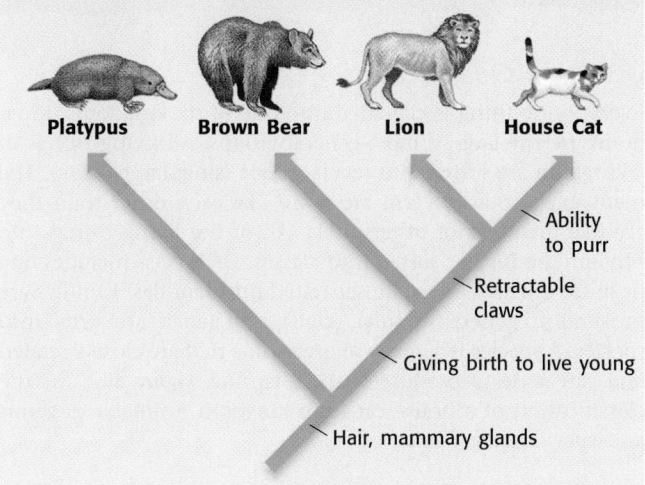

Platypus   Brown Bear   Lion   House Cat

— Ability to purr

— Retractable claws

— Giving birth to live young

— Hair, mammary glands

Figure 2 *This branching diagram shows the similarities and differences between four mammals.*

How Do Scientists Classify Organisms?

Before the 1600s, many scientists divided organisms into two groups: plants and animals. But, as more organisms were discovered, some organisms did not fit into either group. In the 1700s, a Swedish scientist named Carolus Linnaeus (KAR uh luhs li NAY uhs) founded modern taxonomy. **Taxonomy** (taks AHN uh mee) is the science of describing, classifying, and naming living things. Linnaeus tried to classify all living things based on their shape and structure. He described a seven-level system of classification, which is still used today.

Classification Today

Taxonomists use the seven-level system to classify living things based on shared characteristics. Scientists also use shared characteristics to hypothesize how closely related living things are. The more characteristics the organisms share, the more closely related the organisms may be. For example, the platypus, brown bear, lion, and house cat are thought to be related because they share many characteristics. These animals have hair and mammary glands, so they are grouped together as mammals. But they can be further classified into more-specific groups.

Branching Diagrams

Look at the branching diagram in **Figure 2.** Several characteristics are listed along the line that points to the right. Each characteristic is shared by the animals to the right of it. All of the animals shown have hair and mammary glands. But only the bear, lion, and house cat give birth to live young. The lion and the house cat have retractable claws, but the other animals do not. Thus, the lion and the house cat are more closely related to each other than to the other animals.

taxonomy the science of describing, naming, and classifying organisms

A Branching Diagram

1. Construct a diagram similar to the one in **Figure 2.**
2. Use a frog, a snake, a kangaroo, and a rabbit in your diagram.
3. Think of one major change that happened before the frog evolved.
4. For the last three organisms, think of a change that happened between one of these organisms and the other two. Write all of these changes in your diagram.

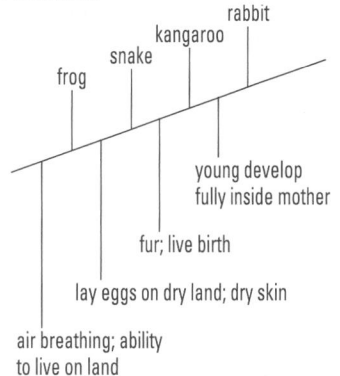

Discussion — BASIC

Classification Drill To help students understand what constitutes a species, genus, family, order, class, phylum, and kingdom, ask them the following questions:

• What does a species contain? (organisms that have the same characteristics)

• What does a genus contain? (similar species)

• What does a family contain? (similar genera)

• What does an order contain? (similar families)

• What does a class contain? (similar orders)

• What does a phylum contain? (similar classes)

• What does a kingdom contain? (similar phyla)

LS Logical/Auditory

Using the Figure — GENERAL

Classification Refer students to **Figure 3**. Have them answer these questions:

• Which animals are pictured at the kingdom level? (beetle, bird, lion, lynx, bear, human, house cat)

• Which of these pictured animals does not fit the description of a chordate? (the beetle)

• Which of the animals pictured at the chordate level does not fit the description of a mammal? (the bird)

English Language Learners

LS Visual

INTERNET ACTIVITY

For another activity related to this chapter, go to **go.hrw.com** and type in the keyword **HL5CLSW**.

Levels of Classification

Every living thing is classified into one of six kingdoms. Kingdoms are the largest, most general groups. All living things in a kingdom are sorted into several phyla (singular, *phylum*). The members of one phylum are more like each other than they are like members of other phyla. All of the living things in a phylum are further sorted into classes. Each class includes one or more orders. Orders are separated into families. Families are broken into genera (singular, *genus*). And genera are sorted into species. A species is a group of organisms that are closely related and can mate to produce fertile offspring. **Figure 3** shows the classification of a house cat from kingdom Animalia to genus and species, *Felis domesticus*.

Scientific Names

By classifying organisms, biologists are able to give organisms scientific names. A scientific name is always the same for a specific kind of organism no matter how many common names there might be. Before Linnaeus's time, scholars used names that were as long as 12 words to identify species. The names were hard to work with because they were so long. And different scientists named organisms differently, so an organism could have more than one name.

Figure 3 *The seven levels of classification are kingdom, phylum, class, order, family, genus, and species.*

Kingdom Animalia	Phylum Chordata	Class Mammalia	Order Carnivora
All animals are in the **kingdom Animalia**.	All animals in the **phylum Chordata** have a hollow nerve cord. Most have a backbone.	Animals in the **class Mammalia** have a backbone. They also nurse their young.	Animals in the **order Carnivora** have a backbone and nurse their young. They also have special teeth for tearing meat.

CHAPTER RESOURCES

Technology

Transparencies
• Levels of Classification

Is That a Fact!

The term *dinosaur* wasn't coined until the 19th century. Until then, as dinosaur fossils were uncovered all over the world, the most widely accepted view was that the fossils were the remains of dragons.

Two-Part Names

Linnaeus simplified the naming of living things by giving each species a two-part scientific name. For example, the scientific name for the Asian elephant is *Elephas maximus* (EL uh fuhs MAK suh muhs). The first part of the name, *Elephas,* is the genus name. The second part, *maximus,* is the species name. No other species has both this genus name and this species name. Naming rules help scientists communicate clearly about living things.

All genus names begin with a capital letter. All species names begin with a lowercase letter. Usually, both words are underlined or italicized. But if the surrounding text is italicized, the genus and species names are not italicized, as shown in **Figure 4.** These printing styles show a reader which names are genus and species names.

Scientific names, which are usually in Latin or Greek, contain information about an organism. The name of the animal shown in **Figure 4** is *Tyrannosaurus rex. Tyrannosaurus* is a combination of two Greek words and means "tyrant lizard." The word *rex* is Latin for "king." The name tells you that this animal was probably not a passive grass eater! Sometimes, *Tyrannosaurus rex* is referred to as *T. rex.* The species name is not correct without the genus name or its abbreviation.

Figure 4 *You would never call* Tyrannosaurus rex *just* rex!

✓ **Reading Check** What are the two parts of a scientific name?

Family *Felidae*	Genus *Felis*	Species *Felis domesticus*
Animals in the **family Felidae** are cats. They have a backbone, nurse their young, have special teeth for tearing meat, and have retractable claws.	Animals in the **genus Felis** have traits of other animals in the same family. However, these cats cannot roar; they can only purr.	The **species Felis domesticus** is the common house cat. The house cat shares traits with all of the organisms in the levels above the species level, but it also has unique traits.

Is That a Fact!

If you put all of the insects in the world together, they would weigh more than all of the people and the rest of the animals combined.

Close

Reteaching — **BASIC**

Name That Bird Display a picture of a bird whose common name is not well known to your students. Ask students to give the bird a name. List students' answers on the board. Help students understand that scientists would have difficulty sharing information about the bird if they used more than one name for it. **LS** Visual

Quiz — GENERAL

1. Why do scientists classify animals? (to make studying them easier)

2. What is the basis of modern classification systems? (shared characteristics)

Alternative Assessment — GENERAL

Cartooning Have students create a cartoon that shows how using different common names for an animal instead of its scientific name creates confusion. Students must include scientific names in their cartoon. **LS** Visual   *English Language Learners*

Answer to Dichotomous Key

Mammal on the top left: 1b, 2b, 4b, 6a, 7a, longtail weasel

Mammal on the top right: 1b, 2b, 4b, 6b, 8b, 9b, woodchuck

Answer to Reading Check

A dichotomous key is an identification aid that helps identify organisms.

Dichotomous Keys

You might someday turn over a rock and find an organism that you don't recognize. How would you identify the organism? Taxonomists have developed special guides to help scientists identify organisms. A **dichotomous key** (die KAHT uh muhs KEE) is an identification aid that uses sequential pairs of descriptive statements. There are only two alternative responses for each statement. From each pair of statements, the person trying to identify the organism chooses the statement that describes the organism. Either the chosen statement identifies the organism or the person is directed to another pair of statements. By working through the statements in the key in order, the person can eventually identify the organism. Using the simple dichotomous key in **Figure 5**, try to identify the two animals shown.

dichotomous key an aid that is used to identify organisms and that consists of the answers to a series of questions

✓ *Reading Check* What is a dichotomous key?

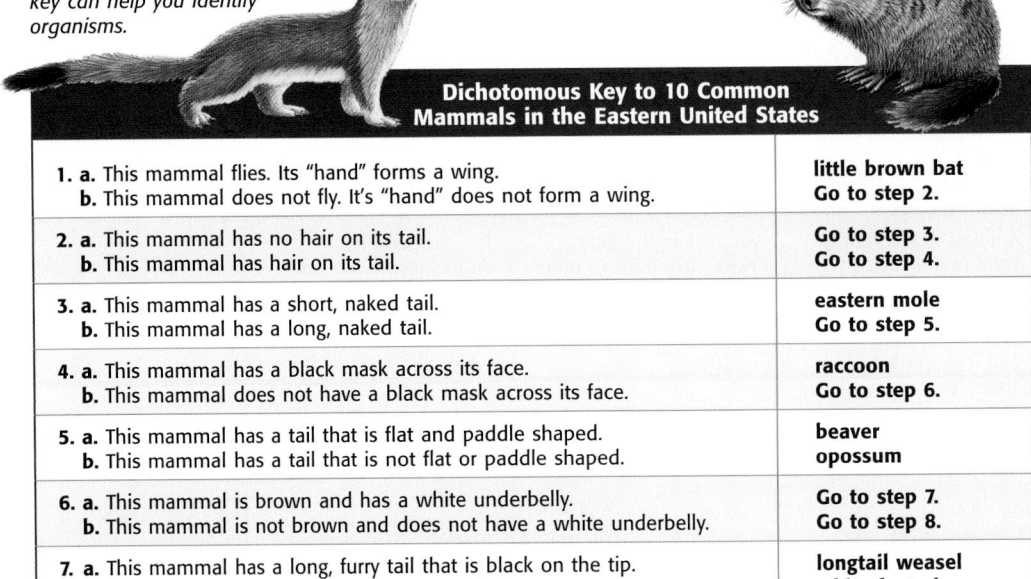

Figure 5 *A dichotomous key can help you identify organisms.*

Dichotomous Key to 10 Common Mammals in the Eastern United States

1. a. This mammal flies. Its "hand" forms a wing. **b.** This mammal does not fly. It's "hand" does not form a wing.	**little brown bat** Go to step 2.
2. a. This mammal has no hair on its tail. **b.** This mammal has hair on its tail.	Go to step 3. Go to step 4.
3. a. This mammal has a short, naked tail. **b.** This mammal has a long, naked tail.	**eastern mole** Go to step 5.
4. a. This mammal has a black mask across its face. **b.** This mammal does not have a black mask across its face.	**raccoon** Go to step 6.
5. a. This mammal has a tail that is flat and paddle shaped. **b.** This mammal has a tail that is not flat or paddle shaped.	**beaver** **opossum**
6. a. This mammal is brown and has a white underbelly. **b.** This mammal is not brown and does not have a white underbelly.	Go to step 7. Go to step 8.
7. a. This mammal has a long, furry tail that is black on the tip. **b.** This mammal has a long tail that has little fur.	**longtail weasel** **white-footed mouse**
8. a. This mammal is black and has a narrow white stripe on its forehead and broad white stripes on its back. **b.** This mammal is not black and does not have white stripes.	**striped skunk** Go to step 9.
9. a. This mammal has long ears and a short, cottony tail. **b.** This mammal has short ears and a medium-length tail.	**eastern cottontail** **woodchuck**

INCLUSION Strategies

- *Developmentally Delayed*
- *Hearing Impaired*

Use this activity to clarify the procedure. Place the following six objects on a table: stapler, marker, zipper bag of ice, book, roll of tape, and piece of wadded-up paper. Use the following questions to identify the items by their physical characteristics.

1. Is it very cold and could melt? If yes, it is ice. If no, go to step 2.

2. Is it made of metal? If yes, it is a stapler. If no, go to step 3.

3. Is it made of paper? If yes, go to step 4. If no, go to step 5.

4. Is it intended to be read? If yes, it is a book. Is it intended to be thrown? If yes, it is a paper wad.

5. Is it used for writing? If yes, it is a marker. Does it have a sticky side? If yes, it is tape.   *English Language Learners*

LS Logical

A Growing System

You may think that all of the organisms on Earth have already been classified. But people are still discovering and classifying organisms. Some newly discovered organisms fit into existing categories. But sometimes, someone discovers new evidence or an organism that is so different from other organisms that it does not fit existing categories. For example, in 1995, scientists studied an organism named *Symbion pandora* (SIM bee AHN pan DAWR uh). Scientists found *S. pandora* living on lobster lips! Scientists learned that *S. pandora* had some characteristics that no other known organism had. In fact, scientists trying to classify *S. pandora* found that it didn't fit in any existing phylum. So, taxonomists created a new phylum for *S. pandora*.

SECTION Review

Summary

- Classification refers to the arrangement of living things into orderly groups based on their similarities.
- Today's living things are classified by using a seven-level system of organization. The seven levels are kingdom, phylum, class, order, family, genus, and species.
- An organism has only one correct scientific name.
- Dichotomous keys are tools for identifying organisms.

Using Key Terms

1. In your own words, write a definition for each of the following terms: *classification* and *taxonomy*.

Understanding Key Ideas

2. The two parts of a scientific name are the names of the genus and the
   a. species.   c. family.
   b. phylum.   d. order.

3. Why do scientists use scientific names for organisms?

4. List the seven levels of classification.

5. Describe how a dichotomous key helps scientists identify organisms.

Critical Thinking

6. **Analyzing Processes** Biologists think that millions of species are not classified yet. Why do you think so many species have not been classified yet?

7. **Applying Concepts** Both dolphins and sharks have a tail and fins. How can you determine if dolphins and sharks are closely related?

Interpreting Graphics

Use the figure below to answer the questions that follow.

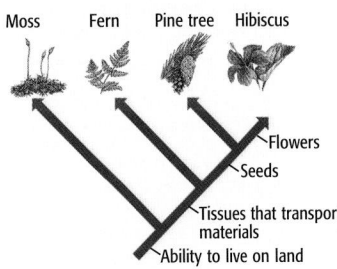

Moss   Fern   Pine tree   Hibiscus

Flowers
Seeds
Tissues that transport materials
Ability to live on land

8. Which plant is most similar to the hibiscus?

9. Which plant is least similar to the hibiscus?

SCILINKS

Developed and maintained by the National Science Teachers Association

For a variety of links related to this chapter, go to www.scilinks.org

Topic: Basis for Classification; Levels of Classification
SciLinks code: HSM0138; HSM0870

Focus

Overview

This section explains how improved understanding of organisms leads to revisions in our system of biological classification. Students are introduced to the six kingdoms:

Archaebacteria, Eubacteria, Protista, Fungi, Plantae, and Animalia.

They learn how organisms from each kingdom are distinguished.

🔔 Bellringer

Have students list seven musical artists, bands, or acts. Then have students categorize the names on their lists by style of music. Ask them to describe in their **science journal** the categories they chose and to explain which bands might fit into more than one category.

Motivate

ACTiViTY ———— GENERAL

Grouping Animals Have students write letters to zoos requesting a copy of their visitors' map. Students could then compare the layouts of many zoos and the ways that animals are grouped. Be sure to have students include a stamped, self-addressed envelope with their letter describing the project.
LS Logical

READING WARM-UP

Objectives

- Explain how classification schemes for kingdoms developed as greater numbers of different organisms became known.
- Describe each of the six kingdoms.

Terms to Learn

Archaebacteria	Fungi
Eubacteria	Plantae
Protista	Animalia

READING STRATEGY

Reading Organizer As you read this section, make a table comparing the six classification kingdoms to each other.

Figure 1 *How would you classify this organism? This member of the genus* Euglena, *which is shown here highly magnified, has characteristics of both plants and animals.*

The Six Kingdoms

What do you call an organism that is green, makes its own food, lives in pond water, and moves? Is it a plant, an animal, or something in between?

For hundreds of years, all living things were classified as either plants or animals. But over time, scientists discovered species that did not fit easily into these two kingdoms. For example, an organism of the genus *Euglena,* such as the one shown in **Figure 1,** has characteristics of both plants and animals. How would you classify such an organism?

What Is It?

Organisms are classified by their characteristics. For example, organisms of the genus *Euglena* are

- single celled and live in pond water
- green and make their own food through photosynthesis

These two characteristics might lead you to conclude that the genus of *Euglena* are plants. However, you should consider the following other characteristics before you form your conclusion:

- Members of the genus *Euglena* move by whipping their "tails," which are called *flagella.*
- *Euglena* can feed on other organisms.

Plants don't move themselves around and usually do not eat other organisms. So, are organisms of the genus *Euglena* animals? As you can see, *Euglena* does not fit into the category of plants or animals. Scientists solved this classification problem by adding another kingdom, the kingdom Protista, to classify organisms such as *Euglena.*

As scientists continued to learn about living things, they added kingdoms that account for the characteristics of different organisms. Currently, most scientists agree that the six-kingdom classification system works best. However, scientists will continue to adjust the system as they learn more.

CHAPTER RESOURCES

Chapter Resource File

- **Lesson Plan**
- **Directed Reading A** BASIC
- **Directed Reading B** SPECIAL NEEDS

Technology

Transparencies
- Bellringer
- *LINK TO EARTH SCIENCE* Intrusive Igneous Rock Formations

CONNECTION to
Earth Science ——— GENERAL

Rocky Habitats Bacteria have been found living in igneous rocks deep in the Earth's crust. The rocks contain little water and no organic matter. The bacteria subsist on carbon dioxide and hydrogen gas dissolved in the rock and slowly make their own organic compounds. Use the teaching transparency entitled "Intrusive Igneous Rock Formations" to introduce information about igneous rocks that may be unfamiliar to students. **LS** Visual

---

Figure 2 *The Grand Prismatic Spring in Yellowstone National Park contains water that is about 90°C (194°F). The spring is home to archaebacteria that thrive in its hot water.*

Archaebacteria a kingdom made up of bacteria that live in extreme environments

Eubacteria a kingdom that contains all prokaryotes except archaebacteria

The Two Kingdoms of Bacteria

Bacteria are extremely small, single-celled organisms that differ from all other living things. Bacteria are *prokaryotes* (proh KAYR ee OHTS), organisms that lack nuclei. Many biologists divide bacteria into two kingdoms: Archaebacteria (AHR kee bak TEER ee uh) and Eubacteria (YOO bak TEER ee uh).

Archaebacteria

Prokaryotes that can live in extreme environments are in the kingdom **Archaebacteria.** The prefix *archae-* comes from a Greek word meaning "ancient." Today, most archaebacteria can be found living in places where most organisms could not survive. **Figure 2** shows a hot spring in Yellowstone National Park. The yellow and orange rings around the edge of the hot spring are made up of the billions of archaebacteria that live there.

Eubacteria

Bacteria that are not in the kingdom Archaebacteria are in the kingdom **Eubacteria.** Eubacteria are prokaryotes that live in the soil, in water, and even on and inside the human body! For example, *Escherichia coli,* pictured in **Figure 3,** is present in large numbers in human intestines, where it produces vitamin K. One kind of eubacterium converts milk into yogurt. Another kind of eubacterium causes pneumonia.

✔ Reading Check **Name a type of eubacterium that lives in your body.** (*See the Appendix for answers to Reading Checks.*)

Figure 3 *Specimens of* E. coli *are shown on the point of a pin under a scanning electron microscope. These eubacteria live in the intestines of animals and decompose undigested food.*

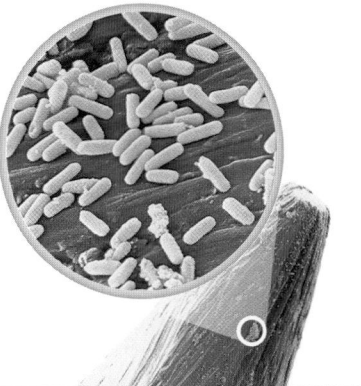

CONNECTION ACTIVITY
Environmental Science — GENERAL

Penguin Problem Recently, signs of *Salmonella* infection were found in the droppings of an Antarctic gentoo penguin. The bacteria were most likely introduced from outside the Antarctic. The bacterium, *Salmonella enteritidis,* is not endemic to penguins. Scientists think that sewage dumped from passing ships or visiting albatrosses that feed on waste-contaminated squid in the oceans surrounding South America might be the sources of the bacteria. The bacterium could kill the penguins if it becomes infectious and pathogenic. Have students create a poster that could inform ship owners of the danger human wastes pose to native wildlife. **LS** Visual

Researching Protists
Have students research
protists, such as
Paramecium, slime mold, and
giant kelp. Have them write
descriptions about each protist,
including information about its
size, form, method of obtaining
nutrients, method of reproduction, and, in the case of the
giant kelp and other algae, the
commercial uses of the
organism. **LS Verbal**

CONNECTION ACTiViTY
Real World ——— **ADVANCED**

Exploring Mushrooms Tell students that Pennsylvania, which
has many caves, is one of the
major mushroom-growing
regions of the United States.
Caves are ideal places in which
to grow some kinds of edible
mushrooms. Ask students to
research and write a report on
mushroom farming in the United
States. What kinds of mushrooms
are grown commercially, and
what special conditions does
each species require? Inexpensive
kits are available for growing
mushrooms, and interested students might enjoy the experience
of raising their own. Caution students not to attempt to cultivate
or eat mushrooms that they find
in the wild. Some toxic species
are difficult to distinguish from
nontoxic ones. Accidental ingestion of toxic mushrooms can
be fatal. **LS Kinesthetic/Verbal**

Figure 4 *This slime mold is a protist.*

Protista a kingdom of mostly one-
celled eukaryotic organisms that are
different from plants, animals, bacteria, and fungi

Fungi a kingdom made up of
nongreen, eukaryotic organisms
that have no means of movement,
reproduce by using spores, and get
food by breaking down substances in
their surroundings and absorbing the
nutrients

Figure 5 *This beautiful fungus of
the genus* Amanita *is poisonous.*

Kingdom Protista

Members of the kingdom **Protista** (proh TIST uh),
commonly called *protists* (PROH tists), are single-
celled or simple multicellular organisms that don't
fit into any other kingdom. Unlike bacteria, protists
are *eukaryotes,* organisms whose cells have a nucleus
and membrane-bound organelles. The kingdom Protista contains all eukaryotes that are not plants,
animals, or fungi. Scientists think the first protists
evolved from ancient bacteria about 2 billion years
ago. Much later, protists gave rise to plants, fungi,
and animals as well as to modern protists.

The kingdom Protista contains many kinds of
organisms. Animal-like protists are called *protozoans.* Plantlike protists are called *algae.* Slime molds,
such as the one shown in **Figure 4,** and water molds
are fungus-like protists. Members of *Euglena* are also
members of the kingdom Protista.

Kingdom Fungi

Molds and mushrooms are examples of the complex multicellular members of the kingdom Fungi (FUHN JIE). Unlike plants,
fungi do not perform photosynthesis, and unlike animals, fungi
do not eat food. Instead, members of the kingdom **Fungi** absorb
nutrients from substances in their surroundings. Fungi use
digestive juices to break down the substances. **Figure 5** shows
a very poisonous fungus. Never eat wild fungi.

Scientists At Odds

To Be or Not to Be a Fungus Is a slime
mold a fungus? Slime molds were traditionally classified as fungi because despite other
differences, they exhibit a similar life cycle,
including the formation of spores on sporangia. But critics point out that some bacteria also exhibit a similar life cycle and
those organisms are not reclassified
as fungi.

Is That a Fact!

Farmers on the Orkney Islands of
Scotland have historically used seaweed
as fertilizer and food for their sheep.

Figure 6 *Giant sequoias can measure 30 m around at the base and can grow to more than 91.5 m tall.*

▲ **Figure 7** *Plants such as these are common in the Tropics.*

Kingdom Plantae

Although plants vary remarkably in size and form, most people easily recognize the members of the kingdom Plantae. **Plantae** consists of organisms that are eukaryotic, have cell walls, and make food through photosynthesis. For photosynthesis to occur, plants must be exposed to sunlight. Plants can therefore be found on land and in water that light can penetrate.

The food that plants make is important not only for the plants but also for all of the organisms that get nutrients from plants. Most life on Earth is dependent on plants. For example, some members of the kingdoms Fungi, Protista, and Eubacteria consume plants. When these organisms digest the plant material, they get energy and nutrients made by the plants.

Plants also provide habitat for other organisms. The giant sequoias in **Figure 6** and the flowering plants in **Figure 7** provide birds, insects, and other animals with a place to live.

✓ **Reading Check** How do members of the kingdom Plantae provide energy and nutrients to members of other kingdoms?

Plantae a kingdom made up of complex, multicellular organisms that are usually green, have cell walls made of cellulose, cannot move around, and use the sun's energy to make sugar by photosynthesis

MATH PRACTICE

Ring-Around-the-Sequoia
How many students would have to join hands to form a human chain around a giant sequoia that is 30 m in circumference? Assume for this calculation that the average student can extend his or her arms about 1.3 m.

Close

Reteaching ———— BASIC

New Kingdom Have students describe and illustrate in their **science journal** an organism that might require the formation of a seventh kingdom. Students should explain why they think the organism should be classified in its own kingdom. **LS** Visual/Logical

Quiz ———————— GENERAL

1. What causes increases in the number of kingdoms in the modern classification system? (discovery of some organisms that do not fit into established kingdoms)

2. Which of the six kingdoms have prokaryotic organisms, and which have eukaryotic organisms? (prokaryotic: Archaebacteria, Eubacteria, Protista; eukaryotic: Protista, Plantae, Fungi, Animalia)

Alternative Assessment ——— GENERAL

Making a Chart
PORTFOLIO Have students construct a chart of the six kingdoms. They should list the major characteristics of each kingdom on the chart and include a representative organism for each kingdom. English Language Learners
LS Visual/Logical

Animalia a kingdom made up of complex, multicellular organisms that lack cell walls, can usually move around, and quickly respond to their environment

Kingdom Animalia

The kingdom **Animalia** contains complex, multicellular organisms that don't have cell walls, are usually able to move around, and have specialized sense organs. These sense organs help most animals quickly respond to their environment. Organisms in the kingdom Animalia are commonly called *animals*. You probably recognize many of the organisms in the kingdom Animalia. All of the organisms in **Figure 8** are animals.

Animals depend on the organisms from other kingdoms. For example, animals depend on plants for food. Animals also depend on bacteria and fungi to recycle the nutrients found in dead organisms.

Figure 8 *The kingdom Animalia contains many different organisms, such as eagles, tortoises, and beetles.*

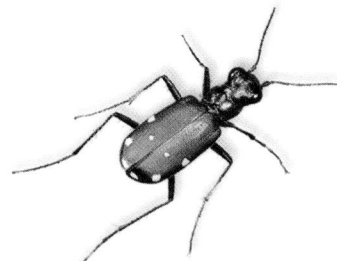

CONNECTION TO Social Studies

WRITING SKILL **Animals That Help** Humans have depended on animals for thousands of years. Many people around the world still use oxen to farm. Camels, horses, donkeys, goats, and llamas are all still used as pack animals. Dogs still help herd sheep, protect property, and help people hunt. Scientists are even discovering new ways that animals can help us. For example, scientists are training bees to help find buried land mines. Using the library or the Internet, research an animal that helps people. Make a poster describing the animal and the animal's scientific name. The poster should show who uses the animal, how the animal is used, and how long people have depended on the animal. Find or draw pictures to put on your poster.

ACTIVITY

MISCONCEPTION ALERT

Misleading Similarities Physical similarities can be misleading indicators of the relatedness of two organisms. For example, a small lizard, such as a skink, may look more like a salamander than like a turtle, but the skink is more closely related to the turtle. Both the lizard and turtle are reptiles, and the salamander is an amphibian.

Simple Animals

When you think of an animal, what do you imagine? You may think of a dog, a cat, or a parrot. All of those organisms are animals. But the animal kingdom also includes some members that might surprise you, such as worms, insects, and corals.

The red cup sponge shown in **Figure 9** is also an animal. Sponges are usually thought of as the simplest animals. They don't have sense organs. Most sponges cannot move. Sponges used to be considered plants. But sponges cannot make food. They must eat other organisms to get nutrients, which is one reason that sponges are classified as animals.

Reading Check Why were sponges once thought to be plants?

Figure 9 *This red cup sponge is a simple animal.*

SECTION Review

Summary

- Most biologists recognize six kingdoms: Archaebacteria, Eubacteria, Protista, Fungi, Plantae, and Animalia.

- Archaebacteria live in extreme environments. Eubacteria live almost everywhere else.

- Plants, animals, fungi, and protists are eukaryotic organisms. Plants perform photosynthesis. Animals eat food and digest it inside their body. Fungi absorb nutrients from material that they break down outside of their body. Protists are organisms that don't fit in other kingdoms.

Using Key Terms

For each pair of terms, explain how the meanings of the terms differ.

1. *Archaebacteria* and *Eubacteria*

2. *Plantae* and *Fungi*

Understanding Key Ideas

3. Biological classification schemes change
   a. as new evidence and more kinds of organisms are discovered.
   b. every 100 years.
   c. when scientists disagree.
   d. only once.

4. Explain the different ways in which plants, fungi, and animals obtain nutrients.

5. Why are protists placed in their own kingdom?

6. Describe the six kingdoms.

Math Skills

7. A certain eubacterium can divide every 30 min. If you begin with 1 eubacterium, when will you have more than 1,000 eubacteria?

Critical Thinking

8. **Identifying Relationships** How are bacteria similar to fungi? How are fungi similar to animals?

9. **Analyzing Methods** Why do you think Linnaeus did not include classification kingdoms for categories of bacteria?

10. **Applying Concepts** The Venus' flytrap does not move around. It can make its own food by using photosynthesis. It can also trap insects and digest the insects to get nutrients. The flytrap also has a cell wall. Into which kingdom would you place the Venus' flytrap? What makes this organism unusual in the kingdom you chose?

SCiLINKS
Developed and maintained by the National Science Teachers Association

For a variety of links related to this chapter, go to www.scilinks.org

Topic: The Six Kingdoms
SciLinks code: HSM1397

Answer to Reading Check

Sponges don't have sense organs, and they usually can't move around.

CHAPTER RESOURCES

Chapter Resource File

- Section Quiz GENERAL
- Section Review GENERAL
- Vocabulary and Section Summary GENERAL
- Reinforcement Worksheet BASIC
- SciLinks Activity GENERAL

Answers to Section Review

1. Sample answer Archaebacteria live in extreme environments. Eubacteria are bacteria that usually live in environments that are not extreme.

2. Sample answer: The kingdom Plantae contains organisms that can make their own food. The kingdom Fungi contains organisms that can't make their own food.

3. a

4. Plants make food using the energy in sunlight. Fungi absorb nutrients from their surroundings after breaking them down with digestive juices. Animals eat plants and other animals to obtain food.

5. The kingdom Protista includes organisms that don't fit in the other kingdoms. Although protists are eukaryotes, they are not plants, animals, or fungi.

6. Sample answer: Archaebacteria includes prokaryotes that live in extreme environments. Eubacteria includes prokaryotes that live in soil, water, and other organisms. Protista includes eukaryotes don't fit into the other kingdoms. Fungi includes eukaryotic organisms that make spores, don't make their own food, and don't move. Plantae includes eukaryotes that use photosynthesis and have cells with cell walls. Animalia includes multicellular organisms that have cells without cell walls, can usually move around, and have specialized sense organs.

7. after 5 h

8. Sample answer: Bacteria and fungi are both decomposers; Fungi and animals are both unable to make their own food.

9. Sample answer: Linnaeus may not have had access to microscopes that could allow him to study bacteria.

10. Sample answer: Plantae; Most plants are not consumers.

Shape Island

Teacher's Notes

Time Required
One 45-minute class period

Lab Ratings

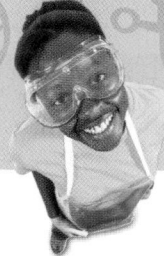

EASY —————————→ HARD

Teacher Prep 🧪
Student Set-Up 🧪
Concept Level 🧪🧪
Clean Up 🧪

Lab Notes

This lab will help students demonstrate an understanding of binomial nomenclature by using a key to assign scientific names to fictional organisms. After completing the lab, students should be able to explain the function of the scientific naming system. This chapter on classification uses the term *two-part scientific name* instead of *binomial nomenclature.* You may wish to introduce the latter here. This activity may be more successful if you review prefixes, suffixes, and root words briefly before beginning. Remind students that the genus name is capitalized but the species name is not and that both words are underlined or italicized.

Skills Practice Lab

Shape Island

OBJECTIVES

Classify organisms.

Name organisms.

You are a biologist exploring uncharted parts of the world to look for new animal species. You sailed for days across the ocean and finally found Shape Island hundreds of miles south of Hawaii. Shape Island has some very unusual organisms. The shape of each organism is a variation of a geometric shape. You have spent more than a year collecting and classifying specimens. You have been able to assign a two-part scientific name to most of the species that you have collected. Now, you must assign a two-part scientific name to each of the last 12 specimens collected before you begin your journey home.

Procedure

1. Draw each of the organisms pictured on the facing page. Beside each organism, draw a line for its name, as shown on the top left of the following page. The first organism pictured has already been named, but you must name the remaining 12. Use the glossary of Greek and Latin prefixes, suffixes, and root words in the table to help you name the organisms.

Greek and Latin roots, prefixes, and suffixes	Meaning
ankylos	angle
antennae	external sense organs
bi-	two
cyclo-	circular
macro-	large
micro-	small
mono-	one
peri-	around
-plast	body
-pod	foot
quad-	four
stoma	mouth
tri-	three
uro-	tail

Analyze Results

1. **Analyzing Results** If you gave species 1 a common name, such as *round-face-no-nose,* would any other scientist know which of the newly discovered organisms you were referring to? Explain. How many others have a round face and no nose?

2. **Organizing Data** Describe two characteristics that are shared by all of your newly discovered specimens.

Maurine Marchani
Raymond Park Middle School
Indianapolis, Indiana

CHAPTER RESOURCES

Chapter Resource File

- Datasheet for Chapter Lab
- Lab Notes and Answers

Technology

 Classroom Videos
- Lab Video

- The Voyage of the USS *Adventure*

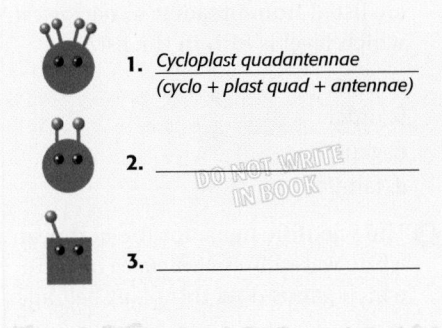

1. *Cycloplast quadantennae*
   (cyclo + plast quad + antennae)

2. _DO NOT WRITE IN BOOK_

3. _____

Draw Conclusions

❸ **Applying Conclusions** One more organism exists on Shape Island, but you have not been able to capture it. However, your supplies are running out, and you must start sailing for home. You have had a good look at the unusual animal and can draw it in detail. Draw an animal that is different from all of the others, and give it a two-part scientific name.

Applying Your Data

Look up the scientific names *Mertensia virginica* and *Porcellio scaber.* Answer the following questions as they apply to each organism: Is the organism a plant or an animal? How many common names does the organism have? How many scientific names does it have?

Think of the name of your favorite fruit or vegetable. Find out if it has other common names, and find out its two-part scientific name.

1

2

3

4

5

6

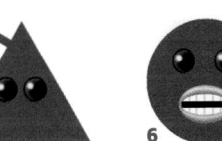
7

8

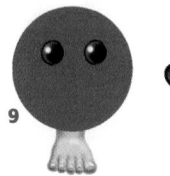
9

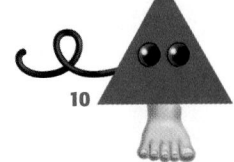
10

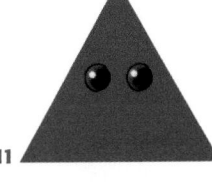
11

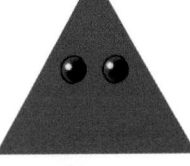
12

13

CHAPTER RESOURCES

Workbooks

📖 **EcoLabs & Field Activities**
• Water Wigglers GENERAL

📖 **Long-Term Projects & Research Ideas**
• The Panda Mystery ADVANCED

Procedure

1. Students' answers may vary, but students should demonstrate an understanding of the key provided. Each name should consist of two words. The first describes the organism generally, and the second describes it more specifically. Sample answer:
   1. *Cycloplast quadantennae*
   2. *Cycloplast biantennae*
   3. *Quadankylosplast monoantenna*
   4. *Quadankylosplast bipod*
   5. *Triankylosplast triantennae*
   6. *Cycloplast stoma*
   7. *Triankylosplast stoma*
   8. *Quadankylosplast periantennae*
   9. *Cycloplast monopod*
   10. *Triankylosplast uromonopod*
   11. *Triankylos macroplast*
   12. *Quadankylos microplast*
   13. *Cycloplast uro*

Analyze the Results

1. no; Five species have round faces and lack noses.

2. Sample answer: All have geometric shapes and two eyes. All are the same color. All are animals. All are living organisms.

Draw Conclusions

3. Answers may vary. Students should demonstrate an understanding of binomial nomenclature.

Applying Your Data

Mertensia virginica, commonly known as the Virginia bluebell, is a plant; Other common names for this species include Virginia-cowslip, Roanoke-bells, lungwort, and oysterleaf. These wildflowers are found in April and May in shady areas, mostly in moist spots near streams. Flower buds are pink but turn blue when the flower is fully opened. This wildflower is very common in western Kentucky. *Porcellio scaber* is a species of wood louse. Common names for *Porcellio scaber* include dooryard sowbug and common rough woodlouse. Wood lice are crustaceans related to shrimps, crabs, and lobsters, and they belong to a class of arthropods called *Isopoda.*

Chapter Review

Assignment Guide

Section	Questions
1	1, 4, 6–9, 12–13, 15, 17–18, 20–23
2	2–3, 5, 10–11, 14, 16, 19

ANSWERS

Using Key Terms

1. taxonomy
2. Archaebacteria
3. Animalia
4. classification
5. Eubacteria

Understanding Key Ideas

6. a
7. d
8. a
9. b
10. b
11. c

USING KEY TERMS

Complete each of the following sentences by choosing the correct term from the word bank.

Animalia	Protista
Eubacteria	Plantae
Archaebacteria	classification
taxonomy	

1 Linnaeus founded the science of ___.

2 Bacteria that live in extreme environments are in the kingdom ___.

3 Complex multicellular organisms that can usually move around and respond to their environment are in the kingdom ___.

4 A system of ___ can help group animals into categories.

5 Prokaryotes that are not archaebacteria are in the kingdom ___.

UNDERSTANDING KEY IDEAS

Multiple Choice

6 Scientists classify organisms by
  a. arranging the organisms in orderly groups.
  b. giving the organisms many common names.
  c. deciding whether the organisms are useful.
  d. using only existing categories of classification.

7 When the seven levels of classification are listed from broadest to narrowest, which level is fifth in the list?
  a. class
  b. order
  c. genus
  d. family

8 The scientific name for the European white waterlily is *Nymphaea alba*. To which genus does this plant belong?
  a. *Nymphaea*   c. water lily
  b. *alba*   d. alba lily

9 *Animalia, Protista, Fungi, Archaebacteria, Eubacteria,* and *Plantae* are the
  a. scientific names of different organisms.
  b. names of kingdoms.
  c. levels of classification.
  d. scientists who organized taxonomy.

10 Bacteria that live in your intestines are classified in the kingdom
  a. Protista.   c. Archaebacteria.
  b. Eubacteria.   d. Fungi.

11 What kind of organism thrives in hot springs and other extreme environments?
  a. fungus   c. archaebacterium
  b. eubacterium   d. protist

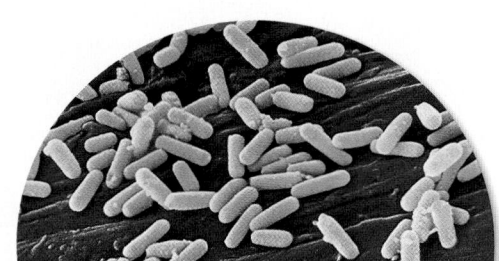

Short Answer

12 Why is the use of scientific names important in biology?

13 What kind of evidence is used by modern taxonomists to classify organisms based on evolutionary relationships?

14 Is a eubacterium a type of eukaryote? Explain your answer.

15 Scientists used to classify organisms as either plants or animals. Why doesn't that classification system work?

CRITICAL THINKING

16 **Concept Mapping** Use the following terms to create a concept map: *kingdom, fern, lizard, Animalia, Fungi, algae, Protista, Plantae,* and *mushroom.*

17 **Analyzing Methods** Explain how the levels of classification depend on the similarities and differences between organisms.

18 **Making Inferences** Explain why two species that belong to the same genus, such as white oak (*Quercus alba*) and cork oak (*Quercus suber*), also belong to the same family.

19 **Identifying Relationships** What characteristic do the members of all six kingdoms have in common?

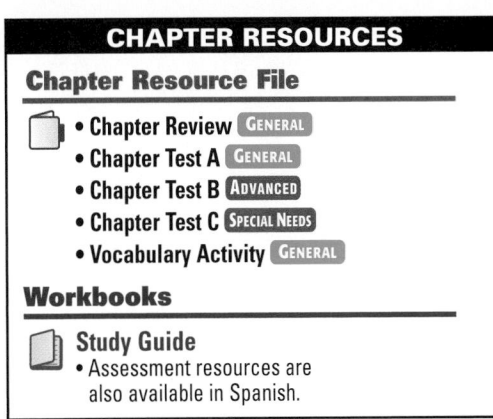

INTERPRETING GRAPHICS

Use the branching diagram of selected primates below to answer the questions that follow.

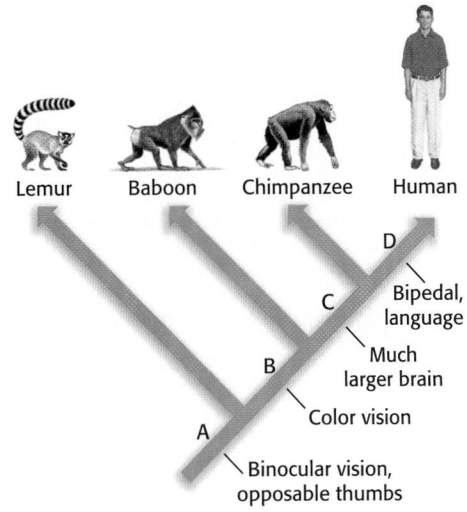

20 Which primate is the closest relative to the common ancestor of all primates?

21 Which primate shares the most traits with humans?

22 Do both lemurs and humans have the characteristics listed at point D? Explain your answer.

23 What characteristic do baboons have that lemurs do not have? Explain your answer.

CHAPTER RESOURCES

Chapter Resource File

- Chapter Review **GENERAL**
- Chapter Test A **GENERAL**
- Chapter Test B **ADVANCED**
- Chapter Test C **SPECIAL NEEDS**
- Vocabulary Activity **GENERAL**

Workbooks

Study Guide
- Assessment resources are also available in Spanish.

---

12. Sample answer: Each species is unique, and scientific names make it possible for scientists to know specifically which organism is being discussed without the confusion of common names.

13. Taxonomists classify organisms based on their shared characteristics.

14. no, A eubacterium is a prokaryote because it does not have a nucleus.

15. Sample answer: Some organisms, such as slime molds and mushrooms, have characteristics that neither plants nor animals have.

Critical Thinking

16. 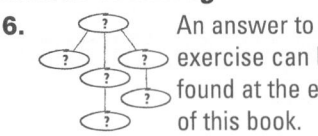 An answer to this exercise can be found at the end of this book.

17. Sample answer: Each level of classification groups organisms according to characteristics they share. At broader levels of classification, such as kingdom and phylum, organisms share fewer characteristics than they do at more specific levels, such as genus and species.

18. Sample answer: The family level of classification contains genera and all the species in those genera. All of the *Quercus* genera are in the same family because of shared characteristics.

19. Sample answer: All members of the six kingdoms are living organisms. They all have DNA.

Interpreting Graphics

20. lemur

21. chimpanzee

22. no; Lemurs branched off between points A and B.

23. Baboons have color vision, but lemurs do not. Color vision appears on the diagram after lemurs branched off and before baboons branched off.

Standardized Test Preparation

Teacher's Note

To provide practice under more realistic testing conditions, give students 20 minutes to answer all of the questions in this Standardized Test Preparation.

MISCONCEPTION ///ALERT

Answers to the standardized test preparation can help you identify student misconceptions and misunderstandings.

READING

Passage 1

1. A
2. I
3. C

✚ **TEST DOCTOR**

Question 1: Students selecting an incorrect answer may benefit from a review of how context can help a reader understand new terms. The words *equally* and *categories* offer clues to the reader that the word *distributed* indicates that the organisms are divided into the categories.

Question 3: Answer B is arguably true, but it is not stated in the passage. The correct answer is found in the last sentence of the paragraph.

READING

Read each of the passages below. Then, answer the questions that follow each passage.

Passage 1 When organizing life on Earth into categories, we must remember that organisms are not equally <u>distributed</u> throughout the categories of our classification system. We often think of Earth's living things as only the plants and animals that live on Earth's surface. However, the largest kingdoms in terms of the number of individuals and total mass are the kingdoms Archaebacteria and Eubacteria. And a common home of bacteria may be deep within the Earth's crust.

1. In the passage, what does *distributed* mean?
   A divided
   B important
   C visible
   D variable

2. According to the passage, what are most of the organisms living on Earth?
   F plants
   G animals
   H fungi
   I bacteria

3. Which of the following statements is a fact according to the passage?
   A All organisms are equally distributed over Earth's surface.
   B Plants are the most important organisms on Earth.
   C Many bacteria may live deep within Earth's crust.
   D Bacteria are equally distributed over Earth's surface.

Passage 2 When you think of an animal, what do you imagine? You may think of a dog, a cat, or a parrot. All of those organisms are animals. But the animal kingdom also includes some <u>members</u> that might surprise you, such as worms, insects, <u>corals</u>, and sponges.

1. In the passage, what is coral?
   A a kind of animal
   B a kind of insect
   C a color similar to pink
   D an organism found in lakes and streams

2. What can you infer from the passage?
   F All members of the animal kingdom are visible.
   G Parrots make good pets.
   H Not all members of the animal kingdom have DNA.
   I Members of the animal kingdom come in many shapes and sizes.

3. Which of the following can you infer from the passage?
   A Worms and corals make good pets.
   B Corals and cats have some traits in common.
   C All organisms are animals.
   D Worms, corals, insects, and sponges are in the same family.

4. In the passage, what does *members* mean?
   F teammates
   G limbs
   H individuals admitted to a club
   I components

Passage 2

1. A
2. I
3. B
4. I

✚ **TEST DOCTOR**

Question 2: Students may struggle with the task of inferring. None of the answers offered are explicitly stated in the passage. But the fourth sentence links corals, sponges, worms, and insects to dogs, cats, and parrots. Because the passage indicates that both groups are in the animal kingdom, students can conclude that all the organisms mentioned share characteristics.

The Venn diagrams below show two classification systems. Use the diagrams to answer the questions that follow.

Classification system A

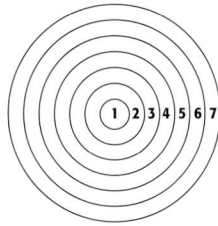

Classification system B

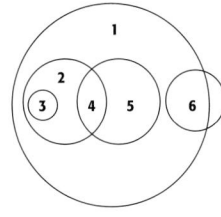

1. For Classification system A, which of the following statements is true?

A All organisms in group 6 are in group 7.

B All organisms in group 5 are in group 4.

C All organisms in group 6 are in group 1.

D All organisms in group 2 are in group 1.

2. For Classification system A, which of the following statements is true?

F All organisms in group 3 are in group 2.

G All organisms in group 3 are in group 4.

H All organisms in group 3 are in group 1.

I All organisms in group 3 are in every other group.

3. For Classification system B, which of the following statements is true?

A All organisms in group 1 are in group 6.

B All organisms in group 6 are in group 1.

C All organisms in group 3 are in group 1.

D All organisms in group 2 are in group 5.

4. For Classification system B, which of the following statements is true?

F All organisms in group 4 are in group 1, 2, and 5.

G All organisms in group 4 are in groups 3 and 5.

H All organisms in group 4 are in groups 5 and 6.

I All organisms in group 4 are in groups 1, 5, and 6.

5. In Classification system B, which group contains organisms that are not in group 1?

A 2

B 4

C 5

D 6

MATH

Read each question below, and choose the best answer.

1. Scientists estimate that millions of species have not yet been discovered and classified. About 1.8 million species have been discovered and classified. If scientists think that this 1.8 million makes up only 10% of the total number of species on Earth, how many species do scientists think exist on Earth?

A 180 million

B 18 million

C 1.8 million

D 180,000

2. Sequoia trees can grow to more than 90 m in height. There are 3.28 feet in 1 meter. How many feet are in 90 m?

F 27.4 ft

G 95.2 ft

H 270 ft

I 295.2 ft

Standardized Test Preparation

---

1. A

2. G

3. C

4. F

5. D

 TEST DOCTOR

Question 1: In Classification system A, the larger number contains all of the organisms in the groups smaller than it. So, the correct answer to this question will have to be the answer that lists a smaller group in a larger group. Answer option A is the only answer with that characteristic.

Question 5: In Classification system B, the only organisms that are not in group 1 are those outside the circle marking group 1. The only organisms outside that circle are in group 6.

MATH

1. B

2. I

 TEST DOCTOR

Question 1: Students who select incorrect answers here may benefit from a review of how percentages are calculated. Showing students how to transfer the written problem into an equation may help them solve for the correct variable.

CHAPTER RESOURCES

Chapter Resource File

 • Standardized Test Preparation GENERAL

State Resources

 For specific resources for your state, visit **go.hrw.com** and type in the keyword **HSMSTR.**

Scientific Debate

Background

A 1997 find in Argentina gives some support to the proponents of the birds-from-dinosaurs hypothesis. A 6 ft long fossil found in Argentina shows the most birdlike dinosaur ever discovered. Its skeletal structure indicates it had arms that could flap and fold like wings. It had a birdlike pelvis as well. The sediments in which the dinosaur fossil was found suggest that it is 90 million years old. But this fossil, too, has fueled the debate. Some experts say the dinosaur existed long after the development of modern birds. Birds, they argue, evolved from another line of reptiles.

Scientific Discovery

Background

In basic research, entomologists study insect classification, distribution, and behavior. Entomologists work with farmers and ranchers to help them produce crops or livestock more efficiently. They may also work in forestry to protect trees from insect pests. Forensic entomologists use their knowledge of insect physiology, behavior, and distribution to help law enforcement officials solve crimes or resolve legal issues.

Science in Action

Scientific Debate

Birds and Dinosaurs

Did birds evolve from dinosaurs? Some scientists think that birds evolved from small, carnivorous dinosaurs such as *Velociraptor* about 115 million to 150 million years ago. This idea is based on similarities of modern birds and these small dinosaurs. These similarities include the size, shape, and number of toes and "fingers," the location and shape of the breastbone and shoulder, and the presence of a hollow bone structure. Many scientists find this evidence convincing.

However, some scientists think that birds developed 100 million years before *Velociraptor* and its relatives did. These scientists point out that *Velociraptor* and its relatives were ground dwellers and were the wrong shape and size for flying.

Math ACTIVITY

Velociraptor lived between 115 million and 150 million years ago. Find the average of these two numbers. Use that average to answer the following questions: How many weeks ago did *Velociraptor* live on Earth? How many days ago did *Velociraptor* live on Earth?

Scientific Discovery

A New Insect Order

In 2001, Oliver Zompro was studying a fossil insect preserved in amber. Although the fossil insect resembled a grasshopper or a walking stick, it was unique and could not be classified in the same group as either one. Zompro wondered if he might be seeing a new type of insect or an insect that was now thought to be extinct. The fossil insect was less than 4 cm long. Its spiny appearance earned the insect the nickname "gladiator." The gladiator bug that Zompro discovered is so unusual that it cannot be classified in any of the 30 existing orders of insects. Instead, the gladiator bug constitutes its own new order, which has been named *Mantophasmatodea*.

Language Arts ACTIVITY

WRITING SKILL Give the gladiator bug a new nickname. Write a short essay about why you chose that particular name for the insect.

Answer to Math Activity

115 million years + 150 million years =
265 million years,
265 million years ÷ 2 =
132.5 million years;

132.5 million years × 52 weeks/year =
927.5 million weeks;

927.5 million weeks × 7 days/week =
6.49 billion days

Answer to Language Arts Activity

Nicknames may vary, but essays should all give clear reasons for the name chosen for the insect.

Michael Fay

Crossing Africa Finding and classifying wild animals takes a great deal of perseverance. Just ask Michael Fay, who spent 15 months crossing 2,000 miles of uninhabited rain forest in the Congo River Basin of West Africa. He used video, photography, and old-fashioned note taking to record the types of animals and vegetation that he encountered along the way.

To find and classify wild animals, Fay often had to think like an animal. When coming across a group of monkeys swinging high above him in the emerald green canopy, Fay would greet the monkeys with his imitation of the crowned eagle's high-pitched, whistling cry. When the monkeys responded with their own distinctive call, Fay could identify exactly what species they were and would jot it down in one of his 87 waterproof notebooks. Fay also learned other tricks, such as staying downwind of an elephant to get as close to the elephant as possible. He could then identify its size, its age, and the length of its tusks.

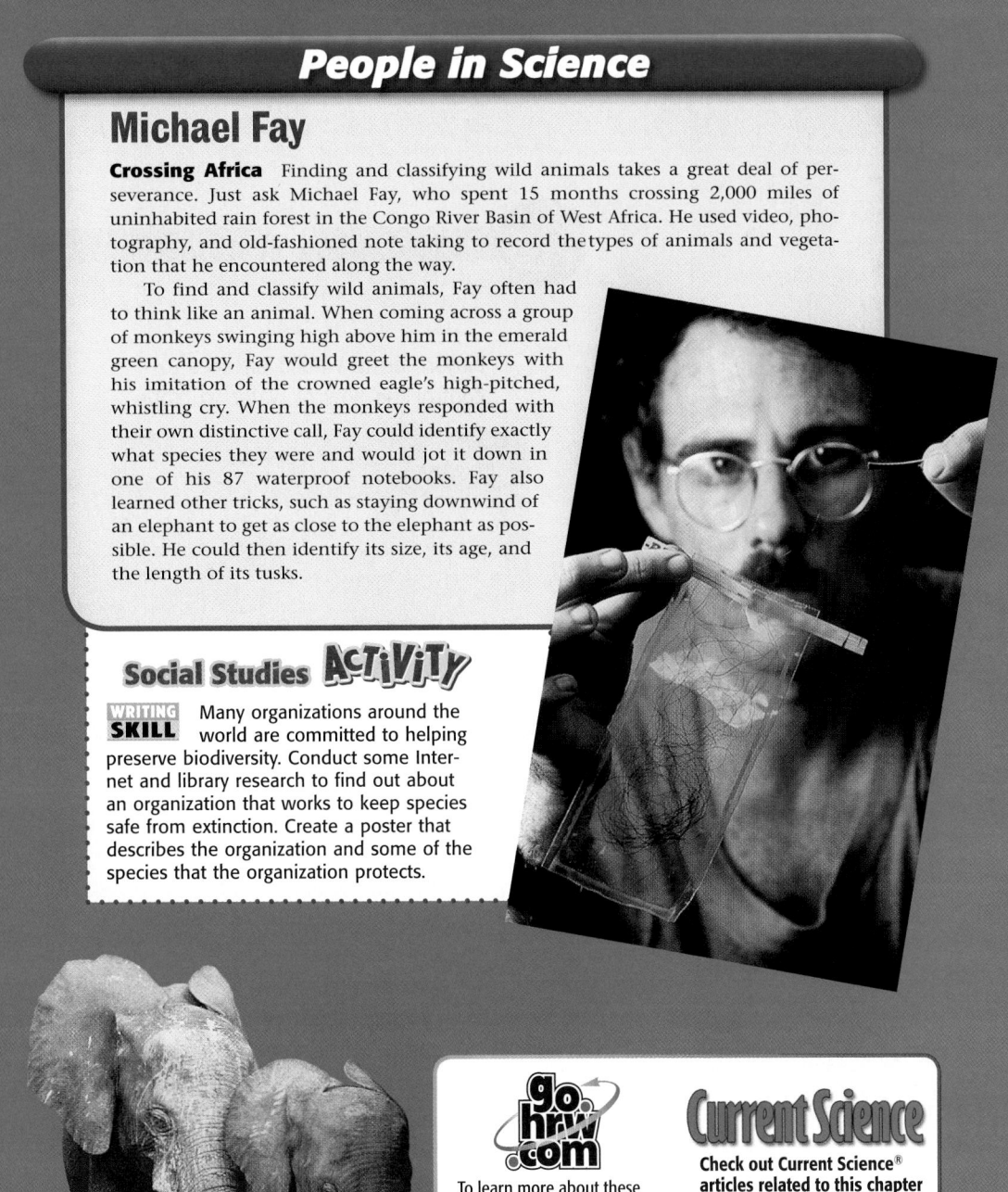

Social Studies ACTIVITY

WRITING SKILL Many organizations around the world are committed to helping preserve biodiversity. Conduct some Internet and library research to find out about an organization that works to keep species safe from extinction. Create a poster that describes the organization and some of the species that the organization protects.

go.hrw.com
To learn more about these Science in Action topics, visit go.hrw.com and type in the keyword **HL5CLSF**.

Current Science
Check out Current Science® articles related to this chapter by visiting go.hrw.com. Just type in the keyword **HL5CS09**.

Simple Organisms, Fungi, and Plants

Do you know how important plants are? Plants provide oxygen and food for other living things.

Throughout history, people have been trying to under-stand plants. In this unit, you will join them. You'll also learn about, some other fascinating organ-isms—bacteria, protists, and fungi. Some of these organisms cause disease, but others provide food and medicines. Read on, and be amazed!

Around 250

Mayan farmers build terraces to control the flow of water to crops.

1864

Louis Pasteur uses heat to eliminate microbes. This process is later called *pasteurization*.

1897

Beatrix Potter, the author of *The Tale of Peter Rabbit*, completes her collection of 270 watercolors of fungi. Today, she is considered an expert in mycology, the study of fungi.

1971

Ananda Chakrabarty uses genetics to design bacteria that can break down oil in oil spills.

1580

Prospero Alpini discovers that plants have both male structures and female structures.

1683

Anton van Leeuwenhoek is the first person to describe bacteria.

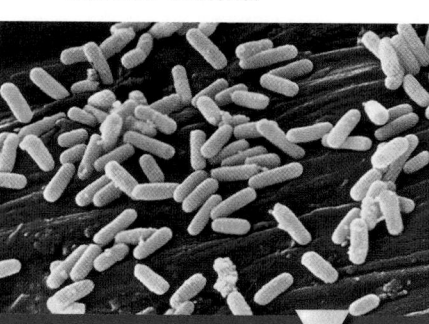

E. coli under an electron microscope

1763

Joseph Kolreuter studies orchid pollination and discovers that both parent plants contribute traits to the offspring.

1898

Martinus Beijerinck gives the name *virus* to infectious material that is smaller than a bacterium.

1928

Alexander Fleming observes that certain molds can eliminate bacterial growth, and he discovers penicillin.

1955

A vaccine for the polio virus developed by Dr. Jonas Salk becomes widely used.

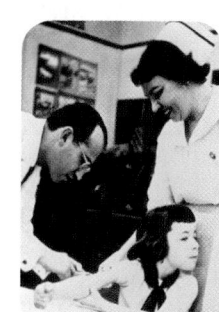

1983

HIV, the virus responsible for AIDS, is isolated.

1995

An outbreak of the deadly Ebola virus occurs in Zaire.

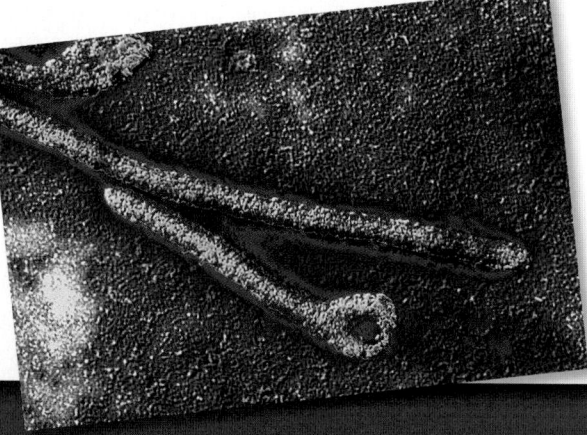

Ebola virus

2002

An international team decodes the DNA sequences for both the protist that causes malaria and the mosquito that carries this protist. As a result, the door to more-effective antimalaria drugs is opened.

10

Bacteria and Viruses
Chapter Planning Guide

Compression guide:
To shorten instruction because of time limitations, omit Section 2.

OBJECTIVES	LABS, DEMONSTRATIONS, AND ACTIVITIES	TECHNOLOGY RESOURCES
PACING • 90 min pp. 244–251 **Chapter Opener**	SE **Start-up Activity**, p. 245 GENERAL	OSP **Parent Letter** ■ GENERAL CD **Student Edition on CD-ROM** CD **Guided Reading Audio CD** ■ TR **Chapter Starter Transparency*** VID **Brain Food Video Quiz**
Section 1 Bacteria • Describe the characteristics of bacteria. • Explain how bacteria reproduce. • Compare and contrast eubacteria and archaebacteria.	SE **Quick Lab** Spying on Spirilla, p. 247 GENERAL CRF **Datasheet for Quick Lab*** TE **Connection Activity** Math, p. 248 GENERAL TE **Activity** Bacteria in the Air, p. 249 GENERAL SE **Connection to Language Arts** Colorful Names, p. 250 GENERAL	CRF **Lesson Plans*** TR **Bellringer Transparency*** TR **The Most Common Shapes of Bacteria*** TR **Binary Fission*** TR **LINK TO PHYSICAL SCIENCE** Parts of an Atom*** CRF **SciLinks Activity*** GENERAL
PACING • 90 min pp. 252–255 **Section 2 Bacteria's Role in the World** • Explain how life on Earth depends on bacteria. • List three ways bacteria are useful to people. • Describe two ways in which bacteria can be harmful to people.	SE **School-to-Home Activity** Make a Meal Plan, p. 253 GENERAL TE **Connection Activity** Real World, p. 253 GENERAL SE **Inquiry Lab** Aunt Flossie and the Intruder, p. 260 GENERAL CRF **Datasheet for Chapter Lab*** LB **EcoLabs & Field Activities** Ditch's Brew*** GENERAL LB **Labs You Can Eat** Bacterial Buddies*** GENERAL LB **Inquiry Labs** It's an Invasion!*** GENERAL LB **Long-Term Projects & Research Ideas** Bacteria to the Rescue!*** ADVANCED	CRF **Lesson Plans*** TR **Bellringer Transparency*** TE **Internet Activity** p. 258 GENERAL VID **Lab Videos for Life Science** CD **Interactive Explorations CD-ROM** Scope It Out! GENERAL
PACING • 45 min pp. 256–259 **Section 3 Viruses** • Explain how viruses are similar to and different from living things. • List the four major virus shapes. • Describe the two kinds of viral reproduction.	TE **Demonstration** Flame Tulips, p. 256 GENERAL TE **Connection Activity** History, p. 257 GENERAL SE **Connection to Chemistry** Viral Crystals, p. 258 GENERAL SE **Science in Action** Math, Social Studies, and Language Arts Activities, p. 266–267 GENERAL SE **Model-Making Lab** Viral Decorations, p. 772 GENERAL CRF **Datasheet for LabBook***	CRF **Lesson Plans*** TR **Bellringer Transparency*** TR **The Basic Shapes of Viruses*** TR **The Lytic Cycle***

PACING • 90 min

CHAPTER REVIEW, ASSESSMENT, AND STANDARDIZED TEST PREPARATION

CRF **Vocabulary Activity*** GENERAL
SE **Chapter Review**, pp. 262–263 GENERAL
CRF **Chapter Review*** ■ GENERAL
CRF **Chapter Tests A*** ■ GENERAL, **B*** ADVANCED, **C*** SPECIAL NEEDS
SE **Standardized Test Preparation**, pp. 264–265 GENERAL
CRF **Standardized Test Preparation*** GENERAL
CRF **Performance-Based Assessment*** GENERAL
OSP **Test Generator** GENERAL
CRF **Test Item Listing*** GENERAL

Online and Technology Resources

Visit **go.hrw.com** for a variety of free resources related to this textbook. Enter the keyword **HL5VIR**.

Students can access interactive problem-solving help and active visual concept development with the *Holt Science and Technology* Online Edition available at **www.hrw.com**.

 Guided Reading Audio CD
Also in Spanish

A direct reading of each chapter for auditory learners, reluctant readers, and Spanish-speaking students.

 Science Tutor CD-ROM

Excellent for remediation and test practice.

SKILLS DEVELOPMENT RESOURCES	SECTION REVIEW AND ASSESSMENT	STANDARDS CORRELATIONS
SE Pre-Reading Activity, p. 244 `GENERAL` **OSP** Science Puzzlers, Twisters & Teasers* `GENERAL`		National Science Education Standards UCP 2; SAI 1; LS 1b, 1c, 2a, 3a, 3b, 4b
CRF Directed Reading A* ■ `BASIC`, B* `SPECIAL NEEDS` **CRF** Vocabulary and Section Summary* ■ `GENERAL` **SE** Reading Strategy Prediction Guide, p. 246 `GENERAL` **TE** Inclusion Strategies, p. 247 **TE** Reading Strategy Prediction Guide, p. 248 `BASIC` **CRF** Reinforcement Worksheet Bacteria Bonanza* `GENERAL`	**SE** Reading Checks, pp. 246, 248 `GENERAL` **TE** Homework, p. 247 `ADVANCED` **TE** Reteaching, p. 250 `BASIC` **TE** Quiz, p. 250 `GENERAL` **TE** Alternative Assessment, p. 250 `GENERAL` **SE** Section Review,* p. 251 ■ `GENERAL` **CRF** Section Quiz* ■ `GENERAL`	UCP 1, 3, 5; SAI 1; LS 1b, 1c, 2a, 3a, 3b, 4b
CRF Directed Reading A* ■ `BASIC`, B* `SPECIAL NEEDS` **CRF** Vocabulary and Section Summary* ■ `GENERAL` **SE** Reading Strategy Reading Organizer, p. 252 `GENERAL` **TE** Inclusion Strategies, p. 254 **CRF** Critical Thinking Bacterial Blastoff* `ADVANCED`	**SE** Reading Checks, pp. 252, 254 `GENERAL` **TE** Reteaching, p. 254 `BASIC` **TE** Quiz, p. 254 `GENERAL` **TE** Alternative Assessment, p. 254 `ADVANCED` **SE** Section Review,* p. 255 ■ `GENERAL` **CRF** Section Quiz* ■ `GENERAL`	UCP 2, 3, 4, 5; ST 1, 2; SPSP 5; HNS 3; LS 1f; *Chapter Lab:* UCP 2; SAI 1, 2; LS 1c
CRF Directed Reading A* ■ `BASIC`, B* `SPECIAL NEEDS` **CRF** Vocabulary and Section Summary* ■ `GENERAL` **SE** Reading Strategy Discussion, p. 256 `GENERAL` **SE** Math Practice Sizing Up a Virus, p. 257 `GENERAL` **MS** Math Skills for Science Multiplying Whole Numbers* `GENERAL` **CRF** Reinforcement Worksheet The Lytic Cycle* `BASIC`	**SE** Reading Checks, pp. 257, 258 `GENERAL` **TE** Reteaching, p. 258 `BASIC` **TE** Quiz, p. 258 `GENERAL` **TE** Alternative Assessment, p. 258 `GENERAL` **SE** Section Review,* p. 259 ■ `GENERAL` **TE** Homework, p. 259 `ADVANCED` **CRF** Section Quiz* ■ `GENERAL`	UCP 1, 2, 5; SAI 1, 2; SPSP 4, 5; LS 1f, 2a

One-Stop Planner® CD-ROM

This convenient CD-ROM includes:
- Lab Materials QuickList Software
- Holt Calendar Planner
- Customizable Lesson Plans
- Printable Worksheets
- ExamView® Test Generator

cnnstudentnews.com

Find the latest news, lesson plans, and activities related to important scientific events.

SCI LINKS.
NSTA

www.scilinks.org

Maintained by the **National Science Teachers Association.** See Chapter Enrichment pages for a complete list of topics.

Current Science®

Check out *Current Science* articles and activities by visiting the HRW Web site at **go.hrw.com.** Just type in the keyword **HL5CS10T.**

Classroom Videos

- **Lab Videos** demonstrate the chapter lab.
- **Brain Food Video Quizzes** help students review the chapter material.
- **CNN Videos** bring science into your students' daily life.

Visual Resources

CHAPTER STARTER TRANSPARENCY

Bacteria and Viruses — CHAPTER STARTER

Imagine . . .

It was a dark and stormy night—the kind of night where bizarre things happen. Suzanne sat quietly in her bedroom reading her science book. She tried to concentrate, but the constant patter of rain against her window soon lulled her to sleep.

Thunder roared through the air. Suzanne looked down at her hands and suddenly screamed in horror. She was covered from head to toe with creeping, crawling creatures! They clung to her hair, her back, and even her eyelashes! There was nowhere she could go to escape them!

Suzanne woke with a start. What a strange dream! Were these creatures real? Then she remembered what she had just read in her science book. The things she had dreamed about were called bacteria and viruses.

Bacteria and viruses are all around you. Suzanne, just as they are all around you. They are in the air you breathe and the food you eat. They are inside your body and all over the ground. Most of them are so small that you can only be seen with a high-powered microscope. Despite their tiny size, bacteria and viruses have a huge impact on the world around you. You'll read all about them in this chapter.

BELLRINGER TRANSPARENCIES

Bacteria and Viruses — BELLRINGER TRANSPARENCY

Section: Bacteria
If you can't see bacteria without a microscope, how do you know when you have come into contact with them? What kinds of things do you do to avoid bacteria? Do you know of any foods that have *good* bacteria in them?

Write your answers in your **science journal.**

Section: Bacteria's Role in the World
Are harmful bacteria more of a problem or less of a problem to people now than they were 200 years ago? Name some major historical events involving the spread of bacteria. How would your life change if you had to worry about getting clean water each day?

Record your answers in your **science journal.**

TEACHING TRANSPARENCIES

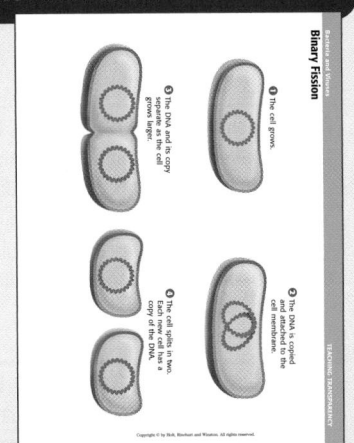

The Most Common Shapes of Bacteria

Bacilli (buh-SIL-y) are rod shaped. They have a large surface area, which helps them take in nutrients. But a large surface area can cause them to dry out easily.

Cocci (KAHK-sy) are round. They do not dry out as quickly as rod-shaped bacteria.

Spirilla (spie-RIL-uh) are long and spiral shaped. They use flagella at both ends to move like a corkscrew.

Binary Fission

1. The DNA and its copy separate as the cell grows larger.

2. The cell grows.

3. The cell splits in two. Each new cell has a copy of the DNA.

TEACHING TRANSPARENCIES

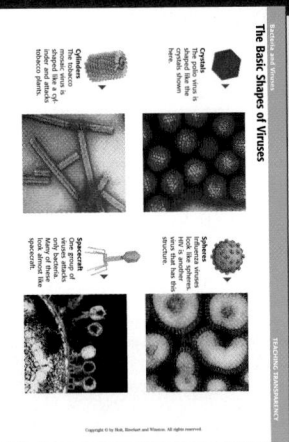

The Basic Shapes of Viruses

Cylinders The tobacco mosaic virus is shaped like a cylinder and attacks tobacco plants.

Crystals The polio virus is shaped like the crystals shown here.

Spacecraft One group of viruses attacks only bacteria. Many of these look almost like spacecraft.

Spheres Some viruses look like spheres. The influenza viruses that give you the flu share this structure.

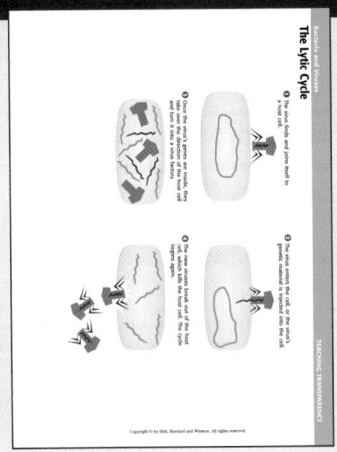

The Lytic Cycle

1. The new virus body and gene itself to a host cell.

2. Once the virus's genes are inside, they take over the direction of the host cell and turn it into a virus factory.

3. The new viruses influence use the host cell, which breaks the host cell. The new viruses break out of the host cell, ready to infect other cells. Then the cycle begins again.

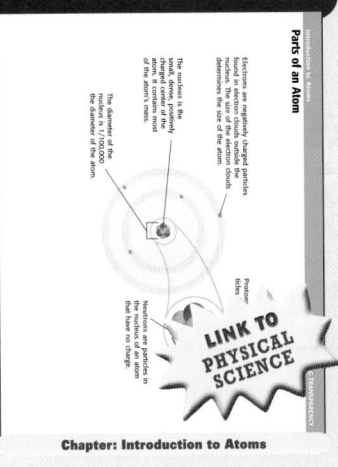

Parts of an Atom

The nucleus is the small, densely packed, positively charged center of the atom. It contains most of the atom's mass.

Electrons are negatively charged particles found in electron clouds outside the nucleus. The size of the electron clouds determines the size of the atom.

The diameter of the nucleus is 1/100,000 of the diameter of the atom.

Protons

Neutrons are particles in that atom that have no charge.

LINK TO PHYSICAL SCIENCE

Chapter: Introduction to Atoms

CONCEPT MAPPING TRANSPARENCY

Bacteria and Viruses — CONCEPT MAPPING TRANSPARENCY

Use the following terms to complete the concept map below:
bacteria, archaebacteria, decomposers, eubacteria, prokaryotes, nucleus, consumers, producers

are divided into two kingdoms

which means they do not contain a

which are classified by the way they get food into

which make their own food

which obtain nutrients from other organisms and may be

parasites

Planning Resources

LESSON PLANS

Lesson Plan — SAMPLE

Section: Waves

Pacing
Regular Schedule: with lab(s):2 days   without lab(s)1 day
Block Schedule: with lab(s):1 1/2 days   without lab(s)1 day

Objectives
1. Relate the seven properties of life to a living organism.
2. Describe seven themes that can help you to organize what you learn about biology.
3. Identify the tiny structures that make up all living organisms.
4. Differentiate between reproduction and heredity and between metabolism and homeostasis.

National Science Education Standards Covered
LSInter1:Cells have particular structures that underlie their functions.
LSMat1:Most cell functions involve chemical reactions.
LSBeh1:Cells store and use information to guide their functions.
UCP1:Cell functions are regulated.
SI1: Cells can differentiate and form complete multicellular organisms.
PS1:Species evolve over time.
ESS1: The great diversity of organisms is the result of more than 3.5 billion years of evolution.
ESS2: Natural selection and its evolutionary consequences provide a scientific explanation for the fossil record of ancient life forms as well as for the striking molecular similarities observed among the diverse species of living organisms.
ST1: The millions of different species of plants, animals, and microorganisms that live on Earth today are related by descent from common ancestors.
ST2: The energy for life primarily comes from the sun.
SPSP1: The complexity and organization of organisms accommodates the need for obtaining, transforming, transporting, releasing, and eliminating the matter and energy used to sustain the organism.
SPSP4: Matter and energy flows through different levels of organization of living systems—cells, organs, communities—and between living systems and the physical environment, chemical elements in different ways.
HNS1: Organisms have behavioral responses to internal changes and to external stimuli.

PARENT LETTER

SAMPLE

Dear Parent,

Your son's or daughter's science class will soon begin exploring the chapter entitled "The World of Physical Science." In this chapter, students will learn about how the scientific method applies to the world of physical science and the role of physical science in the world. By the end of the chapter, students should demonstrate a clear understanding of the chapter's main ideas and be able to discuss the following topics:

1. physical science is the study of energy and matter (Section 1)
2. the role of physical science in the world around them (Section 1)
3. careers that rely on physical science (Section 1)
4. the steps used in the scientific method (Section 2)
5. examples of technology (Section 2)
6. how the scientific method is used to answer questions and solve problems (Section 2)
7. how our knowledge of science changes over time (Section 2)
8. how models represent real objects or systems (Section 3)
9. examples of different ways models are used in science (Section 3)
10. the importance of the International System of Units (Section 4)
11. the appropriate units to use for particular measurements (Section 4)
12. how area and density are derived quantities (Section 4)

Questions to Ask Along the Way

You can help your son or daughter learn about these topics by asking interesting questions such as the following:

• What are some surprising careers that use physical science?
• What is a characteristic of a good hypothesis?
• When is it a good idea to use a model?
• Why do Americans measure things in terms of inches and yards and meters ?

ALSO IN SPANISH

TEST ITEM LISTING

TEST ITEM LISTING
The World of Science — SAMPLE

MULTIPLE CHOICE

1. A limitation of models is that
a. they are large enough to see.
b. they do not act exactly like the things that they model.
c. they are smaller than the things that they model.
d. they model unfamiliar things.
Answer: B   Difficulty: 1   Section: 3   Objective: 2

2. The length 10 m is equal to
a. 100 cm.   c. 10,000 mm.
b. 1,000 cm.   d. Both (b) and (c)
Answer: D   Difficulty: 1   Section: 3   Objective: 2

3. To be valid, a hypothesis must be
a. testable.   c. made into a test.
b. supported by evidence.   d. Both (a) and (b)
Answer: D   Difficulty: 1   Section: 2   Objective: 2 | 1

4. The statement "Sheila has a stain on her shirt" is an example of a(n)
a. law.   c. observation.
b. hypothesis.   d. prediction.
Answer: B   Difficulty: 1   Section: 2   Objective: 2

5. A hypothesis is often developed out of
a. observations.   c. laws.
b. experiments.   d. Both (a) and (b)
Answer: D   Difficulty: 1   Section: 2   Objective: 2

6. How many milliliters are in 3.5 kL?
a. 3,500 mL   c. 3,500, 000 mL
b. 0.0035 mL   d. 35,000 mL
Answer: C   Difficulty: 1   Section: 3   Objective: 2

7. A map of Seattle is an example of a
a. law.   c. model.
b. theory.   d. unit.
Answer: B   Difficulty: 1   Section: 3   Objective: 2

8. A lab has the safety icons shown below. These icons mean that you should wear
a. only safety goggles.   c. safety goggles and a lab apron.
b. only a lab apron.   d. safety goggles, a lab apron, and gloves.
Answer: B   Difficulty: 1   Section: 1   Objective: 2

9. The law of conservation of mass says the tot al mass before a chemical change is
a. more than the total mass after the change.
b. less than the total mass after the change.
c. the same as the total mass after the change.
d. not the same as the total mass after the change.
Answer: B   Difficulty: 1   Section: 3   Objective: 2

10. In which of the following areas might you find a geochemist at work?
a. studying the chemistry of rocks   c. studying fishes
b. studying forestry   d. studying the atmosphere
Answer: A   Difficulty: 1   Section: 1   Objective: 2

One-Stop Planner® CD-ROM

This CD-ROM includes all of the resources shown here and the following time-saving tools:

• **Lab Materials QuickList Software**
• **Customizable lesson plans**
• **Holt Calendar Planner**
• **The powerful ExamView® Test Generator**

For a preview of available worksheets covering math and science skills, see pages T26–T33. All of these resources are also on the One-Stop Planner®.

Meeting Individual Needs

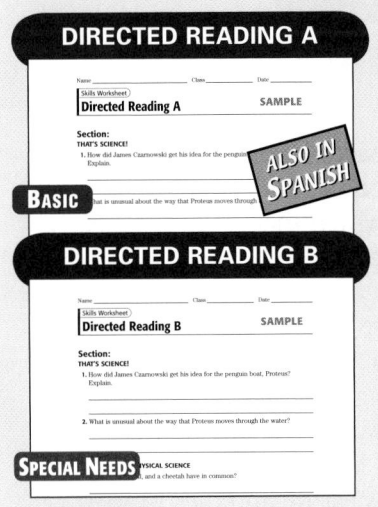

DIRECTED READING A

Skills Worksheet
Directed Reading A — SAMPLE

Section:
THAT'S SCIENCE!
1. How did James Czarnowski get his idea for the penguin boat, Proteus? Explain.

ALSO IN SPANISH

BASIC
2. What is unusual about the way that Proteus moves through

DIRECTED READING B

Skills Worksheet
Directed Reading B — SAMPLE

Section:
THAT'S SCIENCE!
1. How did James Czarnowski get his idea for the penguin boat, Proteus? Explain.

2. What is unusual about the way that Proteus moves through the water?

SPECIAL NEEDS PHYSICAL SCIENCE

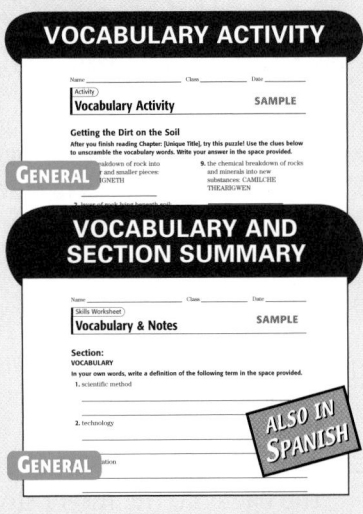

VOCABULARY ACTIVITY

Skills Worksheet
Vocabulary Activity — SAMPLE

Getting the Dirt on the Soil
After you finish reading Chapter [Unique Title], try this puzzle! Use the clues below to unscramble the vocabulary words. Write your answer in the space provided.

GENERAL

VOCABULARY AND SECTION SUMMARY

Skills Worksheet
Vocabulary & Notes — SAMPLE

Section:
VOCABULARY
In your own words, write a definition of the following term in the space provided.
1. scientific method

GENERAL

ALSO IN SPANISH

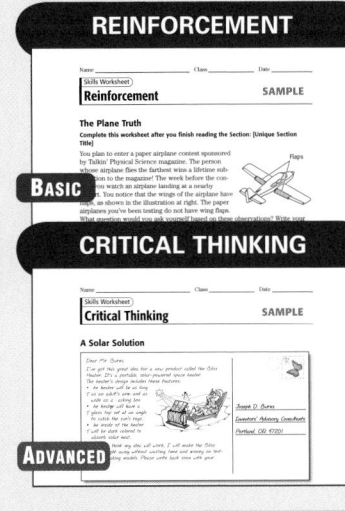

REINFORCEMENT

Activity
Reinforcement — SAMPLE

The Plane Truth
Complete this worksheet after you finish reading the Section: [Unique Section Title]

BASIC

CRITICAL THINKING

Skills Worksheet
Critical Thinking — SAMPLE

A Solar Solution

ADVANCED

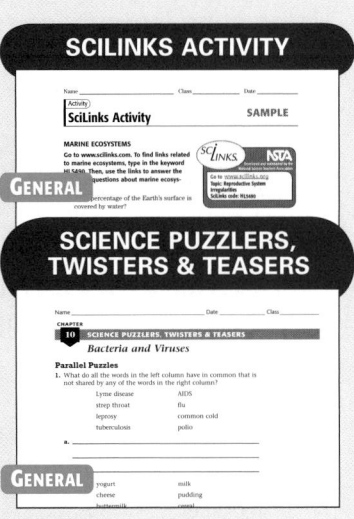

SCILINKS ACTIVITY

Activity
SciLinks Activity — SAMPLE

MARINE ECOSYSTEMS
Go to www.scilinks.org. To find links related to marine ecosystems, type in the keyword HL5490. Then, use the links to answer the questions about marine ecosys-

GENERAL

SCIENCE PUZZLERS, TWISTERS & TEASERS

CHAPTER 10 — SCIENCE PUZZLERS, TWISTERS & TEASERS
Bacteria and Viruses

Parallel Puzzles
1. What do all the words in the left column have in common that is not shared by any of the words in the right column?

Lyme disease	AIDS
strep throat	flu
leprosy	common cold
tuberculosis	polio

GENERAL

Labs and Activities

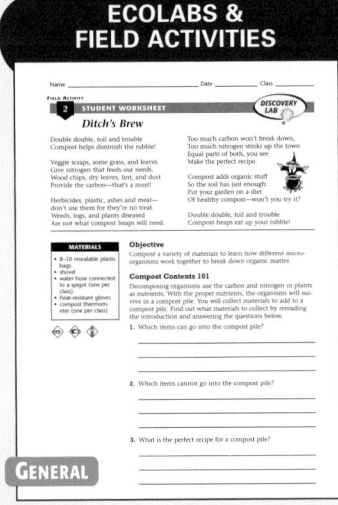

ECOLABS & FIELD ACTIVITIES

FIELD ACTIVITY
2 **STUDENT WORKSHEET** — DISCOVERY LAB
Ditch's Brew

Objective

MATERIALS

GENERAL

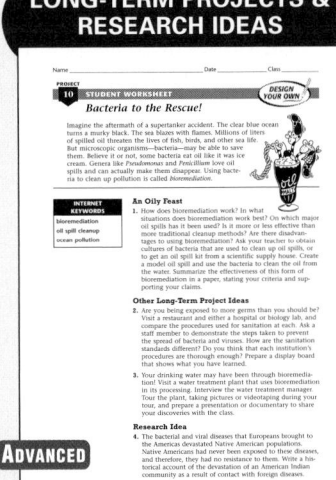

LONG-TERM PROJECTS & RESEARCH IDEAS

PROJECT
10 **STUDENT WORKSHEET** — DESIGN YOUR OWN
Bacteria to the Rescue!

INTERNET KEYWORDS
bioremediation
oil spill cleanup
ocean pollution

An Oily Feast

Compost Contents 101

Other Long-Term Project Ideas

Research Idea

ADVANCED

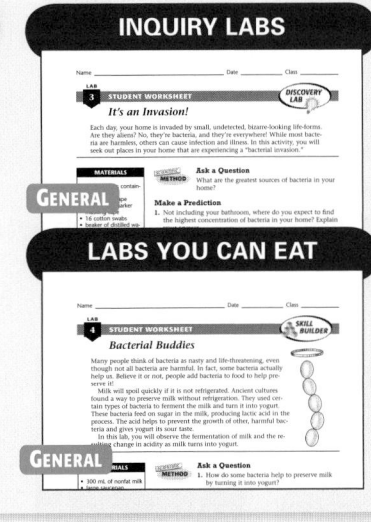

INQUIRY LABS

LAB
3 **STUDENT WORKSHEET** — DISCOVERY LAB
It's an Invasion!

MATERIALS

Ask a Question

Make a Prediction

GENERAL

LABS YOU CAN EAT

LAB
4 **STUDENT WORKSHEET** — SKILL BUILDER
Bacterial Buddies

Ask a Question

GENERAL

DATASHEETS FOR QUICK LABS

TEACHER RESOURCE PAGE
Quick Lab — DATASHEET FOR QUICK LAB
Reaction to Stress — SAMPLE

Background

DATASHEETS FOR CHAPTER LABS

TEACHER RESOURCE PAGE
Skills Practice Lab — DATASHEET FOR CHAPTER LAB
Using Scientific Methods — SAMPLE

Teacher's Notes
TIME REQUIRED

DATASHEETS FOR LABBOOK

TEACHER RESOURCE PAGE
Skills Practice Lab — DATASHEET FOR LABBOOK LAB
Does It All Add Up? — SAMPLE

Teacher's Notes
TIME REQUIRED
One 45-minute class period.

Review and Assessments

SECTION QUIZ

Assessment
Section Quiz — SAMPLE

Section:
In the space provided, write the letter of the description that best matches the term or best answers each question.

ALSO IN SPANISH

GENERAL

SECTION REVIEW

Skills Worksheet
Section Review — SAMPLE

Section:
KEY TERMS
1. What do paleontologists study?

2. How does a trace fossil differ from petrified wood?

GENERAL

ALSO IN SPANISH

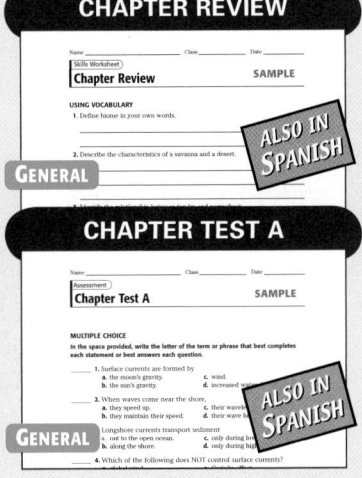

CHAPTER REVIEW

Skills Worksheet
Chapter Review — SAMPLE

USING VOCABULARY
1. Define biome in your own words.

2. Describe the characteristics of a savanna and a desert.

GENERAL

ALSO IN SPANISH

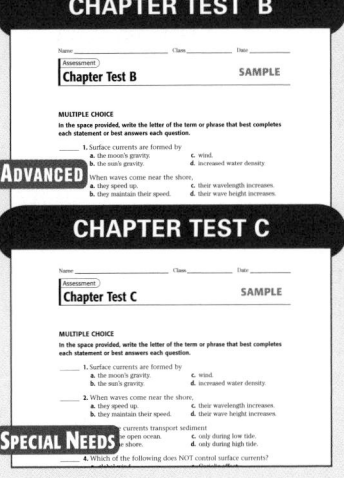

CHAPTER TEST B

Assessment
Chapter Test B — SAMPLE

MULTIPLE CHOICE
In the space provided, write the letter of the term or phrase that best completes each statement or best answers each question.

1. Surface currents are formed by
   a. the moon's gravity.   c. wind.
   b. the sun's gravity.   d. increased water density.
2. When waves come near the shore,
   a. they speed up.   c. their wavelength increases.
   b. they maintain their speed. d. their wave height increases.

ADVANCED

CHAPTER TEST C

Assessment
Chapter Test C — SAMPLE

MULTIPLE CHOICE
In the space provided, write the letter of the term or phrase that best completes each statement or best answers each question.

1. Surface currents are formed by
   a. the moon's gravity.   c. wind.
   b. the sun's gravity.   d. increased water density.
2. When waves come near the shore,
   a. they speed up.   c. their wavelength increases.
   b. they maintain their speed. d. their wave height increases.

SPECIAL NEEDS

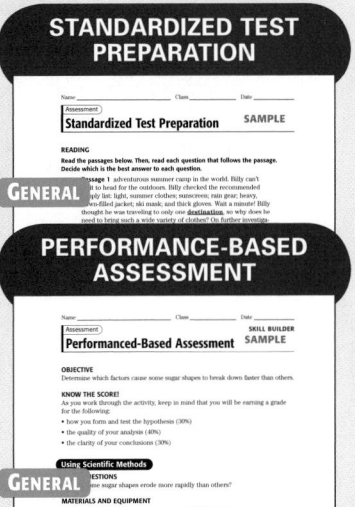

STANDARDIZED TEST PREPARATION

Assessment
Standardized Test Preparation — SAMPLE

READING
Read the passages below. Then, read each question that follows the passage. Decide which is the best answer to each question.

GENERAL

PERFORMANCE-BASED ASSESSMENT

Assessment
Performanced-Based Assessment — SKILL BUILDER SAMPLE

OBJECTIVE
Determine which factors cause some sugar shapes to break down faster than others.

KNOW THE SCORE!
As you work through the activity, keep in mind that you will be earning a grade for the following:
• how you form and test the hypothesis (30%)
• the quality of your analysis (40%)
• the clarity of your conclusions (30%)

Using Scientific Methods

MATERIALS AND EQUIPMENT
• 1 regular sugar cube

GENERAL

This Chapter Enrichment provides relevant and interesting information to expand and enhance your presentation of the chapter material.

Section 1

Bacteria

Kingdoms of Bacteria

- The classification of living things is an ever-changing process. This book uses a six-kingdom system of classification. Bacteria are divided into two kingdoms: Eubacteria and Archaebacteria. In five-kingdom systems of classification, all bacteria are classified in the kingdom Monera.

- Bacteria are sometimes classified by shape or by how they live (for example, *saprophytes* decompose dead matter and *symbionts* live on or in living matter). Many eubacteria are also classified as Gram positive or Gram negative. Gram-positive bacteria have a thick peptidoglycan cell wall that appears purple when stained with crystal violet, iodine, and safranine. Gram-negative bacteria have a much thinner peptidoglycan cell wall as well as additional layers of lipids and polysaccharides that are not found in gram-positive cells. Gram-negative bacteria appear red when stained with the same combination of dyes.

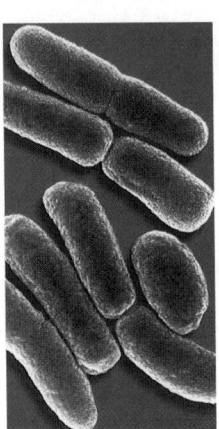 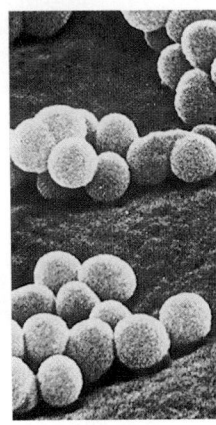 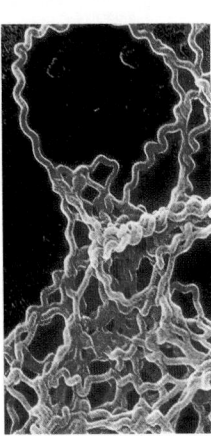

Mistaken Identity

- Cyanobacteria were once classified as blue-green algae because they use photosynthesis and sometimes grow together in long filaments that resemble algae. However, cyanobacteria are prokaryotes, which do not have nuclei or membrane-bound organelles. Blue-green algae, in contrast, are eukaryotes, which have nuclei and membrane-bound organelles.

Section 2

Bacteria's Role in the World

Bacteria and Plants

- When the nitrogen-fixing bacteria *Rhizobium* enters a plant's roots, it forms a nodule. *Rhizobium* inhabits only the roots of legumes, which include beans, peas, soybeans, alfalfa, clover, peanuts, and vetch.

- One example of the effective biological control of insects involves the bacteria *Bacillus thuringiensis*. When ingested by leaf-eating insects, the bacteria begin to secrete enzymes that dissolve the insects' digestive system. Within 24 hours after ingesting the bacteria, the insect stops eating and dies.

Is That a Fact!

◆ Bacteria are used in a number of industrial applications. They can peel and eat the paint off old aircraft. Bacteria are also being used to remove the sulfur from coal before it is burned, which helps reduce acid rain.

Poison Producers

- Botulism, a type of food poisoning, is caused by a toxin produced by the bacteria *Clostridium botulinum*. Consumption of very small amounts—sometimes as little as one-millionth of a gram—can cause paralysis and eventually death. *C. botulinum* grows in foods that have been improperly canned and sterilized.

- The intestinal disorder that many travelers refer to as traveler's diarrhea is frequently caused by a strain of the common intestinal bacteria *Escherichia coli*, commonly called *E. coli*. In many countries, contraction of the disease can be avoided by not drinking tap water and by not eating uncooked fruits and vegetables.

Is That a Fact!

◆ The water droplets in the air produced in a sneeze can carry between 10,000 and 100 million bacteria. The bacteria that cause whooping cough, tuberculosis, diphtheria, and scarlet fever can be carried through the air from one person to another on droplets such as these.

Section 3

Viruses

The Discovery of Viruses

● Viruses were discovered when scientists were trying to find the cause of tobacco mosaic disease, a disease in which the leaves of tobacco plants become wrinkled, blotchy, and yellow and have stunted growth.

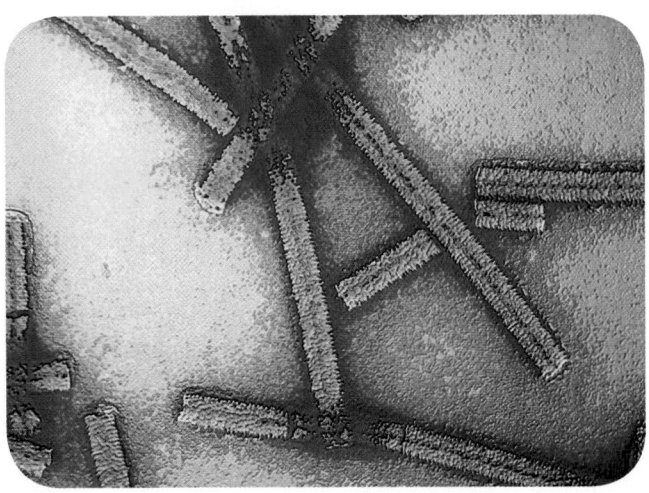

● In 1883, a German scientist named Adolf Mayer discovered that tobacco mosaic disease was contagious, and he suspected that "very small" bacteria caused the disease. Russian biologist Dmitri Ivanovsky tested Mayer's hypothesis in 1892. Ivanovsky passed the liquid from a diseased plant through extremely fine filters to isolate the small bacteria. He found no bacteria but discovered that the filtered sap from an infected plant caused the disease in a healthy plant. He concluded that "poison" from the bacteria was the cause of the disease. In 1897, Dutch biologist Martinus Beijernick discovered that the disease-causing agent was something smaller and simpler than bacteria. In 1898, Beijernick used the word *virus* to describe these tiny disease-causing agents.

● American biochemist Wendell Stanley (1904–1971) first isolated the tobacco mosaic virus in 1935. He treated the sap from infected plants in such a way that the viruses formed needle-shaped crystals. When Stanley spread the crystals from the diseased plant onto the leaves of a healthy plant, the healthy plant developed the disease. Even though Stanley isolated and chemically analyzed viruses in 1935, viruses were not seen until 1940, when the electron microscope was invented.

Smallpox

● Vaccines eliminated smallpox infections from the world. Smallpox causes permanent disfigurement and, in many cases, death. The use of smallpox vaccines began in the 1700s and rapidly spread in industrialized countries around the world.

● Some of the smallpox virus still exists in labs around the world, and there is debate over whether this virus should be eliminated completely so that it could never be used for the purposes of bioterrorism. However, many scientists and health officials hesitate to destroy the virus completely because if any were to escape, the disease would be much harder to control without the laboratory stock of the virus.

Is That a Fact!

◆ A man named Ali Maow Maalin of Merka, Somalia, contracted the last known naturally occurring case of smallpox in the world in 1977.

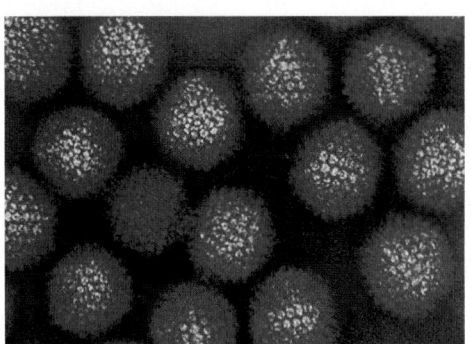

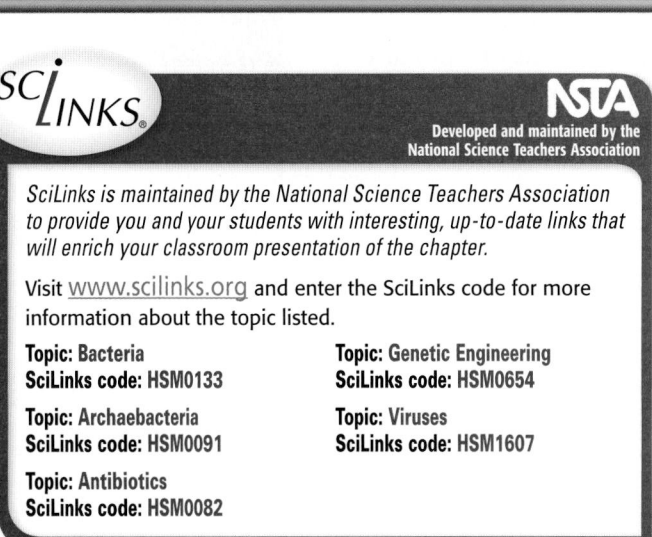

SCiLINKS.

NSTA
Developed and maintained by the
National Science Teachers Association

SciLinks is maintained by the National Science Teachers Association to provide you and your students with interesting, up-to-date links that will enrich your classroom presentation of the chapter.

Visit www.scilinks.org and enter the SciLinks code for more information about the topic listed.

Topic: Bacteria
SciLinks code: HSM0133

Topic: Genetic Engineering
SciLinks code: HSM0654

Topic: Archaebacteria
SciLinks code: HSM0091

Topic: Viruses
SciLinks code: HSM1607

Topic: Antibiotics
SciLinks code: HSM0082

Overview

Tell students that this chapter will help them learn about bacteria and viruses. The chapter discusses the characteristics of bacteria, three types of archaebacteria, and bacteria's role in the world. Finally, the chapter describes viruses, how they are classified, how they reproduce, and how they are treated.

Assessing Prior Knowledge

Students should be familiar with the following topics:

• cells

• classification

Identifying Misconceptions

Students may be confused by the idea that viruses are not considered living organisms by many scientists. Help them understand the characteristics of living things—living things have cells, they sense and respond to change, they reproduce, they have DNA, they use energy, and they grow and develop. Then, explain to students that viruses do not meet all of these criteria. For example, viruses do not grow, and they cannot reproduce on their own. Viruses must use the living cells of other organisms to reproduce. A simple way to think of viruses is that they are capsules filled with genetic material.

10

Bacteria and Viruses

About the PHOTO

Bacteria are everywhere. Some provide us with medicines, and some make foods we eat. Others, such as the one pictured here, can cause illness. This bacterium is a kind of *Salmonella*, and it can cause food poisoning. *Salmonella* can live inside chickens and other birds. Cooking eggs and chicken properly helps make sure that you don't get sick from *Salmonella*.

PRE-READING ACTIVITY

FOLDNOTES **Double Door** Before you read the chapter, create the FoldNote entitled "Double Door" described in the **Study Skills** section of the Appendix. Write "Bacteria" on one flap of the double door and "Viruses" on the other flap. As you read the chapter, compare the two topics, and write characteristics of each on the inside of the appropriate flap.

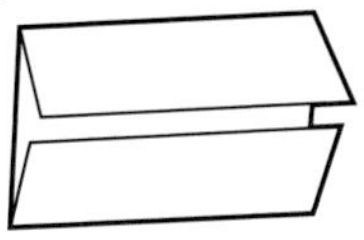

Standards Correlations

National Science Education Standards

The following codes indicate the National Science Education Standards that correlate to this chapter. The full text of the standards is at the front of the book.

Chapter Opener
UCP 2; SAI 1; LS 1b, 1c, 2a, 3a, 3b, 4b

Section 1 Bacteria
UCP 1, 3, 5; SAI 1; LS 1b, 1c, 2a, 3a, 3b, 4b

Section 2 Bacteria's Role in the World
UCP 2, 3, 4, 5; ST 1, 2; SPSP 5; HNS 3; LS 1f

Section 3 Viruses
UCP 1, 2, 5; SAI 1, 2; SPSP 4, 5; LS 1f, 2a

Chapter Lab
UCP 2; SAI 1, 2; LS 1c

Chapter Review
UCP 1, 2, 3, 4, 5; SAI 1, 2; ST 1, 2; SPSP 4, 5; HNS 3; LS 1b, 1c, 1f, 2a, 3a, 3b, 4b

Science in Action
SAI 2; SPSP 5; HNS 1, 2, 3

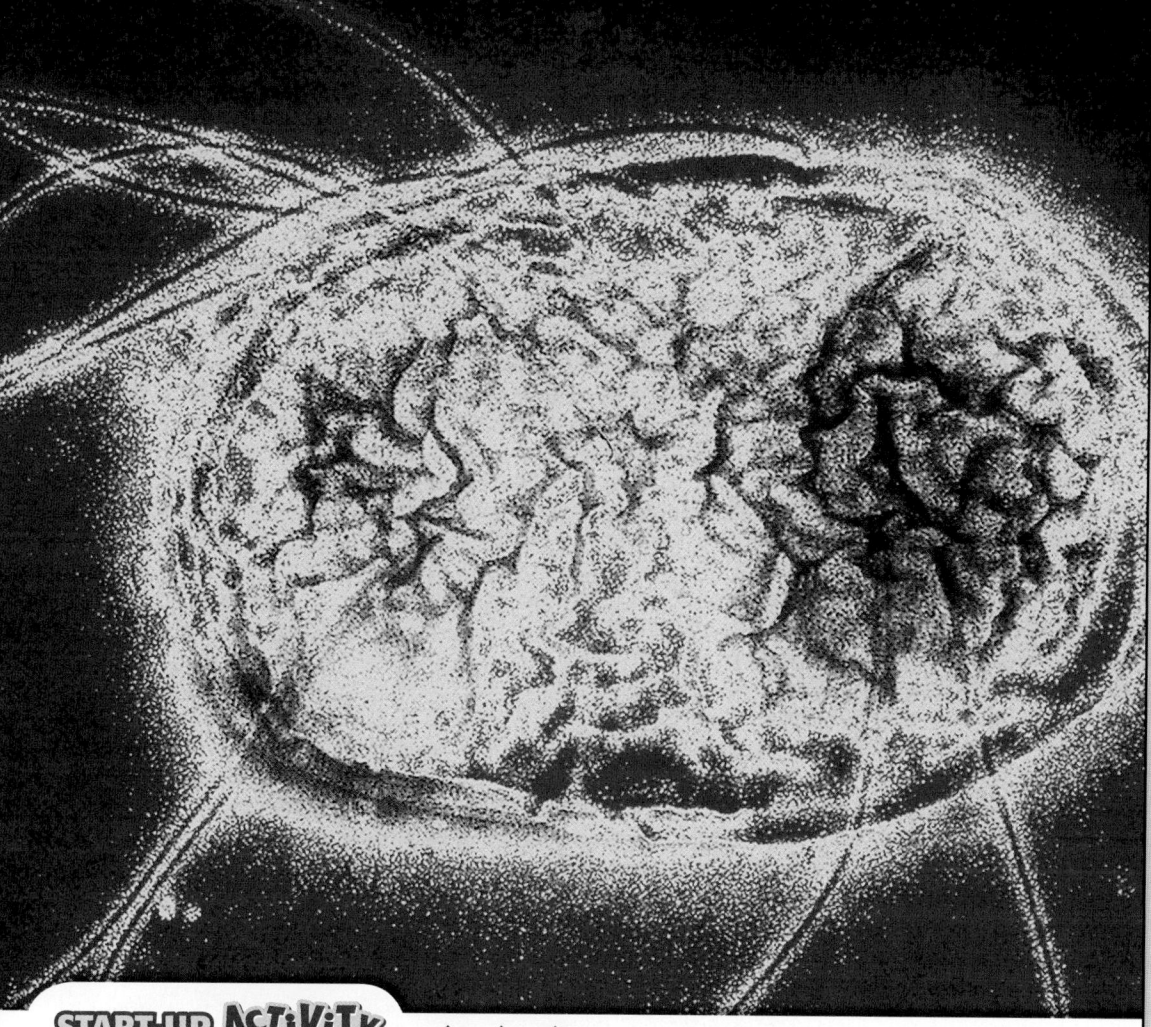

Safety Caution: Plastic dishes are safer than glass dishes.

Teacher's Notes: Prepoured agar plates can be purchased from a biological supply house.

To minimize the risk of contamination from airborne bacteria, have students lift the Petri dish lids only slightly when treating the agar. Do not allow students to open the Petri dishes after the dishes have been inoculated and sealed.

Tell students to label the Petri dishes on the bottom rather than the lid, because lids can easily be switched.

Answers

1. Answers may vary, but students should mention color differences, variations in colony shapes and sizes, and differing amounts of growth.

2. Answers may vary. Most likely, the Petri dish that is exposed to soil will have the most bacterial growth.

START-UP **ACTIVITY**

Our Constant Companions

Bacteria are in the soil, in the air, and even inside your body. When grown in a laboratory, microscopic bacteria form colonies that you can see. In this activity, you will observe some of the bacteria that share your world.

Procedure

1. Get **three plastic Petri dishes containing nutrient agar** from your teacher. Label one dish "Hand," another "Breath," and another "Soil."

2. Wipe your finger across the agar in the dish labeled "Hand." Breathe into the dish labeled "Breath." Place a **small amount of soil** in the dish labeled "Soil."

3. Secure the Petri dish lids with **transparent tape.** Wash your hands. Keep the dishes upside down in a warm, dark place for about one week. **Caution:** Do not open the Petri dishes after they are sealed.

4. Observe the Petri dishes each day. What do you see? Record your observations.

Analysis

1. How does the appearance of the colonies growing on the agar in each dish differ? What do bacterial colonies look like?

2. Which source caused the most bacterial growth—your hand, your breath, or the soil? Why do you think this source caused the most growth?

Chapter Starter Transparency
Use this transparency to help students begin thinking about bacteria and viruses.

Focus

Overview

This section introduces students to bacteria. Students will compare eubacteria and archaebacteria. They will distinguish between bacterial producers and consumers. Finally, students will describe the three main groups of archaebacteria.

🔊 Bellringer

Pose the following questions to your students:

- What are the two kingdoms of bacteria? (Eubacteria and Archaebacteria)
- What are three shapes of bacteria? (bacilli, cocci, and spirilla)

Motivate

Discussion —————— GENERAL

Types of Cells Ask students, "What is the difference between eukaryotic and prokaryotic cells?" (Prokaryotic cells don't have a nucleus, and eukaryotic cells do have a nucleus.) "Are bacteria prokaryotes or eukaryotes?" (prokaryotes) Remind students that prokaryotic cells are usually much smaller than eukaryotic cells. **LS Verbal**

Answer to Reading Check

Bacteria make up the kingdoms Eubacteria and Archaebacteria.

Bacteria

How many bacteria are in a handful of soil? Would you believe that a single gram of soil—which is about the mass of a pencil eraser—may have more than 2.5 billion bacteria? A handful of soil may contain trillions of bacteria!

There are more types of bacteria on Earth than all other living things combined. Most bacteria are too small to be seen without a microscope. But not all bacteria are the same size. In fact, the largest known bacteria are 1,000 times larger than the average bacterium. One of these giant bacteria was first found inside a surgeonfish and is shown in **Figure 1.**

Characteristics of Bacteria

All living things fit into one of six kingdoms: Protista, Plantae, Fungi, Animalia, Eubacteria, or Archaebacteria. Bacteria make up the kingdoms Eubacteria (YOO bak TIR ee uh) and Archaebacteria (AHR kee bak TIR ee uh). These two kingdoms contain the oldest forms of life on Earth. All bacteria are single-celled organisms. Bacteria are usually one of three main shapes: bacilli, cocci, or spirilla.

✔ Reading Check What two kingdoms are made up of bacteria? *(See the Appendix for answers to Reading Checks.)*

READING WARM-UP

Objectives
- Describe the characteristics of bacteria.
- Explain how bacteria reproduce.
- Compare and contrast eubacteria and archaebacteria.

Terms to Learn
prokaryote
binary fission
endospore

READING STRATEGY

Prediction Guide Before reading this section, predict whether each of the following statements is true or false:
- There are only a few kinds of bacteria.
- Most bacteria are too small to see.

Figure 1 *The giant bacteria inside this fish are 0.6 mm long, which is big enough to see without a microscope.*

CHAPTER RESOURCES

Chapter Resource File

- **Lesson Plan**
- **Directed Reading A** BASIC
- **Directed Reading B** SPECIAL NEEDS

Technology

Transparencies
- Bellringer
- The Most Common Shapes of Bacteria

Answer to Reading Strategy

- false; There are more types of bacteria on Earth than all other living things combined.
- true; Most bacteria can only be seen with a microscope.

Figure 2 The Most Common Shapes of Bacteria

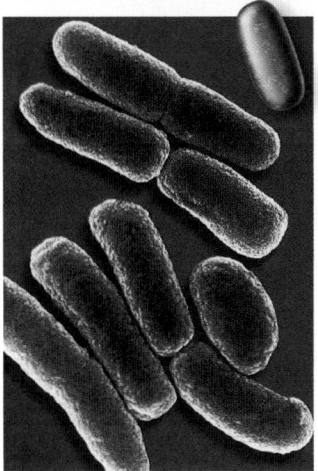

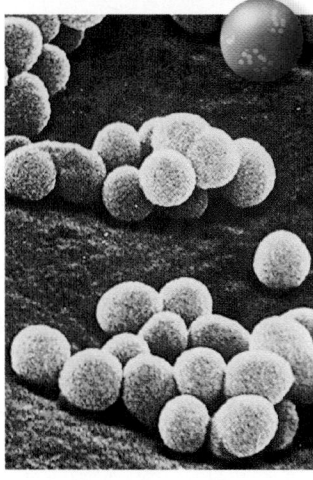

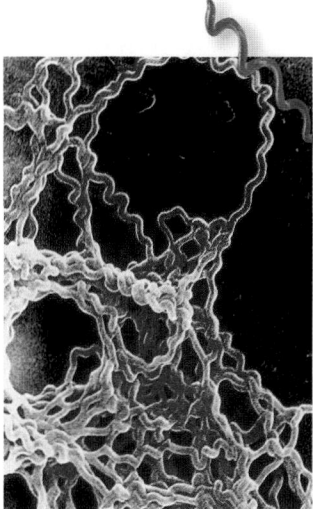

Bacilli (buh SIL ie) are rod shaped. They have a large surface area, which helps them take in nutrients. But a large surface area can cause them to dry out easily.

Cocci (KAHK sie) are spherical. They do not dry out as quickly as rod-shaped bacteria.

Spirilla (spie RIL uh) are long and spiral shaped. They use flagella at both ends to move like a corkscrew.

The Shape of Bacteria

Most bacteria have a rigid cell wall that gives them their shape. **Figure 2** shows the three most common shapes of bacteria. Bacilli (buh SIL ie) are rod shaped. Cocci (KAHK sie) are spherical. Spirilla (spie RIL uh) are long and spiral shaped. Each shape helps bacteria in a different way.

Some bacteria have hairlike parts called *flagella* (fluh JEL uh) that help them move around. Flagella spin to push a bacterium through water or other liquids.

No Nucleus!

All bacteria are single-celled organisms that do not have a nucleus. An organism that does not have a nucleus is called a **prokaryote** (proh KAR ee OHT). A prokaryote is able to move, get energy, and reproduce like cells that have a nucleus, which are called *eukaryotes* (yoo KAR ee OHTZ).

Prokaryotes function as independent organisms. Some bacteria stick together to form strands or films, but each bacterium is still functioning as a single organism. Most prokaryotes are much simpler and smaller than eukaryotes. Prokaryotes also reproduce differently than eukaryotes do.

prokaryote an organism that consists of a single cell that does not have a nucleus

Spying on Spirilla

1. Using a **microscope,** observe prepared **slides of bacteria.** Draw each type of bacteria you see.
2. What different shapes do you see? What are these shapes called?

 **SCIENCE**

Bacteria called *Thiobacillus ferrooxidans* are used to mine copper from copper ore. Copper ore contains metal sulfides. The bacteria take in copper sulfides and separate them into copper and sulfur. The bacteria excrete the purified copper as a waste product.

Prediction Guide Before students read this page, ask the following question: "What do you think happens to the DNA inside a bacterium before it reproduces?" (Accept all reasonable answers. Students should infer that the DNA replicates before the cell divides.)

Have students evaluate their answer after they read about bacterial reproduction. **LS** Verbal

Using the Figure — GENERAL

Binary Fission Discuss the stages of bacterial cell division by binary fission, shown in **Figure 3.** Ask students to describe what takes place during each step of this process. Have them point out the key structures involved. **LS** Visual/Verbal

CONNECTION ACTIVITY
Math ———————— GENERAL

Bacterial Reproduction Some species of bacteria undergo binary fission every 30 min. If they began with one bacterium, have students calculate how many bacteria there would be after 1 h (4 bacteria), after 2 h (16 bacteria), after 3 h (64 bacteria), after 4 h (256 bacteria), and after 5 h (1,024 bacteria). **LS** Logical

---

Figure 3 Binary Fission

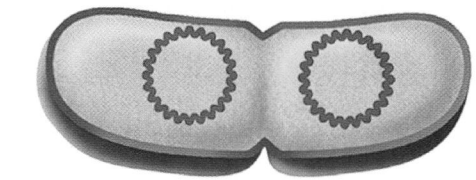

❶ The cell grows.

❷ The DNA is copied and attached to the cell membrane.

❸ The DNA and its copy separate as the cell grows larger.

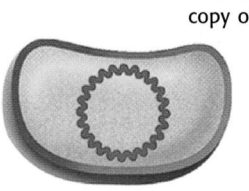

❹ The cell splits in two. Each new cell has a copy of the DNA.

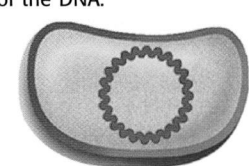

binary fission a form of asexual reproduction in single-celled organisms by which one cell divides into two cells of the same size

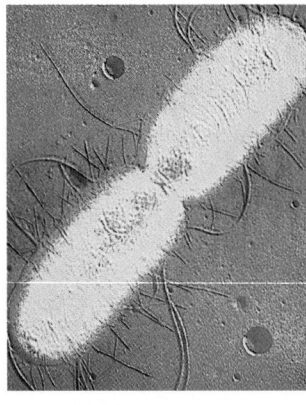

Bacterial Reproduction

Bacteria reproduce by the process shown in **Figure 3.** This process is called binary fission (BIE nuh ree FISH uhn). **Binary fission** is reproduction in which one single-celled organism splits into two single-celled organisms.

Prokaryotes have no nucleus, so their DNA is not surrounded by a membrane. The DNA of bacteria is in circular loops. In the first step of binary fission, the cell's DNA is copied. The DNA and its copy then bind to different places on the inside of the cell membrane. As the cell and its membrane grow bigger, the loops of DNA separate. Finally, when the cell is about double its original size, the membrane pinches inward as shown in **Figure 4.** A new cell wall forms and separates the two new cells. Each new cell has one exact copy of the parent cell's DNA.

✔ **Reading Check** What is binary fission?

Figure 4 *This bacterium is about to complete binary fission.*

 CHAPTER RESOURCES

Technology

🖳 **Transparencies**
• Binary Fission
• *LINK TO PHYSICAL SCIENCE* Parts of an Atom

Answer to Reading Check

Binary fission is a process of cell division in which one cell splits into two. All bacteria reproduce by binary fission.

Endospores

Most species of bacteria do well in warm, moist places. In dry or cold surroundings, some species of bacteria will die. In these conditions, other bacteria become inactive and form endospores (EN doh SPAWRZ). An **endospore** contains genetic material and proteins and is covered by a thick, protective coat. Many endospores can survive in hot, cold, and very dry places. When conditions improve, the endospores break open, and the bacteria become active again. Scientists found endospores inside an insect that was preserved in amber for 30 million years. When the endospores were moistened in a laboratory, bacteria began to grow! A similar piece of amber can be seen in **Figure 5.**

Kingdom Eubacteria

Most bacteria are eubacteria. The kingdom Eubacteria has more individuals than all of the other five kingdoms combined. Scientists think that eubacteria have lived on Earth for more than 3.5 billion years.

Eubacteria Classification

Eubacteria are classified by the way they get food. Most eubacteria, such as those breaking down the leaf in **Figure 6,** are consumers. Consumers get their food by eating other organisms. Many bacteria are decomposers, which feed on dead organisms. Other consumer bacteria live in or on the body of another organism. Eubacteria that make their own food are called *producers.* Like plants, producer bacteria use the energy from sunlight to make food. These bacteria are often green.

Figure 5 *Endospores found in a preserved insect like this one showed scientists that bacteria can survive for millions of years.*

endospore a thick-walled protective spore that forms inside a bacterial cell and resists harsh conditions

Figure 6 *Decomposers, such as the ones helping to decay this leaf, return nutrients to the soil for other living things to use.*

BRAIN FOOD

Largest Species of Bacteria
Thiomargarita namibiensis is a bacterial species so large that an individual bacterium is visible to the naked eye. It is the largest known bacterium, with cells as large as 750 μm (0.03 in.) in diameter. Even large bacteria are single-celled organisms, and their surface-area-to-volume ratio is far less than that of smaller bacteria. Ask students, "What problems might a small surface-area-to-volume ratio cause in an organism?" (A small surface-area-to-volume ratio makes it difficult to take in a sufficient quantity of nutrients and to eliminate wastes efficiently.)

ACTIVITY ———— GENERAL

Bacteria in the Air Tell students that air typically has around 4,000 bacteria per cubic meter. Ask students to measure the dimensions of your classroom and then calculate the number of bacteria in the air of the classroom. (Answers may vary depending on the size of the classroom. Students should measure the length, width, and height of the classroom in meters and then calculate the volume of the classroom. The volume of the classroom in cubic meters multiplied by 4,000 will give the number of bacteria in the air of the classroom.) You may want to point out that not all bacteria cause diseases and that our bodies have many defenses to protect us from harmful bacteria. **LS Logical**

CONNECTION to Physical Science—ADVANCED

Breaking It Down We often try to understand the size of bacteria by comparing them to bigger things. However, comparing them to smaller components may also be helpful. Use the teaching transparency entitled "Parts of an Atom" to give students another way to understand the size of bacteria. **LS Verbal**

Close

Bacterial Trivia Have the class work in two teams, and provide each team with 10 large index cards. Have each team look through this section and write 10 questions, one per index card, about the characteristics of bacteria. Bring the teams together to play a trivia game about bacteria.
LS Verbal Co-op Learning

Quiz — GENERAL

1. How are prokaryotes different from eukaryotes? (Prokaryotes lack a nucleus, are smaller and simpler than eukaryotes, and reproduce in a different way from eukaryotes.)

2. What are the three main types of archaebacteria? (methane makers, heat lovers, and salt lovers)

Alternative Assessment — GENERAL

Concept Mapping After students read this section, have them create a concept map using the following terms: *bacteria, Eubacteria, Archaebacteria, prokaryotes, nucleus, binary fission, endospore, eukaryotes,* and *harsh environments.*
LS Logical

CONNECTION TO Language Arts

Colorful Names *Cyanobacteria* means "blue bacteria." Many other names also refer to colors. You might not recognize these colors because the words for the colors are in another language. Look at the list of Greek color words below. Write down two English words that have one of the color roots in them. (Hint: Many words have the color as the first part of the word.)

melano = black
chloro = green
erythro = red
leuko = white

Cyanobacteria

Cyanobacteria (SIE uh noh bak TIR ee uh) are producers. Cyanobacteria usually live in water. These bacteria contain the green pigment chlorophyll. Chlorophyll is important to photosynthesis (the process of making food from the energy in sunlight). Many cyanobacteria have other pigments as well. Some have a blue pigment that helps in photosynthesis. This pigment gives those cyanobacteria a blue tint. Other cyanobacteria have red pigment. Flamingos get their pink color from eating red cyanobacteria.

Some scientists think that billions of years ago, bacteria similar to cyanobacteria began to live inside larger cells. According to this theory, the bacteria made food, and the cells provided protection. This combination may have given rise to the first plants on Earth.

Kingdom Archaebacteria

The three main types of archaebacteria are *heat lovers, salt lovers,* and *methane makers.* Heat lovers live in ocean vents and hot springs. They live in very hot water, usually from 60°C to 80°C, but they can survive temperatures of more than 250°C. Salt lovers live in environments that have high levels of salt, such as the Dead Sea and Great Salt Lake. Methane makers give off methane gas and live in swamps and animal intestines. **Figure 7** shows one type of methane maker found in the mud of swamps.

Figure 7 *These bacteria are methane makers. This micrograph shows two bacteria sliced across their narrow side and a dividing bacterium sliced lengthwise.*

Answer to Connection to Language Arts

Sample answer:
- *melano:* melanoma (dark-colored skin cancer), melanin (pigment that makes skin dark)
- *chloro:* chlorophyll (green pigment found in photosynthetic organisms), chloroplast (in plants, organelle that contains chlorophyll)
- *erythro:* erythrocyte (red blood cell), erythroblast (cells in bone marrow from which red blood cells form)
- *leuko:* leukocyte (white blood cell), leukemia (a disease that causes an overproduction of white blood cells)

Harsh Environments

Archaebacteria often live where nothing else can. Most archaebacteria prefer environments where there is little or no oxygen. Scientists have found them in the hot springs at Yellowstone National Park and beneath 430 m of ice in Antarctica. Archaebacteria have even been found living 8 km below the Earth's surface! Even though they are often found in these harsh environments, many archaebacteria can also be found in moderate environments in Earth's oceans.

Archaebacteria are very different from eubacteria. Not all archaebacteria have cell walls. When they do have them, the cell walls are chemically different from those of eubacteria.

SECTION Review

Summary

- Bacteria are single-celled organisms that are the smallest and simplest living things on Earth.
- Most bacteria have a rigid cell wall that gives them their shape. The main shapes of bacteria are rod shaped (bacilli), spherical (cocci), and spiral shaped (spirilla).
- Bacteria reproduce by binary fission. In binary fission, one cell divides into two cells.
- Eubacteria have cell walls and are either producers (bacteria that make their own food) or consumers (bacteria that get food from other organisms).
- Archaebacteria often live in harsh environments.

Using Key Terms

The statements below are false. For each statement, replace the underlined term to make a true statement.

1. Bacteria are <u>eukaryotes.</u>

2. Bacteria reproduce by <u>primary fission.</u>

Understanding Key Ideas

3. The structure that helps some bacteria survive harsh conditions is called a(n)
   - **a.** endospore.
   - **c.** exospore.
   - **b.** shell.
   - **d.** exoskeleton.

4. How are eubacteria and archaebacteria different?

5. Draw and label the four stages of binary fission.

6. Describe one advantage of each shape of bacteria.

7. What two things do producer bacteria and plants have in common?

Math Skills

8. An ounce (oz) is equal to about 28 g. If 1 g of soil contains 2.5 billion bacteria, how many bacteria are in 1 oz of soil?

Critical Thinking

9. **Applying Concepts** Many bacteria cannot reproduce in cooler temperatures and are destroyed at high temperatures. How do humans take advantage of this fact when preparing and storing food?

10. **Making Comparisons** Scientists are studying cold and dry environments on Earth that are like the environment on Mars. What kind of bacteria do you think they might find in these environments on Earth? Explain.

11. **Forming Hypotheses** You are studying a lake and the bacteria that live in it. What conditions of the lake would you measure to form a hypothesis about what kind of bacteria may live there?

For a variety of links related to this chapter, go to www.scilinks.org

Topic: Bacteria; Archaebacteria
SciLinks code: HSM0133; HSM0091

CHAPTER RESOURCES

Chapter Resource File

- Section Quiz **GENERAL**
- Section Review **GENERAL**
- Vocabulary and Section Summary **GENERAL**
- Reinforcement Worksheet **BASIC**
- SciLinks Activity **GENERAL**
- Datasheet for Quick Lab

Answers to Section Review

1. prokaryotes

2. binary fission

3. a

4. Sample answer: Archaebacteria do not always have cell walls, and when they do, the cell walls are different from those of eubacteria. Also, archaebacteria often live where nothing else can live.

5. Students' drawings should show four basic stages: the cell grows, the DNA is copied and attached to the cell membrane, the DNA and its copy separate as the cell grows larger, and the cell splits in two.

6. Sample answer: Bacilli have a large surface area, which helps them take in nutrients. Cocci do not dry out as quickly as bacilli. Spirilla can move easily.

7. Sample answer: Like plants, producer bacteria use sunlight to make their own food. Like most plants, many of these bacteria are green.

8. 70 billion bacteria; (28 g × 2,500,000,000 bacteria/g = 70,000,000,000 bacteria)

9. Sample answer: Humans store food in a refrigerator or freezer, which keeps bacteria from reproducing. Humans also cook many foods, which destroys bacteria that might be living in the uncooked food.

10. Sample answer: They will probably find archaebacteria because archaebacteria can live in harsh environments such as those found on Mars.

11. Sample answer: I would measure the level of salt, methane, and the temperature of the lake to form a hypothesis about what kind of bacteria might live in the lake.

Focus

Overview

This section explains how life on Earth depends on bacteria. Students learn how bacteria are both beneficial and harmful to people and other organisms.

🎙 Bellringer

Ask students the following question, "Are harmful bacteria more of a problem or less of a problem to people now than they were 200 years ago?" (Students should recognize that harmful bacteria usually cause fewer problems today because people now maintain more hygienic conditions, which eliminate many bacteria. The discovery of antibiotics and vaccines has also helped people overcome some of the health problems posed by bacteria.)

Motivate

Discussion ——— GENERAL

Bacterial Products Ask students to name products that are made by using bacteria. (Sample answer: yogurt, cheese, sour cream, sauerkraut, and some medicines)

 Verbal

READING WARM-UP

Objectives
- Explain how life on Earth depends on bacteria.
- List three ways bacteria are useful to people.
- Describe two ways in which bacteria can be harmful to people.

Terms to Learn
bioremediation
antibiotic
pathogenic bacteria

READING STRATEGY

Reading Organizer As you read this section, create an outline of the section. Use the headings from the section in your outline.

Bacteria's Role in the World

Have you ever had strep throat or a cavity in your tooth? Did you know that both are caused by bacteria?

Bacteria live in our water, our food, and our bodies. Much of what we know about bacteria was learned by scientists fighting bacterial diseases. But of the thousands of types of bacteria, only a few hundred cause disease. Many bacteria do things that are important and even helpful to us.

Good for the Environment

Life as we know it could not exist without bacteria. Bacteria are very important to the health of Earth. They help recycle dead animals and plants. Bacteria also play an important role in the nitrogen cycle.

Nitrogen Fixation

Most living things depend on plants. Plants need nitrogen to grow. Nitrogen gas makes up about 78% of the air, but most plants cannot use nitrogen directly from the air. They need to take in a different form of nitrogen. Nitrogen-fixing bacteria take in nitrogen from the air and change it to a form that plants can use. This process, called *nitrogen fixation*, is described in **Figure 1.**

✓ **Reading Check** What is nitrogen fixation? (*See the Appendix for answers to Reading Checks.*)

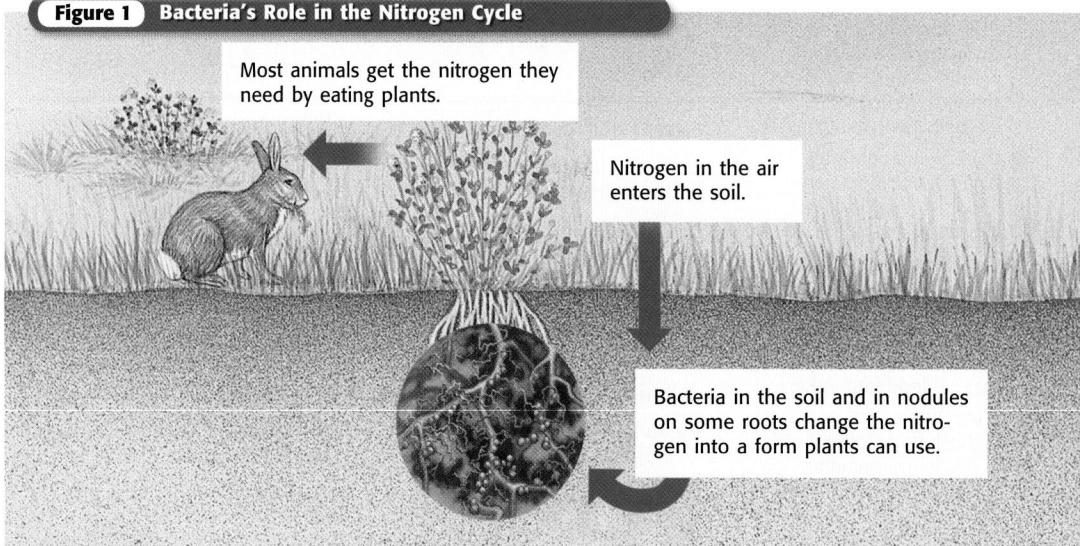

Figure 1 Bacteria's Role in the Nitrogen Cycle

Most animals get the nitrogen they need by eating plants.

Nitrogen in the air enters the soil.

Bacteria in the soil and in nodules on some roots change the nitrogen into a form plants can use.

CHAPTER RESOURCES

Chapter Resource File
- Lesson Plan
- Directed Reading A **BASIC**
- Directed Reading B **SPECIAL NEEDS**

Technology
- Transparencies
  - Bellringer

Answer to Reading Check

Nitrogen fixing is the process by which nitrogen gas in the air is transformed into a form that plants can use.

Recycling

Have you ever seen dead leaves and twigs on a forest floor? These leaves and twigs are recycled over time with the help of bacteria. Decomposer bacteria break down dead plant and animal matter. Breaking down dead matter makes nutrients available to other living things.

Cleaning Up

Bacteria and other microorganisms are also used to fight pollution. **Bioremediation** (BIE oh ri MEE dee AY shuhn) means using microorganisms to change harmful chemicals into harmless ones. Bioremediation is used to clean up hazardous waste from industries, farms, and cities. It is also used to clean up oil spills. The workers in **Figure 2** are using bacteria to remove pollutants from the soil.

Good for People

Bacteria do much more than help keep our environment clean. Bacteria also help produce many of the foods we eat every day. They even help make important medicines.

Bacteria in Your Food

Believe it or not, people raise bacteria for food! Every time you eat cheese, yogurt, buttermilk, or sour cream, you are also eating bacteria. Lactic acid-producing bacteria break down the sugar in milk, which is called *lactose*. In the process, the bacteria change lactose into lactic acid. Lactic acid preserves and adds flavor to the food. All of the foods shown in **Figure 3** were made with the help of bacteria.

Figure 2 *Bioremediating bacteria are added to soil to eat pollutants. The bacteria then release the pollutants as harmless waste.*

bioremediation the biological treatment of hazardous waste by living organisms

Make a Meal Plan

With a parent, create a week's meal plan without any foods made with bacteria. What would your diet be like without bacteria?

Figure 3 *Bacteria are used to make many kinds of foods.*

Bacterial Review On the board, write the headings "Helpful bacteria" and "Harmful bacteria." Have volunteers go to the board and write an example of how bacteria can be either helpful or harmful. **LS** Verbal

Quiz ———————— GENERAL

1. How is bioremediation helpful? (Sample answer: Bioremediation is helpful because it uses microorganisms to treat hazardous waste and pollution in the environment.)

2. Explain why bacteria are important in helping plants obtain nitrogen. (Sample answer: Nitrogen-fixing bacteria that live in the soil or in a plant's roots consume nitrogen gas and change it into a form that can be used by plants.)

Alternative Assessment ——— ADVANCED

Writing **Short Story** Have students imagine what it was like before people realized that bacteria existed. Then, have students research what life was like before people knew how to deal with bacteria and write a creative story using their research. **LS** Verbal

Figure 4 *Genes from the Xenopus frog were used to produce the first genetically engineered bacteria.*

antibiotic medicine used to kill bacteria and other microorganisms

pathogenic bacteria bacteria that cause disease

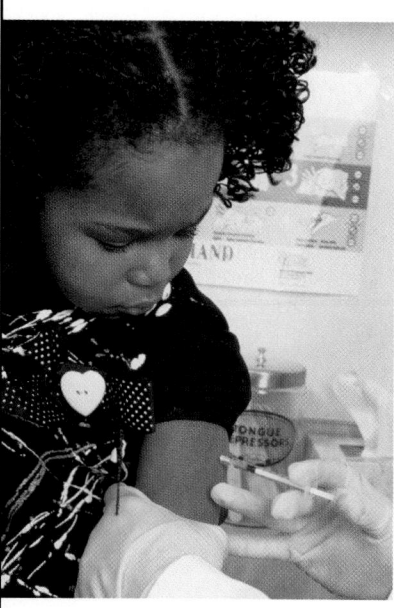

Figure 5 *Vaccines can protect you from bacterial diseases such as tetanus and diptheria.*

Making Medicines

What's the best way to fight disease-causing bacteria? Would you believe that the answer is to use other bacteria? **Antibiotics** are medicines used to kill bacteria and other microorganisms. Many antibiotics are made by bacteria.

Insulin

The human body needs insulin to break down and use sugar and carbohydrates. People who have diabetes do not make enough insulin. In the 1970s, scientists discovered how to put genes into bacteria so that the bacteria would make human insulin. The insulin can then be separated from the bacteria and given to people who have diabetes.

Genetic Engineering

When scientists change the genes of bacteria, or any other living thing, the process is called *genetic engineering*. Scientists have been genetically engineering bacteria since 1973. In that year, researchers put genes from a frog like the one in **Figure 4** into the bacterium *Escherichia coli* (ESH uh RIK ee uh KOH LIE). The bacterium then started making copies of the frog genes. Scientists can now engineer bacteria to make many products, such as insecticides, cleansers, and adhesives.

✓ *Reading Check* What is genetic engineering?

Harmful Bacteria

Humans couldn't live without bacteria, but bacteria can also cause harm. Scientists learned in the 1800s that some bacteria are pathogenic (PATH uh JEN ik). **Pathogenic bacteria** are bacteria that cause disease. Pathogenic bacteria get inside a host organism and take nutrients from the host's cells. In the process, they harm the host. Today, we are protected from many bacterial diseases by vaccination, as shown in **Figure 5.** Many bacterial diseases can also be treated with antibiotics.

● INCLUSION Strategies

- *Learning Disabled*
- *Developmentally Delayed*
- *Hearing Impaired*

Many students can handle new vocabulary words better if they are given a chance to work with the words. Have students create a crossword puzzle using the bacterial diseases mentioned in the section. Then, have students trade papers and solve each other's puzzles. **LS** Verbal

Answer to Reading Check

In genetic engineering, scientists change the genes of bacteria and other living things.

Diseases in Other Organisms

Bacteria cause diseases in other organisms as well as in people. Have you ever seen a plant with odd-colored spots or soft rot? If so, you've seen bacterial damage to plants. Pathogenic bacteria attack plants, animals, protists, fungi, and even other bacteria. They can cause damage to grain, fruit, and vegetable crops. The branch of the pear tree in **Figure 6** shows the effects of pathogenic bacteria. Plants are sometimes treated with antibiotics. Scientists have also genetically engineered certain plants to be resistant to disease-causing bacteria.

Figure 6 *This branch of a pear tree has a bacterial disease called* fire blight.

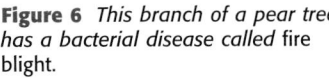

SECTION Review

Summary

- Bacteria are important to life on Earth because they fix nitrogen and decompose dead matter.
- Bacteria are useful to people because they help make foods and medicines.
- Scientists have genetically engineered bacteria to make medicines.
- Pathogenic bacteria are harmful to people. Bacteria can also harm the crops we grow for food.

Using Key Terms

1. In your own words, write a definition for the term *bioremediation*.

2. Use the following terms in the same sentence: *pathogenic bacteria* and *antibiotic*.

Understanding Key Ideas

3. What are two ways that bacteria affect plants?

4. How can bacteria both cause and cure diseases?

5. Explain two ways in which bacteria are crucial to life on Earth.

6. Describe two ways your life was affected by bacteria today.

Math Skills

7. Nitrogen makes up about 78% of air. If you have 2 L of air, how many liters of nitrogen are in the air?

Critical Thinking

8. **Identifying Relationships** Legumes, which include peas and beans, are efficient nitrogen fixers. Legumes are also a good source of amino acids. What chemical element would you expect to find in amino acids?

9. **Applying Concepts** Design a bacterium that will be genetically engineered. What do you want it to do? How would it help people or the environment?

For a variety of links related to this chapter, go to www.scilinks.org

Topic: Antibiotics; Genetic Engineering
SciLinks code: HSM0082; HSM0654

Answers to Section Review

1. Sample answer: During bioremediation, bacteria are used to clean up hazardous waste.

2. Sample answer: Antibiotics are medicines used to fight infections caused by pathogenic bacteria.

3. Sample answer: Bacteria help plants by changing nitrogen in the air to a form that plants can use. Bacteria can also cause diseases in plants.

4. Sample answer: Bacteria can cause diseases by taking nutrients from an organism's cells, but bacteria can also be used to fight diseases by making antibiotics.

5. Sample answer: Bacteria fix nitrogen for plants, and they act as decomposers, making nutrients available to other living things.

6. Sample answer: I ate cheese, and someone in my family used insulin, which may have been made by bacteria.

7. 1.56 L of nitrogen (2 L × 0.78 = 1.56 L)

8. Sample answer: Because legumes are good nitrogen fixers, I would expect to find nitrogen in the amino acids.

9. Sample answer: I would genetically engineer a bacterium that would eat carbon dioxide and change it into water. The bacterium could be used to supply clean water to places that need it and remove carbon dioxide from the air.

CHAPTER RESOURCES

Chapter Resource File

- Section Quiz **GENERAL**
- Section Review **GENERAL**
- Vocabulary and Section Summary **GENERAL**
- Critical Thinking **ADVANCED**

Technology

- Interactive Explorations CD-ROM
  - Scope It Out! **GENERAL**

SECTION
3

Focus

Overview

This section describes the characteristics of viruses. Students will learn that viruses can be classified by their shape, the disease that they cause, their life cycle, or the kind of genetic material they contain. Students will also learn how viruses reproduce.

Bellringer

Ask students to answer the following question: "Are viruses living?" (Students should recognize that viruses do not have all the characteristics of living things. They do not grow, eat, or reproduce on their own.)

Motivate

Demonstration — GENERAL

Characteristics of Viruses Show students a picture or diagram of a typical plant or animal cell (whose organelles are labeled). Then, show students pictures of one or more viruses (especially a bacteriophage). Help students compare the parts of the plant or animal cell with the parts of the viruses. Review with students parts of a cell or virus that may not be visible, such as DNA. Ask students to predict whether viruses are alive and how viruses cause disease.

LS Visual   English Language Learners

SECTION
3

READING WARM-UP

Objectives

- Explain how viruses are similar to and different from living things.
- List the four major virus shapes.
- Describe the two kinds of viral reproduction.

Terms to Learn

virus
host

READING STRATEGY

Discussion Read this section silently. Write down questions that you have about this section. Discuss your questions in a small group.

virus a microscopic particle that gets inside a cell and often destroys the cell

host an organism from which a parasite takes food or shelter

Viruses

One day, you discover red spots on your skin. More and more spots appear, and they begin turning into itchy blisters. What do you have?

The spots could be chickenpox. Chickenpox is a disease caused by a virus. A **virus** is a microscopic particle that gets inside a cell and often destroys the cell. Many viruses cause diseases, such as the common cold, flu, and acquired immune deficiency syndrome (AIDS).

It's a Small World

Viruses are tiny. They are smaller than the smallest bacteria. About 5 billion virus particles could fit in a single drop of blood. Viruses can change rapidly. So, a virus's effect on living things can also change. Because viruses are so small and change so often, scientists don't know exactly how many types exist. These properties also make them difficult to fight.

Are Viruses Living?

Like living things, viruses contain protein and genetic material. But viruses, such as the ones shown in **Figure 1,** don't act like living things. They can't eat, grow, break down food, or use oxygen. In fact, a virus cannot function on its own. A virus can reproduce only inside a living cell that serves as a host. A **host** is a living thing that a virus or parasite lives on or in. Using a host's cell as a tiny factory, the virus forces the host to make viruses rather than healthy new cells.

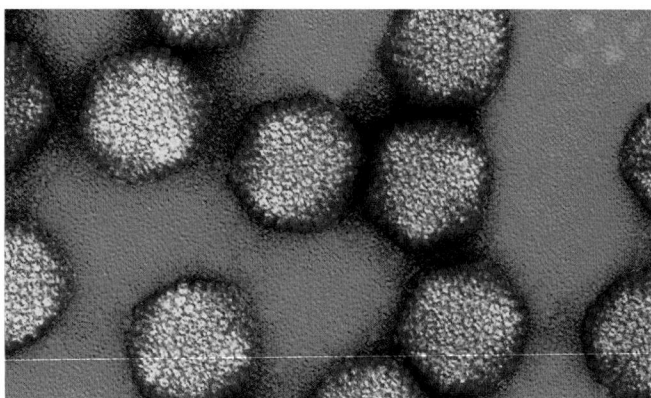

Figure 1 *Viruses are not cells. They do not have cytoplasm or organelles.*

Is That a Fact!

Bacteria are small, but viruses are even smaller. Millions of viruses can fit inside a single bacterium.

Figure 2 The Basic Shapes of Viruses

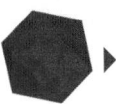

Crystals
The polio virus is shaped like the crystals shown here.

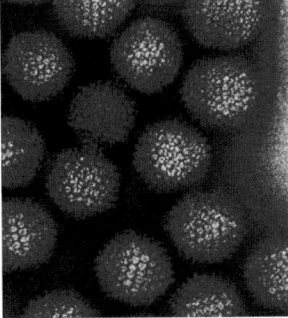

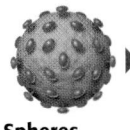

Spheres
Influenza viruses look like spheres. HIV is another virus that has this structure.

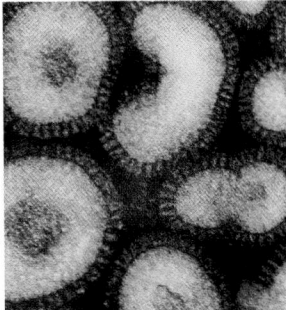

Cylinders
The tobacco mosaic virus is shaped like a cylinder and attacks tobacco plants.

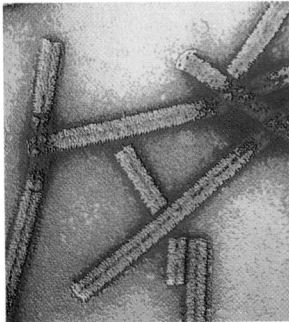

Spacecraft
One group of viruses attacks only bacteria. Many of these look almost like spacecraft.

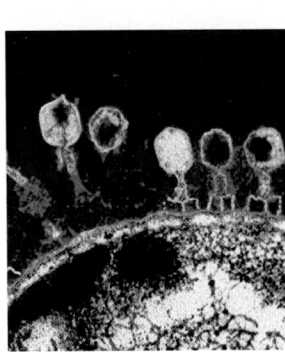

Classifying Viruses

Viruses can be grouped by their shape, the type of disease they cause, their life cycle, or the kind of genetic material they contain. The four main shapes of viruses are shown in **Figure 2**. Every virus is made up of genetic material inside a protein coat. The protein coat protects the genetic material and helps a virus enter a host cell. Many viruses have a protein coat that matches characteristics of their specific host.

The genetic material in viruses is either DNA or RNA. Most RNA is made up of one strand of nucleotides. Most DNA is made up of two strands of nucleotides. Both DNA and RNA contain information for making proteins. The viruses that cause warts and chickenpox contain DNA. The viruses that cause colds and the flu contain RNA. The virus that causes AIDS, which is called the *human immunodeficiency virus* (HIV), also contains RNA.

Reading Check What are two ways in which viruses can be classified? (*See the Appendix for answers to Reading Checks.*)

Sizing Up a Virus
If you enlarged an average virus 600,000 times, it would be about the size of a small pea. How tall would you be if you were enlarged 600,000 times?

Answer to Reading Check

Viruses can be classified by shape or by the type of genetic material they contain. Other possible answers are that viruses can be classified by life cycle or by the kind of disease that they cause.

Answer to Math Practice

This answer will vary depending on the student's height. Sample answer: If a student is 1.6 m (5 ft 4 in.) tall, he or she would be 960,000 m (3,149,606 ft) tall if enlarged 600,000 times. (1.6 m × 600,000 = 960,000 m)

Reteaching — BASIC

Lytic Cycle Have students work in pairs to review the lytic cycle. Students should take turns summarizing the cycle to each other. Students should stop each other if they find a concept confusing or need clarification. **LS Verbal/Interpersonal**

Quiz — GENERAL

1. List three shapes of viruses, and give an example of each. (Sample answer: crystals—polio virus; spheres—influenza virus; cylinders—tobacco mosaic virus)

2. How are viruses like and unlike living things? (Sample answer: Like living things, viruses contain protein and genetic material, but unlike living things, viruses don't eat, grow, break down food, or use oxygen.)

Alternative Assessment — GENERAL

Writing **New Virus** Have students write a short story in which they discover a new type of disease-causing virus. Ask students to include specific details about the structure of the new virus and the way it reproduces. **LS Verbal**

Answer to Reading Check

when a virus attacks living cells and turns them into virus factories

---

Figure 3 The Lytic Cycle

❶ The virus finds and joins itself to a host cell.

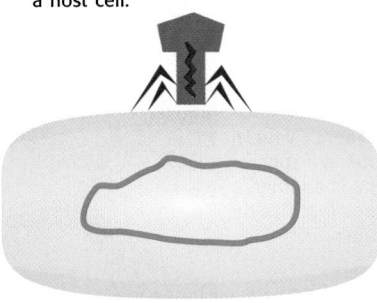

❷ The virus enters the cell, or the virus's genetic material is injected into the cell.

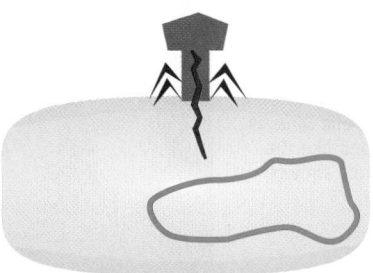

❸ Once the virus's genes are inside, they take over the direction of the host cell and turn it into a virus factory.

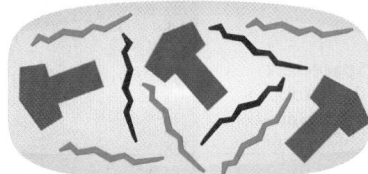

❹ The new viruses break out of the host cell, which kills the host cell. The cycle begins again.

CONNECTION TO Chemistry

Viral Crystals Many viruses can form into crystals. Scientists can study X rays of these crystals to learn about the structure of viruses. Why do you think scientists want to learn more about viruses?

A Destructive House Guest

The one thing that viruses do that living things also do is make more of themselves. Viruses attack living cells and turn them into virus factories. This cycle is called the *lytic cycle* (LIT ik SIE kuhl), and it is shown in **Figure 3.**

✓ Reading Check What is the lytic cycle?

A Time Bomb

Some viruses don't go straight into the lytic cycle. These viruses also put their genetic material into the host cell. But new viruses are not made right away. In the lysogenic (LIE soh JEN ik) cycle, each new cell gets a copy of the virus's genes when the host cell divides. The genes can stay inactive for a long time. When the genes do become active, they begin the lytic cycle and make copies of the virus.

Answer to Connection to Chemistry

Sample answer: Scientists want to learn more about viruses so they can design new ways of fighting viral diseases.

INTERNET ACTiViTy Essay — GENERAL

For an internet activity related to this chapter, have students go to **go.hrw.com** and type in the keyword **HL5VIRW.**

Treating a Virus

Antibiotics do not kill viruses. But scientists have recently developed antiviral (AN tie VIE ruhl) medications. Many of these medicines stop viruses from reproducing. Because many viral diseases do not have cures, it is best to prevent a viral infection from happening in the first place. Childhood vaccinations give your immune system a head start in fighting off viruses. Having current vaccinations can prevent you from getting a viral infection. It is also a good practice to wash your hands often and never to touch wild animals. If you do get sick from a virus, like the boy in **Figure 4,** it is often best to rest and drink extra fluids. As with any sickness, you should tell your parents or a doctor.

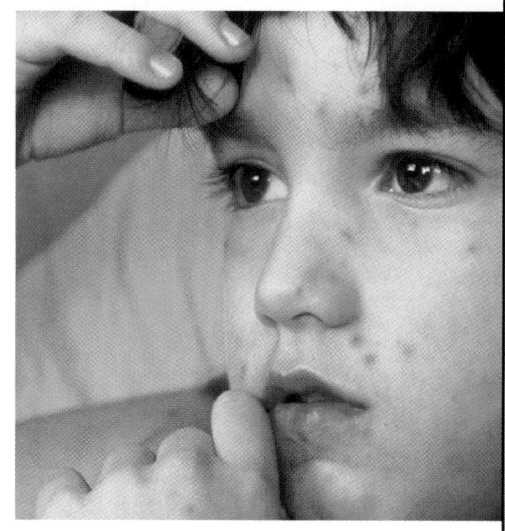

Figure 4 *The chickenpox virus resides inside your body even after the red spots are gone.*

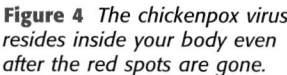
SECTION Review

Summary

- Viruses have characteristics of living and nonliving things. They reproduce in living cells.
- Viruses may be classified by their shape, the kind of disease they cause, or their life cycle.
- To reproduce, a virus must enter a cell, reproduce itself, and then break open the cell. This is called the lytic cycle.
- In the lysogenic cycle, the genes of a virus are incorporated into the genes of the host cell.

Using Key Terms

1. Use the following terms in the same sentence: *virus* and *host*.

Understanding Key Ideas

2. One characteristic viruses have in common with living things is that they
   a. eat.   c. sleep.
   b. reproduce.   d. grow.

3. Describe the four steps in the lytic cycle.

4. Explain how the lytic cycle and the lysogenic cycle are different.

Math Skills

5. A bacterial cell infected by a virus divides every 20 min. After 10,000 divisions, the new viruses are released from their host cell. About how many weeks will this process take?

Critical Thinking

6. **Making Inferences** Do you think modern transportation has had an effect on the way viruses spread? Explain.

7. **Identifying Relationships** What characteristics of viruses do you think have made finding drugs to attack them difficult?

8. **Expressing Opinions** Do you think that vaccinations are important even in areas where a virus is not found?

SCILINKS®

NSTA
Developed and maintained by the National Science Teachers Association

For a variety of links related to this chapter, go to www.scilinks.org

Topic: Viruses
SciLinks code: HSM1607

Homework —— ADVANCED

Viral Diseases After students read this section, have them research three viruses that cause disease. Have them make a chart that includes the name of the disease, the symptoms of the disease, and the treatment for the disease. **L$_S$ Logical**

CHAPTER RESOURCES

Chapter Resource File

- Section Quiz **GENERAL**
- Section Review **GENERAL**
- Vocabulary and Section Summary **GENERAL**
- Reinforcement Worksheet **BASIC**

Technology

Transparencies
- The Lytic Cycle

Answers to Section Review

1. Sample answer: A virus infects a host, forcing the host's cells to make more viruses.

2. b

3. Sample answer: The virus joins itself to a host cell. The virus enters the cell or injects its genetic material into the host cell. The virus's genes take over the host cell, and the host starts making copies of the virus. The new viruses break out of the host cell, killing the host cell. These viruses look for new host cells.

4. Sample answer: In the lysogenic cycle, a virus invades a host cell but does not start making copies of itself right away. The genes stay inactive for a long time. When the genes do become active, the lytic cycle begins.

5. 19.8 weeks (10,000 divisions × 20 min/division = 200,000 min; 200,000 min ÷ 60 min/h = 3,333 h; 3,333 h ÷ 24 h/d = 139 days; 139 days ÷ 7 days/week = 19.8 wk)

6. Sample answer: Modern transportation makes it possible for a virus to spread to a larger area faster. Airplanes can travel halfway around the world in less than a day. A virus carried by someone on the plane could also travel halfway around the world in that period of time.

7. Sample answer: Viruses reproduce very quickly, and viruses can change rapidly.

8. Sample answer: Vaccinations are important because people travel and a virus can turn up in places where it has not historically been found.

Aunt Flossie and the Intruder

Teacher's Notes

Time Required

Three 20-minute brainstorming and design sessions and five 5-minute observation periods on successive days

Lab Ratings

EASY ——————→ HARD

Teacher Prep 🧪🧪
Student Set-Up 🧪🧪🧪
Concept Level 🧪🧪🧪
Clean Up 🧪🧪

MATERIALS

Students will need to submit a list of supplies and equipment they will need for their experiment to you for approval.

Safety Caution

Be sure students address any safety concerns in the design of their experiments.

OBJECTIVES

Design an experiment that will answer a specific question.

Investigate what kind of organisms make food spoil.

MATERIALS

- gloves, protective
- items, such as sealable plastic bags, food samples, a scale, or a thermometer, to be determined by the students and approved by the teacher as needed for each experiment

SAFETY

Aunt Flossie and the Intruder

Aunt Flossie is a really bad housekeeper! She never cleans the refrigerator, and things get really gross in there. Last week she pulled out a plastic bag that looked like it was going to explode! The bag was full of gas that she did not put there! Aunt Flossie remembered from her school days that gases are released from living things as waste products. Something had to be alive in the bag!

Aunt Flossie became very upset that there was an intruder in her refrigerator. She refuses to bake another cookie until you determine the nature of the intruder.

Ask a Question

1. How did gas get into Aunt Flossie's bag?

Form a Hypothesis

2. Write a hypothesis which answers the question above. Explain your reasoning.

Test the Hypothesis

3. Design an experiment that will determine how gas got into Aunt Flossie's bag. Make a list of the materials you will need, and prepare all the data tables you will need for recording your observations.

4. Get your teacher's approval of your experimental design and your list of materials before you begin.

5. Dispose of your materials according to your teacher's instructions at the end of your experiment. **Caution:** Do not open any bags of spoiled food or allow any of the contents to escape.

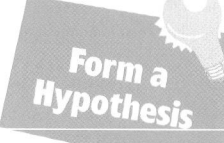

Ask a Question

Form a Hypothesis

Test the Hypothesis

Elizabeth Rustad
Crane Junior High School
Yuma, Arizona

CHAPTER RESOURCES

Chapter Resource File

- Datasheet for Chapter Lab
- Lab Notes and Answers

Technology

- Classroom Videos
  - Lab Video

Lab Book

- Viral Decorations

Analyze the Results

❶ **Organizing Data** What data did you collect from your experiment?

Draw Conclusions

❷ **Drawing Conclusions** What conclusions can you draw from your investigation? Where did the gas come from?

❸ **Evaluating Methods** If you were going to perform another investigation, what would you change in the experiment to give better results? Explain your answer.

Communicating Your Data

WRITING SKILL Write a letter to Aunt Flossie describing your experiment. Explain what produced the gas in the bag and your recommendations for preventing these intruders in her refrigerator in the future.

Analyze the Results

1. Answers may vary depending on the student's design.

Draw Conclusions

2. Answers may vary. Students should conclude that living organisms from the food or air produce gas.

3. Answers may vary.

Communicating Your Data

Students should explain (in a letter to Aunt Flossie) that mold or bacteria in the bag produced the gas. The gas was a product of the respiration of the mold or bacteria on the food. Preventing future intruders could be as simple as lowering the temperature of the refrigerator or freezing food.

Analyze the Results

Draw Conclusions

Do they support your hypothesis?

No

Yes

CHAPTER RESOURCES

Workbooks

Labs You Can Eat
• Bacterial Buddies GENERAL

Inquiry Labs
• It's an Invasion! GENERAL

EcoLabs & Field Activities
• Ditch's Brew GENERAL

Long-Term Projects & Research Ideas
• Bacteria to the Rescue! ADVANCED

Chapter Review

Assignment Guide

Section	Questions
1	2, 7–10, 18, 22–25
2	1, 3, 5, 12, 13, 16, 19–21
3	4, 6, 11, 14–15, 17

ANSWERS

Using Key Terms

1. Sample answer: Pathogenic bacteria are bacteria that cause disease.
2. binary fission
3. antibiotics
4. virus

Understanding Key Ideas

5. d
6. a
7. b
8. b
9. c
10. d
11. c
12. d

USING KEY TERMS

1 In your own words, write a definition for the term *pathogenic bacteria*.

Complete each of the following sentences by choosing the correct term from the word bank.

binary fission	endospore
antibiotic	bioremediation
virus	bacteria

2 Most bacteria reproduce by ___.

3 Bacterial infections can be treated with ___.

4 A(n) ___ needs a host to reproduce.

UNDERSTANDING KEY IDEAS

Multiple Choice

5 Bacteria are used for all of the following EXCEPT

  a. making certain foods.

  b. making antibiotics.

  c. cleaning up oil spills.

  d. preserving fruit.

6 In the lytic cycle, the host cell

  a. is destroyed.

  b. destroys the virus.

  c. becomes a virus.

  d. undergoes cell division.

7 A bacterial cell

  a. is an endospore.

  b. has a loop of DNA.

  c. has a distinct nucleus.

  d. is a eukaryote.

8 Eubacteria

  a. include methane makers.

  b. include decomposers.

  c. all have chlorophyll.

  d. are rod-shaped.

9 Cyanobacteria

  a. are consumers.

  b. are parasites.

  c. contain chlorophyll.

  d. are decomposers.

10 Archaebacteria

  a. are a special type of eubacteria.

  b. live only in places without oxygen.

  c. are lactic acid-producing bacteria.

  d. can live in hostile environments.

11 Viruses

  a. are about the same size as bacteria.

  b. have nuclei.

  c. can reproduce only within a host cell.

  d. do not infect plants.

12 Bacteria are important to the planet as

  a. decomposers of dead organic matter.

  b. processors of nitrogen.

  c. makers of medicine.

  d. All of the above

Short Answer

13 How are the functions of nitrogen-fixing bacteria and decomposers similar?

14 Which cycle takes more time, the lytic cycle or the lysogenic cycle?

15 Describe two ways in which viruses do not act like living things.

16 What is bioremediation?

17 Describe how doctors can treat a viral infection.

CRITICAL THINKING

18 **Concept Mapping** Use the following terms to create a concept map: *eubacteria, bacilli, cocci, spirilla, consumers, producers,* and *cyanobacteria.*

19 **Predicting Consequences** Describe some of the problems you think bacteria might face if there were no humans.

20 **Applying Concepts** Many modern soaps contain chemicals that kill bacteria. Describe one good outcome and one bad outcome of the use of antibacterial soaps.

21 **Identifying Relationships** Some people have digestive problems after they take a course of antibiotics. Why do you think these problems happen?

INTERPRETING GRAPHICS

The diagram below illustrates the stages of binary fission. Match each statement with the correct stage.

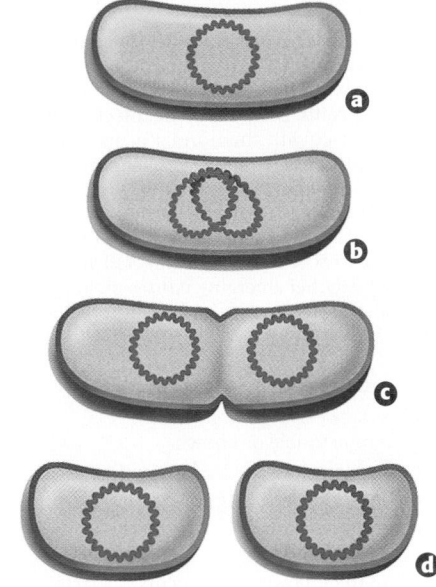

22 The DNA loops separate.

23 The DNA loop replicates.

24 The parent cell starts to expand.

25 The DNA attaches to the cell membrane.

---

13. Nitrogen-fixing bacteria and decomposers both perform functions that are critical for life on Earth.

14. the lysogenic cycle; In the lysogenic cycle, the virus injects its genetic material into the host but does not immediately begin to reproduce.

15. Viruses do not grow or eat as living things do.

16. Bioremediation is the process by which bacteria or other organisms turn toxic substances into harmless ones.

17. Sample answer: Doctors can treat some viral infections with antiviral medicines that stop viruses from reproducing.

Critical Thinking

18. An answer to this exercise can be found at the end of this book.

19. Sample answer: Most bacteria would face no problems at all. The only bacteria that might have a problem are pathogenic bacteria that infect only humans.

20. Sample answer: Antibacterial soaps can prevent bacterial infection. But these soaps might also lead to bacteria changing and becoming harder to fight with antibiotics available today.

21. Sample answer: Antibiotics kill all bacteria, even the good bacteria that live in your digestive tract. Your digestive system does not work properly without healthy colonies of beneficial bacteria.

Interpreting Graphics

22. stage c
23. stage b
24. stage a
25. stage b

CHAPTER RESOURCES

Chapter Resource File

- Chapter Review `GENERAL`
- Chapter Test A `GENERAL`
- Chapter Test B `ADVANCED`
- Chapter Test C `SPECIAL NEEDS`
- Vocabulary Activity `GENERAL`

Workbooks

Study Guide
- Assessment resources are also available in Spanish.

Teacher's Note

To provide practice under more realistic testing conditions, give students 20 minutes to answer all of the questions in this Standardized Test Preparation.

MISCONCEPTION ALERT

Answers to the standardized test preparation can help you identify student misconceptions and misunderstandings.

READING

Passage 1

1. A
2. F
3. D

+ TEST DOCTOR

Question 2: Students who chose answers G and I may be confused because the passage states that 40% to 50% of infected humans die. If the percentage of people who die is between 40 and 50, the answer must be over 40% and under 50%. Therefore, the correct answer must be F.

READING

Read each of the passages below. Then, answer the questions that follow each passage.

Passage 1 Viruses that evolve in isolated areas and that can infect human beings are called *emerging* viruses. These new viruses are dangerous to public health. People become infected when they have contact with the normal hosts of these viruses. In the United States, the hantavirus is considered an emerging virus. First detected in the southwestern United States, the hantavirus occurs in wild rodents and can infect and kill humans. Roughly 40% to 50% of humans infected with the hantavirus die. Other emerging viruses include the Ebola (Africa), Lassa (Africa), and Machupo (South America) viruses.

1. In the passage, what does the word *emerging* mean?
   - **A** to become visible or known
   - **B** to fade away into the background
   - **C** to melt from two things into one
   - **D** to become urgent

2. Which of the following statements is a fact from the passage?
   - **F** Hantavirus causes death in more than 40% of its victims.
   - **G** Hantavirus causes death in more than 50% of its victims.
   - **H** Hantavirus causes death in fewer than 30% of its victims.
   - **I** Hantavirus causes death in fewer than 40% of its victims.

3. Which of the following is an emergent virus in South America?
   - **A** Ebola virus
   - **B** Lassa virus
   - **C** SARS virus
   - **D** Machupo virus

Passage 2 Less than 100 years ago, people had no way to treat bacterial infections. But in 1928, a Scottish scientist named Alexander Fleming discovered the first antibiotic, or bacteria-killing drug. This first antibiotic was called *penicillin*. The discovery of antibiotics improved healthcare dramatically. However, scientists are now realizing that many bacteria are becoming resistant to existing antibiotics. Scientists are hoping that a particular type of virus called a bacteriophage (bak TIR ee uh FAHJ) might hold the key to fighting bacteria in the future. Bacteriophages destroy bacteria cells. Each kind of bacteriophage can infect only a particular species of bacteria.

1. In what year was penicillin discovered?
   - **A** 1905
   - **B** 1928
   - **C** 1969
   - **D** 1974

2. According to the passage, what might be the key to fighting bacteria in the future?
   - **F** antibiotics
   - **G** bacteriophages
   - **H** penicillin
   - **I** antibiotic-resistant bacteria

3. According to the passage, what can each kind of bacteriophage infect?
   - **A** viruses that cause disease
   - **B** only antibiotic-resistant bacteria
   - **C** all kinds of bacteria
   - **D** only a particular species of bacteria

Passage 2

1. B
2. G
3. D

+ TEST DOCTOR

Question 3: Students who chose answer A may mistakenly think that bacteriophages kill viruses, but bacteriophages are in fact viruses. Students who chose answer B may be confused because the passage mentions antibiotic-resistant bacteria as a problem and bacteriophages as a solution. However, bacteriophages do not kill only resistant bacteria. The correct answer is D, because each bacteriophage infects only a particular species of bacteria.

The images below show the four main shapes of viruses. Use these pictures to answer the questions that follow.

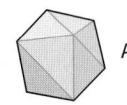 A

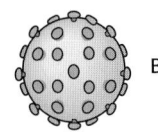 B

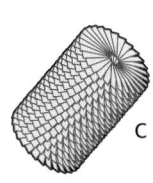

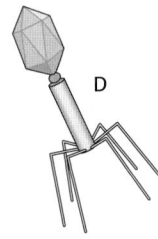 D

C

1. Which viral shape attacks only bacteria?
A virus A
B virus B
C virus C
D virus D

2. Which viral shape is the cylinder?
F virus A
G virus B
H virus C
I virus D

3. Which viral shape would you expect to have the largest surface area–to-volume ratio?
A virus A
B virus B
C virus C
D virus D

MATH

Read each question below, and choose the best answer.

1. Reagan spent $26 for four equally priced CDs. Which of the following equations could be used to find how much each CD costs?
A $4 \times \$26 = n$
B $n = \$26 - 4$
C $4 \times n = \$26$
D $n \times \$26 = 4$

2. What is $5 + (-8)$ equal to?
F -13
G -3
H 3
I 13

3. What is $-9 - 2$ equal to?
A -11
B -7
C -4
D 7

4. What is the solution to $45 \div 0.009$?
F $5,000$
G 500
H 50
I 5

5. What is $-9 + 2$ equal to?
A -11
B -7
C -4
D 7

6. Jennifer, Beth, and Sienna live 8 km, 2.2 km, and 7.4 km from the school. Which of the following is a reasonable estimate of the average distance these friends live from the school?
F 6 km
G 7.4 km
H 9 km
I 18 km

Standardized Test Preparation

1. D
2. H
3. D

 TEST DOCTOR

Question 3: A spherical shape has less surface area relative to volume than other shapes such as cones and pyramids. This shape helps spherical viruses and bacteria to keep from drying out. Students who chose B may have mistakenly thought that spheres have larger surface area relative to volume. Students who chose answers A or C may have felt less familiar with the shapes that make up the virus in answer D. However, answer D probably has the highest surface area relative to its volume.

MATH
1. C
2. G
3. A
4. F
5. B
6. F

 **TEST DOCTOR**

Question 6: Students who chose answer G may be confused about what an average is and decide that the middle number, 7.4, is the answer. Students who chose answer I may have estimated the sum of the three distances and then not divided the sum by 3 to find an average. The correct answer, F, is found by adding the three distances and then dividing the sum by 3.

CHAPTER RESOURCES

Chapter Resource File

 • Standardized Test Preparation **GENERAL**

State Resources

 For specific resources for your state, visit **go.hrw.com** and type in the keyword **HSMSTR**.

Science, Technology, and Society

Discussion ——— GENERAL

The milk of transgenic animals is also being tested as a potential edible vaccine. Scientists hope that goat's milk containing malaria-like proteins will prevent millions of malaria deaths. Ask students how they think scientists could do this. Then, tell students that scientists put genes for the proteins in the goat's genome. When the mammary cells express the proteins into the milk, the scientists can then milk the goats, isolate the malaria-like proteins, and use the proteins to make a vaccine.

Scientific Discoveries

Background

Influenza, or the flu, is a highly contagious disease that causes fever, chills, sore throats, coughing, and even death. The flu has been a fact of life since as early as 412 BCE. For many years, no one knew how this disease worked. In the 15th century, people believed that epidemics were influenced by stars and, because of this, they named the disease *influenza*. Only recently have scientists discovered that this disease is a virus. Scientists today continue to do research in order to understand how the flu virus attacks our bodies.

Science in Action

Science, Technology, and Society

Edible Vaccines

Vaccines protect you from life-threatening diseases. But vaccinations are expensive, and the people who give them must go through extensive training. These and other factors often prevent people in developing countries from getting vaccinations. But help may be on the way. Scientists are developing edible vaccines. Imagine eating a banana and getting the same protection you would from several painful injections. These vaccines are made from DNA that encodes a protein in the disease-causing particles. This DNA can then be inserted into the banana's genes. Researchers are still working on safe and effective edible vaccines.

Language Arts ACTIVITY

WRITING SKILL Write an advertisement for an edible vaccine. Be sure to describe the benefits of vaccinations.

Scientific Discoveries

Spanish Flu and the Flu Cycle

In 1918, a version of the influenza (the flu) virus killed millions of people worldwide. This disease, mistakenly called the Spanish Flu (it probably started in China), was one of the worst epidemics in history. Doctors and scientists realized that the large movement of people during the First World War probably made it easier for the Spanish Flu to spread. But the question of how this common disease could become so deadly remained unknown. One important factor is that the influenza virus is constantly changing. Many scientists now think that the influenza virus mutates into a more deadly form about every 30 years. There were flu epidemics in 1918, 1957, and 1968, which leads some scientists to believe that we are overdue for another flu epidemic.

Social Studies ACTIVITY

WRITING SKILL Conduct an interview with an older member of your family. Ask them how the flu, smallpox, tuberculosis, or polio has affected their lives. Write a report that includes information on how doctors deal with the disease today.

Answer to Language Arts Activity
Answers may vary. Advertisements should show an understanding of the benefits of edible vaccines, such as the cost savings and reduced training required for administering the vaccinations.

Answer to Social Studies Activity
Answers may vary. Students should include information on how the disease in their report is dealt with today.

People in Science

Laytonville Middle School

Composting Project In 1973, Mary Appelhof tried an experiment. She knew that bacteria can help break down dead organic matter. In her basement, she set up a bin with worms and dumped her food scraps in there. Her basement didn't smell like garbage because her worms were eating the food scraps! Composting uses heat, bacteria, and, sometimes, worms to break down food wastes. Composting turns these wastes into fertilizer.

Binet Payne, a teacher at the Laytonville Middle School in California, decided to try Appelhof's composting system. Ms. Payne asked her students to separate their school cafeteria's trash into different categories: veggie wastes (worm food), protein foods (meat, milk, and cheese), bottles, cans, bags (to be recycled), and "yucky trash" (napkins and other nonrecyclables). The veggie waste was placed into the worm bins, and the protein foods were used to feed a local farm's chickens and pigs. In the first year, the Garden Project saved the school $6,000, which otherwise would have been used to dump the garbage into a landfill.

Math ACTIVITY

If the school saved $6,000 the first year, how much money did the school save each day of the year?

To learn more about these Science in Action topics, visit **go.hrw.com** and type in the keyword **HL5VIRF**.

Check out Current Science® articles related to this chapter by visiting go.hrw.com. Just type in the keyword **HL5CS10.**

Answer to Math Activity
$16.44 per day ($6,000 ÷ 365 days)

People in Science
Teaching Strategy GENERAL

Explain to students that there are two types of decomposition: aerobic and anaerobic. In aerobic decomposition, organic material combines with oxygen to produce carbon dioxide, water, heat, and energy. In anaerobic decomposition, there is no oxygen present. Organic matter combines with water to produce carbon dioxide, methane, hydrogen sulfide, and energy. If you are composting and the pile starts to smell rotten, the smell is probably due to the hydrogen sulfide being made by anaerobic decomposition. This smell signals that the pile needs more oxygen. The easiest way to add oxygen is by turning the pile.

ACTIVITY GENERAL

Have students follow these steps to make their own compost bin: Drill 8 holes into the bottom of a 2 ft × 2 ft plastic bin (at least 8 in. deep). Add water to several pounds of shredded paper until it feels moist. Spread the bedding in the bottom of the bin, and cover it with a few handfuls of soil. Place some red worms in the bin. Add some veggie wastes, and leave the bin covered for a week. After a week, discuss what is happening in the bin. **Note:** If the compost will be used to help grow food, you should research whether there are any toxins in the kind of paper you plan to use as bedding for the bin.

Protists and Fungi
Chapter Planning Guide

Compression guide:
To shorten instruction because of time limitations, omit Section 2.

OBJECTIVES	LABS, DEMONSTRATIONS, AND ACTIVITIES	TECHNOLOGY RESOURCES
PACING • 90 min pp. 268–273 **Chapter Opener**	**SE** Start-up Activity, p. 269 (GENERAL)	**OSP** Parent Letter ■ (GENERAL) **CD** Student Edition on CD-ROM **CD** Guided Reading Audio CD ■ **TR** Chapter Starter Transparency* **VID** Brain Food Video Quiz
Section 1 Protists • Describe the characteristics of protists. • Describe four ways that protists get food. • Describe three ways that protists reproduce.	**TE** Activity Methods of Moving, p. 270 (GENERAL) **SE** School-to-Home Activity Food for Thought, p. 271 (GENERAL) **TE** Group Activity Making a Hypothesis, p. 271 (ADVANCED) **TE** Connection Activity Math, p. 272 (GENERAL) **SE** Science in Action Math, Social Studies, and Language Arts Activities, p. 296–297 (GENERAL) **SE** Model-Making Lab Making a Protist Mobile, p. 773 (GENERAL) **CRF** Datasheet for LabBook*	**CRF** Lesson Plans* **TR** Bellringer Transparency* **TR** The Life Cycle of *P. vivax**
PACING • 45 min pp. 274–281 **Section 2 Kinds of Protists** • Describe how protists can be organized into three groups based on their shared traits. • List an example for each group of protists.	**TE** Demonstration Algae as Food, p. 274 ◆ (GENERAL) **TE** Activity Organizing Algae Information, p. 275 (BASIC) **TE** Connection Activity Art, p. 276 (ADVANCED) **TE** Activity Concept Mapping, p. 276 (GENERAL) **TE** Activity Observing Live Amoebas, p. 277 ◆ (GENERAL) **SE** Connection to Geology Shell Deposits, p. 278 (GENERAL) **SE** Connection to Social Studies Malaria, p. 279 (GENERAL) **TE** Connection Activity Social Studies, p. 279 (ADVANCED) **TE** Group Activity Make a Slime Mold, p. 280 ◆ (ADVANCED) **LB** Long-Term Projects & Research Ideas Algae for All!* (ADVANCED)	**CRF** Lesson Plans* **TR** Bellringer Transparency* **TR** *Euglena, Paramecium** **TR** **LINK TO EARTH SCIENCE** The Geologic Time Scale* **SE** Internet Activity, p. 280 (GENERAL)
PACING • 90 min pp. 282–289 **Section 3 Fungi** • Describe the characteristics of fungi. • Distinguish between the four main groups of fungi. • Explain how lichens affect their environment.	**SE** Quick Lab Moldy Bread, p. 284 (GENERAL) **CRF** Datasheet for Quick Lab* **TE** Activity Making Models, p. 285 ◆ (GENERAL) **TE** Connection Activity Math, p. 285 (ADVANCED) **SE** Quick Lab Observe a Mushroom, p. 286 ◆ (GENERAL) **CRF** Datasheet for Quick Lab* **TE** Activity Fungus Reproduction, p. 286 (BASIC) **SE** Connection to Language Arts Beatrix Potter, p. 287 (GENERAL) **SE** Skills Practice Lab There's a Fungus Among Us!, p. 290 (GENERAL) **CRF** Datasheet for Chapter Lab* **LB** Whiz-Bang Demonstrations Unleash the Yeast!* ◆ (GENERAL) **LB** Labs You Can Eat Knot Your Average Yeast Lab* (BASIC)	**CRF** Lesson Plans* **TR** Bellringer Transparency* **CRF** SciLinks Activity* (GENERAL) **VID** Lab Videos for Life Science

PACING • 90 min

CHAPTER REVIEW, ASSESSMENT, AND STANDARDIZED TEST PREPARATION

CRF Vocabulary Activity* (GENERAL)
SE Chapter Review, pp. 292–293 (GENERAL)
CRF Chapter Review* ■ (GENERAL)
CRF Chapter Tests A* ■ (GENERAL), B* (ADVANCED), C* (SPECIAL NEEDS)
SE Standardized Test Preparation, pp. 294–295 (GENERAL)
CRF Standardized Test Preparation* (GENERAL)
CRF Performance-Based Assessment* (GENERAL)
OSP Test Generator (GENERAL)
CRF Test Item Listing* (GENERAL)

Online and Technology Resources

Visit **go.hrw.com** for a variety of free resources related to this textbook. Enter the keyword **HL5PRO**.

Holt Online Learning

Students can access interactive problem-solving help and active visual concept development with the *Holt Science and Technology* Online Edition available at **www.hrw.com**.

 Guided Reading Audio CD Also in Spanish

A direct reading of each chapter for auditory learners, reluctant readers, and Spanish-speaking students.

 Science Tutor CD-ROM

Excellent for remediation and test practice.

SKILLS DEVELOPMENT RESOURCES	SECTION REVIEW AND ASSESSMENT	STANDARDS CORRELATIONS
SE Pre-Reading Activity, p. 268 `GENERAL` **OSP** Science Puzzlers, Twisters & Teasers* `GENERAL`		National Science Education Standards UCP 2; SAI 1; LS 1b
CRF Directed Reading A* ■ `BASIC`, B* `SPECIAL NEEDS` **CRF** Vocabulary and Section Summary* ■ `GENERAL` **SE** Reading Strategy Discussion, p. 270 `GENERAL` **TE** Reading Strategy Prediction Guide, p. 271 `BASIC` **SE** Math Practice Pairs of Paramecia, p. 272 `GENERAL` **SS** Science Skills Organizing Your Research* `GENERAL` **MS** Math Skills for Science A Shortcut for Multiplying Large Numbers* `GENERAL` **CRF** Reinforcement Worksheet Protists on Parade* `BASIC` **CRF** Critical Thinking Protist Pop Culture* `ADVANCED`	**SE** Reading Checks, pp. 271, 272 `GENERAL` **TE** Reteaching, p. 272 `BASIC` **TE** Quiz, p. 272 `GENERAL` **TE** Alternative Assessment, p. 272 `GENERAL` **SE** Section Review,* p. 273 ■ `GENERAL` **TE** Homework, p. 273 `GENERAL` **CRF** Section Quiz* ■ `GENERAL`	UCP 5; SAI 2; LS 1b, 1c, 1f, 2a, 4b, 5a
CRF Directed Reading A* ■ `BASIC`, B* `SPECIAL NEEDS` **CRF** Vocabulary and Section Summary* ■ `GENERAL` **SE** Reading Strategy Reading Organizer, p. 274 `GENERAL` **TE** Reading Strategy Prediction Guide, p. 275 `BASIC` **TE** Inclusion Strategies, p. 279	**SE** Reading Checks, pp. 275, 276, 278, 280 `GENERAL` **TE** Reteaching, p. 280 `BASIC` **TE** Quiz, p. 280 `GENERAL` **TE** Alternative Assessment, p. 280 `BASIC` **SE** Section Review,* p. 281 ■ `GENERAL` **CRF** Section Quiz* ■ `GENERAL`	UCP 5; LS 1a, 1b, 1f, 3a, 5a; *LabBook:* UCP 2
CRF Directed Reading A* ■ `BASIC`, B* `SPECIAL NEEDS` **CRF** Vocabulary and Section Summary* ■ `GENERAL` **SE** Reading Strategy Paired Summarizing, p. 282 `GENERAL` **TE** Reading Strategy Prediction Guide, p. 283 `GENERAL` **TE** Inclusion Strategies, p. 288 **CRF** Reinforcement Worksheet An Ode to a Fungus* `BASIC`	**SE** Reading Checks, pp. 283, 284, 286, 288 `GENERAL` **TE** Reteaching, p. 288 `BASIC` **TE** Quiz, p. 288 `GENERAL` **TE** Alternative Assessment, p. 288 `GENERAL` **SE** Section Review,* p. 289 ■ `GENERAL` **CRF** Section Quiz* ■ `GENERAL`	UCP 5; SAI 1; SPSP 5; LS 1a, 1b, 1d, 1f, 2a, 4b, 5a; *Chapter Lab:* UCP 5; SAI 1; LS 1a

One-Stop Planner® CD-ROM

This convenient CD-ROM includes:
- **Lab Materials QuickList Software**
- **Holt Calendar Planner**
- **Customizable Lesson Plans**
- **Printable Worksheets**
- **ExamView® Test Generator**

CNN student News™

cnnstudentnews.com

Find the latest news, lesson plans, and activities related to important scientific events.

SCILINKS® NSTA

www.scilinks.org

Maintained by the **National Science Teachers Association.** See Chapter Enrichment pages for a complete list of topics.

Current Science®

Check out *Current Science* articles and activities by visiting the HRW Web site at **go.hrw.com.** Just type in the keyword **HL5CS11T.**

Classroom Videos

- **Lab Videos** demonstrate the chapter lab.
- **Brain Food Video Quizzes** help students review the chapter material.
- **CNN Videos** bring science into your students' daily life.

Visual Resources

CHAPTER STARTER TRANSPARENCY

The Potato Eaters, van Gogh, 1885

This Really Happened!

The year is 1846, and the country is Ireland. The weather is cold and rainy, and the situation is desperate. Disease has swept through the potato fields. In just a few weeks, it destroyed almost the entire crop.

The Irish depend on potatoes for food. Every day, hundreds of people die of starvation. With no other hope for survival, tens of thousands are fleeing their country. Most head for the United States.

During the hungry years of the Great Potato Famine, from 1845–1852, Ireland lost one-third of its population. Two million people left the country. One million people died. What was the cause of all this death and devastation? A simple organism called a water mold was to blame.

Water molds are protists. This particular water mold changed the course of Irish history. It also changed the American population. Do you have Irish ancestry? If so, a water mold may have brought your family to this country.

But don't get the wrong idea. Not all protists are harmful. Some are very helpful. You'll learn about protists in this chapter.

BELLRINGER TRANSPARENCIES

Section: Protists

Have you ever heard of a protist? How many examples of protists can you think of? Why do you suppose protists are not as well known as fungi?

Record your answers in your **science journal**.

Section: Kinds of Protists

Do you know what algae are? Have you ever seen algae? If so, describe what it looks like. Algae need a lot of water in order to live. Where do you suppose most algae live?

Record your answers in your **science journal**.

TEACHING TRANSPARENCIES

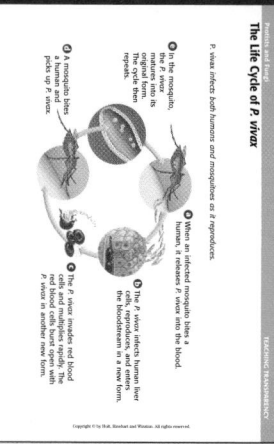

The Life Cycle of P. vivax

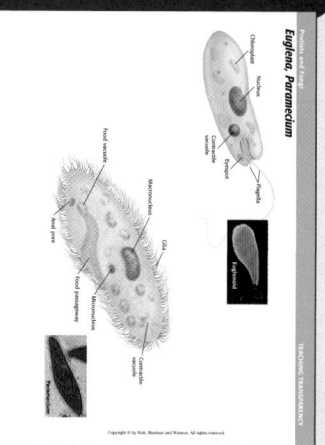

Euglena, Paramecium

TEACHING TRANSPARENCIES

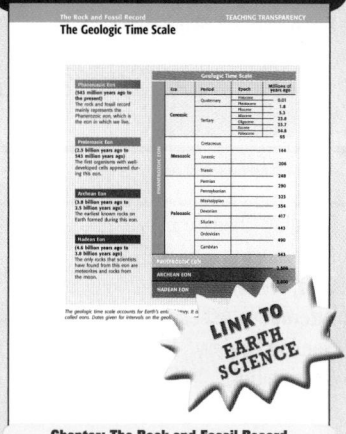

The Geologic Time Scale

LINK TO EARTH SCIENCE

Chapter: The Rock and Fossil Record

CONCEPT MAPPING TRANSPARENCY

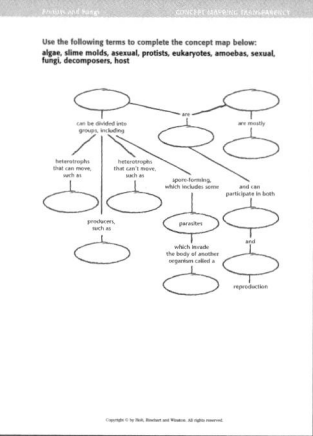

Use the following terms to complete the concept map below: algae, slime molds, asexual, protists, eukaryotes, amoebas, sexual, fungi, decomposers, host

Planning Resources

LESSON PLANS

Lesson Plan SAMPLE

Section: Waves

Pacing

Regular Schedule: with lab(s):2 days   without lab(s):2 days
Block Schedule: with lab(s): 1 1/2 days   without lab(s):1 day

Objectives

1. Relate the seven properties of life to a living organism.
2. Describe seven themes that can help you to organize what you learn about biology.
3. Identify the tiny structures that make up all living organisms.
4. Differentiate between reproduction and heredity and between metabolism and homeostasis.

National Science Education Standards Covered

LSInter6:Cells have particular structures that underlie their functions.
LSMat1:Most cell functions involve chemical reactions.
LSBeh1:Cells store and use information to guide their functions.
UCP1:Cell functions are regulated.
St1: Cells can differentiate and form complete multicellular organisms.
PS1: Species evolve over time.
ESS1: The great diversity of organisms is the result of more than 3.5 billion years of evolution.
ESS2: Natural selection and its evolutionary consequences provide a scientific explanation for the fossil record of ancient life forms as well as for the striking molecular similarities observed among the diverse species of living organisms.
ST1: The millions of different species of plants, animals, and microorganisms that live on Earth today are related by descent from common ancestors.
ST2: The energy for life primarily comes from the sun.
SPSP1: The complexity and organization of organisms accommodates the need for obtaining, transforming, transporting, releasing, and eliminating the matter and energy used to sustain the organism.
SPSP6: As matter and energy flows through different levels of organization of living systems—cells, organs, communities—and between living species, the physical environment, chemical elements are recombined in different ways.
HNS1: Organisms have behavioral responses to internal changes and to external stimuli.

PARENT LETTER

SAMPLE

Dear Parent,

Your son's or daughter's science class will soon begin exploring the chapter entitled "The World of Physical Science." In this chapter, students will learn about how the scientific method applies to the world of physical science and the role of physical science in the world. By the end of the chapter, students should demonstrate a clear understanding of the chapter's main ideas and be able to discuss the following topics:

1. physical science as the study of energy and matter (Section 1)
2. the role of physical science in the world around them (Section 1)
3. careers that rely on physical science (Section 1)
4. the steps used in the scientific method (Section 2)
5. examples of technology (Section 2)
6. how the scientific method is used to answer questions and solve problems (Section 2)
7. how our knowledge of science changes over time (Section 2)
8. how models represent real objects or systems (Section 3)
9. examples of different ways models are used in science (Section 3)
10. the importance of the International System of Units (Section 4)
11. how area and density are derived quantities (Section 4)

Questions to Ask Along the Way

You can help your son or daughter learn about these topics by asking interesting questions such as the following:

- What are some surprising careers that use physical science?
- What is a characteristic of a good hypothesis?
- When is it a good idea to use a model?
- Why do Americans measure things in terms of inches and yards and meters?

ALSO IN SPANISH

TEST ITEM LISTING

TEST ITEM LISTING
The World of Science SAMPLE

MULTIPLE CHOICE

1. A limitation of models is that
   a. they are large enough to see.
   b. they do not act exactly like the things that they model.
   c. they are smaller than the things that they model.
   d. they model unfamiliar things.
   Answer: B   Difficulty: 1   Section: 3   Objective: 2

2. The length 10 m is equal to
   a. 100 cm.   c. 10,000 mm.
   b. 1,000 cm.   d. Both (b) and (c)
   Answer: B   Difficulty: 1   Section: 3   Objective: 2

3. To be valid, a hypothesis must be
   a. testable.   c. made into a law.
   b. supported by evidence.   d. Both (a) and (b)
   Answer: B   Difficulty: 1   Section: 3   Objective: 2 1

4. The statement "Sheila has a stain on her shirt" is an example of a(n)
   a. law.   c. observation.
   b. hypothesis.   d. prediction.
   Answer: B   Difficulty: 1   Section: 2   Objective: 2

5. A hypothesis is often developed out of
   a. observations.   c. laws.
   b. experiments.   d. Both (a) and (b)
   Answer: B   Difficulty: 1   Section: 2   Objective: 2

6. How many milliliters are in 3.5 kL?
   a. 3,500 mL   c. 3,500,000 mL
   b. 0.0035 mL   d. 35,000 mL
   Answer: B   Difficulty: 1   Section: 3   Objective: 2

7. A map of Seattle is an example of a
   a. model.   c. unit.
   b. law.   d. quantity.
   Answer: B   Difficulty: 1   Section: 3   Objective: 2

8. A lab has the safety icons shown below. These icons mean that you should wear
   a. only safety goggles.   c. safety goggles and a lab apron.
   b. only a lab apron.   d. safety goggles, a lab apron, and gloves.
   Answer: B   Difficulty: 1   Section: 3   Objective: 2

9. The law of conservation of mass says the total mass before a chemical change is
   a. more than the total mass after the change.
   b. less than the total mass after the change.
   c. the same as the total mass after the change.
   d. not the same as the total mass after the change.
   Answer: B   Difficulty: 1   Section: 3   Objective: 2

10. To which of the following areas might you find a geochemist at work?
    a. studying the chemistry of rocks   c. studying fishes
    b. studying forestry   d. studying the atmosphere
    Answer: B   Difficulty: 1   Section: 3   Objective: 2

One-Stop Planner® CD-ROM

This CD-ROM includes all of the resources shown here and the following time-saving tools:

- *Lab Materials QuickList Software*
- *Customizable lesson plans*
- *Holt Calendar Planner*
- *The powerful ExamView® Test Generator*

Meeting Individual Needs

DIRECTED READING A
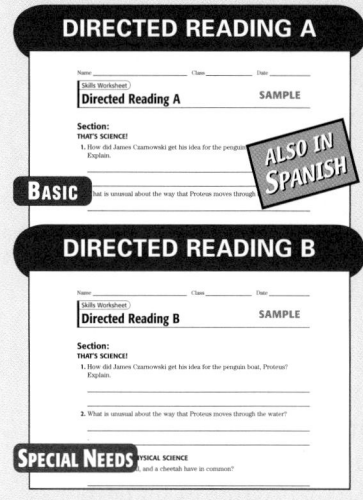

BASIC — ALSO IN SPANISH

DIRECTED READING B

SPECIAL NEEDS

VOCABULARY ACTIVITY
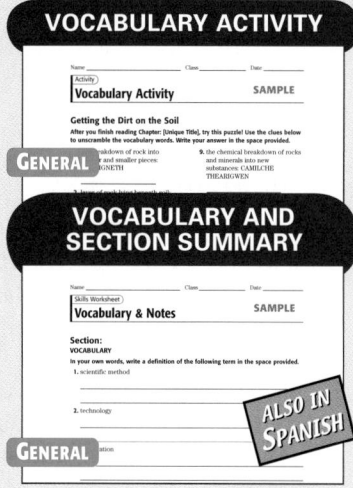

GENERAL

VOCABULARY AND SECTION SUMMARY

GENERAL — ALSO IN SPANISH

REINFORCEMENT
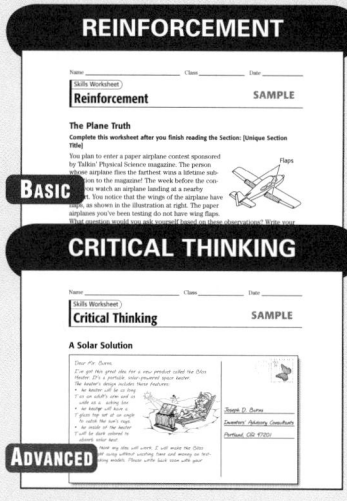

BASIC

CRITICAL THINKING

ADVANCED

SCILINKS ACTIVITY

GENERAL

SCIENCE PUZZLERS, TWISTERS & TEASERS

GENERAL

Labs and Activities

LONG-TERM PROJECTS & RESEARCH IDEAS
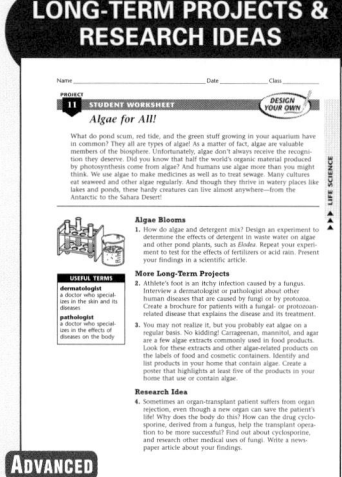

ADVANCED

WHIZ-BANG DEMONSTRATIONS
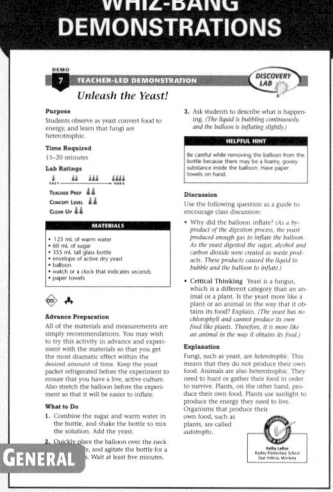

GENERAL

LABS YOU CAN EAT
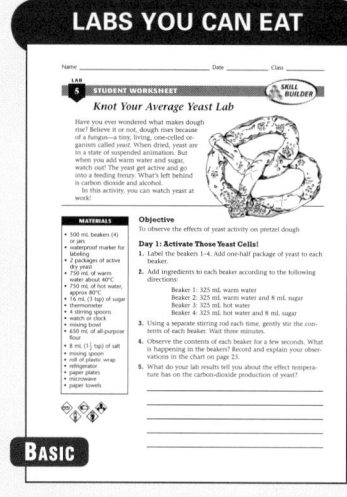

BASIC

DATASHEETS FOR QUICK LABS

DATASHEETS FOR CHAPTER LABS

DATASHEETS FOR LABBOOK

Review and Assessments

SECTION QUIZ
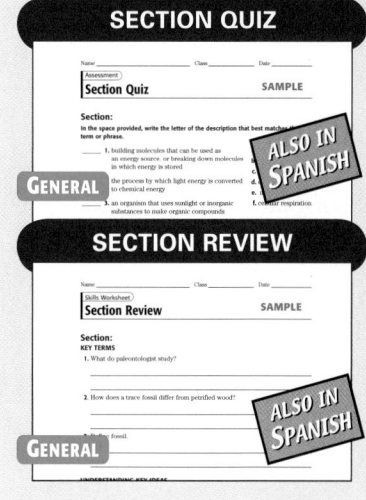

GENERAL — ALSO IN SPANISH

SECTION REVIEW

GENERAL — ALSO IN SPANISH

CHAPTER REVIEW
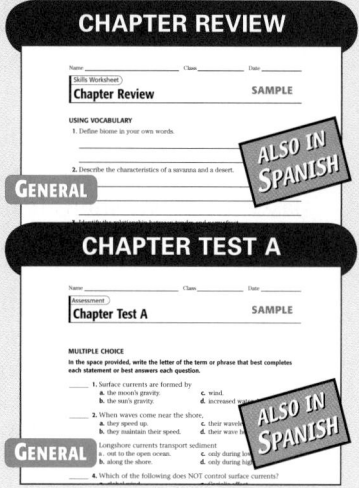

GENERAL — ALSO IN SPANISH

CHAPTER TEST A

GENERAL — ALSO IN SPANISH

CHAPTER TEST B
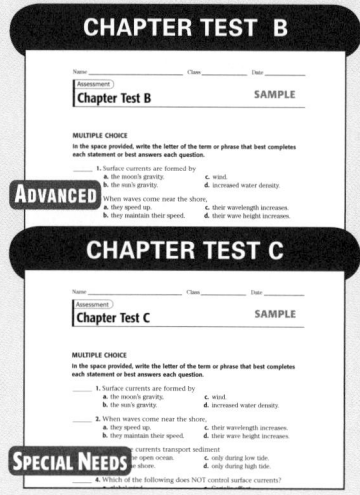

ADVANCED

CHAPTER TEST C

SPECIAL NEEDS

STANDARDIZED TEST PREPARATION
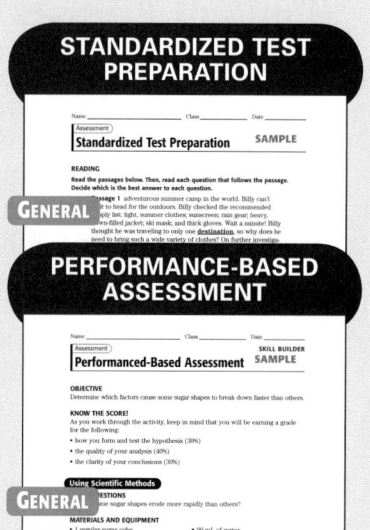

GENERAL

PERFORMANCE-BASED ASSESSMENT

GENERAL

This Chapter Enrichment provides relevant and interesting information to expand and enhance your presentation of the chapter material.

Section 1

Protists

Protists, Protists, Everywhere

- Most protists are aquatic. Some live in marine environments; others live in fresh water or in the water that surrounds soil particles. Still other protists live in the body fluids of other organisms. Some even live in snow.

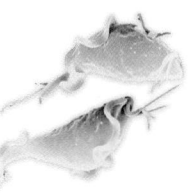

Is That a Fact!

◆ A harmless species of symbiotic amoebas called *Entamoeba gingivalis* lives in the mouths of many people and feeds on loose cells and organic debris.

The Need to Conjugate

- Laboratory experiments have shown that some species of *Paramecium* must conjugate periodically to survive. If these paramecia are not allowed to conjugate, they have the capacity for only a limited number of asexual divisions (about 350) before they die.

Section 2

Kinds of Protists

Products from Algae

- The cell walls of red algae contain a substance that gives the algae a slippery texture. Agar, which is derived from this substance, has the consistency of gelatin and is used worldwide as a culture medium for growing bacteria, fungi, and plant tissue.

- Giant kelp and other brown algae are the source of algin, which has hundreds of uses. For example, it is used as a thickening and stabilizing agent in ice cream, milkshakes, pie fillings, and weight-control drinks; as an additive in paper and a coating on frozen food packages; as a smoothing agent in lotions and creams; and as an ingredient in latex paints and adhesives.

Is That a Fact!

◆ During the Irish potato famine of 1846, people ate a red alga called *dulse* as a substitute for potatoes.

Slime Molds

- There are two types of slime molds: cellular slime molds (about 70 species in the phylum Acrasiomycota) and plasmodial or acellular slime molds (about 800 species in the phylum Mycetozoa).

- Plasmodial slime molds are named for their slimy, often large and colorful plasmodia. A plasmodium is the feeding phase of the slime mold, and it engulfs bacteria, yeast, and bits of organic matter in its path. A plasmodium can flow around obstacles and will even flow through the meshwork of a piece of cloth.

Is That a Fact!

◆ Many students who have kept fish in an aquarium have seen *Saprolegnia,* the common water mold that forms a fuzzy white mass as it grows over the surface of a dead or an injured fish.

Diatoms

- The word *diatom* comes from the Greek word *diatomos,* which means "cut in two." The meaning refers to the glassy, two-part shells (called *frustules*) that enclose these single-celled organisms.

- The frustules of diatoms have complex and strikingly beautiful markings that are different for each species and are therefore important in diatom identification.

- One liter of sea water may contain almost a million diatoms.

Section 3

Fungi

Fungi Functions

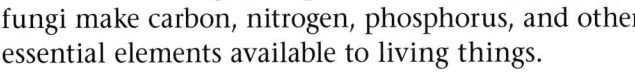

- Fungi are extremely important as decomposers; they break down complex organic material to simple organic compounds and inorganic molecules. Through this process, fungi make carbon, nitrogen, phosphorus, and other essential elements available to living things.

- Fungi are also essential in the making of bread, cheeses, wine, beer, and soy sauce; in the production of many antibiotics; and as research organisms for biochemists, cytologists, microbiologists, and mycologists.

- Most plant roots have mutualistic symbiotic associations with fungi, which are called _mycorrhizae._ The mycorrhizae often greatly enhance plant mineral nutrient uptake.

- Fungi are the major cause of plant diseases. At least 5,000 kinds of fungi attack crops, garden plants, and wild plants. Some fungi also cause disease, such as ringworm, in animals. A toxic fungus from the genus _Stachybotrys_ has made some houses unlivable for humans.

Sac Fungi

- There are more than 30,000 known species of sac fungi (class Ascomycota), about 500 of which are single-celled yeasts.

- Morels and truffles are multicellular sac fungi. For hundreds of years, the only way to enjoy truffles, which grow underground on the roots of oak and hazelnut trees, was to unearth wild ones with the help of specially trained pigs and dogs. Today, truffles can be cultivated commercially, but doing so is very difficult.

A Predatory Fungus

- One of the imperfect fungi (_Arthrobotrys dactyloides_) preys on tiny roundworms (nematodes) in soil. The filaments of the fungi produce minute loops that swell rapidly when nematodes try to crawl through them. The loops hold the nematodes tightly while hyphae grow into the nematodes' bodies and kill them.

Lichens

- Lichens are a symbiotic association between a fungus—in most cases a sac fungus, or ascomycete—and either a photosynthetic alga or a cyanobacterium. The term _lichen_ is often defined without mentioning cyanobacteria, the name now used for blue-green algae.

- In severe growing conditions, lichens grow extremely slowly. Even small lichens may be hundreds or even thousands of years old.

Is That a Fact!

- ◆ Lichens are an important food for caribou. During winter on the tundra, other foods are not available and caribou eat almost exclusively lichens.

SciLinks is maintained by the National Science Teachers Association to provide you and your students with interesting, up-to-date links that will enrich your classroom presentation of the chapter.

Visit www.scilinks.org and enter the SciLinks code for more information about the topic listed.

Topic: Protists
SciLinks code: HSM1245

Topic: Fungi
SciLinks code: HSM0628

Topic: Algae
SciLinks code: HSM0042

Topic: Lichens
SciLinks code: HSM0871

Topic: Protozoans
SciLinks code: HSM1247

Overview

Tell students that this chapter will help them learn about protists and fungi. The chapter describes how protists and fungi get food and reproduce. It also describes several different kinds of protists and fungi.

Assessing Prior Knowledge

Students should be familiar with the following topics:

- characteristics of living things
- classification
- cells

Identifying Misconceptions

As students learn the material in this chapter, some of them may be confused about what characteristics unite the organisms in the kingdom Protista. You may want to stress that this group is unique in that the organisms in kingdom Protista are united more by their differences from other groups than by their similarities with each other. Many of the organisms in kingdom Protista are only distantly related to each other, and scientists do not agree on how to classify the members of this kingdom.

11

Protists and Fungi

About the PHOTO

These glowing disks may look like spaceships, but they are mushrooms! Some fungi—and some protists—glow with bioluminescence (BIE oh LOO muh NES uhns), just as fireflies do. Bioluminescence is the production of light from chemical reactions in an organism. The function of bioluminescence in fungi is not known. Some scientists think that the glow attracts insects that help spread the fungi's spores. Other scientists think that the light is just a way to release energy.

PRE-READING ACTIVITY

FOLDNOTES **Booklet** Before you read the chapter, create the FoldNote entitled "Booklet" described in the **Study Skills** section of the Appendix. Label each page of the booklet with a main idea from the chapter. As you read the chapter, write what you learn about each main idea on the appropriate page of the booklet.

Standards Correlations

National Science Education Standards

The following codes indicate the National Science Education Standards that correlate to this chapter. The full text of the standards is at the front of the book.

Chapter Opener
UCP 2; SAI 1; LS 1b

Section 1 Protists
UCP 5; SAI 2; LS 1b, 1c, 1f, 2a, 4b, 5a

Section 2 Kinds of Protists
UCP 5; LS 1a, 1b, 1f, 3a, 5a; LabBook: UCP 2

Section 3 Fungi
UCP 5; SAI 1; SPSP 5; LS 1a, 1b, 1d, 1f, 2a, 4b, 5a

Chapter Lab
UCP 5; SAI 1; LS 1a

Chapter Review
SAI 1; LS 1a, 2a

Science in Action
SAI 2; ST 2; SPSP 5; HNS 2; LS 1f

START-UP ACTIVITY
MATERIALS
FOR EACH STUDENT
• microscope
• microscope slide
• plastic coverslip
• plastic dropper
• pond water or hay infusion
• ProtoSlo™

Safety Caution: Tell students not to taste the solution. Care should be taken handling microscope slides and coverslips. Check for known mold or fungi allergies among students before conducting this lab. Have an eyewash available, and instruct students to wipe up all spills immediately.

Answers

1. Answers may vary. Pond water may contain protist producers, such as members of the genera *Spirogyra* and *Volvox,* and protist heterotrophs, such as members of the genera *Stentor, Vorticella, Euglena,* and *Paramecium* and amoebas. Students may also see nematode worms and small, fast-moving, multicellular animals called *rotifers.*

2. Sample answer: The organisms are moving, which suggests that they are alive. Also, green pigments suggest that algae are going through photosynthesis.

3. Answers may vary, but most of these microscopic organisms, if not all, are single-celled organisms.

START-UP ACTIVITY

A Microscopic World

In this activity, you will find some common protists in pond water or in a solution called a *hay infusion.*

Procedure

1. Use a **plastic eyedropper** to place **one drop of pond water or hay infusion** onto a **microscope slide.**

2. Add a **drop of ProtoSlo™** to the slide.

3. Add a **plastic coverslip** by putting one edge on the slide and then slowly lowering the coverslip over the drop to prevent air bubbles.

4. Observe the slide under low power of a **microscope.**

5. Find an organism in the liquid on the slide.

6. Observe the organism under high power to get a closer look.

7. Sketch the organism as you see it under high power. Then, return the microscope to low power, and find other organisms to sketch. Return the microscope to high power, and sketch the new organisms.

Analysis

1. How many kinds of organisms do you see?

2. Are the organisms alive? Support your answer with evidence.

3. How many cells does each organism appear to have?

This Really Happened!

The year is 1846, and the country is Ireland. The weather is cold and rainy, and the situation is desperate. Disease has swept through the potato fields. In just a few weeks, it destroyed almost the entire crop.

The Irish depend on potatoes for food. Every day, hundreds of people die of starvation. With no other hope for survival, tens of thousands are fleeing their

Water molds are protists. This particular water mold changed the course of Irish history. It also changed the American population. Do you have Irish ancestry? If so, a water mold may have brought your family to this country.

But don't get the wrong idea. Not all protists are harmful. Some are very helpful. You'll learn about protists

Chapter Starter Transparency
Use this transparency to help students begin thinking about the relationships between protists and humans.

CHAPTER RESOURCES

Technology

Transparencies
• Chapter Starter Transparency

READING SKILLS

Student Edition on CD-ROM

Guided Reading Audio CD
• English or Spanish

Classroom Videos
• Brain Food Video Quiz

Workbooks

Science Puzzlers, Twisters & Teasers
• Protists and Fungi GENERAL

Focus

Overview

This section introduces students to protists. Students will learn that protists share few characteristics but that they are all eukaryotic. Students will also learn that protists get food as producers or heterotrophs and that protists reproduce asexually or sexually.

📶 Bellringer

Ask students if they have heard of protists before reading this chapter. Students should make a list of examples of protists. Then, have students read the lists aloud and discuss why protists are not well known.

Motivate

ACTIVITY ——————— GENERAL

Methods of Moving Ask students to imagine that an organism needs to move itself without using arms, fins, wings, or legs. Ask students, "How would the organism move? What environments could the organism live in?" Have students write their answers in their **science journal.** Encourage students to illustrate their answers whenever possible. (Accept all reasonable responses. Tell students that many protists live in water and move by using flagella and cilia.) **LS Verbal**

READING WARM-UP

Objectives

- Describe the characteristics of protists.
- Describe four ways that protists get food.
- Describe three ways that protists reproduce.

Terms to Learn

protist   parasite
heterotroph   host

READING STRATEGY

Discussion Read this section silently. Write down questions that you have about this section. Discuss your questions in a small group.

protist an organism that belongs to the kingdom Protista

Protists

Some are so tiny that they cannot be seen without a microscope. Others grow many meters long. Some are poisonous. And some provide food for people.

What are they? The organisms described above are protists. A **protist** is a member of the kingdom Protista. Protists differ from other living things in many ways. Look at **Figure 1** to see a variety of protists.

General Characteristics

Protists are very diverse and have few traits in common. Most protists are single-celled organisms, but some are made of many cells, and others live in colonies. Some protists produce their own food, and some eat other organisms or decaying matter. Some protists can control their own movement, and others cannot. However, protists do share a few characteristics. For example, all protists are *eukaryotic* (yoo KAR ee AHT ik), which means that their cells each have a nucleus.

Members of the kingdom Protista are related more by how they differ from members of other kingdoms than by how they are similar to other protists. Protists are less complex than other eukaryotic organisms are. For example, protists do not have specialized tissues. Fungi, plants, and animals have specialized tissues that have specific functions. Most scientists agree that fungi, plants, and animals evolved from early protists.

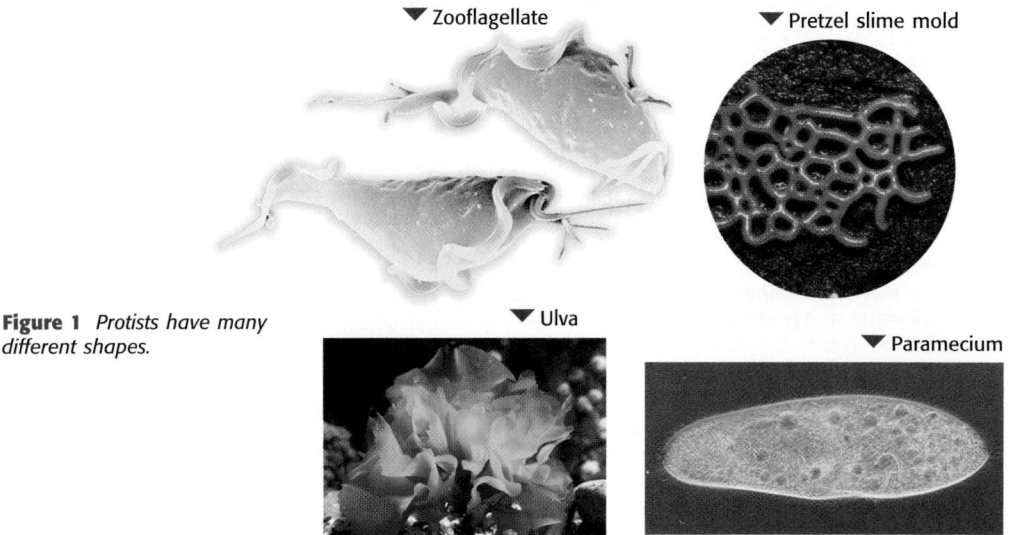

▼ Zooflagellate   ▼ Pretzel slime mold

▼ Ulva   ▼ Paramecium

Figure 1 *Protists have many different shapes.*

CHAPTER RESOURCES

Chapter Resource File

- Lesson Plan
- Directed Reading A **BASIC**
- Directed Reading B **SPECIAL NEEDS**

Technology

Transparencies
- Bellringer

Protists and Food

Protists get food in many ways. Some protists can make their own food. Other protists eat other organisms, parts or products of other organisms, or the remains of other organisms. Some protists use more than one method of getting food.

Producing Food

Some protists are *producers.* Like green plants, these protists make their own food. Protist producers have special structures called *chloroplasts* (KLAWR uh PLASTS) in their cells. These structures capture energy from the sun. Protists use this energy to produce food in a process called *photosynthesis* (FOHT oh SIN thuh sis). Plants use this same process to make their own food.

✓ **Reading Check** How do protist producers get their food? (*See the Appendix for answers to Reading Checks.*)

Finding Food

Some protists must get food from their environment. These protists are heterotrophs (HET uhr oh TROHFS). **Heterotrophs** are organisms that cannot make their own food. These organisms eat other organisms, parts or products of other organisms, or the remains of other organisms.

Many protist heterotrophs eat small living organisms, such as bacteria, yeast, or other protists. The way that these heterotrophs get food is similar to how many animals get food. Some protist heterotrophs are decomposers. *Decomposers* get energy by breaking down dead organic matter. Some protists get energy in more than one way. For example, slime molds, such as the one in **Figure 2,** get energy by engulfing both small organisms and particles of organic matter.

Some protist heterotrophs are parasites. A **parasite** invades another organism to get the nutrients that it needs. An organism that a parasite invades is called a **host.** Parasites cause harm to their host. Parasitic protists may invade fungi, plants, or animals. During the mid-1800s, a parasitic protist wiped out most of the potatoes in Ireland. Without potatoes to eat, many people died of starvation. Today, people know how to protect crops from many such protists.

Food for Thought

With your family, review how producers, consumers, decomposers, and parasites get energy. Think of organisms that live near your home and that get their food in these different ways. Then, make a poster to display your examples. Be sure that the poster describes each way of getting food.

heterotroph an organism that gets food by eating other organisms or their byproducts and that cannot make organic compounds from inorganic materials

parasite an organism that feeds on an organism of another species (the host) and that usually harms the host; the host never benefits from the presence of the parasite

host an organism from which a parasite takes food or shelter

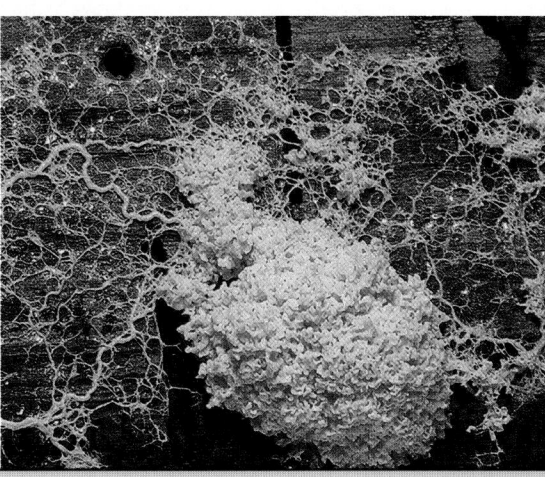

Figure 2 *Slime molds get energy from small organisms and particles of organic matter.*

Answer to Reading Check

Protist producers make their own food through photosynthesis.

WEIRD SCIENCE

At the 1933 Chicago World's Fair, an exhibit of "hair growing on wood" was displayed in the Believe It or Not pavilion. Although the "hair" amazed many fair-goers, it was actually the clustered fruiting bodies of a slime mold.

Teach

📖 **READING STRATEGY** ── BASIC

Prediction Guide Before students read about how protists get food, ask them to brainstorm ways in which organisms get food. (Answers may include photosynthesis, consuming plants or animals, decomposing, and parasitism.) Tell students that protists are very diverse and that there is probably a protist that uses every method of getting food listed by the class. Ask students to look for the methods they brainstormed as they read about how protists get food. **LS Verbal**

Group ACTIVITY ── ADVANCED

Making a Hypothesis Amoebas sometimes ignore food that is close to them and move toward food that is farther away. Scientists are not sure why amoebas behave in this way. Ask students to work in groups to come up with a hypothesis about this behavior. Have groups design experiments that could test their hypotheses. **LS Interpersonal**

CONNECTION to Environmental Science ──── GENERAL

Rain-Forest Soil The rain forests of Guatemala contain great and diverse populations of slime molds that keep the soil of the rain forests healthy. Unfortunately, when the trees of the rain forest are cut down, the slime molds are no longer protected from sunlight and rain. Without this protection, the molds die. Without slime molds, the soil is no longer enriched, and regrowth of the forest becomes very unlikely. Ask students, "How do you think slime molds enrich the soil?" **LS Verbal**

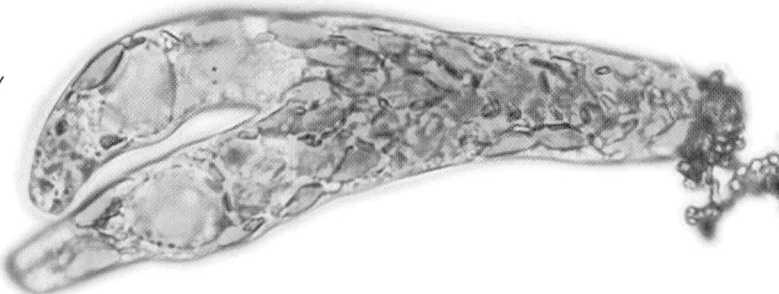

Figure 3 *Members of the genus* Euglena *reproduce by dividing lengthwise during fission.*

Close

Reteaching — BASIC

Sunshine Help students get used to the idea that plants are not the only organisms that use photosynthesis by telling them that some bacteria use photosynthesis. This may help them remember that protist producers use photosynthesis. **LS Logical**

Quiz — GENERAL

1. How do protist producers differ from plants? (Plants have specialized tissues that have specific functions, but protist producers do not have specialized tissues.)

2. When might protists switch from asexual to sexual reproduction? (Sample answer: Some protists switch methods each generation, and other protists use sexual reproduction only when conditions are stressful.)

Alternative Assessment — GENERAL

Making a Pop-up Book Ask students to make a pop-up book in which they devote a chapter to each of three groups of protists. Encourage students to be creative and write text for their protist books. **LS Verbal/Kinesthetic**

Answer to Reading Check
binary fission and multiple fission

Answer to Math Practice
24 protists (3 pairs results in 12 protists. 6 pairs results in 24 protists.)

MATH PRACTICE

Pairs of Paramecia

Suppose that three pairs of protists from the genus *Paramecium* are conjugating at one time. Each pair successfully results in four protists that have new combinations of genetic material. Then, the new individuals pair up for another successful round of conjugation. How many protists will there be after this round of conjugation?

Figure 4 *Members of the genus* Paramecium *can reproduce by conjugation, a type of sexual reproduction.*

Producing More Protists

Like all living things, protists reproduce. Protists reproduce in several ways. Some protists reproduce asexually, and some reproduce sexually. Some protists even reproduce asexually at one stage in their life cycle and sexually at another stage.

Asexual Reproduction

Most protists reproduce asexually. In asexual reproduction, the offspring come from just one parent. These offspring are identical to the parent. **Figure 3** shows a member of the genus *Euglena* reproducing asexually by fission. In *binary fission,* a single-celled protist divides into two cells. In some cases, single-celled protists use *multiple fission* to make more than two offspring from one parent. Each new cell is a single-celled protist.

Reading Check What are two ways that protists can reproduce asexually by fission?

Sexual Reproduction

Some protists can reproduce sexually. Sexual reproduction requires two parents. Members of the genus *Paramecium* (PAR uh MEE see uhm) sometimes reproduce sexually by a process called *conjugation.* During conjugation, two individuals join together and exchange genetic material by using a small, second nucleus. Then, they divide to produce four protists that have new combinations of genetic material. **Figure 4** shows two paramecia in the process of conjugation.

Many protists can reproduce asexually and sexually. In some protist producers, the kind of reproduction alternates by generation. For example, a parent will reproduce asexually, and its offspring will reproduce sexually. Other protists reproduce asexually until environmental conditions become stressful, such as when there is little food or water. When conditions are stressful, these protists will use sexual reproduction until conditions improve.

CONNECTION ACTIVITY
Math — GENERAL

Malaria Math Many protists reproduce asexually by fission, or dividing in two. Students are probably familiar with this form of division, which can result in a population growing exponentially over time; that is, 1 cell divides to produce 2 cells, which in turn divide to produce 4 cells, which in turn produces 8 cells, and so on. *Plasmodium vivax* and some other parasitic, spore-forming protozoa can divide asexually by a process known as *schizogony,* or multiple fission. For example, a single spore, or a sporozoite of a *P. vivax* organism can produce 40,000 offspring. Researchers have determined that when a mosquito that is infected with *P. vivax* inserts its proboscis into a human blood vessel, the mosquito injects about a thousand spores. Have students calculate how many *P. vivax* spores could be present in a person's body after just one division by multiple fission. (1,000 spores × 40,000 offspring = 40,000,000 spores) **LS Logical**

Reproductive Cycles

Some protists have complex reproductive cycles. These protists may change forms many times. **Figure 5** shows the life cycle of *Plasmodium vivax* (plaz MOH dee uhm VIE vaks), the protist that causes the disease malaria. *P. vivax* depends on both humans and mosquitoes to reproduce.

Figure 5 *P. vivax infects both humans and mosquitoes as it reproduces.*

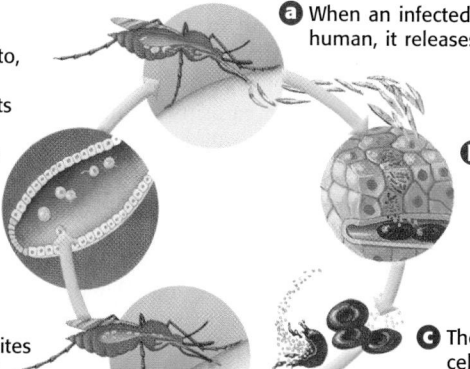

ⓐ When an infected mosquito bites a human, it releases *P. vivax* into the blood.

ⓑ The *P. vivax* infects human liver cells, reproduces, and enters the bloodstream in a new form.

ⓒ The *P. vivax* invades red blood cells and multiplies rapidly. The red blood cells burst open with *P. vivax* in another new form.

ⓓ A mosquito bites a human and picks up *P. vivax*.

ⓔ In the mosquito, the *P. vivax* matures into its original form. The cycle then repeats.

SECTION Review

Summary

- Protists are a diverse group of single-celled and many-celled organisms.
- Protists are grouped in their own kingdom because they differ from other organisms in many ways.
- Protists get food by producing it or by getting it from their environment.
- Some protists reproduce asexually, some reproduce sexually, and some reproduce both asexually and sexually.

Using Key Terms

1. Use the following terms in the same sentence: *parasite* and *host*.

2. In your own words, write a definition for each of the following terms: *protist* and *heterotroph*.

Understanding Key Ideas

3. What is one way that protists differ from plants and animals?
   a. Protists are eukaryotic.
   b. All protists have many cells.
   c. Protists do not have specialized tissues.
   d. Protists are not eukaryotic.

4. Name a characteristic shared by all protists.

5. Name three ways that protists can differ from each other.

6. Describe four ways that protists get food.

7. Describe three ways that protists reproduce.

Math Skills

8. If seven individuals of the genus *Euglena* reproduce at one time, how many individuals result?

Critical Thinking

9. **Identifying Relationships** How is conjugation similar to fission?

10. **Applying Concepts** The spread of malaria depends on both human and mosquito hosts. Use this fact to think of a way to stop the spread of malaria.

SCiLINKS.

NSTA
Developed and maintained by the National Science Teachers Association

For a variety of links related to this chapter, go to www.scilinks.org

Topic: Protists
SciLinks code: HSM1245

Answers to Section Review

1. Sample answer: An organism that is invaded by a parasite is called a *host*.

2. Sample answer: A protist is a eukaryotic organism that is a member of the kingdom Protista. A heterotroph is an organism that gets food by eating other organisms or organic matter.

3. c

4. All protists are eukaryotic.

5. Sample answer: Protists can differ in whether they are single-celled or multicellular, how they get food (as producers or as heterotrophs), how they move (with pseudopodia, flagella, or cilia), and how they reproduce (sexually, asexually, or both at different stages of life).

6. Protists get food by producing it, by eating other organisms, by consuming dead organic matter, or by invading other organisms as parasites.

7. Protists can reproduce asexually by fission, sexually by conjugation, and in complex reproductive cycles.

8. 14 individual protists

9. Sample answer: In both conjugation and fission, the number of protists resulting from reproduction is double the number that reproduced.

10. Sample answer: If populations of mosquitoes infected by malaria were controlled, malaria could not spread between infected people because the steps of the *P. vivax* reproductive cycle that depend on the mosquito could not happen.

Homework ———— GENERAL

Writing **Research** Encourage students to research and report on malaria and the work currently being done to develop malaria vaccines. **LS** Verbal

CHAPTER RESOURCES

Chapter Resource File

- Section Quiz **GENERAL**
- Section Review **GENERAL**
- Vocabulary and Section Summary **GENERAL**
- Reinforcement Worksheet **BASIC**
- Critical Thinking **ADVANCED**

Technology

Transparencies
- The Life Cycle of *P. vivax*

Focus

Overview

This section describes what different kinds of protists look like, where they live, and how they move. Protists are organized into three groups: protist producers, heterotrophic protists that can move, and heterotrophic protists that cannot move.

Bellringer

Ask students where they think algae live. (Students may think of algae that live in the ocean.) Tell them that algae also live in fresh water, moist soil, melting snow, and other environments.

Motivate

Demonstration —— GENERAL

Algae as Food Display the following on a table: ice cream, salad dressing, jelly beans, chocolate milk, instant pudding, and dry gravy mix. Tell students that two substances taken from algae—alginate and carrageenan—are common ingredients in many foods. Alginate comes from brown algae, while carrageenan comes from a red alga. Both are used as thickeners, stabilizers, and emulsifiers. Have students read the ingredients on the packages. **LS Visual**

READING WARM-UP

Objectives

● Describe how protists can be organized into three groups based on their shared traits.

● List an example for each group of protists.

Terms to Learn

algae
phytoplankton

READING STRATEGY

Reading Organizer As you read this section, make a table comparing protist producers, heterotrophs that can move, and heterotrophs that can't move.

algae eukaryotic organisms that convert the sun's energy into food through photosynthesis but that do not have roots, stems, or leaves (singular, *alga*)

phytoplankton the microscopic, photosynthetic organisms that float near the surface of marine or fresh water

Figure 1 *Some kinds of algae, such as this giant kelp, can grow to be many meters in length.*

Kinds of Protists

Would you believe that there is an organism that lives in the forest and looks like a pile of scrambled eggs? This organism exists, and it's a protist.

Slimy masses of protists can look like spilled food. Smears of protists on the walls of a fish tank may look like dirt. Few of the many kinds of protists look alike.

These unique organisms are hard to classify. Scientists are always learning more about protist relationships. So, organizing protists into groups is not easy. One way that protists are grouped is based on shared traits. Using this method, scientists can place protists into three groups: producers, heterotrophs that can move, and heterotrophs that can't move. These groups do not show how protists are related to each other. But these groups do help us understand how protists can differ.

Protist Producers

Many protists are producers. Like plants, protist producers use the sun's energy to make food through photosynthesis. These protist producers are known as **algae** (AL JEE). All algae (singular, *alga*) have the green pigment chlorophyll, which is used for making food. But most algae also have other pigments that give them a color. Almost all algae live in water.

Some algae are made of many cells, as shown in **Figure 1.** Many-celled algae generally live in shallow water along the shore. You may know these algae as *seaweeds*. Some of these algae can grow to many meters in length.

Free-floating single-celled algae are called **phytoplankton** (FIET oh PLANGK tuhn). These algae cannot be seen without a microscope. They usually float near the water's surface. Phytoplankton provide food for most other organisms in the water. They also produce much of the world's oxygen.

CHAPTER RESOURCES

Chapter Resource File

• Lesson Plan
• Directed Reading A BASIC
• Directed Reading B SPECIAL NEEDS

Technology

Transparencies
• Bellringer

Red Algae

Most of the world's seaweeds are red algae. Most red algae live in tropical oceans, attached to rocks or to other algae. Red algae are usually less than 1 m in length. Their cells contain chlorophyll, but a red pigment gives them their color. Their red pigment allows them to absorb the light that filters deep into the clear water of the Tropics. Red algae can grow as deep as 260 m below the surface of the water. An example of a red alga can be seen in **Figure 2.**

Reading Check If red algae have chlorophyll in their cells, why aren't they green? (*See the Appendix for answers to Reading Checks.*)

Green Algae

The green algae are the most diverse group of protist producers. They are green because chlorophyll is the main pigment in their cells. Most live in water or moist soil. But others live in melting snow, on tree trunks, and inside other organisms.

Many green algae are single-celled organisms. Others are made of many cells. These many-celled species may grow to be 8 m long. Individual cells of some species of green algae live in groups called *colonies*. **Figure 3** shows colonies of *Volvox*.

Brown Algae

Most of the seaweeds found in cool climates are brown algae. They attach to rocks or form large floating beds in ocean waters. Brown algae have chlorophyll and a yellow-brown pigment. Many are very large. Some grow 60 m—as long as about 20 cars—in just one season! Only the tops of these gigantic algae are exposed to sunlight. These parts of the algae make food through photosynthesis. This food is transported to parts of the algae that are too deep in the water to receive sunlight.

Figure 2 *This* Sebdenia *(seb DEE nee uh) is a red alga.*

Figure 3 Volvox *is a green alga that grows in round colonies.*

Is That a Fact!

Giant kelp, a type of brown alga, is anchored to the ocean bottom. It has air bladders that help keep it floating upward, toward the water's surface, where the sunlight is the strongest.

Answer to Reading Check

Red algae also have a red pigment in their cells that gives the algae a red color.

Art with Algae Anna Atkins (1799–1871) was an amateur botanist. Atkins specialized in making photographic blueprints called *cyanotypes*, or sunprints. Over a 10-year period, Atkins created hundreds of cyanotypes of algae from the British Isles. Her book, *British Algae: Cyanotype Impressions,* was published in 1843 and is thought to be the first book illustrated with photographic images. Interested students may wish to create their own cyanotypes of algae to accompany their reports. Students may use leaves, fern fronds, or other plant parts if algae are not available. Cyanotype paper can be obtained from biological supply houses. **LS Visual**

ACTIVITY ───────── GENERAL

Concept Mapping Have students construct a concept map using the following terms: *brown algae, algae, phytoplankton, protists, red algae, green algae, diatoms, dinoflagellates,* and *producers.* **LS Visual/Verbal**

Answer to Reading Check
salt water, fresh water, and snow

Diatoms

Diatoms (DIE e TAHMZ) are single celled. They are found in both salt water and fresh water. Diatoms get their energy from photosynthesis. They make up a large percentage of phytoplankton. **Figure 4** shows some diatoms' many unusual shapes. The cell walls of diatoms contain a glasslike substance called *silica.* The cells of diatoms are enclosed in a two-part shell.

Dinoflagellates

Most dinoflagellates (DIE noh FLAJ uh lits) are single celled. Most live in salt water, but a few species live in fresh water. Some dinoflagellates even live in snow. Dinoflagellates have two whiplike strands called *flagella* (singular, *flagellum*). The beating of these flagella causes the cells to spin through the water. Most dinoflagellates get their energy from photosynthesis, but a few are consumers, decomposers, or parasites.

✓ Reading Check Name three places where dinoflagellates live.

Euglenoids

Euglenoids (yoo GLEE NOYDZ) are single-celled protists. Most euglenoids live in fresh water. They use their flagella to move through the water. Many euglenoids are producers and so make their own food. But when there is not enough light to make food, these euglenoids can get food as heterotrophs. Other euglenoids do not contain chlorophyll and cannot make food. These euglenoids are full-time consumers or decomposers. Because euglenoids can get food in several ways, they do not fit well into any one protist group. **Figure 5** shows the structure of a euglenoid.

Figure 4 *Although most diatoms are free floating, some cling to plants, shellfish, sea turtles, and whales.*

Figure 5 The Structure of Euglenoids

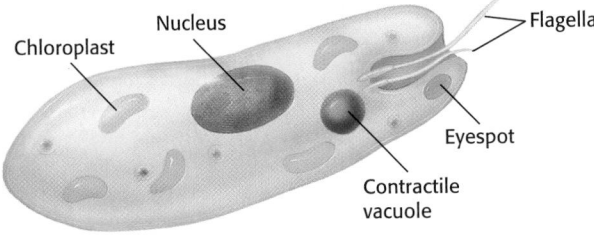
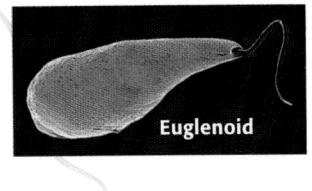

Photosynthesis takes place in **chloroplasts.** These structures contain the green pigment chlorophyll.

Most euglenoids have two **flagella,** one long and one short. Euglenoids use flagella to move through water.

Euglenoids can't see, but they have **eyespots** that sense light.

A special structure called a **contractile vacuole** holds excess water and removes it from the cell.

Chloroplast — Nucleus — Flagella — Eyespot — Contractile vacuole — Euglenoid

CHAPTER RESOURCES
Technology
Transparencies • *Euglena, Paramecium*

SCIENTISTS AT ODDS

Which Phylum? Euglenoids pose a classification problem for taxonomists. Many euglenoids have plastids containing pigments that the euglenoids can use for photosynthesis, as algae do. But euglenoid cell walls are made up mainly of protein, and euglenoids use flagella to move. In the dark, a euglenoid feeds as a heterotroph. But in sunlight, it photosynthesizes. Biologists once classified euglenoids in the phylum Zoomastigophora. Now, euglenoids are classified in the phylum Euglenophyta.

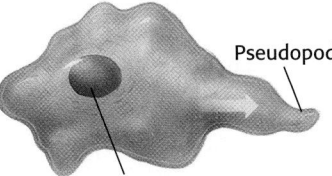

Figure 6 Amoebic Movement

❶ An amoeba extends a new pseudopod from part of its cell.

❷ The rest of the cell flows into the new pseudopod.

❸ Other pseudopodia retract.

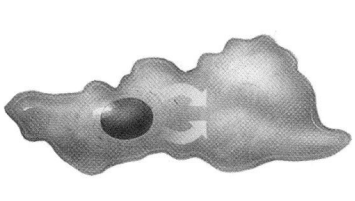

Pseudopod

Contractile vacuole

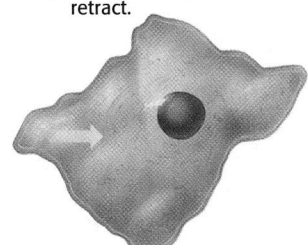

Heterotrophs That Can Move

Some heterotrophic protists have special traits that allow them to move. Other heterotrophic protists cannot move on their own. Those that can move are usually single-celled consumers or parasites. These mobile protists are sometimes called *protozoans* (PROHT oh ZOH uhnz).

Amoebas

Amoebas (uh MEE buhs) and similar amoeba-like protists are soft, jellylike protozoans. They are found in both fresh and salt water, in soil, and as parasites in animals. Although amoebas look shapeless, they are highly structured cells. Amoebas have contractile vacuoles to get rid of excess water. Many amoebas eat bacteria and small protists. But some amoebas are parasites that get food by invading other organisms. Certain parasitic amoebas live in human intestines and cause amoebic dysentery (uh MEE bik DIS uhn TER ee). This painful disease causes internal bleeding.

Amoebic Movement

Amoebas and amoeba-like protists move with pseudopodia (SOO doh POH dee uh). *Pseudopodia* means "false feet." To move, an amoeba stretches a pseudopod out from the cell. The cell then flows into the pseudopod. **Figure 6** shows how an amoeba uses pseudopodia to move.

Amoebas and amoeba-like protists use pseudopodia to catch food, too. When an amoeba senses a food source, it moves toward the food. The amoeba surrounds the food with its pseudopodia. This action forms a *food vacuole*. Enzymes move into the vacuole to digest the food, and the digested food passes into the amoeba. **Figure 7** shows an amoeba catching food. To get rid of wastes, an amoeba reverses the process. A waste-filled vacuole is moved to the edge of the cell and is released.

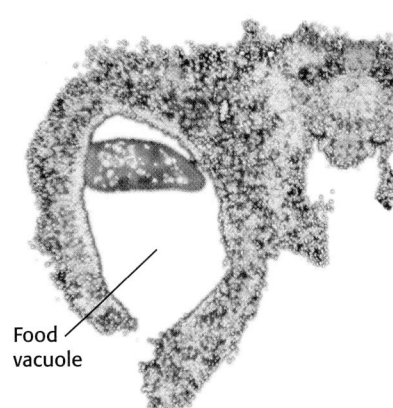

Food vacuole

Figure 7 *An amoeba engulfs its prey with its pseudopodia.*

Q: Knock, Knock!

A: Who's there?

Q: *Euglena.*

A: *Euglena* who?

Q: *Euglena* your room, or you're grounded!

WEIRD SCIENCE

People may have more in common with amoebas than they think. Researchers have discovered that very similar contractile proteins are used in both amoeboid movement and the movement of animal muscles. The cytoplasm of an amoeba contains thick and thin filaments that are almost identical to the thick myosin filaments and the thin actin filaments found in the striated muscle of humans.

Discussion — GENERAL

Protists and Pyramids Ask students the following questions:

• What are the great pyramids of Egypt made of? (Accept all reasonable responses.)

• How is it possible that the pyramids are made, in part, of protist shells? (Accept all reasonable responses.)

Tell students that tiny, single-celled protists called *foraminiferans* make shells. When the foraminiferans die, the shells fall to the ocean floor. Over millions of years, the shells collect and mix with other minerals in the ocean water. Under the pressure of the ocean water, these components form the type of limestone that was used to make the great pyramids of Egypt. **LS** Verbal

CONNECTION to Earth Science — GENERAL

Foraminiferans For millions of years, different species of foraminiferans flourished and then died out, leaving distinctive layers in sea-floor deposits. Some of those deposits are now exposed as thick outcroppings of limestone. These fossils provide clues about the age of rock layers and the relationship between limestone deposits in different parts of the world. Use the teaching transparency titled "The Geologic Time Scale" to discuss the geologic time scale. **LS** Visual

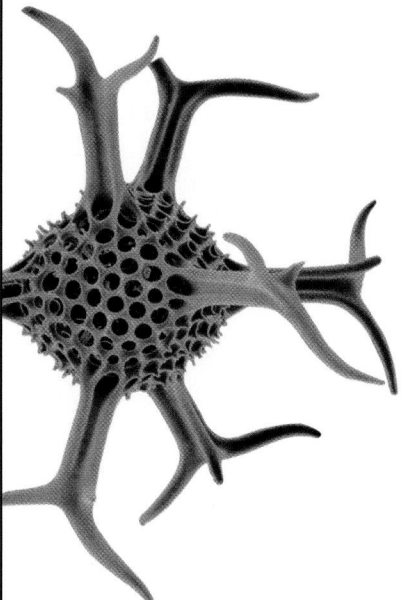

Figure 8 Radiolarians are amoeba-like protists that have shells.

CONNECTION TO Geology

Shell Deposits Foraminiferans have existed for more than 600 million years. During this time, shells of dead foraminiferans have been sinking to the bottom of the ocean. Millions of years ago, foraminiferan shells formed a thick layer of sediment of limestone and chalk deposits. The chalk deposits in England that are known as the White Cliffs of Dover formed in this way. Use geology books to find examples of sedimentary rocks formed from protist shells. Make a poster that explains the process by which shells become sedimentary rock.

ACTIVITY

Shelled Amoeba-Like Protists

Not all amoeba-like protists look shapeless. Some have an outer shell. *Radiolarian* (RAY dee oh LER ee uhn) shells look like glass ornaments, as shown in **Figure 8**. *Foraminiferans* (fuh RAM uh NIF uhr uhnz) have snail-like shells. These protists move by poking pseudopodia out of pores in the shells.

✓ **Reading Check** Name two shelled, amoeba-like protists.

Zooflagellates

Zooflagellates (ZOH uh FLAJ uh LAYTS) are protists that wave flagella back and forth to move. Some zooflagellates live in water. Others live in the bodies of other organisms.

Some zooflagellates are parasites that cause disease. The parasite *Giardia lamblia* (jee AWR dee uh LAM blee uh) can live in the digestive tract of many vertebrates. One form of *G. lamblia* lives part of its life in water. People who drink water infected with *G. lamblia* can get severe stomach cramps.

Some zooflagellates live in mutualism with other organisms. In *mutualism,* one organism lives closely with another organism. Each organism helps the other live. The zooflagellate in **Figure 9** lives in the gut of termites. This zooflagellate digests the cell walls of the wood that the termites eat. Both organisms benefit from the arrangement. The protist helps the termite digest wood. The termite gives the protist food and a place to live.

Figure 9 The Structure of Flagellates

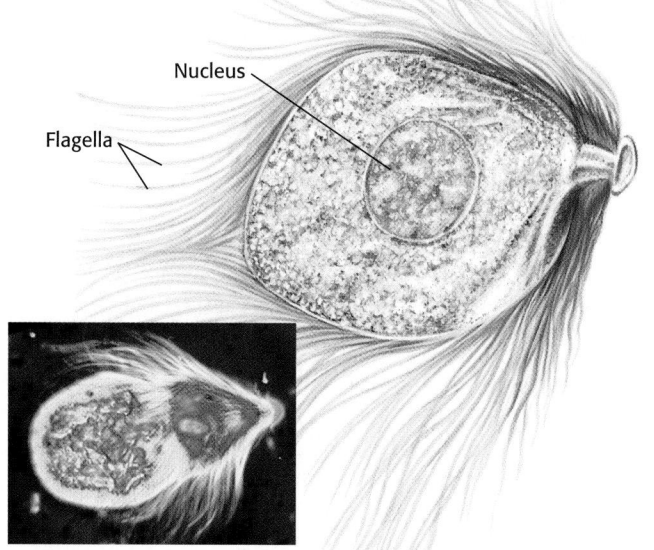

Nucleus

Flagella

Answer to Reading Check
radiolarians and foraminiferans

Figure 10 The Structure of a Paramecium

Members of the genus *Paramecium* eat by using cilia to sweep food into a **food passageway.**

Food enters a **food vacuole,** where enzymes digest the food.

Food waste is removed from the cell through the **anal pore.**

A **contractile vacuole** pumps out excess water.

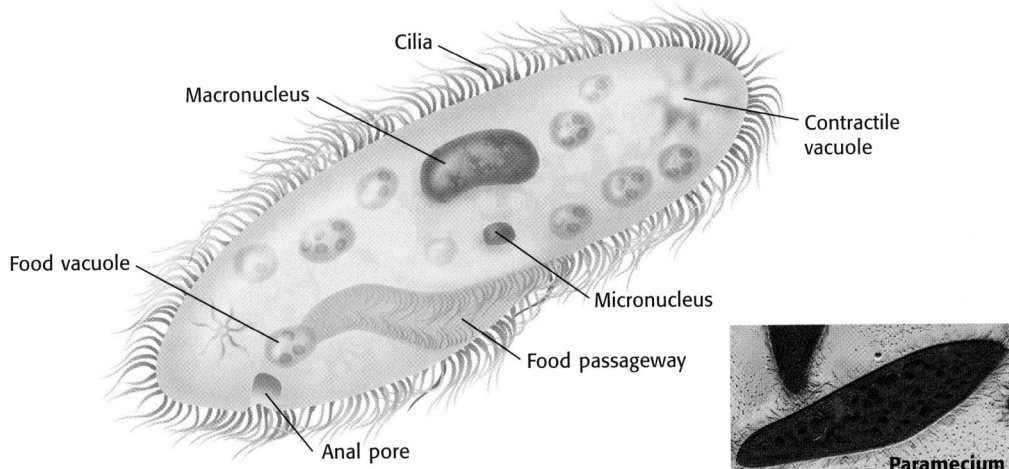

- Cilia
- Macronucleus
- Contractile vacuole
- Food vacuole
- Micronucleus
- Food passageway
- Anal pore

Paramecium

Ciliates

Ciliates (SIL ee its) are complex protists. They have hundreds of tiny, hairlike structures known as *cilia*. The cilia move a protist forward by beating back and forth. Cilia can beat up to 60 times a second! Ciliates also use their cilia for feeding. The cilia sweep food toward the protist's food passageway. The best-known genus of ciliates is *Paramecium*, shown in **Figure 10.**

The cell of a paramecium has two kinds of nuclei. A large nucleus called a *macronucleus* controls the functions of the cell. A smaller nucleus, the *micronucleus*, passes genes to another paramecium during sexual reproduction.

Heterotrophs That Can't Move

Not all protist heterotrophs have features that help them move. Some of these protists are parasites that do not move about. Others can move only at certain phases in their life cycle.

Spore-Forming Protists

Many spore-forming protists are parasites. They absorb nutrients from their hosts. They have no cilia or flagella, and they cannot move on their own. Spore-forming protists have complicated life cycles that usually include two or more hosts. For example, the spore-forming protist that causes malaria uses both mosquitoes and humans as hosts.

CONNECTION TO Social Studies

Malaria *Plasmodium vivax* is a spore-forming protist that causes malaria. People get malaria in tropical areas when they are bitten by mosquitoes carrying *P. vivax*. Malaria can be treated with drugs, but many people do not have access to these drugs. Millions of people die from malaria each year. Research malaria rates in different parts of the world, and give a presentation of your findings to the class.

ACTIVITY

Research ——— **ADVANCED**

PORTFOLIO

Animalcules Anton van Leeuwenhoek (1632–1723) called the tiny, active organisms he viewed under his handmade microscopes *animalcules*. The ciliated protozoans undoubtedly are the most animal-like members of the kingdom Protista. Have students research a ciliate protozoan of their choice. Encourage students to make posters of their ciliate. Posters should include a large, detailed drawing of the ciliate, information about where it lives, what it eats, and how it moves, and other interesting information about its biology.
LS Visual

INCLUSION Strategies

- *Hearing Impaired*
- *Developmentally Delayed*
- *Learning Disabled*

Students can better understand and remember new information when they relate it to familiar information. Ask students to look at the pictures of protists throughout this section and identify familiar items that look like the different kinds of protists. Some possibilities include giant kelp: wide noodles; *Sebdenia*: a branching plant; colonies of *Volvox*: rubber balls; paramecium: a removable shoe liner; and slime mold sporangia: cherry tomatoes.   English Language Learners
LS Visual

Is That a Fact!

Deposits of foraminiferan shells on the sea floor are thousands of meters thick and cover millions of square kilometers. The sand of some beaches is also mostly made from the remains of foraminiferans. There are nearly 50,000 of these foraminiferan shells in 1 g of sand.

CONNECTION ACTIVITY Social Studies ——— ADVANCED

Researching Malaria Malaria is an enormous world health problem. According to the World Health Organization, 500 million people contract malaria each year and 2.7 million people die from it each year. Have students conduct library or Internet research on the nature of the disease and modern efforts to combat it. **LS Verbal**

Phytoplankton To help students remember what phytoplankton are, tell them that the word *phytoplankton* comes from the roots *phyto,* which means "plant," and *planktos,* which means "wandering." Remind students that phytoplankton are protist producers. **LS** Verbal

Quiz ——————— GENERAL

1. Why are euglenoids difficult to classify? (Sample answer: Many euglenoids can be producers or heterotrophs.)

2. Name three protists that are producers. (red, brown, and green algae; diatoms; and many euglenoids)

Alternative Assessment ——— BASIC

Pretty Protists Ask students to find pictures of magnified protists on the Internet or at a library. Students should choose five pretty or interesting organisms and draw those protists on a poster that describes each organism. **LS** Visual

Answer to Reading Check

as decomposers or as parasites

Figure 11 *Parasitic water molds attack various organisms, including fish.*

For another activity related to this chapter, go to **go.hrw.com** and type in the keyword **HL5PROW.**

Water Molds

Water molds are also heterotrophic protists that can't move. Most water molds are small, single-celled organisms. Water molds live in water, moist soil, or other organisms. Some of them are decomposers and thus eat dead matter. But many are parasites. Their hosts can be living plants, animals, algae, or fungi. A parasitic water mold is shown in **Figure 11.**

✓ Reading Check Name two ways that water molds get food.

Slime Molds

Slime molds are heterotrophic protists that can move only at certain phases of their life cycle. They look like thin, colorful, shapeless globs of slime. Slime molds live in cool, moist places in the woods. They use pseudopodia to move and to eat bacteria and yeast. They also decompose small bits of rotting organic matter by surrounding small pieces of the matter and then digesting them.

Some slime molds live as a giant cell that has many nuclei and a single cytoplasm at one stage of life. As long as food and water are available, the cell will continue to grow. One cell may be more than 1 m across! Other slime molds live as single-celled individuals that can come together as a group when food or water is hard to find.

When environmental conditions are stressful, slime molds grow stalklike structures with rounded knobs at the top, as shown in **Figure 12.** The knobs contain spores. *Spores* are small reproductive cells covered by a thick cell wall. The spores can survive for a long time without water or nutrients. As spores, slime molds cannot move. When conditions improve, the spores will develop into new slime molds.

Figure 12 *The spore-containing knobs of a slime mold are called* sporangia *(spoh RAN jee uh).*

Group ACTiViTY — ADVANCED

Make a Slime Mold For this activity, students should wear safety goggles, an apron, and protective gloves. They should not put any of the materials in their mouths. Food coloring is nontoxic but can stain skin and clothing. Students can make a substance that behaves much like a slime mold. Have students work in groups of four or five. Each group should have a 25 × 25 cm (9 × 9 in.) pan, cornstarch, food coloring, a small container of water, a measuring cup, and a tablespoon. Instruct the students to place 240 mL (1 cup) of cornstarch in the pan. Then, have them add 15 mL (1 Tbsp) of water at a time to the cornstarch until the mixture has the consistency of a slime that flows slowly. Then, have them mix a few drops of food coloring into the mixture, and allow students to explore moving the slime around in the pan. They can put small objects, such as paper clips, in the path of the slime and let the substance surround the objects. **LS** Kinesthetic

English Language Learners

Summary

- Protists can be organized into the following groups: producers, heterotrophs that can move, and heterotrophs that cannot move.
- Protist producers make their own food through photosynthesis. They are known as *algae*, and most live in water. Free-floating single-celled algae are phytoplankton.
- Red algae, green algae, brown algae, diatoms, dinoflagellates, and some euglenoids are producers.

- Heterotrophic protists cannot make their own food. They are consumers, decomposers, or parasites. Those that can move are sometimes called *protozoans*.
- Amoeba-like protists, shelled amoeba-like protists, flagellates, and ciliates are heterotrophs that can move.
- Spore-forming protists, water molds, and slime molds are protists that cannot move or can move only in certain phases of their life cycle.

Using Key Terms

1. Use the following terms in the same sentence: *phytoplankton* and *algae*.

Understanding Key Ideas

2. Which of the following kinds of protists are producers?
   - **a.** diatoms
   - **b.** amoebas
   - **c.** slime molds
   - **d.** ciliates

3. How do many amoeba-like protists eat?
   - **a.** They secrete digestive juices onto food.
   - **b.** They produce food from sunlight.
   - **c.** They engulf food with pseudopodia.
   - **d.** They use cilia to sweep food toward them.

4. Give an example of one protist from each of the three groups of protists.

5. Explain why it makes sense to group protists based on shared traits rather than by how they are related to each other.

Critical Thinking

6. **Making Comparisons** How do protist producers, heterotrophs that can move, and heterotrophs that can't move differ?

7. **Making Inferences** You learned how shelled amoeba-like protists move. How do you think they get food into their shells in order to eat?

Interpreting Graphics

Use the photo below to answer the questions that follow.

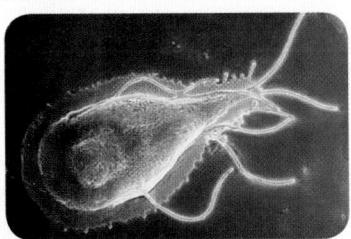

8. How does this protist move?

9. Identify what kind of protist is shown. To do so, first make a list of the kinds of protists that this organism could not be.

Developed and maintained by the
National Science Teachers Association

For a variety of links related to this chapter, go to www.scilinks.org

Topic: Algae; Protozoans
SciLinks code: HSM0042; HSM1247

CHAPTER RESOURCES

Chapter Resource File

- Section Quiz GENERAL
- Section Review GENERAL
- Vocabulary and Section Summary GENERAL

Answers to Section Review

1. Sample answer: Phytoplankton are single-celled, freefloating algae.

2. a

3. c

4. Sample answer: protist producer: diatom; heterotrophic protist that can move: radiolarian; heterotrophic protist that can't move: water mold

5. Scientists are not sure how protists are related to each other. Protists are a very diverse group of organisms. So, grouping them by their shared traits is a helpful way to organize protists.

6. The three groups of protists differ from each other in the ways that they get food and the ways that they move. Protist producers make food by photosynthesis. A few of them have flagella and can move. Heterotrophs get food by eating other organisms or organic matter. The two groups of heterotrophs differ in whether they can move. One group can move throughout the entire life cycle, and the other group can move only at certain parts of the life cycle or not at all.

7. Sample answer: Shelled amoebalike protists can use their pseudopodia to eat. They can poke the pseudopodia out of the pores in their shells and engulf food outside the shell.

8. Sample answer: This protist has flagella, so we can assume it moves with its flagella.

9. The protist cannot be an amoebalike protist because it does not have pseudopodia. It can't be a ciliate because it has no cilia. It can't be a euglenoid or a dinoflagellate, because it has more than two flagella. It can't be a protist producer, because it has no chloroplasts. Based on the photo, it must be a zooflagellate.

Overview

In this section, students will learn about fungi—eukaryotic consumers that obtain their food by absorbing nutrients from other organisms. Students will be introduced to the four main groups of fungi: threadlike fungi, sac fungi, club fungi, and imperfect fungi. Finally, students will learn about lichens.

🔊 Bellringer

Ask students to answer the following questions:

• What are mushrooms?

• What is the function of a mushroom's cap? (The umbrella-shaped mushrooms that students may be most familiar with are club fungi. The above-ground part of the mushroom produces spores.)

Discussion ——— GENERAL

Fungi Ask students to describe a world without fungi. (Accept all reasonable responses. Explain that without fungi, there would be no leavened bread, penicillin, blue cheese, or mushroom pizza. Also, many plant species would grow poorly without help from mycorrhizae. And because fungi are decomposers, dead organic matter might collect without fungi.) **LS Verbal**

SECTION
3

Fungi

How are cheese, bread, and soy sauce related to fungi? A fungus can help make each of these foods.

Fungi (singular, *fungus*) are everywhere. The mushrooms on pizza are a type of fungus. The yeast used to make bread is a fungus. And if you've ever had athlete's foot, you can thank a fungus for that, too.

Characteristics of Fungi

Fungi are eukaryotic heterotrophs that have rigid cell walls and no chlorophyll. They are so different from other organisms that they are placed in their own kingdom. As you can see in **Figure 1,** fungi come in a variety of shapes, sizes, and colors.

Food for Fungi

Fungi are heterotrophs, but they cannot catch or surround food. Fungi must live on or near their food supply. Most fungi are consumers. These fungi get nutrients by secreting digestive juices onto a food source and then absorbing the dissolved food. Many fungi are decomposers, which feed on dead plant or animal matter. Other fungi are parasites.

Some fungi live in mutualism with other organisms. For example, many types of fungi grow on or in the roots of a plant. The plant provides nutrients to the fungus. The fungus helps the root absorb minerals and protects the plant from some disease-causing organisms. This relationship between a plant and a fungus is called a *mycorrhiza* (MIE koh RIE zuh).

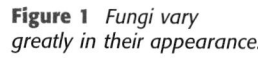

fungus an organism whose cells have nuclei, rigid cell walls, and no chlorophyll and that belongs to the kingdom Fungi

Figure 1 *Fungi vary greatly in their appearance.*

▼ Straight coral fungus

▲ Bird's nest fungus

▼ Witch's hat fungus

Is That a Fact!

There are about 350 species of yeasts. The most economically important species of yeasts is *Saccharomyces cerevisiae*, which has been used by humans in the production of bread, beer, and wine for thousands of years.

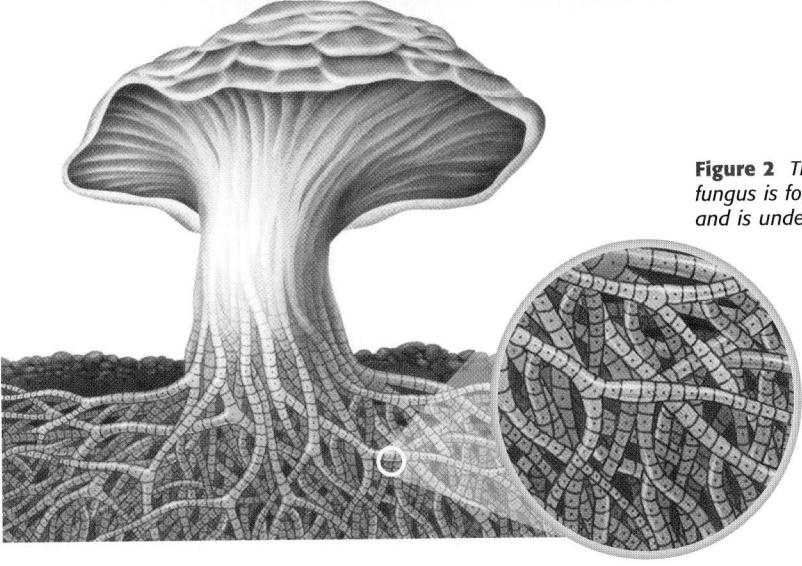

Figure 2 *The mycelium of a fungus is formed by hyphae and is underground.*

Prediction Guide Before students read the rest of this section, ask them if each of the following statements is true or false. Students will learn the answers as they read the section.

- Unlike protists, fungi can reproduce only asexually. (false)
- Morels and truffles are highly prized fungi. (true)
- Lichens are a combination of a fungus and an alga. (true)

LS Verbal

Hidden from View

All fungi are made of eukaryotic cells, which have nuclei. Some fungi are single celled, but most fungi are made of many cells. These many-celled fungi are made up of chains of cells called hyphae (HIE fee). **Hyphae** (singular, *hypha*) are threadlike fungal filaments. These filaments are made of cells that have openings in their cell walls. These openings allow cytoplasm to move freely between the cells.

Most of the hyphae that make up a fungus grow together to form a twisted mass called the **mycelium** (mie SEE lee uhm). The mycelium makes up the major part of the fungus. However, this mass is hidden from view underneath the ground. **Figure 2** shows the hyphae of a fungus.

hypha a nonreproductive filament of a fungus

mycelium the mass of fungal filaments, or hyphae, that forms the body of a fungus

spore a reproductive cell or multicellular structure that is resistant to stressful environmental conditions and that can develop into an adult without fusing with another cell

Making More Fungi

Reproduction in fungi may be either asexual or sexual. Asexual reproduction in fungi occurs in two ways. In one type of asexual reproduction, the hyphae break apart, and each new piece becomes a new fungus. Asexual reproduction can also take place by the production of spores. **Spores** are small reproductive cells that are protected by a thick cell wall. Spores are light and easily spread by wind. When the growing conditions where a spore lands are right, the spore will grow into a new fungus.

Sexual reproduction in fungi happens when special structures form to make sex cells. The sex cells join to produce sexual spores that grow into a new fungus. **Figure 3** shows a fungus releasing sexual spores into the air.

✔ **Reading Check** What are two ways that fungi can reproduce asexually? (*See the Appendix for answers to Reading Checks.*)

Discussion —— GENERAL

Allergies and Molds Ask students if they or people that they know are allergic to molds. As a class, encourage students to discuss why mold allergies are so common. Then, have students discuss what types of environments or substances mold-sensitive people might want to avoid and why. (Sample answer: One reason mold allergies are common is that molds and mold spores are so common. Mold-sensitive individuals might want to avoid caves, damp basements, damp soil, leaf litter, and other decaying organic matter because molds flourish in such places and materials.)

LS Verbal/Auditory

Figure 3 *This puffball is releasing sexual spores that can produce new fungi.*

Is That a Fact!

Yeasts are widely used in genetic research. Yeasts were the first eukaryotic organisms to have their DNA manipulated through the techniques of genetic engineering. Today, they are the organisms of choice for many types of experiments in molecular and cell biology. Experiments on species of yeasts such as *Saccharomyces cerevisiae,* the common bread yeast, have provided enormous insight into the functioning of eukaryotic cells.

Answer to Reading Check

hyphae breaking apart so that each piece becomes a new fungus or fungi producing spores

Tempeh Centuries ago, Indonesians found that the bread mold of the genus *Rhizopus* can be used to make a food called *tempeh*. Soybeans that have been stripped of their skins and boiled are inoculated with this mold and left to sit for 24 hours. A mycelium grows around the soybeans, holding them together in a mass and producing enzymes that increase the level of B vitamins in the mixture. Tempeh is very nutritious and is prepared daily in many Indonesian homes, just as bread is in many other countries. Tempeh can be fried, baked, steamed, or roasted. Ask interested students to find a recipe that uses tempeh. **LS Verbal**

MATERIALS

FOR EACH GROUP
• bag, plastic, sealable
• bread, 1 slice
• water

Answers

4. After a week, the bread should have become moldy.

5. Answers may vary. The mold spores likely came from the air and grew using the nutrients in the bread and water.

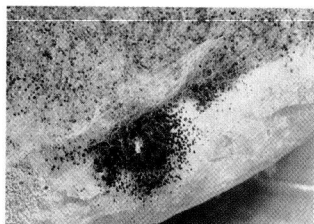

Figure 4 *Black bread mold is a soft, cottony mass that grows on bread and fruit.*

mold a fungus that looks like wool or cotton

Quick Lab

Moldy Bread

1. Dampen a **slice of bread** with a **few drops of water,** and then seal it in a **plastic bag** for 1 week.

2. Draw a picture of the bread in the plastic bag.

3. Predict what you think will happen during the week. Will the bread get moldy?

4. After the week has passed, check on the bread in the plastic bag. Compare it with your original drawing. What happened? Were your predictions correct?

5. With a partner, discuss where you think mold spores come from and how they grow.

WEIRD SCIENCE

The mold of the genus *Pilobolus* grows on animal manure. This mold produces little sacs of spores on top of stalked structures that swell. As the spores mature, pressure builds up in the swollen structures until the sacs are shot up to 8 m into the air! The spore sacs stick to grass and leaves. When animals eat the plants, the spores pass through their digestive track and end up in their dung, where the spores germinate.

Kinds of Fungi

Fungi are classified based on their shape and the way that they reproduce. There are four main groups of fungi. Most species of fungi fit into one of these groups. These groups are threadlike fungi, sac fungi, club fungi, and imperfect fungi.

Threadlike Fungi

Have you ever seen fuzzy mold growing on bread? A **mold** is a shapeless, fuzzy fungus. **Figure 4** shows a black bread mold. This particular mold belongs to a group of fungi called *threadlike fungi*. Most of the fungi in this group live in the soil and are decomposers. However, some threadlike fungi are parasites.

Threadlike fungi can reproduce asexually. Parts of the hyphae grow into the air and form round spore cases at the tips. These spore cases are called *sporangia* (spoh RAN jee uh). **Figure 5** shows some magnified sporangia. When the sporangia break open, many tiny spores are released into the air. New fungi will develop from these spores if they land in an area with good growing conditions.

Threadlike fungi can also reproduce sexually. Threadlike fungi reproduce sexually when a hypha from one individual joins with a hypha from another individual. The hyphae grow into specialized sporangia that can survive times of cold or little water. When conditions improve, these specialized sporangia release spores that can grow into new fungi.

✓ **Reading Check** Describe two ways that threadlike fungi can reproduce.

Figure 5 *Each of the round sporangia contains thousands of spores.*

Answer to Reading Check

asexually by releasing spores from sporangia or sexually by different individuals growing together into specialized sporangia

Figure 6 *Morels are only part of a larger fungus. They are the sexual reproductive part of a fungus that lives under the soil.*

Sac Fungi

Sac fungi are the largest group of fungi. Sac fungi include yeasts, powdery mildews, truffles, and morels. Some morels are shown in **Figure 6.**

Sac fungi can reproduce both asexually and sexually during their life cycles. Most of the time, they use asexual reproduction. When they reproduce sexually, they form a sac called an *ascus.* This sac gives the sac fungi their name. Sexually produced spores develop within the ascus.

Most sac fungi are made of many cells. However, *yeasts* are single-celled sac fungi. When yeasts reproduce asexually, they use a process called *budding.* In budding, a new cell pinches off from an existing cell. **Figure 7** shows a yeast that is budding. Yeasts are the only fungi that reproduce by budding.

Some sac fungi are very useful to humans. For example, yeasts are used in making bread and alcohol. Yeasts use sugar as food and produce carbon dioxide gas and alcohol as waste. Trapped bubbles of carbon dioxide cause bread dough to rise. This process is what makes bread light and fluffy. Other sac fungi are sources of antibiotics and vitamins. And some sac fungi, such as truffles and morels, are prized as human foods.

Not all sac fungi are helpful. In fact, many sac fungi are parasites. Some cause plant diseases, such as chestnut blight and Dutch elm disease. The effects of Dutch elm disease are shown in **Figure 8.**

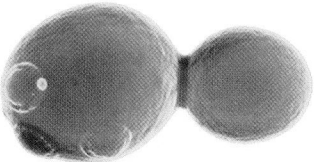

Figure 7 *Yeasts reproduce by budding. A round scar forms where a bud breaks off from a parent cell.*

Figure 8 *Dutch elm disease is a fungal disease that has killed millions of elm trees.*

Is That a Fact!

Some yeasts produce an enzyme called *invertase.* This enzyme is used by commercial candy makers to soften or liquefy the centers of chocolate candies after the coating has been applied. The invertase takes several weeks to liquefy the centers, so it can be added before the candy is coated with chocolate.

Quick Lab

MATERIALS

FOR EACH STUDENT
- knife, plastic
- magnifying lens
- mushroom

Safety Caution: Remind students to review all safety cautions and icons before beginning this lab activity. You may want to ask students to wear protective gloves, especially students with allergies to fungi.

Answer

4. Students should be able to find and label the stalk, cap, and gills. Spores and hyphae may or may not be visible.

ACTIVITY — BASIC

Writing

Fungus Reproduction
Have students write out the following words: *threadlike fungi, sac fungi, club fungi, ascus, gills,* and *sporangia.* Then, have students match the type of fungus with its appropriate reproductive structure. Finally, have students use each correctly matched pair in a sentence. (threadlike fungi, sporangia; sac fungi, ascus; club fungi, gills)
LS Verbal

Answer to Reading Check

the spore-forming structures, called *basidia*

Figure 9 *A ring of mushrooms can appear overnight. In European folk legends, these were known as "fairy rings."*

Quick Lab

Observe a Mushroom

1. Identify the stalk, cap, and gills on a **mushroom** that your teacher has provided.

2. Carefully twist or cut off the cap, and cut it open with a **plastic knife**. Use a **magnifying lens** to observe the gills. Look for spores.

3. Use the magnifying lens to observe the other parts of the mushroom. The mycelium begins at the bottom of the stalk. Try to find individual hyphae.

4. Sketch the mushroom, and label the parts.

Club Fungi

The umbrella-shaped mushrooms are the most familiar fungi. Mushrooms belong to a group of fungi called *club fungi.* This group gets its name from structures that the fungi grow during reproduction. Club fungi reproduce sexually. During reproduction, they grow special hyphae that form clublike structures. These structures are called *basidia* (buh SID ee uh), the Greek word for "clubs." Sexual spores develop on the basidia.

When you think of a mushroom, you probably picture only the spore-producing, above-ground part of the organism. But most of the organism is underground. The mass of hyphae from which mushrooms are produced may grow 35 m across. That's about as long as 18 adults lying head to toe! Mushrooms usually grow at the edges of the mass of hyphae. As a result, mushrooms often appear in circles, as shown in **Figure 9.**

The most familiar mushrooms are known as *gill fungi.* The basidia of these mushrooms develop in structures called *gills,* under the mushroom cap. Some varieties are grown commercially and sold in supermarkets. However, not all gill fungi are edible. For example, the white destroying angel is a very poisonous fungus. Simply a taste of this mushroom can be fatal. See if you can pick out the poisonous fungus in **Figure 10.**

✓ Reading Check What part of a club fungus grows above the ground?

Figure 10 *Many poisonous mushrooms look just like edible ones. Never eat a mushroom from the wild unless a professional identifies it in person.*

WEIRD SCIENCE

Mushrooms consist mostly of water (about 90%). But some fungi are nutritious. The shiitake mushroom has been grown for centuries in Japan and China. In ancient China, people believed that eating shiitake mushrooms promoted good health. They were right—shiitake mushrooms are rich in iron, phosphorus, calcium, and vitamins B, D, and C. Shiitake mushrooms also have twice the protein content of most other commercially grown mushrooms.

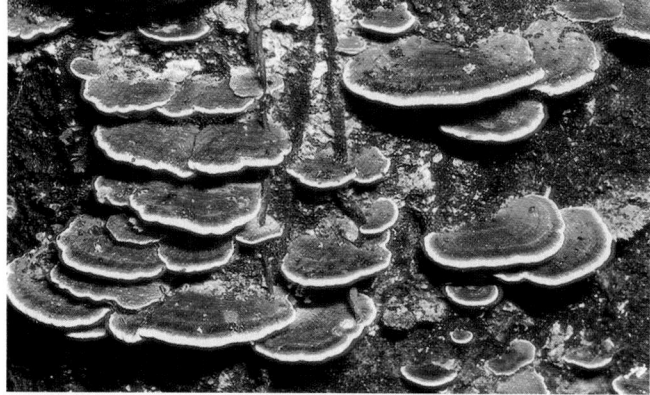

Figure 11 *Bracket fungi look like shelves on trees. The underside of the bracket contains spores.*

Nonmushroom Club Fungi

Mushrooms are not the only club fungi. Bracket fungi, puffballs, smuts, and rusts are also club fungi. Bracket fungi grow outward from wood and form small shelves or brackets, as shown in **Figure 11.** Smuts and rusts are common plant parasites. They often attack crops such as corn and wheat. The corn in **Figure 12** has been infected with a smut.

Figure 12 *This corn is infected with a club fungus called* smut.

Imperfect Fungi

The *imperfect fungi* group includes all of the species of fungi that do not quite fit in the other groups. These fungi do not reproduce sexually. Most are parasites that cause diseases in plants and animals. One common human disease caused by these fungi is athlete's foot, a skin disease. Another fungus from this group produces a poison called *aflatoxin* (AF luh TAHKS in), which can cause cancer.

Some imperfect fungi are useful. *Penicillium,* shown in **Figure 13,** is the source of the antibiotic penicillin. Other imperfect fungi are also used to produce medicines. Some imperfect fungi are used to produce cheeses, soy sauce, and the citric acid used in cola drinks.

Figure 13 *The fungus* Penicillium *produces a substance that kills certain bacteria.*

Beatrix Potter Beatrix Potter (1866–1943) is best known for writing children's stories, such as *The Tale of Peter Rabbit* and *The Tale of Two Bad Mice*. Potter lived and worked in England and had a scholarly interest in fungi. She was a shy person, and she was not taken seriously by fungi scholars of her time. But today, she is widely respected as a mycologist (a scientist who studies fungi). She wrote many valuable papers about fungi and made detailed drawings of more than 270 fungi. Research Potter's life, and present a report to your class.

ACTIVITY

Is That a Fact!

If you are allergic to penicillin, you will probably be allergic to Camembert and Roquefort cheeses, too. These cheeses get their flavor from molds of the genus *Penicillium*.

CONNECTION to Real World — GENERAL

Fungal Medicines Cyclosporin is a chemical compound that was discovered in an imperfect fungus in the 1980s. Cyclosporin suppresses immune reactions that lead to the rejection of transplanted organs. This fungal drug has led to much greater success in organ transplants. Interested students should research other fungal medicines. **LS Verbal**

Using the Figure — GENERAL

Dirty Fungi? Tell students that the word *smut*, which describes a non-mushroom club fungus, comes from the same root word that led to the words *mud* and *moss*. In fact, another definition for the word *smut* is the following: a mark made by something dirty; a spoiled spot. Ask students to look at the photo of a smut in **Figure 12** and write a few sentences about possible reasons why the name of this fungus relates to dirt. **LS Verbal**

MISCONCEPTION ALERT

Lawn Care Students may think that they can rid a lawn or a garden of mushrooms by pulling the mushrooms out like they pull out weeds or by chopping the mushrooms up with a hoe. Tell students that because the largest part of a club fungus lives underground, this approach will not work. In fact, chopping up mushrooms with a hoe may help release and spread fungal spores, which could grow into additional mycelia.

Close

Reteaching — BASIC

Drawing Fungi Ask students to draw an example of each of the four kinds of fungi. Then, ask students why some fungi are hard to draw. (Many fungi do not have a defined shape.) Remind them that much of a club fungus is underground. **LS** Visual

Quiz — GENERAL

1. Why should you never eat wild mushrooms that haven't been identified by an expert? (Many poisonous mushrooms closely resemble mushrooms that are safe to eat.)

2. From what kind of a fungus is the antibiotic penicillin derived? (an imperfect fungus from the genus *Penicillium*)

3. Where are lichens found? (on bare rocks, soil, tree trunks, and mountain peaks in environments ranging from dry deserts to cold, polar regions)

Alternative Assessment — GENERAL

 Describing Fungi Have students write a story in which they find several fungi on a walk through a temperate forest. Students should identify each fungus' group and its role in the forest ecosystem. **LS** Verbal

Answer to Reading Check
Lichens make acids that break down rocks, which causes cracks.

▲ Wolf lichen

British soldier ▶ lichen

▼ Christmas lichen

Figure 14 *These are some of the many types of lichens.*

lichen a mass of fungal and algal cells that grow together in a symbiotic relationship and that are usually found on rocks or trees

Lichens

A **lichen** (LIE kuhn) is a combination of a fungus and an alga that grow together. The alga actually lives inside the protective walls of the fungus. The resulting organism is different from either organism growing alone. The lichen is a result of a mutualistic relationship. But the merging of the two organisms to form a lichen is so complete that scientists give lichens their own scientific names. **Figure 14** shows some examples of lichens.

Unlike fungi, lichens are producers. The algae in the lichens produce food through photosynthesis. And unlike algae, lichens can keep from drying out. The protective walls of the fungi keep water inside the lichens. Lichens are found in almost every type of land environment. They can even grow in dry environments, such as deserts, and cold environments, such as the Arctic.

Because lichens need only air, light, and minerals to grow, they can grow on rocks. As lichens grow, the changes that they make to their surroundings allow other organisms to live there, too. For example, lichens make acids that break down rocks and cause cracks. When bits of rock and dead lichens fill the cracks, soil is made. Other organisms then grow in this soil.

Lichens absorb water and minerals from the air. As a result, lichens are easily affected by air pollution. So, the presence or absence of lichens can be a good measure of air quality in an area.

Reading Check How can lichens affect rocks?

INCLUSION Strategies

- *Attention Deficit Disorder*
- *Behavior Control Issues*
- *Hearing Impaired*

Many students are more successful when some movement is built into a class period. Give students a chance to move around while they explore the meaning of *intertwined* as it is used to describe how lichens grow. Ask half of the students to select one textbook and the other half to select another textbook. Use several copies of each text book for the following exercise. Have students place a mixture of the two textbooks flat on the floor in a random arrangement. Then, ask them to consider the mass of textbooks as one object made of many small ones. Discuss how the arrangement of the two kinds of textbooks making up a separate object is similar to the arrangement of the alga and fungus making up a separate organism, a lichen. **LS** Kinesthetic — English Language Learners

SECTION Review

Summary

- Fungi can be consumers, decomposers, or parasites, or they can live in mutualistic relationships with other organisms.
- Most fungi are made up of chains of cells called *hyphae*. Many hyphae join together to form a mycelium.
- The four main groups of fungi are threadlike fungi, sac fungi, club fungi, and imperfect fungi.
- Threadlike fungi are primarily decomposers that form sporangia containing spores.

- During sexual reproduction, sac fungi form little sacs in which sexual spores develop.
- Club fungi form structures called *basidia* during sexual reproduction.
- The imperfect fungi include all of the species that do not quite fit in the other groups. Many are parasites that reproduce only by asexual reproduction.
- A lichen is a combination of a specific fungus and a specific alga. The lichen is different from either organism growing alone.

Using Key Terms

1. In your own words, write a definition for each of the following terms: *spore* and *mold*.

For each pair of terms, explain how the meanings of the terms differ.

2. *fungus* and *lichen*

3. *hyphae* and *mycelium*

Understanding Key Ideas

4. Which of the following statements about fungi is true?
   a. All fungi are eukaryotic.
   b. All fungi are decomposers.
   c. All fungi reproduce by sexual reproduction.
   d. All fungi are producers.

5. What are the four main groups of fungi? Give a characteristic of each group.

6. How are fungi able to withstand periods of cold or drought?

Critical Thinking

7. **Analyzing Processes** Many fungi are decomposers. Imagine what would happen to the natural world if decomposers no longer existed. Write a description of how a lack of decomposers might affect the processes of nature.

8. **Identifying Relationships** Explain how two organisms make up a lichen.

Interpreting Graphics

Use the photo below to answer the questions that follow.

9. To which group of fungi does this organism belong? How can you be sure?

10. What part of the organism is shown in this photo? What part is not shown? Explain.

SCi LINKS®

NSTA
Developed and maintained by the
National Science Teachers Association

For a variety of links related to this chapter, go to www.scilinks.org

Topics: Fungi; Lichens
SciLinks codes: HSM0628; HSM0871

Answers to Section Review

1. Sample answer: A spore is a reproductive cell that is protected by a thick wall. A mold is a shapeless, fuzzy fungus.

2. Sample answer: Fungi are decomposers that break down dead organic material. A lichen is a fungus and an alga living in a close symbiotic relationship. The lichen gets food through the alga's photosynthesis.

3. Sample answer: Hyphae are threadlike filaments. A large mass of hyphae make up the body of a fungus, which is the mycelium.

4. a

5. Sample answer: Threadlike fungi have hyphae that end in sporangia. Sac fungi have spores in a sac called an *ascus*. Club fungi produce clublike structures called *basidia*. Imperfect fungi do not reproduce sexually.

6. Sample answer: During periods of extreme cold, heat, or drought, some fungi form spores or sporangia, which can survive difficult environmental conditions.

7. Sample answer: If fungi and other decomposers ceased to exist, the dead matter would not break down. The forest floors would be littered with dead matter that would never decompose.

8. Sample answer: Lichens are a combination of a fungus and an alga. Each organism benefits from the other, and the relationship is so close that the lichen is considered to be a unique organism.

9. Sample answer: This organism is a club fungus. You could be sure by looking for club-shaped basidia on gills under the cap.

10. Sample answer: We can see the basidia, which is the reproductive structure of the fungus. We cannot see the mycelium, which makes up the bulk of the organism, because the mycelium is underground.

CHAPTER RESOURCES

Chapter Resource File

- **Section Quiz** `GENERAL`
- **Section Review** `GENERAL`
- **Vocabulary and Section Summary** `GENERAL`
- **Reinforcement Worksheet** `BASIC`
- **SciLinks Activity** `GENERAL`
- **Datasheet for Quick Lab**

There's a Fungus Among Us!

Teacher's Notes

Time Required

15 minutes of one class period and one 45-minute class period the next day

Lab Ratings

EASY ——————→ HARD

Teacher Prep 🧪🧪🧪
Student Set-Up 🧪🧪🧪
Concept Level 🧪🧪🧪
Clean Up 🧪🧪

Preparation Notes

Do not use mushrooms gathered from the wild. Suitable mushrooms can be found in the produce section of a grocery store. Have protective gloves available for students who wish to wear them. This lab works well with groups of 2 to 4 students per mushroom. If you do not have an incubator, place the Petri dishes in a warm place, out of drafts and direct sunlight.

Safety Caution

Remind students to review all safety cautions and icons before beginning this lab activity. Before beginning this lab, check for any mushroom allergies among students. Caution students not to eat any of the mushrooms.

OBJECTIVES

Examine the parts of a mushroom.

Describe your observations of the mushroom.

MATERIALS

- gloves, protective
- incubator
- microscope or magnifying lens
- mushroom
- paper, white (2 sheets)
- Petri dish with fruit-juice agar plate
- tape, masking
- tape, transparent
- tweezers

SAFETY

There's a Fungus Among Us!

Fungi share many characteristics with plants. For example, most fungi live on land and cannot move from place to place. But fungi have several unique features that suggest that they are not closely related to any other kingdom of organisms. In this activity, you will observe some of the unique structures of a mushroom, a member of the kingdom Fungi.

Procedure

1 Put on your safety goggles and gloves. Get a mushroom from your teacher. Carefully pull the cap of the mushroom from the stem.

2 Using tweezers, remove one of the gills from the underside of the cap. Place the gill on a sheet of white paper.

3 Place the mushroom cap gill-side down on the other sheet of paper. Use masking tape to keep the mushroom cap in place. Place the paper aside for at least 24 hours.

4 Use tweezers to take several 1 cm pieces from the stem, and place these pieces in your Petri dish. Record the appearance of the plate by drawing the plate in a notebook. Cover the Petri dish, and incubate it overnight.

5 Use tweezers to gently pull the remaining mushroom stem apart lengthwise. The individual fibers or strings that you see are the hyphae, which form the structure of the fungus. Place a thin strand on the same piece of paper on which you placed the gill that you removed from the cap.

6 Use a magnifying lens or microscope to observe the gill and the stem hyphae.

7 After at least 24 hours, record any changes that occurred in the Petri dish.

8 Carefully remove the mushroom cap from the paper. Place a piece of transparent tape over the print left behind on the paper. Record your observations.

Jason Marsh
Montevideo High and Country School
Montevideo, Minnesota

CHAPTER RESOURCES

Chapter Resource File

- **Datasheet for Chapter Lab**
- **Lab Notes and Answers**

Technology

 Classroom Videos
- Lab Video

- Making a Protist Mobile

Analyze the Results

1 **Describing Events** Describe the structures that you saw on the gill and hyphae.

2 **Explaining Events** What makes up the print that was left on the white paper?

3 **Examining Data** Describe the structures on the mushroom gill. Explain how these structures are connected to the print.

4 **Analyzing Data** Compare your original drawing of the Petri dish to your observations of the dish after leaving it for 24 hours.

Draw Conclusions

5 **Evaluating Results** Explain how the changes that occurred in your Petri dish are related to methods of fungal reproduction.

Applying Your Data

Fungi such as mushrooms and yeast are used in cooking and baking in many parts of the world. Bread is a staple food in many cultures. There are thousands of kinds of bread. Conduct library and Internet research on how yeast makes bread rise. Find a bread recipe, and show how the recipe involves the care and feeding of yeast. Ask an adult to help you bake a loaf of bread to share with your class during your presentation.

Analyze the Results

1. Sample answer: Gills look like knife blades. Hyphae are string-like.
2. The print on the white paper is a spore print produced by basidio-spores being released from the gills.
3. The structures on the mushroom gill contain the nuclei that will develop into spores like the ones that were released as the spore print.
4. After 24 hours, students may see mycelia growth on the Petri dish. (It may take a little longer.)

Draw Conclusions

5. The mycelia grow to form the main body of the mushroom and develop from germinating spores.

Applying Your Data

As the yeast fungus metabolizes sugars through cellular respiration, it produces carbon dioxide gas that makes the bread rise. Most bread recipes will include food for the yeast and conditions that encourage yeast growth (moisture and warmth).

Assignment Guide

Section	Questions
1	5, 14, 17, 19
2	6–8, 11, 13, 15–16, 18, 23
3	1, 3–4, 9–10, 12, 20–22, 24–28
1 and 2	2

ANSWERS

Using Key Terms

1. Sample answer: The mycelium is the mass of hyphae that makes up the body of a fungus. A lichen is an organism that is made up of a fungus and an alga living intertwined. A heterotroph is an organism that cannot make its own food.

2. Sample answer: Algae, including free-floating phytoplankton, are protists that produce food from the sun's energy.

3. Sample answer: Molds, like all threadlike fungi, reproduce by releasing spores into the air.

4. Sample answer: A fungus is an organism that is made up of hyphae. A hypha is a threadlike filament that grows together with many other hyphae to form the mycelium.

5. A parasite is an organism that invades the body of another living organism to get food from it. A host is the organism that is invaded by a parasite.

USING KEY TERMS

1 In your own words, write a definition for each of the following terms: *mycelium, lichen,* and *heterotroph.*

2 Use the following terms in the same sentence: *protists, algae,* and *phytoplankton.*

3 Use the following terms in the same sentence: *spore* and *mold.*

For each pair of terms, explain how the meanings of the terms differ.

4 *fungus* and *hypha*

5 *parasite* and *host*

UNDERSTANDING KEY IDEAS

Multiple Choice

6 Protist producers include
  a. euglenoids and ciliates.
  b. lichens and zooflagellates.
  c. spore-forming protists and smuts.
  d. dinoflagellates and diatoms.

7 Protists can be
  a. parasites or decomposers.
  b. made of chains of cells called *hyphae.*
  c. divided into four major groups.
  d. only parasites.

8 A euglenoid has
  a. a micronucleus.
  b. pseudopodia.
  c. two flagella.
  d. cilia.

9 Which statement about fungi is true?
  a. Fungi are producers.
  b. Fungi cannot eat or engulf food.
  c. Fungi are found only in the soil.
  d. Fungi are primarily single celled.

10 A lichen is made up of
  a. a fungus and a funguslike protist that live together.
  b. an alga and a fungus that live together.
  c. two kinds of fungi that live together.
  d. an alga and a funguslike protist that live together.

11 Heterotrophic protists that can move
  a. are also known as *protozoans.*
  b. include amoebas and paramecia.
  c. may be either free living or parasitic.
  d. All of the above

Short Answer

12 How are fungi helpful to humans?

13 What is the function of cilia in a paramecium?

14 How are fungi different from protists that get food as decomposers?

15 How are slime molds and amoebas similar?

16 What is a contractile vacuole?

17 Compare how *Paramecium, Plasmodium vivax,* and *Euglena* reproduce.

Understanding Key Ideas

6. d
7. a
8. c
9. b
10. b
11. d
12. Some fungi recycle nutrients as decomposers, provide food for humans, or are used to make medicines.
13. Members of the genus *Paramecium* use cilia to move and to get food.

14. Sample answer: Fungi cannot move, but protists that get food as decomposers, such as slime molds, can move in certain phases of life.

15. Both slime molds and amoebas are protists, and both move (slime molds move during certain phases of life) and feed by using pseudopodia.

16. a structure that holds excess water and removes water from a protist cell

17. *Paramecium* uses conjugation, *P. vivax* uses a complex cycle, and *Euglena* uses fission.

18 Compare how phytoplankton, amoebas, and *Giardia lamblia* get food.

19 Explain how protists differ from other organisms.

20 Give an example of where you might find each of the following fungi: threadlike fungi, sac fungi, club fungi, and imperfect fungi.

CRITICAL THINKING

21 Concept Mapping Use the following terms to create a concept map: *yeast, basidia, threadlike fungi, mushrooms, fungi, bread mold, ascus,* and *club fungi.*

22 Applying Concepts Why do you think bread turns moldy less quickly when it is kept in a refrigerator than when it is kept at room temperature?

23 Making Inferences Some protozoans, such as radiolarians and foraminiferans, have shells around their bodies. How might these shells be helpful to the protists that live in them?

24 Predicting Consequences Suppose a forest where many threadlike fungi live goes through a very dry summer and fall and then a very cold winter. How could this extreme weather affect the reproductive patterns of these fungi?

INTERPRETING GRAPHICS

Use the pictures of fungi below to answer the questions that follow.

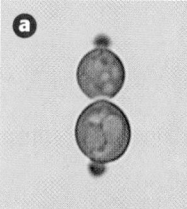 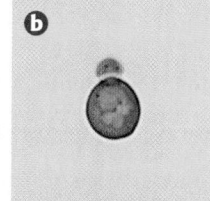

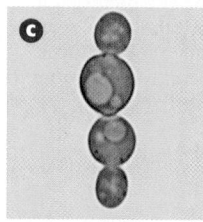 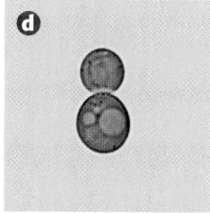

25 What kind of fungus is shown here?

26 What cellular process is shown in these pictures?

27 Which picture was taken first? Which was taken last? Arrange the pictures in order.

28 Which is the original parent cell? How do you know?

18. Amoebas use pseudopodia to engulf food, phytoplankton produce their own food, and *G. lamblia* is a parasite that feeds on a host.

19. Protists do not have specialized tissues, so they are different from fungi, plants, and animals. And unlike bacteria, protists are eukaryotic.

20. Sample answer: threadlike fungi: old bread; sac fungi: under the soil; club fungi: in the supermarket; imperfect fungi: in an animal as a parasite

Critical Thinking

21. 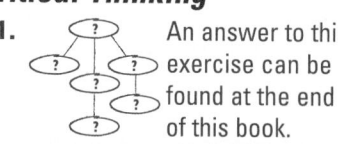 An answer to this exercise can be found at the end of this book.

22. Bread mold is a threadlike fungus. These fungi grow best in warm, moist conditions. The refrigerator's cool temperature keeps the fungi from growing.

23. Sample answer: These protozoans are probably protected from danger by their shells because the shells are hard and their bodies are soft.

24. These fungi may respond to the difficult environmental conditions by changing from asexual reproduction to sexual reproduction. They would likely form sporangia that would release spores when the environmental conditions improved.

Interpreting Graphics

25. yeast , which is a sac fungus

26. budding

27. b; c; b, d, a, c

28. The large cell in picture b is the original cell because it is the first to bud.

Teacher's Note

To provide practice under more realistic testing conditions, give students 20 minutes to answer all of the questions in this Standardized Test Preparation.

MISCONCEPTION ALERT

Answers to the standardized test preparation can help you identify student misconceptions and misunderstandings.

READING

Passage 1

1. A
2. I
3. C

➕ TEST DOCTOR

Question 2: The correct answer is A. This fact is revealed in the second sentence. Students may choose answer G because the first sentence implies that the people near the cave do not pay attention to the dripping slime. However, the sentence does not state that they ignore the slime globs. Students may choose answer F if they exaggerate the point that these slime globs are made up of organisms. While the passage states that billions of organisms live in the caves, the passage says nothing about many different kinds of organisms living there.

READING

Read each of the passages below. Then, answer the questions that follow each passage.

Passage 1 For centuries, people living near Cueva de Villa Luz (the Cave of the Lighted House) in Mexico have walked past slimy globs that drip from the cave's ceiling without thinking much about them. When scientists decided to analyze these slime balls, they discovered that the formations are home to billions of microscopic organisms! Scientists nicknamed these colonies "snot-tites" because the colonies <u>resemble</u> mucus. Actually, the "snot-tites" are a mixture of fungi and bacteria.

1. In the passage, what does *resemble* mean?
   A to look like
   B to feel like
   C to smell like
   D to sound like

2. Which of the following statements is a fact according to the passage?
   F Many kinds of organisms live in Cueva de Villa Luz.
   G The people of Mexico ignore the snot-tites.
   H Scientists found no explanation for the slime balls that are in Cueva de Villa Luz.
   I Cueva de Villa Luz's ceiling is dripping with microscopic organisms.

3. The microscopic organisms discovered by scientists
   A are fungi.
   B are bacteria.
   C are a mixture of fungi and bacteria.
   D are a mixture of protists and fungi.

Passage 2 Between 1845 and 1852, Ireland lost one-third of its population. In 1846, a disease swept through the potato fields of Ireland. In just a few weeks, it destroyed almost the entire crop of potatoes. Because the Irish depended on potatoes for food, people were dying of starvation each day. About 2 million people fled the country to find a place to live where they could find enough food. The cause of all of these deaths and this devastation was a simple organism. The disease was caused by a water mold, which is a kind of protist.

1. What caused the population of Ireland to decline between 1845 and 1852?
   A a fungus
   B a water mold
   C a potato
   D poisonous potatoes

2. According to the passage, why did the population of Ireland decline?
   F A disease swept through the people of Ireland.
   G Some people died of starvation, and others fled the country.
   H A simple organism infected the people of Ireland.
   I When people ate potatoes, they became sick.

3. Which of the following statements is a fact according to the passage?
   A People in Ireland have always depended on potatoes for food.
   B Protists are parasitic and cause disease.
   C About 2 million people fled Ireland between 1845 and 1852.
   D Food is more readily available in the United States than it is in Ireland.

Passage 2

1. B
2. G
3. C

Question 2: The correct answer is G. The fourth and fifth sentences reveal that some people died of starvation and others fled the country because of the potato famine. Students may choose answer F or H if they misread the passage and think the water mold infects people instead of potatoes. They may choose answer I if they assume that the water mold was passed from potatoes to people when people ate potatoes. Instead, the water mold caused problems because it killed the potatoes and then left people without enough to eat.

The table below shows the number of species in different phyla of protists. Use this table to answer the questions that follow.

Protist Phyla	
Phylum	Number of Species
Rhizopoda	300
Foraminifera	300
Chlorophyta	7,000
Rhodophyta	4,000
Phaeophyta	1,500
Bacillariophyta	11,500
Dinoflagellata	2,100
Euglenophyta	1,000
Kinetoplastida	3,000
Ciliophora	8,000
Acrasiomycota	70
Myxomycota	800
Oomycota	580
Apicomplexa	3,900

1. Which phylum has the largest number of species?
 A Rhizopoda
 B Bacillariophyta
 C Ciliophora
 D Euglenophyta

2. Which phylum has the smallest number of species?
 F Acrasiomycota
 G Rhizopoda
 H Chlorophyta
 I Bacillariophyta

3. If the total number of species of protists is 43,000, what percentage of species are in the phylum Bacillariophyta?
 A 0.27%
 B 3.7%
 C 27%
 D 374%

4. If the total number of species of protists is 43,000, what percentage of species are in the phylum Rhizopoda?
 F 0.7%
 G 1.4%
 H 7%
 I 143%

MATH

Read each question below, and choose the best answer.

1. Beth had $300 in her savings account when she started her summer job as an assistant to a commercial mushroom grower. If she put $25 into her savings account each month, which equation could be used to find n, the number of months it took Beth to increase her savings to $1,000?
 A $1{,}000 = 300 + n$
 B $1{,}000 = 25n$
 C $1{,}000 = 25n + 300$
 D $1{,}000 = 300n + 25$

2. If you want to determine whether a polygon-shaped protist has the shape of a pentagon, which of the following pieces of information do you need to know?
 F the area
 G the length of the diagonal
 H the number of sides
 I the number of faces

3. Marcus had an average score of 90% on two biology tests about protists. If his first test score was 96%, which score did he receive on the second test?
 A 45%
 B 84%
 C 90%
 D 102%

Standardized Test Preparation

1. B
2. F
3. C
4. F

 **TEST DOCTOR**

Question 3: The correct answer is C and is found by noting that there are approximately 11,500 species in the phylum Bacillariophyta and by dividing this number by the total species, 43,000 species, to get the figure 27%. Students may choose answer A if they forget how to change a decimal answer to a percentage. They may choose B or D if they forget how to find a percentage and divide 43,000 by the number of species of Bacillariophyta.

MATH

1. C
2. H
3. B

 **TEST DOCTOR**

Question 1: Because Beth begins with $300 in her account, the answer will have to include that as a starting point. She will add $25 to the original $300 each month for n months until the total is $1,000. So, the answer equation must set 1,000 equal to 300 plus 25 times n months, as shown in answer C. Students may choose answer B if they forget to account for the original $300. They may choose answer D if they confuse the original money with the money earned each month. They may choose answer A if they forget to account for how much money is added each month.

CHAPTER RESOURCES

Chapter Resource File

• Standardized Test Preparation GENERAL

State Resources

For specific resources for your state, visit **go.hrw.com** and type in the keyword **HSMSTR**.

Science in Action

Science, Technology, and Society

Weird Science

Algae Ice Cream

If someone offered you a bowl of algae ice cream, would you eat it? Would you eat algae pudding? These foods may not sound appetizing, but algae are a central ingredient in these foods. You eat many kinds of algae every day. Parts of brown algae help thicken ice cream and other dairy products. Red algae help keep breads and pastries from drying out. They are also used in chocolate, milk, eggnog, ice cream, sherbet, instant pudding, and frosting. Green algae contain a pigment that is used as yellow and orange food coloring. Algae are all around you!

Social Studies ACTIVITY

Food products are not the only products that use protist producers. In groups, research how people take advantage of the shiny shells of diatoms. Then, present your findings to the class.

Weird Science

Glowing Protists

As your kayak drifts silently through the night, it leaves a trail of swirling green light in the water behind it. You jump in the water to swim, and your hands turn into glowing underwater comets, which leave sparkling trails that slowly fade away. This may sound like a dream, but it happens every night for swimmers at Mosquito Bay on the island of Vieques in Puerto Rico. The source of this green glow is a protist. The waters of this bay contain millions of dinoflagellates that glow when the water around them is disturbed.

The species of dinoflagellates in Mosquito Bay is *Pyrodinium bahamense,* which means "whirling fire." These spherical single-celled protists are covered by armored plates. Each individual has two flagella that spin it through the water. The light is produced by a chemical reaction that is similar to the reaction in fireflies.

Math ACTIVITY

Living in every gallon of water in Mosquito Bay are 750,000 dinoflagellates. Suppose you took a gallon of water from this bay and dumped it into a bathtub full of 6 gal of fresh water that didn't contain any dinoflagellates. Then, you mixed up the water and turned out the lights to see if the bathtub would glow in the dark. How many dinoflagellates would be in each gallon of water in the bathtub after you mixed up the water?

Terrie Taylor

Fighting Malaria Malaria claims about 2 million victims each year. A person gets malaria when the blood is infected by protists from the genus *Plasmodium*. Dr. Terrie Taylor of Michigan State University's College of Osteopathic Medicine has devoted her life to malaria research. Since 1987, Dr. Taylor has spent six months of every year in Malawi, a small African country in which malaria is widespread.

When Dr. Taylor first traveled to Malawi, she did not have a particular interest in malaria. However, she quickly started to realize that the majority of her patients were infected with the deadly disease. The patients who were suffering the most were children. For every 100 children infected with malaria and treated by Dr. Taylor, between 20 and 25 would die from a malaria-induced coma. When a malaria coma starts, the patient becomes confused and sleepy. The patient then falls into a coma, which may lead to death. Dr. Taylor worked with other doctors at the hospital to develop a coma scale so that doctors could have a standardized way to assess patients moving toward coma. This scale is now used around the world.

Dr. Taylor wanted to find out why malaria victims fell into a coma. She took blood samples from malaria patients. She realized that severe malaria often led to a rapid fall in the patient's blood-sugar level. Dr. Taylor hypothesizes that the drop in blood sugar is related to the fact that the protists that cause malaria primarily infect a person's liver. The liver is the organ responsible for releasing sugar into the blood. Dr. Taylor has used this information to create a new treatment. Whenever she treats children who have a severe case of malaria, she gives them glucose, the type of sugar that is found in the bloodstream. This simple treatment has already saved hundreds of lives!

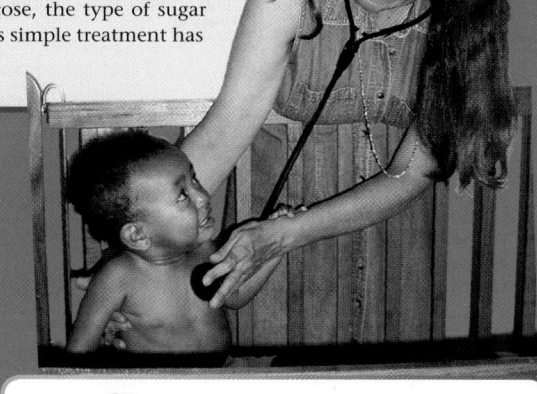

Language Arts ACTIVITY

The word *malaria* is a combination of two words. *Mala* means "bad," and *aria* means "air." Why do you think that people would use these words to describe the disease? Note that people did not realize that malaria was transmitted to people by mosquitoes until about 1899.

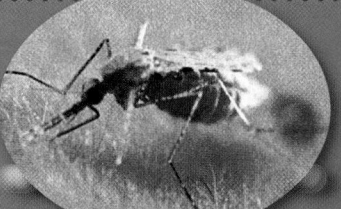

go.hrw.com
To learn more about these Science in Action topics, visit **go.hrw.com** and type in the keyword **HL5PROF.**

Current Science
Check out Current Science® articles related to this chapter by visiting **go.hrw.com.** Just type in the keyword **HL5CS11.**

Malaria is not very common in North America, but there are many other diseases caused by protists or fungi that are common in North America. Have students find out what protist or fungal diseases are prevalent in your area. Have students produce a chart showing the different diseases that they learn about. Ask students to state the most common ways a person can become infected with the disease, what treatments exist for the disease, and how common the disease is.

Background

Malaria is difficult to diagnose because the symptoms vary greatly between individuals and can resemble the symptoms of other diseases. The only way to make an accurate diagnosis is to examine the patient's red blood cells for signs of infection by protists from the genus *Plasmodium*. Recently, tests have been developed that allow for the detection of the parasite's genetic material in the blood stream. These new tests can verify a malaria infection several days faster than previous tests.

Answers to Language Arts Activity

Sample answer: Before people understood what caused malaria, they may have noticed that people became sick after spending time outdoors (where mosquitoes were present). Because people lacked a better explanation, they may have thought that the disease was caused by breathing bad air while they were outside.

12

Introduction to Plants
Chapter Planning Guide

Compression guide:
To shorten instruction because of time limitations, omit Section 4.

OBJECTIVES	LABS, DEMONSTRATIONS, AND ACTIVITIES	TECHNOLOGY RESOURCES
PACING • 90 min pp. 298–303 **Chapter Opener**	**SE** Start-up Activity, p. 299 ◆ GENERAL	**OSP** Parent Letter ■ GENERAL **CD** Student Edition on CD-ROM **TR** Chapter Starter Transparency* **CD** Guided Reading Audio CD ■ **VID** Brain Food Video Quiz
Section 1 What Is a Plant? • Identify four characteristics that all plants share. • Describe the four main groups of plants. • Explain the origin of plants.	**TE** Activity Water Travel in Plants, p. 300 GENERAL **TE** Group Activity Baby-Powder Cuticle, p. 301 GENERAL **TE** Activity Life Cycles, p. 301 ADVANCED	**CRF** Lesson Plans* **TR** Bellringer Transparency* **TR** The Main Groups of Plants* **CRF** SciLinks Activity* GENERAL **CD** Interactive Explorations CD-ROM Shut Your Trap! GENERAL
PACING • 45 min pp. 304–307 **Section 2 Seedless Plants** • List three nonvascular plants and three seedless vascular plants. • Explain how seedless plants are important to the environment. • Describe the relationship between seedless vascular plants and coal.	**TE** Activity Identifying Plant Parts, p. 304 ◆ GENERAL **SE** Quick Lab Moss Mass, p. 305 GENERAL **CRF** Datasheet for Quick Lab* **TE** Connection Activity Real World, p. 305 GENERAL **SE** Science in Action Math, Social Studies, and Language Arts Activities, pp. 328–329 GENERAL	**CRF** Lesson Plans* **TR** Bellringer Transparency*
PACING • 45 min pp. 308–313 **Section 3 Seed Plants** • Describe three ways that seed plants differ from seedless plants. • Describe the structure of seeds. • Compare angiosperms and gymnosperms. • Explain the economic and environmental importance of gymnosperms and angiosperms.	**TE** Activity Seed Types, p. 308 GENERAL **SE** Quick Lab Dissecting Seeds, p. 309 GENERAL **TE** Group Activity Seed Dispersal, p. 309 ◆ GENERAL **TE** Connection Activity Earth Science, p. 310 ADVANCED **SE** Skills Practice Lab Travelin' Seeds, p. 776 ◆ GENERAL **LB** EcoLabs & Field Activities The Case of the Ravenous Radish* ◆ GENERAL **LB** Long-Term Projects & Research Ideas Plant Planet ADVANCED	**CRF** Lesson Plans* **TR** Bellringer Transparency* **TR** Two Classes of Angiosperms* **TE** Internet Activity, p. 312 GENERAL
PACING • 90 min pp. 314–321 **Section 4 Structures of Seed Plants** • List three functions of roots and three functions of stems. • Describe the structure of a leaf. • Identify the parts of a flower and their functions.	**TE** Demonstration Roots, p. 314 ◆ GENERAL **TE** Group Activity Root Growth, p. 315 ◆ BASIC **TE** Activity Stem Functions, p. 316 BASIC **TE** Connection Activity History, p. 316 ADVANCED **TE** Activity Analyzing Tree Rings, p. 317 GENERAL **SE** School-to-Home Activity Looking at Leaves, p. 318 GENERAL **TE** Group Activity Leaf Collecting, p. 318 GENERAL **SE** Model-Making Lab Build a Flower, p. 322 ◆ GENERAL **SE** Skills Practice Lab Leaf Me Alone!, p. 774 GENERAL **LB** Whiz-Bang Demonstrations Inner Life of a Leaf* ◆ BASIC	**CRF** Lesson Plans* **TR** Bellringer Transparency* **TR** The Structures of a Root* **TR** Cross Section of an Herbaceous Stem; Cross Section of a Woody Stem* **TR** The Structure of a Leaf* **TR** *LINK TO EARTH SCIENCE* The Electromagnetic Spectrum* **TR** The Structure of a Flower* **VID** Lab Videos for Life Science

PACING • 90 min

CHAPTER REVIEW, ASSESSMENT, AND STANDARDIZED TEST PREPARATION

CRF Vocabulary Activity* GENERAL
 SE Chapter Review, pp. 324–325 GENERAL
CRF Chapter Review* ■ GENERAL
 SE Standardized Test Preparation, pp. 326–327 GENERAL
CRF Standardized Test Preparation* GENERAL
CRF Performance-Based Assessment* GENERAL
OSP Test Generator GENERAL
CRF Test Item Listing* GENERAL
CRF Chapter Tests A* ■ GENERAL, B* ADVANCED, C* SPECIAL NEEDS

Online and Technology Resources

Visit **go.hrw.com** for a variety of free resources related to this textbook. Enter the keyword **HL5PL1**.

Holt Online Learning

Students can access interactive problem-solving help and active visual concept development with the *Holt Science and Technology* Online Edition available at **www.hrw.com**.

 Guided Reading Audio CD
Also in Spanish

A direct reading of each chapter for auditory learners, reluctant readers, and Spanish-speaking students.

 Science Tutor CD-ROM

Excellent for remediation and test practice.

SKILLS DEVELOPMENT RESOURCES	SECTION REVIEW AND ASSESSMENT	STANDARDS CORRELATIONS
SE Pre-Reading Activity, p. 298 GENERAL **OSP** Science Puzzlers, Twisters & Teasers GENERAL		National Science Education Standards SAI 1, 2; LS 1c, 3a
CRF Directed Reading A* ■ BASIC, B* SPECIAL NEEDS **CRF** Vocabulary and Section Summary* ■ GENERAL **SE** Reading Strategy Reading Organizer, p. 300 GENERAL **SE** Connection to Social Studies Countries and Crops, p. 301 GENERAL	**SE** Reading Checks, pp. 301, 302, 303 GENERAL **TE** Homework, p. 301 GENERAL **TE** Reteaching, p. 302 BASIC **TE** Quiz, p. 302 GENERAL **TE** Alternative Assessment, p. 302 ADVANCED **SE** Section Review,* p. 303 ■ GENERAL **CRF** Section Quiz* ■ GENERAL	UCP 1, 2, 4; SAI 1, 2; ST 2; HNS 2; LS 1a, 2b, 4c, 5a
CRF Directed Reading A* ■ BASIC, B* SPECIAL NEEDS **CRF** Vocabulary and Section Summary* ■ GENERAL **SE** Reading Strategy Paired Summarizing, p. 304 GENERAL **TE** Inclusion Strategies, p. 306 ◆ **SE** Connection to Language Arts Selling Plants, p. 307 GENERAL	**SE** Reading Checks, pp. 305, 307 GENERAL **TE** Reteaching, p. 306 BASIC **TE** Quiz, p. 306 GENERAL **TE** Alternative Assessment, p. 306 GENERAL **TE** Homework, p. 306 GENERAL **SE** Section Review,* p. 307 ■ GENERAL **CRF** Section Quiz* ■ GENERAL	UCP 1, 2, 3, 4; SAI 1; LS 1a, 1c, 2b, 5c
CRF Directed Reading A* ■ BASIC, B* SPECIAL NEEDS **CRF** Vocabulary and Section Summary* ■ GENERAL **SE** Reading Strategy Reading Organizer, p. 308 GENERAL **SE** Connection to Environmental Science Animals That Help Plants, p. 309 **TE** Inclusion Strategies, p. 311 **SS** Science Skills Science Writing* GENERAL **CRF** Reinforcement Worksheet Classifying Plants* GENERAL **CRF** Reinforcement Worksheet Drawing Dicots* GENERAL	**SE** Reading Checks, pp. 308, 309, 311, 312, 313 GENERAL **TE** Homework, p. 310 ADVANCED **TE** Reteaching, p. 312 BASIC **TE** Quiz, p. 312 GENERAL **TE** Alternative Assessment, p. 312 ADVANCED **SE** Section Review,* p. 313 ■ GENERAL **CRF** Section Quiz* ■ GENERAL	UCP 1, 2, 4; SAI 1; SPSP 4; LS 1a, 1d, 2b, 2c, 2d, 4b, 4c, 4d, 5b; *LabBook:* UCP 2, 5; SAI 1, 2; LS 2b
CRF Directed Reading A* ■ BASIC, B* SPECIAL NEEDS **CRF** Vocabulary and Section Summary* ■ GENERAL **SE** Reading Strategy Mnemonics, p. 314 GENERAL **SE** Math Practice Practice with Percentages, p. 315 GENERAL **SS** Science Skills Taking Notes* GENERAL **CRF** Critical Thinking The Voodoo Lily* ADVANCED	**SE** Reading Checks, pp. 315, 316, 318, 320 GENERAL **TE** Homework, p. 319 GENERAL **SE** Section Review,* p. 321 ■ GENERAL **TE** Reteaching, p. 320 BASIC **TE** Quiz, p. 320 GENERAL **TE** Alternative Assessment, p. 320 GENERAL **CRF** Section Quiz* ■ GENERAL	UCP 1, 2, 4; SAI 1; SPSP 5; LS 1a, 1d, 2b, 3d, 4c, 5b; *Chapter Lab:* UCP 1, 2, 5; SAI 1, 2; ST 2; HNS 1, 2; LS 1a, 2a, 2b; *LabBook:* UCP 1, 5; SAI 1

One-Stop Planner® CD-ROM

This convenient CD-ROM includes:
- Lab Materials QuickList Software
- Holt Calendar Planner
- Customizable Lesson Plans
- Printable Worksheets
- ExamView® Test Generator

cnnstudentnews.com

Find the latest news, lesson plans, and activities related to important scientific events.

www.scilinks.org

Maintained by the **National Science Teachers Association.** See Chapter Enrichment pages for a complete list of topics.

Check out **Current Science** articles and activities by visiting the HRW Web site at go.hrw.com. Just type in the keyword **HL5CS12T.**

Classroom Videos
- **Lab Videos** demonstrate the chapter lab.
- **Brain Food Video Quizzes** help students review the chapter material.
- **CNN Videos** bring science into your students' daily life.

Visual Resources

CHAPTER STARTER TRANSPARENCY

This Really Happened!

A lone scientist trudges through a remote rain forest. Peering into a steep, narrow canyon, he notices something unusual. On closer inspection, he discovers that it is a species of tree that has survived from the days when *Tyrannosaurus rex* and *Velociraptor* walked the Earth!

No, this isn't a scene out of *Jurassic Park*. This really happened in an Australian rain forest in 1994. The scientist's name was David Noble. He discovered a tree species that dates back to the Cretaceous period, between 144 million and 65 million years ago.

The trees, called Wollemi pines, have large, bladelike leaves and knobby brown bark. They grow as tall as 35 m, and their trunks can grow as wide as 1 m.

Since the discovery of the trees, scientists at the Royal Botanic Gardens in Sydney, Australia, have been planting seeds of the Wollemi pines and growing seedlings. Soon Wollemi pines will be made available to gardeners so they can transform their yards into their own Cretaceous parks.

In this chapter, you will learn more about the mysterious world of plants. You will see that plants are complex organisms that challenge our understanding of nature.

BELLRINGER TRANSPARENCIES

Section: What Is a Plant?
There are four major types of plants. Try to identify all four types, and give at least two examples for each one. Do all four types of plants grow near your home? Where will you most likely find each type of plant?

Write your responses in your **science journal.**

Section: Seedless Plants
If plants can make their own food, why do people add fertilizer to soil? What happens when you plant crops in the same field over and over again? Does fertilizer ever stop working?

Write your answers in your **science journal.**

TEACHING TRANSPARENCIES

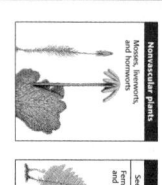
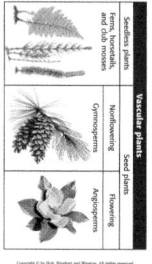

The Main Groups of Plants

Two Classes of Angiosperms

The Structure of a Leaf

TEACHING TRANSPARENCIES

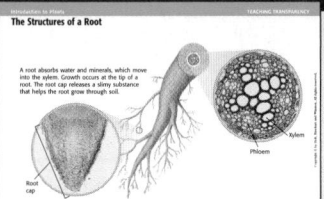
The Structures of a Root

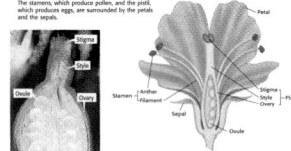
The Structure of a Flower

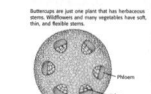
Cross Section of a Herbaceous Stem

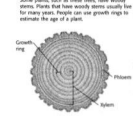
Cross Section of a Woody Stem

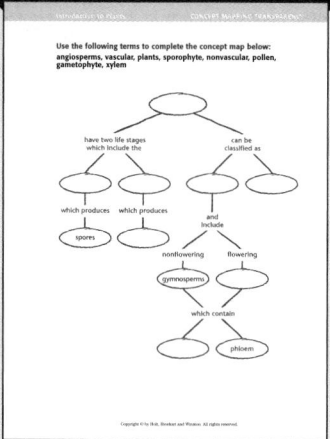
The Electromagnetic Spectrum

LINK TO EARTH SCIENCE

Chapter: The Nature of Light

CONCEPT MAPPING TRANSPARENCY

Use the following terms to complete the concept map below: angiosperms, vascular, plants, sporophyte, nonvascular, pollen, gametophyte, xylem

Planning Resources

LESSON PLANS

Lesson Plan — SAMPLE

Section: Waves

Pacing
Regular Schedule: with lab(s):2 days without lab(s):2 days
Block Schedule: with lab(s): 1 1/2 days without lab(s):1 day

Objectives
1. Relate the seven properties of life to a living organism.
2. Describe seven themes that can help you to organize what you learn about biology.
3. Identify the tiny structures that make up all living organisms.
4. Differentiate between reproduction and heredity and between metabolism and homeostasis.

National Science Education Standards Covered
LS1nter6:Cells have particular structures that underlie their functions.
LS1Ma1: Most cell functions involve chemical reactions.
LSBeh1:Cells store and use information to guide their functions.
UCP1:Cell functions are regulated.
S1: Cells can differentiate and form complete multicellular organisms.
PS1: Species evolve over time.
ESS1: The great diversity of organisms is the result of more than 3.5 billion years of evolution.
ESS2: Natural selection and its evolutionary consequences provide a scientific explanation for the fossil record of ancient life forms as well as for the striking molecular similarities observed among the diverse species of living organisms.
ST1: The millions of different species of animals, plants, and microorganisms that live on Earth today are related by descent from common ancestors.
ST2: The energy for life ultimately comes from the sun.
SPSP1: The complexity and organization of organisms accommodates the need for obtaining, transforming, transporting, releasing, and eliminating the matter and energy used to sustain the organism.
SPSP6: As matter and energy flows through different levels of organization of living systems—cells, organs, communities—and between living systems and the physical environment, chemical elements are recombined in different ways.
HNS1: Organisms have behavioral responses to internal changes and to external stimuli.

PARENT LETTER

Dear Parent,

Your son's or daughter's science class will soon begin exploring the chapter entitled "The World of Physical Science." In this chapter, students will learn about how the scientific method applies to the world of physical science and the role of physical science in the world. By the end of the chapter, students should demonstrate a clear understanding of the chapter's main ideas and be able to discuss the following topics:

1. physical science is the study of energy and matter (Section 1)
2. the role of physical science in the world around them (Section 1)
3. careers that rely on physical science (Section 1)
4. the steps used in the scientific method (Section 2)
5. examples of technology (Section 2)
6. how the scientific method is used to answer questions and solve problems (Section 2)
7. how our knowledge of science changes over time (Section 2)
8. how models represent real objects or systems (Section 3)
9. examples of different ways models are used in science (Section 3)
10. the importance of the International System of Units (Section 4)
11. the appropriate units to use for particular measurements (Section 4)
12. how area and density are derived quantities (Section 4)

Questions to Ask Along the Way
You can help your son or daughter learn about these topics by asking interesting questions such as the following:
• What are some surprising careers that use physical science?
• What is a characteristic of a good hypothesis?
• When is it a good idea to use a model?
• Why do Americans measure things in terms of inches and yards and meters?

ALSO IN SPANISH

TEST ITEM LISTING

The World of Science — SAMPLE

MULTIPLE CHOICE
(sample test items listing)

One-Stop Planner® CD-ROM

This CD-ROM includes all of the resources shown here and the following time-saving tools:
• Lab Materials QuickList Software
• Customizable lesson plans
• Holt Calendar Planner
• The powerful ExamView® Test Generator

Meeting Individual Needs

DIRECTED READING A
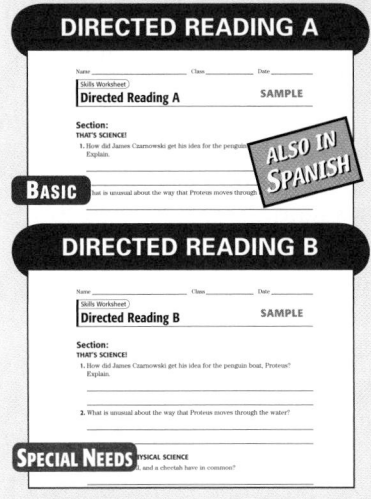
BASIC — ALSO IN SPANISH

VOCABULARY ACTIVITY
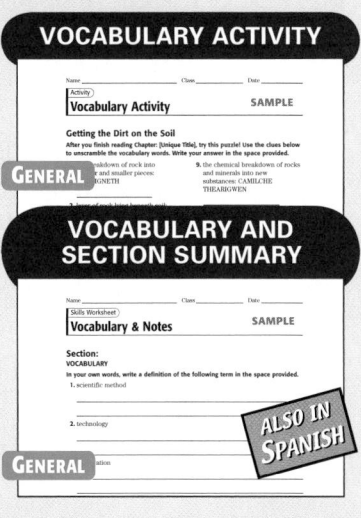
GENERAL

VOCABULARY AND SECTION SUMMARY
GENERAL — ALSO IN SPANISH

REINFORCEMENT
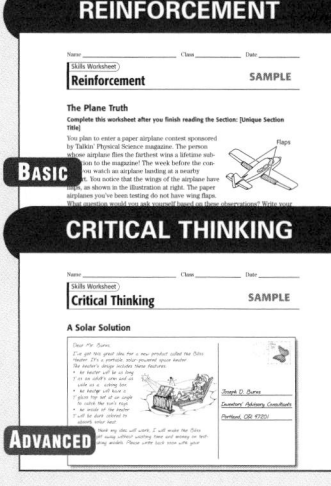
BASIC

CRITICAL THINKING
ADVANCED

SCILINKS ACTIVITY
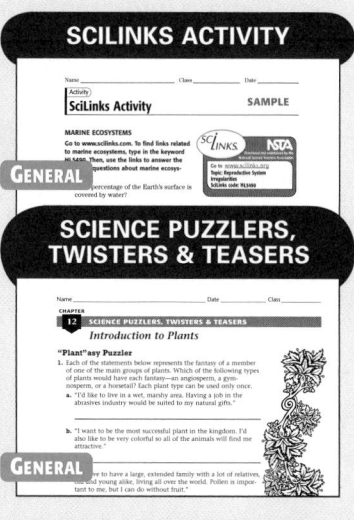
GENERAL

SCIENCE PUZZLERS, TWISTERS & TEASERS
GENERAL

DIRECTED READING B
SPECIAL NEEDS

Labs and Activities

ECOLABS & FIELD ACTIVITIES
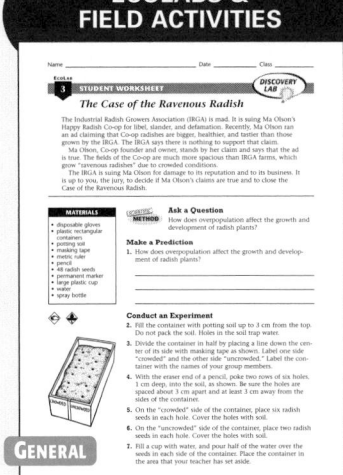
GENERAL

WHIZ-BANG DEMONSTRATIONS
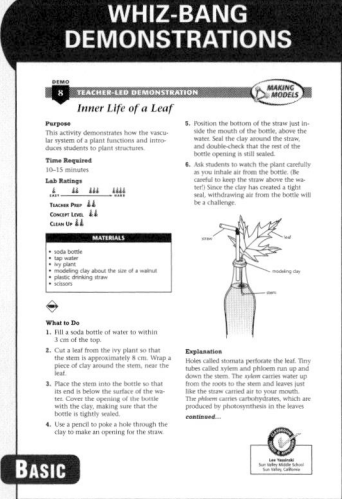
BASIC

LONG-TERM PROJECTS & RESEARCH IDEAS
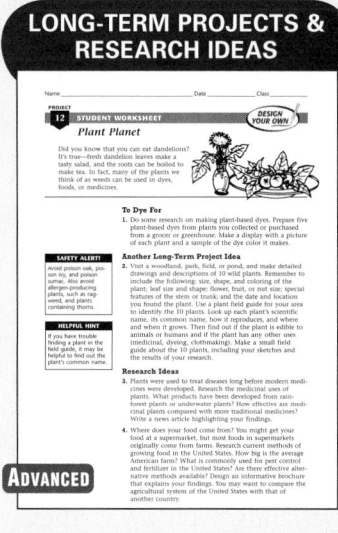
ADVANCED

DATASHEETS FOR QUICK LABS

DATASHEETS FOR CHAPTER LABS
DATASHEETS FOR LABBOOK

Review and Assessments

SECTION QUIZ
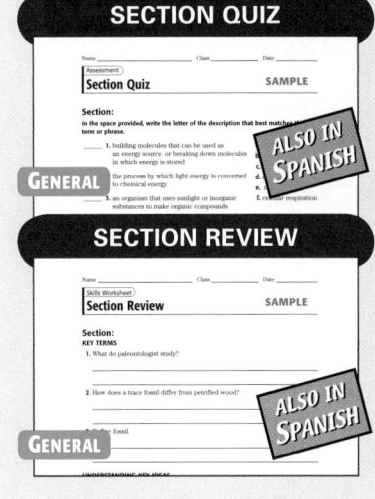
GENERAL — ALSO IN SPANISH

SECTION REVIEW
GENERAL — ALSO IN SPANISH

CHAPTER REVIEW
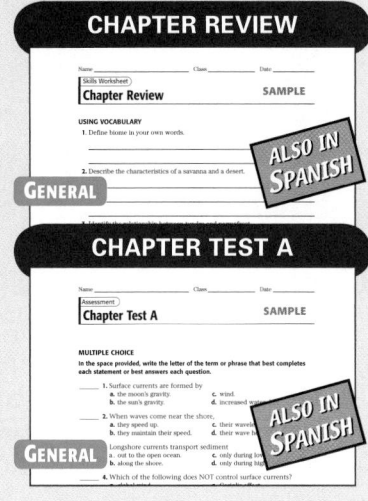
GENERAL — ALSO IN SPANISH

CHAPTER TEST A
GENERAL — ALSO IN SPANISH

CHAPTER TEST B
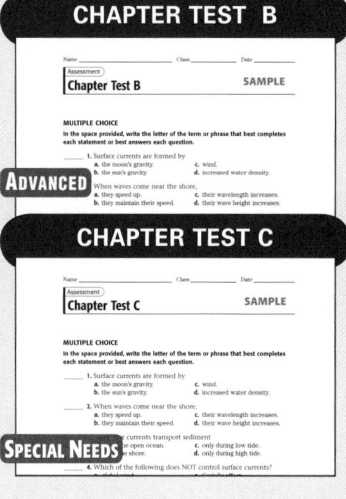
ADVANCED

CHAPTER TEST C
SPECIAL NEEDS

STANDARDIZED TEST PREPARATION
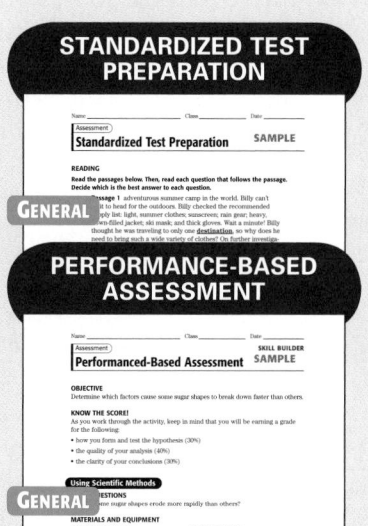
GENERAL

PERFORMANCE-BASED ASSESSMENT
GENERAL

This Chapter Enrichment provides relevant and interesting information to expand and enhance your presentation of the chapter material.

Section 1

What Is a Plant?

Theophrastus

● Theophrastus (c. 372–287 BCE) was Aristotle's student and one of the first botanists. He wrote two books about plants, *Inquiry into Plants* and *Growth of Plants*. He described the morphology, uses, propagation, and pollination of 500 plants and described sexual reproduction in plants. Theophrastus directed the Lyceum, a school and center of learning in Athens. The Lyceum housed the first botanical garden. Theophrastus's writings were the standard for botanical study until the 16th century.

Carnivorous Plants

● Carnivorous plants photosynthesize and are true plants. They often grow in wetlands, such as marshes, where soil is waterlogged. Bacteria and fungi cannot thrive in these soils, so little organic matter is decomposed to provide minerals to plants. The small invertebrates that carnivorous plants catch provide additional minerals, especially nitrogen. The insects are digested by enzymes secreted by the leaves or by bacteria and fungi living in the cupped leaves of the plant.

Is That a Fact!

◆ The leaves of a pitcher plant form tall, narrow cups that hold rainwater. The tip of the plant is colorful and has nectar-secreting glands that attract insects. The insects follow a path of tiny hairs down into the cup, where the walls are smooth. The insects lose their grip and drown.

Section 2

Seedless Plants

Bryophytes

● Bryophytes, which include mosses, hornworts, and liverworts, make up more than 15,000 described species worldwide. Various species tend to be restricted to particular environments because of sensitivities to temperature, light, water availability, and chemical composition of the substrate. So, bryophytes are good indicator species for ecologists and conservation biologists. These experts can characterize an environment by identifying the bryophytes present in an area.

Is That a Fact!

◆ Before the invention of flashbulbs and strobe lights for indoor and low-light photography, photographers created an explosive flash of light with a powder. The powder contained spores from club mosses, seedless vascular plants that are related to ferns and horsetails.

● Bryophytes are small and are easy to culture in the lab. Field biologists, however, usually observe bryophytes year-round under natural conditions.

Evolution of Ferns

● Ferns are an ancient group of plants with fossil records dating to the middle of the Devonian period, 408 to 345 million years ago. Nearly all of those early fern groups are now extinct. Few modern fern genera can be traced directly to their Carboniferous ancestors.

Section 3

Seed Plants

The Millennium Seed Bank

- The Royal Botanic Gardens in Kew, England, has launched a project to collect seeds from 24,000 plant species around the world. As many as 50,000 species of plants might become extinct in the next 30 years, but the seed bank will ensure the survival of plants that help stabilize soil and provide food, medicine, and building materials. The collected seeds are dried and stored in subzero temperatures. Scientists believe the seeds will grow even hundreds of years in the future.

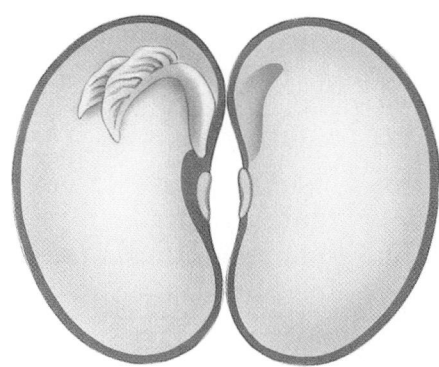

The Economic Importance of Plants

- Farming originated thousands of years ago. Today, three of the earliest cultivated crops—wheat, rice, and corn—feed more than half of the people in the world.

- Herbs and spices were valued commodities on ancient trade routes. In medieval times, explorers and merchants brought spices to Europe by camel caravan from east Asia.

- Perfume makers use essential oils from a variety of flowers, including rose, orange, lavender, and jasmine.

- The ancient Egyptians made paper from papyrus reeds. Paper can also be made from nettles, bamboo, cotton, hemp, and other plants. Today, most paper is made from wood pulp.

Is That a Fact!

- The sea bean (genus *Mucuna*) is one of the largest seed pods in the world. When a sea bean pod falls into a river, it floats to the ocean, where it may travel for thousands of miles before it is washed onto shore.

Section 4

Structures of Seed Plants

Inflorescences

- The cluster of flowers that develops on many plants is called an *inflorescence*, of which there are two types. In a determinate inflorescence, the peduncle, or main axis, terminates in a flower bud, which prevents the peduncle from continued growth. In indeterminate inflorescences, the lower buds open first. As the peduncle continues to grow, the youngest flowers are always at the top. There are several forms of inflorescences, including the following:

  - raceme: each flower of the cluster is on a pedicel, or short stem, that extends from the peduncle (snapdragon)
  - spike: resembles a raceme but has no pedicels (gladiolus)
  - panicle: branched raceme in which each branch has multiple flowers (lilac)
  - head: short, dense spike with flowers in a circular mass (dandelion)
  - umbel: all the pedicels grow from the same point at the top of the peduncle (onion)

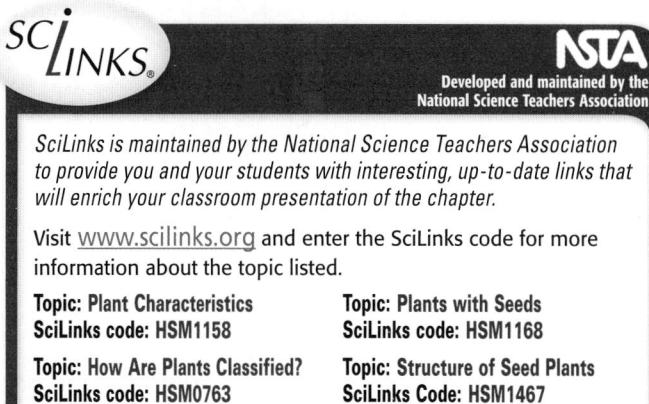

Developed and maintained by the National Science Teachers Association

SciLinks is maintained by the National Science Teachers Association to provide you and your students with interesting, up-to-date links that will enrich your classroom presentation of the chapter.

Visit www.scilinks.org and enter the SciLinks code for more information about the topic listed.

Topic: Plant Characteristics
SciLinks code: HSM1158

Topic: How Are Plants Classified?
SciLinks code: HSM0763

Topic: Seedless Plants
SciLinks code: HSM1368

Topic: Plants with Seeds
SciLinks code: HSM1168

Topic: Structure of Seed Plants
SciLinks Code: HSM1467

Overview

Tell students that this chapter will help them learn about plants. The chapter describes the four basic groups of plants. The chapter also discusses the structures of flowering plants.

Assessing Prior Knowledge

Students should be familiar with the following topics:

• cells

• photosynthesis

Identifying Misconceptions

As students learn the material in this chapter, some of them may think that plants get all of their food from soil. Plants do get water and some water-soluble minerals from soil, but the mass of plants—even large plants, such as trees—is derived from the carbon dioxide gas that plants take in from the air for photosynthesis. This carbon dioxide is combined with water to make larger molecules, such as glucose. In turn, glucose is used to make storage molecules, such as sucrose and starch.

Introduction to Plants

About the PHOTO

In Costa Rica's Monteverde Cloud Forest Preserve, a green coil begins to unfold. It is hidden from all but the most careful observer. The coil looks alien, but it is very much of this Earth. The coil is the leaf of a fern, a plant that grows in moist areas. Soon, the coil will unfold into a lacy, delicate frond.

PRE-READING ACTIVITY

FOLDNOTES **Pyramid** Before you read the chapter, create the FoldNote entitled "Pyramid" described in the **Study Skills** section of the Appendix. Label the sides of the pyramid with "Nonvascular plants," "Seedless vascular plants," and "Seed plants." As you read the chapter, define each kind of plant, and write characteristics of each kind of plant on the appropriate pyramid side.

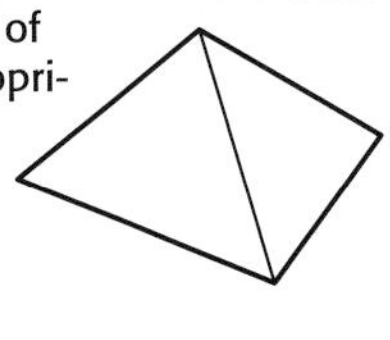

Standards Correlations

National Science Education Standards

The following codes indicate the National Science Education Standards that correlate to this chapter. The full text of the standards is at the front of the book.

Chapter Opener
SAI 1, 2; LS 1c, 3a

Section 1 What Is a Plant?
UCP 1, 2, 4; SAI 1, 2; ST 2; HNS 2; LS 1a, 2b, 4c, 5a

Section 2 Seedless Plants
UCP 1, 2, 3, 4; SAI 1; LS 1a, 1c, 2b, 5c

Section 3 Seed Plants
UCP 1, 2, 4; SAI 1; SPSP 4; LS 1a, 1d, 2b, 2c, 2d, 4b, 4c, 4d, 5b;
LabBook: UCP 2, 5; SAI 1, 2; LS 2b

Section 4 Structures of Seed Plants
UCP 1, 2, 4; SAI 1; SPSP 5; LS 1a, 1d, 2b, 3d, 4c, 5b;
LabBook: UCP 1, 5; SAI 1

Chapter Lab
UCP 1, 2, 5; SAI 1, 2; ST 2; HNS 1, 2; LS 1a, 2a, 2b

Chapter Review
UCP 1, 2, 3, 4; SAI 1; ST 2; SPSP 4, 5; HNS 2; LS 1a, 1c, 1d, 2b, 2c, 2d, 3d, 4b, 4c, 4d, 5a, 5b, 5c

START-UP ACTIVITY

MATERIALS

FOR EACH GROUP
- aluminum foil
- bean seeds (3–4)
- bottle, soda, clear plastic, with neck cut off, 2 L
- potting soil, moist
- water, 60 mL

Safety Caution: Some students—particularly those who suffer from allergies—may wish to wear protective gloves while handling the soil and seeds. Have students wash their hands when they are finished with the activity.

Teacher's Notes: Cut off the neck of each bottle before distributing bottles to students. Soaking the seeds overnight in advance will decrease the number of days until germination.

Answers

1. Answers may vary. Students may report that not all of their seeds grew.

2. Answers may vary. Germination times vary depending on the seeds used.

3. Sample answer: The seed contains stored food that is used for energy to grow.

START-UP ACTIVITY

Observing Plant Growth

When planting a garden, you bury seeds and water them. What happens to the seeds below the soil? How do seeds grow into plants?

Procedure

1. Fill a clear **2 L soda bottle** to within 8 cm of the top with **moist potting soil.** Your teacher will have already cut off the neck of the bottle.

2. Press **three or four bean seeds** into the soil and against the wall of the bottle. Add enough additional potting soil to increase the depth by 5 cm.

3. Cover the sides of the bottle with **aluminum foil** to keep out light. Leave the top of the bottle uncovered.

4. Water the seeds with about **60 mL of water,** or water them until the soil is moist. Add more water when the soil dries out.

5. Place the bottle in an area that receives sunshine. Check on your seeds each day, and record your observations.

Analysis

1. How many seeds grew?

2. How long did the seeds take to start growing?

3. From where did the seeds most likely get the energy to grow?

Science in Action
ST 2; SPSP 1, 3, 4, 5; HNS 1, 2, 3; LS 1f

This Really Happened!

A lone scientist trudges through a remote rain forest. Peering into a steep, narrow canyon, he notices something unusual. On closer inspection, he discovers that it is a species of tree that has survived from the days when *Tyrannosaurus rex* and *Velociraptor* walked the Earth! No, this isn't a scene out of *Jurassic Park.* This really happened in an Australian rain forest in 1994. The scientist's name

bark. They grow as tall as 35 m, and their trunks can grow as wide as 1 m.

Since the discovery of the trees, scientists at the Royal Botanic Gardens in Sydney, Australia, have been planting seeds of the Wollemi pines and growing seedlings. Soon Wollemi pines will be made available to gardeners so they can transform their yards into their own Cretaceous parks.

Chapter Starter Transparency
Use this transparency to help students begin thinking about the world of plants.

CHAPTER RESOURCES

Technology

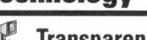 **Transparencies** — Chapter Starter Transparency   READING SKILLS

 Student Edition on CD-ROM

Guided Reading Audio CD
- English or Spanish

 **Classroom Videos**
- Brain Food Video Quiz

Workbooks

 Science Puzzlers, Twisters & Teasers
- Introduction to Plants GENERAL

Focus

Overview

In this section, students will learn the shared characteristics of plants. Plants make their own food, have a cuticle, reproduce with spores and sex cells, and have cells with cell walls. Finally, students will learn about the four main groups of plants.

 Bellringer

Tell students that there are four major types of plants. Ask them to try to identify those types and to give at least two examples for each one. (Students likely will not classify plants according to the section information. Students may name flowers, trees, weeds, grasses, fruits, and vegetables.)
LS Verbal

Motivate

ACTiViTY ──────── GENERAL

Water Travel in Plants Slice a stalk of celery lengthwise to just below the leaves. Place the two halves in separate beakers, each containing a different color of water. Red and blue food colorings work best. Students should be able to see the veins in the leaves change color after the colored liquids have traveled up the stalk. English Language Learners
LS Visual

READING WARM-UP

Objectives
- Identify four characteristics that all plants share.
- Describe the four main groups of plants.
- Explain the origin of plants.

Terms to Learn
nonvascular plant
vascular plant
gymnosperm
angiosperm

READING STRATEGY

Reading Organizer As you read this section, create an outline of the section. Use the headings from the section in your outline.

What Is a Plant?

Imagine spending a day without plants. What would you eat? It would be impossible to make chocolate chip cookies and many other foods.

Without plants, you couldn't eat much. Almost all food is made from plants or from animals that eat plants. Life would be very different without plants!

Plant Characteristics

Plants come in many different shapes and sizes. So, what do cactuses, water lilies, ferns, and all other plants have in common? One plant may seem very different from another. But most plants share certain characteristics.

Photosynthesis

Take a look at **Figure 1.** Do you know why this plant is green? Plant cells contain chlorophyll (KLAWR uh FIL). *Chlorophyll* is a green pigment that captures energy from sunlight. Chlorophyll is found in chloroplasts (KLAWR uh PLASTS). Chloroplasts are organelles found in many plant cells and some protists. Plants use energy from sunlight to make food from carbon dioxide and water. This process is called *photosynthesis* (FOHT oh SIN thuh sis). Because plants make their own food, they are called *producers.*

Cuticles

Most plants live on dry land and need sunlight to live. But why don't plants dry out? Plants are protected by a cuticle. A *cuticle* is a waxy layer that coats most of the surfaces of plants that are exposed to air. The cuticle keeps plants from drying out.

Figure 1 *Chlorophyll makes the leaves of this plant green. Chlorophyll helps plants make their own food by capturing energy from sunlight.*

CHAPTER RESOURCES

Chapter Resource File

- Lesson Plan
- Directed Reading A **BASIC**
- Directed Reading B **SPECIAL NEEDS**

Technology

 **Transparencies**
- Bellringer

Cultural Awareness ── GENERAL

Breadnut Ancient Maya and Aztec people made extensive use of the fruit of the breadnut tree. It was boiled and eaten like potatoes or mashed into a gruel and sweetened. Breadnuts were ground, cooked, and mixed with corn to make tortillas. Diluted breadnut sap was fed to babies when their mother's milk was not available. Breadnut leaves were also fed to female animals to increase their milk supply.

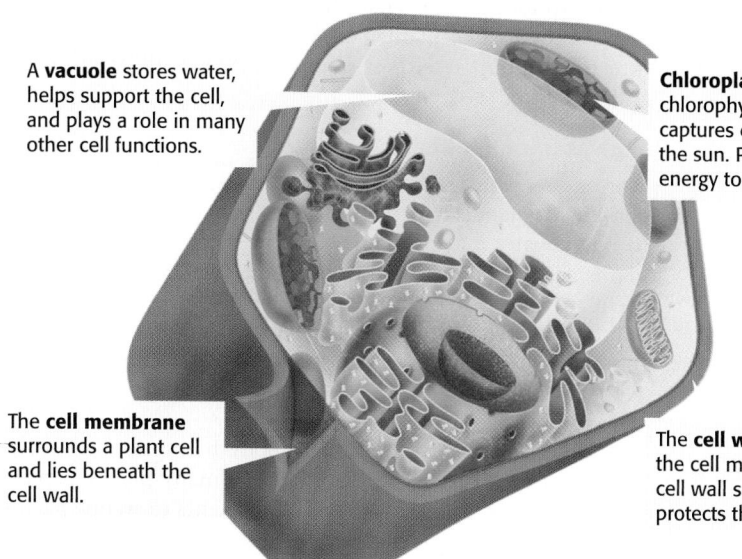

Figure 2 Some Structures of a Photosynthetic Plant Cell

A **vacuole** stores water, helps support the cell, and plays a role in many other cell functions.

Chloroplasts contain chlorophyll. Chlorophyll captures energy from the sun. Plants use this energy to make food.

The **cell membrane** surrounds a plant cell and lies beneath the cell wall.

The **cell wall** surrounds the cell membrane. The cell wall supports and protects the plant cell.

Cell Walls

How do plants stay upright? They do not have skeletons like many animals do. Instead, plant cells are surrounded by a rigid cell wall. The cell wall lies outside the cell membrane, as shown in **Figure 2.** Carbohydrates and proteins in the cell wall form a hard material. Cell walls support and protect the plant cell. Some plant cells also have a secondary cell wall that forms after the cell is mature. When this wall has formed, a plant cell cannot grow larger.

Reproduction

Plants have two stages in their life cycle—the sporophyte (SPAWR uh FIET) stage and the gametophyte (guh MEET uh FIET) stage. In the sporophyte stage, plants make spores. In a suitable environment, such as damp soil, the spores of some plants grow. These new plants are called *gametophytes*.

During the gametophyte stage, female gametophytes produce eggs. Male gametophytes produce sperm. Eggs and sperm are sex cells. Sex cells cannot grow directly into new plants. Instead, a sperm must fertilize an egg. The fertilized egg grows into a sporophyte. The sporophyte makes more spores. So, the cycle starts again.

✓ Reading Check How do plants reproduce? (*See the Appendix for answers to Reading Checks.*)

CONNECTION TO Social Studies

Countries and Crops Without plants, most life on land couldn't survive. But plants are important for more than the survival of living things. Many countries rely on plants for income. Identify five major food crops. Then, find out which countries are the main producers of these crops and how much the countries produce each year. Make a table to show your findings.

Plant Groups Ask students to list the four main groups of plants and to give an example of a plant from each group. Be sure that students understand the characteristics of each plant group. **LS** Logical

Quiz — GENERAL

1. How is a plant's size related to its method of transporting water and nutrients? (Sample answer: Nonvascular plants rely on diffusion, which is efficient only in small plants. Vascular plants have conducting tissues, which enable the plant to be very large.)

2. What is required for a spore to grow into a new plant? (It must land in a suitable environment, such as damp soil.)

Alternative Assessment — ADVANCED

Interview Have students interview one another about the characteristics common to all plants. Have students ask, "How do plants make their own food?" "Why are cell walls necessary?" "What is the purpose of the cuticle?" "What are gametophytes and sporophytes, and what roles do they play in a plant's life cycle?" **LS** Verbal/Interpersonal

nonvascular plant the three groups of plants (liverworts, hornworts, and mosses) that lack specialized conducting tissues and true roots, stems, and leaves

vascular plant a plant that has specialized tissues that conduct materials from one part of the plant to another

gymnosperm a woody, vascular seed plant whose seeds are not enclosed by an ovary or fruit

angiosperm a flowering plant that produces seeds within a fruit

Plant Classification

Although all plants share basic characteristics, they can be classified into four groups. First, they are classified as nonvascular plants and vascular plants. Vascular plants are further divided into three groups—seedless plants, nonflowering seed plants, and flowering seed plants.

Nonvascular Plants

Mosses, liverworts, and hornworts are nonvascular plants. A **nonvascular plant** is a plant that doesn't have specialized tissues to move water and nutrients through the plant. Nonvascular plants depend on diffusion to move materials from one part of the plant to another. Diffusion is possible because nonvascular plants are small. If nonvascular plants were large, the cells of the plants would not get enough water and nutrients.

Vascular Plants

In the same way that the human body has special tissues to move materials through the body, so do many plants. A plant that has tissues to deliver water and nutrients from one part of the plant to another is called a **vascular plant.** These tissues are called *vascular tissues*. Vascular tissues can move water to any part of a plant. So, vascular plants can be almost any size.

Vascular plants are divided into three groups—seedless plants and two types of seed plants. Seedless vascular plants include ferns, horsetails, and club mosses. Nonflowering seed plants are called **gymnosperms** (JIM noh SPUHRMZ). Flowering seed plants are called **angiosperms** (AN jee oh SPUHRMZ). The four main groups of plants are shown in **Figure 3.**

✓ **Reading Check** What are the four main groups of plants?

Figure 3 The Main Groups of Plants

Nonvascular plants	Vascular plants		
	Seedless plants	Seed plants	
Mosses, liverworts, and hornworts	Ferns, horsetails, and club mosses	Nonflowering	Flowering
		Gymnosperms	Angiosperms

Answer to Reading Check
nonvascular plants, seedless vascular plants, gymnosperms, and angiosperms

The Origin of Plants

Imagine that you traveled back in time about 440 million years. The Earth seems like a strange, bare, and unfriendly place. For one thing, no plants live on land. So, where did plants come from?

Take a look at **Figure 4.** The photo on the left shows a green alga. The photo on the right shows a fern. The green alga may look like a plant, such as a fern, but it isn't a plant. However, green algae and plants have many similarities. Green algae cells and plant cells have the same kind of chlorophyll. They have similar cell walls. Green algae and plants make their own food through photosynthesis. Both store energy in the form of starch. Like plants, green algae have a two-stage life cycle. Because of these similarities, some scientists think that green algae and plants share a common ancestor.

Reading Check What are some characteristics that green algae and plants have in common?

Figure 4 *The similarities between a modern green alga (left) and plants, such as ferns (right), suggest that both may have originated from an ancient species of green algae.*

SECTION Review

Summary

● All plants make their own food and have cuticles, cells walls, and a two-stage life cycle.

● Plants are first classified into two groups: nonvascular plants and vascular plants. Vascular plants are further divided into seedless plants, gymnosperms, and angiosperms.

● Similarities between green algae and plants suggest they may have a common ancestor.

Using Key Terms

For each pair of terms, explain how the meanings of the terms differ.

1. *nonvascular plants* and *vascular plants*

2. *gymnosperms* and *angiosperms*

Understanding Key Ideas

3. Which of the following plants is nonvascular?
   - **a.** ferns
   - **b.** mosses
   - **c.** gymnosperms
   - **d.** club mosses

4. What are four characteristics that all plants share?

5. What do green algae and plants have in common?

6. Describe the plant life cycle.

Math Skills

7. A plant produced 200,000 spores and one-third as many eggs. How many eggs did the plant produce?

Critical Thinking

8. **Making Inferences** One difference between green algae and plants is that green algae do not have a cuticle. Why don't green algae have a cuticle?

9. **Applying Concepts** Imagine an environment that is very dry and receives a lot of sunlight. Water is found deep below the soil. Which of the four groups of plants could survive in this environment? Explain your answer.

SCiLINKS **NSTA** Developed and maintained by the National Science Teachers Association

For a variety of links related to this chapter, go to www.scilinks.org
Topic: Plant Characteristics; How Are Plants Classified?
SciLinks code: HSM1158; HSM0763

Answer to Reading Check

Sample answer: Green algae and plant cells have the same kind of chlorophyll, have similar cell walls, and make their own food through photosynthesis. Both store energy in the form of starch and have a two-stage life cycle.

CHAPTER RESOURCES

Chapter Resource File

- • Section Quiz GENERAL
- • Section Review GENERAL
- • Vocabulary and Section Summary GENERAL
- • SciLinks Activity GENERAL

Technology

Transparencies
- • The Main Groups of Plants

**Interactive Explorations CD-ROM**
- • Shut Your Trap! GENERAL

Focus

Overview

In this section, students will learn that seedless plants include nonvascular plants (mosses, liverworts, and hornworts) and vascular plants (ferns, horsetails, and club mosses). Finally, students will learn about the importance of these plants to the environment and to humans.

 Bellringer

Ask students the following question: "If plants can make their own food, why do people add fertilizer to the soil?" (Sample answer: Fertilizers add minerals to the soil that plants cannot make for themselves.)

Motivate

ACTiViTY ———————— GENERAL

Identifying Plant Parts Before students read this section, let them view a moss and a fern. Ask students to compare the two plants. (Sample answer: The moss is much smaller than the fern.) Ask students to identify the sporophyte and gametophyte. (Help students recognize these structures. Depending on the stage of the plant, the sporophyte or gametophyte may not be visible.) **LS** **Visual**

READING WARM-UP

Objectives

- List three nonvascular plants and three seedless vascular plants.
- Explain how seedless plants are important to the environment.
- Describe the relationship between seedless vascular plants and coal.

Terms to Learn

rhizoid
rhizome

READING STRATEGY

Paired Summarizing Read this section silently. In pairs, take turns summarizing the material. Stop to discuss ideas that seem confusing.

rhizoid a rootlike structure in nonvascular plants that holds the plants in place and helps plants get water and nutrients

---

Seedless Plants

When you think of plants, you probably think of plants, such as trees and flowers, that make seeds. But two groups of plants don't make seeds.

One group of seedless plants is the nonvascular plants—mosses, liverworts, and hornworts. The other group is seedless vascular plants—ferns, horsetails, and club mosses.

Nonvascular Plants

Mosses, liverworts, and hornworts are small. They grow on soil, the bark of trees, and rocks. These plants don't have vascular tissue. So, nonvascular plants usually live in places that are damp. Each cell of the plant must get water from the environment or from a nearby cell.

Mosses, liverworts, and hornworts don't have true stems, roots, or leaves. They do, however, have structures that carry out the activities of stems, roots, and leaves.

Mosses

Mosses often live together in large groups. They cover soil or rocks with a mat of tiny green plants. Mosses have leafy stalks and rhizoids (RIE ZOYDZ). A **rhizoid** is a rootlike structure that holds nonvascular plants in place. Rhizoids help the plants get water and nutrients. As you can see in **Figure 1,** mosses have two stages in their life cycle.

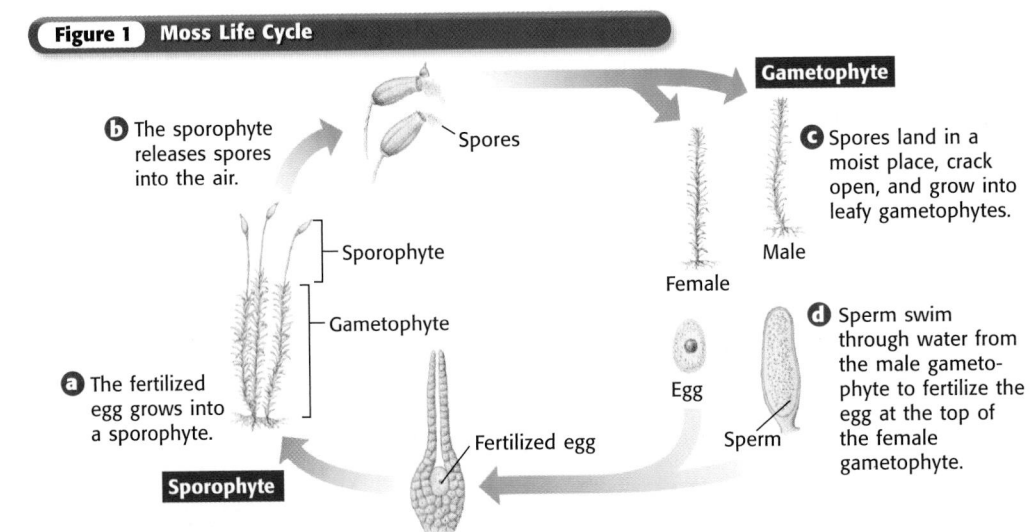

Figure 1 Moss Life Cycle

b The sporophyte releases spores into the air.

Spores

Sporophyte

Gametophyte

a The fertilized egg grows into a sporophyte.

Sporophyte

Gametophyte

c Spores land in a moist place, crack open, and grow into leafy gametophytes.

Male

Female

Egg

Fertilized egg

Sperm

d Sperm swim through water from the male gametophyte to fertilize the egg at the top of the female gametophyte.

CHAPTER RESOURCES

Chapter Resource File

- **Lesson Plan**
- **Directed Reading A** BASIC
- **Directed Reading B** SPECIAL NEEDS

Technology

- **Transparencies**
  - Bellringer

CONNECTION to

History ———————— ADVANCED

Writing **Elizabeth Knight Britton** Elizabeth Knight Britton was a botanist when female scientists faced many obstacles. She was the unofficial curator of mosses at Columbia University in New York and published 346 scientific papers between 1881 and 1930. Britton was especially active in the conservation of plants. Have students identify one of her accomplishments in this area and write a magazine article about their findings. **LS** **Verbal**

Liverworts and Hornworts

Like mosses, liverworts and hornworts are small, nonvascular plants that usually live in damp places. The life cycles of liverworts and hornworts are similar to the life cycle of mosses. The gametophytes of liverworts can be leafy and mosslike or broad and flattened. Hornworts also have broad, flattened gametophytes. Both liverworts and hornworts have rhizoids.

The Importance of Nonvascular Plants

Nonvascular plants have an important role in the environment. They are usually the first plants to live in a new environment, such as newly exposed rock. When these nonvascular plants die, they form a thin layer of soil. New plants can grow in this soil. More nonvascular plants may grow and hold the soil in place. This reduces soil erosion. Some animals eat nonvascular plants. Other animals use these plants for nesting material.

Peat mosses are important to humans. Peat mosses grow in bogs and other wet places. In some places, dead peat mosses have built up over time. This peat can be dried and burned as a fuel. Peat mosses are also used in potting soil.

Reading Check How are nonvascular plants important to the environment? (*See the Appendix for answers to Reading Checks.*)

Seedless Vascular Plants

Ancient ferns, horsetails, and club mosses grew very tall. Club mosses grew to 40 m in ancient forests. Horsetails once grew to 18 m tall. Some ferns grew to 8 m tall. Today, ferns, horsetails, and club mosses are usually much smaller. But because they have vascular tissue, they are often larger than nonvascular plants. **Figure 2** shows club mosses and horsetails.

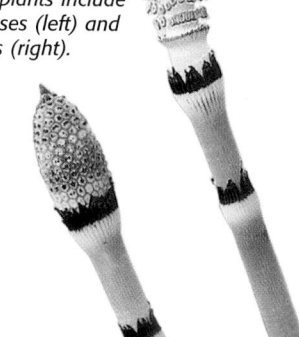

Figure 2 *Seedless vascular plants include club mosses (left) and horsetails (right).*

Quick Lab

Moss Mass

1. Determine the mass of a small sample of **dry sphagnum moss.**

2. Observe what happens when you put a small piece of the moss in **water.** Predict what will happen if you put the entire sample in water.

3. Place the moss sample in a **large beaker of water** for 10 to 15 minutes.

4. Remove the wet moss from the beaker, and determine the mass of the moss.

5. How much mass did the moss gain? Compare your result with your prediction.

6. What could this plant be used for?

MISCONCEPTION ALERT

Moss to the North Folklore says that moss grows on the north side of trees. But often, the green alga *Pleurococcus*, not moss, thrives on the moist, shaded (usually north) side of trees, stone walls, and fences.

MATERIALS

FOR EACH GROUP
• balance or scale
• sphagnum moss, dry
• water, in large beaker

Teacher's Notes: It may be helpful to use a dry beaker of predetermined mass to hold the wet moss for weighing.

Answers

4. Answers may vary.

5. Answers may vary. Students will likely underestimate how much water the moss can absorb.

6. Sample answer: The moss could be used to wipe up spills.

CONNECTION ACTIVITY
Real World — GENERAL

Sphagnum Moss Sphagnum moss was used during World War I as a dressing for wounds. Its hollow cells enable it to absorb up to 20 times its own weight in fluid. Sphagnum moss was also once used for diapers, lamp wicks, and bedding. Have students research how sphagnum moss is used today. (Sample answer: Sphagnum moss is used as protection for plants during shipping and for potting material.) Have students make posters describing their findings. **LS Visual**

Answer to Reading Check

Sample answer: Nonvascular plants are usually the first plants to live in a new environment. They form a thin layer of soil, where new plants can grow. Nonvascular plants also prevent erosion.

Close

Reteaching —— BASIC

Plant Life Cycles Help students review the life cycles of mosses and ferns. Ask students to come up to the board individually and diagram a single step of the life cycle for each plant. **LS** Visual

Quiz —— GENERAL

1. What is the difference between a rhizoid and a rhizome? (Sample answer: A rhizoid is a rootlike structure that holds a nonvascular plant in place. A rhizome is a horizontal underground stem from which new roots and shoots can grow.)

2. Describe the environmental importance of mosses, liverworts, and hornworts. (Sample answer: They are usually the first plants to live in a new area. When they die, they form a thin layer of soil in which other plants can grow. They also prevent soil erosion, are eaten by some animals, and are used for nesting material.)

Alternative Assessment —— GENERAL

Organizational Chart Have students make a chart or Venn diagram that describes the differences and similarities between the seedless nonvascular and seedless vascular plants discussed in this section. Have students present their chart to the class. **LS** Logical/Verbal

Ferns

Ferns grow in many places, from the cold Arctic to warm, humid tropical forests. Many ferns are small plants. But some tropical tree ferns grow as tall as 24 m. Most ferns have a rhizome. A **rhizome** is an underground stem from which new leaves and roots grow. At first, fern leaves, or fronds, are tightly coiled. These fronds look like the end of a violin, or fiddle. So, they are called *fiddleheads*. You are probably most familiar with the leafy fern sporophyte. The fern gametophyte is a tiny plant about half the size of one of your fingernails. The fern gametophyte is green and flat. It is usually shaped like a tiny heart. The life cycle of ferns is shown in **Figure 3**.

Horsetails and Club Mosses

Modern horsetails can be as tall as 8 m. But many horsetails are smaller. They usually grow in wet, marshy places. Their stems are hollow and contain silica. The silica gives horsetails a gritty texture. In fact, early American pioneers referred to horsetails as *scouring rushes*. They used horsetails to scrub pots and pans. Horsetails and ferns have similar life cycles.

Club mosses are often about 20 cm tall. They grow in woodlands. Club mosses are not actually mosses. Unlike mosses, club mosses have vascular tissue. The life cycle of club mosses is similar to the fern life cycle.

rhizome a horizontal, underground stem that produces new leaves, shoots, and roots

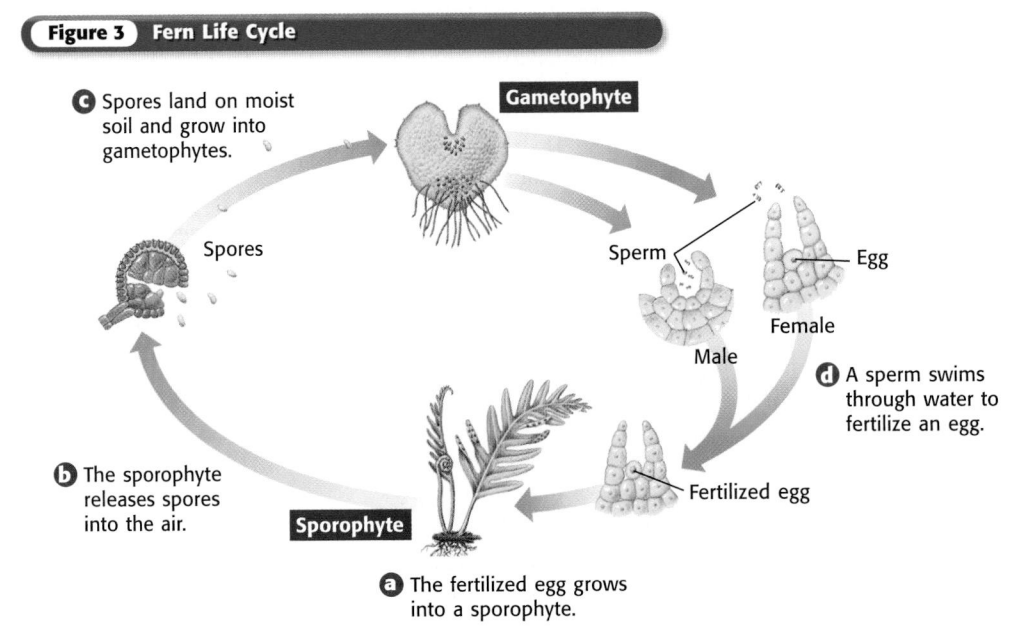

Figure 3 **Fern Life Cycle**

G Spores land on moist soil and grow into gametophytes.

Gametophyte

Spores

Sperm

Egg

Female

Male

d A sperm swims through water to fertilize an egg.

b The sporophyte releases spores into the air.

Sporophyte

Fertilized egg

a The fertilized egg grows into a sporophyte.

INCLUSION Strategies

- *Developmentally Delayed*
- *Learning Disabled*
- *Visually Impaired*

Many students learn best when they use their hands. Have students work in groups of three or four. Assign a sporophyte to each group. Give each group brown and green construction paper and pipe cleaners. Have each group create a model of their assigned sporophyte. **LS** Kinesthetic

Homework —— GENERAL

The Incredible, Edible Fern
Fiddleheads are a delicacy found in the forests of the northeastern United States during the spring. Edible fiddleheads are actually the tightly coiled, emerging fronds of the ostrich fern, *Matteuccia struthiopteris*. Fiddleheads are also available commercially. Have interested students research recipes for fiddleheads or prepare some dishes for the class. **LS** Verbal/Kinesthetic

The Importance of Seedless Vascular Plants

Seedless vascular plants play important roles in the environment. Ferns, horsetails, and club mosses help form soil. They also help prevent soil erosion. In rocky areas, ferns can play a role in the formation of communities. After lichens and mosses create a layer of soil, ferns may take over. Ferns add to soil depth, which allows other plants to grow.

Ferns and some club mosses are popular houseplants. The fiddleheads of some ferns can be cooked and eaten. Young horsetail shoots and their roots are also edible. Horsetails are used in some dietary supplements, shampoos, and skin-care products.

Seedless vascular plants that lived and died about 300 million years ago are among the most important to humans. The remains of these ancient ferns, horsetails, and club mosses formed coal. Coal is a fossil fuel that humans mine from the Earth's crust. Humans rely on coal for energy.

✓ Reading Check How are seedless vascular plants important to the environment?

CONNECTION TO Language Arts

WRITING SKILL **Selling Plants** Imagine that you work for an advertising agency. Your next assignment is to promote seedless vascular plants. Write an advertisement describing seedless vascular plants and ways people benefit from them. Your advertisement should be exciting and persuasive.

SECTION Review

Summary

- Nonvascular plants include mosses, liverworts, and hornworts.
- Seedless vascular plants include ferns, horsetails, and club mosses.
- The rhizoids and rhizomes of seedless plants prevent erosion by holding soil in place.
- The remains of seedless vascular plants that lived and died about 300 million years ago formed coal. Humans rely on coal for energy.

Using Key Terms

1. Use each of the following terms in a separate sentence: *rhizoid* and *rhizome*.

Understanding Key Ideas

2. Seedless plants
   a. help form communities.
   b. reduce soil erosion.
   c. add to soil depth.
   d. All of the above

3. Describe six kinds of seedless plants.

4. What is the relationship between coal and seedless vascular plants?

Math Skills

5. Club mosses once grew as tall as 40 m. Now, they grow no taller than 20 cm. What is the difference in height between ancient and modern club mosses?

Critical Thinking

6. **Making Inferences** Imagine a very damp area. Mosses cover the rocks and trees in this area. Liverworts and hornworts are also very abundant. What might happen if the area dries out? Explain your answer.

7. **Applying Concepts** Modern ferns, horsetails, and club mosses are smaller than they were millions of years ago. Why might these plants be smaller?

For a variety of links related to this chapter, go to www.scilinks.org

Topic: Seedless Plants
SciLinks code: HSM1368

Answer to Reading Check

Sample answer: Seedless vascular plants prevent erosion. They can grow in new soil and add to the soil's depth.

CHAPTER RESOURCES

Chapter Resource File

- Section Quiz GENERAL
- Section Review GENERAL
- Vocabulary and Section Summary GENERAL

Answers to Section Review

1. Sample answer: A moss plant has a rhizoid, which anchors the plant in soil. A fern has a rhizome, or underground stem, from which new leaves and roots can grow.

2. d

3. Sample answer: Mosses cover soil or rocks with a mat of tiny green plants. Mosses have leafy stalks and rhizoids. The gametophytes of liverworts are leafy and mosslike or broad and flattened. Hornworts also have broad, flattened gametophytes. Most ferns are small, but some tree ferns grow as tall as 24 m. The fern gametophyte is often very small and heart shaped. Horsetails grow in wet, marshy places and have hollow stems that contain silica. Club mosses are often about 20 cm tall and grow in woodlands.

4. Sample answer: The remains of seedless vascular plants that lived about 300 million years ago formed coal.

5. 3,980 cm (40 m $\times$ 100 cm/m = 4,000 cm; 4,000 cm $-$ 20 cm = 3,980 cm)

6. Sample answer: Mosses, liverworts, and hornworts live in damp areas. If the area dried out, these plants would likely die.

7. Sample answer: Ferns, horsetails, and club mosses need moisture. They may be smaller today because there is less moisture available. Also, competition from other plants might have led to smaller ferns, horsetails, and club mosses.

SECTION

3

Focus

Overview

Students will learn the characteristics of seed plants and the advantages of seeds over spores. Students will also learn about gymnosperms and angiosperms, as well as the environmental and economic importance of these plants.

🔔 Bellringer

Use the board or an overhead projector to pose the following question to students: "If plants cannot move, how do they disperse their seeds?" (Sample answer: Plants spread their seeds by wind, water, and animals.)

Motivate

ActiVity ——— GENERAL

Seed Types Give students gray-stripe sunflower seeds, pumpkin seeds, and wildflower seeds to examine. Tell students to compare the seeds. Ask students how seeds differ from spores. (Sample answer: Seeds contain stored food.) Ask students if they think it would be easier to introduce seed plants or seedless plants to a new plot of land. (Sample answer: If the land is dry, seed plants would be more successful than seedless plants.) **LS** Visual

---

READING WARM-UP

Objectives

● Describe three ways that seed plants differ from seedless plants.

● Describe the structure of seeds.

● Compare angiosperms and gymnosperms.

● Explain the economic and environmental importance of gymnosperms and angiosperms.

Terms to Learn

pollen
pollination

READING STRATEGY

Reading Organizer As you read this section, make a table comparing angiosperms and gymnosperms.

pollen the tiny granules that contain the male gametophyte of seed plants

Figure 1 *Dandelion fruits, which each contain a seed, are spread by wind.*

Seed Plants

Think about the seed plants that you use during the day. You likely use dozens of seed plants, from the food you eat to the paper you write on.

The two groups of vascular plants that produce seeds are gymnosperms and angiosperms. Gymnosperms are trees and shrubs that do not have flowers or fruit. Angiosperms have flowers and seeds that are protected by fruit.

Characteristics of Seed Plants

As with seedless plants, the life cycle of seed plants alternates between two stages. But seed plants, such as the plant in **Figure 1,** differ from seedless plants in the following ways:

● Seed plants produce seeds. Seeds nourish and protect young sporophytes.

● Unlike the gametophytes of seedless plants, the gametophytes of seed plants do not live independently of the sporophyte. The gametophytes of seed plants are tiny. The gametophytes form within the reproductive structures of the sporophyte.

● The sperm of seedless plants need water to swim to the eggs of female gametophytes. The sperm of seed plants do not need water to reach an egg. Sperm form inside tiny structures called **pollen.** Pollen can be transported by wind or by animals.

These three characteristics of seed plants allow them to live just about anywhere. For this reason, seed plants are the most common plants on Earth today.

✓ **Reading Check** List three characteristics of seed plants. (*See the Appendix for answers to Reading Checks.*)

CHAPTER RESOURCES

Chapter Resource File

 • Lesson Plan
• Directed Reading A **BASIC**
• Directed Reading B **SPECIAL NEEDS**

Technology

 Transparencies
• Bellringer

Answer to Reading Check

Sample answer: Seed plants produce seeds. The gametophytes of seed plants do not live independently of the sporophyte. The sperm of seed plants don't need water to fertilize eggs.

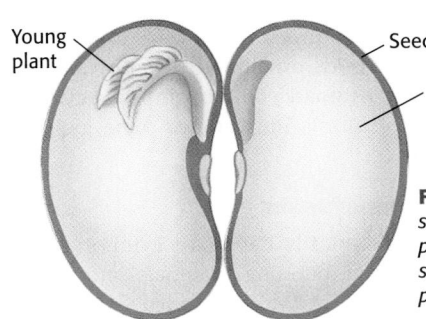

Young plant

Seed coat

Stored food in cotyledon

Figure 2 *A seed contains stored food and a young plant, or sporophyte. A seed is surrounded and protected by a seed coat.*

The Structure of Seeds

A seed forms after fertilization, when sperm and eggs are joined. A seed is made up of three parts, as shown in **Figure 2.** The first part is a young plant, or the sporophyte. The second part is stored food. It is often found in the cotyledons (KAHT uh LEED uhnz), or the seed leaves of the young plant. Finally, a seed coat surrounds and protects the young plant.

Seed plants have some advantages over seedless plants. For example, when a seed begins to grow, the young plant uses the food stored in the seed. The spores of seedless plants don't have stored food to help a new plant grow. Another advantage of seed plants is that seeds can be spread by animals. The spores of seedless plants are usually spread by wind. Animals spread seeds more efficiently than the wind spreads spores.

Reading Check Describe two advantages that seed plants have over seedless plants.

CONNECTION TO Environmental Science

WRITING SKILL **Animals That Help Plants** Animals need plants to live, but some plants benefit from animals, too. These plants produce seeds with tough seed coats. An animal's digestive system can wear down these seed coats and speed the growth of a seed. Identify a plant that animals help in this way. Then, find out how being eaten by animals makes it possible for seeds to grow. Write about your findings in your **science journal.**

Dissecting Seeds

1. Soak a **lima bean seed** in **water** overnight. Draw the seed before placing it in the water.

2. Remove the seed from the water. Draw what you see.

3. The seed will likely look wrinkly. This is the seed coat. Use a **toothpick** to gently remove the seed coat from the lima bean seed.

4. Gently separate the halves of the lima bean seed. Draw what you see.

5. What did you see after you split the lima bean seed in half?

6. What part of the seed do you think provides the lima bean plant with the energy to grow?

WEIRD SCIENCE

A large number of plants in the heath-land of South Africa produce seeds with a very tasty covering called an *elaio-some*—tasty, that is, to ants, which carry seeds into their underground colonies. The ants nibble off the outside covering and then leave the seed alone. The ants plant the seed at just the right depth for it to germinate successfully. Eventually, the seed begins to grow.

Answer to Reading Check

Sample answer: Seeds have stored food to nourish a young plant while spores do not. Seeds can be spread by animals while spores are spread by wind. Animals spread seeds more efficiently than the wind does.

Teach

Group ACTIVITY — GENERAL

MATERIALS

FOR EACH GROUP
• cotton balls
• fan
• paper, construction
• scissors
• table
• tape, clear or masking

Seed Dispersal Have students shred the cotton balls and place the pieces on a table in front of the fan. Turn on the fan, and have students observe how far the cotton "seeds" travel. Have students wad a strip of tape into a marble-sized ball and attach it to the table. How far does the ball move when subjected to the "wind"? Ask students how they think the seeds in this type of fruit might best be transported. (Sample answer: on an animal's fur) Have students cut a "maple fruit" from construction paper. Have students observe how this "fruit" behaves in the wind.
LS Kinesthetic/Visual

MATERIALS

FOR EACH GROUP
• lima bean seed
• toothpick
• water

Teacher's Notes: Use lima bean seeds sold in packets for use in gardens. Otherwise, students may not see young sporophytes.

Answers

5. Students will likely see the young sporophyte.

6. Sample answer: Food is stored in the two halves of the seed.

Discussion — BASIC

Gymnosperms Many students are already familiar with conifers, such as pine trees but may suddenly feel confused when the term *gymnosperm* is introduced. Encourage these students to list the characteristics they have observed in pine trees. (Sample answers: stay green all year; thin, needle-shaped leaves; pine cones) Stress that even though this section provides additional information about gymnosperms, students already know a great deal about them. **LS** Verbal

Using the Figure — GENERAL

Some Common Gymnosperms Have students work in pairs. Ask students to examine **Figure 3.** Students should take turns summarizing the information in the figure aloud. Their partners should stop them if they find the information confusing or need clarification. **LS** Verbal/ Interpersonal

Homework — ADVANCED

Writing **Gnetophytes** Gnetophytes have many things in common with angiosperms. Some scientists believe that the two are closely related. Ask interested students to research and write a report about the similarities between gnetophytes and angiosperms and about the theories for these similarities. **LS** Verbal

Gymnosperms

Seed plants that do not have flowers or fruit are called *gymnosperms*. Gymnosperm seeds are usually protected by a cone. The four groups of gymnosperms are conifers, ginkgoes, cycads, and gnetophytes (NEE toh FIETS). You can see some gymnosperms in **Figure 3.**

The Importance of Gymnosperms

Conifers are the most economically important gymnosperms. People use conifer wood for building materials and paper products. Pine trees produce a sticky fluid called *resin*. Resin is used to make soap, turpentine, paint, and ink. Some conifers produce an important anticancer drug. Some gnetophytes produce anti-allergy drugs. Conifers, cycads, and ginkgoes are popular in gardens and parks.

Figure 3 Examples of Gymnosperms

◀ **Conifers** The conifers, such as this ponderosa pine, are the largest group of gymnosperms. There are about 550 species of conifers. Most conifers are evergreens that keep their needle-shaped leaves all year. Conifer seeds develop in cones.

◀ **Ginkgoes** Today, there is only one living species of ginkgo, the ginkgo tree. Ginkgo seeds are not produced in cones. The seeds have fleshy seed coats and are attached directly to the branches of the tree.

◀ **Cycads** The cycads were more common millions of years ago. Today, there are only about 140 species of cycads. These plants grow in the Tropics. Like conifer seeds, cycad seeds develop in cones.

◀ **Gnetophytes** About 70 species of gnetophytes, such as this joint fir, exist today. Many gnetophytes are shrubs that grow in dry areas. The seeds of most gnetophytes develop in cones.

CONNECTION ACTiViTY
Earth Science — ADVANCED

Growth Rings Geochronology, the interpretation and dating of the geologic record, includes dendrochronology, which is the study of trees' growth rings. Bristlecone pines have been particularly useful in this endeavor because many of them are very old. Ask interested students to research how scientists date trees and use them for geochronology. Ask students to present their findings to the class. **LS** Verbal

WEIRD SCIENCE

When scientists compared radiocarbon dates of bristlecone pines with dates obtained from tree-ring patterns, they discovered that their calibrations for carbon-14 analysis were incorrect. The new data indicated that some wooden artifacts found in Europe were 1,000 years older than originally thought. The bristlecone pines became known as the "trees that rewrote history."

The Importance of Angiosperms

Flowering plants provide many land animals with the food they need to survive. A field mouse that eats seeds and berries is using flowering plants directly as food. An owl that eats a field mouse is using flowering plants indirectly as food.

People use flowering plants in many ways. Major food crops, such as corn, wheat, and rice, are flowering plants. Some flowering plants, such as oak trees, are used for building materials. Flowering plants, such as cotton and flax, are used to make clothing and rope. Flowering plants are also used to make medicines, rubber, and perfume oils.

Reading Check How are flowering plants important to humans?

SECTION Review

Summary

- Seeds nourish the young sporophyte of seed plants. Seed plant gametophytes rely on the sporophyte. Also, they do not need water for fertilization.
- Seeds nourish a young plant until it can make food by photosynthesis.
- Gymnosperms do not have flowers or fruits. Gymnosperm seeds are usually protected by cones. Gymnosperms are used for building materials, paper, resin, and medicines.
- Angiosperms have flowers and fruits. Angiosperms are used for food, medicines, fibers for clothing, rubber, and building materials.

Using Key Terms

1. In your own words, write a definition for each of the following terms: *pollen* and *pollination*.

Understanding Key Ideas

2. One advantage of seed plants is that
   a. seed plants grow in few places.
   b. they can begin photosynthesis as soon as they begin to grow.
   c. they need water for fertilization.
   d. young plants are nourished by food stored in the seed.

3. The gametophytes of seed plants
   a. live independently of the sporophytes.
   b. are very large.
   c. are protected in the reproductive structures of the sporophyte.
   d. None of the above

4. Describe the structure of seeds.

5. Briefly describe the four groups of gymnosperms. Which group is the largest and most economically important?

6. Compare angiosperms and gymnosperms.

Math Skills

7. More than 265,000 species of plants have been discovered. Approximately 235,000 of those species are angiosperms. What percentage of plants are NOT angiosperms?

Critical Thinking

8. **Making Inferences** In what ways are flowers and fruits adaptations that help angiosperms reproduce?

9. **Applying Concepts** An angiosperm lives in a dense rainforest, close to the ground. It receives little wind. Several herbivores live in this area of the rainforest. What are some ways the plant can ensure its seeds are carried throughout the forest?

SciLINKS® Developed and maintained by the National Science Teachers Association

For a variety of links related to this chapter, go to www.scilinks.org

Topic: Plants with Seeds
SciLinks code: HSM1168

Answer to Reading Check

Sample answer: Major food crops are flowering plants. Flowering plants provide building material, are used to make clothing and rope, and are used to make medicines, rubber, and perfume oils.

Answers to Section Review

1. Sample answer: Pollen contains the male gametophyte of seed plants. Pollination happens when pollen is transferred from male structures to female structures.

2. d

3. c

4. Sample answer: Seeds are made up of three parts. The first part is the young plant. The second part is stored food, often found in the cotyledons. The third part is the seed coat, which surrounds and protects the young plant.

5. Sample answer: Most conifers are evergreens that have seeds in cones. Cycads grow in the tropics and have seeds in cones. There is only one species of gingko, which produces its seeds in fleshy seed coats attached to the branches of the tree. Gnetophytes are often shrubs that grow in dry areas, and most gnetophytes have seeds in cones. Conifers are the largest and most economically important group of gymnosperms.

6. Sample answer: Gymnosperms and angiosperms are both seed plants, but gymnosperms do not have flowers or fruits as angiosperms do. Instead, gymnosperms often have cones.

7. $265,000 - 235,000 = 30,000$ plants; $30,000 \div 265,000 \times 100 = 11.3\%$

8. Sample answer: Flowers attract pollinators, which carry pollen to the flowers. Some flowers are adapted for the wind to spread pollen. Fruits protect the seeds, but fruits also attract animals or stick to animals' fur. Being eaten and sticking to fur both help to spread seeds.

9. Sample answer: The plant does not get much wind to spread its seeds, so it likely relies on animals to spread its seeds. Because there are herbivores in the area, the plant may have sweet fruits to attract the animals. The animals could eat the fruits and spread the seeds.

READING WARM-UP

Objectives

- List three functions of roots and three functions of stems.
- Describe the structure of a leaf.
- Identify the parts of a flower and their functions.

Terms to Learn

xylem   stamen
phloem   pistil
sepal   ovary
petal

READING STRATEGY

Mnemonics As you read this section, create a mnemonic device to help you remember the parts of a plant.

xylem the type of tissue in vascular plants that provides support and conducts water and nutrients from the roots

phloem the tissue that conducts food in vascular plants

Figure 1 *The roots of these plants provide the plants with water and minerals.*

Structures of Seed Plants

You have different body systems that carry out many functions. Plants have systems too—a root system, a shoot system, and a reproductive system.

A plant's root system and shoot system supply the plant with what it needs to survive. The root system is made up of roots. The shoot system includes stems and leaves.

The vascular tissues of the root and shoot systems are connected. There are two kinds of vascular tissue—xylem (ZIE luhm) and phloem (FLOH em). **Xylem** is vascular tissue that transports water and minerals through the plant. Xylem moves materials from the roots to the shoots. **Phloem** is vascular tissue that transports food molecules to all parts of a plant. Xylem and phloem are found in all parts of vascular plants.

Roots

Most roots are underground, as shown in **Figure 1.** So, many people do not realize how extensive root systems can be. For example, a corn plant that is 2.5 m tall can have roots that grow 2.5 m deep and 1.2 m out and away from the stem!

Root Functions

The following are the three main functions of roots:

- Roots supply plants with water and dissolved minerals. These materials are absorbed from the soil. The water and minerals are transported to the shoots in the xylem.
- Roots hold plants securely in the soil.
- Roots store surplus food made during photosynthesis. The food is produced in the leaves. Then, it is transported in the phloem to the roots. In the roots, the surplus food is usually stored as sugar or starch.

Onion   **Dandelion**   **Carrots**

Is That a Fact!

The deepest roots ever discovered belonged to a wild fig tree in South Africa. The roots had penetrated the soil to a depth of more than 120 m.

Root Structure

The structures of a root are shown in **Figure 2.** The layer of cells that covers the surface of roots is called the *epidermis*. Some cells of the epidermis extend from the root. These cells, or root hairs, increase the surface area of the root. This surface area helps the root absorb water and minerals. After water and minerals are absorbed by the epidermis, they diffuse into the center of the root, where the vascular tissue is located.

Roots grow longer at their tips. A group of cells called the *root cap* protects the tip of a root. The root cap produces a slimy substance. This substance makes it easier for the root to push through soil as it grows.

Root Systems

There are two kinds of root systems—taproot systems and fibrous root systems. A taproot system has one main root, or a taproot. The taproot grows downward. Many smaller roots branch from the taproot. Taproots can reach water deep underground. Dicots and gymnosperms usually have taproot systems.

A fibrous root system has several roots that spread out from the base of a plant's stem. The roots are usually the same size. Fibrous roots usually get water from close to the soil surface. Monocots usually have fibrous roots.

✔ **Reading Check** What are two types of root systems? (*See the Appendix for answers to Reading Checks.*)

Practice with Percentages

The following table gives an estimate of the number of species in each plant group.

Plant Species	
Plant group	**Number of species**
Mosses, liverworts, and hornworts	15,600
Ferns, horsetails, and club mosses	12,000
Gymnosperms	760
Angiosperms	235,000

What percentage of plants do not produce seeds?

Figure 2   The Structures of a Root

A root absorbs water and minerals, which move into the xylem. Growth occurs at the tip of a root. The root cap releases a slimy substance that helps the root grow through soil.

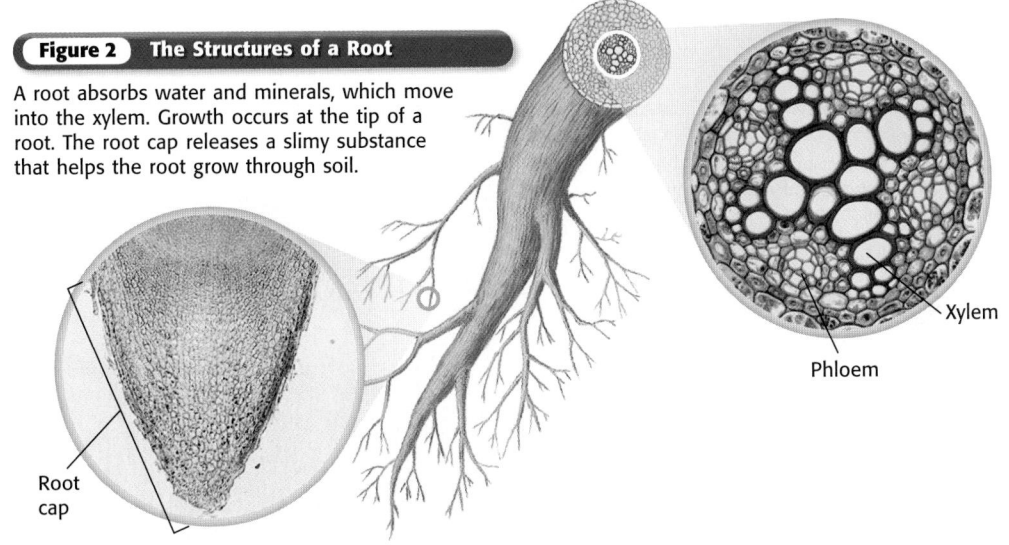

Root cap

Xylem

Phloem

Answer to Reading Check

taproot systems and fibrous root systems

Teach

Answer to Math Practice

about 10% (15,600 + 12,000 = 27,600 seedless plants; 15,600 + 12,000 + 760 + 235,000 = 263,360 total plants; 27,600 ÷ 263,360 × 100 = 10.4%)

Group Activity — BASIC

MATERIALS

FOR EACH GROUP
- bags, plastic, resealable (4)
- ruler, metric
- seed, four varieties, 1 seed each
- towels, paper (4)
- water

Root Growth   Have students work in groups of four. Tell students to fold a paper towel in quarters, placing a seed in the fold of the towel. Students should moisten the paper towel thoroughly, but the paper towel should not be dripping. Tell students to place paper towels in a plastic bag. For each day of the next week, have students measure the length of the roots that develop. Students should moisten the paper towel as needed during the week. Students should also observe the roots each day for changes in appearance. Ask students to make a chart of their measurements. Then, ask students the following questions: "What did you notice about the appearance of your roots at they grew?" (Students may notice that the roots grew root hairs or became more numerous. Some students may also note that the tips of the roots seemed slimy.) "Which of your seeds grew the fastest?" (Answers may vary depending on the varieties of seeds used.) At the end of the experiment, consider asking students to plant their seeds in potting soil to see how the roots continue to develop. **LS Kinesthetic**

Stem Functions Have students draw pictures that illustrate the functions of stems. Tell them to write captions for each illustration. **LS** Visual/Verbal

CONNECTION ACTIVITY
History ─────── ADVANCED

Using Stems The stems of many large aquatic grasses are called *reeds*. After reeds are harvested and dried, they can be used to construct many useful products. For thousands of years, arrows, pens, baskets, musical instruments, furniture, and houses have been made out of reeds. Building boats from reeds is an ancient craft that is still practiced in some places where reeds are plentiful. Ancient Egyptian buildings include friezes of oceangoing ships made of reeds. In the 1960s, a Norwegian explorer named Thor Heyerdahl wondered if a reed ship could have provided ancient peoples with transportation across the Atlantic Ocean. To demonstrate that such a journey was possible, he had Bolivian craftspersons build a traditional reed vessel, the *Ra II*. Ask students to research Heyerdahl and the *Ra II*. Have interested students make a model of Heyerdahl's reed vessel. **LS** Kinesthetic

Figure 3 *The stem, or trunk, of this valley oak keeps the tree upright, which helps leaves get sunlight for photosynthesis.*

Stems

Stems vary greatly in shape and size. Stems are usually located above ground. However, many plants have underground stems. The trunk of the valley oak in **Figure 3** is a stem.

Stem Functions

A stem connects a plant's roots to its leaves and flowers. A stem also has the following functions:

- Stems support the plant body. Leaves are arranged along stems or on the ends of stems. This arrangement helps leaves get sunlight for photosynthesis. Stems hold up flowers, which helps pollinators, such as bees, see the flowers.
- Stems transport materials between the root system and the shoot system. Xylem carries water and dissolved minerals from the roots to the leaves and other shoot parts. Phloem carries the food made during photosynthesis to roots and other parts of the plant.
- Some stems store materials. For example, the stems of cactuses and some trees are adapted for water storage.

Herbaceous Stems

Many plants have stems that are soft, thin, and flexible. These stems are called *herbaceous stems* (huhr BAY shuhs STEMZ). Examples of plants that have herbaceous stems include wildflowers, such as clovers and poppies. Many crops, such as beans, tomatoes, and corn, have herbaceous stems. A cross section of an herbaceous stem is shown in **Figure 4.**

✓ Reading Check What are herbaceous stems? Give an example of a plant that has an herbaceous stem.

Figure 4   Cross Section of an Herbaceous Stem

Buttercups are just one plant that has herbaceous stems. Wildflowers and many vegetables have soft, thin, and flexible stems.

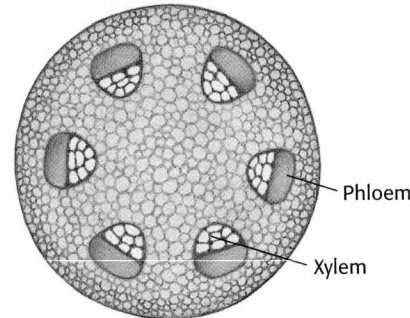

Phloem

Xylem

Is That a Fact!

Linen is a fabric woven from the long fibers harvested from the stems of flax plants. Humans have used linen fabrics for over 10,000 years.

Answer to Reading Check

Sample answer: Herbaceous stems are soft, thin, and flexible. Poppies have herbaceous stems.

Figure 5 Cross Section of a Woody Stem

Some plants, such as these trees, have woody stems. Plants that have woody stems usually live for many years. People can use growth rings to estimate the age of a plant.

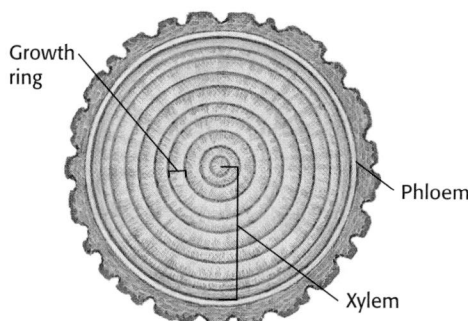

Growth ring

Phloem

Xylem

ACTIVITY — GENERAL

Analyzing Tree Rings Have students examine preserved cross sections of trees that clearly show growth rings. Ask students to identify the xylem and phloem rings. (Students should recognize that phloem compose the innermost part of bark. Xylem form the growth rings of the center of the stem.) Ask students to measure the width of each ring and to interpret the measurements. Have them take into account the growing conditions in the spring and summer. (Students may recognize dry years and wet years based on these measurements.) **LS Visual** English Language Learners

Woody Stems

Trees and shrubs have rigid stems made of wood and bark. These stems are called *woody stems*. **Figure 5** shows a cross section of a woody stem. Trees or shrubs that live in areas with cold winters have a growing period during the spring and summer. These plants have a dormant period during the winter. At the beginning of each growing period, large xylem cells are produced. As fall approaches, the plants produce smaller xylem cells, which appear darker. In the fall and winter, the plants stop producing new cells. The cycle begins again the next spring. A ring of dark cells surrounding a ring of light cells makes up a growth ring.

Leaves

Leaves vary greatly in shape. They may be round, narrow, heart-shaped, or fan-shaped. Leaves also vary in size. The raffia palm has leaves that may be six times longer than you are tall. The leaves of duckweed, a tiny aquatic plant, are so small that several of the leaves can fit on your fingernail. **Figure 6** shows a poison ivy leaf.

Leaf Functions

The main function of leaves is to make food for the plant. Chloroplasts in the cells of leaves capture energy from sunlight. The leaves also absorb carbon dioxide from the air. The leaves use the captured energy to make food, or sugar, from carbon dioxide and water.

Figure 6 *The leaves of poison ivy are very distinctive. They make food to help the plant survive.*

WEIRD SCIENCE

Garlic bulbs are fleshy, nutrient-storing structures composed of modified leaves and a stem. Garlic has a pungent flavor and is often used to season foods. Sometimes, garlic is used as a nutritional supplement. At the annual Gilroy Garlic Festival in Gilroy, California, visitors can purchase garlic ice cream and garlic candy.

CHAPTER RESOURCES

Technology

Transparencies
• Cross Section of an Herbaceous Stem; Cross Section of a Woody Stem

Teach, continued

Group ACTiViTY — GENERAL

MATERIALS

FOR EACH GROUP
• books, heavy
• leaves
• newspapers
• notebook or index cards
• paper towels
• tape, transparent

Safety Caution: Tell students to avoid plants such as poison ivy and poison oak during this activity. You may want to show students pictures of these plants.

Leaf Collecting Challenge students to see how many different types of leaves they can collect. Students should press the leaves for a few days after collecting them. They can do this by placing each leaf between two paper towels and several sheets of newspaper on each side. Then, students should stack heavy books on top of the leaf. When the leaf is flat and dry, have students tape the leaves to cards or to the pages of a notebook. Have students use reference books to identify the names of the plants from which they collected the leaves. Have students label each leaf with the common name, the scientific name, the date, and the location where the leaf was found. **English Language Learners**

LS Kinesthetic

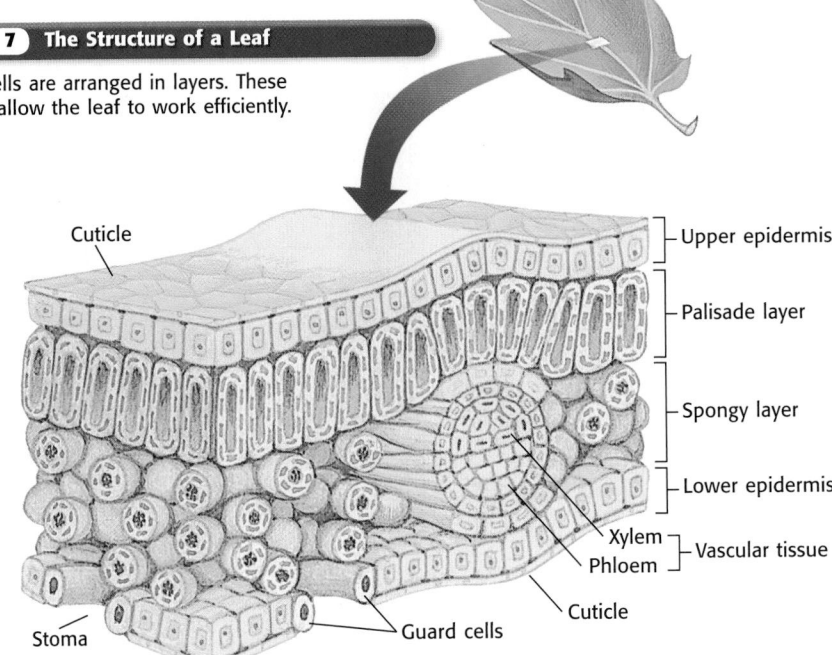

Figure 7 The Structure of a Leaf
Leaf cells are arranged in layers. These layers allow the leaf to work efficiently.

Cuticle
Upper epidermis
Palisade layer
Spongy layer
Lower epidermis
Xylem
Phloem — Vascular tissue
Cuticle
Stoma
Guard cells

Leaf Structure

The structure of leaves, shown in **Figure 7,** is related to their main function—photosynthesis. The outer surfaces of a leaf are covered by a cuticle. The cuticle prevents water loss from the leaf. A single layer of cells, the epidermis, lies beneath the cuticle. Light passes through the epidermis. Tiny openings in the epidermis, called *stomata* (singular, *stoma*), let carbon dioxide enter the leaf. Guard cells open and close the stomata.

Most photosynthesis takes place in the middle of a leaf. This part of a leaf often has two layers. Cells in the upper layer, the palisade layer, contain many chloroplasts. Photosynthesis takes place in the chloroplasts. Carbon dioxide moves freely in the space between the cells of the second layer, the spongy layer. Xylem and phloem are also found in the spongy layer.

✓ Reading Check What are the cell layers of a leaf?

Leaf Adaptations

Some leaves have functions other than photosynthesis. For example, the leaves of many cactuses are modified as spines. These spines keep animals from eating the cactuses. The leaves of another plant, the sundew, are modified to catch insects. Sundews grow in soil that does not contain enough nitrogen to meet the plants' needs. By catching and digesting insects, a sundew is able to get enough nitrogen.

SCHOOL to HOME

Looking at Leaves

Leaves are many shapes and sizes. They are also arranged on a stem in many ways. Walk around your home. In your **science journal,** sketch the leaves of the plants you see. Notice how the leaves are arranged on the stem, the shapes of the leaves, and the veins in the leaves. Use a ruler to measure the size of the leaves.

ACTiViTY

Is That a Fact!

Duckweed, which lives on the surfaces of ponds, is the smallest flowering plant in the world. A duckweed plant can be less than 1 mm long and have a mass of about 150 μg, or the equivalent of two grains of table salt. It's a good thing animals like to eat duckweed. One species reproduces every 30–36 hours. Left unchecked, one duckweed plant could produce 1 nonillion plants (1 followed by 30 zeros) in 4 months!

Answer to Reading Check

epidermis, palisade layer, and spongy layer

Flowers

Most people admire the beauty of flowers, such as the wildflowers in **Figure 8.** But why do plants have flowers? Flowers are adaptations for sexual reproduction.

Flowers come in many shapes, colors, and fragrances. Brightly colored and fragrant flowers usually rely on animals for pollination. For example, some flowers look and smell like rotting meat. These flowers attract flies. The flies pollinate the flowers. Plants that lack brightly colored flowers and fragrances, such as grasses, depend on the wind to spread pollen.

Many flowers also produce nectar. Nectar is a fluid that contains sugar. Nectar attracts birds and insects. These animals move from flower to flower and drink the nectar. As they do so, they often carry pollen to the flowers.

Sepals and Petals

Flowers usually have the following basic parts: sepals, petals, stamens, and one or more pistils. The flower parts are usually arranged in rings around the central pistil.

Sepals are modified leaves that make up the outermost ring of flower parts and protect the bud. Sepals are often green like other leaves. Sepals cover and protect the flower while it is a bud. As the blossom opens, the sepals fold back. Then, the petals can unfold and become visible. **Petals** are broad, flat, thin leaflike parts of a flower. Petals vary greatly in color and shape. Petals attract insects or other animals to the flower. These animals help plants reproduce by carrying pollen from flower to flower.

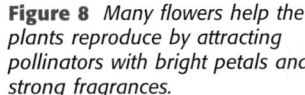

sepal in a flower, one of the outermost rings of modified leaves that protect the flower bud

petal one of the ring or rings of the usually brightly colored, leaf-shaped parts of a flower

Figure 8 *Many flowers help the plants reproduce by attracting pollinators with bright petals and strong fragrances.*

Is That a Fact!

The more water-repellent a leaf is, the healthier it may be, according to some scientists. Dirt, which contains disease-causing microbes, has a stronger attraction to water droplets than to a leaf's surface. When the water rolls off the leaf, so do the dirt and microbes. Water repellency thus helps prevent infection.

CHAPTER RESOURCES

Technology

Transparencies
- The Structure of a Leaf
- *LINK TO EARTH SCIENCE* The Electromagnetic Spectrum

Reteaching — BASIC

Flower Parts Ask student volunteers to describe a flower part and to draw that part on the board. Continue until students have drawn a complete flower.
LS Visual

Quiz — GENERAL

1. Why do some plants have brightly colored flowers and other plants do not? (Sample answer: Plants with brightly colored flowers usually attract animals for pollination. Plants without showy flowers usually rely on the wind for pollination.)

2. Describe the two types of root systems, and list one plant that has each type. (A taproot system has one main root. Carrots have a taproot. Fibrous root systems include many roots of a similar size that grow from the base of the stem. Onions have fibrous roots.)

Alternative Assessment — GENERAL

Eating Plants Have students list ingredients for a salad. (Sample answers: lettuce, tomato, cucumber, carrot, cabbage, broccoli, alfalfa sprouts, and garbanzo beans) Ask students to identify the part of the plant that is eaten. (Sample answer: Lettuce and cabbage come from leaves. Tomato and cucumber are fruits. Carrots are roots. Broccoli are flowers. Alfalfa sprouts are root, stem, and leaf. Garbanzo beans are seeds.)
LS Logical/Verbal

Figure 9 The Structure of a Flower

The stamens, which produce pollen, and the pistil, which produces eggs, are surrounded by the petals and the sepals.

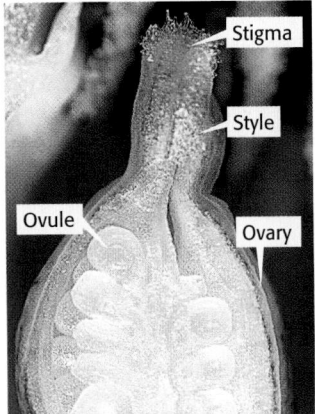

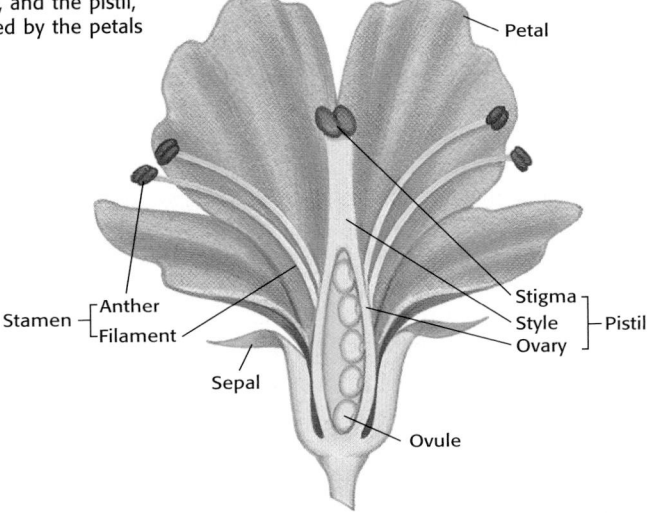

stamen the male reproductive structure of a flower that produces pollen and consists of an anther at the tip of a filament

pistil the female reproductive part of a flower that produces seeds and consists of an ovary, style, and stigma

ovary in flowering plants, the lower part of a pistil that produces eggs in ovules

Stamens and Pistils

As you can see in **Figure 9,** the stamens of flowers are usually found just above the petals. A **stamen** is a male reproductive structure of flowers. Each stamen has a thin stalk called a *filament*. The filament is topped by an anther. Anthers are saclike structures that produce pollen.

Found in the center of most flowers is one or more pistils. A **pistil** is the female reproductive structure of flowers. The tip of the pistil is called the *stigma*. Pollen grains collect on stigmas, which are often sticky or feathery. The long, slender part of the pistil is the style. The rounded base of a pistil that contains one or more ovules is called the **ovary.** Each ovule contains an egg. When the egg is fertilized, the ovule develops into a seed. The ovary develops into a fruit.

✓ *Reading Check* **Describe stamens and pistils. Which are the female parts of a flower? the male parts of a flower?**

The Importance of Flowers

Flowers help plants reproduce. Humans also use flowers for many things. Roses and many other flowers are used for floral arrangements. Some flowers, such as artichokes, broccoli, and cauliflower, can be eaten. Other flowers, such as hibiscus and chamomile flowers, are used to make tea. Flowers used as spices include cloves and saffron. Flowers are also used in perfumes, lotions, and shampoos.

Answer to Reading Check

Sample answer: Stamens, which have filaments topped by anthers, are the male reproductive parts of flowers. A pistil is the female part of a flower. A pistil has a stigma, style, and ovary.

SECTION Review

Summary

- Roots supply plants with water and dissolved minerals. They support and anchor plants. Roots also store surplus food made during photosynthesis.

- Stems support the body of a plant. They allow transport of material between the root system and shoot system. Some stems store materials, such as water.

- A leaf has a thin epidermis on its upper and lower surfaces. The epidermis allows sunlight to pass through to the center of the leaf.

- Most photosynthesis takes place in the palisade layer of a leaf. The spongy layer of a leaf allows the movement of carbon dioxide and contains the xylem and phloem.

- The four main parts of a flower are the sepals, the petals, the stamens, and one or more pistils.

- Flowers are usually arranged around the pistil. The ovary of a pistil contains ovules. When the eggs are fertilized, ovules develop into seeds and the ovary becomes a fruit.

Using Key Terms

1. In your own words, write a definition for each of the following terms: *xylem, phloem, stamen,* and *pistil*.

2. Use each of the following terms in a separate sentence: *sepal, petal, pistil,* and *ovary.*

Understanding Key Ideas

3. Which of the following flower structures produces pollen?
   a. pistil
   c. anther
   b. filament
   d. stigma

4. The ___ of a leaf allows carbon dioxide to enter.
   a. stoma
   c. palisade layer
   b. epidermis
   d. spongy layer

5. Compare xylem and phloem.

6. Describe the internal structure of a leaf.

7. What are the functions of stems?

8. Identify the two types of stems, and briefly describe them.

9. How do people use flowers?

Critical Thinking

10. **Making Inferences** Describe two kinds of root systems. How does the structure of each system help the roots perform their three functions?

11. **Applying Concepts** Pampas grass flowers are found at the top of tall stems, are light-colored, and are unscented. Explain how pampas grass flowers are most likely pollinated.

Interpreting Graphics

Use the table below to answer the questions that follow.

Age of Trees in a Small Forest	
Number of trees	**Number of growth rings**
5	71
1	73
3	68

12. How many trees are older than 70 years?

13. What is the average age of these trees, in years?

For a variety of links related to this chapter, go to www.scilinks.org

Topic: Structure of Seed Plants
SciLinks code: HSM1467

Answers to Section Review

1. Sample answer: Xylem transports water and minerals. Phloem transports food molecules. A stamen is the male reproductive part of a flower. A pistil is the female reproductive structure of a flower.

2. Sample answer: A flower bud is protected by sepals. The petals of a flower attract pollinators. The pistil of a flower is often found at the center of the flower. The ovary of a flower protects the ovules and develops into a fruit.

3. c

4. a

5. Sample answer: Xylem transports water and nutrients from the roots to the shoots. Phloem transports food molecules throughout the plant.

6. Sample answer: A leaf often has two middle layers. The cells of the palisade layer have many chloroplasts. The spongy layer lies beneath the palisade layer and includes the xylem and phloem.

7. Sample answer: Stems support the plant body, transport materials between the root and shoot systems, and store materials.

8. Herbaceous stems are soft, thin, and flexible. Woody stems are rigid and made of wood and bark.

9. Sample answer: Flowers are used for floral arrangements. Some flowers can be eaten, used to make tea, or used as spices. Flowers are also used in perfumes, lotions, and shampoos.

10. Sample answer: A taproot system has one main root, the taproot. Taproots may grow very deep to reach water and minerals. They also hold the plant in the soil. Taproots can also store surplus food, as carrot plants do. A fibrous root system has several roots of a similar size that spread out from the base of the plant. Fibrous roots may absorb water from the soil surface. Fibrous roots spread out from the stem and hold the plant in place. They also store some surplus food.

11. Sample answer: Pampas grass flowers are pollinated by the wind. They don't have brightly colored petals to attract pollinators, nor do they have a fragrance. Also, they are at the top of a tall stem where they might best catch the wind.

12. 6 trees

13. $5 \times 71 = 355$; $3 \times 68 = 204$; $355 + 204 + 73 = 632$; $632 \div 9 = 70.2$ years

CHAPTER RESOURCES

Chapter Resource File

- Section Quiz GENERAL
- Section Review GENERAL
- Vocabulary and Section Summary GENERAL
- Critical Thinking ADVANCED

Technology

Transparencies
- The Structure of a Flower

Model-Making Lab

Build a Flower

Teacher's Notes

Time Required
One 45-minute class period

Lab Ratings
EASY ————————————→ HARD

Teacher Prep △
Student Set-Up △△
Concept Level △△
Clean Up △

MATERIALS
The materials listed on the student page include enough supplies for one student or group of students.

Safety Caution
Remind students to review all safety cautions and icons before beginning this lab activity.

Model-Making Lab

OBJECTIVES

Build a model of a flower.

Explain how the model represents an actual flower.

Describe the basic parts of a flower.

MATERIALS

- art materials such as colored paper, pipe cleaners, beads, and yarn
- card, index, 3 × 5 in.
- glue
- recycled items such as paper plates and cups, yogurt containers, wire, string, buttons, cardboard, and bottles
- scissors
- tape

SAFETY

Build a Flower

Scientists often make models in the laboratory. Models help scientists understand processes and structures. Models are especially useful when scientists are trying to understand processes that are too small to be seen easily, such as pollination, or processes that are too large to be examined in a laboratory, such as the growth of a tree. Models also make it possible to examine the structures of objects, such as flowers.

In this activity, you will use your creativity and your understanding of the structure of a flower to make a model of a flower from recycled materials and art supplies.

Procedure

1. Draw a flower similar to the one shown in the figure below. This flower has both male and female parts. Not all flowers have this structure. The flowers of many species of plants have only male parts or only female parts, not both.

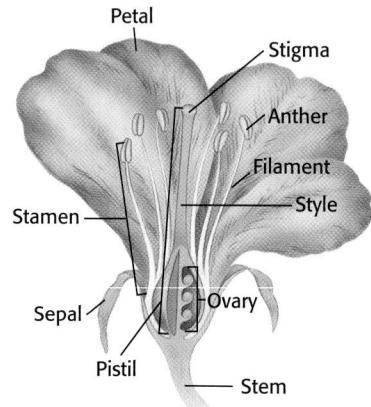

2. Decide which materials you will use to represent each flower part. Then, build a three-dimensional model of a flower that looks like one of the flowers shown on the next page. The model you build should contain each of the following parts: stem, sepals, petals, stamens (anther and filament), and pistil (stigma, style, and ovary).

Jane Lemons
Western Rockingham Middle School
Madison, North Carolina

CHAPTER RESOURCES

Chapter Resource File

- Datasheet for Chapter Lab
- Lab Notes and Answers

Technology

Classroom Videos
- Lab Video

LabBook

- Leaf Me Alone!
- Travelin' Seeds

Lily

Tulip

Hibiscus

3 After you build your model, draw a key for your flower model on an index card. Label each of the structures represented on your flower.

Analyze the Results

1 **Organizing Data** List the structures of a flower, and explain the function of each part.

2 **Identifying Patterns** What is the outermost part of your flower? the innermost part of your flower?

3 **Analyzing Data** How are your flower model and an actual flower alike? How are they different?

Draw Conclusions

4 **Drawing Conclusions** How might your flower attract pollinators? What modifications could you make to your flower to attract a greater number of pollinators?

5 **Evaluating Models** Is your model an accurate representation of a flower? Why or why not?

6 **Making Predictions** If you based your flower model on a plant species that had flowers that did not have both male and female parts, how would that model be different from your current model?

Applying Your Data

Research flowering plants whose flowers do not have both male and female reproductive parts. Build models of the male flower and the female flower for one of these flowering plants. Then, compare the new models to your original model, which includes both male and female reproductive parts.

CHAPTER RESOURCES

Workbooks

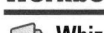 **Whiz-Bang Demonstrations**
• Inner Life of a Leaf ADVANCED

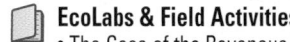 **EcoLabs & Field Activities**
• The Case of the Ravenous Radish GENERAL

Long-Term Projects & Research Ideas
• Plant Planet ADVANCED

Applying Your Data

Students should demonstrate an understanding of how flowers with both male and female parts differ from flowers with only male or only female parts. Students' models should reflect this understanding. Some students may also note that in some species, both male and female flowers can be found on one plant, but in other species, they are found on different plants.

Analyze the Results

1. **petal:** the often colorful leaf-shaped part of a flower that attracts pollinators

   sepal: the modified leaves that form the base of the flower and that enclose and protect the bud before the flower opens

   stem: the main stalk of the plant from which leaves, flowers, and fruits develop; water and nutrients move through the stem between the leaves and roots

   pistil: the female reproductive structure of a flower

   stigma: the upper tip of the pistil, which receives pollen

   style: the stalklike part of the pistil between the stigma and ovary

   ovary: the enlarged part of the pistil in which ovules are formed

   stamen: the male reproductive structure of flowers

   anther: the top of the stamen that produces pollen

   filament: the threadlike part of the stamen that holds the anther

2. sepals; pistil

3. Sample answer: My flower model and an actual flower have the same parts: sepals, petals, stamens, and pistils. Unlike real flowers, my flower cannot be pollinated, nor can it produce seeds.

Draw Conclusions

4. Sample answer: My flower will attract pollinators because it has bright petals. I could give my flower a fragrance to attract more pollinators.

5. Sample answer: My flower is accurate in appearance, but it is not accurate in function. My model looks like a flower, but it cannot be pollinated or fertilized.

6. Sample answer: My flower would have only stamen or only pistils if it were modeled after a plant that had flowers without both male and female parts.

Assignment Guide

SECTION	QUESTIONS
1	5, 9, 11–12, 14, 19
2	3, 13
3	7
4	1–2, 4, 6, 8, 10, 16–18, 20, 22–25
1 and 4	21
2 and 3	15

ANSWERS

Using Key Terms

1. stamen
2. Xylem
3. rhizome
4. pollen
5. nonvascular plant
6. Phloem

Understanding Key Ideas

7. a
8. d
9. a
10. a
11. Plants make their own food by photosynthesis. Plants also have cuticles. Plant cells have rigid cell walls. Plants have a two-stage life cycle.
12. nonvascular plants, seedless vascular plants, gymnosperms, and angiosperms
13. Mosses, liverworts, and hornworts are nonvascular plants. Ferns, horsetails, and club mosses are seedless vascular plants.

Complete each of the following sentences by choosing the correct term from the word bank.

pistil   rhizoid
vascular plant   rhizome
xylem   phloem
pollen   stamen
nonvascular plant

1. A ___ is the male part of a flower.

2. ___ transports water and nutrients through a plant.

3. An underground stem that produces new leaves and roots is called a ___.

4. The male gametophytes of flowers are contained in structures called ___.

5. A ___ does not have specialized tissues for transporting water.

6. ___ transports food through a plant.

Multiple Choice

7. Which of the following statements about angiosperms is NOT true?
   a. Their seeds are protected by cones.
   b. They produce seeds.
   c. They provide animals with food.
   d. They have flowers.

8. Roots
   a. supply water and nutrients.
   b. anchor and support a plant.
   c. store surplus food.
   d. All of the above

9. Which of the following statements about plants and green algae is true?
   a. Plants and green algae may have a common ancestor.
   b. Green algae are plants.
   c. Plants and green algae have cuticles.
   d. None of the above

10. In which part of a leaf does most photosynthesis take place?
    a. palisade layer   c. xylem
    b. phloem   d. epidermis

Short Answer

11. List four characteristics that all plants share.

12. List the four main groups of plants.

13. Name three nonvascular plants and three seedless vascular plants.

14. Why do scientists think green algae and plants have a common ancestor?

15. How are seedless plants, gymnosperms, and angiosperms important to the environment?

16. What are two advantages that seeds have over spores?

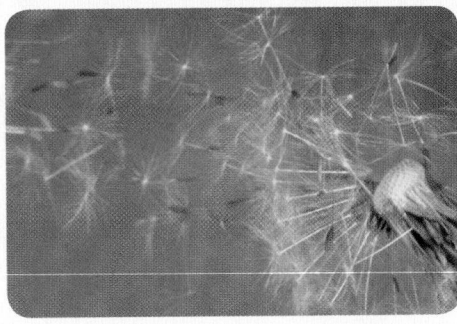

14. Sample answer: Plants and green algae have many similarities, so scientists think they are related. Both have the same kind of chlorophyll and cell walls. Both store food in the form of starch, and both have a two-stage life cycle.

15. Sample answer: Nonvascular plants are often the first plants to live in a new environment. They form a thin layer of soil, to which seedless vascular plants add. Seedless plants also prevent soil erosion. Gymnosperms are often found in gardens and parks, and angiosperms provide most of the food that animals need to survive.

16. Sample answer: When the young plant begins to grow, it can use stored food in the seed. Spores do not have stored food to help a plant grow. Another advantage is that seeds can be spread by animals, while spores are spread by wind. Animals spread seeds more efficiently than the wind spreads spores.

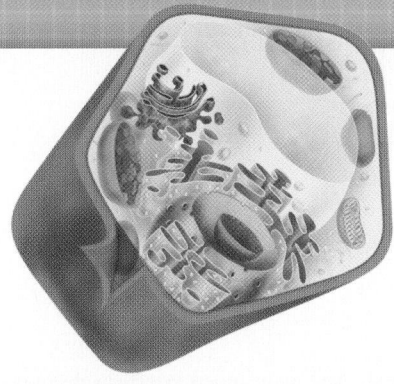

CRITICAL THINKING

17 **Concept Mapping** Use the following terms to create a concept map: *flowers, pollen, stamens, ovaries, pistils, stigmas, filaments, anthers, ovules, petals,* and *sepals.*

18 **Making Comparisons** Imagine that a seed and a spore are beginning to grow in a deep, dark crack in a rock. Which of the two is more likely to grow into an adult plant? Explain your answer.

19 **Identifying Relationships** Grass flowers do not have strong fragrances or bright colors. How might these characteristics be related to the way by which grass flowers are pollinated?

20 **Analyzing Ideas** Plants that are pollinated by wind produce more pollen than plants pollinated by animals do. Why might wind-pollinated plants produce more pollen?

21 **Applying Concepts** A scientist discovered a new plant. The plant has vascular tissue and produces seeds. It has brightly colored and strongly scented flowers. It also has sweet fruits. Based on this information, which of the four main types of plants did the scientist discover? How is the plant most likely pollinated? How does the plant most likely spread its seeds?

INTERPRETING GRAPHICS

22 Look at the cross section of a woody stem below. Use the diagram to determine the age of the tree.

Use the diagram of the flower below to answer the questions that follow.

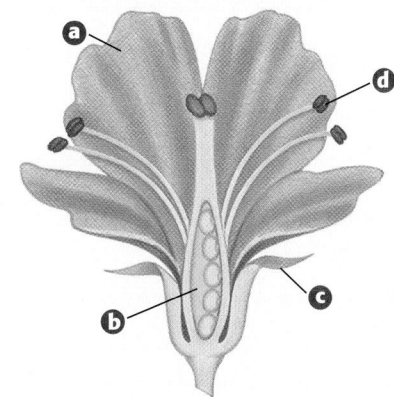

23 Which letter corresponds to the structure in which pollen is produced? What is the name of this structure?

24 Which letter corresponds to the structure that contains the ovules? What is the name of this structure?

25 Which letter corresponds to the structure that protects the flower bud? What is the name of this structure?

 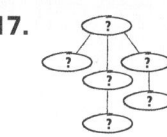

Standardized Test Preparation

Standardized Test Preparation

Teacher's Note

To provide practice under more realistic testing conditions, give students 20 minutes to answer all of the questions in this Standardized Test Preparation.

Answers to the standardized test preparation can help you identify student misconceptions and misunderstandings.

READING

Passage 1

1. B
2. H
3. B

 TEST DOCTOR

Question 2: Some students may think the word *species* refers to DNA or genes because members of a species share similar genes and DNA. However, this fact is not in the passage. As the word *species* is used in the passage, it can only mean "group of organisms."

Question 3: Some students may select answer D, but the two items in this answer are part of a single process, not two. Bacteria and a gene gun are the two distinct means of introducing new DNA discussed in the passage. Fungi are not mentioned in the passage.

READING

Read each of the passages below. Then, answer the questions that follow each passage.

Passage 1 Through genetic engineering, scientists are now able to duplicate one organism's DNA and place a certain gene from the DNA into the cells of another <u>species</u> of plant or animal. This technology enables scientists to give plants and animals a new trait that can then be passed on to future generations. There are two methods to introduce new DNA into plant cells. In one method, DNA is first placed inside a special bacterium, which carries the DNA into the plant cell. In the second method, microscopic particles of metal are coated with the new DNA and fired into the plant cells with a device called a *gene gun*.

1. Based on the passage, what does genetic engineering allow scientists to do?
   A to breed better plants
   B to move genes from one organism to another
   C to see a very small object without a microscope
   D to grow plants without soil

2. In the passage, what does the word *species* most likely mean?
   F DNA
   G future generations
   H group of organisms
   I genes

3. Based on the passage, what are the two most common ways genes are moved to plant cells?
   A by bacteria and fungi
   B by bacteria and a gene gun
   C by fungi and a gene gun
   D by particles of metal and a gene gun

Passage 2 The main function of leaves is photosynthesis, or the production of food. However, some leaves have functions other than photosynthesis. For example, the leaves on a cactus plant are modified as spines. These spines discourage animals from eating the cactus. The leaves of another plant, the sundew, are modified to catch insects. Sundews live in areas with nitrogen-poor soil. They don't get enough nitrogen from the soil to meet their needs. So, the plants use their modified leaves to catch insects. Then, the sundews digest the insects to get the nitrogen they need to survive.

1. Based on the passage, which of the following statements about photosynthesis is true?
   A Photosynthesis produces modified leaves.
   B Photosynthesis is how plants catch insects for food.
   C Photosynthesis discourages animals from eating plants.
   D Photosynthesis is how plants get food.

2. Based on the passage, what do the modified leaves of cactuses do?
   F They discourage animals from eating them.
   G They catch insects for nitrogen.
   H They function mainly for photosynthesis.
   I They help cactuses get enough nitrogen from the soil.

3. Based on the passage, what can be concluded about pitcher plants if they capture insects?
   A They grow in areas with nitrogen-poor soil.
   B They are trying to discourage animals from eating them.
   C They don't need nitrogen from insects to survive.
   D They have leaves that are modified as spines.

Passage 2

1. D
2. F
3. A

 TEST DOCTOR

Question 2: Some students may think that the modified leaves of cactuses catch insects, function for photosynthesis, or help the plants get enough nitrogen. Although all of these things are mentioned in the passage, the spines of cactuses are not designed to catch insects, nor do they contain chlorophyll for photosynthesis. In the passage, sundews need nitrogen from insects, but cactuses are not described as needing nitrogen from insects.

The pie graph below shows the distribution of four types of plants. Use the pie graph below to answer the questions that follow.

Distribution of Plants

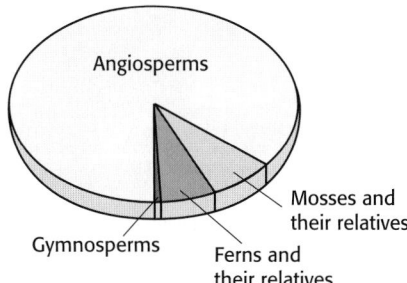

1. Which of the following types of plants is the least common?
   A ferns and their relatives
   B mosses and their relatives
   C angiosperms
   D gymnosperms

2. About what percentage of plants are angiosperms?
   F 1%
   G 10%
   H 20%
   I 80%

3. About what percentage of plants are mosses, ferns, and their relatives?
   A 1%
   B 10%
   C 20%
   D 80%

4. If there are about 265,000 species of plants, about how many of the species are mosses and relatives of mosses?
   F 2,650 species
   G 13,250 species
   H 26,500 species
   I 212,000 species

Read each question below, and choose the best answer.

1. Sophie wants to plant a garden. Her garden is 25 m wide. She puts a row of plants every half meter. Every fifth row is a row of flowers. If the rest of the rows are vegetables, about how many rows of vegetables are in the garden?
   A 10 rows
   B 25 rows
   C 40 rows
   D 50 rows

2. The area of a garden is 50 m². If the garden is 12 m long, which of the following equations expresses the value of w, the width of the garden?
   F $w = 12 \times 50$
   G $w = 50 \times 12$
   H $w = 50 \div 12$
   I $w = 12 \div 12$

3. There are 140 species of cycads. If 18% of gymnosperms are cycads, about how many gymnosperms are there?
   A 25 gymnosperms
   B 165 gymnosperms
   C 775 gymnosperms
   D 2,520 gymnosperms

4. A packet of cabbage seeds that contains enough seeds for two rows costs $2.00. A packet of carrots that contains enough seeds for three rows costs $2.25. If Katy wants to plant five rows of cabbage and seven rows of carrots, how much will the seeds cost?
   F $12.75
   G $12.00
   H $8.50
   I $6.00

Standardized Test Preparation

1. D
2. I
3. C
4. H

TEST DOCTOR

Question 3: Some students may think that the answer to this question is 10%. However, the question asks for both mosses and their relatives and ferns and their relatives. Together, these two groups comprise about 20% of plants.

1. C
2. H
3. C
4. F

TEST DOCTOR

Question 1: Some students may answer 50 rows if they don't notice that every fifth row in the garden is flowers. Other students may answer 10 rows if they calculate the number of rows of flowers instead of the rows of vegetables. Some students may answer 25 rows because the number 25 appears in the question. However, 40 rows is the best answer. You may want to diagram this problem on the board to help students understand it.

Question 3: Some students may answer 25 gymnosperms if they calculate 18% of 140. Other students will answer 165 gymnosperms if they multiply 140 by 1.18. Some students will answer 2,520 if they multiply 140 by 18. However, to find the total number of gymnosperms, students should divide 140 by 0.18, which yields 778. So, the best answer is 775 gymnosperms.

CHAPTER RESOURCES

Chapter Resource File

 • Standardized Test Preparation GENERAL

State Resources

 For specific resources for your state, visit **go.hrw.com** and type in the keyword **HSMSTR**.

Science in Action

Scientific Debate

Background

The risks of taking herbal supplements can increase when supplements contain more than one ingredient. Steve Bechler, a 23-year-old minor-league baseball player, was a regular user of a weight-loss dietary supplement containing ephedra and caffeine. During spring training with the Baltimore Orioles in 2003, Bechler collapsed and died. After his death, minor league baseball joined professional and college football in banning ephedra use by its athletes.

Science, Technology, and Society

ACTiViTY ——— GENERAL

Have students research plant poaching in your area. Have them identify which plants are being stolen and why, and have them identify steps being taken to control poaching. Ask students to contact local park managers or state and federal natural resources agencies, such as the National Park Service. Other sources of information include the Internet, newspapers, and magazines. Students should makes posters about their findings, including pictures of the plants that poachers steal and a description of the plants' habitats.

Scientific Debate

Are Herbal Supplements Safe?

Humans have always used plants for food, for shelter, or for medicine. In fact, one of our most common medicines, aspirin, is similar to a chemical found in the bark of a willow tree. Today, many people still use natural plant products, such as pills or teas, as medicine. These products are often called *herbal supplements*. Echinacea, St. John's wort, and ma huang are just a few examples of the herbal supplements that people use to treat a variety of health problems. People spend billions of dollars on herbal supplements each year. But are herbal supplements safe to use?

Social Studies ACTiViTY

Make a poster illustrating a plant used for medicine by native cultures and the health problems the plant is used to treat.

Science, Technology, and Society

Plant Poachers

Imagine you're walking through a swamp. The swamp is full of life. You're surrounded by trees, vines, and water lilies. You can hear frogs singing and mosquitoes buzzing. Then, you notice a ghost orchid hanging from a tree branch. The flower of this orchid looks like a ghost or like a white frog leaping. For some people, this orchid is worth stealing. These people, called *plant poachers*, steal orchids and other plants from the wild. Many plant species and natural areas are threatened by plant theft.

Math ACTiViTY

A plant poacher stole 100 plants from a nature preserve. He planned on selling each plant for $50, but he was caught and was fined $300 for each plant he stole. What is the difference between the total fine and the total amount of money the plant poacher planned on selling the plants for?

Answer to Social Studies Activity

Students should demonstrate an understanding of the medicinal uses of plants by native cultures in places such as South America and Asia. Students may also research traditional plant use by Native Americans from North America and by ancient Europeans. Posters should include comprehensive information about the plant, how it is used, and what it is used to treat. Some students may also include information about the effectiveness of the plant.

Answer to Math Activity

$25,000 (100 × $50 = $5,000; 100 × $300 = $30,000; $30,000 − $5,000 = $25,000)

Careers

Paul Cox

Ethnobotanist Paul Cox is an ethnobotanist. He travels to remote places to look for plants that can help treat diseases. He seeks the advice of native healers in his search. In Samoan cultures, the healer is one of the most valued members of the community. In 1984, Cox met a 78-year-old Samoan healer named Epenesa. Epenesa understood human anatomy, and she dispensed medicines with great accuracy.

After Cox spent months observing Epenesa, she gave him her treatment for yellow fever. Cox brought the yellow-fever remedy to the United States. In 1986, researchers at the National Cancer Institute found that the plant contains a virus-fighting chemical called *prostratin*, which may have potential as a treatment for AIDS.

When two of the Samoan healers that Cox observed died in 1993, generations of medical knowledge was lost with them. The healers' deaths show the urgency of recording this knowledge before all of the healers are gone. Cox and other ethnobotanists work hard to gather knowledge from healers before their knowledge is lost.

Language Arts ACTIVITY

WRITING SKILL Imagine that you are a healer. Write a letter to an ethnobotanist describing some of the plants you use to treat diseases.

go.hrw.com
To learn more about these Science in Action topics, visit **go.hrw.com** and type in the keyword **HL5PL1F.**

Current Science
Check out Current Science® articles related to this chapter by visiting go.hrw.com. Just type in the keyword **HL5CS12.**

Careers

Background
Some biologists estimate that there are 235,000 species of flowering plants in the world. Of these, less than half of 1% have been studied for their potential medicinal qualities. Because there are so many species, efficient strategies are necessary to find the plants most likely to have medicinal value. One strategy used by ethnobotanists is to assume that if native people use a local plant for medicine, then the plant probably has some medicinal value. Many ethnobotanists seek out native healers or shamans. Ethnobotanists hope to acquire the knowledge that has taken the shamans years to accumulate. With these insights, the researchers can then decide which plants they should collect and study.

Some of the most useful drugs developed from plants used by indigenous peoples include aspirin, for reducing pain and inflammation; codeine, for decreasing pain and suppressing coughs; and quinine, for combating malaria.

Answer to Language Arts Activity
In their letters, students should demonstrate an understanding of how important native healers are to ethnobotanists. Students should also demonstrate an understanding of the fact that although native cultures may seem primitive, the knowledge that many native healers have is actually very sophisticated. In some cases, this knowledge may rival that of modern medicine.

Plant Processes
Chapter Planning Guide

Compression guide:
To shorten instruction because of time limitations, omit Section 3.

OBJECTIVES	LABS, DEMONSTRATIONS, AND ACTIVITIES	TECHNOLOGY RESOURCES
PACING • 135 min pp. 330–335 **Chapter Opener**	**SE** Start-up Activity, p. 331 `GENERAL`	**OSP** Parent Letter ■ `GENERAL` **CD** Student Edition on CD-ROM **CD** Guided Reading Audio CD ▨ **TR** Chapter Starter Transparency* **VID** Brain Food Video Quiz
Section 1 Photosynthesis • Describe photosynthesis. • Compare photosynthesis and cellular respiration. • Describe how gas is exchanged in the leaves of plants. • Describe two ways in which photosynthesis is important.	**TE** Group Activity Modeling Molecules, p. 333 `GENERAL` **SE** Connection to Chemistry Transpiration, p. 334 `GENERAL` **SE** Skills Practice Lab Food Factory Waste, p. 344 `GENERAL` **CRF** Datasheet for Chapter Lab* **SE** Skills Practice Lab Weepy Weeds, p. 777 `GENERAL` **CRF** Datasheet for LabBook* **LB** Calculator-Based Labs Power of the Sun* `ADVANCED`	**CRF** Lesson Plans* **TR** Bellringer Transparency* **TR** Photosynthesis* **TR** Gas Exchange in Leaves* **TR** *LINK TO PHYSICAL SCIENCE* Balancing a Chemical Equation* **VID** Lab Videos for Life Science
PACING • 45 min pp. 336–339 **Section 2 Reproduction of Flowering Plants** • Describe pollination and fertilization in flowering plants. • Explain how fruits and seeds are formed from flowers. • List three reasons why a seed might be dormant. • List three examples of asexual reproduction in plants.	**TE** Demonstration Parts of a Flower, p. 336 `GENERAL` **TE** Group Activity Concept Mapping, p. 337 `ADVANCED` **TE** Activity Germination, p. 337 `BASIC` **TE** Connection Activity Art, p. 337 `ADVANCED` **SE** Quick Lab Thirsty Seeds, p. 338 `GENERAL` **CRF** Datasheet for Quick Lab* **LB** Labs You Can Eat Not Just Another Nut* `GENERAL`	**CRF** Lesson Plans* **TR** Bellringer Transparency* **TR** Pollination and Fertilization* **TR** Seed Production*
PACING • 45 min pp. 340–343 **Section 3 Plant Responses to the Environment** • Describe how plants may respond to light and gravity. • Explain how some plants respond to night length. • Describe how some plants respond to changes of season.	**SE** School-to-Home Activity Earth's Orbit and the Seasons, p. 342 `GENERAL` **SE** Science in Action Math, Social Studies, and Language Arts Activities, pp. 350–351 `GENERAL` **LB** EcoLabs & Field Activities Recycle! Make Your Own Paper* `GENERAL` **LB** Long-Term Projects & Research Ideas Plant Partners* `ADVANCED` **LB** Calculator-Based Labs What Causes the Seasons?* `ADVANCED`	**CRF** Lesson Plans* **TR** Bellringer Transparency* **TR** Night Length and Blooming; Amount of Pigment Based on Season* **SE** Internet Activity, p. 341 `GENERAL` **CRF** SciLinks Activity* `GENERAL` **CD** Interactive Explorations CD-ROM How's It Growing? `GENERAL`

PACING • 90 min

CHAPTER REVIEW, ASSESSMENT, AND STANDARDIZED TEST PREPARATION

CRF Vocabulary Activity* `GENERAL`
SE Chapter Review, pp. 346–347 `GENERAL`
CRF Chapter Review* ■ `GENERAL`
CRF Chapter Tests A* ■ `GENERAL`, B* `ADVANCED`, C* `SPECIAL NEEDS`
SE Standardized Test Preparation, pp. 348–349 `GENERAL`
CRF Standardized Test Preparation* `GENERAL`
CRF Performance-Based Assessment* `GENERAL`
OSP Test Generator `GENERAL`
CRF Test Item Listing* `GENERAL`

Online and Technology Resources

Visit **go.hrw.com** for a variety of free resources related to this textbook. Enter the keyword **HL5PL2.**

Students can access interactive problem-solving help and active visual concept development with the *Holt Science and Technology* Online Edition available at **www.hrw.com.**

 Guided Reading Audio CD
Also in Spanish

A direct reading of each chapter for auditory learners, reluctant readers, and Spanish-speaking students.

 Science Tutor CD-ROM

Excellent for remediation and test practice.

SKILLS DEVELOPMENT RESOURCES	SECTION REVIEW AND ASSESSMENT	STANDARDS CORRELATIONS
SE Pre-Reading Activity, p. 330 `GENERAL` **OSP Science Puzzlers, Twisters & Teasers** `GENERAL`		National Science Education Standards UCP 1, 2, 5; SAI 1, 2; LS 1c, 3a, 3b
CRF Directed Reading A* ■ `BASIC`, **B*** `SPECIAL NEEDS` **CRF Vocabulary and Section Summary*** ■ `GENERAL` **SE Reading Strategy** Discussion, p. 332 `GENERAL` **SE Connection to Social Studies** Sugar, p. 333 `GENERAL` **TE Inclusion Strategies,** p. 333 **CRF Reinforcement Worksheet** A Leaf's Work Is Never Done* `BASIC` **MS Math Skills for Science** Balancing Chemical Equations* `GENERAL`	**SE Reading Checks,** pp. 332, 335 `GENERAL` **TE Reteaching,** p. 334 `BASIC` **TE Quiz,** p. 334 `GENERAL` **TE Alternative Assessment,** p. 334 `GENERAL` **SE Section Review,*** p. 335 ■ `GENERAL` **CRF Section Quiz*** ■ `GENERAL`	UCP 1, 2, 3, 4, 5; SAI 1, 2; SPSP 3; HNS 1, 2; LS 1a, 1c, 3c, 4c; *LabBook:* UCP 2, 3, 5; SAI 1, 2; LS 3a; *Chapter Lab:* UCP 2, 3, 5; SAI 1, 2; LS 1c, 1d, 3a, 4c
CRF Directed Reading A* ■ `BASIC`, **B*** `SPECIAL NEEDS` **CRF Vocabulary and Section Summary*** ■ `GENERAL` **SE Reading Strategy** Reading Organizer, p. 336 `GENERAL` **CRF Reinforcement Worksheet** Fertilizing Flowers* `BASIC`	**SE Reading Checks,** pp. 337, 338 `GENERAL` **TE Reteaching,** p. 338 `BASIC` **TE Quiz,** p. 338 `GENERAL` **TE Alternative Assessment,** p. 338 `GENERAL` **SE Section Review,*** p. 339 ■ `GENERAL` **CRF Section Quiz*** ■ `GENERAL`	UCP 2, 3, 4, 5; SAI 1, 2; SPSP 4; HNS 1; LS 1a, 2a, 2b, 2d, 5b
CRF Directed Reading A* ■ `BASIC`, **B*** `SPECIAL NEEDS` **CRF Vocabulary and Section Summary*** ■ `GENERAL` **SE Reading Strategy** Discussion, p. 340 `GENERAL` **SE Math Practice** Bending by Degrees, p. 341 `GENERAL` **TE Inclusion Strategies,** p. 342 **CRF Reinforcement Worksheet** How Plants Respond to Change* `BASIC` **CRF Critical Thinking** Space Plants* `ADVANCED`	**SE Reading Checks,** pp. 340, 341, 342 `GENERAL` **TE Homework,** p. 341 `ADVANCED` **TE Reteaching,** p. 342 `BASIC` **SE Section Review,*** p. 343 ■ `GENERAL` **TE Quiz,** p. 343 `GENERAL` **TE Alternative Assessment,** p. 343 `GENERAL` **CRF Section Quiz*** ■ `GENERAL`	UCP 1, 2, 3; SAI 1, 2; SPSP 2, 3, 5; HNS 2; LS 2b, 2c, 3a, 3c, 3d, 5b

One-Stop Planner® CD-ROM

This convenient CD-ROM includes:
- Lab Materials QuickList Software
- Holt Calendar Planner
- Customizable Lesson Plans
- Printable Worksheets
- ExamView® Test Generator

cnnstudentnews.com

Find the latest news, lesson plans, and activities related to important scientific events.

www.scilinks.org

Maintained by the **National Science Teachers Association.** See Chapter Enrichment pages for a complete list of topics.

Current Science®

Check out *Current Science* articles and activities by visiting the HRW Web site at **go.hrw.com.** Just type in the keyword **HL5CS13T.**

Classroom Videos
- **Lab Videos** demonstrate the chapter lab.
- **Brain Food Video Quizzes** help students review the chapter material.
- **CNN Videos** bring science into your students' daily life.

Visual Resources

CHAPTER STARTER TRANSPARENCY

Strange but True!

BELLRINGER TRANSPARENCIES

Section: Photosynthesis
Where do you get the energy you need to stay alive? Where do the things you eat get their energy from get their energy? Is there an ultimate source of energy for most life on earth?

Write your response in your **science journal**.

Section: Reproduction of Flowering Plants
What are pollination and fertilization? Draw a diagram in your **science journal** of a flowering plant's reproductive system. Do you think there are plants with only male reproductive parts and plants with only female reproductive parts? Explain your answer.

Write your answers in your **science journal**.

TEACHING TRANSPARENCIES

Photosynthesis

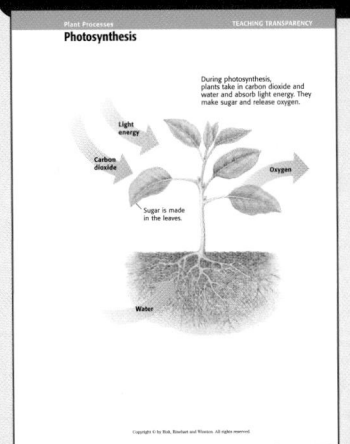

During photosynthesis, plants take in carbon dioxide and water and absorb light energy. They make sugar and release oxygen.

Gas Exchange in Leaves

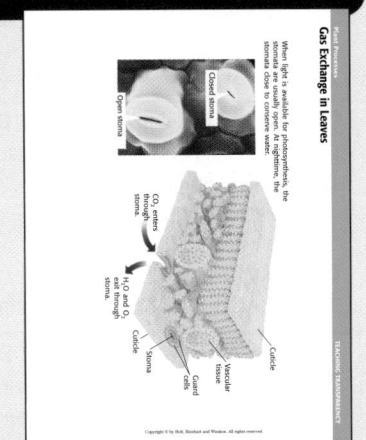

TEACHING TRANSPARENCIES

Seed Production

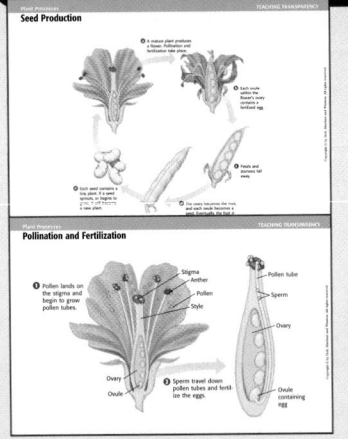

Pollination and Fertilization

Amount of Pigment Based on Season

Night Length and Blooming

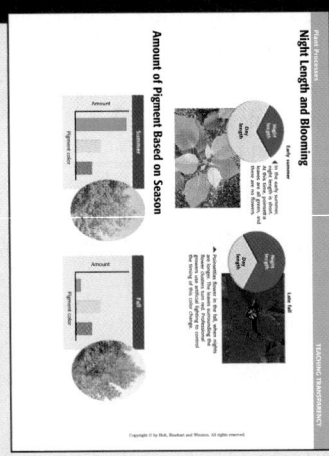

Balancing a Chemical Equation

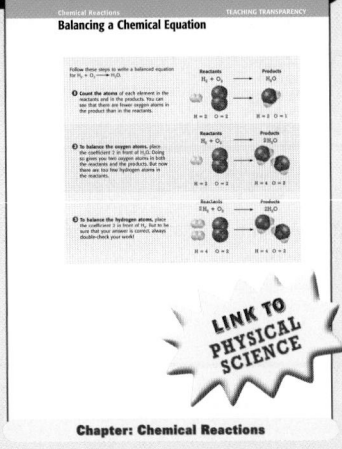

LINK TO PHYSICAL SCIENCE

Chapter: Chemical Reactions

CONCEPT MAPPING TRANSPARENCY

Use the following terms to complete the concept map below: evergreen, plants, stimulus, deciduous, gravitropism, phototropism, seasonal changes

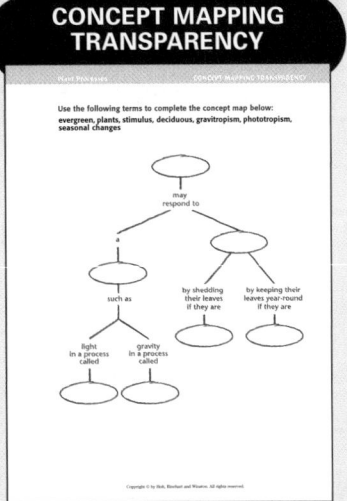

Planning Resources

LESSON PLANS

Lesson Plan   SAMPLE

Section: Waves

Pacing
Regular Schedule: with lab(s):2 days   without lab(s):2 days
Block Schedule: with lab(s):1 1/2 days   without lab(s):1 day

Objectives
1. Relate the seven properties of life to a living organism.
2. Describe seven themes that can help you to organize what you learn about biology.
3. Identify the tiny structures that make up all living organisms.
4. Differentiate between reproduction and heredity and between metabolism and homeostasis.

National Science Education Standards Covered
LSInter6:Cells have particular structures that underlie their functions.
LSMat1:Most cell functions involve chemical reactions.
LSBeh1:Cells store and use information to guide their functions.
UCP1:Cell functions are regulated.
SI1: Cells can differentiate and form complete multicellular organisms.
PS1: Species evolve over time.
ESS1: The great diversity of organisms is the result of more than 3.5 billion years of evolution.
ESS2: Natural selection and its evolutionary consequences provide a scientific explanation for the fossil record of ancient life forms as well as for the striking molecular similarities observed among the diverse species of living organisms.
ST1: The millions of different species of plants, animals, and microorganisms that live on Earth today are related in descent from common ancestors.
ST2: The energy for life primarily comes from the sun.
SPSP1: The complexity and organization of organisms accommodates the need for obtaining, transforming, transporting, releasing, and eliminating the matter and energy used to sustain the organism.
SPSP6: As matter and energy flows through different levels of organization of living systems—cells, organs, communities—and between living systems and the physical environment, chemical elements are recombined in different ways.
HNS1: Organisms have behavioral responses to internal changes and to external stimuli.

PARENT LETTER

SAMPLE

Dear Parent,

Your son's or daughter's science class will soon begin exploring the chapter entitled "The World of Physical Science." In this chapter, students will learn about how the scientific method applies to the world of physical science and the role of physical science in the world. By the end of the chapter, students should demonstrate a clear understanding of the chapter's main ideas and be able to discuss the following topics:

1. physical science as the study of energy and matter (Section 1)
2. the role of physical science in the world around them (Section 1)
3. careers that rely on physical science (Section 1)
4. the steps used in the scientific method (Section 2)
5. examples of technology (Section 2)
6. how the scientific method is used to answer questions and solve problems (Section 2)
7. how our knowledge of science changes over time (Section 2)
8. how models represent real objects or systems (Section 3)
9. examples of different ways models are used in science (Section 3)
10. the importance of the International System of Units (Section 4)
11. the appropriate units to use for particular measurements (Section 4)
12. how area and density are derived quantities (Section 4)

Questions to Ask Along the Way

You can help your son or daughter learn about these topics by asking interesting questions such as the following:

- What are some surprising careers that use physical science?
- What is a characteristic of a good hypothesis?
- When is it a good idea to use a model?
- Why do Americans measure things in terms of inches and yards and meters?

ALSO IN SPANISH

TEST ITEM LISTING

TEST ITEM LISTING
The World of Science   SAMPLE

MULTIPLE CHOICE

1. A limitation of models is that
   a. they are large enough to see.
   b. they do not act exactly like the things that they model.
   c. they are smaller than the things that they model.
   d. they model unfamiliar things.
   Answer: B   Difficulty: 1   Section: 3   Objective: 2

2. The length 10 m is equal to
   a. 100 cm.   c. 10,000 mm.
   b. 1,000 cm.   d. Both (b) and (c)
   Answer: B   Difficulty: 1   Section: 3   Objective: 2

3. To be valid, a hypothesis must be
   a. testable.   c. made into a law.
   b. supported by evidence.   d. Both (a) and (b)
   Answer: B   Difficulty: 1   Section: 3   Objective: 2

4. The statement "Sheila has a stain on her shirt" is an example of a(n)
   a. law.   c. observation.
   b. hypothesis.   d. prediction.
   Answer: B   Difficulty: 1   Section: 3   Objective: 2

5. A hypothesis is often developed out of
   a. observations.   c. laws.
   b. experiments.   d. Both (a) and (b)
   Answer: D   Difficulty: 1   Section: 3   Objective: 2

6. How many milliliters are in 3.5 kL?
   a. 3,500 mL   c. 3,500,000 mL
   b. 0.0035 mL   d. 35,000 mL
   Answer: C   Difficulty: 1   Section: 3   Objective: 2

7. A map of Seattle is an example of a
   a. law.   c. model.
   b. theory.   d. unit.
   Answer: B   Difficulty: 1   Section: 3   Objective: 2

8. A lab has five safety icons shown below. These icons mean that you should wear
   a. only safety goggles.   c. safety goggles and a lab apron.
   b. only a lab apron.   d. safety goggles, a lab apron, and gloves.
   Answer: B   Difficulty: 1   Section: 3   Objective: 2

9. The law of conservation of mass says the lot of mass before a chemical change is
   a. more than the total mass after the change.
   b. less than the total mass after the change.
   c. the same as the total mass after the change.
   d. not the same as the total mass after the change.
   Answer: B   Difficulty: 1   Section: 3   Objective: 2

10. In which of the following areas might you find a geochemist at work?
    a. studying the chemistry of rocks   c. studying fishes
    b. studying forestry   d. studying the atmosphere
    Answer: B   Difficulty: 1   Section: 3   Objective: 2

One-Stop Planner® CD-ROM

This CD-ROM includes all of the resources shown here and the following time-saving tools:

- *Lab Materials QuickList Software*
- *Customizable lesson plans*
- *Holt Calendar Planner*
- *The powerful ExamView® Test Generator*

Meeting Individual Needs

DIRECTED READING A
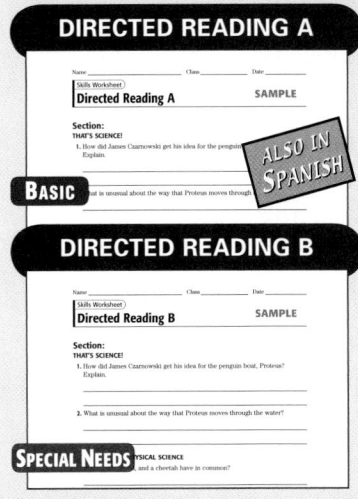

Directed Reading A   SAMPLE

Section:
THAT'S SCIENCE!
1. How did James Czarnowski get his idea for the penguin boat, Proteus? Explain.

ALSO IN SPANISH

BASIC

DIRECTED READING B
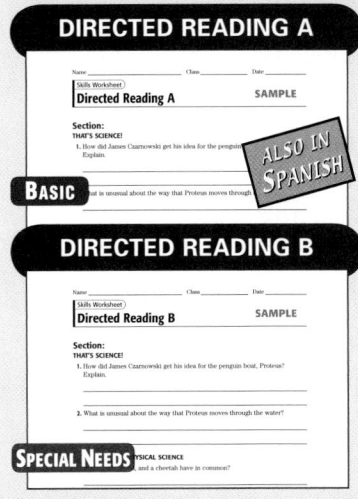

Directed Reading B   SAMPLE

Section:
THAT'S SCIENCE!
1. How did James Czarnowski get his idea for the penguin boat, Proteus? Explain.

2. What is unusual about the way that Proteus moves through the water?

SPECIAL NEEDS

VOCABULARY ACTIVITY
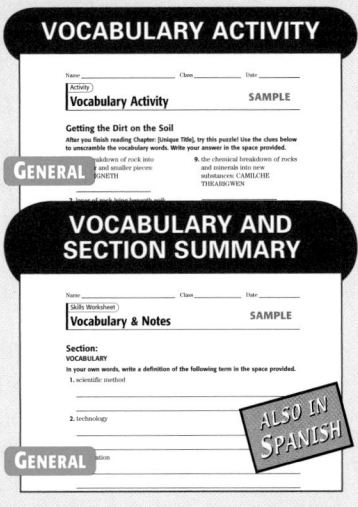

Vocabulary Activity   SAMPLE

Getting the Dirt on the Soil

GENERAL

VOCABULARY AND SECTION SUMMARY
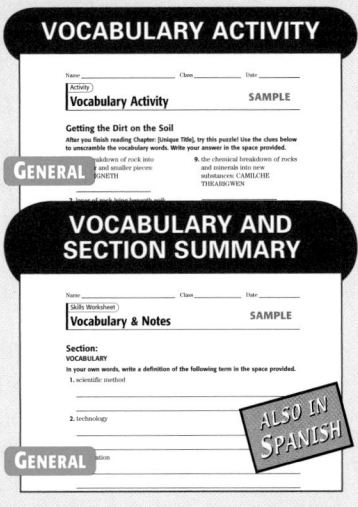

Vocabulary & Notes   SAMPLE

Section:
VOCABULARY
In your own words, write a definition of the following term in the space provided.
1. scientific method

2. technology

ALSO IN SPANISH

GENERAL

REINFORCEMENT
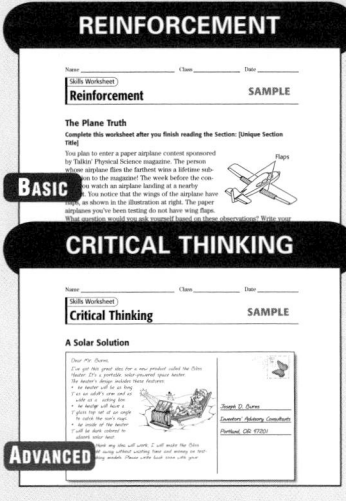

Reinforcement   SAMPLE

The Plane Truth

BASIC

CRITICAL THINKING
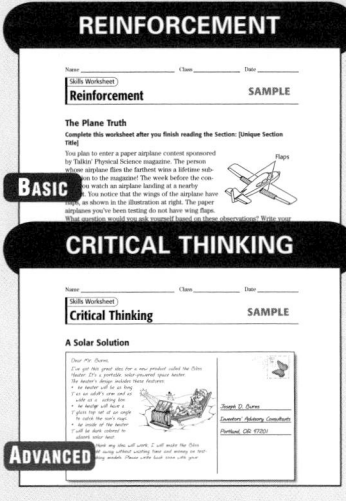

Critical Thinking   SAMPLE

A Solar Solution

ADVANCED

SCILINKS ACTIVITY

SciLinks Activity   SAMPLE

MARINE ECOSYSTEMS

GENERAL

SCIENCE PUZZLERS, TWISTERS & TEASERS

CHAPTER 13   SCIENCE PUZZLERS, TWISTERS & TEASERS
Plant Processes

Greg's Gravitropic Greenhouse Gremlins

a. Mon.
b. Tues.
c. Wed.
d. Thurs.

GENERAL

Labs and Activities

ECOLABS & FIELD ACTIVITIES
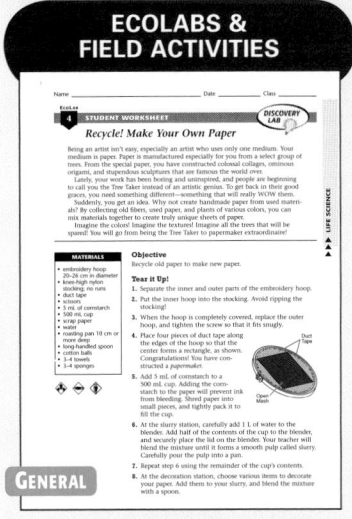

Recycle! Make Your Own Paper

GENERAL

LONG-TERM PROJECTS & RESEARCH IDEAS

PROJECT 13   STUDENT WORKSHEET
Plant Partners

ADVANCED

LABS YOU CAN EAT

LAB 6   STUDENT WORKSHEET
Not Just Another Nut

GENERAL

CALCULATOR-BASED LABS
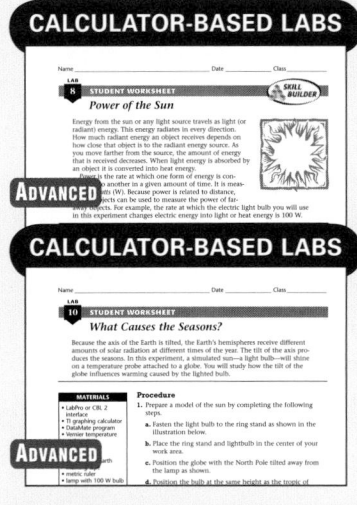

LAB 8   STUDENT WORKSHEET
Power of the Sun

ADVANCED

CALCULATOR-BASED LABS
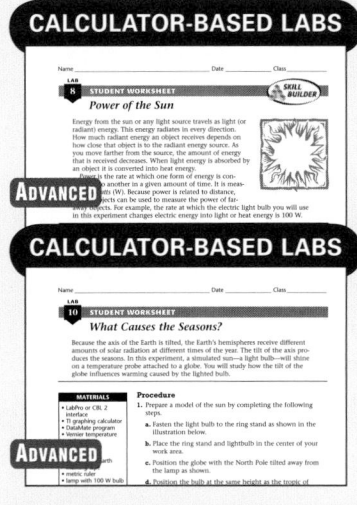

LAB 10   STUDENT WORKSHEET
What Causes the Seasons?

ADVANCED

DATASHEETS FOR QUICK LABS

Quick Lab   DATASHEET FOR QUICK LAB
Reaction to Stress   SAMPLE

DATASHEETS FOR CHAPTER LABS

Skills Practice Lab   DATASHEET FOR CHAPTER LAB
Using Scientific Methods   SAMPLE

Teacher's Notes
TIME REQUIRED
One 45-minute class period.

DATASHEETS FOR LABBOOK

Skills Practice Lab   DATASHEET FOR LABBOOK LAB
Does It All Add Up?   SAMPLE

Teacher's Notes
TIME REQUIRED
One 45-minute class period.

Review and Assessments

SECTION QUIZ
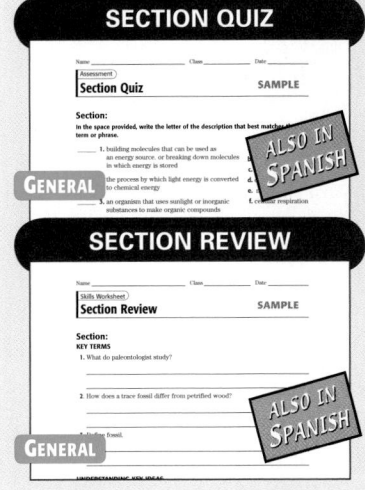

Section Quiz   SAMPLE

ALSO IN SPANISH

GENERAL

SECTION REVIEW
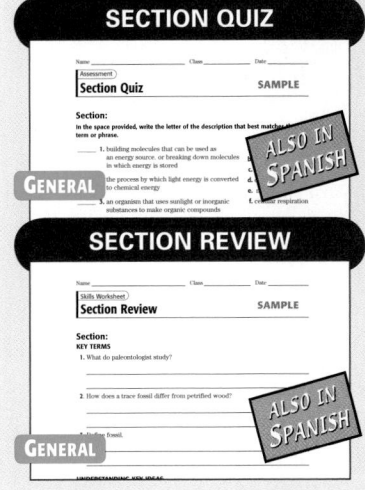

Section Review   SAMPLE

Section:
KEY TERMS
1. What do paleontologist study?

2. How does a trace fossil differ from petrified wood?

ALSO IN SPANISH

GENERAL

CHAPTER REVIEW
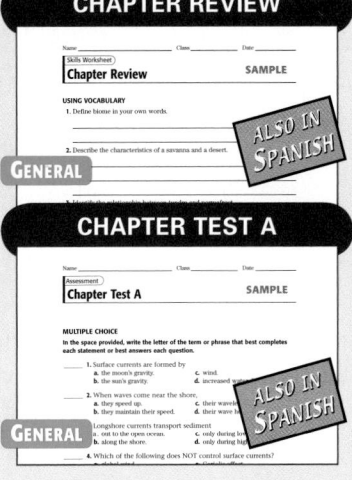

Chapter Review   SAMPLE

USING VOCABULARY
1. Define biome in your own words.

2. Describe the characteristics of a savanna and a desert.

ALSO IN SPANISH

GENERAL

CHAPTER TEST A

Chapter Test A   SAMPLE

MULTIPLE CHOICE
1. Surface currents are formed by
a. the moon's gravity.   c. wind.
b. the sun's gravity.   d. increased water density.
2. When waves come near the shore,
a. they speed up.   c. their wavelength increases.
b. they maintain their speed.   d. their wave height increases.

ALSO IN SPANISH

GENERAL

CHAPTER TEST B
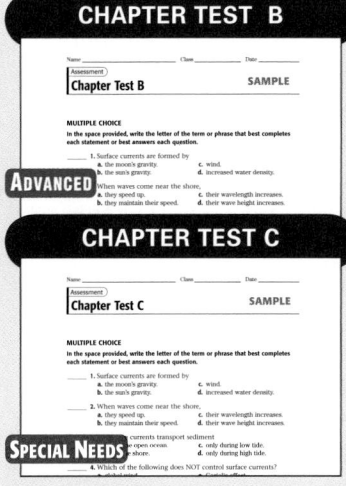

Chapter Test B   SAMPLE

MULTIPLE CHOICE
1. Surface currents are formed by
a. the moon's gravity.   c. wind.
b. the sun's gravity.   d. increased water density.
2. When waves come near the shore,
a. they speed up.   c. their wavelength increases.
b. they maintain their speed.   d. their wave height increases.

ADVANCED

CHAPTER TEST C
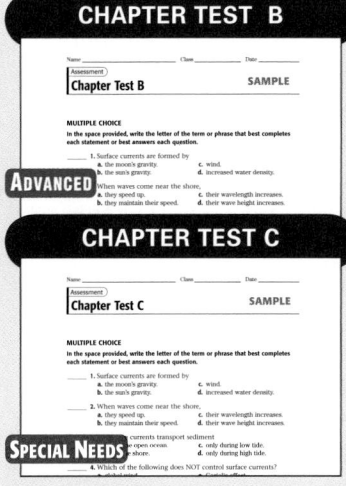

Chapter Test C   SAMPLE

MULTIPLE CHOICE
1. Surface currents are formed by
a. the moon's gravity.   c. wind.
b. the sun's gravity.   d. increased water density.
2. When waves come near the shore,
a. they speed up.   c. their wavelength increases.
b. they maintain their speed.   d. their wave height increases.

SPECIAL NEEDS

STANDARDIZED TEST PREPARATION
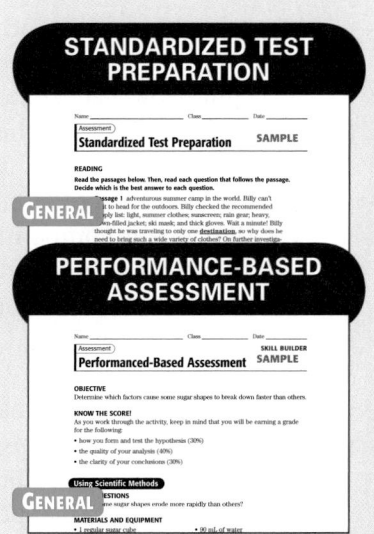

Standardized Test Preparation   SAMPLE

READING

GENERAL

PERFORMANCE-BASED ASSESSMENT
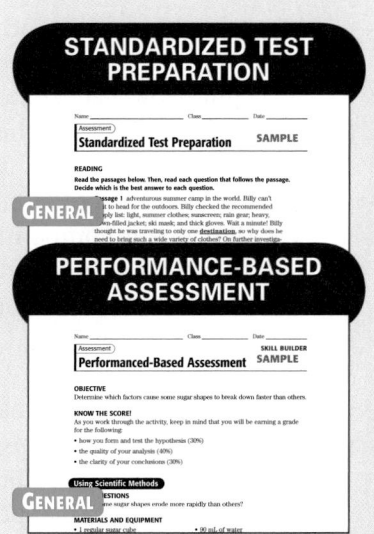

Performanced-Based Assessment   SKILL BUILDER   SAMPLE

OBJECTIVE
Determine which factors cause some sugar shapes to break down faster than others.

GENERAL

This Chapter Enrichment provides relevant and interesting information to expand and enhance your presentation of the chapter material.

Section 1

Photosynthesis

Sunlight

- While sunlight is used for photosynthesis, too much sunlight—specifically, too much ultraviolet radiation—can damage a plant. Ultraviolet radiation damages plant DNA, bleaches leaves yellow, and stunts growth.

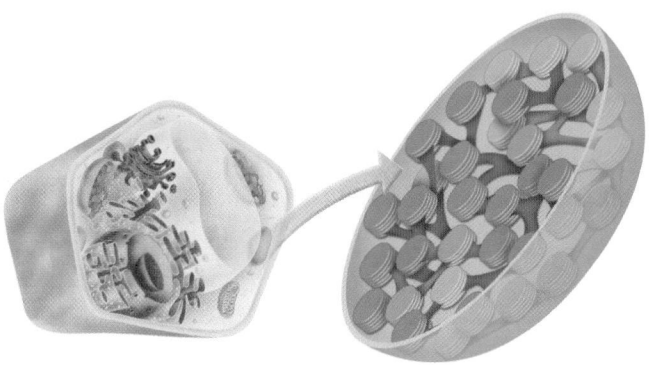

Water

- Water conservation is as important for alpine plants as it is for cactuses. In the Alps, the mountain aven and the mountain kidney vetch have hairlike coverings on their leaves to reduce water loss. These coverings also provide insulation.

Air

- Ozone, O_3, is a gas found in Earth's atmosphere. Ozone in the stratosphere protects Earth from harmful UV light. However, ozone found in the troposphere, or at ground level, can harm plants. Ground-level ozone is a byproduct of a reaction between two types of human-made pollutants—nitrogen oxides and volatile organic compounds. Sunlight and heat facilitate the reaction between these molecules. For this reason, there is often more ground-level ozone on hot days.

- Ground-level ozone damages the leaves of plants. It reduces the yield of crops, stunts the growth of plants, and reduces the survivability of seedlings. Ozone makes some plants more susceptible to disease and pests.

Section 2

Reproduction of Flowering Plants

Vegetative Reproduction

- *Vegetative reproduction* is another term for asexual reproduction in which a piece of a plant grows into a complete plant. For example, each year, tulip bulbs produce one or two new bulbs, which can be broken off the parent plant and used to produce new plants.

- Succulents, such as jade plants, have fleshy leaves full of water. This water sustains the leaves if they fall off the parent plant, often long enough for the leaves to send down roots and develop into new plants.

Is That a Fact!

- ◆ Night-blooming flowers rely on nocturnal animals, such as bats and hawkmoths, to pollinate their flowers. The flowers are usually white for increased visibility and often have a strong fragrance to attract pollinators.

- ◆ The oldest known fossil seeds are approximately 350 million years old, from the late Devonian period. They belong to plants called *seed ferns*.

The Perfect Flower?

- Flowers can be either perfect or imperfect. Perfect flowers have both male parts (stamens) and female parts (pistils). Imperfect flowers have one or the other—stamens or pistils—but not both.

Section 3

Plant Responses to the Environment

Plant Pigments

- In addition to containing the green pigment chlorophyll, plants contain other pigments that account for the colorful changes in autumn leaves. Xanthophylls are yellow, carotenes are yellowish orange, anthocyanins are red and purple, and tannins are brown.

- Carotenes and xanthophylls are always present in leaves. Anthocyanins are synthesized in late summer and autumn. They are not always present in leaves.

- In some years, the autumn colors of leaves—especially reds—are bright and colorful; in other years, they are dull. Two factors affect autumn leaf color: warm, sunny days followed by cool nights and the amount of moisture in the soil contribute to the production of bright colors.

Is That a Fact!

◆ In 2001, the U.S. Department of Agriculture reported that more than 67 million poinsettias (*Euphorbia pulcherrima*) were sold in the United States. Even though poinsettias are sold only during the late fall and early winter, poinsettias are the country's most popular potted plants.

Discovery of Auxins

- Charles Darwin (1809–1882) is credited with making the first recorded observations that led to the discovery of plant hormones called *auxins.* Auxins control the elongation of plant cells. In 1881, Darwin and his son, Francis, described phototropism, the bending of a plant toward a light source. The Darwins placed caps on the growing tips of grass seedlings and noted that the growing tips did not bend. When the caps were removed, the tips bent toward the light source. Other scientists furthered Darwin's research and discovered auxins in the early 1900s.

Is That a Fact!

◆ Plant hormones occur in very small quantities. In a pineapple plant, for example, only 6 μg of auxins are present for 1 kg of plant material. In terms of weight, this is equivalent to a needle in a truckload of hay that weighs 20 metric tons.

SciLINKS **NSTA**

Developed and maintained by the
National Science Teachers Association

SciLinks is maintained by the National Science Teachers Association to provide you and your students with interesting, up-to-date links that will enrich your classroom presentation of the chapter.

Visit www.scilinks.org and enter the SciLinks code for more information about the topic listed.

Topic: Photosynthesis
SciLinks code: HSM1140

Topic: Plant Tropisms
SciLinks code: HSM1166

Topic: Reproduction of Plants
SciLinks code: HSM1295

Topic: Plant Growth
SciLinks code: HSM1159

Overview

Tell students that this chapter will help them learn about photosynthesis, reproduction in flowering plants, and plant responses to the environment. The chapter describes pollination, fertilization, asexual reproduction, and tropisms in plants.

Assessing Prior Knowledge

Students should be familiar with the following topics:

• seed plants

• asexual reproduction

Identifying Misconceptions

Students may have several misconceptions about photosynthesis and the way that plants get energy. First, help students understand that while plants produce glucose during photosynthesis, most of this glucose is immediately converted to sucrose or starch for storage. Then, help students understand that plants produce oxygen as a byproduct of photosynthesis but that plants also need oxygen. Plants use oxygen for cellular respiration, which releases energy from glucose and other food molecules. During this process, plants give off carbon dioxide. This carbon dioxide can exit the plant in the same way that oxygen and water vapor exit the plant—through the stomata.

13

Plant Processes

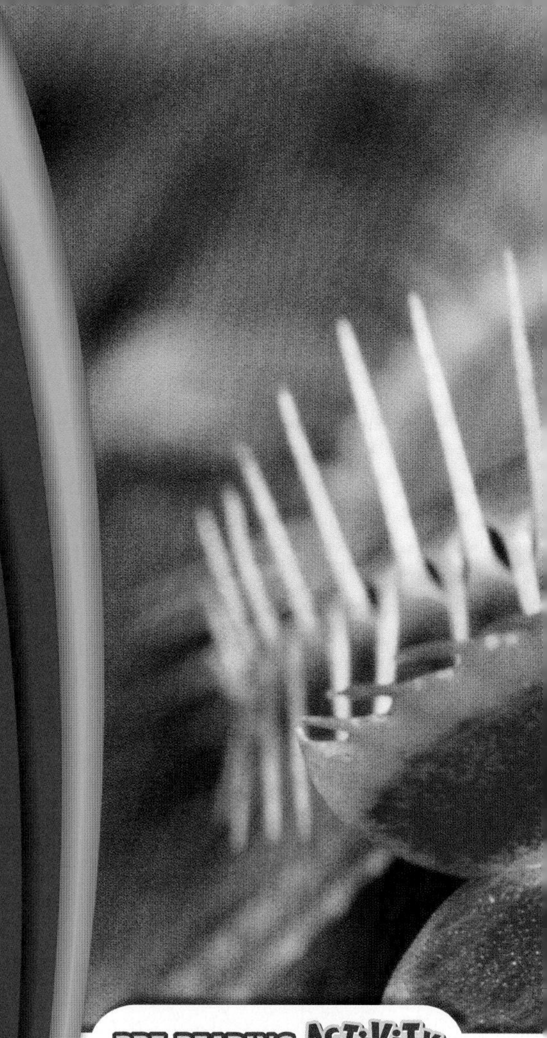

About the PHOTO

The plant in this photo is a Venus' flytrap. Those red and green spiny pads are its leaves. Like other plants, Venus' flytraps rely on photosynthesis to get energy. What is so unusual about the Venus' flytrap? Unlike most plants, the Venus' flytrap gets important nutrients, such as nitrogen, by capturing and digesting insects or other small animals.

PRE-READING ACTIVITY

FOLDNOTES Booklet Before you read the chapter, create the FoldNote entitled "Booklet" described in the **Study Skills** section of the Appendix. Label each page of the booklet with a main idea from the chapter. As you read the chapter, write what you learn about each main idea on the appropriate page of the booklet.

Standards Correlations

National Science Education Standards

The following codes indicate the National Science Education Standards that correlate to this chapter. The full text of the standards is at the front of the book.

Chapter Opener
UCP 1, 2, 5; SAI 1, 2; LS 1c, 3a, 3b

Section 1 Photosynthesis
UCP 1, 2, 3, 4, 5; SAI 1, 2; SPSP 3; HNS 1, 2; LS 1a, 1c, 3c, 4c;
LabBook: UCP 2, 3, 5; SAI 1, 2; LS 3a

Section 2 Reproduction of Flowering Plants
UCP 2, 3, 4, 5; SAI 1, 2; SPSP 4; HNS 1; LS 1a, 2a, 2b, 2d, 5b

Section 3 Plant Responses to the Environment
UCP 1, 2, 3; SAI 1, 2; SPSP 2, 3, 5; HNS 2; LS 2b, 2c, 3a, 3c, 3d, 5b

Chapter Lab
UCP 2, 3, 5; SAI 1, 2; LS 1c, 1d, 3a, 4c

START-UP ACTIVITY

MATERIALS

FOR EACH GROUP
- corn seeds (5–6)
- cup, clear plastic, medium-sized
- marker
- paper towels
- water

Teacher's Notes: To minimize the effect of light on the growth of the stems, students should rotate the cups every day. Students can also wrap the sides of the cups in aluminum foil.

Be sure that students keep the paper towels moist throughout the activity.

To further emphasize the effect of gravity on plant growth, have students turn their cups upside down after the plants have grown for several days.

Answers

1. Students should observe that the stems of all the germinating seeds grow upward, or away from the force of gravity, no matter what the original orientation of the seeds was.

2. Sample answer: The shoots grew upward because plants grow away from the force of gravity.

START-UP ACTIVITY

Which End Is Up?

If you plant seeds with their "tops" facing in different directions, will their stems all grow upward? Do this activity to find out.

Procedure

1. Pack a **clear, medium-sized plastic cup** with slightly moistened **paper towels.**

2. Place **five or six corn seeds,** equally spaced, around the cup between the side of the cup and the paper towels. Point the tip of each seed in a different direction.

3. Using a **marker,** draw arrows on the outside of the cup to show the direction each seed tip points.

4. Place the cup in a well-lit location for 1 week. Keep the seeds moist by adding **water** to the paper towels as needed.

5. After 1 week, observe the seeds. Record the direction in which each shoot grew.

Analysis

1. In which direction did each of your shoots grow?

2. What might explain why your shoots grew the way they did?

Chapter Review
UCP 1, 2, 3, 4, 5; SAI 1, 2; SPSP 2, 3, 4, 5; HNS 1, 2; LS 1a, 1c, 2a, 2b, 2c, 2d, 3a, 3c, 3d, 4c, 5b

Science in Action
UCP 5; HNS 1, 2, 3; LS 1d, 2a, 2b, 4d, 5c

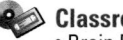
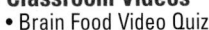

Strange but True!

It's war every day in the cornfield. When beet armyworm caterpillars attack the corn, the corn fights back. The corn somehow sends out SOS signals. Soon, parasitic wasps swoop in, attack the caterpillars, and save the day!

How can a plant send out a distress signal? When a corn plant is being munched on by a caterpillar, chemicals in the mouth of the caterpillar cause the corn plant to release a second chemical into the air. Wasps sense the corn's response and make a beeline for the infested plant.

Like an airborne cavalry, the wasps dive for the caterpillars and lay eggs under their skin. The eggs hatch in a short time, and the wasp larvae devour the insides of the caterpillars.

Jim Tumlinson, the scientist who discovered this partnership between corn and wasps, says it probably occurred by chance. Many plants release special chemicals when attacked by pests. The wasps have a natural attraction for the chemical released by corn plants.

Tumlinson hopes to breed other plants so that they release insect-attracting chemicals. Attracting plant-friendly wasps could decrease the need for poisonous pesticides.

Making and releasing special chemicals are processes that occur in many plants. In this chapter you will learn about other plant processes.

Chapter Starter Transparency
Use this transparency to help students begin thinking about plant processes.

CHAPTER RESOURCES

Technology

Transparencies   READING SKILLS
- Chapter Starter Transparency

Student Edition on CD-ROM

Guided Reading Audio CD
- English or Spanish

Classroom Videos
- Brain Food Video Quiz

Workbooks

Science Puzzlers, Twisters & Teasers
- Plant Processes   GENERAL

Focus

Overview

This section describes photosynthesis. Students will learn about the relationship between photosynthesis and cellular respiration. In addition, they will learn about the importance of stomata in transpiration.

Bellringer

Write the following question on the board or overhead projector: "Where do you get the energy you need to stay alive?" (Students will likely answer that they get their energy from the foods that they eat.) **LS** Verbal

Motivate

Discussion — GENERAL

Food and Energy Before students begin reading this section, ask them the following questions:

• Where do the animals that are used for food get their energy to survive? (Sample answer: The animals eat plants or other animals that eat plants.)

• Where do plants get their energy to survive? (Plants get their energy from sunlight.)

Explain to students that plants use energy from the sun to make their own food in a process called *photosynthesis*. **LS** Verbal

READING WARM-UP

Objectives
● Describe photosynthesis.
● Compare photosynthesis and cellular respiration.
● Describe how gas is exchanged in the leaves of plants.
● Describe two ways in which photosynthesis is important.

Terms to Learn
photosynthesis   stoma
chlorophyll   transpiration
cellular respiration

READING STRATEGY

Discussion Read this section silently. Write down questions that you have about this section. Discuss your questions in a small group.

Photosynthesis

Plants don't have lungs. But like you, plants need air. Air contains oxygen, carbon dioxide, and other gases. Your body needs oxygen, and plants need oxygen. But what other gas is important to plants?

If you guessed *carbon dioxide*, you are correct. Plants use carbon dioxide for photosynthesis (FOHT oh SIN thuh sis). **Photosynthesis** is the process by which plants make their own food. Plants capture energy from sunlight during photosynthesis. This energy is used to make the sugar glucose ($C_6H_{12}O_6$) from carbon dioxide (CO_2) and water (H_2O).

Capturing Light Energy

Plant cells have organelles called *chloroplasts* (KLAWR uh PLASTS), shown in **Figure 1.** Chloroplasts are surrounded by two membranes. Inside the chloroplast, another membrane forms stacks called *grana* (GRAY nuh). Grana contain a green pigment, called **chlorophyll** (KLAWR uh FIL), that absorbs light energy.

Sunlight is made up of many different wavelengths of light. Chlorophyll absorbs many of these wavelengths. But it reflects more wavelengths of green light than wavelengths of other colors of light. So, most plants look green.

✓ **Reading Check** Why are most plants green? (*See the Appendix for answers to Reading Checks.*)

Figure 1 Chloroplast Structure

The grana found in chloroplasts contain chlorophyll, which captures energy from sunlight.

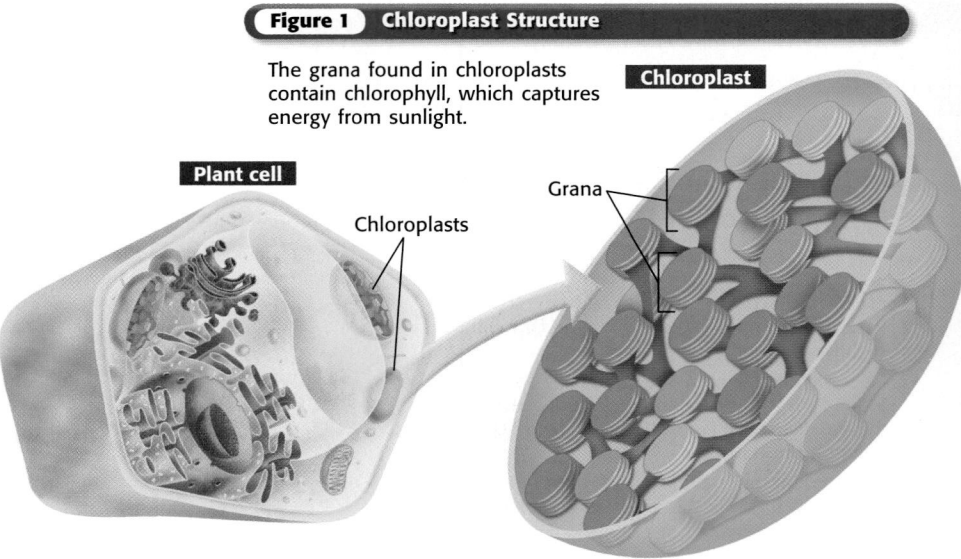

Plant cell

Chloroplast

Chloroplasts

Grana

CHAPTER RESOURCES

Chapter Resource File

• Lesson Plan
• Directed Reading A **BASIC**
• Directed Reading B **SPECIAL NEEDS**

Technology

Transparencies
• Bellringer
• Photosynthesis
• *LINK TO PHYSICAL SCIENCE* Balancing a Chemical Equation

Answer to Reading Check

Chlorophyll reflects more wavelengths of green light than wavelengths of other colors of light. So, most plants look green.

Making Sugar

The light energy captured by chlorophyll is used to help form glucose molecules. In turn, oxygen gas (O_2) is given off by plant cells. Photosynthesis is a complicated process made up of many steps. But photosynthesis can be summarized by the following chemical equation:

$$6CO_2 + 6H_2O \xrightarrow{\text{light energy}} C_6H_{12}O_6 + 6O_2$$

Six molecules of carbon dioxide and six molecules of water are needed to form one molecule of glucose and six molecules of oxygen. **Figure 2** shows where plants get the materials for photosynthesis.

Getting Energy from Sugar

Glucose molecules store energy. Plant cells use this energy for their life processes. To get energy, plant cells break down glucose and other food molecules in a process called **cellular respiration.** During this process, plant cells use oxygen. The cells give off carbon dioxide and water. Excess glucose is converted to another sugar called *sucrose* or stored as starch.

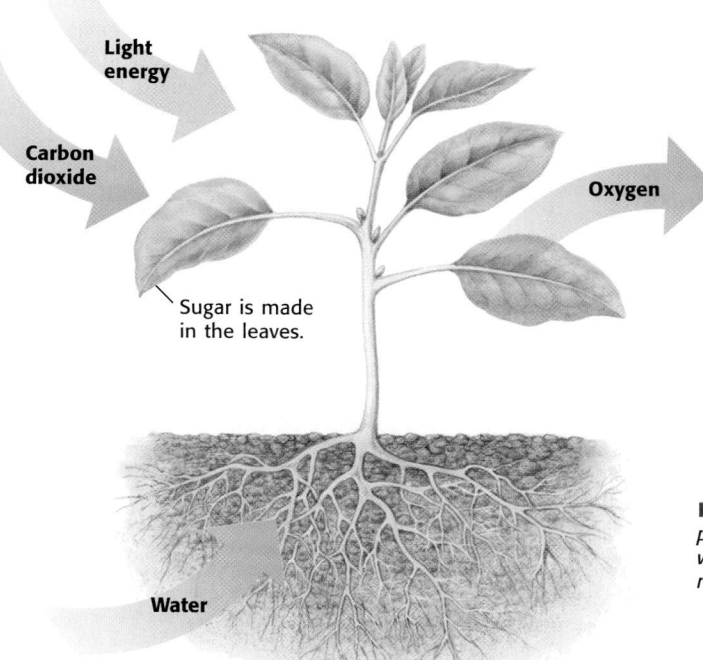

Light energy

Carbon dioxide

Oxygen

Sugar is made in the leaves.

Water

Figure 2 *During photosynthesis, plants take in carbon dioxide and water and absorb light energy. They make sugar and release oxygen.*

photosynthesis the process by which plants, algae, and some bacteria use sunlight, carbon dioxide, and water to make food

chlorophyll a green pigment that captures light energy for photosynthesis

cellular respiration the process by which cells use oxygen to produce energy from food

Definitions Have students read the definitions of *photosynthesis, cellular respiration,* and *transpiration* aloud and then write a definition of each term in their own words.
LS Verbal
English Language Learners

Quiz — GENERAL

1. What molecules do plants use to make sugar? (carbon dioxide and water)

2. What substances enter and exit a leaf through the stomata? (Sample answer: Carbon dioxide enters the leaf while oxygen and water exit the leaf.)

3. How is oxygen an important byproduct of photosynthesis? (Sample answer: The oxygen produced by photosynthesis is used by animals and plants for cellular respiration.)

Alternative Assessment — GENERAL

Writing
Stomata Have students write about stomata. Students should describe the appearance of stomata and the passage of materials through the stomata. **LS** Verbal

---

Figure 3 Gas Exchange in Leaves

When light is available for photosynthesis, the stomata are usually open. At nighttime, the stomata close to conserve water.

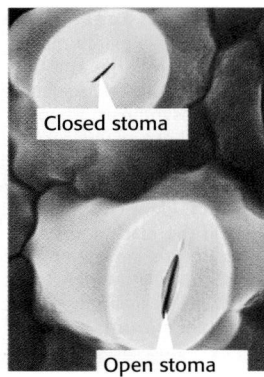
Closed stoma
Open stoma

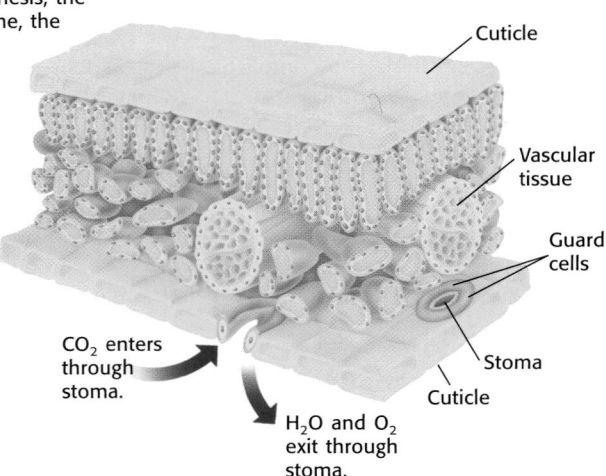
Cuticle
Vascular tissue
Guard cells
Stoma
Cuticle
CO_2 enters through stoma.
H_2O and O_2 exit through stoma.

stoma one of many openings in a leaf or a stem of a plant that enable gas exchange to occur (plural, *stomata*)

transpiration the process by which plants release water vapor into the air through stomata

Gas Exchange

Many above-ground plant surfaces are covered by a waxy cuticle. The cuticle protects the plant from water loss. How does a plant get carbon dioxide through this barrier? Carbon dioxide enters the plant's leaves through stomata (singular, *stoma*). A **stoma** is an opening in the leaf's epidermis and cuticle. Each stoma is surrounded by two *guard cells*. The guard cells act like double doors, opening and closing the stoma. You can see stomata in **Figure 3.**

When stomata are open, carbon dioxide enters the leaf. The oxygen produced during photosynthesis exits the leaf through the stomata. Water vapor also exits the leaf in this way. The loss of water from leaves is called **transpiration.** Most of the water absorbed by a plant's roots replaces the water lost during transpiration. Sometimes, more water is lost through a plant's leaves than is absorbed by the plant's roots. When this happens, the plant wilts.

CONNECTION TO Chemistry

Transpiration Wrap a plastic bag around the branch of a tree or a portion of a potted plant. Secure the bag closed with a piece of tape or a rubber band, but be sure not to injure the plant. Record what happens over the next few days. What happened to the bag? How does this illustrate transpiration?

ACTIVITY

Answer to Connection to Chemistry

Students should note that water droplets form on the inside of the plastic bag. These water droplets demonstrate transpiration because the water comes from the plant. The water vapor that exits the leaves through the stomata condenses on the inside of the bag.

WEIRD SCIENCE

Some leaves have more than 100,000 stomata per square centimeter of leaf surface.

The Importance of Photosynthesis

Plants and other photosynthetic organisms, such as some bacteria and many protists, form the base of nearly all food chains on Earth. An example of one food chain is shown in **Figure 4.** During photosynthesis, plants store light energy as chemical energy. Some animals use this chemical energy when they eat plants. Other animals get energy from plants indirectly. These animals eat animals that eat plants. Most organisms could not survive without photosynthetic organisms.

Plants, animals, and most other organisms rely on cellular respiration to get energy. Cellular respiration requires oxygen. Oxygen is a byproduct of photosynthesis. So, photosynthesis provides the oxygen that animals and plants need for cellular respiration.

✓ Reading Check What are two ways in which photosynthesis is important?

Figure 4 *Mice rely on plants for food. In turn, cats get energy from mice.*

SECTION Review

Summary

- During photosynthesis, plants use energy from sunlight, carbon dioxide, and water to make food.
- Plants get energy from food by cellular respiration, which uses oxygen and releases carbon dioxide and water.
- Transpiration, or the loss of water through the leaves, happens when stomata are open.
- Photosynthesis provides oxygen. Most animals rely on photosynthetic organisms for food.

Using Key Terms

1. In your own words, write a definition for each of the following terms: *photosynthesis*, *chlorophyll*, and *cellular respiration*.

Understanding Key Ideas

2. During photosynthesis, plants
   a. absorb energy from sunlight.
   b. use carbon dioxide and water.
   c. make food and oxygen.
   d. All of the above

3. How is cellular respiration related to photosynthesis?

4. Describe gas exchange in plants.

Math Skills

5. Plants use 6 carbon dioxide molecules and 6 water molecules to make 1 glucose molecule. How many carbon dioxide and water molecules would be needed to make 12 glucose molecules?

Critical Thinking

6. **Predicting Consequences** Predict what might happen if plants and other photosynthetic organisms disappeared.

7. **Applying Concepts** Light filters let through certain colors of light. Predict what would happen if you grew a plant under a green light filter.

SCiLINKS® **NSTA** Developed and maintained by the National Science Teachers Association

For a variety of links related to this chapter, go to www.scilinks.org

Topic: Photosynthesis
SciLinks code: HSM1140

CHAPTER RESOURCES

Chapter Resource File

- Section Quiz **GENERAL**
- Section Review **GENERAL**
- Vocabulary and Section Summary **GENERAL**
- Reinforcement Worksheet **BASIC**

Technology

Transparencies
- Gas Exchange in Leaves

Workbooks

Math Skills for Science
- Balancing Chemical Equations **GENERAL**

Focus

Overview

This section describes pollination and fertilization. Students will be able to explain how fruits are formed from flowers and differentiate between sexual and asexual reproduction in flowering plants.

🔊 Bellringer

Ask students the following question: "What are pollination and fertilization?" (Sample answer: Pollination happens when a pollen grain reaches the stigma. Fertilization happens when a sperm joins with an egg.)

Motivate

Demonstration — GENERAL

Parts of a Flower Show students a variety of fresh flowers, and ask them to compare the flowers. Point out the stamens, stigmas, petals, and sepals in each flower. Remove the petals, and shake the flower over paper. (Pollen can stain skin and clothing. You may wish to wear protective gloves.) Ask students to identify the powder on the paper. (pollen) Explain that pollen contain the flower's male reproductive cells.

English Language Learners

LS Visual

READING WARM-UP

Objectives

● Describe pollination and fertilization in flowering plants.

● Explain how fruits and seeds are formed from flowers.

● List three reasons why a seed might be dormant.

● List three examples of asexual reproduction in plants.

Terms to Learn

dormant

READING STRATEGY

Reading Organizer As you read this section, make a table comparing sexual reproduction and asexual reproduction in plants.

Reproduction of Flowering Plants

Imagine you are standing in a field of wildflowers. You're surrounded by bright colors and sweet fragrances. You can hear bees buzzing from flower to flower.

Flowering plants are the largest and most diverse group of plants. Their success is partly due to their flowers. Flowers are adaptations for sexual reproduction. During sexual reproduction, an egg is fertilized by a sperm.

Fertilization

In flowering plants, fertilization takes place within flowers. *Pollination* happens when pollen is moved from anthers to stigmas. Usually, wind or animals move pollen from one flower to another flower. Pollen contains sperm. After pollen lands on the stigma, a tube grows from each pollen grain. The tube grows through the style to an ovule. Ovules are found inside the ovary. Each ovule contains an egg. Sperm from the pollen grain move down the pollen tube and into an ovule. Fertilization happens when a sperm fuses with the egg inside an ovule. **Figure 1** shows pollination and fertilization.

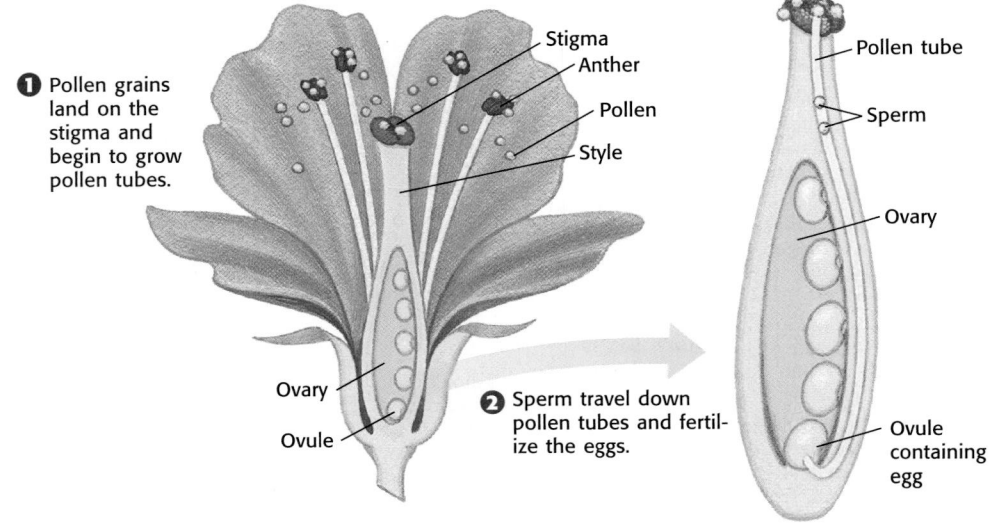

Figure 1 **Pollination and Fertilization**

❶ Pollen grains land on the stigma and begin to grow pollen tubes.

Stigma
Anther
Pollen
Style

Ovary
Ovule

❷ Sperm travel down pollen tubes and fertilize the eggs.

Pollen tube
Sperm
Ovary
Ovule containing egg

CHAPTER RESOURCES

Chapter Resource File

 • Lesson Plan
• Directed Reading A **BASIC**
• Directed Reading B **SPECIAL NEEDS**

Technology

 Transparencies
• Bellringer
• Pollination and Fertilization
• Seed Production

CONNECTION to
History —————— GENERAL

Cacao In 1519, the explorer Hernando Cortez brought cacao beans and a recipe from Montezuma's court back to Spain. The recipe was for a new drink called *xocoatl*, or chocolate. Invite students to research the history of chocolate. Have students make posters of their findings. **LS Verbal/Visual**

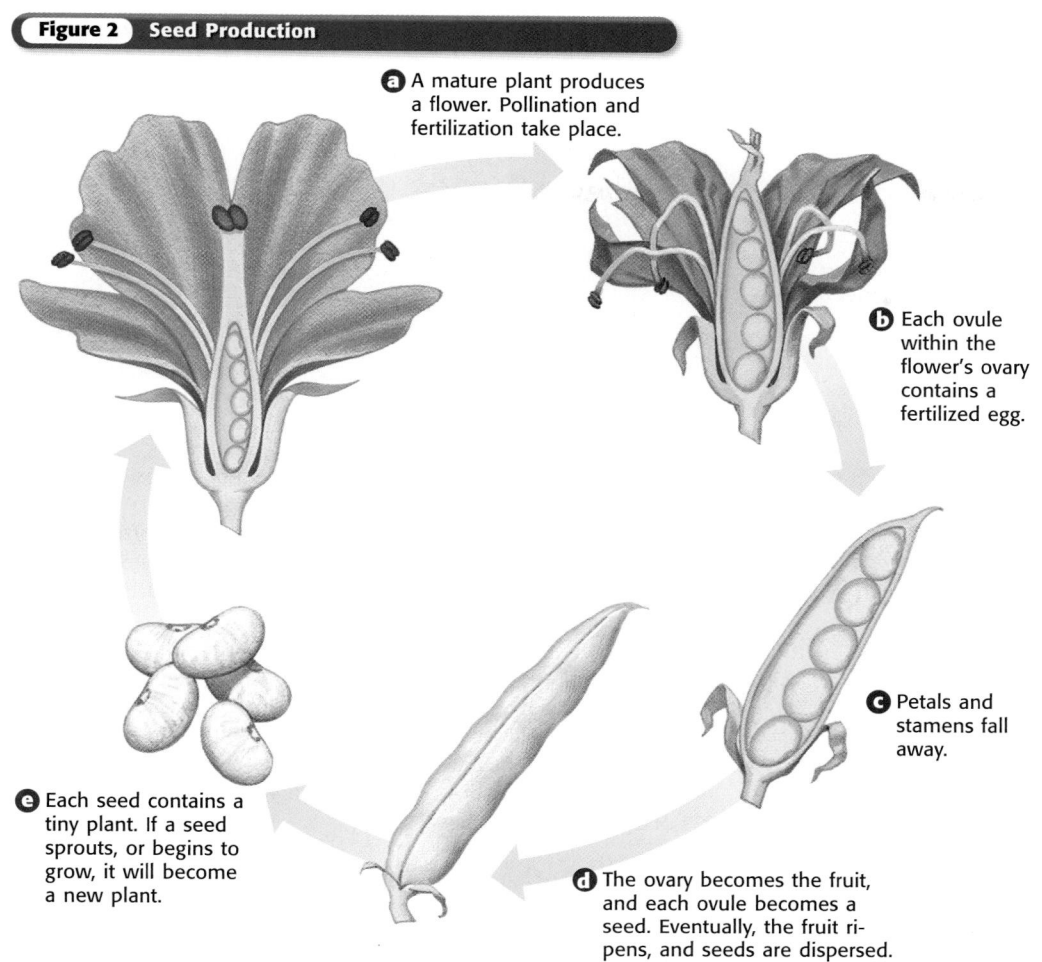

Figure 2 Seed Production

ⓐ A mature plant produces a flower. Pollination and fertilization take place.

ⓑ Each ovule within the flower's ovary contains a fertilized egg.

ⓒ Petals and stamens fall away.

ⓓ The ovary becomes the fruit, and each ovule becomes a seed. Eventually, the fruit ripens, and seeds are dispersed.

ⓔ Each seed contains a tiny plant. If a seed sprouts, or begins to grow, it will become a new plant.

From Flower to Fruit

After fertilization takes place, the ovule develops into a seed. The seed contains a tiny, undeveloped plant. The ovary surrounding the ovule becomes a fruit, as shown in **Figure 2.**

As a fruit swells and ripens, it protects the developing seeds. **Figure 3** shows a common fruit. Fruits often help a plant spread its seeds. Many fruits are edible. Animals may eat these fruits. Then, the animals discard the seeds away from the parent plant. Other fruits, such as burrs, get caught in an animal's fur. Some fruits are carried by the wind.

✔ **Reading Check** How do fruits help a plant spread its seeds? (*See the Appendix for answers to Reading Checks.*)

Fruit from ovary

Seed from ovule

Figure 3 *Tomatoes develop from a flower's ovary and ovules.*

Answer to Reading Check

Sample answer: Animals may eat fruits and discard the seeds away from the parent plant. Other fruits, such as burrs, get caught in an animal's fur. Some fruits are carried by the wind.

CONNECTION ACTIVITY

Art ———————————— **ADVANCED**

Flowers in Art Have students find examples of how artists and illustrators throughout history have represented flowers and fruits in their work. You might want to show students reproductions of works by Pierre Redoute, Claude Monet, or Georgia O'Keeffe to encourage their interest in this activity. Ask students to create their own art of flowers. English Language Learners
LS Kinesthetic

Group ACTIVITY — **GENERAL**

Concept Mapping Have students work together in groups of four to create a concept map that details the process of sexual reproduction in plants from the time that pollen grains reach the stigma until a seed develops inside a fruit. Encourage students to illustrate their work.
LS Verbal/Logical Co-op Learning

ACTIVITY ———————— **BASIC**

MATERIALS

FOR EACH GROUP
• bean seeds (1 packet)
• container, plastic, small, with snap-on caps (2)
• water

Germination Show students that plant germination can push the caps off bottles. This demonstration will take a few days. Fill a container, such as a plastic film canister, with bean seeds. Fill another container with bean seeds and water. Snap the caps onto the bottles. (Don't use child-proof bottles that lock.) Place the bottles where they can be observed. In a few days, the germinating bean seeds will knock the caps off or even split the bottles apart. Ask students to note which beans are more powerful—the beans with water or the beans without water. (The beans with water are expanding as they absorb water for germination. They are producing CO_2 because they have begun cellular respiration.) English Language Learners
LS Visual

Close

Reteaching — BASIC

Making Comparisons Ask students to compare sexual and asexual reproduction in flowering plants. Students should recognize the structures involved and the ways in which pollination and fertilization differ from asexual reproduction. **LS** Logical

Quiz — GENERAL

Ask students whether each of the following statements is true or false.

1. Pollination happens when a sperm joins with an egg. (false)

2. Tubers, plantlets, and runners are structures used for asexual reproduction. (true)

3. *Dormant* describes the active state of a seed or other plant part. (false)

Alternative Assessment — GENERAL

Drawing Flowers Have students make a drawing of a flower and label the anthers, stigmas, style, ovary, and ovule. Students should also show pollination and fertilization. **LS** Visual   English Language Learners

Answer to Reading Check

plantlets, tubers, and runners

Figure 4 *Seeds grow into new plants. The roots begin to grow first. Then, the shoot grows up through the soil.*

dormant describes the inactive state of a seed or other plant part when conditions are unfavorable to growth

Quick Lab

Thirsty Seeds

1. Fill a **Petri dish** two-thirds full of **water,** and add **six dry bean seeds.** Using a **wax pencil,** label the dish "Water."

2. Add **six dry bean seeds** to a dry **Petri dish.** Label this dish "Control."

3. The next day, compare the size of the two sets of seeds. Record your observations.

4. What caused the size of the seeds to change? Why might this be important to the seed's survival?

From Seed to Plant

Once a seed is fully developed, the young plant inside the seed stops growing. The seed may become dormant. When seeds are **dormant,** they are inactive. Dormant seeds often survive long periods of drought or freezing temperatures. Some seeds need extreme conditions, such as cold winters or forest fires, to break their dormancy.

When seeds are dropped or planted in a suitable environment, the seeds sprout. To sprout, most seeds need water, air, and warm temperatures. Each plant species has an ideal temperature at which most of its seeds will begin to grow. For many plants, the ideal temperature for growth is about 27°C (80.6°F). **Figure 4** shows the *germination* (JUHR muh NAY shuhn), or sprouting, of a bean seed.

Other Methods of Reproduction

Flowering plants may also reproduce asexually. For asexual reproduction, plants do not need flowers. Part of a plant, such as a stem or root, produces a new plant. The following are three structures plants use to reproduce asexually:

- **Plantlets** Tiny plants grow along the edges of a plant's leaves. These plantlets fall off and grow on their own.
- **Tubers** Underground stems, or tubers, can produce new plants after a dormant season.
- **Runners** Above-ground stems from which new plants can grow are called *runners*.

You can see an example of each kind of asexual reproduction in **Figure 5.**

Reading Check What are three structures plants use to reproduce asexually?

Quick Lab

MATERIALS

FOR EACH GROUP
- bean seed (12)
- marker or wax pencil
- Petri dish (2)
- water

Answers

3. Students should note that the seeds in water increased in size or cracked open.

4. The seeds swell because they are absorbing water. Once a seed absorbs enough water, the seed coat ruptures, which allows the root and shoot to emerge.

Figure 5 Three Structures for Asexual Reproduction

Kalanchoe plants produce **plant-lets** along the edges of their leaves. The plantlets eventually fall off and root in the soil to grow on their own.

A potato is a **tuber,** or underground stem. The "eyes" of potatoes are buds that can grow into new plants.

The strawberry plant produces **runners,** or stems that grow horizontally along the ground. Buds along the runners take root and grow into new plants.

SECTION Review

Summary

- After pollination, a pollen tube forms from the stigma to an ovule. This tube allows a sperm to fertilize an egg.
- After fertilization, seeds and fruit form. The seeds are protected by fruit.
- A dormant seed can survive drought and freezing temperatures. Some seeds need extreme conditions to break their dormancy.
- Some plants use plantlets, tubers, or runners to reproduce asexually.

Using Key Terms

1. In your own words, write a definition for the term *dormant*.

Understanding Key Ideas

2. Pollination happens when
   a. a pollen tube forms.
   b. a sperm cell fuses with an egg.
   c. pollen is transferred from the anther to the stigma.
   d. None of the above

3. Which part of a flower develops into a fruit? into a seed?

4. Why do seeds become dormant?

5. Describe how plants reproduce asexually.

Math Skills

6. A seed sprouts when the temperature is 27°C. If the temperature is now 20°C and it rises 1.5°C per week, in how many weeks will the seed sprout?

Critical Thinking

7. **Making Inferences** What do flowers and runners have in common? How do they differ?

8. **Identifying Relationships** When might asexual reproduction be important for the survival of some flowering plants?

9. **Analyzing Ideas** Sexual reproduction produces more genetic variety than asexual reproduction. Why is variety important?

SCI**LINKS**.

NSTA

Developed and maintained by the National Science Teachers Association

For a variety of links related to this chapter, go to www.scilinks.org

Topic: Reproduction of Plants
SciLinks code: HSM1295

WEIRD SCIENCE

The oldest known living seed was a lotus seed that was more than 1,200 years old. When plant physiologist Jane Shen-Miller tried to germinate the seed, it grew! Unfortunately, the plant did not survive for long. However, discovering why the seed survived for so long may benefit agriculture if the knowledge can be used to produce crop seeds that can live for a long period of time.

CHAPTER RESOURCES

Chapter Resource File

- Section Quiz **GENERAL**
- Section Review **GENERAL**
- Vocabulary and Section Summary **GENERAL**
- Reinforcement Worksheet **BASIC**
- Datasheet for Quick Lab

Answers to Section Review

1. Sample answer: A seed or plant part that doesn't grow when conditions are unfavorable is dormant.

2. c

3. ovary; ovule

4. Sample answer: Dormant seeds can survive unfavorable conditions, such as long periods of drought and freezing temperatures. Some seeds need extreme conditions, such as cold winters or forest fires, to break their dormancy.

5. Sample answer: Plantlets are tiny plants that grow along the edges of a plant's leaves, fall to the ground, and grow on their own. Tubers are underground stems that can produce new plants. Runners are above-ground stems from which new plants can grow.

6. in about 5 weeks
   (27°C − 20°C = 7°C;
   7°C ÷ 1.5°C/week = 4.7 weeks)

7. Sample answer: Both flowers and runners are used for reproduction, but flowers are involved in sexual reproduction, whereas runners are used for asexual reproduction.

8. Sample answer: A flowering plant produces seeds, but conditions may not be favorable for the seeds to grow. However, these same conditions may not affect asexual reproduction, so the plant can continue reproducing in this way. Also, if there are no pollinators in an area, sexual reproduction would be difficult for some plants. So, these plants may reproduce asexually.

9. Sample answer: Genetic variety may improve the ability of the plant to survive. For example, the offspring produced by asexual reproduction have the same weaknesses that the parent plant does. The offspring of sexual production differ from a parent plant, so the offspring may survive diseases or unfavorable conditions that would have affected the parent plant.

Focus

Overview

This section describes how plants respond to light and gravity and how some plants flower in response to night length.

Bellringer

Have students answer the following questions:

• How does the direction of light affect the growth of plants? (Sample answer: Plants may grow toward light.)

• How does gravity affect the growth of plants? (Sample answer: A plant's shoots grow away from the force of gravity, and a plant's roots grow toward the force of gravity.)

Motivate

Discussion ——— GENERAL

Plant Responses Bring to class a touch-sensitive plant, such as *Mimosa pudica*. Show students how the leaves of the plant "fold up" when they are touched. You also can demonstrate plant movement with a Venus' flytrap. Explain to students that while these movements are plant responses, they are not tropisms. They are nastic movements. Nastic movements are plant responses that happen independently of the direction of a stimulus. **LS** Visual

---

READING WARM-UP

Objectives

● Describe how plants may respond to light and gravity.

● Explain how some plants respond to night length.

● Describe how some plants respond to the changes of season.

Terms to Learn

tropism

READING STRATEGY

Discussion Read this section silently. Write down questions that you have about this section. Discuss your questions in a small group.

tropism the growth of all or part of an organism in response to an external stimulus, such as light

---

Plant Responses to the Environment

What happens when you get really cold? Do your teeth chatter? Or do you shiver? Anything that causes a reaction in your body is a stimulus (plural, stimuli). But would a plant respond to a stimulus?

Plants do respond to stimuli! For example, they respond to light, gravity, and changing seasons.

Plant Tropisms

Some plants respond to an environmental stimulus by growing in a particular direction. Growth in response to a stimulus is called a **tropism** (TROH PIZ uhm). Tropisms are either positive or negative. Plant growth toward a stimulus is a positive tropism. Plant growth away from a stimulus is a negative tropism.

Light

What happens if you place a houseplant so that it gets light from only one direction, such as from a window? The shoot tips probably bend toward the light. Bending toward the light is a positive tropism. A change in the direction a plant grows that is caused by light is called *phototropism* (FOH toh TROH PIZ uhm). The result of phototropism is shown in **Figure 1.** Shoots bend because cells on one side of the shoot grow longer than cells on the other side of the shoot.

Reading Check What happens when a plant gets light from only one direction? (*See the Appendix for answers to Reading Checks.*)

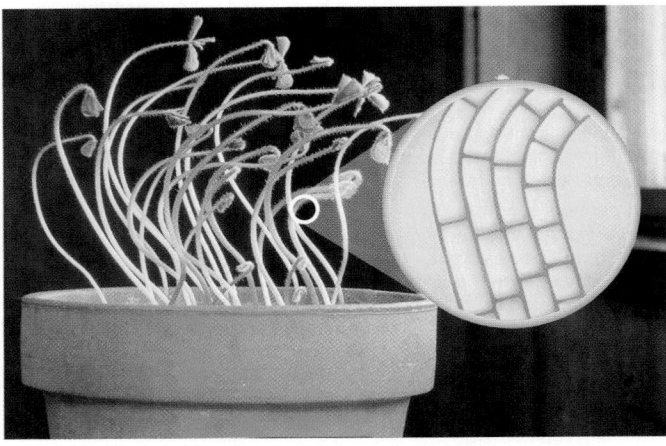

Figure 1 *The plant cells on the dark side of the shoot grow longer than the cells on the other side. So, the shoot bends toward the light.*

CHAPTER RESOURCES

Chapter Resource File

• **Lesson Plan**
• **Directed Reading A** BASIC
• **Directed Reading B** SPECIAL NEEDS

Technology

 Transparencies
• Bellringer

● **Interactive Explorations CD-ROM**
• How's It Growing? GENERAL

Answer to Reading Check

Sample answer: The shoot tips will probably bend toward the light.

Figure 2 Gravitropism

▼ To grow away from the pull of gravity, this plant has grown upward.

▼ This plant has recently been upside down.

MATH PRACTICE

Bending by Degrees

Suppose a plant has a positive phototropism and bends toward light at a rate of 0.3° per minute. In how many hours will the plant bend 90°?

Gravity

Plant growth also changes in response to the direction of gravity. This change is called *gravitropism* (GRAV i TROH PIZ uhm). The effect of gravitropism is demonstrated by the plants in **Figure 2.** A few days after a plant is placed on its side or turned upside down, the roots and shoots change direction of growth. Most shoot tips have negative gravitropism. They grow upward, away from the center of the Earth. In contrast, most root tips have positive gravitropism. Roots grow downward, toward the center of the Earth.

Seasonal Responses

What would happen if a plant living in an area that has very cold winters flowered in December? Would the plant be able to successfully produce seeds and fruits? Probably not. The plant's flowers would likely freeze and die. So, the flowers would never produce mature seeds.

Plants living in regions with cold winters can detect the change in seasons. How do plants do this? As fall and winter approach, the days get shorter, and the nights get longer. The opposite happens when spring and summer approach. Plants respond to the change in the length of day.

INTERNET ACTIVITY

For another activity related to this chapter, go to **go.hrw.com** and type in the keyword **HL5PL2W.**

✓ **Reading Check** How do plants detect seasonal changes?

Answer to Reading Check

Sample answer: Plants respond to the change in the length of day.

Cultural Awareness — GENERAL

Writing **Harvest Festivals** Many ancient and traditional cultures have festivals during harvest time, often in the fall. Ask interested students to research a harvest festival. Have students write a magazine article about their findings. **LS** Verbal

Teach

Answer to Math Practice

5 h (90° ÷ 0.3°/min = 300 min; 300 min ÷ 60 min/h = 5 h)

Using the Figure — GENERAL

Phototropism and Gravitropism
Have students look closely at **Figure 1** and **Figure 2.** Point out that after a few days, the leaves of the plants in the photos grow toward light or away from the force of gravity. Roots are not affected by light, but they grow toward the force of gravity. Ask students to describe these tropisms as positive or negative. (Growth toward a stimulus is a positive tropism, while growth away from a stimulus is a negative tropism. Growth by shoots toward light and growth by roots toward gravity are positive tropisms. The growth of shoots away from gravity is a negative tropism.) English Language Learners
LS Verbal

Homework — ADVANCED

Investigating Plant Growth
Have students research how the lifespan of a plant is measured in one-year growing seasons. Ask students to describe the life cycle of plants in each of the following categories and to give examples of each:

• annuals (plants whose life cycle is completed in one growing season; corn, marigolds, beans, and sunflowers)

• biennials (plants that require two growing seasons to complete their life cycle; hollyhocks, foxgloves, carrots, and onions)

• perennials (plants that live year after year for more than two years; trees, roses, asparagus, and irises)

Encourage students to include drawings that illustrate when each plant begins to grow, produces seeds, and dies.
LS Verbal/Visual

Teach, *continued*

INCLUSION Strategies

- *Developmentally Delayed*
- *Learning Disabled*

The idea that leaves do not turn colors but that one of the colors is removed is probably in opposition to what most students think. Using a leaf pattern, trace two leaves onto green construction paper and one each onto yellow and orange construction paper. Cover each of the yellow and orange leaves with a green leaf. Discuss and show that the yellow and orange colors are there but are covered by the green. Then, remove the green leaf and discuss that the other colors in leaves become visible when the green color decreases in the fall. You may want to explain to students that red pigments are an exception—these pigments are made in the fall.
LS Visual

Close

Reteaching — BASIC

Organizing Information Write the following heads on the board: "Phototropism," "Gravitropism," and "Seasonal responses." Ask student volunteers to add information under the appropriate head.
LS Verbal/Logical

Figure 3 Night Length and Flower Color

Early summer

Night length

Day length

◀ In the early summer, night length is short. At this time, poinsettia leaves are all green, and there are no flowers.

Late fall

Night length

Day length

▲ Poinsettias flower in the fall, when nights are longer. The leaves surrounding the flower clusters turn red. Professional growers use artificial lighting to control the timing of this color change.

Length of Day

The difference between day length and night length is an important environmental stimulus for many plants. This stimulus can cause plants to begin reproducing. For example, some plants flower in fall or winter. At this time, night length is long. These plants are called *short-day plants*. Poinsettias, such as those shown in **Figure 3,** are short-day plants. Chrysanthemums are also short-day plants. Other plants flower in spring or early summer, when night length is short. These plants are called *long-day plants*. Clover, spinach, and lettuce are examples of long-day plants.

Seasons and Leaf Loss

All trees lose their leaves. Some trees, such as pine and holly, shed some of their leaves year-round so that some leaves are always on the tree. These trees are called *evergreen trees*. Evergreen trees have leaves adapted to survive throughout the year. The leaves are often covered with a thick cuticle. This cuticle protects the leaves from cold and dry weather.

Other trees, such as maple, oak, and elm trees, are called *deciduous* (dee SIJ oo uhs) *trees*. These trees lose all of their leaves around the same time each year. In colder areas, deciduous trees usually lose their leaves before winter begins. In warmer climates that have wet and dry seasons, deciduous trees lose their leaves before the dry season. The loss of leaves helps plants survive low temperatures or long periods without rain.

 **Reading Check** Compare evergreen trees and deciduous trees.

SCHOOL to HOME

Earth's Orbit and the Seasons

The seasons are caused by Earth's tilt and its orbit around the sun. Research how Earth's orbit determines the seasons. With a parent, make a model of the Earth's orbit around the sun to illustrate your findings.

ACTIVITY

Answer to School-to-Home Activity

Students' models should illustrate an understanding of how Earth's orbit and tilt affect the amount of sunlight that an area receives at a particular time of year.

Answer to Reading Check

Sample answer: Evergreen trees always have some leaves on them. Deciduous trees lose all of their leaves around the same time each year.

Figure 4   Amount of Pigment Based on Season

Summer

Amount

Pigment color

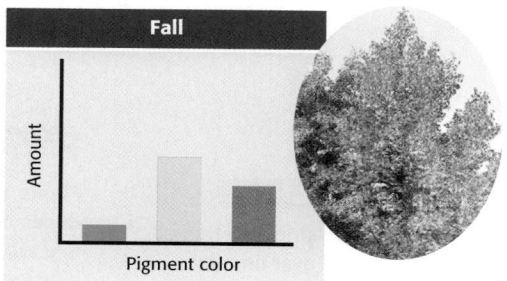

Fall

Amount

Pigment color

Seasons and Leaf Color

As shown in **Figure 4,** the leaves of deciduous trees may change color before they are lost. As fall approaches, green chlorophyll breaks down. Orange or yellow pigments in the leaves are then revealed. These pigments were always present in the leaves. But they were hidden by green chlorophyll.

SECTION Review

Summary

- Plant growth in response to a stimulus is called a tropism. Tropisms are positive or negative.
- Plants react to light, gravity, and changing seasons.
- Short-day plants flower when night length is long. Long-day plants flower when night length is short.
- Evergreen trees do not lose all their leaves at one time. Deciduous trees lose their leaves at the same time each year.

Using Key Terms

1. In your own words, write a definition for the term *tropism*.

Understanding Key Ideas

2. Deciduous trees lose their leaves
   a. to conserve water during the dry season.
   b. around the same time each year.
   c. to survive low winter temperatures.
   d. All of the above

3. How do light and gravity affect plants?

4. Describe how day length can affect the flowering of plants.

Math Skills

5. A certain plant won't bloom until it is dark for 70% of a 24 h period. How long is the day when the plant will bloom?

Critical Thinking

6. **Making Inferences** Many evergreen trees live in areas with long, cold winters. Why might these evergreen trees keep their leaves all year?

7. **Analyzing Ideas** Some short-day plants bloom during the winter. If cold weather reduces the chances that a plant will produce seeds, what might you conclude about where these short-day plants are found?

SCLINKS®

NSTA
Developed and maintained by the
National Science Teachers Association

For a variety of links related to this chapter, go to www.scilinks.org

Topic: Plant Tropisms; Plant Growth
SciLinks code: HSM1166; HSM1159

Quiz   GENERAL

1. Why do some leaves change color in the fall? (Sample answer: Green chlorophyll in the leaves breaks down, and other pigments become visible.)

2. What is the difference between an evergreen tree and a deciduous tree? (Sample answer: An evergreen tree has leaves adapted to survive throughout the year. It sheds some of its leaves year-round. A deciduous tree loses all of its leaves at around the same time each year.)

3. Define *tropism*. (A tropism is growth in response to an external stimulus, such as light or gravity.)

Alternative Assessment   GENERAL

 Writing **Length of Day** Have students write a short article about how plants, such as poinsettias, respond to the length of day. **LS** Verbal

Answers to Section Review

1. Sample answer: A tropism is growth in response to a stimulus.

2. d

3. Sample answer: Plant shoots usually grow toward light. Plant shoots grow away from the force of gravity, and plant roots grow toward the force of gravity.

4. Sample answer: Short-day plants, such as poinsettias, flower in fall or winter, when night length is long. Long-day plants flower in spring and summer, when night length is short.

5. 7.2 h (100% − 70% = 30%; 24 h × 0.3 = 7.2 h)

6. Sample answer: If the trees live in areas that have long winters, the growing season is likely too short for the trees to make all new leaves each year. So, the trees keep their leaves year-round to conduct photosynthesis during the winter.

7. Sample answer: These short-day plants are likely found in areas that don't have cold winters.

Food Factory Waste

Teacher's Notes

Time Required
One 45-minute class period and about 5 minutes per day for 5 days

Lab Ratings

EASY ——————————————→ HARD

Teacher Prep 🔺🔺
Student Set-Up 🔺🔺🔺
Concept Level 🔺🔺🔺
Clean Up 🔺🔺

MATERIALS

The materials listed on the student page are enough for a pair or small group of students. *Elodea* (whose common name is *waterweed*) is a common aquarium plant and can be found at some pet stores and most places that sell aquarium fish. A 5% solution of baking soda and water can be made by adding water to 5 g of baking soda until the volume is 100 mL. (You would add about 95 mL of water.)

Safety Caution
Remind students to review all safety cautions and icons before beginning this lab activity.

Skills Practice Lab

Food Factory Waste

Plants use photosynthesis to make food. Photosynthesis produces oxygen gas. Humans and many other organisms cannot live without this oxygen. Oxygen is necessary for cellular respiration. In this activity, you will determine the rate of oxygen production for an *Elodea* plant.

Procedure

❶ Add 450 mL of baking-soda-and-water solution to a beaker.

❷ Put two or three sprigs of *Elodea* in the beaker. The baking soda will provide the *Elodea* with the carbon dioxide it needs for photosynthesis.

❸ Place the wide end of the funnel over the *Elodea*. The small end of the funnel should be pointing up. The *Elodea* and the funnel should be completely under the solution.

❹ Fill a test tube with the remaining baking-soda-and-water solution. Place your thumb over the end of the test tube, and turn the test tube upside down. Make sure no air enters the test tube. Hold the opening of the test tube under the solution. Place the test tube over the small end of the funnel. Try not to let any solution out of the test tube.

OBJECTIVES

Measure the amount of gas produced over time by photosynthesis.

Draw a graph of the amount of gas produced versus time.

MATERIALS

- baking-soda-and-water solution, 5% (500 mL)
- beaker (600 mL)
- *Elodea* sprigs, 20 cm long (2–3)
- funnel
- gloves, protective
- ruler, metric
- test tube

SAFETY

David Sparks
Redwater Junior High School
Redwater, Texas

CHAPTER RESOURCES

Chapter Resource File

 • **Datasheet for Chapter Lab**
• **Lab Notes and Answers**

Technology

 Classroom Videos
• Lab Video

• Weepy Weeds

5 Place the beaker setup in a well-lit area.

6 Prepare a data table similar to the one below.

Amount of Gas Present in the Test Tube		
Days of exposure to light	Total amount of gas present (mm)	Amount of gas produced per day (mm)
0		
1		
2		
3		
4		
5		

DO NOT WRITE IN BOOK

7 If no air entered the test tube, record that there was 0 mm of gas in the test tube on day 0. If air got into the tube while you were placing it, measure the height of the column of air in the test tube in millimeters. Measure the gas in the test tube from the middle of the curve on the bottom of the upside-down test tube to the level of the solution. Record this number for day 0.

8 As described in the previous step, measure the amount of gas in the test tube each day for the next 5 days. Record your measurements in the second column of your data table.

9 Calculate the amount of gas produced each day. Subtract the amount of gas present on the previous day from the amount of gas present on the current day. Record these amounts in the third column of your data table.

Analyze the Results

1 Constructing Graphs Make a graph similar to the one below. Based on your measurements, your graph should show the amount of gas produced versus time.

Amount of Gas Produced by Photosynthesis

Total amount of gas produced (mm) — vertical axis 0–11
Day — horizontal axis 1–5

DO NOT WRITE IN BOOK

2 Describing Events Based on your graph, what happened to the amount of gas in the test tube?

Draw Conclusions

3 Interpreting Information Write the equation for photosynthesis. Then, relate each part of your experiment to the part of the equation it represents.

Applying Your Data

As you can see from your results, *Elodea* produces oxygen gas as a byproduct of photosynthesis. Research photosynthesis. Find out if there are factors that affect the rate of photosynthesis. Then, predict what would happen to the production of oxygen gas.

Lab Notes

You may want to have students practice placing the test tube over the inverted funnel using water before students do so with the baking-soda solution. It may take two or three tries to get the test tube over the funnel stem without letting any air into the tube. Tell students the following: "First, fill the test tube with the solution. Place your thumb over the opening tightly so that air cannot get in. Submerge your thumb and the top of the test tube. Once the top of the test tube is underwater, you can remove your thumb from the opening of the test tube and maneuver the test tube over the stem of the funnel. Be sure that you have the *Elodea* in place under the funnel before you begin!"

Analyze the Results

1. Students' graphs should show a gradual increase in the amount of gas in the test tube.

2. Sample answer: The amount of gas in the test tube increased over time.

Draw Conclusions

3. $6CO_2 + 6H_2O + \text{light energy} \rightarrow C_6H_{12}O_6 + 6O_2$
CO_2 is carbon dioxide, which comes from the baking-soda-and-water solution. H_2O is water, which is also found in the baking-soda-and-water solution. Light energy comes from the sun. $C_6H_{12}O_6$ is glucose, and O_2 is oxygen. Glucose and oxygen are products of photosynthesis. The oxygen is released by *Elodea* and fills the test tube. The glucose is stored by the *Elodea*.

CHAPTER RESOURCES

Workbooks

 **Labs You Can Eat**
• Not Just Another Nut **GENERAL**

EcoLabs & Field Activities
• Recycle! Make Your Own Paper **GENERAL**

Long-Term Projects & Research Ideas
• Plant Partners **ADVANCED**

Calculator Based Labs
• Power of the Sun **ADVANCED**
• What Causes the Seasons? **ADVANCED**

Applying Your Data

Students should demonstrate an understanding of the factors that affect the rate of photosynthesis. Students will find that among those factors, color of light and the amount of carbon dioxide and water present can affect the rate of photosynthesis. Students should indicate that factors that increase the rate of photosynthesis lead to the production of more oxygen while factors that decrease the rate of photosynthesis decrease the amount of oxygen produced.

Chapter Review

Assignment Guide

SECTION	QUESTIONS
1	1, 3–5, 7–8, 16–18
2	6, 10, 13–15, 19, 22–25
3	2, 9, 11–12, 20–21

ANSWERS

Using Key Terms

1. transpiration
2. tropism
3. Chlorophyll
4. cellular respiration
5. stoma
6. dormant
7. Photosynthesis

Understanding Key Ideas

8. b
9. b
10. c
11. Sample answer: Short-day plants bloom when nights are long, during the fall and winter. Long-day plants bloom when nights are short, during the spring and summer.
12. Sample answer: The shoots would bend upward, away from the force of gravity, while the roots would bend downward, toward the force of gravity.

USING KEY TERMS

Complete each of the following sentences by choosing the correct term from the word bank.

stoma	photosynthesis
dormant	cellular respiration
tropism	chlorophyll
transpiration	

1 The loss of water from leaves is called ___.

2 A plant's response to light or gravity is called a ___.

3 ___ is a green pigment found in plant cells.

4 To get energy from the food made during photosynthesis, plants use ___.

5 A ___ is an opening in the epidermis and cuticle of a leaf.

6 An inactive seed is ___.

7 ___ is the process by which plants make their own food.

UNDERSTANDING KEY IDEAS

Multiple Choice

8 During gas exchange in plants,
  a. carbon dioxide exits while oxygen and water enter the leaf.
  b. oxygen and water exit while carbon dioxide enters the leaf.
  c. carbon dioxide and water enter while oxygen exits the leaf.
  d. carbon dioxide and oxygen enter while water exits the leaf.

9 Plants often respond to light from one direction by
  a. bending away from the light.
  b. bending toward the light.
  c. wilting.
  d. None of the above

10 Which of the following is NOT a way that plants reproduce asexually?
  a. runners
  b. tubers
  c. flowers
  d. plantlets

Short Answer

11 Compare short-day plants and long-day plants.

12 How do potted plants respond to gravity if placed on their sides?

13 Describe the pollination and fertilization of flowering plants.

14 What three things do seeds need before they will sprout?

15 Explain how fruits and seeds form from flowers.

16 Compare photosynthesis and cellular respiration.

17 What are two ways in which photosynthesis is important?

13. Sample answer: Pollination happens when pollen is transferred from the anthers to the stigma. After the pollen lands on the stigma, a tube grows from each pollen grain. The tube grows through the style to an ovule. A sperm travels down the tube and fertilizes an egg in the ovule.

14. water, air, and warm temperatures

15. Sample answer: After the egg is fertilized, the ovule forms a seed. The ovary becomes a fruit, which protects the seeds.

16. Sample answer: Photosynthesis is the process by which plants make glucose. It uses carbon dioxide and water and produces oxygen. Cellular respiration is the process by which plants get energy from glucose and other food molecules. Cellular respiration uses oxygen and gives off carbon dioxide and water.

17. Sample answer: Photosynthetic organisms form the base of nearly all food chains on Earth. Photosynthesis also produces the oxygen that animals and plants need for cellular respiration.

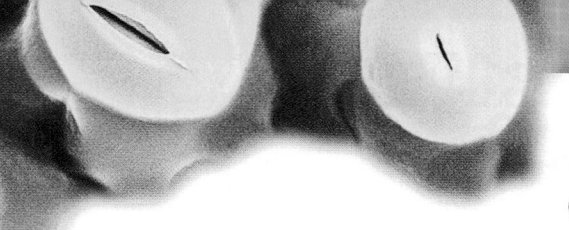

CRITICAL THINKING

18 Concept Mapping Use the following terms to create a concept map: *plants, cellular respiration, light energy, photosynthesis, chemical energy, carbon dioxide,* and *oxygen.*

19 Making Inferences Many plants live in areas that have severe winters. Some of these plants have seeds that will not germinate unless the seeds have first been exposed to a long period of cold. How might this characteristic help new plants survive?

20 Analyzing Ideas Most plant shoots have positive phototropism. Plant roots have positive gravitropism. What might be the benefits of each of these characteristics?

21 Applying Concepts If you wanted to make poinsettias bloom and the leaves turn red in the summer, what would you have to do?

22 Making Inferences Imagine that someone discovered a new flowering plant. The plant has yellow flowers and underground stems. How might this plant reproduce asexually?

INTERPRETING GRAPHICS

The graph below shows seed germination rates for different seed companies. Use the graph below to answer the questions that follow.

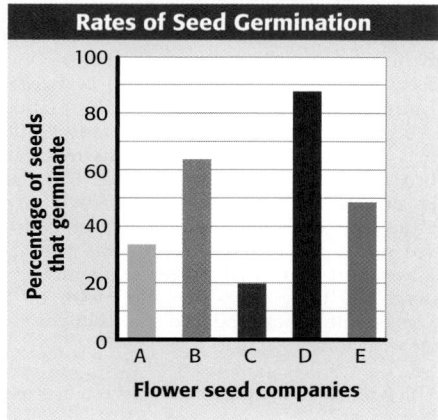

23 Which seed company had the highest rate of seed germination? the lowest rate of seed germination?

24 Which seed companies had seed germination rates higher than 50%?

25 If Elaine wanted to buy seeds that had a germination rate higher than 60%, which seed companies would she buy seeds from? Why might Elaine want to buy seeds with a higher germination rate?

Critical Thinking

18. An answer to this exercise can be found at the end of this book.

19. Sample answer: If the seeds germinate before they have been exposed to a long period of cold, they may germinate too early. The cold temperatures may not be over, so the young plants may be exposed to freezing temperatures that may kill the plants.

20. Sample answer: Positive phototropism can ensure that plant shoots get the sunlight that they need for photosynthesis. The positive gravitropism of plant roots ensures that the roots can reach water.

21. Sample answer: I would have to grow the poinsettias under controlled lights. Instead of exposing the poinsettias to long periods of darkness during the winter, I would expose the poinsettias to short periods of darkness and long periods of light. To bloom in the summer, the poinsettias should be exposed to long nights and short days during the summer.

22. Sample answer: Underground stems, such as tubers, can grow into new plants, so the plant likely reproduces asexually in this way.

Interpreting Graphics

23. D; C

24. B and D

25. B and D; More seeds will grow if Elaine buys seeds that have higher germination rates.

CHAPTER RESOURCES

Chapter Resource File

- Chapter Review GENERAL
- Chapter Test A GENERAL
- Chapter Test B ADVANCED
- Chapter Test C SPECIAL NEEDS
- Vocabulary Activity GENERAL

Workbooks

Study Guide
- Assessment resources are also available in Spanish.

Standardized Test Preparation

Teacher's Note

To provide practice under more realistic testing conditions, give students 20 minutes to answer all of the questions in this Standardized Test Preparation.

MISCONCEPTION ALERT

Answers to the standardized test preparation can help you identify student misconceptions and misunderstandings.

READING

Passage 1

1. C
2. I
3. A

✚ TEST DOCTOR

Question 1: Students may answer that crossbreeding has produced colored cotton with short fibers if they misread the passage or the answer responses. It would be correct if the statement said that the fibers were long. The statement that colored cotton is better than white cotton is an opinion. Native Americans may have harvested white cotton, but the passage states that Native Americans harvested different shades of cotton.

READING

Read each of the passages below. Then, answer the questions that follow each passage.

Passage 1 Cotton fibers are contained in the plant's seed pods, or bolls. Bolls open at maturity to reveal a fuzzy mass of fibers and seeds. Once the seeds are removed, the fibers can be twisted into yarn and used to make many kinds of fabric. The fibers in cotton plants are naturally white, so they must be dyed with chemicals to create the bright colors seen in many fabrics. Different shades of cotton have been harvested by Native Americans for centuries. These types of cotton showed some resistance to insect pests but had fibers too short to be used by the textile industry. Crossbreeding these types of cotton with other varieties of cotton has produced strains of colored cotton with long fibers.

1. Which of the following statements is a fact in the passage?
   A Crossbreeding colored cotton has produced colored cotton with short fibers.
   B Colored cotton is better than white cotton.
   C Cotton fibers can be used to make fabrics.
   D Native Americans harvested only white cotton.

2. Based on the passage, how are bright fabric colors produced?
   F The cotton fibers are twisted into a yarn.
   G Crossbreeding different varieties of cotton produces brightly colored fabrics.
   H Cotton with long fibers is always brightly colored.
   I Cotton must be dyed with chemicals.

3. Based on the passage, how has crossbreeding benefited the textile industry?
   A It produced colored cotton with long fibers.
   B It produced white cotton with long fibers.
   C It produced cotton yarn.
   D It produced brightly colored cotton.

Passage 2 Most above-ground plant surfaces are covered by a waxy <u>cuticle</u>. The cuticle protects the plant from water loss. Carbon dioxide enters the plant's leaves through stomata (singular, *stoma*). A stoma is an opening in the leaf's epidermis and cuticle. Each stoma is surrounded by two guard cells, which act like double doors, opening and closing the gap. When stomata are open, carbon dioxide enters the leaf. The oxygen produced during photosynthesis diffuses out of leaf cells and exits the leaf through stomata. Water vapor also exits the leaf in this way. The loss of water from leaves is called *transpiration*.

1. In the passage, the word *cuticle* most likely means which of the following?
   A protective covering
   B double doors
   C water vapor
   D transpiration

2. Based on the passage, which of the following is true about stomata?
   F Oxygen enters the leaf through the stomata.
   G Stomata are always open.
   H Stomata are surrounded by two guard cells.
   I Carbon dioxide exits the leaf through the stomata.

3. Which of the following statements about water vapor is a fact in the passage?
   A Water vapor enters the leaf through the stomata.
   B Water vapor is produced during photosynthesis.
   C Water vapor is lost through transpiration.
   D Water vapor does not enter or exit the leaf.

Passage 2

1. A
2. H
3. C

✚ TEST DOCTOR

Question 2: Students may answer that water vapor enters through the stomata, but the passage states that water vapor exits the leaf through the stomata during transpiration. The passage also states that stomata are surrounded by guard cells that open and close the stomata, so stomata are not always open. Finally, the passage states that carbon dioxide enters through the stomata rather than exiting through the stomata.

The graph below shows the pollen counts for three kinds of plants over a 5-day period. Use the graph below to answer the questions that follow.

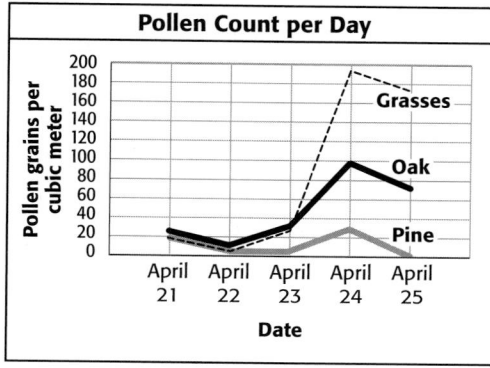

Pollen Count per Day

1. On which of the following days was grass pollen the most common type of pollen?
   A April 21
   B April 22
   C April 23
   D April 24

2. What was the total pollen count for April 24?
   F 30 pollen grains per cubic meter
   G 100 pollen grains per cubic meter
   H 190 pollen grains per cubic meter
   I 320 pollen grains per cubic meter

3. On what days were the total pollen counts lower than 100 pollen grains per cubic meter?
   A April 21, April 22, and April 23
   B April 22 and April 23
   C April 23, April 24, and April 25
   D April 24 and April 25

4. What was the pollen count for grasses on April 25?
   F 0 pollen grains per cubic meter
   G 75 pollen grains per cubic meter
   H 175 pollen grains per cubic meter
   I 250 pollen grains per cubic meter

Read each question below, and choose the best answer.

1. Choose the list in which the numbers are in order from smallest to greatest.
   A 0.123, 0.132, 0.321, 0.231
   B 0.321, 0.231, 0.132, 0.123
   C 0.123, 0.132, 0.231, 0.321
   D 0.123, 0.231, 0.132, 0.321

2. If a plant stem takes 6 h to bend 90° toward the light coming from a window, about how many degrees does the stem bend each minute?
   F 0.07°
   G 0.25°
   H 4°
   I 15°

3. If $50 = 3x + 20$, what is x?
   A 10
   B 23
   C 73
   D 90

4. In a swamp that is 20 km long and 15 km wide, there are 1,200 orchid plants. On average, how many orchids are there per square kilometer in this swamp?
   F 4
   G 35
   H 60
   I 80

5. A certain plant grows 0.12 cm per day. About how many meters will the plant grow in a year?
   A 0.044 m
   B 0.44 m
   C 4.4 m
   D 44 m

Standardized Test Preparation

1. D
2. I
3. A
4. H

 TEST DOCTOR

Question 4: For April 25, 0 pollen grains per cubic meter is the pollen count for pine, 75 pollen grains per cubic meter is the pollen count for oak, and 250 pollen grains per cubic meter is the total pollen count.

1. C
2. G
3. A
4. F
5. B

 **TEST DOCTOR**

Question 2: Students should convert 6 h to minutes and divide 90 by that number (360 min). If students divide 6 by 90, they will get the incorrect answer of 0.07°. If they divide 360 by 90, they will get the incorrect answer of 4°. If students divide 90 by 6, they will get the incorrect answer of 15°. A protractor may help students visualize 90° and some of the increments listed as answers.

Question 5: Students should multiply 0.12 cm by 365 days, but they will need to convert the answer from centimeters to meters. If they forget to do so, students will incorrectly answer 44 m. If students divide the answer by a factor of 10 rather than a factor of 100 (there are 100 cm in a meter), they will incorrectly answer 4.4 m. If students divide by 1,000, they will incorrectly answer 0.044 m.

CHAPTER RESOURCES

Chapter Resource File

 • Standardized Test Preparation **GENERAL**

State Resources

 For specific resources for your state, visit **go.hrw.com** and type in the keyword **HSMSTR**.

Weird Science

Background

The corpse flower, or titan arum (*Amorphophallus titanum*), generates heat to disperse malodorous sulfuric compounds across a great distance. This metabolic burn of the plant's stored carbohydrates uses up an enormous amount of energy. This is one reason that the titan arum seldom blooms—in the wild, it may bloom only three to four times within 40 years.

Scientific Debate

ACTIVITY ———— GENERAL

Have an ecologist or a landscaper come to the classroom and talk to your class about how to plan, plant, and take care of a native plant garden. Then, have students research and design a native plant garden. After students design their native plant gardens, consider choosing one of the designs and having the class plant the garden in the schoolyard or on an empty lot. Be sure to get the appropriate permission before planting the garden. Your community may have other native plant gardens that your class can visit for inspiration.

Science in Action

Weird Science

What's That Smell?

Imagine that you are walking through a tropical rain forest. You're surrounded by green—green leaves, green vines, and green trees. You can hear monkeys and birds calling to each other. When you touch the plants nearby, they are wet from a recent rain shower. But what's that horrible smell? You don't see any rotting garbage around, but you do see a huge flower spike. As you get closer, the smell gets stronger. Then, you realize the flower is what smells so bad! The flower is called a *corpse flower*. The corpse flower is just one plant that uses bad odors to attract pollinators.

Math ACTIVITY

A corpse flower sprouts and grows to a maximum height of 2.35 m in 28 days. In centimeters, what is the average growth of the corpse flower per day?

Scientific Debate

Are Exotic Species Helpful or Harmful?

Have you visited the coast of California? If so, you may have seen large eucalyptus trees. You may be surprised to know that those trees are an exotic species. An *exotic species* is an organism that makes a new home for itself in a new place. People brought eucalyptus trees to California to use them in their yards and gardens. Since then, eucalyptus trees have spread to other areas. Exotic species often take over areas. Exotic species may compete with native species. Sometimes, exotic species keep native species from surviving. But in urban areas, exotic species are sometimes the only plants that will grow. So, are exotic species helpful or harmful?

Social Studies ACTIVITY

Identify an exotic species that people imported to grow in their gardens. Find out where the exotic species came from and the effect it is having on the environment.

Answer to Math Activity
8.4 cm per day (2.35 m × 100 cm/m = 235 cm; 235 cm ÷ 28 days = 8.4 cm/day)

Answer to Social Studies Activity
Students may be surprised to discover that many of the plants that they are familiar with are exotic species. Some of these plants include alfalfa, bamboo, catnip, kudzu, and dandelion. Students should recognize that exotic species can have an adverse effect on native species.

Careers

Nalini Nadkarni

Canopy Scientist As a child, Nalini Nadkarni loved to climb trees. She still does. Nadkarni is a biologist who studies the forest canopy. The canopy is the uppermost layer of the trees. It includes leaves, twigs, and branches and the air among them. Far above the ground, the canopy is home to many different plants, birds, insects, and other animals.

Canopy science was a new field of study when Nadkarni started her research 20 years ago. Because most canopies are tall, few scientists visited them. Most field biologists did their research with both feet planted firmly on the ground. Today, scientists know that the canopy is an important habitat for wildlife.

Nadkarni tells others about the importance of forests. As she puts it, "I can have a real impact in raising public awareness of the need to save forests." Nadkarni has invited artists and musicians to visit the canopy. "In my job, I try to understand the science of the canopy, but artists and musicians help capture the aesthetic value of the canopy."

Language Arts ACTIVITY

WRITING SKILL Imagine that you are a canopy scientist. Then, write a creative story about something that you would like to study in the canopy.

go.hrw.com

To learn more about these Science in Action topics, visit **go.hrw.com** and type in the keyword **HL5PL2F**.

Current Science

Check out Current Science® articles related to this chapter by visiting go.hrw.com. Just type in the keyword **HL5CS13**.

UNIT 5

TIMELINE

Animals

Have you ever been to a zoo or watched a wild-animal program on TV? If so, you have some idea of how many types of animals—from tiny insects to massive whales—are found on Earth.

Animals are fascinating, in part because of their variety in appearance and behavior. They also teach us about ourselves because humans are also classified as animals.

In this unit, you will learn about many types of animals—maybe even some that you never knew existed. So, get ready for an animal adventure!

1610
Galileo Galilei uses a compound microscope to study insect anatomy.

1681
The Mauritius Dodo, a flightless bird, becomes extinct.

1827
John James Audubon publishes the first edition of *Birds of America*.

1839
The first bicycle is constructed.

1983
The U.S. Space Shuttle *Challenger* is launched. Sally Ride, the first American woman in space, is on board.

1987
The last wild California condor is captured in an effort to save the species from extinction.

1995
Fourteen Canadian gray wolves are reintroduced into Yellowstone National Park.

1693
John Ray correctly identifies whales as mammals.

1761
The first veterinary school is founded in Lyons, France.

1775
J. C. Fabricius develops a system for the classification of insects.

1882
Research on the ship *The Albatross* helps increase our knowledge of marine life.

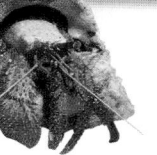

1935
Francis B. Sumner studies the protective coloration of fish.

1960
Jane Goodall, an English zoologist, begins her research on chimpanzees in Tanzania.

1998
Keiko, the killer-whale star of the movie *Free Willy,* is taught to catch fish so that he can be released from captivity.

2003
Researchers find that individual cloned pigs behave in very different ways. This finding shows that environmental conditions affect behavior.

Animals and Behavior
Chapter Planning Guide

Compression guide:
To shorten instruction because of time limitations, omit the Chapter Lab.

OBJECTIVES	LABS, DEMONSTRATIONS, AND ACTIVITIES	TECHNOLOGY RESOURCES
PACING • 90 min pp. 354–359 **Chapter Opener**	**SE Start-up Activity,** p. 355 `GENERAL`	**OSP Parent Letter** ■ `GENERAL` **CD Student Edition on CD-ROM** **CD Guided Reading Audio CD** ■ **TR Chapter Starter Transparency*** **VID Brain Food Video Quiz**
Section 1 What Is an Animal? • Describe the difference between vertebrates and invertebrates. • Describe the five characteristics that all animals share.	**SE School-to-Home Activity** Explore Your Home, p. 357 `GENERAL` **TE Group Activity** Animal Diversity, p. 357 `GENERAL` **TE Activity** Animal Traits, p. 358 `BASIC`	**CRF Lesson Plans*** **TR Bellringer Transparency*** **TR Organs of a Shark***
PACING • 90 min pp. 360–365 **Section 2 Animal Behavior** • Explain the difference between learned and innate behavior. • Describe five kinds of behaviors that help animals survive. • Name three cycles that are influenced by biological clocks.	**TE Demonstration** Sign Language, p. 361 ◆ `GENERAL` **SE Quick Lab** Migration Mapping, p. 363 `GENERAL` **CRF Datasheet for Quick Lab*** **TE Activity** Observing Animals, p. 363 `BASIC` **SE Connection to Environmental Science** Do Not Disturb, p. 364 `GENERAL` **SE Inquiry Lab** Aunt Flossie and the Bumblebee, p. 370 `GENERAL` **CRF Datasheet for Chapter Lab*** **SE Skills Practice Lab** Wet, Wiggly Worms!,* p. 779 `GENERAL` **CRF Datasheet for LabBook*** **LB Inquiry Labs** Follow the Leader* `GENERAL` **LB Whiz-Bang Demonstrations** Six-Legged Thermometer* `ADVANCED`	**CRF Lesson Plans*** **TR Bellringer Transparency*** **TR LINK TO EARTH SCIENCE** Cylindrical Projection/Conic Projection/Azimuthal Projection*** **SE Internet Activity,** p. 361 `GENERAL` **CRF SciLinks Activity*** `GENERAL` **VID Lab Videos for Life Science**
PACING • 45 min pp. 366–369 **Section 3 Social Relationships** • Describe four ways that animals communicate. • List the advantages and disadvantages of living in groups.	**TE Activity** Nonverbal Communication, p. 366 `GENERAL` **TE Connection Activity** Geography, p. 367 `GENERAL` **TE Demonstration** Whale Songs, p. 367 ◆ `BASIC` **LB Long-Term Projects & Research Ideas** Animal-Myth Behaviors* `ADVANCED` **SE Science in Action** Math, Social Studies, and Language Arts Activities, pp. 376–377 `GENERAL`	**CRF Lesson Plans*** **TR Bellringer Transparency*** **TR The Dance of the Bees***

PACING • 90 min

CHAPTER REVIEW, ASSESSMENT, AND STANDARDIZED TEST PREPARATION

CRF Vocabulary Activity* `GENERAL`
SE Chapter Review, pp. 372–373 `GENERAL`
CRF Chapter Review* ■ `GENERAL`
CRF Chapter Tests A* ■ `GENERAL`, **B*** `ADVANCED`, **C*** `SPECIAL NEEDS`
SE Standardized Test Preparation, pp. 374–375 `GENERAL`
CRF Standardized Test Preparation,* `GENERAL`
CRF Performance-Based Assessment* `GENERAL`
OSP Test Generator `GENERAL`
CRF Test Item Listing* `GENERAL`

Online and Technology Resources

Visit **go.hrw.com** for a variety of free resources related to this textbook. Enter the keyword **HL5ANM.**

Holt Online Learning

Students can access interactive problem-solving help and active visual concept development with the *Holt Science and Technology* Online Edition available at **www.hrw.com.**

Guided Reading Audio CD
Also in Spanish

A direct reading of each chapter for auditory learners, reluctant readers, and Spanish-speaking students.

Science Tutor CD-ROM

Excellent for remediation and test practice.

SKILLS DEVELOPMENT RESOURCES	SECTION REVIEW AND ASSESSMENT	STANDARDS CORRELATIONS
SE Pre-Reading Activity, p. 354 `GENERAL` **OSP** Science Puzzlers, Twisters & Teasers `GENERAL`		National Science Education Standards UCP 1, 2; SAI 1, 2; LS 3a, 3c
CRF Directed Reading A* ■ `BASIC`, B* `SPECIAL NEEDS` **CRF** Vocabulary and Section Summary* ■ `GENERAL` **SE** Reading Strategy Prediction Guide, p. 356 `GENERAL` **SS** Science Skills Introduction to Graphs* `GENERAL` **CRF** Reinforcement Worksheet What Makes an Animal an Animal?* `BASIC`	**SE** Reading Checks, pp. 357, 358 `GENERAL` **TE** Homework, p. 357 `GENERAL` **TE** Reteaching, p. 358 `BASIC` **TE** Quiz, p. 358 `GENERAL` **TE** Homework, p. 358 `ADVANCED` **TE** Alternative Assessment, p. 359 `BASIC` **SE** Section Review,* p. 359 ■ `GENERAL` **CRF** Section Quiz* ■ `GENERAL`	UCP 1; SAI 1; HNS 3; LS 1a, 1b, 1d, 2a, 2b, 4b, 5a
CRF Directed Reading A* ■ `BASIC`, B* `SPECIAL NEEDS` **CRF** Vocabulary and Section Summary* ■ `GENERAL` **SE** Reading Strategy Discussion, p. 360 `GENERAL` **TE** Reading Strategy Paired Summarizing, p. 361 `BASIC` **TE** Reading Strategy Prediction Guide, p. 362 `GENERAL` **TE** Inclusion Strategies, p. 363 **SE** Connection to Social Studies Defensive Tools, p. 364 `GENERAL` **MS** Math Skills for Science Average, Mode, and Median* `GENERAL` **CRF** Reinforcement Worksheet Animal Interviews* `BASIC` **CRF** Critical Thinking Masters of Navigation* `ADVANCED`	**SE** Reading Checks, pp. 361, 362, 364 `GENERAL` **TE** Reteaching, p. 364 `BASIC` **TE** Quiz, p. 364 `GENERAL` **TE** Alternative Assessment, p. 364 `GENERAL` **SE** Section Review,* p. 365 ■ `GENERAL` **CRF** Section Quiz* ■ `GENERAL`	UCP 1, 3, 5; SAI 1; LS 1a, 3a, 3b, 3c, 3d, 5b; *Chapter Lab:* UCP 2; SAI 1, 2; LS 3c; *LabBook:* UCP 2, 3; SAI 1, 2; HNS 2; LS 3c
CRF Directed Reading A* ■ `BASIC`, B* `SPECIAL NEEDS` **CRF** Vocabulary and Section Summary* ■ `GENERAL` **SE** Reading Strategy Paired Summarizing, p. 366 `BASIC` **TE** Inclusion Strategies, p. 368	**SE** Reading Checks, pp. 366, 368 `GENERAL` **TE** Homework, p. 367 `ADVANCED` **TE** Reteaching, p. 368 `BASIC` **TE** Quiz, p. 368 `GENERAL` **TE** Alternative Assessment, p. 368 `GENERAL` **TE** Homework, p. 369 `ADVANCED` **SE** Section Review,* p. 369 ■ `GENERAL` **CRF** Section Quiz* ■ `GENERAL`	UCP 1; SAI 1; LS 1a, 3c, 3d, 4a

One-Stop Planner® CD-ROM

This convenient CD-ROM includes:
- Lab Materials QuickList Software
- Holt Calendar Planner
- Customizable Lesson Plans
- Printable Worksheets
- ExamView® Test Generator

cnnstudentnews.com

Find the latest news, lesson plans, and activities related to important scientific events.

www.scilinks.org

Maintained by the **National Science Teachers Association.** See Chapter Enrichment pages for a complete list of topics.

Current Science®

Check out *Current Science* articles and activities by visiting the HRW Web site at **go.hrw.com.** Just type in the keyword **HL5CS14T.**

Classroom Videos

- **Lab Videos** demonstrate the chapter lab.
- **Brain Food Video Quizzes** help students review the chapter material.
- **CNN Videos** bring science into your students' daily life.

Visual Resources

CHAPTER STARTER TRANSPARENCY

This Really Happened!

Robert S. Ridgely and Lelis Navarrete are ornithologists, people who study birds. In November 1992, they were hiking in the Andes mountains of Ecuador and recording bird songs. Suddenly they heard a sound that was a cross between the hoot of an owl and the bark of a dog. Even though they both had spent a lot of time in the woods, neither of the scientists had ever heard such a sound before.

What was in the woods? They kept hiking, and almost 40 minutes later, they heard the sound again. This time, Ridgely, shown below, taped the sound and quickly played it back. The creature answered and came rushing through the woods toward them. It was a bird! But neither of the experts had ever seen a bird like it.

It turned out to be a species that no one had ever seen before! The bird is about 25 cm long, with long legs and a short tail. It has a broad white stripe across its face and a crown of black.

It hops on the forest floor and eats large insects. So far, the bird does not have a name, but Ridgely and Navarrete have been studying it and will name it soon.

For centuries, people like Robert Ridgely and Lelis Navarrete have used their observation skills to study animals and their behavior. We now know of over over 1 million animal species, and we have learned much about how animals live and interact with other animals. But there are always more discoveries to be made!

BELLRINGER TRANSPARENCIES

Section: What Is an Animal?
What is the best material for washing a car—a cotton rag, a scratch pad, or an animal skeleton?

Explain your answer in your **science journal**.

Section: Animal Behavior
Write a sentence to describe each of the following terms:
predator
prey
List three animals that are predators and three that are prey. Are humans predators or prey? Explain your answer.

Write your answers in your **science journal**.

TEACHING TRANSPARENCIES

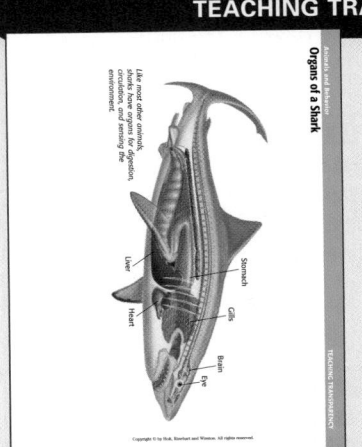

Organs of a Shark

The Dance of the Bees

TEACHING TRANSPARENCIES

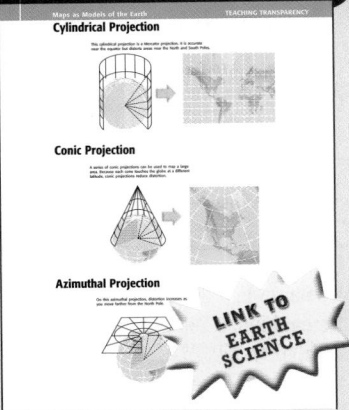

Cylindrical Projection

Conic Projection

Azimuthal Projection

LINK TO EARTH SCIENCE

Chapter: Maps as Models of the Earth

CONCEPT MAPPING TRANSPARENCY

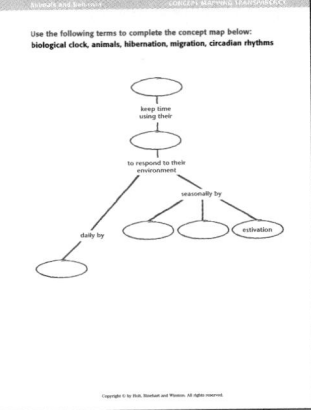

Use the following terms to complete the concept map below:
biological clock, animals, hibernation, migration, circadian rhythms

Planning Resources

LESSON PLANS

Lesson Plan SAMPLE

Section: Waves

Pacing
Regular Schedule: with lab(s):2 days without lab(s):2 days
Block Schedule: with lab(s):1 1/2 days without lab(s):1 day

Objectives
1. Relate the seven properties of life to a living organism.
2. Describe seven themes that can help you to organize what you learn about biology.
3. Identify the tiny structures that make up all living organisms.
4. Differentiate between reproduction and heredity and between metabolism and homeostasis.

National Science Education Standards Covered
LSInter6:Cells have particular structures that underlie their functions.
LSMat1: Most cell functions involve chemical reactions.
LSBeh1: Cells store and use information to guide their functions.
UCP1:Cell functions are regulated.
SI1: Cells can differentiate and form complete multicellular organisms.
PS1: Species evolve over time.
ESS1: The great diversity of organisms is the result of more than 3.5 billion years of evolution.
ESS2: Natural selection and its evolutionary consequences provide a scientific explanation for the fossil record of ancient life forms as well as for the striking molecular similarities observed among the diverse species of living organisms.
ST1: The millions of different species of plants, animals, and microorganisms that live on Earth today are related by descent from common ancestors.
ST2: The energy for life primarily comes from the sun.
SPSP1: The complexity and organization of organisms accommodates the need for obtaining, transforming, transporting, releasing, and eliminating the matter and energy used to sustain the organism.
SPSP6: As matter and energy flows through different levels of organization of living systems—cells, organs, communities—and between living systems and the physical environment, chemical elements are recombined in different ways.
HNS1: Organisms have behavioral responses to internal changes and to external stimuli.

PARENT LETTER

SAMPLE

Dear Parent,

Your son's or daughter's science class will soon begin exploring the chapter entitled "The World of Physical Science." In this chapter, students will learn about how the scientific method applies to the world of physical science and the role of physical science in the world. By the end of the chapter, students should demonstrate a clear understanding of the chapter's main ideas and be able to discuss the following topics:

1. physical science as the study of energy and matter (Section 1)
2. the role of physical science in the world around them (Section 1)
3. careers that rely on physical science (Section 1)
4. the steps used in the scientific method (Section 2)
5. examples of technology (Section 2)
6. how the scientific method is used to answer questions and solve problems (Section 2)
7. how our knowledge of science changes over time (Section 2)
8. how models represent real objects or systems (Section 3)
9. examples of different ways models are used in science (Section 3)
10. the importance of the International System of Units (Section 4)
11. the appropriate units to use for particular measurements (Section 4)
12. how area and density are derived quantities (Section 4)

Questions to Ask Along the Way

You can help your son or daughter learn about these topics by asking interesting questions such as the following:

- What are some surprising careers that use physical science?
- What is a characteristic of a good hypothesis?
- When is it a good idea to use a model?
- Why do Americans measure things in terms of inches and yards and meters ?

ALSO IN SPANISH

TEST ITEM LISTING

TEST ITEM LISTING
The World of Science SAMPLE

MULTIPLE CHOICE

1. A limitation of models is that
a. they are large enough to see.
b. they do not act exactly like the things that they model.
c. they are smaller than the things that they model.
d. they model unfamiliar things.
Answer: B   Difficulty: 1   Section: 3   Objective: 2

2. The length 10 m is equal to
a. 100 cm.   c. 10,000 mm.
b. 1,000 cm.   d. Both (b) and (c)
Answer: B   Difficulty: 1   Section: 3   Objective: 2

3. To be valid, a hypothesis must be
a. testable.   c. made into a law.
b. supported by evidence.   d. Both (a) and (b)
Answer: D   Difficulty: 1   Section: 3   Objective: 2

4. The statement "Sheila has a stain on her shirt" is an example of a(n)
a. law.   c. observation.
b. hypothesis.   d. prediction.
Answer: B   Difficulty: 1   Section: 2   Objective: 2

5. A hypothesis is often developed out of
a. observations.   c. laws.
b. experiments.   d. Both (a) and (b)
Answer: B   Difficulty: 1   Section: 3   Objective: 2

6. How many milliliters are in 3.5 kL?
a. 3,500 mL.   c. 3,500, 000 mL.
b. 0.0035 mL.   d. 35,000 mL.
Answer: B   Difficulty: 1   Section: 3   Objective: 2

7. A map of Seattle is an example of a
a. law.   c. model.
b. theory.   d. unit.
Answer: B   Difficulty: 1   Section: 3   Objective: 2

8. A lab that has safety issues shown below: These icons mean that you should wear
a. only safety goggles.   c. safety goggles and a lab apron.
b. only a lab apron.   d. safety goggles, a lab apron, and gloves.
Answer: B   Difficulty: 1   Section: 3   Objective: 2

9. The law of conservation of mass says the lot al mass before a chemical change is
a. more than the total mass after the change.
b. less than the total mass after the change.
c. the same as the total mass after the change.
d. not the same as the total mass after the change.
Answer: B   Difficulty: 1   Section: 3   Objective: 2

10. In which of the following areas might you find a geochemist at work?
a. studying the chemistry of rocks   c. studying fishes
b. studying forestry   d. studying the atmosphere

One-Stop Planner® CD-ROM

This CD-ROM includes all of the resources shown here and the following time-saving tools:

- *Lab Materials QuickList Software*
- *Customizable lesson plans*
- *Holt Calendar Planner*
- *The powerful ExamView® Test Generator*

Meeting Individual Needs

DIRECTED READING A
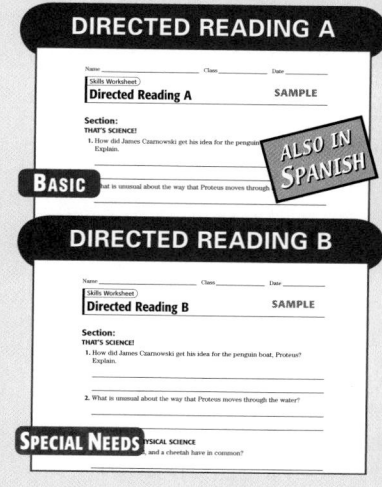

VOCABULARY ACTIVITY
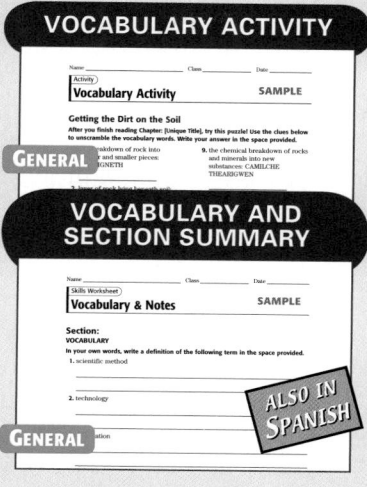

REINFORCEMENT
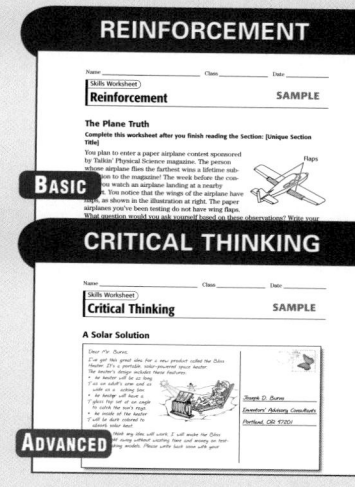

SCILINKS ACTIVITY

Labs and Activities

LONG-TERM PROJECTS & RESEARCH IDEAS
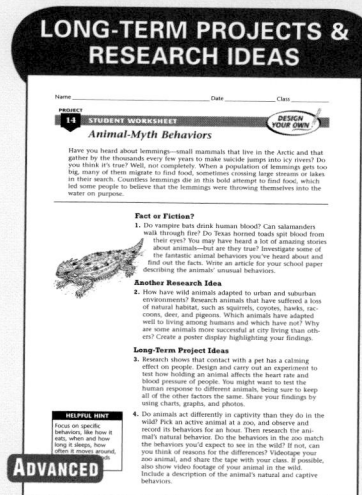

WHIZ-BANG DEMONSTRATIONS
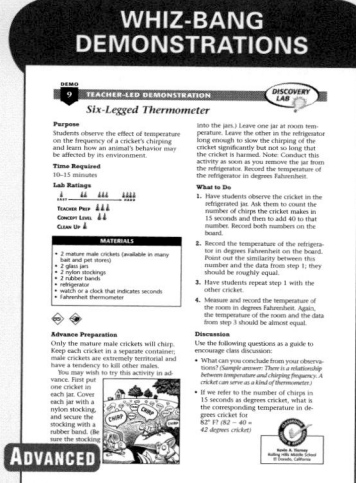

INQUIRY LABS
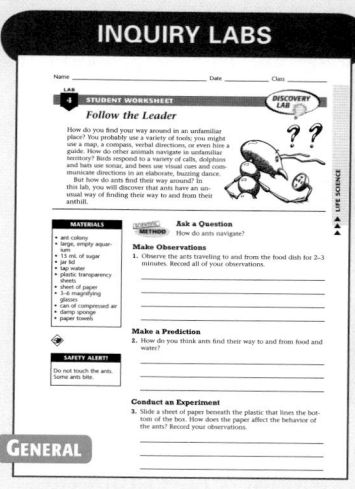

DATASHEETS FOR QUICK LABS

Review and Assessments

SECTION QUIZ
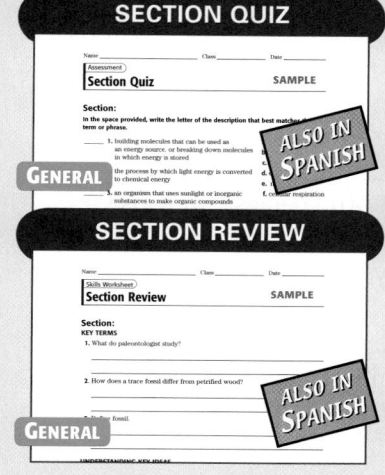

CHAPTER REVIEW
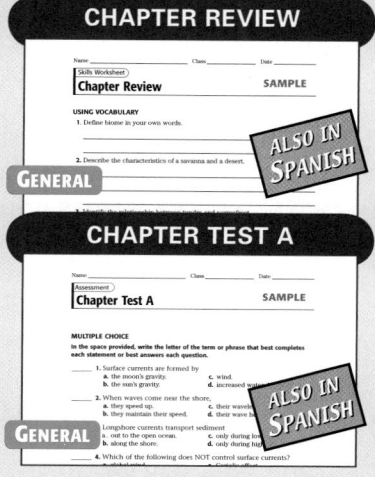

CHAPTER TEST B
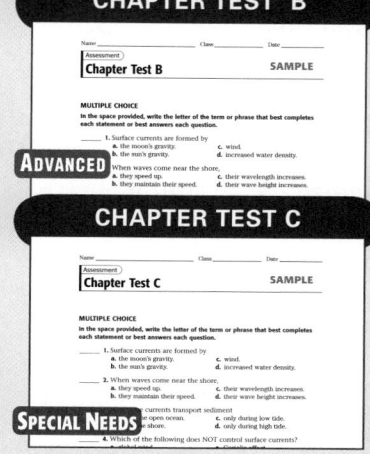

STANDARDIZED TEST PREPARATION
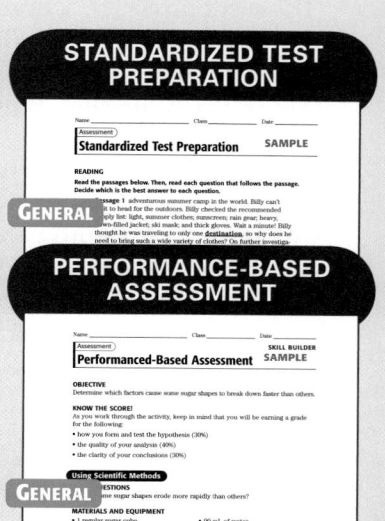

This Chapter Enrichment provides relevant and interesting information to expand and enhance your presentation of the chapter material.

Section 1

What Is an Animal?

Animal Classifications

- Zoologists classify members of the animal kingdom based on their similarities and differences. One major distinction is whether an animal has no ceolom, a false coelom, or a true coelom. A coelom is a body cavity that contains internal organs. Animals with a true coelom are divided into two groups based on how they develop: protostomes and deuterostomes.

- The animal kingdom has about 35 phyla, and each phylum may be divided into subphyla and other subgroups. The phylum Chordata (meaning "cord") has three subphyla: Urochordata (including tunicates), Cephalochordata (including lancelets), and Vertebrata (the vertebrates). Vertebrates include fish, amphibians, reptiles, birds, and mammals.

- The vast majority of animals are invertebrates. Major invertebrate phyla include Arthropoda (meaning "jointed foot"), Porifera (meaning "hole bearers"), Nematoda (meaning "thread"), and Echinodermata (meaning "spiny skin"). Arthropoda, which includes crustaceans, spiders, millipedes, and insects, is by far the largest phylum. It includes more than 1 million living species.

Animal Reproduction

- Some animals can reproduce both sexually and asexually. The adult jellyfish, or medusa, releases sperm and eggs into the water. Fertilization results in a planula larva. When the planula matures into a polyp, it grows and buds off new medusas. These medusas then grow into adult jellyfish and start sexual reproduction again.

Moving Around

- Animals use a variety of techniques to move from place to place. Cephalopods, which include the squid and the octopus, have a unique way of moving. They can move quickly to escape from predators by forcing a powerful jet of water from a siphon near their head.

- Kangaroo rats have powerful hind legs that help them quickly leap away from predators. Their tail, which acts like a rudder, enables them to change course while in midair.

Section 2

Animal Behavior

Animal Survival Strategies

- Animals use a variety of methods to defend themselves and sometimes their families from predators. Many species emit toxic chemicals. Others have ways to confuse predators, such as releasing a cloud of ink or spraying a terrible scent.

- Jellyfish eject poison-tipped barbs from stinging cells, called *nematocysts,* on their bodies. Although most jellyfish stings can't penetrate human skin, the stings of the Portuguese man-of-war and the box jellyfish are exceptions. Stings from both species can cause extreme pain and even death. Don't ever step on a dead jellyfish. The nematocysts can still sting!

- A type of Chrysomelid beetle has such a toxic poison that the San, a tribe living mainly in Africa's Kalahari Desert, tip their arrows with it. The poison causes death by paralysis.

Learned and Innate Behaviors

- All behaviors, innate or learned, represent an interplay of genes and the environment. An innate behavior may appear in its fully functional form the first time it is performed. Innate behavior expresses itself without prior experience. Learned behavior depends on experience.

Animal Migration

- Ruby-throated hummingbirds, which live as far north as Canada during the summer, fly to Central America in the fall. Their route requires them to fly 833 km (500 mi) nonstop over the Gulf of Mexico.

Human Seasonal Rhythms

- Although humans don't hibernate or estivate, our biological rhythms are affected by seasonal changes. Seasonal affective disorder (SAD) is a form of depression that many people, especially those in northern countries, experience during the winter. Common symptoms include feeling fatigued, sleeping more than usual, craving carbohydrates, and experiencing an increase in appetite and sudden weight gain. Researchers have found that many people who have SAD improve when they undergo light therapy, or phototherapy.

Section 3

Social Relationships

Animal Communication

- Some kinds of animals live together, and others maintain a solitary existence. Both situations offer advantages and disadvantages. Regardless of how animals live, they communicate with each other to protect themselves, to find food, to display dominance, to find mates, and for many other reasons.

- Although both octopuses and squids are cephalopods, their social habits are quite different. Octopuses are solitary creatures, whereas squids are frequently found in schools.

- Besides using a "waggle dance" to communicate the location of nectar, honeybees communicate information about the taste and smell of food resources. They communicate this information through the process of trophallaxis, or the regurgitation of food into the mouths of members of the colony.

Is That a Fact!

- Elephants have several distinct vocal calls, including the familiar trumpet that elephants make when they are excited. Elephants can also communicate dozens of messages through low-frequency, infrasonic rumbles. Such sounds can travel about 5 km.

- Some antelopes have glands on their hooves that release a scent onto the ground. Individuals that get separated from the group can follow this scent to find their way back to the group.

SciLinks — Developed and maintained by the National Science Teachers Association

SciLinks is maintained by the National Science Teachers Association to provide you and your students with interesting, up-to-date links that will enrich your classroom presentation of the chapter.

Visit www.scilinks.org and enter the SciLinks code for more information about the topic listed.

Topic: Vertebrates and Invertebrates
SciLinks code: HSM1603

Topic: Animal Behavior
SciLinks code: HSM0069

Topic: Rhythms of Life
SciLinks code: HSM1311

Topic: Communication in the Animal Kingdom
SciLinks code: HSM0320

Overview

Tell students that this chapter will help them learn about animal characteristics, including behavior. The chapter describes what makes an organism an animal and discusses a variety of animal behaviors.

Assessing Prior Knowledge

Students should be familiar with the following topics:

- cells
- classification

Identifying Misconceptions

As students learn the material in this chapter, some of them may be surprised to learn that most animals in the world are invertebrates. Some students may have the misconception that all animals are organisms that have two eyes, a nose, and a mouth. Emphasize that the animal kingdom is very diverse and that vertebrates make up a small portion of the world's animals.

Animals and Behavior

About the

This spider needs to eat in order to survive. On the other hand, this hover fly needs to avoid being eaten in order to survive. How do the spider, the fly, and other animals get what they need to live? Animals use many behaviors to compete with each other for survival.

PRE-READING ACTIVITY

Graphic
Organizer

Spider Map Before you read the chapter, create the graphic organizer entitled "Spider Map" described in the **Study Skills** section of the Appendix. Label the circle "Animal Behavior." Create a leg for each type of animal behavior. As you read the chapter, fill in the map with details about each type of animal behavior.

Standards Correlations

National Science Education Standards

The following codes indicate the National Science Education Standards that correlate to this chapter. The full text of the standards is at the front of the book.

Chapter Opener
UCP 1, 2; SAI 1, 2; LS 3a, 3c

Section 1 What Is an Animal?
UCP 1; SAI 1; HNS 3; LS 1a, 1b, 1d, 2a, 2b, 4b, 5a

Section 2 Animal Behavior
UCP 1, 3, 5; SAI 1; LS 1a, 3a, 3b, 3c, 3d, 5b

Section 3 Social Relationships
UCP 1; SAI 1; LS 1a, 3c, 3d, 4a

Chapter Lab
UCP 2; SAI 1, 2; LS 3c; *LabBook:* UCP 2, 3; SAI 1, 2; HNS 2; LS 3c

Chapter Review
UCP 1; SAI 1; LS 1a, 3c

Science in Action
SAI 1, 2; HNS 3; LS 3c, 3d

START-UP ACTIVITY

Go on a Safari!

You don't have to travel far to see interesting animals. If you look closely, you can find many animals nearby. **Caution:** Always be careful around wild or unfamiliar animals, because they may bite or sting. Do not handle wild animals or any animals that are unfamiliar to you.

Procedure

1. Go outside, and find **two different kinds of animals** to observe.
2. Without disturbing the animals, watch them quietly for a few minutes from a distance. You may want to use **binoculars** or a **magnifying lens.**
3. Write down everything you notice about each animal. Do you know what kind of animal each is? Where did you find them? What do they look like? How big are they? What are they doing? You may want to draw a picture of them.

Analysis

1. Compare the two animals that you studied. Do they look alike? Do they have similar behaviors?
2. How do the animals move? Did you see them communicating with other animals or defending themselves?
3. Can you tell what each animal eats? What characteristics of each animal help it find or catch food?

Chapter Starter Transparency
Use this transparency to help students begin thinking about animals that are not yet known to scientists.

Focus

Overview

This section provides students with an introduction to the animal kingdom. Students will find out the difference between vertebrates and invertebrates. Students will also discover the characteristics that set animals apart from all other living things.

🔊 Bellringer

While you are taking attendance, ask students to ponder this question: "What is the best material for washing a car—a cotton rag, a scratch pad, or an animal skeleton? Explain your answer." Have students take a few moments to record their answer in their **science journal.** Before you begin the section, call on individual students to give their answer and reasoning. (It may surprise some students to learn that genuine sponges—ones that some people use for washing cars—are animal skeletons. During the process of preparing sponges for sale, all tissue is removed from the animals, leaving only skeletal remains. Although there are thousands of sponge species, fewer than 20 of them have any commercial value.)

SECTION
1

What Is an Animal?

What do you think of when you hear the word animal*? You may think of your dog or cat. You may think about giraffes or grizzly bears. But would you think of a sponge?*

The natural sponges that people use for washing are the remains of an animal. Animals come in many shapes and sizes. Some have four legs and fur, but most do not. Some are too small to be seen without a microscope, and others are bigger than a school bus. They are all part of the animal kingdom.

Animal Diversity

How many different kinds of animals do you see in **Figure 1**? You may be surprised to learn that feather stars and corals are animals. Spiders, fish, and birds are also animals. And slugs, kangaroos, and monkeys are animals, too. Scientists have named more than 1 million species of animals. Many species that exist have not yet been named. Some scientists estimate that more than 3 million species of animals live on the Earth.

Vertebrates

Most animals look nothing like humans. However, we share many characteristics with a group of animals called vertebrates (VUHR tuh brits). A *vertebrate* is an animal that has a backbone. Vertebrates include fishes, amphibians, reptiles, birds, and mammals. Humans are one of about 5,000 species of mammals.

Figure 1 *All of the living things in this picture are animals.*

Feather star

Fish

Coral

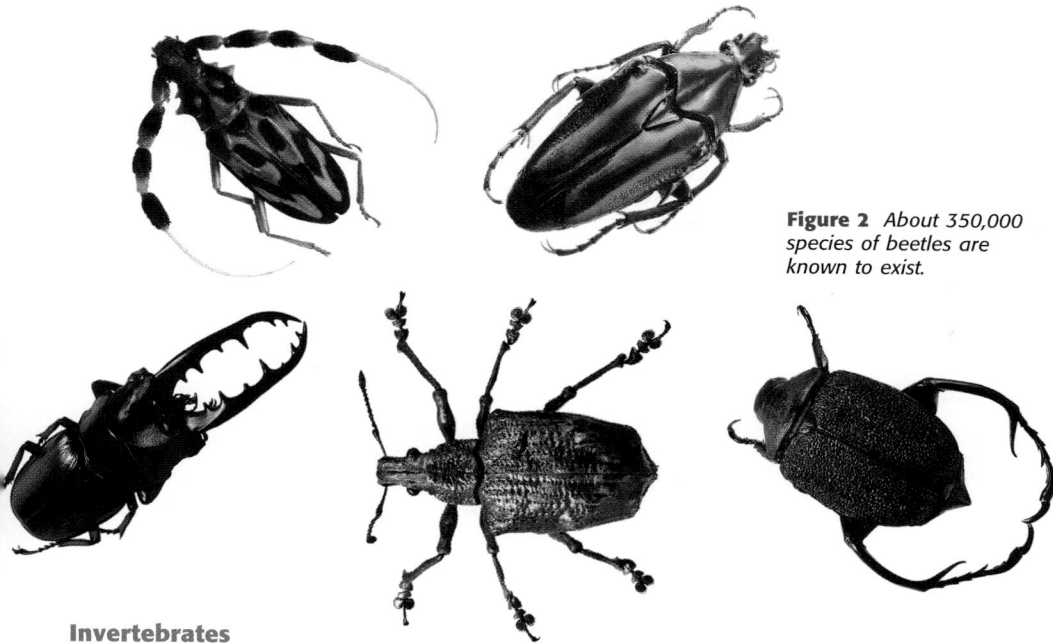

Figure 2 *About 350,000 species of beetles are known to exist.*

Invertebrates

You are probably more familiar with vertebrates than inverte-brates, but vertebrates are definitely the minority among living things. Less than 5% of known animal species are vertebrates. Most animal species are insects, snails, jellyfish, worms, and other *invertebrates* (in VUHR tuh brits), or animals without backbones. In fact, beetles make up more than 30% of all animal species! **Figure 2** shows a few species of beetles.

Reading Check Are people vertebrates or invertebrates? (*See the Appendix for answers to Reading Checks.*)

Animal Characteristics

Sponges, worms, penguins, and lions are animals. But until about 200 years ago, most people thought sponges were plants. And worms don't look anything like penguins or lions. So why do we say all these things are animals? What determines whether a living thing is an animal, a plant, or something else? There is no single answer. But all animals share characteristics that set them apart from all other living things.

Multicellular Makeup

All animals are *multicellular,* which means they are made of many cells. Your own body has trillions of cells. Animal cells are *eukaryotic,* which means they have a nucleus. Unlike plant cells, animal cells do not have cell walls. Animal cells are sur-rounded by only cell membranes.

SCHOOL to HOME

Explore Your Home

With your family, list all the animals that you find around your home. Do you have pets? Do any spiders spin webs outside your front door? Can you see any ani-mals outside your window? Remember that cats, spiders, and birds are animals. When you have finished writing your list, make a poster about the animals you found.

ACTIVITY

Motivate

Group ACTIVITY — GENERAL

Animal Diversity Have students work in groups of four to explore the diversity of animals. Each group should write down two exam-ples for each of the following:

- Arctic animals ("penguin" is incorrect, and "polar bear" is correct)
- Antarctic animals ("polar bear" is incorrect, and "penguin" is correct)
- animals that crawl
- animals that fly
- animals that lack bones
- African animals
- North American animals
- animals that live in the soil
- ocean animals
- animals that have more than four legs

Answers should be as specific as possible. For example, students should answer "garter snake," not "snake," or "praying man-tis" instead of "insect." Have each group share its answers while other groups cross out matches on their own page. How many animals did the class think of? That's diversity!

LS Interpersonal

Answer to Reading Check
vertebrates

Homework ——— GENERAL

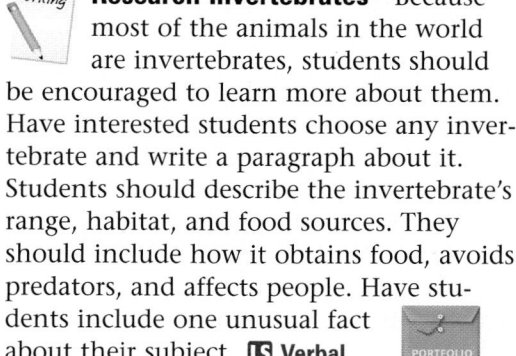

Research Invertebrates Because most of the animals in the world are invertebrates, students should be encouraged to learn more about them. Have interested students choose any inver-tebrate and write a paragraph about it. Students should describe the invertebrate's range, habitat, and food sources. They should include how it obtains food, avoids predators, and affects people. Have stu-dents include one unusual fact about their subject. **LS Verbal** **PORTFOLIO**

Science BLOopers

Platypus Prank? In 1798, when English scholars first observed the duck-billed platypus that had been sent to them by a scientist in Australia, they thought they were the victims of a joke. The English scholars cut and sliced the dead animal for signs of stitches holding the bill and webbed feet to its mammal-like body. Eventually, they came to the con-clusion that the animal was indeed real.

Animal Traits On the board, make a chart with column headings that list the shared animal traits. Label the rows "Tree," "Slug," "Fungus," "Coati," "Snapdragon," "Kookaburra," and "Serval." Tell students to copy this chart. Have them check off which traits are found in each organism. Students may need to check additional resources to identify some of the organisms. **LS** Visual — English Language Learners

Answer to Reading Check
Sample answer: heart, lungs, and kidneys

Close

Reteaching ‎ BASIC

Plants That Eat Animals Help students remember the traits of an animal by asking, "Why aren't pitcher plants, Venus' fly traps, and other plants that eat animals classified as animals?" (They have cell walls, cannot move about, and get some food from photosynthesis.) **LS** Logical

Quiz ‎ GENERAL

1. What do vertebrates have that invertebrates don't? (a skull and a backbone)

2. What are collections of similar cells called? (tissues)

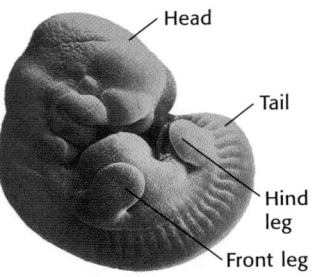

Figure 3 *Embryos are very small. When mouse embryos like this one are 10 days old, they are about 4.5 mm long.*

Head
Tail
Hind leg
Front leg

embryo a plant or animal at an early stage of development

Reproduction and Development

Almost all animals reproduce sexually. These animals make sex cells—eggs or sperm. When an egg and a sperm join during fertilization, they form the first cell of a new organism. This cell divides into many cells to form an embryo (EM bree OH). An **embryo** is an organism at an early stage of development. A mouse embryo is shown in **Figure 3.** Many stages of development follow the embryo stage as an animal grows.

A few animals can reproduce asexually. For example, hydras can reproduce by budding. In *budding,* part of an organism breaks off and develops as a new organism.

Many Specialized Parts

An animal's body has distinct parts that do different things. When a fertilized egg cell divides into many cells to form an embryo, the cells become different from each other. Some of the cells may become skin cells. Other cells may become muscle cells, nerve cells, or bone cells. These different kinds of cells form *tissues,* which are collections of similar cells. For example, muscle cells form muscle tissue, and nerve cells form nerve tissue.

Most animals also have organs. An *organ* is a group of tissues that carry out a special function of the body. Your heart, lungs, and kidneys are all organs. Each organ in an animal's body has a unique job. The shark shown in **Figure 4** has organs that allow the shark to digest food, pump blood, and sense the environment.

> **✓ Reading Check** Name three organs that are inside your body.

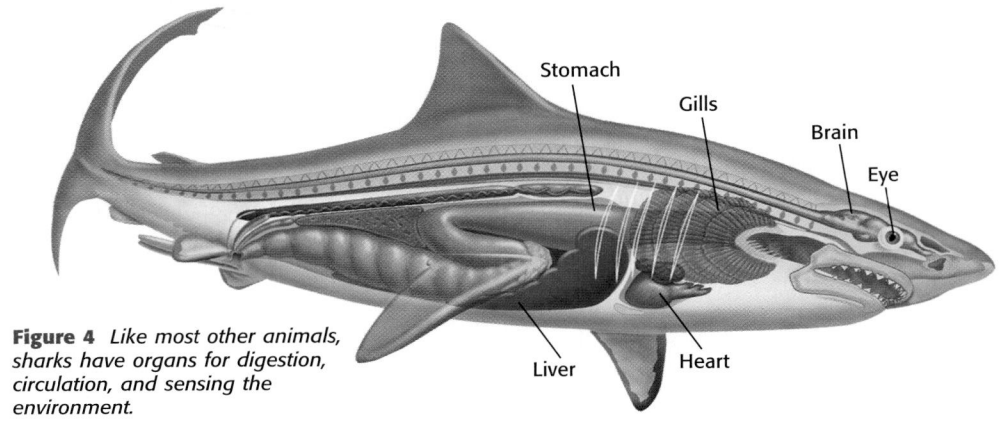

Stomach
Gills
Brain
Eye
Liver
Heart

Figure 4 *Like most other animals, sharks have organs for digestion, circulation, and sensing the environment.*

SCIENCE HUMOR

Q: What lies on the forest floor, 100 feet in the air?

A: a dead centipede

Homework ‎ ADVANCED

Traits by Gender Sometimes, male and female animals develop differently. For example, all lions have hair, but only the male lion has a bushy mane. Have students research unusual physical characteristics of animals that differ between adult males and females. Tell students to prepare a poster with photographs or drawings of their research results. Suggest that students investigate a peacock's feathers, an elephant's tusks, or the coloration in many bird species. **LS** Visual

Movement

Most animals can move from place to place. They may fly, run, swim, or jump. Nearly all animals use movement to search for food, shelter, or mates at some stage of life. However, some animals are less active at certain stages of life than at other stages. For example, young sea anemones swim through the ocean to find their food. But adult sea anemones attach to rocks or the ocean floor and wait for food to arrive.

Consuming

Animals cannot make their own food. All animals survive by eating other organisms or parts and products of other organisms. In other words, animals are consumers. A **consumer** is an organism that eats other organisms. This trait sets animals apart from plants. Though there are a few exceptions, most plants do not eat other organisms. Plants make their own food.

Animals eat a great variety of foods. As shown in **Figure 5,** pandas eat bamboo. Spiders eat other animals. Mosquitoes drink blood. Butterflies drink nectar from flowers. All animals need to eat to survive.

Figure 5 *Pandas eat about 30 pounds of bamboo every day.*

consumer an organism that eats other organisms or organic matter

---

SECTION Review

Summary

- Scientists have named over 1 million animal species. Humans are vertebrates, but most animals are invertebrates.

- Animals are multicellular, reproduce sexually (usually), have many specialized parts, are able to move, and consume other organisms. Only animals have all of these characteristics.

Using Key Terms

1. In your own words, write a definition for each of the following terms: *embryo* and *consumer*.

Understanding Key Ideas

2. Which of the following must be true if a sponge is an animal?
   a. Sponges eat other organisms.
   b. Sponges make their own food.
   c. Sponges move all of the time.
   d. Sponges have a backbone.

3. What five characteristics distinguish animals from other organisms?

4. How are vertebrates different from invertebrates?

Math Skills

5. If a fish can swim short distances at 48 km/h, how long would the fish take to reach a smaller fish that is 3 m away?

Critical Thinking

6. **Applying Concepts** Choose an animal that interests you. Explain how you know that this organism is an animal.

7. **Identifying Relationships** Suppose that a certain fish tank contains the following: water, chemicals, fish, snails, algae, plants, and gravel. Which of these items are alive? Which are animals? Why aren't some of the living organisms classified as animals?

SCiLINKS®

NSTA
Developed and maintained by the
National Science Teachers Association

For a variety of links related to this chapter, go to www.scilinks.org

Topic: Vertebrates and Invertebrates
SciLinks code: HSM1603

CHAPTER RESOURCES

Chapter Resource File

- Section Quiz GENERAL
- Section Review GENERAL
- Vocabulary and Section Summary GENERAL
- Reinforcement Worksheet BASIC

Alternative Assessment ── BASIC

Writing **Animal Examples** Have students write a summary of the characteristics shared by all animals. Tell them not to repeat the boldface paragraph headings in the text. Instead, students must explain each characteristic by first giving an example. (Sample answer: Monkeys run, climb, and swing in trees. Animals move.) **LS Verbal**

Answers to Section Review

1. Sample answer: An embryo is an organism at an early stage of development. A consumer is an organism that eats other organisms or organic matter.

2. a

3. being multicellular, using sexual reproduction (usually), having many specialized parts, being able to move, and being a consumer

4. Vertebrates have a backbone. Invertebrates do not have a backbone.

5. 0.225 s (48 km/h $\times$ 1,000 m/km = 48,000 m/h; 3m $\div$ 48,000 m/h = 0.0000625 h; 0.0000625 h $\times$ 60 min/h $\times$ 60 s/min = 0.225 s)

6. Answers may vary. Sample answer: A fox is an animal. It is multicellular, reproduces sexually, has organs made of specialized tissues, can walk and run, and eats other organisms.

7. Sample answer: Fish, snails, algae, and plants are alive. Fish and snails are animals. Algae and plants are not animals because they can't move and they are not consumers.

Overview

This section introduces students to animal behavior. Students will discover the difference between innate and learned behavior. They will see how animals find food and defend themselves from predators. Finally, they will learn why animal behaviors change at different times of the year and how an animal's biological clock controls its biological cycles.

Bellringer

Ask students to write a sentence that uses each of the following terms: *predator* and *prey*.

Have students list three animals at the end of each sentence that are predators and three that are prey.

Predators hunt for their food. (alligators, sharks, spiders, lions, wolves, rattlesnakes, and eagles)

Prey stay alert to avoid being eaten. (mice, rabbits, pigeons, flies, and deer) English Language Learners

READING WARM-UP

Objectives
● Explain the difference between learned and innate behavior.
● Describe five kinds of behaviors that help animals survive.
● Name three cycles that are influenced by biological clocks.

Terms to Learn
innate behavior
learned behavior
territory
hibernation
estivation
circadian rhythm

READING STRATEGY

Discussion Read this section silently. Write down questions that you have about this section. Discuss your questions in a small group.

Animal Behavior

Suppose that you look out a window and see a bird flying away from a tree. Could the bird be leaving a nest in search of food? Or could the bird be escaping from danger?

Though the bird's purpose may not be clear, the bird is flying away for a specific reason. Animals run from enemies, search for food, battle for territory, and build homes. All of these activities are known as *behavior*.

Kinds of Behavior

How do animals know when a situation is dangerous? How do they know where to find food? Sometimes animals instinctively know how to behave, but sometimes they learn how.

Innate Behavior

Behavior that doesn't depend on learning or experience is known as **innate behavior.** Innate behaviors are inherited through genes. Puppies inherit the tendency to chew, and bees inherit the tendency to fly. The male bird in **Figure 1** inherited the tendency to collect colorful objects for its nest. Some innate behaviors are present at birth. Newborn whales have the innate ability to swim. Other innate behaviors develop months or years after birth. For example, walking is innate for humans. But we do not walk until we are about one year old.

Learned Behavior

Innate behaviors can be modified. Animals can use learning to change a behavior. **Learned behavior** is behavior that has been learned from experience or from observing other animals. Humans inherit the tendency to speak. But the language we use is not inherited. We might learn English, Spanish, or sign language. Humans are not the only animals that change behaviors through learning. All animals can learn.

Figure 1 *The male bowerbird collected colorful objects for its nest to attract the female bowerbird to be his mate.*

CHAPTER RESOURCES

Chapter Resource File

• Lesson Plan
• Directed Reading A BASIC
• Directed Reading B SPECIAL NEEDS

Technology

Transparencies
• Bellringer

Figure 2 *Chimpanzees make and use tools to get ants and other food out of hard-to-reach places.*

Survival Behavior

Animals depend on their behaviors to survive. To stay alive, an animal has to do many things. It must avoid being eaten, and it must find food, water, and a place to live.

Finding Food

Animals find food in many ways. Bees fly from flower to flower collecting nectar. Koala bears climb trees to get eucalyptus leaves. Some animals, such as the chimpanzee shown in **Figure 2,** use tools to get food. Many animals hunt for their food. For example, owls hunt mice.

Animals that eat other animals are known as *predators*. The animal being eaten is the *prey*. Animals that are predators can also be the prey for another animal. For example, a frog eats insects. So the frog is a predator. But a frog may be eaten by a snake. In this case, the frog is the prey.

 **Reading Check** What is the relationship between a predator and its prey? (*See the Appendix for answers to Reading Checks.*)

Marking Territory

Sometimes, members of the same species must compete for food and mates. Some animals claim territories to save energy by avoiding this competition. A **territory** is an area that is occupied by one animal or by a group of animals that do not allow other members of the species to enter. Some birds mark a territory by singing. The song lets other birds know not to enter the area. If other birds do enter the area, the first bird may chase them away. Animals use their territories for mating, raising young, and finding food.

innate behavior an inherited behavior that does not depend on the environment or experience

learned behavior a behavior that has been learned from experience

territory an area that is occupied by one animal or a group of animals that do not allow other members of the species to enter

INTERNET ACTIVITY

For another activity related to this chapter, go to **go.hrw.com** and type in the keyword **HL5ANMW**.

Is That a Fact!

Fun with Food Zoo keepers and pet owners have found that when they challenge their animals to search for food, the animals' appetites improve and activity levels and alertness increase. In addition, the animals genuinely seem to enjoy the search. At one zoo, the polar bears appeared downright depressed until keepers began to hide the bears' food and freeze their fish in big buckets of solid ice. Working for their food simulated the hunting that the bears would have done in the wild, perhaps alleviating some of the stress of captivity.

Teach, continued

Discussion ——— GENERAL

Yawning Begin a discussion by yawning at the front of the classroom. Record how many students yawn as a result. Tell them that yawning is one of the few specific behaviors shared by different animal groups. Reptiles, fish, amphibians, birds, and mammals yawn. Ask students, "Why do we yawn?" (We yawn to rid our body of excess carbon dioxide in order to speed oxygen to our brain when we are tired or nervous. We also yawn when we observe someone else yawning.)
 **Kinesthetic**

Answer to Reading Check

A rabbit can "freeze" to hide from predators, or it can try to outrun predators.

📖 READING STRATEGY ——— GENERAL

Prediction Guide Before students read about seasonal behavior, ask them whether the following statements are true or false.

- Bears sleep through the entire winter. (false)
- Animals that live in hot places such as the desert do not have to deal with seasonal food shortages. (false)
- Frogs can survive through the winter by burying themselves in the mud. (true)

LS Logical

CONNECTION TO Social Studies

WRITING SKILL **Defensive Tools** People use tools to help defend their homes. Some people build homes on stilts to stay safe from floods. Others build smoky fires to force biting insects from their homes. Write a paragraph in your **science journal** about how houses in your area are built to defend people from animals or bad weather.

Figure 3 *Skunks spray irritating chemicals at attackers to protect themselves.*

Defensive Action

Defensive behavior allows animals to protect resources, including territories, from other animals. Animals defend food, mates, and offspring. Have you ever heard a pet dog growl when a person approached while it was eating? Many male animals, such as lions, fight violently to defend mates. Some birds use distraction to defend their young. When a predator is near, a mother killdeer may pretend to have a broken wing and move away from her young. This action distracts the predator's attention from the young so they will remain safe.

Defensive behavior also helps animals protect themselves from predators. One way animals avoid predators is to make themselves hard to see. For example, a rabbit often "freezes" so that its color blends into a background of shrubs or grass. But once a predator is aware of its prey, the prey needs another way to defend itself. Rabbits try to outrun predators. Bees, ants, and wasps inject a powerful acid into their attackers. As seen in **Figure 3,** skunks spray irritating chemicals at predators. Has an animal ever defended itself against you?

✔ **Reading Check** What are two ways a rabbit can defend itself?

Courtship

Animals need to find mates to reproduce. Reproduction is essential for the survival of an individual's genes. Animals have special behaviors that help them find a mate. These behaviors are referred to as *courtship*. Some birds and fish build nests to attract a mate. Other animals use special movements and sounds to attract a mate. **Figure 4** shows two cranes performing a courtship display.

Figure 4 *These Japanese ground cranes use an elaborate courtship dance to tell each other when they are ready to mate.*

CONNECTION to Math ——— GENERAL

Slow Sloths It's hard not to perceive sloths as lazy. However, their slow movement makes them almost invisible to predators and saves energy, too. You may envy the sleeping patterns of sloths; they sleep 15 to 18 hours per day! Ask students this question: "What percentage of the day does the sloth spend asleep?" (63% to 75%) **Logical**
English Language Learners

CHAPTER RESOURCES
Workbooks
📖 **Math Skills for Science** • Average, Mode, and Median GENERAL

Figure 5 *Adult killer whales teach their young how to hunt in the first years of life.*

Parenting

Some animals, such as caterpillars, begin life with the ability to take care of themselves. But many young animals depend on their parents for survival. Some adult birds bring food to their young because they cannot feed themselves at hatching. Other animals, such as the killer whales in **Figure 5,** spend years teaching their young how to hunt for food.

Seasonal Behavior

Humans bundle up when it is cold outside. Many other animals have to deal with bitter cold during the winter, too. They may even face winter food shortages. Frogs hide from the cold by burrowing in mud. Squirrels store food to prepare for winter. Seasonal behaviors help animals adjust to the environment.

Migration

Many animals avoid cold weather by traveling to warmer places. These animals migrate to find food, water, or safe nesting grounds. To *migrate* is to travel from one place to another. Whales, salmon, bats, and even chimpanzees migrate. Each winter, the monarch butterflies shown in **Figure 6** migrate to central Mexico from all over North America. And each fall, birds in the Northern Hemisphere fly south thousands of kilometers. In the spring, they return north to nest.

If you were planning a trip, you would probably use a map. But how do animals know which way to go? For short trips, many animals use landmarks to find their way. *Landmarks* are fixed objects that an animal uses to find its way. Birds use landmarks such as mountain ranges, rivers, and coastlines to find their way.

Migration Mapping

1. Pair up with a classmate to draw a map of your school. Include at least five landmarks.
2. Use a **compass** to label North, South, East, and West on your map.
3. Draw the path you would travel if you were migrating from north to south.
4. Use the landmarks and compass directions to describe the path of your migration.

Figure 6 *When monarch butterflies gather in Mexico for the winter, there can be as many as 4 million butterflies per acre!*

Section 2 • Animal Behavior 363

Reteaching ——— BASIC

Animal Adaptations Have students list as many behaviors or adaptations for winter survival as they can. (Answers may include hibernating, migrating, and collecting and storing food.) **LS** Verbal

Quiz ——— GENERAL

1. How does hibernation help animals? (It helps them save energy when there are food and water shortages.)

2. How do landmarks help animals? (They help animals navigate during short trips.)

Alternative Assessment ——— GENERAL

Writing **Species Reports** Have each student write a brief report about an animal species. Reports should describe the traits that make the species an animal. **LS** Verbal

Answer to Reading Check

mice, squirrels, and skunks

Figure 7 *Bears slow down for the winter, but they do not enter deep hibernation.*

hibernation a period of inactivity and lowered body temperature that some animals undergo in winter as a protection against cold weather and lack of food

estivation a period of inactivity and lowered body temperature that some animals undergo in summer as a protection against hot weather and lack of food

circadian rhythm a biological daily cycle

CONNECTION TO Environmental Science

Do Not Disturb Many bats avoid food shortages during winter by hibernating in caves. Visiting a cave of hibernating bats may sound like fun, but people can endanger the bats by visiting their caves. The bats sleep with a lowered heart rate that allows them to save their energy until food is available. When people visit the caves, the bats may wake up. Waking up requires a lot of energy and makes it harder for the bats to survive until spring to find more food. If the bats lose too much energy, they can die. Make a poster that explains how people can help bats survive winters by avoiding their caves. **ACTIVITY**

Slowing Down

Some animals deal with food and water shortages by hibernating. **Hibernation** is a period of inactivity and decreased body temperature that some animals experience in winter. Hibernating animals survive on stored body fat. Many animals hibernate, including mice, squirrels, and skunks. While an animal hibernates, its temperature, heart rate, and breathing rate drop. Some hibernating animals drop their body temperature to a few degrees above freezing and do not wake for weeks at a time. Other animals, such as the bear in **Figure 7,** slow down but do not enter deep hibernation. The bear's body temperature does not drop to just above freezing. Also, bears sleep for shorter periods of time than hibernating animals sleep.

Winter is not the only time that resources can be hard to find. Many desert squirrels and mice experience a similar internal slowdown in the hottest part of the summer, when they run low on water and food. This period of reduced activity in the summer is called **estivation.**

Reading Check Name three animals that hibernate.

A Biological Clock

Animals need to keep track of time so that they know when to store food and when to migrate. The internal control of an animal's natural cycles is called a *biological clock*. Animals may use clues such as the length of the day and the temperature to set their clocks.

Some biological clocks keep track of daily cycles. These daily cycles are called **circadian rhythms.** Most animals wake up and get sleepy at about the same time each day and night. This is an example of a circadian rhythm.

Cycles of Change

Some biological clocks control long cycles. Seasonal cycles are nearly universal among animals. Many animals hibernate at certain times of the year and reproduce at other times. Reproducing during a particular season takes advantage of environmental conditions that help the young survive. Migration patterns are also controlled by seasonal cycles.

Biological clocks also control cycles of internal changes. For example, treehoppers, such as the one in **Figure 8,** go through several stages in life. They begin as an egg, then hatch as a nymph, and then develop into an adult. Finally, the adult emerges from the skin of its nymph form.

Figure 8 *The treehopper's biological clock signals the animal to shed the skin of its nymph form.*

SECTION Review

Summary

- Behavior may be classified as innate or learned. The potential for innate behavior is inherited. Learned behavior depends on experience.
- Behaviors that help animals survive include finding food, marking a territory, defensive action, courtship, and parenting.
- Animals have internal biological clocks that control daily, seasonal, and internal natural cycles.

Using Key Terms

1. Use each of the following terms in a separate sentence: *territory, innate behavior,* and *circadian rhythm.*

2. In your own words, write a definition for each of the following terms: *hibernation* and *estivation.*

Understanding Key Ideas

3. An animal that lives in a hot, dry environment might spend the summer
   a. hibernating.
   b. estivating.
   c. migrating to a warmer climate.
   d. None of the above

4. Biological clocks control
   a. seasonal cycles.
   b. circadian rhythms.
   c. internal cycles.
   d. All of the above

5. How do innate behaviors and learned behaviors differ?

6. Do bears hibernate? Explain your answer.

7. Name five behaviors that help animals survive.

Math Skills

8. Suppose that an animal's circadian rhythms tell it to eat a meal every 4 h. How many meals will the animal eat each day?

Critical Thinking

9. **Applying Concepts** People who travel to different time zones often suffer from *jet lag.* Jet lag makes people have trouble waking up and going to sleep at appropriate times. Why do you think people experience jet lag? Explain.

10. **Making Inferences** Many children are born with the tendency to make babbling sounds. But few adults make these sounds. How could you explain this change in an innate behavior?

Answers to Section Review

1. Sample answer: Male birds often sing to protect a territory. Speaking is an innate behavior in humans. Circadian rhythms control an animals' sleep cycles.

2. Sample answer: Hibernation is a period of inactivity and lowered body temperature that some animals go through during winter. Estivation is a period of inactivity and lowered body temperature that some animals go through during summer.

3. b

4. d

5. Innate behavior is influenced by genes and does not depend on learning. Learned behavior results from experience or observation.

6. Sample answer: Bears do not hibernate. They do have reduced activity in the winter, but their body temperature and heart rate do not drop low enough to be considered to be in a state of hibernation.

7. finding food, marking territory, defensive action, courtship, and parenting

8. six meals

9. Sample answer: Because of circadian rhythms, a person tends to wake up and go to sleep at about the same time every day. When people switch time zones, their bodies are ready to wake up and go to sleep at times that may not be appropriate in the new time zone.

10. Sample answer: Innate behaviors can be influenced by learning. The given example could be explained if children are born with an innate tendency to make vocal sounds, but as they grow, they learn to control those sounds so that they make the sounds of language instead of babbling.

CONNECTION to Earth Science — GENERAL

Finding the Way Use the teaching transparency "Cylindrical Projection/Conic Projection/Azimuthal Projection" to guide a student discussion about how humans navigate by using different kinds of maps.

 **Visual/Logical**

CHAPTER RESOURCES

Chapter Resource File

- **Section Quiz** GENERAL
- **Section Review** GENERAL
- **Vocabulary and Section Summary** GENERAL
- **Reinforcement Worksheet** BASIC
- **Critical Thinking** ADVANCED
- **SciLinks Activity** GENERAL

Technology

Transparencies
- **LINK TO EARTH SCIENCE** Cylindrical Projection / Conic Projection / Azimuthal Projection

Focus

Overview

In this section, students will discover some of the ways that animals communicate with each other. They will explore how animals signal information to other animals through sound, touch, chemicals, and sight. Students will also learn about the advantages and disadvantages of living in a group.

Bellringer

Tell students that humans use many cues to get information. Ask students what information can be learned from these cues:

- smell (what's cooking, dangerous fumes, spoiled food)
- sound (someone approaching, a train's warning whistle, school bells, fire alarms)

Motivate

ACTIVITY ——— GENERAL

Nonverbal Communication
Play a game of charades with students to demonstrate the importance of nonverbal communication among humans and other animals.

English Language Learners

LS Visual

Answer to Reading Check

defend territory, find food, warn others of danger, identify family, frighten predators, and find mates

READING WARM-UP

Objectives
- Describe four ways that animals communicate.
- List the advantages and disadvantages of living in groups.

Terms to Learn
social behavior
communication
pheromone

READING STRATEGY

Paired Summarizing Read this section silently. In pairs, take turns summarizing the material. Stop to discuss ideas that seem confusing.

social behavior the interaction between animals of the same species

communication a transfer of a signal or message from one animal to another that results in some type of response

Social Relationships

Have you ever noticed a pair of squirrels chattering and chasing each other through the branches of a tree? Though it may not be clear why they behave this way, it is clear that they are interacting.

Animals often interact with each other—in groups and one on one. They may work together, or they may compete. All of this behavior is called social behavior. **Social behavior** is the interaction among animals of the same species. Animals depend on communication for their social interactions.

Communication

Imagine what life would be like if people could not talk or read. There would be no telephones, no books, and no Internet. The world would certainly be different! Language is an important way for humans to communicate. In **communication,** a signal must travel from one animal to another, and the receiver of the signal must respond in some way. Animals do not use a language with complex words and grammar, but they communicate in many ways.

Communication helps animals survive. Many animals, such as the wolves in **Figure 1,** communicate to defend a territory from other members of the species. Animals also communicate to find food, to warn others of danger, to identify family members, to frighten predators, and to find mates.

Reading Check What are six reasons that animals communicate with each other? (*See the Appendix for answers to Reading Checks.*)

Figure 1 These wolves are howling to discourage neighboring wolves from invading their territory.

CHAPTER RESOURCES

Chapter Resource File

 - Lesson Plan
- Directed Reading A **BASIC**
- Directed Reading B **SPECIAL NEEDS**

Technology

- Transparencies
- Bellringer

Is That a Fact!

Vampire bats will share food with unrelated colony members. Vampire bats eat 50% to 100% of their weight in blood each night (usually from cows or horses). If a bat misses a meal two nights in a row, it will die. As many as a third of the bats miss a meal each night, yet few starve. A hungry bat licks the wings of another bat, which in response usually regurgitates some of its meal to help the hungry bat survive.

Ways to Communicate

Animals communicate by signaling information to other animals through sound, touch, chemicals, and sight. Each of these methods can be used to convey specific information.

Sound

Many animals communicate by making noises. Wolves howl. Dolphins use whistles and complex clicking noises to communicate with other dolphins. Male birds may sing songs in the spring to claim their territory or to attract a mate.

Sound is a signal that can reach many animals over a large area. As described in **Figure 2,** elephants use low frequency rumbles to communicate with other elephants that are kilometers away. Humpback whales sing songs that can be heard for many kilometers. Both species use these sounds to convey information about their locations.

Touch

Animals may also use touch to communicate. For example, chimpanzees often groom each other. Grooming involves animals resting together while picking bits of skin from each other's fur. This activity is an important way for primates to communicate. Chimpanzees use grooming to calm and comfort one another. Through touch, they may communicate friendship or support.

Chemicals

One way to communicate is through chemicals. The chemicals that animals use to communicate are called **pheromones** (FER uh MOHNZ). Ants and other insects secrete a variety of pheromones. For example, alarm chemicals can warn other ants of danger. Recognition chemicals announce which colony an ant is from to both friends and enemies.

Many animals use pheromones to find a mate. Amazingly, elephants and insects use some of the same pheromones to attract mates. Fire ants, such as the ones in **Figure 3,** use pheromones to control which colony members can reproduce.

Figure 2 *Elephants communicate with low-pitched sounds that humans cannot hear. When an elephant is communicating this way, the skin on its forehead flutters.*

pheromone a substance that is released by the body and that causes another individual of the same species to react in a predictable way

Figure 3 *This fire ant queen can make pheromones that other ants in the colony cannot make.*

Teach

CONNECTION ACTIVITY
Geography ——— GENERAL

River Dolphins Dolphins are usually thought of as ocean animals, but there are small dolphins that live in fresh water in many of the world's largest rivers. River dolphins are different from their marine relatives in that they have poor eyesight and huge numbers of pointed teeth. In addition, they swim on their sides or even upside down. Have students locate on a map or globe the following rivers and coastal areas where river dolphins live:

- the Ganges River (India)
- the Indus River (Pakistan)
- the Yangtze River (China)
- the Amazon River (Brazil)
- the estuaries of the La Plata River (the Atlantic coast of South America)
- the estuaries of the Tucuxi River (the northeastern coast of South America)

LS Visual

Demonstration ——— BASIC

Whale Songs Play a tape of humpback-whale songs. Ask students to offer suggestions about what information the whales might be communicating. Your library might be a good source for whale tapes. Examples of whale songs can also be found on the Internet. **LS Auditory**

Homework ——— ADVANCED

Writing **Ant Behavior** Have students research the behavior of ants. How do ants organize the work of their colony? Several ant species enslave other species. Have students investigate how one ant species manages to capture and control another species. Students can present their findings as a report or in a poster. **LS Logical**

Figure 4 **The Dance of the Bees**

Reteaching — BASIC

Living in Groups Help students remember the benefits and costs of living in groups by asking them to brainstorm the benefits and costs to the individuals living in the following social groups: a group of musk oxen (benefit: working together to defend their young; cost: attracting predators), a group of lions (benefit: working together to kill large prey; cost: competing with each other for mates), and a group of ground squirrels (benefit: spotting a predator quickly; cost: attracting predators). **LS Verbal**

Quiz — GENERAL

1. What two things must happen for communication to occur? (a signal and a response)

2. List two kinds of information that animals communicate. (Sample answer: information about food and territory)

Alternative Assessment — GENERAL

Concept Mapping Have students create a concept map, including linking words, using the following words: *communication, identify family members, pheromones, making noises, touch, courtship, defend a territory, warn about danger,* and *body language.* **LS Verbal**

Answer to Reading Check

They use body language to communicate where to find food sources.

ⓐ A honeybee leader does a "waggle dance" to tell other bees where it has found food. Other worker bees—followers—gather closely around the dancing bee to learn the details about the food source.

Followers can tell what kind of food was found by smelling the pollen on the leader's body. Or the leader may spit out some nectar for the followers to smell.

ⓑ The leader dances a figure eight, beating its wings rapidly and waggling its abdomen. The wings make sounds that communicate information about the food's distance from the hive.

As the bee goes through the center, it waggles its abdomen. The number of waggles tells the other bees how far away the nectar is.

The direction of the center line of the figure eight tells the other bees the direction from the hive to the nectar.

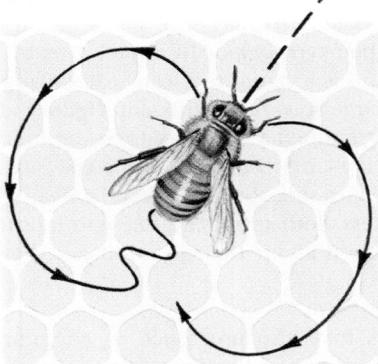

Sight

Animals also use visual communication. When we smile at a friend, we are sending a visual message with *body language.* As shown in **Figure 4,** bees use body language, along with other forms of communication, to spread news about food.

Body language can communicate many ideas. An animal that wants to scare another animal may ruffle its feathers to look bigger, or it may show its teeth as a threat. Visual displays are also used in courtship. For example, fireflies blink signals to attract each other. Animals also use body language when playing. The dog in **Figure 5** is play bowing to show that it wants to play.

✓ *Reading Check* How do honeybees use body language?

Living Together

Tigers live alone. Except for the time a mother tiger spends with her cubs, a tiger meets other tigers rarely. Yet the tiger's closest relative, the lion, is rarely alone. Lions live in groups called *prides.* The members of a pride sleep together, hunt together, and raise their cubs together. Why do some animals live in groups, while others live apart?

Figure 5 *When dogs want to play, they drop down on their forelegs.*

• **Developmentally Delayed**   • **Learning Disabled**
• **Attention Deficit Disorder**

Make sure that students understand the idea of body language. Ask each team to come up with five examples of body language used by humans. Have the teams act out their five examples, and have the rest of the class guess what messages the team is sending. Some messages they could use include "Hi" (wave), "Look at that" (point), "I'm angry" (fist), "I smell something" (wiggle nose), "Come here!" (wiggle finger), "Stop!" (raise hand, palm out), "Yes!" (nod head), "Bad idea" (wrinkle nose and eyebrows), "Is anyone looking?" (turn eyes from side to side with head still), "Do you mean me?" (point to self with a questioning look on face), "Be quiet!" (put finger over lip), and "Move back" (sweep arms away from body). **LS Visual**

English Language Learners

The Benefits of Living in Groups

Living in groups can be safer than living alone. Large groups can spot a predator quickly because they have so many pairs of eyes watching for danger. As shown in **Figure 6,** one animal can warn many others of danger. Also, groups can work together to defend themselves. For example, threatened musk oxen will circle their young with their horns pointed outward.

Living together can also help animals find food. Animals that hunt alone can usually kill only animals that are smaller than themselves. In contrast, predators such as lions and wolves, which hunt in groups, can kill larger prey.

The Downside of Living in Groups

Living in groups causes problems as well. Animals living in large groups must compete with each other for food and mates. An area that has enough food for one animal may not have enough food for a group of animals. In these cases, groups must move around in search of food. Also, animals in groups attract predators, so they must always be on the lookout. Living as a group can also help diseases spread.

Figure 6 *A ground squirrel whistles a loud alarm to alert other ground squirrels that danger is near.*

SECTION Review

Summary

- Animals communicate with each other. Communication must include both a signal and a response.
- Animals communicate through chemicals, touch, sound, and sight.
- Animals that live in groups can spot both prey and predators more easily. But living in a group increases competition for food and mates and attracts the attention of predators.

Using Key Terms

1. Use each of the following terms in a separate sentence: *social behavior* and *communication.*

2. In your own words, write a definition for the following term: *pheromone.*

Understanding Key Ideas

3. Which of the following is NOT an example of social behavior?
   a. a wolf howling at distant wolves to protect its territory
   b. a rabbit hiding from a predator
   c. a ground squirrel calling to signal danger to other squirrels
   d. a group of lions working together to hunt prey

4. Describe four ways that animals communicate with each other. Give an example of each type of communication.

5. Compare the costs and benefits of living in a group of animals.

Math Skills

6. How fast could a bee that flies 6 km/h reach a flower that is 1.2 km from the hive?

Critical Thinking

7. **Applying Concepts** Why do you think humans live together?

8. **Identifying Relationships** Language is not the only way that humans communicate. Describe how we use sound, touch, chemicals, and sight to communicate.

For a variety of links related to this chapter, go to www.scilinks.org

Topic: Communication in the Animal Kingdom

SciLinks code: HSM0320

Homework — ADVANCED

 Writing **Social Weavers** Students might enjoy researching social weavers of the family Ploceidae. These small African birds cooperatively build and maintain huge thatched-roof, apartment-like structures with as many as 300 chambers. Each chamber is occupied by one pair of birds. Students can prepare an illustrated report of their findings or can write a fictional story about the birds and the value of cooperation.

 LS Verbal

 PORTFOLIO

CHAPTER RESOURCES

Chapter Resource File

- Section Quiz **GENERAL**
- Section Review **GENERAL**
- Vocabulary and Section Summary **GENERAL**

Technology

Transparencies
- The Dance of the Bees

Answers to Section Review

1. Sample answer: Social behavior is the interaction between animals of the same species. Chimpanzees use grooming as a type of communication.

2. Sample answer: A pheromone is a chemical that animals use to communicate information to each other.

3. b

4. Sample answer: sound (birds sing to mark territory), touch (chimpanzees groom to comfort each other), chemicals (elephants use pheromones to attract mates), and sight (dogs bow down to show that they want to play)

5. Answers may vary. Some possible benefits are protection and the ability to work together. Some possible costs are increased competition, the attraction of predators, and the spread of disease.

6. 12 min

7. Answers may vary. Some of the benefits for humans living in groups are similar to those for all animals. Groups can work together for protection and help each other find food. Humans can also work together to accomplish major tasks, such as building elaborate structures and planning cities and government.

8. Answers may vary. Humans can communicate with sound without using language. Laughter and crying can be used as communication. We use touch when we hug someone or tap someone on the shoulder. We sometimes use chemicals by wearing perfume or cologne. We use sight to interpret sign language and body language.

Aunt Flossie and the Bumblebee

Teacher's Notes

Time Required
One to three 45-minute class periods

Lab Ratings

EASY ———————— HARD

Teacher Prep 🧪🧪
Student Set-Up 🧪🧪🧪
Concept Level 🧪🧪
Clean Up 🧪🧪

MATERIALS
Materials that students may need include construction paper in several bright colors, shoe boxes, scents, honey or some other sweet spread, twine, and binoculars or a magnifying lens. Encourage students to use recycled materials and to bring in their own supplies.

Safety Caution
Remind students to review all safety cautions and icons before beginning this lab activity.

Tell students to avoid wearing bright floral clothing and perfume or cologne while performing this lab.

All students should be cautious when working with wildlife. Students who are allergic to insect and bee stings should be excused from this exercise.

Lab Notes
This lab may need to be done during a favorable season in your geographical area. Some students may want to extend their data collection period to several days or weeks.

Aunt Flossie and the Bumblebee

Last week Aunt Flossie came to watch the soccer game, and she was chased by a big, yellow-and-black bumblebee. Everyone tried not to laugh, but Aunt Flossie did look pretty funny. She was running and screaming, and she was wearing perfume and dressed in a bright floral dress, shiny jewelry, and a huge hat with a big purple bow. No one could understand why the bumblebee bugged Aunt Flossie and left everyone else alone. She told you that she would not come to another game until you figure out why the bee chased her.

Your job is to design and carry out an experiment that will determine why the bee was attracted to Aunt Flossie. You may simulate the situation by using objects that contain the same sensory clues that Aunt Flossie wore that day—bright, shiny colors and strong scents.

OBJECTIVES
Plan a way to test bumblebee behavior.

Conduct your own experiment on bumblebees.

Describe materials that attract bumblebees.

MATERIALS
- items to be determined by the students and approved by the teacher

SAFETY

Ask a Question

1. Use the information in the story above to ask a question that would lead you to a hypothesis about the bee's behavior. For example, your question may be one of the following: What was Aunt Flossie wearing? What did she look like to a bumblebee? What scent was she wearing? Which characteristics may have affected the bee's behavior? What characteristic of Aunt Flossie affected the bee's behavior?

CHAPTER RESOURCES

Chapter Resource File
 • Datasheet for Chapter Lab
• Lab Notes and Answers

Technology
 Classroom Videos
• Lab Video

 LabBook

• Wet, Wiggly Worms!

Form a Hypothesis

2 Form a testable hypothesis about insect behavior based on your observations of Aunt Flossie and the bumblebee at the soccer game. One possible hypothesis is the following: Insects are attracted to strong floral scents. Write out your own hypothesis.

Test the Hypothesis

3 Plan a procedure for your experiment. Be sure to follow the steps of the scientific methods. Design your procedure to answer specific questions. For example, if you want to know if insects are attracted to different colors, you might want to hang up pieces of paper of different colors.

4 Make a list of materials for your experiment. You may want to include colored paper, pictures from magazines, or strong perfumes as bait. You may not use living things as bait in your experiment. Your teacher must approve your experimental design before you begin.

5 Decide what safety procedures are necessary for your experiment. Add them to your written procedure.

6 Find a place to conduct your experiment. For example, you may want to place your materials in a box on the ground, or you may want to hang items from a tree branch.

7 Using graph paper or a computer, construct tables to organize your data. Be sure that your data tables fit your investigation.

8 Have your teacher approve your plans. Carry out your procedure using the materials and safety procedures that you selected. **Caution:** Be sure to remain at a safe distance from your experimental setup. Do not touch any insects. Have an adult help you release any insects that are trapped or collected.

9 When you are finished, clean and store your equipment. Recycle or dispose of all materials properly.

Analyze the Results

1 **Describing Events** Describe your experimental procedure. How did bumblebees and other insects behave in your experiment?

2 **Analyzing Results** Did your results support your original hypothesis? Explain.

Draw Conclusions

3 **Evaluating Results** Compare your results with those of your classmates. Which hypotheses were supported? What conclusions can you draw from the class results?

4 **Applying Conclusions** Write a letter to Aunt Flossie telling her what you have learned. Tell her what you think caused the bee attack. Invite her to attend another soccer game, and tell her what you think she should or should not wear!

Analyze the Results

1. Answers may vary. Students should describe their experimental procedure. All answers will depend on students' procedures and observations.

2. Answers may vary. Answers will depend on students' hypotheses and observations.

Draw Conclusions

3. Answers may vary. Students should consider whether results from different groups show similar trends in insect behavior.

4. Letters may vary but should demonstrate what students have learned about insect behavior.

CHAPTER RESOURCES

Workbooks

📖 **Whiz-Bang Demonstrations**
• Six-Legged Thermometer ADVANCED

📖 **Inquiry Labs**
• Follow the Leader GENERAL

📖 **Long-Term Projects & Research Ideas**
• Animal-Myth Behaviors ADVANCED

CLASSROOM TESTED & APPROVED

Barry Bishop
San Rafael Junior High
Ferron, Utah

Assignment Guide

Section	Questions
1	5, 14, 22–25
2	2, 4, 6–8, 10–13, 16, 20
3	3, 9, 15, 17–19, 21
1 and 3	1

ANSWERS

Using Key Terms

1. Sample answer: An embryo is an organism at an early stage of development. A consumer is an organism that gets food from other organisms or their by-products. A pheromone is a chemical that is produced by animals and that is used to communicate.

2. Sample answer: An animal's biological clock controls not only its circadian rhythms but also its seasonal behaviors, such as estivation and hibernation.

3. Sample answer: Social behavior is interaction between animals of the same species. Communication is a certain kind of interaction that can happen between animals that are or are not the same species.

4. Sample answer: Learned behaviors depend on experience and learning, while innate behaviors do not depend on learning.

USING KEY TERMS

1. In your own words, write a definition for each of the following terms: *embryo, consumer,* and *pheromone.*

2. Use the following terms in the same sentence: *estivation, hibernation,* and *circadian rhythm.*

For each pair of terms, explain how the meanings of the terms differ.

3. *social behavior* and *communication*

4. *learned behavior* and *innate behavior*

UNDERSTANDING KEY IDEAS

Multiple Choice

5. Which of the following is a characteristic of all animals?
   a. asexual reproduction
   b. producing their own food
   c. having many specialized parts
   d. being unable to move

6. An innate behavior
   a. cannot change.
   b. must be learned from parents.
   c. is always present from birth.
   d. does not depend on learning or experience.

7. Migration
   a. occurs only in birds.
   b. helps animals escape cold and food shortages in winter.
   c. always refers to moving southward for the winter.
   d. is a way to defend against predators.

8. A biological clock controls
   a. circadian rhythms.
   b. defensive behavior.
   c. learned behavior.
   d. being a consumer.

9. For animals, living as part of a group
   a. is always safer than living alone.
   b. can attract attention from predators.
   c. keeps them from killing large prey.
   d. decreases competition for mates and food.

Short Answer

10. What is a territory? Give an example of a territory from your environment.

11. What landmarks help you find your way home from school?

12. What are five behaviors that animals may use to survive?

13. What do migration and hibernation have in common?

14. Describe the differences between vertebrates and invertebrates.

15. Describe four ways that an animal could communicate a message to other animals about where to find food.

Understanding Key Ideas

5. c
6. d
7. b
8. a
9. b
10. A territory is an area occupied by one animal or a group of animals of the same species. Other members of the species are excluded from the area. Examples may vary and may include a bedroom, a home, or a school.

11. Sample answer: the big oak tree, the red house, and the school

12. finding food, marking territory, taking defensive action, courtship, and parenting

13. Both are seasonal behaviors controlled by biological clocks.

14. Vertebrates have a backbone, and invertebrates do not.

15. Sample answer: The animal could make a sound, touch the other animal, produce chemicals (pheromones), or use body language that the other animal would see.

CRITICAL THINKING

16 **Concept Mapping** Use the following terms to create a concept map: *animals, survival behavior, finding food, migration, defensive action, seasonal behavior, marking a territory, estivation, parenting, hibernation,* and *courtship.*

17 **Analyzing Processes** If you see a skunk raise its tail toward you while you are hiking and you turn around to take a different path, has the skunk communicated with you? Explain your answer.

18 **Making Inferences** Ants depend on pheromones and touch for communication, but birds depend more on sight and sound. Why might these two types of animals have different forms of communication?

19 **Making Comparisons** Dogs use visual communication in many situations. They may arch their back and raise their fur to look threatening. When they want to play, they may bow down on their front legs. How are these two visual signals different from each other? How do the different visual signals relate to the different information they are meant to communicate?

20 **Analyzing Ideas** People have internal biological clocks. However, people are used to keeping track of time by using clocks and calendars. Why do you think people use these tools if they have internal clocks?

21 **Applying Concepts** Imagine that you are taking care of a friend's cat for a few days but that the friend forgot to tell you where to find the cat food. When you arrive at the friend's house, the cat meows and runs to the door that leads to the garage. Where would you look for the cat food? What kind of communication led you to this conclusion?

INTERPRETING GRAPHICS

The diagram below shows some internal organs of a fish. Use the diagram below to answer the questions that follow.

22 What characteristics suggest that this organism is an animal?

23 Which labels point to the animal's organs? Name any organs that you can recognize.

24 Do any labels point to the animal's tissues? Explain.

25 Is this animal a vertebrate or an invertebrate? Explain.

CHAPTER RESOURCES

Chapter Resource File

- • Chapter Review GENERAL
- • Chapter Test A GENERAL
- • Chapter Test B ADVANCED
- • Chapter Test C SPECIAL NEEDS
- • Vocabulary Activity GENERAL

Workbooks

Study Guide
- • Assessment resources are also available in Spanish.

Critical Thinking

16. 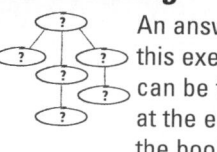 An answer to this exercise can be found at the end of the book.

17. yes; The skunk sent me a message (raising its tail shows that it may spray you), and I have responded (by turning to take a different path).

18. Sample answer: Ants are small and cannot see or hear over great distances, so they depend on pheromones and touch for communication. Birds have good eyesight, can hear well, and can sing, so they can communicate by sound and sight.

19. These visual signals use opposite motions (back and fur up to threaten and back and body down to play). This relationship as opposites is appropriate because the information communicated is nearly opposite as well. Playing is not meant to be a threat, and a threat is not meant to be playful.

20. Sample answer: Biological clocks do help people keep track of time, but mechanical clocks and calendars are more precise. A biological clock is probably not able to distinguish between exact times.

21. Sample answer: I would probably look for cat food in the garage. The cat used visual communication to show me where it wanted to go, and I reacted by looking for food there.

Interpreting Graphics

22. This organism is multicellular and has many specialized tissues and organs. Also, it has fins, which are used to move.

23. Each label points to an organ. Label a is the eye. Label b is the stomach. Label c is the liver.

24. Any label pointing to an organ also points to tissues, because organs are made up of tissues. So, all three labels point to tissues.

25. This animal is a vertebrate. It has a backbone.

Teacher's Note

To provide practice under more realistic testing conditions, give students 20 minutes to answer all of the questions in this Standardized Test Preparation.

Answers to the standardized test preparation can help you identify student misconceptions and misunderstandings.

READING

Passage 1

1. B
2. F
3. D

Question 2: This fact is mentioned in the last sentence: "But if conditions in their small pond include intense competition with members of their own species, certain larger salamanders may begin to eat other salamanders!" Some students may assume that cannibalism is often used by animals to survive because it is mentioned here as a way for salamanders to compete for survival. No factual statements about spiders or tadpoles are made in the passage.

READING

Read each of the passages below. Then, answer the questions that follow each passage.

Passage 1 Competing, surviving, and reproducing are all part of life. And in some species, cannibalism (eating members of one's own species) is part of life. But how does cannibalism relate to competing, surviving, and reproducing? It turns out that sometimes competition for survival can lead to cannibalism. Young tiger salamanders eat zooplankton, aquatic insect larvae, and sometimes tadpoles. But if conditions in their small pond include <u>intense</u> competition with members of their own species, certain larger salamanders may begin to eat other salamanders!

1. In the passage, what does the term *intense* mean?
   - **A** weak
   - **B** strong
   - **C** some
   - **D** furious

2. Based on the passage, which of the following statements is a fact?
   - **F** Large tiger salamanders sometimes eat other tiger salamanders.
   - **G** Animals often use cannibalism to help themselves survive.
   - **H** Female spiders sometimes eat male spiders.
   - **I** Tadpoles do not practice cannibalism.

3. What do young salamanders eat?
   - **A** other small salamanders
   - **B** large salamanders
   - **C** frogs and small fish
   - **D** zooplankton, aquatic insect larvae, and tadpoles

Passage 2 Unlike many birds, most bat species in the northern and central parts of the United States don't fly south for the winter. Instead of migrating, many bat species go into hibernation. Hibernation is usually a safe way to pass the cold winter. However, if their deep sleep is disturbed too often, the bats may die. People visiting bat caves sometimes force hibernating bats to wake up. When the bats wake up, they use up their stored fat too quickly. For example, each time a little brown bat wakes up, it consumes stored fat that would have lasted for 67 days of deep sleep. And because few insects live in the caves during the winter, the bats cannot build up fat <u>reserves</u> during the winter.

1. According to the passage, what is one reason that it is harmful for people to visit bat caves in the winter?
   - **A** Bats migrate south for the winter.
   - **B** People wake up the bats, which forces the bats to use much of their stored fat.
   - **C** People spread diseases to hibernating bats.
   - **D** People may scare insects away from the bat caves and leave the bats with no food.

2. In the passage, what does the term *reserve* mean?
   - **F** needs
   - **G** days
   - **H** supply
   - **I** weight

3. Why do many bats from the northern and central parts of the United States hibernate?
   - **A** to survive the winter
   - **B** to store fat
   - **C** to compete with birds
   - **D** to be near people that visit their caves

Passage 2

1. B
2. H
3. A

Question 1: A lack of insects in bat caves during the winter can be harmful to bats, but the lack of insects is not the result of humans visiting the caves. And although people may spread diseases to bats, this issue is not discussed in the passage. The harmful effects of people visiting bats' caves are a result of the bats' waking up, which causes them to use up their fat reserves and could eventually cause their death. Bats that migrate south for the winter are mentioned only briefly in the passage and do not apply to this question.

The graphs below show the average high and low temperatures for 1 year at two locations. Use the graphs to answer the questions that follow.

Average High and Low Temperatures at Glacier National Park

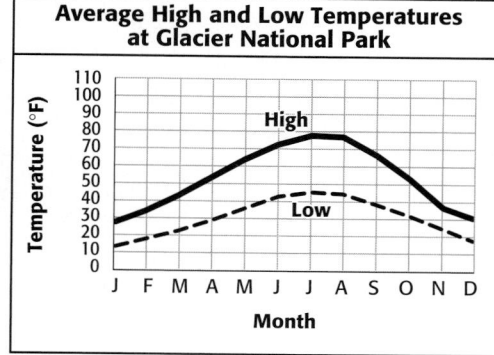

Average High and Low Temperatures Inside the Grand Canyon

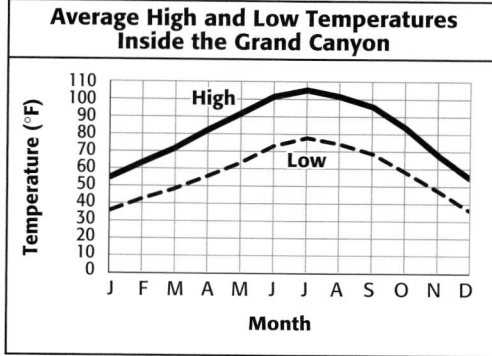

1. What is the average high temperature for each location in July?

A Glacier Park: 79°F; Grand Canyon: 106°F
B Glacier Park: 47°F; Grand Canyon: 78°F
C Glacier Park: 63°F; Grand Canyon: 92°F
D Glacier Park: 70°F; Grand Canyon: 100°F

2. What is the average low temperature for each location in January?

F Glacier Park: 15°F; Grand Canyon: 56°F
G Glacier Park: 30°F; Grand Canyon: 36°F
H Glacier Park: 15°F; Grand Canyon: 36°F
I Glacier Park: 22°F; Grand Canyon: 46°F

3. In which location would animals be more likely to estivate? to hibernate?

A Glacier Park; Grand Canyon
B Glacier Park; Glacier Park
C Grand Canyon; Grand Canyon
D Grand Canyon; Glacier Park

4. During which three months would animals be most likely to estivate?

F May, June, and July
G June, July, and August
H December, January, and February
I January, February, and March

MATH

Read each question below, and choose the best answer.

1. Manuel wants to build a fence so that he can let his pet dog out in the backyard without worrying about it wandering away from home. If he builds the fence to be 3 m long and 4.5 m wide, what will the size of the fenced area be?

A 7.5 m
B 7.5 m²
C 13.5 m²
D 135 m²

2. A bird gathers insects for its three baby birds each day. If each baby eats three bugs per day, how do you express the number of bugs that the mother bird gathers for her babies over a period of 3 weeks in exponential notation?

F $3^3 \times 7^3$
G $3^3 + 7^1$
H $3^3 \times 7^1$
I $3^1 \times 7^3$

3. In which of the following lists are the numbers in order from smallest to largest?

A 0.027, 0.072, 0.270, 0.720
B 0.027, 0.072, 0.720, 0.270
C 0.072, 0.027, 0.270, 0.720
D 0.720, 0.270, 0.072, 0.027

Standardized Test Preparation

INTERPRETING GRAPHICS

1. A
2. H
3. D
4. G

 **TEST DOCTOR**

Question 1: The average high temperature for each location is shown in the line labeled "High." The average high temperature in July is found by finding where the high temperature line intersects with the month of July. Some students may mistakenly look at the low temperature line and choose B. Other students may look at the line for June instead of the line for July and choose D. The correct answer is A.

MATH

1. C
2. H
3. A

TEST DOCTOR

Question 2: The mother bird gathers three bugs for three babies each day for three weeks. There are seven days per week. So, the number of bugs gathered equals $3 \times 3 \times 3 \times 7$. For this number to be expressed in exponential notation, the 3s are expressed as 3 with the exponent 3, and the 7 is given the exponent 1. These numbers are then multiplied. Some students may not multiply the 3s and the 7 but may add them instead, as in G. Other students may forget how to find an exponent and choose F or I. However, H is the correct answer.

CHAPTER RESOURCES

Chapter Resource File

 • Standardized Test Preparation **GENERAL**

State Resources

 For specific resources for your state, visit **go.hrw.com** and type in the keyword **HSMSTR**.

Science, Technology, and Society

ACTIVITY — GENERAL

Students can learn how Kanzi communicates by creating their own lexigram boards. Organize students into four groups. Have students use markers to divide a poster board into equal squares. Tell them to draw a unique symbol and a corresponding English word within each square. Ask students to make lexigrams for objects in the classroom and for verbs that could be used with those objects, such as *to give* and *to hide*. When boards are finished, have students communicate by using only the board.

Background

Scientists at the Language Research Center aren't just interested in chimps. They want to create technology that can help severely retarded people communicate. People who are unable to speak or use sign language can touch a lexigram on the board that represents a word they'd like to say. The lexigram keyboard gives people who cannot speak a way to share their thoughts and needs with the rest of the world.

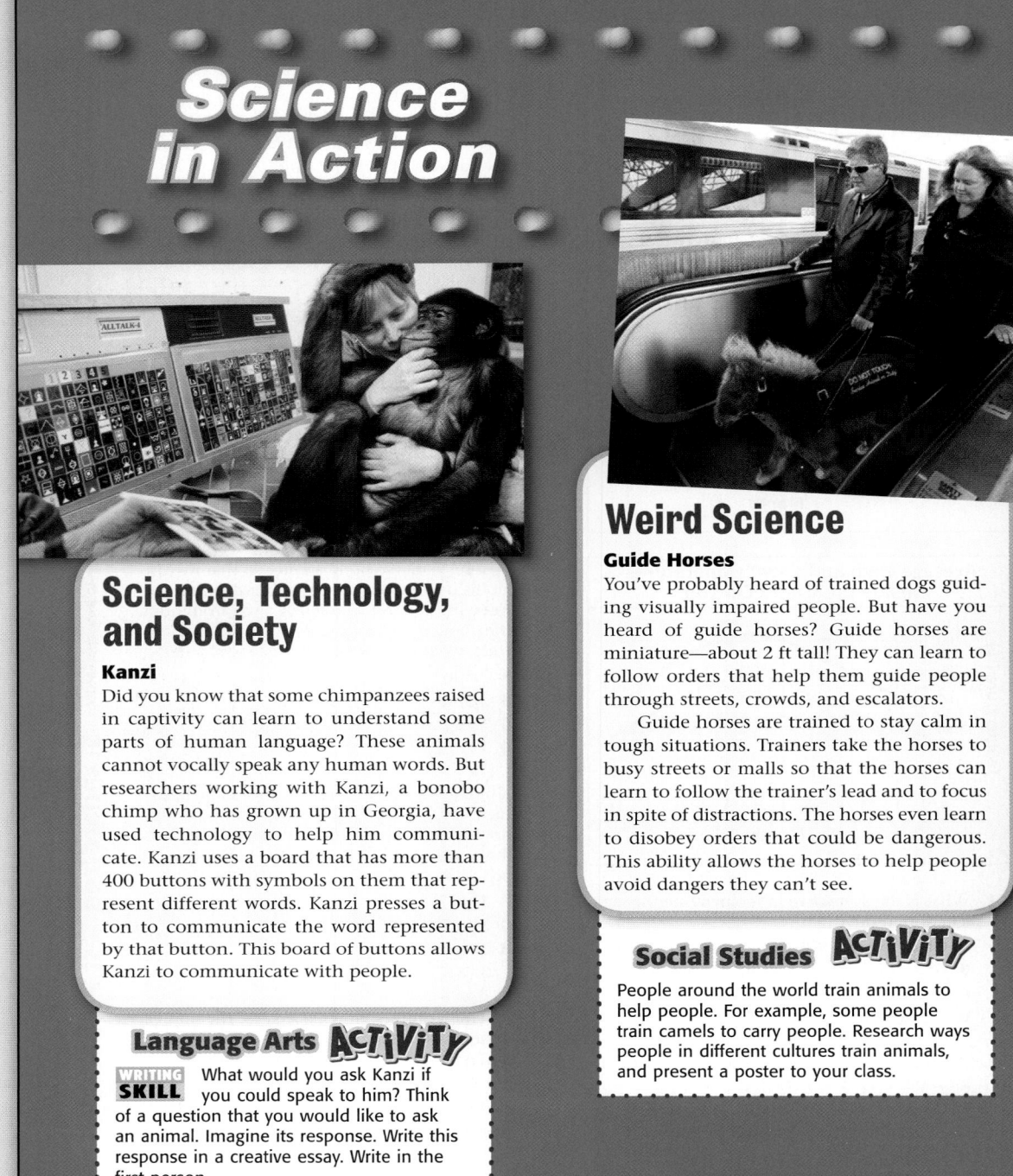

Science in Action

Science, Technology, and Society

Kanzi

Did you know that some chimpanzees raised in captivity can learn to understand some parts of human language? These animals cannot vocally speak any human words. But researchers working with Kanzi, a bonobo chimp who has grown up in Georgia, have used technology to help him communicate. Kanzi uses a board that has more than 400 buttons with symbols on them that represent different words. Kanzi presses a button to communicate the word represented by that button. This board of buttons allows Kanzi to communicate with people.

Language Arts ACTIVITY

WRITING SKILL What would you ask Kanzi if you could speak to him? Think of a question that you would like to ask an animal. Imagine its response. Write this response in a creative essay. Write in the first person.

Weird Science

Guide Horses

You've probably heard of trained dogs guiding visually impaired people. But have you heard of guide horses? Guide horses are miniature—about 2 ft tall! They can learn to follow orders that help them guide people through streets, crowds, and escalators.

Guide horses are trained to stay calm in tough situations. Trainers take the horses to busy streets or malls so that the horses can learn to follow the trainer's lead and to focus in spite of distractions. The horses even learn to disobey orders that could be dangerous. This ability allows the horses to help people avoid dangers they can't see.

Social Studies ACTIVITY

People around the world train animals to help people. For example, some people train camels to carry people. Research ways people in different cultures train animals, and present a poster to your class.

Answer to Language Arts Activity

Essays will vary. Students should include a question and a response written from the animal's point of view.

Answer to Social Studies Activity

Posters will vary. Students should clearly show how a particular culture uses animals' ability to learn in ways that are valuable to humans.

People in Science

George Archibald

Dancing with Cranes Imagine a man flapping his arms in a dance with a whooping crane. Does this sound funny? When Dr. George Archibald danced with a crane named Tex, he wasn't joking around. To help this endangered species survive, Archibald wanted cranes to mate in captivity so that he could release cranes into the wild. But the captive cranes wouldn't do their courtship dance. Archibald's cranes had imprinted on the humans that raised them. *Imprinting* is a process in which birds learn to recognize their species by looking at their parents. The birds saw humans as their own species, and could only reproduce if a human did the courtship dance. So, Archibald decided to dance. His plan worked! After some time, Tex hatched a baby crane.

After that, Archibald found a way to help the captive cranes imprint on other cranes. He and his staff now feed baby cranes with hand puppets that look like crane heads. They play recordings of real crane sounds for the young cranes. They even wear crane suits when they are near older birds. These cranes are happy to do their courtship dance with each other instead of with Archibald.

Math ACTIVITY

Suppose you want to drive a group of cranes from Madison, Wisconsin, to Orlando, Florida. Find and measure this distance on a map. If your truck goes 500 km per gas tank and a tank costs $30, how much would gas cost on your trip?

To learn more about these Science in Action topics, visit **go.hrw.com** and type in the keyword **HL5ANMF**.

Current Science

Check out Current Science® articles related to this chapter by visiting go.hrw.com. Just type in the keyword **HL5CS14**.

Invertebrates
Chapter Planning Guide

Compression guide:
To shorten instruction because of time limitations, omit Section 2.

OBJECTIVES	LABS, DEMONSTRATIONS, AND ACTIVITIES	TECHNOLOGY RESOURCES
PACING • 90 min pp. 378–387 **Chapter Opener**	**SE Start-up Activity,** p. 379 `GENERAL`	**OSP Parent Letter** ■ `GENERAL` **CD Student Edition on CD-ROM** **CD Guided Reading Audio CD** ■ **TR Chapter Starter Transparency*** **VID Brain Food Video Quiz**
Section 1 Simple Invertebrates • Describe the body plans, nervous systems, and guts of invertebrates. • Explain how sponges get food. • Describe three cnidarian traits. • Describe the three kinds of flatworms. • Describe the body of a roundworm.	**TE Group Activity** Determining Symmetry, p. 380 `GENERAL` **TE Connection Activity** Real World, p. 382 `GENERAL` **TE Demonstration** Sponge Expansion, p. 382 `BASIC` **SE Connection to Environmental Science** Threatened Reefs, p. 383 `GENERAL` **TE Activity** Observing Hydras, p. 383 `GENERAL` **TE Demonstration** Stinging Cells, p. 384 ◆ `GENERAL` **SE School-to-Home Activity** A Walk in the Park, p. 385 `GENERAL` **TE Connection Activity** Real World, p. 385 `GENERAL` **SE Connection to Social Studies** Tapeworms, p. 386 `GENERAL` **SE Skills Practice Lab** Soaking Sponges, p. 402 ◆ `GENERAL` **CRF Datasheet for Chapter Lab***	**CRF Lesson Plans*** **TR Bellringer Transparency*** **VID Lab Videos for Life Science**
PACING • 45 min pp. 388–391 **Section 2 Mollusks and Annelid Worms** • Explain how mollusks eat, control body functions, and circulate blood. • Describe the four body parts that most mollusks have in common. • Describe three annelid worms.	**TE Group Activity** Mollusk Menus, p. 388 `GENERAL` **TE Group Activity** Earthworms in Action, p. 390 `GENERAL` **LB Inquiry Labs** At a Snail's Pace* ◆ `ADVANCED` **LB Labs You Can Eat** Here's Looking at You, Squid* ◆ `GENERAL`	**CRF Lesson Plans*** **TR Bellringer Transparency***
PACING • 45 min pp. 392–397 **Section 3 Arthropods** • List the four main characteristics of arthropods. • Describe the different body parts of the four kinds of arthropods. • Describe the two types of metamorphosis in insects.	**TE Connection Activity** Math, p. 393 `ADVANCED` **TE Activity** Making Models, p. 394 ◆ `GENERAL` **TE Group Activity** Spider Webs, p. 394 `GENERAL` **SE Quick Lab** Sticky Webs, p. 395 `GENERAL` **CRF Datasheet for Quick Lab*** **TE Activity** Insecticide Alternatives, p. 396 `ADVANCED` **SE Inquiry Lab** The Cricket Caper, p. 781 `GENERAL` **CRF Datasheet for LabBook***	**CRF Lesson Plans*** **TR Bellringer Transparency*** **TR** The Stages of Complete Metamorphosis* **TR** Incomplete Metamorphosis* **TE Internet Activity** p. 394 `GENERAL` **CRF SciLinks Activity*** `GENERAL`
PACING • 45 min pp. 398–401 **Section 4 Echinoderms** • Describe the endoskeleton, nervous system, and water vascular system of echinoderms. • Explain how an echinoderm's body symmetry changes with age. • Describe five classes of echinoderms.	**TE Activity** Sea Star Hypotheses, p. 398 `GENERAL` **SE Science in Action** Math, Social Studies, and Language Arts Activities, p. 408–409 `GENERAL` **LB Long-Term Projects & Research Ideas** Creepy, Crawly Food? `ADVANCED`	**CRF Lesson Plans*** **TR Bellringer Transparency*** **TR** The Water Vascular System* **TR** *LINK TO EARTH SCIENCE* The Three Groups of Marine Life*

PACING • 90 min

CHAPTER REVIEW, ASSESSMENT, AND STANDARDIZED TEST PREPARATION

- **CRF Vocabulary Activity*** `GENERAL`
- **SE Chapter Review,** pp. 404–405 `GENERAL`
- **CRF Chapter Review*** ■ `GENERAL`
- **CRF Chapter Tests A*** ■ `GENERAL`, **B*** `ADVANCED`, **C*** `SPECIAL NEEDS`
- **SE Standardized Test Preparation,** pp. 406–407 `GENERAL`
- **CRF Standardized Test Preparation*** `GENERAL`
- **CRF Performance-Based Assessment*** `GENERAL`
- **OSP Test Generator** `GENERAL`
- **CRF Test Item Listing*** `GENERAL`

Online and Technology Resources

Visit **go.hrw.com** for a variety of free resources related to this textbook. Enter the keyword **HL5INV.**

Students can access interactive problem-solving help and active visual concept development with the *Holt Science and Technology* Online Edition available at **www.hrw.com.**

 Guided Reading Audio CD
Also in Spanish

A direct reading of each chapter for auditory learners, reluctant readers, and Spanish-speaking students.

 Science Tutor
CD-ROM

Excellent for remediation and test practice.

SKILLS DEVELOPMENT RESOURCES	SECTION REVIEW AND ASSESSMENT	STANDARDS CORRELATIONS
SE Pre-Reading Activity, p. 378 `GENERAL` **OSP Science Puzzlers, Twisters & Teasers*** `GENERAL`		National Science Education Standards UCP 1; SAI 1; LS 5a
CRF Directed Reading A* ■ `BASIC`**, B*** `SPECIAL NEEDS` **CRF Vocabulary and Section Summary*** ■ `GENERAL` **SE Reading Strategy** Reading Organizer, p. 380 `GENERAL` **TE Inclusion Strategies,** p. 381 **SE Math Practice** Several Sponges, p. 382 `GENERAL` **TE Reading Strategy** Mnemonics, p. 383 `GENERAL` **CRF Reinforcement Worksheet** Life Without a Backbone* `BASIC` **CRF Critical Thinking** A New Form of Danger in the Deep* `ADVANCED`	**SE Reading Checks,** pp. 381, 382, 385, 386 `GENERAL` **TE Reteaching,** p. 386 `BASIC` **TE Quiz,** p. 386 `GENERAL` **TE Homework,** p. 386 `GENERAL` **TE Alternative Assessment,** p. 387 `GENERAL` **SE Section Review,*** p. 387 ■ `GENERAL` **CRF Section Quiz*** ■ `GENERAL`	UCP 1, 4, 5; LS 1a, 1d, 1f, 2a, 3a, 3c, 5a; *Chapter Lab:* UCP 3; SAI 1; LS 1a
CRF Directed Reading A* ■ `BASIC`**, B*** `SPECIAL NEEDS` **CRF Vocabulary and Section Summary*** ■ `GENERAL` **SE Reading Strategy** Discussion, p. 388 `GENERAL` **TE Inclusion Strategies,** p. 391	**SE Reading Checks,** pp. 389, 391 `GENERAL` **TE Reteaching,** p. 390 `BASIC` **TE Quiz,** p. 390 `GENERAL` **TE Alternative Assessment,** p. 390 `GENERAL` **SE Section Review,*** p. 391 ■ `GENERAL` **CRF Section Quiz*** ■ `GENERAL`	UCP 1, 2, 3, 5; LS 1a, 1d, 3a, 5a
CRF Directed Reading A* ■ `BASIC`**, B*** `SPECIAL NEEDS` **CRF Vocabulary and Section Summary*** ■ `GENERAL` **SE Reading Strategy** Prediction Guide, p. 392 `GENERAL` **TE Connection to Chemistry** Chitin, p. 394 `GENERAL` **MS Math Skills for Science** Dividing Whole Numbers with Long Division* `GENERAL` **MS Math Skills for Science** Checking Division with Multiplication* `GENERAL`	**SE Reading Checks,** pp. 393, 395, 397 `GENERAL` **TE Reteaching,** p. 396 `BASIC` **TE Quiz,** p. 396 `GENERAL` **TE Alternative Assessment,** p. 396 `GENERAL` **SE Section Review,*** p. 397 ■ `GENERAL` **CRF Section Quiz*** ■ `GENERAL`	UCP 2, 3, 5; SAI 2; LS 1a, 1d, 1f, 5a; *LabBook:* SAI 1; LS 3c
CRF Directed Reading A* ■ `BASIC`**, B*** `SPECIAL NEEDS` **CRF Vocabulary and Section Summary*** ■ `GENERAL` **SE Reading Strategy** Paired Summarizing, p. 398 `GENERAL` **TE Connection to Earth Science** Marine Life, p. 398 `GENERAL` **TE Reading Strategy** Prediction Guide, p. 399 `GENERAL` **CRF Reinforcement Worksheet** Spineless Variety* `BASIC`	**SE Reading Checks,** pp. 399, 401 `GENERAL` **TE Reteaching,** p. 400 `BASIC` **TE Quiz,** p. 400 `GENERAL` **TE Alternative Assessment,** p. 400 `GENERAL` **SE Section Review,*** p. 401 ■ `GENERAL` **CRF Section Quiz*** ■ `GENERAL`	UCP 5; LS 1a, 1d, 3a, 5a

One-Stop Planner® CD-ROM

This convenient CD-ROM includes:
• Lab Materials QuickList Software
• Holt Calendar Planner
• Customizable Lesson Plans
• Printable Worksheets
• ExamView® Test Generator

cnnstudentnews.com

Find the latest news, lesson plans, and activities related to important scientific events.

www.scilinks.org

Maintained by the **National Science Teachers Association.** See Chapter Enrichment pages for a complete list of topics.

Current Science®

Check out *Current Science* articles and activities by visiting the HRW Web site at **go.hrw.com.** Just type in the keyword **HL5CS15T.**

 **Classroom Videos**

• **Lab Videos** demonstrate the chapter lab.
• **Brain Food Video Quizzes** help students review the chapter material.
• **CNN Videos** bring science into your students' daily life.

Visual Resources

CHAPTER STARTER TRANSPARENCY

Invertebrates — CHAPTER STARTER

Strange but True!

In 1995, researchers in Germany made a computer chip that could send signals to a single nerve cell in a living leech. Even more amazing, the leech's nerve cell could send signals back to the computer chip. What is so amazing about having a "mind link" with a leech? The answer may surprise you.

In the United States alone, accidents result in more than 10,000 spinal-cord injuries a year. In severe cases, a person can lose muscle control, particularly in the arms and legs. But what does this have to do with leeches?

Giant leeches from South America, like the one shown here on the scientist's arm, have only a few nerve cells. By studying leech nerves, biologists are learning how to communicate directly with nerve cells.

The scientists hope that communicating with leech nerves using a computer chip will one day help them communicate with human nerve cells. In the future, people with spinal-cord injuries may be able to use computers to communicate with the nerve cells in their body and move their muscles.

Scientists still have a lot to learn, but who would have expected such a promising breakthrough with an animal that doesn't even have a backbone? In this chapter, you will learn about many spineless critters, the invertebrates.

BELLRINGER TRANSPARENCIES

Invertebrates — BELLRINGER TRANSPARENCY

Section: Simple Invertebrates
Think of all the beautiful or interesting invertebrates that you have heard of, such as jellyfish, butterflies, beetles, earthworms, sea shells, and sea stars. Then describe your favorite invertebrate in your **science journal**. What special features does your favorite invertebrate have that will help it survive in its environment?

Section: Mollusks and Annelid Worms
Unscramble the following words:
gluss
isalns
sdusqi
klomssul

Write a sentence in your **science journal** using each word. Your sentences should describe where and when you might find each organism.

TEACHING TRANSPARENCIES

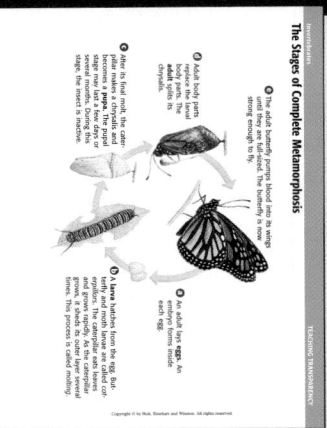

The Stages of Complete Metamorphosis

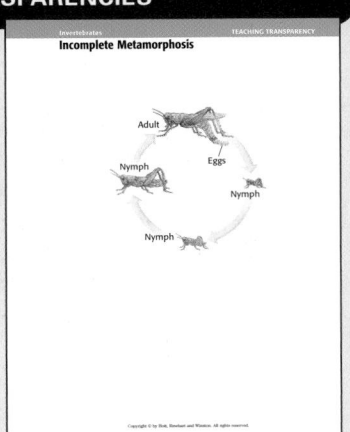

Incomplete Metamorphosis

Adult
Nymph
Eggs
Nymph
Nymph

TEACHING TRANSPARENCIES

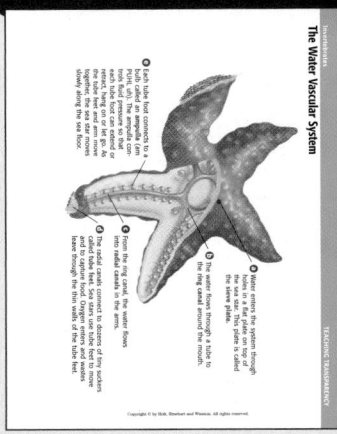

The Water Vascular System

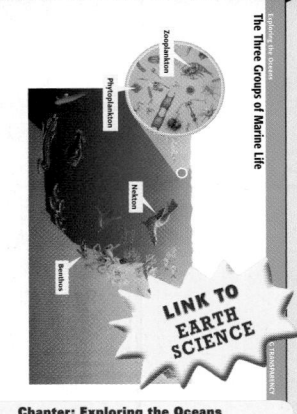

The Three Groups of Marine Life

Zooplankton
Phytoplankton
Nekton
Benthos

LINK TO EARTH SCIENCE

Chapter: Exploring the Oceans

CONCEPT MAPPING TRANSPARENCY

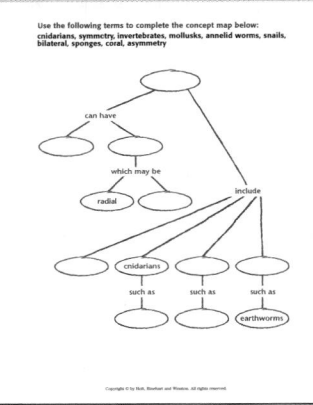

Use the following terms to complete the concept map below: cnidarians, symmetry, invertebrates, mollusks, annelid worms, snails, bilateral, sponges, coral, asymmetry

Planning Resources

LESSON PLANS

Lesson Plan — SAMPLE

Section: Waves

Pacing
Regular Schedule: with lab(s):2 days / without lab(s):2 days
Block Schedule: with lab(s):1 1/2 days / without lab(s):1 day

Objectives
1. Relate the seven properties of life to a living organism.
2. Describe several themes that can help you to organize what you learn about biology.
3. Identify the tiny structures that make up all living organisms.
4. Differentiate between reproduction and heredity and between metabolism and homeostasis.

National Science Education Standards Covered
LSInter6:Cells have particular structures that underlie their functions.
LSMat1:Most cell functions involve chemical reactions.
LSBeh1:Cells store and use information to guide their functions.
UCP1:Cell functions are regulated.
SI1: Cells can differentiate and form complete multicellular organisms.
PS1: Species evolve over time.
ESS1: The great diversity of organisms is the result of more than 3.5 billion years of evolution.
ESS2: Natural selection and its evolutionary consequences provide a scientific explanation for the fossil record of ancient life forms as well as for the striking molecular similarities observed among the diverse species of living organisms.
ST1: The millions of different species of plants, animals, and microorganisms that live on Earth today are related by descent from common ancestors.
ST2: The energy for life primarily comes from the sun.
SPSP1: The complexity and organization of organisms accommodates the need for obtaining, transforming, transporting, releasing, and eliminating the matter and energy used to sustain the organism.
SPSP6: As matter and energy flows through different levels of organization of living systems—cells, organs, communities—and between living systems and the physical environment, chemical elements are recombined in different ways.
HNS1: Organisms have behavioral responses to internal and external stimuli.

PARENT LETTER

SAMPLE

Dear Parent,

Your son's or daughter's science class will soon begin exploring the chapter entitled "The World of Physical Science." In this chapter, students will learn about how the scientific method applies to the world of physical science and the role of physical science in the world. By the end of the chapter, students should demonstrate a clear understanding of the chapter's main ideas and be able to discuss the following topics:

1. physical science as the study of energy and matter (Section 1)
2. the role of physical science in the world around them (Section 1)
3. careers that rely on physical science (Section 1)
4. the steps used in the scientific method (Section 2)
5. examples of technology (Section 2)
6. how the scientific method is used to answer questions and solve problems (Section 2)
7. how our knowledge of science changes over time (Section 2)
8. how models represent real objects or systems (Section 3)
9. examples of different ways models are used in science (Section 3)
10. the importance of the International System of Units (Section 4)
11. the appropriate units to use for particular measurements (Section 4)
12. how area and density are related (Section 4)

Questions to Ask Along the Way

You can help your son or daughter learn about these topics by asking interesting questions such as the following:

• What are some surprising careers that use physical science?
• What is a characteristic of a good hypothesis?
• Why is it a good idea to use a model?
• Why do Americans measure things in terms of inches and yards and meters ?

ALSO IN SPANISH

TEST ITEM LISTING

TEST ITEM LISTING
The World of Science — SAMPLE

MULTIPLE CHOICE

1. A limitation of models is that
a. they are large enough to see.
b. they do not act exactly like the things that they model.
c. they are smaller than the things that they model.
d. they model unfamiliar things.
Answer: B   Difficulty: 1   Section: 3   Objective: 2

2. The length 10 m is equal to
a. 100 cm.   c. 10,000 mm.
b. 1,000 cm.   d. Both (a) and (c)
Answer: B   Difficulty: 1   Section: 3   Objective: 2

3. To be valid, a hypothesis must be
a. testable.   c. made into a law.
b. supported by evidence.   d. Both (a) and (b)
Answer: B   Difficulty: 1   Section: 3   Objective: 2 1

4. The statement "Sheila has a stain on her shirt" is an example of a(n)
a. law.   c. observation.
b. hypothesis.   d. prediction.
Answer: B   Difficulty: 1   Section: 3   Objective: 2

5. A hypothesis is often developed out of
a. observations.   c. laws.
b. experiments.   d. theories.
Answer: B   Difficulty: 1   Section: 3   Objective: 2

6. How many milliliters are in 3.5 kL?
a. 3,500 mL.   c. 3,500, 300 mL.
b. 0.0035 mL.   d. 35,000 mL.
Answer: B   Difficulty: 1   Section: 3   Objective: 2

7. A map of Seattle is an example of a
a. law.   c. model.
b. theory.   d. unit.
Answer: B   Difficulty: 1   Section: 3   Objective: 2

8. A lab has the safety icons shown below. These icons mean that you should wear
a. only safety goggles.   c. safety goggles and a lab apron.
b. only a lab apron.   d. safety goggles, a lab apron, and gloves.
Answer: B   Difficulty: 1   Section: 3   Objective: 2

9. The law of conservation of mass says the total mass before a chemical change is
a. more than the total mass after the change.
b. less than the total mass after the change.
c. the same as the total mass after the change.
d. not the same as the total mass after the change.
Answer: B   Difficulty: 1   Section: 3   Objective: 2

10. In which of the following areas might you find a geochemist at work?
a. studying the chemistry of rocks   c. studying fishes
b. studying forestry   d. studying the atmosphere
Answer: B   Difficulty: 1   Section: 3   Objective: 2

One-Stop Planner® CD-ROM

This CD-ROM includes all of the resources shown here and the following time-saving tools:

• *Lab Materials QuickList Software*
• *Customizable lesson plans*
• *Holt Calendar Planner*
• *The powerful ExamView® Test Generator*

For a preview of available worksheets covering math and science skills, see pages T26–T33. All of these resources are also on the One-Stop Planner®.

Meeting Individual Needs

DIRECTED READING A
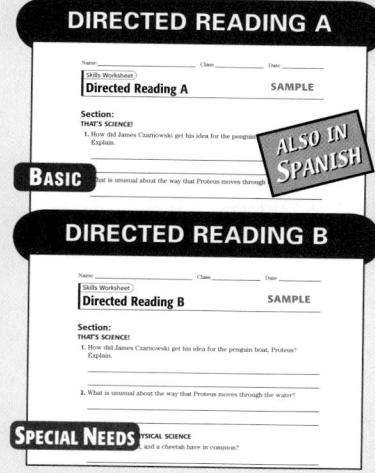
Skills Worksheet
Directed Reading A — SAMPLE
Section: THAT'S SCIENCE!
1. How did James Czarnowski get his idea for the penguin boat, Proteus? Explain.
...that is unusual about the way that Proteus moves through...
BASIC — ALSO IN SPANISH

DIRECTED READING B
Skills Worksheet
Directed Reading B — SAMPLE
Section: THAT'S SCIENCE!
1. How did James Czarnowski get his idea for the penguin boat, Proteus? Explain.
2. What is unusual about the way that Proteus moves through the water?
SPECIAL NEEDS ...PHYSICAL SCIENCE
...and a cheetah have in common?

VOCABULARY ACTIVITY
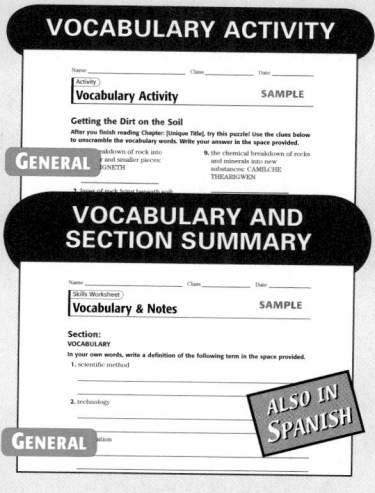
Activity
Vocabulary Activity — SAMPLE
Getting the Dirt on the Soil
After you finish reading Chapter: [Unique Title], try this puzzle! Use the clues below to unscramble the vocabulary. Write your answer in the space provided.
...breakdown of rock into... NGNETH
9. the chemical breakdown of rocks and minerals into new substances: CAMILCHE THEARGWEN
...layer of rock lying beneath soil...
GENERAL

VOCABULARY AND SECTION SUMMARY
Skills Worksheet
Vocabulary & Notes — SAMPLE
Section: VOCABULARY
In your own words, write a definition of the following term in the space provided.
1. scientific method
2. technology
GENERAL — ALSO IN SPANISH

REINFORCEMENT
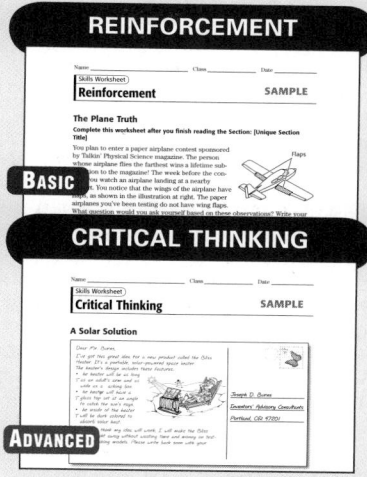
Skills Worksheet
Reinforcement — SAMPLE
The Plane Truth
Complete this worksheet after you finish reading the Section: [Unique Section Title]
You plan to enter a paper airplane contest sponsored by Talkin' Physical Science magazine. The person whose airplane flies the farthest wins a lifetime subscription to the magazine! The week before the contest, you watch an airplane landing at a nearby airport. You notice that the wings of the airplane have flaps, as shown in the illustration at right. The paper airplanes you've been testing do not have wing flaps.
What question would you ask yourself based on these observations? Write your...
BASIC

CRITICAL THINKING
Skills Worksheet
Critical Thinking — SAMPLE
A Solar Solution
Dear Mr. Burns,
I've got this great idea for a new product called the Solar Heater. It's a portable, solar-powered space heater...
Joseph D. Burns
Granoters' Advisory Consultants
Portland, OR 97201
ADVANCED

SCILINKS ACTIVITY

Activity
SciLinks Activity — SAMPLE
MARINE ECOSYSTEMS
Go to www.scilinks.com. To find links related to marine ecosystems, type in the keyword to text. Then, use the links to answer the questions about marine ecosystems.
...percentage of the Earth's surface is covered by water?
GENERAL

SCIENCE PUZZLERS, TWISTERS & TEASERS
CHAPTER 15 SCIENCE PUZZLERS, TWISTERS & TEASERS
Invertebrates
Odd One Out
1. For each group of terms, circle the one that doesn't belong and explain why not.
a. earthworm, bristle worm, roundworm, leech.
b. dog, sponge, planarian, human
...squid, crab, pillbug
GENERAL

Labs and Activities

LONG-TERM PROJECTS & RESEARCH IDEAS
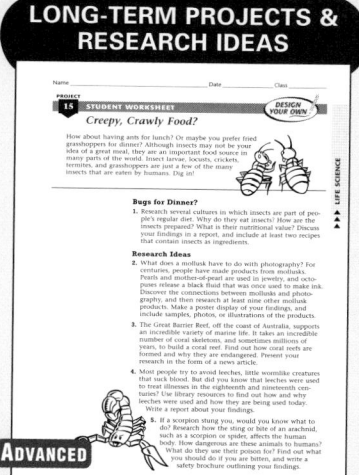
PROJECT 15 STUDENT WORKSHEET — DESIGN YOUR OWN
Creepy, Crawly Food?
How about having ants for lunch? Or maybe you prefer fried grasshoppers for dinner? Although insects may not be your idea of a great meal, they are an important food source in many parts of the world. Insect larvae, locusts, crickets, termites, and grasshoppers are just a few of the many insects that are eaten by humans. Dig in!
Bugs for Dinner?
1. Research several cultures in which insects are part of people's regular diet. Why do they eat insects? How are the insects prepared? What is their nutritional value? Discuss your findings in a report, and include at least two recipes that contain insects as ingredients.
Research Ideas
2. What does a mollusk have to do with photography? For centuries, people have made products from mollusks. Pearls and mother-of-pearl are used in jewelry, and octopuses release a black fluid that was once used to make ink. Discover the connections between mollusks and photography, and then research at least nine other mollusk products. Make a poster display of your findings, and include samples, photos, or illustrations of the products.
3. The Great Barrier Reef, off the coast of Australia, supports an incredible variety of marine life. It takes an incredible number of coral skeletons, and sometimes millions of years, to build a coral reef. Find out how coral reefs are formed and why they are endangered. Present your research in the form of a news article.
4. Most people try to avoid leeches, little wormlike creatures that suck blood. But did you know that leeches were used to treat illnesses in the eighteenth and nineteenth centuries? Use library resources to find out how and why leeches were used and how they are being used today. Write a report about your findings.
5. If a scorpion stung you, would you know what to do? Research how the sting or bite of an arachnid, such as a scorpion or spider, affects the human body. How dangerous are these animals to humans? What do they use their poison for? Find out what you should do if you are bitten, and write a safety brochure outlining your findings.
ADVANCED

LABS YOU CAN EAT
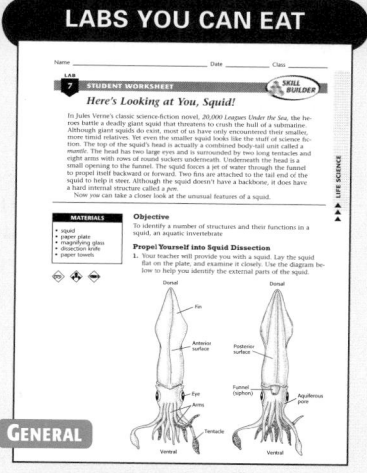
LAB 7 STUDENT WORKSHEET — SKILL BUILDER
Here's Looking at You, Squid!
In Jules Verne's classic science-fiction novel, 20,000 Leagues Under the Sea, the heroes battle a deadly giant squid that threatens to crush the hull of a submarine. Although giant squids do exist, most of us have only encountered their smaller, more timid relatives. Yet even the smaller squid looks like the stuff of science fiction. The top of the squid's head is actually a combined body-tail unit called a mantle. The head has two large eyes and is surrounded by two long tentacles and eight arms with rows of round suckers underneath. Underneath the head is a small opening to the funnel. The squid forces a jet of water through the funnel to propel itself backward or forward. Two fins are attached to the tail end of the squid to help it steer. Although the squid doesn't have a backbone, it does have a hard internal structure called a pen.
Now you can take a closer look at the unusual features of a squid.
MATERIALS
• squid
• paper plate
• magnifying glass
• dissection knife
• paper towels
Objective
To identify a number of structures and their functions in a squid, an aquatic invertebrate
Propel Yourself Into Squid Dissection
1. Your teacher will provide you with a squid. Lay the squid flat on the plate, and examine it closely. Use the diagram below to help you identify the external parts of the squid.
GENERAL

INQUIRY LABS
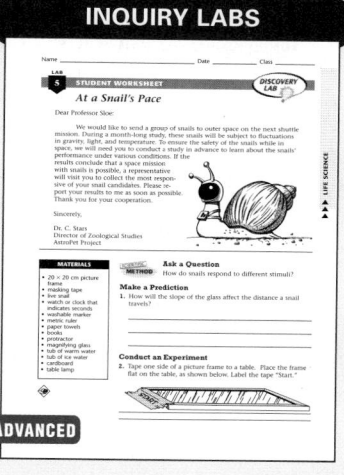
LAB 5 STUDENT WORKSHEET — DISCOVERY LAB
At a Snail's Pace
Dear Professor Sine,
We would like to send a group of snails to outer space on the next shuttle mission. During a month-long study, these snails will be subject to fluctuations in gravity, light, and temperature. To ensure the safety of the snails while in space, we will need you to conduct a study in advance to learn about the snails' performance under various conditions. If the results conclude that a space mission with snails is possible, a representative will visit you to collect the most responsive of your snail candidates. Please report your results to me as soon as possible. Thank you for your cooperation.
Sincerely,
Dr. C. Stars
Director of Zoological Studies
AstroPet Project
MATERIALS
• 20 × 20 cm picture frame
• masking tape
• watch or clock that indicates seconds
• washable marker
• metric ruler
• paper towels
• books
• protractor
• magnifying glass
• tub of warm water
• tub of ice water
• cardboard
• table lamp
SCIENTIFIC METHOD
Ask a Question How do snails respond to different stimuli?
Make a Prediction
1. How will the slope of the glass affect the distance a snail travels?
Conduct an Experiment
2. Tape one side of a picture frame to a table. Place the frame flat on the table, as shown below. Label the tape "Start."
ADVANCED

DATASHEETS FOR QUICK LABS

TEACHER RESOURCE PAGE
Quick Lab — DATASHEET FOR QUICK LAB
Reaction to Stress — SAMPLE
Background
The graph below illustrates changes that occur in the membrane potential of a neuron during an action potential. Use the graph to answer the following questions. Refer to Figure 3 as needed.

DATASHEETS FOR CHAPTER LABS
TEACHER RESOURCE PAGE
Skills Practice Lab — DATASHEET FOR CHAPTER LAB
Using Scientific Methods — SAMPLE
Teacher's Notes
TIME REQUIRED
One 45-minute class period.

DATASHEETS FOR LABBOOK
TEACHER RESOURCE PAGE
Skills Practice Lab — DATASHEET FOR LABBOOK LAB
Does It All Add Up? — SAMPLE
Teacher's Notes
TIME REQUIRED

Review and Assessments

SECTION QUIZ

Assessment
Section Quiz — SAMPLE
Section:
In the space provided, write the letter of the description that best matches the term or phrase.
1. building molecules that can be used as an energy source, or breaking down molecules in which energy is stored
2. the process by which light energy is converted to chemical energy
3. an organism that uses sunlight or inorganic substances to make organic compounds
f. cellular respiration
GENERAL — ALSO IN SPANISH

SECTION REVIEW
Skills Worksheet
Section Review — SAMPLE
Section:
KEY TERMS
1. What do paleontologist study?
2. How does a trace fossil differ from petrified wood?
...fossil.
GENERAL — ALSO IN SPANISH

CHAPTER REVIEW
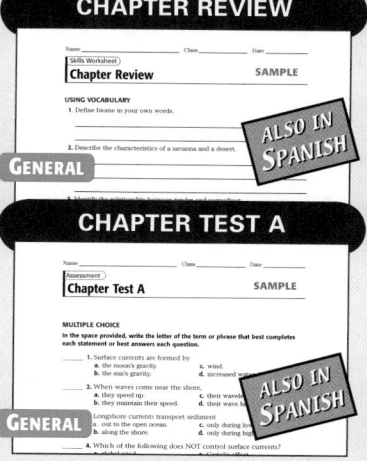
Skills Worksheet
Chapter Review — SAMPLE
USING VOCABULARY
1. Define biome in your own words.
2. Describe the characteristics of a savanna and a desert.
GENERAL — ALSO IN SPANISH

CHAPTER TEST A
Assessment
Chapter Test A — SAMPLE
MULTIPLE CHOICE
In the space provided, write the letter of the term or phrase that best completes each statement or best answers each question.
1. Surface currents are formed by
a. the moon's gravity.   c. wind.
b. the sun's gravity.   d. increased w...
2. When waves come near the shore,
a. they speed up.   c. their wave...
b. they maintain their speed. d. their wave...
...currents transport sediment
...out to the open ocean.   c. only during low...
...along the shore.   d. only during hig...
4. Which of the following does NOT control surface currents?
GENERAL — ALSO IN SPANISH

CHAPTER TEST B
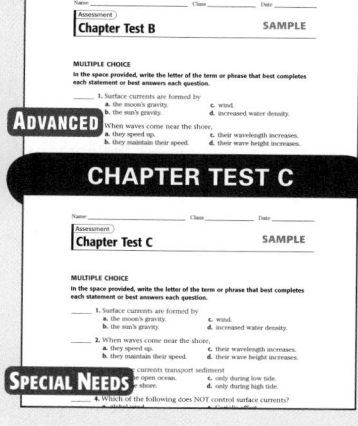
Assessment
Chapter Test B — SAMPLE
MULTIPLE CHOICE
In the space provided, write the letter of the term or phrase that best completes each statement or best answers each question.
1. Surface currents are formed by
a. the moon's gravity.   c. wind.
b. the sun's gravity.   d. increased water density.
When waves come near the shore,
a. they speed up.   c. their wavelength increases.
b. they maintain their speed. d. their wave height increases.
ADVANCED

CHAPTER TEST C
Assessment
Chapter Test C — SAMPLE
MULTIPLE CHOICE
In the space provided, write the letter of the term or phrase that best completes each statement or best answers each question.
1. Surface currents are formed by
a. the moon's gravity.   c. wind.
b. the sun's gravity.   d. increased water density.
2. When waves come near the shore,
a. they speed up.   c. their wavelength increases.
b. they maintain their speed. d. their wave height increases.
...currents transport sediment
...out to the open ocean.   c. only during low tide.
...along the shore.   d. only during high tide.
4. Which of the following does NOT control surface currents?
SPECIAL NEEDS

STANDARDIZED TEST PREPARATION
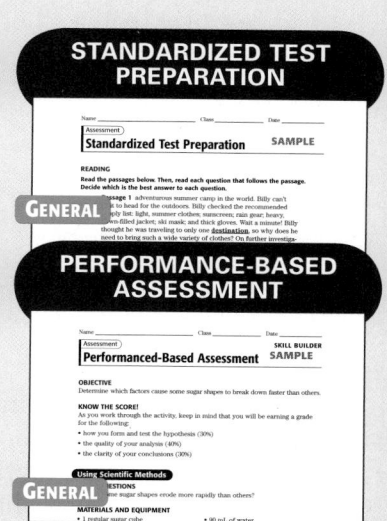
Assessment
Standardized Test Preparation — SAMPLE
READING
Read the passages below. Then, read each question that follows the passage. Decide which is the best answer to each question.
Passage 1 adventurous summer camp in the world. Billy can't wait to head for the outdoors. Billy checked the recommended supply list: light, summer clothes; sunscreen; rain gear; heavy, down-filled jacket; ski mask; and thick gloves. Wait a minute! Billy thought he was traveling to only one destination, so why does he need to bring such a wide variety of clothes? On further investiga...
GENERAL

PERFORMANCE-BASED ASSESSMENT
Assessment — SKILL BUILDER
Performanced-Based Assessment — SAMPLE
OBJECTIVE
Determine which factors cause some sugar shapes to break down faster than others.
KNOW THE SCORE!
As you work through the activity, keep in mind that you will be earning a grade for the following:
• how you form and test the hypothesis (30%)
• the quality of your analysis (40%)
• the clarity of your conclusions (30%)
Using Scientific Methods
...some sugar shapes erode more rapidly than others?
MATERIALS AND EQUIPMENT
• 1 regular sugar cube   • 80 mL of water
GENERAL

This Chapter Enrichment provides relevant and interesting information to expand and enhance your presentation of the chapter material.

Section 1

Simple Invertebrates

Aristotle

- The Greek philosopher Aristotle (384–322 BCE) was particularly interested in marine invertebrates; he made detailed observations of sea stars, crustaceans, and mollusks—especially cuttlefish, which are related to squids.

Sponges are Animals

- Sponges were not completely accepted as animals until the early 1800s, when Scottish zoologist R. E. Grant conducted experiments in which he added fine, colored particles to the water around sponges. Grant watched under a microscope as the particles were taken into the sponges through microscopic pores and then "vomited forth" from the central cavity.

Is That a Fact!

- Coral has a skeletal structure that is remarkably similar to human bone. Coral is now being used to speed up the growth of bone grafts.

- Tapeworms can reach enormous sizes. Some can grow to be longer than a school bus!

Medusa

- The free-swimming form of a jellyfish has tentacles and is called the *medusa*. It gets its name from Medusa, a character in Greek mythology. Medusa was a monster whose long, curly "hair" was made of snakes.

Section 2

Mollusks and Annelid Worms

Useful, Edible Mollusks

- More than any other invertebrates, mollusks are consumed as food by people worldwide. Oysters, mussels, clams, snails, squids, and octopuses are just a few edible mollusks.

Is That a Fact!

- Giant clams are the largest living bivalves. Shells of the giant clam *Tridacna gigas* can be 1.5 m long and can have a mass of more than 225 kg.

Earth Movers

- Charles Darwin (1809–1882) spent many years studying earthworms and calculating their remarkable earth-moving abilities.

- Scientists estimate that the amount of soil brought to the surface by earthworms each year can be as much as 90 metric tons per hectare in temperate regions and considerably more in tropical regions. Earthworm activity aerates the soil and in some environments this activity improves growing conditions for plants.

Is That a Fact!

- Australia is home to the world's longest earthworms, which can exceed 3 m in length.

Terrestrial Leeches

- Most leeches are aquatic, but tropical rain forests are home to terrestrial leeches. The body heat of mammals attracts these blood-sucking leeches. The leeches will quickly move over vegetation and converge on any unlucky animal that stands in one place for more than a few minutes.

Section 3

Arthropods

Diversity

- Nearly 1 million species of arthropods have been identified. Scientists estimate that millions more are yet to be named. Arthropods are more densely and widely distributed than members of any other animal group are.

- Arthropods are found in every imaginable type of environment, from mountain peaks to deep-sea trenches and from equatorial rain forests to polar  regions. Some arthropods are adapted for life on land, others for life in the air, and still others for life in salty, brackish, or fresh water.

Beetles

- The order Coleoptera (meaning "sheathed wings"), which contains beetles, fireflies, and weevils, is the largest order in the animal kingdom. There are more than 300,000 known species of beetles.

Is That a Fact!

◆ All known species of spiders are predators. Their chelicerae (anterior pair of appendages) end in fangs that inject venom that kills or paralyzes their prey. When a spider bites, it also pumps digestive enzymes into its victims. A spider can then suck up the resulting predigested "broth" from its prey.

Section 4

Echinoderms

How Sea Stars Feed

- The mouth of a sea star is located on the underside of its body. A short esophagus leads to a large stomach that, in many species, can be pushed out, or everted, through the sea star's mouth. When a sea star, such as *Asterias*, comes upon a clam, for example, it uses its tube feet and muscular arms to pull the clam's shell apart just enough so that the sea star can push its everted stomach through the opening. The stomach then wraps around the soft parts of the clam's body, and digestion begins.

Class Crinoidea

- The echinoderm class Crinoidea is less familiar to most people than the other classes in the phylum Echinodermata are. Crinoids include sea lilies and feather stars. Sea lilies have a stalked body topped by feathery arms that are used to snare small plankton from the water. Most sea lilies live in deep water. Feather stars are colorful, free-moving animals that have long, many-branched arms. Feather stars are common inhabitants of coral reefs.

Is That a Fact!

◆ When disturbed, many types of sea cucumbers will expel parts of their internal organs through the cloaca. This defense mechanism is quite effective in discouraging potential predators. The lost parts are quickly regenerated.

Overview

Tell students that this chapter will help them learn about invertebrates, which are animals that do not have backbones. The chapter describes several groups of invertebrates, including simple invertebrates, mollusks, annelid worms, arthropods, and echinoderms.

Assessing Prior Knowledge

Students should be familiar with the following topics:

• cells

• classification

• animals and behavior

Identifying Misconceptions

As students learn the material in this chapter, some of them may have the mistaken impression that invertebrates—especially insects—are creepy pests that harm people. You may want to explain to students that most invertebrates are harmless and many are extremely helpful to people. Few spiders, for example, can harm people. But many spiders eat insects that are pests. Also, many invertebrates are beautiful creatures, such as butterflies, starfish, and mollusks that make elegant shells. Encourage students to observe invertebrates that live nearby so that students overcome such misconceptions.

15

Invertebrates

About the PHOTO

No, this creature isn't an alien! It's a sea slug, a relative of garden slugs and snails. This sea slug lives in the cold Pacific Ocean, near the coast of California. Its bright coloring comes from the food that the slug eats. This animal doesn't breathe with lungs. Instead, it brings oxygen into its body through the orange clubs on its back. Like all invertebrates, sea slugs don't have a backbone.

PRE-READING ACTIVITY

FOLDNOTES **Tri-Fold** Before you read the chapter, create the FoldNote entitled "Tri-Fold" described in the **Study Skills** section of the Appendix. Write what you know about invertebrates in the column labeled "Know." Then, write what you want to know in the column labeled "Want." As you read the chapter, write what you learn about invertebrates in the column labeled "Learn."

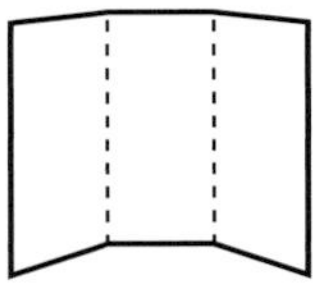

Standards Correlations

National Science Education Standards

The following codes indicate the National Science Education Standards that correlate to this chapter. The full text of the standards is at the front of the book.

Chapter Opener
UCP 1; SAI 1; LS 5a

Section 1 Simple Invertebrates
UCP 1, 4, 5; LS 1a, 1d, 1f, 2a, 3a, 3c, 5a

Section 2 Mollusks and Annelid Worms
UCP 1, 2, 3, 5; LS 1a, 1d, 3a, 5a

Section 3 Arthropods
UCP 2, 3, 5; SAI 2; LS 1a, 1d, 1f, 5a; *LabBook:* SAI 1; LS 3c

Section 4 Echinoderms
UCP 5; LS 1a, 1d, 3a, 5a

Chapter Lab
UCP 3; SAI 1; LS 1a

Chapter Review
SAI 1; LS 1a, 5a

Science in Action
SAI 1, 2; ST 2; SPSP 5; LS 1a, 4d

Teacher's Notes: Provide each student with 6 to 12 pictures of invertebrates. Each student should receive some pictures of invertebrates that have unique features and some pictures of invertebrates that have common features.

Answers

1. Answers may vary according to the animal pictures provided to students. Students should explain the logic of their groupings. Sample answer: I grouped animals by the number of their legs and wings.

2. Answers may vary according to the animal pictures provided to students. Students should explain the logic of their groupings. Sample answer: I grouped animals by how many legs, antennae, wings, and eyes they have as well as by where they live and what their body shape is.

3. Answers may vary. Look for logical, well-reasoned answers. Students may find that not everyone used the same features to classify the animals.

START-UP ACTIVITY

Classify It!

Animals are classified according to their different traits. In this activity, you will classify invertebrates.

Procedure

1. Look at the **pictures** that your teacher has provided. These animals do not have a backbone.

2. Which animals are the most alike? Organize them into groups according to their shared traits.

3. Decide which animals within each group are the most alike. Put these animals into smaller groups inside of their larger group.

4. Construct a table that organizes your classification groups.

Analysis

1. What features did you use to classify the animals into the larger groups? Explain why you think these features are the most important.

2. What features did you use to place the animals in smaller groups? Explain your reasoning.

3. Compare your table with those of your classmates. What similarities or differences do you find?

Strange but True!

In 1995, researchers in Germany made a computer chip that could send signals to a single nerve cell in a living leech. Even more amazing, the leech's nerve cell could send signals back to the computer chip. What is so amazing about having a "mind link" with a leech? The answer may surprise you.

In the United States alone, accidents result in more than 10,000 spinal-cord injuries a year. In severe cases, a person can lose muscle control, particularly in the arms and legs. But what does this have to do with leeches?

Giant leeches from South America, like the one shown here on the scientist's arm, have only a few nerve cells. By studying leech nerves, biologists are learning how to communicate directly with nerve cells.

The scientists hope that communicating with leech nerves using a computer chip will one day help them communicate with human nerve cells. In the future, people with spinal-cord injuries may be able to use computers to communicate with the nerve cells in their body and move their muscles.

Scientists still have a lot to learn, but who would have expected such a promising breakthrough with an animal that doesn't even have a backbone? In this chapter, you will learn about many spineless critters, the invertebrates.

Chapter Starter Transparency
Use this transparency to help students begin thinking about why humans study invertebrates.

CHAPTER RESOURCES

Technology

Transparencies
• Chapter Starter Transparency

READING SKILLS

Student Edition on CD-ROM

Guided Reading Audio CD
• English or Spanish

Classroom Videos
• Brain Food Video Quiz

Workbooks

Science Puzzlers, Twisters & Teasers
• Invertebrates GENERAL

Focus

Overview

This section introduces students to some simple invertebrates: sponges, cnidarians, flatworms, and roundworms. Students learn about the different body plans and important characteristics of these animals.

🔊 Bellringer

Have students write down their answers to the following questions:

• What is an invertebrate? (an animal that lacks a backbone)

• What is your favorite invertebrate? (Answers may vary.)

• What special features help your favorite invertebrate survive? (Answers may vary.)

Motivate

Group ACTIVITY — GENERAL

Determining Symmetry Divide students into cooperative groups of three or four. Give each group a small, rectangular hand mirror and copies of simple, top-view drawings of a butterfly and a sea urchin. Challenge students to use the mirror to demonstrate that the butterfly has bilateral symmetry and that the sea urchin has radial symmetry. **English Language Learners**
 Kinesthetic

Simple Invertebrates

Humans and snakes have them, but octopuses and butterflies don't. What are they? Backbones!

Animals that don't have backbones are called **invertebrates** (in VUHR tuh brits). They make up about 96% of all animal species. So far, more than 1 million invertebrates have been named. Most biologists think that millions more have not been identified yet.

Invertebrate Characteristics

Invertebrates come in many different shapes and sizes. Grasshoppers, clams, earthworms, and jellyfish are examples of invertebrates. They are all very different from each other. Some invertebrates have heads, and others do not. Some invertebrates eat food through their mouths. Others absorb food particles through their tissues. But all invertebrates are similar because they do not have backbones.

Invertebrates have three basic body plans, or types of *symmetry*. Symmetry can be bilateral (bie LAT uhr uhl) or radial (RAY dee uhl). Some animals have no symmetry at all. Animals that don't have symmetry are *asymmetrical* (AY suh MEH tri kuhl). Most animals have bilateral symmetry. **Figure 1** shows examples of each kind of symmetry.

📋 READING WARM-UP

Objectives

● Describe the body plans, nervous systems, and guts of invertebrates.
● Explain how sponges get food.
● Describe three cnidarian traits.
● Describe the three kinds of flatworms.
● Describe the body of a roundworm.

Terms to Learn

invertebrate   gut
ganglion   coelom

📋 READING STRATEGY

Reading Organizer As you read this section, create an outline of the section. Use the headings from the section in your outline.

Figure 1	Animal Body Plans

Bilateral Symmetry   **Radial Symmetry**   **Asymmetry**

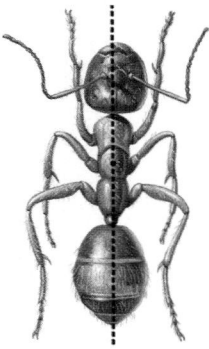 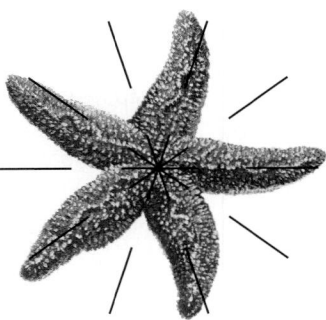 

This ant has **bilateral symmetry.** The two sides of its body mirror each other. On each side of its body, the ant has one eye, one antenna, and three legs.

This sea star has **radial symmetry.** Its body is organized around the center, like spokes on a wheel.

This sponge is **asymmetrical.** You cannot draw a straight line to divide its body into two or more equal parts. Its body is not organized around a center.

CHAPTER RESOURCES

Chapter Resource File

• Lesson Plan
• Directed Reading A **BASIC**
• Directed Reading B **SPECIAL NEEDS**

Technology

Transparencies
• Bellringer

🌐 Cultural Awareness   ADVANCED

Spicule Strength The silica spicules from many freshwater sponges are sharp, abrasive, and strong. In Russia, dried freshwater sponges have long been used to polish silver, brass, and other metals. People who live along the Amazon River in South America add sponge spicules to clay to strengthen the clay pots that they make. Have students research other uses of spicules or whole sponges and create a poster based on their findings. **Visual**

Neurons and Ganglia

All animals except sponges have special tissues that make fibers called *neurons*. Neurons allow animals to sense their environment. Neurons also carry messages around the body to control an animal's actions. Simple invertebrates have neurons arranged in networks or in nerve cords. *Nerve cords* are packs of neurons that carry messages along a single path.

In some invertebrates, many nerve cells come together as ganglia (singular, *ganglion*). A **ganglion** (GANG glee uhn) is a concentrated mass of nerve cells. Each ganglion controls different parts of the body. Ganglia are connected by nerve cords. In complex invertebrates, ganglia are controlled by a brain. The *brain* is an organ that controls nerves throughout the body.

Guts

Almost all animals digest food in a gut. A **gut** is a pouch lined with cells that release chemicals that break down food into small particles. The cells in the gut then absorb the food particles. In complex animals, the gut is inside a coelom (SEE luhm). A **coelom** is the body cavity that surrounds the gut. The coelom contains many organs, such as the heart and lungs. But these organs are separated from the gut. This arrangement keeps gut movement from disturbing other body processes. **Figure 2** shows an earthworm's coelom.

> ✓ **Reading Check** How is the coelom related to the gut? (*See the Appendix for answers to Reading Checks.*)

Sponges

Sponges are the simplest invertebrates. They are asymmetrical and have no tissues, gut, or neurons. Adult sponges move only millimeters per day—if they move at all. In fact, sponges were once thought to be plants! But sponges can't make their own food. That's one reason they are classified as animals. **Figure 3** shows a sponge.

invertebrate an animal that does not have a backbone

ganglion a mass of nerve cells

gut the digestive tract

coelom a body cavity that contains the internal organs

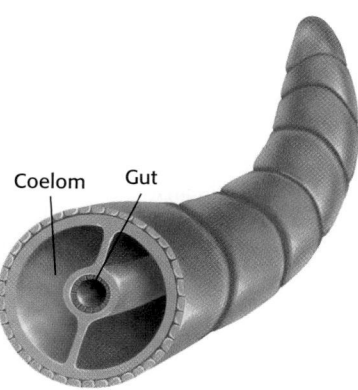

Coelom   Gut

Figure 2 *Earthworms have a fluid-filled coelom that contains the gut.*

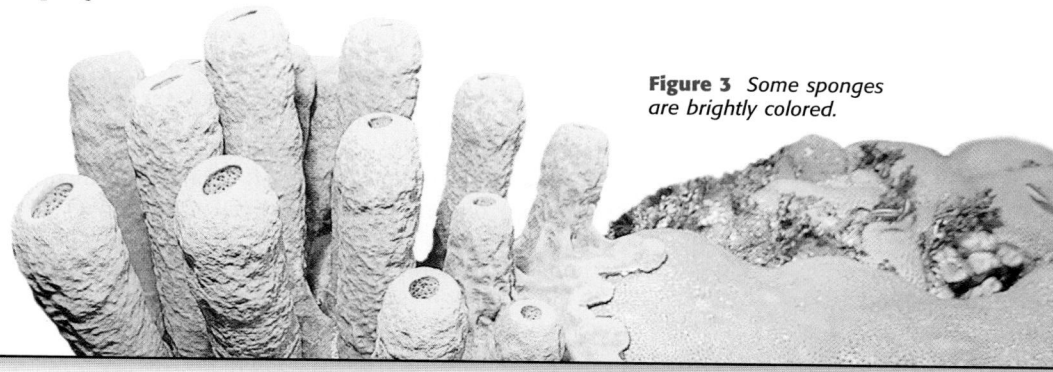

Figure 3 *Some sponges are brightly colored.*

INCLUSION Strategies

- *Visually Impaired*
- *Developmentally Delayed*

Some students learn best when ideas are both concrete and personal. Make the meanings of the different symmetries both concrete and personal by having students label each of the following body parts as having bilateral symmetry, radial symmetry, or asymmetry:

- the human body (bilateral)
- ear (asymmetry)
- hand with fingers and thumb (asymmetry)
- eyeball (radial)
- foot with toes (asymmetry)
- thumb (bilateral)

LS Kinesthetic   English Language Learners

Helpful Sponges Sponges have few predators. The sharp spicules and tough fibers in the bodies of sponges discourage fish and other aquatic organisms from eating sponges. Many sponges also produce toxic chemicals that deter predators and keep other sponges from growing too close. A chemical from a Caribbean sponge, *Cryptotethya crypta,* was one of the first marine compounds to be used in chemotherapy. Currently, many other compounds produced by sponges are being tested as anticancer and antiviral drugs. Have students use the Internet to research other modern uses for chemicals produced by sponges. **LS Verbal**

Demonstration —————— BASIC

Sponge Expansion Place a thin, dry slice of a natural sponge under a microscope, and allow students to examine the spongin-fiber network. Next, add a few drops of water to the sponge, and have students examine the slice again. Students should be able to see clearly how the water is taken up by the fibers (the fibers will swell slightly) and taken into the spaces between the fibers. **LS Visual**

Answer to Math Practice
35 sponges

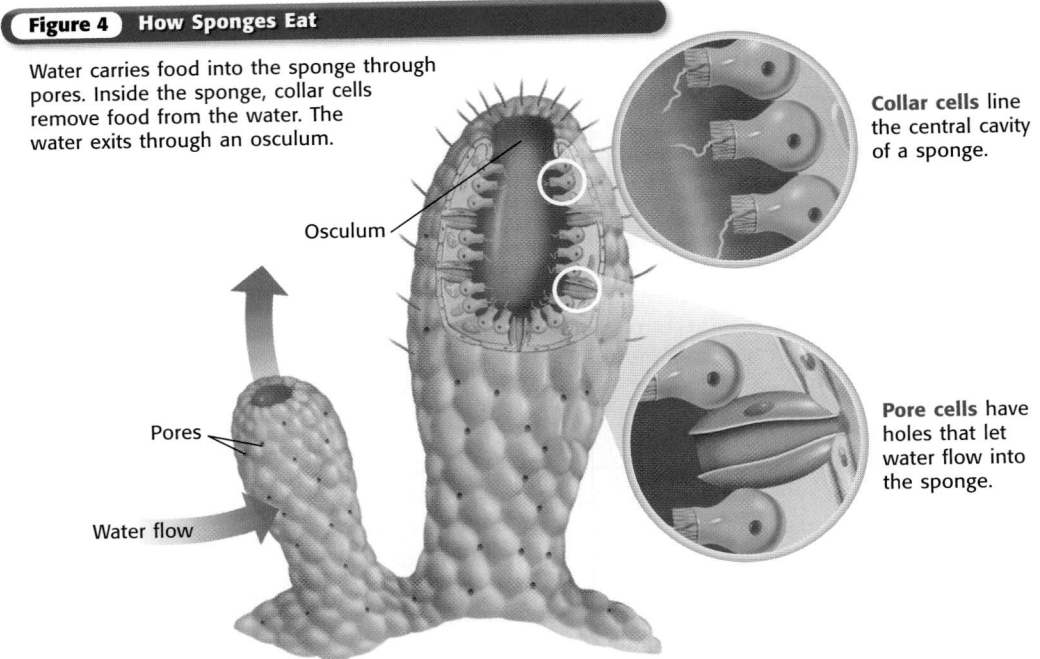

Figure 4 How Sponges Eat

Water carries food into the sponge through pores. Inside the sponge, collar cells remove food from the water. The water exits through an osculum.

Osculum

Pores

Water flow

Collar cells line the central cavity of a sponge.

Pore cells have holes that let water flow into the sponge.

MATH PRACTICE

Several Sponges

Suppose that a big sponge breaks into seven pieces. Each piece begins to grow into a new sponge. Then, each new sponge breaks into five smaller pieces, and each of these new pieces forms a new sponge. How many sponges would you have?

How Do Sponges Eat?

Sponges feed on tiny plants and animals. Because sponges cannot move in search of food and do not have a gut, they have a special way of getting food. A sponge sweeps water into its body through its pores. *Pores* are the holes on the outside of a sponge's body. Water flows into a cavity in the middle of the body, bringing oxygen and food. Special cells called *collar cells* line this cavity. Collar cells filter and digest food from the water that enters the body. Water leaves the body through a hole at the top of the sponge. This hole is called an *osculum* (AHS kyoo luhm). **Figure 4** shows this process.

✓ **Reading Check** How does water enter a sponge's body?

Body Part Abilities

Sponges have some unusual abilities. If you forced a sponge's body through a strainer, the separated cells could come back together and re-form into a new sponge. If part of a sponge is broken off, the missing part can *regenerate,* or grow back. And if a sponge is broken into pieces, or fragmented, new sponges may form from each fragment. Though sponges can use regeneration as a form of reproduction, they also use sexual reproduction.

WEIRD SCIENCE

Nearly all sponges are sessile—they live attached to a surface and cannot move from place to place. *Tethya seychellensis,* a species that lives in the Red Sea, is an exception. Young sponges of this species can move very slowly—about 10 mm to 15 mm a day—by extending long, sticky projections from their body wall. The projections attach to the substrate and then contract to pull the sponge forward.

Answer to Reading Check
Water enters a sponge's body through pores.

Kinds of Sponges

All sponges live in water, and most live in the ocean. As shown in **Figure 5,** sponges come in many different shapes and sizes. Most sponges have a skeleton made of small, hard fibers called *spicules* (SPIK YOOLZ). Some spicules are straight, some are curved, and others have complex star shapes. A sponge's skeleton supports its body and helps protect it from predators. Sponges are divided into groups according to the kinds of skeletons they have.

Cnidarians

Do you know anyone who has been stung by a jellyfish? It is a very painful experience! Jellyfish are members of a group of invertebrates that have stinging cells. Animals in this group are called *cnidarians* (ni DER ee uhns).

Cnidarians are more complex than sponges. Cnidarians have complex tissues and a gut for digesting food. They also have a simple network of nerve cells. Most cnidarians can move more quickly than sponges can. But some cnidarians do share a special trait with sponges. If the body cells are separated, they can come back together to re-form the cnidarian.

Two Body Forms

A cnidarian body can have one of two forms—the *medusa* or the *polyp* form. These body forms are shown in **Figure 6.** Medusas swim through the water. Polyps usually attach to a surface. Some cnidarians change forms at different times in their lives. But many cnidarians are polyps for their whole lives.

Figure 5 *Sponges come in many shapes and sizes.*

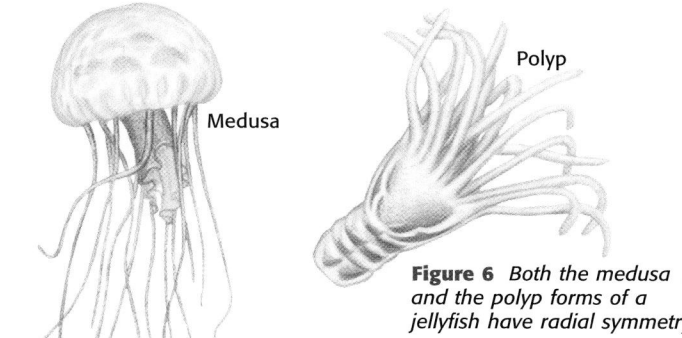

Polyp

Medusa

Figure 6 *Both the medusa and the polyp forms of a jellyfish have radial symmetry.*

Demonstration —— GENERAL

Stinging Cells After students have studied **Figure 7,** perform the following demonstration. Invert the fingers of a rubber glove, and use duct tape to attach the top of the glove securely to the head of a water faucet. Tell students that the inverted fingers of the glove represent nematocysts coiled within stinging cells. Scientists have discovered that nematocysts "fire" as a result of a sudden change in water pressure inside stinging cells. When a nematocyst is stimulated to discharge, the nematocyst membrane becomes highly permeable to water. As water rushes in, the sudden increase in water pressure pushes the nematocyst out with explosive force and turns the nematocyst inside out in the process. Demonstrate this phenomenon by briefly turning on the faucet. The sudden pressure increase will cause the inverted fingers of the rubber glove to evert quickly and forcefully. **LS Visual**   English Language Learners

Research —— GENERAL

Writing **Jellyfish** Have students research *Aurelia,* a genus of jellyfish. Then, have students write a story in which they discuss how the jellyfish move, what jellyfish eat, and how jellyfish sense their environment. **LS Verbal**   PORTFOLIO

Figure 7 *Each stinging cell contains a tiny spear.*

Before Firing
Coiled inside each stinging cell is a tiny, barbed spear.

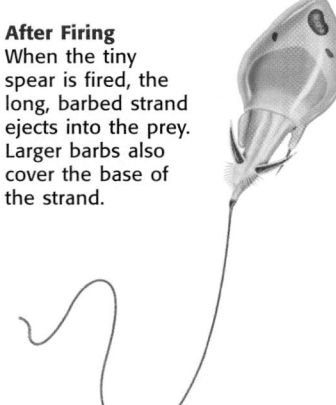

After Firing
When the tiny spear is fired, the long, barbed strand ejects into the prey. Larger barbs also cover the base of the strand.

Stinging Cells

All cnidarians have tentacles covered with stinging cells. When an organism brushes against the tentacles, it activates hundreds of stinging cells. Each stinging cell uses water pressure to fire a tiny, barbed spear into the organism. **Figure 7** shows a stinging cell before and after firing. The tiny spears can release a painful—and sometimes paralyzing—poison into their targets. Cnidarians use their stinging cells to protect themselves and to catch food.

Kinds of Cnidarians

There are three major classes of cnidarians: hydrozoans (HIE dro ZOH uhn), jellyfish, and sea anemones and corals. **Figure 8** shows each kind of cnidarian. Hydrozoans are common cnidarians that live in both freshwater and marine environments. Most spend their entire lives as polyps. Jellyfish catch other invertebrates and fish in their tentacles. They spend most of their lives as medusas. Sea anemones and corals spend their lives as polyps. They are often brightly colored.

Most corals are small and live in colonies. The colonies build huge skeletons that are made of calcium carbonate. Each new generation of corals builds on top of the last generation. Over thousands of years, these tiny animals build massive underwater reefs. Coral reefs can be found in warm, tropical waters throughout the world.

Figure 8   Kinds of Cnidarians

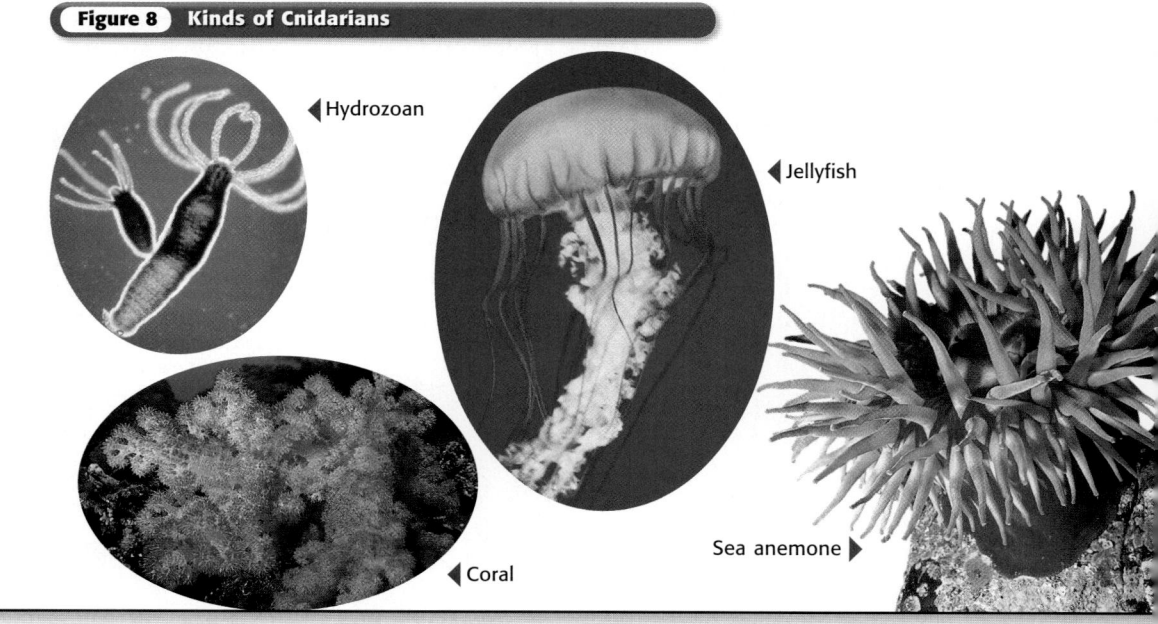

◄ Hydrozoan

◄ Jellyfish

◄ Coral

Sea anemone ▶

BRAIN FOOD

Transparent Trappers Many jellyfish that capture and eat small fish have transparent or nearly transparent bodies and long, trailing tentacles that are very difficult to see in the water. Ask students to speculate about how these features are an advantage to jellyfish as predators. **LS Verbal**

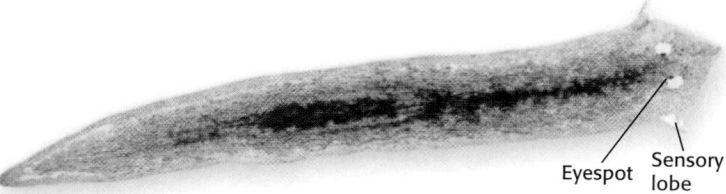

Figure 9 *This planarian has a head with eyespots and sensory lobes. Planarians are often about 15 mm long.*

Eyespot

Sensory lobe

Flatworms

When you think of worms, you probably think of earthworms. But there are many other kinds of worms. Many of them are too tiny to see without a microscope. The simplest worms are the flatworms. Flatworms are divided into three major classes: planarians (pluh NER ee uhnz) and marine flatworms, flukes, and tapeworms.

All flatworms have bilateral symmetry. Many flatworms also have a clearly defined head and two large eyespots. Even though the eyespots cannot focus, a flatworm knows the direction that light is coming from. Some flatworms also have a bump on each side of their head. These bumps are *sensory lobes*. Sensory lobes are used for detecting food. You can see these traits in the planarian shown in **Figure 9.**

✓ Reading Check What are the three major classes of flatworms?

Planarians

Planarians live in freshwater lakes and streams or on land in damp places. Most planarians are predators. They eat other animals or parts of other animals and digest food in a gut. They find food by using their sensory lobes. The planarian's head, eyespots, and sensory lobes are clues that it has a well-developed nervous system. Planarians even have a brain for processing information about their surroundings.

Flukes

Flukes are parasites. A *parasite* is an organism that invades and feeds on the body of another living organism that is called a *host*. Most flukes live and reproduce inside the bodies of other animals. A fluke's fertilized eggs pass out of the other animal's body with waste products. If these fertilized eggs infect drinking water or food, animals may eat them. The fertilized eggs will develop into new flukes inside the animals.

Flukes have tiny heads without eyespots or sensory lobes. They have special suckers and hooks for attaching to animals. **Figure 10** shows a fluke.

SCHOOL to HOME

A Walk in the Park

With your family, take a walk around your neighborhood or a nearby park and make a list of all the invertebrates you find. If you can't recognize some of the invertebrates, draw them, and try to identify them later using a local guide to invertebrates.

ACTIVITY

Figure 10 *Flukes use suckers to attach to their host. Most flukes are just a few millimeters long.*

Is That a Fact!

The adult broad-fish tapeworm, which can infect humans, grows 10 to 20 m in length and may consist of 3,000 to 4,000 sections. A mature fish tapeworm can shed a million eggs a day.

Reteaching — BASIC

Table of Traits To help students remember the differences between sponges, cnidarians, flatworms, and roundworms, make a table on the board. Label the rows with the four kinds of invertebrates, and label the columns "No backbone," "Gut," "Bilateral symmetry," and "Simple brain." Ask the class to tell you which traits to check off for each invertebrate. **LS** Visual

Quiz — GENERAL

1. Describe the nervous system of most simple invertebrates. (Simple invertebrates have nerves arranged in networks or in nerve cords throughout their body. In some invertebrates, nerve cells are grouped into ganglia that control different body parts.)

2. List three kinds of cnidarians. (Answer may include: corals, hydras, jellyfish, and sea anemones)

3. What is the relationship between a parasite and its host? (A parasite is an organism that invades and feeds on another living creature; the organism that the parasite feeds on is the parasite's host.)

CONNECTION TO Social Studies

Tapeworms People and animals can become infected by tapeworms when they swallow something that contains tapeworm eggs or larvae. These eggs or larvae can come from unclean food, water, or surfaces. Animals can even get tapeworms by swallowing infected fleas. In a group, research one of the following topics: What are some different kinds of tapeworms? What are the effects of tapeworm infection? How can tapeworm infection be prevented? Then, present your research to the rest of the class.

ACTiViTY

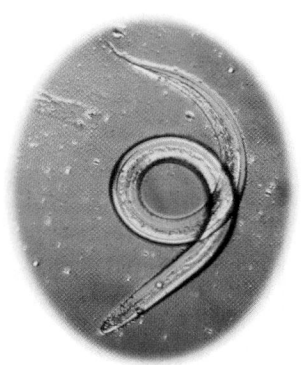

Figure 12 *This hookworm is a tiny larva. Even as an adult, it will be less than 15 mm long.*

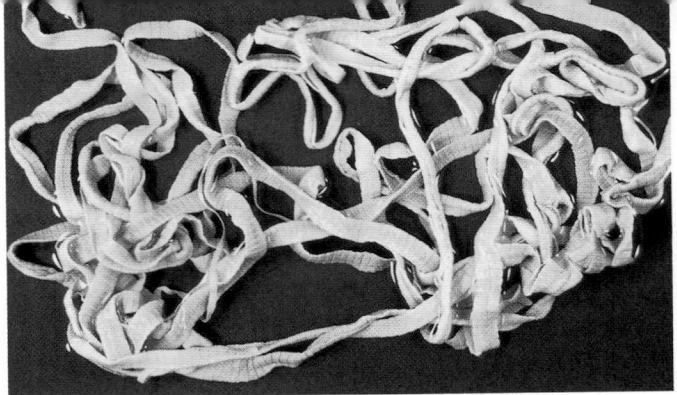

Figure 11 *Tapeworms can reach enormous sizes. Some can grow to be longer than a school bus!*

Tapeworms

Tapeworms are similar to flukes. Like flukes, they have a small head with no eyespots or sensory lobes. They live and reproduce in other animals. They also feed on these animals as parasites. But tapeworms have a unique body that is very specialized for their internal environment. Tapeworms do not have a gut. These organisms simply attach to the intestines of another animal and absorb nutrients. The nutrients move directly through the tapeworm's tissues. **Figure 11** shows a tapeworm that can infect humans.

Roundworms

Roundworms have bodies that are long, slim, and round, like spaghetti. Like other worms, they have bilateral symmetry. Roundworms have a simple nervous system. A ring of ganglia forms a simple brain. Parallel nerve cords connect the two ends of their body. **Figure 12** shows one kind of roundworm.

Most species of roundworms are very small. A single rotten apple could contain 100,000 roundworms! These tiny worms break down the dead tissues of plants and animals. This process helps make soil rich and healthy.

Not all roundworms eat dead tissues. Many roundworms are parasites. Some of these roundworms, including pinworms and hookworms, infect humans. *Trichinella spiralis* (TRIK i NEL uh spuh RAL is) is a parasitic roundworm that is passed to people from infected pork. This roundworm causes the disease trichinosis (TRIK i NOH sis). This illness causes fever, fatigue, and digestive problems. Cooking pork thoroughly will kill any roundworms living in the meat.

✓ **Reading Check** Name three roundworms that are parasites and that can affect humans.

Homework — GENERAL

Writing **Roundworm Reality** Have students research the life cycle of *Trichinella spiralis*, a species of roundworm parasites, and write a persuasive paragraph on the importance of cooking pork thoroughly to prevent the contraction of trichinosis. **LS** Verbal

Answer to Reading Check

pinworms, hookworms, and *Trichinella spiralis*

SECTION Review

Summary

- Invertebrates are animals that do not have a backbone. Most invertebrates have neurons and a gut. The gut is surrounded by the coelom.

- Almost all animals have radial or bilateral symmetry. But some animals, including sponges, are asymmetrical.

- Sponges filter food from water with collar cells. Collar cells also digest food. Sponges can regenerate body parts. They are classified by the kinds of skeletons they have.

- Cnidarians have stinging cells and have two body forms: the medusa and the polyp. Hydrozoans, jellyfish, and sea anemones and corals are cnidarians.

- Planarians, flukes, and tapeworms are three classes of flatworms. Planarians have eyespots and sensory lobes. Flukes and tapeworms are parasites.

- Roundworms are tiny worms that break down dead plant and animal tissue. Some roundworms are parasites.

Using Key Terms

Complete each of the following sentences by choosing the correct term from the word bank.

invertebrate	gut
ganglion	coelom

1. A(n) ___ is a mass of nerve cells that controls an animal's actions.

2. A(n) ___ does not have a backbone.

3. The ___ is a special space in an animal's body that surrounds the ___ and other organs.

Understanding Key Ideas

4. Which of the following is a trait shared by all invertebrates?
   a. having no backbone
   b. having radial symmetry
   c. having a brain
   d. having a gut

5. What do sponges use to digest food?
   a. an osculum
   b. pores
   c. collar cells
   d. a gut

6. Describe cnidarian body forms and stinging cells.

7. How is a roundworm similar to a piece of spaghetti?

Interpreting Graphics

All invertebrate nervous systems are made up of some or all of the same basic parts. The drawing below shows the nervous system of a segmented worm. Use this drawing to answer the questions that follow.

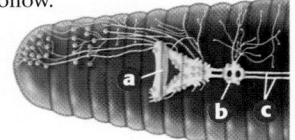

8. The letters in the drawing point to nerve cords, a ganglion, and a brain. Which letter points to the brain? How can you tell?

9. How is the brain connected to the ganglion?

Critical Thinking

10. **Making Inferences** Explain why it would be important for a parasite that its host survive.

  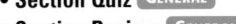

CHAPTER RESOURCES

Chapter Resource File

- Section Quiz **GENERAL**
- Section Review **GENERAL**
- Vocabulary and Section Summary **GENERAL**
- Reinforcement Worksheet **BASIC**
- Critical Thinking **ADVANCED**

Alternative Assessment —— GENERAL

Invertebrate Feeding
Ask students to create an illustrated book about the ways that sponges, cnidarians, and flatworms obtain food. Students should label the invertebrates' body structures on the illustration and may wish to draw internal views or cross sections to show special cells, internal organs, or body systems. Students should also include text in which they discuss the feeding adaptations of the invertebrates. **LS** Verbal/Visual

Answers to Section Review

1. ganglion

2. invertebrate

3. coelom, gut

4. a

5. c

6. Sample answer: Cnidarian body forms include the polyp and the medusa. Both have radial symmetry. Polyps are often sessile, but medusas can move around in the water. Cnidarian stinging cells are cells that contain tiny spears that are shot as a defense or as a way to catch food.

7. Roundworms are shaped like a piece of spaghetti. Both are long, slim, and round.

8. a points to the brain, b points to a ganglion, and c points to a nerve cord. A nerve cord is thick and straight, a ganglion is a mass of many nerve cells, and a brain is a mass that is more complex than a ganglion.

9. by nerve cords

10. Sample answer: A parasite gets its food from its host. If the parasite killed the host right away, the parasite would lose its food source. If the host survives, the parasite has a stable food supply.

SECTION

2

Focus

Overview

In this section, students are introduced to three major classes of mollusks: gastropods, bivalves, and cephalopods. Students learn about mollusks' bodies, feeding habits, and circulatory systems. Students will also study annelid worms, including earthworms, marine worms, and leeches.

Bellringer

Have students unscramble the following words and write a sentence that uses all of the words.

• gluss (slugs)

• isalns (snails)

• sdusqi (squids)

• klomssul (mollusks)

(Sample answer: Slugs, snails, and squids are mollusks.)

Motivate

Group ACTIVITY — GENERAL

Mollusk Menus Organize students into groups that will research how people in different countries use mollusks for food. Students can look for recipes for snails, clams, squids, and other mollusks. Ask each group to make a menu that consists of an appetizer and a main dish made from mollusks.

LS Verbal

READING WARM-UP

Objectives

● Explain how mollusks eat, control body functions, and circulate blood.

● Describe the four body parts that most mollusks have in common.

● Describe three annelid worms.

Terms to Learn

open circulatory system
closed circulatory system
segment

READING STRATEGY

Discussion Read this section silently. Write down questions that you have about this section. Discuss your questions in a small group.

CHAPTER RESOURCES

Chapter Resource File

• Lesson Plan
• Directed Reading A **BASIC**
• Directed Reading B **SPECIAL NEEDS**

Technology

📽 Transparencies
• Bellringer

Mollusks and Annelid Worms

Have you ever eaten clams or calamari? Have you ever seen earthworms on the sidewalk after it rains?

If you have, then you already know a thing or two about mollusks and annelid worms. These animals are more complex than sponges, cnidarians, flatworms, and roundworms. For example, mollusks and annelid worms have a circulatory system that carries materials throughout their bodies.

Mollusks

Snails, slugs, clams, oysters, squids, and octopuses are all mollusks. Most of these animals live in the ocean. But some live in fresh water, and some live on land.

Most mollusks fit into three classes. The *gastropods* (GAS troh PAHDZ) include slugs and snails. The *bivalves* include clams and other shellfish that have two shells. *Cephalopods* (SEF uh loh PAHDZ) include squids and octopuses.

How Do Mollusks Eat?

Each kind of mollusk has its own way of eating. Snails and slugs eat with a ribbonlike organ—a tongue covered with curved teeth. This organ is called a *radula* (RAJ u luh). **Figure 1** shows a close-up of a slug's radula. Slugs and snails use the radula to scrape algae from rocks, chunks of tissue from seaweed, or pieces of leaves from plants. Clams and oysters attach to one place and use gills to filter tiny plants, bacteria, and other particles from the water. Octopuses and squids use tentacles to grab their food and to place it in their powerful jaws.

Figure 1 *The rows of teeth on a slug's radula help scrape food from surfaces. The radula here has been magnified 2,000 times.*

WEIRD SCIENCE

The blue-ringed octopus of the South Pacific is deadly. When the octopus is provoked, the blue rings on its skin turn so blue that they almost glow. The saliva in its bite contains a powerful toxin for which there is no known antidote! This toxin paralyzes the victim. If a person bitten by this octopus arrives at the hospital in time, he or she is put on a respirator until the toxin wears off.

Ganglia and Brains

All mollusks have complex ganglia. They have special ganglia to control breathing, movement, and digestion. But octopuses and squids have the most advanced nervous system of all invertebrates. Cephalopods, such as the octopus in **Figure 2,** have large brains that connect all of their ganglia. Cephalopods are thought to be the smartest invertebrates.

Pumping Blood

Unlike simple invertebrates, mollusks have a circulatory system. The circulatory system transports materials through the body in the blood. Most mollusks have an open circulatory system. In an **open circulatory system,** a simple heart pumps blood through blood vessels that empty into *sinuses*, or spaces in the animal's body. Squids and octopuses have a closed circulatory system. In a **closed circulatory system,** a heart pumps blood through a network of blood vessels that form a closed loop.

Reading Check What is the difference between an open circulatory system and a closed circulatory system? (*See the Appendix for answers to Reading Checks.*)

Mollusk Bodies

A snail, a clam, and a squid look quite different from one another. Yet if you look closely, you will see that their bodies all have similar structures. The body parts of mollusks are described in **Figure 3.**

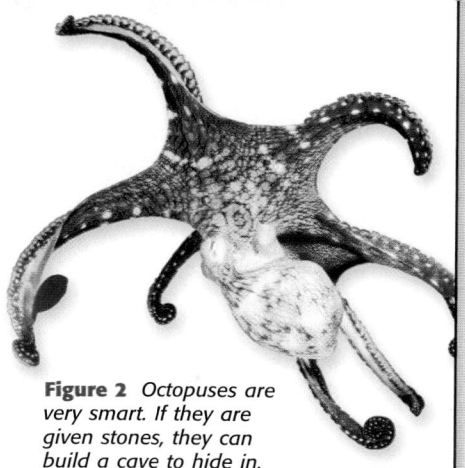

Figure 2 *Octopuses are very smart. If they are given stones, they can build a cave to hide in.*

open circulatory system a circulatory system in which the circulatory fluid is not contained entirely within vessels

closed circulatory system a circulatory system in which the heart circulates blood through a network of blood vessels that form a closed loop

Success Story Giant clams live in tropical waters of the Pacific Ocean. They are a staple in the diet of many Pacific islanders and are a delicacy in many Asian countries. Recently, giant clams have been threatened by overfishing. Scientists have been working to restore giant clam populations by raising thousands of these mollusks on giant clam "farms" along protected coasts. When farmed clams are big enough, they are transplanted to the wild. As a result, giant clams are once again common around many Pacific islands. Ask students to research other efforts to help restore threatened invertebrate populations. **LS Verbal**

Answer to Reading Check

An open circulatory system has a heart that pumps blood through blood vessels that empty into sinuses. A closed circulatory system has a heart that pumps blood through a closed loop of blood vessels.

BRAIN FOOD

Mutualism Giant clams and most corals contain mutualistic algae in their tissues. These photosynthetic algae produce food for themselves and their hosts. In return, giant clams and corals provide the algae with a safe place to live. Ask students to hypothesize why giant clams and corals that contain algae are found only in clear, relatively shallow ocean waters. (Clear, shallow water allows sunlight to reach the algae.)

Figure 3 **Body Parts of Mollusks**

Mollusks are known for their broad, muscular **foot.** The foot helps the animal move. In gastropods, the foot makes mucus that the animal slides along.

The gills, gut, and other organs form the **visceral mass** (VIS uhr uhl MAS). It lies in the center of a mollusk's body.

A layer of tissue called the **mantle** covers the visceral mass. The mantle protects the bodies of mollusks that do not have a shell.

In most mollusks, the outside of the mantle secretes a **shell.** The shell protects the mollusk from predators and keeps land mollusks from drying out.

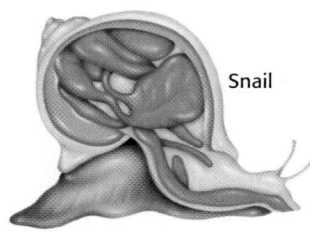

Snail

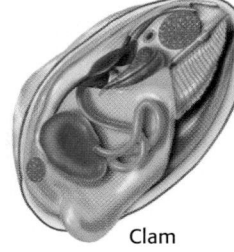

Clam

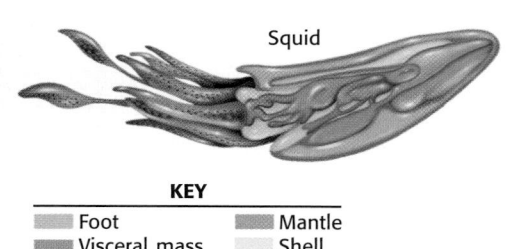

Squid

KEY

▬ Foot	▬ Mantle
▬ Visceral mass	▬ Shell

Science Bloopers

Hungry Snails Nearly 30 cm long, the giant African snail is native to east Africa, where it eats decaying plants. When introduced onto Pacific islands, African snails ate crops and became pests. A misguided attempt to solve the problem involved releasing several new snail species onto the islands. But the predatory snails ate the islands' native snails instead of the African snails. Now some of the native snails are endangered.

Is That a Fact!

The large fleshy lobe to the right of the octopus's eyes in **Figure 2** is not the head. It contains the visceral mass.

Reteaching — BASIC

Mollusk Names Help students remember the difference between gastropods, bivalves, and cephalopods by teaching them the following root words: *gastro*, which means "stomach," *cephalo*, which means "head," *pod*, which means "foot," *bi*, which means "two," and *valve*, which means "door." Ask students to explain why "stomach foot," "two doors," and "head foot" are appropriate names for each group. **LS Verbal**

Quiz — GENERAL

1. What are the three main classes of mollusks? (gastropods, bivalves, and cephalopods)

2. How do herbivorous snails and slugs use their radula to obtain food? (They use their radula to scrape algae off rocks, chunks of tissue from seaweed, or pieces from plant leaves.)

Alternative Assessment — GENERAL

Writing **Worms Gone Wild** Have students research how earthworms introduced into forests in the Midwest by the dumping of bait by fishers are endangering the forests. Students can write a one-page report explaining how worms can be good for gardens, but bad for forests in the Midwest. **LS Verbal**

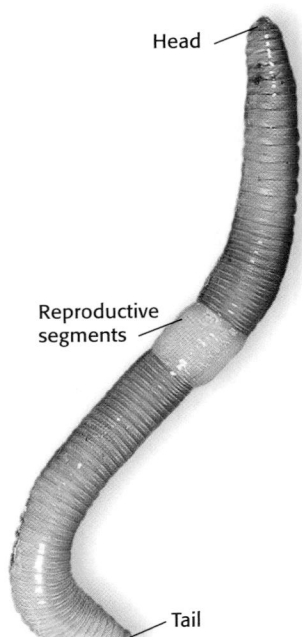

Figure 4 *Except for the head, tail, and reproductive segments, all of the segments of this earthworm are identical.*

Head

Reproductive segments

Tail

segment any part of a larger structure, such as the body of an organism, that is set off by natural or arbitrary boundaries

Figure 5 *This marine worm is a predator that eats small animals. Can you see the segments of this worm?*

Annelid Worms

Annelid worms are often called segmented worms because their bodies have segments. A **segment** is an identical, or almost identical, repeating body part. You can see the segments of an earthworm in **Figure 4.**

Like roundworms and flatworms, annelid worms have bilateral symmetry. But annelid worms are more complex than other worms. Annelid worms have a closed circulatory system. They also have a complex nervous system with a brain. A nerve cord connects the brain to a ganglion in each segment.

Annelid worms live in salt water, in fresh water, or on land. They eat plant material or animals. Three major groups of annelid worms are earthworms, marine worms, and leeches.

Earthworms

Earthworms are the most familiar annelid worms. Each earthworm has 100 to 175 segments. Most of these segments are identical, but some look different from the others. These segments have special jobs, such as eating or reproducing.

Earthworms eat material in the soil. They break down plant and animal matter in the soil and leave behind wastes called *castings*. Castings help gardens by making the soil richer. Earthworms also improve garden soil by digging tunnels. The tunnels allow air and water to reach deep into the soil.

To move, earthworms use stiff hairs, or bristles, on the outside of their body. The bristles hold the back part of the worm in place while the front part pushes through the soil.

Marine Worms

If there were a beauty contest for worms, marine worms would win. These worms are called *polychaetes* (PAHL ih KEETS), which means "many bristles." They are covered in bristles and come in many colors. **Figure 5** shows a marine worm. Most of these worms live in the ocean. Some eat mollusks and other small animals. Others filter small pieces of food from the water.

Group ACTiViTY — GENERAL

Earthworms in Action To demonstrate earthworms' ability to mix soil, have the class work cooperatively to fill the bottom half of a large glass jar with sand and the top half with potting soil. Add enough water to moisten the soil and the sand, and add 5 to 10 large earthworms (available from sporting goods or hardware stores) to the jar. Punch air holes in the lid, and place it securely on the jar. Put the jar in a cool, dimly lit location in the classroom. Add water periodically to keep the soil moist. Encourage students to observe how the earthworms gradually mix the soil and sand during the next few weeks. **LS Visual** **Co-op Learning** English Language Learners

Leeches

Leeches are known as parasites that suck other animals' blood. This is true of some leeches. But other leeches are not parasites. Some leeches are scavengers that eat dead animals. Others are predators that eat insects, slugs, and snails.

Leeches that suck blood can be useful in medicine. After surgery, doctors sometimes use leeches to prevent dangerous swelling near a wound. **Figure 6** shows two leeches being used for this purpose. Leeches also make a chemical that keeps blood thin so that it does not form clots. The leech uses the chemical to keep blood flowing from its host. Doctors use this chemical to prevent blood clots in people with circulation problems. This chemical can also help break down blood clots that already exist.

Reading Check What are two ways that doctors use leeches to help people?

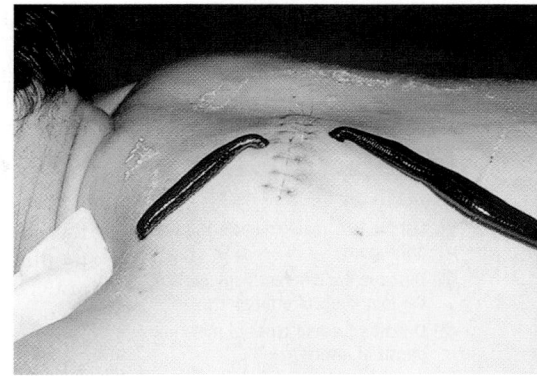

Figure 6 *Doctors sometimes use leeches to reduce swelling after surgery.*

SECTION Review

Summary

- Mollusks get food with gills, a radula, or tentacles and jaws.
- Mollusks have a complex nervous system.
- Mollusks have either an open circulatory system or a closed circulatory system.
- All mollusks have a foot, a visceral mass, and a mantle. Most mollusks also have a shell.
- The three major groups of annelid worms are earthworms, marine worms, and leeches.

Using Key Terms

1. Use the following terms in the same sentence: *open circulatory system* and *closed circulatory system*.

2. In your own words, write a definition for the term *segment*.

Understanding Key Ideas

3. Some mollusks use a radula to
   a. scrape algae off rocks.
   b. filter food from water.
   c. grab food from water.
   d. place food in their jaws.

4. What trait do all mollusk nervous systems share? What is unique about squids' and octopuses' nervous systems?

5. What are the four main body parts of most mollusks?

6. Describe three different kinds of annelid worms.

Math Skills

7. If a squid swims at 30 km/h, how far can it swim in 1 min?

Critical Thinking

8. **Predicting Consequences** Clams use gills to filter food from water. How could water pollution affect clams?

9. **Analyzing Ideas** Cephalopods do not have shells. What other traits do they have to help make up for this lack of protection?

SCI LINKS
Developed and maintained by the National Science Teachers Association

For a variety of links related to this chapter, go to www.scilinks.org

Topic: Mollusks and Annelid Worms
SciLinks code: HSM0986

Overview

In this section, students learn that arthropods have jointed limbs, a segmented body, an exoskeleton, a well-developed brain, and specialized sense organs. Students are introduced to four major groups of arthropods—centipedes and millipedes, crustaceans, arachnids, and insects. The section describes insect bodies and patterns of development.

Bellringer

Have students pretend that they can undergo metamorphosis. Ask students the following questions:

• What might you look like when you emerge?

• How might you find food, and what might you eat?

• What adaptations that you do not have now might you have after metamorphosis?

Motivate

Discussion ——— GENERAL

Arthropods Introduce the general characteristics of arthropods. Have students discuss how these characteristics may have helped arthropods adapt to nearly all environments and to diversify such that arthropods make up the largest group of animals on Earth. **LS** Verbal

---

SECTION

3

Arthropods

Have you ever explored a park or field, looking for living things? How many animals do you think can live on one acre of land? If you could find all the arthropods in that area, you could count more than a million animals!

Arthropods have lived for hundreds of millions of years. They have adapted to nearly every environment. You are probably familiar with many of them, such as insects, spiders, crabs, and centipedes. Arthropods are the largest group of animals on Earth. At least 75% of all animal species are arthropods.

Characteristics of Arthropods

All arthropods share four characteristics: a segmented body with specialized parts, jointed limbs, an exoskeleton, and a well-developed nervous system.

Segmented and Specialized

Like annelid worms, arthropods are segmented. In some arthropods, such as centipedes, nearly every segment is identical. Only the segments that make up the head and tail are different from the rest. But most species of arthropods have segments that include specialized structures, such as wings, antennae, gills, pincers, and claws. During an arthropod's development, some segments grow together. This process forms three main body parts. These body parts are the *head,* the *thorax,* and the *abdomen.* You can see these three body parts in **Figure 1.**

Figure 1 *Like most arthropods, this dragonfly has a head, a thorax, and an abdomen.*

READING WARM-UP box:

Science BIOOperS

Spreading Silk In 1869, the gypsy moth was introduced into the United States in an attempt to breed a better silkworm. The results were disastrous. Some moths escaped, and the species spread throughout the northeastern part of the country. Gypsy moth caterpillars eat the leaves of deciduous trees. In years in which there are especially large numbers of caterpillars, millions of acres of trees can be stripped of their leaves.

Jointed Limbs

Jointed limbs give arthropods their name. *Arthro* means "joint," and *pod* means "foot." Jointed limbs are legs or other body parts that bend at the joints. Having jointed limbs makes it easier for arthropods to move.

An External Skeleton

Arthropods have a hard outer covering. The hard, external structure that covers the outside of the body is an **exoskeleton.** You can see a crab's yellow and white exoskeleton in **Figure 2.** This structure is made of protein and a special substance called *chitin* (KIE tin). An exoskeleton does some of the same things that an internal skeleton does. Like your bones, it serves as a stiff frame that supports the body. It also allows the animal to move. An arthropod's muscles connect to different parts of the skeleton. When the muscles contract, they move the exoskeleton, which moves parts of the animal.

But the exoskeleton also does things that an internal skeleton doesn't do well. The exoskeleton acts like a suit of armor to protect organs inside the body. The exoskeleton also keeps water inside the animal's body. This feature allows arthropods to live on land without drying out.

✔ **Reading Check** How is an exoskeleton similar to an internal skeleton? (*See the Appendix for answers to Reading Checks.*)

Sensing Surroundings

All arthropods have a head and a well-developed brain and nerve cord. The nervous system receives information from sense organs, including eyes and bristles. Some arthropods, such as the tarantula, use external bristles to sense their surroundings. The bristles detect motion, vibration, pressure, and chemicals.

Some arthropods have very simple eyes. These arthropods can detect light but cannot see images. But most arthropods have compound eyes. Arthropods that have compound eyes can see images. A **compound eye** is an eye that is made of many identical, light-sensitive units. The fruit fly in **Figure 3** has two compound eyes.

Figure 2 *A ghost crab's exoskeleton protects its body from drying out on land.*

exoskeleton a hard, external, supporting structure

compound eye an eye composed of many light detectors

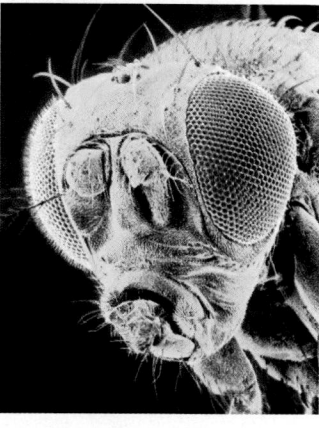

Figure 3 *Compound eyes are made of many identical, light-sensitive units that work together.*

WEIRD SCIENCE

Compass termites from Australia can air-condition their mounds! These insects build towers that are up to 2.5 m long and 3 m high but are narrow and tall. Up to 2 million termites may live inside. These termites build their towers so that large, broad sides face east and west, and narrow sides face north and south. This design allows the nest to maintain a steady temperature. In the morning and evening, the rising and setting sun hits the broad sides of the nest. But the hot midday sun does not strike a large part of the nest. That way, the nest gets a steady supply of moderate heat throughout the day.

Making Models It is a common misconception that spiders are insects. Challenge students to disprove this misconception by using modeling clay and pipe cleaners to create models of a spider and an insect. Have students read this section before they begin. Students' models should reflect that spiders have two main body parts, four pairs of legs, and no antennae, whereas insects have three main body parts, three pairs of legs, and one pair of antennae. **LS Kinesthetic**

English Language Learners

Group ACTIVITY — GENERAL

Have students work in cooperative groups of three or four to research web-building spiders. Each group should investigate one spider species. Have each group use string or yarn to create an example of the type of web that the chosen species builds. Guide students in a class discussion in which they compare the web shapes and designs. **LS Kinesthetic/ Interpersonal**

Co-op Learning   English Language Learners

INTERNET ACTIVITY
Sequence Board — GENERAL

For an internet activity related to this chapter, have students go to **go.hrw.com** and type in the keyword **HL5INVW**.

Centipede

Millipede

Figure 4 *Centipedes eat other animals. Millipedes eat plants.*

antenna a feeler that is on the head of an invertebrate, such as a crustacean or an insect, that senses touch, taste, or smell

Kinds of Arthropods

Arthropods are classified by the kinds of body parts they have. You can tell the difference between arthropods by looking at the number of legs, eyes, and antennae they have. An **antenna** is a feeler that senses touch, taste, or smell.

Centipedes and Millipedes

Centipedes and millipedes have one pair of antennae, a hard head, and one pair of mandibles. *Mandibles* are mouthparts that can pierce and chew food. One way to tell these animals apart is to count the number of legs on each segment. Centipedes have one pair of legs on each segment. They can have 30 to 354 legs. Millipedes have two pairs of legs on each segment. The record number of legs on a millipede is 752! **Figure 4** shows a centipede and a millipede. How many legs can you count on each?

Crustaceans

Shrimps, barnacles, crabs, and lobsters are crustaceans. Most crustaceans live in water. They have gills for breathing in the water, mandibles for eating, and two compound eyes. Each eye is located on the end of an eyestalk. Unlike all other arthropods, crustaceans have two pairs of antennae. The crustaceans in **Figure 5** show some of these traits. The lobster's gills are located under the exoskeleton.

Figure 5 *Water fleas and lobsters are two kinds of crustaceans.*

Antenna
Eyestalk
Antenna

CONNECTION to Chemistry ——————— GENERAL

Chitin Chitin is a strong, flexible, waterproof polysaccharide (a polymer of glucose). Chitin molecules bond readily with proteins, such as those found in the exoskeletons of arthropods. A Japanese textile and fiber manufacturing company has exploited chitin's unique chemical properties to create chitin sutures for surgery and chitin-based artificial skin. Chitin sutures don't have to be removed because they dissolve in the body; they also bind so well with proteins that they may promote healing. Ask students to research how chitin is used in modern medical practices. They can present their results to the class in an oral presentation. **LS Verbal**

Arachnids

Spiders, scorpions, mites, and ticks are arachnids (uh RAK nidz). **Figure 6** shows the two main body parts of an arachnid: the *cephalothorax* (SEF uh loh THAWR AKS) and the abdomen. The cephalothorax is made of both a head and a thorax. Most arachnids have four pairs of legs. They have no antennae. Instead of mandibles, they have a pair of clawlike mouthparts called *chelicerae* (kuh LIS uhr EE). And instead of compound eyes, they have simple eyes. The number of eyes varies—some spiders have eight eyes!

Though some people fear spiders, these arachnids are more helpful than harmful. A few kinds of spider bites do need medical treatment. But the chelicerae of many spiders cannot even pierce human skin. And spiders usually use their chelicerae to catch small insects. Spiders kill more insect pests than any other animal does.

Ticks live in forests, brushy areas, and even grassy lawns. Their bodies can be just a few millimeters long. The segments of these small bodies are joined as one part. Ticks are parasites that use chelicerae to slice into a host's skin. These parasites attach onto the host and feed on the host's blood. A few ticks that bite humans can carry diseases, such as Lyme disease. But most people who are bitten by ticks do not get sick.

✔ **Reading Check** How are spiders helpful to humans?

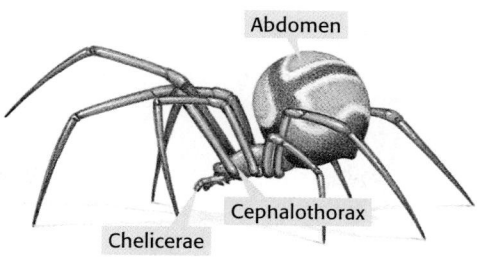

Figure 6 *Arachnids have two main body parts and special mouthparts called chelicerae.*

Insects

Insects make up the largest group of arthropods. If you put all the insects in the world together, they would weigh more than all the other animals combined! **Figure 7** shows a few kinds of insects. Although they look different, they all have three main body parts, six legs, and two antennae.

Sticky Webs

1. Place a **piece of tape** on your desk, sticky side up. The tape represents a web. Your fingers will represent an insect's legs, and then they will represent a spider's legs.

2. Holding the tape in place by the edges, "walk" your fingers across the tape. What happens?

3. Dip your fingers in **cooking oil,** and "walk" them across the tape again. What happens this time?

4. Use the results to explain why spiders don't get stuck in webs.

▲ Bumblebee

◀ Praying mantis

▲ Dragonfly

Figure 7 *These are just a few of the many different insects. Can you see any traits that they have in common?*

Is That a Fact!

The hind legs of the human flea, *Pulex irritans,* are especially adapted for jumping. How high can a flea jump? *P. irritans* can leap 33 cm horizontally and 20 cm vertically, which is comparable to an 85 m high jump for a human!

Answer to Reading Check

Spiders are helpful because they catch small insects that are pests to humans.

Sneaky and Strong

Trapdoor spiders construct silk-lined burrows topped with a hinged lid that acts like a trapdoor. They wait beneath the door for isopods, crickets, or other prey to pass by, and then they bound up from below with remarkable speed. If the trapdoor is disturbed, the spiders use their chelicerae to pull their burrow doors shut. Using a small spring scale, researchers have found that a trapdoor spider can exert an inward pull on its trapdoor that is 140 times the spider's body weight. Calculate what your pulling strength would be if you could exert a force 140 times your weight. (Sample answer for a student who weighs 40 kg: 40 kg × 140 = pulling strength of 5,600 kg)

LS Logical English Language Learners

MATERIALS

FOR EACH STUDENT
• oil, cooking
• tape, transparent

Answers

2. Students' fingers should stick to the tape.

3. Students' fingers should not stick to the tape.

4. The oil makes the fingers slippery so that they will not stick to the tape. Some spiders secrete a nonstick substance that keeps their legs from sticking to their webs. (Note: Some spiders avoid sticking to their webs by stepping only on certain nonstick parts of the web. Others do not have sticky webs, but catch food when insects get tangled in a mess of nonstick silk strands.)

Reteaching ──── BASIC

Writing **Crustaceans** Have students describe a lobster and list the characteristics that make the lobster a crustacean. **LS Verbal**

Quiz ──── GENERAL

Ask students whether each of the following statements is true or false:

1. The cephalothorax of a spider consists of a head and a thorax. (true)

2. The legs of most insects attach to the abdomen. (false)

3. Some types of insects live deep in ocean waters. (false)

4. The stages of complete metamorphosis are egg, nymph, and adult. (false)

Alternative Assessment ──── GENERAL

Writing **Arthropod Encounters** Have students write a narrative in which they describe a walk along a rocky ocean shore or through a tropical rain forest. Have them describe at least a dozen different arthropods that they are likely to encounter. Students should research the two ecosystems before they begin writing. Some students may wish to create illustrations or collages to accompany their narratives. **LS Verbal** PORTFOLIO

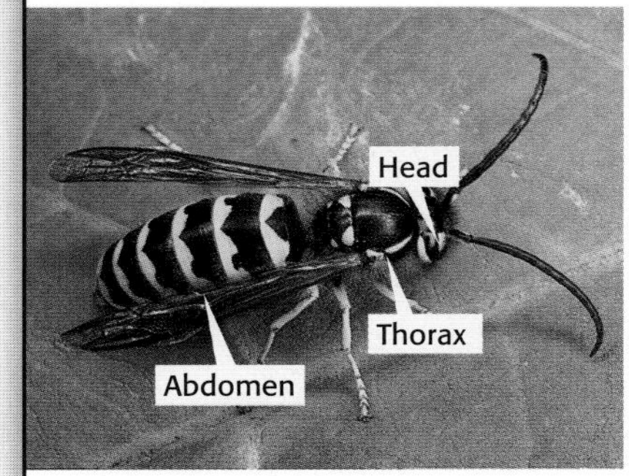

Figure 8 *All insect bodies have these three main parts.*

metamorphosis a phase in the life cycle of many animals during which a rapid change from the immature form of an organism to the adult form takes place

The World of Insects

The only place on Earth where insects do not live is in ocean water. They live on land, in fresh water, and near the sea in beach areas. Many insects are helpful. Most flowering plants depend on insects to carry pollen between plants. Farmers depend on insects to pollinate fruit crops. But some insects are pests that destroy crops or spread disease. And others, such as fleas, ticks, and mosquitoes, bite us and suck our blood.

Insect Bodies

As shown in **Figure 8,** an insect's body has three parts: the head, the thorax, and the abdomen. On the head, insects have one pair of antennae, one pair of compound eyes, and mandibles. The thorax is made of three segments, each of which has one pair of legs. Some insects have no wings. Others may have one or two pairs of wings on the thorax.

Complete Metamorphosis

As an insect develops, it changes form. This process is called **metamorphosis** (MET uh MAWR fuh sis). Most insects go through a complex change called complete metamorphosis. As shown in **Figure 9,** complete metamorphosis has four main stages: egg, larva, pupa (PYOO puh), and adult. Butterflies, beetles, flies, bees, wasps, and ants go through this change.

Figure 9 The Stages of Complete Metamorphosis

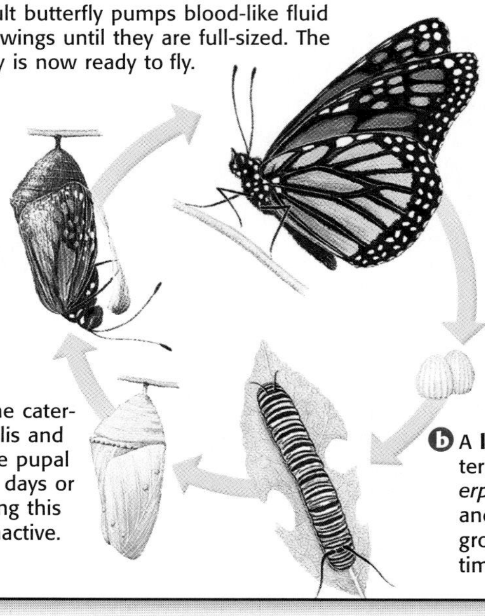

e The adult butterfly pumps blood-like fluid into its wings until they are full-sized. The butterfly is now ready to fly.

d Adult body parts replace the larval body parts. The **adult** splits its chrysalis.

a An adult lays **eggs.** An embryo forms inside each egg.

c After its final molt, the caterpillar makes a chrysalis and becomes a **pupa.** The pupal stage may last a few days or several months. During this stage, the insect is inactive.

b A **larva** hatches from the egg. Butterfly and moth larvae are called *caterpillars.* The caterpillar eats leaves and grows rapidly. As the caterpillar grows, it sheds its outer layer several times. This process is called *molting.*

ACTiViTy ──── ADVANCED

PORTFOLIO **Insecticide Alternatives** Insecticides are routinely sprayed on lawns and gardens to kill insect pests. Unfortunately, these chemicals also kill many beneficial insects, remain in the environment for long periods of time, and accumulate in the bodies of animals (including people) that are higher up the food chain. In recent years, a variety of biological controls that are much more environmentally safe have been developed to control insect pests. Have students investigate different biological controls and create a poster on the topic that could be displayed at a local garden center. **LS Verbal/Visual**

Incomplete Metamorphosis

Grasshoppers and cockroaches are some of the insects that go through incomplete metamorphosis. Incomplete metamorphosis is less complicated than complete metamorphosis. As shown in **Figure 10,** incomplete metamorphosis has three main stages: egg, nymph, and adult. Some nymphs shed their exoskeleton several times in a process called *molting*.

An insect in the nymph stage looks very much like an adult insect. But a nymph does not have wings and is very small. Through molting, it develops into an adult.

✔ **Reading Check** What are the three stages of incomplete metamorphosis?

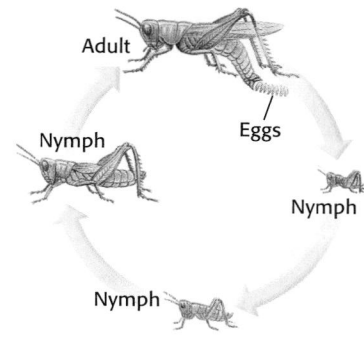

Figure 10 *The grasshopper nymphs look like smaller versions of the adult.*

SECTION Review

Summary

● At least 75% of all animal species are arthropods.

● The four main characteristics shared by arthropods are jointed limbs, a hard exoskeleton, body segments, and a well-developed nervous system.

● The four kinds of arthropods are centipedes and millipedes, crustaceans, arachnids, and insects. Insects are the largest group.

● Insects can go through complete or incomplete metamorphosis.

Using Key Terms

1. Use the following terms in the same sentence: *compound eye* and *antenna*.

2. In your own words, write a definition for each of the following terms: *exoskeleton* and *metamorphosis*.

Understanding Key Ideas

3. Which of the following is NOT a trait shared by all arthropods?
   a. exoskeleton
   b. body segments
   c. antennae
   d. jointed limbs

4. Which of the following arthropods is an arachnid?
   a. butterfly
   b. tick
   c. centipede
   d. lobster

5. What is the difference between complete metamorphosis and incomplete metamorphosis?

6. Name the four kinds of arthropods. How do their bodies differ?

7. Which arthropods have chelicerae? Which have mandibles?

Math Skills

8. How many segments does a millipede with 752 legs have? How many segments does a centipede with 354 legs have?

Critical Thinking

9. **Applying Concepts** Suppose that you find an arthropod in a swimming pool. The organism has compound eyes, antennae, and wings. Is it a crustacean? Why or why not?

10. **Forming Hypotheses** Suppose you have found several cocoons on a plant outside your school. Develop a hypothesis about what animal is inside the cocoon. How could you find out if your hypothesis is correct?

For a variety of links related to this chapter, go to www.scilinks.org

Topic: Arthropods
SciLinks code: HSM0098

Answer to Reading Check

egg, nymph, and adult

CHAPTER RESOURCES

Chapter Resource File

● **Section Quiz** GENERAL
● **Section Review** GENERAL
● **Vocabulary and Section Summary** GENERAL
● **SciLinks Activity** GENERAL
● **Datasheet for Quick Lab**

Technology

Transparencies
• The Stages of Complete Metamorphosis
• Incomplete Metamorphosis

Answers to Section Review

1. Sample answer: Insects use their compound eyes and antennae to sense their surroundings.

2. Sample answer: An exoskeleton is a hard, supporting outer covering. Metamorphosis is a phase during which an organism changes from an immature form to an adult.

3. c

4. b

5. Incomplete metamorphosis has three stages: egg, nymph, and adult. Nymphs look like smaller adults. Complete metamorphosis has four stages: egg, larva, pupa, and adult. Larvae look much different than adults.

6. Sample answer: centipedes and millipedes, crustaceans, arachnids, and insects; Centipedes and millipedes have one pair of antennae, mandibles, and one or two pairs of legs per segment. Crustaceans have mandibles, compound eyes, and two pairs of antennae. Arachnids have an abdomen and a cephalothorax, chelicerae, and no antennae. Insects have a head, thorax, and abdomen, and they have one pair of antennae and mandibles. Some insects have wings.

7. Arachnids have chelicerae. Centipedes, millipedes, crustaceans, and insects have mandibles.

8. A millipede that has 752 legs has 188 segments. A centipede that has 354 legs has 177 segments.

9. No, the arthropod is not a crustacean because crustaceans do not have wings.

10. Sample answer: You could hypothesize that the animal is an insect in the pupa stage of complete metamorphosis. Thus, the animal could be a butterfly, beetle, fly, bee, wasp, or ant. To find out if you were correct, you could wait for the cocoon to continue developing through metamorphosis and see what animal emerges as an adult.

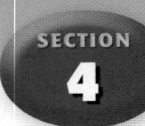
Focus

Overview

In this section, students are introduced to echinoderms, including sea stars, brittle stars and basket stars, sea urchins and sand dollars, sea lilies and feather stars, and sea cucumbers. Students learn that echinoderms have an endoskeleton, spiny skin, radial symmetry in adulthood, a simple nervous system, and a water vascular system.

📻 Bellringer

Have students write down their thoughts about the following question: "Echinoderms include marine animals such as sea stars, sea urchins, and sea cucumbers. All these organisms are slow-moving bottom dwellers. How do you think that they protect themselves from predators?"

Motivate

ACTiViTY ——————— GENERAL

Sea Star Hypotheses Display an example of an echinoderm, such as a sea star. Have students draw the echinoderm in their **science journal** and write a brief hypothesis describing what it eats, how it moves, and where it most likely lives. Discuss students' answers before beginning the section.
LS Verbal/Visual   English Language Learners

SECTION
4

READING WARM-UP

Objectives
● Describe the endoskeleton, nervous system, and water vascular system of echinoderms.
● Explain how an echinoderm's body symmetry changes with age.
● Describe five classes of echinoderms.

Terms to Learn
endoskeleton
water vascular system

READING STRATEGY

Paired Summarizing Read this section silently. In pairs, take turns summarizing the material. Stop to discuss ideas that seem confusing.

endoskeleton an internal skeleton made of bone or cartilage

Echinoderms

Would you touch an object that was covered in sharp spines? Probably not—the spines could hurt you! Some invertebrates are covered in spines that protect them from predators. The predators avoid spines, just like you do.

These spiny invertebrates are called *echinoderms* (ee KIE noh DUHRMZ). Sea stars (starfish), sea urchins, and sand dollars are some familiar members of this group. All echinoderms are marine animals. That means they live in the ocean. Echinoderms live on the sea floor in all parts of the world's oceans. Some of them eat shellfish, some eat dead plants and animals, and others eat algae that they scrape off rocks.

Spiny Skinned

The name *echinoderm* means "spiny skinned." But the animal's skin is not the spiny part. The spines are on the animal's skeleton. An echinoderm's internal skeleton is called an **endoskeleton** (EN doh SKEL uh tuhn). Endoskeletons can be hard and bony or stiff and flexible. The spines covering these skeletons can be long and sharp. They can also be short and bumpy. The animal's skin covers the endoskeleton.

Bilateral or Radial?

Adult echinoderms have radial symmetry. But they develop from larvae that have bilateral symmetry. **Figure 1** shows a sea urchin larva and an adult sea urchin. Notice how the symmetry is different in the two forms.

Figure 1 *The sea urchin larva has bilateral symmetry. The adult sea urchin has radial symmetry.*

Larva   Adult

CHAPTER RESOURCES

Chapter Resource File

● Lesson Plan
● Directed Reading A **BASIC**
● Directed Reading B **SPECIAL NEEDS**

Technology

Transparencies
● Bellringer
● The Water Vascular System
● *LINK TO EARTH SCIENCE* The Three Groups of Marine Life

CONNECTION to
Earth Science ——————— GENERAL

Marine Life Echinoderms are members of the *benthos*, the organisms that live on the ocean floor. Use the teaching transparency "The Three Groups of Marine Life" to illustrate the ocean context of echinoderms.
LS Visual

The Nervous System

All echinoderms have a simple nervous system similar to that of a jellyfish. Around the mouth is a circle of nerve fibers called the *nerve ring*. In sea stars, a *radial nerve* runs from the nerve ring to the tip of each arm, as shown in **Figure 2**. The radial nerves control the movements of the sea star's arms.

At the tip of each arm is a simple eye that senses light. The rest of the body is covered with cells that sense touch and chemical signals in the water.

✔ *Reading Check* **How are the movements of a sea star's arms controlled?** (*See the Appendix for answers to Reading Checks.*)

Water Vascular System

One characteristic that is unique to echinoderms is the water vascular system. The **water vascular system** is a system of canals filled with fluid. It uses water pumps to help the animal move, eat, breathe, and sense its environment. **Figure 3** shows the water vascular system of a sea star. Notice how water pressure from the system is used for many functions.

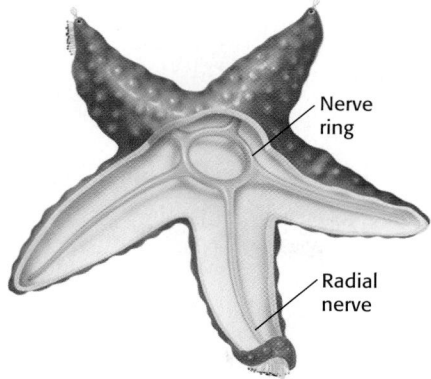

Figure 2 *Sea stars have a simple nervous system.*

water vascular system a system of canals filled with a watery fluid that circulates throughout the body of an echinoderm

| Figure 3 | The Water Vascular System |

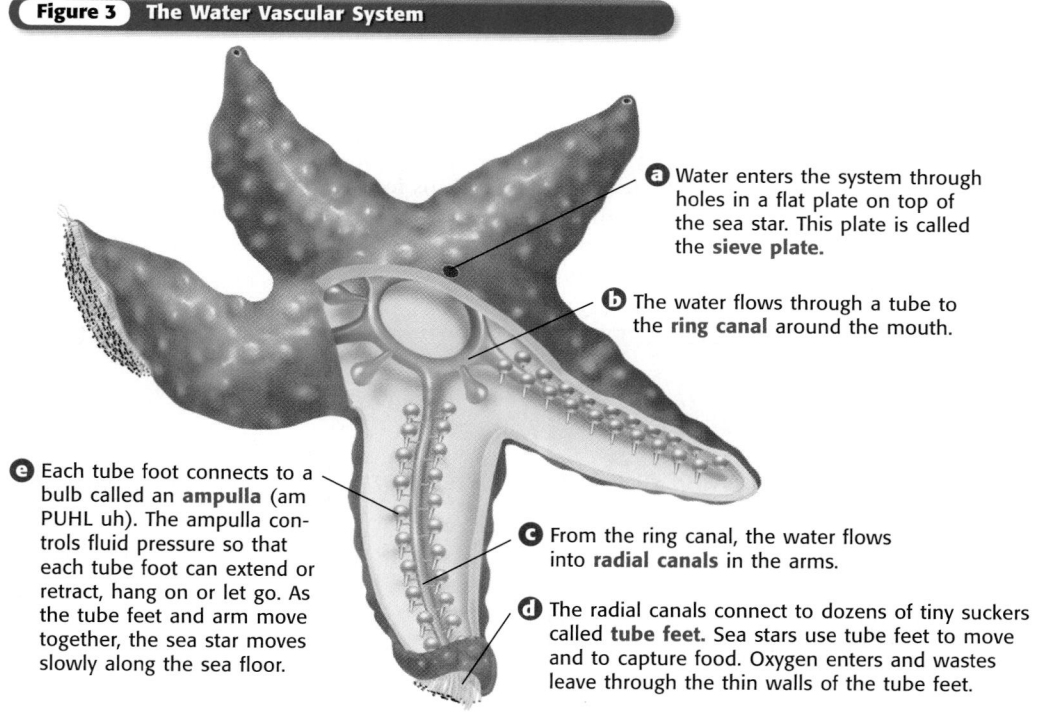

ⓐ Water enters the system through holes in a flat plate on top of the sea star. This plate is called the **sieve plate**.

ⓑ The water flows through a tube to the **ring canal** around the mouth.

ⓔ Each tube foot connects to a bulb called an **ampulla** (am PUHL uh). The ampulla controls fluid pressure so that each tube foot can extend or retract, hang on or let go. As the tube feet and arm move together, the sea star moves slowly along the sea floor.

ⓒ From the ring canal, the water flows into **radial canals** in the arms.

ⓓ The radial canals connect to dozens of tiny suckers called **tube feet.** Sea stars use tube feet to move and to capture food. Oxygen enters and wastes leave through the thin walls of the tube feet.

Is That a Fact!

Sea stars typically have five arms, but some species may have 40 or even 50 arms!

Answer to Reading Check

Radial nerves control the movements of a sea star's arms.

Teach

📖 **READING STRATEGY** — GENERAL

Prediction Guide Before students read this page, ask the following question: "How does a starfish move from place to place?"

a. It curls up its arms and rolls across the sea floor.

ⓑ. It uses suction cup–like tube feet that systematically attach and release to move along.

c. It uses its spines to dig into the sea floor and pull itself forward.

d. By using its long arms, a starfish swims slowly through the water.

LS Verbal

ACTIVITY — GENERAL

Writing **Concept Mapping** Have students make a concept map in their **science journal** by using the terms that describe echinoderms' physical characteristics and nervous and water vascular systems. Students should connect at least 12 terms and link the terms with meaningful phrases. Encourage students to share their concept maps with the class. **LS Verbal/Visual**

BRAIN FOOD

Echinoderm Metamorphosis Most adult echinoderms either are sessile or move slowly over the sea floor. But echinoderm larvae are able to swim, and with the help of ocean currents, they often travel great distances before they settle and change into adults. Ask students why it is an advantage for echinoderm larvae to have bilateral symmetry and for adults to have radial symmetry.

◄ Basket star

▲ Brittle star

Reteaching — BASIC

Reinforcing Knowledge Ask students to write down a type of echinoderm. Collect the papers, shuffle them, and redistribute them so that each student has one. Students should draw a representative specimen of the echinoderm, label its features, and note important facts about that echinoderm. **LS** Verbal

Quiz — GENERAL

1. Name five major groups of echinoderms. (sea stars, brittle stars and basket stars, sea urchins and sand dollars, sea cucumbers, and sea lilies and feather stars)

2. What does the water vascular system enable echinoderms to do? (Echinoderms use the water vascular system to move, eat, breathe, and sense their environment.)

Alternative Assessment — GENERAL

Compare and Contrast Have students compare and contrast the members of the five main classes of echinoderms discussed in the text. Students may wish to include a chart that lists characteristics that all echinoderms have in common and characteristics that are unique to each class of echinoderms. **LS** Verbal

Figure 4 *Brittle stars and basket stars move around more than other echinoderms do.*

Kinds of Echinoderms

Scientists divide echinoderms into five major classes. Sea stars are the most familiar echinoderms, and they make up one class. But there are other classes of echinoderms that may not be as familiar to you.

Brittle Stars and Basket Stars

Brittle stars and basket stars look like their close relatives, sea stars. But these echinoderms have long, slim arms and are often smaller than sea stars. Also, they don't have suckers on their tube feet. **Figure 4** shows a brittle star and a basket star.

Sea Urchins and Sand Dollars

Sea urchins and sand dollars are round. Their endoskeletons form a solid, shell-like structure. As shown in **Figure 5,** they have no arms. But they use their tube feet to move in the same way that sea stars move. Some sea urchins can also walk on their spines. Sea urchins feed on algae they scrape from rocks and other objects. They chew the algae with special teeth. Sand dollars burrow into soft sand or mud. They eat tiny particles of food they find there.

Figure 5 *Sea urchins and sand dollars use their spines for defense and for movement.*

Sea urchin

Sand dollars

Cultural Awareness — GENERAL

What's Cooking? Sea cucumbers are a prized ingredient in many Asian foods. Organize the class into groups, and assign each group one of the following research topics: cultures that use sea cucumbers as a cooking ingredient, types of sea cucumbers that are most popular as food, recipes that include sea cucumbers, and ways in which sea cucumbers are harvested and prepared for market. Have each group report its findings to the class. **LS** Verbal

Is That a Fact!

The long-spined black urchin found in Caribbean waters can rotate its spines to point at any moving object above it.

Sea Lilies and Feather Stars

Sea lilies and feather stars may have 5 to 200 feathery arms. Their arms stretch away from their body and trap small pieces of food. A sea lily's cup-shaped body sits on top of a long stalk, which sticks to a rock. Feather stars, such as the one shown in **Figure 6,** do not have a stalk.

✓ Reading Check What is the difference between a feather star and a sea lily?

Sea Cucumbers

Like sea urchins and sand dollars, sea cucumbers have no arms. A sea cucumber has a soft, leathery body. Unlike other echinoderms, sea cucumbers are long and have a wormlike shape. **Figure 7** shows a sea cucumber.

Figure 7 *Like other echinoderms, sea cucumbers move with tube feet.*

Figure 6 *Like sea stars, brittle stars, and basket stars, feather stars can regrow lost arms.*

SECTION Review

Summary

- Echinoderms are marine animals that have an endoskeleton, a water vascular system, and a nerve ring with radial nerves.
- Echinoderms start life with bilateral symmetry and then develop radial symmetry.
- The different classes of echinoderms include sea stars, sea urchins and sand dollars, brittle stars and basket stars, feather stars and sea lilies, and sea cucumbers.

Using Key Terms

1. Use each of the following terms in a separate sentence: *endoskeleton* and *water vascular system*.

Understanding Key Ideas

2. Which of the following is NOT a trait found in echinoderms?
   a. an endoskeleton
   b. spiny skin
   c. a water vascular system
   d. a nerve ring

3. What is the path taken by water as it flows through the parts of the water vascular system?

4. How are sea cucumbers different from other echinoderms?

5. How does an echinoderm's body symmetry change with age?

6. Name five different classes of echinoderms. List at least one trait for each group.

Math Skills

7. A sea lily lost 12 of its 178 arms in a hurricane. What percentage of its arms were NOT damaged?

Critical Thinking

8. **Making Comparisons** How are echinoderms different from and similar to other invertebrates?

9. **Making Inferences** Suppose you found a sea star with four long arms and one short arm. What might explain the difference?

SCiLINKS® NSTA
Developed and maintained by the
National Science Teachers Association

For a variety of links related to this chapter, go to www.scilinks.org

Topic: Echinoderms
SciLinks code: HSM0458

Answer to Reading Check

A sea lily's body is at the end of a long stalk, while a feather star does not have a stalk.

Answers to Section Review

1. Sample answer: An echinoderm's endoskeleton is underneath its skin. A sea star uses its water vascular system to move, eat, breathe, and sense its environment.

2. b

3. Water enters through a sieve plate and flows into a ring canal. From there, water flows down radial canals that are connected to tube feet. Water pressure in the tube feet is regulated by bulbs called *ampullae*.

4. Sea cucumbers have a long and wormlike shape.

5. As larvae, echinoderms have bilateral symmetry. As adults, echinoderms have radial symmetry.

6. Sea stars have suckers on tube feet. Brittle stars and basket stars have long, slim arms. Sea urchins and sand dollars are round. Sea lilies and feather stars may have 5 to 200 arms. Sea cucumbers have a wormlike shape.

7. 93% ($178 - 12 = 166$; $166 \div 178 = 0.93$)

8. Sample answer: Echinoderms differ from other invertebrates in that echinoderms have an endoskeleton and a water vascular system, whereas other invertebrates do not. Echinoderms are similar to other invertebrates because echinoderms do not have a backbone.

9. Sample answer: Sea stars can regrow lost arms. The sea star that has four long arms and one short arm is probably in the process of regrowing a lost arm.

Soaking Sponges

Teacher's Notes

Time Required
One 45-minute class period

Lab Ratings

EASY ——————→ HARD

Teacher Prep 🧪🧪
Student Set-Up 🧪
Concept Level 🧪
Clean Up 🧪

Safety Caution
Remind students to review all safety cautions and icons before beginning this lab activity.

Preparation Notes
Many students have never touched a natural sponge. Allow them a few moments to experience the feel of a natural sponge, and help them identify the structures. Tell them that sponges are animals even though they don't appear animal-like. Discuss how sponges obtain food. This activity is not designed to produce one "right" answer. Instead, it is designed to teach students the value of experimentation. Students may learn that experiments can produce unexpected results.

Soaking Sponges

Early biologists thought sponges were plants because sponges are like plants in some ways. In many species, the adults attach to a surface and stay there. They cannot chase their food. Instead, sponges absorb and filter a lot of water to get food. In this activity, you will observe the structure of a sponge. You will also consider how the size of the sponge's holes affects the amount of water the sponge can absorb.

OBJECTIVES

Observe the structure of a sponge.

Determine how the size of a sponge's holes affect the amount of water the sponge can absorb.

MATERIALS

- beaker
- bowl (large enough for sponge and water)
- calculator (optional)
- kitchen sponge
- natural sponge
- paper towel
- water

SAFETY

Ask a Question

1 Look at the natural sponge. Identify the pores on the outside of the sponge. See if you can find the sponge's central cavities and oscula.

2 Notice the size and shape of the sponge's holes. Look at the holes in the kitchen sponge and the paper towel. Think of a question about how the holes in each item affect its ability to absorb water.

Form a Hypothesis

3 Formulate a testable hypothesis to answer your question. Record your hypothesis.

Kathy LaRoe
East Valley Middle School
East Helena, Montana

Test the Hypothesis

4️⃣ Read steps 5–9. Design and draw a data table for the data that you will collect. Remember, you will collect data for the natural sponge, the kitchen sponge, and the paper towel.

5️⃣ Use a balance to measure the mass of the natural sponge. Record the mass.

6️⃣ Place the natural sponge in the bowl. Use the graduated cylinder to add water to the sponge, 10 mL at a time, until the sponge is completely soaked. Record the amount of water added.

7️⃣ Gently remove the sponge from the bowl. Measure the amount of water left in the bowl. How much water did the sponge absorb? Record your data.

8️⃣ Calculate how many milliliters of water your sponge holds per gram of dry sponge. For example, if your sponge's dry mass is 12 g and it holds 59.1 mL of water, then your sponge holds 4.9 mL of water per gram (59.1 mL ÷ 12 g = 4.9 mL/g).

9️⃣ Repeat steps 5–8 with the kitchen sponge and the paper towel.

Analyze the Results

1️⃣ **Analyzing Results** Compare your results from steps 5–9. Which item held the most water per gram of dry mass?

Draw Conclusions

2️⃣ **Evaluating Data** Did your results support your hypothesis? Explain your answer.

3️⃣ **Evaluating Results** Do you see a connection between the size of an item's holes and its ability to hold water?

4️⃣ **Analyzing Results** What can you conclude about how the size and shape of a sponge's holes affect its feeding ability?

Applying Your Data

WRITING SKILL Use the Internet to see if scientists have done research that backs up your ideas about how the size and shape of a sponge affect its feeding abilities. Write your findings in a report to present to the class.

Analyze the Results

1. Answers may vary depending on the materials used.

Draw Conclusions

2. Answers may vary depending on each student's hypothesis. In some cases, results will support the hypothesis. In other cases, they will not.

3. Answers may vary depending on the materials used.

4. Answers may vary. Students should explain that the characteristics that allow for more water absorbtion would result in sponges having a greater opportunity for feeding because more water would pass through their osculum and pass by their collar cells.

Applying Your Data

Answers may vary depending on students' hypotheses about how the size and shape of a sponge's holes affect its feeding ability. Accept any reasonable answers that are based on scientific research.

Chapter Review

Assignment Guide

Section	Questions
1	3, 10, 14, 16, 22
2	13, 17, 20, 23, 26
3	5–6, 8–9, 15, 18, 25, 27–30
4	7, 11, 19
1 and 2	2, 12, 24
1 and 4	1
2 and 3	4
1, 2, 3, and 4	21

ANSWERS

Using Key Terms

1. Sample answer: A ganglion is a mass of nerves. A water vascular system is a series of canals that are filled with fluids. A coelom is a space in the body that surrounds the internal organs.
2. Sample answer: Most invertebrates have an open circulatory system.
3. gut
4. segments
5. exoskeleton
6. compound eyes
7. endoskeleton
8. antennae
9. metamorphosis

Understanding Key Ideas

10. d
11. b
12. b
13. d

USING KEY TERMS

1 In your own words, write a definition for each of the following terms: *ganglion, water vascular system,* and *coelom.*

2 Use the following terms in the same sentence: *open circulatory system* and *invertebrate.*

Complete each of the following sentences by choosing the correct term from the word bank.

antennae	exoskeleton
coelom	gut
compound eyes	metamorphosis
endoskeleton	segments

3 Almost all invertebrates digest food in a(n) ___.

4 Repeating ___ make up the bodies of annelid worms and arthropods.

5 A crab's ___ keeps it from losing water.

6 Arthropods use ___ to see images.

7 Echinoderms have spines on their ___.

8 Arthropods use ___ to touch, taste, and smell.

9 Insects change form during ___.

UNDERSTANDING KEY IDEAS

Multiple Choice

10 No invertebrates have
  a. a brain.
  b. a gut.
  c. ganglia.
  d. a backbone.

11 Which animals have a nerve ring?
  a. sponges
  b. echinoderms
  c. crustaceans
  d. flatworms

12 Which of the following is NOT a flatworm?
  a. a tapeworm
  b. an earthworm
  c. a planarian
  d. a fluke

13 Which body part is NOT present in all mollusks?
  a. foot
  b. visceral mass
  c. mantle
  d. shell

Short Answer

14 Describe how a sponge eats.

15 What are the four main characteristics of arthropods?

16 Describe the body of a roundworm.

17 What are three ways that different mollusks eat?

18 Which insects go through complete metamorphosis? go through incomplete metamorphosis?

19 How is an adult echinoderm different from an echinoderm larva?

20 How are cephalopod nervous systems unique among mollusks?

14. Sample answer: Water enters the sponge through its pores. Collar cells that line the osculum filter and then digest small particles from the water.

15. Arthropods have jointed limbs, an exoskeleton, segmented bodies, and a well-developed brain that receives information from sense organs.

16. A roundworm's body is long, slender, and round.

17. by scraping food with a radula, by filtering food with gills, and by grabbing food with tentacles that carry food to the jaws

18. complete metamorphosis: butterflies, beetles, flies, bees, wasps, and ants; incomplete metamorphosis: grasshoppers and cockroaches

19. Adult echinoderms are radially symmetrical and usually remain in one place. Larvae are bilaterally symmetrical and move around.

20. Cephalopods have large brains that connect all of their ganglia.

CRITICAL THINKING

21. Concept Mapping Use the following terms to create a concept map: *segments, invertebrates, endoskeleton, antennae, exoskeleton, water vascular system, metamorphosis,* and *compound eyes.*

22. Applying Concepts You have discovered a new animal that has radial symmetry and tentacles with stinging cells. Can this animal be classified as a cnidarian? Explain.

23. Making Inferences Unlike other mollusks, cephalopods can move quickly. Based on what you know about the structure and function of mollusks, why do you think that cephalopods have this ability?

24. Making Comparisons Why don't roundworms, flatworms, and annelid worms belong to the same group of invertebrates?

25. Analyzing Processes Butterflies mate as adults and spend time eating and growing in their other stages. They have no wings during the larval or pupal stage of metamorphosis. Can you think of a reason that they would need wings in their adult form more than in the other stages of development? Explain your answer.

26. Predicting Consequences How do earthworms affect gardens? What do you think would happen to a garden if the gardener removed all the earthworms from it?

INTERPRETING GRAPHICS

The picture below shows an arthropod. Use the picture to answer the questions that follow.

27 Name the body segments labeled a, b, and c.

28 How many legs does this arthropod have?

29 To which segment are the arthropod's legs attached?

30 What kind of arthropod is this?

Critical Thinking

21. An answer to this exercise can be found at the end of this book.

22. Sample answer: Yes, it can be classified as a cnidarian. Cnidarians have radial symmetry, tentacles, and stinging cells.

23. Sample answer: Cephalopods need to move rapidly to catch prey and to avoid predators. The lack of a bulky shell probably helps them move quickly. Their advanced nervous system probably helps them move quickly, too.

24. Sample answer: The worms are not grouped together because they have different characteristics. Annelid worms are segmented, while the others are not. Annelid worms have a closed circulatory system, whereas other worms do not. Flatworms have eyespots and sensory lobes, and the other worms do not.

25. Sample answer: Butterflies need to find a mate when they are ready to reproduce. Wings would allow them to search for a mate in a broader area.

26. Sample answer: Earthworms dig holes in soil and thus allow air to reach more parts of the soil. They also digest parts of the soil and leave castings as waste. The castings make the soil rich. If a gardener removed all earthworms from a garden, the soil would not be as fertile.

Interpreting Graphics

27. a: head; b: thorax; c: abdomen

28. 6

29. the thorax (b)

30. an insect

READING

Passage 1

1. A
2. H
3. C

TEST DOCTOR

Question 2: Students who choose answer F may have misread the last sentence of the first paragraph, which states that it is hard to imagine that giant squids have enemies. Students who choose answer G may be confused by the third sentence in the second paragraph, which mentions that thousands of beaks have been found in the stomach of a single sperm whale. While the passage does imply that squids and sperm whales fight each other, the implication is that squids defend themselves from sperm whales (answer H) rather than that squids and sperm whales fight each other in competition for food (answer I). The correct answer is H.

READING

Read each of the passages below. Then, answer the questions that follow each passage.

Passage 1 Giant squids are very similar to their smaller relatives. They have a torpedo-shaped body, two tentacles, eight arms, a mantle, and a beak. All of their body parts are much larger, though. A giant squid's eye may be as large as a volleyball! Given the size of giant squids, it's hard to imagine that they have any enemies in the ocean, but they do.

Toothed sperm whales eat giant squids. How do we know this? Thousands of squid beaks have been found in the stomach of a single sperm whale. The hard beaks of giant squids are <u>indigestible</u>. Also, many whales bear ring marks on their forehead and fins that match the size of the suckers found on giant squids.

1. Based on the passage, what do you think the word *indigestible* describes?
   - **A** something that cannot be digested
   - **B** something that causes indigestion
   - **C** something that one cannot dig out
   - **D** something that one cannot guess

2. What can you infer from this passage?
   - **F** Giant squids only imagine that they have enemies.
   - **G** A toothed sperm whale can eat 10,000 giant squids in one meal.
   - **H** Giant squids defend themselves against toothed sperm whales.
   - **I** Giant squids and sperm whales compete with each other for food.

3. How are giant squids different from other kinds of squids?
   - **A** Giant squids have a torpedo-shaped body, a mantle, and a beak.
   - **B** Giant squids have enemies in the ocean.
   - **C** Giant squids have larger body parts.
   - **D** Giant squids are the size of a volleyball.

Passage 2 Water bears are microscopic invertebrates that are closely related to arthropods. Most water bears live on wet mosses and lichens. Some of them eat roundworms and other tiny animals, but most feed on mosses. What makes water bears unique is their ability to shut down their body processes. They do this when their environment becomes too hot, too cold, or too dry. Shutting down body processes means that the organism doesn't eat, move, or breathe. But it doesn't die, either. It just dries out. When conditions improve, the water bear returns to normal life. Scientists think that the water bear's cells become coated with sugar when its body shuts down. This sugar may keep the cells from breaking down while they are inactive.

1. How do scientists think sugar helps water bears survive while their body processes are shut down?
   - **A** Sugar coats their cells, keeping the cells from breaking down.
   - **B** Sugar coats their cells, trapping moisture inside the cells.
   - **C** Sugar coats their cells, keeping moisture from entering the cells.
   - **D** Sugar provides water bears with nutrients.

2. What do water bears eat?
   - **F** sugar
   - **G** mosses
   - **H** lichens
   - **I** arthropods

3. Which is a unique characteristic of water bears?
   - **A** They are related to arthropods.
   - **B** They often live on mosses or lichens.
   - **C** They can live at the bottom of the ocean.
   - **D** They can shut down their body processes without dying.

Passage 2

1. A
2. G
3. D

TEST DOCTOR

Question 3: Although all four answers state characteristics of water bears, the only unique characteristic is provided in answer D. The passage clearly states this idea in the fourth sentence: "What makes water bears unique is their ability to shut down their body processes."

The bar graph below shows the number of monarchs in a population from 1990 to 1994. Use the graph to answer the questions that follow.

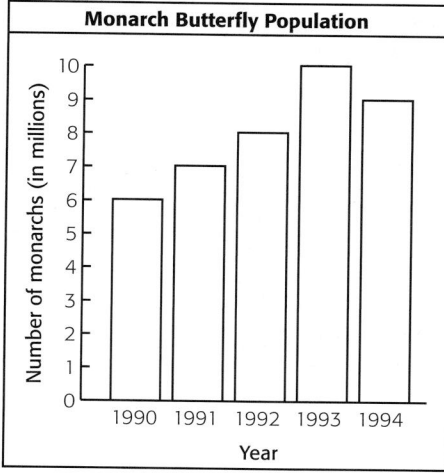

Monarch Butterfly Population

1. Compare the number of butterflies in the population during 1990, 1991, 1992, and 1993. Identify the statement that best describes how the population changed during those years.
   - **A** The population increased.
   - **B** The population remained the same.
   - **C** The population decreased.
   - **D** The population doubled yearly.

2. Why might butterfly scientists be surprised about the 1994 monarch population?
   - **F** The 1994 population was the first population of 9 million ever recorded.
   - **G** The 1994 population was the first decreased population recorded in 4 years.
   - **H** The 1994 population was the first increased population recorded in 4 years.
   - **I** The 1994 population was the first decreased population ever recorded.

3. What can you infer from the graph about how the monarch's environmental conditions changed between 1993 and 1994?
   - **A** Conditions were worse in 1994.
   - **B** Conditions did not change between 1993 and 1994.
   - **C** Conditions were better in 1994.
   - **D** This graph does not contain enough information to determine how conditions changed between 1993 and 1994.

4. What was the average population of monarchs during these 5 years?
   - **F** 7 million
   - **G** 8 million
   - **H** 9 million
   - **I** 40 million

MATH

Read each question below, and choose the best answer.

1. Raymond wanted to arrange his shell collection in order of size. Which group of shell lengths is listed in order from smallest to largest?
   - **A** 1.6 cm, 0.25 dm, 0.017 m, 5.0 cm
   - **B** 0.017 m, 0.25 dm, 1.6 cm, 5.0 cm
   - **C** 1.6 cm, 5.0 cm, 0.25 dm, 0.017 m
   - **D** 1.6 cm, 0.017 m, 0.25 dm, 5.0 cm

2. Raquelle wants to buy some earthworms to put in her garden. The earthworms are sold in containers that each hold 8 worms. How many containers will Raquelle need to buy if she wants 75 earthworms?
   - **F** 9 containers
   - **G** 10 containers
   - **H** 15 containers
   - **I** 83 containers

3. Maxwell found a huge basket star while he was scuba diving. The basket star had five arms, and each arm branched into three pieces. Each of these pieces branched into two more tips. How many tips did the basket star have?
   - **A** 2 tips
   - **B** 5 tips
   - **C** 15 tips
   - **D** 30 tips

Standardized Test Preparation

INTERPRETING GRAPHICS

1. A
2. G
3. D
4. G

TEST DOCTOR

Question 2: Students who answer this question incorrectly may be confused by having to take into account that the graph shows only 5 years of data. We cannot assume that any part of the graph is the only time such data were ever recorded. Therefore, answers F and I cannot be true. Answer H is incorrect because it states that the population decreases rather than increases. So, the correct answer is G.

MATH

1. D
2. G
3. D

TEST DOCTOR

Question 1: Students who are confused by this question may find converting all of the numbers into the same unit helpful. If all of the numbers are listed in centimeters, it becomes clear that answer D is the only one that shows the lengths arranged from smallest to largest.

CHAPTER RESOURCES

Chapter Resource File

 • Standardized Test Preparation GENERAL

State Resources

 For specific resources for your state, visit **go.hrw.com** and type in the keyword **HSMSTR**.

Science, Technology, and Society

Discussion ———— GENERAL

Tell students that for centuries, physicians used leeches to remove blood from patients in a process called *bloodletting*. The physicians thought that an excess of blood in the body was responsible for several illnesses, including head-aches, fevers, and heart disease. Supposedly, the leeches would remove the bad blood from a patient's body. However, this idea was discredited in the late 1800s. Ask students to brainstorm how people may have realized that ill-ness was not caused by excess blood in the body. Discuss how science depends on challenging old ideas and testing new ideas.

Weird Science

Background

The forelimbs of the mantis shrimp usually stay strong and intact despite their violent and repetitive usage. One reason that the forelimbs stay strong is that they undergo a periodic molt, which replaces their shell. Also, the forelimbs of the "smashers" are especially thick and calcified. When a mantis shrimp is found to be missing a forelimb, the problem is usually due to another mantis shrimp rather than to a feeding accident.

Science in Action

Science, Technology, and Society

Leeches to the Rescue

Bloodsucking leeches may sound scary, but they could save your toes! Leeches are used in operations to reattach lost limbs, fingers, or toes. During these operations, doctors can reconnect arteries, but not small veins, which are more delicate. As a result, blood flow in the limb, finger, or toe is impaired. The tissues may become full of loose blood. If this happens, the tissues of the reattached parts die. But if leeches suck the extra blood from the reattached part, the tissues can remain healthy until the veins grow back.

Math ACTIVITY

Measure the widest and narrowest parts of the leech in the photo. Calculate how many times wider the wide part is than the narrow part. Which end of the leech do you think is the head? Why do you think so?

Weird Science

A Powerful Punch

The mantis shrimp packs a powerful punch! This animal is nick-named "killer shrimp" and "thumb-splitter." These crustaceans can be divided into two groups: the *smashers* and the *spearers*. The smashers have large front limbs that they use to club their prey with great speed and power. They can easily smash through the shells of clams, snails, and crabs. Larger species have been known to break double-walled aquarium glass! The spearers have sharp spines on their front limbs, and lash out with incredible speed— at about 1,000 cm/sec. That is one of the fastest animal movements known!

Language Arts ACTIVITY

The words *crustacean* and *crust* both come from the same Latin root—*crusta*. Think of how crustaceans are similar to crusts, and then guess the meaning of the Latin root.

Answer to Math Activity

The widest part of the leech is about 2.7 cm and its narrowest part is about 0.5 cm. So, 2.7 cm ÷ 0.5 cm = 5.4. The wide part is about 5.4 times wider than the narrow part. Accept all reason-able answers about which end of the leech is the head. Two important parts of the answer are that the student may use the measurements as a basis for an answer and that the student dem-onstrates some rational basis for the answer.

Answer to Language Arts Activity

Sample answer: A crust is a hard covering on bread, and a crustacean has a hard exoskeleton surrounding its body. So, the root *crusta* prob-ably refers to a hard covering.

Careers

George Matsumoto

Marine Biologist Dr. George Matsumoto is a marine biologist at the Monterey Bay Aquarium in California. A seventh-grade snorkeling class first sparked his interest in ocean research. Since then, he's studied the deep seas by snorkeling, scuba diving, and using research vessels, remotely operated vehicles (ROVs), and deep-sea submersibles. On the Johnson Sea Link submersible, he traveled down to 1,000 m (3,281 ft) below sea level!

Marine biology is a field full of strange and wonderful creatures. Matsumoto focuses on marine invertebrates, particularly the delicate animals called comb jellies. These invertebrates are beautiful animals that have not been studied very much. Comb jellies are also called *ctenophores* (TEN uh FAWRZ), which means "comb-bearers." They have eight rows of cilia that look like the rows of a comb. These cilia help ctenophores move through the water. By studying ctenophores and similar marine invertebrates, Matsumoto and other marine scientists can learn about the ecology of ocean communities.

Social Studies ACTIVITY

WRITING SKILL One ctenophore from the United States took over both the Black Sea and the Sea of Azov by eating small fish and other food. This crowded out bigger fish, changing the ecosystem and ruining the fisheries. Write a paragraph about how Matsumoto's work as a marine biologist could help solve problems like this one.

To learn more about these Science in Action topics, visit **go.hrw.com** and type in the keyword **HL5INVF**.

Current Science

Check out Current Science® articles related to this chapter by visiting go.hrw.com. Just type in the keyword **HL5CS15**.

Careers ACTIVITY ⎯⎯ GENERAL

If your town or a neighboring town has an aquarium, arrange a class field trip to the aquarium. Be sure to ask a scientist at the aquarium to talk to students about careers in marine biology. If you aren't close to an aquarium, have the class visit the Monterey Bay E-quarium on the Internet. Ask each student to read about the marine science careers on this Web site. Have students pick the career that most interests them and write a short report about that career.

Answer to Social Studies Activity

Sample answer: Marine biologists who study ctenophores could think of ways to control the foreign ctenophores that were disrupting the Black Sea and Sea of Azov ecosystems. For example, scientists such as Matsumoto may know how to remove the ctenophores, how to balance ctenophore populations by protecting natural ctenophore predators that live in the Black Sea and Sea of Azov, or how to stop the transfer of ctenophores from the United States to the Black Sea and Sea of Azov.

16 Fishes, Amphibians, and Reptiles
Chapter Planning Guide

Compression guide:
To shorten instruction
because of time limitations,
omit the Chapter Lab.

OBJECTIVES	LABS, DEMONSTRATIONS, AND ACTIVITIES	TECHNOLOGY RESOURCES
PACING • 90 min pp. 410–419 **Chapter Opener**	SE **Start-up Activity**, p. 411 ◆ GENERAL	OSP **Parent Letter** ■ GENERAL CD **Student Edition on CD-ROM** CD **Guided Reading Audio CD** ■ TR **Chapter Starter Transparency*** VID **Brain Food Video Quiz**
Section 1 Fishes: The First Vertebrates • List the four common body parts of chordates. • Describe the two main characteristics of vertebrates. • Explain the difference between an ectotherm and an endotherm. • Describe four traits that fishes share. • Describe the three classes of living fishes, and give an example of each.	TE **Demonstration** Identifying Backbones, p. 412 ◆ GENERAL TE **Connection Activity** Paleontology, p. 413 ADVANCED SE **Quick Lab** Body Temperature, p. 414 GENERAL CRF **Datasheet for Quick Lab*** SE **Connection to Physics** How Fish See the World, p. 415 GENERAL TE **Activity** Researching Lampreys, p. 416 ADVANCED SE **Skills Practice Lab** Floating a Pipe Fish, p. 432 GENERAL CRF **Datasheet for Chapter Lab*** LB **Whiz-Bang Demonstrations** The Fish in the Abyss* BASIC	CRF **Lesson Plans*** TR **Bellringer Transparency*** TR Chordate Body Parts* TR Body Parts of a Fish* TR *LINK TO PHYSICAL SCIENCE* How a Cell Produces an Electric Current* SE **Internet Activity**, p. 416 GENERAL VID **Lab Videos for Life Science**
PACING • 45 min pp. 420–425 **Section 2 Amphibians** • Explain how amphibians breathe. • Describe amphibian metamorphosis. • Describe the three groups of amphibians, and give an example of each. • Explain why amphibians are ecological indicators.	TE **Demonstration** Fossils, p. 420 ◆ GENERAL SE **Connection to Social Studies** Troublesome Toads, p. 421 GENERAL TE **Activity** Research Cloning, p. 421 ADVANCED TE **Activity** Observing Development, p. 422 ◆ GENERAL SE **School-to-Home Activity** Looking for Locals, p. 423 GENERAL TE **Connection Activity** Geography, p. 423 BASIC TE **Activity** Visit the Zoo, p. 423 BASIC SE **Skills Practice Lab** A Prince of a Frog, p. 784 GENERAL CRF **Datasheet for LabBook***	CRF **Lesson Plans*** TR **Bellringer Transparency*** TR Amphibian Metamorphosis*
PACING • 45 min pp. 426–431 **Section 3 Reptiles** • Explain the traits that allow reptiles to live on land. • Describe the characteristics of an amniotic egg. • Name the four groups of modern reptiles, and give an example of each.	TE **Activity** Organizing Reptiles, p. 427 BASIC TE **Connection Activity** Math, p. 428 GENERAL TE **Demonstration** Reptile Exhibit, p. 428 ◆ GENERAL SE **Science in Action** Math, Social Studies, and Language Arts Activities, pp. 438–439 GENERAL LB **Long-Term Projects & Research Ideas** Go Fish!* ADVANCED	CRF **Lesson Plans*** TR **Bellringer Transparency*** TR An Amniotic Egg* CRF **SciLinks Activity*** GENERAL

PACING • 90 min

CHAPTER REVIEW, ASSESSMENT, AND STANDARDIZED TEST PREPARATION

CRF **Vocabulary Activity*** GENERAL
SE **Chapter Review**, pp. 434–435 GENERAL
CRF **Chapter Review*** ■ GENERAL
CRF **Chapter Tests A*** ■ GENERAL, **B*** ADVANCED, **C*** SPECIAL NEEDS
SE **Standardized Test Preparation**, pp. 436–437 GENERAL
CRF **Standardized Test Preparation*** GENERAL
CRF **Performance-Based Assessment*** GENERAL
OSP **Test Generator** GENERAL
CRF **Test Item Listing*** GENERAL

Online and Technology Resources

Visit **go.hrw.com** for a variety of free resources related to this textbook. Enter the keyword **HL5VR1**.

Holt Online Learning

Students can access interactive problem-solving help and active visual concept development with the *Holt Science and Technology* Online Edition available at **www.hrw.com**.

 Guided Reading Audio CD Also in Spanish

A direct reading of each chapter for auditory learners, reluctant readers, and Spanish-speaking students.

 Science Tutor CD-ROM

Excellent for remediation and test practice.

SKILLS DEVELOPMENT RESOURCES	SECTION REVIEW AND ASSESSMENT	STANDARDS CORRELATIONS
SE Pre-Reading Activity, p. 410 `GENERAL` **OSP** Science Puzzlers, Twisters & Teasers `GENERAL`		National Science Education Standards UCP 2, 5; SAI 1; LS 1a, 1d, 3b
CRF Directed Reading A* ■ `BASIC`, B* `SPECIAL NEEDS` **CRF** Vocabulary and Section Summary* ■ `GENERAL` **SE** Reading Strategy Reading Organizer, p. 412 `GENERAL` **TE** Reading Strategy Prediction Guide, p. 413 `BASIC` **TE** Inclusion Strategies, p. 415 **TE** Reading Strategy Prediction Guide, p. 416 `GENERAL` **TE** Connection to Math Shark Teeth, p. 417 `ADVANCED` **SE** Math Practice A Lot of Bones, p. 418 `GENERAL`	**SE** Reading Checks, pp. 413, 414, 416, 418 `GENERAL` **TE** Homework, p. 414 `ADVANCED` **TE** Reteaching, p. 418 `BASIC` **TE** Quiz, p. 418 `GENERAL` **TE** Alternative Assessment, p. 418 `GENERAL` **SE** Section Review,* p. 419 `GENERAL` **TE** Homework, p. 419 `GENERAL` **CRF** Section Quiz* ■ `GENERAL`	UCP 1, 3, 5; SAI 1; LS 1a, 1d, 2a, 3a, 3b, 3c, 5a, 5c; *Chapter Lab:* UCP 1, 2, 3, 5; SAI 1, 2; LS 1a, 1d, 3b
CRF Directed Reading A* ■ `BASIC`, B* `SPECIAL NEEDS` **CRF** Vocabulary and Section Summary* ■ `GENERAL` **SE** Reading Strategy Reading Organizer, p. 420 `GENERAL` **TE** Reading Strategy Prediction Guide, p. 421 `GENERAL` **TE** Inclusion Strategies, p. 424	**SE** Reading Checks, pp. 420, 423, 424 `GENERAL` **TE** Reteaching, p. 424 `BASIC` **TE** Quiz, p. 424 `GENERAL` **TE** Alternative Assessment, p. 424 `GENERAL` **SE** Section Review,* p. 425 ■ `GENERAL` **CRF** Section Quiz* ■ `GENERAL`	UCP 1, 5; SAI 1; LS 1a, 2a, 3a, 3c, 3d, 5a, 5b; *LabBook:* UCP 2, 4, 5; SAI 1; LS 1a, 3c, 3d, 5b
CRF Directed Reading A* ■ `BASIC`, B* `SPECIAL NEEDS` **CRF** Vocabulary and Section Summary* ■ `GENERAL` **SE** Reading Strategy Brainstorming, p. 426 `GENERAL` **MS** Math Skills for Science Using Temperature Scales* `GENERAL` **CRF** Reinforcement Worksheet Coldblooded Critters* `BASIC` **CRF** Critical Thinking Frogs Aren't Breathing Easy* `ADVANCED`	**SE** Reading Checks, pp. 427, 428, 431 `GENERAL` **TE** Reteaching, p. 430 `BASIC` **TE** Quiz, p. 430 `GENERAL` **TE** Alternative Assessment, p. 430 `GENERAL` **TE** Homework, p. 430 `ADVANCED` **SE** Section Review,* p. 431 ■ `GENERAL` **CRF** Section Quiz* ■ `GENERAL`	UCP 1, 2, 5; SAI 1; 1a, 1d, 2a, 2b, 3a, 3c, 3d, 5a, 5b, 5c

Visual Resources

CHAPTER STARTER TRANSPARENCY

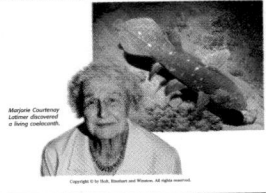

Would You Believe...?

BELLRINGER TRANSPARENCIES

Section: Fishes: The First Vertebrates
What are some of the physical characteristics shared by dinosaurs and humans? What are the major physical differences between dinosaurs and humans?

Record your responses in your **science journal**.

Section: Amphibians
Amphibians are notable for their thin, moist skin. What are some advantages and disadvantages of thin, moist skin? Do you think human skin is more or less useful than amphibian skin? What might be some advantages of skin that is covered in thick fur or dry scales?

Write your answers in your **science journal**.

TEACHING TRANSPARENCIES

Chordate Body Parts

Body Parts of a Fish

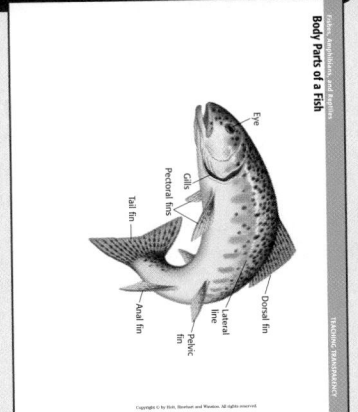

TEACHING TRANSPARENCIES

Amphibian Metamorphosis

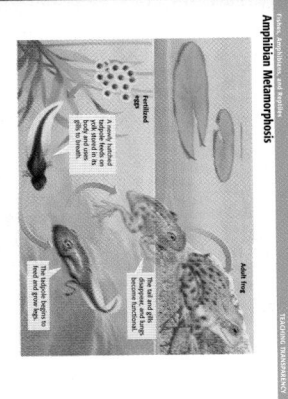

An Amniotic Egg

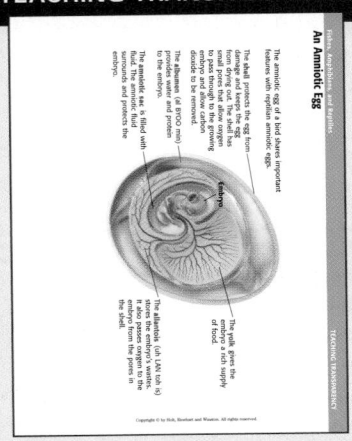

How a Cell Produces an Electric Current

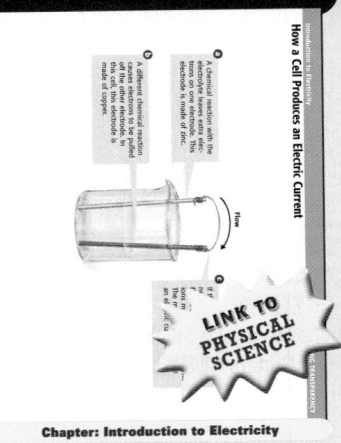

LINK TO PHYSICAL SCIENCE

Chapter: Introduction to Electricity

CONCEPT MAPPING TRANSPARENCY

Use the following terms to complete the concept map below:
ectotherms, lungs, vertebrates, endotherms, reptiles, fishes, amphibians, metamorphosis

Planning Resources

LESSON PLANS

Lesson Plan SAMPLE

Section: Waves

Pacing
Regular Schedule: with lab(s):2 days without lab(s):2 days
Block Schedule: with lab(s): 1 1/2 days without lab(s): 1 day

Objectives
1. Relate the seven properties of life to a living organism.
2. Describe seven themes that can help you to organize what you learn about biology.
3. Identify the tiny structures that make up all living organisms.
4. Differentiate between reproduction and heredity and between metabolism and homeostasis.

National Science Education Standards Covered
LSInter6:Cells have particular structures that underlie their functions.
LSMat1:Most cell functions involve chemical reactions.
LSBeh1:Cells store and use information to guide their functions.
UCP1:Cell functions are regulated.
SI1: Cells can differentiate and form complete multicellular organisms.
PS1:Species evolve over time.
ESS1: The great diversity of organisms is the result of more than 3.5 billion years of evolution.
ESS2: Natural selection and its evolutionary consequences provide a scientific explanation for the fossil record of ancient life forms as well as for the striking molecular similarities observed among the diverse species of living organisms.
ST1: The millions of different species of plants, animals, and microorganisms that live on Earth today are related by descent from common ancestors.
ST2: The energy for life primarily comes from the sun.
SPSP1: The complexity and organization of organisms accommodates the need for obtaining, transforming, transporting, releasing, and eliminating the matter and energy used to sustain the organism.
SPSP6: As matter and energy flows through different levels of organization of living systems—cells, organs, communities—and between living systems and the physical environment, chemical elements are recombined in different ways.
HNS1: Organisms have behavioral responses to internal changes and to external stimuli.

PARENT LETTER

SAMPLE

Dear Parent,

Your son's or daughter's science class will soon begin exploring the chapter entitled "The World of Physical Science." In this chapter, students will learn about how the scientific method applies to the world of physical science and the role of physical science in the world. By the end of the chapter, students should demonstrate a clear understanding of the chapter's main ideas and be able to discuss the following topics:

1. physical science is the study of energy and matter (Section 1)
2. the role of physical science in the world around them (Section 1)
3. careers that rely on physical science (Section 1)
4. examples of technology (Section 2)
5. how our scientific method is used to answer questions and solve problems (Section 2)
6. how our knowledge of science changes over time (Section 2)
7. how models represent real objects or systems (Section 3)
8. examples of different ways models are used in science (Section 3)
9. the importance of the International System of Units (Section 4)
10. the appropriate units to use for particular measurements (Section 4)
11. how area and density are derived quantities (Section 4)

Questions to Ask Along the Way

You can help your son or daughter learn about these topics by asking interesting questions such as the following:

• What are some surprising careers that use physical science?
• What is a characteristic of a good hypothesis?
• When is it a good idea to use a model?
• Why do Americans measure things in terms of inches and yards and meters ?

ALSO IN SPANISH

TEST ITEM LISTING

TEST ITEM LISTING
The World of Science SAMPLE

MULTIPLE CHOICE

1. A limitation of models is that
   a. they are large enough to see
   b. they do not act exactly like the things that they model.
   c. they are smaller than the things that they model.
   d. they model unfamiliar things.
   Answer: B   Difficulty: 1   Section: 3   Objective: 2
2. The length 10 m is equal to
   a. 100 cm.   c. 10,000 mm.
   b. 1,000 cm.   d. Both (b) and (c)
   Answer: B   Difficulty: 1   Section: 3   Objective: 2
3. To be valid, a hypothesis must be
   a. testable.   c. made into a law
   b. supported by evidence.   d. Both (a) and (b)
   Answer: B   Difficulty: 1   Section: 3   Objective: 2
4. The statement "Sharks has a stain on her shirt" is an example of a(n)
   a. law.   c. observation.
   b. hypothesis.   d. prediction.
   Answer: B   Difficulty: 1   Section: 3   Objective: 2
5. A hypothesis is often developed out of
   a. observations   c. laws.
   b. experiments.   d. Both (a) and (b)
   Answer: B   Difficulty: 1   Section: 3   Objective: 2
6. How many milliliters are in 3.5 kL?
   a. 3,500 mL.   c. 3,500,000 mL.
   b. 0.0035 mL.   d. 35,000 mL.
   Answer: B   Difficulty: 1   Section: 3   Objective: 2
7. A map of Seattle is an example of a
   a. law.   c. model.
   b. theory.   d. unit
   Answer: B   Difficulty: 1   Section: 3   Objective: 2
8. A lab has the safety icons shown below. These icons mean that you should wear
   a. only safety goggles.   c. safety goggles and a lab apron.
   b. only a lab apron.   d. safety goggles, a lab apron, and gloves
   Answer: B   Difficulty: 1   Section: 3   Objective: 2
9. The law of conservation of mass says the the ad mass before a chemical change is
   a. more than the total mass after the change
   b. less than the total mass after the change
   c. the same as the total mass after the change
   d. not the same as the total mass after the change
   Answer: B   Difficulty: 1   Section: 3   Objective: 2
10. In which of the following areas might you find a geochemist at work?
    a. studying the chemistry of rocks   c. studying forestry
    b. studying forestry   d. studying the atmosphere
    Answer: B   Difficulty: 1   Section: 3   Objective: 2

One-Stop Planner® CD-ROM

This CD-ROM includes all of the resources shown here and the following time-saving tools:

• *Lab Materials QuickList Software*
• *Customizable lesson plans*
• *Holt Calendar Planner*
• *The powerful ExamView® Test Generator*

Meeting Individual Needs

DIRECTED READING A
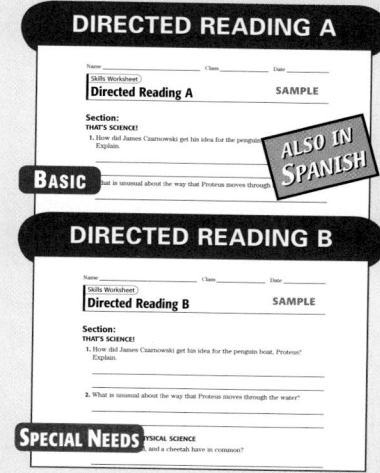

Skills Worksheet
Directed Reading A SAMPLE

Section:
THAT'S SCIENCE!

1. How did James Czarnowski get his idea for the penguin boat, Proteus? Explain.

BASIC

ALSO IN SPANISH

DIRECTED READING B

Skills Worksheet
Directed Reading B SAMPLE

Section:
THAT'S SCIENCE!

1. How did James Czarnowski get his idea for the penguin boat, Proteus? Explain.

2. What is unusual about the way that Proteus moves through the water?

SPECIAL NEEDS

VOCABULARY ACTIVITY
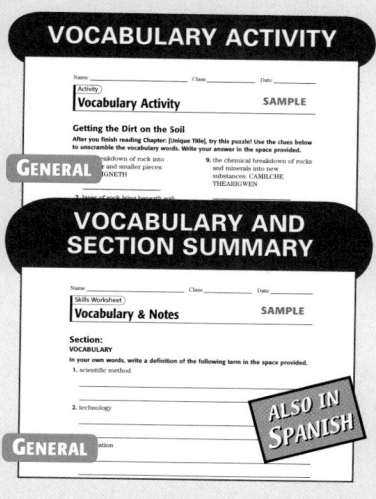

Activity
Vocabulary Activity SAMPLE

Getting the Dirt on the Soil
After you finish reading Chapter: [Unique Title], try this puzzle! Use the clues below to unscramble the vocabulary words. Write your answer in the space provided.

9. the chemical breakdown of rocks and minerals into smaller pieces
substance: CAMICHE
THEARIGWEN

GENERAL

VOCABULARY AND SECTION SUMMARY

Skills Worksheet
Vocabulary & Notes SAMPLE

Section:
VOCABULARY

In your own words, write a definition of the following term in the space provided.

1. scientific method

2. technology

GENERAL

ALSO IN SPANISH

REINFORCEMENT
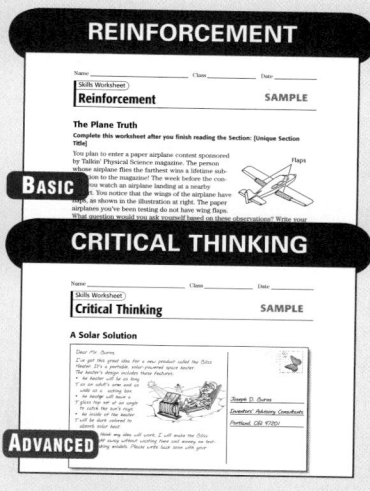

Skills Worksheet
Reinforcement SAMPLE

The Plane Truth
Complete this worksheet after you finish reading the Section: [Unique Section Title]

You plan to enter a paper airplane content sponsored by Talins' Physical Science magazine. The person whose airplane flies the farthest wins a lifetime subscription to the magazine! The week before the contest, you watch an airplane landing at a nearby airport. You notice that the wings of the airplane have flaps. As shown in the illustration at right. The paper airplanes you've been testing do not have wing flaps. What question would you ask yourself based on these observations? Write your

Flaps

BASIC

CRITICAL THINKING

Skills Worksheet
Critical Thinking SAMPLE

A Solar Solution

Dear Mr. Burns,
...

Joseph D. Burns
Dwellers' Advisory Consultants
Portland, OR 97201

ADVANCED

SCILINKS ACTIVITY

Activity
SciLinks Activity SAMPLE

MARINE ECOSYSTEMS
Go to www.scilinks.com. To find links related to marine ecosystems, type in the keyword in text. Then, use the links to answer the questions about marine ecosystems.

percentage of the Earth's surface is covered by water?

GENERAL

SCIENCE PUZZLERS, TWISTERS & TEASERS

CHAPTER 16 SCIENCE PUZZLERS, TWISTERS & TEASERS
Fishes, Amphibians, and Reptiles

Chordate Code
1. Use the clue that is given to help you find several terms found in this chapter. Write your answers in the spaces provided.
If the phrase:
V E R T E B R A T E S A R E C H O R D A T E S
is represented as:
3 8 1 6 8 10 15 6 8 4 5 18 2 20 9 17 5 6 8 4
what are the following vertebrate-related terms?

a. 18 9 6 9 2 20 4
b. 6 5 12 14
c. 8 5 12 14 5 11 8
d. 5 6 9 20 8 1 15
e. 22 22 10 9 18 8
f. 4 19 12 18 5 14 2 9 1 7

GENERAL

Labs and Activities

LONG-TERM PROJECTS & RESEARCH IDEAS
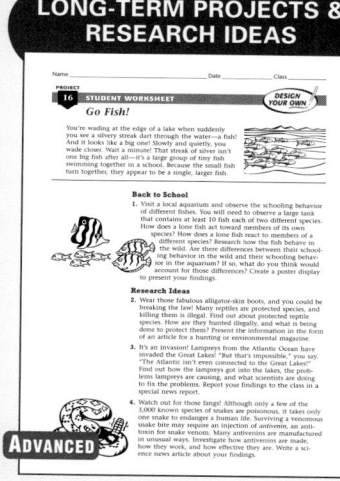

PROJECT 16 STUDENT WORKSHEET
Go Fish!

DESIGN YOUR OWN

You're wading at the edge of a lake when suddenly you see a silvery streak dart through the water—a fish! And it looks like a big one! Slowly and quietly, you wade closer. Wait a minute! That streak of silver isn't one big fish after all—it's a large group of tiny fish swimming together in a school. Because the small fish turn together, they appear to be a single, larger fish.

Back to School
1. Visit a local aquarium and observe the schooling behavior of different fishes. You will need to observe a large tank that contains at least 10 fish each of two different species. How does a lone fish act toward members of its own species? How does a lone fish react to members of a different species? Research how the fish behave in the wild. Are there differences between their schooling behavior in the wild and their schooling behavior in the aquarium? If so, what do you think would account for those differences? Create a poster display to present your findings.

Research Ideas
2. Wear these fabulous alligator-skin boots, and you could be breaking the law! Many reptiles are protected species, and killing them is illegal. Find out about protected reptile species. How are they hunted illegally, and what is being done to protect them? Present the information in the form of an article for a hunting or environmental magazine.

3. It's an invasion! Lampreys from the Atlantic Ocean have invaded the Great Lakes! "That isn't impossible," you say. "The Atlantic isn't even connected to the Great Lakes!" Find out how the lampreys got into the lakes, the problems lampreys are causing, and what scientists are doing to fix the problems. Report your findings to the class in a special news report.

4. Watch out for those fangs! Although only a few of the 3,000 known species of snakes are poisonous, it takes only one snake to endanger a human life. Surviving a venomous snake bite may require an injection of antivenin, an antitoxin for snake venom. Many antivenins are manufactured in unusual ways. Investigate how antivenins are made, how they work, and how effective they are. Write a science news article about your findings.

ADVANCED

WHIZ-BANG DEMONSTRATIONS
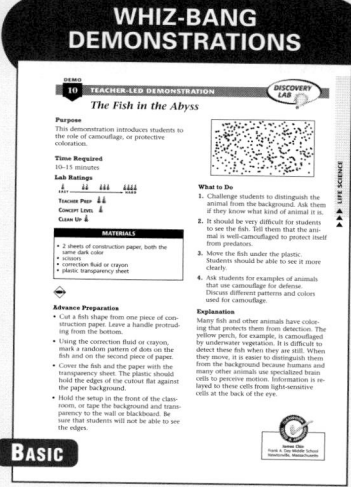

DEMO 10 TEACHER-LED DEMONSTRATION
The Fish in the Abyss

DISCOVERY LAB

Purpose
This demonstration introduces students to the role of camouflage, or protective coloration.

Time Required
10–15 minutes

Lab Ratings
TEACHER PREP
CONCEPT LEVEL

MATERIALS
• 2 sheets of construction paper, both the same dark color
• scissors
• correction fluid or crayon
• plastic transparency sheet

Advance Preparation
• Cut a fish shape from one piece of construction paper. Leave a handle protruding from the bottom.
• Using the correction fluid or crayon, mark a random pattern of dots on the fish and on the second piece of paper.
• Cover the fish and the paper with the transparency sheet. The plastic should hold the edges of the cutout flat against the paper background.
• Hold the setup in the front of the classroom, or tape the background and transparency to the wall or blackboard. Be sure that students will not be able to see the edges.

What to Do
1. Challenge students to distinguish the animal from the background. Ask them if they know what kind of animal it is.
2. It should be very difficult for students to see the fish. Tell them that the animal is well-camouflaged to protect itself from predators.
3. Move the fish under the paper. Students should be able to see it more clearly.
4. Ask students for examples of animals that use camouflage for defense. Discuss different patterns and colors used for camouflage.

Explanation
Many fish and other animals have coloring that protects them from detection. The yellow perch, for example, is camouflaged by underwater vegetation. It is difficult to detect these fish when they are still. When they move, it is easier to distinguish them from the background because humans and many other animals use specialized brain cells to perceive motion. Information is relayed to these cells from light-sensitive cells at the back of the eye.

LIFE SCIENCE

BASIC

DATASHEETS FOR QUICK LABS

TEACHER RESOURCE PAGE

Quick Lab
Reaction to Stress DATASHEET FOR QUICK LAB SAMPLE

Background
The graph below illustrates changes that occur in the membrane potential of a neuron during an action potential. Use the graph to answer the following questions. Refer to Figure 3 as needed.

DATASHEETS FOR CHAPTER LABS

TEACHER RESOURCE PAGE

Skills Practice Lab
Using Scientific Methods DATASHEET FOR CHAPTER LAB SAMPLE

Teacher's Notes
TIME REQUIRED
One 45-minute class period.

DATASHEETS FOR LABBOOK

TEACHER RESOURCE PAGE

Skills Practice Lab
Does It All Add Up? DATASHEET FOR LABBOOK LAB SAMPLE

Teacher's Notes
TIME REQUIRED
One 45-minute class period.

Review and Assessments

SECTION QUIZ
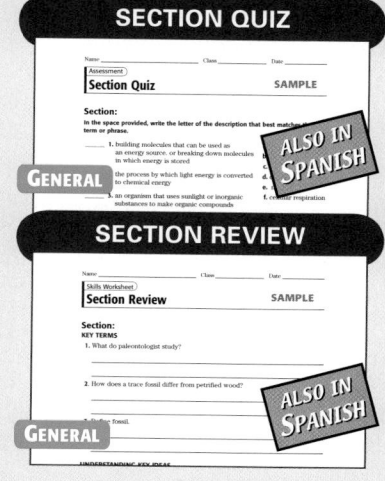

Assessment
Section Quiz SAMPLE

Section:
In the space provided, write the letter of the description that best matches the term or phrase.

1. building molecules that can be used as an energy source, or breaking down molecules in which energy is stored

2. the process by which light energy is converted to chemical energy

3. an organism that uses sunlight or inorganic substances to make organic compounds

a.
b.
c.
d.
e.
f. cellular respiration

GENERAL

ALSO IN SPANISH

SECTION REVIEW

Skills Worksheet
Section Review SAMPLE

Section:
KEY TERMS

1. What do paleontologist study?

2. How does a trace fossil differ from petrified wood?

3. Define fossil.

GENERAL

ALSO IN SPANISH

CHAPTER REVIEW
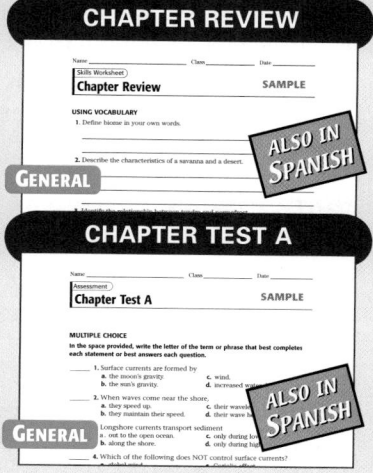

Skills Worksheet
Chapter Review SAMPLE

USING VOCABULARY
1. Define biome in your own words.

2. Describe the characteristics of a savanna and a desert.

GENERAL

ALSO IN SPANISH

CHAPTER TEST A

Assessment
Chapter Test A SAMPLE

MULTIPLE CHOICE
In the space provided, write the letter of the term or phrase that best completes each statement or best answers each question.

1. Surface currents are formed by
a. the moon's gravity.   c. wind.
b. the sun's gravity.   d. increased water density.

2. When waves come near the shore,
a. they speed up.   c. their wavelength increases.
b. they maintain their speed.   d. their wave height increases.

Longshore currents transport sediment
a. out to the open ocean.   c. only during low tide.
b. along the shore.   d. only during high tide.

4. Which of the following does NOT control surface currents?

GENERAL

ALSO IN SPANISH

CHAPTER TEST B
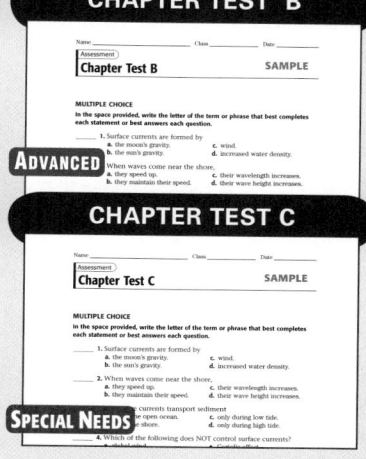

Assessment
Chapter Test B SAMPLE

MULTIPLE CHOICE
In the space provided, write the letter of the term or phrase that best completes each statement or best answers each question.

1. Surface currents are formed by
a. the moon's gravity.   c. wind.
b. the sun's gravity.   d. increased water density.

When waves come near the shore,
a. they speed up.   c. their wavelength increases.
b. they maintain their speed.   d. their wave height increases.

ADVANCED

CHAPTER TEST C

Assessment
Chapter Test C SAMPLE

MULTIPLE CHOICE
In the space provided, write the letter of the term or phrase that best completes each statement or best answers each question.

1. Surface currents are formed by
a. the moon's gravity.   c. wind.
b. the sun's gravity.   d. increased water density.

2. When waves come near the shore,
a. they speed up.   c. their wavelength increases.
b. they maintain their speed.   d. their wave height increases.

currents transport sediment
e open ocean.   c. only during low tide.
e shore.   d. only during high tide.

4. Which of the following does NOT control surface currents?

SPECIAL NEEDS

STANDARDIZED TEST PREPARATION
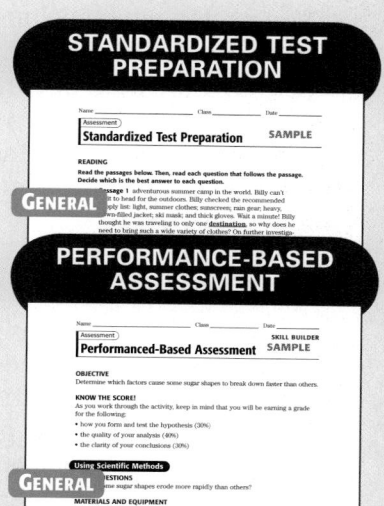

Assessment
Standardized Test Preparation SAMPLE

READING
Read the passages below. Then, read each question that follows the passage. Decide which is the best answer to each question.

Passage 1 adventurous summer camp in the woods. Billy can't wait for the outdoors. Billy checked the recommended supply list: light, summer clothes, sunscreen, rain gear, heavy, down-filled jacket, ski mask, and thick gloves. Wait a minute! Billy thought he was traveling to only one destination, so why does he need to bring such a wide variety of clothes? On further investiga-

GENERAL

PERFORMANCE-BASED ASSESSMENT

Assessment
Performanced-Based Assessment SKILL BUILDER SAMPLE

OBJECTIVE
Determine which factors cause some sugar shapes to break down faster than others.

KNOW THE SCORE!
As you work through the activity, keep in mind that you will be earning a grade for the following:
• how you form and test the hypotheses (30%)
• the quality of your analysis (40%)
• the clarity of your conclusions (30%)

Using Scientific Methods
QUESTIONS
sugar shapes erode more rapidly than others?

MATERIALS AND EQUIPMENT
• 1 regular sugar cube   • 90 mL of water

GENERAL

This Chapter Enrichment provides relevant and interesting information to expand and enhance your presentation of the chapter material.

Section 1

Fishes: The First Vertebrates

Chordates

- Chordate embryos have four basic features that distinguish them from other animals. The first is the notochord, a semiflexible rod that runs along the length of the body. Chordates also have a hollow dorsal nerve cord, which consists of nerve fibers that make contact with the muscles; pharyngeal pouches, which are openings between the pharynx and the outside of the animal; and a postanal tail, which is an extension of the notochord and dorsal nerve cord.

Is That a Fact!

- Cephalochordates (lancelets) have more than 100 pharyngeal pouches that are used to strain food particles from water.

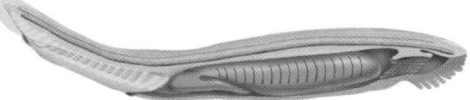

Vertebrates

- Vertebrates, which belong to the phylum Chordata, first appeared on Earth during the late Cambrian period, more than 500 million years ago. The first vertebrates were jawless; jaws appeared about 100 million years later. Vertebrates include fishes, amphibians, reptiles, birds, and mammals.

Is That a Fact!

- Hagfishes are jawless fishes that make large amounts of slime in mucus glands. In fact, they are sometimes called slime eels. Scientists think hagfish may use the slime to help kill their prey, protect themselves from predators, repel competitors, or build burrow walls.

Is That a Fact!

- Some ray-finned fishes have unusual traits. For example, Siamese fighting fish are able to take oxygen from the air through their gills in addition to taking oxygen from water through their gills. Fish such as the walking catfish and mudskipper can even crawl on land!

Cartilaginous Fishes

- Sharks, skates, and rays are all Chondrichthyes, or cartilaginous fishes. Cartilaginous fishes are an amazingly diverse group both behaviorally and physically. For example, sharks range in size from the 12 m (40 ft) whale shark to the 0.6 m (2 ft) dogshark. Shark diets differ greatly too. Although most sharks eat other fish, great white sharks have been known to eat seals and other marine mammals. Some sharks, such as the gentle basking shark, eat nothing but plankton.

- Nurse sharks have barbels, which are special sensory organs beneath their nose that help them locate food on the bottom of the ocean.

Bony Fishes

- Bony fishes are the largest class of fishes. There are more than 25,000 species of bony fishes, which makes them by far the largest group of aquatic vertebrates as well.

- The first bony fish appeared during the Devonian period.

Section 2

Amphibians

Salamanders

● Salamanders belong to the order Caudata. These carnivorous amphibians have a visible tail as adults, two pairs of legs of approximately the same size, ribs, and teeth on both jaws. Salamanders live in cool, moist habitats in tropical and northern temperate areas.

Is That a Fact!

◆ Some salamanders can extend their sticky, mucus-coated tongues as far as 80% of their body length.

◆ Most salamanders can regenerate lost toes and even entire limbs. As a defense mechanism, they sometimes shed their tail. Muscle contractions in the detached tail distract a predator long enough to enable the salamander to make a quick getaway.

Frogs and Toads

● How do toads and frogs differ? Toads are types of frogs. Many toads belong to the family Bufonidae. These "true toads" generally have stubby bodies, short hind legs, and dry and warty skin, and they tend to lay their eggs in long chains. "True frogs," which are members of the family Ranidae, generally have bulging eyes, strong and long webbed feet, and smooth skin, and they tend to lay their eggs in clusters. There are many exceptions to these generalizations, however; for example, there are some warty frogs and some smooth-skinned toads.

Section 3

Reptiles

Reptile Characteristics

● Most reptiles live in tropical areas. Reptile species include snakes, lizards, crocodiles, turtles, and tuataras, which are lizardlike animals that can be found only on some of the islands of New Zealand. Reptiles range in size from the tiny gecko lizard (3 cm long) to the anaconda snake (thought to reach 11.5 m long).

Crocodiles and Alligators

● Crocodiles and alligators are closely related carnivorous reptiles that belong to the order Crocodylia. How are they different from each other? Alligators have  broader snouts than crocodiles. Also, the fourth tooth on either side of a crocodile's jaw protrudes when the crocodile's mouth is closed.

Is That a Fact!

◆ Estuarine crocodiles can live more than 100 years.

◆ The Chinese alligator, a relatively small animal once found in China's Yangtze River region, is an endangered species and may even be extinct in the wild.

SCI LINKS®

NSTA

Developed and maintained by the National Science Teachers Association

SciLinks is maintained by the National Science Teachers Association to provide you and your students with interesting, up-to-date links that will enrich your classroom presentation of the chapter.

Visit www.scilinks.org and enter the SciLinks code for more information about the topic listed.

Topic: Vertebrates
SciLinks code: HSM1602

Topic: Amphibians
SciLinks code: HSM0058

Topic: Fishes
SciLinks code: HSM0579

Topic: Reptiles
SciLinks code: HSM1299

Overview

Tell students that this chapter will help them learn about three kinds of vertebrates. The chapter describes the characteristics of fishes, amphibians, and reptiles.

Assessing Prior Knowledge

Students should be familiar with the following topics:
• animals and behavior
• classification

Identifying Misconceptions

As students learn the material in this chapter, some of them may be confused that the word "fish" is sometimes used in common non-fish animal names such as jellyfish and starfish. It may be helpful to point out that jellyfish and starfish are not fish! You might use this idea to talk about the value of scientific names and some of the problems that arise when using only common names to discuss an animal.

16

Fishes, Amphibians, and Reptiles

About the PHOTO

This unlucky caiman must have been quite a match for the snake. But somehow the snake's body strength overcame the caiman's muscular jaws. Each of these animals has a unique trait that makes the animal a strong predator. But as reptiles, these animals have many traits in common. For example, both animals are covered in thick skin, and both use lungs to breathe.

PRE-READING ACTIVITY

Graphic Organizer

Comparison Table Before you read the chapter, create the graphic organizer entitled "Comparison Table" described in the **Study Skills** section of the Appendix. Label the columns with "Fishes," "Amphibians," and "Reptiles." Label the rows with "Characteristics" and "Kinds." As you read the chapter, fill in the table with details about the characteristics and kinds of each animal.

Standards Correlations

National Science Education Standards

The following codes indicate the National Science Education Standards that correlate to this chapter. The full text of the standards is at the front of the book.

Chapter Opener
UCP 2, 5; SAI 1; LS 1a, 1d, 3b

Section 1 Fishes: The First Vertebrates
UCP 1, 3, 5; SAI 1; LS 1a, 1d, 2a, 3a-3c, 5a, 5c

Section 2 Amphibians
UCP 1, 5; SAI 1; LS 1a, 3a, 3c, 3d, 5a, 5b; *LabBook*: UCP 2, 4, 5; SAI 1; LS 1a, 3c, 3d, 5b

Section 3 Reptiles
UCP 1, 2, 5; SAI 1; LS 1a, 1d, 2a, 2b, 3a, 3c, 3d, 5a-5c

Chapter Lab
UCP 1, 2, 3, 5; SAI 1, 2; LS 1a, 1d, 3b

Chapter Review
UCP 1, 2, 3, 5; SAI 1, 2; LS 1a, 3b

Science in Action
UCP 4, 5; SAI 1; SPSP 2, 5; LS 4d, 5b, 5c

START-UP ACTIVITY

MATERIALS

FOR EACH GROUP
- balloons, two
- beakers, two
- cooking oil
- fish tank
- funnel
- water

Answers

1. The balloon filled with water will eventually settle about halfway to the bottom of the tank. The oil-filled balloon will float.

2. Sample answer: The oil in an oily liver is less dense than water. This property provides buoyancy to a cartilaginous fish and helps it keep from sinking.

3. Sample answer: The air would change the density of the balloon. If the air was not removed, the balloons would float more easily.

START-UP ACTIVITY

Oil and Water

A shark stores a lot of oil in its liver. In this activity, you will build a model of an oily liver to see how an oily liver can help keep a shark from sinking.

Procedure

1. Use **two beakers** to measure equal amounts of **water** and **cooking oil.**

2. Use a **funnel** to fill **one balloon** with the water that you measured.

3. Using the funnel, fill a **second balloon** with the cooking oil.

4. Tie the balloons so that no air remains inside. Be careful not to squeeze the oil or water out of the balloons while tying them.

5. Put each balloon in a **fish tank** that is full of **water.** Observe what happens to each of the balloons.

Analysis

1. Compare where the two balloons come to rest in the tank of water.

2. A shark's oily liver helps keep the shark from sinking. How does the structure of the shark's oily liver help achieve this result?

3. Why do you think it was important to remove the air from the balloons before putting them in the water? What might have happened if you did not remove the air from the balloons?

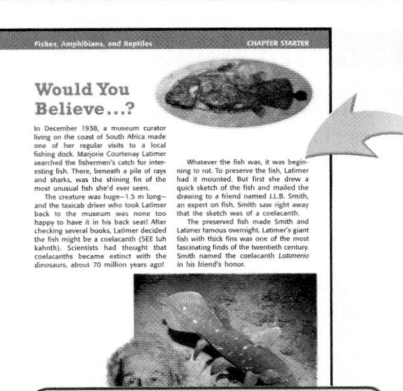

Chapter Starter Transparency
Use this transparency to help students begin thinking about why humans study invertebrates.

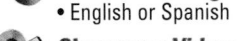
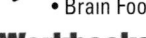

CHAPTER RESOURCES

Technology

Transparencies
- Chapter Starter Transparency

READING SKILLS

Student Edition on CD-ROM

Guided Reading Audio CD
- English or Spanish

Classroom Videos
- Brain Food Video Quiz

Workbooks

Science Puzzlers, Twisters & Teasers
- Invertebrates GENERAL

Focus

Overview

This section introduces students to vertebrates and other chordates. Students will learn about the characteristics of vertebrates and the traits that set them apart from other chordates. The section also introduces fishes, the first vertebrates. Students will learn about three classes of fishes. They will also learn the differences between ectotherms and endotherms.

🔔 Bellringer

While you are taking attendance, ask students to think about this question:

What are some of the physical characteristics shared by dinosaurs and people?

Have each student write down two or three ideas. Then briefly discuss students' lists before beginning the section.

Motivate

Demonstration — GENERAL

Identifying Backbones Extract a skeleton from an owl pellet. Ask students to find the backbone. Students may understand the structure of vertebrae better if they are able to manipulate the parts of the skeleton to see how the vertebrae interlock.
LS Kinesthetic

Fishes: The First Vertebrates

You may have seen a dinosaur skeleton at a museum. And you've probably seen a lot of fish. Have you ever thought about what you might have in common with these animals or what they might have in common with each other?

The skeletons of humans and fish have many bones that are similar to dinosaur bones. Dinosaur bones are just bigger. For example, all of these skeletons have a backbone. Animals that have a backbone are called **vertebrates** (VUHR tuh brits).

Chordates

Vertebrates belong to the phylum Chordata. Members of this phylum are called *chordates* (KAWR DAYTS). Vertebrates make up the largest group of chordates. But there are two other groups of chordates—lancelets (LANS lits) and tunicates (TOO ni kits). These chordates are much simpler than vertebrates. They do not have a backbone or a well-developed head. **Figure 1** shows an example of each group of chordates.

The three groups of chordates share certain characteristics. All chordates have each of four particular body parts at some point in their life. These parts are shown in the lancelet in **Figure 2** on the next page.

vertebrate an animal that has a backbone

Figure 1 *Tunicates (right), lancelets (lower right), and vertebrates, such as the fish (lower left), are chordates.*

CHAPTER RESOURCES

Chapter Resource File

- Lesson Plan
- Directed Reading A **BASIC**
- Directed Reading B **SPECIAL NEEDS**

Technology

Transparencies
- Bellringer
- Chordate Body Parts

🌐 Cultural Awareness GENERAL

Lancelets for Lunch? In many parts of Asia, lancelets are commercially harvested and are an important food source. Have students research the use of lancelets as food. They should examine things such as taste, price per pound, and availability in the United States. Students could present their findings in an oral or written report or use the information they have gathered to develop recipes using lancelets. **LS Verbal**

Figure 2 Chordate Body Parts

Tail
Chordates have a tail that begins behind the anus. Some chordates have a tail only in the embryo stage.

Notochord
A stiff but flexible rod called a notochord (NOHT uh KAWRD) gives the body support. In most vertebrates, the embryo's notochord is replaced by a backbone.

Hollow Nerve Cord
A hollow nerve cord runs along the back and is full of fluid. In vertebrates, this nerve cord is called the *spinal cord.*

Pharyngeal Pouches
All chordate embryos have pharyngeal (fuh RIN jee uhl) pouches. These pouches develop into gills or other body parts as the embryo matures.

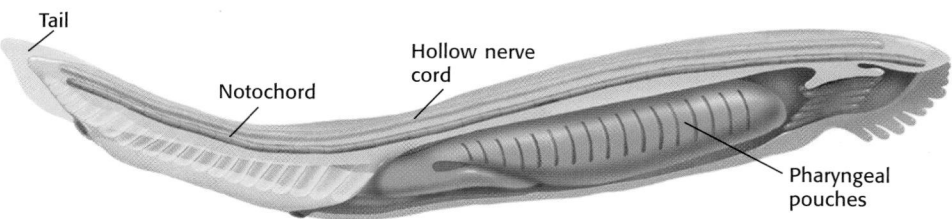

Tail

Notochord

Hollow nerve cord

Pharyngeal pouches

Vertebrate Characteristics

Fishes, amphibians, reptiles, birds, and mammals are vertebrates. Many things set vertebrates apart from lancelets and tunicates. One major difference is that only vertebrates have a backbone. The backbone is a strong but flexible column of bones that are called *vertebrae* (VUHR tuh BRAY). **Figure 3** shows the vertebrae of a human. The vertebrae surround and protect the spinal cord. They also help support the rest of the body.

Another difference between vertebrates and other chordates is the head. Vertebrates have a well-developed head protected by a skull. The skull is made of either cartilage or bone. *Cartilage* is the tough material that the flexible parts of our ears and nose are made of. The skeletons of all vertebrate embryos are made of cartilage. But as most vertebrates grow, the cartilage is replaced by bone. Bone is much harder than cartilage.

Because bone is so hard, it can be easily fossilized. Scientists have discovered many fossils of vertebrates. These fossils give scientists valuable clues about how organisms are related to each other. For example, fossil evidence indicates that fish appeared about 500 million years ago. These fossils show that fish were the first vertebrates on Earth.

✓ Reading Check What material makes up the skeleton of a human embryo? (*See the Appendix for answers to Reading Checks.*)

Figure 3 *The vertebrae interlock to form the backbone.*

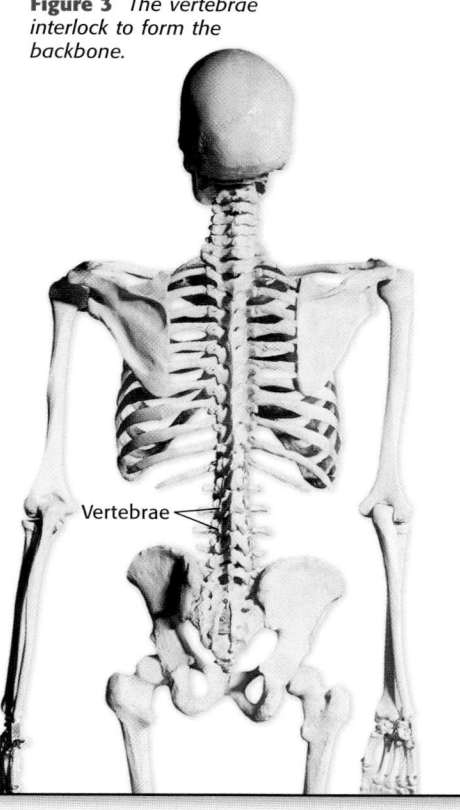

Vertebrae

WEIRD SCIENCE

Tunicates are actually more well developed as young larvae than they are when they "mature" into adults! As larvae, tunicates have many chordate features, look much like tadpoles, and are able to swim. As they reach adulthood, however, tunicates lose their tail (and therefore their ability to swim) and their nervous system largely disintegrates.

Teach

CONNECTION ACTIVITY
Paleontology — ADVANCED

Careers Have students research the field of paleontology and report their findings to the class. The report could be part of a special "career day" during which students present reports on a variety of scientific fields. Suggest that students answer questions such as the following:

• What do paleontologists do?

• What type of education do paleontologists need?

• What types of career opportunities exist for paleontologists?

LS Verbal

READING STRATEGY — BASIC

Prediction Guide Before students read the passage about fishes, ask them whether the following statements are true or false:

• Sharks are fish. (true)

• Some fish will suffocate if they stop swimming. (true)

• All fish need to swim continuously to stay alive. (false)

Students will discover the answers as they read the section. **LS Verbal**

Writing **Researching Fishes** Have students visit the supermarket and write down each type of canned fish for sale and each type of frozen or fresh fish for sale. Students should then choose one of the fishes and write a brief, half-page paper describing the fish, its natural habitat, areas where it can be found, what makes it suitable for selling to consumers, and the amount of the fish harvested each year. Students should also identify whether the fish is jawless, cartilaginous, or bony.
LS Visual/Verbal

Quick Lab

MATERIALS

FOR EACH STUDENT
• thermometer

Answers

3. Students should find that their body temperature does not fluctuate more than a few tenths of a degree during the day.

4. Human body temperature does not change drastically, even after exercise. Interested students may want to test this by measuring their temperature before and after exercising.

5. An ectotherm's body temperature fluctuates more dramatically, depending on the temperature of its environment.

Figure 4 *Most fishes, including this leafy sea dragon, are ectotherms.*

endotherm an animal that can use body heat from chemical reactions in the body's cells to maintain a constant body temperature

ectotherm an organism that needs sources of heat outside of itself

Quick Lab

Body Temperature

1. Use a **thermometer** to take your temperature every hour for 6 h.

2. Make a graph of your body temperature. Place the time of day on the x-axis and your temperature on the y-axis.

3. Does your temperature change throughout the day? How much does it change?

4. Do you think exercise changes your body temperature?

5. How do you think your results would be different if you were an ectotherm?

Answer to Reading Check

Because most fishes are ectotherms, the body temperature of most fishes would increase as the temperature of their environment increased.

Are Vertebrates Warm or Cold?

All vertebrates need to live at the proper temperature. An animal's cells work properly only at certain temperatures. If an animal's body temperature is too high or too low, its body cannot function well. Some animals heat their own bodies. Others depend on the environment to control their temperature.

Staying Warm

The body temperature of birds and mammals does not change much as the temperature of the environment changes. Birds and mammals use energy released by the chemical reactions in their cells to warm their bodies. Animals that have a stable body temperature are called **endotherms** (EN doh THUHRMZ). They are sometimes called *warmblooded animals*. Because of their stable temperature, endotherms can stay warm in cold weather.

Cold Blood?

Some animals depend on their surroundings to stay warm. Their body temperature changes as the temperature of the environment changes. Animals that do not control body temperature through activity in their cells are called **ectotherms** (EK toh THUHRMZ). They are sometimes called *coldblooded animals*. Nearly all amphibians and reptiles are ectotherms. Most fishes, such as the one in **Figure 4,** are also ectotherms. Being an ectotherm is one of many traits that most fishes share.

✓ Reading Check How would the body temperature of most fishes change if the temperature of the environment increased?

Fish Characteristics

Fishes come in many shapes, sizes, and colors. There are more than 25,000 species of fishes, and many look very different from each other. But all fishes share several characteristics. Some traits help fishes live in the water. Other traits, such as a strong body and a brain, help fishes catch or find food.

MISCONCEPTION /// ALERT \\\

Oxygen in Water Fish take in oxygen gas that is dissolved in the water. They do not use the oxygen that is part of the water molecule itself. Each molecule of water contains one atom of oxygen, but it is unavailable to the fish.

Born to Swim

Fishes have many body parts that help them swim. Strong muscles attached to the backbone allow many fishes to swim quickly after their prey. To steer, stop, and balance, fishes use *fins*, which are fan-shaped structures that help fishes move. And many fishes have bodies covered by bony structures called *scales*. Scales protect the body and lower friction as fishes swim through the water. **Figure 5** shows some body parts of a fish.

Making Sense of the World

Fishes have a brain that keeps track of information coming in from the senses. All fishes have the senses of vision, hearing, and smell. Most fishes also have a lateral line system. The **lateral line** is a row or rows of tiny sense organs that detect water vibrations, such as those caused by another fish swimming by. These organs are found along each side of the body and usually extend onto the head.

Underwater Breathing

Fishes use their gills to breathe. A **gill** is an organ that removes oxygen from the water. Oxygen in the water passes through the thin membrane of the gills to the blood. The blood then carries oxygen through the body. Gills are also used to remove carbon dioxide from the blood.

Making More Fish

Most fishes reproduce by *external fertilization*. The female lays unfertilized eggs in the water, and the male drops sperm on them. But some species of fish use *internal fertilization*. In this case, the male deposits sperm inside the female. Usually, the female then lays fertilized eggs that have embryos inside. But in some species, the embryos develop inside the female.

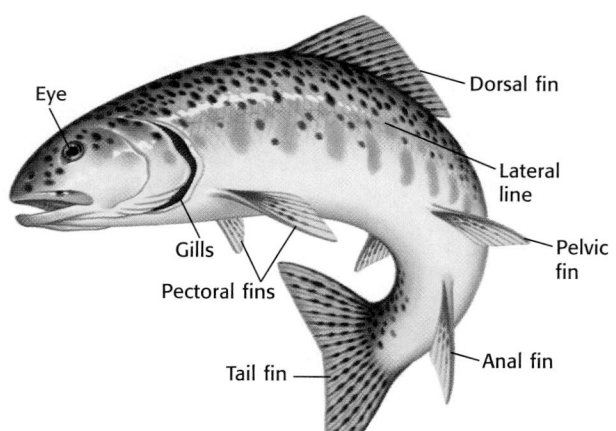

Eye

Dorsal fin

Lateral line

Gills

Pectoral fins

Pelvic fin

Tail fin

Anal fin

CONNECTION TO
Physics

How Fish See the World You have to move a magnifying lens back and forth to bring an object into focus. Fish eyes focus on objects in the same way. Fish use muscles to change the position of the lenses in their eyes. By moving the eye lenses, fish can bring objects into focus. To understand how fish see the world, use a magnifying lens to look at objects in your classroom.

ACTIVITY

lateral line a faint line visible on both sides of a fish's body that runs the length of the body and marks the location of sense organs that detect vibrations in water

gill a respiratory organ in which oxygen from the water is exchanged with carbon dioxide from the blood

Figure 5 *Fishes have many shapes and sizes, but all fishes have gills, fins, and a tail.*

Is That a Fact!

Air has 26 times more oxygen than water at the same temperature. Consequently, fish expend much more energy breathing than most mammals do.

📖 **READING STRATEGY** — GENERAL

Prediction Guide Ask students to name the three types of fishes alive in the world today. (jawless, cartilaginous, and bony)
LS Verbal

CONNECTION to Environmental Science — GENERAL

Nile Perch Once home to between 200 and 500 species of fishes, Lake Victoria, in East Africa, is now home to the Nile perch. This perch has reduced the number of other types of fishes. Most of the native fishes were small cichlids, and each species was unique in appearance and habit. But the native fishes were hard to fish commercially. The Nile perch was being tested in a nearby lake for introduction into Lake Victoria for commercial fishing when it mysteriously appeared in the lake. It has since nearly wiped out the native fishes in this huge lake. The Nile perch is now largely feeding on shrimp and its own young. Ask students, "What are the commercial and ecological costs and benefits of the Nile perch's appearance in Lake Victoria?" **LS** Verbal

Answer to Reading Check
Hagfish eat dead fishes on the ocean floor. Lampreys suck other animals' blood and flesh through a toothed suction cup-like mouth.

Kinds of Fishes

There are five very different classes of fishes. Two classes are now extinct. But scientists have been able to study the fossils of the extinct fishes. The three classes of fishes living today are *jawless fishes, cartilaginous* (KART'l AJ uh nuhs) *fishes,* and *bony fishes.*

Jawless Fishes

The first fishes did not have jaws. You might think that having no jaws would make eating difficult and would lead to extinction. But the jawless fishes have thrived for half a billion years.

The two kinds of modern jawless fishes are hagfish and lampreys, as shown in **Figure 6.** These fishes are eel-like. They have smooth, slimy skin and a round, jawless mouth. Their skeleton is made of cartilage, and they have a notochord but no backbone. These fishes have a skull, a brain, and eyes.

Jawless fishes do not need jaws to eat. Hagfish eat dead fishes on the ocean floor. For this reason, they are sometimes called *vultures of the sea.* Lampreys suck other animals' blood and flesh. They have a suction cup–like mouth that has teeth. They don't need jaws because they don't bite or chew.

✓ **Reading Check** Describe how jawless fishes eat.

INTERNET ACTIVITY
For another activity related to this chapter, go to **go.hrw.com** and type in the keyword **HL5VR1W.**

Figure 6 Jawless Fishes

▼ **Hagfish** can tie their flexible bodies into knots. They slide the knot from their tail end to their head to remove slime from their skin or to escape from predators.

▼ **Lampreys** can live in salt water or fresh water, but they must reproduce in fresh water.

Is That a Fact!

Some scientists think that hagfishes produce slime in order to help kill their prey. Slime produced near a dying fish may suffocate the fish by clogging its gills, keeping the fish from getting oxygen. But a hagfish's slime can also suffocate the hagfish itself if the hagfish does not clean the slime from its body! Hagfish slide a knot down the length of the body to remove the slime they produce.

ACTIVITY — ADVANCED

Researching Lampreys Lampreys became a problem in the Great Lakes in the 1950s. These fish preyed on trout, whitefish, and other lake fishes. By the late 1950s, the lampreys had nearly wiped out the trout population in the Great Lakes. Ask students to research the different ways that scientists have tried to control the lamprey population since the 1950s. (Answers may include chemical sprays that kill lampreys and electric fences that prevent the lampreys from spawning.) **LS** Verbal

Figure 7   Cartilaginous Fishes

▲ Unlike rays, **skates** have a small dorsal fin.

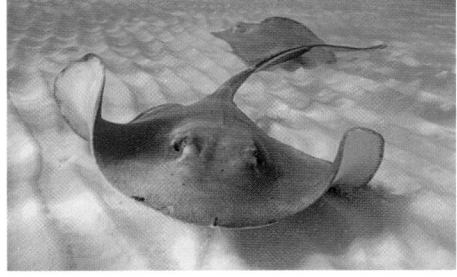

▲ Rays, such as this **stingray,** feed on shell-fish and worms on the sea floor. A ray swims by moving its fins up and down.

◀ Sharks, such as this **hammerhead shark,** rarely prey on humans. They usually eat other fish.

Cartilaginous Fishes

Did you know that a shark is a fish? Sharks belong to a class of fishes called cartilaginous fishes. In most vertebrates, soft cartilage in the embryo is slowly replaced by bone. But in sharks, skates, and rays, the skeleton never changes to bone. So, they are called *cartilaginous fishes.*

Cartilaginous fishes have fully functional jaws. These fishes are strong swimmers and expert predators. Many have excellent senses of sight and smell, and they have a lateral line system. **Figure 7** shows some cartilaginous fishes.

To stay afloat, cartilaginous fishes store a lot of oil in their liver. The oil helps the fishes be more buoyant because the oil is less dense than water. But even with oily livers, these fishes are denser than water. They have to keep moving to stay afloat. When they stop swimming, they slowly sink.

Some cartilaginous fishes also swim to keep water moving over their gills. If these fishes stop swimming, they will suffocate. Other cartilaginous fishes do not have to swim. They can lie on the ocean floor and pump water across their gills.

Answer to Math Practice

28,500 species of bony fishes
$(30{,}000 \times 0.95 = 28{,}500)$

Reteaching ——— BASIC

Recognizing Roots Help students remember the difference between endotherms and ectotherms by knowing the words' roots. Explain that *therm* refers to temperature, *ecto* refers to outside, and *endo* refers to inside. Ask them to underline these three roots where used in the following words, and then look up the words' meanings: *thermometer, ectoderm,* and *endoskeleton.* **LS** Verbal

Quiz ——— GENERAL

1. What is the segmented column of bones that supports the body of a vertebrate called? (backbone)

2. Which kinds of fishes have scales? (bony fishes)

3. Sharks are a member of what class of fishes? (cartilaginous)

4. What are the two kinds of modern jawless fishes? (lampreys and hagfish)

Alternative Assessment ——— GENERAL

Concept Mapping Create a concept map using the following terms:

   vertebrate, chordate, notochord, tail, hollow nerve chord, pharyngeal pouches
LS Verbal

A Lot of Bones
If there are 30,000 species of fishes and 95% of all fishes are bony fishes, how many species of bony fishes are there?

swim bladder a gas-filled sac that is used to control buoyancy; also known as a *gas bladder*

Bony Fishes

When you hear the word *fish,* you probably think of a bony fish. Goldfish, tuna, trout, catfish, and cod are bony fishes. This class of fishes is the largest. Ninety-five percent of all fishes are bony fishes. They range in size from about 1 cm to 8.6 m long. Some bony fishes are shown in **Figure 8.**

Bony fishes are very different from other fishes. As their name suggests, bony fishes have a skeleton made of bone. Also, their bodies are covered by bony scales. Unlike other fishes, bony fishes can rest in one place without swimming. They have a swim bladder that keeps them from sinking. The **swim bladder** is a balloonlike organ that is filled with oxygen and other gases. These gases are lighter than water, so they help the fish be more buoyant. The swim bladder is sometimes called a *gas bladder.*

There are two main groups of bony fishes. Almost all bony fishes are *ray-finned fishes.* Ray-finned fishes have paired fins supported by thin rays of bone. Ray-finned fishes include many familiar fishes, such as eels, herrings, trout, minnows, and perch.

Lobe-finned fishes make up the second group of bony fishes. Lobe-finned fishes have fins that are muscular and thick. There are seven living species of lobe-finned fishes. Six of these species are lungfishes. Lungfishes have air sacs. Because air sacs can gulp air, they are like lungs. Scientists think that ancient fishes from this group were the ancestors of amphibians.

✓ **Reading Check** How do bony fishes differ from cartilaginous fishes?

Figure 8 Bony Fishes

▼ **Lungfishes** live in shallow waters that often dry up in the summer.

▼ **Masked butterfly fish** live in warm waters around coral reefs.

▼ **Pikes** are fast predators that move in quick bursts of speed to catch fish and invertebrates.

Answer to Reading Check

Bony fishes have skeletons made of bone, have bodies covered in bony scales, and can rest in one place without swimming.

SECTION Review

Summary

- Chordates include lancelets, tunicates, and vertebrates. At some point during their development, chordates have a notochord, a hollow nerve cord, pharyngeal pouches, and a tail.

- Most chordates are vertebrates. Vertebrates differ from other chordates in that they have a backbone composed of vertebrae.

- Endotherms control body temperature through the chemical reactions of their cells. Ectotherms do not.

- Fishes share many characteristics. Most have fins and scales to help them swim. Many have a lateral line system to sense water movement. Fishes breathe with gills.

- There are three groups of living fishes: jawless fishes, cartilaginous fishes, and bony fishes. Jawless fishes do not have a backbone. Cartilaginous fishes have an oily liver. Bony fishes have a swim bladder.

- The oily liver and the swim bladder both help fishes keep from sinking.

Using Key Terms

1. Use each of the following terms in a separate sentence: *vertebrate, lateral line system, gill,* and *swim bladder.*

2. In your own words, write a definition for each of the following terms: *endotherm* and *ectotherm.*

Understanding Key Ideas

3. At some point in its life, every chordate has each of the following EXCEPT
   a. a tail.
   b. a notochord.
   c. a hollow nerve cord.
   d. a backbone.

4. Which vertebrates are ectotherms?

5. What are four characteristics shared by most fishes?

6. What are the three classes of living fish? Give an example of each.

7. Most bony fishes reproduce by external fertilization. What does this mean?

Critical Thinking

8. **Analyzing Relationships** Describe the ways that cartilaginous fishes and bony fishes maintain buoyancy. Why do you think that jawless fishes do not use one of these methods?

9. **Applying Concepts** How could moving a fishbowl from a cold window sill to a warmer part of the house affect a pet fish?

Interpreting Graphics

Use the bar graph below to answer the questions that follow.

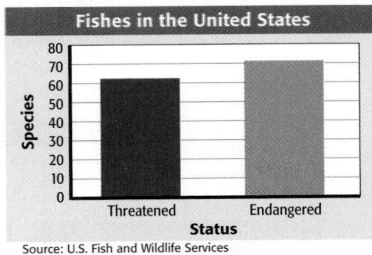

Source: U.S. Fish and Wildlife Services

10. How many fish species in the United States are threatened? How many are endangered?

11. What is the total number of threatened and endangered fish species in the United States?

Developed and maintained by the National Science Teachers Association

For a variety of links related to this chapter, go to www.scilinks.org

Topic: Vertebrates; Fishes
SciLinks code: HSM1602; HSM0579

CHAPTER RESOURCES

Chapter Resource File

- **Section Quiz** GENERAL
- **Section Review** GENERAL
- **Vocabulary and Section Summary** GENERAL
- **Datasheet for Quick Lab**

Homework —— GENERAL

Classifying Fish Have students indicate which class (or classes) of fishes have the following characteristics. *J* stands for jawless, *C* for cartilaginous, and *B* for bony.

gills (J, C, B)

oily liver (C)

swim bladder (B)

LS Logical

Answers to Section Review

1. Sample answer: Fishes are vertebrates. The lateral line system is a row or rows of sense organs along the side of a fish's body. Fishes get oxygen through their gills. A swim bladder is a balloon-shaped organ that fills with gases to help keep bony fishes afloat.

2. Sample answer: An endotherm is an animal that can generate body heat from chemical changes in its cells. An ectotherm is an animal that needs sources of heat outside of itself.

3. d

4. most fishes, amphibians, and reptiles

5. body parts that help them swim, a nervous system, gills, and sexual reproduction

6. Sample answer: jawless fishes, hagfish; cartilaginous fishes, shark; bony fishes, goldfish

7. In external fertilization, a female's eggs are fertilized in the water when a male drops sperm on them.

8. Sample answer: Cartilaginous fishes use an oily liver to be buoyant. Bony fishes use a swim bladder that is filled with gases to be buoyant. Hagfish do not need these structures because they live on the ocean's floor so they do not need buoyancy. Lampreys may have a special way of swimming that allows them to be buoyant without help from an oily liver or a swim bladder.

9. Sample answer: Because most fishes are ectotherms, moving the pet fish to a warmer part of the house will increase its body temperature.

10. threatened: about 62 species; endangered: about 70 species

11. about 132 species

Focus

Overview

In this section, students will learn how vertebrates moved to land as amphibians. They will learn how amphibians breathe, reproduce, and develop through metamorphosis. Students will explore three groups of amphibians and learn how amphibians can be ecological indicators.

 Bellringer

Ask students to name an advantage and a disadvantage to the thin, moist skin of amphibians. (They can absorb oxygen and water through skin, but they also lose moisture through skin.)

Motivate

Demonstration —— GENERAL

Fossils Explain that we know about early amphibians from fossils. To show how fossils form, fill a bucket halfway with sand. Put a sponge on the sand and pour more sand over it. Dissolve salt in a bucket of warm water. Pour the salt water over the sand. A few days later, uncover the sponge. The water should have evaporated or drained. The salt should have hardened the sponge. Explain that fossils form as dissolved minerals enter spaces in plant or animal material and harden.
LS Visual

SECTION

2

Amphibians

Did you know that some animals are able to breathe through their skin? Do these animals live on land or in the water? Actually, they live both on land and in the water.

About 350 million years ago, fishes lived wherever there was water. But no vertebrates lived on land. The land had many resources for vertebrates. It had plants and insects for vertebrates to eat, and there were few predators. But to live on land, vertebrates needed lungs for breathing and legs for walking.

Moving to Land

Amphibians (am FIB ee uhnz) are animals that can live in water and have lungs and legs. Scientists think that amphibians evolved from the ancestors of lungfish-like fishes. These ancient fishes developed lungs that got oxygen from the air. A **lung** is a saclike organ that takes oxygen from the air and delivers oxygen to the blood. These fishes also had strong fins that could have evolved into legs.

Most of today's amphibians are frogs or salamanders, such as those in **Figure 1.** But early amphibians looked different. Fossils show that the first amphibians looked like a cross between a fish and a salamander. Many were very large—up to 10 m long. Early amphibians could stay on dry land longer than today's amphibians can. But they still had to return to the water to keep from drying out or overheating. They also returned to the water to mate and to lay eggs.

Reading Check How do amphibians get oxygen from the air? *(See the Appendix for answers to Reading Checks.)*

Figure 1 *Frogs and salamanders are two kinds of the amphibians on Earth today.*

READING WARM-UP

Objectives
● Explain how amphibians breathe.
● Describe amphibian metamorphosis.
● Describe the three groups of amphibians, and give an example of each.
● Explain why amphibians are ecological indicators.

Terms to Learn
lung
tadpole
metamorphosis

READING STRATEGY

Reading Organizer As you read this section, create an outline of the section. Use the headings from the section in your outline.

CHAPTER RESOURCES

Chapter Resource File

• Lesson Plan
• Directed Reading A BASIC
• Directed Reading B SPECIAL NEEDS

Technology

Transparencies
• Bellringer

Answer to Reading Check

Most amphibians get oxygen through lungs.

Characteristics of Amphibians

Amphibian means "double life." Most amphibians live part of their lives in water and part of their lives on land. Amphibian eggs do not have a shell or a membrane that prevents water loss. For this reason, embryos must develop in a wet environment. Most amphibians live in the water after hatching and then later develop into adults that can live on land.

But even adult amphibians are only partly adapted to life on land. Amphibians are ectotherms. So, their body temperature depends on the temperature of their environment. Water helps amphibians keep their bodies at a stable temperature. Also, water helps adults keep from losing too much moisture through their skin.

Thin Skin

Amphibian skin is thin, smooth, and moist. The skin is so thin that amphibians absorb water through it instead of drinking. But they can also lose water through their skin and easily become dehydrated. Their thin skin is one reason that most amphibians live in water or in damp habitats.

Amphibians can breathe by gulping air into their lungs. But many also absorb oxygen through their skin, which is full of blood vessels. In fact, a few amphibians, such as the salamander in **Figure 2,** breathe only through their skin.

Many amphibians also have brightly colored skin. The colors often warn predators that the skin contains poison glands. These poisons may simply be irritating, or they may be deadly. The skin of the poison arrow frog, shown in **Figure 3,** has one of the most deadly toxins known.

Figure 3 *The skin of this poison arrow frog is full of poison glands. Hunters in South America rub the tips of their arrows in the deadly toxin.*

lung a respiratory organ in which oxygen from the air is exchanged with carbon dioxide from the blood

Figure 2 *The four-toed salamander has no lungs. It gets all of its oxygen through its skin.*

CONNECTION TO Social Studies

WRITING SKILL **Troublesome Toads** In the 1930s, cane toads were shipped from Hawaii to Australia to eat cane grubs that were destroying sugar cane crops. But the toad populations grew out of control, and the toads did not eat the grubs. Native species that ate the toads were killed by the toads' poison glands. Research another animal that has caused disastrous effects in a new environment. In your **science journal,** write three paragraphs about this animal.

WEIRD SCIENCE

Most toads leave their fertilized eggs to develop unguarded. But the Surinam toad of South America is different. In a strange mating encounter that involves somersaults, fertilized eggs are attached to the back of the female. The eggs grow into pockets for each developing embryo. Depending on the species, young emerge from the pockets either as tadpoles or as young toads.

ACTIVITY ——— ADVANCED

Research Cloning Tell students that amphibians were the first vertebrates to be successfully cloned. Have students use library or Internet resources to locate information about the history of cloning and report their findings to the class. **LS Verbal**

📖 READING STRATEGY ——— GENERAL

Prediction Guide Before students read this section, tell them that *amphibian* means "double life." Then ask them to answer the following question in their **science journal:**

> Why would we give amphibians a name that means "double life?"

Ask students to evaluate their answers after reading this section. **LS Logical**

CONNECTION to Physical Science — GENERAL

Loud Little Lungs The Puerto Rican coqui frog is a very loud little animal. This amphibian can belt out its song at an amazing 120 decibels (db), as measured a few centimeters from the frog. (Noise is classified as physically painful to humans above 130 db.) At a distance where humans would hear it, the coqui's call may be about 90 db. This small frog has been accidentally introduced in Florida, Louisiana, and Hawaii. In Hawaii the coqui has become a pest because coquis there eat large amounts of native insects, forcing native birds to compete for this source of food. In addition, its loud calls keep people awake at night! Interested students can research loud animals and other loud sounds and then make a graph comparing the decibel levels that these sounds reach. **LS Auditory**

Observing Development Obtain frog or salamander eggs either locally or from a biological supply company. Set up an aquarium, and allow students to observe the metamorphosis that follows. Students should sketch the process each step of the way. (Note: If the animals were not collected locally, they cannot be released into the wild.) **LS** Visual

English Language Learners

MISCONCEPTION ///ALERT\\\\

Worrying about Warts Some students may have the mistaken impression that they can get warts from touching frogs and toads. Explain that warts are caused by human viruses.

Research ———————— ADVANCED

Writing **Herpetology** Have interested students conduct research about the field of herpetology, the branch of zoology that deals with amphibians and reptiles. Students could prepare reports and present them to the class. **LS** Verbal

PORTFOLIO

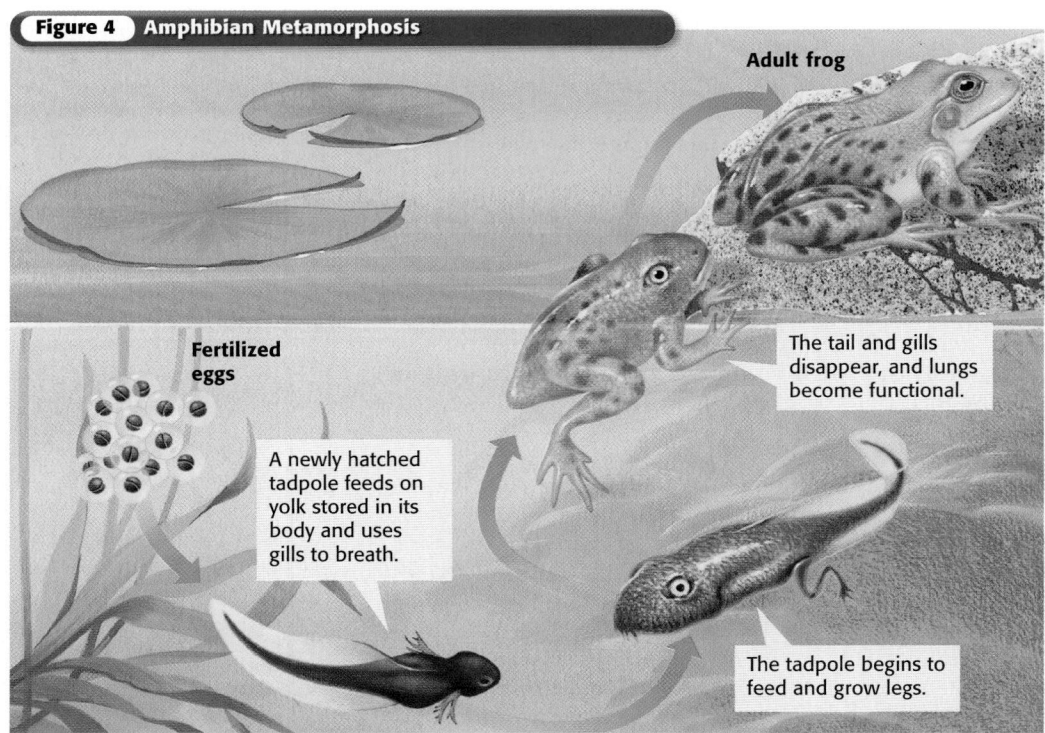

Figure 4 Amphibian Metamorphosis

Adult frog

Fertilized eggs

The tail and gills disappear, and lungs become functional.

A newly hatched tadpole feeds on yolk stored in its body and uses gills to breath.

The tadpole begins to feed and grow legs.

tadpole the aquatic, fish-shaped larva of a frog or toad

metamorphosis a phase in the life cycle of many animals during which a rapid change from the immature form of an organism to the adult form takes place

Figure 5 *Darwin's frogs live in Chile and Argentina. A male frog may carry 5 to 15 embryos in its vocal sacs.*

Leading a Double Life

Most amphibians don't just get bigger as they grow into adults. They change form as they grow. After hatching, a frog or toad embryo becomes a tadpole. A **tadpole** is an immature frog or toad that must live in the water. It gets oxygen through gills and uses its long tail to swim. Later, the tadpole loses its gills and develops structures such as lungs and limbs that allow it to live on land. This change from an immature form to an adult form is called **metamorphosis** (MET uh MAWR fuh sis) and is shown in **Figure 4.** Most adult amphibians can live on land. However, they still need to keep their skin moist.

A few amphibians develop in other ways. Some do not go through full metamorphosis. They hatch as tiny versions of adults, but they have gills. Some develop on land in wet places. For example, Darwin's frogs lay eggs on moist ground. When an embryo begins to move, an adult male Darwin's frog takes it into his mouth and protects it inside his vocal sacs. When the embryo has finished developing, the adult opens his mouth and a tiny frog jumps out. **Figure 5** shows a Darwin's frog.

CHAPTER RESOURCES

Technology

 **Transparencies**
• Amphibian Metamorphosis

WEIRD SCIENCE

Foam-nest tree frogs mate in trees that hang over ponds and streams. Females lay their eggs in large foamy, cocoonlike masses that harden for protection from the sun. After a few days of development, the tadpoles are ready to emerge, but they can do so only after a rain moistens the foam. Once moistened, the foam, carrying the young tadpoles, drips into the water below.

Kinds of Amphibians

More than 5,400 species of amphibians are alive today. They belong to three groups: caecilians (see SIL ee uhnz), salamanders, and frogs and toads.

Caecilians

Most people are not familiar with caecilians. However, scientists have discovered more than 160 species of caecilians. These amphibians live in tropical areas of Asia, Africa, and South America. They look like earthworms or snakes, but they have the thin, moist skin of amphibians. Several traits distinguish caecilians from other amphibians. For example, caecilians do not have legs, as shown in **Figure 6.** And unlike other amphibians, some caecilians have bony scales in their skin.

Salamanders

There are about 500 known species of salamanders. As adults, most salamanders live under stones and logs in the woods of North America. Two salamanders are shown in **Figure 7.** Of modern amphibians, salamanders are the most like prehistoric amphibians in overall form. Although salamanders are much smaller than their ancestors, they have a similar body shape, a long tail, and four strong legs. They range in size from a few centimeters long to 1.5 m long.

Salamanders do not develop as tadpoles. But most of them do lose gills and grow lungs during their development. A few species, such as the axolotl (AK suh LAHT'l), never lose their gills. These species live their entire life in the water.

✔ **Reading Check** How does a salamander's body change during development?

Figure 6 *Caecilians do not have legs. They live in damp soil in the Tropics and eat small invertebrates in the soil.*

SCHOOL to HOME

Looking for Locals

Talk with your family about whether amphibians might live near your home. Are there any ponds, streams, or lakes nearby? Do moist leaves cover the ground outside? Then, go outside to look for amphibians around your home. Be careful not to disturb any animals that you find. Were your predictions correct? Record your observations in your **science journal.**

ACTIVITY

Figure 7 | Salamanders

▼ The **marbled salamander** lives in damp places, such as under rocks or logs or among leaves.

▼ This **axolotl** is an unusual salamander. It keeps its gills and never leaves the water.

Is That a Fact!

Although caecilians are more closely related to frogs and salamanders than they are to snakes, the scientific name for caecilians, *Gymnophiona*, means "naked snakes."

ACTIVITY — BASIC

Visit the Zoo Encourage interested students to visit their local zoo's amphibian exhibit. Suggest that students take photographs of some of the animals and arrange them in an album with captions. Students could then present their albums to the class. **LS Visual**

English Language Learners

Figure 8   Frogs and Toads

▼ Frogs, such as this **bull frog,** have smooth, moist skin.

▼ Toads, such as this **Fowler's toad,** spend less time in water than frogs do. Their skin is drier and bumpier.

Close

Reteaching ——— BASIC

Poster Project Have students create a poster with captions that show how a tadpole changes into a frog. **LS** Visual   English Language Learners

Quiz ——————— GENERAL

1. Where do most amphibians start their lives? (in water)

2. What does the word amphibian actually mean? (double life)

3. What is the largest group of amphibians? (frogs and toads)

Alternative Assessment ——— GENERAL

Writing **Amphibian Inspiration** Have students compose a song or poem that accurately describes the life cycle of an amphibian of their choice. Students may want to write lyrics about the stages of metamorphosis to the melody of a familiar song. The familiar melody may help them remember the different stages of metamorphosis. **LS** Auditory

Frogs and Toads

About 90% of all amphibians are frogs or toads. Frogs and toads are very similar. In fact, toads are a type of frog. You can see a frog and a toad in **Figure 8.**

Frogs and toads live all over the world, except for very cold places. They are found in deserts and rain forests. They are highly adapted for life on land. Adults have strong leg muscles for jumping. They have well-developed ears for hearing and vocal cords for calling. They also have a long, sticky tongue. The tongue is attached to the front of the mouth so that it can be flipped out quickly to catch insects.

Singing Frogs

Frogs are well known for their nighttime choruses, but many frogs sing in the daytime, too. Like humans, they force air from their lungs across vocal cords in the throat to make sounds. But frogs have something we lack. A thin-walled sac of skin called the *vocal sac* surrounds their vocal cords. When frogs sing, the sac inflates with vibrating air. The frog in **Figure 9** has an inflated vocal sac. The sac increases the volume of the song so that the song can be heard over long distances.

Frogs sing to communicate messages that help in attracting mates and marking territories. Usually, frogs sing songs that they know without having to learn the songs. But some frogs can change the notes they sing. For example, to make its voice louder, one frog uses a tree's acoustics. It sits in a hole in a tree trunk and tries many notes until it finds the loudest one. Then, it sings this note repeatedly to be as loud as possible.

Figure 9 *Most frogs that sing are males. Their songs communicate messages to other frogs.*

✓ **Reading Check**   How does a frog use its vocal sac?

◉ INCLUSION Strategies

• *Hearing Impaired*   • *Learning Disabled*
• *Developmentally Delayed*

Many students can gain from additional visual aids. Draw a circle on the board (about 20 inch diameter). Create a pie chart that shows the relative numbers of amphibians that are caecilians (about 2%), salamanders (about 8%), and frogs and toads (about 90%). **LS** Visual   English Language Learners

Answer to Reading Check

Frogs use vocal sacs to sing, which helps frogs mark territories and attract mates.

Amphibians as Ecological Indicators

Amphibians are often called *ecological indicators*. In other words, unhealthy amphibians can be an early sign of changes in an ecosystem. When large numbers of amphibians begin to die or show deformities, a problem with the environment may exist. For example, the disappearance of the golden toad, shown in **Figure 10,** caused concern about the toad's environment.

Amphibians are ecological indicators because they are very sensitive to changes in their environment. Their thin skin absorbs any chemicals in the water or air. And their lungs take in chemicals from the air. Climate change is another factor that may affect amphibians. As ectotherms, their body temperature depends on the temperature of their environment.

Figure 10 *Golden toads were seen regularly in Costa Rica until 1989. After that year, they disappeared.*

SECTION Review

Summary

- Amphibians were the first vertebrates to live on land.
- Amphibians breathe by gulping air into the lungs and by absorbing oxygen through the skin.
- Amphibians start life in water, where they use gills to breathe. During metamorphosis, they lose their gills and grow legs that allow them to live on land as adults.
- The three groups of amphibians are caecilians, salamanders, and frogs and toads.
- Because amphibians are very sensitive to environmental changes, they are sometimes called *ecological indicators*.

Using Vocabulary

1. Use each of the following terms in a separate sentence: *lung, tadpole,* and *metamorphosis.*

Understanding Key Ideas

2. The first vertebrates to live on land were
   a. fish.
   b. dinosaurs.
   c. amphibians.
   d. reptiles.

3. Many adult amphibians breathe by using
   a. only their gills.
   b. only their lungs.
   c. only their skin.
   d. their lungs and skin.

4. Describe metamorphosis in amphibians.

5. Why do adult amphibians have to live near water or in a very wet habitat?

6. Why are amphibians sometimes called *ecological indicators*?

7. Name the three types of amphibians. How are they similar? How are they different?

8. How are frogs and toads similar? How are they different?

Math Skills

9. A certain toad species spends 2 months of its life as a tadpole and 3 years of its life as an adult. What percentage of its life is spent in the water? What percentage is spent on land?

Critical Thinking

10. **Analyzing Relationships** Describe the relationship between lungfishes and amphibians. How are these animals alike? How are they different?

11. **Evaluating Conclusions** Scientists think that climate change may have caused the golden toad to become extinct. What other causes are possible, and how could scientists test these ideas?

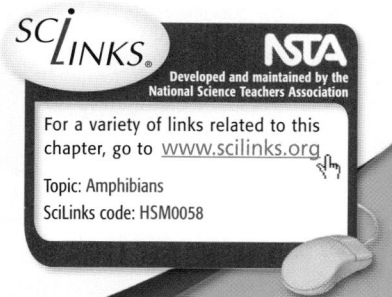

SCILINKS

NSTA
Developed and maintained by the
National Science Teachers Association

For a variety of links related to this chapter, go to www.scilinks.org

Topic: Amphibians
SciLinks code: HSM0058

CHAPTER RESOURCES

Chapter Resource File
- Section Quiz GENERAL
- Section Review GENERAL
- Vocabulary and Section Summary GENERAL

Answers to Section Review

1. Sample answer: Amphibians use lungs to get oxygen from air. A tadpole develops into a frog. Many amphibians develop through metamorphosis.

2. c

3. d

4. Sample answer: After fertilization of an egg, the embryo develops into a tadpole that lives in water. The tadpole loses its gills and develops lungs and legs and becomes an adult.

5. Sample answer: Amphibians must live near water because they have very thin, moist skin and can dehydrate easily. Also, their fertilized eggs must be kept wet or the embryo will die.

6. Sample answer: Amphibians are sensitive to changes in their environment because they have lungs, thin skin, and are ectothermic. For this reason, the health of amphibians may indicate the health of an ecosystem.

7. frogs and toads, salamanders, and caecilians; All three have thin, moist skin. Salamanders and frogs and toads have legs, but caecilians do not. Some caecilians have scales in their skin.

8. Sample answer: Frogs and toads both have strong leg muscles, ears, vocal cords, and a long tongue. Most frogs have smooth skin, and most toads have dry, bumpy skin.

9. percentage of life in the water: about 5.3%; percentage of life on land: about 94.7%

10. Sample answer: Lungfishes and amphibians are similar because they both have lungs. They are different because lungfish have fins while amphibians have legs.

11. Sample answer: Because amphibians are sensitive to chemicals in the air and water, it is possible that air or water pollution caused the golden toads to disappear. Scientists could check for pollution in the ecosystem where the golden toads lived to test this idea.

SECTION

3

Focus

Overview

This section introduces students to reptiles. Students will learn about the four major groups: turtles and tortoises, crocodiles and alligators, lizards and snakes, and tuataras. They will also learn about reptiles' physical characteristics and behaviors.

 Bellringer

Have students list three adjectives they associate with reptiles. After students read the section, have them list three new adjectives and then compare the lists.

Motivate

Discussion ——— GENERAL

Exploring Fears Ask students to list several of the most feared creatures on Earth. Likely, many of these animals will be reptiles, especially snakes. Ask students:

Why are reptiles so feared? Is their reputation deserved?

(While many reptiles are capable of killing humans—about 400 of the 1,600 species of snakes are poisonous—more people die from insect bites each year than from reptile bites. In the United States, only 5 to 15 deaths per year result from snake bites. However, worldwide, snakes are the second-deadliest animals—they kill as many as 40,000 people each year.)
LS Verbal

READING WARM-UP

Objectives
- Explain the traits that allow reptiles to live on land.
- Describe the characteristics of an amniotic egg.
- Name the four groups of modern reptiles, and give an example of each.

Terms to Learn
amniotic egg

READING STRATEGY

Brainstorming The key idea of this section is reptiles. Brainstorm words and phrases related to reptiles.

Reptiles

How are reptiles different from amphibians? Amphibians need to spend part of their lives in or near the water. But most reptiles can spend their whole lives on land.

Living on Land

About 35 million years after amphibians moved onto land, some of them began to change. They grew thick, dry skin that reduced water loss. Their legs changed and grew stronger, so they could walk easily. They also laid eggs that did not dry out on dry land. They had become reptiles, the first animals to live out of the water.

Many reptiles are now extinct. Dinosaurs that lived on land are the most well known prehistoric reptiles. But there were many other ancient reptiles. Some could swim, others could fly, and many were similar to reptiles that are alive today. A few living reptiles are shown in **Figure 1.**

Figure 1 *These animals are just a few of the many kinds of reptiles on Earth today.*

▲ Crocodile

▼ South American emerald boa

▲ Giant tortoise

CHAPTER RESOURCES

Chapter Resource File
- **Lesson Plan**
- **Directed Reading A** BASIC
- **Directed Reading B** SPECIAL NEEDS

Technology
 Transparencies
- Bellringer

Is That a Fact!

Turtles may migrate very long distances between their feeding grounds and their breeding grounds. For example, one group of green sea turtles feeds along the coast of Brazil and migrates to Ascension Island off the coast of Africa to breed. This trip is more than 1000 km (621 mi) each way!

Characteristics of Reptiles

Reptiles are well adapted for life on land. For example, all reptiles—even reptiles that live in water—have lungs to breathe air. Reptiles also have thick skin, use their surroundings to control their temperature, and have a special kind of egg that is laid on land.

Thick Skin

Thick, dry skin is a very important adaptation for life on land. This skin forms a watertight layer that keeps cells from losing water by evaporation. Unlike amphibians, most reptiles cannot breathe through their skin. Most reptiles, such as the snake in **Figure 2,** depend on only their lungs for oxygen.

Body Temperature

Nearly all reptiles are ectotherms. They cannot keep their bodies at a stable temperature. They are active when it is warm outside, and they slow down when it is cool. A few reptiles can get some heat from their own body cells. But most reptiles live in mild climates. They cannot handle the cold polar regions, where mammals and birds can thrive.

The Amazing Amniotic Egg

The most important adaptation to life on land is the amniotic (AM nee AHT ik) egg. An **amniotic egg** is an egg that holds fluid that protects the embryo. Reptiles, birds, and mammals have amniotic eggs. Reptiles' amniotic eggs have a shell, as shown in **Figure 3.** The amniotic eggs of birds and egg-laying mammals also have a shell. The shell protects the embryo and keeps the egg from drying out. A reptile's amniotic egg can be laid under rocks, in the ground, or even in the desert.

✓ **Reading Check** Why don't reptile eggs dry out on land? (*See the Appendix for answers to Reading Checks.*)

Figure 2 *Many people think snakes are slimy, but the skin of snakes and other reptiles is scaly and dry.*

amniotic egg a type of egg that is surrounded by a membrane, the amnion, and that in reptiles, birds, and egg-laying mammals contains a large amount of yolk and is surrounded by a shell

Amphibian eggs   Reptile eggs

Figure 3 *Compare these amphibian and reptile eggs. The reptile eggs are amniotic, but the amphibian eggs are not.*

Answer to Reading Check

Reptile eggs have a shell that keeps the embryo from drying out on land.

Teach

ACTIVITY ——————— BASIC

Organizing Reptiles Before students read about the types of reptiles, have them take a moment to try to put the following reptiles into their groups. Students should match the animal on the left with its closest relative on the right. They should check their answers after reading.

turtle	crocodile
snake	tortoise
alligator	lizard

(turtle—tortoise; snake—lizard; alligator—crocodile)

LS Visual

Using the Figure — BASIC

Eggs Encourage students to make comparisons between the reptile eggs and the amphibian eggs shown on the student page. (Amphibian eggs don't have shells and must be laid in water or moist ground. Reptile eggs do have shells and can be laid in the dry earth.)

Ask students how these facts might favor reptile reproduction over amphibian reproduction during a drought. (Dehydration would kill off amphibian embryos, but reptile embryos would be more likely to survive.)

LS Logical/Visual   English Language Learners

CONNECTION ACTiViTY
Math ——————— GENERAL

Temperature Conversions

Scientists use the Celsius scale when measuring temperature, while most Americans use the Fahrenheit scale in daily life. To convert Celsius to Fahrenheit, multiply the degrees Celsius by 1.8 (or 9/5) and add 32. Ask students to try the following exercises:

> Some reptiles are able to keep their body at 34°C even when the environment is cool. Convert 34°C to degrees Fahrenheit. (93.2°F)

Convert the following:

100°C	(212°F)	8°C	(46.4°F)
0°C	(32°F)	72°C	(161.6°F)
27°C	(80.6°F)	37°C	(98.6°F)

LS Logical

Answer to Reading Check

turtles and tortoises, crocodiles and alligators, lizards and snakes, and tuataras

Demonstration ——— GENERAL

Reptile Exhibit Invite a reptile expert from the local zoo or an amateur reptile enthusiast to bring several safe reptiles to the class for a hands-on presentation. Afterward, have students describe in their impressions of the reptiles, including the reptiles' physical characteristics and the way the reptiles felt to the touch. English Language Learners

LS Kinesthetic

Figure 4 An Amniotic Egg

The amniotic egg of a bird shares important features with reptilian amniotic eggs.

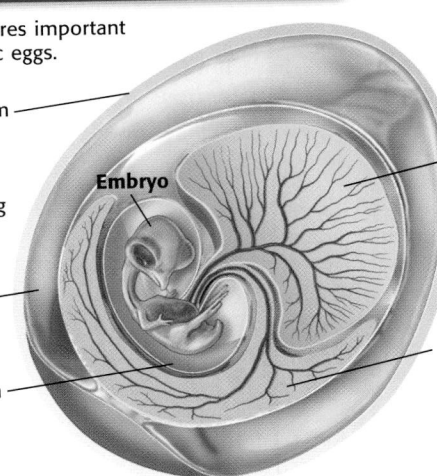

The **shell** protects the egg from damage and keeps the egg from drying out. The shell has small pores that allow oxygen to pass through to the growing embryo and allow carbon dioxide to be removed.

Embryo

The **yolk** gives the embryo a rich supply of food.

The **albumen** (al BYOO min) provides water and protein to the embryo.

The **allantois** (uh LAN toh is) stores the embryo's wastes. It also passes oxygen to the embryo from the pores in the shell.

The **amniotic sac** is filled with fluid. The amniotic fluid surrounds and protects the embryo.

Parts of the Amniotic Egg

The shell is just one important part of the amniotic egg of a reptile, bird, or egg-laying mammal. All of the parts of the amniotic egg are described in **Figure 4.** Together, these parts protect the embryo from predators, infections, and water loss.

Reptile Reproduction

Reptiles usually reproduce by internal fertilization. After the egg is fertilized inside the female, a shell forms around the egg. Then, the female lays the egg. Most reptiles lay their eggs in soil or sand. But a few reptiles do not lay their eggs. Instead, the embryos develop inside the mother, and the young are born live. In either case, the embryo develops into a tiny young reptile that looks like a small adult. Reptiles do not go through metamorphosis.

Kinds of Reptiles

The Age of Dinosaurs lasted from 300 million years ago until about 65 million years ago. During this time, most land vertebrates were reptiles. But today, about 8,000 species of living reptiles are known to exist. This number is much smaller than the number of reptile species that lived in the past. Turtles and tortoises, crocodiles and alligators, lizards and snakes, and tuataras are the four groups of reptiles that still live today. **Figure 5** shows one example of a modern reptile.

✓ **Reading Check** What are the four groups of living reptiles?

Figure 5 This panther chameleon is a modern lizard.

CHAPTER RESOURCES

Technology

 Transparencies
• An Amniotic Egg

Workbooks

 Math Skills for Science
• Using Temperature Scales GENERAL

Is That a Fact!

Like modern reptiles and birds, dinosaurs laid their eggs on land. There is a rich fossil record of these eggs. According to the National Geographic Society, eggs (some of which contain embryos) and nests have been discovered at over 199 sites. Most of the sites are in Asia. Eggs have been found in at least 39 locations in North America.

Figure 6 Turtles and Tortoises

▼ This **green sea turtle** has a streamlined shell that helps the turtle swim and turn rapidly.

▼ The **Texas tortoise** is one of four living species of tortoises native to North America.

Turtles and Tortoises

Turtles and tortoises are distantly related to other living reptiles. Generally, tortoises live on land, and turtles spend all or much of their lives in the water. However, even sea turtles come on land to lay their eggs. **Figure 6** shows a turtle and a tortoise.

The trait that makes turtles and tortoises so unique is their shell. The shell makes them slow and inflexible, so outrunning predators is unlikely. But many turtles can draw their head and limbs into the armorlike shell to protect themselves.

Crocodiles and Alligators

Crocodiles and alligators spend most of their time in the water. Their eyes and nostrils are on the top of their flat head. So, they can watch their surroundings while most of their body is hidden underwater. Hiding in this way gives them a great advantage over their prey. Crocodiles and alligators are meat eaters. They eat invertebrates, fish, turtles, birds, and mammals. **Figure 7** shows how to tell the difference between an alligator and a crocodile.

Figure 7 Crocodiles and Alligators

▼ A crocodile, such as this **American crocodile,** has a narrow head and a pointed snout.

▼ An alligator, such as this **American alligator,** has a broad head and a rounded snout.

SCIENCE HUMOR

Q: Why does a turtle live in a shell?

A: because it can't afford an apartment

MISCONCEPTION ALERT

Urban Alligator Legends Despite lingering urban legends, there has never been a confirmed sighting of an alligator living in the sewers of New York City.

CONNECTION to Real World — GENERAL

Gerontology Gerontologists—scientists who study aging in humans—are looking to the animal world to better understand the aging process. Why do some animals, such as turtles, live so long? Turtles not only live long, but also show almost no signs of aging until the very end. Tortoises grow throughout their lives, so there may be a slight size difference between tortoises of different ages. But other than this size difference, there is little different between a 30-year-old tortoise and a 70-year-old tortoise. Ask interested students to research the ages of the oldest reptiles ever known and then share their results with the class.
 Verbal

Cultural Awareness — GENERAL

Finding Water People of Indonesia, Sri Lanka, the Philippines, and Southeast Asia have learned that they can use the water monitor, a carnivorous lizard nearly 2 m long, to find water. If the lizard is seen walking about, it is almost always heading for water.

Research — ADVANCED

Writing **Comparing Carnivores** Have students investigate and write a report on the differences between the diet of an alligator and the diet of a similarly sized carnivorous mammal (a lion or tiger). Which of these animals eats more food? Why? (The mammal needs to eat more because mammals are endotherms that use a large amount of energy to keep themselves warm. Also, mammals are usually more active than reptiles, and this activity requires more energy.) 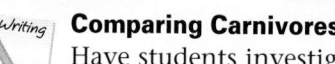 Logical

Close

Reteaching — BASIC

Lizards and the Tuatara Help students understand the difference between lizards and the tuatara by asking them to list two differences between lizards and tuataras. (Most lizards are active in the day, but tuataras are active at night. Also, tuataras do not have visible ear openings on the outside of the body.) **LS** Verbal

Quiz — GENERAL

1. How are crocodiles and alligators different? (Alligators have a broad head and a rounded snout. Crocodiles have a narrow head and a pointed snout.)

2. What kind of egg holds fluid that protects the embryo and is usually surrounded by a shell? (amniotic egg)

Alternative Assessment — GENERAL

Writing **Make a Menu** Have students imagine that they are one of the reptiles in this section. They also own a restaurant, and they are trying to attract other reptiles to their restaurant. Have students prepare accurate menus containing delectables that will surely please their thick-skinned, ectothermic customers. **LS** Verbal *PORTFOLIO*

Figure 8 Snakes

▼ **Cape cobras** are famous for their deadly venom. These aggressive snakes live in very dry areas.

▲ **Sinaloan milk snakes** are not poisonous, but they look a lot like poisonous coral snakes.

Snakes and Lizards

Today, the most common reptiles are snakes and lizards. Snakes are carnivores. They have special organs in the mouth that help them smell prey. When a snake flicks its tongue out, tiny molecules in the air stick to its tongue. The snake then touches its tongue to the organs in its mouth. The molecules on the tongue tell the snake what prey is nearby. Some snakes kill their prey by squeezing it until it suffocates. Other snakes have fangs for injecting venom. But no matter how snakes kill their prey, they eat it in the same way. Snakes can open their mouths very wide. So, snakes can eat animals and eggs by swallowing them whole. **Figure 8** shows two kinds of snakes.

Most lizards eat small insects and worms, but some lizards eat plants. One giant lizard—the Komodo dragon—eats deer, pigs, and goats! Lizards have a loosely connected lower jaw, but they do not swallow large prey whole. Lizards do have other eye-catching abilities, though. For example, many lizards can break their tails off to escape predators and then grow new tails. **Figure 9** shows two kinds of lizards.

Figure 9 Lizards

The **frilled lizard** ▶ puffs out its frills to look threatening.

◀ The **thorny devil** is a harmless lizard that eats ants.

Homework — ADVANCED

Writing **Reporting on Reptiles** Have students choose their favorite reptile and write a brief report about the animal. Students should include the following information: size, appearance, range, habitat, diet, adaptations to its particular way of life, relationship to people, and whether or not it is endangered. **LS** Verbal

Tuataras

Tuataras (TOO uh TAH ruhs) live on only a few islands off the coast of New Zealand. **Figure 10** shows a tuatara in the wild. Tuataras look similar to lizards and can grow to be about 60 cm long.

Although tuataras look like lizards, the two reptiles are classified in different groups. Unlike many lizards, tuataras do not have visible ear openings on the outside of the body. Also, unlike many reptiles, tuataras are most active when the temperature is low. During the day, tuataras rest and absorb sunlight. At night, they search for food.

Reading Check Name two unique traits of tuataras.

Figure 10 *Tuataras have survived without changing for about 150 million years.*

SECTION Review

Summary

- Reptiles have thick, scaly skin that protects them from drying out. They also have lungs, and they depend on their surroundings to control their body temperature.
- A tough shell keeps the amniotic egg of a reptile from drying out and protects the embryo.
- Reptiles reproduce by internal fertilization.
- There are four groups of modern reptiles. The groups are: turtles and tortoises, crocodiles and alligators, lizards and snakes, and tuataras.

Using Vocabulary

1. In your own words, write a definition for the term *amniotic egg*.

Understanding Key Ideas

2. Reptiles are well adapted to living on land because they
   a. have thick, scaly skin.
   b. have lungs.
   c. lay amniotic eggs.
   d. All of the above

3. A reptile can lay its egg on land because
   a. the egg's shell prevents fertilization.
   b. the egg's shell keeps moisture inside the egg.
   c. the egg's shell keeps carbon dioxide inside the egg.
   d. the egg's shell allows water to leave the egg.

4. Name three ways that an amniotic egg protects reptile embryos.

5. Explain how most reptiles reproduce.

6. Name the four groups of modern reptiles, and give an example of each kind.

7. What special adaptations do snakes have for eating?

Math Skills

8. Suppose that a sea turtle lays 104 eggs. If 50% of the hatchlings reach the ocean alive and 25% of those survivors reach adulthood, how many adults result from the eggs?

Critical Thinking

9. **Applying Concepts** Mammals give birth to live young. The embryo develops inside the female's body. Which parts of a reptilian amniotic egg could a mammal do without? Explain.

10. **Analyzing Ideas** Rattlesnakes can't see well, but they can detect temperature changes of three-thousandths of a degree Celsius. How could this ability be useful to the snakes?

Developed and maintained by the National Science Teachers Association

For a variety of links related to this chapter, go to www.scilinks.org

Topic: Reptiles
SciLinks code: HSM1299

Answer to Reading Check

Tuataras are most active at low temperatures, and they have no visible ear openings on the outside of the body.

Answers to Section Review

1. Sample answer: An amniotic egg is an egg that holds fluid that protects the embryo.

2. d

3. b

4. The amniotic egg protects embryos from predators, infections, and water loss.

5. Most reptiles reproduce sexually by internal fertilization. After fertilization, most females lay amniotic eggs.

6. Sample answer: turtles and tortoises, green sea turtle; crocodiles and alligators, american alligator; snakes and lizards, cape cobra; and tuataras, the tuatara

7. Snakes can open their mouths wide and swallow their prey whole. They also have special organs in the mouth that help them smell prey. Some can squeeze prey tightly, and some have fangs that inject venom.

8. 13 adult turtles
   ($104 \times 0.5 = 52$; $52 \times 0.25 = 13$)

9. Sample answer: Most mammals do not need the shell of the amniotic egg because their egg does not need to be protected from the outside environment. Students might also realize that mammals do not need the yolk because mammal embryos develop inside the mother and receive nutrients directly from her body.

10. Sample answer: Rattlesnakes could use the ability to detect heat changes as they search for prey. They could sense a change in temperature when prey is near because of the prey's body heat.

Floating a Pipe Fish

Teacher's Notes

Time Required
One 45-minute class period

Lab Ratings

EASY ——————————→ HARD

Teacher Prep 🧪🧪
Student Set-Up 🧪🧪
Concept Level 🧪
Clean Up 🧪

MATERIALS

The materials listed on the student page are enough for 1 or 2 students. PVC pipe (3/4 in.) is available at hardware stores and is relatively inexpensive. The pieces should be cut in advance. If your school has a shop or industrial arts classroom, perhaps you could get the pieces cut there. The hardware store may cut them for you. For water containers, students may use anything that is at least 15 cm deep. Helium-quality party balloons will work best with this activity. Be sure that the corks fit snugly in the neck of the balloons.

Safety Caution

Before you give students the pieces of PVC pipe, make sure that the edges are not jagged or sharp. Also, remind students to review all safety cautions and icons before beginning this lab activity.

Christopher Wood
Western Rockingham Middle School
Madison, North Carolina

Floating a Pipe Fish

Bony fishes control how deep or shallow they swim by using a special structure called a *swim bladder*. As gases are absorbed and released by the swim bladder, the fish's body rises or sinks in the water. In this activity, you will make a model of a fish that has a swim bladder. Your challenge will be to make the fish rest in one place, without rising or sinking, halfway between the top of the water and the bottom of the container. You will probably need to do several trials and a lot of observing and analyzing.

OBJECTIVES

Make a model of a fish that has a swim bladder.

Describe how swim bladders help fish maintain buoyancy.

MATERIALS

- balloon, slender
- container for water at least 15 cm deep
- cork, small
- PVC pipe, 12 cm in length, 3/4 in. diameter
- rubber band
- water

SAFETY

Ask a Question

1 Think of a question about the amount of gases needed to keep a pipe fish model resting halfway between the top of the water and the bottom of the container.

Form a Hypothesis

2 Formulate a testable hypothesis that answers your question. Estimate how much air you will need in the balloon so that your pipe fish will come to rest halfway between the top of the water and the bottom of the container. Will you need to inflate the balloon halfway, a small amount, or all the way?

CHAPTER RESOURCES

Chapter Resource File
- Datasheet for Chapter Lab
- Lab Notes and Answers

Technology
 Classroom Videos
- Lab Video

- A Prince of a Frog

Test the Hypothesis

③ Inflate your balloon. Hold the neck of the balloon so that no air escapes, and push the cork into the end of the balloon. If the cork is properly placed, no air should leak out when the balloon is held underwater.

④ Place your swim bladder inside the pipe, and place a rubber band along the pipe as shown. The rubber band will keep the swim bladder from coming out of either end of the pipe.

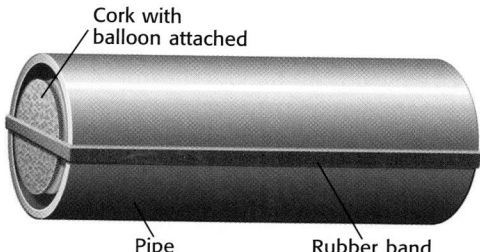

Cork with balloon attached

Pipe

Rubber band

⑤ Place your pipe fish in the water, and note where the fish rests without sinking or rising. Record your observations.

⑥ If the pipe fish does not rest at the halfway point, take it out of the water, adjust the amount of air in the balloon, and try again.

⑦ You can release small amounts of air from the bladder by carefully lifting the neck of the balloon away from the cork. You can add more air by removing the cork and blowing more air into the balloon. Keep adjusting and testing until your fish rests, without sinking or rising, halfway between the bottom of the container and the top of the water.

Analyze the Results

① **Analyzing Results** Was the estimate you made in your hypothesis the correct amount of air your balloon needed to rest at the halfway point? Explain your answer.

② **Examining Data** Consider the length and volume of the entire pipe fish. How much air was needed to make the fish rest at the correct place? State your answer as a proportion or percentage. (Remember that the volume of a cylinder is equal to the height or length of the cylinder multiplied by the area of its base.)

③ **Evaluating Data** Analyze the information you gathered in this activity to explain how the structure of a fish's swim bladder complements its function. What are some limitations to your model?

Draw Conclusions

④ **Interpreting Information** Some fast-swimming fishes, such as sharks, and marine mammals, such as whales and dolphins, do not have a swim bladder. Do research at a library or on the Internet to find out how these animals keep from sinking to the bottom of the ocean. Can you find any reasons why a swim bladder would be helpful to them? How could a swim bladder cause problems for these animals?

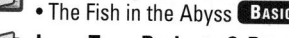
Analyze the Results

1. Answers may vary. Students may tend to inflate the balloon too much, causing the pipe to float on the surface. They may be surprised to find out how little air is needed in the balloon to make it rest in the middle of the water column. Remind students that the cork has some buoyancy of its own. You may want to substitute something less buoyant for the cork.

2. Answers may vary. Filling less than 10% of the internal volume of the pipe with air will make the pipe rest in the middle of the water column.

3. Sample answer: The structure of a fish's swim bladder complements its function because it can maintain an amount of gases that keeps the fish from sinking or floating. A few limitations of this model are the fact that the cork has some buoyancy of its own, and the fact that the PVC pipe is denser than a real fish.

Draw Conclusions

4. Sample answer: Many sharks and marine mammals, such as dolphins and whales, must swim almost constantly to keep from sinking to the bottom. Also, sharks have oily livers that help keep them from sinking. However, a swim bladder may not be helpful for these animals. Dolphins and whales must come to the surface frequently to breathe. Many sharks must constantly move or lie in moving water to keep water moving past their gills. These animals do not rest in one place for long, as bony fishes do. Also, sharks and marine mammals are able to dive to great depths because they don't have a swim bladder that would rupture under pressure.

Assignment Guide

SECTION	QUESTIONS
1	3–6, 9, 11, 15, 21–22, 24–26
2	8, 10, 14, 16–17, 20
3	12–13, 19, 23
1 and 2	2
2 and 3	7
1, 2, and 3	1, 18

ANSWERS

Using Key Terms

1. Sample answer: Metamorphosis is the process of an animal changing form as it becomes an adult. An amniotic egg is an egg that protects the embryo and keeps it from drying out. A vertebrate is an animal that has a backbone.

2. Sample answer: A tadpole loses its gills when it forms lungs and becomes an adult.

3. Endotherms and ectotherms heat their bodies differently. Endotherms get heat from cell activity and ectotherms usually get heat from the environment.

4. The swim bladder and the lateral line are both parts of some fishes, but these parts have different functions. The swim bladder helps bony fishes maintain buoyancy, and the lateral line helps fishes sense their surroundings.

Understanding Key Ideas

5. b
6. b
7. a
8. b
9. a

USING KEY TERMS

1. In your own words, write a definition for each of the following terms: *metamorphosis*, *amniotic egg*, and *vertebrate*.

2. Use the following terms in the same sentence: *lung*, *gills*, and *tadpole*.

For each pair of terms, explain how the meanings of the terms differ.

3. *endotherm* and *ectotherm*

4. *swim bladder* and *lateral line*

UNDERSTANDING KEY IDEAS

Multiple Choice

5. Which of the following structures is not present in some chordates?
   a. a tail
   b. a backbone
   c. a notochord
   d. a hollow nerve cord

6. Which fishes do not have jaws?
   a. sharks, skates, and rays
   b. hagfish and lampreys
   c. bony fishes
   d. None of the above

7. Both amphibians and reptiles
   a. have lungs.
   b. have gills.
   c. breathe only through their skin.
   d. have amniotic eggs.

8. Metamorphosis occurs in
   a. fishes and amphibians.
   b. amphibians.
   c. fishes, amphibians, and reptiles.
   d. amphibians and reptiles.

9. Both bony fishes and cartilaginous fishes have
   a. fins.
   b. an oily liver.
   c. a swim bladder.
   d. skeletons made of bone.

Short Answer

10. How do amphibians breathe?

11. What characteristics allow fishes to live in the water?

12. What characteristics allow reptiles to live on land?

13. How does a reptile embryo in an amniotic egg get oxygen?

14. Describe the stages of metamorphosis in a frog.

15. What two things are present in all vertebrates but not in some chordates?

16. Describe the three kinds of amphibians.

17. Explain why amphibians can be effective ecological indicators.

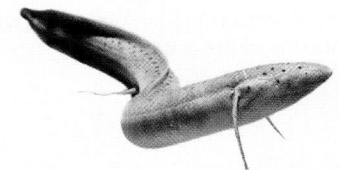

---

10. Amphibians may breathe through lungs, skin, and gills.

11. Fish have gills to get oxygen from the water and fins and tails that help them swim.

12. Reptiles have thick skin to keep moisture in the body, lungs to get oxygen from air, and amniotic eggs with shells to keep moisture in the egg.

13. Air passes through pores in the shell.

14. A tadpole hatches from an egg. It grows legs and then the tail and gills disappear. It begins to use lungs as it becomes an adult.

15. a backbone and a skull

16. Salamanders have a long tail and four legs. Caecilians are legless and some have bony scales in the skin. Adult frogs and toads have four legs and no tail.

17. Amphibians are sensitive to environmental change because they are ectotherms and because they have thin skin and lungs.

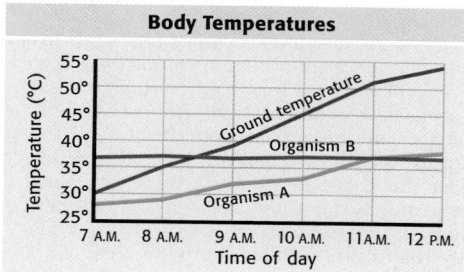

CRITICAL THINKING

18 Concept Mapping Use the following terms to create a concept map: *dinosaur, turtle, reptiles, amphibians, fishes, shark, salamander,* and *vertebrates*.

19 Applying Concepts If the air temperature outside is 43°C and the ideal body temperature of a lizard is 38°C, would you most likely find that lizard in the sun or in the shade? Explain your answer.

20 Identifying Relationships Describe three characteristics of amphibian skin. How do amphibians use their skin? How does the structure of amphibian skin relate to its function?

21 Making Inferences Suppose that you have found an animal that has a backbone and gills, but the animal does not seem to have a notochord. Is the animal a chordate? How can you be sure of your answer?

22 Analyzing Processes If you found a shark that lacks the muscles needed to pump water over its gills, what would that information tell you about how the shark lives?

23 Forming Hypotheses If you found a reptile that you did not recognize, what questions would you need to ask to determine which of the four reptile groups the reptile belongs to? Explain how you could form a hypothesis about the reptile's group based on the answers to these questions.

INTERPRETING GRAPHICS

The graph below shows body temperatures of two organisms and the ground temperature of their environment. Use the graph to answer the questions that follow.

24 How do the body temperatures of organism A and organism B change as the ground temperature changes?

25 Which of these organisms is most likely an ectotherm? Explain your answer.

26 Which of these organisms is most likely an endotherm? Explain your answer.

20. Amphibian skin is thin, smooth, and moist. These characteristics allow many amphibians to absorb oxygen and water through their skin.

21. yes; Animals with a backbone are vertebrates, and all vertebrates are chordates. The notochord is replaced by the backbone as a vertebrate develops.

22. Sample answer: If the shark cannot pump water over its gills, the shark would have to keep moving through the water constantly to ensure that water flowed over the gills.

23. Sample answer: I would ask: Does it have a shell? Does it have legs? How much time does it spend in water? What does it eat? When is it active? If the animal is active at night, it's a tuatara. If the animal has a shell, it's a turtle or a tortoise. If the animal has no legs, it's probably a snake. If the animal spends most of its time near water, has legs, has no shell, and eats meat it's probably a crocodile or alligator. If the animal has legs, has no shell, and spends its time on land it's probably a lizard.

Interpreting Graphics

24. The body temperature of organism A increases as ground temperature increases. The body temperature of organism B does not change with ground temperature. The graph shows a slight change in the body temperature of organism B, but this change is not related to the ground temperature.

25. Organism A is probably an ectotherm. Its body temperature seems to depend on the temperature of the environment.

26. Organism B is probably an endotherm. Its body temperature stays constant though the environmental temperature changes.

Critical Thinking

18. 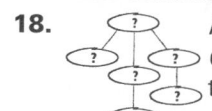 An answer to this exercise can be found at the end of the book.

19. The lizard would be in the shade. Because it is an ectotherm, its body temperature will respond to the environmental temperature. Because the air temperature is higher than the lizard's normal body temperature, the lizard will try to find cool shade.

Standardized Test Preparation

Teacher's Note

To provide practice under more realistic testing conditions, give students 20 minutes to answer all of the questions in this Standardized Test Preparation.

MISCONCEPTION ALERT

Answers to the standardized test preparation can help you identify student misconceptions and misunderstandings.

READING

Passage 1

1. B

2. H

3. B

✚ TEST DOCTOR

Question 3: Some students may think A is the answer because the passage focused on the fishes that can heat parts of their bodies. However, few fishes can heat their bodies. Some students may think C is the answer because they remember that most fishes do not heat part of their bodies. However, there are some fishes that do heat parts of their bodies. The correct answer, B, can be found in the seventh sentence: "For this reason, some fishes, such as swordfish, marlin, and sailfish, have adaptations that let the fishes heat only a few body parts."

READING

Read each of the passages below. Then, answer the questions that follow each passage.

Passage 1 Only a few kinds of fishes are endotherms. These fishes depend on their environment for most of their body heat but can heat parts of their bodies by internal cell activity. Because they can produce heat within their bodies, endothermic fishes can hunt for prey in extremely chilly water. As a result, they face limited competition with other fishes because few species of fishes can live in cold areas. Yet endothermic fishes pay a high price for their ability to <u>inhabit</u> very cold areas. Producing heat by internal cell activity uses a lot of energy. For this reason, some fishes, such as swordfish, marlin, and sailfish, have adaptations that let the fishes heat only a few body parts. These fishes warm only their eyes and brain. Heating just these parts of the body uses less energy than heating the entire body does.

1. In this passage, what does *inhabit* mean?

  A to use energy in
  B to live in
  C to heat up
  D to eat in

2. Which of the following statements is a fact according to the passage?

  F Tuna always live in very cold areas.
  G Most prey live in extremely chilly water.
  H Some fishes that heat parts of their body can hunt for prey in cold water.
  I The eyes and the brain are the most important parts of a fish's body.

3. Which fishes can heat certain parts of their bodies and hunt in extremely cold waters?

  A most fishes
  B swordfish, marlin, and sailfish
  C no fishes
  D tropical fishes

Passage 2 Fishes are quicker and much more <u>maneuverable</u> than most ships and submarines. So, why aren't ships and submarines built more like fishes—with tails that flap back and forth? This question caught the attention of some scientists at MIT, and they decided to build a robot model of a bluefin tuna. This robot fish is 124 cm long. It contains six motors and has a skeleton made of aluminum ribs and hinges. These scientists think that if ships were designed more like the bodies of fishes, the ships would use much less energy than they currently use. If the new design does require less energy—and thus less fuel—the ships will save money.

1. According to the passage, what is one reason that scientists are designing a robot model of a fish?

  A Designing ships to work more like fishes' bodies might save energy.
  B Fishes' bodies do not use much energy.
  C Bluefin tuna have tails that move back and forth.
  D Designing ships to work more like fishes' bodies could reduce ocean pollution levels.

2. What does *maneuverable* probably mean?

  F able to move easily
  G able to move like a robot
  H made of aluminum
  I fuel efficient

3. Which of the following statements is a fact according to the passage?

  A Fueling ships is very expensive.
  B Some MIT scientists built a robot fish.
  C Designing a ship that moves like a fish will save money.
  D Fishes are 124 cm long.

Passage 2

1. A

2. F

3. B

✚ TEST DOCTOR

Question 3: Students may chose A because the passage implies that fuel is expensive, but this statement is not given as a fact in the passage. The passage also implies that ships built like fishes will save money, but this is not a fact, either. And while the passage does mention that a robot fish is 124 cm long, that fact does not apply to all fishes. The correct answer, B, can be found in the third sentence: "This question caught the imagination of some scientists at MIT, and they decided to build a robot model of a bluefin tuna."

The chart below shows the kinds of amphibians that are threatened or endangered in the United States. Use the chart below to answer the questions that follow.

Threatened and Endangered Amphibian Species in the United States

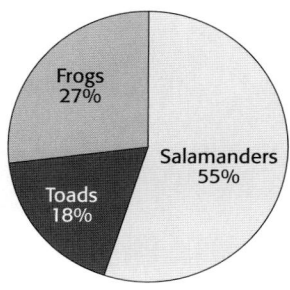

Source: U.S. Fish and Wildlife Service.

1. Which amphibian group has the most threatened and endangered species in the United States?

A frogs

B salamanders

C toads

D caecilians

2. If the total number of threatened and endangered amphibian species in the United States is 22, how many species of salamanders are threatened or endangered?

F 4

G 6

H 12

I 22

3. If the total number of threatened and endangered amphibian species in the United States is 22, how many more species of salamanders are threatened or endangered than species of frogs and toads?

A 12

B 10

C 6

D 2

4. Which of the following statements about the pie chart is true?

F The chart does not have any information about amphibians outside of the United States.

G The chart shows that amphibians outside of the United States are also endangered and threatened.

H The chart shows that frogs are more sensitive to environmental pollution than toads are.

I The chart shows that amphibians are ecological indicators.

MATH

Read each question below, and choose the best answer.

1. Suppose that a snake eats a mouse that has one-third more mass than the snake does. If the snake has a mass of 4.2 kg, what is the mass of the mouse?

A 1.4 kg

B 2.8 kg

C 4.2 kg

D 5.6 kg

2. One year, there were 2,000 salamanders in a state park. If the population decreased by 8% each year for 3 years, what would the salamander population be after the 3-year period?

F 1,520 salamanders

G 1,557 salamanders

H 1,840 salamanders

I 1,898 salamanders

3. What is the volume of a rectangular fish tank that is 1 m wide, 2 m long, and 1.5 m tall?

A 3 m²

B 3 m³

C 4.5 m

D 4.5 m³

1. B

2. H

3. D

4. F

✚ TEST DOCTOR

Question 2: The correct answer, H, is figured by finding 55% of 22. Students who choose answer F or G may have mistakenly found the number of frogs or toads instead of salamanders.

MATH

1. D

2. G

3. B

✚ TEST DOCTOR

Question 1: The correct answer, D, is found by finding a third of the snake's mass (1.4 kg) and adding it to the snake's mass (1.4 kg + 4.2 kg) to get 5.6 kg. Students who choose answer A may have found one third the mass of the snake and then forgot to finish the question by finding the mass of the mouse. Students who choose answer B may have subtracted one third of the snake's mass rather than adding it to find the mouse's mass. Students who have trouble with this problem may find it helpful to read through each sentence carefully and write down relevant information as it comes up.

Question 2: To find the correct answer, G, students will need to round the numbers of individual salamanders in each generation's population.

Standardized Test Preparation

CHAPTER RESOURCES

Chapter Resource File

 • Standardized Test Preparation GENERAL

State Resources

 For specific resources for your state, visit **go.hrw.com** and type in the keyword **HSMSTR**.

Weird Science

Discussion — ADVANCED

Tell students that one adaptation that allows fish to eat fruit is large, flat molars. Then ask them if they know what other animals have flat molars, and what those animals usually eat.

(Rodents such as mice and squirrels have flat molars. They eat seeds and grass. Rabbits and hoofed animals, such as deer and cows, also have flat molars, and they eat grass and other plants. Omnivores, such as bears, have molars like humans. They eat fruit, seeds, plants, and some meat.)

Scientific Discoveries

ACTiViTy — GENERAL

Obtain or borrow several animal skulls from a fellow teacher, local nature center, natural history museum, or biological supply catalog. The skulls may include mammals, reptiles, and birds. Have students work in groups to sketch the skulls and then attempt to sketch and identify the entire animal. They will need to imagine muscle, fur, scales, feathers, and other features to complete the picture. Students should pay close attention to the teeth, and attempt to identify each animal's diet. Explain that this activity is similar to the process of identifying new fossils.

Science in Action

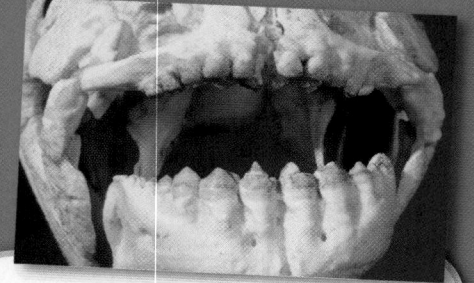

Weird Science

Fish That Eat Fruit

Have you ever thought about fish teeth? You probably know what shark teeth look like. So, you shouldn't be surprised that fish teeth are usually very different from your own teeth. But take a look at the fish shown above. This fish is *frugivorous* (froo JIV uh ruhs), which means that it eats fruit. Some frugivorous fishes live in the Amazon River in Brazil. Parts of the Amazon River basin flood for much of the year, which causes the water level to rise and spread under fruit trees. Fruit falls from the trees into the water, so these fishes have evolved to eat fruit. Eating fruit requires teeth that can bite and chew, just like human teeth. So, these fishes' teeth have evolved into a form that is similar to human teeth!

Math ACTiViTy

Suppose the water level in a river rose 8 m when it was flooded. At this time, 4 meters of a certain tree are above water. This tree is 16 m tall. What was the original depth of the river before it was flooded?

Scientific Discoveries

Giant Crocodiles

Have you ever watched a crocodile at a zoo or on TV? Even when crocodiles are resting and not moving, we instinctively know to be wary of them. Most crocodiles today are about 3.5 m long. But Paul Sereno recently discovered a fossil in the Sahara that shows how big crocodiles used to be. The fossil crocodile that Sereno found is 12 m—about the length of seven adult humans lying head to toe! This crocodile lived 110 million years ago. Sereno's find answered many questions raised by other crocodile fossils that had been found before. Now scientists can estimate the animal's huge size with accuracy.

Language Arts ACTiViTy

WRITING SKILL Imagine that you discovered an animal living today that was 4 times the size of an average organism of that species. For example, imagine discovering a rattlesnake that was 4 times the size of an average rattlesnake. Write a story about your discovery, and include your ideas about how size affected the life of the organism.

Answers to Math Activity

The original depth of the river equals the tree's height (16m) minus the height above water (4m) minus the amount the water rose (8m). So, the original depth of the river was 4 m.

Answers to Language Arts Activity

Students' stories will vary. They should include a discussion of how the animal's large size affects its life.

Dagmar Werner

Raising Iguanas At the Carara Biological Preserve in Costa Rica, thousands of iguana eggs sit just below the surface of the Earth in sun-heated incubators. Why would anyone bother to incubate thousands of iguana eggs? Dr. Dagmar Werner leads this project in an attempt to restore an iguana population that has been severely reduced in the past several decades. The lizards have suffered from the effects of hunting, pollution, and habitat destruction by people who clear the rain forest for farming.

Dr. Werner combined her captive-breeding program at the preserve with an education program that shows farmers that there is more than one way to make a profit from the rain forest. She encourages local farmers to raise iguanas, which can be released into the wild or sold for food, instead of raising cattle (and cutting down the rain forest to do so). Known as the "chicken of the trees," the iguana has been a favored source of meat among native rain-forest inhabitants for thousands of years. Farmers not only profit from the sale of iguana meat but also produce iguana leather and other handicrafts.

According to Dr. Werner, "Many locals have never thought of wild animals as creatures that must be protected in order to survive. That's why so many go extinct." To get her message across, Dr. Werner has established an organization that sponsors festivals and education seminars in local communities. These activities promote the traditional appeal of the iguana, increase civic pride in the animal, and heighten awareness about the iguana's economic importance.

Social Studies ACTIVITY

WRITING SKILL Dr. Werner's project helps the iguanas because it takes hunting pressure off the iguana population. But it also helps farmers by increasing their income and preventing habitat destruction. Can you think of a project that could help both the people and the environment in your own community? Write a three-paragraph description of an environmental project that could work for your community.

.com

To learn more about these Science in Action topics, visit go.hrw.com and type in the keyword HL5VR1F.

Current Science

Check out Current Science® articles related to this chapter by visiting go.hrw.com. Just type in the keyword HL5CS16.

Answers to Social Studies Activity
Students' projects may vary. The projects should be related to the students' community needs.

The green iguana (*Iguana iguana*) is found throughout Central America. In some parts of its habitat, it has been hunted to extinction. The green iguana has been used for centuries as a food source. It is called *chicken of the trees,* or *gallina de palo* in Spanish. The name comes from the fact that iguanas have a white meat that tastes like chicken. The demand for iguanas and iguana eggs for food has caused them to nearly become extinct.

Releasing iguanas into the wild is a key part of Dr. Werner's program. Attempting to raise the iguanas to a marketable size in captivity would be a costly process because iguanas constantly need food and require large habitats. By releasing the iguanas into the wild, much of the expense is reduced. However, to increase the productivity of the iguanas, feeding stations are set up in the jungle.

By supplying extra food for the iguanas—rice, meat, bone, fish meal, papayas, mangos, bananas, avocados, and a variety of leaves and flowers—many more iguanas can grow to maturity than could be naturally supported by the habitat. In fact, scientists estimate that 6 to 10 times more iguanas can be raised by supplied food.

17 Birds and Mammals
Chapter Planning Guide

Compression guide:
To shorten instruction because of time limitations, omit Sections 2, 4, and 5.

OBJECTIVES	LABS, DEMONSTRATIONS, AND ACTIVITIES	TECHNOLOGY RESOURCES
PACING • 135 min pp. 440–447 **Chapter Opener**	SE **Start-up Activity**, p. 441 GENERAL	OSP **Parent Letter** ■ GENERAL CD **Student Edition on CD-ROM** CD **Guided Reading Audio CD** ■ TR **Chapter Starter Transparency*** VID **Brain Food Video Quiz**
Section 1 Characteristics of Birds • Describe two kinds of feathers. • Describe how a bird's diet, breathing, muscles, and skeleton help it fly. • Explain how lift works. • Describe how birds raise their young.	TE **Activity** Light as a Feather, p. 442 GENERAL TE **Group Activity** Constructing Feathers, p. 443 BASIC TE **Demonstration** Observing Bird Bones, p. 445 ◆ GENERAL TE **Activity** Jump Up and Down, p. 445 GENERAL SE **Model-Making Lab** What? No Dentist Bills?, p. 468 ◆ GENERAL CRF **Datasheet for Chapter Lab***	CRF **Lesson Plans*** TR **Bellringer Transparency*** TR **The Digestive System of a Bird*** TR **Flight Adaptations of Birds: A*** TR **Flight Adaptations of Birds: B*** TR *LINK TO PHYSICAL SCIENCE* **Wing Design and Lift*** VID **Lab Videos for Life Science**
PACING • 45 min pp. 448–451 **Section 2 Kinds of Birds** • Identify the differences between flightless birds, water birds, perching birds, and birds of prey.	TE **Activity** Raptors, p. 450 GENERAL LB **Labs You Can Eat** Why Birds of a Beak Eat Together* GENERAL SE **Science in Action** Math, Social Studies, and Language Arts Activities, pp. 474–75 GENERAL	CRF **Lesson Plans*** TR **Bellringer Transparency*** SE **Internet Activity**, p. 449 GENERAL CRF **SciLinks Activity*** GENERAL
PACING • 45 min pp. 452–455 **Section 3 Characteristics of Mammals** • Explain how early mammals lived. • Describe seven common characteristics of mammals.	SE **Quick Lab** Diaphragm Demo, p. 453 GENERAL CRF **Datasheet for Quick Lab*** TE **Activity** Offspring Number, p. 453 GENERAL TE **Activity** Comparing Skulls, p. 454 ◆ BASIC	CRF **Lesson Plans*** TR **Bellringer Transparency***
PACING • 45 min pp. 456–463 **Section 4 Placental Mammals** • Explain how placental mammals develop. • Give an example of each type of placental mammal.	TE **Connection Activity** Archeology, p. 456 GENERAL TE **Activity** Comparing Footprints, p. 459 ADVANCED TE **Connection Activity** Real Life, p. 460 GENERAL SE **Connection to Language Arts** Funky Monkey, p. 462 GENERAL LB **Long-Term Projects & Research Ideas** Look Who's Coming to Dinner* ADVANCED	CRF **Lesson Plans*** TR **Bellringer Transparency***
PACING • 45 min pp. 464–467 **Section 5 Monotremes and Marsupials** • Describe the difference between monotremes and marsupials. • Name the two kinds of monotremes. • Give three examples of marsupials. • Explain why many marsupials are endangered or extinct.	TE **Group Activity** Amphibious Mammals, p. 464 GENERAL TE **Connection Activity** Anthropology, p. 464 ADVANCED SE **Connection to Environmental Science** Pouches in Peril, p. 465 GENERAL TE **Connection Activity** Math, p. 467 GENERAL	CRF **Lesson Plans*** TR **Bellringer Transparency***

PACING • 90 min

CHAPTER REVIEW, ASSESSMENT, AND STANDARDIZED TEST PREPARATION

CRF **Vocabulary Activity*** GENERAL
SE **Chapter Review**, pp. 470–471 GENERAL
CRF **Chapter Review*** ■ GENERAL
CRF **Chapter Tests A*** ■ GENERAL, **B*** ADVANCED, **C*** SPECIAL NEEDS
SE **Standardized Test Preparation**, pp. 472–473 GENERAL
CRF **Standardized Test Preparation*** GENERAL
CRF **Performance-Based Assessment*** GENERAL
OSP **Test Generator** GENERAL
CRF **Test Item Listing*** GENERAL

Online and Technology Resources

Visit **go.hrw.com** for a variety of free resources related to this textbook. Enter the keyword **HL5VR2.**

Holt Online Learning

Students can access interactive problem-solving help and active visual concept development with the *Holt Science and Technology* Online Edition available at **www.hrw.com.**

Guided Reading Audio CD
Also in Spanish

A direct reading of each chapter for auditory learners, reluctant readers, and Spanish-speaking students.

Science Tutor CD-ROM

Excellent for remediation and test practice.

SKILLS DEVELOPMENT RESOURCES	SECTION REVIEW AND ASSESSMENT	STANDARDS CORRELATIONS
SE Pre-Reading Activity, p. 440 GENERAL **OSP Science Puzzlers, Twisters & Teasers*** GENERAL		National Science Education Standards UCP 2; SAI 1; ST 2; LS 1a, 3c, 5b
CRF Directed Reading A* ■ BASIC, **B*** SPECIAL NEEDS **CRF Vocabulary and Section Summary*** ■ GENERAL **SE Reading Strategy** Prediction Guide, p. 442 GENERAL **TE Reading Strategy** Prediction Guide, p. 444 GENERAL **TE Inclusion Strategies**, p. 444 **SE Math Practice** Flying Far, p. 445 GENERAL **TE Connection to Physical Science** Wing Design, p. 446 ADVANCED **CRF Critical Thinking** A Puzzling Piece of Paleontology* ADVANCED	**SE Reading Checks**, pp. 443, 444, 446 GENERAL **TE Homework**, p. 442 BASIC **TE Homework**, p. 445 GENERAL **TE Reteaching**, p. 446 BASIC **TE Quiz**, p. 446 GENERAL **TE Alternative Assessment**, p. 446 ADVANCED **SE Section Review,*** p. 447 ■ GENERAL **CRF Section Quiz*** ■ GENERAL	UCP 1, 2, 5; LS 1a, 1d, 2a, 3a, 3b, 3c, 5a, 5b; *Chapter Lab:* UCP 2, 5; SAI 1; LS 1a, 1d
CRF Directed Reading A* ■ BASIC, **B*** SPECIAL NEEDS **CRF Vocabulary and Section Summary*** ■ GENERAL **SE Reading Strategy** Discussion, p. 448 GENERAL **TE Inclusion Strategies**, p. 449	**SE Reading Checks**, pp. 449, 450 GENERAL **TE Reteaching**, p. 450 BASIC **TE Quiz**, p. 450 GENERAL **TE Alternative Assessment**, p. 450 GENERAL **SE Section Review,*** p. 451 ■ GENERAL **CRF Section Quiz*** ■ GENERAL	UCP 5; LS 1a, 3a, 3b, 3c, 5a, 5b
CRF Directed Reading A* ■ BASIC, **B*** SPECIAL NEEDS **CRF Vocabulary and Section Summary*** ■ GENERAL **SE Reading Strategy** Reading Organizer, p. 452 GENERAL **TE Reading Strategy** Paired Summarizing, p. 453 BASIC	**SE Reading Checks**, pp. 453, 455 GENERAL **TE Homework**, p. 453 ADVANCED **TE Reteaching**, p. 454 BASIC **TE Quiz**, p. 454 GENERAL **TE Alternative Assessment**, p. 455 GENERAL **SE Section Review,*** p. 455 ■ GENERAL **CRF Section Quiz*** ■ GENERAL	UCP 5; LS 1a, 1d, 2a, 3a, 3b, 3c, 5a
CRF Directed Reading A* ■ BASIC, **B*** SPECIAL NEEDS **CRF Vocabulary and Section Summary*** ■ GENERAL **SE Reading Strategy** Brainstorming, p. 456 GENERAL **MS Math Skills for Science** The Unit Factor and Dimensional Analysis* GENERAL **CRF Reinforcement Worksheet** Mammals Are Us* BASIC	**SE Reading Checks**, pp. 457, 458, 461, 462 GENERAL **TE Homework**, p. 457, 459, 461 ADVANCED **TE Reteaching**, p. 462 BASIC **TE Quiz**, p. 462 GENERAL **TE Alternative Assessment**, p. 462 BASIC **SE Section Review,*** p. 463 ■ GENERAL **CRF Section Quiz*** ■ GENERAL	UCP 5; LS 1a, 1d, 2a, 3a, 3c, 5a
CRF Directed Reading A* ■ BASIC, **B*** SPECIAL NEEDS **CRF Vocabulary and Section Summary*** ■ GENERAL **SE Reading Strategy** Paired Summarizing, p. 464 GENERAL **TE Reading Strategy** Prediction Guide, p. 465 BASIC	**SE Reading Checks**, pp. 465, 466 GENERAL **TE Reteaching**, p. 466 BASIC **TE Quiz**, p. 466 GENERAL **TE Alternative Assessment**, p. 466 BASIC **SE Section Review,*** p. 467 ■ GENERAL **CRF Section Quiz*** ■ GENERAL	UCP 5; SPSP 5; LS 1a, 1d, 2a, 3a, 3c, 5a, 5c

One-Stop Planner® CD-ROM

This convenient CD-ROM includes:
- Lab Materials QuickList Software
- Holt Calendar Planner
- Customizable Lesson Plans
- Printable Worksheets
- ExamView® Test Generator

CNN student news

cnnstudentnews.com

Find the latest news, lesson plans, and activities related to important scientific events.

SCI LINKS
NSTA

www.scilinks.org

Maintained by the **National Science Teachers Association.** See Chapter Enrichment pages for a complete list of topics.

Current Science®

Check out *Current Science* articles and activities by visiting the HRW Web site at **go.hrw.com.** Just type in the keyword **HL5CS17T.**

Classroom Videos

- **Lab Videos** demonstrate the chapter lab.
- **Brain Food Video Quizzes** help students review the chapter material.
- **CNN Videos** bring science into your students' daily life.

Visual Resources

CHAPTER STARTER TRANSPARENCY

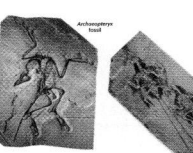

Birds and Mammals — CHAPTER STARTER

Would You Believe...?

Would it surprise you to know that the pigeons in your schoolyard are related to velociraptors? A pigeon's waddling gait might not make you think of the fierce prehistoric animal, but most biologists now agree that birds are descendants of dinosaurs.

The first piece of evidence to link reptiles and birds was the fossil of *Archaeopteryx* (ark ee AHP tuhr iks). *Archaeopteryx* fossils were first discovered in Germany almost 150 years ago. Like a dinosaur, *Archaeopteryx* had heavy bones and teeth, but like a bird, it had feathered wings.

Many scientists were skeptical about the link between dinosaurs and birds. For one thing, some research suggested that *Archaeopteryx* wasn't a true dinosaur.

Then in 1998, Chinese scientists discovered fossils of true dinosaurs that had wings and feathers. These feathers share some characteristics of modern bird feathers. So far, no one knows how feathers might have helped the dinosaurs. Their wings were too short for flight. The feathers may have been insulation against cold. Or maybe males used them to attract female dinosaurs.

The discovery of these winged dinosaurs helped to convince some scientists that birds are descendants of dinosaurs. A few scientists go even further. They say the dinosaurs never went extinct because birds are dinosaurs.

You'll learn more about birds in this chapter. You'll also learn about another group of vertebrates—mammals.

BELLRINGER TRANSPARENCIES

Birds and Mammals — BELLRINGER TRANSPARENCY

Section: Characteristics of Birds
What are some ways that birds are beneficial to people? Are birds ever harmful or annoying? Where and when do you most often see birds in your daily life?

Write your observations in your **science journal.**

Section: Kinds of Birds
What traits do you think scientists use to classify animals as birds? Would you guess that flying is the only characteristic? If so, remember that moths, bats, and flying squirrels also fly, but they are not birds. Why do you think scientists don't classify them as birds? Can you think of any animals that do not fly but are classified as birds? What traits are used to classify these flightless animals as birds?

Record your thoughts in your **science journal.**

TEACHING TRANSPARENCIES

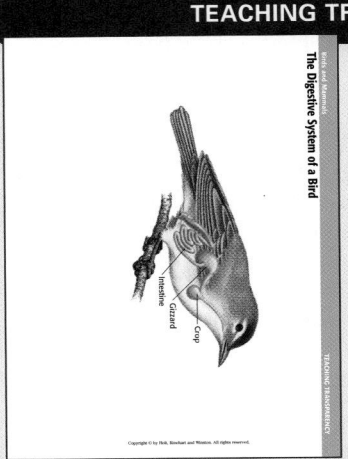

The Digestive System of a Bird

Flight Adaptations of Birds: A

Most birds have **large eyes** and excellent eyesight. Large eyes allow birds to see objects and food from a distance. Some birds, such as hawks and eagles, can see 8 times better than humans can see!

Birds have a **rapidly beating heart.** The heart pumps a hot, steady stream of oxygen-rich blood to the flight muscles. In small birds, the heart beats about 1,000 times a minute! (Your heart beats about 70 times a minute.)

Birds have special organs called **air sacs** attached to their lungs. The air sacs store air. Because of the stored air, a bird's lungs have a continuous supply of air—whether the bird is inhaling or exhaling.

TEACHING TRANSPARENCIES

Flight Adaptations of Birds: B

Wing shape is related to how a bird flies. Short, rounded wings allow a bird to quickly turn, drop, and pull up, much like the way a fighter plane moves. Long, narrow wings are best for soaring, just as a glider does.

Bird skeletons are compact and strong. Some of the vertebrae, ribs, and hipbones are fused together. For this reason, bird skeletons are more rigid than those of other vertebrates. A **rigid skeleton** allows a bird to move its wings powerfully and efficiently.

Birds that fly have **powerful flight muscles** that move the wings. These muscles are attached to a large breast-bone called a **keel.** The keel anchors the flight muscles. It allows the bird to flap its wings with force and speed.

Birds have **hollow bones.** So, birds have much lighter skeletons than other vertebrates do. The bones have thin cross supports that give strength, much like the cross supports of many bridges.

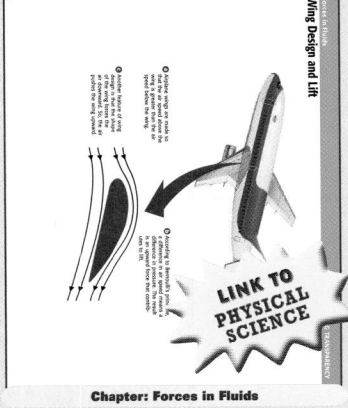

Wing Design and Lift

LINK TO PHYSICAL SCIENCE

Chapter: Forces in Fluids

CONCEPT MAPPING TRANSPARENCY

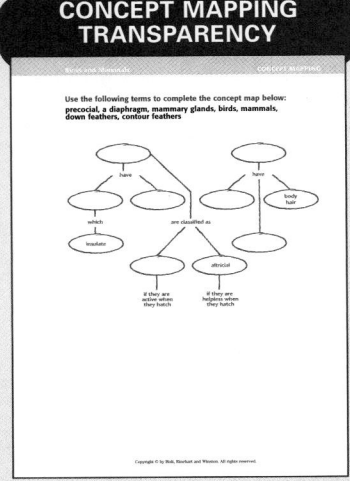

Use the following terms to complete the concept map below: **precocial, a diaphragm, mammary glands, birds, mammals, down feathers, contour feathers**

Planning Resources

LESSON PLANS

Lesson Plan — SAMPLE

Section: Waves

Pacing
Regular Schedule: with lab(s)2 days / without lab(s)2 days
Block Schedule: with lab(s)1 1/2 days / without lab(s)1 day

Objectives
1. Relate the seven properties of life to a living organism.
2. Describe seven themes that can help you to organize what you learn about biology.
3. Identify the tiny structures that make up all living organisms.
4. Differentiate between reproduction and heredity and between metabolism and homeostasis.

National Science Education Standards Covered
LSInter4: Cells have particular structures that underlie their functions.
LSMat1: Most cell functions involve chemical reactions.
LSBeh1: Cells store and use information to guide their functions.
UCP1: Cell functions are regulated.
SI1: Cells can differentiate and form complete multicellular organisms.
PS1: Species evolve over time.
ESS1: The great diversity of organisms is the result of more than 3.5 billion years of evolution.
ESS2: Natural selection and its evolutionary consequences provide a scientific explanation for the fossil record of ancient life forms as well as for the striking molecular similarities observed among the diverse species of living organisms.
ST1: The millions of different species of plants, animals, and microorganisms that live on Earth today are related by descent from common ancestors.
ST2: The energy for life primarily comes from the sun.
SPSP1: The complexity and organization of organisms accommodates the need for obtaining, transforming, transporting, releasing, and eliminating the matter and energy used to sustain the organism.
SPSP6: As matter and energy flow through different levels of organization of living systems—cells, organs, communities—and between living systems and the physical environment, chemical elements are recombined in different ways.
HNS1: Organisms have behavioral responses to internal changes and to external stimuli.

PARENT LETTER

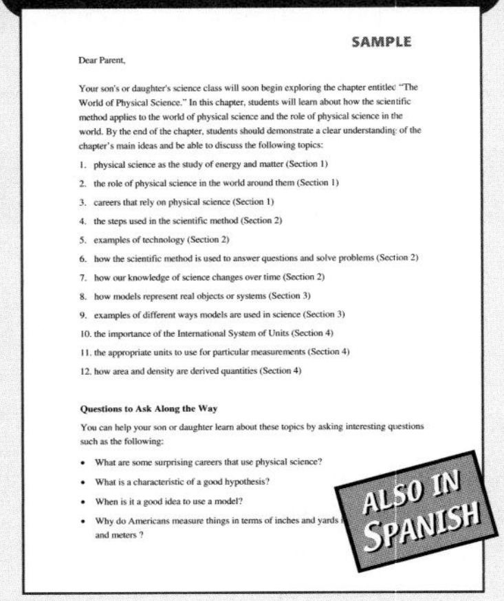

SAMPLE

Dear Parent,

Your son's or daughter's science class will soon begin exploring the chapter entitled "The World of Physical Science." In this chapter, students will learn about how the scientific method applies to the world of physical science and the role of physical science in the world. By the end of the chapter, students should demonstrate a clear understanding of the chapter's main ideas and be able to discuss the following topics:

1. physical science is the study of energy and matter (Section 1)
2. the role of physical science in the world around them (Section 1)
3. careers that rely on physical science (Section 1)
4. the steps used in the scientific method (Section 2)
5. examples of technology (Section 2)
6. how the scientific method is used to answer questions and solve problems (Section 2)
7. how our knowledge of science changes over time (Section 2)
8. how models represent real objects or systems (Section 3)
9. examples of different ways models are used in science (Section 3)
10. the importance of the International System of Units (Section 4)
11. the appropriate units to use for particular measurements (Section 4)
12. how area and density are derived quantities (Section 4)

Questions to Ask Along the Way

You can help your son or daughter learn about these topics by asking interesting questions such as the following:

• What are some surprising careers that use physical science?
• What is a characteristic of a good hypothesis?
• When is it a good idea to use a model?
• Why do Americans measure things in terms of inches and yards and meters ?

ALSO IN SPANISH

TEST ITEM LISTING

TEST ITEM LISTING
The World of Science — SAMPLE

MULTIPLE CHOICE

1. A limitation of models is that
   a. they are large enough to see.
   b. they do not act exactly like the things that they model.
   c. they are smaller than the things that they model.
   d. they model unfamiliar things.
   Answer: B   Difficulty: 1   Section: 3   Objective: 2

2. The length 10 m is equal to
   a. 100 cm.   c. 10,000 mm.
   b. 1,000 cm.   d. Both (b) and (c)
   Answer: D   Difficulty: 1   Section: 3   Objective: 2

3. To be valid, a hypothesis must be
   a. testable.   c. made into a law.
   b. supported by evidence. d. Both (a) and (b)
   Answer: D   Difficulty: 1   Section: 2   Objective: 1

4. The statement "Sheila has a stain on her shirt" is an example of a(n)
   a. law.   c. observation.
   b. hypothesis.   d. prediction.
   Answer: C   Difficulty: 1   Section: 3   Objective: 2

5. A hypothesis is often developed out of
   a. observations.   c. laws.
   b. experiments.   d. Both (a) and (b)
   Answer: D   Difficulty: 1   Section: 3   Objective: 2

6. How many milliliters are in 3.5 kL?
   a. 3,500 mL   c. 3,500, 000 mL.
   b. 0.0035 mL.   d. 35,000 mL.
   Answer: C   Difficulty: 1   Section: 3   Objective: 2

7. A map of Seattle is an example of a
   a. law.   c. model.
   b. theory.   d. unit.
   Answer: C   Difficulty: 1   Section: 3   Objective: 2

8. A lab has the safety icons shown below. These icons mean that you should wear
   a. only safety goggles.   c. safety goggles and a lab apron.
   b. only a lab apron.   d. safety goggles, a lab apron, and gloves.
   Answer: D   Difficulty: 1   Section: 3   Objective: 2

9. The law of conservation of mass says that the tot al mass before a chemical change is
   a. more than the total mass after the change.
   b. less than the total mass after the change.
   c. the same as the total mass after the change.
   d. not the same as the total mass after the change.
   Answer: C   Difficulty: 1   Section: 3   Objective: 2

10. In which of the following areas might you find a geochemist at work?
    a. studying the chemistry of rocks   c. studying fishes
    b. studying forestry   d. studying the atmosphere
    Answer: A   Difficulty: 1   Section: 3   Objective: 2

One-Stop Planner® CD-ROM

This CD-ROM includes all of the resources shown here and the following time-saving tools:

• *Lab Materials QuickList Software*
• *Customizable lesson plans*
• *Holt Calendar Planner*
• *The powerful ExamView® Test Generator*

Meeting Individual Needs

DIRECTED READING A
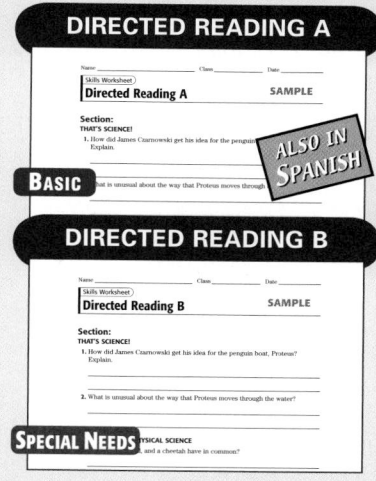
BASIC · ALSO IN SPANISH

VOCABULARY ACTIVITY
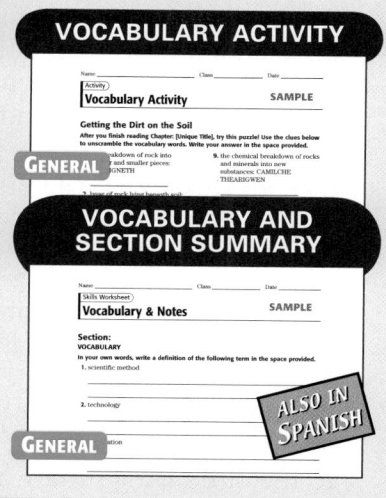
GENERAL

REINFORCEMENT
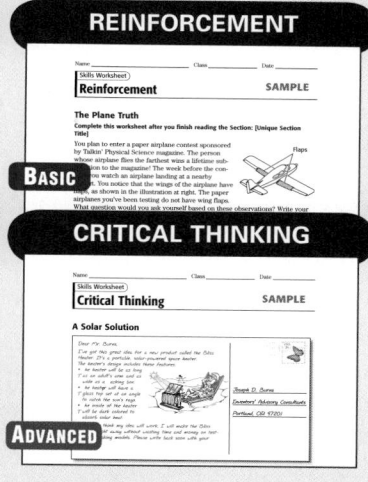
BASIC

SCILINKS ACTIVITY

GENERAL

DIRECTED READING B
Directed Reading B — SAMPLE
SPECIAL NEEDS

VOCABULARY AND SECTION SUMMARY
Vocabulary & Notes — SAMPLE
GENERAL · ALSO IN SPANISH

CRITICAL THINKING
Critical Thinking — SAMPLE
ADVANCED

SCIENCE PUZZLERS, TWISTERS & TEASERS
Birds and Mammals
GENERAL

Labs and Activities

LONG-TERM PROJECTS & RESEARCH IDEAS
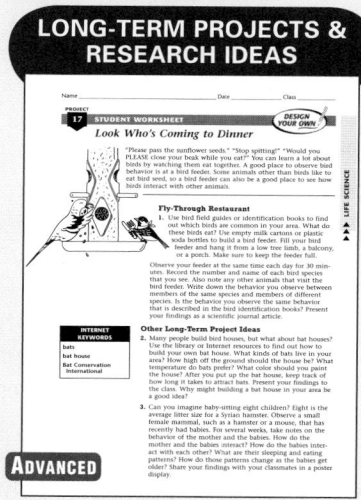
Look Who's Coming to Dinner
ADVANCED

LABS YOU CAN EAT
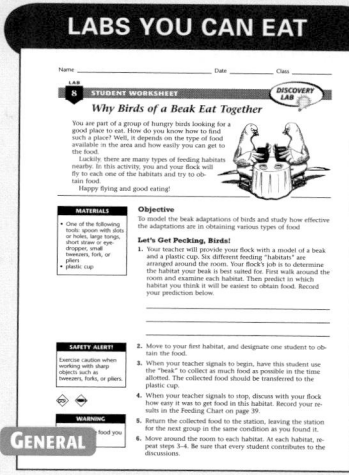
Why Birds of a Beak Eat Together
GENERAL

DATASHEETS FOR QUICK LABS

Reaction to Stress — DATASHEET FOR QUICK LAB — SAMPLE

DATASHEETS FOR CHAPTER LABS
Using Scientific Methods — DATASHEET FOR CHAPTER LAB — SAMPLE

DATASHEETS FOR LABBOOK
Does It All Add Up? — DATASHEET FOR LABBOOK LAB — SAMPLE

Review and Assessments

SECTION QUIZ

GENERAL · ALSO IN SPANISH

CHAPTER REVIEW
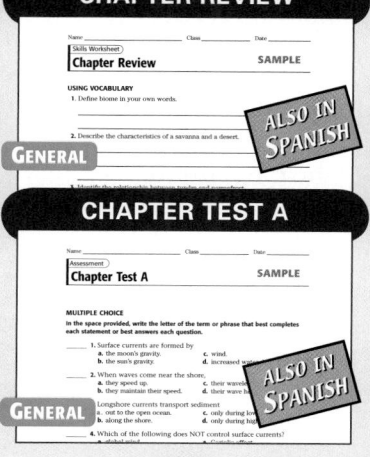
GENERAL · ALSO IN SPANISH

CHAPTER TEST B
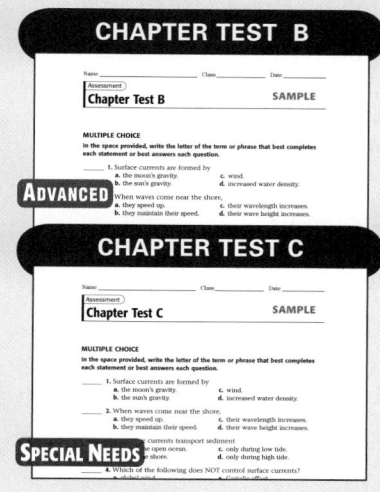
Chapter Test B — SAMPLE
ADVANCED

STANDARDIZED TEST PREPARATION
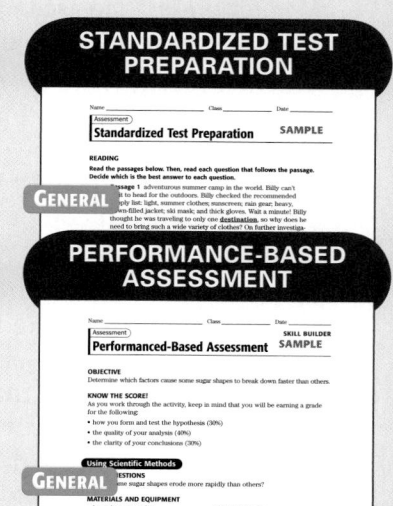
Standardized Test Preparation — SAMPLE
GENERAL

SECTION REVIEW
Section Review — SAMPLE
GENERAL · ALSO IN SPANISH

CHAPTER TEST A
Chapter Test A — SAMPLE
GENERAL · ALSO IN SPANISH

CHAPTER TEST C
Chapter Test C — SAMPLE
SPECIAL NEEDS

PERFORMANCE-BASED ASSESSMENT
Performanced-Based Assessment — SKILL BUILDER SAMPLE
GENERAL

This Chapter Enrichment provides relevant and interesting information to expand and enhance your presentation of the chapter material.

Section 1

Characteristics of Birds

Feathers

- Ornithologists classify feathers based on their function and location on the bird's body.

  - **Contour feathers** have a stiff shaft and firm barbs on the inner and outer vanes, although the base is often downy. Contour feathers include the feathers on the outer surface of the body and the flight feathers of the wings (remiges) and the tail (rectrices). The auriculars, which cover the ears, are small, modified contour feathers.

  - **Semiplumes** are small but have a relatively large shaft and downy vanes. Semiplumes, which lie hidden beneath body feathers, fill the spaces between larger contour feathers, provide insulation, and, in water birds, increase buoyancy. Some birds, such as herons, have showy semiplumes that attract mates.

  - **Down feathers** are tiny and fluffy and do not have a shaft, and are important for insulation. Down feathers are the sole body covering for newly hatched birds. In adult birds, down feathers are hidden beneath contour feathers. Down feathers are most abundant in water birds.

- Thin, stiff *barbs* branch from the shaft of typical contour feathers. Hundreds of smaller branches, called *barbules*, grow out from either side of the barbs. Each barbule has tiny hooks that wrap around barbules of adjacent barbs and tightly bind all parts of the feather to each other, which makes the feathers firmer and better able to insulate and waterproof a bird.

Forms of Flight

- During flapping flight, a bird's inner wing functions as an anchor for the outer portion and helps provide lift. At the bottom of the downstroke, which propels the bird, the "wrist" flexes and begins the upstroke.

- Soaring flight allows a bird to gain and maintain altitude without flapping its wings. Instead of flapping, some birds "ride" on warm air currents called *thermals*. Vultures, hawks, and eagles can use soaring flight because they have a low wing loading. A wing loading is the ratio of a bird's weight to the bird's wing surface area.

- No other bird can match the hummingbird in its ability to maintain a position in midair. Hummingbirds move their wings only from the shoulder, which provides unusual flexibility and maneuverability.

Section 2

Kinds of Birds

Diving and Hovering

- Cormorants and anhingas are fish-eating birds that must dive to catch their food. To decrease their buoyancy and enhance their ability to dive deep, they have bones that are unusually heavy for a bird, smaller air sacs, and nonwaterproof plumage. To dry off after a dive, they must find a perch and spread their wings.

- The ruby-throated hummingbird has about 940 feathers. The whistling swan has about 25,000. But the hummingbird has more feathers per unit of body weight than the swan does. Small birds have a greater need for efficient heat retention.

Is That a Fact!

- ◆ Hummingbirds are the only birds that can fly backward.

Section 3

Characteristics of Mammals

Fur

- All mammals have hair, but not all mammals have thick fur. Thick fur consists of two layers: a dense undergrowth of short ground hairs, which provide insulation, and longer guard hairs, which protect the skin and the ground hairs from rain or snow.

Is That a Fact!

◆ Shrews and other small mammals have a high metabolic rate to compensate for the large amount of body heat that they lose because of their large body surface–to–volume ratio. A captive shrew (genus *Sorex*) consumed 3.3 times its body weight in food in a 24-hour period.

Section 4

Placental Mammals

Beneficial Bats

- Guano from insectivorous bats is a valuable fertilizer in many countries. In some caves, the guano covers and helps preserve archeological artifacts and fossils.

- Although some fruit-eating bats can reduce a farmer's harvest, many of them are essential to dispersing seeds that are responsible for new plant growth. Other bats eat only pollen and nectar and are the primary or exclusive pollinators of various plants.

Rodent Teeth

- Rodents have evolved a unique jaw articulation to use their huge incisors effectively. The upper and the lower incisors are separated from the cheek teeth by a large gap. When the cheek teeth are chewing, the lower jaw is pulled back and the incisors do not meet. When the animal is gnawing with its incisors, the lower jaw is pulled forward and downward so that the incisors meet. Rodents spend a lot of time gnawing, and their ever-growing incisors are worn to a sharp cutting edge.

Is That a Fact!

◆ A three-toed sloth has nine cervical vertebrae and can turn its head 270°. Most mammals have seven neck vertebrae.

Section 5

Monotremes and Marsupials

Australian Adaptations

- Male duckbill platypuses have sharp spurs on the back of their hind legs. These spurs can inject poison into another platypus competing for a mate or into an attacker.

- Tree kangaroos can move around easily in and spend time in trees. They use their thick tail to brace themselves and to maintain balance. But tree kangaroos spend time on the ground, too.

Developed and maintained by the National Science Teachers Association

SciLinks is maintained by the National Science Teachers Association to provide you and your students with interesting, up-to-date links that will enrich your classroom presentation of the chapter.

Visit www.scilinks.org and enter the SciLinks code for more information about the topic listed.

Topic: Bird Characteristics
SciLinks code: HSM0167

Topic: Kinds of Mammals
SciLinks code: HSM0832

Topic: Kinds of Birds
SciLinks code: HSM0831

Topic: Monotremes and Marsupials
SciLinks code: HSM0990

Topic: Characteristics of Mammals
SciLinks code: HSM0259

Overview

Tell students that this chapter will help them learn about birds and mammals. The chapter describes several characteristics of both kinds of animals. Students will learn about flightless birds, water birds, perching birds, and birds of prey. Students will also learn about placental mammals, monotremes, and marsupials.

Assessing Prior Knowledge

Students should be familiar with the following topics:

• classification

• vertebrates

Identifying Misconceptions

As students learn the material in this chapter, some of them may be confused by broad generalizations that people tend to make about birds and mammals. It may be helpful to remind students that not all birds can fly and that not all mammals give birth to live young. This reminder may provide a good opportunity to discuss how exceptions to the rule occur throughout the field of biology.

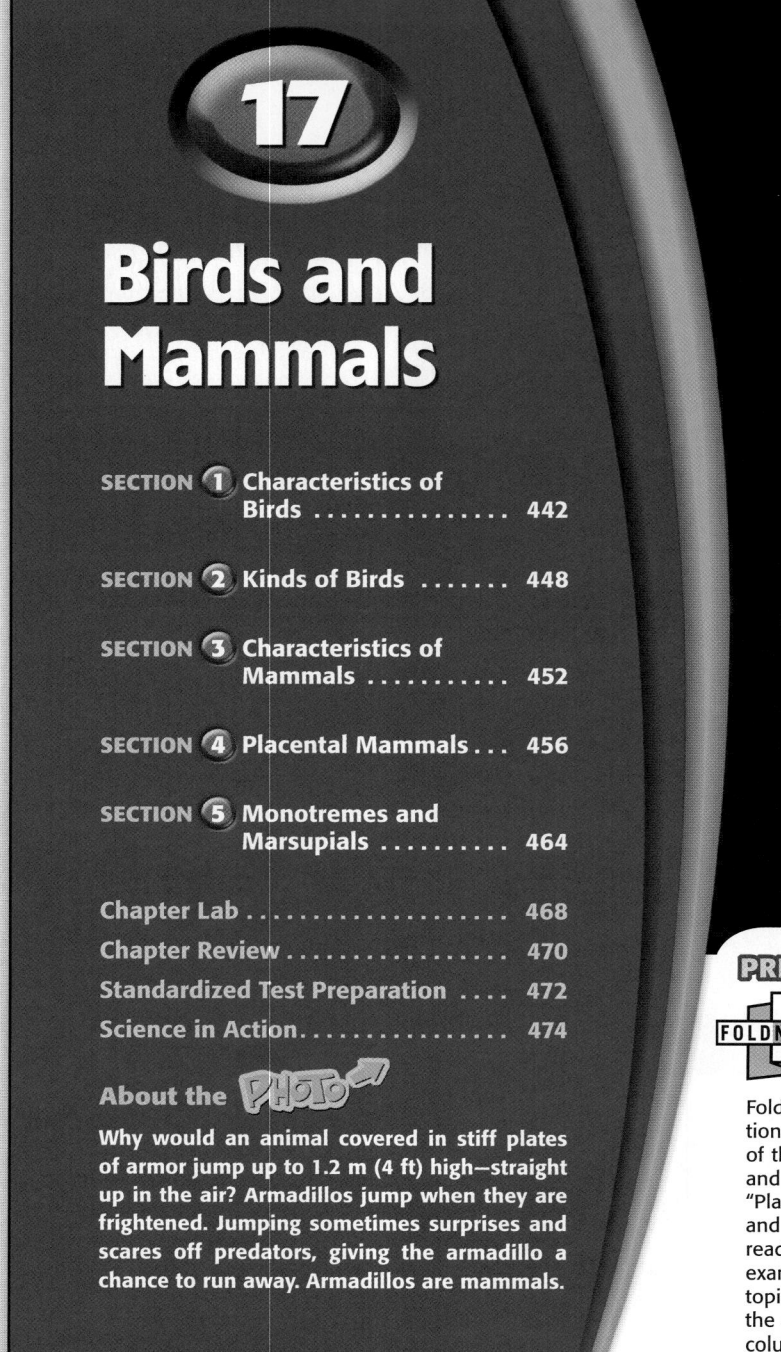

17

Birds and Mammals

About the PHOTO

Why would an animal covered in stiff plates of armor jump up to 1.2 m (4 ft) high—straight up in the air? Armadillos jump when they are frightened. Jumping sometimes surprises and scares off predators, giving the armadillo a chance to run away. Armadillos are mammals.

PRE-READING ACTIVITY

FOLDNOTES **Table Fold** Before you read the chapter, create the FoldNote entitled "Table Fold" described in the **Study Skills** section of the Appendix. Label the columns of the table fold with "Characteristics" and "Kinds." Label the rows with "Birds," "Placental mammals," and "Monotremes and marsupials." As you read the chapter, write examples of each topic under the appropriate column.

Standards Correlations

National Science Education Standards

The following codes indicate the National Science Education Standards that correlate to this chapter. The full text of the standards is at the front of the book.

Chapter Opener
UCP 2, 5; SAI 1; ST 2; LS 1a, 3c, 5b

Section 1 Characteristics of Birds
UCP 1, 2, 5; LS 1a, 1d, 2a, 3a, 3b, 3c, 5a, 5b

Section 2 Kinds of Birds
UCP 5; LS 1a, 3a, 3c, 5a, 5b

Section 3 Characteristics of Mammals
UCP 5; LS 1a, 1d, 2a, 3a, 3b, 3c, 5a

Section 4 Placental Mammals
UCP 5; LS 1a, 1d, 2a, 3a, 3c, 5a

Section 5 Monotremes and Marsupials
UCP 5; SPSP 5; LS 1a, 1d, 2a, 3a, 3c, 5a, 5c

Chapter Lab
UCP 2, 5; SAI 1; LS 1a, 1d

Chapter Review
UCP 2, 5; SAI 1; LS 1a, 1d, 2a, 3a, 3c, 5a, 5b, 5c

START-UP ACTiViTY

MATERIALS

FOR EACH STUDENT
• paper, 8 1/2 in. × 11 in.

Safety Caution: Instruct students to throw their planes only into areas where other people are not present.

Answers

1. Answers may vary, but forcefully thrown planes probably went farther. Students should realize that forces probably have similar effects on bird flight, although bird flight is affected not only by the strength of forces but also by more-complex factors.

2. Answers may vary. Smaller wings make the plane more maneuverable but less able to glide; longer wings offer more surface area to keep the plane (or bird) in the air. These differences suggest that wing size would indeed affect the way that a bird flies.

3. Answers may vary, but a good design will depend on what kind of flight is desired.

START-UP ACTiViTY

Let's Fly!

How do birds fly? This activity will give you a few hints.

Procedure

1. Carefully fold a **piece of paper** to make a paper airplane. Make the folds even and the creases sharp.

2. Throw the plane through the air very gently. What happened?

3. Take the same plane, and throw it more forcefully. Did anything change?

4. Reduce the size of the wings by folding them inward toward the center crease. Make sure the two wings are the same size and shape.

5. Throw the airplane two more times. Throw it gently at first, and then throw it with more force. What happened each time?

Analysis

1. Analyze what effect the force of your throw has on the paper airplane's flight. Do you think forces of different strengths affect bird flight in a similar way? Explain your answer.

2. What happened when the wings were made smaller? Why do you think this happened? Do you think wing size affects the way a bird flies? Explain your answer.

3. Based on your results, how would you design and throw the perfect paper airplane?

Science in Action
SAI 1; SPSP 5; LS 3a, 3c, 5b

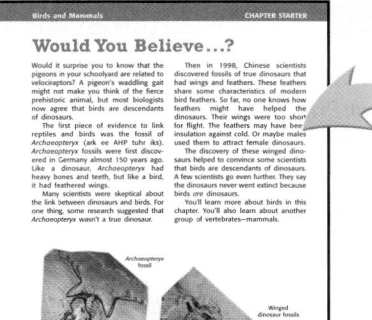

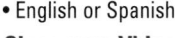

Chapter Starter Transparency
Use this transparency to help students begin thinking about the relationship between birds and other vertebrates.

CHAPTER RESOURCES

Technology

Transparencies
• Chapter Starter Transparency

READING SKILLS

Student Edition on CD-ROM

Guided Reading Audio CD
• English or Spanish

Classroom Videos
• Brain Food Video Quiz

Workbooks

Science Puzzlers, Twisters & Teasers
• Birds and Mammals GENERAL

Chapter 17 • Birds and Mammals **441**

Focus

Overview

In this section, students learn about several characteristics of birds. Students will learn about feathers, a unique digestive system, several adaptations for flight, and the ways that birds raise their young.

🔔 Bellringer

Ask students, "What are some ways that birds are beneficial to people?" (Birds provide meat, eggs, and feathers; provide natural and cost-saving insect and rodent control; pollinate plants; spread plant seeds; and consume decaying animals.)

Motivate

ACTIVITY ——————— GENERAL

Light as a Feather Organize the class into small groups. Provide each group with a wing feather, a paper clip, a small scale, and a meterstick. Tell students to weigh the feather and the paper clip. Next, tell the class to let group members take turns dropping the feather and the paper clip from a height of 1 m. Challenge groups to discuss how the fall of the feather differs from the fall of the paper clip and how feather shape has a role in bird flight. **English Language Learners**
LS Visual

READING WARM-UP

Objectives

● Describe two kinds of feathers.
● Describe how a bird's diet, breathing, muscles, and skeleton help it fly.
● Explain how lift works.
● Describe how birds raise their young.

Terms to Learn

preening
molting
down feather
contour feather
lift
brooding

READING STRATEGY

Prediction Guide Before reading this section, write the title of each heading in this section. Next, under each heading, write what you think you will learn.

preening in birds, the act of grooming and maintaining their feathers

molting the shedding of an exoskeleton, skin, feathers, or hair to be replaced by new parts

Characteristics of Birds

What do a powerful eagle, a lumbering penguin, and a dainty finch have in common? They all have feathers, wings, and a beak, which means they are all birds.

Birds share many characteristics with reptiles. Like reptiles, birds are vertebrates. Birds' feet and legs are covered by thick scales like those that cover reptiles' bodies. Also, bird eggs have an amniotic sac and a shell, just as reptile eggs do.

Birds also have many unique characteristics. For example, bird eggs have harder shells than reptile eggs do. And as shown in **Figure 1,** birds have feathers and wings. They also have a horny beak instead of jaws with teeth. Also, birds can use heat from activity in their cells to maintain a constant body temperature.

Feathers

One familiar characteristic of birds is their feathers. Feathers help birds stay dry and warm, attract mates, and fly.

Preening and Molting

Birds take good care of their feathers. They use their beaks to spread oil on their feathers in a process called **preening.** The oil is made by a gland near the bird's tail. The oil helps waterproof the feathers and keeps them clean. When feathers wear out, birds replace them by molting. **Molting** is the process of shedding old feathers and growing new ones. Most birds shed their feathers at least once a year.

▼ Hummingbird

▲ Great blue heron

▼ Toucan

Figure 1 *There are about 10,000 known species of birds on Earth today.*

CHAPTER RESOURCES

Chapter Resource File

 • Lesson Plan
• Directed Reading A **BASIC**
• Directed Reading B **SPECIAL NEEDS**

Technology

 Transparencies
• Bellringer
• The Digestive System of a Bird

Homework ——————— BASIC

 Writing **Researching Bird Breeding** Tell students that biologists have used their understanding of parent-offspring relationships in birds to breed birds in captivity. Have students research ways that some scientists mimic parent birds in order to feed and nurture chicks. Students can also research the success of these captive-breeding efforts. **LS Verbal**

Two Kinds of Feathers

Birds have two main kinds of feathers—down feathers and contour feathers. **Down feathers** are fluffy feathers that lie next to a bird's body. These feathers help birds stay warm. When a bird fluffs its down feathers, air is trapped close to the body. Trapping air keeps body heat near the body. **Contour feathers** are stiff feathers that cover a bird's body and wings. Their colors and shapes help some birds attract mates. Contour feathers have a stiff central shaft with many side branches, called *barbs*. The barbs link together to form a smooth surface, as shown in **Figure 2**. This streamlined surface helps birds fly.

Reading Check What is the function of a bird's down feathers? (*See the Appendix for answers to Reading Checks.*)

High-Energy Animals

Birds need a lot of energy to fly. To get this energy, their bodies break down food quickly. This process generates a lot of body heat. In fact, the average body temperature of a bird is 40°C—three degrees warmer than yours. Birds cannot sweat to cool off if they get too hot. Instead, they lay their feathers flat and pant like dogs do.

Fast Digestion

Because birds need a lot of energy, they eat a lot. Hummingbirds need to eat almost constantly to get the energy they need! Most birds eat insects, nuts, seeds, or meat. These foods are high in protein and fat. A few birds, such as geese, eat grass, leaves, and other plants. Birds have a unique digestive system to help them get energy quickly. **Figure 3** shows this system. Modern birds don't have teeth, so they can't chew. Instead, food goes from the mouth to the crop. The *crop* stores food until it moves to the gizzard. Many *gizzards* have small stones inside. These stones grind up the food so that it can be easily digested in the intestine. This grinding action is similar to what happens when we chew our food.

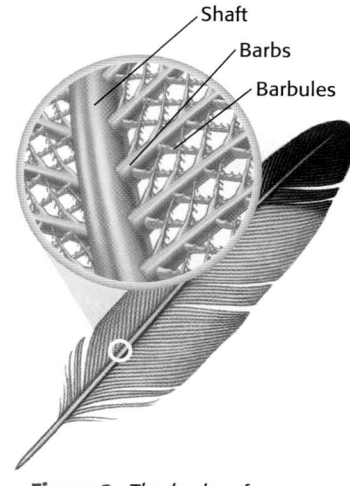

Shaft
Barbs
Barbules

Figure 2 *The barbs of a contour feather have cross branches called* barbules. *Barbs and barbules give the feather strength and shape.*

down feather a soft feather that covers the body of young birds and provides insulation to adult birds

contour feather one of the most external feathers that cover a bird and that help determine its shape

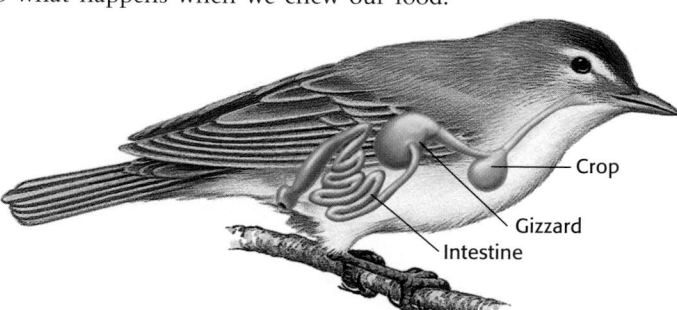

Crop
Gizzard
Intestine

Figure 3 *A bird's digestive system helps the bird rapidly change food into usable energy.*

Answer to Reading Check
Down feathers help birds stay warm.

Prediction Guide Before students read these pages, ask them, "Why do you think that birds are such successful flyers?" (Birds have feathers, a high rate of metabolism, wings, lightweight bones, and air sacs.)

Have students review their answers after they read the text. **LS** Verbal

Answer to Reading Check
The heart beats rapidly so that it can pump enough blood to power the flight muscles.

Using the Figure — ADVANCED

Writing **Flightless Birds** Remind students that several bird species, including ostriches, kiwis, and emus, are flightless. Tell students to use a library or the Internet to research the body and wing structure of flightless birds and to write a new paragraph for each caption in **Figure 4**. The new paragraphs should explain how the characteristics of flightless birds differ from the characteristics of birds that fly. **LS** Verbal   *English Language Learners*

Flying

Most birds can fly. Even flightless birds, such as ostriches, have ancestors that could fly. So, it is not surprising that birds have many adaptations for flight. The most obvious characteristic related to flight is the wings. But birds also have lightweight bodies. And they have powerful flight muscles and a rapidly beating heart. The fast heart rate helps birds get plenty of oxygen-rich blood to the flight muscles. **Figure 4** describes many bird characteristics that are important for flight.

✔ **Reading Check** How does a bird's heart help the bird fly?

Figure 4 Flight Adaptations of Birds

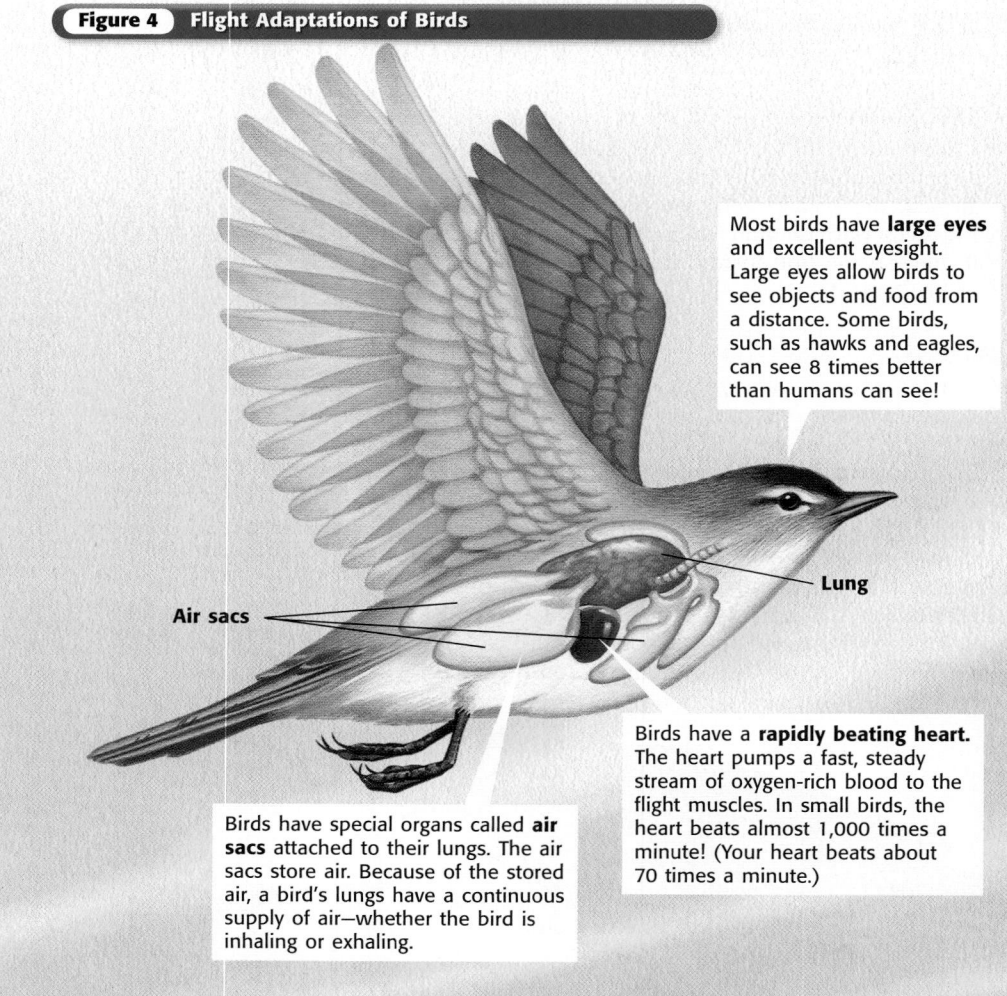

Most birds have **large eyes** and excellent eyesight. Large eyes allow birds to see objects and food from a distance. Some birds, such as hawks and eagles, can see 8 times better than humans can see!

Lung

Air sacs

Birds have special organs called **air sacs** attached to their lungs. The air sacs store air. Because of the stored air, a bird's lungs have a continuous supply of air—whether the bird is inhaling or exhaling.

Birds have a **rapidly beating heart.** The heart pumps a fast, steady stream of oxygen-rich blood to the flight muscles. In small birds, the heart beats almost 1,000 times a minute! (Your heart beats about 70 times a minute.)

INCLUSION Strategies

• *Developmentally Delayed* • *Behavior Control Issues*
• *Attention Deficit Disorder*

Help students understand the effort that birds go through to build nests. Organize the students into teams of four or five. Ask each team to build a bird nest. Tell students that they may pick up only one item, such as one piece of grass, one leaf, or one twig, at a time. Only after an item is added to the nest can another item can be picked up. Remind students to weave the items together so the nest will remain intact. Give teams about 20 minutes to work on their nests. (They will probably finish only a small part of a nest.) Discuss that one nest requires thousands of trips from the ground to the nest. *English Language Learners* **LS** Kinesthetic

Wing shape is related to how a bird flies. Short, rounded wings allow a bird to quickly turn, drop, and pull up, much like the way a fighter plane moves. Long, narrow wings are best for soaring, just as a glider does.

MATH PRACTICE

Flying Far

A certain bird flies 970 km (600 mi) when it goes south for the winter. It flies north each summer. If this bird lives for 8 years, how many total kilometers will it fly during migrations in its lifetime?

Bird skeletons are compact and strong. Some of the vertebrae, ribs, and hipbones are fused together. For this reason, bird skeletons are more rigid than those of other vertebrates. A **rigid skeleton** allows a bird to move its wings powerfully and efficiently.

Keel

Birds that fly have **powerful flight muscles** that move the wings. These muscles are attached to a large breastbone called a **keel**. The keel anchors the flight muscles. It allows the bird to flap its wings with force and speed.

Cross supports

Birds have **hollow bones.** So, birds have much lighter skeletons than other vertebrates do. The bones have thin cross supports that give strength, much like the cross supports of many bridges.

Demonstration — GENERAL

Observing Bird Bones Obtain several chicken or turkey bones, such as the lower leg bones (drumsticks) and thigh bones, that have been cooked and thoroughly cleaned. Carefully break open the bones so that students can examine the air spaces inside. **LS Visual** *English Language Learners*

Homework — GENERAL

Writing **Researching Falconry** Falconry is an ancient sport that may date back to the eighth century BCE in Assyria. Falconry was immensely popular among the European upper classes in the Middle Ages. Today, the sport is strictly regulated by the U.S. Fish and Wildlife Service, which issues permits that allow individuals to trap and train hawks, falcons, and some eagles. Have students conduct research and write a report about the history of falconry. Their report should include information about the role of falconry in raptor conservation. **LS Verbal**

ACTIVITY — GENERAL

Jump Up and Down Ask students to measure their heart rate while seated (they can take their pulse at the wrist or neck). Then, ask them to jump up and down or move their arms vigorously and measure their heart rate again. Ask them to explain why the heart beats faster as a person's activity level increases. (The body needs more oxygen, so the heart pumps blood more quickly.) Then, ask them to use this information to explain why birds have fast heart rates. (Birds need a lot of oxygen to power their flight muscles, so their hearts beat rapidly to pump blood quickly.) **LS Kinesthetic**

Is That a Fact!

A bird's common name may describe features of the bird, but it may not tell you what kind of bird it is. For example, the nighthawk is not a hawk, although it appears hawklike in flight. Nighthawks are in the Caprimulgidae family, most members of which are insect eaters. *Caprimulgidae* is from the Latin *caper*, "goat," and *mulgeo*, "to milk." According to legend, these birds sucked milk from goats at night!

CHAPTER RESOURCES

Technology

 Transparencies
- Flight Adaptations of Birds: A
- Flight Adaptations of Birds: B

Workbooks

 Science Skills
- Organizing Your Research **BASIC**
- Researching on the Web **GENERAL**

Comparing Coverings Bring a fuzzy sweater and a sleek windbreaker to class. Ask students to describe ways in which people use each item, and ask which item is similar to a layer of down feathers and which item is similar to a layer of contour feathers. (The sweater insulates as down feathers do. The windbreaker forms a streamlined surface as contour feathers do.) **LS** Kinesthetic

Quiz — GENERAL

1. List three flight adaptations of birds. (Sample answer: wings, hollow bones, and a keel that anchors flight muscles)

2. Describe the two types of feathers. (Contour feathers are stiff and have a shaft and many barbs. Down feathers are fluffy and do not have a shaft.)

Alternative Assessment — ADVANCED

Courtship Many birds, such as the whooping crane, the bird of paradise, the prairie chicken, the mockingbird, and the emperor penguin, have elaborate courtship behaviors. Have students work in groups of four to research the courtship behavior of a particular species. Groups will present their findings to the class. Have group members designate who will do research, who will write the presentation, who will make a poster, and who will present the material. **LS** Verbal/ Visual Co-op Learning

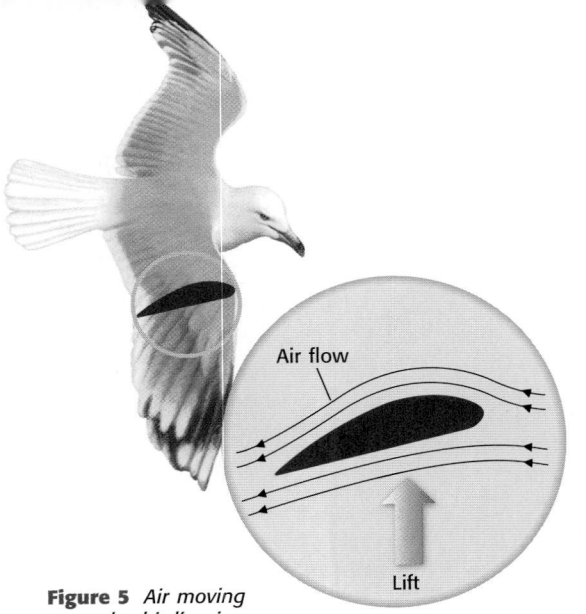

Figure 5 *Air moving around a bird's wing changes in speed and direction, creating an upward force that keeps a bird in the air.*

lift an upward force on an object that moves in a fluid

brooding to sit on and cover eggs to keep them warm until they hatch; to incubate

Figure 6 *This robin's nest is only one example of a bird's nest. Birds build nests of many different shapes and sizes.*

CONNECTION to Physical Science — ADVANCED

Wing Design For both birds and aircraft, the shape of a wing creates differences in maneuverability and air speed. Designing an airplane wing requires taking into account what kind of flying the plane will do. Selective pressures have led to a vast array of wing shapes in birds. These wing shapes enable species to fly in a variety of ways. Use the teaching transparency "Wing Design and Lift" to illustrate the effect of wingshape on air speed and lift. **LS** Visual

Getting off the Ground

How do birds overcome gravity to fly? Birds flap their wings to get into the air. They keep flapping to push themselves through the air. They are able to stay in the air because their wings cause lift. **Lift** is an upward force on a bird's wings.

As a bird flies through the air, some of the air is forced over the top of its wings. Some air is forced underneath the wings. **Figure 5** shows this airflow. A bird's wings are curved on top. The shape of the wings affects the air around them. As air flows over and under a bird's wings, the air's speed and direction change. These changes in the air's speed and direction affect the wings in a way that creates lift, the upward force that acts on the wings.

Lift is affected by flying speed and by wing shape. The faster a bird flies, the greater the lift. Also, the larger the wing is, the greater the lift. Birds with large wings can glide for long distances.

Raising Baby Birds

The way that birds reproduce is similar to the way that reptiles reproduce. Like reptiles, birds reproduce sexually by internal fertilization. Both birds and reptiles lay amniotic eggs in which there is a growing embryo. But unlike most reptiles, birds must keep their eggs warm for the embryos to live and grow.

Nests

Most birds build nests in which they lay their eggs. **Figure 6** shows a bird's nest with eggs in it. Birds keep their eggs warm by brooding. **Brooding** is the act of sitting on eggs and using body heat to keep them warm. Birds sit on their eggs until the eggs hatch. For some birds, such as gulls, the job of brooding is shared by both males and females. In many species of songbirds, the female broods the eggs, and the male brings food to the brooding female. In a few species, the male broods the eggs.

✓ **Reading Check** How does the process of brooding keep a bird's eggs warm?

Answer to Reading Check
A bird's body heat warms the eggs.

Precocial and Altricial

Some birds, such as chickens and ducks, are active soon after they hatch. These active chicks are *precocial* (pree KOH shuhl). Precocial chicks are covered with downy feathers. As soon as they can stand up, the chicks follow their parents around. These chicks depend on a mother for warmth and protection, but they can walk, swim, and feed themselves.

Some birds, such as hawks and songbirds, are weak and helpless for a while after hatching. These weak chicks are *altricial* (al TRISH uhl). When they hatch, they have no feathers and their eyes are closed. They cannot walk or fly. Their parents must keep them warm and feed them for several weeks. **Figure 7** shows a parent feeding its altricial chicks.

Figure 7 *Parents of altricial chicks bring food to the nest.*

SECTION Review

Summary

- Birds have feathers, a beak, wings, and a constant body temperature.
- Down feathers keep birds warm. Contour feathers help birds fly and attract mates.
- Birds must eat a high-energy diet to get energy for flying.
- Lightweight bodies and strong muscles help birds fly. Air sacs help them get enough oxygen to fly.
- Wings create lift as they cut through the air. Lift pushes the wings up to keep a bird in the air.
- Birds keep their eggs warm in a nest by brooding. When the chicks hatch, they are precocial or altricial.

Using Key Terms

1. Use each of the following terms in a separate sentence: *lift* and *brooding.*

For each pair of terms, explain how the meanings of the terms differ.

2. *down feather* and *contour feather*

3. *preening* and *molting*

Understanding Key Ideas

4. Which of the following is NOT a flight adaptation in birds?
   a. hollow bones
   b. air sacs
   c. down feathers
   d. rapidly beating heart

5. What do birds eat? Describe the path taken by a bird's food as it moves through the bird's digestive system.

6. How does the air around a bird's wings cause lift?

7. Explain the difference between precocial chicks and altricial chicks.

8. Name two ways that birds use their contour feathers. Name one way that birds use their down feathers.

Math Skills

9. Suppose that a bird that weighs 325 g loses 40% of its body weight during migration. What is the bird's weight when it reaches its destination?

Critical Thinking

10. **Analyzing Ideas** Why can't people fly without the help of technology? Name at least four human body characteristics that are poorly adapted for flight.

11. **Applying Concepts** Some people use the phrase "eats like a bird" to describe someone who does not eat very much. Does using the phrase in this way show an accurate understanding of a bird's eating habits? Why or why not?

SCI LINKS®

Developed and maintained by the National Science Teachers Association

For a variety of links related to this chapter, go to www.scilinks.org

Topic: Bird Characteristics
SciLinks code: HSM0167

Answers to Section Review

1. Sample answer: Lift is an upward force on a bird's wings. Birds keep their eggs warm by brooding.

2. Sample answer: These two kinds of feathers differ in form and function. Down feathers are small and soft. They help keep birds warm. Contour feathers are stiff and smooth. They help give birds a streamlined surface.

3. Sample answer: Preening is a process in which birds spread oil on their feathers. Molting is a process through which birds replace old feathers.

4. c

5. Sample answer: Most birds eat insects, nuts, seeds, or meat. Food moves from a bird's mouth to the crop, where the food can be stored. Food then moves to the gizzard, where small stones grind up the food before it moves to the intestine.

6. Sample answer: Air moving over and under a bird's wings changes speed and direction in a way that causes an upward force, called *lift,* on the wings.

7. Sample answer: Precocial chicks are active soon after they hatch. Altricial chicks are weak for a while after they hatch.

8. Sample answer: Colorful contour feathers can attract mates because of their color and help birds fly because they form a streamlined surface. Down feathers trap air close to the body to keep a bird warm.

9. 195 g (40% of 325 g = 130 g; 325 g − 130 g = 195 g)

10. Sample answer: The human body is poorly adapted for flight. Our hearts beat more slowly than bird hearts do. We do not have air sacs attached to our lungs. We do not have wings, hollow bones, or a rigid skeleton. We do not have a keel to anchor flight muscles.

11. No, birds eat a tremendous amount of food in relation to their mass.

Is That a Fact!

The wandering albatross's wings are 3 to 3.5 m long but are barely 23 cm wide. The wings are inefficient for flapping flight, but the unusual shape of the wings enables albatrosses to soar for months at a time. Albatrosses alight only when they need to nest and feed and when winds are too calm for soaring.

CHAPTER RESOURCES

Chapter Resource File

- Section Quiz **GENERAL**
- Section Review **GENERAL**
- Vocabulary and Section Summary **GENERAL**
- Critical Thinking **ADVANCED**

Technology

Transparencies
- *LINK TO PHYSICAL SCIENCE* Wing Design and Lift

Focus

Overview

This section introduces students to four kinds of birds: flightless birds, water birds, perching birds, and birds of prey.

🔊 Bellringer

To reinforce the concept that feathers are the defining characteristic of birds, ask students the following questions:

• Why are hawk moths, bats, and flying squirrels not classified as birds? (These animals don't have feathers.)

• Why are penguins and ostriches classified as birds? (Sample answer: These birds do not fly, but they do have feathers.)

Motivate

Discussion ——— GENERAL

The National Bird Ask students the following questions:

• What bird is our nation's symbol? (the bald eagle)

• Why? (Throughout history, eagles have been symbols of strength and power. An eagle was the emblem of the Babylonian god Ashur. An eagle adorned the staff of Zeus. In Norse myths, Odin, the king of the gods, often assumed the shape of an eagle.)

LS Verbal

Objectives

● Identify the differences between flightless birds, water birds, perching birds, and birds of prey.

READING STRATEGY

Discussion Read this section silently. Write down questions that you have about this section. Discuss your questions in a small group.

Kinds of Birds

There are about 10,000 species of birds on Earth. Birds vary in color, shape, and size. They range in mass from the 1.6 g bee hummingbird to the 125 kg North African ostrich. The ostrich is almost 80,000 times more massive than the hummingbird!

Scientists group living bird species into 28 different orders. Songbirds, such as robins or bluebirds, make up the largest order. This order includes about 60% of all bird species. But birds are often grouped into four nonscientific categories: flightless birds, water birds, perching birds, and birds of prey. These categories don't include all birds. But they do show how different birds can be.

Flightless Birds

Not all birds fly. Most flightless birds do not have the large keel that anchors birds' flight muscles. Instead of flying, some flightless birds run quickly to move around. Others are skilled swimmers. **Figure 1** shows three kinds of flightless birds.

Figure 1 **Flightless Birds**

▼ Unlike other flightless birds, **penguins** have a large keel and very strong flight muscles. Their wings have changed over time to become flippers. They flap these wings to "fly" underwater.

◄ The **ostrich** is the largest living bird. It can reach a height of 2.5 m and a mass of 125 kg. An ostrich's two-toed feet look almost like hoofs. These birds can run up to about 60 km/h.

The **kiwi** is a small, chicken-sized bird from New Zealand. Kiwis sleep during the day. At night, they hunt for worms, caterpillars, and berries. ▶

MISCONCEPTION
/// ALERT

Feathers, Not Fur Some birds appear to be covered with fur. Help students understand that these birds are actually covered with tiny feathers. Feathers of most birds grow in lines called *tracts*. Between the tracts are gaps called *apteria*. If you blow on the belly of a bird that can fly, such as a robin, the feathers separate to reveal patches of bare skin. But on ostriches and penguins, feathers cover every bit of skin.

Figure 2   Water Birds

The **blue-footed booby** is a tropical water bird. These birds have an elaborate court-ship dance that includes raising their feet one at a time.

Male **wood ducks** have beautiful plumage to attract females. Like all ducks, they are strong swim-mers and flyers.

The **common loon** can make very deep dives and remain underwater for several minutes while searching for fish.

Water Birds

Many flying birds are also comfortable in the water. These water birds include cranes, ducks, geese, swans, pelicans, and loons. These birds usually have webbed feet for swimming or long legs for wading. **Figure 2** above shows three different water birds.

Water birds find food both in the water and on land. Many of these birds eat plants, invertebrates, or fish. Some water birds have a rounded, flat beak for eating plants or small inverte-brates. Others have a long, sharp beak for catching fish.

 Reading Check   What are the two kinds of beaks that are com-mon in water birds? (*See the Appendix for answers to Reading Checks.*)

INTERNET ACTIVITY

For another activity related to this chapter, go to **go.hrw.com** and type in the keyword **HL5VR2W**.

WEIRD SCIENCE

Some oceanic birds, such as fulmars, can eject a smelly oil from their stomachs. Fulmars can spew the oil as a defensive weapon. Elimination of the oil can also reduce a bird's weight before flight. The behavior is instinctive—newly hatched fulmars have been observed regurgitat-ing the oil while emerging from the shell. During courtship, adult fulmars exchange the oil with each other.

Answer to Reading Check
rounded, flat beaks and long, sharp beaks

Teach

Debate ──────── ADVANCED
Destroying Wildlife to Save It?
The artist John James Audubon (1785–1851) painted pictures of birds that he shot. This was the only way that he could get close enough to see the level of detail he needed in his paintings. Although modern cameras and binoculars provide researchers with excellent detail, scientists have sometimes killed birds for study and museum collections. This close study allows scientists to place the birds in the proper evolutionary context, to confirm the discovery of new species, and to develop specific conser-vation measures. Ask students to debate the pros and cons of this scientific technique.
LS Verbal/Logical

◉ INCLUSION *Strategies*

• *Gifted and Talented*
• *Behavior Control Issues*
Some students can benefit from exploring classroom topics in greater depth and from making choices about their learning. Challenge these students to research the gestation periods and length of brooding for 10 bird spe-cies of the students' choos-ing. Ask students to present their results in a bar graph. **LS** Verbal

Making Comparisons Have students make tables comparing the four major groups of birds. **LS Verbal**

Quiz ——————— GENERAL

1. What are four groups of birds? (flightless birds, water birds, perching birds, and birds of prey)

2. What do flightless birds do to move around instead of flying? (Some flightless birds run quickly. Other flightless birds are skilled swimmers.)

3. Compare perching birds and birds of prey. (Perching birds have feet that automatically close around branches. Birds of prey have sharp talons; sharp, curved beaks; and good vision.)

Alternative Assessment ——— GENERAL

Classifying Birds Display pictures of birds for the class. Have students make charts that have three columns. Tell them to put the number of the bird in the first column and the general type of the bird (flightless, water, perching, or bird of prey) in the second column. Have students list the reasons that each bird was classified as it was in the third column.   English Language Learners
LS Visual

Answer to Reading Check
The perching bird's feet will remain closed around the branch.

Perching Birds

Perching birds have special adaptations for resting on branches. Songbirds, such as robins, warblers, and sparrows, make up a large part of this group of birds. When a perching bird lands in a tree, its feet automatically close around a branch. If the bird falls asleep while it is perching, its feet will stay closed. The sleeping bird will not fall off the branch. **Figure 3** shows three kinds of perching birds.

✓**Reading Check** What happens to a perching bird that falls asleep while it is perching on a branch?

| Figure 3 | Perching Birds |

▼ **Parrots** have special feet for perching and climbing. They open seeds and slice fruit with their strong, hooked beak.

▲ **Chickadees** are lively, little birds that often visit garden feeders. They can dangle underneath a branch while hunting for insects, seeds, or fruits.

Most tanagers are tropical birds, but the **scarlet tanager** spends the summer in North America. The male is red, but the female is a yellow green color that blends into the trees. ▶

ACTIVITY ——————— GENERAL

Raptors Birds of prey, such as eagles, owls, falcons, and hawks, are called *raptors*. There are raptor centers throughout the United States. Many specialize in the care and rehabilitation of injured birds. Many house and display birds that are too wounded or too accustomed to people to survive on their own. The centers frequently serve as wildlife education centers, too. Have students research and contact these centers to obtain more information about raptors and their care. Have students make an informative pamphlet about what they learn. If a raptor center is nearby, encourage students to work with the school administration to arrange a visit by a naturalist and a bird or two from the raptor center.
LS Verbal/Interpersonal

Birds of Prey

Birds of prey hunt and eat other vertebrates. These birds may eat insects or other invertebrates in addition to mammals, fish, reptiles, and birds. Take a look at the birds in **Figure 4.** Birds of prey have sharp claws on their feet and a sharp, curved beak. These traits help the birds catch and eat their prey. Birds of prey also have very good vision. Most of them hunt during the day, as the osprey does. But most owls hunt at night.

Figure 4 Birds of Prey

◀ Owls, such as this **northern spotted owl,** are the only birds of prey that hunt at night. They have a strong sense of hearing to help them find their prey in the dark.

◀ **Ospreys** eat fish. They fly over the water and catch fish with their clawed feet.

SECTION Review

Summary

- Some flightless birds do not have a large keel as other birds do. Many flightless birds are fast runners or swimmers.
- Many water birds have webbed feet for swimming or long legs for wading.
- Perching birds have feet that automatically close around a branch.
- Birds of prey have a sharp beak and claws for catching and eating their prey.

Understanding Key Ideas

1. Which of the following groups of birds includes birds that do NOT have a large keel?
   a. flightless birds
   b. water birds
   c. perching birds
   d. birds of prey

2. Why do some water birds have long legs?
   a. for swimming
   b. for wading
   c. for running
   d. for flying

3. Most birds of prey have very good eyesight. Why do you think good vision is important for these birds?

4. To which group of birds do songbirds belong? Name three examples of songbirds.

Math Skills

5. How quickly could an ostrich, running at a speed of 60 km/h, run a 400 m track event?

Critical Thinking

6. **Predicting Consequences** Would it be helpful for a duck to have the feet of a perching bird? Explain why or why not.

7. **Making Inferences** How could being able to run 60 km/h be helpful for an ostrich?

For a variety of links related to this chapter, go to www.scilinks.org

Topic: Kinds of Birds
SciLinks code: HSM0831

CHAPTER RESOURCES

Chapter Resource File

- Section Quiz GENERAL
- Section Review GENERAL
- Vocabulary and Section Summary GENERAL
- SciLinks Activity GENERAL

SECTION
3

Focus

Overview

This section introduces students to seven common characteristics of mammals.

Bellringer

Have students answer the following question, "What are the characteristics of mammals?" (Students may not be able to list all general mammal characteristics, but these characteristics include the ability to make milk, using a diaphragm for breathing, an endothermic body temperature, hair, specialized teeth, the ability to reproduce sexually, and a large brain.)

Motivate

Discussion ——— GENERAL

Domestication of Animals

Ask students to describe how humans have interacted with wild mammals over time. (Sample answer: Humans have hunted mammals and used their meat for food, their hides for clothing and shelter, and their bones for tools.) Ask students how the domestication of mammals, such as horses, pigs, and cats, changed the lives of early humans. (Domestication of mammals allowed early humans to cultivate larger areas and carry supplies longer distances. It also provided early humans with food, clothing, and pest control.) **LS** Verbal

READING WARM-UP

Objectives

● Explain how early mammals lived.
● Describe seven common characteristics of mammals.

Terms to Learn

mammary gland
diaphragm

READING STRATEGY

Reading Organizer As you read this section, create an outline of the section. Use the headings from the section in your outline.

Characteristics of Mammals

What do you have in common with a bat, a donkey, a giraffe, and a whale? You're all mammals!

Mammals live in the coldest oceans, the hottest deserts, and almost every place in between. The tiniest bats weigh less than a cracker, and the blue whale can weigh more than twenty school buses. Though mammals vary in many ways, all of the approximately 5,000 modern species share certain characteristics. **Figure 1** shows a few of the many types of mammals.

The First Mammals

Fossil evidence indicates that about 280 million years ago, reptiles called *therapsids* (thuh RAP sihdz) existed. These animals had characteristics of both reptiles and mammals. True mammals appeared soon after. Mammals appeared in the fossil record more than 225 million years ago. They were about the size of mice. These animals were endotherms, so they were able to keep their body temperature constant. They did not depend on their surroundings to keep warm. This trait allowed them to look for food at night and to avoid being eaten by dinosaurs during the day.

When the dinosaurs died out, more land and food were available for the mammals. These resources allowed mammals to spread out and live in many different environments.

Figure 1 *Even though they look very different, all of these animals are mammals.*

▼ Beluga whale

 Mandrill baboon

 Rhinoceros

CHAPTER RESOURCES

Chapter Resource File

- Lesson Plan
- Directed Reading A **BASIC**
- Directed Reading B **SPECIAL NEEDS**

Technology

Transparencies
- Bellringer

WEIRD SCIENCE

The world's smallest flying mammal is the bumblebee bat, which has a mass of only 2 g. It weighs less than a penny does! The bumblebee bat is about 33 mm long. This tiny bat lives in limestone caves in southwest Thailand.

Figure 2 Like all mammals, this calf drinks its mother's milk for its first meals.

Common Characteristics

Dolphins, monkeys, and elephants have hair and specialized teeth, just as you do! Mammals share these and many other characteristics that make them unlike other animals.

Making Milk

All mammals have mammary glands. No other animal has these glands. **Mammary glands** are structures that make milk. However, only mature females produce milk in their mammary glands. All female mammals feed their young with this milk. **Figure 2** shows a cow nursing her calf.

All milk is made of water, proteins, fats, and sugars. But the amount of each nutrient is different in different milk. For example, human milk has half the fat and twice the sugar of cow's milk.

Reading Check What is milk made of? (*See the Appendix for answers to Reading Checks.*)

Breathing Air

All animals need oxygen to get energy from their food. Like birds and reptiles, mammals use lungs to get oxygen from the air. But mammals have a muscle that helps them get air. The **diaphragm** (DIE uh FRAM) is a large muscle that helps bring air into the lungs. It lies at the bottom of the rib cage.

Endothermic

As oxygen helps to break down a mammal's food, energy is released. This energy keeps mammals warm. Has a dog or cat ever sat in your lap? If so, then you have felt how warm a mammal's body is. Like birds, mammals are endotherms. Their internal chemical changes keep their body temperature constant. The ability to stay warm helps them survive in cold areas and stay active when the weather is cool.

mammary gland in a female mammal, a gland that secretes milk

diaphragm a dome-shaped muscle that is attached to the lower ribs and that functions as the main muscle in respiration

Diaphragm Demo

1. Place your hand under your rib cage to feel your abdominal muscles (which are indirectly connected to your diaphragm). Breathe in and out.
2. Write down what your hand feels as you breathe.
3. Place your hand under your rib cage again. Contract your abdominal muscles, and try breathing. Then, relax your abdominal muscles, and breathe.
4. Write down what happens.
5. Explain your observations. Then, draw a picture of how the diaphragm moves.

Flashcards Have students make flashcards to help them remember the seven characteristics of mammals. **LS** Verbal

Quiz — GENERAL

1. What are two features that help keep mammals warm? (fur and a layer of fat)

2. When did the first mammals appear in the fossil record? (more than 225 million years ago)

3. What are large cutting teeth called? (incisors)

Alternative Assessment — GENERAL

Concept Mapping Have students use the following terms and phrases to create a concept map: *canines, mammary glands, mammals, endothermic, incisors, breathe air, diaphragm, hair, specialized teeth, sexual reproduction, large brains, make milk,* and *molars.* **LS** Logical

Figure 3 *The thick fur of this arctic fox helps its body stay warm in the coldest winters.*

Hair

Mammals have a few characteristics that keep them from losing their body heat. One way they stay warm is by having hair. Mammals are the only animals that have hair. All mammals—even whales—have hair. Mammals that live in cold climates, such as the fox in **Figure 3,** usually have thick coats of hair. These thick coats are called *fur.* Large mammals that live in warm climates, such as elephants, do not need warm fur. Humans have hair all over their bodies, as apes do. But human body hair is shorter and more fine than ape hair.

Most mammals also have a layer of fat under their skin to keep them warm. This fat helps trap heat in the body. Whales and other mammals that live in cold oceans have an especially thick layer of fat. This thick layer of fat is called *blubber.*

Specialized Teeth

Another unique mammal characteristic is specialized teeth. Modern birds don't have teeth. Fish and reptiles have teeth, but usually all of their teeth are identical. Mammals have teeth with different shapes and sizes for different jobs. Also, mammals replace their original baby teeth with a permanent set.

Your own mouth has three kinds of teeth. You have cutting teeth, called *incisors,* in the front of your mouth. Most people have four incisors on top and four on the bottom. Next to them are stabbing teeth, called *canines.* These help you grab and hold on to food. Your flat, grinding back teeth are *molars.*

Each kind of tooth helps mammals eat a certain kind of food. Meat-eating mammals have large canines to help them eat prey. Plant-eating mammals have larger incisors and molars to help them bite and grind plants. **Figure 4** shows the teeth of a meat-eating mammal and a plant-eating mammal.

Figure 4 *Mountain lions have sharp canine teeth for grabbing their prey. Horses have sharp incisors in front for cutting plants and flat molars in the back for grinding plants.*

ACTiViTY — BASIC

Comparing Skulls Display several skulls for students to study. Include mammal skulls, a reptile skull, a bird skull, and an amphibian skull. Tell students to carefully examine the skulls and to describe similarities and differences between the kinds of animals. Ask students to describe differences in dentition and speculate about advantages and disadvantages of the tooth arrangements that they observe. English Language Learners **LS** Verbal/Visual

Sexual Reproduction

All mammals reproduce sexually. Sperm fertilize eggs inside the female's body. Though there are a few exceptions, most mammals give birth to live young. Newborn mammals stay with at least one parent until they are grown. Mammal parents care for and protect their young during this time. **Figure 5** shows a brown bear with her young.

> ✓ **Reading Check** How long does a young mammal stay with at least one parent?

Large Brains

A mammal's brain is much larger than that of most other animals that are the same size. This large brain allows mammals to learn and think quickly. It also allows mammals to respond quickly to events around them.

Mammals use vision, hearing, smell, touch, and taste to find out about the world around them. The importance of each sense often depends on a mammal's surroundings. For example, mammals that are active at night depend on their hearing more than on their vision.

Figure 5 *A mother bear will attack anything that threatens her cubs.*

SECTION Review

Summary

- Early mammals were small. Being endothermic helped them survive.
- Mammals have mammary glands, a diaphragm, and hair.
- All mammals are endotherms. Most have a layer of fat under their skin for extra warmth.
- Mammals have specialized teeth.
- Mammals reproduce sexually and raise young.
- Mammals have large brains and learn quickly.

Using Key Terms

1. Use each of the following terms in a separate sentence: *mammary gland* and *diaphragm*.

Understanding Key Ideas

2. Large brains help mammals survive by allowing them
   a. to think and learn quickly.
   b. to maintain their body temperature.
   c. to have hair all over their body.
   d. to depend on all of the senses equally.

3. What does a diaphragm do?

4. Name three characteristics that are unique to mammals.

5. Describe three characteristics that help mammals stay warm.

6. How are mammal teeth different from reptile and fish teeth?

7. How do mammals reproduce?

Math Skills

8. What is the mass of a 90,000 kg whale in grams? in milligrams?

Critical Thinking

9. **Making Inferences** Early endothermic mammals could be active at night. If this protected them from certain dinosaurs, were the dinosaurs endothermic? Explain.

10. **Applying Concepts** How could the teeth of a skull give you clues about a mammal's diet?

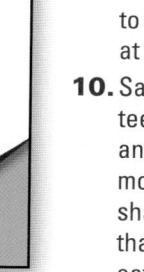

Developed and maintained by the National Science Teachers Association

For a variety of links related to this chapter, go to www.scilinks.org

Topic: Characteristics of Mammals
SciLinks code: HSM0259

 **Cultural Awareness** **GENERAL**

Staying Warmer Native peoples of the Arctic region, such as the Inuit, have traditionally hunted marine mammals, such as seals, whales, and walruses. Ask interested students to research how these cultures use mammals to survive cold temperatures. Have students make a poster showing their findings. **LS Visual**

CHAPTER RESOURCES

Chapter Resource File

- Section Quiz **GENERAL**
- Section Review **GENERAL**
- Vocabulary and Section Summary **GENERAL**

Focus

Overview

This section describes the development of placental mammals and gives several examples of placental mammals.

🔊 Bellringer

Ask students to list 25 mammals and organize them into groups based on their similarities. (Students should find basic similarities between mammals, but they will likely not sort mammals into the groups described in this section.) As students read the section, they will see whether scientists group mammals based on similarities.

Motivate

CONNECTION ACTIVITY
Archeology————— GENERAL

Mammal Evidence When archeologists study the homes of prehistoric peoples, they sometimes find animal remains. Archeologists discovered that ancient South American Indians used the shells of early armadillos to build roofs for homes. These ancestors of modern armadillos had shells up to 3 m long. Ask students to research other mammal remains that have been found in the homes of prehistoric peoples. **LS Verbal**

READING WARM-UP

Objectives
- Explain how placental mammals develop.
- Give an example of each type of placental mammal.

Terms to Learn
placental mammal
gestation period

READING STRATEGY

Brainstorming The key idea of this section is kinds of placental mammals. Brainstorm words and phrases related to placental mammals.

CHAPTER RESOURCES

Chapter Resource File
- Lesson Plan
- Directed Reading A **BASIC**
- Directed Reading B **SPECIAL NEEDS**

Technology
- Transparencies
  - Bellringer

Placental Mammals

Both elephants and mice begin life by developing inside a mother. Elephants need up to 23 months to develop inside the mother. But mice need only a few weeks!

Mammals are divided into groups based on how they develop. The groups are placental mammals, monotremes, and marsupials. Most mammals are placental mammals. A **placental mammal** is a mammal whose embryos develop inside the mother's body. The embryos grow in an organ called the *uterus*. An organ called the *placenta* attaches the embryos to the uterus. The placenta carries food and oxygen from the mother's blood to the embryo and carries wastes away from the embryo.

The time in which an embryo develops within the mother is called a **gestation period** (jes TAY shuhn PIR ee uhd). This period lasts a different amount of time for each kind of placental mammal. In humans, this period lasts about 9 months.

Living placental mammals are divided into 18 orders. The most common orders are described on the following pages.

Anteaters, Armadillos, and Sloths

A few mammals have unique backbones that have special connections between the vertebrae. This group includes anteaters, armadillos, and sloths. These mammals are sometimes called "toothless mammals," but only anteaters have no teeth. The others have small teeth. Most mammals in this group eat insects they catch with their long, sticky tongues. **Figure 1** shows two mammals from this group.

Figure 1 Anteaters, Armadillos, and Sloths

 Armadillos eat insects, frogs, mushrooms, and roots. Threatened armadillos roll up into a ball, or they may jump to scare a predator. They are protected by their tough plates.

▼ **Giant anteaters** never destroy the nests of the insects they eat. They open a nest and eat a few insects. Then, they move on to another nest.

MISCONCEPTION ///ALERT\\\

Placentas Both placental mammals and marsupials have a placenta. So, why is only one group called *placental*? The difference is that in marsupials, the placenta nourishes the fetus only for the short period before its early birth. But in placental mammals, the placenta plays a major role in nourishing the fetus throughout its development.

Figure 2   Insectivores

The **star-nosed mole** has sensitive feelers on its nose. These help the mole find earthworms to eat. Moles have poor vision.

Hedgehogs live throughout Europe, Asia, and Africa. Their spines keep them safe from most predators.

Insectivores

Insectivores make up another group of mammals that eat insects. This group includes moles, shrews, and hedgehogs. Most insectivores are small and have long, pointed noses that help them smell their food. They have small brains and simple teeth. Some eat worms, fish, frogs, lizards, and small mammals in addition to insects. **Figure 2** shows two insectivores.

Rodents

More than one-third of mammal species are rodents. Rodents live on every continent except Antarctica. They include squirrels, mice, rats, guinea pigs, porcupines, and chinchillas. Most rodents have sensitive whiskers. They all have one set of incisors in the upper jaw. Rodents gnaw and chew so much that these teeth wear down. But that doesn't stop their chewing—their incisors grow continuously! **Figure 3** shows two rodents.

placental mammal a mammal that nourishes its unborn offspring through a placenta inside its uterus

gestation period in mammals, the length of time between fertilization and birth

Reading Check   What do rodents do with their sharp incisors? *(See the Appendix for answers to Reading Checks.)*

Figure 3   Rodents

▲ Like all rodents, **porcupines** have gnawing teeth.

▼ The **capybara** (KAP i BAH ruh) of South America is the largest rodent in the world. Females have a mass of up to 70 kg—as much as a grown man.

Teach

Cultural Awareness   GENERAL

Writing   **Shrews** Shrews have been objects of fear and adoration. Some Native American lore holds that red-toothed shrews (genus *Sorex*) kill people by burrowing through the body to the heart. Some central Africans worship the hero shrew (*Scutisorex congicus*). Because the vertebrae in the hero shrew's backbone are arched and fused, the backbone is strong enough to protect the shrew from being crushed. Some people believe that eating the shrew's heart will endow them with that same strength. Ask students to research beliefs about shrews. Then, have students write a creative story about their findings. **LS Verbal**

Homework   ADVANCED

Orders of Placental Mammals Not all orders of placental mammals are represented in this section. Have students research and draw a diagram depicting a hypothesis for the genetic relationships between the 18 orders of placental mammals. **LS Visual**

Science BlOopers

Tree Shrews Tree shrews are tiny animals that look like squirrels that have long, cone-shaped noses. Although they are insectivores and have shrewlike noses, tree shrews are not true shrews. Until the late 20th century, zoologists thought that tree shrews were primates. Recently, taxonomists recognized the uniqueness of tree shrews and placed them in a new order, Scandentia.

Answer to Reading Check
They gnaw and chew.

BRAIN FOOD

Making Tracks In the snow, the four footprints of a single rabbit or hare are aligned or the prints from the back feet are in front of those from the front feet. When moving quickly, rabbits and hares rely on their powerful back legs to propel them forward. Their jump distance is increased when they swing their back legs forward until they touch down nearly in line with the front feet and then push off. Rabbits and hares are very efficient animals because of this type of locomotion. Cheetahs can also run this way.

Discussion ——— GENERAL

Bat Fact and Fiction Ask students whether each of the following statements is true or false:

1. Some bats have wing spans of more than 1.5 m. (true, giant flying foxes can have a wing span of over 1.5 m)

2. A single little brown bat can catch 1,200 mosquito-sized insects in 1 h. (true)

3. Bats present a serious disease threat to humans. (false, less than one-half of 1% of bats carry rabies, and most bats bite only when threatened)

LS Verbal

Figure 4 Rabbits, Hares, and Pikas

▲ The large ears of this **black-tailed jack rabbit** help it hear well and keep cool. They also work with a sensitive nose and large eyes to detect predators.

◀ **Pikas** are small animals that live high in the mountains. Pikas gather plants and pile them into "haystacks" to dry. In the winter, pikas use the dry plants for food and insulation.

Rabbits, Hares, and Pikas

Rodents are similar to a group of mammals that includes rabbits, hares, and pikas (PIE kuhz). **Figure 4** shows two members of this group. Like rodents, they have sharp gnawing teeth. But unlike rodents, they have two sets of incisors in their upper jaw. Also, their tails are shorter than rodents' tails.

✓ **Reading Check** How are rabbits different from rodents?

Flying Mammals

Bats are the only mammals that fly. **Figure 5** shows two kinds of bats. Bats are active at night. They sleep in protected areas during the day. Most bats eat insects or other small animals. But some bats eat fruit or plant nectar. A few bats, called *vampire bats,* drink the blood of birds or mammals.

Most bats use echoes to find their food and their way. Using echoes to find things is called *echolocation.* Bats make clicking noises as they fly. The clicks echo off trees, rocks, and insects. Bats know what is around them by hearing these echoes.

Figure 5 Flying Mammals

◀ **Fruit bats,** also called *flying foxes,* live in tropical regions. They pollinate plants as they go from one plant to another, eating fruit.

▲ The **spotted bat** is found in parts of the American Southwest. Like most bats, it eats flying insects. It uses its large ears during echolocation.

Is That a Fact!

Of the known mammal species, nearly 25% are bats.

Answer to Reading Check

Rabbits have two sets of sharp front teeth in their upper jaw, and they have a short tail.

Figure 6   Carnivores

▼ **Coyotes** are members of the dog family. They live throughout North America and in parts of Central America.

▼ **Walruses,** like all pinnipeds, eat in the ocean but sleep and mate on land. They use their huge canines in courtship displays, for defense, and to climb onto ice.

Carnivores

Mammals that have large canine teeth and special molar teeth for slicing meat are called *carnivores.* Many mammals in this group eat only meat. But some mammals in this group are omnivores or herbivores that eat plants. For example, black bears eat grass, nuts, and berries and rarely eat meat. The carnivore group includes cats, dogs, otters, bears, raccoons, and hyenas. *Pinnipeds,* a group of fish-eating ocean mammals, are also carnivores. Seals, sea lions, and walruses are pinnipeds. **Figure 6** shows two carnivores.

Trunk-Nosed Mammals

Elephants are the only living mammals that have a trunk. The trunk is a combination of an upper lip and a nose. An elephant uses its trunk in the same ways we use our hands, lips, and nose. An elephants uses its trunk to put food in its mouth. It also uses its trunk to spray water on its back to cool off. **Figure 7** shows two species of elephants.

Figure 7   Trunk-Nosed Mammals

◀ Elephants are social. The females live in herds of mothers, daughters, and sisters. These elephants are **African elephants.**

These **Indian elephants** have smaller ears and tusks than African elephants do. ▶

Homework ──── ADVANCED

PORTFOLIO   **Elephant Populations** Have students examine the wild populations of African and Asian elephants. Students should identify approximately how many elephants are in these populations today, where these populations are found, and whether the populations are protected. Students should also identify ways in which elephant populations have changed over time. Students should create a map showing the current and past distributions of wild elephants. **LS** Visual

ACTIVITY ──── ADVANCED
Comparing Footprints Have students compare footprints or foot casts of two common carnivores: the domestic dog and the domestic cat. Students can make footprints by having a pet step on damp, claylike soil. They can make casts by pouring plaster of Paris in a dried footprint. Have students study the casts and hypothesize the reasons for the features and differences that they notice. **LS** Visual/Verbal   English Language Learners

Debate ──── GENERAL
Carnivore Conservation
Explain to students that many carnivores are endangered because of habitat loss, hunting, and poaching. Historically, persuading people to preserve animals that they considered dangerous to themselves and to livestock has been difficult. Some carnivores are endangered because people hunt them for their fur or for body parts that are believed to have medicinal qualities. Have students work in teams to debate the extent to which large carnivores, such as wolves and tigers, should be preserved and the steps that people should take to deal with these large carnivores. **LS** Verbal/Logical   Co-op Learning

Water Buffaloes Many kinds of hoofed mammals are used for draft work. In the United States, small farms still rely on horses or mules to pull some farm equipment. Oxen, llamas, goats, elephants, and camels are used in various parts of the world for pulling or carrying. But perhaps no animal is as widely used as the water buffalo is. Water buffaloes are large, strong, and relatively docile animals. They are hardy and can eat rough, native vegetation. They were originally domesticated in Asia thousands of years ago and are still vital to the farms of southern China and Southeast Asia. The water buffalo was introduced to Africa about 1,400 years ago and is still used for draft work there. More recently, the water buffalo was introduced to Central and South America. Have interested students research and present to the class an oral report on the importance of water buffaloes or other draft animals to farmers around the world. **LS Verbal**

Hoofed Mammals

Horses, pigs, deer, and rhinoceroses are some of the many mammals that have thick hoofs. A *hoof* is a thick, hard pad that covers a mammal's toe. The hoof is similar to a toenail or a claw, but it covers the entire toe. Most hoofed mammals are fast runners. They also have large, flat molars. These teeth help hoofed mammals grind the plants that they eat.

Hoofed mammals include two orders—odd-toed and even-toed. Odd-toed hoofed mammals have one or three toes on each foot. Horses and zebras have one large, hoofed toe. Rhinoceroses have three toes. Even-toed hoofed mammals have two or four toes on each foot. Pigs, cattle, camels, deer, and giraffes are even-toed. **Figure 8** shows some hoofed mammals.

Figure 8 Hoofed Mammals

► **Tapirs** are large, odd-toed mammals. They live in forests in Central America, South America, and Southeast Asia. Tapirs are active mostly at night.

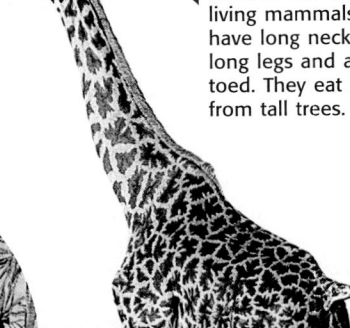

◄ **Giraffes** are the tallest living mammals. They have long necks and long legs and are even-toed. They eat leaves from tall trees.

Camels are even-toed mammals. The hump of a camel is a large lump of fat that provides energy for the camel when food is scarce. Camels can live without drinking water for a long time, so they can live in very dry places. ►

Horses Hernando Cortez reintroduced the horse into North America during the 1500s. The arrival of the horse changed the lives of Native Americans forever. Ask students to research Native American ways of life before and after the reintroduction of the horse. Have students make posters comparing ways of life during the two time periods. **LS Verbal/Visual**

Is That a Fact!

The limbs of hoofed mammals are adapted for running and walking long distances over open terrain. These animals have between one and four toes and very long foot bones. If we compare the way that hoofed animals walk with the human skeleton and human methods of walking, one would say that hoofed animals balance on the tips of their toes.

Figure 9   Cetaceans

▼ **Spinner dolphins** spin like a football when they leap from the water. Like all dolphins, they are intelligent and highly social.

▼ **Humpback whales** are toothless. Like all toothless whales, they strain sea water through special plates in their mouth. These plates are made of a substance called *baleen*. The baleen traps tiny sea life for the whale to eat.

Cetaceans

Cetaceans (suh TAY shuhnz) are a group of mammals made up of whales, dolphins, and porpoises. All cetaceans live in the water. **Figure 9** shows two kinds of cetaceans. At first glance, they may look more like fish than like mammals. But unlike fish, cetaceans have lungs and nurse their young.

Most of the largest whales are toothless. They strain tiny, shrimplike animals from sea water. However, dolphins, porpoises, sperm whales, and killer whales all have teeth to help them eat. Like bats, these animals use echolocation to find fish and other animals.

Manatees and Dugongs

The smallest group of mammals that live in the water are manatees (MAN uh TEEZ) and dugongs (DOO gawngz). This group includes three species of manatees and the dugong. Manatees and dugongs use their front flippers and a tail to swim slowly through the water. **Figure 10** shows a manatee.

Manatees and dugongs live along ocean coasts and in rivers. They are large animals that eat mostly seaweed and water plants. These animals spend all of their time in the water, but they lift their noses from the water to breathe air.

✔ **Reading Check** How much of their time do dugongs and manatees spend in the water?

Figure 10 *Manatees are also called* sea cows.

Reteaching — BASIC

Making Tables Have students make tables listing the major characteristics of the groups of mammals described in the section. Students should include examples of animals from each group in their tables. **LS Logical**

Quiz — GENERAL

1. What is a carnivore? (an animal that has large canine teeth and special molar teeth for slicing)

2. How do placental mammals develop? (Sample answer: The embryos develop in the uterus. The placenta attaches embryos to the uterus and carries food and oxygen from the mother's blood to the embryos. The placenta also removes wastes from the embryos.)

3. What are three characteristics of primates? (Sample answer: eyes that face forward, five fingers on each hand and five toes on each foot, and flat fingernails instead of claws)

Alternative Assessment — BASIC

Poster Project Have students create a poster that shows an animal from each of the mammal groups discussed in the section. Students should list the general characteristics of each mammal group on their posters. **LS Visual**

CONNECTION TO Language Arts

WRITING SKILL **Funky Monkey** In many parts of the world, cities have taken over natural, nonhuman primate habitat. Some nonhuman primates have moved into the city and adopted new lifestyles. Macaques have been known to steal ice-cream cones from children or hop on a bus for a short ride! Write a story in your **science journal** about people living with monkeys in a city.

Primates

Scientists classify prosimians, monkeys, apes, and humans as *primates*. These animals have five fingers on each hand and five toes on each foot. Most have flat fingernails instead of claws. Primates have a larger brain than most other mammals the same size have. They are considered highly intelligent mammals. Primates also have unique arrangements of body parts that help them do complicated things. For example, all primates have forward-facing eyes that can focus on a single point. And primates have opposable thumbs, which allow them to hold objects.

Many primates live in trees. They climb with their grasping hands and feet. Flexible shoulder joints allow them to swing between branches. They eat leaves and fruits, and some primates even hunt animals. **Figure 11** shows some primates.

✓ Reading Check What traits help many primates live in trees?

Figure 11 Primates

◀**Orangutans** and other apes often walk upright. Apes usually have larger brains and bodies than monkeys do.

Spider monkeys, like ▶ many monkeys, have grasping tails. Their long arms, legs, and tails help them move among the trees.

▲ The **proboscis monkey** has an enormous nose! The males have larger noses than the females do. That difference makes some scientists wonder if the male's nose is used to attract females.

Answer to Connection to Language Arts
Students' stories should be creative and should demonstrate an understanding of how monkeys have adapted to life in cities.

Answer to Reading Check
large brains, grasping hands and feet, flexible shoulder joints, and forward-facing eyes

Summary

- Placental mammals develop inside the mother during a gestation period. Placental mothers nurse their young after birth.
- Anteaters, armadillos, and sloths have unique backbones.
- Moles, shrews, and hedgehogs eat insects.
- Squirrels, rats, and porcupines are rodents.
- Rabbits, hares, and pikas are similar to rodents but have an extra pair of incisors.
- Bats are flying mammals.

- Cats, dogs, otters, bears, sea lions, and walruses are in the carnivore group.
- Horses, zebras, pigs, deer, rhinoceroses, and giraffes are hoofed mammals.
- Elephants are trunk-nosed mammals.
- Whales and porpoises are cetaceans.
- Manatees and dugongs are large, slow mammals that live in the water.
- Prosimians, monkeys, apes, and humans are primates.

Using Key Terms

1. Use the following terms in the same sentence: *placental mammal* and *gestation period*.

Understanding Key Ideas

2. Which mammals live entirely in the water?
   a. manatees, dugongs, cetaceans, and pinnipeds
   b. only manatees and dugongs
   c. only cetaceans
   d. manatees, dugongs, and cetaceans

3. A placental mammal's embryo
   a. develops in the uterus.
   b. develops in the placenta.
   c. develops in a pouch.
   d. develops in a leathery egg.

4. Could you tell a horse from a deer just by looking at their feet? Explain.

5. Give one example of each type of placental mammal described in the section.

Critical Thinking

6. **Making Inferences** What is a gestation period? Why do you think elephants have a longer gestation period than mice do?

7. **Identifying Relationships** Manatees may look a little like pinnipeds, but they are more closely related to elephants. In what ways is a manatee more like an elephant than like a pinniped?

Interpreting Graphics

Use the picture of the animal below to answer the questions that follow.

8. To which placental mammal group does this animal belong? How can you tell?

9. Why can't this animal be a rodent?

10. Why can't this animal be a primate?

Developed and maintained by the National Science Teachers Association

For a variety of links related to this chapter, go to www.scilinks.org

Topic: Kinds of Mammals
SciLinks code: HSM0832

CONNECTION to
Anthropology——ADVANCED

Organizing Primates Ask interested students to examine the taxonomic organization of primate species. Students should identify the major groups of primates, such as lemurs, lorises, tarsiers, New World monkeys, Old World monkeys, apes, and hominids. Encourage students to examine extinct primates as a part of their research. Have students create a poster showing the taxonomy of primates. **LS Visual**

CHAPTER RESOURCES

Chapter Resource File

- Section Quiz GENERAL
- Section Review GENERAL
- Vocabulary and Section Summary GENERAL
- Reinforcement Worksheet BASIC

Answers to Section Review

1. Sample answer: In placental mammals, the amount of time in which the embryo develops within the uterus is called a *gestation period*.

2. d

3. a

4. Sample answer: Yes, horses have an odd number of toes, while deer have an even number of toes.

5. Sample answer: An anteater is a mammal that is part of a mammal group sometimes called *toothless mammals*. A hedgehog is an insectivore. Porcupines are rodents. Rabbits are part of a group of animals that are similar to rodents but have two sets of sharp incisors in their top jaw and have shorter tails than most rodents do. Bats are flying mammals. Wolves are carnivores. Elephants are trunk-nosed mammals. Giraffes are hoofed animals. Dolphins are cetaceans. Manatees are mammals that live in the water. Monkeys are primates.

6. Sample answer: A gestation period is the amount of time an embryo takes to develop. Elephants are much larger than mice, so elephant embryos likely need more time to develop. For this reason, elephant embryos have a longer gestation period.

7. Sample answer: Unlike pinnipeds, manatees do not eat meat. Like elephants, manatees are herbivores: manatees eat water plants and seaweeds.

8. Sample answer: The animal is a carnivore. It is eating meat, and it has large canine teeth.

9. Sample answer: This animal doesn't have a set of large incisors in its upper jaw, so it cannot be a rodent.

10. Sample answer: This animal has claws instead of flat fingernails and does not have opposable thumbs, so the animal cannot be a primate.

Focus

Overview

This section describes the three species of monotremes and several species of marsupials. Students will learn how monotremes and marsupials differ from placental mammals.

Bellringer

Before students read the section, ask students to name a monotreme. (Sample answer: platypus) Then, ask students to name three marsupials. (Sample answer: kangaroo, wallaby, and opossum)

Motivate

Group ACTiViTY — GENERAL

Amphibious Mammals The platypus is an amphibious mammal. Tell students to look up the word *amphibious* in a dictionary if they do not know what the word means. Then, have students list examples of other amphibious mammals. (Sample answer: river otters, hippopotamuses, beavers, and muskrats)
LS Verbal

Monotremes and Marsupials

Did you know that some mammals hatch from eggs and that others spend the first months of life in a mother's pouch? Only a few kinds of mammals develop this way.

Placental mammals are born as well-developed young. But monotremes hatch from eggs. And newborn marsupials still need months of development in a mother's pouch.

Monotremes

A **monotreme** (MAHN oh TREEM) is a mammal that lays eggs. Monotremes have all the traits of mammals, including mammary glands, a diaphragm, and hair. And like other mammals, they keep their body temperature constant.

A female monotreme lays eggs with thick, leathery shells. She uses her body's energy to keep the eggs warm. After the young hatch, the mother takes care of them and feeds them milk. Monotremes do not have nipples as other mammals do. Baby monotremes lick milk from the skin and hair around their mother's mammary glands.

Echidnas

There are only three living species of monotremes. Two of these species are echidnas (ee KID nuhz). Echidnas are about the size of a house cat. Their large claws and long snouts help them dig ants and termites out of insect nests. **Figure 1** shows the two species of echidnas.

Figure 1 Echidnas

 The **long-beaked echidna** lives in New Guinea.

The **short-beaked echidna** lives in Australia and New Guinea.

CONNECTION ACTiViTY
Anthropology — ADVANCED

Aboriginal Art The artwork of Australia's Aborigines often depicts Australia's unique and varied wildlife. Have students research the history of Aboriginal art and the symbolism of the animals in the Aborigines' paintings. Students should use what they learn to create their own piece of art. **LS** Kinesthetic/Visual

English Language Learners

Figure 2 *When underwater, a duckbill platypus closes its eyes and ears. It uses its bill to find food.*

The Platypus

The only other living monotreme is the platypus. Only one species of platypus lives today. This animal lives in Australia. It looks very different from other mammals. In fact, when scientists outside Australia were first sent the remains of a platypus, they thought they were the victims of a practical joke. **Figure 2** shows a platypus.

The platypus is a swimming mammal that lives and feeds in rivers and ponds. It has webbed feet and a flat tail to help it move through the water. It uses its flat, rubbery bill to search for food. It uses its claws to dig tunnels in riverbanks. The platypus lays its eggs in these tunnels.

Reading Check How does a platypus use its bill? (*See Appendix for answers to Reading Checks.*)

Marsupials

You probably know that kangaroos carry their young in a pouch. Kangaroos and other mammals with pouches are **marsupials** (mahr SOO pee uhlz). Like all mammals, marsupials have mammary glands, hair, and specialized teeth. Unlike monotremes, marsupials give birth to live young. Marsupial development is unique because newborn marsupials continue their development in a mother's pouch. The newborns stay in the pouch for several months.

There are about 280 species of marsupials living today. Most of them live in Australia, New Guinea, and South America. The only living marsupial native to North America is the opossum (uh PAHS uhm).

CONNECTION TO Environmental Science

Pouches in Peril Australia's marsupials are in danger. Many other species have been artificially introduced into Australia's unique ecosystems. These new species are competing with native marsupials for food and living space. One way to stop the introduction of new species into Australia is to educate people about the dangers of species introduction. Make a poster that explains why people should be careful not to release pets or foreign animals into the wild.

marsupial a mammal that carries and nourishes its young in a pouch

Reteaching — BASIC

Trivia Game Have students work in groups of four. Have each group write 10 questions about monotremes and marsupials. Collect the questions, and use them to lead the groups in a trivia game. **LS** Verbal
Co-op Learning

Quiz — GENERAL

Ask students whether each of the statements below is true or false. Then, ask students to correct false statements.

1. There are no marsupials in North America. (false, the opossum is the only marsupial species in North America)

2. There are three species of monotremes. (true)

3. Marsupials lay eggs. (false, monotremes lay eggs)

4. Monotremes do not have nipples. (true)

Alternative Assessment — BASIC

Concept Mapping Have students use the following terms to create a concept map about monotremes and marsupials: *monotremes, extinction, pouches, kangaroos, platypus, marsupials, koalas, echidnas, eggs,* and *Tasmanian tiger.* **LS** Verbal/Logical

Figure 3 *This newborn kangaroo will stay in its mother's pouch for several months as it continues developing.*

The Pouch

Marsupials are born at an early stage of development. They are born just days or weeks after fertilization. At birth, kangaroos are as small as bumblebees. **Figure 3** shows a newborn kangaroo. Newborn marsupials are hairless, and only their front limbs are well developed. They use these limbs to drag themselves through their mother's fur to the pouch on her belly. Many do this without any help from their parents. Inside the pouch are mammary glands. The newborn climbs in, latches onto a nipple, and starts drinking milk. Young kangaroos, called *joeys,* stay in the mother's pouch for several months. When joeys first leave the pouch, they do so for only short periods of time.

✓ **Reading Check** How big is a newborn kangaroo?

Kinds of Marsupials

You may be familiar with the well-known marsupials shown in **Figure 4.** But many marsupials are not as familiar. Have you heard of wallabies, bettongs, and numbats? Most marsupials live in and around Australia. Tasmanian devils, which are marsupials that eat other animals, live on the island of Tasmania. Tree kangaroos, which spend much of their time in trees, live in the rain forests of Queensland and New Guinea.

Figure 4 **Kinds of Marsupials**

▼ **Koalas** sleep for about 18 hours each day. They eat eucalyptus leaves.

◄ Young **kangaroos** that no longer live in their mother's pouch return to the pouch if there is any sign of danger.

When in danger, an ▶ **opossum** will lie perfectly still. It "plays dead" so predators will ignore it.

Answer to Reading Check
as small as a bumblebee

MISCONCEPTION ALERT

Partial Pouches Not all marsupials have a fully developed pouch. Some species have an incomplete fold of abdominal skin that only partially covers the nursing young, and some smaller species have no pouch at all. But these marsupials still have a brief gestation period and the young are nearly embryonic at birth. The tiny, blind baby must crawl through the mother's fur and attach itself to a nipple.

Endangered and Extinct Marsupials

The number of living marsupial species is decreasing. At least 22 of Australia's native mammal species have become extinct in the last 400 years. Many more are currently in danger. When Europeans came to Australia in the 18th and 19th centuries, they brought animals such as rabbits, cats, and foxes. Many of these species escaped into the wild. Some, such as rabbits, now compete with marsupials for food. Others, such as foxes, now prey on marsupials. The marsupials have no adaptations to protect themselves from these exotic species.

Exotic species are not the only threat to marsupials in Australia. Habitat destruction also threatens marsupials. And the Tasmanian tiger, shown in **Figure 5,** was hunted by people who saw it as a threat to their livestock. Today, conservation efforts across Australia are helping to protect the unique marsupials that live there.

Figure 5 *The Tasmanian tiger, a marsupial carnivore, is probably extinct. There have been no official sightings since 1936.*

SECTION Review

Summary

- Monotremes lay eggs instead of bearing live young. They produce milk but do not have nipples.
- The three living species of monotremes are two kinds of echidnas and the platypus.
- Marsupials give birth to live young, but the young are not fully developed when born. They finish developing in a mother's pouch.
- Many marsupials are endangered or extinct.

Using Key Terms

1. Use each of the following terms in a separate sentence: *monotreme* and *marsupial.*

Understanding Key Ideas

2. Which of the following characteristics is shared by monotremes and marsupials?
   a. The young hatch from eggs.
   b. Some species of both live in South America.
   c. Females have no nipples.
   d. Females produce milk.

3. What are the two kinds of monotremes?

4. Name three kinds of marsupials.

5. What has caused many marsupials in Australia to become endangered or extinct?

6. How are monotremes different from all other mammals? How are they similar?

Math Skills

7. What percentage of the approximately 5,000 known species of mammals are monotremes?

Critical Thinking

8. **Making Comparisons** How are monotremes similar to birds? How are they different?

9. **Making Inferences** Why do you think opossums play dead when they are in danger?

For a variety of links related to this chapter, go to www.scilinks.org

Topic: Monotremes and Marsupials
SciLinks code: HSM0990

CONNECTION ACTIVITY Math — GENERAL

Rapid Roo Tell students that red kangaroos can attain a maximum speed of 65 km/h. Then, ask students how many meters a red kangaroo could travel in 2 min.

(65 km/h ÷ 60 min = 1.08 km/min

1.08 km/min × 2 min = 2.16 km

2.16 km × 1,000 m/km = 2,160 m)

LS Logical

CHAPTER RESOURCES

Chapter Resource File
- Section Quiz GENERAL
- Section Review GENERAL
- Vocabulary and Section Summary GENERAL

Model-Making Lab

What? No Dentist Bills?

Teacher's Notes

Time Required

Two 45-minute class periods

Lab Ratings

EASY ————————→ HARD

Teacher Prep 🧪🧪
Student Set-Up 🧪🧪
Concept Level 🧪🧪
Clean Up 🧪🧪

MATERIALS

A 60 g supply of birdseed should be sufficient. Pea gravel is an acceptable substitute for aquarium gravel. It can be obtained from most local hardware stores and is much less expensive than aquarium gravel is. A 4:1 ratio of gravel to birdseed works best.

Safety Caution

Remind students to review all safety cautions and icons before beginning this lab activity.

Using Scientific Methods

Model-Making Lab

OBJECTIVES

Make a model of a bird's digestive system.

Test your model, using birdseed.

MATERIALS

- bags, plastic, sealable, various sizes (several)
- birdseed
- gravel, aquarium
- scissors (or other materials as needed)
- straw, plastic drinking
- string
- tape, transparent
- water

SAFETY

What? No Dentist Bills?

When you and I eat, we must chew our food well. Chewing food into small bits is the first part of digestion. But birds don't have teeth. How do birds make big chunks of food small enough to begin digestion? In this activity, you will develop a hypothesis about how birds digest their food. Then, you will build a model of a bird's digestive system to test your hypothesis.

Ask a Question

1. Formulate a question about how a bird's digestive system can break down food even though the bird has no teeth. Your question may be something such as, "How are birds able to begin digestion without using teeth?"

Form a Hypothesis

2. Look at the diagram below of a bird's digestive system. Form a hypothesis about how birds digest their food without using teeth.

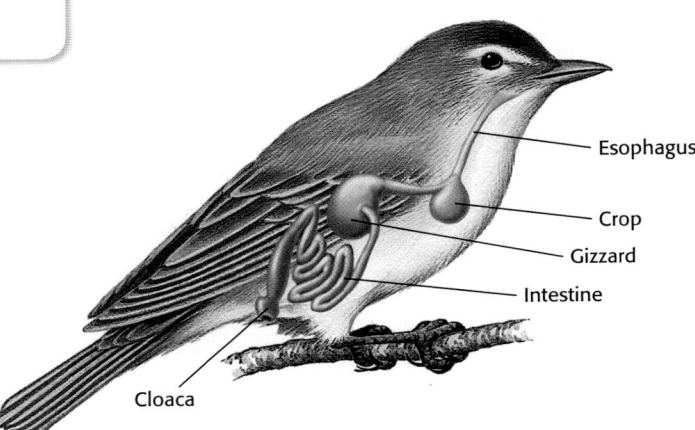

Esophagus
Crop
Gizzard
Intestine
Cloaca

Randy Christian
Stovall Junior High School
Houston, Texas

CHAPTER RESOURCES

Chapter Resource File

 • Datasheet for Chapter Lab
• Lab Notes and Answers

Technology

 Classroom Videos
• Lab Video

---

468 **Chapter 17 • Birds and Mammals**

Test the Hypothesis

❸ Design a model of a bird's digestive system. Include in your design as many of the following parts as possible: esophagus, crop, gizzard, intestine, and cloaca.

❹ Obtain a plastic bag and the other materials you need from your teacher. Build your model.

❺ Test your hypothesis by sending birdseed through your model digestive system.

Analyze the Results

❶ **Describing Events** Did your model digestive system grind the birdseed? Describe what happened to the birdseed as it moved through the system.

❷ **Analyzing Results** Which part of your model was most helpful in grinding? Which part of a real bird's digestive system is represented by this part of your model?

❸ **Recognizing Patterns** Does the amount of material added to your model gizzard change the gizzard's ability to work effectively? Explain your answer.

Draw Conclusions

❹ **Drawing Conclusions** Birds can break down food without using teeth. What conclusions can you draw about how they do this?

❺ **Evaluating Results** Analyze the strengths and weaknesses of your hypothesis based on your results. Was your hypothesis correct? Explain your answer.

❻ **Evaluating Models** What are some limitations of your model? How do you think you could improve it?

Applying Your Data

Did you know that scientists have found "gizzard stones" with fossilized dinosaur skeletons? Look in the library or on the Internet for information about the evolutionary relationship between dinosaurs and birds. List the similarities you find between the two types of animals.

Analyze the Results

1. Answers may vary. If their model gizzards work, students should be able to demonstrate how their model gizzard grinds birdseed.

2. Gizzard stones are small pebbles that some birds swallow. The stones settle in a bird's gizzard, where they help grind food. Students should recognize that structures similar to a bird's gizzard should be most helpful in grinding birdseed.

3. Model gizzards that are no more than three-quarters full will probably be most effective.

Draw Conclusions

4. Sample answer: The gizzard stones help the birds break down food.

5. Answers may vary. Students should describe the strengths and weaknesses of their original hypothesis.

6. Answers may vary.

Applying Your Data

Scientists have long recognized similarities between birds and some dinosaurs. These similarities include an S-shaped neck, an unusual ankle joint structure, and hollow bones. Fossil evidence suggests that some dinosaurs had beaks without teeth, and some had feathers. Today, many scientists think that birds should be classified as a kind of dinosaur. This classification would mean that birds are reptiles!

CHAPTER RESOURCES

Workbooks

📖 **Labs You Can Eat**
• Why Birds of a Beak Eat Together **GENERAL**

📖 **Long-Term Projects & Research Ideas**
• Look Who's Coming to Dinner **ADVANCED**

Chapter Review

Assignment Guide

SECTION	QUESTIONS
1	4–8, 12–13, 19
2	14, 24–28
3	2, 9, 15, 20
4	3, 10, 18, 23
5	11, 16–17
4 and 5	1, 22
1, 3, 4, and 5	21

ANSWERS

Using Key Terms

1. Sample answer: Placental mammals, monotremes, and marsupials have mammary glands.
2. diaphragm
3. gestation period
4. molting
5. Down feathers
6. brooding
7. Contour feathers

Understanding Key Ideas

8. a
9. b
10. c
11. c
12. c
13. Sample answer: Down feathers trap air close to the bird's body to help the bird stay warm. Contour feathers can help some birds attract mates. Contour feathers form a streamlined surface that helps birds fly.

USING KEY TERMS

1. Use the following terms in the same sentence: *mammary gland*, *placental mammal*, *marsupial*, and *monotreme*.

Complete each of the following sentences by choosing the correct term from the word bank.

brooding	gestation period
contour feathers	lift
diaphragm	molting
down feathers	preening

2. The ___ is a muscle that helps animals breathe.

3. The embryos of placental mammals develop during a ___.

4. Birds grow new feathers as a part of the ___ process.

5. ___ help keep birds warm by trapping air near the body.

6. Birds use the ___ process to keep their eggs warm.

7. ___ form a streamlined surface that helps birds fly.

UNDERSTANDING KEY IDEAS

Multiple Choice

8. Both birds and reptiles
   a. lay eggs.
   b. brood their young.
   c. have air sacs.
   d. have feathers.

9. Only mammals
   a. use internal fertilization.
   b. nurse their young.
   c. lay eggs.
   d. have teeth.

10. Which of the following is NOT a primate?
    a. a lemur
    b. a human
    c. a pika
    d. a chimpanzee

11. Monotremes do NOT
    a. have mammary glands.
    b. care for their young.
    c. give birth to live young.
    d. have hair.

12. What is lift?
    a. air that travels over the top of a wing
    b. a force provided by a bird's air sacs
    c. the upward force on a wing that keeps a bird in the air
    d. a force created by pressure from the diaphragm

Short Answer

13. How are contour feathers and down feathers helpful to birds?

14. How do flightless birds, water birds, perching birds, and birds of prey differ from each other?

15. Which trait allowed early mammals to look for food at night?

14. Sample answer: Many flightless birds do not have large keels, which anchor flight muscles. Flightless birds can run quickly to move around or are skilled swimmers. Water birds are flying birds that are comfortable in water. These birds often have webbed feet for swimming or long legs for wading. Perching birds have feet that automatically close when they land on branches. Birds of prey hunt and eat other vertebrates. Birds of prey have sharp claws; a sharp, curved beak; and very good vision.

15. Sample answer: The ability to keep their body temperature constant allowed early mammals to hunt at night.

16. Sample answer: Exotic species threaten marsupials by competing with marsupials for food and by preying on marsupials.

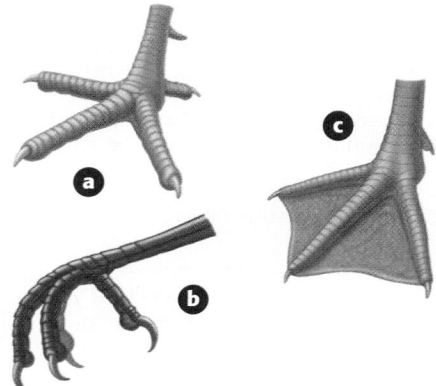

16 Describe two ways that animals introduced to Australia threaten its native marsupials.

17 Which kind of marsupial lives in North America?

18 Which group of placental mammals includes the pinnipeds?

19 How is a bird's digestive system related to its ability to fly?

20 How can mammalian milks differ?

CRITICAL THINKING

21 **Concept Mapping** Use the following terms to create a concept map: *monotremes, endotherms, birds, mammals, mammary glands, placental mammals, marsupials, feathers,* and *hair.*

22 **Making Comparisons** The embryos of birds and monotremes get energy from the yolk of the egg. How do developing embryos of marsupials and placental mammals get the nutrition they need?

23 **Making Inferences** Most bats and cetaceans use echolocation. Why don't these mammals rely solely on sight to hunt and sense their surroundings?

24 **Applying Concepts** Suppose you are making a museum display of bird skeletons, but the skeletons have lost their labels. How can you separate the skeletons of flightless birds from those of birds that fly? Will you be able to tell which birds flew rapidly and which birds could soar? Explain your answer.

25 **Making Inferences** Suppose that you saw a bird flying above you. The bird has long, skinny legs and a long, sharp beak. To which group of birds do you think this bird probably belongs? Explain your answer.

INTERPRETING GRAPHICS

The illustrations below show three different kinds of bird feet. Use these illustrations to answer the questions that follow.

26 Which foot most likely belongs to a water bird? Explain your choice.

27 Which foot most likely belongs to a perching bird? Explain your choice.

28 To what kind of bird do you think the remaining foot could belong? Explain your answer.

Critical Thinking

21. An answer to this exercise can be found at the end of this book.

22. Sample answer: Embryos of marsupials get nutrition from their mother's milk. Embryos of placental mammals get nutrition from the mother's body through the placenta.

23. Sample answer: Bats and cetaceans are active in environments where seeing is difficult.

24. Skeletons that have a large keel are from birds that fly. Wing bones of birds that fly are larger than those of flightless birds. Skeletons that have large keels and wing bones of short or average length are probably from birds that fly rapidly. Long wings provide the lift needed for soaring, so skeletons that have long wing bones are probably from birds that soar.

25. Sample answer: This bird is probably a water bird. It uses its long, skinny legs when it wades through water. The sharp beak helps it catch fish.

Interpreting Graphics

26. c; Many water birds have webbed feet to help them swim.

27. b; Perching birds have feet that are adapted to perching. These feet automatically grasp and hold onto a branch even when the bird is sleeping.

28. Accept all reasonable answers. The foot does not belong to a bird of prey (the foot lacks a bird of prey's large, sharp claws), perching bird (the foot lacks a perching bird's grasping adaptation), or water bird (wading birds have longer toes), so students may answer that the foot belongs to a flightless bird through the process of elimination. Some students may recognize that the foot resembles the feet of chickens or pheasants, which belong to a group of birds that is not described in the chapter (fowl or game birds).

17. opossum

18. carnivores

19. Sample answer: Birds need a lot of energy to fly. So, their digestive system breaks down food very quickly.

20. Sample answer: All milk is made of water, proteins, fats, and sugars. The amount of each nutrient present in milk differs between species.

CHAPTER RESOURCES

Chapter Resource File

- Chapter Review **GENERAL**
- Chapter Test A **GENERAL**
- Chapter Test B **ADVANCED**
- Chapter Test C **SPECIAL NEEDS**
- Vocabulary Activity **GENERAL**

Workbooks

Study Guide
- Assessment resources are also available in Spanish.

Standardized Test Preparation

Teacher's Note

To provide practice under more realistic testing conditions, give students 20 minutes to answer all of the questions in this Standardized Test Preparation.

MISCONCEPTION ALERT

Answers to the standardized test preparation can help you identify student misconceptions and misunderstandings.

READING

Passage 1

1. C
2. G
3. D

TEST DOCTOR

Question 1: The hair between the naked mole rat's toes helps sweep dirt from tunnels. Whiskers help the naked mole rat find its way. Its skin allows the naked mole rat to move easily through the tunnels. The hair on the naked mole rat's lips keeps dirt from getting into its mouth.

Question 2: Students may answer that the naked mole rat is hairless because of its name, but it does have some hair. The only correct answer could be that the naked mole rat has poor eyesight because the passage states that it is nearly blind.

READING

Read each of the passages below. Then, answer the questions that follow the passage.

Passage 1 A naked mole rat is a rodent that looks like an overcooked hot dog. This nearly blind mammal is 7 cm long and lives in hot, dry regions of Kenya, Ethiopia, and Somalia. This animal has some strange characteristics. Its grayish pink skin hangs loosely on its body. The loose skin allows the naked mole rat to move easily through its home of narrow underground tunnels. At first glance, a naked mole rat appears to be hairless. Though the naked mole rat doesn't have fur, it does have hair. Its sensitive whiskers guide it through the dark tunnels. Hair between its toes acts as tiny brooms to sweep up loose dirt. The naked mole rat even has hair on its lips that keeps dirt from getting into its mouth while it digs.

1. Why does the naked mole rat have hair on its lips?

   A to sweep loose dirt from its tunnels

   B to find its way through the tunnels

   C to keep dirt from getting into its mouth

   D to move easily through its tunnels

2. Which of the following is a characteristic of naked mole rats?

   F thick fur

   G poor eyesight

   H large toes

   I hairless bodies

3. How do naked mole rats navigate through their tunnels?

   A strong sense of hearing

   B sensitive grayish pink skin

   C tasting the dirt along their tunnel walls

   D sensitive whiskers

Passage 2

1. B
2. G
3. C

Passage 2 For centuries, people have tried to imitate a spectacular feat that birds perfected millions of years ago—flight. The Wright brothers were not able to fly in a heavier-than-air flying machine until 1903. Their first flight lasted only 12 s, and they traveled only 37 m. Although modern airplanes are much more sophisticated, they still rely on the same principles of flight. The sleek body of a jet is shaped to battle drag, while the wings are shaped to battle Earth's gravity. In order to take off, airplanes must pull upward with a force greater than gravitational force. This upward force is called lift.

1. According to the passage, how are modern airplanes similar to the flying machine invented by the Wright brothers?

   A Both look like birds.

   B Both rely on the same principles of flight.

   C Both are sophisticated.

   D Both have sleek body shapes.

2. Which part of a jet's design works against Earth's gravity?

   F the sleek shape

   G the wings

   H the heavier-than-air weight

   I the tail

3. Based on the passage, which of the following statements is a fact?

   A The Wright brothers were the first people to try building a flying machine.

   B Modern airplanes can fly more easily than birds can fly.

   C The Wright brothers' first flight lasted for only 12 s.

   D Overcoming gravity with lift is the only force needed to fly an airplane.

TEST DOCTOR

Question 3: If students make incorrect conclusions based on information that is not in the passage, they may answer that the Wright brothers were the first people to try building a flying machine. Students may answer that modern airplanes can fly more easily than birds can, but this is not a fact in the passage. Students may answer that lift is the only force needed for flight, but the passage states that the plane must also combat drag. So, the only correct answer is that the Wright brothers' flight lasted 12 s.

The graph below shows how many Calories a small dog uses while running at different speeds. Use this graph to answer the questions that follow.

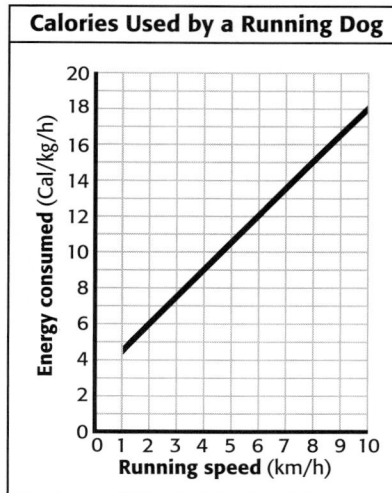

Calories Used by a Running Dog

1. As the dog runs faster, how does the amount of energy it consumes per hour change?

   A The energy consumed increases.

   B The energy consumed decreases.

   C The energy consumed remains the same.

   D Changes in the energy consumed are not related to changes in the dog's speed.

2. How much energy per hour will this dog consume if it is running at 4 km/h?

   F 1 Cal/kg/h

   G 6 Cal/kg/h

   H 9 Cal/kg/h

   I 10 Cal/kg/h

3. How much energy per hour will this dog consume if it is running at 9 km/h?

   A 4 Cal/kg/h

   B 16 Cal/kg/h

   C 16.5 Cal/kg/h

   D 18 Cal/kg/h

4. Energy consumed is given in Calories per kilogram of body mass per hour. If the dog has a mass of 6 kg and is running at 7 km/h, how many Calories per hour will it use?

   F 2.25 Cal/h

   G 19.5 Cal/h

   H 72 Cal/h

   I 81 Cal/h

Read each question below, and choose the best answer.

1. A bird flying at 35 km/h consumes 60 Cal per gram of body mass per hour. If the bird has a mass of 50 g, how many Calories will it use if it flies for 30 min at this speed?

   A 1,050 Cal

   B 1,500 Cal

   C 1,750 Cal

   D 3,000 Cal

2. Cecilia's kitten weighed 2 lb when she got him. The kitten gained about 0.5 lb each month for the next 11 months. How much did the kitten weigh at the end of the 11 months?

   F less than 6 lb

   G between 6 lb and 7 lb

   H between 7 lb and 8 lb

   I more than 8 lb

3. Gina bought two birds for $31.96, a box of birdseed for $1.69, and some bird treats for $3.98. What is the best estimate of the total cost of Gina's purchase?

   A between $35 and $36

   B between $36 and $37

   C between $37 and $38

   D more than $38

4. On each of 5 days, Leo saw 5 rabbits. He saw 3 rabbits on each of 2 other days. How could you find C, the total number of rabbits he saw?

   F $C = (5 \times 5) + (2 \times 3)$

   G $C = (5 + 5) \times (2 + 3)$

   H $C = 5 + 5 + 2 + 3$

   I $C = (5 \times 5) - (2 \times 3)$

Standardized Test Preparation

1. A

2. H

3. C

4. I

 TEST DOCTOR

Question 4: The correct answer is 81 Cal/h (13.5 Cal/kg/h × 6 kg = 81 Cal/h). At 7 km/h, a dog uses 13.5 Cal/kg/h. If students divide this number by 6, they will incorrectly answer 2.25 Cal/h. If students add 13.5 and 6, they will incorrectly answer 19.5 Cal/h. If they mistakenly look at the Calories consumed for a dog running 6 km/h (12 Cal/kg/h), they will incorrectly answer 72 Cal/h.

1. B

2. H

3. C

4. F

 TEST DOCTOR

Question 2: To find the answer, students must multiply 11 by 0.5 and add the product to 2 lb. If they forget to add, they will incorrectly choose answer F. If students incorrectly round their answers down, they will incorrectly choose answer G. If students incorrectly round their answers up, they will incorrectly choose answer I. You may want to calculate this problem on the board so that students understand where the correct answer, between 7 lb and 8 lb, comes from.

Question 3: Students should round amounts to the nearest dollar to find the answer. If students round down rather than rounding up, they will incorrectly choose answer A, between $35 and $36, or answer B, between $36 and $37. When students round up, they will get the answer of $38, but the actual cost would be somewhat less than $38. For this reason, answer D, more than $38, is incorrect.

CHAPTER RESOURCES

Chapter Resource File

 • Standardized Test Preparation `GENERAL`

State Resources

 For specific resources for your state, visit **go.hrw.com** and type in the keyword **HSMSTR.**

Science, Technology, and Society

ACTiViTY — ADVANCED

Each dolphin that works for the Navy costs, including training and care, about a million dollars. The Secretary of the Navy oversees the treatment of the dolphins. There is an order that "marine mammals will be provided the highest quality of humane care and treatment." The engineers, scientists, and veterinarians that work with the dolphins provide them with carefully balanced diets, extensive healthcare, and proper stimulation. However, some people think that the military should not use dolphins. Ask students to research and debate these points of view.

Weird Science

Background

In 1934, scientists brought 22 lyrebirds to the island of Tasmania to protect the birds from extinction. Lyrebirds have spread through the island and their number is now estimated to be 8,200. Some people are concerned about the impact that lyrebirds are having on the island. People enjoy the presence of the lyrebirds and their songs. But some people note that lyrebirds are changing the Tasmanian forest ecosystems.

Science in Action

Science, Technology, and Society

Dolphins in the Navy

Did you know that some dolphins work for the Navy? One way that dolphins help the Navy's Marine Mammal Program is by detecting underwater mines, which are bombs that drift underwater. Most mines explode when a large object bumps into them. Dolphins can find mines safely by using a natural sonar system, called *echolocation,* which allows them to sense their surroundings even in murky waters. When dolphin finds a mine and alerts a person, experts can deactivate the mine.

Math ACTiViTY

Suppose that each dolphin in the Navy's program is trained for 5 years and each trained dolphin works for 25 years. If 10 dolphins began training each year for 10 years, how many would be working at the end of those 10 years? How many would still be in training?

Weird Science

Sounds of the Lyrebird

Imagine that you are hiking in an Australian forest. You hear many different bird calls, beaks snapping, and wings rustling. There must be many species of birds around, right? Not if a lyrebird is nearby—all those sounds could be coming from just one bird! The lyrebird imitates the songs of other birds. In fact, lyrebirds can imitate just about any sound they hear. Many Australians have heard lyrebirds singing the sounds of chainsaws, car engines, and dog barks. Supposedly, a lyrebird once confused timber-mill workers when it sang the sound of the mill's whistle, causing the workers to quit for the day.

Language Arts ACTiViTY

WRITING SKILL A lyrebird's ability to imitate noises could lead to a lot of humorous confusion for people who hear its songs. Think about how lyrebirds could mimic human-made sounds, causing confusion for the people nearby, and then write a short story about the situation.

Answer to Math Activity

50 dolphins (The total number of dolphins in the program after 10 years would be 100 dolphins. However, half of those dolphins would still be in the 5-year training period. So, only 50 dolphins would be working.)

Answer to Language Arts Activity

Answers may vary. Students' stories should illustrate an understanding that lyrebirds' vocal impersonations can cause confusion.

Irene Pepperberg

Bird Brains Dr. Irene Pepperberg studies bird brains. She works with a little African Grey parrot named Alex. Pepperberg began her work with Alex because she wanted to see if birds that could talk could also understand what they were saying.

Pepperberg developed a new kind of communication training, with Alex as her pupil. First, Alex was rewarded with the object that he identified—not with food. This reinforced that the word represented the object. Next, two trainers acted out a kind of play to teach Alex words. One trainer would ask a question, and the other would respond with the right or wrong answer. The first trainer would reward the second for a right answer but take the object away for a wrong answer. This training showed Alex what would happen when he gave an answer.

Pepperberg's experiment has been very successful. Not only can Alex say the names of objects but he can tell you what they are made of, what their shape is, and how one object is different from another. Pepperberg has shown that at least one parrot can pass intelligence tests at the same level as some nonhuman primates and marine mammals. She has discovered that with the right training, animals can teach us a lot about themselves.

Social Studies ACTIVITY

WRITING SKILL People train pets all the time. See if you can train your pet or a friend's pet to learn a simple behavior, such as following a command. Write up your results in a report.

To learn more about these Science in Action topics, visit **go.hrw.com** and type in the keyword **HL5VR2F.**

Current Science

Check out Current Science® articles related to this chapter by visiting **go.hrw.com.** Just type in the keyword **HL5CS17.**

People in Science
ACTIVITY ——————— GENERAL

Invite students to research other studies of animal intelligence. Students should identify the types of animals being used in the studies and the results that scientists are getting from these studies. Examples of animals that students could research include parrots, crows, dogs, chimpanzees and gorillas, and marine mammals. Have students give an oral presentation of their findings.

Answer to Social Studies Activity

Answers may vary. Students will have varied results with their training.

TIMELINE

Ecology

What did you have for breakfast this morning? Your breakfast was a result of living things working together. For example, milk comes from a cow. The cow eats plants to gain energy. Bacteria help the plants obtain nutrients from the soil. And the soil has nutrients because fungi break down dead trees.

All living things on Earth are interconnected. Our actions have an impact on our environment, and our environment has an impact on us. In this unit, you will study ecology, the interaction of living things. This timeline shows some of the ways that humans have studied and affected the Earth.

1661

John Evelyn publishes a book condemning air pollution in London, England.

1771

In his experiments with plants, Joseph Priestley finds that plants use carbon dioxide and release oxygen.

1933

The Civilian Conservation Corps is established. The corps plants trees, fights forest fires, and builds dams to control floods.

1990

To save dolphins from being caught in fishing nets, U.S. tuna processors announce that they will not accept tuna caught in nets that can kill dolphins.

1851

The United States imports sparrows from Germany to defend against crop-damaging caterpillars.

1854

Henry David Thoreau's *Walden* is published. In it, Thoreau asserts that people should live in harmony with nature.

1872

The first U.S. national park, Yellowstone, is established by Congress.

1962

Rachel Carson's book *Silent Spring,* which describes the wasteful use of pesticides and their destruction of the environment, is published.

1970

The Environmental Protection Agency (EPA) is formed to set and enforce pollution-control standards in the United States.

1973

The United States Congress passes the Endangered Species Act.

1993

Americans recycle 59.5 billion aluminum cans (two out of every three cans).

1996

The Glen Canyon Dam is opened, purposefully flooding the Grand Canyon. The flooding helps maintain the ecological balance by restoring beaches and sandbars and rejuvenating marshes.

2002

The U.S. Fish and Wildlife Service installs red neon lights along the Florida coast to replace lights that distract baby sea turtles from finding the ocean when they hatch.

Compression guide:
To shorten instruction
because of time limitations,
omit Section 3.

OBJECTIVES	LABS, DEMONSTRATIONS, AND ACTIVITIES	TECHNOLOGY RESOURCES
PACING • 90 min pp. 478–483 **Chapter Opener**	**SE** Start-up Activity, p. 479 GENERAL	**OSP** Parent Letter ■ GENERAL **CD** Student Edition on CD-ROM **CD** Guided Reading Audio CD ■ **TR** Chapter Starter Transparency* **VID** Brain Food Video Quiz
Section 1 Everything Is Connected • Distinguish between the biotic and abiotic parts of the environment. • Explain how populations and communities are related. • Describe how the abiotic parts of the environment affect ecosystems.	**TE** Group Activity Exploring, p. 480 GENERAL **SE** Quick Lab Meeting the Neighbors, p. 481 GENERAL **CRF** Datasheet for Quick Lab* **SE** Skills Practice Lab Capturing the Wild Bean, p. 498 ◆ GENERAL **CRF** Datasheet for Chapter Lab* **SE** Science in Action Math, Social Studies, and Language Arts Activities, pp. 504–505 GENERAL	**CRF** Lesson Plans* **TR** Bellringer Transparency* **TR** The Five Levels of Environmental Organization* **SE** Internet Activity, p. 483 GENERAL **CRF** SciLinks Activity* GENERAL **VID** Lab Videos for Life Science
PACING • 45 min pp. 484–489 **Section 2 Living Things Need Energy** • Describe the functions of producers, consumers, and decomposers in an ecosystem. • Distinguish between a food chain and a food web. • Explain how energy flows through a food web. • Describe how the removal of one species affects the entire food web.	**TE** Activity Definitions, p. 484 GENERAL **SE** School-to-Home Activity A Chain Game, p. 485 GENERAL **TE** Activity Inferring Information, p. 487 BASIC **LB** EcoLabs & Field Activities Survival Is Just a Roll of the Dice* GENERAL **LB** Whiz-Bang Demonstrations Voracious Fly Catcher* ◆ BASIC	**CRF** Lesson Plans* **TR** Bellringer Transparency* **TR** Energy Pyramid* **TR** *LINK TO EARTH SCIENCE* Porous Rocks Are Reservoirs for Fossil Fuels
PACING • 45 min pp. 490–497 **Section 3 Types of Interactions** • Explain the relationship between carrying capacity and limiting factors. • Describe the two types of competition. • Distinguish between mutualism, commensalism, and parasitism. Give an example of coevolution.	**TE** Activity Predators and Prey, p. 492 GENERAL **TE** Connection Activity Real World, p. 494 GENERAL **TE** Activity Symbiosis, p. 495 BASIC **SE** Model-Making Lab Adaptation: It's a Way of Life, p. 786 ◆ GENERAL **CRF** Datasheet for LabBook* **LB** Long-Term Projects & Research Ideas Out of House and Home* ADVANCED	**CRF** Lesson Plans* **TR** Bellringer Transparency* **CD** Interactive Explorations CD-ROM What's Bugging You? GENERAL

PACING • 90 min

CHAPTER REVIEW, ASSESSMENT, AND STANDARDIZED TEST PREPARATION

CRF Vocabulary Activity* GENERAL
SE Chapter Review, pp. 500–501 GENERAL
CRF Chapter Review* ■ GENERAL
CRF Chapter Tests A* ■ GENERAL, B* ADVANCED, C* SPECIAL NEEDS
SE Standardized Test Preparation, pp. 502–503 GENERAL
CRF Standardized Test Preparation* GENERAL
CRF Performance-Based Assessment* GENERAL
OSP Test Generator GENERAL
CRF Test Item Listing* GENERAL

Online and Technology Resources

Visit **go.hrw.com** for a variety of free resources related to this textbook. Enter the keyword **HL5INT**.

Students can access interactive problem-solving help and active visual concept development with the *Holt Science and Technology* Online Edition available at **www.hrw.com**.

 Guided Reading Audio CD
Also in Spanish

A direct reading of each chapter for auditory learners, reluctant readers, and Spanish-speaking students.

 Science Tutor CD-ROM

Excellent for remediation and test practice.

SKILLS DEVELOPMENT RESOURCES	SECTION REVIEW AND ASSESSMENT	STANDARDS CORRELATIONS
SE **Pre-Reading Activity**, p. 478 `GENERAL` OSP **Science Puzzlers, Twisters & Teasers** `GENERAL`		National Science Education Standards UCP 1, 5; SAI 1
CRF **Directed Reading A*** ■ `BASIC`, **B*** `SPECIAL NEEDS` CRF **Vocabulary and Section Summary*** ■ `GENERAL` SE **Reading Strategy** Reading Organizer, p. 480 `GENERAL` TE **Inclusion Strategies**, p. 481	TE **Reteaching**, p. 482 `BASIC` TE **Quiz**, p. 482 `GENERAL` TE **Alternative Assessment**, p. 482 `GENERAL` SE **Reading Checks**, pp. 483 `GENERAL` SE **Section Review,*** p. 483 ■ `GENERAL` CRF **Section Quiz*** ■ `GENERAL`	UCP 1; SAI 1; SPSP 2; LS 1a, 4a, 4c, 4d; *Chapter Lab:* UCP1, 4; SAI 1; LS 1a, 3d, 4d
CRF **Directed Reading A*** ■ `BASIC`, **B*** `SPECIAL NEEDS` CRF **Vocabulary and Section Summary*** ■ `GENERAL` SE **Reading Strategy** Reading Organizer, p. 484 `GENERAL` TE **Connection to Math** Energy Loss, p. 486 `GENERAL` SE **Math Practice** Energy Pyramids, p. 489 `GENERAL` MS **Math Skills for Science** Working with Percentages and Proportions* `GENERAL` CRF **Reinforcement Worksheet** Weaving a Food Web* `GENERAL` CRF **Critical Thinking** A Struggle to Survive* `ADVANCED`	SE **Reading Checks**, pp. 485, 487, 488 `GENERAL` TE **Reteaching**, p. 488 `BASIC` TE **Quiz**, p. 488 `GENERAL` TE **Alternative Assessment**, p. 488 `GENERAL` SE **Section Review,*** p. 489 ■ `GENERAL` CRF **Section Quiz*** ■ `GENERAL`	UCP 1; SAI 1; LS 1a, 4a, 4b, 4c, LS 4d
CRF **Directed Reading A*** ■ `BASIC`, **B*** `SPECIAL NEEDS` CRF **Vocabulary and Section Summary*** ■ `GENERAL` SE **Reading Strategy** Reading Organizer, p. 490 `GENERAL` TE **Inclusion Strategies**, p. 491 SE **Connection to Environmental Science** Pretenders, p. 493 TE **Connecction to Math** Species Numbers, p. 493 SE **Connection to Social Studies** Rabbits in Australia, p. 496 CRF **Reinforcement Worksheet** Symbiotic Relationships* `GENERAL`	SE **Reading Checks**, pp. 491, 493, 494, 496 `GENERAL` TE **Reteaching**, p. 496 `BASIC` TE **Quiz**, p. 496 `GENERAL` TE **Alternative Assessment**, p. 496 `GENERAL` SE **Section Review,*** p. 497 ■ `GENERAL` CRF **Section Quiz*** ■ `GENERAL`	UCP 1, 4; SAI 1; LS 3a, 3c, 3d, 4a,b, 4c, 4d; *LabBook:* UCP1, 4; SAI 1, LS 1a, 3d

One-Stop Planner® CD-ROM

This convenient CD-ROM includes:
- Lab Materials QuickList Software
- Holt Calendar Planner
- Customizable Lesson Plans
- Printable Worksheets
- ExamView® Test Generator

cnnstudentnews.com

Find the latest news, lesson plans, and activities related to important scientific events.

www.scilinks.org

Maintained by the **National Science Teachers Association.** See Chapter Enrichment pages for a complete list of topics.

Check out *Current Science* articles and activities by visiting the HRW Web site at **go.hrw.com.** Just type in the keyword **HL5CS18.**

Classroom Videos

- **Lab Videos** demonstrate the chapter lab.
- **Brain Food Video Quizzes** help students review the chapter material.
- **CNN Videos** bring science into your students' daily life.

Chapter Resources

Visual Resources

CHAPTER STARTER TRANSPARENCY

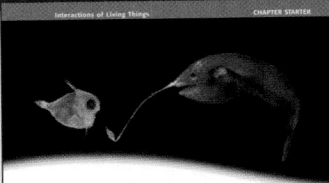

Strange but True!

BELLRINGER TRANSPARENCIES

Section: Everything Is Connected
Think of all the things that make up a pond in the countryside. List all the parts of the pond's ecosystem in your **science journal**. Then draw an illustration of a pond ecosystem. Are all the parts of the ecosystem living? Explain your answer.

Section: Living Things Need Energy
Indian pipe is a plant that is completely white—it has no chlorophyll or chloroplasts to give it a green color. Do you think this plant could be a producer? If not, where do you think it could get the energy it needs to survive?

Write your answers in your **science journal**.

TEACHING TRANSPARENCIES

The Five Levels of Environmental Organization

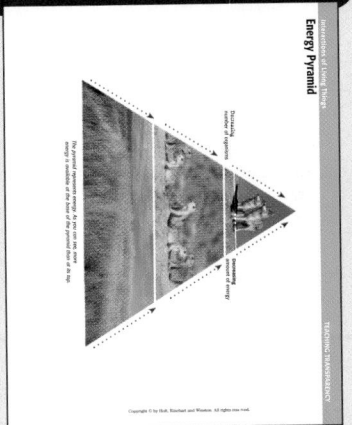

Energy Pyramid

TEACHING TRANSPARENCIES

Porous Rocks as Reservoirs for Fossil Fuels

LINK TO EARTH SCIENCE

Chapter: Rocks: Mineral Mixtures

CONCEPT MAPPING TRANSPARENCY

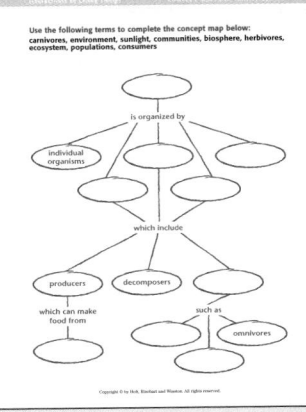

Use the following terms to complete the concept map below: carnivores, environment, sunlight, communities, biosphere, herbivores, ecosystem, populations, consumers

Planning Resources

LESSON PLANS

Lesson Plan SAMPLE

Section: Waves

Pacing
Regular Schedule: with lab(s):2 days without lab(s)2 days
Block Schedule: with lab(s) 1 1/2 days without lab(s)1 day

Objectives
1. Relate the seven properties of life to a living organism.
2. Describe seven themes that can help you to organize what you learn about biology.
3. Identify the tiny structures that make up all living organisms.
4. Differentiate between reproduction and heredity and between metabolism and homeostasis.

National Science Education Standards Covered
LSInter4:Cells have particular structures that underlie their functions.
LSBeh1:Most cell functions involve chemical reactions.
LSBeh1:Cells store and use information to guide their functions.
UCP1:Cell functions are regulated.
SI1: Cells can differentiate and form complete multicellular organisms.
PS1: Species evolve over time.
ESS1: The great diversity of organisms is the result of more than 3.5 billion years of evolution.
ESS2: Natural selection and its evolutionary consequences provide a scientific explanation for the fossil record of ancient life forms as well as for the striking molecular similarities observed among the diverse species of living organisms.
ST1: The millions of different species of plants, animals, and microorganisms that live on Earth today are related by descent from common ancestors.
ST2: The energy for life primarily comes from the sun.
SPSP1: The complexity and organization of organisms accommodates the need for obtaining, transforming, transporting, releasing, and eliminating the matter and energy used to sustain the organism.
SPSP6: As matter and energy flows through different levels of organization of living systems—cells, organs, communities—and between living systems and the physical environment, chemical elements are recombined in different ways.
HNS1: Organisms have behavioral responses to internal changes and to external stimuli.

PARENT LETTER

SAMPLE

Dear Parent,

Your son's or daughter's science class will soon begin exploring the chapter entitled "The World of Physical Science." In this chapter, students will learn about how the scientific method applies to the world of physical science and the role of physical science in the world. By the end of the chapter, students should demonstrate a clear understanding of the chapter's main ideas and be able to discuss the following topics:

1. physical science as the study of energy and matter (Section 1)
2. the role of physical science in the world around them (Section 1)
3. careers that rely on physical science (Section 1)
4. the steps used in the scientific method (Section 2)
5. examples of technology (Section 2)
6. how the scientific method is used to answer questions and solve problems (Section 2)
7. how our knowledge of science changes over time (Section 2)
8. how models represent real objects or systems (Section 3)
9. examples of different ways models are used in science (Section 3)
10. the importance of the International System of Units (Section 4)
11. the appropriate units to use for particular measurements (Section 4)
12. how area and density are derived quantities (Section 4)

Questions to Ask Along the Way

You can help your son or daughter learn about these topics by asking interesting questions such as the following:

• What are some surprising careers that use physical science?
• What is a characteristic of a good hypothesis?
• When is it a good idea to use a model?
• Why do Americans measure things in terms of inches and yards and meters?

ALSO IN SPANISH

TEST ITEM LISTING

TEST ITEM LISTING
The World of Science SAMPLE

MULTIPLE CHOICE

1. A limitation of models is that
   a. they are large enough to see.
   b. they do not act exactly like the things that they model.
   c. they are smaller than the things that they model.
   d. they model unfamiliar things.
   Answer: B   Difficulty: 1   Section: 3   Objective: 2
2. The length 10 m is equal to
   a. 100 cm.   c. 10,000 mm.
   b. 1,000 cm.   d. Both (b) and (c).
   Answer: B   Difficulty: 1   Section: 3   Objective: 2
3. To be valid, a hypothesis must be
   a. testable.   c. made into a law.
   b. supported by evidence. d. Both (a) and (b).
   Answer: D   Difficulty: 1   Section: 3   Objective: 2
4. The statement "Sheila has a stain on her shirt" is an example of a(n)
   a. law.   c. observation.
   b. hypothesis.   d. prediction.
   Answer: B   Difficulty: 1   Section: 3   Objective: 2
5. A hypothesis is often developed out of
   a. observations.   c. laws.
   b. experiments.   d. Both (a) and (b)
   Answer: D   Difficulty: 1   Section: 3   Objective: 2
6. How many milliliters are in 3.5 kL?
   a. 3,500 mL   c. 3,500, 000 mL
   b. 0.0035 mL   d. 35,000 mL.
   Answer: B   Difficulty: 1   Section: 3   Objective: 2
7. A map of Seattle is an example of a
   a. law.   c. model.
   b. theory.   d. unit.
   Answer: B   Difficulty: 1   Section: 3   Objective: 2
8. A lab has the safety icons shown below. These icons mean that you should wear
   a. only safety goggles.   c. safety goggles and a lab apron.
   b. only a lab apron.   d. safety goggles, a lab apron, and gloves.
   Answer: B   Difficulty: 1   Section: 3   Objective: 2
9. The law of conservation of mass says the tot of mass before a chemical change is
   a. more than the total mass after the change.
   b. less than the total mass after the change.
   c. the same as the total mass after the change.
   d. not the same as the total mass after the change.
   Answer: B   Difficulty: 1   Section: 3   Objective: 2
10. In which of the following areas might you find a geochemist at work?
    a. studying the chemistry of rocks   c. studying fishes
    b. studying forestry   d. studying the atmosphere
    Answer: B   Difficulty: 1   Section: 3   Objective: 2

One-Stop Planner® CD-ROM

This CD-ROM includes all of the resources shown here and the following time-saving tools:

• *Lab Materials QuickList Software*
• *Customizable lesson plans*
• *Holt Calendar Planner*
• *The powerful ExamView® Test Generator*

477C Chapter 18 • Interactions of Living Things

Meeting Individual Needs

DIRECTED READING A

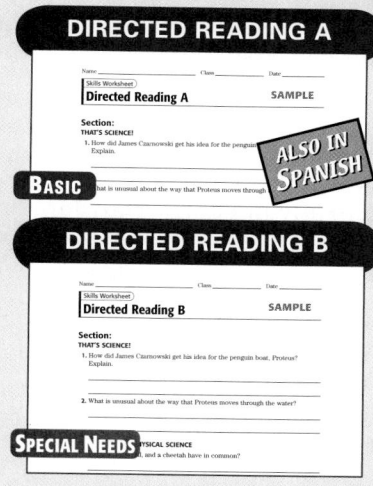

Skills Worksheet
Directed Reading A — SAMPLE

Section:
THAT'S SCIENCE!
1. How did James Czarnowski get his idea for the penguin boat, Proteus? Explain.

BASIC

ALSO IN SPANISH

DIRECTED READING B

Skills Worksheet
Directed Reading B — SAMPLE

Section:
THAT'S SCIENCE!
1. How did James Czarnowski get his idea for the penguin boat, Proteus? Explain.

2. What is unusual about the way that Proteus moves through the water?

SPECIAL NEEDS

VOCABULARY ACTIVITY

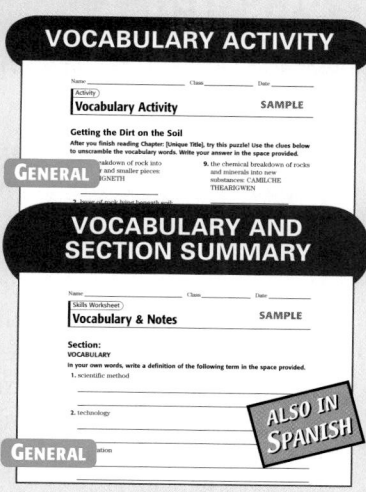

Activity
Vocabulary Activity — SAMPLE

Getting the Dirt on the Soil
After you finish reading Chapter: [Unique Title], try this puzzle! Use the clues below to unscramble the vocabulary words. Write your answer in the space provided.

GENERAL

VOCABULARY AND SECTION SUMMARY

Skills Worksheet
Vocabulary & Notes — SAMPLE

Section:
VOCABULARY
In your own words, write a definition of the following term in the space provided.
1. scientific method

2. technology

GENERAL

ALSO IN SPANISH

REINFORCEMENT

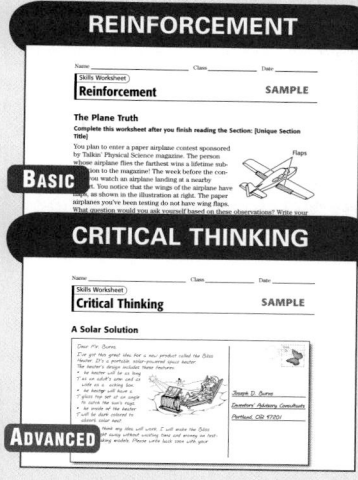

Skills Worksheet
Reinforcement — SAMPLE

The Plane Truth
Complete this worksheet after you finish reading the Section: [Unique Section Title]

BASIC

CRITICAL THINKING

Skills Worksheet
Critical Thinking — SAMPLE

A Solar Solution

ADVANCED

SCILINKS ACTIVITY

Activity
SciLinks Activity — SAMPLE

MARINE ECOSYSTEMS

GENERAL

SCIENCE PUZZLERS, TWISTERS & TEASERS

CHAPTER 18 SCIENCE PUZZLERS, TWISTERS & TEASERS
Interactions of Living Things

Nature's Philosophers
1. A group of astronauts has discovered amazing new life-forms on a distant planet. Each life-form was asked to describe its philosophy of life in a sentence or two. Help the astronauts categorize each as a producer, carnivore, omnivore, scavenger, or decomposer by writing the appropriate term in the space provided.
   a. "To kill is wrong. To let food go to waste is worse."

   b. "The swift receive the most satisfying reward."

   d. "Self-reliance is the path to contentment. Always seek the light

GENERAL

Labs and Activities

ECOLABS & FIELD ACTIVITIES

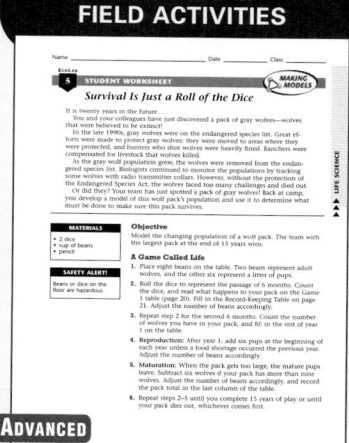

EcoLab
5 STUDENT WORKSHEET
MAKING MODELS

Survival Is Just a Roll of the Dice

ADVANCED

WHIZ-BANG DEMONSTRATIONS

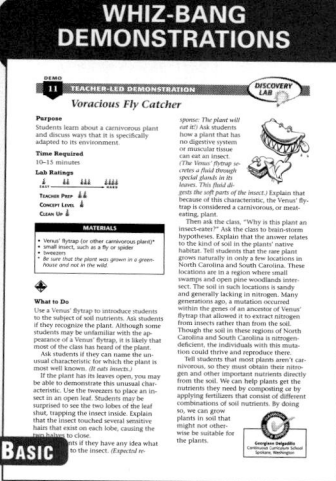

DEMO
11 TEACHER-LED DEMONSTRATION
DISCOVERY LAB

Voracious Fly Catcher

Purpose

Time Required
10–15 minutes

Lab Ratings

MATERIALS

What to Do

BASIC

LONG-TERM PROJECTS & RESEARCH IDEAS

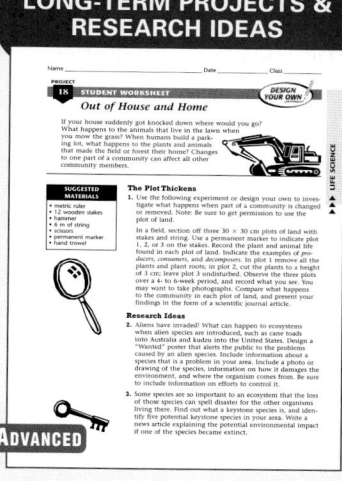

PROJECT
18 STUDENT WORKSHEET
DESIGN YOUR OWN

Out of House and Home

The Plot Thickens

Research Ideas

ADVANCED

DATASHEETS FOR QUICK LABS

TEACHER RESOURCE PAGE
Quick Lab — DATASHEET FOR QUICK LAB
Reaction to Stress

Background

DATASHEETS FOR CHAPTER LABS

TEACHER RESOURCE PAGE
Skills Practice Lab — DATASHEET FOR CHAPTER LAB
Using Scientific Methods — SAMPLE

Teacher's Notes
TIME REQUIRED
One 45-minute class period.

DATASHEETS FOR LABBOOK

TEACHER RESOURCE PAGE
Skills Practice Lab — DATASHEET FOR LABBOOK LAB
Does It All Add Up? — SAMPLE

Teacher's Notes
TIME REQUIRED
One 45-minute class period.

Review and Assessments

SECTION QUIZ

Assessment
Section Quiz — SAMPLE

Section:
In the space provided, write the letter of the description that matches the term or phrase.

GENERAL

ALSO IN SPANISH

SECTION REVIEW

Skills Worksheet
Section Review — SAMPLE

Section:
KEY TERMS
1. What do paleontologist study?

GENERAL

ALSO IN SPANISH

CHAPTER REVIEW

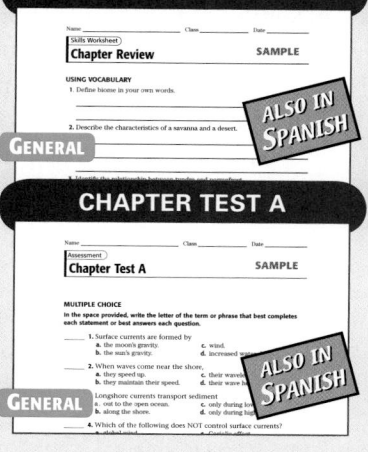

Skills Worksheet
Chapter Review — SAMPLE

USING VOCABULARY
1. Define biome in your own words.

2. Describe the characteristics of a savanna and a desert.

GENERAL

ALSO IN SPANISH

CHAPTER TEST A

Assessment
Chapter Test A — SAMPLE

MULTIPLE CHOICE
In the space provided, write the letter of the term or phrase that best completes each statement or best answers each question.
1. Surface currents are formed by
   a. the moon's gravity.   c. wind.
   b. the sun's gravity.   d. increased
2. When waves come near the shore,
   a. they speed up.   c. their wave
   b. they maintain their speed.   d. their wave

GENERAL

ALSO IN SPANISH

CHAPTER TEST B

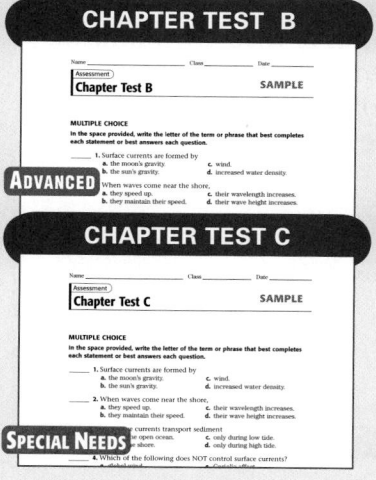

Assessment
Chapter Test B — SAMPLE

MULTIPLE CHOICE
In the space provided, write the letter of the term or phrase that best completes each statement or best answers each question.
1. Surface currents are formed by
   a. the moon's gravity.   c. wind.
   b. the sun's gravity.   d. increased water density.
2. When waves come near the shore,
   a. they speed up.   c. their wavelength increases.
   b. they maintain their speed.   d. their wave height increases.

ADVANCED

CHAPTER TEST C

Assessment
Chapter Test C — SAMPLE

MULTIPLE CHOICE
In the space provided, write the letter of the term or phrase that best completes each statement or best answers each question.
1. Surface currents are formed by
   a. the moon's gravity.   c. wind.
   b. the sun's gravity.   d. increased water density.
2. When waves come near the shore,
   a. they speed up.   c. their wavelength increases.
   b. they maintain their speed.   d. their wave height increases.

SPECIAL NEEDS

STANDARDIZED TEST PREPARATION

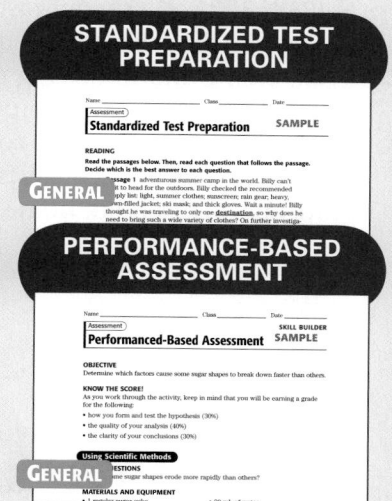

Assessment
Standardized Test Preparation — SAMPLE

READING
Read the passages below. Then, read each question that follows the passage. Decide which is the best answer to each question.

GENERAL

PERFORMANCE-BASED ASSESSMENT

Assessment
SKILL BUILDER
Performanced-Based Assessment — SAMPLE

OBJECTIVE
Determine which factors cause some sugar shapes to break down faster than others.

KNOW THE SCORE!
As you work through the activity, keep in mind that you will be earning a grade for the following:
• how you form and test the hypothesis (30%)
• the quality of your analysis (40%)
• the clarity of your conclusions (30%)

Using Scientific Methods

MATERIALS AND EQUIPMENT

GENERAL

This Chapter Enrichment provides relevant and interesting information to expand and enhance your presentation of the chapter material.

Section 1

Everything Is Connected

Indicator Species

● An indicator species is a plant or animal that, by its presence in a particular area, indicates the environmental conditions of the site. This information tells scientists what other species might thrive in the locale. For example, mosses usually indicate acidic soil, which can limit the types of plants that can survive in the area. This, in turn, affects the variety of herbivores and other animals that can live there.

Is That a Fact!

◆ The Australian mallee fowl regulates the temperature of its nest mound with the help of other organisms. A healthy population of fungus and bacteria inhabit the leaf-and-twig mound built by the birds. As the bacteria decompose the leaves, they give off heat. When the temperature reaches 34°C (the birds can tell by sticking their beak into the mound), it's egg-laying time! The birds work hard to keep the mound and their eggs at a constant temperature by adding more material or digging ventilation shafts.

Ecology

● Ecology as an academic discipline can be traced to Theophrastus (c. 372–287 BCE), a student of Aristotle (384–322 BCE). Theophrastus offered the first descriptions of the relationships between organisms and the living and nonliving parts of their environment. The term *ecology* was coined in 1858 by Ernst Haeckel (1834–1919), a German zoologist. *Ökologie*, the German word for ecology, comes from the Greek *oikos*, which means "household, home, or place to live."

Section 2

Living Things Need Energy

Systems Ecology

● Some early ecologists focused on communities and populations, but others looked at the energy transfer between organisms. Today the study of energy transfer is called *systems ecology*. It involves the analysis of the flow of energy and the recycling of nutrients within an ecosystem to answer the question, "How does the ecosystem function?" The use of modern materials and techniques, such as radioisotopes, computer science, and applied mathematics, has enabled scientists to quantify the movement of nutrients and energy through ecosystems.

Is That a Fact!

◆ Kelp is a marine alga, often called *seaweed*, anchored to the ocean floor. Sea urchins and many other organisms eat this primary producer. Kelp also provides shelter for animals, such as the bronze kelp perch. Sea otters sometimes wrap themselves in a blade of kelp to keep from drifting while they nap.

◆ Some animals build a home within their habitat. The trapdoor spider digs a burrow in the ground and constructs a "trap door" of silk and mud with silk hinges. It waits until an insect walks by, then quickly opens the door and grabs its prey. Trapdoor spiders inject venom into their prey, but they are harmless to people.

◆ Different habitats provide different materials for animals to use when constructing a home. These homes have different names. A squirrel's nest of leaves and sticks is called a *drey*. A badger's burrow is called a *sett*. A river otter's burrow in a river bank is called a *holt*.

Section 3

Types of Interactions

Mimicry

- Batesian mimicry was named for Henry Walter Bates (1825–1892), who described it in 1862. The mimic assumes the form of its model to take advantage of the model's defenses. For example, the snake caterpillar's movements resemble those of a real snake and thus help prevent attack by predators fearful of snakes.

- In 1878, Fritz Müller (1821–1897) described Müllerian mimicry, in which the resemblance of two species gives them mutual defense benefits. Both the sand wasp and the yellow jacket can sting. A predator that avoids one will avoid the other.

- Camouflage, an adaptation illustrated by the praying mantis's resemblance to a leaf, is a form of mimicry.

The Joke's on You: Prey Adaptations

- The killdeer is a ground-nesting bird that distracts a predator from its nest or chicks with a "broken-wing" display. It will limp and drag a wing on the ground to make itself appear to be an easy catch. But because it is actually quite healthy, the killdeer always stays one step ahead of the predator.

Plants and Ants

- Symbiotic relationships between animals and plants are often a marvel to behold. Some epiphytes (plants that grow without soil) have coevolved with ants. The plants provide knobby, chambered tubers in which the ants live, while the ants' excrement provides vital nutrition for the plant.

- Some tree-dwelling tropical ants collect and plant seeds in "gardens" they tend in their homes. The ants nourish the seeds with feces they collect and bring to the garden. The plants then grow and provide the ants with food.

- In West Africa, stinging ants protect the *Barteria*, the small tree in which the ants live. The sting of this ant can numb a human for several days and can penetrate even the tough skin of an elephant.

Mutualism

- Corals live in a mutualistic relationship with the algae that live inside them. Humans benefit from the mutualistic relationship we have with the *Escherichia coli* that live inside of us. We provide the bacteria with food and comfortable growing conditions, and the bacteria help us digest our food and provide us with nutrients.

Overview

This chapter explains how organisms are connected to each other and to the environment and discusses the way the environment is organized. This chapter also describes how energy moves through an ecosystem and how an ecosystem is changed by the disappearance of organisms.

Assessing Prior Knowledge

Students should be familiar with the following topics:

- photosynthesis
- energy
- bacteria

Identifying Misconceptions

Most students understand that photosynthesis requires air, water, and sunlight but do not understand that plant mass increases because the plant incorporates the carbon from from carbon dioxide gas. They may also be confused about the importance of green plants to other organisms as a major food source. Students also often think that dead things gradually break down and go away but fail to grasp that decaying matter is converted and used by other organisms.

18

Interactions of Living Things

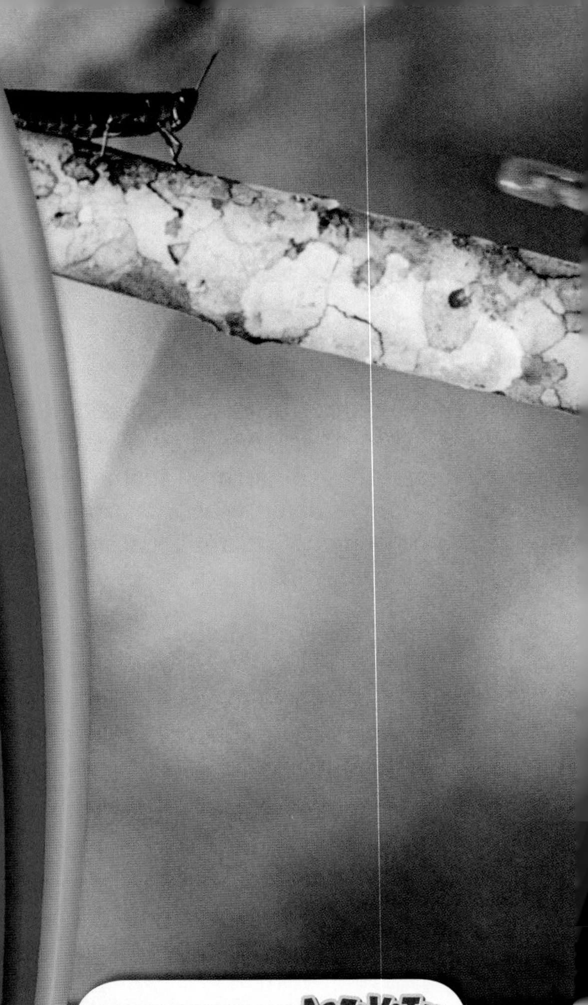

About the PHOTO

A chameleon is about to grab an insect using its long tongue. A chameleon's body can change color to match its surroundings. Blending in helps the chameleon sneak up on its prey and also keeps the chameleon safe from animals that would like to make a snack out of a chameleon.

PRE-READING ACTIVITY

FOLDNOTES **Tri-Fold** Before you read the chapter, create the FoldNote entitled "Tri-Fold" described in the **Study Skills** section of the Appendix. Write what you know about the interactions of living things in the column labeled "Know." Then, write what you want to know in the column labeled "Want." As you read the chapter, write what you learn about the interactions of living things in the column labeled "Learn."

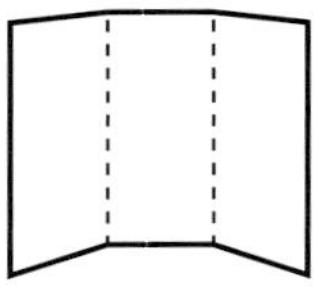

Standards Correlations

National Science Education Standards

The following codes indicate the National Science Education Standards that correlate to this chapter. The full text of the standards is at the front of the book.

Chapter Opener
UCP 1, 5; SAI 1

Section 1 Everything Is Connected
UCP 1; SAI 1; SPSP 2; LS 1a, 4a, 4c, 4d

Section 2 Living Things Need Energy
UCP 1; SAI 1; LS 1a, 4a, 4b, 4c, LS 4d

Section 3 Types of Interactions
UCP 1, 4; SAI 1; LS 3a, 3c, 3d, 4a,b, 4c, 4d

Chapter Lab
UCP 1, 4; SAI 1; LS 1a, 3d, 4d

Chapter Review
LS 1a, 3a, 3b, 3c, 3d, 4a, 4b, 4c, 4d

Science in Action
UCP 2; LS 5a

Answer to Procedure

4. cod

Answers to Analysis

1. Sample answer: The other organisms might starve if algae were removed. If the killer whale was removed, there would be more seals because fewer seals would be eaten by whales. More seals would make for fewer krill shrimp and cod.

2. Sample answer: Cod eat algae and krill shrimp; leopard seals eat both krill shrimp and cod; and killer whales eat krill shrimp, cod, and seals. This is a true food web, and it contains more than the five organisms discussed here. The arrangement of cards should show that there are several predator-prey relationships. The pieces of string could be used to connect all of the organisms that feed on each other.

START-UP ACTIVITY

Who Eats Whom?

In this activity, you will learn how organisms interact when finding (or becoming) the next meal.

Procedure

1. On each of **five index cards,** print the name of one of the following organisms: killer whale, cod fish, krill shrimp, algae, and leopard seal.

2. On your desk, arrange the cards in a chain to show who eats whom.

3. Record the order of your cards.

4. In nature, would you expect to see more killer whales or cod? Arrange the cards in order of most individuals in an organism group to fewest.

Analysis

1. What might happen to the other organisms if algae were removed from this group? What might happen if the killer whales were removed?

2. Are there any organisms in this group that eat more than one kind of food? (Hint: What else might a seal, a fish, or a killer whale eat?) How could you change the order of your cards to show this information? How could you use pieces of string to show these relationships?

Strange but True!

A small fish swims through the darkest part of the ocean in search of its next meal. Food is scarce at this depth, but suddenly a glowing morsel comes into view. The tiny fish swims quickly to it, but just as the little fish is about to nab its meal, large jaws rimmed with needle-sharp teeth appear out of nowhere. Before the fish can escape, it is swallowed whole.

This is how the deep-sea anglerfish—the one with the needle-sharp teeth—catches its food. The anglerfish has a unique way of fooling unsuspecting prey. The anglerfish is equipped with its own "fishing pole," a special branchlike body

The anglerfish and the glowing bacteria are involved in a relationship that benefits both of them. In exchange for providing the anglerfish with a lure to catch fish, the bacteria get to live in a protected and mobile home. In this chapter you will learn more about the diverse ways living things interact with each other and with their environment. Some of these relationships are almost too strange to believe!

Chapter Starter Transparency
Use this transparency to help students begin thinking about the interactions between organisms.

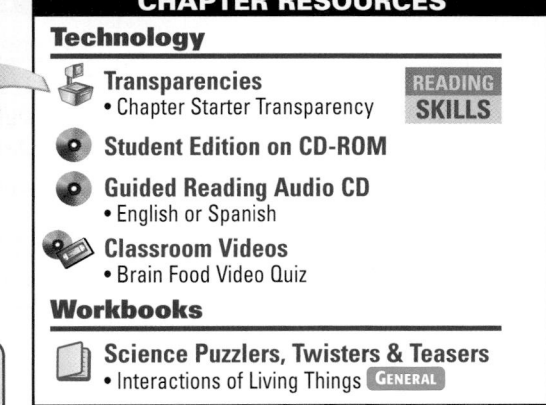

CHAPTER RESOURCES

Technology

📽 **Transparencies**
 • Chapter Starter Transparency   **READING SKILLS**

💿 **Student Edition on CD-ROM**

💿 **Guided Reading Audio CD**
 • English or Spanish

📼 **Classroom Videos**
 • Brain Food Video Quiz

Workbooks

📖 **Science Puzzlers, Twisters & Teasers**
 • Interactions of Living Things **GENERAL**

Focus

Overview

In this section, students will learn that the natural environment is a system of parts that must work together to function properly. Students will also learn to identify the biotic and abiotic parts of an environment. Finally, students will learn how environments are organized into the various levels.

Bellringer

Ask students to make a list of all the things they can think of that are found in a pond ecosystem. When they have completed their lists, have them indicate which of the things are living and which are nonliving.

LS Logical/Verbal

Motivate

Group ACTiViTy — GENERAL

Exploring Take the class outside to explore the school grounds. Have students work in groups to describe the different levels of organization found on the grounds. They should describe an organism, a population, the community of populations, and the abiotic parts of the school-grounds ecosystem.

LS Kinesthetic/Interpersonal

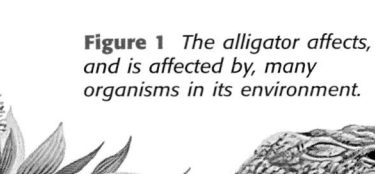

READING WARM-UP

Objectives
- Distinguish between the biotic and abiotic parts of the environment.
- Explain how populations and communities are related.
- Describe how the abiotic parts of the environment affect ecosystems.

Terms to Learn

ecology	community
biotic	ecosystem
abiotic	biosphere
population	

READING STRATEGY

Reading Organizer As you read this section, create an outline of the section. Use the headings from the section in your outline.

Everything Is Connected

An alligator drifts in a weedy Florida river, watching a long, thin fish called a gar. The gar swims too close to the alligator. Then, in a rush of murky water, the alligator swallows the gar whole and slowly swims away.

It is clear that two organisms have interacted when one eats the other. But organisms have many interactions other than simply "who eats whom." For example, alligators dig underwater holes to escape from the heat. After the alligators abandon these holes, fish and other aquatic organisms live in the holes during the winter dry period.

Studying the Web of Life

All living things are connected in a web of life. Scientists who study the web of life specialize in the science of ecology. **Ecology** is the study of the interactions of organisms with one another and with their environment.

The Two Parts of an Environment

An organism's environment consists of all the things that affect the organism. These things can be divided into two groups. All of the organisms that live together and interact with one another make up the **biotic** part of the environment. The **abiotic** part of the environment consists of the nonliving factors, such as water, soil, light, and temperature. How many biotic parts and abiotic parts do you see in **Figure 1**?

Figure 1 *The alligator affects, and is affected by, many organisms in its environment.*

CHAPTER RESOURCES

Chapter Resource File

- Lesson Plan
- Directed Reading A **BASIC**
- Directed Reading B **SPECIAL NEEDS**

Technology

 Transparencies
- Bellringer
- The Five Levels of Environmental Organization

Answer to question on student page

biotic parts: alligator, fishes, plants, and clams; abiotic parts: water, soil, and sunlight

Organization in the Environment

At first glance, the environment may seem disorganized. However, the environment can be arranged into different levels, as shown in **Figure 2.** The first level is made of an individual organism. The second level is larger and is made of similar organisms, which form a population. The third level is made of different populations, which form a community. The fourth level is made of a community and its abiotic environment, which form an ecosystem. The fifth and final level contains all ecosystems, which form the biosphere.

ecology the study of the interactions of living organisms with one another and with their environment

biotic describes living factors in the environment

abiotic describes the nonliving part of the environment, including water, rocks, light, and temperature

Figure 2 The Five Levels of Environmental Organization

Biosphere

Ecosystem

Community

Population

Organism

Meeting the Neighbors

1. Explore two or three blocks of your neighborhood.

2. Draw a map of the area's biotic and abiotic features. For example, map the location of sidewalks, large rocks, trees, water features, and any animals you see. Remember to approach all plants and animals with caution. Use your map to answer the following questions.

3. How are the biotic factors affected by the abiotic factors?

4. How are the abiotic factors affected by the biotic factors?

Writing **Biotic and Abiotic** Ask students to list biotic and abiotic factors in their neighborhood. Write these factors on the board. Then ask students to describe how biotic factors change when abiotic factors change. (For example, if it rains a lot, plants will likely grow more.) **LS** Verbal

Quiz ──────── GENERAL

1. A caterpillar, a deer, and a rabbit all want to drink from the same puddle, eat the same plant, and bask in the same spot of sunshine. Are they competing members of a population? Why or why not? (No; each is a different species. Therefore, they are competing members of a community.)

2. Using the salt-marsh example, explain why ecologists state that saving a large animal, such as the heron or egret, can also save an ecosystem. (The heron and the egret can survive only if the salt marsh remains intact to provide shelter and food for the organisms that the birds need to eat.)

Alternative Assessment ──── GENERAL

Poster Project Have students create a poster that shows at least five biotic and five abiotic factors of either an aquatic or a terrestrial ecosystem. **LS** Visual

population a group of organisms of the same species that live in a specific geographical area

community all the populations of species that live in the same habitat and interact with each other

Populations

A salt marsh, such as the one shown in **Figure 3,** is a coastal area where grasslike plants grow. Within the salt marsh are animals. Each animal is a part of a **population,** or a group of individuals of the same species that live together. For example, all of the seaside sparrows that live in the same salt marsh are members of a population. The individuals in the population often compete with one another for food, nesting space, and mates.

Communities

A **community** consists of all of the populations of species that live and interact in an area. The animals and plants you see in **Figure 3** form a salt-marsh community. The populations in a community depend on each other for food, shelter, and many other things.

Figure 3 *Examine the picture of a salt marsh. Try to find examples of each level of organization in this environment.*

Laughing gull

Egret

Cordgrass

Seaside sparrows eat insects, spiders, and small crabs. A male and his mate weave a nest out of cordgrass stalks.

Heron

Juvenile sea croaker

The little marsh crab eats cordgrass as well as tiny shrimp.

Jellyfish

Some animals eat cordgrass, along with the microscopic algae that grow on the surface of its leaves and stems.

The periwinkle snail eats the algae that grow on the cordgrass. The periwinkle snail also uses the cordgrass as a place to hide from predators.

Cultural Awareness GENERAL

Ethnobotany In Hawaii, officials of the Ethnobotanical Garden are working with scientists to develop wetland habitats that will support makaloa, a wetland sedge once used by Hawaiians to weave mats. The wetlands will be part of a wastewater treatment system and will support the resurgence of makaloa. Encourage students to research the weaving traditions of Hawaii and present their findings to the class. **LS** Visual

Ecosystems

An **ecosystem** is made up of a community of organisms and the abiotic environment of the community. An ecologist studying the ecosystem could examine how organisms interact as well as how temperature, precipitation, and soil characteristics affect the organisms. For example, the rivers that empty into the salt marsh carry nutrients, such as nitrogen, from the land. These nutrients affect the growth of the cordgrass and algae.

The Biosphere

The **biosphere** is the part of Earth where life exists. It extends from the deepest parts of the ocean to high in the air where plant spores drift. Ecologists study the biosphere to learn how organisms interact with the abiotic environment—Earth's atmosphere, water, soil, and rock. The water in the abiotic environment includes fresh water and salt water as well as water that is frozen in polar icecaps and glaciers.

✓ **Reading Check** What is the biosphere? (*See the Appendix for answers to Reading Checks.*)

ecosystem a community of organisms and their abiotic environment

biosphere the part of Earth where life exists

INTERNET ACTIVITY

For another activity related to this chapter, go to **go.hrw.com** and type in the keyword **HL5INTW.**

SECTION Review

Summary

- All living things are connected in a web of life.
- The biotic part of an environment is made up of all of the living things found within it.
- The abiotic part of an environment is made up of all of the nonliving things found within it, such as water and light.
- An ecosystem is made up of a community of organisms and its abiotic environment.

Using Key Terms

1. In your own words, write a definition for the term *ecology*.

2. Use the following terms in the same sentence: *biotic* and *abiotic*.

Understanding Key Ideas

3. Which one of the following is the highest level of environmental organization?
   a. ecosystem   c. population
   b. community   d. organism

4. What makes up a community?

5. Give two examples of how abiotic factors can affect an ecosystem.

Math Skills

6. From sea level, the biosphere goes up about 9 km and down about 19 km. What is the thickness of the biosphere in meters?

Critical Thinking

7. **Analyzing Relationships** What would happen to the other organisms in the salt-marsh ecosystem if the cordgrass suddenly died?

8. **Identifying Relationships** Explain in your own words what people mean when they say that everything is connected.

9. **Analyzing Ideas** Do ecosystems have borders? Explain your answer.

SCILINKS

NSTA

Developed and maintained by the National Science Teachers Association

For a variety of links related to this chapter, go to www.scilinks.org

Topic: Biotic and Abiotic Factors; Organization in the Environment
SciLinks code: HSM0164; HSM1079

Answer to Reading Check

The biosphere is the part of Earth where life exists.

Answers to Section Review

1. Sample answer: Ecology is the study of the interactions of organisms with each other and with their environment.

2. Sample answer: An ecosystem is made up of biotic and abiotic parts.

3. a

4. A community is made up of all of the populations that interact in an area.

5. Sample answer: Temperature affects which animals can live in an ecosystem. Water and its abundance affect whether certain plants grow easily in an area.

6. 28,000 m (9 − ⁻19 = 28 km; 28 × 1000 = 28,000 m)

7. Sample answer: The populations of organisms that fed on the cordgrass would decrease. The populations of organisms that fed on the organisms that ate the cordgrass would also decrease.

8. Sample answers: All living things depend on other living and nonliving things to survive.

9. Sample answer: No, ecosystems do not have borders. Some ecosystems are partially contained, but water, light, and many organisms move freely from one ecosystem to the next.

Focus

Overview
In this section, students will learn how producers, consumers, and decomposers obtain energy to survive. They will also learn the difference between a food chain and a food web and how energy is transferred among members of a food chain or a food web.

 Bellringer
Tell students that a flowering plant called *Indian pipe* is completely white—it has no chlorophyll or chloroplasts. Ask: "Can this plant still be a producer? If not, where does it get the energy it needs to survive?" (This plant is a consumer. It lives off the roots of rotting trees with the help of a fungus.)

Motivate

ACTIVITY———— GENERAL
Before reading this section, students should use prior knowledge to write a definition for *producer* and *consumer*. They should also define *carnivore*, *omnivore*, and *herbivore* in their own words. After reading the section, students should revise their definitions. **LS Verbal**

Living Things Need Energy

Do you think you could survive on only water and vitamins? Eating food satisfies your hunger because it provides something you cannot live without—energy.

Living things need energy to survive. For example, black-tailed prairie dogs, which live in the grasslands of North America, eat grass and seeds to get the energy they need. Everything a prairie dog does requires energy. The same is true for the plants that grow in the grasslands where the prairie dogs live.

The Energy Connection
Organisms, in a prairie or any community, can be divided into three groups based on how they get energy. These groups are producers, consumers, and decomposers. Examine **Figure 1** to see how energy passes through an ecosystem.

Producers
Organisms that use sunlight directly to make food are called *producers*. They do this by using a process called *photosynthesis*. Most producers are plants, but algae and some bacteria are also producers. Grasses are the main producers in a prairie ecosystem. Examples of producers in other ecosystems include cordgrass and algae in a salt marsh and trees in a forest. Algae are the main producers in the ocean.

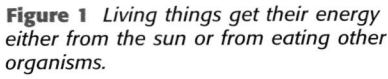

READING WARM-UP

Objectives
- Describe the functions of producers, consumers, and decomposers in an ecosystem.
- Distinguish between a food chain and a food web.
- Explain how energy flows through a food web.
- Describe how the removal of one species affects the entire food web.

Terms to Learn

herbivore	food chain
carnivore	food web
omnivore	energy pyramid

READING STRATEGY

Reading Organizer As you read this section, make a table comparing producers, consumers, and decomposers.

Figure 1 *Living things get their energy either from the sun or from eating other organisms.*

Energy Sunlight is the source of energy for almost all living things.

Producer Plants use the energy in sunlight to make food.

Consumer The black-tailed prairie dog (herbivore) eats seeds and grass in the grasslands of western North America.

Consumer All of the prairie dogs in a colony watch for enemies, such as coyotes (carnivore), hawks, and badgers. Occasionally, a prairie dog is killed and eaten by a coyote.

CHAPTER RESOURCES

Chapter Resource File

- • Lesson Plan
- • Directed Reading A **BASIC**
- • Directed Reading B **SPECIAL NEEDS**

Technology

- • Transparencies
  - • Bellringer
  - • *LINK TO EARTH SCIENCE* Porous Rocks Are Reservoirs for Fossil Fuels

---

CONNECTION to
Earth Science———— GENERAL

Fossil Fuels Fossil fuels store solar energy gathered by ancient plants. Students may be interested to learn where fossil fuels exist underground. Use the teaching transparency titled "Porous Rocks Are Reservoirs for Fossil Fuels" to illustrate where fossil fuels are located. **LS Visual**

Consumers

Organisms that eat other organisms are called *consumers*. They cannot use the sun's energy to make food like producers can. Instead, consumers eat producers or other animals to obtain energy. There are several kinds of consumers. A consumer that eats only plants is called a **herbivore.** Herbivores found in the prairie include grasshoppers, prairie dogs, and bison. A **carnivore** is a consumer that eats animals. Carnivores in the prairie include coyotes, hawks, badgers, and owls. Consumers known as **omnivores** eat both plants and animals. The grasshopper mouse is an example of an omnivore. It eats insects, lizards, and grass seeds.

Scavengers are omnivores that eat dead plants and animals. The turkey vulture is a scavenger in the prairie. A vulture will eat what is left after a coyote has killed and eaten an animal. Scavengers also eat animals and plants that have died from natural causes.

✓ **Reading Check** What are organisms that eat other organisms called? (*See the Appendix for answers to Reading Checks.*)

Decomposers

Organisms that get energy by breaking down dead organisms are called *decomposers*. Bacteria and fungi are decomposers. These organisms remove stored energy from dead organisms. They produce simple materials, such as water and carbon dioxide, which can be used by other living things. Decomposers are important because they are nature's recyclers.

herbivore an organism that eats only plants

carnivore an organism that eats animals

omnivore an organism that eats both plants and animals

SCHOOL to HOME

A Chain Game

With the help of your parent, make a list of the foods you ate at your most recent meal. Trace the energy of each food back to the sun. Which foods on your list were consumers? How many were producers?

ACTIVITY

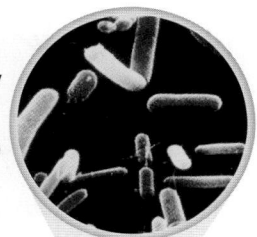

Consumer A turkey vulture (scavenger) may eat some of the coyote's leftovers. A scavenger can pick bones completely clean.

Decomposer Any prairie dog remains not eaten by the coyote or the turkey vulture are broken down by bacteria (decomposer) and fungi that live in the soil.

WEIRD SCIENCE

Turkey vultures have an acute sense of smell. A biologist put decaying carcasses in metal containers, hid the containers in the California foothills, and used a fan to diffuse the odor. Turkey vultures were soon soaring overhead. Engineers once pumped ethyl mercaptan, which smells like rotting flesh, into natural-gas lines. They located leaks by watching for turkey vultures attracted to the pipeline.

Answer to School-to-Home Activity

Answers may vary. Answers should reflect student understanding that consumers get energy from producers. For example, a student consuming yogurt is getting energy that a cow got from grass or grain. The grass or grain got its energy from the sun.

CONNECTION to Real World ——— GENERAL

Cockroaches Having survived for 300 million years, the common cockroach may be the most successful and well-adapted scavenger of all time. Cockroaches scavenged dinosaur leftovers long before they survived on the crumbs and kitchen scraps of humans. Dead skin and fingernails are a real treat for them; leftover food is a delicacy. If these tasty morsels aren't available, cockroaches can survive on such unlikely food sources as shoe polish, paint, and soap. Have interested students research cockroaches and present their findings to the class. **LS Verbal**

Answer to Reading Check

Organisms that eat other organisms are called *consumers*.

Using the Figure — BASIC

Energy Transfer Have students write new captions for **Figure 1.** Then, have students draw a similar diagram showing the transfer of energy within an aquatic ecosystem. **LS Visual**

MISCONCEPTION ALERT

Bears The North American black bear and the grizzly are not carnivores. They are omnivores. Besides eating mammals and fish, both bears eat berries and roots. Black bears also eat pine cones, acorns, and insects. Sometimes, grizzlies even eat grass.

Energy Loss There are 12,000 units of the sun's energy available to grass, which occupies the base of an energy pyramid. Grass stores this 10% of available energy in its tissues. This energy becomes available to the next consumer, a prairie dog. In turn, the prairie dog, a consumer of grass, stores 10% of the energy that was stored in the grass. A coyote, a consumer of prairie dogs, stores 10% of the energy that was stored in the prairie dog. Calculate the units of food energy stored in the grass, the prairie dog, and the coyote.

(The grass stores 10% of the sun's energy:

$0.1 \times 12,000 = 1,200$ units of energy stored in the grass

The prairie dog stores 10% of the grass' stored energy:

$0.1 \times 1,200 = 120$ units of energy stored in the prairie dog

The coyote stores 10% of the prairie dog's stored energy:

$0.1 \times 120 = 12$ units of energy stored in the coyote)

LS Logical

---

food chain the pathway of energy transfer through various stages as a result of the feeding patterns of a series of organisms

food web a diagram that shows the feeding relationships between organisms in an ecosystem

---

Food Chains and Food Webs

Figure 1 on the previous page, shows a food chain. A **food chain** is a diagram that shows how energy in food flows from one organism to another. Because few organisms eat just one kind of food, simple food chains are rare.

The energy connections in nature are more accurately shown by a food web than by a food chain. A **food web** is a diagram that shows the feeding relationships between organisms in an ecosystem. **Figure 2** shows a simple food web. Notice that an arrow goes from the prairie dog to the coyote, showing that the prairie dog is food for the coyote. The prairie dog is also food for the mountain lion. Energy moves from one organism to the next in a one-way direction, even in a food web. Any energy not immediately used by an organism is stored in its tissues. Only the energy stored in an organism's tissues can be used by the next consumer. There are two main food webs on Earth: a land food web and an aquatic food web.

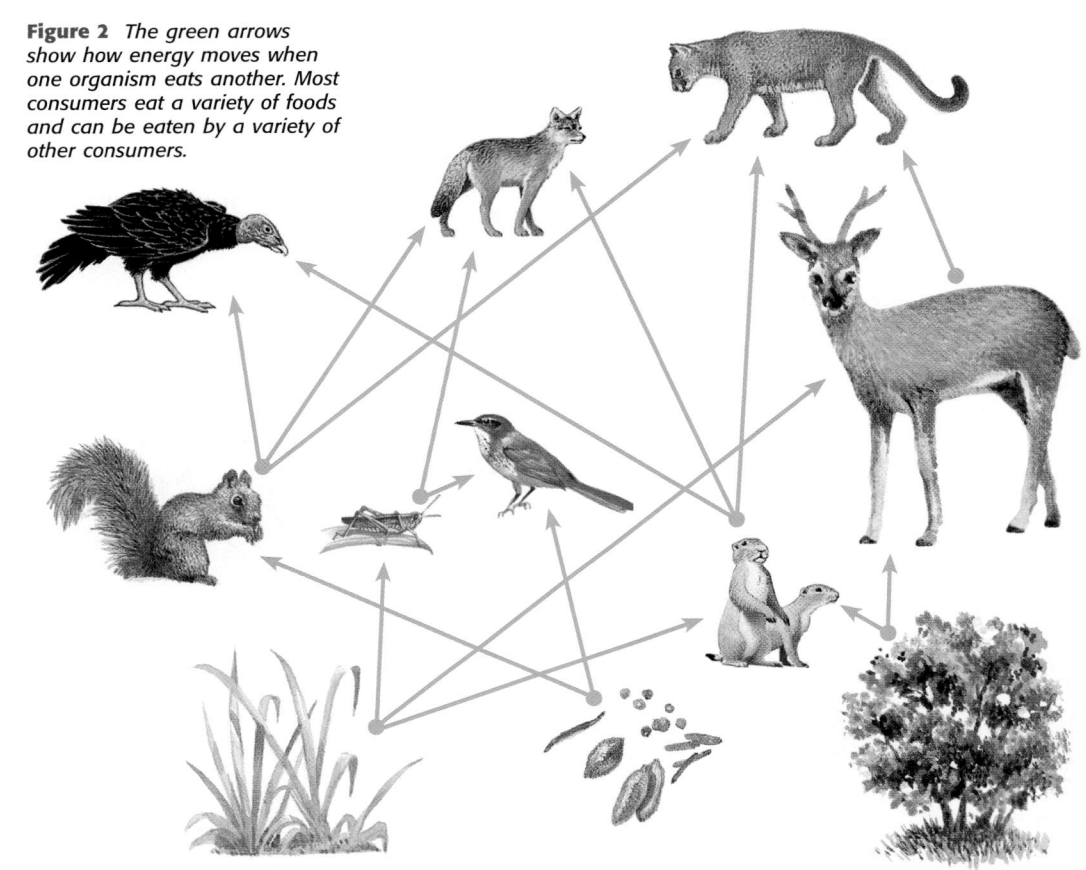

Figure 2 *The green arrows show how energy moves when one organism eats another. Most consumers eat a variety of foods and can be eaten by a variety of other consumers.*

SCIENCE HUMOR

Customer: Waiter! Waiter! There's a fly in my soup!

Waiter: Don't worry, sir. The spider in your salad will get it!

Is That a Fact!

In 1989, the Nature Conservancy purchased 30,000 acres of grassland in Oklahoma. Their goal was to restore the land to a grass-prairie ecosystem. The restoration will allow the more than 700 prairie plant species to reestablish themselves. A healthy prairie is also home to 300 bird species, 80 mammal species, and hundreds of thousands of insect species. Biologists also have reintroduced bison, whose grazing is integral to the prairie food web.

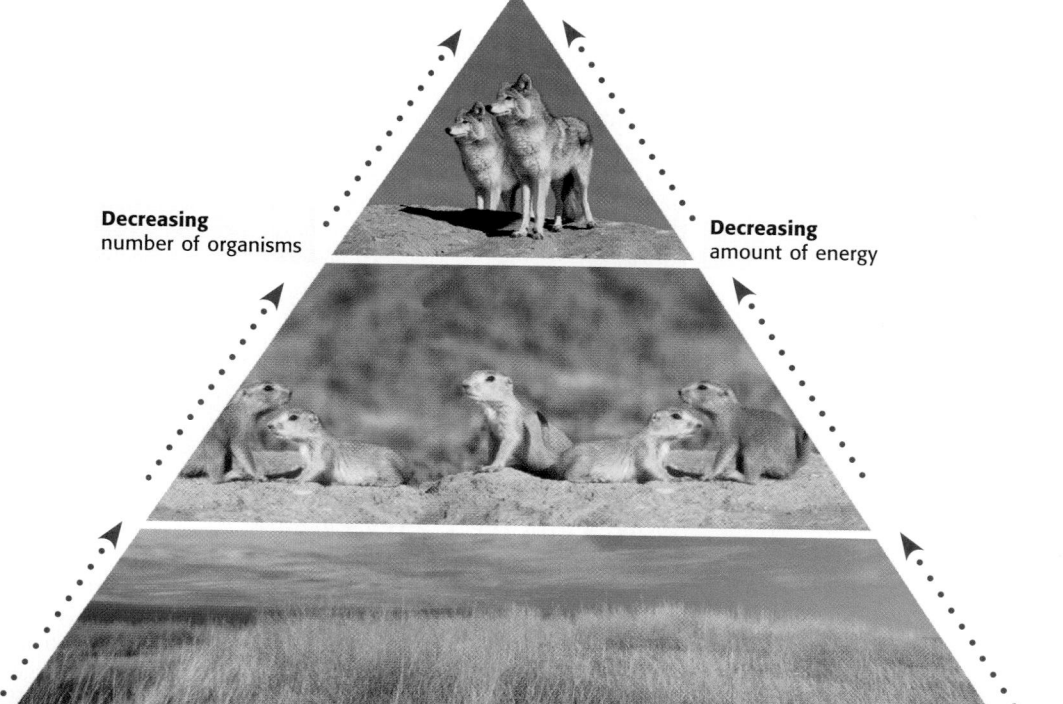

Decreasing number of organisms

Decreasing amount of energy

Energy Pyramids

Grass uses most of the energy it gets from sunlight for its own life processes. But some of the energy is stored in the grass' tissues. This energy is used by the prairie dogs and other animals that eat the grass. Prairie dogs use most of the energy they get from eating grass and store only a little in their tissues. Therefore, a population of prairie dogs can support only a few coyotes. In the community, there must be more grass than prairie dogs and more prairie dogs than coyotes.

The energy at each level of the food chain can be seen in an energy pyramid. An **energy pyramid** is a diagram that shows an ecosystem's loss of energy. An example of an energy pyramid is shown in **Figure 3.** You can see that the energy pyramid has a large base and a small top. Less energy is available at higher levels because only energy stored in the tissues of an organism can be transferred to the next level.

 Reading Check What is an energy pyramid?

Figure 3 *The pyramid represents energy. As you can see, more energy is available at the base of the pyramid than at its top.*

energy pyramid a triangular diagram that shows an ecosystem's loss of energy, which results as energy passes through the ecosystem's food chain

Answer to Reading Check

An energy pyramid is a diagram that shows an ecosystem's energy loss.

CHAPTER RESOURCES

Technology

Transparencies
• Energy Pyramid

Reviewing Food Webs Make a label for each of the 11 organisms in **Figure 2** of this section, and give the labels to individual students. Then, have students use string to connect themselves to the other "foods" in the food web. **LS** Kinesthetic/Interpersonal

Quiz ———— GENERAL

1. How might an omnivore be a link both at the beginning of a food web and near the end? (Sample answer: An omnivore can be at the beginning because it eats plants. It also can be near the end because it eats other consumers or can be eaten by other consumers.)

2. How does the energy in a fish get into the fish? How does the energy stored in the fish get released from the fish? (Sample answer: The fish stores some of the energy it gets from the food it eats. The energy in the fish is released when the fish is eaten by another organism.)

Alternative Assessment ———— GENERAL

Writing **Recipe** Have students write an eight-step recipe for a decomposer's dinner. Tell students that the first ingredient is sunlight. **LS** Verbal

Figure 4 *As the wilderness was settled, the gray wolf population in the United States declined.*

Wolves and the Energy Pyramid

One species can be very important to the flow of energy in an environment. Gray wolves, which are shown in **Figure 4,** are consumers that control the populations of many other animals. The diet of gray wolves can include anything from a lizard to an elk. Because gray wolves are predators that prey on large animals, their place is at the top of the food pyramid.

Once common throughout much of the United States, gray wolves were almost wiped out as the wilderness was settled. Without wolves, some species, such as elk, were no longer controlled. The overpopulation of elk in some areas led to overgrazing. The overgrazing left too little grass to support the elk and other populations who depended on the grass for food. Soon, almost all of the populations in the area were affected by the loss of the gray wolves.

✓ *Reading Check* How were other animals affected by the disappearance of the gray wolf?

Gray Wolves and the Food Web

Gray wolves were brought back to Yellowstone National Park in 1995. The reintroduced wolves soon began to breed. **Figure 5** shows a wolf caring for pups. The U.S. Fish and Wildlife Service thinks the return of the wolves will restore the natural energy flow in the area, bring populations back into balance, and help restore the park's natural integrity.

Not everyone approves, however. Ranchers near Yellowstone are concerned about the safety of their livestock. Cows and sheep are not the natural prey of wolves. However, the wolves will eat cows and sheep if they are given the chance.

Figure 5 *In small wolf packs, only one female has pups. They are cared for by all of the males and females in the pack.*

WEIRD SCIENCE

In certain tropical areas, the dry season can last several months. Some frogs, such as the African bullfrog, burrow into the mud before the mud dries out. The frog then sheds several intact layers of skin, which harden and form a protective covering. Only the frog's nostrils are exposed, so it can breathe. When the rains return, the frog breaks through the moist soil and returns to the surface.

Answer to Reading Check

Other animals in Yellowstone National Park were affected by the disappearance of the gray wolf because the food web was interrupted. Animals that would normally be prey for the gray wolf were more plentiful. These larger populations ate more vegetation.

Balance in Ecosystems

As wolves become reestablished in Yellowstone National Park, they kill the old, injured, and diseased elk. This process is reducing the number of elk. The smaller elk population is letting more plants grow. So, the numbers of animals that eat the plants, such as snowshoe hares, and the animals that eat the hares, such as foxes, are increasing.

All organisms in a food web are important for the health and balance of all other organisms in the food web. But the debate over the introduction of wolves to Yellowstone National Park will most likely continue for years to come.

Energy Pyramids

Draw an energy pyramid for a river ecosystem that contains four levels—aquatic plants, insect larvae, bluegill fish, and a largemouth bass. The plants obtain 10,000 units of energy from sunlight. If each level uses 90% of the energy it receives from the previous level, how many units of energy are available to the bass?

SECTION Review

Summary

- Producers use the energy in sunlight to make their own food.
- Consumers eat producers and other organisms to gain energy.
- Food chains represent how energy flows from one organism to another.
- All organisms are important to maintain the balance of energy in the food web.
- Energy pyramids show how energy is lost at each food chain level.

Using Key Terms

1. Use each of the following terms in a separate sentence: *herbivores, carnivores,* and *omnivores.*

2. In your own words, write a definition for each of the following terms: *food chain, food web,* and *energy pyramid.*

Understanding Key Ideas

3. Herbivores, carnivores, and scavengers are all examples of
   a. producers.   c. consumers.
   b. decomposers. d. omnivores.

4. Explain the importance of decomposers in an ecosystem.

5. Describe how producers, consumers, and decomposers are linked in a food chain.

6. Describe how energy flows through a food web.

Math Skills

7. The plants in each square meter of an ecosystem obtained 20,810 Calories of energy from sunlight per year. The herbivores in that ecosystem ate all the plants but obtained only 3,370 Calories of energy. How much energy did the plants use?

Critical Thinking

8. **Identifying Relationships** Draw two food chains, and depict how they link together to form a food web.

9. **Applying Concepts** Are consumers found at the top or bottom of an energy pyramid? Explain your answer.

10. **Predicting Consequences** What would happen if a species disappeared from an ecosystem?

For a variety of links related to this chapter, go to www.scilinks.org

Topic: Food Chains and Food Webs
SciLinks code: HSM0594

Answer to Math Practice

10 units of energy (10,000 × 0.1 = 1,000 units of energy for insect larvae; 1,000 × 0.1 = 100 units of energy for bluegill fish; 100 × 0.1 = 10 units of energy for largemouth bass)

Answers to Section Review

1. Sample answer: Herbivores are consumers that eat only plants. Carnivores are consumers that eat only animals. Omnivores are consumers that eat both plants and animals.

2. Sample answer: A food chain is a diagram that shows which animals feed on other animals. A food web is many food chains linked together. An energy pyramid shows how energy is lost in an ecosystem.

3. c

4. Decomposers remove energy from dead organisms and produce materials that can be used by other organisms. Decomposers are nature's recyclers.

5. Sample answer: Consumers feed on producers and other consumers. Decomposers feed on producers and other consumers after they are dead.

6. Sample answer: Energy flows into the consumers from the plants and animals that the consumers eat.

7. 17,440 Calories (20,810 − 3,370 = 17,440 Calories)

8. Answers may vary. Chains and webs should show that students understand how producers provide food for consumers and understand that most food sources are interrelated.

9. Sample answer: Consumers are found at the top of an energy pyramid because they require energy from the producers below them.

10. Sample answer: The food web might be changed greatly if a species disappeared from an ecosystem. The organisms that fed on that species would have to find new sources of energy.

CHAPTER RESOURCES

Chapter Resource File

- Section Quiz GENERAL
- Section Review GENERAL
- Vocabulary and Section Summary GENERAL
- Reinforcement Worksheet BASIC
- Critical Thinking ADVANCED

Focus

Overview

In this section, students will learn about the types of interactions that organisms have with each other and with their environment. Students will learn to distinguish the two types of competition and to identify predator and prey species. They will also learn to recognize mutualism, commensalism, and parasitism. Finally, students will learn about coevolution.

 ### Bellringer

On the board or overhead projector, write the following:

Make a list of predators that are also prey.

(Sample answers: salamanders, frogs, shrews, snakes, lizards, and weasels)

READING WARM-UP

Objectives
- Explain the relationship between carrying capacity and limiting factors.
- Describe the two types of competition.
- Distinguish between mutualism, commensalism, and parasitism. Give an example of coevolution.

Terms to Learn

carrying capacity   mutualism
prey   commensalism
predator   parasitism
symbiosis   coevolution

READING STRATEGY

Reading Organizer As you read this section, make a concept map by using the terms above.

Types of Interactions

Look at the seaweed forest shown in **Figure 1** *below. How many fish do you see? How many seaweed plants do you count? Why do you think there are more members of the seaweed population than members of the fish population?*

In natural communities, the sizes of populations of different organisms can vary greatly. This variation happens because everything in the environment affects every other thing. Populations also affect every other population.

Interactions with the Environment

Most living things produce more offspring than will survive. A female frog, for example, might lay hundreds of eggs in a small pond. In a few months, the population of frogs in that pond will be about the same as it was the year before. Why won't the pond become overrun with frogs? An organism, such as a frog, interacts with biotic and abiotic factors in its environment that can control the size of its population.

Limiting Factors

Populations cannot grow without stopping, because the environment contains a limited amount of food, water, living space, and other resources. A resource that is so scarce that it limits the size of a population is called a *limiting factor*. For example, food becomes a limiting factor when a population becomes too large for the amount of food available. Any single resource can be a limiting factor to a population's size.

Figure 1 *This seaweed forest is home to a large number of interacting species.*

CHAPTER RESOURCES

Chapter Resource File

- **Lesson Plan**
- **Directed Reading A** BASIC
- **Directed Reading B** SPECIAL NEEDS

Technology

- **Transparencies**
  - Bellringer

 **WEIRD SCIENCE**

In Japan, green herons make interesting use of the biotic and abiotic parts of their environment. They will drop sticks and even bread crumbs into the water to attract fish. Sometimes, they will catch a fish within 2 or 3 seconds of dropping the bait.

Carrying Capacity

The largest population that an environment can support is known as the **carrying capacity.** When a population grows larger than its carrying capacity, limiting factors in the environment cause individuals to die off or leave. As individuals die or leave, the population decreases.

For example, after a rainy season, plants may produce a large crop of leaves and seeds. This large amount of food may cause an herbivore population to grow. If the next year has less rainfall, there won't be enough food to support the large herbivore population. In this way, a population may become larger than the carrying capacity, but only for a little while. A limiting factor will cause the population to die back. The population will return to a size that the environment can support.

carrying capacity the largest population that an environment can support at any given time

Interactions Between Organisms

Populations contain individuals of a single species that interact with one another, such as a group of rabbits feeding in the same area. Communities contain interacting populations, such as a coral reef with many species of corals trying to find living space. Ecologists have described four main ways that species and individuals affect each other: competition, predators and prey, symbiotic relationships, and coevolution.

✓ **Reading Check** **What are four main ways organisms affect one another?** (*See the Appendix for answers to Reading Checks.*)

Competition

When two or more individuals or populations try to use the same resource, such as food, water, shelter, space, or sunlight, it is called *competition.* Because resources are in limited supply in the environment, their use by one individual or population decreases the amount available to other organisms.

Competition happens between individuals *within* a population. The elks in Yellowstone National Park are herbivores that compete with each other for the same food plants in the park. This competition is a big problem in winter when many plants die.

Competition also happens *between* populations. The different species of trees in **Figure 2** are competing with each other for sunlight and space.

Figure 2 *Some of the trees in this forest grow tall to reach sunlight, which reduces the amount of sunlight available to shorter trees nearby.*

ACTIVITY ———————— GENERAL

Predators and Prey Organize students into six groups. Then, divide each group into subgroups of two or three, and designate each subgroup as Predator or Prey. Instruct each Predator group to name a prey animal and the adaptations the predator uses to catch the prey. (Sample answers: speed, talons, and strength) Tell each Prey group to name a predator animal and the prey's adaptations to evade capture. (Sample answers: camouflage, speed, protective armor, and flight) Have students write down the adaptations and share their information with the other groups.

LS Kinesthetic/ Interpersonal   English Language Learners

MISCONCEPTION //ALERT

Balance The phrase *balance of nature* should not be taken to mean that the components of an environment are static. Populations are in balance when their sizes are stable. That stability is the result of constant interactions between individuals of a population, between populations in a community, and between populations and environmental factors.

---

prey an organism that is killed and eaten by another organism

predator an organism that eats all or part of another organism

Figure 3 *The goldenrod spider is difficult for its insect prey to see. Can you see it?*

Figure 4 *Many predators know better than to eat the fire salamander! This colorful animal will make a predator very sick.*

Predators and Prey

Many interactions between species consist of one organism eating another. The organism that is eaten is called the **prey.** The organism that eats the prey is called the **predator.** When a bird eats a worm, the worm is prey and the bird is the predator.

Predator Adaptations

To survive, predators must be able to catch their prey. Predators have a wide variety of methods and abilities for doing so. The cheetah, for example, is able to run very quickly to catch its prey. The cheetah's speed gives it an advantage over other predators competing for the same prey.

Other predators, such as the goldenrod spider, shown in **Figure 3,** ambush their prey. The goldenrod spider blends in so well with the goldenrod flower that all it has to do is wait for its next insect meal to arrive.

Prey Adaptations

Prey have their own methods and abilities to keep from being eaten. Prey are able to run away, stay in groups, or camouflage themselves. Some prey are poisonous. They may advertise their poison with bright colors to warn predators to stay away. The fire salamander, shown in **Figure 4,** sprays a poison that burns. Predators quickly learn to recognize its *warning coloration.*

Many animals run away from predators. Prairie dogs run to their underground burrows when a predator approaches. Many small fishes, such as anchovies, swim in groups called *schools.* Antelopes and buffaloes stay in herds. All the eyes, ears, and noses of the individuals in the group are watching, listening, and smelling for predators. This behavior increases the likelihood of spotting a potential predator.

Is That a Fact!

Pancake tortoises live on rocky hillsides in Africa. They are very flat and can wedge themselves into cracks in the rocks for protection from predators. Their bottom shells are pliable and can "inflate" so that a predator can't pry out the tortoises.

Camouflage

One way animals avoid being eaten is by being hard to see. A rabbit often freezes so that its natural color blends into a background of shrubs or grass. Blending in with the background is called *camouflage*. Many animals mimic twigs, leaves, stones, bark, or other materials in their environment. One insect, called a walking stick, looks just like a twig. Some walking sticks even sway a bit, as though a breeze were blowing.

Reading Check What is camouflage, and how does it prevent an animal from being eaten?

Defensive Chemicals

The spines of a porcupine clearly signal trouble to a potential predator, but other defenses may not be as obvious. Some animals defend themselves with chemicals. The skunk and the bombardier beetle both spray predators with irritating chemicals. Bees, ants, and wasps inject a powerful acid into their attackers. The skin of both the poison arrow frog and a bird called the *hooded pitohui* contains a deadly toxin. Any predator that eats, or tries to eat, one of these animals will likely die.

Warning Coloration

Animals that have a chemical defense need a way to warn predators that they should look elsewhere for a meal. Their chemical weapons are often advertised by warning colors, as shown in **Figure 5.** Predators will avoid any animal that has the colors and patterns they associate with pain, illness, or unpleasant experiences. The most common warning colors are bright shades of red, yellow, orange, black, and white.

Figure 5 *The warning coloration of the yellow jacket (left) and the pitohui (above) warns predators that they are dangerous.*

Teach, *continued*

Discussion ── BASIC

Honeyguide The honeyguide, a small African bird, lives up to its name. The purpose of its song is to lure nearby creatures to a nest of honeybees it has found. Many animals have learned to listen for this bird! Baboons, mongooses, ratels (or honey badgers), and even people will follow the bird in order to claim the honey. Out of harm's way, the bird waits for the leftovers: bee larvae. The bird's unique digestive system allows it to eat wax as well. Ask students the following questions:

• Which animals in this story are in a mutualistic relationship? (The honeyguide and the animals that eat the honey.)

• Which animals are prey, and which are predators? (The bees are prey. All of the other animals are predators.)

LS Logical

CONNECTION ACTIVITY
Real World ── GENERAL

Interaction To help students understand the differences between mutualism, commensalism, and parasitism, ask them about their relationships with other species. Interactions with pets, backyard animals, and annoying insects can shed light on these relationships. Are any of these interactions examples of mutualism? parasitism? commensalism? **LS Logical**

---

symbiosis a relationship in which two different organisms live in close association with each other

mutualism a relationship between two species in which both species benefit

commensalism a relationship between two organisms in which one organism benefits and the other is unaffected

Figure 6 *In the smaller photo above, you can see the gold-colored algae inside the coral.*

Answer to Reading Check
In a mutualistic relationship, both organisms benefit from the relationship.

Symbiosis

Some species have very close interactions with other species. **Symbiosis** is a close, long-term association between two or more species. The individuals in a symbiotic relationship can benefit from, be unaffected by, or be harmed by the relationship. Often, one species lives in or on the other species. The thousands of symbiotic relationships in nature are often classified into three groups: mutualism, commensalism, and parasitism.

Mutualism

A symbiotic relationship in which both organisms benefit is called **mutualism** (MYOO choo uhl IZ uhm). For example, you and a species of bacteria that lives in your intestines benefit each other! The bacteria get food from you, and you get vitamins that the bacteria produce.

Another example of mutualism happens between corals and algae. Coral near the surface of the water provide a home for algae. The algae produce food for the coral by photosynthesis. When a coral dies, its skeleton is used by other corals. Over a long time, these skeletons build up large formations that lie under the surface of warm seas, as shown in **Figure 6.**

✓ *Reading Check* Which organism benefits in mutualism?

Commensalism

A symbiotic relationship in which one organism benefits and the other is unaffected is called **commensalism.** One example of commensalism is the relationship between sharks and smaller fish called *remoras*. **Figure 7** shows a shark with a remora attached to its body. Remoras "hitch a ride" and feed on scraps of food left by sharks. The remoras benefit from this relationship, while sharks are unaffected.

Figure 7 *The remora attached to the shark benefits from the relationship. The shark neither benefits from nor is harmed by the relationship.*

MISCONCEPTION ///ALERT\\\

Types of Relationships You will often hear the word *symbiosis* used when *mutualism* is meant. Mutualism is one type of symbiosis; commensalism and parasitism are the other two types.

Parasitism

A symbiotic association in which one organism benefits while the other is harmed is called **parasitism** (PAR uh SIT iz uhm). The organism that benefits is called the *parasite*. The organism that is harmed is called the *host*. The parasite gets nourishment from its host while the host is weakened. Sometimes, a host dies. Parasites, such as ticks, live outside the host's body. Other parasites, such as tapeworms, live inside the host's body.

Figure 8 shows a bright green caterpillar called a *tomato hornworm*. A female wasp laid tiny eggs on the caterpillar. When the eggs hatch, each young wasp will burrow into the caterpillar's body. The young wasps will actually eat the caterpillar alive! In a short time, the caterpillar will be almost completely eaten and will die. When that happens, the adult wasps will fly away.

In this example of parasitism, the host dies. Most parasites, however, do not kill their hosts. Most parasites don't kill their hosts because parasites depend on their hosts. If a parasite were to kill its host, the parasite would have to find a new host.

Coevolution

Relationships between organisms change over time. Interactions can also change the organisms themselves. When a long-term change takes place in two species because of their close interactions with one another, the change is called **coevolution.**

The ant and the acacia tree shown in **Figure 9** have a mutualistic relationship. The ants protect the tree by attacking other organisms that come near the tree. The tree has special structures that make food for the ants. The ants and the acacia tree may have coevolved through interactions between the two species. Coevolution can take place between any organisms that live close together. But changes happen over a very long period of time.

Figure 8 *The tomato hornworm is being parasitized by young wasps. Do you see their cocoons?*

parasitism a relationship between two species in which one species, the parasite, benefits from the other species, the host, which is harmed

coevolution the evolution of two species that is due to mutual influence, often in a way that makes the relationship more beneficial to both species

Figure 9 *Ants collect food made by the acacia tree and store the food in their shelter, which is also made by the tree.*

Reteaching — BASIC

Organizing Information Have students make a table that shows how the following relationships are different:

predator and prey relationships, mutualism, parasitisim, and commensalism.

🔲 Logical

Quiz — GENERAL

1. Explain the difference between mutualism and coevolution. (Mutualism is a close relationship between two species in which both benefit. Coevolution is the gradual change in two species' physical characteristics as a result of a symbiotic relationship.)

2. Can a predator ever be the prey for another species? (Yes; field mice eat insects and are sometimes eaten by snakes and hawks. Small fish are consumed by larger fish, which are eaten by even larger fish.)

Alternative Assessment — GENERAL

Concept Mapping Have students organize the following terms into a concept map:

competition, predator, individuals, population, symbiosis, commensalism, prey, mutualism, interactions

🔲 Logical/Visual

CONNECTION TO
Social Studies

Rabbits in Australia In 1859, settlers released 12 rabbits in Australia. There was plenty of food and no natural predators for the rabbits. The rabbit population increased so fast that the country was soon overrun by rabbits. Then, the Australian government introduced a rabbit virus to control the population. The first time the virus was used, more than 99% of the rabbits died. The survivors reproduced, and the rabbit population grew large again. The second time the virus was used, about 90% of the rabbits died. Once again, the rabbit population increased. The third time the virus was used, only about 50% of the rabbits died. Suggest what changes might have occurred in the rabbits and the virus.

Coevolution and Flowers

A *pollinator* is an organism that carries pollen from one flower to another. Pollination is necessary for reproduction in most plants.

Flowers have changed over millions of years to attract pollinators. Pollinators such as bees, bats, and hummingbirds can be attracted to a flower because of its color, odor, or nectar. Flowers pollinated by hummingbirds make nectar with the right amount of sugar for the bird. Hummingbirds have long beaks, which help them drink the nectar.

Some bats, such as the one shown in **Figure 10,** changed over time to have long, thin tongues and noses to help them reach the nectar in flowers. As the bat feeds on the nectar, its nose becomes covered with pollen. The next flower it eats from will be pollinated with the pollen it is gathering from this flower. The long nose helps it to feed and also makes it a better pollinator.

Because flowers and their pollinators have interacted so closely over millions of years, there are many examples of coevolution between them.

✔ Reading Check Why do flowers need to attract pollinators?

Figure 10 *This bat is drinking nectar with its long, skinny tongue. The bat has coevolved with the flower over millions of years.*

Answer to Connection to Social Studies

Sample answer: Viruses that kill all of their hosts have no place to live. The viruses in Australia became less virulent, no longer killing rabbits, which the viruses use as hosts. The rabbits, on the other hand, began to produce more survivors with immunity. The survivors bred, producing a population of rabbits that included more individuals that were immune to the virus.

Answer to Reading Check

Flowers need to attract pollinators to help the flowers reproduce with other members of their species.

SECTION Review

Summary

- Limiting factors in the environment keep a population from growing without limit.
- Two or more individuals or populations trying to use the same resource is called *competition.*
- A predator is an organism that eats all or part of another organism. The organism that is eaten is called *prey.*
- Prey have developed features such as camouflage, chemical defenses, and warning coloration, to protect them from predators.
- Symbiosis occurs when two organisms form a very close relationship with one another over time.
- Close relationships over a very long time can result in coevolution. For example, flowers and their pollinators have evolved traits that benefit both.

Using Key Terms

1. In your own words, write a definition for the term *carrying capacity.*

2. Use each of the following terms in a separate sentence: *mutualism, commensalism,* and *parasitism.*

Understanding Key Ideas

3. Which of the following is NOT a prey adaptation?
   a. camouflage   c. warning coloration
   b. chemical defenses   d. parasitism

4. Identify two things organisms compete with one another for.

5. Briefly describe one example of a predator-prey relationship. Identify the predator and the prey.

Critical Thinking

6. **Making Comparisons** Compare coevolution with symbiosis.

7. **Identifying Relationships** Explain the probable relationship between the giant *Rafflesia* flower, which smells like rotting meat, and the carrion flies that buzz around it. (Hint: *Carrion* means "rotting flesh.")

8. **Predicting Consequences** Predict what might happen if all of the ants were removed from an acacia tree.

Interpreting Graphics

The population graph below shows the growth of a species of *Paramecium* (single-celled microorganism) over 18 days. Food was added to the test tube occasionally. Use this graph to answer the questions that follow.

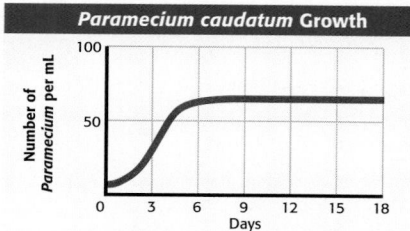

Paramecium caudatum Growth

9. What is the carrying capacity of the test tube as long as food is added?

10. Predict what will happen if no more food is added?

11. What keeps the number of *Paramecium* at a steady level?

 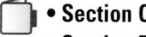

Developed and maintained by the National Science Teachers Association

For a variety of links related to this chapter, go to www.scilinks.org

Topic: Predator/Prey; Coevolution
SciLinks code: HSM1205; HSM0309

CHAPTER RESOURCES

Chapter Resource File
- **Section Quiz** GENERAL
- **Section Review** GENERAL
- **Vocabulary and Section Summary** GENERAL
- **Reinforcement Worksheet** BASIC

Technology
- **Interactive Explorations CD-ROM**
  - What's Bugging You? GENERAL

Answers to Section Review

1. Sample answer: Carrying capacity is the maximum number of individuals that can live in an environment.

2. Sample answer: Mutualism is when two organisms that are interacting both benefit from the relationship. Commensalism is when one organism is helped and the other is not affected. Parasitism is when one organism is helped and the other is harmed by the relationship.

3. d

4. Sample answer: Organisms compete with one another for space and for resources such as food and water.

5. Answers may vary. Sample answer: A bird (predator) eats a worm (prey).

6. Sample answer: Coevolution happens when a symbiotic relationship occurs over a very long period of time and changes the structure or behavior of the organisms involved in the relationship. However, symbiosis does not always cause a change in the structure or behavior of an organism.

7. Sample answer: The relationship between the flower and the flies is probably coevolution brought about by symbiosis.

8. Sample answer: The tree would not thrive as much as it would have if the ants had remained, because it would be vulnerable to more attacks by other organisms.

9. about 65 paramecia

10. The carrying capacity will drop and eventually all of the organisms will die.

11. Sample answer: limiting factors such as food supply

Capturing the Wild Bean

Teacher's Notes

Time Required

One 45-minute class period

Lab Ratings

EASY ──────────────→ HARD

Teacher Prep 🧪🧪🧪
Student Set-Up 🧪🧪
Concept Level 🧪🧪
Clean Up 🧪🧪

MATERIALS

The materials listed on the student page are enough for a group of 4 or 5 students. Large, dried beans of any kind will work well in this exercise.

Lab Notes

Explain to students that this is a very common method used in field biology by scientists who need to count a population that is on the move, such as a flock of migratory birds. Explain that scientists always mark their captures in a way that neither harms the organism nor alters its behavior.

Skills Practice Lab

OBJECTIVES

Estimate the size of a "population" of beans.

Calculate the difference between your estimation and the actual number of beans.

MATERIALS

- bag, paper lunch, small
- beans, pinto
- calculator (optional)
- marker, permanent

Capturing the Wild Bean

When wildlife biologists study a group of organisms in an area, they need to know how many organisms live there. Sometimes, biologists worry that a certain organism is outgrowing the environment's carrying capacity. Other times, scientists need to know if an organism is becoming rare so that steps can be taken to protect it. However, animals can be difficult to count because they can move around and hide. Because of this challenge, biologists have developed methods to estimate the number of animals in a specific area. One of these counting methods is called the *mark-recapture method*.

In this activity, you will enter the territory of the wild pinto bean to estimate the number of beans that live in the paper-bag habitat.

Procedure

1 Prepare a data table like the one below.

Mark-Recapture Data Table				
Number of animals in first capture	Total number of animals in recapture	Number of marked animals in recapture	Calculated estimate of population	Actual total population
	DO NOT WRITE IN BOOK			

2 Your teacher will provide you with a paper bag containing an unknown number of beans. Carefully reach into the bag, and remove a handful of beans.

Jason Marsh
Montevideo High and
Country School
Montevideo, Minnesota

CHAPTER RESOURCES

Chapter Resource File

- **Datasheet for Chapter Lab**
- **Lab Notes and Answers**

Technology

 Classroom Videos
- Lab Video

- Adaptation: It's a Way of Life

3 Count the number of beans you have "captured." Record this number in your data table under "Number of animals in first capture."

4 Use the permanent marker to carefully mark each bean that you have just counted. Allow the marks to dry completely. When all the marks are dry, place the marked beans back into the bag.

5 Gently mix the beans in the bag so that the marks won't rub off. Once again, reach into the bag. "Capture" and remove a handful of beans.

6 Count the number of beans in your "recapture." Record this number in your data table under "Total number of animals in recapture."

7 Count the beans in your recapture that have marks from the first capture. Record this number in your data table under "Number of marked animals in recapture."

8 Calculate your estimation of the total number of beans in the bag by using the following equation:

$$\frac{\text{number of beans in recapture} \times \text{number of beans marked}}{\text{number of marked beans in recapture}} = \begin{array}{c}\text{calculated estimate}\\\text{of population}\end{array}$$

Enter this number in your data table under "Calculated estimate of population."

9 Place all the beans in the bag. Then empty the bag on your work table. Be careful that no beans escape! Count each bean as you place them one at a time back into the bag. Record the number in your data table under "Actual total population."

Analyze the Results

① **Evaluating Results** How close was your estimate to the actual number of beans?

Draw Conclusions

② **Evaluating Methods** If your estimate was not close to the actual number of beans, how might you change your mark-recapture procedure? If you did not recapture any marked beans, what might be the cause?

Applying Your Data

How could you use the mark-recapture method to estimate the population of turtles in a small pond? Explain your procedure.

Analyze the Results

1. Have students evaluate their estimate. Ask students if they think their estimate was close enough to the actual number of beans in the bag.

Draw Conclusions

2. Samples that are too small can lead to incorrect estimates. If no marked beans were recaptured, then the sample was too small and increasing the sample size would improve the procedure. A sample should be large enough to allow a scientist to accurately estimate the number of organisms in the population without having to count every single organism.

Applying Your Data

Have students state the size of the pond and form a reasonable hypothesis that includes the number of animals that should be in the sample size. Students should describe a way to capture turtles without harming them and should recommend a marking method that will not harm the turtles or alter the turtles' behavior. The turtles should be returned to their environment immediately and given a day or two to recover from the trauma.

Assignment Guide

Section	Questions
1	2–6
2	7, 10, 12–14, 16, 17, 22, 23, 25–28
3	1, 8, 9, 11, 18–20, 24
1 and 2	21

ANSWERS

Using Key Terms

1. In symbiosis, two organisms have a close relationship with each other. In mutualism, two organisms that are interacting both benefit from the relationship. In commensalism, one organism is helped and the other is not affected. In parasitism, one organism is helped and the other is harmed by the relationship.

2. abiotic

3. biotic

4. ecosystem

5. Sample answer: A community is made up of populations.

6. Sample answer: All ecosystems are a part of the biosphere.

7. Sample answer: Producers make their own food while consumers must eat other organisms to get energy.

USING KEY TERMS

1 Use each of the following terms in a separate sentence: *symbiosis, mutualism, commensalism,* and *parasitism.*

Complete each of the following sentences by choosing the correct term from the word bank.

biotic   abiotic
ecosystem   community

2 The environment includes _____ factors including water, rocks, and light.

3 The environment also includes _____, or living, factors.

4 A community of organisms and their environment is called a(n) _____.

For each pair of terms, explain how the meanings of the terms differ.

5 *community* and *population*

6 *ecosystem* and *biosphere*

7 *producers* and *consumers*

UNDERSTANDING KEY IDEAS

Multiple Choice

8 A tick sucks blood from a dog. In this relationship, the tick is the _____ and the dog is the _____.

a. parasite, prey   c. parasite, host
b. predator, host   d. host, parasite

---

9 Resources such as water, food, or sunlight are likely to be limiting factors

a. when population size is decreasing.
b. when predators eat their prey.
c. when the population is small.
d. when a population is approaching the carrying capacity.

10 Nature's recyclers are

a. predators.   c. producers.
b. decomposers.   d. omnivores.

11 A beneficial association between coral and algae is an example of

a. commensalism. c. mutualism.
b. parasitism.   d. predation.

12 The process by which energy moves through an ecosystem can be represented by

a. food chains.
b. energy pyramids.
c. food webs.
d. All of the above

13 Which organisms does the base of an energy pyramid represent?

a. producers   c. herbivores
b. carnivores   d. scavengers

14 Which of the following is the correct order in a food chain?

a. sun→producers→herbivores→scavengers→carnivores
b. sun→consumers→predators→parasites→hosts
c. sun→producers→decomposers→consumers→omnivores
d. sun→producers→herbivores→carnivores→scavengers

Understanding Key Ideas

8. c
9. d
10. b
11. c
12. d
13. a
14. d
15. b

16. Sample answer: Energy flows from the sun to plants, or other producers. The energy stored in the cells of producers flows to consumers when the plants are eaten. In this way, energy flows from consumer to consumer and then finally to decomposers.

17. Sample answer: When the gray wolf disappeared, populations of its prey increased. This change caused overgrazing, which affected many of the populations in the park.

15 Remoras and sharks have a relationship that is best described as

a. mutualism.　　**c.** predator and prey.

b. commensalism.　**d.** parasitism.

Short Answer

16 Describe how energy flows through a food web.

17 Explain how the food web changed when the gray wolf disappeared from Yellowstone National Park.

18 How are the competition between two trees of the same species and the competition between two different species of trees similiar?

19 How do limiting factors affect the carrying capacity of an environment?

20 What is coevolution?

CRITICAL THINKING

21 **Concept Mapping** Use the following terms to create a concept map: *herbivores, organisms, producers, populations, ecosystems, consumers, communities, carnivores,* and *biosphere*.

22 **Identifying Relationships** Could a balanced ecosystem contain producers and consumers but not decomposers? Why or why not?

23 **Predicting Consequences** Some biologists think that certain species, such as alligators and wolves, help maintain biological diversity in their ecosystems. Predict what might happen to other organisms, such as gar fish or herons, if alligators were to become extinct in the Florida Everglades.

24 **Expressing Opinions** Do you think there is a carrying capacity for humans? Why or why not?

INTERPRETING GRAPHICS

Use the energy pyramid below to answer the questions that follow.

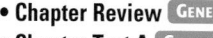

25 According to the energy pyramid, are there more prairie dogs or plants?

26 What level has the most energy?

27 Would an energy pyramid such as this one exist in nature?

28 How could you change this pyramid to look like one representing a real ecosystem?

18. Sample answer: All trees might compete for sunlight, water, or space.

19. Sample answer: Limiting factors generally define an environment's carrying capacity. Populations cannot grow without limits because all environments contain a limited amount of food, water, living space, and other needed resources.

20. Coevolution is a long-term change that takes place in two species that have a close relationship with each other.

Critical Thinking

21. An answer to this exercise can be found at the end of this book.

22. Sample answer: An ecosystem with no decomposers could not exist very long because the ecosystem would soon become buried in dead organisms. Decomposers are needed to return raw materials to the environment.

23. Sample answer: Species such as gar fish and herons would not be as healthy without alligators to eat sick or old individuals. Herons might experience a population increase, which would lead to fewer gar. Eventually, the herons may die off if the gar population becomes too small.

24. Answers may vary.

Interpreting Graphics

25. prairie dogs

26. the top level

27. No, an energy pyramid like this could not exist in nature.

28. Sample answer: The pyramid should be widened at the bottom and narrowed at the top.

CHAPTER RESOURCES

Chapter Resource File

- Chapter Review **GENERAL**
- Chapter Test A **GENERAL**
- Chapter Test B **ADVANCED**
- Chapter Test C **SPECIAL NEEDS**
- Vocabulary Activity **GENERAL**

Workbooks

Study Guide
- Assessment resources are also available in Spanish.

Standardized Test Preparation

Teacher's Note

To provide practice under more realistic testing conditions, give students 20 minutes to answer all of the questions in this Standardized Test Preparation.

MISCONCEPTION ALERT

Answers to the standardized test preparation can help you identify student misconceptions and misunderstandings.

READING

Passage 1

1. A
2. I
3. B

TEST DOCTOR

Question 2: The reason for listing food, shelter, water, space and sunlight in the passage is to specify the resources organisms compete for. These resources are found in Yellowstone National Park, but they are offered in this passage as examples of resources found wherever organisms live, so the best answer is "I."

Question 3: Some students may think that competition can only happen between two different populations. However, competition can occur between any two organisms competing for the same resource.

READING

Read each of the passages below. Then, answer the questions that follow each passage.

Passage 1 Two or more individuals trying to use the same resource, such as food, water, shelter, space, or sunlight is called *competition*. Because resources are in limited supply in the environment, the use of them by one individual or population decreases the amount available to other organisms. Competition also occurs between individuals within a population. The elk in Yellowstone National Park are herbivores that compete with each other for the same food plants in the park.

1. According to the passage, competition occurs between which of the following?
   - **A** individuals trying to use the same resource
   - **B** elk and carnivores
   - **C** food and shelter
   - **D** individuals trying to use different resources

2. According to the passage, food, water, shelter, space, and sunlight are examples of
   - **F** populations.
   - **G** things found in Yellowstone National Park.
   - **H** competition.
   - **I** resources.

3. Based on the passage, which of the following statements is a fact?
   - **A** Competition occurs only between individuals of different populations.
   - **B** Competition occurs between individuals within a population and between individuals of different populations.
   - **C** Competition increases the amount of resources available to individuals.
   - **D** Because resources are abundant in the environment, competition rarely happens between individuals of different populations.

Passage 2 In the deserts of northern Africa and the Middle East, water is a scarce and valuable resource. In this area, no permanent streams flow except for the Nile. More than 1.6 million square kilometers of this region typically have no rainfall for years at a time. However, much of this area has large aquifers. The water that these aquifers contain dates back to much wetter times thousands of years ago. Occasionally, water reaches the surface to form an oasis. Wells supply the rest of the water used throughout the region. In some regions of Saudi Arabia and Kuwait, wells drilled for water more often strike oil.

1. According to the passage, an aquifer contains what resource?
   - **A** oil
   - **B** water
   - **C** wells
   - **D** oasis

2. Based on the passage, which of the following statements is a fact?
   - **F** The Nile no longer flows through northern Africa and the Middle East.
   - **G** The water found in aquifers is from recent rainfall.
   - **H** Wells drilled in Saudi Arabia and Kuwait are more likely to strike oil than water.
   - **I** The desert regions of northern Africa and the Middle East receive rainfall almost every day.

3. According to the passage, an oasis forms under what conditions?
   - **A** when water stays beneath the surface
   - **B** when water is drilled from a well
   - **C** when it rains
   - **D** when water reaches the surface

Passage 2

1. B
2. H
3. D

TEST DOCTOR

Question 1: One way to help students check this answer is to help them recognize that the word *aquifer* is closely related to the words *aquatic* and *aquarium*. All three words contain the root word for water.

The graphs below show the population growth for two populations. Use these graphs to answer the questions that follow.

Growth of Population A

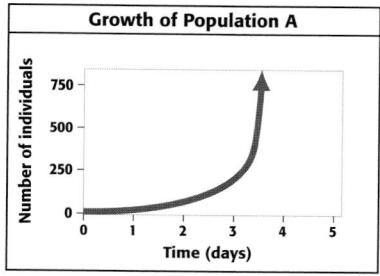

Growth of Population B

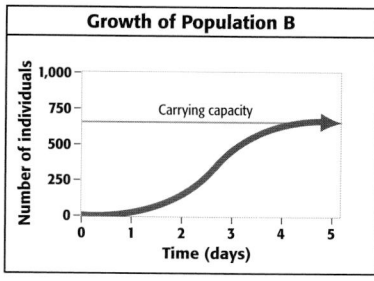

1. After 2 days, which population has more individuals?

A Population A has more individuals.
B Population B has more individuals.
C The populations are the same.
D There is not enough information to determine the answer.

2. After 5 days, which population has more individuals?

F Population A has more individuals.
G Population B has more individuals.
H The populations are the same.
I There is not enough information to determine the answer.

3. On day 10, which statement is probably true?

A Population B is larger than population A.
B Population A is the same as it was on day 5.
C Population A and B are the same.
D Population B is the same as it was on day 5.

Read each question below, and choose the best answer.

1. The figure below is a map of a forest ecosystem. What is the area of this ecosystem?

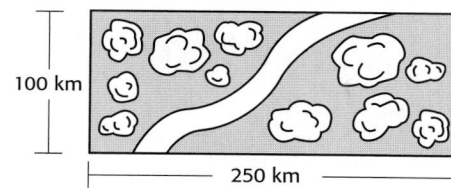

A 25,000 km²
B 32,000 km
C 1,200 km²
D 2,500 km

2. If an antelope eats 7 kg of vegetation in 2 days, how many kilograms of vegetation does it eat per day?

F 2/7 kg
G 3/5 kg
H 3 1/2 kg
I 7 1/2 kg

3. If $x = 3$ and $y = x + 2$, what is y?

A 2
B 4
C 5
D 8

4. If $x = 4$ and $y = x + 2$, what is y?

F 2
G 5
H 6
I 8

Standardized Test Preparation

1. B
2. F
3. D

✚ TEST DOCTOR

Question 2: Some students may be confused about the fact that the line is not visible at day 5. Explain to them that the line exists but is too high to show on the graph.

Question 3: Students who struggle with predicting what will happen may benefit from actually plotting the graph out to 10 days.

1. A
2. H
3. C
4. H

✚ TEST DOCTOR

Question 2: Answer F is wrong because the numerator and the denominator are switched. Answer I is wrong because it is an incorrect simplification of the fraction 7/2. Students struggling with fractions may benefit from using a visual aid, such as a pie graph or a piece of paper cut into pieces, that can illustrate how fractions represent parts of a whole.

CHAPTER RESOURCES

Chapter Resource File

 • Standardized Test Preparation GENERAL

State Resources

 For specific resources for your state, visit **go.hrw.com** and type in the keyword **HSMSTR**.

Scientific Debate

ACTIVITY ——————— GENERAL

Many of your students may be dog owners. Encourage these students to bring pictures of their pets to class. If they wish, they can also share a story about how they interact with their pet or something amazing that their pet can do.

Weird Science

Background

Follicle mites are harmless, but other kinds of mites are not benign. Mites are responsible for the devastation of honeybee populations in the United States. In the last few decades, tracheal mites and varroa mites have cut the number of domesticated honeybee colonies in half. There are almost no wild honeybees left in parts of the United States.

Scientists and beekeepers are trying various solutions to deal with the mite infestations. Some chemicals seem to help. More promising solutions are found in new strains of honeybees bred to be resistant to mites and in those honeybees that have developed the ability to groom mites off each other.

Science in Action

Scientific Debate

How Did Dogs Become Pets?

Did humans change dogs to be the social and helpful creatures they are today? Or were dogs naturally social? Did dogs start moving closer to our campfires long ago? Or did humans find dogs and bring them into our homes? The way in which dogs became our friends, companions, and helpers is still a question. Some scientists think humans and training are the reasons for many of our dogs' best features. Other scientists think dogs and humans have both changed over time to form their strong and unique bond.

Math ACTIVITY

Scientists have found fossils of dogs that are 15,000 years old. Generation time is the time between the birth of one generation and the next. If the generation time for dogs is 1.5 years, how many generations have there been in the last 15,000 years?

Weird Science

Follicle Mites

What has a tiny tubelike body and short stumpy legs and lives in your eyebrows and eyelashes? Would you believe a small animal lives there? It's called a follicle mite, and humans are its host. Studies show that more than 97% of adults have these mites. Except in rare cases, follicle mites are harmless.

Like all large animals, human beings are hosts to a variety of smaller creatures that live in or on our bodies and share our bodies' resources. Bacteria that live in our lower digestive tracks help to produce vitamins such as folic acid and vitamin K. Other bacteria may help maintain proper pH levels in our bodies.

Language Arts ACTIVITY

WRITING SKILL Imagine that you were shrunk to the size of a follicle mite. How would you get food? Where would you sleep? Write a short story describing one day in your new, tiny life.

Answer to Math Activity
10,000 generations (15,000 ÷ 1.5 = 10,000 generations)

Answer to Language Arts Activity
Answers may vary. Students may also illustrate their story, make a poster, or use their story as the basis for a book for a young reader.

Dalton Dockery

Horticulture Specialist Did you know that instead of using pesticides to get rid of insects that are eating the plants in your garden, you can use other insects? "It is a healthy way of growing vegetables without the use of chemicals and pesticides, and it reduces the harmful effects pesticides have on the environment," says Dalton Dockery, a horticulture specialist in North Carolina. Some insects, such as ladybugs and praying mantises, are natural predators of many insects that are harmful to plants. They will eat other bugs but leave your precious plants in peace. Using bugs to drive off pests is just one aspect of natural gardening. Natural gardening takes advantage of relationships that already exist in nature and uses these interactions to our benefit. For Dockery, the best parts about being a horticultural specialist are teaching people how to preserve the environment, getting to work outside regularly, and having the opportunity to help people on a daily basis.

Social Studies ACTIVITY

WRITING SKILL Research gardening or farming techniques in other cultures. Do other cultures use any of the same aspects of natural gardening as horticultural specialists? Write a short report describing your findings.

To learn more about these Science in Action topics, visit go.hrw.com and type in the keyword HL5INTF.

Current Science

Check out Current Science® articles related to this chapter by visiting go.hrw.com. Just type in the keyword HL5CS18.

Careers
Teaching Strategy — GENERAL
The insect shown at the bottom of the page is a praying mantis, which is often used by organic gardeners to eat harmful pests. Ask students if they have ever heard of "organic" produce. Then, ask them to research organic vegetables and to differentiate between the ways in which organic and nonorganic vegetables are grown.

Answer to Social Studies Activity
Answers may vary. Ideas that may help students begin researching include the following: rice farming in Asia, the ancient farming techniques used in Latin America, and the use of donkeys for farming in Africa.

Cycles in Nature
Chapter Planning Guide

Compression guide:
To shorten instruction because of time limitations, omit Section 2.

OBJECTIVES	LABS, DEMONSTRATIONS, AND ACTIVITIES	TECHNOLOGY RESOURCES
PACING • 90 min pp. 506–511 **Chapter Opener**	SE **Start-up Activity**, p. 507 ◆ GENERAL	OSP **Parent Letter** ■ GENERAL CD **Student Edition on CD-ROM** CD **Guided Reading Audio CD** ■ TR **Chapter Starter Transparency*** VID **Brain Food Video Quiz**
Section 1 The Cycles of Matter • Diagram the water cycle, and explain its importance to living things. • Diagram the carbon cycle, and explain its importance to living things. • Diagram the nitrogen cycle, and explain its importance to living things.	TE **Activity** Matter Matters, p. 508 ◆ GENERAL TE **Demonstration** Water Cycle, p. 509 ◆ GENERAL SE **Quick Lab** Combustion, p. 510 ◆ GENERAL CRF **Datasheet for Quick Lab*** SE **Connection to Environmental Science** Global Warming, p. 511 GENERAL SE **Skills Practice Lab** Nitrogen Needs, p. 516 ◆ GENERAL CRF **Datasheet for Chapter Lab*** LB **Calculator-Based Labs** Keeping Things Cool ◆ ADVANCED	CRF **Lesson Plans*** TR **Bellringer Transparency*** TR **The Water Cycle*** TR **The Carbon Cycle*** TR *LINK TO PHYSICAL SCIENCE* Changing the State of Water* TR **The Nitrogen Cycle*** VID **Lab Videos for Life Science** CRF **SciLinks Activity*** GENERAL
PACING • 45 min pp. 512–515 **Section 2 Ecological Succession** • Describe the process of succession. • Contrast primary and secondary succession. • Explain how mature communities develop.	TE **Connection Activity** Math, p. 513 GENERAL TE **Connection Activity** Earth Science, p. 513 GENERAL SE **Model-Making Lab** A Passel o' Pioneers, p. 788 ◆ GENERAL CRF **Datasheet for LabBook*** LB **Long-Term Projects & Research Ideas** Smokey Says* GENERAL LB **Calculator-Based Labs** A Soil Study ◆ ADVANCED SE **Science in Action** Math, Social Studies, and Language Arts Activities, pp. 522–523	CRF **Lesson Plans*** TR **Bellringer Transparency*** TR **An Example of Primary Succession*** TR **An Example of Secondary Succession*** SE **Internet Activity**, p. 514 GENERAL

PACING • 90 min

CHAPTER REVIEW, ASSESSMENT, AND STANDARDIZED TEST PREPARATION

CRF **Vocabulary Activity*** GENERAL
SE **Chapter Review**, pp. 518–519 GENERAL
CRF **Chapter Review*** ■ GENERAL
CRF **Chapter Tests A*** ■ GENERAL, **B*** ADVANCED, **C*** SPECIAL NEEDS
SE **Standardized Test Preparation**, pp. 520–521 GENERAL
CRF **Standardized Test Preparation*** GENERAL
CRF **Performance-Based Assessment*** GENERAL
OSP **Test Generator** GENERAL
CRF **Test Item Listing*** GENERAL

Online and Technology Resources

Visit **go.hrw.com** for a variety of free resources related to this textbook. Enter the keyword **HL5CYC**.

Holt Online Learning

Students can access interactive problem-solving help and active visual concept development with the *Holt Science and Technology* Online Edition available at **www.hrw.com**.

 Guided Reading Audio CD Also in Spanish

A direct reading of each chapter for auditory learners, reluctant readers, and Spanish-speaking students.

 Science Tutor CD-ROM

Excellent for remediation and test practice.

SKILLS DEVELOPMENT RESOURCES	SECTION REVIEW AND ASSESSMENT	STANDARDS CORRELATIONS
SE Pre-Reading Activity, p. 506 `GENERAL` **OSP** Science Puzzlers, Twisters & Teasers* `GENERAL`		National Science Education Standards UCP 1, 3, 4; SAI 1, 2
CRF Directed Reading A* ■ `BASIC`, B* `SPECIAL NEEDS` **CRF** Vocabulary and Section Summary* ■ `GENERAL` **SE** Reading Strategy Mnemonics, p. 508 `GENERAL` **SE** Math Practice Where's the Water?, p. 509 `GENERAL` **TE** Inclusion Strategies, p. 509 **CRF** Reinforcement Worksheet What Goes Around....* `BASIC` **CRF** Critical Thinking Pass the Salt, Please* `ADVANCED`	**SE** Reading Checks, pp. 509, 511 `GENERAL` **TE** Reteaching, p. 510 `BASIC` **TE** Quiz, p. 510 `GENERAL` **TE** Alternative Assessment, p. 510 `GENERAL` **SE** Section Review,* p. 511 ■ `GENERAL` **CRF** Section Quiz* ■ `GENERAL`	UCP 1, 3, 4; SAI 1, 2; SPSP 2, 4, 5; LS 1c, 4b, 4c, 5a; *Chapter Lab:* UCP 2, 3; SAI 1; LS 1c, 4b, 5a
CRF Directed Reading A* ■ `BASIC`, B* `SPECIAL NEEDS` **CRF** Vocabulary and Section Summary* ■ `GENERAL` **SE** Reading Strategy Reading Organizer, p. 512 `GENERAL`	**SE** Reading Checks, pp. 512, 514 `GENERAL` **TE** Reteaching, p. 514 `BASIC` **TE** Quiz, p. 514 `GENERAL` **TE** Alternative Assessment, p. 514 `GENERAL` **TE** Homework, p. 514 `GENERAL` **TE** Homework, p. 515 `ADVANCED` **SE** Section Review,* p. 515 ■ `GENERAL` **CRF** Section Quiz* ■ `GENERAL`	UCP 1, 3, 4; SAI 2; SPSP 2, 3; LS 1a, 4d; UCP 1, 2, 3; *LabBook:* SAI 1, 2; LS 1a, 4d

 **One-Stop Planner® CD-ROM**

This convenient CD-ROM includes:
- Lab Materials QuickList Software
- Holt Calendar Planner
- Customizable Lesson Plans
- Printable Worksheets
- ExamView® Test Generator

 **cnnstudentnews.com**

Find the latest news, lesson plans, and activities related to important scientific events.

 **www.scilinks.org**

Maintained by the **National Science Teachers Association.** See Chapter Enrichment pages for a complete list of topics.

Current Science®

Check out **Current Science** articles and activities by visiting the HRW Web site at **go.hrw.com.** Just type in the keyword **HL5CS19T.**

 Classroom Videos
- **Lab Videos** demonstrate the chapter lab.
- **Brain Food Video Quizzes** help students review the chapter material.
- **CNN Videos** bring science into your students' daily life.

Chapter Resources

Visual Resources

CHAPTER STARTER TRANSPARENCY

This Really Happened!

BELLRINGER TRANSPARENCIES

Section: The Cycles of Matter
What are the three different physical states in which water can commonly be found on Earth? Name one way that you use water in each of these states in your daily life.

Write your answers in your science journal.

Section: Ecological Succession
Imagine that you have been hired to oversee the maintenance of a public forest. Answer the following questions to describe how you would approach the task:
• How would you evaluate the health of the forest?
• What actions would you take to keep the forest healthy?
• What factors might pose a threat to the health of the forest? How would you prevent these factors from causing harm?

Write your answers in your science journal.

TEACHING TRANSPARENCIES

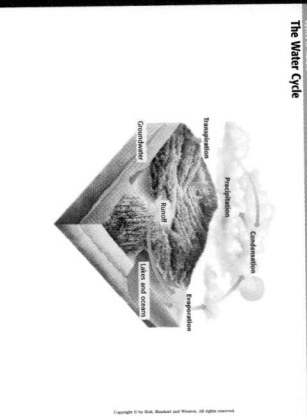

The Water Cycle

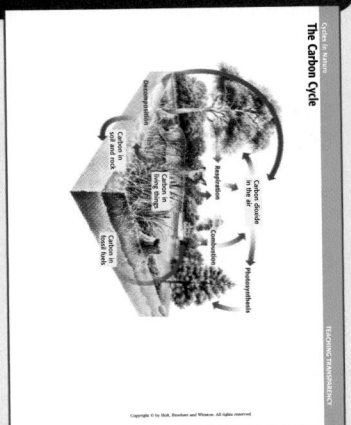

The Carbon Cycle

TEACHING TRANSPARENCIES

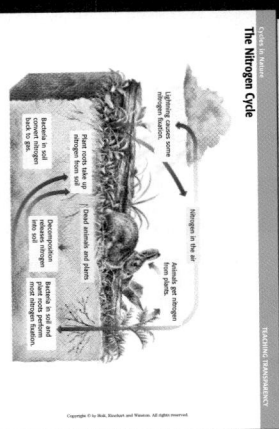

The Nitrogen Cycle

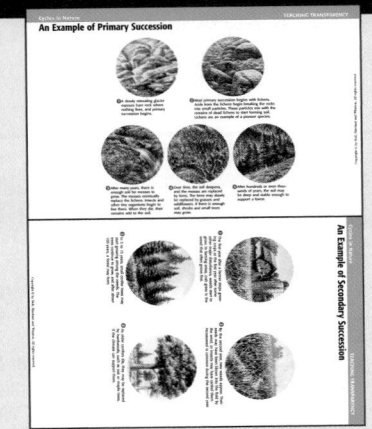

An Example of Primary Succession

An Example of Secondary Succession

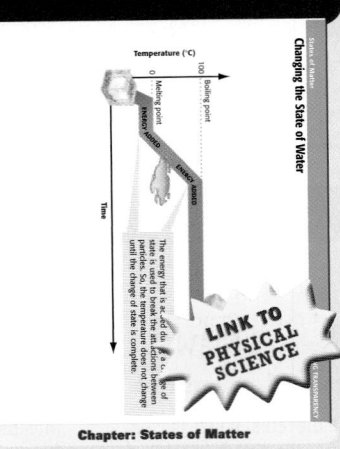

Changing the State of Water

Chapter: States of Matter

CONCEPT MAPPING TRANSPARENCY

Use the following terms to complete the concept map below: water cycle, precipitation, decomposition, carbon, combustion, condensation, carbon cycle, photosynthesis

Planning Resources

LESSON PLANS

Lesson Plan — SAMPLE

PARENT LETTER

SAMPLE

TEST ITEM LISTING

TEST ITEM LISTING
The World of Science — SAMPLE

One-Stop Planner® CD-ROM

This CD-ROM includes all of the resources shown here and the following time-saving tools:

• Lab Materials QuickList Software
• Customizable lesson plans
• Holt Calendar Planner
• The powerful ExamView® Test Generator

Meeting Individual Needs

DIRECTED READING A
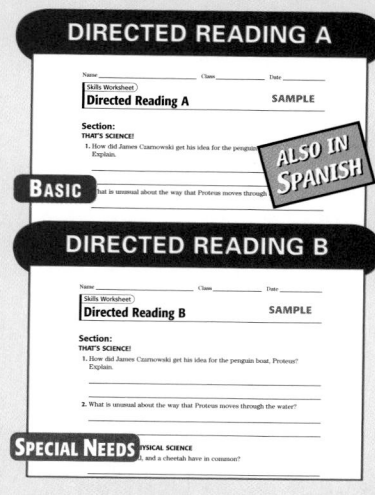
BASIC · ALSO IN SPANISH

DIRECTED READING B
SPECIAL NEEDS

VOCABULARY ACTIVITY
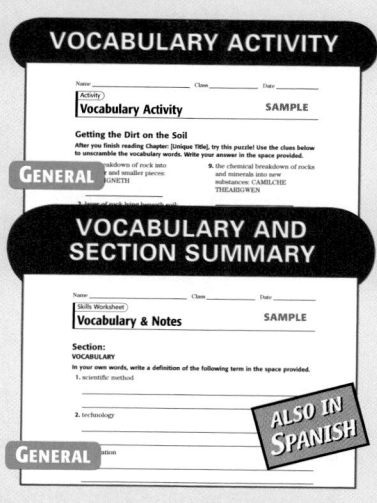
GENERAL

VOCABULARY AND SECTION SUMMARY
GENERAL · ALSO IN SPANISH

REINFORCEMENT
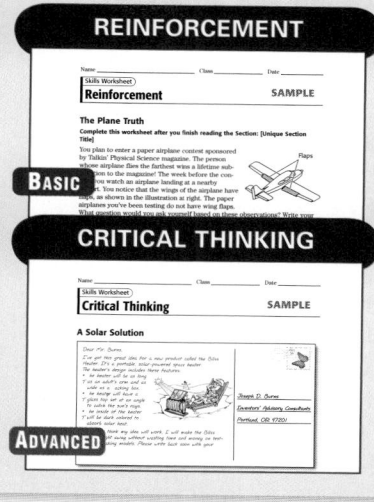
BASIC

CRITICAL THINKING
ADVANCED

SCILINKS ACTIVITY

GENERAL

SCIENCE PUZZLERS, TWISTERS & TEASERS
GENERAL

Labs and Activities

LONG-TERM PROJECTS & RESEARCH IDEAS
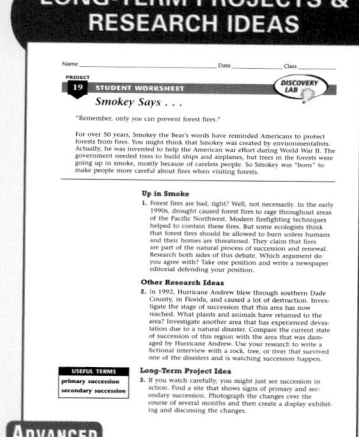
ADVANCED

CALCULATOR-BASED LABS
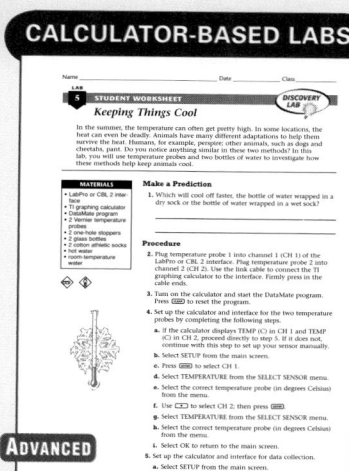
Keeping Things Cool
ADVANCED

CALCULATOR-BASED LABS
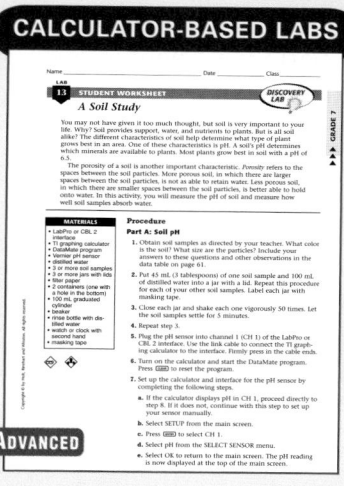
A Soil Study
ADVANCED

DATASHEETS FOR QUICK LABS

DATASHEETS FOR CHAPTER LABS

DATASHEETS FOR LABBOOK

Review and Assessments

SECTION QUIZ

GENERAL · ALSO IN SPANISH

SECTION REVIEW
GENERAL · ALSO IN SPANISH

CHAPTER REVIEW
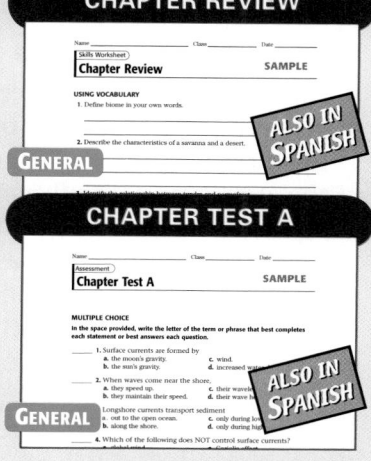
GENERAL · ALSO IN SPANISH

CHAPTER TEST A
GENERAL · ALSO IN SPANISH

CHAPTER TEST B
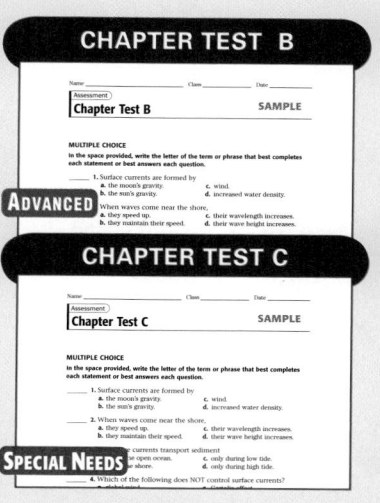
ADVANCED

CHAPTER TEST C
SPECIAL NEEDS

STANDARDIZED TEST PREPARATION
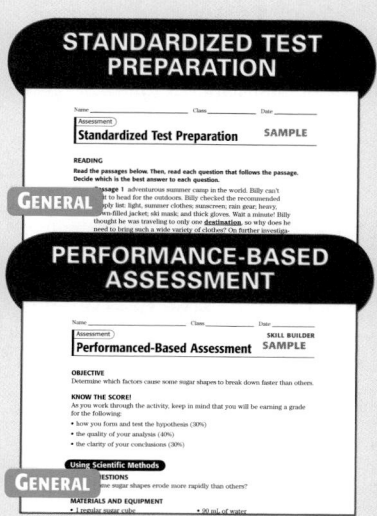
GENERAL

PERFORMANCE-BASED ASSESSMENT
GENERAL

This Chapter Enrichment provides relevant and interesting information to expand and enhance your presentation of the chapter material.

Section 1

The Cycles of Matter

Blue Icebergs

● Snow and ice usually appear white in color because full spectrum light is scattered and reflected at the boundary between air spaces and ice crystals. The bubbles atop a dark carbonated beverage appear white for the same reason. However, ice appears blue when it has been so tightly compressed that most air spaces have been squeezed out. This is usually true of the ice in glaciers and icebergs. As light travels through ice, the absorption of wavelengths at the red end of the spectrum is six times greater than at the blue end. Thus, as light travels deeper into a glacier or an iceberg, more red light is absorbed and primarily blue light is reflected and perceived by the human eye.

The Water Cycle

● There are about 1.4 billion cubic kilometers of water in the Earth system (1 cubic kilometer = more than 264 billion gallons). Although that is an enormous volume of water, only a small fraction of it—3,000 km³— exists in the atmosphere. In other words, if all of the water in the atmosphere fell to the Earth's surface at one time, the land on Earth would be covered with about 2.5 cm of water.

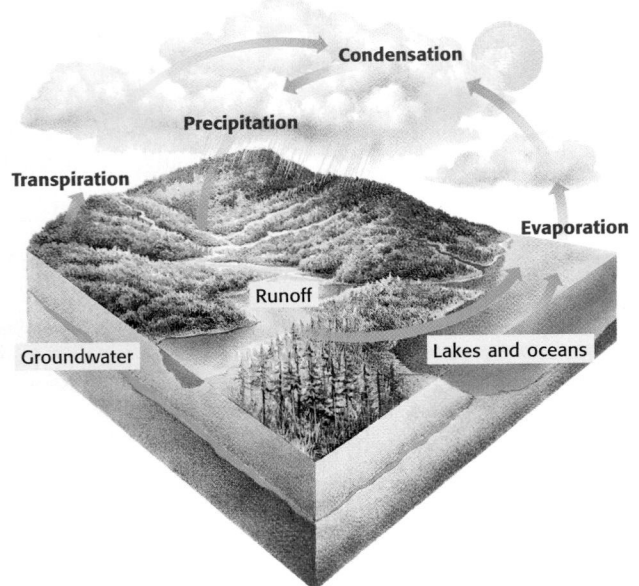

● Plants play an important role in the water cycle. Of the 1,200 km³ of water that enters the atmosphere every day, as much as 120 km³ is released by plants as they transpire. Plants take in water through their roots and release it through *stomates,* which are small pores located on the undersides of their leaves. Through this process, a one-acre cornfield can transpire as much as 15,000 L of water every day.

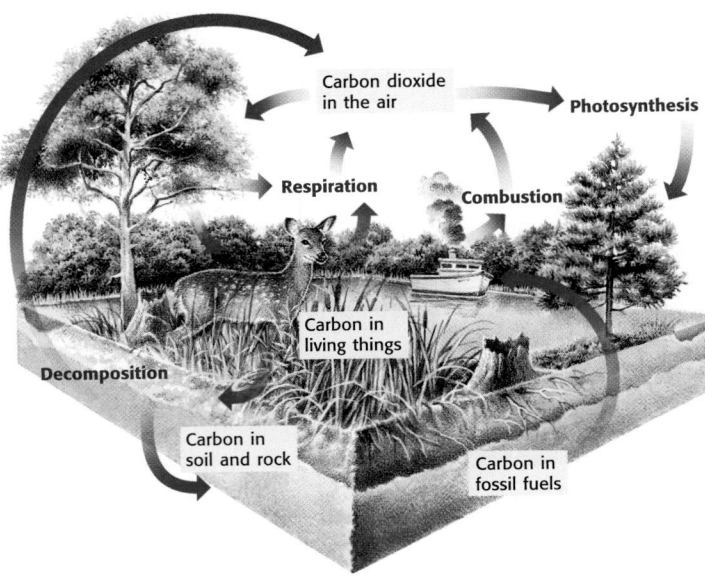

The Carbon Cycle

● Like water, carbon is recycled in the natural world. The respiration of living things releases carbon dioxide, which is taken up by plants and converted to sugars. The carbon that accumulates in plants as carbohydrates circulates in nature in a number of ways. When animals eat plants, the carbon from the plants is transferred to animals. The waste products of the animals' metabolism—including carbon dioxide—are returned to nature. Finally, when living things die, their decomposition releases carbon.

Carbon Dioxide in the Atmosphere

● Human activities can alter the historical balance of the global carbon cycle. The burning of carbon-containing fossil fuels, for example, releases carbon dioxide into the atmosphere. Fossil fuels are currently being extracted and used by humans more rapidly than the fuels form. Within the past 100 years, the amount of carbon dioxide in the atmosphere has been increasing. Scientists are concerned that this phenomenon may be causing the temperature on Earth to rise. Carbon dioxide is a type of *greenhouse gas,* or a gas that traps heat within Earth's atmosphere.

Nitrogen-Poor Soils

● Carnivorous plants, such as the venus fly trap and the pitcher plant, are adapted to grow in soils that are low in nitrogen. Because these plants are carnivorous, they can get nitrogen from a source besides the soil where they grow.

Section 2

Ecological Succession

The Nature of Ecosystems

● Like living things, ecosystems are born, develop, and mature. Events such as fires, storms, and volcanic eruptions can disrupt ecosystems and set into action a chain of events known as succession. Though discussions of succession generally center on forests, all ecosystems undergo succession.

Forest Management

● The branch of forestry concerned with the life cycle of trees and the forest is known as forest management. Forest managers try to balance multiple uses of forests, such as timber logging, recreation, and wildlife habitat. Balancing these demands is sometimes difficult. Forest managers need an understanding of ecological processes along with some skills in engineering and business management.

Is That a Fact!

◆ Records were set in the years 2000 and 2002 for the largest areas of the United States burned by wildfire in 50 years. More than 4 million acres were burned in 2002 during a period of severe drought.

● One controversial activity carried out by forest managers is known as *prescribed burning*. Though dangerous and often destructive, fire is a necessary part of the life cycle of forest communities. Its effects on wildlife are complex; fire can assist in the recycling of nutrients, regulate plant succession, help maintain biological diversity, reduce biomass, and help control insect populations and disease. In 1998, the U.S. Forest Service burned between 850,000 acres and 1 million acres.

Succession Around the Great Lakes

● During the last several thousand years, the water level of the Great Lakes has gradually decreased. As the lake shores expanded, sand dunes formed. These dunes are communities. Like a forest, a sand dune community follows a pattern of succession. Bare sand is unstable, infertile, and inhospitable. At first, only the hardiest plants might survive there. These pioneer plants may stabilize the sand and enrich the soil as they decay. This makes a more hospitable environment for other living things. Grasses may grow, then shrubs and pines may grow, and then trees such as oaks, maples, and elms may appear.

Plant Competition and Succession

● Plant succession is affected by competition between plants for resources. Plants compete with one another for sunlight, water, nitrogen, and other resources. As in other forms of ecological competition, the more-successful plants are those that are able to defend resources or use resources more quickly or efficiently.

SCiLINKS®

NSTA

Developed and maintained by the National Science Teachers Association

SciLinks is maintained by the National Science Teachers Association to provide you and your students with interesting, up-to-date links that will enrich your classroom presentation of the chapter.

Visit www.scilinks.org and enter the SciLinks code for more information about the topic listed.

Topic: Cycles of Matter
SciLinks code: HSM0373

Topic: Succession
SciLinks code: HSM1475

Overview

Tell students that this chapter will help them learn about processes in nature that happen in cycles. The chapter describes three cycles of matter and two types of ecological succession.

Assessing Prior Knowledge

Students should be familiar with the following topics:

• interactions of living things
• cellular processes

Identifying Misconceptions

As students learn the material in this chapter, they may overlook or forget connections between processes such as the carbon cycle and what they have learned about cellular processes such as photosynthesis. Whenever possible, help students recall these connections. Students may have difficulty making sense of the complex diagrams of cycles of matter unless they understand what is meant by the label of each step. Remind students that they can witness the results of each of these processes, such as photosynthesis, decomposition, and evaporation, in action around them every day.

19

Cycles in Nature

About the PHOTO

These penguins have a unique playground on this iceberg off the coast of Antarctica. Icebergs break off from glaciers and float out to sea. A glacier is a giant "river" of ice that slides slowly downhill. Glaciers are formed from snow piling up in mountains. Eventually, glaciers and icebergs melt and become liquid water. Water in oceans and lakes rises into the air and then falls down again as rain or snow. There is a lot of water on Earth, and most of it is constantly moving and changing form.

PRE-READING ACTIVITY

FOLDNOTES **Pyramid** Before you read the chapter, create the FoldNote entitled "Pyramid" described in the **Study Skills** section of the Appendix. Label the sides of the pyramid with "Water cycle," "Carbon cycle," and "Nitrogen cycle." As you read the chapter, define each cycle, and write the steps of each cycle on the appropriate pyramid side.

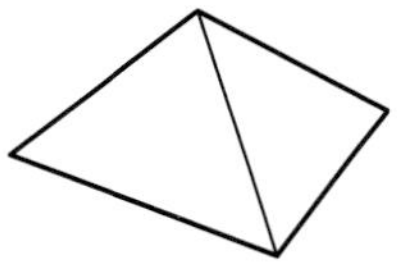

Standards Correlations

National Science Education Standards

The following codes indicate National Science Education Standards that correlate to this chapter. The full text of the standards is at the front of the book.

Chapter Opener
UCP 1, 3, 4; SAI 1, 2

Section 1 The Cycles of Matter
UCP 1, 3, 4; SAI 1, 2; SPSP 2, 4, 5; LS 1c, 4b, 4c, 5a

Section 2 Ecological Succession
UCP 1, 3, 4; SAI 2; SPSP 2, 3; LS 1a, 4d;
LabBook: UCP 1, 2, 3; SAI 1, 2; LS 1a, 4d

Chapter Lab
UCP 2, 3; SAI 1; LS 1c, 4b, 5a

Chapter Review
SAI 2; SPSP 2, 5; LS 1a, 1c, 4b, 4c, 4d, 5a

Science in Action
UCP 1, 5; ST 1, 2; SPSP 1, 2, 4; HNS 1

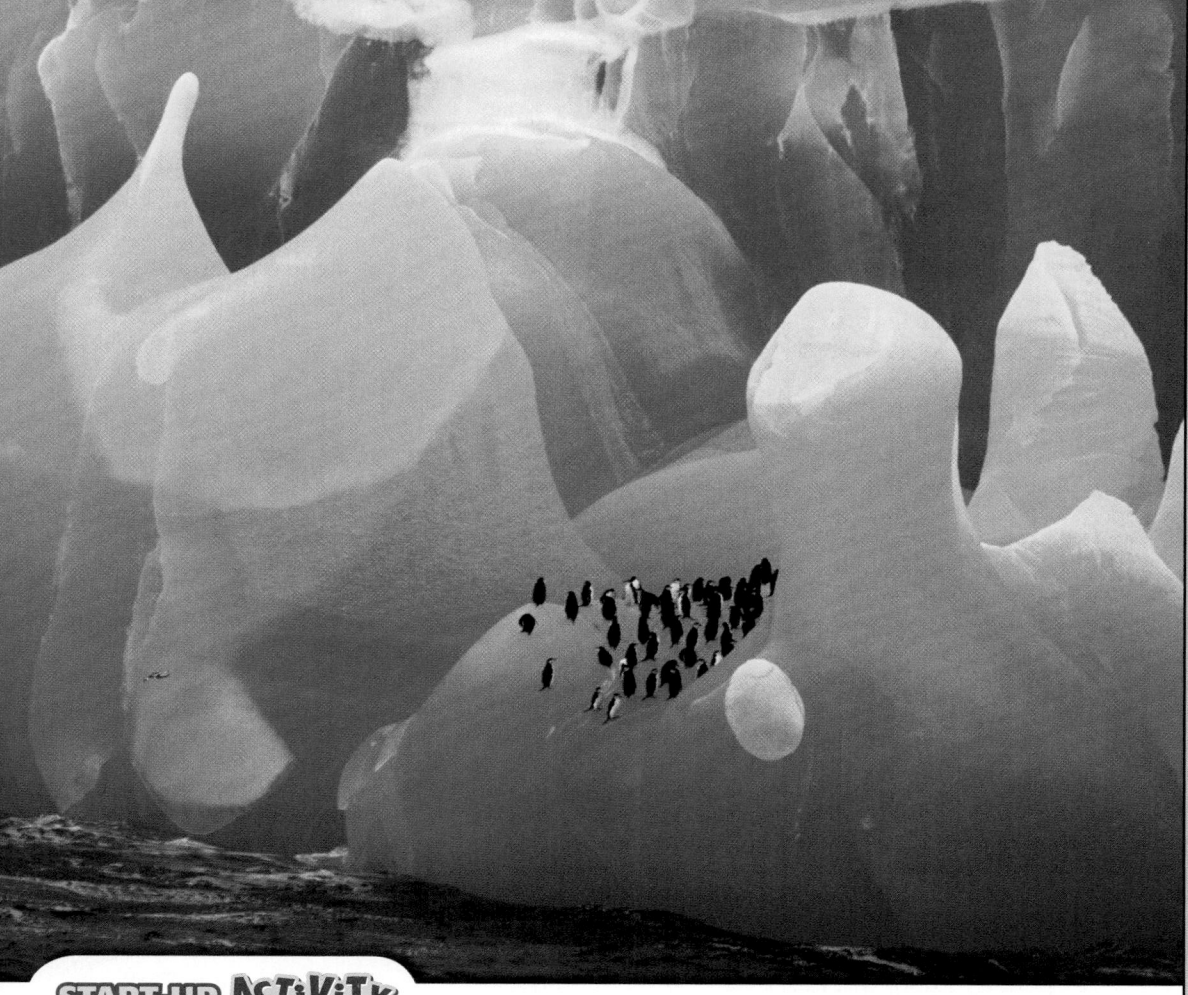

START-UP ACTIVITY

Making Rain

Do you have the power to make rain? Yes!—on a small scale. In this activity, you will cause water to change state in the same way that rain is formed. This process is one way that water is reused on Earth.

Procedure

1. Start with a **large, sealable, plastic freezer bag.** Be sure that the bag is clean and dry and has no leaks. Place a **small, dark-colored bowl** inside the bag. Position the bowl with the opening at the top.
2. Fill the bowl halfway with water. Place a few drops of **red food coloring** in the water. Seal the bag.
3. Place the bowl and bag under a strong, warm **light source,** such as a lamp or direct sunlight.
4. Leave the bag in the light for as long as possible. Observe the bag at regular time intervals.

Analysis

1. Each time you observe the bag, describe what you see. Explain what you think is happening.
2. After observing the bag several times, carefully remove the bowl from the bag. Observe and describe any water that is now in the bag. Where did this water come from? How does it differ from the water in the bowl?

START-UP ACTIVITY

MATERIALS

FOR EACH GROUP
- bag, plastic, sealable, 1 gal
- bowl, dark-colored, 1 qt or 1 L
- food coloring, red
- lamp or other strong light source, 100 W or more
- water, about 0.5 pt or 0.25 L

Teacher's Notes: Before having students attempt this activity, check that you have a strong enough light source and can keep the bowl warm enough to get results within one class period. If not, consider having the students make observations over several class periods. Encourage students to make a data table to record their observations.

Answers

1. Sample answers: The inside of the bag is getting steamy; water droplets are forming around the top and edges; water is dripping down the edges of the bag; a puddle is collecting at the bottom of the bag; and the water level in the bowl is getting lower.

2. Sample answers: The water in the bottom of the bag is clear and warm; it has no color, unlike the water in the bowl. The water in the bag must have come from the bowl. The heat made the water change to steam. The steam cooled on the inside surface of the bag and changed into water that then dripped down the sides of the bag.

This Really Happened!

The sun came up over the desert horizon and woke the scientist. She had a full day ahead of her. Today she would start out working in the fields with the other seven scientists. The small fields of food crops had to recycle all of the water and nutrients that the plants used. These crops were the scientists' only source of food in this tightly sealed environment. Later, the scientist would jog over to the rain forest, where she would observe

important to the scientists because their lives depended on the health of their sealed environment. Several weeks ago, the sensors began to detect trouble ...

This was an actual day in the life of one of eight scientists who lived in the largest artificial biosphere ever constructed, called Biosphere 2. The goal was to develop an enclosed system where water and air could be recycled and food could be grown and harvested.

Chapter Starter Transparency
Use this transparency to help students begin thinking about cycles in nature.

CHAPTER RESOURCES

Technology

 **Transparencies**
- Chapter Starter Transparency

READING SKILLS

 Student Edition on CD-ROM

 **Guided Reading Audio CD**
- English or Spanish

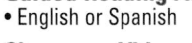 **Classroom Videos**
- Brain Food Video Quiz

Workbooks

 **Science Puzzlers, Twisters & Teasers**
- Cycles in Nature **GENERAL**

SECTION 1

Focus

Overview

This section explains that matter is limited and thus reused on Earth. Materials in the environment are constantly recycled, especially those needed by living things. The water, carbon, and nitrogen cycles are examined.

Bellringer

Ask students "What are the three states in which water can commonly be found on Earth?" (solid: ice, liquid: water, gas: water vapor or steam)

Motivate

ACTIVITY ——— GENERAL

Matter Matters Remind students of the properties of matter with the following definitions and simple investigations:

- Matter is anything that has mass and takes up space, even though we may not see it. Show students this property by weighing a large, deflated balloon and then by weighing the balloon when filled with air (not helium).

- Matter is always conserved (never created nor destroyed). Show students this property by causing ice to melt and then evaporate in a sealed jar and by weighing it at each stage.

LS Visual/Kinesthetic

SECTION 1

READING WARM-UP

Objectives

- Diagram the water cycle, and explain its importance to living things.
- Diagram the carbon cycle, and explain its importance to living things.
- Diagram the nitrogen cycle, and explain its importance to living things.

Terms to Learn

evaporation decomposition
condensation combustion
precipitation

READING STRATEGY

Mnemonics As you read this section, create a mnemonic device to help you remember the parts of the water cycle.

evaporation the change of a substance from a liquid to a gas

condensation the change of state from a gas to a liquid

precipitation any form of water that falls to the Earth's surface from the clouds

---

The Cycles of Matter

The matter in your body has been on Earth since the planet formed billions of years ago!

Matter on Earth is limited, so the matter is used over and over again. Each kind of matter has its own cycle. In these cycles, matter moves between the environment and living things.

The Water Cycle

The movement of water between the oceans, atmosphere, land, and living things is known as the *water cycle*. The parts of the water cycle are shown in **Figure 1.**

How Water Moves

During **evaporation,** the sun's heat causes water to change from liquid to vapor. In the process of **condensation,** the water vapor cools and returns to a liquid state. The water that falls from the atmosphere to the land and oceans is **precipitation.** Rain, snow, sleet, and hail are forms of precipitation. Most precipitation falls into the ocean. Some of the precipitation that falls on land flows into streams, rivers, and lakes and is called *runoff.* Some precipitation seeps into the ground and is stored in spaces between or within rocks. This water, known as *groundwater,* will slowly flow back into the soil, streams, rivers, and oceans.

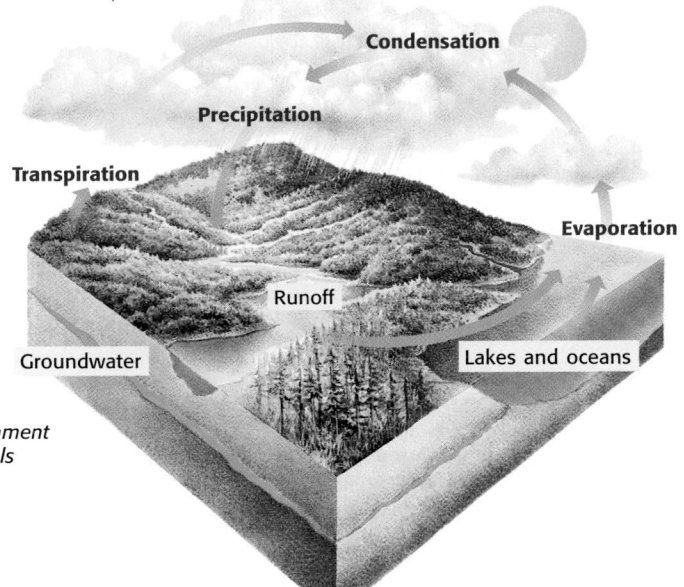

Figure 1 *Water from the environment moves through plants and animals and back to the environment.*

CHAPTER RESOURCES

Chapter Resource File

- **Lesson Plan**
- **Directed Reading A** BASIC
- **Directed Reading B** SPECIAL NEEDS

Technology

Transparencies
- Bellringer
- The Water Cycle
- The Carbon Cycle
- *LINK TO PHYSICAL SCIENCE* Changing the State of Water

CONNECTION to
Physical Science— GENERAL

States of Matter Reinforce the idea that evaporation and condensation are changes in the physical state of water. Use the teaching transparency entitled "Changing the State of Water." **LS Visual/Logical**

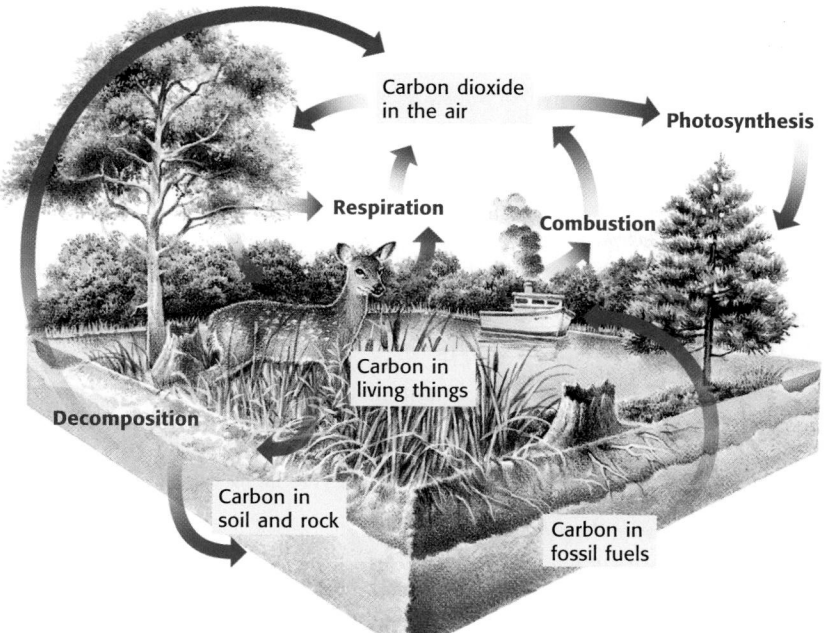

Carbon in living things

Carbon dioxide in the air

Photosynthesis

Respiration

Combustion

Decomposition

Carbon in soil and rock

Carbon in fossil fuels

Figure 2 *Carbon may remain in the environment for millions of years before becoming available to living things.*

Water and Life

Without water, there would be no life on Earth. All organisms, from bacteria to animals and plants, are composed mostly of water. Water helps transport nutrients and wastes within an organism. Water also helps regulate temperature. For example, when you sweat, water evaporates from your skin and cools your body. Eventually, all the water taken in by organisms is returned to the environment. For example, plants release a large amount of water vapor in a process called *transpiration*.

✔ **Reading Check** Why is water important? (*See the Appendix for answers to Reading Checks.*)

The Carbon Cycle

Besides water, the most common molecules in living things are *organic* molecules, or molecules that contain carbon. The exchange of carbon between the environment and living things is known as the *carbon cycle*, as shown in **Figure 2.**

Photosynthesis and Respiration

Photosynthesis is the basis of the carbon cycle. During photosynthesis, plants use carbon dioxide from air to make sugars. Most animals get the carbon and energy they need by eating plants. How does carbon return to the environment? It returns when sugar molecules are broken down to release energy. This process, called *respiration*, uses oxygen. Carbon dioxide and water are released as byproducts of respiration.

MATH PRACTICE

Where's the Water?
There are about 37.5 million cubic kilometers of fresh water on Earth. Of this fresh water, about 8.3 million cubic kilometers is groundwater. What percentage of Earth's fresh water is groundwater?

Reteaching — BASIC

Diagrams Display diagrams of each of the cycles of matter, with the labels covered or omitted. Have students state the label for each part.
LS Visual/Auditory

Quiz — GENERAL

1. What do both the water cycle and the carbon cycle have in common? (Sample answers: Each cycle involves plants and animals; in each cycle, matter is re-used.)

Alternative Assessment — GENERAL

Writing **Concept Mapping** Have students create a concept map using the terms from this section, the section title, and extra terms that may be needed. Remind them to include connecting words and phrases to link the terms. **LS** Visual/Logical — PORTFOLIO

decomposition the breakdown of substances into simpler molecular substances

combustion the burning of a substance

Combustion

1. Place a **candle** on a **jar lid,** and secure the candle with **modeling clay.** Have your teacher light the candle.
2. Hold the jar near the candle flame. Do not cover the flame with the jar. Describe the jar. Where did the substance on the jar come from?
3. Now, place the jar over the candle. What is deposited inside the jar? Where did this substance come from?

Decomposition and Combustion

The breakdown of substances into simpler molecules is called **decomposition.** For example, when fungi and bacteria decompose organic matter, carbon dioxide and water are returned to the environment. You may have witnessed another way to break down organic matter—using fire. **Combustion** is the process of burning a substance, such as wood or fossil fuels. Like decomposition, combustion of organic matter releases carbon dioxide into the atmosphere.

The Nitrogen Cycle

Nitrogen is also important to living things. Organisms need nitrogen to build proteins and DNA for new cells. The movement of nitrogen between the environment and living things is called the *nitrogen cycle.* This cycle is shown in **Figure 3.**

Converting Nitrogen Gas

About 78% of the Earth's atmosphere is nitrogen gas. Most organisms cannot use nitrogen gas directly. However, bacteria in the soil are able to change nitrogen gas into forms that plants can use. This process is called *nitrogen fixation.* Other organisms may then get the nitrogen they need by eating plants or eating organisms that eat plants.

Figure 3 *Without bacteria, nitrogen could not enter living things or be returned to the atmosphere.*

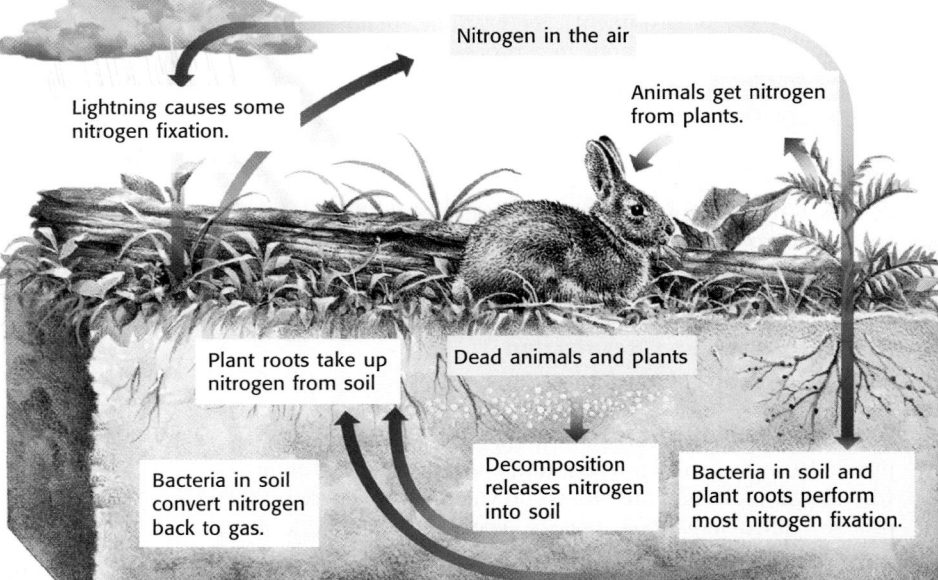

Nitrogen in the air

Lightning causes some nitrogen fixation.

Animals get nitrogen from plants.

Plant roots take up nitrogen from soil

Dead animals and plants

Bacteria in soil convert nitrogen back to gas.

Decomposition releases nitrogen into soil

Bacteria in soil and plant roots perform most nitrogen fixation.

Safety Caution: Remind students to review all safety cautions and icons before beginning this lab activity. Students should stand back from the flame.

Answers

2. The substance on the side of the jar is water. The warm air contains moisture, which condenses when it contacts the cool glass. Therefore, some of the water comes from the warm air. Additionally, some of the water is from the combustion of the candle wax. Combustion releases carbon dioxide and water.

3. The substance inside the jar is soot. Soot is carbon and is the product of the combustion of the candle wax and the wick.

Passing It On

When organisms die, decomposers break down the remains. Decomposition releases a form of nitrogen into the soil that plants can use. Finally, certain types of bacteria in the soil convert nitrogen to a gas, which is returned to the atmosphere.

Many Cycles

Other forms of matter on Earth also pass through cycles. Many of the minerals that living cells need, such as calcium and phosphorous, are cycled through the environment. When an organism dies, every substance in its body is likely to be recycled or reused.

Each of the cycles is connected in many ways. For example, some forms of nitrogen and carbon are carried through the environment by water. Many nutrients pass from soil to plants to animals and back. Living organisms play a part in each of the cycles.

✔ Reading Check Give an example of a form of matter—other than carbon, water, or nitrogen—that is cycled through the environment.

CONNECTION TO Environmental Science

Global Warming The quantity of carbon dioxide being released into the atmosphere is increasing. Carbon dioxide can cause the atmosphere to hold heat. A warmer atmosphere would cause the temperatures of the land and ocean to increase. Scientists think that this situation, known as *global warming*, may be happening. Research data on changes in average global temperature and carbon dioxide levels for the past 50 years, and summarize your findings.

SECTION Review

Summary

- Precipitation, evaporation, transpiration, and condensation are parts of the water cycle.
- Photosynthesis, respiration, decomposition, and combustion are parts of the carbon cycle.
- In the nitrogen cycle, nitrogen gas is converted into other forms and back to gas again.
- Many forms of matter on Earth pass through cycles. These cycles may be connected in many ways.

Using Key Terms

For each pair of terms, explain how the meanings of the terms differ.

1. *evaporation* and *condensation*
2. *decomposition* and *combustion*

Understanding Key Ideas

3. Nitrogen fixation
   a. is done only by plants.
   b. is done mostly by bacteria.
   c. is how animals make proteins.
   d. is a form of decomposition.
4. Describe the water cycle.
5. Describe the carbon cycle.

Math Skills

6. The average person in the United States uses about 78 gal of water each day. How many liters of water does this equal? How many liters of water will the average person use in a year?

Critical Thinking

7. **Analyzing Processes** Draw a simple diagram of each of the cycles discussed in this section. Draw lines between the cycles to show how parts of each cycle are related.

8. **Applying Concepts** Give an example of how the calcium in an animal's bones might be cycled back into the environment.

For a variety of links related to this chapter, go to www.scilinks.org

Topic: Cycles of Matter
SciLinks code: HSM0373

Answer to Reading Check

Sample answer: calcium

CHAPTER RESOURCES

Chapter Resource File

- Section Quiz **GENERAL**
- Section Review **GENERAL**
- Vocabulary and Section Summary **GENERAL**
- Reinforcement Worksheet **BASIC**
- Critical Thinking **ADVANCED**
- SciLinks Activity **GENERAL**

Technology

Transparencies
- The Nitrogen Cycle

Answer to Connection to Environmental Science

Between 1960 and 2000, average annual global temperatures and carbon dioxide levels increased steadily.

Answers to Section Review

1. Sample answer: Evaporation is a change from liquid to gas, but condensation is the opposite change—from gas to liquid.

2. Sample answer: Decomposition is the breakdown of dead materials by organisms, but combustion is the breakdown of materials by burning.

3. b

4. Sample answer: In the water cycle, water falls to Earth's surface as precipitation. Some water reenters the atmosphere by evaporation from the surface and by transpiration from plants. Water condenses and falls as precipitation. Precipitation may run off and be stored in rivers, lakes, oceans, and groundwater.

5. Sample answer: The carbon cycle starts with photosynthesis in plants. Then, carbon moves through other living things such as animals and microorganisms. Some carbon moves from organisms into the air or soil through respiration, decomposition, or combustion.

6. 78 gal/d $\times$ 3.8 L/gal $\times$ 365 d/y = 108,186 L/y = 110,000 L/y

7. Student drawings should resemble the cycle diagrams in this section. Lines should be drawn connecting related parts, such as air (atmosphere), soil, animals, and plants (which play a role in each cycle). Also, students should note that decomposition plays a role in both the carbon and nitrogen cycles.

8. Sample answer: Animals might get calcium by chewing on bones; weather might break down bones and release the calcium back into the soil or water.

Focus

Overview

In this section, students are introduced to the development of communities by succession. Students will learn the difference between primary and secondary succession and some organisms characteristic of each process. Students will examine the gradual formation of a mature community.

🔊 Bellringer

Ask students to imagine that they have been hired to manage a publicly owned forest area, and then ask students the following questions:

• How would you evaluate the health of the forest?

• What actions would you take to keep the forest healthy?

Motivate

Discussion —— GENERAL

Pine Forests Tell students that in deciduous forest areas, hardwood trees sometimes replace the pines that grew first. Point out that pine forests provide valuable resources. Encourage students to speculate how forest managers might prevent hardwood trees from replacing pine trees in managed forests.

LS Logical/Intrapersonal

READING WARM-UP

Objectives

● Describe the process of succession.

● Contrast primary and secondary succession.

● Explain how mature communities develop.

Terms to Learn

succession
pioneer species

READING STRATEGY

Reading Organizer As you read this section, make a table comparing primary succession and secondary succession.

---

succession the replacement of one type of community by another at a single place over a period of time

---

Ecological Succession

Imagine you have a time machine that can take you back to the summer of 1988. If you had visited Yellowstone National Park during that year, you would have seen fires raging throughout the area.

By the end of that summer, large areas of the park were burned to the ground. When the fires were put out, a layer of gray ash blanketed the forest floor. Most of the trees were dead, although many of them were still standing.

Regrowth of a Forest

The following spring, the appearance of the "dead" forest began to change. **Figure 1** shows the changes after just one year. Some of the dead trees fell over, and small, green plants grew in large numbers. Within 10 years, scientists reported that many trees were growing and the forest community was coming back.

A gradual development of a community over time, such as the regrowth of the burned areas of Yellowstone National Park, is called **succession.** Succession takes place in all communities, not just those affected by disturbances such as forest fires.

✓ **Reading Check** What happened after the Yellowstone fires? *(See the Appendix for answers to Reading Checks.)*

Figure 1 *Huge areas of Yellowstone National Park were burned in 1988 (left). By the spring of 1989, regrowth was evident in the burned parts of the park (right).*

CHAPTER RESOURCES

Chapter Resource File

• **Lesson Plan**
• **Directed Reading A** BASIC
• **Directed Reading B** SPECIAL NEEDS

Technology

Transparencies
• Bellringer
• An Example of Primary Succession
• An Example of Secondary Succession

Answer to Reading Check
Plants grew back, and the area is recovering.

Primary Succession

Sometimes, a small community starts to grow in an area where other organisms had not previously lived. There is no soil in this area. And usually, there is just bare rock. Over a very long time, a series of organisms live and die on the rock. The rock is slowly transformed into soil. This process is called *primary succession,* as shown in **Figure 2.** The first organisms to live in an area are called **pioneer species.**

pioneer species a species that colonizes an uninhabited area and that starts a process of succession

---

Figure 2 An Example of Primary Succession

❶ A slowly retreating glacier exposes bare rock where nothing lives, and primary succession begins.

❷ Most primary succession begins with lichens. Acids from the lichens begin breaking the rocks into small particles. These particles mix with the remains of dead lichens to start forming soil. Lichens are an example of a pioneer species.

❸ After many years, there is enough soil for mosses to grow. The mosses eventually replace the lichens. Insects and other tiny organisms begin to live there. When they die, their remains add to the soil.

❹ Over time, the soil deepens, and the mosses are replaced by ferns. The ferns may slowly be replaced by grasses and wildflowers. If there is enough soil, shrubs and small trees may grow.

❺ After hundreds or even thousands of years, the soil may be deep and stable enough to support a forest.

Cultural Awareness GENERAL

Lichen Chemistry Lichens contain unique chemicals that help them survive in harsh environments and deter bacteria, herbivores, and competing fungi from consuming the lichens. These chemicals have been used by cultures around the world, mostly as dyes and medicines. Scottish tweedmakers, Navaho weavers, and the Chilkats have historically used lichen for dyes. The wolf lichen was used by the Blackfoot as a medicinal tea and as a cure for skin problems. Chemicals from the lichen genus *Usnea* have been extracted by cultures throughout the world to make medicinal teas and healing creams.

Close

Reteaching ——— BASIC

Two Types of Succession

Call on students to help fill in a large table comparing primary and secondary succession. Have each student create a copy of the table. **English Language Learners**

LS Logical

Quiz ——————— GENERAL

1. Describe the main difference between primary and secondary succession. (Primary succession takes place on newly exposed surfaces with little soil, where nothing has lived before; secondary succession takes place where soil has been developed by a previous community.)

2. Describe how pioneer species prepare an area for other living things. (Pioneer species may create or enrich soil, or provide shelter or protection from the elements to other species.)

Alternative Assessment ——— GENERAL

 Eco-Acting Organize the class into small groups. Challenge each group to create a song, dance, or drama that reenacts either primary or secondary succession. Direct them to include how succession begins as well as the organisms characteristic of each stage. Encourage students to perform their creations for the class.

LS Auditory/ Kinesthetic **PORTFOLIO**

INTERNET ACTIVITY

For another activity related to this chapter, go to **go.hrw.com** and type in the keyword **HL5CYCW.**

Secondary Succession

Sometimes, an existing community is destroyed by a natural disaster, such as a fire or a flood. Sometimes, a community is affected by another type of disturbance. For example, a farmer might stop growing crops in an area that had been cleared. In either case, if soil is left intact, the original community may regrow through a series of stages called *secondary succession.* **Figure 3** shows an example of secondary succession.

✓ **Reading Check** How does secondary succession differ from primary succession?

Figure 3 **An Example of Secondary Succession**

❶ The first year after a farmer stops growing crops or the first year after some other major disturbance, weeds start to grow. In farming areas, crab grass is the weed that often grows first.

❷ By the second year, new weeds appear. Their seeds may have been blown into the field by the wind, or insects may have carried them. Horseweed is common during the second year.

❸ In 5 to 15 years, small conifer trees may start growing among the weeds. The trees continue to grow, and after about 100 years, a forest may form.

❹ As older conifers die, they may be replaced by hardwoods, such as oak or maple trees, if the climate can support them.

Answer to Reading Check

Primary succession happens in an area where organisms did not previously exist; secondary succession happens where organisms already exist.

Homework ——— GENERAL

PORTFOLIO **Local Succession** Have students identify areas where ecological succession has happened in the history of their local city, country, or state. Students should write a brief description of the history of the area, identify the succession as primary or secondary, and include maps or pictures if possible. **LS** Intrapersonal

Mature Communities and Biodiversity

In the early stages of succession, only a few species grow in an area. These species grow quickly and make many seeds that scatter easily. But all species are vulnerable to disease, disturbances, and competition. As a community matures, it may be dominated by well-adapted, slow-growing *climax species*.

Furthermore, as succession proceeds, more species may become established. The variety of species that are present in an area is referred to as *biodiversity*. Biodiversity is important to communities of organisms. For example, a forest that has a high degree of biodiversity is less likely to be destroyed by an invasion of insects. Most plant-damaging insects prefer to attack only one species of plants. The presence of a variety of plants will lessen the impact and spread of invading insects.

Keep in mind that a mature community may not always be a forest. A mature community simply has organisms that are well adapted to live together in the same area over time. For example, the plants of the Sonoran Desert, shown in **Figure 4,** are well-adapted to the desert's conditions.

Figure 4 *This area of the Sonoran Desert in Arizona is a mature community.*

SECTION Review

Summary

- Ecological succession is the gradual development of communities over time. Often a series of stages is observed during succession.
- Primary succession occurs in an area that was not previously inhabited by living things; no soil is present.
- Secondary succession takes place in an area where an earlier community was disturbed by fire, landslides, floods, or plowing for crops and where soil is present.

Using Key Terms

1. In your own words, write a definition for the term *succession*.

Understanding Key Ideas

2. An area where a glacier has just melted away will begin the process of
   a. primary succession.
   b. secondary succession.
   c. stability.
   d. regrowth.

3. Describe succession that takes place in an abandoned field.

4. Describe a mature community. How does a mature community develop?

Math Skills

5. The fires in 1988 burned 739,000 of the 2.2 million acres that make up Yellowstone National Park. What percentage of the park was burned?

Critical Thinking

6. **Applying Concepts** Give an example of a community that has a high degree of biodiversity, and an example of one that has a low degree of biodiversity.

7. **Analyzing Ideas** Explain why soil formation is always the first stage of primary succession. Does soil formation ever stop? Explain your answer.

For a variety of links related to this chapter, go to www.scilinks.org

Topic: Succession
SciLinks code: HSM1475

Homework ADVANCED

Other Communities Remind students that succession occurs in every ecosystem. Encourage students to select an ecosystem to investigate. Have them use library or Internet resources to find out how succession occurs in their chosen ecosystem. Have them prepare brief reports, and encourage them to share their findings with the class. **LS** Verbal/Logical

CHAPTER RESOURCES

Chapter Resource File
- Section Quiz GENERAL
- Section Review GENERAL
- Vocabulary and Section Summary GENERAL

Skills Practice Lab

Nitrogen Needs

Teacher's Notes

Time Required
One 45-minute class period

Lab Ratings

EASY ——————————→ HARD

Teacher Prep 🧪🧪
Student Set-Up 🧪🧪🧪
Concept Level 🧪🧪🧪
Clean Up 🧪🧪

MATERIALS

The materials listed on the student page are enough for groups of 4–5 students. Dead insects may or may not be easy to find. You may want to go to a pet store and buy crickets. They are usually small and very inexpensive. If the insects you use are small, you will need more than five of them. If you obtain live insects, you can kill them humanely by placing them in a plastic container in a freezer for a few hours.

Safety Caution

Remind students to review all safety cautions and icons before beginning this lab activity. Spills should be cleaned up immediately. Caution students to collect insects carefully by wearing gardening gloves, shoes, and socks. Tell them to wash their hands thoroughly after all lab activities.

OBJECTIVES

Investigate the nitrogen cycle inside a closed system.

Discover how decomposers return nitrogen to the soil.

MATERIALS

- balance or scale
- beaker, 50 mL
- funnel
- gloves, protective
- graduated cylinder, 25 mL
- insects from home or schoolyard, large, dead (5)
- jar with lid, 1 pt (or 500 mL)
- paper, filter (2 pieces)
- pH paper
- soil, potting, commercially prepared without fertilizer
- water, distilled, 60 mL

SAFETY

Nitrogen Needs

The nitrogen cycle is one of several cycles that are vital to living organisms. Without nitrogen, living organisms cannot make amino acids, the building blocks of proteins. Animals obtain nitrogen by eating plants that contain nitrogen and by eating animals that eat those plants. When animals die, decomposers return the nitrogen to the soil in the form of a nitrogen-containing chemical called *ammonia*.

In this activity, you will investigate the nitrogen cycle inside a closed system to discover how decomposers return nitrogen to the soil.

Procedure

1. Fit a piece of filter paper into a funnel. Place the funnel inside a 50 mL beaker, and pour 5 g of soil into the funnel. Add 25 mL of distilled water to the soil.

2. Test the filtered water with pH paper, and record your observations.

3. Place some soil in a jar to cover the bottom with about 5 cm of soil. Add 10 mL of distilled water to the soil.

4. Place the dead insects in the jar, and seal the jar with the lid.

5. Check the jar each day for 5 days for an ammonia odor. (If you do not know what ammonia smells like, ask your teacher.) Record your observations. **Caution:** Your teacher will demonstrate how to check for a chemical odor by wafting. Notice how to gently wave the chemical fumes toward your nose with your hand. Do not put your nose in the jar and inhale!

CHAPTER RESOURCES

Chapter Resource File

- Datasheet for Chapter Lab
- Lab Notes and Answers

Technology

 Classroom Videos
- Lab Video

 LabBook
- A Passel o' Pioneers

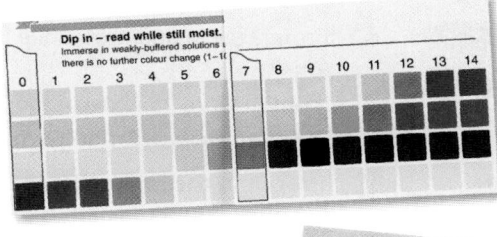

6 On the fifth day, place a second piece of filter paper into the funnel, and place the funnel inside a 50 mL beaker. Remove about 5 g of soil from the jar, and place it in the funnel. Add 25 mL of distilled water to the soil.

7 Once again, test the filtered water with pH paper, and record your observations.

Analyze the Results

1 **Examining Data** What was the pH of the water in the beaker in the first trial? A pH of 7 indicates that the water is neutral. A pH below 7 indicates that the water is acidic, and a pH above 7 indicates that the water is basic. Was the water in the beaker neutral, acidic, or basic?

2 **Analyzing Data** What was the pH of the water in the beaker in the second trial? Explain the difference, if any, between the results of the first trial and the results of the second trial.

Draw Conclusions

3 **Drawing Conclusions** Based on the results of your pH tests, do you think ammonia is acidic or basic?

4 **Evaluating Results** On which days in your investigation were you able to detect an ammonia odor? Explain what caused the odor.

5 **Applying Conclusions** Describe the importance of decomposers in the nitrogen cycle.

Applying Your Data

Test the importance of nitrogen to plants. Fill two 12 cm flowerpots with commercially prepared potting soil and water. Be sure to use soil that has had no fertilizer added. Obtain a dozen tomato or radish seeds. Plant six seeds in each pot. Water your seeds so that the soil is constantly damp but not soaked. Keep your pots in a sunny window. Use a nitrogen-rich liquid plant fertilizer to fertilize one of the pots once a week. Dilute or mix the fertilizer with water according to the directions on the container. Water the other pot once a week with plain tap water.

1. After the seedlings appear, use a metric ruler to measure the growth of the plants in both pots. Measure the plants once a week, and record your results.

2. You may plant other seeds of your choice, but do not use legume (bean) seeds. Research to find out why!

Background

The chemical formula for ammonia is NH_3. Commercial fertilizers often contain nitrogen in the form of ammonium nitrate, NH_4NO_3, derived from ammonia. Fertilizers are usually labeled with *NPK* values—a series of numbers indicating the included percentages of Nitrogen, N, Phosphorous, P, and Potassium, K. Synthetic ammonia is widely produced in factories by placing nitrogen and hydrogen gases together under high pressure.

Procedure

2. Answers may vary, but the pH of the water should be about 7, or neutral.

7. Answers may vary, but the pH of the water should be higher than 7, or basic.

Analyze the Results

1. The filtered water in the first trial should be slightly acidic, but its acidity will depend on the type of potting soil you are using.

2. If ammonia is present, the filtered water will be more basic than the filtered water in the first trial. Decomposition of the dead insects should be the only difference between the first and second trials.

Draw Conclusions

3. Ammonia is basic.

4. Answers may vary. Students should understand that the odor is from bacterial conversion of nitrogen to ammonia.

5. Decomposers convert nitrogen to a form that plants can use. Nitrogen is essential for plants.

Applying Your Data

The plants grown with fertilizer should be bigger and fuller. The plants grown without fertilizer may grow slowly, lack color, or die sooner. The only difference between the two pots should be the amount of nutrients present in the soil.

Chapter Review

Assignment Guide

Section	Questions
1	1, 3–6, 7–11, 15–19, 22–25, 28–29
2	2, 12–14, 20, 21, 26, 27

ANSWERS

Using Key Terms

1. decomposition
2. succession
3. evaporation
4. Combustion
5. precipitation
6. condensation

Understanding Key Ideas

7. c
8. b
9. a
10. c
11. c
12. d
13. b
14. d

USING KEY TERMS

Complete each of the following sentences by choosing the correct term from the word bank.

evaporation   condensation
precipitation   decomposition
combustion   succession

1 The breakdown of dead materials into carbon dioxide and water is called ___.

2 The gradual development of a community over time is called ___.

3 During ___, the heat causes water to change from liquid to vapor.

4 ___ is the process of burning a substance.

5 Water that falls from the atmosphere to the land and oceans is ___.

6 In the process of ___, water vapor cools and returns to a liquid state.

UNDERSTANDING KEY IDEAS

Multiple Choice

7 Clouds form in the atmosphere through the process of
   a. precipitation.   c. condensation.
   b. respiration.   d. decomposition.

8 Which of the following statements about groundwater is true?
   a. It stays underground for a few days.
   b. It is stored in underground caverns or porous rock.
   c. It is salty like ocean water.
   d. It never reenters the water cycle.

9 Burning gas in an automobile is a type of
   a. combustion.   c. decomposition.
   b. respiration.   d. photosynthesis.

10 Nitrogen in the form of a gas can be used directly by some kinds of
   a. plants.   c. bacteria.
   b. animals.   d. fungi.

11 Bacteria are most important in the process of
   a. combustion.   c. nitrogen fixation.
   b. condensation.   d. evaporation.

12 The pioneer species on bare rock are usually
   a. ferns.   c. mosses.
   b. pine trees.   d. lichens.

13 Which of the following is an example of primary succession?
   a. the recovery of Yellowstone National Park following the fires of 1988
   b. the appearance of lichens and mosses in an area where a glacier has recently melted away
   c. the growth of weeds in a field after a farmer stops using the field
   d. the growth of weeds in an empty lot that is no longer being mowed

14 One of the most common plants in a recently abandoned farm field is
   a. oak or maple trees.
   b. pine trees.
   c. mosses.
   d. crabgrass.

15. Sample answer: streams, ditches, and rivers, lakes

16. solid (ice), liquid, and gas (vapor)

17. Animals obtain carbon from the food they eat. Then, they give off carbon dioxide through respiration and contribute carbon to the soil through feces and decomposition.

18. Humans have the same roles animals do and also cause the release of carbon dioxide into the atmosphere through the combustion of fossil fuels.

19. nitrogen gas

20. The main difference between primary and secondary succession is that primary succession begins with the formation of soil. Secondary succession begins on preexisting soil. Pioneer species in primary succession are usually lichens, which begin the formation of soil. In secondary succession, there are no pioneer species but species such as seed plants may quickly germinate and take root in the soil.

Short Answer

15 List four places where water can go after it falls as precipitation.

16 In what forms can water on Earth be found?

17 What role do animals have in the carbon cycle?

18 What roles do humans have in the carbon cycle?

19 Earth's atmosphere is mostly made up of what substance?

20 Compare and contrast the two forms of succession.

CRITICAL THINKING

21 **Concept Mapping** Use the following terms to create a concept map: *abandoned farmland, lichens, bare rock, soil formation, horseweed, succession, forest fire, primary succession, secondary succession,* and *pioneer species.*

22 **Identifying Relationships** Is snow a part of the water cycle? Why or why not?

23 **Analyzing Processes** Make a list of several places where water might be found on Earth. For each item on your list, state how it is part of the water cycle.

24 **Forming Hypotheses** Predict what would happen if the water on Earth suddenly stopped evaporating.

25 **Forming Hypotheses** Predict what would happen if all of the bacteria on Earth suddenly disappeared.

26 **Making Inferences** Describe why a lawn usually doesn't go through succession.

27 **Making Inferences** Can one scientist observe all of the stages of secondary succession on an abandoned field? Explain your answer.

INTERPRETING GRAPHICS

The graph below shows how water is used each day by an average household in the United States. Use the graph to answer the questions that follow.

Average Household Daily Water Use

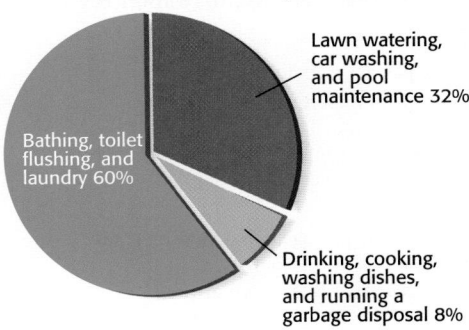

Lawn watering, car washing, and pool maintenance 32%

Bathing, toilet flushing, and laundry 60%

Drinking, cooking, washing dishes, and running a garbage disposal 8%

28 According to this graph, which of the following activities uses the greatest amount of water?

a. bathing

b. toilet flushing

c. washing laundry

d. There is not enough information to determine the answer.

29 An average family used 380 L of water per day, until they stopped washing their car, stopped watering their lawn, and stopped using their pool. Now, how much water per day do they use?

Critical Thinking

21. 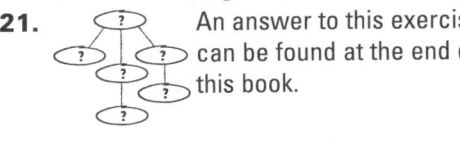 An answer to this exercise can be found at the end of this book.

22. All water on Earth is part of the water cycle, even the water frozen in snow. This frozen water is part of the water cycle by evaporation or by becoming liquid that flows into the ocean.

CHAPTER RESOURCES

Chapter Resource File

 • **Chapter Review** GENERAL
• **Chapter Test A** GENERAL
• **Chapter Test B** ADVANCED
• **Chapter Test C** SPECIAL NEEDS
• **Vocabulary Activity** GENERAL

Workbooks

Study Guide
• Assessment resources are also available in Spanish.

23. Sample answer: under the city as groundwater from runoff precipitation; in the clouds as condensation; in glaciers and polar icecaps as what was once precipitation that may become recycled if it melts.

24. Sample answer: The Earth would soon be covered with water. The water cycle would be interrupted. It would no longer rain. Land organisms would probably go extinct.

25. Sample answer: The carbon and nitrogen cycles would be interrupted. Dead organisms might not decays, and nutrients would be locked in their bodies. Nitrogen might be locked in the atmosphere in an unusable form. All other types of organisms might eventually be unable to survive.

26. A lawn does not go through the stages of succession because it is constantly being disturbed by mowing and other activities.

27. A scientist would probably require a life span of more than 100 years to observe all of the stages of secondary succession on an abandoned field. Scientists can photograph changes for future scientists to observe. We know about past changes in certain areas because of historical records of disturbances. One scientist is able to observe several stages but not all stages.

Interpreting Graphics

28. d

29. 100% − 32 % =
68% of previous water use
380 L × 68 ÷ 100 = 258 L
or about 260 L

Teacher's Note

To provide practice under more realistic testing conditions, give students 20 minutes to answer all of the questions in this Standardized Test Preparation.

MISCONCEPTION ///ALERT

Answers to the standardized test preparation can help you identify student misconceptions and misunderstandings.

Passage 1

1. B

2. F

3. B

+ TEST DOCTOR

Question 1: The meaning of the word *aspen* can be deduced from its use in context as a modifier of the word *forest*.

Question 3: The strategy to solving a question like this is to look for statements in the passage that support the possible facts. Answer B is directly supported by the fifth and sixth sentences in the passage.

READING

Read each of the passages below. Then, answer the questions that follow each passage.

Passage 1 The scientist woke up and jogged over to the rain forest. There she observed the water-recycling experiment. She took a swim in the ocean, and she walked through the <u>aspen</u> forest on her way home. At home, she ate lunch and then went to the computer lab. From the lab, she could monitor the sensors that would alert her if any part of the ecosystem failed to cycle properly. This monitoring was very important to the scientist and her research team because their lives depended on the health of their sealed environment. Several weeks ago, the sensors began to detect trouble.

1. In the passage, what does *aspen* mean?
   A a type of experiment
   B a type of tree
   C beautiful
   D ugly

2. Based on the passage, what can the reader conclude?
   F The scientist lives in an artificial environment.
   G The scientist lives by herself.
   H The scientist and her research team are studying a newly discovered island.
   I The scientist does not rely on the sensors to detect trouble.

3. Based on the passage, which of the following statements is a fact?
   A The scientist is scared that her environment is being destroyed.
   B The scientists depend on the sensors to alert them of trouble.
   C The scientists live on an island.
   D The scientist eats lunch at home every day.

Passage 2 Every summer, millions of fish are killed in an area in the Gulf of Mexico called a *hypoxia region*. Hypoxia is a condition that occurs when there is an unusually low level of oxygen in the water. The area is often referred to as the *dead zone* because almost every fish and crustacean in the area dies. In 1995, this zone covered more than $18,000 \text{ km}^2$, and almost 1 million fish were killed in a single week. Why does this happen? Can it be stopped?

1. Based on the passage, what is the **best** definition of a hypoxia region?
   A a region where millions of fish are killed
   B a region where there is a low level of oxygen
   C a region that creates a "dead zone"
   D a region that is $18,000 \text{ km}^2$

2. Why is the hypoxia region called a *dead zone*?
   F because the oxygen in the region is dead
   G because the region covers more area than fish can live in
   H because the Gulf of Mexico is not a popular fishing zone anymore
   I because almost every fish and crustacean in the area dies

3. What information would the paragraph following the passage provide?
   A an explanation of the definition of hypoxia
   B a description of how hypoxia occurs in other parts of the world
   C a list all of the animals that died in the Gulf of Mexico in 1995
   D an explanation of how the hypoxia region is formed in the Gulf of Mexico

Passage 2

1. B

2. I

3. D

+ TEST DOCTOR

Question 3: This question requires the student to predict which of the topics given would make most sense to follow this passage. For these kinds of questions, encourage students to consider the main idea and to reread the last two sentences of the preceding passage. In this case, these sentences ask questions that one may reasonably expect to be answered in a paragraph that would follow. Thus, D is the best answer.

The illustration below shows what an area looked like when visited on several successive occasions. Use the illustration to answer the questions that follow.

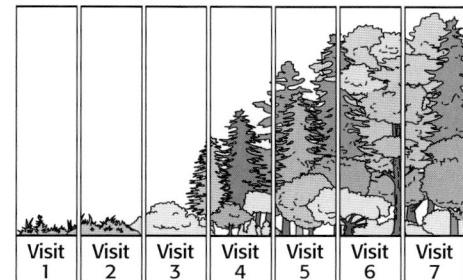

Visit 1 | Visit 2 | Visit 3 | Visit 4 | Visit 5 | Visit 6 | Visit 7

1. In the area illustrated, what process is evident over time?

A ecological succession
B combustion of fossil fuels
C pioneer speciation
D ecological organization

2. During which of the following visits would you see the **most** mature community?

F visit 1
G visit 3
H visit 5
I visit 7

3. Assume that a forest fire happened after the seventh visit. If the scientist were to visit again within 1 year after the fire, the area would most likely look like it did during which visit?

A visit 1
B visit 3
C visit 5
D visit 7

Read each question below, and choose the best answer.

1. Flushing the toilet accounts for almost half the water a person uses in a day. Some toilets use up to 6 gal per flush. More-efficient toilets use about 1.5 gal per flush. How many liters of water can you save each day by using a more-efficient toilet if you flush five times a day?

A 4.5 gal
B 20 gal
C 80 L
D 85 L

2. About 15 m of topsoil covers the eastern plains of the United States. If topsoil forms at the rate of 2.5 cm per 500 years, how long did it take for the 15 m of topsoil to form?

F 3,000 years
G 18,750 years
H 30,000 years
I 300,000 years

3. If $16 = 2x + 10$, what is x?

A 2
B 3
C 4
D 8

4. What is the area of the rectangle below?

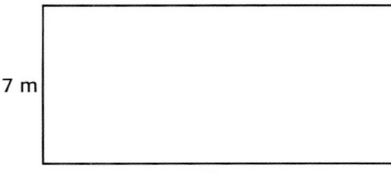

7 m

15 m

F 22 m
G 22 m^2
H 105 m
I 105 m^2

Standardized Test Preparation

1. A
2. I
3. A

TEST DOCTOR

Question 3: This question requires careful examination of the picture, careful reading of the question and potential answers, and deductive reasoning to determine which of the options is *most* likely to meet the conditions stated. A forest fire would most likely prompt a new cycle of secondary succession much like the succession that was already witnessed by the scientist. Thus, the beginning of the sequence (answer A) is the best answer.

1. D
2. I
3. B
4. I

TEST DOCTOR

Question 1: The calculation is as follows:

(6.0 − 1.5) gal/flush ×
5.0 flushes/day× 3.79 L/gal =
85.3 L/day or 85 L/day when
rounded to two significant figures

Question 2: The calculation is as follows:

15 m × 100 cm/m × 500 y / 2.5 cm=
300,000 y

Question 4: The calculation is as follows:

7 m × 15 m = 105 m^2

Students need to know the formula for area of a rectangle (*length* × *width*). Students also need to understand that units of area are usually square units, such as square meters (m^2). Remind students that whenever more than one unit is offered as an answer, they should double-check that the units in their calculations make sense.

Science, Technology, and Society

ACTIVITY — GENERAL

Have students make a simple solar water distiller. They will need a large plastic bowl, plastic wrap, masking tape, a small glass, a small rock, water, and two tablespoons of salt. Pour a shallow pool of water in the bottom of the bowl, and stir in the salt. Place the glass in the middle of the bowl, but make sure it remains empty. Cover the bowl with plastic wrap, and seal it with tape. Then, place the rock on the wrap directly over the glass so that the plastic wrap slopes toward the glass but does not touch the glass. Place the bowl in the sun for several hours, and examine the water that collects in the glass.

Scientific Discoveries

Background

Before humans altered the Mississippi watershed, runoff often carried nutrients downstream, but numerous wetlands acted as "sponges" to absorb excess nutrients. When the hypoxia region doubled in size after the Mississippi flood of 1993, scientists and government representatives began to propose efforts to restore wetlands and reduce runoff in the watershed.

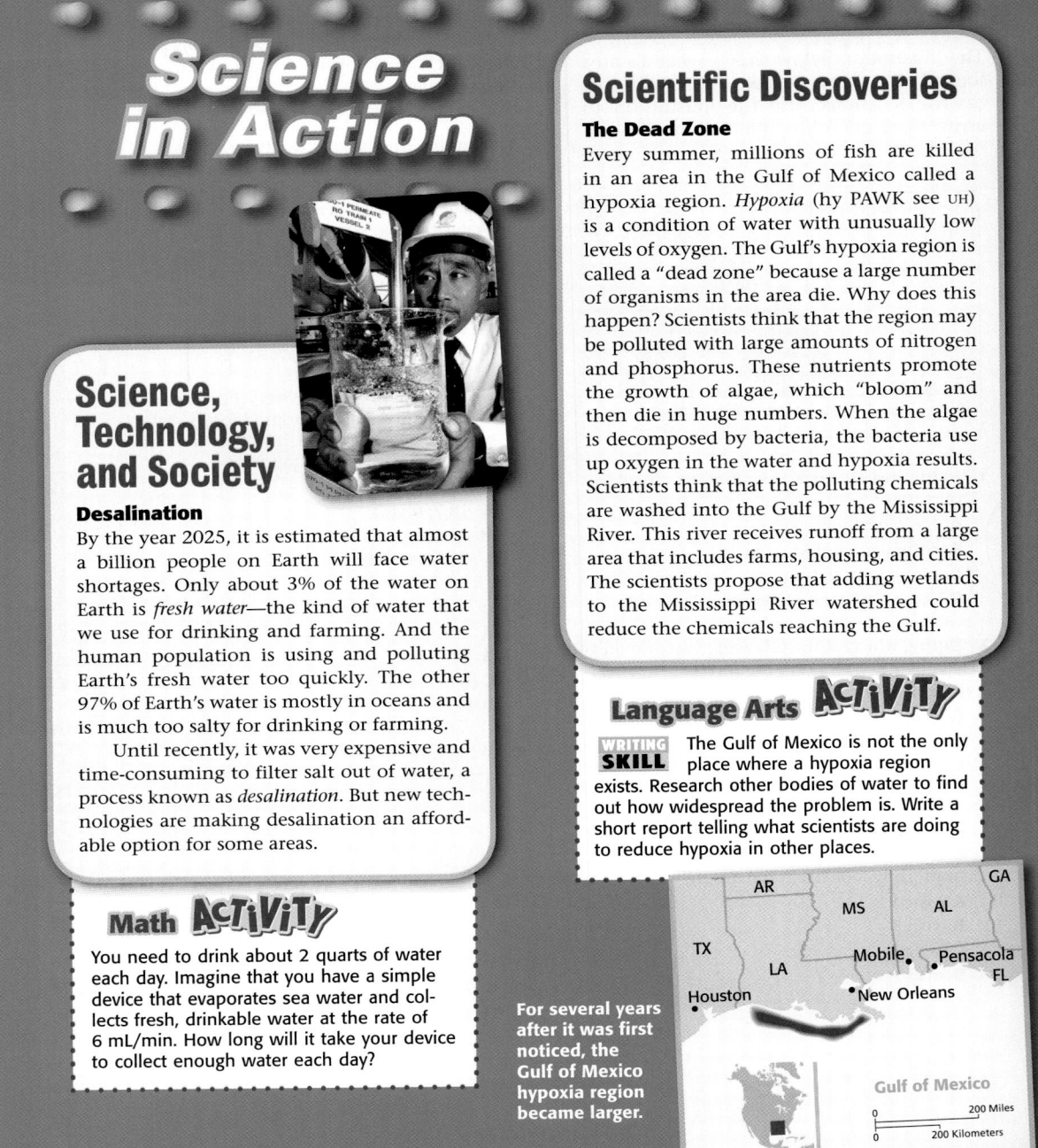

Science in Action

Science, Technology, and Society

Desalination

By the year 2025, it is estimated that almost a billion people on Earth will face water shortages. Only about 3% of the water on Earth is *fresh water*—the kind of water that we use for drinking and farming. And the human population is using and polluting Earth's fresh water too quickly. The other 97% of Earth's water is mostly in oceans and is much too salty for drinking or farming.

Until recently, it was very expensive and time-consuming to filter salt out of water, a process known as *desalination*. But new technologies are making desalination an affordable option for some areas.

Math ACTIVITY

You need to drink about 2 quarts of water each day. Imagine that you have a simple device that evaporates sea water and collects fresh, drinkable water at the rate of 6 mL/min. How long will it take your device to collect enough water each day?

Scientific Discoveries

The Dead Zone

Every summer, millions of fish are killed in an area in the Gulf of Mexico called a hypoxia region. *Hypoxia* (hy PAWK see UH) is a condition of water with unusually low levels of oxygen. The Gulf's hypoxia region is called a "dead zone" because a large number of organisms in the area die. Why does this happen? Scientists think that the region may be polluted with large amounts of nitrogen and phosphorus. These nutrients promote the growth of algae, which "bloom" and then die in huge numbers. When the algae is decomposed by bacteria, the bacteria use up oxygen in the water and hypoxia results. Scientists think that the polluting chemicals are washed into the Gulf by the Mississippi River. This river receives runoff from a large area that includes farms, housing, and cities. The scientists propose that adding wetlands to the Mississippi River watershed could reduce the chemicals reaching the Gulf.

Language Arts ACTIVITY

WRITING SKILL The Gulf of Mexico is not the only place where a hypoxia region exists. Research other bodies of water to find out how widespread the problem is. Write a short report telling what scientists are doing to reduce hypoxia in other places.

For several years after it was first noticed, the Gulf of Mexico hypoxia region became larger.

Gulf of Mexico

0 — 200 Miles
0 — 200 Kilometers

Answer to Math Activity

2 qt × 0.95 L/qt × 1,000 mL/L ÷ 6 mL/min = 317 min or 5 h 17 min

Answer to Language Arts Activity

The places about which students report may vary. Another location where a hypoxia region exists is in Long Island Sound. There, the plan for managing hypoxia will require a large amount of money and the coordinated efforts of many states and people. The nitrogen loads deposited into the sound are being identified, monitored, and gradually reduced over time.

Michael Fan

Wastewater Manager If you are concerned about clean water and you like to work both in a laboratory and outdoors, you might like a career in wastewater management. The water cycle helps to keep water in nature pure enough for most organisms. But when humans use water in houses, factories, and farms, we create *wastewater*, often faster than natural processes can clean it up. To make the water safe again, we can imitate the ways water gets cleaned up in nature—and speed up the process.

Michael M. Fan is the Assistant Superintendent of wastewater operations at the Wastewater Treatment Plant at the University of California in Davis, California. This plant has one of the most advanced wastewater management systems in the country. Mr. Fan finds his job exciting. The plant operates 24 hours a day, and there are many tasks to manage. Running the plant requires skills in chemistry, physics, microbiology, and engineering. Many organisms in the Davis area are counting on Mr. Fan to make sure that the water used by the University campus is safely returned to nature.

Social Studies
ACTiViTy

Research the ways that the ancient Romans managed their wastewater. Make a poster that illustrates some of their methods and technologies.

go.hrw.com

To learn more about these Science in Action topics, visit **go.hrw.com** and type in the keyword **HL5CYCF**

Current Science

Check out Current Science® articles related to this chapter by visiting **go.hrw.com**. Just type in the keyword **HL5CS19**.

Careers
Background

Biosolids are the undiluted material that remains after wastewater is treated. Traditionally, biosolids were simply disposed of in landfills. Newer methods of recycling biosolids may have less impact on the environment. At water treatment facilities that use these newer methods, the biosolids are collected and processed separately. After being separated from the water, the biosolids are composted at a high temperature, or otherwise treated, to destroy dangerous pathogens. Treated biosolids can be used in a variety of ways: applied as fertilizer for agricultural or horticultural use, burned to produce energy, incorporated into certain products, or used as landfill cover material.

ACTiViTy —————— GENERAL

Take the class on a field trip to your local wastewater treatment facility. Focus on the different methods used to clean the waste stream. The emphasis of modern wastewater technologies is on minimizing the use of chemicals and maximizing the use of biological processes. Expose the students to the different types of jobs people do at the facility: the cleanup process, operation and maintenance of equipment, analytical studies, microbiology procedures, regulatory compliance (a critical aspect), administrative aspects (day-to-day management of the facility), and budgeting.

The Earth's Ecosystems
Chapter Planning Guide

Compression guide:
To shorten instruction because of time limitations, omit the Chapter Lab.

OBJECTIVES	LABS, DEMONSTRATIONS, AND ACTIVITIES	TECHNOLOGY RESOURCES
PACING • 90 min pp. 524–533 **Chapter Opener**	SE **Start-up Activity**, p. 525 GENERAL	OSP **Parent Letter** ■ GENERAL CD **Student Edition on CD-ROM** CD **Guided Reading Audio CD** ■ TR **Chapter Starter Transparency*** VID **Brain Food Video Quiz**
Section 1 Land Biomes • Distinguish between abiotic factors and biotic factors in biomes. • Identify seven land biomes on Earth.	TE **Activity** Describing Biomes, p. 526 GENERAL TE **Connection Activity** Language Arts, p. 527 ADVANCED TE **Group Activity** Rainfall and Temperature, p. 528 ADVANCED TE **Connection Activity** Math, p. 528 GENERAL TE **Connection Activity** Real World, p. 529 GENERAL TE **Group Activity** What Biome Am I?, p. 531 BASIC SE **School-to-Home Activity** Local Ecosystems, p. 532 GENERAL SE **Inquiry Lab** Life in the Desert, p. 790 GENERAL CRF **Datasheet for LabBook*** SE **Inquiry Lab** Discovering Mini-Ecosystems, p. 791 GENERAL CRF **Datasheet for LabBook***	CRF **Lesson Plans*** TR **Bellringer Transparency*** TR **Land Biomes*** TR **Coniferous Forest*** TR **Tropical Rain Forest***
PACING • 45 min pp. 534–539 **Section 2 Marine Ecosystems** • List three abiotic factors that shape marine ecosystems. • Describe four major ocean zones. • Describe five marine ecosystems.	TE **Connection Activity** Real World, p. 536 GENERAL TE **Group Activity** Coral Reef, p. 537 BASIC LB **Calculator-Based Labs** Ocean Floor Mapping* ADVANCED	CRF **Lesson Plans*** TR **Bellringer Transparency*** TR *LINK TO EARTH SCIENCE* Ocean Salinity* TR **Ocean Zones A*** TR **Ocean Zones B*** CRF **SciLinks Activity*** GENERAL CD **Interactive Explorations CD-ROM** Sea Sick GENERAL
PACING • 90 min pp. 540–543 **Section 3 Freshwater Ecosystems** • Describe one abiotic factor that affects freshwater ecosystems. • Describe the three zones of a lake. • Describe two wetland ecosystems. • Explain how a lake becomes a forest.	SE **Quick Lab** Pond-Food Relationships, p. 541 GENERAL CRF **Datasheet for Quick Lab*** TE **Activity** Water Distribution, p. 541 GENERAL SE **Skills Practice Lab** Too Much of a Good Thing?, p. 544 GENERAL CRF **Datasheet for Chapter Lab*** SE **Science in Action** Math, Social Studies, and Language Arts Activities, pp. 550–551 GENERAL LB **EcoLabs & Field Activities** Biome Adventure Travel* GENERAL LB **Long-Term Projects & Research Ideas** Tropical Medicine* ADVANCED	CRF **Lesson Plans*** TR **Bellringer Transparency*** TR **Rivers*** TR **Lake Zones*** SE **Internet Activity**, p. 543 GENERAL VID **Lab Videos for Life Science**

PACING • 90 min

CHAPTER REVIEW, ASSESSMENT, AND STANDARDIZED TEST PREPARATION

CRF **Vocabulary Activity*** GENERAL
SE **Chapter Review**, pp. 546–547 GENERAL
CRF **Chapter Review*** ■ GENERAL
CRF **Chapter Tests A*** ■ GENERAL, **B*** ADVANCED, **C*** SPECIAL NEEDS
SE **Standardized Test Preparation**, pp. 548–549 GENERAL
CRF **Standardized Test Preparation*** GENERAL
CRF **Performance-Based Assessment*** GENERAL
OSP **Test Generator** GENERAL
CRF **Test Item Listing*** GENERAL

Online and Technology Resources

Visit **go.hrw.com** for a variety of free resources related to this textbook. Enter the keyword **HL5ECO**.

Holt Online Learning

Students can access interactive problem-solving help and active visual concept development with the *Holt Science and Technology* Online Edition available at **www.hrw.com**.

Guided Reading Audio CD
Also in Spanish

A direct reading of each chapter for auditory learners, reluctant readers, and Spanish-speaking students.

Science Tutor CD-ROM

Excellent for remediation and test practice.

SKILLS DEVELOPMENT RESOURCES	SECTION REVIEW AND ASSESSMENT	STANDARDS CORRELATIONS
SE **Pre-Reading Activity,** p. 524 GENERAL **OSP** **Science Puzzlers, Twisters & Teasers** GENERAL		National Science Education Standards UCP 1, 2; SAI 1, 2; ST 2; SPSP 2; LS 4b, 4c, 4d
CRF **Directed Reading A*** ■ BASIC, **B*** SPECIAL NEEDS **CRF** **Vocabulary and Section Summary*** ■ GENERAL **SE** **Reading Strategy** Reading Organizer, p. 526 GENERAL **SE** **Connection to Environmental Science** Mountains and Climate, p. 530 GENERAL **TE** **Inclusion Strategies,** p. 531 **MS** **Math Skills for Science** Subtraction Review* GENERAL **MS** **Math Skills for Science** Rain-Forest Math* GENERAL **CRF** **Reinforcement Worksheet** Know Your Biomes* BASIC	**SE** **Reading Checks,** pp. 527, 528, 530, 531, 532 GENERAL **TE** **Reteaching,** p. 532 BASIC **TE** **Quiz,** p. 532 GENERAL **TE** **Alternative Assessment,** p. 532 GENERAL **SE** **Section Review,*** p. 533 ■ GENERAL **CRF** **Section Quiz*** ■ GENERAL	UCP 2, 4, 5; SAI 1; ST 1; SPSP 2, 3; LS 1a, 3a, 3c, 3d, 4b, 4c, 4d, 5a, 5b; *LabBook:* UCP 1, 2, 4, 5; SAI 1, 2; SPSP 2; LS 3a, 3b, 3c, 4a, 4b, 4d
CRF **Directed Reading A*** ■ BASIC, **B*** SPECIAL NEEDS **CRF** **Vocabulary and Section Summary*** ■ GENERAL **SE** **Reading Strategy** Prediction Guide, p. 534 GENERAL **TE** **Reading Strategy** Prediction Guide, p. 535 GENERAL **SS** **Science Skills** Being Flexible* GENERAL	**SE** **Reading Checks,** pp. 534, 535, 537, 538 GENERAL **TE** **Homework,** p. 537 GENERAL **TE** **Reteaching,** p. 538 BASIC **TE** **Quiz,** p. 538 GENERAL **TE** **Alternative Assessment,** p. 538 GENERAL **SE** **Section Review,*** p. 539 ■ GENERAL **CRF** **Section Quiz*** ■ GENERAL	UCP 2, 3; SAI 1, 2; SPSP 2; LS 1a, 3d, 4a, 4b, 4c, 4d
CRF **Directed Reading A*** ■ BASIC, **B*** SPECIAL NEEDS **CRF** **Vocabulary and Section Summary*** ■ GENERAL **SE** **Reading Strategy** Paired Summarizing, p. 540 GENERAL **SE** **Connection to Language Arts** Compound Words, p. 542 GENERAL **TE** **Inclusion Strategies,** p. 542 **CRF** **Critical Thinking** Risky Development?* ADVANCED	**SE** **Reading Checks,** pp. 541, 542, 543 GENERAL **TE** **Reteaching,** p. 542 BASIC **TE** **Quiz,** p. 542 GENERAL **TE** **Alternative Assessment,** p. 542 GENERAL **SE** **Section Review,*** p. 543 ■ GENERAL **CRF** **Section Quiz*** ■ GENERAL	UCP 2, 3, 4; SAI 1; SPSP 2; LS 1a, 3d, 4a, 4b, 4c, 4d; *Chapter Lab:* UCP 1, 2, 3, 4; SAI 1, 2; ST 2; SPSP 2, 4, 5; LS 4a, 4b, 4c, 4d

One-Stop Planner® CD-ROM

This convenient CD-ROM includes:
• Lab Materials QuickList Software
• Holt Calendar Planner
• Customizable Lesson Plans
• Printable Worksheets
• ExamView® Test Generator

cnnstudentnews.com

Find the latest news, lesson plans, and activities related to important scientific events.

NSTA

www.scilinks.org

Maintained by the **National Science Teachers Association.** See Chapter Enrichment pages for a complete list of topics.

Check out *Current Science* articles and activities by visiting the HRW Web site at **go.hrw.com.** Just type in the keyword **HL5CS20T.**

Classroom Videos

• **Lab Videos** demonstrate the chapter lab.
• **Brain Food Video Quizzes** help students review the chapter material.
• **CNN Videos** bring science into your students' daily life.

Visual Resources

CHAPTER STARTER TRANSPARENCY

BELLRINGER TRANSPARENCIES

Section: Land Biomes
What is a biome? List seven land biomes and an organism that can be found in each.

Write your answers in your **science journal.**

Section: Marine Ecosystems
What are some abiotic factors in marine ecosystems? Are these abiotic factors different from the abiotic factors in land biomes?

Record your responses in your **science journal.**

TEACHING TRANSPARENCIES

Land Biomes

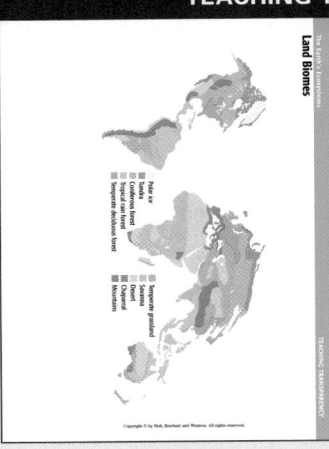

Coniferous Forest

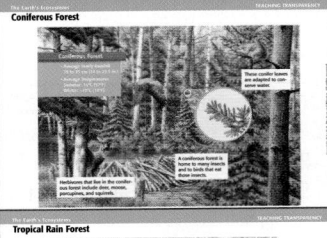

Tropical Rain Forest

TEACHING TRANSPARENCIES

Rivers

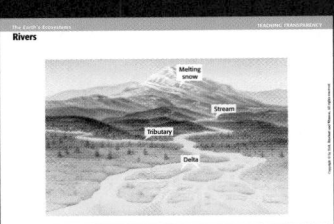

Lake Zones

Ocean Zones: A

Ocean Zones: B

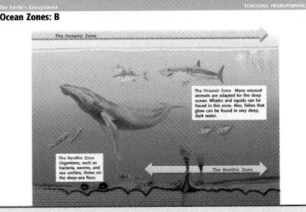

Ocean Salinity

LINK TO EARTH SCIENCE

Chapter: Exploring the Oceans

CONCEPT MAPPING TRANSPARENCY

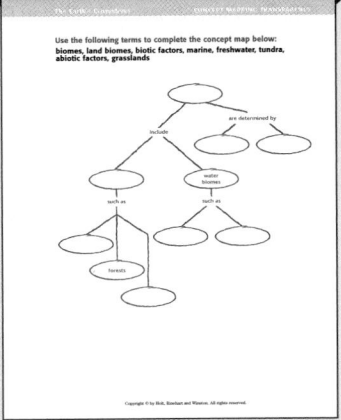

Use the following terms to complete the concept map below: biomes, land biomes, biotic factors, marine, freshwater, tundra, abiotic factors, grasslands

Planning Resources

LESSON PLANS

Lesson Plan SAMPLE

Section: Waves

Pacing
Regular Schedule: with lab(s):2 days   without lab(s):2 days
Block Schedule: with lab(s):1 1/2 days without lab(s):1 day

Objectives
1. Relate the seven properties of life to a living organism.
2. Describe seven themes that can help you to organize what you learn about biology.
3. Identify the tiny structures that make up all living organisms.
4. Differentiate between reproduction and heredity and between metabolism and homeostasis.

National Science Education Standards Covered
LSInter6:Cells have particular structures that underlie their functions.
LSMat1:Most cell functions involve chemical reactions.
LSBeh1:Cells store and use information to guide their functions.
UCP1:Cell functions are regulated.
S11: Cells can differentiate and form complete multicellular organisms.
PS1: Species evolve over time.
ESS1: The great diversity of organisms is the result of more than 3.5 billion years of evolution.
ESS2: Natural selection and its evolutionary consequences provide a scientific explanation for the fossil record of ancient life forms as well as for the striking molecular similarities observed among the diverse species of living organisms.
ST1: The millions of different species of plants, animals, and microorganisms that live on Earth today are related by descent from common ancestors.
ST2: The energy for life primarily comes from the sun.
SPSP1: The complexity and organization of organisms accommodates the need for obtaining, transforming, transporting, releasing, and eliminating the matter and energy used to sustain the organism.
SPSP6: As matter and energy flows through different levels of organization of living systems—cells, organs, communities—and between living systems and the physical environment, chemical elements are recombined in different ways.
HNS1: Organisms have behavioral responses to internal changes and to external stimuli.

PARENT LETTER

SAMPLE

Dear Parent,

Your son's or daughter's science class will soon begin exploring the chapter entitled "The World of Physical Science." In this chapter, students will learn about how the scientific method applies to the world of physical science and the role of physical science in the world. By the end of the chapter, students should demonstrate a clear understanding of the chapter's main ideas and be able to discuss the following topics:

1. physical science as the study of energy and matter (Section 1)
2. the role of physical science in the world around them (Section 1)
3. careers that rely on physical science (Section 1)
4. the steps used in the scientific method (Section 2)
5. examples of technology (Section 2)
6. how the scientific method is used to answer questions and solve problems (Section 2)
7. how our knowledge of science changes over time (Section 2)
8. how models represent real objects or systems (Section 3)
9. examples of different ways models are used in science (Section 3)
10. the importance of the International System of Units (Section 4)
11. the appropriate units to use for particular measurements (Section 4)
12. how area and density are derived quantities (Section 4)

Questions to Ask Along the Way

You can help your son or daughter learn about these topics by asking interesting questions such as the following:

- What are some surprising careers that use physical science?
- What is a characteristic of a good hypothesis?
- When is it a good idea to use a model?
- Why do Americans measure things in terms of inches and yards and meters ?

ALSO IN SPANISH

TEST ITEM LISTING

TEST ITEM LISTING
The World of Science SAMPLE

MULTIPLE CHOICE

1. A limitation of models is that
   a. they are large enough to see.
   b. they do not act exactly like the things that they model.
   c. they are smaller than the things that they model.
   d. they model unfamiliar things.
   Answer: B   Difficulty: 1   Section: 3   Objective: 2

2. The length 10 m is equal to
   a. 100 cm.   c. 10,000 mm.
   b. 1,000 cm.   d. Both (b) and (c)
   Answer: B   Difficulty: 1   Section: 3   Objective: 2

3. To be valid, a hypothesis must be
   a. testable.   c. made into a law.
   b. supported by evidence.   d. Both (a) and (b)
   Answer: B   Difficulty: 1   Section: 3   Objective: 2 1

4. The statement "Sheila has a stain on her shirt" is an example of a(n)
   a. law.   c. observation.
   b. hypothesis.   d. prediction.
   Answer: B   Difficulty: 1   Section: 3   Objective: 2

5. A hypothesis is often developed out of
   a. observations.   c. laws.
   b. experiments.   d. Both (a) and (b)
   Answer: B   Difficulty: 1   Section: 3   Objective: 2

6. How many milliliters are in 3.5 kL?
   a. 3,500 mL   c. 3,500, 000 mL
   b. 0.0035 mL.   d. 35,000 mL.
   Answer: B   Difficulty: 1   Section: 3   Objective: 2

7. A map of Seattle is an example of a
   a. law.   c. model.
   b. theory.   d. unit.
   Answer: B   Difficulty: 1   Section: 3   Objective: 2

8. A lab has the safety icons shown below. These icons mean that you should wear
   a. only safety goggles.   c. safety goggles and a lab apron.
   b. only a lab apron.   d. safety goggles, a lab apron, and gloves.
   Answer: B   Difficulty: 1   Section: 3   Objective: 2

9. The law of conservation of mass says the tot al mass before a chemical change is
   a. more than the total mass after the change.
   b. less than the total mass after the change.
   c. the same as the total mass after the change.
   d. not the same as the total mass after the change.
   Answer: B   Difficulty: 1   Section: 3   Objective: 2

10. In which of the following areas might you find a geochemist at work?
    a. studying the chemistry of rocks   c. studying fishes
    b. studying forestry   d. studying the atmosphere
    Answer: B   Difficulty: 1   Section: 3   Objective: 2

One-Stop Planner® CD-ROM

This CD-ROM includes all of the resources shown here and the following time-saving tools:

- *Lab Materials QuickList Software*
- *Customizable lesson plans*
- *Holt Calendar Planner*
- *The powerful ExamView® Test Generator*

Meeting Individual Needs

DIRECTED READING A
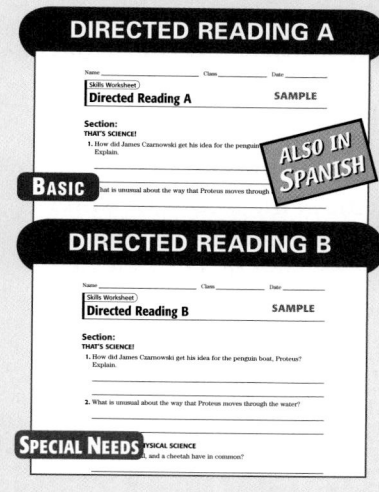

BASIC — ALSO IN SPANISH

VOCABULARY ACTIVITY
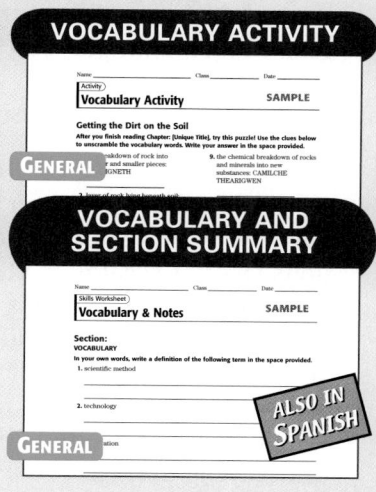

GENERAL

REINFORCEMENT
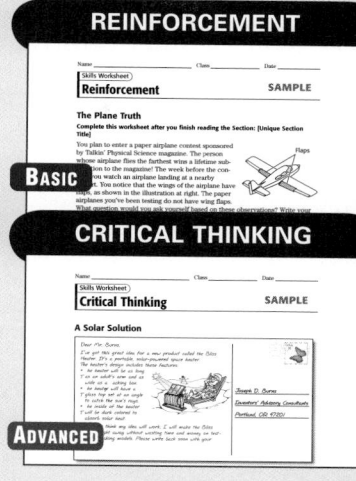

BASIC

SCILINKS ACTIVITY

GENERAL

DIRECTED READING B

SPECIAL NEEDS

VOCABULARY AND SECTION SUMMARY

GENERAL — ALSO IN SPANISH

CRITICAL THINKING

ADVANCED

SCIENCE PUZZLERS, TWISTERS & TEASERS

GENERAL

Labs and Activities

ECOLABS & FIELD ACTIVITIES
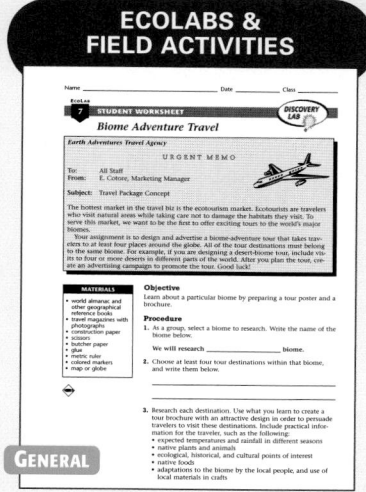

GENERAL

LONG-TERM PROJECTS & RESEARCH IDEAS
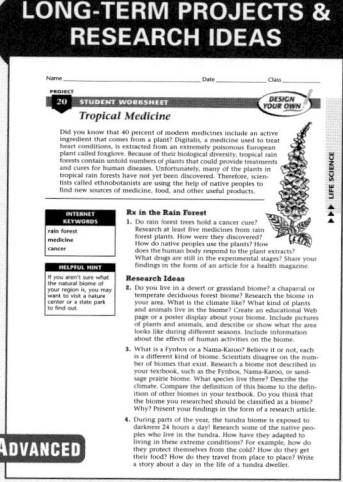

ADVANCED

CALCULATOR-BASED LABS
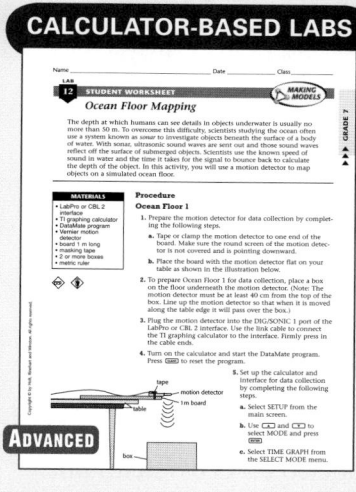

ADVANCED

DATASHEETS FOR QUICK LABS

DATASHEETS FOR CHAPTER LABS

DATASHEETS FOR LABBOOK

Review and Assessments

SECTION QUIZ
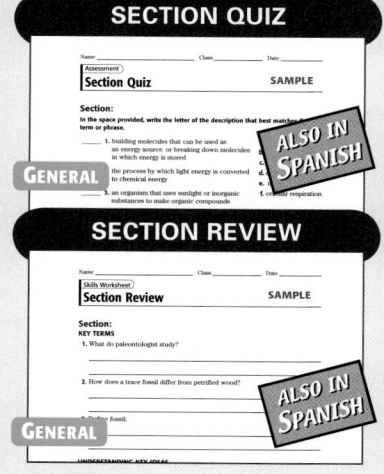

GENERAL — ALSO IN SPANISH

CHAPTER REVIEW
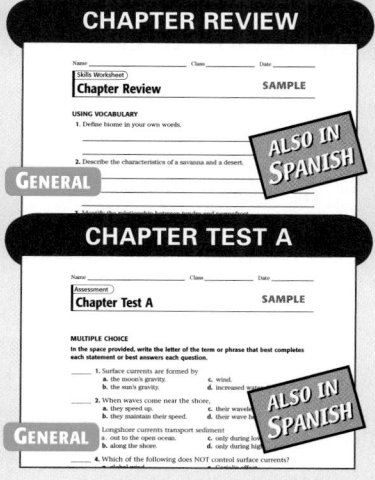

GENERAL — ALSO IN SPANISH

CHAPTER TEST B
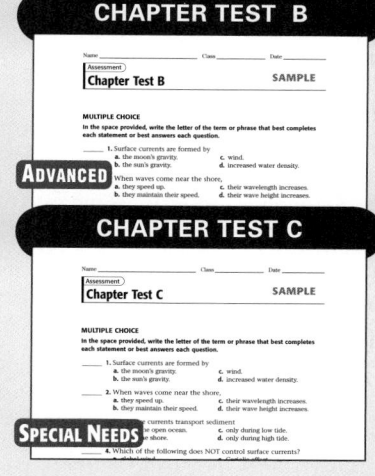

ADVANCED

STANDARDIZED TEST PREPARATION
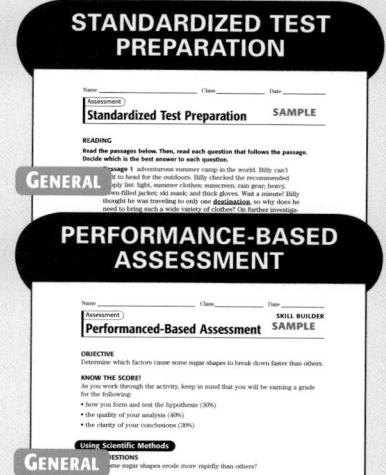

GENERAL

SECTION REVIEW

GENERAL — ALSO IN SPANISH

CHAPTER TEST A

GENERAL — ALSO IN SPANISH

CHAPTER TEST C

SPECIAL NEEDS

PERFORMANCE-BASED ASSESSMENT

GENERAL

This Chapter Enrichment provides relevant and interesting information to expand and enhance your presentation of the chapter material.

Section 1

Land Biomes

The Biosphere

- All of the parts of Earth that are inhabited by organisms make up the biosphere. The biosphere is a relatively thin layer encircling the planet. Today, aquatic habitats dominate the biosphere.

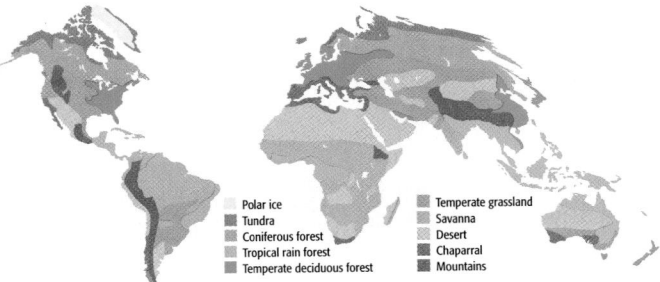

Polar ice	Temperate grassland
Tundra	Savanna
Coniferous forest	Desert
Tropical rain forest	Chaparral
Temperate deciduous forest	Mountains

- Earth can be divided into gas, liquid, and solid parts. The atmosphere is the layer of gases that envelops Earth. The hydrosphere is the portion of Earth's surface that is covered by water. The lithosphere is the soil and rock on Earth's surface.

Biotic and Abiotic Factors

- An ecosystem encompasses all of the biotic and abiotic factors in a particular area. Anything from a rotten log to the entire Earth can be labeled an ecosystem, but when discussing very large areas, scientists often use the term *biome* rather than the term *ecosystem*.

- Biotic factors include all organisms—plants, animals, protists, fungi, and bacteria. Abiotic factors include climate, water, sunlight, wind, rocks, and soil.

- Almost all ecosystems are driven by energy from the sun. Thus, the amount of sunlight a region receives has a large effect on the number of producers and consumers that can be supported by an ecosystem.

- Just as chemical reactions are limited by a limiting reagent, populations within ecosystems are limited by limiting factors. The lack of any single abiotic factor can prevent the survival of a population. Limiting factors include the amount of light received, water, temperature, and nutrients in the soil.

Tropical Rain Forests

- Students may think that tropical rain forests are jungles. In fact, a jungle is an area of dense undergrowth within a tropical rain forest. Jungles grow in areas that receive large amounts of sunlight and are near rivers.

- A tropical rain forest can be divided into four strata, or layers. The emergent layer includes the trees that tower over the forest canopy. The canopy layer is the continuous layer of vegetation that is formed by the tops of trees. Below the canopy is the understory layer, which receives little sunlight and is home to leafy plants and young trees. The fourth layer is the forest floor, which receives so little sunlight that few plants grow here. The forest floor is often covered with a very thin layer of decaying matter.

- Tropical rain forests cover about 7% of Earth's surface. This small portion of Earth contains more than 50% of the species that inhabit the planet.

Tundra

- A tundra may receive as little rainfall as a desert does. But the soil in a tundra region remains wet due to permafrost, low temperatures, and a low rate of evaporation.

Is That a Fact!

- ◆ Antarctica has been accumulating ice for more than 25 million years. It contains about 90% of Earth's ice and about 70% of Earth's fresh water.

- ◆ In summer, when ice begins to melt and break off into icebergs, Antarctica shrinks. In winter, Antarctica expands to twice its summer size.

Section 2
Marine Ecosystems
Oceans

- The Earth's oceans include the Pacific Ocean, the Atlantic Ocean, the Indian Ocean, and the Arctic Ocean. Although these oceans have different names, they are all connected.

- Because the oceans are connected, a change in one marine environment may eventually affect other marine environments.

Underwater Exploration

- New technology for remote-operated vehicles has broadened scientists' ability to explore ocean depths. Using vehicles equipped with cameras, mechanical arms, and remote sensors, scientists have discovered a new world that includes deep-sea animals, underwater volcanoes, thermal vents, and ecosystems that do not directly depend on light for energy.

- Early diving suits consisted of a hard helmet, a canvas-and-rubber tunic, boots with lead-weighted soles, and 13 kg in weights. This suit, called a *standard diving suit*, was invented by Augustus Siebe in the 1830s.

- In the early 1940s, Jacques-Yves Cousteau invented the Aqua Lung®, the precursor to SCUBA (**S**elf-**C**ontained **U**nderwater **B**reathing **A**pparatus).

Section 3
Freshwater Ecosystems
Wetlands

- Sometimes, wetlands are drained so that the land can be used for agriculture or urban development. Wetlands are breeding grounds for mosquitoes, which can be a health problem. However, wetlands play an important role in flood control, replenish water supplies, and support many organisms.

- Two types of wetlands are introduced in the text: the marsh and the swamp. However, there are many different kinds of wetlands, including inland freshwater wetlands, coastal freshwater wetlands, and coastal saltwater wetlands.

Is That a Fact!
- About 5% of the land in the United States is wetlands.
- Wetland areas in the contiguous United States have shrunk from about 890,000 km² (in the early 1600s) to about 430,000 km² (in 1997).

SciLinks is maintained by the National Science Teachers Association to provide you and your students with interesting, up-to-date links that will enrich your classroom presentation of the chapter.

Visit www.scilinks.org and enter the SciLinks code for more information about the topic listed.

Topic: Forests
SciLinks code: HSM0609

Topic: Freshwater Ecosystems
SciLinks code: HSM0621

Topic: Marine Ecosystems
SciLinks code: HSM0911

Overview

Tell students that this chapter will help them learn about Earth's ecosystems. The chapter describes several different land biomes and discusses a variety of marine and freshwater ecosystems.

Assessing Prior Knowledge

Students should be familiar with the following topics:
- interactions of living things
- cycles in nature

Identifying Misconceptions

As students learn the material in this chapter, some of them may be confused about the difference between a *biome* and an *ecosystem*. The concept of ecosystem can be used at almost any scale, including the entire Earth. However, applying the concept of ecosystem to Earth and large areas can be confusing. So, scientists often refer to large areas with similar vegetation, animals, and climate as *biomes*. You may want to stress the difference between these two concepts by explaining that a biome is generally larger than areas described as ecosystems and that biomes can contain many different ecosystems.

20

The Earth's Ecosystems

About the PHOTO

Is this animal a movie monster? No! The thorny devil is a lizard that lives in the desert of Australia. The thorny devil's rough skin is an adaptation that helps it survive in the hot, dry desert. Grooves in the thorny devil's skin collect water that the lizard later drinks. Water lands on its back and runs along the tiny grooves to the thorny devil's mouth.

PRE-READING ACTIVITY

FOLDNOTES **Three-Panel Flip Chart**
Before you read the chapter, create the FoldNote entitled "Three-Panel Flip Chart" described in the **Study Skills** section of the Appendix. Label the flaps of the three-panel flip chart with "Land biomes," "Marine ecosystems," and "Freshwater ecosystems." As you read the chapter, write information you learn about each category under the appropriate flap.

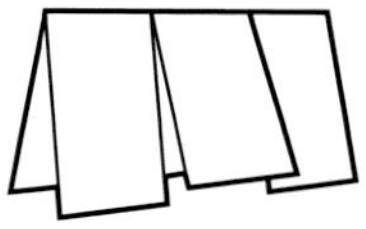

Standards Correlations

National Science Education Standards

The following codes indicate the National Science Education Standards that correlate to this chapter. The full text of the standards is at the front of the book.

Chapter Opener
UCP 1, 2; SAI 1, 2; ST 2; SPSP 2; LS 4b, 4c, 4d

Section 1 Land Biomes
UCP 2, 4, 5; SAI 1; ST 1; SPSP 2, 3; LS 1a, 3a, 3c, 3d, 4b, 4c, 4d, 5a, 5b; *LabBook:* UCP 1, 2, 4, 5; SAI 1, 2; SPSP 2; LS 3a, 3b, 3c, 4a, 4b, 4d

Section 2 Marine Ecosystems
UCP 2 , 3; SAI 1, 2; SPSP 2; LS 1a, 3d, 4a, 4b, 4c, 4d

Section 3 Freshwater Ecosystems
UCP 2, 3, 4; SAI 1; SPSP 2; LS 1a, 3d, 4a, 4b, 4c, 4d

Chapter Lab
UCP 1, 2, 3, 4; SAI 1, 2; ST 2; SPSP 2, 4, 5; LS 4a, 4b, 4c, 4d

Chapter Review
UCP 2, 3, 4, 5; SAI 1, 2; ST 1; SPSP 2, 3; LS 1a, 3a, 3c, 3d, 4a, 4b, 4c, 4d, 5a, 5b

Science in Action
UCP 1, 3; ST 2; SPSP 2, 4, 5; HNS 1, 2, 3; LS 4d, 5c

START-UP ACTIVITY

A Mini-Ecosystem

In this activity, you will build and observe a miniature ecosystem.

Procedure

1. Place a layer of **gravel** at the bottom of a **container,** such as a **large, wide-mouthed jar** or a **2 L soda bottle** with the top cut off. Then, add a layer of **soil.**

2. Add a variety of **plants** that need similar growing conditions. Choose small plants that will not grow too quickly.

3. Spray **water** inside the container to moisten the soil.

4. Loosely cover the container with a **lid** or **plastic wrap.** Place the container in indirect light.

5. Describe the appearance of your ecosystem.

6. Let your mini-ecosystem grow for 6 weeks. Add more water when the soil is dry.

7. Observe your mini-ecosystem every week. Record your observations.

Analysis

1. List the nonliving factors that make up the ecosystem that you built.

2. List the living factors that make up your ecosystem.

3. How is your mini-ecosystem similar to a real ecosystem? How is it different?

START-UP ACTIVITY

MATERIALS

FOR EACH GROUP
- gravel
- jar (large, wide-mouthed) or soda bottle (2 L)
- lid or plastic wrap
- plants
- soil
- water

Safety Caution: For additional safety, you may want to consider asking students to wear gloves while handling plants. Plants and plant parts should be kept away from the face and eyes because they may cause injury or otherwise cause irritation. Have students wash their hands after handling plants and soil.

Answers

1. Sample answers: gravel, soil, jar (or bottle), lid (or plastic wrap), water, and light

2. plants

3. Sample answer: Like a real ecosystem, my mini-ecosystem has biotic and abiotic factors. My mini-ecosystem differs from a real ecosystem because my mini-ecosystem likely doesn't have as many organisms as a real ecosystem does.

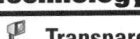

Would You Believe . . . ?

A Venus' flytrap waits. Before long, an unsuspecting fly bumps into one of the flytrap's sensitive hairs. Whack! The flytrap's two hinged doors snap shut! The victim is trapped. The more it struggles, the tighter the trap closes. The creature's fate is sealed.

Is this some weird animal? No, the Venus' flytrap is a plant, although an unusual one. As you know, most plants get nutrients they need to survive from the soil. In areas known as wetlands, the soil contains few of the nutrients plants need. Yet plants such as the Venus' flytrap thrive there. They get their

The Venus' flytrap is a very vulnerable organism, in spite of its tough appearance. The Venus' flytrap's range is very small; it grows only in certain areas of North Carolina and South Carolina. Lawn and farm fertilizers cause problems for the Venus' flytrap because it is adapted to areas of low nutrients.

In this chapter you will learn that the Earth contains many areas that are very different from one another. Different plants and animals are especially adapted for survival in each area.

Chapter Starter Transparency
Use this transparency to help students begin thinking about biomes and ecosystems.

CHAPTER RESOURCES

Technology

Transparencies
- Chapter Starter Transparency

READING SKILLS

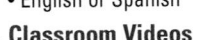
Student Edition on CD-ROM

Guided Reading Audio CD
- English or Spanish

Classroom Videos
- Brain Food Video Quiz

Workbooks

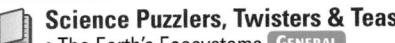
Science Puzzlers, Twisters & Teasers
- The Earth's Ecosystems GENERAL

Focus

Overview

This section introduces the concept of a *biome* and describes several land biomes. Students will learn about forests, grasslands, deserts, and tundras.

◉ Bellringer

Ask students the following questions about biomes.

- What is a biome? (a large area characterized by climate and the plants and animals that live in the area)

- List seven land biomes. (temperate deciduous forest, coniferous forest, tropical rain forest, temperate grassland, savanna, desert, and tundra)

Motivate

ACTiViTy ——————— GENERAL

Describing Biomes Have students work in pairs to brainstorm which characteristics distinguish different land biomes from each other. Have students write down their ideas and read them to the class.

LS Verbal/Interpersonal

READING WARM-UP

Objectives
- ● Distinguish between abiotic factors and biotic factors in biomes.
- ● Identify seven land biomes on Earth.

Terms to Learn
biome	desert
savanna	tundra

READING STRATEGY

Reading Organizer As you read this section, create an outline of the section. Use the headings from the section in your outline.

biome a large region characterized by a specific type of climate and certain types of plant and animal communities

---

Land Biomes

What do you think of when you think of polar bears? You probably imagine them in a snow-covered setting. Why don't polar bears live in the desert?

Different ecosystems are home to different kinds of organisms. Polar bears don't live in the desert because they are adapted to very cold environments. Polar bears have thick fur. This fur keeps polar bears warm. It also hides them in the snow.

The Earth's Land Biomes

Imagine yourself in a hot, dry, dusty place. You see a cactus on your right. A lizard sits on a rock to your left. Where are you? You may not know exactly, but you probably think you are in a desert.

A desert is different from other places because of its abiotic (AY bie AHT ik) factors and biotic (bie AHT ik) factors. *Abiotic factors* are the nonliving parts of an environment. Soil, water, and climate are abiotic factors. Climate is the average weather conditions for an area over a long period of time. *Biotic factors* are the living parts of an environment. Plants and animals are biotic factors. Areas that have similar abiotic factors usually have similar biotic factors. A **biome** (BIE OHM) is a large area characterized by its climate and the plants and animals that live in the area. A biome contains related ecosystems. For example, a tropical rain forest biome contains treetop ecosystems and forest-floor ecosystems. The major land biomes on Earth are shown in **Figure 1.**

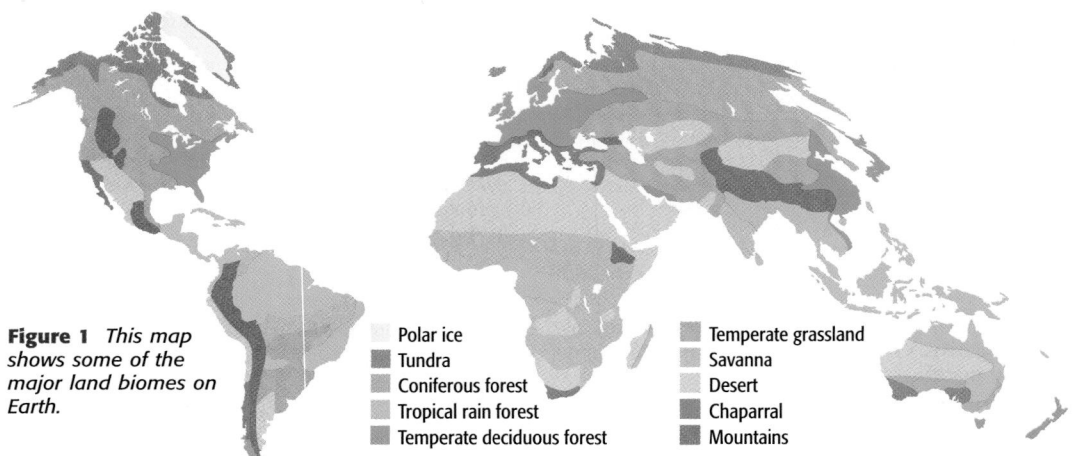

Figure 1 *This map shows some of the major land biomes on Earth.*

▢ Polar ice	▢ Temperate grassland
▢ Tundra	▢ Savanna
▢ Coniferous forest	▢ Desert
▢ Tropical rain forest	▢ Chaparral
▢ Temperate deciduous forest	▢ Mountains

CHAPTER RESOURCES

Chapter Resource File

- Lesson Plan
- Directed Reading A BASIC
- Directed Reading B SPECIAL NEEDS

Technology

Transparencies
- Bellringer
- Land Biomes

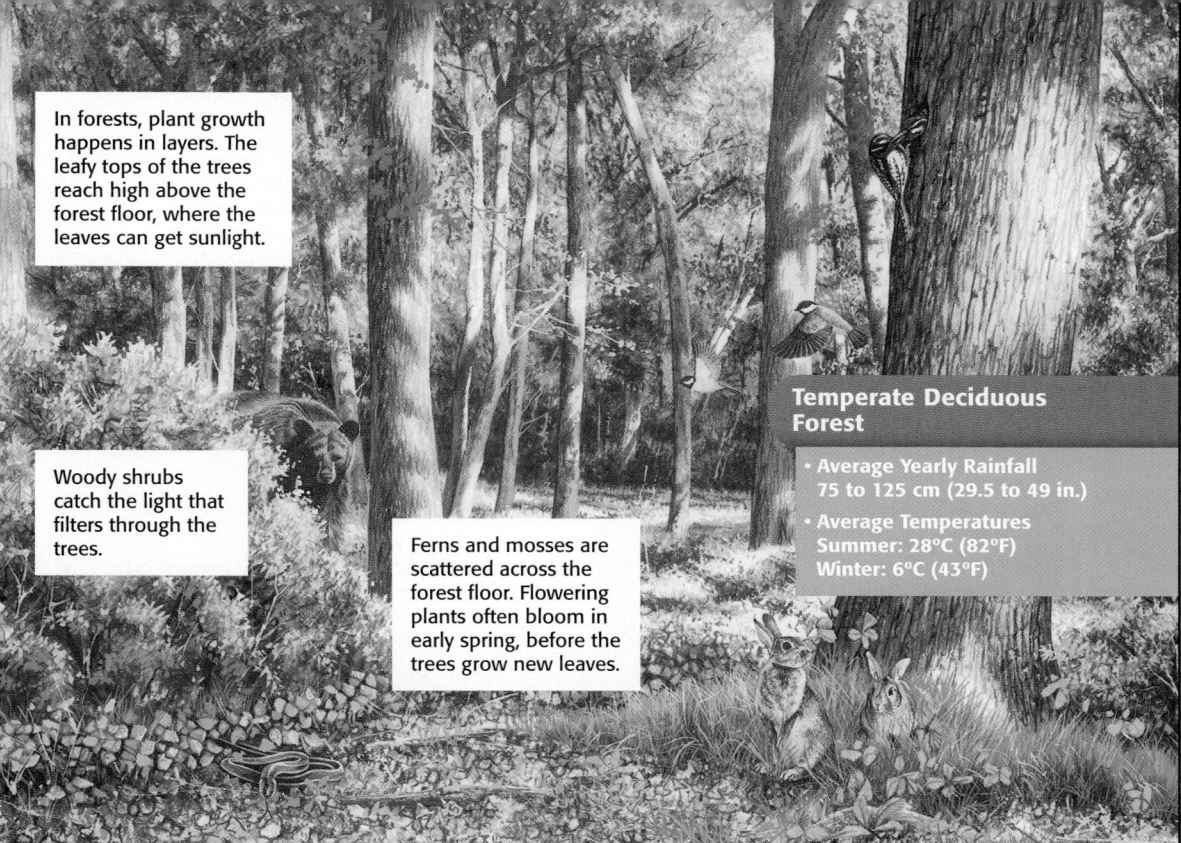

In forests, plant growth happens in layers. The leafy tops of the trees reach high above the forest floor, where the leaves can get sunlight.

Woody shrubs catch the light that filters through the trees.

Ferns and mosses are scattered across the forest floor. Flowering plants often bloom in early spring, before the trees grow new leaves.

Temperate Deciduous Forest

- **Average Yearly Rainfall** 75 to 125 cm (29.5 to 49 in.)
- **Average Temperatures** Summer: 28°C (82°F) Winter: 6°C (43°F)

Figure 2 *In a temperate deciduous forest, mammals, birds, and reptiles thrive on the many leaves, seeds, nuts, and insects.*

Forests

Forest biomes are often found in areas that have mild temperatures and plenty of rain. The kind of forest biome that develops depends on an area's temperatures and rainfall. Three forest biomes are temperate deciduous (dee SIJ oo uhs) forests, coniferous (koh NIF uhr uhs) forests, and tropical rain forests.

Temperate Deciduous Forests

Have you seen leaves change colors in the fall? Have you seen trees lose all of their leaves? If so, you have seen trees that are deciduous. The word *deciduous* comes from a Latin word that means "to fall off." Deciduous trees shed their leaves to save water during the winter or during the dry season. As shown in **Figure 2**, a variety of animals, such as bears, snakes, and woodpeckers, live in temperate deciduous forests.

✓ **Reading Check** How does the word *deciduous* describe temperate deciduous forests? (*See the Appendix for answers to Reading Checks.*)

Answer to Reading Check

Sample answer: *Deciduous* comes from a Latin word that means "to fall off." In temperate deciduous forests, the trees lose their leaves in the fall.

Teach

Using the Figure—GENERAL

Land Biomes Have students examine the map of biomes in **Figure 1.** Ask students the following questions: "Does every continent include a biome?" (Students will likely note that Antarctica is not shown on the map.) "What kind of biome would you likely find in Antarctica?" (Sample answer: polar ice) Point out that many of the organisms that inhabit Antarctica are part of a marine biome rather than a land biome. **LS** Visual

CONNECTION ACTIVITY
Language Arts—ADVANCED

Temperate and Tropical Have students look up the words *temperate* and *tropical*. Then, ask students to define *temperate ecosystem* and *tropical ecosystem* in their own words. Tell students to look at the map in **Figure 1** and at a globe. Ask students to generalize where tropical and temperate ecosystems might be found. (Students should infer that tropical ecosystems are likely found near the equator, between the Tropic of Cancer and the Tropic of Capricorn. Temperate ecosystems are often found north of the Tropic of Cancer and south of the Tropic of Capricorn.) **LS** Verbal/Visual

Group ACTIVITY —ADVANCED

Rainfall and Temperature

Have students work in groups of four. Give each group an almanac and graph paper. Ask groups to graph the average monthly rainfall and the average monthly temperature for your area. Then, ask students to compare the climate of the region in which you live with the climate of one of the biomes discussed in the section. **LS** Interpersonal/ Logical   Co-op Learning

CONNECTION ACTIVITY

Math —————————— GENERAL

Rainfall   Have students compare the amount of rainfall in each of the forest biomes described in the section. Then, ask students the following questions:

• Which forest biome receives the most rain? (tropical rain forest)

• How much more rain does this biome receive than the forest biome that receives the least amount of rain? (The coniferous forest receives a minimum of 35 cm of rain per year. The tropical rain forest receives as much as 400 cm of rain per year. The difference between the two is 365 cm of rain.)

LS Logical/Auditory

Coniferous Forest
• Average Yearly Rainfall 35 to 75 cm (14 to 29.5 in.)
• Average Temperatures Summer: 14°C (57°F) Winter: −10°C (14°F)

These conifer leaves are adapted to conserve water.

A coniferous forest is home to many insects and to birds that eat those insects.

Herbivores that live in the coniferous forest include deer, moose, porcupines, and squirrels.

Figure 3 *Many animals that live in a coniferous forest survive the harsh winters by hibernating or migrating to a warmer climate for the winter.*

Coniferous Forests

Most of the trees in a coniferous forest are called *conifers*. Conifers produce seeds in cones. Conifers also have special leaves that are shaped like needles. The leaves have a thick, waxy coating. This waxy coating has three functions. First, it helps keep conifer leaves from drying out. Second, the waxy coating protects needles from being damaged by cold winter temperatures. Finally, the waxy coating allows most conifers to keep many of their leaves year-round. So, most conifers do not change very much from summer to winter. Trees that stay green all year and do not lose all of their leaves at one time are known as *evergreen trees*.

Figure 3 shows a coniferous forest and some of the animals that live there. Squirrels and insects live in coniferous forests. Birds, such as finches, chickadees, and jays, are common in these forests. Herbivores, such as porcupines, elk, and moose, also live in coniferous forests. The ground beneath large conifers is often covered by a thick layer of needles. Also, very little light reaches the ground. So, few large plants can grow beneath these trees.

✓ **Reading Check** What is another name for most conifers? What are some animals that live in coniferous forests?

Answer to Reading Check
evergreen trees; squirrels, insects, finches, chickadees, jays, porcupines, elk, and moose

Is That a Fact!

The coniferous forest is also known as *boreal forest* or *taiga*. More land on Earth can be categorized as a coniferous forest biome than can be categorized as any other land biome.

Tropical Rain Forests

Tropical rain forests have more biological diversity than other places on Earth have. This means that rain forests have more kinds of plants and animals than any other land biome. For example, more than 100 different kinds of trees may grow in an area about one-fourth the size of a football field. Many animals live on the ground. But most animals live in the *canopy,* or the treetops. Many different animals live in the canopy. For example, nearly 1,400 species of birds live in the rain-forest canopy. **Figure 4** shows some of the diversity of the tropical rain forest.

Because of its diversity, the rain forest may seem as if it has nutrient-rich soil. But most of the nutrients in the tropical rain forest are found in the plants. The soil is actually very thin and poor in nutrients. Because the soil is so thin, many trees grow above-ground roots for extra support.

Figure 4 *Tropical rain forests have a greater variety of organisms than any other biome.*

Trees form a continuous green roof, or canopy, that may extend 60 m above the forest floor.

Woody vines climb the tree trunks to reach sunlight.

Little light reaches the ground. Low-growing plants in the rain forest don't need a lot of light.

Tropical Rain Forest

- **Average Yearly Rainfall** up to 400 cm (157.5 in.)
- **Average Temperatures** Daytime: 34°C (93°F) Nighttime: 20°C (68°F)

Using Science Fiction ——— GENERAL

The Greatest Asset Encourage students to read "The Greatest Asset," by Isaac Asimov. It can be found in the *Holt Anthology of Science Fiction*. Ask students to write a short report about the story. ⑮ Verbal

Discussion ——— ADVANCED

Eating in the Dry Season
During the dry season, the roots of savanna plants survive but the structures above the ground often die back. Ask students to discuss how herds of large herbivores might survive when savanna vegetation dies back. (Students may suggest that the animals migrate to an area where food and water are more plentiful. Point out that migration is a behavioral adaptation for survival.)
⑮ Verbal/Auditory

Cultural Awareness ——— GENERAL

Farmland Temperate grasslands provide almost ideal growing conditions for most grain crops. For this reason, few temperate grasslands remain today. Ask interested students to identify areas in the United States and in other countries where temperate grasslands are used to grow crops. Have students make a map of their findings. ⑮ Visual

Temperate Grassland
- Average Yearly Rainfall 25 to 75 cm (10 to 29.5 in.)
- Average Temperatures
  Summer: 30°C (86°F)
  Winter: 0°C (32°F)

Figure 5 *Bison once roamed North American temperate grasslands in great herds.*

savanna a grassland that often has scattered trees and that is found in tropical and subtropical areas where seasonal rains, fires, and drought happen

CONNECTION TO Environmental Science

WRITING SKILL
Mountains and Climate
Mountains can affect the climate of the land around them. Research the ecosystems around a mountain range. In your **science journal,** write a report describing how the mountains affect the climate of the surrounding land.

Grasslands

Grasslands have many names, such as *steppes, prairies,* and *pampas.* Grasslands are found on every continent but Antarctica. They are often flat or have gently rolling hills.

Temperate Grasslands

Temperate grassland plants include grasses and other flowering plants. Temperate grasslands have few trees. Fires, drought, and grazing prevent the growth of trees and shrubs. Temperate grasslands support small seed-eating animals, such as prairie dogs and mice. Large grass eaters, such as the North American bison shown in **Figure 5,** also live in temperate grasslands.

Savannas

A grassland that has scattered clumps of trees and seasonal rains is called a **savanna.** Savannas are found in parts of Africa, India, and South America. During the dry season, savanna grasses dry out and turn yellow. But the grasses' deep roots survive for many months without water. The African savanna is home to many large herbivores, such as elephants, giraffes, zebras, and wildebeests. Some of these animals are shown in **Figure 6.**

✓ **Reading Check** What happens to grasses on a savanna during the dry season?

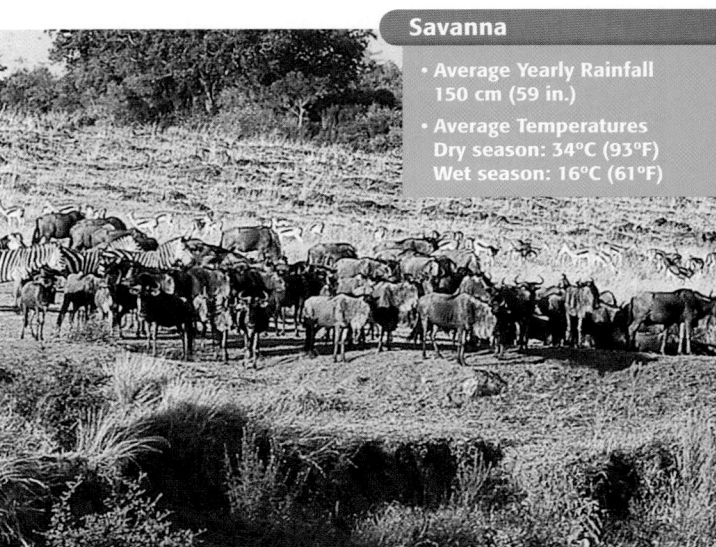

Savanna
- Average Yearly Rainfall 150 cm (59 in.)
- Average Temperatures
  Dry season: 34°C (93°F)
  Wet season: 16°C (61°F)

Figure 6 *In the African savanna, lions and leopards hunt zebras and wildebeests.*

Answer to Connection to Environmental Science

Students should recognize the rain-shadow effect, which causes one side of the mountain range to receive more rain than the other side does. Some students may note that the rain-shadow effect contributes to desertification.

Answer to Reading Check

During the dry season, grasses on the savanna dry out and turn yellow. But their deep roots survive for many months without water.

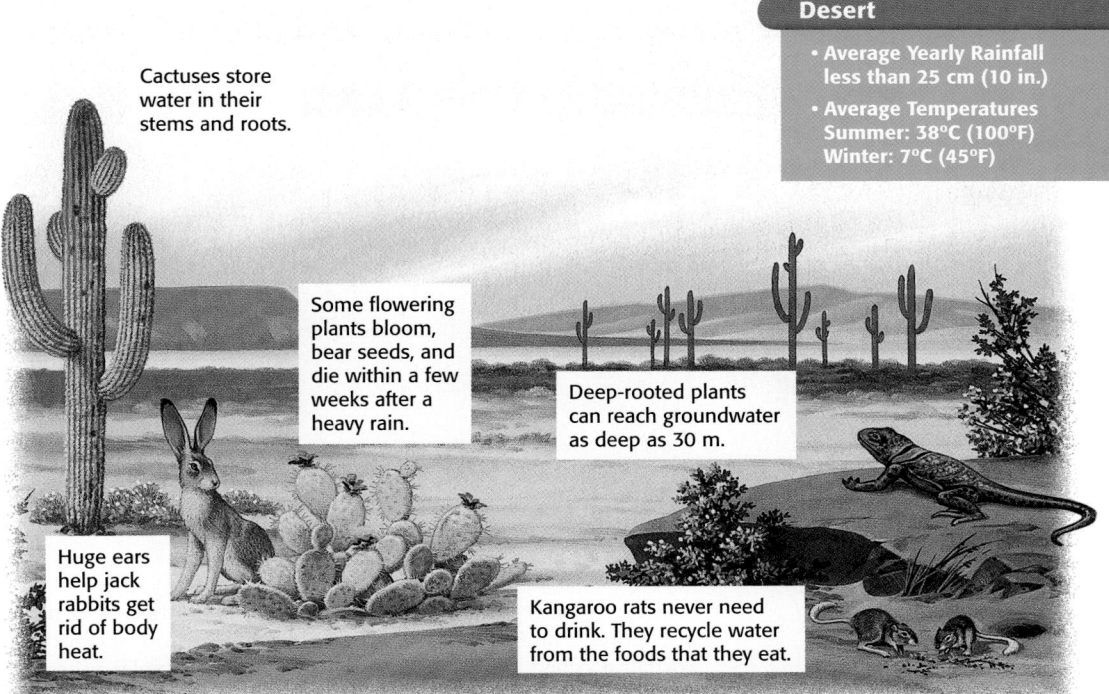

Cactuses store water in their stems and roots.

Some flowering plants bloom, bear seeds, and die within a few weeks after a heavy rain.

Deep-rooted plants can reach groundwater as deep as 30 m.

Huge ears help jack rabbits get rid of body heat.

Kangaroo rats never need to drink. They recycle water from the foods that they eat.

Figure 7 *The residents of the desert biome have special adaptations to survive in a dry climate.*

Deserts

Biomes that are very dry and often very hot are called **deserts**. Many kinds of plants and animals are found only in deserts. These organisms have special adaptations to live in a hot, dry climate. For example, plants grow far apart so that the plants won't have to compete with each other for water. Some plants have shallow, widespread roots that grow just under the surface. These roots let plants take up water during a storm. Other desert plants, such as cactuses, have fleshy stems and leaves. These fleshy structures store water. The leaves of desert plants also have a waxy coating that helps prevent water loss.

Animals also have adaptations for living in the desert. Most desert animals are active only at night, when temperatures are cooler. Some animals, such as the spadefoot toad, bury themselves in the ground and are dormant during the dry season. Doing so helps these animals escape the heat of summer. Animals such as desert tortoises eat flowers or leaves and store the water under their shells. **Figure 7** shows how some desert plants and animals live in the heat with little water.

desert a region that has little or no plant life, long periods without rain, and extreme temperatures; usually found in hot climates

 **Reading Check** What are some adaptations of desert plants?

Answer to Reading Check

Sample answer: Desert plants grow far apart. Some plants have shallow, widespread roots to take up water after a storm. Some desert plants have fleshy stems and leaves to store water. They also have waxy coatings to prevent water loss.

What Biome Am I? Have students work in groups of four. Have each student choose a land biome. Then, have students take turns describing the biome they chose to the other members of the group. Members of the group should try to guess which biome the student is describing. The successful guesser takes the next turn. Allow students to play the game until everyone has had a chance to describe a biome. **LS Verbal/Kinesthetic**

INCLUSION Strategies

- *Developmentally Delayed*
- *Hearing Impaired*
- *Learning Disabled*

Many students are more likely to understand information that is presented in a graphic format. On the board, create a table with these headings: "Temperate grasslands," "Savannas," and "Deserts." On the side of the table, write the following: "Examples of plants and animals," "Amount of rainfall," and "Average temperatures." Ask volunteers to come up to the board and fill in the empty boxes. (For temperate grasslands: grasses, other flowering plants, prairie dogs, and mice; 25 to 75 cm rain per year; average summer temperature 30°C and average winter temperature 0°C. For savannas: grasses, trees, elephants, giraffes, zebras, and wildebeests; 150 cm of rain per year; average dry season temperature 34°C and average wet season temperature 16°C. For deserts: cactuses, jack rabbits, tortoises, and kangaroo rats; less than 25 cm of rain per year; average summer temperature 38°C and average winter temperature 7°C.) **LS Visual/Logical**

Reteaching — BASIC

Paired Summarizing Have students work in pairs to review the seven biomes described in the chapter. **LS** Verbal/Interpersonal

Quiz — GENERAL

Ask students whether each of the following statements is true or false. Have students correct any false statements.

1. Permafrost thaws only briefly in the summer. (false; Only the top layer of soil thaws; permafrost stays frozen all of the time.)

2. Tropical rain forests have more species than any other land biome. (true)

3. Tropical rain forests have very poor soil. (true)

Alternative Assessment — GENERAL

Poster Project Have students choose a biome and make a poster that displays facts about the biome and images of the biome. Posters should indicate where the biome is found. **LS** Visual

Tundra
- Average Yearly Rainfall 30 to 50 cm (12 to 20 in.)
- Average Temperatures Summer: 12°C (54°F) Winter: −26°C (−15°F)

Figure 8 *During winters in the tundra, caribou migrate to grazing grounds that have a more-plentiful supply of food.*

tundra a treeless plain found in the Arctic, in the Antarctic, or on the tops of mountains that is characterized by very low winter temperatures and short, cool summers

Local Ecosystems

WRITING SKILL With a parent, explore the ecosystems around your home. What kinds of plants and animals live in your area? In your **science journal**, write a short essay describing the plants and animals in the ecosystems near your home.

Tundra

Imagine a place on Earth where it is so cold that trees do not grow. A biome that has very cold temperatures and little rainfall is called a **tundra.** Two types of tundra are polar tundra and alpine tundra.

Polar Tundra

Polar tundra is found near the North and South Poles. In polar tundra, the layer of soil beneath the surface soil stays frozen all the time. This layer is called *permafrost*. During the short, cool summers, only the surface soil thaws. The layer of thawed soil is too shallow for deep-rooted plants to live. So, shallow-rooted plants, such as grasses and small shrubs, are common. Mosses and lichens (LIE kuhnz) grow beneath these plants. The thawed soil above the permafrost becomes muddy. Insects, such as mosquitoes, lay eggs in the mud. Birds feed on these insects. Other tundra animals include musk oxen, wolves, and caribou, such as the one shown in **Figure 8.**

Alpine Tundra

Alpine tundra is similar to arctic tundra. Alpine tundra also has permafrost. But alpine tundra is found at the top of tall mountains. Above an elevation called the *tree line*, trees cannot grow on a mountain. Alpine tundra is found above the tree line. Alpine tundra gets plenty of sunlight and precipitation.

Reading Check What is alpine tundra?

Answer to School-to-Home Activity
Accept all reasonable answers. Students should recognize local flora and fauna.

Answer to Reading Check
Sample answer: Alpine tundra is tundra found at the top of tall mountains, above the tree line.

Summary

- A biome is characterized by abiotic factors, such as climate, and biotic factors, such as plant and animal communities.
- Three forest biomes are temperate deciduous forests, coniferous forests, and tropical rain forests.
- Grasslands are areas where grasses are the main plants. Temperate grasslands have hot summers and cold winters. Savannas have wet and dry seasons.

- Deserts are very dry and often very hot. Desert plants and animals competing for the limited water supply have special adaptations for survival.
- Tundras are cold areas that have very little rainfall. Permafrost, the layer of frozen soil below the surface of arctic tundra, determines the kinds of plants and animals that live on the tundra.

Using Key Terms

1. Use each of the following terms in a separate sentence: *biome* and *tundra*.

2. In your own words, write a definition for each of the following terms: *savanna* and *desert*.

Understanding Key Ideas

3. If you visited a savanna, you would most likely see
   a. large herds of grazing animals, such as zebras, gazelles, and wildebeests.
   b. dense forests stretching from horizon to horizon.
   c. snow and ice throughout most of the year.
   d. trees that form a continuous green roof, called the *canopy*.

4. Components of a desert ecosystem include
   a. a hot, dry climate.
   b. plants that grow far apart.
   c. animals that are active mostly at night.
   d. All of the above

5. List seven land biomes that are found on Earth.

6. What are two things that characterize a biome?

Critical Thinking

7. **Making Inferences** While excavating an area in the desert, a scientist discovers the fossils of very large trees and ferns. What might the scientist conclude about biomes in this area?

8. **Analyzing Ideas** Tundra receives very little rainfall. Could tundra accurately be called a *frozen desert*? Explain your answer.

Interpreting Graphics

Use the bar graph below to answer the questions that follow.

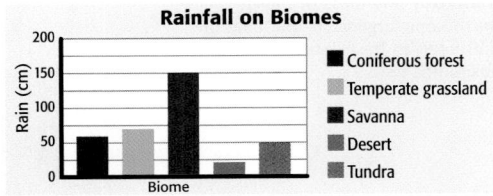

Rainfall on Biomes

Legend:
- Coniferous forest
- Temperate grassland
- Savanna
- Desert
- Tundra

9. Which biomes receive 50 cm or more of rain each year?

10. Which biome receives the smallest amount of rain? the largest amount of rain?

SCiLINKS
NSTA
Developed and maintained by the
National Science Teachers Association

For a variety of links related to this chapter, go to www.scilinks.org

Topic: Forests
SciLinks code: HSM0609

Answers to Section Review

1. Sample answer: A biome is characterized by biotic and abiotic factors. Tundra is found in polar regions and at the tops of mountains.

2. Sample answer: A savanna is a grassland that has scattered clumps of trees, seasonal rains, fires, and drought. A desert is a biome that is very dry and often very hot.

3. a

4. d

5. temperate deciduous forest, coniferous forest, tropical rain forest, temperate grassland, savanna, desert, and tundra

6. Sample answer: A biome is a large region characterized by its climate and by the plants and animals that live in the region.

7. Sample answer: The scientist might conclude that the area was once a forest biome and that the area received more rain in the past.

8. Sample answer: no; Deserts receive less than 25 cm of rain per year. Tundra receives 30 to 50 cm of rain per year. Also, the plants on the tundra are not spread far apart, as plants are in a desert, and tundra plants do not have adaptations to a dry and hot climate, such as deep roots.

9. coniferous forest, temperate grassland, savanna, and tundra

10. desert; savanna

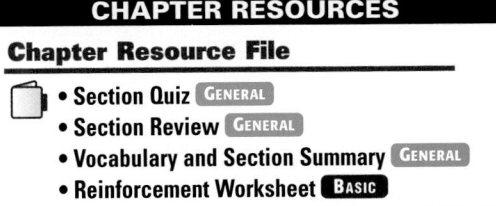

CHAPTER RESOURCES

Chapter Resource File

- Section Quiz **GENERAL**
- Section Review **GENERAL**
- Vocabulary and Section Summary **GENERAL**
- Reinforcement Worksheet **BASIC**

Focus

Overview

This section introduces and describes marine ecosystems. Students will learn about abiotic factors in marine ecosystems and about ocean zones.

 Bellringer

Ask students the following question: "What are abiotic factors in marine ecosystems?" (water temperature, the amount of sunlight that passes into the water, and water depth)

Motivate

Discussion ── GENERAL

Oceans Students may not realize how connected their lives are to the oceans, especially if students live far from the coast. Ask students the following question: "If marine life were to die off, how would humans be affected?" (There would be less food available for human consumption. There would be less oxygen in the atmosphere because marine phytoplankton produce one-third to one-half of atmospheric oxygen. Jobs would be lost. Marine nature preserves would not be available to enjoy for recreation.) **LS** Verbal

READING WARM-UP

Objectives

● List three abiotic factors that shape marine ecosystems.
● Describe four major ocean zones.
● Describe five marine ecosystems.

Terms to Learn
plankton
estuary

READING STRATEGY

Prediction Guide Before reading this section, write the title of each heading in this section. Next, under each heading, write what you think you will learn.

plankton the mass of mostly microscopic organisms that float or drift freely in freshwater and marine environments

Figure 1 *Marine ecosystems support a broad diversity of life. Humpback whales rely on plankton for food.*

Marine Ecosystems

What covers almost three-fourths of Earth's surface? What holds both the largest animals and some of the smallest organisms on Earth?

If your answer to both questions is *oceans,* you are correct! Earth's oceans contain many different ecosystems. Scientists call ecosystems in the ocean *marine ecosystems.*

Life in the Ocean

Marine ecosystems are shaped by abiotic factors. These factors include water temperature, water depth, and the amount of sunlight that passes into the water. The animals and plants that live in the ocean come in all shapes and sizes. The largest animals on Earth, blue whales, live in the ocean. So do trillions of tiny plankton. **Plankton** are tiny organisms that float near the surface of the water. Many plankton are producers. They use photosynthesis to make their own food. Plankton form the base of the ocean's food chains. **Figure 1** shows plankton and an animal that relies on plankton for food.

Reading Check What are plankton? How are they important to marine ecosystems? (*See the Appendix for answers to Reading Checks.*)

CHAPTER RESOURCES

Chapter Resource File

 • Lesson Plan
• Directed Reading A **BASIC**
• Directed Reading B **SPECIAL NEEDS**

Technology

 Transparencies
• Bellringer
• *LINK TO EARTH SCIENCE* Ocean Salinity

Answer to Reading Check

Sample answer: Plankton are tiny organisms that float near the surface of the water. They form the base of the ocean's feeding relationships.

Temperature

The temperature of ocean water decreases as the depth of the water increases. However, the temperature change is not gradual. **Figure 2** shows the three temperature zones of ocean water. Notice that the temperature of the water in the surface zone is much warmer than in the rest of the ocean. Temperatures in the surface zone vary with latitude. Areas of the ocean along the equator are warmer than areas closer to the poles. Surface zone temperatures also vary with the time of year. During the summer, the Northern Hemisphere is tilted toward the sun. So, the surface zone is warmer than it is during the winter.

Temperature affects the animals that live in marine ecosystems. For example, fishes that live near the poles have adaptations to live in near-freezing water. In contrast, animals that live in coral reefs need warm water to live. Some animals, such as whales, migrate from cold areas to warm areas of the ocean to reproduce. Water temperature also affects whether some animals, such as barnacles, can eat. If the water is too hot or too cold, these animals may not be able to eat. A sudden change in temperature may cause these animals to die.

✓ Reading Check How does temperature affect marine animals?

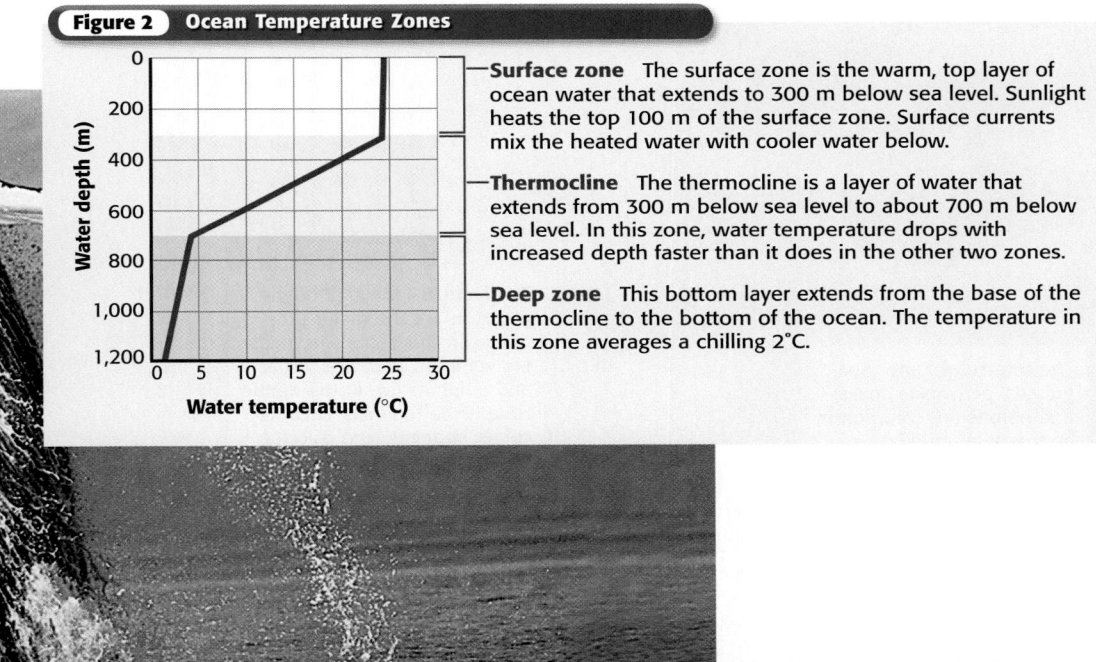

Figure 2 | **Ocean Temperature Zones**

Surface zone The surface zone is the warm, top layer of ocean water that extends to 300 m below sea level. Sunlight heats the top 100 m of the surface zone. Surface currents mix the heated water with cooler water below.

Thermocline The thermocline is a layer of water that extends from 300 m below sea level to about 700 m below sea level. In this zone, water temperature drops with increased depth faster than it does in the other two zones.

Deep zone This bottom layer extends from the base of the thermocline to the bottom of the ocean. The temperature in this zone averages a chilling 2°C.

(Graph axes: Water depth (m), 0 to 1,200; Water temperature (°C), 0 to 30)

CONNECTION to Earth Science — ADVANCED

Salinity Tell students that salinity is an abiotic factor that can have an effect on the organisms living in a marine ecosystem. For example, organisms living in estuaries must be able to adjust to changing concentrations of salt. Then, tell students that salinity varies throughout the ocean. Use the teaching transparency titled "Ocean Salinity" to illustrate this point. **LS Visual**

Answer to Reading Check

Sample answer: Fishes that live near the poles have adaptations for the near-freezing water. Animals in coral reefs need warm water to live. Some animals migrate to warmer waters to reproduce. Water temperature affects whether some animals can eat.

📖 READING STRATEGY — GENERAL

Prediction Guide Before students read this page, ask them the following questions:

1. What are three ocean temperature zones? (surface zone, thermocline, and deep zone)

2. How do water temperatures vary in the surface zone? (Sample answer: In the surface zone, water temperature varies with latitude and time of year. Water is warmer near the equator, and water is warmer during the summer.)

3. How does temperature affect marine animals? (Sample answer: Fishes near the poles have adaptations to the near-freezing water. Animals that live in coral reefs need warm water to survive. Some animals migrate to warmer waters to reproduce. Temperature also affects the ability of some animals to eat.)

Have students evaluate their responses after they read about temperature zones in marine ecosystems. **LS Verbal**

🌐 Cultural Awareness — ADVANCED

Algal Food People in Japan and Korea use brown seaweed to make *kombu* soup. A red alga called *nori* is dried in sheets and wrapped around rice to make sushi. Seaweed provides iodine and other nutrients, but it is often used for the flavor and texture that it adds to foods. Ask interested students to research foods made with algae. Encourage students to prepare some of the dishes that they learn about for the class. **LS Verbal/Kinesthetic**

Using the Figure — BASIC

Ocean Zones Help students understand the information in **Figure 3** by pointing out how it is organized. You may want to point out that the oceanic zone and the benthic zone continue extending into the ocean. Also, point out how the depth of the ocean changes farther away from shore. You may also want to interpret the magnified views of the ocean for students. **LS Visual**   English Language Learners

CONNECTION ACTiViTY
Real World — GENERAL

 The Bends A diving condition called the *bends*, or decompression sickness, can occur when a person who is using underwater breathing devices dives very deeply into the water, ascends to the water's surface too quickly after diving, or stays under the water for a long period of time. Ask interested students to research what happens when a person gets decompression sickness. Students should also research ways to prevent and treat decompression sickness. Have students write an informative magazine article about their findings. Ask students to relate their findings to modern SCUBA practices. **LS Verbal**

Depth and Sunlight

In addition to water temperature, life in the ocean is affected by water depth and the amount of sunlight that passes into the water. The major ocean zones are shown in **Figure 3.**

The Intertidal Zone

The intertidal zone is the place where the ocean meets the land. This area is exposed to the air for part of the day. Waves are always crashing on the rock and sand. The animals that live in the intertidal zone have adaptations to survive exposure to air and to keep from being washed away by the waves.

The Neritic Zone

As you move farther away from shore, into the neritic zone (nee RIT ik ZOHN), the water becomes deeper. The ocean floor starts to slope downward. The water is warm and receives a lot of sunlight. Many interesting plants and animals, such as corals, sea turtles, fishes, and dolphins, live in this zone.

Figure 3 *The life in a marine ecosystem depends on water temperature, water depth, and the amount of sunlight the area receives.*

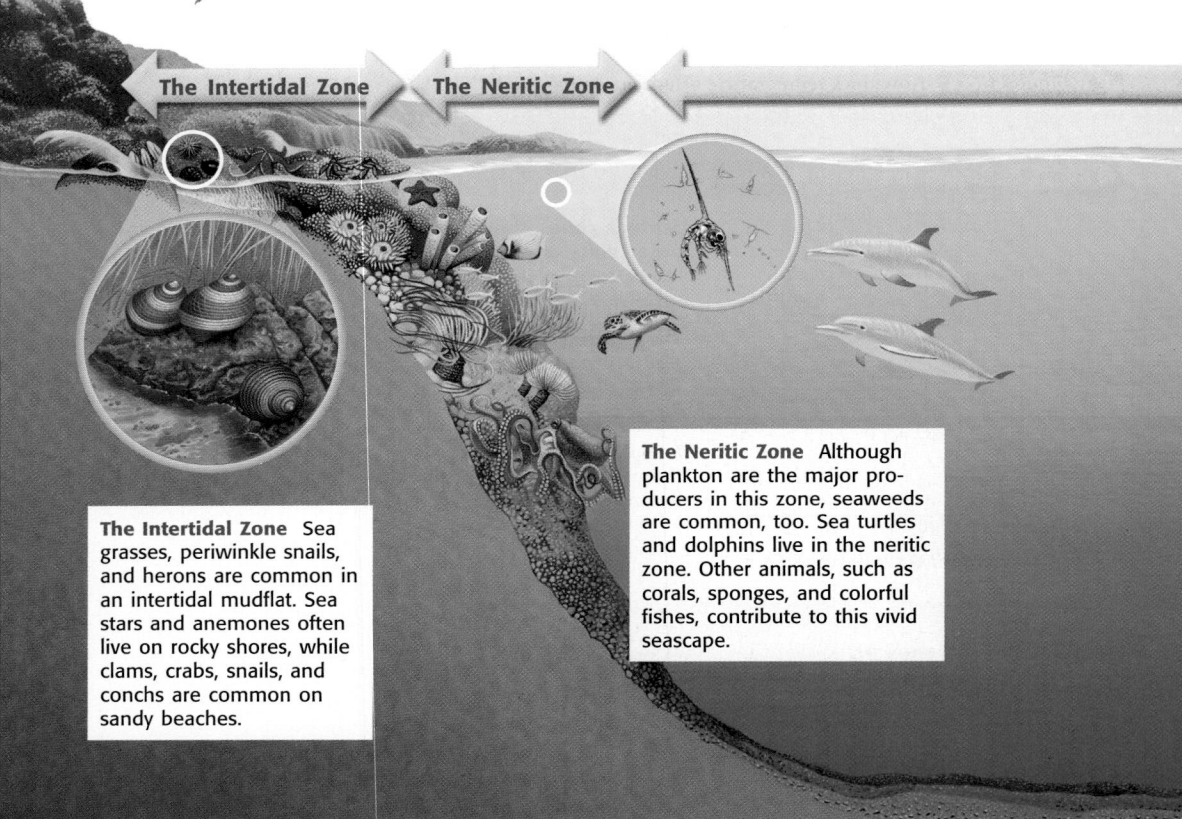

The Intertidal Zone   **The Neritic Zone**

The Intertidal Zone Sea grasses, periwinkle snails, and herons are common in an intertidal mudflat. Sea stars and anemones often live on rocky shores, while clams, crabs, snails, and conchs are common on sandy beaches.

The Neritic Zone Although plankton are the major producers in this zone, seaweeds are common, too. Sea turtles and dolphins live in the neritic zone. Other animals, such as corals, sponges, and colorful fishes, contribute to this vivid seascape.

CHAPTER RESOURCES
Technology
Transparencies
• Ocean Zones A
• Ocean Zones B

CONNECTION to
Physical Science — ADVANCED

Light Red, orange, and yellow wavelengths of light that strike the surface of the water are absorbed more easily than blue and green wavelengths of light are. Blue and green wavelengths can penetrate the water more deeply. Thus, producers that are capable of using blue and green wavelengths of light for photosynthesis can live at greater depths. Ask interested students to research and diagram how light reacts with water. **LS Visual**

The Oceanic Zone

In the oceanic zone, the sea floor drops sharply. This zone contains the deep water of the open ocean. Plankton can be found near the water surface. Animals, such as fishes, whales, and sharks, are found in the oceanic zone. Some animals in this zone live in very deep water. These animals often get food from material that sinks down from the ocean surface.

The Benthic Zone

The benthic zone is the ocean floor. The deepest parts of the benthic zone do not get any sunlight. They are also very cold. Animals, such as fishes, worms, and crabs, have special adaptations to the deep, dark water. Many of these organisms get food by eating material that sinks from above. Some organisms, such as bacteria, get energy from chemicals that escape from thermal vents on the ocean floor. Thermal vents form at cracks in the Earth's crust.

Reading Check How do animals in the benthic zone get food?

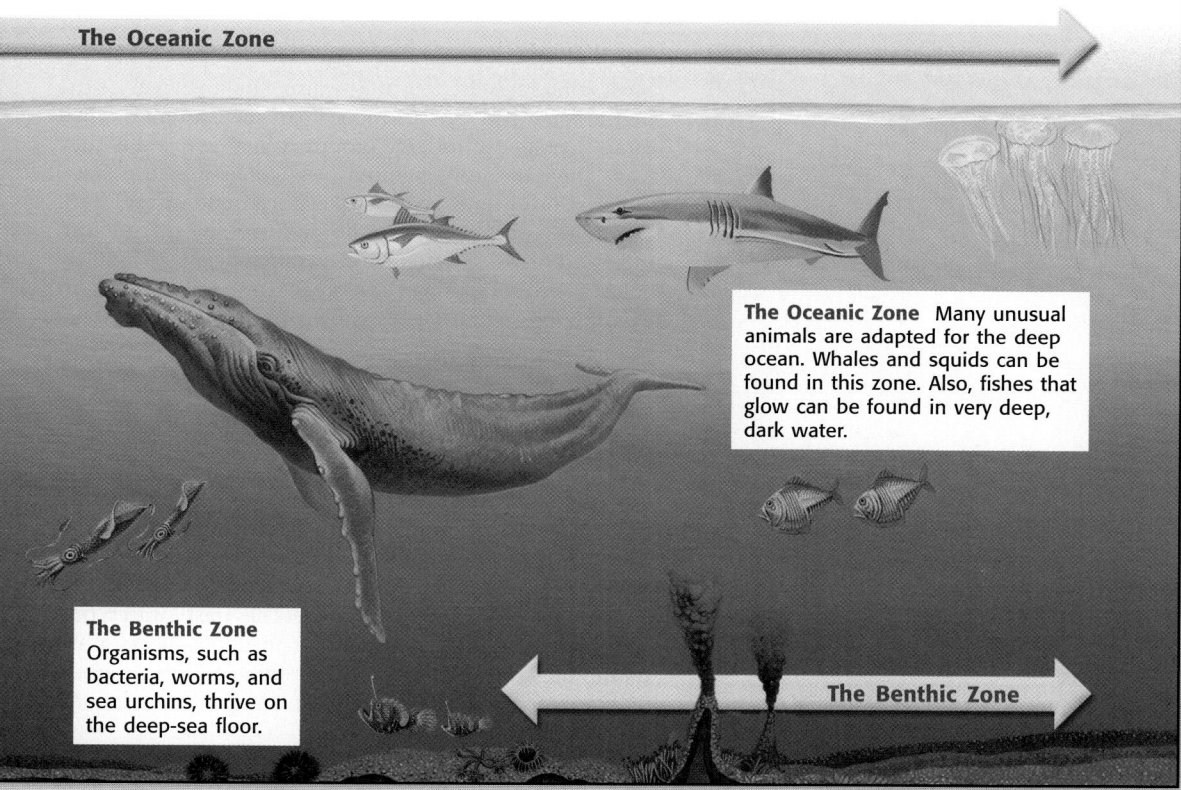

The Oceanic Zone

The Oceanic Zone Many unusual animals are adapted for the deep ocean. Whales and squids can be found in this zone. Also, fishes that glow can be found in very deep, dark water.

The Benthic Zone Organisms, such as bacteria, worms, and sea urchins, thrive on the deep-sea floor.

The Benthic Zone

Is That a Fact!

Deep-sea-vent ecosystems depend on neither sunlight nor photosynthesis for energy. Many of these ecosystems rely on chemicals released by the vents.

Answer to Reading Check

Sample answer: Some animals get food from material that sinks to the bottom from the surface. Other animals get energy from chemicals released by thermal vents.

A Closer Look

Life on Earth depends on the ocean. Through evaporation, the ocean provides most of the water that makes up Earth's precipitation. Ocean temperatures and currents can affect world climates and wind patterns. Humans and many animals depend on the ocean for food.

Many ecosystems exist in the ocean. Some of these ecosystems are found on or near the shore. Other ecosystems are found in the middle of the ocean or near the poles.

Intertidal Areas

Intertidal areas are found near the shore. These areas include mudflats, sandy beaches, and rocky shores. Intertidal organisms must be able to live both underwater and out of water. The organisms that live in mudflats include worms and crabs. Shorebirds feed on these animals. Organisms that live on sandy beaches include worms, clams, crabs, and plankton. On rocky shores, organisms have adaptations to keep from being swept away by crashing waves. Some organisms use rootlike structures called *holdfasts* to attach themselves to the rocks. Other organisms attach themselves to rocks by releasing a special glue.

Coral Reefs

Most coral reefs are found in warm, shallow areas of the neritic zone. The reefs are made up of small animals called *corals.* Corals live in large groups. When corals die, they leave their skeletons behind. New corals grow on these remains. Over time, layers of skeletons build up and form a reef. This reef provides a home for many marine animals and plants. These organisms include algae, brightly colored fishes, sponges, sea stars, and sea urchins. An example of a coral reef is shown in **Figure 4.**

✓ Reading Check How do coral reefs develop?

Estuaries

An area where fresh water from streams and rivers spills into the ocean is called an **estuary** (ES tyoo er ee). In estuaries, the fresh water from rivers and the salt water from the ocean are always mixing. Therefore, the amount of salt in the water is always changing. Plants and animals that live in estuaries must be able to survive the changing concentrations of salt. The fresh water that spills into an estuary is rich in nutrients. Because estuaries are so nutrient rich, they support large numbers of plankton. The plankton, in turn, provide food for many animals.

estuary an area where fresh water from rivers mixes with salt water from the ocean

Figure 4 A coral reef is one of the most biologically diverse ecosystems on Earth.

The Sargasso Sea

An ecosystem called the *Sargasso Sea* (sahr GAS oh SEE) is found in the middle of the Atlantic Ocean. This ecosystem contains floating rafts of algae called *sargassum* (sahr GAS uhm). Many of the animals that live in the Sargasso Sea are the same color as sargassum, which helps the animals hide from predators.

Polar Ice

The Arctic Ocean and the ocean around Antarctica make up another marine ecosystem. These icy waters are rich in nutrients, which support large numbers of plankton. Many fishes, birds, and mammals rely on the plankton for food. Animals, such as polar bears and penguins, live on the polar ice.

SECTION Review

Summary

- Abiotic factors that affect marine ecosystems are water temperature, water depth, and the amount of light that passes into the water.

- Plankton form the base of the ocean's food chains.

- Four ocean zones are the intertidal zone, the neritic zone, the oceanic zone, and the benthic zone.

- The ocean contains unique ecosystems, including intertidal areas, coral reefs, estuaries, the Sargasso Sea, and polar ice.

Using Key Terms

1. Use each of the following terms in a separate sentence: *plankton* and *estuary*.

Understanding Key Ideas

2. Water temperature
   a. has no effect on the animals in a marine ecosystem.
   b. affects the types of organisms that can live in a marine ecosystem.
   c. decreases gradually as water gets deeper.
   d. increases as water gets deeper.

3. What are three abiotic factors that affect marine ecosystems?

4. Describe four major ocean zones.

5. Describe five marine ecosystems. For each ecosystem, list an organism that lives there.

Math Skills

6. The ocean covers about 71% of the Earth's surface. If the total surface area of the Earth is about 510 million square kilometers, how many square kilometers are covered by the ocean?

Critical Thinking

7. **Making Inferences** Animals in the Sargasso Sea hide from predators by blending in with the sargassum. Color is only one way to blend in. What is another way that animals can blend in with sargassum?

8. **Identifying Relationships** Many fishes and other organisms that live in the deep ocean produce light. What are two ways in which this light might be useful?

9. **Applying Concepts** Imagine that you are studying animals that live in intertidal zones. You just discovered a new animal. Describe the animal and adaptations the animal has to survive in the intertidal zone.

For a variety of links related to this chapter, go to www.scilinks.org

Topic: Marine Ecosystems
SciLinks code: HSM0911

SCiLINKS®
NSTA
Developed and maintained by the National Science Teachers Association

---

CHAPTER RESOURCES

Chapter Resource File

- **Section Quiz** GENERAL
- **Section Review** GENERAL
- **Vocabulary and Section Summary** GENERAL
- **SciLinks Activity** GENERAL

Technology

Interactive Explorations CD-ROM
- Sea Sick GENERAL

Answers to Section Review

1. Sample answer: Plankton are tiny organisms that form the base of many of the ocean's food chains. An estuary is an area where fresh water from rivers mixes with salt water from the ocean.

2. b

3. water temperature, water depth, and the amount of sunlight that passes into the water

4. Sample answer: The intertidal zone is the place where the ocean meets the land. This area is exposed to air for part of the day. The neritic zone is farther from shore, where the water starts to get deeper. This water is often warm and sunny. The oceanic zone starts where the sea floor drops sharply. It includes the deepest part of the ocean. The benthic zone is the ocean floor.

5. Sample answer: Intertidal areas include mudflats, sandy beaches, and rocky shores. Worms live in intertidal areas. Coral reefs are found in the shallow waters of the neritic zone. Corals are small animals that make up the reefs. Estuaries are areas where fresh water meets salt water. Plankton are abundant in estuaries. The Sargasso Sea is found in the middle of the Atlantic Ocean. Sargassum is an alga found in this ecosystem. Polar ice is found at the poles. Plankton thrive on the nutrients found in this near-freezing water.

6. $510,000,000 \text{ km}^2 \times 0.71 = 362,100,000 \text{ km}^2$

7. Sample answer: Animals in the Sargasso Sea could look like or be shaped like the leaves of the sargassum.

8. Sample answer: The light may attract prey. The light may also confuse a predator.

9. Accept all reasonable answers. Students should recognize that intertidal organisms must have adaptations for exposure to air and for the effect of surf.

Focus

Overview

This section introduces fresh-water ecosystems. Students will learn about the characteristics of rivers, streams, ponds, and lakes. Students will also learn about two types of wetlands and how a lake can become a forest.

🔔 Bellringer

Ask students the following question: "What are four freshwater ecosystems?" (Sample answers: streams, rivers, lakes, marshes, ponds, swamps, bogs, and creeks)

Motivate

Discussion —— GENERAL

Water Sources Ask students, "What is the source for river water?" (Sample answers: springs, melting snow and ice, and rainfall) Tell students that the sources of river water can vary. In addition to springs and precipitation, lakes and ponds can serve as sources for river water.
LS Auditory/Logical

READING WARM-UP

Objectives
- Describe one abiotic factor that affects freshwater ecosystems.
- Describe the three zones of a lake.
- Describe two wetland ecosystems.
- Explain how a lake becomes a forest.

Terms to Learn

littoral zone	wetland
open-water zone	marsh
deep-water zone	swamp

READING STRATEGY

Paired Summarizing Read this section silently. In pairs, take turns summarizing the material. Stop to discuss ideas that seem confusing.

Freshwater Ecosystems

A brook bubbles over rocks. A mighty river thunders through a canyon. A calm swamp echoes with the sounds of frogs and birds. What do these places have in common?

Brooks, rivers, and swamps are examples of freshwater ecosystems. The water in brooks and rivers is often fast moving. In swamps, water moves very slowly. Also, water in swamps is often found in standing pools.

Stream and River Ecosystems

The water in brooks, streams, and rivers may flow from melting ice or snow. Or the water may come from a spring. A spring is a place where water flows from underground to the Earth's surface. Each stream of water that joins a larger stream is called a *tributary* (TRIB yoo TER ee). As more tributaries join a stream, the stream contains more water. The stream becomes stronger and wider. A very strong, wide stream is called a *river*. **Figure 1** shows how a river develops.

Like other ecosystems, freshwater ecosystems are characterized by their abiotic factors. An important abiotic factor in freshwater ecosystems is how quickly water moves.

Streams and rivers are full of life. Plants line the edges of streams and rivers. Fish live in the open waters. And clams and snails live in the mud at the bottom of a stream or river. Organisms that live in fast-moving water have adaptations to keep from being washed away. Some producers, such as algae and moss, are attached to rocks. Consumers, such as tadpoles, use suction disks to hold themselves to rocks. Other consumers, such as insects, live under rocks.

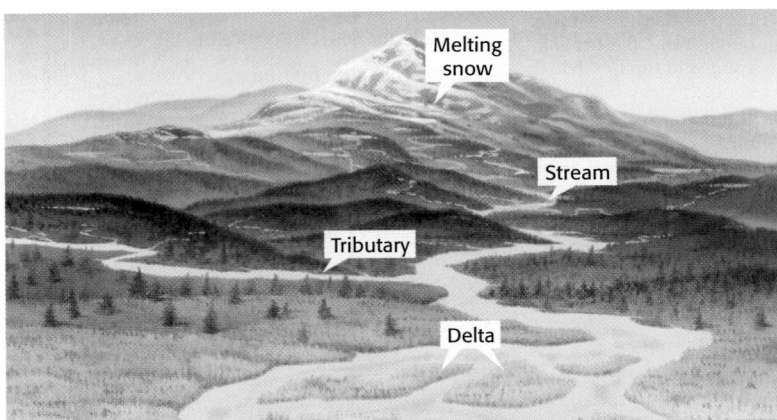

Figure 1 *Rivers become larger as more tributaries flow into them.*

CHAPTER RESOURCES

Chapter Resource File

- Lesson Plan
- Directed Reading A **BASIC**
- Directed Reading B **SPECIAL NEEDS**

Technology

Transparencies
- Bellringer
- Rivers
- Lake Zones

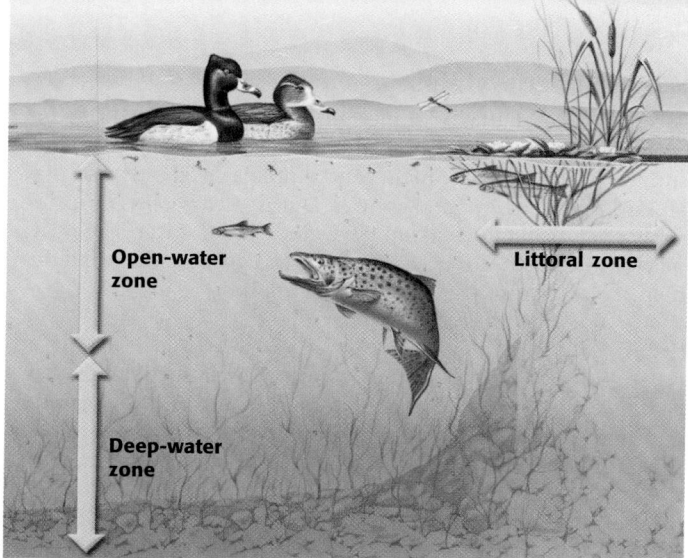

Figure 2 *Ponds and lakes can be divided into three zones. Each zone has different organisms and abiotic factors.*

Pond and Lake Ecosystems

Ponds and lakes have different ecosystems than streams and rivers do. **Figure 2** shows the zones of a typical lake.

Life near Shore

The area of water closest to the edge of a lake or pond is called the **littoral zone** (LIT uh ruhl ZOHN). Sunlight reaches the bottom of the littoral zone. This sunlight makes it possible for algae and plants to grow in the littoral zone. Algae grow beneath the surface of the water in the littoral zone. Plants that grow near the shore include cattails and rushes. Floating leaf plants, such as water lilies, grow farther from the shore. The plants of the littoral zone are home to small animals, such as snails and insects. Clams and worms bury themselves in the mud. Frogs, salamanders, turtles, fish, and snakes also live in this zone.

Life Away from Shore

The area of a lake or pond that extends from the littoral zone across the top of the water is called the **open-water zone.** The open-water zone goes as deep as sunlight can reach. This zone is home to bass, lake trout, and other fishes. Many photosynthetic plankton also live in this area. Beneath the open-water zone is the **deep-water zone,** where no sunlight reaches. Catfish, carp, worms, crustaceans, fungi, and bacteria live here. These organisms often feed on dead organisms that sink from above.

✓ Reading Check Describe the three zones of a lake. (*See the Appendix for answers to Reading Checks.*)

littoral zone the shallow zone of a lake or pond where light reaches the bottom and nurtures plants

open-water zone the zone of a pond or lake that extends from the littoral zone and that is only as deep as light can reach

deep-water zone the zone of a lake or pond below the open-water zone, where no light reaches

Quick Lab

Pond-Food Relationships

1. On **index cards,** write the names of some of the plants and animals that live in a typical freshwater pond or small lake. Write one type of organism on each card.

2. Use **yarn** or **string** to connect each organism to its food sources.

3. Describe the food relationships in a pond.

Answer to Reading Check

Sample answer: The littoral zone is the zone closest to shore in which light reaches the lake bottom. The open zone extends from the littoral zone and goes as deep as sunlight can reach. The deep-water zone lies beneath the open-water zone.

Teach

Making Models — ADVANCED

Lake Model Have students design and construct a three-dimensional model of a lake. Students' models should show the three lake zones and show examples of plants and animals found in these zones. **English Language Learners**

LS Kinesthetic

Quick Lab

MATERIALS

FOR EACH GROUP
- index cards
- yarn or string

Answer

3. Students should recognize that photosynthetic organisms form the base of most freshwater food chains. Students should also recognize predator-prey relationships.

ACTIVITY — GENERAL

Water Distribution Tell students that 97.6% of the water on Earth is found in the oceans. Then, ask students to make a bar graph that shows the relative amounts of non-ocean water in the world based on the following list.

Ice and snow	29,000 km³
Ground water	4,000 km³
Lakes and reservoirs	125 km³
Atmosphere	113 km³
Salt lakes	104 km³
Surface soils	65 km³
Organisms	65 km³
Swamps, marshes	3.6 km³
Rivers and streams	1.7 km³

LS Visual/Logical

Figure 3 *This painted turtle suns itself on a log in a freshwater marsh.*

wetland an area of land that is periodically underwater or whose soil contains a great deal of moisture

marsh a treeless wetland ecosystem where plants such as grasses grow

swamp a wetland ecosystem in which shrubs and trees grow

Wetland Ecosystems

An area of land that is sometimes underwater or whose soil contains a great deal of moisture is called a **wetland.** Wetlands support many different plants and animals. Wetlands also play an important role in flood control. During heavy rains or spring snow melt, wetlands soak up large amounts of water. The water in wetlands also moves deeper into the ground. So, wetlands help replenish underground water supplies.

Marshes

A treeless wetland ecosystem where plants, such as grasses, grow is called a **marsh.** A freshwater marsh is shown in **Figure 3.** Freshwater marshes are often found in shallow areas along the shores of lakes, ponds, rivers, and streams. The plants in a marsh vary depending on the depth of the water and the location of the marsh. Grasses, reeds, bulrushes, and wild rice are common marsh plants. Muskrats, turtles, frogs, and birds also live in marshes.

Swamps

A wetland ecosystem in which trees and vines grow is called a **swamp.** Swamps, as shown in **Figure 4,** are found in low-lying areas and beside slow-moving rivers. Most swamps are flooded part of the year, depending on rainfall. Willows, bald cypresses, and oaks are common swamp trees. Vines, such as poison ivy, grow up tree trunks. Plants, such as orchids, may hang from tree branches. Water lilies and other plants grow in standing water. Many fishes, snakes, and birds also live in swamps.

✔ **Reading Check** What is a swamp?

Figure 4 *The trunks of these trees are adapted to give the trees more support in the wet, soft soil of a swamp.*

From a Lake to a Forest

Did you know that a lake or pond can disappear? How can this happen? Water entering a standing body of water usually carries nutrients and sediment. These materials settle to the bottom of the pond or lake. Dead leaves from overhanging trees and decaying plant and animal life also settle to the bottom. Then, bacteria decompose this material. This process uses oxygen in the water. The loss of oxygen affects the kinds of animals that can survive in the pond or lake. For example, many fishes would not be able to survive with less oxygen in the water.

Over time, the pond or lake is filled with sediment. Plants grow in the new soil. Shallow areas fill in first. So, plants slowly grow closer and closer to the center of the pond or lake. What is left of the lake or pond becomes a wetland, such as a marsh or swamp. Eventually, the wetland can become a forest.

✓ Reading Check What happens to some of the animals in a pond as the pond becomes a forest?

INTERNET ACTIVITY

For another activity related to this chapter, go to **go.hrw.com** and type in the keyword **HL5ECOW**.

SECTION Review

Summary

- An important abiotic factor in freshwater ecosystems is how quickly water moves.
- The three zones of a pond or lake are the littoral zone, the open-water zone, and the deep-water zone.
- Wetlands include marshes and swamps.
- Sediments and decaying plant and animal matter build up in a pond. Over time, the pond may fill completely and become a forest.

Using Key Terms

1. Use the following terms in the same sentence: *wetland, marsh,* and *swamp.*

Understanding Key Ideas

2. A major abiotic factor in freshwater ecosystems is the
   a. source of the water.
   b. speed of the water.
   c. width of the stream or river.
   d. None of the above

3. Describe the three zones of a lake.

4. Explain how a lake can become a forest over time.

Math Skills

5. Sunlight can penetrate a certain lake to a depth of 15 m. The lake is five and a half times deeper than the depth to which light can penetrate. In meters, how deep is the lake?

Critical Thinking

6. **Making Inferences** When bacteria decompose material in a pond, the oxygen in the water may be used up. So, fishes in the pond die. How might the absence of fish lead to a pond filling faster?

7. **Applying Concepts** Imagine a steep, rocky stream. What kinds of adaptations might animals living in this stream have? Explain your answer.

SCiLINKS

NSTA
Developed and maintained by the
National Science Teachers Association

For a variety of links related to this chapter, go to www.scilinks.org

Topic: Freshwater Ecosystems
SciLinks code: HSM0621

Answer to Reading Check

Sample answer: Many fishes will die as the pond fills in because bacteria that decompose material in the pond use up the oxygen in the water.

Answers to Section Review

1. Sample answer: Both a marsh and a swamp are wetlands.
2. b
3. Sample answer: The area of water closest to the edge of the lake is the littoral zone. Sunlight reaches the bottom of the littoral zone. The open-water zone stretches across the surface of the water from the edge of the littoral zone. The open-water zone goes as deep as sunlight can reach. The deep-water zone lies beneath the open-water zone. It stretches to the bottom of the lake.
4. Sample answer: Materials settle to the bottom of the lake. Bacteria decompose these materials and use oxygen in the water. The loss of oxygen affects the survival of animals in the water. Many fishes die because of the loss of oxygen. As the pond fills in, plants grow in the filled areas. Over time, the pond becomes a swamp or marsh. Eventually, the swamp or marsh becomes a forest.
5. 82.5 m (15 m × 5.5 = 82.5 m)
6. Sample answer: If the fishes die, the bodies of the fishes will contribute to the material on the bottom of the pond. Also, while the fishes were alive, they may have eaten plankton, algae, or water plants. Without fishes, these plankton, algae, and plants may multiply, adding to the material in the pond.
7. Answers may vary. Students should mention adaptations to moving water, such as attaching to rocks, using suction disks, and living under rocks.

CHAPTER RESOURCES

Chapter Resource File

- Section Quiz GENERAL
- Section Review GENERAL
- Vocabulary and Section Summary GENERAL
- Critical Thinking ADVANCED

Too Much of a Good Thing?

Teacher's Notes

Time Required
One 45-minute class period and one 10-minute observation time every 3 days for 3 weeks

Lab Ratings

EASY ———————→ HARD

Teacher Prep 🧪🧪
Student Set-Up 🧪🧪
Concept Level 🧪🧪🧪
Clean Up 🧪🧪

MATERIALS

The materials listed on the student page are enough for 1–2 students. This lab is a good opportunity to recycle glass jars or clear plastic 2 L soda bottles. Any container that is transparent and will hold at least 1 L of water will do.

Safety Caution
Remind students to review all safety cautions and icons before beginning this lab activity.

Lab Notes
A review of the causes of eutrophication might be helpful before beginning this lab.

Skills Practice Lab

OBJECTIVES

Draw common pond-water organisms.

Observe the effect of fertilizer on pond-water organisms.

Describe how fertilizer affects the number and type of pond-water organisms over time.

MATERIALS

- beaker, 500 mL
- distilled water, 2.25 L
- eyedropper
- fertilizer
- gloves, protective
- graduated cylinder, 100 mL
- jars, 1 qt or 1 L (3)
- microscope
- microscope slides with coverslips
- pencil, wax
- plastic wrap
- pond water containing living organisms, 300 mL
- stirring rod

SAFETY

Too Much of a Good Thing?

Plants need nutrients, such as phosphates and nitrates, to grow. Phosphates are often found in detergents. Nitrates are often found in animal wastes and fertilizers. When large amounts of these nutrients enter rivers and lakes, algae and plants grow rapidly and then die off. Microorganisms that decompose the dead matter use up oxygen in the water. Without oxygen, fish and other animals die. In this activity, you will observe the effect of fertilizers on organisms that live in pond water.

Procedure

1. Label one jar "Control," the second jar "Fertilizer," and the third jar "Excess fertilizer."

2. Pour 750 mL of distilled water into each jar. To the "Fertilizer" jar, add the amount of fertilizer recommended for 750 mL of water. To the "Excess fertilizer" jar, add 10 times the amount recommended for 750 mL of water. Stir the contents of each jar to dissolve the fertilizer.

3. Obtain a sample of pond water. Stir it gently to make sure that the organisms in it are evenly distributed. Pour 100 mL of pond water into each of the three jars.

4. Observe a drop of water from each jar under the microscope. Draw at least four of the organisms. Determine whether the organisms you see are producers, which are usually green, or consumers, which are usually able to move. Describe the number and type of organisms in the pond water.

Common Pond-Water Organisms

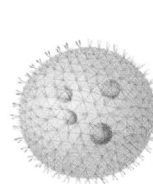   

Volvox (producer) **Spirogyra** (producer) **Daphnia** (consumer) **Vorticella** (consumer)

Jason Marsh
Montevideo High and Country School
Montevideo, Minnesota

CHAPTER RESOURCES

Chapter Resource File

- **Datasheet for Chapter Lab**
- **Lab Notes and Answers**

Technology

 Classroom Videos
- Lab Video

- Life in the Desert
- Discovering Mini-Ecosystems

5 Cover each jar loosely with plastic wrap. Place the jars near a sunny window but not in direct sunlight.

6 Make a prediction about how the pond organisms will grow in each of the three jars.

7 Make three data tables. Title one table "Control," as shown below. Title another table "Fertilizer," and title the third table "Excess fertilizer."

Control			
Date	Color	Odor	Other observations
DO NOT WRITE IN BOOK			

8 Observe the jars when you first set them up and once every 3 days for the next 3 weeks. Note the color, the odor, and the presence of organisms. Record your observations.

9 When organisms become visible in the jars, use an eyedropper to remove a sample from each jar. Observe the sample under the microscope. How have the number and type of organisms changed since you first looked at the pond water?

10 At the end of the 3-week period, observe a sample from each jar under the microscope. Draw at least four of the most abundant organisms, and describe how the number and type of organisms have changed since your last microscope observation.

Analyze the Results

1 **Describing Events** After 3 weeks, which jar has the most abundant growth of algae?

2 **Analyzing Data** Did you observe any effects on organisms (other than algae) in the jar with the most abundant algal growth? Explain your answer.

Draw Conclusions

3 **Drawing Conclusions** What may have caused increased growth in the jars?

4 **Evaluating Results** Did your observations match your predictions? Explain your answer.

5 **Interpreting Information** Decaying plant and animal life contribute to the filling of lakes and ponds. How might the rapid filling of lakes and ponds be prevented or slowed?

Analyze the Results

1. Answers may vary. Students should note increased algal growth in the jars containing fertilizer.

2. Answers may vary. Increased algal growth may lead to increased bacterial growth because of the decomposition of dead algae. The bacteria consume oxygen in the water, which kills organisms that need oxygen to survive. Eventually, this loss of oxygen will also affect algae because algae use oxygen.

Draw Conclusions

3. Sample answer: Algae need nitrates and phosphates to grow. Fertilizer contains nitrates. Adding fertilizer increased the amount of nitrates in the water. So, the algae grew more.

4. Accept all reasonable answers.

5. Sample answer: When more algae grow, they contribute to the filling of the pond. So, preventing detergents and fertilizers from entering a pond will likely prevent algal growth that contributes to the filling of a pond.

CHAPTER RESOURCES

Workbooks

 **EcoLabs & Field Activities**
• Biome Adventure Travel **GENERAL**

 Long-Term Projects & Research Ideas
• Tropical Medicine **GENERAL**

Calculator-Based Labs
• Ocean Floor Mapping **ADVANCED**

Assignment Guide

Section	Questions
1	1, 3, 6, 10, 12, 16, 19–24
2	2, 7–9, 17
3	4–5, 11, 13–14, 18
1, 2, and 3	15

ANSWERS

Using Key Terms

1. Sample answer: A biome is a large area characterized by climate and the plants and animals that live in the area. Tundra is a biome with cold temperatures, little rainfall, and no trees.

2. Sample answer: Organisms that live in the intertidal zone are exposed to the air for part of the day. In the neritic zone, water is warm and receives a lot of sunlight. The oceanic zone includes the deep areas of the ocean.

3. Sample answer: A savanna is a biome characterized by grasses and seasonal rains. A desert is a biome that is very dry and often very hot.

4. Sample answer: The open-water zone receives sunlight, but the deep-water zone does not receive sunlight.

5. Sample answer: Marshes do not have trees, while swamps do have trees.

USING KEY TERMS

1. In your own words, write a definition for the following terms: *biome* and *tundra*.

2. Use each of the following terms in a separate sentence: *intertidal zone, neritic zone,* and *oceanic zone*.

For each pair of terms, explain how the meanings of the terms differ.

3. *savanna* and *desert*

4. *open-water zone* and *deep-water zone*

5. *marsh* and *swamp*

UNDERSTANDING KEY IDEAS

Multiple Choice

6. Trees that lose their leaves in the winter are called
   a. evergreen trees.
   b. coniferous trees.
   c. deciduous trees.
   d. None of the above

7. In which major ocean zone are plants and animals exposed to air for part of the day?
   a. intertidal zone
   b. neritic zone
   c. oceanic zone
   d. benthic zone

8. An abiotic factor that affects marine ecosystems is
   a. the temperature of the water.
   b. the depth of the water.
   c. the amount of sunlight that passes through the water.
   d. All of the above

9. _____ is a marine ecosystem that includes mudflats, sandy beaches, and rocky shores.
   a. An intertidal area
   b. Polar ice
   c. A coral reef
   d. The Sargasso Sea

Short Answer

10. What are seven land biomes?

11. Explain how a small lake can become a forest.

12. What are two factors that characterize biomes?

13. Describe the three zones of a lake.

14. How do rivers form?

15. What are three abiotic factors in land biomes? three abiotic factors in marine ecosystems? an abiotic factor in fresh-water ecosystems?

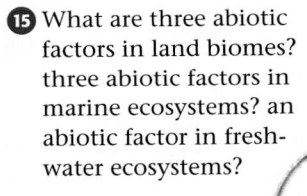

Understanding Key Ideas

6. c   7. a

8. d   9. a

10. temperate deciduous forests, coniferous forests, tropical rain forests, temperate grasslands, savannas, deserts, and tundras

11. Sample answer: Materials that are washed into the lake build up. To decompose these materials, bacteria use oxygen in the water, which affects the animals that live in the lake. The shallow areas fill in, and plants begin to grow. The lake becomes a marsh or swamp. Eventually, the marsh or swamp becomes a forest.

12. Sample answer: climate and the plants and animals that live in an area

13. Sample answer: The littoral zone is the area of a lake closest to shore, where sunlight reaches the bottom of the lake. The open-water zone extends from the littoral zone and is as deep as sunlight can reach. The deep-water zone lies beneath the open-water zone.

14. Sample answer: Water in rivers may come from springs or melting snow. Each stream of water joins another stream. As more water is added, the stream eventually becomes a river.

CRITICAL THINKING

16 Concept Mapping Use the following terms to create a concept map: *plants and animals, tropical rain forest, tundra, biomes, permafrost, canopy, desert,* and *abiotic factors.*

17 Making Inferences Plankton use photosynthesis to make their own food. They need sunlight for photosynthesis. Which of the four major ocean zones can support plankton growth? Explain your answer.

18 Predicting Consequences Wetlands, such as marshes and swamps, play an important role in flood control. Wetlands also help replenish underground water supplies. Predict what might happen if a wetland dries out.

19 Analyzing Ideas A scientist has a new hypothesis. He or she thinks that savannas and deserts are part of one biome rather than two separate biomes. Based on what you've learned, decide if the scientist's hypothesis is correct. Explain your answer.

20 Applying Concepts Imagine that you are a scientist. You are studying an area that gets about 100 cm of rain each year. The average summer temperatures are near 30°C. What biome are you in? What are some plants and animals you will likely encounter? If you stayed in this area for the winter, what kind of preparations might you need to make?

INTERPRETING GRAPHICS

Use the graphs below to answer the questions that follow.

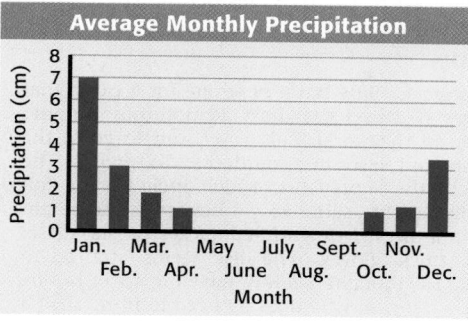

Average Monthly Precipitation

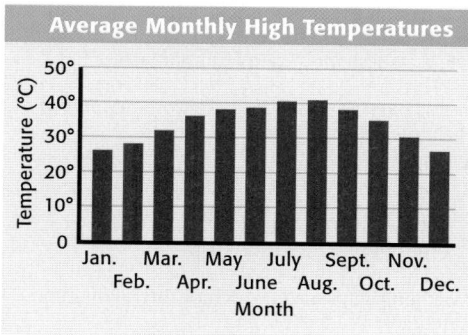

Average Monthly High Temperatures

21 Which biome is most likely found in the region described by the graphs above? Explain your answer.

22 How many centimeters of rain fell in the region during the course of the year?

23 Which month is the hottest in the region? the coolest in the region?

24 What is the average monthly precipitation for the month that has the highest average high temperature?

Critical Thinking

16. 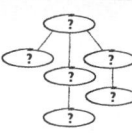 An answer to this exercise can be found at the end of this book.

17. Sample answer: Plankton can live in the intertidal zone, the neritic zone, and the oceanic zone. All of these areas receive sunlight, which is necessary for photosynthesis.

18. Sample answer: The area may be more likely to flood if the wetland dries out. Also, because wetlands store water, there may be a shortage of water in the area.

19. Sample answer: The hypothesis is incorrect. Savannas and deserts have different climates. Savannas get more rain than deserts do. Also, the plants and animals that live in each area are different. Savannas have grasses and scattered trees, while the plants in the desert grow far apart and are adapted to a very dry climate.

20. Sample answer: The biome is likely a deciduous forest. I would see deciduous trees, bears, deer, and woodpeckers. Winters are likely cold, so I will need warm clothing and shelter.

Interpreting Graphics

21. Sample answer: The biome is likely a desert because the region receives less than 25 cm of rain during the year and is warm.

22. about 19 cm

23. August; January

24. 0 cm

15. climate, water, and rocks; water temperature, water depth, and the amount of sunlight that passes through the water; the speed at which water moves

Standardized Test Preparation

Teacher's Note

To provide practice under more realistic testing conditions, give students 20 minutes to answer all of the questions in this Standardized Test Preparation.

MISCONCEPTION ALERT

Answers to the standardized test preparation can help you identify student misconceptions and misunderstandings.

READING

Passage 1

1. C
2. G
3. C

TEST DOCTOR

Question 1: Some students may think that the word *destination* refers to a camp, vacation, or mountain because those words are used in the passage. However, as it is used in the sentence, *destination* means "place."

Question 2: The last sentence of the passage states that Kilimanjaro is Africa's tallest mountain. Because the brochure indicates that Billy needs to bring warm clothing, students may incorrectly choose answers concerning the weather conditions on Kilimanjaro. However, no factual statements about weather conditions are made in the passage.

READING

Read each of the passages below. Then, answer the questions that follow each passage.

Passage 1 Billy has a brochure for a camp that boasts of being the most adventurous summer camp in the world. Billy can't wait to go to the camp and have fun outdoors. To prepare, he checks the supply list, which includes the following: light, summer clothes; sunscreen; rain gear; a heavy, down-filled jacket; a ski mask; and thick gloves. The list seems strange to Billy. He thought he was traveling to only one <u>destination</u>, so why does he need to bring such a wide variety of clothes? Billy rereads the brochure and learns that the campers will "climb the biomes of the world in just three days." The destination is Africa's tallest mountain, Kilimanjaro.

1. In this passage, what does the word *destination* likely mean?
   - **A** camp
   - **B** vacation
   - **C** place
   - **D** mountain

2. Based on the passage, which of the following statements is a fact?
   - **F** People ski on Kilimanjaro.
   - **G** Kilimanjaro is Africa's tallest mountain.
   - **H** It rains a lot on Kilimanjaro.
   - **I** The summers are cold on Kilimanjaro.

3. Why might Billy wonder if the brochure was advertising only one location?
   - **A** The brochure called the camp the most adventurous summer camp in the world.
   - **B** The brochure said that he would need light, summer clothes and sunscreen.
   - **C** The brochure said that he would need light, summer clothes and a heavy, down-filled jacket.
   - **D** The brochure said that the summers are cold on Kilimanjaro.

Passage 2 The layer of soil above the permafrost is too shallow for plants with deep roots to live. Grasses and shrubs can survive there because they have shallow roots. A sheet of mosses and lichens grows beneath these plants. When the soil above the permafrost thaws, the soil becomes muddy. Muddy soil is an excellent place for insects, such as mosquitoes, to lay eggs. Many birds spend the summer in the tundra to feed on these insects. Tundra animals include caribou, musk oxen, wolves, and other large mammals. Smaller animals, such as lemmings, shrews, and hares, also live in the tundra.

1. Based on the passage, what is one reason for the lack of trees on the tundra?
   - **A** Trees need more sunlight than is available.
   - **B** The roots of trees need more room than is available.
   - **C** The soil above the permafrost becomes too muddy for trees.
   - **D** Trees need more water than is available.

2. Based on the passage, which of the following statements about permafrost is true?
   - **F** It is a thawed layer of soil.
   - **G** It is always moist.
   - **H** It is always frozen.
   - **I** It is shallow.

3. Based on the passage, which of the following statements is a fact?
   - **A** Muddy soil is an excellent place for mosses and lichens to grow.
   - **B** Birds fly north to reach the tundra in the summer.
   - **C** Caribou and oxen are some of the large mammals that live in the tundra.
   - **D** The tundra is a beautiful biome that is home to diverse communities.

Passage 2

1. B
2. H
3. C

TEST DOCTOR

Question 3: Some students may answer that muddy soil is an excellent place for mosses and lichens to grow, but this is not a fact in the passage. Other students may infer that birds fly north to reach the tundra in the summer, but this is not stated in the passage. The fourth answer, that the tundra is a beautiful biome, is partially an opinion, and the passage does not state that the tundra is home to diverse communities.

The map below shows the biomes of Australia. Use the map to answer the questions that follow.

Biomes of Australia

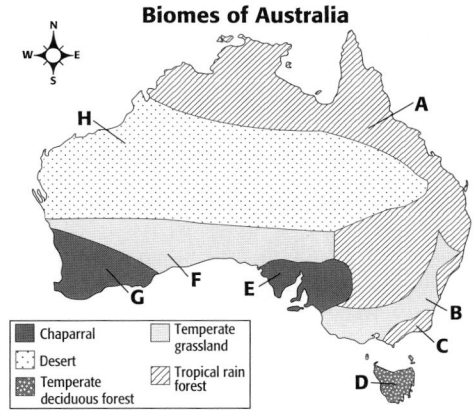

Legend:
- Chaparral
- Desert
- Temperate deciduous forest
- Temperate grassland
- Tropical rain forest

1. Which letters on the map correspond to areas that are chaparral?
   A A and C
   B B and F
   C C and E
   D E and G

2. If you lived in the area marked F, which biome would you live in?
   F desert
   G temperate grassland
   H temperate deciduous forest
   I tropical rain forest

3. If you wanted to live in a forest, which letters correspond to areas where you could live?
   A A, B, and D
   B A, C, and D
   C B, C, and D
   D C, D, and E

4. Which letter corresponds to desert?
   F A
   G D
   H F
   I H

Read each question below, and choose the best answer.

1. Larry wants to buy a glass tabletop for his science lab at home. The glass tabletop is 1 m wide and 2 m long. How many square meters is the surface of the glass tabletop?
   A 2 m
   B 2 m^2
   C 3 m^2
   D 6 m^2

2. A scuba diver was exploring a coral reef. She spent 1.5 h exploring on Friday and spent twice as many hours exploring on Saturday. Which equation could be used to find n, the total number of hours that the scuba diver spent exploring on Friday and Saturday?
   F $n = 2 \div 1.5$
   G $n = 1.5 + (2 \times 1.5)$
   H $n = 1.5 + 1.5 + 2$
   I $n = 2 \times 1.5$

3. How do you express $5 \times 5 \times 5 \times 5 \times 2 \times 2 \times 2$ in exponential notation?
   A $(5 \times 4) + (2 \times 3)$
   B $5^4 \times 2^3$
   C $4^5 \times 3^2$
   D $5^7 \times 2^7$

4. The tropical rain forest receives up to 400 cm of rain per year. The desert receives up to 25 cm of rain per year. Which of the following simplified fractions compares rainfall in the desert to rainfall in the rain forest?
   F 1/400
   G 1/25
   H 1/16
   I 16

Standardized Test Preparation

1. D
2. G
3. B
4. I

✚ TEST DOCTOR

Question 3: On the map, labels A and C correspond to tropical rain forest, label D corresponds to temperate deciduous forest, label B corresponds to temperate grassland, and label E corresponds to chaparral. Temperate grasslands and chaparral are not forest biomes, so labels A, C, and D are the labels that indicate forest biomes on the map.

MATH

1. B
2. G
3. B
4. H

✚ TEST DOCTOR

Question 1: The first answer, 2 m, is incorrect because meters should be squared. Students may have selected the third answer, 3 m^2, if they added the two lengths rather than multiplying them. Students may have selected the fourth answer, 6 m^2, if they calculated the perimeter instead of the area.

Question 2: Answer choice F is incorrect because there is no need to divide in the equation. In answer choice H, 2 and 1.5 should be multiplied to find the time spent diving on Saturday, but they are added. Answer choice I does not include the time spent diving on Friday.

CHAPTER RESOURCES

Chapter Resource File

- Standardized Test Preparation GENERAL

State Resources

For specific resources for your state, visit **go.hrw.com** and type in the keyword **HSMSTR**.

Scientific Debate

ACTiViTy — GENERAL

Invite an ecologist to your classroom to discuss local wetlands. Ask the ecologist to show on a map where local wetlands are located. Also, have the ecologist discuss any pending developments of local wetlands. Afterwards, you may wish to lead students in a debate over whether they support or oppose the proposed developments.

Scientific Discoveries

Background

The first black smoker was found off the Galápagos Islands in 1977. Since then, several black smokers have been found on the floor of the Pacific Ocean. The heat generated by one of these black smokers was so intense that water at the surface was nearly boiling when the chimney was lifted out. While few organisms could survive under such conditions, one species of tubeworm can withstand temperatures up to 80°C (176°F) and some microorganisms can withstand temperatures up to 113°C (235°F)!

Science in Action

Scientific Debate

Developing Wetlands

Wetlands are home to many flowering plants, birds, and turtles. Wetlands also play important roles in flood control and maintaining water quality. However, as more people need homes, grocery stores, and other facilities, some wetlands are being developed for construction. State governments often regulate the development of wetlands. Development is not allowed on many environmentally sensitive wetlands. But it is sometimes allowed on wetlands that are less sensitive. However, some people think that all wetlands should be protected, regardless of how sensitive an area is.

Language Arts ACTiViTy

WRITING SKILL Research wetland development on your own. Then, write a letter in which you describe your opinion about the development of wetlands.

Scientific Discoveries

Ocean Vents

Imagine the deepest parts of the ocean. There is no light at all, and it is very cold. Some of the animals that live here have found a unique place to live—vents on the ocean floor. Water seeps into the Earth between plates on the ocean floor. The water is heated and absorbs sulfuric gases. When the water blasts up through ocean vents, it raises the temperature of the ocean hundreds of degrees! Bacteria use the gases from the ocean vents to survive. In turn, mussels and clams feed on the bacteria. Without ocean vents, it would be much more difficult for these organisms to survive.

Math ACTiViTy

A thermal vent increases the temperature of the water around it to 360°C. If the temperature of the water was 2°C, what is the difference in temperature? By what percentage did the water temperature increase?

Answer to Language Arts Activity

Answers may vary. Accept any response that is well researched, thoughtful, and articulate.

Answer to Math Activity

358°C (360°C − 2°C = 358°C);
17,900% (358°C ÷ 2°C × 100 = 17,900%)

Alfonso Alonso-Mejía

Ecologist During the winter, ecologist Alfonso Alonso-Mejía visits sites in central Mexico where millions of monarch butterflies spend the winter. Unfortunately, the monarchs' winter habitat is threatened by human activity. Only nine of the monarchs' wintering sites remain. Five of the sites are set aside as sanctuaries for monarchs, but these sites are threatened by people who cut down fir trees for firewood or for commercial purposes.

Alonso-Mejía discovered that monarchs depend on understory vegetation, bushlike plants that grow beneath fir trees, to survive. When the temperature is low, monarchs can climb understory vegetation until they are at least 10 cm above the ground. This tiny difference in elevation can ensure that monarchs are warm enough to survive. Because of Alonso-Mejía's discovery, Mexican conservationists are working to protect understory vegetation and monarchs.

Social Studies ACTIVITY

Use your school library or the Internet to research the routes that monarchs use to migrate to Mexico. Draw a map illustrating your findings.

go.hrw.com

To learn more about these Science in Action topics, visit go.hrw.com and type in the keyword HL5ECOF.

Current Science

Check out Current Science® articles related to this chapter by visiting go.hrw.com. Just type in the keyword HL5CS20.

Environmental Problems and Solutions
Chapter Planning Guide

Compression guide:
To shorten instruction because of time limitations, omit the Chapter Lab.

OBJECTIVES	LABS, DEMONSTRATIONS, AND ACTIVITIES	TECHNOLOGY RESOURCES
PACING • 90 min pp. 552–559 **Chapter Opener**	**SE Start-up Activity**, p. 553 (GENERAL)	**OSP Parent Letter** ■ (GENERAL) **CD Student Edition on CD-ROM** **CD Guided Reading Audio CD** ■ **TR Chapter Starter Transparency*** **VID Brain Food Video Quiz**
Section 1 Environmental Problems • List five kinds of pollutants. • Distinguish between renewable and nonrenewable resources. • Describe the impact of exotic species. • Explain why human population growth has increased. • Describe how habitat destruction affects biodiversity. • Give two examples of how pollution affects humans.	**TE Group Activity** Environmental Problems, p. 554 (GENERAL) **SE Connection to Chemistry** Ozone Holes, p. 555 (GENERAL) **TE Connection Activity** Math, p. 555 (GENERAL) **TE Activity** Oil Spills and Seabird Eggs, p. 556 (GENERAL) **SE Connection to Social Studies** Wood, p. 558 (GENERAL)	**CRF Lesson Plans*** **TR Bellringer Transparency*** **TR *LINK TO EARTH SCIENCE*** The Greenhouse Effect*
PACING • 90 min pp. 560–567 **Section 2 Environmental Solutions** • Explain the importance of conservation. • Describe the three Rs. • Explain how biodiversity can be maintained. • List five environmental strategies.	**TE Group Activity** Reusing Trash, p. 560 (GENERAL) **TE Activity** Friendly Cleaner, p. 561 (GENERAL) **TE Connection Activity** Math, p. 561 (BASIC) **TE Demonstration** Reuse and Recycle, p. 562 (BASIC) **TE Connection Activity** Real World, p. 563 (ADVANCED) **TE Connection Activity** Carpentry, p. 565 (GENERAL) **TE Activity** Environmental Protection, p. 565 (GENERAL) **SE Inquiry Lab** Biodiversity—What a Disturbing Thought!, p. 568 (GENERAL) **CRF Datasheet for Chapter Lab*** **SE Science in Action** Math, Social Studies, and Language Arts Activities, pp. 574–575 **SE Skills Practice Lab** Deciding About Environmental Issues, p. 792 (GENERAL) **CRF Datasheet for LabBook*** **LB EcoLabs & Field Activities** A Filter with Culture* (GENERAL) **LB Long-Term Projects & Research Ideas** Let's Talk Trash* (ADVANCED) **LB Calculator-Based Labs** Solar Homes* (ADVANCED)	**CRF Lesson Plans*** **TR Bellringer Transparency*** **TR Conservation*** **VID Lab Videos for Life Science** **CRF SciLinks Activity*** (GENERAL) **CD Interactive Explorations CD-ROM** Moose Malady (GENERAL) **SE Internet Activity**, p. 565 (GENERAL)

PACING • 90 min

CHAPTER REVIEW, ASSESSMENT, AND STANDARDIZED TEST PREPARATION

CRF Vocabulary Activity* (GENERAL)
SE Chapter Review, pp. 570–571 (GENERAL)
CRF Chapter Review* ■ (GENERAL)
CRF Chapter Tests A* ■ (GENERAL), **B*** (ADVANCED), **C*** (SPECIAL NEEDS)
SE Standardized Test Preparation, pp. 572–573 (GENERAL)
CRF Standardized Test Preparation* (GENERAL)
CRF Performance-Based Assessment* (GENERAL)
OSP Test Generator (GENERAL)
CRF Test Item Listing* (GENERAL)

Online and Technology Resources

Visit **go.hrw.com** for a variety of free resources related to this textbook. Enter the keyword **HL5ENV**.

Students can access interactive problem-solving help and active visual concept development with the *Holt Science and Technology* Online Edition available at **www.hrw.com**.

 Guided Reading Audio CD
Also in Spanish

A direct reading of each chapter for auditory learners, reluctant readers, and Spanish-speaking students.

 Science Tutor CD-ROM

Excellent for remediation and test practice.

SKILLS DEVELOPMENT RESOURCES	SECTION REVIEW AND ASSESSMENT	STANDARDS CORRELATIONS
SE Pre-Reading Activity, p. 552 `GENERAL` **OSP** Science Puzzlers, Twisters & Teasers* `GENERAL`		National Science Education Standards SAI 1, 2; ST 2; SPSP 2, 5
CRF Directed Reading A* ■ `BASIC`, B* `SPECIAL NEEDS` **CRF** Vocabulary and Section Summary* ■ `GENERAL` **SE** Reading Strategy Reading Organizer, p. 554 `GENERAL` **TE** Reading Strategy Prediction Guide, p. 555 `GENERAL` **SE** Math Practice Water Depletion, p. 556 `GENERAL` **TE** Inclusion Strategies, p. 557 **MS** Math Skills for Science A Formula for SI Catch-up* `GENERAL` **MS** Math Skills for Science Rain-Forest Math* `GENERAL`	**SE** Reading Checks, pp. 554, 557, 558 `GENERAL` **TE** Reteaching, p. 558 `BASIC` **TE** Quiz, p. 558 `GENERAL` **TE** Alternative Assessment, p. 558 `BASIC` **SE** Section Review,* p. 559 ■ `GENERAL` **CRF** Section Quiz* ■ `GENERAL`	UCP 3; SAI 1, 2; ST 2; SPSP 2, 3, 4, 5; HNS 3; LS 3a, 4d
CRF Directed Reading A* ■ `BASIC`, B* `SPECIAL NEEDS` **CRF** Vocabulary and Section Summary* ■ `GENERAL` **SE** Reading Strategy Discussion, p. 560 `GENERAL` **TE** Inclusion Strategies, p. 563 **TE** Reading Strategy Prediction Guide, p. 563 `GENERAL` **CRF** Reinforcement Worksheet It's "R" Planet!* `BASIC` **CRF** Critical Thinking Dave Goodman Has a Plan* `ADVANCED`	**SE** Reading Checks, pp. 560, 562, 565 `GENERAL` **TE** Homework, p. 565 `ADVANCED` **TE** Reteaching, p. 566 `BASIC` **TE** Quiz, p. 566 `GENERAL` **TE** Alternative Assessment, p. 566 `GENERAL` **SE** Section Review,* p. 567 ■ `GENERAL` **CRF** Section Quiz* ■ `GENERAL`	UCP 2, 3, 4; SAI 1; ST 2; SPSP 2, 4, 5; HNS 2; LS 5c; *LabBook:* UCP 1, 3; SAI 1, 2; SPSP 2; LS 4a, 4b, 4c, 4d; *Chapter Lab:* UCP 1, 2, 3; SAI 1, 2; ST 1, 2; SPSP 2; HNS 1

One-Stop Planner® CD-ROM

This convenient CD-ROM includes:
- Lab Materials QuickList Software
- Holt Calendar Planner
- Customizable Lesson Plans
- Printable Worksheets
- ExamView® Test Generator

cnnstudentnews.com

Find the latest news, lesson plans, and activities related to important scientific events.

NSTA

www.scilinks.org

Maintained by the **National Science Teachers Association.** See Chapter Enrichment pages for a complete list of topics.

Current Science®

Check out *Current Science* articles and activities by visiting the HRW Web site at **go.hrw.com.** Just type in the keyword **HL5CS21T**.

 Classroom Videos
- **Lab Videos** demonstrate the chapter lab.
- **Brain Food Video Quizzes** help students review the chapter material.
- **CNN Videos** bring science into your students' daily life.

Visual Resources

CHAPTER STARTER TRANSPARENCY

Imagine . . .

Fifteen-year-old Haifa Aldonasi loves science and is concerned about the environment. She knows that today's paper is made by cutting down trees, making them into a pulp, and adding chemicals. Haifa is also fascinated by American history. She knows that the colonists made paper from linen and cotton rags. Their paper had no ink, yet some of it is still in good condition today. Haifa knows that today's paper will not last nearly as long as the colonists' paper did.

At age 15, Haifa put her knowledge of history, her love of science, and her concern about the environment together with a variety of vegetables, two years of research and experiments, and a whole lot of patience. The result? Haifa

produced good-quality paper without cutting a single branch from a tree or using a single chemical. Her paper will last for centuries.

Haifa hasn't stopped her research. Hoping to develop a process that can be used to manufacture large amounts of paper without cutting any trees, she continues to perfect her technique. She hopes to eventually present her product to major companies. In the meantime, Haifa sells a papermaking kit she developed so that other people can make a good quality paper without using wood or chemicals.

In this chapter, you will learn about some environmental problems and what you can do to help, including making your own paper!

BELLRINGER TRANSPARENCIES

Section: Environmental Problems
What is the difference between a renewable resource and a nonrenewable resource? What nonrenewable resources do you use? Could you use a renewable resource in place of any of these nonrenewable resources?

Write your answers in your **science journal.**

Section: Environmental Solutions
Imagine that you have just finished reading a magazine. Write down at least two things you can do with the magazine that would be preferable to throwing it in the trash.

Write your responses in your **science journal.**

TEACHING TRANSPARENCIES

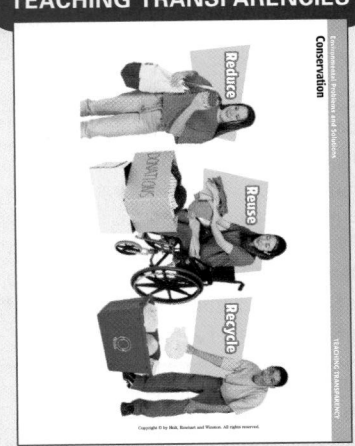

TEACHING TRANSPARENCIES

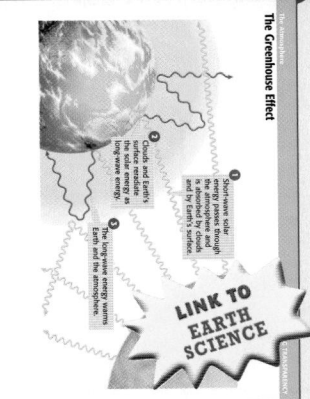

Chapter: The Atmosphere

CONCEPT MAPPING TRANSPARENCY

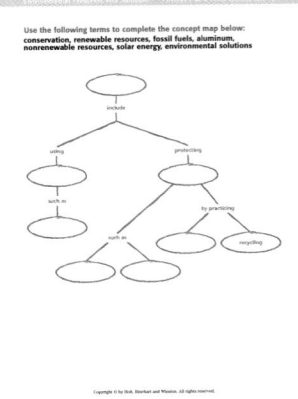

Use the following terms to complete the concept map below: **conservation, renewable resources, fossil fuels, aluminum, nonrenewable resources, solar energy, environmental solutions**

Planning Resources

LESSON PLANS

Lesson Plan   SAMPLE

Section: Waves

Pacing
Regular Schedule: with lab(s):2 days   without lab(s):1 days
Block Schedule: with lab(s):1 1/2 days without lab(s):1 day

Objectives
1. Relate the seven properties of life to a living organism.
2. Describe seven themes that can help you to organize what you learn about biology.
3. Identify the tiny structures that make up all living organisms.
4. Differentiate between reproduction and heredity and between metabolism and homeostasis.

National Science Education Standards Covered
LSInter6:Cells have particular structures that underlie their functions.
LSMat1:Most cell functions involve chemical reactions.
LSBeh1:Cells store and use information to guide their functions.
UCP1:Cell functions are regulated.
SI1: Cells can differentiate and form complete multicellular organisms.
PS1:Species evolve over time.
ESS1: The great diversity of organisms is the result of more than 3.5 billion years of evolution.
ESS2: Natural selection and its evolutionary consequences provide a scientific explanation for the fossil record of ancient life forms as well as for the striking molecular similarities observed among the diverse species of living organisms.
ST1: The millions of different species of plants, animals, and microorganisms that live on Earth today are related by descent from common ancestors.
ST2: The energy for life primarily comes from the sun.
SPSP1: The complexity and organization of organisms accommodates the need for obtaining, transforming, transporting, releasing, and eliminating the matter and energy used to sustain the organism.
SPSP6: As matter and energy flows through different levels of organization of living systems—cells, organs, communities—and between living systems and the physical environment, chemical elements are recombined in different ways.
HNS1: Organisms have behavioral responses to internal changes and to external stimuli.

PARENT LETTER

SAMPLE

Dear Parent,

Your son's or daughter's science class will soon begin exploring the chapter entitled "The World of Physical Science." In this chapter, students will learn about how the scientific method applies to the world of physical science and the role of physical science in the world. By the end of the chapter, students should demonstrate a clear understanding of the chapter's main ideas and be able to discuss the following topics:

1. physical science as the study of energy and matter (Section 1)
2. the role of physical science in the world around them (Section 1)
3. careers that rely on physical science (Section 1)
4. the steps used in the scientific method (Section 2)
5. examples of technology (Section 2)
6. how the scientific method is used to answer questions and solve problems (Section 2)
7. how our knowledge of science changes over time (Section 2)
8. how models represent real objects or systems (Section 3)
9. examples of different ways models are used in science (Section 3)
10. the importance of the International System of Units (Section 4)
11. the appropriate units to use for particular measurements (Section 4)
12. how area and density are derived quantities (Section 4)

Questions to Ask Along the Way

You can help your son or daughter learn about these topics by asking interesting questions such as the following:

• What are some surprising careers that use physical science?
• What is a characteristic of a good hypothesis?
• When is it a good idea to use a model?
• Why do Americans measure things in terms of inches and yards and meters ?

ALSO IN SPANISH

TEST ITEM LISTING

TEST ITEM LISTING
The World of Science   SAMPLE

MULTIPLE CHOICE
1. A limitation of models is that
   a. they are large enough to see.
   b. they do not act exactly like the things that they model.
   c. they are smaller than the things that they model.
   d. they model unfamiliar things.
   Answer: B   Difficulty: 1   Section: 3   Objective: 2

2. The length 10 m is equal to
   a. 100 cm.   c. 10,000 mm.
   b. 1,000 cm.   d. Both (b) and (c)
   Answer: B   Difficulty: 1   Section: 3   Objective: 2

3. To be valid, a hypothesis must be
   a. testable.   c. made into a law.
   b. supported by evidence. d. Both (a) and (b)
   Answer: D   Difficulty: 3   Section: 3   Objective: 2

4. The statement "Sheila has a stain on her shirt" is an example of a(n)
   a. law.   c. observation.
   b. hypothesis.   d. prediction.
   Answer: B   Difficulty: 1   Section: 3   Objective: 2

5. A hypothesis is often developed out of
   a. observations.   c. laws.
   b. experiments.   d. Both (a) and (b)
   Answer: B   Difficulty: 1   Section: 3   Objective: 2

6. How many milliliters are in 3.5 kL?
   a. 3,500 mL.   c. 3,500, 000 mL.
   b. 0.0035 mL.   d. 35,000 mL.
   Answer: B   Difficulty: 1   Section: 3   Objective: 2

7. A map of Seattle is an example of a
   a. law.   c. model.
   b. theory.   d. unit.
   Answer: B   Difficulty: 1   Section: 3   Objective: 2

8. A lab has the safety icons shown below. These icons mean that you should wear
   a. only safety goggles.   c. safety goggles and a lab apron.
   b. only a lab apron.   d. safety goggles, a lab apron, and gloves.
   Answer: B   Difficulty: 1   Section: 3   Objective: 2

9. The law of conservation of mass says the tot al mass before a chemical change is
   a. more than the total mass after the change.
   b. less than the total mass after the change.
   c. the same as the total mass after the change.
   d. not the same as the total mass after the change.
   Answer: B   Difficulty: 1   Section: 3   Objective: 2

10. In which of the following areas might you find a geochemist at work?
    a. studying the chemistry of rocks   c. studying fishes
    b. studying forestry   d. studying the atmosphere
    Answer: B   Difficulty: 1   Section: 3   Objective: 2

One-Stop Planner® CD-ROM

This CD-ROM includes all of the resources shown here and the following time-saving tools:

• *Lab Materials QuickList Software*
• *Customizable lesson plans*
• *Holt Calendar Planner*
• *The powerful ExamView® Test Generator*

Meeting Individual Needs

DIRECTED READING A
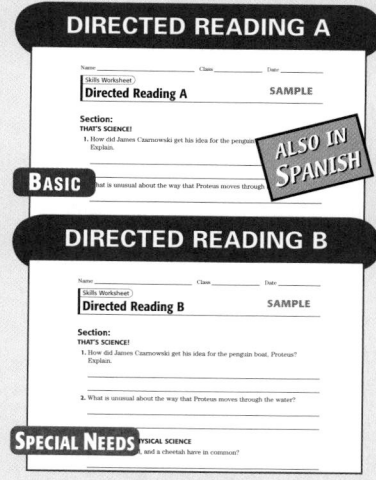
BASIC

DIRECTED READING B
SPECIAL NEEDS

VOCABULARY ACTIVITY
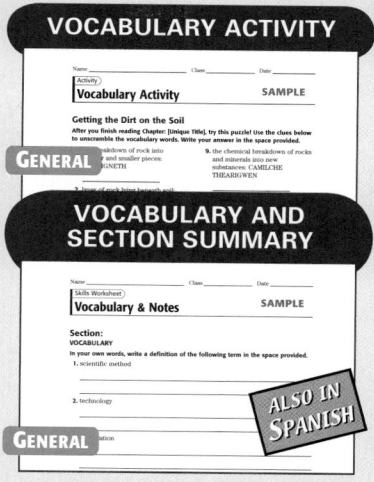
GENERAL

VOCABULARY AND SECTION SUMMARY
GENERAL

REINFORCEMENT
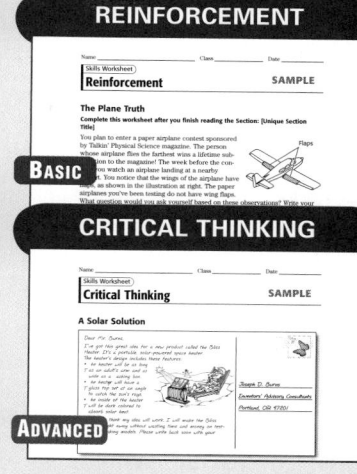
BASIC

CRITICAL THINKING
ADVANCED

SCILINKS ACTIVITY

GENERAL

SCIENCE PUZZLERS, TWISTERS & TEASERS
GENERAL

Labs and Activities

ECOLABS & FIELD ACTIVITIES
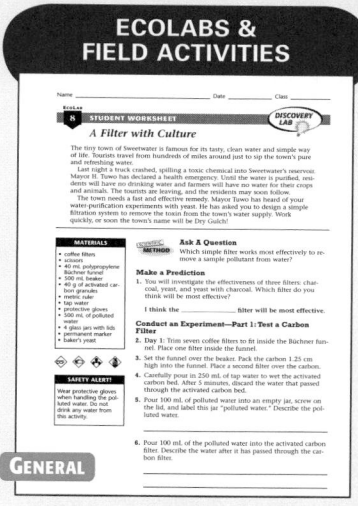
GENERAL

LONG-TERM PROJECTS & RESEARCH IDEAS
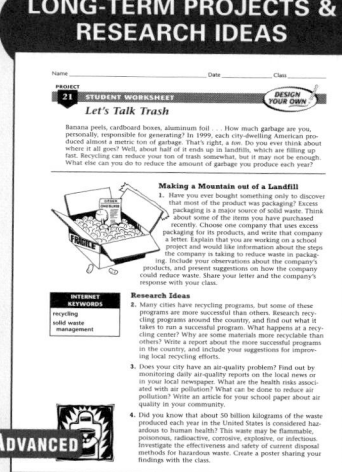
ADVANCED

CALCULATOR-BASED LABS
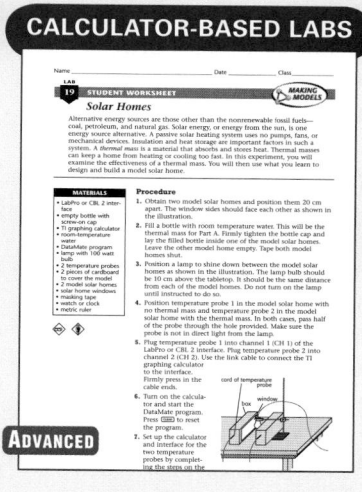
ADVANCED

DATASHEETS FOR CHAPTER LABS

DATASHEETS FOR LABBOOK

Review and Assessments

SECTION QUIZ
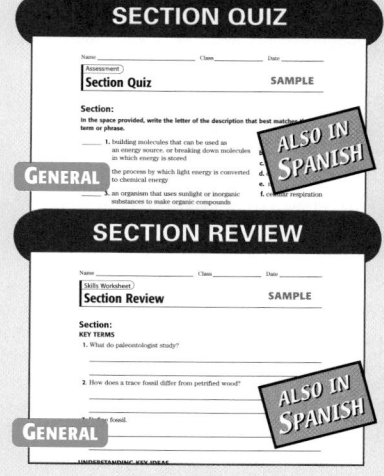
GENERAL

SECTION REVIEW
GENERAL

CHAPTER REVIEW
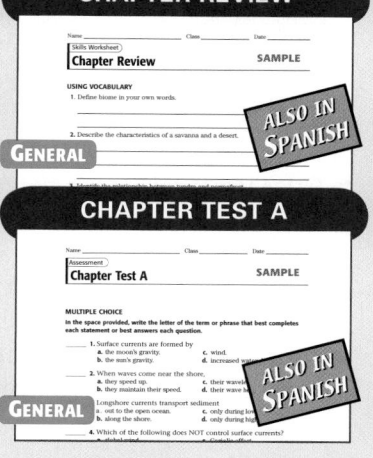
GENERAL

CHAPTER TEST A
GENERAL

CHAPTER TEST B
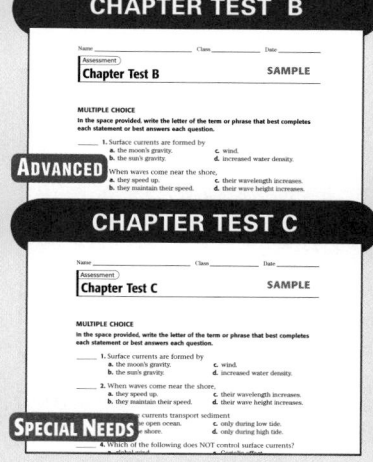
ADVANCED

CHAPTER TEST C
SPECIAL NEEDS

STANDARDIZED TEST PREPARATION
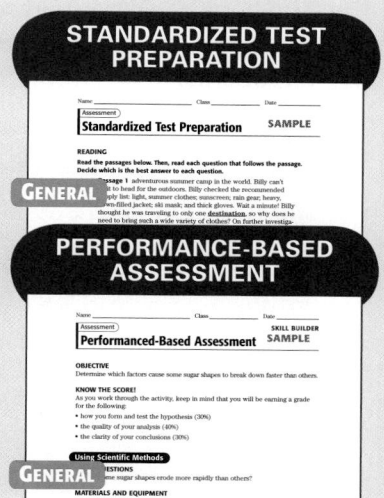
GENERAL

PERFORMANCE-BASED ASSESSMENT
GENERAL

This Chapter Enrichment provides relevant and interesting information to expand and enhance your presentation of the chapter material.

Section 1

Environmental Problems

Rachel Carson (1907–1964)

- Rachel Carson was an American biologist and environmentalist. In 1932, she received a master's degree from Johns Hopkins University, and she later worked as an aquatic biologist with the U.S. Bureau of Fisheries. In 1941, she published her first book, *Under the Sea-Wind*. Her second book, *The Sea Around Us*, was published in 1951 and was extremely well received. It became a bestseller, won the National Book Award, and established Carson as an outstanding science writer.

- Carson was apprehensive about the use of the pesticide DDT as early as 1945, but at that time, few other people shared her concern. By the late 1950s, DDT use had increased enormously. It was routinely used to kill crop pests and mosquitoes, but unfortunately it killed nontargeted animals, such as birds, fish, crabs, grasshoppers, and bees.

- Carson began to research pesticides and found alarming evidence that pesticides contaminated soil, water, and air; that pesticides became increasingly concentrated as they moved up the food chain; and that such chemicals are so stable that they persist as toxins for a very long time. In the meantime, chemical companies were zealously promoting the success of pesticides such as DDT. Carson compiled her evidence against chemical pesticides in her book *Silent Spring* (1962). The book's release sparked an immediate controversy. Chemical companies were Carson's most vociferous opponents.

- Many scientists, however, praised Carson's book. The American public took Carson's warnings to heart, and by the end of 1962, more than 40 bills concerning pesticide regulation had been introduced in state legislatures. The formation of the Environmental Protection Agency in 1970 was due partly to Carson's efforts. The United States began to phase out the use of DDT in 1972.

Is That a Fact!

◆ Upon the release of *Silent Spring*, representatives of chemical manufacturers did not shrink from attacking Carson personally. Carson was accused of being a "high priestess of nature," and her book was said to be part of a "communist plot" to destroy the economies of noncommunist countries.

Problems with Landfills

- Landfills take up valuable land, smell bad, and attract pests. Landfills are responsible for a host of less obvious but equally troublesome problems as well. Decades ago, little thought was given to landfills. They were established wherever cheap or seemingly useless land existed. For years, household trash—some of which contained toxic chemicals—was plowed into landfills.

- Over time, rainwater percolated through the mountains of garbage and picked up dissolved metals and chemical and bacterial wastes. This rainwater forms a poisonous concoction known as *leachate*. Leachate can seep into groundwater. Eventually, leachate can contaminate drinking water. Today, landfills are lined with clay or plastic to keep leachate from reaching groundwater.

Section 2

Environmental Solutions

John Muir (1838–1914)

- Scottish-born naturalist John Muir is often considered the father of the conservation movement in the United States. When Muir was 11, he and his family moved to the United States and settled on a farm in Wisconsin. In 1867, Muir set out to walk from Indianapolis to the Gulf of Mexico, an experience he described in his classic book, *A Thousand-Mile Walk to the Gulf* (1916). The walk was a turning point in Muir's life. He moved to Yosemite Valley in California and devoted himself to the study of the wilderness areas of the West.

- Muir wrote a number of natural-history articles for national magazines. In 1876, he proposed to the federal government that it take measures to preserve forests. His efforts facilitated the establishment of Sequoia National Park and Yosemite National Park in 1890.

- Two years later, Muir founded the Sierra Club, whose purpose was to "explore, enjoy, and render accessible the mountain regions of the Pacific Coast." Today, the Sierra Club is a national organization whose goals have broadened to include advocating the responsible use, protection, and restoration of the world's ecosystems.

A Heritage of Reuse and Recycling

- Before the 1950s in the United States, recycling and reuse were routine practices. Relatively few disposable items existed, and most products were not wrapped and sealed in layers of packaging. A few items, such as sugar and flour, were packaged, but people reused the large cotton sacks in which those items came. Some of the sacks had decorative prints, which encouraged people to use the sacks for clothing.

Reuse   Recycle

Is That a Fact!

◆ In 1955, *Life* magazine published an article that described the new "throwaway" lifestyle and how it liberated Americans from tedious cleanup chores. Among the noteworthy items that the article highlighted were disposable curtains, hunting decoys, and barbecue grills.

◆ The conventional recycling of paper uses harsh de-inking chemicals and requires that the paper be repulped and reprocessed into new paper. Most paper can be recycled only about three times before its cellulose fibers lose their integrity. In 1996, a mechanical engineer named Sameer Madanshetty devised a very gentle, chemical-free de-inking method that uses focused sound waves to "explode" ink off of paper. When paper is placed in water, tiny bubbles form around the inked portions of the paper. Sound waves directed at the bubbles blast the bubbles and remove the ink, which can then be filtered out of the water. The paper itself is undamaged and can be dried and reused repeatedly.

SciLinks is maintained by the National Science Teachers Association to provide you and your students with interesting, up-to-date links that will enrich your classroom presentation of the chapter.

Visit www.scilinks.org and enter the SciLinks code for more information about the topic listed.

Topic: Air Pollution
SciLinks code: HSM0033

Topic: Recycling
SciLinks code: HSM1277

Topic: Resource Depletion
SciLinks code: HSM1304

Topic: Maintaining Biodiversity
SciLinks code: HSM0902

Overview

Tell students that this chapter will help them learn about environmental problems and environmental solutions. Students will learn about how human activity has affected the environment and how people are dealing with these effects.

Assessing Prior Knowledge

Students should be familiar with the following topics:

• interactions of living things
• cycles in nature
• ecosystems

Identifying Misconceptions

As students learn about environmental problems, they may come to the conclusion that humans cause all environmental problems. However, students should recognize that while humans are largely responsible for environmental problems, natural events can contribute to environmental problems. Natural events, such as volcanic eruptions, storms, earthquakes, and landslides, can cause air pollution and habitat destruction.

21

Environmental Problems and Solutions

About the PHOTO

After an oil spill, volunteers try to capture oil-covered penguins. The oil affects the penguins' ability to float. So, oil-covered penguins often won't go into the water to get food. The penguins may also swallow oil, harming their stomach, kidneys, and lungs. Once captured, the penguins are fed activated charcoal. The charcoal helps the penguins get rid of any oil they have swallowed. Then, the birds are washed to remove oil from their feathers.

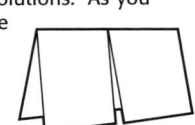 **Two-Panel Flip Chart**
Before you read the chapter, create the FoldNote entitled "Two-Panel Flip Chart" described in the **Study Skills** section of the Appendix. Label the flaps of the two-panel flip chart with "Environmental problems" and "Environmental solutions." As you read the chapter, write information you learn about each category under the appropriate flap.

Standards Correlations

National Science Education Standards

The following codes indicate the National Science Education Standards that correlate to this chapter. The full text of the standards is at the front of the book.

Chapter Opener
SAI 1, 2; ST 2; SPSP 2, 5

Section 1 Environmental Problems
UCP 3; SAI 1, 2; ST 2; SPSP 2, 3, 4, 5; HNS 3; LS 3a, 4d

Section 2 Environmental Solutions
UCP 2, 3, 4; SAI 1; ST 2; SPSP 2, 4, 5; HNS 2; LS 5c;
LabBook: UCP 1, 3; SAI 1, 2; SPSP 2; LS 4a, 4b, 4c, 4d

Chapter Lab
UCP 1, 2, 3; SAI 1, 2; ST 1, 2; SPSP 2; HNS 1

Chapter Review
UCP 2, 3, 4; SAI 1, 2; ST 2; SPSP 2, 3, 4, 5; HNS 2, 3;
LS 3a, 4d, 5c

Science in Action
ST 1, 2; SPSP 1, 2, 5; HNS 1, 2, 3

START-UP ACTIVITY

Recycling Paper

In this activity, you will be making paper without cutting down trees. You will be reusing paper that has already been made.

Procedure

1. Tear **two sheets of old newspaper** into small pieces, and put them in a **blender**. Add **1 L of water.** Cover and blend until the mixture is soupy.

2. Fill a **square pan** with **water** to a depth of 2 cm to 3 cm. Place a **wire screen** in the pan. Pour 250 mL of the paper mixture onto the screen, and spread the mixture evenly.

3. Lift the screen out of the water with the paper on it. Drain excess water into the pan.

4. Place the screen inside a **section of newspaper.** Close the newspaper, and turn it over so that the screen is on top of the paper mixture.

5. Cover the newspaper with a **flat board.** Press on the board to squeeze out excess water.

6. Open the newspaper, and let your paper mixture dry overnight. Use your recycled paper to write a note to a friend!

Analysis

1. How is your paper like regular paper? How is it different?

2. What could you do to improve your papermaking methods?

START-UP ACTIVITY
MATERIALS

FOR EACH GROUP
- blender
- board, flat
- newspaper (2 sheets and 1 section)
- pan, square
- water
- wire screen

Safety Caution: Cover all work surfaces, and have students wear aprons or smocks to protect their clothing. Tell students to wipe up any spills right away.

Teacher's Notes: Students are supposed to let their paper dry overnight, but the paper may need additional time to dry, depending on how warm and moist the air in your classroom is. To ensure the quickest drying time, students should squeeze as much excess water out of the paper as they can.

Answers

1. Sample answer: My paper looks similar to regular paper, and both regular paper and my paper can be used for writing or drawing. The handmade paper is not as smooth as regular paper, is easier to tear than regular paper, and is thicker than regular paper.

2. Answers may vary. Some students might suggest using less water or squeezing more water out of the mixture.

Imagine . . .

Fifteen-year-old Haifa Aldorasi loves science and is concerned about the environment. She knows that today's paper is made by cutting down trees, making them into a pulp, and adding chemicals. Haifa is also fascinated by American history. She knows that the colonists made paper from linen and cotton rags. Their paper had no chemicals, yet some of it is still in good condition today. Haifa knows that today's paper will not last nearly as long as the colonists' paper did.

At age 13, Haifa put her knowledge of history, her love of science, and her concern about the environment together with a variety of vegetables, two years of research and experiments, and a whole lot of patience. The result? Haifa produced good-quality paper without cutting a single branch from a tree or using a single chemical. Her paper will last for centuries.

Haifa hasn't stopped her research. Hoping to develop a process that can be used to manufacture large amounts of paper without cutting any trees, she continues to perfect her technique. She hopes to eventually present her product to major paper companies. In the meantime, Haifa sells a papermaking kit she developed so that other people can make a good quality paper without using wood or chemicals.

In this chapter, you will learn about some environmental problems and what you can do to help, including making your own paper!

Chapter Starter Transparency
Use this transparency to help students begin thinking about the environment.

CHAPTER RESOURCES

Technology

 Transparencies
- Chapter Starter Transparency

READING SKILLS

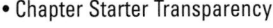 **Student Edition on CD-ROM**

 Guided Reading Audio CD
- English or Spanish

 **Classroom Videos**
- Brain Food Video Quiz

Workbooks

 Science Puzzlers, Twisters & Teasers
- Environmental Problems and Solutions GENERAL

Chapter 21 • Environmental Problems and Solutions 553

Focus

Overview

In this section, students will learn about five types of pollutants. Students also distinguish between renewable and non-renewable resources and explore how increases in human population and human activities affect the environment.

 Bellringer

Ask students the following question: "What is the difference between a renewable resource and a nonrenewable resource?" (Sample answer: A renewable resource can be used over and over or has an unlimited supply. A non-renewable resource cannot be replaced or can be replaced only over thousands or millions of years.)

Motivate

Group ACTIVITY — GENERAL

Environmental Problems Have students work in groups of four to come up with a list of environmental problems. Have groups pick from that list the four problems that they think are most important, and have the groups explain why they think that these problems are important. **LS Verbal**

READING WARM-UP

Objectives

● List five kinds of pollutants.
● Distinguish between renewable and nonrenewable resources.
● Describe the impact of exotic species.
● Explain why human population growth has increased.
● Describe how habitat destruction affects biodiversity.
● Give two examples of how pollution affects humans.

Terms to Learn

pollution · overpopulation
renewable · biodiversity
 resource
nonrenewable
 resource

READING STRATEGY

Reading Organizer As you read this section, make a concept map by using the terms above.

---

pollution an unwanted change in the environment caused by substances or forms of energy

---

Figure 1 *Every year, Americans throw away about 200 million metric tons of garbage.*

Environmental Problems

Maybe you've heard warnings about dirty air, water, and soil. Or you've heard about the destruction of rain forests. Do these warnings mean our environment is in trouble?

In the late 1700s, the Industrial Revolution began. People started to rely more and more on machines. As a result, more harmful substances entered the air, water, and soil.

Pollution

Today, machines don't produce as much pollution as they once did. But there are more sources of pollution today than there once were. **Pollution** is an unwanted change in the environment caused by substances, such as wastes, or forms of energy, such as radiation. Anything that causes pollution is called a *pollutant*. Some pollutants are produced by natural events, such as volcanic eruptions. Many pollutants are human-made. Pollutants may harm plants, animals, and humans.

Garbage

The average American throws away more trash than the average person in any other nation—about 12 kg of trash a week. This trash often goes to a landfill like the one in **Figure 1.** Other landfills contain medical waste, lead paint, and other hazardous wastes. *Hazardous waste* includes wastes that can catch fire; corrode, or eat through metal; explode; or make people sick. Many industries, such as paper mills and oil refineries, produce hazardous wastes.

✓ **Reading Check** What is hazardous waste? (*See the Appendix for answers to Reading Checks.*)

CHAPTER RESOURCES

Chapter Resource File

• Lesson Plan
• Directed Reading A **BASIC**
• Directed Reading B **SPECIAL NEEDS**

Technology

Transparencies
• Bellringer
• *LINK TO EARTH SCIENCE* The Greenhouse Effect

Answer to Reading Check

Sample answer: Hazardous waste is waste that can catch fire, wear through metal, explode, or make people sick.

Figure 2 *Fertilizer promotes the growth of algae. As dead algae decompose, oxygen in the water is used up. So, fish die because they cannot get oxygen.*

Chemicals

People need and use many chemicals. Some chemicals are used to treat diseases. Other chemicals are used in plastics and preserved foods. Sometimes, the same chemicals that help people may harm the environment. As shown in **Figure 2,** fertilizers and pesticides may pollute soil and water.

CFCs and PCBs are two groups of harmful chemicals. Ozone protects Earth from harmful ultraviolet light. CFCs destroy ozone. CFCs were used in aerosols, refrigerators, and plastics. The second group, PCBs, was once used in appliances and paints. PCBs are poisonous and may cause cancer. Today, the use of CFCs and PCBs is banned. But CFCs are still found in the atmosphere. And PCBs are still found in even the most remote areas on Earth.

High-Powered Wastes

Nuclear power plants provide electricity to many homes and businesses. The plants also produce radioactive wastes. *Radioactive wastes* are hazardous wastes that give off radiation. Some of these wastes take thousands of years to become harmless.

Gases

Earth's atmosphere is made up of a mixture of gases, including carbon dioxide. The atmosphere acts as a protective blanket. It keeps Earth warm enough for life to exist. Since the Industrial Revolution, however, the amount of carbon dioxide in the atmosphere has increased. Carbon dioxide and other air pollutants act like a greenhouse, trapping heat around the Earth. Many scientists think the increase in carbon dioxide has increased global temperatures. If temperatures continue to rise, the polar icecaps could melt. Then, the level of the world's oceans would rise. Coastal areas could flood as a result.

CONNECTION TO Chemistry

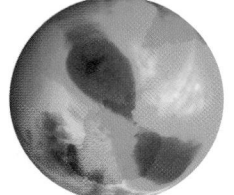

Ozone Holes This image of two holes in the ozone layer (the purple areas over Antarctica) was taken in 2002. Ozone in the stratosphere absorbs most of the ultraviolet light that comes from the sun. Ozone is destroyed by CFCs. Research how CFCs destroy ozone. Make a model demonstrating this process. Then, identify the effects of too much ultraviolet light.

ACTiViTY

Answer to Connection to Chemistry

Students should recognize that CFCs interfere with the bonds between the oxygen atoms in ozone, O_3. The ozone breaks down into oxygen gas, O_2. Students should also recognize that too much UV light can cause skin cancer and can damage plants. Some students may have the misconception that the ozone hole is responsible for global warming. However, greenhouse gases are responsible for a possible increase in global temperatures. Also, emphasize to students that although stratospheric ozone protects Earth, ozone near Earth's surface is considered pollution.

CONNECTION Math **ACTiViTY** — GENERAL

Carbon Dioxide Ask students the following question: "On average, for each 1.6 km (1 mi) a car travels, 0.4 kg (0.9 lb) of carbon dioxide is added to the atmosphere. If the average trip to work is 18 km (11.2 mi), how much carbon dioxide is added to the air per trip?" (18 km ÷ 1.6 km = 11.25; 11.25 × 0.4 kg = 4.5 kg CO_2 per trip) **LS Logical**

📖 **READING STRATEGY** — GENERAL

Prediction Guide Before students begin to read the section, ask them whether the following statements are true or false.

• The average American produces more garbage than the average citizen of any other nation in the world does. (true)

• Noise can be a form of pollution. (true)

• All natural resources can be reused. (false)

• The destruction of animal habitats has a negative effect on animals but no effect on humans. (false)

LS Verbal

CONNECTION to Earth Science — GENERAL

The Greenhouse Effect About 20% of the radiation that enters Earth's atmosphere is absorbed by certain atmospheric gases, such as CO_2, and is transferred to the rest of Earth's atmosphere and to Earth's surface in the form of heat. But these gases can capture heat in other ways. When land and water absorb radiation, the molecules in them move faster, increasing the temperature of land and water. This energy is transferred to gas molecules in the atmosphere before the energy can escape into space. As a result, the atmosphere warms. Earth's heating process, in which gases in the atmosphere absorb radiation and transfer the energy in the form of heat, is known as the *greenhouse effect.* Earth's atmosphere works much like a greenhouse, as shown in the teaching transparency titled "The Greenhouse Effect." Ask interested students to research how excess CO_2 contributes to the greenhouse effect. Have them present their findings to the class. **LS Visual/Verbal**

Teach, continued

MATERIALS

FOR EACH GROUP
• bowl
• egg, hardboiled (4)
• gloves, protective
• oil, vegetable, colored with oil-soluble red food coloring (250 mL)

Oil Spills and Seabird Eggs

Have students work in groups of four. Tell students to put eggs in a bowl filled with 250 mL of vegetable oil that has been dyed with oil-soluble red food coloring. (You can color vegetable oil by adding powdered food coloring for cake decorating, which is available from hobby stores, to the oil or by simmering 0.5 cup of annatto seeds, which are available from natural foods stores, in a cup of vegetable oil for 10 min.) Students should remove one egg from the bowl every 5 min, and shell the egg. Have students record how much time elapses before a shelled egg shows red coloring, which indicates that the oil has permeated the shell. Have students draw conclusions about how oil spills might affect unborn seabirds and seabird populations. (Sample answer: The oil might kill developing birds or might interfere with their development. The birds' chance of survival would be compromised. The survival of seabird species could be threatened if fewer birds survive to reproduce.)
LS Kinesthetic English Language Learners

Water Depletion

In one day, millions of liters of water are removed from a water supply. Of this volume, 30 million liters cannot be replaced naturally. Today, the water supply has 60 billion liters of water. In years, how long would the water supply last if water continued to be removed at this rate? If water were removed at the same rate as it was replaced, how long would the water supply last?

renewable resource a natural resource that can be replaced at the same rate at which the resource is consumed

nonrenewable resource a resource that forms at a rate that is much slower than the rate at which it is consumed

Figure 3 *This area has been mined for iron using a method called* strip mining.

Noise

Some pollutants affect the senses. These pollutants include loud noises. Too much noise is not just annoying. Noise pollution affects your ability to hear and think clearly. And it may damage your hearing. People who work in noisy environments, such as in construction zones, must protect their ears.

Resource Depletion

Some of Earth's resources are renewable. But other resources are nonrenewable. A **renewable resource** is one that can be used over and over or has an unlimited supply. Solar and wind energy are renewable resources, as are some kinds of trees. A **nonrenewable resource** is one that cannot be replaced or that can be replaced only over thousands or millions of years. Most minerals and fossil fuels, such as oil and coal, are nonrenewable resources.

Nonrenewable resources cannot last forever. These resources will become more expensive as they become harder to find. The removal of some materials from the Earth also carries a high price tag. This removal may lead to oil spills, loss of habitat, and damage from mining, as shown in **Figure 3**.

Renewable or Nonrenewable?

Some resources once thought to be renewable are becoming nonrenewable. For example, scientists used to think that fresh water was a renewable resource. However, in some areas, water supplies are being used faster than they are being replaced. Eventually, these areas may run out of fresh water. So, scientists are working on ways to keep these water supplies from being used up.

Answers to Math Practice

5.5 years (60,000,000,000 L ÷ 30,000,000 L/day = 2,000 days; 2,000 days ÷ 365 days/year = 5.5 years)
If the water were removed at the same rate as it was replaced, the water supply would last forever.

MISCONCEPTION ALERT

Tropical Rain Forests Although rain forests are lush, their soil contains very few nutrients. When organisms die in a rain forest, they decompose quickly and the nutrients that are released by this decomposition are quickly taken up by other organisms.

Exotic Species

People are always on the move. Without knowing it, people carry other species with them. Plant seeds, animal eggs, and adult organisms are carried from one part of the world to another. An organism that makes a home for itself in a new place outside its native home is an *exotic species.* Exotic species often thrive in new places. One reason is that they are free from the predators found in their native homes.

Exotic species can become pests and compete with native species. In 2002, the northern snakehead fish was found in a Maryland pond. This fish, shown in **Figure 4,** is from Asia. Scientists are concerned because the northern snakehead eats other fish, amphibians, small birds, and some mammals. It can also move across land. The northern snakehead could invade more lakes and ponds.

✓ Reading Check What are exotic species?

Human Population Growth

Look at **Figure 5.** In 1800, there were 1 billion people on Earth. By 2000, there were more than 6 billion people. Advances in medicine, such as immunizations, and advances in farming have made human population growth possible. Overall, these advances are beneficial. But some people argue that there may eventually be too many people on Earth. **Overpopulation** happens when the number of individuals becomes so large that the individuals can't get the resources they need to survive. However, many scientists think that human population growth will slow down or level off before it reaches that point.

Figure 4 *Northern snakehead fish can move across land in search of water. These fish can survive out of water for up to four days!*

overpopulation the presence of too many individuals in an area for the available resources

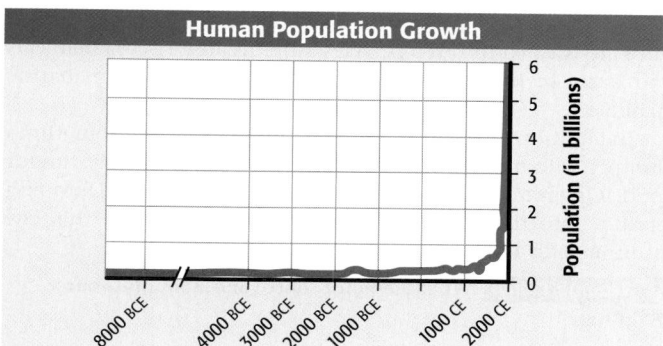

Human Population Growth

Figure 5 *Recently, the human population has been doubling every few decades.*

Is That a Fact!

During the 1930s, soil conservationists in the southern United States recommended planting kudzu to hold soil in place. This vine is native to Asia, where frosts keep its growth in check. In the South, frosts are infrequent. By the 1960s, kudzu had spread throughout the South. Eradicating the vine is difficult. A single plant may have 50 or more vines attached to a giant root, which can weigh as much as 181 kg!

Answer to Reading Check

Exotic species are organisms that make a home for themselves in a new place.

Section 1 • Environmental Problems **557**

Pollution Ask students to make tables describing five pollutants, including how each pollutant affects the environment. Then, ask students to relate what they know about resources, exotic species, overpopulation, and habitat destruction. **LS** Verbal

Quiz — GENERAL

1. Why is hazardous waste dangerous? (Hazardous waste can catch fire, wear through metal, explode, or make people sick.)

2. Why is coal considered a nonrenewable resource? (Coal is a nonrenewable resource because coal can be replaced only after millions of years.)

3. What are two ways that pollution can harm people? (Sample answer: Polluted air affects people who have respiratory problems. Drinking polluted water can make people sick.)

Alternative Assessment — BASIC

Future Pollution Have students draw a picture of what their community might look like in the year 2100 if pollution and habitat destruction happen at a rapid rate. Then, have students draw a picture of their community in the year 2100 if pollution and habitat destruction are prevented. **LS** Visual/Kinesthetic   English Language Learners

Figure 6 *Deforestation can leave soil exposed to erosion.*

biodiversity the number and variety of organisms in a given area during a specific period of time

CONNECTION TO Social Studies

Wood Identify a country that is a major exporter of wood. List some of the ways this wood is used. Research the impact this exportation is having on that country's forests. Make a poster describing your findings.

ACTIVITY

Habitat Destruction

People need homes. People also need food and building materials. But when land is cleared for construction, crops, mines, or lumber, the topsoil may erode. Chemicals may pollute nearby streams and rivers. The organisms that were living in these areas may be left without food and shelter. These organisms may die.

An organism's *habitat* is where it lives. Every habitat has its own number and variety of organisms, or **biodiversity**. If a habitat is damaged or destroyed, biodiversity is lost.

Forest Habitats

Trees provide humans with oxygen, lumber, food, rubber, and paper. For some of these products, such as lumber and paper, trees must be cut down. *Deforestation* is the clearing of forest lands, as shown in **Figure 6.** At one time, many of these cleared forests were not replanted. Today, lumber companies often plant new trees to replace the trees that were cut down. However, some biodiversity is still lost.

Tropical rain forests, the most diverse habitats on Earth, are sometimes cleared for farmland, roads, and lumber. But after a tropical rain forest is cleared, the area cannot grow to be as diverse as it once was. Also, thin tropical soils are often badly damaged.

Marine Habitats

Many people think of oil spills when they think of pollution in marine habitats. This is an example of *point-source pollution*, or pollution that comes from one source. Spilled oil pollutes both open waters and coastal habitats.

A second kind of water pollution is *nonpoint-source pollution*. This kind of pollution comes from many different sources. Nonpoint-source pollution often happens when chemicals on land are washed into rivers, lakes, and oceans. These chemicals can harm or kill many of the organisms that live in marine habitats.

In addition to oil and chemicals, plastics are also sometimes dumped into marine habitats. Animals may mistake plastics for food. Or animals may become tangled in plastics. Dumping plastics into the ocean is against the law. However, this law is difficult to enforce.

✓ Reading Check What are point-source and nonpoint-source pollution?

Answer to Reading Check

Point-source pollution is pollution that comes from one place. Nonpoint-source pollution is pollution that comes from many places.

Answer to Connection to Social Studies

Answers may vary. Students will likely find that some countries carefully maintain their forests while other countries are less successful at protecting forest resources. Reasons for the latter may include a need for land for agriculture or development, economic pressure, or ineffective ways of controlling illegal harvesting.

Effects on Humans

Trees and marine life are not the only organisms affected by pollution and habitat destruction. Pollution and habitat destruction affect humans, too. Sometimes, the effect is immediate. Polluted air affects people with respiratory problems. If you drink polluted water, you may get sick. Sometimes, the damage is not apparent right away. Some chemicals cause cancers many years after a person is exposed to them. Over time, natural resources may be hard to find or used up. Your children or grandchildren may have to deal with these problems.

Anything that harms other organisms may eventually harm people, too. Caring for the environment means being aware of what is happening now and looking ahead to the future.

SECTION Review

Summary

- Pollutants include garbage, chemicals, high-energy wastes, gases, and noise.
- Renewable resources can be used over and over. Nonrenewable resources cannot be replaced or are replaced over thousands or millions of years.
- Exotic species can become pests and compete with native species.
- Overpopulation happens when a population is so large that it can't get what it needs to survive.
- Habitat destruction can lead to soil erosion, water pollution, and decreased biodiversity.
- In addition to harming the environment, pollution can harm humans.

Using Key Terms

The statements below are false. For each statement, replace the underlined term to make a true statement.

1. Coal is a <u>renewable resource</u>.
2. <u>Overpopulation</u> is the number and variety of organisms in an area.

Understanding Key Ideas

3. Which of the following can cause pollution?
   a. noise
   b. garbage
   c. chemicals
   d. All of the above
4. Pollution
   a. does not affect humans.
   b. can make humans sick.
   c. makes humans sick only after many years.
   d. None of the above
5. Compare renewable and nonrenewable resources.
6. Why has human population growth increased?
7. What is an exotic species?
8. How does habitat destruction affect biodiversity?

Math Skills

9. Jodi's family produces 48 kg of garbage each week. What is the percentage decrease if they reduce the amount of garbage to 40 kg per week?

Critical Thinking

10. **Applying Concepts** Explain how each of the following can help people but harm the environment: hospitals, old refrigerators, and road construction.
11. **Making Inferences** Explain how human population growth is related to pollution problems.
12. **Predicting Consequences** How can the pollution of marine habitats affect humans?

For a variety of links related to this chapter, go to www.scilinks.org

Topic: Air Pollution; Resource Depletion
SciLinks code: HSM0033; HSM1304

Developed and maintained by the National Science Teachers Association

Answers to Section Review

1. nonrenewable resource
2. Biodiversity
3. d
4. b
5. A renewable resource is a resource that can be used over and over or that has an unlimited supply. A nonrenewable resource cannot be replaced or can be replaced only over thousands or millions of years.
6. Sample answer: Advances in medicine, such as immunizations, and advances in farming have made human population growth possible.
7. An exotic species is a species that makes a home for itself in a new area outside its native home.
8. Sample answer: Habitat destruction may cause erosion and pollute streams and rivers. Habitat destruction may also leave some organisms without food or a place to live. Some of these organisms may die. So, habitat destruction causes the loss of biodiversity.
9. 17% decrease
   (48 kg − 40 kg = 8 kg;
   8 kg ÷ 48 kg × 100 = 17%)
10. Sample answer: Hospitals save people's lives but produce medical waste, which is hazardous waste. Old refrigerators kept food cold but used CFCs, which destroy protective ozone. Road construction makes it easier for people to travel from one place to another but causes habitat destruction.
11. Sample answer: Each person causes pollution. As the population grows, more pollution is produced.
12. Sample answer: Pollution of marine habitats could kill many of the organisms that humans collect for food or could make those organisms unfit for humans to eat. Pollution also harms coral reefs, which are places that people like to visit for recreation.

Focus

Overview

In this section, students will learn about conservation. Students will also learn about the importance of protecting habitats. Finally, students will explore specific strategies that they can use to help protect the environment.

 Bellringer

Have students imagine that they've finished reading a magazine. Then, ask students to describe at least two things they can do instead of throwing the magazine away. (Sample answer: I can give the magazine to a friend or relative, donate the magazine to a library or homeless shelter, use the magazine to make a collage, or recycle the magazine.)

Motivate

Group ACTiViTy — GENERAL

Reusing Trash Organize students into groups of four, and give each group a plastic grocery bag. Have students list at least five ways that the bag can be reused. (Sample answer: It can be reused for groceries, used as a waterproof covering for books, used to line a wastebasket, used to hold wet items, used to wrap sandwiches, or used to protect surfaces.) **LS Verbal**

READING WARM-UP

Objectives
- Explain the importance of conservation.
- Describe the three Rs.
- Explain how biodiversity can be maintained.
- List five environmental strategies.

Terms to Learn
conservation
recycling

READING STRATEGY

Discussion Read this section silently. Write down questions that you have about this section. Discuss your questions in a small group.

conservation the preservation and wise use of natural resources

---

Environmental Solutions

As the human population grows, it will need more resources. People will need food, healthcare, transportation, and waste disposal. What does this mean for the Earth?

All of these needs will have an impact on the Earth. If people don't use resources wisely, people will continue to pollute the air, soil, and water. More natural habitats could be lost. Many species could die out as a result. But there are many things people can do to protect the environment.

Conservation

One way to care for the Earth is conservation (KAHN suhr VAY shuhn). **Conservation** is the preservation and wise use of natural resources. You can ride your bike to conserve fuel. At the same time, you prevent air pollution. You can use organic compost instead of chemical fertilizer in your garden. Doing so conserves the resources needed to make the fertilizer. Also, you may reduce soil and water pollution.

Practicing conservation means using fewer natural resources. Conservation helps reduce waste and pollution. Also, conservation can help prevent habitat destruction. The three Rs are shown in **Figure 1.** They describe three ways to conserve resources: Reduce, Reuse, and Recycle.

✓ **Reading Check** What are the three Rs? (*See the Appendix for answers to Reading Checks.*)

Figure 1 *By reducing, reusing, and recycling, these teens are conserving resources.*

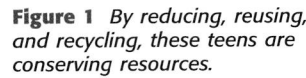  

CHAPTER RESOURCES

Chapter Resource File

 • Lesson Plan
• Directed Reading A **BASIC**
• Directed Reading B **SPECIAL NEEDS**

Technology

 Transparencies
• Bellringer
• Conservation

Answer to Reading Check
reduce, reuse, and recycle

Reduce

What is the best way to conserve the Earth's natural resources? Use less of them! Doing so also helps reduce pollution.

Reducing Waste and Pollution

As much as one-third of the waste produced by some countries is packaging material. Products can be wrapped in less paper and plastic to reduce waste. For example, fast-food restaurants used to serve sandwiches in large plastic containers. Today, sandwiches are usually wrapped in thin paper instead. This paper is more biodegradable than plastic. Something that is *biodegradable* can be broken down by living organisms, such as bacteria. Scientists, such as the ones in **Figure 2,** are working to make biodegradable plastics.

Many people and companies are using less-hazardous materials in making their products. For example, some farmers don't use synthetic chemicals on their crops. Instead, they practice organic farming. They use mulch, compost, manure, and natural pest control. Agricultural specialists are also working on farming techniques that are better for the environment.

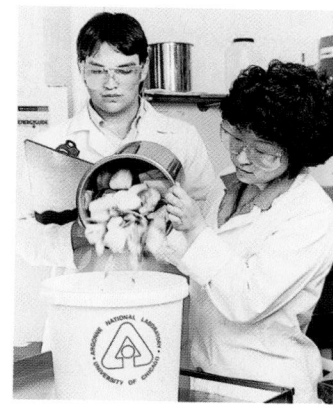

Figure 2 *These scientists are studying ways to make biodegradable plastics.*

Reducing the Use of Nonrenewable Resources

Some scientists are looking for sources of energy that can replace fossil fuels. For example, solar energy can be used to power homes, such as the home shown in **Figure 3.** Scientists are studying power sources such as wind, tides, and falling water. Car companies have developed electric and hydrogen-fueled automobiles. Driving these cars uses fewer fossil fuels and produces less pollution than driving gas-fueled cars does.

Figure 3 *The people who live in this home use solar panels to get energy from the sun.*

SCIENCE HUMOR

Dan and Eddie made a great plan,
to recycle all that they can.
They reduced lots of waste
with a bit too much haste,
and recycled their mother's new van.

CONNECTION to Language Arts —— GENERAL

Biodegradable Plastics
Biodegradable plastics contain substances such as starch that can be broken down by microorganisms. Tell students to imagine that they work for a company that uses nonbiodegradable plastic in the packaging of its products. Have students write a persuasive letter advocating a changeover to biodegradable plastics.
LS Verbal

Demonstration — BASIC

Reuse and Recycle To help students distinguish the meaning of the word *reuse* from the meaning of the word *recycle*, point out that *reuse* most often refers to using a particular item again and again. You might indicate this graphically by drawing a series of horizontal arrows and drawing a lunchbox (or other reusable item) between each of the arrows to indicate that the lunchbox can be used many times. Explain that the word *recycle* usually indicates that an item undergoes a process that transforms the item into another item or another version of the same item. To depict recycling, you could display three items that are made from the same material (such as a newspaper, a piece of writing paper, and a cardboard box). **English Language Learners**

LS Visual

Research — GENERAL

Local Recycling Ask students to find out what specific materials are recycled in your community. Students should find out how your community handles recyclables. Have students create an informative brochure about local recycling resources.

LS Verbal/Visual

Figure 4 *This home was built with reused tires and aluminum cans.*

Reuse

Do you get hand-me-down clothes from an older sibling? Do you try to fix broken sports equipment instead of throwing it away? If so, you are helping conserve resources by *reusing* products.

Reusing Products

Every time you reuse a plastic bag, one bag fewer needs to be made. Reusing the plastic bag at the grocery store is just one way to reuse the bag. Reusing products is an important way to conserve resources.

You might be surprised at how many materials can be reused. For example, building materials can be reused. Wood, bricks, and tiles can be used in new structures. Old tires can be reused, too. They can be reused for playground surfaces. As shown in **Figure 4,** some tires are even reused to build new homes!

Figure 5 *This golf course is being watered with reclaimed water.*

Reusing Water

About 100 billion liters of water are used each day in American homes. Most of this water goes down the drain. Many communities are experiencing water shortages. Some of these communities are experimenting with reusing, or reclaiming, wastewater.

One way to reclaim water is to use organisms to clean the water. These organisms include plants and filter-feeding animals, such as clams. Often, reclaimed water isn't pure enough to drink. But it can be used to water crops, lawns, and golf courses, such as the one shown in **Figure 5.** Sometimes, reclaimed water is returned to underground water supplies.

✓ Reading Check Describe how water is reused.

Answer to Reading Check

Sample answer: Water is reclaimed with plants or filter-feeding animals. Then, it can be used to water crops, parks, lawns, and golf courses.

Recycle

Another example of reuse is recycling. **Recycling** is the recovery of materials from waste. Sometimes, recyclable items, such as paper, are used to make the same kinds of products. Other recyclable items are made into different products. For example, yard clippings can be recycled into a natural fertilizer.

Recycling Trash

Plastics, paper, aluminum, wood, glass, and cardboard are examples of materials that can be recycled. Every week, about half a million trees are used to make Sunday newspapers. Recycling newspapers could save millions of trees. Recycling aluminum saves 95% of the energy needed to change raw ore into aluminum. Glass can be recycled over and over again to make new bottles and jars.

Many communities make recycling easy. Some cities provide containers for glass, plastic, aluminum, and paper. People can leave these containers on the curb. Each week, the materials are picked up for recycling, as shown in **Figure 6**. Other cities have centers where people can take materials for recycling.

Recycling Resources

Waste that can be burned can also be used to generate electricity. Electricity is generated in waste-to-energy plants, such as the one shown in **Figure 7**. Using garbage to make electricity is an example of *resource recovery*. Some companies are beginning to make electricity with their own waste. Doing so saves the companies money and conserves resources.

About 16% of the solid waste in the United States is burned in waste-to-energy plants. But some people are concerned that these plants pollute the air. Other people worry that the plants reduce recycling.

recycling the process of recovering valuable or useful materials from waste or scrap

Figure 6 *In some communities, recyclable materials are picked up each week.*

Figure 7 *A waste-to-energy plant can provide electricity to many homes and businesses.*

INBio Although Costa Rica is a small country (about 51,000 km²), it is home to an estimated 505,660 species, which is about 4% of all living species. In 1989, the Costa Rican government set up the National Institute of Biodiversity (Instituto Nacional de Biodiversidad, or INBio) to catalog native species and to educate residents about the importance of preserving biodiversity. Some of the collecting and cataloging is done by local people who have been trained by scientists. Invite interested students to use the Internet to find out how INBio shares information about beneficial and sustainable uses for some of the unique species found in Costa Rica. **LS** Verbal

MISCONCEPTION ALERT

Extinctions In the recent past, humans caused extinction primarily by overhunting and overharvesting. Today, extinction of species is more likely to result from habitat loss and the introduction of exotic species. Saving species today requires protecting not only the organisms but also the ecosystems that support the organisms.

Figure 8 *What could happen if a fungus attacks a banana field? Biodiversity is low in fields of crops such as bananas.*

Maintaining Biodiversity

You know the three Rs. What else can you do to help the environment? You can help maintain biodiversity! So, how does biodiversity help the environment?

Imagine a forest with only one kind of tree. If a disease hit that species, the entire forest might die. Now, imagine a forest with 10 species of trees. If a disease hits one species, 9 other species will remain. Bananas, shown in **Figure 8,** are an important crop. But banana fields are not very diverse. Fungi threaten the survival of bananas. Farmers often use chemicals to control fungi. Growing other plants among the bananas, or increasing biodiversity, can also prevent the spread of fungi.

Biodiversity is also important because each species has a unique role in an ecosystem. Losing one species could disrupt an entire ecosystem. For example, if an important predator is lost, its prey will multiply. The prey might eat the plants in an area, keeping other animals from getting food. Eventually, even the prey won't have food. So, the prey will starve.

Protecting Species

One way to maintain biodiversity is to protect individual species. In the United States, a law called the *Endangered Species Act* was designed to do just that. Endangered species are put on a special list. The law forbids activities that would harm a species on this list. The law also requires the development of recovery programs for each endangered species. Some endangered species, such as the California condor in **Figure 9,** are now increasing in number.

Anyone can ask the government to add a species to or remove a species from the endangered species list. This process can take years to complete. The government must study the species and its habitat before making a decision.

Figure 9 *Thanks to captive-breeding programs, the California condor population is increasing.*

Is That a Fact!

Just outside Detroit, Michigan, looms a former landfill that was once known as *Mount Trashmore*. From the 1970s to the mid-1990s, Mount Trashmore was used as a ski slope! Also, methane gas tapped from decomposing wastes within the landfill was converted to electricity. Today, the former landfill, renamed *Riverview Highlands*, is used for ice skating, tubing (using recycled tire tubes), and other recreational activities.

Protecting Habitats

Waiting until a species is almost extinct to begin protecting it is like waiting until your teeth are rotting to begin brushing them. Scientists want to prevent species from becoming endangered and from becoming extinct.

Plants, animals, and microorganisms depend on each other. Each organism is part of a huge, interconnected web of organisms. The entire web should be protected to protect these organisms. To protect the web, complete habitats, not just individual species, must be preserved. Nature preserves, such as the one shown in **Figure 10,** are one way to protect entire habitats.

Environmental Strategies

Laws have been passed to help protect the Earth's environment. By following those laws, people can help the environment. People can also use the following environmental strategies:

- **Reduce pollution.** Recycle as much as possible, and buy recycled products. Don't dump wastes on farmland, in forests, or into rivers, lakes, and oceans. Participate in a local cleanup project.

- **Reduce pesticide use.** Use only pesticides that are targeted specifically for harmful insects. Avoid pesticides that might harm beneficial insects, such as ladybugs or spiders. Use natural pesticides that interfere with how certain insects grow, develop, and reproduce.

- **Protect habitats.** Preserve entire habitats. Conserve wetlands. Reduce deforestation. Use resources at a rate that allows them to be replenished naturally.

- **Learn about local issues.** Attend local meetings about laws and projects that may affect your local environment. Research the impact of the project, and let people know about your concerns.

- **Develop alternative energy sources.** Increase the use of renewable energy, such as solar power and wind power.

The *Environmental Protection Agency* (EPA) is a government organization that helps protect the environment. The EPA works to help people have a clean environment in which to live, work, and play. The EPA keeps people informed about environmental issues and helps enforce environmental laws.

Reading Check What is the EPA?

Figure 10 *Setting aside public lands for wildlife is one way to protect habitats.*

INTERNET ACTIVITY

For another activity related to this chapter, go to **go.hrw.com** and type in the keyword **HL5ENVW**.

Answer to Reading Check

Sample answer: The EPA is a government organization that helps protect the environment.

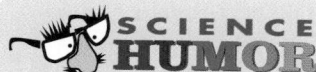

SCIENCE HUMOR

Q: What are people who damage the habitat of endangered birds engaging in?

A: fowl play

Homework — ADVANCED

Volunteering for the Environment There are many volunteer organizations that seek to protect and maintain animal and plant habitats. These organizations sponsor activities, such as cleanups of beaches or riverfronts; tree planting; or the removal of exotic species from a forest, prairie, or wetland. Have interested students contact local environmental organizations to find out how they can help organize and lead a group of classmates in volunteer field work. **LS Verbal/Interpersonal**

CONNECTION ACTIVITY
Carpentry — GENERAL

For the Birds As their habitat disappears, many birds have difficulty obtaining food and shelter. Have students research, design, and build a simple birdhouse or bird feeder. Birdhouses and bird feeders help birds survive and are a good way to reuse scrap lumber. English Language Learners **LS Kinesthetic**

ACTIVITY — GENERAL

Environmental Protection
Have students examine environmental legislation such as the Clean Air Act, the Clean Water Act, or the Superfund Act (CERCLA). Have students examine why the law was passed and what it does to protect the environment. Then, have students give oral presentations about their finding. **LS Verbal**

Close

Reteaching ———— BASIC

Recycling Triangle Have students draw a triangle. Ask them to write *reduce*, *reuse*, and *recycle* each at a point of the triangle. Then, tell students to define each term in the corner of the triangle and to give three examples for each term. **LS** Verbal/Visual

Quiz ———— GENERAL

1. Give one example each of how you could reduce the use of, reuse, and recycle a natural resource. (Sample answer: To reduce the use of a resource, I could ride a bike to a friend's house instead of getting a ride in a car. To reuse a resource, I could use refillable water jugs. To recycle a resource, I could recycle aluminum cans.)

2. How does the Endangered Species Act protect endangered organisms? (The Endangered Species Act forbids activities that would harm species on the endangered species list. The act also requires the development of recovery programs for each endangered species.)

Alternative Assessment ———— GENERAL

Writing **PSA** Ask students to write a public service announcement encouraging people to follow the five environmental strategies discussed in the text. **LS** Verbal

What You Can Do

Reduce, reuse, and recycle. Protect the Earth. These are jobs for everyone. Children as well as adults can help clean up the Earth. By doing so, people can improve their environment. And they can improve their quality of life.

The list in **Figure 11** offers some suggestions for how *you* can help. How many of these things do you already do? What can you add to the list?

Figure 11   How You Can Help the Environment

1. Volunteer at a local preserve or nature center, and help other people learn about conservation.
2. Give away your old toys.
3. Use recycled paper.
4. Fill up both sides of a sheet of paper.
5. Start an environmental awareness club at your school or in your neighborhood.
6. Recycle glass, plastics, paper, aluminum, and batteries.
7. Don't buy any products made from an endangered plant or animal.
8. Turn off electrical devices when you are not using them.
9. Wear hand-me-downs.
10. Share books with friends, or use the library.
11. Walk, ride a bicycle, or use public transportation.
12. Carry a reusable cloth shopping bag to the store.
13. Use a lunch box, or reuse your paper lunch bags.
14. Turn off the water while you brush your teeth.
15. Buy products made from biodegradable and recycled materials.
16. Use cloth napkins and kitchen towels.
17. Buy things in packages that can be recycled.
18. Use rechargeable batteries.
19. Make a compost heap.

THIS BAG IS BIODEGRADABLE

Summary

- Conservation is the preservation and wise use of natural resources. Conservation helps reduce pollution, ensures that resources will be available in the future, and protects habitats.
- The three Rs are Reduce, Reuse, and Recycle. Reducing means using fewer resources. Reusing means using materials and products over and over. Recycling is the recovery of materials from waste.

- Biodiversity is vital for maintaining healthy ecosystems. A loss of one species can affect an entire ecosystem.
- Biodiversity can be preserved by protecting endangered species and entire habitats.
- Environmental strategies include reducing pollution, reducing pesticide use, protecting habitats, enforcing the Endangered Species Act, and developing alternative energy resources.

Using Key Terms

1. Use each of the following terms in a separate sentence: *conservation* and *recycling*.

Understanding Key Ideas

2. Which of the following is NOT a strategy to protect the environment?
   a. preserving entire habitats
   b. using pesticides that target all insects
   c. reducing deforestation
   d. increasing the use of solar power

3. Conservation
   a. has little effect on the environment.
   b. is the use of more natural resources.
   c. involves using more fossil fuels.
   d. can prevent pollution.

4. Describe the three Rs.

5. Describe why biodiversity is important. How can biodiversity be protected?

Critical Thinking

6. **Applying Concepts** Liza rode her bike to the store. She bought items that had little packaging and put her purchases into her backpack. Describe how Liza practiced conservation.

7. **Identifying Relationships** How does conservation of resources also reduce pollution and protect habitats?

Interpreting Graphics

Use the pie graph below to answer the questions that follow.

Land Use in the United States

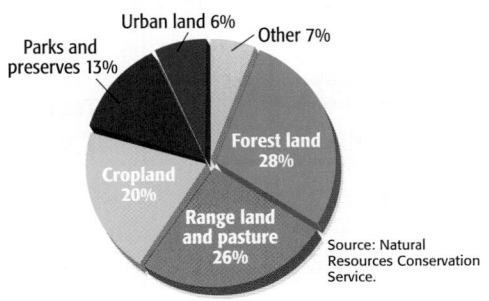

Urban land 6%   Other 7%
Parks and preserves 13%
Forest land 28%
Cropland 20%
Range land and pasture 26%

Source: Natural Resources Conservation Service.

8. If half of the forest land were made into preserves, what percentage of total land would be parks and preserves?

9. If 10% of the cropland were not planted, what percentage of land would be used for crops?

SCiLINKS®

NSTA
Developed and maintained by the
National Science Teachers Association

For a variety of links related to this chapter, go to www.scilinks.org

Topic: Recycling; Maintaining Biodiversity
SciLinks code: HSM1277; HSM0902

Answers to Section Review

1. Sample answer: Conservation protects the environment by reducing pollution. Someone who is recycling is conserving resources.

2. b

3. d

4. Sample answer: *Reduce* means "to use fewer natural resources." *Reuse* means "to use something over and over." *Recycle* means "to reclaim materials from waste."

5. Sample answer: Biodiversity is important to the survival of species in an ecosystem. For example, the loss of a predator can cause an increase in a prey population that causes other species to starve. Biodiversity is protected by protecting species and by protecting habitats.

6. Sample answer: Liza reduced the use of resources by riding her bike, which saves gas; by buying products with little packaging, which reduces trash; and by using a backpack instead of a plastic bag, which also reduces trash.

7. Sample answer: Conserving resources means that you are using less of them, so you won't be producing as much trash. If you conserve resources, fewer habitats will be destroyed by activities such as mining, harvesting, or construction.

8. 27% (28% ÷ 2 = 14%; 13% + 14% = 27%)

9. 18% (20% × 0.9 = 18%)

Biodiversity—What a Disturbing Thought!

Teacher's Notes

Time Required

One or two 45-minute class periods

Lab Ratings

EASY ————————————— HARD

Teacher Prep 🧪🧪
Student Set-Up 🧪🧪
Concept Level 🧪🧪🧪
Clean Up 🧪🧪

MATERIALS

Binoculars may not be available in your classroom. Ask students if they have some at home that they could get permission to bring to class for this activity.

Lab Notes

The lab should be reviewed ahead of time. This lab can be extended to a field trip that can involve parents. Your school may be in a city where there is no suitable undisturbed area. If you are unable to take students on a field trip, help them understand the difference between a severely disturbed area (a paved parking lot) and an area that is less disturbed (an unimproved lot). Some biodiversity should exist in every area.

Terry Rakes
Elmwood Junior High School
Rogers, Arkansas

OBJECTIVES

Examine biodiversity in your community.

Identify which areas in your community have the greatest biodiversity.

MATERIALS

- items to be determined by the students and approved by the teacher (Possible field equipment includes a meterstick, binoculars, a magnifying lens, and forceps.)
- stakes (4)
- twine

SAFETY

Biodiversity—What a Disturbing Thought!

Biodiversity is important for the stability of an ecosystem. Microorganisms, plants, and animals all have a role in an ecosystem. In this activity, you will investigate areas outside your school to determine which areas contain the greatest biodiversity.

Ask a Question

❶ Based on your understanding of biodiversity, do you expect a forest or an area planted with crops to be more diverse?

Form a Hypothesis

❷ Select an area that is highly disturbed (such as a yard) and an area that is relatively undisturbed (such as a vacant lot). Make a hypothesis about which area contains the greater biodiversity. Get your teacher's approval of your selected locations.

Test the Hypothesis

❸ Design a procedure to determine which area contains the greater biodiversity. Have your plan approved by your teacher before you begin.

CHAPTER RESOURCES

Chapter Resource File

- **Datasheet for Chapter Lab**
- **Lab Notes and Answers**

Technology

 Classroom Videos
- Lab Video

- Deciding About Environmental Issues

Prairie

Wheat Field

4 To discover smaller organisms, measure off a square meter, set stakes at the corners, and mark the area with twine. Use a magnifying lens to observe organisms. When you record your observations, refer to organisms in the following way: Ant A, Ant B, and so on. Make note of any visits by larger organisms.

5 Create any data tables that you might need for recording your data. If you observe your areas on more than one occasion, make data tables for each observation period. Organize your data into clear and understandable categories.

Analyze the Results

1 Explaining Events What factors did you consider before deciding which habitats were disturbed or undisturbed?

2 Constructing Maps Draw a map of the land around your school. Label areas of high biodiversity and those of lower biodiversity.

3 Analyzing Data What problems did you have while making observations and recording data for each habitat? How did you solve these problems?

Draw Conclusions

4 Drawing Conclusions Review your hypothesis. Did your data support your hypothesis? Explain your answer.

5 Evaluating Methods Describe possible errors in your investigation. What are ways you could improve your procedure to eliminate errors?

6 Applying Conclusions Do you think that the biodiversity around your school increased or decreased since the school was built? Explain your answer.

Applying Your Data

The photographs of the prairie and of the wheat field on this page are beautiful. One of these areas, however, is very low in biodiversity. Describe each photograph, and explain the difference in biodiversity.

CHAPTER RESOURCES

Workbooks

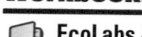

EcoLabs & Field Activities
• A Filter with Culture **GENERAL**

Long-Term Projects & Research Ideas
• Let's Talk Trash **ADVANCED**

Calculator-Based Labs
• Solar Homes **ADVANCED**

Applying Your Data

A wheat field is less diverse than a prairie because a wheat field is highly disturbed. Only one kind of plant grows in a wheat field, and it provides little habitat for animals. Some animals may visit and feed in a wheat field, but their nests or dens would be in danger at harvest time. A prairie is undisturbed, so it will have greater biodiversity.

Analyze the Results

1. Students should recognize that areas in which there has been a great deal of human activity are disturbed and that areas in which there has been little human activity are relatively undisturbed.

2. Answers may vary. Areas that are disturbed should have less biodiversity than areas that are undisturbed do. Some areas that are disturbed might have a high diversity of plant species. Many of these plant species will be weedy, undesirable, or exotic.

3. Answers may vary. Students may mention problems with their experimental set-up; with conditions on the day of the survey, such as bad weather; and with human error.

Draw Conclusions

4. Most students' data should match their hypothesis if their hypothesis states that undisturbed areas will have greater biodiversity than disturbed areas will. If students' data do not support this hypothesis, students may have examined an area that was disturbed, thinking it was undisturbed.

5. A possible error might be deciding that an area is undisturbed when in fact it is highly disturbed and has little biodiversity. To avoid this error, students should research the history of an area to make sure that the area is not highly disturbed.

6. Answers may vary. Students should discuss construction and growth in the neighborhood that have occurred since the school was built. Most likely, biodiversity in the area around the school has decreased.

Assignment Guide

SECTION	QUESTIONS
1	1–3, 5, 7–8, 10–11, 14–16, 18–22
2	4, 6, 9, 12–13, 17

ANSWERS

Using Key Terms

1. nonrenewable resource
2. overpopulation
3. Pollution
4. conservation
5. Biodiversity

Understanding Key Ideas

6. d
7. b
8. a
9. Sample answer: *Reduce* means "to use fewer resources." *Reuse* means "to use something over and over instead of throwing it away." *Recycle* means "to recover useful materials from trash."
10. garbage, chemicals, radioactive wastes, gases, and noise
11. Advances in medicine, such as vaccines, and advances in farming have made human population growth possible.

USING KEY TERMS

Complete each of the following sentences by choosing the correct term from the word bank.

conservation pollution
recycling biodiversity
overpopulation
renewable resource
nonrenewable resource

❶ A(n) ___ is a resource that is replaced at a much slower rate than it is used.

❷ The presence of too many individuals in a population for available resources is called ___.

❸ ___ is an unwanted change in the environment caused by wastes.

❹ The preservation and wise use of natural resources is called ___.

❺ ___ is the number and variety of organisms in an area.

UNDERSTANDING KEY IDEAS

Multiple Choice

❻ Preventing habitat destruction is important because

a. organisms do not live independently of each other.

b. protection of habitats is a way to promote biodiversity.

c. the balance of nature could be disrupted if habitats were destroyed.

d. All of the above

❼ Exotic species

a. do not affect native species.

b. are species that make a home for themselves in a new place.

c. are not introduced by human activity.

d. do not take over an area.

❽ A renewable resource

a. is a natural resource that can be replaced as quickly as it is used.

b. is a natural resource that takes thousands or millions of years to be replaced.

c. includes fossil fuels, such as coal or oil.

d. will eventually run out.

Short Answer

❾ Describe how you can use the three Rs to conserve resources.

❿ What are five kinds of pollutants?

⓫ Explain why human population growth has increased.

⓬ What are two things that can be done to maintain biodiversity?

⓭ List five environmental strategies.

12. Sample answer: To maintain biodiversity, species can be protected and habitats can be preserved.

13. Sample answer: Five environmental strategies are to reduce pollution, to reduce pesticide use, to protect habitats, to learn about local issues, and to develop alternative energy sources.

CRITICAL THINKING

14 Concept Mapping Use the following terms to create a concept map: *pollution, radioactive wastes, gases, pollutants, CFCs, PCBs, hazardous wastes, chemicals, noise,* and *garbage.*

15 Analyzing Ideas How may deforestation have contributed to the extinction of some species?

16 Predicting Consequences Imagine that the supply of fossil fuels is going to run out in 50 years. What will happen if people are not prepared when the supply runs out? What might be done to prepare for such an event?

17 Evaluating Conclusions A scientist thinks that farms should be planted with many different kinds of crops instead of a single crop. Based on what you learned about biodiversity, evaluate the scientist's conclusion. What problems might this cause?

18 Applying Concepts Imagine that a new species has moved into a local habitat. The species feeds on some of the same plants that the native species do, but it has no natural predators. Describe what might happen to local habitats as a result.

19 Making Inferences Many scientists think that forests are nonrenewable resources. Explain why they might have this opinion.

INTERPRETING GRAPHICS

The line graph below shows the concentration of carbon dioxide in the atmosphere between 1958 and 1994. Use this graph to answer the questions that follow.

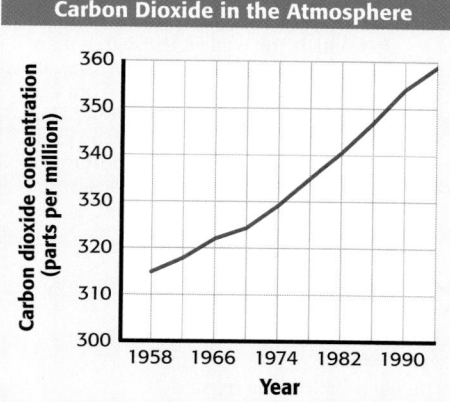

Carbon Dioxide in the Atmosphere

20 What was the concentration of carbon dioxide in parts per million in 1960? in 1994?

21 What is the average change in carbon dioxide concentration every 4 years?

22 If the concentration of carbon dioxide continues to change at the rate shown in the graph, what will the concentration be in 2010?

Critical Thinking

14. 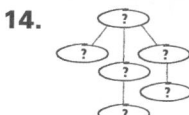 An answer to this exercise can be found at the end of this book.

15. Sample answer: Deforestation is the removal of all trees from an area. Without the trees, many species don't have shelter or food, so some species may die.

CHAPTER RESOURCES

Chapter Resource File

- Chapter Review **GENERAL**
- Chapter Test A **GENERAL**
- Chapter Test B **ADVANCED**
- Chapter Test C **SPECIAL NEEDS**
- Vocabulary Activity **GENERAL**

Workbooks

Study Guide
- Assessment resources are also available in Spanish.

16. Sample answer: If people weren't prepared, there would be an energy shortage. To prepare for the exhaustion of fossil fuel supplies, people can develop alternative sources of energy, such as energy from sunlight, wind, and water.

17. Sample answer: A farm that has many kinds of crops is less likely to be wiped out by a plant disease than a farm that has a single crop is. A plant disease could destroy the entire crop of a single-crop farm, whereas the disease likely would not kill all of the crops on a multi-crop farm. However, a farm that has many crops often doesn't produce as much of a single crop as a farm that grows that crop alone does.

18. Sample answer: The new species will compete with the local species for food, but without predators to thin the population of the new species, the population of the new species will continue to grow. Eventually, the new species may take over the area.

19. Sample answer: To get big, trees often need to grow for many years. Some trees take hundreds of years to grow. So, these trees could easily be used faster than they recover. Also, if a forest is cut down, the biodiversity of the area will likely never be restored and some species may be lost.

Interpreting Graphics

20. 317 parts per million; 359 parts per million

21. about 5 parts per million every four years (360 ppm − 315 ppm = 45 ppm; 45 ppm ÷ 9 four-year periods = 5 ppm per four-year period)

22. about 380 parts per million (2010 − 1994 = 16 years; 16 ÷ 4 = 4 four-year periods; 4 four-year periods × 5 ppm = 20 ppm increase; 360 ppm + 20 ppm = 380 ppm)

Standardized Test Preparation

Teacher's Note

To provide practice under more realistic testing conditions, give students 20 minutes to answer all of the questions in this Standardized Test Preparation.

MISCONCEPTION
**/// ALERT **

Answers to the standardized test preparation can help you identify student misconceptions and misunderstandings.

READING

Passage 1
1. A
2. G
3. B

 TEST DOCTOR

Question 1: Based on the statement from the passage that mentions a "sealed environment," students should infer that the scientist lives in an artificial environment. Students may answer that the scientist is by herself if they missed the statement about the scientist and her research team. Students may think that the scientist is on an island because she swims in the ocean, but a person doesn't have to be on an island to swim in the ocean. Finally, the passage states that the scientist's life depends on the health of her environment, so students should infer that the final answer choice is incorrect.

Standardized Test Preparation

READING

Read the passages below. Then, answer the questions that follow each passage.

Passage 1 The scientist woke up and jogged over to the rain forest. There she observed the water-recycling experiment. She took a swim in the ocean, after which she walked through a mangrove forest on her way home. At home, she ate lunch and went to the computer lab. From the lab, she could monitor the sensors that would alert her if any part of the ecosystem failed to cycle properly. This monitoring was very important to the scientist and her research team because their lives depended on the health of their sealed environment.

1. Based on the passage, the reader can conclude which of the following?
   A The scientist lives in an artificial environment.
   B The scientist lives by herself.
   C The scientist and her research team are studying a newly discovered island.
   D The scientist does not rely on the health of her environment.

2. Which of the following statements is a fact in the passage?
   F The scientist is scared that her environment is being destroyed.
   G The scientist depends on sensors to alert her to trouble.
   H The scientist lives in an open environment.
   I The scientist eats lunch at home every day.

3. Based on the passage, which of the following events happened first?
   A The scientist walked through the mangrove forest.
   B The scientist checked the water-recycling experiment.
   C The scientist swam in the ocean.
   D The scientist ate lunch.

Passage 2 All along the Gulf Coast, marine scientists and Earth scientists are trying to find methods to reduce or eliminate the dead zone. They have made models of the Mississippi River ecosystem that have accurately predicted the data that have since been collected. The scientists have changed the models to see what happens. For example, wetlands are one of nature's best filters. Wetlands take up a lot of the chemicals present in water. Scientists predict that adding wetlands to the Mississippi River watershed could reduce the chemicals reaching the Gulf of Mexico, possibly reducing the dead zone.

1. Based on the passage, what can you conclude about the dead zone?
   A It is found in the Mississippi River.
   B It may be prevented by adding wetlands to the Mississippi River watershed.
   C It reduces the chemicals reaching the Gulf of Mexico.
   D It is not caused by chemicals.

2. Based on the passage, which of the following statements about models is true?
   F Models do not accurately predict data.
   G Scientists do not change models.
   H Scientists use models to make predictions.
   I Models are always used for research.

3. Based on the passage, why did the scientists change their models?
   A to predict the effects of adding wetlands to the Mississippi River watershed
   B to find out why the dead zone happened
   C to eliminate the dead zone
   D to predict why there are a lot of chemicals in the Gulf of Mexico

Passage 2
1. B
2. H
3. A

 TEST DOCTOR

Question 1: Students may answer that the dead zone is in the Mississippi River because the river is mentioned in the passage, but the dead zone is in the Gulf of Mexico. Students may answer that the dead zone reduces the chemicals reaching the gulf if they misread the statement that wetlands may reduce chemicals. Finally, because the scientists are trying to find ways to reduce the chemicals reaching the Gulf of Mexico, students should infer that the dead zone is caused by chemicals and that the final answer choice is incorrect.

The table below shows the change in ozone levels between 1960 and 1990 above Halley Bay, Antarctica. Use the table to answer the questions that follow.

October Ozone Levels Above Halley Bay, Antarctica, in Dobson Units (DU)	
Year	Ozone level (DU)
1960	300
1970	280
1980	235
1990	190

1. According to the table, which of the following is the most likely ozone level for October 2000?

A 120 DU

B 150 DU

C 235 DU

D 280 DU

2. According to the table, the ozone level above Halley Bay is doing which of the following?

F It steadily increased between 1960 and 1990.

G It fell by 37% between 1960 and 1990.

H It decreased by an average of 37 DU per year.

I It decreased by about 25% every 10 years.

3. What is the percent decrease in ozone level between 1980 and 1990?

A 16%

B 19%

C 24%

D 81%

4. What is the average loss of ozone level per year in DU?

F 4 DU

G 6 DU

H 37 DU

I 63 DU

Read each question below, and choose the best answer.

1. About 15 m of topsoil covers the western plains of the United States. If topsoil forms at the rate of 2.5 cm per 500 years, how long did it take for 15 m of topsoil to form?

A 3,000 years

B 7,500 years

C 18,750 years

D 300,000 years

2. The dimensions of a habitat are 16 km by 6 km. If these dimensions are decreased by 50%, what will the area of the habitat be?

F 22 km^2

G 24 km^2

H 48 km^2

I 96 km^2

3. If each person in a city of 500,000 people throws away 12 kg of trash each week, how many metric tons of trash does the city produce per year? (There are 1,000 kg in a metric ton.)

A 6,000 metric tons

B 26,000 metric tons

C 312,000 metric tons

D 312,000,000 metric tons

4. Producing one ton of new glass creates about 175 kg of mining waste. Using 50% recycled glass cuts this rate by 75%. Which of the following equations calculates y, the mass of mining waste produced using 50% recycled glass?

F $y = 175 \times 0.25$

G $y = 175 \times 0.75$

H $y = 175 \times 0.5$

I $y = 175 \div 0.75$

Standardized Test Preparation

1. B

2. G

3. B

4. F

 TEST DOCTOR

Question 3: To find the answer, students should find the difference between 235 and 190, divide the difference by 235, and multiply by 100. Students will answer 16% if they calculate the answer for 1970 to 1980 instead of 1980 to 1990. Students will answer 24% if they divide the difference by 190 instead of 235. Students will answer 81% if they divide 190 by 235.

 **MATH**

1. D

2. G

3. C

4. F

 TEST DOCTOR

Question 1: To find the answer, students should convert 15 m to centimeters, divide by 2.5 cm, and multiply this quotient by 500 years. Students will answer 3,000 years if they forget to convert 15 m to centimeters. Students will answer 7,500 years if they multiply 15 by 500. Students will answer 18,750 years if they multiply 15 by 2.5 and by 500.

Question 3: To find the answer, students should multiply 500,000 by 12 and by 52 and divide by 1,000. Students will answer 6,000 metric tons if they calculate the tons of trash produced in 1 week and forget to multiply by 52 weeks. Students will answer 26,000 metric tons if they forget to include 12 kg in their calculations. Finally, students will answer 312,000,000 metric tons if they forget to divide by 1,000 kg per metric ton.

CHAPTER RESOURCES

Chapter Resource File

 • Standardized Test Preparation GENERAL

State Resources

For specific resources for your state, visit **go.hrw.com** and type in the keyword **HSMSTR**.

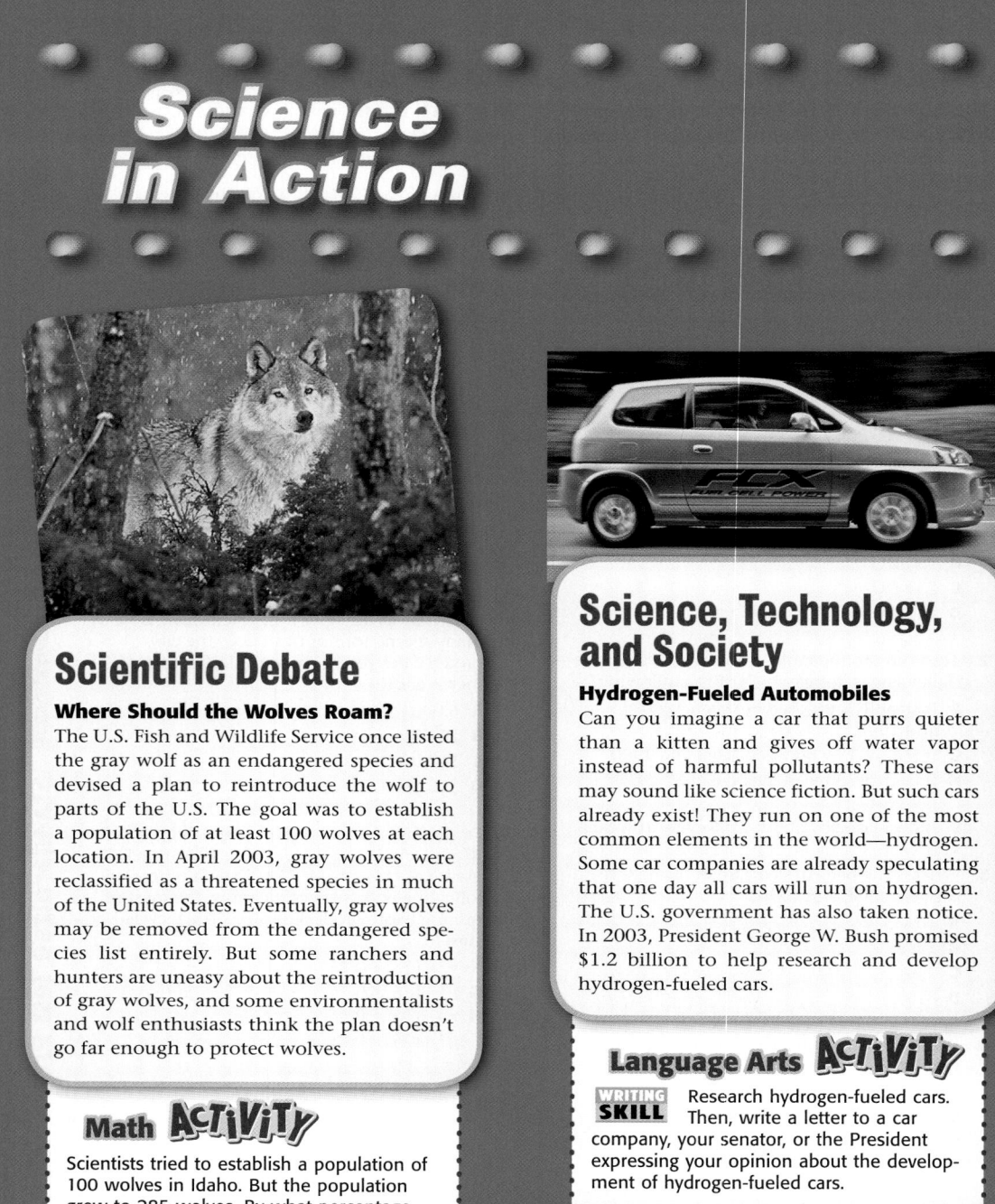

Science in Action

Scientific Debate

Background

In the 1920s, the gray wolf was exterminated from much of the United States. Wolves were killed to protect livestock and game animals. People in favor of wolf reintroduction cite biologists' claims that wolf attacks on livestock are not as widespread as is generally believed. Some opponents of wolf reintroduction argue that wolves should not be classified as endangered at all. According to data from biologists, there are 1,500 to 2,000 wolves in Minnesota, 6,000 to 10,000 wolves in Alaska, and 40,000 to 50,000 wolves in Canada. Many people feel that wolves should not receive the special treatment given to endangered species.

Science, Technology, and Society

ACTIVITY ——————— GENERAL

Have students research the fuel efficiency of several types of hydrogen-fueled automobiles as well as that of standard and hybrid automobiles. Ask students, "How much do these cars and trucks cost? What are the advantages of owning a fuel-efficient automobile? Are there any disadvantages to hybrid or hydrogen-fueled automobiles?"

Scientific Debate

Where Should the Wolves Roam?

The U.S. Fish and Wildlife Service once listed the gray wolf as an endangered species and devised a plan to reintroduce the wolf to parts of the U.S. The goal was to establish a population of at least 100 wolves at each location. In April 2003, gray wolves were reclassified as a threatened species in much of the United States. Eventually, gray wolves may be removed from the endangered species list entirely. But some ranchers and hunters are uneasy about the reintroduction of gray wolves, and some environmentalists and wolf enthusiasts think the plan doesn't go far enough to protect wolves.

Math ACTIVITY

Scientists tried to establish a population of 100 wolves in Idaho. But the population grew to 285 wolves. By what percentage did the population exceed expectations?

Science, Technology, and Society

Hydrogen-Fueled Automobiles

Can you imagine a car that purrs quieter than a kitten and gives off water vapor instead of harmful pollutants? These cars may sound like science fiction. But such cars already exist! They run on one of the most common elements in the world—hydrogen. Some car companies are already speculating that one day all cars will run on hydrogen. The U.S. government has also taken notice. In 2003, President George W. Bush promised $1.2 billion to help research and develop hydrogen-fueled cars.

Language Arts ACTIVITY

WRITING SKILL Research hydrogen-fueled cars. Then, write a letter to a car company, your senator, or the President expressing your opinion about the development of hydrogen-fueled cars.

Answer to Math Activity

185% (285 wolves − 100 wolves = 185 wolves; 185 wolves ÷ 100 wolves × 100 = 185%)

Answer to Language Arts Activity

Answers may vary. Students should write letters that clearly state their opinions and the reasoning behind their opinions.

Phil McCrory

Hairy Oil Spills Phil McCrory, a hairdresser in Huntsville, Alabama, asked a brilliant question when he saw an otter whose fur was drenched with oil from the *Exxon Valdez* oil spill. If the otter's fur soaked up all the oil, why wouldn't human hair do the same? McCrory gathered hair from the floor of his salon and took it home to perform his own experiments. He stuffed hair into a pair of his wife's pantyhose and tied the ankles together to form a bagel-shaped bundle. McCrory floated the bundle in his son's wading pool and poured used motor oil into the center of the ring. When he pulled the ring closed, not a drop of oil remained in the water!

McCrory approached the National Aeronautics and Space Administration (NASA) with his discovery. Based on tests performed by NASA, scientists estimated that 64 million kilograms of hair in reusable mesh pillows could have cleaned up all of the oil spilled by the *Exxon Valdez* within a week! Unfortunately, the $2 billion spent on the cleanup removed only about 12% of the oil.

Social Studies ACTIVITY

Make a map of an oil spill. Show the areas that were affected. Indicate some of the animal populations affected by the spill, such as penguins.

go.hrw.com

To learn more about these Science in Action topics, visit **go.hrw.com** and type in the keyword **HL5ENVF**.

Current Science

Check out Current Science® articles related to this chapter by visiting go.hrw.com. Just type in the keyword **HL5CS21**.

People in Science
Background

Bioremediation is the use of biological processes and products to eliminate organic contaminants from soils. Hair is a biological waste product that doesn't degrade well in landfills. Using hair for the bioremediation of oil spills would reduce the amount of waste in landfills. Also, because hair adsorbs the oil, wringing the hair out means that the oil can be recovered and that the hair can be used again. As a last resort, the oil-saturated mesh pillows can be burned as fuel to recover the value of the oil that they contain.

Answer to Social Studies Activity

Answers may vary. Students' maps should show the areas affected by an oil spill and should indicate some of the animal populations affected by the spill. Students are likely to make maps of the *Exxon Valdez* spill, but there are more recent spills that students can illustrate.

Human Body Systems

Like a finely tuned machine, your body is made up of many systems that work together. Your lungs take in oxygen. Your brain reacts to things you see, hear, and smell and sends signals through your nervous system that cause you to react to those things. Your digestive system converts the food you eat into energy that the cells of your body can use. And those are just a few things that your body can do!

In this unit, you will study the systems of your body. You'll discover how the parts of your body work together.

Around 3000 BCE

Ancient Egyptian doctors are the first to study the human body scientifically.

1824

Jean Louis Prevost and Jean Batiste Dumas prove that sperm is essential for fertilization.

1766

Albrecht von Haller determines that nerves control muscle movement and that all nerves are connected to the spinal cord or to the brain.

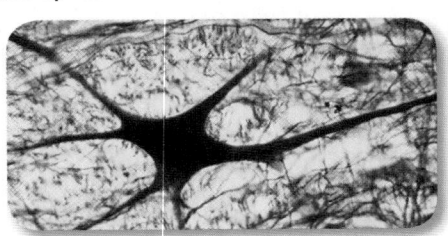

1940

During World War II in Italy, Rita Levi-Montalcini is forced to leave her work at a medical school laboratory because she is Jewish. She sets up a laboratory in her bedroom and studies the development of the nervous system.

Around 500 BCE
Indian surgeon Susrata performs operations to remove cataracts.

1492
Christopher Columbus lands in the West Indies.

1543
Andreas Vesalius publishes the first complete description of the structure of the human body.

1616
William Harvey discovers that blood circulates and that the heart acts as a pump.

1893
Daniel Hale Williams, an African American surgeon, becomes the first person to repair a tear in the pericardium, the sac around the heart.

1922
Frederick Banting, Charles Best, and John McLeod discover insulin.

1930
Karl Landsteiner receives a Nobel Prize for his discovery of the four human blood types.

1982
Dr. William DeVries implants an artificial heart in Barney Clark.

1998
The first sucessful hand transplant is performed in France.

2001
Drs. Laman A. Gray, Jr. and Robert D. Dowling at Jewish Hospital in Louisville, Kentucky, implant the first self-contained mechanical human heart.

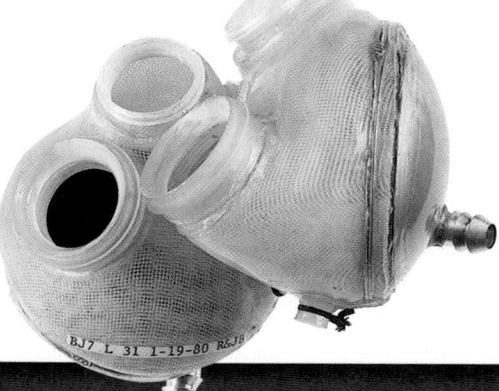

Body Organization and Structure
Chapter Planning Guide

Compression guide:
To shorten instruction because of time limitations, omit Section 1.

OBJECTIVES	LABS, DEMONSTRATIONS, AND ACTIVITIES	TECHNOLOGY RESOURCES
PACING • 90 min pp. 578–583 **Chapter Opener**	SE **Start-up Activity**, p. 579 `GENERAL`	OSP **Parent Letter** ■ `GENERAL` CD **Student Edition on CD-ROM** CD **Guided Reading Audio CD** ■ TR **Chapter Starter Transparency*** VID **Brain Food Video Quiz**
Section 1 Body Organization • Describe how tissues, organs, and organ systems are related. • List 12 organ systems. • Identify how organ systems work together to maintain homeostasis.	TE **Connection Activity** History, p. 581 `ADVANCED`	CRF **Lesson Plans*** TR **Bellringer Transparency*** TR **Organ Systems*** CRF **SciLinks Activity*** `GENERAL`
PACING • 45 min pp. 584–587 **Section 2 The Skeletal System** • Identify the major organs of the skeletal system. • Describe four functions of bones. • Describe three joints. • List three injuries and two diseases that affect bones and joints.	TE **Activity** Locating Bones, p. 584 `GENERAL` SE **Quick Lab** Pickled Bones, p. 585 ◆ `GENERAL` CRF **Datasheet for Quick Lab*** TE **Demonstration** Bone Dissection, p. 585 ◆ `BASIC`	CRF **Lesson Plans*** TR **Bellringer Transparency*** TR **The Skeleton*** TR ***LINK TO PHYSICAL SCIENCE*** Machines Change the Size and/or Direction of a Force*
PACING • 45 min pp. 588–591 **Section 3 The Muscular System** • List three kinds of muscle tissue. • Describe how skeletal muscles move bones. • Compare aerobic exercise with resistance exercise. • Describe two muscular system injuries.	TE **Group Activity** Poster Project, p. 588 `GENERAL` SE **School-to-Home Activity** Power in Pairs, p. 589 `GENERAL` TE **Demonstration** Muscle Contraction, p. 589 `BASIC` SE **Connection to Chemistry** Muscle Function, p. 590 `GENERAL` SE **Inquiry Lab** Muscles at Work, p. 794 ◆ `GENERAL` CRF **Datasheet for LabBook*** LB **Inquiry Labs** On a Wing and a Layer* ◆ `GENERAL`	CRF **Lesson Plans*** TR **Bellringer Transparency*** TR **A Pair of Muscles in the Arm***
PACING • 90 min pp. 592–595 **Section 4 The Integumentary System** • List four functions of skin. • Describe the two layers of skin. • Describe the structure and function of hair and nails. • Describe two kinds of damage that can affect skin.	TE **Activity** Measuring Temperature, p. 593 ◆ `GENERAL` TE **Connection Activity** Real World, p. 594 `GENERAL` SE **Skills Practice Lab** Seeing Is Believing, p. 596 `GENERAL` CRF **Datasheet for Chapter Lab*** SE **Science in Action** Math, Social Studies, and Language Arts Activities, pp. 602–603 `GENERAL` LB **Long-Term Projects & Research Ideas** Mapping the Human Body* `ADVANCED`	CRF **Lesson Plans*** TR **Bellringer Transparency*** TR **Structures of the Skin*** VID **Lab Videos for Life Science** TE **Internet Activity**, p. 593 `GENERAL`

PACING • 90 min

CHAPTER REVIEW, ASSESSMENT, AND STANDARDIZED TEST PREPARATION

CRF **Vocabulary Activity*** `GENERAL`
SE **Chapter Review**, pp. 598–599 `GENERAL`
CRF **Chapter Review*** ■ `GENERAL`
CRF **Chapter Tests A*** ■ `GENERAL`, **B*** `ADVANCED`, **C*** `SPECIAL NEEDS`
SE **Standardized Test Preparation**, pp. 600–601 `GENERAL`
CRF **Standardized Test Preparation*** `GENERAL`
CRF **Performance-Based Assessment*** `GENERAL`
OSP **Test Generator** `GENERAL`
CRF **Test Item Listing*** `GENERAL`

Online and Technology Resources

Visit **go.hrw.com** for a variety of free resources related to this textbook. Enter the keyword **HL5BD1**.

Holt Online Learning

Students can access interactive problem-solving help and active visual concept development with the *Holt Science and Technology* Online Edition available at **www.hrw.com**.

 Guided Reading Audio CD
Also in Spanish

A direct reading of each chapter for auditory learners, reluctant readers, and Spanish-speaking students.

 Science Tutor CD-ROM

Excellent for remediation and test practice.

SKILLS DEVELOPMENT RESOURCES	SECTION REVIEW AND ASSESSMENT	STANDARDS CORRELATIONS
SE Pre-Reading Activity, p. 578 GENERAL **OSP** Science Puzzlers, Twisters & Teasers GENERAL		National Science Education Standards UCP 1, 3,4 5; SAI 1, 2; SPSP 1; LS 1d, 1e, 3a, 3b
CRF Directed Reading A* ■ BASIC, B* SPECIAL NEEDS **CRF** Vocabulary and Section Summary* ■ GENERAL **SE** Reading Strategy Reading Organizer, p. 580 GENERAL **TE** Reading Strategy Prediction Guide, p. 581 BASIC **TE** Inclusion Strategies, p. 582	**SE** Reading Checks, pp. 581, 582 GENERAL **TE** Reteaching, p. 582 BASIC **TE** Quiz, p. 582 GENERAL **TE** Alternative Assessment, p. 582 GENERAL **SE** Section Review,* p. 583 ■ GENERAL **CRF** Section Quiz* ■ GENERAL	UCP 1, 3, 4; LS 1a, 1d, 3a
CRF Directed Reading A* ■ BASIC, B* SPECIAL NEEDS **CRF** Vocabulary and Section Summary* ■ GENERAL **SE** Reading Strategy Reading Organizer, p. 584 GENERAL **SE** Connection to Environmental Science Bones from the Ocean, p. 586 GENERAL **MS** Math Skills for Science Mechanical Advantage* GENERAL **CRF** Reinforcement Worksheet The Hipbone's Connected to the… BASIC **CRF** Critical Thinking The Tissue Engineering Debate* ADVANCED	**SE** Reading Checks, pp. 585, 586 GENERAL **TE** Reteaching, p. 586 BASIC **TE** Quiz, p. 586 GENERAL **SE** Section Review,* p. 587 ■ GENERAL **TE** Alternative Assessment, p. 587 GENERAL **CRF** Section Quiz* ■ GENERAL	UCP 2, 3, 5; SAI 1; SPSP 1, 4; LS 1d, 1e
CRF Directed Reading A* ■ BASIC, B* SPECIAL NEEDS **CRF** Vocabulary and Section Summary* ■ GENERAL **SE** Reading Strategy Discussion, p. 588 GENERAL **SE** Math Practice Runner's Time, p. 591 GENERAL **MS** Math Skills for Science The Unit Factor and Dimensional Analysis* GENERAL **CRF** Reinforcement Worksheet Muscle Map* BASIC	**SE** Reading Checks, pp. 589, 591 GENERAL **TE** Reteaching, p. 590 BASIC **TE** Quiz, p. 590 GENERAL **TE** Alternative Assessment, p. 590 GENERAL **TE** Homework, p. 590 ADVANCED **SE** Section Review,* p. 591 ■ GENERAL **CRF** Section Quiz* ■ GENERAL	UCP 1, 2, 3, 4; SAI 1, 2; SPSP 1; LS 1d, 1e; *LabBook:* UCP 3; SAI 1, 2; LS 1a, 1d, 1e, 3b
CRF Directed Reading A* ■ BASIC, B* SPECIAL NEEDS **CRF** Vocabulary and Section Summary* ■ GENERAL **SE** Reading Strategy Paired Summarizing, p. 592 GENERAL **TE** Inclusion Strategies, p. 593 **SE** Connection to Social Studies Using Hair, p. 594 GENERAL	**SE** Reading Checks, pp. 593, 594 GENERAL **TE** Reteaching, p. 594 BASIC **TE** Quiz, p. 594 GENERAL **TE** Alternative Assessment, p. 594 ADVANCED **SE** Section Review,* p. 595 ■ GENERAL **CRF** Section Quiz* ■ GENERAL	UCP 3, 5; SAI 2; SPSP 1; LS 1c, 1d, 1e, 1f, 3a, 3b; *Chapter Lab:* UCP 1, 2, 3, 5; SAI 1, 2; SPSP 1; LS 1d

 **One-Stop Planner® CD-ROM**

This convenient CD-ROM includes:
- Lab Materials QuickList Software
- Holt Calendar Planner
- Customizable Lesson Plans
- Printable Worksheets
- ExamView® Test Generator

 **cnnstudentnews.com**

Find the latest news, lesson plans, and activities related to important scientific events.

 **SCiLINKS® NSTA**

www.scilinks.org

Maintained by the **National Science Teachers Association.** See Chapter Enrichment pages for a complete list of topics.

 **Current Science®**

Check out *Current Science* articles and activities by visiting the HRW Web site at **go.hrw.com.** Just type in the keyword **HL5CS22T.**

 **Classroom Videos**

- **Lab Videos** demonstrate the chapter lab.
- **Brain Food Video Quizzes** help students review the chapter material.
- **CNN Videos** bring science into your students' daily life.

Visual Resources

CHAPTER STARTER TRANSPARENCY

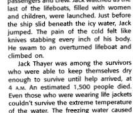

Body Organization and Structure   CHAPTER STARTER

This Really Happened!

On April 14, 1912, at 11:40 P.M., the British steamship *Titanic*, the largest and most luxurious steamship ever built, struck an iceberg. Jack Thayer, a 17-year-old from Pennsylvania, felt the impact in his cabin and went on deck to see what had happened. To his horror, he found that the ship was sinking and that there were not enough lifeboats for the 2,207 passengers and crew. Jack watched as the last of the lifeboats, filled with women and children, were launched. Just before the ship descended into the icy water, Jack jumped. The pain of the cold felt like knives stabbing every inch of his body. He swam to an overturned lifeboat and climbed on.

Jack Thayer was among the survivors who were able to keep themselves dry enough to survive until help arrived, at 4 A.M. An estimated 1,500 people died. Even those who were wearing life jackets couldn't survive the extreme temperature of the water. The freezing water caused their body systems to fail. Breathing became difficult, and muscles no longer functioned. Finally, they lost consciousness and their hearts stopped.

The water around the *Titanic* was just too cold for human survival.

Under normal circumstances, our bodies are able to maintain a constant internal temperature. Read on to find out about this and other interesting information on how our bodies work.

BELLRINGER TRANSPARENCIES

Body Organization and Structure   BELLRINGER TRANSPARENCY

Section: Body Organization
Match the body system in the first column with the correct function in the second column:
1. respiratory system   a. regulates body functions
2. muscular system   b. breaks down food
3. digestive system   c. pumps blood
4. circulatory system   d. absorbs oxygen
5. endocrine system   e. moves bones

Record your answers in your **science journal.**

Section: The Skeletal System
Brainstorm some problems you would have if you lacked bones. Do you know any kinds of animals that don't have bones? Do you know of any animals that wear their "skeletons" on the outside of their bodies?

Record your answers in your **science journal.**

TEACHING TRANSPARENCIES

Body Organization and Structure   TEACHING TRANSPARENCY

Organ Systems

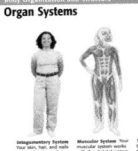
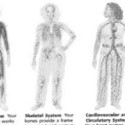
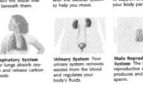

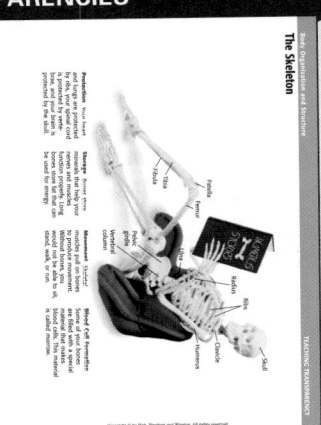

The Skeleton

TEACHING TRANSPARENCIES

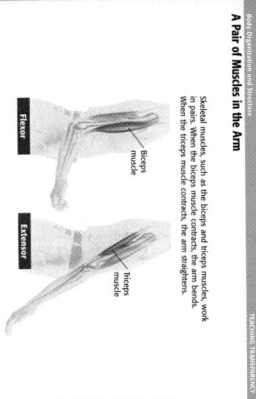

A Pair of Muscles in the Arm

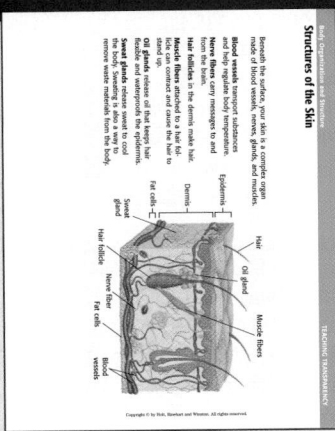

Structures of the Skin

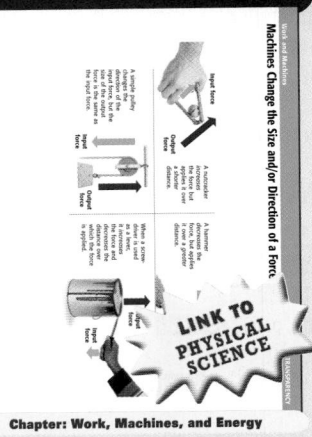

Machines Change the Size and/or Direction of a Force

LINK TO PHYSICAL SCIENCE

Chapter: Work, Machines, and Energy

CONCEPT MAPPING TRANSPARENCY

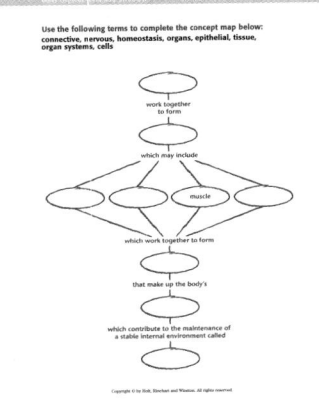

Body Organization and Structure   CONCEPT MAPPING TRANSPARENCY

Use the following terms to complete the concept map below: connective, nervous, homeostasis, organs, epithelial, tissue, organ systems, cells

Planning Resources

LESSON PLANS

Lesson Plan   SAMPLE

Section: Waves

Pacing
Regular Schedule: with lab(s):2 days   without lab(s):1 days
Block Schedule: with lab(s): 1 1/2 days without lab(s):1 day

Objectives
1. Relate the seven properties of life to a living organism.
2. Describe seven themes that can help you to organize what you learn about biology.
3. Identify the tiny structures that make up all living organisms.
4. Differentiate between reproduction and heredity and between metabolism and homeostasis.

National Science Education Standards Covered
LSInter6:Cells have particular structures that underlie their functions.
LSMat1:Most cell functions involve chemical reactions.
LSBeh1:Cells store and use information to guide their functions.
UCP1:Cell functions are regulated.
SI1: Cells can differentiate and form complete multicellular organisms.
PS1: Species evolve over time.
ESS1: The great diversity of organisms is the result of more than 3.5 billion years of evolution.
ESS2: Natural selection and its evolutionary consequences provide a scientific explanation for the fossil record of ancient life forms as well as for the striking molecular similarities observed among the diverse species of living organisms.
ST1: The millions of different species of plants, animals, and microorganisms that live on Earth today are related by descent from common ancestors.
ST2: The energy for life primarily comes from the sun.
SPSP1: The complexity and organization of organisms accommodates the need for obtaining, transforming, transporting, releasing, and eliminating the matter and energy used to sustain the organism.
SPSP6: As matter and energy flows through different levels of organization of living systems—cells, organs, communities—and between living systems and the physical environment, chemical elements are recombined in different ways.
HNS1: Organisms have behavioral responses to internal changes and to external stimuli.

PARENT LETTER

SAMPLE

Dear Parent,

Your son's or daughter's science class will soon begin exploring the chapter entitled "The World of Physical Science." In this chapter, students will learn about how the scientific method applies to the world of physical science and the role of physical science in the world. By the end of the chapter, students should demonstrate a clear understanding of the chapter's main ideas and be able to discuss the following topics:

1. physical science as the study of energy and matter (Section 1)
2. the role of physical science and themes in science (Section 1)
3. careers that rely on physical science (Section 1)
4. the steps used in the scientific method (Section 2)
5. examples of technology (Section 2)
6. how the scientific method is used to answer questions and solve problems (Section 2)
7. how our knowledge of science changes over time (Section 3)
8. how models represent real objects or systems (Section 3)
9. examples of different ways models are used in science (Section 3)
10. the importance of the International System of Units (Section 4)
11. the appropriate units to use for particular measurements (Section 4)
12. how area and density are derived quantities (Section 4)

Questions to Ask Along the Way

You can help your son or daughter learn about these topics by asking interesting questions such as the following:

• What are some surprising careers that use physical science?
• What is a characteristic of a good hypothesis?
• When is it a good idea to use a model?
• Why do Americans measure things in terms of inches and yards and meters?

ALSO IN SPANISH

TEST ITEM LISTING

TEST ITEM LISTING
The World of Science   SAMPLE

MULTIPLE CHOICE
1. A limitation of models is that
   a. they are large enough to see.
   b. they do not act exactly like the things that they model.
   c. they are smaller than the things that they model.
   d. they model unfamiliar things.
   Answer: B   Difficulty: 1   Section: 3   Objective: 2
2. The length 10 m is equal to
   a. 100 cm.   c. 10,000 mm.
   b. 1,000 cm.   d. Both (b) and (c)
   Answer: B   Difficulty: 1   Section: 3   Objective: 2
3. To be valid, a hypothesis must be
   a. testable.   c. made into a law.
   b. supported by evidence.   d. Both (a) and (b)
   Answer: B   Difficulty: 1   Section: 3   Objective: 2 1
4. The statement "Sheila has a stain on her shirt" is an example of a(n)
   a. law.   c. observation.
   b. hypothesis.   d. prediction.
   Answer: 7   Difficulty: 1   Section: 2   Objective: 2
5. A hypothesis is often developed out of
   a. observations.   c. laws.
   b. experiments.   d. Both (a) and (b)
   Answer: 9   Difficulty: 1   Section: 3   Objective: 2
6. How many milliliters are in 3.5 kL?
   a. 3,500 mL   c. 3,500, 000 mL
   b. 0.0035 mL   d. 35,000 mL.
   Answer: 8   Difficulty: 1   Section: 3   Objective: 2
7. A map of Seattle is an example of a
   a. law.   c. model.
   b. theory.   d. unit.
   Answer: 8   Difficulty: 1   Section: 3   Objective: 2
8. A lab has the safety icons shown below. These icons mean that you should wear
   a. only safety goggles. c. safety goggles and a lab apron.
   b. only a lab apron.   d. safety goggles, a lab apron, and gloves.
   Answer: 8   Difficulty: 1   Section: 3   Objective: 2
9. The law of conservation of mass says the total mass before a chemical change is
   a. more than the total mass after the change.
   b. less than the total mass after the change.
   c. the same as the total mass after the change.
   d. not the same as the total mass after the change.
   Answer: 8   Difficulty: 1   Section: 3   Objective: 2
10. In which of the following areas might you find a geochemist at work?
   a. studying the chemistry of rocks   c. studying fishes
   b. studying forestry   d. studying the atmosphere
   Answer: 8   Difficulty: 1   Section: 3   Objective: 2

One-Stop Planner® CD-ROM

This CD-ROM includes all of the resources shown here and the following time-saving tools:

• *Lab Materials QuickList Software*
• *Customizable lesson plans*
• *Holt Calendar Planner*
• *The powerful ExamView® Test Generator*

Meeting Individual Needs

DIRECTED READING A
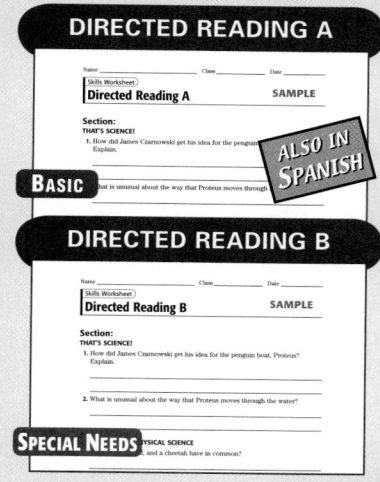
BASIC · ALSO IN SPANISH

DIRECTED READING B
SPECIAL NEEDS

VOCABULARY ACTIVITY
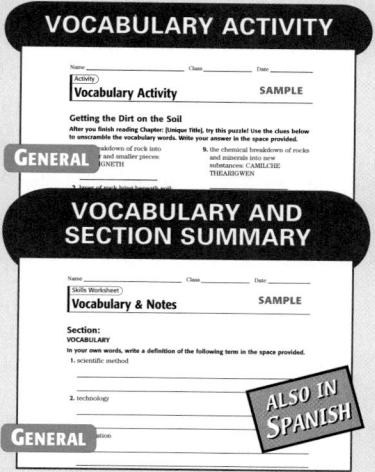
Getting the Dirt on the Soil
GENERAL

VOCABULARY AND SECTION SUMMARY
Vocabulary & Notes
GENERAL · ALSO IN SPANISH

REINFORCEMENT
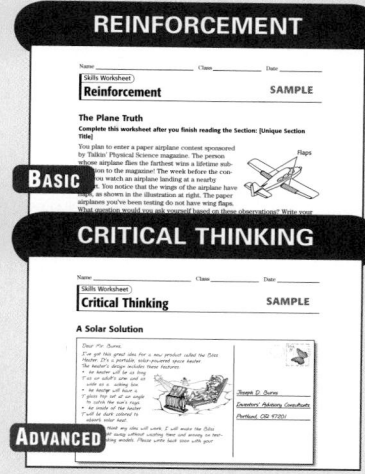
The Plane Truth
BASIC

CRITICAL THINKING
A Solar Solution
ADVANCED

SCILINKS ACTIVITY

MARINE ECOSYSTEMS
GENERAL

SCIENCE PUZZLERS, TWISTERS & TEASERS
Body Organization and Structure
Find the Oddballs and Decode the Message
GENERAL

Labs and Activities

LONG-TERM PROJECTS & RESEARCH IDEAS
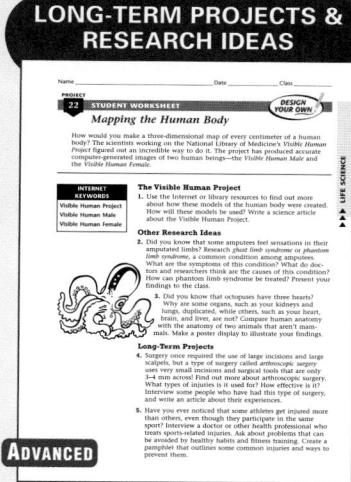
Mapping the Human Body
ADVANCED

INQUIRY LABS
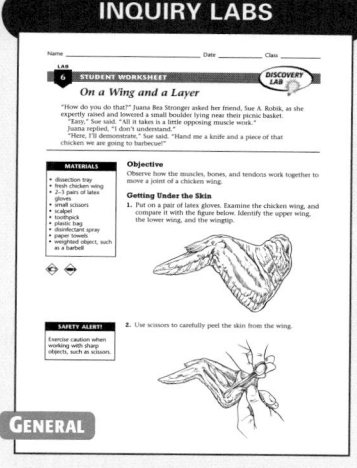
On a Wing and a Layer
GENERAL

DATASHEETS FOR QUICK LABS

Reaction to Stress

DATASHEETS FOR CHAPTER LABS
Using Scientific Methods

DATASHEETS FOR LABBOOK
Does It All Add Up?

Review and Assessments

SECTION QUIZ
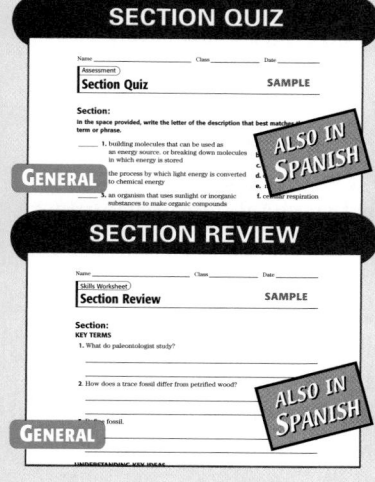
GENERAL · ALSO IN SPANISH

SECTION REVIEW
GENERAL · ALSO IN SPANISH

CHAPTER REVIEW
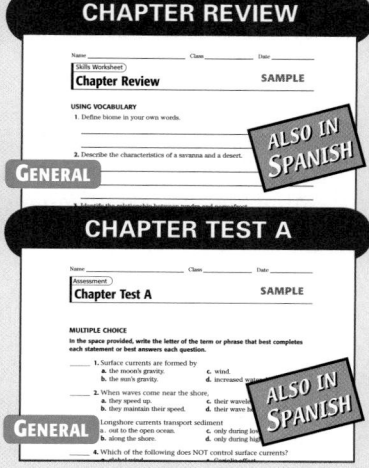
GENERAL · ALSO IN SPANISH

CHAPTER TEST A
GENERAL · ALSO IN SPANISH

CHAPTER TEST B
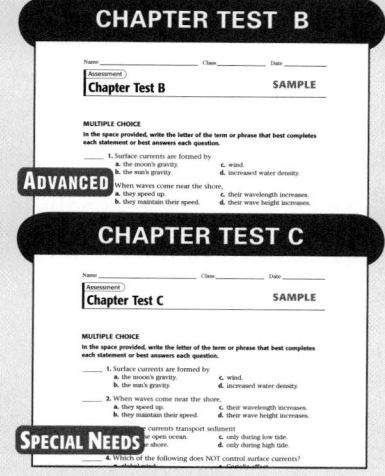
ADVANCED

CHAPTER TEST C
SPECIAL NEEDS

STANDARDIZED TEST PREPARATION
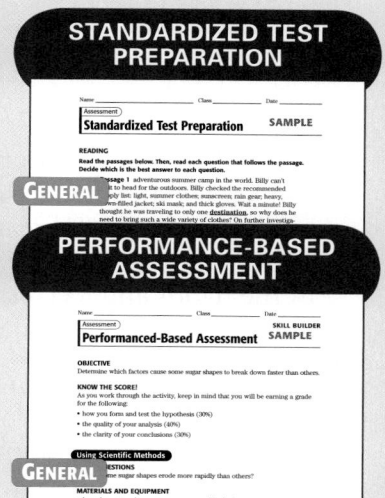
GENERAL

PERFORMANCE-BASED ASSESSMENT
Performanced-Based Assessment
GENERAL

This Chapter Enrichment provides relevant and interesting information to expand and enhance your presentation of the chapter material.

Section 1

Body Organization

Tissues

- Tissues differ from each other in terms of the shape and size of cells, the amount and kind of material between the cells, and the special functions the tissues perform to maintain proper functioning of the body.

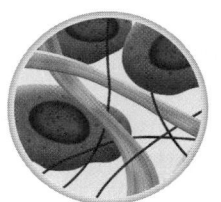 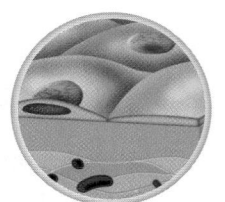

- Connective tissue is the most abundant tissue in the body. It displays the most variety in form and type. All connective tissue, however, can be classified into one of four types: dense connective tissue (cartilage and bone), loose connective tissue (found beneath the skin and around nerves, blood vessels, and organs), liquid connective tissue (blood and lymph), and adipose tissue (where the body stores energy as droplets of fat).

- Although bone is considerably harder than other body tissues, it accounts for only about 14% of a person's total body weight.

Section 2

The Skeletal System

The Human Skeleton

- The skeleton provides support for soft tissue. Also, it regulates body minerals and produces both red and white blood cells. There are typically 206 bones in the adult human body, but extra bones, particularly those in the hands and feet, can increase that number. The number of bones in children varies with age.

- The skeleton forms from more than 800 centers of ossification. All of the bony elements are generally not completely united to form an adult skeleton until a person reaches his or her mid-20s.

- The skeletons of male and female humans are slightly different. The most pronounced differences are in the pelvis. A female's pelvis is adapted for childbearing and thus has a larger pelvic inlet. Women who are malnourished during childhood typically do not develop the wider pelvis, which can make natural childbirth dangerous or even fatal for them.

- An individual's age can be determined by looking at the skeleton alone. A younger individual's dentition and bone fusion patterns indicate his or her age. In adults, age determination is more difficult because one must rely solely on signs of skeletal deterioration.

Bones

- Each bone is surrounded by a strong fibrous covering called a *periosteum*. Articular surfaces are covered in cartilage.

- Bones are made of three types of cells: osteoblasts, osteocytes, and osteoclasts. Osteoblasts are bone-producing cells. Osteocytes are bone-maintaining cells. Osteoclasts are bone-destroying cells.

- For its weight, bone is 5 times stronger than steel.

Joints

- Doctors typically classify joints by structure rather than movement. The three types of joint structures are called *fibrous*, *cartilaginous*, and *synovial*. Fibrous joints (such as those in the skull) are immovable joints in which a fibrous tissue or a hyaline cartilage connects the bones. Cartilaginous joints (such as those in the rib cage) are slightly moveable joints in which cartilage connects the bones. Synovial joints (such as the knee) are freely moving joints in which synovial membranes cover the cartilage and ligaments connecting the bone.

Section 3

The Muscular System

Skeletal Muscles

- There are more than 600 skeletal muscles in the human body. They are often organized into the following groups: muscles of the head and the neck, muscles of the trunk, muscles of the upper limbs, and muscles of the lower limbs.

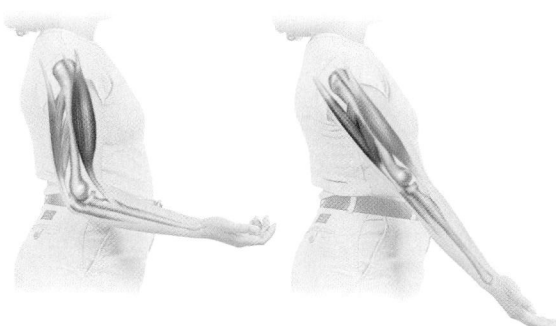

Types of Muscle Cells

- When observed through a microscope, the three types of muscles are clearly identifiable. Cells of smooth muscles have a long, tapered shape; no clearly defined striations; and a large central nucleus. Skeletal muscle cells are long and tapered and characterized by distinct light- and dark-colored bands. Each cell has multiple nuclei because several skeletal muscle cells merge, and the cell membranes become indistinct. The cells of cardiac muscle have one or more nuclei and have an irregular, branched shape.

Section 4

The Integumentary System

Skin

- One square inch of skin can hold as many as 650 sweat glands, 20 blood vessels, and more than 1,000 nerve endings.

- Each person has a unique series of ridges and indentations called *fingerprints* on the tips of his or her fingers. No two people have the same fingerprints. Fingerprints help the fingers to grip slippery surfaces. Each person also has unique patterns on the tips of his or her toes.

Is That a Fact!

- ◆ More than three-fourths of the dust in some homes is made up of dead skin cells!

Hair and Nails

- Only mammals have true hair. All mammals have hair somewhere on their bodies.

- The body's most visible signs of aging occur in the integumentary system. Skin becomes thin, dry, wrinkled, and less supple. Dark-colored age spots may develop. Hair turns gray or white and may begin to fall out. Hair follicles decrease in number. Sweat glands become less active, so older people are less tolerant to extremely hot weather.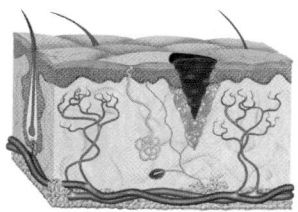

- Hair that is kept short grows an average of 2 cm per month. Growth slows to about 1 cm per month when hair reaches about 30 cm long. Fingernails grow about 2 cm each year. The fastest-growing nail is on the middle finger. Fingernails grow three to four times more quickly than toenails do.

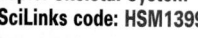

Overview

Tell students that this chapter will help them learn about human body systems. In particular, the chapter will introduce students to the skeletal, muscular, and integumentary systems.

Assessing Prior Knowledge

Students should be familiar with the following topics:

- cells
- body organization

Identifying Misconceptions

As students learn the material in this chapter, some of them may be confused about the concept of homeostasis. Students should understand that homeostasis is a state in which the internal environment of the human body is stable. Help students understand that because the external environment is always changing, the human body must adjust to these changes to maintain homeostasis within the body. Students should also understand that all cells in the body play a role in homeostasis, but because there are many kinds of cells, no single cell has to do all of the jobs necessary for homeostasis.

22

Body Organization and Structure

About the PHOTO

Lance Armstrong has won the Tour de France several times. These victories are especially remarkable because he was diagnosed with cancer in 1996. But with medicine and hard work, he grew strong enough to win one of the toughest events in all of sports.

PRE-READING ACTIVITY

FOLDNOTES **Four-Corner Fold**
Before you read the chapter, create the FoldNote entitled "Four-Corner Fold" described in the **Study Skills** section of the Appendix. Label the flaps of the four-corner fold with "The skeletal system," "The muscular system," and "The integumentary system." Write what you know about each topic under the appropriate flap. As you read the chapter, add other information that you learn.

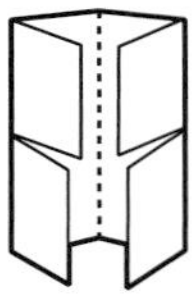

Standards Correlations

National Science Education Standards

The following codes indicate the National Science Education Standards that correlate to this chapter. The full text of the standards is at the front of the book.

Chapter Opener
UCP 1, 3, 4, 5; SAI 1, 2; SPSP 1; LS 1d, 1e, 3a, 3b

Section 1 Body Organization
UCP 1, 3, 4; LS 1a, 1d, 3a

Section 2 The Skeletal System
UCP 2, 3, 5; SAI 1; SPSP 1, 4; LS 1d, 1e

Section 3 The Muscular System
UCP 1, 2, 3, 4; SAI 1, 2; SPSP 1; LS 1d, 1e; *LabBook:* UCP 3; SAI 1, 2; LS 1a, 1d, 1e, 3b

Section 4 The Integumentary System
UCP 3, 5; SAI 2; SPSP 1; LS 1c, 1d, 1e, 1f, 3a, 3b

Chapter Lab
UCP 1, 2, 3, 5; SAI 1, 2; SPSP 1; LS 1d

Chapter Review
UCP 1, 2, 3, 4, 5; SAI 1, 2; SPSP 1, 4; LS 1a, 1c, 1d, 1e, 1f, 3a, 3b

Science in Action
UCP 1, 5; ST 1, 2; SPSP 1, 4, 5; LS 1d, 1e

START-UP ACTIVITY

Too Cold for Comfort

Your nervous system sends you messages about your body. For example, if someone steps on your toe, your nervous system sends you a message. The pain you feel is a message that tells you to move your toe to safety. Try this exercise to watch your nervous system in action.

Procedure

1. Hold **a few pieces of ice** in one hand. Allow the melting water to drip into a **dish.** Hold the ice until the cold is uncomfortable. Then, release the ice into the dish.

2. Compare the hand that held the ice with your other hand. Describe the changes you see.

Analysis

1. What message did you receive from your nervous system while you held the ice?

2. How quickly did the cold hand return to normal?

3. What organ systems do you think helped restore your hand to normal?

4. Think of a time when your nervous system sent you a message, such as an uncomfortable feeling of heat, cold, or pain. How did your body react?

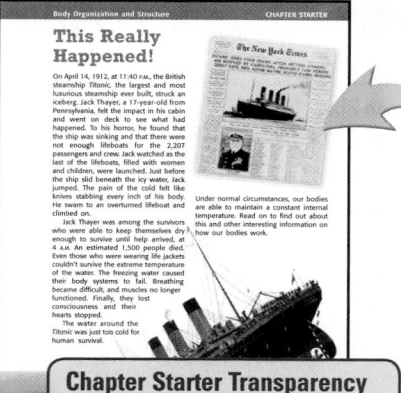

This Really Happened!

   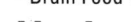

Chapter Starter Transparency
Use this transparency to help students begin thinking about human body systems.

CHAPTER RESOURCES

Technology

Transparencies
- Chapter Starter Transparency

READING SKILLS

Student Edition on CD-ROM

Guided Reading Audio CD
- English or Spanish

Classroom Videos
- Brain Food Video Quiz

Workbooks

Science Puzzlers, Twisters & Teasers
- Body Organization and Structure GENERAL

Focus

Overview

This section introduces the basic organization of the human body. Students will learn about the four major tissues of the body and that the body's organs are arranged by function into 12 organ systems.

🔘 Bellringer

Write the names of the following organ systems on the board or an overhead projector: *respiratory system, muscular system, digestive system, cardiovascular system,* and *endocrine system.* Then, write the following functions: *to pump blood, to enable movement, to send out chemical messages, to absorb oxygen,* and *to break down food.* Ask students to match each organ system with its correct function. (The respiratory system absorbs oxygen. The muscular system enables movement. The digestive system breaks down food. The cardiovascular system pumps blood. The endocrine system sends out chemical messages.)

READING WARM-UP

Objectives

● Describe how tissues, organs, and organ systems are related.

● List 12 organ systems.

● Identify how organ systems work together to maintain homeostasis.

Terms to Learn

homeostasis   organ
tissue

READING STRATEGY

Reading Organizer As you read this section, make a concept map by using the terms above.

homeostasis the maintenance of a constant internal state in a changing environment

tissue a group of similar cells that perform a common function

Body Organization

Imagine jumping into a lake. At first, your body feels very cold. You may even shiver. But eventually you get used to the cold water. How?

Your body gets used to cold water because of homeostasis (HOH mee OH STAY sis). **Homeostasis** is the maintenance of a stable internal environment in the body. When you jump into a lake, homeostasis helps your body adapt to the cold water.

Cells, Tissues, and Organs

Maintaining homeostasis is not easy. Your internal environment is always changing. Your cells need nutrients and oxygen to survive. Your cells need wastes removed. If homeostasis is disrupted, cells may not get the materials they need. So, cells may be damaged or may die.

Your cells must do many jobs to maintain homeostasis. Fortunately, each of your cells does not have to do all of those jobs. Just as each person on a soccer team has a role during a game, each cell in your body has a job in maintaining homeostasis. Your cells are organized into groups. A group of similar cells working together forms a **tissue.** Your body has four main kinds of tissue. The four kinds of tissue are shown in **Figure 1.**

Figure 1   **Four Kinds of Tissue**

Epithelial tissue covers and protects underlying tissue. When you look at the surface of your skin, you see epithelial tissue. The cells form a continuous sheet.

Nervous tissue sends electrical signals through the body. It is found in the brain, nerves, and sense organs.

CHAPTER RESOURCES

Chapter Resource File

📁   • **Lesson Plan**
     • **Directed Reading A** BASIC
     • **Directed Reading B** SPECIAL NEEDS

Technology

🖥️   **Transparencies**
     • Bellringer

Is That a Fact!

The Pompeii worm, *Alvinella pompejana,* can survive a temperature difference of 60°C between its head and its tail! Scientists theorize that a coating of furry bacteria living on the worm's back allows the worm to endure such extreme temperature differences.

Figure 2 Organization of the Stomach

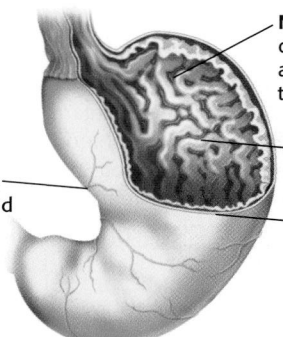

The stomach is an organ. The four kinds of tissue work together so that the stomach can carry out digestion.

Nervous tissue in the stomach partly controls the production of acids that aid in the digestion of food. Nervous tissue signals when the stomach is full.

Epithelial tissue lines the stomach.

Blood and another **connective tissue** called *collagen* are found in the wall of the stomach.

Layers of **muscle tissue** break up stomach contents.

Tissues Form Organs

One kind of tissue alone cannot do all of the things that several kinds of tissue working together can do. Two or more tissues working together form an **organ.** Your stomach, shown in **Figure 2,** uses all four kinds of tissue to carry out digestion.

Organs Form Systems

Your stomach does a lot to help you digest your food. But the stomach doesn't do it all. Your stomach works with other organs, such as the small and large intestines, to digest your food. Organs that work together make up an *organ system.*

✓ Reading Check How is the stomach part of an organ system? (*See the Appendix for answers to Reading Checks.*)

organ a collection of tissues that carry out a specialized function of the body

Muscle tissue is made of cells that contract and relax to produce movement.

Connective tissue joins, supports, protects, insulates, nourishes, and cushions organs. It also keeps organs from falling apart.

CONNECTION ACTiViTY
History —————— ADVANCED

Organ Transplants The first transplant of a human heart was performed in Cape Town, South Africa, on December 3, 1967, by Dr. Christiaan Barnard and a team of 30 physicians. Have interested students research when other organs, such as kidneys, livers, and lungs, were first transplanted. Have students make posters about their findings. **LS Visual**

Answer to Reading Check

The stomach works with other organs, such as the small and large intestines, to digest food.

Section 1 • Body Organization  **581**

Reteaching — **BASIC**

Organizing Information To help students understand and identify the 12 major organ systems of the body, have them make a table with the following headings: "Name of organ system," "Function(s)," and "Main organs." Have students use the table to review the information presented on these pages. **LS** Logical

Quiz — **GENERAL**

Ask students whether each of the following statements is true or false. Have students correct false statements.

1. Homeostasis is the maintenance of a stable internal environment. (true)

2. Epithelial tissue sends electrical signals throughout the body. (false; Nervous tissue sends electrical signals throughout the body and epithelial tissue covers and protects underlying tissue.)

3. Blood is a type of connective tissue. (true)

Alternative Assessment — **GENERAL**

 **Organ Systems** In their **science journal,** have students describe three of the organ systems introduced in this section. Have them describe the functions and primary organs of each system and include drawings of each system. **LS** Verbal

Working Together

Organ systems work together to maintain homeostasis. Your body has 12 major organ systems, as shown in **Figure 3.** The circulatory and cardiovascular systems are shown together. The cardiovascular system includes your heart and blood vessels. Additionally, these organs are part of the circulatory system, which also includes blood. Together, these two systems deliver the materials your cells need to survive. This is just one example of how organ systems work together to keep you healthy.

✓ **Reading Check** Give an example of how organ systems work together in the body.

Figure 3 Organ Systems

 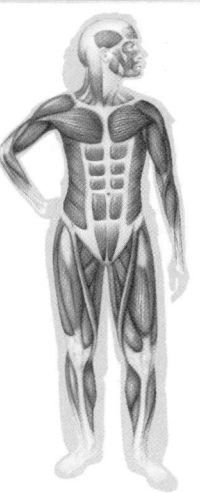 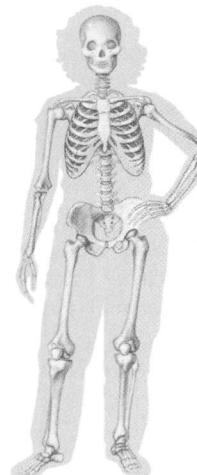 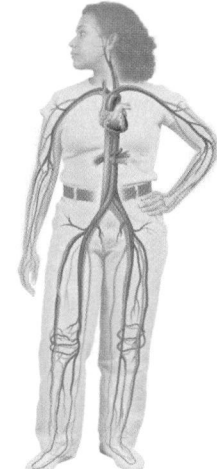

Integumentary System Your skin, hair, and nails protect the tissue that lies beneath them.

Muscular System Your muscular system works with the skeletal system to help you move.

Skeletal System Your bones provide a frame to support and protect your body parts.

Cardiovascular and Circulatory Systems Your heart pumps blood through all of your blood vessels.

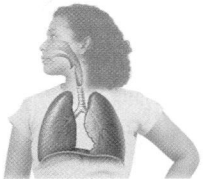 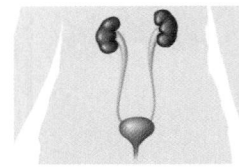 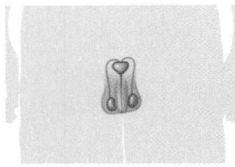 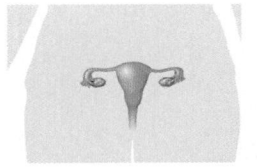

Respiratory System Your lungs absorb oxygen and release carbon dioxide.

Urinary System Your urinary system removes wastes from the blood and regulates your body's fluids.

Male Reproductive System The male reproductive system produces and delivers sperm.

Female Reproductive System The female reproductive system produces eggs and nourishes and protects the fetus.

⬤ INCLUSION *Strategies*

• *Attention Deficit Disorder* • *Visually Impaired*
• *Developmentally Delayed*

Kinesthetic activities can help students learn more easily. Ask 11 students to hold signs identifying each student as an organ system (exclude the reproductive system). Ask the students to step forward if their system is involved in the following activities: snoring (respiratory and muscular), sweating (lymphatic and integumentary),

jumping in fear (muscular, skeletal, nervous, and endocrine), drinking (muscular, digestive, and urinary), eating an apple (digestive and muscular), running (muscular, skeletal, circulatory, cardiovascular, and respiratory). You may want to tell students that some body systems, such as the nervous system and the endocrine system, play a role in nearly all of the body's functions. **LS** Kinesthetic/Visual

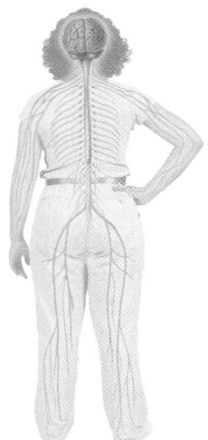

Nervous System Your nervous system receives and sends electrical messages throughout your body.

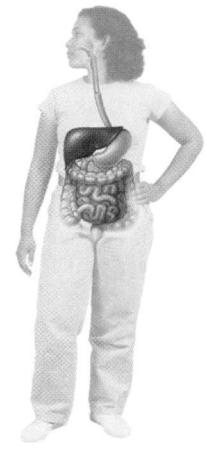

Digestive System Your digestive system breaks down the food you eat into nutrients that your body can absorb.

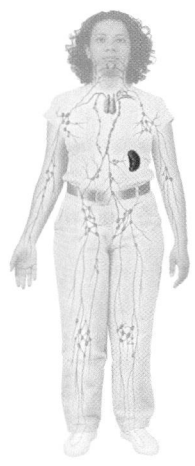

Lymphatic System The lymphatic system returns leaked fluids to blood vessels and helps get rid of bacteria and viruses.

Endocrine System Your glands send out chemical messages. Ovaries and testes are part of this system.

SECTION Review

Summary

- A group of cells that work together is a tissue. Tissues form organs. Organs that work together form organ systems.
- There are four kinds of tissue in the human body.
- There are 12 major organ systems in the human body.
- Organ systems work together to help the body maintain homeostasis.

Using Key Terms

1. Use the following terms in the same sentence: *homeostasis*, *tissue*, and *organ*.

Understanding Key Ideas

2. Which of the following statements describes how tissues, organs, and organ systems are related?
   a. Organs form tissues, which form organ systems.
   b. Organ systems form organs, which form tissues.
   c. Tissues form organs, which form organ systems.
   d. None of the above

3. List the 12 organ systems.

Math Skills

4. The human skeleton has 206 bones. The human skull has 22 bones. What percentage of human bones are skull bones?

Critical Thinking

5. **Applying Concepts** Tanya went to a restaurant and ate a hamburger. Describe how Tanya used five organ systems to eat and digest her hamburger.

6. **Predicting Consequences** Predict what might happen if the human body did not have specialized cells, tissues, organs, and organ systems to maintain homeostasis.

Developed and maintained by the National Science Teachers Association

For a variety of links related to this chapter, go to www.scilinks.org

Topic: Tissues and Organs; Body Systems
SciLinks code: HSM1530; HSM0184

Answers to Review

1. Sample answer: Homeostasis is maintained by cells, tissues, and organs.

2. c

3. integumentary system, muscular system, skeletal system, cardiovascular system, circulatory system, respiratory system, urinary system, reproductive system, nervous system, digestive system, lymphatic system, and endocrine system

4. about 11% (22 bones ÷ 206 bones × 100 = 10.7%)

5. Sample answer: The nervous system sends messages to Tanya's muscular system to bite into the hamburger. Tanya's jaws, which are part of the skeletal system, help grind up the food. The food moves into Tanya's stomach, which is part of her digestive system. The digestive system breaks down the food, and the circulatory system picks up nutrients from the digestive system to take throughout the body.

6. Sample answer: The body would be unable to maintain homeostasis because the cells of the body would have too many jobs to do. The cells likely would not be able to do all of these jobs.

Answer to Reading Check

Sample answer: The cardiovascular system includes the heart and blood vessels. These organs are also part of the circulatory system, which includes blood. Together, these systems deliver the materials cells need to survive.

CHAPTER RESOURCES

Chapter Resource File

- Section Quiz GENERAL
- Section Review GENERAL
- Vocabulary and Section Summary GENERAL
- SciLinks Activity GENERAL

Technology

Transparencies
- Organ Systems

SECTION
2

Focus

Overview

This section introduces the skeletal system and describes the functions of bones. The section also illustrates the internal structure of bones and three types of joints.

🔘 Bellringer

Have students brainstorm problems that they would have if they lacked bones. (Students should understand that they would have no defined structure, mineral storage, organ protection, blood cells, or mobility.)

Motivate

ACTiViTY ——————— GENERAL

Locating Bones Review with students that the skeletal system supports the body and protects delicate body parts. Encourage students to press the skin in various parts of their body to feel their bones. Ask students to describe any parts of their body where they cannot feel their bones. (Answers may vary but should include the abdomen, nose, and ears.) As you point to various parts of the body, ask students what organs the bones protect. (Sample answers: The skull protects the brain. The ribs protect the heart and lungs.) **LS Kinesthetic/Visual**

READING WARM-UP

Objectives

● Identify the major organs of the skeletal system.
● Describe four functions of bones.
● Describe three joints.
● List three injuries and two diseases that affect bones and joints.

Terms to Learn

skeletal system
joint

READING STRATEGY

Reading Organizer As you read this section, create an outline of the section. Use the headings from the section in your outline.

skeletal system the organ system whose primary function is to support and protect the body and to allow the body to move

The Skeletal System

When you hear the word skeleton, *you may think of the remains of something that has died. But your skeleton is not dead. It is very much alive.*

You may think your bones are dry and brittle. But they are alive and active. Bones, cartilage, and the connective tissue that holds bones together make up your **skeletal system.**

Bones

The average adult human skeleton has 206 bones. Bones help support and protect parts of your body. They work with your muscles so you can move. Bones also help your body maintain homeostasis by storing minerals and making blood cells. **Figure 1** shows the functions of your skeleton.

| Figure 1 | The Skeleton |

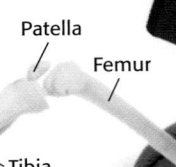
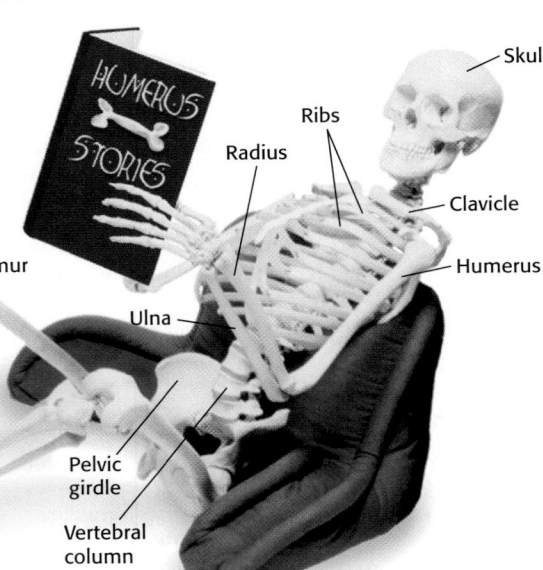

Skull
Ribs
Radius
Clavicle
Patella
Femur
Humerus
Ulna
Tibia
Fibula
Pelvic girdle
Vertebral column

Protection Your heart and lungs are protected by ribs, your spinal cord is protected by vertebrae, and your brain is protected by the skull.

Storage Bones store minerals that help your nerves and muscles function properly. Long bones store fat that can be used for energy.

Movement Skeletal muscles pull on bones to produce movement. Without bones, you would not be able to sit, stand, walk, or run.

Blood Cell Formation Some of your bones are filled with a special material that makes blood cells. This material is called *marrow.*

CHAPTER RESOURCES

Chapter Resource File

• Lesson Plan
• Directed Reading A BASIC
• Directed Reading B SPECIAL NEEDS

Technology

Transparencies
• Bellringer
• The Skeleton

SCIENCE HUMOR

Q: Why didn't the skeleton cross the road?

A: It didn't have the guts.

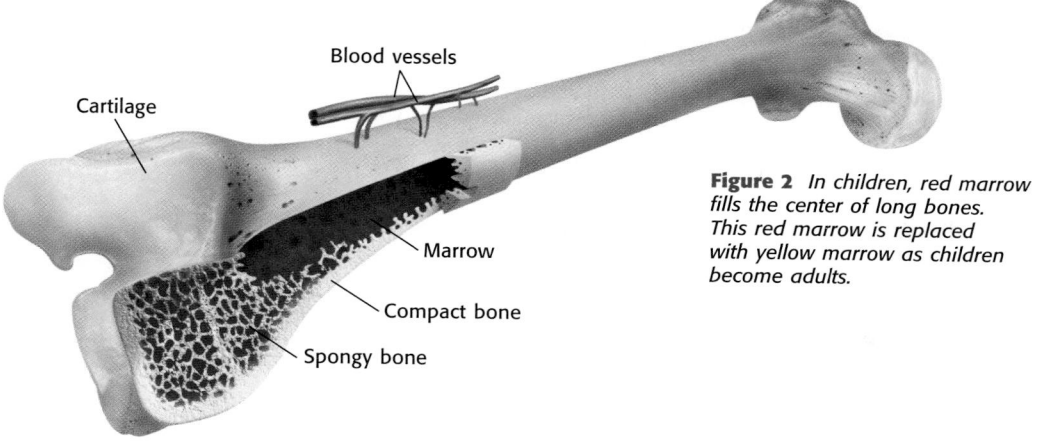

Cartilage

Blood vessels

Marrow

Compact bone

Spongy bone

Figure 2 *In children, red marrow fills the center of long bones. This red marrow is replaced with yellow marrow as children become adults.*

Bone Structure

A bone may seem lifeless. But a bone is a living organ made of several different tissues. Bone is made of connective tissue and minerals. These minerals are deposited by living cells called *osteoblasts* (AHS tee oh BLASTS).

If you look inside a bone, you will notice two kinds of bone tissue. If the bone tissue does not have any visible open spaces, it is called *compact bone*. Compact bone is rigid and dense. Tiny canals within compact bone contain small blood vessels. Bone tissue that has many open spaces is called *spongy bone*. Spongy bone provides most of the strength and support for a bone.

Bones contain a soft tissue called *marrow*. There are two types of marrow. Red marrow produces both red and white blood cells. Yellow marrow, found in the central cavity of long bones, stores fat. **Figure 2** shows a cross section of a long bone, the femur.

Bone Growth

Did you know that most of your skeleton used to be soft and rubbery? Most bones start out as a flexible tissue called *cartilage*. When you were born, you didn't have much true bone. But as you grew, most of the cartilage was replaced by bone. During childhood, most bones still have growth plates of cartilage. These growth plates provide a place for bones to continue to grow.

Feel the end of your nose. Or bend the top of your ear. These areas are two places where cartilage is never replaced by bone. These areas stay flexible.

Reading Check How do bones grow? (*See the Appendix for answers to Reading Checks.*)

Pickled Bones
1. Place a **clean chicken bone** in a **jar of vinegar.**
2. After 1 week, remove the bone and rinse it with **water.**
3. Describe the changes that you can see or feel.
4. How has the bone's strength changed?
5. What did the vinegar remove?

Discussion ——— GENERAL

Joints After students read about the different kinds of joints, ask them the following questions.

• What kind of joint do you use when you bend your knee? (hinge joint)

• What kind of joint moves when you swing your arm back and forth? (ball-and-socket joint) Name another location in your body where this type of joint is located. (hip)

LS Verbal

Close

Reteaching ——— BASIC

Skeletal System Have students work in pairs to review the functions of the skeletal system. Students should stop each other if a concept is confusing or if they need clarification.

LS Interpersonal

Quiz ——— GENERAL

1. What is the difference between compact bone and spongy bone? (Sample answer: Compact bone has no visible, open spaces. Spongy bone has many visible spaces.)

2. Where in the body are ball-and-socket joints found? (hip and shoulder) Where are hinge joints? (knee) Where are gliding joints? (wrist and ankle)

Figure 3 Three Joints

Gliding Joint
Gliding joints allow bones in the hand and wrist to glide over one another and give some flexibility to the area.

Ball-and-Socket Joint
As a video-game joystick lets you move your character all around, the shoulder lets your arm move freely in all directions.

Hinge Joint
As a hinge allows a door to open and close, the knee enables you to flex and extend your lower leg.

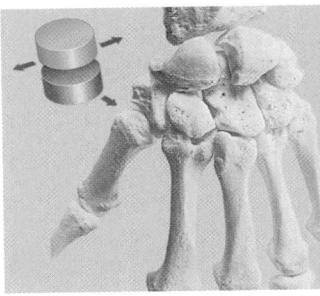 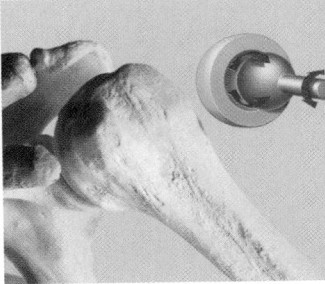 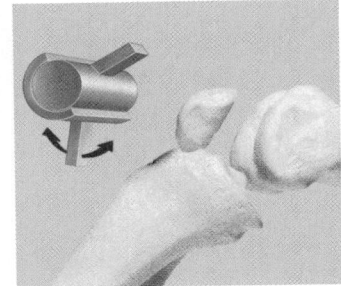

Joints

A place where two or more bones meet is called a **joint.** Your joints allow your body to move when your muscles contract. Some joints, such as fixed joints, allow little or no movement. Many of the joints in the skull are fixed joints. Other joints, such as your shoulder, allow a lot of movement. Joints can be classified based on how the bones in a joint move. For example, your shoulder is a ball-and-socket joint. Three joints are shown in **Figure 3.**

Joints are held together by *ligaments* (LIG uh muhnts). Ligaments are strong elastic bands of connective tissue. They connect the bones in a joint. Also, cartilage covers the ends of many bones. Cartilage helps cushion the area in a joint where bones meet.

joint a place where two or more bones meet

✓ **Reading Check** Describe the basic structure of joints.

CONNECTION TO Environmental Science

WRITING SKILL **Bones from the Ocean** Sometimes, a bone or joint may become so damaged that it needs to be repaired or replaced with surgery. Often, replacement parts are made from a metal, such as titanium. However, some scientists have discovered that coral skeletons from coral reefs in the ocean can be used to replace human bone. Research bone surgery. Identify why doctors use metals such as titanium. Then, identify the advantages that coral may offer. Write a report discussing your findings.

Answer to Reading Check

Sample answer: Joints are held together by ligaments. Cartilage cushions the area in a joint where bones meet.

Answer to Connection to Environmental Science

Answers may vary. Students should understand that titanium is a relatively nonreactive metal, so it is used for bone replacement. Students should also demonstrate an understanding that coral easily binds to existing bone. You may want to ask students to examine the impact of coral bone replacement on the environment.

Skeletal System Injuries and Diseases

Sometimes, parts of the skeletal system are injured. As shown in **Figure 4,** bones may be fractured, or broken. Joints can also be injured. A dislocated joint is a joint in which one or more bones have been moved out of place. Another joint injury, called a *sprain*, happens if a ligament is stretched too far or torn.

There are also diseases of the skeletal system. *Osteoporosis* (AHS tee OH puh ROH sis) is a disease that causes bones to become less dense. Bones become weak and break more easily. Age and poor eating habits can make it more likely for people to develop osteoporosis. Other bone diseases affect the marrow or make bones soft. A disease that affects the joints is called *arthritis* (ahr THRIET is). Arthritis is painful. Joints may swell or stiffen. As they get older, some people are more likely to have some types of arthritis.

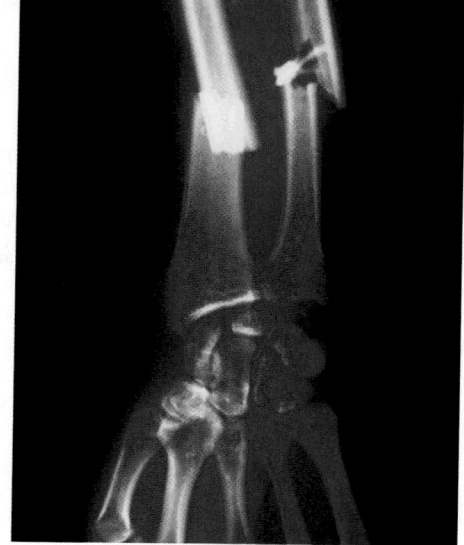

Figure 4 *This X ray shows that the two bones of the forearm have been fractured, or broken.*

SECTION Review

Summary

- The skeletal system includes bones, cartilage, and the connective tissue that connects bones.
- Bones protect the body, store minerals, allow movement, and make blood cells.
- Joints are places where two or more bones meet.
- Skeletal system injuries include fractures, dislocations, and sprains. Skeletal system diseases include osteoporosis and arthritis.

Using Key Terms

1. In your own words, write a definition for the term *skeletal system.*

Understanding Key Ideas

2. Which of the following is NOT an organ of the skeletal system?
   a. bone
   b. cartilage
   c. muscle
   d. None of the above

3. Describe four functions of bones.

4. What are three joints?

5. Describe two diseases that affect the skeletal system.

Math Skills

6. A broken bone usually heals in about six weeks. A mild sprain takes one-third as long to heal. In days, about how long does it take a mild sprain to heal?

Critical Thinking

7. **Identifying Relationships** Red bone marrow produces blood cells. Children have red bone marrow in their long bones, while adults have yellow bone marrow, which stores fat. Why might adults and children have different kinds of marrow?

8. **Predicting Consequences** What might happen if children's bones didn't have growth plates of cartilage?

For a variety of links related to this chapter, go to www.scilinks.org

Topic: Skeletal System
SciLinks code: HSM1399

CONNECTION to Physical Science — GENERAL

Levers Students may be surprised to learn that their arms and legs are machines. Human limbs are levers, and levers are the simplest kind of machine. Levers allow people to apply, increase, and change the direction of force. Use the teaching transparency titled "Machines Change the Size and/or Direction of a Force" to illustrate this point. **LS** Visual

Alternative Assessment — GENERAL

Writing **Bone Essays** Have students write an essay about bones. Essays should address what bones do, how they are specialized, and how they are joined. **LS** Verbal

Answers to Section Review

1. Sample answer: The skeletal system includes bones, cartilage, and connective tissue, and it provides support to the body.

2. c

3. Sample answer: Bones protect organs. Bones store materials that help nerves and muscles function properly. Along with skeletal muscles, bones make it possible to move. Finally, marrow in bones produces blood cells.

4. gliding joints, hinge joints, and ball-and-socket joints

5. Sample answer: Osteoporosis is a disease that causes bones to become less dense. Bones become weak and break more easily. Arthritis is a painful joint disease that causes joints to swell or stiffen.

6. 14 days (6 weeks × 7 days/week = 42 days; 42 days × 1/3 = 14 days)

7. Sample answer: Children are still growing, so they need more blood cells as their bodies get bigger. After children become adults, they don't need as many new blood cells, so long bones store fat instead.

8. Sample answer: Growth plates are places where bones continue to grow. If children did not have growth plates, their bones would not continue to grow.

Focus

Overview

This section introduces students to the major parts of the muscular system and describes three types of muscle. This section also describes movement, aerobic exercise, and resistance exercise. The section discusses muscular system injuries and ways to prevent them.

Bellringer

On the board or an overhead projector, write the following: "List at least five parts of your body that you use to drink a glass of water." (Sample answer: fingers, hands, arm, lips, and tongue) Remind students that all of the parts that they use, including the eyes that they use to see the glass, are controlled by muscles.

Motivate

Group ACTIVITY — GENERAL

Poster Project Have students create a poster illustrating the three types of muscle. Students should include information about where the muscle is found, what it looks like, and whether it is involuntary or voluntary. Have students present their posters to the class.

LS Verbal/Visual

READING WARM-UP

Objectives
- List three kinds of muscle tissue.
- Describe how skeletal muscles move bones.
- Compare aerobic exercise with resistance exercise.
- Describe two muscular system injuries.

Terms to Learn
muscular system

READING STRATEGY

Discussion Read this section silently. Write down questions that you have about this section. Discuss your questions in a small group.

The Muscular System

Have you ever tried to sit still, without moving any muscles at all, for one minute? It's impossible! Somewhere in your body, muscles are always working.

Your heart is a muscle. Muscles make you breathe. And muscles hold you upright. If all of your muscles rested at the same time, you would collapse. The **muscular system** is made up of the muscles that let you move.

Kinds of Muscle

Figure 1 shows the three kinds of muscle in your body. *Smooth muscle* is found in the digestive tract and in the walls of blood vessels. *Cardiac muscle* is found only in your heart. *Skeletal muscle* is attached to your bones for movement. Skeletal muscle also helps protect your inner organs.

Muscle action can be voluntary or involuntary. Muscle action that is under your control is *voluntary*. Muscle action that is not under your control is *involuntary*. Smooth muscle and cardiac muscle are involuntary muscles. Skeletal muscles can be both voluntary and involuntary muscles. For example, you can blink your eyes anytime you want to. But your eyes will also blink automatically.

Figure 1 **Three Kinds of Muscle**

Skeletal muscle enables bones to move.

Smooth muscle moves food through the digestive system.

Cardiac muscle pumps blood around the body.

CHAPTER RESOURCES

Chapter Resource File

- Lesson Plan
- Directed Reading A BASIC
- Directed Reading B SPECIAL NEEDS

Technology

Transparencies
- Bellringer
- A Pair of Muscles in the Arm

Is That a Fact!

Horses can sleep standing up. Their legs can support their weight on their bones without the use of muscles. When horses fall asleep and their muscles relax, their leg bones lock in place underneath them and hold them upright for the duration of their nap.

Figure 2 A Pair of Muscles in the Arm

Skeletal muscles, such as the biceps and triceps muscles, work in pairs. When the biceps muscle contracts, the arm bends. When the triceps muscle contracts, the arm straightens.

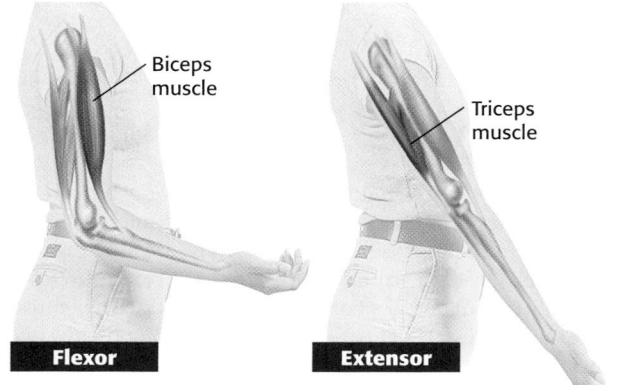

Biceps muscle

Triceps muscle

Flexor

Extensor

muscular system the organ system whose primary function is movement and flexibility

Movement

Skeletal muscles can make hundreds of movements. You can see many of these movements by watching a dancer, a swimmer, or even someone smiling or frowning. When you want to move, signals travel from your brain to your skeletal muscle cells. The muscle cells then contract, or get shorter.

Muscles Attach to Bones

Strands of tough connective tissue connect your skeletal muscles to your bones. These strands are called *tendons*. When a muscle that connects two bones gets shorter, the bones are pulled closer to each other. For example, tendons attach the biceps muscle to a bone in your shoulder and to a bone in your forearm. When the biceps muscle contracts, your forearm bends toward your shoulder.

Muscles Work in Pairs

Your skeletal muscles often work in pairs. Usually, one muscle in the pair bends part of the body. The other muscle straightens part of the body. A muscle that bends part of your body is called a *flexor* (FLEKS uhr). A muscle that straightens part of your body is an *extensor* (ek STEN suhr). As shown in **Figure 2,** the biceps muscle of the arm is a flexor. The triceps muscle of the arm is an extensor.

✓ **Reading Check** Describe how muscles work in pairs. (*See the Appendix for answers to Reading Checks.*)

SCHOOL to HOME

Power in Pairs

Ask a parent to sit in a chair and place a hand palm up under the edge of a table. Tell your parent to apply gentle upward pressure. Feel the front and back of your parent's upper arm. Next, ask your parent to push down on top of the table. Feel your parent's arm again. What did you notice about the muscles in your parent's arm when he or she was pressing up? pushing down?

ACTiViTY

Muscle Contraction Ask a student to stand in a doorway with his or her arms and hands relaxed and palms turned inward. Ask the student to raise his or her hands against the door frame (backs of the hands on the frame) and press steadily against the frame for about 30 to 40 seconds. Then, ask the student to relax and step away from the door. Have the rest of the class observe what happens to the student's arms. (The student's arms should rise slowly without obvious effort by the student.) Explain that the student's arms rise because the muscles that were pushing against the door frame are still shortened, or contracted. **English Language Learners**
LS Kinesthetic/Visual

CONNECTION to Real World ──── ADVANCED

Polio In the early 1900s, tens of thousands of people, mostly children, were stricken with polio, a viral disease that paralyzes muscles. Often, polio would leave its victims unable to walk or move. An Australian nurse, Sister Elizabeth Kenny, treated patients by using flexible hot wraps and exercise instead of immobilizing casts. Using her treatments, patients avoided paralysis. Largely because Kenny had no formal medical education, the doctors and hospital administrators of the time fought against her practices. Eventually, her successes became well known, and her contributions began the field of physical therapy. Have students research Kenny's story and the opposition that she faced. Have them give a report to the class. **LS Verbal**

Answer to Reading Check

Sample answer: One muscle, the flexor, bends part of the body. Another muscle, the extensor, straightens part of the body.

Answer to School-to-Home Activity

Sample answer: While my parent pushes down, the muscles in the back of my parent's arm contract, and while my parent pushes up, the muscles in the front of the arm contract.

Exercise Ask students to demonstrate different resistance and aerobic exercises. Then, ask students to explain the benefits of each exercise. Make sure students have warmed up before their demonstrations.

LS Kinesthetic

Quiz — GENERAL

1. What is the difference between voluntary muscle action and involuntary muscle action? (Sample answer: Voluntary muscle action is action that you can control. Involuntary muscle action is not under your control.)

2. What kind of muscle bends part of your body? (flexor) What kind of muscle straightens part of your body? (extensor)

3. What are the risks of using anabolic steroids? (Anabolic steroids can damage the heart, liver, and kidneys and can cause high blood pressure. They can cause bones to stop growing.)

Alternative Assessment — GENERAL

Crossword Puzzle Have students work in groups of four. Have groups make crossword puzzles using the vocabulary terms and other important terms in this section. Have groups exchange puzzles with each other.

LS Verbal   English Language Learners

Figure 3 *This girl is strengthening her heart and improving her endurance by doing aerobic exercise. This boy is doing resistance exercise to build strong muscles.*

Use It or Lose It

What happens when someone wears a cast for a broken arm? Skeletal muscles around the broken bone become smaller and weaker. The muscles weaken because they are not exercised. Exercised muscles are stronger and larger. Strong muscles can help other organs, too. For example, contracting muscles squeeze blood vessels. This action increases blood flow without needing more work from the heart.

Certain exercises can give muscles more strength and endurance. More endurance lets muscles work longer without getting tired. Two kinds of exercise can increase muscle strength and endurance. They are resistance exercise and aerobic exercise. You can see an example of each kind in **Figure 3.**

Resistance Exercise

Resistance exercise is a great way to strengthen skeletal muscles. During resistance exercise, people work against the resistance, or weight, of an object. Some resistance exercises, such as curl-ups, use your own weight for resistance.

Aerobic Exercise

Steady, moderately intense activity is called *aerobic exercise*. Jogging, cycling, skating, swimming, and walking are aerobic exercises. This kind of exercise can increase muscle strength. However, aerobic exercise mostly strengthens the heart and increases endurance.

CONNECTION TO Chemistry

Muscle Function Body chemistry is very important for healthy muscle function. Spasms or cramps happen if too much sweating, poor diet, or illness causes a chemical imbalance in muscles. Identify three chemicals that the body needs for muscles to work properly. Make a poster explaining how people can make sure that they have enough of each chemical.

ACTIVITY

Homework — ADVANCED

Injuries For one month, have students read the sports section in a local newspaper or look for articles in sports magazines about injuries sustained by athletes. Ask students to identify and count the types of injuries, such as sprains and strains. Have students compile their information on bar graphs in which they record the kinds of injuries on the *x*-axis and the number of injuries on the *y*-axis.

LS Logical

Answer to Connection to Chemistry

Students should discuss the importance of minerals, such as magnesium, calcium, potassium, or sodium, to muscle function. Students should identify important dietary sources of these minerals.

Muscle Injury

Any exercise program should be started slowly. Starting slowly means you are less likely to get hurt. You should also warm up for exercise. A *strain* is an injury in which a muscle or tendon is overstretched or torn. Strains often happen because a muscle has not been warmed up. Strains also happen when muscles are worked too hard.

People who exercise too much can hurt their tendons. The body can't repair an injured tendon before the next exercise session. So, the tendon becomes inflamed. This condition is called *tendinitis*. Often, a long rest is needed for the injured tendon to heal.

Some people try to make their muscles stronger by taking drugs. These drugs are called *anabolic steroids* (A nuh BAH lik STER oidz). They can cause long-term health problems. Anabolic steroids can damage the heart, liver, and kidneys. They can also cause high blood pressure. If taken before the skeleton is mature, anabolic steroids can cause bones to stop growing.

Reading Check What are the risks of using anabolic steroids?

Runner's Time

Jan has decided to enter a 5 km road race. She now runs 5 km in 30 min. She would like to decrease her time by 15% before the race. What will her time be when she reaches her goal?

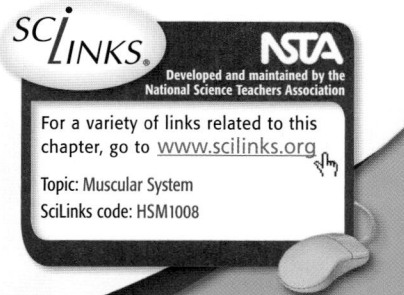

SECTION Review

Summary

- The three kinds of muscle tissue are smooth muscle, cardiac muscle, and skeletal muscle.
- Skeletal muscles work in pairs. Skeletal muscles contract to move bones.
- Resistance exercise improves muscle strength. Aerobic exercise improves heart strength and muscle endurance.
- Strains are injuries that affect muscles and tendons. Tendinitis affects tendons.

Using Key Terms

1. In your own words, write a definition for the term *muscular system*.

Understanding Key Ideas

2. Muscles
   a. work in pairs.
   b. move bones by relaxing.
   c. get smaller when exercised.
   d. All of the above

3. Describe three kinds of muscle.

4. List two kinds of exercise. Give an example of each.

5. Describe two muscular system injuries.

Math Skills

6. If Trey can do one curl-up every 2.5 s, about how long will it take him to do 35 curl-ups?

Critical Thinking

7. **Applying Concepts** Describe some of the muscle action needed to pick up a book. Include flexors and extensors in your description.

8. **Predicting Consequences** If aerobic exercise improves heart strength, what likely happens to heart rate as the heart gets stronger? Explain your answer.

Developed and maintained by the National Science Teachers Association

For a variety of links related to this chapter, go to www.scilinks.org

Topic: Muscular System
SciLinks code: HSM1008

Answer to Reading Check

Sample answer: Anabolic steroids can damage the heart, liver, and kidneys. They can also cause high blood pressure. Anabolic steroids can cause bones to stop growing.

CHAPTER RESOURCES

Chapter Resource File

- Section Quiz GENERAL
- Section Review GENERAL
- Vocabulary and Section Summary GENERAL
- Reinforcement Worksheet BASIC

Workbooks

Math Skills for Science
- The Unit Factor and Dimensional Analysis GENERAL

Answer to Math Practice

25 min, 30 s (30 min × 0.85 = 25.5 min)

Answers to Section Review

1. Sample answer: The muscular system is the group of muscles that allow people to move.

2. a

3. Sample answer: Smooth muscle is found in the digestive tract and in the walls of blood vessels. Cardiac muscle is found only in the heart. Skeletal muscle is attached to bones for movement.

4. Sample answer: Curl-ups are a resistance exercise. Jogging is an aerobic exercise.

5. Sample answer: A strain is an injury in which a muscle or tendon is overstretched or torn. Tendinitis is a condition in which a tendon becomes inflamed when the body doesn't have enough time to repair the tendon between exercise sessions.

6. 87.5 s (35 curl-ups × 2.5 curl-ups/s = 87.5 s)

7. Sample answer: An extensor in the back of my arm straightens out my arm as I reach for the book. Flexors in my hand let me close my fingers on the book, and a flexor in my arm bends my arm as I pick up the book.

8. Sample answer: As the heart gets stronger, the heart likely will pump more blood with each beat. The heart will not need to work as hard to pump the same amount of blood. So, heart rate will likely decrease.

Focus

Overview

This section introduces students to the major functions of the integumentary system and describes the major parts of skin and their functions. Students will also learn about common skin injuries.

Bellringer

Write the following questions on the board or an overhead projector: "When do you see dogs panting?" (Sample answer: on hot days or after they have run) "Why do you think dogs pant?" (Sample answer: Dogs don't sweat the way humans do. Dogs pant to regulate their body temperature.)

Motivate

Discussion ——— GENERAL

Homeostasis Relay the following story to students: "More than 200 years ago, Dr. Charles Blagden tested how mammals regulate body temperature. He spent 45 min in a room with an uncooked steak. The temperature in the room measured 126°C (260°F)." Ask students what they think happened to Dr. Blagden and the steak. (Dr. Blagden emerged from the room unharmed, but the steak was cooking! Living people and mammals can regulate their body temperature.)
LS Logical

READING WARM-UP

Objectives

- List four functions of skin.
- Describe the two layers of skin.
- Describe the structure and function of hair and nails.
- Describe two kinds of damage that can affect skin.

Terms to Learn

integumentary system
epidermis
dermis

READING STRATEGY

Paired Summarizing Read this section silently. In pairs, take turns summarizing the material. Stop to discuss ideas that seem confusing.

integumentary system the organ system that forms a protective covering on the outside of the body

The Integumentary System

What part of your body has to be partly dead to keep you alive? Here are some clues: It comes in many colors, it is the largest organ in the body, and it is showing right now!

Did you guess your skin? If you did, you guessed correctly. Your skin, hair, and nails make up your **integumentary system** (in TEG yoo MEN tuhr ee SIS tuhm). The integumentary system covers your body and helps you maintain homeostasis.

Functions of Skin

Why do you need skin? Here are four good reasons:

- Skin protects you by keeping water in your body and foreign particles out of your body.
- Skin keeps you in touch with the outside world. Nerve endings in your skin let you feel things around you.
- Skin helps regulate your body temperature. Small organs in the skin called *sweat glands* make sweat. Sweat is a salty liquid that flows to the surface of the skin. As sweat evaporates, the skin cools.
- Skin helps get rid of wastes. Several kinds of waste chemicals can be removed in sweat.

As shown in **Figure 1,** skin comes in many colors. Skin color is determined by a chemical called *melanin*. If a lot of melanin is present, skin is very dark. If little melanin is present, skin is very light. Melanin absorbs ultraviolet light from the sun. So, melanin reduces damage that can lead to skin cancer. However, all skin, even dark skin, is vulnerable to cancer. Skin should be protected from sunlight whenever possible.

Figure 1 *Variety in skin color is caused by the pigment melanin. The amount of melanin varies from person to person.*

CHAPTER RESOURCES

Chapter Resource File

- Lesson Plan
- Directed Reading A BASIC
- Directed Reading B SPECIAL NEEDS

Technology

Transparencies
- Bellringer
- Structures of the Skin

Is That a Fact!

In an average adult, the skin has a surface area of about 2 m² and has a mass of about 4 kg. The skin on the human body varies in thickness from about 5 mm on the soles of the feet to about 0.5 mm on the eyelids.

Figure 2 Structures of the Skin

Beneath the surface, your skin is a complex organ made of blood vessels, nerves, glands, and muscles.

Blood vessels transport substances and help regulate body temperature.

Nerve fibers carry messages to and from the brain.

Hair follicles in the dermis make hair.

Muscle fibers attached to a hair follicle can contract and cause the hair to stand up.

Oil glands release oil that keeps hair flexible and waterproofs the epidermis.

Sweat glands release sweat to cool the body. Sweating is also a way to remove waste materials from the body.

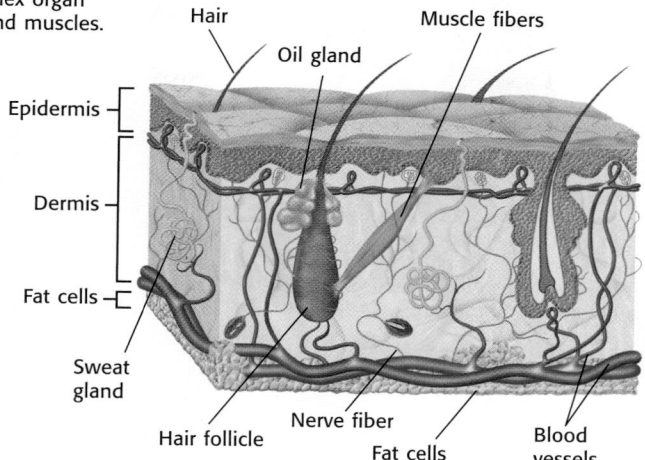

Hair
Oil gland
Muscle fibers
Epidermis
Dermis
Fat cells
Sweat gland
Hair follicle
Nerve fiber
Fat cells
Blood vessels

Layers of Skin

Skin is the largest organ of your body. In fact, the skin of an adult covers an area of about 2 m²! However, there is more to skin than meets the eye. Skin has two main layers: the epidermis (EP uh DUHR mis) and the dermis. The **epidermis** is the outermost layer of skin. You see the epidermis when you look at your skin. The thicker layer of skin that lies beneath the epidermis is the **dermis.**

Epidermis

The epidermis is made of epithelial tissue. Even though the epidermis has many layers of cells, it is as thick as only two sheets of paper over most of the body. It is thicker on the palms of your hands and on the soles of your feet. Most cells in the epidermis are dead. These cells are filled with a protein called *keratin*. Keratin helps make the skin tough.

Dermis

The dermis lies beneath the epidermis. The dermis has many fibers made of a protein called *collagen*. These fibers provide strength. They also let skin bend without tearing. The dermis contains many small structures, as shown in **Figure 2.**

✓ **Reading Check** Describe the dermis. How does it differ from the epidermis? (*See the Appendix for answers to Reading Checks.*)

epidermis the surface layer of cells on a plant or animal

dermis the layer of skin below the epidermis

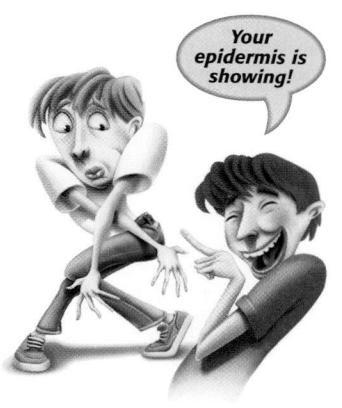

Your epidermis is showing!

Answer to Reading Check

The dermis is the layer of skin that lies beneath the epidermis. It is composed of a protein called *collagen*, while the epidermis contains keratin.

 **INCLUSION Strategies**

- *Learning Disabled*
- *Developmentally Delayed*
- *Hearing Impaired*

Students can often better retain information if they create a visual image. Have students work in groups of four. Give each group a sheet of poster board. Have students divide the poster board into four sections and draw memory clues to help them remember the four functions of the skin. **LS** Visual

 **Teach**

ACTIVITY — GENERAL

MATERIALS

FOR EACH GROUP
- clock or watch
- cotton balls
- fan
- thermometers, Celsius (2)
- water at room temperature

Measuring Temperature Have students work in groups of four students. Have students wrap the bulb of each thermometer with a cotton ball and then wet one of the cotton balls. Have students record the beginning temperature of each thermometer and then hold both thermometers in front of a fan. Students should record the temperature of each thermometer every minute for 5 min. Ask students: "How do the temperatures of the thermometers differ?" (Sample answer: The thermometer with the wet cotton has a lower temperature.) "Why?" (Sample answer: Evaporation lowers the temperature.) "How does this process relate to what happens when you sweat?" (Sample answer: As sweat evaporates from the body, the skin becomes cooler.) **LS** Kinesthetic

INTERNET ACTIVITY
Brochure — GENERAL

For an internet activity related to this chapter, have students go to **go.hrw.com** and type in the keyword **HL5BD1W.**

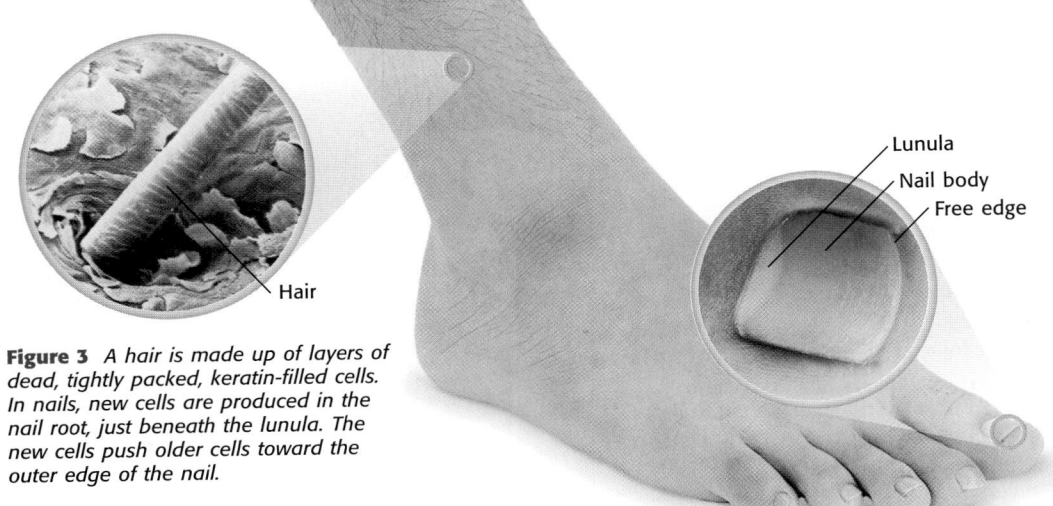

Figure 3 *A hair is made up of layers of dead, tightly packed, keratin-filled cells. In nails, new cells are produced in the nail root, just beneath the lunula. The new cells push older cells toward the outer edge of the nail.*

Lunula
Nail body
Free edge
Hair

Close

Reteaching — BASIC

Hair and Nails Ask students to relate the functions of hair and nails. Then, ask students to describe how hair and nails form. **LS Verbal**

Quiz — GENERAL

1. What are four functions of skin? (to keep moisture in and foreign particles out, to provide information about the outside world, to help regulate body temperature, and to remove wastes)

2. Describe the two layers of skin. (The epidermis is the outermost layer of skin and contains epithelial tissue and mostly dead cells. The dermis lies beneath the epidermis and contains collagen.)

Alternative Assessment — ADVANCED

Skin Art Have students make a colorful drawing of a cross section of skin. Have students make their drawings from memory and label and describe the function of blood vessels, nerve fibers, muscle fibers, hair follicles, oil glands, and sweat glands. **LS Visual**

CONNECTION TO
Social Studies

WRITING SKILL **Using Hair** Many traditional cultures use animal hair to make products, such as rugs and blankets. Identify a culture that uses animal hair. In your **science journal,** write a report describing how the culture uses animal hair.

Hair and Nails

Hair and nails are important parts of the integumentary system. Like skin, hair and nails are made of living and dead cells. **Figure 3** shows hair and nails.

A hair forms at the bottom of a tiny sac called a *hair follicle.* The hair grows as new cells are added at the hair follicle. Older cells get pushed upward. The only living cells in a hair are in the hair follicle. Like skin, hair gets its color from melanin.

Hair helps protect skin from ultraviolet light. Hair also keeps particles, such as dust and insects, out of your eyes and nose. In most mammals, hair helps regulate body temperature. A tiny muscle attached to the hair follicle contracts. If the follicle contains a hair, the hair stands up. The lifted hairs work like a sweater. They trap warm air around the body.

A nail grows from living cells in the *nail root* at the base of the nail. As new cells form, the nail grows longer. Nails protect the tips of your fingers and toes. So, your fingers and toes can be soft and sensitive for a keen sense of touch.

✓ Reading Check **Describe how nails grow.**

Skin Injuries

Skin is often damaged. Fortunately, your skin can repair itself, as shown in **Figure 4.** Some damage to skin is very serious. Damage to the genetic material in skin cells can cause skin cancer. Skin may also be affected by hormones that cause oil glands in skin to make too much oil. This oil combines with dead skin cells and bacteria to clog hair follicles. The result is acne. Proper cleansing can help but often cannot prevent this problem.

CONNECTION ACTIVITY
Real World — GENERAL

Protection from the Sun Skin cancer is the most common kind of cancer. Hundreds of thousands of new cases of skin cancer are reported each year. Ask interested students to research ways people can prevent skin cancer. Have students create informative brochures about their findings. **LS Verbal/Visual**

Answer to Reading Check

Sample answer: A nail grows from living cells in the nail root at the base of the nail. As new cells form, the nail grows longer.

Figure 4 How Skin Heals

❶ A blood clot forms over a cut to stop bleed-ing and to keep bacteria from entering the wound. Bacteria-fighting cells then come to the area to kill bacteria.

❷ Damaged cells are replaced through cell division. Eventually, all that is left on the surface is a scar.

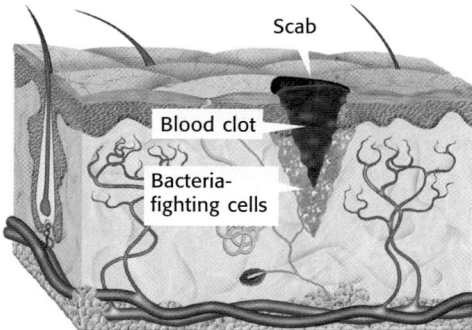

Scab

Blood clot

Bacteria-fighting cells

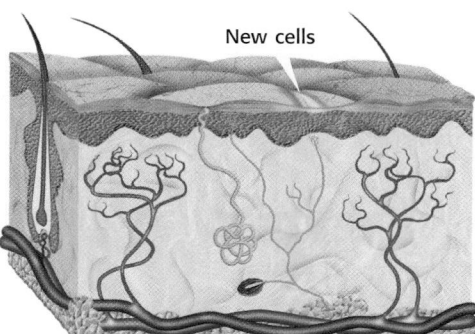

New cells

SECTION Review

Summary

● Skin keeps water in the body, keeps foreign par-ticles out of the body, lets people feel things around them, regu-lates temperature, and removes wastes.

● The two layers of skin are the epidermis and the dermis.

● Hair grows from hair fol-licles. Nails grow from nail roots.

● Skin may develop skin cancer. Acne may develop if skin produces too much oil.

Using Key Terms

1. In your own words, write a defi-nition for each of the following terms: *integumentary system, epidermis,* and *dermis.*

Understanding Key Ideas

2. Which of the following is NOT a function of skin?
   a. to regulate body temperature
   b. to keep water in the body
   c. to move your body
   d. to get rid of wastes

3. Describe the two layers of skin.

4. How do hair and nails develop?

5. Describe how a cut heals.

Math Skills

6. On average, hair grows 0.3 mm per day. How many millimeters does hair grow in 30 days? in a year?

Critical Thinking

7. **Making Inferences** Why do you feel pain when you pull on your hair or nails, but not when you cut them?

8. **Analyzing Ideas** The epider-mis on the palms of your hands and on the soles of your feet is thicker than it is anywhere else on your body. Why might this skin need to be thicker?

SC_LINKS.

NSTA

Developed and maintained by the National Science Teachers Association

For a variety of links related to this chapter, go to www.scilinks.org

Topic: Integumentary System
SciLinks code: HSM0803

CHAPTER RESOURCES

Chapter Resource File

● Section Quiz GENERAL
● Section Review GENERAL
● Vocabulary and Section Summary GENERAL

Answers to Section Review

1. Sample answer: The integumen-tary system is the organ system that forms a protective covering over the body. The epidermis is the outer layer of skin. The der-mis lies beneath the epidermis.

2. c

3. Sample answer: The epidermis is the outermost layer of skin. It is made of epithelial tissue. Most of the cells of the epidermis are dead cells that contain keratin. The dermis lies beneath the epi-dermis and contains sweat glands, hair follicles, nerve fibers, muscle fibers, and blood vessels. The dermis also con-tains collagen.

4. Sample answer: A hair grows as new cells are added in the hair follicle, which is where the only living cells are located. Nails grow from living cells in the nail root at the base of the nail.

5. Sample answer: A blood clot forms over a cut to stop bleeding and to keep bacteria out of the cut. Bacteria-fighting cells come to the area to kill bacteria. Damaged skin cells are replaced through cell division. Eventually, all that is left is a scar.

6. 9 mm (0.3 mm/day × 30 days = 9 mm); 109.5 mm (0.3 mm/day × 365 days = 109.5 mm)

7. Sample answer: Except in the hair follicle and in the nail root, hair and nails are made of dead cells, so cutting them does not hurt. Pulling on them, however, affects the living areas of hair and nails in the dermis, where nerve fibers are located.

8. Sample answer: The epidermis forms a protective covering of dead cells. The hands and the feet are areas that are often used, so the epidermis in these areas needs to be thicker for better protection.

Seeing Is Believing

Teacher's Notes

Time Required

One 45-minute class period and 5 to 10 minutes every other day for 2 weeks

Lab Ratings

EASY ————————— HARD

Teacher Prep 🧪
Student Set-Up 🧪
Concept Level 🧪
Clean Up 🧪

MATERIALS

The materials listed on the student page are enough for 1–2 students. This lab may be done with several different types of marking methods. The fingernail is very hard and is not very porous. Marking the nail permanently is a challenge. A permanent marker, such as a laundry-marking pen, may need to be refreshed only once a day. Fingernail polish may be an acceptable alternative. Acrylic paint may also be used.

Safety Caution

Remind students to review all safety cautions and icons before beginning this lab activity.

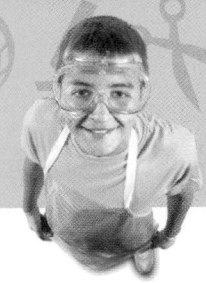

Skills Practice Lab

OBJECTIVES

Measure nail growth over time.

Draw a graph of nail growth.

MATERIALS

- graph paper (optional)
- metric ruler
- permanent marker

SAFETY

Seeing Is Believing

Like your hair and skin, fingernails are part of your body's integumentary system. Nails, shown in the figure below, are a modification of the outer layer of the skin. Nails grow from the nail bed and will grow continuously throughout your life. In this activity, you will measure the rate at which fingernails grow.

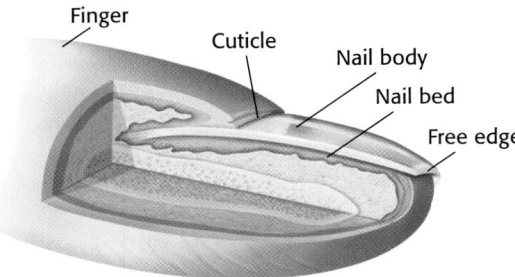

Finger • Cuticle • Nail body • Nail bed • Free edge

Procedure

1. Use a permanent marker to mark the center of the nail bed on your right index finger, as shown in the figure below. **Caution:** Do not get ink on your clothing.

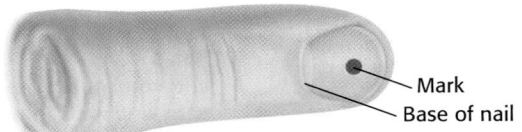

Mark — Base of nail

2. Measure from the mark to the base of your nail. Record the measurement, and label the measurement "Day 1."

3. Repeat steps 1 and 2 for your left index finger.

4. Let your fingernails grow for 2 days. Normal daily activity will not wash away the mark completely, but you may need to freshen the mark.

5. Measure the distance from the mark on your nail to the base of your nail. Record this distance, and label the measurement "Day 3."

Kathy LaRoe
East Valley Middle School
East Helena, Montana

CHAPTER RESOURCES

Chapter Resource File
 • Datasheet for Chapter Lab
• Lab Notes and Answers

Technology
 Classroom Videos
• Lab Video

• Muscles at Work

6 Continue measuring and recording the growth of your nails every other day for 2 weeks. Refresh the mark as necessary. You may continue to file or trim your nails as usual throughout the course of the lab.

7 After you have completed your measurements, use them to create a graph similar to the graph below.

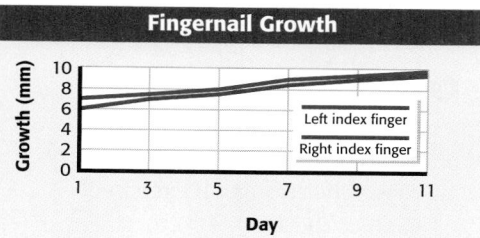

Fingernail Growth

Growth (mm) vs Day

Left index finger
Right index finger

Analyze the Results

1 **Describing Events** Did the nail on one hand grow faster than the nail on the other hand?

2 **Examining Data** Did your nails grow at a constant rate, or did your nails grow more quickly at certain times?

Draw Conclusions

3 **Making Predictions** If one nail grew more quickly than the other nail, what might explain the difference in growth?

4 **Analyzing Graphs** Compare your graph with the graphs of your classmates. Do you notice any differences in the graphs based on gender or physical characteristics, such as height? If so, describe the difference.

Applying Your Data

Do additional research to find out how nails are important to you. Also, identify how nails can be used to indicate a person's health or nutrition. Based on what you learn, describe how your nail growth indicates your health or nutrition.

CHAPTER RESOURCES

Workbooks

📘 **Inquiry Labs**
  • On a Wing and a Layer **GENERAL**

📘 **Long-Term Projects & Research Ideas**
  • Mapping the Human Body **ADVANCED**

Applying Your Data
Students should discover that the appearance of a nail can reflect the health of an individual. Abnormalities in color, such as white, yellow, or red nail beds, can indicate serious problems such as liver, lung, and heart diseases. Other problems indicated by nail appearance are bacterial or fungal infections of the nails and poor nutrition.

Lab Notes
Few topics are as important to students as gaining knowledge and understanding of their own body. As they develop, students can't help but observe how they are changing physically. In this lab, students witness the growth of their own fingernails.

Tell students that the graphed data shown in this lab are only an example and will not be the same as their own data.

Analyze the Results
1. Answers may vary. Many students may note that rates of growth vary.
2. Answers may vary. Some students will answer that their nails did not grow at a constant rate.

Draw Conclusions
3. The nails of the dominant hand grow faster than those of the other hand. Damage to the nail root can affect how quickly a nail grows. Also, circulation to the area affects growth. If one hand receives poor circulation, the nail will grow at a slower rate.
4. Some students may note differences in nail growth. While these differences likely are not related to height, they are related to nutrition. Someone who does not have enough of certain minerals, such as calcium and magnesium, in his or her diet will have slower nail growth. Nail growth is also affected by age, time of year, and gender. Nail growth slows as people get older. Nails grow faster in the summer than they do in the winter. Often, men's nails grow faster than women's nails do.

Assignment Guide

Section	Questions
1	2, 5, 7, 13, 17
2	1, 6, 12, 14, 18, 20–21
3	8, 10–11, 15
4	3–4, 9, 16, 19, 23–27
2 and 3	22

ANSWERS

Using Key Terms

1. joint
2. Homeostasis
3. epidermis
4. integumentary system
5. organ
6. skeletal system

Understanding Key Ideas

7. c
8. c
9. a
10. d
11. Sample answer: Muscles are connected to bones by tendons. When a muscle that connects two bones contracts, the bones are pulled closer together. Muscles often work in pairs.
12. Sample answer: The skeletal system includes the bones, cartilage, and connective tissue whose primary function is to support the body. The skeletal system protects organs, stores minerals, allows movement, and produces blood cells.

USING KEY TERMS

Complete each of the following sentences by choosing the correct term from the word bank.

homeostasis   organ
joint   skeletal system
tissue   muscular system
epidermis   dermis
integumentary system

1 A(n) ___ is a place where two or more bones meet.

2 ___ is the maintenance of a stable internal environment.

3 The outermost layer of skin is the ___.

4 The organ system that includes skin, hair, and nails is the ___.

5 A(n) ___ is made up of two or more tissues working together.

6 The ___ supports and protects the body, stores minerals, and allows movement.

UNDERSTANDING KEY IDEAS

Multiple Choice

7 Which of the following lists shows the way in which the body is organized?

a. cells, organs, organ systems, tissues
b. tissues, cells, organs, organ systems
c. cells, tissues, organs, organ systems
d. cells, tissues, organ systems, organs

---

8 Which muscle tissue can be both voluntary and involuntary?

a. smooth muscle
b. cardiac muscle
c. skeletal muscle
d. All of the above

9 The integumentary system

a. helps regulate body temperature.
b. helps the body move.
c. stores minerals.
d. None of the above

10 Muscles

a. work in pairs.
b. can be voluntary or involuntary.
c. become stronger if exercised.
d. All of the above

Short Answer

11 How do muscles move bones?

12 Describe the skeletal system, and list four functions of bones.

13 Give an example of how organ systems work together.

14 List three injuries and two diseases that affect the skeletal system.

---

13. Sample answer: The circulatory and cardiovascular systems work closely together to maintain homeostasis. The cardiovascular system includes the heart and blood vessels. These structures are also part of the circulatory system, which includes blood. These two systems work together to deliver the materials that cells need to survive.
14. fractures, dislocations, sprains, osteoporosis, and arthritis

15 Compare aerobic exercise and resistance exercise.

16 What are two kinds of damage that may affect skin?

CRITICAL THINKING

17 Concept Mapping Use the following terms to create a concept map: *tissues, muscle tissue, connective tissue, cells, organ systems, organs, epithelial tissue,* and *nervous tissue.*

18 Making Comparisons Compare the shapes of the bones of the human skull with the shapes of the bones of the human leg. How do the shapes differ? Why are the shapes important?

19 Making Inferences Compare your elbows and fingertips in terms of the texture and sensitivity of the skin on these parts of your body. Why might the skin on these body parts differ?

20 Making Inferences Imagine that you are building a robot. Your robot will have a skeleton similar to a human skeleton. If the robot needs to be able to move a limb in all directions, what kind of joint would be needed? Explain your answer.

21 Analyzing Ideas Human bones are dense and are often filled with marrow. But many bones of birds are hollow. Why might birds have hollow bones?

22 Identifying Relationships Why might some muscles fail to work properly if a bone is broken?

INTERPRETING GRAPHICS

Use the cross section of skin below to answer the questions that follow.

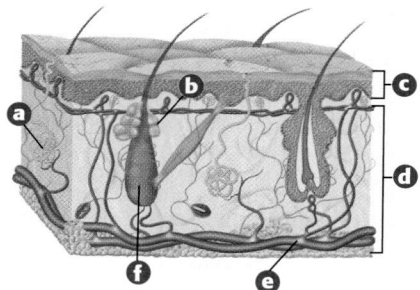

23 What is d called? What substance is most abundant in this layer?

24 What is the name and function of a?

25 What is the name and function of b?

26 Which letter corresponds to the part of the skin that is made up of epithelial tissue that contains dead cells?

27 Which letter corresponds to the part of the skin from which hair grows? What is this part called?

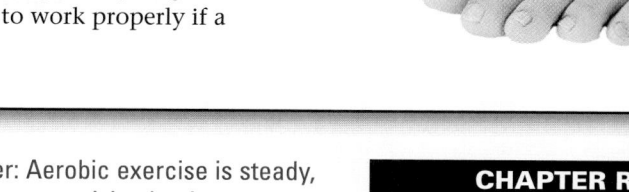

Critical Thinking

17. 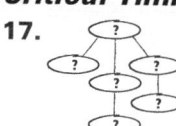 An answer to this exercise can be found at the end of the book.

18. Sample answer: Leg bones are long and skinny, while skull bones are thin and wide. Many skull bones are curved. Leg bones enable walking and standing, while skull bones are designed to protect the brain.

19. Sample answer: The skin on the elbows is thin, loose, and sometimes rough. The skin on the fingertips is thicker, but more sensitive to touch. The skin on elbows allows elbows to bend because it is loose and can stretch. The skin on the fingers is important for the sense of touch.

20. Sample answer: The robot would need a ball-and-socket joint. A ball-and-socket joint allows movement in all directions.

21. Sample answer: Dense bones that are filled with marrow weigh more than hollow bones. Because most birds fly, they need lighter bones. So, birds' bones are hollow.

22. Sample answer: If a bone is broken, flexors or extensors likely will not work properly. These muscles will not be able to pull on a bone in the way that they do when a bone is not broken. Also, if the area where the muscle attaches is damaged, the ability of the muscle to pull on the bone may be affected.

Interpreting Graphics

23. dermis; collagen

24. Sample answer: Sweat glands release sweat to cool the body.

25. Sample answer: Oil glands release oil to keep hair flexible and to waterproof the epidermis.

26. c

27. f; hair follicle

---

15. Sample answer: Aerobic exercise is steady, moderately intense activity that improves endurance. Resistance exercise strengthens skeletal muscles. During resistance exercise, muscles work against resistance, or weight.

16. Sample answer: Damage to genetic material in skin cells can cause skin cancer. If oil glands in skin produce too much oil, hair follicles may be clogged, which causes acne.

CHAPTER RESOURCES

Chapter Resource File

- Chapter Review GENERAL
- Chapter Test A GENERAL
- Chapter Test B ADVANCED
- Chapter Test C SPECIAL NEEDS
- Vocabulary Activity GENERAL

Workbooks

Study Guide
- Assessment Resources are also available in Spanish.

To provide practice under more realistic testing conditions, give students 20 minutes to answer all of the questions in this Standardized Test Preparation.

MISCONCEPTION ALERT

Answers to the standardized test preparation can help you identify student misconceptions and misunderstandings.

READING

Passage 1

1. C

2. F

3. B

➕ **TEST DOCTOR**

Question 2: Some students may answer that a skin graft is skin made of plastic because plastic bandages are discussed in the passage. Some students may think that a skin graft is damaged skin that has been removed, but it is undamaged skin that has been removed to replace damaged skin. Finally, some students may think that a skin graft is burned skin because burns are mentioned in the passage.

READING

Read the passages below. Then, answer the questions that follow each passage.

Passage 1 Sometimes, doctors perform a skin graft to transfer some of a person's healthy skin to an area where skin has been damaged. Doctors perform skin grafts because skin is often the best "bandage" for a wound. Like cloth or plastic bandages, skin protects the wound. Skin allows the wound to breathe. Unlike cloth or plastic bandages, skin can regenerate itself as it covers a wound. But sometimes a person's skin is so severely damaged (by burns, for example) that the person doesn't have enough skin to spare.

1. Based on the passage, what can skin do that manufactured bandages can't do?
  A Skin can protect a wound.
  B Skin can stop more skin from being damaged.
  C Skin can regenerate itself.
  D Skin can prevent burns.

2. In the passage, what does the term *skin graft* most likely mean?
  F a piece of skin transplanted from one part of the body to another
  G a piece of skin made of plastic
  H a piece of damaged skin that has been removed from the body
  I burned skin

3. Based on the passage, why might a severe burn victim not receive a skin graft?
  A Manufactured bandages are better.
  B He or she doesn't have enough healthy skin.
  C There isn't enough damaged skin to repair.
  D Skin is the best bandage for a wound.

Passage 2 Making sure that your body maintains homeostasis is not an easy task. The task is difficult because your internal environment is always changing. Your body must do many different jobs to maintain homeostasis. Each cell in your body has a specific job in maintaining homeostasis. Your cells are organized into groups. A group of similar cells working together forms a tissue. Your body has four main kinds of tissue—epithelial tissue, connective tissue, muscle tissue, and nervous tissue. These tissues work together to form organs, which help maintain homeostasis.

1. Based on the passage, which of the following statements about tissues is true?
  A Tissues do not help maintain homeostasis.
  B Tissues form organ systems.
  C Tissues are changing because the body's internal environment is always changing.
  D There are four kinds of tissue.

2. According to the passage, which of the following statements about homeostasis is true?
  F It is easy for the body to maintain homeostasis.
  G The body must do different jobs to maintain homeostasis.
  H Your internal environment rarely changes.
  I Organs and organ systems do not help maintain homeostasis.

3. Which of the following statements about cells is false?
  A Cells are organized into different groups.
  B Cells form tissues.
  C Cells work together.
  D Cells don't maintain homeostasis.

Passage 2

1. D

2. G

3. D

➕ **TEST DOCTOR**

Question 1: Some students may answer that tissues do not help maintain homeostasis. However, because all cells in the body have a role in homeostasis, so do tissues. Some students may answer that tissues form organ systems, but tissues form organs. Some students may answer that tissues are always changing, but this is not mentioned in the passage.

The line graph below shows hair growth over time. Use the graph to answer the questions that follow.

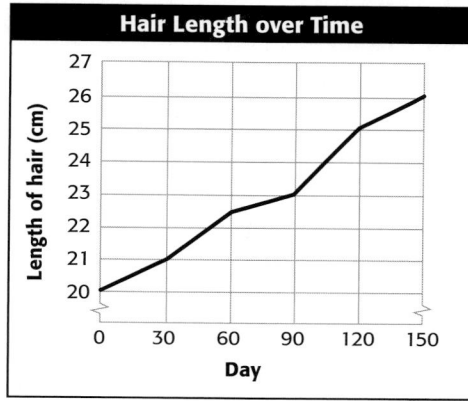

Hair Length over Time

1. How long was the hair on day 60?
   A 20.0 cm
   B 21.0 cm
   C 22.5 cm
   D 23.0 cm

2. On which day was hair length 23 cm?
   F day 60
   G day 90
   H day 120
   I day 150

3. From day 0 to day 150, what is the average amount that hair grows every 30 days?
   A 0.5 cm
   B 1.2 cm
   C 1.5 cm
   D 2.0 cm

4. Based on the average amount of hair growth per 30-day period, how long would it take the hair to grow another 3.6 cm?
   F 30 days
   G 60 days
   H 90 days
   I 120 days

Read each question below, and choose the best answer.

1. About 40% of a person's mass is muscle tissue. If Max has a mass of 40 kg, about how much muscle tissue does he have?
   A 16 kg
   B 20 kg
   C 24 kg
   D 30 kg

2. When running, an adult inhales about 72 L of air per minute. That amount is 12 times the amount that an adult needs while resting. How much air does an adult inhale while resting?
   F 6 L/min
   G 12 L/min
   H 60 L/min
   I 64 L/min

3. Maggie likes to do bench presses, a resistance exercise. She bench presses 10 kg. If Maggie added 2 kg every 2 weeks, how long would it take her to reach 20 kg?
   A 4 weeks
   B 5 weeks
   C 10 weeks
   D 12 weeks

4. A box of 25 bandages costs $4.00. A roll of tape costs $1.50. Troy needs 125 bandages and 3 rolls of tape for a first-aid kit. Which of the following equations shows the cost of first-aid supplies, x?
   F $x = (125 \times 4.00) + (3 \times 1.50)$
   G $x = (25 \times 4.00) + (3 \times 1.50)$
   H $x = [(25 \times 4.00) \div 125] + (3 \times 1.50)$
   I $x = [(125 \div 25) \times 4.00] + (3 \times 1.50)$

5. Stephen wants to run a 10 K race. Right now, he can run 5 K. What is the percentage increase from 5 K to 10 K?
   A 50%
   B 100%
   C 200%
   D 500%

Standardized Test Preparation

1. C
2. G
3. B
4. H

 TEST DOCTOR

Question 3: Students can calculate average hair growth by examining the total hair growth (6 cm) and the number of 30-day periods (5). In calculating the average growth, students should find that hair grows about 1.2 cm every 30 days (6 cm ÷ 5 = 1.2 cm). If students round their answers, they may incorrectly answer 1.0 cm or 1.5 cm.

1. A
2. F
3. C
4. I
5. B

 **TEST DOCTOR**

Question 2: Students may answer 12 L because the number 12 is introduced in the question. Students may answer 60 L if they subtract 12 from 72 L. Students may answer 64 L if they assume that people need 12% less air rather than 12 times less air.

Question 5: To find percentage increase, students must find the difference between 10 K and 5 K, divide it by 5 K, and multiply by 100. If students divide 5 K by 10 K, they will get the incorrect answer of 50%. If they divide 10 K by 5 K, they will get the incorrect answer of 200%. Finding the difference between 10 K and 5 K and multiplying the answer by 100 without dividing first will yield the incorrect answer of 500%.

CHAPTER RESOURCES

Chapter Resource File

• Standardized Test Preparation GENERAL

State Resources

For specific resources for your state, visit **go.hrw.com** and type in the keyword **HSMSTR**.

Weird Science

Background

The way that a wound heals when engineered skin is used is far better than the way that a wound heals when engineered skin is not used—more scar tissue forms. Scar tissue is weaker and more brittle than the skin that the scar tissue replaces. Scar tissue does not stretch and grow, which is a particularly difficult problem for children suffering from burns. Engineered skin also helps reduce the disfigurement associated with scarring. One significant limitation of the engineered skin is that when it is new, it lacks sweat glands. Patients who have large skin grafts need to be cautious about overexercising and exposure to the sun.

Science, Technology, and Society

ACTIVITY ——— GENERAL

Have students model having a prosthetic hand by using a clothespin to pick up papers, hold a pencil to write their name, and tie their shoes. Have them discuss how it feels, and have them try to imagine what having an artificial hand would be like. Then, ask students to brainstorm ways that they might improve their "prosthetic hand" (the clothespin).

Science in Action

Weird Science

Engineered Skin

Your skin is your first line of defense against the outside world. Your skin keeps you safe from dehydration and infection, helps regulate body temperature, and helps remove some wastes. But what happens if a large portion of skin is damaged? Skin may not be able to function properly. For someone who has a serious burn, a doctor often uses skin from an undamaged part of the person's body to repair the damaged skin. But some burn victims don't have enough undamaged skin to spare. Doctors have discovered ways to engineer skin that can be used in place of human skin.

Math ACTIVITY

A doctor repaired 0.35 m² of an adult patient's skin with engineered skin. If an adult has about 2 m² of skin, what percentage of the patient's skin was repaired?

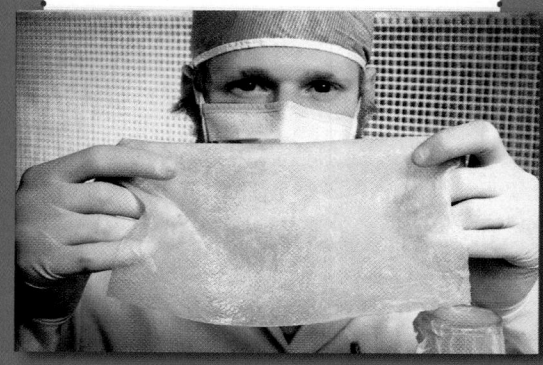

Science, Technology, and Society

Beating the Odds

Sometimes, people are born without limbs or lose limbs in accidents. Many of these people have prostheses (prahs THEE SEEZ), or human-made replacements for the body parts. Until recently, many of these prostheses made it more difficult for many people to participate in physical activities, such as sports. But new designs have led to lighter, more comfortable prostheses that move the way that a human limb does. These new designs have allowed athletes with physical disabilities to compete at higher levels.

Social Studies ACTIVITY

Research the use of prostheses throughout history. Create a timeline showing major advances in prosthesis use and design.

Answer to Math Activity
17.5% (0.35 m² ÷ 2 m² × 100 = 17.5%)

Answer to Social Studies Activity
Students' timelines should display an understanding of how modern technology has improved prosthesis design. Timelines should include the use of wooden prostheses, expand into the use of metal and the development of plastics and other synthetics in prosthesis construction, and discuss modern ergonomic designs.

Zahra Beheshti

Physical Therapist A physical therapist is a licensed professional who helps people recover from injuries by using hands-on treatment instead of medicines. Dr. Zahra Beheshti is a physical therapist at the Princeton Physical Therapy Center in New Jersey. She often helps athletes who suffer from sports injuries.

After an injury, a person may go through a process called *rehabilitation* to regain the use of the injured body part. The most common mistake made by athletes is that they play sports before completely recovering from injuries. Dr. Beheshti explains, "Going back to their usual pre-injury routine could result in another injury."

Dr. Beheshti also teaches patients about preventing future sports injuries. "Most injuries happen when an individual engages in strenuous activities without a proper warm-up or cool-down period." Being a physical therapist is rewarding work. Dr. Beheshti says, "I get a lot of satisfaction when treating patients and see them regain their function and independence and return to their normal life."

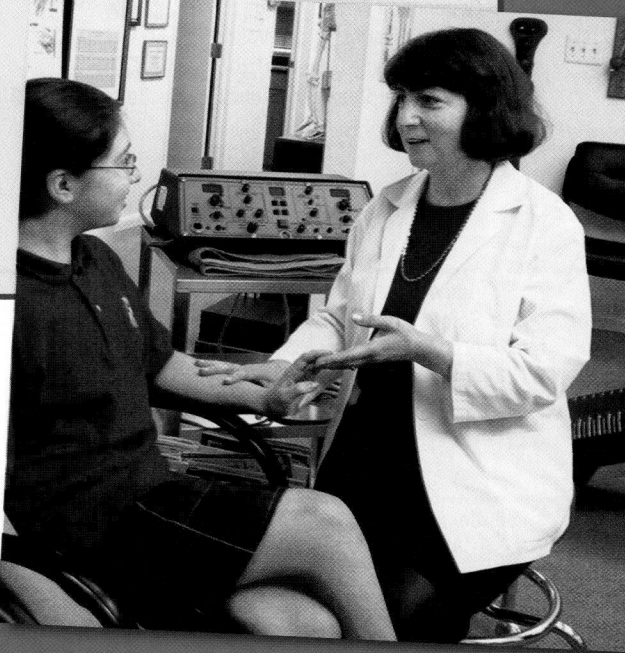

Language Arts
ACTIVITY

WRITING SKILL Interview a physical therapist who works in or near your community. Write a newspaper article about your interview.

go.hrw.com
To learn more about these Science in Action topics, visit go.hrw.com and type in the keyword HL5BD1F.

Current Science
Check out Current Science® articles related to this chapter by visiting go.hrw.com. Just type in the keyword HL5CS22.

Circulation and Respiration
Chapter Planning Guide

Compression guide:
To shorten instruction because of time limitations, omit the Chapter Lab.

OBJECTIVES	LABS, DEMONSTRATIONS, AND ACTIVITIES	TECHNOLOGY RESOURCES
PACING • 90 min pp. 604–611 **Chapter Opener**	SE **Start-up Activity**, p. 605 GENERAL	OSP **Parent Letter** ■ GENERAL CD **Student Edition on CD-ROM** CD **Guided Reading Audio CD** ■ TR **Chapter Starter Transparency*** VID **Brain Food Video Quiz**
Section 1 The Cardiovascular System • List four main parts of the cardiovascular system, and describe their functions. • Describe the two types of circulation of blood in the body. • List four cardiovascular problems.	TE **Connection Activity** Math, p. 607 GENERAL TE **Activity** Viewing Blood Vessels, p. 608 ◆ GENERAL TE **Group Activity** Circulate!, p. 609 ◆ GENERAL LB **Whiz-Bang Demonstrations** Get the Beat* ◆ BASIC	CRF **Lesson Plans*** TR **Bellringer Transparency*** TR **The Flow of Blood Through the Heart*** TR **The Flow of Blood Through the Body*** TE **Internet Activity,** p. 611 GENERAL
PACING • 45 min pp. 612–615 **Section 2 Blood** • Identify the four main components of blood. • Describe three functions of blood. • Explain how blood pressure is measured. • Explain what the ABO blood types are and why they are important.	TE **Activity** Making a Model of Blood, p. 613 ◆ BASIC SE **Science in Action** Math, Social Studies, and Language Arts Activities, pp. 630–631 GENERAL LB **Calculator-Based Labs** A Hot Hand* ◆ ADVANCED	CRF **Lesson Plans*** TR **Bellringer Transparency***
PACING • 45 min pp. 616–619 **Section 3 The Lymphatic System** • Describe the relationship between the lymphatic system and the circulatory system. • Identify six parts of the lymphatic system, and describe their functions.	SE **Connection to Social Studies** Vent Your Spleen, p. 618 GENERAL	CRF **Lesson Plans*** TR **Bellringer Transparency*** CRF **SciLinks Activity*** GENERAL
PACING • 90 min pp. 620–623 **Section 4 The Respiratory System** • Describe the parts of the respiratory system and their functions. • Explain how breathing happens. • Discuss the relationship between the respiratory system and the cardiovascular system. • Identify two respiratory disorders.	TE **Activity** Deep Breathing, p. 620 GENERAL TE **Activity** Investigating Speech, p. 621 GENERAL SE **Connection to Chemistry** Oxygen and Blood, p. 622 GENERAL SE **Quick Lab** Why Do People Snore?, p. 623 GENERAL SE **Skills Practice Labs** Carbon Dioxide Breath, p. 624 ◆ GENERAL SE **Model-Making Lab**s Build a Lung, p. 795 ◆ GENERAL LB **Whiz-Bang Demonstrations** Take a Deep Breath* ◆ GENERAL LB **EcoLabs & Field Activities** There's Something in the Air* ◆ GENERAL LB **Long-Term Projects & Research Ideas** Getting to the Heart* ◆ ADVANCED	CRF **Lesson Plans*** TR **Bellringer Transparency*** TR **The Role of Blood in Respiration*** TR *LINK TO PHYSICAL SCIENCE* Exhaling, Pressure, and Fluid Flow* VID **Lab Videos for Life Science**

PACING • 90 min

CHAPTER REVIEW, ASSESSMENT, AND STANDARDIZED TEST PREPARATION

CRF **Vocabulary Activity*** GENERAL
SE **Chapter Review**, pp. 626–627 GENERAL
CRF **Chapter Review*** ■ GENERAL
CRF **Chapter Tests A*** ■ GENERAL, **B*** ADVANCED, **C*** SPECIAL NEEDS
SE **Standardized Test Preparation**, pp. 628–629 GENERAL
CRF **Standardized Test Preparation*** GENERAL
CRF **Performance-Based Assessment*** GENERAL
OSP **Test Generator** GENERAL
CRF **Test Item Listing*** GENERAL

Online and Technology Resources

Visit **go.hrw.com** for a variety of free resources related to this textbook. Enter the keyword **HL5BD2**.

Students can access interactive problem-solving help and active visual concept development with the *Holt Science and Technology* Online Edition available at **www.hrw.com**.

 Guided Reading Audio CD Also in Spanish

A direct reading of each chapter for auditory learners, reluctant readers, and Spanish-speaking students.

 Science Tutor CD-ROM

Excellent for remediation and test practice.

SKILLS DEVELOPMENT RESOURCES	SECTION REVIEW AND ASSESSMENT	STANDARDS CORRELATIONS
SE Pre-Reading Activity, p. 604 `GENERAL` **OSP** Science Puzzlers, Twisters & Teasers `GENERAL`		National Science Education Standards UCP 1, 2; SAI 1; ST 2; SPSP 5; LS 1e, 3b
CRF Directed Reading A* ■ `BASIC`, B* `SPECIAL NEEDS` **CRF** Vocabulary and Section Summary* ■ `GENERAL` **SE** Reading Strategy Paired Summarizing, p. 606 `GENERAL` **TE** Reading Strategy Mnemonics, p. 608 `GENERAL` **SE** Math Practice The Beat Goes On, p. 610 `GENERAL` **MS** Math Skills for Science Multiplying Whole Numbers* `BASIC` **CRF** Reinforcement Worksheet Matchmaker, Matchmaker* `GENERAL` **CRF** Reinforcement Worksheet Colors of the Heart* `BASIC` **CRF** Critical Thinking Doctor for a Day* `ADVANCED`	**SE** Reading Checks, pp. 606, 608, 610 `GENERAL` **TE** Homework, p. 607 `GENERAL` **TE** Homework, p. 607 `GENERAL` **TE** Reteaching, p. 610 `BASIC` **TE** Quiz, p. 610 `GENERAL` **TE** Alternative Assessment, p. 610 `GENERAL` **SE** Section Review,* p. 611 ■ `GENERAL` **CRF** Section Quiz* ■ `GENERAL`	UCP 1, 2, 3, 5; SPSP 1, 4, 5; LS 1a, 1b, 1c, 1d, 1e, 1f, 3b
CRF Directed Reading A* ■ `BASIC`, B* `SPECIAL NEEDS` **CRF** Vocabulary and Section Summary* ■ `GENERAL` **SE** Reading Strategy Reading Organizer, p. 612 `GENERAL` **TE** Discussion Blood, p. 612 `GENERAL` **TE** Reading Strategy Asking Questions, p. 613 `GENERAL` **TE** Inclusion Strategies, p. 614	**SE** Reading Checks, pp. 612, 613, 614, 615 `GENERAL` **TE** Reteaching, p. 614 `BASIC` **TE** Quiz, p. 614 `GENERAL` **TE** Alternative Assessment, p. 614 `GENERAL` **SE** Section Review,* p. 615 ■ `GENERAL` **CRF** Section Quiz* ■ `GENERAL`	UCP 1; SPSP 1, 5; LS 1a, 1b, 1c, 1d, 1e, 1f, 3a, 3b
CRF Directed Reading A* ■ `BASIC`, B* `SPECIAL NEEDS` **CRF** Vocabulary and Section Summary* ■ `GENERAL` **SE** Reading Strategy Prediction Guide, p. 616 `GENERAL` **TE** Research Lymphatic System and Disease, p. 617 `ADVANCED` **TE** Reading Strategy Paired Summarizing, p. 617 `GENERAL`	**SE** Reading Checks, pp. 616, 618 `GENERAL` **TE** Reteaching, p. 618 `BASIC` **TE** Quiz, p. 618 `GENERAL` **TE** Alternative Assessment, p. 618 `ADVANCED` **SE** Section Review,* p. 619 ■ `GENERAL` **CRF** Section Quiz* ■ `GENERAL`	UCP 1, 5; LS 1a, 1c, 1d, 1e, 1f
CRF Directed Reading A* ■ `BASIC`, B* `SPECIAL NEEDS` **CRF** Vocabulary and Section Summary* ■ `GENERAL` **SE** Reading Strategy Reading Organizer, p. 620 `GENERAL` **TE** Inclusion Strategies, p. 621	**SE** Reading Checks, pp. 621, 622 `GENERAL` **TE** Reteaching, p. 622 `BASIC` **TE** Quiz, p. 622 `GENERAL` **TE** Alternative Assessment, p. 622 `ADVANCED` **SE** Section Review,* p. 623 ■ `GENERAL` **CRF** Section Quiz* ■ `GENERAL`	UCP 1, 2, 4, 5; LS 1a, 1b, 1c, 1d, 1e, 1f; UCP 2, 5; SAI 1, 2; LS 1a; *Chapter Lab:* UCP 2, 5; SAI 1, 2; LS 1a; *LabBook:* UCP 2, 5; SAI 1, 2; LS 1a

One-Stop Planner® CD-ROM

This convenient CD-ROM includes:
• Lab Materials QuickList Software
• Holt Calendar Planner
• Customizable Lesson Plans
• Printable Worksheets
• ExamView® Test Generator

cnnstudentnews.com

Find the latest news, lesson plans, and activities related to important scientific events.

www.scilinks.org

Maintained by the **National Science Teachers Association.** See Chapter Enrichment pages for a complete list of topics.

Current Science®

Check out *Current Science* articles and activities by visiting the HRW Web site at go.hrw.com. Just type in the keyword **HL5CS23T.**

Classroom Videos

• **Lab Videos** demonstrate the chapter lab.

• **Brain Food Video Quizzes** help students review the chapter material.

• **CNN Videos** bring science into your students' daily life.

Visual Resources

CHAPTER STARTER TRANSPARENCY

This Really Happened!

The human heart is normally a very dependable organ. It may beat more than 100,000 times per day for a person's entire life. During this time it pumps millions of liters of blood through the body. When there is a serious problem with the heart, it is life threatening.

In the past, heart failure resulted in immediate death. But in 1969, Dr. Denton Cooley, of the Texas Heart Institute, kept a patient alive for 5 days after the patient's heart failed. How did he do it? He used an artificial heart that he designed himself.

The design of artificial hearts has improved considerably since Dr. Cooley's first model. The electric artificial heart

shown above right is one of the more recent test models. Its mass is about 680 g—only a little heavier than a real human heart. Newer test models are even smaller and lighter. These artificial hearts have special sensors and microprocessors that regulate the beat and respond to changes in blood pressure.

Currently, there is no artificial heart that can permanently replace the human heart. The human heart is a sophisticated organ that serves the cardiovascular system, one of the body's pathways for circulating fluids. In this chapter you will also read about the lymphatic system and the respiratory system and how all of these systems are related.

BELLRINGER TRANSPARENCIES

Section: The Cardiovascular System

In 2 to 3 minutes, list as many song titles and lyrics as you can that contain the word *heart*. What ideas are associated with the heart? Why do you think the heart is part of so many songs?

Write your answers in your **science journal.**

Section: Blood

What does blood do? List as many functions of blood as you can think of in your **science journal.** Think about the following phrase: "Blood is thicker than water." Have you ever heard someone use this phrase? What do you think it means?

TEACHING TRANSPARENCIES

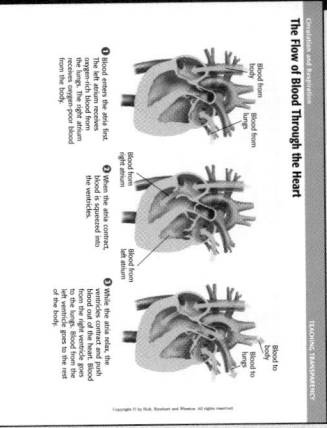

The Flow of Blood Through the Heart

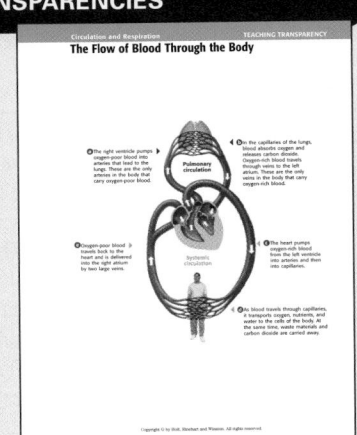

The Flow of Blood Through the Body

TEACHING TRANSPARENCIES

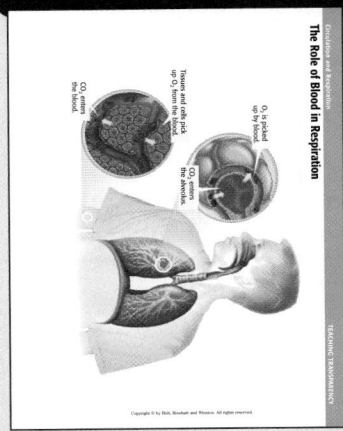

The Role of Blood in Respiration

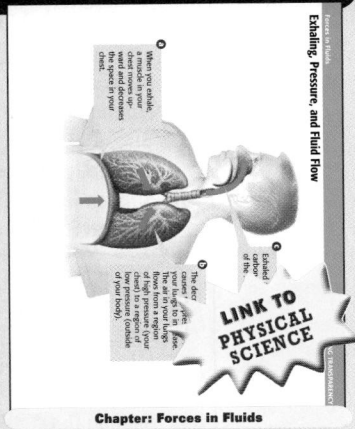

Exhaling, Pressure, and Fluid Flow

Chapter: Forces in Fluids

CONCEPT MAPPING TRANSPARENCY

Use the following terms to complete the concept map below: arteries, cardiovascular system, bronchi, alveoli, capillaries, respiratory system, cellular respiration, blood

Planning Resources

LESSON PLANS

Lesson Plan   SAMPLE

Section: Waves

Pacing
Regular Schedule: with lab(s):2 days   without lab(s)2 days
Block Schedule: with lab(s):1 1/2 days without lab(s)1 day

Objectives
1. Relate the seven properties of life to a living organism.
2. Describe seven themes that can help you to organize what you learn about biology.
3. Identify the tiny structures that make up all living organisms.
4. Differentiate between reproduction and heredity and between metabolism and homeostasis.

National Science Education Standards Covered
LSInter/x:Cells have particular structures that underlie their functions.
LSMat1: Most cell functions involve chemical reactions.
LSBeh1: Cells store and use information to guide their functions.
UCP1:Cell functions are regulated.
SI1: Cells can differentiate and form complete multicellular organisms.
PS1: Species evolve over time.
ESS1: The great diversity of organisms is the result of more than 3.5 billion years of evolution.
ESS2: Natural selection and its evolutionary consequences provide a scientific explanation for the fossil record of ancient life forms as well as for the striking molecular similarities observed among the diverse species of living organisms.
ST1: The millions of different species of plants, animals, and microorganisms that live on Earth today are related by descent from common ancestors.
ST2: The energy for life primarily comes from the sun.
SPSP1: The complexity and organization of organisms accommodates the need for obtaining, transforming, transporting, releasing, and eliminating the matter and energy used to sustain the organism.
SPSP6: As matter and energy flows through different levels of organization of living systems—cells, organs, communities—and between living organisms and the physical environment, chemical elements are recombined in different ways.
HNS1: Organisms have behavioral responses to internal changes and to external stimuli.

PARENT LETTER

SAMPLE

Dear Parent,

Your son's or daughter's science class will soon begin exploring the chapter entitled "The World of Physical Science." In this chapter, students will learn about how the scientific method applies to the world of physical science and the role of physical science in the world. By the end of the chapter, students should demonstrate a clear understanding of the chapter's main ideas and be able to discuss the following topics:

1. physical science as the study of energy and matter (Section 1)
2. the role of physical science in the world around them (Section 1)
3. careers that rely on physical science (Section 1)
4. the steps used in the scientific method (Section 2)
5. examples of technology (Section 2)
6. how the scientific method is used to answer questions and solve problems (Section 2)
7. how our knowledge of science changes over time (Section 2)
8. how models represent real objects or systems (Section 3)
9. examples of different ways models are used in science (Section 3)
10. the importance of the International System of Units (Section 4)
11. the appropriate units to use for particular measurements (Section 4)
12. how area and density are derived quantities (Section 4)

Questions to Ask Along the Way

You can help your son or daughter learn about these topics by asking interesting questions such as the following:

• What are some surprising careers that use physical science?
• What is a characteristic of a good hypothesis?
• When is it a good idea to use a model?
• Why do Americans measure things in terms of inches and yards and meters ?

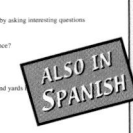
ALSO IN SPANISH

TEST ITEM LISTING

TEST ITEM LISTING
The World of Science   SAMPLE

MULTIPLE CHOICE
1. A limitation of models is that
   a. they are large enough to see.
   b. they do not act exactly like the things that they model.
   c. they are smaller than the things that they model.
   d. they model unfamiliar things
   Answer: B   Difficulty: 1   Section: 3   Objective: 2
2. The length 10 m is equal to
   a. 100 cm.   c. 10,000 mm.
   b. 1,000 cm.   d. Both (b) and (c)
   Answer: B   Difficulty: 1   Section: 3   Objective: 2
3. To be valid, a hypothesis must be
   a. testable.   c. made into a law.
   b. supported by evidence. d. Both (a) and (b)
   Answer: B   Difficulty: 1   Section: 3   Objective: 2 1
4. The statement "Sheila has a stain on her shirt" is an example of a(n)
   a. law.   c. observation.
   b. hypothesis.   d. prediction.
   Answer: B   Difficulty: 1   Section: 2   Objective: 2
5. A hypothesis is often developed out of
   a. observations.   c. laws.
   b. experiments.   d. Both (a) and (b)
   Answer: B   Difficulty: 1   Section: 2   Objective: 2
6. How many milliliters are in 3.5 kL?
   a. 3,500 mL.   c. 3,500, 000 mL.
   b. 0.0035 mL.   d. 35,000 mL.
   Answer: B   Difficulty: 1   Section: 3   Objective: 2
7. A map of Seattle is an example of a
   a. law.   c. model.
   b. theory.   d. unit.
   Answer: B   Difficulty: 1   Section: 3   Objective: 2
8. A lab has the safety icons shown below. These icons mean that you should wear
   a. only safety goggles.   c. safety goggles and a lab apron.
   b. only a lab apron.   d. safety goggles, a lab apron, and gloves.
   Answer: B   Difficulty: 1   Section: 3   Objective: 2
9. The law of conservation of mass says the t=t of mass before a chemical change to
   a. the total mass after the change.
   b. less than the total mass after the change.
   c. the same as the total mass after the change.
   d. not the same as the total mass after the change.
   Answer: B   Difficulty: 1   Section: 3   Objective: 2
10. In which of the following areas might you find a geochemist at work?
   a. studying the chemistry of rocks   c. studying fishes
   b. studying forestry   d. studying the atmosphere
   Answer: B   Difficulty: 1   Section: 3   Objective: 2

One-Stop Planner® CD-ROM

This CD-ROM includes all of the resources shown here and the following time-saving tools:

• *Lab Materials QuickList Software*
• *Customizable lesson plans*
• *Holt Calendar Planner*
• *The powerful ExamView® Test Generator*

Meeting Individual Needs

DIRECTED READING A
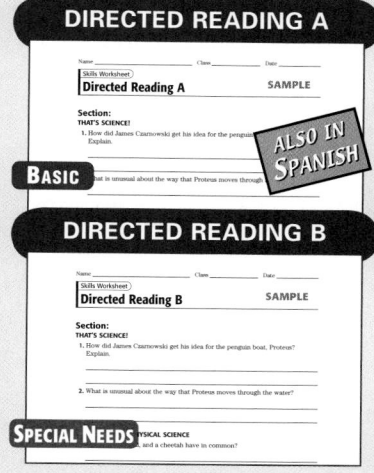
BASIC · ALSO IN SPANISH

DIRECTED READING B
SPECIAL NEEDS

VOCABULARY ACTIVITY
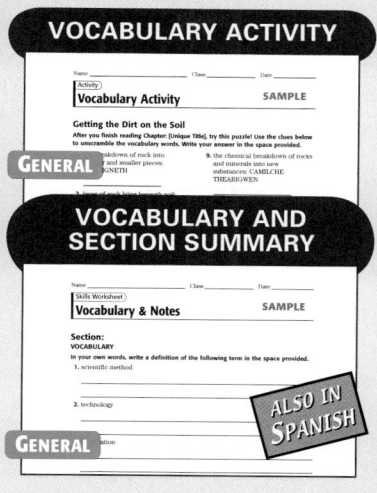
GENERAL

Getting the Dirt on the Soil

VOCABULARY AND SECTION SUMMARY
GENERAL · ALSO IN SPANISH

REINFORCEMENT
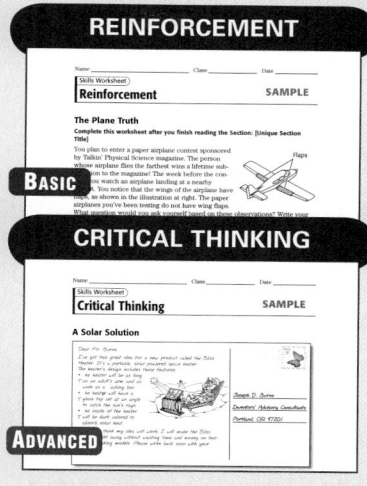
BASIC

The Plane Truth

CRITICAL THINKING
ADVANCED

A Solar Solution

SCILINKS ACTIVITY

GENERAL

MARINE ECOSYSTEMS

SCIENCE PUZZLERS, TWISTERS & TEASERS
GENERAL

Circulation and Respiration
The Rat Workout

Labs and Activities

ECOLABS & FIELD ACTIVITIES
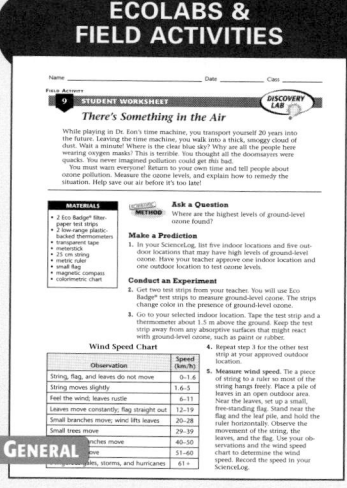
GENERAL

There's Something in the Air

WHIZ-BANG DEMONSTRATIONS
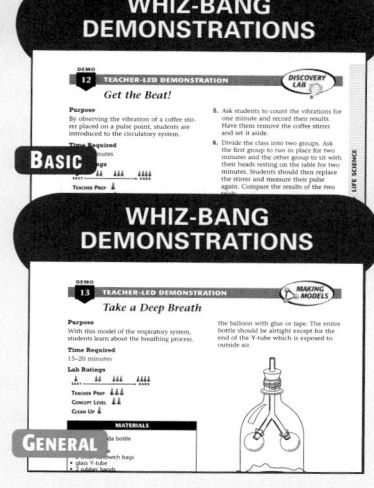
BASIC

Get the Beat!

WHIZ-BANG DEMONSTRATIONS
GENERAL

Take a Deep Breath

LONG-TERM PROJECTS & RESEARCH IDEAS
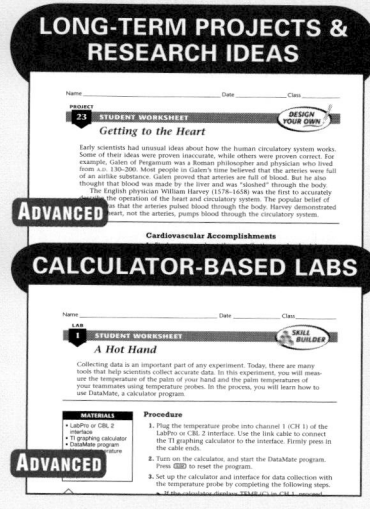
ADVANCED

Getting to the Heart

CALCULATOR-BASED LABS
ADVANCED

A Hot Hand

DATASHEETS FOR QUICK LABS

Reaction to Stress

DATASHEETS FOR CHAPTER LABS

Using Scientific Methods

DATASHEETS FOR LABBOOK

Does It All Add Up?

Review and Assessments

SECTION QUIZ

GENERAL · ALSO IN SPANISH

SECTION REVIEW
GENERAL · ALSO IN SPANISH

CHAPTER REVIEW
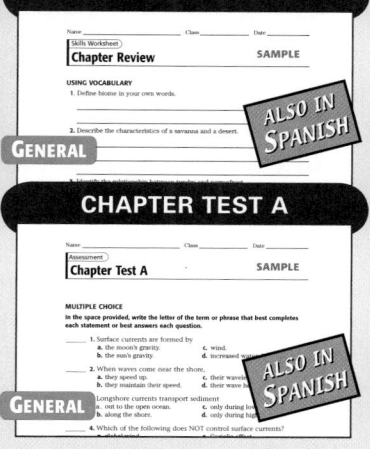
GENERAL · ALSO IN SPANISH

CHAPTER TEST A
GENERAL · ALSO IN SPANISH

CHAPTER TEST B
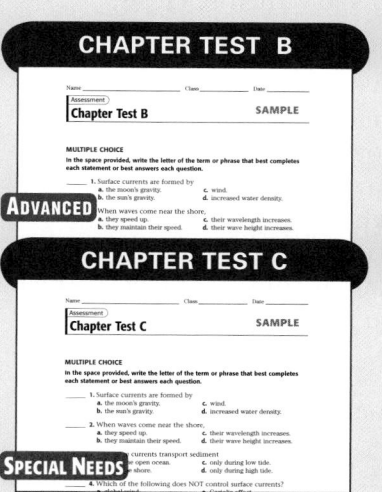
ADVANCED

CHAPTER TEST C
SPECIAL NEEDS

STANDARDIZED TEST PREPARATION
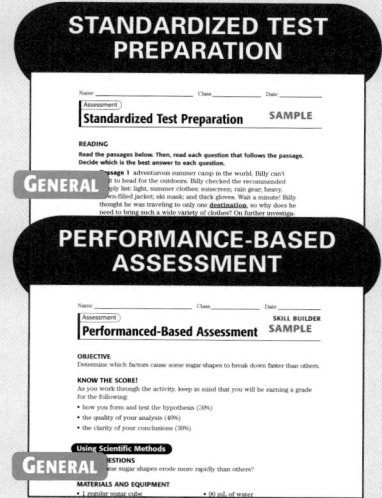
GENERAL

PERFORMANCE-BASED ASSESSMENT
GENERAL

Performanced-Based Assessment

This Chapter Enrichment provides relevant and interesting information to expand and enhance your presentation of the chapter material.

Section 1

The Cardiovascular System

The Flow of Blood

- William Harvey (1578–1657) is credited with being the first European to discover the circulation of the blood through the body.

- Based on his dissections of animals, Harvey rightly concluded that the heart was a muscle that served to pump blood through the body. Harvey correctly maintained that arteries carry blood away from the heart and veins carry blood toward the heart. His views, for which many other physicians ridiculed him, contradicted conventional wisdom and theories of the famous physician Galen (129–c. 201 CE).

Atherosclerosis

- Atherosclerosis is a disease of the arteries in which the inside layer of the arterial walls thickens with plaque. Plaque forms in areas where the inner arterial wall has been damaged. As the walls of an artery thicken, the diameter of the vessel narrows, which impedes blood flow.

- Cigarette smoking, high blood pressure, obesity, inactivity, high cholesterol level, and a family history of heart disease are risk factors for atherosclerosis.

Hypertension

- Like people who have atherosclerosis, people afflicted with hypertension may not exhibit symptoms of the disease for years. In fact, hypertension is often called "the silent killer." Although blood pressure varies within a wide range across the population, a person whose resting blood pressure is consistently at the high end of that range is said to have hypertension.

- Smoking, obesity, stress, excessive consumption of alcohol, and diabetes mellitus exacerbate high blood pressure.

Stroke

- A stroke occurs when the brain is damaged because of an interruption in the blood flow or the leakage of blood from the blood vessels. Atherosclerosis and hypertension are some of the causes of strokes.

Heart Attack

- A heart attack occurs when part of the heart muscle dies because of blood and oxygen deprivation. About 1 million people in the United States have a heart attack each year.

Section 2

Blood

Blood Types and Rh Factor

- Human blood has four ABO types (A, B, AB, and O), which are determined by surface antigens on red blood cells (RBCs). Blood is also either Rh+ or Rh−. If RBCs have an Rh antigen (a protein on the surface of the cells), the blood is Rh+. If an Rh antigen is not present, the blood is Rh−. People have one of the following blood types: A+, A−, B+, B−, AB+, AB−, O+, or O−.

- People make antibodies against the antigens that their RBCs do not have. People who have Rh− blood (no Rh antigens) make antibodies against the Rh antigen only after being exposed to Rh+ blood. For example, people who have type B− blood make A antibodies that attack any blood cell that has an A antigen. They may also make Rh antibodies that will attack any blood cell that has an Rh antigen on it. So, people who have type B− blood who have been exposed to Rh+ blood cannot be given A+, A−, B+, AB+, or AB− blood.

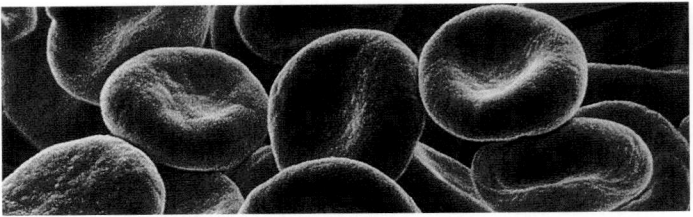

- Type O− blood can be given to anyone because its RBCs do not have any A, B, or Rh antigens that a recipient's antibodies could attack. For this reason, a type O− person is said to be a universal donor. Type AB+ people are called *universal recipients*; they can be given any type of blood because they do not make any antibodies against A, B, or Rh antigens.

Section 3

The Lymphatic System

Lymphocytes

- Lymphocytes are white blood cells that specialize in fighting pathogens. The two main kinds of lymphocytes are B cells and T cells.

- About 10 % of lymphocytes are B cells. When confronted with foreign antigens, B cells produce antibodies that destroy the antigens. This process is called *humoral immunity.*

- About 90 % of lymphocytes are T cells, which form in the bones and mature in the thymus. Cells called *killer T cells* locate and attack cells on whose surface are foreign antigens. This type of immunity is called *cell-mediated immunity.*

- HIV infects and destroys lymphocytes called *helper T cells.* When a person's helper T cell count falls below 200 cells per cubic millimeter of blood, the person is diagnosed with AIDS.

Is That a Fact!

◆ The tonsils reach their largest size when a person is about seven years old. Then, the tonsils begin to shrink.

Section 4

The Respiratory System

Control of Breathing

- Unless a person consciously holds his or her breath or changes the rate of his or her breathing, breathing is controlled automatically by breathing control centers in the base of the brain (in the medulla oblongata and in the pons).

- Hiccups are a result of a sudden, jerky contraction of the diaphragm. When a person eats too much food, the full stomach may irritate the diaphragm muscle and cause the muscle to contract jerkily. However, other causes of hiccups are unknown.

Is That a Fact!

◆ Each day, about 2,000 adolescents in the United States become regular daily smokers each day. The habit will eventually kill one-third of these children.

◆ Children who have asthma are particularly at risk from their parents' second-hand smoke. Each year, second-hand smoke increases the number of asthma attacks and the severity of the symptoms in 200,000 to 1 million children who have asthma.

Smoking

- Tobacco smoking has been implicated in more than 90% of lung cancers among men. Among people who do not smoke, 3,000 cases of lung cancer are linked to second-hand cigarette smoke each year.

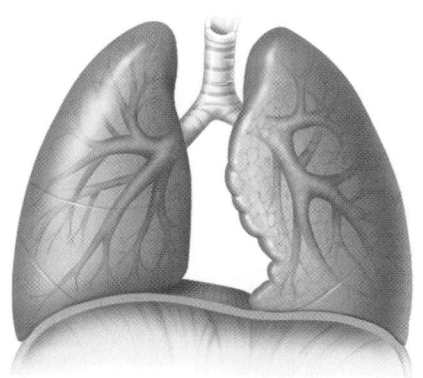

SciLINKS.

NSTA
Developed and maintained by the
National Science Teachers Association

SciLinks is maintained by the National Science Teachers Association to provide you and your students with interesting, up-to-date links that will enrich your classroom presentation of the chapter.

Visit www.scilinks.org and enter the SciLinks code for more information about the topic listed.

Topic: The Cardiovascular System
SciLinks code: HSM0221

Topic: The Lymphatic System
SciLinks code: HSM0891

Topic: Cardiovascular Problems
SciLinks code: HSM0220

Topic: The Immune System
SciLinks code: HSM0786

Topic: Blood
SciLinks code: HSM0175

Topic: The Respiratory System
SciLinks code: HSM1307

Topic: Blood Donations
SciLinks code: HSM0178

Topic: Respiratory Disorders
SciLinks code: HSM1306

Overview

Tell students that this chapter will help them learn about their cardiovascular, lymphatic, and respiratory systems. The chapter has a separate section about blood and a clear description of the way that the cardiovascular system and blood make up the circulatory system.

Assessing Prior Knowledge

Students should be familiar with the following topics:
- the basic life processes
- cells

Identifying Misconceptions

As students learn the material in this chapter, some of them may be confused about the difference between cells and molecules. When asked to draw a molecule, many students will draw something that resembles a cell. Instruction should describe the relationship between molecules and cells. Also, many students may think that proteins and molecules are bigger than cells. The concepts of the cell and the molecule are important when studying the way that blood transports materials to cells and the way that gases are exchanged in the lungs. Use a Venn diagram to help clarify the relationship between atoms, molecules and cells.

23
Circulation and Respiration

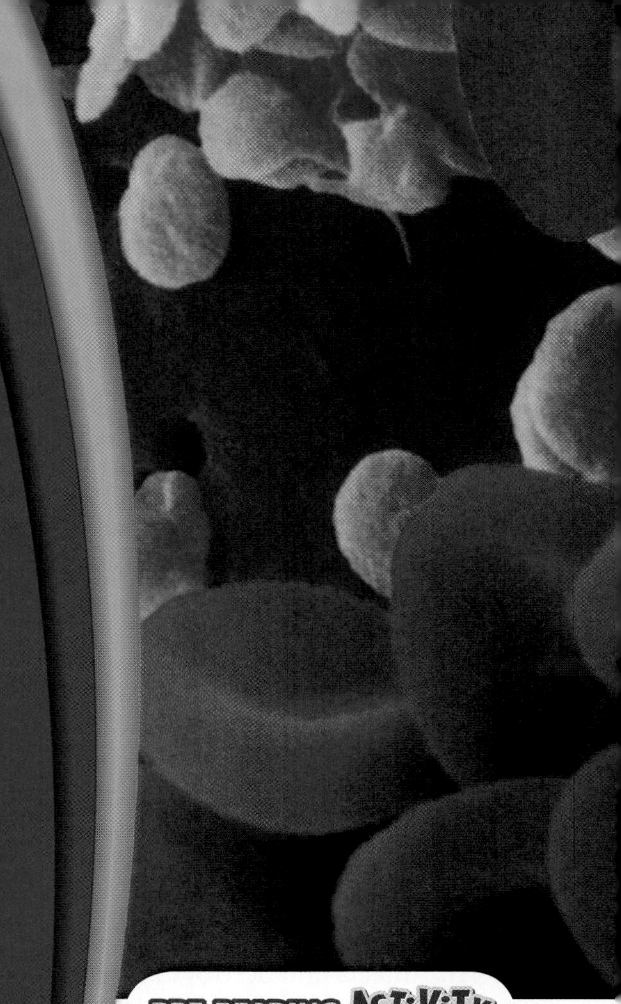

About the PHOTO

Your circulatory system is made up of the heart, blood vessels, and blood. This picture is a colored scanning electron micrograph of red and white blood cells and cell fragments called *platelets*. Red blood cells are disk shaped, white blood cells are rounded, and platelets are the small green fragments. There are millions of blood cells in a drop of blood. Blood cells are so important that your body makes about 200 billion red blood cells every day.

PRE-READING ACTIVITY

FOLDNOTES **Four-Corner Fold**
Before you read the chapter, create the FoldNote entitled "Four-Corner Fold" described in the **Study Skills** section of the Appendix. Label the flaps of the four-corner fold with the section titles "Cardiovascular system," "Blood," Lymphatic system," and "Respiratory system." Write what you know about each topic under the appropriate flap. As you read the chapter, add other information that you learn.

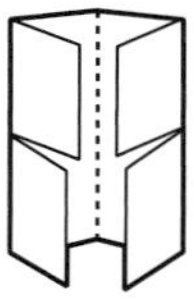

Standards Correlations

National Science Education Standards

The following codes indicate the National Science Education Standards that correlate to this chapter. The full text of the standards is at the front of the book.

Chapter Opener
UCP 1, 2; SAI 1; ST 2; SPSP 5; LS 1e, 3b

Section 1 The Cardiovascular System
UCP 1, 2, 3, 5; SPSP 1, 4, 5; LS 1a, 1b, 1c, 1d, 1e, 1f, 3b

Section 2 Blood
UCP 1; SPSP 1, 5; LS 1a, 1b, 1c, 1d, 1e, 1f, 3a, 3b

Section 3 The Lymphatic System
UCP 1, 5; LS 1a, 1c, 1d, 1e, 1f

Section 4 The Respiratory System
UCP 1, 2, 4, 5; LS 1a, 1b, 1c, 1d, 1e, 1f; *LabBook:* UCP 2, 5; SAI 1, 2; LS 1a

Chapter Lab
UCP 2, 5; SAI 1, 2; LS 1a

Chapter Review
UCP 1; SAI 1; LS 1a, 1c, 1d, 1e, 3a

Science in Action
SAI 1, 2; ST 2; SPSP 4, 5; HNS 1; LS 1e

Safety Caution: Have students bring in a signed permission slip for this activity. Any students who have a health problem that may be worsened by exercise should be excused from the exercise portion of this activity. Instruct students who feel pain or become dizzy or tired to stop exercising immediately. Some students may feel embarrassed to exercise in front of their peers. You may want to invite a few volunteers to perform the exercise portion instead of having all of the students exercise.

Answers

1. Students should notice that their heart rate goes up when they are exercising. Explanations may vary, but students should understand that during exercise an increase in circulation rate is needed to ensure delivery of sufficient oxygen and fuel to the body.

2. Sample answer: An increased heart rate increases the rate of blood flow and delivers red blood cells to the body more quickly.

3. Sample answer: When I stop exercising, my body no longer needs extra oxygen and fuel, so my heart rate returns to normal after a period of rest.

START-UP ACTIVITY

Exercise Your Heart

How does your heart respond to exercise? You can see this reaction by measuring your pulse.

Procedure

1. Take your pulse while remaining still. (Take your pulse by placing your fingers on the inside of your wrist just below your thumb.)

2. Using a **watch with a second hand,** count the number of heart beats in 15 s. Then, multiply this number by 4 to calculate the number of beats in 1 minute.

3. Do some moderate physical activity, such as jumping jacks or jogging in place, for 30 s.

4. Stop and calculate your heart rate again.
   Caution: Do not perform this exercise if you have difficulty breathing, if you have high blood pressure or asthma, or if you get dizzy easily.

5. Rest for 5 min.

6. Take your pulse again.

Analysis

1. How did exercise affect your heart rate? Why do you think this happened?

2. How does your heart rate affect the rate at which red blood cells travel throughout your body?

3. Did your heart rate return to normal (or almost normal) after you rested? Why or why not?

This Really Happened!

The human heart is normally a very dependable organ. It may beat more than 100,000 times per day for a person's entire life. During this time it pumps millions of liters of blood through the body. When there is a serious problem with the heart, it is life threatening.

In the past, heart failure resulted in immediate death. But in 1969, Dr. Denton Cooley, of the Texas Heart Institute, kept a patient alive for 5 days after the patient's heart failed. How did he do it? He used an artificial heart that he designed himself.

shown above right is one of the more recent test models. Its mass is about 680 g—only a little heavier than a real human heart. Newer test models are even smaller and lighter. These artificial hearts have special sensors and microprocessors that regulate the beat and respond to changes in blood pressure.

Currently, there is no artificial heart that can permanently replace the human heart. The human heart is a sophisticated organ that serves the cardiovascular system, one of the body's pathways for circulating fluids. In this chapter you will

Chapter Starter Transparency
Use this transparency to help students begin thinking about their circulatory system and its functions.

CHAPTER RESOURCES

Technology

 **Transparencies**
• Chapter Starter Transparency

READING SKILLS

 Student Edition on CD-ROM

 Guided Reading Audio CD
• English or Spanish

 Classroom Videos
• Brain Food Video Quiz

Workbooks

Science Puzzlers, Twisters & Teasers
• Circulation and Respiration GENERAL

Focus

Overview

This section introduces the structures and functions of the cardiovascular and circulatory systems. Students study the three types of blood vessels, trace the path of blood in the body, and learn about blood types.

🔊 Bellringer

Ask students to list as many song titles, phrases, and slogans that contain the word *heart* as they can in two to three minutes. Ask for examples, and list the examples on the board. Ask for reasons that the word *heart* is the focus of so many songs and slogans.

Motivate

Discussion ——— GENERAL

Cardiovascular System Ask students to describe or diagram the flow of blood through their body. Remind students that their body is made up of trillions of cells. Ask students how they think that oxygen and nutrients get to each cell. Give a general description of the roles of the heart and the blood vessels, and discuss how sturdy these structures must be to work for a lifetime. **LS** Verbal/Logical

---

READING WARM-UP

Objectives
- List four main parts of the cardiovascular system, and describe their functions.
- Describe the two types of circulation of blood in the body.
- List four cardiovascular problems.

Terms to Learn

cardiovascular system	pulmonary circulation
artery	systemic circulation
capillary	
vein	

READING STRATEGY

Paired Summarizing Read this section silently. In pairs, take turns summarizing the material. Stop to discuss ideas that seem confusing.

cardiovascular system a collection of organs that transport blood throughout the body

---

The Cardiovascular System

When you hear the word heart, *what do you think of first? Many people think of romance. Some people think of courage. But the heart is much more than a symbol of love or bravery. Your heart is an amazing pump.*

The heart is an organ that is part of your circulatory system. The *circulatory system* includes your heart; your blood; your veins, capillaries, and arteries; and your lymphatic system.

Your Cardiovascular System

Your heart creates pressure every time it beats. This pressure moves blood to every cell in your body through your cardiovascular system (KAR dee OH VAS kyoo luhr SIS tuhm). The **cardiovascular system** consists of the heart and the three types of blood vessels that carry blood throughout your body. The word *cardio* means "heart," and *vascular* means "blood vessel." The blood vessels—arteries, capillaries, and veins—carry blood pumped by the heart. **Figure 1** shows the major arteries and veins.

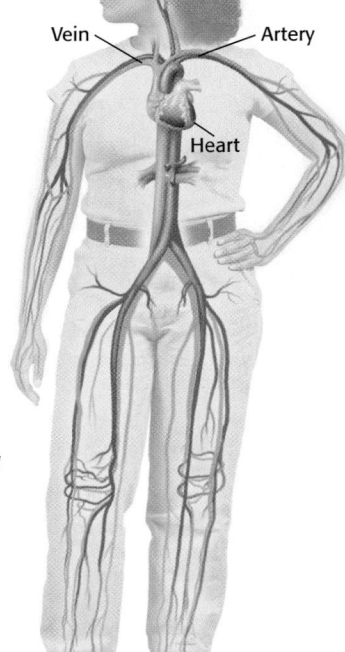

Vein — Artery

Heart

✓ **Reading Check** What are the four main parts of the cardiovascular system? (*See the Appendix for answers to Reading Checks.*)

Figure 1 *The cardiovascular system carries blood to every cell in your body.*

CHAPTER RESOURCES

Chapter Resource File

- **Lesson Plan**
- **Directed Reading A** BASIC
- **Directed Reading B** SPECIAL NEEDS

Technology

Transparencies
- Bellringer
- The Flow of Blood Through the Heart

Workbooks

Math Skills for Science
- The Unit Factor and Dimensional Analysis

Answer to Reading Check

The four main parts of the cardiovascular system are the heart and the arteries, capillaries, and veins.

The Heart

Your *heart* is an organ made mostly of cardiac muscle tissue. It is about the size of your fist and is almost in the center of your chest cavity. Like hearts of all mammals, your heart has a left side and a right side that are separated by a thick wall. The right side of the heart pumps oxygen-poor blood to the lungs. The left side pumps oxygen-rich blood to the body. As you can see in **Figure 2,** each side has an upper chamber and a lower chamber. Each upper chamber is called an *atrium* (plural, *atria*). Each lower chamber is called a *ventricle*.

Flaplike structures called *valves* are located between the atria and ventricles and in places where large arteries are attached to the heart. As blood moves through the heart, these valves close to prevent blood from going backward. The "lub-dub, lub-dub" sound of a beating heart is caused by the valves closing. **Figure 3** shows the flow of blood through the heart.

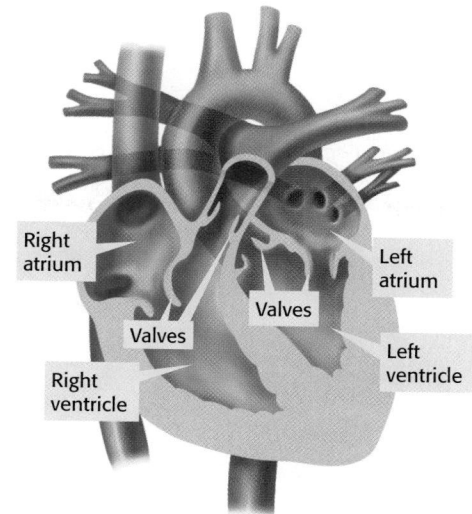

Right atrium
Valves
Right ventricle
Left atrium
Valves
Left ventricle

Figure 2 *The heart pumps blood through blood vessels. The vessels carrying oxygen-rich blood are shown in red. The vessels carrying oxygen-poor blood are shown in blue.*

Figure 3 — The Flow of Blood Through the Heart

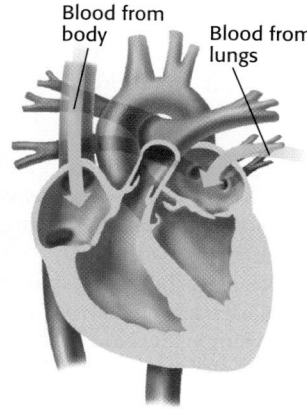

Blood from body
Blood from lungs

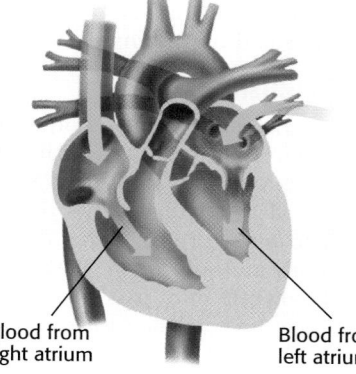

Blood from right atrium
Blood from left atrium

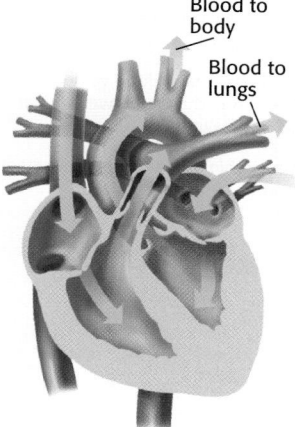

Blood to body
Blood to lungs

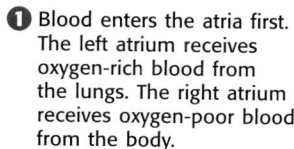

❶ Blood enters the atria first. The left atrium receives oxygen-rich blood from the lungs. The right atrium receives oxygen-poor blood from the body.

❷ When the atria contract, blood is squeezed into the ventricles.

❸ While the atria relax, the ventricles contract and push blood out of the heart. Blood from the right ventricle goes to the lungs. Blood from the left ventricle goes to the rest of the body.

MISCONCEPTION ///ALERT\\\

Left Side, Right Side The words *left* and *right* as used to diagram the anatomy of the heart might confuse students. When students are looking at a picture of the heart, the left atrium appears on their right and the right atrium appears on their left. Help students understand anatomical left and right by facing them and asking them to identify your left and right hands in relation to their own.

Homework —— GENERAL

Poster Project Have students make a poster showing a diagram of the heart. Remind students to label each chamber of the heart properly and to use arrows to indicate the flow of blood. Students can also include diagrams of the lungs and of the rest of the body to show how blood flows to and from the heart. **LS Visual**

Teach

CONNECTION ACTiViTY
Math —— GENERAL

The Pump in Your Chest Your heart beats about 100,800 times per day. With every beat, about 70 mL of blood is pumped out of your heart. In 1 h, how many liters of blood does your heart pump out? (294 L)

About how many liters of blood does your heart pump out in a day? (7,056 L) Help students visualize this amount by showing them a liter of water. **LS Logical/Visual**

Homework —— GENERAL

Making Models Have students make a model of the human heart that shows the path of blood through the heart. Models can be drawings or three-dimensional constructions. Have students present their completed models to the class. Provide yarn or a pen light so that students can demonstrate to the class the flow of blood through their model heart. **LS Visual** English Language Learners

CONNECTION to
Chemistry —— ADVANCED

Pacemaker Contraction of the heart is started by a structure called the *sinoatrial node,* a small cluster of cells embedded in the upper wall of the right atrium. Have students research the sinoatrial node (and the atrioventricular node, which stimulates the ventricles to contract) and make a model or a poster showing how these special cells control the heartbeat.

(Students should find that the heartbeat is not triggered by the nervous system, that the atria contract almost simultaneously, and that the contraction spreads to the ventricles but that there is a short delay during which the atria empty blood into the ventricles.)

READING STRATEGY — GENERAL

Mnemonics Challenge students to create mnemonic devices to help them recall the flow of blood in the body. For example, arteries carry blood away from the heart, and both *artery* and *away* begin with the letter *a*.
LS Verbal

CONNECTION to Real World — BASIC

Blood Vessels Have students rank blood vessels in order from thickest vessel wall to thinnest vessel wall. Have students explain why wall thicknesses vary. (arteries—blood is under pressure; veins—blood is not under as much pressure as in arteries, but walls do not need to be as thin as capillaries; capillaries—their walls are thinnest because the walls must allow for gas, nutrient, and waste exchange with cells) English Language Learners
LS Logical

ACTIVITY — GENERAL

Viewing Blood Vessels Set up microscope stations that have prepared slides of an artery and a vein. Have students view the slides and match them with the descriptions of arteries and veins in the textbook. Have students sketch what they see under the microscope and write descriptive words beside each sketch. English Language Learners
LS Visual

From heart

To heart

Vein

Capillaries

Wall of vein

Artery

Wall of artery

Figure 4 *Large arteries branch into smaller arteries, which branch into capillaries. Capillaries join small veins, which join to form large veins.*

artery a blood vessel that carries blood away from the heart to the body's organs

capillary a tiny blood vessel that allows an exchange between blood and cells in other tissue

vein in biology, a vessel that carries blood to the heart

Blood Vessels

Blood travels throughout your body in hollow tubes called *blood vessels*. The three types of blood vessels—arteries, capillaries, and veins—are shown in **Figure 4.**

Arteries

A blood vessel that carries blood away from the heart is an **artery.** Arteries have thick walls, which contain a layer of smooth muscle. Each heartbeat pumps blood into your arteries at high pressure. This pressure is your *blood pressure*. Artery walls stretch and are usually strong enough to stand the pressure. Your *pulse* is caused by the rhythmic change in your blood pressure.

Capillaries

Nutrients, oxygen, and other substances must leave blood and get to your body's cells. Carbon dioxide and other wastes leave body cells and are carried away by blood. A **capillary** is a tiny blood vessel that allows these exchanges between body cells and blood. These exchanges can take place because capillary walls are only one cell thick. Capillaries are so narrow that blood cells must pass through them in single file. No cell in the body is more than three or four cells away from a capillary.

Veins

After leaving capillaries, blood enters veins. A **vein** is a blood vessel that carries blood back to the heart. As blood travels through veins, valves in the veins keep the blood from flowing backward. When skeletal muscles contract, they squeeze nearby veins and help push blood toward the heart.

✓ Reading Check Describe the three types of blood vessels.

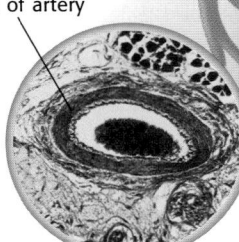

WEIRD SCIENCE

Babies that have certain congenital heart defects are blue at birth. The condition, called *cyanosis,* can be caused by low levels of oxygen in the blood. Oxygen-poor blood may be a result of defects in the heart. These defects cause oxygen-poor blood to be pumped to the body before it is pumped to the lungs. These defects can be repaired surgically.

Answer to Reading Check

Arteries have thick, stretchy walls and carry blood away from the heart. Capillaries are tiny blood vessels that allow the exchange of oxygen, carbon dioxide, and nutrients between cells and blood. Veins are blood vessels that carry blood back to the heart.

Two Types of Circulation

Where does blood get the oxygen to deliver to your body? From your lungs! Your heart pumps blood to the lungs. In the lungs, carbon dioxide leaves the blood and oxygen enters the blood. The oxygen-rich blood then flows back to the heart. This circulation of blood between your heart and lungs is called **pulmonary circulation** (PUL muh NER ee SUHR kyoo LAY shuhn).

The oxygen-rich blood returning to the heart from the lungs is then pumped to the rest of the body. The circulation of blood between the heart and the rest of the body is called **systemic circulation** (sis TEM ik SUHR kyoo LAY shuhn). Both types of circulation are shown in **Figure 5.**

pulmonary circulation the flow of blood from the heart to the lungs and back to the heart through the pulmonary arteries, capillaries, and veins

systemic circulation the flow of blood from the heart to all parts of the body and back to the heart

---

Figure 5 The Flow of Blood Through the Body

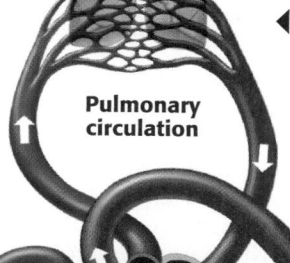
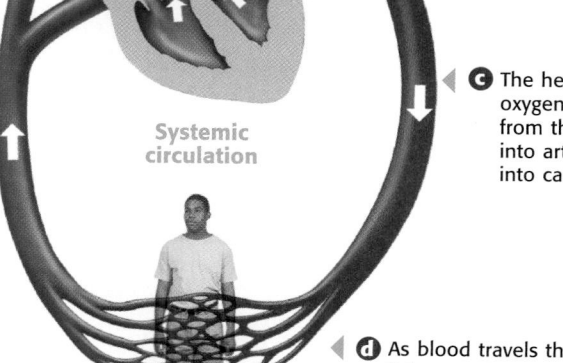

ⓐ The right ventricle pumps oxygen-poor blood into arteries that lead to the lungs. These are the only arteries in the body that carry oxygen-poor blood.

ⓑ In the capillaries of the lungs, blood takes up oxygen and releases carbon dioxide. Oxygen-rich blood travels through veins to the left atrium. These are the only veins in the body that carry oxygen-rich blood.

Pulmonary circulation

Systemic circulation

ⓔ Oxygen-poor blood travels back to the heart and is delivered into the right atrium by two large veins.

ⓒ The heart pumps oxygen-rich blood from the left ventricle into arteries and then into capillaries.

ⓓ As blood travels through capillaries, it transports oxygen, nutrients, and water to the cells of the body. At the same time, waste materials and carbon dioxide are carried away.

MISCONCEPTION ///ALERT\\\

Pulmonary Circulation Students may think that blood from the heart enters one lung and leaves from the other. However, each lung is serviced by its own vessels that carry blood to and from the heart.

CHAPTER RESOURCES

Technology

🔲 **Transparencies**
• The Flow of Blood Through the Body

Circulate! Organize the class into five teams for a relay race. The race should proceed as follows:

1. Students begin in the left ventricle carrying a red balloon, which represents an oxygenated blood cell.

2. They travel through the aorta.

3. After passing through the aorta, students carry oxygenated blood to the muscles and exchange the red balloon for a blue one.

4. From the muscles, students carry blood loaded with CO_2 to the right atrium.

5. From the right atrium, students travel into the right ventricle.

6. Students travel through the pulmonary artery.

7. From the pulmonary artery, students travel into the lungs, where they exchange their CO_2 for oxygen (they exchange blue balloons for red ones).

8. Carrying oxygenated blood (red balloons), students enter the left atrium and are ready to begin again or hand off their balloons.

Walk one student at a time through the pathway; then, have the teams send students through in a relay race. **LS Kinesthetic/ Interpersonal**
Co-op Learning   **English Language Learners**

Answer to Math Practice

1. 100,800 beats per day
2. 2,759,400,000 beats per 75 years
3. 864,000 fewer beats

Reteaching ── BASIC

Writing **Owner's Guide** Have students make an owner's guide for their cardiovascular system. The guide should include a description of the various components of the system as well as information about the care and maintenance of the system. Encourage students to include a diagram or flowchart to illustrate their guide. **LS Verbal**

Quiz ── GENERAL

Ask students whether each of the statements below is true or false. Have students correct false statements.

1. High blood pressure makes arteries stronger. (false)
2. Capillaries and veins have the same function. (false)
3. A major cause of heart disease is atherosclerosis. (true)
4. Arteries carry blood to the body and to the lungs. (true)

Alternative Assessment ── GENERAL

Spider Map Have students make a spider map using the key terms in this chapter. Have them label the circle "Cardiovascular system," and have them make a leg for each of the other key terms. **LS Logical**

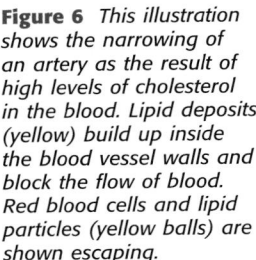

MATH PRACTICE

The Beat Goes On

A person's heart averages about 70 beats per minute.

1. Calculate how many times a heart beats in a day.
2. If a person lives for 75 years, how many times will his or her heart beat?
3. If an athlete's heart beats 50 times a minute, how many fewer times than an average heart will his or her heart beat in 30 days?

Cardiovascular Problems

More than just your heart and blood vessels are at risk if you have cardiovascular problems. Your whole body may be harmed. Cardiovascular problems can be caused by smoking, high levels of cholesterol in the blood, stress, physical inactivity, or heredity. Eating a healthy diet and getting plenty of exercise can reduce the risk of having cardiovascular problems.

Atherosclerosis

Heart diseases are the leading cause of death in the United States. A major cause of heart diseases is a cardiovascular disease called *atherosclerosis* (ATH uhr OH skluh ROH sis). Atherosclerosis happens when cholesterol (kuh LES tuhr AWL) builds up inside of blood vessels. This cholesterol buildup causes the blood vessels to become narrower and less elastic. **Figure 6** shows how clogged the pathway through a blood vessel can become. When an artery that supplies blood to the heart becomes blocked, the person may have a heart attack.

✓ **Reading Check** Why is atherosclerosis dangerous?

High Blood Pressure

Atherosclerosis may be caused by hypertension. *Hypertension* is abnormally high blood pressure. The higher the blood pressure, the greater the risk of a heart attack, heart failure, kidney disease, and stroke. A *stroke* is when a blood vessel in the brain becomes clogged or ruptures. As a result, that part of the brain receives no oxygen. Without oxygen, brain cells die.

Figure 6 *This illustration shows the narrowing of an artery as the result of high levels of cholesterol in the blood. Lipid deposits (yellow) build up inside the blood vessel walls and block the flow of blood. Red blood cells and lipid particles (yellow balls) are shown escaping.*

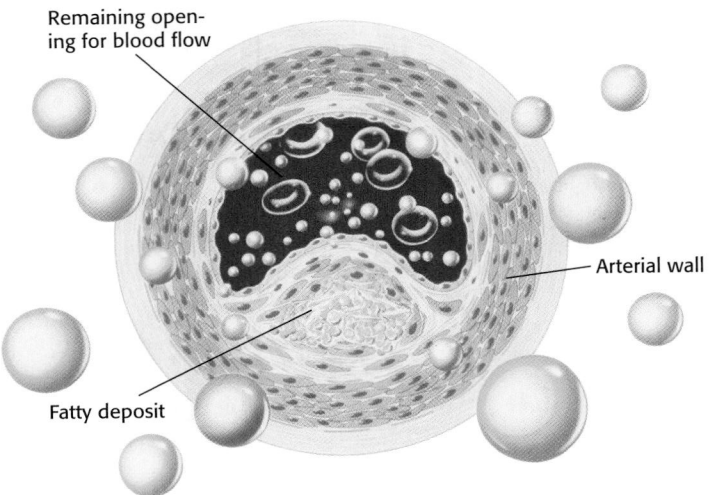

Remaining opening for blood flow

Arterial wall

Fatty deposit

Answer to Reading Check

Atherosclerosis is dangerous because it is the buildup of material inside an artery. When the artery becomes blocked, blood can't flow and can't reach the cells. In some cases, a person can have a heart attack from a blocked artery.

CHAPTER RESOURCES

Workbooks

 Math Skills for Science
- Multiplying Whole Numbers **BASIC**
- Counting the Zeros **GENERAL**
- Creating Exponents **GENERAL**
- Multiplying and Dividing in Scientific Notation **ADVANCED**

Heart Attacks and Heart Failure

Two cardiovascular problems are heart attacks and heart failure. A *heart attack* happens when heart muscle cells die and part of the heart muscle is damaged. As shown in **Figure 7,** arteries that deliver oxygen to the heart may be blocked. Without oxygen, heart muscle cells die quickly. When enough heart muscle cells die, the heart may stop.

Heart failure is different. *Heart failure* happens when the heart cannot pump enough blood to meet the body's needs. Organs, such as the brain, lungs, and kidneys, may be damaged by lack of oxygen or nutrients, or by the buildup of fluids or wastes.

Figure 7 Heart Attack

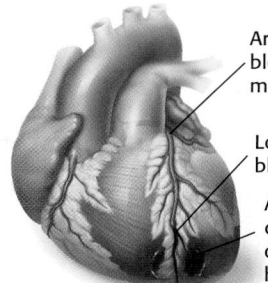

Artery delivering blood to heart muscle

Location of blocked artery

Area of heart damaged by lack of oxygen to heart muscle

SECTION Review

Summary

- The cardiovascular system is made up of the heart and three types of blood vessels.
- The three types of blood vessels are arteries, veins, and capillaries.
- Oxygen-poor blood flows from the heart through the lungs, where it picks up oxygen.
- Oxygen-rich blood flows from the heart to the rest of the body.
- Cardiovascular problems include atherosclerosis, hypertension, heart attacks, and strokes.

Using Key Terms

For each pair of terms, explain how the meanings of the terms differ.

1. *artery* and *vein*

2. *systemic circulation* and *pulmonary circulation*

Understanding Key Ideas

3. Which of the following is true of blood in the pulmonary veins?
   a. The blood is going to the body.
   b. The blood is oxygen poor.
   c. The blood is going to the lungs.
   d. The blood is oxygen rich.

4. What are the four parts of the cardiovascular system? Describe the functions of each part.

5. What is the difference between a heart attack and heart failure?

Math Skills

6. An adult male's heart pumps about 2.8 million liters of blood a year. If his heart beats 70 times a minute, how much blood does his heart pump with each beat?

Critical Thinking

7. **Identifying Relationships** How is the structure of capillaries related to their function?

8. **Making Inferences** One of aspirin's effects is that it prevents platelets from being too "sticky." Why might doctors prescribe aspirin for patients who have had a heart attack?

9. **Analyzing Ideas** Veins and arteries are everywhere in your body. When a pulse is taken, it is usually taken at an artery in the neck or wrist. Explain why.

10. **Making Comparisons** Why is the structure of arteries different from the structure of capillaries?

SCLINKS. **NSTA**
Developed and maintained by the National Science Teachers Association

For a variety of links related to this chapter, go to www.scilinks.org
Topic: The Cardiovascular System; Cardiovascular Problems
SciLinks code: HSM0221; HSM0220

Answers to Section Review

1. Arteries have stretchy, thick walls and carry blood away from the heart. Veins have valves and carry blood toward the heart.

2. Blood travels to and from the lungs in pulmonary circulation. Blood travels to and from the body in systemic circulation.

3. d

4. Sample answer: heart: to pump blood to lungs and to all parts of the body; arteries: to carry blood from the heart to the lungs and to all parts of the body; capillaries: to allow the exchange of gases, nutrients, and wastes between cells and blood; veins: to carry blood back to the heart

5. Sample answer: A heart attack happens when heart muscle cells get insufficient oxygen and die, which may cause the heart to stop beating. Heart failure is when the heart cannot pump enough blood to meet the needs of the body.

6. about 76 mL per beat

7. Sample answer: Capillaries are very small and have very thin walls. This structure lets capillaries be near every cell and allows oxygen, nutrients, and carbon dioxide and other wastes to pass into and out of the capillaries and to and from cells.

8. Sample answer: A doctor might prescribe aspirin to keep platelets from sticking together and blocking an artery or vein, especially one in the heart. Such a blockage might cause another heart attack.

9. The wrist and the neck are two places where a large artery is close to the surface of the skin and the pulse can be felt.

10. Arteries and capillaries have different functions: arteries carry blood under pressure away from the heart, and capillaries allow the exchange of gases, nutrients and wastes in cells.

INTERNET ACTIVITY
Short Story ──────── GENERAL

For an Internet activity related to this chapter, have students go to **go.hrw.com** and type in the keyword **HL5BD2W.**

CHAPTER RESOURCES

Chapter Resource File

- **Section Quiz** GENERAL
- **Section Review** GENERAL
- **Vocabulary and Section Summary** GENERAL
- **Reinforcement Worksheet** BASIC
- **Critical Thinking** ADVANCED

Focus

Overview

In this section, students learn about blood, the parts of blood, and blood types.

 Bellringer

Ask students to list three things that they know about blood, such as the parts of blood, the places where blood cells form, the function of blood in the body, and the way in which blood is donated.

Motivate

Discussion ——— GENERAL

Blood Have students describe a time when their skin was cut and describe what their blood looked like. List the words that students use to describe their blood. Based on students' experiences with blood and bleeding, lead a discussion about the structure and functions of blood. Have students read these pages and compare their descriptions of blood with the one in the textbook. Ask students the following questions: "Can you see individual blood cells when you bleed?" (no) "Why or why not?" (They are too small.) "How are red blood cells important to other cells in the body?" (They have hemoglobin, which helps red blood cells carry oxygen to other cells in the body.) **LS** Verbal

READING WARM-UP

Objectives
- Identify the four main components of blood.
- Describe three functions of blood.
- Explain how blood pressure is measured.
- Explain what the ABO blood types are and why they are important.

Terms to Learn

blood
blood pressure

READING STRATEGY

Reading Organizer As you read this section, create an outline of the section. Use the headings from the section in your outline.

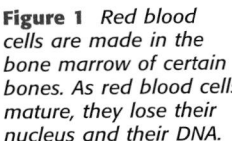

blood the fluid that carries gases, nutrients, and wastes through the body and that is made up of plasma, red blood cells, platelets, and white blood cells

Blood

Blood is part of the circulatory system. It travels through miles and miles of blood vessels to reach every cell in your body. So, you must have a lot of blood, right?

Well, actually, an adult human body has about 5 L of blood. Your body probably has a little less than that. All the blood in your body would not fill two 3 L soda bottles.

What Is Blood?

Your *circulatory system* is made up of your heart, your blood vessels, and blood. **Blood** is a connective tissue made up of plasma, red blood cells, platelets, and white blood cells. Blood carries oxygen and nutrients to all parts of your body.

✓ **Reading Check** What are the four main components of blood? *(See the Appendix for answers to Reading Checks.)*

Plasma

The fluid part of the blood is called plasma (PLAZ muh). *Plasma* is a mixture of water, minerals, nutrients, sugars, proteins, and other substances. Red blood cells, white blood cells, and platelets are found in plasma.

Red Blood Cells

Most blood cells are *red blood cells,* or RBCs. RBCs, such as the ones shown in **Figure 1,** take oxygen to every cell in your body. Cells need oxygen to carry out their functions. Each RBC has hemoglobin (HEE moh GLOH bin). *Hemoglobin* is an oxygen-carrying protein. Hemoglobin clings to the oxygen you inhale. RBCs can then transport oxygen throughout the body. Hemoglobin also gives RBCs their red color.

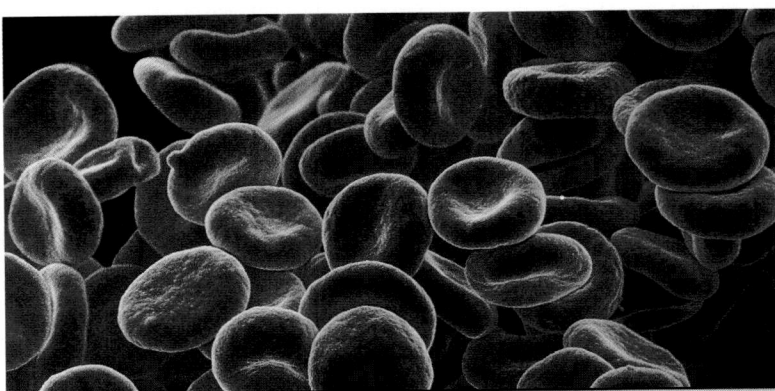

Figure 1 *Red blood cells are made in the bone marrow of certain bones. As red blood cells mature, they lose their nucleus and their DNA.*

CHAPTER RESOURCES

Chapter Resource File

- **Lesson Plan**
- **Directed Reading A** BASIC
- **Directed Reading B** SPECIAL NEEDS

Technology

Transparencies
- Bellringer

Answer to Reading Check

plasma, red blood cells, white blood cells, and platelets

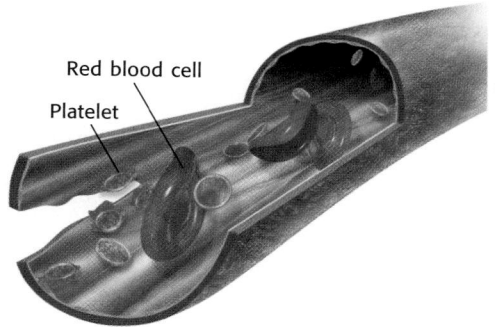

Red blood cell

Platelet

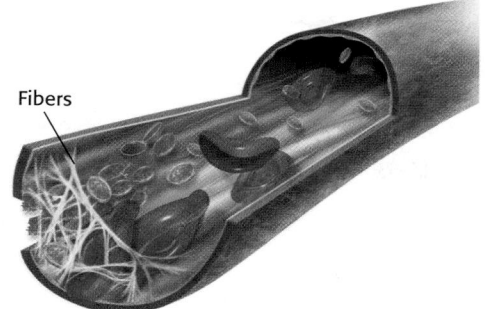

Fibers

Figure 2 *Platelets release chemicals in damaged vessels and cause fibers to form. The fibers make a "net" that traps blood cells and stops bleeding.*

Platelets

Drifting among the blood cells are tiny particles called platelets. *Platelets* are pieces of larger cells found in bone marrow. These larger cells remain in the bone marrow, but fragments are pinched off and enter the bloodstream as platelets. Platelets last for only 5 to 10 days, but they are an important part of blood. When you cut or scrape your skin, you bleed because blood vessels have been opened. As soon as bleeding starts, platelets begin to clump together in the damaged area. They form a plug that helps reduce blood loss, as shown in **Figure 2.** Platelets also release chemicals that react with proteins in plasma. The reaction causes tiny fibers to form. The fibers help create a blood clot.

White Blood Cells

Sometimes *pathogens* (PATH uh juhnz)—bacteria, viruses, and other microscopic particles that can make you sick—enter your body. When they do, they often meet *white blood cells,* or WBCs. WBCs, shown in **Figure 3,** help keep you healthy by destroying pathogens. WBCs also help clean wounds.

WBCs fight pathogens in several ways. Some WBCs squeeze out of blood vessels and move around in tissues, searching for pathogens. When they find a pathogen, they destroy it. Other WBCs release antibodies. *Antibodies* are chemicals that identify or destroy pathogens. WBCs also keep you healthy by destroying body cells that have died or been damaged. Most WBCs are made in bone marrow. Some WBCs mature in the lymphatic system.

✔️ **Reading Check** Why are WBCs important to your health?

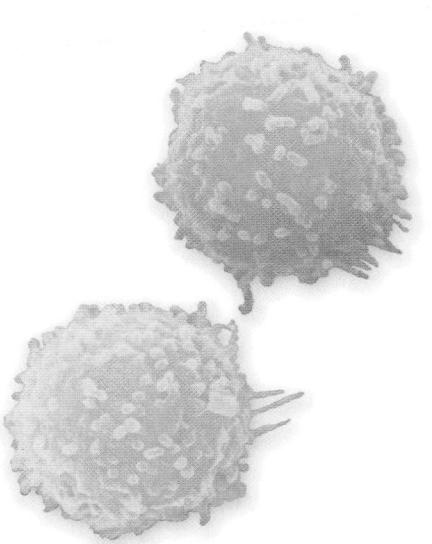

Figure 3 *White blood cells defend the body against pathogens. These white blood cells have been colored yellow to make their shape easier to see.*

Answer to Reading Check
White blood cells identify and attack pathogens that may make you sick.

Close

Reteaching ——————— BASIC

Blood Types The subject of blood types may be confusing. Review the material in **Figure 4** to reinforce the material presented in the text. Help students compare the shapes of the antigens on each red blood cell with the shapes of the antibodies that bind to the antigens. **LS Verbal**

Quiz ——————————— GENERAL

1. Which antibodies will a person who has type AB blood produce? (none)

2. Can a person who has type O blood receive blood from a person who has type AB blood? Why or why not? (No, the type O blood will have antibodies that attack the A and B antigens in the AB blood.)

3. In your own words, define the term *transfusion*. (A transfusion occurs when a person is given an injection of blood to replace blood that has been lost.)

Alternative Assessment ——— GENERAL

Blood Groups Have students write a report about Karl Landsteiner (1868–1943), a Nobel Prize-winning scientist. (Landsteiner discovered that some mixtures of blood are compatible and others are not and that he could divide the population into different groups based on how blood from one group of people reacted with blood from another group.) **LS Verbal**

---

blood pressure the force that blood exerts on the walls of the arteries

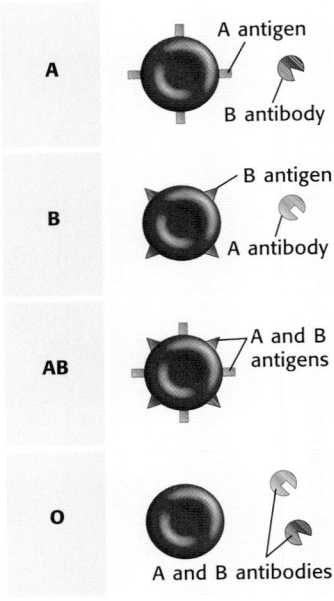

Figure 4 *This figure shows which antigens and antibodies may be present in each blood type.*

INCLUSION Strategies

• *Learning Disabled* • *Developmentally Delayed*
Some students may have difficulty remembering a variety of details, such as the functions of different types of blood cells. Help students develop hints or clues, such as mnemonic or visual clues, that will help them remember the main jobs of red and white blood cells.

(Examples of clues include <u>RE</u>d = <u>RE</u>spiration and <u>WhI</u>te = <u>WI</u>pe out problems.)
LS Verbal

Body Temperature Regulation

Your blood does more than supply your cells with oxygen and nutrients. It also helps regulate your body temperature. When your brain senses that your body temperature is rising, it signals blood vessels in your skin to enlarge. As the vessels enlarge, heat from your blood is transferred to your skin. This transfer helps lower your temperature. When your brain senses that your temperature is normal, it instructs your blood vessels to return to their normal size.

Blood Pressure

Every time your heart beats, it pushes blood out of the heart and into your arteries. The force exerted by blood on the inside walls of arteries is called **blood pressure.**

Blood pressure is expressed in millimeters of mercury (mm Hg). For example, a blood pressure of 110 mm Hg means the pressure on the artery walls can push a narrow column of mercury to a height of 110 mm.

Blood pressure is usually given as two numbers, such as 110/70 mm Hg. Systolic (sis TAHL ik) pressure is the first number. *Systolic pressure* is the pressure inside large arteries when the ventricles contract. The surge of blood causes the arteries to bulge and produce a pulse. The second number, *diastolic* (DIE uh STAHL ik) *pressure,* is the pressure inside arteries when the ventricles relax. For adults, a blood pressure of 120/80 mm Hg or below is considered healthy. High blood pressure can cause heart or kidney damage.

✓ Reading Check What is the difference between systolic pressure and diastolic pressure?

Blood Types

Every person has one of four blood types: A, B, AB, or O. Your blood type refers to the type of chemicals you have on the surface of your RBCs. These surface chemicals are called *antigens* (AN tuh juhnz). Type A blood has A antigens; type B has B antigens; and type AB has both A and B antigens. Type O blood has neither the A nor the B antigen.

The different blood types have different antigens on their RBCs. They may also have different antibodies in the plasma. These antibodies react to antigens of other blood types as if the antigens were pathogens. As shown in **Figure 4,** type A blood has antibodies that react to type B blood. If a person with type A blood receives type B blood, the type B antibodies attach themselves to the type B RBCs. These RBCs begin to clump together, and the clumps may block blood vessels. A reaction to the wrong blood type may be fatal.

Answer to Reading Check

Systolic pressure is the pressure inside arteries when the ventricles contract. Diastolic pressure is the pressure inside the arteries when the ventricles are relaxed.

Blood Types and Transfusions

Sometimes, a person must be given a blood transfusion. A *transfusion* is the injection of blood or blood components into a person to replace blood that has been lost because of surgery or an injury. **Figure 5** shows bags of blood that may be given in a transfusion. The blood type is clearly marked. Because the ABO blood types have different antigen-antibody reactions, a person receiving blood cannot receive blood from just anyone. **Table 1** shows blood transfusion possibilities.

Table 1 **Blood Transfusion Possibilities**

Type	Can receive	Can donate to
A	A, O	A, AB
B	B, O	B, AB
AB	all	AB only
O	O	all

Reading Check People with type O blood are sometimes called universal donors. Why might this be true?

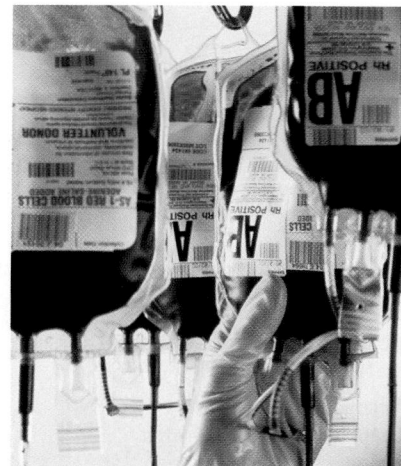

Figure 5 *The blood type must be clearly labeled on blood stored for transfusions.*

SECTION Review

Summary

- Blood's four main components are plasma, red blood cells, platelets, and white blood cells.
- Blood carries oxygen and nutrients to cells, helps protect against disease, and helps regulate body temperature.
- Blood pressure is the force blood exerts on the inside walls of arteries.
- Every person has one of four ABO blood types.
- Mixing blood types may be fatal.

Using Key Terms

1. Use each of the following terms in a separate sentence: *blood* and *blood pressure.*

Understanding Key Ideas

2. A person with type B blood can donate blood to people with which type(s) of blood?
   a. B, AB
   b. A, AB
   c. AB only
   d. All types

3. List the four main components of blood and tell what each component does.

4. Why is it important for a doctor to know a patient's blood type?

Math Skills

5. A person has a systolic pressure of 174 mm Hg. What percentage of normal (120 mm Hg) is this?

Critical Thinking

6. **Identifying Relationships** How does the body use blood and blood vessels to help maintain proper body temperature?

7. **Predicting Consequences** Some blood conditions and diseases affect the ability of red blood cells to deliver oxygen to cells of the body. Predict what might happen to a person with a disease of that type.

SCILINKS

NSTA
Developed and maintained by the National Science Teachers Association

For a variety of links related to this chapter, go to www.scilinks.org

Topic: Blood; Blood Donations
SciLinks code: HSM0175; HSM0178

The Lymphatic System

Every time your heart pumps, a little fluid is forced out of the thin walls of the capillaries. Some of this fluid collects in the spaces around your cells. What happens to this fluid?

Focus

Overview

This section introduces students to the lymphatic system. Students will also learn about the relationship between blood and lymph.

🔊 Bellringer

Ask students, "Do you know people who have had their tonsils out? What are tonsils? What is their function? Where are they located in the body?" Have students write the answers to these questions in their **science journal.** Tell students that if they are not sure of the answers to make an educated guess at them: (Tonsils are small masses of lymphatic tissue at the back of the tongue and in the throat. Their function is to trap pathogens that might otherwise get into the body and cause disease.)

Motivate

Discussion ——— GENERAL

Swollen Glands Ask students if a doctor has ever felt their neck or under their jaw when they were sick. Ask them if they know what the doctor was checking. Encourage students who have had this experience to share it with the class. Then, invite students to explore the purpose of this type of examination. English Language Learners
LS Verbal

READING WARM-UP

Objectives

● Describe the relationship between the lymphatic system and the circulatory system.

● Identify six parts of the lymphatic system, and describe their functions.

Terms to Learn

lymphatic system	thymus
lymph	spleen
lymph node	tonsils

READING STRATEGY

Prediction Guide Before reading this section, write the title of each heading in this section. Next, under each heading, write what you think you will learn.

lymphatic system a collection of organs whose primary function is to collect extracellular fluid and return it to the blood

lymph the fluid that is collected by the lymphatic vessels and nodes

Most of the fluid is reabsorbed through the capillaries into your blood. But some is not. Your body has a second circulatory system called the lymphatic (lim FAT ik) system.

The **lymphatic system** is the group of organs and tissues that collect the excess fluid and return it to your blood. The lymphatic system also helps your body fight pathogens.

Vessels of the Lymphatic System

The fluid collected by the lymphatic system is carried through vessels. The smallest vessels of the lymphatic system are *lymph capillaries*. Lymph capillaries absorb some of the fluid and particles from between the cells. These particles are too large to enter blood capillaries. Some of these particles are dead cells or pathogens. The fluid and particles absorbed into lymph capillaries are called **lymph.**

As shown in **Figure 1,** lymph capillaries carry lymph into larger vessels called *lymphatic vessels*. Skeletal muscles squeeze these vessels to force lymph through the lymphatic system. Valves inside lymphatic vessels stop backflow. Lymph drains into the large neck veins of the cardiovascular system.

✓ **Reading Check** How is the lymphatic system related to the cardiovascular system? (*See the Appendix for answers to Reading Checks.*)

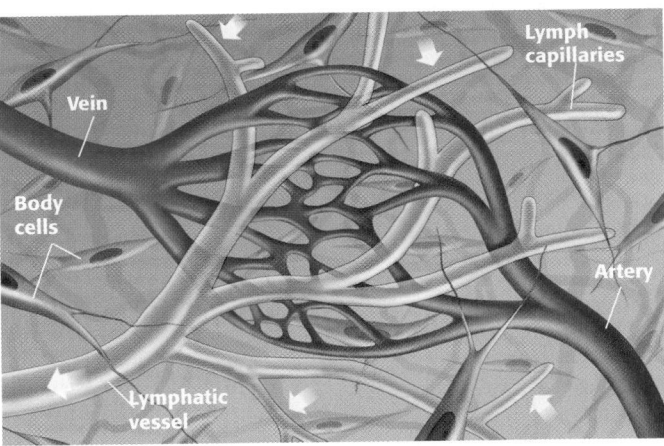

Figure 1 *The white arrows show the movement of lymph into lymph capillaries and through lymphatic vessels.*

CHAPTER RESOURCES

Chapter Resource File

 • **Lesson Plan**
• **Directed Reading A** BASIC
• **Directed Reading B** SPECIAL NEEDS

Technology

 Transparencies
• Bellringer

Answer to Reading Check

The lymphatic system is a secondary circulatory system in the body. The lymphatic system collects fluid and particles from between the cells and returns them to the cardiovascular system.

Other Parts of the Lymphatic System

In addition to vessels and capillaries, several organs and tissues are part of the lymphatic system. These organs and tissues are shown in **Figure 2.** Bone marrow plays an important role in your lymphatic system. The other parts of the lymphatic system are the lymph nodes, the thymus gland, the spleen, and the tonsils.

Bone Marrow

Bones—part of your skeletal system—are very important to your lymphatic system. *Bone marrow* is the soft tissue inside of bones. Bone marrow is where most red and white blood cells, including lymphocytes (LIM foh SIETS), are produced. *Lymphocytes* are a type of white blood cell that helps your body fight pathogens.

Lymph Nodes

As lymph travels through lymphatic vessels, it passes through lymph nodes. **Lymph nodes** are small, bean-shaped masses of tissue that remove pathogens and dead cells from the lymph. Lymph nodes are concentrated in the armpits, neck, and groin.

Lymph nodes contain lymphocytes. Some lymphocytes—called *killer T cells*—surround and destroy pathogens. Other lymphocytes—called *B cells*—produce antibodies that attach to pathogens. These marked pathogens clump together and are then destroyed by other cells.

When bacteria or other pathogens cause an infection, WBCs may multiply greatly. The lymph nodes fill with WBCs that are fighting the infection. As a result, some lymph nodes may become swollen and painful. Your doctor may feel these swollen lymph nodes to see if you have an infection. In fact, if your lymph nodes are swollen and sore, you or your parent can feel them, too. Swollen lymph nodes are sometimes an early clue that you have an infection.

Thymus

T cells develop from immature lymphocytes produced in the bone marrow. Before these cells are ready to fight infections, they develop further in the thymus. The **thymus** is the gland that produces T cells that are ready to fight infection. The thymus is located behind the breastbone, just above the heart. Mature lymphocytes from the thymus travel through the lymphatic system to other areas of your body.

lymph node an organ that filters lymph and that is found along the lymphatic vessels

thymus the main gland of the lymphatic system; it produces mature T lymphocytes

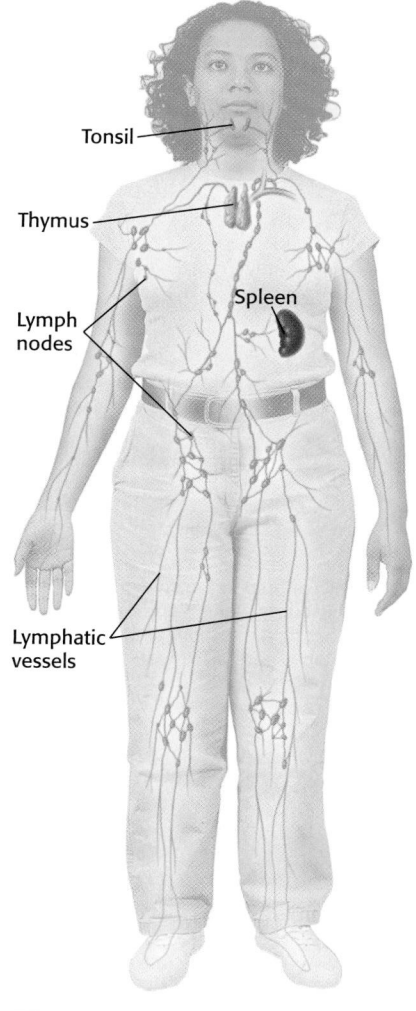

Figure 2   The Lymphatic System

Tonsil

Thymus

Spleen

Lymph nodes

Lymphatic vessels

SCIENTISTS AT ODDS

First to Publish? The Danish physician Thomas Bartholin (1616–1680) is often credited with being the first person to describe the lymphatic system. His Swedish contemporary Olof Rudbeck (1630–1702), known as Rudbeck the Elder, also studied the lymphatic system and published his own description of the lymphatic system. For several years, Bartholin and Rudbeck engaged in a bitter dispute over who deserved the credit for discovering lymph glands and the lymphatic system.

Reteaching — BASIC

Planning a Brochure Ask students to outline and plan a brochure or pamphlet explaining the lymphatic system. Students do not have to make the brochure; they must only plan it. The brochure or pamphlet should be similar to one that you might find in a doctor's office. **LS** Verbal

Quiz — GENERAL

1. What is one function of the tonsils? (The tonsils contain white blood cells, which help fight pathogens.)

2. How is the lymphatic system a circulatory system? (The lymphatic system collects fluid that is not reabsorbed by the capillaries and returns it to the bloodstream.)

Alternative Assessment — ADVANCED

Model of Lymphatic System
Have students make a life-sized model of the lymphatic system. Provide students with butcher paper, dried beans, glue, and markers. Then, have students use their model to demonstrate the way that the lymphatic system and the cardiovascular system interact. English Language **LS** Visual/Kinesthetic Learners

---

spleen the largest lymphatic organ in the body

CONNECTION TO Social Studies

WRITING SKILL **Vent Your Spleen** Why do we say that someone is "venting his spleen"? What does it mean? Conduct library or Internet research about this phrase. Write a report on what you have learned.

Spleen

Your spleen is the largest lymphatic organ. The **spleen** stores and produces lymphocytes. It is a purplish organ about the size of your fist. Your spleen is soft and spongy. It is located in the upper left side of your abdomen. As blood flows through the spleen, lymphocytes attack or mark pathogens in the blood. If pathogens cause an infection, the spleen may also release lymphocytes into the bloodstream.

In addition to being part of the lymphatic system, the spleen produces, monitors, stores, and destroys blood cells. When red blood cells (RBCs) are squeezed through the spleen's capillaries, the older and more fragile cells burst. These damaged RBCs are then taken apart by some of the cells in the spleen. Some parts of these RBCs may be reused. For this reason, you can think of the spleen as the red-blood-cell recycling center.

The spleen has two important functions. The *white pulp*, shown in **Figure 3,** is part of the lymphatic system. It helps to fight infections. The *red pulp*, also shown in **Figure 3,** removes unwanted material, such as defective red blood cells, from the blood. However, it is possible to lead a healthy life without your spleen. If the spleen is damaged or removed, other organs in the body take over many of its functions.

✓ Reading Check What are two important functions of the spleen?

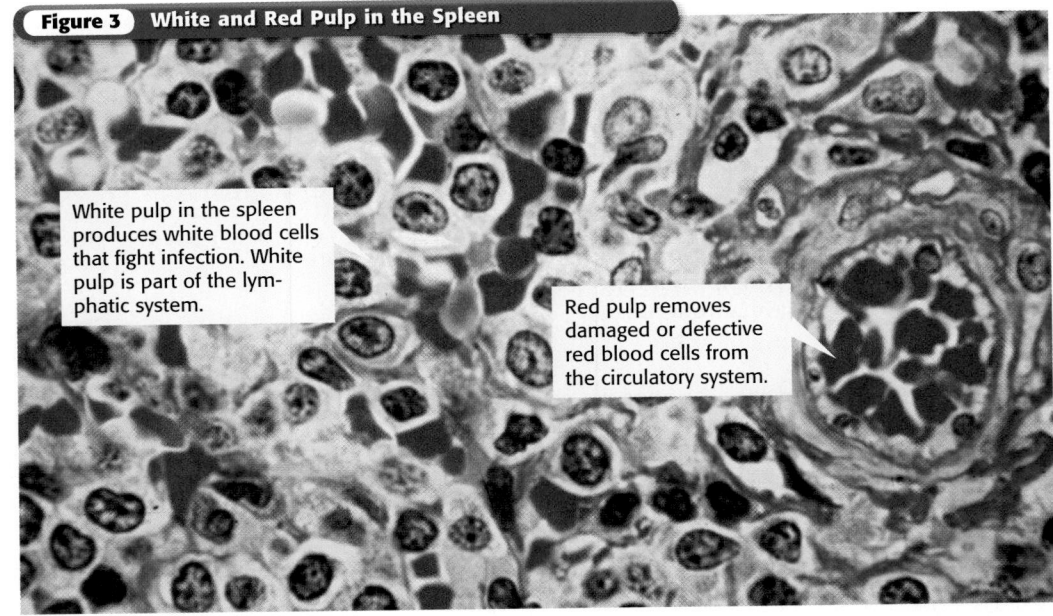

Figure 3 White and Red Pulp in the Spleen

White pulp in the spleen produces white blood cells that fight infection. White pulp is part of the lymphatic system.

Red pulp removes damaged or defective red blood cells from the circulatory system.

Answer to Reading Check

The white pulp of the spleen is part of the lymphatic system. It helps fight infections by storing and producing lymphocytes. The red pulp of the spleen removes unwanted material, such as defective red blood cells, from the circulatory system.

Tonsils

The lymphatic system includes your tonsils. **Tonsils** are lymphatic tissue in the nasal cavity and at the back of the mouth on either side of the tongue. Each tonsil is about the size of a large olive.

Tonsils help defend the body against infection. Lymphocytes in the tonsils trap pathogens that enter the throat. Sometimes, tonsils become infected and are red, swollen, and very sore. Severely infected tonsils may be covered with patches of white, infected tissue. Sore, swollen tonsils, such as those in **Figure 4,** make swallowing difficult.

Sometimes, a doctor will suggest surgery to remove the tonsils. In the past, this surgery was frequently done in childhood. It is less common today. Surgery is now done only if a child has frequent, severe tonsil infections or if a child's tonsils are so enlarged that breathing is difficult.

tonsils small, rounded masses of lymphatic tissue located in the pharynx and in the passage from the mouth to the pharynx

Figure 4 *Tonsils help protect your throat and lungs from infection by trapping pathogens.*

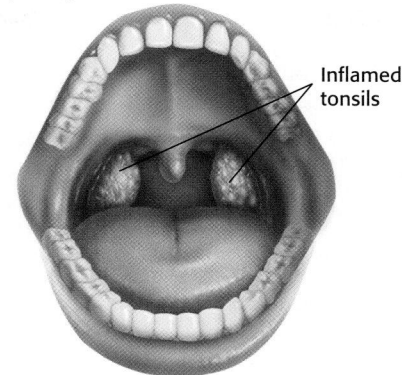

Inflamed tonsils

SECTION Review

Summary

- The lymphatic system collects fluid from between the cells and returns it to the blood.
- The lymphatic system contains cells that help the body fight disease.
- The lymphatic system consists of lymphatic vessels, lymph, and tissues and organs throughout the body.
- The thymus, spleen, and tonsils contain lymphocytes that help fight pathogens.

Using Key Terms

1. Use each of the following terms in a separate sentence: *lymph nodes, spleen,* and *tonsils.*

Understanding Key Ideas

2. Lymph
   a. is the same as blood.
   b. is fluid in the cells.
   c. drains into your muscles.
   d. is fluid collected by lymphatic vessels.

3. Name six parts of the lymphatic system. Tell what each part does.

4. How are your cardiovascular and lymphatic systems related?

Math Skills

5. One cubic millimeter of blood contains 5 million RBCs and 10,000 WBCs. How many times more RBCs are there than WBCs?

Critical Thinking

6. **Expressing Opinions** Some people have frequent, severe tonsil infections. These infections can be treated with medicine, and the infections usually go away after a few days. Do you think removing tonsils in such a case is a good idea? Explain.

7. **Analyzing Ideas** Why is it important that lymphatic tissue is spread throughout the body?

SCiLINKS

Developed and maintained by the National Science Teachers Association

For a variety of links related to this chapter, go to www.scilinks.org

Topic: The Lymphatic System
SciLinks code: HSM0891

Answers to Section Review

1. Sample answer: Sometimes, when you are sick, your lymph nodes get swollen. Your spleen is an organ that is part of the circulatory system and the lymphatic system. Tonsils are lymphatic tissue at the back of your throat.

2. d

3. lymph vessels and capillaries, bone marrow, lymph nodes, thymus, spleen, and tonsils; lymph vessels and capillaries: they carry lymph from the body to the cardiovascular system; bone marrow: it is the tissue in which white blood cells are produced; lymph nodes: they remove pathogens and dead cells from lymph; thymus: it is the gland in which killer T cells mature; spleen: it produces and stores lymphocytes; tonsils: they trap pathogens

4. The lymphatic system collects particles and excess fluid from around your cells and returns them to the bloodstream, which is part of your cardiovascular system. The two systems work together to help the body fight pathogens: both lymph and blood carry white blood cells around the body to fight pathogens.

5. There are 500 times as many RBCs as WBCs.

6. Answers may vary as students offer their opinions. The most important part of the answer is the reasoning and the way in which the ideas that lead to the opinion are supported.

7. Sample answer: It is important for lymphatic tissue to be spread throughout the body so that fluid and particles from around every cell can be removed and pathogens in any part of the body can be identified and attacked.

Focus

Overview

This section introduces students to the respiratory system. Students will learn about the flow of air in the respiratory system and about the way that the respiratory and the circulatory systems are related.

Bellringer

Ask students, "Are breathing and respiration the same thing?" (No, breathing is only one part of respiration. Respiration also includes cellular respiration.)

Motivate

ACTIVITY _____ GENERAL

Deep Breathing Have students place their hands on either side of their rib cage and breathe deeply several times. Then, ask students to describe what they felt while they breathed in and out. (Students should feel their rib cage moving up and expanding during inhalation and moving down and returning to its initial size during exhalation.)

LS Kinesthetic | English Language Learners

READING WARM-UP

Objectives

- Describe the parts of the respiratory system and their functions.
- Explain how breathing happens.
- Discuss the relationship between the respiratory system and the cardiovascular system.
- Identify two respiratory disorders.

Terms to Learn

respiration   trachea
respiratory system   bronchus
pharynx   alveoli
larynx

READING STRATEGY

Reading Organizer As you read this section, make a flowchart of the steps of the process of respiration.

respiration the exchange of oxygen and carbon dioxide between living cells and their environment; includes breathing and cellular respiration

respiratory system a collection of organs whose primary function is to take in oxygen and expel carbon dioxide

---

The Respiratory System

Breathing—you do it all the time. You're doing it right now. You hardly ever think about it, though, unless you suddenly can't breathe.

Then, it becomes very clear that you have to breathe in order to live. But why is breathing important? Your body needs oxygen in order to get energy from the foods you eat. Breathing makes this process possible.

Respiration and the Respiratory System

The words *breathing* and *respiration* are often used to mean the same thing. However, breathing is only one part of respiration. **Respiration** is the process by which a body gets and uses oxygen and releases carbon dioxide and water. Respiration is divided into two parts. The first part is breathing, which involves inhaling and exhaling. The second part is cellular respiration, which involves chemical reactions that release energy from food.

Breathing is made possible by your respiratory system. The **respiratory system** is the group of organs that take in oxygen and get rid of carbon dioxide. The nose, throat, lungs, and passageways that lead to the lungs make up the respiratory system. **Figure 1** shows the parts of the respiratory system.

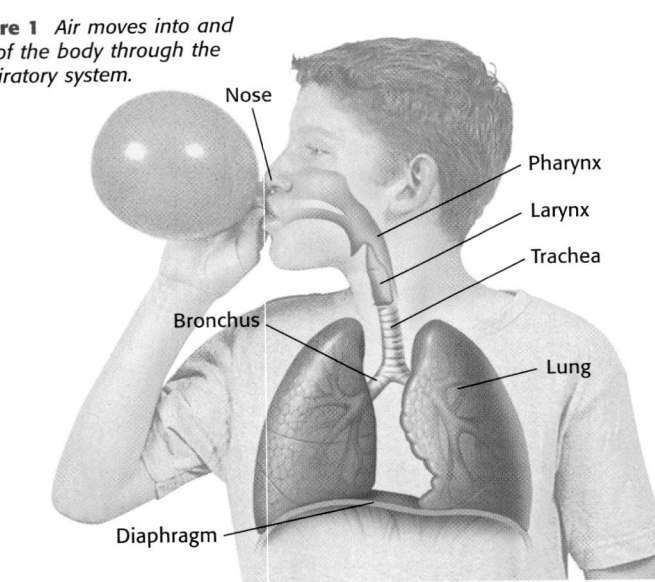

Figure 1 *Air moves into and out of the body through the respiratory system.*

Nose
Pharynx
Larynx
Trachea
Bronchus
Lung
Diaphragm

CHAPTER RESOURCES

Chapter Resource File

- **Lesson Plan**
- **Directed Reading A** BASIC
- **Directed Reading B** SPECIAL NEEDS

Technology

Transparencies
- Bellringer
- The Role of Blood in Respiration

Cultural Awareness   GENERAL

Adapting to High Altitudes Newcomers to Peruvian villages in the Andes Mountains may get headaches, feel nauseated, and be short of breath. Why? The newcomer is suffering from a lack of oxygen. Villagers don't have these problems; they have adapted to the elevation. Over time, villagers develop lungs that are larger than those of a newcomer. Villagers also have more red blood cells than newcomers have.

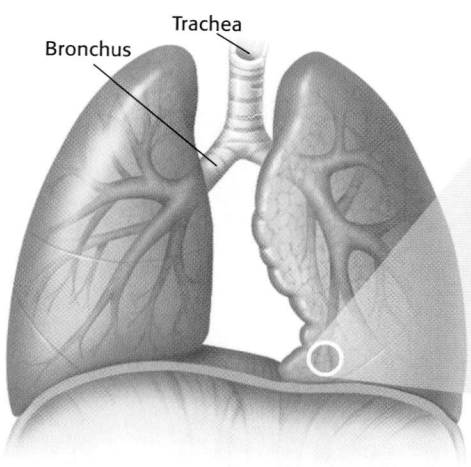

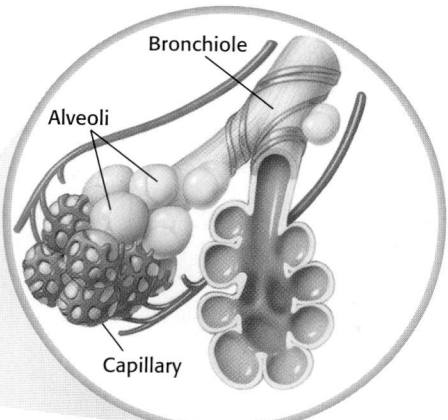

Figure 2 *Inside your lungs, the bronchi branch into bronchioles. The bronchioles lead to tiny sacs called alveoli.*

Nose, Pharynx, and Larynx

Your *nose* is the main passageway into and out of the respiratory system. Air can be breathed in through and out of the nose. Air can also enter and leave through the mouth.

From the nose, air flows into the **pharynx** (FAR ingks), or throat. Food and drink also travel through the pharynx on the way to the stomach. The pharynx branches into two tubes. One tube, the *esophagus,* leads to the stomach. The other tube is the larynx (LAR ingks). The larynx leads to the lungs.

The **larynx** is the part of the throat that contains the vocal cords. The *vocal cords* are a pair of elastic bands that stretch across the larynx. Muscles connected to the larynx control how much the vocal cords are stretched. When air flows between the vocal cords, the cords vibrate. These vibrations make sound.

Trachea

The larynx guards the entrance to a large tube called the **trachea** (TRAY kee uh), or windpipe. Your body has two large, spongelike lungs. The trachea, shown in **Figure 2,** is the passageway for air traveling from the larynx to the lungs.

Bronchi and Alveoli

The trachea splits into two branches called **bronchi** (BRAHNG KIE) (singular, *bronchus*). One bronchus connects to each lung. Each bronchus branches into smaller tubes that are called *bronchioles* (BRAHNG kee OHLZ). In the lungs, each bronchiole branches to form tiny sacs that are called **alveoli** (al VEE uh LIE) (singular, *alveolus*).

Reading Check Describe the flow of air from your nose to your alveoli. (*See the Appendix for answers to Reading Checks.*)

pharynx the passage from the mouth to the larynx and esophagus

larynx the area of the throat that contains the vocal cords and produces vocal sounds

trachea the tube that connects the larynx to the lungs

bronchus one of the two tubes that connect the lungs with the trachea

alveoli any of the tiny air sacs of the lungs where oxygen and carbon dioxide are exchanged

Figure 3   The Role of Blood in Respiration

Close

Reteaching — BASIC

Section Outline Have students make an outline of this section by using the chapter title, sub-heads, and key terms as topics. Help them fill in their outline to make a useful study tool.

LS Logical

Quiz — GENERAL

Ask students whether each of the statements below is true or false. Have students correct false statements.

1. SARS is caused by air pollution. (false)

2. There are two main bronchi —one for each lung— in the human body. (true)

3. The lungs are made of muscle tissue. (false)

Alternative Assessment — ADVANCED

Lung Models Have students make models of healthy lungs and lungs damaged by smoking. Photographs of healthy lungs and damaged lungs can be found in literature from the American Lung Association and the American Cancer Society and in various science and health textbooks.

English Language Learners

LS Visual/Kinesthetic

Answer to Connection to Chemistry

Because there is less oxygen in the air at high altitudes, it is difficult for the body to get the oxygen needed.

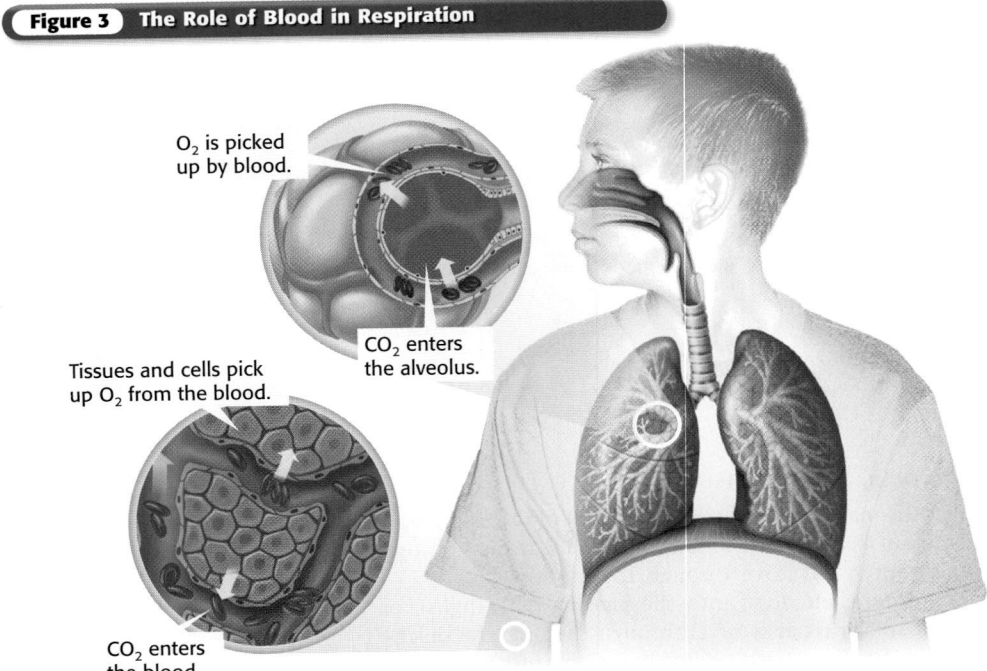

O_2 is picked up by blood.

CO_2 enters the alveolus.

Tissues and cells pick up O_2 from the blood.

CO_2 enters the blood.

CONNECTION TO Chemistry

Oxygen and Blood When people who live at low elevations travel up into the mountains, they may find themselves breathing heavily even when they are not exerting themselves. Why might this happen?

Breathing

When you breathe, air is sucked into or forced out of your lungs. However, your lungs have no muscles of their own. Instead, breathing is done by the diaphragm (DIE uh FRAM) and rib muscles. The *diaphragm* is a dome-shaped muscle beneath the lungs. When you inhale, the diaphragm contracts and moves down. The chest cavity's volume increases. At the same time, some of your rib muscles contract and lift your rib cage. As a result, your chest cavity gets bigger and a vacuum is created. Air is sucked in. Exhaling is this process in reverse.

Breathing and Cellular Respiration

In *cellular respiration,* oxygen is used by cells to release energy stored in molecules of glucose. Where does the oxygen come from? When you inhale, you take in oxygen. This oxygen diffuses into red blood cells and is carried to tissue cells. The oxygen then diffuses out of the red blood cells and into each cell. Cells use the oxygen to release chemical energy. During the process, carbon dioxide (CO_2) and water are produced. Carbon dioxide is exhaled from the lungs. **Figure 3** shows how breathing and blood circulation are related.

✓ **Reading Check** What is cellular respiration?

Answer to Reading Check

Cellular respiration is the process inside a cell in which oxygen is used to release energy stored in molecules of glucose. During the process, carbon dioxide (CO_2) and water are released.

CONNECTION to Physical Science — GENERAL

Air Pressure and Breathing Lead a discussion about the ways in which the body creates changes in air pressure to make breathing possible. The teaching transparency "Exhaling, Pressure, and Fluid Flow" is a helpful illustration of the process of breathing. **LS** Visual/Logical

Respiratory Disorders

Millions of people suffer from respiratory disorders. Respiratory disorders include asthma, emphysema, and severe acute respiratory syndrome (SARS). Asthma causes the bronchioles to narrow. A person who has asthma has difficulty breathing. An asthma attack may be triggered by irritants such as dust or pollen. SARS is caused by a virus. A person who has SARS may have a fever and difficulty breathing. Emphysema happens when the alveoli have been damaged. People who have emphysema have trouble getting the oxygen they need. **Figure 4** shows a lung damaged by emphysema.

Figure 4 *The photo on the left shows a healthy lung. The photo on the right shows the lung of a person who had emphysema.*

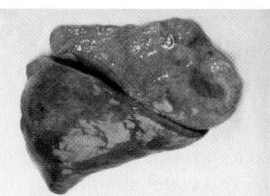 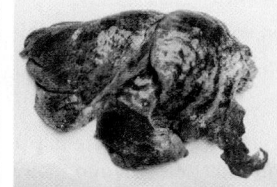

Why Do People Snore?

1. Get a **15 cm² sheet of wax paper.**
2. Hum your favorite song.
3. Then, take the wax paper and press it against your lips. Hum the song again.
4. How was your humming different when wax paper was pressed to your mouth?
5. Use your observations to guess what might cause snoring.

SECTION Review

Summary

- Air travels to the lungs through the nose or mouth, pharynx, larynx, trachea, and bronchi.
- In the lungs, the bronchi branch into bronchioles, which branch into alveoli.
- Breathing involves lungs, muscles in the rib cage, and the diaphragm.
- Oxygen enters the blood through the alveoli in the lungs. Carbon dioxide leaves the blood and is exhaled.
- Respiratory disorders include asthma, SARS, and emphysema.

Using Key Terms

For each pair of terms, explain how the meanings of the terms differ.

1. *pharynx* and *larynx*

Understanding Key Ideas

2. Which of the following are respiratory disorders?
   a. SARS, alveoli, and asthma
   b. alveoli, emphysema, and SARS
   c. larynx, asthma, and SARS
   d. SARS, emphysema, and asthma

3. Explain how breathing happens.

4. Describe how your cardiovascular and respiratory systems work together.

Math Skills

5. Total lung capacity (TLC) is about 6 L. A person can exhale about 3.6 L. What percentage of TLC cannot be exhaled?

Critical Thinking

6. **Interpreting Statistics** About 6.3 million children in the United States have asthma. About 4 million of them had an asthma attack last year. What do these statistics tell you about the relationship between asthma and asthma attacks?

7. **Identifying Relationships** If a respiratory disorder causes lungs to fill with fluid, how might this affect a person's health?

For a variety of links related to this chapter, go to www.scilinks.org
Topic: The Respiratory System; Respiratory Disorders
SciLinks code: HSM1307; HSM1306

Answers

4. A strong vibrating sound was made when the paper was pressed against the lips.
5. Sample answer: Most snoring happens when soft tissues in the mouth block a person's airway and vibrate.

Answers to Section Review

1. The pharynx is the passage from the mouth to the larynx and esophagus, while the larynx is the part of the throat that contains the vocal cords.

2. d

3. When you breathe, air is sucked into or forced out of your lungs. A muscle called the *diaphragm* contracts and increases chest-cavity volume, which creates a vacuum. The vaccum pulls air in through the nose or mouth. Then, the air travels through the pharynx, larynx, trachea, and bronchi to reach the lungs.

4. The respiratory system brings in oxygen and expels carbon dioxide, and the cardiovascular system transports those gases to and from the lungs.

5. 6 L − 3.6 L = 2.4 L unexhaled
   2.4 L ÷ 6 L = 0.40, or 40% of TLC cannot be exhaled

6. Sample answer: These statistics tell us that last year not every child who had asthma had an asthma attack.

7. Sample answer: The alveoli in the lungs are made for the exhange of gases, not liquids. Fluids in the lungs would prevent a person from getting all of the oxygen needed to maintain regular activity. The person might feel weak or tired. Also, the person could not get rid of the carbon dioxide from the cells, which might cause a problem, too.

Is That a Fact!

The lungs contain about 300 million alveoli. The alveoli provide a tremendous surface area for gas exchange. In fact, because of this large capacity for gas exchange, a person can breathe easily with only one lung.

Carbon Dioxide Breath

Teacher's Notes

Time Required
One 45-minute class period

Lab Ratings

EASY ⟶ HARD

Teacher Prep 🧪🧪
Student Set-Up 🧪🧪
Concept Level 🧪🧪
Clean Up 🧪🧪

MATERIALS

You may wish to substitute bromthymol blue indicator solution for the phenol red indicator. The bromthymol blue will turn green in the presence of CO_2. Clear plastic cups (6 oz or 8 oz) may be used instead of 150 mL flasks if glassware is in short supply or if you have concerns about breakage.

Safety Caution
Remind students to review all safety cautions and icons before beginning this lab activity.

Lab Notes
Tell students that carbon dioxide is in the air in the classroom. They may need to cover their indicator solution to delay the reaction with the air. Tell them not to leave the indicator solution sitting exposed for several minutes before it is used.

Skills Practice Lab

OBJECTIVES

Detect the presence of carbon dioxide in your breath.

Compare the data for carbon dioxide in your breath with the data from your classmates.

MATERIALS

- calculator (optional)
- clock with a second hand, or a stopwatch
- Erlenmeyer flask, 150 mL
- eyedropper
- gloves, protective
- graduated cylinder, 150 mL
- paper towels
- phenol red indicator solution
- plastic drinking straw
- water, 100 mL

SAFETY

Carbon Dioxide Breath

Carbon dioxide is important to both plants and animals. Plants take in carbon dioxide during photosynthesis and give off oxygen as a byproduct of the process. Animals—including you—take in oxygen during respiration and give off carbon dioxide as a byproduct of the process.

Procedure

1. Put on your gloves, safety goggles, and apron.

2. Use the graduated cylinder to pour 100 mL of water into a 150 mL flask.

3. Using an eyedropper, carefully place four drops of phenol red indicator solution into the water. The water should turn orange.

4. Place a plastic drinking straw into the solution of phenol red and water. Drape a paper towel over the flask to prevent splashing.

5. Carefully blow through the straw into the solution.
   Caution: Do not inhale through the straw. Do not drink the solution, and do not share a straw with anyone.

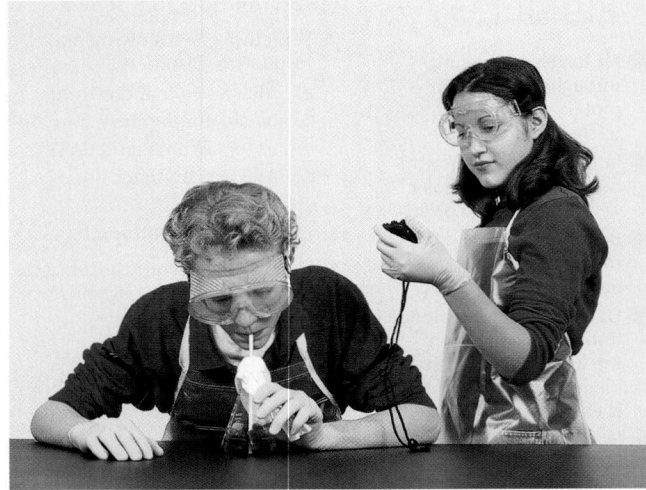

Yvonne Brannum
Hine Junior High School
Washington, D.C.

CHAPTER RESOURCES

Chapter Resource File

- **Datasheet for Chapter Lab**
- **Lab Notes and Answers**

Technology
 Classroom Videos
- Lab Video

- Build a Lung

6 Your lab partner should begin keeping time as soon as you start to blow through the straw. Have your lab partner time how long the solution takes to change color. Record the time.

Analyze the Results

1 **Describing Events** Describe what happens to the indicator solution.

2 **Examining Data** Compare your data with those of your classmates. What was the longest length of time it took to see a color change? What was the shortest? How do you account for the difference?

3 **Constructing Graphs** Make a bar graph that compares your data with the data of your classmates.

Draw Conclusions

4 **Interpreting Information** Do you think that there is a relationship between the length of time the solution takes to change color and the person's physical characteristics, such as which gender the tester is or whether the tester has an athletic build? Explain your answer.

5 **Making Predictions** Predict how exercise might affect the results of your experiment. For example, would you predict that the level of carbon dioxide in the breath of someone who was exercising would be higher or lower than the carbon dioxide level in the breath of someone who was sitting quietly? Would you predict that the level of carbon dioxide in the breath would affect the timing of any color change in the phenol solution?

Applying Your Data

Do jumping jacks or sit-ups for 3 minutes, and then repeat the experiment. Did the phenol solution still change color? Did your exercising change the timing? Describe and explain any change.

CHAPTER RESOURCES

Workbooks

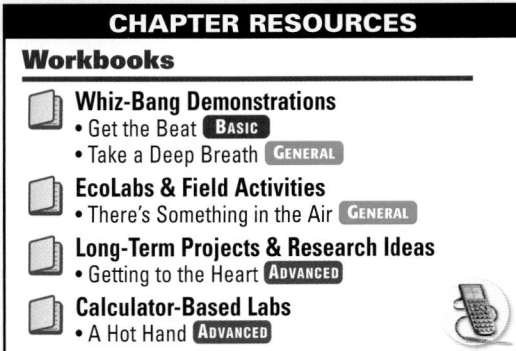

Whiz-Bang Demonstrations
• Get the Beat **BASIC**
• Take a Deep Breath **GENERAL**

EcoLabs & Field Activities
• There's Something in the Air **GENERAL**

Long-Term Projects & Research Ideas
• Getting to the Heart **ADVANCED**

Calculator-Based Labs
• A Hot Hand **ADVANCED**

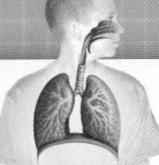

Assignment Guide

Section	Questions
1	2, 6, 8, 10, 24–26
2	1, 7, 13, 21–22
3	3, 8, 16, 23
4	4–5, 9, 11–12, 14, 18, 20
1, 2, and 3	15, 19
1, 2, and 4	17

ANSWERS

Using Key Terms

1. Red blood cells
2. Arteries
3. lymphatic system
4. larynx
5. alveoli

Understanding Key Ideas

6. b
7. d
8. a
9. c
10. b
11. a
12. Pulmonary circulation carries blood to the lungs and back to the heart. Systemic circulation carries blood from the heart to the rest of the body and then returns the blood to the heart.
13. The first number, systolic pressure, is pressure in arteries when ventricles contract. The second number, diastolic pressure, is pressure in arteries when ventricles relax.

USING KEY TERMS

Complete each of the following sentences by choosing the correct term from the word bank.

red blood cells	veins
white blood cells	arteries
lymphatic system	larynx
alveoli	bronchi
respiratory system	trachea

1 ___ deliver oxygen to the cells of the body.

2 ___ carry blood away from the heart.

3 The ___ helps the body fight pathogens.

4 The ___ contains the vocal cords.

5 The pathway of air through the respiratory system ends at the tiny sacs called ___.

UNDERSTANDING KEY IDEAS

Multiple Choice

6 Blood from the lungs enters the heart at the
  a. left ventricle.
  b. left atrium.
  c. right atrium.
  d. right ventricle.

7 Blood cells are made
  a. in the heart.
  b. from plasma.
  c. from lymph.
  d. in the bones.

8 Which of the following activities is a function of the lymphatic system?
  a. returning excess fluid to the circulatory system
  b. delivering nutrients to the cells
  c. bringing oxygen to the blood
  d. pumping blood to all parts of the body

9 Alveoli are surrounded by
  a. veins.
  b. muscles.
  c. capillaries.
  d. lymph nodes.

10 What prevents blood from flowing backward in veins?
  a. platelets
  b. valves
  c. muscles
  d. cartilage

11 Air moves into the lungs when the diaphragm muscle
  a. contracts and moves down.
  b. contracts and moves up.
  c. relaxes and moves down.
  d. relaxes and moves up.

Short Answer

12 What is the difference between pulmonary circulation and systemic circulation in the cardiovascular system?

13 Walton's blood pressure is 110/65. What do the two numbers mean?

14 What body process produces the carbon dioxide you exhale?

15 Describe how the circulatory system and the lymphatic system work together to keep your body healthy.

16 How is the spleen important to both the lymphatic system and the circulatory system?

17 Briefly describe the path that oxygen follows in your respiratory system and your circulatory system.

CRITICAL THINKING

18 **Concept Mapping** Use the following terms to create a concept map: *blood, oxygen, alveoli, capillaries,* and *carbon dioxide.*

19 **Making Comparisons** Compare and contrast the functions of the circulatory system and the lymphatic system.

20 **Identifying Relationships** Why do you think there are hairs in your nose?

21 **Applying Concepts** After a person donates blood, the blood is stored in one-pint bags until it is needed for a transfusion. A healthy person has about 5 million RBCs in each cubic millimeter (1 mm³) of blood.

   a. How many RBCs are in 1 mL of blood? (One milliliter is equal to 1 cm³ and to 1,000 mm³.)

   b. How many RBCs are there in 1 pt? (One pint is equal to 473 mL.)

22 **Predicting Consequences** What would happen if all of the red blood cells in your blood disappeared?

23 **Identifying Relationships** When a person is not feeling well, a doctor may examine samples of the person's blood to see how many white blood cells are present. Why would this information be useful?

INTERPRETING GRAPHICS

The diagram below shows how the human heart would look in cross section. Use the diagram to answer the questions that follow.

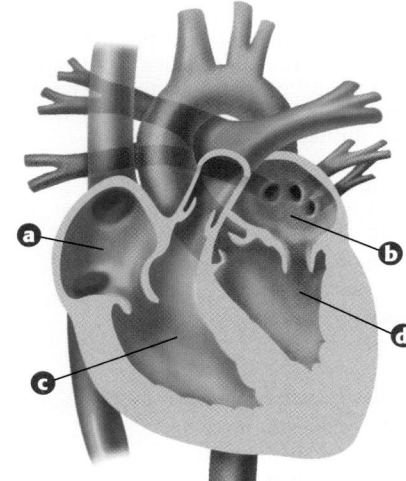

24 Which letter identifies the chamber that receives blood from systemic circulation? What is this chamber's name?

25 Which letter identifies the chamber that receives blood from the lungs? What is this chamber's name?

26 Which letter identifies the chamber that pumps blood to the lungs? What is this chamber's name?

16. The spleen is important to the circulatory system because it removes old or damaged red blood cells. It is important to the lymphatic system because it stores white blood cells, which help fight disease.

17. Oxygen comes into the body through the nose or mouth, travels to the lungs, and enters the alveoli. In the alveoli, oxygen moves through the capillary walls and enters the blood. The circulatory system carries the blood from the lungs to the heart, which pumps the blood to all parts of the body. Oxygen is carried by red blood cells to every body cell.

Critical Thinking

18. 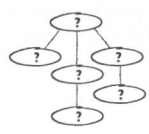 An answer to this exercise can be found at the end of the book.

19. Sample answer: The circulatory system and the lymphatic system use fluids to carry substances to and from all parts of the body. The circulatory system delivers oxygen and nutrients to the cells and removes wastes from the cells. The lymphatic system helps fight disease and infection.

20. The hairs catch dust and other foreign particles, which helps keep your lungs clean.

21. a. 5 billion (5,000,000,000) cells

   b. 2.365 trillion (2,365,000,000,000) cells

22. Sample answer: In a short time, I would probably die because my body could not get the oxygen it needs.

23. The immune system produces white blood cells to fight pathogens. A high white blood cell count tells the doctor that the person may have an infection.

Interpreting Graphics

24. a, the right atrium

25. b, the left atrium

26. c, the right ventricle

---

14. Carbon dioxide is a product of cellular respiration, which occurs in the body's cells.

15. Sample answer: The circulatory system delivers oxygen, nutrients, and white blood cells to all parts of the body. The lymphatic system returns excess fluid from between the cells to the circulatory system.

CHAPTER RESOURCES

Chapter Resource File

- Chapter Review **GENERAL**
- Chapter Test A **GENERAL**
- Chapter Test B **ADVANCED**
- Chapter Test C **SPECIAL NEEDS**
- Vocabulary Activity **GENERAL**

Workbooks

Study Guide
- Assessment resources are also available in Spanish.

Teacher's Note

To provide practice under more realistic testing conditions, give students 20 minutes to answer all of the questions in this Standardized Test Preparation.

MISCONCEPTION ALERT

Answers to the standardized test preparation can help you identify student misconceptions and misunderstandings.

READING

Passage 1

1. C
2. I
3. C

TEST DOCTOR

Question 2: Students may select the incorrect answers F or H because the passage is about sneezing and mentions heredity. Students may select incorrect answer G because they may recall that some plants show phototropism, or a response to light.

Standardized Test Preparation

READING

Read each of the passages below. Then, answer the questions that follow each passage.

Passage 1 For some reason, about one in five people sneeze when they step from a dimly lit area into a brightly lit area. In fact, some may sneeze a dozen times or more! Fortunately, the sneezing usually stops relatively quickly. This sneeze reaction is called a photic sneeze reflex (FOHT ik SNEEZ REE fleks). No one knows for certain why it happens. A few years ago, some geneticists studied the photic sneeze reflex. They named it the *ACHOO syndrome*. Scientists know that the ACHOO syndrome runs in families. So, the photic sneeze may be hereditary and can be passed from parent to child. Sometimes, even the number of times in a row that each person sneezes is the same throughout a family.

1. According to the passage, the ACHOO syndrome is most likely to be which of the following?
   A contagious
   B photosynthetic
   C hereditary
   D allergic

2. In the passage, what does *photic* mean?
   F having to do with sneezing
   G having to do with plants
   H having to do with genetics
   I having to do with light

3. Which of the following statements is one clue that the photic sneeze reflex can be passed from parent to child?
   A The reflex is triggered by bright light.
   B Sneezing usually stops after a few sneezes.
   C Family members even sneeze the same number of times.
   D Scientists do not know what causes the ACHOO syndrome.

Passage 2 The two main functions of blood are transporting nutrients and oxygen from the lungs to cells and carrying carbon dioxide and other waste materials away from cells to the lungs or other organs. Blood also transfers body heat to the body surface and plays a role in defending the body against disease. The respiratory system transports gases to and from blood. The respiratory system and blood work together to carry out external respiration and internal respiration. External respiration is the exchange of gases between the atmosphere and blood. Internal respiration is the exchange of gases between blood and the cells of the body.

1. In the passage, what does *external respiration* mean?
   A the exchange of gases outdoors
   B the inhalation of gases as you breathe in
   C the exchange of gases between blood and the atmosphere
   D the exhalation of gases as you breathe out

2. Which of the following statements is a fact in the passage?
   F The respiratory system transports oxygen to all the cells of the body.
   G The respiratory system is part of the circulatory system.
   H Blood is a kind of cardiac tissue.
   I Blood transports oxygen to cells.

3. According to the passage, what are two of the roles blood plays in the human body?
   A transferring body heat and defending against disease
   B defending against disease and transporting gases to the circulatory system
   C transporting carbon dioxide to body cells and transferring body heat
   D external respiration and atmosphere

Passage 2

1. C
2. I
3. A

TEST DOCTOR

Question 3: Students may select incorrect answers B or C if they do not read the passage carefully. Blood does not transport gases to the circulatory system (answer B) or transport carbon dioxide to the body cells (answer C). Students may select incorrect answer D if they do not see that the question asks for two roles.

Use the graph below to answer the questions that follow.

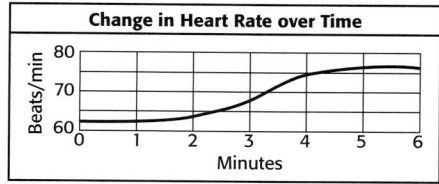

Change in Heart Rate over Time

1. What is the most likely explanation for the change seen after the two-minute mark?

 A The person started exercising.

 B The person fell asleep.

 C The person inhaled.

 D The person sat down.

2. How much faster is the heart beating during minute 5 than during minute 2?

 F 10 beats per minute more

 G 12 beats per minute more

 H 15 beats per minute more

 I 17 beats per minute more

3. About how many minutes did it take for this person's heart rate to go from 65 beats per minute to 75 beats per minute?

 A 0.7 minute

 B 1.0 minute

 C 1.7 minutes

 D 4.0 minutes

4. After how many minutes does this person's heart rate return to its resting rate?

 F 1.0 minute

 G 2.0 minutes

 H 5.0 minutes

 I There is not enough information to determine the answer.

MATH

Read each question below, and choose the best answer.

1. If Jim's heart beats 73 times every minute, Jen's heart beats 68 times every minute, and Leigh's heart beats 81 times every minute, what is the average heart rate for these 3 people?

 A 73 beats per minute

 B 74 beats per minute

 C 141 beats per minute

 D 222 beats per minute

2. The Griffith family has 4 dogs. Each of the dogs eats between 0.9 kg and 1.3 kg of food every day. Which is a reasonable estimate of the total amount of food all 4 dogs eat every day?

 F 1 kg of food

 G 3 kg of food

 H 4 kg of food

 I 8 kg of food

3. Assume that the average person's resting heart rate is 70 beats per minute. The resting heart rate of a particular person is 10 beats per minute more than the average person's. If a person with the higher heart rate lives 75 years, about how many more times will his or her heart beat than the average person's heart in that time?

 A 3,942

 B 394,200

 C 3,942,000

 D 394,200,000

4. At rest, the cells of the human body use about 250 mL of oxygen per minute. At that rate, how much oxygen would the cells of the human body use every 24 hours?

 F about 36 L

 G about 360 L

 H about 36,000 L

 I about 360,000 L

Standardized Test Preparation

 1. A

 2. G

 3. C

 4. I

TEST DOCTOR

Question 2: Students may select any of the incorrect answers if they do not look closely at the graph. The heart rate increases from about 64 beats per minute to 76 beats per minute.

Question 4: Students may select answer F, G, or H by guessing because they think that they should be able to find on the graph the point at which the heart rate returns to normal. However, the heart rate does not return to normal during the time period shown on the graph.

MATH

 1. B

 2. H

 3. D

 4. G

TEST DOCTOR

Question 3: Students may select any of the incorrect answers because they have not kept track of the proper number of decimal places in this two-step problem.

Question 4: Students may select incorrect answer I if they forget to convert milliliters to liters in their final answer.

CHAPTER RESOURCES

Chapter Resource File

 • Standardized Test Preparation GENERAL

State Resources

 For specific resources for your state, visit **go.hrw.com** and type in the keyword **HSMSTR**.

Science, Technology, and Society

Background

Because of the dangers associated with giving someone blood of the wrong type, people have searched for safe blood substitutes for hundreds of years. At one time, even wine was proposed as a substitute! Four substances are in advanced clinical trials in the United States. PolyHeme and Hemolink are derived from modified human hemoglobin. Hemopure is made from modified bovine hemoglobin. Oxygent is entirely synthetic and is made from an emulsion of perfluorocarbon molecules.

Weird Science

Background

Drawings of men playing an instrument that appears to be a didjeridu appear in caves in Australia. Evidence indicates that the didjeridu has been in Australia for about 1,000 years. Aboriginals, though, trace the history of the instrument back to the "Dreamtime," the very beginning of their people. The first reference by Westerners comes from a man named T. B. Wilson in 1835. Wilson described an aboriginal man playing an instrument that was made of bamboo and was about 1 m long.

Science in Action

Science, Technology, and Society

Artificial Blood

What happens when someone loses blood rapidly? Loss of blood can be fatal in a very short time, so lost blood must be replaced as quickly as possible. But what if enough blood, or blood of the right type, is not immediately available? Scientists are developing different types of artificial blood—including one based on cow hemoglobin—that may soon be used to save lives that would otherwise be lost.

Language Arts ACTIVITY

WRITING SKILL Imagine that you are a doctor and one of your patients needs surgery. Create a pamphlet or brochure that explains what artificial blood is and how it may be used in surgical procedures.

Weird Science

Circular Breathing and the Didgeridoo

Do you play a musical instrument such as a clarinet, flute, or tuba? How long can you blow into it before you have to take a breath? Can you blow into it for one minute? two minutes? And what happens when you stop to breathe? The Aboriginal people of Australia have a musical instrument called the *didgeridoo* (DIJ uh ree DOO). Didgeridoo players can play for hours without stopping to take a breath. They use a technique called *circular breathing* that lets them inhale and exhale at the same time. Circular breathing lets a musician play music without having to take breaths as often. With a little practice, maybe you can do it, too.

Social Studies ACTIVITY

WRITING SKILL Select a country from Africa or Asia. Research that country's traditional musical instruments or singing style. Write a description of how the instruments or singing style of that country differs from those of the United States. Illustrate your report.

Answer to Language Arts Activity

Students' brochures should be attractive, well illustrated, and informative. Brochures should explain which type of artificial blood the patient may receive and whether the patient or the doctor (or student) recommends the type of artificial blood to be used.

Answer to Social Studies Activity

Students' reports will vary depending on the country or region, the instrument, and the musical or singing style that the students have selected. Reports should be clear, interesting, and informative. Students should provide sources and references for their report, and their report should include illustrations that enhance the report.

People in Science

Anthony Roberts, Jr.

Leader in Training Anthony Roberts, Jr., has asthma. When he was in the 5th grade, his school counselor told him about a summer camp—The Boggy Creek Gang Camp—that was just being built. His counselor said that the camp was designed to serve kids who have asthma or other disabilities and diseases, such as AIDS, cancer, diabetes, epilepsy, hemophilia, heart disease, kidney disease, rheumatic diseases, and sickle cell anemia. Kids, in other words, who might otherwise never go to summer camp. Anthony jumped at the chance to go. Now, Anthony is too old to be a camper, and he is too young to be a regular counselor. But he can be a *Leader in Training* (LIT). Some camps have LIT programs that help young people make the transition from camper to counselor.

For Anthony, the chance to be an LIT fit perfectly with his love of camping and with his desire to work with kids with disabilities. Anthony remembers the fun he had and wants to help other kids have the same summer fun he did.

Math

Research how many children under 17 years of age in the United States have asthma. Make a bar graph that shows how the number of children who have asthma has changed since 1981. What does this graph tell you about rates of asthma among children in the United States?

go.hrw.com

To learn more about these Science in Action topics, visit **go.hrw.com** and type in the keyword **HL5BD2F**.

Current Science

Check out Current Science® articles related to this chapter by visiting go.hrw.com. Just type in the keyword **HL5CS23**.

People in Science
Teaching Strategy – GENERAL

If appropriate for your class, begin by talking in a general way about summer vacation: what students like to do, how they spend their time, whether they go to summer camp (day camp or residence camp), and whether they know of anyone (no names) who has asthma or another disability that might make summer camp activities difficult. Then, discuss the Boggy Creek Gang Camp and Anthony Roberts, Jr., and his role as a leader in training. Your class may be interested to know that the Boggy Creek Gang Camp is one of the Hole in the Wall camps started by actor Paul Newman. The Hole in the Wall Gang was the outlaw gang of which Butch Cassidy was a member. Newman portrayed Cassidy in the 1969 film *Butch Cassidy and the Sundance Kid.*

Answers to Math Activity

Students should find that asthma rates for children under 17 have increased from 3.2% in 1981 to 5.7% in 2001. Students should be able to update the figures each year as more-current data is published. Bar graphs should reflect the growth in the rate from the 1980s to the present. As an extension, students can research the costs associated with asthma in children or can research the ways in which asthma rates differ between races.

The Digestive and Urinary Systems
Chapter Planning Guide

Compression guide:
To shorten instruction because of time limitations, omit Section 2.

OBJECTIVES	LABS, DEMONSTRATIONS, AND ACTIVITIES	TECHNOLOGY RESOURCES
PACING • 90 min pp. 632–641 **Chapter Opener**	SE **Start-up Activity**, p. 633 ◆ GENERAL	OSP **Parent Letter** ■ GENERAL CD **Student Edition on CD-ROM** CD **Guided Reading Audio CD** ■ TR **Chapter Starter Transparency*** VID **Brain Food Video Quiz**
Section 1 The Digestive System • Compare mechanical digestion with chemical digestion. • Describe the parts and functions of the digestive system.	SE **Quick Lab** Break It Up!, p. 635 ◆ GENERAL CRF **Datasheet for Quick Lab*** TE **Demonstration** Measuring Saliva, p. 635 ◆ BASIC TE **Demonstration** Peristalsis, p. 637 ◆ GENERAL TE **Connection Activity** Chemistry, p. 638 ◆ GENERAL TE **Activity** Examining Tissue, p. 638 ◆ ADVANCED TE **Activity** Digestive Tract, p. 639 BASIC SE **School-to-Home Activity** Bile Model, p. 639 GENERAL SE **Connection to Environmental Science** Waste Away, p. 640 GENERAL SE **Skills Practice Lab** As the Stomach Churns, p. 646 ◆ GENERAL CRF **Datasheet for Chapter Lab*** SE **Skills Practice Lab** Enzymes in Action, p. 800 ◆ GENERAL CRF **Datasheet for LabBook*** LB **Whiz-Bang Demonstrations** Liver Let Live* ◆ GENERAL	CRF **Lesson Plans*** TR **Bellringer Transparency*** TR **The Digestive System*** TR **The Role of Enzymes in Protein Digestion*** TR **The Stomach; The Small Intestine and Villi*** TR **LINK TO EARTH SCIENCE** Mohs' Hardness Scale*** CRF **SciLinks Activity*** GENERAL TE **Internet Activity**, p. 639 GENERAL VID **Lab Videos for Life Science**
PACING • 45 min pp. 642–645 **Section 2 The Urinary System** • Explain how the kidneys filter blood. • Describe three disorders of the urinary system.	SE **Science in Action** Math, Social Studies, and Language Arts Activities, pp. 652–653 GENERAL TE **Activity** Defining Terms, p. 643 BASIC TE **Demonstration** Kidney Structure, p. 643 ◆ GENERAL LB **Long-Term Projects & Research Ideas** Copying the Kidney* ADVANCED	CRF **Lesson Plans*** TR **Bellringer Transparency*** TR **How the Kidneys Filter Blood***

PACING • 90 min

CHAPTER REVIEW, ASSESSMENT, AND STANDARDIZED TEST PREPARATION

CRF **Vocabulary Activity*** GENERAL
SE **Chapter Review**, pp. 648–649 GENERAL
CRF **Chapter Review*** ■ GENERAL
CRF **Chapter Tests A*** ■ GENERAL, **B*** ADVANCED, **C*** SPECIAL NEEDS
SE **Standardized Test Preparation**, pp. 650–651 GENERAL
CRF **Standardized Test Preparation*** GENERAL
CRF **Performance-Based Assessment*** GENERAL
OSP **Test Generator** GENERAL
CRF **Test Item Listing*** GENERAL

Online and Technology Resources

Visit **go.hrw.com** for a variety of free resources related to this textbook. Enter the keyword **HL5BD3.**

Holt Online Learning

Students can access interactive problem-solving help and active visual concept development with the *Holt Science and Technology* Online Edition available at **www.hrw.com.**

 Guided Reading Audio CD Also in Spanish

A direct reading of each chapter for auditory learners, reluctant readers, and Spanish-speaking students.

 Science Tutor CD-ROM

Excellent for remediation and test practice.

SKILLS DEVELOPMENT RESOURCES	SECTION REVIEW AND ASSESSMENT	STANDARDS CORRELATIONS
SE Pre-Reading Activity, p. 632 GENERAL **OSP** Science Puzzlers, Twisters & Teasers GENERAL		National Science Education Standards UCP2, SAI 1; SPSP 5; HNS 2; LS 1e
CRF Directed Reading A* ■ BASIC, B* SPECIAL NEEDS **CRF** Vocabulary and Section Summary* ■ GENERAL **SE** Reading Strategy Prediction Guide, p. 634 GENERAL **TE** Reading Strategy Activity, p. 636 BASIC **SE** Math Practice Tooth Truth, p. 637 GENERAL **TE** Inclusion Strategies, p. 637 **TE** Connection to Math Liver Regeneration, p. 639 GENERAL **CRF** Critical Thinking Frankenstein's Food* ADVANCED	**SE** Reading Checks, pp. 635, 637, 639, 640 GENERAL **TE** Homework, p. 635 GENERAL **TE** Homework, p. 639 GENERAL **TE** Reteaching, p. 640 BASIC **TE** Quiz, p. 640 GENERAL **TE** Alternative Assessment, p. 640 ADVANCED **SE** Section Review,* p. 641 ■ GENERAL **CRF** Section Quiz* ■ GENERAL	UCP 1, 2, 5; SAI 1; SPSP1, 5; HNS 1; LS 1a, 1d, 1e, 1f, 3b; *Chapter Lab:* UCP 2, 5; SAI 1; LS 1a, 1e; *LabBook:* UCP 2, 5; SAI 1; LS 1a, 1e
CRF Directed Reading A* ■ BASIC, B* SPECIAL NEEDS **CRF** Vocabulary and Section Summary* ■ GENERAL **SE** Reading Strategy Reading Organizer, p. 642 GENERAL **TE** Inclusion Strategies, p. 644 **CRF** Reinforcement Worksheet Annie Apple's Amazing Adventure* BASIC	**SE** Reading Checks, pp. 643, 644 GENERAL **TE** Reteaching, p. 644 BASIC **TE** Quiz, p. 644 GENERAL **TE** Alternative Assessment, p. 644 GENERAL **SE** Section Review,* p. 645 ■ GENERAL **CRF** Section Quiz* ■ GENERAL	UCP 1, 2, 3, 4, 5; HNS 1; LS la, 1c, 1d, 1e, 1f, 3a, 3b

One-Stop Planner® CD-ROM

This convenient CD-ROM includes:
- Lab Materials QuickList Software
- Holt Calendar Planner
- Customizable Lesson Plans
- Printable Worksheets
- ExamView® Test Generator

CNN student News™

cnnstudentnews.com

Find the latest news, lesson plans, and activities related to important scientific events.

SCILINKS® NSTA

www.scilinks.org

Maintained by the **National Science Teachers Association.** See Chapter Enrichment pages for a complete list of topics.

Current Science®

Check out *Current Science* articles and activities by visiting the HRW Web site at **go.hrw.com.** Just type in the keyword **HL4CS24T.**

Classroom Videos

- **Lab Videos** demonstrate the chapter lab.
- **Brain Food Video Quizzes** help students review the chapter material.
- **CNN Videos** bring science into your students' daily life.

Visual Resources

CHAPTER STARTER TRANSPARENCY

This Really Happened!

BELLRINGER TRANSPARENCIES

Section: The Digestive System
How does your circulatory system get the nutrients that it carries to your cells? Describe as best you can the process that turns food into nutrients that cells can use.

Write your answers in your **science journal.**

Section: The Urinary System
Your blood must be cleaned regularly. Without looking in your textbook, guess how the body cleans the blood. Think about what organs might be used to clean your blood. Do you know what medical procedure you must undergo if your body is no longer able to clean its own blood?

Write your answers in your **science journal,** and then check your answer against the textbook.

TEACHING TRANSPARENCIES

The Digestive System

The Role of Enzymes in Protein Digestion
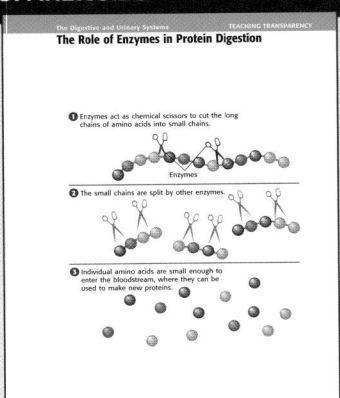

TEACHING TRANSPARENCIES

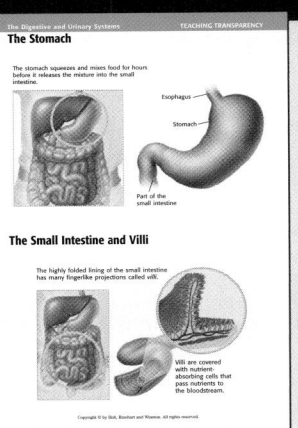
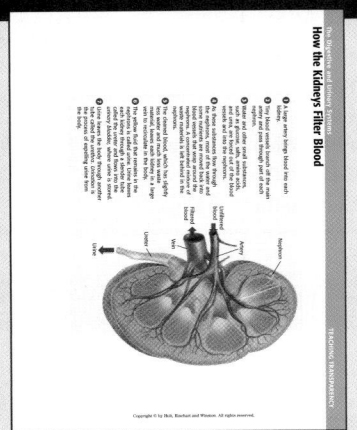
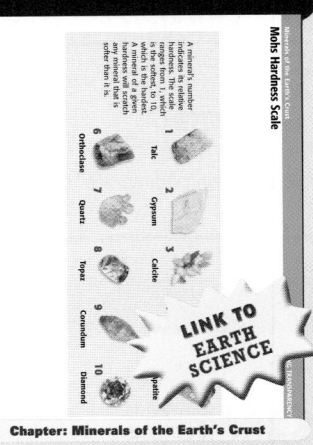

Chapter: Minerals of the Earth's Crust

CONCEPT MAPPING TRANSPARENCY

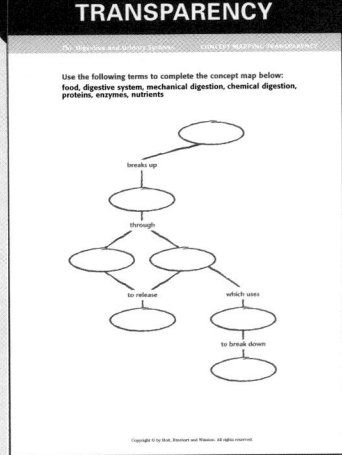

Planning Resources

LESSON PLANS

PARENT LETTER

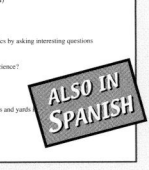
ALSO IN SPANISH

TEST ITEM LISTING

One-Stop Planner® CD-ROM

This CD-ROM includes all of the resources shown here and the following time-saving tools:

- Lab Materials QuickList Software
- Customizable lesson plans
- Holt Calendar Planner
- The powerful ExamView® Test Generator

For a preview of available worksheets covering math and science skills, see pages T26–T33. All of these resources are also on the One-Stop Planner®.

Meeting Individual Needs

DIRECTED READING A
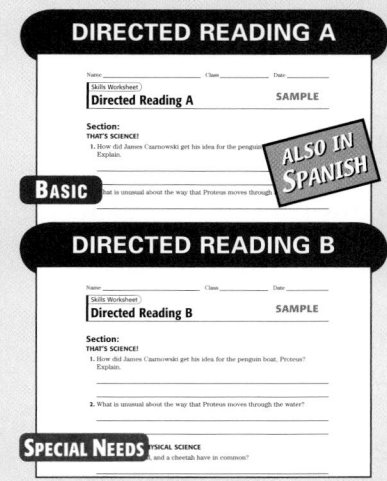
BASIC · **ALSO IN SPANISH**

DIRECTED READING B
SPECIAL NEEDS

VOCABULARY ACTIVITY
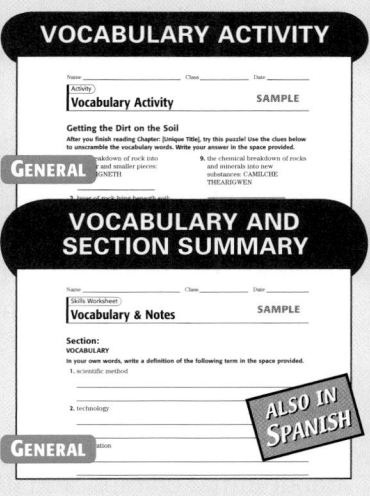
GENERAL · **ALSO IN SPANISH**

VOCABULARY AND SECTION SUMMARY
GENERAL · **ALSO IN SPANISH**

REINFORCEMENT
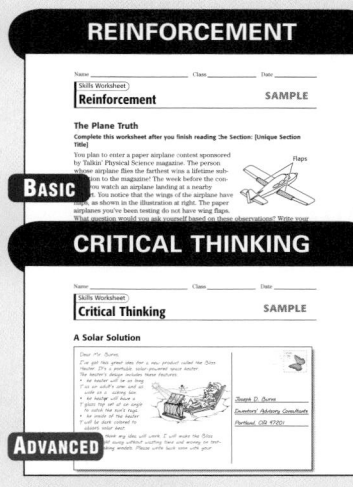
BASIC

CRITICAL THINKING
ADVANCED

SCILINKS ACTIVITY

GENERAL

SCIENCE PUZZLERS, TWISTERS & TEASERS
GENERAL

Labs and Activities

LONG-TERM PROJECTS & RESEARCH IDEAS
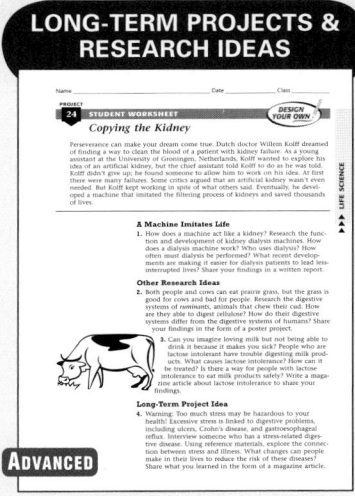
ADVANCED

WHIZ-BANG DEMONSTRATIONS
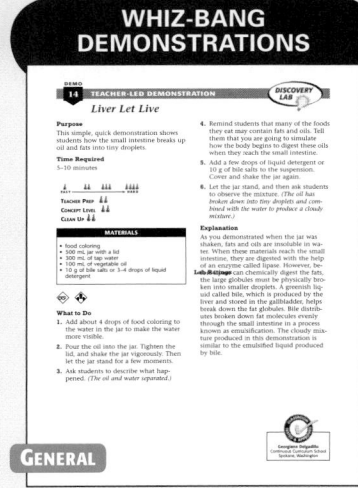
GENERAL

DATASHEETS FOR QUICK LABS

DATASHEETS FOR CHAPTER LABS

DATASHEETS FOR LABBOOK

Review and Assessments

SECTION QUIZ

GENERAL · **ALSO IN SPANISH**

SECTION REVIEW
GENERAL · **ALSO IN SPANISH**

CHAPTER REVIEW
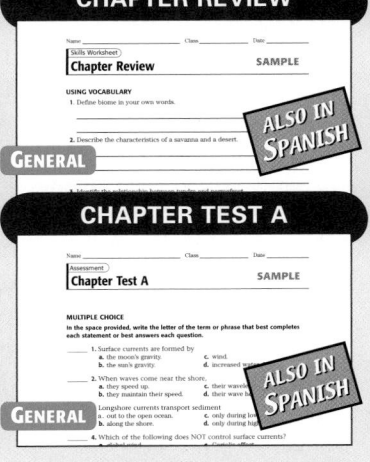
GENERAL · **ALSO IN SPANISH**

CHAPTER TEST A
GENERAL · **ALSO IN SPANISH**

CHAPTER TEST B
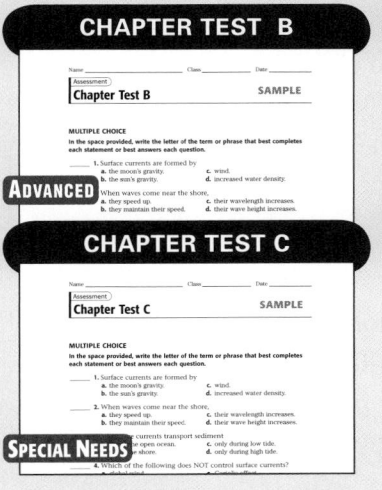
ADVANCED

CHAPTER TEST C
SPECIAL NEEDS

STANDARDIZED TEST PREPARATION
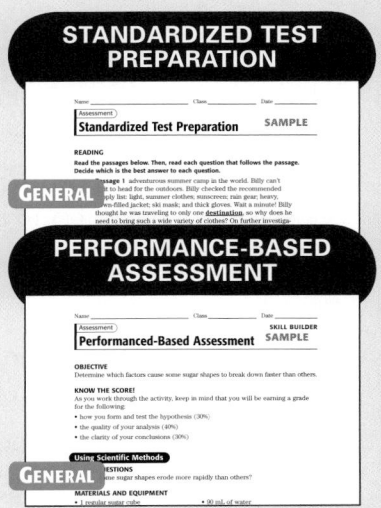
GENERAL

PERFORMANCE-BASED ASSESSMENT
GENERAL

This Chapter Enrichment provides relevant and interesting information to expand and enhance your presentation of the chapter material.

Section 1

The Digestive System

Parts of the System

- The digestive system is composed of two sets of organs: those that make up the digestive tract and those that are called *accessory organs*. The digestive tract is a continuous tube consisting of the mouth, including the teeth and the tongue, the pharynx, the esophagus, the stomach, the small intestine, the large intestine, rectum, and anus.

- The accessory digestive organs include the salivary glands, the gallbladder, the liver, and the pancreas.

Is That a Fact!

- The digestive tract in a cadaver is about 9 m long. However, because of muscle tone, the digestive tract of a living person is considerably shorter.

The Stomach

- In short people, the stomach is found high in the abdomen and runs horizontally. In tall people, the stomach tends to run vertically, forming a **J** shape.

Is That a Fact!

- It takes from about four to eight seconds for food to pass from the top of the throat to the stomach.
- It takes less than two seconds for liquids to pass from the top of the throat to the stomach.

The Intestines

- The small intestine is the longest portion of the digestive tract. It is about 6 m long and 2.5 cm in diameter.

- Unlike the small intestine, the large intestine does not have villi and does not secrete digestive enzymes.

The Appendix

- The appendix is an offshoot of the large intestine and is 5 to 10 cm long. Like the tonsils, the appendix contains a large amount of lymphoid tissue.

- Occasionally, doctors begin an appendectomy on patients misdiagnosed with appendicitis. Instead of having appendicitis, however, the patients have had holes in the lining of their intestines made by parasitic worms. The incidence of intestinal parasitic worms is increasing as eating raw fish, such as sushi and sashimi, becomes more popular.

Food Poisoning

- Food poisoning is characterized by nausea, vomiting, abdominal cramps, and diarrhea. The two most common culprits are the bacteria *Salmonella* and *Shigella*.

- *Salmonella* is typically spread by poorly cooked meat and feces-contaminated hands. *Salmonella* infects the microvilli in the intestinal lining, causing blisters. If *Salmonella* poisoning is not treated promptly, the bacteria may spread throughout the body.

- *Shigella* is commonly found among people who have visited developing countries. It is spread via food, feces, fingers, flies, and contaminated public bodies of water, such as swimming pools.

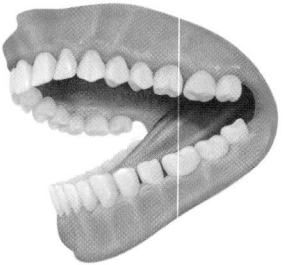

Eating Disorders

- Anorexia nervosa and bulimia nervosa are two common eating disorders that are characterized by an obsessive fear of gaining weight. Often, underlying psychological factors initiate these disorders.

- Anorexia nervosa is an eating disorder characterized by self-induced starvation. People with this condition refuse to eat and often exercise obsessively. Although the disorder can affect anyone, adolescent girls and young women are commonly afflicted. Boys, especially those involved in weight-conscious sports such as wrestling, can also suffer from anorexia nervosa.

- Bulimia nervosa is a binge-purge syndrome in which those afflicted binge on enormous amounts of food and then force themselves to vomit or use laxatives to eliminate the food. The binge-purge cycle may be repeated several times per day or only a couple of times per week.

- Although bulimics generally maintain a normal body weight and appear to be healthy, they are not healthy. They tend to have swollen salivary glands, pancreatitis, and liver and kidney problems. In addition, they are at risk of heart failure and stomach rupture, both of which can result in death. Excessive vomiting damages the esophagus and the stomach and wears away tooth enamel.

- Treatment for eating disorders may include diet control, often by means of hospitalization, behavior modification, nutrition education, and use of antidepressants.

Section 2

The Urinary System

Filtering Wastes

- The urinary system functions primarily to maintain the correct balance of salts and water and to remove metabolic, nitrogen-containing wastes, such as urea, from the body in the form of urine.

- The digestive system, the circulatory system, and the respiratory system also excrete wastes. The digestive system excretes food wastes in the form of feces. The circulatory and respiratory systems work together to rid the body of carbon dioxide.

- The yellow color of urine comes from the yellow pigment urochrome.

The Kidneys

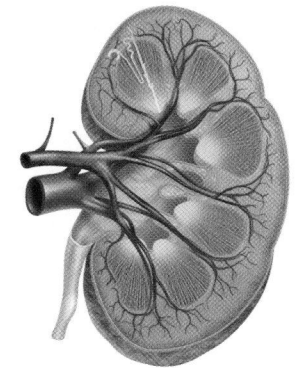

- The kidneys are surrounded and kept in their proper place in the body by fat. People who become too thin risk damage to the kidneys and other related urinary problems. As much as 1,200 mL of blood passes through the nephrons each minute.

Is That a Fact!

- ◆ Urinary bladders of average size can contain as much as 1 L of urine!

- ◆ The kidneys require up to one-fourth of the body's oxygen supply to carry out their functions.

- ◆ The kidneys filter about 180 L of fluid from the blood each day. About 99% of this fluid is returned to the bloodstream. The other 1% leaves the body in the form of urine.

- ◆ A person who donates a kidney can maintain normal kidney functions. The remaining kidney enlarges and carries out the functions previously performed by two kidneys.

The Urinary Bladder

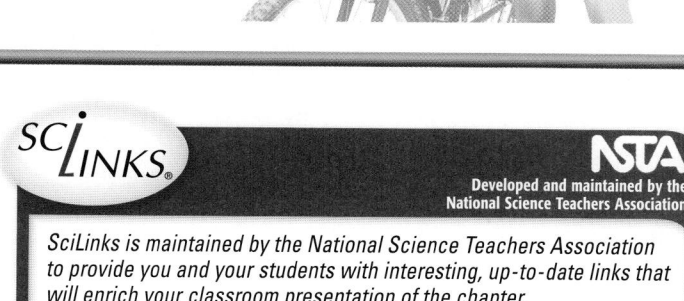

- Like the stomach, the size of the bladder varies with the amount of its contents. The bladder can hold 300 mL of urine without increasing its internal pressure significantly. At 500 mL of urine, the bladder is fairly full and may be 12.5 cm in length.

SCiLINKS

NSTA

Developed and maintained by the National Science Teachers Association

SciLinks is maintained by the National Science Teachers Association to provide you and your students with interesting, up-to-date links that will enrich your classroom presentation of the chapter.

Visit www.scilinks.org and enter the SciLinks code for more information about the topic listed.

Topic: The Digestive System
SciLinks code: HSM0409

Topic: Urinary System Ailments
SciLinks code: HSM1584

Topic: Problems in the Digestive System
SciLinks code: HSM1218

Topic: Tapeworms
SciLinks code: HSM1492

Topic: The Urinary System
SciLinks code: HSM1583

Overview

In this chapter, students will learn about the digestive and urinary systems of the human body. Students will learn how the digestive system breaks down food into building blocks the body can use and how the digestive and urinary systems eliminate wastes from the body.

Assessing Prior Knowledge

Students should be familiar with the following topics:

• cellular structure and function

• body organization

Identifying Misconceptions

Students may have misconceptions regarding the digestive and urinary systems. Many people commonly refer only to the stomach when discussing eating and digestion. So, some students may not know other organs are also part of the digestive system. Students may also mistakenly think that all digestion is mechanical. Though mechanical digestion is important, chemical digestion reduces food into subunits the body can use.

24
The Digestive and Urinary Systems

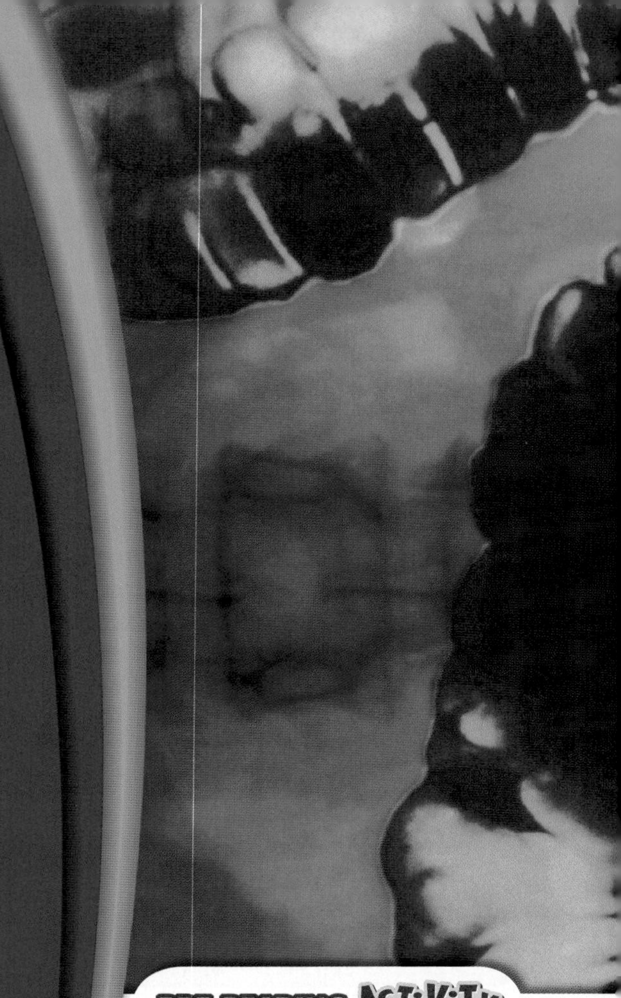

About the PHOTO

Is this a giant worm? No, it's an X ray of a healthy large intestine! Your large intestine helps your body preserve water. As mostly digested food passes through your large intestine, water is drawn out of the food. This water is returned to the bloodstream. The gray shadow behind the intestine is the spinal column. The areas that look empty are actually filled with organs. A special liquid helps this large intestine show up on the X ray.

PRE-READING ACTIVITY

Graphic Organizer

Chain-of-Events Chart Before you read the chapter, create the graphic organizer entitled "Chain-of-Events Chart" described in the **Study Skills** section of the Appendix. As you read the chapter, fill in the chart with details about each step of the processes that your body uses to digest food.

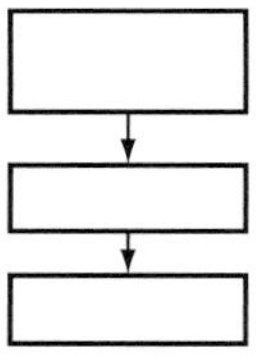

Standards Correlations

National Science Education Standards

The following codes indicate the National Science Education Standards that correlate to this chapter. The full text of the standards is at the front of the book.

Chapter Opener
UCP2, SAI 1; SPSP 5; HNS 2, 3; LS 1e

Section 1 The Digestive System
UCP 1, 2, 5; SAI 1; SPSP1, 5; HNS 1, 3; LS 1a, 1d, 1e, 1f, 3b;
LabBook: UCP 2, 5; SAI 1; LS 1a, 1e

Section 2 The Urinary System
UCP 1, 2, 3, 4, 5; HNS 1; LS 1a, 1c, 1d, 1e, 1f, 3a, 3b

Chapter Lab
UCP 2, 5; SAI 1; LS 1a, 1e

Chapter Review
LS1 a, 1c, 1d, 1e, 1f, 3a, 3b

Science in Action
HNS 1; SPSP 5; LS 1f

START-UP ACTiViTY
MATERIALS
FOR EACH STUDENT
- bag, plastic, sealable
- flour, 200 mL
- vegetable oil, 100 mL
- water, 100 mL

Safety Caution: Tell students not to ingest any of the materials used in this investigation. Using strong bags or doubling the bags works best. Have paper towels on hand, and clean up any spills immediately. Spilled liquids are a slipping hazard.

Answers

1. Sample answer: Before I squeezed the bag, the contents were well dispersed. Once I began squeezing the bag, the oil was mixed into the flour mixture.

2. Sample answer: The stomach is a muscular, baglike organ that is involved in the physical and chemical digestion of food. By squeezing the bag, I am modeling the muscular contractions of the stomach. (Note: This activity does not model the chemical digestion that occurs in the stomach.)

3. Sample answer: This is a good model of how the stomach works. Squeezing the bag helps show how the stomach mechanically mashes food. But the model does not have acids and enzymes that also help a real stomach break down food.

START-UP ACTiViTY

Changing Foods

The stomach breaks down food by, in part, squeezing the food. You can model the action of the stomach in the following activity.

Procedure

1. Add **200 mL of flour** and **100 mL of water** to a **resealable plastic bag.**
2. Mix **100 mL of vegetable oil** with the flour and water.
3. Seal the plastic bag.
4. Shake the bag until the flour, water, and oil are well mixed.
5. Remove as much air from the bag as you can, and reseal the bag carefully.
6. Knead the bag carefully with your hands for 5 min. Be careful to keep the bag sealed.

Analysis

1. Describe the mixture before and after you kneaded the bag.
2. How might the changes you saw in the mixture relate to how your stomach digests food?
3. Do you think this activity is a good model of how your stomach works? Explain your answer.

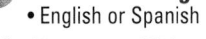

This Really Happened!

In 1822, a Canadian fur trader named Alexis St. Martin accidentally shot himself in his left side. An army surgeon named Dr. William Beaumont was able to save St. Martin's life, but the wound never completely healed. A hole approximately 6 cm in diameter remained open in his side, leading through skin and muscle right into his stomach.

Dr. Beaumont seized the opportunity

stomach squeeze and relax as it digested the bits of food. When he removed the food, he could see that it had changed. He also found that food changed when he placed it in a test tube with juices from St. Martin's stomach. Beaumont was able to determine that the stomach's juices, not just its squeezing action, were responsible for turning the food to mush.

What began as an unfortunate acci-

Chapter Starter Transparency
Use this transparency to help students begin thinking about how the human body digests food.

CHAPTER RESOURCES

Technology

 Transparencies
- Chapter Starter Transparency

READING SKILLS

Student Edition on CD-ROM

Guided Reading Audio CD
- English or Spanish

Classroom Videos
- Brain Food Video Quiz

Workbooks

Science Puzzlers, Twisters & Teasers
- The Digestive and Urinary Systems **GENERAL**

Focus

Overview

This section introduces the structures and functions of the digestive system. Students will compare mechanical digestion with chemical digestion and will learn to trace the path of food through the digestive system.

Bellringer

Ask students to answer the following questions:

- How does your circulatory system obtain the nutrients that it brings to your cells? (from the digestive system)

- Describe as best you can the process that turns food into nutrients that cells can use. (Sample answer: Food is broken down into smaller pieces by chewing and by the muscles of the digestive system. Chemicals in the digestive system then break these smaller pieces into nutrients that cells can use.)

READING WARM-UP

Objectives

- Compare mechanical digestion with chemical digestion.
- Describe the parts and functions of the digestive system.

Terms to Learn

digestive system
esophagus
stomach
pancreas
small intestine
liver
gallbladder
large intestine

READING STRATEGY

Prediction Guide Before reading this section, write the title of each heading in this section. Next, under each heading, write what you think you will learn.

digestive system the organs that break down food so that it can be used by the body

The Digestive System

It's your last class before lunch, and you're starving! Finally, the bell rings, and you get to eat!

You feel hungry because your brain receives signals that your cells need energy. But eating is only the beginning of the story. Your body must change a meal into substances that you can use. Your **digestive system,** shown in **Figure 1,** is a group of organs that work together to digest food so that it can be used by the body.

Digestive System at a Glance

The most obvious part of your digestive system is a series of tubelike organs called the *digestive tract.* Food passes through the digestive tract. The digestive tract includes your mouth, pharynx, esophagus, stomach, small intestine, large intestine, rectum, and anus. The human digestive tract can be more than 9 m long! The liver, gallbladder, pancreas, and salivary glands are also part of the digestive system. But food does not pass through these organs.

Figure 1 **The Digestive System**

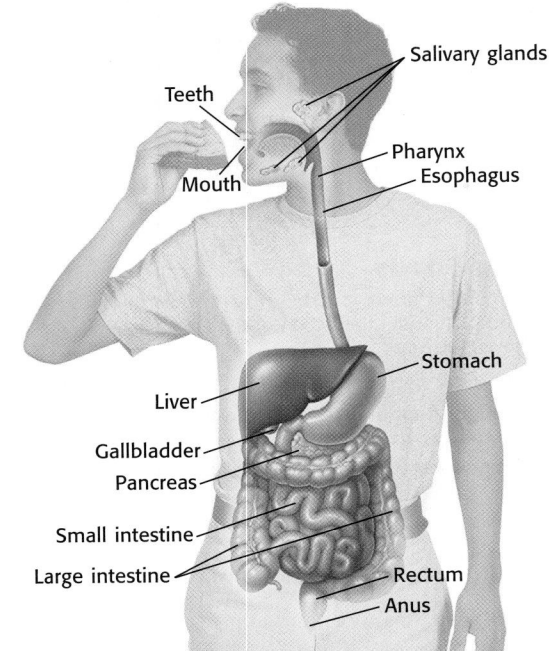

- Teeth
- Mouth
- Salivary glands
- Pharynx
- Esophagus
- Stomach
- Liver
- Gallbladder
- Pancreas
- Small intestine
- Large intestine
- Rectum
- Anus

CHAPTER RESOURCES

Chapter Resource File

- Lesson Plan
- Directed Reading A BASIC
- Directed Reading B SPECIAL NEEDS

Technology

Transparencies
- Bellringer
- The Role of Enzymes in Protein Digestion

Cultural Awareness GENERAL

World Diets Have students research the diets of people in countries such as Japan, India, Israel, Egypt, Mexico, and Russia. Encourage students to discover strategies that people in these countries use to obtain a nutritious diet, and have students compare the diets of people in each country with the diets of people in the United States. You may also want to have students compare the diets based on fat or cholesterol intake. **LS Verbal/Logical**

Breaking Down Food

Digestion is the process of breaking down food, such as a peanut butter and jelly sandwich, into a form that can pass from the digestive tract into the bloodstream. There are two types of digestion—mechanical and chemical. The breaking, crushing, and mashing of food is called *mechanical digestion*. In *chemical digestion,* large molecules are broken down into nutrients. Nutrients are substances in food that the body needs for normal growth, maintenance, and repair.

Three major types of nutrients—carbohydrates, proteins, and fats—make up most of the food you eat. In fact, a peanut butter and jelly sandwich contains all three of these nutrients. Substances called *enzymes* break some nutrients into smaller particles that the body can use. For example, proteins are chains of smaller molecules called *amino acids.* Proteins are too large to be absorbed into the bloodstream. So, enzymes cut up the chain of amino acids. The amino acids are small enough to pass into the bloodstream. This process is shown in **Figure 2.**

✓ Reading Check How do enzymes help digestion? (*See the Appendix for answers to Reading Checks.*)

Figure 2   The Role of Enzymes in Protein Digestion

❶ Enzymes act as chemical scissors to cut the long chains of amino acids into small chains.

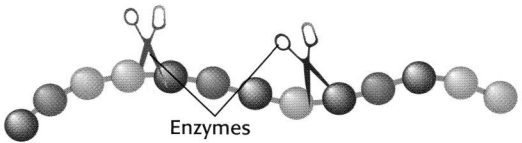

Enzymes

❷ The small chains are split by other enzymes.

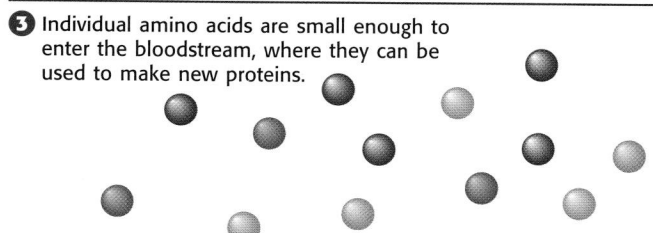

❸ Individual amino acids are small enough to enter the bloodstream, where they can be used to make new proteins.

Quick Lab

Break It Up!

1. Drop **one piece of hard candy** into a **clear plastic cup of water.**

2. Wrap an **identical candy** in a **towel,** and crush the candy with a **hammer.** Drop the candy into a **second clear cup of water.**

3. The next day, examine both cups. What is different about the two candies?

4. What type of digestion is represented by breaking the hard candy?

5. How does chewing your food help the process of digestion?

Answer to Reading Check

Enzymes cut proteins into amino acids that the body can use.

✏️ *Writing*

Activity Before students read the text on these pages, have them read the headings aloud. Then ask students to formulate one question that they expect the text under each heading to answer. Have students write their questions down. Possible questions include the following:

- "What happens in the mouth?"
- "Why is chewing important?"
- "What makes the stomach's environment harsh?"

LS Verbal

CONNECTION to
Ear—— GENERAL
Earth Science

Enamel Tooth enamel is made primarily of carbonated calcium hydroxyapatite. Fluoride compounds, taken internally while the teeth are growing, strengthen the enamel by forming the enamel out of fluoroapatite, an apatite material more acid resistant than natural enamel. Applying fluoride to the outside of teeth after the teeth have formed can also help strengthen the enamel by changing the natural hydroxyapatite in the tooth to fluoroapatite. Use the teaching transparency "Mohs' Hardness Scale" to illustrate that in geology, apatite is in the middle of the hardness scale for minerals. **LS** Visual

Digestion Begins in the Mouth

Chewing is important for two reasons. First, chewing creates small, slippery pieces of food that are easier to swallow than big, dry pieces are. Second, small pieces of food are easier to digest.

Teeth

Teeth are very important organs for mechanical digestion. With the help of strong jaw muscles, teeth break and grind food. The outermost layer of a tooth, the *enamel*, is the hardest material in the body. Enamel protects nerves and softer material inside the tooth. **Figure 3** shows a cross section of a tooth.

Have you ever noticed that your teeth have different shapes? Look at **Figure 4** to locate the different kinds of teeth. The molars are well suited for grinding food. The *premolars* are perfect for mashing food. The sharp teeth at the front of your mouth, the *incisors* and *canines,* are for shredding food.

Saliva

As you chew, the food mixes with a liquid called *saliva*. Saliva is made in salivary glands located in the mouth. Saliva contains an enzyme that begins the chemical digestion of carbohydrates. Saliva changes complex carbohydrates into simple sugars.

Leaving the Mouth

Once the food has been reduced to a soft mush, the tongue pushes it into the throat, which leads to a long, straight tube called the **esophagus** (i SAHF uh guhs). The esophagus squeezes the mass of food with rhythmic muscle contractions called *peristalsis* (PER uh STAL sis). Peristalsis forces the food into the stomach.

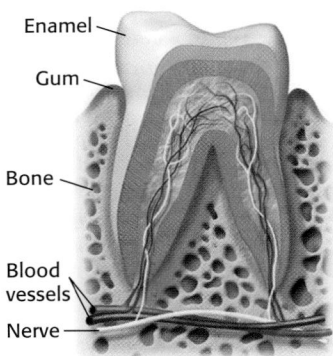

Enamel
Gum
Bone
Blood vessels
Nerve

Figure 3 *A tooth, such as this molar, is made of many kinds of tissue.*

esophagus a long, straight tube that connects the pharynx to the stomach

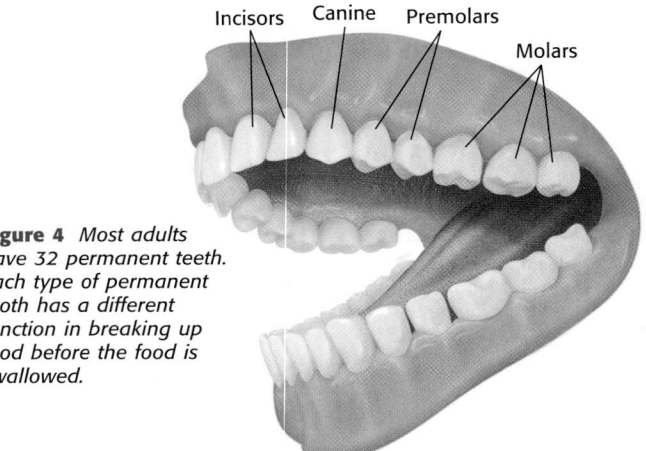

Incisors Canine Premolars Molars

Figure 4 *Most adults have 32 permanent teeth. Each type of permanent tooth has a different function in breaking up food before the food is swallowed.*

MISCONCEPTION ALERT

Teeth and Bones Students may mistakenly assume that teeth are made of bone. Point out that although enamel and dentin are similar to bone in appearance and calcium content, they are not bone. Bone contains blood vessels, but enamel and dentin do not.

Figure 5 The Stomach

The stomach squeezes and mixes food for hours before it releases the mixture into the small intestine.

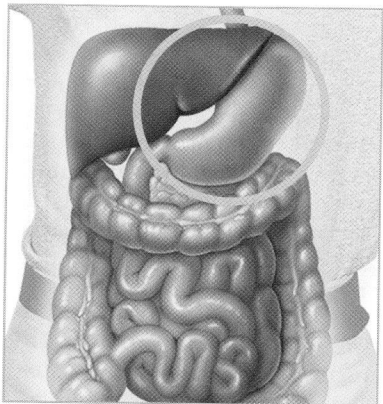

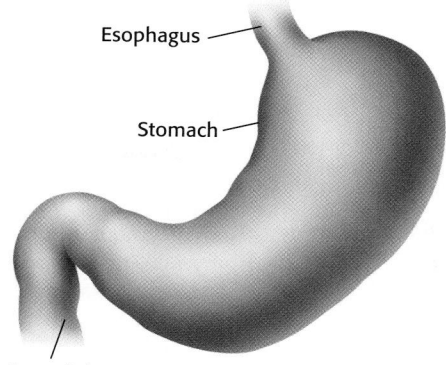

Esophagus

Stomach

Part of the small intestine

The Harsh Environment of the Stomach

The **stomach** is a muscular, saclike, digestive organ attached to the lower end of the esophagus. The stomach is shown in **Figure 5.** The stomach continues the mechanical digestion of your meal by squeezing the food with muscular contractions. While this squeezing is taking place, tiny glands in the stomach produce enzymes and acid. The enzymes and acid work together to break food into nutrients. Stomach acid also kills most bacteria that you might swallow with your food. After a few hours of combined mechanical and chemical digestion, your peanut butter and jelly sandwich has been reduced to a soupy mixture called *chyme* (KIEM).

stomach the saclike, digestive organ between the esophagus and the small intestine that breaks down food into a liquid by the action of muscles, enzymes, and acids

✓ **Reading Check** What is chyme?

Leaving the Stomach

The stomach slowly releases the chyme into the small intestine through a small ring of muscle that works like a valve. This valve keeps food in the stomach until the food has been thoroughly mixed with digestive fluids. Each time the valve opens and closes, it lets a small amount of chyme into the small intestine. Because the stomach releases chyme slowly, the intestine has more time to mix the chyme with fluids from the liver and pancreas. These fluids help digest food and stop the harsh acids in chyme from hurting the small intestine.

Tooth Truth

Young children get a first set of 20 teeth called *baby teeth*. These teeth usually fall out and are replaced by 32 permanent teeth. How many more permanent teeth than baby teeth does a person have? What is the ratio of baby teeth to permanent teeth? Be sure to express the ratio in its most reduced form.

Changes As food is digested, it undergoes both physical and chemical changes. Ask students to categorize the following activities as either physical changes or chemical changes:

• chewing food (physical change)

• enzymes in saliva breaking down carbohydrates (chemical change)

• squeezing and churning food in the stomach (physical change)

• breaking down food with pancreatic juice (chemical change)

LS Logical

ACTIVITY — ADVANCED

Examining Tissue Provide students with a compound light microscope and prepared slides of several different digestive organs. You might want to include cross sections of tissue from the stomach, the small intestine, the liver, and the pancreas. Review the proper use of microscopes before allowing students to operate them, and make sure that students do not work with broken or cracked slides. Have students observe the specimens, compare the different cross sections, and make sketches. **LS** Visual

pancreas the organ that lies behind the stomach and that makes digestive enzymes and hormones that regulate sugar levels

small intestine the organ between the stomach and the large intestine where most of the breakdown of food happens and most of the nutrients from food are absorbed

CONNECTION TO Social Studies

WRITING SKILL **Parasites** Intestinal parasites are organisms, such as roundworms and hookworms, that infect people and live in their digestive tract. Worldwide, intestinal parasites infect more than 1 billion people. Some parasites can be deadly. Research intestinal parasites in a library or on the Internet. Then, write a report on a parasite, including how it spreads, what problems it causes, how many people have it, and what can be done to stop it.

The Pancreas and Small Intestine

Most chemical digestion takes place after food leaves the stomach. Proteins, carbohydrates, and fats in the chyme are digested by the small intestine and fluids from the pancreas.

The Pancreas

When the chyme leaves the stomach, the chyme is very acidic. The pancreas makes fluids that protect the small intestine from the acid. The **pancreas** is an oval organ located between the stomach and small intestine. The chyme never enters the pancreas. Instead, the pancreatic fluid flows into the small intestine. This fluid contains enzymes that chemically digest chyme and contains bicarbonate, which neutralizes the acid in chyme. The pancreas also functions as a part of the endocrine system by making hormones that regulate blood sugar.

The Small Intestine

The **small intestine** is a muscular tube that is about 2.5 cm in diameter. Other than having a small diameter, it is really not that small. In fact, if you stretched the small intestine out, it would be longer than you are tall—about 6 m! If you flattened out the surface of the small intestine, it would be larger than a tennis court! How is this possible? The inside wall of the small intestine is covered with fingerlike projections called *villi*, shown in **Figure 6.** The surface area of the small intestine is very large because of the villi. The villi are covered with tiny, nutrient-absorbing cells. Once the nutrients are absorbed, they enter the bloodstream.

Figure 6 The Small Intestine and Villi

The highly folded lining of the small intestine has many fingerlike projections called *villi*.

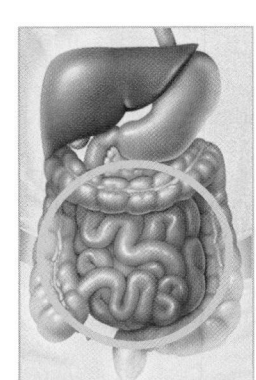
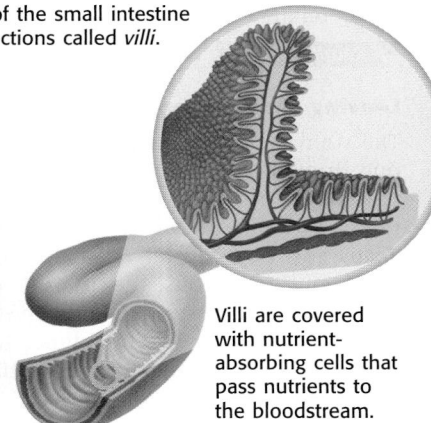

Villi are covered with nutrient-absorbing cells that pass nutrients to the bloodstream.

Answer to Connection to Social Studies
Sample answer: The World Health Organization reports that the intestinal parasite *Ascaris lumbricodes* (a kind of roundworm) kills 60,000 people every year. Symptoms include abdominal pain, intestinal blockage, and vomiting. The disease can be treated with medicines. Roundworms are spread by poor sanitary practices, such as using untreated human waste as fertilizer. Improved sanitary practices help control the spread of roundworms.

SCIENCE HUMOR

A man walks into a doctor's office with a stalk of celery in one ear and a carrot in the other. The man says, "Doc, I'm just not feeling well these days." The doctor replies, "I think that's because you haven't been eating right."

Figure 7 The Liver and the Gallbladder

Food does not move through the liver, gallbladder, and pancreas even though these organs are linked to the small intestine.

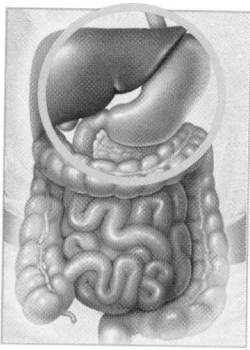
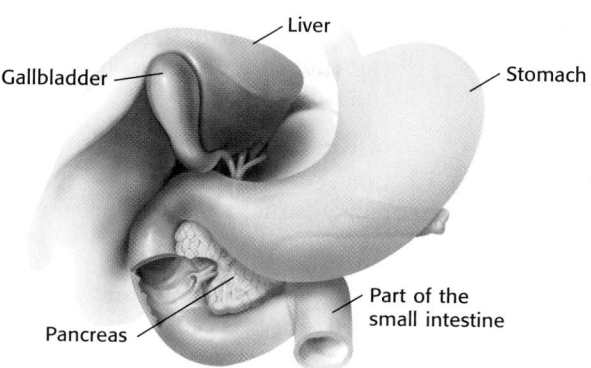

Liver

Gallbladder

Stomach

Pancreas

Part of the small intestine

The Liver and Gallbladder

The **liver** is a large, reddish brown organ that helps with digestion. A human liver can be as large as a football. Your liver is located toward your right side, slightly higher than your stomach, as shown in **Figure 7**. The liver helps with digestion in the following ways:

- It makes bile to break up fat.
- It stores nutrients.
- It breaks down toxins.

Breaking Up Fat

Although bile is made by the liver, bile is temporarily stored in a small, saclike organ called the **gallbladder**, shown in **Figure 7**. Bile is squeezed from the gallbladder into the small intestine, where the bile breaks large fat droplets into very small droplets. This mechanical process allows more fat molecules to be exposed to digestive enzymes.

 **Reading Check** How does bile help digest fat?

Storing Nutrients and Protecting the Body

After nutrients are broken down, they are absorbed into the bloodstream and carried through the body. Nutrients that are not needed right away are stored in the liver. The liver then releases the stored nutrients into the bloodstream as needed. The liver also captures and detoxifies many chemicals in the body. For instance, the liver produces enzymes that break down alcohol and many other drugs.

liver the largest organ in the body; it makes bile, stores and filters blood, and stores excess sugars as glycogen

gallbladder a sac-shaped organ that stores bile produced by the liver

SCHOOL to HOME

Bile Model

You can model the way bile breaks down fat and oil by using dish soap. At home with a parent, put a small amount of water in a small jar. Then, add a few drops of vegetable oil to the water. Notice that the two liquids separate. Draw a picture of the jar and its contents. Next, add a few drops of dishwashing soap to the water, tighten the lid securely onto the jar, and shake the jar. What happened to the three liquids in the jar? Draw another picture of the jar and its contents.

ACTIVITY

Answer to School-to-Home Activity

Sample answer: Before the dishwashing soap was added, the liquids separated. After the soap was added and the jar was shaken, the oil and water mixed.

ACTIVITY — BASIC

Digestive Tract Help students remember the route that food takes through the digestive tract by providing them with additional practice. Begin by showing students a model or illustration of the digestive tract. Then have students take turns naming and identifying, in order, the organs through which food travels through the digestive tract. (The proper sequence is as follows: mouth, pharynx, esophagus, stomach, small intestine, and large intestine.) LS Logical/Visual

Homework — GENERAL

Concept Mapping List the following terms on the board:

digestive system, mouth, stomach, liver, pancreas, gallbladder, teeth, salivary glands, saliva, digestive tract, esophagus, throat, tongue, small intestine

Then have students copy the terms onto a piece of paper and construct a concept map using these terms and linking words between them. LS Logical

Answer to Reading Check

Bile breaks large fat droplets into very small droplets. This process allows more fat molecules to be exposed to digestive enzymes.

CONNECTION to Math — GENERAL

Liver Regeneration Tell students that as much as 75% of a person's liver can be removed or impaired before the liver stops functioning. Ask students to calculate how much of a 1 kg liver must remain for it to function. (25% × 1,000 g = 250 g or 0.25 kg) LS Logical

Creating Graphs Provide students with the following average lengths of the digestive organs:

esophagus—25 cm, stomach—25 cm, small intestine—6 m, large intestine—1.5 m

Then have students prepare a bar graph to compare the average lengths of each digestive organ listed.

LS Logical

English Language Learners

Quiz ———— GENERAL

Ask students whether each of the statements below is true or false.

1. Digestion begins when food reaches the stomach. (false)

2. Breaking, crushing, and mashing food is an example of chemical digestion. (false)

3. Saliva contains enzymes, which begin the chemical digestion of food. (true)

4. The esophagus connects the mouth with the small intestine directly. (false)

Alternative Assessment ———— ADVANCED

Writing **Owner's Guide** Have students develop an owner's guide for their digestive system. The guide should include information about the structures of the digestive system and a diagram of the location of these body structures.

LS Verbal

---

large intestine the wider and shorter portion of the intestine that removes water from mostly digested food and that turns the waste into semisolid feces, or stool

CONNECTION TO Environmental Science

Waste Away Feces and other human wastes contain microorganisms and other substances that can contaminate drinking water. Every time you flush a toilet, the water and wastes go through the sewer to a wastewater treatment plant. At the wastewater treatment plant, the disease-causing microorganisms are removed, and the clean water is released back to rivers, lakes, and streams. Find out where the wastewater treatment plants are in your area. Report to your class where their wastewater goes.

 ACTIVITY

The End of the Line

Material that can't be absorbed into the blood is pushed into the large intestine. The **large intestine** is the organ of the digestive system that stores, compacts, and then eliminates indigestible material from the body. The large intestine, shown in **Figure 8,** has a larger diameter than the small intestine. The large intestine is about 1.5 m long, and has a diameter of about 7.5 cm.

In the Large Intestine

Undigested material enters the large intestine as a soupy mixture. The large intestine absorbs most of the water in the mixture and changes the liquid into semisolid waste materials called *feces,* or *stool.*

Whole grains, fruits, and vegetables contain a carbohydrate, called *cellulose,* that humans cannot digest. We commonly refer to this material as *fiber.* Fiber keeps the stool soft and keeps material moving through the large intestine.

✓ *Reading Check* **How does eating fiber help digestion?**

Leaving the Body

The *rectum* is the last part of the large intestine. The rectum stores feces until they can be expelled. Feces pass to the outside of the body through an opening called the *anus.* It has taken your sandwich about 24 hours to make this journey through your digestive system.

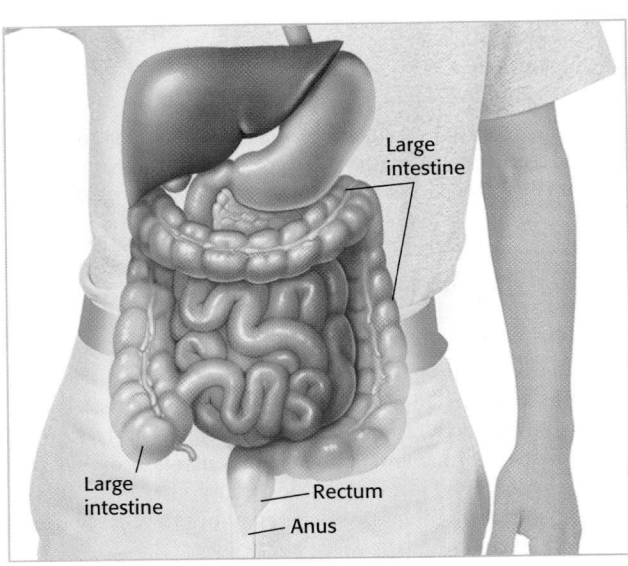

Figure 8 *The large intestine is the final organ of digestion.*

Is That a Fact!

Scientists once thought that only stress and heredity caused peptic ulcers. But in 1982, Australian scientists Robin Warren and Barry Marshall discovered a species of bacterium that was common to many ulcer patients. By infecting himself with the bacterium, succumbing to peptic ulcers, and then curing himself with antibiotics, Dr. Marshall proved that this species of bacterium was responsible for some ulcers.

Answer to Reading Check

Fiber keeps the stool soft and keeps material moving through the large intestine.

Summary

- Your digestive system is a group of organs that work together to digest food so that the nutrients from food can be used by the body.
- The breaking and mashing of food is called *mechanical digestion*. Chemical digestion is the process that breaks large food molecules into simpler molecules.
- The stomach mixes food with acid and enzymes that break down nutrients. The mixture is called *chyme*.
- In the small intestine, pancreatic fluid and bile are mixed with chyme.
- From the small intestine, nutrients enter the bloodstream and are circulated to the body's cells.
- The liver makes bile, stores nutrients, and breaks down toxins.
- The large intestine absorbs water, changing liquid waste into semisolid stool, or feces.

Using Key Terms

1. Use each of the following terms in a separate sentence: *digestive system, large intestine,* and *small intestine.*

Understanding Key Ideas

2. Which of the following is NOT a function of the liver?
   a. to secrete bile
   b. to store nutrients
   c. to detoxify chemicals
   d. to compact wastes

3. What is the difference between mechanical digestion and chemical digestion?

4. What happens to the food that you eat when it gets to your stomach?

5. Describe the role of the liver, gallbladder, and pancreas in digestion.

6. Put the following steps of digestion in order.
   a. Food is chewed by the teeth in the mouth.
   b. Water is absorbed by the large intestine.
   c. Food is reduced to chyme in the stomach.
   d. Food moves down the esophagus.
   e. Nutrients are absorbed by the small intestine.
   f. The pancreas releases enzymes.

Critical Thinking

7. **Evaluating Conclusions** Explain the following statement: "Digestion begins in the mouth."

8. **Identifying Relationships** How would the inability to make saliva affect digestion?

Interpreting Graphics

9. Label and describe the function of each of the organs in the diagram below.

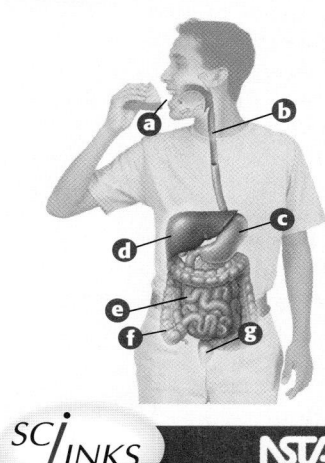

For a variety of links related to this chapter, go to www.scilinks.org

Topic: The Digestive System
SciLinks code: HSM0409

CHAPTER RESOURCES

Chapter Resource File

- **Section Quiz** GENERAL
- **Section Review** GENERAL
- **Vocabulary and Section Summary** GENERAL
- **Critical Thinking** ADVANCED
- **SciLinks Activity** GENERAL
- **Datasheet for Quick Lab**

Answers to Section Review

1. Sample answer: The digestive system breaks down food so that cells can use the nutrients. The large intestine reabsorbs water from digested food. The small intestine absorbs nutrients from digested food.

2. d

3. Mechanical digestion usually involves the crushing and mashing of whole bites of food. Mechanical digestion prepares the food for chemical digestion, which is the process of changing large molecules of food into smaller molecules that can be absorbed into the bloodstream.

4. The contractions of the stomach break food into smaller pieces. Chemical digestion by enzymes, water, and acids breaks bonds in the food molecules.

5. The liver stores nutrients and makes bile, which is used in the digestion of fat. Bile is stored in a small, baglike organ called the gallbladder. The pancreas makes pancreatic juice, which contains enzymes for digesting chyme and contains bicarbonate for neutralizing the acid in chyme.

6. a, d, c, f, e, b

7. Mechanical and chemical digestion begin in the mouth. As you chew, you are physically breaking down food. Saliva contains an enzyme that begins the chemical digestion of carbohydrates.

8. Sample answer: Without saliva, swallowing would be more difficult and the chemical digestion of carbohydrates would not begin until the food reached the stomach.

9. Sample answer: a: The mouth and teeth chew food, beginning mechanical digestion. b: The esophagus squeezes food into the stomach. c: The stomach kneads food and adds acids and enzymes. d: The liver creates bile, which helps break down fat. e: The small intestine absorbs nutrients. f: The large intestine compacts wastes. g: The rectum passes food from the body.

Focus

Overview

This section introduces the structures and the functions of the urinary system. Students will learn how the kidneys filter blood. Students will also learn about some major problems of the urinary system and their causes.

 Bellringer

Tell students that the blood must be cleaned regularly. Then ask students to speculate, without looking in the textbook, how the body cleans blood. Once students have written a description of the cleaning process, allow them to check their answers in their textbook.

Motivate

Discussion ——— GENERAL

Mongolian Gerbils Tell students that Mongolian gerbils are desert animals that never drink. Ask students how they think Mongolian gerbils obtain water. (They get water from the foods they eat.) Ask students how they think the gerbils have adapted to their habitat. (These animals have adapted to use water very efficiently, losing little or none from their lungs, skin, and urine.)

LS Verbal/Logical

READING WARM-UP

Objectives

- Describe the parts and functions of the urinary system.
- Explain how the kidneys filter blood.
- Describe three disorders of the urinary system.

Terms to Learn

urinary system
kidney
nephron

READING STRATEGY

Reading Organizer As you read this section, create an outline of the section. Use the headings from the section in your outline.

The Urinary System

As blood travels through the tissues, it picks up waste produced by the body's cells. Your blood is like a train that comes to town to drop off supplies and take away garbage. If the waste is not removed, your body can actually be poisoned.

Excretion is the process of removing waste products from the body. Three of your body systems have a role in excretion. Your integumentary system releases waste products and water when you sweat. Your respiratory system releases carbon dioxide and water when you exhale. Finally, the **urinary system** contains the organs that remove waste products from your blood.

Cleaning the Blood

As your body performs the chemical activities that keep you alive, waste products, such as carbon dioxide and ammonia, are made. Your body has to get rid of these waste products to stay healthy. The urinary system, shown in **Figure 1,** removes these waste products from the blood.

urinary system the organs that produce, store, and eliminate urine

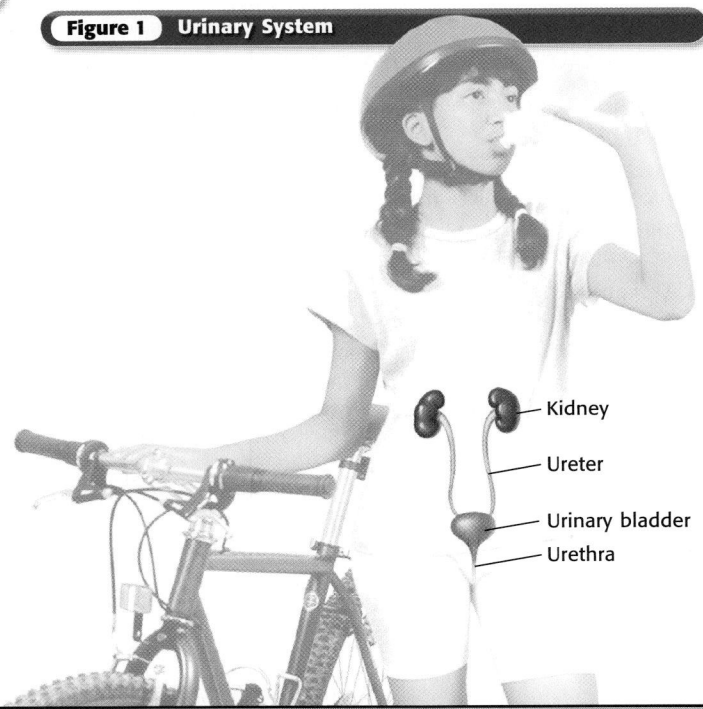

Figure 1 Urinary System

Kidney
Ureter
Urinary bladder
Urethra

CHAPTER RESOURCES

Chapter Resource File

- **Lesson Plan**
- **Directed Reading A** BASIC
- **Directed Reading B** SPECIAL NEEDS

Technology

Transparencies
- Bellringer
- How the Kidneys Filter Blood

SCIENCE HUMOR

Q: What does the kidney say when it plays baseball with the other urinary organs?

A: Bladder up!

The Kidneys as Filters

The **kidneys** are a pair of organs that constantly clean the blood. Your kidneys filter about 2,000 L of blood each day. Your body holds only 5.6 L of blood, so your blood cycles through your kidneys about 350 times per day!

Inside each kidney, shown in **Figure 2,** are more than 1 million nephrons. **Nephrons** are microscopic filters in the kidney that remove wastes from the blood. Nephrons remove many harmful substances. One of the most important substances removed by nephrons is urea (yoo REE uh), which contains nitrogen and is formed when cells use protein for energy.

✔ **Reading Check** How are nephrons related to kidneys? (*See the Appendix for answers to Reading Checks.*)

kidney one of the pair of organs that filter water and wastes from the blood and that excrete products as urine

nephron the unit in the kidney that filters blood

Figure 2   How the Kidneys Filter Blood

❶ A large artery brings blood into each kidney.

❷ Tiny blood vessels branch off the main artery and pass through part of each nephron.

❸ Water and other small substances, such as glucose, salts, amino acids, and urea, are forced out of the blood vessels and into the nephrons.

❹ As these substances flow through the nephrons, most of the water and some nutrients are moved back into blood vessels that wrap around the nephrons. A concentrated mixture of waste materials is left behind in the nephrons.

❺ The cleaned blood, which has slightly less water and much less waste material, leaves each kidney in a large vein to recirculate in the body.

❻ The yellow fluid that remains in the nephrons is called *urine.* Urine leaves each kidney through a slender tube called the *ureter* and flows into the *urinary bladder,* where urine is stored.

❼ Urine leaves the body through another tube called the *urethra. Urination* is the process of expelling urine from the body.

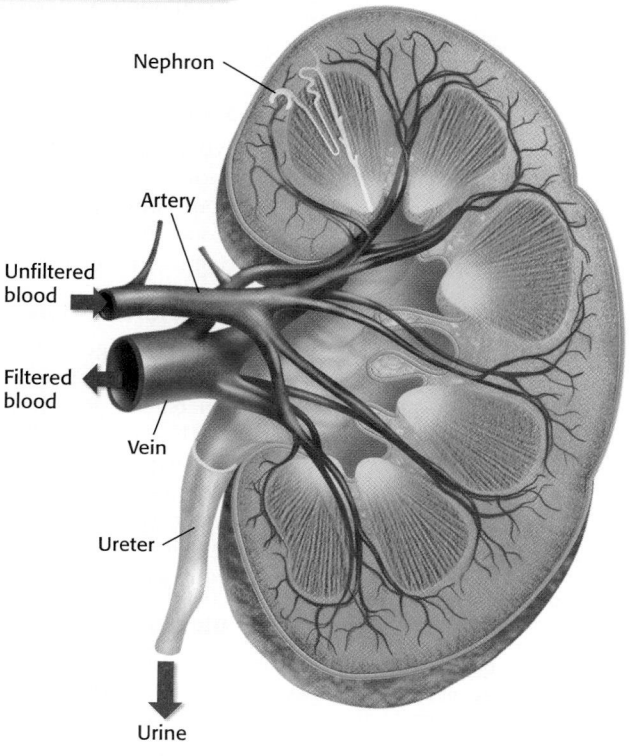

Nephron

Artery

Unfiltered blood

Filtered blood

Vein

Ureter

Urine

Answer to Reading Check
Nephrons are microscopic filters inside the kidney.

Figure 3 *Drinking water when you exercise helps replace the water you lose when you sweat.*

Reteaching — BASIC

Cooling You can demonstrate how sweat helps cool the body. Have students put a few drops of water on one arm. Tell students to blow air on their dry arm and then to blow air over the water on the other arm. Ask students: "Which arm was cooler?" (The arm with water was probably cooler. As the water evaporates from the arm, it takes thermal energy away from the skin on the arm.) **LS Kinesthetic** English Language Learners

Quiz — GENERAL

Ask students whether these statements are true or false.

1. The main function of the urinary system is to remove wastes from the blood. (true)

2. The kidneys are made up of small filtering factories called *ureas*. (false)

Alternative Assessment — GENERAL

Concept Mapping Have students define the new terms in this section and use the terms to construct a concept map. Make sure the maps contain appropriate words and phrases linking the terms. **LS Logical**

Answer to Reading Check

Diuretics are chemicals that cause the kidneys to make more urine.

Water In, Water Out

You drink water every day. You lose water every day in sweat and urine. You need to get rid of as much water as you drink. If you don't, your body will swell up. So, how does your body keep the water levels in balance? The balance of fluids is controlled by chemical messengers in the body called *hormones*.

Sweat and Thirst

When you are too warm, as the boy in **Figure 3** is, you lose a lot of water in the form of sweat. The evaporation of water from your skin cools you down. As the water content of the blood drops, the salivary glands produce less saliva. This is one of the reasons you feel thirsty.

Antidiuretic Hormone

When you get thirsty, other parts of your body react to the water shortage, too. A hormone called *antidiuretic hormone* (AN tee DIE yoo RET ik HAWR MOHN), or ADH, is released. ADH signals the kidneys to take water from the nephrons. The nephrons return the water to the bloodstream. Thus, the kidneys make less urine. When your blood has too much water, small amounts of ADH are released. The kidneys react by allowing more water to stay in the nephrons and leave the body as urine.

Diuretics

Some beverages contain caffeine, which is a *diuretic* (DIE yoo RET ik). Diuretics cause the kidneys to make more urine, which decreases the amount of water in the blood. When you drink a beverage that contains water and caffeine, the caffeine increases fluid loss. So, your body gets to use less of the water from the caffeinated beverage than from a glass of water.

✓ Reading Check What are diuretics?

CONNECTION TO Language Arts

WRITING SKILL **Beverage Ban** During football season, a football coach insists that all members of the team avoid caffeinated beverages. Many of the players are upset by the news. Pretend that you are the coach. Write a letter to the members of the team explaining why it is better for them to drink water than to drink beverages that contain caffeine. Read the letter aloud to members of your family. Ask them how you could make your letter more convincing.

🔵 INCLUSION Strategies

• *Behavior Control Issues* • *Attention Deficit Disorder*
Divide the class into teams of three. Assign these roles within each team: "record keeper," "balloon emptier," and "discharge watcher." Give each team a balloon and a very small pebble. Have students predict how many times out of 5 the "kidney stone" will pass. Tell students:

1. Place the pebble inside the balloon.

2. Have an adult fill the balloon with water.

3. Pinch the neck of the balloon so that the water can spray out in only a small spray.

4. While pinching the neck, empty the balloon into a bowl or bucket.

5. Record whether the pebble came out.

6. Repeat the above steps four times.

7. Compare the results with your predictions. **LS Kinesthetic** English Language Learners

Urinary System Problems

The urinary system regulates body fluids and removes wastes from the blood. Any problems with water regulation can become dangerous for your body. Some common urinary system problems are described below.

- **Bacterial Infections** Bacteria can get into the bladder and ureters through the urethra and cause painful infections. Infections should be treated early, before they spread to the kidneys. Infections in the kidneys can permanently damage the nephrons.

- **Kidney Stones** Sometimes, salts and other wastes collect inside the kidneys and form kidney stones like the one in **Figure 4.** Some kidney stones interfere with urine flow and cause pain. Most kidney stones pass naturally from the body, but sometimes they must be removed by a doctor.

- **Kidney Disease** Damage to nephrons can prevent normal kidney functioning and can lead to kidney disease. If a person's kidneys do not function properly, a kidney machine can be used to filter waste from the blood.

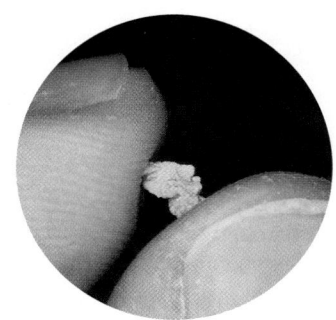

Figure 4 *This kidney stone had to be removed from a patient's urinary system.*

SECTION Review

Summary

- The urinary system removes liquid waste as urine. The filtering structures in the kidney are called *nephrons*.

- Most of the water in the blood is returned to the bloodstream. Urine passes through the ureter, into the bladder, and out of the body through the urethra.

- Disorders of the urinary system include infections, kidney stones, and kidney disease.

Using Key Terms

1. In your own words, write a definition for the term *urinary system*.

Understanding Key Ideas

2. Which event happens first?
   a. Water is absorbed into blood.
   b. A large artery brings blood into the kidney.
   c. Water enters the nephrons.
   d. The nephron separates water from wastes.

3. How do kidneys filter blood?

4. Describe three disorders of the urinary system.

Math Skills

5. A study has shown that 75% of teenage boys drink 34 oz of soda per day. How many 12 oz cans of soda would a boy drink in a week if he drank 34 oz per day?

Critical Thinking

6. **Applying Concepts** Which of the following contains more water: the blood going into the kidney or the blood leaving it?

7. **Predicting Consequences** When people have one kidney removed, their other kidney can often keep their blood clean. But the remaining kidney often changes. Predict how the remaining kidney may change to do the work of two kidneys.

For a variety of links related to this chapter, go to www.scilinks.org
Topic: The Urinary System; Urinary System Ailments
SciLinks code: HSM1583; HSM1584

Developed and maintained by the National Science Teachers Association

CHAPTER RESOURCES

Chapter Resource File
- Section Quiz GENERAL
- Section Review GENERAL
- Vocabulary and Section Summary GENERAL
- Reinforcement Worksheet BASIC

As the Stomach Churns

Teacher's Notes

Time Required

One 45-minute class period and another 15 minutes after 24 hours

Lab Ratings

EASY ——————————→ HARD

Teacher Prep 🧪🧪
Student Set-Up 🧪🧪
Concept Level 🧪🧪
Clean Up 🧪🧪

MATERIALS

The materials listed on the student page are enough for one student or a group of 2–4 students. The two tenderizers should be available at the grocery store. You will need to examine the different brands of powdered or liquid tenderizers. You may substitute fresh papaya or pineapple juices if they are available, if both types of the other tenderizers cannot be found.

Using Scientific Methods

Skills Practice Lab

As the Stomach Churns

The stomach, as you know, performs not only mechanical digestion but also chemical digestion. As the stomach churns, which moves the food particles around, the digestive fluids—acid and enzymes—are added to begin protein digestion.

Commercially prepared meat tenderizers contain enzymes from plants that break down, or digest, proteins. Two types of meat tenderizer are commonly available at grocery stores. One type of tenderizer contains an enzyme called *papain,* from papaya. Another type of tenderizer contains an enzyme called *bromelain,* from pineapple. In this lab, you will test the effects of these two types of meat tenderizers on beef stew meat.

OBJECTIVES

Demonstrate chemical digestion in the stomach.
Investigate three forms of chemical digestion.

MATERIALS

- beef stew meat, 1 cm cubes (3)
- eyedropper
- gloves, protective
- graduated cylinder, 25 mL
- hydrochloric acid, very dilute, 0.1 M
- measuring spoon, 1/4 tsp
- meat tenderizer, commercially prepared, containing bromelain
- meat tenderizer, commercially prepared, containing papain
- tape, masking
- test tubes (4)
- test-tube marker
- test-tube rack
- water

SAFETY

Ask a Question

❶ Determine which question you will answer through your experiment. That question may be one of the following: Which meat tenderizer will work faster? Which one will make the meat more tender? Will the meat tenderizers change the color of the meat or water? What might these color changes, if any, indicate?

Form a Hypothesis

❷ Form a hypothesis from the question you formed in step 1. **Caution:** Do not taste any of the materials in this activity.

Test the Hypothesis

❸ Identify all variables and controls present in your experiment. In your notebook, make a data table that includes these variables and controls. Use this data table to record your observations and results.

❹ Label one test tube with the name of one tenderizer, and label the other test tube with the name of the other tenderizer. Label the third test tube "Control." What will the test tube labeled "Control" contain?

Safety Caution

Remind students to review all safety cautions and icons before beginning this lab activity. Caution students that HCl is a chemical they should handle very carefully. You may choose to dispense the HCl yourself. Tell students that if any HCl comes in contact with their skin, they should wash the area with plenty of water immediately and they should notify you as they wash. Tell students not to taste any materials used in this or any lab.

CHAPTER RESOURCES

Chapter Resource File

- Datasheet for Chapter Lab
- Lab Notes and Answers

Technology

Classroom Videos
- Lab Video

LabBook

- Enzymes in Action

5 Pour 20 mL of water into each test tube.

6 Use the eyedropper to add four drops of very dilute hydrochloric acid to each test tube. **Caution:** Hydrochloric acid can burn your skin. If any acid touches your skin, rinse the area with running water and tell your teacher immediately.

7 Use the measuring spoon to add 1/4 tsp of each meat tenderizer to its corresponding test tube.

8 Add one cube of beef to each test tube.

9 Record your observations for each test tube immediately, after 5 min, after 15 min, after 30 min, and after 24 h.

Analyze the Results

1 **Describing Events** Did you immediately notice any differences in the beef in the three test tubes? At what time interval did you notice a significant difference in the appearance of the beef in the test tubes? Explain the differences.

2 **Examining Data** Did one meat tenderizer perform better than the other? Explain how you determined which performed better.

Draw Conclusions

3 **Evaluating Results** Was your hypothesis supported? Explain your answer.

4 **Applying Conclusions** Many animals that sting have venom composed of proteins. Explain how applying meat tenderizer to the wound helps relieve the pain of such a sting.

Test the Hypothesis

4. The "Control" tube will contain everything that goes into the other tubes except the meat tenderizer.

Analyze the Results

1. There should be very little difference in the three test tubes at first. Differences will be mild until after 24 hours, when a significant difference will be noticed between the "Control" tube and the experimental tubes.

2. Both tenderizers should work in a similar way. If one tenderizer is noted to be more efficient, students should be able to describe how they tested the stew meat to demonstrate the difference.

Draw Conclusions

3. Answers will vary, but students should be able to explain how their hypothesis was supported or how their experimental results did not support their hypothesis.

4. Students may conclude that certain digestive enzymes break down proteins. Breaking down the protein in venom often makes the venom less harmful and less painful. Explain to students that using meat tenderizer on an insect bite is only first aid and is not intended to substitute for medical attention. Emphasize that snakebites require immediate medical attention.

CHAPTER RESOURCES

Workbooks

Whiz-Bang Demonstrations
• Liver Let Live GENERAL

Long-Term Projects & Research Ideas
• Copying the Kidney ADVANCED

Yvonne Brannum
Hine Junior High School
Washington, D.C.

Chapter Review

Assignment Guide

SECTION	QUESTIONS
1	1–2, 5–6, 8, 10–17, 19–26
2	3–4, 7, 9, 18

ANSWERS

Using Key Terms

1. pancreas
2. stomach
3. kidney
4. urinary system
5. digestive system
6. large intestine

Understanding Key Ideas

7. c
8. d
9. c
10. d
11. b
12. a
13. d
14. c
15. a

USING KEY TERMS

Complete each of the following sentences by choosing the correct term from the word bank.

pancreas	digestive system
large intestine	stomach
kidney	small intestine
nephron	urinary system

1 The _____ secretes juices into the small intestine.

2 The saclike organ at the end of the esophagus is called the _____.

3 The _____ is an organ that contains millions of nephrons.

4 A group of organs that removes waste from the blood and excretes it from the body is called the _____.

5 The _____ is a group of organs that work together to break down food.

6 Indigestible material is formed into feces in the _____.

UNDERSTANDING KEY IDEAS

Multiple Choice

7 The hormone that signals the kidneys to make less urine is

a. urea.
b. caffeine.
c. ADH.
d. ATP.

8 Which of the following organs aids digestion by producing bile?

a. stomach
b. pancreas
c. small intestine
d. liver

9 The part of the kidney that filters the blood is the

a. artery.
b. ureter.
c. nephron.
d. urethra.

10 The fingerlike projections that line the small intestine are called

a. emulsifiers.
b. fats.
c. amino acids.
d. villi.

11 Which of the following is NOT part of the digestive tract?

a. mouth
b. kidney
c. stomach
d. rectum

12 The soupy mixture of food, enzymes, and acids in the stomach is called

a. chyme.
b. villi.
c. urea.
d. vitamins.

13 The stomach helps with

a. storing food.
b. chemical digestion.
c. physical digestion.
d. All of the above

14 The gall bladder stores

a. food.
b. urine.
c. bile.
d. villi.

15 The esophagus connects the

a. pharynx to the stomach.
b. stomach to the small intestine.
c. kidneys to the nephrons.
d. stomach to the large intestine.

Short Answer

16 Why is it important for the pancreas to release bicarbonate into the small intestine?

17 How does the structure of the small intestine help the small intestine absorb nutrients?

18 What is a kidney stone?

19 **Concept Mapping** Use the following terms to create a concept map: *teeth, stomach, digestion, bile, saliva, mechanical digestion, gallbladder,* and *chemical digestion.*

20 **Predicting Consequences** How would digestion be affected if the liver were damaged?

21 **Analyzing Processes** When you put a piece of carbohydrate-rich food, such as bread, a potato, or a cracker, into your mouth, the food tastes bland. But if this food sits on your tongue for a while, the food will begin to taste sweet. What digestive process causes this change in taste?

22 **Making Comparisons** The recycling process for one kind of plastic begins with breaking the plastic into small pieces. Next, chemicals are used to break the small pieces of plastic down to its building blocks. Then, those building blocks are used to make new plastic. How is this process both like and unlike human digestion?

INTERPRETING GRAPHICS

The bar graph below shows how long the average meal spends in each portion of your digestive tract. Use the graph below to answer the questions that follow.

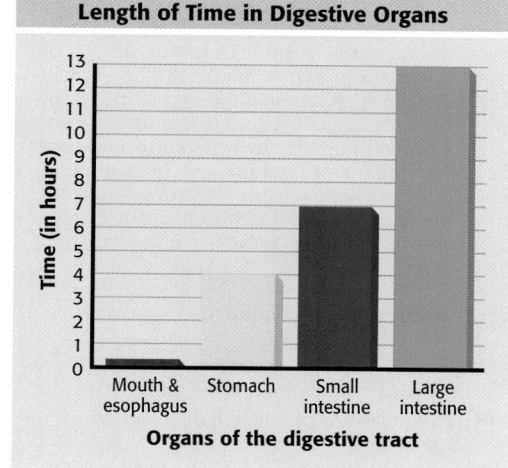

Length of Time in Digestive Organs

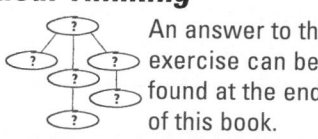

23 In which part of your digestive tract does the food spend the longest amount of time?

24 On average, how much longer does food stay in the small intestine than in the stomach?

25 Which organ mixes food with special substances to make chyme? Approximately how long does food remain in this organ?

26 Bile breaks large fat droplets into very small droplets. How long is the food in your body before it comes into contact with bile?

CHAPTER RESOURCES

Chapter Resource File

- Chapter Review **GENERAL**
- Chapter Test A **GENERAL**
- Chapter Test B **ADVANCED**
- Chapter Test C **SPECIAL NEEDS**
- Vocabulary Activity **GENERAL**

Workbooks

Study Guide
- Assessment resources are also available in Spanish.

---

16. Bicarbonate neutralizes the acidic chyme coming in from the stomach. By neutralizing the acid, the bicarbonate protects the lining of the small intestine.

17. The long length, folds, and villi increase the surface area that comes into contact with the food that is being digested in the small intestine, allowing more nutrients to be absorbed.

18. a stone made of salts and the wastes that sometimes collect in the kidney

Critical Thinking

19. 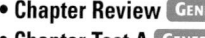 An answer to this exercise can be found at the end of this book.

20. Sample answer: Digestion would be poor. The liver makes bile, which aids in the digestion of fats. If the liver were damaged, it might not make bile, and so the body could not digest fats well.

21. Sample answer: Saliva causes chemical digestion of the carbohydrate-rich food, breaking it down into simple sugars, which taste sweet.

22. Sample answer: The process of breaking down the plastic mechanically and chemically so that its building blocks can be reused is similar to the way the body digests food. But the recycling process does not result in the growth or repair of a living organism, so recycling is different from digestion.

Interpreting Graphics

23. in the large intestine

24. 3 hours

25. The stomach mixes food with enzymes and acid to make a soupy mixture called chyme. Food stays in the stomach for approximately 4 hours.

26. just over 4 hours

Teacher's Note

To provide practice under more realistic testing conditions, give students 20 minutes to answer all of the questions in this Standardized Test Preparation.

MISCONCEPTION ALERT

Answers to the standardized test preparation can help you identify student misconceptions and misunderstandings.

READING

Passage 1

1. D
2. F

 TEST DOCTOR

Question 1: Students may not understand that solutions have higher concentrations when the amount of dissolved material is the same in less liquid. Students may think the reverse is true: increasing the amount of liquid increases the concentration.

Question 2: Only answer F contains information contained in the passage. Though the other answers may be true, they are not facts from the passage.

READING

Read the passage below. Then, read each question that follows the passage. Decide which is the best answer to each question.

Passage 1 When you lose water, your blood becomes <u>more concentrated</u>. Think about how you make a powdered drink, such as lemonade. If you use the same amount of powder in 1 L of water as you do in 2 L of water, the drinks will taste different. The lemonade made with 1 L of water will be stronger because it is more concentrated. Losing water through sweating increases the concentration of sodium and potassium in your blood. The kidneys force the extra potassium out of the blood stream and into nephrons. From the nephrons, the potassium is eliminated from the body in urine.

1. The words *more concentrated* in this passage refer to
   - A the same amount of water with different amounts of material dissolved in it.
   - B small amounts of material dissolved in small amounts of water.
   - C large amounts of material dissolved in large amounts of water.
   - D a given amount of material dissolved in a smaller amount of water.

2. Which of the following statements is a fact from the passage?
   - F Blood contains both potassium and sodium.
   - G Losing too much sodium is dangerous.
   - H Potassium and sodium can be replaced by drinking an exercise drink.
   - I Tears contain sodium.

Passage 2 Three major types of nutrients—<u>carbohydrates</u>, proteins, and fats—make up most of the food you eat. Chemical substances called *enzymes* break these nutrients into smaller particles for the body to use. For example, proteins, which are chains of smaller molecules called *amino acids,* are too large to be absorbed into the bloodstream. So, enzymes cut the chain of amino acids. These amino acids are small enough to pass into the bloodstream to be used by the body.

1. According to the passage, what is a carbohydrate?
   - A an enzyme
   - B a substance made of amino acids
   - C a nutrient
   - D the only substance in a healthy diet

2. Which of the following statements is a fact from the passage?
   - F Carbohydrates, fats, and proteins are three major types of nutrients.
   - G Proteins are made of fats and carbohydrates.
   - H Some enzymes create chains of proteins.
   - I Fats are difficult to digest.

3. Which of the following can be inferred from the passage?
   - A To be useful to the body, nutrients must be small enough to enter the bloodstream.
   - B Carbohydrates are made of amino acids.
   - C Amino acids are made of proteins.
   - D Without enough protein, the body cannot grow.

Passage 2

1. C
2. F
3. A

 TEST DOCTOR

Question 3: In the passage, students are told that proteins need to be broken down because they are too large to be absorbed into the bloodstream. So, students may infer that, to be useful, nutrients have to be small enough to enter the bloodstream.

Use the figure below to answer the questions that follow.

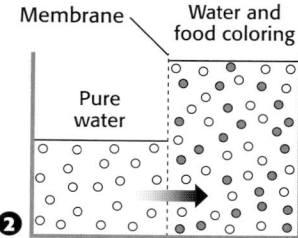

Membrane

Pure water | Water and food coloring

❶

Membrane | Water and food coloring

Pure water

❷

1. The container is divided by a membrane. What can you conclude from the diagram?

 A Water molecules can pass through the membrane.

 B Food-coloring molecules can pass through the membrane.

 C Both water molecules and food-coloring molecules can pass through the membrane.

 D Neither water molecules nor food-coloring molecules can pass through the membrane.

2. If the membrane has holes that separate molecules by size,

 F food-coloring molecules are larger than water molecules.

 G water molecules are larger than food-coloring molecules.

 H water molecules and food-coloring molecules are the same size.

 I the holes are smaller than both water molecules and food-coloring molecules.

3. The concentration of food-coloring molecules in the columns labeled "Water and food coloring"

 A is greater in 2 than in 1.

 B is greater in 1 than in 2.

 C is the same in 1 and 2.

 D cannot change.

MATH

Read each question below, and choose the best answer.

1. Cora is 1.5 m tall. Cora's small intestine is 6 m long. How many times longer is Cora's small intestine than her height?

 A 3 times longer

 B 4 times longer

 C 5 times longer

 D 6 times longer

2. During a water-balance study that was performed for one day, a woman drank 1,500 mL of water. The food she ate contained 750 mL of water, and her body produced 250 mL of water internally during normal body processes. She lost 900 mL of water in sweat, 1,500 mL in urine, and 100 mL in feces. Overall, how much water did she gain or lose during the day?

 F She gained 1,500 mL of water.

 G She lost 900 mL of water.

 H She gained as much water as she lost.

 I She lost twice as much water as she gained.

3. There are 6 blue marbles, 2 red marbles, and 4 green marbles in a bag. If someone selects 1 marble at random from the bag, what is the probability that the marble will be blue?

 A 1/5

 B 1/4

 C 1/3

 D 1/2

Standardized Test Preparation

INTERPRETING GRAPHICS

1. A
2. F
3. B

✚ TEST DOCTOR

Question 1: Students interpreting the graphic may not understand that the arrow indicates that water molecules pass from one side of the membrane to the other. Students also may not realize that some membranes have holes small enough to separate molecules.

Question 3: Students may not realize that as water passes through the membrane, the water is diluting the food coloring. Increasing the number of water molecules without increasing the number of food-coloring molecules decreases the concentration of food-coloring.

MATH

1. B
2. H
3. D

✚ TEST DOCTOR

Question 2: Students struggling with this type of question may benefit from practicing organizing information. This type of gain-and-loss question is best answered by setting up a table with gains in one column and losses in another. After adding up all the gains and losses separately, students can subtract the sum of the losses column from the sum of the gains column. This final number is the net loss or gain. A positive answer represents a gain; a negative answer represents a loss.

CHAPTER RESOURCES

Chapter Resource File

 • **Standardized Test Preparation** GENERAL

State Resources

 For specific resources for your state, visit **go.hrw.com** and type in the keyword **HSMSTR**.

Science in Action

Weird Science

Background

In many parts of the world, dangerous parasitic infections are common health problems. For example, onchocerciasis, or river blindness, is a parasitic disease spread by flies. Worldwide, almost 18 million people suffer from this disease. And dracunculiasis, or Guinea worm disease, is a painful parasitic illness caused by a long, thin worm that infests many tissues and ulcerates the skin as the worm leaves the body.

Science, Technology, and Society

Teaching Strategy—GENERAL

Invite students to brainstorm the ways that doctors diagnose diseases. List their ideas on the board. Have students identify diseases with each diagnostic method. Then have students read the feature and compare this method of diagnosis with the others on their list. Have them discuss the advantages and disadvantages of the pill camera and other diagnostic tools with which they are familiar.

Weird Science

Tapeworms

What if you found out that you had a constant mealtime companion who didn't want just a bite but wanted it all? And what if that companion never asked for your permission? This mealtime companion might be a tapeworm. Tapeworms are invertebrate flatworms. These flatworms are parasites. A parasite is an organism that obtains its food by living in or on another organism. A tapeworm doesn't have a digestive tract of its own. Instead, a tapeworm absorbs the nutrients digested by the host. Some tape worms can grow to be over 10 m long. Cooking beef, pork, and fish properly can help prevent people from getting tapeworms. People or animals who get tapeworms can be treated with medicines.

Social Studies ACTIVITY

WRITING SKILL The World Health Organization and the Pan American Health Organization have made fighting intestinal parasites in children a high priority. Conduct library or Internet research on Worm Busters, which is a program for fighting parasites. Write a brief report of your findings.

Science, Technology, and Society

Pill Cameras

Open wide and say "Ahhhh." When you have a problem with your mouth or teeth, doctors can examine you pretty easily. But when people have problems that are further down their digestive tract, examination becomes more difficult. So, some doctors have recently created a tiny, disposable camera that patients can swallow. As the camera travels down the digestive tract, the camera takes pictures and sends them to a tiny recorder that patients wear on their belt. The camera takes about 57,000 images during its trip. Later, doctors can review the pictures and see the pictures of the patient's entire digestive tract.

Math ACTIVITY

If a pill camera takes 57,000 images while it travels through the digestive system and takes about two pictures per second, how many hours is the camera in the body?

Answer to Social Studies Activity

Sample answer: The Worm Busters program helps eliminate parasites in Latin America. The program provides medicine to millions of children who suffer from intestinal parasites.

Answer to Math Activity

57,000 images at 2 images per second means the camera is in the body for 28,500 seconds, or 475 minutes, or almost 8 hours.

Careers

Christy Krames

Medical Illustrator Christy Krames is a medical illustrator. For 19 years, she has created detailed illustrations of the inner workings of the human body. Medical illustrations allow doctors and surgeons to share concepts, theories, and techniques with colleagues and allow students to learn about the human body.

Medical illustrators often draw tiny structures or body processes that would be difficult or impossible to photograph. For example, a photograph of a small intestine can show the entire organ. But a medical illustrator can add to the photograph an enlarged drawing of the tiny villi inside the intestine. Adding details helps to better explain how small parts of organs work together so that the organs can function.

Medical illustration requires knowledge of both art and science. So, Christy Krames studied both art and medicine in college. Often, Krames must do research before she draws a subject. Her research may include reading books, observing surgical procedures, or even dissecting a pig's heart. This research results in accurate and educational drawings of the inner body.

Language Arts ACTiViTY

WRITING SKILL Pretend you are going to publish an atlas of the human body. Write a classified advertisement to hire medical illustrators. Describe the job, and describe the qualities that the best candidates will have. As you write the ad, remember you are trying to persuade the best illustrators to contact you.

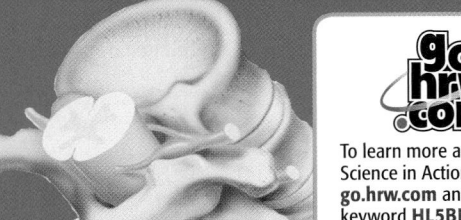

go.hrw.com
To learn more about these Science in Action topics, visit **go.hrw.com** and type in the keyword **HL5BD3F.**

Current Science
Check out Current Science® articles related to this chapter by visiting **go.hrw.com. Just type in the keyword HL5CS24.**

Compression guide:
To shorten instruction because of time limitations, omit Section 2.

OBJECTIVES	LABS, DEMONSTRATIONS, AND ACTIVITIES	TECHNOLOGY RESOURCES
PACING • 90 min pp. 654–663 **Chapter Opener**	SE **Start-up Activity**, p. 655 `GENERAL`	OSP **Parent Letter** ■ `GENERAL` CD **Student Edition on CD-ROM** CD **Guided Reading Audio CD** ▧ TR **Chapter Starter Transparency*** VID **Brain Food Video Quiz**
Section 1 The Nervous System • Describe the relationship between the central nervous system and the peripheral nervous system. • Compare the somatic nervous system with the autonomic nervous system. • List one function of each part of the brain.	TE **Activity** Nerve Cells and Other Cells, p. 657 `ADVANCED` TE **Group Activity** Simulating Neuronal Impulses, p. 658 `BASIC` TE **Group Activity** Model the PNS, p. 659 `ADVANCED` TE **Group Activity** Reteaching the Brain, p. 660 `BASIC` TE **Connection Activity** Language Arts, p. 661 `GENERAL` TE **Connection Activity** Real World, p. 661 `GENERAL` SE **Quick Lab** Building a Neuron, p. 662 ◆ `GENERAL` CRF **Datasheet for Quick Lab***	CRF **Lesson Plans*** TR **Bellringer Transparency*** TR **A Typical Neuron*** TR **What Is a Nerve?*** TR **Regions of the Brain*** TR **The Spinal Cord*** CRF **SciLinks Activity*** `GENERAL`
PACING • 90 min pp. 664–669 **Section 2 Responding to the Environment** • List five sensations that are detected by receptors in the skin. • Describe how a feedback mechanism works. • Describe how light relates to sight. • Describe how the senses of hearing, taste, and smell work.	TE **Group Activity** Losing Your Senses, p. 664 `GENERAL` TE **Activity** "Ol' Three Eyes," p. 665 `BASIC` TE **Activity** Do You Hear Colors?, p. 665 `ADVANCED` TE **Activity** Pupil Action, p. 666 ◆ `GENERAL` SE **Quick Lab** Where's the Dot?, p. 667 `GENERAL` CRF **Datasheet for Quick Lab*** SE **Connection to Physics**, p. 668 `GENERAL` SE **Skills Practice Lab** You've Gotta Lotta Nerve, p. 674 ◆ `GENERAL` CRF **Datasheet for Chapter Lab*** LB **Whiz-Bang Demonstrations** Now You See It, Now You Don't* ◆ `GENERAL` LB **Labs You Can Eat** A Salty Sweet Experiment* ◆ `GENERAL`	CRF **Lesson Plans*** TR **Bellringer Transparency*** TR ***LINK TO PHYSICAL SCIENCE*** Measuring Wavelengths; Measuring Frequency*** SE **Internet Activity**, p. 666 `GENERAL` VID **Lab Videos for Life Science**
PACING • 45 min pp. 670–673 **Section 3 The Endocrine System** • Explain why the endocrine system is important to the body. • Identify five glands of the endocrine system, and describe what their hormones do. • Describe how feedback mechanisms stop and start hormone release. • Name two hormone imbalances.	SE **Connection to Language Arts** Fight or Flight?, p. 671 `GENERAL` LB **Long-Term Projects & Research Ideas** Man Versus Machine* ◆ `ADVANCED` SE **Science in Action** Math, Social Studies, and Language Arts Activities, pp. 680–681 `GENERAL`	CRF **Lesson Plans*** TR **Bellringer Transparency***

PACING • 90 min

CHAPTER REVIEW, ASSESSMENT, AND STANDARDIZED TEST PREPARATION

CRF **Vocabulary Activity*** `GENERAL`
SE **Chapter Review**, pp. 676–677 `GENERAL`
CRF **Chapter Review*** ■ `GENERAL`
CRF **Chapter Tests A*** `GENERAL`, **B*** `ADVANCED`, **C*** `SPECIAL NEEDS`
SE **Standardized Test Preparation**, pp. 678–679 `GENERAL`
CRF **Standardized Test Preparation*** `GENERAL`
CRF **Performance-Based Assessment*** `GENERAL`
OSP **Test Generator** `GENERAL`
CRF **Test Item Listing*** `GENERAL`

Online and Technology Resources

Visit **go.hrw.com** for a variety of free resources related to this textbook. Enter the keyword **HL5BD4**.

Holt Online Learning

Students can access interactive problem-solving help and active visual concept development with the *Holt Science and Technology* Online Edition available at **www.hrw.com.**

 Guided Reading Audio CD
Also in Spanish

A direct reading of each chapter for auditory learners, reluctant readers, and Spanish-speaking students.

 Science Tutor CD-ROM

Excellent for remediation and test practice.

KEY

SE Student Edition
TE Teacher Edition

CRF Chapter Resource File
OSP One-Stop Planner
LB Lab Bank
TR Transparencies

SS Science Skills Worksheets
MS Math Skills for Science Worksheets
CD CD or CD-ROM
VID Classroom Video/DVD

* Also on One-Stop Planner
◆ Requires advance prep
■ Also available in Spanish

SKILLS DEVELOPMENT RESOURCES	SECTION REVIEW AND ASSESSMENT	STANDARDS CORRELATIONS
SE **Pre-Reading Activity**, p. 654 GENERAL OSP **Science Puzzlers, Twisters & Teasers** GENERAL		National Science Education Standards SAI 1; HNS 3; LS 1e
CRF **Directed Reading A*** ■ BASIC, **B*** SPECIAL NEEDS CRF **Vocabulary and Section Summary*** ■ GENERAL SE **Reading Strategy** Discussion, p. 656 GENERAL SE **Math Practice** Time to Travel, p. 657 GENERAL TE **Reading Strategy** Formulating Questions, p. 657 BASIC TE **Inclusion Strategies**, p. 657 SE **Connection to Chemistry** Keeping Your Balance, p. 659 GENERAL TE **Reading Strategy** Prediction Guide, p. 660 GENERAL CRF **Reinforcement Worksheet** This System is Just "Two" Nervous!* BASIC	SE **Reading Checks**, pp. 656, 657, 658, 659, 660, 661, 662 GENERAL TE **Homework**, p. 660 GENERAL TE **Homework**, p. 661 BASIC TE **Reteaching**, p. 662 BASIC TE **Quiz**, p. 662 GENERAL TE **Alternative Assessment**, p. 662 GENERAL SE **Section Review,*** p. 663 ■ GENERAL CRF **Section Quiz*** ■ GENERAL	UCP 1, 2, 3, 4, 5; SAI 1, 2; SPSP 1; LS 1a, 1d, 1e, 3a, 3b, 3c
CRF **Directed Reading A*** ■ BASIC, **B*** SPECIAL NEEDS CRF **Vocabulary and Section Summary*** ■ GENERAL SE **Reading Strategy** Reading Organizer, p. 664 GENERAL MS **Math Skills for Science** Multiplying and Dividing in Scientific Notation* ADVANCED CRF **Reinforcement Worksheet** The Eyes Have It* BASIC CRF **Critical Thinking** There's a Microchip in My Eye!* ADVANCED	SE **Reading Checks**, pp. 664, 665, 666, 667, 668 GENERAL TE **Homework**, p. 665 ADVANCED TE **Reteaching**, p. 668 BASIC TE **Quiz**, p. 668 GENERAL TE **Alternative Assessment**, p. 668 GENERAL SE **Section Review,*** p. 669 ■ GENERAL CRF **Section Quiz*** ■ GENERAL	UCP 2, 4, 5; SAI 1; LS 1a, 1d, 1e, 3a; *Chapter Lab:* UCP 2; SAI 1; LS 3a
CRF **Directed Reading A*** ■ BASIC, **B*** SPECIAL NEEDS CRF **Vocabulary and Section Summary*** ■ GENERAL SE **Reading Strategy** Discussion, p. 670 GENERAL TE **Inclusion Strategies**, p. 672 CRF **Reinforcement Worksheet** Every Gland Lends a Hand* BASIC	SE **Reading Checks**, pp. 671, 672 GENERAL TE **Reteaching**, p. 672 BASIC TE **Quiz**, p. 672 GENERAL TE **Alternative Assessment**, p. 672 GENERAL SE **Section Review,*** p. 673 ■ GENERAL TE **Homework**, p. 673 GENERAL CRF **Section Quiz*** ■ GENERAL	UCP 1; LS 1e, 1f, 3a, 3b, 3c

One-Stop Planner® CD-ROM

This convenient CD-ROM includes:
• Lab Materials QuickList Software
• Holt Calendar Planner
• Customizable Lesson Plans
• Printable Worksheets
• ExamView® Test Generator

cnnstudentnews.com

Find the latest news, lesson plans, and activities related to important scientific events.

www.scilinks.org

Maintained by the **National Science Teachers Association.** See Chapter Enrichment pages for a complete list of topics.

Current Science®

Check out *Current Science* articles and activities by visiting the HRW Web site at **go.hrw.com.** Just type in the keyword **HL5CS25T.**

Classroom Videos

• **Lab Videos** demonstrate the chapter lab.
• **Brain Food Video Quizzes** help students review the chapter material.
• **CNN Videos** bring science into your students' daily life.

Visual Resources

CHAPTER STARTER TRANSPARENCY

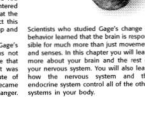

This Really Happened!

About 150 years ago, a bizarre accident changed the way scientists view the role of the brain. The accident involved a railroad worker named Phineas Gage. One day in 1848, Gage was using a long metal rod to pack explosives into a hole to clear a path for some railroad track. A spark caused an explosion that blew the rod through Gage's head. The rod entered through his left cheek and exited at the top of his skull. You would expect this injury to be fatal, but Gage stood up and was able to speak.

In a little over 2 months, Gage's wounds were healed, but he was not quite the same. The Phineas Gage that people knew before the accident was calm, responsible, and considerate of others. But after the accident he became irresponsible and quick to anger.

The arrow shows the path of the tamping rod.

BELLRINGER TRANSPARENCIES

Section: The Nervous System
List as many functions of the brain as you can. Don't forget that in addition to controlling your body, your brain is also occupied with thinking. How do you suppose your brain can coordinate all these functions?

Record your ideas in your **science journal**.

Section: Responding to the Environment
List the five senses, and draw the organ associated with each sense. Then, list an object detected by more than one of the senses? How could it be helpful to use more than one sense to get information about an object?

Record your answers in your **science journal**.

TEACHING TRANSPARENCIES

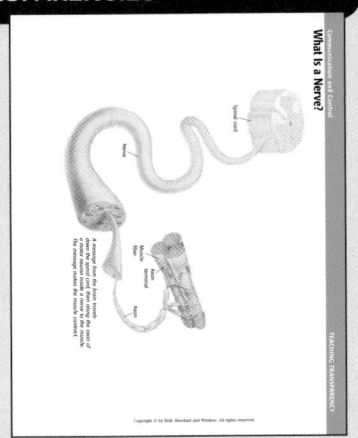

A Typical Neuron

What Is a Nerve?

TEACHING TRANSPARENCIES

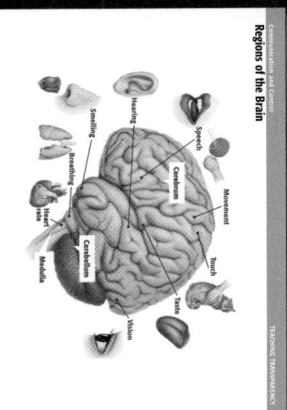

Regions of the Brain

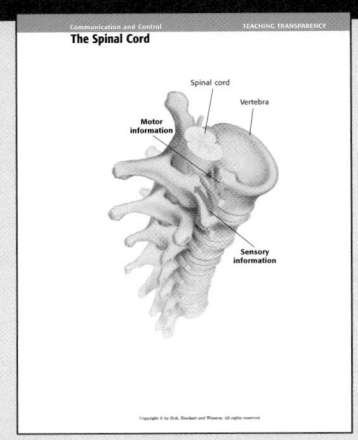

The Spinal Cord

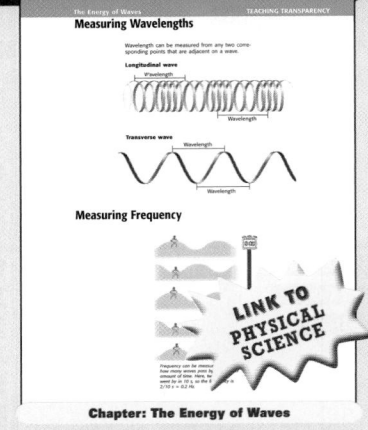

Measuring Wavelengths

Measuring Frequency

LINK TO PHYSICAL SCIENCE

Chapter: The Energy of Waves

CONCEPT MAPPING TRANSPARENCY

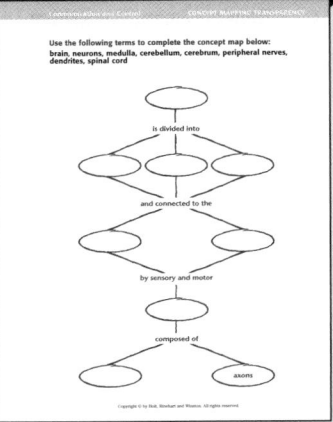

Use the following terms to complete the concept map below: brain, neurons, medulla, cerebellum, cerebrum, peripheral nerves, dendrites, spinal cord.

Planning Resources

LESSON PLANS

Lesson Plan   SAMPLE

Section: Waves

Pacing

Regular Schedule: with lab(s):2 days   without lab(s):2 days
Block Schedule: with lab(s): 1 1/2 days without lab(s):1 day

Objectives
1. Relate the seven properties of life to a living organism.
2. Describe seven themes that can help you to organize what you learn about biology.
3. Identify the tiny structures that make up all living organisms.
4. Differentiate between reproduction and heredity and between metabolism and homeostasis.

National Science Education Standards Covered
LSInter6:Cells have particular structures that underlie their functions.
LSMat1:Most cell functions involve chemical reactions.
LSBeh1:Cells store and use information to guide their functions.
UCP1:Cell functions are regulated.
SI1: Cells can differentiate and form complete multicellular organisms.
PS1: Species evolve over time.
ESS1: The great diversity of organisms is the result of more than 3.5 billion years of evolution.
ESS2: Natural selection and its evolutionary consequences provide a scientific explanation for the fossil record of ancient life forms as well as for the striking molecular similarities observed among the diverse species of living organisms.
ST1: The millions of different species of plants, animals, and microorganisms that live on Earth today are related by descent from common ancestors.
ST2: The energy for life primarily comes from the sun.
SPSP1: The complexity and organization of organisms accommodates the need for obtaining, transforming, transporting, releasing, and eliminating the matter and energy used to sustain the organism.
SPSP6: As matter and energy flows through different levels of organization of living systems—cells, organs, communities—and between living systems and the physical environment, chemical elements are recombined in different ways.
HNS1: Organisms have behavioral responses to internal changes and to external stimuli.

PARENT LETTER

SAMPLE

Dear Parent,

Your son's or daughter's science class will soon begin exploring the chapter entitled "The World of Physical Science." In this chapter, students will learn about how the scientific method applies to the world of physical science and the role of physical science in the world. By the end of the chapter, students should demonstrate a clear understanding of the chapter's main ideas and be able to discuss the following topics:

1. physical science as the study of energy and matter (Section 1)
2. the role of physical science in the world around them (Section 1)
3. careers that rely on physical science (Section 1)
4. the steps used in the scientific method (Section 2)
5. examples of technology (Section 2)
6. how the scientific method is used to answer questions and solve problems (Section 2)
7. how our knowledge of science changes over time (Section 2)
8. how models represent real objects or systems (Section 3)
9. examples of different ways models are used in science (Section 3)
10. the importance of the International System of Units (Section 4)
11. the appropriate units to use for physical measurements (Section 4)
12. how area and density are derived quantities (Section 4)

Questions to Ask Along the Way

You can help your son or daughter learn about these topics by asking interesting questions such as the following:
- What are some surprising careers that use physical science?
- What is a characteristic of a good hypothesis?
- When is it a good idea to use a model?
- Why do Americans measure things in terms of inches and yards and meters ?

ALSO IN SPANISH

TEST ITEM LISTING

TEST ITEM LISTING
The World of Science   SAMPLE

MULTIPLE CHOICE

1. A limitation of models is that
   a. they are large enough to see.
   b. they do not act exactly like the things that they model.
   c. they are smaller than the things that they model.
   d. they model unfamiliar things.
   Answer: B   Difficulty: 1   Section: 3   Objective: 2

2. The length 10 m is equal to:
   a. 100 cm.   c. 10,000 mm.
   b. 1,000 cm   d. Both (b) and (c)
   Answer: B   Difficulty: 1   Section: 3   Objective: 2

3. To be valid, a hypothesis must be
   a. testable.   c. made into a law.
   b. supported by evidence. d. Both (a) and (b)
   Answer: B   Difficulty: 1   Section: 2   Objective: 2 1

4. The statement "Sheila has a stain on her shirt" is an example of a(n)
   a. law.   c. observation.
   b. hypothesis.   d. prediction.
   Answer: B   Difficulty: 1   Section: 3   Objective: 2

5. A hypothesis is often developed out of
   a. observations.   c. laws.
   b. experiments.   d. Both (a) and (b)
   Answer: B   Difficulty: 1   Section: 3   Objective: 2

6. How many milliliters are in 3.5 kL?
   a. 3,500 mL   c. 3,500, 000 mL
   b. 0.0035 mL   d. 35,000 mL
   Answer: B   Difficulty: 1   Section: 3   Objective: 2

7. A map of Seattle is an example of a
   a. law.   c. model.
   b. theory.   d. unit.
   Answer: B   Difficulty: 1   Section: 3   Objective: 2

8. A lab has the safety icons shown below. These icons mean that you should wear
   a. only safety goggles.   c. safety goggles and a lab apron.
   b. only a lab apron.   d. safety goggles, a lab apron, and gloves.
   Answer: B   Difficulty: 1   Section: 3   Objective: 2

9. The law of conservation of mass says the tot al mass before a chemical change is
   a. more than the total mass after the change.
   b. less than the total mass after the change.
   c. the same as the total mass after the change.
   d. not the same as the total mass after the change.
   Answer: B   Difficulty: 1   Section: 3   Objective: 2

10. In which of the following areas might you find a geochemist at work?
    a. studying the chemistry of rocks   c. studying fishes
    b. studying forestry   d. studying the atmosphere
    Answer: B   Difficulty: 1   Section: 3   Objective: 2

One-Stop Planner® CD-ROM

This CD-ROM includes all of the resources shown here and the following time-saving tools:

- *Lab Materials QuickList Software*
- *Customizable lesson plans*
- *Holt Calendar Planner*
- *The powerful ExamView® Test Generator*

Meeting Individual Needs

DIRECTED READING A
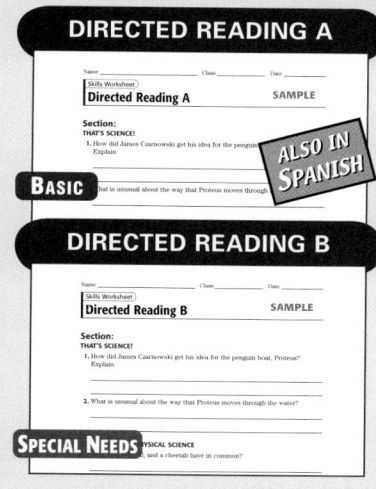
BASIC — ALSO IN SPANISH

VOCABULARY ACTIVITY
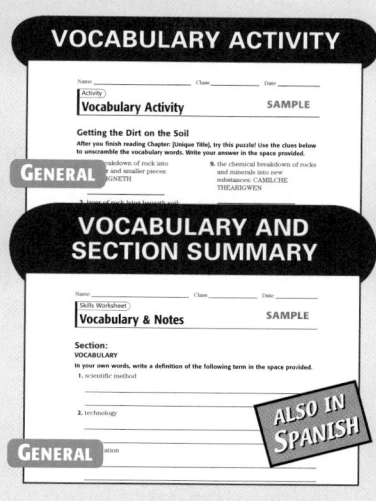
GENERAL

REINFORCEMENT
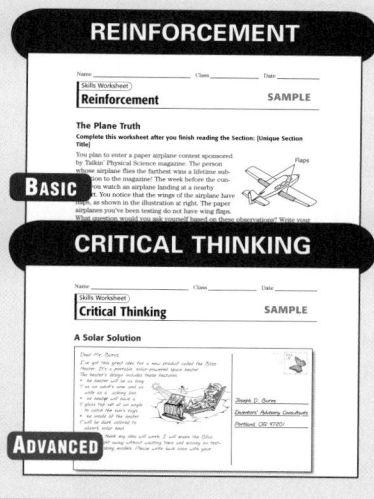
BASIC

SCILINKS ACTIVITY

GENERAL

DIRECTED READING B
SPECIAL NEEDS

VOCABULARY AND SECTION SUMMARY
GENERAL — ALSO IN SPANISH

CRITICAL THINKING
ADVANCED

SCIENCE PUZZLERS, TWISTERS & TEASERS
GENERAL

Labs and Activities

LONG-TERM PROJECTS & RESEARCH IDEAS
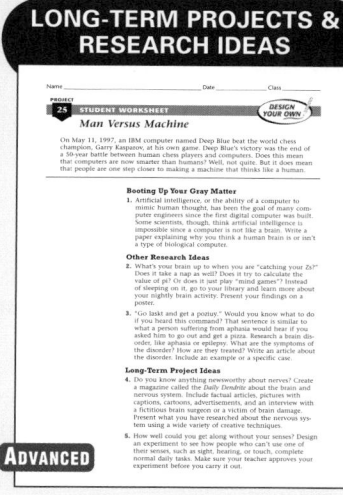
ADVANCED

WHIZ-BANG DEMONSTRATIONS
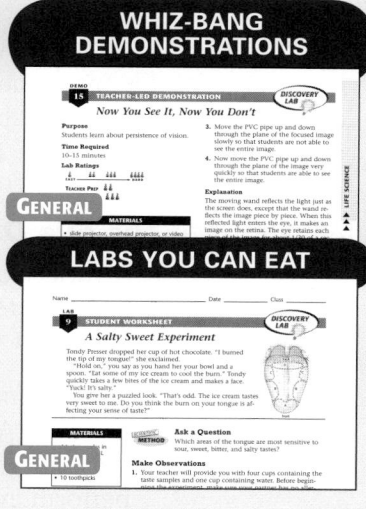
GENERAL

LABS YOU CAN EAT
GENERAL

DATASHEETS FOR QUICK LABS

DATASHEETS FOR CHAPTER LABS

DATASHEETS FOR LABBOOK

Review and Assessments

SECTION QUIZ
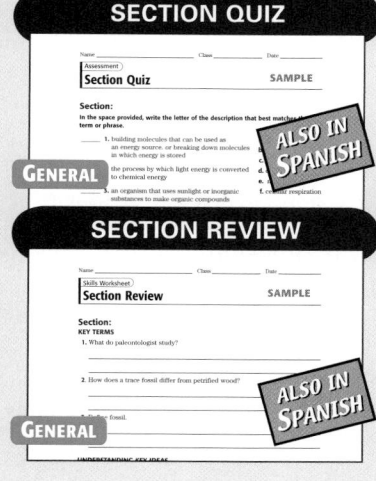
GENERAL — ALSO IN SPANISH

CHAPTER REVIEW
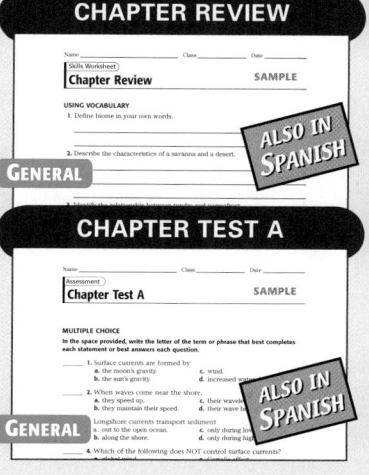
GENERAL — ALSO IN SPANISH

CHAPTER TEST B
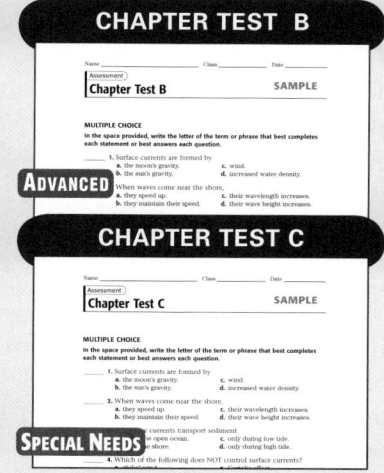
ADVANCED

STANDARDIZED TEST PREPARATION
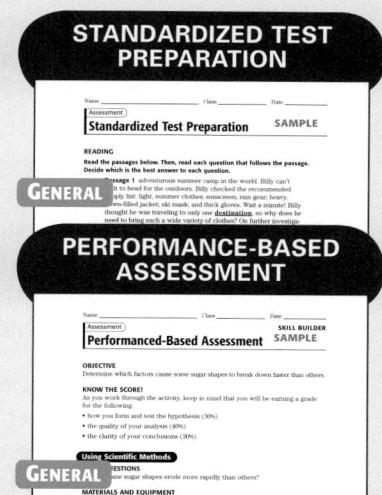
GENERAL

SECTION REVIEW
GENERAL — ALSO IN SPANISH

CHAPTER TEST A
GENERAL — ALSO IN SPANISH

CHAPTER TEST C
SPECIAL NEEDS

PERFORMANCE-BASED ASSESSMENT
GENERAL

This Chapter Enrichment provides relevant and interesting information to expand and enhance your presentation of the chapter material.

Section 1

The Nervous System

The Brain

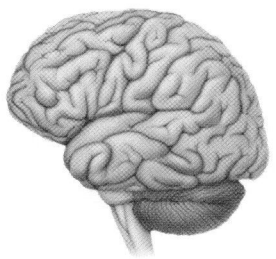

- The cerebral cortex is the main part of the exterior surface of the brain. The surface area of the brain is about 1,500 cm² to 2,000 cm², or about the size of 1 to 2 pages of a newspaper. To fit within the skull, the cortex is folded, forming *gyri* (folds) and *sulci* (grooves). Several large sulci divide the cortex into lobes: the frontal lobe, parietal lobe, occipital lobe, and temporal lobe. Each lobe has a different function.

- Computerized scanning techniques allow physicians to observe the brain in action and to detect brain abnormalities. Scanning techniques include CAT scanning, MRI scanning, radionucleotide scanning, ultrasound scanning, and PET scanning.

Is That a Fact!

◆ The cerebral cortex makes up more than 80% of the total human brain mass.

The Spinal Cord

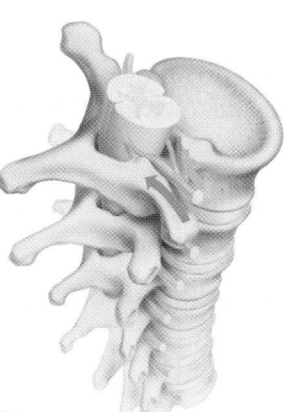

- Like the brain, the spinal cord contains both gray matter and white matter. The center of the spinal cord is made up of neuron cell bodies and is called *gray matter*. The outer layer of the spinal cord is made up of axons that traverse the spinal cord. This outer part of the spinal cord is called *white matter*.

- The spinal cord is protected by 25 bones, including the vertebrae and the sacrum. These bones are connected by joints and are separated by cartilaginous disks.

Section 2

Responding to the Environment

Hearing Loss

- There are two principal kinds of deafness: conductive deafness and sensorineural deafness.

- Conductive deafness results when transmission of sound from the outer ear to the inner ear fails. It may occur as a result of earwax buildup or damage to the middle ear.

- Sensorineural deafness results when sounds reach the inner ear but are not transmitted to the brain because of damaged inner ear structures or damaged nerves that carry information from the ear to the brain.

Is That a Fact!

◆ Sensorineural deafness occurs in 1 out of every 1,000 babies.

The Eye Doctor

- A variety of healthcare professionals have qualifications to treat different aspects of eye disorders and to correct vision problems.

- Ophthalmologists are physicians who specialize in the eyes. An ophthalmologist can examine eyes, prescribe corrective lenses, treat eye disorders, and perform eye surgery.

- An optometrist can examine and test eyes and can prescribe corrective lenses in the form of glasses or contact lenses.

- An optician may only fit and adjust glasses and contact lenses.

Is That a Fact!

◆ Using contact lenses to correct poor vision was first recorded in 1508 by Leonardo da Vinci (1452–1519).

◆ The first contact lens was made of glass. It covered the entire frontal surface of the eyeball. This first contact lens was made by Adolf Fick in 1887.

The Sense of Taste

- The water and enzymes in saliva break down the food and drink that we consume into small molecules and ions. After passing through pores in the taste buds, these molecules and ions stimulate small nerve endings, which send messages to the brain. These messages form our sense of taste.

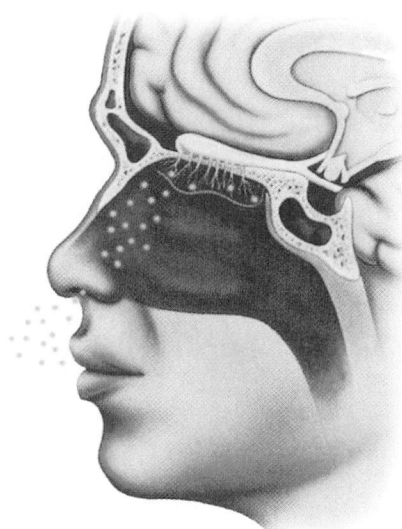

- People often lose their sense of taste when they lose their sense of smell. This loss occurs when olfactory bulbs are damaged or when the person has a stuffy nose. It is rare for a person to maintain the sense of smell and to lose the sense of taste.

Section 3

The Endocrine System

Exocrine and Endocrine Glands

- There are two main types of glands in the body: exocrine glands and endocrine glands. Exocrine glands, such as sweat glands and salivary glands, secrete substances through ducts to a local area.

- Unlike exocrine glands, endocrine glands secrete substances directly into the bloodstream (no ducts are involved). The substances secreted by endocrine glands—called hormones—are carried by the bloodstream to all parts of the body. A hormone may affect just a few cells or may have an effect on several organs or tissues.

The Pituitary Gland

- The pituitary gland is often called the *master gland* because its secretions regulate several other endocrine glands.

- About 10% of brain tumors affect the pituitary gland. Although usually benign, these tumors can have a great effect on the body because they can affect the production of the pituitary hormones.

- Because of the pituitary gland's location in the brain, enlargement of the gland can cause vision disorders by creating pressure on the optic nerve.

Diabetes

- The term *diabetes* refers to more than one disorder. The three kinds of diabetes include *diabetes insipidus* (a rare condition) and two types of *diabetes mellitus* (called *type 1* and *type 2 diabetes*). Type 1 diabetes requires regular injections of insulin. Type 2 diabetes can often be controlled by changes in diet and plenty of exercise, although insulin injections may be necessary.

Is That a Fact!

- ◆ Approximately one in every 400 to 500 children and adolescents in the United States has type 1 diabetes.

- ◆ About 16.9 million people age 20 years or older have diabetes. Of these 16.9 million people, 90% to 95% have type 2 diabetes.

SciLINKS. | NSTA
Developed and maintained by the National Science Teachers Association

SciLinks is maintained by the National Science Teachers Association to provide you and your students with interesting, up-to-date links that will enrich your classroom presentation of the chapter.

Visit www.scilinks.org and enter the SciLinks code for more information about the topic listed.

Topic: Nervous System
SciLinks code: HSM1023

Topic: Sensory Receptors
SciLinks code: HSM1379

Topic: The Senses
SciLinks code: HSM1378

Topic: Hormones
SciLinks code: HSM0758

Topic: The Eye
SciLinks code: HSM0560

Topic: Endocrine System
SciLinks code: HSM0504

Overview

In this chapter, students will learn how the body receives, processes, and responds to information. The chapter describes the nervous system and how senses respond to stimuli. The chapter also describes how the endocrine system is part of the body's communication and control system.

Assessing Prior Knowledge

Students should be familiar with the following topics:

- cells and the activities of cells
- sensory interactions with the environment
- body structure and organization

Identifying Misconceptions

Some students may be confused about the different levels of the nervous system. A large diagram or other visual aid may help you teach this chapter by showing the central and peripheral nervous systems and the parts of the peripheral nervous system. Also, many students associate a stimulus with its source (i.e., light comes from the bulb) and do not understand that some stimuli travel as energy from one place to another. So, students may have difficulty understanding how vision works.

25
Communication and Control

About the PHOTO

This picture may look like it shows a flower garden or a coral reef. But it really shows something much closer to home. It shows the human tongue (magnified thousands of times, of course). Those round bumps are taste buds. You use taste and other senses to gather information about your surroundings.

PRE-READING ACTIVITY

Graphic Organizer

Concept Map Before you read the chapter, create the graphic organizer entitled "Concept Map" described in the **Study Skills** section of the Appendix. As you read the chapter, fill in the concept map with details about each part or division of the nervous system. Include details about what each part or division does.

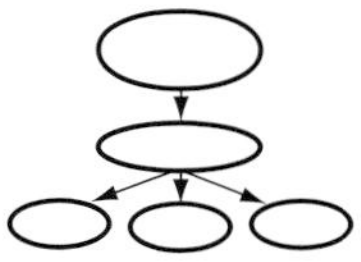

Standards Correlations

National Science Education Standards

The following codes indicate the National Science Education Standards that correlate to this chapter. The full text of the standards is at the front of the book.

Chapter Opener
SAI 1; HNS 3; LS 1e

Section 1 The Nervous System
UCP 1, 2, 3, 4, 5; SAI 1, 2; SPSP 1; LS 1a, 1d, 1e, 3a, 3b, 3c

Section 2 Responding to the Environment
UCP 2, 4, 5; SAI 1; LS 1a, 1d, 1e, 3a

Section 3 The Endocrine System
UCP 1; LS 1e, 1f, 3a, 3b, 3c

Chapter Lab
UCP 2; SAI 1; LS 3a

Chapter Review
UCP 1; LS 1a, 1d, 1e, 3b

Science in Action
UCP 2; SAI 2; ST 2; SPSP 4, 5; HNS 1, 2; LS 1a, 1d, 1e, 3a, 3b, 3c

Safety Caution: Remind students to handle the meterstick carefully and to keep it away from their face and far away from the faces and eyes of their classmates.

Teacher's Notes: Allow students to have a practice trial. Instruct students to look only at the ruler and not at their partner. Point out that looking at their partner could distort the results of the investigation because the partner might give a clue about when he or she will drop the meterstick.

Answers

1. Sample answer: I am right handed, and I use each hand differently. Each hand has different abilities.

2. Sample answer: One person might respond more quickly than another depending on how rested a person is, how well a person can concentrate on the activity, and how strong a person's hands are.

START-UP ACTIVITY

Act Fast!

If you want to catch an object, your brain sends a message to the muscles in your arm. In this exercise, you will see how long sending that message takes.

Procedure

1. Sit in a **chair** with one arm in a "handshake" position. Your partner should stand facing you, holding a **meterstick** vertically. The stick should be positioned so that it will fall between your thumb and fingers.

2. Tell your partner to let go of the meterstick without warning you. Catch the stick between your thumb and fingers. Your partner should catch the meterstick if it tips over.

3. Record the number of centimeters that the stick dropped before you caught it. That distance represents your reaction time.

4. Repeat steps 1–3 three times. Calculate the average distance.

5. Repeat steps 1–4 with your other hand.

6. Trade places with your partner, and repeat steps 1–5.

Analysis

1. Compare the reaction times of your own hands. Why might one hand react more quickly than the other?

2. Compare your results with your partner's. Why might one person react more quickly than another?

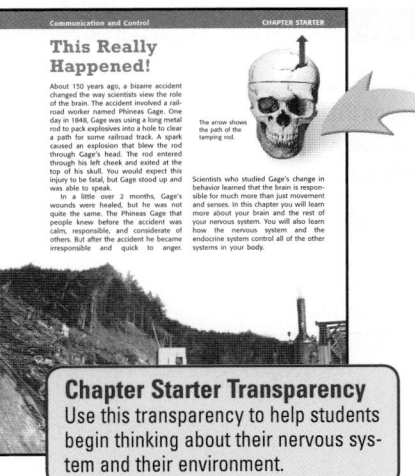

Communication and Control — **CHAPTER STARTER**

This Really Happened!

About 150 years ago, a bizarre accident changed the way scientists view the role of the brain. The accident involved a railroad worker named Phineas Gage. One day in 1848, Gage was using a long metal rod to pack explosives into a hole to clear a path for some railroad track. A spark caused an explosion that blew the rod through Gage's head. The rod entered through his left cheek and exited at the top of his skull. You would expect this injury to be fatal, but Gage stood up and was able to speak.

In a little over 2 months, Gage's wounds were healed, but he was not quite the same. The Phineas Gage that people knew before the accident was calm, responsible, and considerate of others. But after the accident he became irresponsible and quick to anger.

The arrow shows the path of the tamping rod.

Scientists who studied Gage's change in behavior learned that the brain is responsible for much more than just movement and senses. In this chapter you will learn more about your brain and the rest of your nervous system. You will also learn how the nervous system and the endocrine system control all of the other systems in your body.

Chapter Starter Transparency
Use this transparency to help students begin thinking about their nervous system and their environment.

CHAPTER RESOURCES

Technology

 **Transparencies**
- Chapter Starter Transparency

READING SKILLS

 Student Edition on CD-ROM

 **Guided Reading Audio CD**
- English or Spanish

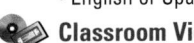 **Classroom Videos**
- Brain Food Video Quiz

Workbooks

 Science Puzzlers, Twisters & Teasers
- Communication and Control GENERAL

Focus

Overview

This section introduces the structures and functions of the nervous system. Students will learn the differences between the central nervous system and the peripheral nervous system, and will learn about the parts of the peripheral nervous system.

 Bellringer

Have students list as many different functions of the brain as they can. Have students predict how the brain coordinates all the different activities.

Motivate

Discussion ——— GENERAL

Reacting to Stimuli Ask students to describe a time when they reacted quickly to something. Have them describe not only what happened but also how quickly they were able to react and what they were thinking about as they reacted. Sample experiences include jerking a hand away from a hot object, quickly catching a falling object, and extending one's hand out to brace for a fall. Based on students' experiences, lead a discussion about how quickly the nervous system is able to respond to a stimulus.

LS Intrapersonal

READING WARM-UP

Objectives
- Describe the relationship between the central nervous system and the peripheral nervous system.
- Compare the somatic nervous system with the autonomic nervous system.
- List one function of each part of the brain.

Terms to Learn
central nervous system
peripheral nervous system
neuron
nerve
brain

READING STRATEGY

Discussion Read this section silently. Write down questions that you have about this section. Discuss your questions in a small group.

central nervous system (CNS) the brain and the spinal cord

peripheral nervous system (PNS) all of the parts of the nervous system except for the brain and the spinal cord

The Nervous System

Which of the following activities do NOT involve your nervous system: eating, playing a musical instrument, reading a book, running, or sleeping?

This is a trick question. All of these activities involve your nervous system. In fact, your nervous system controls almost everything you do.

Two Systems Within a System

The nervous system acts as the body's central command post. It has two basic functions. First, it gathers and interprets information. This information comes from inside your body and from the world outside your body. Then, the nervous system responds to that information as needed.

The nervous system has two parts: the central nervous system and the peripheral (puh RIF uhr uhl) nervous system. The **central nervous system** (CNS) is your brain and spinal cord. The CNS processes and responds to all messages coming from the peripheral nervous system. The **peripheral nervous system** (PNS) is all of the parts of the nervous system except for the brain and the spinal cord. The PNS connects all parts of the body to the CNS. The PNS uses specialized structures, called *nerves*, to carry information between your body and your CNS. **Figure 1** shows the major divisions of the nervous system.

Reading Check Explain the difference between the CNS and the PNS. (*See the Appendix for answers to Reading Checks.*)

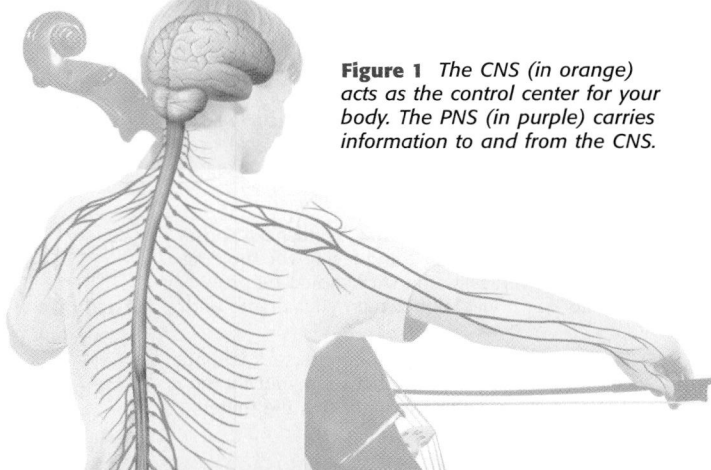

Figure 1 The CNS (in orange) acts as the control center for your body. The PNS (in purple) carries information to and from the CNS.

CHAPTER RESOURCES

Chapter Resource File

- **Lesson Plan**
- **Directed Reading A** BASIC
- **Directed Reading B** SPECIAL NEEDS

Technology

Transparencies
- Bellringer
- A Typical Neuron

Answer to Reading Check

The CNS is the brain and the spinal cord. The PNS is all of the parts of the nervous system except the brain and the spinal cord.

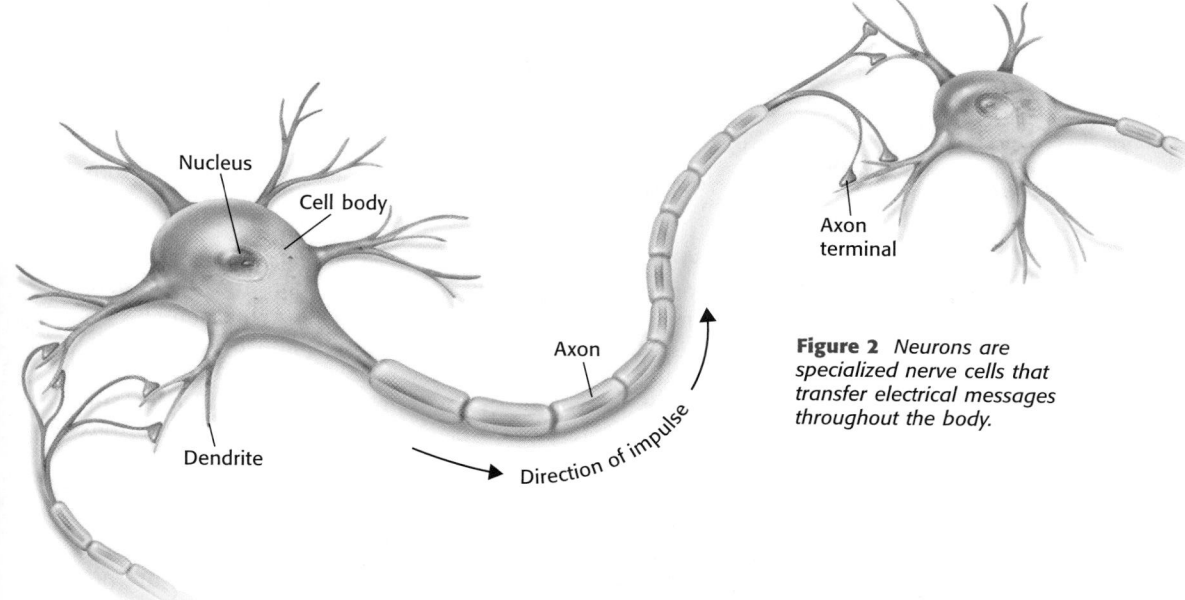

Nucleus

Cell body

Axon terminal

Axon

Dendrite

Direction of impulse

Figure 2 *Neurons are specialized nerve cells that transfer electrical messages throughout the body.*

The Peripheral Nervous System

Messages about your environment travel through the nervous system along neurons. A **neuron** (NOO RAHN) is a nerve cell that is specialized to transfer messages in the form of fast-moving electrical energy. These electrical messages are called *impulses.* Impulses may travel as fast as 150 m/s or as slow as 0.2 m/s. **Figure 2** shows a typical neuron transferring an impulse.

Neuron Structure

In many ways, a neuron is similar to other cells. A neuron has a large region in its center called the *cell body.* The cell body has a nucleus and cell organelles. But neurons also have special structures called dendrites and axons. *Dendrites* are usually short, branched extensions of the cell. Neurons receive information from other cells through their dendrites. A neuron may have many dendrites, which allows it to receive impulses from thousands of other cells.

Impulses are carried away from the cell body by axons. *Axons* are elongated extensions of a neuron. They can be very short or quite long. Some long axons extend almost 1 m from your lower back to your toes. The end of an axon often has branches that allow information to pass to other cells. The tip of each branch is called an *axon terminal.*

✔ **Reading Check** In your own words, describe a neuron.

neuron a nerve cell that is specialized to receive and conduct electrical impulses

MATH PRACTICE

Time to Travel

To calculate how long an impulse takes to travel a certain distance, you can use the following equation:

$$time = \frac{distance}{speed}$$

If an impulse travels 100 m/s, about how long would it take an impulse to travel 10 m?

Is That a Fact!

Male canaries sing a new song every year. Male canaries replace old brain cells related to song production with new neurons each spring. In the spring, the brain-cell clusters associated with vocalization grow larger. So, males compose their new melodies and females learn to recognize the males by their new songs. In the fall, when the birds stop singing, the brain clusters shrink.

Answer to Reading Check

A neuron is a cell that has a cell body and a nucleus. A neuron also has dendrites that receive signals from other neurons and axons that send signals to other neurons.

Simulating Neuronal Impulses
Ask students to form a circle and hold hands. Explain that each person in the circle represents a neuron. Every left hand represents a dendrite, every body represents a cell body, and every right hand represents an axon. Join the circle, and initiate a nerve impulse by gently squeezing the hand of the student to your right. Instruct students to pass the nerve impulse to the person to their right by gently squeezing his or her hand. Once students understand the mechanics of the activity, have them call out *dendrite, cell body,* and *axon* as the impulse is passed along the circle.

LS Kinesthetic/ Interpersonal English Language Learners

Discussion —— GENERAL

Following an Impulse Ask students to imagine that an electrical impulse is sent from the brain along neurons, similar to the one shown in **Figure 2,** and along a nerve, as shown in **Figure 3.** Discuss with students the path of the impulse from the brain, along the neuron to the spinal cord, and then along the nerve to the muscle. Draw a diagram on the board. Then, ask students to predict what will happen in the muscle next. (The muscle will move and send a message back to the brain to tell the brain of its new position.)

LS Visual/Verbal

nerve a collection of nerve fibers (axons) through which impulses travel between the central nervous system and other parts of the body

Information Collection

Remember that neurons are a type of nerve cell that carries impulses. Some neurons are *sensory neurons*. These neurons gather information about what is happening in and around your body. They have specialized nerve endings called *receptors*. Receptors detect changes inside and outside the body. For example, receptors in your eyes detect light. Sensory neurons then send this information to the CNS for processing.

Delivering Orders

Neurons that send impulses from the brain and spinal cord to other systems are called *motor neurons*. When muscles get impulses from motor neurons, they respond by contracting. For example, motor neurons cause muscles around your eyes to contract when you are in bright light. These muscles make you squint. Squinting lets less light enter the eyes. Motor neurons also send messages to your glands, such as sweat glands. These messages tell sweat glands to start or stop making sweat.

Nerves

The central nervous system is connected to the rest of your body by nerves. A **nerve** is a collection of axons bundled together with blood vessels and connective tissue. Nerves are everywhere in your body. Most nerves have axons of both sensory neurons and motor neurons. Axons are parts of nerves, but nerves are more than just axons. **Figure 3** shows the structure of a nerve. The axon in this nerve transmits information from the spinal cord to muscle fibers.

Reading Check What is a nerve?

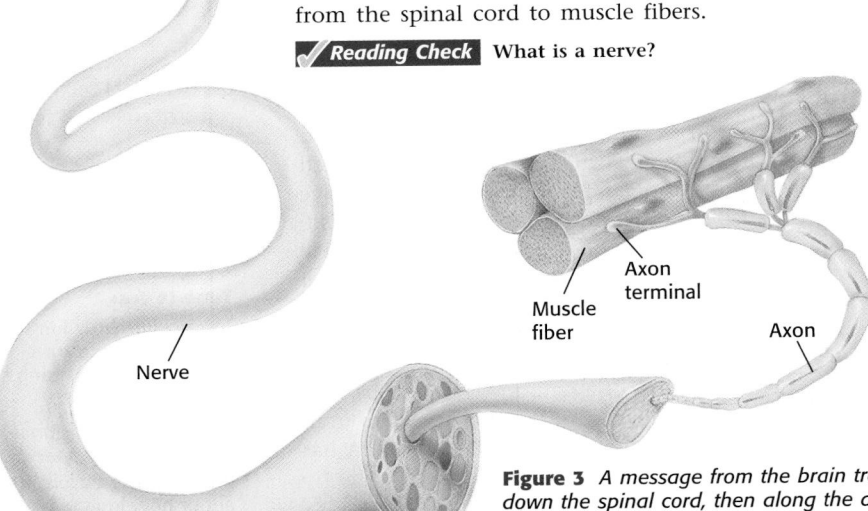

Spinal cord

Nerve

Muscle fiber

Axon terminal

Axon

Figure 3 *A message from the brain travels down the spinal cord, then along the axon of a motor neuron inside a nerve to the muscle. The message makes the muscle contract.*

CHAPTER RESOURCES

Technology

 Transparencies
• What Is a Nerve?

Answer to Reading Check

A nerve is a collection of nerve fibers, or axons, bundled together with blood vessels through which impulses travel between the central nervous system and other parts of the body.

Somatic and Autonomic Nervous Systems

Remember, the PNS connects your CNS to the rest of your body. And the PNS has two main parts—the sensory part (sensory neurons) and the motor part (motor neurons). You know that sensory nerves collect information from your senses and send that information to the CNS. You also know that motor nerves carry out the CNS's responses to that sensory information. To carry those responses, the motor part of the PNS has two kinds of nerves: somatic nerves and autonomic nerves.

Somatic Nervous System

Most of the neurons that are part of the *somatic nervous system* are under your conscious control. These are the neurons that stimulate skeletal muscles. They control voluntary movements, such as writing, talking, smiling, or jumping.

Autonomic Nervous System

Autonomic nerves do not need your conscious control. These neurons are part of the autonomic nervous system. The *autonomic nervous system* controls body functions that you don't think about, such as digestion and heart rate (the number of times your heart beats per minute).

The main job of the autonomic nervous system is to keep all the body's functions in balance. Depending on the situation, the autonomic nervous system can speed up or slow down these functions. The autonomic nervous system has two divisions: the *sympathetic nervous system* and the *parasympathetic nervous system.* These two divisions work together to keep your internal environment stable. This is called *homeostasis.* Some of these functions are shown in **Table 1.**

Reading Check Describe three functions of the PNS.

Table 1 Effects of the Autonomic Nervous System on the Body

Organ	Effect of sympathetic division	Effect of parasympathetic division
Eyes	pupils dilate (grow larger; makes it easier to see objects)	pupils constrict (vision normal)
Heart	heart rate increases (increases blood flow)	heart rate slows (blood flow slows)
Lungs	bronchioles dilate (grow larger; increases oxygen in blood)	bronchioles constrict
Blood vessels	blood vessels dilate (increases blood flow except to digestion)	little or no effect
Intestines	digestion slows (reduces blood flow to stomach and intestines)	digestion returns to normal

CONNECTION TO Chemistry

Keeping Your Balance The autonomic nervous system has two parts—the sympathetic division and the parasympathetic division. These parts of your nervous system help keep all of your body systems in balance. Research these two parts of the nervous system, and make a poster showing how they keep your body healthy. **ACTIVITY**

SCIENCE HUMOR

Q: How do nerves shop?

A: They buy only on impulse.

Prediction Guide Before students read about the central nervous system, ask them whether the following statements are true or false.

1. The brain is the body's largest organ. (false)

2. The largest part of the brain is the cerebrum. (true)

3. The medulla is responsible for speech and balance. (false)

4. The spinal cord is about as big around as your thumb. (true)

Have students evaluate their answers after they have read this section. **LS** Verbal

Group ACTiViTy ——— BASIC

Reteaching the Brain If students have difficulty distinguishing the structures of the brain, have them make a life-size model of the brain. Organize the class into groups of two or three. Give each group modeling clay of different colors. Each group should have enough clay to make a life-size model of the brain. Instruct students to make labels for the parts of the brain. They should include the cerebrum, cerebellum, medulla, and the top of the spinal cord. Also, have students label the hemispheres. Allow students to use their models as you finish teaching about the brain. English Language Learners **LS** Kinesthetic

brain the mass of nerve tissue that is the main control center of the nervous system

The Central Nervous System

The central nervous system receives information from the sensory neurons. Then it responds by sending messages to the body through motor neurons in the PNS.

The Control Center

The largest organ in the nervous system is the brain. The **brain** is the main control center of the nervous system. Many processes that the brain controls happen automatically. These processes are called *involuntary.* For example, you couldn't stop digesting food even if you tried. On the other hand, some actions controlled by your brain are *voluntary.* When you want to move your arm, your brain sends signals along motor neurons to muscles in your arm. Then, the muscles contract, and your arm moves. The brain has three main parts—the cerebrum (suh REE bruhm), the cerebellum (SER uh BEL uhm), and the medulla (mi DUHL uh). Each part has its own job.

✓ **Reading Check** What is the difference between a voluntary action and an involuntary action?

The Cerebrum

The largest part of your brain is called the *cerebrum.* It looks like a mushroom cap. This dome-shaped area is where you think and where most memories are stored. It controls voluntary movements and allows you to sense touch, light, sound, odors, taste, pain, heat, and cold.

The cerebrum has two halves, called *hemispheres.* The left hemisphere directs the right side of the body, and the right hemisphere directs the left side of the body. **Figure 4** shows some of the activities that each hemisphere controls. However, most brain activities use both hemispheres.

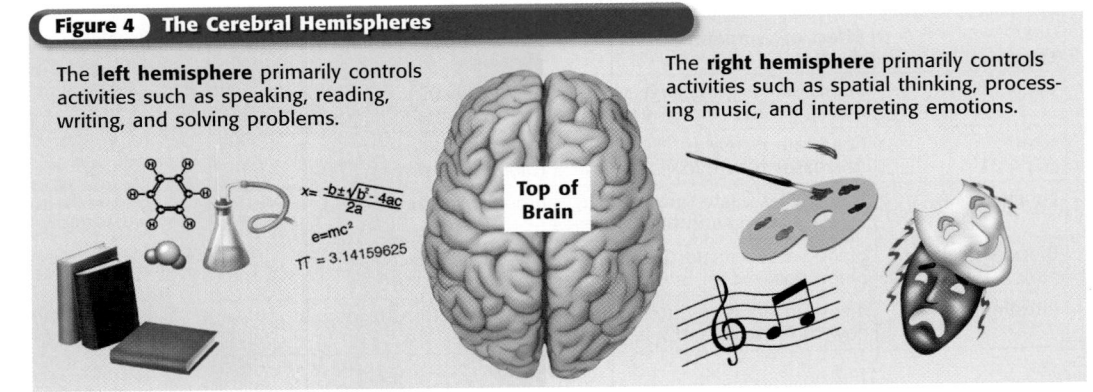

Figure 4 **The Cerebral Hemispheres**

The **left hemisphere** primarily controls activities such as speaking, reading, writing, and solving problems.

The **right hemisphere** primarily controls activities such as spatial thinking, processing music, and interpreting emotions.

Top of Brain

Homework ——— GENERAL

Writing **Dream Research** Dreaming, sleepwalking, and daydreaming are all phenomena of the brain. Have students research one of these topics and give group presentations to the class. They may use posters, signs, songs, skits, oral reports, and other techniques for their presentations. **LS** Verbal/Visual

Answer to Reading Check

A voluntary action is an action over which you have conscious control. Voluntary activities include throwing a ball, playing a video game, talking to your friends, taking a bite of food, and raising your hand to answer a question in class. An involuntary action is an action that happens automatically. It is an action or process over which you have no conscious control.

The Cerebellum

The second-largest part of your brain is the *cerebellum*. It lies beneath the back of the cerebrum. The cerebellum processes sensory information from your body, such as from skeletal muscles and joints. This allows the brain to keep track of your body's position. If you begin to lose your balance, the cerebellum sends impulses telling different skeletal muscles to contract. Those muscles shift a person's weight and keep a person, such as the girl in **Figure 5,** from losing her balance.

The Medulla

The *medulla* is the part of your brain that connects to your spinal cord. The medulla is about 3 cm long, and you can't live without it. The medulla controls involuntary processes, such as blood pressure, body temperature, heart rate, and involuntary breathing.

Your medulla constantly receives sensory impulses from receptors in your blood vessels. It uses this information to regulate your blood pressure. If your blood pressure gets too low, the medulla sends out impulses that tell blood vessels to tighten up. As a result, blood pressure rises. The medulla also sends impulses to the heart to make the heart beat faster or slower. **Figure 6** shows the location of the parts of the brain and some of the functions of each part.

Reading Check Explain why the medulla is important.

Figure 5 *Your cerebellum causes skeletal muscles to make adjustments so that you will stay upright.*

Figure 6 Areas of the Brain at Work

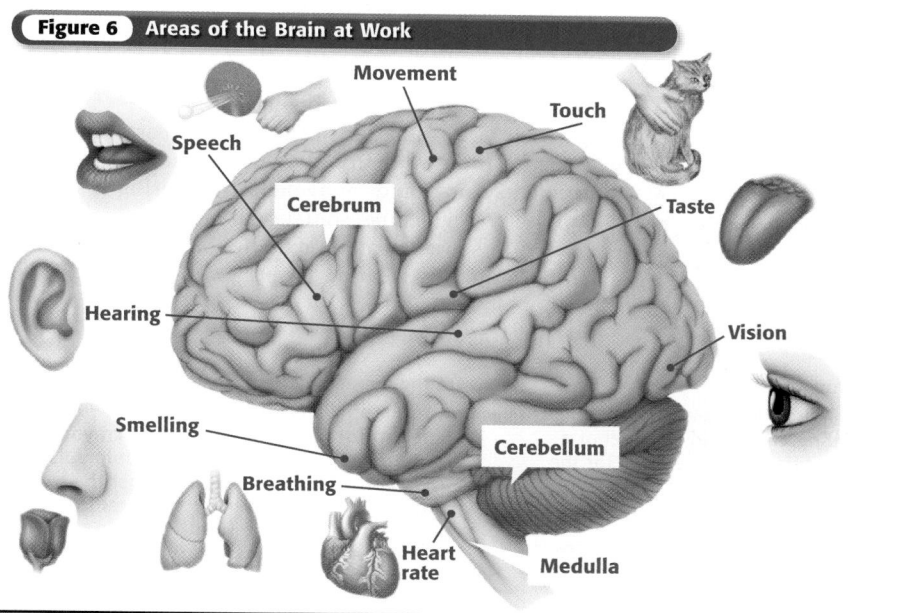

Movement
Touch
Speech
Cerebrum
Taste
Hearing
Vision
Smelling
Cerebellum
Breathing
Heart rate
Medulla

CHAPTER RESOURCES

Technology

Transparencies
• Regions of the Brain

Nervous Systems Have students work in pairs to trace the outline of one student's body on butcher paper. Next, have each pair fill in the outline, using different colors for each of the parts of the nervous systems.

LS Kinesthetic/ English Language
Visual   Learners

Quiz   GENERAL

Ask students whether each of the statements below is true or false. Have students correct false statements.

1. An axon transmits an electrical impulse to a dendrite. (true)

2. Most neurons are made up of either axons or dendrites; few neurons have both. (false)

3. The central nervous system is made up of the brain and the spinal cord. (true)

Alternative Assessment   GENERAL

Writing **Owner's Guide** Have students develop an owner's guide for their central nervous system. The guide should include information about the various components of the central nervous system and a diagram showing their location in the body. Encourage students to share their guide with the class in the form of a presentation or a poster.
LS Verbal

The Spinal Cord

Your spinal cord, which is part of your central nervous system, is about as big around as your thumb. The spinal cord is made of neurons and bundles of axons that pass impulses to and from the brain. As shown in **Figure 7,** the spinal cord is surrounded by protective bones called *vertebrae* (VUHR tuh BRAY).

The nerve fibers in your spinal cord allow your brain to communicate with your peripheral nervous system. Sensory neurons in your skin and muscles send impulses along their axons to your spinal cord. The spinal cord carries impulses to your brain. The brain interprets these impulses as pain, temperature, or other sensations. The brain then responds to the situation. Impulses moving from the brain down the spinal cord are relayed to motor neurons. Motor neurons carry the impulses along their axons to muscles and glands all over your body.

✓ Reading Check Describe the path of an impulse from the skin to the brain and the path of the response.

Spinal Cord Injury

A spinal cord injury may block all information to and from the brain. Sensory information coming from below the injury may not get to the brain. For example, a spinal cord injury may block all sensory impulses from the feet and legs. People with such an injury would not be able to sense pain, touch, or temperature with their feet. And motor commands from the brain to the injured area may not reach the peripheral nerves. So, the person would not be able to move his or her legs.

Each year, thousands of people are paralyzed by spinal cord injuries. Many of these injuries happen in car accidents and could be avoided by wearing a seat belt. Among young people, spinal cord injuries are sometimes related to sports or other activities. These injuries might be prevented by wearing proper safety equipment.

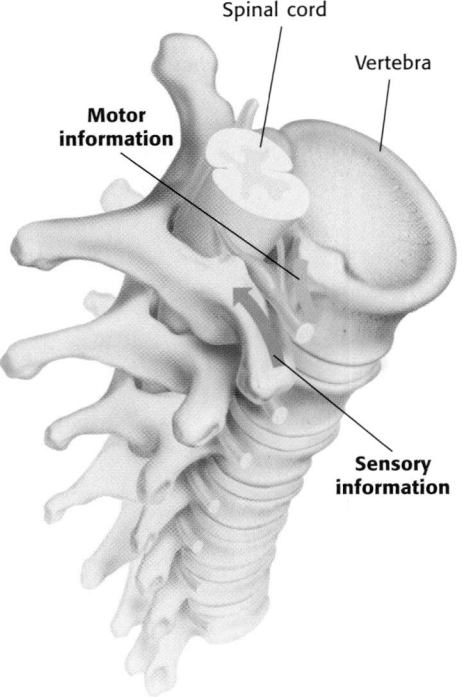

Figure 7 *The spinal cord carries information to and from the brain. Vertebrae protect the spinal cord.*

Building a Neuron

1. Your teacher will provide at least four different colors of **modeling clay.** Build a model of a neuron by using different-colored clay for the various parts of the neuron.

2. Use **tape** to attach your model neuron to a **piece of plain white paper.**

3. On the paper, label each part of the neuron. Draw an arrow from the label to the part.

4. Using a **colored pencil, marker,** or **crayon,** draw arrows showing the path of an impulse traveling in your neuron. Tell whether the impulse is a sensory impulse or a motor impulse. Then, describe what will happen when the impulse reaches its destination.

MATERIALS

FOR EACH GROUP
- clay, modeling
- colored pencil, marker, or crayon
- paper, white (1 piece)
- tape

Safety Caution: Students should wear a safety apron while doing this Quick Lab.

Answer to Reading Check

When someone touches your skin, an impulse that travels along a sensory neuron to your spinal cord and then to your brain is created. The response travels back from your brain to your spinal cord and then along a motor neuron to a muscle.

Summary

- The central nervous system (CNS) includes the brain and the spinal cord.
- The peripheral nervous system (PNS) is all the parts of the nervous system except the brain and spinal cord.
- The peripheral nervous system has nerves made up of axons of neurons.
- Sensory neurons have receptors that detect information about the body and its environment. Motor neurons carry messages from the brain and spinal cord to other parts of the body.

- The PNS has two types of motor nerves—somatic nerves and autonomic nerves.
- The cerebrum is the largest part of the brain and controls thinking, sensing, and voluntary movement.
- The cerebellum is the part of the brain that keeps track of the body's position and helps maintain balance.
- The medulla controls involuntary processes, such as heart rate, blood pressure, body temperature, and breathing.

Using Key Terms

1. In your own words, write a definition for each of the following terms: *neuron* and *nerve*.

2. Use the following terms in the same sentence: *brain* and *peripheral nervous system*.

Understanding Key Ideas

3. Someone touches your shoulder and you turn around. Which sequence do your impulses follow?
   a. motor neuron, sensory neuron, CNS response
   b. motor neuron, CNS response, sensory neuron
   c. sensory neuron, motor neuron, CNS response
   d. sensory neuron, CNS response, motor neuron

4. Describe one function of each part of the brain.

5. Compare the somatic nervous system with the autonomic nervous system.

6. Explain how a severe injury to the spinal cord can affect other parts of the body.

Critical Thinking

7. **Applying Concepts** Some medications slow a person's nervous system. These drugs are often labeled "May cause drowsiness." Explain why a person needs to know about this side effect.

8. **Predicting Consequences** Explain how your life would change if your autonomic nervous system suddenly stopped working.

Interpreting Graphics

Use the figure below to answer the questions that follow.

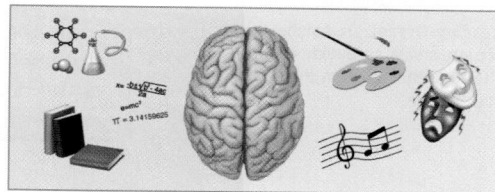

9. Which hemisphere of the brain recognizes and processes words, numbers, and letters? faces, places, and objects?

10. For a person whose left hemisphere is primarily in control, would it be easier to learn to play a new computer game by reading the rules and following instructions or by watching a friend play and imitating his actions?

SCiLINKS

NSTA
Developed and maintained by the
National Science Teachers Association

For a variety of links related to this chapter, go to www.scilinks.org

Topic: Nervous System
SciLinks code: HSM1023

CHAPTER RESOURCES

Chapter Resource File

- **Section Quiz** GENERAL
- **Section Review** GENERAL
- **Vocabulary and Section Summary** GENERAL
- **Reinforcement Worksheet** BASIC
- **SciLinks Activity** GENERAL
- **Datasheet for Quick Lab**

Technology

Transparencies
- The Spinal Cord

Focus

Overview

This section introduces the five senses: touch, sight, hearing, taste, and smell. Students will learn about the receptor cells that are unique to each sense.

Bellringer

Ask students to list the five senses and draw an organ associated with each sense as well as an object detected by each sense. For example, students may draw an ear and a bell to represent the sense of hearing.

Motivate

Group ACTiViTY — GENERAL

Losing Your Senses

Organize the class into groups of three or four students, and assign each group a sense. Each group should imagine what it would be like to live without that sense. Allow students 10 to 15 minutes to develop a skit or example of life without the assigned sense. **LS** Intrapersonal/

Kinesthetic

Co-op Learning   English Language Learners

Answer to Reading Check

Skin can detect pressure, temperature, pain, and vibration.

READING WARM-UP

Objectives

● List four sensations that are detected by receptors in the skin.
● Describe how a feedback mechanism works.
● Describe how light relates to sight.
● Describe how the senses of hearing, taste, and smell work.

Terms to Learn

integumentary system
reflex
feedback mechanism
retina
cochlea

READING STRATEGY

Reading Organizer As you read this section, create an outline of the section. Use the headings from the section in your outline.

integumentary system the organ system that forms a protective covering on the outside of the body

Figure 1 *Each type of receptor in your skin has its own structure and function.*

Responding to the Environment

You feel a tap on your shoulder. Who tapped you? You turn to look, hoping to see a friend. Your senses are on the job!

The tap produces impulses in sensory receptors on your shoulder. These impulses travel to your brain. Once the impulses reach your brain, they create an awareness called a *sensation*. In this case, the sensation is of your shoulder being touched. But you still do not know who tapped you. So, you turn around. The sensory receptors in your eyes send impulses to your brain. Now, your brain recognizes your best friend.

Sense of Touch

Touch is what you feel when sensory receptors in the skin are stimulated. It is the sensation you feel when you shake hands or feel a breeze. As shown in **Figure 1,** skin has different kinds of receptors. Each kind of receptor responds mainly to one kind of stimulus. For example, *thermoreceptors* respond to temperature change. Each kind of receptor produces a specific sensation of touch, such as pressure, temperature, pain, or vibration. Skin is part of the integumentary (in TEG yoo MEN tuhr ee) system. The **integumentary system** protects the body from damage. It includes hair, skin, and nails.

✔ **Reading Check** List four sensations that your skin can detect. *(See the Appendix for answers to Reading Checks.)*

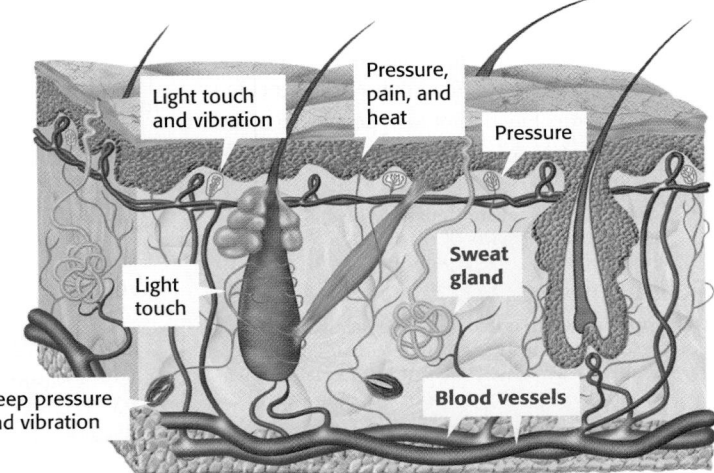

Light touch and vibration
Pressure, pain, and heat
Pressure
Light touch
Sweat gland
Deep pressure and vibration
Blood vessels

CHAPTER RESOURCES

Chapter Resource File

- Lesson Plan
- Directed Reading A BASIC
- Directed Reading B SPECIAL NEEDS

Technology

Transparencies
• Bellringer

Workbooks

Study Guide
• Multilplying and Dividing in Scientific Notation GENERAL

Responding to Sensory Messages

When you step on something sharp, as the man in **Figure 2** did, pain receptors in your foot or toe send impulses to your spinal cord. Almost immediately, a message to move your foot travels back to the muscles in your leg and foot. Without thinking, you quickly lift your foot. This immediate, involuntary action is called a **reflex.** Your brain isn't telling your leg to move. In fact, by the time the message reaches your brain, your leg and foot have already moved. If you had to wait for your brain to act, you toes might be seriously hurt!

✓ Reading Check Why are reflexes important?

Feedback Mechanisms

Most of the time, the brain processes information from skin receptors. For example, on a hot day, heat receptors in your skin detect an increase in your temperature. The receptors send impulses to the brain. Your brain responds by sending messages to your sweat glands to make sweat. As sweat evaporates, it cools your body. Your brain also tells the blood vessels in your skin to dilate (open wider). Blood flow increases. Thermal energy from the blood in your skin moves to your surroundings. This also cools your body. As your body cools, it sends messages to your brain. The brain responds by sending messages to sweat glands and blood vessels to reduce their activity.

This cooling process is one of your body's feedback mechanisms. A **feedback mechanism** is a cycle of events in which information from one step controls or affects a previous step. The temperature-regulating feedback mechanism helps keep your body temperature within safe limits. This cooling mechanism works like a thermostat on an air conditioner. Once a room reaches the right temperature, the thermostat sends a message to the air conditioner to stop blowing cold air.

reflex an involuntary and almost immediate movement in response to a stimulus

feedback mechanism a cycle of events in which information from one step controls or affects a previous step

Figure 2 *A reflex, such as lifting your foot when you step on something sharp, is one way your nervous system responds to your environment.*

ACTIVITY ———— GENERAL

Writing **Pupil Action** Ask students to write a paragraph that explains what happens to their eyes and vision when they first leave a dark movie theater on a sunny day. Students should discuss the change from dim to bright light and its effects on the pupils as well as on their ability to see. **LS Verbal**

Discussion ———— GENERAL

Eye Strain For us to see objects within a distance of 6 m, the muscles in the eye must work constantly to focus. Long periods of focusing on very near objects, such as a book, can tire the eye muscles and cause eyestrain. Ask students to suggest ways to avoid straining the eye muscles during these activities. (Answers may include taking breaks from the activity once an hour and looking up and allowing the eyes to relax occasionally.) **LS Logical**

Answer to Reading Check

Light strikes cells on the retina and triggers impulses in those cells. The impulses are carried to the brain, which interprets the impulses as images that you "see."

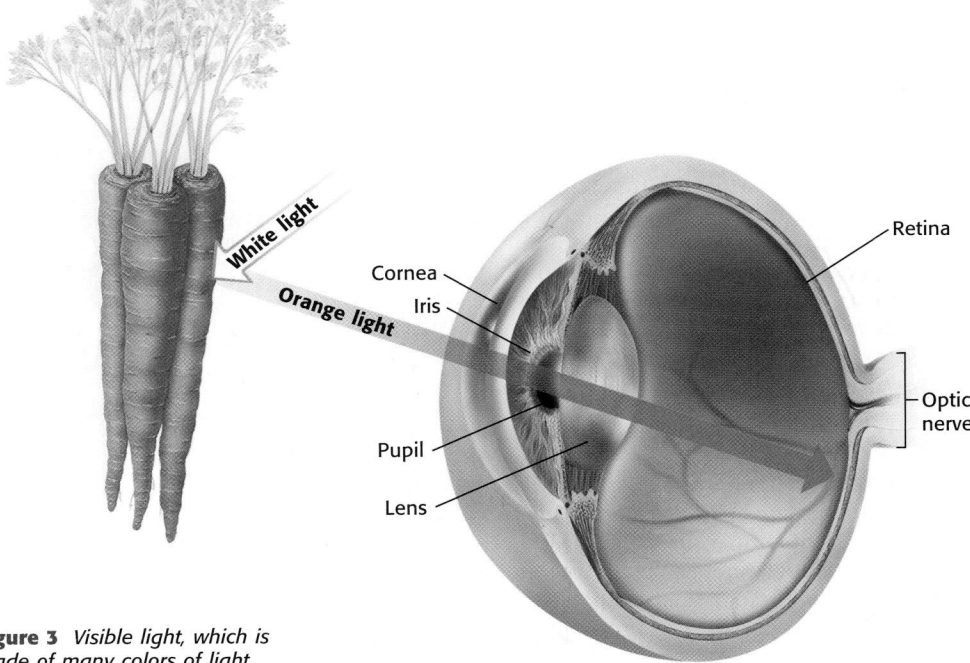

Figure 3 *Visible light, which is made of many colors of light, hits the carrots. Carrots look orange because they reflect orange light to your eyes.*

retina the light-sensitive inner layer of the eye; it receives images formed by the lens and transmits them through the optic nerve to the brain

INTERNET ACTIVITY

For another activity related to this chapter, go to **go.hrw.com** and type in the keyword **HL5BD4W.**

Sense of Sight

Sight is the sense that allows you to see the size, shape, motion, and color of objects around you. You see an object when it sends or reflects visible light toward your eyes. Your eyes detect this light, which enables your brain to form visual images.

Your eyes are complex sensory organs, as you can see in **Figure 3.** The front of the eye is covered by a clear membrane called the *cornea*. The cornea protects the eye but allows light to enter. Light from an object enters the front of your eye through an opening called the *pupil*. The light then travels through the lens to the back of the eye. There, the light strikes the **retina,** a layer of light-sensitive cells.

The retina is packed with photoreceptors. A *photoreceptor* is a special neuron that changes light into electrical impulses. The retina has two kinds of photoreceptors: rods and cones. Rods are very sensitive to dim light. They are important for night vision. Impulses from rods are interpreted as black-and-white images. Cones are very sensitive to bright light. Impulses from cones allow you to see fine details and colors.

Impulses from the rods and cones travel along axons. The impulses leave the back of each eye through an optic nerve. The optic nerve carries the impulses to your brain, where the impulses are interpreted as the images that you see.

Reading Check Describe how light and sight are related.

CHAPTER RESOURCES

Technology

Transparencies
- **LINK TO PHYSICAL SCIENCE** Measuring Wavelengths

MISCONCEPTION ALERT

Colorblindness Students may think that people who are colorblind see in black and white. People who are colorblind can usually perceive colors, but certain colors may appear very similar to one another. This similarity is caused by a lack of at least one of the three cones in the eye. Many people do not know that they are colorblind because they have learned to distinguish other differences in their perception of colors.

Reacting to Light

Your pupil looks like a black dot in the center of your eye. In fact, it is an opening that lets light enter the eye. The pupil is surrounded by the *iris,* a ring of muscle. The iris controls the amount of light that enters the eye and gives the eye its color. In bright light, the iris contracts, which makes the pupil smaller. A smaller pupil reduces the amount of light entering the eye and passing onto the retina. In dim light, the iris opens the pupil and lets in more light.

Reading Check How does your iris react to bright light?

Focusing the Light

Light travels in straight lines until it passes through the cornea and the lens. The *lens* is an oval-shaped piece of clear, curved material behind the iris. Muscles in the eye change the shape of the lens in order to focus light onto the retina. When you look at objects close to the eye, the lens becomes more curved. When you look at objects far away, the lens gets flatter.

Figure 4 shows some common vision problems. In some eyes, the lens focuses the light in front of the retina, which results in nearsightedness. If the lens focuses the light just behind the retina, the result is farsightedness. Glasses, contact lenses, or surgery can usually correct these vision problems.

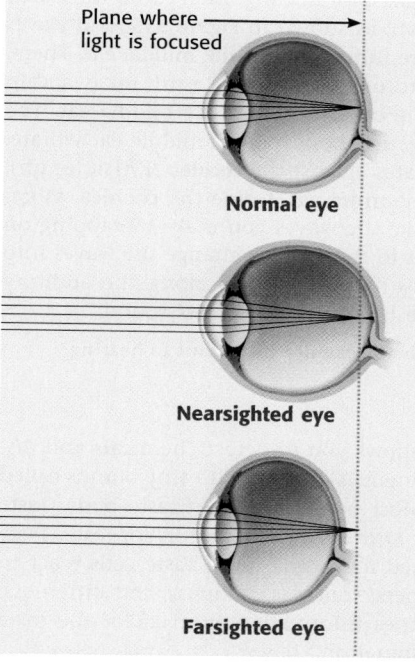

Plane where light is focused

Normal eye

Nearsighted eye

Farsighted eye

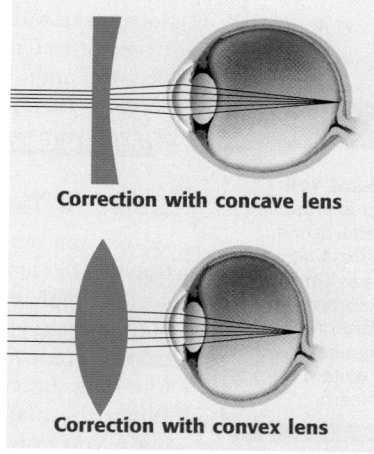

Figure 4 *A concave lens bends light rays outward to correct nearsightedness. A convex lens bends light rays inward to correct farsightedness.*

Correction with concave lens

Correction with convex lens

Where's the Dot?

1. Hold your **book** at arm's length, and close your right eye. Focus your left eye on the black dot below.

○   ●

2. Slowly move the book toward your face until the white dot disappears. You may need to try a few times to get this result. The white dot doesn't always disappear for every person.
3. Describe your observations.
4. Use the library or the Internet to research the optic nerve and to find out why the white dot disappears.

Is That a Fact!

Young people often hold a book close to their face when reading, while adults hold a book farther away. The closest point on which a person can focus, called the *near point of vision,* changes with age. A typical child can focus on an object about 10 cm from his or her eyes (objects closer than the near point of vision can be seen but appear fuzzy). The change in the near point of vision is caused by the lens's decreasing elasticity over time.

Answers to Quick Lab

3. Students should observe that the white dot disappears when the image is held about 10 cm from their face. The exact point where this happens will vary from person to person. Have students try this activity several times until the dot disappears.
4. Students should discover that the area where the optic nerve leaves the back of the eyeball does not contain any photoreceptors and is called the blind spot. So, when the white dot is focused on the eye's blind spot, the dot disappears.

CONNECTION to Physical Science— GENERAL

Wavelength and Color Vision

In the retina, there are three types of cones that respond maximally to red, blue, or green light. When red cones and green cones are stimulated at the same time, the color yellow is perceived. White is perceived when all three kinds of cones are equally stimulated. Different colors of visible light have different wavelengths. Red has the longest wavelength, and violet has the shortest. Use the teaching transparency entitled "Measuring Wavelengths" to illustrate how wavelengths are measured. LS Visual

Answer to Reading Check

In bright light, your iris contracts and reduces the amount of light entering the eye.

Reteaching — BASIC

Model of a Sense Organ Have students choose one of the sense organs and make a model that shows how the organ interacts with the brain. Allow students to choose from an assortment of materials for their model. Ask students to explain their model to the class. **English Language Learners**

LS Kinesthetic

Quiz — GENERAL

Ask students whether each of the statements below is true or false. Have students correct false statements.

1. Rods help you see color and detail in bright light. (false)

2. Cones provide a colorful view of the world. (true)

3. Your brain combines signals from the senses of smell and hearing to give you a sensation of flavor. (false)

Alternative Assessment — GENERAL

Writing **Making Sense of It**
Have students write and illustrate a pamphlet or brochure that explains each of the senses. The pamphlet or brochure should be written for somone who does not know much about science. **English Language Learners**

LS Verbal/Visual

Answer to Reading Check

Neurons in the cochlea convert waves into electrical impulses that the brain interprets as sound.

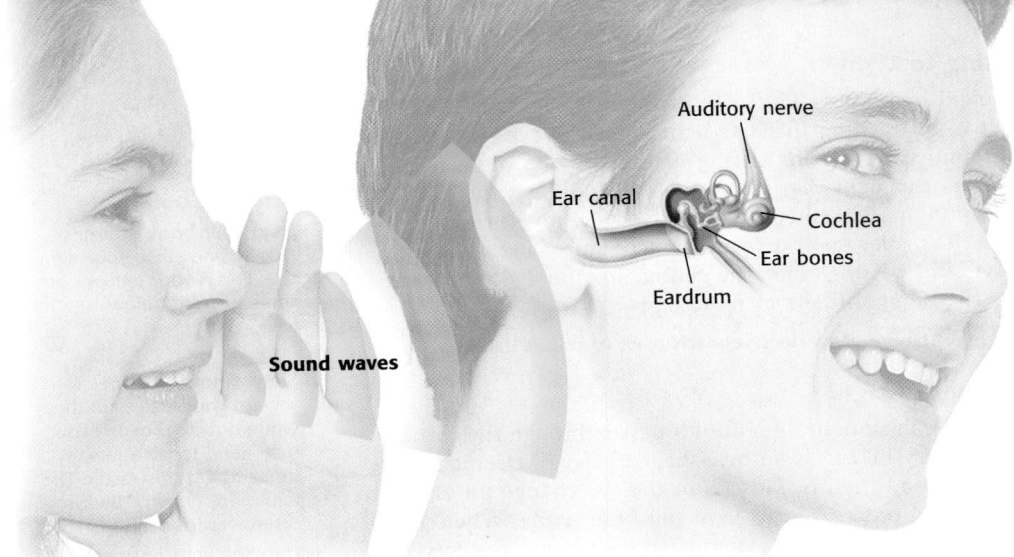

Figure 5 *A sound wave travels into the outer ear. It is converted into bone vibrations in the middle ear, then into liquid vibrations in the inner ear, and finally, into nerve impulses that travel to the brain.*

cochlea a coiled tube that is found in the inner ear and that is essential to hearing

CONNECTION TO Physics

WRITING SKILL **Elephant Talk** Sound is produced by vibrating objects. Some sounds, called *infrasonic sounds*, are too low for human ears to detect. Research how elephants use infrasonic sounds to communicate with each other, and write a report about what you learn.

Sense of Hearing

Sound is produced when something, such as a drum, vibrates. Vibrations push on nearby air particles, which push on other air particles. The vibrations create waves of sound energy. Hearing is the sense that allows you to experience sound energy.

Ears are organs specialized for hearing. Each ear has an outer, middle, and inner portion, as shown in **Figure 5.** Sound waves reaching the outer ear are funneled into the middle ear. There, the waves make the eardrum vibrate. The eardrum is a thin membrane separating the outer ear from the middle ear. The vibrating eardrum makes tiny bones in the middle ear vibrate. One of these bones vibrates against the **cochlea** (KAHK lee uh), a fluid-filled organ of the inner ear. Inside the cochlea, vibrations make waves just like the waves you make by tapping on a glass of water. Neurons in the cochlea change the waves into electrical impulses. These impulses travel along the auditory nerve to the area of the brain that interprets sound.

✓ Reading Check Why is the cochlea important to hearing?

Sense of Taste

Taste is the sense that allows you to detect chemicals and distinguish flavors. Your tongue is covered with tiny bumps called *papillae* (puh PIL ee). Most papillae contain taste buds. Taste buds contain clusters of *taste cells*, the receptors for taste. Taste cells respond to dissolved food molecules. Taste cells react to four basic tastes: sweetness, sourness, saltiness, and bitterness. When the brain combines information from all of the taste buds, you taste a "combination" flavor.

CONNECTION to Physical Science — ADVANCED

Owls Hunting by Hearing Students are probably familiar with the idea that owls see well in the dark. Students may not know that some owls actually hunt by listening for mice tunneling under the snow. Have students research the many adaptations that help owls hear well. Students can present their findings on a poster or by making a model of an owl's head that shows how an owl uses its hearing to hunt. **LS Verbal**

WEIRD SCIENCE

Some spicy foods, such as chile peppers, contain a chemical compound called *capsaicin*. Capsaicin triggers the pain receptors in the mouth. These receptors react to capsaicin exactly as they would to heat. This is why spicy foods, such as jalapeño peppers, feel like they are burning your mouth. In fact, no damage from heat actually happens—the burning is all in your mind!

Sense of Smell

As you can see in **Figure 6,** receptors for smell are located on *olfactory cells* in the upper part of your nasal cavity. An olfactory cell is a nerve cell that responds to chemical molecules in the air. You smell something when the receptors react to molecules that have been inhaled. The molecules dissolve in the moist lining of the nasal cavity and trigger an impulse. Olfactory cells send those impulses to the brain, which interprets the impulses as odors.

Taste buds and olfactory cells both detect dissolved molecules. Your brain combines information from both senses to give you sensations of flavor.

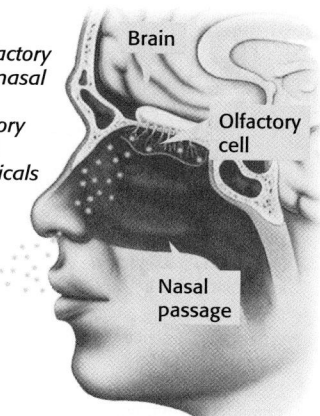

Figure 6 *Olfactory cells line the nasal cavity. These cells are sensory receptors that react to chemicals in the air.*

SECTION Review

Summary

- Touch allows you to respond to temperature, pressure, pain, and vibration on the skin.
- Reflexes and feedback mechanisms help you respond to your environment.
- Sight allows you to respond to light energy.
- Hearing allows you to respond to sound energy.
- Taste allows you to distinguish flavors.
- Smell allows you to perceive different odors.

Using Key Terms

1. In your own words, write a definition for each of the following terms: *reflex* and *feedback mechanism.*

2. Use each of the following terms in a separate sentence: *retina* and *cochlea.*

Understanding Key Ideas

3. Three sensations that receptors in the skin detect are
   a. light, smell, and sound.
   b. touch, pain, and odors.
   c. temperature, pressure, and pain.
   d. pressure, sound, and touch.

4. Explain how light and sight are related.

5. Describe how your senses of hearing, taste, and smell work.

6. Explain why you might have trouble seeing bright colors at a candlelit dinner.

7. How is your sense of taste similar to your sense of smell, and how do these senses work together?

8. Describe how the feedback mechanism that regulates body temperature works.

Math Skills

9. Suppose a nerve impulse must travel 0.90 m from your toe to your central nervous system. If the impulse travels at 150 m/s, calculate how long it will take the impulse to arrive. If the impulse travels at 0.2 m/s, how long will it take the impulse to arrive?

Critical Thinking

10. **Making Inferences** Why is it important for the human body to have reflexes?

11. **Applying Concepts** Rods help you detect objects and shapes in dim light. Explain why it is important for human eyes to have both rods and cones.

Developed and maintained by the National Science Teachers Association

For a variety of links related to this chapter, go to www.scilinks.org

Topic: The Senses; The Eye
SciLinks code: HSM1378; HSM0560

Answers to Section Review

1. Sample answer: A reflex is an unconscious, immediate response to a stimulus. A feedback mechanism is a series of steps in which one step affects a previous step.

2. Sample answer: The retina converts light to electrical impulses. The cochlea converts sound to electrical impulses.

3. c

4. Sample answer: Light enters the eye and strikes the retina. Cells in the retina are triggered by light and produce electrical impulses that are sent to the brain, where they are interpreted as images you see.

5. Sample answer: The ear converts sound waves into electrical impulses. The brain interprets these impulses as sounds. Taste buds in the papillae respond to four basic tastes (sweetness, bitterness, sourness, and saltiness) and send messages to the brain, which produces a "flavor." Smell receptors on olfactory cells respond to chemicals in the air and send impulses to the brain, which interprets them as odors.

6. Sample answer: Cones in the retina, which produce impulses that are interpreted as colors, do not work as well in dim light.

7. Sample answer: Receptors for smell detect chemicals in air. Receptors for taste detect chemicals in your mouth. The chemicals trigger impulses that the brain interprets as smells or tastes. The brain combines information from the mouth and the nose to give you a sensation of flavor.

8. Sample answer: The brain receives information about body temperature. If body temperature is too high or too low, the brain tells the body to take steps to correct its temperature. The brain receives information about the adjustments. When body temperature is correct, the brain tells the body to stop what it was doing to raise or lower the temperature.

9. 0.90 m ÷ 150 m/s = 0.006 s; 0.90 m ÷ 0.2 m/s = 4.5 s

10. Sample answer: Reflexes are important becaus they protect us by acting faster than the body would act if the brain had to process information and send a message.

11. In bright light, cones trigger impulses that are interpreted as images that provide information about color, shape, and motion. At night, rods allow you to detect something in the dark, even if you can't tell much about its color or shape. Together, cones and rods give you information about your environment.

Focus

Overview

In this section, students will learn about the endocrine system and how endocrine glands control the body's slower, long-term processes via hormones. They will also learn the location and function of specific endocrine glands.

Bellringer

Write the following on the board:

Unscramble the following words, and write them on a piece of paper:

nalgd	(gland)
meornoh	(hormone)
noclotr	(control)

Motivate

Discussion ———— GENERAL

Endocrine System Ask students to think of a time when they were suddenly frightened. Discuss with students how their pulse rate and breathing rate were different before and after being scared. (Both rates should be elevated after the scare.) Tell students that the endocrine system, along with the autonomic nervous system, is responsible for the changes that occurred in their pulse rate and breathing rate. Verbal

---

READING WARM-UP

Objectives

● Explain why the endocrine system is important to the body.
● Identify five glands of the endocrine system, and describe what their hormones do.
● Describe how feedback mechanisms stop and start hormone release.
● Name two hormone imbalances.

Terms to Learn

endocrine system
gland
hormone

READING STRATEGY

Discussion Read this section silently. Write down questions that you have about this section. Discuss your questions in a small group.

endocrine system a collection of glands and groups of cells that secrete hormones that regulate growth, development, and homeostasis

gland a group of cells that make special chemicals for the body

---

The Endocrine System

Have you ever heard of an epinephrine (EP uh NEPH rin) rush? You might have had one without realizing it. Exciting situations, such as riding a roller coaster or watching a scary movie, can cause your body to release epinephrine.

Epinephrine is one of the body's chemical messengers made by the endocrine system. Your endocrine system regulates body processes, such as fluid balance, growth, and development.

Hormones as Chemical Messengers

The **endocrine system** controls body functions by using chemicals that are made by the endocrine glands. A **gland** is a group of cells that make special chemicals for your body. Chemical messengers made by the endocrine glands are called hormones. A **hormone** is a chemical messenger made in one cell or tissue that causes a change in another cell or tissue in another part of the body. Hormones flow through the bloodstream to all parts of the body. Thus, an endocrine gland near your brain can control an organ that is somewhere else in your body.

Endocrine glands may affect many organs at one time. For example, in the situation shown in **Figure 1,** the adrenal glands release the hormone *epinephrine*, which is sometimes called *adrenaline*. Epinephrine increases your heartbeat and breathing rate. This response is called the "fight-or-flight" response. When you are frightened, angry, or excited, the "fight-or-flight" response prepares you to fight the danger or to run from it.

Figure 1 *When you have to move quickly to avoid danger, your adrenal glands make more blood glucose available for energy.*

CHAPTER RESOURCES

Chapter Resource File

- **Lesson Plan**
- **Directed Reading A** BASIC
- **Directed Reading B** SPECIAL NEEDS

Technology

Transparencies
- Bellringer

Is That a Fact!

Epinephrine occurs naturally in the human body, but it is also administered as a drug by doctors. It can be injected into the heart to help revive a person who has suffered a heart attack. Epinephrine is also sometimes used to dilate the bronchioles in the lungs of people who have asthma or who have severe allergic reactions, such as reactions to bee stings.

More Endocrine Glands

Your body has several other endocrine glands. Some of these glands have many functions. For example, your pituitary gland stimulates skeletal growth and helps the thyroid gland work properly. It also regulates the amount of water in the blood. And the pituitary gland stimulates the birth process in women.

Your thyroid gland is very important during infancy and childhood. Thyroid hormones control the secretion of growth hormones for normal body growth. Thyroid hormones also control the development of the central nervous system. And they control your metabolism. *Metabolism* is the sum of all the chemical processes that take place in an organism.

Your thymus gland is important to your immune system. Cells called *killer T cells* grow and mature in the thymus gland. These T cells help destroy or neutralize cells or substances that invade your body. The names and some of the functions of endocrine glands are shown in **Figure 2**.

✔ **Reading Check** Name two endocrine glands, and explain why they are important to your body. *(See the Appendix for answers to Reading Checks.)*

hormone a substance that is made in one cell or tissue and that causes a change in another cell or tissue in a different part of the body

CONNECTION TO Language Arts

WRITING SKILL **Fight or Flight?** Write a paragraph describing a time when you had a fight-or-flight experience. Include in your description the following terms: *hormones, fight-or-flight,* and *epinephrine.* If you cannot think of a personal experience, write a short story describing someone else's fight-or-flight experience.

Figure 2	**Endocrine Glands and Their Functions**

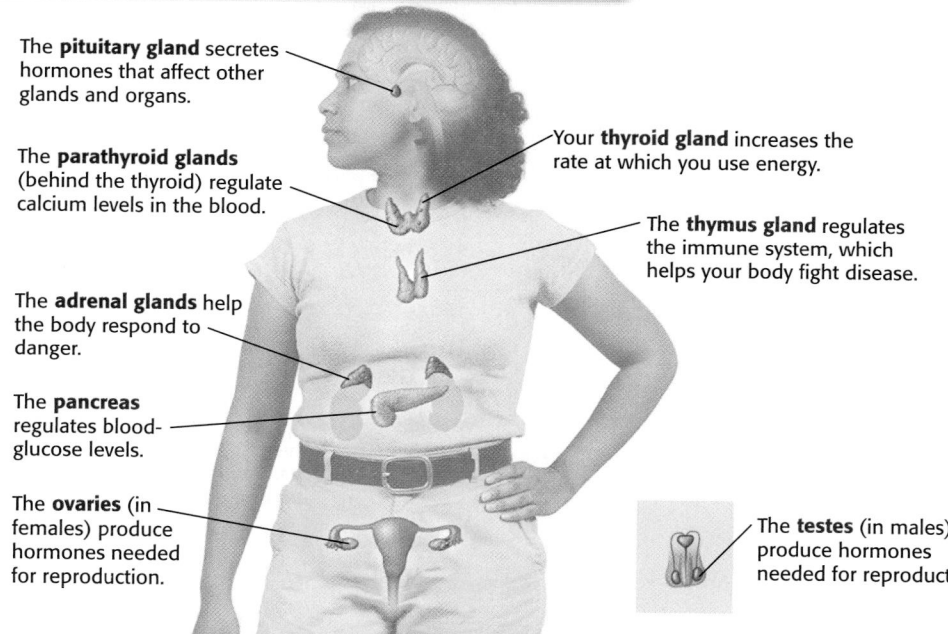

The **pituitary gland** secretes hormones that affect other glands and organs.

The **parathyroid glands** (behind the thyroid) regulate calcium levels in the blood.

The **adrenal glands** help the body respond to danger.

The **pancreas** regulates blood-glucose levels.

The **ovaries** (in females) produce hormones needed for reproduction.

Your **thyroid gland** increases the rate at which you use energy.

The **thymus gland** regulates the immune system, which helps your body fight disease.

The **testes** (in males) produce hormones needed for reproduction.

Is That a Fact!

Since the mid-1980s research at Rutgers University shows that some potent hormones produced in the last trimester of pregnancy prepare and motivate mothers to care for their young. The most important of these hormones is oxytocin. Oxytocin causes the uterus to contract, so oxytocin is in the mother's brain at the time the mother meets her newborn. Some scientists believe oxytocin helps the mother to bond with her new baby.

Answer to Reading Check

Sample answer: The thyroid gland increases the rate at which the body uses energy. The thymus gland regulates the immune system, which helps your body fight disease.

Reteaching — BASIC

Fight-or-Flight Have students work in pairs. Ask students to tell each other about a time when they were frightened and to describe the physical responses they had. Make a list of all responses. Discuss with students how one hormone causes all these changes. Ask students, "How are the changes related?" (They all get the body ready to fight or run from danger.)
LS Interpersonal/Intrapersonal

Quiz — GENERAL

Ask students whether each of the statements below is true or false. Have students correct false statements.

1. Hormones are chemicals secreted into the bloodstream. (true)

2. All endocrine glands come in pairs. (false)

3. Hormones are regulated by feedback mechanisms. (true)

Alternative Assessment — GENERAL

Writing **New Hormone** Have students write a story about a new hormone that controls a function, such as the ability to tell jokes, not discussed in this lesson. Students should describe a feedback control of this hormone. **LS Verbal**

Answer to Reading Check

Insulin helps regulate the amount of glucose in the blood.

Controlling the Endocrine Glands

Do you remember the feedback mechanisms at work in the nervous system? Endocrine glands control similar feedback mechanisms. For example, the pancreas has specialized cells that make two different hormones, *insulin* and *glucagon*. As shown in **Figure 3,** these two hormones control the level of glucose in the blood. Insulin lowers blood-glucose levels by telling the liver to convert glucose into glycogen and to store glycogen for future use. Glucagon has the opposite effect. It tells the liver to convert glycogen into glucose and to release the glucose into the blood.

✓ *Reading Check* What does insulin do?

Figure 3 Blood-Glucose Feedback Control

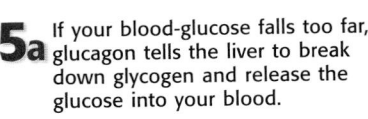

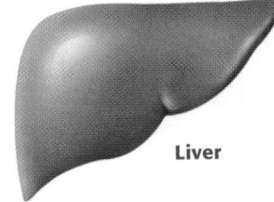

5b Sometimes, to raise your blood-glucose level, you must eat something.

5a If your blood-glucose falls too far, glucagon tells the liver to break down glycogen and release the glucose into your blood.

Pancreas

1 Glucose is fuel for your body. Glucose is absorbed into the bloodstream from the small intestine.

2 When the glucose level in the blood is high, such as after a meal, the pancreas releases the hormone insulin into the blood.

Pancreas

4 When the pancreas detects that your blood-glucose level has returned to normal, it stops releasing insulin.

3 Insulin signals the liver to take in glucose from the blood, convert the glucose into glycogen, and to store glycogen for future energy needs.

Liver

INCLUSION Strategies

• *Gifted and Talented* • *Hearing Impaired*
Some students benefit from exploring topics in greater depths. Ask students to divide a large piece of poster board in half. On one half, have them show a healthy pancreas with healthy insulin production and usage. On the other half, have them show a pancreas that could belong to a person with *diabetes mellitus.* English Language Learners
LS Visual

Hormone Imbalances

Occasionally, an endocrine gland makes too much or not enough of a hormone. For example, when a person's blood-glucose level rises, the pancreas secretes insulin. Insulin sends a message to the liver to convert glucose into glycogen. The liver stores glycogen for future use. But a person whose body does not use insulin properly or whose pancreas does not make enough insulin has a condition called *diabetes mellitus* (DIE uh BEET EEZ muh LIET uhs). A person who has diabetes may need daily injections of insulin to keep his or her blood-glucose levels within safe limits. Some patients, such as the woman in **Figure 4,** receive their insulin automatically from a small machine worn next to the body.

Another hormone imbalance is when a child's pituitary gland doesn't make enough growth hormone. As a result, the child's growth is stunted. Fortunately, if the problem is detected early, a doctor can prescribe growth hormone and monitor the child's growth. If the pituitary makes too much growth hormone, a child may grow taller than expected.

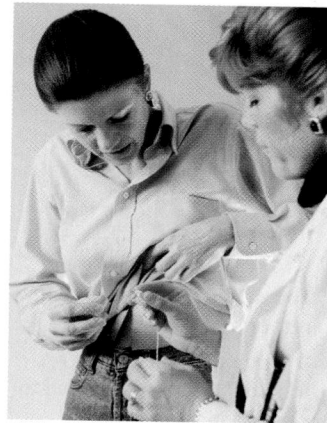

Figure 4 *This woman has diabetes and receives insulin from a device that monitors her blood-glucose level.*

SECTION Review

Summary

- Glands in the endocrine system use chemical messengers called *hormones*.
- Hormones regulate body functions by causing changes in cells or tissues.
- Feedback mechanisms tell endocrine glands when to turn hormones on and off.
- A hormone imbalance is when a gland releases too much or too little of a hormone.

Using Key Terms

1. Use the following terms in the same sentence: *endocrine system, glands,* and *hormone.*

Understanding Key Ideas

2. Identify five endocrine glands, and explain why their hormones are important to your body.

3. Hormone imbalances may cause
   a. feedback and insulin.
   b. diabetes and stunted growth.
   c. thyroid and pituitary.
   d. glucose and glycogen.

4. How do feedback mechanisms control hormone production?

Math Skills

5. One's bedtime blood-glucose level is normally 140 mg/dL. Ty's blood-glucose level is 189 mg/dL at bedtime. What percentage above 140 mg/dL is Ty's level?

Critical Thinking

6. **Making Inferences** Glucose is a source of energy. Epinephrine quickly increases the blood-glucose level. Why is epinephrine important in times of stress?

7. **Applying Concepts** The hormone glucagon is released when glucose levels fall below normal. Explain how the hormones glucagon and insulin work together to control blood-glucose levels.

SCiLINKS

Developed and maintained by the National Science Teachers Association

For a variety of links related to this chapter, go to www.scilinks.org

Topic: Hormones
SciLinks code: HSM0758

You've Gotta Lotta Nerve

Teacher's Notes

Time Required

One 45-minute class period

Lab Ratings

EASY ——————————→ HARD

Teacher Prep 🧪
Student Set-Up 🧪
Concept Level 🧪🧪
Clean Up 🧪

MATERIALS

The materials listed on the student page are enough for a group of 3 students. If more appropriate for your class, substitute fine point ball point pens for the dissecting pins.

Safety Caution

Remind students to review all safety cautions and icons before beginning this lab activity. Remind students to be safe and gentle with each other in this exercise and to respect the sensitivity and comfort of their peers. Tell students that they will not be testing for pain. The protective cover on the sharp end of the dissecting pin must remain in place at all times.

Skills Practice Lab

OBJECTIVES

Locate areas on the skin that respond to certain stimuli.

Determine which areas on the skin are more sensitive to certain kinds of stimuli.

MATERIALS

- dissecting pin with a small piece of cork or a small rubber stopper covering the sharp end
- eyedropper, plastic
- paper, graphing
- pens or markers, washable, fine point
- ruler, metric
- tap water, hot
- water, very cold

SAFETY

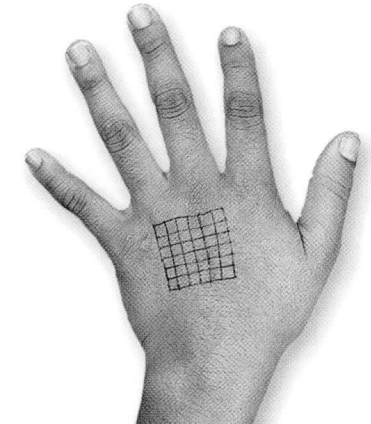

You've Gotta Lotta Nerve

Your skin has thousands of nerve receptors that detect sensations, such as temperature, pain, and pressure. Your brain is designed to filter out or ignore most of the input it receives from these skin receptors. If the brain did not filter input, simply wearing clothes would trigger so many responses that you couldn't function.

Some areas of the skin, such as the back of your hand, are more sensitive than others. In this activity, you will map the skin receptors for heat, cold, and pressure on the back of your hand.

Procedure

1. Form a group of three. One of you will volunteer the back of your hand for testing, one will do the testing, and the third will record the results.

2. Use a fine-point, washable marker or pen and a metric ruler to mark a 3 cm × 3 cm square on the back of one person's hand. Draw a grid within the area. Space the lines approximately 0.5 cm apart. You will have 36 squares in the grid when you are finished, as shown in the photograph below.

3. Mark off three 3 cm × 3 cm areas on a piece of graph paper. Make a grid in each area exactly as you did on the back of your partner's hand. Label one grid "Cold," another grid "Hot," and the third grid "Pressure."

Lab Notes

This activity works best if the student whose hand is being tested looks away or is loosely blindfolded while his or her hand is being tested. Often, students will say they feel something when they think they should feel something. Students should be given the choice of being blindfolded or looking away.

4 Use the eyedropper to apply one small droplet of cold water on each square in the grid on your partner's hand. Your partner should turn away while being tested. On your graph paper, mark an X on the "Cold" grid to show where your partner felt the cold droplet. Carefully blot the water off your partner's hand after several drops.

5 Repeat the test using hot-water droplets. The hot water should not be hot enough to hurt your partner. Mark an X on the "Hot" grid to indicate where your partner felt the hot droplet.

6 Repeat the test by using the head (not the point!) of the pin. Touch the skin to detect pressure receptors. Use a very light touch. On the graph paper, mark an X on the "Pressure" grid to indicate where your partner felt the pressure.

Analyze the Results

1 **Organizing Data** Count the number of Xs in each grid. How many heat receptor responses are there per 3 cm²? How many cold receptor responses are there? How many pressure receptor responses are there?

2 **Explaining Events** Do you have areas on the back of your hand where the receptors overlap? Explain your answer.

3 **Recognizing Patterns** How do you think the results of this experiment would be similar or different if you mapped an area of your forearm? of the back of your neck? of the palm of your hand?

Draw Conclusions

4 **Interpreting Information** Prepare a written report that includes a description of your investigation and a discussion of your answers to items 1–3. What conclusions can you draw from your results?

> ### Applying Your Data
>
> Use the library or the Internet to research what happens if a receptor is continuously stimulated. Does the kind of receptor make a difference? Does the intensity or strength of the stimulus make a difference? Explain your answers.

CHAPTER RESOURCES
Workbooks

📖 **Whiz-Bang Demonstrations**
 • Now You See It, Now You Don't **GENERAL**

📖 **Labs You Can Eat**
 • A Salty Sweet Experiment **GENERAL**

📖 **Long-Term Projects & Research Ideas**
 • Man Versus Machine **ADVANCED**

Disposal Information
Provide receptacles for used dissecting pins and eyedroppers. Be sure students know the location of the receptacles and deposit their sharp items in the designated containers. Dispose of sharp items properly to eliminate the risk of injury.

Analyze the Results
1. Answers may vary. Some groups will have more receptors in each category than others.
2. Students may notice that receptors in the same square on the grid can sense heat, cold, and pressure. Students may explain this reaction by noting that they have different kinds of receptors in the same spot. Students may also explain this by noting that the same receptor responds to more than one stimulus. Some students may interpret hot and cold as variations of a single sensation—temperature. They may also determine that the blunt head of the pin might have been cold and that they felt its temperature instead of the pressure.
3. Answers may vary. Different areas of the body are more sensitive than others.

Draw Conclusions
4. Answers may vary. Students should provide logical, well-reasoned conclusions that are supported by the details and results of the experiment. Students should discuss the answers to items 1–3.

Applying Your Data
Students will find that responses to a constant stimulus differ depending on the type and intensity of the stimulus. A person may become insensitive to an odor or even mild pain over time. Intense, sudden, or continued stimuli, such as heat, pain, or noise, may do much damage to a person over time.

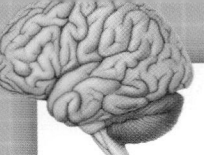

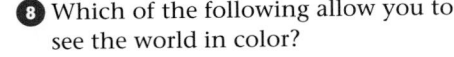

Assignment Guide

SECTION	QUESTIONS
1	1–2, 6, 10–11, 13, 15, 18, 22
2	4, 7, 8, 16, 19–21
3	3, 5, 9, 12, 14, 17, 23–26

ANSWERS

Using Key Terms

1. central nervous system
2. retina
3. hormone
4. reflex
5. feedback mechanism
6. neuron

Understanding Key Ideas

7. c
8. a
9. d
10. a
11. d
12. d
13. Sample answer: The main difference is that the somatic nervous system controls voluntary movements and activities, and the autonomic nervous system controls body functions that you do not need to think about. Both systems are important because together they keep your body active and alive. You are able to do all of your voluntary activities while your body functions are controlled by the autonomic nervous system.

USING KEY TERMS

Complete each of the following sentences by choosing the correct term from the word bank.

insulin   axon
hormone   nerve
retina   central nervous
neuron   system
reflex

1 The two parts of your _____ are your brain and spinal cord.

2 Sensory receptors in the _____ detect light.

3 Epinephrine is a(n) _____ that triggers the fight-or-flight response.

4 A(n) _____ is an involuntary and almost immediate movement in response to a stimulus.

5 One hormone that helps to regulate blood-glucose levels is _____ .

6 A(n) _____ is a specialized cell that receives and conducts electrical impulses.

UNDERSTANDING KEY IDEAS

Multiple Choice

7 Which of the following has receptors for smelling?
  a. cochlea cells
  b. thermoreceptors
  c. olfactory cells
  d. optic nerve

8 Which of the following allow you to see the world in color?
  a. cones
  b. rods
  c. lenses
  d. retinas

9 Which of the following glands makes insulin?
  a. adrenal gland
  b. pituitary gland
  c. thyroid gland
  d. pancreas

10 The peripheral nervous system does NOT include
  a. the spinal cord.
  b. axons.
  c. sensory receptors.
  d. motor neurons.

11 Which part of the brain regulates blood pressure?
  a. right cerebral hemisphere
  b. left cerebral hemisphere
  c. cerebellum
  d. medulla

12 The process in which the endocrine system, the digestive system, and the circulatory system control the level of blood glucose is an example of
  a. a reflex.
  b. an endocrine gland.
  c. the fight-or-flight response.
  d. a feedback mechanism.

---

14. Sample answer: The endocrine system is important because it produces chemical messengers called *hormones* that regulate body processes such as growth, fluid balance, and development.

15. Sample answer: The PNS receives stimuli from inside and outside the body and sends messages to the CNS. The CNS processes the messages and sends responses. The PNS carries the responses to the part of the body that will respond to a stimulus.

Short Answer

13 What is the difference between the somatic nervous system and the autonomic nervous system? Why are both systems important to the body?

14 Why is the endocrine system important to your body?

15 What is the relationship between the CNS and the PNS?

16 What is the function of the bones in the middle ear?

17 Describe two interactions between the endocrine system and the body that happen when a person is frightened.

CRITICAL THINKING

18 Concept Mapping Use the following terms to create a concept map: *nervous system, spinal cord, medulla, peripheral nervous system, brain, cerebrum, central nervous system,* and *cerebellum.*

19 Making Comparisons Compare a feedback mechanism with a reflex.

20 Analyzing Ideas Why is it important to have a lens that can change shape inside the eye?

21 Applying Concepts Why it is important that reflexes happen without thinking about them?

22 Predicting Consequences What would happen if your autonomic nervous system stopped working?

23 Making Comparisons How are the nervous system and the endocrine system similar? How are they different?

INTERPRETING GRAPHICS

Use the diagram below to answer the questions that follow.

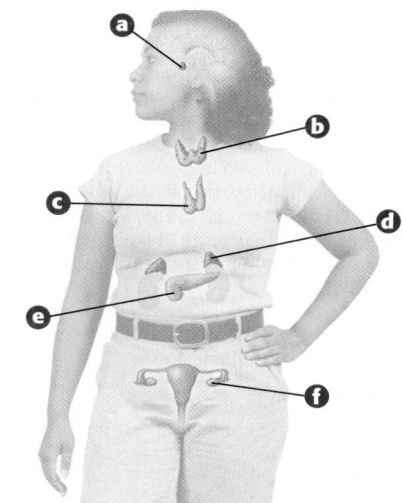

24 Which letter identifies the gland that regulates blood-glucose level?

25 Which letter identifies the gland that releases a hormone that stimulates the birth process?

26 Which letter identifies the gland that helps the body fight disease?

CHAPTER RESOURCES

Chapter Resource File

- **Chapter Review** GENERAL
- **Chapter Test A** GENERAL
- **Chapter Test B** ADVANCED
- **Chapter Test C** SPECIAL NEEDS
- **Vocabulary Activity** GENERAL

Workbooks

Study Guide
- Assessment resources are also available in Spanish.

 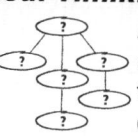

Standardized Test Preparation

Teacher's Note

To provide practice under more realistic testing conditions, give students 20 minutes to answer all of the questions in this Standardized Test Preparation.

MISCONCEPTION ALERT

Answers to the standardized test preparation can help you identify student misconceptions and misunderstandings.

READING

Passage 1
1. B
2. H
3. D

TEST DOCTOR

Question 1: The correct answer, B, is not explicitly stated in the passage. Students must read the passage to find out that a synapse is the gap between an axon and another cell. Students may select answer A if they confuse the neurotransmitters with the gap across which neurotransmitters work.

Question 3: Students may select incorrect answers A or C if they are not clear about what a synapse is. A synapse is not part of a cell; a synapse is a space between nerve cells. Impulses cannot just a synapse; they are transmitted by neurotransmitters.

READING

Read each of the passages below. Then, answer the questions that follow each passage.

Passage 1 The axon terminals of neurons usually do not touch the other cells. There is a small gap between an axon terminal and another cell. This space where a neuron meets another cell is called a *synapse*. When a nerve impulse arrives at an axon terminal, the impulse cannot cross the gap. Instead, the impulse triggers the release of chemicals called *neurotransmitters*. These neurotransmitters cross the synapse between the axon terminal and the cell. When neurotransmitters reach the next cell, they signal the cell to react in a certain way. There are many kinds of neurotransmitters. Some neurotransmitters tell cells to start an action. Other neurotransmitters tell cells to stop an action.

1. What is the space between a neuron terminal and a receiving cell called?
   A a neurotransmitter
   B a synapse
   C an axon
   D a nerve

2. Why are neurotransmitters necessary?
   F They tell muscle cells to contract or relax.
   G They create a gap that axons must cross.
   H They carry messages across the synapse.
   I They release chemical signals called *impulses*.

3. Which of the following statements is a fact in the passage?
   A A synapse is an extension of a nerve cell.
   B The space between an axon terminal and another cell is filled with neurons.
   C Nerve impulses jump from an axon to another cell.
   D There are many kinds of neurotransmitters.

Passage 2 Hormones are chemical messengers released by cells that <u>regulate</u> other cells in the body. Hormones regulate many body processes. Hormones control growth, direct the production and use of energy, keep body temperature within normal limits, and direct responses to stimuli outside the body. Hormones carry chemical messages that tell cells to change their activities. For example, one hormone tells the heart to beat faster. Another hormone tells certain cells to make proteins and stimulates bone and muscle growth. Each hormone communicates with specific cells. Each hormone is like a key that opens only one kind of lock. A hormone's message can be received only by cells that have the right kind of lock. Hormones control many important body functions, so their messages must be delivered properly.

1. According to the passage, which of the following statements about hormones is true?
   A Hormones tell cells to change their activities.
   B Hormones are electrical messengers.
   C Hormones are like locks.
   D Hormones are not important to your body.

2. What does the word *regulate* mean?
   F to control or direct
   G to beat faster
   H to raise your temperature
   I to reverse

3. According to the passage, what are two ways that one particular hormone affects the body?
   A controls your temperature and heart rate
   B responds to stimuli and makes proteins
   C stimulates bone growth and makes proteins
   D coordinates energy production and use and decreases temperature

Passage 2
1. A
2. F
3. C

TEST DOCTOR

Question 2: This question asks students to determine the meaning of the word *regulate* from the context of the passage. Students may select incorrect answers G, H, or I if they confuse a specific type of command or regulation with the more general definition of the word.

Question 3: Students may select incorrect answers A, B, or D if they read only the general list of hormone effects. Only one sentence in the passage refers to a particular hormone that has two effects, so the correct answer is C.

The diagram below shows a typical neuron. Use the diagram below to answer the questions that follow.

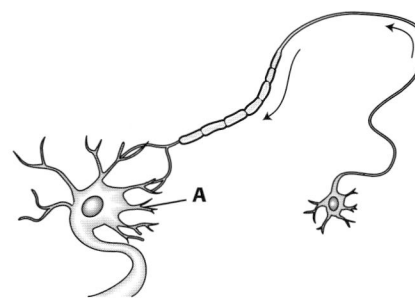

1. What does A represent?

  A a cell body   **C** a dendrite

  B an axon   **D** an axon terminal

2. Which of the following represents the path that an impulse in a neuron travels?

  F dendrite, cell body, axon, axon terminal

  G axon, axon terminal, cell body, dendrite

  H dendrite, nucleus, cell body, axon

  I nucleus, cell body, nucleus, axon

3. To where is an impulse that reaches an axon terminal transmitted?

  A another axon terminal

  B the brain

  C a reflex

  D dendrites of another neuron

4. What does having many dendrites allow a neuron to do?

  F to be locked into place in the body

  G to receive impulses from many other cells

  H to send impulses to surrounding cells

  I to get necessary nutrition

5. Which of the following statements about an axon is true?

  A An axon is part of a gland.

  B An axon connects the cell body to the axon terminal.

  C An axon detects sights and sounds.

  D An axon carries chemical messages.

MATH

Read each question below, and choose the best answer.

1. Sound travels about 335 m/s. How many kilometers would a sound travel in 1 min? (One kilometer is equal to 1,000 meters.)

  A 335,000 km

  B 20,100 km

  C 20.1 km

  D 0.335 km

2. Some axons send one impulse every 2.5 milliseconds. How many impulses could one of these axons send every second? (One second is equal to 1,000 milliseconds.)

  F 4 impulses

  G 40 impulses

  H 400 impulses

  I 4,000 impulses

3. The table below shows the results of Miguel's blood-glucose tests. Miguel ate lunch at 12:00 noon. His blood glucose was measured every hour after that time. What was the average hourly decrease in blood-glucose level?

Blood Glucose	
Time tested	Blood-glucose level (mg/1,000 mL)
1:00 P.M.	178
2:00 P.M.	112
3:00 P.M.	100
4:00 P.M.	89

  A approximately 160 mg/1,000 mL

  B approximately 120 mg/1,000 mL

  C approximately 30 mg/1,000 mL

  D approximately 22 mg/1,000 mL

4. Your brain has about 1 billion neurons. How is 1 billion expressed in scientific notation?

  F 1×10^3

  G 1×10^6

  H 1×10^9

  I 1×10^{12}

Standardized Test Preparation

CHAPTER RESOURCES

Chapter Resource File

• Standardized Test Preparation GENERAL

State Resources

 For specific resources for your state, visit **go.hrw.com** and type in the keyword **HSMSTR**.

INTERPRETING GRAPHICS

1. C

2. F

3. D

4. G

5. B

✚ TEST DOCTOR

Question 3: Answer D is correct because when an impulse reaches an axon terminal, it is carried across the synapse by neurotransmitters to the dendrites of another neuron. Students may select incorrect answer A if they forget the difference between a dendrite and an axon terminal.

Question 5: Answer B is correct because an axon is the part of the nerve cell that runs from the nerve cell body and ends in an axon terminal. Students may select incorrect answer D if they confuse the chemical messages carried across a synapse by neurotransmitters with the electrical impulses carried by axons.

MATH

1. C

2. H

3. C

4. H

✚ TEST DOCTOR

Question 1: Students may select incorrect answers A or D if they simply multiply or divide 335 by 1,000. They will have neglected to include the factor of 60 s/min. Students may select incorrect answer B if they forget to convert meters to kilometers.

Question 4: Students may select incorrect answers F, G, or I if they count the wrong number of decimal places when figuring the exponent.

Scientific Discoveries

Discussion ——— GENERAL

Encourage a class discussion on the placebo effect by asking students the following questions:

- Do you think other therapies, such as acupuncture, homeopathy, or chiropractic care could act as placebos? (Answers may vary.)

- Do you think it would ever be ethical for a doctor to give a patient a placebo? (Answers may vary.)

- Do you think a person could become addicted to a placebo? (Answers may vary.)

Science, Technology, and Society

Discussion ——— GENERAL

If a disabled person could be hooked up to a computer, then so could anyone. Discuss the possibilities of having computers directly connected to the human brain. Ask students the following questions: What are some things that computers can do that humans can't? (Answers may vary.) What are some of the possibilities for memory, information retrieval, and new sorts of senses? (Answers may vary.) What can humans do that computers can't? (Answers may vary.)

Science in Action

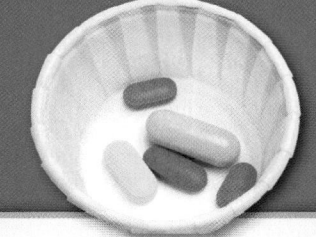

Scientific Discoveries

The Placebo Effect

A placebo (pluh SEE boh) is an inactive substance, such as a sugar pill, used in experimental drug trials. Some of the people who are test subjects are given a placebo as if it were the drug being tested. Usually, neither the doctor conducting the trial nor the test subjects know whether a person is taking a placebo or the test drug. In theory, any change in a subject's condition should be the result of the test drug. But for many years, scientists have known about the *placebo effect,* the effect of feeling better after taking the placebo pill. What makes someone who takes the placebo feel better? By studying brain activity, scientists are beginning to understand the placebo effect.

Social Studies ACTIVITY

Research the differences and similarities between ancient Chinese medical practices and traditional Western medical treatment. Both types of treatment rely in part on a patient's mental and emotional response to treatment. How might the placebo effect be part of both medical traditions? Create a poster showing the results of your research.

Science, Technology, and Society

Robotic Limbs

Cyborgs, or people that are part human and part robot, have been part of science fiction for many years and usually have super-human strength and X-ray vision. Meanwhile there are ordinary people on Earth who have lost the use of their arms and legs and could use some robot power. However, until recently, they have had to settle for clumsy mechanical limbs that were not a very good substitute for a real arm or hand. Today, thanks to advances in technology, scientists are developing artificial limbs—and eyes and ears—that can be wired directly into the nervous system and can be controlled by the brain. In the near future, artificial limbs and some artificial organs will be much more like the real thing.

Language Arts ACTIVITY

WRITING SKILL At the library or on the Internet, find examples of optical or visual illusions. Research how the brain processes visual information and how the brain "sees" and interprets these illusions. Write a report about why the brain seems to be fooled by visual tricks. How can understanding the brain's response to illusions help scientists create artificial vision?

Answer to Social Studies Activity

Students' posters may include a variety of ancient medical practices, including acupuncture, acupressure, and herbal medicines. The student should indicate that, in addition to the physical effect of the treatment, any medical treatment always includes a mental or emotional component that may be strengthened or weakened by the treatment being employed.

Answer to Language Arts Activity

Current brain research is still trying to find the answers to why the brain is fooled by optical or visual illusions. Students may find information in a variety of places, including science magazines such as *Scientific American* and a number of Internet Web sites.

Bertha Madras

Studying Brain Activity The brain is an amazing organ. Sometimes, though, drugs or disease keep the brain from working properly. Bertha Madras is a biochemist who studies drug addiction. Dr. Madras studies brain activity to see how substances, such as cocaine, target cells or areas in the brain. Using a variety of brain scanning techniques, Dr. Madras can observe a brain on drugs. She can see how a drug affects the normal activity of the brain. During her research, Dr. Madras realized that some of her results could be applied to Parkinson's disease and to attention deficit hyperactivity disorder (ADHD) in adults. Her research has led to new treatments for both problems.

Math ACTIVITY

Using a search engine on a computer connected to the Internet, search the Internet for "reaction time experiment." Go to one of the Web sites and take the response-time experiment. Record the time that it took you to respond. Repeat the test nine more times, and record your response time for each trial. Then, make a line graph or a bar graph of your response times. Did your response times change? In what way did they change?

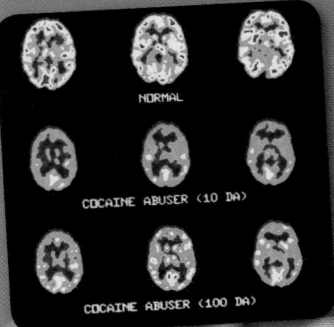

NORMAL

COCAINE ABUSER (10 DA)

COCAINE ABUSER (100 DA)

go.hrw.com

To learn more about these Science in Action topics, visit **go.hrw.com** and type in the keyword **HL5BD4F.**

Current Science

Check out Current Science® articles related to this chapter by visiting go.hrw.com. Just type in the keyword HL5CS25.

People in Science

Background

Bertha Madras, Ph.D., is a Professor of Psychobiology in the Department of Psychiatry at Harvard Medical School. She also serves as Chair of the Division of Neurochemistry at the New England Regional Primate Research Center (part of Harvard Medical School).

Madras has published more than 100 articles and served on a number of committees dedicated to brain and drug research. Madras also volunteers her time as a science teacher and regularly speaks to groups about the impact of drugs on the brain. To help people understand how drugs affect the brain, Madras has developed an exhibit and a CD-ROM called "Changing Your Mind: Drugs in the Brain."

Answer to Math Activity

Students will find several response-time experiments on the Internet. Students may find that their response times improved as they repeated the experiment, perhaps indicating that they were improving their ability to anticipate the cue and to respond to it. Other students may find that their response times declined as they played, indicating that their brains and muscles had become fatigued. Students' graphs should indicate what kind of experiment they took and should reflect their response times.

Reproduction and Development
Chapter Planning Guide

Compression guide:
To shorten instruction because of time limitations, omit the Chapter Lab.

OBJECTIVES	LABS, DEMONSTRATIONS, AND ACTIVITIES	TECHNOLOGY RESOURCES
PACING • 90 min pp. 682–687 **Chapter Opener**	**SE** Start-up Activity, p. 683 ◆ GENERAL	**OSP** Parent Letter ■ GENERAL **CD** Student Edition on CD-ROM **CD** Guided Reading Audio CD ■ **TR** Chapter Starter Transparency* **VID** Brain Food Video Quiz
Section 1 Animal Reproduction • Distinguish between asexual and sexual reproduction. • Explain the difference between external and internal fertilization. • Identify the three different types of mammalian reproduction.	**TE** Activity Asexual or Sexual Reproduction?, p. 685 BASIC **TE** Demonstration The Amazing Egg, p. 685 ◆ GENERAL **TE** Connection Activity Chemistry, p. 685 ADVANCED **SE** Science in Action Math, Social Studies, and Language Arts Activities, pp. 704–705 ◆ GENERAL	**CRF** Lesson Plans* **TR** Bellringer Transparency* **TE** Internet Activity, p. 687 GENERAL
PACING • 45 min pp. 688–691 **Section 2 Human Reproduction** • Identify the structures and functions of the male and female reproductive systems. • Describe two reproductive system problems.	**TE** Connection Activity Language Arts, p. 689 GENERAL **SE** School-to-Home Activity Twins and More, p. 690 GENERAL **TE** Group Activity Reproductive System Cancer, p. 690 GENERAL **SE** Connection to Social Studies Understanding STDs, p. 691 GENERAL **TE** Connection Activity Language Arts, p. 690 ADVANCED	**CRF** Lesson Plans* **TR** Bellringer Transparency* **TR** The Male Reproductive System* **TR** The Female Reproductive System*
PACING • 90 min pp. 692–697 **Section 3 Growth and Development** • Summarize the processes of fertilization and implantation. • Describe the development of the embryo and the fetus. • Identify the stages of human development from birth to death.	**SE** School-to-Home Activity Growing Up, p. 693 GENERAL **TE** Activity Making Models, p. 693 ◆ GENERAL **SE** Connection to Physics Using Ultrasound, p. 694 GENERAL **TE** Connection Activity Language Arts, p. 695 GENERAL **TE** Connection Activity Earth Science, p. 695 GENERAL **SE** Quick Lab Life Grows On, p. 696 GENERAL **CRF** Datasheet for Quick Lab* **SE** Skills Practice Lab It's a Comfy, Safe World!, p. 698 ◆ GENERAL **CRF** Datasheet for Chapter Lab* **SE** Skills Practice Lab My, How You've Grown!, p. 798 ◆ GENERAL **CRF** Datasheet for LabBook* **LB** Long-Term Projects & Research Ideas Get a Whiff of This!* ◆ ADVANCED	**CRF** Lesson Plans* **TR** Bellringer Transparency* **TR** Stages of Human Development* **TR** *LINK TO PHYSICAL SCIENCE* How Sonar Works* **CRF** SciLinks Activity* GENERAL **VID** Lab Videos for Life Science

PACING • 90 min

CHAPTER REVIEW, ASSESSMENT, AND STANDARDIZED TEST PREPARATION

CRF Vocabulary Activity* GENERAL
SE Chapter Review, pp. 700–701 GENERAL
CRF Chapter Review* ■ GENERAL
CRF Chapter Tests A* ■ GENERAL, B* ADVANCED, C* SPECIAL NEEDS
SE Standardized Test Preparation, pp. 702–703 GENERAL
CRF Standardized Test Preparation* GENERAL
CRF Performance-Based Assessment* GENERAL
OSP Test Generator GENERAL
CRF Test Item Listing* GENERAL

Online and Technology Resources

Visit **go.hrw.com** for a variety of free resources related to this textbook. Enter the keyword **HL5BD5**.

Holt Online Learning

Students can access interactive problem-solving help and active visual concept development with the *Holt Science and Technology* Online Edition available at **www.hrw.com**.

Guided Reading Audio CD
Also in Spanish

A direct reading of each chapter for auditory learners, reluctant readers, and Spanish-speaking students.

Science Tutor CD-ROM

Excellent for remediation and test practice.

SKILLS DEVELOPMENT RESOURCES	SECTION REVIEW AND ASSESSMENT	STANDARDS CORRELATIONS
SE Pre-Reading Activity, p. 682 GENERAL **OSP Science Puzzlers, Twisters & Teasers** GENERAL		National Science Education Standards UCP 3; SAI 1; LS 2a, 3a
CRF Directed Reading A* ■ BASIC, **B*** SPECIAL NEEDS **CRF Vocabulary and Section Summary*** ■ GENERAL **SE Reading Strategy** Prediction Guide, p. 684 GENERAL **SE Connection to Language Arts** Nature or Nurture, p. 685 GENERAL **TE Inclusion Strategies,** p. 686 GENERAL **SS Science Skills** Organizing Your Research BASIC	**TE Homework,** p. 684 GENERAL **SE Reading Checks,** pp. 685, 686, 687 GENERAL **TE Reteaching,** p. 686 BASIC **TE Quiz,** p. 686 GENERAL **TE Alternative Assessment,** p. 686 GENERAL **TE Homework,** p. 686 GENERAL **SE Section Review,*** p. 687 ■ GENERAL **CRF Section Quiz*** ■ GENERAL	UCP 5; SAI 2; LS 2a, 2b, 2c, 2d, 2e
CRF Directed Reading A* ■ BASIC, **B*** SPECIAL NEEDS **CRF Vocabulary and Section Summary*** ■ GENERAL **SE Reading Strategy** Reading Organizer, p. 688 GENERAL **SE Math Practice** Counting Eggs, p. 689 GENERAL **TE Reading Strategy** Activity, p. 689 GENERAL **MS Math Skills for Science** Multiplying Whole Numbers* GENERAL **MS Math Skills for Science** Dividing Whole Numbers with Long Division* GENERAL **MS Math Skills for Science** Parts of 100: Calculating Percentages* GENERAL	**SE Reading Checks,** pp. 688, 690 GENERAL **TE Reteaching,** p. 690 BASIC **TE Quiz,** p. 690 GENERAL **TE Alternative Assessment,** p. 690 GENERAL **SE Section Review,*** p. 691 ■ GENERAL **CRF Section Quiz*** ■ GENERAL	UCP 1, 5; SAI 1; SPSP 1, 4; LS 1d, 1e, 1f, 2b
CRF Directed Reading A* ■ BASIC, **B*** SPECIAL NEEDS **CRF Vocabulary and Section Summary*** ■ GENERAL **SE Reading Strategy** Discussion, p. 692 GENERAL **TE Reading Strategy** Answering Questions, p. 693 GENERAL **TE Inclusion Strategies,** p. 693 GENERAL **TE Connection to Math** Factor of Increase, p. 694 GENERAL **CRF Reinforcement Worksheet** The Beginning of a Life* GENERAL **CRF Critical Thinking** One to Grow On!* ADVANCED	**SE Reading Checks,** pp. 692, 693, 694, 696 GENERAL **TE Reteaching,** p. 696 BASIC **TE Quiz,** p. 696 GENERAL **TE Alternative Assessment,** p. 696 ADVANCED **SE Section Review,*** p. 697 ■ GENERAL **CRF Section Quiz*** ■ GENERAL	UCP 1, 2, 3; SAI 1; ST 2; LS 1a, 1b, 1c, 1e, 2b; *Chapter Lab:* SAI 1, 2; ST 2; SPSP 4; HNS 1; LS 1a, 2b; *LabBook:* UCP 2, 3; SAI 1; ST 1

One-Stop Planner® CD-ROM

This convenient CD-ROM includes:
- **Lab Materials QuickList Software**
- **Holt Calendar Planner**
- **Customizable Lesson Plans**
- **Printable Worksheets**
- **ExamView® Test Generator**

cnnstudentnews.com

Find the latest news, lesson plans, and activities related to important scientific events.

SCLINKS. NSTA

www.scilinks.org

Maintained by the **National Science Teachers Association.** See Chapter Enrichment pages for a complete list of topics.

Current Science®

Check out **Current Science** articles and activities by visiting the HRW Web site at **go.hrw.com.** Just type in the keyword **HL5CS26T.**

Classroom Videos

- **Lab Videos** demonstrate the chapter lab.
- **Brain Food Video Quizzes** help students review the chapter material.
- **CNN Videos** bring science into your students' daily life.

Visual Resources

CHAPTER STARTER TRANSPARENCY

Strange but True!

A tiny animal is resting peacefully in a warm, dark space. Suddenly it finds itself driven out into the cold and light. The chilly temperature is almost unbearable for its hairless body. The glaring light is disorienting to its blurry vision. Driven by instinct, the animal starts crawling up and up to the promise of warmth and security. If it slips and falls to the ground, it will die. Almost 30 minutes pass before it reaches its destination—a pouch in its mother's abdomen. Inside the pouch, it finds a nipple that will supply milk for several months as the animal grows and develops.

Can you guess what animal has just been born? That's right, a baby kangaroo, called a joey. Joeys are born in a very early stage of development. They continue to develop inside their mother's pouch until they are able to eat solid food such as grasses and other plants.

Like all living things, kangaroos eventually grow old and die. They must reproduce to pass on their genetic heritage. There are many ways of reproducing, as you will discover in this chapter. But reproduction is only part of the story. Development, or the way organisms grow, is also an important part of the cycle of life.

BELLRINGER TRANSPARENCIES

Section: Animal Reproduction
Do you know how birds, ants, humans, and sea stars reproduce? Write down any differences that you are aware of in how these animals reproduce. Also write down any differences that you know of in how these animals raise their young.

Write your answers in your **science journal.**

Section: Human Reproduction
You may have heard of *cloning* in recent news stories. Do you know what cloning is? If so, write out a definition for cloning. Would cloning be considered asexual or sexual reproduction? Do you think that cloning human beings could be considered as a kind of reproduction? Why or why not? Do you know of any organisms that naturally reproduce by cloning? If so, write out a few examples of these animals.

Record your answers in your **science journal.**

TEACHING TRANSPARENCIES

The Male Reproductive System

The Female Reproductive System

TEACHING TRANSPARENCIES

Stages of Human Development
Infant, 4 years, 7 years, 11 years, Adult

How Sonar Works
A fish finder sends ultrasonic waves down into the water. The time it takes for the echo to return helps determine the location of the fish.

LINK TO PHYSICAL SCIENCE

Chapter: The Nature of Sound

CONCEPT MAPPING TRANSPARENCY

Use the following terms to complete the concept map below: fragmentation, reproduction, sexual reproduction, internal fertilization, an embryo, zygote, egg, budding, asexual reproduction

Planning Resources

LESSON PLANS

Lesson Plan — SAMPLE

Section: Waves

Pacing
Regular Schedule: with lab(s):2 days | without lab(s)2 days
Block Schedule: with lab(s): 1 1/2 days | without lab(s)1 day

Objectives
1. Relate the seven properties of life to a living organism.
2. Describe seven themes that can help you to organize what you learn about biology.
3. Identify the tiny structures that make up all living organisms.
4. Differentiate between reproduction and heredity and between metabolism and homeostasis.

National Science Education Standards Covered
LSInter6:Cells have particular structures that underlie their functions.
LSMat1:Most cell functions involve chemical reactions.
LSBeh1:Cells store and use information to guide their functions.
UCP1:Cell functions are regulated.
SI1: Cells can differentiate and form complete multicellular organisms.
PS1: Species evolve over time.
ESS1: The great diversity of organisms is the result of more than 3.5 billion years of evolution.
ESS2: Natural selection and its evolutionary consequences provide a scientific explanation for the fossil record of ancient life forms as well as for the striking molecular similarities observed among the diverse species of living organisms.
ST1: The millions of different species of plants, animals, and microorganisms that live on Earth today are related by descent from common ancestors.
ST2: The energy for life primarily comes from the sun.
SPSP1: The complexity and organization of organisms accommodates the need for obtaining, transforming, transporting, releasing, and eliminating the matter and energy used to sustain the organism.
SPSP6: As matter and energy flows through different levels of organization of living systems—cells, organs, communities—and between living systems and the physical environment, chemical elements are recombined in different ways.
HNS1: Organisms have behavioral responses to internal changes and to external stimuli.

PARENT LETTER

SAMPLE

Dear Parent,

Your son's or daughter's science class will soon begin exploring the chapter entitled "The World of Physical Science." In this chapter, students will learn about how the scientific method applies to the world of physical science and the role of physical science in the world. By the end of the chapter, students should demonstrate a clear understanding of the chapter's main ideas and be able to discuss the following topics:

1. physical science as the study of energy and matter (Section 1)
2. the role of physical science in the world around them (Section 1)
3. careers that rely on physical science (Section 1)
4. the steps used in the scientific method (Section 2)
5. examples of technology (Section 2)
6. how the scientific method is used to answer questions and solve problems (Section 2)
7. how our knowledge of science changes over time (Section 2)
8. how models represent real objects or systems (Section 3)
9. examples of different ways models are used in science (Section 3)
10. the importance of the International System of Units (Section 4)
11. the appropriate units to use for particular measurements (Section 4)
12. how area and density are derived quantities (Section 4)

Questions to Ask Along the Way

You can help your son or daughter learn about these topics by asking interesting questions such as the following:
- What are some surprising careers that use physical science?
- What is a characteristic of a good hypothesis?
- When is it a good idea to use a model?
- Why do Americans measure things in terms of inches and yards and meters?

ALSO IN SPANISH

TEST ITEM LISTING

TEST ITEM LISTING
The World of Science — SAMPLE

MULTIPLE CHOICE
1. A limitation of models is that
  a. they are large enough to see.
  b. they do not act exactly like the things that they model.
  c. they are smaller than the things that they model.
  d. they model unfamiliar things
  Answer: B   Difficulty: 1   Section: 3   Objective: 2
2. The length 10 m is equal to
  a. 100 cm.   c. 10,000 mm.
  b. 1,000 cm.   d. Both (b) and (c)
  Answer: B   Difficulty: 1   Section: 3   Objective: 2
3. To be valid, a hypothesis must be
  a. testable.   c. made into a law.
  b. supported by evidence.   d. Both (a) and (b)
  Answer: D   Difficulty: 1   Section: 3   Objective: 2 1
4. The statement "Sheila has a stain on her shirt" is an example of a(n)
  a. law.   c. observation.
  b. hypothesis.   d. prediction.
  Answer: B   Difficulty: 1   Section: 3   Objective: 2
5. A hypothesis is often developed out of
  a. observations.   c. laws.
  b. experiments.   d. Both (a) and (b)
  Answer: B   Difficulty: 1   Section: 3   Objective: 2
6. How many milliliters are in 3.5 kL?
  a. 3,500 mL   c. 3,500, 000 mL.
  b. 0.0035 mL   d. 35,000 mL.
  Answer: B   Difficulty: 1   Section: 3   Objective: 2
7. A map of Seattle is an example of a
  a. law.   c. model.
  b. theory.   d. unit.
  Answer: B   Difficulty: 1   Section: 3   Objective: 2
8. A lab has the safety icons shown below. These icons mean that you should wear
  a. only safety goggles.   c. safety goggles and a lab apron.
  b. only a lab apron.   d. safety goggles, a lab apron, and gloves.
  Answer: B   Difficulty: 1   Section: 3   Objective: 2
9. The law of conservation of mass says that no mass before a chemical change is
  a. more than the total mass after the change.
  b. less than the total mass after the change.
  c. the same as the total mass after the change.
  d. not the same as the total mass after the change.
  Answer: B   Difficulty: 1   Section: 3   Objective: 2
10. In which of the following areas might you find a geochemist at work?
  a. studying the chemistry of rocks   c. studying fishes
  b. studying forestry   d. studying the atmosphere
  Answer: B   Difficulty: 1   Section: 3   Objective: 2

One-Stop Planner® CD-ROM

This CD-ROM includes all of the resources shown here and the following time-saving tools:

- Lab Materials QuickList Software
- Customizable lesson plans
- Holt Calendar Planner
- The powerful ExamView® Test Generator

Meeting Individual Needs

DIRECTED READING A

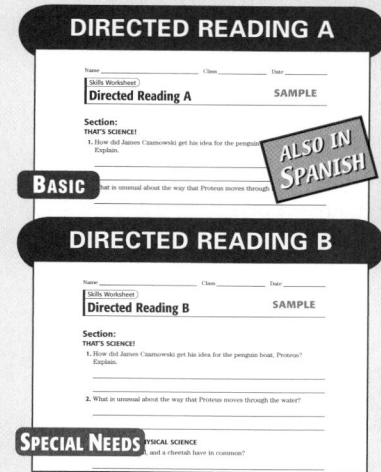

Skills Worksheet
Directed Reading A — SAMPLE

Section:
THAT'S SCIENCE!
1. How did James Czarnowski get his idea for the penguin...
Explain.

... at is unusual about the way that Proteus moves through...

BASIC

ALSO IN SPANISH

VOCABULARY ACTIVITY

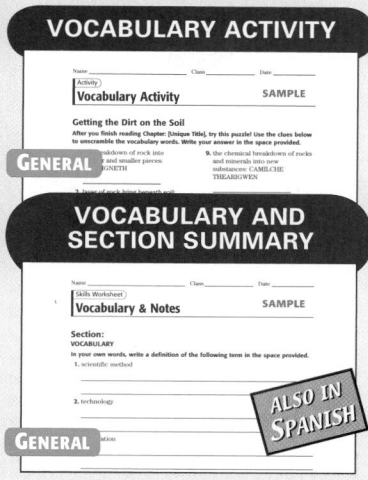

Activity
Vocabulary Activity — SAMPLE

Getting the Dirt on the Soil
After you finish reading Chapter: [Unique Title], try this puzzle! Use the clues below to unscramble the vocabulary words. Write your answer in the space provided.

... and smaller pieces. ... RGNETH

... layer of rock being beneath soil
... 9. the chemical breakdown of rocks and material into new substances: CAMILCHE THEAIRGWEN

GENERAL

REINFORCEMENT

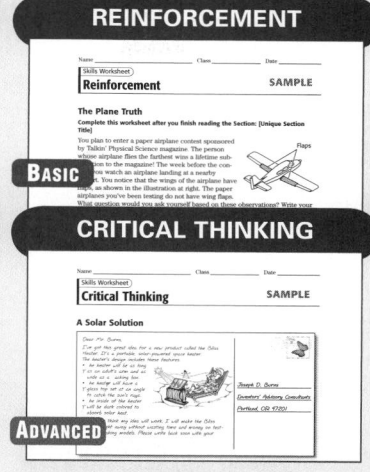

Skills Worksheet
Reinforcement — SAMPLE

The Plane Truth
Complete this worksheet after you finish reading the Section: [Unique Section Title]

You plan to enter a paper airplane contest sponsored by Talkin' Physical Science magazine. The person whose airplane flies the farthest wins a lifetime subscription to the magazine! The week before the contest, you watch an airplane landing at a nearby ... You notice that the wings of the airplane have flaps, as shown in the illustration at right. The paper airplanes you've been testing do not have wing flaps.
What question would you ask yourself based on these observations? Write your...

Flaps

BASIC

SCILINKS ACTIVITY

Activity
SciLinks Activity — SAMPLE

MARINE ECOSYSTEMS
Go to www.scilinks.com. To find links related to marine ecosystems, type in the keyword HL5400. Then, use the links to answer the questions about marine ecosys...

... percentage of the Earth's surface is covered by water?

GENERAL

Go to www.scilinks.org
Topic: Reproductive System
Sropination:
SciLinks code: HL5400

DIRECTED READING B

Skills Worksheet
Directed Reading B — SAMPLE

Section:
THAT'S SCIENCE!
1. In your own words, how did James Czarnowski get his idea for the penguin boat, Proteus? Explain.

2. What is unusual about the way that Proteus moves through the water?

SPECIAL NEEDS ... PHYSICAL SCIENCE

... and, and a cheetah have in common?

VOCABULARY AND SECTION SUMMARY

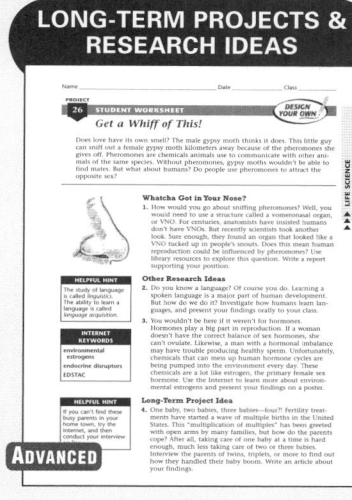

Skills Worksheet
Vocabulary & Notes — SAMPLE

Section:
VOCABULARY
In your own words, write a definition of the following term in the space provided.

1. scientific method

2. technology

GENERAL

ALSO IN SPANISH

CRITICAL THINKING

Skills Worksheet
Critical Thinking — SAMPLE

A Solar Solution

Dear Mr. Burns,
I've got this great idea for a new product called the Silos Insulator. It's a portable, solar-powered space heater...

Joseph D. Burns
Inventors' Advisory Consultants
Portland, OR 97201

ADVANCED

SCIENCE PUZZLERS, TWISTERS & TEASERS

Name ___ Date ___ Class ___
CHAPTER
26 SCIENCE PUZZLERS, TWISTERS & TEASERS
Reproduction and Development

Crossing Words
1. The following is a list of first generation words. As they are, the words are nonsense. If you find the right mate for each word, however, they will produce offspring that are vocabulary words from the chapter. Consider the letters on each word to be genetic material. As you have learned from the chapter, parent organisms each contribute one-half of their genes to the offspring. Match each of these words with another from the list that can be divided and recombined in such a way as to produce two vocabulary words.

Example: ___ infertile ___ + ___ menstruie ___ produce
___ infertale ___ + ___ menstruation

The Vocabulary Gene Pool
egmentation embryo epiding fetryo
flagg implanenta manseme monotrupial overty

GENERAL

Labs and Activities

LONG-TERM PROJECTS & RESEARCH IDEAS

Name ___ Date ___ Class ___
PROJECT
26 STUDENT WORKSHEET
Get a Whiff of This!

DESIGN YOUR OWN

Does love have its own smell? The male gypsy moth thinks it does. This little guy can smell a female gypsy moth kilometers away because of the pheromones she gives off. Pheromones are chemicals animals use to communicate with other animals of the same species. Without pheromones, gypsy moths wouldn't be able to find mates. But what about humans? Do people use pheromones to attract the opposite sex?

Whatcha Got in Your Nose?
1. How would you go about sniffing pheromones? Well, you would need to use a structure called a vomeronasal organ, or VNO. For centuries, anatomists have insisted humans don't have VNOs. But recently scientists took another look. Sure enough, they found an organ that looked like a VNO tucked up in people's mouth. Does this mean human reproduction could be influenced by pheromones? Use library resources to explore this question. Write a report supporting your position.

Other Research Ideas
2. Do you know a language? Of course you do. Learning a spoken language is a major part of human development. But how do we do it? Investigate how humans learn languages, and present your findings orally to your class.

3. You wouldn't be here if it weren't for hormones. Hormones play a big part in reproduction. If a woman doesn't have the correct balance of sex hormones, she can't ovulate. Likewise, a man with a hormonal imbalance may have trouble producing healthy sperm. Unfortunately, chemicals that can mess up human hormone cycles are being pumped into the environment every day. These chemicals are a lot like estrogen, the primary female sex hormone. Use the Internet to learn more about environmental estrogens and present your findings on a poster.

Long-Term Project Idea
4. One baby, two babies, three babies—four?! Fertility treatments have started a wave of multiple births in the United States. This "multiplication of multiples" has been greeted with open arms by many families, but how do the parents cope? After all, taking care of one baby at a time is hard enough, much less taking care of two or three babies. Interview the parents of twins, triplets, or more to find out how they handled their baby booms. Write an article about your findings.

HELPFUL HINT
The study of language is called linguistics. The ability to learn a language is called language acquisition.

INTERNET KEYWORDS
environmental estrogens
endocrine disruptors
EDSTAC

HELPFUL HINT
If you can't find these busy parents in your home town, try the Internet, and then conduct your interview.

LIFE SCIENCE

ADVANCED

DATASHEETS FOR QUICK LABS

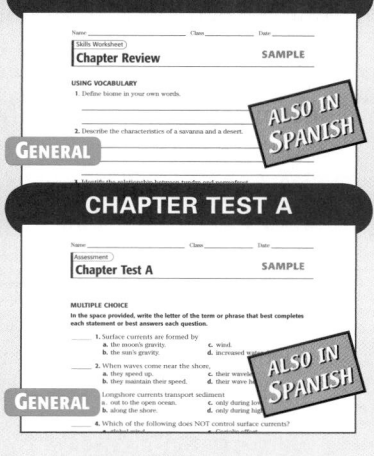

TEACHER RESOURCE PAGE

Quick Lab
Reaction to Stress — DATASHEET FOR QUICK LAB
SAMPLE

Background
The graph below illustrates changes that occur in the membrane potential of a neuron during an action potential. Use the graph to answer the following questions. Refer to Figure 3 as needed.

DATASHEETS FOR CHAPTER LABS

TEACHER RESOURCE PAGE

Skills Practice Lab
Using Scientific Methods — DATASHEET FOR CHAPTER LAB
SAMPLE

Teacher's Notes
TIME REQUIRED
One 45-minute class period.

DATASHEETS FOR LABBOOK

TEACHER RESOURCE PAGE

Skills Practice Lab
Does It All Add Up? — DATASHEET FOR LABBOOK LAB
SAMPLE

Teacher's Notes
TIME REQUIRED
One 45-minute class period.

Review and Assessments

SECTION QUIZ

Assessment
Section Quiz — SAMPLE

Section:
In the space provided, write the letter of the description that best matches the term or phrase.

___ 1. building molecules that can be used as an energy source, or breaking down molecules in which energy is stored

___ the process by which light energy is converted to chemical energy

___ an organism that uses sunlight or inorganic substances to make organic compounds

f. cellular respiration

GENERAL

ALSO IN SPANISH

CHAPTER REVIEW

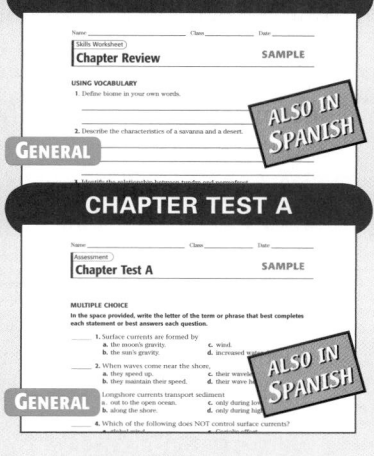

Skills Worksheet
Chapter Review — SAMPLE

USING VOCABULARY
1. Define biome in your own words.

2. Describe the characteristics of a savanna and a desert.

... Identify the relationship between tundra and permafrost

GENERAL

ALSO IN SPANISH

CHAPTER TEST B

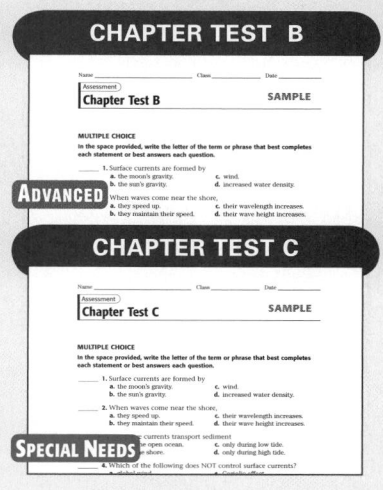

Assessment
Chapter Test B — SAMPLE

MULTIPLE CHOICE
In the space provided, write the letter of the term or phrase that best completes each statement or best answers each question.

___ 1. Surface currents are formed by
a. the moon's gravity.   c. wind.
b. the sun's gravity.   d. increased water density.

When waves come near the shore,
a. they speed up.   c. their wavelength increases.
b. they maintain their speed.   d. their wave height increases.

ADVANCED

STANDARDIZED TEST PREPARATION

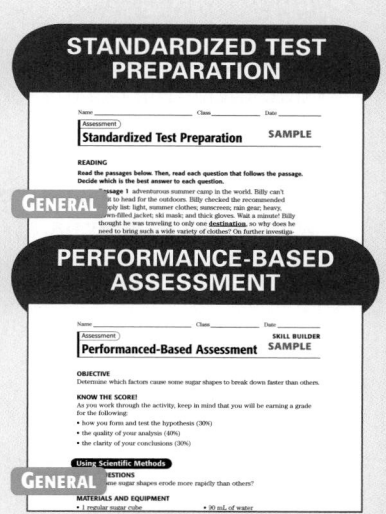

Assessment
Standardized Test Preparation — SAMPLE

READING
Read the passages below. Then, read each question that follows the passage. Decide which is the best answer to each question.

Passage 1 ... adventurous summer camp in the world. Billy can't ... to head for the outdoors. Billy checked the recommended ... list: light, summer clothes, sunscreen; rain gear; heavy, ... filled jacket; ski mask; and thick gloves. Wait a minute! Billy thought he was traveling to only one destination, so why does he need to bring such a wide variety of clothes? On further investiga-

GENERAL

SECTION REVIEW

Skills Worksheet
Section Review — SAMPLE

Section:
KEY TERMS
1. What do paleontologists study?

2. How does a trace fossil differ from petrified wood?

... fossil.

GENERAL

... UNDERSTANDING KEY IDEAS

ALSO IN SPANISH

CHAPTER TEST A

Assessment
Chapter Test A — SAMPLE

MULTIPLE CHOICE
In the space provided, write the letter of the term or phrase that best completes each statement or best answers each question.

___ 1. Surface currents are formed by
a. the moon's gravity.   c. wind.
b. the sun's gravity.   d. increased water density.

___ 2. When waves come near the shore,
a. they speed up.   c. their wavelength increases.
b. they maintain their speed.   d. their wave height increases.

Longshore currents transport sediment
... out to the open ocean.   c. only during low tide.
... along the shore.   d. only during high tide.

___ 4. Which of the following does NOT control surface currents?

GENERAL

ALSO IN SPANISH

CHAPTER TEST C

Assessment
Chapter Test C — SAMPLE

MULTIPLE CHOICE
In the space provided, write the letter of the term or phrase that best completes each statement or best answers each question.

___ 1. Surface currents are formed by
a. the moon's gravity.   c. wind.
b. the sun's gravity.   d. increased water density.

___ 2. When waves come near the shore,
a. they speed up.   c. their wavelength increases.
b. they maintain their speed.   d. their wave height increases.

... currents transport sediment
... to the open ocean.   c. only during low tide.
... along the shore.   d. only during high tide.

___ 4. Which of the following does NOT control surface currents?

SPECIAL NEEDS

PERFORMANCE-BASED ASSESSMENT

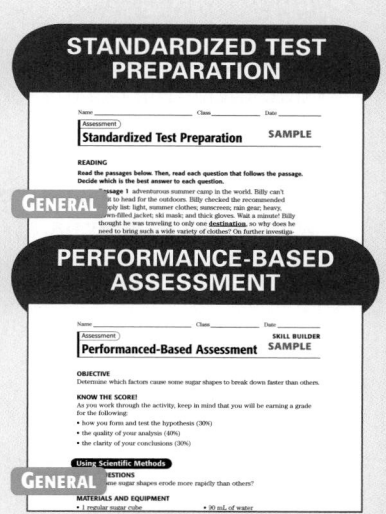

Assessment
Performanced-Based Assessment — SAMPLE

SKILL BUILDER

OBJECTIVE
Determine which factors cause some sugar shapes to break down faster than others.

KNOW THE SCORE!
As you work through the activity, keep in mind that you will be earning a grade for the following:
• how you form and test the hypothesis (20%)
• the quality of your analysis (30%)
• the clarity of your conclusions (30%)

Using Scientific Methods
... STIONS
... sugar shapes erode more rapidly than others?

MATERIALS AND EQUIPMENT
• 1 regular sugar cube   • 30 mL of water

GENERAL

This Chapter Enrichment provides relevant and interesting information to expand and enhance your presentation of the chapter material.

Section 1

Animal Reproduction

Asexual Reproduction

- The most common forms of asexual reproduction are binary fission, budding, and fragmentation. Binary fission is used mainly by bacteria.

- A major advantage of asexual reproduction is that it does not require a mate. Asexual reproduction also allows animals to produce many offspring in a 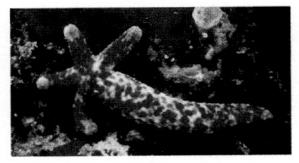 short period of time. Many animals that do not move around, such as sea sponges, reproduce asexually.

Sexual Reproduction

- Because sexual reproduction brings together genetic material from two parents, there is greater variation among animals that reproduce sexually versus those that reproduce asexually.

Fertilization

- In external fertilization, eggs can be fertilized without physical contact between the parents. Instead, chemical signals coordinate the fertilization process, ensuring that the parents release their sex cells at the appropriate time.

- Internal fertilization requires a more sophisticated reproductive system, including organs for delivering and storing sperm. Fertilized eggs can develop externally, as with birds, or internally, as with placental mammals. Internally protected embryos are more likely to survive, but placental females do not usually produce as many offspring as do egg-laying females.

Is That a Fact!

- Some animal species that reproduce sexually don't have separate sexes. Instead, every individual contains male and female sexual characteristics. This situation is known as *hermaphrodism*. Hermaphrodites, such as earthworms, usually exchange sex cells with one another. Some hermaphrodites can reproduce by themselves as well.

Section 2

Human Reproduction

The Male Reproductive System

- Male reproductive functions mainly concern sperm production. The head of a sperm contains DNA, and the tail region contains mitochondria. The mitochondria are "engines" for the sperm, providing the sperm's tail with the energy to whip back and forth.

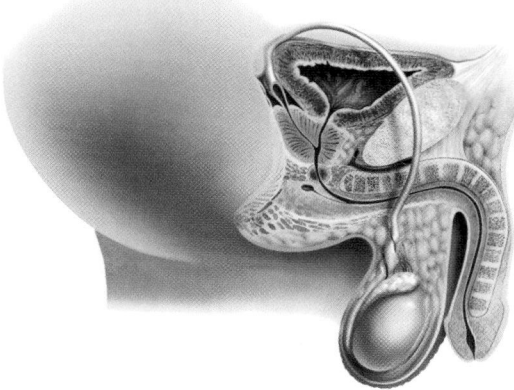

- The process of maturation of sperm from germ cells to spermatozoa takes about 74 days. Even then, they cannot yet penetrate an ovum. First they must "ripen" in the epididymis, a process that takes about 10 days. Though the maturation process is lengthy, once sperm are fully mature, they can remain viable for about 6 weeks.

Is That a Fact!

- If the seminiferous tubules—the bundle of tubes that makes up each testicle—were joined together and extended, they would be more than 200 m long!

The Female Reproductive System

- The ovaries are the primary female reproductive organs. About the size of large almonds, the ovaries are located on either side of the uterus, each anchored by an ovarian ligament. These tiny organs secrete the hormones largely responsible for development during puberty. They are also responsible for releasing eggs.

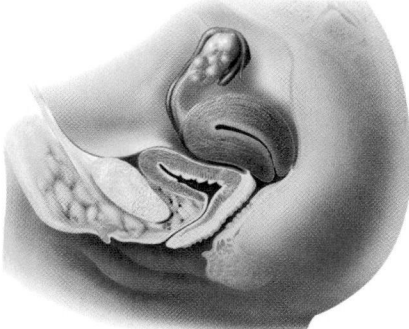

- Every menstrual cycle, several ova begin to ripen. In most cases, however, only one egg reaches maturity at a time. This mature, ripened ovum, encased in a Graafian follicle, travels to the surface of the ovary, where it remains until midcycle, when ovulation occurs. Then, the Graafian follicle, distended with fluid, ruptures, sending the egg into the abdominal cavity. The fallopian tube then captures the ovum, and the ovum begins its descent to the uterus.

Sexually Transmitted Diseases

- Chlamydia is the most prevalent bacterial sexually transmitted disease (STD) in North America. Caused by an organism called *Chlamydia trachomatis,* its symptoms include a frequent desire to urinate, pain with urination, and penile or vaginal discharge. In women, there are often few symptoms in the early stages. Troublesome as the symptoms are, the consequences are worse: chlamydia is a major cause of infertility. If left untreated, it can cause *pelvic inflammatory disease* and, in women, the subsequent inability to conceive. In men, infection that reaches the testes results in infertility.

- Also known as *salpingitis,* pelvic inflammatory disease (PID) is an infection of the fallopian tubes, uterus, and cervix. While a number of bacteria can cause PID, the usual culprits are chlamydia and gonorrhea. Although these infections can be completely cured with antibiotics, PID often leaves the fallopian tubes—the conduits between the ovaries and the uterus—scarred, making conception difficult or impossible. Other potential consequences of PID include ectopic pregnancy, peritonitis, and death.

Section 3

Growth and Development

Sex Determination

- One pair of human chromosomes determines the sex of a baby. There are two types of these sex chromosomes: X and Y. Because the egg contains only the X chromosome, the gender of the baby is determined by the father's sperm, which may contain either an X or a Y chromosome. If a sperm containing an X chromosome joins with an egg, the baby will be a girl. If a sperm containing a Y chromosome fertilizes the egg, the baby will be a boy.

Fetal Development

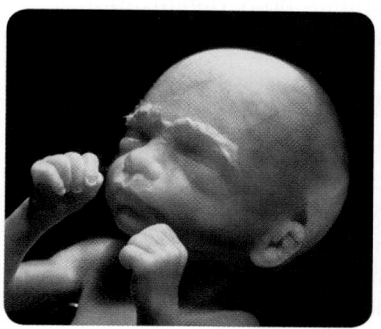

- The development of a baby from a single cell progresses at an astounding rate. Early in development, the embryo resembles a tiny tadpole, with a rounded body and tail. About 4 weeks after fertilization (the 6th week of pregnancy), however, limb buds—with knee and elbow joints evident—form, and facial features are recognizable. By the ninth week, nerves and muscles have developed enough that the fetus can move independently. By 12 weeks, the fetus is about 7.6 cm long and has a mass of about 28 g.

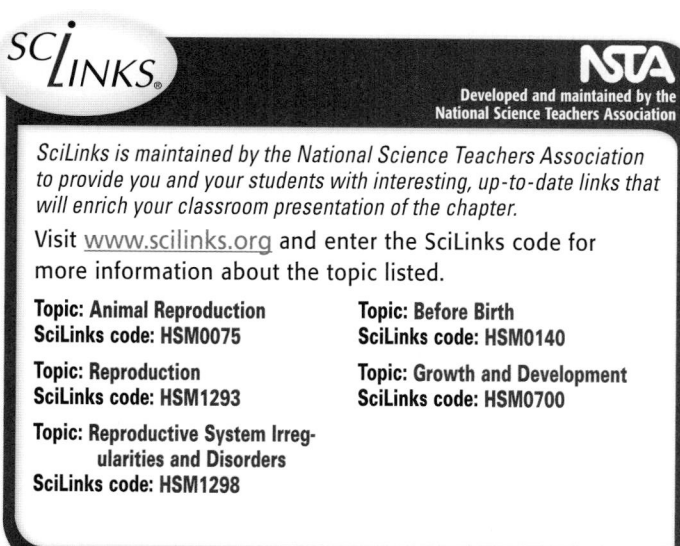

SciLinks Developed and maintained by the National Science Teachers Association

SciLinks is maintained by the National Science Teachers Association to provide you and your students with interesting, up-to-date links that will enrich your classroom presentation of the chapter.

Visit www.scilinks.org and enter the SciLinks code for more information about the topic listed.

Topic: Animal Reproduction
SciLinks code: HSM0075

Topic: Before Birth
SciLinks code: HSM0140

Topic: Reproduction
SciLinks code: HSM1293

Topic: Growth and Development
SciLinks code: HSM0700

Topic: Reproductive System Irregularities and Disorders
SciLinks code: HSM1298

Overview

Tell students that this chapter will help them learn about how animals, including people, reproduce. The chapter describes asexual and sexual reproduction in animals. The chapter also describes human reproduction and development.

Assessing Prior Knowledge

Students should be familiar with the following topics:
- cells and cellular activities
- mammals
- human body organization and structure

Identifying Misconceptions

Students may have some confusion about forms of reproduction that do not involve "mating," such as asexual reproduction or external fertilization. Students may also be confused that offspring inherit traits from both parents equally. Girls may believe they get more of their traits from their mother, and boys may believe they share more with their father. Students may or may not be familiar with the words *gene* and *chromosome*. Very few students have a good grasp of the chemical basis for inheritance.

26

Reproduction and Development

About the PHOTO

If someone had taken your picture when your mother was about 13 weeks pregnant with you, that picture would have looked much like this photograph. You have changed a lot since then, haven't you? You started out as a single cell, and you became a complete person. And you haven't stopped growing and changing yet. In fact, you will continue to change for the rest of your life.

PRE-READING ACTIVITY

Graphic Organizer

Spider Map Before you read the chapter, create the graphic organizer entitled "Spider Map" described in the **Study Skills** section of the Appendix. Label the circle "Reproduction and Development." Create a leg for each section title. As you read the chapter, fill in the map with details about reproduction and development from each section.

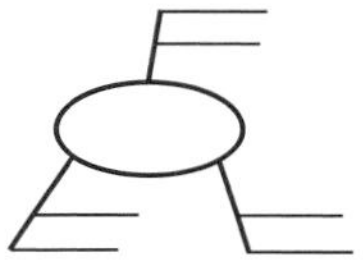

Standards Correlations

National Science Education Standards

The following codes indicate the National Science Education Standards that correlate to this chapter. The full text of the standards is at the front of the book.

Chapter Opener
UCP 3; SAI 1; LS 2a, 3a

Section 1 Animal Reproduction
UCP 5; SAI 2; LS 2a, 2b, 2c, 2d, 2e

Section 2 Human Reproduction
UCP 1, 5; SAI 1; SPSP 1, 4; LS 1d-1f, 2b

Section 3 Growth and Development
UCP 1, 2, 3; SAI 1; ST 2; LS 1a, 1c, 1d, 1e, 2b;
Labbook: UCP2, 3; SAI 1; ST 1

Chapter Lab
SAI 1, 2; ST 2; SPSP 3, 4; HNS 1; LS 1a, 2b

Chapter Review
LS 2a, 2b

Science in Action
SAI 1; ST 2; SPSP 2, 5; HNS 1; LS 1e, 1f

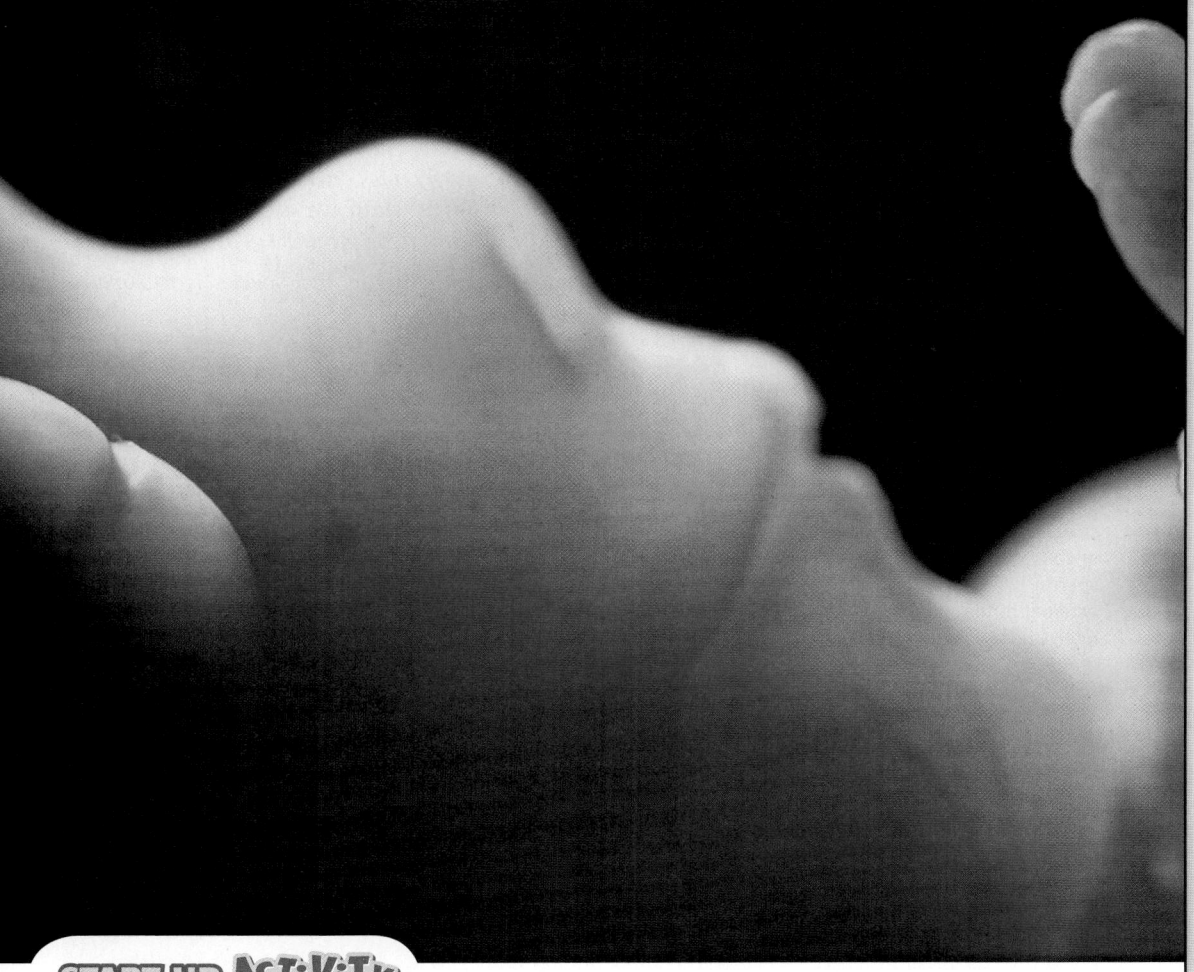

Teacher's Notes: Instructions for taking measurements (demonstrate these techniques for your students): Measure head height by standing next to the board with one ear against it. On the board, mark the top of the head and the bottom of the chin. Measure the distance between the marks. Find the total body height by measuring the distance from the top-of-the-head mark to the ground. Leg length should be measured from the hip where the leg bends when you sit down. Hold a meterstick parallel to the floor at your hips. Have someone then use the tape measure to measure the distance from the meterstick to the floor. Prior to class, write the measurements of at least three adults, such as yourself and two other teachers, on the board.

Answer

1. The student's head height will probably be a greater proportion of his or her overall height than the adults' head height. The student's leg length should be about 50% of his or her overall height, which should match the leg-length proportion of adults.

START-UP ACTIVITY

How Grows It?

As you read this paragraph, you are slowly aging. Your body is growing into the body of an adult. But does your body have the same proportions that an adult's body has? Complete this activity to find out.

Procedure

1. Have a classmate use a **tape measure** and **meterstick** to measure your total height, head height, and leg length. Your teacher will tell you how to take these measurements.

2. Use the following equations to calculate your head height–to–total body height proportion and your leg length–to–total body height proportion.

$$\text{head proportion} = \frac{\text{head height}}{\text{body height}} \times 100$$

$$\text{leg proportion} = \frac{\text{leg length}}{\text{body height}} \times 100$$

3. Your teacher will give you the head, body, and leg measurements of three adults. Calculate the head-body and leg-body proportions of each of the three adults. Record all of the measurements and calculations.

Analysis

1. Compare your proportions with the proportions of the three adults.

Reproduction and Development   CHAPTER STARTER

Strange but True!

A tiny animal is resting peacefully in a warm, dark space. Suddenly it finds itself driven out into the cold and light. The chilly temperature is almost unbearable for its hairless body. The glaring light is disorienting to its blurry vision. Driven by instinct, the animal starts crawling up and up to the promise of warmth and security. If it slips and falls to the ground, it will die. Almost 30 minutes pass before it reaches its destination—a pouch in its mother's abdomen. Inside the pouch, it finds a nipple that will supply milk for several months as the animal grows and develops.

Can you guess what animal has just been born? That's right, a baby kangaroo, called a joey. Joeys are born in a very early stage of development. They continue to develop inside their mother's pouch until they are able to eat solid food such as grasses and other plants.

Like all living things, kangaroos eventually grow old and die. They must reproduce to pass on their genetic heritage. There are many ways of reproducing, as you will discover in this chapter. But reproduction is only part of the story. Development, or the way organisms grow, is also an important part of the cycle of life.

Chapter Starter Transparency
Use this transparency to help students begin thinking about reproduction and human growth and development.

CHAPTER RESOURCES

Technology

 **Transparencies**
• Chapter Starter Transparency

`READING SKILLS`

 Student Edition on CD-ROM

 Guided Reading Audio CD
• English or Spanish

 Classroom Videos
• Brain Food Video Quiz

Workbooks

 Science Puzzlers, Twisters & Teasers
• Reproduction and Development `GENERAL`

Focus

Overview

In this section, students learn about asexual and sexual reproduction. Students also learn about internal and external fertilization. Finally, students learn about differences in mammalian reproduction.

🔔 Bellringer

Write the following list on the board:

a. bird   **c.** ants

b. human   **d.** sea stars

Ask students to write a paragraph explaining how they think reproduction differs between these four animals.

Motivate

Discussion ——— GENERAL

Reproduction If appropriate for your students, lead a discussion and ask students to think about the similarities and differences between the ways animals, such as the ones listed above, reproduce. Birds and ants lay eggs, but humans and sea stars don't. Females and males mate to reproduce in humans, ants, and birds, but not in sea stars. Help them understand that the end result of reproduction is the same for all animal species, but the means differ widely. **LS Verbal**

READING WARM-UP

Objectives

● Distinguish between asexual and sexual reproduction.

● Explain the difference between external and internal fertilization.

● Identify the three different types of mammalian reproduction.

Terms to Learn

asexual reproduction
sexual reproduction
egg
sperm
external fertilization
internal fertilization

READING STRATEGY

Prediction Guide Before reading this section, write the title of each heading in this section. Next, under each heading, write what you think you will learn.

---

asexual reproduction reproduction that does not involve the union of sex cells and in which a single parent produces offspring that are genetically identical to the parent

---

Animal Reproduction

The life span of some living things is short compared with ours. For example, a fruit fly lives only about 40 days. Other organisms live much longer than we do. Some bristlecone pine trees, for example, are nearly 5,000 years old.

But all living things eventually die. If a species is to survive, its members must reproduce.

Asexual Reproduction

Some animals, particularly simpler ones, reproduce asexually. In **asexual reproduction,** a single parent has offspring that are genetically identical to the parent.

One kind of asexual reproduction is called budding. *Budding* happens when a part of the parent organism pinches off and forms a new organism. The new organism separates from the parent and lives independently. The hydra, shown in **Figure 1,** reproduces by budding. The new hydra is genetically identical to its parent.

Fragmentation is a second kind of asexual reproduction. In *fragmentation,* parts of an organism break off and then develop into a new individual that is identical to the original one. Certain organisms, such as flatworms called *planaria,* reproduce by fragmentation. A third type of asexual reproduction, similar to fragmentation, is *regeneration.* When an organism capable of regeneration, such as the sea star in **Figure 2,** loses a body part, that part may develop into an entirely new organism.

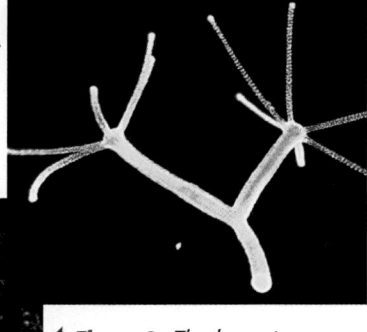

Figure 1 *The hydra bud will separate from its parent. Buds from other organisms, such as certain corals, remain attached to the parent.*

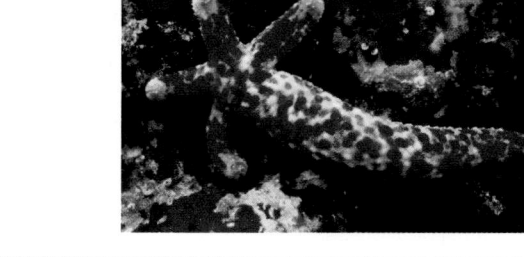

Figure 2 *The largest arm on this sea star was a fragment, from which a new sea star will regenerate. In time, all of the sea star's arms will grow to the same size.*

CHAPTER RESOURCES

Chapter Resource File

- Lesson Plan
- Directed Reading A **BASIC**
- Directed Reading B **SPECIAL NEEDS**

Technology

Transparencies
- Bellringer

Workbooks

Science Skills
- Organizing Your Research **BASIC**

Homework ——— GENERAL

Making Tables Ask students to make a table in their **science journal.** In one column, they will list 10 mammals. In the next column, they will indicate how each mammal produces young. From the information in this section, students should be able to indicate whether the animal is a monotreme, a marsupial, or a placental. Students should fill in the table to the best of their knowledge, research the correct answers, and put them in an additional column. **LS Logical**

Sexual Reproduction

Most animals reproduce sexually. In **sexual reproduction,** offspring are formed when genetic information from more than one parent combines. Sexual reproduction in animals usually requires two parents—a male and a female. The female parent produces sex cells called **eggs.** The male parent produces sex cells called **sperm.** When an egg's nucleus and a sperm's nucleus join, a fertilized egg, called a *zygote* (ZIE GOHT), is created. This joining of an egg and sperm is known as *fertilization.*

Human cells—except eggs and sperm and mature red blood cells—contain 46 chromosomes. Eggs and sperm are formed by a process called *meiosis.* In humans, meiosis is the division of one cell that has 46 chromosomes into four cells that have 23 chromosomes each. When an egg and a sperm join to form a zygote, the original number of 46 chromosomes is restored.

Genetic information is found in *genes.* Genes are located on *chromosomes* (KROH muh SOHMZ) made of the cell's DNA. During fertilization, the egg and sperm each contribute chromosomes to the zygote. The combination of genes from the two parents results in a zygote that grows into a unique individual. **Figure 3** shows how genes mix through three generations.

Reading Check What is sexual reproduction? (*See the Appendix for answers to Reading Checks.*)

sexual reproduction reproduction in which sex cells from two parents unite to produce offspring that share traits from both parents

egg a sex cell produced by a female

sperm the male sex cell

Figure 3 Inheriting Genes

Eggs and sperm contain chromosomes. You inherit chromosomes—and the genes on them—from both of your parents. Your parents each inherited chromosomes from their parents.

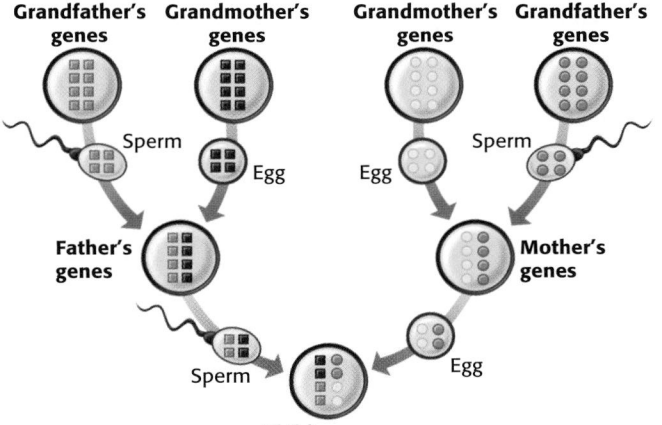

Grandfather's genes Grandmother's genes Grandmother's genes Grandfather's genes
Sperm Egg Egg Sperm
Father's genes Mother's genes
Sperm Egg
Child's genes

CONNECTION TO Language Arts

WRITING SKILL **Nature or Nurture?** Scientists debate whether genetics or upbringing is more important in shaping people. Use the Internet or library to research the issue of "nature versus nurture." Find information about identical twins who were raised apart. When you finish your research, write a persuasive essay supporting one side of the debate. Include evidence to support your argument.

Teach

Demonstration — GENERAL

The Amazing Egg Bird eggs are fertilized internally but develop externally, which requires good packaging. The egg shell gives the developing embryo a stable, safe environment. Using an ordinary chicken egg, demonstrate that the shape of the egg keeps it from rolling away from the mother. Next, wrap your hand around the egg. Demonstrate that the shape of the egg is protective against squeezing pressure from the outside. Tell students that the egg is shaped to withstand the pressures of passing through the chicken and of incubation. It is designed to be easy to break from within so that even a young chick can peck its way out. **LS** Visual English Language Learners

Answer to Reading Check

Sexual reproduction is reproduction in which the sex cells (egg and sperm) of two parents unite to form a new individual.

Answer to Connection to Language Arts

Opinions may vary. Make sure students have provided information to support their answers. Sources of information may include journals such as *Scientific American* and reputable studies of twins.

ACTIVITY — BASIC

Asexual or Sexual Reproduction? Help students differentiate between sexual and asexual reproduction by having them make a poster that includes all the pertinent information. Students should use a different primary color for sexual and asexual reproduction and include artwork depicting the cells involved. The diagrams should state whether or not the resulting offspring are genetically identical to their parent(s). English Language Learners **LS** Visual

CONNECTION ACTIVITY Chemistry — ADVANCED

PORTFOLIO Encourage interested students to use the library or the Internet to research the role that incubation temperature plays in the reproductive process of some reptile and amphibian species. Have students draw diagrams or make a poster illustrating the effect of temperature on reproduction and development. Give students time to present their findings to the class. **LS** Visual

External fertilization is when sex cells unite outside of the female's body. Internal fertilization is when sex cells unite inside the female's body.

Reteaching —————— BASIC

Outline Discuss with students how to make an outline of this section. Ask students to volunteer to share their outline to reteach the class. **LS** Logical

Quiz —————— GENERAL

1. How do the offspring created by asexual reproduction differ from those created by sexual reproduction? (Offspring from asexual reproduction are genetically identical to the parent. Offspring from sexual reproduction have genetic material from two parents and are genetically different from their parents.)

2. Why does external fertilization usually take place in moist environments? (External fertilization usually takes place in moist environments so that the delicate zygotes do not dry out.)

Alternative Assessment —————— GENERAL

Concept Mapping Have students create a concept map using the new terms in this section and the section title. **LS** Verbal

Figure 4 *Some fish, such as these clownfish, fertilize their eggs externally. The eggs are the orange mass on the rock.*

external fertilization the union of sex cells outside the bodies of the parents

internal fertilization fertilization of an egg by sperm that occurs inside the body of a female

Figure 5 *This zebra has just been born, but he is already able to stand. Within an hour, he will be able to run.*

Internal and External Fertilization

Fertilization can happen either outside or inside the female's body. When the sperm fertilizes the eggs outside the female's body, the process is called **external fertilization.** External fertilization must take place in a moist environment so that the delicate zygotes won't dry out. Some fishes, such as those in **Figure 4,** reproduce by external fertilization.

Many amphibians, such as frogs, use external fertilization. For example, the female frog releases her eggs. At the same time, the male frog releases his sperm over the eggs to fertilize them. Frogs usually leave the zygotes to develop on their own. In about two weeks, the fertilized eggs hatch into tadpoles.

Internal Fertilization

When the egg and sperm join inside the female's body, the process is called **internal fertilization.** Internal fertilization allows the female animal to protect the developing egg inside her body. Reptiles, birds, mammals, and some fishes reproduce by internal fertilization. Many animals that use internal fertilization can lay fertilized eggs. Female chickens, for example, usually lay one or two eggs after internal fertilization has taken place.

In most mammals, one or more fertilized eggs develop inside the mother's body. Many mammals give birth to young that are well developed. Young zebras, such as the one in **Figure 5,** can stand up and nurse almost immediately after birth.

✓ **Reading Check** What is the difference between external and internal fertilization?

Homework —————— GENERAL

Montremes Encourage students to research an egg-laying mammal. Then, have them write and illustrate a short story about how the egg develops into a new individual. **LS** Verbal

INCLUSION Strategies

- **Behavior Control Issues** • **Visually Impaired**
- **Attention Deficit Disorder**

Organize the students into teams of two or three. Have each team find an animal that has a pouch for its babies. Ask the teams to create a presentation giving what the name of the animal is, where the animal lives, how the baby gets into the pouch, and how long the baby stays in the pouch. Make sure no animal choices are repeated. **LS** Verbal

Mammals

All mammals reproduce sexually. All mammals nurture their young with milk. And all mammals reproduce in one of the following three ways:

- **Monotreme** *Monotremes* (MAHN oh TREEMZ) are mammals that lay eggs. After the eggs are incubated and hatch, the young are nourished by milk that oozes from pores on the mother's belly. Echidnas and platypuses are monotremes.

- **Marsupial** Mammals that give birth to partially developed live young, such as the kangaroo in **Figure 6,** are *marsupials* (mahr SOO pee uhlz). Most marsupials have pouches where their young continue to develop after birth. Opossums, koalas, wombats, and Tasmanian devils are marsupials.

- **Placental Mammal** There are more than 4,000 species of placental mammals, including armadillos, humans, and bats. Placental mammals are nourished inside their mother's body before birth. Newborn placental mammals are more developed than newborn monotremes or marsupials are.

Reading Check Name two ways that all mammals are alike.

Figure 6 *The red kangaroo is a marsupial. A young kangaroo, such as this one in its mother's pouch, is called a* joey.

SECTION Review

Summary

- In asexual reproduction, a single parent produces offspring that are genetically identical to the parent.
- In sexual reproduction, an egg from one parent combines with a sperm from the other parent.
- Fertilization can be external or internal.
- All mammals reproduce sexually and nurture their young with milk.

Using Key Terms

For each pair of terms, explain how the meanings of the terms differ.

1. *internal fertilization* and *external fertilization*

2. *asexual reproduction* and *sexual reproduction*

Understanding Key Ideas

3. In humans, each egg and each sperm contain
   a. 23 chromosomes.
   b. 46 chromosomes.
   c. 69 chromosomes.
   d. 529 chromosomes.

4. List three types of asexual reproduction.

5. How do monotremes differ from marsupials?

6. Describe the process of meiosis.

7. Are humans placental mammals, monotremes, or marsupials? Explain.

Math Skills

8. Some bristlecone pine needles last 40 years. If a tree lives for 3,920 years, how many sets of needles might it grow?

Critical Thinking

9. **Making Inferences** Why is reproduction as important to a bristlecone pine as it is to a fruit fly?

10. **Applying Concepts** Describe one advantage of internal fertilization over external fertilization.

Developed and maintained by the National Science Teachers Association

For a variety of links related to this chapter, go to www.scilinks.org

Topic: Reproduction
SciLinks code: HSM1293

Answers to Section Review

1. Internal fertilization occurs inside the female's body, while external fertilization occurs outside the female's body.

2. Asexual reproduction is when a single parent produces offspring that are genetically identical to the parent. Sexual reproduction requires sex cells from two parents to unite.

3. a

4. budding, fragmentation, and regeneration

5. Monotremes lay eggs; marsupials give birth to live young.

6. Meiosis is when a male or a female sex cell that has 46 chromosomes divides into 4 eggs or 4 sperm that have 23 chromosomes each.

7. Humans are placental mammals because they nourish their young internally before giving birth to live young.

8. 3,920 ÷ 40 = 98 sets of needles

9. Every living organism is a member of a species. Every living organism eventually dies. In order for a species to survive, individual organisms must reproduce.

10. Internal fertilizaton allows the female to protect the developing egg inside her body.

Answer to Reading Check

All mammals reproduce sexually and nurture their young with milk.

INTERNET ACTIVITY

Sequence Board — GENERAL

For an internet activity related to this chapter, have students go to **go.hrw.com** and type in the keyword **HL5BD5W.**

CHAPTER RESOURCES

Chapter Resource File

- **Section Quiz** GENERAL
- **Section Review** GENERAL
- **Vocabulary and Section Summary** GENERAL
- **Reinforcement Worksheet** BASIC

Section 1 · Animal Reproduction **687**

Focus

Overview

In this section, students learn about the male and female reproductive systems. Students also learn about multiple births and some problems of the reproductive system.

 Bellringer

Have students write answers to these questions: Do you think that cloning human beings could be considered reproduction? Why or why not? What kind of reproduction is it?

Motivate

Discussion —— GENERAL

Bird and Human Ask students to compare reproduction in birds with reproduction in humans. (Both birds and humans fertilize their eggs internally. Birds lay eggs and protect them. Birds keep the eggs warm while obtaining food for themselves. Human mothers carry a baby inside their body, so the baby is always protected. After eggs hatch or the baby is born, parents protect and care for the baby. Humans take care of their offspring for much longer than birds care for theirs.) **LS Verbal**

Answer to Reading Check

testes, epididymis, vas deferens, urethra, penis

SECTION 2

Human Reproduction

About nine months after a human sperm and egg combine, a mother gives birth to her baby. But how do humans make eggs and sperm?

READING WARM-UP

Objectives
- Identify the structures and functions of the male and female reproductive systems.
- Describe two reproductive system problems.

Terms to Learn

testes   uterus
penis   vagina
ovary

READING STRATEGY

Reading Organizer As you read this section, create an outline of the section. Use the headings from the section in your outline.

The Male Reproductive System

The male reproductive system, shown in **Figure 1,** produces sperm and delivers it to the female reproductive system. The **testes** (singular, *testis*) are a pair of organs that make sperm and testosterone (tes TAHS tuhr OHN). Testosterone is the main male sex hormone. It helps regulate the production of sperm and the development of male characteristics.

As sperm leave a testis, they are stored in a tube called an *epididymis* (EP uh DID i mis). Sperm mature in the epididymis. Another tube, called a *vas deferens* (vas DEF uh RENZ), passes from the epididymis into the body and through the *prostate gland*. The prostate gland surrounds the neck of the bladder. As sperm move through the vas deferens, they mix with fluids from several glands, including the prostate gland. This mixture of sperm and fluids is called *semen*.

To leave the body, semen passes through the vas deferens into the *urethra* (yoo REE thruh). The urethra is the tube that runs through the penis. The **penis** is the external organ that transfers semen into the female's body.

✓ Reading Check Describe the path that sperm take from the testes to the penis. (*See the Appendix for answers to Reading Checks.*)

testes the primary male reproductive organs, which produce sperm and testosterone (singular, *testis*)

penis the male organ that transfers sperm to a female and that carries urine out of the body

Figure 1   The Male Reproductive System

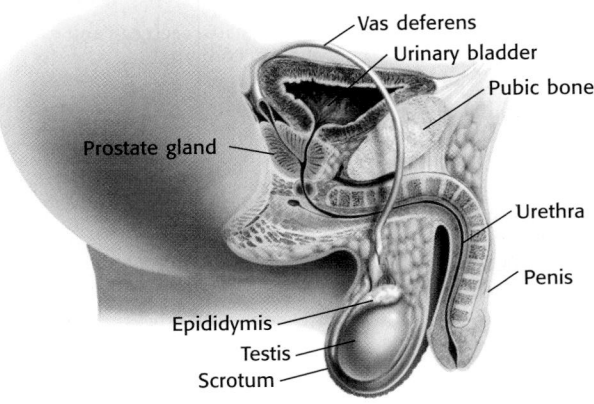

Vas deferens
Urinary bladder
Pubic bone
Prostate gland
Urethra
Penis
Epididymis
Testis
Scrotum

CHAPTER RESOURCES

Chapter Resource File

- Lesson Plan
- Directed Reading A **BASIC**
- Directed Reading B **SPECIAL NEEDS**

Technology

Transparencies
- Bellringer
- The Male Reproductive System

Is That a Fact!

Mumps, a common childhood disease, poses a risk to males who contract it during puberty or adulthood. When mumps occurs after childhood, it can cause inflammation of the testes, known as *acute orchitis,* which, in rare cases, can result in sterility.

Figure 2   The Female Reproductive System

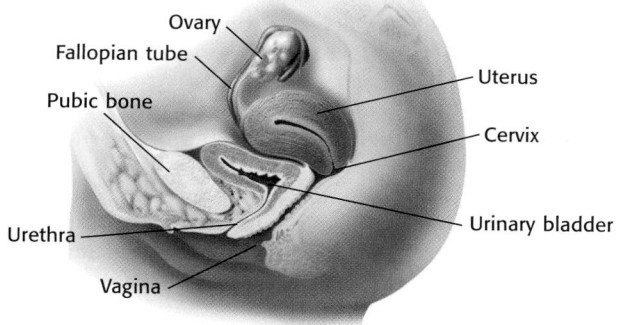

Ovary
Fallopian tube
Pubic bone
Urethra
Vagina
Uterus
Cervix
Urinary bladder

The Female Reproductive System

The female reproductive system, shown in **Figure 2,** produces eggs, nurtures fertilized eggs (zygotes), and gives birth. The two **ovaries** are the organs that make eggs. Ovaries also release estrogen (ES truh juhn) and progesterone (proh JES tuhr OHN), the main female sex hormones. These hormones regulate the release of eggs and development of female characteristics.

The Egg's Journey

During *ovulation* (AHV yoo LAY shuhn), an egg is released from an ovary and passes into a *fallopian* (fuh LOH pee uhn) *tube.* A fallopian tube leads from each ovary to the uterus. The egg passes through the fallopian tube into the uterus. Fertilization usually happens in the fallopian tube. If the egg is fertilized, the resulting zygote enters the uterus. The zygote may become embedded in the thickened lining of the uterus. The **uterus** is the organ in which a zygote develops into a baby.

When a baby is born, he or she passes from the uterus through the vagina and emerges outside the body. The **vagina** is the canal between the outside of the body and the uterus.

Menstrual Cycle

From puberty through her late 40s or early 50s, a woman's reproductive system goes through monthly changes. These changes prepare the body for pregnancy and are called the *menstrual cycle* (MEN struhl SIE kuhl). The first day of *menstruation* (MEN STRAY shuhn), the monthly discharge of blood and tissue from the uterus, is counted as the first day of the cycle. Menstruation lasts about 5 days. When menstruation ends, the lining of the uterus thickens. Ovulation occurs on about the 14th day of the cycle. If the egg is not fertilized within a few days, menstruation begins and flushes the egg away. The cycle—which usually takes about 28 days—starts again.

ovary in the female reproductive system of animals, an organ that produces eggs

uterus in female mammals, the hollow, muscular organ in which a fertilized egg is embedded and in which the embryo and fetus develop

vagina the female reproductive organ that connects the outside of the body to the uterus

Counting Eggs

1. The average woman ovulates each month from about age 12 to about age 50. How many mature eggs could she produce from age 18 to age 50?

2. A female's ovaries typically contain 2 million immature eggs. If she ovulates regularly from age 12 to age 50, what percentage of her eggs will mature?

CONNECTION ACTIVITY
Language Arts —— GENERAL

Word Origins The words *male* and *female* actually originate from two unrelated Latin words. *Female* comes from *femella,* meaning "girl," while *male* comes from *masculus,* meaning "male." Have students select the names of any five parts of the male and female reproductive systems. Then, have students find the origins of those terms and write a brief history of each one.
LS Verbal

CHAPTER RESOURCES

Technology

Transparencies
• The Female Reproductive System

Workbooks

Math Skills for Science
• Multiplying Whole Numbers GENERAL
• Dividing Whole Numbers with Long Division GENERAL
• Parts of 100: Calculating Percentages GENERAL

Teach

READING STRATEGY —— GENERAL

Activity Draw students' attention to **Figures 1** and **2.** Have them write the new terms in their **science journal,** leaving a few lines between each term. As students read the section, have them fill in definitions that explain the new terms in their own words. **LS** Verbal

Discussion —— GENERAL

Multiple Births A Russian woman in the 18th century gave birth to 69 children, with 67 living to reach adulthood. Ask students: "If this woman began ovulation at age 12 and stopped ovulating at age 50, and pregnancy lasts 9 months, how could she have had so many children?" Write the following answer on the board to demonstrate how it is possible that she had 69 children: She had 27 pregnancies, all of them producing 2 or more children. She had 16 pairs of twins, 7 sets of triplets, 4 sets of quadruplets.
$(16 \times 2) + (7 \times 3) + (4 \times 4) = 69$
LS Logical

Answers to Math Practice

1. $50 \text{ y} - 12 \text{ y} = 38 \text{ y}$
   $38 \text{ y} \times 12 \text{ eggs/year} = 456 \text{ eggs}$
   She can produce about 456 mature eggs in her lifetime.

2. 456 mature eggs/2,000,000 possible eggs $= 0.000228 \times 100 = 0.0228\%$ of her eggs may possibly mature.

Reteaching — BASIC

Puzzle Making Organize the
class into small groups. Challenge each group to create a
crossword puzzle using the
Terms to Learn and italicized
terms from the section. Have
each group write appropriate
clues and construct a puzzle.
Then, have groups exchange
puzzles. Allow time for students
to solve the puzzles. **LS Logical/
Interpersonal**

Quiz — GENERAL

1. What purpose does the epididymis serve? (the site where
sperm mature and are stored
before sperm leave the testes)

2. What is menstruation? (the
monthly discharge of blood and
tissue from the uterus)

Alternative
Assessment — GENERAL

Tracing the Path If appropriate
for your class, ask students to
make diagrams that illustrate
the path an egg or sperm must
travel before fertilization. Have
them label anatomical structures
and indicate, with arrows, the
direction in which the sex
cell travels. English Language
LS Visual Learners

Figure 3 *Identical twins have
genes that are exactly the
same. Many identical twins who
are raised apart have similar
personalities and interests.*

Twins and More

With a parent, discuss some
challenges that are created
by the birth of twins, triplets,
quadruplets, or other multiples. Include financial, mental, emotional, and physical
challenges.

Create a poster that shows
these challenges and ways to
meet them.

If twins or other multiples
are in your family, discuss
how the individuals differ and
how they are alike.

Multiple Births

Have you ever seen identical twins? Sometimes, they are so
similar that even their parents have trouble telling them apart.
The boys in **Figure 3** are identical twins. Fraternal twins, the
other type of twins, are more common than identical twins
are. Fraternal twins can look very different from each other.
In every 1,000 births, there are about 30 sets of twins. About
one-third of all twin births are identical twins.

Twins are the most common multiple births. But humans
sometimes have triplets (3 babies). In the United States, there
are about two sets of triplets in every 1,000 births. Humans also
have quadruplets (4 babies), quintuplets (5 babies), and more.
These types of multiple births are rare. Births of quintuplets
or more happen only once in about 53,000 births.

Reading Check What is the frequency of twin births?

Reproductive System Problems

In most cases, the reproductive system functions flawlessly. But
like any body system, the reproductive system sometimes has
problems. These problems include disease and infertility.

STDs

Chlamydia, herpes, and hepatitis B are common sexually
transmitted diseases. A *sexually transmitted disease,* or STD, is
a disease that can pass from a person who is infected with the
STD to an uninfected person during sexual contact. STDs are
also called *sexually transmitted infections,* or STIs. These diseases
affect many people each year, as shown in **Table 1.**

An STD you may have heard of is *acquired immune deficiency
syndrome* (AIDS). AIDS is caused by *human immunodeficiency
virus* (HIV). But you may not have heard of the STD *hepatitis B,*
a liver disease also caused by a virus. This virus is spread in
several ways, including sexual contact. In the United States,
about 140,000 new cases of hepatitis B happen each year.

Table 1 The Spread of STDs in the United States	
STD	**Approximate number of new cases each year**
Chlamydia	3 to 10 million
Genital HPV (human papillomavirus)	5.5 million
Genital herpes	1 million
Gonorrhea	650,000
Syphilis	70,000
HIV/AIDS	40,000 to 50,000

CONNECTION ACTIVITY
Language Arts — ADVANCED

Writing **Fertility Drugs and Multiple Births**
Have students conduct Internet or
library research and write a report
on how fertility drugs may have affected
the number and frequency of multiple
births in the last 15 years. **LS Verbal**

Group ACTIVITY — GENERAL

Reproductive System Cancer Have students work in small groups to research
breast, testicular, ovarian, prostate, or cervical cancer. Students should focus on the
incidence of the disease, its risk factors,
and the importance of early detection.
Have students use the information they
gather to design and create a public service
brochure—complete with artwork—
designed to educate the public about the
disease. Allow students time to present and
discuss their brochures in class. **LS Visual**

Cancer

Sometimes, cancer happens in reproductive organs. *Cancer* is a disease in which cells grow at an uncontrolled rate. Cancer cells start out as normal cells. Then, something triggers uncontrolled cell growth. Different kinds of cancer have different triggers.

In men, the two most common reproductive system cancers are cancer of the testes and cancer of the prostate gland. In women, the two most common reproductive system cancers are breast cancer and cancer of the cervix. The *cervix* is the lower part, or neck, of the uterus. The cervix opens to the vagina.

Infertility

In the United States, about 15% of married couples have difficulty producing offspring. Many of these couples are *infertile*, or unable to have children. Men may be infertile if they do not produce enough healthy sperm. Women may be infertile if they do not ovulate normally.

Sexually transmitted diseases, such as gonorrhea and chlamydia, can lead to infertility in women. STD-related infertility occurs in men, but not as commonly as it does in women.

CONNECTION TO Social Studies

Understanding STDs Select one of the STDs in **Table 1**. Make a poster or brochure that identifies the cause of the disease, describes its symptoms, explains how it affects the body, and tells how it can be treated. Include a bar graph that shows the number of cases in different age groups.

ACTIVITY

SECTION Review

Summary

- The male reproductive system produces sperm and delivers it to the female reproductive system.
- The female reproductive system produces eggs, nurtures zygotes, and gives birth.
- Humans usually have one child per birth, but multiple births, such as those of twins or triplets, are possible.
- Human reproduction can be affected by cancer, infertility, and disease.

Using Key Terms

1. Use the following terms in the same sentence: *uterus* and *vagina*.

Understanding Key Ideas

2. Describe two problems of the reproductive system.

3. Identify the structures and functions of the male and female reproductive systems.

4. Identical twins happen once in 250 births. How many pairs of these twins might be at a school with 2,750 students?
   - **a.** 1
   - **b.** 11
   - **c.** 22
   - **d.** 250

Math Skills

5. In one country, 7 out of 1,000 infants die before their first birthday. Convert this figure to a percentage. Is your answer greater than or less than 1%?

Critical Thinking

6. **Making Inferences** What is the purpose of the menstrual cycle?

7. **Applying Concepts** Twins can happen when a zygote splits in two or when two eggs are fertilized. How can these two ways of twin formation explain how identical twins differ from fraternal twins?

8. **Predicting Consequences** How might cancer of the testes affect a man's ability to make sperm?

For a variety of links related to this chapter, go to www.scilinks.org

Topic: Reproduction System Irregularities or Disorders

SciLinks code: HSM1298

CHAPTER RESOURCES

Chapter Resource File

- Section Quiz GENERAL
- Section Review GENERAL
- Vocabulary and Section Summary GENERAL

Answers to Section Review

1. Sample answer: A woman's vagina is the canal that connects the uterus to the outside world.

2. One reproductive system problem is infertility. Infertility is when a man or a woman is unable to have children. Sexually transmitted diseases (STDs) are a second reproductive system problem. STDs can infect the reproductive system and may cause infertility.

3. testes (males): make sperm and produce testosterone (helps regulate sperm production and the development of male characteristics); penis (males): the external male organ that transfers semen into the female's body; ovaries (females): organs that make eggs and release estrogen and progesterone (which regulate the release of eggs and the development of female characteristics); uterus (females): the organ in which the fertilized egg develops; vagina (females): the canal that connects the uterus to the outside world, through which a baby passes when it is born

4. b

5. $7/1{,}000 = 0.007$; Then, convert to a percentage by moving the decimal point two places to the right: 0.7%; This is less than 1%.

6. The menstrual cycle is the series of changes through which a female's reproductive system goes in order to prepare the female for pregnancy. The cycle usually takes about 28 days.

7. When a single fertilized egg splits in two, each cell contains identical genes. If each cell develops into a separate baby, they will be identical twins. When two separate eggs are fertilized, their genes are different. This results in fraternal twins.

8. Sample answer: Cancer is uncontrolled cell growth. In the testes, this uncontrolled growth could destroy cells and damage the production of sperm and the production of testosterone.

Overview

In this section, students learn about fertilization and implantation. Students are also introduced to the different stages of growth of a fetus in utero, culminating in the birth of a baby. Finally, students learn about stages of human development, from birth through adulthood.

 **Bellringer**

Write the following on the board:

Name the stages of physical development you have passed through thus far in your life.

Have students list the stages in their **science journal.** Remind students that their growth and development began while they were still in the uterus. (Students may list stages such as the following: crawling, walking, talking, growing taller, and puberty.)

Motivate

Discussion — GENERAL

Life Stages Ask students to list as many characteristics of each of the following as they can: infancy, childhood, adolescence, and adulthood. Tell students that while there are individual differences, all people go through these stages. LS Logical

---

SECTION

3

Growth and Development

Every one of us started out as a single cell. How did that cell become a person made of trillions of cells?

A single cell divides many times and develops into a baby. But the development of a baby from a single cell is only the first stage of human development. Think about how you will change between now and when you become a grandparent!

From Fertilization to Embryo

Ordinarily, the process of human development starts when a man deposits millions of sperm into a woman's vagina. A few hundred sperm make it through the uterus into a fallopian tube. There, a few sperm cover the egg. Usually, only one sperm gets through the outer coating of the egg. When this happens, it triggers a response—a membrane forms around the egg to keep other sperm from entering. When the sperm's nucleus joins with the nucleus of the egg, the egg becomes fertilized.

The fertilized egg (zygote) travels down the fallopian tube toward the uterus. This journey takes 5 to 6 days. During the trip, the zygote undergoes cell division many times. Eleven to 12 days after fertilization, the zygote has become a tiny ball of cells called an **embryo.** The embryo implants itself in the uterus. *Implantation* happens when the zygote embeds itself in the thick, nutrient-rich lining of the uterus. Fertilization and implantation are outlined in **Figure 1.**

✓ Reading Check Describe the process of fertilization and implantation. (*See the Appendix for answers to Reading Checks.*)

Figure 1 **Fertilization and Implantation**

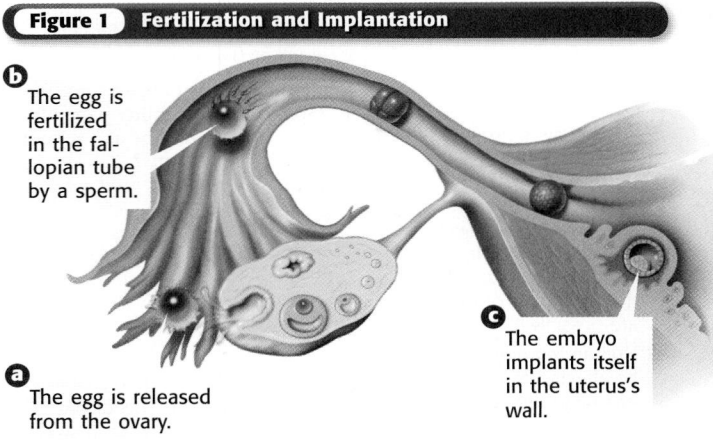

b The egg is fertilized in the fallopian tube by a sperm.

a The egg is released from the ovary.

c The embryo implants itself in the uterus's wall.

Answer to Reading Check

Fertilization happens when the nucleus of a sperm unites with the nucleus of an egg. Implantation happens after the fertilized egg travels down the fallopian tube to the uterus and embeds itself in the wall of the uterus.

From Embryo to Fetus

After implantation, the placenta (pluh SEN tuh) begins to grow. The **placenta** is a special two-way exchange organ. It has a network of blood vessels that provides the embryo with oxygen and nutrients from the mother's blood. Wastes produced by the embryo are removed in the placenta. They are carried by the mother's blood so that her body can excrete them. The embryo's blood and the mother's blood flow very near each other in the placenta, but they normally do not mix.

 **Reading Check** Why is the placenta important?

Weeks 1 and 2

Doctors commonly count the time of a woman's pregnancy as starting from the first day of her last menstrual period. Even though fertilization has not yet taken place, that day is a convenient date from which to start counting. A normal pregnancy lasts about 280 days, or 40 weeks, from that day.

Weeks 3 and 4

Fertilization takes place at about the end of week 2. In week 3, after fertilization, the zygote moves to the uterus. As the zygote travels, it divides many times. It becomes a ball of cells that implants itself in the wall of the uterus. The zygote is now called an *embryo*. At the end of week 4, implantation is complete and the woman is pregnant. The embryo's blood cells begin to form. At this point, the embryo is about 0.2 mm long.

Weeks 5 to 8

Weeks 5 to 8 of pregnancy are weeks 3 to 6 of embryonic development. In this stage, the embryo becomes surrounded by a thin membrane called the *amnion* (AM nee AHN). The amnion is filled with amniotic fluid and protects the growing embryo from bumps and injury. During week 5, the umbilical cord forms. The **umbilical cord** (uhm BIL i kuhl KAWRD) is a cord that connects the embryo to the placenta. **Figure 2** shows the umbilical cord, amnion, and placenta.

In this stage, the heart, brain, other organs, and blood vessels start to form. They grow quickly. In weeks 5 and 6, eyes and ears take shape. The spinal cord begins to develop. In week 6, tiny limb buds appear. These buds will become arms and legs. In week 8, muscles start developing. Nerves grow into the shoulders and upper arms. Fingers and toes start to form. The embryo, now about 16 mm long, can swallow and blink.

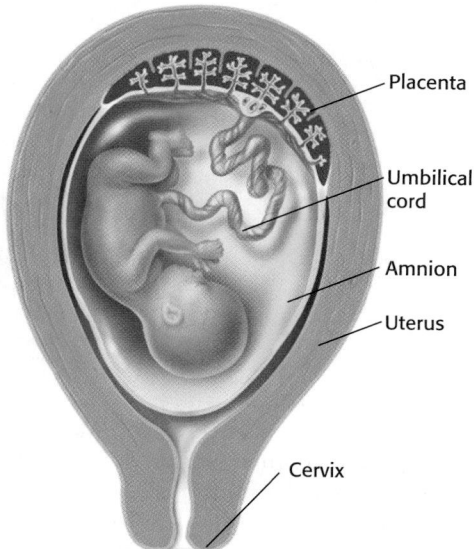

Placenta

Umbilical cord

Amnion

Uterus

Cervix

Figure 2 *The placenta, amnion, and umbilical cord are the life support system for the fetus. This fetus is about 20 to 22 weeks old.*

umbilical cord the structure that connects the fetus to the placenta

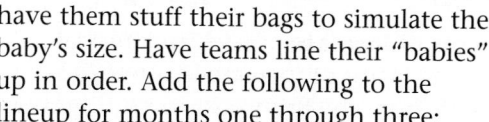

Growing Up

With a parent, discuss the physical and mental changes that you went through between your birth and your first day of school. Make a poster illustrating those changes.

BRAIN FOOD

Writing **Seahorses** Seahorses are one of very few kinds of organisms in which the male carries the fertilized eggs. Ask students to research the reproductive and parenting behaviors of seahorses. Have them make a poster showing their findings. (After courtship, the female deposits eggs into the pouch of her male mate. The male then fertilizes the eggs and carries them until they develop. After a gestation period of between 10 and 60 days, depending on the species, tiny, fully formed sea horses emerge from an opening in the pouch.)

Answer to Reading Check

The embryo is now called a *fetus;* the fetus's face begins to look more human and it can swallow, the fetus grows rapidly (it triples in size), and the fetus begins to make movements that the mother can feel.

Research ———— GENERAL

Writing **FAS** Drinking alcohol during the first few weeks of pregnancy can lead to birth defects and miscarriages. Have students research the causes and consequences of fetal alcohol syndrome (FAS) and present their findings in a short report. **LS Verbal**

---

fetus a developing human from seven or eight weeks after fertilization until birth

CONNECTION TO
Physics

Using Ultrasound Doctors often use ultrasound to view a fetus in the uterus. Research how an ultrasound machine works, and make a poster explaining how sound waves can show what is happening inside a human body.

ACTIVITY

CONNECTION to
Math ———— GENERAL

Factor of Increase Have students calculate the factor of increase in a fetus's body length from the 8th week, when it is about 2.5 cm long, to the 5th month, when it is about 25 cm long, to birth, when it is about 50 cm long. (2.5 cm to 25 cm is an increase by a factor of 10, 25 cm to 50 cm is an increase by a factor of 2, and 2.5 cm to 50 cm is an increase by a factor of 20) **LS Logical**

Weeks 9 to 16

At week 9, the fetus may begin to make tiny movements. After week 10, the embryo is called a **fetus** (FEET uhs). In about week 13, the fetus's face begins to look more human. During this stage, fetal muscles grow stronger. As a result, the fetus can make a fist and begins to move. The fetus grows rapidly during this stage. It doubles, and then triples, its size within a month. For example, in week 10, the fetus is about 36 mm long. A little later, at week 16, the fetus is about 108 mm to 116 mm long. Use **Figure 3** to follow some of the changes that take place in the fetus as it develops.

✓ **Reading Check** Describe three changes the fetus undergoes during weeks 9 to 16.

Weeks 17 to 24

By week 17, the fetus can make faces. Usually, in week 18, the fetus starts to make movements that the mother can feel. By week 18, the fetus can hear sounds through the mother's uterus. It may even jump at loud noises. By week 23, the fetus's movements may be quite vigorous! If the fetus were born after week 24, it might survive. But babies born at 24 weeks require a lot of help. In weeks 17 to 24, the fetus grows to between 25 cm and 30 cm in length.

Weeks 25 to 36

At about 25 or 26 weeks, the fetus's lungs are well developed but not fully mature. The fetus still gets oxygen from its mother through the placenta. The fetus will not take its first breath of air until it is born. By the 32nd week, the fetus's eyes can open and close. Studies of fetal heart rate and brain activity show that fetuses respond to light. Some scientists have observed brain activity and eye movements in sleeping fetuses that resemble those activities in sleeping children or adults. These scientists think that a sleeping fetus may dream. After 36 weeks, the fetus is almost ready to be born.

Birth

At 37 to 38 weeks, the fetus is fully developed. A full-term pregnancy usually lasts about 40 weeks. Typically, as birth begins, the mother's uterus begins a series of muscular contractions called *labor*. Usually, these contractions push the fetus through the mother's vagina, and the baby is born. The newborn is still connected to the placenta by its umbilical cord, which is tied and cut. All that will remain of the point where the umbilical cord was attached is the baby's navel. Soon, the mother expels the placenta, and labor is complete.

Is That a Fact!

Between conception and birth, the developing fetus increases in size from a single cell to 6 trillion cells! After birth, infants and children continue to grow rapidly. For example, girls attain three-quarters of their adult height by the age of 7 1/2. Boys attain three-quarters of their adult height by the age of 9.

Figure 3   Pregnancy Timeline

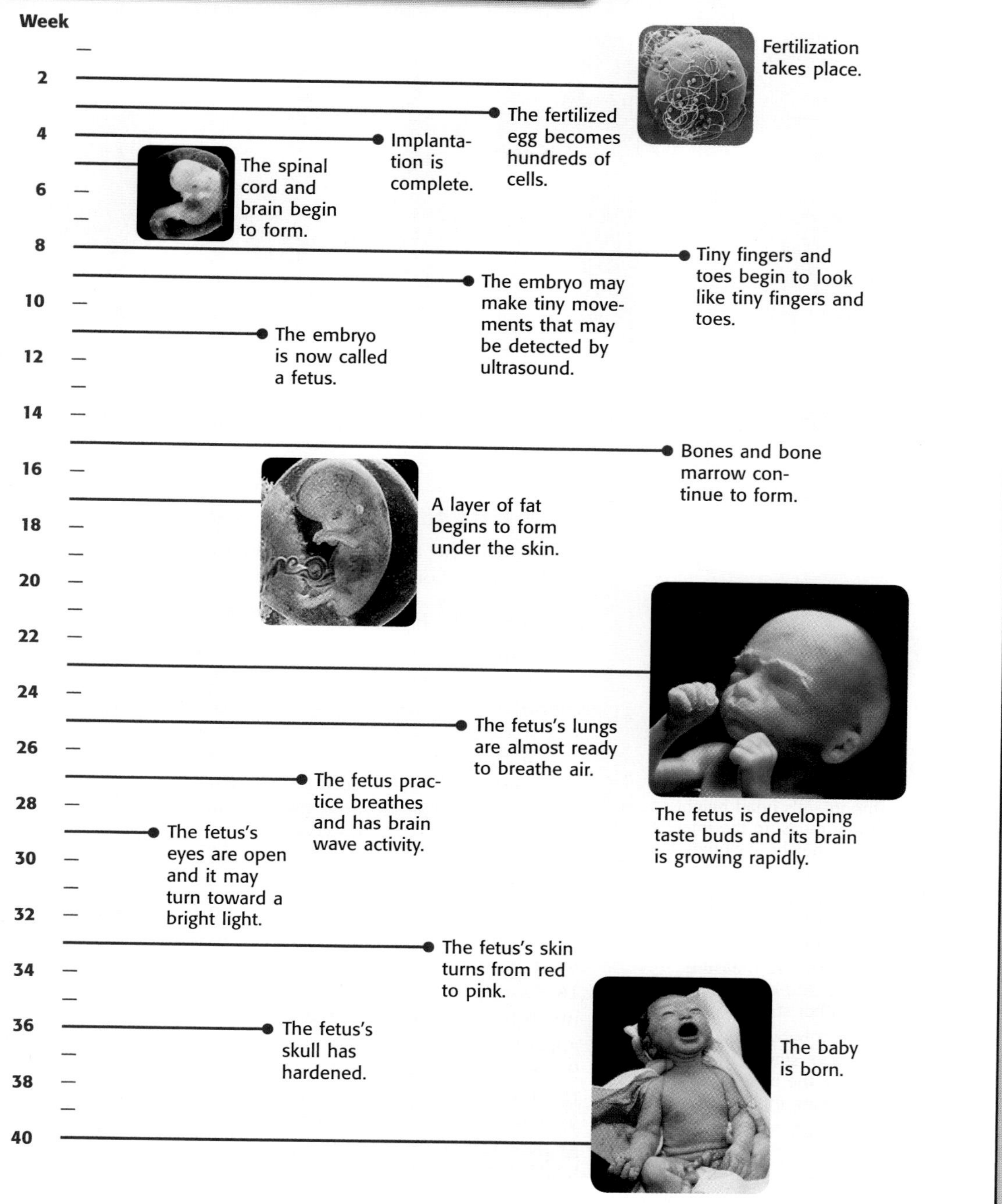

Week

— Fertilization takes place.

2 —

4 — The fertilized egg becomes hundreds of cells.

Implantation is complete.

6 — The spinal cord and brain begin to form.

8 — Tiny fingers and toes begin to look like tiny fingers and toes.

The embryo may make tiny movements that may be detected by ultrasound.

10 —

12 — The embryo is now called a fetus.

14 —

16 — Bones and bone marrow continue to form.

A layer of fat begins to form under the skin.

18 —

20 —

22 —

24 —

26 — The fetus's lungs are almost ready to breathe air.

28 — The fetus practice breathes and has brain wave activity.

The fetus's eyes are open and it may turn toward a bright light.

30 —

32 —

The fetus is developing taste buds and its brain is growing rapidly.

34 — The fetus's skin turns from red to pink.

36 — The fetus's skull has hardened.

38 —

The baby is born.

40 —

Figure 4 Stages of Human Development

Close

Reteaching ——— BASIC

From Birth to Adulthood
Have students work in pairs to design, create, and illustrate a pamphlet or brochure that briefly describes human growth and development from birth to old age.
LS Interpersonal

Quiz ——— GENERAL

1. What is implantation? (It is the process by which an embryo embeds itself in the uterus.)

2. What functions does the placenta serve? (It is a two-way exchange organ that allows oxygen and nutrients to travel to the fetus from the mother and allows wastes to travel from the fetus to the mother.)

Alternative Assessment ——— ADVANCED

Life as a Fetus Ask students to imagine that they have not yet been born. Have them write first-person stories describing their time in utero. Encourage creativity, but direct students to include the stages of development they went through as a fetus. Allow time for students to share their stories with the class.

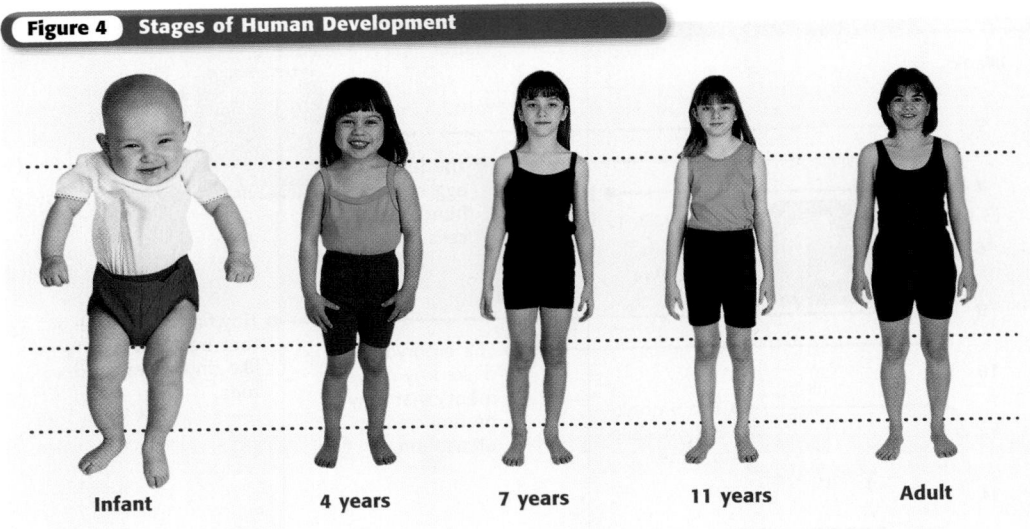

Infant   4 years   7 years   11 years   Adult

Life Grows On

Use **Figure 4** to complete this activity.

1. Use a **ruler** to measure the infant's head height. Then, measure the infant's entire height, including the head.

2. Calculate the ratio of the infant's head height to the infant's total height.

3. Repeat these measurements and calculations for the other stages.

4. Does a baby's head grow faster or slower than the rest of the body? Why do you think this is so?

From Birth to Death

After birth, the human body goes through several stages of development. Some of those stages are shown in **Figure 4.**

Infancy and Childhood

Generally, infancy is the stage from birth to age 2. During infancy, you grew quickly and your baby teeth appeared. As your nervous system developed, you became more coordinated and started to walk.

Childhood—another period of fast growth—lasts from age 2 to puberty. Your baby teeth were replaced by permanent teeth. And your muscles became more coordinated, which allowed you to ride a bicycle, jump rope, and do other activities.

Adolescence

The stage from puberty to adulthood is adolescence. During puberty, a person's reproductive system becomes mature. In most boys, puberty takes place between the ages of 11 and 16. During this time, the young male's body becomes more muscular, his voice becomes deeper, and body and facial hair appear. In most girls, puberty takes place between the ages of 9 and 14. During puberty in females, the amount of fat in the hips and thighs increases, the breasts enlarge, body hair appears, and menstruation begins.

Reading Check Name an important change that takes place during adolescence.

Answer to Reading Check
A person's reproductive system becomes mature.

MATERIALS

FOR EACH STUDENT
• calculator, if available
• ruler

Answers

Slower; Newborns have large heads to hold the large brains that enable them to learn quickly. In infancy, their bodies begin to catch up in size.

Adulthood

From about age 20 to age 40, you will be a young adult. You will be at the peak of your physical development. Beginning around age 30, changes associated with aging begin. These changes are gradual and different for everyone. Some early signs of aging include loss of flexibility in muscles, deterioration of eyesight, increase in body fat, and some loss of hair.

The aging process continues in middle age (between 40 and 65 years old). During this time, hair may turn gray, athletic abilities will decline, and skin may wrinkle. A person who is more than 65 years old is considered an older adult. Although the aging process continues, many older adults lead very active lives, as is shown in **Figure 5.**

Figure 5 *Older adults can still enjoy activities that they enjoyed when they were younger.*

SECTION Review

Summary

- Fertilization occurs when a sperm from the male joins with an egg from the female.
- The embryo and fetus undergo many changes between implantation and birth.
- The first stage of human development lasts from fertilization to birth.
- After birth, a human goes through four more stages of growth and development.

Using Key Terms

1. In your own words, write a definition for the term *umbilical cord.*

2. Use the following terms in the same sentence: *embryo* and *fetus.*

Understanding Key Ideas

3. After birth, the two periods of most rapid growth are
   a. infancy and adolescence.
   b. childhood and adulthood.
   c. infancy and childhood.
   d. adolescence and adulthood.

4. After birth, which stage of human development is the longest?
   a. infancy
   b. childhood
   c. adolescence
   d. adulthood

5. Describe the development of the embryo and the fetus.

6. What is the function of the placenta?

7. Summarize the processes of fertilization and implantation.

8. What are five stages of human development?

Math Skills

9. Suppose a person is 80 years old and that puberty took place when he or she was 12 years old.
   a. Calculate the percentage of the person's life that he or she spent in each of the four stages of development that follow birth.
   b. Make a bar graph showing the percentage for each stage.

Critical Thinking

10. **Applying Concepts** Why does the egg's covering change after a sperm has entered the egg?

11. **Analyzing Ideas** Do you think any one stage of development is more important than other stages? Explain your answer.

Developed and maintained by the National Science Teachers Association

For a variety of links related to this chapter, go to www.scilinks.org
Topic: Before Birth; Growth and Development
SciLinks code: HSM0140; HSM0700

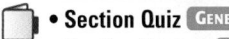

It's a Comfy, Safe World!

Teacher's Notes

Time Required

Two 45-minute class periods

Lab Ratings

EASY — HARD

Teacher Prep 🧪🧪
Student Set-Up 🧪
Concept Level 🧪
Clean Up 🧪🧪🧪

MATERIALS

This lab may require some large plastic bags, a meterstick, and various other materials depending on the students' designs. Soft-boiled eggs will simplify the cleanup. Students may wear gloves.

Safety Caution

Remind students to review all safety cautions and icons before beginning this lab activity. Students should wash their hands after handling the eggs.

Lab Notes

Students will be dropping their models, so this lab should be done over a large plastic sheet. You may want to do this lab outside because it is may be quite messy. Students can modify their models in any way they feel will improve the protection.

OBJECTIVES

Construct a model of a human uterus protecting a fetus.

Compare the protection that a bird's egg gives a developing baby bird with the protection that a human uterus gives a fetus.

MATERIALS

- computer (optional)
- cotton, soft fabric, or other soft materials
- eggs, soft-boiled and in the shell (2 to 4)
- eggs, soft-boiled and peeled (3 or 4)
- gloves, protective
- mineral oil, cooking oil, syrup, or other thick liquid
- plastic bags, sealable
- water

SAFETY

It's a Comfy, Safe World!

Before birth, baby birds live inside a hard, protective shell until the baby has used up all the food supply. Most mammal babies develop within their mother's uterus, in which they are surrounded by fluid and connected to a placenta, before they are born. Before human babies are born, they lead a comfy life. By the seventh month, they lie around sucking their thumb, blinking their eyes, and perhaps even dreaming.

Ask a Question

1 Inside which structure is a developing organism better protected from bumps and blows: the uterus of a placental mammal or the egg of a bird?

Form a Hypothesis

2 A placental mammal's uterus protects a developing organism from bumps and blows better than a bird's egg does.

Test the Hypothesis

3 Brainstorm several ideas about how you will construct and test your model of a mammalian uterus. Then, use the materials provided by your teacher to build your model. A peeled, soft-boiled egg will represent the fetus inside your model uterus.

4 Make a data table similar to **Table 1** below. Test your model, examine the egg for damage, and record your results.

Table 1 First Model Test	
Original model	**Modified model**
DO NOT WRITE IN BOOK	

5 Modify your model as necessary; test this modified model using another peeled, soft-boiled egg; and record your results.

Randy Christian
Stovall Junior High School
Houston, Texas

CHAPTER RESOURCES

Chapter Resource File

 • Datasheet for Chapter Lab
• Lab Notes and Answers

Technology

 Classroom Videos
• Lab Video

• My, How You've Grown!

6. When you are satisfied with the design of your model, obtain another peeled, soft-boiled egg and an egg in the shell. The egg in the shell represents the baby bird inside the egg.

7. Make a data table similar to **Table 2** below. Test your new eggs, examine them for damage, and record your results in your data table.

Table 2 Final Model Test	
	Test Results
Model	DO NOT WRITE IN BOOK
Egg in shell	

Analyze the Results

1. **Explaining Events** Explain any differences in the test results for the model and the egg in a shell.

2. **Analyzing Results** What modification to your model was the most effective in protecting the fetus?

Draw Conclusions

3. **Evaluating Data** Review your hypothesis. Did your data support your hypothesis? Why or why not?

4. **Evaluating Models** What modifications to your model might make it more like a uterus?

Applying Your Data

Use the Internet or the library to find information about the development of monotremes, such as the echidna or the platypus, and marsupials, such as the koala or the kangaroo. Then, using what you have learned in this lab, compare the development of placental mammals with that of marsupials and monotremes.

Analyze the Results

1. Answers may vary, but an egg inside a viscous liquid in a plastic bag, wrapped in soft cotton and placed inside another bag, should not be damaged when dropped from a height of 1 m. An egg protected only by a shell should break. In general, the more protected the fetus or egg, the more resistant to damage it is and the less damage it will suffer when dropped from a height of 1 m.

2. Answers may vary according to students' modifications. Most students will observe that the more soft wrapping and/or viscous fluid protecting the egg, the better the egg survived the drop from 1 m.

Draw Conclusions

3. Students' answers may vary depending on their hypothesis and the data collected. Accept all reasonable answers.

4. Students' answers may vary depending on their model and the data collected. Accept all reasonable answers.

Applying Your Data

Students should recognize that all mammals have internal fertilization of eggs. Students should include the ideas that monotreme mammals lay eggs with leathery shells and, after the eggs hatch, nurture their young with milk that oozes from pores in the mother's skin. Marsupial mammals give birth to live young that are very underdeveloped; the young move to a pouch and continue their development in the pouch. Placental mammals also give birth to live young, but their young are more developed than those of marsupial mammals. Even so, placental mammals may have to care for their young for several years.

Assignment Guide

SECTION	QUESTIONS
1	1, 3, 6, 10, 18–19, 21
2	2, 4–5, 7–8, 11, 12, 13 16–17, 20, 21
3	9, 12, 14–15
2 and 3	22–25

ANSWERS

Using Key Terms

1. Internal fertilization means that the eggs are fertilized inside the female's body. External fertilization is when the eggs are fertilized outside the female's body.

2. Testes are male organs that produce sperm. Ovaries are female organs that produce eggs.

3. Asexual reproduction is when a single parent has offspring that are genetically identical to the parent. Sexual reproduction happens when sex cells from two parents unite.

4. Fertilization happens when the nucleus of a sperm unites with the nucleus of an egg. Implantation is when the embryo embeds itself in the wall of the uterus.

5. The umbilical cord links the fetus with the placenta. The placenta is the organ that helps the fetus get oxygen and nutrients and get rid of wastes.

USING KEY TERMS

For each pair of terms, explain how the meanings of the terms differ.

1. *internal fertilization* and *external fertilization*

2. *testes* and *ovaries*

3. *asexual reproduction* and *sexual reproduction*

4. *fertilization* and *implantation*

5. *umbilical cord* and *placenta*

UNDERSTANDING KEY IDEAS

Multiple Choice

6. The sea star reproduces asexually by
   a. fragmentation.
   b. budding.
   c. external fertilization.
   d. internal fertilization.

7. Which list shows in order sperm's path through the male reproductive system?
   a. testes, epididymis, urethra, vas deferens
   b. epididymis, urethra, testes, vas deferens
   c. testes, vas deferens, epididymis, urethra
   d. testes, epididymis, vas deferens, urethra

8. Identical twins are the result of
   a. a fertilized egg splitting in two.
   b. two separate eggs being fertilized.
   c. budding in the uterus.
   d. external fertilization.

9. If the onset of menstruation is counted as the first day of the menstrual cycle, on what day of the cycle does ovulation typically occur?
   a. 2nd day
   b. 5th day
   c. 14th day
   d. 28th day

10. How do monotremes differ from placental mammals?
    a. Monotremes are not mammals.
    b. Monotremes have hair.
    c. Monotremes nurture their young with milk.
    d. Monotremes lay eggs.

11. All of the following are sexually transmitted diseases EXCEPT
    a. chlamydia.
    b. AIDS.
    c. infertility.
    d. genital herpes.

12. Where do fertilization and implantation, respectively, take place?
    a. uterus, fallopian tube
    b. fallopian tube, vagina
    c. uterus, vagina
    d. fallopian tube, uterus

Short Answer

13. Which human reproductive organs produce sperm? produce eggs?

14. Explain how the fetus gets oxygen and nutrients and how it gets rid of waste.

15. What are four stages of human life following birth?

Understanding Key Ideas

6. a
7. d
8. a
9. c
10. d
11. c
12. d
13. The testes produce sperm, and the ovaries produce eggs.
14. The placenta is a specialized organ that allows the fetus to get oxygen and get rid of wastes.

15. infancy, childhood, adolescence, adulthood

16. Sample answer: Infertility is a problem because it may prevent people from having babies. STDs are a problem because they can damage a person's reproductive system, and they may also cause infertility. Cancer is a problem because it can damage a person's reproductive system.

17. Drawings should resemble the images in Section 2, Figure 1, The Male Reproductive System, and Figure 2, The Female Reproductive System.

16 Name three problems that can affect the human reproductive system, and explain why each is a problem.

17 Draw a diagram showing the structures of the male and female reproductive systems. Label each structure, and explain how each structure contributes to fertilization and implantation.

CRITICAL THINKING

18 Concept Mapping Use the following terms to create a concept map: *asexual reproduction, budding, external fertilization, fragmentation, reproduction, internal fertilization,* and *sexual reproduction.*

19 Identifying Relationships The environment in which organisms live may change over time. For example, a wet, swampy area may gradually become a grassy area with a small pond. Explain how sexual reproduction may give species that live in a changing environment a survival advantage.

20 Applying Concepts What is the function of the uterus? How is this function related to the menstrual cycle?

21 Making Inferences In most human body cells, the 46 chromosomes are duplicated during cell division so that each new cell receives 46 chromosomes. Cells that make eggs and sperm also split and duplicate their 46 chromosomes. But then, in the process of meiosis, the two cells split again to form four cells (egg or sperm) that each have 23 chromosomes. Why is meiosis important to human reproduction and to the human species?

INTERPRETING GRAPHICS

The following graph illustrates the cycles of the female hormone estrogen and the male hormone testosterone. The blue line shows the estrogen level in a female over 28 days. The red line shows the testosterone level in a male over the same amount of time. Use the graph below to answer the questions that follow.

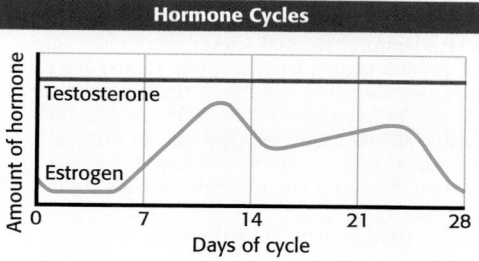

Hormone Cycles

22 What is the major difference between the levels of the two hormones over the 28 days?

23 What cycle do you think estrogen affects?

24 Why might the level of testosterone stay the same?

25 Do you think that the above estrogen cycle would change in a pregnant woman? Explain your answer.

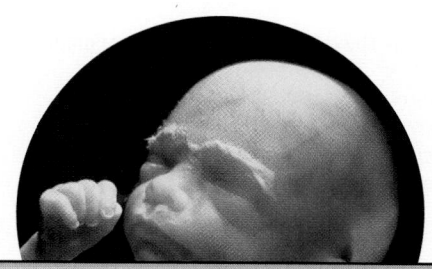

Critical Thinking

18. 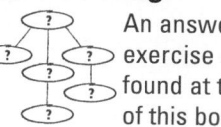 An answer to this exercise can be found at the end of this book.

19. Sample answer: Sexual reproduction produces offspring that have genetic information from two different parents. Some of that information may enable the offspring to do better in a changing environment than other members of the species. As a result, there is a greater chance that the beneficial information will be passed on to the next generation.

20. The uterus, an organ in the female reproductive system, is where an embryo develops into a fetus. Every month, it builds up tissue that can help nourish a developing embryo. If no embryo implants, the tissue will discharge in menstruation.

21. Meiosis ensures that the characteristic human chromosome number remains the same. Because sex cells from two separate parents combine to form a zygote, each sex cell needs only half the 46 chromosomes that all other human body cells have. Meiosis also ensures that offspring will have a mix of genetic information.

Interpreting Graphics

22. Estrogen levels fluctuate, but testosterone stays at the same level throughout the month.

23. Estrogen affects the menstrual cycle.

24. Testosterone levels stay the same because men continually produce sperm and do not prepare for a possible pregnancy.

25. Sample answer: Yes, I think it might change because estrogen affects the menstrual cycle. During pregnancy, the menstrual cycle stops, so the level of estrogen will level off until the pregnancy is over.

Standardized Test Preparation

Teacher's Note

To provide practice under more realistic testing conditions, give students 20 minutes to answer all of the questions in this Standardized Test Preparation.

MISCONCEPTION ///**ALERT**\\\

Answers to the standardized test preparation can help you identify student misconceptions and misunderstandings.

READING

Passage 1

1. B
2. H
3. C

✚ **TEST DOCTOR**

Question 2: This fact is mentioned in the following sentences: "Normal human body temperature is about 37°C. Normal sperm production and development cannot take place at that high temperature." Students may not put the two sentences together to extract the fact. Some students may choose answer I because they have mistakenly read "37°F" for the correct "37°C."

Question 3: Students may skip over the word "tubes" in the question and answer the more general question "Where are sperm made?" by choosing answer A.

READING

Read each of the passages below. Then, answer the questions that follow each passage.

Passage 1 The male reproductive system is made up of internal and external organs. The <u>external</u> organs of this system are the penis and the scrotum. The scrotum is a skin-covered sac that hangs outside the body. Normal human body temperature is about 37°C. Normal sperm production and development cannot take place at that temperature. Normal sperm production and development takes place at lower temperatures. That is why the testes rest in the scrotum, outside the body. The scrotum is about 2°C cooler than the body. Inside each testis are masses of tightly coiled tubes, called *seminiferous tubules,* in which sperm are produced when conditions are right.

1. In this passage, what does the word *external* mean?
   - **A** not part of the body
   - **B** outside the body
   - **C** inside the body
   - **D** lasting a long time

2. Which of the following statements is a fact according to the passage?
   - **F** The temperature in the scrotum is higher than body temperature.
   - **G** Testes are internal organs of the male reproductive system.
   - **H** Normal sperm production cannot take place at normal body temperature.
   - **I** Normal human body temperature is about 37°F.

3. What are the tubes in which sperm are made called?
   - **A** testes
   - **B** scrotum
   - **C** seminiferous tubules
   - **D** external organs

Passage 2 In a normal pregnancy, the fertilized egg travels to the uterus and implants itself in the uterus's wall. But, in about 7 out of 1,000 pregnancies in the United States, a woman has an <u>ectopic pregnancy</u>. The term *ectopic* is from two Greek words meaning "out of place." In an ectopic pregnancy, the fertilized egg implants itself in an ovary, a fallopian tube, or another area of the female reproductive system that is not the lining of the uterus. Because the zygote cannot develop properly outside of the uterus, an ectopic pregnancy can be very dangerous for both the mother and zygote. As the zygote grows, it causes the mother pain and bleeding. For example, an ectopic pregnancy in a fallopian tube can rupture the tube and cause abdominal bleeding. If an ectopic pregnancy is not treated quickly enough, the mother may die.

1. In the passage, what does the term *ectopic pregnancy* probably mean?
   - **A** a pregnancy that takes place at the wrong time
   - **B** a type of pregnancy that happens about 7 out of 100 times in the United States
   - **C** a type of pregnancy caused by a problem with a fallopian tube
   - **D** a pregnancy in which the zygote implants itself in the wrong place

2. Which of the following statements is a fact according to the passage?
   - **F** Ectopic pregnancies take place in about 7% of all pregnancies.
   - **G** The ectopic pregnancy rate in the United States is less than 1%.
   - **H** Ectopic pregnancies take place in the uterus.
   - **I** An ectopic pregnancy is harmless.

Passage 2

1. D
2. G

✚ **TEST DOCTOR**

Question 2: The passage states that ectopic pregnancies happen in about 7 out of 1,000 pregnancies, which is 0.7%. The correct answer is therefore answer G. Students may read "7 out of 1000" as "7 out of 100," and would pick incorrect answer F.

Use the diagrams below to answer the questions that follow.

A.

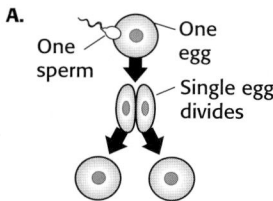

One sperm — One egg — Single egg divides

B. Two sperm

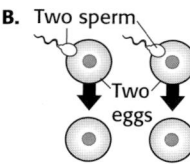

Two eggs

1. Which diagram of cell division would produce identical twins: A or B?

A diagram B, because each egg is fertilized by a separate sperm cell

B both diagram A and diagram B, because twins result in both cases

C diagram A, because a single fertilized egg separates into two halves

D diagram B, because two eggs are released by an ovary

2. Which of the following could describe fraternal twins?

F both boys

G both girls

H one girl and one boy

I any of these combinations

3. Which diagram of cell division could explain triplets, two of whom are identical and one of whom is fraternal?

A diagram A

B diagram B

C either diagram A or diagram B

D neither diagram A or diagram B

Read each question below, and choose the best answer.

1. Identify the group that contains equivalent fractions, decimals, and percents.

A 7/10, 0.7, 7%

B 1/2, 0.5, 50%

C 3/8, 0.38, 38%

D 3/100, 0.3, 33%

2. A geologist was exploring a cave. She spent 2.7 h exploring on Saturday and twice as many hours exploring on Sunday. Which equation could be used to find n, the total number of hours the geologist spent exploring the cave on those 2 days?

F $n = 2 \div 2.7$

G $n = 2.7 + (2 \times 2.7)$

H $n = 2.7 + 2.7 + 2$

I $n = 2 \times 2.7$

3. Which of the following story problems can be solved by the equation below?

$$(60 + 70 + 68 + 80 + x) \div 5 = 70$$

A The heights of four buildings in South Braintree are 60 ft, 70 ft, 68 ft, and 80 ft. Find x, the average height of the buildings.

B The weights of four dogs Jason is raising are 60 lb, 70 lb, 68 lb, and 80 lb. Find x, the sum of the weights of the four dogs.

C Kayla's first four handmade bracelets sold for $60, $70, $68, and $80. Find x, the amount for which Kayla needs to sell her fifth bracelet to have an average selling price of $70.

D The times it took Taylor to complete each of four 100 m practice swims were 60 s, 70 s, 68 s, and 80 s. Find x, the average time it took Taylor to complete his practice swims.

Standardized Test Preparation

1. C

2. I

3. D

➕ **TEST DOCTOR**

Question 1: Students may select answer B because twins do result in both cases. However, identical twins happen only when a single fertilized egg splits in two.

Question 2: Students may think that fraternal twins, even if they are not identical, must still be of the same sex. The correct answer is I; fraternal twins may be two boys, two girls, or one of each, because fraternal twins develop from two separate fertilized eggs, not from the splitting of one egg.

1. B

2. G

3. C

➕ **TEST DOCTOR**

Question 2: Students often have trouble converting a word problem into a number statement. Students may select answer H or I because those answers are similar to the correct answer. Students who have problems writing number statements often overlook an important clue in the word problem, and their statement is incomplete.

Question 3: This is another word problem, but it is a little more complex than question 2. Students must realize that the average has already been calculated and that what they are seeking is the quantity that gives the average. Answer C is the only answer in which the average is given; the other three answers ask to solve for the average.

CHAPTER RESOURCES

Chapter Resource File

📁 • Standardized Test Preparation GENERAL

State Resources

 For specific resources for your state, visit **go.hrw.com** and type in the keyword **HSMSTR**.

Science in Action

Science, Technology, and Society

Discussion — ADVANCED

Lead students in a discussion about the implications of fetal-surgery technology for treating fetal disorders. What sorts of disorders might be successfully treated? (anatomical disorders and discrete tumors) What types of disorders would be more difficult to treat? (genetic disorders and disorders affecting the entire fetus)

Scientific Discoveries

Background

The word *laser* is actually an abbreviation for **l**ight **a**mplification by **s**timulated **e**mission of **r**adiation. Lasers can pump energy into a solid, liquid, gas, or semiconductor to produce a beam. Carbon dioxide and helium-neon are common gas lasers. Ruby is a common solid-state laser. Each medium produces a laser with a different wavelength. Semiconductor (or diode) lasers emit a wavelength of 630 nm. They are so weak that they can be used as pointers. Carbon dioxide lasers, emitting a wavelength of 10,600 nm, are so strong that they can cut through steel!

Doctors operated on a fetus, whose hand is visible in this photo, to correct spina bifida.

Science, Technology, and Society

Fetal Surgery

Sometimes, a developing fetus has a serious medical problem. In many cases, surgery after birth can correct the problem. But some problems can be treated while the fetus is still in the uterus. For example, fetal surgery may be used to correct spina bifida (part of the spinal cord is exposed because the backbone doesn't form properly). Doctors now can fix several types of problems before a baby is born.

Social Studies ACTIVITY

WRITING SKILL Research the causes of spina bifida. Write a brochure telling expectant mothers what precautions they can take to prevent spina bifida.

Scientific Discoveries

Lasers and Acne

Many people think that acne affects only teenagers, but acne can strike at any age. Some acne is mild, but some is severe. Now, for some severe cases of acne, lasers may provide relief. That's right—lasers can be used to treat acne! Surgeons who specialize in the health and diseases of the skin use laser light to treat the skin disease known as *acne*.

In addition, laser treatments may stimulate the skin cells that produce collagen. Collagen is a protein found in connective tissue. Increased production of collagen in the skin improves the skin's texture and helps smooth out acne scars.

Language Arts ACTIVITY

WRITING SKILL Write a story about how severe acne affects a teen's life. Tell what happens when a doctor refers the teen to a specialist for laser treatment and how the successful treatment changes the teen's life.

Answer to Social Studies Activity

Spina bifida (a Latin term meaning *split spine*) is a group of congenital birth defects that affect the development of the central nervous system—the brain and the spinal cord—and nerve tissues. Spina bifida occurs about 10 to 20 times per 1,000 births. With severe spina bifida, a person's legs and feet are paralyzed. There are often problems with bowel and bladder control. The long-term effects of spina bifida depend on the type and severity of the defect. Up to 75% of the cases of spina bifida could be prevented if the mother takes folic acid daily before pregnancy and during the first trimester.

Answer to Language Arts Activity

Students' stories may reflect the emotional, social, and psychological impact that severe acne can have and the positive effects laser treatments may have for the acne sufferer. Improved self-confidence, a better self-image, and more-successful social interactions may be some of the benefits.

Reva Curry

Diagnostic Medical Sonographer Sounds are everywhere in our world. But only some of those sounds—such as your favorite music playing on the stereo or the dog barking next door—are sounds that we can hear. There are sound waves whose frequency is too high for us to hear. These high-pitched sounds are called *ultrasound*. Some animals, such as bats, use ultrasound to hunt and to avoid midair collisions.

Humans use ultrasound, too. Ultrasound machines can peer inside the human body to look at hearts, blood vessels, and fetuses. Diagnostic medical sonographers are people who use sonography equipment to diagnose medical problems and to follow the growth and development of a fetus before it is born. One of the leading professionals in the field of diagnostic medical sonography is Dr. Reva Curry. Dr. Curry spent many years as a sonographer. Her primary job was to use high-tech instruments to create ultrasound images of parts of the body and interpret the results for other medical professionals. Today, Dr. Curry works with students as the dean of a community college.

Math ACTIVITY

At 20°C, the speed of sound in water is 1,482 m/s and in steel is 5,200 m/s. How long would it take a sound to travel 815.1 m in water? In that same length of time, how far would a sound travel in a steel beam?

To learn more about these Science in Action topics, visit **go.hrw.com** and type in the keyword **HL5BD5F**.

Current Science

Check out Current Science® articles related to this chapter by visiting go.hrw.com. Just type in the keyword **HL5CS26**.

Careers

Discussion ——— GENERAL

Generate interest in diagnostic medical sonography by inviting a diagnostic medical sonographer from a local hospital or clinic. Before the visit, discuss with the class Dr. Curry's story and any experiences the students may have had with sonography or other diagnostic imaging techniques. Have students prepare questions for the guest speaker prior to the visit. Your guest may show a video of the procedure itself and interpret some actual sonograms. The students should have the opportunity for an open discussion with the practitioner and thereby get first-hand knowledge about the profession.

Answers to Math Activity
1. 0.55 s
2. 2,860 m

TIMELINE

Human Health

In many ways, living in the 21st century is good for your health. Many deadly diseases that plagued our ancestors now have cures. Some diseases, such as smallpox, have been wiped out entirely. And others can be prevented by vaccines and other methods. Many researchers, including the people on this timeline, have worked to understand diseases and to find cures.

But people still get sick, and many diseases have no cure. In this unit, you will learn how your body protects itself and fights illness. You will also learn about ways to keep yourself healthy so that your body can operate in top form.

1403

The first quarantine is imposed in Venice, Italy, to stop the spread of the plague, or Black Death.

1717

Lady Mary Wortley Montague introduces a smallpox vaccine in England.

1854

Nurse Florence Nightingale introduces hygienic standards into military hospitals during the Crimean War.

1895

X rays are discovered by Wilhelm Roentgen.

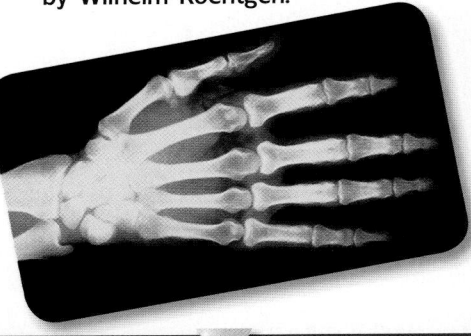

1953

Cigarette smoking is linked to lung cancer.

1816

R. T. Laënnec invents the stethoscope.

1853

Charles Gerhardt synthesizes aspirin for the first time.

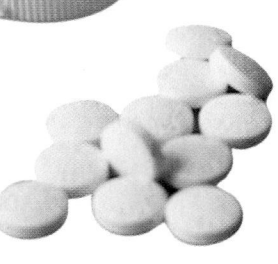

1900

Walter Reed discovers that yellow fever is carried by mosquitoes.

1906

Upton Sinclair writes *The Jungle*, which describes unsanitary conditions in the Chicago stockyards and leads to the creation of the Pure Food and Drug Act.

1921

A tuberculosis vaccine is produced.

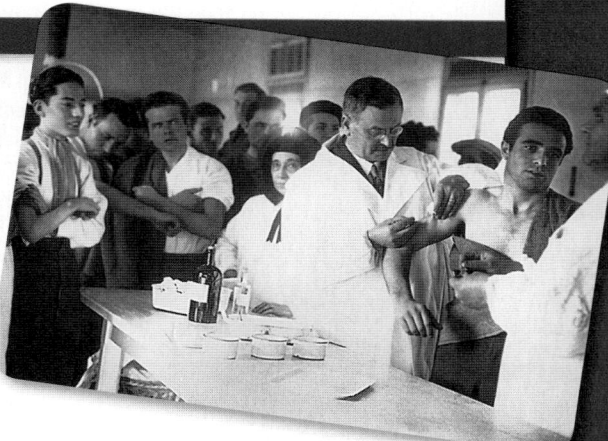

1979

Smallpox is eradicated.

1997

Researchers discover that high doses of alcohol in early pregnancy switch off a gene that controls brain, heart, limb, and skull development in the fetus.

2003

More than 8,000 people are infected with severe acute respiratory syndrome (SARS), which is caused by a newly discovered virus.

Body Defenses and Disease
Chapter Planning Guide

Compression guide:
To shorten instruction
because of time limitations,
omit the Chapter Lab.

OBJECTIVES	LABS, DEMONSTRATIONS, AND ACTIVITIES	TECHNOLOGY RESOURCES
PACING • 90 min pp. 708–713 **Chapter Opener**	SE **Start-up Activity**, p. 709 `GENERAL`	OSP **Parent Letter** ■ `GENERAL` CD **Student Edition on CD-ROM** CD **Guided Reading Audio CD** ■ TR **Chapter Starter Transparency*** VID **Brain Food Video Quiz**
Section 1 **Disease** • Explain the difference between infectious diseases and noninfectious diseases. • Identify five ways that you might come into contact with a pathogen. • Discuss four methods that have helped reduce the spread of disease.	SE **Connection to Social Studies** Disease and History, p. 711 `GENERAL` TE **Activity** Using Microscopes, p. 711 `BASIC` SE **School-to-Home Activity** Label Check, p. 712 `GENERAL` TE **Connection to Physical Science** Pasteurization, p. 712 SE **Skills Practice Lab** Passing the Cold, p. 722 ◆ `GENERAL` CRF **Datasheet for Chapter Lab*** SE **Science In Action** Math, Social Studies and Language Arts Activites, pp. 728–729	CRF **Lesson Plans*** TR **Bellringer Transparency*** TR ***LINK TO PHYSICAL SCIENCE*** Thermal Energy in Water*** VID **Lab Videos for Life Science**
PACING • 45 min pp. 714–721 **Section 2** **Your Body's Defenses** • Describe how your body keeps out pathogens. • Explain how the immune system fights infections. • Describe four challenges to the immune system.	TE **Activity** Reactions to Illness, p. 714 `GENERAL` SE **Quick Lab** Only Skin Deep, p. 715 `GENERAL` CRF **Datasheet for Quick Lab*** TE **Activity** Follow the Path, p. 716 `BASIC` TE **Group Activity** Immunity Skit, p. 717 `ADVANCED` SE **Connection to Chemistry** Bent out of Shape, p. 718 `GENERAL` TE **Connection Activity** Real World, p. 718 `GENERAL` TE **Activity** Concept Mapping, p. 720 `GENERAL` SE **Model-Making Lab** Antibodies to the Rescue, p. 799 `GENERAL` CRF **Datasheet for LabBook*** LB **Long-Term Projects & Research Ideas** A Chuckle a Day Keeps the Doctor Away* `ADVANCED`	CRF **Lesson Plans*** TR **Bellringer Transparency*** TR **An Antibody's Shape Fits an Antigen*** TR **Immune Response: A*** TR **Immune Response: B*** SE **Internet Activity**, p. 716 `GENERAL` CRF **SciLinks Activity*** `GENERAL`

PACING • 90 min

CHAPTER REVIEW, ASSESSMENT, AND STANDARDIZED TEST PREPARATION

CRF **Vocabulary Activity*** `GENERAL`
SE **Chapter Review**, pp. 724–725 `GENERAL`
CRF **Chapter Review*** ■ `GENERAL`
CRF **Chapter Tests A*** ■ `GENERAL`, **B*** `ADVANCED`, **C*** `SPECIAL NEEDS`
SE **Standardized Test Preparation**, pp. 726–727 `GENERAL`
CRF **Standardized Test Preparation*** `GENERAL`
CRF **Performance-Based Assessment*** `GENERAL`
OSP **Test Generator** `GENERAL`
CRF **Test Item Listing*** `GENERAL`

Online and Technology Resources

Visit **go.hrw.com** for a variety of free resources related to this textbook. Enter the keyword **HL5BD6.**

Holt Online Learning

Students can access interactive problem-solving help and active visual concept development with the *Holt Science and Technology* Online Edition available at **www.hrw.com.**

 Guided Reading Audio CD
Also in Spanish

A direct reading of each chapter for auditory learners, reluctant readers, and Spanish-speaking students.

 **Science Tutor
CD-ROM**

Excellent for remediation and test practice.

SKILLS DEVELOPMENT RESOURCES	SECTION REVIEW AND ASSESSMENT	STANDARDS CORRELATIONS
SE Pre-Reading Activity, p. 708 `GENERAL` **OSP** Science Puzzlers, Twisters & Teasers* `GENERAL`		National Science Education Standards SAI 1, 2; LS 1f
CRF Directed Reading A* ■ `BASIC`, B* `SPECIAL NEEDS` **CRF** Vocabulary and Section Summary* ■ `GENERAL` **SE** Reading Strategy Paired Summarizing, p. 710 `GENERAL` **TE** Inclusion Strategies, p. 711 **SE** Math Practice Epidemic!, p. 713 `GENERAL` **CRF** Critical Thinking Vaccine for Super Bug Found!* `ADVANCED`	**SE** Reading Checks, pp. 711, 713 `GENERAL` **TE** Reteaching, p. 712 `BASIC` **TE** Quiz, p. 712 `GENERAL` **TE** Alternative Assessment, p. 712 `GENERAL` **SE** Section Review,* p. 713 ■ `GENERAL` **CRF** Section Quiz* ■ `GENERAL`	SAI 1, 2; ST 2; SPSP 1, 5; HNS 1, 3; LS 1f; *Chapter Lab:* UCP 2, SAI 1
CRF Directed Reading A* ■ `BASIC`, B* `SPECIAL NEEDS` **CRF** Vocabulary and Section Summary* ■ `GENERAL` **SE** Reading Strategy Reading Organizer, p. 714 `GENERAL` **TE** Inclusion Strategies, p. 718 **CRF** Reinforcement Worksheet Immunity Teamwork* `GENERAL`	**SE** Reading Checks, pp. 715, 716, 719, 720 `GENERAL` **TE** Homework, p. 719 `GENERAL` **TE** Reteaching, p. 720 `BASIC` **TE** Quiz, p. 720 `GENERAL` **TE** Alternative Assessment, p. 720 `ADVANCED` **SE** Section Review,* p. 721 ■ `GENERAL` **CRF** Section Quiz* ■ `GENERAL`	UCP 1, 2, 3, 4, 5; SAI 1; HNS 3; LS 1b, 1d, 1e, 1f, 3a, 3b; *LabBook:* UCP 2; SAI 1

One-Stop Planner® CD-ROM

This convenient CD-ROM includes:
- Lab Materials QuickList Software
- Holt Calendar Planner
- Customizable Lesson Plans
- Printable Worksheets
- ExamView® Test Generator

cnnstudentnews.com

Find the latest news, lesson plans, and activities related to important scientific events.

www.scilinks.org

Maintained by the **National Science Teachers Association.** See Chapter Enrichment pages for a complete list of topics.

Check out *Current Science* articles and activities by visiting the HRW Web site at **go.hrw.com.** Just type in the keyword **HL5CS27T.**

Classroom Videos

- **Lab Videos** demonstrate the chapter lab.
- **Brain Food Video Quizzes** help students review the chapter material.
- **CNN Videos** bring science into your students' daily life.

Visual Resources

CHAPTER STARTER TRANSPARENCY

BELLRINGER TRANSPARENCIES

TEACHING TRANSPARENCIES

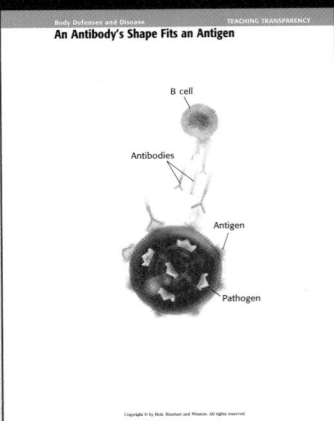 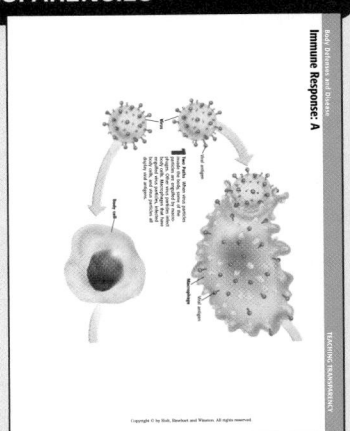

TEACHING TRANSPARENCIES

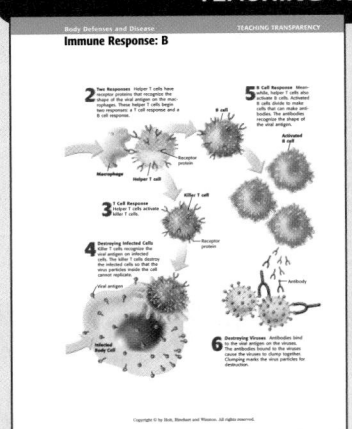 

CONCEPT MAPPING TRANSPARENCY

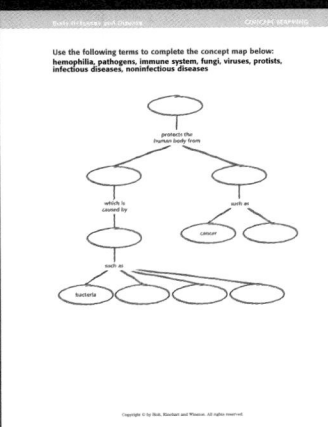

Planning Resources

LESSON PLANS

PARENT LETTER

ALSO IN SPANISH

TEST ITEM LISTING

One-Stop Planner® CD-ROM

This CD-ROM includes all of the resources shown here and the following time-saving tools:

- *Lab Materials QuickList Software*
- *Customizable lesson plans*
- *Holt Calendar Planner*
- *The powerful ExamView® Test Generator*

Meeting Individual Needs

DIRECTED READING A
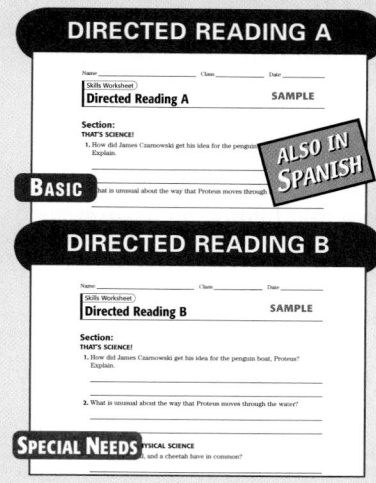
BASIC — ALSO IN SPANISH

DIRECTED READING B
SPECIAL NEEDS

VOCABULARY ACTIVITY
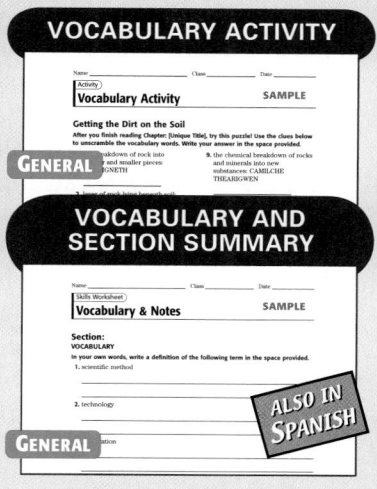
GENERAL

VOCABULARY AND SECTION SUMMARY
GENERAL — ALSO IN SPANISH

REINFORCEMENT
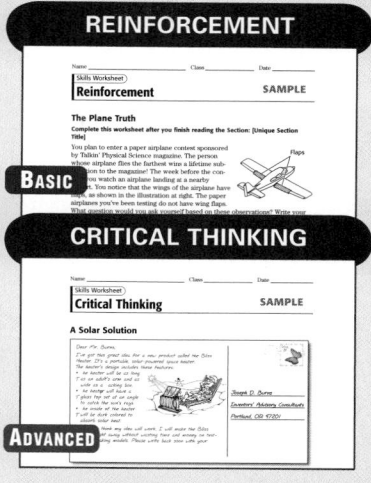
BASIC

CRITICAL THINKING
ADVANCED

SCILINKS ACTIVITY

GENERAL

SCIENCE PUZZLERS, TWISTERS & TEASERS
GENERAL

Labs and Activities

LONG-TERM PROJECTS & RESEARCH IDEAS
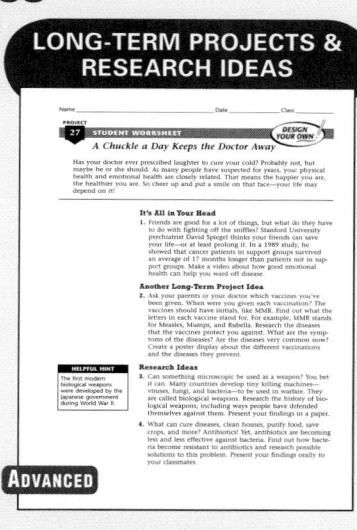
ADVANCED

DATASHEETS FOR QUICK LABS

DATASHEETS FOR CHAPTER LABS

DATASHEETS FOR LABBOOK

Review and Assessments

SECTION QUIZ
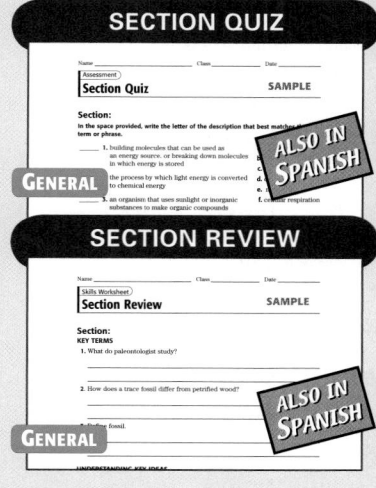
GENERAL — ALSO IN SPANISH

SECTION REVIEW
GENERAL — ALSO IN SPANISH

CHAPTER REVIEW
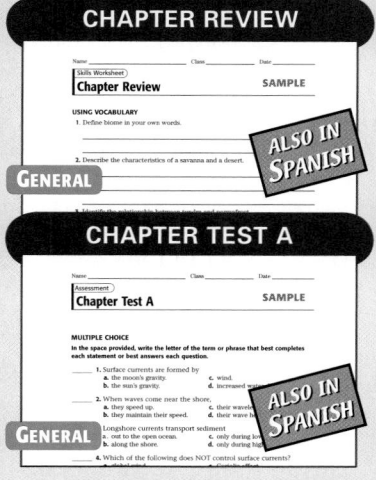
GENERAL — ALSO IN SPANISH

CHAPTER TEST A
GENERAL — ALSO IN SPANISH

CHAPTER TEST B
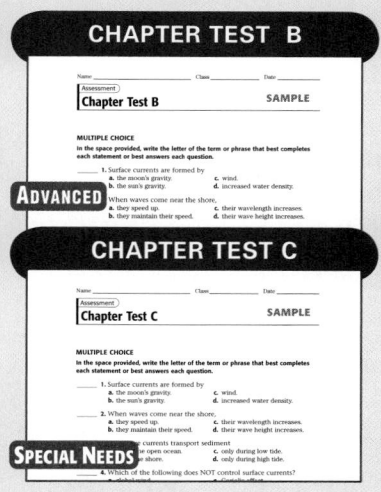
ADVANCED

CHAPTER TEST C
SPECIAL NEEDS

STANDARDIZED TEST PREPARATION
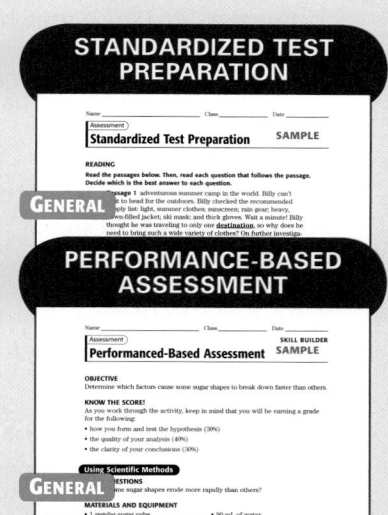
GENERAL

PERFORMANCE-BASED ASSESSMENT
GENERAL

This Chapter Enrichment provides relevant and interesting information to expand and enhance your presentation of the chapter material.

Section 1

Disease

Pathogens and the Diseases That They Cause

- Pathogens are agents that cause disease. Pathogens can be living or nonliving. Living pathogens include bacteria, protists, fungi, worms, and insects. Nonliving pathogens include viruses, viroids, and prions.

- Bacterial diseases include bubonic plague, cholera, dental caries, Lyme disease, pneumonia, and typhoid fever.

- Viral diseases include colds, influenza, chickenpox, measles, rubella, mumps, smallpox, infectious hepatitis, polio, and AIDS.

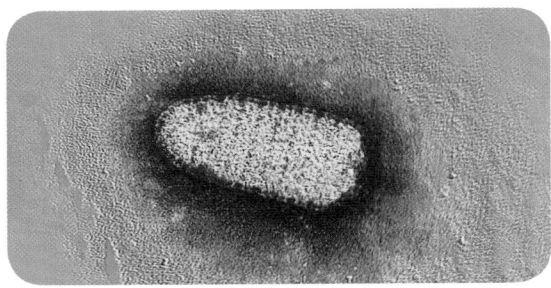

- Protists cause malaria, Chagas' disease, toxoplasmosis, and giardiasis. Common fungal diseases include ringworm, athlete's foot, vaginal yeast infections, jock itch, and histoplasmosis.

Is That a Fact!

- ◆ Bacteria were the first organisms to inhabit Earth. They are thought to have been the only organisms on Earth for about 1 billion years.

- ◆ All other life-forms are thought to have evolved from ancestral forms of bacteria.

- ◆ Some species of bacteria can reproduce every 20 min. Given unlimited resources, one bacterium could produce 1 million kilograms of bacteria in a day!

Emerging Viruses

- The news is full of instances in which new viruses have suddenly begun to infect people. Examples include HIV, which became common in the 1980s, hantavirus, which caused an outbreak in 1993, new strains of Ebola, which were announced in the 1990s, and a corona virus causing SARS, which became common in 2003. Such viruses are called *emerging viruses.*

- Emerging viruses can evolve or mutate from an existing virus that was not infectious. They can also spread from one species to another. Another way that a virus can suddenly emerge is through globalization. When people build roads through a previously isolated area or travel to new places, viruses can spread.

Types of Vaccines

- Vaccines are generally harmless forms of a pathogen or parts of a pathogen that are introduced into the body to help the immune system develop antibodies against the pathogen should the disease-causing form enter the body in the future.

- There are several ways that vaccines are prepared today. One way to make a vaccine is to inactivate the viruses or to kill the bacteria that cause the disease. Another way is to use a similar strain of pathogen or an attenuated or weakened version of the pathogen. The latter kind of vaccine is sometimes called a *live attenuated vaccine.*

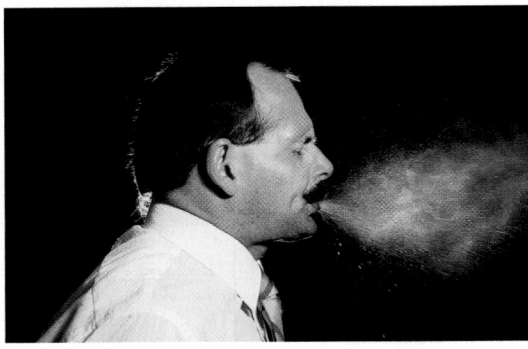

Section 2

Your Body's Defenses

The Body's Defenses Against Pathogens

- The body has two main kinds of defenses against disease—specific and nonspecific defenses.

- The body's so-called first and second lines of defense are its nonspecific defense mechanisms. The first line of defense consists of the skin, the mucous membranes, and the secretions of the mucous membranes. Oil, sweat, tears, mucus, and saliva wash pathogens away and contain enzymes that digest the cell walls of microbes.

- The body's second line of defense includes white blood cells that ingest or destroy foreign agents detected in the body. The second line of defense also includes proteins that help cells avoid infection by foreign agents. Antimicrobial proteins include complement proteins and interferons. Also part of the body's second line of defense is its inflammatory response, which occurs in response to cuts or other incisions through the skin.

Fever

- A fever occurs when the body's temperature rises above 98.6°F (37°C) when measured orally.

- Fevers, which commonly accompany infectious diseases, help the body thwart invading pathogens. However, fevers may also accompany noninfectious conditions, such as dehydration and heart attack.

Is That a Fact!

◆ A very high fever can cause a coma, seizures, or brain damage.

AIDS

- AIDS is the final stage in an HIV infection. Upon infection, the viruses first multiply quickly and are quickly fought off by immune system cells. Some viruses remain in the body and replicate slowly over time. Immune system cells continue the fight, sometimes for many years. HIV attacks helper T cells, and when the number of helper T cells falls below a certain level, a person is said to have AIDS.

- HIV is spread through the exchange of blood and other body fluids. It is not spread through casual contact.

- There is no cure for AIDS at this time. There are only drug regimens that may prolong the life of some patients.

- The best way to avoid contracting AIDS is to avoid the behaviors known to put one at risk for acquiring HIV. These behaviors include sharing needles and engaging in unprotected sexual contact.

Allergic Reactions

- The first time a person is exposed to an allergen, such as pollen, he or she usually shows no allergic response. As when a vaccine is administered, the body produces antibodies against the allergen. Thus prepared, the body develops the allergic response upon subsequent exposures to the allergen.

Is That a Fact!

◆ Allergic responses may be a defense mechanism left over from the body's defenses against parasitic worms. This hypothesis comes from the observation that the body's method of combating parasitic worms is very similar to the allergic response seen in hay fever and asthma.

SciLINKS

NSTA
Developed and maintained by the National Science Teachers Association

SciLinks is maintained by the National Science Teachers Association to provide you and your students with interesting, up-to-date links that will enrich your classroom presentation of the chapter.

Visit www.scilinks.org and enter the SciLinks code for more information about the topic listed.

opic: What Causes Diseases?
SciLinks code: HSM1653

Topic: Pathogens
SciLinks code: HSM1118

Topic: Body Defenses
SciLinks code: HSM0181

Topic: Allergies
SciLinks code: HSM0048

Topic: Cancer and HIV
SciLinks code: HSM0208

Overview

Tell students that this chapter will help them learn about diseases, including how infectious diseases are spread, how the body defends against diseases, and what problems can arise with the immune system.

Assessing Prior Knowledge

Students should be familiar with the following topics:

- bacteria and viruses
- body systems

Identifying Misconceptions

As students learn the material in this chapter, some of them may be confused about how diseases are spread. For example, warnings to bundle up during cold weather may lead students to think that cold weather causes infectious disease. Help them understand that pathogens cause infectious disease. Furthermore, some students may think that all microorganisms are harmful. Emphasize that although some microorganisms can cause disease, life as we know it would be impossible without microbes.

27

Body Defenses and Disease

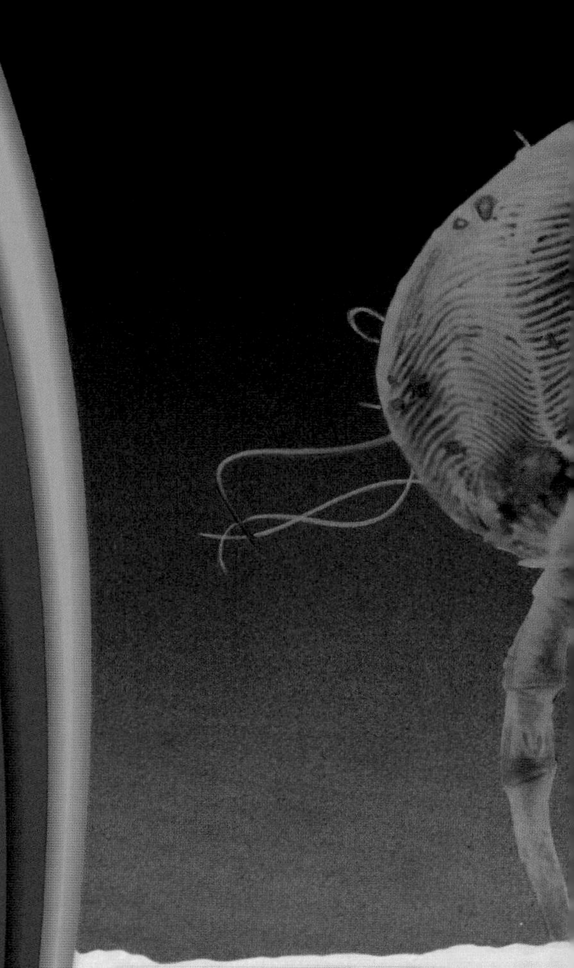

About the PHOTO

No, this photo is not from a sci-fi movie. It is not an alien insect soldier. This is, in fact, a greatly enlarged image of a house dust mite that is tinier than the dot of an *i*. Huge numbers of these creatures live in carpets, beds, and sofas in every home. Dust mites often cause problems for people who have asthma or allergies. The body's immune system fights diseases and alien factors, such as dust mites, that cause allergies.

PRE-READING ACTIVITY

FOLDNOTES **Tri-Fold** Before you read the chapter, create the FoldNote entitled "Tri-Fold" described in the **Study Skills** section of the Appendix. Write what you know about the body's defenses in the column labeled "Know." Then, write what you want to know in the column labeled "Want." As you read the chapter, write what you learn about the body's defenses in the column labeled "Learn."

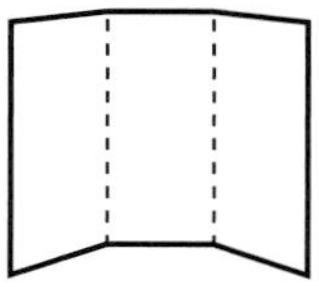

Standards Correlations

National Science Education Standards

The following codes indicate the National Science Education Standards that correlate to this chapter. The full text of the standards is at the front of the book.

Chapter Opener
SAI 1, 2; LS 1f

Section 1 Disease
SAI 1, 2; ST 2; SPSP 1, 5; HNS 1, 3; LS 1f

Section 2 Your Body's Defenses
UCP 1, 2, 3, 4, 5; SAI 1; HNS 3; LS 1b, 1d, 1e, 1f, 3a, 3b;
LabBook: UCP2; SAI 1

Chapter Lab
UCP 1; SAI 1

Chapter Review
LS 1b, 1d, 1e, 1f, 3a, 3b

Science in Action
HNS 1; LS 1f

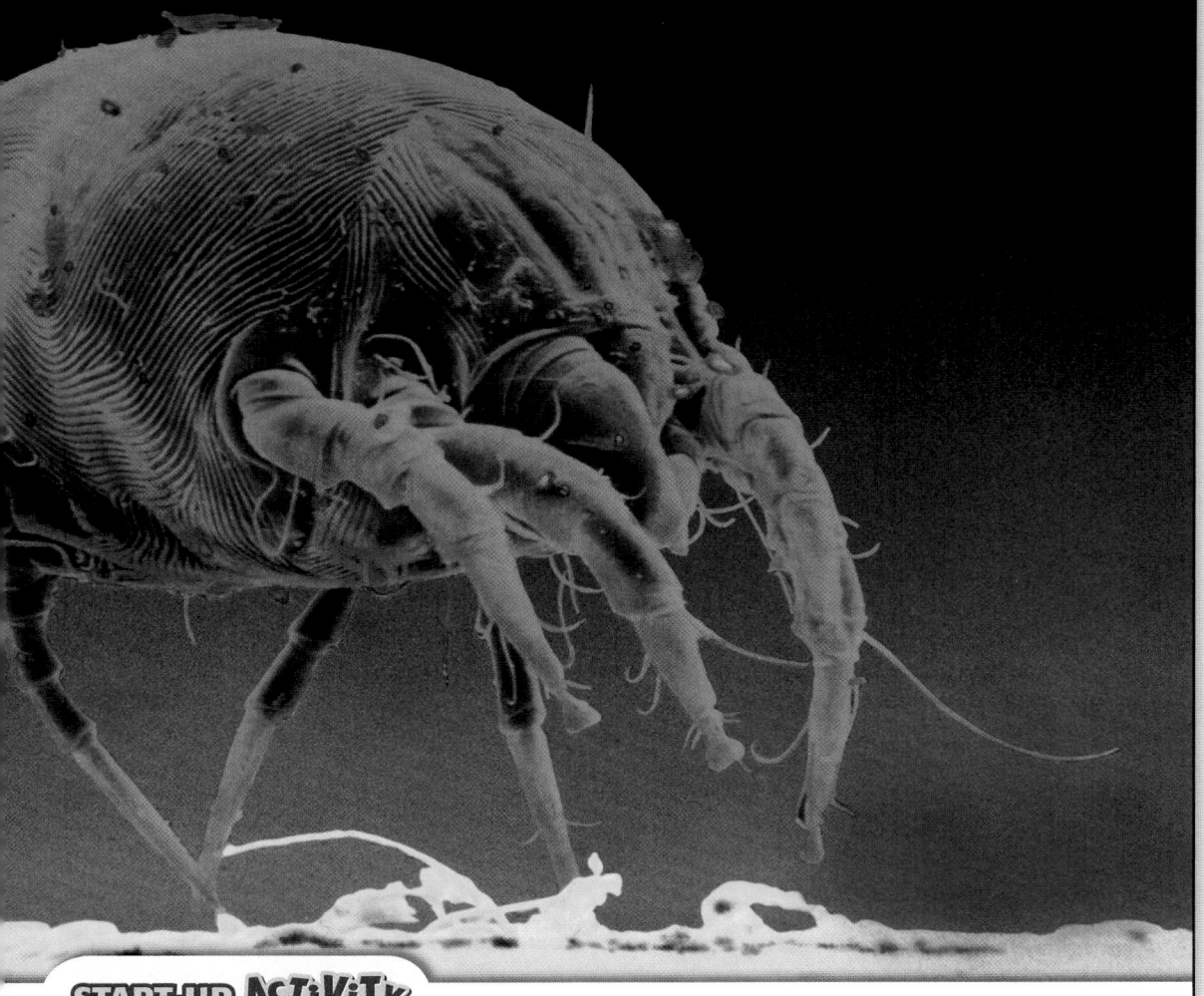

START-UP ACTIVITY

MATERIALS

FOR EACH GROUP
• agar, nutrient
• gloves, protective
• marbles (2)
• Petri dishes (2)
• soap
• tape, transparent
• water, warm

Safety Caution: Remind students to review all safety cautions and icons before beginning this lab activity. Tell students not to open the Petri dishes once they are sealed. Treat all growth in the Petri dishes as pathogenic, and dispose of the dishes as you would any other biohazard.

Teacher's Notes: Keep the lids on the Petri dishes except when rolling the marble on the agar. Doing so will help keep outside contamination to a minimum. In step 6, it might be helpful to use an incubator set at 37°C.

Answers

1. Descriptions may vary. The Petri dish labeled "Unwashed" should have the most bacterial growth.

2. Sample answer: It is important to wash my hands to help decrease the number of microorganisms I put in my mouth.

START-UP ACTIVITY

Invisible Invaders

In this activity, you will see tiny organisms grow.

Procedure

1. Obtain **two Petri dishes containing nutrient agar.** Label them "Washed" and "Unwashed."

2. Rub **two marbles** between the palms of your hands. Observe the appearance of the marbles.

3. Roll one marble in the Petri dish labeled "Unwashed."

4. Put on a pair of **disposable gloves.** Wash the other marble with **soap** and **warm water** for 4 min.

5. Roll the washed marble in the Petri dish labeled "Washed."

6. Secure the lids of the Petri dishes with **transparent tape.** Place the dishes in a warm, dark place. Do not open the Petri dishes after they are sealed.

7. Record changes in the Petri dishes for 1 week.

Analysis

1. How did the washed and unwashed marbles compare? How did the Petri dishes differ after several days?

2. Why is it important to wash your hands before eating?

Chapter Starter Transparency
Use this transparency to help students begin thinking about the way that vaccines help defend the body.

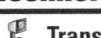

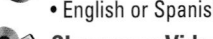

Focus

Overview

This section introduces the difference between noninfectious diseases and infectious diseases. Students will learn how they can come into contact with pathogens and how cleanliness, pasteurization, vaccines, and antibiotics can help reduce the spread of pathogens.

🔊 Bellringer

 Writing Ask students to list as many diseases as they can. After students have completed their lists, you may want to make a master list on the board or on a transparency. The list might include physical illnesses as well as mental illnesses. Explain that in this chapter, students will learn how pathogens cause illnesses and how illnesses can be prevented.

READING WARM-UP

Objectives

● Explain the difference between infectious diseases and noninfectious diseases.

● Identify five ways that you might come into contact with a pathogen.

● Discuss four methods that have helped reduce the spread of disease.

Terms to Learn

noninfectious disease
infectious disease
pathogen
immunity

READING STRATEGY

Paired Summarizing Read this section silently. In pairs, take turns summarizing the material. Stop to discuss ideas that seem confusing.

noninfectious disease a disease that cannot spread from one individual to another

infectious disease a disease that is caused by a pathogen and that can be spread from one individual to another

pathogen a virus, microorganism, or other organism that causes disease

---

Disease

You've probably heard it before: "Cover your mouth when you sneeze!" "Wash your hands!" "Don't put that in your mouth!"

What is all the fuss about? When people say these things to you, they are concerned about the spread of disease.

Causes of Disease

When you have a *disease,* your normal body functions are disrupted. Some diseases, such as most cancers and heart disease, are not spread from one person to another. They are called **noninfectious diseases.**

Noninfectious diseases can be caused by a variety of factors. For example, a genetic disorder causes the disease hemophilia (HEE moh FIL ee uh), in which a person's blood does not clot properly. Smoking, lack of physical activity, and a high-fat diet can greatly increase a person's chances of getting certain noninfectious diseases. Avoiding harmful habits may help you avoid noninfectious diseases.

A disease that can be passed from one living thing to another is an **infectious disease.** Infectious diseases are caused by agents called **pathogens.** Viruses and some bacteria, fungi, protists, and worms may all cause diseases. **Figure 1** shows some enlarged images of common pathogens.

Figure 1 Pathogens

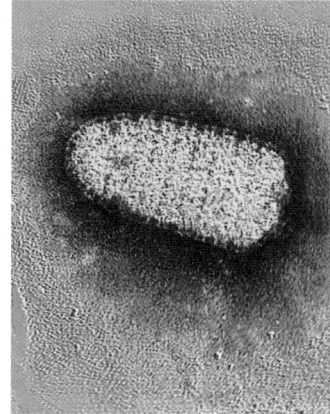
▲ This virus causes rabies.

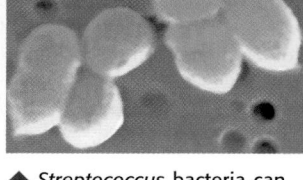
▲ *Streptococcus* bacteria can cause strep throat.

CHAPTER RESOURCES

Chapter Resource File

● Lesson Plan
● Directed Reading A BASIC
● Directed Reading B SPECIAL NEEDS

Technology

Transparencies
• Bellringer

MISCONCEPTION ///ALERT\\\

Helpful Bacteria Students may think that all bacteria are pathogens. Point out that very few bacteria are pathogenic. Bacteria serve many useful—and, in some cases, essential—functions. Bacteria fix nitrogen and assist in digestion. They are used to make foods such as yogurt and cheese, to clean up oil spills, and to recycle wastes. Also, they can be genetically engineered to produce insulin and other human proteins that are needed to treat disease.

Pathways to Pathogens

There are many ways pathogens can be passed from one person to another. Being aware of them can help you stay healthy.

Air

Some pathogens travel through the air. For example, a single sneeze, such as the one shown in **Figure 2,** releases thousands of tiny droplets of moisture that can carry pathogens.

Contaminated Objects

You may already know that if you drink from a glass that an infected person has just used, you could become infected with a pathogen. A person who is sick may leave bacteria or viruses on many other objects, too. For example, contaminated doorknobs, keyboards, combs, and towels can pass pathogens.

Person to Person

Some pathogens are spread by direct person-to-person contact. You can become infected with some illnesses by kissing, shaking hands, or touching the sores of an infected person.

Animals

Some pathogens are carried by animals. For example, humans can get a fungus called *ringworm* from handling an infected dog or cat. Also, ticks may carry bacteria that cause Lyme disease or Rocky Mountain spotted fever.

Food and Water

Drinking water in the United States is generally safe. But water lines can break, or treatment plants can become flooded. These problems may allow microorganisms to enter the public water supply. Bacteria growing in foods and beverages can cause illness, too. For example, meat, fish, and eggs that are not cooked enough can still contain dangerous bacteria or parasites. Even leaving food out at room temperature can give bacteria such as salmonella the chance to grow and produce toxins in the food. Refrigerating foods can slow the growth of many of these pathogens. Because bacteria grow in food, washing all used cooking surfaces and tools is also important.

 **Reading Check** Why must you cook meat and eggs thoroughly? (*See the Appendix for answers to Reading Checks.*)

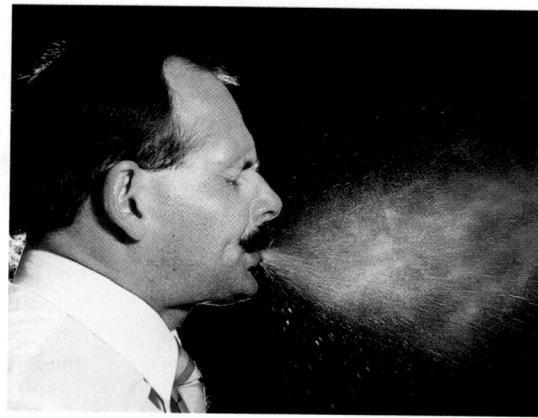

Figure 2 *A sneeze can force thousands of pathogen-carrying droplets out of your body at up to 160 km/h.*

CONNECTION TO Social Studies

Disease and History Many diseases have shaped history. For example, yellow fever, which is caused by a virus that is spread by mosquitoes, was one of the obstacles in building the Panama Canal. Only after people learned how to prevent the spread of the yellow fever virus could the canal be completed.

Use information from Internet and library research to create a poster describing how one infectious disease affected history.

ACTIVITY

Close

Answer to School-to-Home Activity

Most products that require pasteurization also require refrigeration because once the products are opened, they are vulnerable to getting bacteria in them. Refrigeration helps slow the growth of the bacteria.

Reteaching — **BASIC**

Reviewing Pathways Have students make a chart titled "How to Stay Healthy." In one column, they can list the ways that pathogens are encountered. In a second column, students can list ways to prevent becoming infected. **LS** Logical

Quiz — **GENERAL**

Ask students whether the following statements are true or false.

1. All diseases are caused by pathogens. (false)

2. You can become infected with some pathogens by shaking hands with an infected person. (true)

3. Pasteurization uses very cold temperatures to kill bacteria. (false)

Alternative Assessment — **GENERAL**

Pamphlet Have students develop a disease-prevention pamphlet. Encourage students to include illustrations. **LS** Verbal

SCHOOL to HOME

Label Check
At home or in a local store, find a product that has been pasteurized. In your **science journal**, write down other safety information you find on the label, including the product's refrigeration needs. Why do you think most products that require pasteurization also require refrigeration?

ACTIVITY

immunity the ability to resist or to recover from an infectious disease

Figure 3 *Today, pasteurization is used to kill pathogens in many different types of food, including dairy products, shellfish, and juices.*

Putting Pathogens in Their Place

Until the twentieth century, surgery patients often died of bacterial infections. But doctors learned that simple cleanliness could help prevent the spread of some diseases. Today, hospitals and clinics use a variety of technologies to prevent the spread of pathogens. For example, ultraviolet radiation, boiling water, and chemicals are used to kill pathogens in health facilities.

Pasteurization

During the mid-1800s, Louis Pasteur, a French scientist, discovered that microorganisms caused wine to spoil. The uninvited microorganisms were bacteria. Pasteur devised a method of using heat to kill most of the bacteria in the wine. This method is called *pasteurization* (PAS tuhr i ZAY shuhn), and it is still used today. The milk that the girl in **Figure 3** is drinking has been pasteurized.

Vaccines and Immunity

In the late 1700s, no one knew what a pathogen was. During this time, Edward Jenner studied a disease called *smallpox*. He observed that people who had been infected with cowpox seemed to have protection against smallpox. These people had a resistance to the disease. The ability to resist or recover from an infectious disease is called **immunity.** Jenner's work led to the first modern vaccine. A *vaccine* is a substance that helps your body develop immunity to a disease.

Today, vaccines are used all over the world to prevent many serious diseases. Modern vaccines contain pathogens that are killed or specially treated so that they can't make you very sick. The vaccine is enough like the pathogen to allow your body to develop a defense against the disease.

CONNECTION to Physical Science — **GENERAL**

Pasteurization Pasteurization is the process of killing harmful bacteria by using thermal energy. Milk is pasteurized in one of two ways: by heating it to 63°C for 30 min or by heating it to 72°C for 16 s. The organisms that can survive pasteurization will eventually spoil the milk, but they are generally not harmful to people.

Boiling the milk would kill even more of the bacteria —not just the harmful ones—but would also change the milk. Use the teaching transparency titled "Thermal Energy in Water" to illustrate how increasing the temperature of a substance increases the substance's thermal energy. **LS** Visual

Antibiotics

Have you ever had strep throat? If so, you have had a bacterial infection. Bacterial infections can be a serious threat to your health. Fortunately, doctors can usually treat these kinds of infections with antibiotics. An *antibiotic* is a substance that can kill bacteria or slow the growth of bacteria. Antibiotics may also be used to treat infections caused by other microorganisms, such as fungi. You may take an antibiotic when you are sick. Always take antibiotics according to your doctor's instructions to ensure that all the pathogens are killed.

Viruses, such as those that cause colds, are not affected by antibiotics. Antibiotics can kill only living things, and viruses are not alive. The only way to destroy viruses in your body is to locate and kill the cells they have invaded.

✓ Reading Check Frank caught a bad cold just before the opening night of a school play. He visited his doctor and asked her to prescribe antibiotics for his cold. The doctor politely refused and advised Frank to stay home and get plenty of rest. Why do you think the doctor refused to give Frank antibiotics?

Epidemic!

You catch a cold and return to your school while sick. Your friends don't have immunity to your cold. On the first day, you expose five friends to your cold. The next day, each of those friends passes the virus to five more people. If this pattern continues for 5 more days, how many people will be exposed to the virus?

SECTION Review

Summary

● Noninfectious diseases cannot be spread from one person to another.

● Infectious diseases are caused by pathogens that are passed from one living thing to another.

● Pathogens can travel through the air or can be spread by contact with other people, contaminated objects, animals, food, or water.

● Cleanliness, pasteurization, vaccines, and antibiotics help control the spread of pathogens.

Using Key Terms

1. In your own words, write a definition for each of the following terms: *infectious disease, noninfectious disease,* and *immunity.*

Understanding Key Ideas

2. Vaccines contain
   a. treated pathogens.
   b. heat.
   c. antibiotics.
   d. pasteurization.

3. List five ways that you might come into contact with a pathogen.

4. Name four ways to help keep safe from pathogens.

Math Skills

5. If 10 people with the virus each expose 25 more people to the virus, how many people will be exposed to the virus?

Critical Thinking

6. **Identifying Relationships** Why might the risk of infectious disease be high in a community that has no water treatment facility?

7. **Analyzing Methods** Explain what might happen if a doctor did not wear gloves when treating patients.

8. **Applying Concepts** Why do vaccines for diseases in animals help prevent some illnesses in people?

SCi LINKS Developed and maintained by the National Science Teachers Association

For a variety of links related to this chapter, go to www.scilinks.org

Topic: Pathogens; What Causes Diseases?
SciLinks code: HSM1118; HSM1653

Focus

Overview

In this section, students will learn how the skin keeps pathogens out of the body and how the immune system works. Students will also learn about allergies and other immune system problems.

🔊 Bellringer

Have students make a list of the ways that pathogens might enter the body. (Examples include through the mouth, ears, nose, and cuts in the skin. Pathogens can travel in the water, in the air, and in food.)

Motivate

ACTIVITY ——————— GENERAL

Reactions to Illness Ask students to think of a time when they were ill. Have students list the ways in which their body reacted to the illness. (Answers might include having a fever, chills, a runny nose, a sore throat, a rash, and throbbing pain.) Encourage students to share their lists with a partner. Then, have students skim this lesson and try to link their body's reactions with the reactions of the immune system to pathogenic invasions.

LS Interpersonal

READING WARM-UP

Objectives

- Describe how your body keeps out pathogens.
- Explain how the immune system fights infections.
- Describe four challenges to the immune system.

Terms to Learn

immune system	memory B cell
macrophage	allergy
T cell	autoimmune
B cell	disease
antibody	cancer

READING STRATEGY

Reading Organizer As you read this section, make a flowchart of the steps of how your body responds to a virus.

Your Body's Defenses

Bacteria and viruses can be in the air, in the water, and on all the surfaces around you.

Your body must constantly protect itself against pathogens that are trying to invade it. But how does your body do that? Luckily, your body has its own built-in defense system.

First Lines of Defense

For a pathogen to harm you, it must attack a part of your body. Usually, though, very few of the pathogens around you make it past your first lines of defense.

Many organisms that try to enter your eyes or mouth are destroyed by special enzymes. Pathogens that enter your nose are washed down the back of your throat by mucus. The mucus carries the pathogens to your stomach, where most are quickly digested.

Your skin is made of many layers of flat cells. The outermost layers are dead. As a result, many pathogens that land on your skin have difficulty finding a live cell to infect. As **Figure 1** shows, the dead skin cells are constantly dropping off your body as new skin cells grow from beneath. As the dead skin cells flake off, they carry away viruses, bacteria, and other microorganisms. In addition, glands secrete oil onto your skin's surface. The oil contains chemicals that kill many pathogens.

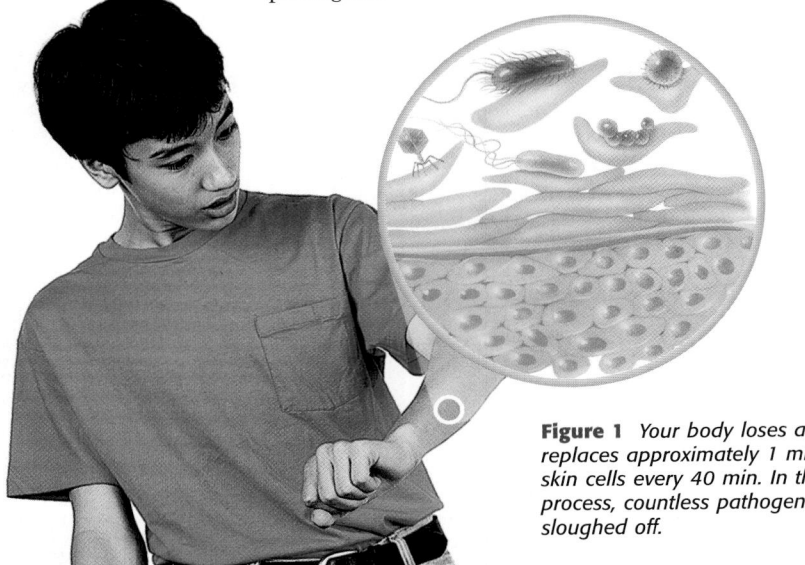

Figure 1 *Your body loses and replaces approximately 1 million skin cells every 40 min. In the process, countless pathogens are sloughed off.*

CHAPTER RESOURCES

Chapter Resource File

- **Lesson Plan**
- **Directed Reading A** BASIC
- **Directed Reading B** SPECIAL NEEDS

Technology

Transparencies
- Bellringer
- An Antibody's Shape Fits an Antigen

 **SCIENCE**

Earwax is one of the body's defenses against foreign invaders. Wax collects dirt, bacteria, fungi, and other foreign matter that could cause an ear infection.

Failure of First Lines

Sometimes, skin is cut or punctured and pathogens can enter the body. The body acts quickly to keep out as many pathogens as possible. Blood flow to the injured area increases. Cell parts in the blood called *platelets* help seal the open wound so that no more pathogens can enter.

The increased blood flow also brings cells that belong to the **immune system,** the body system that fights pathogens. The immune system is not localized in any one place in your body. It is not controlled by any one organ, such as the brain. Instead, it is a team of individual cells, tissues, and organs that work together to keep you safe from invading pathogens.

Cells of the Immune System

The immune system consists mainly of three kinds of cells. One kind is the macrophage (MAK roh FAYJ). **Macrophages** engulf and digest many microorganisms or viruses that enter your body. If only a few microorganisms or viruses have entered a wound, the macrophages can easily stop them.

The other two main kinds of immune-system cells are T cells and B cells. **T cells** coordinate the immune system and attack many infected cells. **B cells** are immune-system cells that make antibodies. **Antibodies** are proteins that attach to specific antigens. *Antigens* are substances that stimulate an immune response. Your body is capable of making billions of different antibodies. Each antibody usually attaches to only one kind of antigen, as illustrated in **Figure 2.**

Reading Check How do macrophages help fight disease? (*See the Appendix for answers to Reading Checks.*)

Only Skin Deep

1. Cut an **apple** in half.
2. Place **plastic wrap** over each half. The plastic wrap will act as skin.
3. Use **scissors** to cut the plastic wrap on one of the apple halves, and then use an **eyedropper** to drip **food coloring** on each apple half. The food coloring represents pathogens coming into contact with your body.
4. What happened to each apple half?
5. How is the plastic wrap similar to skin?
6. How is the plastic wrap different from skin?

immune system the cells and tissues that recognize and attack foreign substances in the body

macrophage an immune system cell that engulfs pathogens and other materials

T cell an immune system cell that coordinates the immune system and attacks many infected cells

B cell a white blood cell that makes antibodies

antibody a protein made by B cells that binds to a specific antigen

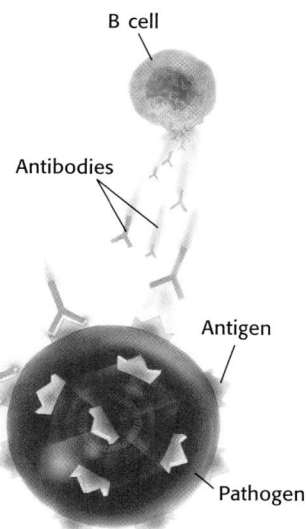

Figure 2 *An antibody's shape is very specialized. It matches an antigen like a key fits a lock.*

Disease and Conquest In the 16th century, Hernando Cortes and the Spanish conquistadors overwhelmed and conquered the flourishing cultures of what is now Mexico. One reason the Europeans were able to overtake the Native Americans so quickly is that the Europeans incidentally brought with them diseases such as smallpox. These diseases were new to the populations in the Americas, and they devastated entire nations. In the span of just two generations, an estimated 12,000,000 to 25,000,000 Native Americans died as a result of European diseases. Have interested students research and report on the role that disease played when the Europeans settled in North and South America. **LS Verbal**

MATERIALS

FOR EACH STUDENT
- apple (cut in half)
- eyedropper
- food coloring
- plastic wrap
- scissors

Safety Caution: Tell students to cut in a direction away from their face and hands. Students should not ingest the apple or the food coloring after the activity. Food coloring can stain hands and clothes.

Teacher's Note: You may want to provide gloves and smocks for this activity. Dark food coloring, such as blue, green, and red, works best in this activity. Yellow does not show up as well as the darker colors. Instruct students to limit themselves to three drops of food coloring per apple half.

Answers

4. The apple half with the uncut wrap was not affected by the food coloring. The apple half with the cut wrap was dyed by the food coloring that seeped through the slits.

5. Sample answer: The plastic wrap is similar to skin because it keeps foreign substances out and protects the soft tissue underneath it.

6. Sample answer: The plastic wrap is different from skin because it cannot heal the wound or swell to help close the wound.

Answer to Reading Check
Macrophages engulf, or eat, any microorganisms or viruses that enter your body.

ACTIVITY ——— BASIC

Follow the Path Have students trace the proper sequence of the pictures across these two pages. Point out that each picture has its own caption that begins with a bold heading. Then, have students outline the information on these two pages by listing the bold headings in order on a sheet of paper. Have pairs of students compare their outlines.
LS Visual   English Language Learners

Using the Figure—GENERAL

Identifying Cells As students look at the pictures on these pages, point out that the pictures are numbered. After students have studied the sequence of events portrayed in the pictures, have them point to each kind of white blood cell shown in the pictures on these two pages as you call out the names of the cells: *helper T cell, killer T cell, B cell,* and *macrophage.* Then, ask students to describe the role of each kind of white blood cell.
LS Visual   English Language Learners

INTERNET ACTIVITY

For another activity related to this chapter, go to **go.hrw.com** and type in the keyword **HL5BD6W.**

Responding to a Virus

If virus particles enter your body, some of the particles may pass into body cells and begin to replicate. Other virus particles will be engulfed and broken up by macrophages. This is just the beginning of the immune response. The process your immune system uses to fight an invading virus is summarized in the figure below.

✓ Reading Check What are two things that can happen to virus particles when they enter the body?

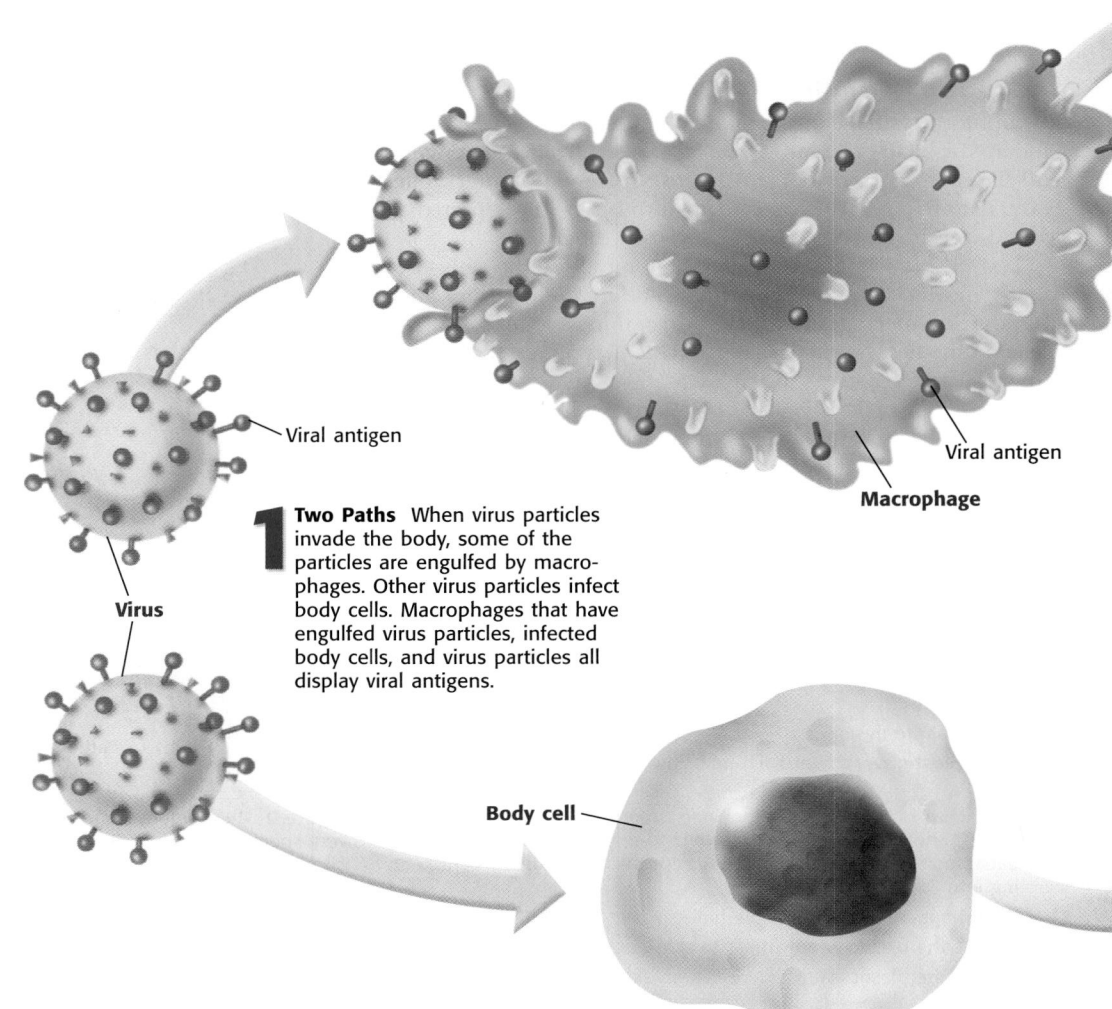

Viral antigen

Viral antigen

Macrophage

Virus

 Two Paths When virus particles invade the body, some of the particles are engulfed by macrophages. Other virus particles infect body cells. Macrophages that have engulfed virus particles, infected body cells, and virus particles all display viral antigens.

Body cell

CHAPTER RESOURCES

Technology

🖴 **Transparencies**
• Immune Response: A
• Immune Response: B

Answer to Reading Check

If a virus particle enters the body, it may pass into body cells and begin to replicate. Or it may be engulfed and broken up by macrophages.

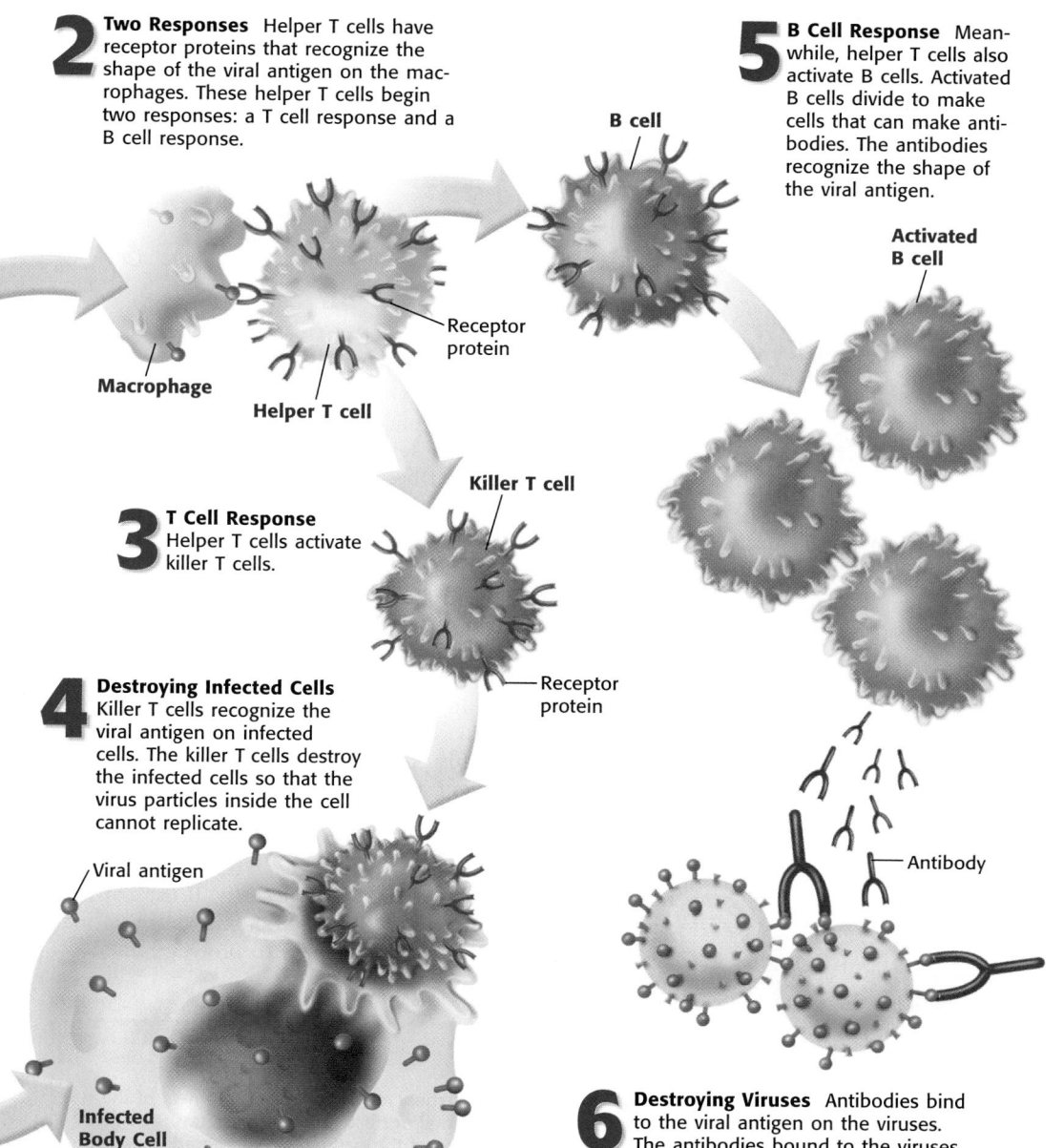

2 **Two Responses** Helper T cells have receptor proteins that recognize the shape of the viral antigen on the macrophages. These helper T cells begin two responses: a T cell response and a B cell response.

Macrophage

Helper T cell

Receptor protein

B cell

3 **T Cell Response** Helper T cells activate killer T cells.

Killer T cell

Receptor protein

4 **Destroying Infected Cells** Killer T cells recognize the viral antigen on infected cells. The killer T cells destroy the infected cells so that the virus particles inside the cell cannot replicate.

Viral antigen

Infected Body Cell

5 **B Cell Response** Meanwhile, helper T cells also activate B cells. Activated B cells divide to make cells that can make antibodies. The antibodies recognize the shape of the viral antigen.

Activated B cell

Antibody

6 **Destroying Viruses** Antibodies bind to the viral antigen on the viruses. The antibodies bound to the viruses cause the viruses to clump together. Clumping marks the virus particles for destruction.

Research —————— GENERAL

Writing **Immune Deficiency**
Have students research the immune problems of "bubble" children, such as David Vetter (the "Bubble Boy"). These children suffer from severe combined immune deficiency (SCID). (Students should find that children afflicted with this disease lack T cells and B cells and have a very weak immune system. Childhood illnesses that most children can shrug off can kill a child who has SCID. People who have SCID must live in a germ-free environment, such as in a sterile plastic bubble or cubicle in which the air is cleaned.) **LS** **Verbal**

Group ACTIVITY — ADVANCED

Immunity Skit Have students perform a skit that demonstrates the immune system's response to an invasion of viruses. Assign a role to each student, and have students study the text to learn about their role. Allow students time to prepare their skit and make any props that they need. For example, the students playing B cells may wish to make antibodies, and the students playing viruses may wish to construct simple body cells to infect. **LS** **Kinesthetic/Interpersonal**

WEIRD SCIENCE

In some cases, a pregnant woman may form antibodies against the blood of the baby she is carrying. The situation is likely to occur when the mother's blood is Rh-negative, meaning it lacks the Rh antigen, and the baby's blood is Rh-positive, meaning it carries the Rh antigen. The mother's immune system recognizes the Rh antigen as foreign and begins to attack the baby's blood cells.

Is That a Fact!

In 1918, a strain of flu viruses called the *Spanish flu* killed at least 20 million people. That number is more than the number of people killed in combat in World War I.

Treating Allergies An allergy is usually treated in two ways once the allergen is identified. An allergist may try to desensitize a patient to the allergen by administering small, periodic doses of the allergen. In addition, an allergist may prescribe drugs to minimize the body's reactions to the allergen. Have interested students contact an allergist and conduct an interview about his or her work. **LS** Interpersonal/Verbal

Research ———— GENERAL

Writing **Immune Disorders** Have students find an article or news report about one of the immune disorders discussed in this lesson. Have students work in small groups to prepare a written or oral report that summarizes one of the articles and links the article it to the concepts presented in this chapter. **LS** Inerpersonal/Verbal

Answer to Connection to Chemistry

As the egg white cooks, the proteins change shape. The change in shape causes the proteins to form a solid mass.

Figure 3 *You may not feel well when you have a fever. But a fever is one way that your body fights infections.*

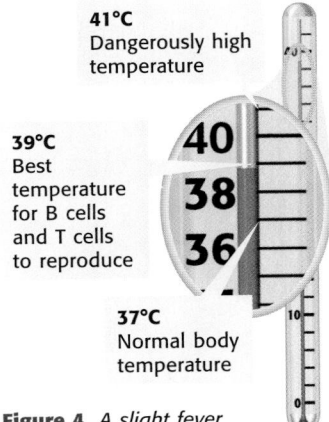

41°C
Dangerously high temperature

39°C
Best temperature for B cells and T cells to reproduce

37°C
Normal body temperature

Figure 4 *A slight fever helps immune cells reproduce. But a fever of more than a few degrees can become dangerous.*

memory B cell a B cell that responds to an antigen more strongly when the body is reinfected with an antigen than it does during its first encounter with the antigen

Fevers

The man in **Figure 3** is sick and has a fever. What is a fever? When macrophages activate the helper T cells, they send a chemical signal that tells your brain to turn up the thermostat. In a few minutes, your body's temperature can rise several degrees. A moderate fever of one or two degrees actually helps you get well faster because it slows the growth of some pathogens. As shown in **Figure 4,** a fever also helps B cells and T cells multiply faster.

Memory Cells

Your immune system can respond to a second encounter faster than it can respond the first time. B cells must have had previous contact with a pathogen before they can make the correct antibodies. During the first encounter with a new pathogen, specialized B cells make antibodies that are effective against that particular invader. This process takes about 2 weeks, which is far too long to prevent an infection. Therefore, the first time you are infected, you usually get sick.

A few of the B cells become memory B cells. **Memory B cells** are cells in your immune system that "remember" how to make an antibody for a particular pathogen. If the pathogen shows up again, the memory B cells produce B cells that make enough antibodies in just 3 or 4 days to protect you.

CONNECTION TO Chemistry

Bent out of Shape When you have a fever, the heat of the fever changes the shape of viral or bacterial proteins, slowing or preventing the reproduction of the pathogen. With an adult present, observe how an egg white changes as it cooks. What do you think happens to the protein in the egg white as it cooks?

ACTIVITY

INCLUSION Strategies

• *Learning Disabled*
• *Attention Deficit Disorder*

Many students have trouble differentiating between allergies and autoimmune diseases. Help students by repeating that autoimmune diseases happen when the body mistakenly attacks its own tissues, and that allergies happen when the immune system mistakenly attacks harmless substances that enter the body. Then, use the following drill:

Which of the following are allergic reactions and which are autoimmune responses?

• sneezing at pollen (allergic reaction)
• the immune system attacking a nerve cell (autoimmune response)
• the immune system attacking the body cells that make insulin (autoimmune response)
• the immune system attacking the proteins in peanut butter (allergic reaction)
LS Verbal

Challenges to the Immune System

The immune system is a very effective body-defense system, but it is not perfect. The immune system is unable to deal with some diseases. There are also conditions in which the immune system does not work properly.

Allergies

Sometimes, the immune system overreacts to antigens that are not dangerous to the body. This inappropriate reaction is called an **allergy.** Allergies may be caused by many things, including certain foods and medicines. Many people have allergic reactions to pollen, shown in **Figure 5.** Symptoms of allergic reactions range from a runny nose and itchy eyes to more serious conditions, such as asthma.

Doctors are not sure why the immune system overreacts in some people. Scientists think allergies might be useful because the mucus draining from your nose carries away pollen, dust, and microorganisms.

Autoimmune Diseases

A disease in which the immune system attacks the body's own cells is called an **autoimmune disease.** In an autoimmune disease, immune-system cells mistake body cells for pathogens. One autoimmune disease is rheumatoid arthritis (ROO muh TOYD ahr THRIET IS), in which the immune system attacks the joints. A common location for rheumatoid arthritis is the joints of the hands, as shown in **Figure 6.** Other autoimmune diseases include type 1 diabetes, multiple sclerosis, and lupus.

Reading Check Name four autoimmune diseases.

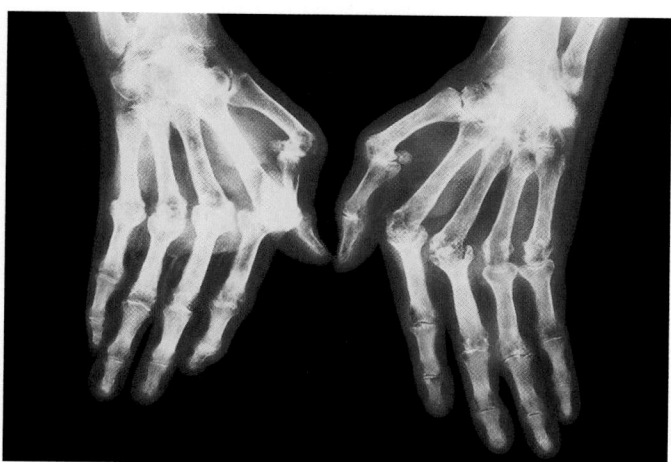

Figure 6 *In rheumatoid arthritis, immune-system cells cause joint-tissue swelling, which can lead to joint deformities.*

allergy a reaction to a harmless or common substance by the body's immune system

autoimmune disease a disease in which the immune system attacks the organism's own cells

Figure 5 *Pollen is one substance that can cause allergic reactions.*

Discussion ——— GENERAL

Allergies Ask students to tell you about any allergies that they know about and the reactions that people experience when exposed to the particular allergens. Write their responses on the board or an overhead transparency, and use this list, especially the body responses, as a way of introducing how the immune system can make peoples's lives miserable—or at least uncomfortable—when it does not function properly.
LS Auditory

Homework ——— GENERAL

Writing **Anaphylactic Shock** Ask students to research and report on the topic of anaphylactic shock. (Students should find that anaphylactic shock is a serious allergic reaction that can result in death. A small amount of an allergen can produce anaphylactic shock. People who are prone to such an allergic reaction may carry with them a syringe containing the hormone epinephrine to combat the onset of anaphylactic shock.) **LS Verbal**

Is That a Fact!

Peanuts are dangerous, even potentially deadly, to people who are allergic to them. A person nearly died from eating a tuna sandwich because the knife used to cut the sandwich had just been used to make a peanut butter sandwich.

Answer to Reading Check

rheumatoid arthritis, diabetes, multiple sclerosis, and lupus

Reteaching — BASIC

Reviewing HIV You can use the figures from this section that illustrate an immune response to help students understand how HIV hurts the immune system. HIV infects and destroys helper T cells. Have students cover and hide the helper T cell illustrated in the figure. Then, ask students how destroying helper T cells would affect the immune response. (Students should be able to see that both the B cell and T cell responses to infection would be stopped if the helper T cells were eliminated.) **LS** Visual/Auditory

Quiz — GENERAL

Ask students whether the following statements are true or false.

1. Antibodies are specific to certain pathogens. (true)

2. An allergy is caused by the immune system attacking the cells of the body. (false)

3. People with AIDS have too many killer T cells. These cells begin to attack the body's cells, and AIDS is the result. (false)

Alternative Assessment — ADVANCED

 Have students choose one of the disorders discussed in this section and prepare a report or a presentation about it. Encourage students to discuss the immune response and the cells of the immune system. **LS** Verbal

Figure 7 Immune Cells Fighting Cancer

❶ A killer T cell attacks an unregulated cell.

Killer T cell

Unregulated cell

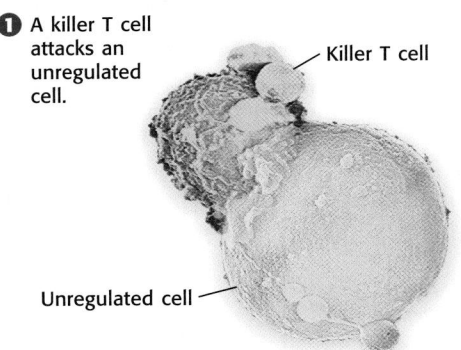

❷ The cell's membrane ruptures as the cell dies.

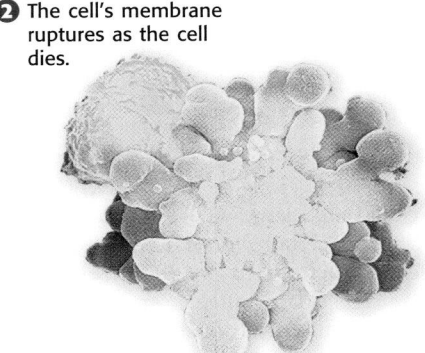

cancer a disease in which the cells begin dividing at an uncontrolled rate and become invasive

Cancer

Healthy cells divide at a carefully regulated rate. Occasionally, a cell doesn't respond to the body's regulation and begins dividing at an uncontrolled rate. As can be seen in **Figure 7,** killer T cells destroy this type of cell. Sometimes, the immune system cannot control the division of these cells. **Cancer** is the condition in which cells divide at an uncontrolled rate.

Many cancers will invade nearby tissues. They can also enter the cardiovascular system or lymphatic system. Cancers can then be transported to other places in the body. Cancers disrupt the normal activities of the organs they have invaded, sometimes leading to death. Today, though, there are many treatments for cancer. Surgery, radiation, and certain drugs can be used to remove or kill cancer cells or slow their division.

AIDS

The human immunodeficiency virus (HIV) causes acquired immune deficiency syndrome (AIDS). Most viruses infect cells in the nose, mouth, lungs, or intestines, but HIV is different. HIV infects the immune system itself, using helper T cells as factories to produce more viruses. You can see HIV particles in **Figure 8.** The helper T cells are destroyed in the process. Remember that the helper T cells put the B cells and killer T cells to work.

People with AIDS have very few helper T cells, so nothing activates the B cells and killer T cells. Therefore, the immune system cannot attack HIV or any other pathogen. People with AIDS don't usually die of AIDS itself. They die of other diseases that they are unable to fight off.

✓ **Reading Check** What virus causes AIDS?

Figure 8 The blue particles on this helper T cell are human immunodeficiency viruses. They replicated inside the T cell.

ACTiViTY — GENERAL

 Concept Mapping Have students define the new terms presented in this chapter and then use the terms in a concept map. Have students use the chapter title as the first concept in their map. **LS** Visual/Logical

SECTION Review

Summary

- Macrophages engulf pathogens, display antigens on their surface, and activate helper T cells. The helper T cells put the killer T cells and B cells to work.
- Killer T cells kill infected cells. B cells make antibodies.
- Fever helps speed immune-cell growth and slow pathogen growth.
- Memory B cells remember how to make an antibody for a pathogen that the body has previously fought.

- An allergy is the overreaction of the immune system to a harmless antigen.
- Autoimmune diseases are responses in which the immune system attacks healthy tissue.
- Cancer cells are cells that undergo uncontrolled division.
- AIDS is a disease that results when the human immunodeficiency virus kills helper T cells.

Using Key Terms

For each pair of terms, explain how the meanings of the terms differ.

1. *B cell* and *T cell*

2. *autoimmune disease* and *allergy*

Understanding Key Ideas

3. Your body's first line of defense against pathogens includes
   a. skin.
   b. macrophages.
   c. T cells.
   d. B cells.

4. List three ways your body defends itself against pathogens.

5. Name three different cells in the immune system, and describe how they respond to pathogens.

6. Describe four challenges to the immune system.

7. What characterizes a cancer cell?

Critical Thinking

8. **Identifying Relationships** Can your body make antibodies for pathogens that you have never been in contact with? Why or why not?

9. **Applying Concepts** If you had chickenpox at age 7, what might prevent you from getting chickenpox again at age 8?

Interpreting Graphics

10. Look at the graph below. Over time, people with AIDS become very sick and are unable to fight off infection. Use the information in the graph below to explain why this occurs.

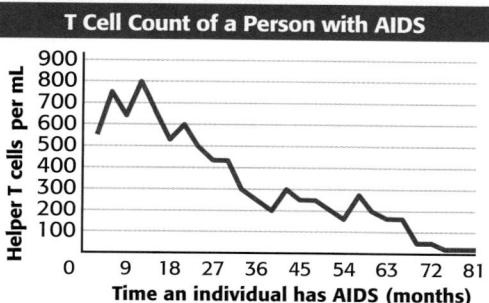

T Cell Count of a Person with AIDS

Helper T cells per mL / Time an individual has AIDS (months)

SCiLINKS

NSTA
Developed and maintained by the
National Science Teachers Association

For a variety of links related to this chapter, go to www.scilinks.org

Topic: Body Defenses; Allergies
SciLinks code: HSM0181; HSM0048

CHAPTER RESOURCES

Chapter Resource File

- Section Quiz GENERAL
- Section Review GENERAL
- Vocabulary and Section Summary GENERAL
- SciLinks Activity GENERAL
- Datasheet for Quick Lab

Answers to Section Review

1. Sample answer: B cells pathogens by making antibodies. T cells fight pathogens by coordinating responses and killing infected cells directly.

2. Sample answer: In an autoimmune disease, the immune system attacks the body's tissues. In an allergy, the immune system overreacts to antigens that are not part of the body.

3. a

4. Sample answer: Skin keeps most pathogens out. Chemical defenses are in your eyes, stomach, and mouth. If you have a cut in your skin, blood platelets help close the wound so that more microorganisms cannot enter. Microorganisms that do enter encounter immune system cells.

5. Sample answer: a macrophage engulfs pathogens and stick antigens on their outer membranes, helper T cells activate killer T cells and B cells, and killer T cells kill any body cell infected with pathogens.

6. allergy, the body has an inappropriate reaction to a harmless antigen; autoimmune disease: the immune system reacts to body tissues; cancer: cells of the body divide uncontrollably; AIDS: HIV reduces the number of helper T cells, so the body cannot mount a defense against pathogens

7. A cell becomes cancerous when it starts dividing at an uncontrolled rate.

8. Sample answer: No, the body makes antibodies against specific pathogens. If a pathogen has never been met, the immune system would not have had any reason to make an antibody against it.

9. Sample answer: memory B cells

10. Sample answer: People who have AIDS become less able to fight infections because their helper T cell count decreases over time.

Passing the Cold

Teacher's Notes

Time Required
One 45-minute class period

Lab Ratings

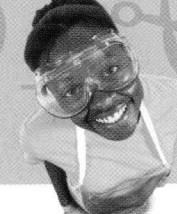

EASY ———————————→ HARD

Teacher Prep 🧪🧪
Student Set-Up 🧪🧪
Concept Level 🧪🧪
Clean Up 🧪🧪

MATERIALS

Prepare a phenolphthalein indicator solution ahead of time. Dilute the indicator solution in water. Add 10 mL of the indicator to 40 mL of water. This solution is enough for one student. Mix a 1.5 % NaOH solution. Mix 15 g NaOH with 1 L of water. All but one student will receive 50 mL of this solution.

Safety Caution: Remind students that although they are working with a very low concentration of an alkaline solution, they should work safely with all materials. All spills should be cleaned up immediately. Skin exposed to solutions should be washed immediately with plenty of running water. Remind students that they must never mix unknown solutions without teacher supervision and approval.

OBJECTIVES

Investigate how diseases spread.

Analyze data about how diseases spread.

MATERIALS

- beaker or a cup, 200 mL
- eyedropper
- gloves, protective
- solution, unknown, 50 mL

SAFETY

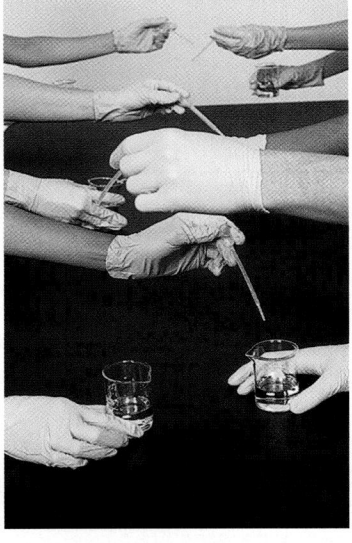

Passing the Cold

There are more than 100 viruses that cause the symptoms of the common cold. Any of the viruses can be passed from person to person—through the air or through direct contact. In this activity, you will track the progress of an outbreak in your class.

Ask a Question

1. With other members of your group, form a question about the spread of disease. For example "How are cold viruses passed from person to person?" or "How can the progress of an outbreak be modeled?"

Form a Hypothesis

2. Form a hypothesis based on the question you asked.

Test the Hypothesis

3. Obtain an empty cup or beaker, an eyedropper, and 50 mL of one of the solutions from your teacher. Only one student will have the "cold virus" solution. You will see a change in your solution when you have become "infected."

4. Your teacher will divide the class into two equal groups. If there is an extra student, that person will record data on the board. Otherwise, the teacher will act as the recorder.

5. The two groups should form straight lines, facing each other.

6. Each time your teacher says the word *mix*, fill your eyedropper with your solution, and place 10 drops of your solution in the beaker of the person in the line opposite you without touching your eyedropper to the other liquid.

7. Gently stir the liquid in your cup with your eyedropper. Do not put your eyedropper in anyone else's solution.

8. If your solution changes color, raise your hand so that the recorder can record the number of students who have been "infected."

9. Your teacher will instruct one line to move one person to the right. Then, the person at the end of the line without a partner should go to the other end of the line.

Edith McAlanis
Socorro Middle School
El Paso, Texas

CHAPTER RESOURCES

Chapter Resource File

 • Datasheet for Chapter Lab
• Lab Notes and Answers

Technology

 **Classroom Videos**
• Lab Video

LabBook

• Antibodies to the Rescue

Results of Experiment			
Trial	Number of infected people	Total number of people	Percentage of infected people
1			
2			
3			
4			
5			
6			
7			
8			
9			
10			

DO NOT WRITE IN BOOK

10. Repeat steps 5–9 nine more times for a total of 10 trials.

11. Return to your desk, and create a data table in your notebook similar to the table above. The column with the title "Total number of people" will remain the same in every row. Enter the data from the board into your data table.

12. Find the percentage of infected people for the last column by dividing the number of infected people by the total number of people and multiplying by 100 in each line.

Analyze the Results

1. **Describing Events** Did you become infected? If so, during which trial did you become infected?

2. **Examining Data** Did everyone eventually become infected? If so, how many trials were necessary to infect everyone?

Draw Conclusions

3. **Interpreting Information** Explain at least one reason why this simulation may underestimate the number of people who might have been infected in real life.

4. **Applying Conclusions** Use your results to make a line graph showing the change in the infection percentage per trial.

Applying Your Data

Do research in the library or on the Internet to find out some of the factors that contribute to the spread of a cold virus. What is the best and easiest way to reduce your chances of catching a cold? Explain your answer.

CHAPTER RESOURCES

Workbooks

 Long-Term Projects & Research Ideas
• A Chuckle a Day Keeps the Doctor Away **ADVANCED**

Applying Your Data

Colds are usually spread by close contact with a person who is infected. Colds may be more prevalent in the winter because people tend to stay indoors, where they are in closer contact with each other. The cold virus is carried on the micro-droplets in a cough or sneeze and by unwashed hands. The best and easiest way to reduce the chances of catching a cold is to avoid crowded places, wash one's hands thoroughly and frequently when people in close proximity have colds, and avoid touching one's face near one's eyes. Eating a healthy diet and getting plenty of rest and exercise will help a person stay in good general health.

Preparation Notes

Phenolphthalein is a base indicator and will turn pink in the presence of NaOH. One student (or two, if your class is large) will be given 50 mL of the indicator. This student will represent the original "infected" individual. (It is more fun if no one knows who the original infected student is at first.) All other students will be given the NaOH solution.

Prepare a results chart similar to the student table on the board. You will need to record results while the students are performing the experiment.

When you switch the students between trials, the student on the end will need to move to the other end of the line so that all students will have a new partner for each trial. In case of an odd number of students, you will need to participate, or you may use one student volunteer to record results on the board.

Analyze the Results

1.–2. If there are 10 students (two rows of 5 students facing each other), it will take six trials for everyone to become infected.

Draw Conclusions

3. In real life, colds are spread by more than one means. Coughing, sneezing, and touching with unwashed hands are ways to spread a cold. More than one person in a classroom may have a cold.

4. The line graphs should accurately reflect student data.

Assignment Guide

Section	Questions
1	1, 7–9, 15, 19
2	2–6, 10–14, 16–18, 20–21

ANSWERS

Using Key Terms

1. infectious disease
2. pathogen
3. T cells
4. antibody
5. allergy
6. Cancer

Understanding Key Ideas

7. b
8. d
9. c
10. d
11. d
12. d
13. Sample answer: When a macrophage engulfs a pathogen, it places pieces of the pathogen called *antigens* on its outer membrane. The antigens attract helper T cells.
14. Helper T cells activate B cells and killer T cells.
15. from animals and from the air

USING KEY TERMS

Complete each of the following sentences by choosing the correct term from the word bank.

antibody   cancer
infectious disease   B cell
noninfectious disease   T cell
pathogen   allergy

1 A(n) _____ is caused by a pathogen.

2 Antibiotics can be used to kill a(n) _____.

3 Macrophages attract helper _____.

4 A(n) _____ binds to an antigen.

5 An immune-system overreaction to a harmless substance is a(n) _____.

6 _____ is the unregulated growth of cells.

UNDERSTANDING KEY IDEAS

Multiple Choice

7 Pathogens are
   a. all viruses and microorganisms.
   b. viruses and microorganisms that cause disease.
   c. noninfectious organisms.
   d. all bacteria that live in water.

8 Which of the following is an infectious disease?
   a. allergies
   b. rheumatoid arthritis
   c. asthma
   d. a common cold

9 The skin keeps pathogens out by
   a. staying warm enough to kill pathogens.
   b. releasing killer T cells onto the surface.
   c. shedding dead cells and secreting oils.
   d. All of the above

10 Memory B cells
   a. kill pathogens.
   b. activate killer T cells.
   c. activate killer B cells.
   d. produce B cells that make antibodies.

11 A fever
   a. slows pathogen growth.
   b. helps B cells multiply faster.
   c. helps T cells multiply faster.
   d. All of the above

12 Macrophages
   a. make antibodies.
   b. release helper T cells.
   c. live in the gut.
   d. engulf pathogens.

Short Answer

13 Explain how macrophages start an immune response.

14 Describe the role of helper T cells in responding to an infection.

15 Name two ways that you come into contact with pathogens.

CRITICAL THINKING

16 **Concept Mapping** Use the following terms to create a concept map: *macrophages, helper T cells, B cells, antibodies, antigens, killer T cells,* and *memory B cells.*

17 **Identifying Relationships** Why does the disappearance of helper T cells in AIDS patients damage the immune system?

18 **Predicting Consequences** Many people take fever-reducing drugs as soon as their temperature exceeds 37°C. Why might it not be a good idea to reduce a fever immediately with drugs?

19 **Evaluating Data** The risk of dying from a whooping cough vaccine is about one in 1 million. In contrast, the risk of dying from whooping cough is about one in 500. Discuss the pros and cons of this vaccination.

INTERPRETING GRAPHICS

The graph below compares the concentration of antibodies in the blood the first time you are exposed to a pathogen with the concentration of antibodies the next time you are exposed to the pathogen. Use the graph below to answer the questions that follow.

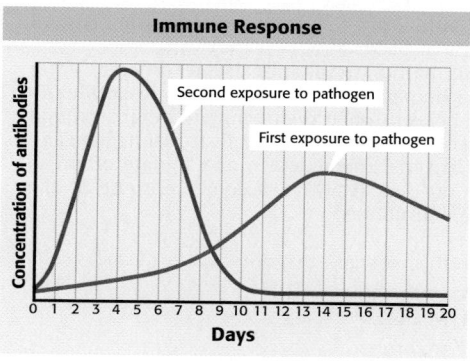

Immune Response

Second exposure to pathogen

First exposure to pathogen

Concentration of antibodies

Days
0 1 2 3 4 5 6 7 8 9 10 11 12 13 14 15 16 17 18 19 20

20 Are there more antibodies present during the first week of the first exposure or the first week of the second exposure? Why do you think this is so?

21 What is the difference in recovery time between the first exposure and second exposure? Why?

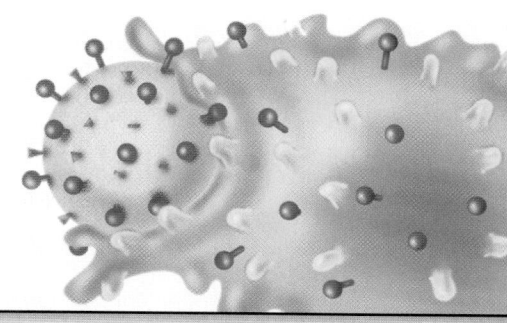

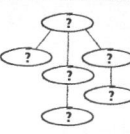

Critical Thinking

16. An answer to this exercise can be found at the end of this book.

17. Sample answer: Helper T cells are needed to activate B cells and killer T cells. Without B cells, the immune system cannot produce antibodies. Without killer T cells, the immune system cannot destroy infected cells.

18. Sample answer: Fevers can help T cells and B cells multiply faster. Fevers can also slow the growth of some pathogens. High fevers can be dangerous, though. If a fever exceeds 40.6°C, fever-reducing drugs can help bring the body's temperature down to a safer temperature.

19. Sample answer: The vaccine gives you an immunity to whooping cough, which is a dangerous disease. However, you may never come into contact with whooping cough and therefore may not need the vaccine. If you receive the vaccine anyway, you will have a small risk of dying from the vaccine. If no one is vaccinated, however, the risk of contracting the disease rises.

Interpreting Graphics

20. Sample answer: There are more antibodies present in the second exposure because memory B cells recognize the pathogen and immediately start to produce antibody-producing B cells.

21. Sample answer: Recovery time is much shorter for the second exposure because memory B cells allow the body to produce more antibodies in less time than the body produced during the first exposure.

Teacher's Note

To provide practice under more realistic testing conditions, give students 20 minutes to answer all of the questions in this Standardized Test Preparation.

MISCONCEPTION ALERT

Answers to the standardized test preparation can help you identify student misconceptions and misunderstandings.

READING

Passage 1

1. A
2. G
3. D

TEST DOCTOR

Question 2: Students may mistakenly select answer H, but the passage does not state that all bacteria mutate. Tell students to be wary of answers that use the words *always* or *never*. Answers framed in absolute terms may be overstating ideas from the passage. Although the word *outside* is not used explicitly in this passage, the passage does use the word *surround*. To surround a cell, the membrane would have to be located outside the cell.

READING

Read each of the passages below. Then, answer the questions that follow each passage.

Passage 1 Bacteria are becoming resistant to many human-made antibiotics, which means that the drugs no longer affect the bacteria. Scientists now face the challenge of developing new antibiotics that can overcome the resistant strains of bacteria.

Antibiotics from animals are different from some human-made antibiotics. These antibiotics bore holes through the membranes that surround bacterial cells, causing the cells to disintegrate and die. Bacterial membranes don't <u>mutate</u> often, so they are less likely to become resistant to the animal antibiotics.

1. In this passage, what does *mutate* mean?
   - **A** to change
   - **B** to grow
   - **C** to form
   - **D** to degrade

2. Based on the passage, which of the following statements is a fact?
   - **F** Bacterial membranes are on the inside of the bacterial cell.
   - **G** Bacterial membranes are on the outside of the bacterial cell.
   - **H** All strains of bacteria mutate.
   - **I** Bacterial membranes never change.

3. Based on the passage, which of the following sentences is false?
   - **A** Antibiotics from animals are different from human-made antibiotics.
   - **B** Antibiotics from animals bore holes in bacterial membranes.
   - **C** Bacterial membranes don't change very often.
   - **D** Bacteria rarely develop resistance to human-made antibiotics.

Passage 2 Drinking water in the United States is generally safe, but water lines can break, or treatment plants can become flooded, allowing microorganisms to enter the public water supply. Bacteria growing in foods and beverages can cause illness, too. Refrigerating foods can slow the growth of many of these <u>pathogens</u>, but meat, fish, and eggs that are not cooked enough can still contain dangerous bacteria or parasites. Leaving food out at room temperature can give bacteria such as *salmonella* time to grow and produce toxins in the food. For these reasons, it is important to wash all used cooking tools.

1. Which of the following statements can you infer from this passage?
   - **A** Treatment plants help keep drinking water safe.
   - **B** Treatment plants never become flooded.
   - **C** Eliminating treatment plants would help keep water safe.
   - **D** New treatment plants are better than old ones.

2. Which of the following statements can you infer from the passage?
   - **F** Bacteria that live in food produce more toxins than molds produce.
   - **G** Cooking food thoroughly kills bacteria living in the food.
   - **H** Some bacteria are helpful to humans.
   - **I** Illnesses caused by bacteria living in food are seldom serious.

3. According to this passage, what do pathogens cause?
   - **A** disease
   - **B** flooding
   - **C** water-line breaks
   - **D** water supplies

Passage 2

1. A
2. G
3. A

TEST DOCTOR

Question 1: Students may mistakenly select answer D, which is a probable answer. But the passage does not distinguish between the effectiveness of new and old plants. Although the passage does not state explicitly that water treatment plants help keep drinking water safe, the first sentence does imply that microorganisms can endanger public health when treatment plants stop working.

INTERPRETING GRAPHICS

The graph below shows the reported number of people living with HIV/AIDS. Use the graph to answer the questions that follow.

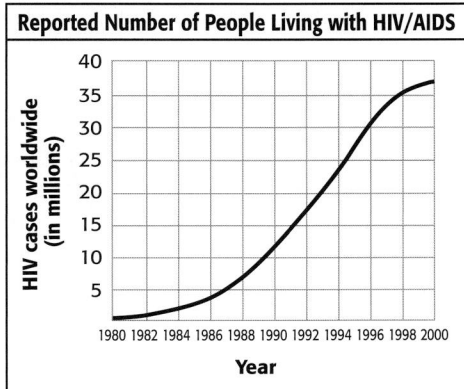

Reported Number of People Living with HIV/AIDS

Source: Joint United Nations Program on HIV/AIDS

1. When did the number of people living with HIV/AIDS reach 5 million?

A 1985
B 1986
C 1987
D 1988

2. When did the number of people living with HIV/AIDS reach 30 million?

F 1996
G 1997
H 1998
I 1999

3. When was the rate of increase of people with HIV/AIDS the **greatest**?

A from 1980 to 1982
B from 1984 to 1986
C from 1988 to 1990
D from 1998 to 2000

4. What percentage of the people who are infected with HIV do not yet have AIDS?

F 10%
G 24%
H 75%
I There is not enough information to determine the answer.

5. If the virus continued to spread as the graph indicates, in the year 2002, about how many people would be infected with HIV?

A 30 million
B 35 million
C 39 million
D 60 million

6. Which part of the graph indicates the rate of infection?

F x-axis
G y-axis
H slope of the line being graphed
I number of years in the sample

MATH

Read each question below, and choose the best answer.

1. Suppose you have 50,000 flu viruses on your fingers and you rub your eyes. Only 20,000 viruses enter your eyes, 10,000 dissolve in chemicals, and 10,000 are washed down into your nose. Of those, you sneeze out 2,000. How many viruses are left to wash down the back of your throat and possibly start an infection?

A 50,000
B 10,000
C 8,000
D 5,000

2. In which of the following lists are the numbers in order from smallest to greatest?

F 0.027, 0.072, 0.270, 0.720
G 0.270, 0.072, 0.720, 0.270
H 0.072, 0.027, 0.270, 0.720
I 0.720, 0.270, 0.072, 0.027

Standardized Test Preparation

INTERPRETING GRAPHICS

1. C
2. F
3. C
4. I
5. C
6. H

✚ TEST DOCTOR

Question 3: Students may struggle to determine when the rate of increase was the greatest. Help them understand that the rate of increase is the same as the number of cases divided by the time in years. Thus, the rate of increase is also the slope of the line. Use a ruler or other straight object to show students how to determine where the line on the graph is steepest.

Question 5: Students may mistakenly choose answer D simply because it is the highest number, but in this case, the highest number is incorrect. Students may struggle to extrapolate information from the graph. Show them how to continue the line at its latest rate to estimate infection rates for years later than the rates shown on the graph.

MATH

1. C
2. F

✚ TEST DOCTOR

Question 1: Students may mistakenly choose answer B because the question states that 10,000 flu viruses are washed into the nose. But show students how to track word problems by using a small chart or table. By keeping track of the parts of the problem, students can isolate the information needed to answer the question.

CHAPTER RESOURCES

Chapter Resource File

 • Standardized Test Preparation GENERAL

State Resources

For specific resources for your state, visit **go.hrw.com** and type in the keyword **HSMSTR**.

Weird Science

Background

Modern scientific study of antibiotics began in the 1800s. Louis Pasteur discovered that bacteria spread infectious diseases, and Robert Koch developed methods for isolating and growing different kinds of bacteria. A breakthrough in treating bacterial diseases came in the early 1900s, when Alexander Fleming discovered penicillin, an antibiotic formed from mold. Streptomycin, a fungal antibiotic, was discovered by Selman A. Waksman in 1943. Doctors now use antibiotics to treat diseases such as strep throat, bacterial meningitis, and tuberculosis.

Scientific Discoveries

Background

The number of people who are allergic to peanuts has increased significantly in recent years, and scientists are not sure why. There has been speculation about the connection between infant creams containing peanut oil and the development of peanut allergies, but nothing has been proven yet. A child is more likely to have a peanut allergy if one of his or her parents is also allergic. Most people who have a peanut allergy also have asthma.

Science in Action

Weird Science

Frogs in the Medicine Cabinet?

Frog skin, mouse intestines, cow lungs, and shark stomachs are all being tested to make more effective medicines to combat harmful bacteria. In 1896, a biologist named Michael Zasloff was studying African clawed frogs. He noticed that cuts in the frogs' skin healed quickly and never became infected. Zasloff decided to investigate further. He found that when a frog was cut, its skin released a liquid antibiotic that killed invading bacteria. Furthermore, sand sharks, moths, pigs, mice, and cows also contain chemicals that kill bacteria and other microorganisms. These useful antibiotics are even found in the small intestines of humans!

Social Studies ACTIVITY

Many medicines were discovered in plants or animals by people living near those plants or animals. Research the origin of one or two common medicines discovered this way. Make a poster showing a world map and the location of the medicines that you researched.

Scientific Discoveries

Medicine for Peanut Allergies

Scientists estimate that 1.5 million people in the United States suffer from peanut allergies. Every year 50 to 100 people in the United States die from an allergic reaction to peanuts. Peanuts and peanut oil are used to make many foods. People who have a peanut allergy sometimes mistakenly eat these foods and suffer severe reactions. A new drug has been discovered to help people control severe reactions. The drug is called TNX-901. The drug is actually an antibody that binds to the antibodies that the body makes during the allergic reaction to the peanuts. By binding these antibodies, the drug controls the allergic response.

Math ACTIVITY

During the testing of the new drug, 84 people were given four injections over the course of 4 months. One-fourth of the people participating received injections of a control that had no medicine in it. The rest of the people participating received different doses of the drug. How many people received the control? How many people received medicine? How many shots containing medicine were administered during the 4-month test?

Answer to Social Studies Activity

Answers may vary but may discuss the origins of the drugs aspirin and digitalis.

Answer to Math Activity

Twenty-one people received a control, and 63 people received medicine. Two hundred fifty-two shots containing medicine were administered.

Careers

Terrel Shepherd III

Nurse Terrel Shepherd III is a registered nurse (RN) at Texas Children's Hospital in Houston, Texas. RNs have many responsibilities. These responsibilities include giving patients their medications, assessing patients' health, and establishing intravenous access. Nurses also serve as a go-between for the patient and the doctor. Although most nurses work in hospitals or clinics, some nurses work for corporations. Pediatric nurses such as Shepherd work specifically with infants, children, and adolescents. The field of nursing offers a wide variety of job opportunities including home-care nurses, traveling nurses, and flight nurses. The hospital alone has many areas of expertise for nurses, including geriatrics (working with the elderly), intensive care, administration, and surgery. Traditionally, nursing has been considered to be a woman's career. However, since nursing began as a profession, men and women have practiced nursing. A career in nursing is possible for anyone who does well in science, enjoys people, and wants to make a difference in people's lives.

Language Arts ACTIVITY

WRITING SKILL Create a brochure that persuades people to consider a career in nursing. Describe nursing as a career, the benefits of becoming a nurse, and the education needed to be a nurse. Illustrate the brochure with pictures of nurses from the Internet or from magazines.

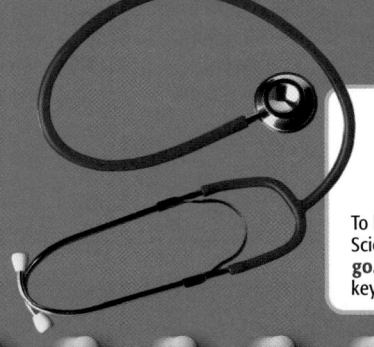

go.hrw.com

To learn more about these Science in Action topics, visit **go.hrw.com** and type in the keyword **HL5BD6F**.

Current Science

Check out Current Science® articles related to this chapter by visiting go.hrw.com. Just type in the keyword **HL5CS27**.

Careers ACTIVITY — GENERAL

Interested students can research any of the following:

1. How did the American Red Cross originate, and what are its responsibilities?
2. What are the responsibilities of nurses who work on emergency helicopter response teams?
3. How does a nurse practitioner differ from other RNs?
4. How has the field of nursing changed during the last 50 years?

Answer to Language Arts Activity

Student brochures should be written in language that persuades people to try nursing. If students struggle to be persuasive, ask them to think about the kind of language that persuades them to try new opportunities. The language should be honest and compelling.

Compression guide:
To shorten instruction because of time limitations, omit Section 3.

OBJECTIVES	LABS, DEMONSTRATIONS, AND ACTIVITIES	TECHNOLOGY RESOURCES
PACING • 90 min pp. 730–737 **Chapter Opener**	SE **Start-up Activity**, p. 731 `GENERAL`	OSP **Parent Letter** ■ `GENERAL` CD **Student Edition on CD-ROM** CD **Guided Reading Audio CD** ■ TR **Chapter Starter Transparency*** VID **Brain Food Video Quiz**
Section 1 Good Nutrition • Identify the six groups of nutrients and explain their importance to good health. • Describe the Food Guide Pyramid. • Understand how to read Nutrition Facts labels. • Explain the dangers of various nutritional disorders.	TE **Activity** Nutrient Table, p. 733 `GENERAL` TE **Connection Activity** Math, p. 733 `ADVANCED` SE **Quick Lab** Brown Bag Test, p. 735 ◆ `GENERAL` CRF **Datasheet for Quick Lab*** TE **Activity** Food Guide Pyramid, p. 735 `BASIC` SE **Inquiry Lab** To Diet or Not to Diet, p. 801 `GENERAL` CRF **Datasheet for LabBook*** LB **Labs You Can Eat** Snack Attack* ◆ `GENERAL` LB **Long-Term Projects & Research Ideas** Breakfast, Lunch, and Dinner of Champions* `ADVANCED`	CRF **Lesson Plans*** TR **Bellringer Transparency*** TR *LINK TO PHYSICAL SCIENCE* Covalent Bonds in a Water Molecule* TR The Food Guide Pyramid* TR Nutrition Facts Label* CRF **SciLinks Activity*** `GENERAL`
PACING • 45 min pp. 738–743 **Section 2 Risks of Alcohol and Other Drugs** • Describe the difference between psychological and physical dependence. • Explain the hazards of tobacco, alcohol, and illegal drugs. • Distinguish between positive and negative uses of drugs.	TE **Activity** Poster Project, p. 738 `GENERAL` TE **Connection Activity** Real World, p. 741 `ADVANCED` SE **School-to-Home Activity** Good Reasons, p. 742 `GENERAL`	CRF **Lesson Plans*** TR **Bellringer Transparency***
PACING • 90 min pp. 744–749 **Section 3 Healthy Habits** • Describe three important aspects of good hygiene. • Explain why exercise and sleep are important to good health. • Describe methods of handling stress. • List three ways to stay safe at home, on the road, and outdoors. • Plan what you would do in the case of an accident.	TE **Activity** Don't Kick These Habits!, p. 744 `GENERAL` TE **Connection Activity** Real World, p. 746 `GENERAL` TE **Group Activity** Poster Project, p. 747 `GENERAL` SE **Skills Practice Lab** Keep It Clean, p. 750 ◆ `GENERAL` CRF **Datasheet for Chapter Lab*** LB **Inquiry Labs** Consumer Challenge* `GENERAL` LB **Calculator-Based Labs** Counting Calories* `ADVANCED`	CRF **Lesson Plans*** TR **Bellringer Transparency*** SE **Internet Activity**, p. 746 `GENERAL` VID **Lab Videos for Life Science**

PACING • 90 min

CHAPTER REVIEW, ASSESSMENT, AND STANDARDIZED TEST PREPARATION

CRF **Vocabulary Activity*** `GENERAL`
SE **Chapter Review**, pp. 752–753 `GENERAL`
CRF **Chapter Review*** ■ `GENERAL`
CRF **Chapter Tests A*** ■ `GENERAL`, **B*** `ADVANCED`, **C*** `SPECIAL NEEDS`
SE **Standardized Test Preparation**, pp. 754–755 `GENERAL`
CRF **Standardized Test Preparation*** `GENERAL`
CRF **Performance-Based Assessment*** `GENERAL`
OSP **Test Generator** `GENERAL`
CRF **Test Item Listing*** `GENERAL`

Online and Technology Resources

Visit **go.hrw.com** for a variety of free resources related to this textbook. Enter the keyword **HL5BD7**.

Students can access interactive problem-solving help and active visual concept development with the *Holt Science and Technology* Online Edition available at **www.hrw.com**.

 Guided Reading Audio CD
Also in Spanish

A direct reading of each chapter for auditory learners, reluctant readers, and Spanish-speaking students.

Science Tutor CD-ROM
Excellent for remediation and test practice.

SKILLS DEVELOPMENT RESOURCES	SECTION REVIEW AND ASSESSMENT	STANDARDS CORRELATIONS
SE Pre-Reading Activity, p. 730 `GENERAL` **OSP** Science Puzzlers, Twisters & Teasers `GENERAL`		National Science Education Standards SAI 1, 2; SPSP 1, 4
CRF Directed Reading A* ■ `BASIC`, B* `SPECIAL NEEDS` **CRF** Vocabulary and Section Summary* ■ `GENERAL` **SE** Reading Strategy Reading Organizer, p. 732 `GENERAL` **SE** Connection to Oceanography Nutritious Seaweed, p. 734 `GENERAL` **SE** Math Practice What Percentage?, p. 736 `GENERAL` **CRF** Critical Thinking A Daily Routine* `ADVANCED` **CRF** Reinforcement Worksheet To Eat or Not to Eat…* `BASIC`	**SE** Reading Checks, pp. 733, 735, 736 `GENERAL` **TE** Homework, p. 734 `GENERAL` **TE** Reteaching, p. 736 `BASIC` **TE** Quiz, p. 736 `GENERAL` **TE** Alternative Assessment, p. 736 `GENERAL` **SE** Section Review,* p. 737 ■ `GENERAL` **CRF** Section Quiz* ■ `GENERAL`	UCP 1, 4; SAI 1; SPSP 1, 4; *LabBook:* SAI 1, 2; SPSP 1, 4
CRF Directed Reading A* ■ `BASIC`, B* `SPECIAL NEEDS` **CRF** Vocabulary and Section Summary* ■ `GENERAL` **SE** Reading Strategy Reading Organizer, p. 738 `GENERAL` **TE** Inclusion Strategies, p. 740	**SE** Reading Checks, pp. 739, 741, 742 `GENERAL` **TE** Homework, p. 739 `GENERAL` **TE** Homework, p. 740 `GENERAL` **TE** Reteaching, p. 742 `BASIC` **TE** Quiz, p. 742 `GENERAL` **TE** Alternative Assessment, p. 742 `GENERAL` **TE** Homework, p. 742 `GENERAL` **SE** Section Review,* p. 743 ■ `GENERAL` **CRF** Section Quiz* ■ `GENERAL`	SAI 1; SPSP 1, 4, 5
CRF Directed Reading A* ■ `BASIC`, B* `SPECIAL NEEDS` **CRF** Vocabulary and Section Summary* ■ `GENERAL` **SE** Reading Strategy Prediction Guide, p. 744 `GENERAL` **SE** Connection to Language Arts Dreamy Poetry, p. 745 `GENERAL` **TE** Reading Strategy Prediction Guide, p. 745 `GENERAL` **TE** Inclusion Strategies, p. 748	**SE** Reading Checks, pp. 745, 747, 749 `GENERAL` **TE** Homework, p. 746 `GENERAL` **TE** Homework, p. 747 `GENERAL` **TE** Reteaching, p. 748 `BASIC` **TE** Quiz, p. 748 `GENERAL` **TE** Alternative Assessment, p. 748 `ADVANCED` **SE** Section Review,* p. 749 ■ `GENERAL` **CRF** Section Quiz* ■ `GENERAL`	UCP 3; SAI 1; SPSP 1, 4, 5; *Chapter Lab:* UCP 2; SAI 1, 2; ST 2, SPSP 1, 3, 4, 5

One-Stop Planner® CD-ROM

This convenient CD-ROM includes:
- Lab Materials QuickList Software
- Holt Calendar Planner
- Customizable Lesson Plans
- Printable Worksheets
- ExamView® Test Generator

cnnstudentnews.com

Find the latest news, lesson plans, and activities related to important scientific events.

www.scilinks.org

Maintained by the **National Science Teachers Association.** See Chapter Enrichment pages for a complete list of topics.

Current Science®

Check out *Current Science* articles and activities by visiting the HRW Web site at **go.hrw.com.** Just type in the keyword **HL5CS28T.**

Classroom Videos

- **Lab Videos** demonstrate the chapter lab.
- **Brain Food Video Quizzes** help students review the chapter material.
- **CNN Videos** bring science into your students' daily life.

Visual Resources

CHAPTER STARTER TRANSPARENCY

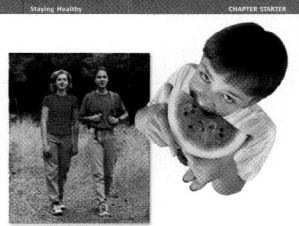

Staying Healthy   CHAPTER STARTER

Imagine . . .

You are part of a nationwide survey of more than 6,000 teenagers. Scientists from the Centers for Disease Control and Prevention are concerned about teen health. They think that certain behaviors put too many teenagers at risk for cancer, heart disease, and other illnesses. The researchers ask you about five health habits: Do you ever smoke cigarettes? Do you exercise regularly? Do you eat plenty of fruits and vegetables? Do you eat a lot of high-fat foods, such as hamburgers, fried foods, and junk foods? Do you sometimes drink alcohol?

This survey of people aged 12 to 17 was actually taken, and 20 percent of those surveyed smoke cigarettes. In addition, 36 percent get little exercise, 85 percent do not eat enough fruits and vegetables, 34 percent eat too many high-fat foods, and 16 percent sometimes drink large amounts of alcohol. Over half of the teenagers (63 percent) engage in two or more of these health-risk behaviors.

Where do you fit into this national survey? Are your habits healthy or risky? This chapter will give you plenty of information about keeping yourself healthy and increasing your chances of having a long, active life.

Copyright © by Holt, Rinehart and Winston. All rights reserved.

BELLRINGER TRANSPARENCIES

Staying Healthy   BELLRINGER TRANSPARENCY

Section: Good Nutrition

Match the terms in the first column with the descriptions in the second column.

1. nutrients   a. units of energy
2. Calories   b. found in vegetable oils
3. carbohydrates   c. necessary for life processes
4. proteins   d. include calcium
5. unsaturated fats   e. build the body
6. minerals   f. main source of energy

Write your answers in your **science journal.**

Section: Risks of Alcohol and Other Drugs

Do you think that drugs are good or bad for you? What are some dangerous drugs, and what makes them dangerous? Are there ever any positive uses for dangerous drugs? Are there any dangers involved with using "good" drugs, such as antibiotics or other medicines?

Explain your thoughts in your **science journal.**

Copyright © by Holt, Rinehart and Winston. All rights reserved.

TEACHING TRANSPARENCIES

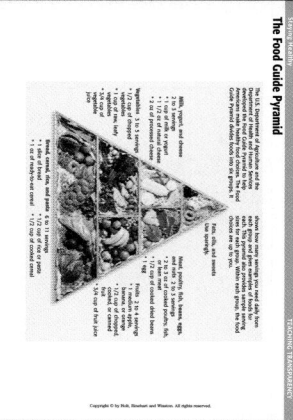

The Food Guide Pyramid

TEACHING TRANSPARENCY

Staying Healthy   TEACHING TRANSPARENCY

Nutrition Facts Label

Nutrition Facts		
Serving Size 1/2 cup (120 ml)		Serving information
Servings per Container 2.5		
Amount per Serving	**Prepared**	
Calories	70	Number of Calories per serving
Calories from Fat	25	
	% Daily Value	
Total Fat 2.5 g		4%
Saturated Fat 1 g		5%
Cholesterol 15 mg		5%
Sodium 960 mg		40%
Total Carbohydrate 8 g		3%
Dietary Fiber less than 1 g		4%
Sugars 1 g		
Protein 3 g		
Vitamin A		15%
Vitamin C		0%
Calcium		0%
Iron		2%

Percentage of daily values

*Percent Daily Values are based on a 2,000 Calorie diet. Your daily values may be higher or lower depending on your Calorie needs:

	Calories	2,000	2,500
Total Fat	Less than	65g	80g
Sat Fat	Less than	20g	25g
Cholesterol	Less than	300mg	300mg
Sodium	Less than	2,400mg	2,400mg
Total Carbohydrate		300g	375g
Dietary Fiber		25g	30g
Protein		50g	60g

Copyright © by Holt, Rinehart and Winston. All rights reserved.

TEACHING TRANSPARENCIES

Covalent Bonds in a Water Molecule

The oxygen atom shares one of its electrons with each of the two hydrogen atoms. It has an outer level filled with 8 electrons.

Each hydrogen atom shares its 1 electron with the oxygen atom. Each hydrogen atom now has an outer level filled with 2 electrons.

This electron-dot diagram for water shows only the outermost level of electrons for each atom. But you still see how the atoms share electrons.

LINK TO PHYSICAL SCIENCE

Chapter: Chemical Bonding

CONCEPT MAPPING TRANSPARENCY

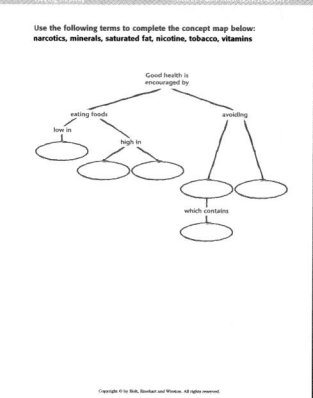

Staying Healthy   CONCEPT MAPPING TRANSPARENCY

Use the following terms to complete the concept map below: **narcotics, minerals, saturated fat, nicotine, tobacco, vitamins**

Good health is encouraged by

eating foods

avoiding

low in

high in

which contains

Copyright © by Holt, Rinehart and Winston. All rights reserved.

Planning Resources

LESSON PLANS

Lesson Plan   SAMPLE

Section: Waves

Pacing
Regular Schedule: with lab(s):2 days   without lab(s):2 days
Block Schedule: with lab(s):1 1/2 days   without lab(s):1 day

Objectives
1. Relate the seven properties of life to a living organism.
2. Describe seven themes that can help you to organize what you learn about biology.
3. Identify the tiny structures that make up all living organisms.
4. Differentiate between reproduction and heredity and between metabolism and homeostasis.

National Science Education Standards Covered
LSInter4:Cells have particular structures that underlie their functions.
LSMat1:Most cell functions involve chemical reactions.
LSBeh1:Cells store and use information to guide their functions.
UCP1:Cell functions are regulated.
SI1: Cells can differentiate and form complete multicellular organisms.
PS1: Species evolve over time.
ESS1: The great diversity of organisms is the result of more than 3.5 billion years of evolution.
ESS2: Natural selection and its evolutionary consequences provide a scientific explanation for the fossil record of ancient life forms as well as for the striking molecular similarities observed among the diverse species of living organisms.
ST1: The millions of different species of plants, animals, and microorganisms that live on Earth today are related by descent from common ancestors.
ST2: The energy for life primarily comes from the sun.
SPSP1: The complexity and organization of organisms accommodate the need for obtaining, transforming, releasing, and eliminating the matter and energy used to sustain the organism.
SPSP6: As matter and energy flows through different levels of organization of living systems—cells, organs, organisms—and between living systems and the physical environment, chemical elements are recombined in different ways.
HNS1: Organisms have behavioral responses to internal changes and to external stimuli.

PARENT LETTER

   SAMPLE

Dear Parent,

Your son's or daughter's science class will soon begin exploring the chapter entitled "The World of Physical Science." In this chapter, students will learn about how the scientific method applies to the world of physical science and the role of physical science in the world. By the end of the chapter, students should demonstrate a clear understanding of the chapter's main ideas and be able to discuss the following topics:

1. physical science as the study of energy and matter (Section 1)
2. the role of physical science in the world around them (Section 1)
3. careers that rely on physical science (Section 1)
4. the steps used in the scientific method (Section 2)
5. examples of technology (Section 2)
6. how the scientific method is used to answer questions and solve problems (Section 2)
7. how our knowledge of science changes over time (Section 2)
8. how models represent real objects or systems (Section 3)
9. examples of different ways models are used in science (Section 3)
10. the importance of the International System of Units (Section 4)
11. the appropriate units to use for particular measurements (Section 4)
12. how area and density are derived quantities (Section 4)

Questions to Ask Along the Way

You can help your son or daughter learn about these topics by asking interesting questions such as the following:

• What are some surprising careers that use physical science?
• What is a characteristic of a good hypothesis?
• When is it a good idea to use a model?
• Why do Americans measure things in terms of inches and yards and meters?

ALSO IN SPANISH

TEST ITEM LISTING

TEST ITEM LISTING
The World of Science   SAMPLE

MULTIPLE CHOICE

1. A limitation of models is that
   a. they are large enough to see.
   b. they do not act exactly like the things that they model.
   c. they are smaller than the things that they model.
   d. they model unfamiliar things.
   Answer: B   Difficulty: 1   Section: 2   Objective: 2

2. The length 10 m is equal to
   a. 100 cm.   c. 10,000 mm.
   b. 1,000 cm.   d. Both (b) and (c)
   Answer: B   Difficulty: 1   Section: 2   Objective: 2

3. To be valid, a hypothesis must be
   a. testable.   c. made into a law.
   b. supported by evidence.   d. Both (a) and (b)
   Answer: B   Difficulty: 1   Section: 3   Objective: 2

4. The statement "Sheila has a stain on her shirt" is an example of a(n)
   a. law.   c. observation.
   b. hypothesis.   d. prediction.
   Answer: B   Difficulty: 1   Section: 3   Objective: 2

5. A hypothesis is often developed out of
   a. observations.   c. laws.
   b. experiments.   d. Both (a) and (b)
   Answer: B   Difficulty: 1   Section: 3   Objective: 2

6. How many milliliters are in 3.5 kL?
   a. 3,500 mL   c. 3,500,000 mL
   b. 0.0035 mL   d. 35,000 mL
   Answer: B   Difficulty: 1   Section: 4   Objective: 2

7. A map of Seattle is an example of a
   a. law.   c. model.
   b. theory.   d. unit.
   Answer: B   Difficulty: 1   Section: 3   Objective: 2

8. A lab has the safety icons shown below. These icons mean that you should wear
   a. safety goggles.   c. safety goggles and a lab apron.
   b. only a lab apron.   d. safety goggles, a lab apron, and gloves.
   Answer: B   Difficulty: 1   Section: 3   Objective: 2

9. The law of conservation of mass says that the total mass before a chemical change is
   a. more than the total mass after the change.
   b. less than the total mass after the change.
   c. the same as the total mass after the change.
   d. not the same as the total mass after the change.
   Answer: B   Difficulty: 1   Section: 3   Objective: 2

10. In which of the following areas might you find a geochemist at work?
    a. studying the chemistry of rocks   c. studying fishes
    b. studying forestry   d. studying the atmosphere
    Answer: B   Difficulty: 1   Section: 3   Objective: 2

One-Stop Planner® CD-ROM

This CD-ROM includes all of the resources shown here and the following time-saving tools:

• *Lab Materials QuickList Software*
• *Customizable lesson plans*
• *Holt Calendar Planner*
• *The powerful ExamView® Test Generator*

Meeting Individual Needs

DIRECTED READING A
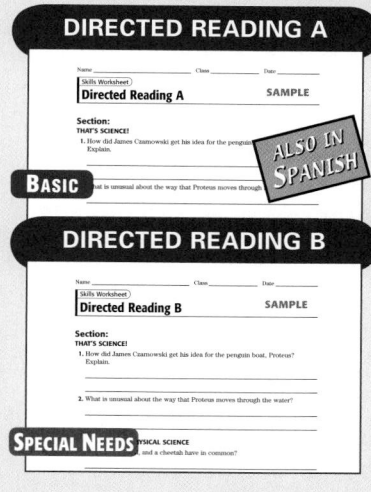
BASIC · ALSO IN SPANISH

DIRECTED READING B
SPECIAL NEEDS

VOCABULARY ACTIVITY
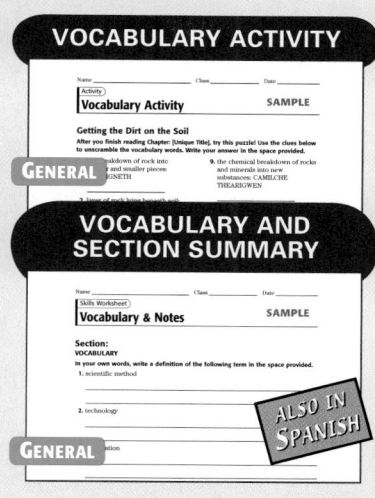
GENERAL

VOCABULARY AND SECTION SUMMARY
GENERAL · ALSO IN SPANISH

REINFORCEMENT
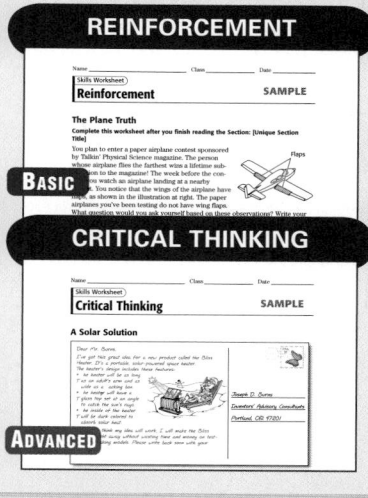
BASIC

CRITICAL THINKING
ADVANCED

SCILINKS ACTIVITY

GENERAL

SCIENCE PUZZLERS, TWISTERS & TEASERS
GENERAL

Labs and Activities

LONG-TERM PROJECTS & RESEARCH IDEAS
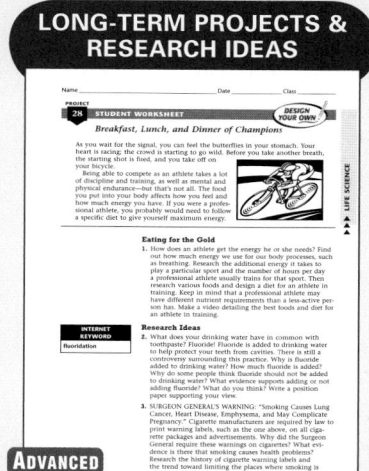
ADVANCED

LABS YOU CAN EAT
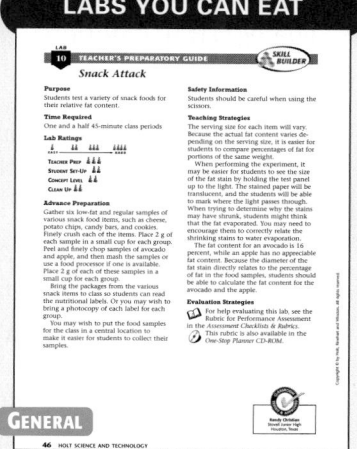
GENERAL

INQUIRY LABS
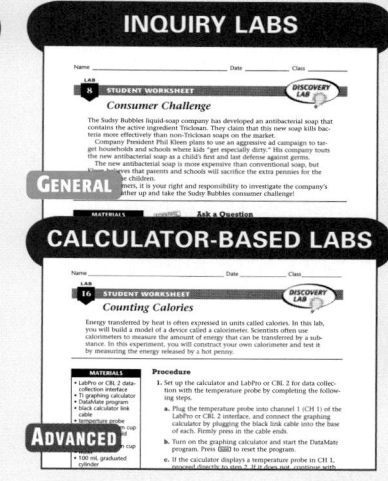
GENERAL

CALCULATOR-BASED LABS
ADVANCED

DATASHEETS FOR QUICK LABS

DATASHEETS FOR CHAPTER LABS

DATASHEETS FOR LABBOOK

Review and Assessments

SECTION QUIZ
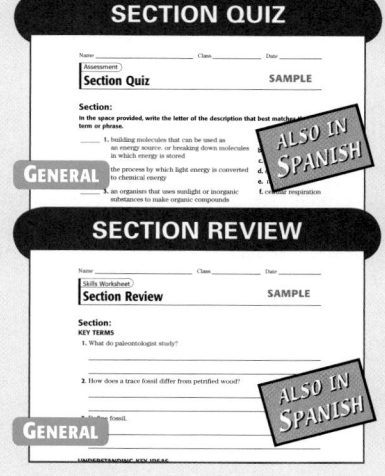
GENERAL · ALSO IN SPANISH

SECTION REVIEW
GENERAL · ALSO IN SPANISH

CHAPTER REVIEW
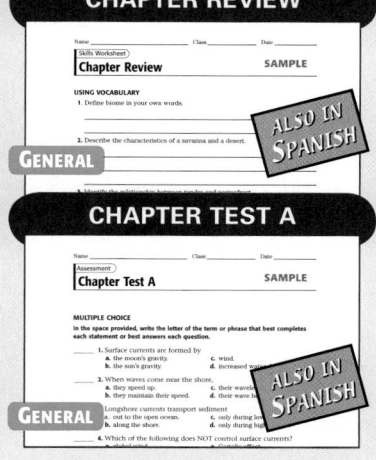
GENERAL · ALSO IN SPANISH

CHAPTER TEST A
GENERAL · ALSO IN SPANISH

CHAPTER TEST B
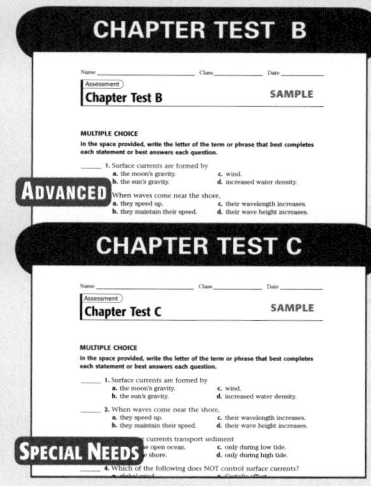
ADVANCED

CHAPTER TEST C
SPECIAL NEEDS

STANDARDIZED TEST PREPARATION
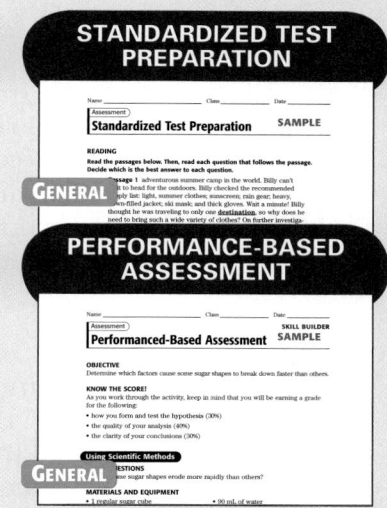
GENERAL

PERFORMANCE-BASED ASSESSMENT
GENERAL

This Chapter Enrichment provides relevant and interesting information to expand and enhance your presentation of the chapter material.

Section 1

Good Nutrition

Nutrient Needs in Adolescence

- Puberty is a period of rapid growth. Changes brought on by puberty affect every organ of the body. Adolescents need extra nutrients to meet their bodies' needs during the growth spurt that accompanies puberty.

- The onset of menstruation in girls and the change in lean body mass in boys increase an adolescent's need for iron. During adolescence, the Recommended Daily Allowance (RDA) for iron is 12–15 mg.

- The increase in skeletal mass that occurs during adolescence boosts the body's calcium needs, which increases the RDA for calcium to 1,200–1,500 mg. About 75 to 80% of the skeleton is built during adolescence.

- Rapid growth during adolescence increases the body's caloric needs. Energy needs vary depending on growth rate, body composition, and activity level. In general, boys have a larger proportion of lean body mass to fat and require more Calories than girls do.

Fiber

- Soluble fiber, found in fruit, beans, peas, and other legumes, can reduce the risk of heart disease by lowering cholesterol levels in the blood. Legume-based fiber also aids in the regulation of blood glucose levels.

- Although fiber contains no vitamins or minerals, it is essential to good health. Insoluble fiber is found in whole-grain foods. Along with fluids, insoluble fiber helps the colon remove waste (fecal matter) from the bowels. A lack of insoluble fiber in a person's diet can increase the risk for constipation, colon and bowel cancer, and diverticulosis, a disorder in which pouches form in the bowel wall.

Is That a Fact!

- ◆ Just before astronauts Neil Armstrong (1930–) and Edwin Aldrin Jr. (1930–1999) embarked on the first moonwalk on July 20, 1969, each astronaut ate four bacon squares, three sugar cookies, and peaches. They drank pineapple-grapefruit juice and coffee.

Adolescence and Nutrition

- The physical, emotional, and social changes of adolescence have a great impact on teen nutrition. Adolescence is typically a period of increased autonomy, so teens have increased opportunity to make food choices. But rather than making food choices based on long-term health, teens tend to be influenced by social pressures to reach cultural ideals of thinness, to gain the acceptance of peers, and to assert their independence from their parents. The characteristic adolescent preoccupation with body image extends to nutrition. If sound nutritional principles are taught and reinforced during adolescence, long-term health can benefit.

Section 2

Risks of Alcohol and Other Drugs

Drug Abuse

- According to yearly surveys conducted by the University of Michigan's Institute for Social Research (funded by the National Institute on Drug Abuse), drug abuse among 8th, 10th, and 12th grade students has decreased over the last few years. That doesn't mean that drug abuse is no longer a problem. The following are some statistics from the 2002 survey:

- About 15% of 8th grade students surveyed indicated that they had tried inhalants in their lifetime.
- About 19% of 8th grade students surveyed indicated that they had tried marijuana in their lifetime.
- About 31% of 8th grade students surveyed indicated that they had tried cigarettes. More than 2% of 8th grade students indicated that they smoked more than half a pack of cigarettes a day.
- About 47% of 8th grade students surveyed indicated that they had tried alcohol in their lifetime.

Is That a Fact!

◆ In the 1800s, scientists learned how to isolate drug compounds from plants. Morphine, cocaine, and heroin became readily available. These drugs were welcomed as safe, powerful pain relievers because, at first, no one knew of their addictive properties. By the early 1900s, there was an epidemic of drug abuse in the United States.

Section 3

Healthy Habits

Safety

- In the United States, accidental injuries are the leading cause of death for children and adolescents between the ages of 1 and 19.

- In 2002, motor-vehicle accidents claimed the lives of almost 43,000 Americans. More than 1,600 victims were between the ages of 8 and 15. Many of these deaths could have been prevented—59% of all motor-vehicle fatalities in 2002 were unrestrained passengers.

Excuse Me?

- When sounds enter the ear, they cause the eardrum to vibrate. Tiny hair cells in the inner ear respond to these vibrations by sending nerve impulses to the brain. Ordinarily, these hair cells slowly die as a person ages. When exposed to loud noises, however, more hair cells die than usual. Fewer impulses are sent to the brain. Once damage occurs, it is irreversible.

- Many teens are at risk for preventable hearing loss. Experts attribute this trend to increased exposure to damaging levels of noise, such as loud music. Sources of loud noise include CD players, concerts, car stereos, video games, and television. Hearing loss can be prevented by turning down the volume on audio devices and by wearing earplugs when loud noise cannot be controlled.

SCiLINKS

NSTA
Developed and maintained by the
National Science Teachers Association

SciLinks is maintained by the National Science Teachers Association to provide you and your students with interesting, up-to-date links that will enrich your classroom presentation of the chapter.

Visit www.scilinks.org and enter the SciLinks code for more information about the topic listed.

Topic: Food Pyramids
SciLinks code: HSM0598

Topic: Drug and Alcohol Abuse
SciLinks code: HSM0428

Topic: Nutritional Disorders
SciLinks code: HSM1057

Topic: Safety
SciLinks code: HSM1339

Overview

Tell students that this chapter will help them learn about good nutrition, the risks of drugs, and how they can take care of themselves to stay healthy.

Assessing Prior Knowledge

Students should be familiar with the following topics:
- body systems
- disease

Identifying Misconceptions

As students learn the material in this chapter, some of them may express misconceptions about drugs. Some students may not recognize that drugs, such as caffeine (found in many sodas, teas, and coffee) or herbal additives (including chamomile, ginseng, and echinacea), are found in some of the foods they eat. You may also want to point out that many of the products that claim to make people think more clearly, control weight, and increase energy contain drugs. Some students may have misconceptions about alcohol, including the belief that alcohol is not a drug, that beer and wine are safer than liquor, and that alcohol is not addictive.

28
Staying Healthy

About the PHOTO

What do you see in this photo? Sure, you can see five students facing the camera, but what else does the picture tell you? The bright eyes, happy smiles, and shiny hair show radiant health. Having a clear mind and a long, active life depend on having a healthy body. Keeping your body healthy depends on eating well; avoiding drugs, cigarettes, and alcohol; and staying safe.

PRE-READING ACTIVITY

FOLDNOTES **Booklet** Before you read the chapter, create the FoldNote entitled "Booklet" described in the **Study Skills** section of the Appendix. Label each page of the booklet with a main idea from the chapter. As you read the chapter, write what you learn about each main idea on the appropriate page of the booklet.

Standards Correlations

National Science Education Standards

The following codes indicate the National Science Education Standards that correlate to this chapter. The full text of the standards is at the front of the book.

Chapter Opener
SAI 1, 2; SPSP 1, 4

Section 1 Good Nutrition
UCP 1, 4; SAI 1; SPSP 1, 4; *LabBook:* SAI 1, 2; SPSP 1, 4

Section 2 Risks of Alcohol and Other Drugs
SAI 1; SPSP 1, 4, 5

Section 3 Taking Care of Your Body
UCP 3; SAI 1; SPSP 1, 4, 5

Chapter Lab
UCP 2; SAI 1, 2; ST 2; SPSP 1, 3, 4, 5

Chapter Review
UCP 1, 3; SAI 1; SPSP 1, 3, 4, 5

Science in Action
SPSP 1, 4, 5

MATERIALS

FOR EACH GROUP
- paper
- pen or pencil
- questionnaire

Teacher's Notes: To ensure privacy, you may want to have students complete their questionnaires at home. Many students will be uncomfortable sharing personal information.

Answers

1. Answers may vary.
2. Answers may vary. Students should recognize that the first four items on the questionnaire are considered good habits, and the fifth item is considered a bad habit.

START-UP ACTIVITY

Conduct a Survey

How healthy are the habits of your classmates? Find out for yourself.

Procedure

1. Copy and answer yes or no to each of the five questions at right. Do not put your name on the survey.

Analysis

1. As a class, record the data from the completed surveys in a chart. For each question, calculate the percentage of your class that answered yes.
2. What good and bad habits do your classmates have?

1. Do you exercise at least three times a week?

2. Do you wear a seat belt every time you ride in a car?

3. Do you eat five or more servings of fruits and vegetables every day?

4. Do you use sunscreen to protect your skin when you are outdoors?

5. Do you eat a lot of high-fat foods?

CHAPTER RESOURCES

Technology

 **Transparencies**
- Chapter Starter Transparency

READING SKILLS

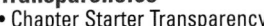 **Student Edition on CD-ROM**

 Guided Reading Audio CD
- English or Spanish

 **Classroom Videos**
- Brain Food Video Quiz

Workbooks

 Science Puzzlers, Twisters & Teasers
- Staying Healthy GENERAL

Imagine . . .
You are part of a nationwide survey of more than 6,000 teenagers. Scientists from the Centers for Disease Control and Prevention are concerned about teen health. They think that certain behaviors put too many teenagers at risk for cancer, heart disease, and other illnesses. The researchers ask you about five health habits: Do you ever smoke cigarettes? Do those surveyed smoke cigarettes. In addition, 36 percent get little exercise, 85 percent do not eat enough fruits and vegetables, 34 percent eat too many high-fat foods, and 16 percent sometimes drink large amounts of alcohol. Over half of the teenagers (63 percent) engage in two or more of these health-risk behaviors.

Chapter Starter Transparency
Use this transparency to help students begin thinking about health and good nutrition.

Focus

Overview

In this section, students will learn about the six essential nutrients and why these nutrients are important for good health. Dietary guidelines and the food pyramid are used to illustrate the principles of sound nutrition, and students will learn how to use these tools. Finally, students will learn about nutritional disorders.

 Bellringer

Post the following lists on the board or an overhead projector:

Column A
1. nutrients
2. Calories
3. carbohydrates
4. proteins
5. unsaturated fats
6. minerals

Column B
a. units of energy
b. found in vegetable oils
c. necessary for life processes
d. include calcium
e. build the body
f. main source of energy

Challenge students to match the terms in column A with the descriptions in column B.
(1. c; 2. a; 3. f; 4. e; 5. b; 6. d)

READING WARM-UP

Objectives
- Identify the six groups of nutrients, and explain their importance to good health.
- Describe the Food Guide Pyramid.
- Understand how to read Nutrition Facts labels.
- Explain the dangers of various nutritional disorders.

Terms to Learn

nutrient	mineral
carbohydrate	vitamin
protein	malnutrition
fat	

READING STRATEGY

Reading Organizer As you read this section, create an outline of the section. Use the headings from the section in your outline.

nutrient a substance in food that provides energy or helps form body tissues and that is necessary for life and growth

carbohydrate a class of energy-giving nutrients that includes sugars, starches, and fiber

Figure 1 *Eating only one food, even a healthy food, will not give you all the substances your body needs.*

Good Nutrition

Does the saying "You are what you eat" mean that you are pizza? No, but substances in pizza help build your body.

Protein in the cheese may become part of your hair. Carbohydrates in the crust can give you energy for your next race.

Nutrients

Are you more likely to have potato chips or broccoli for a snack? If you eat many foods that are high in fat, such as potato chips, your food choices probably are not as healthy as they could be. Broccoli is a healthier food than potato chips. But eating only broccoli, as the person in **Figure 1** is doing, does not give you a balanced diet.

To stay healthy, you need to take in **nutrients,** or substances that provide the materials needed for life processes. Nutrients are grouped into six classes: *carbohydrates, proteins, fats, water, vitamins,* and *minerals.* Carbohydrates, proteins, and fats provide energy for the body in units called *Calories* (Cal).

Carbohydrates

Carbohydrates are your body's main source of energy. A **carbohydrate** is a chemical composed of simple sugars. There are two types of carbohydrates: simple and complex. *Simple carbohydrates* are sugars. They are easily digested and give you quick energy. *Complex carbohydrates* are made up of many sugar molecules linked together. They are digested slowly and give you long-lasting energy. Some complex carbohydrates are good sources of fiber. Fiber is a part of a healthy diet and is found in whole-grain foods, such as brown rice and whole-wheat bread. Many fruits and vegetables also contain fiber.

CHAPTER RESOURCES

Chapter Resource File
- **Lesson Plan**
- **Directed Reading A** BASIC
- **Directed Reading B** SPECIAL NEEDS

Technology

Transparencies
- Bellringer
- *LINK TO PHYSICAL SCIENCE* Covalent Bonds in a Water Molecule

CONNECTION to
Physical Science ——— GENERAL

Water Molecules Water is a very simple molecule that is made up of one oxygen atom and two hydrogen atoms. Water is vital to all living organisms. Remind students that water makes up nearly 70% of the human body. Illustrate the water molecule using the teaching transparency titled "Covalent Bonds in a Water Molecule."
LS Visual

Protein

Proteins are found in body fluids, muscle, bone, and skin. **Proteins** are nutrients used to build and repair your body. Your body makes the proteins it needs, but it must have the necessary building blocks, called *amino acids.* Your digestive system breaks down protein into individual amino acids that are then used to make new proteins. Some foods, such as poultry, fish, milk, and eggs, provide all of the amino acids your body needs. Foods that contain all of these essential amino acids are called *complete proteins. Incomplete proteins* contain only some of the essential amino acids. Most plant foods contain incomplete protein, but eating a variety of plant foods will provide all of the amino acids your body needs.

✔ **Reading Check** What is an incomplete protein? (*See the Appendix for answers to Reading Checks.*)

Figure 2 *This sample meal provides many of the nutrients a growing teenager needs.*

Fats

Another class of nutrients that is important to a healthy meal, such as the meal shown in **Figure 2,** is fat. **Fats** are energy-storage nutrients. Fats are needed to store and transport vitamins, produce hormones, keep skin healthy, and provide insulation. Fats also provide more energy than either proteins or carbohydrates. There are two types of fats: saturated and unsaturated. *Saturated fats* are found in meat, dairy products, coconut oil, and palm oil. Saturated fats raise blood cholesterol levels. Although *cholesterol* is a fat-like substance found naturally in the body, high levels can increase the risk of heart disease. *Unsaturated fats* and foods high in fiber may help reduce blood cholesterol levels. Your body cannot make unsaturated fats. They must come from vegetable oils and fish in your diet. The body needs both kinds of fats.

protein a molecule that is made up of amino acids and that is needed to build and repair body structures and to regulate processes in the body

fat an energy-storage nutrient that helps the body store some vitamins

Water

You cannot survive for more than a few days without water. Your body is about 70% water. Water is in every cell of your body. The main functions of water are to transport substances, regulate body temperature, and provide lubrication. Some scientists think you should drink at least eight glasses of water a day. When you exercise you need more water, as shown in **Figure 3.** You also get water from other liquids you drink and the foods you eat. Fresh fruits and vegetables, juices, soups, and milk are good sources of water.

Figure 3 *When you exercise, you need to drink more water.*

Answer to Reading Check

An incomplete protein does not contain all of the essential amino acids.

Is That a Fact!

Frozen vegetables are often just as nutritious as fresh vegetables are.

Diets Have students examine a popular diet trend. Then, have students evaluate the diet in terms of its ability to meet the body's nutrient and energy needs. If a diet does not meet the body's needs, encourage students to identify changes to the diet that will make the diet healthful. Have students write reports about their findings. **LS Verbal**

Homework — GENERAL

Essential Vitamins
Have students research the physical effects of vitamin deficiencies for at least three essential vitamins. Ask students to create informative brochures about their findings. **LS Verbal**

BRAIN FOOD

Vitamins Point out that many vitamin manufacturers promote their products by claiming that their vitamins are "natural" or "organic," rather than synthetic (manufactured). These vitamins are almost always more expensive than their synthetic counterparts. Point out that most experts agree that organic and synthetic vitamins are identical in both structure and function.

Table 1	Some Essential Vitamins	
Vitamin	**What it does**	**Where you get it**
A	keeps skin and eyes healthy; builds strong bones and teeth	yellow and orange fruits and vegetables, leafy greens, meats, and milk
B (various forms)	helps body use carbohydrates; helps blood, nerves, and heart function	meats, whole grains, beans, peas, nuts, and seafood
C	strengthens tissues; helps the body absorb iron, fight disease	citrus fruits, leafy greens, broccoli, peppers, and cabbage
D	builds strong bones and teeth; helps the body use calcium and phosphorus	sunlight, enriched milk, eggs, and fish
E	protects red blood cells from destruction; keeps skin healthy	oils, fats, eggs, whole grains, wheat germ, liver, and leafy greens
K	assists with blood clotting	leafy greens, tomatoes, and potatoes

mineral a class of nutrients that are chemical elements that are needed for certain body processes

vitamin a class of nutrients that contain carbon and that are needed in small amounts to maintain health and allow growth

Minerals

If you eat a balanced diet, you should get all of the vitamins and minerals you need. **Minerals** are elements that are essential for good health. You need six minerals in large amounts: calcium, chloride, magnesium, phosphorus, potassium, and sodium. There are at least 12 minerals that are required in very small amounts. These include fluorine, iodine, iron, and zinc. Calcium is necessary for strong bones and teeth. Magnesium and sodium help the body use proteins. Potassium is needed to regulate your heartbeat and produce muscle movement, and iron is necessary for red blood cell production.

Vitamins

Vitamins are another class of nutrients. **Vitamins** are compounds that control many body functions. Only vitamin D can be made by the body, so you have to get most vitamins from food. **Table 1** provides information about six essential vitamins.

CONNECTION TO
Oceanography

Nutritious Seaweed Kelp, a type of seaweed, is a good source of iodine. This nutritious food is grown on special farms off the coasts of China and Japan. What other nutritious foods come from the sea?

WEIRD SCIENCE

You are what you eat, and sometimes, you can even look like it! Eating a lot of carrots can give skin a yellowish color, a harmless condition. Tomatoes can give skin a reddish color. In 1960, a doctor examined a patient whose skin was orange. It turned out that the patient was eating a lot of carrots and tomatoes. The two colors mixed, and *voilà*, the patient had orange skin!

Answer to Connection to Oceanography

Sample answer: Other nutritious seafoods include fish and shellfish.

Eating for Good Health

Now you have learned which nutrients you need for good health. But how can you be sure to get all the important nutrients in the right amounts? To begin, keep in mind that most teenage girls need about 2,200 Cal per day, and most boys need about 2,800 Cal. Because different foods contain different nutrients, *where* you get your Calories is as important as *how many* you get. The Food Guide Pyramid, shown in **Figure 4**, can help you make good food choices.

✔ **Reading Check** Using the Food Guide Pyramid below, design a healthy lunch that includes one food from each food group.

ACTIVITY ——————— **BASIC**

Food Guide Pyramid Have students keep track of the food that they eat during a single day. Then, have students determine how many servings from each of the food groups they consumed. Have students determine the percentage of recommended servings these numbers represent. For example, two glasses of milk and a grilled cheese sandwich represent 100% of the recommended daily dairy servings. One apple is 25–50% of the recommended daily fruit servings. Encourage students to identify how they could change their diet to make it more healthful. **LS Logical**

Debate ——————— **ADVANCED**

Changing the Pyramid Many nutrition experts think that the Food Guide Pyramid should be updated to reflect new discoveries about healthy eating habits. Ask students to research the proposed revisions to the Food Guide Pyramid. Then, have students debate whether the Food Guide Pyramid should be changed. **LS Verbal/Logical**

Figure 4 **The Food Guide Pyramid**

The U.S. Department of Agriculture and the Department of Health and Human Services developed the Food Guide Pyramid to help Americans make healthy food choices. The Food Guide Pyramid divides foods into six groups. It shows how many servings you need daily from each group and gives examples of foods for each. This pyramid also provides sample serving sizes for each group. Within each group, the food choices are up to you.

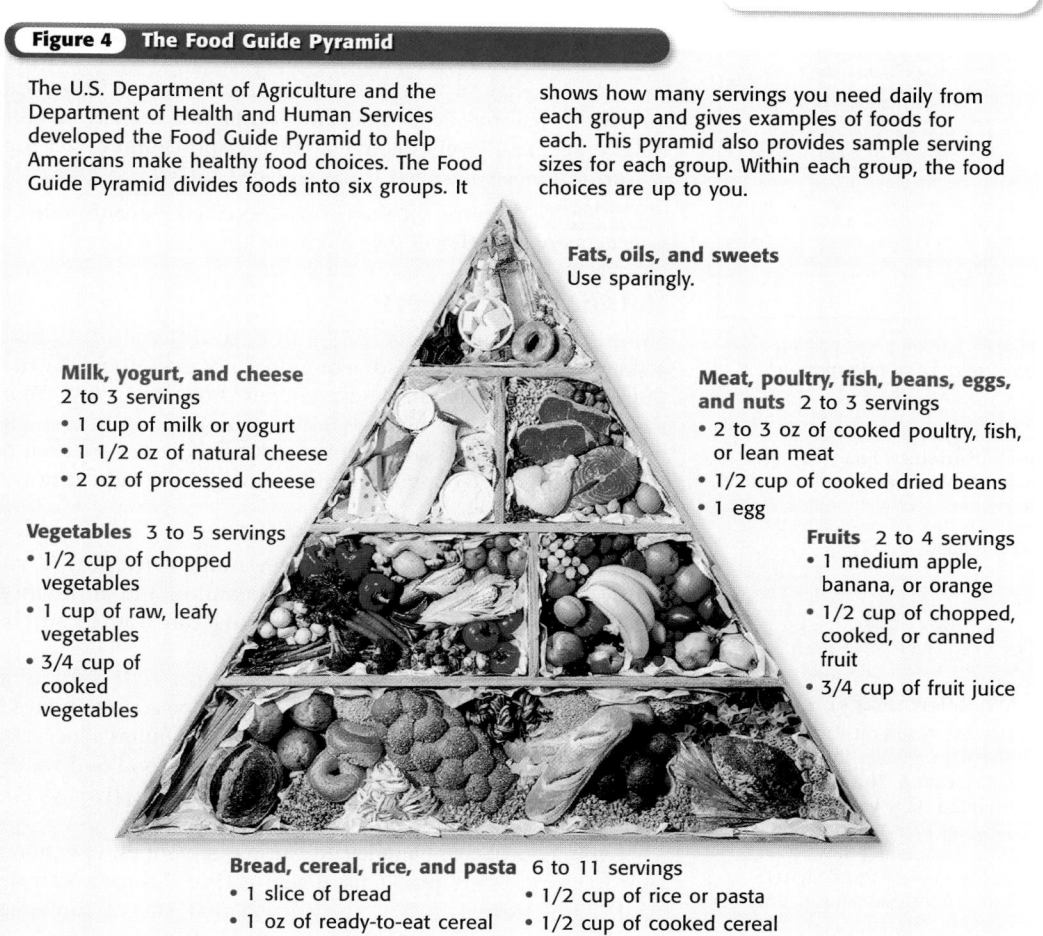

Fats, oils, and sweets
Use sparingly.

Milk, yogurt, and cheese
2 to 3 servings
• 1 cup of milk or yogurt
• 1 1/2 oz of natural cheese
• 2 oz of processed cheese

Meat, poultry, fish, beans, eggs, and nuts 2 to 3 servings
• 2 to 3 oz of cooked poultry, fish, or lean meat
• 1/2 cup of cooked dried beans
• 1 egg

Vegetables 3 to 5 servings
• 1/2 cup of chopped vegetables
• 1 cup of raw, leafy vegetables
• 3/4 cup of cooked vegetables

Fruits 2 to 4 servings
• 1 medium apple, banana, or orange
• 1/2 cup of chopped, cooked, or canned fruit
• 3/4 cup of fruit juice

Bread, cereal, rice, and pasta 6 to 11 servings
• 1 slice of bread
• 1 oz of ready-to-eat cereal
• 1/2 cup of rice or pasta
• 1/2 cup of cooked cereal

Answer to Reading Check

Sample answer: a peanut butter sandwich, a glass of milk, and fresh fruit and vegetable slices

---

CHAPTER RESOURCES

Technology

📠 **Transparencies**
• The Food Guide Pyramid

Reteaching — BASIC

Memory Game Ask students to create a memory game about the six essential nutrients. Give students 12 index cards. On six of the cards, students should list each nutrient. On the other six cards, they should list the role each nutrient plays in the body. Ask students to turn over the cards, scramble them, and turn over cards individually to match each with the appropriate nutrient or function. **LS Kinesthetic/Verbal**

Quiz — GENERAL

1. What are the six essential nutrients? (carbohydrates, proteins, fats, water, vitamins, and minerals)

2. What are the effects of obesity? (Sample answer: Obesity increases the risk of high blood pressure, heart disease, and diabetes. Some obese people may suffer from malnutrition.)

Alternative Assessment — GENERAL

Concept Mapping Have students create a concept map using the new terms from the section and any additional words that are necessary. Have students begin their concept map with the phrase "Good nutrition." **LS Logical**

Nutrition Facts	
Serving Size 1/2 cup (120 ml)	*Serving information*
Servings per Container 2.5	

Amount per Serving	Prepared
Calories	70 ← *Number of Calories per serving*
Calories from Fat	25

	% Daily Value
Total Fat 2.5 g	4%
Saturated Fat 1 g	5%
Cholesterol 15 mg	5%
Sodium 960 mg	40%
Total Carbohydrate 8 g	3%
Dietary Fiber less than 1 g	4%
Sugars 1 g	
Protein 3 g	
Vitamin A	15%
Vitamin C	0%
Calcium	0%
Iron	4%

Percentage of daily values

Percent Daily Values are based on a 2,000 Calorie diet. Your daily values may be higher or lower depending on your Calorie needs:

		Calories	2,000	2,500
Total Fat	Less than		65g	80g
Sat Fat	Less than		20g	25g
Cholesterol	Less than		300mg	300mg
Sodium	Less than		2,400mg	2,400mg
Total Carbohydrate			300g	375g
Dietary Fiber			25g	30g
Protein			50g	60g

Figure 5 *Nutrition Facts labels provide a lot of information.*

malnutrition a disorder of nutrition that results when a person does not consume enough of each of the nutrients that are needed by the human body

What Percentage?

Use the Nutrition Facts label above to answer the following question. The recommended daily value of fat is 72 g for teenage girls and 90 g for teenage boys. What percentage of the daily recommended fat value is provided in one cup of soup?

Reading Food Labels

Packaged foods must have Nutrition Facts labels. **Figure 5** shows a Nutrition Facts label for chicken noodle soup. Nutrition Facts labels show what amount of each nutrient is in one serving of the food. You can tell whether a food is high or low in a nutrient by looking at its daily value. Reading food labels can help you make healthy eating choices. The percentage of daily values shown is based on a diet that consists of 2,000 Cal per day. Most teenagers need more than 2,000 Cal per day. The number of Calories needed depends on factors such as height, weight, age, and level of activity. Playing sports and exercising use up Calories that need to be replaced for you to grow.

✔ **Reading Check** For what nutrients does chicken noodle soup provide more than 10% of the daily value?

Nutritional Disorders

Unhealthy eating habits can cause nutritional disorders. **Malnutrition** occurs when someone does not eat enough of the nutrients needed by the body. Malnutrition can result from eating too few or too many Calories or not taking in enough of the right nutrients. Malnutrition affects how one looks and how quickly one's body can repair damage and fight illness.

Anorexia Nervosa and Bulimia Nervosa

Anorexia nervosa (AN uh REKS ee uh nuhr VOH suh) is an eating disorder characterized by self-starvation and an intense fear of gaining weight. Anorexia nervosa can lead to severe malnutrition.

Bulimia nervosa (boo LEE mee uh nuhr VOH suh) is a disorder characterized by binge eating followed by induced vomiting. Sometimes, people suffering from bulimia nervosa use laxatives or diuretics to rid their bodies of food and water. Bulimia nervosa can damage teeth and the digestive system and can lead to kidney and heart failure.

Both anorexia and bulimia can cause weak bones, low blood pressure, and heart problems. These eating disorders can be fatal if not treated. If you are worried that you or someone you know may have an eating disorder, talk to an adult.

Math Practice

3.5% for girls (2.5 g ÷ 72 g × 100 = 3.5%)
2.8% for boys (2.5 g ÷ 90 g × 100 = 2.8%)

Answer to Reading Check

One serving of chicken noodle soup provides more than 10% of the daily recommended allowance of vitamin A and sodium.

Obesity

Eating too much food that is high in fat and low in other nutrients, such as junk food and fast food, can lead to malnutrition. *Obesity* (oh BEE suh tee) is having an extremely high percentage of body fat. People suffering from obesity may not be eating a variety of foods that provide them with the correct balance of essential nutrients. Having an inactive lifestyle can also contribute to obesity.

Obesity increases the risk of high blood pressure, heart disease, and diabetes. Eating a more balanced diet and exercising regularly can help reduce obesity. Obesity may also be caused by other factors. Scientists are studying the links between obesity and heredity.

SECTION Review

Summary

- A healthy diet has a balance of carbohydrates, proteins, fats, water, vitamins, and minerals.
- The Food Guide Pyramid is a good guide for healthy eating.
- Nutrition Facts labels provide information needed to plan a healthy diet.
- Anorexia nervosa and bulimia nervosa cause malnutrition and damage to many body systems.
- Obesity can lead to heart disease and diabetes.

Using Key Terms

1. In your own words, write a definition for each of the following terms: *nutrient, mineral,* and *vitamin.*

Understanding Key Ideas

2. Malnutrition can be caused by
   a. obesity.
   b. bulimia nervosa.
   c. anorexia nervosa.
   d. All of the above

3. What information is found on a Nutrition Facts label?

4. Give an example of a carbohydrate, a protein, and a fat.

5. If vitamins and minerals do not supply energy, why are they important to a healthy diet?

6. How do anorexia nervosa and bulimia nervosa differ?

7. How can someone who is obese suffer from malnutrition?

Math Skills

8. If you eat 2,500 Cal per day and 20% are from fat, 30% are from protein, and 50% are from carbohydrates, how many Calories of each nutrient do you eat?

Critical Thinking

9. **Applying Concepts** Name some of the nutrients that can be found in a glass of milk.

10. **Identifying Relationships** Explain how eating a variety of foods can help ensure good nutrition.

11. **Predicting Consequences** How would your growth be affected if your diet consistently lacked important nutrients?

12. **Applying Concepts** Explain how you can use the Nutrition Facts label to choose food that is high in calcium.

For a variety of links related to this chapter, go to www.scilinks.org

Topic: Food Pyramids; Nutritional Disorders
SciLinks code: HSM0598; HSM1057

Answers to Section Review

1. Sample answer: A nutrient is a substance that your body needs to keep working. A mineral is nutrient that your body needs for certain body processes. A vitamin is a nutrient that controls many body functions and must be obtained from food.

2. d

3. Sample answer: A Nutrition Facts label shows how much of each nutrient is in a single serving of a packaged food.

4. Sample answer: Bread is a carbohydrate, oil is a fat, and fish contains protein.

5. Sample answer: Vitamins and minerals help control body functions, such as heartbeat and muscle movement, and they help build body parts, such as bones and blood cells.

6. Sample answer: Anorexia nervosa is an eating disorder in which a person starves himself or herself. Bulimia nervosa is an eating disorder in which a person eats and then induces vomiting.

7. Sample answer: A person who is obese can suffer from malnutrition because his or her diet may be high in fat, and he or she does not get enough of the other essential nutrients.

8. 500 Cal from fat (2,500 Cal × 0.2 = 500 Cal), 750 Cal from protein (2,500 Cal × 0.3 = 750 Cal), 1,250 Cal from carbohydrates (2,500 Cal × 0.5 = 1,250 Cal)

9. Accept all reasonable answers. All six types of nutrients can be found in milk.

10. Sample answer: Because different foods contain different nutrients, eating a variety of foods can help people get a variety of nutrients. Many of these nutrients are needed for good nutrition.

11. Sample answer: If your diet lacked Calories, your body would not have the energy to grow. If your diet lacked minerals, such as calcium, your body would not have the building blocks needed to remain healthy and grow.

12. Sample answer: The Nutrition Facts label lists the percentage of daily value for calcium found in a single serving of food. Reading the labels of foods helps people make sure that they eat foods high in calcium.

CHAPTER RESOURCES

Chapter Resource File

- Section Quiz GENERAL
- Section Review GENERAL
- Vocabulary and Section Summary GENERAL
- Reinforcement Worksheet BASIC
- Critical Thinking ADVANCED
- SciLinks Activity GENERAL
- Datasheet for Quick Lab

Technology

Transparencies
- Nutrition Facts Label

Risks of Alcohol and Other Drugs

You see them in movies and on television and read about them in magazines. But what are drugs?

You are exposed to information, and misinformation, about drugs every day. So, how can you make the best decisions?

Focus

Overview

In this section, students will learn that drugs can have positive and negative effects on the body. Students will learn about different types of drugs. Finally, they will learn about the causes, effects, and treatments of drug abuse and addiction.

 Bellringer

Ask students, "Are drugs good or bad for you?" (Explain that a drug is not always inherently good or bad. Any chemical substance that causes a physical or emotional change in a person is a drug.)

Motivate

ACTIVITY ——— GENERAL

Poster Project Have students collect magazine advertisements for prescription drugs, over-the-counter drugs, alcohol, and tobacco. Ask students to make a poster that identifies the drug in each advertisement and the type of person that would find the advertisement appealing.

LS Visual

Figure 1 *All of these products contain drugs.*

What Is a Drug?

Any chemical substance that causes a physical or psychological change is called a **drug.** Drugs come in many forms, as shown in **Figure 1.** Some drugs enter the body through the skin. Other drugs are swallowed, inhaled, or injected. Drugs are classified by their effects. *Analgesics* (AN'l JEE ziks) relieve pain. *Antibiotics* (AN tie bie AHT iks) fight bacterial infections, and *antihistamines* (AN tie HIS tuh MEENZ) control cold and allergy symptoms. *Stimulants* speed up the central nervous system, and *depressants* slow it down. When used correctly, legal drugs can help your body heal. When used illegally or improperly, however, drugs can do great harm.

Dependence and Addiction

The body can develop *tolerance* to a drug. Tolerance means that larger and larger doses of the drug are needed to get the same effect. The body can also form a *physical dependence* or need for a drug. If the body doesn't receive a drug that it is physically dependent on, withdrawal symptoms occur. Withdrawal symptoms include nausea, vomiting, pain, and tremors.

Addiction is the loss of control of drug-taking behavior. Once addicted, a person finds it very hard to stop taking a drug. Sometimes, the need for a drug is not due only to physical dependence. Some people also form *psychological dependence* on a drug, which means that they feel powerful cravings for the drug.

 **SCIENCE**

Humans may not be the only organisms that use drugs. Chimpanzees have been observed swallowing the leaves of a plant that is known to be effective against infections and parasites. Muriqui monkeys of Brazil may be able to control their fertility with certain plants, and howler monkeys may even select the sex of their offspring by eating different plants.

Types of Drugs

There are many kinds of drugs. Some drugs are made from plants, and some are made in a lab. You can buy some drugs at the grocery store, while others can be prescribed only by a doctor. Some drugs are illegal to buy, sell, or possess.

Herbal Medicines

Information about herbal medicines has been handed down for centuries, and some herbs contain chemicals with important healing properties. The tea in **Figure 2** contains chamomile and is made from a plant. Chamomile has chemicals in it that can help you sleep. However, herbs are drugs and should be used carefully. The Federal Drug Administration does not regulate herbal medicines or teas and cannot guarantee their safety.

Over-the-Counter and Prescription Drugs

Over-the-counter drugs can be bought without a prescription. A prescription is written by a doctor and describes the drug, directions for use, and the amount of the drug to be taken.

Many over-the-counter and prescription drugs are powerful healing agents. However, some drugs also produce unwanted side effects. *Side effects* are uncomfortable symptoms, such as nausea, headaches, drowsiness, or more serious problems.

Whether purchased with or without a prescription, all drugs must be used with care. Information on proper use can be found on the label. **Figure 3** shows some general drug safety tips.

Reading Check **What is the difference between an over-the-counter drug and a prescription drug?** *(See the Appendix for answers to Reading Checks.)*

Figure 3 **Drug Safety Tips**

- *Never take another person's prescription medicine.*
- *Read the label before each use. Always follow the instructions on the label and those provided by your doctor or pharmacist.*
- *Do not take more or less medication than prescribed.*
- *Consult a doctor if you have any side effects.*
- *Throw away leftover and out-of-date medicines.*

drug any substance that causes a change in a person's physical or psychological state

addiction a dependence on a substance, such as alcohol or another drug

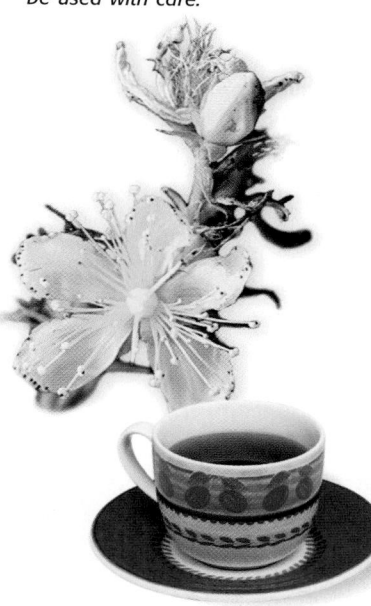

Figure 2 *Some herbs can be purchased in health-food stores. Medicinal herbs should always be used with care.*

Teach

Using the Figure — ADVANCED

Writing **Drug Safety Tips** Refer students to **Figure 3.** Encourage students to research how following each of the drug safety tips listed in the figure can keep them safe. Ask students to write an informative magazine article about their findings. Encourage students to use the tips as headings in their articles. (Students should discover that taking someone else's prescription medicine is risky because they don't know how their bodies are going to react to the medicine. They may have an allergic reaction or the medicine may interfere with their own medications. Students should recognize that reading the label ensures that they take the medicine correctly. Students should discover that taking less medicine than prescribed can make the medicine ineffective. If they take more medicine than prescribed, they may be injured or overdose. Students should recognize that side effects may indicate that they are allergic to the medicine, that the medicine is not effective, or that they might need another medicine to meet their needs. Students should recognize that leftover medicine might be discovered and taken by younger children and that out-of-date medicines likely are no longer effective.) LS **Verbal**

Homework — GENERAL

Pharmacy Encourage students to visit a pharmacy and make a list of 25 over-the-counter drugs. Challenge students to include drugs that have different modes of administration. Have students prepare a table that categorizes the drugs by their active ingredients and by their uses. LS **Verbal**

Cultural Awareness — GENERAL

Aspirin The Chickasaw Indians relieved pain and fever by chewing on the bark of the willow tree. Today many people relieve their minor ills with a chemically related substance—aspirin. Derived from a chemical that is also found in willow bark, aspirin is the most widely used drug in the world. Aspirin relieves pain and fever and prevents blood clotting.

Answer to Reading Check

Over-the-counter drugs can be bought without a prescription. Prescription drugs can be bought only with a prescription from a doctor or other medical professional.

Figure 4 **Effects of Smoking**

▼ Healthy lung tissue of a nonsmoker

▼ Damaged lung tissue of a smoker

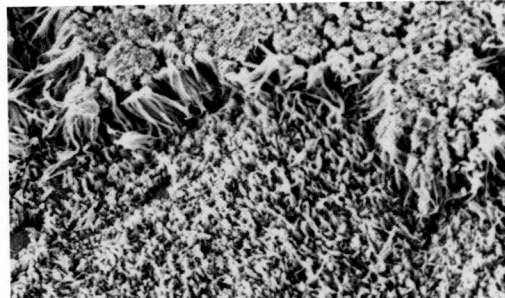

INCLUSION Strategies

- *Behavior Control Issues*
- *Hearing Impaired*
- *Learning Disabled*

Students often benefit from small-group work. Have students work in groups of four. Have them create information webs with large circles in the center and small circles surrounding the large circles. Tell students to write each of the following phrases inside a large circle: "Problems caused by cigarettes" and "Smokeless tobacco hazards." Tell students to add six small circles to the cigarette web and three small circles to the smokeless tobacco web and to write a risk in each of the small circles. **LS Visual**

Discussion —— GENERAL

Advertising Alcohol Tell students that beer, liquor, and wine companies in the United States spend billions of dollars annually on advertising and promotion. Display for students a selection of advertisements for beer, liquor, or wine taken from magazines. Encourage students to identify advertising tactics that might attract youth. (Students might note that the ads often show groups of young, beautiful, and active people in outdoor settings. These ads imply that people cannot have fun without alcohol.) **LS Verbal**

nicotine a toxic, addictive chemical that is found in tobacco and that is one of the major contributors to the harmful effects of smoking

alcoholism a disorder in which a person repeatedly drinks alcoholic beverages in an amount that interferes with the person's health and activities

Figure 5 *This car was in an accident involving a drunk driver.*

Tobacco

Cigarettes are addictive, and smoking has serious health effects. **Nicotine** (NIK uh TEEN) is a chemical in tobacco that increases heart rate and blood pressure and is extremely addictive. Smokers experience a decrease in physical endurance. **Figure 4** shows the effects of smoking on the cilia of your lungs. Cilia clean the air you breathe and prevent debris from entering your lungs. Smoking increases the chances of lung cancer, and it has been linked to other cancers, emphysema, chronic bronchitis, and heart disease. Experts estimate that there are more than 430,000 deaths related to smoking each year in the United States. Secondhand smoke also poses significant health risks.

Like cigarettes, smokeless, or chewing, tobacco is addictive and can cause health problems. Nicotine is absorbed through the lining of the mouth. Smokeless tobacco increases the risk of several cancers, including mouth and throat cancer. It also causes gum disease and yellowing of the teeth.

Alcohol

It is illegal in most of the United States for people under the age of 21 to use alcohol. Alcohol slows down the central nervous system and can cause memory loss. Excessive use of alcohol can damage the liver, pancreas, brain, nerves, and cardiovascular system. In very large quantities, alcohol can cause death. Alcohol is a factor in more than half of all suicides, murders, and accidental deaths. **Figure 5** shows the results of one alcohol-related accident. Alcohol also affects decision making and can lead you to take unhealthy risks.

People can suffer from **alcoholism,** which means that they are physically and psychologically dependent on alcohol. Alcoholism is considered a disease, and genetic factors are thought to influence the development of alcoholism in some people.

Is That a Fact!

About 90% of first-time cigarette smokers will become addicted to cigarettes. Fewer than half of these people are able to quit smoking, which puts their health at great risk. About 90% of people who get lung cancer are smokers or former smokers. Cigarette smokers are also at greater risk of getting cancers of the larynx, lip, esophagus, bladder, pancreas, and kidneys.

Homework —— GENERAL

Avoiding Alcohol Tell students that counteradvertising is an effective technique for deterring alcohol abuse. Have students work in small groups to create a magazine advertisement against alcohol abuse. Consider hanging the advertisements in the classroom or around the school. **LS Verbal**

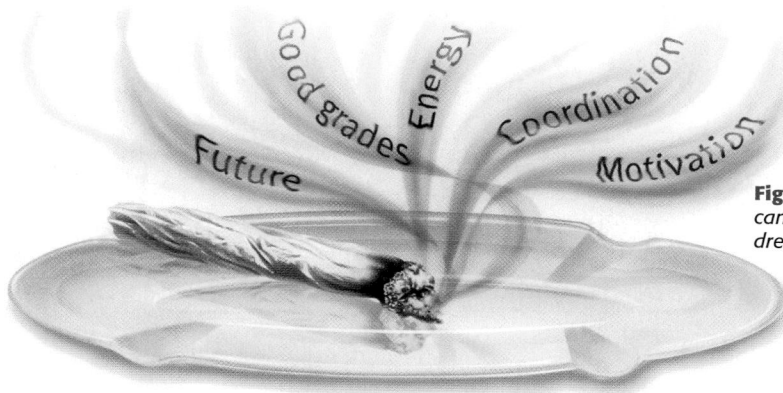

Figure 6 *Smoking marijuana can make your health and dreams go up in smoke.*

Marijuana

Marijuana is an illegal drug that comes from the Indian hemp plant. Marijuana affects different people in different ways. It may increase anxiety or cause feelings of paranoia. Marijuana slows reaction time, impairs thinking, and causes a loss of coordination. Regular use of marijuana can affect many areas of your life, as described in **Figure 6.**

Cocaine

Cocaine and its more purified form, crack, are made from the coca plant. Both drugs are illegal and highly addictive. Users can become addicted to them in a very short time. Cocaine can produce feelings of intense excitement followed by anxiety and depression. Both drugs increase heart rate and blood pressure and can cause heart attacks, even among first-time users.

✓ Reading Check What are two dangers to users of cocaine?

Narcotics and Designer Drugs

Drugs made from the opium plant are called **narcotics.** Some narcotics are used to treat severe pain. Narcotics are illegal unless prescribed by a doctor. Some narcotics are never legal. For example, heroin is one of the most addictive narcotics and is always illegal. Heroin is usually injected, and users often share needles. Therefore, heroin users have a high risk of becoming infected with diseases such as hepatitis and AIDS. Heroin users can also die of an overdose of the drug.

Other illegal drugs include inhalants, barbiturates (bahr BICH uhr itz), amphetamines (am FET uh MEENZ), and *designer drugs.* Designer drugs are made by making small changes to existing drugs. Ecstasy, or "X," is a designer drug that causes feelings of well-being. Over time, the drug causes lesions (LEE zhuhnz), or holes, in a user's brain, as shown in **Figure 7.** Ecstasy users are also more likely to develop depression.

narcotic a drug that is derived from opium and that relieves pain and induces sleep

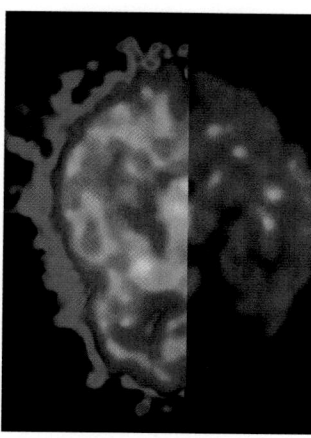

Figure 7 *The brain scan on the left shows a healthy brain. The scan on the right is from a teenager who has regularly used Ecstasy.*

Reteaching — BASIC

Reviewing Drugs Ask students to briefly describe the drugs discussed in the section. Have students identify effects that these drugs can have on the body.
LS Verbal

Quiz — GENERAL

1. What is drug abuse? (Sample answer: Drug abuse is the improper or illegal use of drugs.)

2. What is nicotine? (Nicotine is the drug in tobacco that increases heart rate and blood pressure and is extremely addictive.)

3. What are designer drugs? Give an example. (Sample answer: Designer drugs are drugs made by making small changes to existing drugs. Ecstasy is a designer drug.)

Alternative Assessment — GENERAL

Making Tables Have students prepare tables describing alcohol, tobacco, marijuana, cocaine, LSD, and heroin. Have students define each and describe the effects of the drug on the body. In addition, have students indicate whether the drug is legal and whether it is addictive.
LS Logical/Verbal

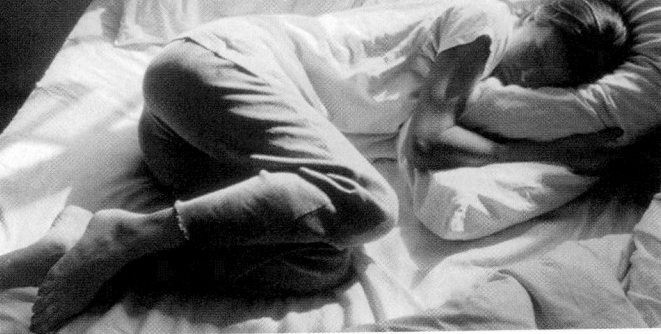

Figure 8 *Drug abuse can leave you depressed and feeling alone.*

Figure 9 Drug Myths

Myth *"It's only alcohol, not drugs."*

Reality Alcohol is a mood-altering and mind-altering drug. It affects the central nervous system and is addictive.

Myth *"I won't get hooked on one or two cigarettes a day."*

Reality Addiction is not related to the amount of a drug used. Some people become addicted after using a drug once or twice.

Myth *"I can quit any time I want."*

Reality Addicts may quit and return to drug usage many times. Their inability to stay drug-free shows how powerful the addiction is.

SCHOOL to HOME

Good Reasons

WRITING SKILL Discuss with your parent the possible effects of drug abuse on your family. Then, write yourself a letter giving reasons why you should stay drug-free. Put your letter in a safe place. If you ever find yourself thinking about using drugs, take out your letter and read it.

ACTIVITY

Hallucinogens

Hallucinogens (huh LOO si nuh juhnz) distort the senses and cause mood changes. Users have hallucinations, which means that they see and hear things that are not real. LSD and PCP are powerful, illegal hallucinogens. Sniffing glue or solvents can also cause hallucinations and serious brain damage.

Drug Abuse

A drug user takes a drug to prevent or improve a medical condition. The drug user obtains the drug legally and uses the drug properly. A drug abuser does not take a drug to relieve a medical condition. An abuser may take drugs for the temporary good feelings they produce, to escape from problems, or to belong to a group. The drug is often obtained illegally, and it is often taken without knowledge of the drug's dangers.

✔ **Reading Check** What is the difference between drug use and drug abuse?

How Drug Abuse Starts

Nicotine, alcohol, and marijuana are sometimes called *gateway drugs* because they are often the first drugs a person abuses. The abuse of other, more dangerous drugs may follow the abuse of gateway drugs. Peer pressure is often the reason that young people begin to use drugs. Teenagers may drink, smoke, or try marijuana to make friends or avoid being teased. Because drug abusers often stand out, it can sometimes be hard to see that many teenagers do not abuse drugs.

Many teenagers begin using illegal drugs to feel part of a group, but drug abuse has many serious consequences. Drug abuse can lead to problems with friends, family, school, and handling money. These problems often lead to depression and social isolation, as shown in **Figure 8.**

Many people who start using drugs do not recognize the dangers. Misinformation about drugs is everywhere. Several common drug myths are discussed in **Figure 9.**

Homework — GENERAL

Writing **Drug Report** Have students write a short paper about one of the following drugs: alcohol, marijuana, cocaine, LSD, PCP, ecstasy, or heroin. Ask students to describe the type of drug, common names for the drug, what the drug is made from, the effects of the drug, the penalty for possession of the drug, and what help is available to those who are addicted to the drug. **LS** Verbal

Answer to Reading Check

Drug use is the proper use of a legal drug. Drug abuse is either the use of an illegal drug or the improper use of a legal drug.

Getting Off Drugs

People who abuse drugs undergo emotional and physical changes. Teenagers who had few problems often begin to have problems with school, family, and money when they start to use drugs.

The first step to quitting drugs is to admit to abusing drugs and to decide to stop. It is important for the addicted person to get the proper medical treatment. There are drug treatment centers, like the one shown in **Figure 10,** available to help. Getting off drugs can be extremely difficult. Withdrawal symptoms are often painful, and powerful cravings for a drug can continue long after a person quits. But people who stop abusing drugs lead happier and healthier lives.

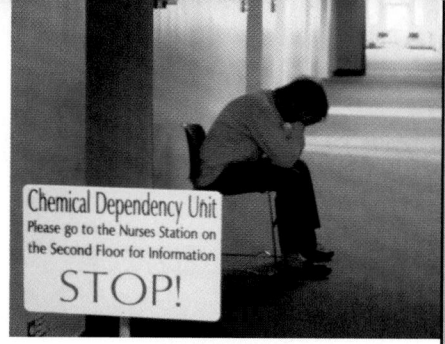

Figure 10 *Drug treatment centers help people get off drugs and back on track to healthier, happier lives.*

SECTION Review

Summary

- Physical dependence causes withdrawal symptoms when a person stops using a drug. Psychological dependence causes powerful cravings.
- There are many types of drugs, including over-the-counter, prescription, and herbal medicines.
- Tobacco contains the highly addictive chemical nicotine.
- Abuse of alcohol can lead to alcoholism.
- Illegal drugs include marijuana, cocaine, hallucinogens, designer drugs, and many narcotics.
- Getting off drugs requires proper medical treatment.

Using Key Terms

1. In your own words, write a definition for the terms *drug, addiction,* and *narcotic.*

Understanding Key Ideas

2. Which of the following products does NOT contain a drug?
   a. cola
   b. fruit juice
   c. herbal tea
   d. cough syrup

3. Describe the difference between physical and psychological dependence.

4. What is the difference between drug use and drug abuse?

5. How does addiction occur, and what are two consequences of drug addiction?

6. Name two different kinds of illegal drugs, and give examples of each.

Math Skills

7. If 2,200 people between the ages of 16 and 20 die every year in alcohol-related car crashes, how many die every day?

Critical Thinking

8. **Analyzing Relationships** How are nicotine, alcohol, heroin, and cocaine similar? How are they different?

9. **Analyzing Ideas** What are two ways that a person who abuses drugs can get in trouble with the law?

10. **Predicting Consequences** How can drug abuse damage family relationships?

11. **Making Inferences** Driving a car while under the influence of drugs can put others in danger. Describe another situation in which one person's drug abuse could put other people in danger.

SCLINKS.

NSTA
Developed and maintained by the
National Science Teachers Association

For a variety of links related to this chapter, go to www.scilinks.org

Topic: Drug and Alcohol Abuse
SciLinks code: HSM0428

Answers to Section Review

1. Sample answer: A drug is any substance that changes a person's physical or emotional state. Addiction happens when someone becomes dependent on a drug. A narcotic is a drug that is derived from opium and that is used to treat pain.

2. b

3. Sample answer: When someone forms a physical dependence, he or she suffers from withdrawal symptoms if he or she stops using a drug. Someone who has a psychological dependence on a drug feels powerful cravings for the drug.

4. Sample answer: Drug use is the legal and proper use of a drug to prevent or improve a medical condition. Drug abuse is the improper and illegal use of drugs, often for the feelings the drugs produce, to escape from problems, and to fit in.

5. Sample answer: Addiction is the loss of control of drug-taking behavior. Addiction can cause problems at school, at home, and with money.

6. Sample answer: Narcotics include opium and heroin. LSD and PCP are hallucinogens.

7. 6 people/day
   (2,200 people ÷ 365 days =
   6 people/day)

8. Sample answer: Nicotine, alcohol, heroin, and cocaine are all addictive. Nicotine and alcohol are legal for many people, but cocaine and heroin are illegal.

9. Sample answers: A person who abuses drugs can get in trouble with the law because many drugs are illegal. Also drug abuse can cause money troubles, which might lead someone to steal. Some people may drink and drive, which is illegal even if a person is old enough to legally drink alcohol.

10. Sample answer: Drug abuse can cause stress in a family because drug abuse causes failing grades and depression.

11. Sample answer: People who abuse drugs often make bad decisions. For example, a drug abuser may try to go swimming in dangerous water. A person who tried to help a drug abuser who makes a bad decision could be hurt.

Focus

Overview

In this section, students will learn how hygiene, exercise, rest, and stress management can enhance their well-being. Students will learn how stress affects the body. Finally, students will learn how injuries can be prevented.

 Bellringer

Tell students the following information: "In the 1800s and earlier, people who sustained simple cuts on their skin often ended up with serious infections. That rarely happens now." Then, ask students to explain why infections are less common now than they once were. (Sample answer: People now understand the importance of washing wounds with soap to keep them clean. People also have antiseptics and antibiotics today.)

Motivate

ACTIVITY ———— GENERAL

Don't Kick These Habits! Ask students to list some of their daily hygienic habits. (Sample answers: washing hands, bathing, brushing teeth, washing dishes, and using clean utensils to eat)

LS Verbal

READING WARM-UP

Objectives

- Describe three important aspects of good hygiene.
- Explain why exercise and sleep are important to good health.
- Describe methods of handling stress.
- List three ways to stay safe at home, on the road, and outdoors.
- Plan what you would do in the case of an accident.

Terms to Learn

hygiene
aerobic exercise
stress

READING STRATEGY

Prediction Guide Before reading this section, write the title of each heading in this section. Next, under each heading, write what you think you will learn.

hygiene the science of health and ways to preserve health

Figure 1 *A slumped posture strains your lower back.*

Healthy Habits

Do you like playing sports or acting in plays? How does your health affect your favorite activities?

Whatever you do, the better your health is, the better you can perform. Keeping yourself healthy is a daily responsibility.

Taking Care of Your Body

The science of preserving and protecting your health is known as **hygiene.** It sounds simple, but washing your hands is the best way to prevent the spread of disease and infection. You should always wash your hands after using the bathroom and before and after handling food. Taking care of your skin, hair, and teeth is important for good hygiene. Good hygiene includes regularly using sunscreen, shampooing your hair, and brushing and flossing your teeth daily.

Good Posture

Posture is also important to health. Good posture helps you look and feel your best. Bad posture strains your muscles and ligaments and makes breathing difficult. To have good posture, imagine a vertical line passing through your ear, shoulder, hip, knee, and ankle when you stand, as shown in **Figure 1.** When working at a desk, you should maintain good posture by pulling your chair forward and planting your feet firmly on the floor.

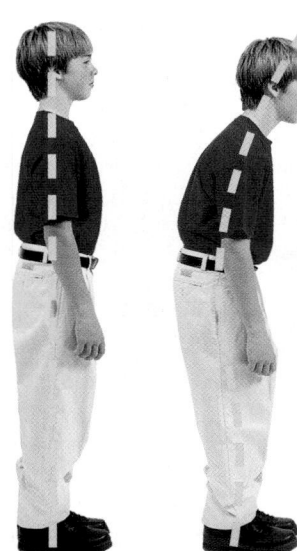

When you have good posture, your ear, shoulder, hip, knee, and ankle are in a straight line.

Bad posture strains your muscles and ligaments and can make breathing difficult.

CHAPTER RESOURCES

Chapter Resource File

 • Lesson Plan
- Directed Reading A **BASIC**
- Directed Reading B **SPECIAL NEEDS**

Technology

 Transparencies
- Bellringer

CONNECTION to
Earth Science ———— ADVANCED

Fossil Hygiene Tell students that they may use fossils as part of their daily hygienic habits. Many toothpastes contain diatomaceous earth, which consists of fossilized diatoms—protist producers with silica shells. The silica in diatomaceous earth polishes the surface of teeth. Ask interested students to research how diatomaceous earth formed and other uses for it. Have students make a poster about their findings. **LS Visual**

Exercise

Aerobic exercise at least three times a week is essential to good health. **Aerobic exercise** is vigorous, constant exercise of the whole body for 20 minutes or more. Walking, running, swimming, and biking are all examples of aerobic exercise. **Figure 2** shows another popular aerobic exercise—basketball.

Aerobic exercise increases the heart rate. As a result, more oxygen is taken in and distributed throughout the body. Over time, aerobic exercise strengthens the heart, lungs, and bones. It burns Calories, helps your body conserve some nutrients, and aids digestion. It also gives you more energy and stamina. Aerobic exercise protects your physical and mental health.

Reading Check What are two benefits of regular exercise? (*See the Appendix for answers to Reading Checks.*)

Sleep

Believe it or not, teenagers actually need more sleep than younger children. Do you ever fall asleep in class, like the girl in **Figure 3,** or feel tired in the middle of the afternoon? If so, you may not be getting enough sleep. Scientists say that teenagers need about 9.5 hours of sleep each night.

At night, the body goes through several cycles of progressively deeper sleep, with periods of lighter sleep in between. If you do not sleep long enough, you will not enter the deepest, most restful period of sleep.

Figure 2 *Aerobic exercise can be fun if you choose an activity you enjoy.*

aerobic exercise physical exercise intended to increase the activity of the heart and lungs to promote the body's use of oxygen

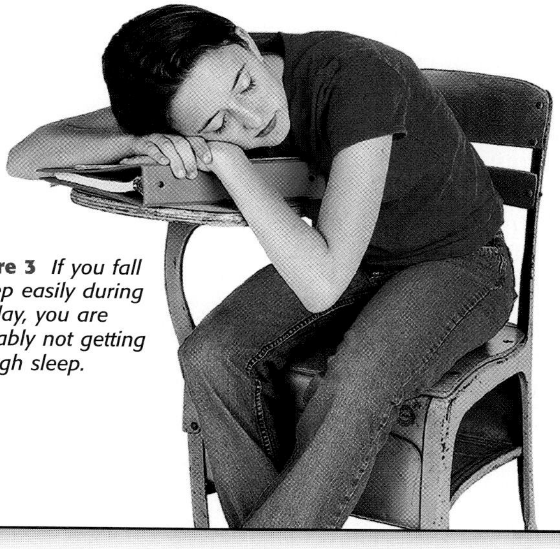

Figure 3 *If you fall asleep easily during the day, you are probably not getting enough sleep.*

CONNECTION TO Language Arts

Dreamy Poetry

You are not wrong, who deem
That my days have been a dream;
Yet if hope has flown away
In a night, or in a day,
In a vision, or in none,
Is it therefore the less gone?
All that we see or seem
Is but a dream within a dream.

(Edgar Allan Poe,
"A Dream Within a Dream")

What do you think Poe means by "a dream within a dream?" Why do you think there are many poems written about dreams or sleep?

WEIRD SCIENCE

Regular, intense exercise decreases body fat. For female athletes who participate in intense exercise frequently, this loss of body fat can restrict the release of estrogen. When this occurs in prepubescent athletes, it delays the onset of puberty. Menstruation is delayed, and the period of bone growth is sometimes extended.

Answer to Connection to Language Arts

Sample answer: "A dream within a dream" could refer to the sense that everything people feel is based on events that have already happened. There are many poems written about dreams because dreams are often strange and can cause strong emotions.

Discussion — GENERAL

Happy Stress Point out to students that although many people think that the term *stress* refers only to the emotional and physical response to negative events, many positive situations also cause stress. Encourage students to identify "happy" events that can create stress. (Sample answers: a new job, the addition of a sibling, and moving to a new house) Point out that stress, whatever its source, produces a physiological reaction that is designed to prepare the body for difficult situations. **LS** Logical/Verbal

CONNECTION ACTIVITY
Real World — GENERAL

Sleep Disorders
Scientists who study people's sleep patterns have learned that about 33% of the general population suffers from a sleep disorder. Ask interested students to research some of these sleep disorders. Students should identify the disorder, characteristics of the disorder, symptoms of the disorder, and ways in which the disorder is treated. Ask students to write a newspaper article about their findings. **LS** Verbal

Figure 4 *Can you identify all of the things in this picture that could cause stress?*

stress a physical or mental response to pressure

For another activity related to this chapter, go to **go.hrw.com** and type in the keyword **HL5BD7W.**

Coping with Stress

You have a big soccer game tomorrow. Are you excited and ready for action? You got a low grade on your English paper. Are you upset or angry? The game and the test are causing you stress. **Stress** is the physical and mental response to pressure.

Some stress is a normal part of life. Stress stimulates your body to prepare for difficult or dangerous situations. However, sometimes you may have no outlet for the stress, and it builds up. Many things are causing stress for the girl shown in **Figure 4.** Excess stress is harmful to your health and can decrease your ability to carry out your daily activities.

You may not even realize you are stressed until your body reacts. Perhaps you get a headache, have an upset stomach, or lie awake at night. You might feel tired all the time or begin an old nervous habit, such as nail-biting. You may become irritable or resentful. All of these things can be signs of too much stress.

Dealing with Stress

Different people are stressed by different things. Once you identify the source of the stress, you can find ways to deal with it. If you cannot remove the cause of stress, here are some ideas for handling stress.

- Share your problems. Talk things over with someone you trust, such as a parent, friend, teacher, or school counselor.
- Make a list of all the things you would like to get done, and rank the things in order of importance. Do the most important things first.
- Exercise regularly, and get enough sleep.
- Pet a friendly animal.
- Spend some quiet time alone, or practice deep breathing or other relaxation techniques.

Homework — GENERAL

Stress Management Ask students, "What are the three things in your life that cause you the most stress?" Have students list the sources of stress in their life and come up with ways of eliminating, reducing, or coping with this stress. Keep in mind that some students are uncomfortable sharing personal information. **LS** Verbal

Injury Prevention

Have you ever fallen off your bike or sprained your ankle? Accidents happen, and they can cause injury and even death. It is impossible to prevent all accidents, but you can decrease your risk by using your common sense and following basic safety rules.

Safety Outdoors

Always dress appropriately for the weather and for the activity. Never hike or camp alone. Tell someone where you are going and when you expect to return. If you do not bring water from home, be sure to purify any water you drink in the wilderness.

Learn how to swim. It could save your life! Never swim alone, and do not dive into shallow water or water of unknown depth. When in a boat, wear a life jacket. If a storm threatens, get out of the water and seek shelter.

✓ **Reading Check** Name three safety tips for the outdoors.

Safety at Home

Many accidents can be avoided. **Figure 5** shows tips for safety around the house.

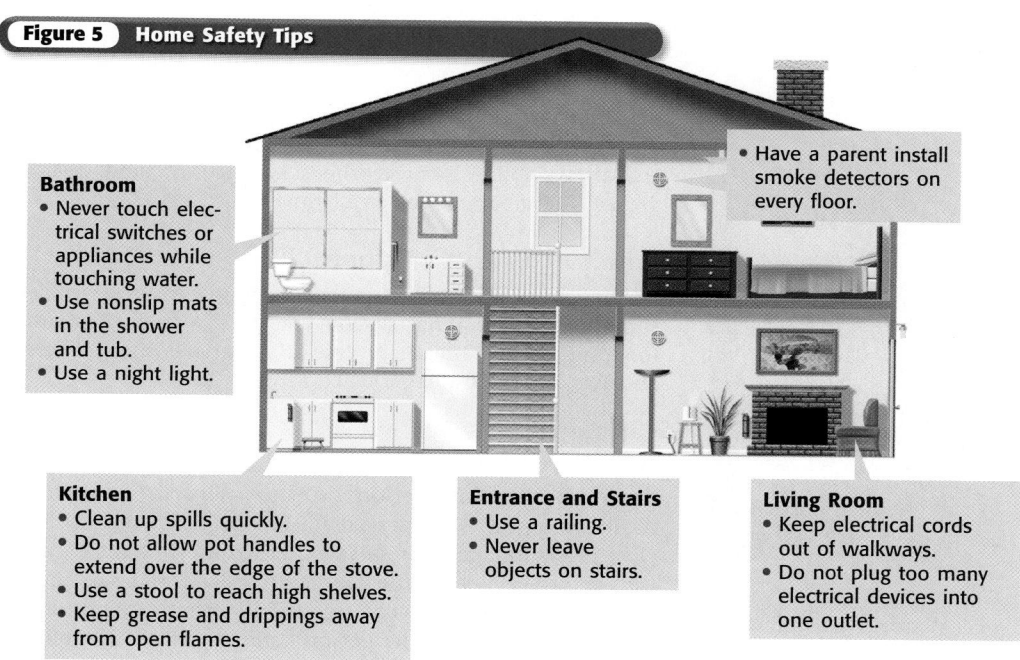

Figure 5 Home Safety Tips

Bathroom
- Never touch electrical switches or appliances while touching water.
- Use nonslip mats in the shower and tub.
- Use a night light.

- Have a parent install smoke detectors on every floor.

Kitchen
- Clean up spills quickly.
- Do not allow pot handles to extend over the edge of the stove.
- Use a stool to reach high shelves.
- Keep grease and drippings away from open flames.

Entrance and Stairs
- Use a railing.
- Never leave objects on stairs.

Living Room
- Keep electrical cords out of walkways.
- Do not plug too many electrical devices into one outlet.

Discussion ⸺ GENERAL

Fatal Injuries Tell students that injuries cause more deaths among children between the ages of 1 and 19 than any major diseases. Point out that bicycle injuries alone cause the death of more than 500 children and teens in the United States each year. Most of these deaths involve head trauma. Remind students that many accidents can be prevented. Experts estimate that the simple act of wearing a bicycle helmet can reduce the risk of head injury by 85%, yet many children don't wear helmets. Ask students why they think people don't wear helmets. (Sample answers: Perhaps some people cannot afford helmets. Some people think that helmets are "funny-looking" or "uncool." Other people may think helmets are uncomfortable.) Ask students if there are other activities in which a helmet protects participants. (Sample answers: skating, snowboarding, football, and hockey) Ask students to brainstorm ways to get more children and teens to wear helmets during physical activity. **LS Verbal**

Group ACTiViTy ⸺ GENERAL

Poster Project Have students work in groups of four, and provide each group with poster board and markers. Have students create posters designed to educate the public about injury prevention. After students present their posters to the class, display the posters in the classroom. **LS Visual**

Homework ⸺ GENERAL

Temperature Injuries Have students research and write a report about the physical symptoms and emergency treatments for hypothermia and heatstroke. **LS Verbal**

Answer to Reading Check

Sample answers: Never hike or camp alone, dress for the weather, learn how to swim, wear a life jacket, and never drink unpurified water.

Taking Care Write the following headings on the board: "Healthy habits," "Coping with stress," and "Preventing injuries." Ask students to write examples of each under the headings. **LS** Logical/Verbal

Quiz — GENERAL

1. List three ways to deal with stress. (Sample answers: Share your problems. Make a list. Exercise regularly. Get enough sleep. Pet a friendly animal. Spend some quiet time alone. Practice relaxation techniques.)

2. What do bicycle helmets and seat belts have in common? (Sample answer: They both decrease the risk of injury from accidents.)

3. When you call for emergency help, what should you tell the operator? (the location of the emergency, the type of accident, the number of people injured, and the types of injuries)

Alternative Assessment — ADVANCED

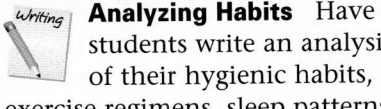 **Analyzing Habits** Have students write an analysis of their hygienic habits, exercise regimens, sleep patterns, and injury risks. Tell students to explain whether their activities and habits are encouraging good health and to describe what changes they might need to make to their routines. **LS** Verbal

Figure 6 *It is always important to use the appropriate safety equipment.*

Safety on the Road

In the car, always wear a seat belt, even if you are traveling only a short distance. Never ride in a car with someone who has been drinking. Safety equipment and common sense are your best defense against injury. When riding a bicycle, always wear a helmet like those shown in **Figure 6.** Ride with traffic, and obey all traffic rules. Be sure to signal when stopping or turning.

Safety in Class

Accidents can happen in school, especially in a lab class or during woodworking class. To avoid hurting yourself and others, always follow your teacher's instructions, and wear the proper safety equipment at all times.

When Accidents Happen

No matter how well you practice safety measures, accidents can still happen. What should you do if a friend chokes on food and cannot breathe? What if a friend is stung by a bee and has a violent allergic reaction?

Figure 7 *When calling 911, stay calm and listen carefully to what the dispatcher tells you.*

Call for Help

Once you've checked for other dangers, call for medical help immediately, as the person shown in **Figure 7** is doing. In most communities, you can dial 911. Speak slowly and clearly. Give the complete address and a description of the location. Describe the accident, the number of people injured, and the types of injuries. Ask what to do, and listen carefully to the instructions. Let the other person hang up first to be sure there are no more questions or instructions for you.

⬤ INCLUSION Strategies

- **Developmentally Delayed** • **Visually Impaired**
- **Learning Disabled**

Students often benefit from verbal activities. Give students a chance to participate by having the class role-play 911 calls. Tell students that the calls should include the following parts:

- slow, clear speech
- description of emergency

- complete address or description of location
- type of injury
- number of people injured
- what has been done to help the victim
- request for instructions
- careful listening

LS Kinesthetic/Verbal

Learn First Aid

If you want to learn more about what to do in an emergency, you can take a first-aid or CPR course, such as the one shown in **Figure 8.** *CPR* can revive a person who is not breathing and has no heartbeat. If you are over 12 years old, you can become certified in both CPR and first aid. Some baby-sitting classes also provide information on first aid. The American Red Cross, community organizations, and local hospitals offer these classes. However, you should not attempt any lifesaving procedure unless you have been trained.

 **Reading Check** What is CPR, and how can you learn it?

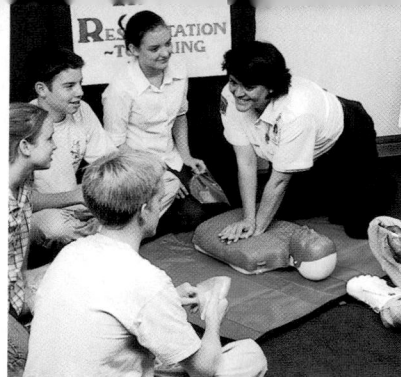

Figure 8 *These teenagers are taking a CPR course to prepare themselves for emergency situations.*

SECTION Review

Summary

- Good hygiene includes taking care of your skin, hair, and teeth.
- Good posture is important to health.
- Exercise keeps your heart, lungs, and bones healthy.
- Teenagers need more than 9 hours of sleep to stay rested and healthy.
- Coping with stress is an important part of staying physically and emotionally healthy.
- It is important to be aware of the possible hazards around your home, outdoors, and at school. Using the appropriate safety equipment can also help keep you safe.

Using Key Terms

Complete each of the following sentences by choosing the correct term from the word bank.

| hygiene | aerobic exercise |
| sleep | stress |

1. The science of protecting your health is called ___.
2. ___ strengthens your heart, lungs, and bones.
3. ___ is the physical and mental response to pressure.

Understanding Key Ideas

4. Which of the following is important for good health?
   a. irregular exercise
   b. getting your hair cut
   c. taking care of your teeth
   d. getting plenty of sun
5. List two things you should do when calling for help in a medical emergency.
6. List three ways to stay safe when you are outside, and three ways to stay safe at home.
7. How do seat belts and safety equipment protect you?

Math Skills

8. It is estimated that only 65% of adults wear their seat belts. If there are 10,000 people driving in your area right now, how many of them are wearing their seat belts?

Critical Thinking

9. **Applying Concepts** What situations cause you stress? What can you do to help relieve the stress you are feeling?
10. **Making Inferences** According to the newspaper, the temperature outside is 61°F right now. Later, it will be 90°F outside. If you and your friends want to play soccer in the park, what should you wear? What should you bring with you?

SCILINKS®

NSTA

Developed and maintained by the National Science Teachers Association

For a variety of links related to this chapter, go to www.scilinks.org

Topic: Safety
SciLinks code: HSM1339

Answer to Reading Check

CPR is a way to revive someone whose heart has stopped beating. CPR classes are available in many places in the community.

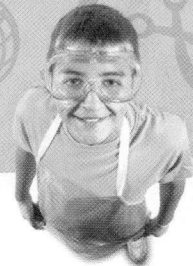

Keep It Clean

Teacher's Notes

Time Required
One 45-minute class period

Lab Ratings

EASY ——————————→ HARD

Teacher Prep 🧪🧪🧪
Student Set-Up 🧪
Concept Level 🧪🧪
Clean Up 🧪🧪

MATERIALS
You can reduce the number of materials needed by having students work in groups and having each group select a volunteer.

Safety Caution
Remind students to review all safety cautions and icons before beginning this lab activity. Check for known allergies to antibacterial soaps or other soaps before beginning the activity. If possible, use plastic Petri dishes.

Skills Practice Lab

OBJECTIVES
Investigate how well antibacterial soap works.
Practice counting bacterial colonies.

MATERIALS
- incubator
- pencil, wax
- Petri dishes, nutrient agar–filled, sterile (3)
- scrub brush, new
- soap, liquid antibacterial
- stopwatch
- tape, transparent

SAFETY

Keep It Clean

One of the best ways to prevent the spread of bacterial and viral infections is to frequently wash your hands with soap and water. Many companies advertise that their soap ingredients can destroy bacteria normally found on the body. In this activity, you will investigate how effective antibacterial soaps are at killing bacteria.

Procedure

1. Keeping the agar plates closed at all times, use the wax pencil to label the bottoms of three agar plates. Label one plate "Control," one plate "No soap," and one plate "Soap."

2. Without washing your hands, carefully press several surfaces of your hands on the agar plate marked "Control." Have your partner immediately put the cover back on the plate. After you touch the agar, do not touch anything with either hand.

3. Hold your right hand under running water for 2 min. Ask your partner to scrub all surfaces of your right hand with the scrub brush throughout these 2 min. Be sure that he or she scrubs under your fingernails. After scrubbing, your partner should turn off the water and open the plate marked "No soap." Touching only the agar, carefully press on the "No soap" plate with the same surfaces of your right hand that you used to press on the "Control" plate.

Elizabeth Rustad
Crane Junior High School
Yuma, Arizona

CHAPTER RESOURCES

Chapter Resource File

- **Datasheet for Chapter Lab**
- **Lab Notes and Answers**

Technology
 Classroom Videos
- Lab Video

 **LabBook**

- To Diet or Not to Diet

4 Repeat step 3, but use your left hand instead of your right. This time, ask your partner to scrub your left hand with liquid antibacterial soap and the scrub brush. Use the plate marked "Soap" instead of the plate marked "No soap."

5 Secure the lid of each plate to its bottom half with transparent tape. Place the plates upside down in the incubator. Incubate all three plates overnight at 37°C.

6 Remove the plates from the incubator, and turn them right side up. Check each plate for the presence of bacterial colonies, and count the number of colonies present on each plate. Record this information. **Caution:** Do not remove the lids on any of the plates.

Analyze the Results

1 **Examining Data** Compare the bacterial growth on the plates. Which plate contained the most growth? Which contained the least?

Draw Conclusions

2 **Drawing Conclusions** Does water alone effectively kill bacteria? Explain.

Applying Your Data

Repeat this experiment, but scrub with regular, not antibacterial, liquid soap. Describe how the results of the two experiments differ.

Analyze the Results
1. Students should observe that the control dish shows the most bacterial growth. Ideally, the dish inoculated after scrubbing hands with antibacterial soap should show the least bacterial growth.

Draw Conclusions
2. Because of chlorine and other agents used to purify drinking water, water alone kills many bacteria. Washing with antibacterial soap for a short time may be only slightly better than washing with water alone.

Applying Your Data
On average, hands must be scrubbed with antibacterial soap for a minimum of 4 minutes to see a significant reduction or absence of bacterial growth in nutrient agar. Ask students if they know how long doctors scrub their hands before surgery. (4–5 min)

Assignment Guide

SECTION	QUESTIONS
1	1–3, 14–15, 17–18
2	4–7, 9, 11–13
3	8, 10, 16, 19–21

ANSWERS

Using Key Terms

1. nutrients
2. Food Guide Pyramid
3. malnutrition
4. addiction
5. drug

Understanding Key Ideas

6. d
7. b
8. c
9. d
10. c
11. a

USING KEY TERMS

Complete each of the following sentences by choosing the correct term from the word bank.

nutrients   Food Guide
addiction   Pyramid
malnutrition   drug

1 Carbohydrates, proteins, fats, vitamins, minerals, and water are the six categories of ___.

2 The ___ divides foods into six groups and gives a recommended number of servings for each group.

3 Both bulimia nervosa and anorexia nervosa cause ___.

4 A physical or psychological dependence on a drug can lead to ___.

5 A(n) ___ is any substance that causes a change in a person's physical or psychological state.

UNDERSTANDING KEY IDEAS

Multiple Choice

6 Which of the following statements about drugs is true?
  a. A child cannot become addicted to drugs.
  b. Smoking just one or two cigarettes is safe for anyone.
  c. Alcohol is not a drug.
  d. Withdrawal symptoms may be painful.

7 What does alcohol do to the central nervous system (CNS)?
  a. It speeds the CNS up.
  b. It slows the CNS down.
  c. It keeps the CNS regulated.
  d. It has no effect on the CNS.

8 To keep your teeth healthy,
  a. brush your teeth as hard as you can.
  b. use a toothbrush until it is worn out.
  c. brush at least twice a day.
  d. floss at least once a week.

9 According to the Food Guide Pyramid, what foods should you eat most?
  a. meats
  b. milk, yogurt, and cheese
  c. fruits and vegetables
  d. bread, cereal, rice, and pasta

10 Which of the following can help you deal with stress?
  a. ignoring your homework
  b. drinking a caffeinated drink
  c. talking to a friend
  d. watching television

11 Tobacco use increases the risk of
  a. lung cancer.
  b. car accidents.
  c. liver damage.
  d. depression.

Short Answer

12 Are all narcotics illegal? Explain.

13 What are three dangers of tobacco and alcohol use?

14 What are the three types of nutrients that provide energy in Calories, and what is the main function of each type in the body?

15 Name two conditions that can lead to malnutrition.

16 Explain why you should always wear safety equipment when you ride your bicycle.

CRITICAL THINKING

17 Concept Mapping Use the following terms to create a concept map: *carbohydrates, water, proteins, nutrients, fats, vitamins, minerals, saturated fats,* and *unsaturated fats.*

18 Applying Concepts You have recently become a vegetarian, and you worry that you are not getting enough protein. Name two foods that you could eat to get more protein.

19 Analyzing Ideas Your two-year-old cousin will be staying with your family. Name three things that you can do to make sure that the house is safe for a young child.

INTERPRETING GRAPHICS

Look at the photos below. The people in the photos are not practicing safe habits. List the unsafe habits shown in these photos. For each unsafe habit, tell what the corresponding safe habit is.

20

21

12. Sample answer: No, not all narcotics are illegal. Some narcotics are prescribed by doctors for the treatment of pain.

13. Sample answer: Alcohol use is a factor in car accidents, and it can cause liver damage. Tobacco use can damage the lungs.

14. Sample answer: Carbohydrates are the body's main source of energy. Fats are energy-storage nutrients. Proteins are used for building and repairing the body.

15. Sample answers: anorexia nervosa, bulimia nervosa, and obesity

16. Sample answer: Safety equipment, such as a helmet, can prevent a head injury if I fall off my bicycle or if I'm involved in an accident.

Critical Thinking

17. 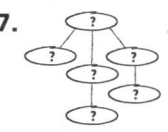 An answer to this exercise can be found at the end of this book.

18. Sample answers: nuts, beans, eggs, and dairy foods

19. Sample answer: Keep objects off the stairs, use a night light, and keep electrical cords out of walkways.

Interpreting Graphics

20. Sample answer: The girl is riding without her seat belt. She needs to fasten her seat belt.

21. Sample answer: A pot handle is hanging over the edge of the stove. The woman should use a pot holder to turn the handle of the pot so that it faces inward.

CHAPTER RESOURCES

Chapter Resource File

- Chapter Review GENERAL
- Chapter Test A GENERAL
- Chapter Test B ADVANCED
- Chapter Test C SPECIAL NEEDS
- Vocabulary Activity GENERAL

Workbooks

Study Guide
- Assessment resources are also available in Spanish.

Standardized Test Preparation

Teacher's Note

To provide practice under more realistic testing conditions, give students 20 minutes to answer all of the questions in this Standardized Test Preparation.

MISCONCEPTION ALERT

Answers to the standardized test preparation can help you identify student misconceptions and misunderstandings.

READING

Passage 1

1. C
2. G
3. B

 **TEST DOCTOR**

Question 3: The passage states that holes in the air sacks of the lungs do not heal. Students may infer that cigarette smoking does not cause all cases of emphysema and bronchitis, but cigarette smoking does cause 80% of cases. Students may think that chronic bronchitis will go away if someone stopped smoking, but the passage states that a chronic disease is a disease that does not go away.

READING

Read each of the passages below. Then, answer the questions that follow each passage.

Passage 1 A <u>chronic</u> disease is a disease that, once developed, is always present and will not go away. Chronic bronchitis is a disease that causes the airways in the lungs to become swollen. This irritation causes a lot of mucus to form in the lungs. As a result, a person who has chronic bronchitis coughs a lot. Another chronic condition is emphysema. Emphysema destroys the tiny air sacs and the walls in the lungs. The holes in the air sacs cannot heal. Eventually, the lung tissue dies, and the lungs can no longer work. Cigarette smoking causes more than 80% of all cases of chronic bronchitis and emphysema.

1. In the passage, what does the word *chronic* mean?
   A disappearing
   B temporary
   C always present
   D mucus filled

2. According to the passage, what disease destroys the tiny air sacs and walls of the lungs?
   F chronic bronchitis
   G emphysema
   H chronic cough
   I cigarette smoking

3. Which of the following is a true statement according to the passage?
   A Holes in the air sacs of lungs heal very quickly.
   B Cigarette smoking causes more than 80% of all cases of chronic bronchitis and emphysema.
   C Cigarette smoking does not cause chronic bronchitis or emphysema.
   D Chronic bronchitis will go away after a person stops smoking cigarettes.

Passage 2 Each body reacts differently to alcohol. Several factors affect how a body reacts to alcohol. A person who has several drinks in a short time is likely to be affected more than a person who has a single drink in the same amount of time. Food in a drinker's stomach can also slow alcohol absorption into the blood. Finally, the way that women absorb and process alcohol differs from the way that men do. If a man and a woman drink the same amount of alcohol, the woman's blood alcohol content (BAC) will be higher than the man's. As BAC increases, mental and physical abilities decline. Muscle coordination, which is especially important for walking and driving, decreases. Vision becomes blurred. Speech and memory are impaired. A high BAC can cause a person to pass out or even die.

1. According to the passage, what does *BAC* stand for?
   A blood alcohol content
   B blood alcohol contaminant
   C blurred alcohol capacity
   D blood alcoholic coordination

2. According to the passage, which of the following factors can affect BAC?
   F time of day
   G food in the stomach
   H age
   I physical activity

3. Which of the following is a fact according to the passage?
   A Alcohol does not affect mood or mental abilities.
   B Men absorb alcohol in the same way that women do.
   C Alcohol decreases muscle coordination.
   D Everybody reacts to alcohol in the same way.

Passage 2

1. A
2. G
3. C

 **TEST DOCTOR**

Question 2: Each body reacts differently to alcohol. However, time of day, age, and physical activity are not mentioned as factors which affect how a person reacts to alcohol. The factors mentioned in the passage include how many drinks a person has over a period of time, whether a person has food in his or her stomach, and gender.

The figure below shows a sample prescription drug label. Use this figure to answer the questions that follow.

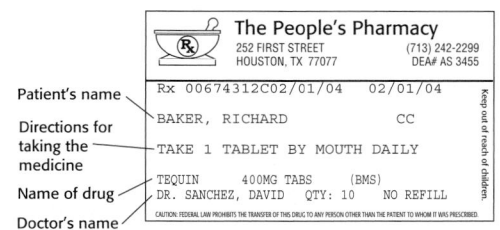

Patient's name	Rx 00674312C02/01/04 02/01/04
Directions for taking the medicine	BAKER, RICHARD CC
	TAKE 1 TABLET BY MOUTH DAILY
Name of drug	TEQUIN 400MG TABS (BMS)
Doctor's name	DR. SANCHEZ, DAVID QTY: 10 NO REFILL

The People's Pharmacy
252 FIRST STREET
HOUSTON, TX 77077
(713) 242-2299
DEA# AS 3455

CAUTION: FEDERAL LAW PROHIBITS THE TRANSFER OF THIS DRUG TO ANY PERSON OTHER THAN THE PATIENT TO WHOM IT WAS PRESCRIBED.

Keep out of reach of children.

1. According to the label, what is the patient's name?
 A Richard Baker
 B Baker Richard
 C David Sanchez
 D James Beard

2. According to the label, how often should the medication be taken?
 F once a day
 G twice a day
 H three times a day
 I once a week

3. According to the label, how many refills remain on the prescription?
 A 0
 B 1
 C 2
 D 3

4. If this patient follows the directions exactly, how long will he need to take this medicine?
 F 1 day
 G 5 days
 H 10 days
 I There is not enough data to determine the answer.

Read each question below, and choose the best answer.

1. Which of the following ratios is equal to 2/4?
 A 1/2
 B 17/18
 C 5/2
 D 7/2

2. If 1 gal = 3.79 L, how many liters are in 3 gal?
 F 3.79 L
 G 7.58 L
 H 11.37 L
 I 15.16 L

3. Approximately how many liters are in 5 gal?
 A 5 L
 B 10 L
 C 20 L
 D 30 L

4. Ada has just built a car for a Pinewood Derby. She wants to find the average speed of her new car. During her first test run, she goes 5 mi/h. During her second run, she goes 4 mi/h, and in her third run, she goes 6 mi/h. What is her average speed?
 F 4 mi/h
 G 5 mi/h
 H 6 mi/h
 I 7 mi/h

5. Which of the following numbers is largest?
 A 1×10^2
 B 1×10^5
 C 3×10^5
 D 5×10^4

6. On Saturday, Mae won a goldfish at the school carnival. On the way home, Mae and her mother bought a fishbowl for $10.25, a container of fish food for $3.75, and a plastic coral for $8.15. How much money did Mae and her mother spend?
 F $11.90
 G $18.40
 H $22.15
 I $30.30

Standardized Test Preparation

 1. A
 2. F
 3. A
 4. H

 TEST DOCTOR

Question 1: Baker Richard is the reversed form of the patient's name. It starts with the patient's last name. David Sanchez is the doctor who prescribed the drug, and James Beard is not a name that appears on the label.

 1. A
 2. H
 3. C
 4. G
 5. C
 6. H

 **TEST DOCTOR**

Question 1: 2/4 can be simplified to 1/2, or one-half of the whole. 17/18 is almost equal to the whole and 5/2 and 7/2 are greater than the whole. Students struggling with fractions may benefit from working with visual aids, such as wooden blocks.

Question 5: 1×10^2 is the smallest number in the answer choices. Some students may base their answer on the power of ten alone and answer 1×10^5, not realizing that 3×10^5 is a larger number. Some students may answer 5×10^4 because 5 is larger than 1 and 3, which are used in the other answer choices. However, a higher power of ten is used in two of the other answer choices.

CHAPTER RESOURCES

Chapter Resource File
 • Standardized Test Preparation GENERAL

State Resources
For specific resources for your state, visit **go.hrw.com** and type in the keyword **HSMSTR**.

Science, Technology, and Society

Teaching Strategy ADVANCED

Explain that a protein consists of a long chain of amino acids. Assign each student one of the 20 common amino acids to investigate. Tell students to find out what foods the amino acid can be found in and what function it serves in the body. Then, on a large index card, have students write information about the amino acid and make illustrations of food sources for the amino acid. Use the index cards to make a poster for the class.

Scientific Discoveries

Background

The female athlete triad is most likely to begin with an attempt to lose weight, which leads to disordered eating. Disordered eating ranges from moderate restriction of food intake to eating disorders, such as anorexia nervosa and bulimia nervosa. Signs that a girl may have disordered eating include a preoccupation with food and weight, a constant expression of being too fat, eating alone, use of laxatives, and trips to the bathroom immediately after eating.

Science in Action

Bones can become severely weakened by the female athlete triad.

Scientific Discoveries

Female Athlete Triad

Getting enough exercise is an important part of staying healthy. But in 1992, doctors learned that too much exercise can be harmful for women. When a girl or woman exercises too much, three things can happen. She may lose too much weight. She may stop having her period. And her bones may become very weak. These three symptoms form the female athlete triad. To prevent this condition, female athletes need to take in enough Calories. Women who exercise heavily and try to lose weight may have a reduction in estrogen. Estrogen is the hormone that helps regulate the menstrual cycle. Low levels of estrogen and inadequate nutrition can cause bones to become weak and brittle. The photo above shows bone that has been weakened greatly.

Science, Technology, and Society

Meatless Munching

Recent studies suggest that a vegetarian diet may reduce the risk of heart disease, adult-onset diabetes, and some forms of cancer. However, a vegetarian diet takes careful planning. Vegetarians must ensure that they get the proper balance of protein and vitamins in their diet. New foods that can help vegetarians remain healthy are being developed constantly. Meat substitutes are now made from soybeans, textured vegetable protein, and tofu. One new food, which is shown above, is made of a fungus that is a relative of mushrooms and truffles.

Social Studies ACTiViTY

WRITING SKILL Research a culture that has a mostly vegetarian diet, such as Hindu or Buddhist. What kinds of food do the people eat? Why don't they eat animals? Write a short report on your findings.

Math ACTiViTY

Some scientists recommend that teenagers get 1,200 to 1,500 mg of calcium every day. A cup of milk has 300 mg of calcium, and a serving of yogurt has 400 mg of calcium. Calculate two combinations of milk and yogurt that would give you the recommended 1,500 mg of calcium.

Answer to Social Studies Activity

Answers may vary. Students should identify some foods eaten by the people in the cultures that they research. Students should also identify reasons such as religious beliefs, cultural traditions, and the availability of meat as reasons why people in these cultures have vegetarian diets.

Answer to Math Activity

Sample answer: 1 serving of yogurt and 4 cups of milk (4 × 300 mg = 1200 mg calcium; 1200 mg + 400 mg = 1600 mg calcium), or 3 cups of milk and 2 servings of yogurt (3 × 300 mg = 900 mg calcium; 2 × 400 mg = 800 mg calcium; 900 mg + 800 mg = 1700 mg calcium)

Russell Selger

Guidance Counselor Guidance counselors help students think about their future by helping them discover their interests. After focusing their interests, a guidance counselor helps students plan a good academic schedule. A guidance counselor might talk to you about taking an art or computer science class that may help you discover a hidden talent. Many skills are vital to being a good guidance counselor. The job requires empathy, which is the ability to understand and sympathize with another person's feelings. Counselors also need patience, good listening skills, and a love of helping young people. Russell Selger, a guidance counselor at Timberlane Middle School, has a great respect for middle school students. "The kids are just alive. They want to learn. There's something about the spark that they have, and it's so much fun to guide them through all of this stuff," he explains.

Language Arts ACTIVITY

WRITING SKILL Visit the guidance counselor's office at your school. What services does your guidance counselor offer? Conduct an interview with a guidance counselor. Ask why he or she became a counselor. Write an article for the school paper about your findings.

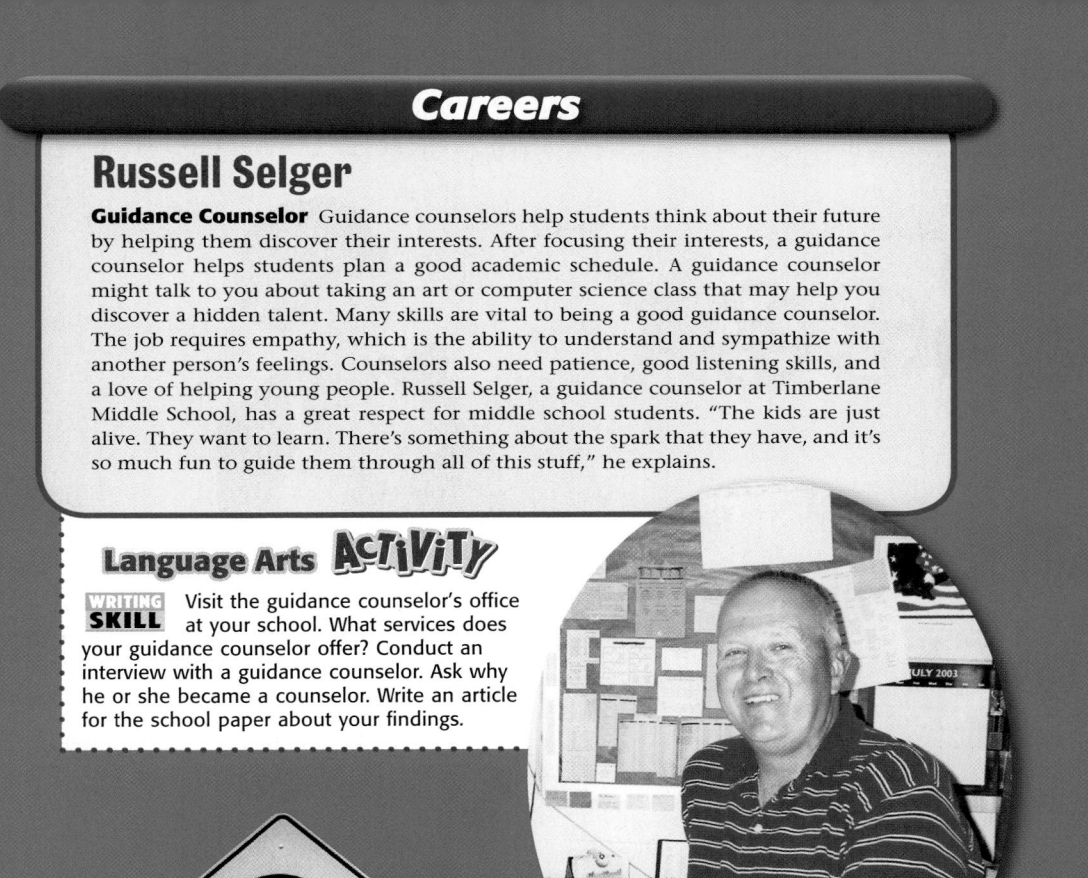

go.hrw.com
To learn more about these Science in Action topics, visit **go.hrw.com** and type in the keyword **HL5BD7F**.

Current Science
Check out Current Science® articles related to this chapter by visiting go.hrw.com. Just type in the keyword **HL5CS28**.

Careers
Discussion ——— GENERAL
Ask students the following questions: "What do you think guidance counselors talk to students about?" (Many students will likely say grades and future career options. Help students understand that guidance counselors can also help them with other problems, such as stress management, conflict management, and mediation.) "What skills does a good guidance counselor need?" (Sample answers: good listening skills, patience, and empathy)

Answer to Language Arts Activity
Answers may vary.

LabBook

Contents

Graphing Data

Teacher's Notes

Time Required
One 45-minute class period

Lab Ratings

EASY —————————→ HARD

Teacher Prep 🧪🧪
Student Set-Up 🧪
Concept Level 🧪
Clean Up 🧪

Safety Caution

Caution students to exercise proper care when handling the beaker of hot water. Also, caution students to be careful when they are moving around an electrical cord. A clip that will hold the thermometer to the side of the beaker and off the bottom of the beaker while it is heating or cooling is safer and more accurate than a thermometer simply propped up inside the beaker.

Analyze the Results

1. Answers may vary according to several factors, including altitude.
2. Answers may vary.

Skills Practice Lab

Graphing Data

When performing an experiment, you usually need to collect data. To understand the data, you can often organize them into a graph. Graphs can show trends and patterns that you might not notice in a table or list. In this exercise, you will practice collecting data and organizing the data into a graph.

Procedure

1. Pour 200 mL of water into a 400 mL beaker. Add ice to the beaker until the waterline is at the 400 mL mark.

2. Place a Celsius thermometer into the beaker. Use a thermometer clip to prevent the thermometer from touching the bottom of the beaker. Record the temperature of the ice water.

3. Place the beaker and thermometer on a hot plate. Turn the hot plate on medium heat, and record the temperature every minute until the water temperature reaches 100°C.

4. Using heat-resistant gloves, remove the beaker from the hot plate. Continue to record the temperature of the water each minute for 10 more minutes. **Caution:** Don't forget to turn off the hot plate.

5. On a piece of graph paper, create a graph similar to the one below. Label the horizontal axis (the x-axis) "Time (min)," and mark the axis in increments of 1 min as shown. Label the vertical axis (the y-axis) "Temperature (°C)," and mark the axis in increments of 10° as shown.

6. Find the 1 min mark on the x-axis, and move up the graph to the temperature you recorded at 1 min. Place a dot on the graph at that point. Plot each temperature in the same way. When you have plotted all of your data, connect the dots with a smooth line.

MATERIALS

- beaker, 400 mL
- clock (or watch) with a second hand
- gloves, heat-resistant
- hot plate
- ice
- paper, graph
- thermometer, Celsius, with a clip
- water, 200 mL

SAFETY

Analyze the Results

1. Examine your graph. Do you think the water heated faster than it cooled? Explain.

2. Estimate what the temperature of the water was 2.5 min after you placed the beaker on the hot plate. Explain how you can make a good estimate of temperature between those you recorded.

Draw Conclusions

3. Explain how a graph may give more information than the same data in a table.

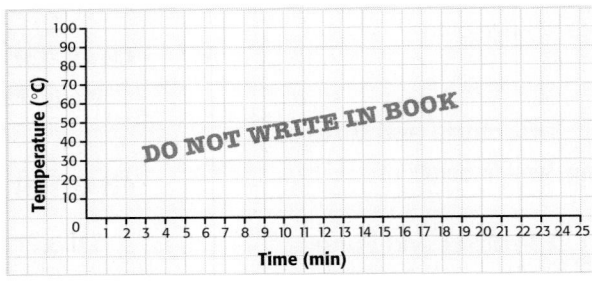

Draw Conclusions

3. A list or a chart is organized information, and sometimes it is necessary to put collected data into one of these forms before graphing. Because a graph is like a picture, it can often help scientists see what is happening when numbers alone would be confusing. A graph can show a trend or a pattern that may not be readily discernible in a list or chart.

CHAPTER RESOURCES

Chapter Resource File

- Datasheet for LabBook
- Lab Notes and Answers

Edith C. McAlanis
Socorro Middle School
El Paso, Texas

Model-Making Lab

A Window to a Hidden World

Have you ever noticed that objects underwater appear closer than they really are? The reason is that light waves change speed when they travel from air into water. Anton van Leeuwenhoek, a pioneer of microscopy in the late 17th century, used a drop of water to magnify objects. That drop of water brought a hidden world closer into view. How did Leeuwenhoek's microscope work? In this investigation, you will build a model of it to find out.

MATERIALS

- eyedropper
- hole punch
- newspaper
- plastic wrap, clear
- poster board, 3 cm × 10 cm
- tape, transparent
- water

Procedure

1. Punch a hole in the center of the poster board with a hole punch, as shown in (a) at right.

2. Tape a small piece of clear plastic wrap over the hole, as shown in (b) at right. Be sure the plastic wrap is large enough so that the tape you use to secure it does not cover the hole.

3. Use an eyedropper to put one drop of water over the hole. Check to be sure your drop of water is dome-shaped (convex), as shown in (c) at right.

4. Hold the microscope close to your eye and look through the drop. Be careful not to disturb the water drop.

5. Hold the microscope over a piece of newspaper, and observe the image.

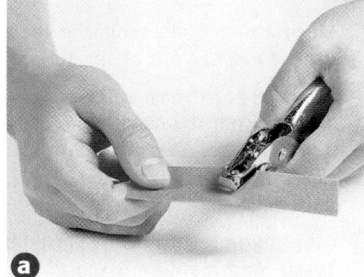

(a)

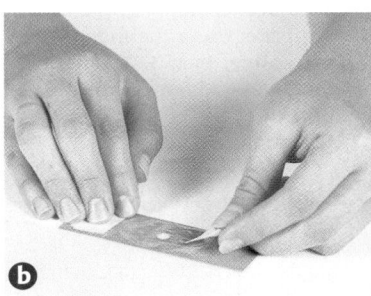

(b)

(c)

Analyze the Results

1. Describe and draw the image you see. Is the image larger than or the same size as it is without the microscope? Is the image clear or blurred? Is the shape of the image distorted?

Draw Conclusions

2. How do you think your model could be improved?

Applying Your Data

Robert Hooke and Zacharias Janssen contributed much to the field of microscopy. Research one of them, and write a paragraph about his contributions.

A Window to a Hidden World

Teacher's Notes

Time Required
One 45-minute class period

Lab Ratings

EASY ————————→ HARD

Teacher Prep 🧪🧪
Student Set-Up 🧪🧪
Concept Level 🧪
Clean Up 🧪

MATERIALS

The materials listed on the student page are enough for a group of 4–5 students. A 3 in. × 5 in. index card cut in half lengthwise can substitute for a stiff piece of poster board. It can be difficult to eliminate wrinkles in the plastic over the hole. Some students may need assistance.

Analyze the Results

1. Answers may vary. Students should see a slightly larger image. It will be blurred, especially around the edges. The image may be distorted.

Draw Conclusions

2. Some students may think their model could be improved by eliminating the wrinkles over the hole.

CHAPTER RESOURCES

Chapter Resource File

- Datasheet for LabBook
- Lab Notes and Answers

CLASSROOM TESTED & APPROVED

Georgiann Delgadillo
East Valley School District
Continuous Curriculum School
Spokane, Washington

Applying Your Data

Robert Hooke (1635–1703), one of the world's great inventors, is famous for his discovery of "cells" in cork tissue as seen through his improved microscope. Hooke was also a keen observer with an interest in fossils and geology. Zacharias Janssen, a Dutch lens grinder, mounted two lenses in a tube to produce the first compound microscope in 1590.

The Best-Bread Bakery Dilemma

Teacher's Notes

Time Required

Two 45-minute class periods

Lab Ratings

EASY ———————————→ HARD

Teacher Prep 🧪🧪
Student Set-Up 🧪
Concept Level 🧪
Clean Up 🧪

MATERIALS

The materials listed on the student page are enough for a group of 3–4 students. Yeast is easily obtained from the local grocery store. The school cafeteria may be willing to donate the amount you need.

You may wish to add other materials in anticipation of students' experimental design. For example, some students may recognize that they could collect CO_2 in a balloon attached to the top of a test tube containing live yeast.

Skills Practice Lab

The Best-Bread Bakery Dilemma

The chief baker at the Best-Bread Bakery thinks that the yeast the bakery received may be dead. Yeast is a central ingredient in bread. Yeast is a living organism, a member of the kingdom Fungi, and it undergoes the same life processes as other living organisms. When yeast grows in the presence of oxygen and other nutrients, yeast produces carbon dioxide. The gas forms bubbles that cause bread dough to rise. Thousands of dollars may be lost if the yeast is dead.

The Best-Bread Bakery has requested that you test the yeast. The bakery has furnished samples of live yeast and some samples of the yeast in question.

Procedure

1. Make a data table similar to the one below. Leave plenty of room to write your observations.

2. Examine each yeast sample with a magnifying lens. You may want to sniff the samples to determine the presence of an odor. (Your teacher will demonstrate the appropriate way to detect odors in this lab.) Record your observations in the data table.

3. Label three test tubes or plastic cups "Live Yeast," "Sample A Yeast," and "Sample B Yeast."

4. Fill a beaker with 125 mL of water, and place the beaker on a hot plate. Use a thermometer to be sure the water does not get warmer than 32°C. Attach the thermometer to the side of the beaker with a clip so the thermometer doesn't touch the bottom of the beaker. Turn off the hot plate when the water temperature reaches 32°C.

MATERIALS

- beaker, 250 mL
- flour
- gloves, heat-resistant
- graduated cylinder
- hot plate
- magnifying lens
- scoopula (or small spoon)
- stirring sticks, wooden (3)
- sugar
- test-tube rack
- test tubes (3) (or clear plastic cups)
- thermometer, Celsius, with clip
- water, 125 mL
- yeast samples (live, A, and B)

SAFETY

Yeast sample	Observations	0 min	5 min	10 min	15 min	20 min	25 min	Dead or alive?
Live								
Sample A			DO NOT WRITE IN BOOK					
Sample B								

Safety Caution

Remind students to review all safety cautions and icons before beginning this lab activity.

Caution students to be careful of the hot plate and the cord. You should demonstrate the proper lab technique for determining the presence of an odor. Hold the container away from your face about 25 cm and just below your nose. Use the other hand to "waft" the odor toward your face. Caution students NEVER to put their noses directly in a container and inhale.

CHAPTER RESOURCES

Chapter Resource File

- Datasheet for LabBook
- Lab Notes and Answers

CLASSROOM TESTED & APPROVED

Susan Gorman
North Ridge Middle School
North Richland Hills, Texas

⑤ Add a small scoop (about 1/2 tsp) of each yeast sample to the correctly labeled container. Add a small scoop of sugar to each container.

⑥ Add 10 mL of the warm water to each container, and stir.

⑦ Add a small scoop of flour to each container, and stir again. The flour will help make the process more visible but is not necessary as food for the yeast.

⑧ Observe the samples carefully. Look for bubbles. Make observations at 5 min intervals. Write your observations in the data table.

⑨ In the last column of the data table, write "alive" or "dead" based on your observations during the experiment.

Analyze the Results

① Describe any differences in the yeast samples before the experiment.

② Describe the appearance of the yeast samples at the conclusion of the experiment.

③ Why was a sample of live yeast included in the experiment?

④ Why was sugar added to the samples?

⑤ Based on your observations, is either Sample A or Sample B alive?

Draw Conclusions

⑥ Write a letter to the Best-Bread Bakery stating your recommendation to use or not use the yeast samples. Give reasons for your recommendation.

Applying Your Data

Based on your observations of the nutrient requirements of yeast, design an experiment to determine the ideal combination of nutrients. Vary the amount of nutrients, or examine different energy sources.

Preparation Notes

At least one of the suspect samples should be killed yeast. To kill the yeast, place the yeast in an oven at 400°F for 10 min or in a microwave oven for a few minutes at high power. Do not allow yeast to become moist before use. Toothpicks, coffee stirrers and so on, may be used for stirring. The amounts of each ingredient used are not definite, and you may wish to vary amounts, depending on the results desired.

Lab Notes

To help students prepare for this activity, you may wish to review cellular respiration and fermentation. The equation for respiration follows: $C_6H_{12}O_6 + 6O_2 \rightarrow 6CO_2 + 6H_2O + energy$.

Analyze Results

1. Answers are based on students' observations and may vary.

2. Answers may vary.

3. Sample answer: Live yeast was included so that bubble formation from the respiration of living organisms could be observed.

4. Sugar was added as a nutrient for the living yeast.

5. Answers may vary according to students' experimental protocol.

Draw Conclusions

6. Student letters may vary but should recommend the optimal samples they determined in their experiment.

Cells Alive!

Teacher's Notes

Time Required
One 45-minute class period

Lab Ratings

EASY ————————→ HARD

Teacher Prep
Student Set-Up
Concept Level
Clean Up

MATERIALS
The materials listed on the student page are enough for a group of 3–4 students. Be sure to keep the algae in a warm, damp place out of direct sunlight; a closed plastic bag with water sprayed into it is ideal.

Procedure
4. Chloroplasts are the parts of the cell that are responsible for photosynthesis.
5. The nucleus of a cell controls most of the activities that take place in that cell and contains the hereditary information.
6. The cytoplasm is a clear gel-like substance that fills the cell and surrounds the organelles. The organelles are floating around in the cytoplasm.

Skills Practice Lab

Cells Alive!
You have probably used a microscope to look at single-celled organisms such as those shown below. They can be found in pond water. In the following exercise, you will look at *Protococcus*—algae that form a greenish stain on tree trunks, wooden fences, flowerpots, and buildings.

MATERIALS
- eyedropper
- microscope
- microscope slide and coverslip
- *Protococcus* (or other algae)
- water

SAFETY

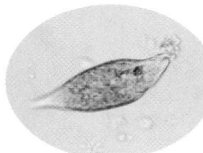
Euglena

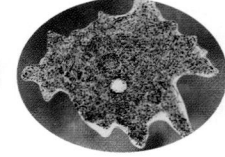
Amoeba

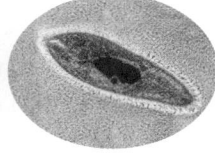
Paramecium

Procedure
1. Locate some *Protococcus*. Scrape a small sample into a container. Bring the sample to the classroom, and make a wet mount of it as directed by your teacher. If you can't find *Protococcus* outdoors, look for algae on the glass in an aquarium. Such algae may not be *Protococcus,* but it will be a very good substitute.

2. Set the microscope on low power to examine the algae. On a separate sheet of paper, draw the cells that you see.

3. Switch to high power to examine a single cell. Draw the cell.

4. You will probably notice that each cell contains several chloroplasts. Label a chloroplast on your drawing. What is the function of the chloroplast?

5. Another structure that should be clearly visible in all the algae cells is the nucleus. Find the nucleus in one of your cells, and label it on your drawing. What is the function of the nucleus?

6. What does the cytoplasm look like? Describe any movement you see inside the cells.

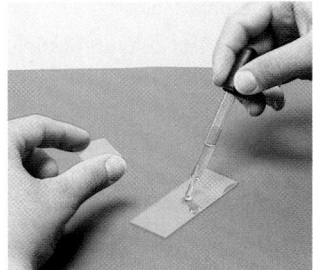

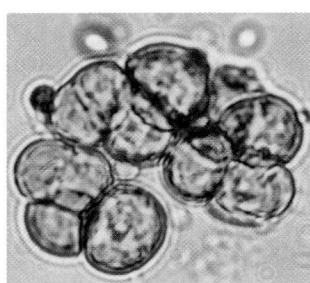
Protococcus

Analyze the Results
1. Are *Protococcus* single-celled organisms or multicellular organisms?

2. How are *Protococcus* different from amoebas?

Analyze the Results
1. *Protococcus* is a genus composed of single-celled algae.
2. Many answers are possible, but the following are most likely: *Protococcus* cannot move about as amoebas can; unlike amoebas, they are green and photosynthesize.

CHAPTER RESOURCES

Chapter Resource File
- Datasheet for LabBook
- Lab Notes and Answers

CLASSROOM TESTED & APPROVED

Terry Rakes
Elmwood Junior High School
Rogers, Arkansas

Skills Practice Lab

Stayin' Alive!

Every second of your life, your body's trillions of cells take in, use, and store energy. They repair themselves, reproduce, and get rid of waste. Together, these processes are called *metabolism*. Your cells use the food that you eat to provide the energy you need to stay alive.

Your Basal Metabolic Rate (BMR) is a measurement of the energy that your body needs to carry out all the basic life processes while you are at rest. These processes include breathing, keeping your heart beating, and keeping your body's temperature stable. Your BMR is influenced by your gender, your age, and many other things. Your BMR may be different from everyone else's, but it is normal for you. In this activity, you will find the amount of energy, measured in Calories, you need every day in order to stay alive.

MATERIALS

- bathroom scale
- tape measure

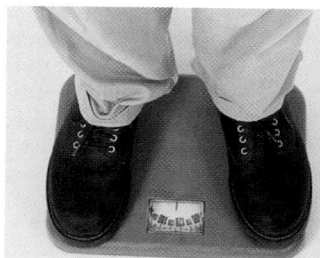

Procedure

1 Find your weight on a bathroom scale. If the scale measures in pounds, you must convert your weight in pounds to your mass in kilograms. To convert your weight in pounds (lb) to mass in kilograms (kg), multiply the number of pounds by 0.454.

Example: If Carlos weighs 125 lb, his mass in kilograms is:

$$
\begin{array}{r}
125 \text{ lb} \\
\times\ \underline{0.454} \\
56.75 \text{ kg}
\end{array}
$$

2 Use a tape measure to find your height. If the tape measures in inches, convert your height in inches to height in centimeters. To convert your height in inches (in.) to your height in centimeters (cm), multiply the number of inches by 2.54.

If Carlos is 62 in. tall, his height in centimeters is:

$$
\begin{array}{r}
62 \text{ in.} \\
\times\ \underline{2.54} \\
157.48 \text{ cm}
\end{array}
$$

CHAPTER RESOURCES

Chapter Resource File

- Datasheet for LabBook
- Lab Notes and Answers

Kathy LaRoe
East Valley Middle School
East Helena, Montana

Teacher's Notes

Time Required
One 45-minute class period

Lab Ratings

EASY ———————————→ HARD

Teacher Prep 🧪
Student Set-Up 🧪
Concept Level 🧪
Clean Up 🧪

MATERIALS

The materials listed on the student page are enough for each group of 5–6 students. You may wish to have your students use a calculator to complete this activity.

Preparation Notes

Some students may consider their height and weight to be personal and won't want to weigh and measure themselves with the others in the class. Give these students the option of using the data of a fictional person, such as one of the following:

Jenny	80 lb	4 ft	age 11
Ben	65 lb	3 ft	age 12
Carlos	110 lb	5 ft 2 in.	age 11
Alexa	120 lb	4 ft 6 in.	age 12
Tasheika	90 lb	4 ft 6 in.	age 13

Lab Notes

Some students will think that their basal metabolic rate, or BMR, is impossibly low. Emphasize that the BMR is the number of Calories a body needs just to keep the heart beating, the lungs breathing, and the cells respiring. The BMR is not the number of Calories a person needs for an active lifestyle.

Of course, a person can consume fewer than that number of Calories for a day, or even for a few days, without dying. Explain that the Calories required to live during starvation conditions are obtained from stored fat. When there is no more fat, then the energy comes from muscle tissue. Under extreme conditions of starvation, the body even begins to shut down some organ functions that use energy but that are not required for survival, such as the uterine cycle in women.

Some students may ask why the BMR numbers are so much higher in males than in females. Explain that before puberty, the numbers are much closer together. But as boys approach puberty, they generally develop a higher muscle-to-fat ratio than girls do. Cellular respiration for muscle tissue requires more energy than for fat tissue.

③ Now that you know your height and mass, use the appropriate formula below to get a close estimate of your BMR. Your answer will give you an estimate of the number of Calories your body needs each day just to stay alive.

Calculating Your BMR	
Females	**Males**
65 + (10 × your mass in kilograms) + (1.8 × your height in centimeters) − (4.7 × your age in years)	66 + (13.5 × your mass in kilograms) + (5 × your height in centimeters) − (6.8 × your age in years)

④ Your metabolism is also influenced by how active you are. Talking, walking, and playing games all take more energy than being at rest. To get an idea of how many Calories your body needs each day to stay healthy, select the lifestyle that best describes yours from the table at right. Then multiply your BMR by the activity factor.

Analyze the Results

❶ In what way could you compare your whole body to a single cell? Explain.

❷ Does an increase in activity increase your BMR? Does an increase in activity increase your need for Calories? Explain your answers.

Draw Conclusions

❸ If you are moderately inactive, how many more Calories would you need if you began to exercise every day?

Activity Factors	
Activity lifestyle	**Activity factor**
Moderately inactive (normal, everyday activities)	1.3
Moderately active (exercise 3 to 4 times a week)	1.4
Very active (exercise 4 to 6 times a week)	1.6
Extremely active (exercise 6 to 7 times a week)	1.8

Applying Your Data

The best energy sources are those that supply the correct amount of Calories for your lifestyle and also provide the nutrients you need. Research in the library or on the Internet to find out which kinds of foods are the best energy sources for you. How does your list of best energy sources compare with your diet?

List everything you eat and drink in 1 day. Find out how many Calories are in each item, and find the total number of Calories you have consumed. How does this number of Calories compare with the number of Calories you need each day for all your activities?

Analyze the Results

1. Sample answer: Just as each cell needs energy on a small scale, your body requires energy on a much larger scale.

2. Sample answer: Technically, the BMR does not change with activity. The BMR is the minimum amount of energy a person needs to stay alive. Activity requires that more energy be added to the BMR, thereby increasing the need for Calories.

Draw Conclusions

3. Students should multiply their own BMR by 1.3 and then multiply their BMR by 1.8. Students should subtract the smaller number from the larger number. This number represents the additional Calories per day the student would expend shifting from a moderately inactive state to an extremely active one.

Inquiry Lab

Tracing Traits

Have you ever wondered about the traits you inherited from your parents? Do you have a trait that neither of your parents has? In this project, you will develop a family tree, or pedigree, similar to the one shown in the diagram below. You will trace an inherited trait through a family to determine how it has passed from generation to generation.

Procedure

❶ The diagram at right shows a family history. On a separate piece of paper, draw a similar diagram of the family you have chosen. Include as many family members as possible, such as grandparents, parents, children, and grandchildren. Use circles to represent females and squares to represent males. You may include other information, such as the family member's name, birth date, or picture.

❷ Draw a table similar to the one on the next page. Survey each of the family members shown in your family tree. Ask them if they have hair on the middle segment of their fingers. Write each person's name in the appropriate square. Explain to each person that it is normal to have either trait. The presence of hair on the middle segment is the dominant form of this trait.

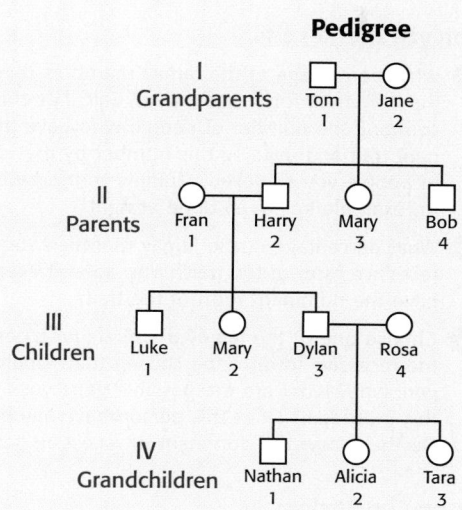

Pedigree

I Grandparents — Tom 1, Jane 2

II Parents — Fran 1, Harry 2, Mary 3, Bob 4

III Children — Luke 1, Mary 2, Dylan 3, Rosa 4

IV Grandchildren — Nathan 1, Alicia 2, Tara 3

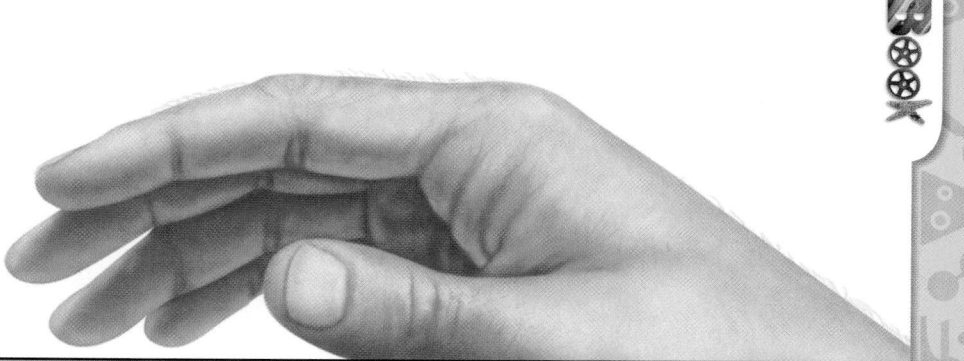

CHAPTER RESOURCES

Chapter Resource File

- Datasheet for LabBook
- Lab Notes and Answers

CLASSROOM TESTED & APPROVED

Kerry Johnson
Isbell Middle School
Santa Paula, California

Tracing Traits

Teacher's Notes

Time Required

Two 45-minute class periods, separated by several days so students have time to complete their surveys

Lab Ratings

EASY ⟶ HARD

Teacher Prep 🧪
Student Set-Up 🧪
Concept Level 🧪🧪
Clean Up 🧪

Lab Notes

Family histories will vary. Encourage students to include at least three generations in their histories.

Survey results will vary. Make sure that students actually surveyed each family member who was available. Responses will vary. You may check family members with shaded symbols against the survey results for accuracy.

Percentages will vary. A family member may receive a recessive allele from the father and a recessive allele from the mother. In such a case, this family member will exhibit the recessive form of the trait rather than the dominant form.

Because so many children are adopted or live in foster homes or group homes, please emphasize to your students that they may choose any family to study.

Analyze the Results

1. Answers may vary.

2. Answers may vary.

3. The genotype of the recessive form of the characteristic must be *hh* (homozygous recessive). Each allele came from one of the individual's parents; Possible genotypes for the parents of the individual expressing the recessive form are *Hh* and *hh*; Does the student know whether either of the parents expresses the recessive form of the trait? Does the student know if the individual chosen has brothers or sisters? Are their genotypes known? If so, have the student decide if each of them has a dominant or recessive genotype. If a dominant genotype is found among the siblings and one of the parents is known to have the recessive form, ask the student what the genotype of the other parent must be (*Hh*).

Draw Conclusions

4. The Punnett square should show *hh* in the bottom right-hand corner. One of the parents must have the genotype *hh*. The other parent must have either *hh* or *Hh*. If any sibling has the dominant trait, the genotype of the other parent must be *Hh*.

Dominant trait	Recessive trait	Family members with the dominant trait	Family members with the recessive trait
Hair present on the middle segment of fingers (*H*)	Hair absent on the middle segment of fingers (*h*)	DO NOT WRITE IN BOOK	

3 Trace this trait throughout the family tree you diagrammed in step 1. Shade or color the symbols of the family members who demonstrate the dominant form of this trait.

Analyze the Results

1 What percentage of the family members demonstrate the dominant form of the trait? Calculate this by counting the number of people who have the dominant trait and dividing this number by the total number of people you surveyed. Multiply your answer by 100. An example has been done at right.

2 What percentage of the family members demonstrate the recessive form of the trait? Why doesn't every family member have the dominant form of the trait?

3 Choose one of the family members who demonstrates the recessive form of the chosen trait. What is this person's genotype? What are the possible genotypes for the parents of this individual? Does this person have any brothers or sisters? Do they show the dominant or recessive trait?

Example: Calculating percentage

$$\frac{10 \text{ people with trait}}{20 \text{ people surveyed}} = \frac{1}{2}$$

$$\frac{1}{2} = 0.50 \times 100 = 50\%$$

Draw Conclusions

4 Draw a Punnett square like the one at right. Use this to determine the genotypes of the parents of the person you chose in step 3. Write this person's genotype in the bottom right-hand corner of your Punnett square. **Hint:** There may be more than one possible genotype for the parents. Don't forget to consider the genotypes of the person's brothers and sisters.

Father

Mother

	?	?
?		
?		

Skills Practice Lab

The Half-life of Pennies

Carbon-14 is a special unstable element used in the absolute dating of material that was once alive, such as fossil bones. Every 5,730 years, half of the carbon-14 in a fossil specimen decays or breaks down into a more stable element. In the following experiment you will see how pennies can show the same kind of "decay."

MATERIALS
- container with a cover, large
- pennies (100)

Procedure

1. Place 100 pennies in a large, covered container. Shake the container several times, and remove the cover. Carefully empty the container on a flat surface making sure the pennies don't roll away.

2. Remove all the coins that have the "head" side of the coin turned upward. Record the number of pennies removed and the number of pennies remaining in a data table similar to the one at right.

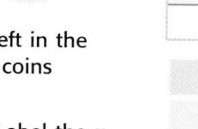

3. Repeat the process until no pennies are left in the container. Remember to remove only the coins showing "heads."

4. Draw a graph similar to the one at right. Label the *x*-axis "Number of shakes," and label the *y*-axis "Pennies remaining." Using data from your data table, plot the number of coins remaining at each shake on your graph.

Analyze the Results

1. Examine the Half-life of Carbon-14 graph at right. Compare the graph you have made for pennies with the one for carbon-14. Explain any similarities that you see.

2. Recall that the probability of landing "heads" in a coin toss is 1/2. Use this information to explain why the remaining number of pennies is reduced by about half each time they are shaken and tossed.

Shake number	Number of coins remaining	Number of coins removed
1		
2	DO NOT WRITE IN BOOK	
3		

Half-life of Pennies

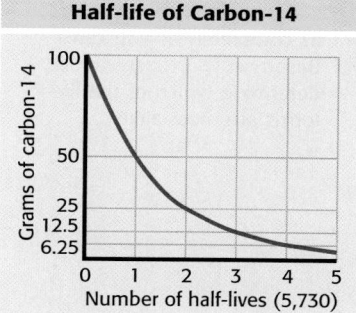

Half-life of Carbon-14

CHAPTER RESOURCES

Chapter Resource File

- Datasheet for LabBook
- Lab Notes and Answers

Karma Houston-Hughes
Kyrene Middle School
Tempe, Arizona

Analyze the Results

1. The graphs should be very similar in shape. With each half-life and each shake, the number remaining will be reduced by half.

2. The remaining number of pennies is reduced by about half each time the pennies are shaken and tossed because there are only two faces on each coin. The rules of probability suggest that half will land heads and half will land tails, and therefore the amount will be reduced by about half with each shake.

The Half-life of Pennies

Teacher's Notes

Time Required
One 45-minute class period

Lab Rating

EASY ————→ HARD

Teacher Prep ⚗
Student Set-Up ⚗
Concept Level ⚗⚗
Clean Up ⚗

Lab Notes

It is useful to use coin tosses to explain half-life because approximately half the coins will land heads and half will land tails. Therefore, about half the entire quantity of coins tossed will be eliminated with each successive toss.

Voyage of the USS *Adventure*

Teacher's Notes

Time Required

One 45-minute class period

Lab Ratings

EASY —————————————→ HARD

Teacher Prep ▲
Student Set-Up ▲
Concept Level ▲▲
Clean Up ▲

Preparation Notes

Some students will find it easier to make the charts on graph paper, so you may wish to supply graph paper to students.

Lab Notes

Students should know that travel outside the solar system is not yet possible. This activity should help students categorize organisms or objects by noticing subtle differences. This activity is a good way to begin a study of classification of animals, rocks, or plants. This lab may be useful before introducing dichotomous keys, for example.

Skills Practice Lab

Voyage of the USS *Adventure*

You are a crew member on the USS *Adventure*. The *Adventure* has been on a 5-year mission to collect life-forms from outside the solar system. On the voyage back to Earth, your ship went through a meteor shower, which ruined several of the compartments containing the extraterrestrial life-forms. Now it is necessary to put more than one life-form in the same compartment.

You have only three undamaged compartments in your starship. You and your crewmates must stay in one compartment, and that compartment should be used for extraterrestrial life-forms only if absolutely necessary. You and your crewmates must decide which of the life-forms could be placed together. It is thought that similar life-forms will have similar needs. You can use only observable characteristics to group the life-forms.

Life-form 1

Life-form 2

Life-form 3

Procedure

❶ Make a data table similar to the one below. Label each column with as many characteristics of the various life-forms as possible. Leave enough space in each square to write your observations. The life-forms are pictured on this page.

Life-form 4

Life-form Characteristics				
	Color	Shape	Legs	Eyes
Life-form 1				
Life-form 2				
Life-form 3		DO NOT WRITE IN BOOK		
Life-form 4				

❷ Describe each characteristic as completely as you can. Based on your observations, determine which of the life-forms are most alike.

Life-form 5

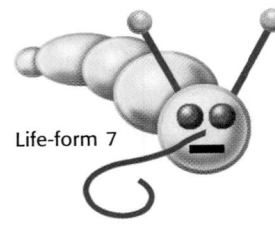

Life-form 7

Life-form 6

CHAPTER RESOURCES

Chapter Resource File

• Datasheet for LabBook
• Lab Notes and Answers

3 Make a data table like the one below. Fill in the table according to the decisions you made in step 2. State your reasons for the way you have grouped your life-forms.

Life-form Room Assignments		
Compartment	Life-forms	Reasons
1		
2		
3		*DO NOT WRITE IN BOOK*

4 The USS *Adventure* has to make one more stop before returning home. On planet X437 you discover the most interesting life-form ever found outside of Earth—the CC9, shown at right. Make a decision, based on your previous grouping of life-forms, about whether you can safely include CC9 in one of the compartments for the trip to Earth.

Analyze the Results

1 Describe the life-forms in compartment 1. How are they similar? How are they different?

2 Describe the life-forms in compartment 2. How are they similar? How do they differ from the life-forms in compartment 1?

3 Are there any life-forms in compartment 3? If so, describe their similarities. In which compartment will you and your crewmates remain for the journey home?

CC9

Draw Conclusions

4 Are you able to transport life-form CC9 safely back to Earth? If so, in which compartment will it be placed? How did you decide?

Applying Your Data

In 1831, Charles Darwin sailed from England on a ship called the HMS *Beagle*. You have studied the finches that Darwin observed on the Galápagos Islands. What were some of the other unusual organisms he found there? For example, find out about the Galápagos tortoise.

Analyze the Results

There are no right or wrong answers in this activity. The objective is to allow students an opportunity to recognize subtle differences and to recognize that organisms may be more alike than they are different. However, you should make sure the students provide good reasons why they grouped certain life-forms together. There are several ways in which these seven organisms are similar. For example, four of them are segmented and have no legs. Three of them are geometrically shaped, and three others have mouths. Have students examine them for less observable characteristics, such as what kind of body plan or symmetry they have, how they might obtain food, or whether they might be land dwelling or aquatic.

Draw Conclusions

4. Answers will depend on how students grouped the life-forms in this lab and which characteristics the students used to classify life-form CC9.

Applying Your Data

The Galápagos tortoise can have a shell length of 1.3 m, have a mass of 180 kg, and live to be 150 years old.

Viral Decorations

Teacher's Notes

Time Required
One 45-minute class period

Lab Ratings

🧪 ━━ 🧪🧪 ━━ 🧪🧪🧪 ━━ 🧪🧪🧪🧪
EASY ──────────────────→ HARD

Teacher Prep 🧪🧪
Student Set-Up 🧪🧪🧪
Concept Level 🧪🧪🧪🧪
Clean Up 🧪🧪

MATERIALS
Enlarge the template at the bottom of this page to provide students with patterns.

Analyze the Results
1–2. Answers may vary.

Communicating Your Data
Influenza virus, of course, causes the flu. HIV is the virus that causes AIDS, and Ebola virus is a rare filovirus that causes a deadly hemorrhagic fever.

Gladys Cherniak
St. Paul's Episcopal School
Mobile, Alabama

Model-Making Lab

Viral Decorations

Although viruses are made of only protein and nucleic acids, their structures have many different shapes that help them attach to and invade living cells. One viral shape can be constructed from the template provided by your teacher. In this activity, you will construct and modify a model of a virus.

Procedure

1 Obtain a virus model template from your teacher. Carefully copy the template on a piece of construction paper. You may make the virus model as large as your teacher allows.

2 Plan how you will modify your virus. For example, you might want to add the tail and tail fibers of a bacteriophage or wrap the model in plastic to represent the envelope that surrounds the protein coat in HIV.

3 Color your virus model, and cut it out by cutting on the solid black lines. Then, fold the virus model along the dotted lines.

4 Glue or tape each lettered tab under the corresponding lettered triangle. For example, glue or tape the large *Z* tab under the *Z*-shaded triangle. When you are finished, you should have a closed box with 20 sides.

5 Apply the modifications that you planned. Give your virus a name, and write it on the model. Decorate your classroom with your virus and those of your classmates.

Analyze the Results

1 Describe the modifications you made to your virus model, and explain how the virus might use them.

2 If your virus causes disease, explain what disease it causes, how it reproduces, and how the virus is spread.

MATERIALS
- glue (or tape)
- markers, colored
- paper, construction
- pipe cleaners, twist ties, buttons, string, plastic wrap, and other scrap materials for making variations of the virus
- scissors
- virus model template

SAFETY

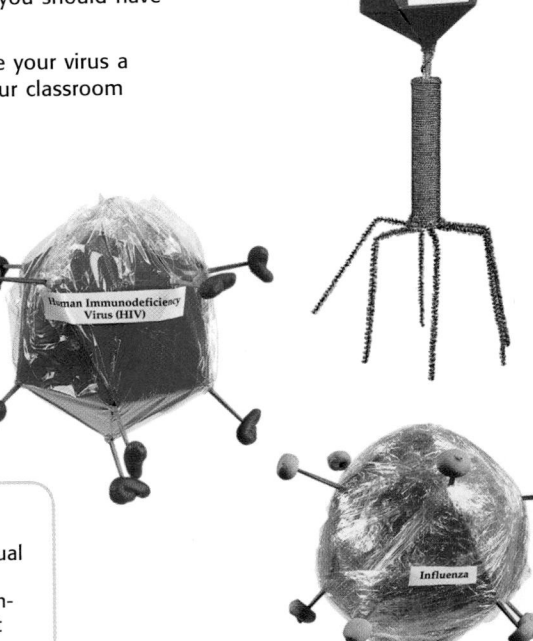

Communicating Your Data

Research in the library or on the Internet an unusual virus that causes an illness, such as the influenza virus, HIV, or Ebola virus. Write a paragraph explaining what is unusual about the virus, what illness it causes, and how it might be avoided.

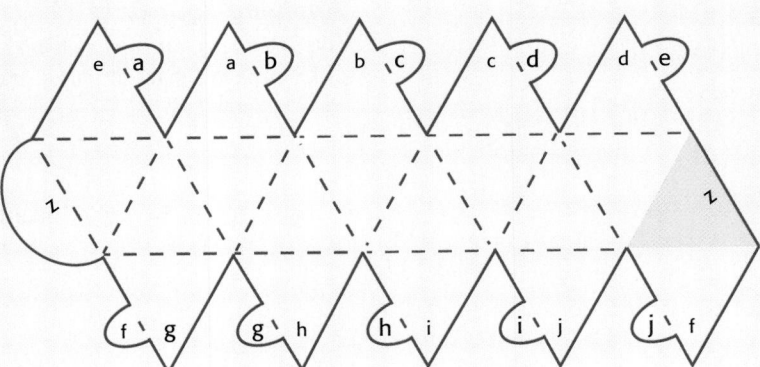

Model-Making Lab

Making a Protist Mobile

You have studied many of the diverse species of organisms within the kingdom Protista. This may be the first time you have ever seen many of these single-celled eukaryotes. In this activity, you will have an opportunity to express a bit of creativity by using what you have learned about these interesting organisms.

Procedure

1. Research the different kinds of protists you have studied. You may cut out pictures of them from magazines, or you may find examples of protists on the Internet. You may want to investigate *Plasmodium, Euglena,* amoebas, slime molds, *Radiolaria, Paramecium, Foraminifera,* various other protozoans, or even algae.

2. Using the paper and recycled materials, make a model of each protist you want to include on your mobile. Be sure to include the special features of each protist, such as vacuoles, pseudopods, shells, cilia, or flagella.

3. Use tape or glue to attach special features to give your protists a three-dimensional look.

4. Provide labels for your protist models. For each protist, provide its name, classification, method of movement (if any), method for obtaining food, and any other interesting facts you have learned about it.

5. Attach your protist models to the wire hanger with wire or string. Use tape or glue to attach your labels to each model.

Analyze the Results

1. What have you learned about the diversity of protists? Include at least three habitats where protists may be found.

Communicating Your Data

Choose a disease-causing protist. Write a report describing the disease, its effect on people or the environment, and the efforts being made to control it.

MATERIALS

- clothes hanger, wire
- markers, colored
- paper (heavyweight construction paper or poster board)
- recycled material of your choice
- scissors
- string, yarn, lightweight wire, or fishing line
- tape, transparent (or glue)

SAFETY

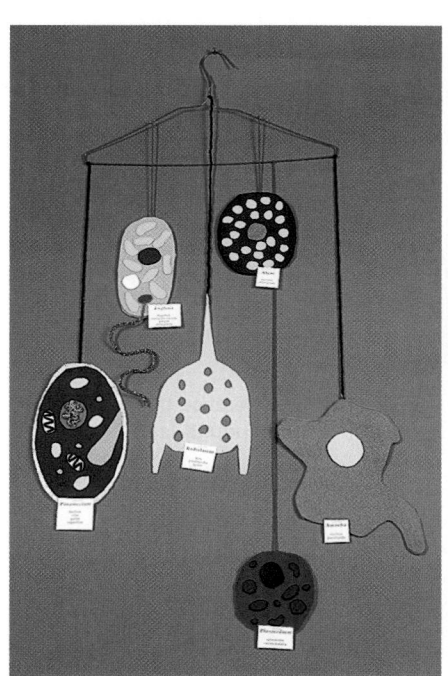

CLASSROOM TESTED & APPROVED

Elizabeth Rustad
Crane Junior High School
Yuma, Arizona

LabBook
Model-Making Lab

Making a Protist Mobile

Teacher's Notes

Time Required
One 45-minute class period

Lab Ratings
EASY ——————→ HARD

Teacher Prep 🧪🧪
Student Set-Up 🧪
Concept Level 🧪🧪
Clean Up 🧪🧪

MATERIALS
Have students bring materials from home, such as buttons, fringe, pipe cleaners, cotton balls, or anything else that can be used to make a model of a protist.

Safety Caution
Remind students to review all safety cautions and icons before beginning this lab activity.

Analyze the Results

1. Sample answer: The kingdom Protista has the greatest diversity of all the eukaryotes with over 65,000 known species. They can live in many different environments. They can drift in the ocean, creep across vegetation in freshwater rivers and ponds, flourish in deep soil, and even reproduce in the bodies of other organisms.

Communicating Your Data
Students may choose from any number of disease-causing protists, from amoebas (amoebic dysentery) to *Plasmodium* (malaria). Students' reports should include some of the symptoms of the disease, how prevalent it is, and how or if it is controlled.

Leaf Me Alone!

Teacher's Notes

Time Required
One 45-minute class period

Lab Ratings

EASY ————→ HARD

Teacher Prep 🧪🧪
Student Set-Up 🧪
Concept Level 🧪🧪
Clean Up 🧪

MATERIALS

The materials listed on the student page are enough for a group of 4–5 students. Collect plant specimens ahead of time, or have students bring in five specimens that they have collected. Students will need to see the leaves as they appear on the stems, so include as much of the plant as possible.

Safety Caution

Remind students to review all safety cautions and icons before beginning this lab activity.

Skills Practice Lab

Leaf Me Alone!

Imagine you are a naturalist all alone on an expedition in a rain forest. You have found several plants that you think have never been seen before. You must contact a botanist, a scientist who studies plants, to confirm your suspicion. Because there is no mail service in the rain forest, you must describe these species completely and accurately by radio. The botanist must be able to draw the leaves of the plants from your description. In this activity, you will carefully describe five plant specimens by using the examples and vocabulary lists in this lab.

MATERIALS
- gloves, protective
- leaf specimens (5)
- plant guidebook (optional)

SAFETY

Procedure

1. Examine the leaf characteristics illustrated on the next page. These examples can be found on the following page. You will notice that more than one term is needed to completely describe a leaf. The leaf shown at right has been labeled for you using the examples and vocabulary lists found in this lab.

2. On a sheet of paper, draw a diagram of a leaf from each plant specimen.

3. Next to each drawing, carefully describe the leaf. Include general characteristics, such as relative size and color. For each plant, identify the following: leaf shape, stem type, leaf arrangement, leaf edge, vein arrangement, and leaf-base shape. Use the terms and vocabulary lists provided to describe each leaf as accurately as possible and to label your drawings.

Analyze the Results

1. What is the difference between a simple leaf and a compound leaf?

2. Describe two different vein arrangements in leaves.

3. Based on what you know about adaptation, explain why there are so many different leaf variations.

Compound Leaf

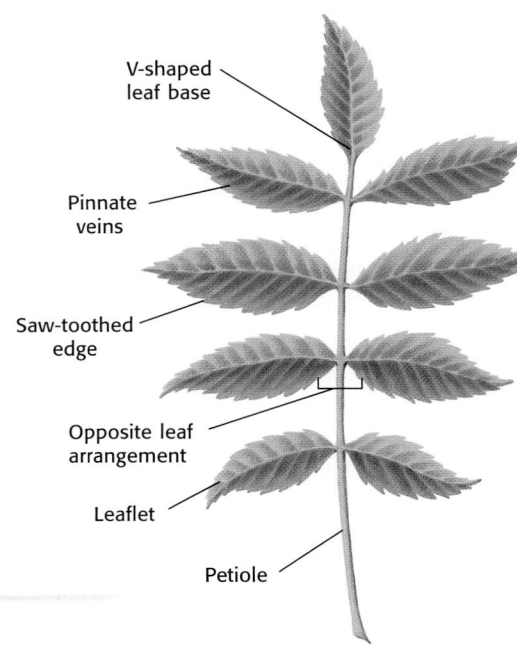

- V-shaped leaf base
- Pinnate veins
- Saw-toothed edge
- Opposite leaf arrangement
- Leaflet
- Petiole

Communicating Your Data

Choose a partner. Using the keys and vocabulary in this lab, describe a leaf, and see if your partner can draw the leaf from your description. Switch roles, and see if you can draw a leaf from your partner's description.

Jane Lemons
Western Rockingham
Middle School
Madison, North Carolina

CHAPTER RESOURCES

Chapter Resource File
- Datasheet for LabBook
- Lab Notes and Answers

Leaf Shapes Vocabulary List

cordate—heart shaped
lanceolate—sword shaped
lobate—lobed
oblong—rounded at the tip
orbicular—disk shaped
ovate—oval shaped, widest at base of leaf
peltate—shield shaped
reniform—kidney shaped
sagittate—arrow shaped

Stems Vocabulary List

herbaceous—green, nonwoody stems
woody—bark or barklike covering on stem

Leaf Arrangements Vocabulary List

alternate—alternating leaves or leaflets along stem or petiole
compound—leaf divided into segments, or several leaflets on a petiole
opposite—compound leaf with several leaflets arranged oppositely along a petiole
palmate—single leaf with veins arranged around a center point
palmate compound—several leaflets arranged around a center point
petiole—leaf stalk
pinnate—single leaf with veins arranged along a center vein
pinnate compound—several leaflets on either side of a petiole
simple—single leaf attached to stem by a petiole

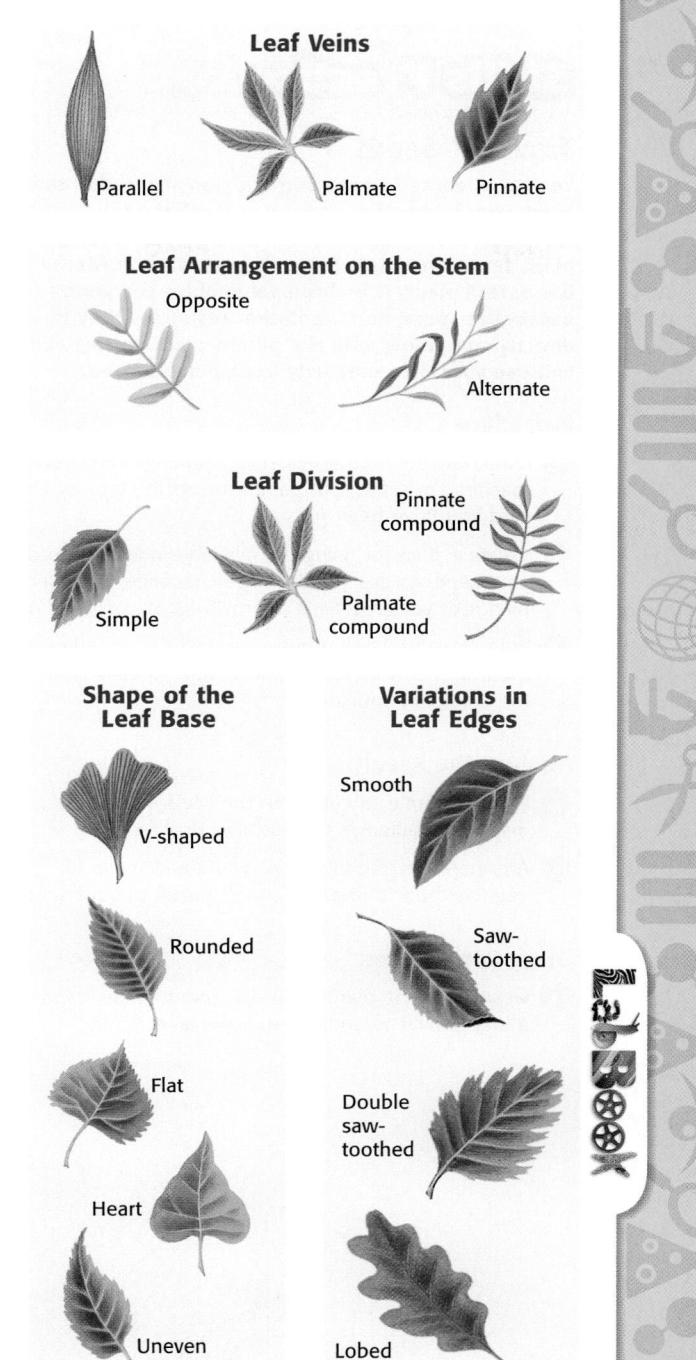

Leaf Veins

Parallel   Palmate   Pinnate

Leaf Arrangement on the Stem

Opposite

Alternate

Leaf Division

Pinnate compound

Simple   Palmate compound

Shape of the Leaf Base

V-shaped
Rounded
Flat
Heart
Uneven

Variations in Leaf Edges

Smooth
Saw-toothed
Double saw-toothed
Lobed

Travelin' Seeds

Teacher's Notes

Time Required

One 45-minute class period

Lab Ratings

🧪　🧪🧪　🧪🧪🧪　🧪🧪🧪🧪
EASY ——————————— HARD

Teacher Prep 🧪🧪
Student Set-Up 🧪🧪
Concept Level 🧪🧪
Clean Up 🧪

Preparation Notes

Five basic challenges are listed below. Copy each as needed so that there is one card per student or group.

1. Modify your seed so that it will be carried on an animal's fur as the animal passes by the plant. The seed must travel for at least 1 m.

2. Modify your seed so that it will be flung safely 1 m away from the parent plant.

3. Modify your seed so that it will glide in the air when it falls off the parent plant. The seed must be dropped, not thrown, at least 1 m.

4. Modify your seed so that animals will find it desirable to eat and digest.

5. Modify your seed so that it will float on water for at least 1 min.

Skills Practice Lab

Travelin' Seeds

You have learned from your study of plants that there are some very interesting and unusual plant adaptations. Some of the most interesting adaptations are modifications that allow plant seeds and fruits to be dispersed, or scattered, away from the parent plant. This dispersal enables the young seedlings to obtain the space, sun, and other resources they need without directly competing with the parent plant. In this activity, you will use your own creativity to disperse a seed.

Procedure

1. Obtain a seed and a dispersal challenge card from your teacher. On a sheet of paper, record the type of challenge card you have been given.

2. Create a plan for using the available materials to disperse your seed, as described on the challenge card. Record your plan. Get your teacher's approval before proceeding.

3. With your teacher's permission, test your seed-dispersal method. Perform several trials. Make a data table, and record the results of your trials.

Analyze the Results

1. Were you able to complete the seed-dispersal challenge successfully? Explain.

2. Are there any modifications you could make to your method to improve the dispersal of your seed?

Draw Conclusions

3. Describe some plants that disperse their seeds in a way similar to your seed-dispersal method.

MATERIALS

- bean seed
- seed-dispersal challenge card
- various household or recycled materials (examples: glue, tape, paper, paper clips, rubber bands, cloth, paper cups and plates, paper towels, and cardboard)

◀ Mangrove seed

◀ Cottonwood

Wild berry ▶

Grass bur ▶

Analyze the Results
1.–2. Answers may vary.

Draw Conclusions
3. Answers may vary.

CHAPTER RESOURCES

Chapter Resource File

- **Datasheet for LabBook**
- **Lab Notes and Answers**

Jane Lemons
Western Rockingham
Middle School
Madison, North Carolina

Skills Practice Lab

Weepy Weeds

You are trying to find a way to drain an area that is flooded with water polluted with fertilizer. You know that a plant releases water through the stomata in its leaves. As water evaporates from the leaves, more water is pulled up from the roots through the stem and into the leaves. By this process, called *transpiration,* water and nutrients are pulled into the plant from the soil. About 90% of the water a plant takes up through its roots is released into the atmosphere as water vapor through transpiration. Your idea is to add plants to the flooded area that will transpire the water and take up the fertilizer in their roots.

How much water can a plant take up and release in a certain period of time? In this activity, you will observe transpiration and determine one stem's rate of transpiration.

Procedure

❶ Make a data table similar to the one below for recording your measurements.

Height of Water in Test Tubes

Time	Test tube with plant	Test tube without plant
Initial		
After 10 min		
After 20 min		
After 30 min		
After 40 min		
Overnight		

DO NOT WRITE IN BOOK

❷ Fill each test tube approximately three-fourths full of water. Place both test tubes in a test-tube rack.

❸ Place the plant stem so that it stands upright in one of the test tubes. Your test tubes should look like the ones in the photograph at right.

❹ Use the glass-marking pen to mark the water level in each of the test tubes. Be sure you have the plant stem in place in its test tube before you mark the water level. Why is this necessary?

MATERIALS

- clock
- coleus or other plant stem cutting
- glass-marking pen
- metric ruler
- paper, graph
- test tube (2)
- test-tube rack
- water

SAFETY

CHAPTER RESOURCES

Chapter Resource File

- **Datasheet for LabBook**
- **Lab Notes and Answers**

CLASSROOM TESTED & APPROVED

David Sparks
Redwater Junior High School
Redwater, Texas

LabBook

Skills Practice Lab

Weepy Weeds

Teacher's Notes

Time Required

One or two 45-minute class periods

Lab Ratings

EASY ——————→ HARD

Teacher Prep 🧪🧪
Student Set-Up 🧪🧪
Concept Level 🧪🧪
Clean Up 🧪🧪

MATERIALS

The materials listed on the student page are enough for 1 student. The plant used in this lab can be any leafy plant, such as a bean plant or a coleus. The plant shown is a coleus with all but the top four leaves trimmed away.

Safety Caution

Remind students to review all safety cautions and icons before beginning this lab activity.

Lab Notes

If your lab period is short, you may want to eliminate the measurement of the height of water in the test tube at 40 min.

Although it is not essential to the activity, you may want to begin with an exact amount of water in each test tube. Students would then know that the difference can be due only to evaporation and transpiration.

Analyze the Results

1. Sample answer: The test tube that held only water was a control; it would lose water only by evaporation.

2. Sample answer: Water in the test tube containing the plant stem was lost through evaporation and transpiration. Evaporation is the only means of water loss in the test tube without the plant stem.

3. Answers may vary according to several variables in the classroom, such as the amount of light and the temperature.

4. Answers may vary. Have students compare and contrast the lines on the graph and explain how the graph is easier to interpret than numbers in a data list.

Applying Your Data

Answers may vary.

---

5. Measure the height of the water in each test tube. Be sure to hold the test tube level, and measure from the waterline to the bottom of the curve at the bottom of the test tube. Record these measurements on the row labeled "Initial."

6. Wait 10 min, and measure the height of the water in each test tube again. Record these measurements in your data table.

7. Repeat step 6 three more times. Record your measurements each time.

8. Wait 24 hours, and measure the height of the water in each test tube. Record these measurements in your data table.

9. Construct a graph similar to the one below. Plot the data from your data table. Draw a line for each test tube. Use a different color for each line, and make a key below your graph.

10. Calculate the rate of transpiration for your plant by using the following operations:

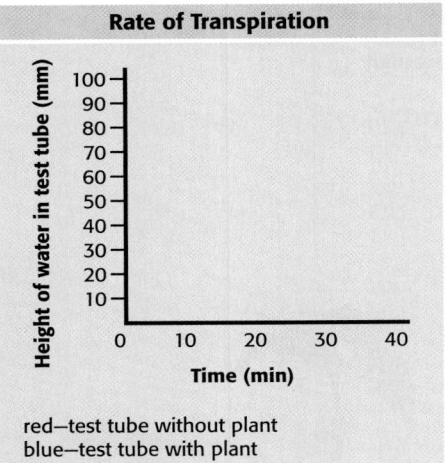

Rate of Transpiration

red—test tube without plant
blue—test tube with plant

Test tube with plant:
Initial height
− Overnight height
Difference in height of water (A)

Test tube without plant:
Initial height
− Overnight height
Difference in height of water (B)

Water height difference due to transpiration:
Difference A
− Difference B
Water lost due to transpiration (in millimeters) in 24 hours

Analyze the Results

1. What was the purpose of the test tube that held only water?

2. What caused the water to go down in the test tube containing the plant stem? Did the same thing happen in the test tube with water only? Explain your answer.

3. What was the calculated rate of transpiration per day?

4. Using your graph, compare the rate of transpiration with the rate of evaporation alone.

5. Prepare a presentation of your experiment for your class. Use your data tables, graphs, and calculations as visual aids.

Applying Your Data

How many leaves did your plant sprigs have? Use this number to estimate what the rate of transpiration might be for a plant with 200 leaves. When you have your answer in millimeters of height in a test tube, pour this amount into a graduated cylinder to measure it in milliliters.

Skills Practice Lab

Wet, Wiggly Worms!

Earthworms have been digging in the Earth for more than 100 million years! Earthworms fertilize the soil with their waste and loosen the soil when they tunnel through the moist dirt of a garden or lawn. Worms are food for many animals, such as birds, frogs, snakes, rodents, and fish. Some say they are good food for people, too!

In this activity, you will observe the behavior of a live earthworm. Remember that earthworms are living animals that deserve to be handled gently. Be sure to keep your earthworm moist during this activity. The skin of the earthworm must stay moist so that the worm can get oxygen. If the earthworm's skin dries out, the worm will suffocate and die. Use a spray bottle to moisten the earthworm with water.

MATERIALS

- celery leaves
- clock
- dissecting pan
- earthworm, live
- flashlight
- paper towels
- probe
- ruler, metric
- shoe box, with lid
- soil
- spray bottle
- water

SAFETY

Procedure

1. Place a wet paper towel in the bottom of a dissecting pan. Put a live earthworm on the paper towel, and observe how the earthworm moves. Record your observations.

2. Use the probe to carefully touch the anterior end (head) of the worm. Gently touch other areas of the worm's body with the probe. Record the kinds of responses you observe.

3. Place celery leaves at one end of the pan. Record how the earthworm responds to the presence of food.

4. Shine a flashlight on the anterior end of the earthworm. Record the earthworm's reaction to the light.

5. Line the bottom of the shoe box with a damp paper towel. Cover half of the shoe box with the box top.

6. Place the worm on the uncovered side of the shoe box in the light. Record your observations of the worm's behavior for 3 min.

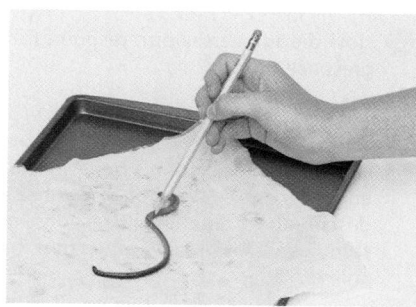

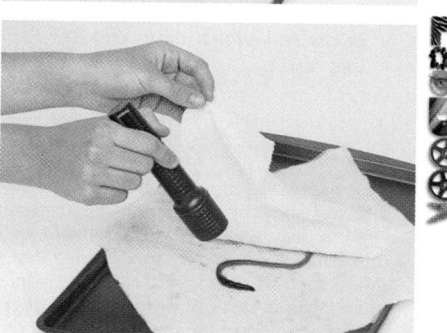

Teacher's Notes

Time Required

One 45-minute class period

Lab Ratings

EASY ——————→ HARD

Teacher Prep 🧪🧪
Student Set-Up 🧪🧪
Concept Level 🧪🧪
Clean Up 🧪🧪

MATERIALS

The materials listed on the student page are enough for a group of 4–5 students.

Safety Caution

Remind students to review all safety cautions and icons before beginning this lab activity. Students may wish to wear protective gloves while handling the worms.

CHAPTER RESOURCES

Chapter Resource File

- Datasheet for LabBook
- Lab Notes and Answers

CLASSROOM TESTED & APPROVED

Gladys Cherniak
St. Paul's Episcopal School
Mobile, Alabama

Lab Notes

Earthworms are scientifically classified as animals belonging to the order Oligochaeta, class Chaetopoda, and phylum Annelida. There are about 1,800 species of earthworms. Only two of these are grown commercially. Earthworms have setae, or bristles, located on each segment, which help them move. Earthworms have both male and female reproductive organs. They usually do not self-fertilize, but they do exchange sperm as they pass in their burrows. Eggs are deposited in the burrow in a cocoon. The cocoon is produced by the clitellum, which encircles the body of the worm. Different segments of the earthworm perform different functions, just as each of our body parts do. Earthworms have from 95 to 150 segments, depending on the species.

7 Place the worm in the covered side of the box. Record your observations for 3 min.

8 Repeat steps 6–7 three times.

9 Spread some loose soil evenly in the bottom of the shoe box so that the soil is about 4 cm deep. Place the earthworm on top of the soil. Observe and record the earthworm's behavior for 3 min.

10 Dampen the soil on one side of the box, and leave the other side dry. Place the earthworm in the center of the box between the wet and dry soil. Cover the box, and wait 3 min. Uncover the box, and record your observations. Repeat this procedure three times. (You may need to search for the worm!)

Analyze the Results

1 How did the earthworm respond to being touched? Were some areas more sensitive than others?

2 How did the earthworm respond to the presence of food?

Draw Conclusions

3 How is the earthworm's behavior influenced by light? Based on your observations, describe how an animal's response to a stimulus might provide protection for the animal.

4 When the worm was given a choice of wet or dry soil, which did it choose? Explain this result.

Communicating Your Data

Based on your observations of an earthworm's behavior, prepare a poster showing where you might expect to find earthworms. Draw a picture with colored markers, or cut out pictures from magazines. Include all the variables that you used in your experiment, such as soil or no soil, wet or dry soil, light or dark, and food. Write a caption at the bottom of your poster describing where earthworms might be found in nature.

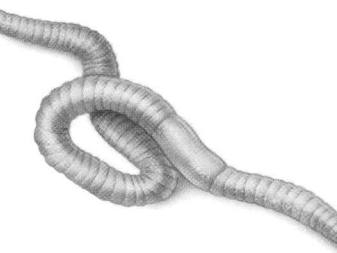

Analyze the Results

1–2. Students' answers may vary according to their own observations. They will probably observe that the worm squirms when touched and that some areas are more sensitive than others, such as the clitellum. Responses to food may vary.

Draw Conclusions

3–4. Students will probably observe that earthworms avoid light and prefer moist soil. Students may describe the worm's behavior as self-protective.

Communicating Your Data

Students' posters should describe warm, moist soil; darkness; and partially decayed organic matter for food.

Skills Practice Lab

The Cricket Caper

Insects are a special class of invertebrates with more than 750,000 known species. Insects may be the most successful group of animals on Earth. In this activity you will observe a cricket's structure and the simple adaptive behaviors that help make it so successful. Remember, you will be handling a living animal that deserves to be treated with care.

Procedure

1 Place a cricket in a clean 600 mL beaker, and quickly cover the beaker with plastic wrap. The supply of oxygen in the container is enough for the cricket to breathe while you complete your work.

2 While the cricket is getting used to the container, make a data table similar to the one below. Be sure to allow enough space to write your descriptions.

Cricket Body Structures

Number	Description
Body segments	
Antennae	*DO NOT WRITE IN BOOK*
Eyes	
Wings	

3 Without making much movement, begin to examine the cricket. Fill in your data table with your observations of the cricket's structure.

4 Place a small piece of apple in the beaker. Set the beaker on a table. Sit quietly for several minutes and observe the cricket. Any movement may cause the cricket to stop what it is doing. Record your observations.

5 Remove the plastic wrap from the beaker, remove the apple, and quickly attach a second beaker. Join the two beakers together at the mouths with masking tape. Handle the beakers carefully. Remember, there is a living animal inside.

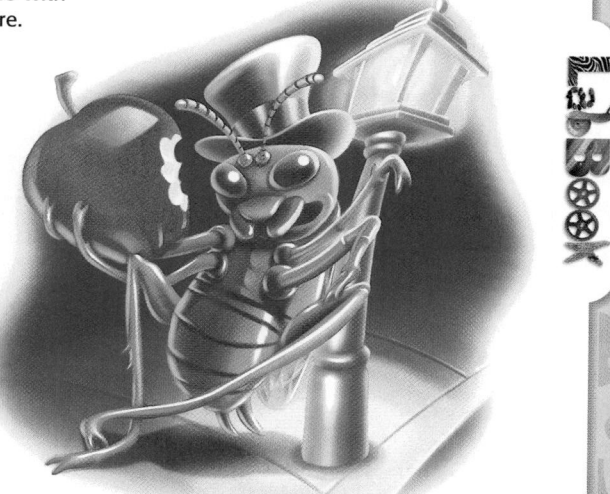

MATERIALS

- aluminum foil
- apple
- bags, plastic, sealable (2)
- beaker, 600 mL (2)
- cricket (2)
- hand lens (optional)
- ice, crushed
- lamp
- plastic wrap
- tape, masking
- water, tap, hot

SAFETY

Alonda Droege
Pioneer Middle School
Steilacom, Washington

Skills Practice Lab

The Cricket Caper

Teacher's Notes

Time Required
One to two 45-minute class periods

Lab Ratings

EASY ———————————→ HARD

Teacher Prep 🜂🜂🜂
Student Set-Up 🜂🜂
Concept Level 🜂🜂
Clean Up 🜂🜂

MATERIALS

The materials listed on the student page are enough for 1 student or a small group of students. Instead of 600 mL beakers, you may use the bottom halves of two clear plastic 2 L bottles. You will need to prepare these ahead of time. The cut on the bottle should be as even as possible to facilitate taping the open ends together in step 5.

Safety Caution
Remind students to review all safety cautions and icons before beginning this lab activity.

Lab Notes
Explain to students that they must move slowly so they won't startle the cricket and alter its behavior. The apple must be removed in step 5 before the containers are taped together. The apple would be an unwanted variable in the tests that follow.

If you decide to extend this activity over two class periods, the cricket will be fine overnight in a covered 500 mL beaker. The cricket will need a slice of potato or apple for food and moisture.

6 Wrap one of the joined beakers with aluminum foil.

7 If the cricket is hiding under the aluminum foil, gently tap the sides of the beaker until the cricket is exposed. Lay the joined beakers on their sides, and shine a lamp on the uncovered side. Record the cricket's location.

8 Record the cricket's location after 5 min. Without disturbing the cricket, carefully move the aluminum foil to the other beaker. After 5 min, record the cricket's location. Repeat this process one more time to see if you get the same result.

9 Fill a sealable plastic bag halfway with crushed ice. Fill another bag halfway with hot tap water. Seal each bag, and arrange them side by side on the table.

10 Remove the aluminum foil from the beakers. Gently rock the joined beakers from side to side until the cricket is in the center. Place the beakers on the plastic bags, as shown below.

11 Observe the cricket's behavior for 5 min. Record your observations.

CHAPTER RESOURCES

Chapter Resource File

• **Datasheet for LabBook**
• **Lab Notes and Answers**

12. Set the beakers on one end for several minutes to allow them to return to room temperature. Repeat steps 10–12 three times. (Why do you think it is necessary to allow the beakers to return to room temperature each time?)

13. Set the beakers on one end. Carefully remove the masking tape, and separate the beakers. Quickly replace the plastic wrap over the beaker containing the cricket. Allow your cricket to rest while you make two data tables similar to those at right.

14. Observe the cricket's movement in the beaker every 15 seconds for 3 min. Fill in the Cricket (alone) data table using the following codes: 0 = no movement, 1 = slight movement, and 2 = rapid movement.

15. Obtain a second cricket from your teacher, and place this cricket in the container with the first cricket. Every 15 seconds, record the movement of each cricket in the Cricket A and Cricket B data table using the codes given in step 14.

Analyze the Results

1. Describe crickets' feeding behavior. Are they lappers, suckers, or chewers?

2. Do crickets prefer light or darkness? Explain.

3. From your observations, what can you infer about a cricket's temperature preferences?

Draw Conclusions

4. Based on your observations of Cricket A and Cricket B, what general statements can you make about the social behavior of crickets?

Applying Your Data

Make a third data table titled "Cricket and Another Species of Insect." Introduce another insect, such as a grasshopper, into the beaker. Record your observations for 3 min. Write a short summary of the cricket's reaction to another species.

Cricket (alone)	
15 s	
30 s	
45 s	
60 s	
75 s	
90 s	DO NOT WRITE IN BOOK
105 s	
120 s	
135 s	
150 s	
165 s	
180 s	

Cricket A and Cricket B		
	A	B
15 s		
30 s		
45 s		
60 s		
75 s		
90 s	DO NOT WRITE IN BOOK	
105 s		
120 s		
135 s		
150 s		
165 s		
180 s		

Procedure

12. If the beakers are still warm, experimental conditions will not be the same for each trial.

Analyze the Results

All answers will depend on the students' observations. The following answers are the expected observations:

1. Crickets are chewers.

2. Crickets generally prefer darkness. They will move from light areas into dark areas.

3. Crickets will prefer the warmer location.

Draw Conclusions

4. Answers may vary, but should reflect that, if well-fed, crickets generally tolerate each other very well. However, they will fight and even eat each other if they are not fed properly.

Applying Your Data

Explain to students that both threatening actions and submissive responses are agonistic behaviors that often result in producing a "winner." For example, wolves that snarl and bare their teeth at a competitor for a mate are displaying agonistic behavior. Ask students to watch this activity carefully. Ask them to be attentive so that they will observe the first signs of agonistic behavior if any arise. If the animals show signs that they are going to fight, tell students to remove one of them from the container immediately.

A Prince of a Frog

Teacher's Notes

Time Required

One 45-minute class period

Lab Ratings

EASY —————→ HARD

Teacher Prep 🧪🧪🧪
Student Set-Up 🧪
Concept Level 🧪🧪
Clean Up 🧪

Safety Caution

Remind students to review all safety cautions and icons before beginning this lab activity.

You will need to provide protective gloves for the students. Students' hands may make the frog vulnerable to infection. Also, frogs are known to carry salmonella. Students should wash their hands thoroughly with soap and warm water after handling the frog.

Skills Practice Lab

A Prince of a Frog

Imagine that you are a scientist interested in amphibians. You have heard in the news about amphibians disappearing all over the world. What a great loss it will be to the environment if all amphibians become extinct! Your job is to learn as much as possible about how frogs normally behave so that you can act as a resource for other scientists who are studying the problem. In this activity, you will observe a normal frog in a dry container and in water.

Procedure

1 Make a table similar to the one below to note all of your observations of the frog in this investigation.

MATERIALS

- beaker, 600 mL
- container half-filled with dechlorinated water
- crickets, live
- frog, live, in a dry container
- gloves, protective
- rock, large (optional)

SAFETY

Observations of a Live Frog	
Characteristic	**Observation**
Breathing	
Eyes	
Legs	DO NOT WRITE IN BOOK
Response to food	
Skin texture	
Swimming behavior	
Skin coloration	

2 Observe a live frog in a dry container. Draw a picture of the frog. Label the eyes, nostrils, front legs, and hind legs.

3 Watch the frog's movements as it breathes air with its lungs. Write a description of the frog's breathing.

4 Look closely at the frog's eyes, and note their location. Examine the upper and lower eyelids as well as the transparent third eyelid. Which of these three eyelids actually moves over the eye?

5 Study the frog's legs. Note in your data table the difference between the front and hind legs

Kerry Johnson
Isbell Middle School
Santa Paula, California

CHAPTER RESOURCES

Chapter Resource File

 • Datasheet for LabBook
• Lab Notes and Answers

6. Place a live insect, such as a cricket, in the container. Observe and record how the frog reacts.

7. Carefully pick up the frog, and examine its skin. How does it feel?
   Caution: Remember that a frog is a living thing and deserves to be handled gently and with respect.

8. Place a 600 mL beaker in the container. Place the frog in the beaker. Cover the beaker with your hand, and carry it to a container of dechlorinated water. Tilt the beaker and gently submerge it in the water until the frog swims out of the beaker.

9. Watch the frog float and swim in the water. How does the frog use its legs to swim? Notice the position of the frog's head.

10. As the frog swims, bend down and look up into the water so that you can see the underside of the frog. Then look down on the frog from above. Compare the color on the top and the underneath sides of the frog. Record your observations in your data table.

Analyze the Results

1. From the position of the frog's eyes, what can you infer about the frog's field of vision? How might the position of the frog's eyes benefit the frog while it is swimming?

2. How can a frog "breathe" while it is swimming in water?

3. How are the hind legs of a frog adapted for life on land and in water?

4. What differences did you notice in coloration on the frog's top side and its underneath side? What advantage might these color differences provide?

5. How does the frog eat? What senses are involved in helping the frog catch its prey?

Applying Your Data

Observe another type of amphibian, such as a salamander. How do the adaptations of other types of amphibians compare with those of the frog you observed in this investigation?

Analyze the Results

1.–5. Have students speculate about the form and function of the frog's structure. Discuss the camouflage coloration of a frog. Ask how the skin of a frog differs from that of a reptile and note that the two different forms have two different functions. Discuss the fact that the frog's skin must stay wet in order for gas exchange to occur.

Applying Your Data

Answers may vary, but students should notice several similar adaptations among amphibians.

Preparation Notes

Frogs collected in the wild are best for this activity because they are easily released. Frogs from pet stores must NOT be released into the wild.

If you can divide the class into groups with several observations going on at the same time, you can use a smaller container for each frog. Containers can be a large glass mixing bowl or something similar. Students may bring containers from home as well. Tree frogs are common in pet stores. They are fun to observe, especially if you can find some small crickets to feed them so that students can observe their feeding behavior.

You may substitute another amphibian, such as water doggies, an immature stage of salamanders. Water doggies are especially interesting if they can be kept in the classroom so students can observe their development into salamanders.

Frogs and water doggies may be obtained in pet stores, in the wild, and in bait shops.

Lab Notes

Several years ago, some students who were out collecting frogs for an activity similar to this lab found severe birth defects and mutations among the frogs they found. A good way to introduce this activity may be to find a news clipping from this event or information about frog deformities taken from the Internet.

Adaptation: It's a Way of Life

Teacher's Notes

Time Required

One or two 45-minute class periods

Lab Ratings

EASY ——————→ HARD

Teacher Prep 🧪🧪
Student Set-Up 🧪🧪
Concept Level 🧪🧪
Clean Up 🧪

MATERIALS

The materials listed on the student page are enough for a group of 4–5 students. Materials for this activity can include recycled materials, glue, buttons, pipe cleaners, poster paints and brushes, and any number of other art or craft supplies. Have students bring in as much as they can to use in their own project and to share.

Model-Making Lab

Adaptation: It's a Way of Life

Since the beginning of life on Earth, species have had special characteristics called *adaptations* that have helped them survive changes in environmental conditions. Changes in a species' environment include climate changes, habitat destruction, or the extinction of prey. These things can cause a species to die out unless the species has a characteristic that helps it survive. For example, a species of bird may have an adaptation for eating sunflower seeds and ants. If the ant population dies out, the bird can still eat seeds and can therefore survive.

In this activity, you will explore several adaptations and design an organism with adaptations you choose. Then, you will describe how these adaptations help the organism survive.

MATERIALS

- arts-and-crafts materials, various
- markers, colored
- magazines for cutouts
- poster board
- scissors

SAFETY

Procedure

1. Study the chart below. Choose one adaptation from each column. For example, an organism might be a scavenger that burrows underground and has spikes on its tail!

Adaptations		
Diet	**Type of transportation**	**Special adaptation**
carnivore	flies	uses sensors to detect heat
herbivore	glides through the air	is active only at night and has excellent night vision
omnivore	burrows underground	changes colors to match its surroundings
scavenger	runs fast	has armor
decomposer	swims	has horns
	hops	can withstand extreme temperature changes
	walks	secretes a terrible and sickening scent
	climbs	has poison glands
	floats	has specialized front teeth
	slithers	has tail spikes
		stores oxygen in its cells so it does not have to breathe continuously
		one of your own invention

Alonda Droege
Pioneer Middle School
Steilacom, Washington

CHAPTER RESOURCES

Chapter Resource File

- Datasheet for LabBook
- Lab Notes and Answers

2 Design an organism that has the three adaptations you have chosen. Use poster board, colored markers, picture cutouts, or craft materials of your choosing to create your organism.

3 Write a caption on your poster describing your organism. Describe its appearance, its habitat, its niche, and the way its adaptations help it survive. Give your organism a two-part "scientific" name that is based on its characteristics.

4 Display your creation in your classroom. Share with classmates how you chose the adaptations for your organism.

Analyze the Results

1 What does your imaginary organism eat?

2 In what environment or habitat would your organism be most likely to survive—in the desert, tropical rain forest, plains, icecaps, mountains, or ocean? Explain your answer.

3 Is your creature a mammal, a reptile, an amphibian, a bird, or a fish? What modern organism (on Earth today) or ancient organism (extinct) is your imaginary organism most like? Explain the similarities between the two organisms. Do some research outside the lab, if necessary, to find out about a real organism that may be similar to your imaginary organism.

Draw Conclusions

4 If there were a sudden climate change, such as daily downpours of rain in a desert, would your imaginary organism survive? What adaptations for surviving such a change does it have?

Applying Your Data

Call or write to an agency such as the U.S. Fish and Wildlife Service to get a list of endangered species in your area. Choose an organism on that list. Describe the organism's niche and any special adaptations it has that help it survive. Find out why it is endangered and what is being done to protect it. Examine the illustration of the animal at right. Based on its physical characteristics, describe its habitat and niche. Is this a real animal?

Analyze the Results

1.–3. All answers will depend on the adaptations that the student chose and the organism the student invented. Students should relate one or more adaptations to what kinds of food the organism eats, where the animal lives, or what kind of animal it is.

Draw Conclusions

4. Answers may vary.

Applying Your Data

This activity is a good way to expand your study of the environment. Students can relate problems in the area where they live to adaptations. Often, people wonder why an organism doesn't just "adapt" to changes in its environment. This activity is a good opportunity to learn firsthand why adaptation can't happen within the span of a single generation and why organisms become endangered. The animal in the illustration is a duck-billed platypus, an actual mammal. The platypus has webbed feet and a flat tail that help it swim through the water. It also uses claws to dig and a flat, rubbery bill to search the mud for worms, crayfish, and other food. The duck-billed platypus lives in the rivers and ponds of Australia.

Lab Notes

This lab provides an opportunity for students to exercise a great deal of creativity and to expand their understanding of adaptations. Most students will probably enjoy choosing the adaptations and inventing a niche where those adaptations are useful. Help them understand that environments and adaptations usually evolve together in the natural world, not one before the other. You may want to make sets of the adaptations and put them in a container and have students select one from the container. This selection process may lessen duplication in the classroom. Someone might be challenged to design a flying decomposer with armor!

A Passel o' Pioneers

Teacher's Notes

Time Required

One 45-minute class and three 5-minute periodic observation periods

Lab Ratings

EASY ———————————→ HARD

Teacher Prep 🧪🧪
Student Set-Up 🧪🧪
Concept Level 🧪🧪🧪
Clean Up 🧪🧪

MATERIALS

The materials listed on the student page are enough for the entire class. You may want to use a large container, such as a 10 gal aquarium, so each student in the class can contribute a small amount of soil from different areas. Students might be able to bring fishbowls from home. If you have enough fishbowls and sunny windows, students really might enjoy seeing what comes up in their own container. If you do not have a sunny window, the containers can be placed where they will get the most light in the classroom. They need warmth for germination to occur, and light is necessary after the seedlings emerge from the soil.

Model-Making Lab

A Passel o' Pioneers

Succession is the natural process of the introduction and development of living things in an area. The area could be one that has never supported life before and has no soil, such as a recently cooled lava flow from a volcano. In an area where there is no soil, the process is called *primary succession.* In an area where soil already exists, such as an abandoned field or a forest after a fire, the process is called *secondary succession.*

In this investigation, you will build a model of secondary succession using natural soil.

Procedure

1 Place the natural soil you brought from home or the schoolyard into the fishbowl, and dampen the soil with 250 mL of water. Cover the top of the fishbowl with plastic wrap, and place the fishbowl in a sunny window.
Caution: Do not touch your face, eyes, or mouth during this activity. Wash your hands thoroughly when you are finished.

2 For 2 weeks, observe the fishbowl for any new growth. Describe and draw any new organisms you observe. Record these and all other observations.

3 Identify and record the names of as many of these new organisms as you can.

MATERIALS

- balance
- graduated cylinder, 250 mL
- large fishbowl
- plastic wrap
- protective gloves
- soil from home or schoolyard, 500 g
- water, 250 mL

SAFETY

Safety Caution

Check for any known allergies to molds before having students begin this lab. There may be molds in the soil.

CHAPTER RESOURCES

Chapter Resource File

- **Datasheet for LabBook**
- **Lab Notes and Answers**

Kerry Johnson
Isbell Middle School
Santa Paula, California

Analyze the Results

1 What kinds of plants sprouted in your model of secondary succession? Were they tree seedlings, grasses, or weeds?

2 Were the plants that sprouted in the fishbowl unusual or common for your area?

Draw Conclusions

3 Explain how the plants that grew in your model of secondary succession can be called pioneer species.

Applying Your Data

Examine each of the photographs on this page. Determine whether each area, if abandoned forever, would undergo primary or secondary succession. You may decide that an area will not undergo succession at all. Explain your reasoning.

Bulldozed land

Eutrophic pond

Mount St. Helens volcano

Shipping port parking lot

Applying Your Data

- Eutrophic pond: A eutrophic pond will eventually fill with sediment. At first, aquatic plants will grow. Later, when the pond is completely filled, the area will undergo secondary succession.

- Bulldozed land: Left abandoned, this area will undergo secondary succession just as abandoned farmland will.

- Shipping port parking lot: If the parking lot is abandoned forever, cracks will appear, exposing the soil underneath, and secondary succession will proceed. Some areas of this vast parking lot may even undergo primary succession, where concrete surfaces can be home to lichens.

- Mount St. Helens volcano: The explosion of Mount St. Helens caused an enormous mudslide and released tons of ash. Areas smothered by ash underwent primary succession. The entire region is now in various stages of secondary succession.

Analyze the Results

1. Plants that sprout should be plants common to the local area. They can be identified using a local-area field guide as soon as dicot seedlings have developed true leaves. Monocots will probably look like grasses.

2. Answers may vary. Students should recognize common plants.

Draw Conclusions

3. All the plants that come up in students' models of succession are pioneers because they are the first plants to grow in an area. Ask students if a tree can be a pioneer. (A tree can be a pioneer if it is one of the first plants to grow in an area. However, pioneers are usually plants that grow rapidly and that produce many seeds that are dispersed over a large area.)

Life in the Desert

Teacher's Notes

Time Required

One 45-minute class period

Lab Ratings

EASY ———————————→ HARD

Teacher Prep 🧪
Student Set-Up 🧪🧪
Concept Level 🧪🧪
Clean Up 🧪

MATERIALS

The sponges used in this lab can be either natural sponges or the synthetic sponges available in grocery stores. Use 3 in. × 6 in. sponges, 1 per student, cut in half.

Analyze the Results

1. Students should describe the kind of covering or protection they provided for their "adapted" sponge. Effectiveness of the adaptation will be measured by the amount of water lost over 24 h. Students will want their sponges to dry out as little as possible.

2. The unprotected sponge represents the organism that has no adaptation for conserving water. The unprotected sponge should dry out far more than the protected sponge.

Life in the Desert

Organisms that live in the desert have some unusual methods for conserving water. Conserving water is a special challenge for animals that live in the desert. In this activity you will invent a water-conserving "adaptation" for a desert animal, represented by a piece of sponge. You will protect your wet desert sponge so it will dry out as little as possible over a 24 h period.

MATERIALS

- balance
- sponge, dry, 8 cm × 8 cm × 2 cm (2 pieces)
- water
- other materials as needed

Ask a Question

❶ How can an animal conserve water in the desert?

Form a Hypothesis

❷ Plan a method for keeping your "desert animal" from drying out. Your "animal" must be in the open for at least 4 h during the 24 h period. Real desert animals expose themselves to the dry desert heat to search for food. Write your plan and predictions about the outcome of your experiment.

❸ Design and draw data tables, if necessary. Have your teacher approve your plan before you begin.

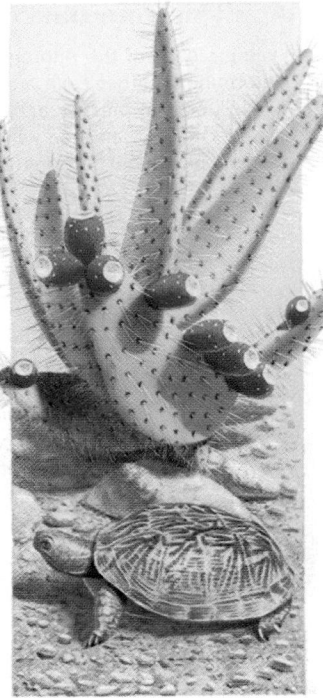

Test the Hypothesis

❹ Soak two pieces of sponge in water until they begin to drip. Place each piece on a balance, and record its mass.

❺ Immediately protect one sponge according to your plan. Place both pieces in an area where they will not be disturbed. You should take your protected "animal" out for feeding for a total of at least 4 h.

❻ At the end of 24 h, place each piece of sponge on the balance again, and record its mass.

Analyze the Results

❶ Describe the adaptation you used to help your "animal" survive. Was it effective? Explain.

❷ What was the purpose of leaving one of the sponges unprotected? How did the water loss in each of your sponges compare?

Communicating Your Data

Conduct a class discussion about other adaptations and results. How can you relate these invented adaptations to adaptations for desert survival among real organisms?

James Chin
Frank A. Day Middle School
Newtonville, Massachusetts

CHAPTER RESOURCES

Chapter Resource File

- Datasheet for LabBook
- Lab Notes and Answers

Discovering Mini-Ecosystems

In your study of ecosystems, you learned that a biome is a very large ecosystem that includes a set of smaller, related ecosystems. For example, a coniferous forest biome may include a river ecosystem, a wetland ecosystem, and a lake ecosystem. Each of those ecosystems may include several other smaller, related ecosystems. Even cities have mini-ecosystems! You may find a mini-ecosystem on a patch of sidewalk, in a puddle of rainwater, under a leaky faucet, in a shady area, or under a rock. In this activity, you will design a method for comparing two different mini-ecosystems found near your school.

MATERIALS
- items to be determined by the students and approved by the teacher

SAFETY

Ask a Question

❶ Examine the grounds around your school, and select two different areas you wish to investigate. Decide what you want to learn about your mini-ecosystems. For example, you may want to know what kind of living things each area contains. Be sure to get your teacher's approval before you begin.

Form a Hypothesis

❷ For each mini-ecosystem, make data tables for recording your observations.

Test the Hypothesis

❸ Observe your mini-ecosystem according to your plan at several different time points throughout the day. Record your observations.

❹ Wait 24 h and observe your mini-ecosystem again at the same times that you observed it the day before. Record your observations.

❺ Wait 1 week, and observe your mini-ecosystem again at the same times. Record your observations.

Analyze the Results

❶ What factors determine the differences between your mini-ecosystems? Identify the factors that set each mini-ecosystem apart from its surrounding area.

❷ How do the populations of your mini-ecosystems compare?

❸ Identify some of the adaptations that the organisms living in your two mini-ecosystems have. Describe how the adaptations help the organisms survive in their environment.

Draw Conclusions

❹ Write a report describing and comparing your mini-ecosystems with those of your classmates.

CHAPTER RESOURCES

Chapter Resource File
- **Datasheet for LabBook**
- **Lab Notes and Answers**

Barry Bishop
San Rafael Junior High
Ferron, Utah

Lab Notes

Even if your school has no area where there is sand, dirt, grass, or trees, ask students to observe puddles, the underside of eaves, the area under drain spouts, and the ground under rocks. Students should observe the areas they have chosen at least twice a day.

Discovering Mini-Ecosystems

Teacher's Notes

Time Required
One to two 45-minute class periods

Lab Ratings
EASY ——→ HARD

Teacher Prep 🧪
Student Set-Up 🧪🧪
Concept Level 🧪🧪🧪
Clean Up 🧪

MATERIALS
Because this is mainly an observation activity, few materials are needed. If binoculars or magnifying lenses are available, however, they may be helpful.

Analyze the Results

1. Students may have many answers, but they should include answers such as different vegetation, organisms that live there, the soil type, density of vegetation, and amount of water present.

2. Students should recognize that the populations present in each area are adapted for life in that area.

3. Adaptations that students name will probably include camouflage, deep roots, and burrowing behavior.

Draw Conclusions

4. Answers may vary according to student observations.

Deciding About Environmental Issues

Teacher's Notes

Time Required

One 45-minute class period

Lab Ratings

EASY ——————————→ HARD

Teacher Prep △
Student Set-Up △△
Concept Level △△△
Clean Up △

MATERIALS

You may want to have students bring in articles for several days prior to doing this activity. You might also want to limit students' choices to those that are age appropriate.

Lab Notes

This lab can be repeated as environmental issues appear in the news.

You may wish to combine this activity with a video that portrays an international environmental issue. Students can also be encouraged to use the Internet as a source of information.

Skills Practice Lab

Deciding About Environmental Issues

You make hundreds of decisions every day. Some of them are complicated, but many of them are very simple, such as what to wear or what to eat for lunch. Deciding what to do about an environmental issue can be very difficult. There are many different factors that must be considered. How will a certain solution affect people's lives? How much will it cost? Is it ethically right?

In this activity, you will analyze an issue in four steps to help you make a decision about it. Find out about environmental issues that are being discussed in your area. Examine newspapers, magazines, and other publications to find out what the issues are. Choose one local issue to evaluate. For example, you could evaluate whether the city should spend the money to provide recycling bins and special trucks for picking up recyclable trash.

MATERIALS

- newspapers, magazines, and other publications containing information about environmental issues

A Four-Step Decision-Making Model

Gather Information
↓
Consider Values
↓
Explore Consequences
↓
Make a Decision

Procedure

1 Write a statement about an environmental issue.

2 Read about your issue in several publications. On a separate sheet of paper, summarize important facts.

3 The values of an issue are the things that you consider important. Examine the diagram below. Several values are given. Which values do you think apply most to the environmental issue you are considering? Are there other values that you believe will help you make a decision about the issue? Consider at least four values in making your decision.

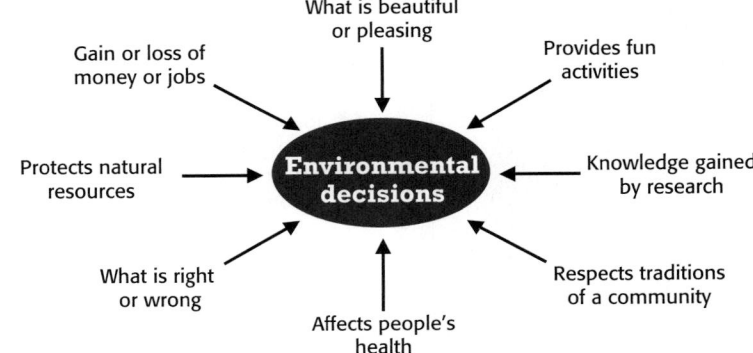

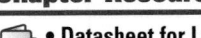

Debra Sampson
Booker T. Washington
Middle School
Elgin, Texas

CHAPTER RESOURCES

Chapter Resource File

- Datasheet for LabBook
- Lab Notes and Answers

4 Consequences are the things that result from a certain course of action. Create a table similar to the one below. Use your table to organize your thoughts about consequences related to your environmental issue. List your values at the top. Fill in each space with the consequences for each value.

Consequences Table				
Consequences	**Values**			
Positive short-term consequences				
Negative short-term consequences	DO NOT WRITE IN BOOK			
Positive long-term consequences				
Negative long-term consequences				

5 Thoroughly consider all of the consequences you have recorded in your table. Evaluate how important each consequence is. Make a decision about what course of action you would choose on the issue.

Analyze the Results

1 In your evaluation, did you consider short-term consequences or long-term consequences to be more important? Why?

2 Which value or values had the greatest influence on your final decision? Explain your reasoning.

Communicating Your Data

Compare your table with your classmates' tables. Did you all make the same decision about a similar issue? If not, form teams, and organize a formal classroom debate of a specific environmental issue.

Analyze the Results

1. Either short- or long-term consequences can be more relevant, depending on the issue.

2. Answers may vary according to students' perspectives.

Communicating Your Data

Encourage students to narrow their topic to a single aspect of an issue, such as the importance of aesthetic value in the preservation of natural areas.

Muscles at Work

Teacher's Notes

Time Required
One 45-minute class period

Lab Ratings

🧪 🧪🧪 🧪🧪🧪 🧪🧪🧪🧪
EASY ——————————→ HARD

Teacher Prep 🧪
Student Set-Up 🧪
Concept Level 🧪🧪
Clean Up 🧪

Safety Caution

A digital thermometer that measures temperature from the ear is recommended.

Because of the vigorous nature of the exercise, you may want to ask for volunteers to do the exercising. Also, you should be aware of any health concerns your students have.

Muscles at Work

Have you ever exercised outside on a cold fall day wearing only a thin warm-up suit or shorts? How did you stay warm? The answer is that your muscle cells contracted, and when contraction takes place, some energy is used to do work, and the rest is converted to thermal energy. This process helps your body maintain a constant temperature in cold conditions. In this activity, you will learn how the release of energy can cause a change in your body temperature.

MATERIALS

- clock (or watch) with a second hand
- thermometer, small, hand held
- other materials as approved by your teacher

Ask a Question

1 Write a question that you can test about how activity affects body temperature.

Form a Hypothesis

2 Form a group of four students. In your group, discuss several exercises that can produce a change in body temperature. Write a hypothesis that could answer the question you asked.

Test the Hypothesis

3 Develop an experimental procedure that includes the steps necessary to test your hypothesis. Be sure to get your teacher's approval before you begin.

4 Assign tasks to individuals in the group, such as note taking, data recording, and timing. What observations and data will you be recording? Design your data tables accordingly.

5 Perform your experiment as planned by your group. Be sure to record all observations in your data tables.

Analyze the Results

1 How did you determine if muscle contractions cause the release of thermal energy? Was your hypothesis supported by your data? Explain your results in a written report. Describe how you could improve your experimental method.

Applying Your Data

Why do humans shiver in the cold? Do all animals shiver? Find out why shivering is one of the first signs that your body is becoming too cold.

Analyze the Results

1. All answers will depend on the students' observations and their own hypotheses.

Applying Your Data

Sample answer: In a process known as *shivering thermogenesis,* muscle tone is gradually increased. Shivering increases the workload of the muscles and elevates oxygen and energy consumption. The heat that is produced warms the deep vessels. Shivering can elevate body temperature effectively. It can increase the rate of heat generation by as much as 400%. Endothermic animals have the capacity to shiver. Shivering is an automatic response of the body to cold.

CHAPTER RESOURCES

Chapter Resource File

- **Datasheet for LabBook**
- **Lab Notes and Answers**

CLASSROOM TESTED & APPROVED

Kathy LaRoe
East Valley Middle School
East Helena, Montana

Model-Making Lab

Build a Lung

When you breathe, you actually pull air into your lungs because your diaphragm muscle causes your chest to expand. You can see this is true by placing your hands on your ribs and inhaling slowly. Did you feel your chest expand?

In this activity, you will build a model of a lung by using some common materials. You will see how the diaphragm muscle works to inflate your lungs. Refer to the diagrams at right as you construct your model.

MATERIALS

- bag, trash, small plastic
- balloon, small
- bottle, top half, 2 L
- clay, golf-ball-sized piece
- rubber bands (2)
- ruler, metric
- straw, plastic
- tape, transparent

Procedure

1. Attach the balloon to the end of the straw with a rubber band. Make a hole through the clay, and insert the other end of the straw through the hole. Be sure at least 8 cm of the straw extends beyond the clay. Squeeze the ball of clay gently to seal the clay around the straw.

2. Insert the balloon end of the straw into the neck of the bottle. Use the ball of clay to seal the straw and balloon into the bottle.

3. Turn the bottle gently on its side. Place the trash bag over the cut end of the bottle. Expand a rubber band around the bottom of the bottle to secure the bag. You may wish to reinforce the seal with tape. Before the plastic is completely sealed, gather the excess material of the bag into your hand, and press toward the inside of the bottle slightly. (You may need to tie a knot about halfway up from the bottom of the bag to take up excess material.) Use tape to finish sealing the bag to the bottle with the bag in this position. The excess air will be pushed out of the bottle.

Analyze the Results

1. What can you do with your model to make the "lung" inflate?

2. What do the balloon, the plastic wrap, and the straw represent in your model?

3. Using your model, demonstrate to the class how air enters the lung and how air exits the lung.

Applying Your Data

Do some research to find out what an "iron lung" is and why it was used in the past. Research and write a report about what is used today to help people who have difficulty breathing.

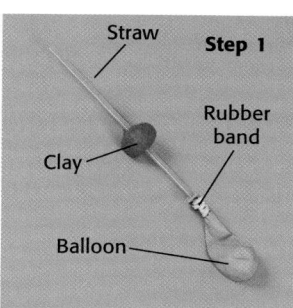

Straw — **Step 1**

Clay

Rubber band

Balloon

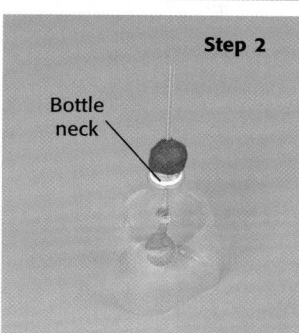

Step 2

Bottle neck

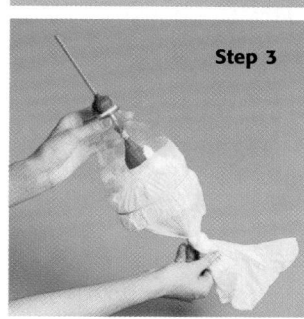
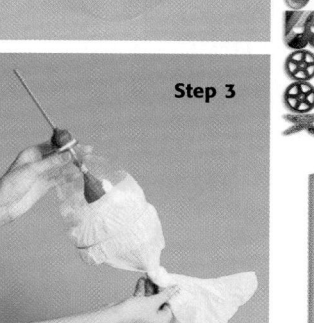

Step 3

CHAPTER RESOURCES

Chapter Resource File

 • Datasheet for LabBook
 • Lab Notes and Answers

CLASSROOM TESTED & APPROVED

Yvonne Brannum
Hine Junior High School
Washington, D.C.

Applying Your Data

From the late 1920s to the 1950s, iron lungs were used to treat respiratory paralysis due to poliomyelitis. The patient was encased within an airtight chamber from the neck down. A large set of leather bellows mounted in a separate pumping unit expanded, causing pressure changes inside the chamber. This, in turn, caused the chest of the patient to expand, drawing fresh air into the lungs through the mouth. Now, several models of portable ventilators allow patients much more freedom to move about.

LabBook
Model-Making Lab

Build a Lung

Teacher's Notes

Time Required
One 45-minute class period

Lab Ratings

EASY ———————→ HARD

Teacher Prep 🧪🧪
Student Set-Up 🧪🧪
Concept Level 🧪
Clean Up 🧪🧪

MATERIALS

You may want to build a model first to use as a reference for students. If so, you may want to substitute a bag smaller than the one that students use to model the diaphragm.

Analyze the Results

1. The balloon will inflate when the plastic bag is pulled down.

2. The balloon represents a lung, the plastic wrap represents a diaphragm, and the straw represents a trachea. (Students may also note that the bottle represents the part of the body in which the lungs are located.)

3. Air enters the lungs when the diaphragm moves down and creates more space inside the chest cavity. Air is forced out of the lungs when the diaphragm moves up. Students should demonstrate this process by moving the plastic bag up and down.

Enzymes in Action

Teacher's Notes

Time Required

One 45-minute class period

Lab Ratings

🧪	🧪🧪	🧪🧪🧪	🧪🧪🧪🧪
EASY			HARD

Teacher Prep 🧪🧪
Student Set-Up 🧪🧪
Concept Level 🧪🧪🧪
Clean Up 🧪🧪

MATERIALS

The materials listed on the student page are enough for 1 student or a group of 2–4 students. If you do not have enough mortar and pestles or small plates, you may have students use any small container to mash the liver with a fork. Beef liver is readily obtained at the grocery store.

Safety Caution

Remind students to review all safety cautions and icons before beginning this lab activity. Use a dilute solution of hydrogen peroxide. Hydrogen peroxide can be harmful to skin and clothing. Caution students to be careful not to spill or splatter the solution while pouring. If hydrogen peroxide comes into contact with skin, wash the skin immediately with plenty of running water.

Skills Practice Lab

Enzymes in Action

You know how important enzymes are in the process of digestion. This lab will help you see enzymes at work. Hydrogen peroxide is continuously produced by your cells. If it is not quickly broken down, hydrogen peroxide will kill your cells. Luckily, your cells contain an enzyme that converts hydrogen peroxide into two nonpoisonous substances. This enzyme is also present in the cells of beef liver. In this lab, you will observe the action of this enzyme on hydrogen peroxide.

Procedure

1. Draw a data table similar to the one below. Be sure to leave enough space to write your observations.

MATERIALS

- beef liver, 1 cm cubes (3)
- gloves, protective
- graduated cylinder, 10 mL
- hydrogen peroxide, fresh (4 mL)
- mortar and pestle (or fork and watch glass)
- plate, small
- spatula
- test tube (3)
- test-tube rack
- tweezers
- water

SAFETY

Data Table		
Size and condition of liver	Experimental liquid	Observations
1 cm cube beef liver	2 mL water	
1 cm cube beef liver	2 mL hydrogen peroxide	DO NOT WRITE IN BOOK
1 cm cube beef liver (mashed)	2 mL hydrogen peroxide	

CHAPTER RESOURCES

Chapter Resource File

- Datasheet for LabBook
- Lab Notes and Answers

② Get three equal-sized pieces of beef liver from your teacher, and use your forceps to place them on your plate.

③ Pour 2 mL of water into a test tube labeled "Water and liver."

④ Using the tweezers, carefully place one piece of liver in the test tube. Record your observations in your data table.

⑤ Pour 2 mL of hydrogen peroxide into a second test tube labeled "Liver and hydrogen peroxide."
Caution: Do not splash hydrogen peroxide on your skin. If you do get hydrogen peroxide on your skin, rinse the affected area with running water immediately, and tell your teacher.

⑥ Using the tweezers, carefully place one piece of liver in the test tube. Record your observations of the second test tube in your data table.

⑦ Pour another 2 mL of hydrogen peroxide into a third test tube labeled "Ground liver and hydrogen peroxide."

⑧ Using a mortar and pestle (or fork and watch glass), carefully grind the third piece of liver.

⑨ Using the spatula, scrape the ground liver into the third test tube. Record your observations of the third test tube in your data table.

Analyze the Results

① What was the purpose of putting the first piece of liver in water? Why was this a necessary step?

② Describe the difference you observed between the liver and the ground liver when each was placed in the hydrogen peroxide. How can you account for this difference?

Applying Your Data

Do plant cells contain enzymes that break down hydrogen peroxide? Try this experiment using potato cubes instead of liver to find out.

Analyze the Results

1. Sample answer: The piece of liver in water is the control. A control is necessary so that differences in reactions to other substances can be observed.

2. Students should observe that the cube of liver produced a quick, foaming reaction to the hydrogen peroxide as the solution came into contact with the cells and destroyed them. The mashed liver should also produce a very quick reaction; however, students should observe that the effervescence subsides faster with the mashed liver than with the cube. The reason is that the mashed liver has a greater surface area than the cube, exposing more liver enzymes to the hydrogen peroxide. There should be no reaction in water.

Applying Your Data

Students will discover that plant cells do contain enzymes that will break down hydrogen peroxide. Have them experiment with different types of plants and vegetables so they can observe the different rates of reaction.

Skills Practice Lab

My, How You've Grown!

Teacher's Notes

Time Required
One 45-minute class period

Lab Ratings

EASY ——————————→ HARD

Teacher Prep
Student Set-Up
Concept Level
Clean Up

Procedure

2. Students' graphs should look like those below.

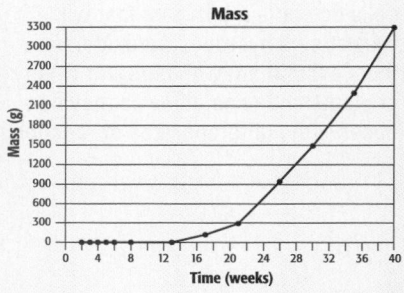

Mass

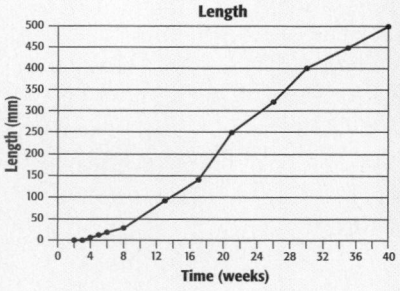

Length

Skills Practice Lab

My, How You've Grown!

In humans, the process of development that takes place between fertilization and birth lasts about 266 days. In 4 weeks, the new individual grows from a single fertilized cell to an embryo whose heart is beating and pumping blood. All of the organ systems and body parts are completely formed by the end of the seventh month. During the last 2 months before birth, the baby grows, and its organ systems mature. At birth, the average mass of a baby is about 33,000 times as much as that of an embryo at 2 weeks of development! In this activity, you will discover just how fast a fetus grows.

MATERIALS
- paper, graph
- pencils, colored

Procedure

1. Using graph paper, make two graphs—one entitled "Length" and one entitled "Mass." On the length graph, use intervals of 25 mm on the *y*-axis. Extend the *y*-axis to 500 mm. On the mass graph, use intervals of 100 g on the *y*-axis. Extend this *y*-axis to 3,300 g. Use 2-week intervals for time on the *x*-axes for both graphs. Both *x*-axes should extend to 40 weeks.

2. Examine the data table at right. Plot the data in the table on your graphs. Use a colored pencil to draw the curved line that joins the points on each graph.

Analyze the Results

1. Describe the change in mass of a developing fetus. How can you explain this change?

2. Describe the change in length of a developing fetus. How does the change in mass compare to the change in length?

Increase of Mass and Length of Average Human Fetus		
Time (weeks)	Mass (g)	Length (mm)
2	0.1	1.5
3	0.3	2.3
4	0.5	5.0
5	0.6	10.0
6	0.8	15.0
8	1.0	30.0
13	15.0	90.0
17	115.0	140.0
21	300.0	250.0
26	950.0	320.0
30	1,500.0	400.0
35	2,300.0	450.0
40	3,300.0	500.0

Applying Your Data

Using the information in your graphs, estimate how tall a child would be at age 3 if he or she continued to grow at the same average rate that a fetus grows.

Analyze the Results

1. The change in mass of a developing fetus is steadily increasing, approximately tripling each month of the first and second trimesters. This period is one of rapid cell division.

2. Fetal length steadily increases, doubling and even tripling each month in the first two trimesters. In the third trimester, the rate of lengthening slows. Mass continues to increase, even in the last trimester.

Applying Your Data
The child would be 2.45 m (8.04 ft) tall!

CHAPTER RESOURCES

Chapter Resource File

- Datasheet for LabBook
- Lab Notes and Answers

CLASSROOM TESTED & APPROVED

Randy Christian
Stovall Junior High School
Houston, Texas

Model-Making Lab

Antibodies to the Rescue

Some cells of the immune system, called *B cells,* make antibodies that attack and kill invading viruses and microorganisms. These antibodies help make you immune to disease. Have you ever had chickenpox? If you have, your body has built up antibodies that can recognize that particular virus. Antibodies will attach themselves to the virus, tagging it for destruction. If you are exposed to the same disease again, the antibodies remember that virus. They will attack the virus even quicker and in greater number than they did the first time. This is the reason that you will probably never have chickenpox more than once.

In this activity, you will construct simple models of viruses and their antibodies. You will see how antibodies are specific for a particular virus.

Procedure

1. Draw the virus patterns shown on this page on a separate piece of paper, or design your own virus models from the craft supplies. Remember to design different receptors on each of your virus models.

2. Write a few sentences describing how your viruses are different.

3. Cut out the viruses, and attach them to a piece of colored paper with tape or glue.

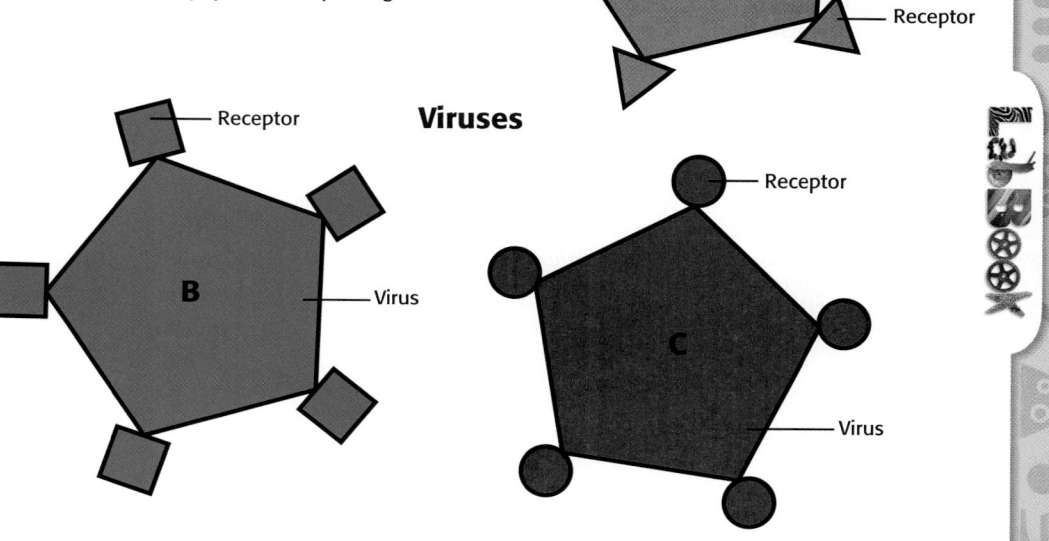

Viruses

CLASSROOM TESTED & APPROVED

Martha Kisiah
Fairview Middle School
Tallahassee, Florida

Antibodies to the Rescue

Teacher's Notes

Time Required
One 45-minute class period

Lab Ratings

EASY ——————→ HARD

Teacher Prep 🧪🧪
Student Set-Up 🧪🧪
Concept Level 🧪🧪
Clean Up 🧪🧪

MATERIALS

You will be able to expand this activity from very simple to a grand art project! Have students bring craft supplies from home. You may want to include poster paper in the materials list.

Preparation Notes
Encourage students to be imaginative in this exercise. Have them come up with interesting shapes for the viruses and the antibodies that fit them. Remind students that the main lesson of this exercise is that the antibodies can fit only a specific pathogen and in only one specific way, just as a key fits only one lock.

Analyze the Results

1. Sample answer: Antibodies recognize and bind to specific pathogens because antibodies are shaped to match the specific three-dimensional shape of the antigen.

2. Sample answer: Antibodies bind to specific pathogens and either inactivate the pathogen or trigger its destruction by macrophages.

3. Sample answer: Vaccines produce immunity because they contain antigens that stimulate an immune response in which memory cells are produced. Students can use their models to demonstrate or give examples.

Draw Conclusions

4. Sample answer: The antibodies that are specific to a pathogen will be ineffective when the pathogen changes its receptors. Students can show this mutation by slightly changing their model so that the virus and the antibody no longer fit as a lock and key do.

---

4 Select the antibodies drawn below, or design your own antibodies that will exactly fit on the receptors on your virus models. Draw or create each antibody enough times to attach one to each receptor site on the virus.

Antibodies

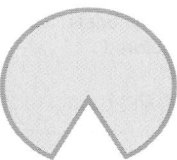  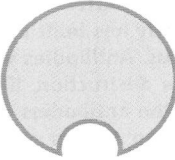

5 Cut out the antibodies you have drawn. Arrange the antibodies so that they bind to the virus at the appropriate receptor. Attach them to the virus with tape or glue.

Analyze the Results

1 Explain how an antibody "recognizes" a particular virus.

2 After the attachment of antibodies to the receptors, what would be the next step in the immune response?

3 Many vaccines use weakened copies of the virus to protect the body. Use the model of a virus and its specific antibody to explain how vaccines work.

Draw Conclusions

4 Use your model of a virus to demonstrate to the class how a receptor might change or mutate so that a vaccine would no longer be effective.

Applying Your Data

Research in the library or on the Internet to find information about the discovery of the Salk vaccine for polio. Include information on how polio affects people today.

Research in the library or on the Internet to find information and write a report about filoviruses. What do they look like? What diseases do they cause? Why are they especially dangerous? Is there an effective vaccine against any filovirus? Explain.

Applying Your Data

Dr. Jonas Edward Salk (1914–1995) was trying to develop an anti-influenza vaccine. This work led him and his colleagues to develop an inactivated vaccine against polio in 1952. Wide-scale testing in 1954 was successful, and the vaccine was distributed nationally. The vaccine greatly reduced the incidence of the polio. Partly because of the Salk vaccine, the number of cases of polio have decreased year after year—the Western Hemisphere was declared polio-free in 1994, and only 4,000 polio cases were reported worldwide in 1996. The World Health Organization is planning to end routine polio vaccination around the year 2005. Filoviruses belong to the family Filoviridae, one of several groups of viruses that can cause hemorrhagic fever, such as Ebola, in animals and humans. When magnified many thousands of times by an electron microscope, filoviruses resemble long filaments or threads. Because filoviruses can be extremely hazardous, laboratory studies of these viruses must be conducted in special maximum-containment facilities. The reservoir and natural history of filoviruses remain unknown. Filoviruses have the highest fatality rates (as high as 90% for epidemics of hemorrhagic fever caused by Ebola-Zaire virus). No vaccine exists to protect against filovirus infection, and no specific treatment is available for diseases caused by these viruses.

Skills Practice Lab

To Diet or Not to Diet

There are six main classes of foods that we need in order to keep our bodies functioning properly: water, vitamins, minerals, carbohydrates, fats, and proteins. In this activity you will investigate the importance of a well-balanced diet in maintaining a healthy body. Then you will create a poster or picture that illustrates the importance of one of the three energy-producing nutrients—carbohydrates, fats, and proteins.

Procedure

1. Draw a table like the one below. Research in the library, on nutrition labels, in nutrition or diet books, or on the Internet to find the information you need to fill out the chart.

Nutrition Data Table			
	Fats	Carbohydrates	Proteins
Found in which foods			
Functions in the body	DO NOT WRITE IN BOOK		
Consequences of deficiency			

2. Choose one of the foods you have learned about in your research, and create a poster or picture that describes its importance in a well-balanced diet.

Analyze the Results

1. Based on what you have learned in this lab, how might you change your eating habits to have a well-balanced diet? Does the nutritional value of foods concern you? Why or why not? Write down your answers, and explain your reasoning.

Communicating Your Data

Write a paragraph explaining why water is a nutrient. Analyze a typical fast-food meal, and determine its overall nutritional value.

LabBook

Skills Practice Lab

To Diet or Not to Diet

Teacher's Notes

Time Required

Two 45-minute class periods

Lab Ratings

EASY ——————→ HARD

Teacher Prep 🧪🧪
Student Set-Up 🧪
Concept Level 🧪🧪
Clean Up 🧪🧪

MATERIALS

A copy of a chart that fast-food restaurants post in their dining rooms outlining the nutritional information of the food they serve would be very helpful in analyzing a fast-food meal.

Analyze the Results

1. Answers may vary. Students may say they might try to eat fewer fatty foods. The nutritional value of foods is a subject that may be new to many students.

Communicating Your Data

Sample answer: Without water, most of the reactions that maintain life could not take place. Water carries the other essential nutrients to all parts of the body and is the medium in which waste products are dissolved and carried away from body tissues.

Answers will vary depending on the type of meal a student chooses. Fast-food restaurants usually post Nutrition Facts in public view. Have students obtain this information and evaluate a fast-food meal based on those Nutrition Facts and daily recommended amounts. Examining the Nutrition Facts labels on food packaging is helpful before beginning this activity.

CHAPTER RESOURCES

Chapter Resource File

- Datasheet for LabBook
- Lab Notes and Answers

CLASSROOM TESTED & APPROVED

Ivora Washington
Hyattsville Middle School
Hyattsville, Maryland

Contents

Appendix

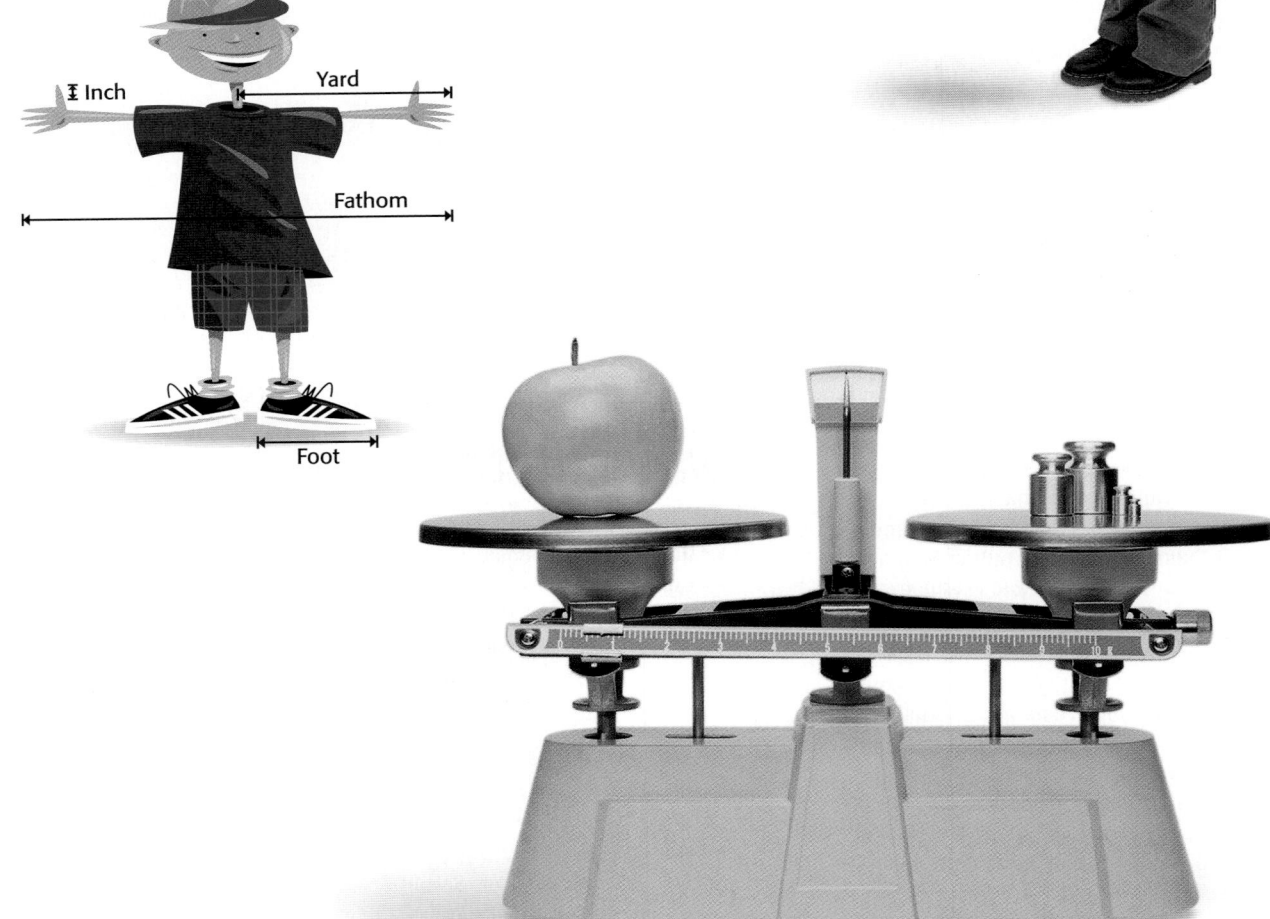

✓ Reading Check Answers

Chapter 1 The World of Life Science

Section 1
Page 6: the study of living things

Page 9: Sample answer: ocean pollution that harms mammals, birds, and fish.

Section 2
Page 10: a series of steps used by scientists to solve problems

Page 12: the possibility that an experiment can be designed to test the hypothesis

Page 14: only one

Page 16: because the scientist has learned something

Section 3
Page 19: a mathematical model

Page 20: to explain a broad range of observations, facts, and tested hypotheses, to predict what might happen, and to organize scientific thinking

Section 4
Page 23: SEMs produce three-dimensional images, and TEMs produce flat images.

Page 25: square units, such as square meters (m^2) and square centimeters (cm^2)

Page 26: how hot or cold it is or how much energy it has

Chapter 2 It's Alive!! Or Is It?

Section 1
Page 39: Sample answer: They control their body temperature by moving from one environment to another. If they get too warm, they move to the shade. If they get too cool, they move out into the sunlight.

Page 40: making food, breaking down food, moving materials into and out of cells, and building cells

Section 2
Page 42: photosynthesis

Page 45: Simple carbohydrates are made of one sugar molecule. Complex carbohydrates are made of many sugar molecules linked together.

Page 46: Most fats are solid, and most oils are liquid.

Chapter 3 Cells: The Basic Units of Life

Section 1
Page 61: Sample answer: All organisms are made of one or more cells, the cell is the basic unit of all living things, and all cells come from existing cells.

Page 62: If a cell's volume gets too large, the cell's surface area will not be able to take in enough nutrients or get rid of wastes fast enough to keep the cell alive.

Page 63: Organelles are structures within a cell that perform specific functions for the cell.

Page 65: One difference between eubacteria and archaea is that bacterial ribosomes are different from archaebacterial ribosomes.

Page 66: The main difference between prokaryotes and eukaryotes is that eukaryotic cells have a nucleus and membrane-bound organelles and prokaryotic cells do not.

Section 2
Page 68: Plant, algae, and fungi cells have cell walls.

Page 69 A cell membrane encloses the cell and separates and protects the cell's contents from the cell's environment. The cell wall also controls the movement of materials into and out of the cell.

Page 70: The cytoskeleton is a web of proteins in the cytoplasm. It gives the cell support and structure.

Page 72: Most of a cell's ATP is made in the cell's mitochondria.

Page 74: Lysosomes destroy worn-out organelles, attack foreign invaders, and get rid of waste material from inside the cell.

Section 3
Page 76: Sample answer: larger size, longer life, and cell specialization

Page 77: An organ is a structure of two or more tissues working together to perform a specific function in the body.

Page 78: cell, tissue, organ, organ system

Chapter 4 The Cell in Action

Section 1
Page 91: Red blood cells would burst in pure water because water particles move from outside, where particles were dense, to inside the cell, where particles were less dense. This movement of water would cause red blood cells to fill up and burst.

Page 93: Exocytosis is the process by which a cell moves large particles to the outside of the cell.

Section 2
Page 95: Cellular respiration is a chemical process by which cells produce energy from food. Breathing supplies oxygen for cellular respiration and removes the carbon dioxide produced by cellular respiration.

Page 97: One kind of fermentation produces CO_2, and the other kind produces lactic acid.

Section 3
Page 99: No, the number of chromosomes is not always related to the complexity of organisms.

Page 100: During cytokinesis in plant cells, a cell plate is formed. During cytokinesis in animal cells, a cell plate does not form.

Chapter 5   Heredity

Section 1
Page 114:   the passing of traits from parents to offspring

Page 117:   During his second set of experiments, Mendel allowed the first-generation plants, which resulted from his first set of experiments, to self-pollinate.

Page 118:   A ratio is a relationship between two different numbers that is often expressed as a fraction.

Section 2
Page 120:   A gene contains the instructions for an inherited trait. The different versions of a gene are called *alleles*.

Page 122:   Probability is the mathematical chance that something will happen.

Page 124:   In incomplete dominance, one trait is not completely dominant over another.

Section 3
Page 127:   23 chromosomes

Page 128:   During meiosis, one parent cell makes four new cells.

Chapter 6   Genes and DNA

Section 1
Page 145:   Guanine and cytosine are always found in DNA in equal amounts, as are adenine and thymine.

Page 147:   every time a cell divides

Section 2
Page 148:   a string of nucleotides that give the cell information about how to make a specific trait

Page 151:   They transfer amino acids to the ribosome.

Page 152:   a physical or chemical agent that can cause a mutation in DNA

Page 153:   Sickle cell disease is caused by a mutation in a single nucleotide of DNA, which then causes a different amino acid to be assembled in a protein used in blood cells.

Page 154:   a near-identical copy of another organism, created with the original organism's genes

Chapter 7   The Evolution of Living Things

Section 1
Page 166:   if they mate with each other and produce more of the same type of organism

Page 168:   by their estimated ages and physical similarities

Page 170:   a four-legged land mammal

Page 172:   that they have common ancestry

Section 2
Page 175:   965 km (600 mi) west of Ecuador

Page 177:   that Earth had been formed by natural processes over a long period of time

Page 178:   *On the Origin of Species by Means of Natural Selection*

Section 3
Page 181:   because they often produce many offspring and have short generation times

Page 182:   Sample answer: A newly formed canyon, mountain range, or lake could divide the members of a population.

Chapter 8   The History of Life on Earth

Section 1
Page 195:   absolute dating

Page 197:   periods of sudden extinction of many species

Page 198:   the idea that the Earth's continents once formed a single landmass surrounded by ocean

Section 2
Page 200:   The early Earth was very different from today—there were violent events and a harsh atmosphere.

Page 203:   a mass extinction

Page 204:   "recent life"

Section 3
Page 207:   the hominid family

Page 208:   Africa

Page 211:   Paleontologists will review their ideas about the evolution of hominids.

Chapter 9   Classification

Section 1
Page 222:   **Sample answer:** How many known species are there? What are the defining characteristics of each species? and What are the relationships between these species?

Page 225:   genus and species

Page 226:   A dichotomous key is an identification aid that uses a series of descriptive statements.

Section 2
Page 229:   *Escherichia coli*

Page 231:   Sample answer: Plants make energy through photosynthesis. Some members of the kingdoms Fungi, Protista, and Eubacteria consume plants. When these organisms digest the plant material, they get energy and nutrients made by the plants.

Page 233:   Sponges don't have sense organs, and they usually can't move around.

Chapter 10   Bacteria and Viruses

Section 1
Page 246:   Bacteria make up the kingdoms Eubacteria and Archaebacteria.

Page 248:   Binary fission is a process of cell division in which one cell splits into two. All bacteria reproduce by binary fission.

Section 2
Page 252:   Nitrogen fixing is the process by which nitrogen gas in the air is transformed into a form that plants can use.

Page 254: In genetic engineering, scientists change the genes of bacteria or other living things.

Section 3
Page 257: Viruses can be classified by shape or by the type of genetic material that they contain. Other possible answers are that viruses can be classified by life cycle or by the kind of disease that they cause.

Page 258: when a virus attacks living cells and turns them into virus factories

Chapter 11 Protists and Fungi
Section 1
Page 271: Protist producers make their own food through photosynthesis.

Page 272: binary fission and multiple fission

Section 2
Page 275: Red algae also have a red pigment in their cells that gives the algae a red color.

Page 276: salt water, fresh water, and snow

Page 278: radiolarians and foraminiferans

Page 280: as decomposers or as parasites

Section 3
Page 283: hyphae breaking apart so that each piece becomes a new fungus or fungi producing spores

Page 284: asexually by releasing spores from sporangia or sexually by different individuals growing together into specialized sporangia

Page 286: the spore-forming structures, called *basidia*

Page 288: Lichens make acids that break down rocks, which causes cracks.

Chapter 12 Introduction to Plants
Section 1
Page 301: In the sporophyte stage, plants make spores, which grow into gametophytes. The gametophytes produce eggs and sperm. A sperm fertilizes an egg. The fertilized egg grows into a sporophyte.

Page 302: nonvascular plants, seedless vascular plants, gymnosperms, and angiosperms

Page 303: Sample answer: Green algae and plant cells have the same kind of chlorophyll, have similar cell walls, and make their own food through photosynthesis. Both store energy in the form of starch and have a two-stage life cycle.

Section 2
Page 305: Sample answer: Nonvascular plants are usually the first plants to live in a new environment. They form a thin layer of soil, where new plants can grow. Nonvascular plants also prevent erosion.

Page 307: Sample answer: Seedless vascular plants prevent erosion. They can grow in new soil and add to the soil's depth.

Section 3
Page 308: Sample answer: Seed plants produce seeds. The gametophytes of seed plants do not live independently of the sporophyte. The sperm of seed plants don't need water to fertilize eggs.

Page 309: Sample answer: Seeds have stored food to nourish a young plant, while spores do not. Seeds can be spread by animals, while spores are spread by wind. Animals spread seeds more efficiently than the wind does.

Page 311: Sample answer: Sperm from the male cone fertilize the eggs of the female cone. A fertilized egg develops into a young sporophyte surrounded by a seed within the female cone. Eventually, seeds are released from the cone.

Page 312: Sample answer: Flowers help angiosperms reproduce. Fruits surround and protect the seeds. Some fruits attract animals, which spread the seeds.

Page 313: Sample answer: Major food crops are flowering plants. Flowering plants provide building material, are used to make clothing and rope, and are used to make medicines, rubber, and perfume oils.

Section 4
Page 315: taproot systems and fibrous root systems

Page 316: Sample answer: Herbaceous stems are soft, thin, and flexible. Poppies have herbaceous stems.

Page 318: epidermis, palisade layer, and spongy layer

Page 320: Sample answer: Stamens, which have filaments topped by anthers, are the male reproductive parts of flowers. A pistil is the female part of a flower. A pistil has a stigma, style, and ovary.

Chapter 13 Plant Processes
Section 1
Page 332: Sample answer: Plants are green because the chlorophyll reflects most wavelengths of green light.

Page 335: Sample answer: Photosynthesis provides the oxygen that organisms need for cellular respiration. Photosynthetic organisms form the base of nearly all food chains on Earth.

Section 2
Page 337: Sample answer: Animals may eat fruits and discard the seeds away from the parent plant. Other fruits, such as burrs, get caught in an animal's fur. Some fruits are carried by the wind.

Page 338: plantlets, tubers, and runners

Section 3
Page 340: Sample answer: The shoot tips will probably bend toward the light.

Page 341: Sample answer: Plants respond to the change in the length of day.

Page 342: Sample answer: Evergreen trees always have some leaves on them. Deciduous trees lose all of their leaves around the same time each year.

Chapter 14　Animals and Behavior

Section 1
Page 357: vertebrates
Page 358: heart, lung, and kidneys

Section 2
Page 361: A predator hunts prey as its food.
Page 362: A rabbit can "freeze" to hide from predators, or it can try to outrun predators.
Page 364: mice, squirrels, and skunks

Section 3
Page 366: defend a territory, find food, warn others of danger, identify family, frighten predators, and find mates
Page 368: They use body language to communicate where to find food sources.

Chapter 15　Invertebrates

Section 1
Page 381: The coelom is the space in the body that surrounds the gut.
Page 382: Water enters a sponge's body through pores.
Page 385: planarians, flukes, and tapeworms
Page 386: pinworms, hookworms, and *Trichinella spiralis*

Section 2
Page 389: An open circulatory system has a heart that pumps blood through blood vessels that empty into sinuses. A closed circulatory system has a heart that pumps blood through a closed loop of blood vessels.
Page 391: Doctors use leeches to prevent swelling and to prevent and break down blood clots.

Section 3
Page 393: Both an exoskeleton and an internal skeleton support an animal's body and allow the animal to move.
Page 395: Spiders are helpful because they catch small insects that are pests to humans.
Page 397: egg, nymph, and adult

Section 4
Page 399: Radial nerves control the movements of a sea star's arms.
Page 401: A sea lily's body is at the end of a long stalk, while a feather star does not have a stalk.

Chapter 16　Fishes, Amphibians, and Reptiles

Section 1
Page 413: cartilage
Page 414: Because most fishes are ectotherms, the body temperature of most fishes would increase as the temperature of their environment increased.
Page 416: Hagfish eat dead fishes on the ocean floor. Lampreys suck other animals' blood and flesh through a toothed suction cup–like mouth.

Page 418: Bony fishes have skeletons made of bone, have bodies covered in bony scales, and can rest in one place without swimming.

Section 2
Page 420: Most amphibians get oxygen through lungs.
Page 423: Most salamanders lose gills and grow lungs but do not go through a tadpole stage.
Page 424: Frogs use vocal sacs to sing, which helps frogs mark territories and attract mates.

Section 3
Page 427: Reptile eggs have a shell that keeps the embryo from drying out on land.
Page 428: turtles and tortoises, crocodiles and alligators, lizards and snakes, and tuataras
Page 431: Tuataras are most active at low temperatures, and they have no visible ear openings on the outside of the body.

Chapter 17　Birds and Mammals

Section 1
Page 443: Down feathers help birds stay warm.
Page 444: The heart beats rapidly so that it can pump enough blood to power the flight muscles.
Page 446: A bird's body heat warms the eggs.

Section 2
Page 449: rounded, flat beaks and long, sharp beaks
Page 450: The perching bird's feet will remain closed around the branch.

Section 3
Page 453: water, protein, fat, and sugar
Page 455: until the young mammal is grown

Section 4
Page 457: They gnaw and chew.
Page 458: Rabbits have two sets of sharp front teeth in their upper jaw, and they have a short tail.
Page 461: all of their time
Page 462: large brains, grasping hands and feet, flexible shoulder joints, and forward-facing eyes

Section 5
Page 465: A platypus uses its bill to dig for food and dig tunnels in the riverbanks where it can lay its eggs.
Page 466: as small as a bumblebee

Chapter 18　Interactions of Living Things

Section 1
Page 483: The biosphere is the part of Earth where life exists.

Section 2
Page 485: Organisms that eat other organisms are called *consumers*.
Page 487: An energy pyramid is a diagram that shows an ecosystem's loss of energy.

Page 488: Other animals in Yellowstone National Park were affected by the disappearance of the gray wolf because the food web was interrupted. The animals that would normally be prey for the gray wolf were more plentiful. These larger populations ate more vegetation.

Section 3

Page 491: The main ways that organisms affect each other are through competition, predator and prey relationships, symbiotic relationships, and coevolution.

Page 493: Camouflage helps an organism blend in with its surroundings because of its coloring. It is harder for a predator to find a camouflaged prey.

Page 494: In a mutualistic relationship, both organisms benefit from the relationship.

Page 496: Flowers need to attract pollinators to help the flowers reproduce with other members of their species.

Chapter 19   Cycles in Nature

Section 1

Page 509: Without water, there would be no life on Earth.

Page 511: Sample answer: calcium

Section 2

Page 512: Plants grew back, and the area is recovering.

Page 514: Primary succession happens in an area where organisms did not previously exist; secondary succession happens where organisms already exist.

Chapter 20   The Earth's Ecosystems

Section 1

Page 527: Sample answer: *Deciduous* comes from a Latin word that means "to fall off." In temperate deciduous forests, the trees lose their leaves in the fall.

Page 528: evergreen trees; squirrels, insects, finches, chickadees, jays, porcupines, elk, and moose

Page 530: During the dry season, grasses on the savanna dry out and turn yellow. But their deep roots survive for many months without water.

Page 531: Sample answer: Desert plants grow far apart. Some plants have shallow, widespread roots to take up water after a storm. Some desert plants have fleshy stems and leaves to store water. They also have waxy coatings to prevent water loss.

Page 532: Sample answer: Alpine tundra is tundra found at the top of tall mountains, above the tree line.

Section 2

Page 534: Sample answer: Plankton are tiny organisms that float near the surface of the water. They form the base of the ocean's feeding relationships.

Page 535: Sample answer: Fishes that live near the poles have adaptations for the near-freezing water. Animals in coral reefs need warm water to live. Some animals migrate to warmer waters to reproduce. Water temperature affects whether some animals can eat.

Page 537: Sample answer: Some animals get food from material that sinks to the bottom from the surface. Other animals get energy from chemicals released by thermal vents.

Page 538: Sample answer: When corals die, they leave behind their skeletons. Other corals grow on these remains. Over time, the layers build up to form a coral reef.

Section 3

Page 541: Sample answer: The littoral zone is the zone closest to shore in which light reaches the lake bottom. The open zone extends from the littoral zone and goes as deep as sunlight can reach. The deep-water zone lies beneath the open-water zone.

Page 542: A swamp is a wetland ecosystem in which trees and vines grow.

Page 543: Sample answer: Many fishes will die as the pond fills in because bacteria that decompose material in the pond use up the oxygen in the water.

Chapter 21   Environmental Problems and Solutions

Section 1

Page 554: Sample answer: Hazardous waste is waste that can catch fire, wear through metal, explode, or make people sick.

Page 557: Sample answer: Exotic species are organisms that make a home for themselves in a new place.

Page 558: Point-source pollution is pollution that comes from one place. Nonpoint-source pollution is pollution that comes from many places.

Section 2

Page 560: reduce, reuse, and recycle

Page 562: Sample answer: Water is reclaimed with plants or filter-feeding animals. Then, it can be used to water crops, parks, lawns, and golf courses.

Page 565: Sample answer: The EPA is a government organization that helps protect the environment.

Chapter 22   Body Organization and Structure

Section 1

Page 581: The stomach works with other organs, such as the small and large intestines, to digest food.

Page 582: Sample answer: The cardiovascular system includes the heart and blood vessels. These organs are also part of the circulatory system, which includes blood. Together, these systems deliver the materials cells need to survive.

Section 2

Page 585: Sample answer: As people grow, most of the cartilage that they start out with is replaced with bone.

Page 586: Sample answer: Joints are held together by ligaments. Cartilage cushions the area in a joint where bones meet.

Section 3

Page 589: Sample answer: One muscle, the flexor, bends part of the body. Another muscle, the extensor, straightens part of the body.

Page 591: Sample answer: Anabolic steroids can damage the heart, liver, and kidneys. They can also cause high blood pressure. Anabolic steroids can cause bones to stop growing.

Section 4

Page 593: The dermis is the layer of skin that lies beneath the epidermis. It is composed of a protein called *collagen*, while the epidermis contains keratin.

Page 594: Sample answer: A nail grows from living cells in the nail root at the base of the nail. As new cells form, the nail grows longer.

Chapter 23 Circulation and Respiration

Section 1

Page 606: The four main parts of the cardiovascular system are the heart and the arteries, capillaries, and veins.

Page 608: Arteries have thick, stretchy walls and carry blood away from the heart. Capillaries are tiny blood vessels that allow the exchange of oxygen, carbon dioxide, and nutrients between cells and blood. Veins are blood vessels that carry blood back to the heart.

Page 610: Atherosclerosis is dangerous because it is the buildup of material inside an artery. When the artery becomes blocked, blood can't flow and can't reach the cells. In some cases, a person can have a heart attack from a blocked artery.

Section 2

Page 612: plasma, red blood cells, white blood cells, and platelets

Page 613: White blood cells identify and attack pathogens that may make you sick.

Page 614: Systolic pressure is the pressure inside arteries when the ventricles contract. Diastolic pressure is the pressure inside the arteries when the ventricles are relaxed.

Page 615: The red blood cells of a person who has type O blood have no A or B antigens. The A or B antibodies in another person's blood will not react to the type O cells. It is safe for anyone to receive type O blood.

Section 3

Page 616: The lymphatic system is a secondary circulatory system in the body. The lymphatic system collects fluid and particles from between the cells and returns them to the cardiovascular system.

Page 618: The white pulp of the spleen is part of the lymphatic system. It helps fight infections by storing and producing lymphocytes. The red pulp of the spleen removes unwanted material, such as defective red blood cells, from the circulatory system.

Section 4

Page 621: nose, pharynx, larynx, trachea, bronchi, bronchioles, alveoli

Page 622: Cellular respiration is the process inside a cell in which oxygen is used to release energy stored in molecules of glucose. During the process, carbon dioxide (CO_2) and water are released.

Chapter 24 The Digestive and Urinary Systems

Section 1

Page 635 Enzymes cut proteins into amino acids that the body can use.

Page 637 Chyme is a soupy mixture of partially digested food in the stomach.

Page 639 Bile breaks large fat droplets into very small droplets. This process allows more fat molecules to be exposed to digestive enzymes.

Page 640 Fiber keeps the stool soft and keeps material moving through the large intestine.

Section 2

Page 643 Nephrons are microscopic filters inside the kidneys.

Page 644 Diuretics are chemicals that cause the kidneys to make more urine.

Chapter 25 Communication and Control

Section 1

Page 656: The CNS is the brain and the spinal cord. The PNS is all of the parts of the nervous system except the brain and the spinal cord.

Page 657: A neuron is a cell that has a cell body and a nucleus. A neuron also has dendrites that receive signals from other neurons and axons that send signals to other neurons.

Page 658: A nerve is a collection of nerve fibers, or axons, bundled together with blood vessels through which impulses travel between the central nervous system and other parts of the body.

Page 659: The PNS connects your CNS to the rest of your body, controls voluntary movements, and keeps your body's functions in balance.

Page 660: A voluntary action is an action over which you have conscious control. Voluntary activities include throwing a ball, playing a video game, talking to your friends, taking a bite of food, and raising your hand to answer a question in class. An involuntary action is an action that happens automatically. It is an action or process over which you do not have conscious control.

Page 661: The medulla is important because it controls your heart rate, blood pressure, and ordinary breathing.

Page 662: When someone touches your skin, an impulse that travels along a sensory neuron to your spinal cord and then to your brain is created. The response travels back from your brain to your spinal cord and then along a motor neuron to a muscle.

Section 2

Page 664: Skin can detect pressure, temperature, pain, and vibration.

Page 665: Reflexes are important because they can protect you from injury.

Page 666: Light strikes cells on the retina and triggers impulses in those cells. The impulses are carried to the brain, which interprets the impulses as images that you "see."

Page 667: In bright light, your iris contracts and reduces the amount of light entering the eye.

Page 668: Neurons in the cochlea convert waves into electrical impulses that the brain interprets as sound.

Section 3

Page 671: Sample answer: The thyroid gland increases the rate at which the body uses energy. The thymus gland regulates the immune system, which helps your body fight disease.

Page 672: Insulin helps regulate the amount of glucose in the blood.

Chapter 26 Reproduction and Development

Section 1

Page 685: Sexual reproduction is reproduction in which the sex cells (egg and sperm) of two parents unite to form a new individual.

Page 686: External fertilization happens when the sex cells unite outside of the female's body. Internal fertilization happens when the sex cells unite inside the female's body.

Page 687: All mammals reproduce sexually and nurture their young with milk.

Section 2

Page 688: testes, epididymis, vas deferens, urethra, penis

Page 690: Twins happen about 30 times in every 1,000 births.

Section 3

Page 692: Fertilization happens when the nucleus of a sperm unites with the nucleus of an egg. Implantation happens after the fertilized egg travels down the fallopian tube to the uterus and embeds itself in the wall of the uterus.

Page 693: The placenta is important because it provides the embryo with oxygen and nutrients from the mother's blood. Wastes from the embryo also travel to the placenta, where they are carried to the mother so that she can excrete them.

Page 694: The embryo is now called a *fetus*. The fetus's face begins to look more human, and the fetus can swallow, grows rapidly (triples in size), and begins to make movements that the mother can feel.

Page 696: A person's reproductive system becomes mature.

Chapter 27 Body Defenses and Disease

Section 1

Page 711: Cooking kills dangerous bacteria or parasites living in meat, fish, and eggs.

Page 713: Frank's doctor did not prescribe antibiotics because Frank had a cold. Colds are caused by viruses. Antibiotics can't stop viruses.

Section 2

Page 715: Macrophages engulf, or eat, any microorganisms or viruses that enter your body.

Page 716: If a virus particle enters the body, it may pass into body cells and begin to replicate. Or it may be engulfed and broken up by macrophages.

Page 719: rheumatoid arthritis, diabetes, multiple sclerosis, and lupus

Page 720: HIV causes AIDS.

Chapter 28 Staying Healthy

Section 1

Page 733: An incomplete protein does not contain all of the essential amino acids.

Page 735: Sample answer: a peanut butter sandwich, a glass of milk, and fresh fruit and vegetable slices

Page 736: One serving of chicken noodle soup provides more than 10% of the daily recommended allowance of vitamin A and sodium.

Section 2

Page 739: Over-the-counter drugs can be bought without a prescription. Prescription drugs can be bought only with a prescription from a doctor or other medical professional.

Page 741: First-time use of cocaine can cause a heart attack or can cause a person to become addicted.

Page 742: Drug use is the proper use of a legal drug. Drug abuse is either the use of an illegal drug or the improper use of a legal drug.

Section 3

Page 745: Aerobic exercise strengthens the heart, lungs, and bones and reduces stress. Regular exercise also burns Calories and can give you more energy.

Page 747: Sample answers: Never hike or camp alone, dress for the weather, learn how to swim, wear a life jacket, and never drink unpurified water.

Page 749: CPR is a way to revive someone whose heart has stopped beating. CPR classes are available in many places in the community.

Study Skills

FoldNote Instructions

Have you ever tried to study for a test or quiz but didn't know where to start? Or have you read a chapter and found that you can remember only a few ideas? Well, FoldNotes are a fun and exciting way to help you learn and remember the ideas you encounter as you learn science!

FoldNotes are tools that you can use to organize concepts. By focusing on a few main concepts, FoldNotes help you learn and remember how the concepts fit together. They can help you see the "big picture." Below you will find instructions for building 10 different FoldNotes.

Pyramid

1. Place a sheet of paper in front of you. Fold the lower left-hand corner of the paper diagonally to the opposite edge of the paper.

2. Cut off the tab of paper created by the fold (at the top).

3. Open the paper so that it is a square. Fold the lower right-hand corner of the paper diagonally to the opposite corner to form a triangle.

4. Open the paper. The creases of the two folds will have created an X.

5. Using scissors, cut along one of the creases. Start from any corner, and stop at the center point to create two flaps. Use tape or glue to attach one of the flaps on top of the other flap.

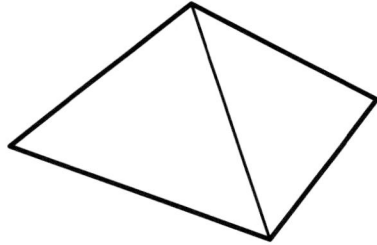

Double Door

1. Fold a sheet of paper in half from the top to the bottom. Then, unfold the paper.

2. Fold the top and bottom edges of the paper to the crease.

Booklet

1. Fold a sheet of paper in half from left to right. Then, unfold the paper.

2. Fold the sheet of paper in half again from the top to the bottom. Then, unfold the paper.

3. Refold the sheet of paper in half from left to right.

4. Fold the top and bottom edges to the center crease.

5. Completely unfold the paper.

6. Refold the paper from top to bottom.

7. Using scissors, cut a slit along the center crease of the sheet from the folded edge to the creases made in step 4. Do not cut the entire sheet in half.

8. Fold the sheet of paper in half from left to right. While holding the bottom and top edges of the paper, push the bottom and top edges together so that the center collapses at the center slit. Fold the four flaps to form a four-page book.

Layered Book

1. Lay one sheet of paper on top of another sheet. Slide the top sheet up so that 2 cm of the bottom sheet is showing.

2. Hold the two sheets together, fold down the top of the two sheets so that you see four 2 cm tabs along the bottom.

3. Using a stapler, staple the top of the FoldNote.

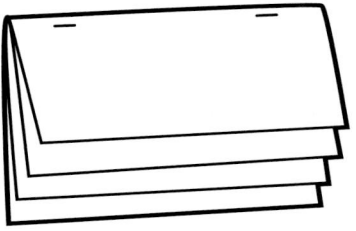

Key-Term Fold

1. Fold a sheet of lined notebook paper in half from left to right.

2. Using scissors, cut along every third line from the right edge of the paper to the center fold to make tabs.

Four-Corner Fold

1. Fold a sheet of paper in half from left to right. Then, unfold the paper.

2. Fold each side of the paper to the crease in the center of the paper.

3. Fold the paper in half from the top to the bottom. Then, unfold the paper.

4. Using scissors, cut the top flap creases made in step 3 to form four flaps.

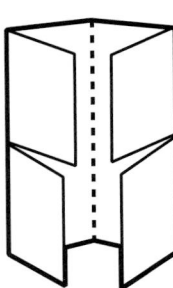

Three-Panel Flip Chart

1. Fold a piece of paper in half from the top to the bottom.

2. Fold the paper in thirds from side to side. Then, unfold the paper so that you can see the three sections.

3. From the top of the paper, cut along each of the vertical fold lines to the fold in the middle of the paper. You will now have three flaps.

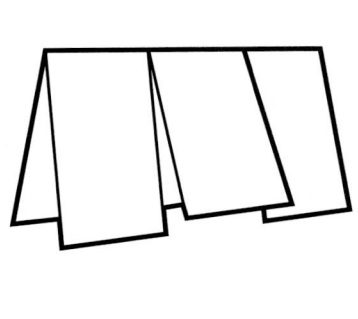

Table Fold

1. Fold a piece of paper in half from the top to the bottom. Then, fold the paper in half again.

2. Fold the paper in thirds from side to side.

3. Unfold the paper completely. Carefully trace the fold lines by using a pen or pencil.

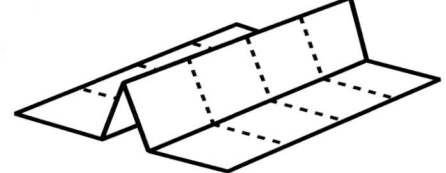

Two-Panel Flip Chart

1. Fold a piece of paper in half from the top to the bottom.

2. Fold the paper in half from side to side. Then, unfold the paper so that you can see the two sections.

3. From the top of the paper, cut along the vertical fold line to the fold in the middle of the paper. You will now have two flaps.

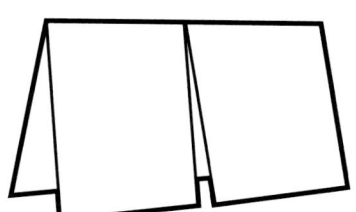

Tri-Fold

1. Fold a piece a paper in thirds from the top to the bottom.

2. Unfold the paper so that you can see the three sections. Then, turn the paper sideways so that the three sections form vertical columns.

3. Trace the fold lines by using a pen or pencil. Label the columns "Know," "Want," and "Learn."

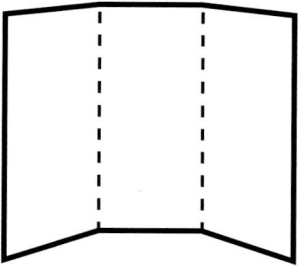

Graphic Organizer Instructions

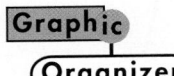 Have you ever wished that you could "draw out" the many concepts you learn in your science class? Sometimes, being able to *see* how concepts are related really helps you remember what you've learned. Graphic Organizers do just that! They give you a way to draw or map out concepts.

All you need to make a Graphic Organizer is a piece of paper and a pencil. Below you will find instructions for four different Graphic Organizers designed to help you organize the concepts you'll learn in this book.

Spider Map

1. Draw a diagram like the one shown. In the circle, write the main topic.

2. From the circle, draw legs to represent different categories of the main topic. You can have as many categories as you want.

3. From the category legs, draw horizontal lines. As you read the chapter, write details about each category on the horizontal lines.

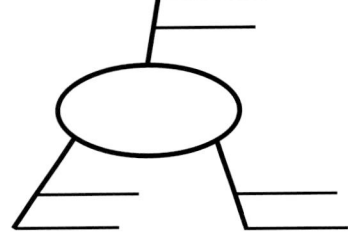

Comparison Table

1. Draw a chart like the one shown. Your chart can have as many columns and rows as you want.

2. In the top row, write the topics that you want to compare.

3. In the left column, write characteristics of the topics that you want to compare. As you read the chapter, fill in the characteristics for each topic in the appropriate boxes.

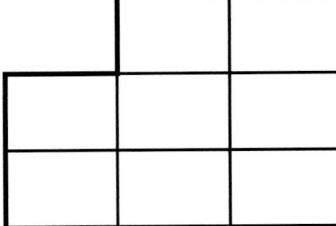

Chain-of-Events-Chart

1. Draw a box. In the box, write the first step of a process or the first event of a timeline.

2. Under the box, draw another box, and use an arrow to connect the two boxes. In the second box, write the next step of the process or the next event in the timeline.

3. Continue adding boxes until the process or timeline is finished.

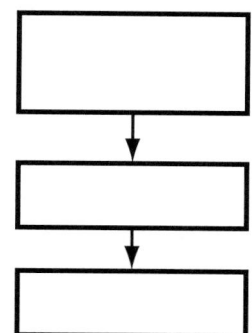

Concept Map

1. Draw a circle in the center of a piece of paper. Write the main idea of the chapter in the center of the circle.

2. From the circle, draw other circles. In those circles, write characteristics of the main idea. Draw arrows from the center circle to the circles that contain the characteristics.

3. From each circle that contains a characteristic, draw other circles. In those circles, write specific details about the characteristic. Draw arrows from each circle that contains a characteristic to the circles that contain specific details. You may draw as many circles as you want.

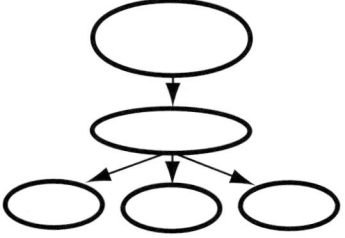

SI Measurement

The International System of Units, or SI, is the standard system of measurement used by many scientists. Using the same standards of measurement makes it easier for scientists to communicate with one another.

SI works by combining prefixes and base units. Each base unit can be used with different prefixes to define smaller and larger quantities. The table below lists common SI prefixes.

SI Prefixes

Prefix	Symbol	Factor	Example
kilo-	k	1,000	kilogram, 1 kg = 1,000 g
hecto-	h	100	hectoliter, 1 hL = 100 L
deka-	da	10	dekameter, 1 dam = 10 m
		1	meter, liter, gram
deci-	d	0.1	decigram, 1 dg = 0.1 g
centi-	c	0.01	centimeter, 1 cm = 0.01 m
milli-	m	0.001	milliliter, 1 mL = 0.001 L
micro-	μ	0.000 001	micrometer, 1 μm = 0.000 001 m

SI Conversion Table

SI units	From SI to English	From English to SI
Length		
kilometer (km) = 1,000 m	1 km = 0.621 mi	1 mi = 1.609 km
meter (m) = 100 cm	1 m = 3.281 ft	1 ft = 0.305 m
centimeter (cm) = 0.01 m	1 cm = 0.394 in.	1 in. = 2.540 cm
millimeter (mm) = 0.001 m	1 mm = 0.039 in.	
micrometer (μm) = 0.000 001 m		
nanometer (nm) = 0.000 000 001 m		
Area		
square kilometer (km^2) = 100 hectares	1 km^2 = 0.386 mi^2	1 mi^2 = 2.590 km^2
hectare (ha) = 10,000 m^2	1 ha = 2.471 acres	1 acre = 0.405 ha
square meter (m^2) = 10,000 cm^2	1 m^2 = 10.764 ft^2	1 ft^2 = 0.093 m^2
square centimeter (cm^2) = 100 mm^2	1 cm^2 = 0.155 in.^{2}	1 in.^{2} = 6.452 cm^2
Volume		
liter (L) = 1,000 mL = 1 dm^3	1 L = 1.057 fl qt	1 fl qt = 0.946 L
milliliter (mL) = 0.001 L = 1 cm^3	1 mL = 0.034 fl oz	1 fl oz = 29.574 mL
microliter (μL) = 0.000 001 L		
Mass		
kilogram (kg) = 1,000 g	1 kg = 2.205 lb	1 lb = 0.454 kg
gram (g) = 1,000 mg	1 g = 0.035 oz	1 oz = 28.350 g
milligram (mg) = 0.001 g		
microgram (μg) = 0.000 001 g		

Appendix

Measuring Skills

Using a Graduated Cylinder

When using a graduated cylinder to measure volume, keep the following procedures in mind:

1 Place the cylinder on a flat, level surface before measuring liquid.

2 Move your head so that your eye is level with the surface of the liquid.

3 Read the mark closest to the liquid level. On glass graduated cylinders, read the mark closest to the center of the curve in the liquid's surface.

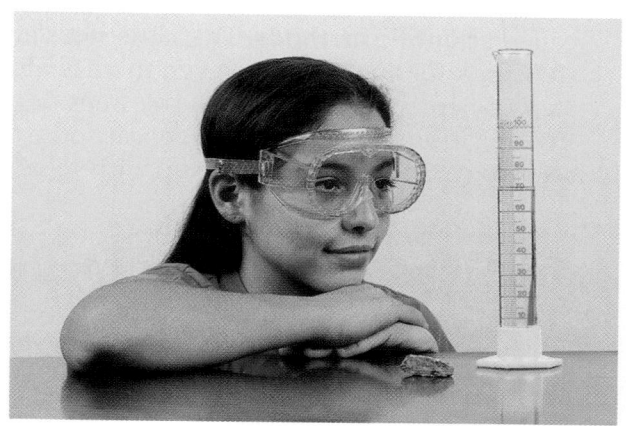

Using a Meterstick or Metric Ruler

When using a meterstick or metric ruler to measure length, keep the following procedures in mind:

1 Place the ruler firmly against the object that you are measuring.

2 Align one edge of the object exactly with the 0 end of the ruler.

3 Look at the other edge of the object to see which of the marks on the ruler is closest to that edge. (Note: Each small slash between the centimeters represents a millimeter, which is one-tenth of a centimeter.)

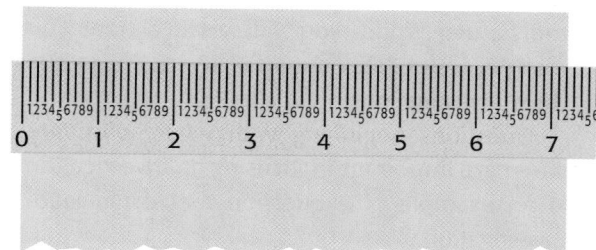

Using a Triple-Beam Balance

When using a triple-beam balance to measure mass, keep the following procedures in mind:

1 Make sure the balance is on a level surface.

2 Place all of the countermasses at 0. Adjust the balancing knob until the pointer rests at 0.

3 Place the object you wish to measure on the pan. **Caution:** Do not place hot objects or chemicals directly on the balance pan.

4 Move the largest countermass along the beam to the right until it is at the last notch that does not tip the balance. Follow the same procedure with the next-largest countermass. Then, move the smallest countermass until the pointer rests at 0.

5 Add the readings from the three beams together to determine the mass of the object.

6 When determining the mass of crystals or powders, first find the mass of a piece of filter paper. Then, add the crystals or powder to the paper, and remeasure. The actual mass of the crystals or powder is the total mass minus the mass of the paper. When finding the mass of liquids, first find the mass of the empty container. Then, find the combined mass of the liquid and container. The mass of the liquid is the total mass minus the mass of the container.

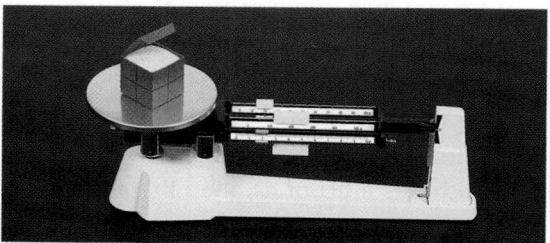

Scientific Methods

The ways in which scientists answer questions and solve problems are called **scientific methods.** The same steps are often used by scientists as they look for answers. However, there is more than one way to use these steps. Scientists may use all of the steps or just some of the steps during an investigation. They may even repeat some of the steps. The goal of using scientific methods is to come up with reliable answers and solutions.

Six Steps of Scientific Methods

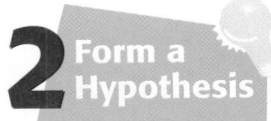
1 Ask a Question

Good questions come from careful **observations.** You make observations by using your senses to gather information. Sometimes, you may use instruments, such as microscopes and telescopes, to extend the range of your senses. As you observe the natural world, you will discover that you have many more questions than answers. These questions drive investigations.

Questions beginning with *what, why, how,* and *when* are important in focusing an investigation. Here is an example of a question that could lead to an investigation.

Question: How does acid rain affect plant growth?

2 Form a Hypothesis

After you ask a question, you need to form a **hypothesis.** A hypothesis is a clear statement of what you expect the answer to your question to be. Your hypothesis will represent your best "educated guess" based on what you have observed and what you already know. A good hypothesis is testable. Otherwise, the investigation can go no further. Here is a hypothesis based on the question, "How does acid rain affect plant growth?"

Hypothesis: Acid rain slows plant growth.

The hypothesis can lead to predictions. A prediction is what you think the outcome of your experiment or data collection will be. Predictions are usually stated in an if-then format. Here is a sample prediction for the hypothesis that acid rain slows plant growth.

Prediction: If a plant is watered with only acid rain (which has a pH of 4), then the plant will grow at half its normal rate.

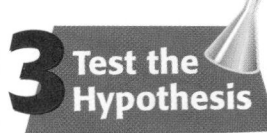
3 Test the Hypothesis

After you have formed a hypothesis and made a prediction, your hypothesis should be tested. One way to test a hypothesis is with a controlled experiment. A **controlled experiment** tests only one factor at a time. In an experiment to test the effect of acid rain on plant growth, the **control group** would be watered with normal rain water. The **experimental group** would be watered with acid rain. All of the plants should receive the same amount of sunlight and water each day. The air temperature should be the same for all groups. However, the acidity of the water will be a variable. In fact, any factor that is different from one group to another is a **variable.** If your hypothesis is correct, then the acidity of the water and plant growth are *dependant variables.* The amount a plant grows is dependent on the acidity of the water. However, the amount of water each plant receives and the amount of sunlight each plant receives are *independent variables.* Either of these factors could change without affecting the other factor.

Sometimes, the nature of an investigation makes a controlled experiment impossible. For example, the Earth's core is surrounded by thousands of meters of rock. Under such circumstances, a hypothesis may be tested by making detailed observations.

4 Analyze the Results

After you have completed your experiments, made your observations, and collected your data, you must analyze all the information you have gathered. Tables and graphs are often used in this step to organize the data.

5 Draw Conclusions

After analyzing your data, you can determine if your results support your hypothesis. If your hypothesis is supported, you (or others) might want to repeat the observations or experiments to verify your results. If your hypothesis is not supported by the data, you may have to check your procedure for errors. You may even have to reject your hypothesis and make a new one. If you cannot draw a conclusion from your results, you may have to try the investigation again or carry out further observations or experiments.

6 Communicate Results

After any scientific investigation, you should report your results. By preparing a written or oral report, you let others know what you have learned. They may repeat your investigation to see if they get the same results. Your report may even lead to another question and then to another investigation.

Scientific Methods in Action

Scientific methods contain loops in which several steps may be repeated over and over again. In some cases, certain steps are unnecessary. Thus, there is not a "straight line" of steps. For example, sometimes scientists find that testing one hypothesis raises new questions and new hypotheses to be tested. And sometimes, testing the hypothesis leads directly to a conclusion. Furthermore, the steps in scientific methods are not always used in the same order. Follow the steps in the diagram, and see how many different directions scientific methods can take you.

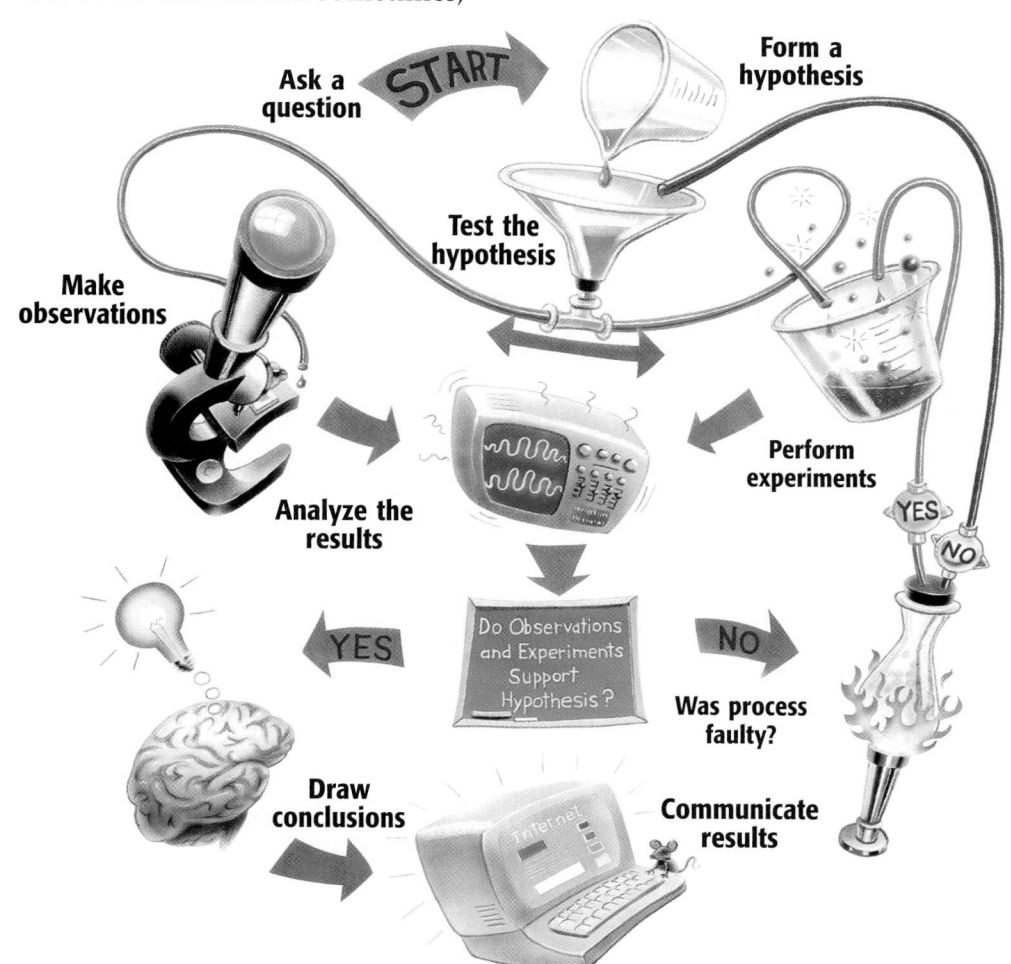

Temperature Scales

Temperature can be expressed by using three different scales: Fahrenheit, Celsius, and Kelvin. The SI unit for temperature is the kelvin (K).

Although 0 K is much colder than 0°C, a change of 1 K is equal to a change of 1°C.

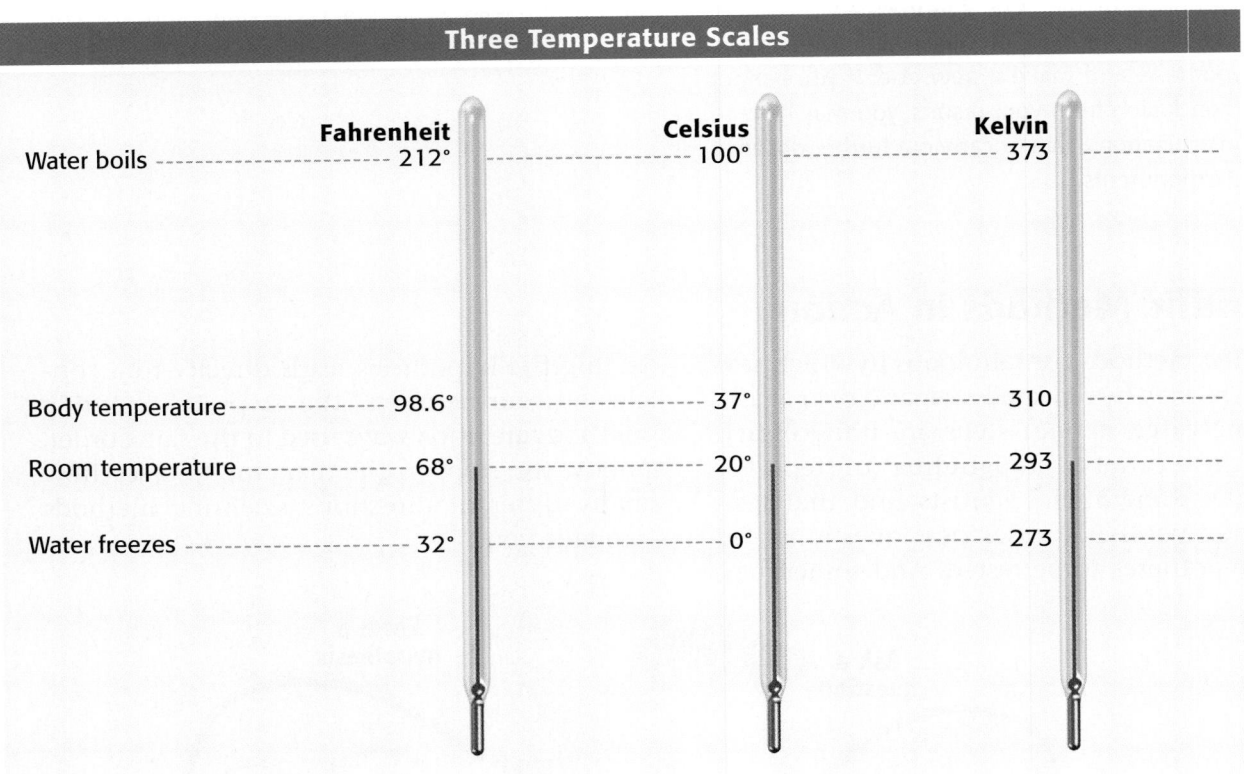

Three Temperature Scales			
	Fahrenheit	**Celsius**	**Kelvin**
Water boils	212°	100°	373
Body temperature	98.6°	37°	310
Room temperature	68°	20°	293
Water freezes	32°	0°	273

Temperature Conversions Table		
To convert	**Use this equation:**	**Example**
Celsius to Fahrenheit °C → °F	$°F = \left(\dfrac{9}{5} \times °C\right) + 32$	Convert 45°C to °F. $°F = \left(\dfrac{9}{5} \times 45°C\right) + 32 = 113°F$
Fahrenheit to Celsius °F → °C	$°C = \dfrac{5}{9} \times (°F - 32)$	Convert 68°F to °C. $°C = \dfrac{5}{9} \times (68°F - 32) = 20°C$
Celsius to Kelvin °C → K	$K = °C + 273$	Convert 45°C to K. $K = 45°C + 273 = 318\ K$
Kelvin to Celsius K → °C	$°C = K - 273$	Convert 32 K to °C. $°C = 32K - 273 = -241°C$

Appendix

Making Charts and Graphs

Pie Charts

A pie chart shows how each group of data relates to all of the data. Each part of the circle forming the chart represents a category of the data. The entire circle represents all of the data. For example, a biologist studying a hardwood forest in Wisconsin found that there were five different types of trees. The data table at right summarizes the biologist's findings.

Wisconsin Hardwood Trees	
Type of tree	Number found
Oak	600
Maple	750
Beech	300
Birch	1,200
Hickory	150
Total	3,000

How to Make a Pie Chart

1 To make a pie chart of these data, first find the percentage of each type of tree. Divide the number of trees of each type by the total number of trees, and multiply by 100.

$$\frac{600 \text{ oak}}{3,000 \text{ trees}} \times 100 = 20\%$$

$$\frac{750 \text{ maple}}{3,000 \text{ trees}} \times 100 = 25\%$$

$$\frac{300 \text{ beech}}{3,000 \text{ trees}} \times 100 = 10\%$$

$$\frac{1,200 \text{ birch}}{3,000 \text{ trees}} \times 100 = 40\%$$

$$\frac{150 \text{ hickory}}{3,000 \text{ trees}} \times 100 = 5\%$$

2 Now, determine the size of the wedges that make up the pie chart. Multiply each percentage by 360°. Remember that a circle contains 360°.

$20\% \times 360° = 72°$ $25\% \times 360° = 90°$

$10\% \times 360° = 36°$ $40\% \times 360° = 144°$

$5\% \times 360° = 18°$

3 Check that the sum of the percentages is 100 and the sum of the degrees is 360.

$20\% + 25\% + 10\% + 40\% + 5\% = 100\%$

$72° + 90° + 36° + 144° + 18° = 360°$

4 Use a compass to draw a circle and mark the center of the circle.

5 Then, use a protractor to draw angles of 72°, 90°, 36°, 144°, and 18° in the circle.

6 Finally, label each part of the chart, and choose an appropriate title.

A Community of Wisconsin Hardwood Trees

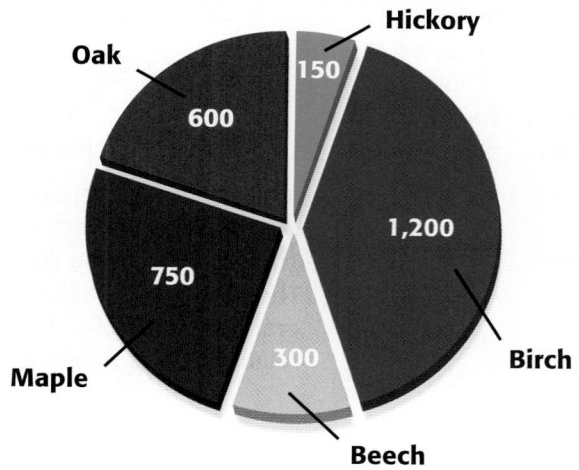

Line Graphs

Line graphs are most often used to demonstrate continuous change. For example, Mr. Smith's students analyzed the population records for their hometown, Appleton, between 1900 and 2000. Examine the data at right.

Because the year and the population change, they are the *variables*. The population is determined by, or dependent on, the year. Therefore, the population is called the **dependent variable,** and the year is called the **independent variable.** Each set of data is called a **data pair.** To prepare a line graph, you must first organize data pairs into a table like the one at right.

Population of Appleton, 1900–2000	
Year	**Population**
1900	1,800
1920	2,500
1940	3,200
1960	3,900
1980	4,600
2000	5,300

How to Make a Line Graph

1 Place the independent variable along the horizontal (*x*) axis. Place the dependent variable along the vertical (*y*) axis.

2 Label the *x*-axis "Year" and the *y*-axis "Population." Look at your largest and smallest values for the population. For the *y*-axis, determine a scale that will provide enough space to show these values. You must use the same scale for the entire length of the axis. Next, find an appropriate scale for the *x*-axis.

3 Choose reasonable starting points for each axis.

4 Plot the data pairs as accurately as possible.

5 Choose a title that accurately represents the data.

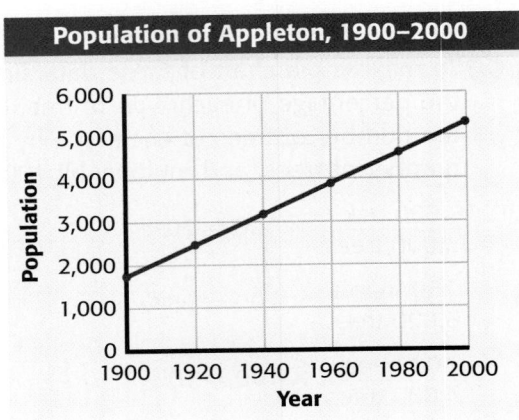

How to Determine Slope

Slope is the ratio of the change in the *y*-value to the change in the *x*-value, or "rise over run."

1 Choose two points on the line graph. For example, the population of Appleton in 2000 was 5,300 people. Therefore, you can define point *a* as (2000, 5,300). In 1900, the population was 1,800 people. You can define point *b* as (1900, 1,800).

2 Find the change in the *y*-value.
(*y* at point *a*) − (*y* at point *b*) =
5,300 people − 1,800 people =
3,500 people

3 Find the change in the *x*-value.
(*x* at point *a*) − (*x* at point *b*) =
2000 − 1900 = 100 years

4 Calculate the slope of the graph by dividing the change in *y* by the change in *x*.

$$slope = \frac{change\ in\ y}{change\ in\ x}$$

$$slope = \frac{3,500\ people}{100\ years}$$

$$slope = 35\ people\ per\ year$$

In this example, the population in Appleton increased by a fixed amount each year. The graph of these data is a straight line. Therefore, the relationship is **linear.** When the graph of a set of data is not a straight line, the relationship is **nonlinear.**

Using Algebra to Determine Slope

The equation in step 4 may also be arranged to be

$$y = kx$$

where y represents the change in the y-value, k represents the slope, and x represents the change in the x-value.

$$slope = \frac{change\ in\ y}{change\ in\ x}$$

$$k = \frac{y}{x}$$

$$k \times x = \frac{y \times x}{x}$$

$$kx = y$$

Bar Graphs

Bar graphs are used to demonstrate change that is not continuous. These graphs can be used to indicate trends when the data cover a long period of time. A meteorologist gathered the precipitation data shown here for Hartford, Connecticut, for April 1–15, 1996, and used a bar graph to represent the data.

Precipitation in Hartford, Connecticut April 1–15, 1996			
Date	Precipitation (cm)	Date	Precipitation (cm)
April 1	0.5	April 9	0.25
April 2	1.25	April 10	0.0
April 3	0.0	April 11	1.0
April 4	0.0	April 12	0.0
April 5	0.0	April 13	0.25
April 6	0.0	April 14	0.0
April 7	0.0	April 15	6.50
April 8	1.75		

How to Make a Bar Graph

1 Use an appropriate scale and a reasonable starting point for each axis.

2 Label the axes, and plot the data.

3 Choose a title that accurately represents the data.

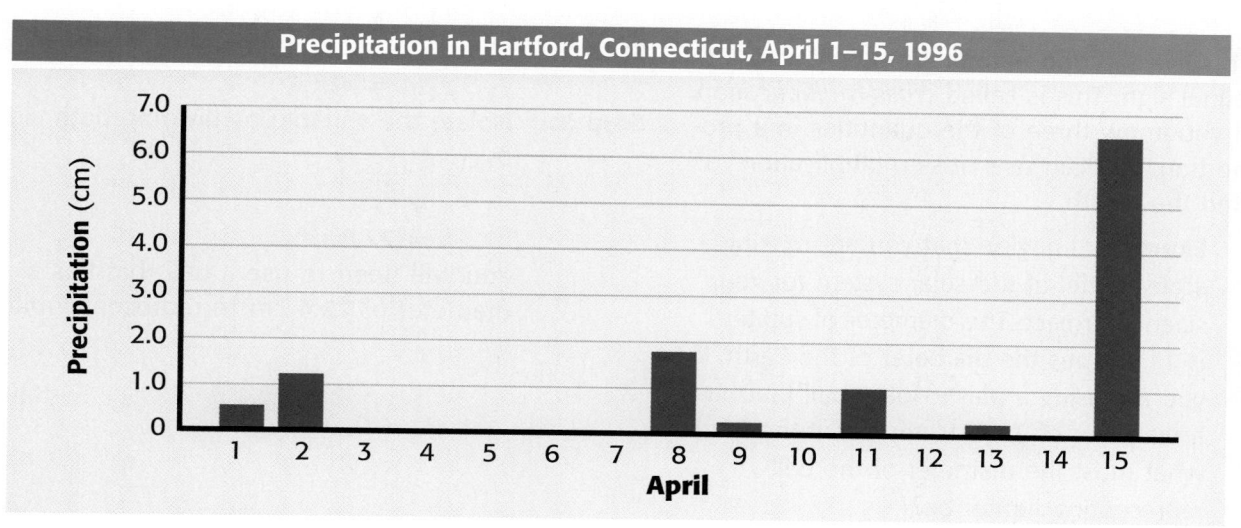

Precipitation in Hartford, Connecticut, April 1–15, 1996

Math Refresher

Science requires an understanding of many math concepts. The following pages will help you review some important math skills.

Averages

An **average,** or **mean,** simplifies a set of numbers into a single number that *approximates* the value of the set.

> **Example:** Find the average of the following set of numbers: 5, 4, 7, and 8.

Step 1: Find the sum.
$$5 + 4 + 7 + 8 = 24$$

Step 2: Divide the sum by the number of numbers in your set. Because there are four numbers in this example, divide the sum by 4.

$$\frac{24}{4} = 6$$

The average, or mean, is **6.**

Ratios

A **ratio** is a comparison between numbers, and it is usually written as a fraction.

> **Example:** Find the ratio of thermometers to students if you have 36 thermometers and 48 students in your class.

Step 1: Make the ratio.
$$\frac{36 \text{ thermometers}}{48 \text{ students}}$$

Step 2: Reduce the fraction to its simplest form.

$$\frac{36}{48} = \frac{36 \div 12}{48 \div 12} = \frac{3}{4}$$

The ratio of thermometers to students is **3 to 4,** or $\frac{3}{4}$. The ratio may also be written in the form 3:4.

Proportions

A **proportion** is an equation that states that two ratios are equal.

$$\frac{3}{1} = \frac{12}{4}$$

To solve a proportion, first multiply across the equal sign. This is called *cross-multiplication.* If you know three of the quantities in a proportion, you can use cross-multiplication to find the fourth.

> **Example:** Imagine that you are making a scale model of the solar system for your science project. The diameter of Jupiter is 11.2 times the diameter of the Earth. If you are using a plastic-foam ball that has a diameter of 2 cm to represent the Earth, what must the diameter of the ball representing Jupiter be?

$$\frac{11.2}{1} = \frac{x}{2 \text{ cm}}$$

Step 1: Cross-multiply.
$$\frac{11.2}{1} \diagdown\!\!\!\!\diagup \frac{x}{2}$$
$$11.2 \times 2 = x \times 1$$

Step 2: Multiply.
$$22.4 = x \times 1$$

Step 3: Isolate the variable by dividing both sides by 1.
$$x = \frac{22.4}{1}$$
$$x = 22.4 \text{ cm}$$

You will need to use a ball that has a diameter of **22.4** cm to represent Jupiter.

Percentages

A **percentage** is a ratio of a given number to 100.

    Example: What is 85% of 40?

Step 1: Rewrite the percentage by moving the decimal point two places to the left.

$$0.\underset{\smile}{85}$$

Step 2: Multiply the decimal by the number that you are calculating the percentage of.

$$0.85 \times 40 = 34$$

85% of 40 is **34.**

Decimals

To **add** or **subtract decimals,** line up the digits vertically so that the decimal points line up. Then, add or subtract the columns from right to left. Carry or borrow numbers as necessary.

    Example: Add the following numbers: 3.1415 and 2.96.

Step 1: Line up the digits vertically so that the decimal points line up.

$$\begin{array}{r} 3.1415 \\ + 2.96 \\ \hline \end{array}$$

Step 2: Add the columns from right to left, and carry when necessary.

$$\begin{array}{r} {\scriptstyle 1\ \ 1} \\ 3.1415 \\ + 2.96 \\ \hline 6.1015 \end{array}$$

The sum is **6.1015.**

Fractions

Numbers tell you how many; **fractions** tell you *how much of a whole*.

    Example: Your class has 24 plants. Your teacher instructs you to put 5 plants in a shady spot. What fraction of the plants in your class will you put in a shady spot?

Step 1: In the denominator, write the total number of parts in the whole.

$$\frac{?}{24}$$

Step 2: In the numerator, write the number of parts of the whole that are being considered.

$$\frac{5}{24}$$

So, $\frac{5}{24}$ of the plants will be in the shade.

Reducing Fractions

It is usually best to express a fraction in its simplest form. Expressing a fraction in its simplest form is called *reducing* a fraction.

    Example: Reduce the fraction $\frac{30}{45}$ to its simplest form.

Step 1: Find the largest whole number that will divide evenly into both the numerator and denominator. This number is called the *greatest common factor* (GCF).

Factors of the numerator 30:
    1, 2, 3, 5, 6, 10, **15,** 30

Factors of the denominator 45:
    1, 3, 5, 9, **15,** 45

Step 2: Divide both the numerator and the denominator by the GCF, which in this case is 15.

$$\frac{30}{45} = \frac{30 \div 15}{45 \div 15} = \frac{2}{3}$$

Thus, $\frac{30}{45}$ reduced to its simplest form is $\frac{2}{3}$.

Adding and Subtracting Fractions

To **add** or **subtract fractions** that have the **same denominator,** simply add or subtract the numerators.

Examples:

$$\frac{3}{5} + \frac{1}{5} = ? \quad \text{and} \quad \frac{3}{4} - \frac{1}{4} = ?$$

Step 1: Add or subtract the numerators.

$$\frac{3}{5} + \frac{1}{5} = \frac{4}{} \quad \text{and} \quad \frac{3}{4} - \frac{1}{4} = \frac{2}{}$$

Step 2: Write the sum or difference over the denominator.

$$\frac{3}{5} + \frac{1}{5} = \frac{4}{5} \quad \text{and} \quad \frac{3}{4} - \frac{1}{4} = \frac{2}{4}$$

Step 3: If necessary, reduce the fraction to its simplest form.

$\frac{4}{5}$ cannot be reduced, and $\frac{2}{4} = \frac{1}{2}$.

To **add** or **subtract fractions** that have **different denominators,** first find the least common denominator (LCD).

Examples:

$$\frac{1}{2} + \frac{1}{6} = ? \quad \text{and} \quad \frac{3}{4} - \frac{2}{3} = ?$$

Step 1: Write the equivalent fractions that have a common denominator.

$$\frac{3}{6} + \frac{1}{6} = ? \quad \text{and} \quad \frac{9}{12} - \frac{8}{12} = ?$$

Step 2: Add or subtract the fractions.

$$\frac{3}{6} + \frac{1}{6} = \frac{4}{6} \quad \text{and} \quad \frac{9}{12} - \frac{8}{12} = \frac{1}{12}$$

Step 3: If necessary, reduce the fraction to its simplest form.

The fraction $\frac{4}{6} = \frac{2}{3}$, and $\frac{1}{12}$ cannot be reduced.

Multiplying Fractions

To **multiply fractions,** multiply the numerators and the denominators together, and then reduce the fraction to its simplest form.

Example:

$$\frac{5}{9} \times \frac{7}{10} = ?$$

Step 1: Multiply the numerators and denominators.

$$\frac{5}{9} \times \frac{7}{10} = \frac{5 \times 7}{9 \times 10} = \frac{35}{90}$$

Step 2: Reduce the fraction.

$$\frac{35}{90} = \frac{35 \div 5}{90 \div 5} = \frac{7}{18}$$

Dividing Fractions

To **divide fractions,** first rewrite the divisor (the number you divide by) upside down. This number is called the *reciprocal* of the divisor. Then multiply and reduce if necessary.

Example:

$$\frac{5}{8} \div \frac{3}{2} = ?$$

Step 1: Rewrite the divisor as its reciprocal.

$$\frac{3}{2} \rightarrow \frac{2}{3}$$

Step 2: Multiply the fractions.

$$\frac{5}{8} \times \frac{2}{3} = \frac{5 \times 2}{8 \times 3} = \frac{10}{24}$$

Step 3: Reduce the fraction.

$$\frac{10}{24} = \frac{10 \div 2}{24 \div 2} = \frac{5}{12}$$

Scientific Notation

Scientific notation is a short way of representing very large and very small numbers without writing all of the place-holding zeros.

Example: Write 653,000,000 in scientific notation.

Step 1: Write the number without the place-holding zeros.

653

Step 2: Place the decimal point after the first digit.

6.53

Step 3: Find the exponent by counting the number of places that you moved the decimal point.

6.53000000

The decimal point was moved eight places to the left. Therefore, the exponent of 10 is positive 8. If you had moved the decimal point to the right, the exponent would be negative.

Step 4: Write the number in scientific notation.

$$6.53 \times 10^8$$

Area

Area is the number of square units needed to cover the surface of an object.

Formulas:

area of a square = side × side
area of a rectangle = length × width
area of a triangle = $\frac{1}{2}$ × base × height

Examples: Find the areas.

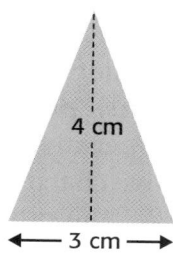

Triangle

area = $\frac{1}{2}$ × base × height

area = $\frac{1}{2}$ × 3 cm × 4 cm

area = **6 cm²**

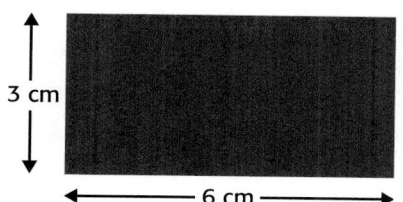

Rectangle

area = length × width
area = 6 cm × 3 cm
area = **18 cm²**

Square

area = side × side
area = 3 cm × 3 cm
area = **9 cm²**

Volume

Volume is the amount of space that something occupies.

Formulas:

volume of a cube =
side × side × side

volume of a prism =
area of base × height

Examples:

Find the volume of the solids.

Cube

volume = side × side × side
volume = 4 cm × 4 cm × 4 cm
volume = **64 cm³**

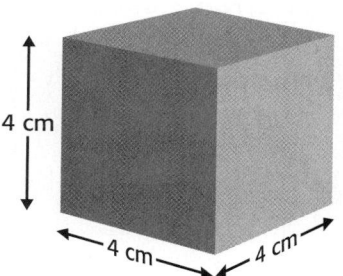

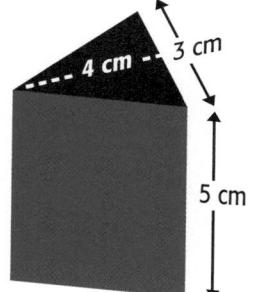

Prism

volume = area of base × height
volume = (area of triangle) × height
volume = ($\frac{1}{2}$ × 3 cm × 4 cm) × 5 cm
volume = 6 cm² × 5 cm
volume = **30 cm³**

Physical Science Refresher

Atoms and Elements

Every object in the universe is made up of particles of some kind of matter. **Matter** is anything that takes up space and has mass. All matter is made up of elements. An **element** is a substance that cannot be separated into simpler components by ordinary chemical means. This is because each element consists of only one kind of atom. An **atom** is the smallest unit of an element that has all of the properties of that element.

Atomic Structure

Atoms are made up of small particles called subatomic particles. The three major types of subatomic particles are **electrons, protons, and neutrons.** Electrons have a negative electric charge, protons have a positive charge, and neutrons have no electric charge. The protons and neutrons are packed close to one another to form the **nucleus.** The protons give the nucleus a positive charge. Electrons are most likely to be found in regions around the nucleus called **electron clouds.** The negatively charged electrons are attracted to the positively charged nucleus. An atom may have several energy levels in which electrons are located.

Atomic Number

To help in the identification of elements, scientists have assigned an **atomic number** to each kind of atom. The atomic number is the number of protons in the atom. Atoms with the same number of protons are all the same kind of element. In an uncharged, or electrically neutral, atom there are an equal number of protons and electrons. Therefore, the atomic number equals the number of electrons in an uncharged atom. The number of neutrons, however, can vary for a given element. Atoms of the same element that have different numbers of neutrons are called **isotopes.**

Periodic Table of the Elements

In the periodic table, the elements are arranged from left to right in order of increasing atomic number. Each element in the table is in a separate box. An uncharged atom of each element has one more electron and one more proton than an uncharged atom of the element to its left. Each horizontal row of the table is called a **period.** Changes in chemical properties of elements across a period correspond to changes in the electron arrangements of their atoms. Each vertical column of the table, known as a **group,** lists elements with similar properties. The elements in a group have similar chemical properties because their atoms have the same number of electrons in their outer energy level. For example, the elements helium, neon, argon, krypton, xenon, and radon all have similar properties and are known as the noble gases.

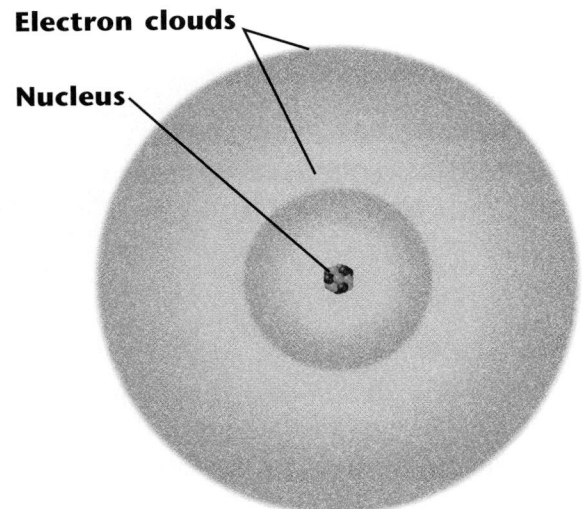

Electron clouds

Nucleus

Molecules and Compounds

When two or more elements are joined chemically, the resulting substance is called a **compound.** A compound is a new substance with properties different from those of the elements that compose it. For example, water, H_2O, is a compound formed when hydrogen (H) and oxygen (O) combine. The smallest complete unit of a compound that has the properties of that compound is called a **molecule.** A chemical formula indicates the elements in a compound. It also indicates the relative number of atoms of each element present. The chemical formula for water is H_2O, which indicates that each water molecule consists of two atoms of hydrogen and one atom of oxygen. The subscript number after the symbol for an element indicates how many atoms of that element are in a single molecule of the compound.

Acids, Bases, and pH

An ion is an atom or group of atoms that has an electric charge because it has lost or gained one or more electrons. When an acid, such as hydrochloric acid, HCl, is mixed with water, it separates into ions. An **acid** is a compound that produces hydrogen ions, H+, in water. The hydrogen ions then combine with a water molecule to form a hydronium ion, H_3O^+. A **base,** on the other hand, is a substance that produces hydroxide ions, OH^-, in water.

To determine whether a solution is acidic or basic, scientists use pH. The **pH** is a measure of the hydronium ion concentration in a solution. The pH scale ranges from 0 to 14. The middle point, pH = 7, is neutral, neither acidic nor basic. Acids have a pH less than 7; bases have a pH greater than 7. The lower the number is, the more acidic the solution. The higher the number is, the more basic the solution.

Chemical Equations

A chemical reaction occurs when a chemical change takes place. (In a chemical change, new substances with new properties are formed.) A chemical equation is a useful way of describing a chemical reaction by means of chemical formulas. The equation indicates what substances react and what the products are. For example, when carbon and oxygen combine, they can form carbon dioxide. The equation for the reaction is as follows: $C + O_2 \rightarrow CO_2$.

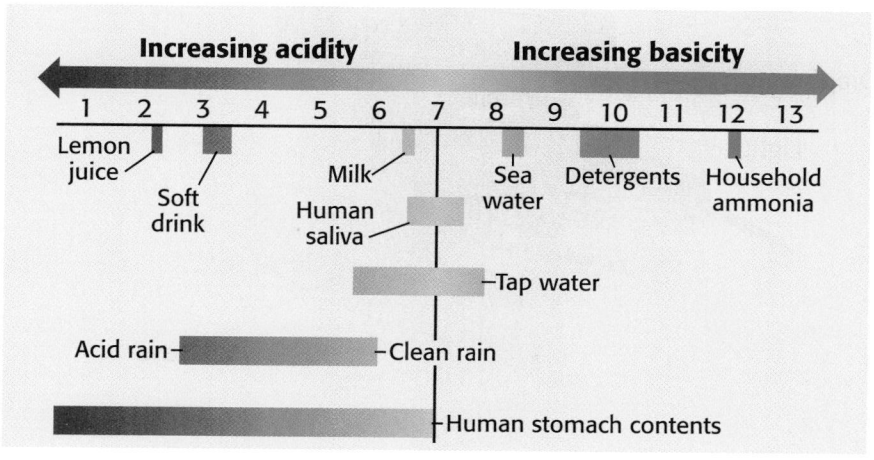

Using the Microscope

Parts of the Compound Light Microscope

- The **ocular lens** magnifies the image 10×.
- The **low-power objective** magnifies the image 10×.
- The **high-power objective** magnifies the image either 40× or 43×.
- The **revolving nosepiece** holds the objectives and can be turned to change from one magnification to the other.
- The **body tube** maintains the correct distance between the ocular lens and objectives.
- The **coarse-adjustment knob** moves the body tube up and down to allow focusing of the image.
- The **fine-adjustment knob** moves the body tube slightly to bring the image into sharper focus.
- The **stage** supports a slide.
- **Stage clips** hold the slide in place for viewing.
- The **diaphragm** controls the amount of light coming through the stage.
- The light source provides a **light** for viewing the slide.
- The **arm** supports the body tube.
- The **base** supports the microscope.

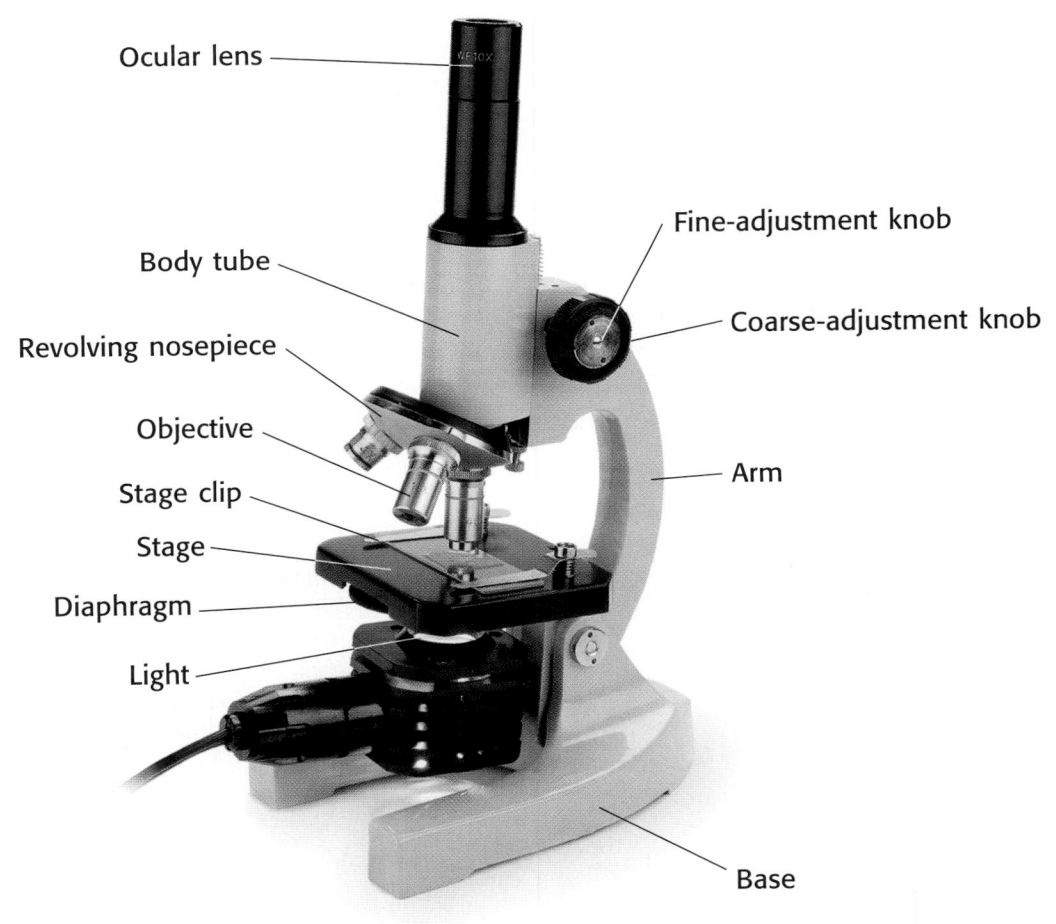

Ocular lens

Body tube

Revolving nosepiece

Objective

Stage clip

Stage

Diaphragm

Light

Fine-adjustment knob

Coarse-adjustment knob

Arm

Base

Proper Use of the Compound Light Microscope

1. Use both hands to carry the microscope to your lab table. Place one hand beneath the base, and use the other hand to hold the arm of the microscope. Hold the microscope close to your body while carrying it to your lab table.

2. Place the microscope on the lab table at least 5 cm from the edge of the table.

3. Check to see what type of light source is used by your microscope. If the microscope has a lamp, plug it in and make sure that the cord is out of the way. If the microscope has a mirror, adjust the mirror to reflect light through the hole in the stage. **Caution:** If your microscope has a mirror, do not use direct sunlight as a light source. Direct sunlight can damage your eyes.

4. Always begin work with the low-power objective in line with the body tube. Adjust the revolving nosepiece.

5. Place a prepared slide over the hole in the stage. Secure the slide with the stage clips.

6. Look through the ocular lens. Move the diaphragm to adjust the amount of light coming through the stage.

7. Look at the stage from eye level. Slowly turn the coarse adjustment to lower the objective until the objective almost touches the slide. Do not allow the objective to touch the slide.

8. Look through the ocular lens. Turn the coarse adjustment to raise the low-power objective until the image is in focus. Always focus by raising the objective away from the slide. Never focus the objective downward. Use the fine adjustment to sharpen the focus. Keep both eyes open while viewing a slide.

9. Make sure that the image is exactly in the center of your field of vision. Then, switch to the high-power objective. Focus the image by using only the fine adjustment. Never use the coarse adjustment at high power.

10. When you are finished using the microscope, remove the slide. Clean the ocular lens and objectives with lens paper. Return the microscope to its storage area. Remember to use both hands when carrying the microscope.

Making a Wet Mount

1. Use lens paper to clean a glass slide and a coverslip.

2. Place the specimen that you wish to observe in the center of the slide.

3. Using a medicine dropper, place one drop of water on the specimen.

4. Hold the coverslip at the edge of the water and at a 45° angle to the slide. Make sure that the water runs along the edge of the coverslip.

5. Lower the coverslip slowly to avoid trapping air bubbles.

6. Water might evaporate from the slide as you work. Add more water to keep the specimen fresh. Place the tip of the medicine dropper next to the edge of the coverslip. Add a drop of water. (You can also use this method to add stain or solutions to a wet mount.) Remove excess water from the slide by using the corner of a paper towel as a blotter. Do not lift the coverslip to add or remove water.

Glossary

A

abiotic describes the nonliving part of the environment, including water, rocks, light, and temperature (480)

absolute dating any method of measuring the age of an event or object in years (195)

active transport the movement of substances across the cell membrane that requires the cell to use energy (92)

adaptation a characteristic that improves an individual's ability to survive and reproduce in a particular environment (166)

addiction a dependence on a substance, such as alcohol or drugs (739)

aerobic exercise physical exercise intended to increase the activity of the heart and lungs to promote the body's use of oxygen (745)

alcoholism a disorder in which a person repeatedly drinks alcoholic beverages in an amount that interferes with the person's health and activities (740)

algae (AL JEE) eukaryotic organisms that convert the sun's energy into food through photosynthesis but that do not have roots, stems, or leaves (singular, *alga*) (274)

allele (uh LEEL) one of the alternative forms of a gene that governs a characteristic, such as hair color (120)

allergy a reaction to a harmless or common substance by the body's immune system (719)

alveoli (al VEE uh LIE) any of the tiny air sacs of the lungs where oxygen and carbon dioxide are exchanged (621)

amniotic egg (AM nee AHT ik EG) a type of egg that is surrounded by a membrane, the amnion, and that in reptiles, birds, and egg-laying mammals contains a large amount of yolk and is surrounded by a shell (427)

angiosperm (AN jee oh SPUHRM) a flowering plant that produces seeds within a fruit (302)

Animalia a kingdom made up of complex, multicellular organisms that lack cell walls, can usually move around, and quickly respond to their environment (232)

antenna a feeler that is on the head of an invertebrate, such as a crustacean or an insect, and that senses touch, taste, or smell (394)

antibiotic medicine used to kill bacteria and other microorganisms (254)

antibody a protein made by B cells that binds to a specific antigen (715)

Archaebacteria (AHR kee bak TEER ee uh) a kingdom made up of bacteria that live in extreme environments (229)

area a measure of the size of a surface or a region (25)

artery a blood vessel that carries blood away from the heart to the body's organs (608)

asexual reproduction reproduction that does not involve the union of sex cells and in which one parent produces offspring that are genetically identical to the parent (40, 684)

ATP adenosine triphosphate, a molecule that acts as the main energy source for cell processes (46)

autoimmune disease a disease in which the immune system attacks the organism's own cells (719)

B

B cell a white blood cell that makes antibodies (715)

binary fission (BIE nuh ree FISH uhn) a form of asexual reproduction in single-celled organisms by which one cell divides into two cells of the same size (248)

biodiversity the number and variety of organisms in a given area during a specific period of time (558)

biome (BIE OHM) a large region characterized by a specific type of climate and certain types of plant and animal communities (526)

bioremediation (BIE oh ri MEE dee AY shuhn) the biological treatment of hazardous waste by living organisms (253)

biosphere the part of Earth where life exists (483)

biotic describes living factors in the environment (480)

bird of prey a bird that hunts and eats other animals (451)

blood the fluid that carries gases, nutrients, and wastes through the body and that is made up of platelets, white blood cells, red blood cells, and plasma (612)

blood pressure the force that blood exerts on the walls of the arteries (614)

brain the mass of nerve tissue that is the main control center of the nervous system (660)

bronchus (BRAHNG kuhs) one of the two tubes that connect the lungs with the trachea (621)

brooding to sit on and cover eggs to keep them warm until they hatch; to incubate (446)

C

cancer a tumor in which the cells begin dividing at an uncontrolled rate and become invasive (720)

capillary a tiny blood vessel that allows an exchange between blood and cells in tissue (608)

carbohydrate a class of energy-giving nutrients that includes sugars, starches, and fiber; contains carbon, hydrogen, and oxygen (45, 732)

cardiovascular system a collection of organs that transport blood throughout the body (606)

carnivore an organism that eats animals (485)

carrying capacity the largest population that an environment can support at any given time (491)

cell in biology, the smallest unit that can perform all life processes; cells are covered by a membrane and contain DNA and cytoplasm (38, 60)

cell cycle the life cycle of a cell (98)

cell membrane a phospholipid layer that covers a cell's surface and acts as a barrier between the inside of a cell and the cell's environment (63)

cellular respiration the process by which cells use oxygen to produce energy from food (95, 333)

cell wall a rigid structure that surrounds the cell membrane and provides support to the cell (68)

Cenozoic era (SEN uh ZOH ik ER uh) the most recent geologic era, beginning 65 million years ago; also called the *Age of Mammals* (204)

central nervous system the brain and the spinal cord; its main function is to control the flow of information in the body (656)

chlorophyll (KLAWR uh FIL) a green pigment that captures light energy for photosynthesis (332)

chromosome in a eukaryotic cell, one of the structures in the nucleus that are made up of DNA and protein; in a prokaryotic cell, the main ring of DNA (98)

circadian rhythm a biological daily cycle (364)

classification the division of organisms into groups, or classes, based on specific characteristics (222)

closed circulatory system a circulatory system in which the heart circulates blood through a network of vessels that form a closed loop; the blood does not leave the blood vessels, and materials diffuse across the walls of the vessels (389)

cochlea (KAHK lee uh) a coiled tube that is found in the inner ear and that is essential to hearing (668)

coelom (SEE luhm) a body cavity that contains the internal organs (381)

coevolution the evolution of two species that is due to mutual influence, often in a way that makes the relationship more beneficial to both species (495)

combustion the burning of a substance (510)

commensalism a relationship between two organisms in which one organism benefits and the other is unaffected (494)

communication a transfer of a signal or message from one animal to another that results in some type of response (366)

community all of the populations of species that live in the same habitat and interact with each other (482)

compound eye an eye composed of many light detectors (393)

compound light microscope an instrument that magnifies small objects so that they can be seen easily by using two or more lenses (23)

condensation the change of state from a gas to a liquid (508)

conservation (KAHN suhr VAY shuhn) the preservation and wise use of natural resources (560)

consumer an organism that eats other organisms or organic matter (43, 359)

contour feather one of the most external feathers that cover a bird and that help determine its shape (443)

controlled experiment an experiment that tests only one factor at a time by using a comparison of a control group with an experimental group (14)

cytokinesis the division of the cytoplasm of a cell (100)

D

decomposer an organism that gets energy by breaking down the remains of dead organisms or animal wastes and consuming or absorbing the nutrients (43)

decomposition the breakdown of substances into simpler molecular substances (510)

deep-water zone the zone of a lake or pond below the open-water zone, where no light reaches (541)

dermis the layer of skin below the epidermis (593)

desert an area that has little or no plant life, long periods without rain, and extreme temperatures; usually found in hot climates (531)

diaphragm (DIE uh FRAM) a dome-shaped muscle that is attached to the lower ribs and that functions as the main muscle in respiration (453)

dichotomous key (die KAHT uh muhs KEE) an aid that is used to identify organisms and that consists of the answers to a series of questions (226)

diffusion (di FYOO zhuhn) the movement of particles from regions of higher density to regions of lower density (90)

digestive system the organs that break down food so that it can be used by the body (634)

DNA deoxyribonucleic acid, a molecule that is present in all living cells and that contains the information that determines the traits that a living thing inherits and needs to live (144)

dominant trait the trait observed in the first generation when parents that have different traits are bred (117)

dormant describes the inactive state of a seed or other plant part when conditions are unfavorable to growth (338)

down feather a soft feather that covers the body of young birds and provides insulation to adult birds (443)

drug any substance that causes a change in a person's physical or psychological state (738)

E

ecology the study of the interactions of living organisms with one another and with their environment (480)

ecosystem a community of organisms and their abiotic, or nonliving, environment (483)

ectotherm (EK toh thuhrm) an organism that needs sources of heat outside of itself (414)

egg a sex cell produced by a female (685)

electron microscope a microscope that focuses a beam of electrons to magnify objects (23)

embryo (EM bree OH) a plant or an animal in an early stage of development (358); a developing human, from fertilization through the first 8 weeks of development (the 10th week of pregnancy) (692)

endocrine system a collection of glands and groups of cells that secrete hormones that regulate growth, development, and homeostasis; includes the pituitary, thyroid, parathyroid, and adrenal glands, the hypothalamus, the pineal body, and the gonads (670)

endocytosis (EN doh sie TOH sis) the process by which a cell membrane surrounds a particle and encloses the particle in a vesicle to bring the particle into the cell (92)

endoplasmic reticulum (EN doh PLAZ mik ri TIK yuh luhm) a system of membranes that is found in a cell's cytoplasm and that assists in the production, processing, and transport of proteins and in the production of lipids (71)

endoskeleton (EN doh SKEL uh tuhn) an internal skeleton made of bone and cartilage (398)

endospore (EN doh SPAWR) a thick-walled protective spore that forms inside a bacterial cell and resists harsh conditions (249)

endotherm (EN doh THUHRM) an animal that can use body heat from chemical reactions in the body's cells to maintain a constant body temperature (414)

energy pyramid a triangular diagram that shows an ecosystem's loss of energy, which results as energy passes through the ecosystem's food chain (487)

epidermis (EP uh DUHR mis) the surface layer of cells on a plant or animal (593)

esophagus (i SAHF uh guhs) a long, straight tube that connects the pharynx to the stomach (636)

estivation a period of inactivity and lowered body temperature that some animals undergo in summer as a protection against hot weather and lack of food (364)

estuary (ES tyoo er ee) an area where fresh water from rivers mixes with salt water from the ocean (538)

Eubacteria (YOO bak TEER ee uh) a kingdom that contains all prokaryotes except archaebacteria (229)

eukaryote an organism made up of cells that have a nucleus enclosed by a membrane; eukaryotes include animals, plants, and fungi but not archaebacteria or eubacteria (66)

evaporation the change of a substance from a liquid to a gas (508)

evolution the process in which inherited characteristics within a population change over generations such that new species sometimes arise (167)

exocytosis (EK soh sie TOH sis) the process in which a cell releases a particle by enclosing the particle in a vesicle that then moves to the cell surface and fuses with the cell membrane (93)

exoskeleton a hard, external, supporting structure (393)

external fertilization the union of sex cells outside the bodies of the parents (686)

extinct describes a species that has died out completely (197)

F

fat an energy-storage nutrient that helps the body store some vitamins (733)

feedback mechanism a cycle of events in which information from one step controls or affects a previous step (665)

fermentation the breakdown of food without the use of oxygen (95)

fetus (FEET uhs) a developing human from seven or eight weeks after fertilization until birth (694)

food chain the pathway of energy transfer through various stages as a result of the feeding patterns of a series of organisms (486)

food web a diagram that shows the feeding relationships between organisms in an ecosystem (486)

fossil the remains or physical evidence of an organism preserved by geological processes (168, 194)

fossil record a historical sequence of life indicated by fossils found in layers of the Earth's crust (168)

function the special, normal, or proper activity of an organ or part (79)

Fungi (FUHN JIE) a kingdom made up of nongreen, eukaryotic organisms that have no means of movement, reproduce by using spores, and get food by breaking down substances in their surroundings and absorbing the nutrients (230)

fungus an organism whose cells have nuclei, rigid cell walls, and no chlorophyll and that belongs to the kingdom Fungi (282)

G

gallbladder a sac-shaped organ that stores bile produced by the liver (639)

ganglion (GANG glee uhn) a mass of nerve cells (381)

gene one set of instructions for an inherited trait (120)

generation time the period between the birth of one generation and the birth of the next generation (181)

genotype the entire genetic makeup of an organism; also the combination of genes for one or more specific traits (121)

geologic time scale the standard method used to divide the Earth's long natural history into manageable parts (196)

gestation period (jes TAY shuhn PIR ee uhd) in mammals, the length of time between fertilization and birth (456)

gill a respiratory organ in which oxygen from the water is exchanged with carbon dioxide from the blood (415)

gland a group of cells that make special chemicals for the body (670)

Golgi complex (GOHL jee KAHM PLEKS) cell organelle that helps make and package materials to be transported out of the cell (73)

gut the digestive tract (381)

gymnosperm (JIM noh SPUHRM) a woody, vascular seed plant whose seeds are not enclosed by an ovary or fruit (302)

H

herbivore an organism that eats only plants (485)

heredity the passing of genetic traits from parent to offspring (40, 114)

heterotroph (HET uhr oh TROHF) an organism that gets food by eating other organisms or their byproducts and that cannot make organic compounds from inorganic materials (271)

hibernation a period of inactivity and lowered body temperature that some animals undergo in winter as a protection against cold weather and lack of food (364)

homeostasis (HOH mee OH STAY sis) the maintenance of a constant internal state in a changing environment (39, 580)

hominid a type of primate characterized by bipedalism, relatively long lower limbs, and lack of a tail; examples include humans and their ancestors (207)

homologous chromosomes (hoh MAHL uh guhs KROH muh SOHMZ) chromosomes that have the same sequence of genes and the same structure (99, 126)

Homo sapiens (HOH moh SAY pee UHNZ) the species of hominids that includes modern humans and their closest ancestors and that first appeared about 100,000 to 150,000 years ago (210)

hormone a substance that is made in one cell or tissue and that causes a change in another cell or tissue in a different part of the body (670)

host an organism from which a parasite takes food or shelter (256, 271)

hygiene the science of health and ways to preserve health (744)

hypha (HIE fuh) a nonreproductive filament of a fungus (283)

hypothesis (hie PAHTH uh sis) an explanation that is based on prior scientific research or observations and that can be tested (12)

I

immune system the cells and tissues that recognize and attack foreign substances in the body (715)

immunity the ability to resist or recover from an infectious disease (712)

infectious disease a disease that is caused by a pathogen and that can be spread from one individual to another (710)

innate behavior an inherited behavior that does not depend on the environment or experience (360)

integumentary system (in TEG yoo MEN tuhr ee SIS tuhm) the organ system that forms a protective covering on the outside of the body (592, 664)

internal fertilization fertilization of an egg by sperm that occurs inside the body of a female (686)

invertebrate (in VUHR tuh brit) an animal that does not have a backbone (380)

J

joint a place where two or more bones meet (586)

K

kidney one of the pair of organs that filter water and wastes from the blood and that excrete products as urine (643)

L

large intestine the wider and shorter portion of the intestine that removes water from mostly digested food and that turns the waste into semi-solid feces, or stool (640)

larynx (LAR ingks) the area of the throat that contains the vocal cords and produces vocal sounds (621)

lateral line a faint line visible on both sides of a fish's body that runs the length of the body and marks the location of sense organs that detect vibrations in water (415)

law a summary of many experimental results and observations; a law tells how things work (20)

learned behavior a behavior that has been learned from experience (360)

lichen (LIE kuhn) a mass of fungal and algal cells that grow together in a symbiotic relationship and that are usually found on rocks or trees (288)

life science the study of living things (6)

lift an upward force on an object that moves in a fluid (446)

lipid a type of biochemical that does not dissolve in water; fats and steroids are lipids (46)

littoral zone (LIT uh ruhl ZOHN) the shallow zone of a lake or pond where light reaches the bottom and nurtures plants (541)

liver the largest organ in the body; it makes bile, stores and filters blood, and stores excess sugars as glycogen (639)

lung a respiratory organ in which oxygen from the air is exchanged with carbon dioxide from the blood (420)

lymph the fluid that is collected by the lymphatic vessels and nodes (616)

lymphatic system (lim FAT ik SIS tuhm) a collection of organs whose primary function is to collect extracellular fluid and return it to the blood; the organs in this system include the lymph nodes and the lymphatic vessels (616)

lymph node an organ that filters lymph and that is found along the lymphatic vessels (617)

lysosome (LIE suh SOHM) a cell organelle that contains digestive enzymes (74)

M

macrophage (MAK roh FAYJ) an immune system cell that engulfs pathogens and other materials (715)

malnutrition a disorder of nutrition that results when a person does not consume enough of each of the nutrients that are needed by the human body (736)

mammary gland in a female mammal, a gland that secretes milk (453)

marsh a treeless wetland ecosystem where plants such as grasses grow (542)

marsupial (mahr SOO pee uhl) a mammal that carries and nourishes its young in a pouch (465)

mass a measure of the amount of matter in an object (26)

meiosis (mie OH sis) a process in cell division during which the number of chromosomes decreases to half the original number by two divisions of the nucleus, which results in the production of sex cells (gametes or spores) (126)

memory B cell a B cell that responds to an antigen more strongly when the body is reinfected with an antigen than it does during its first encounter with the antigen (718)

Mesozoic era (MES oh ZOH ik ER uh) the geologic era that lasted from 248 million to 65 million years ago; also called the *Age of Reptiles* (203)

metabolism (muh TAB uh LIZ uhm) the sum of all chemical processes that occur in an organism (40)

metamorphosis (MET uh MAWR fuh sis) a phase in the life cycle of many animals during which a rapid change from the immature form of an organism to the adult form takes place (396, 422)

mineral a class of nutrients that are chemical elements that are needed for certain body processes (734)

mitochondrion (MIET oh KAHN dree uhn) in eukaryotic cells, the cell organelle that is surrounded by two membranes and that is the site of cellular respiration (72)

mitosis in eukaryotic cells, a process of cell division that forms two new nuclei, each of which has the same number of chromosomes (99)

model a pattern, plan, representation, or description designed to show the structure or workings of an object, system, or concept (18)

mold in biology, a fungus that looks like wool or cotton (284)

molting the shedding of an exoskeleton, skin, feathers, or hair to be replaced by new parts (442)

monotreme (MAHN oh TREEM) a mammal that lays eggs (464)

muscular system the organ system whose primary function is movement and flexibility (588)

mutation a change in the nucleotide-base sequence of a gene or DNA molecule (152)

mutualism (MYOO choo uhl IZ uhm) a relationship between two species in which both species benefit (494)

mycelium (mie SEE lee uhm) the mass of fungal filaments, or hyphae, that forms the body of a fungus (283)

N

narcotic a drug that is derived from opium and that relieves pain and induces sleep; examples include heroine, morphine, and codeine (741)

natural selection the process by which individuals that are better adapted to their environment survive and reproduce more successfully than less well adapted individuals do; a theory to explain the mechanism of evolution (178)

nephron the unit in the kidney that filters blood (643)

nerve a collection of nerve fibers through which impulses travel between the central nervous system and other parts of the body (658)

neuron (NOO RAHN) a nerve cell that is specialized to receive and conduct electrical impulses (657)

nicotine (NIK uh TEEN) a toxic, addictive chemical that is found in tobacco and that is one of the major contributors to the harmful effects of smoking (740)

noninfectious disease a disease that cannot spread from one individual to another (710)

nonrenewable resource a resource that forms at a rate that is much slower than the rate at which it is consumed (556)

nonvascular plant the three groups of plants (liverworts, hornworts, and mosses) that lack specialized conducting tissues and true roots, stems, and leaves (302)

nucleic acid a molecule made up of subunits called *nucleotides* (47)

nucleotide in a nucleic-acid chain, a subunit that consists of a sugar, a phosphate, and a nitrogenous base (144)

nucleus in a eukaryotic cell, a membrane-bound organelle that contains the cell's DNA and that has a role in processes such as growth, metabolism, and reproduction (63)

nutrient a substance in food that provides energy or helps form body tissues and that is necessary for life and growth (732)

O

omnivore an organism that eats both plants and animals (485)

open circulatory system a circulatory system in which the circulatory fluid is not contained entirely within vessels; a heart pumps fluid through vessels that empty into spaces called *sinuses* (389)

open-water zone the zone of a pond or lake that extends from the littoral zone and that is only as deep as light can reach (541)

organ a collection of tissues that carry out a specialized function of the body (77, 581)

organelle one of the small bodies in a cell's cytoplasm that are specialized to perform a specific function (63)

organism a living thing; anything that can carry out life processes independently (78)

organ system a group of organs that work together to perform body functions (78)

osmosis (ahs MOH sis) the diffusion of water through a semipermeable membrane (91)

ovary in flowering plants, the lower part of a pistil that produces eggs in ovules (320); in the female reproductive system of animals, an organ that produces eggs (689)

overpopulation the presence of too many individuals in an area for the available resources (557)

P

Paleozoic era (PAY lee OH ZOH ik ER uh) the geologic era that followed Precambrian time and that lasted from 543 million to 248 million years ago (202)

pancreas the organ that lies behind the stomach and that makes digestive enzymes and hormones that regulate sugar levels (638)

parasite an organism that feeds on an organism of another species (the host) and that usually harms the host; the host never benefits from the presence of the parasite (271)

parasitism (PAR uh SIET iz uhm) a relationship between two species in which one species, the parasite, benefits from the other species, the host, which is harmed (495)

passive transport the movement of substances across a cell membrane without the use of energy by the cell (92)

pathogen a virus, microorganism, or other organism that causes disease (710)

pathogenic bacteria (PATH uh JEN ik bak TIR ee uh) bacteria that cause disease (254)

pedigree a diagram that shows the occurrence of a genetic trait in several generations of a family (132)

penis the male organ that transfers sperm to a female and that carries urine out of the body (688)

peripheral nervous system (puh RIF uhr uhl NUHR vuhs SIS tuhm) all of the parts of the nervous system except for the brain and the spinal cord (656)

petal one of the usually brightly colored, leaf-shaped parts that make up one of the rings of a flower (319)

pharynx (FAR ingks) in flatworms, the muscular tube that leads from the mouth to the gastrovascular cavity; in animals with a digestive tract, the passage from the mouth to the larynx and esophagus (621)

phenotype (FEE noh TIEP) an organism's appearance or other detectable characteristic (120)

pheromone (FER uh MOHN) a substance that is released by the body and that causes another individual of the same species to react in a predictable way (367)

phloem (FLOH EM) the tissue that conducts food in vascular plants (314)

phospholipid (FAHS foh LIP id) a lipid that contains phosphorus and that is a structural component in cell membranes (46)

photosynthesis (FOHT oh SIN thuh sis) the process by which plants, algae, and some bacteria use sunlight, carbon dioxide, and water to make food (94, 332)

phytoplankton (FIET oh PLANGK tuhn) the microscopic, photosynthetic organisms that float near the surface of marine or fresh water (274)

pioneer species a species that colonizes an uninhabited area and that starts a process of succession (513)

pistil the female reproductive part of a flower that produces seeds and consists of an ovary, style, and stigma (320)

placenta (pluh SEN tuh) the structure that attaches a developing fetus to the uterus and that enables the exchange of nutrients, wastes, and gases between the mother and the fetus (693)

placental mammal a mammal that nourishes its unborn offspring through a placenta inside its uterus (456)

plankton the mass of mostly microscopic organisms that float or drift freely in freshwater and marine environments (534)

Plantae a kingdom made up of complex, multicellular organisms that are usually green, have cell walls made of cellulose, cannot move around, and use the sun's energy to make sugar by photosynthesis (231)

plate tectonics the theory that explains how large pieces of the Earth's outermost layer, called *tectonic plates,* move and change shape (198)

pollen the tiny granules that contain the male gametophyte of seed plants (308)

pollination the transfer of pollen from the male reproductive structures to the female structures of seed plants (311)

pollution an unwanted change in the environment caused by substances or forms of energy (554)

population a group of organisms of the same species that live in a specific geographical area (482)

Precambrian time (pree KAM bree uhn TIEM) the period in the geologic time scale from the formation of the Earth to the beginning of the Paleozoic era, from about 4.6 billion to 543 million years ago (200)

precipitation any form of water that falls to the Earth's surface from the clouds (508)

predator an organism that eats all or part of another organism (492)

preening in birds, the act of grooming and maintaining their feathers (442)

prey an organism that is killed and eaten by another organism (492)

primate a type of mammal characterized by opposable thumbs and binocular vision (206)

probability the likelihood that a possible future event will occur in any given instance of the event (122)

producer an organism that can make its own food by using energy from its surroundings (43)

prokaryote (pro KAR ee OHT) an organism that consists of a single cell that does not have a nucleus (64, 247)

protein a molecule that is made up of amino acids and that is needed to build and repair body structures and to regulate processes in the body (44, 733)

protist an organism that belongs to the kingdom Protista (270)

Protista (proh TIST uh) a kingdom of mostly one-celled eukaryotic organisms that are different from plants, animals, bacteria, and fungi (230)

pulmonary circulation (PUL muh NER ee SUHR kyoo LAY shuhn) the flow of blood from the heart to the lungs and back to the heart through the pulmonary arteries, capillaries, and veins (609)

R

recessive trait a trait that is apparent only when two recessive alleles for the same characteristic are inherited (117)

recycling the process of recovering valuable or useful materials from waste or scrap; the process of reusing some items (563)

reflex an involuntary and almost immediate movement in response to a stimulus (665)

relative dating any method of determining whether an event or object is older or younger than other events or objects (195)

renewable resource a natural resource that can be replaced at the same rate at which the resource is consumed (556)

respiration in biology, the exchange of oxygen and carbon dioxide between living cells and their environment; includes breathing and cellular respiration (620)

respiratory system a collection of organs whose primary function is to take in oxygen and expel carbon dioxide; the organs of this system include the lungs, the throat, and the passageways that lead to the lungs (620)

retina the light-sensitive inner layer of the eye, which receives images formed by the lens and transmits them through the optic nerve to the brain (666)

rhizoid (RIE ZOYD) a rootlike structure in nonvascular plants that holds the plants in place and helps plants get water and nutrients (304)

rhizome a horizontal, underground stem that produces new leaves, shoots, and roots (306)

ribosome a cell organelle composed of RNA and protein; the site of protein synthesis (71, 151)

RNA ribonucleic acid, a molecule that is present in all living cells and that plays a role in protein production (150)

S

savanna a grassland that often has scattered trees and that is found in tropical and subtropical areas where seasonal rains, fires, and drought happen (530)

scientific methods a series of steps followed to solve problems (10)

segment any part of a larger structure, such as the body of an organism, that is set off by natural or arbitrary boundaries (390)

selective breeding the human practice of breeding animals or plants that have certain desired characteristics (176)

sepal in a flower, one of the outermost rings of modified leaves that protect the flower bud (319)

sex chromosome one of the pair of chromosomes that determine the sex of an individual (131)

sexual reproduction reproduction in which the sex cells from two parents unite to produce offspring that share traits from both parents (40, 685)

skeletal system the organ system whose primary function is to support and protect the body and to allow the body to move (584)

small intestine the organ between the stomach and the large intestine where most of the breakdown of food happens and most of the nutrients from food are absorbed (638)

social behavior the interaction between animals of the same species (366)

speciation (SPEE shee AY shuhn) the formation of new species as a result of evolution (182)

species a group of organisms that are closely related and can mate to produce fertile offspring (166)

sperm the male sex cell (685)

spleen the largest lymphatic organ in the body; serves as a blood reservoir, disintegrates old red blood cells, and produces lymphocytes and plasmids (618)

spore a reproductive cell or multicellular structure that is resistant to stressful environmental conditions and that can develop into an adult without fusing with another cell (283)

stamen the male reproductive structure of a flower that produces pollen and consists of an anther at the tip of a filament (320)

stimulus anything that causes a reaction or change in an organism or any part of an organism (39)

stoma one of many openings in a leaf or a stem of a plant that enable gas exchange to occur (plural, *stomata*) (334)

stomach the saclike, digestive organ between the esophagus and the small intestine that breaks down food by the action of muscles, enzymes, and acids (637)

stress a physical or mental response to pressure (746)

structure the arrangement of parts in an organism (79)

succession the replacement of one type of community by another at a single location over a period of time (512)

swamp a wetland ecosystem in which shrubs and trees grow (542)

swim bladder in bony fishes, a gas-filled sac that is used to control buoyancy; also known as a *gas bladder* (418)

symbiosis a relationship in which two different organisms live in close association with each other (494)

systemic circulation (sis TEM ik SUHR kyoo LAY shuhn) the flow of blood from the heart to all parts of the body and back to the heart (609)

T

tadpole the aquatic, fish-shaped larva of a frog or toad (422)

taxonomy (taks AHN uh mee) the science of describing, naming, and classifying organisms (223)

T cell an immune system cell that coordinates the immune system and attacks many infected cells (715)

technology the application of science for practical purposes; the use of tools, machines, materials, and processes to meet human needs (22)

temperature a measure of how hot (or cold) something is; specifically, a measure of the average kinetic energy of the particles in an object (26)

territory an area that is occupied by one animal or a group of animals that do not allow other members of the species to enter (361)

testes the primary male reproductive organs, which produce sperm cells and testosterone (singular, *testis*) (688)

theory an explanation that ties together many hypotheses and observations (20)

thymus the main gland of the lymphatic system; it releases mature T lymphocytes (617)

tissue a group of similar cells that perform a common function (77, 580)

tonsils small, rounded masses of lymphatic tissue located in the pharynx and in the passage from the mouth to the pharynx (619)

trachea (TRAY kee uh) in insects, myriapods, and spiders, one of a network of air tubes; in vertebrates, the tube that connects the larynx to the lungs (621)

trait a genetically determined characteristic (176)

transpiration the process by which plants release water vapor into the air through stomata; *also* the release of water vapor into the air by other organisms (334)

tropism (TROH piz uhm) growth of all or part of an organism in response to an external stimulus, such as light (340)

tundra a treeless plain found in the Arctic, in the Antarctic, or on the tops of mountains that is characterized by very low winter temperatures and short, cool summers (532)

U

umbilical cord (uhm BIL i kuhl KAWRD) the structure that connects an embryo and then the fetus to the placenta and through which blood vessels pass (693)

urinary system the organs that make, store, and eliminate urine (642)

uterus in female mammals, the hollow, muscular organ in which a fertilized egg is embedded and in which the embryo and fetus develop (689)

V

vagina the female reproductive organ that connects the outside of the body to the uterus (689)

variable a factor that changes in an experiment in order to test a hypothesis (14)

vascular plant a plant that has specialized tissues that conduct materials from one part of the plant to another (302)

vein in biology, a vessel that carries blood to the heart (608)

vertebrate (VUHR tuh brit) an animal that has a backbone (412)

vesicle (VES i kuhl) a small cavity or sac that contains materials in a eukaryotic cell; forms when part of the cell membrane surrounds the materials to be taken into the cell or transported within the cell (73)

virus a microscopic particle that gets inside a cell and often destroys the cell (256)

vitamin a class of nutrients that contain carbon and that are needed in small amounts to maintain health and allow growth (734)

volume a measure of the size of a body or region in three-dimensional space (25)

W

waterfowl an aquatic bird, such as a duck, goose, or swan (449)

water vascular system a system of canals filled with a watery fluid that circulates throughout the body of an echinoderm (399)

wetland an area of land that is periodically underwater or whose soil contains a great deal of moisture (542)

X

xylem (ZIE luhm) the type of tissue in vascular plants that provides support and conducts water and nutrients from the roots (314)

Spanish Glossary

A

abiotic/abiótico término que describe la parte sin vida del ambiente, incluyendo el agua, las rocas, la luz y la temperatura (480)

absolute dating/datación absoluta cualquier método que sirve para determinar la edad de un suceso u objeto en años (195)

active transport/transporte activo el movimiento de substancias a través de la membrana celular que requiere que la célula gaste energía (92)

adaptation/adaptación una característica que mejora la capacidad de un individuo para sobrevivir y reproducirse en un determinado ambiente (166)

addiction/adicción una dependencia de una substancia, tal como el alcohol o las drogas (739)

aerobic exercise/ejercicio aeróbico ejercicio físico cuyo objetivo es aumentar la actividad del corazón y los pulmones para hacer que el cuerpo use más oxígeno (745)

alcoholism/alcoholismo un trastorno en el cual una persona consume bebidas alcohólicas repetidamente en una cantidad tal que interfiere con su salud y sus actividades (740)

algae/algas organismos eucarióticos que transforman la energía del Sol en alimento por medio de la fotosíntesis, pero que no tienen raíces, tallos ni hojas (274)

allele/alelo una de las formas alternativas de un gene que rige un carácter, como por ejemplo, el color del cabello (120)

allergy/alergia una reacción del sistema inmunológico del cuerpo a una substancia inofensiva o común (719)

alveoli/alveolo cualquiera de las diminutas bolsas de aire de los pulmones, en donde ocurre el intercambio de oxígeno y dióxido de carbono (621)

amniotic egg/huevo amniótico un tipo de huevo que está rodeado por una membrana, el amnios, y que en los reptiles, las aves y los mamíferos que ponen huevos contiene una gran cantidad de yema y está rodeado por una cáscara (427)

angiosperm/angiosperma una planta que da flores y que produce semillas dentro de la fruta (302)

Animalia/Animalia un reino formado por organismos pluricelulares complejos que no tienen pared celular, normalmente son capaces de moverse y reaccionan rápidamente a su ambiente (232)

antenna/antena una estructura ubicada en la cabeza de un invertebrado, como por ejemplo, un crustáceo o un insecto, que percibe sensaciones de tacto, gusto u olor (394)

antibiotic/antibiótico medicina utilizada para matar bacterias y otros microorganismos (254)

antibody/anticuerpo una proteína producida por las células B que se une a un antígeno específico (715)

Archaebacteria/arqueobacteria un reino formado por bacterias que viven en ambientes extremos (229)

area/área una medida del tamaño de una superficie o región (25)

artery/arteria un vaso sanguíneo que transporta sangre del corazón a los órganos del cuerpo (608)

asexual reproduction/reproducción asexual reproducción que no involucra la unión de células sexuales, en la que un solo progenitor produce descendencia que es genéticamente igual al progenitor (40, 684)

ATP/ATP adenosín trifosfato, una molécula orgánica que funciona como la fuente principal de energía para los procesos celulares (46)

autoimmune disease/enfermedad autoinmune una enfermedad en la que el sistema inmunológico ataca las células del propio organismo (719)

B

B cell/célula B un glóbulo blanco de la sangre que fabrica anticuerpos (715)

binary fission/fisión binaria una forma de reproducción asexual de los organismos unicelulares, por medio de la cual la célula se divide en dos células del mismo tamaño (248)

biodiversity/biodiversidad el número y la variedad de organismos que se encuentran en un área determinada durante un período específico de tiempo (558)

biome/bioma una región extensa caracterizada por un tipo de clima específico y ciertos tipos de comunidades de plantas y animales (526)

bioremediation/bioremediación el tratamiento biológico de desechos peligrosos por medio de organismos vivos (253)

biosphere/biosfera la parte de la Tierra donde existe la vida (483)

biotic/biótico término que describe los factores vivientes del ambiente (480)

bird of prey/ave de presa un ave que caza y se alimenta de otros animales (451)

blood/sangre el líquido que lleva gases, nutrientes y desechos por el cuerpo y que está formado por plaquetas, glóbulos blancos, glóbulos rojos y plasma (612)

blood pressure/presión sanguínea la fuerza que la sangre ejerce en las paredes de las arterias (614)

brain/encéfalo la masa de tejido nervioso que es el centro principal de control del sistema nervioso (660)

bronchus/bronquio uno de los dos tubos que conectan los pulmones con la tráquea (621)

brooding/empollar sentarse y cubrir los huevos para mantenerlos calientes hasta que las crías salgan del cascarón; incubar (446)

C

cancer/cáncer un tumor en el cual las células comienzan a dividirse a una tasa incontrolable y se vuelven invasivas (720)

capillary/capilar diminuto vaso sanguíneo que permite el intercambio entre la sangre y las células de los tejidos (608)

carbohydrate/carbohidrato una clase de nutrientes que proporcionan energía; incluye los azúcares, los almidones y las fibras; contiene carbono, hidrógeno y oxígeno (45, 732)

cardiovascular system/aparato cardiovascular un conjunto de órganos que transportan la sangre a través del cuerpo (606)

carnivore/carnívoro un organismo que se alimenta de animales (485)

carrying capacity/capacidad de carga la población más grande que un ambiente puede sostener en cualquier momento dado (491)

cell/célula en biología, la unidad más pequeña que puede realizar todos los procesos vitales; las células están cubiertas por una membrana y tienen ADN y citoplasma (38, 60)

cell cycle/ciclo celular el ciclo de vida de una célula (98)

cell membrane/membrana celular una capa de fosfolípidos que cubre la superficie de la célula y funciona como una barrera entre el interior de la célula y el ambiente de la célula (63)

cellular respiration/respiración celular el proceso por medio del cual las células utilizan oxígeno para producir energía a partir de los alimentos (95, 333)

cell wall/pared celular una estructura rígida que rodea la membrana celular y le brinda soporte a la célula (68)

Cenozoic era/era Cenozoica la era geológica más reciente, que comenzó hace 65 millones de años; también llamada *Edad de los Mamíferos* (204)

central nervous system/sistema nervioso central el cerebro y la médula espinal; su principal función es controlar el flujo de información en el cuerpo (656)

chlorophyll/clorofila un pigmento verde que capta la energía luminosa para la fotosíntesis (332)

chromosome/cromosoma en una célula eucariótica, una de las estructuras del núcleo que está hecha de ADN y proteína; en una célula procariótica, el anillo principal de ADN (98)

circadian rhythm/ritmo circadiano un ciclo biológico diario (364)

classification/clasificación la división de organismos en grupos, o clases, en función de características específicas (222)

closed circulatory system/aparato circulatorio cerrado un aparato circulatorio en el que el corazón hace que la sangre circule a través de una red de vasos que forman un circuito cerrado; la sangre no sale de los vasos sanguíneos y los materiales pasan a través de las paredes de los vasos por difusión (389)

cochlea/cóclea un tubo enrollado que se encuentra en el oído interno y es esencial para poder oír (668)

coelom/celoma una cavidad del cuerpo que contiene los órganos internos (381)

coevolution/coevolución la evolución de dos especies que se debe a su influencia mutua, a menudo de un modo que hace que la relación sea más beneficiosa para ambas (495)

combustion/combustión fenómeno que ocurre cuando una substancia se quema (510)

commensalism/comensalismo una relación entre dos organismos en la que uno se beneficia y el otro no es afectado (494)

communication/comunicación la transferencia de una señal o mensaje de un animal a otro, la cual resulta en algún tipo de respuesta (366)

community/comunidad todas las poblaciones de especies que viven en el mismo hábitat e interactúan entre sí (482)

compound eye/ojo compuesto un ojo compuesto por muchos detectores de luz (393)

compound light microscope/microcopio óptico compuesto un instrumento que magnifica objetos pequeños de modo que se puedan ver fácilmente usando dos o más lentes (23)

condensation/condensación el cambio de estado de gas a líquido (508)

conservation/conservación la preservación y el uso inteligente de los recursos naturales (560)

consumer/consumidor un organismo que se alimenta de otros organismos o de materia orgánica (43, 359)

contour feather/pluma de contorno una las plumas más externas que cubren a un ave y que sirven para determinar su forma (443)

controlled experiment/experimento controlado un experimento que prueba sólo un factor a la vez, comparando un grupo de control con un grupo experimental (14)

cytokinesis/citoquinesis la división del citoplasma de una célula (100)

D

decomposer/descomponedor un organismo que, para obtener energía, desintegra los restos de organismos muertos o los desechos de animales y consume o absorbe los nutrientes (43)

decomposition/descomposición la desintegración de substancias en substancias moleculares más simples (510)

deep-water zone/zona de aguas profundas la zona de un lago o laguna debajo de la zona de aguas abiertas, a donde no llega la luz (541)

dermis/dermis la capa de piel que está debajo de la epidermis (593)

desert/desierto una región con poca vegetación o sin vegetación, largos períodos sin lluvia y temperaturas extremas; generalmente se ubica en climas calientes (531)

diaphragm/diafragma un músculo en forma de cúpula que está unido a las costillas inferiores y que es el músculo principal de la respiración (453)

dichotomous key/clave dicotómica una ayuda para identificar organismos, que consiste en las respuestas a una serie de preguntas (226)

diffusion/difusión el movimiento de partículas de regiones de mayor densidad a regiones de menor densidad (90)

digestive system/aparato digestivo los órganos que descomponen la comida de modo que el cuerpo la pueda usar (634)

DNA/ADN **á**cido **d**esoxirribo**n**ucleico, una molécula que está presente en todas las células vivas y que contiene la información que determina los caracteres que un ser vivo hereda y necesita para vivir (144)

dominant trait/carácter dominante el carácter que se observa en la primera generación cuando se cruzan progenitores que tienen caracteres diferentes (117)

dormant/aletargado término que describe el estado inactivo de una semilla u otra parte de las plantas cuando las condiciones son desfavorables para el crecimiento (338)

down feather/plumón una pluma suave que cubre el cuerpo de las crías de las aves y sirve como aislante en las aves adultas (443)

drug/droga cualquier substancia que produce un cambio en el estado físico o psicológico de una persona (738)

E

ecology/ecología el estudio de las interacciones de los seres vivos entre sí mismos y entre sí mismos y su ambiente (480)

ecosystem/ecosistema una comunidad de organismos y su ambiente abiótico o no vivo (483)

ectotherm/ectotermo un organismo que necesita fuentes de calor fuera de sí mismo (414)

egg/óvulo una célula sexual producida por una hembra (685)

electron microscope/microscopio electrónico microscopio que enfoca un haz de electrones para aumentar la imagen de los objetos (23)

embryo/embrión una planta o un animal en una de las primeras etapas de su desarrollo (358); un ser humano desde la fecundación hasta las primeras 8 semanas de desarrollo (décima semana del embarazo) (692)

endocrine system/sistema endocrino un conjunto de glándulas y grupos de células que secretan hormonas que regulan el crecimiento, el desarrollo y la homeostasis; incluye las glándulas pituitaria, tiroides, paratiroides y suprarrenal, el hipotálamo, el cuerpo pineal y las gónadas (670)

endocytosis/endocitosis el proceso por medio del cual la membrana celular rodea una partícula y la encierra en una vesícula para llevarla al interior de la célula (92)

endoplasmic reticulum/retículo endoplásmico un sistema de membranas que se encuentra en el citoplasma de la célula y que tiene una función en la producción, procesamiento y transporte de proteínas y en la producción de lípidos (71)

endoskeleton/endoesqueleto un esqueleto interno hecho de hueso y cartílago (398)

endospore/endospora una espora protectiva que tiene una pared gruesa, se forma dentro de una célula bacteriana y resiste condiciones adversas (249)

endotherm/endotermo un animal que puede utilizar el calor del cuerpo producido por las reacciones químicas de sus células para mantener una temperatura corporal constante (414)

energy pyramid/pirámide de energía un diagrama triangular que muestra la pérdida de energía en un ecosistema, producida a medida que la energía pasa a través de la cadena alimenticia del ecosistema (487)

epidermis/epidermis la superficie externa de las células de una planta o animal (593)

esophagus/esófago un conducto largo y recto que conecta la faringe con el estómago (636)

estivation/estivación un período de inactividad y menor temperatura corporal por el que pasan algunos animales durante el verano para protegerse del calor y la falta de alimento (364)

estuary/estuario un área donde el agua dulce de los ríos se mezcla con el agua salada del océano (538)

Eubacteria/Eubacteria un reino que agrupa a todos los procariotes, excepto a las arqueobacterias (229)

eukaryote/eucariote un organismo cuyas células tienen un núcleo rodeado por una membrana; entre los eucariotes se encuentran los animales, las plantas y los hongos, pero no las arqueobacterias (66)

evaporation/evaporación el cambio de una substancia de líquido a gas (508)

evolution/evolución el proceso por medio del cual las características heredadas dentro de una población cambian con el transcurso de las generaciones de manera tal que a veces surgen nuevas especies (167)

exocytosis/exocitosis el proceso por medio del cual una célula libera una partícula encerrándola en una vesícula que luego se traslada a la superficie de la célula y se fusiona con la membrana celular (93)

exoskeleton/exoesqueleto una estructura de soporte, dura y externa (393)

external fertilization/fecundación externa la unión de células sexuales fuera del cuerpo de los progenitores (686)

extinct/extinto término que describe a una especie que ha desaparecido por completo (197)

F

fat/grasa un nutriente que almacena energía y ayuda al cuerpo a almacenar algunas vitaminas (733)

feedback mechanism/mecanismo de retroalimentación un ciclo de sucesos en el que la información de una etapa controla o afecta a una etapa anterior (665)

fermentation/fermentación la descomposición de los alimentos sin utilizar oxígeno (95)

fetus/feto un ser humano en desarrollo de las semanas siete a ocho después de la fecundación hasta el nacimiento (694)

food chain/cadena alimenticia la vía de transferencia de energía través de varias etapas, que ocurre como resultado de los patrones de alimentación de una serie de organismos (486)

food web/red alimenticia un diagrama que muestra las relaciones de alimentación entre los organismos de un ecosistema (486)

fossil/fósil los restos o las pruebas físicas de un organismo preservados por los procesos geológicos (168, 194)

fossil record/registro fósil una secuencia histórica de la vida indicada por fósiles que se han encontrado en las capas de la corteza terrestre (168)

function/función la actividad especial, normal o adecuada de un órgano o parte (79)

Fungi/Fungi un reino formado por organismos eucarióticos no verdes que no tienen capacidad de movimiento, se reproducen por esporas y obtienen alimento al descomponer substancias de su entorno y absorber los nutrientes (230)

fungus/hongo un organismo que tiene células con núcleos y pared celular rígida, pero carece de clorofila, perteneciente al reino Fungi (282)

G

gallbladder/vesícula biliar un órgano que tiene la forma de una bolsa y que almacena la bilis producida por el hígado (639)

ganglion/ganglio una masa de células nerviosas (381)

gene/gene un conjunto de instrucciones para un carácter heredado (120)

generation time/tiempo de generación el período entre el nacimiento de una generación y el nacimiento de la siguiente generación (181)

genotype/genotipo la constitución genética completa de un organismo; *también* la combinación genes para uno o más caracteres específicos (121)

geologic time scale/escala de tiempo geológico el método estándar que se usa para dividir la larga historia natural de la Tierra en partes razonables (196)

gestation period/período de gestación en los mamíferos, el tiempo que transcurre entre la fecundación y el nacimiento (456)

gill/branquiaen un órgano respiratorio en el que el oxígeno del agua se intercambia con el dióxido de carbono de la sangre (415)

gland/glándula un grupo de células que elaboran ciertas substancias químicas para el cuerpo (670)

Golgi complex/aparato de Golgi un organelo celular que ayuda a hacer y a empacar los materiales que serán transportados al exterior de la célula (73)

gut/tripa el tracto digestivo (381)

gymnosperm/gimnosperma una planta leñosa vascular que produce semillas que no están contenidas en un ovario o fruto (302)

H

herbivore/herbívoro un organismo que sólo come plantas (485)

heredity/herencia la transmisión de caracteres genéticos de padres a hijos (40, 114)

heterotroph/heterótrofo un organismo que se alimenta comiendo otros organismos o sus productos secundarios y que no puede producir compuestos orgánicos a partir de materiales inorgánicos (271)

hibernation/hibernación un período de inactividad y disminución de la temperatura del cuerpo que algunos animales experimentan en invierno como protección contra el tiempo frío y la escasez de comida (364)

homeostasis/homeostasis la capacidad de mantener un estado interno constante en un ambiente en cambio (39, 580)

hominid/homínido un tipo de primate caracterizado por ser bípedo, tener extremidades inferiores relativamente largas y no tener cola; incluye a los seres humanos y sus ancestros (207)

homologous chromosomes/cromosomas homólogos cromosomas con la misma secuencia de genes y la misma estructura (99, 126)

Homo sapiens/Homo sapiens la especie de homínidos que incluye a los seres humanos modernos y a sus ancestros más cercanos; apareció hace entre 100,000 y 150,000 años (210)

hormone/hormona una substancia que es producida en una célula o tejido, la cual causa un cambio en otra célula o tejido ubicado en una parte diferente del cuerpo (670)

host/huésped el organismo del cual un parásito obtiene alimento y refugio (256, 271)

hygiene/higiene la ciencia de la salud y las formas de preservar la salud (744)

hypha/hifa un filamento no-reproductor de un hongo (283)

hypothesis/hipótesis una explicación que se basa en observaciones o investigaciones científicas previas y que se puede probar (12)

I

immune system/sistema inmunológico las células y tejidos que reconocen y atacan substancias extrañas en el cuerpo (715)

immunity/inmunidad la capacidad de resistir una enfermedad infecciosa o recuperarse de ella (712)

infectious disease/enfermedad infecciosa una enfermedad que es causada por un patógeno y que puede transmitirse de un individuo a otro (710)

innate behavior/conducta innata una conducta heredada que no depende del ambiente ni de la experiencia (360)

integumentary system/sistema integumentario el sistema de órganos que forma una cubierta de protección en la parte exterior del cuerpo (592, 664)

internal fertilization/fecundación interna fecundación de un óvulo por un espermatozoide, la cual ocurre dentro del cuerpo de la hembra (686)

invertebrate/invertebrado un animal que no tiene columna vertebral (380)

J

joint/articulación un lugar donde se unen dos o más huesos (586)

K

kidney/riñón uno de los dos órganos que filtran el agua y los desechos de la sangre y excretan productos en fomra de orina (643)

L

large intestine/intestino grueso la porción más ancha y más corta del intestino, que elimina el agua de los alimentos casi totalmente digeridos y convierte los desechos en heces semisólidas o excremento (640)

larynx/laringe el área de la garganta que contiene las cuerdas vocales y que produce sonidos vocales (621)

lateral line/línea lateral una línea apenas visible que se encuentra a ambos lados del cuerpo de unpez y que recorre la longitud del cuerpo, marcando la ubicación de los órganos de los sentidos que detectan vibraciones en el agua (415)

law/ley un resumen de muchos resultados y observaciones experimentales; una ley dice cómo funcionan las cosas (20)

learned behavior/conducta aprendida una conducta que se ha aprendido por experiencia (360)

lichen/liquen una masa de células de hongos y de algas que crecen juntas en una relación simbiótica y que normalmente se encuentran en rocas o árboles (288)

life science/ciencias de la vida el estudio de los seres vivos (6)

lift/propulsión una fuerza hacia arriba en un objeto que se mueve en un fluido (446)

lipid/lípido un tipo de substancia bioquímica que no se disuelve en agua; las grasas y los esteroides son lípidos (46)

littoral zone/zona litoral la zona poco profunda de un lago o una laguna donde la luz llega al fondo y nutre a las plantas (541)

liver/hígado el órgano más grande del cuerpo; produce bilis, almacena y filtra la sangre, y almacena el exceso de azúcares en forma de glucógeno (639)

lung/pulmón un órgano respiratorio en el que el oxígeno del aire se intercambia con el dióxido de carbono de la sangre (420)

lymph/linfa el fluido que es recolectado por los vasos y nodos linfáticos (616)

lymphatic system/sistema linfático un conjunto de órganos cuya función principal es recolectar el fluido extracelular y regresarlo a la sangre; los órganos de este sistema incluyen los nodos linfáticos y los vasos linfáticos (616)

lymph nodes/nodos linfáticos masas ovaladas de tejido linfático que se encuentran en los vasos linfáticos y filtran la linfa (617)

lysosome/lisosoma un organelo celular que contiene enzimas digestivas (74)

M

macrophage/macrófago una célula del sistema inmunológico que envuelve a los patógenos y otros materiales (715)

malnutrition/desnutrición un trastorno de nutrición que resulta cuando una persona no consume una cantidad suficiente de cada nutriente que el cuerpo humano necesita (736)

mammary gland/glándula mamaria en los mamíferos hembra, una glándula que secreta leche (453)

marsh/pantano un ecosistema pantanoso sin árboles, donde crecen plantas tales como el pasto (542)

marsupial/marsupial un mamífero que lleva y alimenta a sus crías en una bolsa (465)

mass/masa una medida de la cantidad de materia que tiene un objeto (26)

meiosis/meiosis un proceso de división celular durante el cual el número de cromosomas disminuye a la mitad del número original por medio de dos divisiones del núcleo, lo cual resulta en la producción de células sexuales (gametos o esporas) (126)

memory B cell/célula B de memoria una célula B que responde con mayor eficacia a un antígeno cuando el cuerpo vuelve a infectarse con él que cuando lo encuentra por primera vez (718)

Mesozoic era/era Mesozoica la era geológica que comenzó hace 248 millones de años y terminó hace 65 millones de años; también llamada *Edad de los Reptiles* (203)

metabolism/metabolismo la suma de todos los procesos químicos que ocurren en un organismo (40)

metamorphosis/metamorfosis una fase del ciclo de vida de muchos animales durante la cual ocurre un cambio rápido de la forma inmadura del organismo a la adulta (396, 422)

mineral/mineral una clase de nutrientes que son elementos químicos necesarios para ciertos procesos del cuerpo (734)

mitochondrion/mitocondria en las células eucarióticas, el organelo celular rodeado por dos membranas que es el lugar donde se lleva a cabo la respiración celular (72)

mitosis/mitosis en las células eucarióticas, un proceso de división celular que forma dos núcleos nuevos, cada uno de los cuales posee el mismo número de cromosomas (99)

model/modelo un diseño, plan, representación o descripción cuyo objetivo es mostrar la estructura o funcionamiento de un objeto, sistema o concepto (18)

mold/moho en biología, un hongo que tiene la apariencia de lana o algodón (284)

molting/pelechar la muda de un exoesqueleto, piel, plumas o pelo, los cuales son reemplazados por partes nuevas (442)

monotreme/monotrema un mamífero que pone-huevos (464)

muscular system/sistema muscular el sistema de órganos cuya función principal es permitir el movimiento y la flexibilidad (588)

mutation/mutación un cambio en la secuencia de la base de nucleótidos de un gene o de una molécula de ADN (152)

mutualism/mutualismo una relación entre dos especies en la que ambas se benefician (494)

mycelium/micelio una masa de filamentos de hongos, o hifas, que forma el cuerpo de un hongo (283)

N

narcotic/narcótico una droga que proviene del opio, la cual alivia el dolor e induce el sueño; entre los ejemplos se encuentran la heroína, morfina y codeína (741)

natural selection/selección natural el proceso por medio del cual los individuos que están mejor adaptados a su ambiente sobreviven y se reproducen con más éxito que los individuos menos adaptados; una teoría que explica el mecanismo de la evolución (178)

nephron/nefrona la unidad del riñón que filtra la sangre (643)

nerve/nervio un conjunto de fibras nerviosas a través de las cuales se desplazan los impulsos entre el sistema nervioso central y otras partes del cuerpo (658)

neuron/neurona una célula nerviosa que está especializada en recibir y transmitir impulsos eléctricos (657)

nicotine/nicotina una substancia química tóxica y adictiva que se encuentra en el tabaco y que es una de las principales causas de los efectos dañinos de fumar (740)

noninfectious disease/enfermedad no infecciosa una enfermedad que no se contagia de una persona a otra (710)

nonrenewable resource/recurso no renovable un recurso que se forma a una tasa que es mucho más lenta que la tasa a la que se consume (556)

nonvascular plant/planta no vascular los tres tipos de plantas (hepáticas, milhojas y musgos) que carecen de tejidos transportadores y de raíces, tallos y hojas verdaderas (302)

nucleic acid/ácido nucleico una molécula formada por subunidades llamadas *nucleótidos* (47)

nucleotide/nucleótido en una cadena de ácidos nucleicos, una subunidad formada por un azúcar, un fosfato y una base nitrogenada (144)

nucleus/núcleo en una célula eucariótica, un organelo cubierto por una membrana, el cual contiene el ADN de la célula y participa en procesos tales como el crecimiento, metabolismo y reproducción (63)

nutrient/nutriente una substancia de los alimentos que proporciona energía o ayuda a formar tejidos corporales y que es necesaria para la vida y el crecimiento (732)

O

omnivore/omnívoro un organismo que come tanto plantas como animales (485)

open circulatory system/aparato circulatorio abierto un aparato circulatorio en el que el fluido circulatorio no está totalmente contenido en los vasos sanguíneos; un corazón bombea fluido por los vasos sanguíneos, los cuales se vacían en espacios llamados *senos* (389)

open-water zone/zona de aguas superiores la zona de un lago o una laguna que se extiende desde la zona litoral y cuya profundidad sólo alcanza hasta donde penetra la luz (541)

organ/órgano un conjunto de tejidos que desempeñan una función especializada en el cuerpo (77, 581)

organelle/organelo uno de los cuerpos pequeños del citoplasma de una célula que están especializados para llevar a cabo una función específica (63)

organism/organismo un ser vivo; cualquier cosa que pueda llevar a cabo procesos vitales independientemente (78)

organ system/aparato (o sistema) de órganos un grupo de órganos que trabajan en conjunto para desempeñar funciones corporales (78)

osmosis/ósmosis la difusión del agua a través de una membrana semipermeable (91)

ovary/ovario en las plantas con flores, la parte inferior del pistilo que produce óvulos (320); en el aparato reproductor femenino de los animales, un órgano que produce óvulos (689)

overpopulation/sobrepoblación la presencia de demasiados individuos en un área para los recursos disponibles (557)

P

Paleozoic era/era Paleozoica la era geológica que vino después del período Precámbrico; comenzó hace 543 millones de años y terminó hace 248 millones de años (202)

pancreas/páncreas el órgano que se encuentra detrás del estómago y que produce las enzimas digestivas y las hormonas que regulan los niveles de azúcar (638)

parasite/parásito un organismo que se alimenta de un organismo de otra especie (el huésped) y que normalmente lo daña; el huésped nunca se beneficia de la presencia del parásito (271)

parasitism/parasitismo una relación entre dos especies en la que una, el parásito, se beneficia de la otra, el huésped, que resulta perjudicada (495)

passive transport/transporte pasivo el movimiento de substancias a través de una membrana celular sin que la célula tenga que usar energía (92)

pathogen/patógeno un virus, microorganismo u otra substancia que causa enfermedades (710)

pathogenic bacteria/bacteria patogénica bacteria que causa una enfermedad (254)

pedigree/pedigrí un diagrama que muestra la incidencia de un carácter genético en varias generaciones de una familia (132)

penis/pene el órgano masculino que transfiere espermatozoides a una hembra y que lleva la orina hacia el exterior del cuerpo (688)

peripheral nervous system/sistema nervioso periférico todas las partes del sistema nervioso, excepto el encéfalo y la médula espinal (656)

petal/pétalo una de las partes de una flor que normalmente tienen colores brillantes y forma de hoja, las cuales forman uno de los anillos de una flor (319)

pharynx/faringe en los gusanos planos, el tubo muscular que va de la boca a la cavidad gastrovascular; en los animales que tienen tracto digestivo, el conducto que va de la boca a la laringe y al esófago (621)

phenotype/fenotipo la apariencia de un organismo u otra característica perceptible (120)

pheromone/feromona una substancia que el cuerpo libera y que hace que otro individuo de la misma especia reaccione de un modo predecible (367)

phloem/floema el tejido que transporta alimento en las plantas vasculares (314)

phospholipid/fosfolípido un lípido que contiene fósforo y que es un componente estructural de la membrana celular (46)

photosynthesis/fotosíntesis el proceso por medio del cual las plantas, las algas y algunas bacterias utilizan la luz solar, el dióxido de carbono y el agua para producir alimento (94, 332)

phytoplankton/fitoplancton los organismos microscópicos fotosintéticos que flotan cerca de la superficie del agua dulce o marina (274)

pioneer species/especie pionera una especie que coloniza un área deshabitada y empieza un proceso de sucesión (513)

pistil/pistilo la parte reproductora femenina de una flor, la cual produce semillas y está formada por el ovario, estilo y estigma (320)

placenta/placenta la estructura que une al feto en desarrollo con el útero y que permite el intercambio de nutrientes, desechos y gases entre la madre y el feto (693)

placental mammal/mamífero placentario un mamífero que nutre a sus crías aún no nacidas a través de una placenta que se encuentra dentro de su útero (456)

plankton/plancton la masa de organismos en su mayoría microscópicos que flotan o se encuentran a la deriva en ambientes de agua dulce o marina (534)

Plantae/Plantae un reino formado por organismos pluricelulares complejos que normalmente son verdes, tienen una pared celular de celulosa, no tienen capacidad de movimiento y utilizan la energía del Sol para producir azúcar mediante la fotosíntesis (231)

plate tectonics/tectónica de placas la teoría que explica cómo se mueven y cambian de forma las placas tectónicas, que son grandes porciones de la capa más externa de la Tierra (198)

pollen/polen los gránulos diminutos que contienen el gametofito masculino en las plantas con semilla (308)

pollination/polinización la transferencia de polen de las estructuras reproductoras masculinas a las estructuras femeninas de las plantas con semillas (311)

pollution/contaminación un cambio indeseable en el ambiente producido por substancias dañinas, desechos, gases, ruidos o radiación (554)

population/población un grupo de organismos de la misma especie que viven en un área geográfica específica (482)

Precambrian time/tiempo Precámbrico el período en la escala de tiempo geológico que abarca desde la formación de la Tierra hasta el comienzo de la era Paleozoica; comenzó hace aproximadamente 4.6 mil millones de años y terminó hace 543 millones de años (200)

precipitation/precipitación cualquier forma deagua que cae de las nubes a la superficie de la Tierra (508)

predator/depredador un organismo que se alimenta de otro organismo o de parte de él (492)

preening/acicalamiento en las aves, el acto de limpiar y mantener saludables las plumas (442)

prey/presa un organismo al que otro organismo mata para alimentarse de él (492)

primate/primate un tipo de mamífero caracterizado por tener pulgares oponibles y visión binocular (206)

probability/probabilidad la probabilidad de que ocurra un posible suceso futuro en cualquier caso dado del suceso (122)

producer/productor un organismo que puede elaborar sus propios alimentos utilizando la energía de su entorno (43)

prokaryote/procariote un organismo que está formado por una sola célula y que no tiene núcleo (64, 247)

protein/proteína una molécula formada por aminoácidos que es necesaria para construir y reparar estructuras corporales y para regular procesos del cuerpo (44, 733)

protist/protista un organismo que pertenece al reino Protista (270)

Protista/Protista un reino compuesto principalmente por organismo eucarióticos unicelulares que son diferentes de las plantas, animales, bacterias y hongos (230)

pulmonary circulation/circulación pulmonar el flujo de sangre del corazón a los pulmones y de vuelta al corazón a través de las arterias, los capilares y las venas pulmonares (609)

R

recessive trait/carácter recesivo un carácter que se hace aparente sólo cuando se heredan dos alelos recesivos de la misma característica (117)

recycling/reciclar el proceso de recuperar materiales valiosos o útiles de los desechos o de la basura; el proceso de reutilizar algunas cosas (563)

reflex/reflejo un movimiento involuntario y prácticamente inmediato en respuesta a un estímulo (665)

relative dating/datación relativa cualquier método que se utiliza para determinar si un acontecimiento u objeto es más viejo o más joven que otros acontecimientos u objetos (195)

renewable resource/recurso renovable un recurso natural que puede reemplazarse a la misma tasa a la que se consume (556)

respiration/respiración en biología, el intercambio de oxígeno y dióxido de carbono entre células vivas y su ambiente; incluye la respiración y la respiración celular (620)

respiratory system/aparato respiratorio un conjunto de órganos cuya función principal es tomar oxígeno y expulsar dióxido de carbono; los órganos de este aparato incluyen a los pulmones, la garganta y las vías que llevan a los pulmones (620)

retina/retina la capa interna del ojo, sensible a la luz, que recibe imágenes formadas por el lente ocular y las transmite al cerebro por medio del nervio óptico (666)

rhizoid/rizoide una estructura parecida a una raíz que se encuentra en las plantas no vasculares; mantiene a las plantas en su lugar y las ayuda a obtener agua y nutrientes (304)

rhizome/rizoma un tallo horizontal subterráneo que produce nuevas hojas, brotes y raíces (306)

ribosome/ribosoma un organelo celular compuesto de ARN y proteína; el sitio donde ocurre la síntesis de proteínas (71, 151)

RNA/ARN ácido ribonucleico, una molécula que está presente en todas las células vivas y que juega un papel en la producción de proteínas (150)

S

savanna/sabana una región de pastizales que, a menudo, tiene árboles dispersos; se encuentra en áreas tropicales y subtropicales donde se producen lluvias, incendios y sequías estacionales (530)

scientific methods/métodos científicos una serie de pasos que se siguen para solucionar problemas (10)

segment/segmento cualquier parte de una estructura más grande, como el cuerpo de un organismo, que se determina por límites naturales o arbitrarios (390)

selective breeding/reproducción selectiva la práctica humana de cruzar animales o plantas que tienen ciertas características deseadas (176)

sepal/sépalo en una flor, uno de los anillos más externos de hojas modificadas que protegen el capullo de la flor (319)

sex chromosome/cromosoma sexual uno de los dos cromosomas que determinan el sexo de un individuo (131)

sexual reproduction/reproducción sexual reproducción en la que se unen las células sexuales de los dos progenitores para producir descendencia que comparte caracteres de ambos progenitores (40, 685)

skeletal system/sistema esquelético el sistema de órganos cuya función principal es sostener y proteger el cuerpo y permitir que se mueva (584)

small intestine/intestino delgado el órgano que se encuentra entre el estómago y el intestino grueso en el cual se produce la mayor parte de la descomposición de los alimentos y se absorben la mayoría de los nutrientes (638)

social behavior/comportamiento social la interacción entre animales de la misma especie (366)

speciation/especiación la formación de especies nuevas como resultado de la evolución (182)

species/especie un grupo de organismos que tienen un parentesco cercano y que pueden aparearse para producir descendencia fértil (166)

sperm/espermatozoide la célula sexual masculina (685)

spleen/bazo el órgano linfático más grande del cuerpo; funciona como depósito para la sangre, desintegra los glóbulos rojos viejos y produce linfocitos y plásmidos (618)

spore/espora una célula reproductora o estructura pluricelular que resiste las condiciones ambientales adversas y que se puede desarrollar hasta convertirse en un adulto sin necesidad de fusionarse con otra célula (283)

stamen/estambre la estructura reproductora masculina de una flor, que produce polen y está formada por una antera ubicada en la punta del filamento (320)

stimulus/estímulo cualquier cosa que causa una reacción o cambio en un organismo o cualquier parte de un organismo (39)

stoma/estoma una de las muchas aberturas de una hoja o de un tallo de una planta, la cual permite que se lleve a cabo el intercambio de gases (334)

stomach/estómago el órgano digestivo con forma de bolsa ubicado entre el esófago y el intestino delgado, que descompone los alimentos por la acción de músculos, enzimas y ácidos (637)

stress/estrés una respuesta física o mental a la presión (746)

structure/estructura el orden y distribución de las partes de un organismo (79)

succession/sucesión el reemplazo de un tipo de comunidad por otro en un mismo lugar a lo largo de un período de tiempo (512)

swamp/ciénaga un ecosistema de pantano en el que crecen arbustos y árboles (542)

swim bladder/vejiga natatoria en los peces óseos, una bolsa llena de gas que se usa para controlar la flotabilidad; también se llama *vejiga de aire* (418)

symbiosis/simbiosis una relación en la que dos organismos diferentes viven estrechamente asociados uno con el otro (494)

systemic circulation/circulación sistémica el flujo de sangre del corazón a todas las partes del cuerpo y de vuelta al corazón (609)

T

tadpole/renacuajo la larva acuática, parecida a un pez, de una rana o sapo (422)

taxonomy/taxonomía la ciencia de describir, nombrar y clasificar organismos (223)

T cell/célula T una célula del sistema inmunológico que coordina el sistema inmunológico y ataca a muchas células infectadas (715)

technology/tecnología la aplicación de la ciencia con fines prácticos; el uso de herramientas, máquinas, materiales y procesos para satisfacer las necesidades de los seres humanos (22)

temperature/temperatura una medida de qué tan caliente (o frío) está algo; específicamente, una medida de la energía cinética promedio de las partículas de un objeto (26)

territory/territorio un área que está ocupada por un animal o por un grupo de animales que no permiten que entren otros miembros de la especie (361)

testes/testículos los principales órganos reproductores masculinos, los cuales producen espermatozoides y testosterona (688)

theory/teoría una explicación que relaciona muchas hipótesis y observaciones (20)

thymus/timo la glándula principal del sistema linfático; libera linfocitos T maduros (617)

tissue/tejido un grupo de células similares que llevan a cabo una función común (77, 580)

tonsils/amígdalas masas pequeñas y redondas de tejido linfático, ubicadas en la faringe y en el paso de la boca a la faringe (619)

trachea/tráquea en los insectos, miriápodos y arañas, uno de los conductos de una red de conductos de aire; en los vertebrados, el conducto que une la laringe con los pulmones (621)

trait/carácter una característica determinada genéticamente (176)

transpiration/transpiración el proceso por medio del cual las plantas liberan vapor de agua al aire por medio de los estomas; *también,* la liberación de vapor de agua al aire por otros organismos (334)

tropism/tropismo el movimiento de un organismo o de una parte de él en respuesta a un estímulo externo, como por ejemplo, la luz (340)

tundra/tundra una llanura sin árboles situada en la región ártica o antártica o en la cumbre de las montañas; se caracteriza por temperaturas muy bajas en el invierno y veranos cortos y frescos (532)

U

umbilical cord/cordón umbilical la estructura que une al embrión y después al feto con la placenta, a través de la cual pasan vasos sanguíneos (693)

urinary system/sistema urinario los órganos que producen, almacenan y eliminan la orina (642)

uterus/útero en los mamíferos hembras, el órgano hueco y muscular en el que se incrusta el óvulo fecundado y en el que se desarrollan el embrión y el feto (689)

V

vagina/vagina el órgano reproductivo femenino que conecta la parte exterior del cuerpo con el útero (689)

variable/variable un factor que se modifica en un experimento con el fin de probar una hipótesis (14)

vascular plant/planta vascular una planta que tiene tejidos especializados que transportan materiales de una parte de la planta a otra (302)

vein/vena en biología, un vaso que lleva sangre al corazón (608)

vertebrate/vertebrado un animal que tiene columna vertebral (412)

vesicle/vesícula una cavidad o bolsa pequeña que contiene materiales en una célula eucariótica; se forma cuando parte de la membrana celular rodea los materiales que van a ser llevados al interior la célula o transportados dentro de ella (73)

virus/virus una partícula microscópica que se introduce en una célula y a menudo la destruye (256)

vitamin/vitamina una clase de nutrientes que contiene carbono y que es necesaria en pequeñas cantidades para mantener la salud y permitir el crecimiento (734)

volume/volumen una medida del tamaño de un cuerpo o región en un espacio de tres dimensiones (25)

W

waterfowl/aves acuáticas pájaros acuáticos, como por ejemplo, un pato, un ganso o un cisne (449)

water vascular system/sistema vascular acuoso un sistema de canales que están llenos de un fluido acuoso que circula por todo el cuerpo de los equinodermos (399)

wetland/pantano un área de tierra que está periódicamente bajo el agua o cuyo suelo contiene una gran cantidad de humedad (542)

X

xylem/xilema el tipo de tejido que se encuentra en las plantas vasculares, el cual provee soporte y transporta el agua y los nutrientes desde las raíces (314)

Index

Boldface page numbers refer to illustrative material, such as figures, tables, margin elements, photographs, and illustrations.

Index

Index

glowing, 296
as heterotrophs, 271, **271**
in human food, 296
immobile, 279–280, **280**
life cycles of, 273, **273**
mobile, 277–279, **277, 278, 279**
in pond scum, 61, **61**
as producers, **271,** 274–276, **274, 275, 276**
reproduction of, 272–273, **272, 273**
protons, 828
protozoa, 230, 277–279, **277, 278, 279**. *See also* protists
pseudopodia, 277, **277**
psychological dependence, 738
puberty, 689, 696
puffballs, **283**
pulmonary circulation, 609, **609**
pulse, 608
Punnett squares, 19, **19,** 121–122, **121, 122**
pupa (plural, *pupae*), **396**
pupils, 666–667, **666**
pyramid instructions (FoldNote), 810, **810**
Pyrodinium bahamense, 296

Index

Index

Acknowledgments
continued from page ii

Eva Oberdoerster, Ph.D.
Lecturer
Department of Biology
Southern Methodist
 University
Dallas, Texas

Michael H. Renfroe, Ph.D.
Professor of Biology
Department of Biology
James Madison University
Harrisonburg, Virginia

Laurie Santos, Ph.D.
Assistant Professor
Department of Psychology
Yale University
New Haven, Connecticut

Patrick K. Schoff, Ph.D.
Research Associate
Natural Resources Research
 Institute
University of Minnesota—
 Duluth
Duluth, Minnesota

Richard P. Vari, Ph.D.
*Research Scientist and
 Curator*
Division of Fishes
National Museum of
 Natural History
Washington, D.C.

Teacher Reviewers

Diedre S. Adams
Physical Science Instructor
West Vigo Middle School
West Terre Haute, Indiana

Barbara Gavin Akre
*Teacher of Biology, Anatomy-
 Physiology, and Life Science*
Duluth Independent
 School District
Duluth, Minnesota

Sarah Carver
Science Teacher
Jackson Creek Middle
 School
Bloomington, Indiana

Hilary Cochran
Science Teacher
Indian Crest Junior
 High School
Souderton, Pennsylvania

Karen Dietrich, S.S.J., Ph.D.
*Principal and Biology
 Instructor*
Mount Saint Joseph
 Academy
Flourtown, Pennsylvania

Debra S. Kogelman, MAed.
Science Teacher
University of Chicago
 Laboratory Schools
Chicago, Illinois

Augie Maldonado
Science Teacher
Grisham Middle School
Round Rock, Texas

Jean Pletchette
Health Educator
Winterset Community
 Schools
Winterset, Iowa

Elizabeth Rustad
Science Teacher
Higley School District
Gilbert, Arizona

Helen P. Schiller
Instructional Coach
The School District of
 Greenville County
Greenville, South Carolina

Stephanie Snowden
Science Teacher
Canyon Vista Middle
 School
Austin, Texas

Florence Vaughan
Science Teacher
University of Chicago
 Laboratory Schools
Chicago, Illinois

Larry A. Weber, M.S.
Science Teacher
Marshall School
Duluth, Minnesota

Angie Williams
Teacher
Riversprings Middle School
Crawfordville, Florida

Lab Development

Diana Scheidle Bartos
Research Associate
School of Mines
Golden, Colorado

Carl Benson
General Science Teacher
Plains High School
Plains, Montana

Charlotte Blassingame
Technology Coordinator
White Station
 Middle School
Memphis, Tennessee

Marsha Carver
*Science Teacher and
 Department Chair*
McLean County
 High School
Calhoun, Kentucky

Kenneth E. Creese
Science Teacher
White Mountain Junior
 High School
Rock Springs, Wyoming

Linda Culp
*Science Teacher and
 Department Chair*
Thorndale High School
Thorndale, Texas

James Deaver
*Science Teacher and
 Department Chair*
West Point High School
West Point, Nebraska

Frank McKinney, Ph.D.
Professor of Geology
Appalachian State
 University
Boone, North Carolina

Alyson Mike
Science Teacher
East Valley Middle School
East Helena, Montana

C. Ford Morishita
Biology Teacher
Clackamas High School
Milwaukie, Oregon

Patricia D. Morrell, Ph.D.
Associate Professor
School of Education
University of Portland
Portland, Oregon

Hilary C. Olson, Ph.D.
Research Associate
Institute for Geophysics
The University of Texas
 at Austin
Austin, Texas

James B. Pulley
*Science Editor and Former
 Science Teacher*
North Kansas City, Missouri

Denice Lee Sandefur
Science Chairperson
Nucla High School
Nucla, Colorado

Patti Soderberg
Science Writer
The BioQUEST Curriculum
 Consortium
Biology Department
Beloit College
Beloit, Wisconsin

Phillip Vavala
*Science Teacher and
 Department Chair*
Salesianum School
Wilmington, Delaware

Albert C. Wartski, M.A.T.
Biology Teacher
Chapel Hill High School
Chapel Hill, North Carolina

Lynn Marie Wartski
*Science Writer and Former
 Science Teacher*
Hillsborough, North
 Carolina

Ivora D. Washington
*Science Teacher and
 Department Chair*
Hyattsville Middle School
Washington, D.C.

Lab Testing

Barry L. Bishop
*Science Teacher and
 Department Chair*
San Rafael Junior High
 School
Ferron, Utah

Yvonne Brannum
*Science Teacher and
 Department Chair*
Hine Junior High School
Washington, D.C.

Gladys Cherniak
Science Teacher
St. Paul's Episcopal School
Mobile, Alabama

James Chin
Science Teacher
Frank A. Day Middle School
Newtonville, Massachusetts

Randy Christian
Science Teacher
Stovall Junior High School
Houston, Texas

Georgiann Delgadillo
Science Teacher
East Valley Continuous
 Curriculum School
Spokane, Washington

Alonda Droege
Biology Teacher
Evergreen High School
Seattle, Washington

Susan Gorman
Science Teacher
North Ridge Middle
School
North Richland Hills,
Texas

Karma Houston-Hughes
Science Mentor
Kyrene Middle School
Tempe, Arizona

Kerry A. Johnson
Science Teacher
Isbell Middle School
Santa Paula, California

M. R. Penny Kisiah
*Science Teacher and
Department Chair*
Fairview Middle School
Tallahassee, Florida

Kathy LaRoe
Science Teacher
East Valley Middle School
East Helena, Montana

Jane M. Lemons
Science Teacher
Western Rockingham
Middle School
Madison, North Carolina

Maurine O. Marchani
*Science Teacher and
Department Chair*
Raymond Park Middle
School
Indianapolis, Indiana

Jason P. Marsh
Biology Teacher
Montevideo High School
and Montevideo
Country School
Montevideo, Minnesota

Edith C. McAlanis
*Science Teacher and
Department Chair*
Socorro Middle School
El Paso, Texas

Kevin McCurdy, Ph.D.
Science Teacher
Elmwood Junior High
School
Rogers, Arkansas

Terry J. Rakes
Science Teacher
Elmwood Junior High
School
Rogers, Arkansas

Elizabeth Rustad
Science Teacher
Crane Middle School
Yuma, Arizona

Debra A. Sampson
Science Teacher
Booker T. Washington
Middle School
Elgin, Texas

David M. Sparks
Science Teacher
Redwater Junior High
School
Redwater, Texas

Ivora Washington
*Science Teacher and
Department Chair*
Hyattsville Middle School
Washington, D.C.

Christopher Wood
Science Teacher
Western Rockingham
Middle School
Madison, North Carolina

Feature Development

Hatim Belyamani
John A. Benner
David Bradford
Jennifer Childers
Mickey Coakley
Susan Feldkamp
Jane Gardner
Erik Hahn
Christopher Hess
Deena Kalai
Charlotte W. Luongo, MSc
Michael May
Persis Mehta, Ph.D.
Eileen Nehme, MPH
Catherine Podeszwa
Dennis Rathnaw
Daniel B. Sharp
April Smith West
John M. Stokes
Molly F. Wetterschneider

Answer Checking

Hatim Belyamani
Austin, Texas

Staff Credits

Editorial
Robert Todd,
Vice President, Editorial Science
Debbie Starr,
Managing Editor
Kelly Rizk, *Senior Editor*

Editorial Development Team
Karin Akre
Amy Fry
Frieda Gress
Betsy Roll
Marjorie Roueché
Kenneth Shepardson
David Westerberg

Copyeditors
Dawn Marie Spinozza,
Copyediting Manager
Anne-Marie De Witt
Jane A. Kirschman
Kira J. Watkins

Editorial Support Staff
Mary Anderson
Suzanne Krejci
Shannon Oehler

Online Products
Bob Tucek,
Executive Editor
Wesley M. Bain

Design
Book Design
Kay Selke,
Director of Book Design
Sonya Mendeke, *Designer*
Holly Whittaker, *Project Administrator*

Media Design
Richard Metzger,
Design Director
Chris Smith,
Senior Designer

Image Acquisitions
Curtis Riker, *Director*
Jeannie Taylor,
Photo Research Manager
Terry Janecek,
Photo Researcher
Elaine Tate,
Art Buyer Supervisor
Angela Boehm,
Senior Art Buyer

Design New Media
Ed Blake, *Director*
Kimberly Cammerata,
Design Manager
Michael Rinella,
Senior Designer

Cover Design
Bill Smith Studio

Publishing Services
Carol Martin, *Director*

Graphic Services
Bruce Bond, *Director*
Jeff Bowers,
Graphic Services Manager
JoAnn Stringer, *Senior Graphics Specialist II*
Cathy Murphy, *Senior Graphics Specialist*
Nanda Patel,
Graphics Specialist
Katrina Gnader, *Graphics Specialist*

Technology Services
Laura Likon, *Director*
Juan Baquera, *Technology Services Manager*
Lana Kaupp,
Senior Technology Services Analyst
Margaret Sanchez, *Senior Technology Services Analyst*
Sara Buller, *Technology Services Analyst*
Patty Zepeda, *Technology Services Analyst*
Jeff Robinson,
Ancillary Design Manager

New Media
Armin Gutzmer, *Director*
Melanie Baccus,
New Media Coordinator
Lydia Doty,
Senior Project Manager
Cathy Kuhles,
Technical Assistant
Marsh Flournoy,
Quality Assurance Analyst
Tara F. Ross,
Senior Project Manager

Production
Eddie Dawson, *Production Manager*
Sherry Sprague, *Senior Production Coordinator*
Suzanne Brooks,
Production Coordinator

Teacher Edition
Alicia Sullivan
David Hernandez
April Litz

Manufacturing and Inventory
Ivania Quant Lee
Wilonda Ieans

Ancillary Development and Production
General Learning Communications, Northbrook, Illinois

Credits

PHOTOGRAPHY

Front Cover (tr), Corbis; (bl), JH Pete Carmichael/Getty Images; (tl), Dennis Kunkel/Phototake; (br), Victor Englebert; (owl), Kim Taylor/Bruce Coleman

Skills Practice Lab Teens Sam Dudgeon/HRW

Connection to Astrology Corbis Images; **Connection to Biology** David M. Phillips/Visuals Unlimited; **Connection to Chemistry** Digital Image copyright © 2005 PhotoDisc; **Connection to Environment** Digital Image copyright © 2005 PhotoDisc; **Connection to Geology** Letraset Phototone; **Connection to Language** Arts Digital Image copyright © 2005 PhotoDisc; **Connection to Meteorology** Digital Image copyright © 2005 PhotoDisc; **Connection to Oceanography** © ICONOTEC; **Connection to Physics** Digital Image copyright © 2005 PhotoDisc

Table of Contents iii (t), Peter Van Steen/HRW; iii (b), Uniphoto; iv (t), Chip Simmons/Discover Channel; iv (b), Wolfgang Bayer; vi (t), Ned M. Seidler/National Geographic Society Image Collection; vi (b), Sam Dudgeon/HRW; vii (tl), James Beveridge/Visuals Unlimited; vii (tr), © Gail Shumway/Getty Images/FPG International; viii (t), © G. Randall/Getty Images/FPG International; viii (b), CNRI/Science Photo Library/Photo Researchers; viii-ix (t), © Stan Osolinski/Getty Images/FPG International; ix (c), SuperStock; ix (b), Digital Image copyright © 2005 PhotoDisc; x (t), Breck P. Kent/Animals Animals/Earth Scenes; x (b), Ron Kimball; xi (t), © Jeffrey L. Rotman/CORBIS; xi (c), © Kevin Schafer/CORBIS; xi (b), Kenneth Fink/Bruce Coleman, Inc.; xii (t), Sylvain Cordier/Photo Researchers; xiii (t), Kim Heacox/DRK Photo; xiii (bl), © Jeff Hunter/Getty Images/The Image Bank; xiv (tl), © Sindre Ellingsen/Alamy Photos; xiv (b), Sam Dudgeon/HRW; xiv-xv (tc), © Nih/Science Source/Photo Researchers, Inc.; xvi (t), Sam Dudgeon/HRW; xvi (b), Photo Lennart Nilsson/Albert Bonniers Forlag AB, A Child Is Born, Dell Publishing Company; xvii (b), © Rob Van Petten/Getty Images/The Image Bank; xviii-xxxiii (all), Sam Dudgeon/HRW

Unit One 2 (tl), O.S.F./Animals Animals; 2 (cl), Hulton Archive/Getty Images; 2 (bl), Digital Image copyright © 2005 PhotoDisc; 2-3 (br & bl), Peter Veit/DRK Photo; 3 (cl), University of Pennsylvania/Hulton Getty; 3 (t), National Portrait Gallery, Smithsonian Institution/Art Resource; 3 (br), © National Geographic Image Collection/O. Louis Mazzatenta; 3 (cr), Digital Image copyright © 2005 PhotoDisc

Chapter One 4-5 Craig Line/AP/Wide World Photos; 6 (b), Peter Van Steen/HRW 7 (l), NASA; 7 (c), Gerry Gropp; 7 (r), Chip Simmons/Discover Channel; 8 (t), Hank Morgan/Photo Researchers, Inc.; 8 (b), Mark Lennihan/AP/Wide World Photos; 9 © National Geographic Image Collection/Dale Miquelle; 11 (tr), Peter Van Steen/HRW; 11 (b), Sam Dudgeon/HRW; 12 Sam Dudgeon/HRW; 14 John Mitchell/Photo Researchers; 16 (b), Sam Dudgeon/HRW; 17 John Mitchell/Photo Researchers; 18 © Royalty-Free/CORBIS; 20 Art by Christopher Sloan/Photograph by Mark Thiessen both National Geographic Image Collection/© National Geographic Image Collection; 22 (bl), Alfred Pasieka/Photo Researchers; 22 (bl), Howard Sochurek/The Stock Market; 23 (tl), CENCO; 23 (bl), Robert Brons/Biological Photo Service; 23 (tc), Sinclair Stammers/Science Photo Library/Photo Researchers; 23 (tr), RJ Lee Instruments Limited; 23 (bc), Microworks/Phototake; 23 (br), Visuals Unlimited/Karl Aufderheide; 24 (t), Victoria Smith/HRW; 24 (bc), Victoria Smith/HRW; 24 (b), Victoria Smith/HRW; 24 (tc), Sam Dudgeon/HRW; 25 (bl), Peter Van Steen/HRW; 25 (br), Peter Van Steen/HRW; 27 (b), Dr. Jeremy Burgess/Science Photo Library/Photo Researchers, Inc.; 28 Sam Dudgeon/HRW; 29 Sam Dudgeon/HRW; 30 (b), Peter Van Steen/HRW; 30 (t), John Mitchell/Photo Researchers; 34 (l), Craig Fugii/©1988 The Seattle Times; 35 (r), NASA; 35 (l), NASA

Chapter Two 36-37 (t), Rick Friedman/Blackstar Publishing/Picture Quest; 38 (r), Visuals Unlimited/Science Visuals Unlimited; 38 (l), Wolfgang Kaehler Photography; 39 (l), David M. Dennis/Tom Stack and Associates; 39 (r), David M. Dennis/Tom Stack and Associates; 40 (l), Visuals Unlimited/Stanley Flegler; 40 (r), James M. McCann/Photo Researchers, Inc. ; 42 (b), Wolfgang Bayer; 43 (t), Visuals Unlimited/Rob Simpson ; 43 (b), © Alex Kerstitch/Visuals Unlimited, Inc.; 44 (l), William J. Hebert/Stone; 44 (c), SuperStock; 44 (r), Kevin Schafer/Peter Arnold, Inc.; 45 Peter Dean/Grant Heilman Photography; 49 Peter Van Steen/HRW; 50 David M. Dennis/Tom Stack and Associates; 51 (tc), Victoria Smith/HRW; 51 (c), Victoria Smith/HRW; 51 (bc), Victoria Smith/HRW; 51 (t), © Wolfgang Kaehler/Liaison International/Getty News Images; 51 (b), © Alex Kerstitch/Visuals Unlimited, Inc.; 54 (b), Chip East/Reuters/NewsCom; 55 (r), Courtesy Janis Davis-Street/NASA; 55 (l), NASA

Unit Two 56 (c), The National Archives/Corbis; 56 (b), Cold Spring Harbor Laboratory; 56 (t), © Burstein Collection/CORBIS; 57 (t), Ed Reschke/Peter Arnold; 57 (tcr), Keith Porter/Photo Researchers; 57 (bcl), Ed Reschke/Peter Arnold, Inc.; 57 (br), © Dr. Ian Wilmut/Liaison/Getty News Images; 57 (bl), Dan McCoy/Rainbow; 57 (bcr), © Glen Allison/Getty Images/Stone; 57 (tcl), © Bettmann/CORBIS

Chapter Three 58-59, Dennis Kunkel/Phototake; 60 (l), Visuals Unlimited/Kevin Collins; 60 (r), Leonard Lessin/Peter Arnold; 61 (r), T.E. Adams/Visuals Unlimited; 61 (cl), Roland Birke/Peter Arnold, Inc.; 61 (bkgd), Jerome Wexler/Photo Researchers, Inc.; 61 (cr), Biophoto Associates/Photo Researchers, Inc.; 61 (l), M.I. Walker/Photo Researchers, Inc.; 62 Photodisc, Inc.; 63 (t), William Dentler/BPS/Stone; 63 (b), Dr. Gopal Murti/Science Photo Library/Photo Researchers, Inc.; 65 Wolfgang Baumeister/Science Photo Library/Photo Researchers, Inc.; 66 (l), Biophoto Associates/Photo Researchers, Inc.; 70 (bl), Don Fawcett/Visuals Unlimited; 70 (t), Dr. Peter Dawson/Science Photo Library/Photo Researchers, Inc.; 71 (r), R. Bolender-D. Fawcett/Visuals Unlimited; 72 (cl), Don Fawcett/Visuals Unlimited; 72 (bl), Newcomb & Wergin/BPS/Tony Stone Images; 73 (br), Garry T Cole/BPS/Stone; 74 (tl), Dr. Gopal Murti/Science Photo Library/Photo Researchers, Inc.; 74 (cl), Dr. Jeremy Burgess/Science PhotoLibrary/Science Source/Photo Researchers; 76 Quest/Science Photo Library/Photo Researchers, Inc.; 77 Manfred Kage/Peter Arnold, Inc. ; 80 (b), Sam Dudgeon/HRW; 86 (r), Photo Researchers, Inc.; 86 (l), Science Photo Library/Photo Researchers, Inc.; 87 (b), Digital Image copyright © 2005 Artville; 87 (t), Courtesy Caroline Schooley

Chapter Four 88-89 © Michael & Patricia Fogden/CORBIS; 90 Sam Dudgeon/HRW; 92 (br), Photo Researchers; 93 (tr), Birgit H. Satir; 94 (l), Runk/Schoenberger/Grant Heilman; 95 (r), John Langford/HRW Photo; 97 Corbis Images; 98 CNRI/Science Photo Library/Photo Researchers, Inc. ; 99 (t), L. Willatt, East Anglian Regional Genetics Service/Science Photo Library/Photo Researchers, Inc. ; 99 (b), Biophoto Associates/Photo Researchers; 100 (l), Visuals Unlimited/R. Calentine; 100 (l), Ed Reschke/Peter Arnold, Inc.; 100 (c), Ed Reschke/Peter Arnold, Inc.; 100 (cr), Ed Reschke/Peter Arnold, Inc.; 101 (cl), Ed Reschke/Peter Arnold, Inc.; 101 (c), Biology Media/Photo Researchers, Inc.; 101 (cr), Biology Media/Photo Researchers, Inc.; 102 Sam Dudgeon/HRW; 103 Sam Dudgeon/HRW; 104 (l), Runk/Schoenberger/Grant Heilman; 105 (cl), Biophoto Associates/Science Source/Photo Researchers; 105 (cr), Biophoto Associates/Science Source/Photo Researchers; 105 (br), John Langford/HRW Photo; 108 (l), Lee D. Simons/Science Souce/Photo Researchers; 109 (tr), Courtesy Dr. Jarrel Yakel; 109 (tr), David McCarthy/SPL/Photo Researchers, Inc.

Unit Three 110 (t), Library of Congress/Corbis; 110 (c), MBL/WHOI Library; 110 (b), NASA; 111 (cr), John Reader/Science Photo Library/Photo Researchers, Inc.; 111 (bl), John Reader/Science Photo Library/Photo Researchers, Inc.; 111 (br), Ted Thai/Time Magzine; 111 (cl), © Ken Eward/Bio Grafx/Photo Researchers, Inc.; 111 (tl), © John Conrad/CORBIS

Chapter Five 112-113 © Maximilian Weinzierl/Alamy Photos; 114 Ned M. Seidler/National Geographic Society Image Collection; 119 © Andrew Brookes/CORBIS; 120 © Joe McDonald/Visuals Unlimited; 121 (b), Sam Dudgeon/HRW; 123 Digital Image copyright © 2005 PhotoDisc; 124 (b), © Mervyn Rees/Alamy Photos; 125 (b), Image Copyright ©2001 Photodisc, Inc.; 125 (tl), Sam Dudgeon/HRW; 125 (tr), Sam Dudgeon/HRW; 126 (b), Biophoto Associates/Photo Researchers, Inc.; 126 (b), Phototake/CNRI/Phototake NYC; 131 (b), © Rob vanNostrand; 132 (b), © ImageState; 133 © ImageState; 134 (b), Sam Dudgeon/HRW; 135 (b), Sam Dudgeon/HRW; 137 (r), © Mervyn Rees/Alamy Photos; 137 (l), © Rob vanNostrand; 140 (c), Dr. F. R. Turner, Biology Dept., Indiana University; 140 (r), Dr. F. R. Turner, Biology Dept., Indiana University; 140 (l), Hank Morgan/Rainbow; 141, Courtesy of Stacey Wong

Chapter Six 142-143 US Department of Energy/Science Photo Library/Photo Researchers, Inc.; 145 (r), Science Photo Library/Photo Researchers, Inc.; 145 (l), Hulton Archive/Getty Images; 148 (l), Sam Dudgeon/HRW; 148 (l), Sam Dudgeon/HRW; 149 (bl), David M. Phillips/Visuals Unlimited; 149 (cl), J.R. Paulson & U.K. Laemmli/University of Geneva; 153 (br), Jackie Lewin/Royal Free Hospital/Science Photo Library/Photo Researchers, Inc.; 153 (tr), Jackie Lewin/Royal Free Hospital/Science Photo Library/Photo Researchers, Inc.; 154 (t), Visuals Unlimited/Science Visuals Unlimited/Keith Wood ; 154 (b), Volker Steger/Peter Arnold; 155 Sam Dudgeon/HRW; 157 Victoria Smith/HRW; 162 (l), Robert Brook/Science Photo Library/Photo Researchers, Inc.; 163 (r), Photo courtesy of the Whitehead Institute for Biomedical Research at MIT; 163 (l), Garry Watson/Science Photo Library/Photo Researchers, Inc.

Chapter Seven 164-165 (t), © Stuart Westmorland/CORBIS; 166 (bl), James Beveridge/Visuals Unlimited; 166 (tc), © Gail Shumway/Getty Images/FPG International; 166 (br), Doug Wechsler/Animals Animals; 168 (l), Ken Lucas; 168 (r), John Cancalosi/Tom Stack & Associates; 169 (cl), © SuperStock; 169 (bl), © Martin Ruegner/Alamy Photos; 169 (br), © James D. Watt/Stephen Frink Collection/Alamy Photos; 169 (tl), © Ron Kimball/Ron Kimball Stock; 169 (r), © Carl & Ann Purcell/CORBIS; 169 (cr), © Martin B. Withers; Frank Lane Picture Agency/CORBIS; 170 (tr), Illustration by Carl Buell, and taken from http://www.neoucom.edu/Depts/Anat/Pakicetid.html. ; 170 (tl), Courtesy of Research Casting International; 170 (b), Courtesy of Research Casting International; 171 (t), © 1998 Philip Gingerich/Courtesy of the Museum of Paleontology, The University of Michigan; 171 (c), Courtesy of Betsy Webb, Pratt Museum, Homer, Alaska; 171 (b), Courtesy of Betsy Webb, Pratt Museum, Homer, Alaska; 173 (b), Visuals Unlimited/H.W. Robison; 173 (t), James Beveridge/Visuals Unlimited; 174 (l), Christopher Ralling; 174 (r), © William E. Ferguson; 176 (b), Carolyn A. McKeone/Photo Researchers, Inc. ; 180 (b), Getty Images/Stone; 183 (r), Zig Leszczynski/Animals Animals/Earth Scenes; 183 (l), Gary Mezaros/Visuals Unlimited; 185 Victoria Smith/HRW; 186 (t), James Beveridge/Visuals Unlimited; 187 Courtesy of Betsy Webb, Pratt Museum, Homer, Alaska; 190 (l), Doug Wilson/Westlight; 191 (r), Wally Emerson/Courtesy of Raymond Pierotti; 191 (l), George D. Lepp/Photo Researchers, Inc.

878   Credits

Chapter Twenty Six 682-683 Photo Lennart Nilsson/Albert Bonniers Forlag AB, A Child Is Born, Dell Publishing Company; 684 (r), Visuals Unlimited/Cabisco; 684 (l), Innerspace Visions; 686 (b), Photo Researchers; 686 (t), Digital Image copyright © 2005 PhotoDisc Green; 687 © Charles Phillip/CORBIS; 690 Chip Henderson; 695 (tl), Petit Format/Nestle/Science Source/Photo Researchers, Inc.; 695 (cl), Photo Lennart Nilsson/Albert Bonniers Forlag AB, A Child Is Born, Dell Publishing Company; 695 (cr), Photo Lennart Nilsson/Albert Bonniers Forlag AB, A Child Is Born, Dell Publishing Company; 695 (br), Keith/Custom Medical Stock Photo; 695 (tr), David M. Phillips/ Photo Researchers, Inc.; 696 (l), Peter Van Steen/HRW; 696 (cl), Peter Van Steen/ HRW; 696 (c), Peter Van Steen/HRW; 696 (cr), Peter Van Steen/HRW; 696 (r), Peter Van Steen/HRW; 697 © Mark Harmel/Getty Images/FPG International; 699 Digital Image copyright © 2005 PhotoDisc; 700 Peter Van Steen/HRW; 701 Photo Lennart Nilsson/Albert Bonniers Forlag AB, A Child Is Born, Dell Publishing Company; 704 (r), Jim Tunell/Zuma Press/NewsCom; 704 (l), © Michael Clancy; 705 (l), ZEPHYR/ Science Photo Library/Photo Researchers, Inc.; 705 (r), Salem Community College

Unit Eight 706 (c), Erich Schrempp/Photo Researchers, Inc.; 706 (t), Gervase Spencer/E.T. Archive; 707 (tl), Mary Evans Picture Library; 707 (tr), Wayne Floyd/ Unicorn Stock Photos; 707 (cl), © LSHTM/Getty Images/Stone; 707 (cr), UPI/Corbis-Bettmann; 707 (b), Wang Haiyan/China Features/CORBIS

Chapter Twenty Seven 708-709 (t), © K. Kjeldsen/Photo Researchers, Inc.; 710 (br), CNRI/Science Photo Library/Photo Researchers; 710 (bl), Tektoff-RM/CNRI/Science Photo Library/Photo Researchers; 711 (t), Kent Wood/Photo Researchers; 712 (b), Peter Van Steen/HRW ; 714 (b), Peter Van Steen/HRW; 718 (t), John Langford/HRW Photo; 719 (b), Clinical Radiology Dept., Salisbury District Hospital/Science Photo Library/Photo Researchers; 719 (t), SuperStock; 720 (b), Photo Lennart Nilsson/Albert Bonniers Forlag AB; 720 (tl), Dr. A. Liepins/Science Photo Library/Photo Researchers; 720 (tr), Dr. A. Liepins/Science Photo Library/Photo Researchers; 722 Sam Dudgeon/ HRW; 725 (t), Peter Van Steen/HRW ; 728 (l), E. R. Degginger/Bruce Coleman; 728 (r), Chris Rogers/Index Stock Imagery, Inc.; 729 (t), Peter Van Steen/HRW; 729 (b), Corbis

Chapter Twenty Eight 730-731 © Arthur Tilley/Getty Images/Taxi; 732 Peter Van Steen/HRW; 733 (b), Peter Van Steen/HRW; 733 (t), Sam Dudgeon/HRW; 734 (c), Image Copyright ©2004 PhotoDisc, Inc./HRW; 734 (t), Image Copyright ©2004 PhotoDisc, Inc./HRW; 734 (bl), CORBIS Images/HRW; 734 (br), CORBIS Images/HRW; 735 © John Kelly/Getty Images/Stone; 736 John Burwell/FoodPix; 737 Peter Van Steen/HRW; 738 Peter Van Steen/HRW; 739 (b), Peter Van Steen/HRW; 739 (t), ©1999 Steven Foster; 740 (tl), E. Dirksen/Photo Researchers; 740 (b), Spencer Grant/Photo Researchers, Inc.; 740 (tr), Dr. Andrew P. Evans/Indiana University; 742 Jeff Greenberg/PhotoEdit; 743 Mike Siluk/The Image Works; 744 Sam Dudgeon/HRW; 745 (t), © Rob Van Petten/Getty Images/The Image Bank; 745 (b), Peter Van Steen/ HRW; 746 Sam Dudgeon/HRW; 748 (b), Peter Van Steen/HRW; 748 (t), © Mug Shots/CORBIS; 749 Peter Van Steen/HRW; 750 Digital Image copyright © 2005 PhotoDisc; 752 (t), © John Kelly/Getty Images/Stone; 752 (b), Peter Van Steen/HRW; 753 (t), Peter Van Steen/HRW; 753 (b), Peter Van Steen/HRW; 756 (l), Brian Hagiwara/FoodPix; 757 (r), Courtesy Russell Selger; 757 (l), © Eyebyte/Alamy Photos

Lab Book/Appendix "LabBook Header", "L", Corbis Images; "a", Letraset Phototone; "b", and "B", HRW; "o", and "k", images ©2006 PhotoDisc/HRW; 758 (l, tr, br), Sam Dudgeon/HRW; 758 (c), Scott Van Osdol/HRW; 761 (t), Sam Dudgeon/HRW; 761 (b), Sam Dudgeon/HRW; 763 Sam Dudgeon/HRW; 764 (tl), Runk/Schoenberger/Grant Heilman; 764 (tc), Runk/Schoenberger/Grant Heilman; 764 (tr), Michael Abbey/Photo Researchers, Inc.; 764 (tr), Sam Dudgeon/HRW; 764 (br), Runk/Schoenberger/Grant Heilman; 765 (b), Sam Dudgeon/HRW; 765 (c), Sam Dudgeon/HRW; 766 Sam Dudgeon/HRW; 769 (all), Sam Dudgeon/HRW; 772 (tr), Peter Van Steen/HRW; 772 (c), Peter Van Steen/HRW; 772 (br), Peter Van Steen/ HRW; 773 Sam Dudgeon/HRW; 776 (b), Breck P. Kent; 776 (br), Stephen J. Krasemann/Photo Researchers; 776 (c), Visuals Unlimited/R. Calentine; 776 (t), Runk/Schoenberger/Grant Heilman; 777 Sam Dudgeon/HRW; 779 (t), John Langford/ HRW Photo; 779 (b), John Langford/HRW Photo; 780 (t), Sam Dudgeon/HRW; 780 (c), Sam Dudgeon/HRW; 782 (t), Sam Dudgeon/HRW; 782 (b), Sam Dudgeon/HRW; 784 Rod Planck/Photo Researchers; 785 Peter Van Steen/HRW; 788 Peter Van Steen/ HRW; 789 (tr), © Kenneth Gabrielsen; 789 (cl), Visuals Unlimited/Doug Sokell; 789 (br), Larry Nielsen/Peter Arnold; 789 (bl), Phil Degginger; 791 Peter Van Steen/HRW; 793 Peter Van Steen/HRW; 794 Sam Dudgeon/HRW; 795 (t), Sam Dudgeon/HRW; 795 (c), Sam Dudgeon/HRW; 795 (b), Sam Dudgeon/HRW; 796 Sam Dudgeon/HRW; 797 Sam Dudgeon/HRW; 801 Peter Van Steen/HRW; 802 (t), Sam Dudgeon/HRW; 802 (b), Sam Dudgeon/HRW; 811 Sam Dudgeon/HRW; 812 Sam Dudgeon/HRW; 817 (t), Peter Van Steen/HRW; 817 (b), Sam Dudgeon/HRW; 830 CENCO

TEACHER EDITION CREDITS

3E (cl), Craig Line/AP/Wide World Photos; 3E (bl), Chip Simmons/Discover Channel; 3E (br), John Mitchell/Photo Researchers , Inc.; 3F (r), Howard Sochurek/Corbis Stock Market; 3F (r), Art by Christopher Sloan/Photograph by Mark Thiessen both National Geographic Image Collection/National Geographic Image Collection; 35E (l), Visuals Unlimited/Science Visuals Unlimited; 35E (r), Visuals Unlimited/Stanley Flegler; 35F (r), SuperStock; 57E (tl), Visuals Unlimited/Kevin Collins; 57F (l), Quest/Science Photo Library/Photo Researchers, Inc.; 87E (t), Photo Researchers, Inc.; 87F (tl), L. Willatt, East Anglian Regional Genetics Service/Science Photo Library/Photo Researchers, Inc.; 87F (r), Ed Reschke/Peter Arnold, Inc.; 111E (l), Ned M. Seidler/ National Geographic Society Image Collection; 141E (l), Hulton Archive/Getty Images; 141F (l), Visuals Unlimited/Science Visuals Unlimited/Keith Wood; 141F (r), Volker Steger/Peter Arnold; 163E (l), Courtesy of Betsy Webb, Pratt Museum, Homer, Alaska; 191F (r), Neanderthal Museum; 219F (tl), Biophoto Associates/Photo Researchers , Inc.; 219F (bl), Sherrie Jones/Photo Researchers, Inc.; 219F (r), Dr. Tony Brian & David Parker/Science Photo Library/ Photo Researchers, Inc.; 243E (c), Visuals Unlimited/ David M. Phillips; 243E (l), Fran Heyl Associates; 243E (r), CNRI/Science Photo Library/Photo Researchers, Inc.; 243F (r), Visuals Unlimited/Hans Gelderblom; 243F (l), Dr. O. Bradfute/Peter Arnold; 267E (l), Visuals Unlimited/David Phillips; 267E (r), Fred Rhoades/Mycena Consulting; 267F (tl), David M. Dennis/Tom Stack; 267F (bl), Bill Beatty/Minden Pictures; 267F (r), Stephen & Sylvia Duran Sharnoff/National Geographic Society Image Collection; 297E (l), Paul Harris/Stone/Getty Images; 297E (r), Runk/Schoenberger/Grant Heilman; 297F (r), Stephen J. Krasemann/Photo Researchers, Inc.; 329E (r), George Bernard/Earth Scenes; 329F (bl), Visuals Unlimited/E. Webber; 329F (cr),Visuals Unlimited/Bill Beatty; 329F (r), (c) Cathlyn Melloan/Getty Images/Stone; 329F (c), Visuals Unlimited/Bill Beatty; 353E (tl), David B. Fleetham/FPG International/Getty Images; 353E (r), Tom Brakefield/CORBIS; 353E (cr, bl, bc, & br), Digital Image copyright (c) 2005 Artville; 353F (r) Peter Weimann/ Animals Animals; 353F (l), Gerard Lacz/Peter Arnold; 377E (tl), Keith Philpott/Image Bank/Getty Images; 377E (tr), David Fleetham/FPG/Getty Images; 377E (br), Milton Rand/Tom Stack & Associates; 377F (l), M. H. Sharp/Photo Researchers, Inc.; 377F (r), Chesher/Photo Researchers, Inc.; 409E (tl), Randy Morse/Tom Stack; 409E (r), Index Stock; 409F (tl), Stephen Dalton/NHPA; 409F (bl), Telegraph Color Library/FPG/Getty Images; 409F (r), Wayne Lynch/DRK Photo; 439E (l), Gail Shumway/FPG/Getty Images; 439E (br), G. C. Kelley/Photo Researchers, Inc.; 439F (tl), David E. Myers/ Stone/Getty Images; 439F (r), Dave Watts/Nature Picture Library; 439F (bl), Merlin D. Tuttle/Bat Conservation International; 477E (r), Laguna Photo/Liaison International/ Getty Images; 477F (l), Visuals Unlimited/Gerald & Buff Corsi; 477F (tr), Carol Hughes/Bruce Coleman; 477F (br), Telegraph Color Library/FPG/Getty Images; 505F (l), Diana L. Stratton/Tom Stack & Associates; 505F (r), Kim Heacox/DRK Photo; 523F (tl), Stuart Westmorland/Getty Images/Stone; 523F (bl), Jeff Hunter/Image Bank/ Getty Images; 523F (r), (c) Dwight R. Kuhn; 551E (l), J. Roche/Peter Arnold, Inc.; 551E (r), Arthur Tilley/Tony Stone/Getty Images; 551F (l), K. W. Fink/Bruce Coleman; 551F (tl & tr), Peter Van Steen/HRW Photo; 577E (r), Sam Dudgeon/HRW Photo; 577F (tr), Dr. Robert Becker/Custom Medical Stock Photo; 603E (r), SUSUMU NISHINAGA/SCIENCE PHOTO LIBRARY/Photo Researchers, Inc.; 603E (l), John Bavosi /Photo Researchers, Inc.; 681E (tl), Innerspace Visions; 681E (bl), Charles Phillip/ CORBIS; 681F (r), Photo Lennart Nilsson/Albert Bonniers Forlag AB, A Child Is Born, Dell Publishing Company; 707E (l), Tektoff-RM/CNRI/Science Photo Library/Photo Researchers ; 707E (r), Kent Wood/Photo Researchers, Inc.; 707F (l), Peter Van Steen/HRW Photo; 707F (r), SuperStock; 729E (l), Peter Van Steen/HRW Photo; 729E (r), John Kelly/Stone /Getty Images; 729F (r), Spencer Grant/Photo Researchers, Inc.; 729F (l), Peter Van Steen/HRW Photo.

880   Credits

Answers to Concept Mapping Questions

The following pages contain sample answers to all of the concept mapping questions that appear in the Chapter Reviews. Because there is more than one way to do a concept map, your students' answers may vary.

CHAPTER 1 The World of Life Science

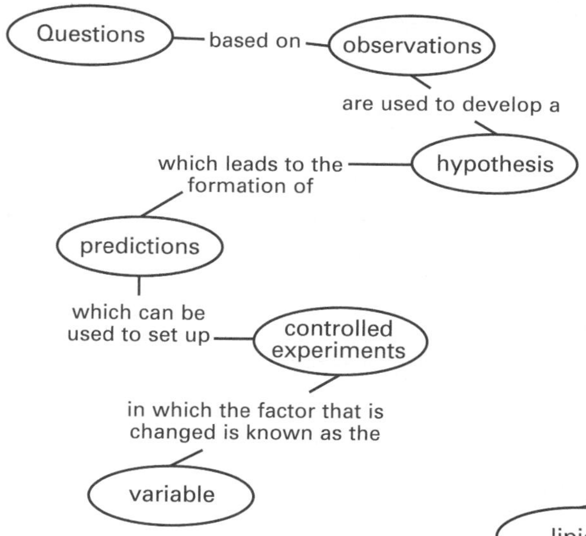

CHAPTER 2 It's Alive!! Or Is It?

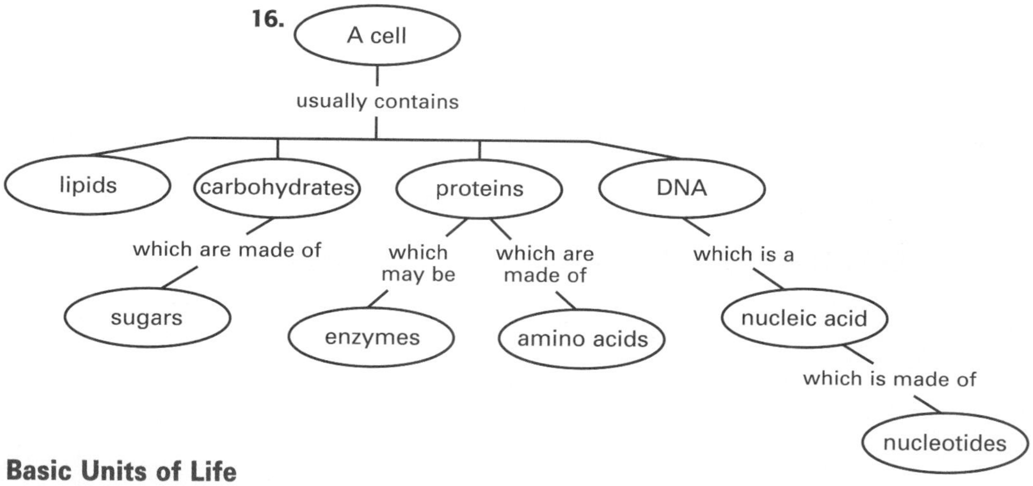

CHAPTER 3 Cells: The Basic Units of Life

CHAPTER 4 The Cell in Action

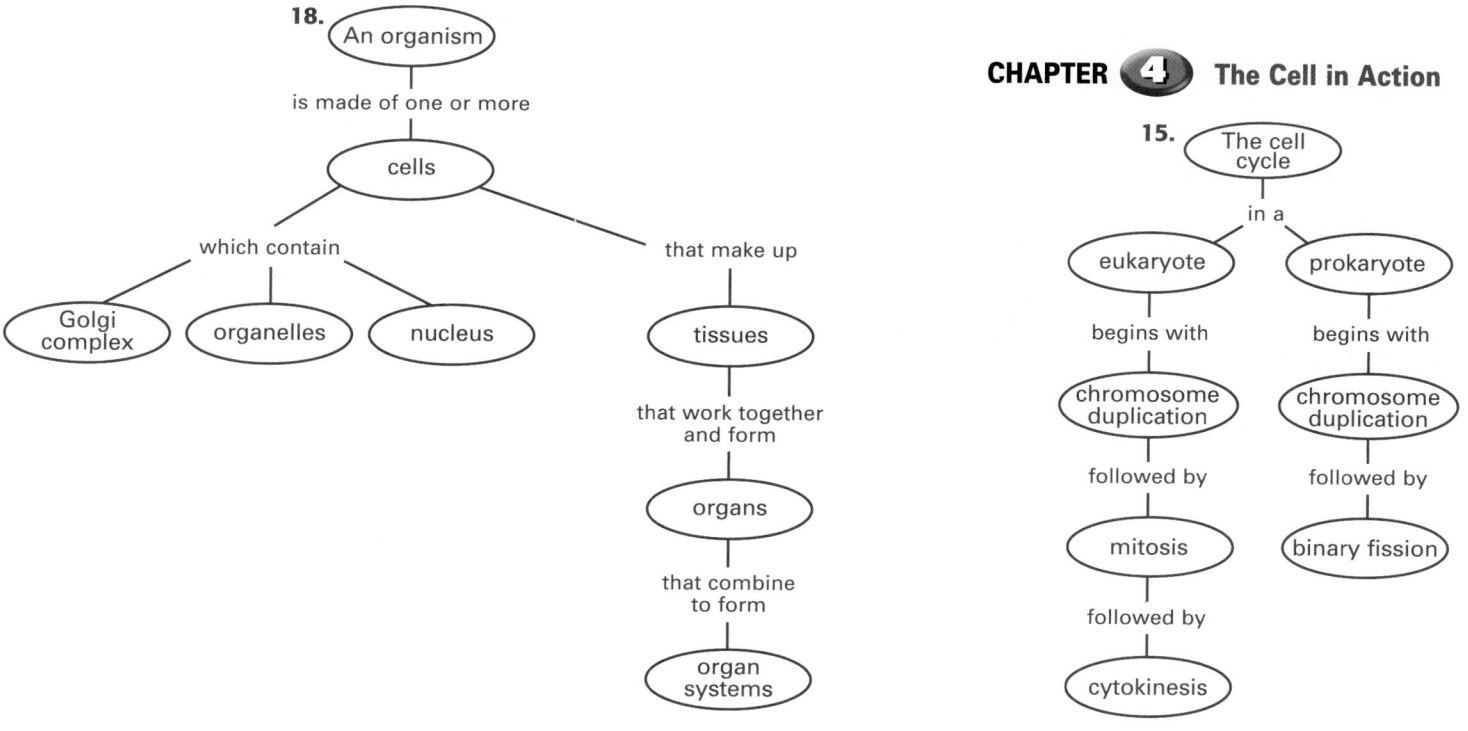

CHAPTER 5 Heredity

16.

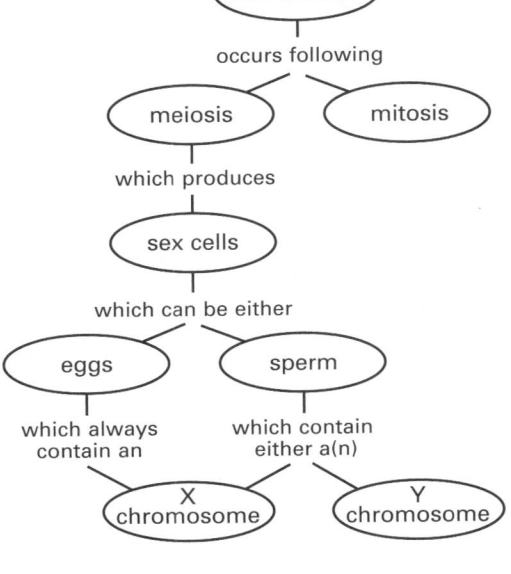

Cell division
occurs following
meiosis
mitosis
which produces
sex cells
which can be either
eggs
sperm
which always contain an
which contain either a(n)
X chromosome
Y chromosome

CHAPTER 6 Genes and DNA

16.

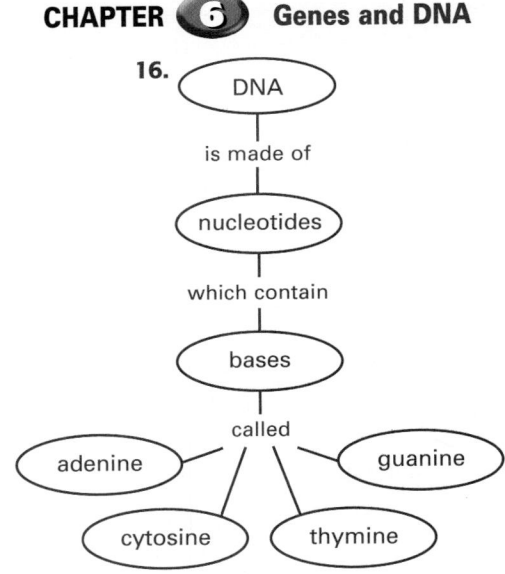

DNA
is made of
nucleotides
which contain
bases
called
adenine
guanine
cytosine
thymine

CHAPTER 7 The Evolution of Living Things

17.

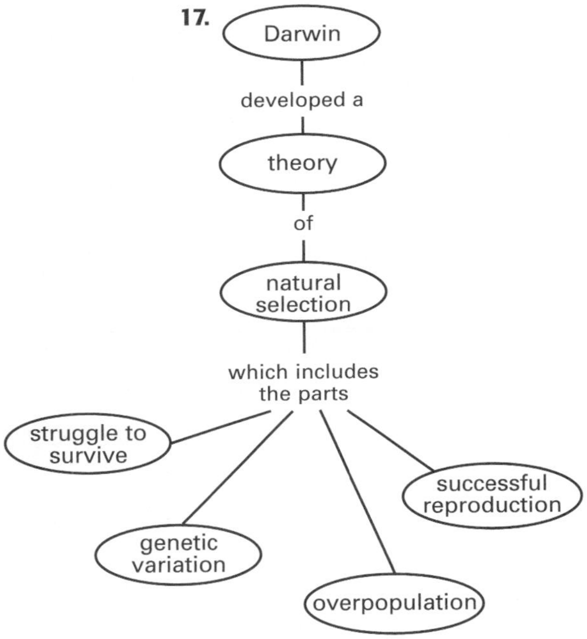

Darwin
developed a
theory
of
natural selection
which includes the parts
struggle to survive
successful reproduction
genetic variation
overpopulation

CHAPTER 8 The History of Life on Earth

19.

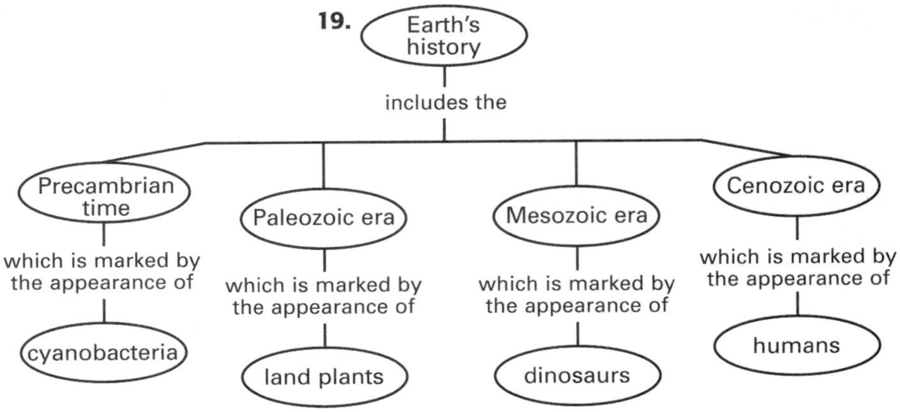

Earth's history
includes the
Precambrian time
Paleozoic era
Mesozoic era
Cenozoic era
which is marked by the appearance of
which is marked by the appearance of
which is marked by the appearance of
which is marked by the appearance of
cyanobacteria
land plants
dinosaurs
humans

CHAPTER 9 Classification

16.

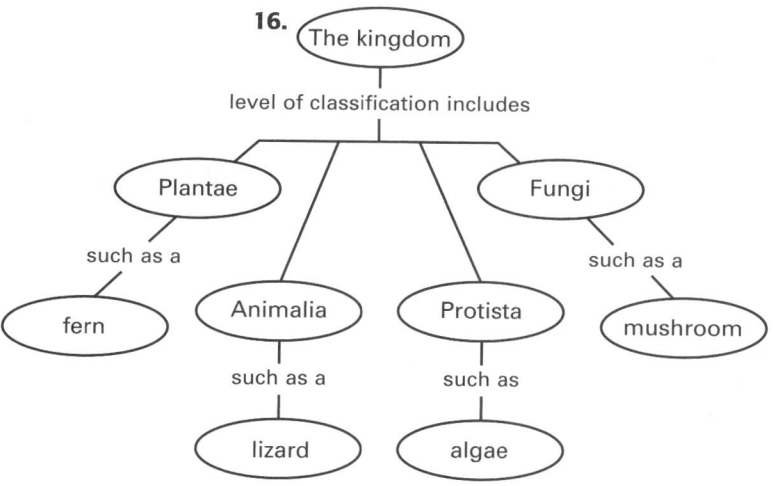

The kingdom
— level of classification includes —

Plantae — such as a — fern

Animalia — such as a — lizard

Protista — such as — algae

Fungi — such as a — mushroom

CHAPTER 10 Bacteria and Viruses

18.

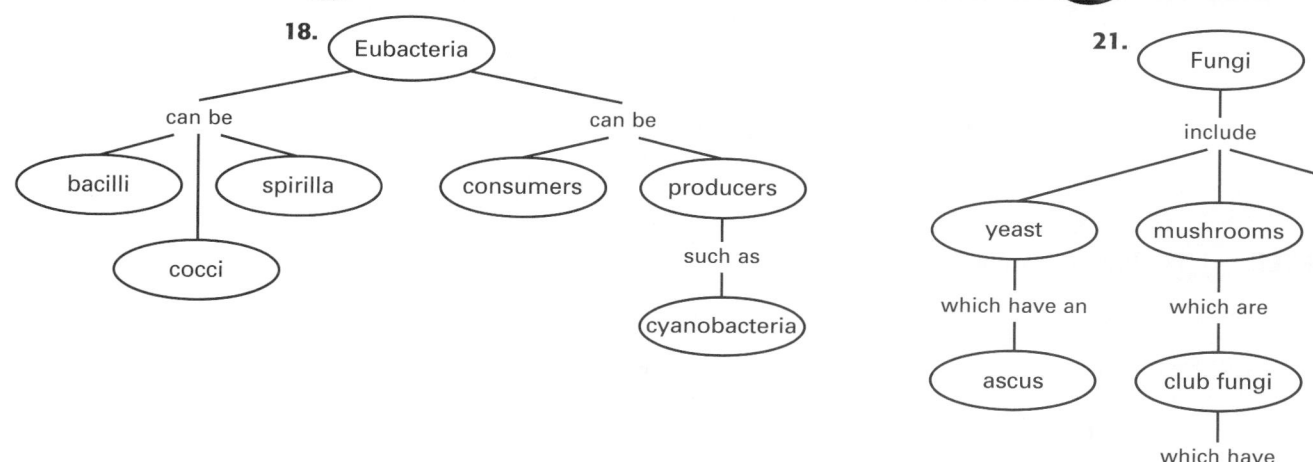

Eubacteria

can be — bacilli, spirilla, cocci

can be — consumers, producers — such as — cyanobacteria

CHAPTER 11 Protists and Fungi

21.

Fungi
— include —

yeast — which have an — ascus

mushrooms — which are — club fungi — which have — basidia

bread mold — which are — threadlike fungi

CHAPTER 12 Introduction to Plants

17.

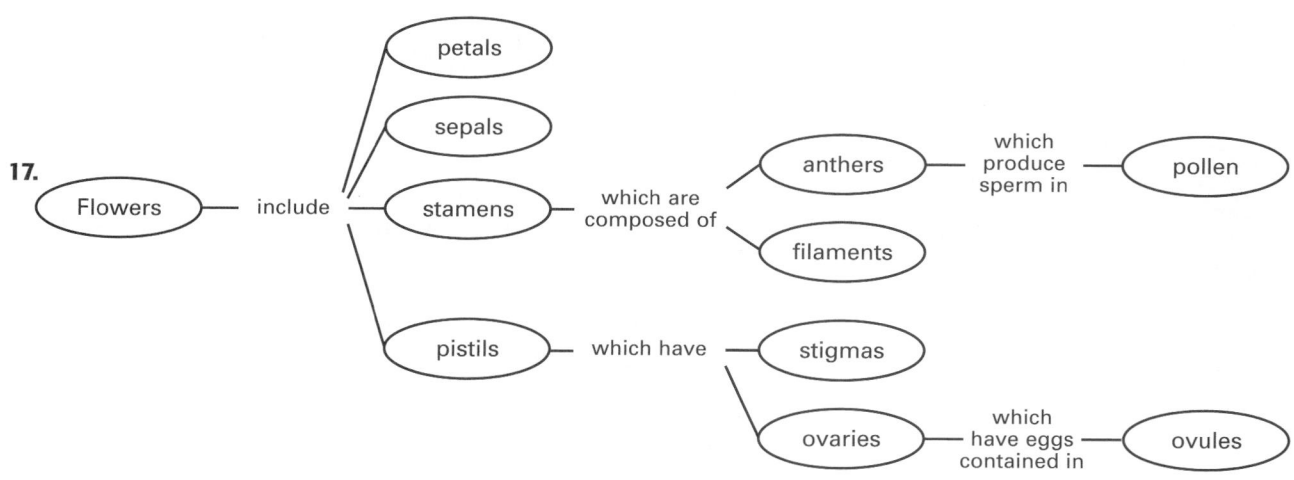

Flowers — include — petals, sepals, stamens, pistils

stamens — which are composed of — anthers — which produce sperm in — pollen

filaments

pistils — which have — stigmas

ovaries — which have eggs contained in — ovules

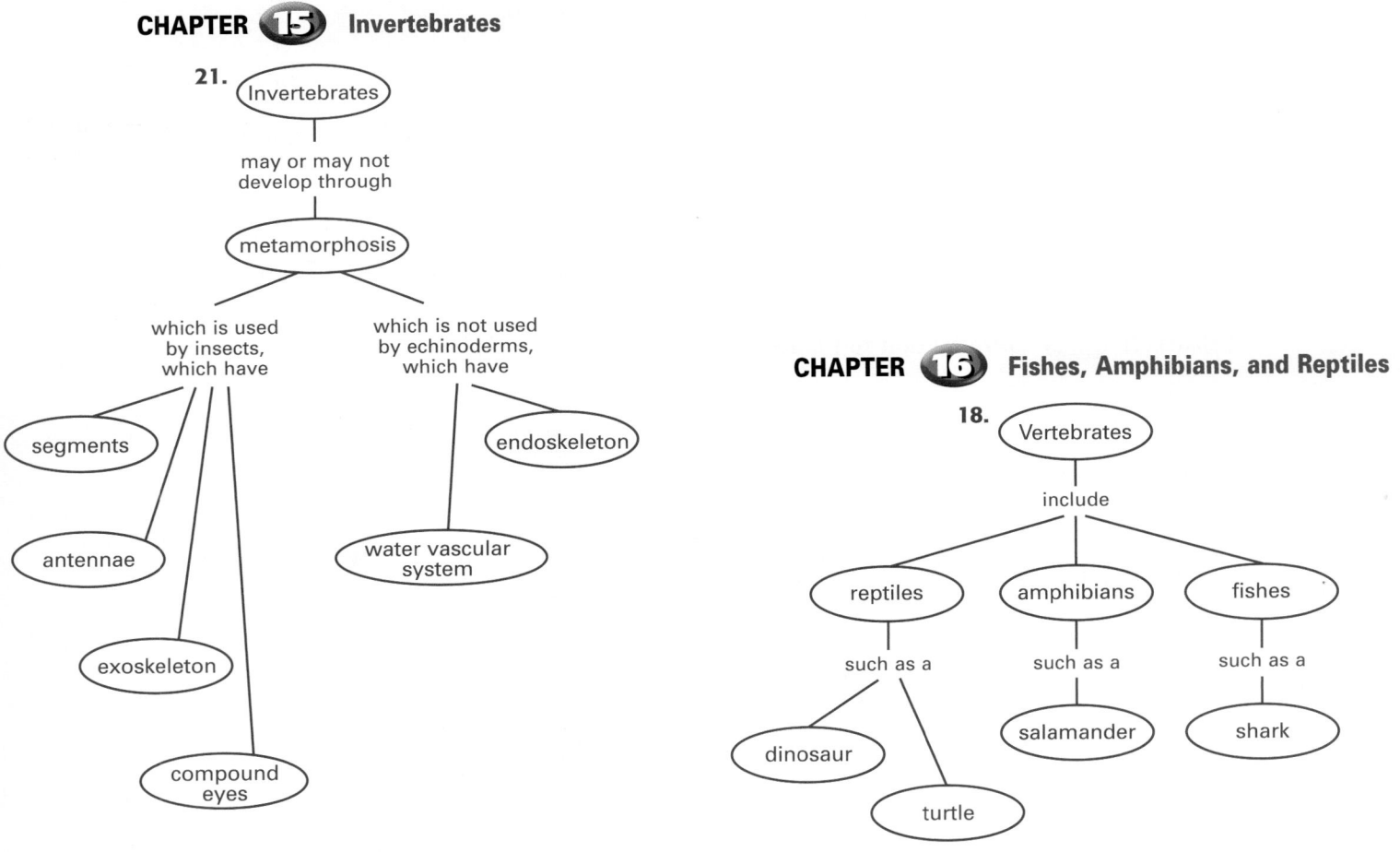

CHAPTER 13 Plant Processes

18.

- Plants
  - convert
    - light energy
      - to
        - chemical energy
  - get food by
    - photosynthesis
      - which uses
        - carbon dioxide
  - get energy from food by
    - cellular respiration
      - which uses
        - oxygen

CHAPTER 14 Animals and Behavior

16.

- Animals
  - use
    - survival behavior
      - such as
        - finding food
        - defensive action
        - marking a territory
        - parenting
        - courtship
    - seasonal behavior
      - such as
        - migration
        - estivation
        - hibernation

CHAPTER 15 Invertebrates

21.

- Invertebrates
  - may or may not develop through
    - metamorphosis
      - which is used by insects, which have
        - segments
        - antennae
        - exoskeleton
        - compound eyes
      - which is not used by echinoderms, which have
        - endoskeleton
        - water vascular system

CHAPTER 16 Fishes, Amphibians, and Reptiles

18.

- Vertebrates
  - include
    - reptiles
      - such as a
        - dinosaur
        - turtle
    - amphibians
      - such as a
        - salamander
    - fishes
      - such as a
        - shark

21.

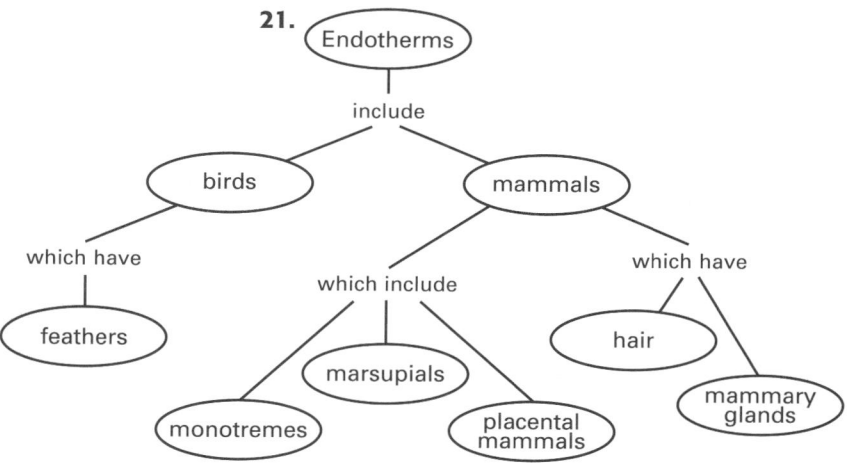

CHAPTER **18** Interactions of Living Things

21.

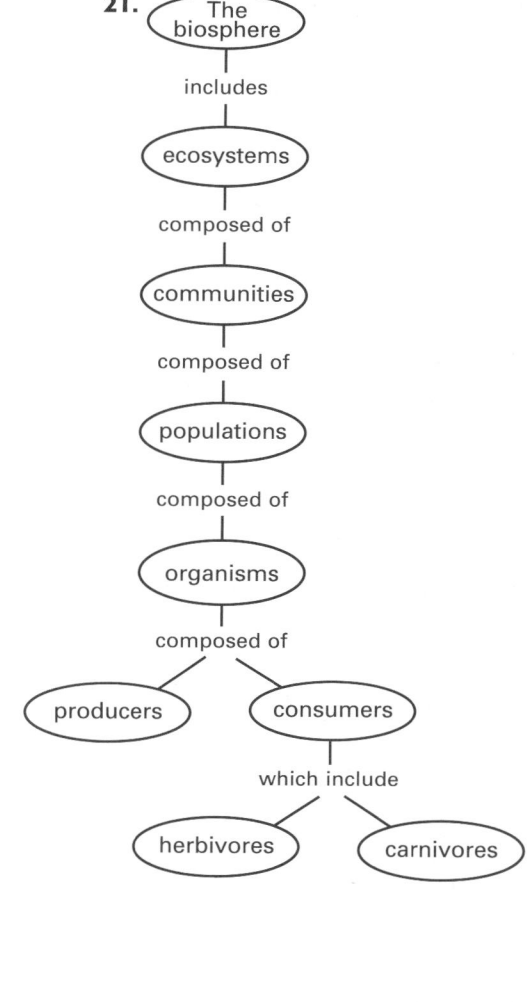

CHAPTER **19** Cycles in Nature

21.

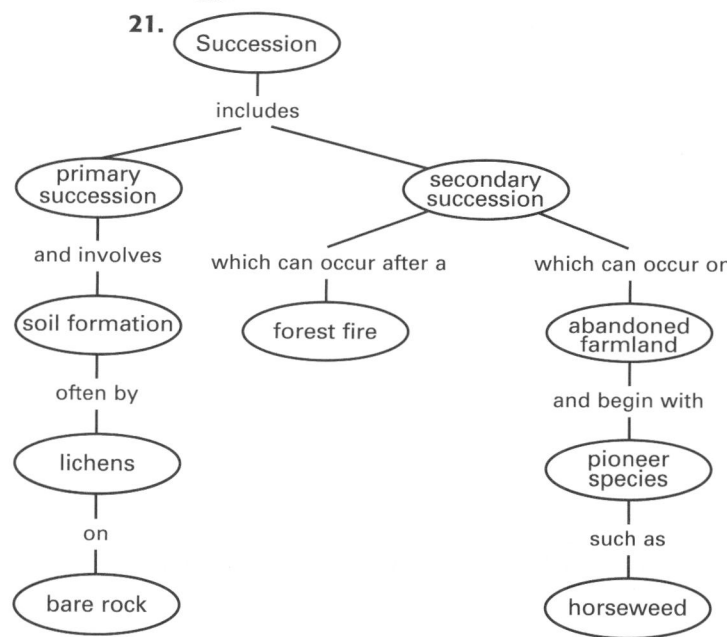

CHAPTER **20** The Earth's Ecosystems

16.

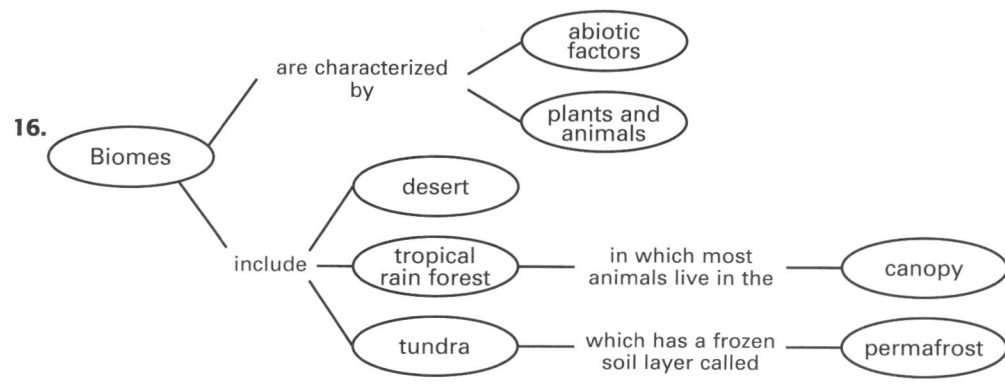

CHAPTER 21 Environmental Problems and Solutions

16.

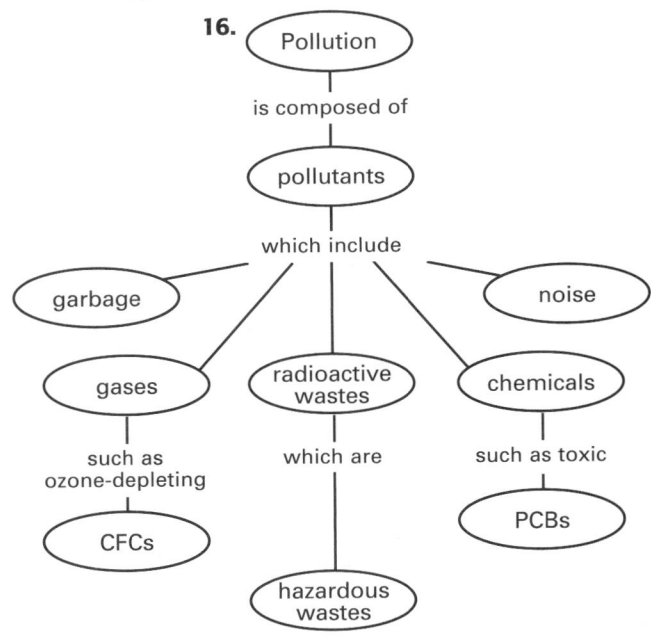

CHAPTER 22 Body Organization and Structure

17.

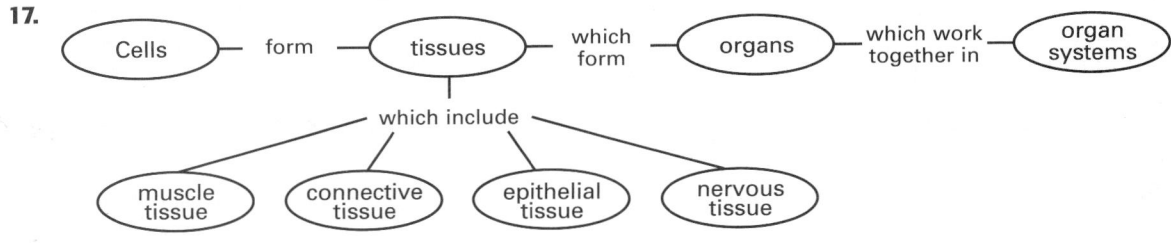

CHAPTER 23 Circulation and Respiration

18.

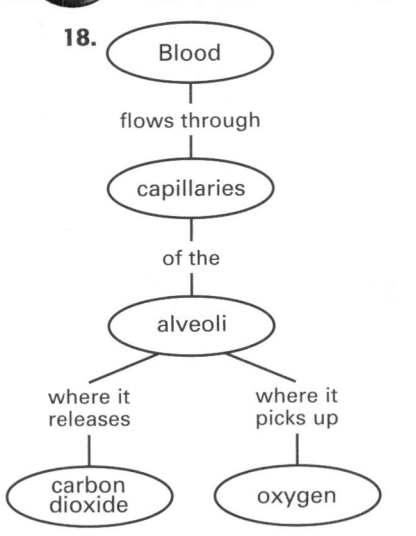

CHAPTER 24 The Digestive and Urinary Systems

19.

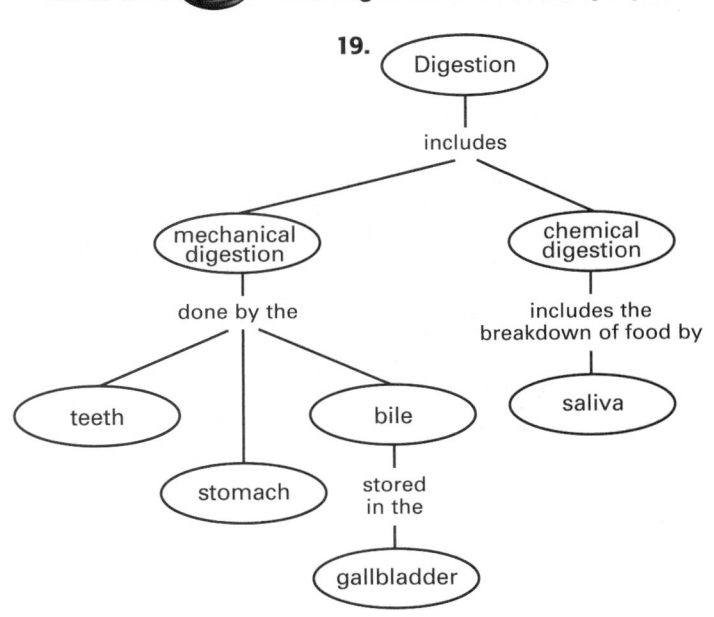

CHAPTER 25   Communication and Control

18.

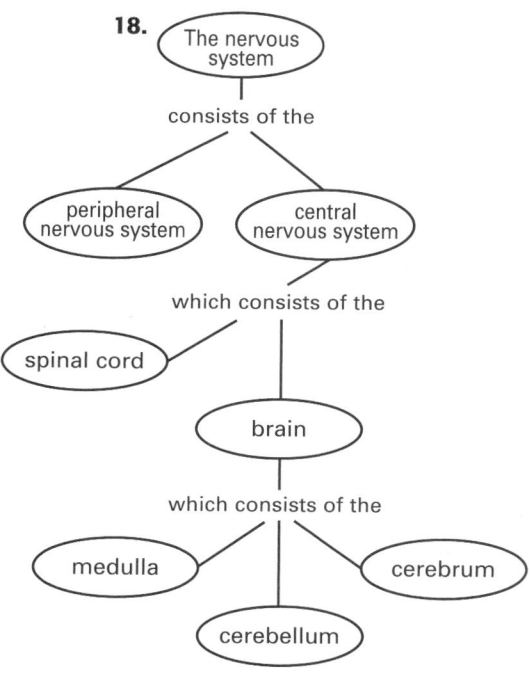

The nervous system
consists of the
- peripheral nervous system
- central nervous system
which consists of the
- spinal cord
- brain
which consists of the
- medulla
- cerebellum
- cerebrum

CHAPTER 26   Reproduction and Development

18.

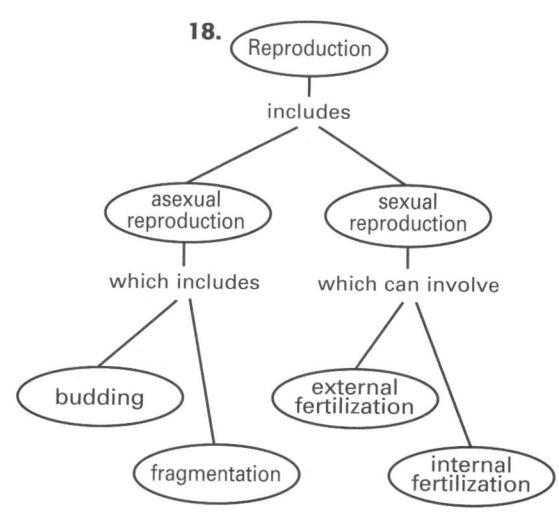

Reproduction
includes
- asexual reproduction
which includes
- budding
- fragmentation
- sexual reproduction
which can involve
- external fertilization
- internal fertilization

CHAPTER 27   Body Defenses and Disease

16.

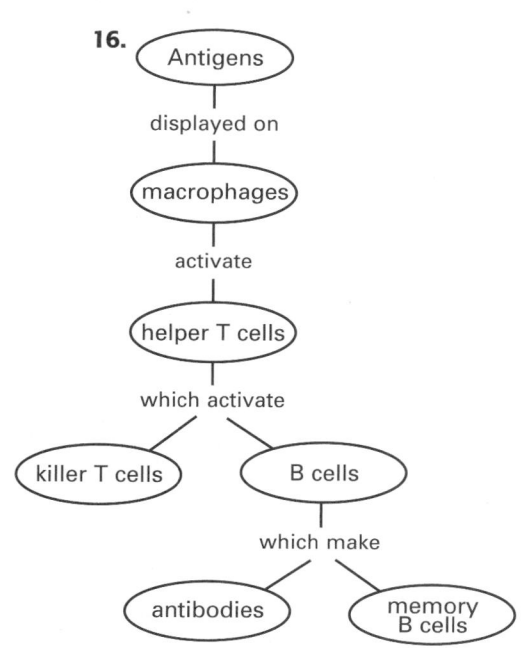

Antigens
displayed on
macrophages
activate
helper T cells
which activate
- killer T cells
- B cells
which make
- antibodies
- memory B cells

CHAPTER 28   Staying Healthy

17.

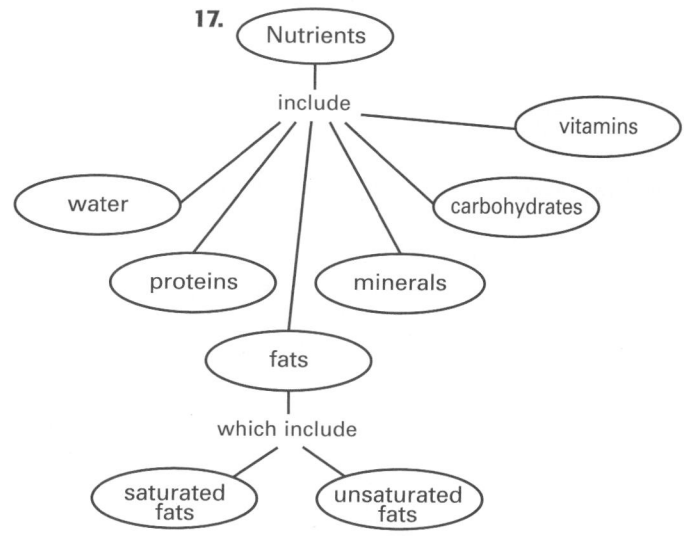

Nutrients
include
- vitamins
- water
- carbohydrates
- proteins
- minerals
- fats
which include
- saturated fats
- unsaturated fats